Auto
Service & Repair

Servicing, Troubleshooting, and Repairing Modern Automobiles.
Applicable to All Makes and Models.

by

Martin W. Stockel
Automotive Writer

Martin T. Stockel
Automotive Writer

Chris Johanson
ASE Certified Master Automobile Technician

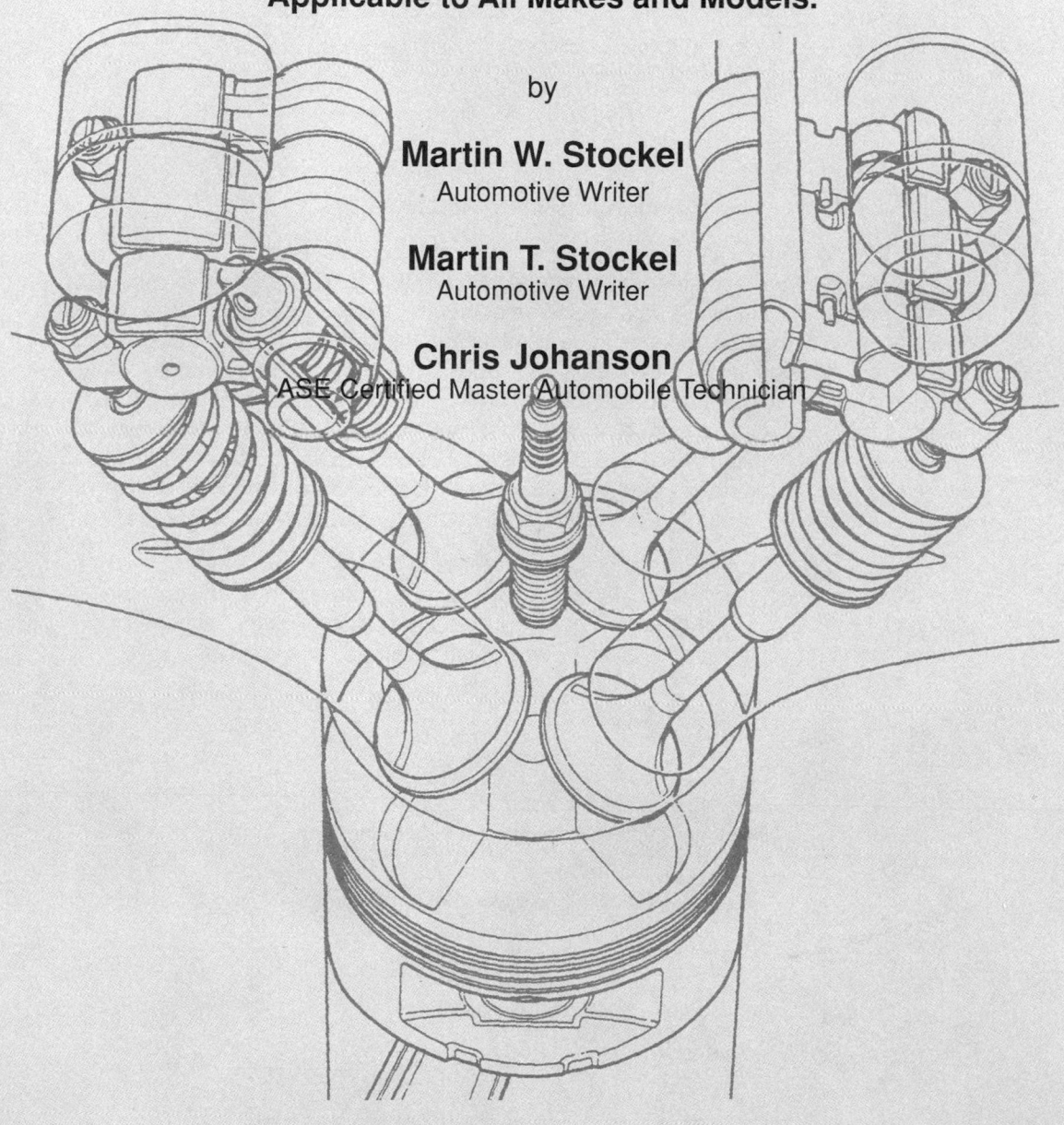

Publisher
The Goodheart-Willcox Company, Inc.
Tinley Park, Illinois

Important Safety Notice

Proper service and repair is important to the safe, reliable operation of motor vehicles. Procedures recommended and described in this book are effective methods of performing service operations. Some require the use of tools specially designed for this purpose and should be used as recommended. Note that this book also contains various safety procedures and cautions, which should be carefully followed to minimize the risk of personal injury or the possibility that improper service methods may damage the engine or render the vehicle unsafe. It is also important to understand that these notices and cautions are not exhaustive. Those performing a given service procedure or using a particular tool must first satisfy themselves that neither their safety nor engine or vehicle safety will be jeopardized by the service method selected.

This book contains the most complete and accurate information that could be obtained from various authoritative sources at the time of publication. Goodheart-Willcox cannot assume responsibility for any changes, errors, or omissions.

Library of Congress Cataloging-in-Publication Data

Stockel, Martin W.
  Auto service and repair / by Martin W. Stockel and Martin T. Stockel.
    p.   cm.
  Includes index.
  ISBN 1-56637-144-9
  1. Automobiles—Maintenance and repair.
I. Stockel, Martin T.   II. Title.
TL152.S7745   1995
629.28'72—dc20   94-30265
                                                  CIP

Introduction

Auto Service and Repair tells and shows how to service, troubleshoot, and repair modern automobiles. It contains information on the latest developments in the automotive field, including computer control, anti-lock brakes, air bags, and refrigerant recovery. The material in this text is easy to understand and is applicable to all automobiles.

The textbook teaches essential automotive repair skills, encourages the development of good work habits, and emphasizes safety. It is comprehensive, detailed, and profusely illustrated. Many of the illustrations were prepared especially for use in this text.

Auto Service and Repair is intended for beginners who need a sound foundation in the fundamentals of automotive repair. It also helps those now engaged in automotive service and repair who want to increase their skills and earnings.

Each chapter of the textbook begins with Learning Objectives that provide focus for the chapter. Technical terms are printed in ***bold italic type*** and are defined when first used. Each chapter also includes a "Tech Talk" section, a Summary, a "Know These Terms" section, Review Questions, ASE-type Questions, and several "Suggested Activities." The Suggested Activities are designed to emphasize reading, math, and communication skills.

A **Workbook for Auto Service and Repair** is also available. It is a convenient study guide and shop activity guide directly related to this textbook.

Martin W. Stockel
Martin T. Stockel
Chris Johanson

Contents

Automotive technicians should follow all applicable safety procedures when performing service and repair operations. This technician is wearing safety goggles to protect his eyes from flying debris. (Hunter Engineering Company)

1

Safety and Environmental Protection

After studying this chapter, you will be able to:
- Identify the major causes of accidents.
- Explain why accidents must be avoided.
- Recognize unsafe conditions in the shop.
- Give examples of unsafe work procedures.
- Use personal protective equipment.
- Describe types of environmental damage caused by improper auto shop practices.
- Identify ways to prevent environmental damage.

This chapter emphasizes the importance of working safely in the automotive shop. It stresses the safety procedures that should be followed when performing service and repair work. It also covers the proper handling and disposal of waste products to safeguard both the technician and the environment.

Preventing Accidents

Accidents are unplanned events that often cause damage or injury. The following sections examine the causes of accidents and explain how knowing what causes accidents can help you avoid them.

Causes of Accidents

There are many causes of accidents. Some accidents occur when technicians try to take shortcuts instead of following proper repair procedures. Other accidents occur when technicians fail to correct dangerous conditions in the work area.

In many cases, accidents happen when two or more unsafe conditions or acts occur simultaneously. For example, many technicians remove the ground prong from the electrical plug of a portable drill because it is too much trouble to find a three-prong extension cord, **Figure 1-1.** Additionally, technicians often use electric tools when standing on a wet concrete floor without wearing insulated rubber–soled shoes because it is too much trouble to change shoes or move to a dry area. Neither of these unsafe acts causes an accident until someone uses the ungrounded drill while standing on a wet floor. If the drill motor develops a short to the drill body, current will flow through the user to ground, **Figure 1-2.** This leads to severe electrical shock, which can cause electrical burns, damage to internal organs, or even death.

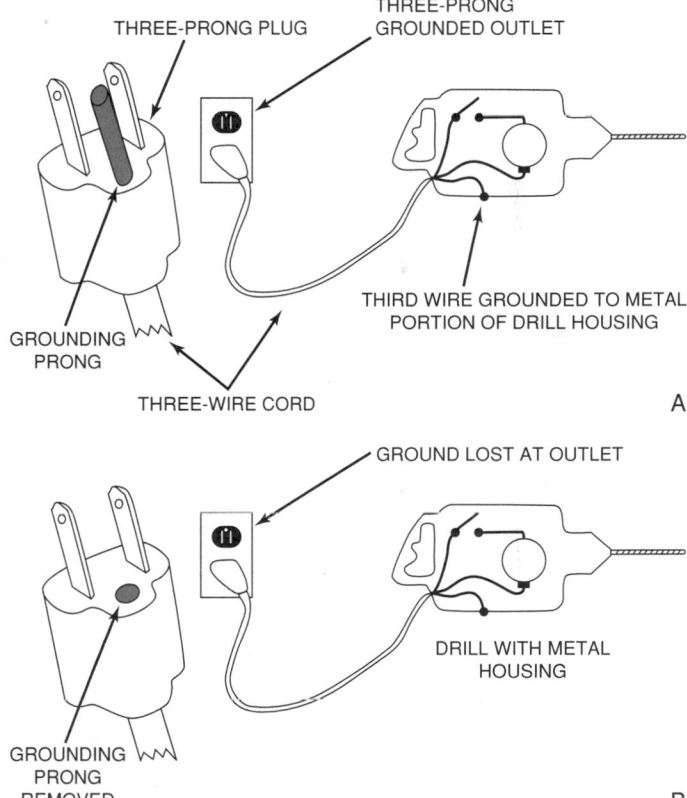

Figure 1-1. A—Properly grounded drill. B—The grounding prong was removed from the plug, making the drill unsafe.

In the above example, no one set out to cause an accident. Instead, it was just too much trouble to do things correctly. The result of this series of unsafe acts was an accident.

Avoiding Accidents

An accident may result in injuries that keep you from working or enjoying your free time. Some accidents can kill. Even slight injuries are painful and annoying. Even if an accident causes no personal injury, it can result in property damage. Repairing damage caused by an accident can be expensive. In some cases, careless accidents can cost you your job.

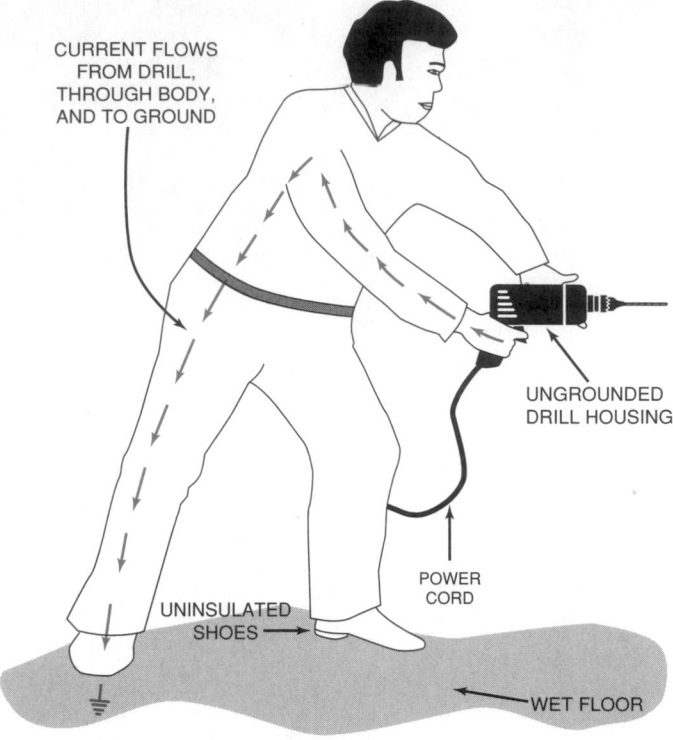

CURRENT FLOWS
FROM DRILL,
THROUGH BODY,
AND TO GROUND

UNGROUNDED
DRILL HOUSING

POWER
CORD

UNINSULATED
SHOES

WET FLOOR

Figure 1-2. If an ungrounded drill with a metal case is used while standing on a wet surface, the technician will receive an electrical shock.

No automotive technician wants to be injured or cause property damage. Sometimes, however, even the most experienced technicians become rushed and careless. As a result, falls, injuries to hands and feet, fires, explosions, electric shocks, and even poisonings occur in auto repair shops. Additionally, carelessness in the shop can lead to long-term bodily harm from prolonged exposure to harmful liquids, vapors, and dust. Lung damage, skin disorders, and even cancer can result from contact from these substances. For this reason, technicians must keep safety in mind at all times, especially when conditions tend to make it the last thing on their minds.

Preventing Accidents

Most accidents occur because of improper shopkeeping, incorrect work procedures, or a combination of both. *Shopkeeping* means maintaining the shop premises in order by keeping all tools and equipment in good working order and storing them in their proper places. Shopkeeping also involves properly disposing of dirt, oil, or other refuse before it piles up. Examples of improper shopkeeping include failing to maintain tools and equipment; allowing old parts, containers, or other trash to accumulate in the shop; and ignoring fluid spills.

Work procedures are the actual diagnosis and repair operations performed in the shop. Improper work procedures include using the wrong tools or methods to perform repairs, using defective tools, not wearing protective equipment when necessary, and not paying close attention while performing the job.

The best way to prevent accidents is to maintain a neat, clean work area, to use safe methods and common sense when making repairs, and to wear protective equipment when needed. The following suggestions will help reduce the possibility of accidents.

Proper Shopkeeping

Shopkeeping does not mean just keeping the shop neat. Instead, shopkeeping refers to the process of identifying and correcting unsafe conditions. Many of the statements covered in this section will seem to be matters of common sense, but they are often disregarded during service operations.

Return all tools and equipment to their proper storage places. This saves time in the long run and reduces the chance of accidents and theft. Do not leave equipment out where others can trip on it.

Keep workbenches clean. This reduces the chances of tools or parts falling from the bench to the floor, where they could be lost or damaged. Of course, this reduces the chances that a tool or part will fall on your foot. A clean workbench also reduces the possibility that critical parts will be lost in the clutter and reduces the chance of a fire from oily debris.

Clean up spills immediately to avoid tracking them through the shop. Many people are injured when they slip on floors coated with oil, antifreeze, or water. Gasoline spills can be extremely dangerous because a flame or spark can ignite the gasoline vapors, causing a major explosion and fire.

Become familiar with the chemicals stored in the shop. Chemicals commonly used in the automotive shop include carburetor cleaners, hot tank solutions, parts cleaners, motor oil, and antifreeze. Chemical manufacturers provide *Material Safety Data Sheets* (MSDS) for every chemical they produce. These sheets list all the known dangers of a specific chemical, as well as first aid procedures for skin or respiratory system contact. There should be an MSDS for every type of chemical used in the shop. Always read the appropriate MSDS before working with an unfamiliar chemical. Store chemicals in properly labeled, approved containers. See **Figure 1-3.**

Make sure that the shop is well lighted. Poor lighting makes it hard to see what you are doing. Not only does poor lighting make the job take longer, it can lead to accidental contact with moving parts or hot surfaces. Overhead lights should be bright and centrally located. Portable droplights should be kept in proper operating condition. Always use a "rough service" bulb in incandescent droplights. These bulbs are more rugged than normal lightbulbs and will not shatter if they break. Do not use a high-wattage bulb in a droplight. High-wattage bulbs get very hot and can melt the light socket or burn anyone who touches the droplight's safety cover.

Do not overload electrical outlets or extension cords by operating several electrical devices from one outlet. Never pair up high-current electrical devices or operate them through extension cords. Examples of high-current electrical devices include drills, grinders, and electric heaters.

Figure 1-3. Chemical wastes produced in the shop should be stored in properly labeled, approved containers. (Dana Corp.)

Periodically inspect electrical cords and compressed air lines to ensure that they are in good condition. Do not close vehicle doors on electrical cords or air lines. Do not run electrical cords through water puddles or use them outside when it is raining.

Make sure that all shop equipment, such as grinders and drill presses, is equipped with appropriate safety guards. These guards should only be removed for service operations, such as changing the grinding wheels.

When servicing any piece of equipment, be sure that it is unplugged. Read the equipment's service literature before beginning repairs.

Closely monitor the condition of tools and equipment, and make repairs when necessary. This includes such varied tasks as replacing damaged leads on test equipment, checking and adding oil to hydraulic jacks, and regrinding the tips on screwdrivers and chisels.

Never leave open containers of antifreeze inside or outside the shop. Ethylene glycol antifreeze will poison any animal (or person) that drinks it, and antifreeze spills will create an extremely slippery floor.

Following Proper Work Procedures

Whenever work is performed, safety should be the primary consideration. The following safe work procedures may seem simple. However, they are often disregarded, with tragic results.

Wear proper clothing and use protective equipment when necessary. Various types of protective equipment are explained in the next section.

Study proper work procedures before beginning any job that is unfamiliar. Never assume that the procedure you have used in the past will work with a different type of vehicle.

Always work carefully. Speed is not as important as doing the job properly and avoiding injury. Avoid people who will not work carefully.

Use the right tool for a given job. Using a screwdriver as a chisel or a wrench as a hammer often leads to an accident. Never use a hand socket (12 point) with an impact wrench. Hand sockets are not designed to withstand the torque produced by an impact wrench and many shatter. If necessary, impact sockets can be used with a hand ratchet.

Learn how to operate new equipment before using it. This is especially true of air-powered tools, such as impact wrenches and chisels, and large electrical devices, such as drill presses, boring bars, and brake lathes. These tools are very powerful and can cause severe injury if used improperly. See **Figure 1-4.** A good way to learn about new equipment is to read the manufacturer's instructions.

When working on electrical systems, avoid creating a short circuit with a jumper wire or a metal tool. Not only will this damage the vehicle components or wiring, but it will generate enough heat to cause a severe burn or to start a fire.

Take proper precautions when lifting objects. Make sure that you are strong enough to lift the object to be moved. Always lift with your legs, not your back. If an object is too heavy to lift by yourself, get help.

Do not smoke in the shop. You may accidentally ignite an undetected gasoline leak. A burning cigarette can also ignite oily rags or paper debris.

Never attempt to raise a vehicle with a jack that is unsafe or too small. Always support a raised vehicle with quality jackstands. Never use boards or cement blocks to support a vehicle. Boards can break and cement blocks can crumble under the weight of the vehicle.

Never run an engine in a closed area without proper ventilation, even for a short time. Carbon monoxide builds up quickly, is odorless, and is deadly.

Figure 1-4. This technician is using an electric on-car brake lathe. Note that he is wearing safety goggles. Also note that the technician is not wearing loose clothing or jewelry, which could become trapped in spinning equipment.

When working on or near a running engine, keep away from moving parts. Never reach between moving engine parts. A rotating engine part can cause serious injury.

Never leave a running vehicle unattended. The vehicle may slip into gear or overheat while you are away. When you must work on a running vehicle, set the parking brake.

When road testing a vehicle, be alert and obey all traffic laws. Do not become so absorbed in diagnosing a problem that you forget to watch the road. Always watch the actions of other drivers carefully. If necessary, take another technician along to assist you during the road test.

Personal Protective Equipment

The proper use of *personal protective equipment* is vital. Some of the equipment described in the following sections not only protects you from immediate injury but also prevents damage and disease caused from long-term exposure to harmful substances. For example, long-term exposure to brake dust, used oil, or exhaust fumes can cause skin cancer, emphysema, and lung cancer. See **Figure 1-5.**

The most basic kind of protective clothing is that which is not dangerous in itself. Do not wear open jackets, scarves, or shirts with long, loose sleeves. Loose clothing can become caught in moving parts of a machine or engine. If you have long hair, keep it away from moving parts by tying it back or securing it under a hat or a headband. Remove rings and other jewelry. Jewelry can be caught in moving parts. Metal jewelry can cause a short circuit if it completes a path between a positive source and ground. The short circuit can generate enough heat to cause serious burns.

Figure 1-6. This technician is inflating a new tire after mounting it on the wheel. Note that he is wearing safety glasses. (Hunter Engineering Company)

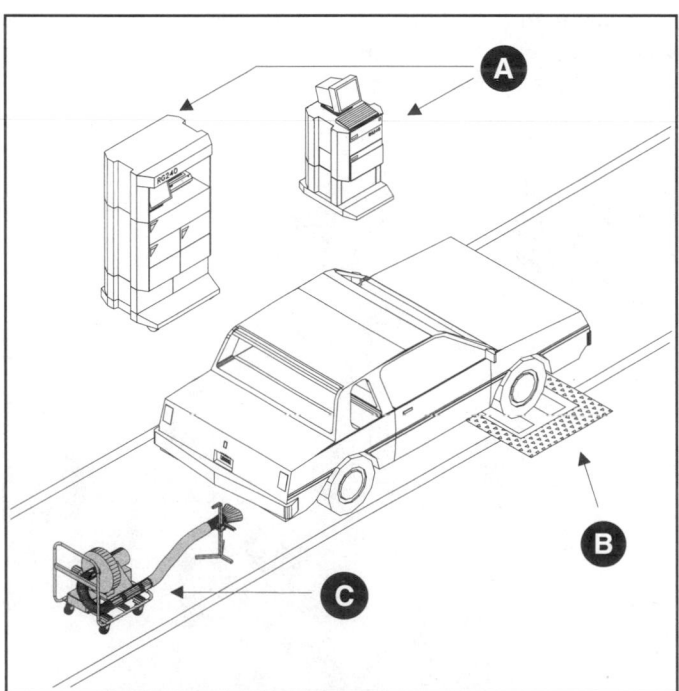

Figure 1-5. Typical setup for testing a vehicle for exhaust emissions. A—Computer. B—Inertia dynamometer. C—Constant volume sampling of exhaust and exhaust remover. (Environmental Systems Products, Inc.)

Eye protection is very important when working in any situation that could result in dirt, metal, or liquids being thrown into your face. This includes working around running engines; using drills, saws, grinders or tire changers; and working around batteries and hot cooling system parts. See **Figure 1-6.**

Safety shoes, preferably with steel toe inserts, should be worn when there is any danger of falling parts or tools. Since such an incident can occur at any time, it is a good idea to wear safety shoes whenever you are in the shop.

Respiratory protection, such as an approved respirator, should be worn whenever you are working on brake systems or clutches. The dust from the friction lining materials used in these devices can cause lung damage or cancer. Respiratory protection is also recommended when working around any equipment that gives off fumes, such as a hot tank or steam cleaner.

Rubber gloves should be worn when working with solvents, such as parts cleaner. If you spill oil, gasoline, cleaning solvents, or any other substance on your skin, clean it off immediately. Prolonged exposure to even mild solvents or petroleum products can cause severe skin rashes or chemical burns. If there is any question about the toxicity of a particular substance, refer to the proper MSDS.

Remember that after all other factors have been figured in, it is still up to you to correct safety hazards, to work safely, and to prevent accidents. Always use common sense when working on vehicles.

Preventing Environmental Damage

Controversy continues over the extent of the environmental damage caused by **pollution.** However, one thing is clear: some damage is definitely occurring as a result of careless disposal of wastes, **Figure 1-7.**

Unfortunately, the automotive service industry is a major source of waste materials. These wastes can be liquids, such as antifreeze and oil; solids, such as scrap parts, tires, and paper containers; or gases, such as refrigerant or carbon monoxide. Preventing the careless disposal of these wastes is important if we are to protect the environment.

It is important to remember that in protecting the earth's environment, we are protecting ourselves. Pollutants can kill—sometimes quickly, sometimes slowly. They will also contaminate the air that we breathe, the water we drink, and the soil in which our food grows. The economic burden of dealing with waste will grow ever larger. If we do not take responsibility for the wastes we generate, our descendants will suffer the effects of our irresponsible acts.

Ways of Damaging the Environment

It is common to identify pollution with large companies. However, anyone can be a polluter. The ways in which the automotive technician can cause environmental damage can be divided into main areas:

- Carelessly disposing of wastes generated in the shop.
- Repairing vehicles in such a way that they cause increased air pollution.

Careless Waste Disposal

One of the most common ways in which automotive technicians cause environmental damage is by improperly disposing of liquid wastes. Pouring oil, transmission fluid, brake fluid, antifreeze, and used cleaning solutions on the ground contaminates the soil. In addition, these liquids sink

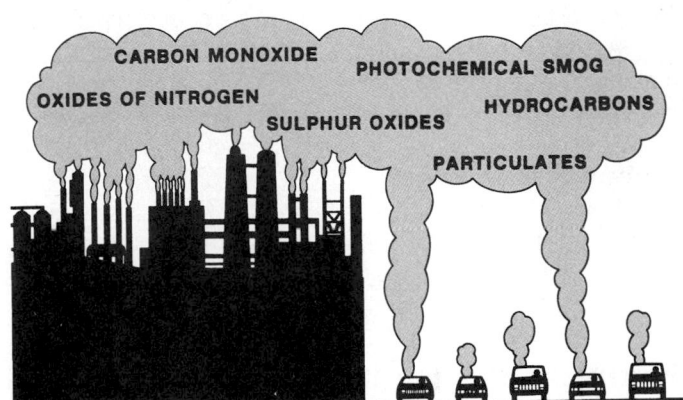

Figure 1-7. Examples of industry and vehicle air pollution. Do your best as an automotive technician to help reduce waste and air pollution. (Sun Electric Corp.)

farther into the ground every time that it rains, eventually contaminating the water table. Your local drinking water may come from this water table. Another way in which liquids can contaminate the soil and the water table is through leaking storage tanks. Although this problem is confined primarily to underground gasoline tanks, any type of tank can leak.

Liquid wastes should never be disposed of by pouring them into the local drainage system. Municipal waste treatment plants cannot handle petroleum products or the heavy metals they absorb from the vehicle during use. In most areas, such dumping is illegal. In addition, the **Environmental Protection Agency** (EPA) has established strict guidelines for disposing of toxic waste. In some cases, you may be liable for cleaning up a contaminated area years after the actual violation occurred.

In many areas, companies exist that specialize in recycling liquid wastes. These companies will accept used oil and used antifreeze for recycling. The oil and antifreeze are re-refined and reused. Some used oil is burned by power plants to produce electricity, eliminating the waste oil and reducing the dependence on imported crude oil.

Another way in which auto technicians improperly dispose of wastes is by discharging air conditioner refrigerant into the atmosphere. Studies have shown that refrigerants, such as R-12, cause extensive damage to the earth's ozone layer, leading to increased ultraviolet ray damage. Even so-called "safe" refrigerants, such as R-22 and R-134a, contribute to ozone layer loss. Therefore, federal and, in some cases, state laws require that all refrigerant be recycled. In addition to damaging the ozone layer, replacing refrigerants can be expensive. For instance, R-12 refrigerant costs over seven times as much as it did just a few years ago. Consequently, it makes good economic sense to recover and reuse refrigerants.

Automotive technicians also increase waste problems by failing to recycle. Parts that can be rebuilt, paper products, old tires, and salable scrap metals are often carelessly discarded, increasing the amount of solid waste that must be disposed of in landfills. Landfill space is becoming scarce. In many parts of the country, local trash departments will not take certain materials for disposal. Burning is illegal in most areas of the country and simply turns solid wastes into airborne wastes. It makes good economic sense to recycle because almost every rebuildable part has a return, or "core," value. The value of paper, old tires, and scrap metals will depend on the current market conditions.

Improper Vehicle Repair Procedures

Another major way in which automotive technicians may cause damage to the environment is by making adjustments or modifications that defeat the purpose of the vehicle emission control systems. This can be done by adjusting the carburetor for a richer mixture, changing the manufacturer's initial timing settings or advance curve, retrofitting older model cylinder heads to a late-model vehicle, disconnecting the engine control computer, or removing the air injection (smog) pump or the catalytic converter. In addition, some seemingly harmless actions, such as installing a lower temperature cooling system thermostat or a nonstock air cleaner, can also cause a rise in emissions. Not only are these actions illegal, but they almost never increase power and mileage as much as hoped.

Any increase in power and economy is almost always offset by increased engine wear, decreased driveability, and other problems. Automobile manufacturers have carefully thought out the function of the emission controls as part of the overall engine and vehicle design, and the technician can rarely outguess them. This is especially true of vehicles with electronic engine controls.

Modifying, disabling, removing, or otherwise tampering with engine emission controls is a federal crime, which carries harsh penalties. Vehicle emission laws are enforced by the Environmental Protection Agency (EPA). The EPA investigates suspected violations and often conducts "sting" operations to catch violators. In addition, some states, such as California, have additional laws protecting the environment.

Following Proper Environmental Procedures

The following basic rules will help make the shop and the vehicles serviced more environmentally responsible. Some of these rules are enforced by federal and state laws.

- Do not make adjustments or modifications to any vehicle system without determining the effect on emissions. It may surprise you to find out how service operations affect emissions.
- Do not discharge any type of air conditioner refrigerant into the atmosphere. Refrigerant recovery equipment should be used at every shop servicing air conditioning systems.
- Recycle parts and scrap materials whenever possible. Check with your local parts supplier to determine which parts can be sent back for rebuilding. Recyclers are often listed in the telephone book and can give you advice on what to do with recyclable materials. If solid wastes cannot be recycled, dispose of them responsibly, not by illegal dumping or burning.
- Do not pour used motor oil, transmission fluid, antifreeze, brake fluid, or gear oil on the ground or into municipal drainage systems. Many recycling companies will pick up used oil and antifreeze. Store these materials in 55-gallon drums until they can be sent to a recycler or disposed of properly.

Additional information about waste disposal and vehicle emissions can be obtained from the Environmental Protection Agency. The EPA has ten regional offices and six field offices. For the address of the nearest EPA office, write or call:

Automotive/Emissions Division
United States Environmental Protection Agency
401 M Street S.W.
Washington, DC 29460
(202) 260-7647

Tech Talk

These days, there is much talk about job security and how you must stay on your toes to keep your job. While many people feel that their jobs are in danger, most automotive technicians are not among them. There is a strong demand for qualified automotive technicians. Whether you want to fix cars, light trucks, tractor-trailers, construction equipment, or boats, you can find a job if you have the necessary skills.

Although the demand for qualified technicians is high, you must remember that no job is 100% guaranteed. Even if your skills are in demand, you must do the work right, show up on time, and meet the minimum standards of attitude and appearance. If you do these things, your boss will figure that you are worth keeping. The only way to get real job security is to do a good job.

Summary

Many accidents occur when technicians try to take shortcuts instead of following proper repair procedures. Another common cause of accidents is failing to correct dangerous conditions in the work area.

An accident may result in personal injuries, long-term bodily harm, or damage to equipment or property. No automotive technician wants to be injured or cause property damage.

There are two major areas of unsafe acts: improper shopkeeping, and improper working procedures. The best way to prevent accidents is to maintain a neat work area, use proper repair methods, and use protective equipment when needed. It is up to the technician to study the job beforehand, work safely, and prevent accidents. Always use common sense when working on vehicles.

Various types of protective equipment are needed to protect the eyes, feet, lungs, and skin. Protective equipment should guard against immediate injury and the long-term effects of exposure to toxic substances.

Much environmental damage is caused by careless production and disposal of wastes. Wastes can take the form of liquids, solids, or gases. Anyone can be a cause of pollution.

Automotive shops are a major source of environmental problems. The two main ways in which an automotive shop can cause environmental damage are carelessly disposing of wastes and repairing vehicles in such a way that they pollute the atmosphere.

Environmental rules should be followed in all instances to prevent damage to the air, water, and soil. In many cases, proper disposal of wastes and proper vehicle repairs are required by federal and state law.

Know These Terms

Accidents	Personal protective
Shopkeeping	equipment
Work procedures	Pollution
Material Safety Data	Environmental Protection
Sheets (MSDS)	Agency (EPA)

Review Questions—Chapter 1

Do not write in this book. Write your answers on a separate sheet of paper.

1. The two major areas of unsafe acts are improper _____ and improper work _____.
2. You should always wear respiratory protection when working on _____ and _____.
3. Creating a short circuit with a jumper wire or a metal tool can cause _____.
   (A) damage to vehicle electrical components
   (B) fires
   (C) personal injury
   (D) All of the above.
4. Technicians should lift heavy objects with their _____, not their backs.
5. If jackstands are not available, is it ever okay to support a vehicle with good quality cement blocks? Explain your answer.
6. Each shop electrical outlet should be used to operate _____ high-current tools?
   (A) 1
   (B) 2
   (C) 3
   (D) 4 or more
7. Material Safety Data Sheets are provided for all dangerous _____.
   (A) procedures
   (B) tools
   (C) chemicals
   (D) working conditions
8. The most important part of working safely is using _____ _____.
9. Waste can take three forms. What are they?
10. State the two main ways in which an automotive technician can cause environmental damage.

ASE-Type Questions

1. Technician A says that accidents occur in auto repair shops when technicians try to take shortcuts. Technician B says that accidents occur in auto repair shops when technicians fail to correct dangerous conditions in the work area. Who is right?
   (A) A only.
   (B) B only.
   (C) Both A & B.
   (D) Neither A nor B.
2. Some of the common accidents that occur in automotive shops are _____.
   (A) falls
   (B) fires
   (C) electric shocks
   (D) All of the above.
3. Technician A says that the best way to prevent accidents is to maintain a neat shop. Technician B says that the best way to prevent accidents is to keep an orderly workplace and to use proper methods of repair. Who is right?
   (A) A only.
   (B) B only.

   (C) Both A & B.
   (D) Neither A nor B.
4. If all equipment and tools are returned to their proper storage places, all of the following will occur, EXCEPT:
   (A) they will be hard to find the next time.
   (B) the chance of tool theft will be reduced.
   (C) the chance of tripping will be reduced.
   (D) All of the above.
5. If the safety guards have been removed from a grinder, what should you do?
   (A) Be very careful when using the grinder.
   (B) Let someone else do the grinding.
   (C) Do not use the grinder until the guards are replaced.
   (D) Wear eye protection.
6. Always use a "rough service" bulb in _____.
   (A) fluorescent droplights
   (B) incandescent droplights
   (C) every light in the shop
   (D) the ceiling lights
7. Technician A says that the technician should never use a hand socket with an impact wrench. Technician B says that the technician should never use an impact socket with a ratchet or pull handle. Who is right?
   (A) A only.
   (B) B only.
   (C) Both A & B.
   (D) Neither A or B.
8. A high-wattage bulb in a droplight can cause _____.
   (A) blindness
   (B) burns
   (C) electric shock
   (D) All of the above.
9. Spilled ethylene glycol antifreeze can cause all of the following, EXCEPT:
   (A) slipping.
   (B) poisoning.
   (C) environmental damage.
   (D) fires.
10. The technician should wear eye protection when _____.
    (A) working around running engines
    (B) using drills, saws, or grinders
    (C) working around batteries
    (D) All of the above.
11. Carbon monoxide can cause all of the following, EXCEPT:
    (A) death from asphyxiation.
    (B) damage to paint and rubber materials.
    (C) long-term respiratory system damage.
    (D) environmental damage.
12. Used antifreeze should be _____.
    (A) poured into municipal drains
    (B) poured into a pit dug in the ground
    (C) left in the sun to evaporate
    (D) stored in drums until it can be recycled
13. Technician A says that the Environmental Protection Agency (EPA) enforces rules concerning waste dis-

posal. Technician B says that the Environmental Protection Agency enforces laws concerning vehicle emissions. Who is right?

(A) A only.

(B) B only.

(C) Both A & B.

(D) Neither A nor B.

14. All of the following actions could cause vehicle emissions to increase, EXCEPT:

(A) adjusting the carburetor.

(B) changing the cooling system thermostat.

(C) changing the alternator.

(D) adjusting the ignition timing.

15. Technician A says that recycling parts makes good economic sense. Technician B says that recycling parts increases waste. Who is right?

(A) A only.

(B) B only.

(C) Both A & B.

(D) Neither A nor B.

Suggested Activities

1. Think back to any minor accidents that you have had in your life, especially accidents that have happened while working on a vehicle or doing another kind of repair work. Based on these accidents, answer the following questions:

    a. What were the results of the accidents in the way of pain and inconvenience?

    b. Was any property damaged?

    c. Could any of the accidents have been prevented if I had recognized an unsafe condition?

    d. Could any of the accidents have been prevented if I had used safe work procedures?

    Discuss your answers to these questions with the other class members.

2. Obtain a copy of the local newspaper and note the types of accidents that are serious enough to make news. Pay particular attention to accidents that occurred in the workplace. Answer the following questions for each accident.

    a. How were people hurt?

    b. How was property damaged?

    c. What caused the accident?

    d. What accident prevention steps covered in this chapter could have prevented the accident?

3. Draw a floor plan of your automotive shop. Decide where equipment should be placed to avoid accidents and provide escape routes in case of fire. Discuss your layout with other class members.

4. Locate every shop fire extinguisher in the shop and list the types of fires each is designed to put out. Draw a "map" showing the location of each fire extinguisher.

Cutaway of a late-model truck. This particular vehicle is equipped with a V-10 engine and four-wheel drive. A top-quality, extensive set of tools is needed to properly service today's complex vehicles. (Dodge)

2

Basic Tools, Equipment, and Manuals

After studying this chapter, you will be able to:
- Identify common automotive hand tools.
- Describe the proper use of automotive hand tools.
- List the safety rules for hand tools.
- Identify commonly used automotive service equipment.
- Describe the proper use of automotive service equipment.
- List the safety rules for automotive service equipment.
- Identify types of service manuals and training materials.
- Select and use the correct tools, equipment, and service manuals for a given job.

This chapter will cover the identification and use of hand tools, shop equipment, and service manuals. The many specialty tools used by automotive technicians will be discussed in the chapters where they apply.

Tools Are Important

Access to a large selection of quality tools will help you work more efficiently. Proper tools enable you to quickly perform the great number of jobs encountered by automotive technicians. The cost of the technician's labor is high. To be fair to their customers and employers, technicians cannot afford to waste time working with inadequate tools.

Buy Top-Quality Tools

If you are, or plan to become, a professional technician, rule out inferior tools. The cheaper grades are usually made of substandard material. They are often thick and cumbersome. They will fail sooner than high-quality tools and will slow your work. Due to poor finishing, inferior tools are often hard to clean.

Top-quality tools are made of alloy steel and are carefully heat-treated for great strength and long wear. They will be less bulky than second-rate tools and will generally have a smooth finish. This makes them easy on the hands and quick to clean. The working surfaces of quality tools are made to close tolerances. Repair parts and service facilities will be available. Quality tools may also be guaranteed.

There are a number of manufacturers that produce excellent tools. Selection of a specific brand must be left to the individual technician. The initial cost of good tools may be high. However, considering pride of ownership, dependability, life span, and ease of use and cleaning, high-quality tools tend to be more economical than tools of lesser quality.

Proper Care Is Essential

Efficiency and confusion cannot exist together. Therefore, it is important to keep your tools clean, orderly, and accessible. A roll cabinet, a tool chest, and a "tote" tray (small tray containing a few selected tools) will provide proper storage and accessibility. See **Figure 2-1.**

Place delicate measuring tools in protective cases. Separate cutting tools (files, chisels, drills) to prevent damage to cutting edges. Tools that rust should be lightly oiled. Place heavy tools by themselves. In general, attempt to keep frequently used tools handy. Keep sockets, open-end wrenches, and box-end wrenches together. The time it takes to keep your tools clean and orderly will be greatly offset by the time saved on the job.

Types of Tools and Equipment

The following sections detail the tools and equipment needed by the average technician. Keep in mind that other tools and equipment will be needed for specialized tasks. In other cases, some of the tools shown here will not be needed if the technician works in a very specialized shop and does only one type of work.

Hammers

A *hammer* is a basic striking tool. Ball peen, plastic, brass, lead, rawhide, and rubber hammers should be included in every technician's selection. See **Figure 2-2.** Various sizes of each type are desirable.

The *ball peen hammer* is used for general striking, installing bushings, and cutting gaskets. *Plastic, lead,* and *brass hammers* are used to prevent marring of part surfaces. When using a hammer, grasp the handle firmly. Place your hand near the handle end. Strike so that the face of the hammer engages the work squarely, **Figure 2-3.**

Figure 2-1.   Keep your tools clean and store them in a roll cabinet tool chest, such as the one shown above. These tools are arranged for display. They will fit neatly into drawers, carry boxes, etc. (Snap-on Tool Co.)

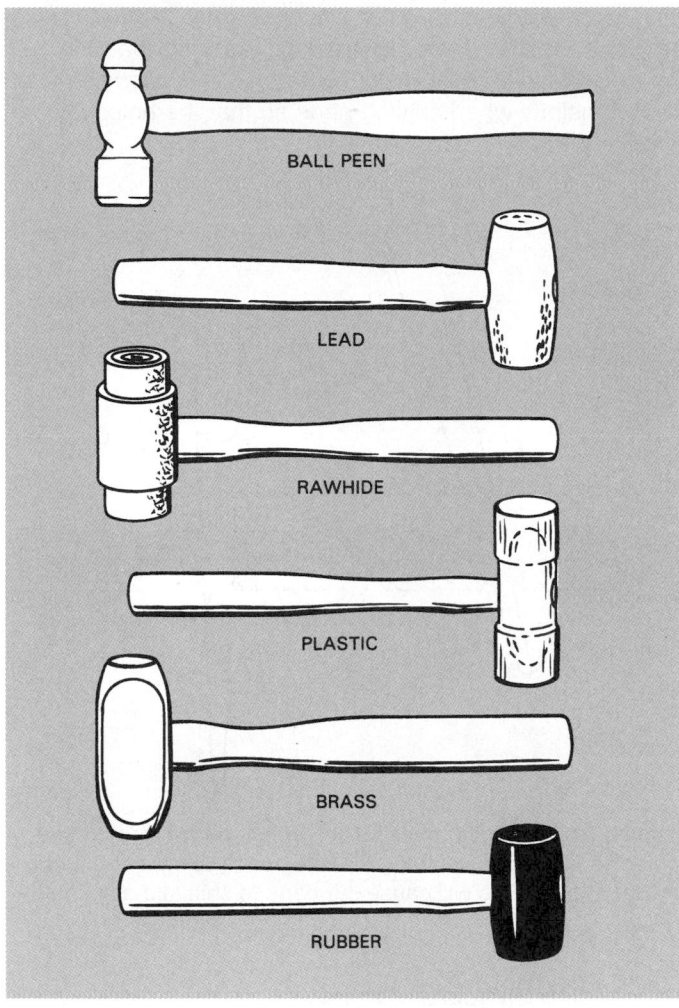

Figure 2-2. These basic hammers will cover all needs. (Deere & Co.)

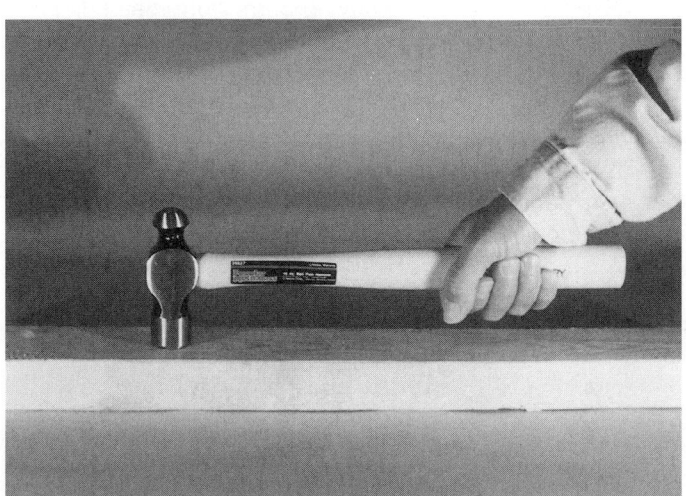

Figure 2-3. The hammer should be held close to the end of the handle. Note that the head contacts the workpiece squarely.

 Warning: Use a hammer with care. Do not swing it in a direction that would allow it to strike someone if it slipped from your grasp. Make certain that the handle is tight in the head and that the handle is clean and dry.

Chisels

Chisels are used for jobs such as cutting off rivet heads, bolts, and rusted nuts. Flat, cape, diamond, half-round, and "rivet buster" chisels should be available, **Figure 2-4.**

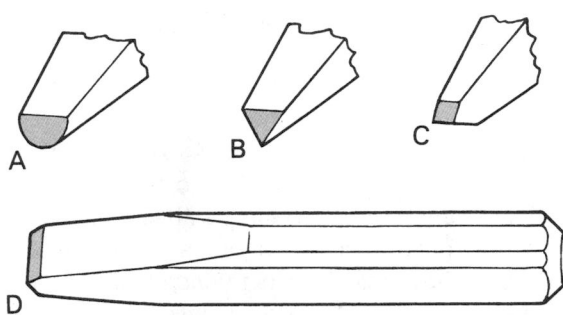

Figure 2-4. Chisels. A—Half-round. B—Diamond. C—Cape. D—Flat.

Hold a chisel securely, but not tightly. Grasp it as far from the top as practical. This will help protect your fingers if the hammer slips from the chisel head. For heavy hammering, a chisel holder should be used, **Figure 2-5.**

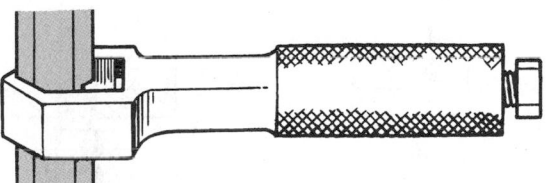

Figure 2-5. Chisel holder. In use, the handle should be kept tight.

Keep the cutting edge of the chisel sharp. Also, make sure that the top of the chisel is chamfered (edges tapered). This reduces the possibility of small chisel segments breaking off and flying outward when struck with the hammer. Wear goggles when using a chisel. Refer to **Figure 2-6.**

Punches

Punches are designed to be used with hammers to install or remove small parts. Starting, drift, and pin punches are essential. A few sections of round brass stock in varying diameters are useful for driving parts that may be damaged with steel punches.

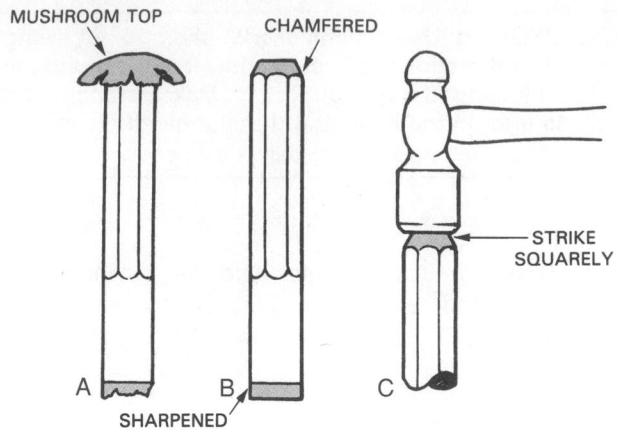

MUSHROOM TOP

CHAMFERED

STRIKE SQUARELY

A   B   C

SHARPENED

Figure 2-6. A—This chisel is dangerous to use. B—Same chisel after chamfering and sharpening. C—Be sure to strike the chisel squarely.

A *starting punch,* **Figure 2-7A,** is used to begin driving rivets, bolts, and pins from a hole. Due to its taper, the starting punch may fill the hole before the part has been completely removed. When this occurs, the job can be completed with a *drift punch,* **Figure 2-7B.** A *pin punch* is similar to a drift punch, but its driving shank is smaller in diameter. Pin punches are useful for removing pins and other fasteners that are installed in small holes, **Figure 2-7C.**

A *center punch* is used to mark work before drilling, **Figure 2-7D.** The small V-shaped indentation created by

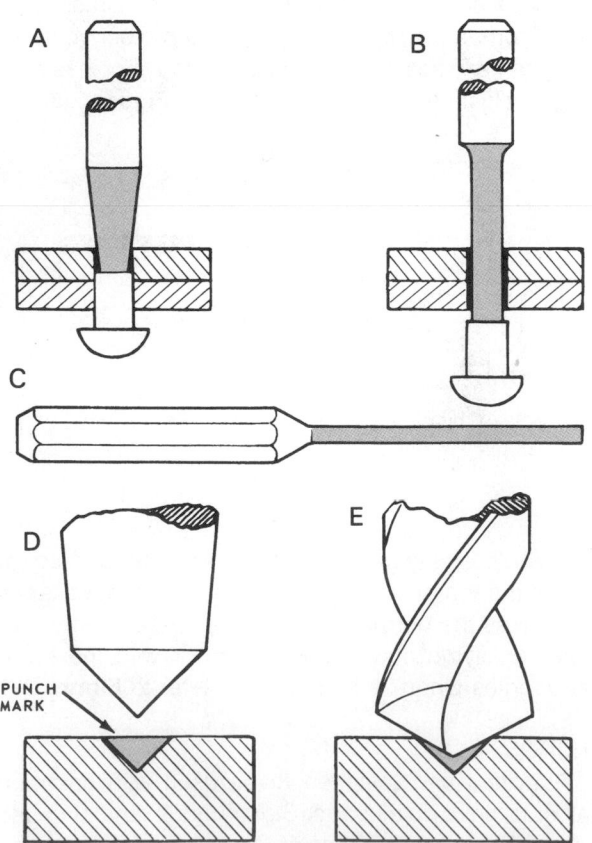

A   B

C

D   E

PUNCH MARK

Figure 2-7. Punches. A—Starting punch. B—Drift punch. C—Pin punch. D—Center punch marking work for drilling. E—Drill ready to make hole.

the punch will help align the drill bit, **Figure 2-7E.** The center punch is also useful for marking parts so that they can be assembled in their original positions. The *aligning punch* is very helpful when shifting parts so that the holes line up, **Figure 2-8.**

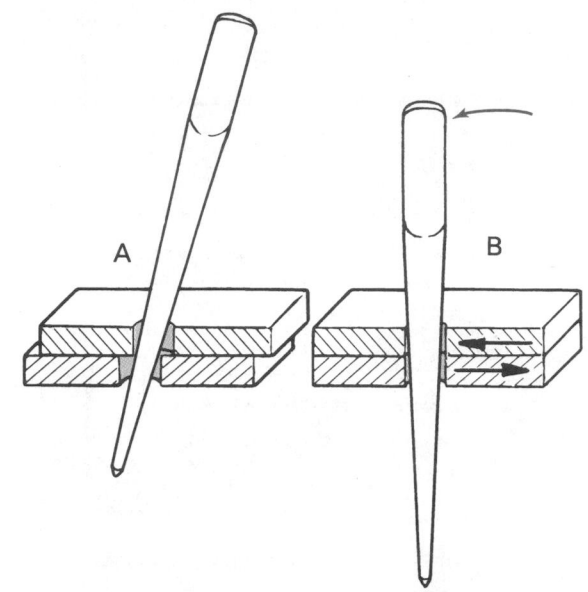

A   B

Figure 2-8. Aligning punch. A—Run the punch through the holes as far as possible. B—Pull the punch upright and force it into the holes. This will cause the parts to shift into alignment.

Sharpening Chisels and Punches

Use care when sharpening chisels and punches. Grind the tools slowly, keeping correct angles, and quench them (dip them in cold water) to prevent drawing the temper (overheating, turning the metal blue and rendering it soft). Wear goggles whenever using grinding equipment.

Files

Files are used for removing burrs from metal, final fitting after hacksawing, and smoothing out surfaces. The most frequently used files are the flat mill, round, square, triangular, and "point" files. Many other special shapes are available, **Figure 2-9.**

A file's relative size and the number of cutting edges per inch determine the file cut. In general, the softer the metal, the coarser the cut needed.

A file may be either single cut (single row of diagonal cutting edges at same angle) or double cut (two rows of

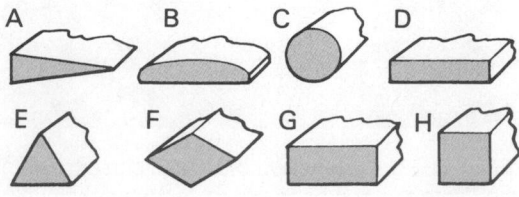

A   B   C   D

E   F   G   H

Figure 2-9. File shapes. A—Knife. B—Half-round. C—Round. D—Flat. E—Triangle. F—Slitting. G—Pillar. H—Square.

diagonal cutting edges that cross each other at an angle). Files may also be rasp cut or curve cut, **Figure 2-10.**

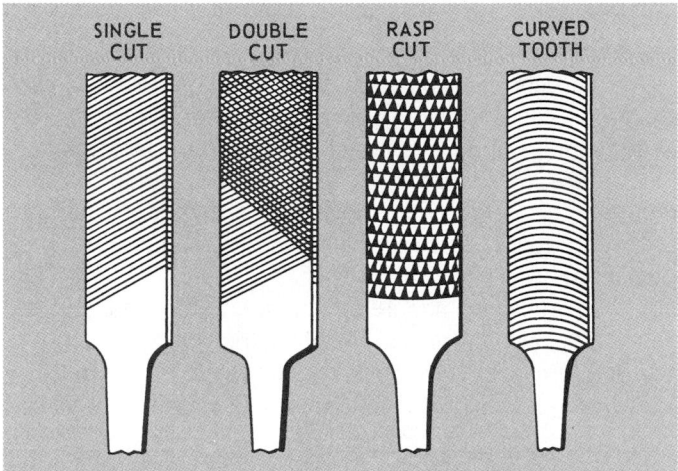

Figure 2-10. File cuts. Each type is designed for certain jobs. (Deere & Co.)

A typical single-cut mill file is pictured in **Figure 2-11.** Note the file handle! Every file should have a handle. Be sure the file handle is firmly affixed to the file's tang before using the tool. This will provide a firm grip and will eliminate the possibility of the tang piercing your hand.

The rotary file is a circular file that is chucked in a drill. This type of file is very handy for blind holes or recesses where a regular file will not work. Several useful shapes are shown in **Figure 2-12.**

Using Files

Grasp the file handle with your right hand (for right-handed persons) and hold the tip of the file with the fingers

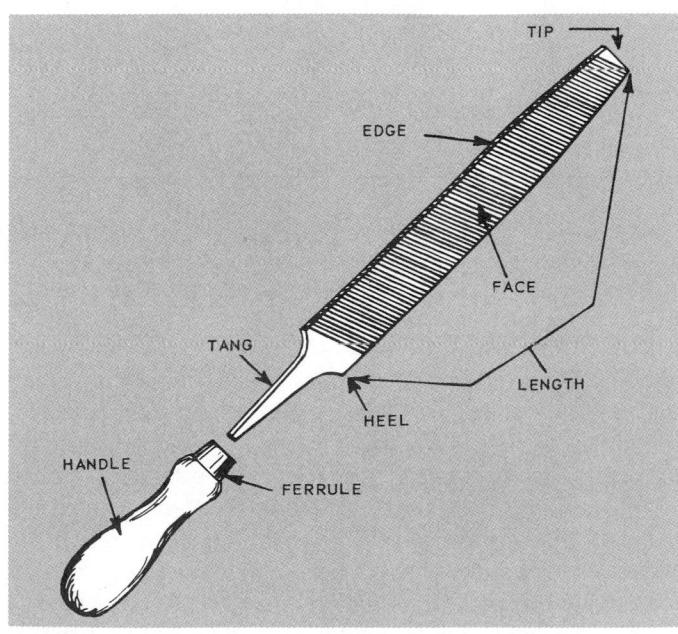

Figure 2-11. Typical single cut mill file.

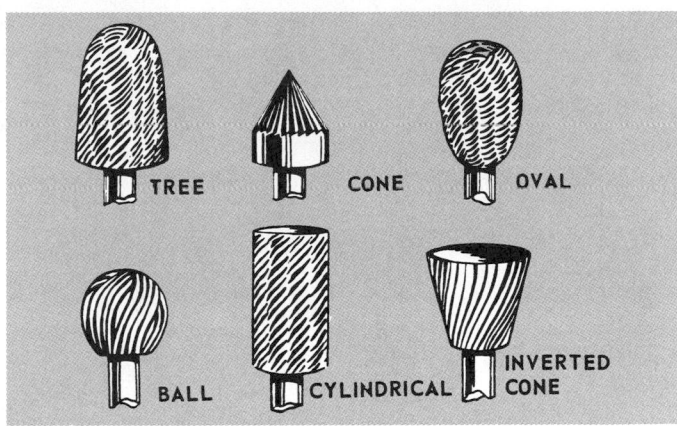

Figure 2-12. Rotary files.

of your left hand. On the forward stroke, bear down with enough pressure to produce a good cutting action. On the return stroke, raise the file to avoid damaging the cutting edges.

Control the file to prevent rocking (unless you are filing round stock). It takes practice to become skilled at filing. In the hands of a professional, a file can be used to do amazingly accurate work.

Keep the file clean and free of oil. A special wire brush, called a card file, should be used to clean the file's teeth. Chalk may be rubbed into the file to help prevent clogging.

Use a cut suitable for the work. Coarse cuts are best for soft metals, such as aluminum, brass, and lead. Finer cuts work well on steel. Your choice will also depend upon the finish desired.

Grinders

The automotive technician will often use a **grinder** to sharpen tools and rework parts. Grinding, like all shop operations, requires skill and patience. Several types of grinders are found in automotive service facilities. You should be familiar with all of them.

The *bench grinder,* **Figure 2-13A,** is mounted on the workbench and is commonly used to sharpen tools and remove stock from various parts. It is often fitted with a grinding wheel on one side and a wire wheel on the other side. A grinder that is mounted on a stand instead of on a bench is called a *pedestal grinder.*

Hand-held grinders and sanders can be fitted with grind stones, wire wheels, or abrasive discs. They are used in body and fender work, carbon and rust removal, weld smoothing and cleaning, etc. **Figure 2-13B** shows several of these power tools.

Other types of specialized grinders (brake grinders, valve grinders, crank grinders) are also found in automotive shops. The use of these tools will be discussed in the chapters relating to the work they are designed to perform.

Safety Rules for Grinders, Sanders, and Wire Wheels

If improperly used, grinders can be extremely dangerous! They can cause many serious injuries to the eyes,

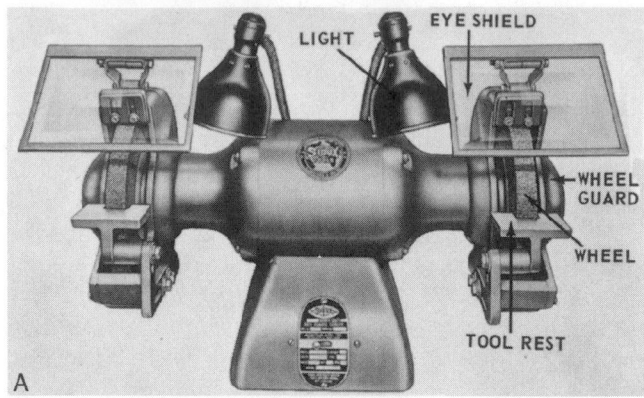

Figure 2-13. A—Bench grinder. B—Hand-held wheel grinders and disk grinders. (Ingersoll-Rand)

hands, and face. Realizing this, the competent technician must *always* observe the following safety rules when using grinding equipment:

- Protect your eyes by wearing an approved face shield or goggles.
- Keep abrasive stones tight, clean, and true.
- Allow the grinder to reach full speed before using it.
- Stand to one side of the grinder until full wheel speed is reached.
- When used, keep the tool rest as close to the wheel as possible.
- Stand to one side of the stone as much as possible.
- Keep persons without goggles away from the tool you are using.
- Hold small objects with vise-grip pliers. This will help you avoid grinding your fingers or having the object seized by the wheel and thrown violently.
- Wear leather gloves for heavy grinding.
- Never strike a grinding wheel while it is rotating. It may shatter and explode.
- Avoid grinding in the presence of explosive vapors, such as gasoline, paint thinner, or the gases from batteries.
- When installing a new stone, make certain that it is designed for the speed of the grinder.

- Keep the grinding wheel guard in place to minimize the danger of flying parts.
- Remember, grinders can be dangerous tools. Always use them with care!

Drill Bits and Power Drills

The technician will often need to drill a hole in a vehicle part. Quality **drill bits,** which are often made of high-speed steel, will do a good job of drilling on most parts of the vehicle. They can be readily ground without drawing their temper. Carbon steel twist drills are cheaper, but they require frequent sharpening and lose their temper if slightly overheated.

The technician should have a set of fractional-size drill bits (1/16″ to 1/2″) and a set of metric drill bits (1 mm to 13 mm). A typical twist drill bit is illustrated in **Figure 2-14.**

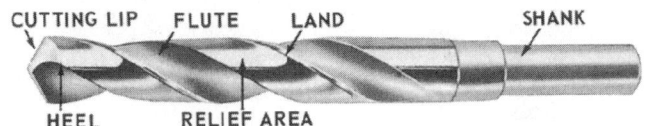

Figure 2-14.   A typical twist drill.

All technicians should have **power hand drills.** These drills can be powered by compressed air, **Figure 2-15,** or by electricity, **Figure 2-16.** The drill contains a chuck to securely hold the drill bit in position. The 3/8″ hand drill is handy for most shop drilling jobs. A 1/2″ drill will handle heavy drilling, honing, and other shop tasks requiring high drill torque.

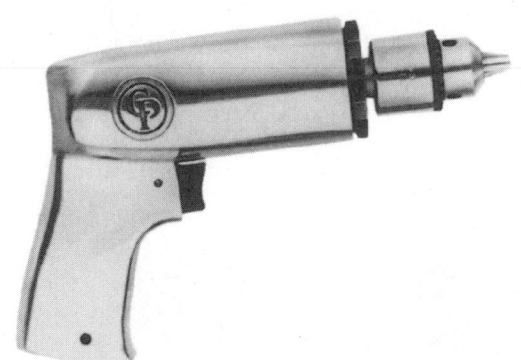

Figure 2-15.   Air-powered hand drill. (Chicago Pneumatics)

The **drill press, Figure 2-17,** is another type of electric drill. The drill motor and chuck are mounted on a stand and can be moved up and down. The workpiece is mounted on a table directly under the drill motor. The drill bit, chuck, and motor are lowered by a lever until the bit contacts the workpiece. The drill press eliminates the need to hold the drill and ensures that the drill bit will produce a hole that is properly aligned and the exact size needed. The disadvantage of the drill press is that it can only accept parts up to a certain size, and it cannot be taken to the vehicle for drilling parts that cannot be removed.

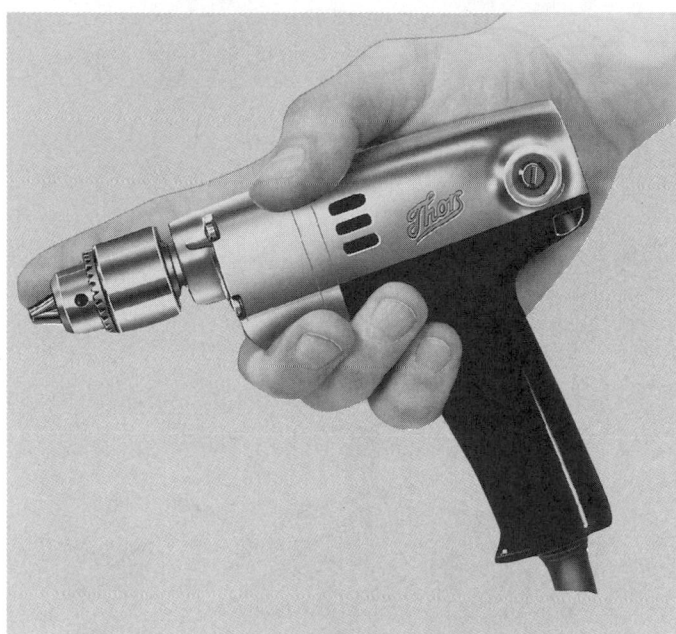

Figure 2-16. Electric hand drill. (Thor Tools)

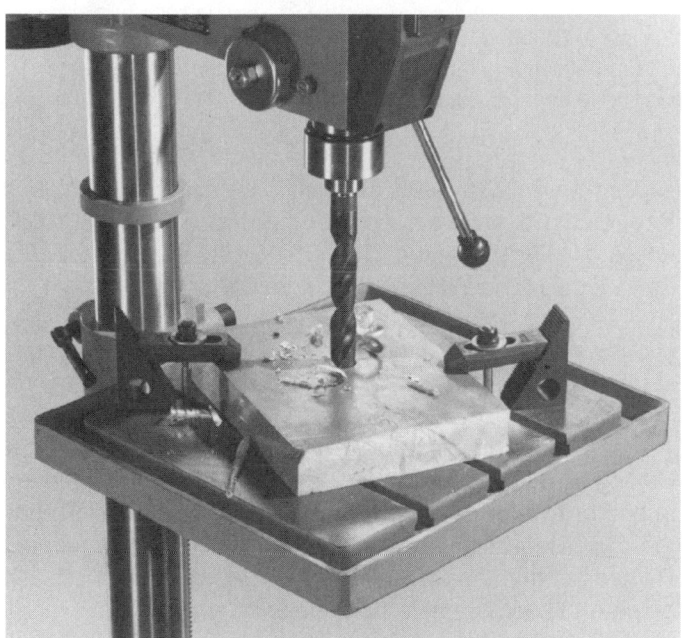

Figure 2-17. Drill press.

Using Drills

Drills are relatively easy to use, but care and attention is required to prevent injury or damage to the bit or the workpiece. Securely fasten the workpiece to the workbench or to the drill press table. Do not try to hold the piece in your hand. When using a hand drill, center punch the spot to be drilled. Chuck the drill bit tightly in the hand drill or drill press. When drilling cast iron, pot metal, aluminum, and thin body metal, cutting oil is not necessary. When drilling steel, however, a small quantity of cutting oil is helpful.

When using a hand drill, keep the drill at the proper angle and apply only enough pressure to produce good cutting action. When drilling thin stock, be careful to hold the

workpiece down, as it has a tendency to climb up the flutes of the drill bit. Just before the bit breaks through, reduce pressure on the drill to prevent grabbing and possible bit breakage.

Safety Rules for the Use of Drills

- Unplug the cord before inserting or removing a drill bit from the chuck. (If the drill starts while you are holding the chuck wrench in the chuck, it might cut your hand badly.)
- Keep loose clothing, ties, jewelry, and hair away from the drill.
- Make certain the drill is properly grounded. All electric drills have the ability to shock you.
- Never use power tools of any kind while standing on a wet surface.
- Properly secure the workpiece to be drilled. (If the drill grabs and the workpiece is loose, it can spin with a vicious cutting force.)
- Wear goggles when grinding drill bits.
- Do not use any power tool in the presence of explosive vapors.

Reamers

Reamers are used to enlarge, shape, and smooth holes. They produce a finish that is much smoother and more accurate than that produced by drilling. Some reamers may be adjusted, and others are of a fixed size. Both straight and tapered reamers are needed. They may use either straight or spiral flutes, **Figure 2-18.**

Use cutting oil when reaming. Turn the reamers in a *clockwise* direction only on entering and leaving the hole.

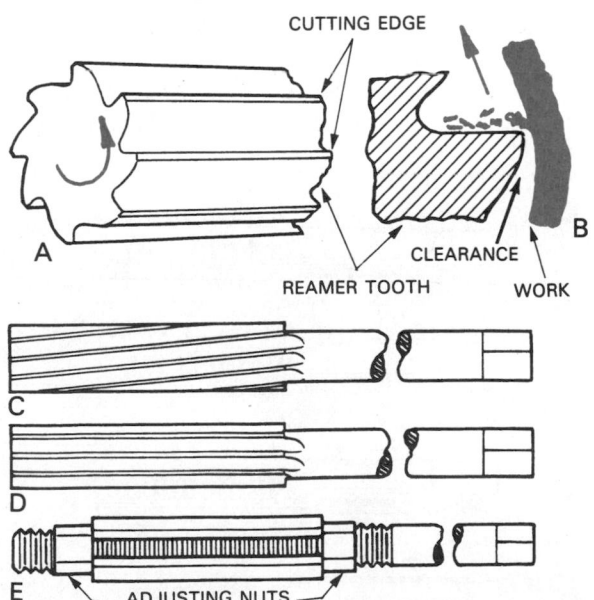

Figure 2-18. Reamers. A—Enlarged section showing reamer tooth construction. B—Reamer tooth removing stock. C—Nonadjustable, spiral flute reamer. D—Nonadjustable, straight flute reamer. E—Adjustable straight reamer. It is opened and closed by removing adjusting nuts.

Take small cuts, removing approximately .001-.002 in. (0.025-0.050 mm) during each pass. Reamers are very hard, and the cutting edges chip readily. Wipe reamers down with oil and keep them in a protective container for storage.

Taps and Dies

Taps are used for cutting internal threads. **Dies** are used to cut external threads on bolts, screws, and pipe. The technician should have a set of taps and dies covering both Unified National Fine threads and Unified National Coarse threads (sometimes called SAE or English sizes) and a full set of fine and coarse metric threads. Thread sizes are covered in the chapter on fasteners.

There are many specialized taps. Taper, plug, bottoming, and pipe taps are commonly needed for automotive service. The *taper tap* has a long chamfer (about 10 threads) that allows it to start easily. It cannot, however, be used when threads must run almost to the bottom of a blind hole. The *plug tap* has a shorter chamfer (about 5 threads). With care, it can be started successfully. It is useful for open holes and for blind holes. The *bottoming tap* has a short chamfer (about 1 thread) and is used in blind holes to finish the thread to the bottom of the hole. The *plug tap* should be used first. When it strikes bottom, the bottoming tap should be used. The *pipe tap* is tapered over its entire length (about 3/4″ per ft.). It is used to tap holes for pipe fittings. Taper, plug, bottoming, and machine screw taps are illustrated in **Figure 2-19**. Taps should always be turned with a tap handle to reduce the chance of tap breakage. See **Figure 2-20**.

Using Taps

To produce a tapped hole, determine the exact number of threads per inch and the diameter of the screw that will enter the hole. Referring to a tap drill size chart, **Figure 2-21,** select the proper tap size drill.

If, for example, you desire a threaded hole for a 7/16″ capscrew with 20 threads per inch, you will find that a 7/16″

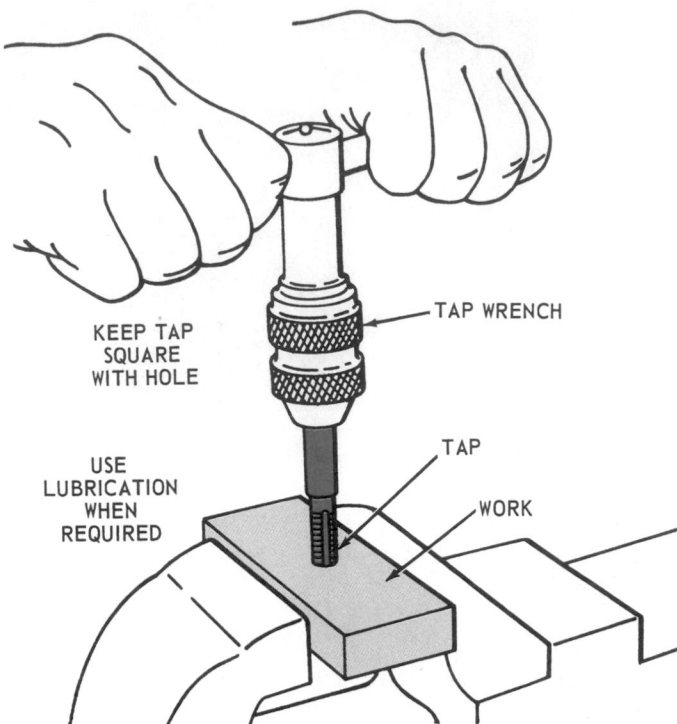

Figure 2-20. The T-handle tap wrench is the best way to turn a tap. It allows the tap to enter easily. The T-handle permits turning in tight quarters. (Deere & Co.)

capscrew with 20 threads per inch is a Unified National Fine size. Going directly across the chart from the 7/16″ UNF, notice a column marked "Tap Drill Size." In this case, the tap drill size for a 7/16″ x 20 is a 25/64″ drill.

Drill the hole with a tap size drill. Holes over 1/4″ should be drilled in at least two operations. Start with a small pilot drill about 1/8″ in diameter. Work up to the appropriate tap drill size.

Using a suitable tap wrench, carefully start the tap. Cutting oil will help when tapping steel. After running the tap in one or two turns, back it up about one half turn to break the chip. Repeat this process until the hole is fully tapped. Remember that taps are very brittle. Do not strain them and be sure to keep the hole from clogging with chips.

Using Dies

The die is used much like the tap. After selecting a die of the correct size, place it in a die stock (handle). Apply cutting oil to the bolt and start the die. Turn the die in the same manner as the tap, backing it up occasionally to break the chip.

Dies are often adjustable so the thread fit can be changed. Adjust the die so that the nut will begin threading smoothly with only light pressure. Keep taps and dies clean, oiled, and in a box.

Special-Purpose Taps and Dies

There are many special-purpose taps and dies, most of which are used to restore existing threads that have been damaged. The axle rethreader is opened up and placed

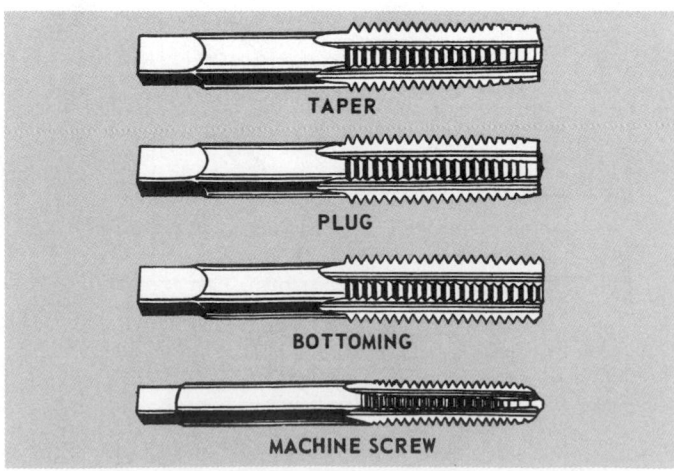

Figure 2-19. Typical taps. Amount of chamfer varies with each type. (Starret Co.)

TAP DRILL SIZES
Recommended for
AMERICAN NATIONAL SCREW THREAD PITCHES

COARSE STANDARD THREAD (N. C.) Formerly U. S. Standard Thread					SPECIAL THREAD (N. S.)				
Sizes	Threads Per Inch	Outside Diameter at Screw	Tap Drill Sizes	Decimal Equivalent of Drill	Sizes	Threads Per Inch	Outside Diameter at Screw	Tap Drill Sizes	Decimal Equivalent of Drill
1	64	.073	53	0.0595	1	56	.0730	54	0.0550
2	56	.086	50	0.0700	4	32	.1120	45	0.0820
3	48	.099	47	0.0785	4	36	.1120	44	0.0860
4	40	.112	43	0.0890	6	36	.1380	34	0.1110
5	40	.125	38	0.1015	8	40	.1640	28	0.1405
6	32	.138	36	0.1065	10	30	.1900	22	0.1570
8	32	.164	29	0.1360	12	32	.2160	13	0.1850
10	24	.190	25	0.1495	14	20	.2420	10	0.1935
12	24	.216	16	0.1770	14	24	.2420	7	0.2010
1/4	20	.250	7	0.2010	1/16	64	.0625	3/64	0.0469
5/16	18	.3125	F	0.2570	3/32	48	.0938	49	0.0730
3/8	16	.375	5/16	0.3125	1/8	40	.1250	38	0.1015
7/16	14	.4375	U	0.3680	5/32	32	.1563	1/8	0.1250
1/2	13	.500	27/64	0.4219	5/32	36	.1563	30	0.1285
9/16	12	.5625	31/64	0.4843	3/16	24	.1875	26	0.1470
5/8	11	.625	17/32	0.5312	3/16	32	.1875	22	0.1570
3/4	10	.750	21/32	0.6562	7/32	24	.2188	16	0.1770
7/8	9	.875	49/64	0.7656	7/32	32	.2188	12	0.1890
1	8	1.000	7/8	0.875	1/4	24	.250	4	0.2090
1 1/8	7	1.125	63/64	0.9843	1/4	27	.250	3	0.2130
1 1/4	7	1.250	1 7/64	1.1093	1/4	32	.250	7/32	0.2187
					5/16	20	.3125	17/64	0.2656
					5/16	27	.3125	J	0.2770
					5/16	32	.3125	9/32	0.2812
					3/8	20	.375	21/64	0.3281
					3/8	27	.375	R	0.3390
					7/16	24	.4375	X	0.3970
					7/16	27	.4375	Y	0.4040
					1/2	12	.500	27/64	0.4219
					1/2	24	.500	29/64	0.4531
					1/2	27	.500	15/32	0.4687
					9/16	27	.5625	17/32	0.5312
					5/8	12	.625	35/64	0.5469
					5/8	27	.625	19/32	0.5937
					11/16	11	.6875	19/32	0.5937
					11/16	16	.6875	5/8	0.6250
					3/4	12	.750	43/64	0.6719
					3/4	27	.750	23/32	0.7187
					7/8	12	.875	51/64	0.7969
					7/8	18	.875	53/64	0.8281
					7/8	27	.875	27/32	0.8437
					1	12	1.000	59/64	0.9219
					1	27	1.000	31/32	0.9687

FINE STANDARD THREAD (N. F.) Formerly S.A.E. Thread

Sizes	Threads Per Inch	Outside Diameter at Screw	Tap Drill Sizes	Decimal Equivalent of Drill
0	80	.060	3/64	0.0469
1	72	.073	53	0.0595
2	64	.086	50	0.0700
3	56	.099	45	0.0820
4	48	.112	42	0.0935
5	44	.125	37	0.1040
6	40	.138	33	0.1130
8	36	.164	29	0.1360
10	32	.190	21	0.1590
12	28	.216	14	0.1820
1/4	28	.250	3	0.2130
5/16	24	.3125	I	0.2720
3/8	24	.375	Q	0.3320
7/16	20	.4375	25/64	0.3906
1/2	20	.500	29/64	0.4531
9/16	18	.5625	0.5062	0.5062
5/8	18	.625	0.5687	0.5687
3/4	16	.750	11/16	0.6875
7/8	14	.875	0.8020	0.8020
1	14	1.000	0.9274	0.9274
1 1/8	12	1.125	1 3/64	1.0468
1 1/4	12	1.250	1 11/64	1.1718

TAP DRILL SIZES (METRIC)

Bolt Diameter (In mm)	Distance Between Threads (in mm)	Diameter of Drill (in mm)	Bolt Diameter (in mm)	Distance Between Threads (in mm)	Diameter of Drill (in mm)
M 2	0.4	1.6	M 22	2.5	19.5
M 2.2	0.45	1.75	M 24	3	21
M 2.5	0.45	2.05	M 27	3	24
			M 30	3.5	26.5
M 3	0.5	2.5			
M 3.5	0.6	2.9	M 33	3.5	29.5
M 4	0.7	3.3	M 36	4	32
M 4.5	0.75	3.7	M 39	4	35
			M 42	4.5	37.5
M 5	0.8	4.2			
M 6	1	5	M 45	4.5	40.5
M 8	1.25	6.8	M 48	5	43
M 10	1.5	8.5	M 52	5	47
M 12	1.75	10.2	M 56	5.5	50.5
M 14	2	12	M 60	5.5	55
M 16	2	14	M 64	6	58
M 18	2.5	15.5	M 68	6	62
M 20	2.5	17.5			

Figure 2-21. Tap drill size chart. (Deere & Co.)

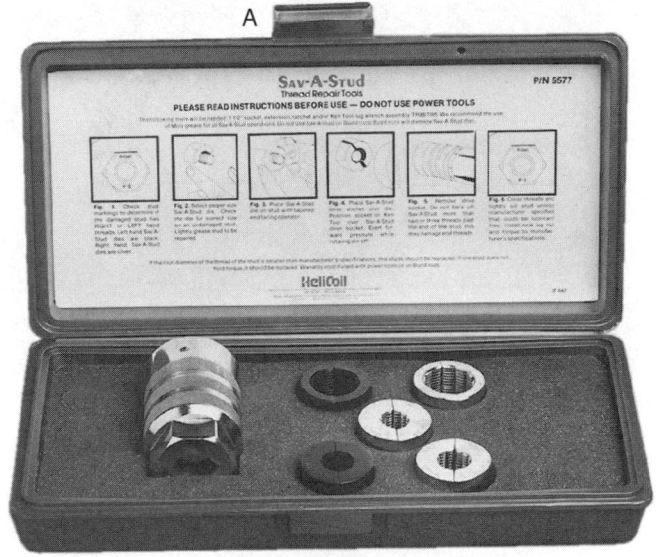

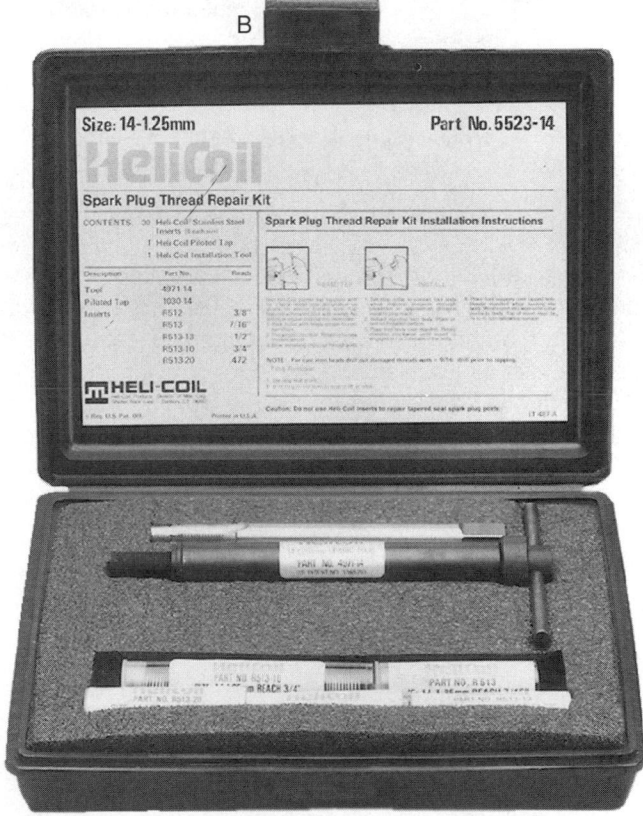

Figure 2-22. Special-purpose taps and dies. A—External rethreading set. B—Internal thread restorer.

around the good threads, **Figure 2-22A.** It is then backed off to restore damaged threads. In addition to repairing damaged threads, spark plug hole thread restorers are handy for removing rust and carbon. See **Figure 2-22B.**

Hacksaws

A **hacksaw** is used to cut tubing, bolts, and other parts. The technician should have blades with 18, 24, and 32 teeth per inch. The 18-tooth blade is used for cutting thick metal, the 24-tooth blade is used for cutting steel of medium thickness, and the 32-tooth blade is used for cut-ting thin sheet metal and tubing. For very thick work, a 14-tooth blade can be used. The blades should be of high-quality steel. High-quality blades will cut faster and last longer than low-quality blades. **Figure 2-23A** illustrates a typical hacksaw frame.

A *jab saw* is a special hacksaw that facilitates cutting in tight quarters. A *hole saw,* which is driven with an electric drill, is handy for cutting large holes in sheet metal. See B and C in **Figure 2-23.**

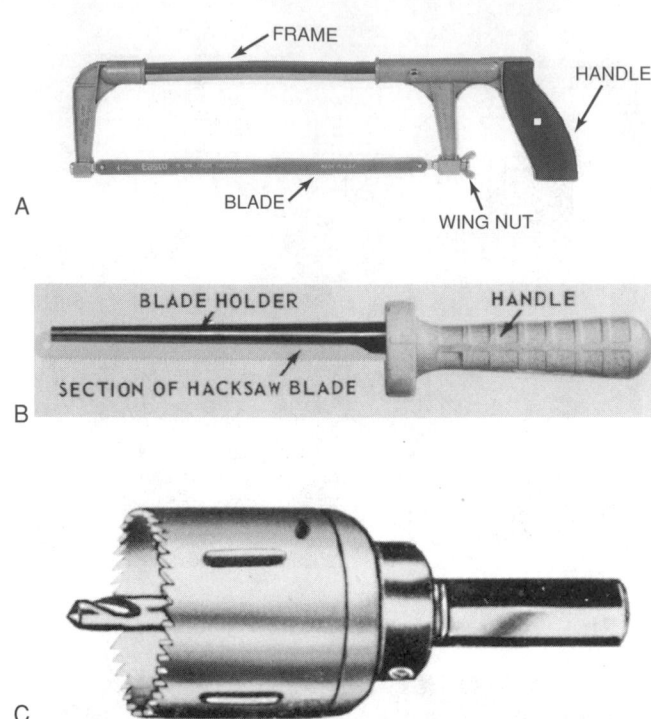

Figure 2-23. Hacksaws. A—Hacksaw frame. B—Jab saw. C—Hole saw. (Owatonna Tool Corp., Snap-on Tools)

Vises

Vises are used to hold parts securely so that other work, such as drilling, cutting, or filing, may be done. A vise suitable for automotive work is pictured in **Figure 2-24.** Keep the vise clean. Use copper, lead, or nylon *jaw covers* for work that is easily marred. Oil the working parts of the vise and avoid hammering on the handle or other surfaces.

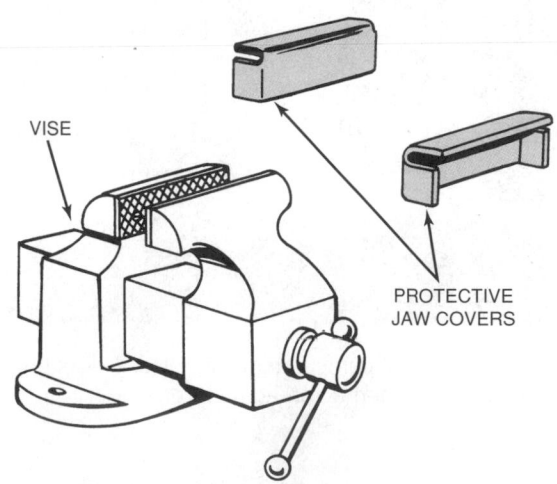

Figure 2-24. Typical bench vise. Note the soft jaw covers.

Cleaning Tools

A number of useful **cleaning tools** are illustrated in **Figure 2-25.** Having a selection of these tools speeds up cleaning work. Scrapers and brushes are used by hand. The wire wheel and power cleaning brushes are mounted in an electric drill.

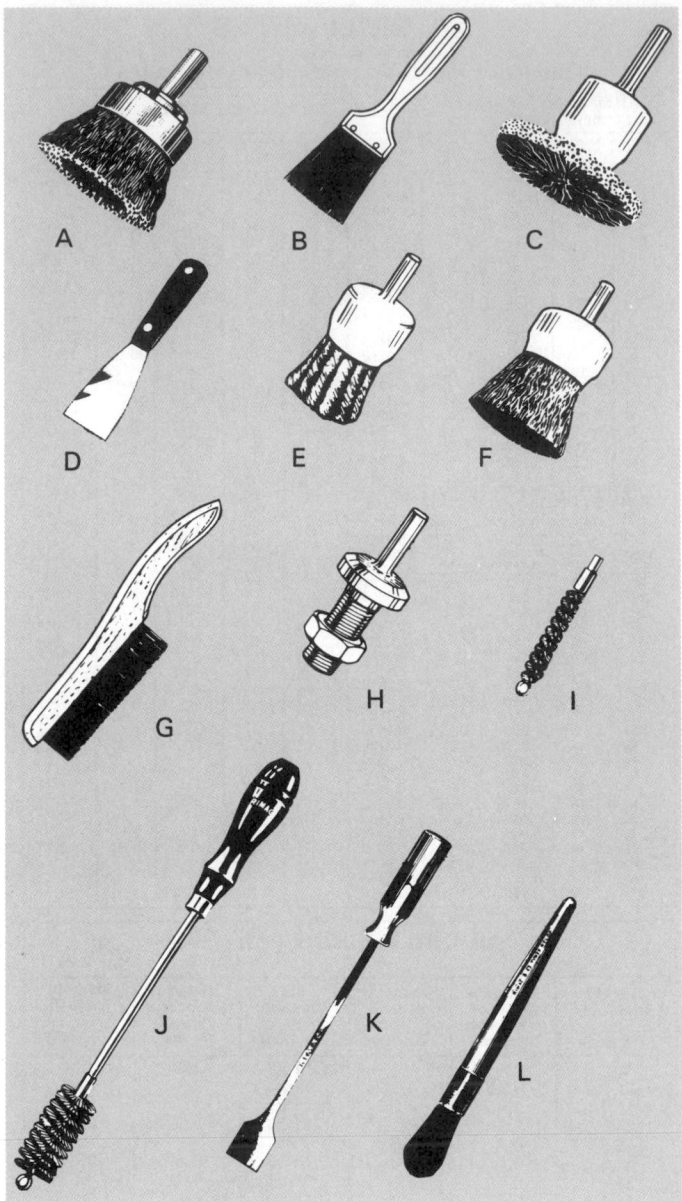

Figure 2-25. Cleaning tools. A—Hollow carbon brush. B—Wire brush. C—Wire wheel. D—Flexible scraper. E—Twisted strand wire brush. F—Bristle head. G—Hand wire scratch brush. H—Arbor for wire wheel. I—Carbon brush. J—Bristle brush and holder. K—Rigid scraper. L—Cleaning brush with nylon bristles.

 Warning: Use goggles when operating the wire wheel and when cleaning with caustic solutions. Small particles and cleaning solutions can cause serious eye damage.

Screwdrivers

The technician should own several different sizes and types of **screwdrivers,** including the *standard, Reed & Prince, Phillips, Torx,* and *clutch* types, **Figure 2-26.** Different lengths are also desirable because screws are often located in areas that are only accessible to long- or short-shank screwdrivers. The *offset screwdriver,* shown in **Figure 2-27,** is useful in tight quarters where even a short-shank screwdriver cannot be used.

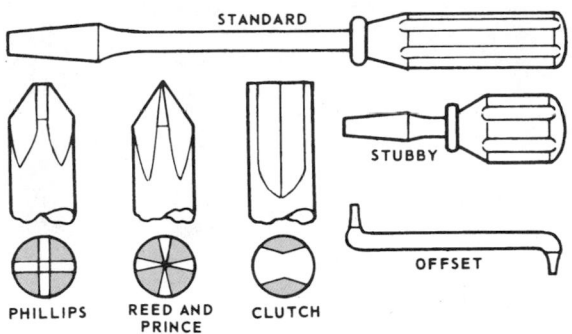

Figure 2-26. Screwdriver types. When using screwdrivers, select right type and size. A good assortment is essential.

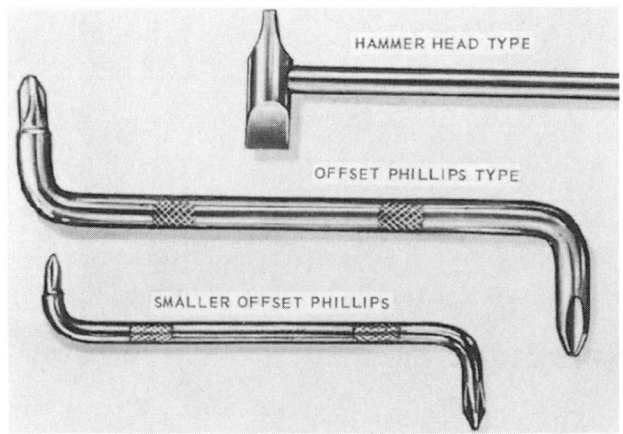

Figure 2-27. Offset screwdrivers.

Using Screwdrivers

Screwdrivers are made to remove and install screws. Avoid prying with or hammering on a screwdriver. However, some very large screwdrivers are made so that minor prying and hammering will not harm them.

 Warning: When holding small screws in your hand, do not push down on the screwdriver handle. The tip of the screwdriver may slip from the fastener and pierce your hand.

When grinding a new tip on a standard tip screwdriver, maintain the original taper. Do not grind it to a sharp point or to a steep taper. This will weaken the tip or allow it to climb out of the slot. See **Figure 2-28.** Avoid overheating the tip.

Pliers

Pliers are commonly used for jobs involving gripping, crimping, and bending. Some types of pliers are also used for cutting wire. The *slip-joint, vise-grip, adjustable, long-nose, needle-nose, diagonal,* and *side-cutter pliers* are most often used, **Figure 2-29.** Other pliers for special purposes, such as removing or installing snap rings, hose clamps, or brake springs, will be covered in later chapters. Two special-purpose pliers are shown in **Figure 2-30.** Avoid using pliers to cut hardened objects. Never use pliers to turn nuts, bolts, or tubing fittings.

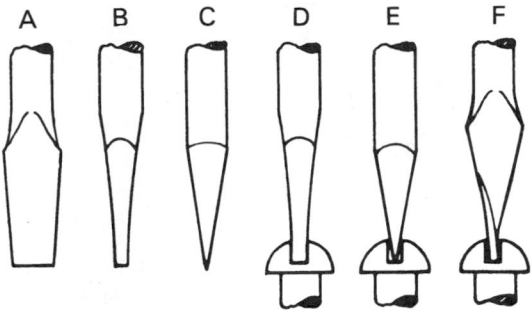

Figure 2-28. Correct sharpening is important. A and B—Front and side view of correct shape. C—Too steep and sharp. D—Correct taper and size. E—Steep angle will "climb out" of screw slot. F—Screwdriver ground too thin; it will twist off.

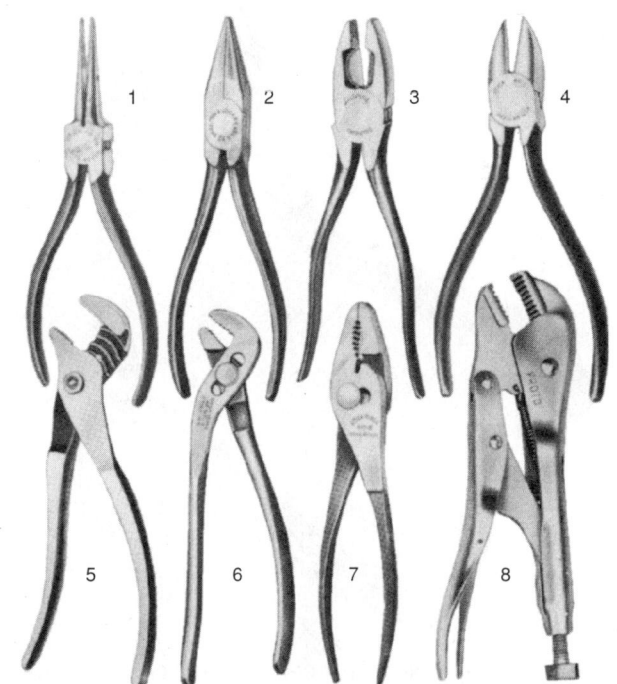

Figure 2-29. Useful pliers. 1—Needle nose. 2—Chain nose. 3—Electrician. 4—Diagonal. 5—Rib joint. 6—Ignition. 7—Combination slip joint. 8—Vise-grips. (Utica and Proto Tools)

Wrenches

The term **wrench** is used to refer to a large group of devices used to remove bolts and capscrews. *Box-end wrenches* are available with 6-point or 12-point openings. Although the 12-point opening allows a shorter swing of the tool, the 6-point opening provides superior holding power. One design uses a double offset to give more handle clearance. Another has a 15° offset. Different lengths and a complete range of opening sizes are needed, **Figure 2-31.** A ratchet tool using a box-end design is shown in **Figure 2-32.** It has many applications and speeds up fastener removal.

The *flare nut wrench,* or *tubing wrench,* is similar to the box-end wrench. However, it has a section cut out so that it may be slipped around tubing and dropped over the tubing nut. The tubing wrench has either 6-point or 12-point openings and is a must for fuel, vacuum, brake, and other fittings. Refer to **Figure 2-33.**

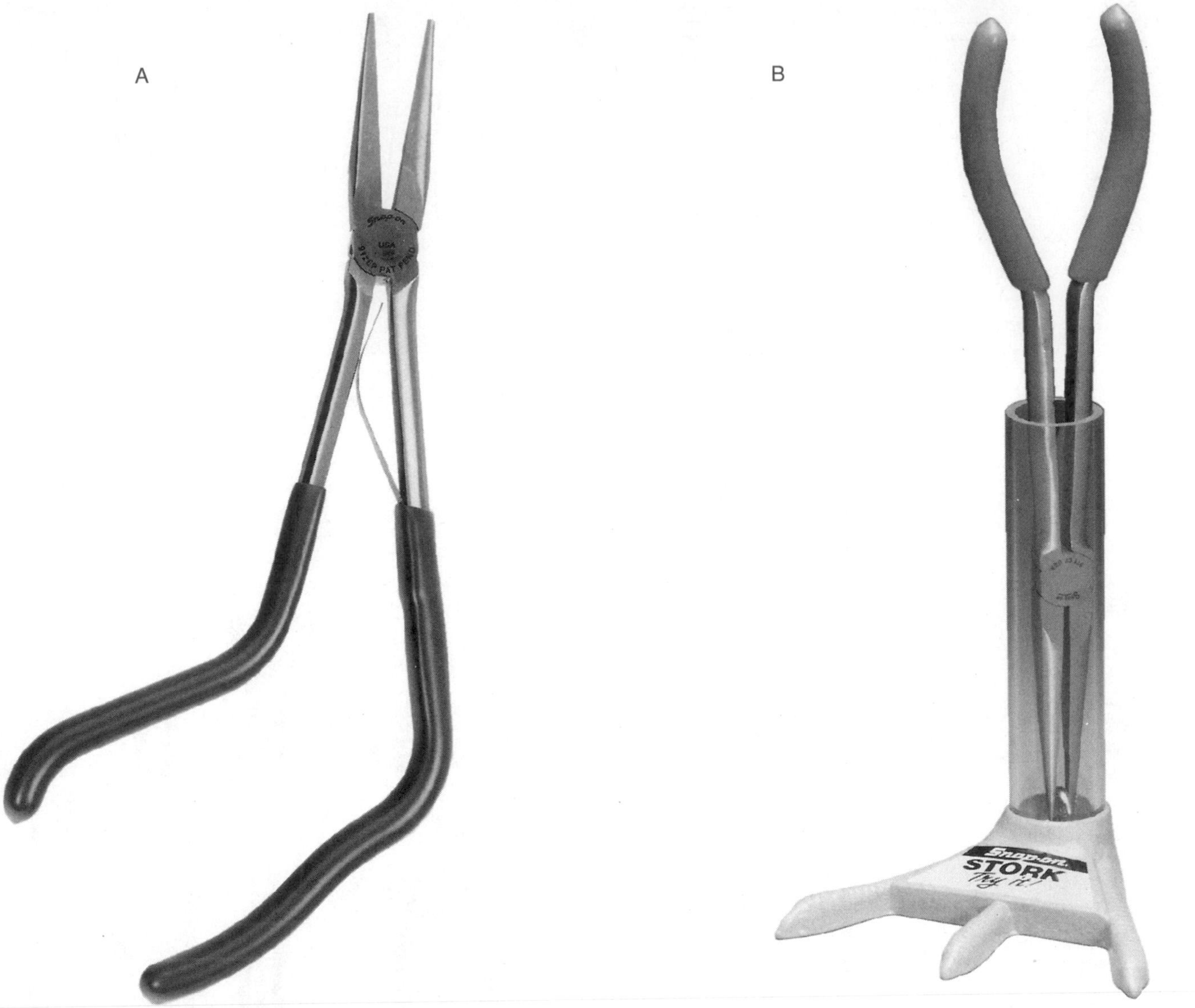

A

B

Figure 2-30.   A—Pistol-grip, needle nose pliers that provide additional hand clearance when using in tight areas. B—Long-reach needle nose pliers. These are handy for retrieving hard-to-reach fasteners, springs, etc.

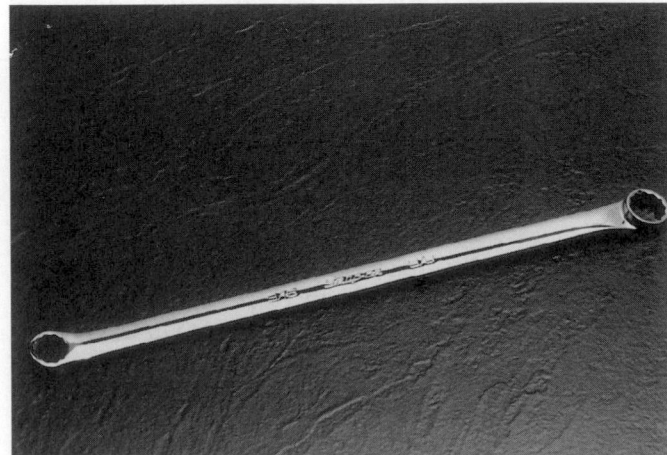

Figure 2-31.   A 12-point box-end wrench with a 15° head offset, which will allow wrench access to fasteners in close groups. (Snap-on Tools)

Figure 2-32.   Ratchet box-end wrench. To reverse ratchet action, flip the wrench over. (Snap-on Tools)

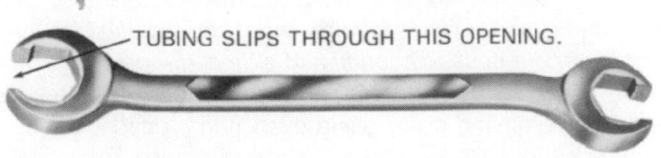

TUBING SLIPS THROUGH THIS OPENING.

Figure 2-33.   Flare nut wrench. Note opening for tubing. (Owatonna Tool Co.)

The *open-end wrench* grasps the nut on only two flats. Unless it fits well, it can slip, rounding off the corners of the nut. There are many places where you can use open-end wrenches. Whenever possible, however, use a box end or socket instead.

The heads of most open-end wrenches are set at an angle, **Figure 2-34.** In tight quarters where handle swing is limited, pull the handle as far as it will go. Then, flip the wrench over and replace it on the fastener. By this method, the open end can operate in a wider arc than it could if the head of the wrench were straight. The *combination wrench* is closed on one end and open on the other. Both ends are the same size, **Figure 2-35.**

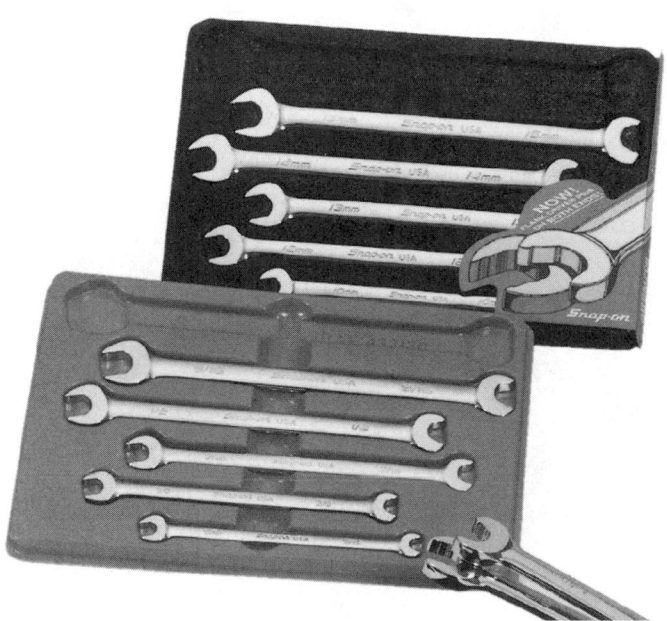

Figure 2-34. This set of open-end wrenches contains both SAE and metric sizes.

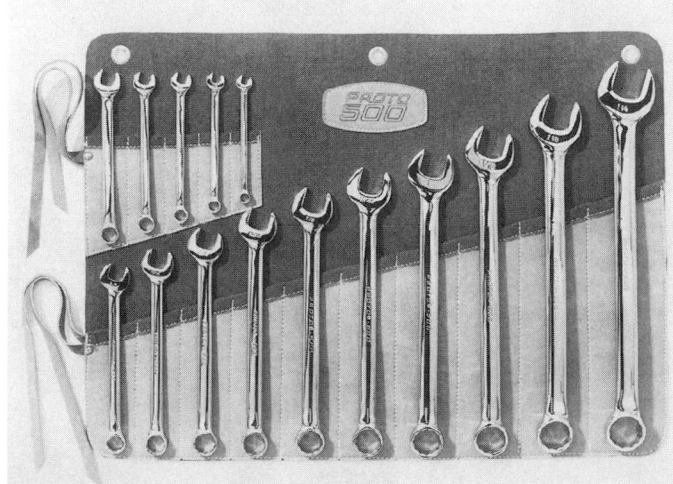

Figure 2-35. Combination wrench.

Sockets

Sockets are used with drive handles, such as a ratchet handle, to loosen and tighten fasteners. One opening of the socket fits over the fastener and the other opening is attached to the drive handle. Sockets are available with 6-point or 12-point fastener openings. *Drive size* indicates the size of the square drive opening in the socket. The technician should have 1/4″ drive sockets for small fasteners, 3/8″ drive sockets to handle the medium sizes, and 1/2″ drive sockets for larger fasteners. The technician may also need a 3/4″ drive set for very large fasteners.

Sockets are manufactured in two depths: standard and deep. Standard sockets will handle the bulk of the work, while the extra reach of the deep socket is occasionally needed for such things as oxygen sensors and oil pressure switches, **Figure 2-36.**

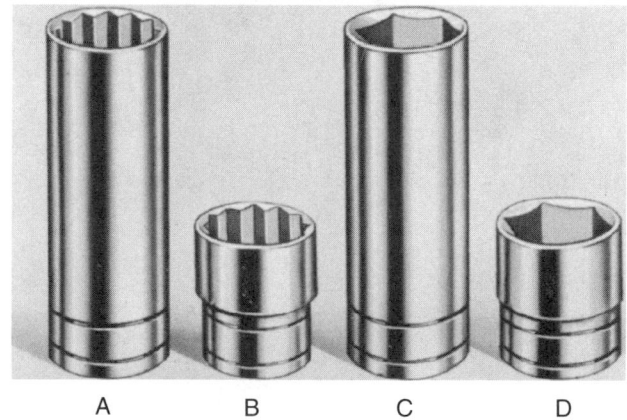

| A | B | C | D |

Figure 2-36. Various sockets. A—12-point deep socket. B—12-point standard socket. C—6-point deep socket. D—6-point standard socket. (Snap-on Tools)

Impact sockets are used with air- or electric-powered impact wrenches. They are available as either six- or twelve-point sockets and are made with heavy sidewalls, **Figure 2-37.** The heavy sidewalls help to protect the socket against the extreme strains caused by using them with an impact wrench. Standard sockets should never be used with impact wrenches because they can break violently.

Figure 2-37. Impact sockets are designed to withstand the tremendous torque produced by the impact wrench. (Snap-on Tools)

Impact sockets can, however, be used with non-powered socket handles.

The *swivel socket* allows the user to turn a fastener that is at an angle other than 90° to the drive handle. As a result, it is handy for many jobs where clearances are tight, **Figure 2-38.**

Drive Handles

Several different **drive handles** are used with sockets. The *ratchet handle* allows both heavy turning force and speed. The fastener can be turned in or out by moving a lever on the ratchet. The ratchet is also useful in areas where a limited swing is necessary, **Figure 2-39.** The *speed handle* is used whenever possible because it can be turned rapidly. See **Figure 2-40.**

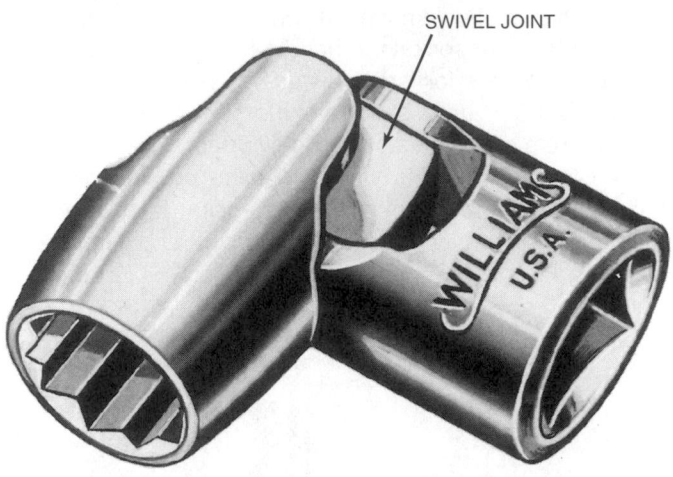

Figure 2-38. A 12-point swivel socket. (Williams Tool Co.)

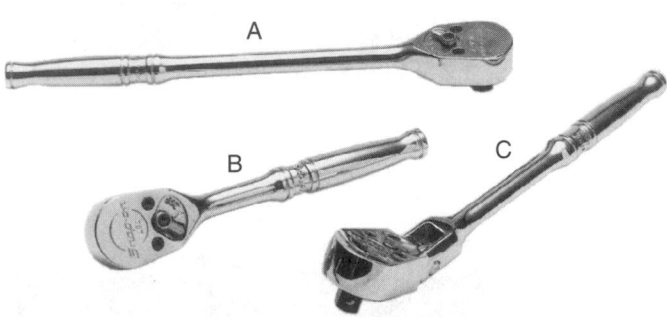

Figure 2-39. A selection of ratchets. A—Standard ratchet handle. B—Short handle. C—Swivel-head ratchet. The swivel head allows 180° of head rotation. (Snap-on Tools)

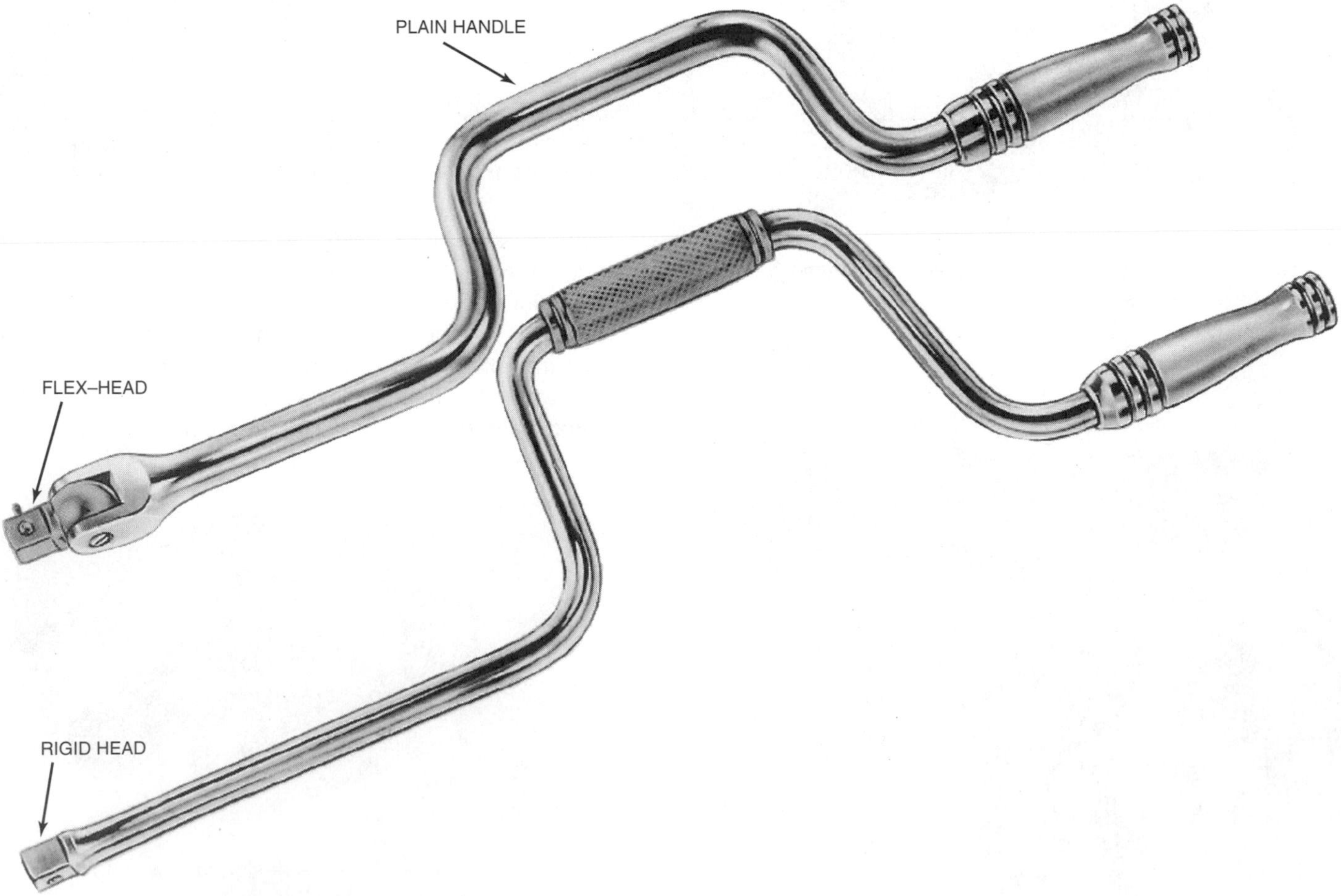

Figure 2-40. Socket speed handles. (J.H. Williams)

Flex handles of different lengths provide heavy turning leverage and may be used at many angles, **Figure 2-41.** The *sliding T handle* has some applications and should be included in a socket set, **Figure 2-42.** *Spinner handles* are used in the same manner as screwdrivers and will accept all sockets or attachments. See **Figure 2-43.**

Figure 2-41.   Socket flex handle. (Owatonna Tool Corp.)

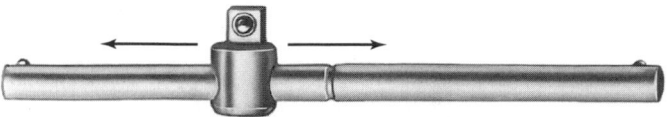

Figure 2-42.   Socket sliding T-handle.

Figure 2-43.   Socket spinner handle.

Impact Wrenches

An **impact wrench,** used in conjunction with impact sockets, speeds up most jobs. Using an impact wrench also makes fastener removal less tiring. Impact wrenches can be the familiar air gun type, **Figure 2-44A,** or the ratchet handle type, **Figure 2-44B.** Most impact wrenches used in shops are pneumatic (powered by air pressure). Some electric impacts are also used, often when there is no handy source of compressed air. See **Figure 2-45.**

Impact wrenches are usually equipped with 3/8″ or 1/2″ drives to accept 3/8″ and 1/2″ drive sockets respectively. Heavy-duty impact wrenches often have 3/4″ or 1″ drives. Always use impact sockets when using an impact wrench. Standard sockets should never be used with impact wrenches.

Socket Attachments

Long, medium, and short **extensions** allow the user to extend the reach of the tool. They may be used singly or snapped together, **Figure 2-46.**

The universal joint will permit driving fasteners at different angles with the various socket handles. See **Figure 2-47.** An adapter allows sockets of one particular drive size to be turned with a drive handle of another size, **Figure 2-48.** Screwdriver, drag link, and crowfoot socket attachments are a few of the many attachments offered. Refer to **Figure 2-49.**

Specialty Wrenches

The **specialty wrenches** described in the following sections are used on nonstandard fasteners or when clearances will not allow the use of the wrenches discussed above. The *flex-head wrench* is a valuable addition to the toolbox. It can be used through various angles and in cramped quarters, **Figure 2-50.**

Several types of *stud wrenches* are available to remove studs from large parts, such as blocks, heads, or exhaust manifolds. When using a stud wrench, be careful not to damage the threads on the stud. See **Figure 2-51.**

A

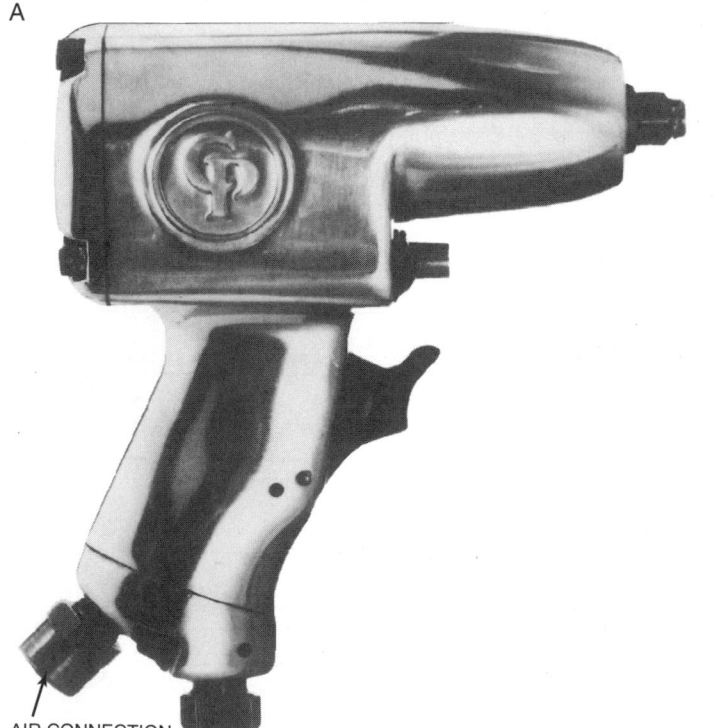

AIR CONNECTION

B

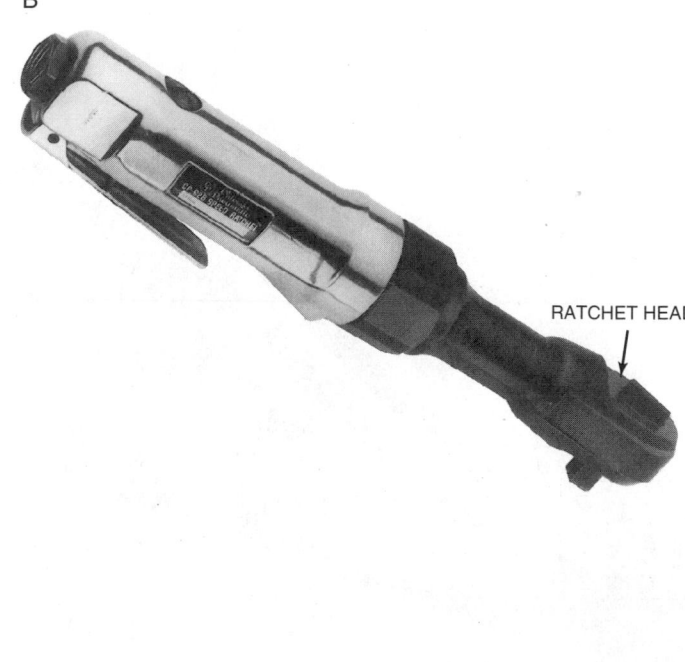

RATCHET HEAD

Figure 2-44. A—Gun-type 1/2″ drive impact wrench. B—Ratchet-type 3/8″ drive impact wrench.

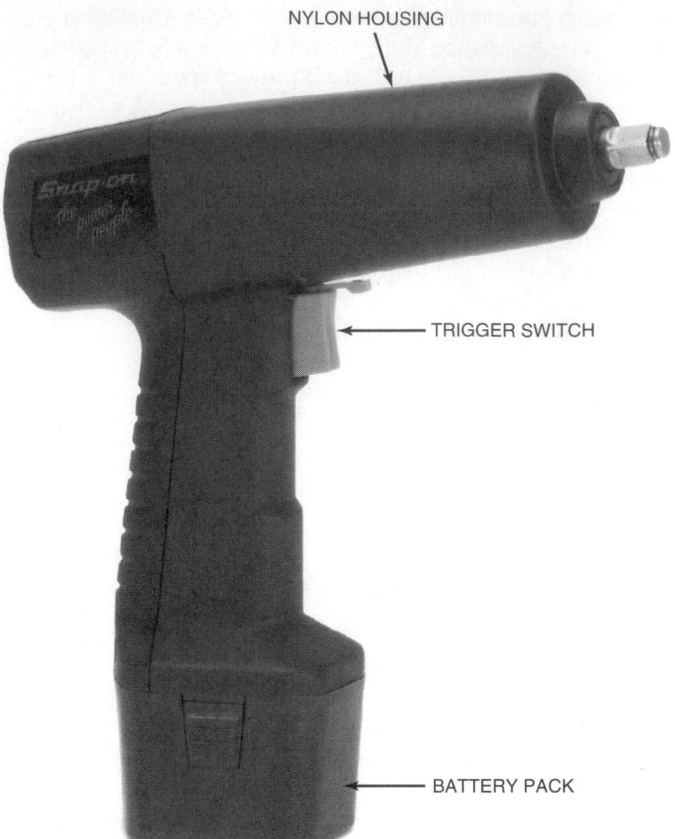

Figure 2-45.   A cordless, 3/8″ drive, electric impact wrench. This wrench produces 50 ft. lb. of torque and has a housing produced from glass-filled reinforced nylon.

Figure 2-46.   Socket extension bars. Note the knurling, which provides additional finger gripping power. (Snap-on Tools)

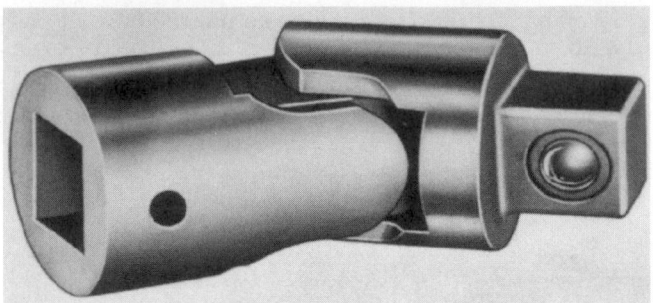

Figure 2-47.   Socket universal joint.

Figure 2-48.   Socket adapter.

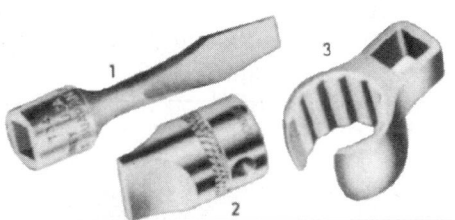

Figure 2-49.   Other socket attachments. 1—Screwdriver. 2—Drag link. 3—Crowfoot. (Bonney Tools)

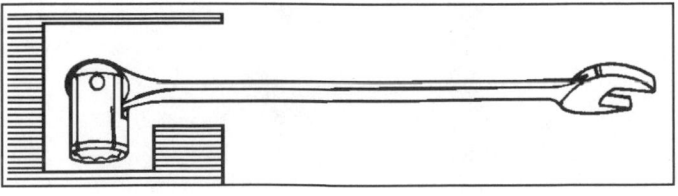

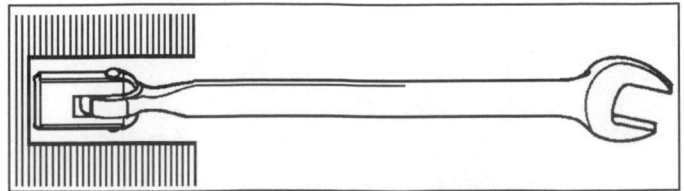

Figure 2-50.   Flex-head wrench. (Snap-on Tools)

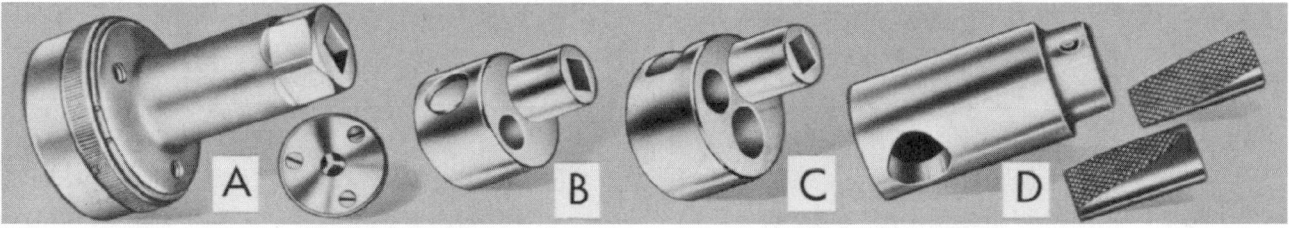

Figure 2-51. Stud wrench types. A—Three jaw. B—Wedge type. C—Rotating lock wheel. D—Wedge type for tight quarters. (Snap-on Tools)

The *adjustable wrench* is a useful tool. Its size may be readily changed to that of the fastener. However, it tends to loosen and slip. When other wrenches are available, use them. Refer to **Figure 2-52.**

The *pipe wrench* is used to grasp irregular or round surfaces. It provides great gripping power. Both inside and outside pipe wrenches are available. Look at **Figure 2-53.**

The *chain wrench* is extremely handy for holding or turning large, irregularly shaped objects, **Figure 2-54.** Similar wrenches employ a fabric strap in place of the chain. These tools are called strap wrenches.

Allen wrenches and *fluted wrenches* are used to turn setscrews and capscrews that have recessed or internal heads. See **Figure 2-55.**

> **STOP** **Warning: When using any wrench, make certain that it is the correct size and is securely engaged. Pull on the wrench handle, do not push. If pushing is absolutely necessary, open your hand and push with your palm. Be careful. If a wrench slips, you can be seriously cut.**

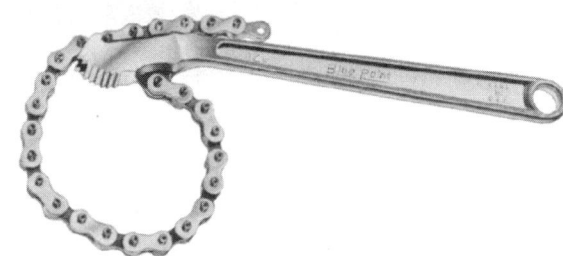

Figure 2-54. Chain wrench. This wrench is very handy for turning large, irregular-shaped objects. (Blue Point)

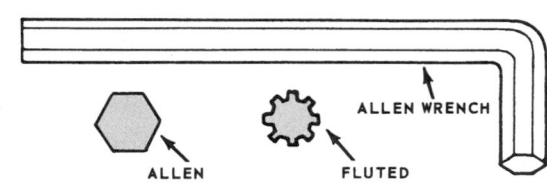

Figure 2-55. Allen and fluted wrenches.

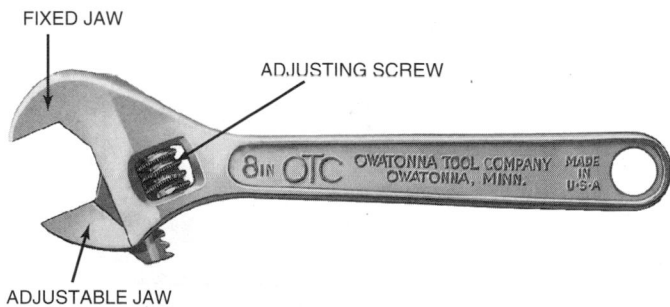

Figure 2-52. Adjustable wrench.

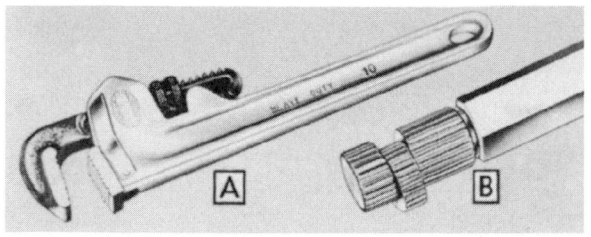

Figure 2-53. Pipe wrenches. A—Outside pipe wrench. B—Inside pipe wrench.

Screw Extractors

A *screw extractor* is often needed to remove the threaded portion of a capscrew that has broken off inside a hole. One type of screw extractor is shown in **Figure 2-56.**

Probing Tools

Probing tools, such as mechanical fingers, extension magnets, and mirror devices, help the technician to retrieve parts and to see in blind areas, **Figure 2-57.**

Hydraulic Presses

Hydraulic presses can be used to remove bearings, straighten shafts, and press bushings. The press is superior to striking tools because the pressure is smooth and controlled. The workpiece is not "upset" by the shock of hammer blows, and enormous pressures can be generated. **Figure 2-58** illustrates a typical hydraulic press with a movable table. When using a hydraulic press, make sure that the table pins are in place and the table winch is slacked off. Failure to do this can break the winch gear or cable.

Portable Hydraulic Power Unit

There are many occasions when heavy, controlled pressures are needed for part alignment and body work. The portable hydraulic power set, **Figure 2-59,** includes a num-

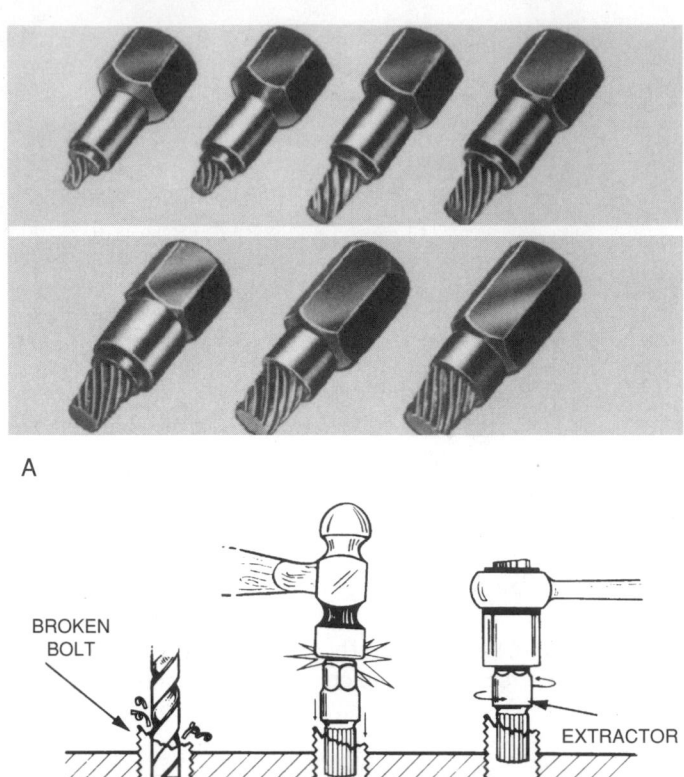

A

B

Figure 2-56. A—Screw extractors are available in various sizes. B—Extractor being used to remove a broken bolt. (Snap-on Tools & Lisle)

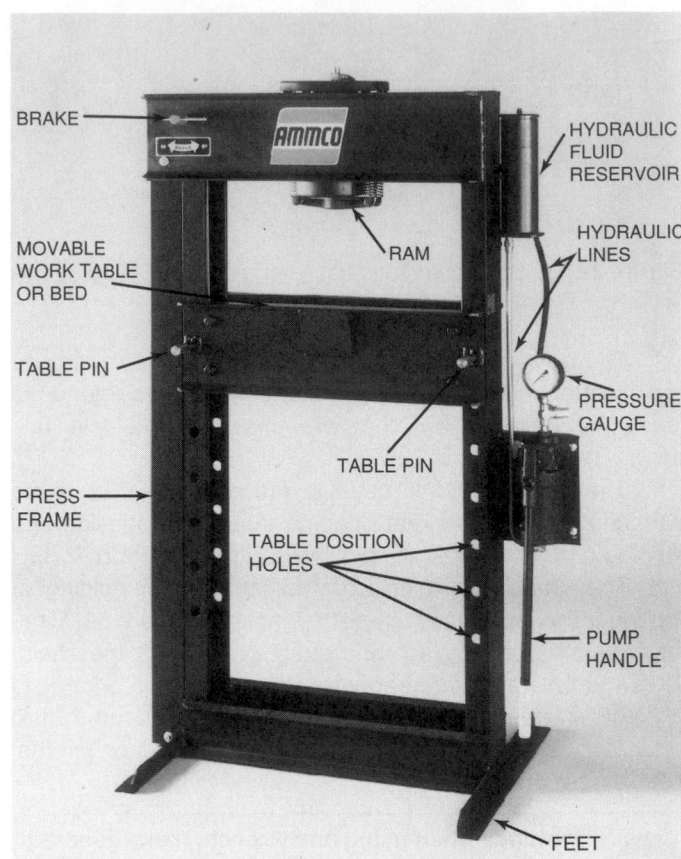

Figure 2-58. Typical hydraulic press with a movable table. (Ammco Tools)

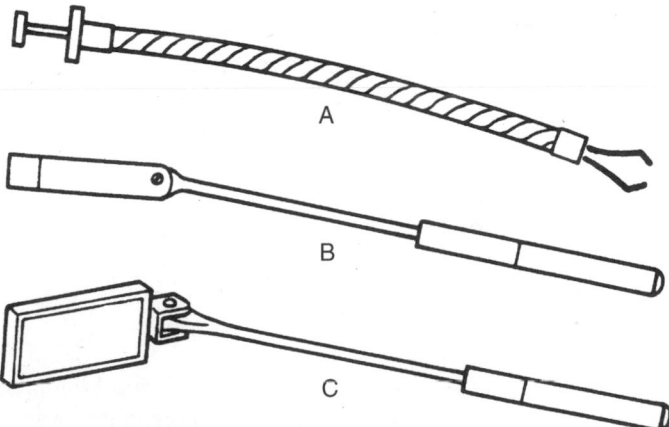

Figure 2-57. Probing tools. A—Mechanical finger pickup. B—Telescoping magnet. C—Telescoping mirror.

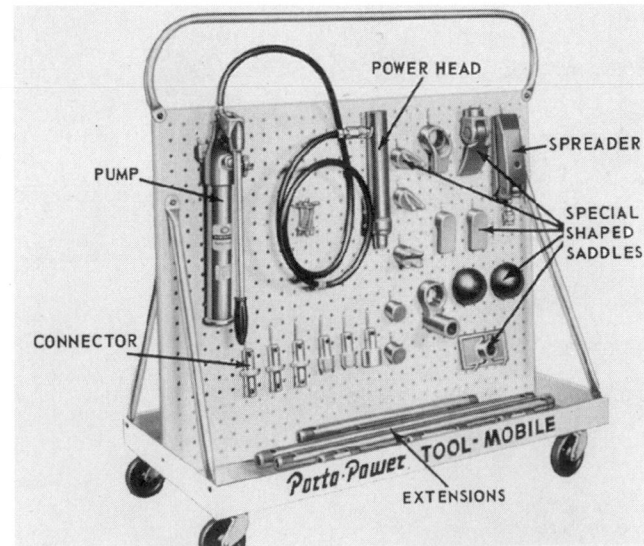

Figure 2-59. Portable hydraulic unit. (Blackhawk)

ber of useful adapters that allow the tool to be used for many jobs. In **Figure 2-60,** a hydraulic set is being used to move vehicle frame members back into position after a collision.

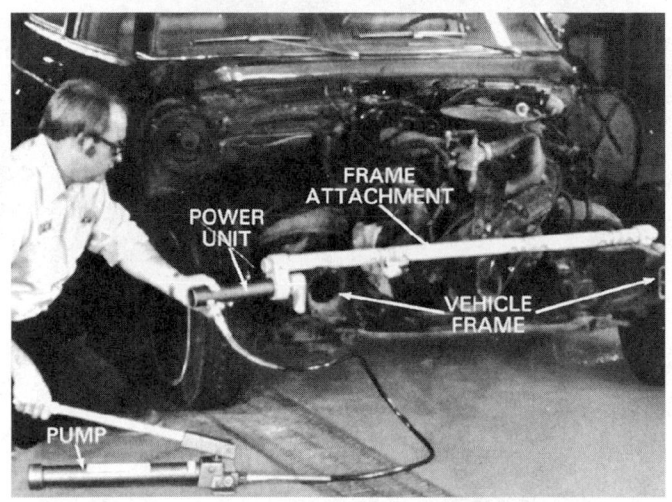

Figure 2-60.   Using portable hydraulic unit to straighten a frame. (Lincoln St. Louis)

Press Safety Precautions

All hydraulic pressing and pulling tools are potentially dangerous if improperly used. General safety rules applicable to all types of hydraulic tools include:

- Stand free while pressure is applied.
- Only apply enough pressure to do the job.
- Shield brittle parts, such as bearings, to protect against flying debris.
- Engage the ram securely and make sure it is in line with the work.
- When any chance of part breakage is present, wear goggles.
- If work must be performed while maintaining pressure, be careful to keep out of line with the tool.
- Be careful of part snap-back if the tool slips.

Hydraulic and Mechanical Pullers

Pullers are used to remove interference-fit (pressed on) parts. Pullers can be manually or hydraulically operated. A good assortment of pullers is important. An attempt to "get by" with a few pullers will result in wasted time and damaged parts. Many jobs are almost impossible without proper pullers.

Three Types of Pulling Jobs

All pulling jobs can be classified as one of three types:

- Pulling an object (such as a gear, pulley, bearing, or retainer) from a shaft.
- Pulling a shaft (such as an axle, transmission, or pinion) from an object.

- Pulling an object (such as bearing outer rings, cylinder sleeves, or camshaft bearings) from a housing bore.

Figures 2-61, 2-62, and **2-63** illustrate the three basic pulling jobs. A typical hydraulic puller is shown in **Figure 2-64.** Several universal-type manual pullers are pictured in **Figure 2-65.** Always store pullers, adapters, and related parts together. Some shops mount individual puller sets on "tote" boards so that all parts may be carried to the job.

Other Tools Will Follow

As mentioned, many more specialty tools will be discussed in this text. When you come across one, pay particular attention to its name and its operating instructions. Many potentially difficult jobs can be made easier if the proper tools are used. Proper tool selection and use is very important; learn all you can about the tools available.

Mark Your Tools

As you obtain tools, scribe your name on them. An electric engraving pencil will do a good job. Mark the tools in an area that will be difficult to grind off.

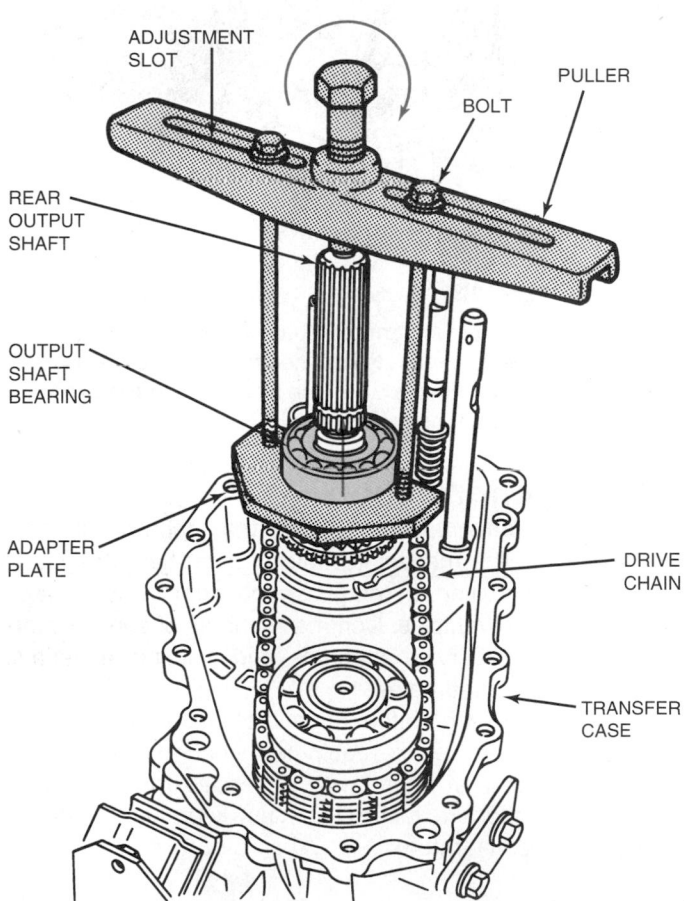

Figure 2-61.   Removing a transfer case rear output shaft bearing with a puller. Note the adjustment slots, which enable the puller to be used on a variety of bearings, gears, etc. (Geo)

A

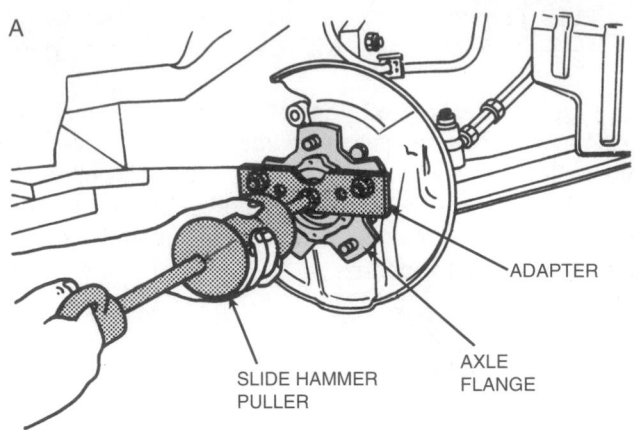

ADAPTER

SLIDE HAMMER
PULLER

AXLE
FLANGE

B

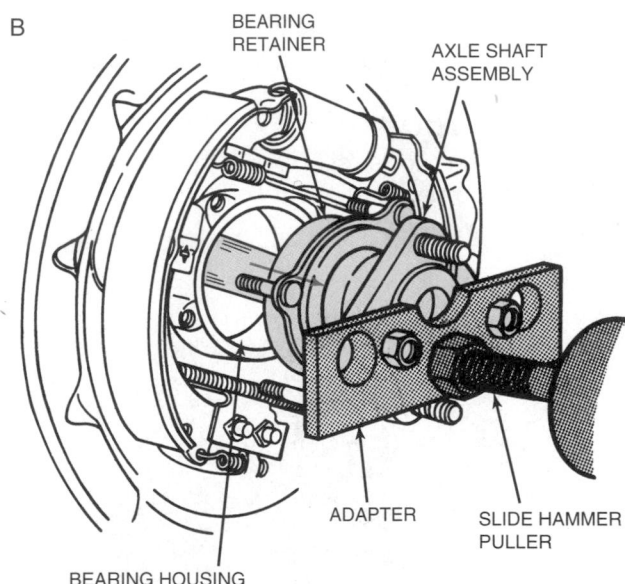

BEARING
RETAINER

AXLE SHAFT
ASSEMBLY

ADAPTER

SLIDE HAMMER
PULLER

BEARING HOUSING

Figure 2-62. Removing an axle shaft with a slide hammer puller. A—The technician has fastened the puller to the axle shaft flange with an adapter. B—The axle is being removed from its housing with the puller. (Geo)

Service Information

Service information is often the technician's most valuable tool. The modern technician must have the latest technical information to diagnose problems and replace parts on today's vehicles. Common sources of service information include service manuals and training materials, which are discussed below.

Available service information is often ignored by technicians. However, vehicle equipment changes every year, and a great deal of information is needed for even basic service. The modern technician must keep up-to-date by reading service literature.

Service Manuals

The *service manual* is a large book that contains text and illustrations showing how to perform service operations. In addition, service manuals contain troubleshooting charts and system schematics. There are three major types of ser-

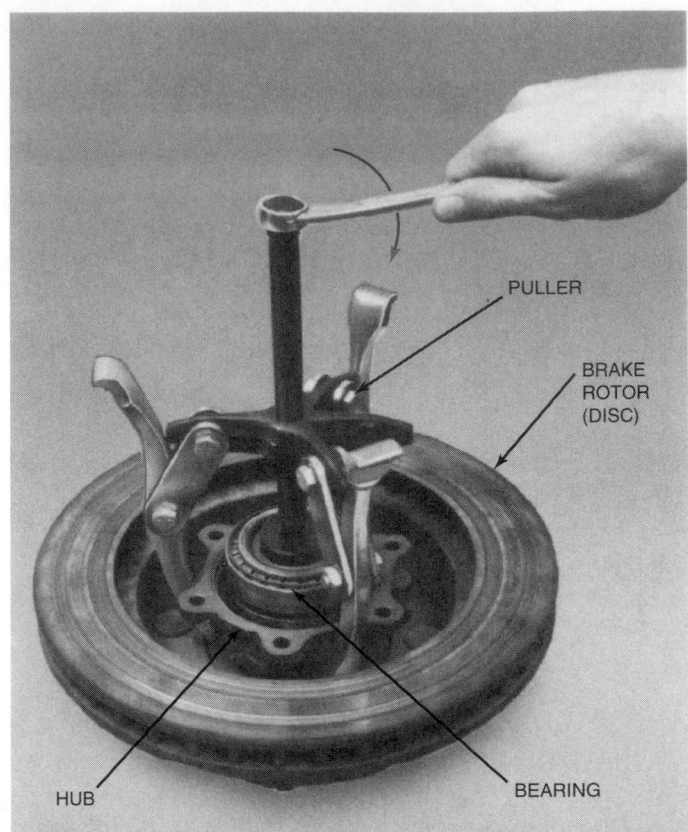

PULLER

BRAKE
ROTOR
(DISC)

HUB

BEARING

Figure 2-63. Pulling a bearing from the hub bore.

vice manuals: the factory manual, the general manual, and the specialized manual.

Factory Manual

The *factory manual,* or *manufacturer's manual,* is dedicated to one make and model of vehicle for a given year. It contains all the needed service information on every part of that vehicle. Some factory manuals are produced in several volumes. Each volume is dedicated to certain vehicle systems. The factory manual is a useful source of detailed procedures for diagnosing specific problems and making repairs to any part of the vehicle. It is also useful for providing detailed replacement and overhaul information for every component on that vehicle. One disadvantage of the factory manual is its relatively high cost, considering the fact that it covers one vehicle for one year.

General Manual

The *general manual* contains service information for many makes of vehicles. General manuals concentrate on information about commonly performed repairs, such as starter and alternator service, brake and suspension repairs, and tune-up procedures. These manuals contain information on preventive maintenance procedures.

There are so many different vehicles available today that general manuals are often divided into automobile and light truck editions. Many automobile manuals cover either

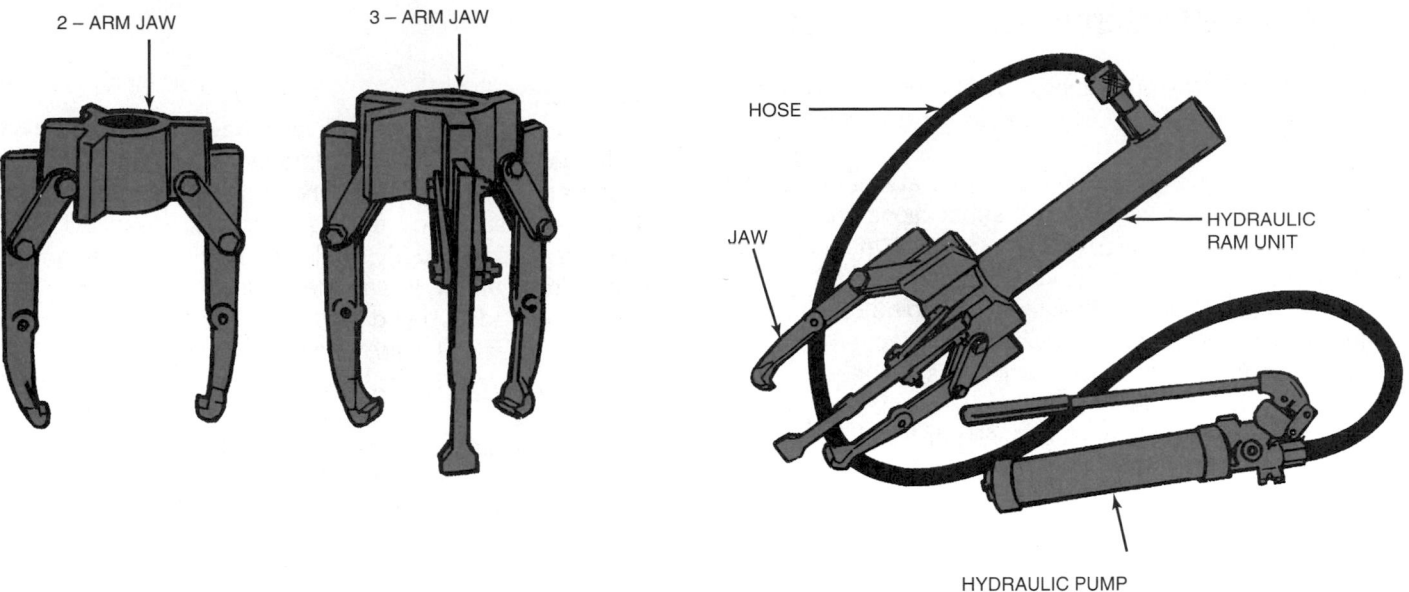

Figure 2-64. Typical hydraulic puller.

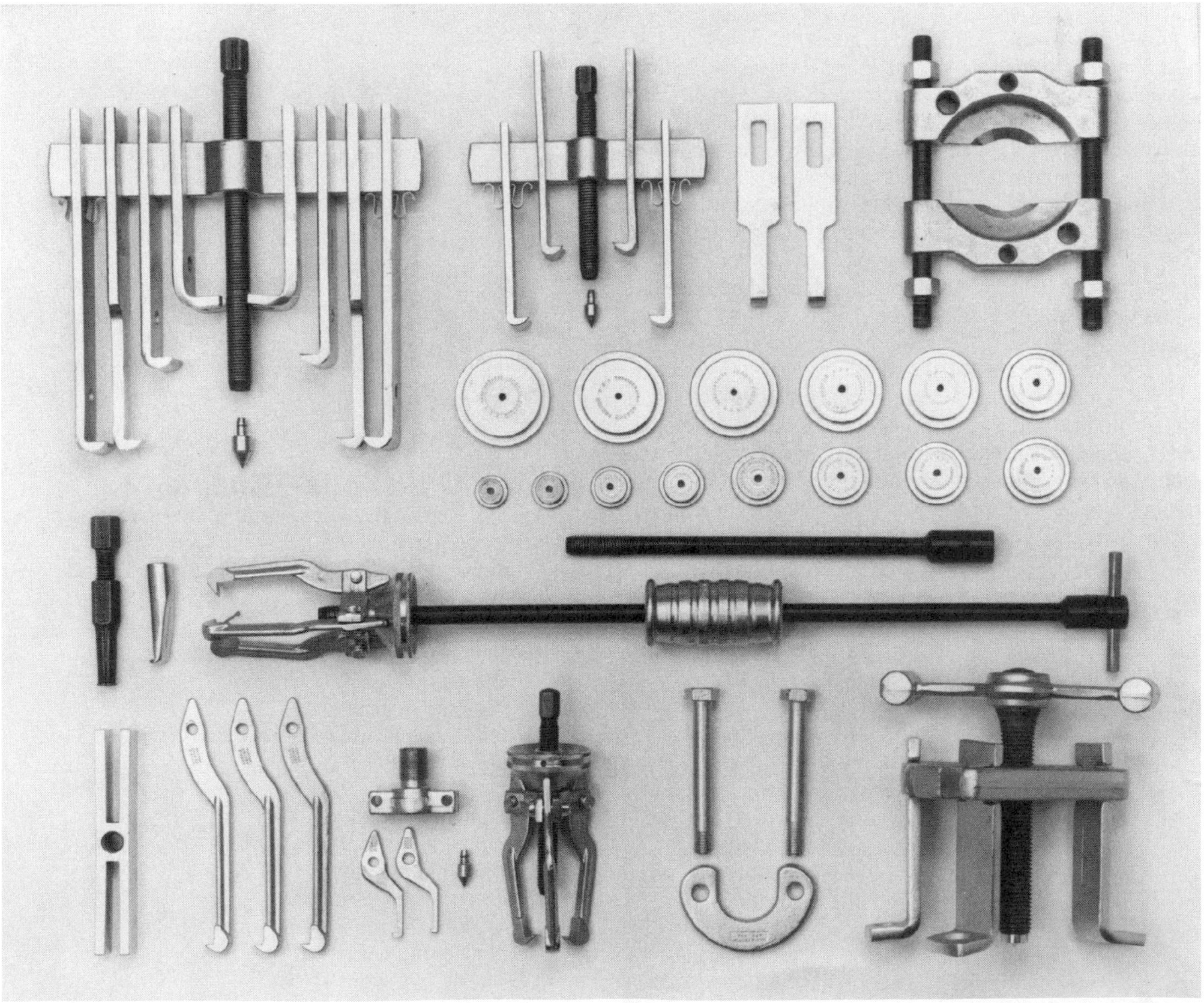

Figure 2-65. Universal manual puller set. (Proto)

all domestic vehicles or all imported vehicles. Some manual publishers further divide their imported car books into European and Asian models.

The individual chapters of general manuals are grouped by vehicle make. Chapter subsections are devoted to particular areas of each make. General manuals also contain separate sections covering general repair procedures that apply to all vehicles, such as engine overhaul, air conditioning service, and starter/alternator overhaul. The major disadvantage of these manuals is the necessity of eliminating most of the information on specialized vehicle equipment, body sheet metal, and interior trim.

Specialized Manual

Specialized manuals cover one common system for many types of vehicles. These manuals often cover such topics as emission controls, automatic transmissions, computerized engine controls, electrical systems, brakes, or suspension systems. They combine some of the best features of factory manuals and general manuals.

Training Materials

Training materials include basic sources of automotive information and update information. Basic information sources include your textbook and related materials, such as workbooks and videotapes, which allow the student to learn about automotive systems and how they operate. Update information is supplied to working technicians to keep them informed of changes that occur as vehicles or their parts are redesigned and improved. Much of the best update information is supplied by vehicle manufacturers and aftermarket (non-factory) parts suppliers.

Care of Service Information

Unlike other tools, service information is in the form of printed pages, and therefore can be damaged by grease, dirt, or rough handling. Always store service manuals and other service information in a clean, dry, and oil-free environment, not on top of the workbench where they can be ruined quickly.

Tech Talk

To keep your tools from rattling and possibly being damaged when you open and close the drawers of your tool cabinet, line the bottom of each drawer with cushioning material. The roughness of the material will keep the tools in place. A piece of cardboard will work, but it is better to use oil-resistant plastic or rubber matting. Cut the matting to fit the drawer and simply lay the tools on the matting.

Many tools are sold in flat plastic display packs. These are excellent for tool storage. Instead of throwing the display pack away after you remove the tools, trim the display pack to fit in the bottom of one of your tool drawers. The original tools will fit perfectly, and they will stay in place when the drawer is opened and closed.

Summary

The automotive technician must have a large selection of high-quality tools to service late-model vehicles properly and efficiently. Quality tools are stronger and less bulky than inferior tools. They are also easier to clean. All tools must be cared for properly. Tools should be kept clean, and they should be stored in an orderly fashion.

Common tools used by the automotive technician include hammers, chisels, punches, files, grinders, drills, saws, vises, screwdrivers, pliers, wrenches, presses, and pullers.

The technician must have access to the latest service information when repairing today's complex vehicles. Service manuals describe service and repair operations. There are three types of service manuals: factory manuals, general manuals, and specialized manuals.

Know These Terms

Hammer	Sockets
Chisels	Drive handles
Punches	Impact wrench
Files	Extensions
Grinder	Specialty wrenches
Drill bits	Screw extractor
Power hand drills	Probing tools
Drill press	Hydraulic presses
Reamers	Pullers
Taps	Service information
Dies	Service manual
Hacksaw	Factory manual
Vises	Manufacturer's manual
Cleaning tools	General manual
Screwdrivers	Specialized manuals
Pliers	Training materials
Wrench	

Review Questions—Chapter 2

Do not write in this book. Write your answers on a separate sheet of paper.

1. All of the following statements about good quality tools are true, EXCEPT:
   (A) they are hard to clean.
   (B) they are less bulky than inferior tools.
   (C) they are made of alloy steel.
   (D) they are guaranteed.
2. Explain how you will store your tools.
3. A hammer handle should be _____.
   (A) clean and dry
   (B) tight in the hammer head
   (C) held firmly
   (D) All of the above.
4. A chisel can be used for _____.
   (A) marking work before drilling
   (B) cutting off rivet heads
   (C) driving pins from holes
   (D) All of the above.
5. If a chisel's edge has become dull, what should be done with it?

6. You should never use a file if it does not have a _____.
   (A) single-cut surface
   (B) double-cut surface
   (C) handle
   (D) None of the above.

7. For storage, files should be _____.
   (A) lightly oiled
   (B) heavily oiled
   (C) clean and dry
   (D) sprayed with penetrating oil

8. A _____ is used to clean files.
   (A) file card
   (B) wire wheel
   (C) wire brush
   (D) soap solution

9. Carbon steel drill bits _____.
   (A) are cheaper than other bits
   (B) stay sharp longer than steel bits
   (C) will not lose their temper if overheated
   (D) All of the above.

10. Air pressure and electricity are two power sources for _____.
    (A) drills
    (B) presses
    (C) pullers
    (D) All of the above.

11. A reamer should remove about _____ of stock with each cut.
    (A) .0001″–.0002″ (.0025 –.005 mm)
    (B) .001″–.002″ (.025 –.05 mm)
    (C) .01″–.02″ (.25 –.5 mm)
    (D) .1″–.2″ (2.5 – 5. mm)

12. What kind of tap would be used in a blind hole when the threads must run almost to the bottom?
    (A) Plug.
    (B) Taper.
    (C) Bottoming.
    (D) Pipe.

13. Cutting oil is helpful when you are trying to cut threads in _____.
    (A) steel
    (B) brass
    (C) cast iron
    (D) aluminum

14. Which of the following hacksaw blades would be best for cutting sheet metal?
    (A) 14 tooth
    (B) 18 tooth
    (C) 24 tooth
    (D) 32 tooth

15. Standard size screwdrivers can be used for which of the following purposes?
    (A) Removing and installing screws.
    (B) Prying of oil pans.
    (C) Hammering on tight parts.
    (D) All of the above.

16. Flare nut wrenches can be used to remove and install _____ fittings.

17. What advantage does a 6-point socket have over a 12-point socket?

18. What advantage does a 12-point socket have over a 6-point socket?

19. Impact sockets are always _____ point sockets.
    (A) 4
    (B) 6
    (C) 12
    (D) Any of the above.

20. Irregularly shaped objects can be turned with a _____.
    (A) pipe wrench
    (B) chain wrench
    (C) pliers
    (D) All of the above.

21. Extractors are used to remove _____.
    (A) stripped tubing fittings
    (B) broken cap screws
    (C) pressed-on bearings
    (D) All of the above.

22. Briefly describe the three types of pulling jobs. (any order)

23. Which of the following types of manuals would you consult if you want to know how to repair heaters and air conditioners on many different makes of vehicles?
    (A) Factory manual.
    (B) General manual.
    (C) Specialized manual.
    (D) Update information manual.

24. Which of the following types of manuals would you consult if you want to find wheel alignment specifications for a 1987 Chrysler LeBaron, a 1992 Chevrolet Cavalier, and a 1994 Toyota Previa?
    (A) Factory manual.
    (B) General manual.
    (C) Specialized manual.
    (D) Update information manual.

25. Which of the following types of manuals would you consult if you want to find the latest information about Ford Motor Company on-board computers?
    (A) Factory manual.
    (B) General manual.
    (C) Specialized manual.
    (D) Update information manual.

ASE-Type Questions

1. Technician A says that chisels, files, drills, and similar tools are very hard and can all be piled together for storage. Technician B says that every type of tool should be carefully stored to prevent damage. Who is right?
   (A) A only.
   (B) B only.
   (C) Both A & B.
   (D) Neither A nor B.

2. All of the following hammers can be used when it is important not to damage the struck surfaces, EXCEPT:
   (A) brass.
   (B) plastic.
   (C) ball peen.
   (D) rubber.

3. Technician A says that chisels can be ruined if they are overheated during sharpening. Technician B says that chisels should be dipped in water as they are being sharpened on a grinder. Who is right?
   (A) A only.
   (B) B only.
   (C) Both A & B.
   (D) Neither A nor B.

4. Which of the following would be the best cut to rough file aluminum?
   (A) Bastard.
   (B) Second cut.
   (C) Smooth cut.
   (D) You must try each one to see which cuts best.

5. All of the following are safety rules for grinding, EXCEPT:
   (A) keep the tool as close to the wheel as possible.
   (B) wear safety glasses.
   (C) hold small objects with pliers.
   (D) stand directly in front of the grinding wheel when grinding.

6. Technician A says that a properly sharpened drill bit can be identified by an equal amount of chip or curl from both lips. Technician B says that a properly sharpened drill can be identified by increased difficulty in cutting through the metal. Who is right?
   (A) A only.
   (B) B only.
   (C) Both A & B.
   (D) Neither A nor B.

7. Technician A says that if you do not have the correct size drill bit for the tap you intend to use, you should use the next largest size drill bit. Technician B says that if you do not have the correct size metric tap, you should use the closest size UNC tap. Who is right?
   (A) A only.
   (B) B only.
   (C) Both A & B.
   (D) Neither A nor B.

8. All of the following statements about dies are true, EXCEPT:
   (A) special dies are used to rethread axle shafts.
   (B) dies are used to cut internal threads.
   (C) when cutting, the die should be backed up to break the chip.
   (D) dies are often adjustable.

9. Technician A says that using an impact wrench will reduce the amount of time that a job takes. Technician B says that impact sockets should always be used with an impact wrench. Who is right?
   (A) A only.
   (B) B only.
   (C) Both A & B.
   (D) Neither A nor B.

10. Pliers can be used for all of the following, EXCEPT:
    (A) tightening tubing fittings.
    (B) bending cotter pins.
    (C) cutting wire.
    (D) crimping connections.

Suggested Activities

1. Obtain a complete set of box end or socket wrenches in both English and metric sizes. Try both sets of wrenches on various bolts or nuts. Which sizes will interchange?
   Sample: Do not write in this book.
   a. _____ inch = _____ mm.
   b. _____ inch = _____ mm.
   c. _____ inch = _____ mm.
   d. _____ inch = _____ mm.
   e. _____ inch = _____ mm.
   Discuss with your instructor or the other members of your class whether it is a good idea to use metric wrenches on English bolts and vice versa.

2. Obtain catalogs from various tool manufacturers and make a list of the tools that you will need to get started as an automotive technician. List additional tools that you would need to become a(n):
   a. drivability technician.
   b. engine overhaul technician.
   c. transmission repair technician.
   d. air conditioning technician.
   e. brake technician.
   f. steering and suspension technician.

3. If possible, figure out the costs of the tools listed in Activity 2. Determine the total investment needed to get started as an automotive technician.

4. Show to your classmates how to look up a particular service operation in one or more factory service manuals.

3

Precision Measurement Tools and Equipment

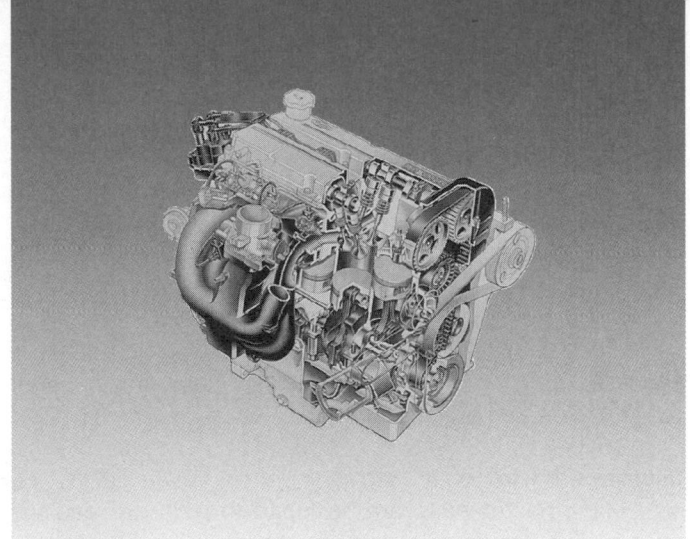

After studying this chapter, you will be able to:
* Identify common measuring tools.
* Select the appropriate measuring tool for a given job.
* Use precision measuring tools.
* Properly maintain precision measuring tools.

The automotive technician must be thoroughly familiar with the precision measuring tools used in the shop. Many jobs involve checking sizes, clearances, and alignments. Other jobs require the technician to check such things as engine vacuum and compression, battery or other electrical system qualities, or various pressures in vehicle components. A careless or inaccurate measurement can be costly in terms of money and customer relations, to say nothing of damaging the technician's reputation. Remember that the top-notch technician must be competent in the use of measuring tools. You can be proud of your ability to make precision measurements—it is the mark of a fine technician!

Buy Quality Tools

When selecting measuring tools that will be used for a period of years, it pays to buy top-quality equipment. The initial cost will obviously be higher. However, considering the importance of accuracy, the longer life span of superior tools easily justifies the extra cost.

Tool Storage

It is advisable to keep your measuring tools in a protective case. See **Figure 3-1.** Also, store them in an area that will not be subjected to excessive moisture or heavy traffic. After each use, wipe the tools down with a lightly oiled, lint-free, clean cloth. Never dip a precision measuring tool in solvent (unless it is being completely dismantled). Do not use an air hose for cleaning precision measuring tools.

Tool Handling

When using a measuring tool, place it in a clean area where it will not fall or be struck by other tools. Never pry, hammer, or force the tools. Remember, measuring tools are precision tools—keep them that way!

Figure 3-1. Precision measuring equipment, such as this dial indicator, should be stored in a protective case. Note that this case also houses the holding fixtures. (Central Tools)

Checking for Accuracy

Precision tools should be checked for accuracy on a regular basis. They may be checked against another tool of known accuracy or by using special gauges. If a tool is accidentally dropped or struck by some object, immediately check it for accuracy. Adjustments for wear or very minor damage are provided on many measuring tools. Follow the manufacturer's instructions.

Types of Precision Measuring Tools

The most common precision measuring tools are described in the following sections. These tools can be used to measure the condition of engine parts and other vehicle components.

Outside Micrometer

The **outside micrometer,** often referred to as a "mike," is used to check the diameter of pistons, pins, crankshafts, and other machined parts. The most commonly used micrometer reads in thousandths of an inch. Some micrometers can measure to within one ten thousandth of an inch. A cutaway view of a typical outside micrometer is shown in **Figure 3-2.** Learn the names of the parts and their relationships to the operation of the tool.

Micrometer Range

Many micrometers are designed to produce readings over a 1″ **range.** Ideally, the automotive technician should obtain a set of six micrometers covering 0″-1″, 1″-2″, 2″-3″, 3″-4″, 4″-5″, and 5″-6″ range. **Figure 3-3** shows a set of 12 micrometers covering 0-12″.

It would be less expensive to purchase only two micrometers with interchangeable anvils, a 0″-4″ micrometer and a 4″-6″ micrometer. However, the multi-range micrometer is bulky and inconvenient, **Figure 3-4.**

Reading the Micrometer

Micrometers are made so that every turn of the **thimble** will move the **spindle** .025″ (twenty-five thousandths of an inch). You will notice that the sleeve is marked with a series of lines. Each of these lines represents .025″. Every fourth one of these .025 markings is marked 1, 2, 3, 4, 5, 6, 7, 8, or 9. These sleeve numbers indicate .100″ (one hundred thousandths), .200″, .300″, and so on. The micrometer **sleeve** then is marked out for one inch in .025″ markings. They will read from .000″ to 1.000″.

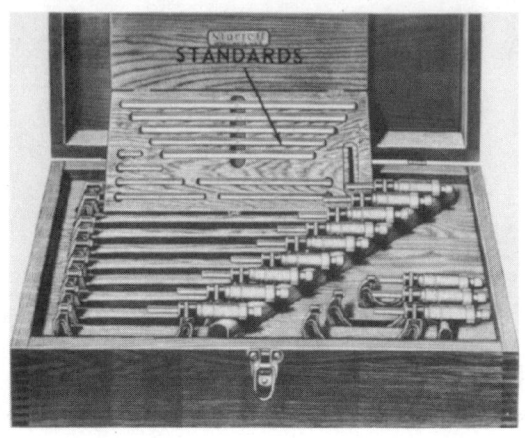

Figure 3-3. Set of 12 outside micrometers. Note the standards, which are used for checking the accuracy of each "mike."

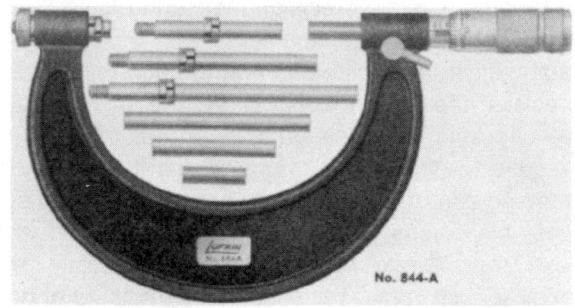

Figure 3-4. A multiple range micrometer. By using the proper anvil, this micrometer covers a range of 0″-4″. (Lufkin)

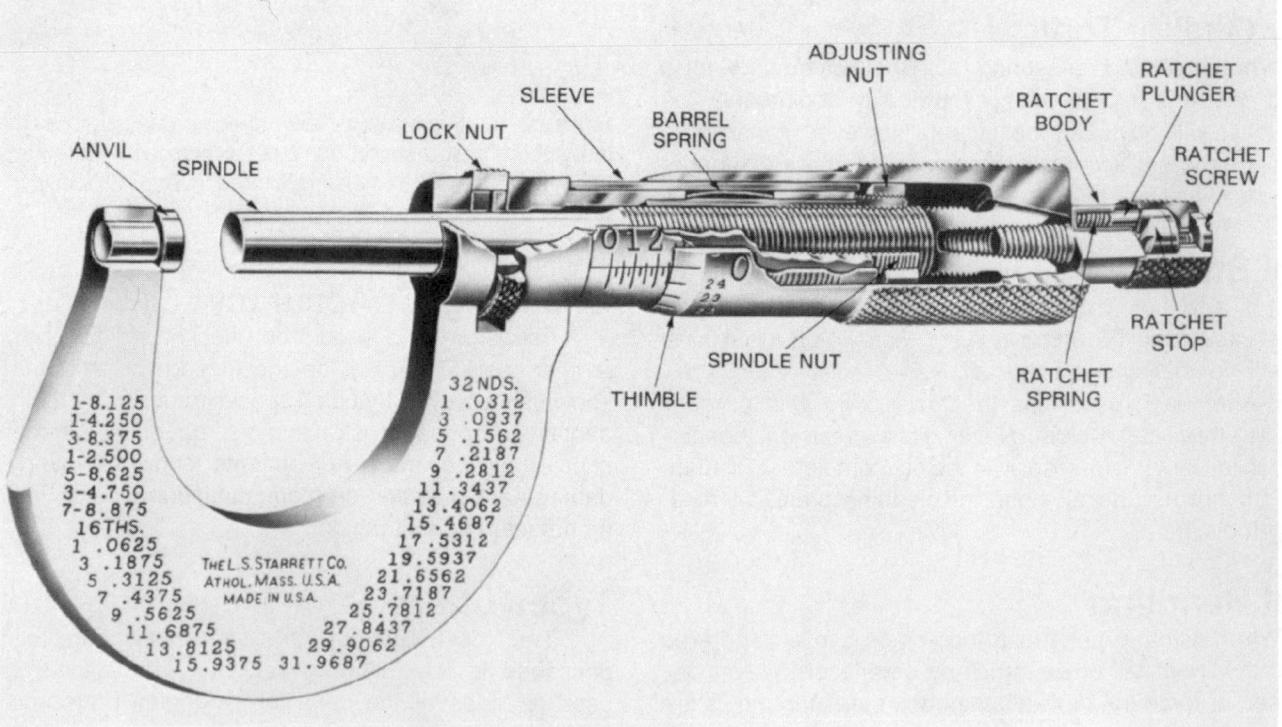

Figure 3-2. Cutaway of an outside micrometer. Learn the names of the various parts.

The tapered end of the thimble has 25 lines around it. Each line represents 1/25 of a revolution. The lines are numbered 1 through 25. One complete turn of the thimble moves the thimble edge exactly .025, or one mark on the sleeve. The distance between marks is determined by reading the thimble line that is even with the long line drawn the length of the sleeve markings. Each line on the thimble edge represents .001″ (one thousandth of an inch), **Figure 3-5.**

Look at the markings on the micrometer section in **Figure 3-6A.** Three numbers are visible on the sleeve. This indicates that the mike is open at least .300″ (three-hundred thousandths of an inch). You can see that the thimble edge is actually past the .300″ mark, but not to the .400″ mark. By careful study, you will see that the thimble edge has moved exactly two additional marks past .300″. This means that the thimble edge is lined up two marks past the .300″ mark. Since each sleeve mark represents .025″, two marks mean that the edge is actually stopped at .300″ plus .050″, or .350″ (three-hundred and fifty thousandths of an inch). Since the thimble edge 0 marking is aligned with the long sleeve line, the mike is set exactly on .350″. If this were a 0″-1″ mike, the reading would be .350″. If this were a 2″-3″ mike, the reading would be 2″ plus .350″, or 2.350″.

In **Figure 3-6B,** the micrometer has been opened to a wider measurement. You will see that the thimble edge is no longer on a sleeve marking, but is somewhere in between.

How many numbers are visible on the sleeve? There are five, or .500″ (five-hundred thousandths). The thimble edge has moved three marks, or .075″, past the .500″ mark. This makes a total of .575″. The thimble edge has moved past the third mark. In that the fourth mark is not visible, we know it is somewhere between the third and fourth marks.

By examining the thimble edge marks shown in **Figure 3-6B,** you will see that the twelfth mark is aligned with the

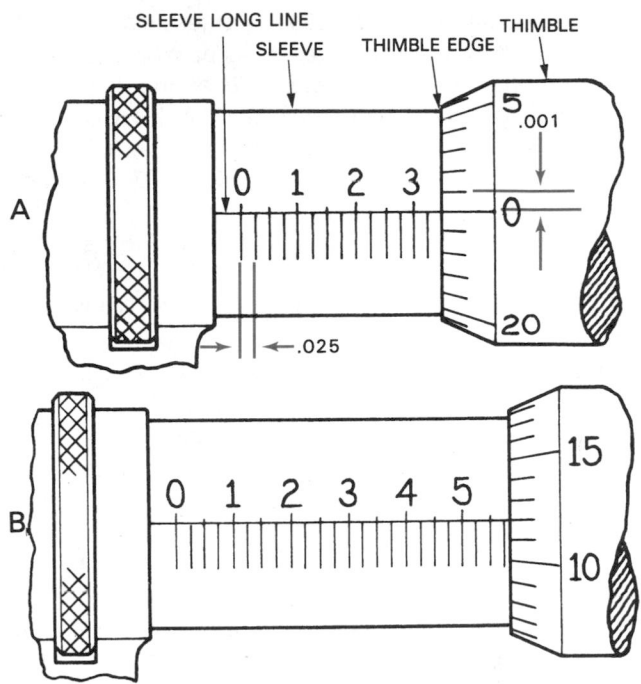

Figure 3-6. Study the numbering system used with an outside micrometer. A—The thimble edge has moved across the sleeve up to the 3 (.300″), plus two more sleeve marks (.050″). The thimble 0 mark is in line with the sleeve long line so the reading is .300″ + .050″ + 0″ = .350″. B—The thimble edge has moved up to the 5 (.500″) plus three more sleeve marks (.075″) plus 12 thimble marks (.012″), resulting in a total reading of .587″.

long line on the sleeve. This means the thimble edge has moved twelve thimble marks past the third sleeve mark. In that each thimble mark equals .001″, the thimble has actually moved .012″ past the third sleeve mark.

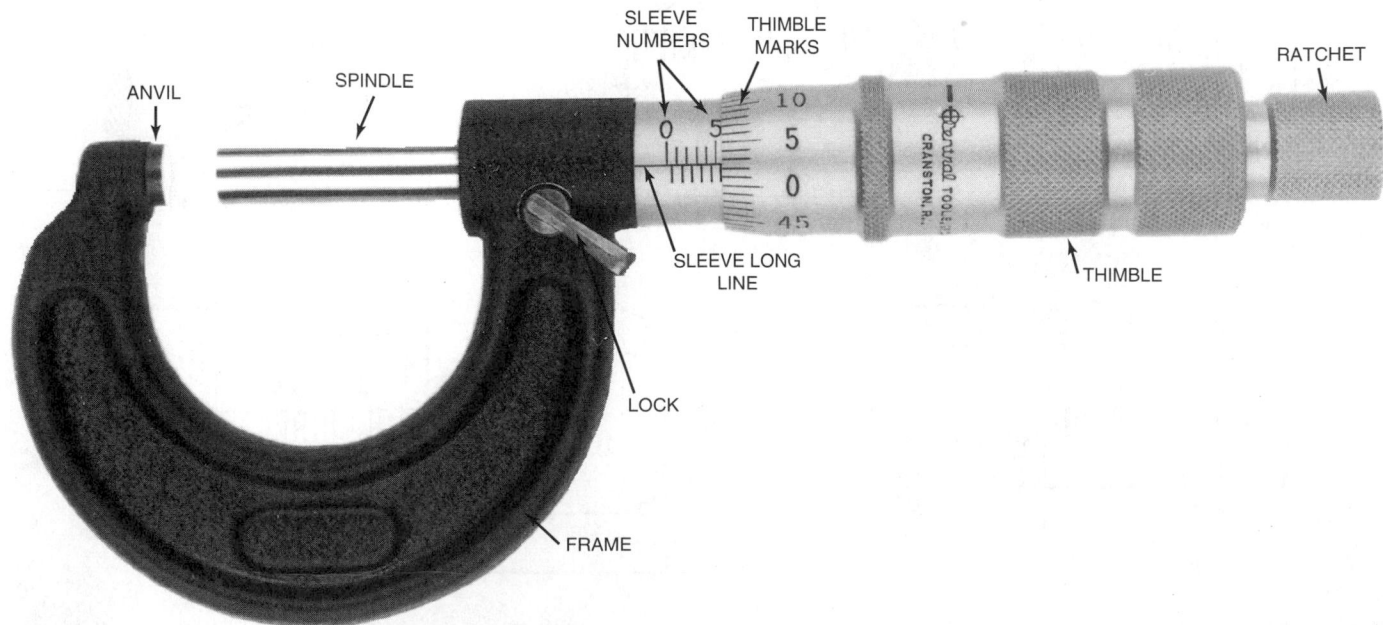

Figure 3-5. A 0-1″ outside micrometer. Study the markings and the part names. (Central Tools, Inc.)

Your reading would be .500″ (largest sleeve number visible) plus .075″ (three sleeve marks past sleeve number) plus .012″ (twelve thimble marks past the third sleeve mark), making a total reading of .587″. If this were a 3-4″ micrometer, the actual measurement would be 3.587″.

Study the readings shown in **Figure 3-7**. Compare your answers with those shown.

Make your readings in four steps. See **Figure 3-8**.

1. Read the largest sleeve number that is visible—each one indicates .100″.
2. Count the number of full sleeve marks past this number—each one indicates .025″.
3. Count the number of thimble marks past this last sleeve number. Each one indicates .001″. If the thimble marks are not quite aligned with the sleeve long line, estimate the fraction of a mark.
4. Add the readings in steps 1, 2, and 3. The total is the correct micrometer reading. Add this reading to the starting size of the micrometer being used. If the mike range was 1-2″, add the total reading to 1.000″.

Reading a Vernier Micrometer

A **vernier micrometer** is similar to a standard micrometer, but it can be used to take accurate readings to one ten-thousandth of an inch. Instead of estimating fractions of a thousandth between thimble marks, a vernier scale on the sleeve is used to accurately divide each thousandth into ten parts, each part equaling one ten-thousandth of an inch (.0001″).

The vernier scale consists of eleven thin lines scribed parallel to the sleeve long line. They are marked 0-10.

When the thimble marks do not fall in line with the long sleeve line, indicating a fraction of one-thousandth of an inch, carefully examine the vernier lines. One of the vernier lines will be aligned with one of the thimble marks. When you locate the vernier line that is aligned, the number of that line indicates the number of ten-thousandths to be added to your initial thimble reading. Look at **Figure 3-9**.

Examine the readings shown in **Figure 3-10**. In both instances, a fraction of a thousandth is obvious by examining the thimble marks. By checking the vernier, you can see that one of the vernier lines is in alignment with a thimble mark, thus indicating the number of ten thousandths over the thimble thousandth reading. Compare your readings with those shown.

Reading a Metric Micrometer

The **metric micrometer** closely resembles the standard type. The basic differences between them are the thimble and sleeve markings. The metric micrometer is marked to measure hundredths of a millimeter instead of thousandths of an inch.

Each line on the sleeve equals 0.5 millimeters (abbreviated mm). Every thimble line equals 0.01 mm. Every two full revolutions of the thimble, the spindle is advanced 1.00 mm. See **Figure 3-11**.

To obtain a reading, follow the following four steps using the micrometer in **Figure 3-11B** as an example.

1. The highest line showing on the sleeve.......................
   10.0 mm
2. The number of lines showing on the sleeve past the highest figure............ 0.5 mm

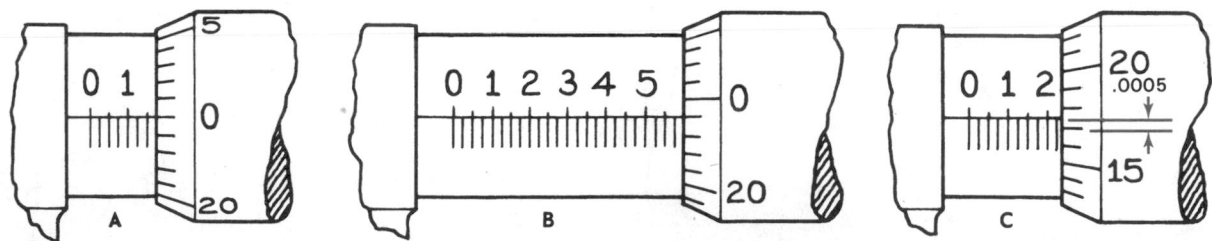

Figure 3-7.   A = .175″. B = .599″. C = .242″ + 1/2 thimble mark, or .2425″. Note that in C, the fraction ten-thousandths is estimated as indicated by the thimble mark.

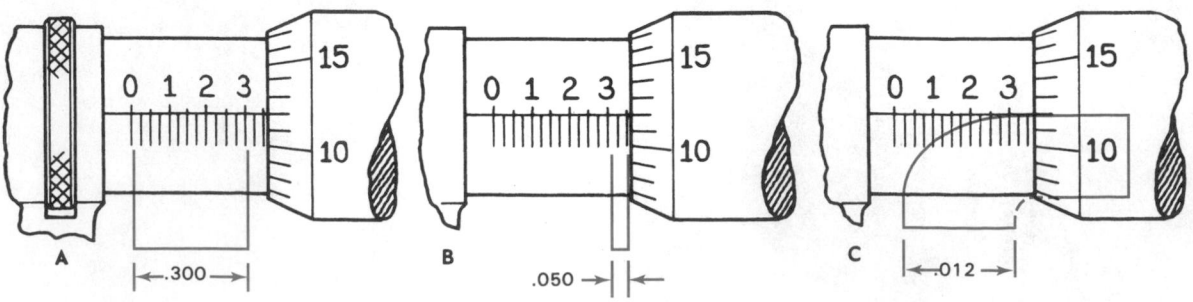

Figure 3-8.   Four steps in reading the micrometer. The first reading in A = .300″. The second reading in B = .050″. The third reading in C = .012″. The total reading is .362″ (three hundred and sixty-two thousandths).

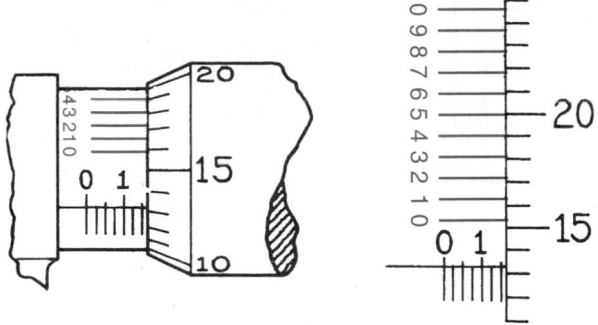

Figure 3-9. Vernier lines are shown in color. Note that vernier line No. 4 is the only one exactly in line with a thimble mark. Your reading would then be .100″ + .050″ + .013″ + .0004″ (four ten-thousandths) = .1634″.

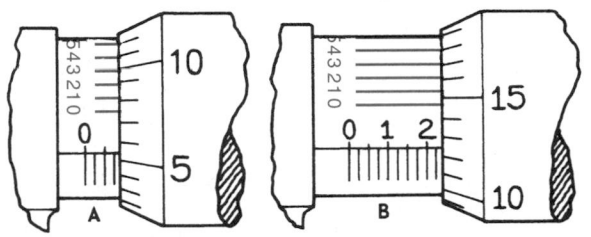

Figure 3-10. A—Vernier line No. 5 is aligned with a thimble mark. Reading is .075″ + .005″ + .0005″ = .0805″. B—Vernier line No. 4 is aligned. Reading is .200″ + .025″ + .0004″ =.2374″.

3. The line on the thimble aligning with the sleeve long line............................ 0.0 mm
4. Add the numbers to obtain the measurement ....10.5 mm

What reading do you get for **Figure 3-11A?**

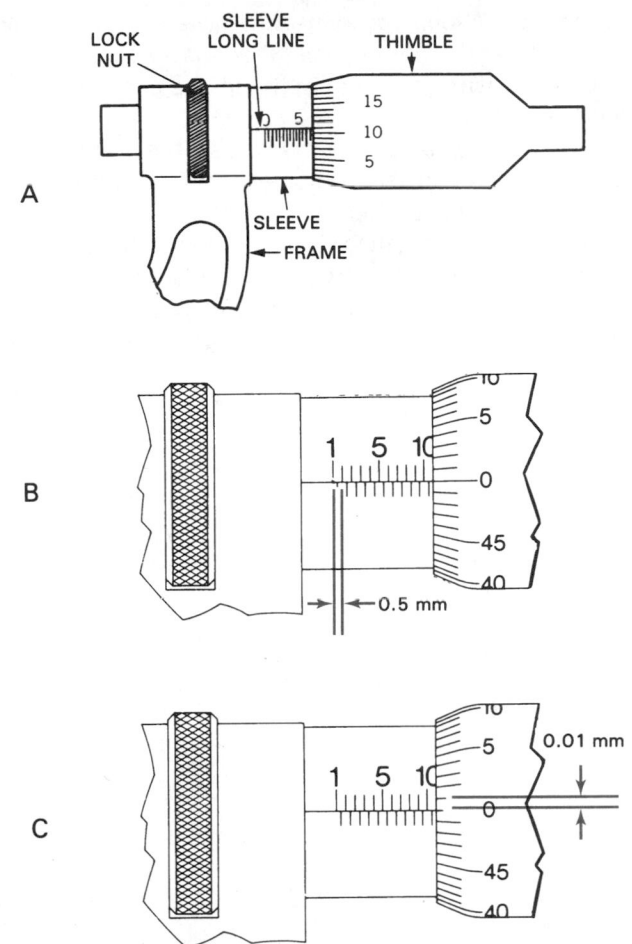

Figure 3-11. Typical outside metric micrometer. Notice that this mike requires two full revolutions of the thimble to equal one millimeter. (TRW, Deere & Co.)

Using an Outside Micrometer

When measuring small objects, grasp the micrometer in your right hand. At the same time, insert the object to be measured between the anvil and spindle.

> **Note: Before using any measuring tool, always thoroughly clean the work to be measured. This ensures accurate readings and reduces wear on the working tips of the tool.**

While holding the work against the anvil, turn the thimble with your thumb and forefinger until the spindle touches the object. Do not clamp the micrometer tightly. Use only enough pressure on the thimble to cause the work to *just fit* between the anvil and spindle. Slip the object in and out of the micrometer while giving the thimble a final adjustment. The work must slip through the micrometer with a very light force. When satisfied that your adjustment is correct, read the micrometer setting. Be careful not to move the adjustment, **Figure 3-12.**

Placing the proper force on the micrometer is often called *feel*. The technician should develop the proper feel by making practice measurements with a micrometer when-

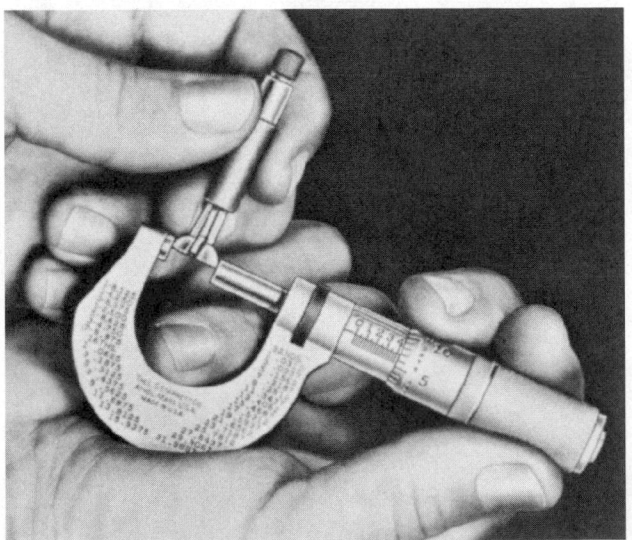

Figure 3-12. Miking a small hole gauge. The heel of the hand supports the micrometer frame while the thumb and forefinger turn the thimble. (L. S. Starrett)

ever possible. Some micrometers have a ratchet clutch knob on the end of the thimble. It allows the user to bring the spindle down against the work with the same amount of tension each time.

To measure larger objects, grasp the frame of the micrometer and slip the micrometer over the work while adjusting the thimble. Slip the micrometer back and forth until very light resistance is felt, **Figure 3-13.** As the micrometer is slipped back and forth over the work, it should be rocked from side to side slightly. This will ensure that the spindle is completely closed against the work, **Figure 3-14.**

Digital Micrometers

The **_digital micrometer_** provides precise measurement readings at a glance. It is similar to a standard micrometer, but the readings appear in a window instead of on the hub and thimble, **Figure 3-15.** Some micrometers provide both standard and digital readings.

 Caution: Handle all micrometers with care. Never store a micrometer with the tips of the anvil and the spindle touching, as this may cause rusting between the tips and warping when the temperature changes.

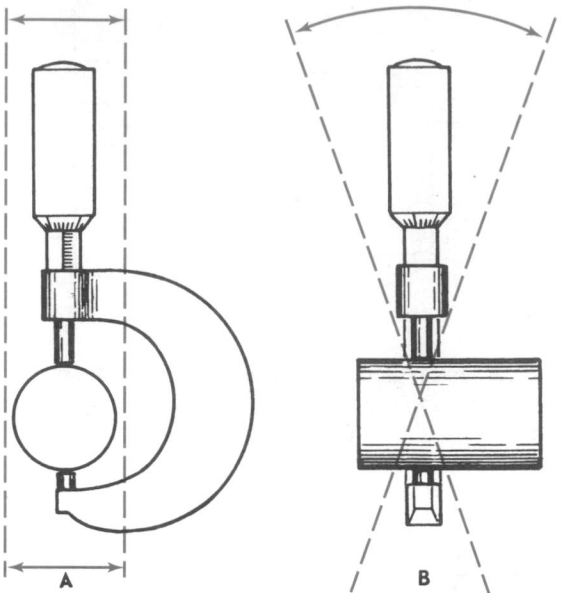

Figure 3-14. A—The micrometer is slipped back and forth over the object. B—The micrometer is rocked from side to side to make certain the smallest diameter is found. Rocking is actually very slight.

Figure 3-13. This technician is miking a crankshaft. Notice how the micrometer is held. (Federal-Mogul)

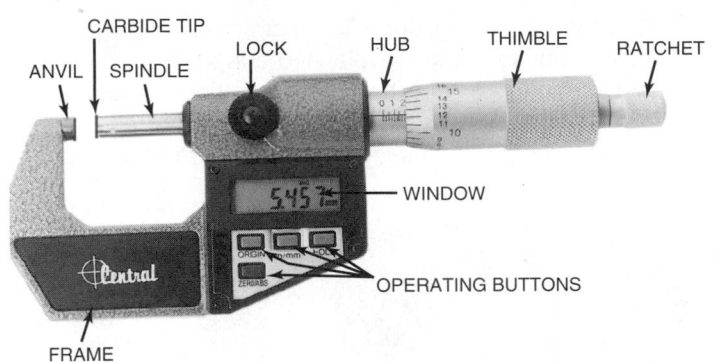

Figure 3-15. On this digital micrometer, four numbers are shown in the window. It can be used to take readings that are accurate to one one-thousandth (.001) of an inch. (Central Tools)

Inside Micrometer

The **inside micrometer** is used to take measurements in cylinder bores, brake drums, large bushings, etc., **Figure 3-16.** An extension handle permits the use of an inside micrometer in a bore that is too small to allow you to hold the tool by hand.

An inside micrometer is read in the same manner as the outside micrometer. The same "feel" is required. When measuring, rock the inside micrometer from side to side. At the same time, keep the anvil firmly against one side of the bore. While the free end is being rocked, it must also be tipped in and out. The rocking allows you to locate the widest part of the bore. The tipping ensures that the micrometer is at right angles to the bore, **Figure 3-17.**

Micrometer Depth Gauge

The **micrometer depth gauge** is a handy tool for reading the depth of slots, splines, counterbores, and holes. To use this tool, press the base against the work (after cleaning) and run the spindle down into the hole to be measured. The depth gauge is read like an outside micrometer.

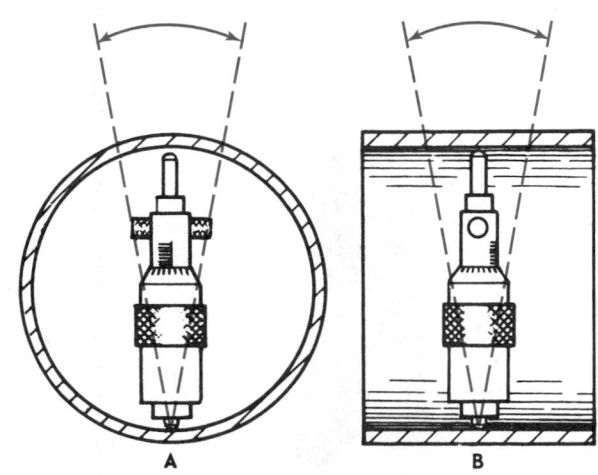

Figure 3-17. A—The inside micrometer must be rocked from side to side. B—At the same time, it must be tipped. Both movements are relatively slight.

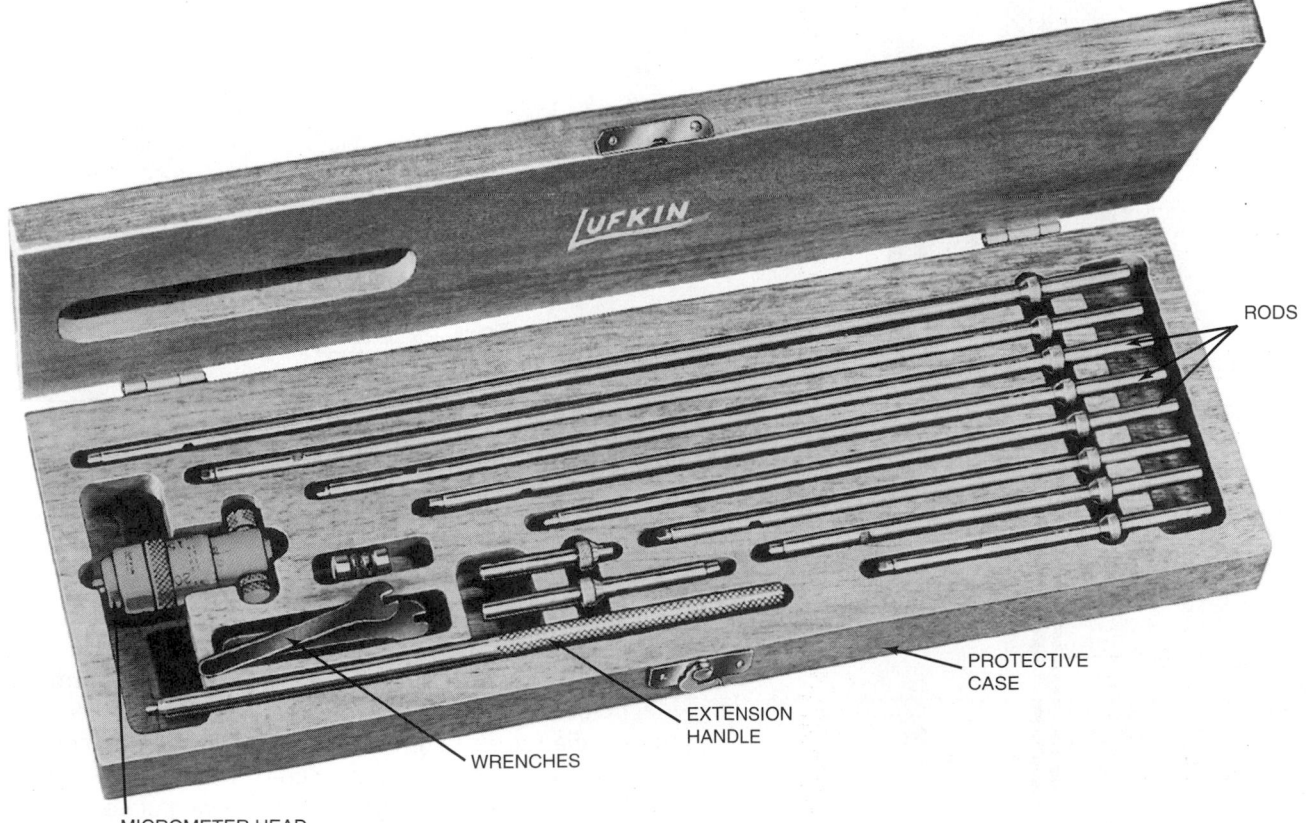

Figure 3-16. Inside micrometer. By changing rods, this set will measure from 2″-8″. (Lufkin)

The only difference is that the sleeve marks run in the reverse direction, **Figure 3-18.**

Dial Indicator

The **dial indicator,** sometimes called a dial gauge, is a precision tool designed to measure movements in thousandths of an inch. Some common uses of the dial indicator include checking shaft end play, gear backlash, valve lift, shaft run-out, and cylinder taper.

Dial indicator faces are calibrated either in thousandths of an inch or in millimeters. Various dial face markings are available. Ranges (distance over which the indicator can be used) vary, depending upon the instrument, **Figure 3-19.** Various mounting arms, swivels, and adapters are provided so that the indicator can be used on various setups. Use care in the handling of this tool. It is sensitive and easily damaged. When not in use, keep it in a protective case.

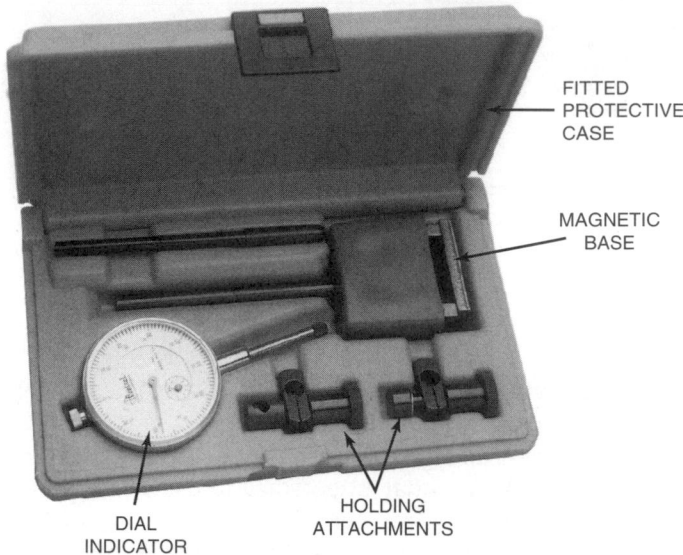

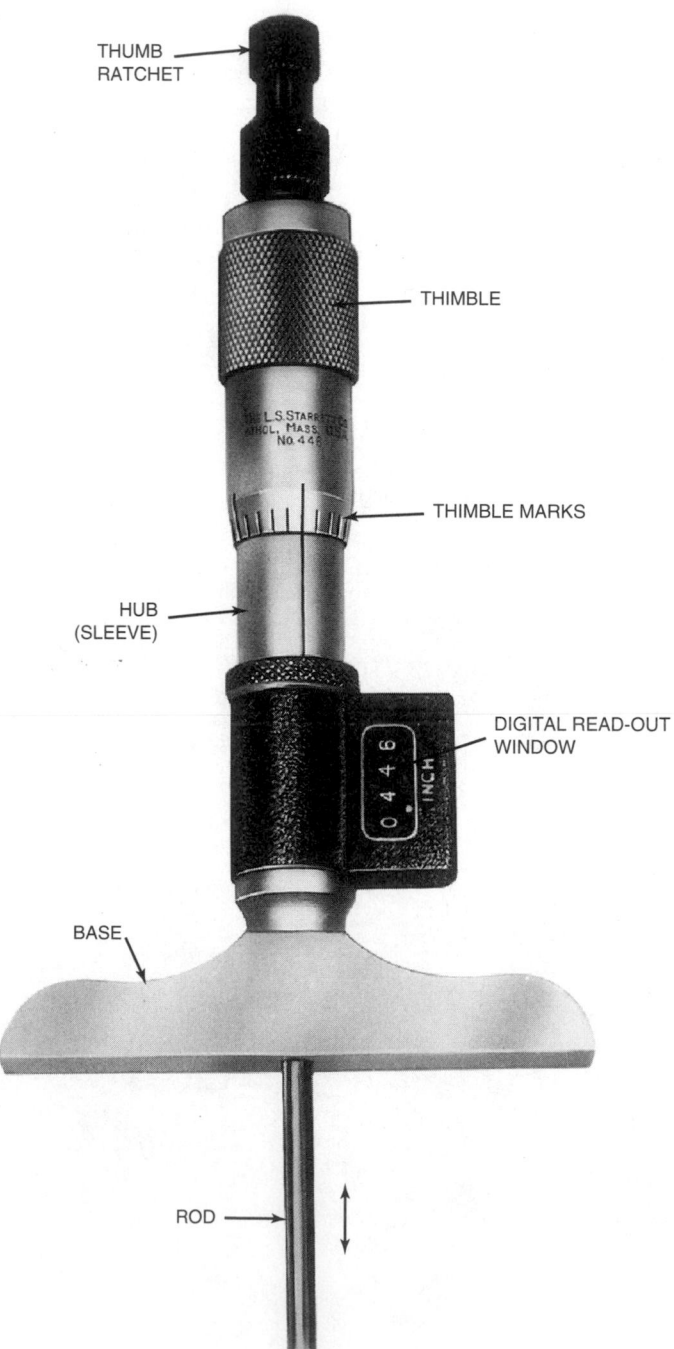

Figure 3-18. Micrometer depth gauge. Note that this particular gauge provides a digital readout. (L. S. Starrett)

Figure 3-19. This dial indicator is available with a magnetic base and holding attachments. (Central Tools)

When using a dial indicator, make sure that it is firmly mounted and that the standard (actuating rod) is parallel to the plane (direction) of movement to be measured, **Figure 3-20.**

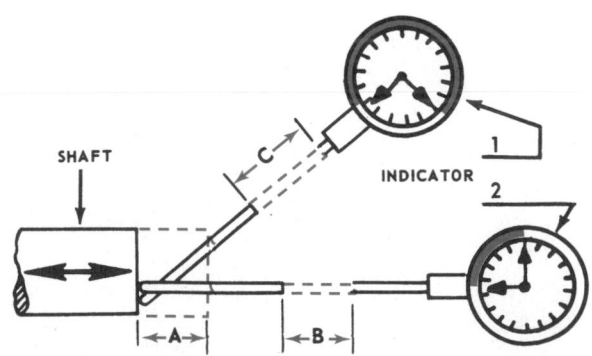

Figure 3-20. Indicator 1 setup is *not* parallel to the movement of the shaft. When the shaft moves distance A, the indicator rod moves distance C, giving a false reading for shaft end play. Indicator 2 is parallel, and shaft movement A causes the indicator rod to move distance B, producing an accurate reading. (OK)

Place the rod end against the work to be measured. Force the indicator toward the work so that the indicator needle travels far enough around the dial that movement in either direction can be measured. The dial face can then be turned to align the 0 mark with the indicator needle. Be sure that the indicator range (limit of travel) will cover the movement anticipated. Ranges usually run from around .200″ to

1.000″ (one inch), depending on the instrument. **Figures 3-21, 3-22,** and **3-23** illustrate typical dial indicator setups.

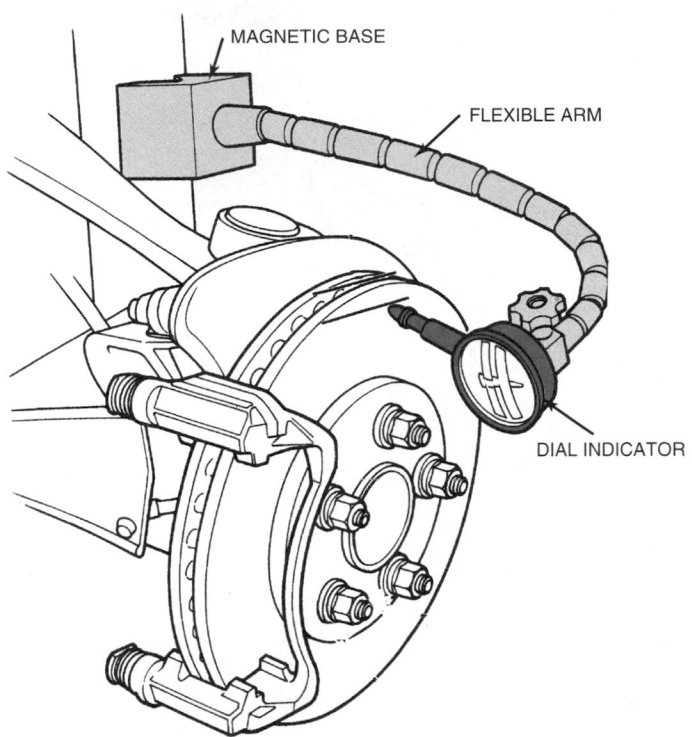

Figure 3-21. Checking brake rotor runout with a dial indicator. Note that a magnetic base and a flexible arm are used to hold the indicator in place. (Honda)

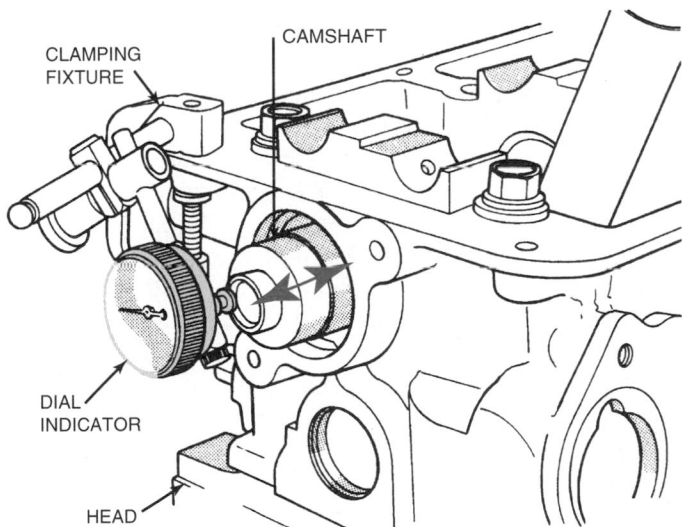

Figure 3-22. In this setup, a dial indicator is used with a clamping fixture to determine camshaft end play. (Chrysler)

Other Dial Indicator Tools

Two other valuable measuring tools utilize a dial indicator as part of their construction. They are the **valve seat runout gauge** and the **cylinder gauge.** The valve seat runout gauge is used to check valve seat concentricity (runout), **Figure 3-24.** The cylinder gauge provides a quick

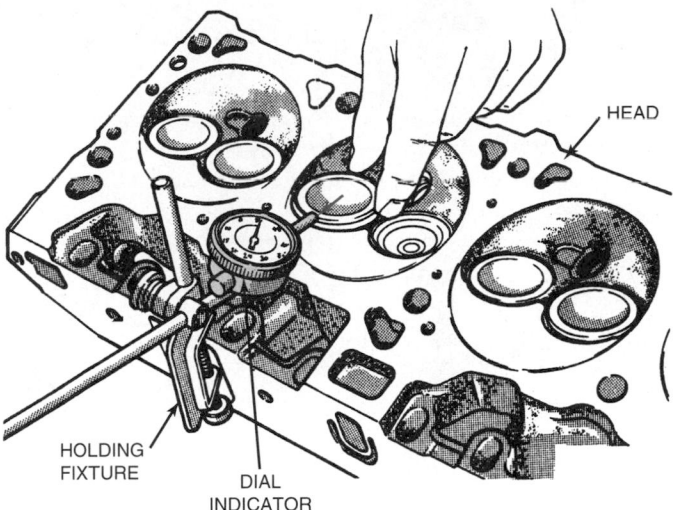

Figure 3-23. This technician is using a dial indicator to measure valve guide wear. (Chrysler)

Figure 3-24. Valve seat runout gauge. (Central Tools)

and accurate way to check cylinder bore size, taper, and out-of-round, **Figure 3-25.**

Other Useful Measuring Tools

In addition to the precision tools already discussed, there are a number of other tools that a technician should own. In your work as an automotive technician, a number of measurements, varying from a few thousandths of an inch to several feet, will be required.

Inside and Outside Calipers

Calipers are useful tools for taking quick measurements when accuracy is not critical. **Figure 3-26** illustrates an outside caliper.

Figure 3-27 shows an inside caliper. The inside caliper is used to measure the diameter of holes. To determine the

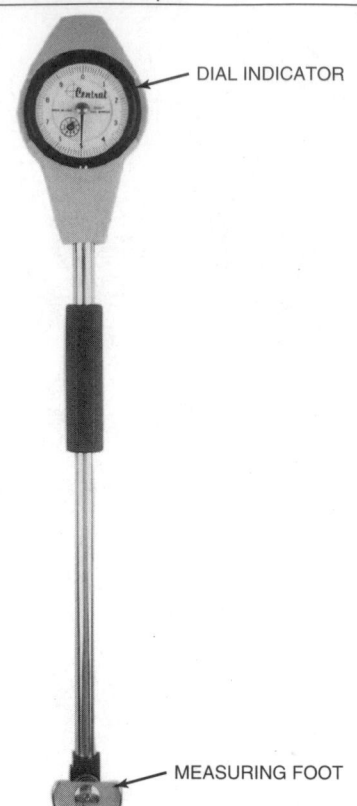

DIAL INDICATOR

MEASURING FOOT

Figure 3-25.   Cylinder gauge. (Central Tools)

Figure 3-27.   Inside caliper. (Central Tools)

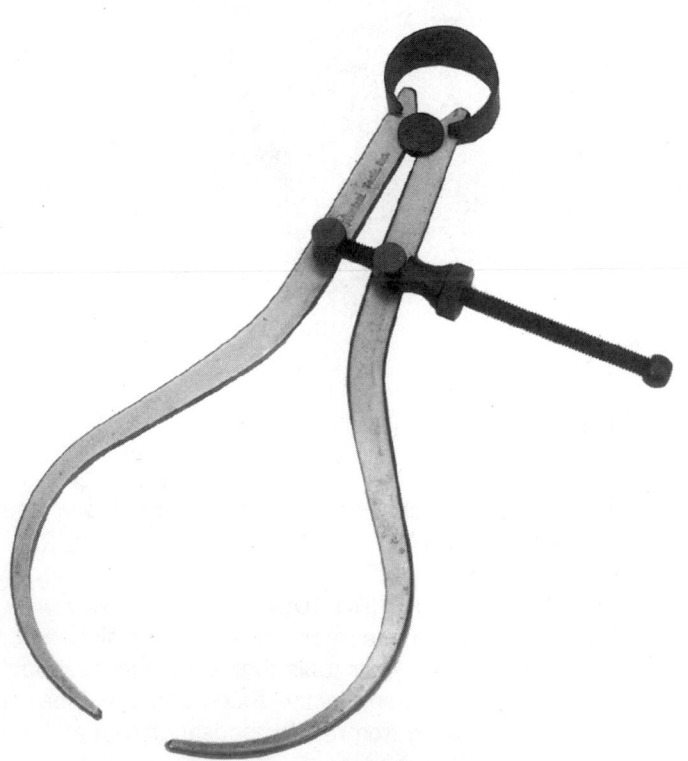

Figure 3-26.   Outside caliper. (Central Tools)

reading, hold the calipers on an accurate steel rule. Carefully measuring across the points (using a very light touch) with an outside micrometer will give a more accurate reading.

Dial Calipers

The *dial caliper* is a very useful precision measuring instrument capable of obtaining inside, outside, and depth readings. Because these calipers are highly accurate, they should be handled with great care. Always store them in protective cases when not in use.

The dial caliper shown in **Figure 3-28A** will measure objects up to 6″ (152.4 mm). The graduation lines on the bar scale (body) are each equal to .100″ (2.54 mm). The dial is calibrated in .001″ (0.025 mm) increments. Every full revolution of the dial needle equals .100″ on the bar scale. The caliper is equipped with a thumb-operated roll knob that aids in obtaining fine adjustments. Once the measurement is taken, the lockscrew can be tightened. This prevents the caliper from opening or closing and altering the reading.

A newer type of caliper is the digital caliper shown in **Figure 3-28B.** Instead of a dial, this caliper uses an electronic digital readout. The digital readout eliminates the chance of making an error and can be easily recalibrated before each use.

Dividers

Dividers are similar to calipers, but they have straight shanks and pointed ends. These tools are handy for making circles and for taking surface measurements. **Figure 3-29** illustrates a pair of dividers.

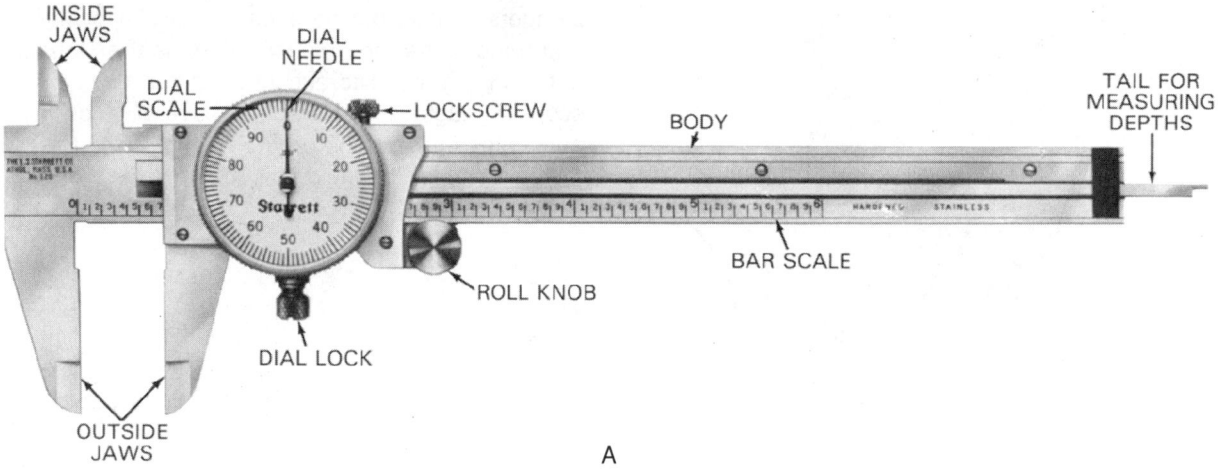

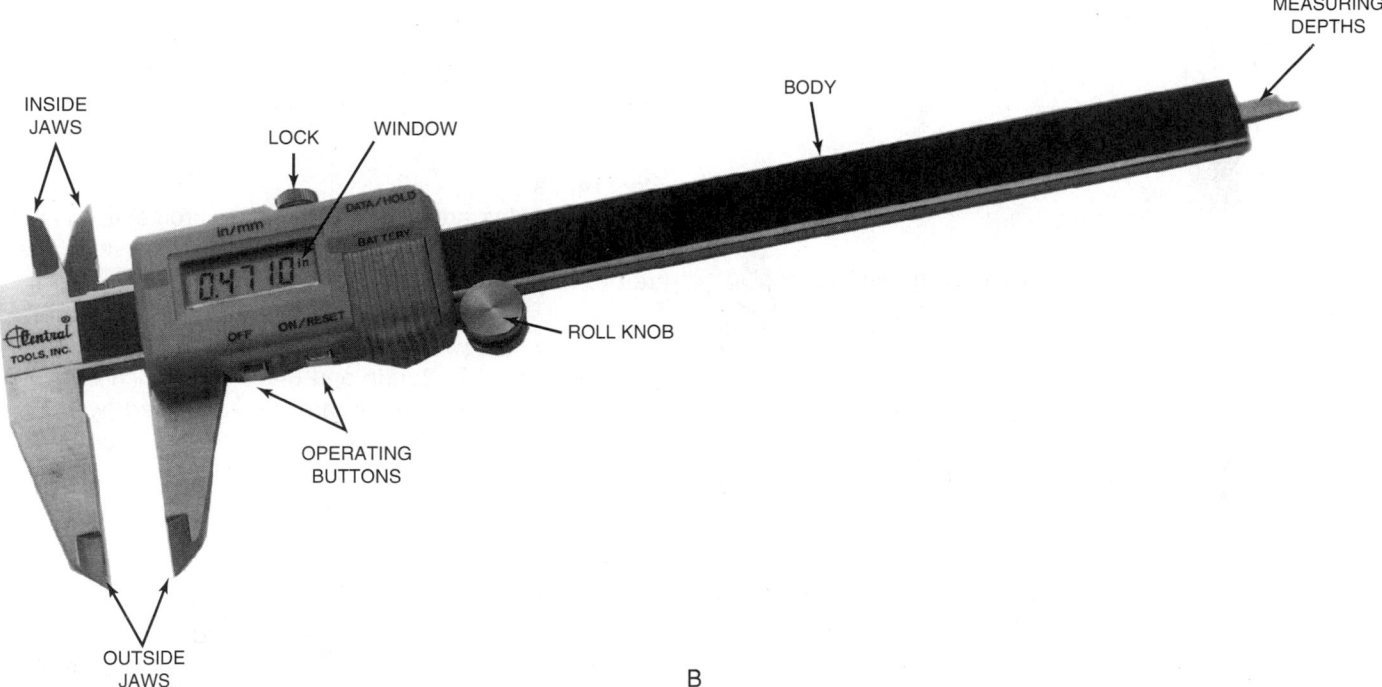

Figure 3-28.   A—Dial caliper. This particular instrument will measure objects, holes, etc., up to 6″ (152.4mm) in diameter and depth. B—Digital caliper. Note that this caliper can provide measurements in either standard or metric units. (Central Tools)

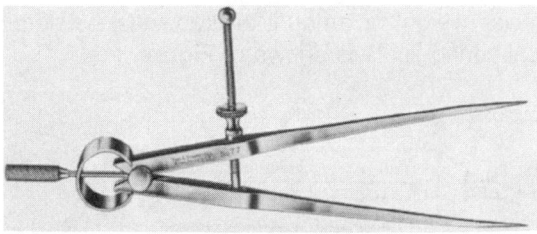

Figure 3-29.   Dividers. Points must be sharp.

Feeler Gauges

Feeler gauges, or *thickness gauges,* consist of specially hardened and ground steel strips. Each strip is marked with its thickness in thousandths of an inch and/or millimeters. Feeler gauges are used to check clearances between two parts, **Figure 3-30.** They come in sets. Some feeler gauges are made of copper or brass for checking clearances in places where a magnetic field would cause a steel feeler gauge to give an inaccurate reading.

Wire Gauge

The *wire gauge* is a thickness gauge using wires of varying diameters instead of thin strips of steel. It is primarily used on older vehicles when checking the gaps of used spark plugs and distributor or voltage regulator point gaps. See **Figure 3-31.**

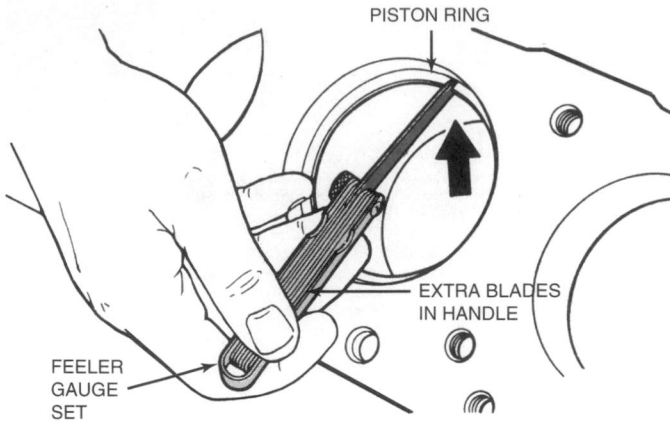

Figure 3-30. This technician is using a feeler gauge to measure piston ring end gap. (Buick)

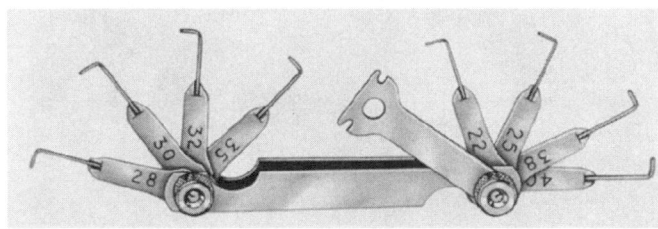

Figure 3-31. This wire gauge set is used to check spark plug gap.

Screw Pitch Gauge

The **screw pitch gauge** is a handy tool for determining the number of threads per inch on bolts, screws, and studs, **Figure 3-32.** It is often used when new threads must be cut. Using a screw pitch gauge will allow the technician to determine which tap or die to use. Taps and dies were discussed in Chapter 2.

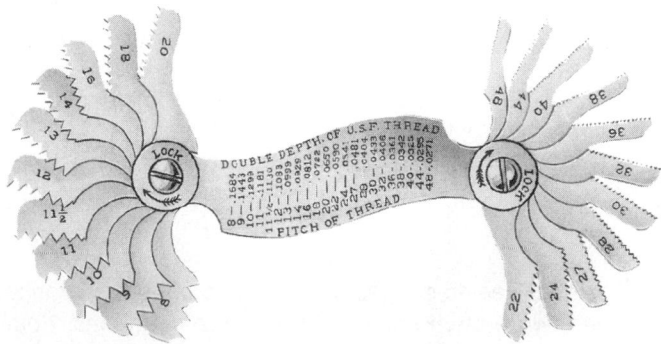

Figure 3-32. Screw pitch gauge. First or small number indicates number of threads per inch. Second number indicates double depth of the threads.

Telescoping Gauge

The **telescoping gauge** is an accurate tool for measuring inside bores of connecting rods and main bearings. To use this tool, compress the plungers and lock them in place by turning the knurled screw on the gauge's handle. Place the gauge in the bore and release the plungers. When the

plungers contact the bore walls, lock the plungers in place and remove the tool. Measure across the plungers with an outside micrometer to accurately determine bore size. Telescoping gauges are available in several ranges and may be purchased in sets. The proper feel for using this tool will be the same as for the inside micrometer, **Figure 3-33.**

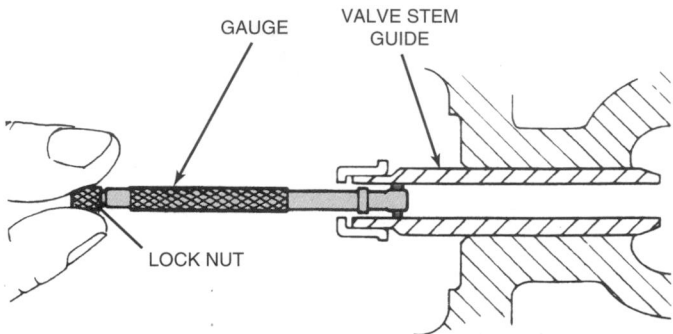

Figure 3-33. This technician is using a telescoping gauge to measure the diameter of a valve guide. (Chrysler)

Steel Rules

Steel rules are handy when measurements must be made quickly and exact precision is not necessary. There are two major types of steel rules:

- A hook rule with a sliding steel head. These are usually marked in 32nds and 64ths of an inch or in millimeters. Some rules are manufactured with inch markings on one side and metric markings on the other. This rule is handy for making quick measurements, such as those taken when comparing old and new parts.
- A steel tape. Most steel tapes can be carried in a pocket or clipped to a belt buckle. Like the hook rule, the steel tape is also marked in 32nds and 64ths of an inch or in millimeters. The tape is handy for making large measurements.

Spring Scale

Spring scales are often used to measure the "pull" on feeler strips when fitting pistons and in any situation where the precise weight or amount of drag must be determined. A typical spring scale is shown in **Figure 3-34.**

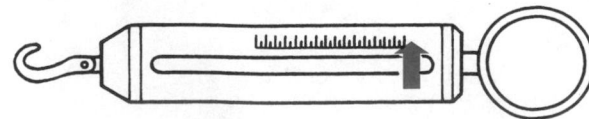

Figure 3-34. A spring scale is a must in every tool kit.

Steel Straightedge

An accurate **steel straightedge** is frequently used when checking parts for warpage. It should be long enough to span the length of an engine block, head, or flywheel. Be careful when handling and storing a straightedge. It must not be damaged, **Figure 3-35.**

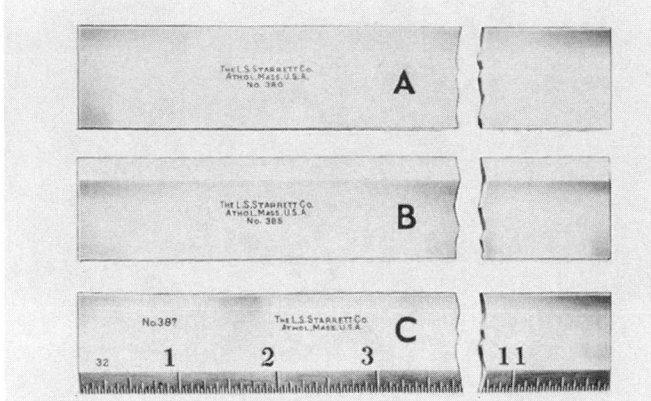

Figure 3-35. Steel straightedge. A—Square edge. B—Bevel edge. C—Bevel and ruled edge. These are available in different lengths.

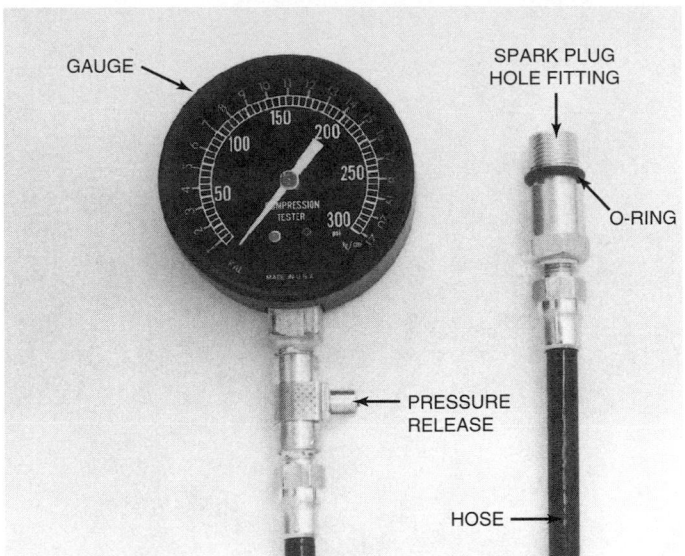

Figure 3-36. Compression gauge. (Ken Tool)

Temperature Is Important

Many specifications for measurements will state that they apply at room temperature, at an exact temperature, or at engine operating temperature. Remember that all metals contract and expand in direct proportion to their temperatures. This makes it imperative that temperature specifications be followed when making precision measurements and settings. Your measuring tools themselves can be affected by extremes of heat and cold. If your tools must be used when very cold or very hot, check them for accuracy before use.

Other Automotive Measuring Equipment

The following section deals with measuring equipment used to perform many diagnostic operations. Additional test and measurement equipment will be covered in later chapters.

Pressure Gauges

When diagnosing many automotive systems, the automotive technician must accurately measure pressures. Therefore, the technician should have several **pressure gauges.** These gauges measure air pressures or the pressure of automotive liquids, such as engine oil, transmission fluid, power steering fluid, and fuel. The most common pressure gauges are discussed below.

Compression Gauge

The **compression gauge, Figure 3-36,** measures the pressure developed in an engine cylinder when the piston moves up on the compression stroke. The compression gauge measures this compression in pounds per square inch, or PSI. By using a compression gauge to check the condition of each cylinder, the technician can identify many engine problems. The gauge is connected to the cylinder through a high-pressure hose that is threaded into the spark

plug hole of a gasoline engine (or the fuel injector hole of a diesel engine). When the engine is cranked, the upward movement of the piston in the cylinder compresses the air, and the pressure created by this action is read on the gauge. Use of the compression tester is covered in detail in Chapter 11.

Vacuum Gauge

The **vacuum gauge, Figure 3-37,** measures vacuum, or negative air pressure. Vacuum is the difference between the air pressure in the engine intake manifold and atmospheric pressure. Vacuum is a reliable indicator of engine load and condition. Variations in vacuum readings indicate various engine problems. Vacuum gauges can also be used to test for proper vacuum to and from vacuum-operated components, such as vacuum-operated heater doors.

The vacuum gauge may be used with a vacuum pump to test various vacuum-operated devices. The pump creates a vacuum on the device to be tested, and the gauge measures the vacuum and indicates if the unit can hold the vacuum. The technician may also be able to observe the action of the vacuum device as the vacuum is applied.

Oil Pressure Tester

An **oil pressure tester** measures the pressure developed by the engine oil pump or by the pumps in automatic transmissions and power steering systems. The oil pressure tester is used to determine whether the pump is providing the specified pressure. The pressure tester is attached to the unit to be tested through a high-pressure hose that threads into a pressure port, **Figure 3-38.** The pressure gauge scale is calibrated according to the output of the system being tested. Engine oil pressure seldom exceeds about 80 PSI, while automatic transmission pressures can reach 300 PSI and power steering pressures can reach 2000 PSI.

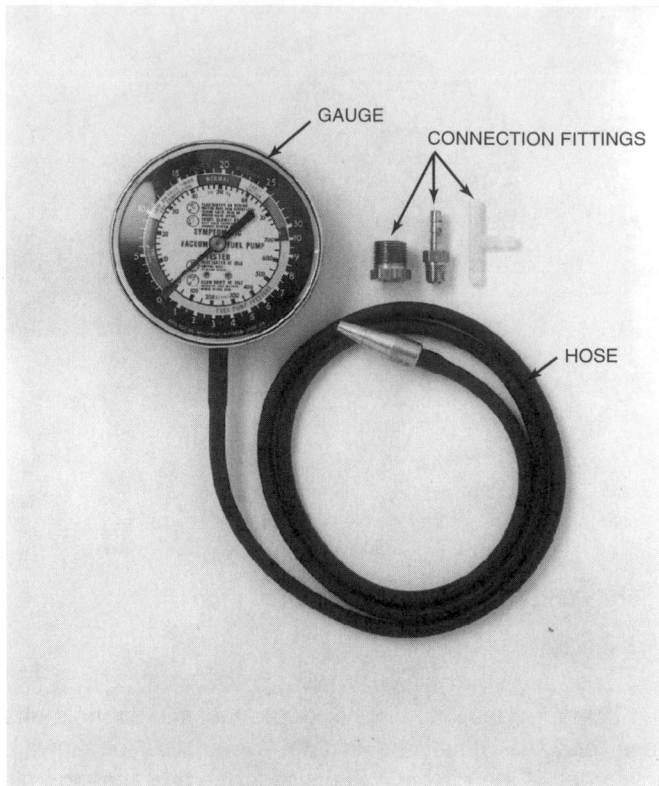

Figure 3-37. Vacuum gauge. (Marquette Tool)

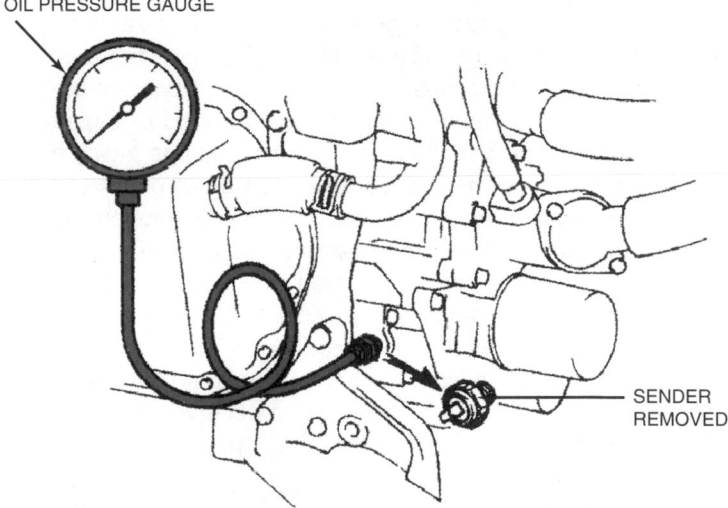

Figure 3-38. Oil pressure gauge. (Toyota)

Fuel Pressure Tester

The *fuel pressure tester* measures the pressure developed by the fuel pump. This tester is used to determine whether the fuel pump is providing enough pressure and flow to keep the engine supplied with fuel. It can also be used to detect clogged fuel filters or other fuel line problems. Pressure testers can be used on both carbureted and fuel-injected engines. A typical fuel pressure tester is shown in **Figure 3-39.**

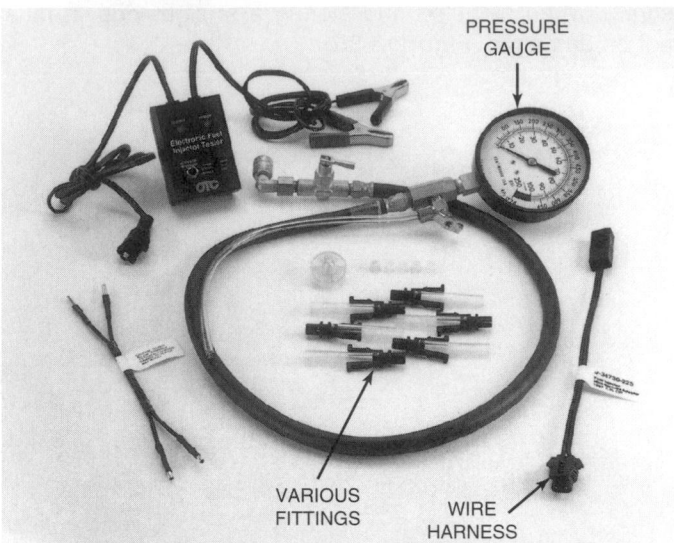

Figure 3-39. Fuel pressure tester. (OTC)

Electrical Testers

The automotive technician must be familiar with several electrical testers in order to troubleshoot electrical systems. Older electrical testers have a needle, or pointer, to indicate the electrical reading. These testers are called analog gauges. Many modern electrical testers are digital and display a number that indicates the electrical reading. Electrical theory and the use of these testers will be covered in detail in later chapters.

Test Light

A *test light* is a simple electrical tester composed of a 12-volt light bulb, two terminals, and connecting wiring, **Figure 3-40.** Using a test light is a quick way to check an electrical device or circuit. However, test lights cannot be used to measure exact electrical units; they only indicate whether electricity is present. A test light should not be used to check computers and other solid-state devices because they can be ruined by the current flowing through the light.

There are two types of test lights. The powered test light contains a battery and is used to check for a complete circuit when no current is flowing in the circuit. The nonpowered test light is connected between a powered circuit and ground. It will light up if power is present in the circuit.

Ohmmeter

Ohmmeters are used to measure electrical resistance. Resistance, which is the opposition to current flow that exists in every electrical circuit or device, is measured in Ohms. Ohmmeters can only check an electrical circuit when no current is flowing in the circuit. An ohmmeter has two leads, which are connected to each side of the unit or circuit to be tested. Polarity (direction of current flow) is not important when checking resistance, except in the case of diodes or some computer circuits. Most ohmmeters have selector knobs for checking various ranges of resistance values. Analog ohmmeters have a special knob to adjust the needle to zero before checking resistance.

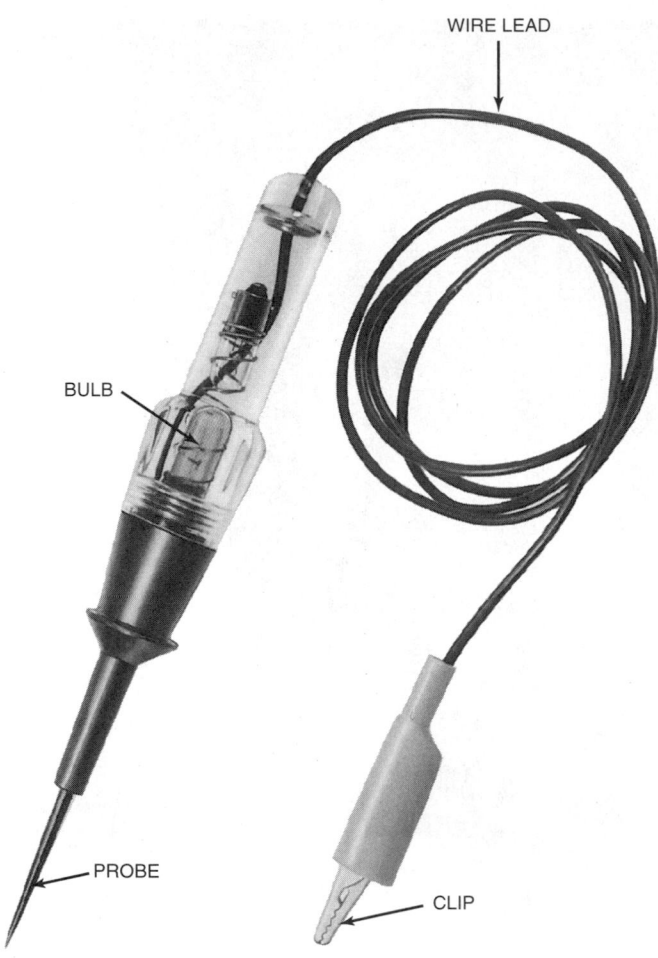

Figure 3-40.   Test light. (S & G Tools)

Voltmeter

Voltmeters are used to check voltage, or electrical potential, between two points in an energized circuit. The circuit to be checked must have a source of electricity available. On some voltmeters, different scales can be selected, depending on the voltage level being measured. Always observe proper polarity when attaching voltmeter leads. The negative lead should always be connected to ground, and the positive lead should be attached to the positive part of the circuit.

Ammeter

An **ammeter** is used to check the amperage (current) in a circuit. The ammeter is used to check the amperage draw of starters or other motors and to check battery condition. Ammeters can also be used to check the amperage draw of ignition coils, solenoids, and other electrical devices.

Multimeter

Multimeters are meters that combine voltmeters, ammeters, ohmmeters, and other testers into one unit. Multimeters usually have at least one positive lead (red) and one negative lead (black). Some multimeters have additional leads for special functions. Polarity should be care-

fully noted when making some tests with multimeters. A typical multimeter is shown in **Figure 3-41.**

Tachometer

Tachometers are used to measure engine speed. Modern tachometers are available in either analog or digital versions. Tachometers have at least two leads. One lead is connected to the distributor side of the ignition coil, and the other lead is connected to ground. Some tachometers have a clamp-on pickup that is placed around a plug wire to obtain the speed reading.

The tachometer may have a low range to set idle speeds and a high range for making various tests at high engine speeds. The ranges may be selected with a control knob, or they may switch automatically as engine speed varies. Some tachometers have a provision for checking distributor dwell, or the amount of time that primary current is flowing in the ignition coil. This is useful when working on older vehicles with point-type ignition systems.

What Is Your Opinion?

A person has just applied for a job as a technician. The garage has a reputation for excellent work. The owner is interested, there is an opening, and the pay is good. The owner introduces the applicant to you, who, as shop supervisor, will be expected to evaluate this person's worth as a technician.

You walk to a nearby service bench, open your tool chest, and lay out a selection of measuring tools. You indicate a specific cylinder bore you would like miked, and inform the applicant to choose the tools and make the measurement.

The applicant picks up an inside caliper and a six inch steel rule, adjusts the caliper in the bore, and then places the caliper on the face of the six inch rule. After some squinting, the applicant informs you that the bore diameter is "just a whisker over four inches." The actual bore diameter is 4.030″. What do you think of the applicant's ability? Will you recommend hiring this person? If not, why?

Tech Talk

An office copier is a handy tool. If you are constantly referring to a certain page of a service manual for engine or electrical specifications, you can copy the page and place it where you can see it, such as on the inside cover of your tool box. This will save time in looking up the specification and will also save wear and tear on the service manual.

Other good subjects for copying are electrical schematics. Instead of tracing out a circuit on the schematic, make a copy and use that to trace the circuit. This saves the original schematic for later use.

Also, when you take a set of measurements, such as compression readings, copy them and give the original to the customer. This allows the customer to see exactly what must be done to the vehicle.

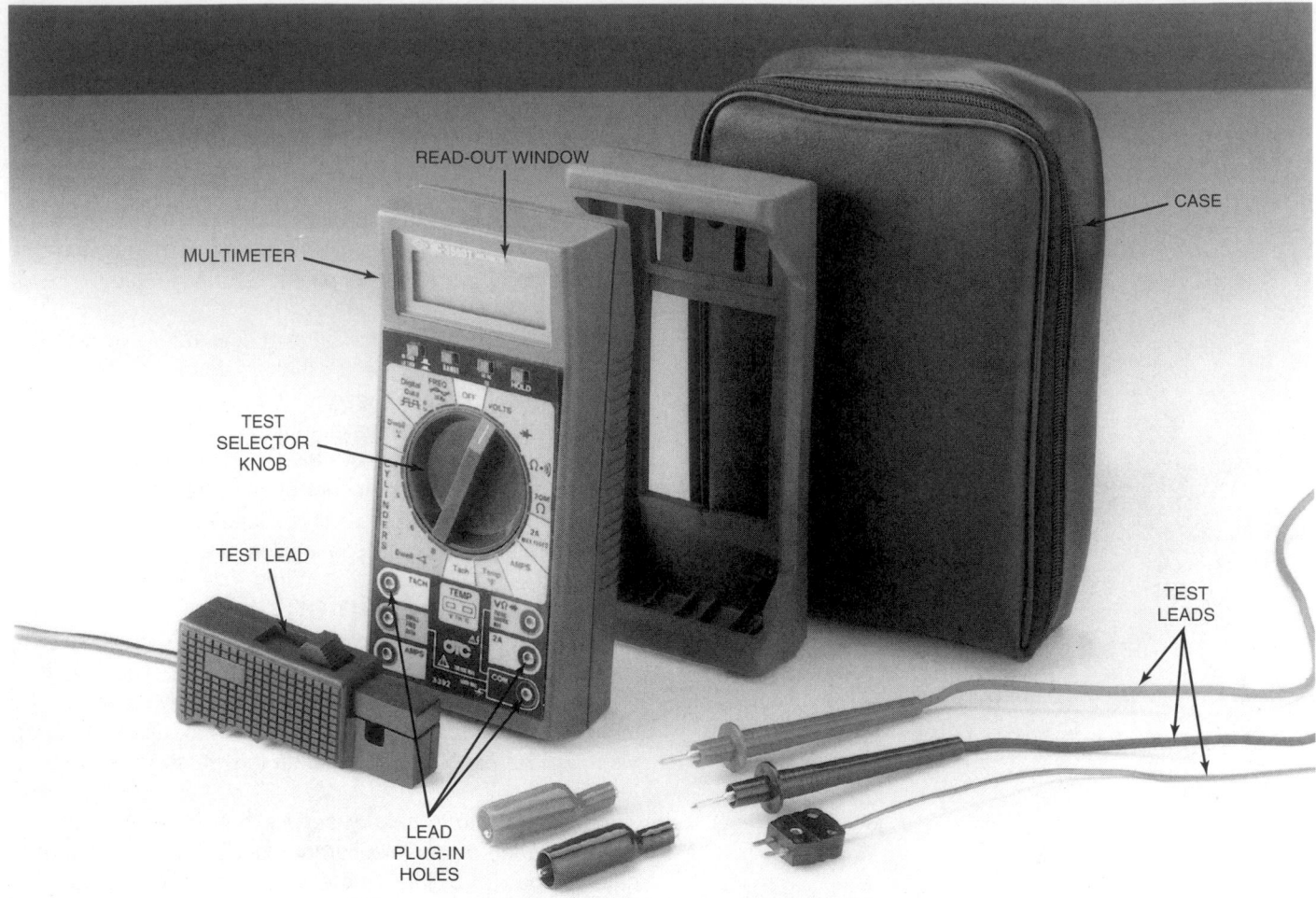

Figure 3-41. Typical multimeter used for automotive applications. (OTC)

Summary

It is important for you to select and correctly use the measuring tools. This will help you take accurate measurements, which are extremely important when servicing late-model vehicles. Precision measuring tools require careful handling and proper storage.

The technician should be able to use outside and inside micrometers, micrometer depth gauges, dial indicators, inside and outside calipers, dial calipers, dividers, feeler gauges, wire gauges, screw pitch gauges, telescoping gauges, steel rules, straightedges, spring scales, and various pressure and electrical testers. Other specialized measuring tools may be acquired as the need dictates.

Know These Terms

Outside micrometer	Feel
Range	Digital micrometer
Thimble	Inside micrometer
Spindle	Micrometer depth gauge
Sleeve	Dial indicator
Vernier micrometer	Valve seat runout gauge
Metric micrometer	Cylinder gauge

Calipers	Pressure gauges
Dial caliper	Compression gauge
Dividers	Vacuum gauge
Feeler gauges	Oil pressure tester
Thickness gauges	Fuel pressure tester
Wire gauge	Test light
Screw pitch gauge	Ohmmeters
Telescoping gauge	Voltmeters
Steel rules	Ammeter
Spring scales	Multimeters
Steel straightedge	Tachometers

Review Questions—Chapter 3

Do not write in this book. Write your answers on a separate sheet of paper.

1. To measure an object that is 3.500″ (88.90 mm) in diameter, you would use a micrometer with a range of _____ to _____.
   (A) 1″ to 2″
   (B) 2″ to 3″
   (C) 3″ to 4″
   (D) 4″ to 5″

Select the correct (some are wrong) readings for the following 0-1″ micrometer settings.

2. _____
3. _____
4. _____
5. _____
6. _____

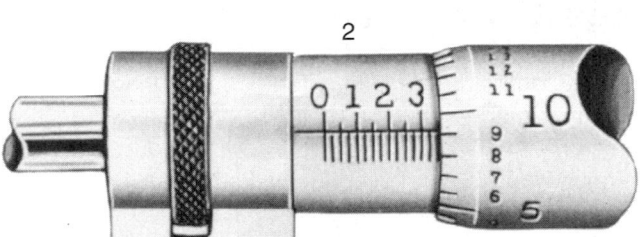

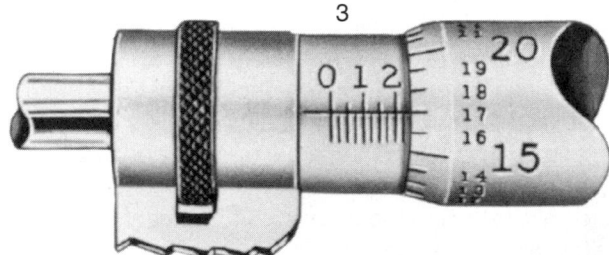

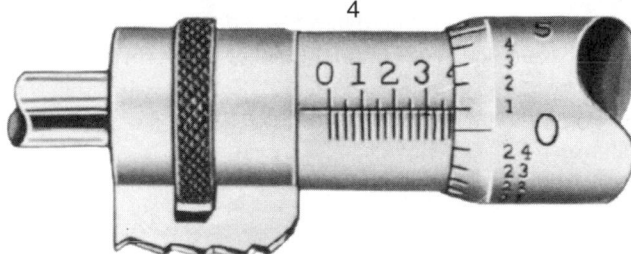

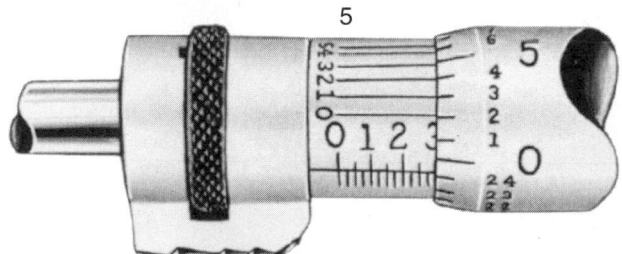

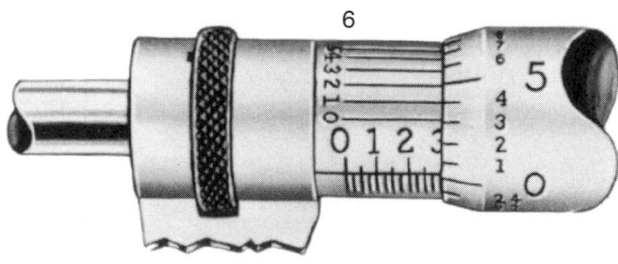

.359   .349   .3001   .3003   .2994
.376   .286   .243   .242   .2991

Name the best tool to handle each of the following measurements:

7. Diameter of a wrist pin.
8. Diameter of a cylinder bore.
9. Distance from face of cylinder head to valve guide top.
10. End play in crankshaft.
11. Diameter of wrist pin bore in a piston.
12. Connecting rod big end bore diameter.
13. Lash (free movement or play) between two gears.
14. Teeth per inch on a bolt.
15. Clearance between the valve stem and rocker.
16. Diameter of an exhaust pipe.
17. Spark plug gap.
18. Disc brake rotor runout.
19. Length of a muffler.
20. Distance between the fan blades and radiator.
21. Engine block surface for warpage.

Write the correct decimal readings for the following:
22. _____ Two and three-hundred and twenty five thousandths inches.
23. _____ Eight-hundred and seventy-eight and one half thousandths inches.
24. _____ Four and six-hundred and thirteen and one-quarter thousandths inches.
25. _____ Three and one-half inches.
26. _____ One ten-thousandth of an inch.
27. _____ One thousandth of an inch.
28. _____ One hundredth of an inch.
29. _____ One tenth of an inch.
30. _____ One inch.

ASE-Type Questions

1. Each line on the sleeve of a standard micrometer represents ___ inch.
(A) 0.0025
(B) 0.025
(C) 0.25
(D) 1
2. Each line on the sleeve of a metric micrometer represents ___ mm.
(A) 0.005
(B) 0.05
(C) 0.5
(D) 5
3. Technician A says that a micrometer should be tightly clamped around the work being measured. Technician B says that a micrometer should be occasionally checked for accuracy. Who is right?
(A) A only.
(B) B only.
(C) Both A & B.
(D) Neither A nor B.
4. Technician A says that dial calipers are very precise and are capable of obtaining inside, outside, and depth readings. Technician B says that dividers are very precise and are capable of obtaining inside, outside, and

depth readings. Who is right?

(A) A only.

(B) B only.

(C) Both A & B.

(D) Neither A nor B.

5. Technician A says that a compression tester is an air pressure gauge. Technician B says that engine compression is negative air pressure. Who is right?

(A) A only.

(B) B only.

(C) Both A & B.

(D) Neither A nor B.

6. A vacuum gauge will not detect which of the following engine conditions?

(A) Burned valve.

(B) Late ignition timing.

(C) Excessive oil consumption.

(D) Clogged exhaust.

7. Which of the following engine problems can be detected with an oil pressure gauge?

(A) Worn rings.

(B) Worn valves.

(C) Worn bearings.

(D) Sticking hydraulic lifter.

8. A fuel pressure tester can measure all of the following fuel pump problems EXCEPT:

(A) pressure.

(B) noise.

(C) vacuum.

(D) volume.

9. A non-powered test light can be used to check all of the following, EXCEPT:

(A) a circuit for presence of voltage.

(B) fuse condition.

(C) an ECU or other solid state components.

(D) resistor continuity.

10. Technician A says that a voltmeter measures resistance to the flow of electricity. Technician B says that a multimeter can measure many kinds of electrical properties. Who is right?

(A) A only.

(B) B only.

(C) Both A & B.

(D) Neither A nor B.

Suggested Activities

1. Obtain several lengths of steel rod, flat stock, and tubing. Measure them with different measuring devices, such a ruler, steel tape, calipers, vernier caliper, and micrometer. Create a chart showing your readings. Which was the most accurate way of measuring? Why? Display your chart in the classroom or shop.

2. List at least three areas of automotive repair where accurate measurements are absolutely necessary. List some areas of automotive repair where accurate measurements are less critical. Discuss your lists with the other members of your class.

3. Explain how to read a micrometer to a friend who does not know how to use one. Have your friend try a reading and continue to help until he or she does it correctly. By doing this, you will reinforce your knowledge.

4. Place a wrist pin in the freezer compartment of a refrigerator. When thoroughly cold, remove the pin, wipe it dry, and quickly measure its diameter and length using an outside micrometer. (Hold the wrist pin with a cloth.) Write down your readings. Now place the wrist pin in boiling water. When the pin is hot, remove it, wipe it dry, and quickly recheck its diameter and length. Is there a difference? If so, how much? What does this indicate? Write a short report summarizing your findings.

4

Jacks, Lifts, and Holding Fixtures

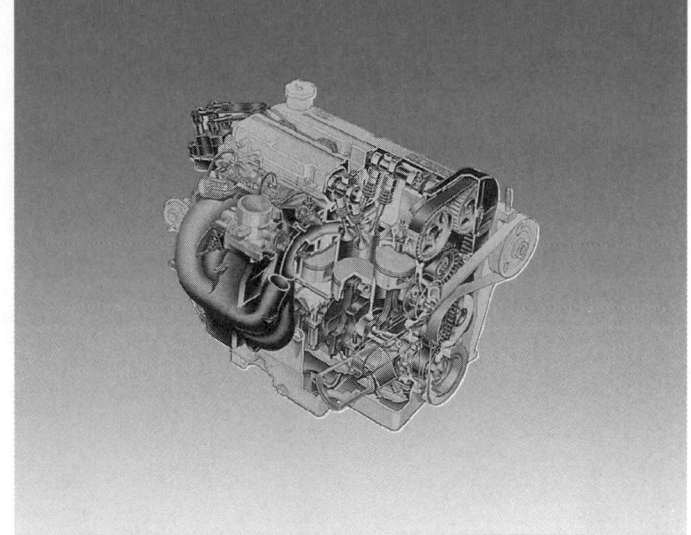

After studying this chapter, you will be able to:
- List the most commonly used lifting and holding equipment.
- Select the correct type of lifting or holding equipment for the job.
- Describe safety precautions for jacks, lifts, and holding fixtures.

A wide assortment of lifting equipment and holding fixtures is available in most automotive shops. Proper use of this equipment will both facilitate and speed up repair work. Extreme care must be used with lifting equipment and all tools capable of developing high pressures, stresses, and tensions. Never use equipment without familiarizing yourself with its use. There are many safety rules in this chapter. Study them carefully.

Lifting Equipment

Lifting equipment includes many devices operated mechanically, hydraulically (oil pressure), or pneumatically (air pressure). In some cases, lifting devices are powered by a combination of hydraulic and pneumatic pressures. The following section details the common types of lifting equipment used in the automotive shop.

Hand Jack

Jacks are often used to raise vehicles when other lifting equipment is not available. The hydraulic *hand jack* is very useful in many applications. It is short, compact, and capable of producing great pressure. It can be used to raise heavy weights, to bend parts, and to pull or push parts into alignment. A hydraulic hand jack is often used as a power source in small presses.

When using a hand jack, make sure it is positioned so that it will not slip as pressure is developed. Be careful not to drop the jack, as it is quite heavy, **Figure 4-1.**

Hydraulic Floor Jack

A *floor jack* is used to raise a portion of a car from the ground. It can be used to raise the entire front, back, or side of a vehicle. It is also handy for maneuvering cars into tight quarters. The jack is placed under the front or back of the car, and the vehicle is lifted. By pulling the jack in the direction desired, the car can be moved forward, backward, or sideways.

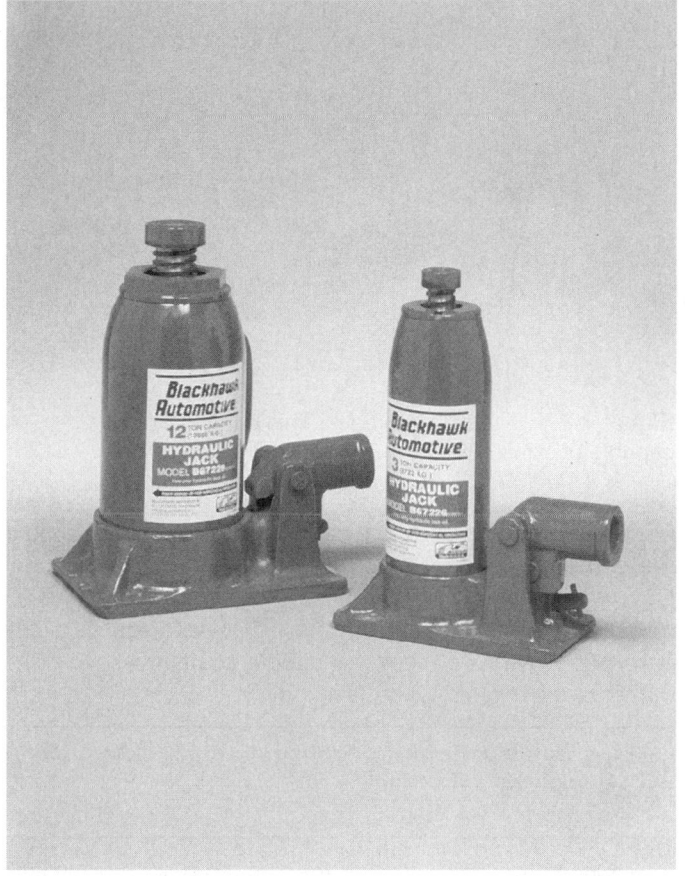

Figure 4-1. Hydraulic hand jacks. (Blackhawk Automotive)

Floor jacks are available in many sizes, with lifting capacities varying from one to twenty tons (900 to 18,000 kg). **Figure 4-2** illustrates a typical floor jack.

Proper Placement Is Important

When positioning the jack saddle for lifting, make certain it is securely engaged. Select a spot that is strong enough to support the load. Never try raising a car by jacking on the oil pan, clutch housing, transmission, tie rods, gas tank, or other weak components.

Proper placement requires care. Get down and take a good look at the jack saddle location before raising a vehicle. If the car is part way up and the jack saddle slips, serious

Figure 4-2. Hydraulic floor jack. This particular jack is capable of lifting 4000 lb. (1814 kilograms).

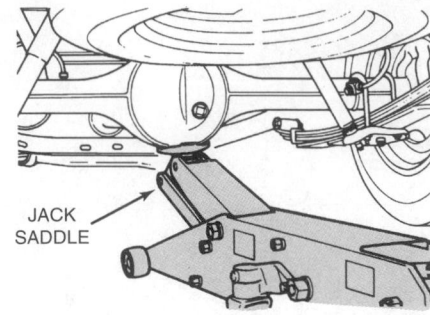

Figure 4-3. Raising a car with a floor jack. Make certain the saddle is properly positioned. (Honda)

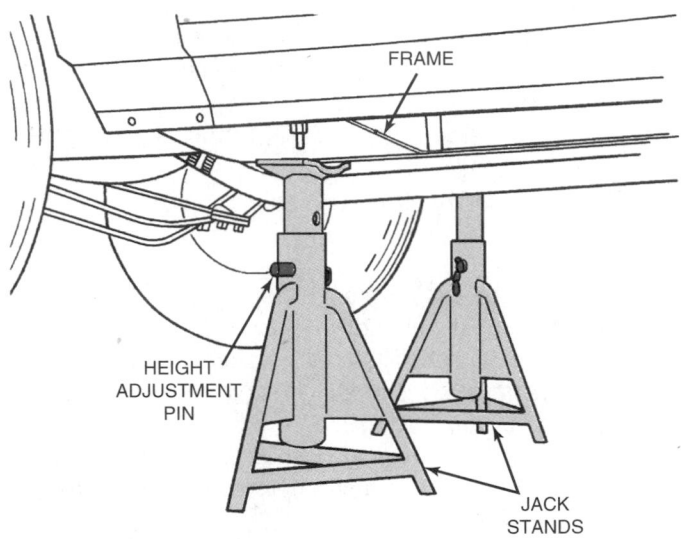

Figure 4-4. Typical adjustable jack stands. Note the height adjusting pin. (Chevrolet)

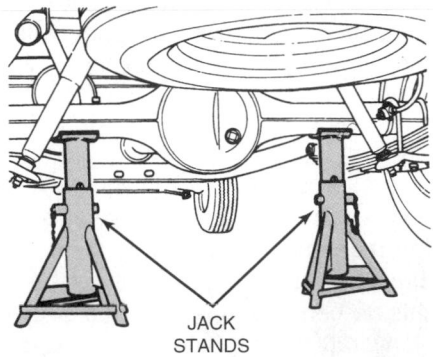

Figure 4-5. Properly placed jack stands provide safe support. (Honda)

damage can occur. On some cars, jacking at a corner or near the center of the chassis on one side can cause damage. Car manufacturers illustrate correct lifting points in their manuals. You must follow the manufacturer's specifications carefully. **Figure 4-3** shows a saddle positioned under the center of the differential housing.

 Warning: Never work under a vehicle supported only by a floor jack.

Once the car is raised to the desired height, place jack stands in the desired locations and lower the weight onto the stands. The jack may then be removed if desired. If not needed in another area, it may be left in position with a very light lifting pressure to keep it positioned.

Jack Stands

Jack stands are made in numerous heights and are usually adjustable. The stands shown in **Figure 4-4** are typical. Note the pin adjustment.

When inserting jack stands, place them in contact with some unit capable of supporting the load. Do not place the jack stand saddles in contact with tapered edges, which may allow them to slip. Make sure the saddles have a secure "bite." **Figure 4-5** shows a pair of jack stands (often called safety stands) in place under a rear axle housing. Note that the saddles are properly positioned.

End Lifts

The *end lift* can be operated by pneumatic pressure or hydraulic pressure. Two basic designs are used. One type will reach far enough under the car to contact the rear axle housing. The other design engages the bumper only.

A pneumatic, long-reach end lift is pictured in **Figure 4-6.** This end lift is capable of raising the vehicle much higher than a floor jack.

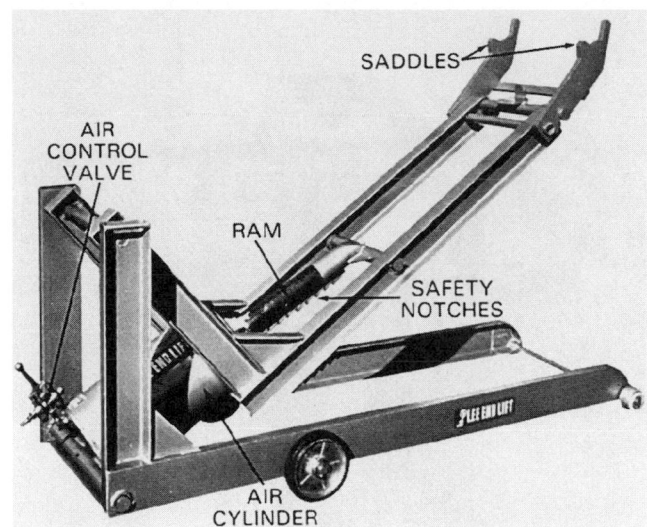

Figure 4-6. One type of long-reach, air-operated end lift. Notice the safety notches on the ram. (Hein-Werner, Lee)

The bumper lift shown in **Figure 4-7** is also air operated. Note the twin rubber-covered *saddles.* The distance between the saddles can be adjusted to engage the bumper where desired. Remember that bumpers may not be very strong, especially near their outer ends. If the bumper can be used, place the saddles at the main bumper-to-frame attachment points.

End lifts are generally provided with strong safety locks, so the technician may safely work beneath the car without jack stands. Make sure the safety lock is fully engaged and the lift contact points are solid. If there is even the slightest doubt, use jack stands for additional protection.

Single-Post Frame Lift

A *single-post frame lift* leaves both the front and rear of the car completely exposed. It does, however, create some obstruction in the central portion of the vehicle. **Figure 4-8** shows a car in the raised position on a single-post frame lift. Note the lift contact points on the frame.

 Note: Proper lift contact points vary from one type of vehicle to another. Follow the manufacturer's instructions.

Double-Post Frame Lift

The *double-post frame lift* eliminates the need for a single, central post. This leaves the center portion of the car more accessible. As with the single-post lift, the car must be carefully centered on a double-post frame lift. In **Figure 4-9,** the technician has centered the car and is adjusting the swivel lift arms.

A vehicle is shown in the raised position in **Figure 4-10.** The equalizer racks ensure that both columns move up and down together. This provides for proper placement of this car on lift.

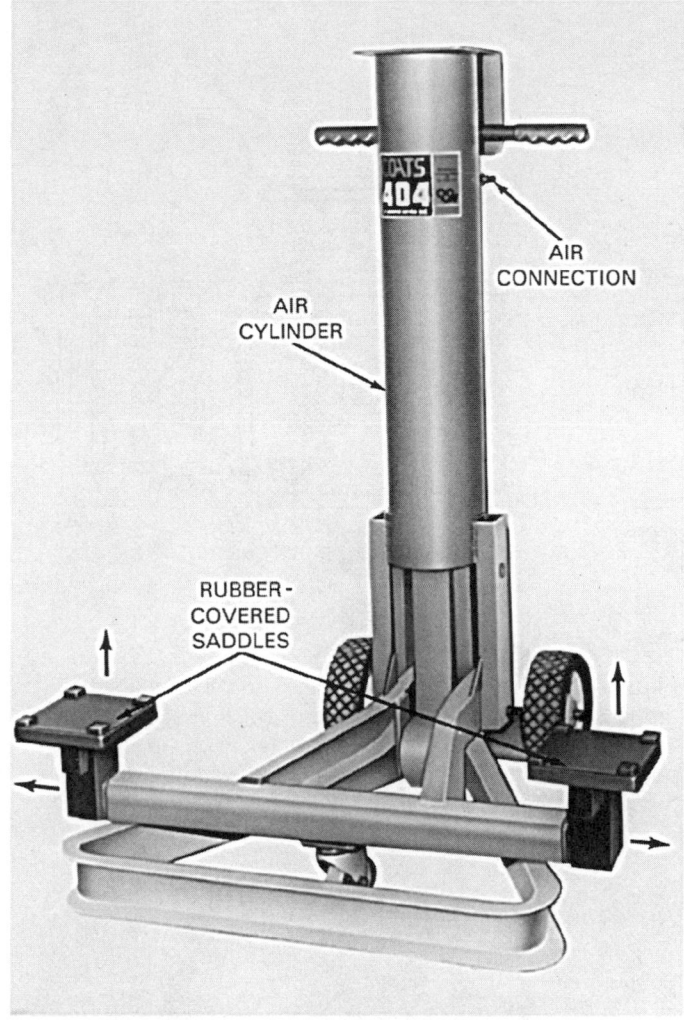

Figure 4-7. A typical air-operated bumper lift. Do not use on cars with energy absorbing bumpers. (Coats)

Double-Post Suspension Lift

The *double-post suspension lift,* pictured in **Figure 4-11,** contacts the front suspension arms and either the rear axle housing or the rear wheels. The front lift column can be moved forward or backward to adjust for various wheelbase lengths. This type of lift presents a minimal amount of under-car obstruction. On some models, a single column can be raised. This allows the lift to be used as an end lift, if desired.

Drive-On Lift

The *drive-on lift,* **Figure 4-12,** offers placement speed, but it does have a relatively large obstruction area. Additionally, the wheels cannot be removed from the vehicle without further jacking of the suspension members—a practice that is not recommended.

Choice of Lifts

As you have noticed, each lift offers certain advantages and disadvantages. The type of lift needed will depend on the work to be performed. Many shops provide

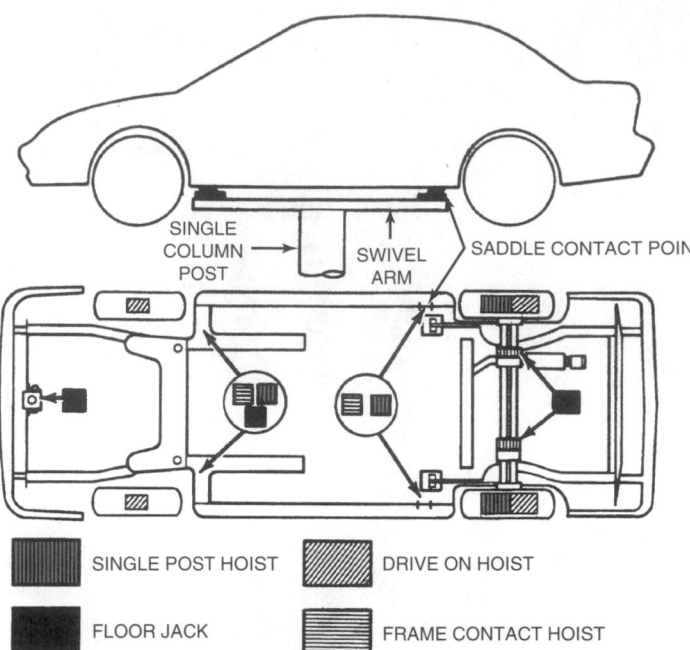

SINGLE POST HOIST   DRIVE ON HOIST

FLOOR JACK   FRAME CONTACT HOIST

Figure 4-8. A single post frame lift. The vehicle must be properly centered and the swivel arm pads must contact the vehicle chassis properly. Always double check the lift contact points *before* lifting the vehicle. A contact pad that is not properly located can allow the vehicle to fall. Be careful!

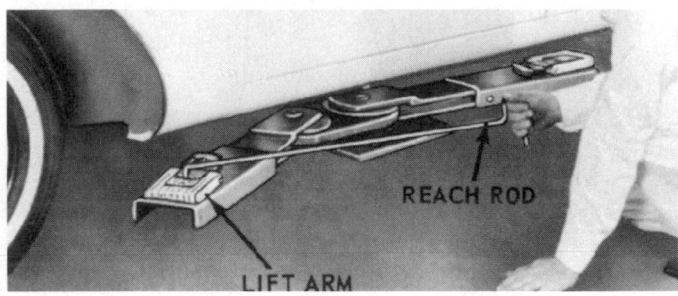

Figure 4-9. Double-post frame lift. Note the reach rod, which is used to position the lift arms.

several types of lifts, allowing the technician to choose the most appropriate lift for the job at hand.

Safety Considerations

Floor jacks, end lifts, and frame lifts must be used with extreme care. Remember that many cars can weigh two tons (1,800 kg) or more. Each year, a number of technicians are killed or injured by the careless use of lift equipment. When using any type of shop equipment, remember to learn and respect the dangers involved. Consistently follow all safety rules and learn to think before you act. Apply these rules to each and every task. Apply them over and over until they become habits that may someday save you from serious injury or death. In addition to following safe operating procedures, it is imperative that lift equipment be kept in sound operating condition. Cracked or bent parts, faulty safety locks, leaking cylinders, and other problems must be corrected.

Figure 4-10. A double-post frame lift. This truck was carefully centered before lifting. Because the lifting posts are on the outside of the vehicle, the undercarriage is completely exposed for service.

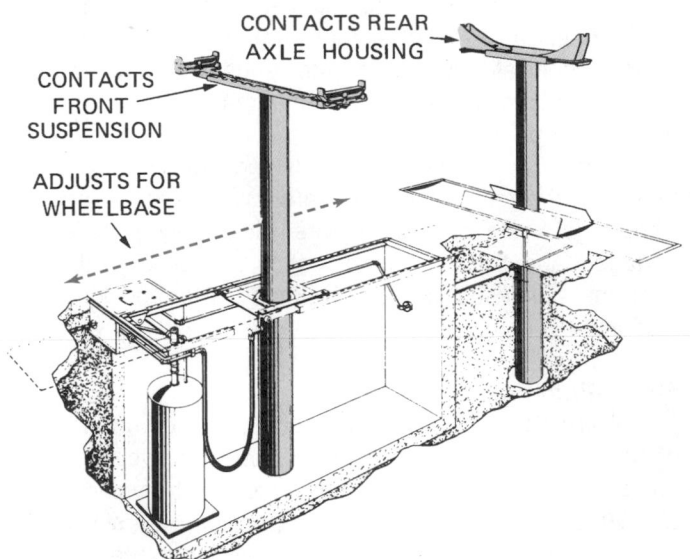

Figure 4-11. Double-post suspension lift. This lift creates very little under-car obstruction.

The following safety precautions apply to all types of lifting equipment. Study the precautions carefully until you remember each one.

1. Position the lift saddles so that they securely contact the vehicle's chassis.
2. When using a floor jack, always use jack stands.
3. Once saddles are located, apply some pressure. Then, stop and examine the saddles again before lifting the car.
4. When raising an entire car, watch for side or overhead obstructions.

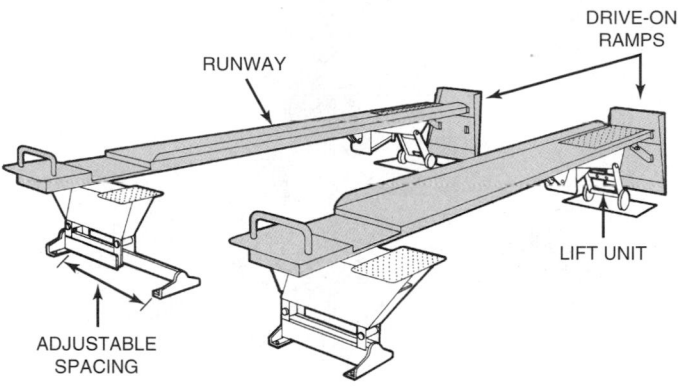

Figure 4-12. Drive-on lift or rack. This particular lift is designed for wheel alignment work. It is shown in the up position. (Ammco)

5. Be sure that the lift safety lock is securely engaged before going under the car.
6. Never remove a lift or jack from another technician's setup without asking permission first.
7. If it is necessary to change the raised height of a car, do not raise or lower the vehicle until all persons are out from under it.
8. Always check for equipment, parts, and personnel beneath a vehicle before lowering it.
9. Lower a vehicle slowly and watch it closely during the entire descent.

Specialty Lifting Equipment

The following section covers some special lifting and holding equipment with which the technician should be familiar.

Power Train Lift

A hydraulic **power train lift** is shown in **Figure 4-13.** The lift can be used to remove or install a complete engine/transaxle assembly from underneath the vehicle. Note the use of the safety straps.

Transmission Jacks

A **transmission jack** is used to remove and install transmissions and transfer cases. The jack's saddle is securely attached to the transmission with a series of adapters and a binder chain or strap. The saddle can be raised and lowered hydraulically, and it can be tipped in any direction through the use of adjusting screws. **Figure 4-14A** shows a typical jack with the transmission in place. **Figure 4-14B** illustrates a high-reach transmission jack. When using a transmission jack, be certain to attach the transmission securely. It is heavy, and if it slips, it could cause serious injury.

Wheel Dolly

Shops doing truck repair find a **wheel dolly** helpful when removing and installing large wheel assemblies.

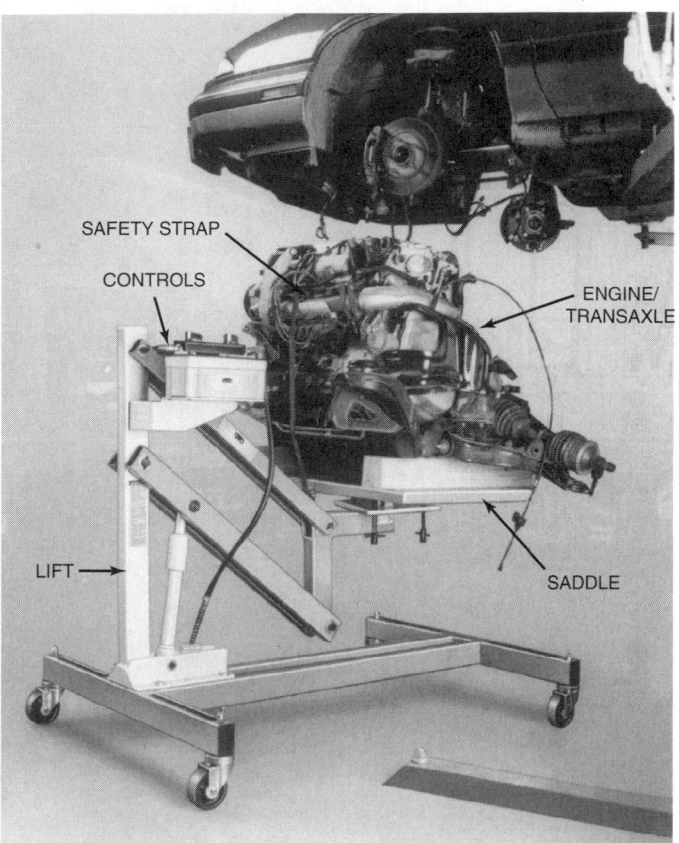

Figure 4-13. Power train lift. (Weaver)

Note the use of a hydraulic hand jack on the dolly in **Figure 4-15.**

Portable Crane and Chain Hoist

The **portable crane** and the **chain hoist** are excellent tools for engine removal. They can also be used to lift heavy parts to bench tops and truck beds. **Figure 4-16** shows a heavy-duty portable crane being used to remove an engine.

Safety Rules to Observe When Using a Crane or Chain Hoist

1. Stand clear of the crane or hoist at all times.
2. Lower the engine as soon as it is clear of the vehicle.
3. Never roll the crane with the load high in the air. Keep it just above the floor.
4. Never leave an engine suspended while working on it. Lower it to the floor or place it on a suitable engine stand.
5. Never leave the crane or hoist with the load suspended. If you must leave, even temporarily, lower the load.
6. When moving heavy loads, alert your fellow technicians.
7. When using a chain hoist attached to an overhead track, never give the load a hard shove and let it coast along the track. Move the load slowly and stay with it.
8. Attaching cables, chains, bolts, and other lifting devices must have ample strength.

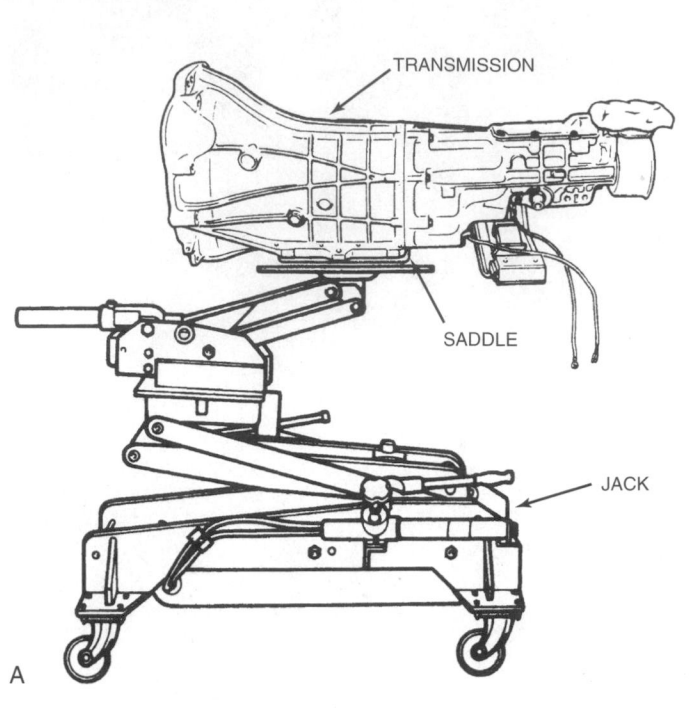

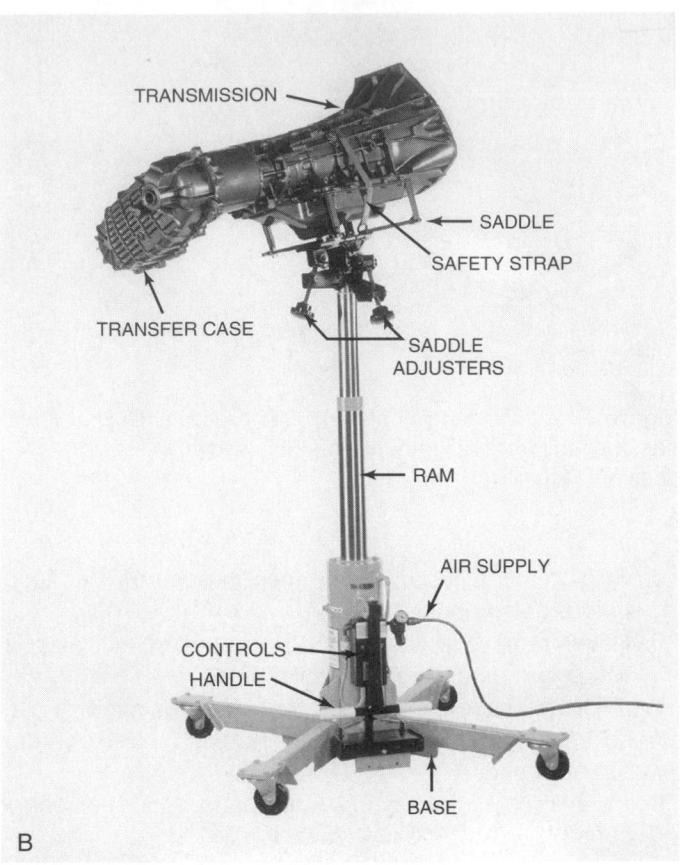

Figure 4-14. Two types of transmission jacks. A—Typical transmission jack, which is constructed like a floor jack. B—High-reach transmission jack. These jacks may also be used to handle engines that are removed from under car. (Weaver)

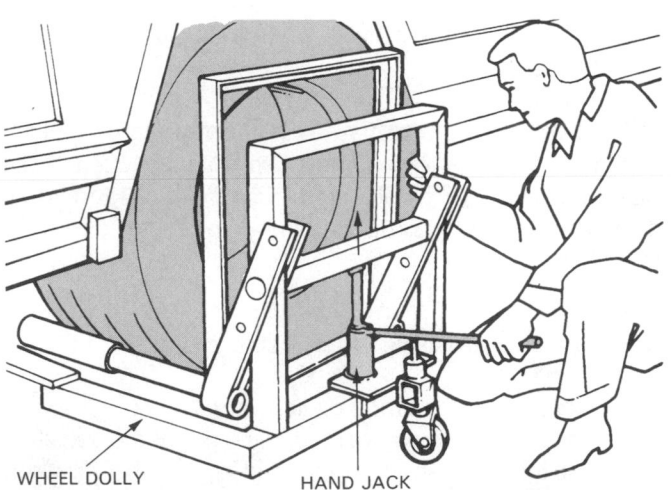

Figure 4-15. One type of hydraulically actuated wheel dolly. These aid greatly when removing and installing heavy wheel and tire assemblies. (Ford)

9. When using nuts to attach lift cables, each nut must be threaded fully on its fastener. When using capscrews, they must have a thread-engagement depth one and one-half times the diameter of the capscrew.

More information on the use of this equipment for engine work will be given in the section on engine removal and installation.

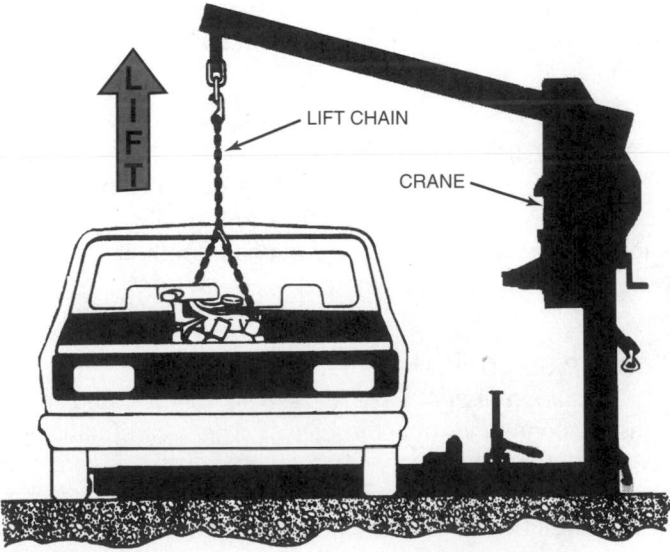

Figure 4-16. This portable crane is being used to pull an engine. (Guy-Chart Systems)

Extension Jack

An **extension jack** is a valuable tool for exerting mild pressure and for holding parts in place. Some extension jacks are adjusted up and down with a screw. Others are hydraulically operated. A hydraulic extension jack is pictured in **Figure 4-17.**

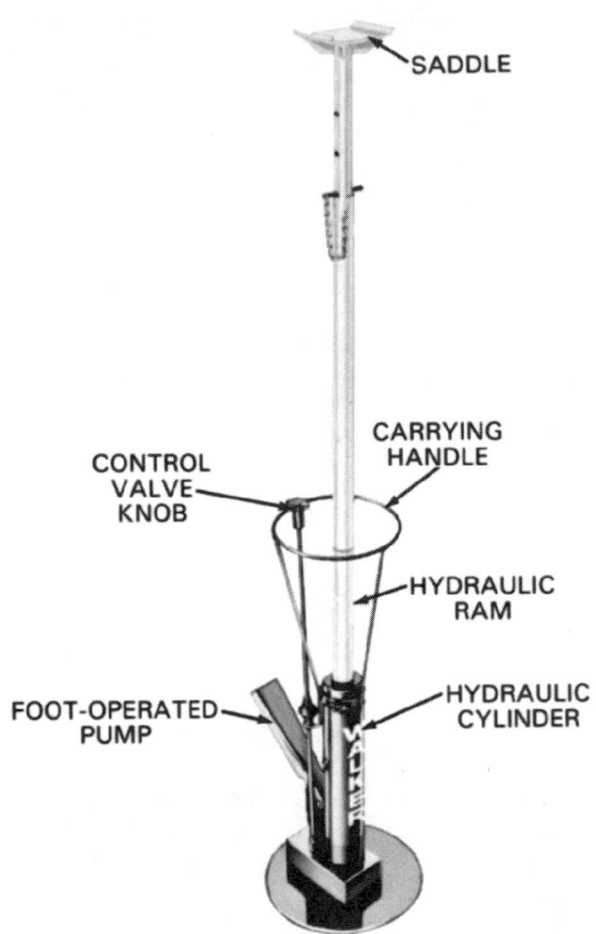

Figure 4-17. One type of extension jack. This jack is raised hydraulically by a foot-operated pump. It has a capacity of 1 ton (900 kg). (Lincoln St. Louis)

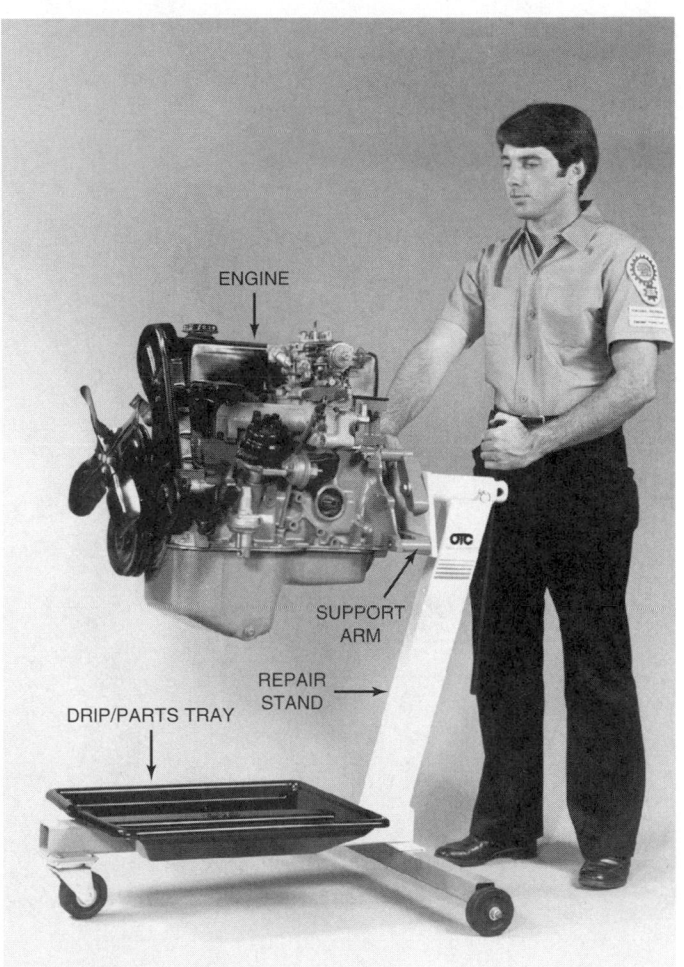

Figure 4-18. One type of movable engine repair stand. The technician can easily roll the engine around to various repair areas. (OTC)

Repair Stands

Engine block, cylinder head, transmission, and differential repairs are greatly facilitated by using a ***repair stand.*** Many types are available. When using repair stands, attach the unit being serviced securely to the stand. Carelessness here can be costly.

Figure 4-18 shows an engine block mounted in a stand. Note that a crank is used to move the block to various positions. A transmission mounted in a similar stand is pictured in **Figure 4-19.** Two cylinder heads are attached to a bench fixture in **Figure 4-20.** As with all stands, tighten the holding screws securely.

Hand Lifting

Occasionally, a technician will want to lift an object by hand. There are several important points to remember in order to avoid injury.

1. Do not "show off" by attempting to lift heavy objects. If necessary, ask for help or use a lift.
2. Keep your back straight and lift with your legs. Keep your legs as close together as possible, **Figure 4-21.**

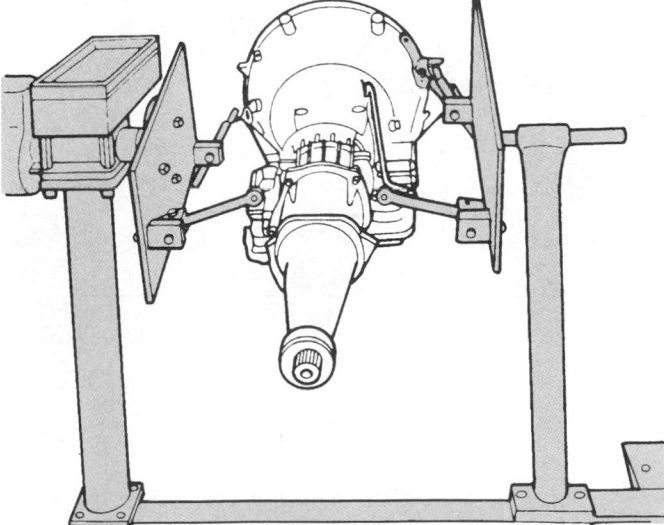

Figure 4-19. Transmission in repair stand. (Ford)

3. Unless you know you can handle the weight, never hold a part with one hand while removing the last fastener with your other hand.
4. Get a firm grip to prevent dropping objects.

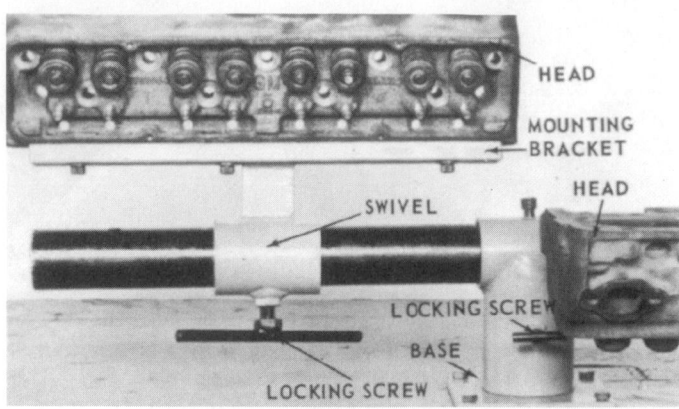

Figure 4-20. This cylinder head holding fixture simplifies repair work. (Storm-Vulcan)

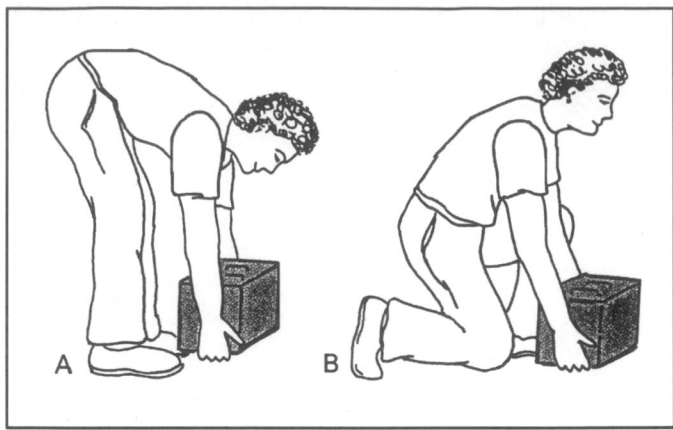

Figure 4-21. When lifting heavy objects, keep your back straight and use your legs to lift the weight. A—Incorrect lifting procedure. B—Correct lifting procedure.

Tech Talk

It is often necessary to operate a vehicle on a lift when checking for oil leaks or problems with the exhaust system or drivetrain. When operating a vehicle in the shop, it is very important to provide proper ventilation to prevent carbon monoxide poisoning. However, many people close the shop doors on cold days and do not realize that they are being poisoned. Symptoms of carbon monoxide poisoning include:

- Headaches or throbbing head.
- Roaring in the ears.
- Nausea.
- Rapid heartbeat.
- Impaired vision.
- Drowsiness.
- Mental confusion.

If you develop any of these symptoms, get out into the fresh air *immediately*. Do not waste time lowering the lift to turn off the engine. Once outside, arrange to open all doors and windows and turn on ventilators until the exhaust gases are removed.

port the car. Be careful not to damage parts when lifting. End lifts have a fairly high reach and support the car safely. Make sure the safety lock is in position. Single- and double-post lifts can be designed to engage either the frame, the suspension system, or the tires. All have advantages and disadvantages.

Vehicles must be centered on the lift, and the lifting brackets should be properly and securely placed. Use care when determining lift points to prevent chassis distortion or part damage.

Transmission jacks, wheel dollies, and portable cranes facilitate the removal and installation of heavy parts.

Repair stands for engines, transmissions, and other assemblies make repairs faster, safer, and easier. Always fasten the unit securely to the stand.

Know These Terms

Lifting equipment	Drive-on lift
Hand jack	Power train lift
Floor jack	Transmission jack
Jack stands	Wheel dolly
End lift	Portable crane
Saddles	Chain hoist
Single-post frame lift	Extension jack
Double-post frame lift	Repair stand
Double-post suspension lift	

Review Questions—Chapter 4

Do not write in this book. Write your answers on a separate sheet of paper.

1. Which of these locations is acceptable for placing a jack saddle?
   (A) Oil pan.
   (B) Transmission housing.
   (C) Differential housing.
   (D) Fuel tank.

2. An end lift is safer to use than most lifting equipment because of what feature?

Summary

Technicians should be familiar with various lifting and holding tools available to make their work easier and more efficient. The tools covered in this chapter must be used with extreme caution. Observe all recommended safety precautions.

Hand jacks have many applications. Floor jacks are very handy for raising and positioning cars. Never get under a car supported only by a floor jack. Use jack stands to sup-

3. What type of lift is most convenient for rear-wheel drive transmission or drive shaft removal?
   (A) Single-post frame lift.
   (B) Double-post frame lift.
   (C) End lift.
   (D) Bumper lift.
4. When attaching lift chains and cables with nuts and studs, how far should the nuts be threaded onto the studs?
   (A) One turn.
   (B) Two turns.
   (C) Three turns.
   (D) All the way.
5. The technician should always stand _____ of heavy loads.
6. Working on engines, transmissions, and cylinder heads is made much easier by the use of _____.
7. List three safety precautions that should be followed when hand lifting.
8. List seven safety rules that should be followed when using jacks and lifts.
9. When replacing a wheel on a heavy truck, it is a good idea to use a _____.
10. List five safety rules regarding portable cranes and chain hoists.

ASE-Type Questions

1. Technician A says that it is safe to work under a vehicle supported on a good, well-placed floor jack. Technician B says end lifts, if properly designed, provide sufficient holding power to allow the technician to work beneath the car without jack stands. Who is right?
   (A) A only.
   (B) B only.
   (C) Both A & B.
   (D) Neither A nor B.
2. Technician A says that lift height should not be varied if anyone is under the vehicle. Technician B says that jack contact points are not important as long as the jack gets a good grip. Who is right?
   (A) A only.
   (B) B only.
   (C) Both A & B.
   (D) Neither A nor B.
3. All of the following lifts make it easy to remove wheels, EXCEPT:
   (A) Low-level air lift.
   (B) End lift.
   (C) Drive-on lift.
   (D) Bumper lift.
4. When placing jack stands under a vehicle, they should be in contact with _____.
   (A) the vehicle frame
   (B) a suspension part capable of supporting the load
   (C) tapered or slanted edges
   (D) Either A or B.

5. Which type of lift does not have to be checked for proper positioning before lifting a vehicle?
   (A) Single-post frame lift.
   (B) Double-post frame lift.
   (C) Drive-on lift.
   (D) Bumper lift.
6. When using a single- or double-post frame lift or a drive-on lift, all the following safety precautions should be followed, EXCEPT:
   (A) Place jack stands under the frame.
   (B) Watch for any side or overhead obstructions when raising the vehicle.
   (C) Make certain that the lift safety lock is engaged before getting under the car.
   (D) Raise and lower the lift slowly.
7. A vehicle that has just been raised is observed to be rocking on the lift. Technician A says that the lift posts can be hammered in their proper positions without lowering the vehicle. Technician B says that the vehicle should be lowered immediately and the lift repositioned before proceeding with any work. Who is right?
   (A) A only.
   (B) B only.
   (C) Both A & B.
   (D) Neither A nor B.
8. Technician A says that when moving an object with a portable crane or chain hoist, the load should be kept as low as possible. Technician B says that it is a good safety practice to work on an engine suspended from a crane or a chain hoist. Who is right?
   (A) A only.
   (B) B only.
   (C) Both A & B.
   (D) Neither A nor B.
9. A chain type engine hoist is usually attached to _____.
   (A) a portable crane
   (B) the building roof supports
   (C) a shop door frame
   (D) Either B or C.
10. An engine has been removed from the vehicle using a portable crane. Technician A says that the engine should be immediately lowered to just above the floor. Technician B says that the engine should be immediately wheeled to a repair stand. Who is right?
   (A) A only.
   (B) B only.
   (C) Both A & B.
   (D) Neither A nor B.

Suggested Activities

1. Send letters requesting up-to-date catalogs to several lifting equipment manufacturers. Study the catalogs carefully. Although your shop may not have all the equipment shown in the catalogs, you should be familiar with the various types of equipment available.

2. Draw a schematic of the hydraulic lift used in your shop, showing how hydraulic pressure is developed and controlled.

3. Make a list of lift safety rules. Make copies of the list and post one copy at each of the shop lifts.

4. List the series of steps that should be performed to correctly raise a vehicle with a floor jack and secure it with safety stands. Discuss the steps with other members of your class.

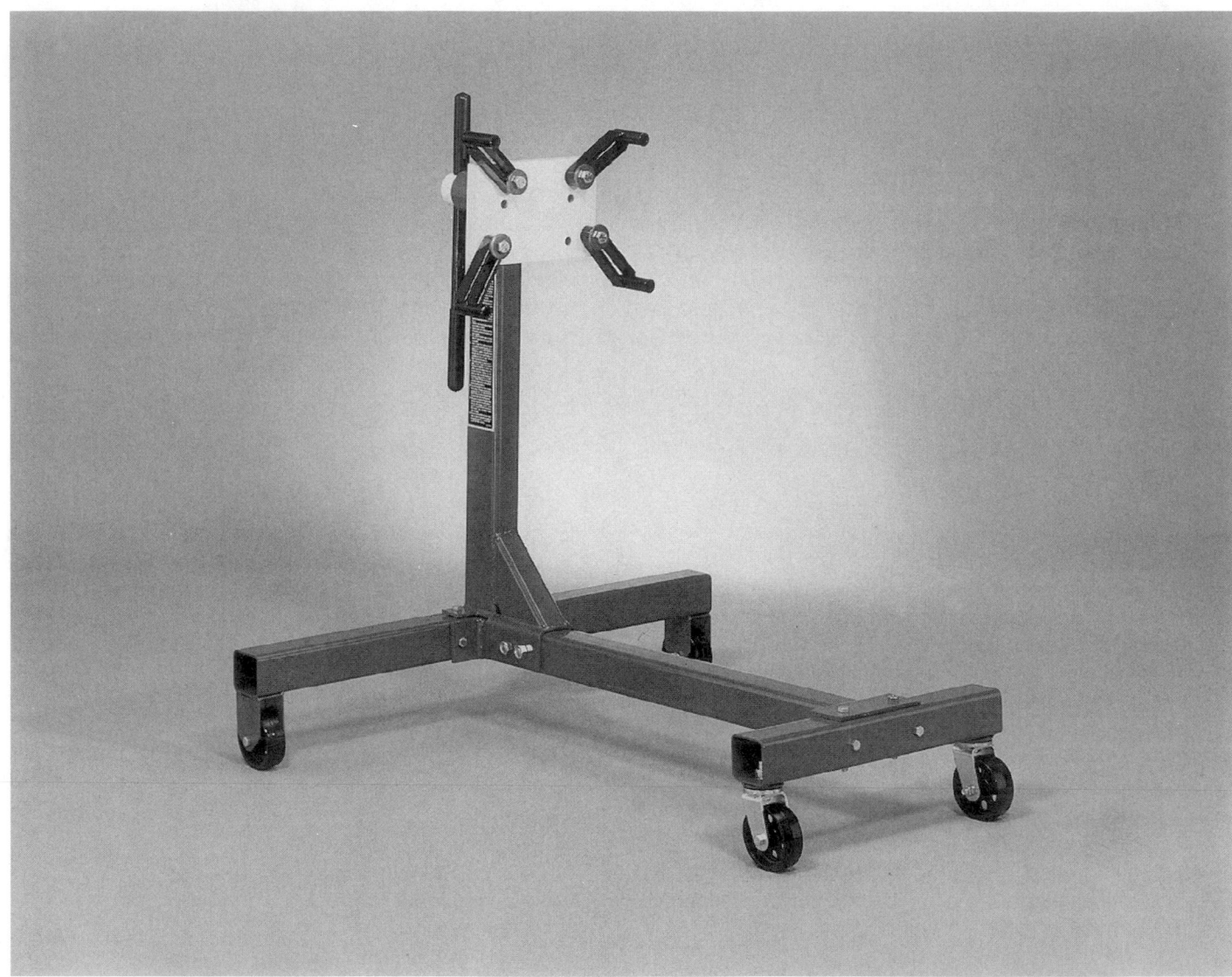

An engine repair stand, such as the one shown above, makes engine repair work easier and faster. This particular stand features a 360° rotating head that can be locked in any position. (Blackhawk Automotive)

5

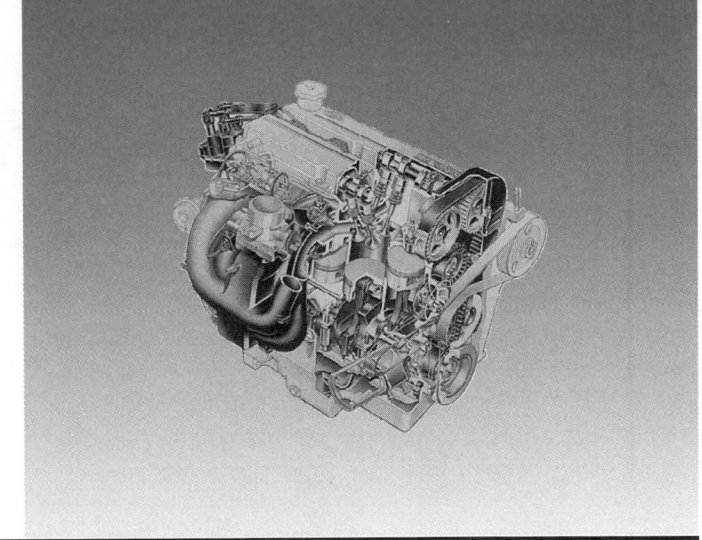

Cleaning Equipment and Techniques

After studying this chapter, you will be able to:
- List the most common automotive cleaning techniques.
- Compare the advantages and disadvantages of different cleaning methods.
- Select the correct cleaning method for a given job.
- Describe the safety rules that apply to various cleaning techniques.

Cleaning parts is a slow, tedious task that can frequently account for nearly half the time spent on a job. Using improper equipment and techniques will make cleaning even more time-consuming. In order to minimize repair charges, the technician must be familiar with the cleaning equipment available.

On an in-car engine cleaning or an undercarriage cleaning job, missing a few spots may displease the customer, but it will not damage the vehicle. On the other hand, careless cleaning of parts during engine, transmission, or rear end teardowns may ruin the job and cause expensive comebacks and angry customers. The only safe course is to be meticulous in your cleaning. Remove *all* foreign materials from the parts and protect them against contamination during storage and handling.

Types of Cleaning Equipment

Cleaning equipment and techniques vary with the size and type of job. You are obviously not going to use a steam cleaner to clean one universal joint when solvent, a brush, and an air hose will handle the task quickly. On the other hand, attempting to clean the outside of an engine before disassembly with a brush and solvent would be equally foolish. You must tailor the equipment and solution to the job at hand. This chapter will deal with the most widely used cleaning techniques. Study them carefully, so that you will be able to choose wisely.

Cleaning with a Wire Brush and Scraper

Engine valves, combustion chambers, piston heads, and piston grooves are subject to accumulations of hard carbon. If these components are not soaked in powerful cleaning solutions, they must be cleaned with scrapers and power brushes. The heavy deposits can be knocked off with

scraping tools and a power wire wheel. A drill-driven rotary brush may also be used for final cleaning.

After thoroughly removing carbon, the part should be washed in solvent and blown dry. **Figure 5-1** shows carbon deposits in a cylinder head combustion chamber being removed with a rotary wire brush that is chucked in an electric drill.

 Caution: Never use a power brush on soft articles, such as pistons, carburetors, or bearing inserts.

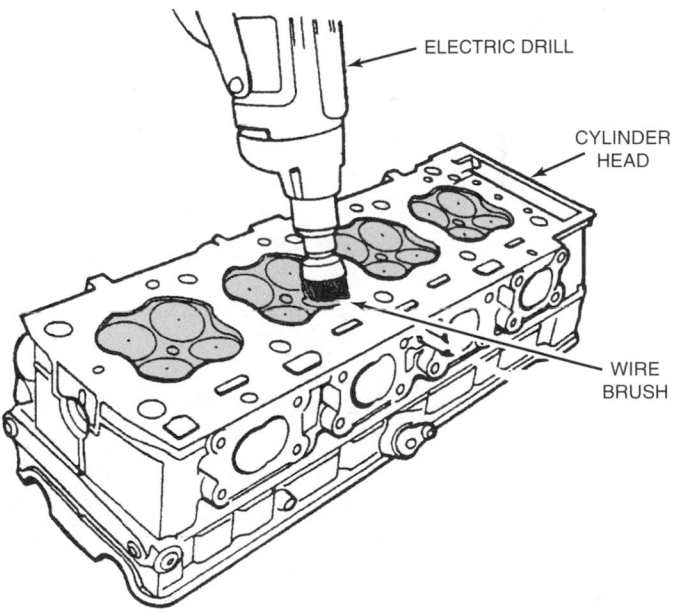

Figure 5-1. A rotary wire brush in an electric drill is being used to clean deposits from this cylinder head.

Get Advice

A number of companies offer various types of cleaning equipment and solutions designed to perform specific tasks, such as car body washing, in-car engine cleaning, carburetor cleaning, block cleaning, hard carbon removal, etc. There are hot solutions, cold solutions, high- and low-pressure sprays, and agitators. So many products are available that it can confuse anyone who is not an expert in the field.

When choosing a cleaning solution or a piece of equipment, it is wise to ask other technicians for their opinions. Also, discuss the problem with sales representatives from reliable companies offering products in this field.

Cleaning Solutions Can Be Dangerous

Many cleaning solutions are *toxic* (poisonous) and *caustic* (will burn skin, eyes). Make sure you know what you are using and follow the manufacturer's recommended handling procedures. General safety rules concerning cleaning solutions include:

* Use cleaning solutions in a well-ventilated area.
* Never use gasoline for cleaning.
* Wear goggles or a face shield when working with the powerful solutions.
* Keep cleaning solutions away from sparks and open flames.
* Do not smoke around solutions.
* Keep solutions covered when not in use. Keep all cleaning solutions in labeled containers.
* Use solutions with relatively high *flash points* (temperature at which vapors will ignite when brought into contact with an open flame).
* Never heat solutions unless specifically recommended by the manufacturer.
* Avoid dampening clothing with solvent.
* Always read and follow the cleaning solution manufacturer's instructions.
* When brushing parts in solvent, use a nylon or brass brush to avoid sparks.
* A large tank of solvent should have a lid that is held open by a fusible link (a holding device that will melt in the event of fire, allowing the lid to drop).
* Wash hands and arms thoroughly when a cleaning job is complete.
* Avoid prolonged skin exposure to all types of solvents.

Parts Washer

Although small parts can be cleaned in cans or buckets, a faster and more efficient job can be done with a regular cold solution *parts washer.* Parts washers hold a lot of solvent. They have soaking trays, solvent agitators, and a filter to remove impurities from the solvent for rinsing. Parts washers are available in many different sizes. See **Figure 5-2.**

Before using the parts washer, the heaviest deposits should be removed with a scraper. Large units, such as engines, should be steam cleaned before disassembly. The parts are placed in the basket and submerged in the solution. Parts with hollow areas should have the hollows facing up, so that an air trap will not prevent solution entry, **Figure 5-3.**

The solution is then agitated (shaken) by air pressure or by the solution passing through nozzles under pressure. The washer shown in **Figure 5-4** has a separate compartment that is air agitated. The main tank is used for soaking, brushing, and rinsing. Some washers have a separate bas-

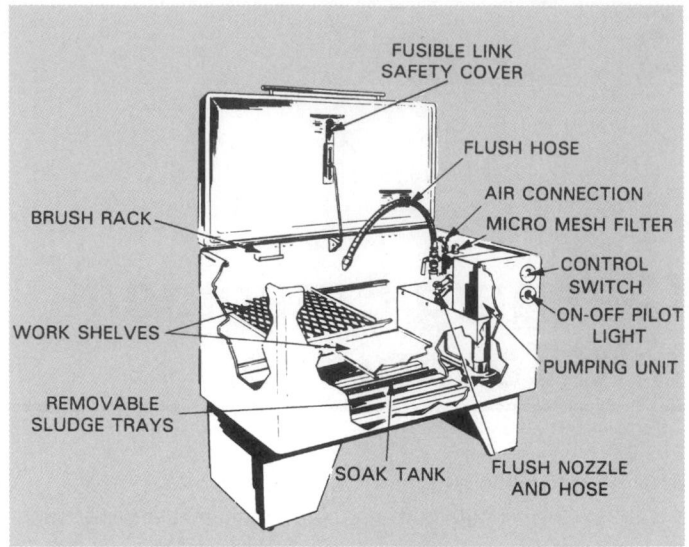

Figure 5-2. Typical cold solution parts washer. (Graymills)

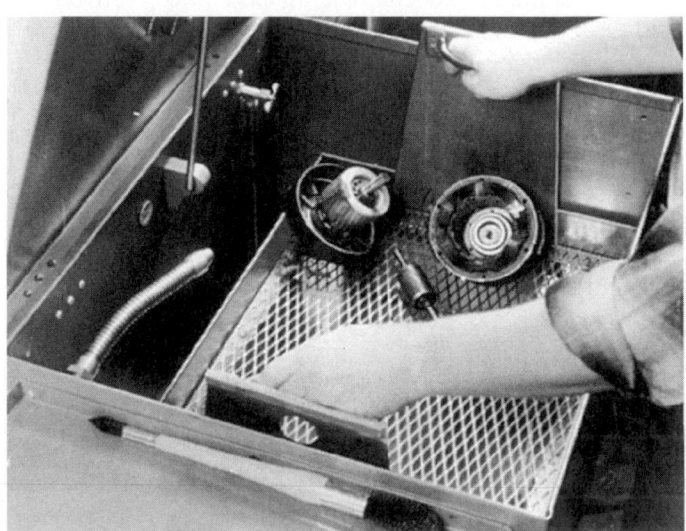

Figure 5-3. Place parts in the basket and submerge them in solvent.

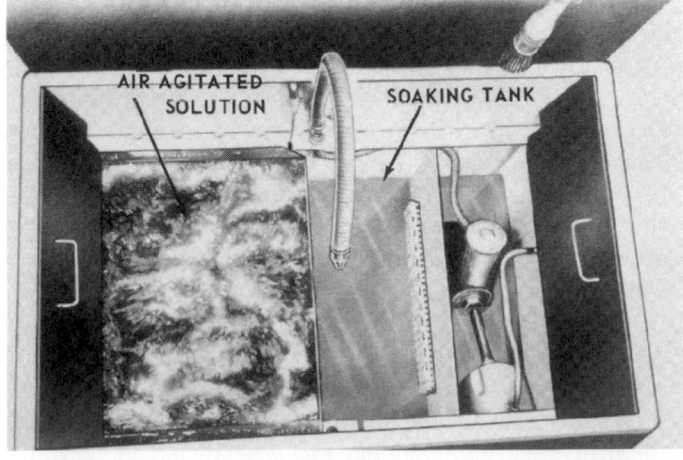

Figure 5-4. Parts washer with both air agitator and soaking tanks. (Kleer-Flo)

ket that is used during the agitation cycle. It will hold a few parts for brushing or rinsing while the remainder are still washing. See **Figure 5-5.**

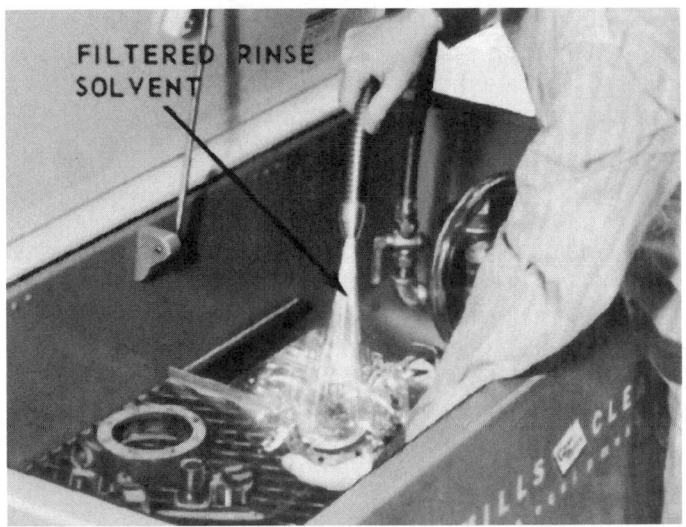

Figure 5-5. This technician is rinsing some parts while others wash.

After a thorough cleaning, the parts should be given a final rinse. The machine shown in **Figure 5-6** has both a soft rinse and a hard spray rinse. After rinsing, let the parts drain and then blow them dry. If there is a possibility of rust formation, oil or grease the parts. Keep parts covered until they are ready to be used. Some shops utilize portable parts washers that can be wheeled to the job or placed on a workbench, **Figure 5-7.**

Figure 5-6. Parts should be given a final rinse in filtered solvent. The solvent must be clean.

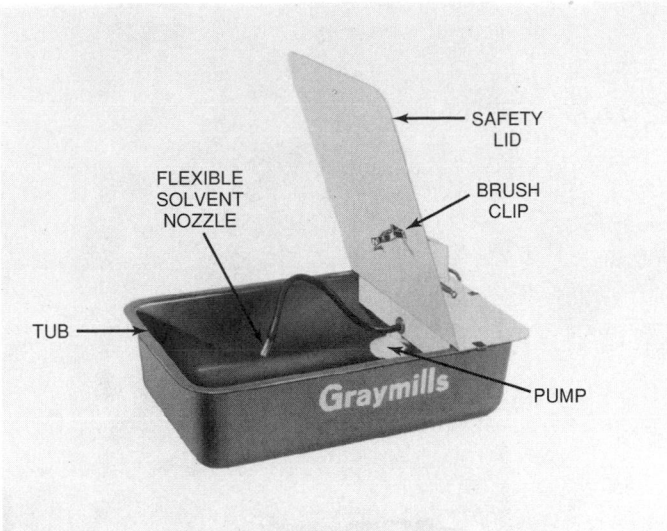

Figure 5-7. This portable parts washer can be placed on the workbench. (Graymills)

Hot Tank Cleaning

Large shops specializing in rebuilding usually have a *hot tank* for heavy cleaning tasks. A hot tank is a large container filled with hot cleaning solution. Many engine blocks, transmission cases, and radiators can be quickly and thoroughly cleaned in the hot tank.

The hot tank usually uses a strong *alkaline compound* mixed with water to form a solution. Temperatures run between 180°-210°F (82°-99°C). The tank may have an agitator to speed cleaning. Most parts are cleaned in thirty minutes or less, depending on tank design, solution strength, solution temperature, and part load.

The alkaline solution is caustic and will attack aluminum. When cleaning aluminum parts, such as modern transmission cases, the solution must be diluted (weakened) to prevent surface erosion of the aluminum.

When the parts are removed from the tank, they should be thoroughly washed, preferably with hot water. Be careful to flush out oil galleries, water jackets, and other internal passages. Parts or surfaces subject to rusting should be oiled after they are dry.

> **STOP** **Warning: Be extremely careful when using the hot tank. Observe all safety precautions. Ask someone skilled in the use of the hot tank to give you instructions before using the tank.**

Figure 5-8 shows engine blocks, heads, and other parts being lowered into two different types of hot tanks. Note the cranes on the tanks, which aid in moving heavy parts.

Steam Cleaning

The *steam cleaner* is an excellent tool for many cleaning tasks. Under-car, engine, and transmission cleaning jobs are handled quickly and thoroughly with a steam cleaner. In operation, a water pump forces a solution of water and a metered amount of cleaning solution through a

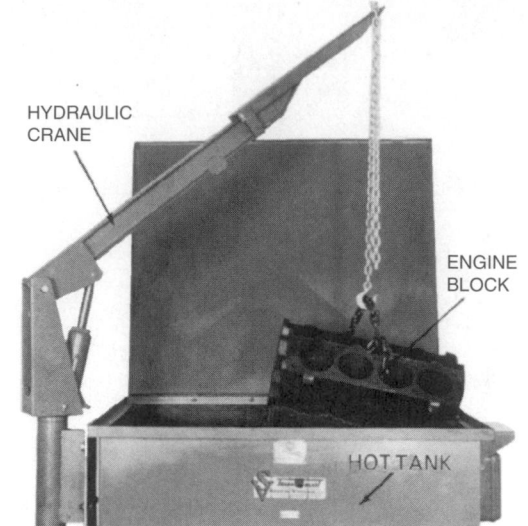

A

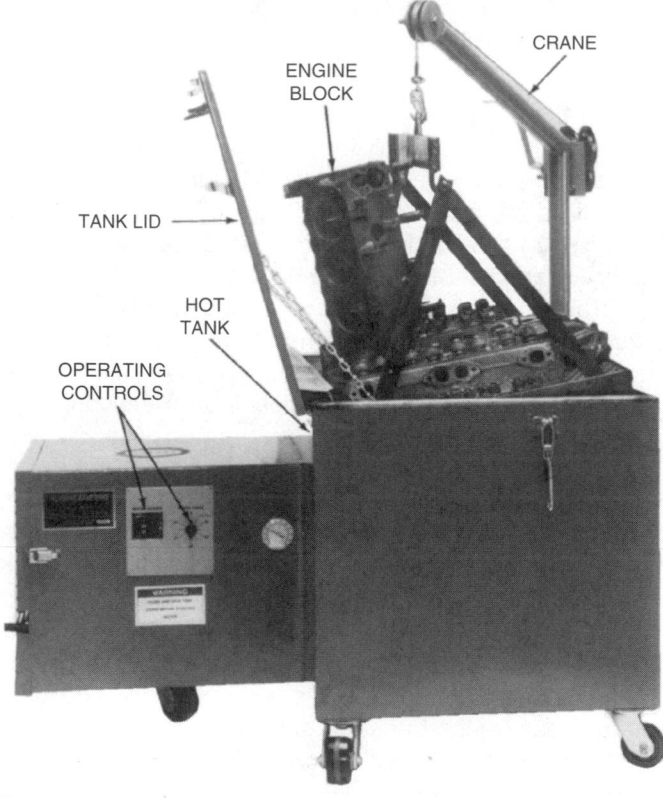

B

Figure 5-8. Hot tanks. A—An engine block being lowered into a hot tank with a hydraulic crane. B—Various engine parts are being placed in a hot tank. This design provides a high degree of agitation to aid cleaning. (Storm-Vulcan and Hurri-Clean)

pipe that is formed into a number of coils. A heat source (oil, gas, or electricity) passes heat quickly through the coils, generating steam pressure. From the coils, the superheated water is passed into a flexible steam hose that is attached to a steam gun. The gun has an insulated handle and an adjustable nozzle. Some units feed the cleaning solution

into the gun instead of into the water supply. **Figure 5-9** shows a typical portable steam cleaner.

General Rules of Operation for Steam Cleaners

There are a number of steam cleaners on the market. As always, the manufacturer's instructions should be followed regarding specific steps and maintenance procedures. There are, however, a number of operational steps that are common to almost all steam cleaners. These will be discussed in the following sections.

Starting the Cleaner

If used indoors, the oil- or gas-operated steam cleaner must have adequate ventilation. Electric units should be properly grounded. Turn on the water source and then activate the water pump. In a short time, you will notice a stream of water flowing from the gun. This indicates that the heating coils are filled with water and that the burner can be ignited without burning the coils.

Next, ignite the burner. When the gun begins to emit steam, adjust the fuel valve to bring the pressure to the desired limit. If the machine utilizes an integral solution tank, check to see if enough solution is present. Mix the solution by opening the stirring valve for about 30 seconds. If no stirring provision is present, place the gun nozzle into the solution and agitate it with steam pressure. If the solution is as desired, open the solution valve.

Using the Steam Cleaner

Cover fenders and windshield area when doing an engine or other under-hood job. Remember that the cleaning

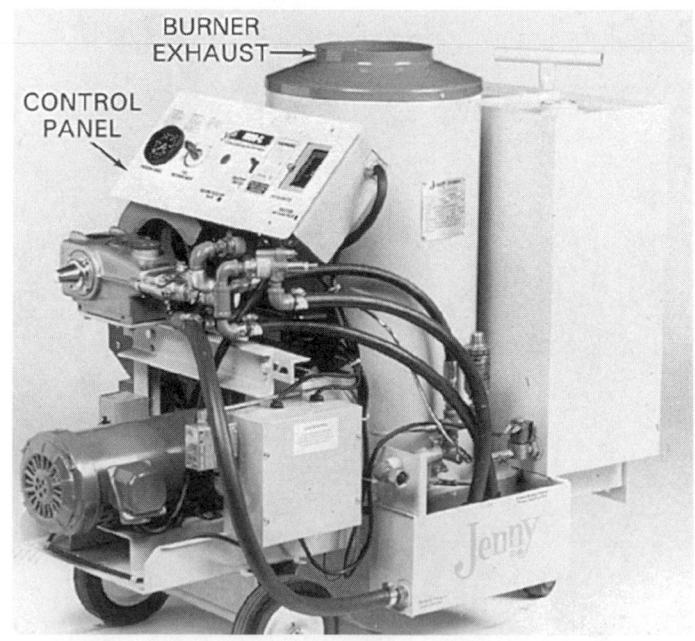

Figure 5-9. Portable steam cleaner. Steam hose and gun are not shown. The exterior cover has been removed to show construction. (Homestead Valve)

solution can damage the paint. When finished, flush all painted surfaces with clean water. Cover all electronic devices, the carburetor or fuel injectors, alternator, distributor, master cylinder, power steering pump, and air conditioning compressor. Avoid prolonged steaming of wiring. Keep spray away from air conditioning lines.

Depending on the nozzle design, the type of dirt to be removed, and the shape of the object being cleaned, hold the gun nozzle from one to four inches (25 to 102 mm) from the surface. If the nozzle is too far from the work, cleaning will be slowed considerably. The steam should be "wet" (ample hot water along with steam). Dry steam will not clean or flush surfaces well.

Avoid applying too much steam to the tie rod ends, suspension knuckles, and other under-car bearing areas. Excessive steaming will melt the lubricant in these components and damage the seals. Do not drive dirt and grease from the brake backing plates into the brake drums. Be careful when using steam cleaner on brake lines and flexible hose.

Remember that steam causes condensation. Part and tool rusting will occur if the steam cleaner is operated in a poorly ventilated area. **Figure 5-10** shows an operator steam cleaning the underside of a car.

Shutting Down the Steam Cleaner

When finished with the cleaner, shut off the solution control valve and allow the cleaner to operate for a short time. Then, shut off the fuel valve, but keep the water pump running. When there is no sign of steam vapor coming from the gun, shut down the water pump. By following this procedure, all solution is removed from the coils and the coils are allowed to cool before the water flow stops. This prevents possible burning and scaling.

Arrange the steam hose so that it is out of the way and will not be kinked or run over. If the surrounding temperature will drop below freezing, the machine should be drained.

Safety Rules for Steam Cleaning

- Do not operate a steam cleaner without proper burner ventilation.
- An electric steam cleaner must have a good ground.
- Keep pressure within specified limits.
- Wear a face shield to keep splatters from entering your eyes.
- Keep other personnel away from the immediate vicinity of the cleaner. When swinging the gun around, watch for bystanders.
- If the machine does not ignite readily, shut off the fuel valve and have a qualified repair person check the burner fuel and ignition system.
- Read the machine instruction book carefully and get "checked out" by an experienced operator.

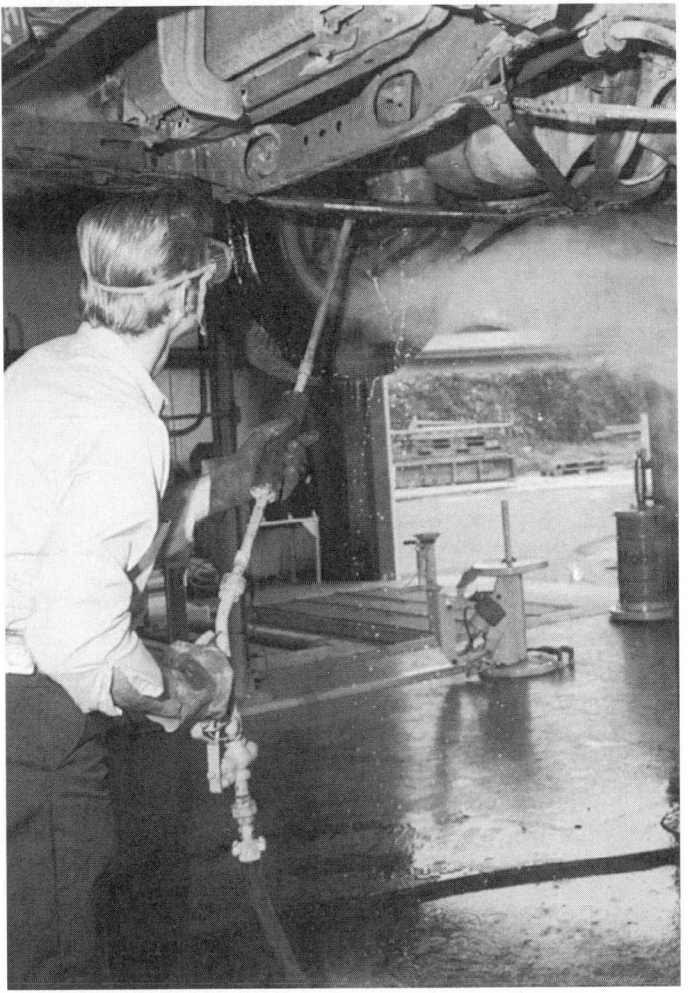

Figure 5-10. Using a steam cleaner for under-body cleaning. Note that the technician is wearing goggles. (Clayton Manufacturing Co.)

- If the machine must be lighted by hand, keep your face and body away from the burner opening.

High-pressure Spray Cleaning

Effective cleaning can be accomplished using **high-pressure spray cleaning equipment.** This type of equipment forces cold water through a spray gun at high pressures. A cleaning solution is injected into the water as it passes through the gun. Pressure at the gun's nozzle can reach approximately 500 psi (3,448 kPa).

By adjusting the gun, a soft mist containing a detergent solution is sprayed over the object to be cleaned until it is thoroughly saturated. Following a short waiting period to allow the deposits to soften, a fine, high-velocity, fan-shaped stream of plain water is used to lift off the dirt. For hard-to-clean corners, the spray can be adjusted to a high-velocity, narrow stream.

When doing an under-hood cleaning job, cover fenders, windshield areas, and sensitive engine and electrical components. **Figure 5-11** illustrates a high-pressure cleaning machine. Note the different spray patterns available.

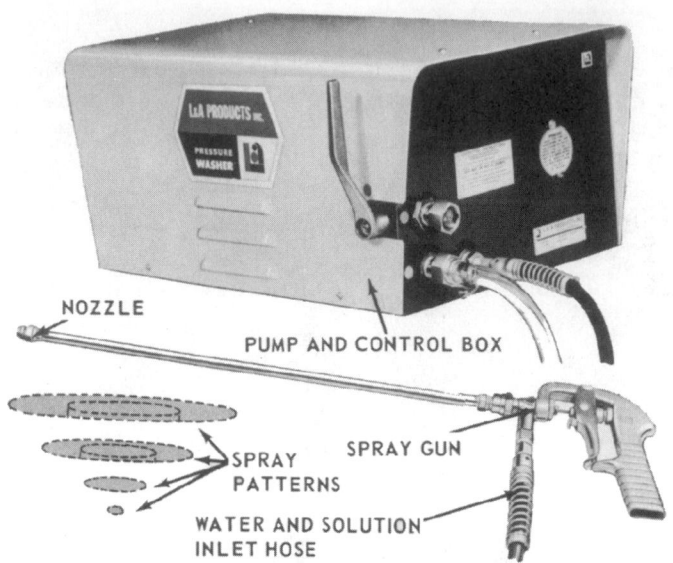

Figure 5-11. High-pressure spray cleaner. (L & A Products)

Low-pressure Spray Cleaning

Low-pressure spray cleaning is another technique involving the use of an air-operated mixing gun. As air passes through the gun, it draws in a metered amount of cleaning solution and sprays it on the object being cleaned. After waiting for deposits to soften, the object can be washed down with a hose. If desired, the cleaning gun suction hose can be placed in a container of water or cleaning solvent.

Special cleaning solutions are generally added to the water or cleaning solvent for the initial cleaning spray. Never use gasoline or any solvent with a low flash point. Spraying atomizes the solvent, rendering it highly explosive. See **Figure 5-12.**

Remove the Battery Ground Cable

Whenever doing under-hood cleaning, it is a good idea to remove the battery ground cable. This prevents possible short circuits caused by grounding a hot wire or terminal with the cleaning gun.

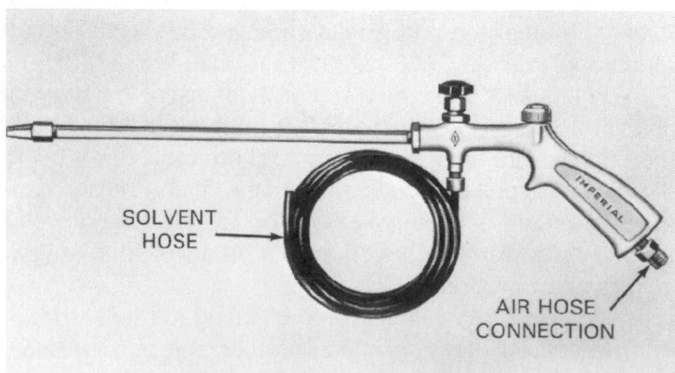

Figure 5-12. Low-pressure spray gun. The hose is placed in a container of solvent. (Imperial Brass)

Cold Soak Cleaning

For **cold soak cleaning,** the dirty part or parts are placed in a basket and lowered into the cleaning solution. Following a period of 10-30 minutes, the parts are removed and rinsed in solvent or water. They are then blown dry with an air gun. Solutions of various kinds are available for specific tasks.

> **STOP** **Warning: Most of the cold soak solutions are extremely caustic. Keep these solutions away from skin and eyes! Wash the soaked parts thoroughly before handling them.**

Cold soak solutions generally come in a special pail or drum that includes a parts basket. The solution is far enough from the top of the pail that a normal load of parts will not cause spillage. A special sealing solution floats on top of the cold soak solution to prevent evaporation and excessive odor. When placing parts in the container, make certain that they are completely submerged and are below the special seal solution. **Figure 5-13** depicts a typical six-gallon (22.8 Liter) pail of cold soak cleaning solution. Notice the parts basket.

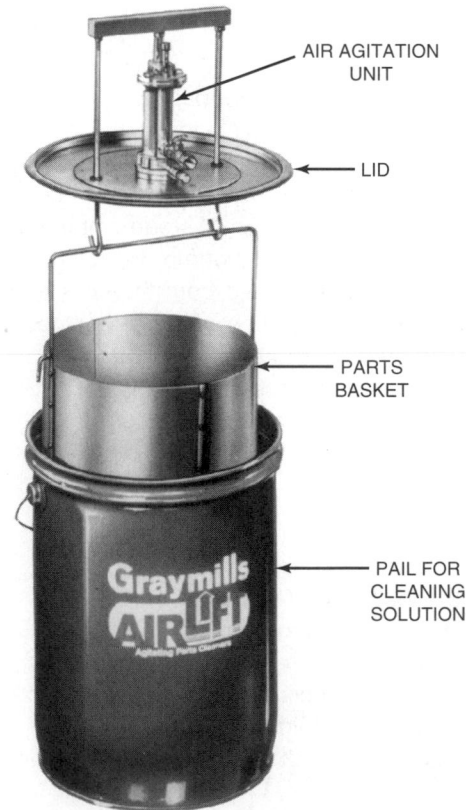

Figure 5-13. This soak-cleaning unit can be air agitated for faster cleaning. This particular solution is specially designed for gum, varnish, and hard carbon removal. (Graymills Co.)

Vapor Cleaning

The **vapor cleaner** illustrated in **Figure 5-14** cleans parts by heating a perchloroethylene solution. The resulting

Figure 5-14. Vapor cleaning unit. Use only recommended solvent.

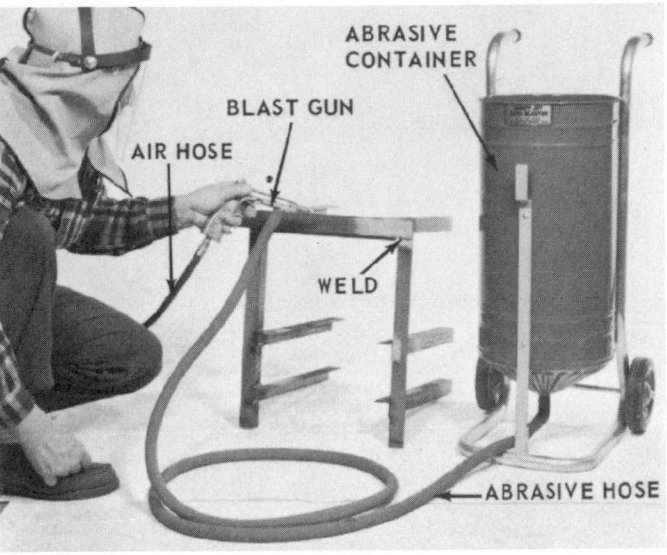

Figure 5-15. Sandblasting a weld to remove slag.

vapors remove deposits from the parts suspended in the metal basket. The solution is nonflammable.

Sandblast Cleaning

Automotive parts are rarely **sandblasted.** The body shop and welding shop occasionally use a sandblaster to quickly remove paint, rust, and welding scale. A special blast gun, operating under air pressure of around 50 to 200 psi (345 to 1379 kPa), draws in a metered amount of abrasive material and propels it against the object to be cleaned with great force. The abrasive material can be silica sand, aluminum oxide, metal shot, or even pulverized walnut shells. Each abrasive has a specific application, and switching between abrasive types makes the sandblaster more versatile.

Always wear a face shield when sandblasting. In addition, a respirator should be worn in situations that are prolonged or produce excessive dust. Never sandblast around a repair area. The abrasive will contaminate parts, with disastrous results. **Figure 5-15** shows a technician sandblasting a weld.

Bead Blast Cleaning

Another type of blast cleaner is the **bead blast cleaner,** or bead blaster. This cleaner consists of a cabinet with an internal blaster. Instead of sand, the blaster uses fine glass beads, which clean the part without removing much of the original material. Some units have a pair of rubber gloves that extends into the cabinet. The gloves allow the technician to handle the parts during the blasting procedure. Bead blast cleaners are often used to remove rust

from small parts and to remove the glaze from automatic transmission clutch plates and drums. One type of bead blaster is shown in **Figure 5-16.**

Tech Talk

Have you ever gone into a restaurant and found the tables sticky and littered with dirty plates? Did you want to eat there? Have you ever walked into a TV repair shop and tripped over disassembled electronic equipment lying around? Did the people who worked there look like they were sleeping out front in the gutter until five minutes before you got there? Did you trust them to fix your television? If you are like most people, you expect a certain level of cleanliness and order and you probably think that work that comes out of a sloppy place will be sloppy, too.

On the other hand, did you ever walk into a repair shop and find everything clean and neat? Your first impression was probably favorable.

This should give you an idea about how you can create a good first impression. If your work area is clean and neat, it will make a good first impression. If you look like you have given some thought to your appearance, it will make an even better impression. If you have made a good first impression, you will not have to spend time overcoming a bad impression.

Elsewhere in this book, we have discussed the importance of good housekeeping and neat clothing to prevent accidents and keep track of tools and parts. Now is a good time to begin thinking about the way that good housekeeping and neat clothing will impress your customers.

Figure 5-16. This bead blaster was used to clean the case of an automatic transmission. (Glassinger)

Summary

Automotive repair and maintenance work procedures require considerable use of cleaning techniques, equipment, and solutions. You will do better work if you select the best cleaning procedure for the job at hand. As with all work, cleaning must be thorough.

Hand brushes and scrapers are occasionally useful. Power brushes are fine for removing hard carbon deposits from some parts. Remember that many cleaning solutions are both toxic and caustic and must be handled with care.

A cold solution parts washer is excellent for many parts not coated with hard carbon. Parts are soaked in an agitated solution, brushed, rinsed, and blown dry. For larger objects or parts that are hard to clean, a hot tank containing a strong alkaline solution is desirable. Aluminum parts will not stand full-strength hot tank solutions.

The steam cleaner is a fast, efficient cleaning tool and is especially good for removing heavy dirt and grease deposits. High-pressure spray cleaning handles dirt and grease very well. Large areas may be cleaned quickly. Low-pressure spray cleaning is effective on many jobs. However, it is generally slower than either steaming or using the high-pressure washer.

Cold soak cleaning solutions are widely used for gum, varnish, and hard carbon removal. Pistons, carburetors, and automatic transmissions are usually cleaned in such a cleaner. A parts basket can be furnished with the pail or drum of solution. Vapor cleaning has some advantages and works particularly well on certain parts. Cleaning solutions can be dangerous. Observe all safety rules.

Sandblast cleaning is useful for removing paint, rust, and weld scale. Do not operate a sandblaster near a repair area. Another type of blast cleaner is the bead blaster. This cleaner consists of a cabinet with an internal blaster.

Know These Terms

Toxic
Caustic
Flash points
Parts washer
Hot tank
Alkaline compound
Steam cleaner

High-pressure spray
  cleaning equipment
Low-pressure spray cleaning
Cold soak cleaning
Vapor cleaner
Sandblasted
Bead blast cleaner

Review Questions—Chapter 5

Do not write in this book. Write your answers on a separate sheet of paper.

1. Cleaning often accounts for one _____ of the total repair time.
   (A) tenth
   (B) fifth
   (C) quarter
   (D) half
2. Give some examples of parts that should not be cleaned with a power brush.
3. A toxic cleaning solution is _____.
4. When should the technician heat a cleaning solution?
   (A) Never.
   (B) Only when specifically recommended.
   (C) At any time.
   (D) When the parts are very dirty.
5. When submerging a part with a hollow compartment, always place the compartment _____, so that the solution will enter.
6. The hot tank solution will attack _____.
7. List six safety rules that should be observed when using the steam cleaner.
8. If gasoline or any flammable solvent with a low flash point is used for cleaning, what could happen?
   (A) Fire.
   (B) Explosion.
   (C) Both A & B.
   (D) Neither A nor B.
9. Most soak-cleaning solutions are extremely _____.
10. A bead blast cleaner is located inside of a _____.

ASE-Type Questions

1. Technician A says that a shop with a steam cleaner really does not need any other cleaning equipment. Technician B says that piston ring grooves are best cleaned with the power wire wheel. Who is right?
   (A) A only.
   (B) B only.
   (C) Both A & B.
   (D) Neither A nor B.
2. Cleaning means removing _____.
   (A) most soft deposits
   (B) every bit of foreign material
   (C) most hard deposits
   (D) Both A and C.

3. Technician A says that a cold solution parts washer is effective for hard carbon removal. Technician B says that a hot tank is excellent for cleaning engine blocks. Who is right?
   (A) A only.
   (B) B only.
   (C) Both A & B.
   (D) Neither A nor B.

4. The solution used for hot tank cleaning is _____.
   (A) toxic
   (B) caustic
   (C) hot
   (D) All of the above.

5. Steam cleaning can be used to clean all of the following, EXCEPT:
   (A) engine blocks.
   (B) alternators.
   (C) transmission cases.
   (D) radiators.

6. Technician A says the water pump should be started before lighting the burner on a steam cleaner. Technician B says that a steam cleaner should be stopped by first shutting off the water pump and, when no water comes from the gun, shutting off the burner. Who is right?
   (A) A only.
   (B) B only.
   (C) Both A & B.
   (D) Neither A nor B.

7. High-pressure spray cleaning will do a good job of removing _____.
   (A) dirt
   (B) grease
   (C) carbon
   (D) Both A & B.

8. It is a good idea to remove the _____ before cleaning under the hood.
   (A) battery cable
   (B) air cleaner
   (C) radiator cap
   (D) drive belts

9. Technician A says that carburetors are best cleaned in a bead blast cabinet. Technician B says that machined engine parts may be cleaned satisfactorily with the sandblaster. Who is right?
   (A) A only.
   (B) B only.
   (C) Both A & B.
   (D) Neither A nor B.

10. Soak-cleaning solutions are usually supplied with a special _____.
    (A) color code
    (B) rinsing solvent
    (C) parts basket
    (D) Both B & C.

Suggested Activities

1. Make a chart showing various cleaning solutions and the systems they are used on (engine, brakes, body, interior, etc.). Display the chart in the shop or classroom.

2. Using a manufacturer's catalog, determine which cleaning tools are needed in the automotive shop. List the prices of these tools and determine how much it would cost to buy all the necessary items.

3. Visit as many repair shops as possible. Using a video camera, record the cleaning techniques used. Narrate the video as you are taping. Before leaving, thank the technicians concerned, as well as the service manager. Present the video to your classmates.

During manufacture, body panels are welded together by robots. These robots produce very accurate, uniform welds. In the field, most automotive welding is confined to the body shop. Nevertheless, the automotive repair technician should have a basic understanding of welding equipment and techniques. (Plymouth)

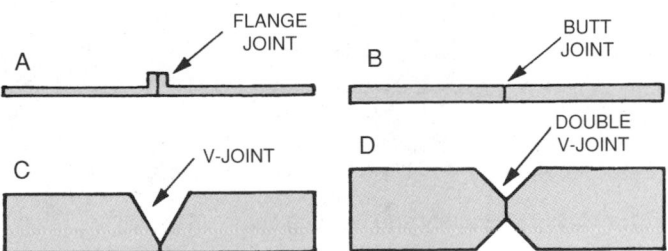

6

Welding Equipment and Techniques

After studying this chapter, you will be able to:
- Describe the equipment needed for welding metal.
- Describe the equipment needed for brazing metal.
- Describe the procedures for brazing metal.

This chapter is designed to provide basic techniques, machine operations, and safety rules pertaining to welding and brazing. The top-level technician must have a number of talents and must be capable of handling the many phases of automotive repair. Numerous basic skills are required, not all of which are commonly associated with automotive work.

Being a successful automotive technician involves much more than disassembly, inspection, replacement, and reassembly. Quite often, parts must be rebuilt, altered, adapted, or welded. To cope successfully with all these demands, the technician must have some knowledge of welding and brazing techniques, as well as machine shop operations, sheet metal work, electrical work, and many other tasks.

Most welding and brazing operations are confined to the body shop. However, you will find that welding skills can be used on many different jobs. Students planning to become automotive technicians will find it helpful to take at least one basic course in welding.

 Warning: Use care when welding, heating, or cutting. Fire or explosion can occur. Keep flames, sparks, and heat away from fuel tanks, batteries, and other flammable items.

Gas Welding

Welding is a *fusion* joining process. This means that a portion of the metal of each part being joined is melted. The melted areas flow together and, upon cooling, form one solid part. Welding rod is often used during the gas welding process to supply a filler metal, which helps to reinforce the joint. The first type of welding to be discussed is gas welding, or *oxyacetylene welding.*

Preparing the Joint for Welding

Before welding, the joint to be welded must be prepared properly. When welding metal that is 1/32" (0.79 mm) thick or less, the joint is often flanged to protect against heat warpage, **Figure 6-1A.** Metals not exceeding 1/8" (3.18 mm) may be welded using a square-edge butt joint, **Figure 6-1B.** When metal thickness ranges from 1/8"-3/8" (3.18-9.53 mm), a V-joint is used, **Figure 6-1C.** Parts over 3/8" (9.53 mm) are usually prepared with a double V-joint , **Figure 6-1D.** In all cases, both the joint and the immediate area must be cleaned of rust, scale, and paint.

Figure 6-1. Weld joint preparation in various thicknesses of metal.

Setting Up Oxyacetylene Equipment

Support both the acetylene and oxygen cylinders securely. The acetylene cylinder should be in the upright position to prevent loss of acetone (acetylene cylinder is filled with an acetone-soaked porous filler material). Keep cylinders away from heat and flames. Protective tank valve caps must be in place when cylinders are stored. Mark empty cylinders with the letters MT. **Figure 6-2** illustrates how cylinders are attached to the welding setup.

The *regulators* reduce cylinder pressures to a controlled and useable amount. **Figures 6-3** and **6-4** illustrate typical regulators. Note the cylinder and hose fittings. The right-hand gauges read cylinder pressures. The left-hand gauges indicate tip operating pressures. Tip pressure is varied by adjusting the handles.

The oxygen regulator has right-hand threads, and the acetylene regulator has left-hand threads. This prevents the technician from installing the regulators on the wrong cylinders.

Before attaching regulators to the cylinders, crack (open slightly) the valve on each cylinder for a second to blow out dust or other foreign material. Do not crack the acetylene near open flames or near a welding operation.

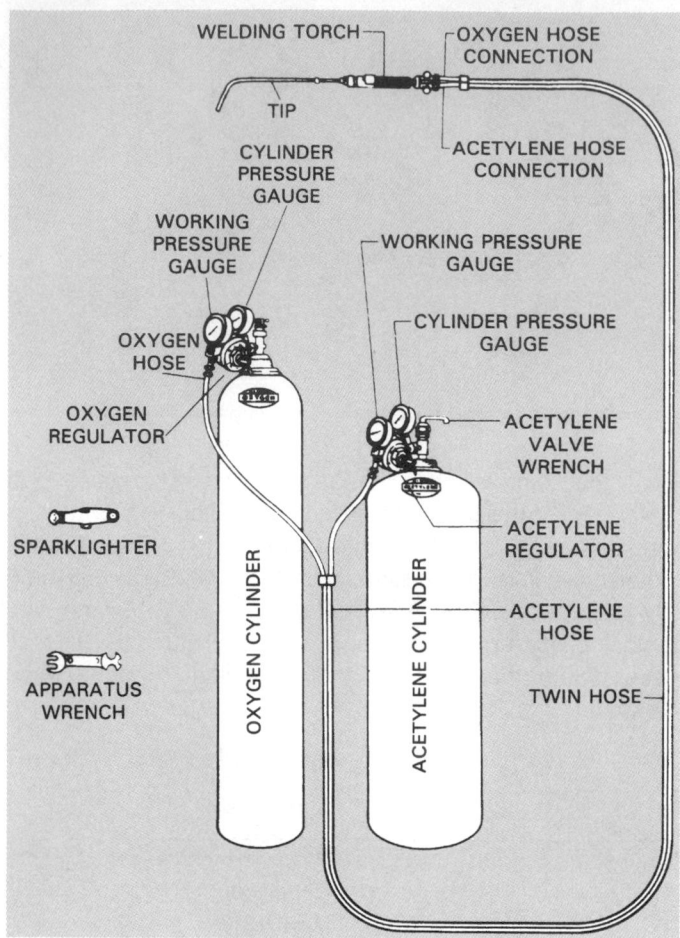

Figure 6-2. Oxyacetylene welding setup. (AIRCO)

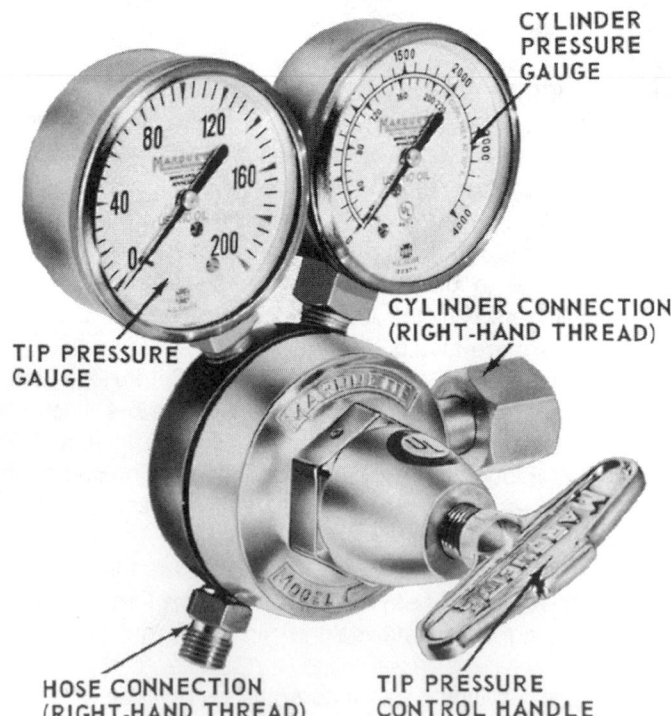

Figure 6-3. Typical oxygen regulator. Note high reading cylinder gauge.

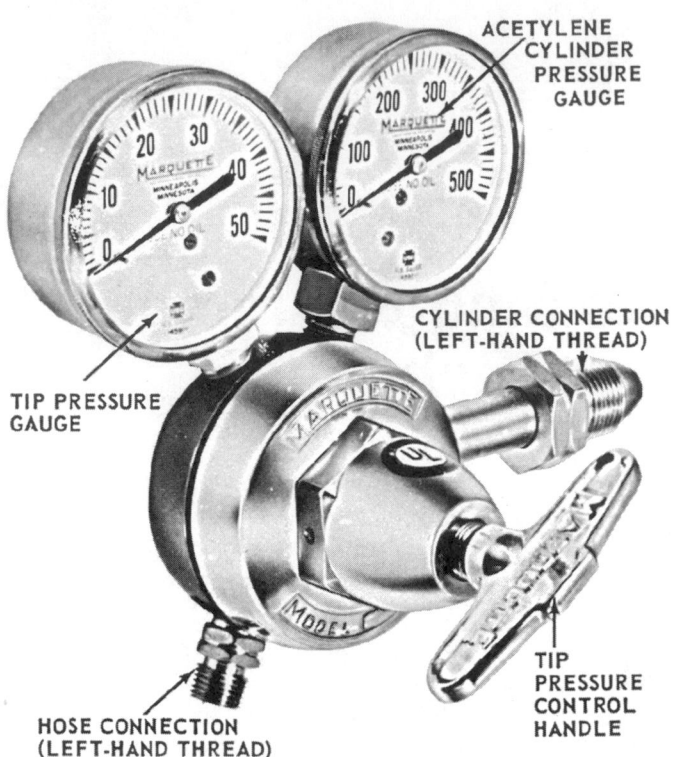

Figure 6-4. Typical acetylene regulator. Note left-hand thread connections.

Attach the regulators to their respective cylinders and tighten them gently. Finally, back out the pressure control handle on each regulator (counterclockwise) until free.

STOP **Warning: Never use oil on regulators. Do not handle gas welding equipment with oily or greasy hands. Do not wear oil-soaked clothing. In the presence of pure oxygen, oil becomes highly flammable.**

Attach the *hoses* to the regulators. The acetylene hose is normally red, and the oxygen hose is green. Acetylene fittings have left-hand threads, and oxygen fittings have right-hand threads. When using the equipment, keep hoses away from hot sparks, flames, oil, and grease. Avoid kinking the hoses, and coil them when you are finished working.

The *torch mixing handle* should be attached to the hose end. Do not overtighten either the mixing handle or the regulator hose connections. Where rubber O-ring seals are used, hand tightening is sufficient. Note the oxygen and acetylene mixing valves in **Figure 6-5**.

Select the proper *tip* and install it on the torch mixing handle. Torch tip size must be suited to the job. **Figure 6-6** gives typical tip sizes and gas pressures for different metal thicknesses.

Adjusting Gas Pressure

After installing the desired tip on the mixing handle, the gas pressure should be adjusted as follows:
1. Make sure the regulator pressure control handles are backed (counterclockwise) completely off.

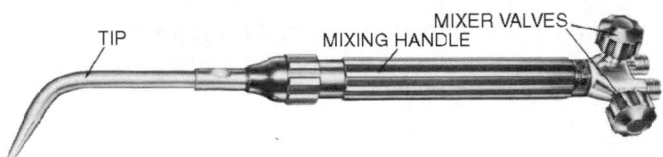

Figure 6-5.   Torch mixing handle with a tip attached. (Marquette)

APPROXIMATE GAS PRESSURES FOR OPERATING AIRCO WELDING TORCHES									
Tip No.	00	0	1	2	3	4	5	6	7
Mixer	00-1	00-1	1-7	1-7	1-7	1-7	1-7	1-7	6-10
Thickness of Metal (In.)	1/64	1/32	1/16	3/32	1/8	3/16	1/4	5/16	3/8
Oxygen Pressure (psi)	1	1	1	2	3	4	5	6	7
Acetylene Pressure (psi)	1	1	1	2	3	4	5	6	7

Figure 6-6.   Typical tip sizes and gas pressures for different metal thicknesses.

2. Slowly open the acetylene valve about 1/4 to 1/2 turn.
3. Slowly open the oxygen valve all the way to prevent leakage around the valve stem. Leave the acetylene wrench in place on the valve to facilitate an emergency shutoff.
4. Shut the acetylene mixing valve and open the oxygen mixing valve.
5. Turn the oxygen regulator handle in (clockwise) until the desired working pressure is obtained (read low-pressure gauge).
6. *Purge* (clear the hose of air or other gases) the oxygen hose line by allowing oxygen to flow from the hose momentarily.
7. Shut off the oxygen mixing valve.
8. Open the acetylene mixing valve (oxygen valve off) and adjust the acetylene regulator to the desired pressure.
9. After purging, close the acetylene mixer valve.

> **Caution: Purging lines is very important. Failure to do so can allow acetylene to enter the oxygen hose and vice versa. This, of course, creates a combustible mixture inside the hose and can cause a flashback (fire burning inside hose).**

Lighting the Torch

Before attempting to light the torch, put on all needed safety equipment, such as goggles, gloves, protective vest, and helmet, before proceeding. This step is extremely important!

To light the torch, open the acetylene mixer valve a small amount while operating a *scratcher,* or spark lighter, in front of the tip. See **Figure 6-7.**

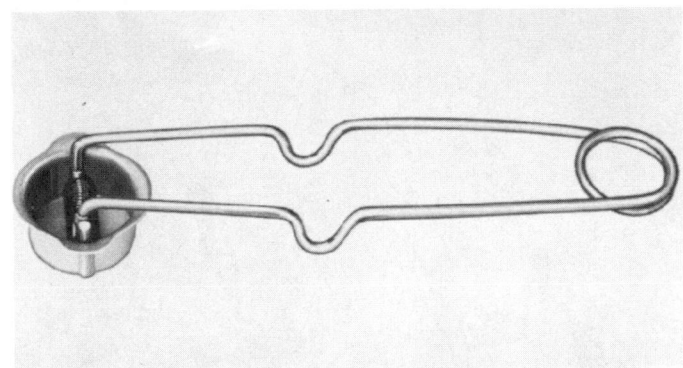

Figure 6-7.   Spark lighter. Squeezing handle moves a flint across a rough metal surface, producing a shower of sparks.

> **Note: Keep the tip facing in a safe direction. Have your welding goggles in position.**

Adjusting the Flame

There are three general types of flames that can be produced by the oxyacetylene torch: the neutral flame, the carburizing flame, and the oxidizing flame. Refer to **Figure 6-8.**

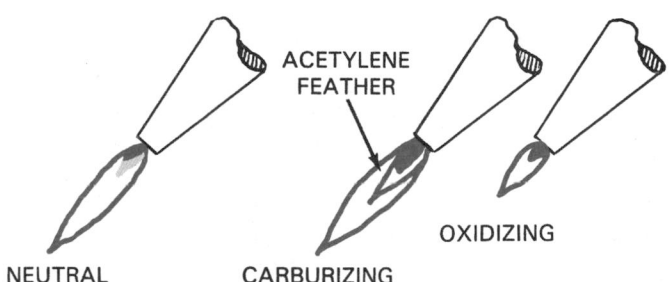

NEUTRAL   CARBURIZING   OXIDIZING

ACETYLENE FEATHER

Figure 6-8.   Neutral, carburizing, and oxidizing flames.

A *neutral flame* should generally be used for gas welding. The neutral flame will permit smooth, dense, strong welds. There will be no foaming, sparking, or other problems. A *carburizing flame* (excess acetylene) will cause molten metal to pick up carbon from the flame. This causes the metal to boil and, upon cooling, to become brittle. An *oxidizing flame* (excess of oxygen) will cause the metal to foam and send off a shower of sparks. Also, the excess oxygen combines with the steel, causing it to burn. The weld will be porous, weak, and brittle.

When the acetylene ignites, adjust the flame until it is hovering about 1/8" (3.2 mm) from the tip, **Figure 6-9A.** Immediately open the oxygen valve and adjust the flame. By starting with a carburizing flame, **Figure 6-9B,** and slowly closing the acetylene valve, **Figure 6-9C,** a neutral flame may be acquired, **Figure 6-9D.** Watch the yellowish acetylene feather to tell when the neutral flame is reached, **Figure 6-9.**

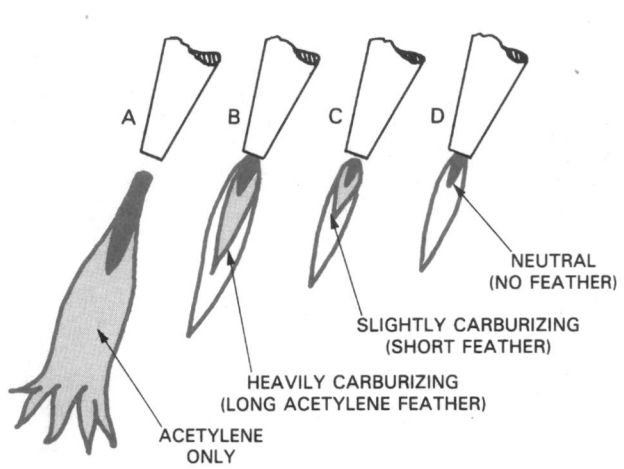

Figure 6-9. Adjusting to a neutral flame. Note acetylene "feather."

Shutting Off the Torch

To shut off the torch, close the acetylene mixer valve. The oxygen will blow out the flame at once. Then, shut off the oxygen mixer valve. When using this technique to shut off the flame, make certain that the acetylene valve is not leaking. If you will be welding again within a few minutes, hang the torch up out of the way. If it will be some time before the torch is needed, drain the lines. To drain the lines, shut off both the acetylene and oxygen cylinder valves. Open one of the mixer valves until the low pressure gauge indicates that there is no pressure left in the line. Back off the regulator adjuster handle, close the mixer valve, and repeat the process on the other line.

Welding Technique—Backhand Method

When using the backhand welding method, the torch is held so that the tip is directed opposite the direction of travel and into the molten puddle. The tip of the welding rod is positioned between the flame and the weld. When the base metal (metal of the parts being joined) melts and forms a puddle, the filler rod is added as the weld progresses. Melt the rod by inserting its end into the puddle. Do not hold the rod above the puddle, allowing it to melt and drip.

 Note: The *inner flame cone* must not touch either the rod or the puddle.

Move the flame along the weld in a steady fashion, causing the base metal to reach the fusion state just ahead of the puddle. The welding rod can be moved from side to side, in small circles, or in half-circles. The weld

should penetrate through the joint. **Figure 6-10** shows both forehand and backhand welding techniques.

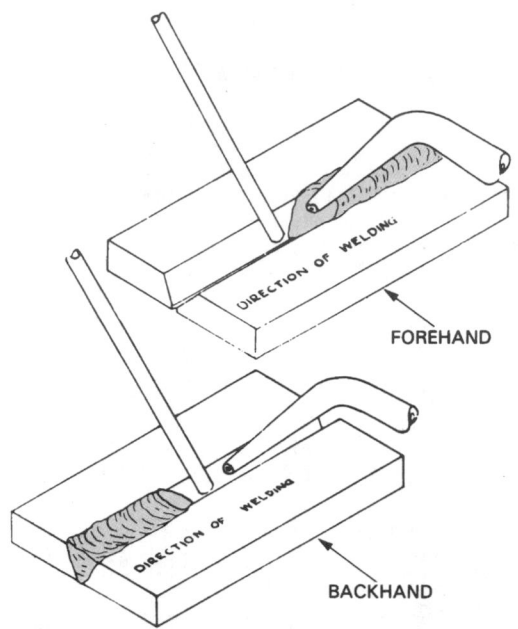

Figure 6-10. Forehand and backhand welding techniques. (AIRCO)

Using the Oxyacetylene Cutting Torch

There are many applications for the *oxyacetylene cutting torch* in the auto shop. The oxyacetylene cutting torch uses a preheating flame, which is maintained at the tip through small orifices, or openings, located around a larger center orifice. To light the cutting torch, set the regulators to give the required pressure and then:

1. Close the cutting attachment oxygen valve.
2. Open the mixer oxygen valve all the way.
3. Open the acetylene mixer valve and light the torch.
4. Open the attachment oxygen valve and adjust the pre-heat flames to neutral.
5. Depress the oxygen jet lever and if preheat flames are altered, readjust them.

After lighting the torch, the preheating flame is held close to the work at the point where the cut is to start. When the spot has been heated to a bright cherry red, press the oxygen jet lever. When the stream of pure oxygen strikes the heated area, it will cut (burn) through the steel.

As soon as the cut starts, move the torch along the work. Move the torch as rapidly as the cutting will allow. Keep the oxygen lever fully depressed. If the cutting action stops, release the oxygen lever. With the preheat flames (they burn continuously), preheat the workpiece again. Hold the torch so that the tip is at right angles to the work and the preheat flames are just above the surface. Refer to **Figure 6-11.** Note that the cutting torch removes a narrow *kerf* (cut) and that the molten metal (slag) is blown out from beneath the work. See **Figure 6-12.**

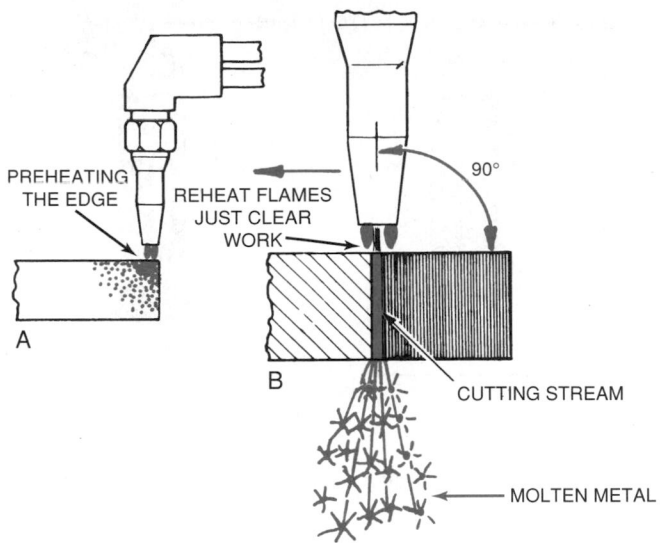

Figure 6-11.   Hold the cutting tip at right angles to the work so the preheat flames just clear the work.

These directions are for the cutting attachment shown in **Figure 6-12.** If another cutting torch is used, follow the manufacturer's instructions.

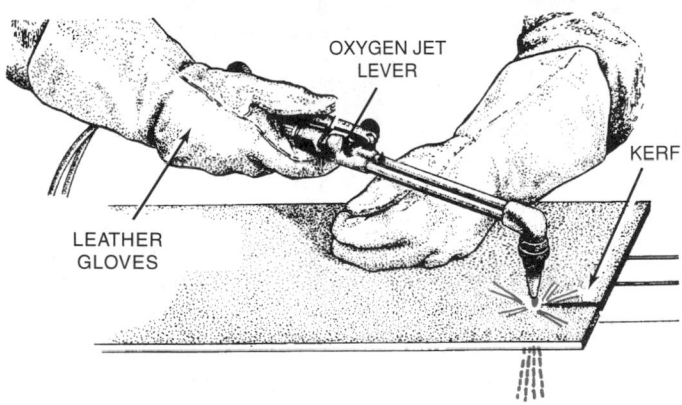

Figure 6-12.   Torch cutting action. Note use of gloves. (Lincoln Electric Co.)

Basic Safety Rules for Oxyacetylene Equipment

The following rules should be observed when using oxyacetylene equipment:

- Wear protective goggles.
- Wear welding gloves and other protective clothing.
- Keep all oil and grease away from equipment.
- Never use equipment with greasy hands or when wearing greasy garments.
- Weld only in well ventilated areas.
- Do not cut, weld, or braze fuel tanks until special precautions have been taken.
- Do not work in an explosive atmosphere.
- Always have a fire extinguisher on the job.

- Open cylinder valves slowly.
- Maintain good hoses and fittings.
- Purge lines before lighting the torch.
- Never use defective regulators.
- Inspect hose for damage following a flashback.
- Never try to repair hose with tape. If a hose leaks, discard it.
- Stand to one side of the regulators when opening cylinder valves.
- Never open the acetylene cylinder valve more than one turn.
- Never use acetylene at pressures exceeding 15 psi (103 kPa).
- When adjusting either oxygen or acetylene pressures, make certain that the other mixer valve is closed. This will prevent flashbacks.
- Point the torch in a safe direction when lighting.
- Know what materials you are cutting or welding. Some coatings produce deadly gases when heated.

Note: There are many more specific safety rules. Study a booklet on safe practices from one of the companies handling gas welding equipment. Have an experienced operator assist you until you have mastered setting up, lighting, and using welding equipment safely.

Arc Welding

Arc welding utilizes the intense heat (6000°-10,000°F or 3318°-5542°C) generated by an electric arc between the end of the welding rod and the workpieces. Both the base metal and the welding rod quickly reach the fusion state. As the work *puddles,* the rod end melts and flows into the molten base metal. The arc force actually causes molten globules of rod metal to travel through the arc to the puddle. This allows the arc welder to be used for overhead welding. See **Figure 6-13.**

Basically, an arc welding machine can be an AC (alternating current) or DC (direct current) machine. Combination AC-DC machines are also available.

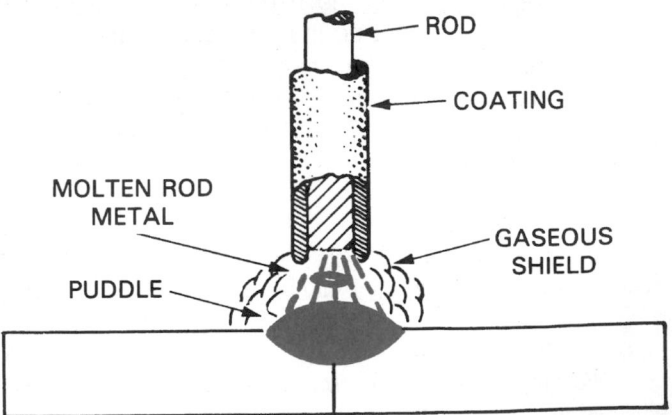

Figure 6-13.   Using the electric arc for welding. Note molten globule traveling from rod to puddle.

The AC or AC-DC machine is generally a power transformer that alters the incoming 220-440 volts (utility line voltage) to a low-voltage, high-amperage current for welding. A typical AC-DC machine is pictured in **Figure 6-14.**

The DC machine is usually driven by an electric motor or a small gas engine. Both types have certain advantages and disadvantages. Arc welding machines are rated by maximum output in amperes. The higher the output, the heavier welding the machine will perform.

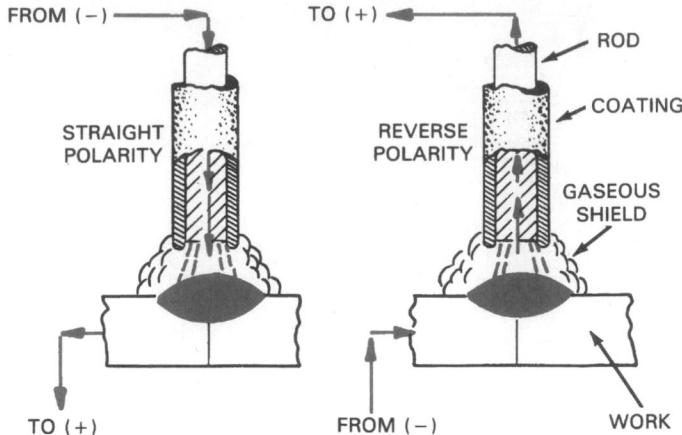

Figure 6-15.   Current travel with both straight and reverse polarity.

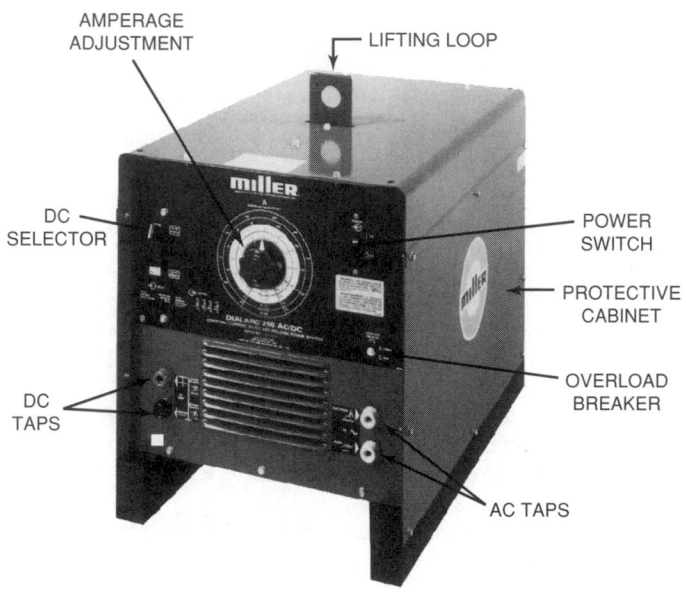

Figure 6-14.   Combination AC-DC arc welding machine. (Miller)

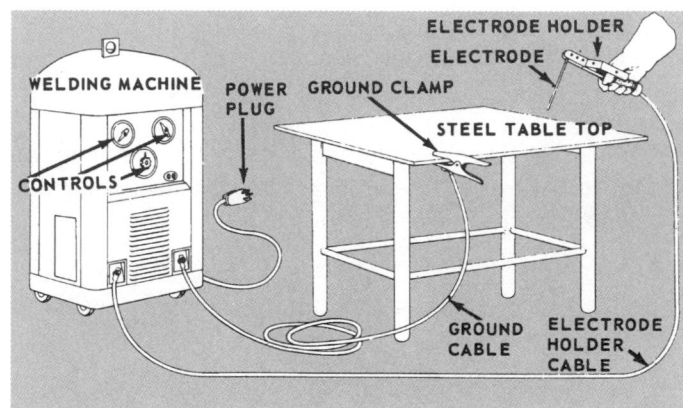

Figure 6-16.   Typical arc welding setup. (Lincoln Electric Co.)

Polarity

Two common terms used in DC arc welding are straight polarity and reverse polarity. **Reverse polarity** means that the current is traveling from the work, through the arc, through the rod, and into the rod holder. **Straight polarity** means that the current is traveling from the rod holder (often called a stringer), through the rod, across the arc, and to the work. For a straight polarity hookup, merely plug (unless a polarity switch is used) the rod holder cable into the hole marked with the negative symbol (-). For a reverse polarity hookup, plug the rod holder cable into the hole with the positive symbol (+).

Polarity is not a factor in AC welding since the direction of alternating current is reversed (or alternated) 60 times per second. See **Figure 6-15.**

Arc Welding Setup

Study **Figure 6-16.** This setup shows the welding machine, rod holder, ground clamp, and connecting cables.

Arc Welding Rods

Welding rods (electrodes) used for arc welding usually range from 12"-14" (305-356 mm) in length and are available in many diameters. They start at 1/16" (0.063 mm) diameter. For general auto shop use, an assortment of rods

in diameters of 1/16", 3/32", 1/8", 5/32", and 3/16" (0.063, 0.094, 0.125, 0.156, and 0.188 mm) will be adequate.

Welding rods used in arc welding are usually coated to provide a gaseous shield around the arc. This shield removes impurities and prevents oxidization. A self-starting, self-spacing rod is offered. The coating is kept in contact with the work and maintains the correct distance between the rod and the work.

Rods are available for welding mild steel, carbon steel, cast iron, aluminum, and other metals. Select a rod suited to the welding job—both in diameter and material.

Protective Equipment

When arc welding, always wear a welding helmet to protect your face and eyes. A welding helmet has a dark glass window that will allow you to watch the blinding arc without eyestrain or damage. **Figure 6-17** shows a welder using protective equipment.

Leather or Kevlar gloves should be used to protect your hands from radiation and from spatter (flying bits of molten metal) burns. Clothing must be heavy and of a hard finished cotton (no wool or synthetics) to shed sparks and spatter without igniting. Overhead and horizontal welding can cause a rain of hot spatter to fall on your arms and shoulders. In these cases, a leather jacket should be worn.

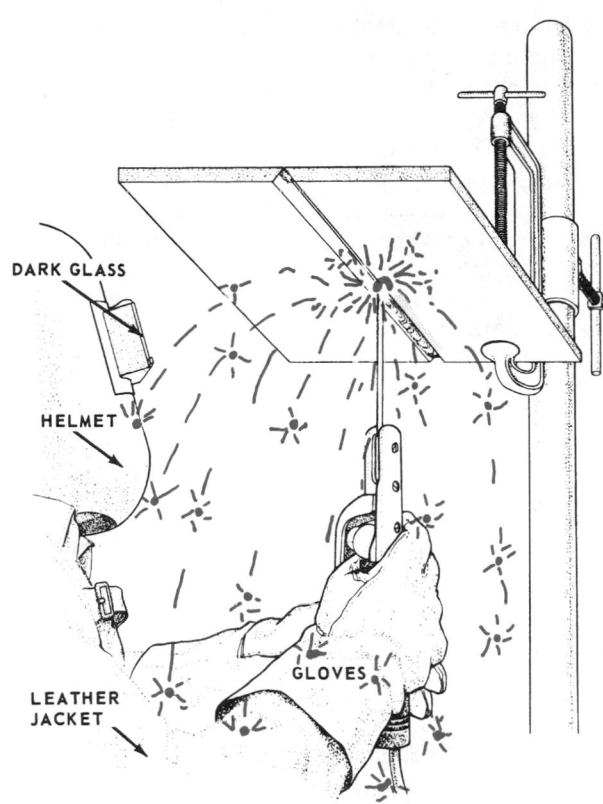

Figure 6-17.   Protective equipment is a must.

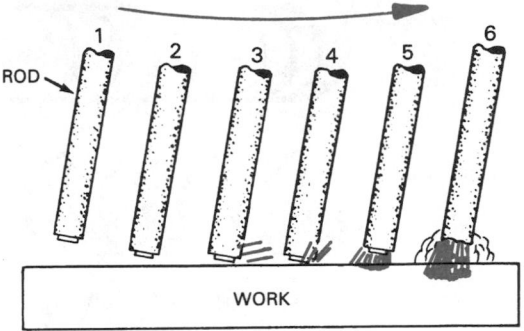

Figure 6-18.   Striking an arc.

See **Figure 6-17.** Pockets must not be open to receive red-hot drops. Shoes must have leather tops and should be high enough to prevent the entry of sparks. When arc welding, rings should not be worn because it is possible to ground a ring between the workpiece and the welding rod. With heavy welding currents, this can heat the ring to a high temperature very quickly.

STOP **Warning: Your eyes can suffer severe burns from the rays produced during arc welding. Never watch the arc (even for a second) without using a helmet or face mask. Never strike an arc when another person is standing nearby unless the person is wearing protective goggles. Eye burns are "sneaky" because the pain does not immediately follow the exposure.**

Arc Welding Techniques

The procedure for producing a weld using arc welding equipment is as follows:
1. Attach the ground clamp securely to a spot on the work that is free of paint, rust, etc.
2. Select the correct size and type of rod.
3. Set the machine as recommended.
4. Insert a rod in the rod holder. The holder jaws must grip the uncoated end of the rod to provide an electrical path.
5. Turn the machine on and strike an arc by striking the end of the rod against the work with a short, scratching motion. When the arc forms, pull the rod away the recommended distance. Look at **Figure 6-18.**

6. When the base metal puddles (melts), move the rod forward slowly. Some rods may be held steady, while others require a whipping motion.

When whipping, move the rod out of the molten puddle until the puddle starts to freeze (solidify and turn from a shiny, wet look to a dull sheen). Then, immediately move it partially back into the puddle. When the puddle is fluid again, hold the rod in place for a split second. Then, whip it out again. Repeat this process. Viewed from the top, the whipping process can form either a straight line or a "C" shape, depending on the need.

Whipping is handy in controlling burn-through in thin metal or when working with wide gaps. The rod should be held so that the top of the rod is tilted 5°-15° toward the direction of travel. See **Figure 6-19.**

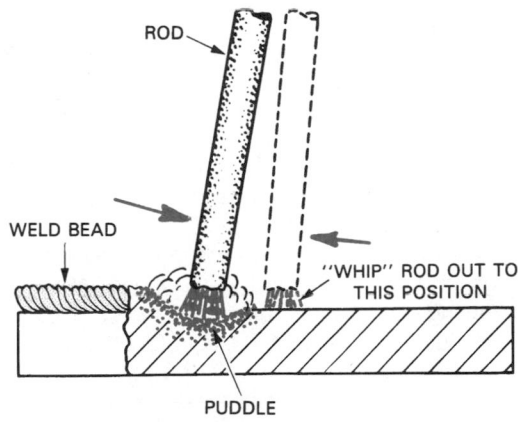

Figure 6-19.   Welding with a whipping motion of the electrode (rod).

Whipping should be done by flexing the wrist. The whipping motion produces a series of circular ridges along the top of the weld. At first, it may be difficult to maintain correct arc length. Continued practice will enable you to develop skill. Always use the recommended machine settings.

Occasionally, a weaving motion will be required. This will help to bridge wider gaps and will deposit weld metal over a wider surface. See **Figure 6-20.**

Study **Figure 6-21.** It pictures a series of welds. All welds were made with the same type and size electrodes.

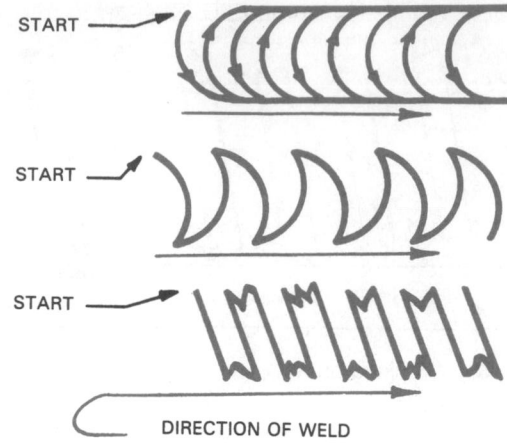

START →

START →

START →

DIRECTION OF WELD

Figure 6-20.   Weaving patterns for arc welding. (Marquette)

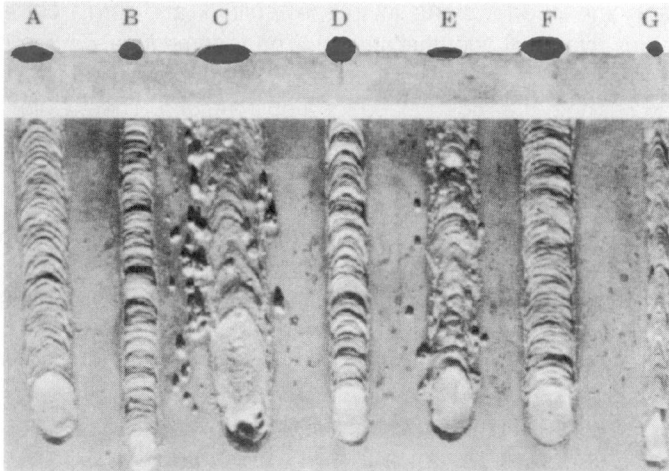

A   B   C   D   E   F   G

Figure 6-21.   Effects of various machine settings, arc lengths, and welding speeds. Rod type and size remained constant. A—A good, smooth weld. Note even whip marks and lack of spatter. B—Machine settings too low. Weld is narrow with little penetration. It is piled high. C—Machine settings too high. Note excessive width, blowholes, and heavy spatter. D—Settings OK but arc too short. E—Settings OK but arc too long. F—Settings OK, arc OK, but speed too slow. G—Arc OK, settings OK, but speed too fast. (Lincoln Electric Co.)

Machine settings and welding speeds were varied to demonstrate the effects.

The sound of the arc is helpful in determining when it is the correct length and of the proper heat. A good arc sounds similar to bacon frying. A short arc will make popping noises and may cause the rod to stick to the work. Excessive arc length will cause a high, humming noise with a lot of spatter. The arc also tends to go out.

Work Should Be Clean

Despite the fact that a good welder can run a bead through rust, paint, and moisture, all weld areas should be dry and clean. The weld will go faster, look better, and be stronger if the surfaces to be welded are clean.

After making the first welding pass, chip the **slag** (brittle coating left on weld from rod coating material) from the bead. Use a wire brush to complete the cleanup job before making the next pass. Some thick parts require a number of passes. If the slag is not removed, the joint may be full of slag **inclusions** (particles) and **blowholes** (air pockets).

 Warning: When chipping or wire brushing, wear protective goggles. Getting a piece of slag in your eye can be serious. Your helmet may be designed so that the dark glass can be tipped up, permitting you to look through a piece of clear glass.

MIG and TIG Welding

There are basically two types of shielded gas arc welding: **metal inert gas (MIG) welding** and **tungsten inert gas (TIG) welding.** In both types, the welding takes place inside a shield of inert gas (helium, argon, neon, krypton). This **gas shield** is used to protect the puddle of molten metal from contamination by nitrogen and oxygen in the air. These two welding techniques are used to repair both ferrous (contains iron) and nonferrous (contains no iron) metals.

A MIG process is shown in **Figure 6-22.** Note that the "filler wire" is passed through the center of the gas nozzle as welding takes place. A TIG welding process is illustrated in **Figure 6-23.** Notice the "filler wire" position.

Safety Rules for Arc Welding

The following safety rules should be observed when using any type of arc welding equipment:

• Never look at the arc unless you are wearing a suitable helmet or face shield.

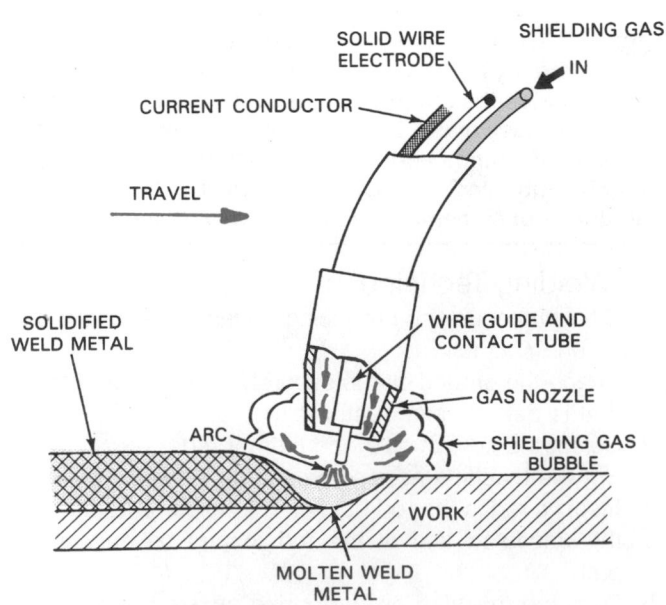

Figure 6-22.   Metal inert gas (MIG) welding procedure. Note shielding gas protective bubble and solid wire electrode being fed through nozzle. (Lincoln Electric Co.)

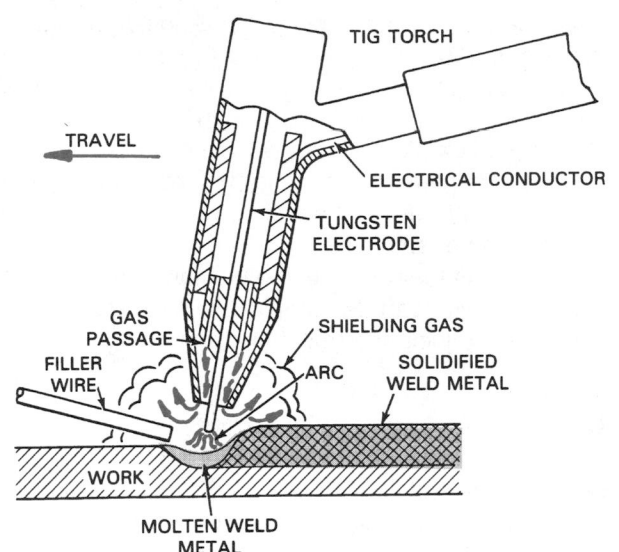

Figure 6-23. Tungsten inert gas (TIG) welding process. Note gas exiting torch nozzle and creating a protective shield. (Lincoln Electric Co.)

- Do not permit bystanders in the work area unless they are wearing protective gear.
- Wear goggles when chipping or wire brushing.
- Wear protective clothing and gloves.
- Make certain that the welding machine is properly grounded.
- Never weld while standing in water or on damp ground.
- Never carelessly strike an arc on a gas tank or on compressed gas cylinders.
- Do not strike an arc on automobile brake lines, gas lines, or other potentially dangerous parts.
- Weld only in areas with adequate ventilation.
- Be careful when welding metal with coatings such as zinc, cadmium, and beryllium. The fumes from these coatings can be deadly.
- Disconnect the welding machine before attempting any repairs.

Preventing Damage to the Arc Welder and the Surrounding Area

To prevent damage to arc welding equipment or to the surrounding area:

- Do not adjust machine settings or attempt to change polarity when the machine is under load (welding). This will damage the switch contacts.
- Keep the ground clamp and the tool holder apart.
- Never start the machine until you are certain that the rod holder is not touching the work.
- Make sure the cables are tight in the sockets, clamp, and rod holder. This will prevent excessive resistance and overheating.
- Protect paint, glass, and upholstery from hot spatter.
- Keep cables coiled when not in use.

- Do not attach the ground clamp to bumpers or other chrome parts. Any looseness will cause arcing that will pit the chrome.

Brazing

Brazing consists of heating the work to a point high enough to melt the brazing material without melting the work itself. Steel, for example, is heated until it is a dull red. A suitable brazing rod is brought into contact with the heated joint and melted. *Capillary action* (attraction between a solid and a liquid) draws the brazing alloy into the joint. This is different from actual welding, where the work is heated enough to melt it together into a single mass. Brazing is similar to soldering (covered in Chapter 11), but the melting temperatures involved are higher. Brazing temperatures are about 800°F (427°C).

For successful brazing, the work must be clean, properly fluxed, and brought to the correct temperature. Parts should be held together securely during the operation and while cooling to avoid internal fractures.

Braze Welding

Braze welding is similar to brazing, but the joint between the parts is loosely fitted. Brazing rod actually flows into the joint and is built up until the joint has sufficient strength. See **Figure 6-24.**

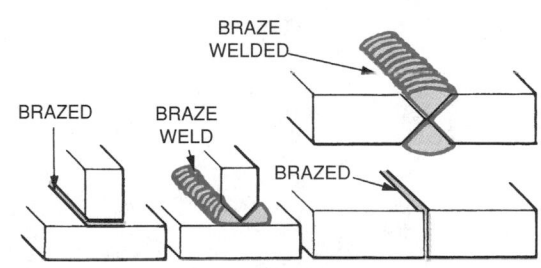

Figure 6-24. Brazed and braze welded joints.

Brazing Rod

Brazing rods come in a wide variety of alloys. A regular bronze or manganese bronze rod is generally acceptable for use on steel, cast iron, and malleable iron. Melting temperature is around 1625°F (886°C), and the rod has a tensile strength (bonded to steel) of around 40,000 psi (275,800 kPa).

Brazing Flux

Numerous *brazing fluxes* are available. Choose a flux that is compatible with the brazing rod being used. Rods are available with flux coatings. Flux is available in either powder or liquid form. The uncoated brazing rod tip is heated and dipped into the flux. Enough flux will adhere to the rod to provide proper fluxing for a short time. The flux helps to remove oxides. It also prevents oxides from forming during the brazing process.

Sources of Heat for Brazing

A Bunsen burner, blowtorch, propane torch, oxyacetylene torch, and carbon arc all produce sufficient heat for brazing and braze welding. Propane and oxyacetylene torches are well suited for the job and are generally available in the shop. The acetylene torch, **Figure 6-25,** is similar to a propane torch. A regulator is attached to a tank of gas, the tank valve is opened, and the regulator is set for the desired flow. Because the brazing torch utilizes oxygen from the air, only one tank (acetylene) is required. Several tip sizes are available. An oxyacetylene brazing setup (uses a tank of oxygen and a tank of acetylene) is shown in **Figure 6-26.** Oxyacetylene flame temperatures exceed 6000°F (3,318°C).

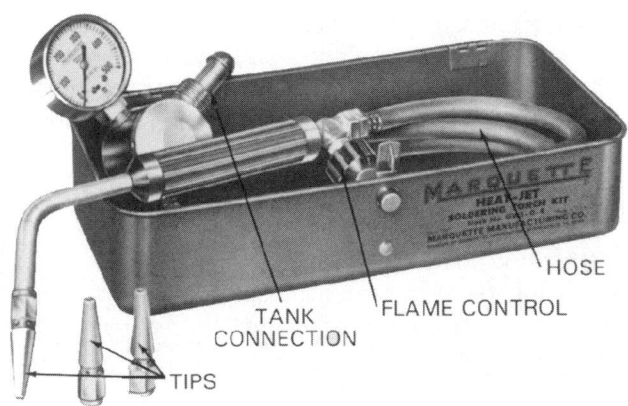

Figure 6-25.   Solder-braze kit. (Marquette)

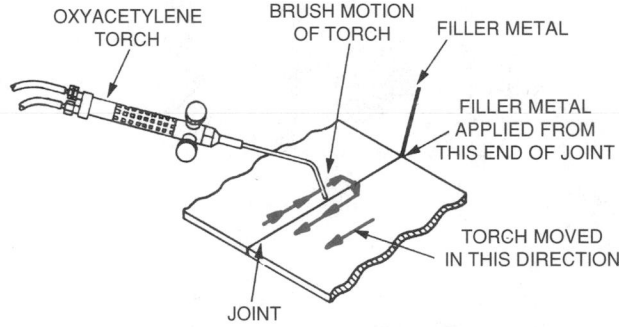

Figure 6-26.   Heat joint prior to applying brazing material. When hot, start applying filler metal from one edge. Use the brushing motion of the flame to draw material along and into the joint. (AIRCO)

Brazing Technique

The technique for brazing is as follows:

1. Select a tip size appropriate to the work. The tip size chart, **Figure 6-6,** will give you an indication of size in relation to metal thickness. Note the recommended gas pressures.
2. Adjust the torch to produce a neutral or slightly carburizing (excess acetylene) flame. Look at **Figure 6-8.**

3. With the parts clean, closely fitted (ideal joint gap for brazing is .0015-.003" or 0.038-0.076 mm), fluxed, and firmly held, apply heat to the joint. Use a brushing motion of the torch tip, **Figure 6-26.**
4. Watch the flux. When it starts to turn watery and clear, a little more heat will be sufficient. Touch the filler wire to the work. When the heat is correct, the wire will melt and tin the parts.
5. Use the tip of the wire to guide the flow of metal (tinning action follows heat). Make sure the filler enters the full length of the joint and that it tins properly.

Tip Distance and Angle Are Important

The distance the torch tip is held from the work affects the rate and extent of heating. Parts with a low melting point will require you to hold the tip farther from the area to be brazed, **Figure 6-27.**

By holding the tip at an angle, **Figure 6-28,** the work is kept at brazing temperature with minimum danger of overheating. Note that the distance is varied to suit the work, but the angle is maintained for all brazing jobs.

Keep the tip in motion to spread the heat. If the flame is kept in one spot too long, overheating may result. A circular motion, **Figure 6-29,** is desirable. The size of the circle should be decreased as the joint becomes heated. When brazing temperature is reached, the circles should be quite small. Using a zigzag motion during the application of the welding rod is also satisfactory.

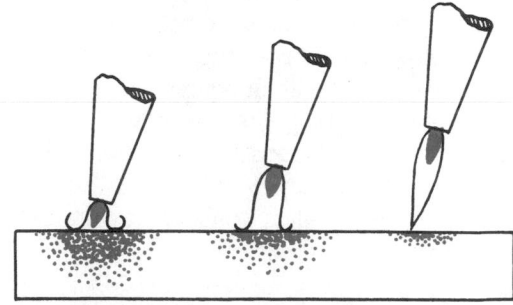

Figure 6-27.   Distance from tip to work affects heat transfer.

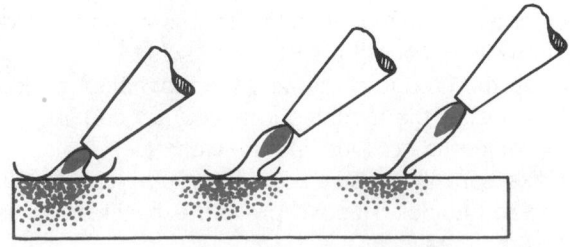

Figure 6-28.   Hold torch tip at an angle to work.

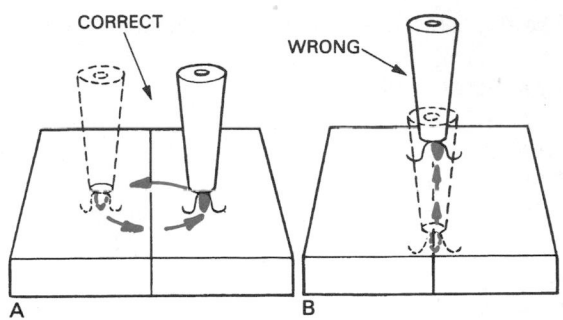

Figure 6-29.   Keep torch tip in motion.

Braze Welding Technique

In braze welding, a groove, fillet, or slot is filled with nonferrous filler metal. The filler metal has a melting point below that of the base metal but above 800°F (427°C). The filler metal is not distributed by capillary attraction.

The technique used for braze welding is similar to brazing. Once the brazing rod has flowed out and the parts have tinned, the heat should be carefully controlled. This allows the braze metal to build up to the desired thickness. As the filler rod is fed, it must mix with the filler added previously, but it must not cause the buildup to flow. See **Figure 6-30**. The rules to follow when braze welding include:

- Workpieces must be clean and well fitted.
- Use gas pressures and a tip appropriate for the job at hand.
- Use a neutral or slightly carburizing flame.
- Keep the tip in motion.
- Hold the tip at an angle to the work.
- Heat may be controlled by changing distance between the tip and the workpiece.
- Braze metal should be suited to the job.
- Use a good flux.
- Braze metal must penetrate the joint and tin the surfaces.
- Parts must be held in position and must not be disturbed until the braze metal sets.
- Materials must not be overheated.

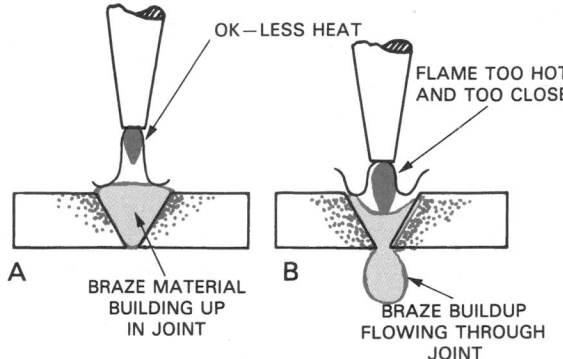

Figure 6-30.   Braze welding. A—Correct. B—Too hot. Note how the braze metal base sags.

Tech Talk

The automotive technician is often called on to do welding when fixing a broken part, sealing a tank, or installing a trailer hitch. Some technicians may even get into specialized areas, such as aluminum welding to repair transmission cases. Therefore, it is a good idea to learn at least the basics of welding. You should always try to develop extra skills, since you never know when they will come in handy.

One way to become good at welding is to take a course in welding. This may already be part of the automotive curriculum at your school. If not, you might want to consider taking such a course for your own benefit. One course will not make you into a welder, but it will enable you to become better at the welding you will do in the automotive repair shop.

Summary

Gas welding involves fusion (melting and mixing) of the metals to be joined. The work should be clean and dry. Thick metals should be beveled. Select a torch tip of the size recommended by the manufacturer. Set gas pressures for the selected tip. Adjust the torch to a neutral flame.

When welding, keep the inner flame from touching either the filler rod or the puddle. Bring the work to the molten state and, if required, add filler rod. The weld must penetrate the work and should be solid and free of slag and blowholes.

Cutting is fast and easy with an oxyacetylene cutting torch. Follow all safety precautions in setting up the equipment and lighting the torch.

Arc welding is fast and applies a minimum amount of heat to the work. Although the arc temperature is high, the welding process is so rapid that the work remains relatively cool. This helps control warpage. Select the appropriate rod size and type.

Adjust the machine to the correct polarity and current settings. Tip the top of the rod in the direction of travel (5°-15°). A whipping motion will help control the heat, direction, and penetration of the weld.

The weld bead should be smooth and even, have good penetration, and be free of slag and blowholes. Remove slag from a bead before welding another pass over the original bead.

Tungsten inert gas (TIG) and metal inert gas (MIG) are two types of shielded gas welding. The material being joined is protected from contamination by an inert gas shield. These welding techniques are used for nonferrous and ferrous metals.

Brazing takes place above a temperature of 800°F (427°C). The work must be clean. Flux the workpieces and heat them until brazing rod melts when in contact with the parts. Capillary action will draw the brazing material into the joints. Do not overheat.

Braze welding requires tinning the work with braze material. Then, build up the brazing material to fill joint irregularities and provide strength. Bronze brazing rod may be used on cast iron, malleable iron, and steel. Either a propane torch or an oxyacetylene torch may be used.

Choose a torch tip that is appropriate for the work. Set the gas pressures as recommended by the torch manufacturer. Use a neutral flame (approximately one-to-one mixture of acetylene and oxygen) to a slightly carburizing flame (one-to-one mixture is varied to give excess of acetylene). Hold the tip at an angle to the work. Vary the distance between the tip and the work as needed. Keep tip in motion to avoid localized overheating.

Know These Terms

Fusion	Reverse polarity
Oxyacetylene welding	Straight polarity
Regulators	Welding rods
Hoses	Slag
Torch mixing handle	Inclusions
Tip	Blowholes
Purge	Metal inert gas (MIG)
Scratcher	welding
Neutral flame	Tungsten inert gas (TIG)
Carburizing flame	welding
Oxidizing flame	Gas shield
Inner flame cone	Brazing
Oxyacetylene cutting torch	Capillary action
Kerf	Braze welding
Arc welding	Brazing rods
Puddles	Brazing fluxes

5. Before opening tank valves, regulator handles should be _____.
   - (A) removed
   - (B) backed out until free
   - (C) tightened securely
   - (D) backed halfway out.

6. Before lighting the oxyacetylene torch, the technician should _____ both lines.
   - (A) purge
   - (B) tighten
   - (C) disconnect
   - (D) None of the above.

7. After the flame is adjusted, the acetylene tank should be opened _____.
   - (A) all the way
   - (B) four turns
   - (C) one turn
   - (D) 1/16 turn

8. The electrical power used by arc welders is _____.
   - (A) AC
   - (B) DC
   - (C) a combination of AC and DC
   - (D) All of the above, depending on the equipment.

9. Nonferrous metals contain no _____.
   - (A) copper
   - (B) aluminum
   - (C) iron
   - (D) zinc

10. Gas shielded (TIG and MIG) welding prevents _____ in the surrounding air from contaminating the weld.
    - (A) nitrogen
    - (B) argon
    - (C) oxygen
    - (D) Both A & C.

Review Questions—Chapter 6

Do not write in this book. Write your answers on a separate sheet of paper.

1. The technician should add filler metal to the weld by _____.
   - (A) touching the rod to the puddle.
   - (B) holding rod above puddle and allowing it to drip in.
   - (C) laying a length of rod flat on the joint.
   - (D) melting and depositing drops of rod all along the joint before melting the base metal.

2. Acetylene tanks should be used in the _____ position.

3. Always open the tank valves _____.

4. Always wear _____ when welding, brazing, or cutting.
   - (A) eye protection
   - (B) gloves
   - (C) vest
   - (D) All of the above.

ASE-Type Questions

1. Technician A says that the flame for braze welding should be an oxidizing flame. Technician B says that the flame for normal welding should be a neutral flame. Who is right?
   - (A) A only.
   - (B) B only.
   - (C) Both A & B.
   - (D) Neither A nor B.

2. Technician A says that the inner flame cone must not touch the weld puddle. Technician B says that the inner flame cone must not touch the rod tip. Who is right?
   - (A) A only.
   - (B) B only.
   - (C) Both A & B.
   - (D) Neither A nor B.

3. Technician A says that the cutting torch uses a jet of oxygen to produce the cutting action. Technician B says that the cutting torch uses a jet of acetylene to produce the cutting action. Who is right?
   (A) A only.
   (B) B only.
   (C) Both A & B.
   (D) Neither A nor B.

4. Technician A says that the cutting torch should be held at a right angle to the work. Technician B says that oil and grease should be kept away from gas welding equipment. Who is right?
   (A) A only.
   (B) B only.
   (C) Both A & B.
   (D) Neither A nor B.

5. Technician A says that arc welding heats the entire workpiece more than gas welding. Technician B says that watching the arc without protective equipment can cause serious eye damage. Who is right?
   (A) A only.
   (B) B only.
   (C) Both A & B.
   (D) Neither A nor B.

6. Technician A says that welding rods are usually coated. Technician B says that some metal coatings will give off poisonous fumes when heated. Who is right?
   (A) A only.
   (B) B only.
   (C) Both A & B.
   (D) Neither A nor B.

7. Technician A says that the hotter the arc, the better. Technician B says that one should never weld or braze fuel tanks until special precautions have been taken. Who is right?
   (A) A only.
   (B) B only.
   (C) Both A & B.
   (D) Neither A nor B.

8. Technician A says that using a whipping motion will help control the heat, direction, and penetration of the weld. Technician B says that one should remove slag from a bead before welding another pass over the original bead. Who is right?
   (A) A only.
   (B) B only.
   (C) Both A & B.
   (D) Neither A nor B.

9. All of the following statements about brazing are true, EXCEPT:
   (A) flux is required for brazing.
   (B) the parent metal does not reach its fusion point.
   (C) brazing and braze welding are one and the same.
   (D) tip size and gas pressures are important.

10. Technician A says that braze welding requires tinning the work with braze material before the actual brazing operation. Technician B says that the tip should be kept in one spot for long periods for maximum heat penetration. Who is right?
    (A) A only.
    (B) B only.
    (C) Both A & B.
    (D) Neither A nor B.

Suggested Activities

1. Check several vehicles and note places where welds are found. Determine what types of welds are used. Make a sketch of a vehicle showing the areas where various welds are used. Be sure to identify the type of welds found.

2. List some situations that might require the automotive technician to weld or braze. Discuss these situations with your instructor or with the other members of your class.

3. Make a poster showing the types of protective clothing that should be used when welding. Display the poster near the welding equipment in your shop.

4. Practice welding on some scrap metal. Write a short description of how you used your mistakes to learn how to weld properly.

Cutaway of a late-model rear-wheel drive vehicle. Modern vehicles make use of a wide variety of gaskets, sealants, seals, and adhesives. (Ford)

7

Fasteners, Gaskets, Sealants

After studying this chapter, you will be able to:
- Identify automotive fasteners.
- Properly select fasteners.
- Torque fasteners to specifications when needed.
- Repair damaged or broken fasteners.
- Describe gasket construction, materials, and application.
- Describe the construction and installation of seals.
- Describe the types and selection of sealants and adhesives.

In the modern car, various components are subjected to heavy loads, high frequency vibration, excessive heat, and severe stress. As a result, fastener design, material, and torque settings are extremely important. Gaskets, seals, sealants, and adhesives are used throughout the car. They confine fuel, oil, water, air, and vacuum to specific units or areas. They keep dust, dirt, water, and other foreign materials out of various parts. They affect torque and tension, part alignment and clearance, temperature, compression ratios, and lubrication. Fasteners, gaskets, and seals play an important part in the proper functioning and service life of all components.

Unfortunately, the importance of the proper selection and installation of fasteners, gaskets, and seals is not always clearly understood. The failure of fasteners, gaskets, sealants, seals, or adhesives can cause extensive damage and expense. Study the material in this chapter carefully and apply the information to your work.

Types of Fasteners

Fasteners hold vehicle parts together. They can be nuts, bolts, screws, or specialized fasteners. The technician must become familiar with the types, uses, and installation of fasteners. Study the various fasteners, their markings, and their uses until you can recognize them immediately.

Machine Screws

Machine screws are used without nuts. They are passed through one part and threaded into another. When the machine screws are tightened, the two parts are then held in firm contact. A capscrew is a machine screw with a hexagonal head. A capscrew is shown in **Figure 7-1.** There

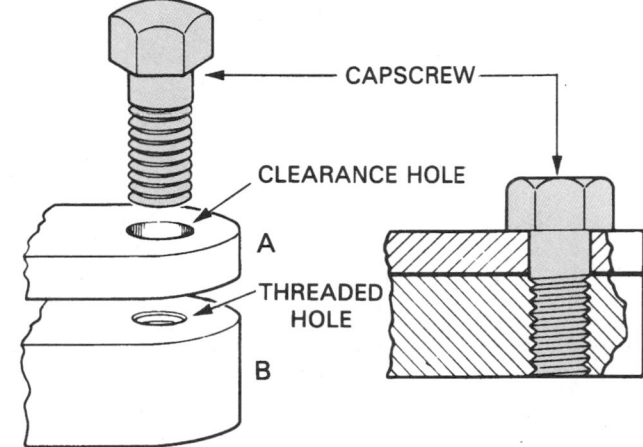

Figure 7-1. Capscrew. The capscrew is passed through a clearance hole in part A and threaded into part B.

are many different types of machine screws and screw heads. See **Figure 7-2.**

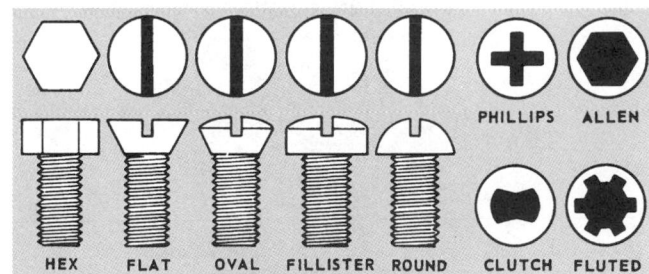

Figure 7-2. Typical machine screws. The four heads on the right illustrate various openings for turning tools.

Sheet Metal Screws

Sheet metal screws are screws with tapering threads. They are used to fasten thin metal pans together and to attach various items to sheet metal. Sheet metal screws can be installed faster and are less expensive than bolts. See **Figure 7-3.** To use a sheet metal screw, simply punch a hole in the sheet metal. The hole should be slightly smaller than the screw's minor diameter (diameter of screw if threads were ground off). A punched hole is better than a drilled hole because the punched hole attempts to close as the screw is tightened. This provides added gripping power, **Figure 7-4.**

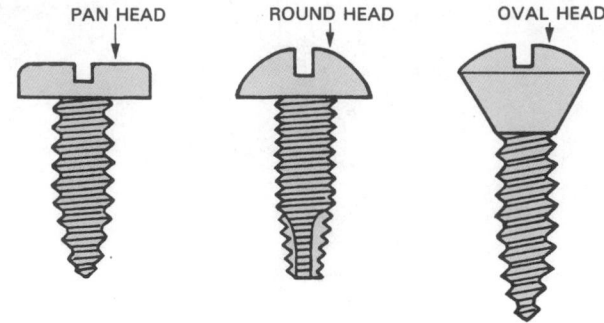

Figure 7-3.   Typical sheet metal screws.

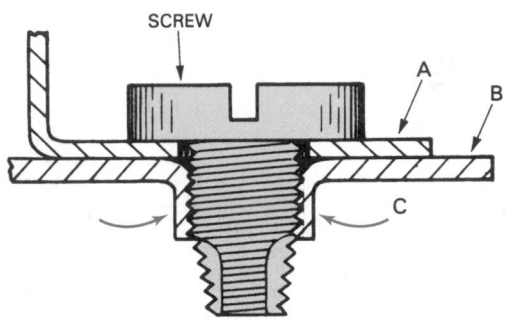

Figure 7-4.   The screw passes freely through A and cuts threads in the punched hole in B. When the screw tightens, the punched metal draws up and in, providing a secure grip, C.

Bolt

A **bolt** is a metal rod that has a head at one end and screw threads for a nut at the other. The bolt is passed through the parts to be joined. Then, the nut is installed and tightened. This holds the parts together, **Figure 7-5.**

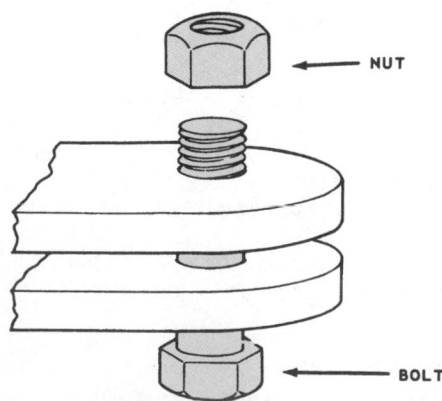

Figure 7-5.   Using a bolt to hold two parts together.

Studs

A **stud** is a metal rod that is threaded on both ends. The stud is turned into a threaded hole in one part, and another part is slipped over the stud. A nut is then turned down on the stud to secure the parts. Studs are available in

many lengths and diameters. Some have a coarse thread on one end and a fine thread on the other. Others have the same thread on both ends. In some cases, this thread may run the full length of the stud, as in **Figure 7-6.**

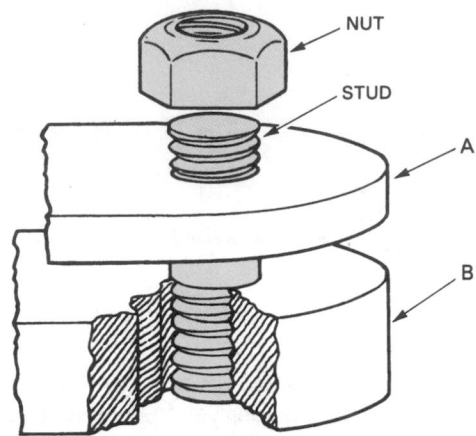

Figure 7-6.   The stud is threaded into B. Part A is slipped over the stud. The nut is placed on the stud and tightened.

A stud wrench should be used to install or remove studs. Be careful not to damage the threads during removal or installation. If a stud wrench is not available, place two nuts on the stud and "jam" them together (turn the top one clockwise and the bottom one counterclockwise until they come together). Place a wrench on the lower nut to remove the stud. See **Figure 7-7.** Place a wrench on the upper nut to install the stud.

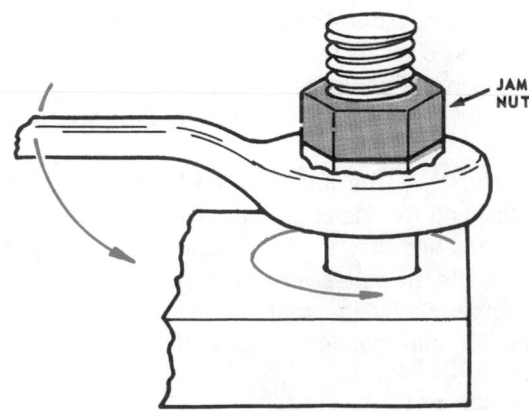

Figure 7-7.   Using jam nuts and a wrench to remove a stud.

Nuts

Nuts are manufactured in a variety of sizes and styles. Nuts for automotive use are generally hexagonal in shape (six sided). They are used on bolts and studs. Nuts must be of the correct diameter and thread pitch (threads per inch), **Figure 7-8.**

Removing Broken Studs or Screws

There are several methods for removing broken fasteners. If a portion of a broken fastener projects above the

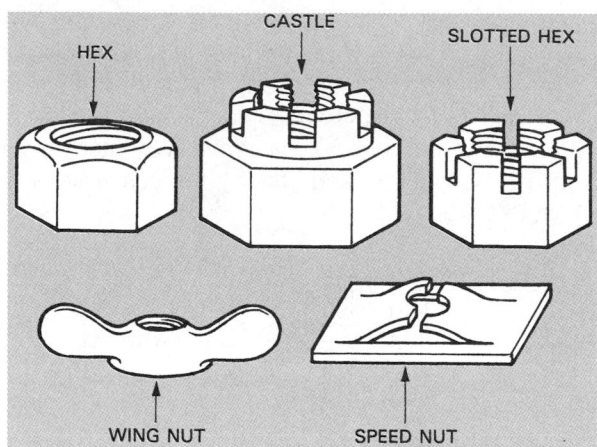

Figure 7-8. Common nuts. A wing nut is installed and removed with fingers. The speed nut is used in fastening sheet metal or other parts not requiring the strength of a regular nut.

work, it may be gripped with vise-grip pliers or a small pipe wrench and backed out.

Where the portion protruding is not sufficient to grasp with pliers or a wrench, flat surfaces may be filed to accept a wrench. Also, a slot may be cut to allow the use of a screwdriver, **Figure 7-9A.** Another method is to drill a hole in a section of flat steel strip. Then place the strip over the broken stud and weld it to the stud. A nut large enough to fit over the stud can also be welded on. The arc welder does this job quickly and with a minimal amount of heating, **Figure 7-9B.**

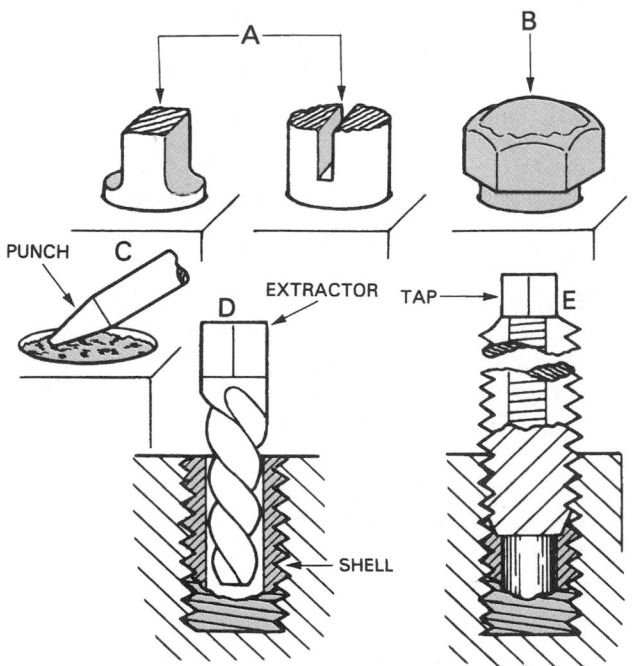

Figure 7-9. Methods used in removing a broken stud. A—Stud slotted or filed flat. B—A nut is welded on the stud. C—A punch is used to unscrew a broken stud. D—Screw extractor. E—Using a tap to remove the shell.

 Warning: Be careful of fire and damage to parts when welding.

When the stud is broken off flush or slightly below the surface, you may use a thin, sharp, pointed punch. Try driving the broken section in a counterclockwise direction. Sometimes the stub will turn out easily, **Figure 7-9C.** If you are not getting results with a punch, stop and try another method.

A *screw extractor* can often be used with good results. Center punch in the exact center of the stub and drill through the stub with a small diameter drill bit. Then, run a bit through that is slightly smaller than the stud's minor diameter. Lightly tap the extractor into the shell that remains and back it out with a wrench. The sharp edges on the flutes will grip the shell. Do not exert enough turning force to break the extractor. If the extractor breaks in the fastener, it could present a problem since it is hardened. See **Figure 7-9D.**

In the event that the methods previously described fail, select the proper tap size drill and, after running the drill through the stub shell, carefully tap out the hole. If done properly, the tap will remove the shell threads, leaving the original threads in the hole undamaged, **Figure 7-9E.**

When drilling, drill through the stub only. Do not drill beyond the stub because you may damage the part. If working on a setup where metal chips may fall into a housing, coat the drill and tap with a heavy coat of sticky grease. The chips will adhere to the grease and tools.

Removing Damaged Nuts

Occasionally, nuts will be difficult to remove due to rust, dirt, and corrosion. When this happens, there are several methods you may use to assist removal: heat (a fire hazard, be careful!), a nut-splitter (cracker), or a chisel and hacksaw. See **Figure 7-10.**

Using Penetrating Oil

Regardless of the method of removal, it is a good idea to apply *penetrating oil* (special light oil used to free rusty and dirty parts) to the damaged fastener and give it a few minutes to work in. If heat will not harm the part, applying heat will also help. Use caution not to overheat. Never use a torch near a gas tank, battery, or other flammable materials.

Repairing Threads

Occasionally, threads are only partially stripped. In such cases, they can be cleaned up using a thread die or a tap. See **Figure 7-11.**

When threads in holes are damaged beyond repair, one of four things can be done:

• The hole may be drilled and tapped to the next suitable oversize. Then, a larger diameter cap screw or stud can be installed. Use a chart to determine the proper size (tap size) to use. A clearance or body drill (drill the size of the bolts major diameter) must be

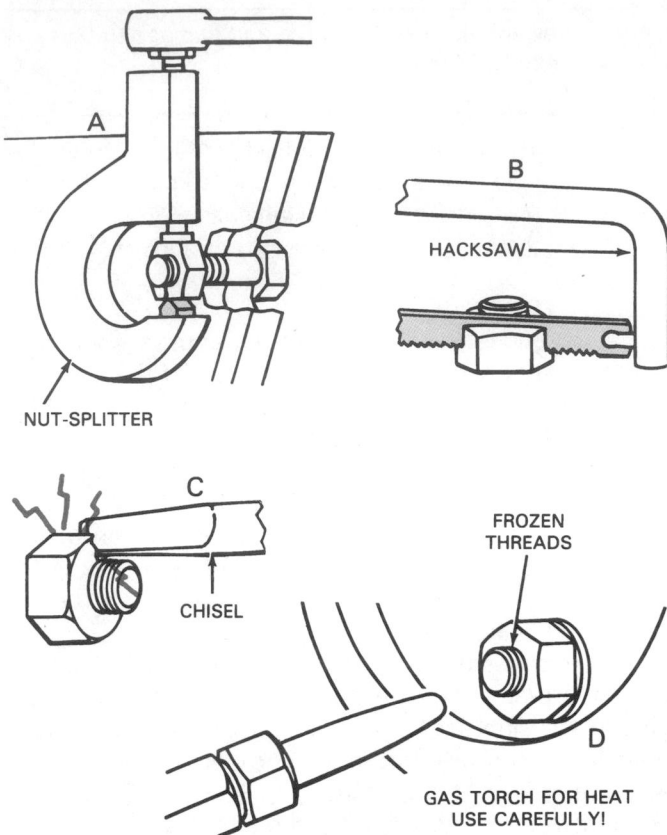

Figure 7-10. Four common methods of removing stubborn nuts. A—Nut-splitter. B—Hacksaw. C—Chisel. D—Torch. (Deere & Co.)

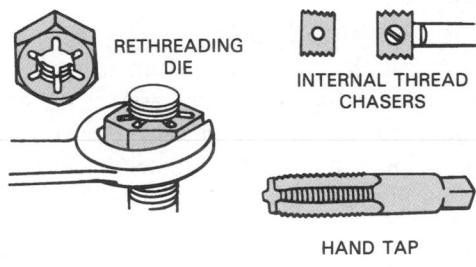

Figure 7-11. Thread restoring tools. (Deere & Co.)

passed through the attaching part to allow an oversize cap screw to be used, **Figure 7-12.**

*   The hole may be drilled and tapped to accept a threaded plug. The plug should also be drilled and

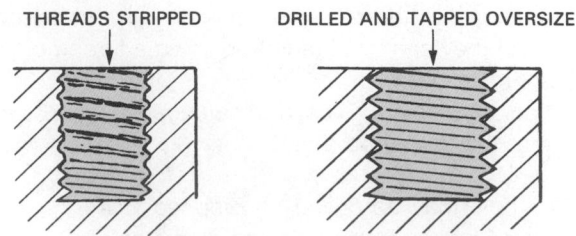

Figure 7-12. Repairing stripped threads by drilling and tapping to next oversize.

tapped to the original screw size. A special self-tapping plug that is already threaded to the original size may be used. You merely drill a hole to the specified size and run the threaded plug into a hole using a cap screw and jam nut. When fully seated, the jam nut is loosened and the cap screw removed, **Figure 7-13.**

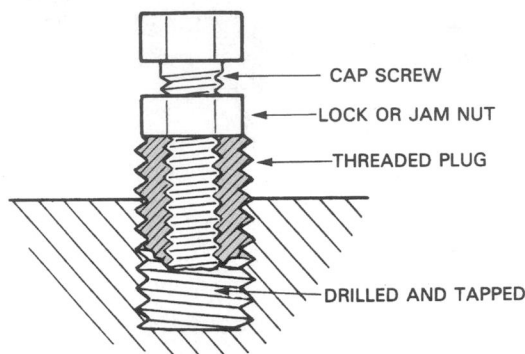

Figure 7-13. Inserting a threaded plug to repair stripped threads.

*   Another method makes use of a patented coil wire insert called a **Heli-Coil®.** A hole is drilled and tapped with a special tap. A Heli-Coil is then inserted. This brings the hole back to its original diameter and thread, **Figure 7-14.**

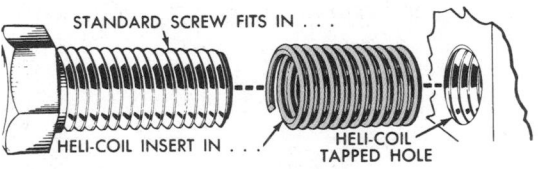

Figure 7-14. Repairing stripped threads using a Heli-Coil. (Chrysler)

*   Another type of thread repair similar to the Heli-Coil is called **Keensert®.** Instead of being an open coil insert, the Keensert is a hollow plug with internal and external threads. The damaged threaded hole is drilled and tapped with a special tap. The Keensert is then installed by hand until it is slightly below the top of the hole. A special punch is then used to force the four locking fingers down the slots that are cut into the insert. The top half of each finger is wider than the bottom, causing it to cut into the threaded hole. This locks the insert firmly into position and brings the hole to the original diameter and thread. See **Figure 7-15.** The insert may be removed using special tools if it becomes damaged.

 Caution: When removing a broken screw or repairing stripped threads, proceed carefully. A frantic or careless attempt at repair can often cause serious and costly trouble.

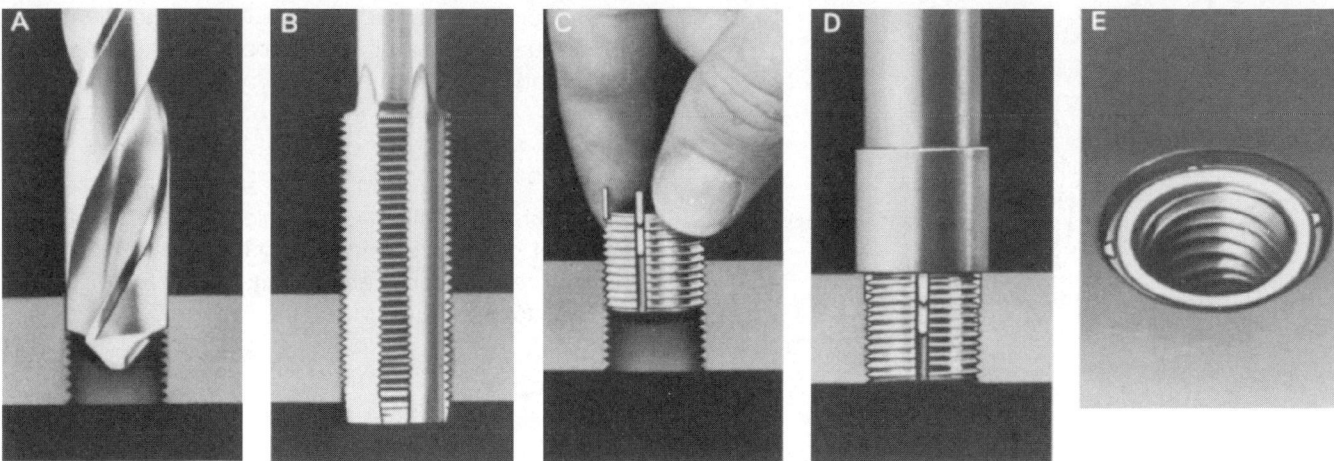

Figure 7-15. Keensert® internal thread repair sequence. A—Drill out damaged threads. B—Cut new threads with the tap. C—Screw insert in until it is slightly below the hole surface. D—Drive the fingers into place with several light taps on the installation tool. E—Installed insert. The hole is now back to the original inside diameter and is ready to be used. (Rexnord)

Bolt and Screw Terminology

Bolts and screws can be identified by type, length, major diameter, pitch (threads per inch), length of thread, class or fit, material, or tensile strength. In some cases, these fasteners are identified by the wrench size needed to install or remove them. The modern technician must learn both the unified, or inch, thread designations and the metric thread classifications. The technician must also be familiar with the torque specifications for various grades and sizes. Look at **Figures 7-16** and **7-17.**

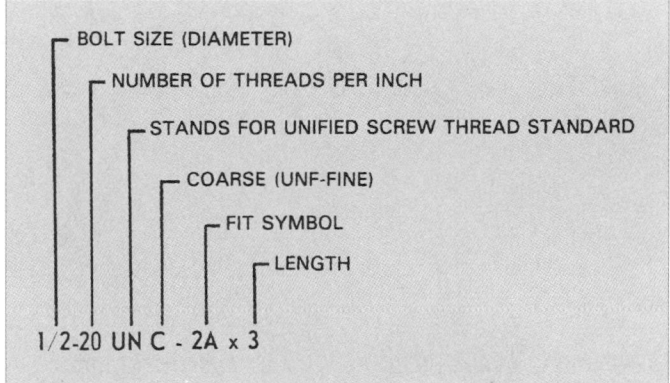

Figure 7-17. Bolt descriptive symbols chart. Learning these symbols and markings will make selecting correct replacement bolts easier and faster. (Deere & Co.)

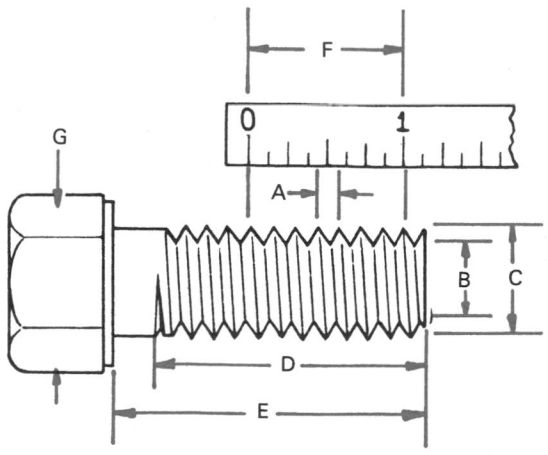

Figure 7-16. Bolt and screw terminology. A—Pitch. B—Minor diameter. C—Major diameter. D—Thread length. E—Screw length. F—Threads per inch. G—Head size measured across flats.

Head Markings

Steel bolts and cap screws are not all made of the same quality material or with the same temper. Current practice utilizes markings on the bolt and screw heads to indicate the **_tensile strength_** of the fastener.

Major Diameter

The **_major diameter_** is the widest diameter as measured from the crest, or top, of the threads on one side to the crest of the threads on the other side. See **Figure 7-16.**

Minor Diameter

The **_minor diameter_** is determined by measuring from the bottom of the threads on one side to the bottom of the threads on the other. If you were to remove all traces of the threads, the diameter of the portion left would be the minor diameter, **Figure 7-16.**

Thread Pitch

Thread pitch is the distance between the crest of one thread to the same spot on the crest of the next thread. The smaller the pitch, the greater number of threads per inch. The pitch, or number of threads per inch, can best be determined by using a thread-pitch gauge. See **Figures 7-18** and **7-19.**

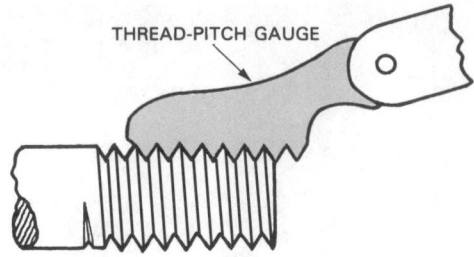

Figure 7-18. Using a thread-pitch gauge to determine the number of threads per inch.

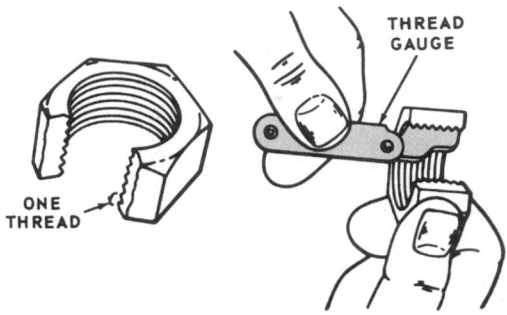

Figure 7-19. This technician is using a thread-pitch gauge to check a nut for the number of threads per inch. (Deere & Co.)

Thread Series

Three kinds of threads are commonly used on modern fasteners:

- Coarse threads (UNC or Unified National Coarse)
- Fine threads (UNF or Unified National Fine)
- Metric threads (SI or Scientific International)

When compared to fine threads, *coarse threads* have a larger and less critical shoulder bearing area, screw in and out faster, and are less subject to stripping and galling (galling occurs when threads rip particles of metal from each other, thereby damaging both threads).

Fine threads have more holding power than coarse threads, even though each thread is smaller. There are more threads per inch, and total gripping area is much more than that of the coarse thread.

The word unified, as used in Unified National Coarse and Unified National Fine, indicates that a thread conforms with thread standards used in the United States, Canada, and England. These threads are sometimes called customary or SAE threads. The UNC and UNF threads have been replaced on modern vehicles by metric fasteners, designated SI. Metric fasteners do not have separate coarse and fine designations. See **Figure 7-20.**

Right and Left Hand Threads

Both right and left hand threads are used. Almost all fasteners use a right hand thread. The left hand thread is reserved for special applications, such as wheel hub nuts or other places where part rotation would tend to loosen a right hand thread fastener.

Nut Terminology

Nuts are used on bolts. They are usually hexagonal in shape. Nuts have the same major thread diameter and number of threads per inch as their corresponding bolt. Wrench size (measured across flats) is standardized, but it does vary for special applications, **Figure 7-21.**

Class and Fit

Thread class indicates the operating clearance between a nut's internal threads and a bolt's external threads. Classes are divided into six categories: 1A, 2A, and 3A, for external threads (bolts, studs, screws) and 1B, 2B, and 3B for internal threads (nuts, threaded holes). This, in effect, gives three classes of fit. A Class 1 fit is a relatively loose fit and would be used for ease of assembly and disassembly under adverse conditions. Class 2 provides a fairly accurate fit, with only a small amount of clearance. Class 2 fasteners are commonly used for automotive applications. Class 3 is an extremely close fit and is used where utmost accuracy is essential.

Locking Devices

As screws, bolts, and nuts are subjected to vibration, expansion, and contraction, they tend to work loose. To prevent this, numerous **locking devices** have been developed. These may be an integral part of the screw or nut, or they may be a part placed under, through, or around the screw or nut. Epoxy cement or special locking compounds are sometimes used to prevent fasteners from loosening.

Self-Locking Nuts

Some nuts are designed to be self-locking or prevailing torque type. This is accomplished in various ways, but all *self-locking nuts* and *prevailing torque nuts* share the same principle. They create friction between the threads of the bolt or stud and the nut, **Figure 7-22.** The term prevailing torque refers to the fact that these nuts have a resistance to turning even before they are tightened. This torque figure must be added to the tightening torque specification for a particular nut.

The nut shown in **Figure 7-22A** utilizes a collar of soft metal, fiber, or plastic. As the bolt threads pass up through the nut, they must force their way through the collar. This jams the collar material tightly into the threads, locking the nut in place.

In **Figure 7-22B,** the upper section of the nut is slotted, and the segments are forced together. When the bolt passes through the nut, it spreads the segments apart, producing a locking action.

Figure 7-22C shows a single slot in the side of a nut. The slot may be forced open or closed during manufacture, distorting the upper thread. This will create a jamming

Recommended for
AMERICAN NATIONAL SCREW THREAD PITCHES

COARSE STANDARD THREAD (N. C.)
Formerly U. S. Standard Thread

Sizes	Threads Per Inch	Outside Diameter at Screw	Tap Drill Sizes	Decimal Equivalent of Drill
1	64	.073	53	0.0595
2	56	.086	50	0.0700
3	48	.099	47	0.0785
4	40	.112	43	0.0890
5	40	.125	38	0.1015
6	32	.138	36	0.1065
8	32	.164	29	0.1360
10	24	.190	25	0.1495
12	24	.216	16	0.1770
1/4	20	.250	7	0.2010
5/16	18	.3125	F	0.2570
3/8	16	.375	5/16	0.3125
7/16	14	.4375	U	0.3680
1/2	13	.500	27/64	0.4219
9/16	12	.5625	31/64	0.4843
5/8	11	.625	17/32	0.5312
3/4	10	.750	21/32	0.6562
7/8	9	.875	49/64	0.7656
1	8	1.000	7/8	0.875
1 1/8	7	1.125	63/64	0.9843
1 1/4	7	1.250	1 7/64	1.1093

SPECIAL THREAD (N. S.)

Sizes	Threads Per Inch	Outside Diameter at Screw	Tap Drill Sizes	Decimal Equivalent of Drill
1	56	.0730	54	0.0550
4	32	.1120	45	0.0820
4	36	.1120	44	0.0860
6	36	.1380	34	0.1110
8	40	.1640	28	0.1405
10	30	.1900	22	0.1570
12	32	.2160	13	0.1850
14	20	.2420	10	0.1935
14	24	.2420	7	0.2010
1/16	64	.0625	3/64	0.0469
3/32	48	.0938	49	0.0730
1/8	40	.1250	38	0.1015
5/32	32	.1563	1/8	0.1250
5/32	36	.1563	30	0.1285
3/16	24	.1875	26	0.1470
3/16	32	.1875	22	0.1570
7/32	24	.2188	16	0.1770
7/32	32	.2188	12	0.1890
1/4	24	.250	4	0.2090
1/4	27	.250	3	0.2130
1/4	32	.250	7/32	0.2187
5/16	20	.3125	17/64	0.2656
5/16	27	.3125	J	0.2770
5/16	32	.3125	9/32	0.2812
3/8	20	.375	21/64	0.3281
3/8	27	.375	R	0.3390
7/16	24	.4375	X	0.3970
7/16	27	.4375	Y	0.4040
1/2	12	.500	27/64	0.4219
1/2	24	.500	29/64	0.4531
1/2	27	.500	15/32	0.4687
9/16	27	.5625	17/32	0.5312
5/8	12	.625	35/64	0.5469
5/8	27	.625	19/32	0.5937
11/16	11	.6875	19/32	0.5937
11/16	16	.6875	5/8	0.6250
3/4	12	.750	43/64	0.6719
3/4	27	.750	23/32	0.7187
7/8	12	.875	51/64	0.7969
7/8	18	.875	53/64	0.8281
7/8	27	.875	27/32	0.8437
1	12	1.000	59/64	0.9219
1	27	1.000	31/32	0.9687

INCHES		DECIMALS	MILLI-METRES
1/32	1/64	.015625	.3969
	3/64	.03125	.7937
1/16	3/64	.046875	1.1906
		.0625	1.5875
3/32	5/64	.078125	1.9844
	7/64	.09375	2.3812
1/8	7/64	.109375	2.7781
	9/64	.125	3.1750
5/32	9/64	.140625	3.5719
	11/64	.15625	3.9687
3/16	11/64	.171875	4.3656
	13/64	.1875	4.7625
7/32	13/64	.203125	5.1594
	15/64	.21875	5.5562
1/4	15/64	.234375	5.9531
	17/64	.25	6.3500
9/32	17/64	.265625	6.7469
	19/64	.28125	7.1437
5/16	19/64	.296875	7.5406
	21/64	.3125	7.9375
11/32	21/64	.328125	8.3344
	23/64	.34375	8.7312
3/8	23/64	.359375	9.1281
	25/64	.375	9.5250
13/32	25/64	.390625	9.9219
	27/64	.40625	10.3187
7/16	27/64	.421875	10.7156
	29/64	.4375	11.1125
15/32	29/64	.453125	11.5094
	31/64	.46875	11.9062
1/2	31/64	.484375	12.3031
	33/64	.5	12.7000
17/32	33/64	.515625	13.0969
	35/64	.53125	13.4937
9/16	35/64	.546875	13.8906
	37/64	.5625	14.2875
19/32	37/64	.578125	14.6844
	39/64	.59375	15.0812
5/8	39/64	.609375	15.4781
	41/64	.625	15.8750
21/32	41/64	.640625	16.2719
	43/64	.65625	16.6687
11/16	43/64	.671875	17.0656
	45/64	.6875	17.4625
23/32	45/64	.703125	17.8594
	47/64	.71875	18.2562
3/4	47/64	.734375	18.6531
	49/64	.75	19.0500
25/32	49/64	.765625	19.4469
	51/64	.78125	19.8437
13/16	51/64	.796875	20.2406
	53/64	.8125	20.6375
27/32	53/64	.828125	21.0344
	55/64	.84375	21.4312
7/8	55/64	.859375	21.8281
	57/64	.875	22.2250
29/32	57/64	.890625	22.6219
	59/64	.90625	23.0187
15/16	59/64	.921875	23.4156
	61/64	.9375	23.8125
31/32	61/64	.953125	24.2094
	63/64	.96875	24.6062
		.984375	25.0031

FINE STANDARD THREAD (N. F.)
Formerly S.A.E. Thread

Sizes	Threads Per Inch	Outside Diameter at Screw	Tap Drill Sizes	Decimal Equivalent of Drill
0	80	.060	3/64	0.0469
1	72	.073	53	0.0595
2	64	.086	50	0.0700
3	56	.099	45	0.0820
4	48	.112	42	0.0935
5	44	.125	37	0.1040
6	40	.138	33	0.1130
8	36	.164	29	0.1360
10	32	.190	21	0.1590
12	28	.216	14	0.1820
1/4	28	.250	3	0.2130
5/16	24	.3125	I	0.2720
3/8	24	.375	Q	0.3320
7/16	20	.4375	25/64	0.3906
1/2	20	.500	29/64	0.4531
9/16	18	.5625	0.5062	0.5062
5/8	18	.625	0.5687	0.5687
3/4	16	.750	11/16	0.6875
7/8	14	.875	0.8020	0.8020
1	14	1.000	0.9274	0.9274
1 1/8	12	1.125	1 3/64	1.0468
1 1/4	12	1.250	1 11/64	1.1718

Figure 7-20. This chart gives the number of threads per inch for various bolts. (Deere & Co.)

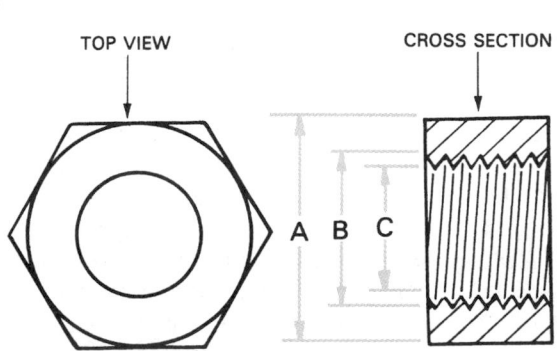

Figure 7-21. Typical nut. A—Size across flats. B—Thread major diameter. C—Thread minor diameter.

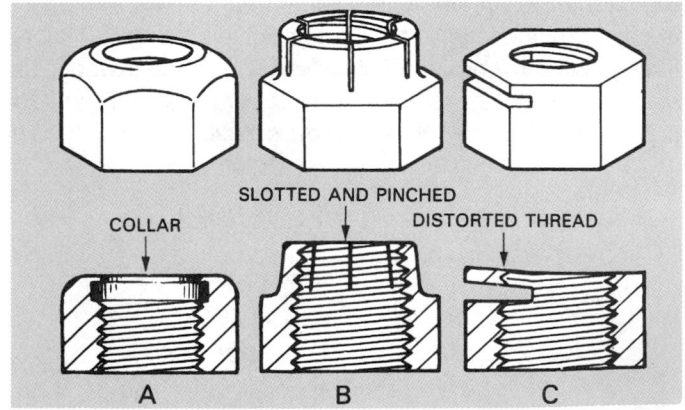

Figure 7-22. Self-locking nuts. A—Soft collar type. B—Top section slotted and pinched together. C—Slot to distort upper thread area.

effect when the bolt threads pull the nut threads back into alignment.

Self-Locking Screws

Some cap screws have heads that are designed to spring when tightened, producing a self-locking effect. Occasionally, the threaded end of a cap screw will be split and the halves will be bent outward slightly. When threaded into a hole, the halves are forced together. This creates friction between the threads.

Lock Washers

A *lock washer* is used under a nut and grips both the nut and the part surface. The three basic lock washer designs are the internal lock washer, the external lock washer, and the plain lock washer. When using lock washers with die cast or aluminum parts, a steel nonlocking washer is frequently used under the lock washer. This practice prevents damage to the part. See **Figure 7-23.**

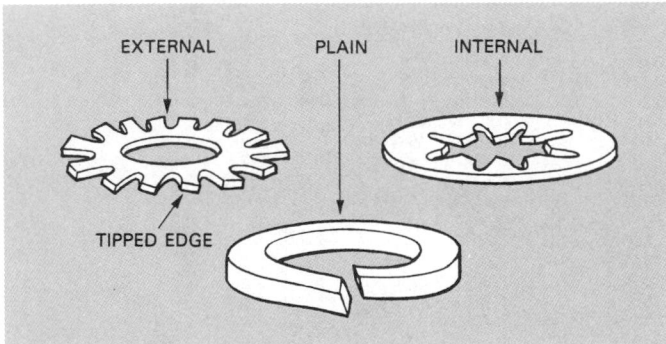

Figure 7-23. Typical lock washers. Tipped edges provide gripping power in the "off" direction.

Palnuts

The *palnut* locking device is constructed of thin, stamped steel. It is designed to bind against the threads of the bolt when installed. In use, the palnut is spun down into contact with the regular nut (open side of palnut away from regular nut). Once firmly in contact with the nut, the palnut is given another half turn. Do not tighten the palnut more than a half turn, or its effectiveness will be destroyed. The half turn draws the steel fingers toward the nut, causing them to jam into the threads, **Figure 7-24.**

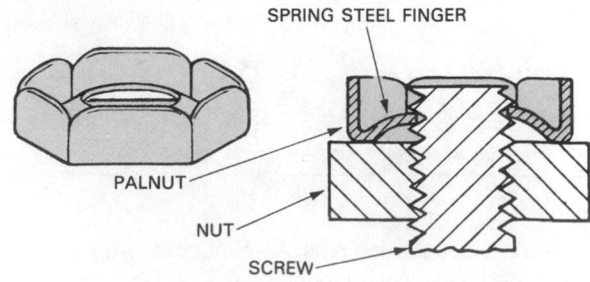

Figure 7-24. Palnut. A half turn jams the steel fingers against the threads.

Cotter Key or Pin

Cotter pins are used both with slotted nuts and castle nuts. They are also used in clevis pins and linkage ends. Use as thick a cotter pin as possible. Cut off the surplus length and bend the ends as shown in **Figure 7-25.** If necessary, the ends may be bent around the sides of the nut. Make certain that the bent ends will not interfere with other parts.

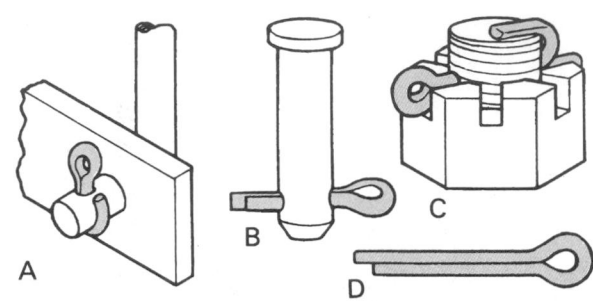

Figure 7-25. Uses of a cotter pin. A—Linkage. B—Clevis pin. C—Slotted hex nut. D—Typical cotter pin.

Special Locking Compounds

Special *locking compounds* are sometimes used to hold fasteners in place. These compounds are applied as liquids and harden to hold the fastener in place. They are often called anaerobic sealers, which means that they remain liquid when exposed to oxygen, but harden after the fastener is tightened and squeezes out all of the air from the threads. A common brand of anaerobic sealer is Locktite®, which is available in many varieties. The type of sealer used will depend on the type of fastener, heat range, or other special circumstances.

Other Types of Fasteners

In addition to the common fasteners described above, the average vehicle uses many special fasteners. Special fasteners are used in situations where there is no room for a normal fastener or where using threaded fasteners would be inconvenient.

Keys, Splines, and Pins

Keys, *splines*, and *pins* are used to attach gears, sprockets, or pulleys to shafts so that they rotate as a unit. When a key or pin is used, the unit being attached to the shaft is generally fixed to eliminate end-to-end, or longitudinal, movement. If desired, splines will allow longitudinal movement while still causing the parts to rotate together. In some cases, pins are used to fix shafts in housings and to prevent end movement and rotation, **Figure 7-26.**

A *locking plate* is made of thin sheet metal. The plate is generally arranged so that two or more screws pass through it. The metal edge or tab is then bent up snugly against the bolt. Various patterns are used.

Occasionally, screws will be locked with *safety wire* (soft or ductile wire). The wire is passed from screw to screw so that it exerts a clockwise pull on the fasteners.

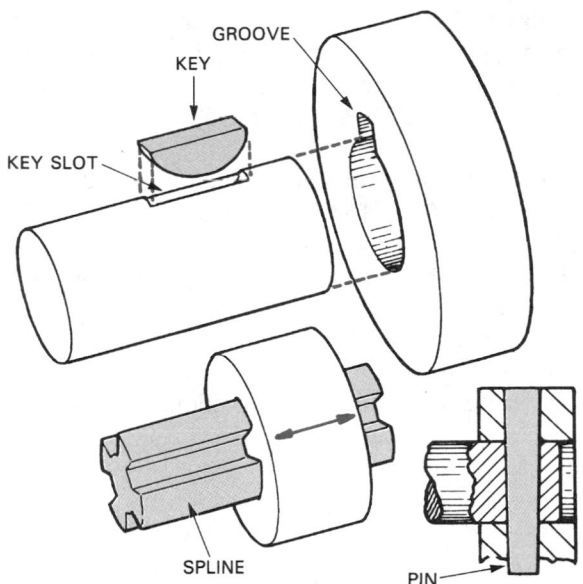

Figure 7-26. Key, spline, and pin. Note that the spline allows end movement. The pin fixes the shaft to the housing, allowing no movement. The key is commonly referred to as a woodruff key or a half-moon key.

Never reuse safety wire and always dispose of locking plates on which the tabs are fatigued (ready to crack), **Figure 7-27.**

Snap Rings

Snap rings are used to position shafts, bearings, gears, and other similar parts. There are both internal and external snap rings of numerous sizes and shapes.

The snap ring is made of spring steel. Depending on the type, it must be expanded or contracted to be removed or installed. Special snap ring pliers are used to remove and install the snap rings.

Be careful when installing or removing snap rings because overexpansion or contraction will distort and ruin them. If a snap ring is sprung out of shape—throw it away.

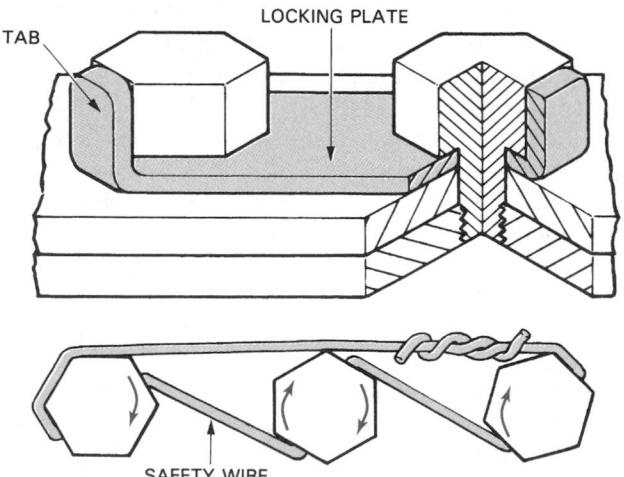

Figure 7-27. A—Locking plate. Tabs must be bent firmly against the cap screw flat to prevent rotation. B—Safety wire.

Never attempt to pound one back into shape. Never compress or expand snap rings any more than necessary. Above all, do not pry one end free of the groove and slide it along the shaft. This may ruin the ring, **Figure 7-28.**

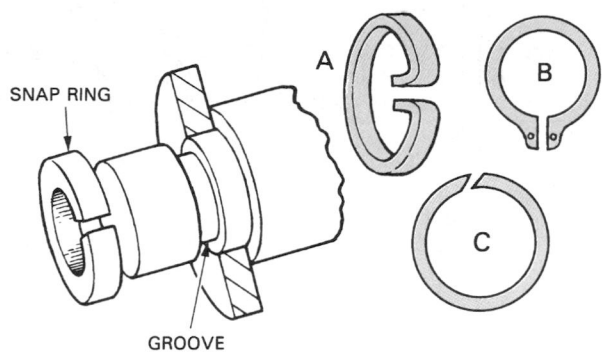

Figure 7-28. Snap rings. A—Flat internal type. B—External. C—Round external. There are many shapes and sizes of rings.

Setscrews

Setscrews are used to both lock and position pulleys and other parts to shafts. The setscrew is hardened and is available with different tips and drive heads.

Keep in mind that setscrews are poor driving devices because they often slip on the shaft. When used in conjunction with a woodruff key, they merely position the unit. As a general rule, do not install any driving unit without a woodruff key.

When a setscrew is used, the shaft will usually have a flat spot to take the screw tip. Make certain this spot is aligned before tightening the screw, **Figure 7-29.**

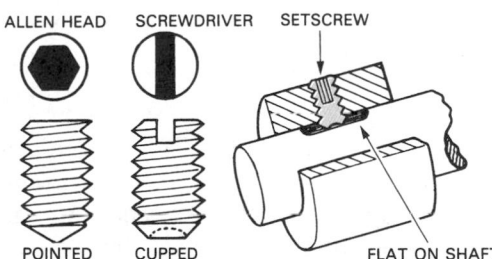

Figure 7-29. Typical setscrews. Setscrews are hardened and they should be run up very tightly.

Rivets

Rivets are made of various metals, including brass, aluminum, and soft steel. They have many applications on an automobile. When using rivets, there are several important considerations. The two parts to be joined must be held tightly together during riveting. The rivet should fit the hole snugly. The rivet material must be in keeping with the job to be done. The rivet must be of the correct type. *Pop rivets* are generally used for automotive applications. **Figure 7-30** illustrates the use of one form of pop rivet.

Figure 7-31 shows pop rivets being used to attach bumper trim. The pop rivet is inserted through the parts to be joined, and a hand-operated setting tool is placed over

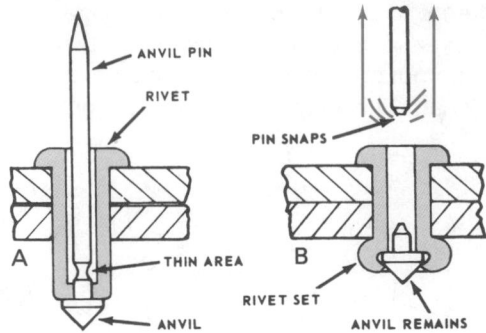

Figure 7-30. Installing a pop rivet. A—Pop rivet in place. B—Rivet tool has pulled the anvil pin outward, pulling the parts together, setting the rivet, and snapping off the pin.

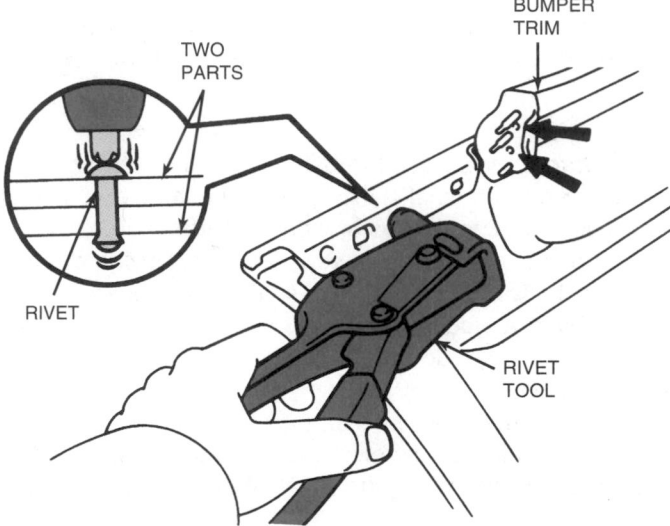

Figure 7-31. Pop rivet tool being used to attach bumper trim parts. (Lexus)

the rivet anvil pin. When the tool's handles are closed, the anvil pin is pulled outward. As the anvil is drawn outward, the rivet head is forced against the work and the hollow stem is set. The setting process draws the two parts tightly together. Further pressure on the tool's handles causes the anvil pin to snap off just ahead of the anvil. The anvil remains in the set area.

Other Fasteners

In addition to fasteners already discussed, there are numerous specialized fasteners, such as hose clamps, C-washers, clevis pins, and spring lock pins. Many types are pictured in **Figure 7-32.**

Fasteners and Torque

To better understand the reason for and proper application of controlled torque, the technician should be familiar with several important terms. Read the definitions that follow carefully. These terms will be used a great deal in this section.

- **Torque**—a turning or twisting force exerted on an object, such as a fastener. Torque is measured in inch-grams, inch-ounces, inch-pounds, foot-pounds, or Newton-meters. See **Figure 7-33**
- **Tension**—a pulling force. When a cap screw is tightened, it actually stretches about .001" (0.025 mm) for every 30,000 lb. (13 500 kg) of tension applied, **Figure 7-34.**
- **Elastic limit**—the amount an object can be distorted (compressed, bent, stretched) and still return to the same dimension when the force is removed, **Figure 7-35.**
- **Distortion**—occurs when the normal shape or configuration of an object is changed or altered due to the application of some force or forces, **Figure 7-36.**
- **Tensile strength**—the amount of pull an object will withstand before breaking, **Figure 7-37.**
- **Residual tension**—the stress remaining in an elastic object that has been distorted and not allowed to return to its original dimension, **Figure 7-38.**
- **Elasticity**—the ability of an object to return, after distortion, to its original shape and dimensions once the distorting force has been removed, **Figure 7-39.**
- **Compression**—a force tending to compress or squeeze an object, **Figure 7-40.**
- **Cold flow**—the tendency of an object under compression to expand outward, thus reducing its thickness in the direction of compression, **Figure 7-41.**
- **Hooke's law**—this law states that as long as distortion is kept within the elastic limits of a material, the amount of distortion (lengthening, shortening, bending, twisting) will be directly proportional to the applied force. This forms the basis for spring scales and torque wrenches, **Figure 7-42.**
- **High-pressure lubricant**—a lubricant that continues to reduce friction between two objects even when they are forced together under heavy pressure.

Torquing Fasteners

To understand the necessity of torquing, we should first establish what we want to accomplish by tightening fasteners. Once this is clear, the reason for the use of a torque wrench becomes obvious.

Technicians tighten fasteners to hold parts together. Once together, the parts should remain that way. The fasteners should not be tightened to the point at which they will break or distort other parts. However, they must be tightened enough to prevent them from working loose or from being sheared or pounded apart. They must also be tightened enough to prevent oil, gas, and water leaks.

Tightening fasteners in a haphazard manner can cause the following problems:

- Out-of-round cylinders.
- Egg-shaped connecting rod and main bearings.
- Warped cylinder head.

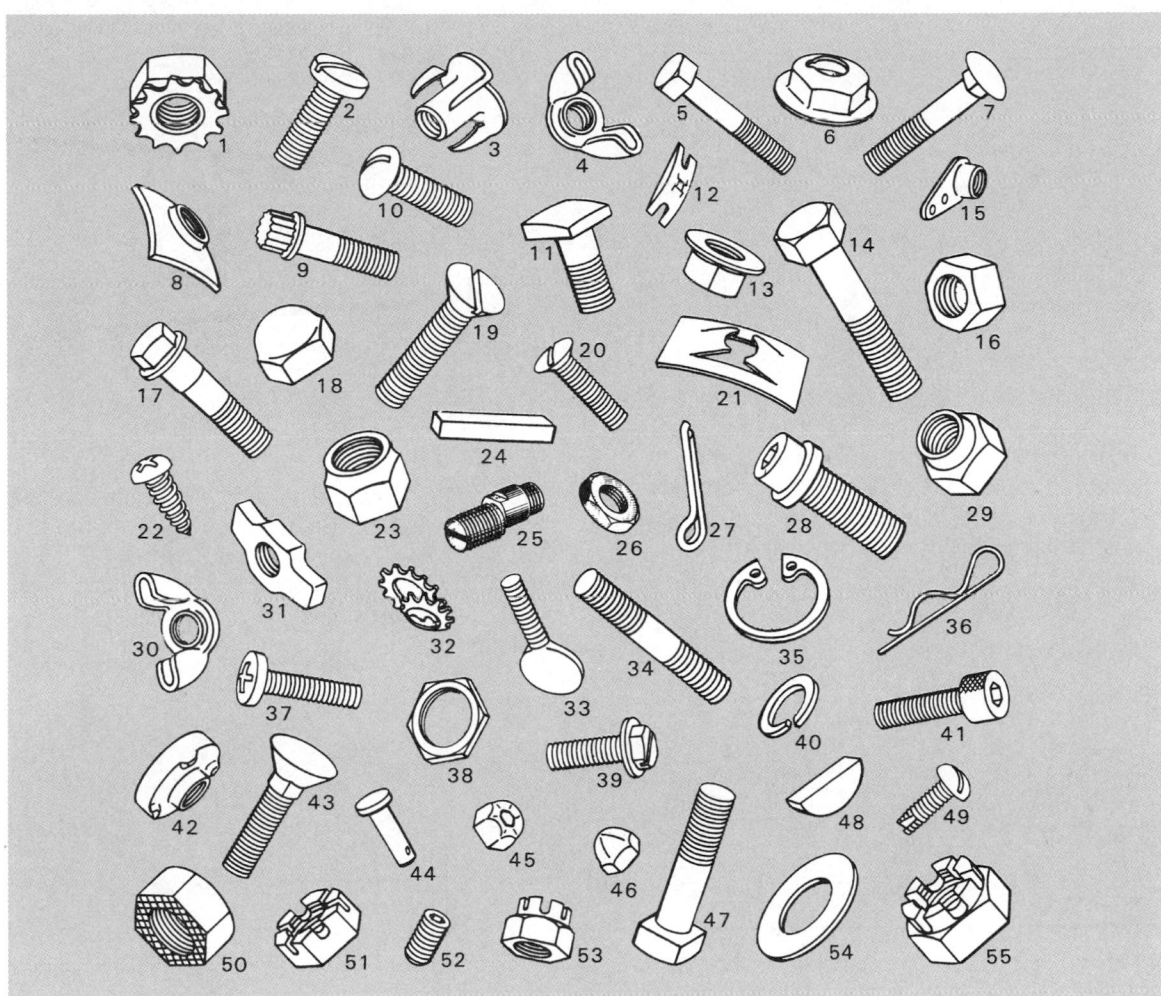

Figure 7-32. An assortment of fasteners. Although terminology can vary somewhat, these are the commonly used names: 1—Flange-lock nut. 2—Fillister-head machine screw. 3—Barrel prong nut. 4—Wing nut. 5—Cap screw. 6—Palnut. 7—Carriage bolt. 8—Spring nut. 9—12-point head bolt. 10—Round-head machine screw. 11—Askew-head bolt. 12—Single-thread nut. 13—Flanged nut. 14—Cap screw. 15—Anchor nut. 16—Plain hex nut. 17—Hex-flange screw. 18—Acorn (cap) nut. 19—Flat-head screw. 20—Small flat-head screw. 21—Speed nut. 22—Sheet metal screw. 23—Locking nut. 24—Key. 25—Offset (eccentric) stud. 26—Thin nut. 27—Cotter pin. 28—Socket-head bolt. 29—Locking nut. 30—Wing nut. 31—Specialty nut. 32—Toothed lock washers. 33—Thumbscrew. 34—Stud. 35—Snap ring. 36—Spring lock pin. 37—Cross-head machine screw. 38—Panel nut. 39—Flanged hex slotted-head screw. 40—Split lock washer. 41—Hex socket-head bolt. 42—Welded nut. 43—Plow bolt. 44—Clevis pin. 45—Open-top acorn nut. 46—Closed-top acorn nut. 47—Square-head cap screw. 48—Woodruff key. 49—Self-tapping screw. 50—Serrated nut. 51—Slotted nut. 52—Set screw. 53—Castle nut. 54—Flat washer. 55—Castle nut.

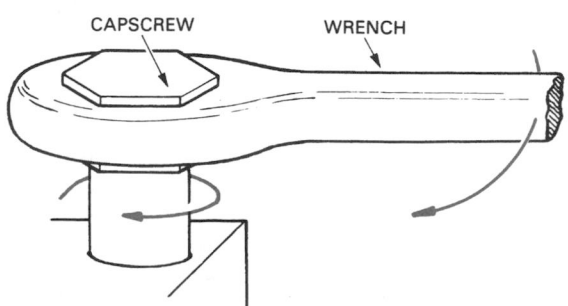

Figure 7-33. Torque, or a twisting force, being applied to a cap screw with a box-end wrench.

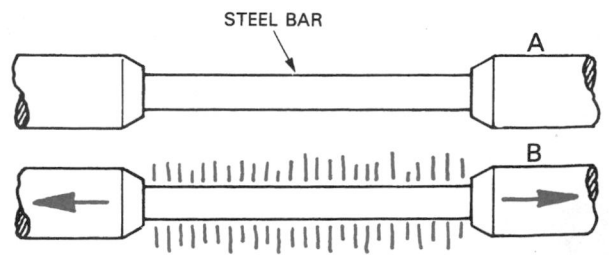

Figure 7-34. Tension. A—A steel bar placed in the jaws of a test machine. B—The jaws are moved apart, creating a pull, or tension, on the bar.

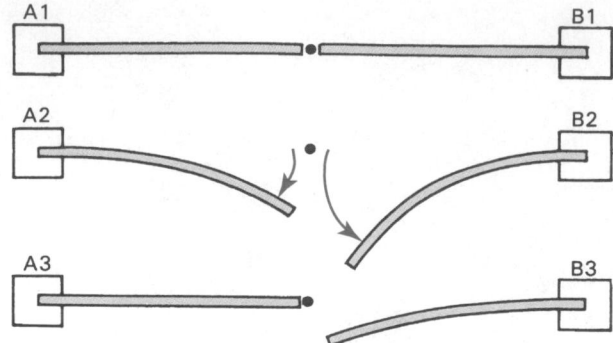

Figure 7-35. Elastic limit. Bars in A1 and B1 are at rest. Note that they are aligned with the black dot. In A2, the bar is bent within its elastic limit. When pressure is removed, it springs back to its normal (A3) position. The bar in B2 is bent beyond its elastic limit. When pressure is removed, the bar springs only part way back, as shown in B3.

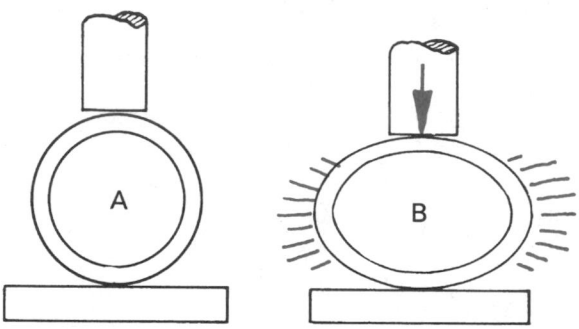

Figure 7-36. Distortion. A—Hydraulic ram about to engage round steel ring. B—Pressure from ram distorts the ring.

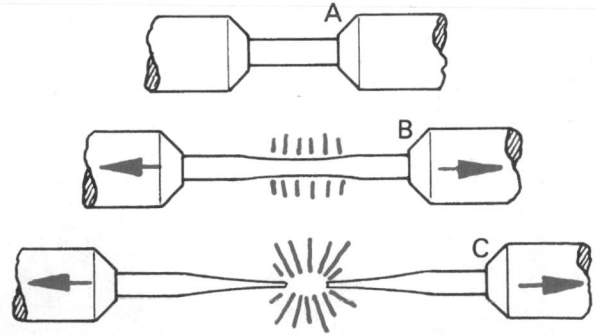

Figure 7-37. Tensile strength. A—Bar of steel in a test machine. B—Heavy tension is applied, exceeding the elastic limit and causing the bar to stretch. C—Increased pull finally snaps the bar as tension exceeds tensile strength.

- Misaligned valve guides.
- Misaligned camshaft bearings.
- Misaligned crankshaft bearings.

In addition, the engine can suffer blown head gaskets, oil, water, and air leaks, and broken connecting rods if fasteners are improperly tightened. Ring, piston, valve, and

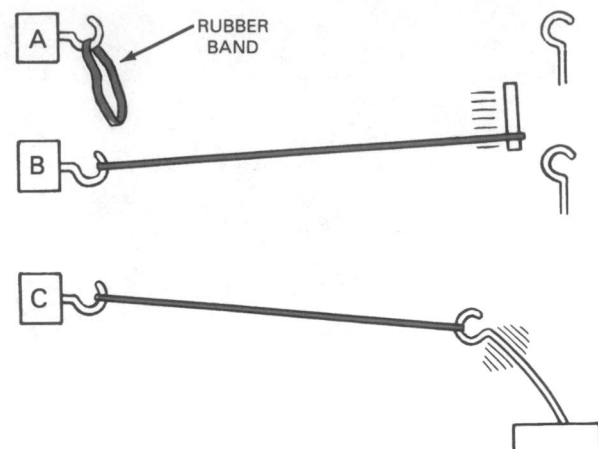

Figure 7-38. Residual tension. A—Rubber band at rest; no residual tension. B—Band being pulled (distorted) out to engage spring steel hook. C—Band attempts to return to original dimensions, creating a pull (residual tension) and bending the hook. Within its elastic limit, steel is more elastic than rubber.

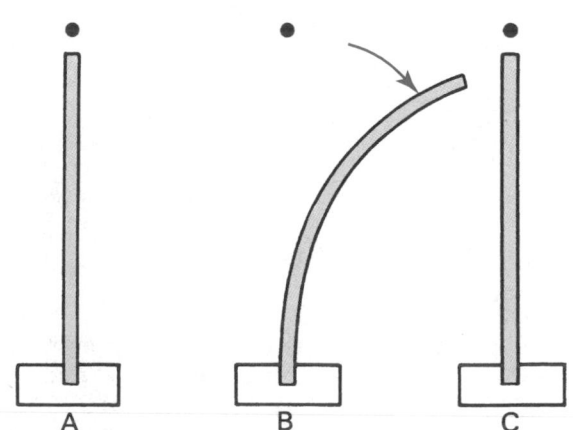

Figure 7-39. Elasticity. A—Original position of bar. B—Bar deflected by pressure. C—Pressure is removed and the bar returns to its original position.

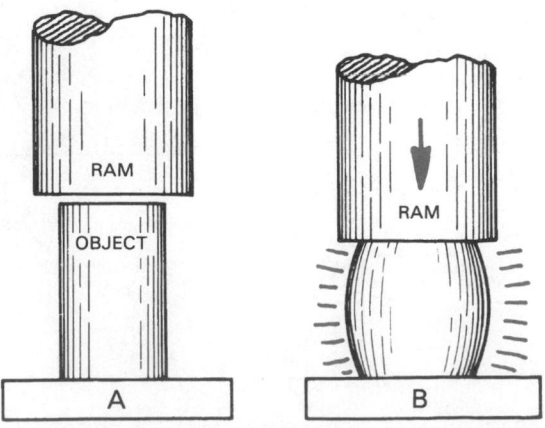

Figure 7-40. Compression. A—Object at rest. B—Object under compression as ram builds up pressure.

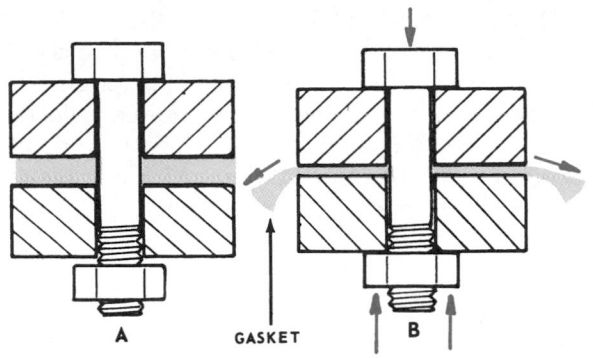

Figure 7-41. Cold flow. A—The nut is not tight and there is no compressive force on the gasket. B—The nut is tightened, compressing the gasket and causing it to flow outward as thickness decreases.

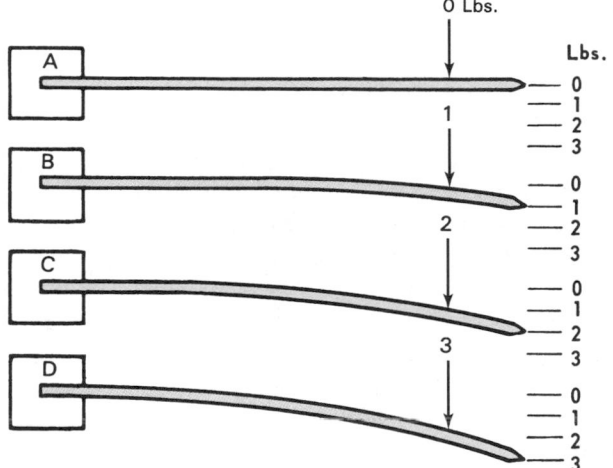

Figure 7-42. Hooke's law. Note that as weight on the spring bar is increased, there is a proportional movement on the scale. This will continue until the bar is deflected past its elastic limit.

bearing wear will be accelerated. The engine will fail in service long before it should.

Proper Fastener Tension

All car manufacturers publish *torque specifications,* which should be closely followed. Each company has spent a great deal of time and money determining the fastener torque for their products that will give the best results. When using torque charts, make sure they pertain to the job at hand.

It has been found that for the vast majority of applications, a fastener should be tightened until it has built up a tension within itself that is around 50%-60% of its elastic limit.

When the fastener has been drawn up to this point, it will not be twisted off. It will retain enough residual tension to continue to exert pressure on the parts and will resist loosening. As mentioned, steel bolts and cap screws will stretch about .001" for each 30,000 pounds of tension. Like

a rubber band, the tendency to return to their normal lengths provides continuous clamping effect.

Fastener Material

As previously mentioned, most bolts and screws have radial lines on their heads that indicate tensile strength. When replacing a fastener, use a fastener that is at least as strong as the original. You will find that the more critical the application (main bearing, connecting rod), the higher the tensile strength of the fastener.

How Fastener Torque Is Measured

To tighten a fastener to a recommended torque, a measuring tool called a *torque wrench* is used. The torque wrench will measure the torque (twisting force) applied to the fastener. Some typical torque wrenches are shown in **Figure 7-43.**

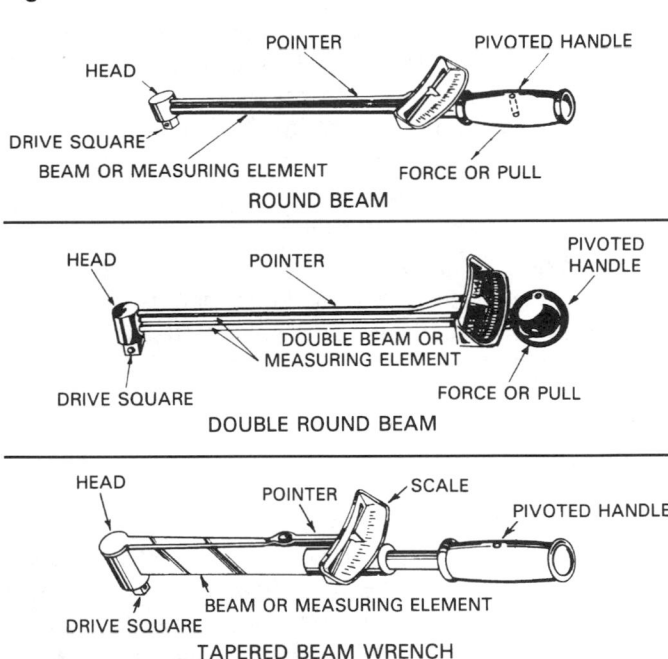

Figure 7-43. Torque wrenches. These beam-type wrenches are widely used, durable, and accurate.

How a Torque Wrench Works

The torque wrench uses Hooke's law in its construction. By deflecting (bending) a part of the torque wrench, the relationship between the pull on the handle (torque) and the amount of deflection is readily established.

When the head is attached to the fastener and the handle is pulled, the flexible part is bent. In a beam-type torque wrench, the pointer rod is attached to the wrench head and is not bent. Since the scale is attached to the handle element, it follows the flexible beam, moving the scale under the pointer end. The scale is calibrated so that the operator can see how much torque is being applied to the fastener. Some torque wrenches provide a digital readout. Other torque wrenches use a device that yields at the preset torque and produces a click that can be both heard and felt. Some torque wrenches use a light to indicate the correct torque. When a torque wrench must be used in a position that makes reading the scale difficult or impossible, these devices are handy.

If the center of pull on the handle is exactly one foot (305 mm) from the center of the head, a one pound (0.45 kg) pull on the handle would produce one foot-pound of torque. One foot-pound equals twelve inch-pounds, or 1.35 Newton-meters.

Torque Wrench Calibration

Torque recommendations can be measured in inch-grams, inch-ounces, inch-pounds, foot-pounds, or Newton-meters. For general automotive use, the inch-pound and foot-pound torque wrenches are common. However, many vehicle makers are giving their torque specifications in Newton-meters. To convert foot-pounds to Newton-meters, multiply by 1.356.

If possible, inch-pound and foot-pound torque wrenches should be used to make direct inch-pound and foot-pound readings. However, if the correct wrench is not available, the readings can be converted. To convert foot-pounds to inch-pounds, multiply the foot-pound reading by 12. To convert inch-pounds to foot-pounds, divide inch-pound reading by 12.

Torque Wrench Range

Torque wrenches are made in different sizes, or *ranges,* as well as in different calibrations. Ideally, the technician should have a 0-200 inch-pound (0-22.60 N.m) wrench, a 0-50 foot-pound (0-67.79 N.m) wrench, a 0-100 foot-pound (0-135.58 N.m) wrench, and a 150 foot-pound (203.37 N.m) wrench.

A torque wrench will produce best results if used for readings that fall near the middle half of its range. For example, a 0-100 foot-pound wrench would give the most accurate readings from 25 to 75 foot-pounds. By having several ranges of wrenches, the technician will also find that this will offer several lengths. The shorter wrenches can be useful in restricted areas.

Range Can Be Altered Using an Adapter

If the technician has a 0-100 foot-pound torque wrench available and the torque recommendation is 150 foot-pounds, the wrench can still be used. However, an *adapter* is needed to lengthen the effective range of the wrench.

If the lever length (distance from the center of wrench head to pivot point on handle) is 19" and you used an adapter bar of equal length, the torque being applied would be double that shown on the scale. If the adapter were 9 1/2" long, or half as long as the lever, the torque would be one and one-half times that shown on the scale. A handy formula to determine applied torque when using an adapter is:

$$\frac{\text{Dial reading} \times (L + A)}{L} = \text{Torque applied to fastener}$$

(L) is length in inches from the center of the handle pivot to the center of the wrench head.

(A) is the length in inches from the center of the wrench head to the end of the adapter. This dimension must be measured parallel to the centerline of the wrench.

Figure 7-44 shows three adapter setups. Notice that the effective length (L + A) is always measured parallel to the centerline of the wrench. When using an adapter, be certain of its exact length. Remember that length and torque are directly related.

Using Torque Wrench

After determining the proper torque and selecting a suitable torque wrench, you are ready to proceed. Be sure to observe the following:

* Threads Must Be Clean. The threads on the bolt or screw and those in the nut or hole must be absolutely clean. Rust, carbon, and dirt will cause galling and improper tension. An accurate torque reading with dirty threads is impossible.
* Use High-Pressure Lubricant. Unless the use of a lubricant is specifically forbidden (due to the possibility of area contamination or the need of a special sealant), always apply a lubricant to the threads and to the area where the nut or cap screw head contacts the part. Refer to manufacturer recommendations to find out which lubricant is suitable.

The use of lubricant will prevent or reduce the possibility of galling, seizing (sticking), or stripping. It will ensure that the fastener torque has created the proper tension. It should be mentioned that the lubricant, while making the fasteners easier to remove at some future date, will not (if torqued properly) cause them to loosen in service. To the contrary, the increased tensioning for the same torque reading will actually cause the fastener to remain more secure.

Use a Proper Locking Device

Unless a self-locking nut or cap screw is being used, make certain the recommended lock washer is in place.

When tightening a fastener up against the softer metals, the use of a plain flat washer between the lock washer and the part is often specified. This prevents the part from being "chewed up" and allows proper torquing without crushing the part.

Check Fasteners

Always check fasteners for correct diameter, thread type, and length. When installing cap screws, make certain that they will not bottom (strike bottom of a threaded hole) in a blind hole (hole not drilled clear through part). Also, make sure that they do not protrude into a housing. This may damage a part of the unit.

 Caution: Stripped threads, broken screws, loose parts, and damaged units can result from failure to use the correct fastener. Be careful!

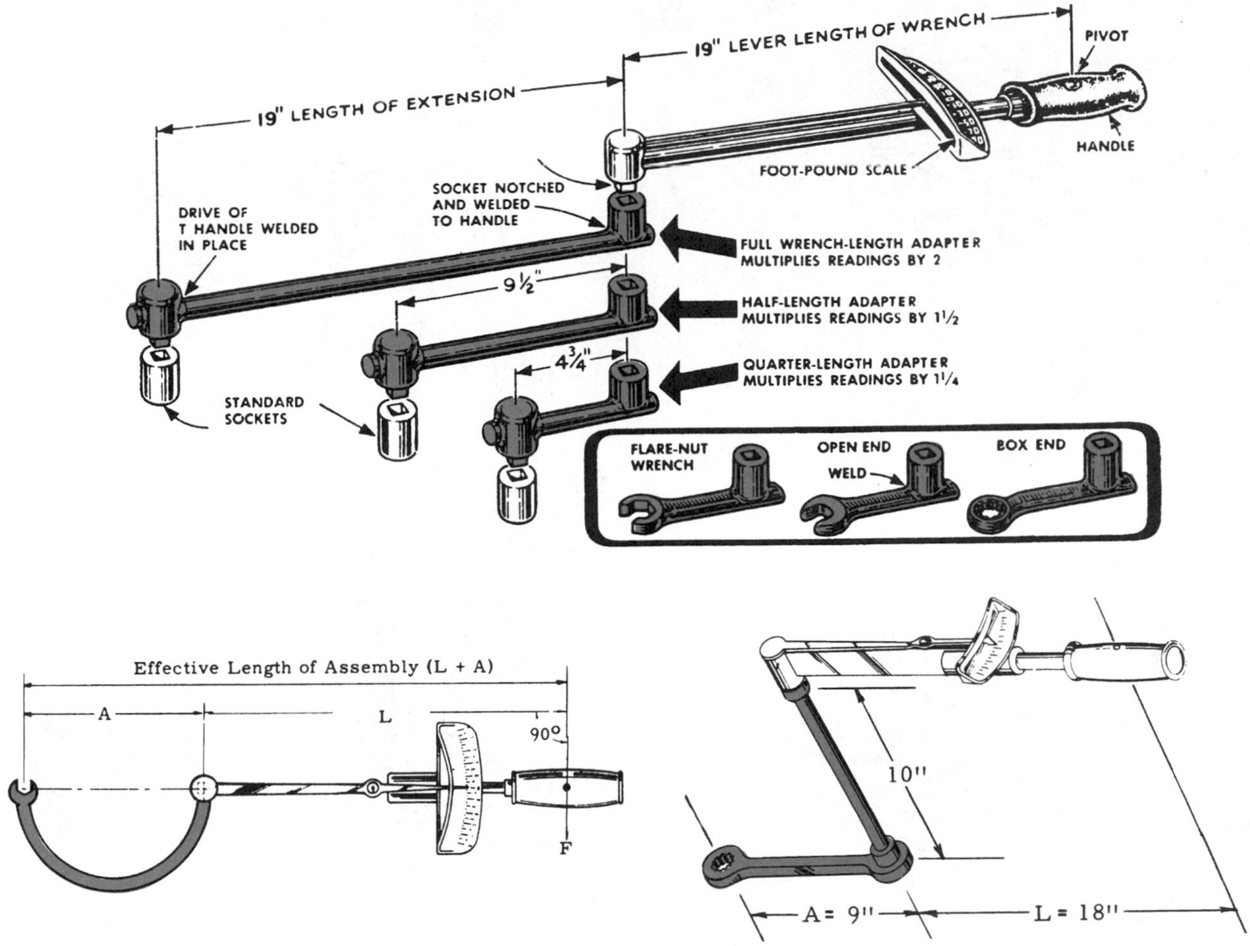

Figure 7-44. Torque wrench adapters. (Popular Science Monthly and P. A. Sturtevant Co.)

In **Figure 7-45A,** the screw has bottomed, leaving the part loose. Continued torquing could twist off the screw head. In **Figure 7-45B,** the screw protruded into the housing and damaged a gear. In **Figure 7-45C,** a coarse thread screw was jammed into a hole with fine threads. This caused the housing to crack.

Some fasteners serve an additional purpose. For instance, a head bolt or cap screw may be drilled for passage of oil, or a cap screw may have a threaded hole in its head to which another assembly is attached. Be careful to insert these fasteners in the correct place.

Follow Recommended Sequence

Where a number of fasteners are used to secure a part (such as a cylinder head), the proper *tightening sequence* (order) should be followed. **Figures 7-46** and **7-47** illustrate the head bolt tightening sequence for two different engines. Always follow the manufacturer's specifications.

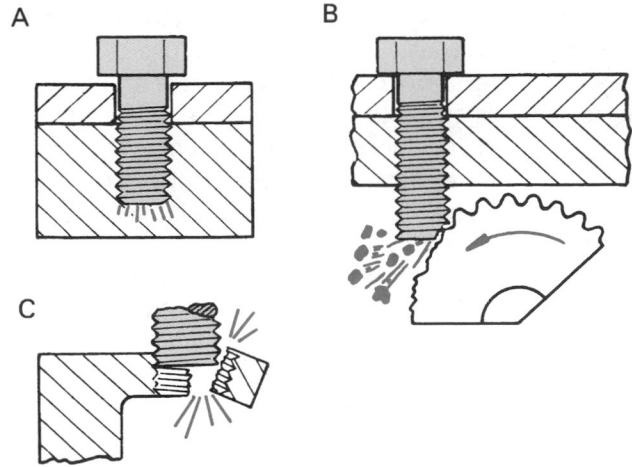

Figure 7-45. Check fasteners! Make certain that the fasteners are of the correct diameter and length and that they have the correct number of threads per inch.

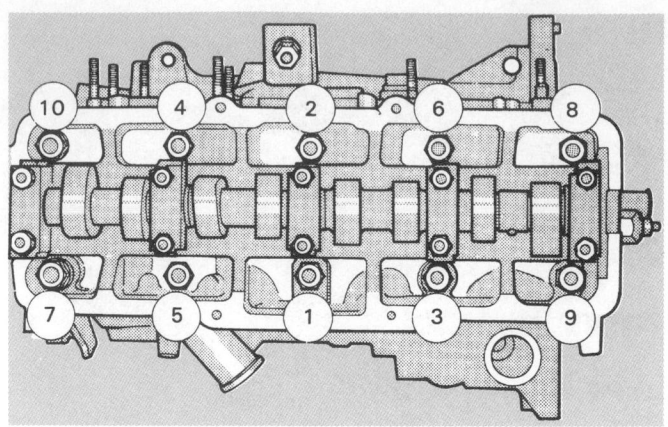

Figure 7-46. Cylinder head bolt tightening sequence for one specific engine. (Chrysler)

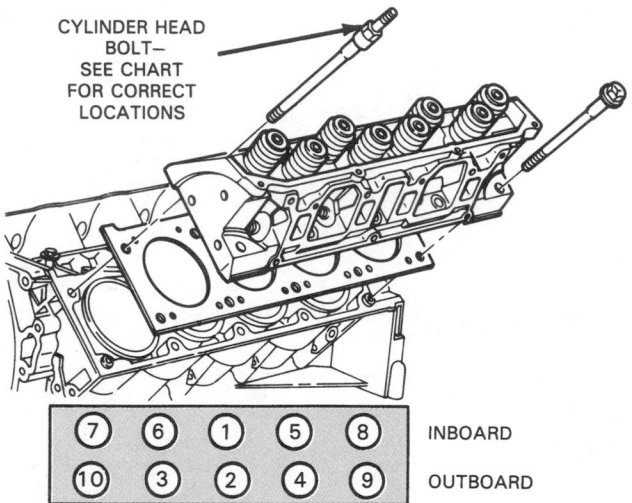

Figure 7-47. Another cylinder head bolt tightening sequence. (Cadillac)

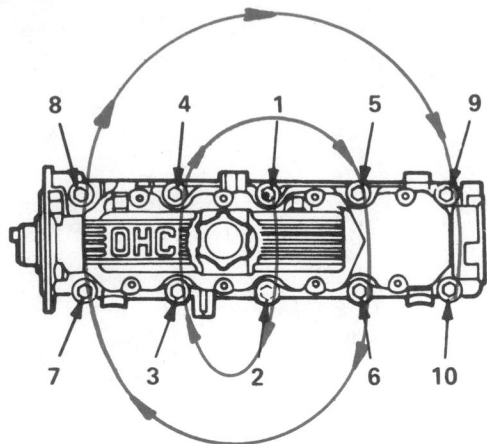

Figure 7-48. Head bolt tightening sequence when no special recommendation is available. (Buick)

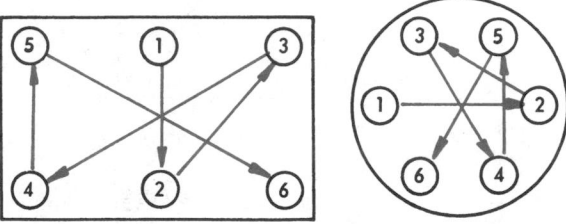

Figure 7-49. Tightening bolts in crisscross sequence.

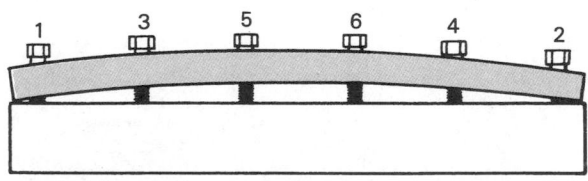

Figure 7-50. Incorrect sequence in tightening fasteners. This sequence would produce a very poor fit!

If no sequence chart can be obtained, it is usually advisable to start in the center of the part and work out to the ends. The chart in **Figure 7-48** illustrates this technique. On some assemblies, it is advisable to use a crisscross sequence. Always avoid starting in one spot and tightening one fastener after another in a row. Remember that the object is to tighten the parts so that an even stress is achieved. At the same time, a crisscross pattern will allow the parts to be drawn together so that their mating surfaces will contact evenly, **Figure 7-49**.

Observe the tightening sequence shown in **Figure 7-50**. Would a good fit be acquired if you followed this sequence? If this sequence is followed, the two ends would be clamped down first. When the center bolts were tightened, the part could not flatten out. In order to flatten, it must spread outward. Therefore, the ends must be free.

Torque in Four Steps

Begin by tightening fasteners snug (do not overtighten) with a regular wrench. Then, observe the following four steps:

1. Tighten each fastener to one-third of the recommended torque setting in the proper sequence.
2. Repeat the process, tightening all fasteners to two-thirds of the full setting.
3. Repeat the process, tightening every fastener to the full torque setting.
4. Repeat step three to be positive you have not missed a fastener.

Step four is very important and frequently overlooked.

Holding the Torque Wrench

Whenever possible, pull on the wrench to prevent skinned knuckles. Keep your hand on the handle. If using a pivoted beam-type handle, keep the handle from tipping in against the wrench. This is important because the pivot is where the pull should be for exact readings. **Figures 7-51A** and **7-51B** show the correct hand position. In **Figure 7-51C**, the technician has placed the right hand on one end of the handle, tipping it and causing interference with wrench

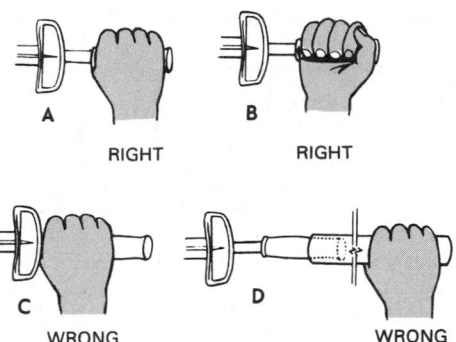

Figure 7-51. Grasp the torque wrench properly.

action. **Figure 7-51D** shows an extension in place on the handle. This should never be done.

Pulling the Wrench

When using a beam-type torque wrench, be careful to pull so that the beam is bent only in the direction of travel. If the wrench is bent up or down while pulling, the indicator point can drag on the scale and impair the reading. Place the palm of the left hand on the head of the wrench to counterbalance the pull on the handle. Allow your palm to turn with the wrench. **Figure 7-52** illustrates the use of the left hand for balance. In this case, both an adapter and extension are being used.

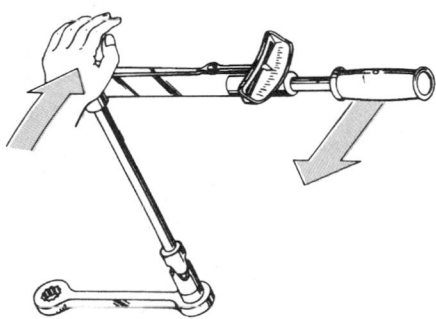

Figure 7-52. Use the palm of your hand on the head of the wrench to balance the pull on the handle. (P. A. Sturtevant Co.)

Sticking

When nearing full torque value, you will often hear a popping sound. The fastener will seem to stick and stop turning. If you increase pressure on the wrench, it may run up to full torque without moving the fastener.

You will find that when a fastener has stuck, the torque required to start it moving (break-away torque) is much higher than that required to keep it moving. This indicates that break-away torque is not a true fastener torque.

When sticking occurs, loosen the fastener (about one-half turn) until it breaks free. Then, with a smooth and steady pull, sweep the wrench handle around in a tightening direction. Stop when the required torque is reached.

Run-Down Torque

Self-locking nuts, slightly damaged threads, or foreign material will cause the fastener to turn with some degree of resistance before it begins drawing parts together. This is called *run-down torque.*

If the run-down torque is noticeable, add it to the recommended torque. Determine run-down torque only during the last one or two turns of the fastener. When a fastener is first started, it may show considerable resistance. However, by the time it reaches bottom, this may have lessened or disappeared.

 Note: Whenever a fastener shows undue resistance, remove it and make sure it is the right length and diameter. Also make sure that it has the proper number of threads per inch.

When Torque Recommendations Are Not Available

The technician should try to secure the car manufacturer's recommended torque for the specific job. If, however, it is not available, consult a chart such as the one in **Figure 7-53.** You will note that by using the head markings and diameter, an approximate torque setting may be determined. Keep in mind that if the fastener is threaded into aluminum, brass, or thin metal, the torque figures may have to be reduced to prevent stripping.

Customary (inch) Bolts—Identification marks correspond to bolt strength. Increasing numbers of lines represent increasing strength.

Metric Bolts—Identification class numbers correspond to bolt strength. Increasing numbers represent increasing strength.

Retorquing

On some assemblies, such as cylinder heads and manifolds, all fasteners should be torqued after a certain period of operation. Cases such as these will be discussed in the textbook sections covering units to which they apply.

Gaskets and Sealants

Gaskets, seals, and sealants are used throughout the vehicle. They confine fuel, oil, water, air, and vacuum to specific units or areas. They also keep dust, dirt, water, and other foreign materials out of various parts. In addition to these duties, they affect torque and tension, part alignment and clearance, temperature, compression ratios, and lubrication. Gaskets, seals, and sealants play an important part in the proper functioning and service life of most components. Unfortunately, the importance of the proper selection, preparation, and installation of gaskets and seals is not always clearly understood.

 Caution: The failure of gaskets, sealants, seals, or adhesives can cause extensive damage and expense. Study the material in this section carefully and apply the information to your work!

Standard Torque Specifications and Capscrew Markings Chart

CAPSCREW HEAD MARKINGS	CAPSCREW BODY SIZE Inches — Thread	SAE GRADE 1 or 2 (Used Infrequently) Torque		SAE GRADE 5 (Used Frequently) Torque		SAE GRADE 6 or 7 (Used at Times) Torque		SAE GRADE 8 (Used Frequently) Torque	
		Ft-Lb	N m	Ft-Lb	N m	Ft-Lb	N m	Ft-Lb	N m
Manufacturer's marks may vary. Three-line markings on heads shown below, for example, indicate SAE Grade 5.	1/4–20 -28	5 6	6.7791 8.1349	8 10	10.8465 13.5582	10	13.5582	12 14	16.2698 18.9815
	5/16–18 -24	11 13	14.9140 17.6256	17 19	23.0489 25.7605	19	25.7605	24 27	32.5396 36 6071
	3/8–16 -24	18 20	24.4047 27.1164	31 35	42.0304 47.4536	34	46.0978	44 49	59.6560 66.4351
	7/16–14 -20	28 30	37.9629 40.6745	49 55	66.4351 74.5700	55	74.5700	70 78	94.9073 105.7538
	1/2–13 -20	39 41	52.8769 55.5885	75 85	101.6863 115.2445	85	115.2445	105 120	142.3609 162.6960
SAE 1 or 2 SAE 5	9/16–12 -18	51 55	69.1467 74.5700	110 120	149.1380 162.6960	120	162.6960	155 170	210.1490 230.4860
	5/8–11 -18	83 95	112.5329 128.8027	150 170	203.3700 230.4860	167	226.4186	210 240	284.7180 325.3920
	3/4–10 -16	105 115	142.3609 155.9170	270 295	366.0660 399.9610	280	379.6240	375 420	508.4250 569.4360
	7/8– 9 -14	160 175	216.9280 237.2650	395 435	535.5410 589.7730	440	596.5520	605 675	820.2590 915.1650
SAE 6 or 7 SAE 8	1– 8 -14	235 250	318.6130 338.9500	590 660	799.9220 894.8280	660	894.8280	910 990	1233.7780 1342.2420

A

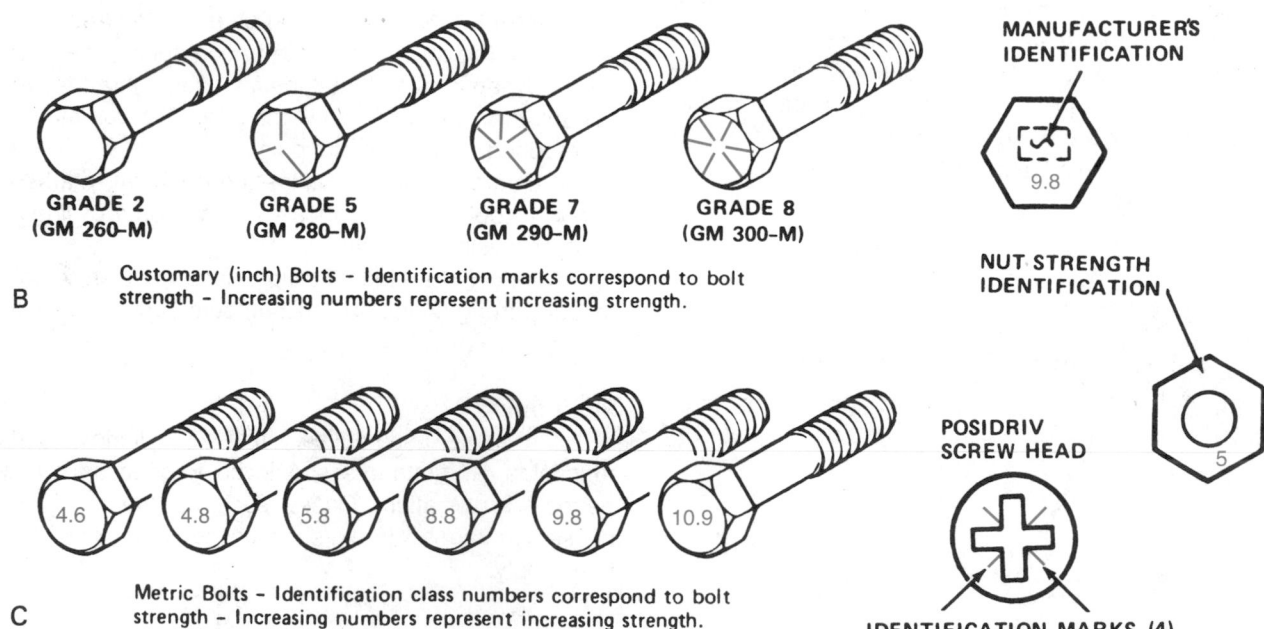

GRADE 2 (GM 260–M) GRADE 5 (GM 280–M) GRADE 7 (GM 290–M) GRADE 8 (GM 300–M)

B   Customary (inch) Bolts – Identification marks correspond to bolt strength – Increasing numbers represent increasing strength.

MANUFACTURER'S IDENTIFICATION

9.8

NUT STRENGTH IDENTIFICATION

5

POSIDRIV SCREW HEAD

IDENTIFICATION MARKS (4)

4.6 4.8 5.8 8.8 9.8 10.9

C   Metric Bolts – Identification class numbers correspond to bolt strength – Increasing numbers represent increasing strength.

Figure 7-53. Chart shows typical torque for cap screws with clean, dry threads. Reduce torque by 10% if the threads are oiled; reduce torque by 20% if new, plated fasteners are used for various fastener grades. Always follow the manufacturer's torque specifications for the exact job at hand. A—Cap screws, bolts, and nuts are marked with lines or numbers to indicate their relative strength. B—Customary (inch) bolt markings. Note that strength (grade) corresponds to the number of lines. There are always two lines less than actual grade. C—Metric bolt markings. The higher the grade (customary) or number (metric), the greater the strength. (Chrysler, General Motors)

Gaskets

A *gasket* is a flexible piece of material or, in some cases, a liquid sealant placed between two or more parts. When the parts are drawn together, any irregularities (warped spots, scratches, dents) will be filled by the gasket material to produce a leakproof joint. See **Figure 7-54.**

Gasket Materials

Many materials are used in gasket construction, such as steel, aluminum, copper, cork, rubber (synthetic), paper,

felt, and liquid silicone. The materials can be used alone or in combination.

Gasket material *compressibility* (how easily it flattens under pressure) varies widely. The gasket must compress to some extent to effect a seal. However, excessive compressibility will cause the gasket to extrude (flow outward and reduce thickness in direction of compression), reducing its thickness beyond a specified point.

The gasket material selected will depend on several variables, including the specific application, temperature,

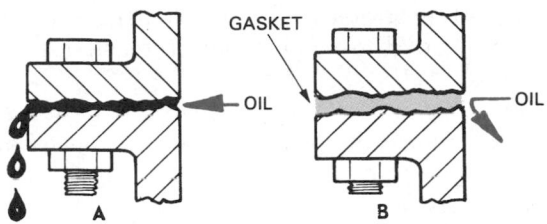

Figure 7-54. Gaskets stop leaks. A—Assembly has no gasket. Irregularities on mating surfaces allow leakage. B—Same assembly is shown with a gasket. Irregularities are filled, and the leak is stopped.

type of fluid to be confined, smoothness of mating parts, fastener tension, pressure of confined fluid, the material used in the construction of mating parts, and the part clearance relationship. All of these affect the choice of gasket material and design.

When constructing or selecting gaskets, give careful thought to these factors and choose wisely. **Figure 7-55** illustrates some of the destructive forces that gaskets must resist to function properly.

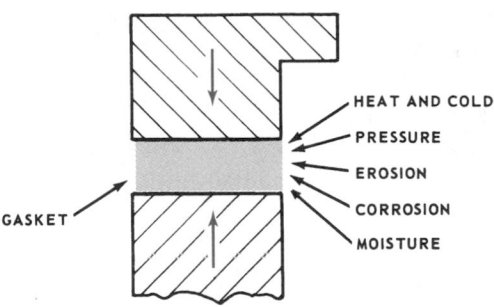

Figure 7-55. Gasket must withstand many forces. The destructive forces shown, in addition to others not illustrated, are constantly attempting to destroy the gasket.

Gasket Construction

Some gaskets are of very simple construction. The engine top water outlet, for example, can use a medium thickness, chemically treated, fibrous-paper gasket. Unit loading (pressure between mating parts) is light, temperature is moderate, and coolant pressure is low, **Figure 7-56.**

As the sealing task becomes more difficult, gasket construction becomes more involved. The exhaust manifold-to-exhaust pipe gasket is more complex than the water outlet gasket. Unit loading pressure is higher. Corrosive flames, gases, and high temperatures attempt to destroy the gasket. This gasket uses a combination of heat-resistant materials and steel in its construction, **Figure 7-57.**

Figure 7-56. Simple paper gasket. The paper is soft, tough, and water resistant.

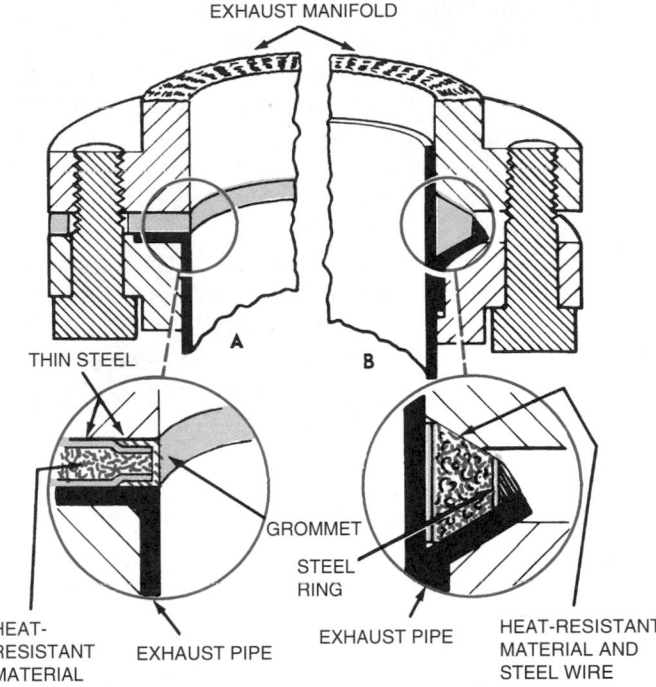

Figure 7-57. Exhaust manifold gaskets. A—Gasket has a heat-resistant center with a thin steel outer layer. Note how the inner edge is protected with a steel grommet. B—This gasket is made up of flexible heat-resistant material and steel wire. A thin steel outer ring can also be used for additional strength.

Perhaps the most complicated gasket in terms of materials used and construction techniques is the cylinder head gasket. Unit pressure is tremendous, and combustion temperatures and pressures are very high. The head gasket must also seal against coolant, oil, corrosive gases, and thermal growth.

There are several basic cylinder head gasket designs in common use. Steel, copper, and rubber may be used in their construction.

One type of multiple-layer gasket is shown in **Figure 7-58A.** A steel center core, which is perforated to produce tiny gripping hooks, is placed between two sheets of heat-resistant flexible material. Steel or copper grommets are placed around the combustion chamber and coolant openings to assist in sealing. The entire gasket is then formed into a one-piece unit.

In **Figure 7-58B,** a heat resistant center core is placed between two sheets of steel or copper. Note that the edges are rolled to produce a grommet.

The single layer beaded, or corrugated, gasket shown in **Figure 7-58C,** is popular on high-compression engines. A single sheet of steel, around .020 in. (0.51 mm) thick, is stamped to produce a beaded edge around combustion chambers and fluid openings. This particular gasket is given an aluminum coating on both sides to assist in sealing and to prevent corrosion. This type of gasket requires accurate and smooth block-to-head surfaces. The aluminum-coated steel gasket will withstand high temperatures and pressures quite successfully. In addition, it will not produce torque loss (gasket becoming thinner under continued fastener tension, thereby reducing bolt tension and torque).

Localized Unit Loading

To produce higher *unit loading* around the combustion chambers or any other opening, a copper wire or other expansion device is inserted between the top and bottom layers of the gasket near the edges of the openings. The remainder of the gasket tends to compress more readily. This creates the desired pressure around the opening, **Figure 7-58D.**

Another technique used to produce localized unit pressure, or loading, is shown in **Figure 7-58E.** This type uses a copper or soft iron grommet around the rolled edges. Coolant and oil openings are sometimes sealed by placing special rubber or neoprene grommets in the gasket openings. These grommets are highly resilient and maintain constant pressure around the openings, **Figure 7-58F.**

Several other techniques employed in head gasket design and construction are shown in **Figures 7-58G, 7-58H,** and **7-58I.** A soft-seal surface composition gasket is shown in **Figure 7-58G.** Note the use of a steel core with a rubber-fiber facing and Teflon® coating over the outside surface for better sealing. The use of a sealer is not recommended with this gasket. An embossed steel gasket (similar to C), also called a "shim" gasket, is pictured in H. It is produced from sheet steel that is approximately .020 in. (0.51 mm) thick. This type of gasket provides good strength in the bead area and fine sealing capabilities when properly installed. The use of a sealer is advised.

Figure 7-58I shows a metal-clad sandwich gasket. It is constructed of sheet steel that is wrapped with a rubber-fiber facing. The gasket has an elastomeric sealing bead around critical areas to aid in sealing. The use of a sealer is not advisable.

Figure 7-59 shows another type of head gasket construction. Note the wire combustion ring and stainless steel armor. This type of gasket is for high-performance and/or high-compression engines.

Gasket Sets

Gaskets are often ordered in sets. For engine work, gaskets are available in a head set (includes all gaskets necessary to remove and replace head or heads), valve grind set (includes all gaskets necessary in doing a valve grind job), and overhaul set (includes all gaskets necessary in doing a complete engine overhaul). See **Figure 7-60.** Gasket sets also include necessary oil seal replacements. Sets for transmissions, carburetors, and differentials are available separately. Single gaskets for some specific parts are also available.

Gasket Installation Techniques

After selecting a gasket material and construction, there are a few important installation considerations. Regardless of the suitability of the gasket, it will fail if not properly installed.

Never Reuse a Gasket

Once a gasket has been in service, it will lose a great deal of its resiliency. When removed, it will not return to its

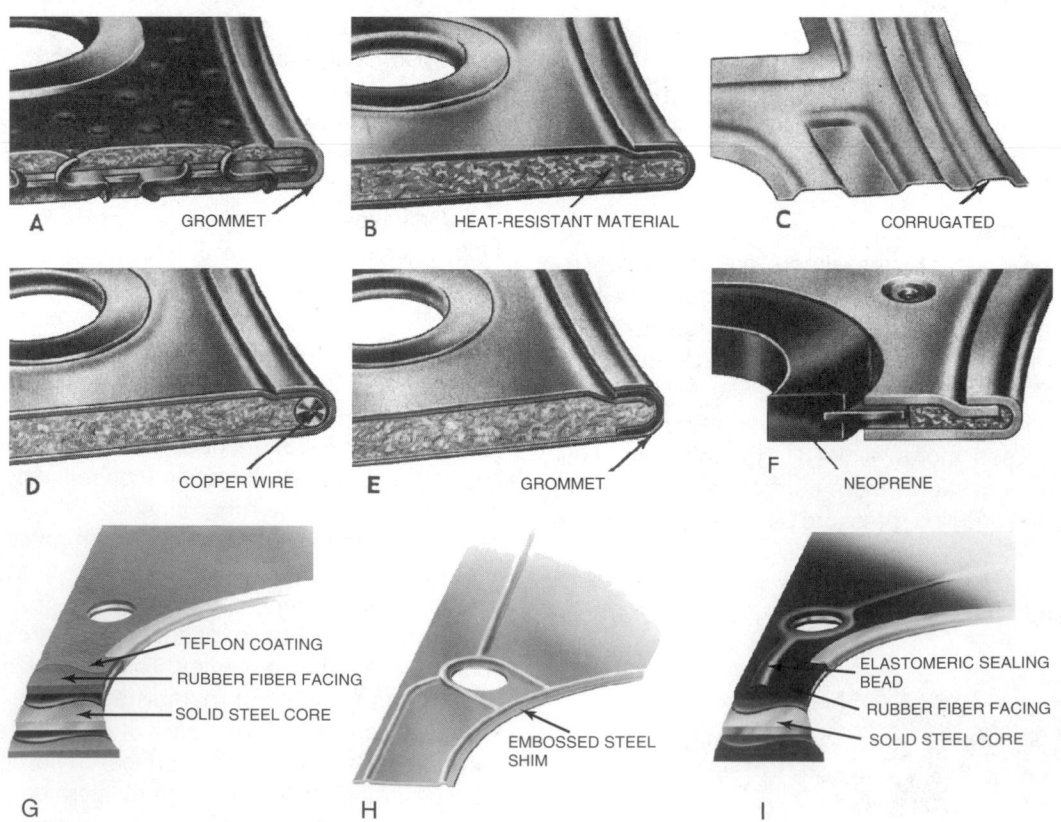

Figure 7-58. Various methods employed in head gasket construction. (Victor, McCord)

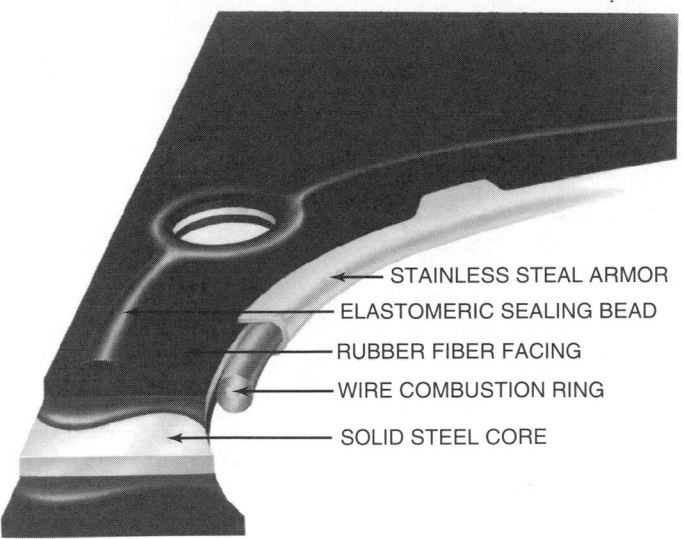

Figure 7-59. One type of head gasket construction. (Fel-Pro)

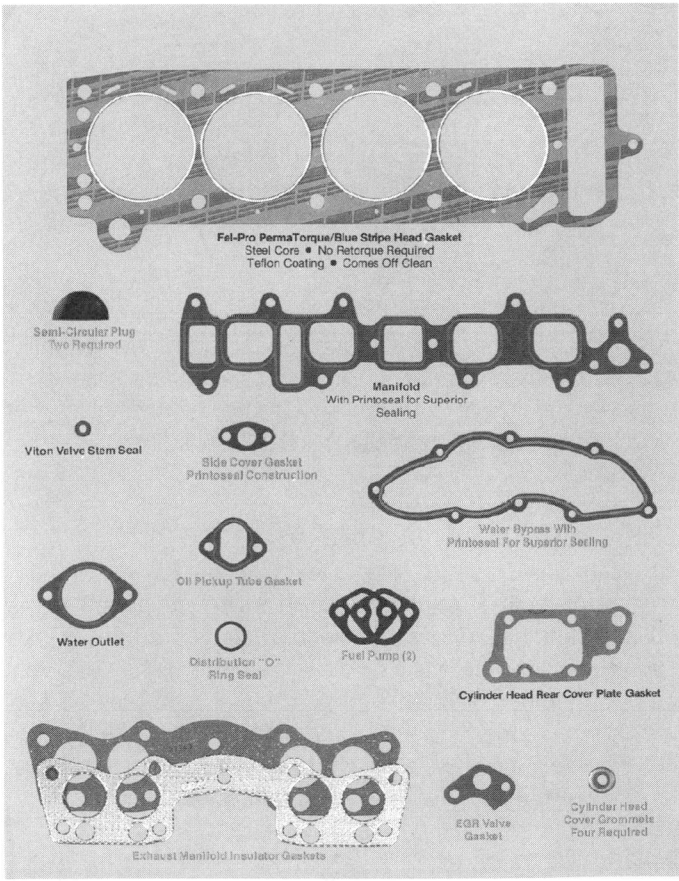

Figure 7-60. Engine overhaul gasket set. This set is for a Toyota four cylinder engine. (Fel-Pro)

original thickness. If reused, it will fail to compress and seal properly. Gasket cost, as related to part and labor costs, is small. The professional technician should not even consider using old gaskets. **Figure 7-61** shows how the use of old gaskets will produce leaks.

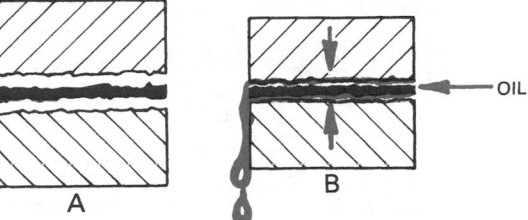

Figure 7-61. Used gaskets will not work! A—Used gasket is positioned. B—When the parts are tightened, old gasket cannot compress and fill irregularities. This results in leaks.

Check Mating Surfaces

After cleaning, inspect the **mating surfaces** for damage. If machined, a 90-110 microinch finish is needed for proper sealing. Refer to **Figure 7-62.**

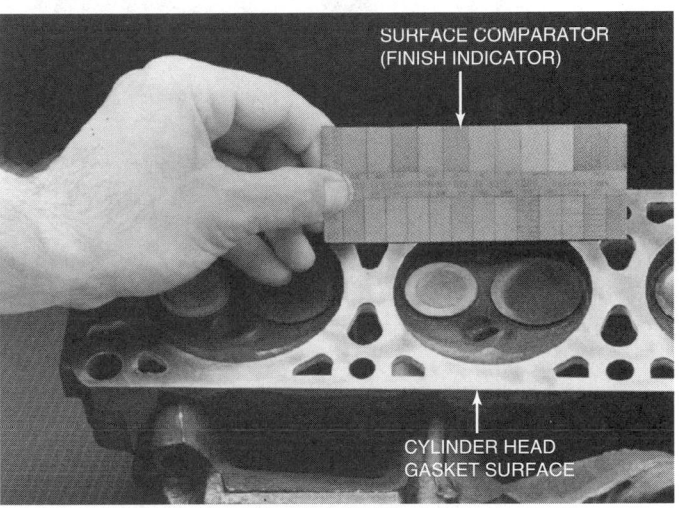

Figure 7-62. Check mating surface. Notice that the head-to-block surface is clean and smooth. All openings must also be clean. (Chevrolet)

Check Gasket for Proper Fit

Place the gasket on the part to determine if it fits properly. On the more complicated setups, such as cylinder head gaskets, make certain that the gasket is right side up, that the proper end is forward, and that bolt, coolant, and other openings are clear and in proper alignment.

Occasionally you may notice that the gasket coolant openings are slightly larger or smaller than the ports in the block or head. This gasket may be designed to fit several models or to restrict or improve coolant circulation. Check out these situations carefully.

Head gaskets for the left and right banks on some V-8 engines are interchangeable; others are not. Many head gaskets have the word top and occasionally the word front stamped on them, **Figure 7-63.**

Some Gaskets Tend to Shrink or Expand

Paper and cork gaskets that have been stored for some time tend to either lose or pick up moisture, depending on storage conditions. Loss of moisture can

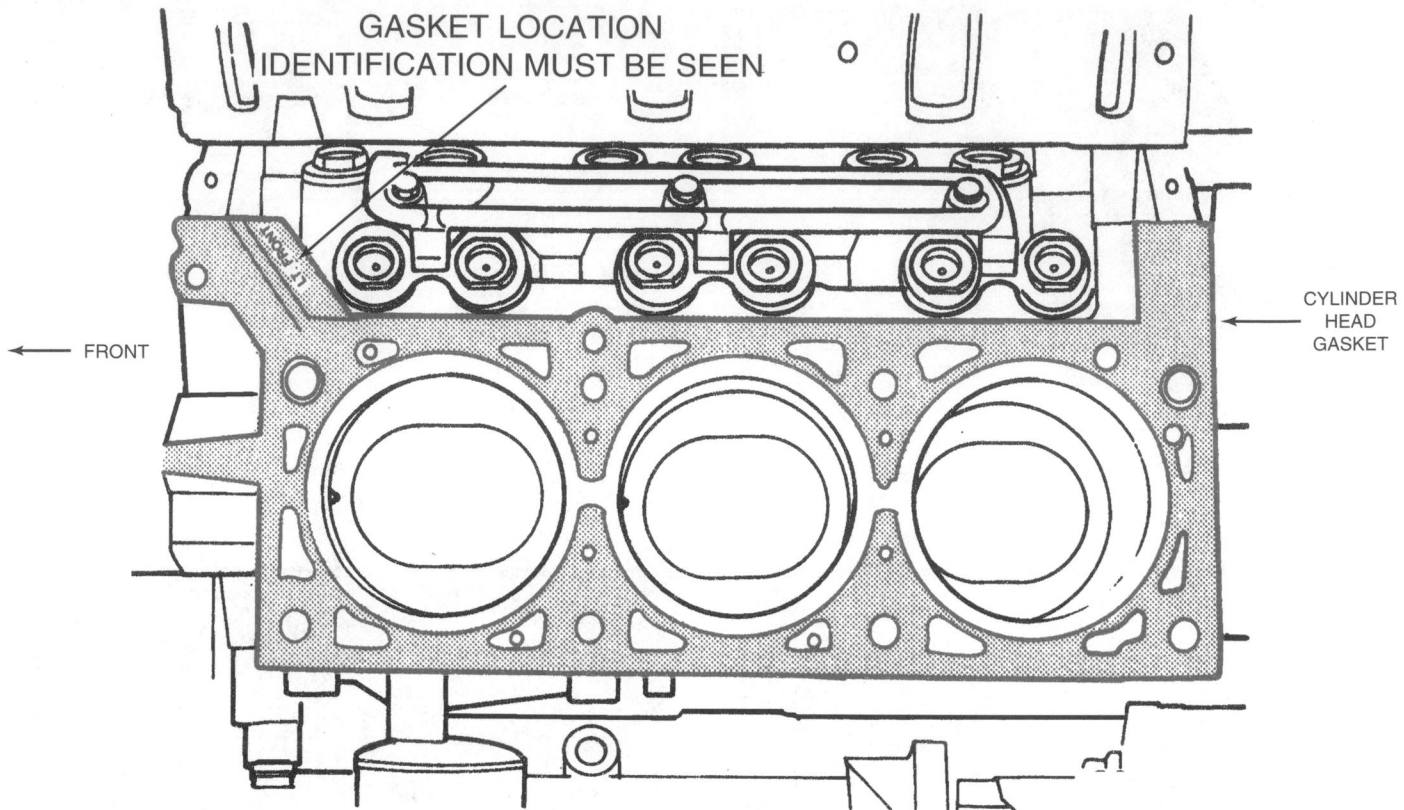

Figure 7-63. This cylinder head gasket is marked with "gasket location identification" and must be installed so that this label faces the technician. All openings must align for a proper fit. (Chrysler)

cause gaskets to shrink. Excess moisture can cause them to expand. In either case, they will show signs of misalignment.

This condition can be corrected by soaking shrunken gaskets in water for a few minutes or by placing expanded gaskets in a warm (150°-200°F or 65.6°-93.4°C) spot. Check them occasionally to prevent overdoing the treatment, **Figure 7-64.**

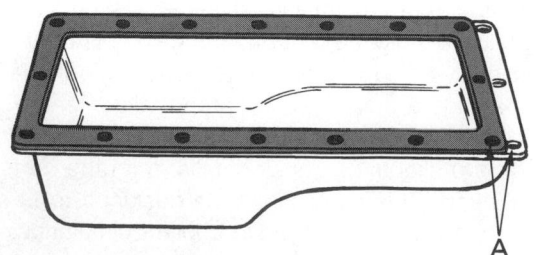

Figure 7-64. This pan gasket has shrunk. The gasket has dried out, producing shrinkage. Note in A that screw holes fail to match. Soaking will salvage this gasket.

Chamfering Screw Holes May Be Necessary

When installing head gaskets, examine the screw holes in the block. If the threads run right up to the very top, it is a good idea to chamfer them lightly.

Then, run the proper size tap in and out of the holes. The chamfer prevents the top thread from being pulled above the block surface. Blow out the holes with compressed air. When using an air hose for cleaning, always wear goggles. Small particles can be thrown into your eyes with great force.

Each Gasket Should Be Checked

Carefully inspect the gasket itself for dents, dirt, cracks, or folds. A minor crease in a cork or paper gasket usually does not render it useless. However, a head gasket should have no creases or other damage. If bent sharply, do not attempt to straighten it. The inner layer may be separated and cause failure. A gentle bend will not ruin the gasket. **Figure 7-65** illustrates what happens when a multiple-layer head gasket is creased and then straightened.

Making a Gasket

If necessary, a simple paper or combination cork-and-rubber gasket can be made. First, trace the pattern. Then, cut the material with scissors or lay the material on the part and gently tap along the edges with a brass hammer. Screw holes can also be tapped lightly with the peen end of the ball peen hammer. Do not tap hard enough to damage the threads. Gasket punches can also be used to make neat screw holes. To help hold the material in place, tap out the corner holes and start these screws before tapping around the edges, **Figure 7-66.**

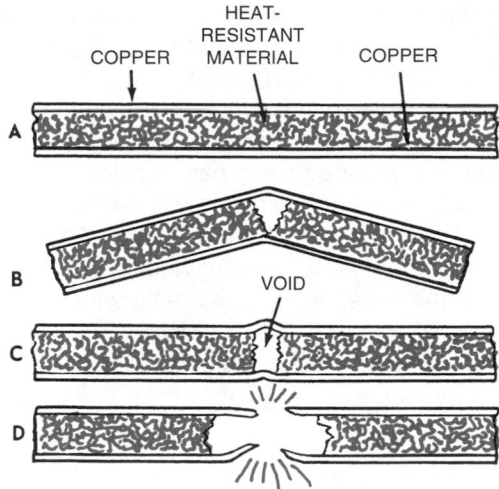

Figure 7-65. Creased gasket. A—Multiple-layer head gasket. B—Gasket has been creased and the center packing pulled apart. C—Gasket straightened, producing void. D—Gasket has "blown" in service.

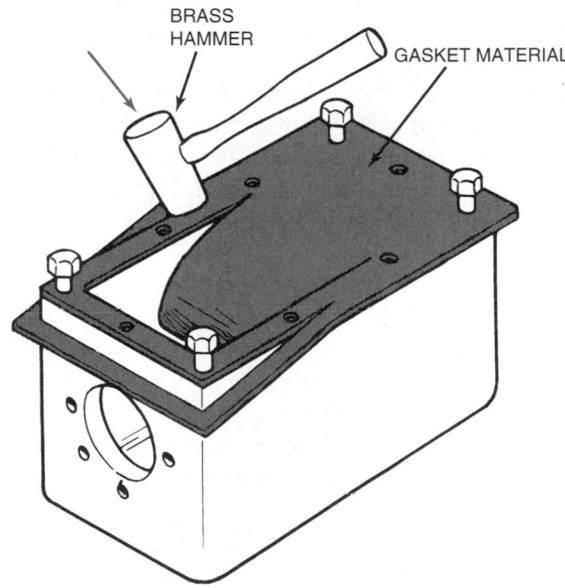

Figure 7-66. Making a gasket. Four corner screws hold the gasket material in place while tapping. A ball peen hammer is used for the holes.

Handle Gaskets With Care

Gaskets should be stored flat, in their containers, and in an area where they will not be bent or crushed. Storage space should not be subjected to extremes of temperature or humidity. Handle gaskets carefully, and do not attempt to force them to fit. If a gasket is accidentally cracked or torn, throw it away.

Use of Sealants

A new, properly installed gasket will usually produce a leakproof joint. However, mating surfaces are not always true. Corners can present problems. Torque loss can reduce pressure on the gasket surface. Gaskets may shrink slightly, and minute part shifting can break the seal. Due to

engine heat, a small amount of oil seepage will spread over a large area. This produces a messy looking job and will deposit oil on the customer's garage floor. For these reasons, *sealant* should be used on some gaskets.

The addition of a sealant helps hold the gaskets in place during assembly. Also, small cracks, indentations, and corner voids are sealed. In short, the use of a good sealant provides additional assurance that the joint will be leakproof. Sealants will be covered in more detail later in this chapter.

Using Rubber Gaskets

Rubber gaskets are highly resilient and will usually do a good job of sealing without the addition of a sealer. In fact, rubber gaskets tend to extrude (squeeze out) under pressure when a sealer is used. Unless a sealant is specifically recommended, a rubber gasket should be installed without sealer.

Holding Gasket during Assembly

Where a sealant is used, the gasket will usually stay in place during assembly. If sealant is not being used and the gasket tends to slip, the gasket can be held in place with a thin coat of grease or quick-drying contact adhesive. On rubber gaskets, the use of grease or sealant is not recommended.

Some parts, such as oil pans, can be difficult to assemble without disturbing gasket position. In some cases, it is advisable to tie the gasket with thin soft string in addition to using a sealant. The parts may be tightened with the string in place. Patented gasket holders are also available and work well.

In other instances, such as cylinder head installation, guide pins are used to hold the gasket in alignment. Make certain the gasket is correctly installed and that it remains in alignment during assembly. See **Figure 7-67.**

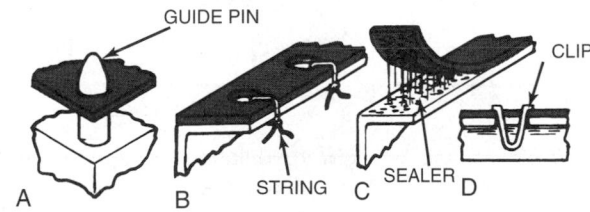

Figure 7-67. Holding gasket in place. It is important that gaskets be held in alignment during assembly.

Use Proper Sequence and Torque

After running all fasteners up snug, tighten them in the proper sequence as recommended in the section on fasteners. In addition to snapping fasteners and producing distortion, improper sequence and torque will very likely cause the gasket to leak. Excessive torque can place the gasket under too much pressure. This can cause it to extrude badly. **Figure 7-68** shows how improper tightening procedures relate to gasket sealing.

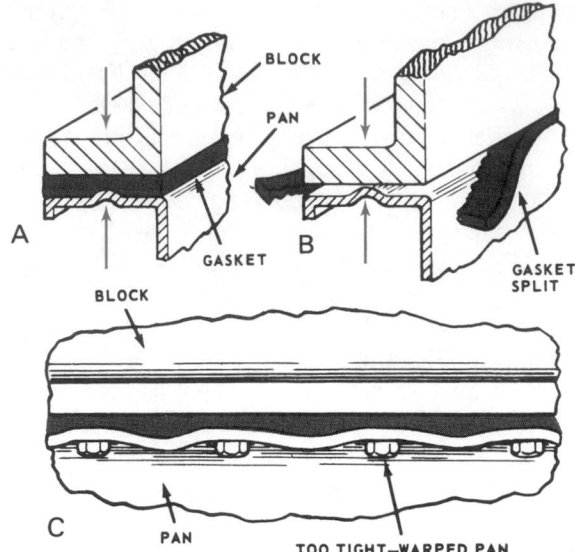

Figure 7-68. Overtightening will cause damage. A—Proper fastener tension. B—Excessive tightening has split this cork pan gasket. C—Excessive tension has warped this oil pan flange.

Stamped Parts Require Extra Care

If bent along the engaging edge, relatively thin stamped parts, such as rocker arm covers, oil pans, and some timing covers, must be straightened before installation. Place the part edge on a smooth, solid metal surface. Gently tap the bent sections to straighten them. When installing thin parts, do not overtighten the fasteners or the parts will bend again, **Figure 7-69.**

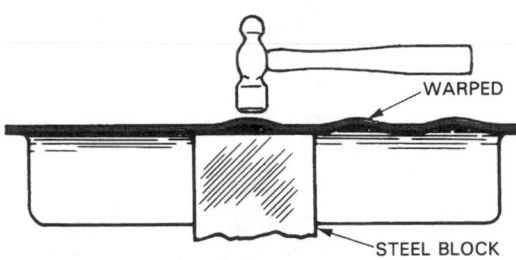

Figure 7-69. Straightening warped flanges. Warped edges cause leaks. Straighten them before installation.

Remember These Steps in Proper Gasket Installation

The following steps should be followed when installing gaskets:

- Clean parts, fasteners, and threaded holes.
- Remove any burrs, bent edges, or excessive warpage and check for dents and scratches.
- Select a new gasket of the correct size and type.
- Check the gasket for fit.
- Where sealant is used, apply a thin coat of the correct sealant on one side of the gasket. Place the gasket

with the coated side against the part. Spread a thin coat on the uncoated side. Do not slop sealant into parts. Wipe off excess sealant.
- If alignment difficulty is anticipated during assembly, secure the gasket by additional means.
- Carefully place the mating part in place.
- Coat the threads of fasteners with anti-seize lubricant (unless prohibited). Install the fasteners in their proper location and tighten them until they are snug.
- Torque the fasteners in proper sequence.
- If necessary, retorque the fasteners after a specified length of time. (These instances will be covered in later chapters.)

Analyze Gasket Failure

When a gasket fails in service, there has to be a reason for the failure. If you do not detect the reason, your own installation might fail also. The following simple steps will help you find the underlying cause of gasket failure:

- Ask the owner about any unusual conditions. Try to determine if the gasket failed suddenly or over a period of time.
- Before disassembly, check fastener torque with a torque wrench. You can loosen each fastener and notice the reading at break-away (point at which the fastener just begins to unscrew). This reading will be somewhat less than true torque. Another method is to carefully mark the position of the head of the screw or nut in relationship to the part (use a sharp scribe). Back the nut off about one-quarter turn. Carefully retighten the nut until the scribed lines are exactly in alignment. If done properly, this will give you a fair indication of torque at the time of failure. If the torque is significantly below or above specifications, or if torque varies widely between fasteners, this could be the cause of failure.
- Following disassembly, carefully blot off any grease, oil, dirt, and carbon from the gasket. Do not rub or wash the gasket immediately, as this may remove telltale signs. Inspect the gasket for signs of uneven pressure, burning, corrosion, cracks, or voids. Check to determine if the gasket is of the correct material and type for the job.
- Inspect the mating parts for warpage and burrs. Always try to find the cause of gasket failure so you may correct the problem when installing a new gasket.

Retorque

Constant fastener tension and the expansion and contraction of parts will tend to further compress a gasket. This will leave the fasteners below proper torque. In a critical application, such as a head gasket installation, it can cause gasket failure unless the fasteners are retorqued after a period of time. Situations requiring retorque will be discussed in later chapters.

Oil Seals

An *oil seal* can be used to confine fluids, prevent the entry of foreign materials, and separate two different fluids. An oil seal is secured to one part, while the sealing lip allows the other part to rotate or reciprocate (move).

Oil seals are used throughout the mechanical parts of the car. The engine, transmission, drive line, differential, wheels, steering, brakes, and accessories all use seals in their construction.

Oil Seal Construction and Materials

Seals are made up of three basic parts: a metal container, or case; a sealing element; and on most seals, a small spiral spring called a garter spring.

Sealing elements are usually made of synthetic rubber or leather. Synthetic rubber seals are replacing leather in most applications. The rubber seal can be made to close tolerances. It can also be given special shapes and heat-resistant properties.

In the rubber oil seal, the sealing element is bonded to the case. The element rubs against the shaft. The case holds the element in place and in alignment. The garter spring forces the seal lip to conform to minor shaft runout (wobble) and maintains constant and controlled pressure on the lip. **Figure 7-70** illustrates typical oil seal construction.

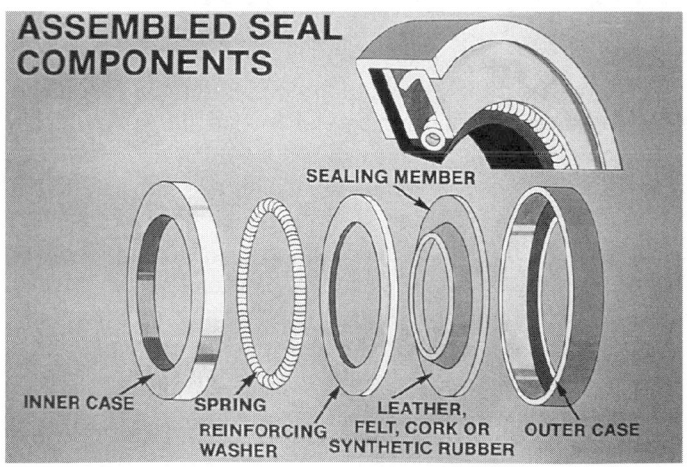

Figure 7-70.   Typical oil seal construction.

Oil Seal Designs

Many different element and lip shapes are provided. Each is designed to provide the best seal for a specific task. **Figure 7-71** shows several designs. Notice that more than one lip can be used. The outside diameter (OD) may be coated with rubber to provide better OD sealing.

Other Types of Oil and Grease Seals

Engine rear main bearing oil seals are available in both one- and two-piece styles. They may be made of graphite-impregnated fiber wicking or synthetic rubber. Some grease (not oil) seals use a felt sealing element. Occasionally, a combination will use an inner rubber seal and a felt outer seal, **Figure 7-72.**

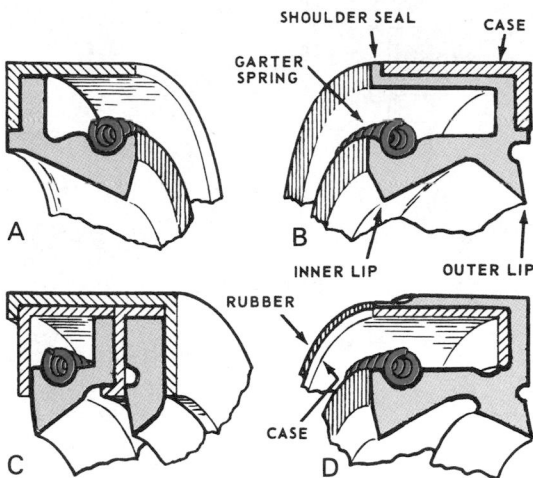

Figure 7-71.   Oil seal designs. A—Single lip. B—Double lip with rubber shoulder seal. Inner lip controls oil, and outer lip keeps out dust and water. C—Double lip. Both lips control oil. D—Double lip with rubber outer coat to assist outside diameter sealing.

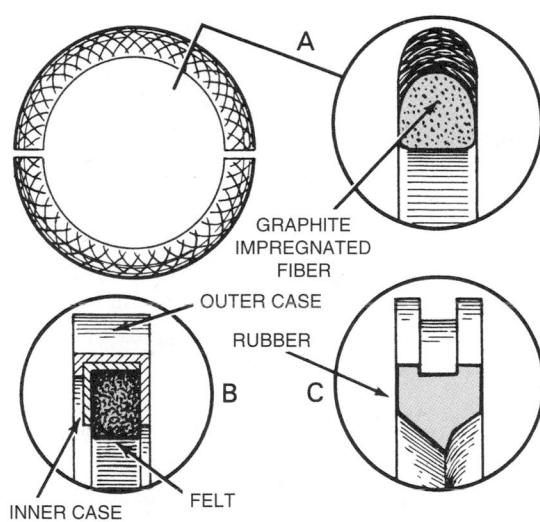

Figure 7-72.   Other seal types. A—Main bearing (rear) seal made of fiber wicking. Both upper and lower halves fit into grooves in block and cap. B—Typical grease seal using a felt sealing ring. C—Synthetic rubber main bearing oil seal. Rubber O-rings (not shown) are used in several areas. They are simple round rubber rings.

Oil Seal Removal

Seals may be removed by prying, driving, or pulling, depending on their location. Use care to avoid damage to the seal bore during seal removal. Such damage can cause leaks and make installation difficult. See **Figure 7-73.** Before removal, notice the depth to which the seal was installed. As with a gasket, inspect the seal after removal for signs of unusual wear or hardening.

 Note: Do not reuse seals. When units are down for service, replace the seals.

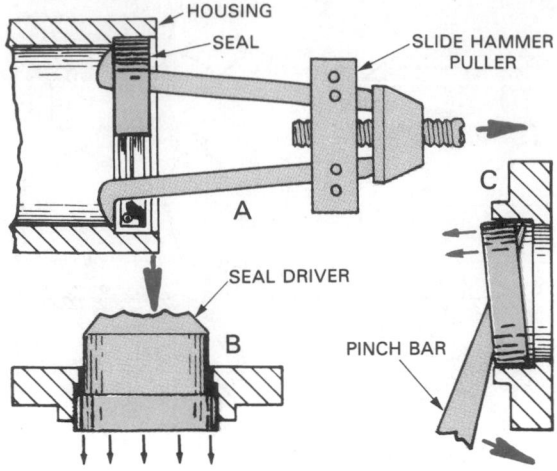

Figure 7-73. Seal removal. A—Slide hammer puller jaws are pushed through the seal and then expanded. Operating the slide hammer will pull the seal out. B—A seal driver can often be used. C—Many seals can be "popped out" with a small pinch bar. When a seal must be removed while a shaft is present, a hollow, threaded cone is threaded into the seal. The cone, which is attached to a slide hammer, will withdraw the seal.

Seal Installation

After removing the old seal, carefully clean the seal recess, or counterbore. Inspect the seal for nicks or burrs. Compare the old seal with the new one to make certain you have the proper replacement. The outside diameter must be the same. The inside diameter may be slightly smaller in the new seal, as it has not been spread and worn. The width can vary somewhat.

If necessary, coat the inside of the seal counterbore with a thin coat of nonhardening sealer. If there is too much sealer, the seal may scrape it off as it enters, causing the surplus to drip down on the shaft and sealing lip. This can cause seal failure, **Figure 7-74.**

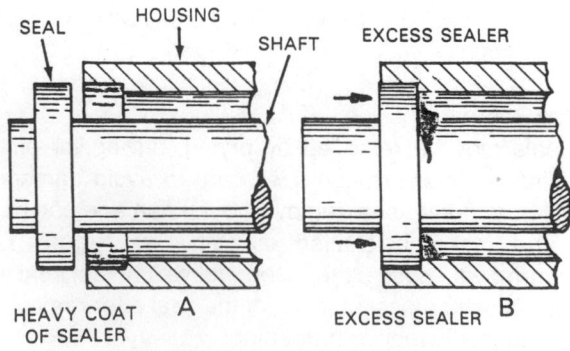

Figure 7-74. Apply sealer sparingly! A—Seal counterbore has been given a heavy coat of sealer. B—When the seal is driven into the counterbore, excess sealer will be forced out onto shaft and seal lips. In addition to ruining the seal, this could clog some opening in the mechanism.

After preparing the seal counterbore, place the seal squarely against the opening with the seal lip facing inward, or toward the area in which the fluid is being confined. If the lip faces the other way, it will probably leak, **Figure 7-75.**

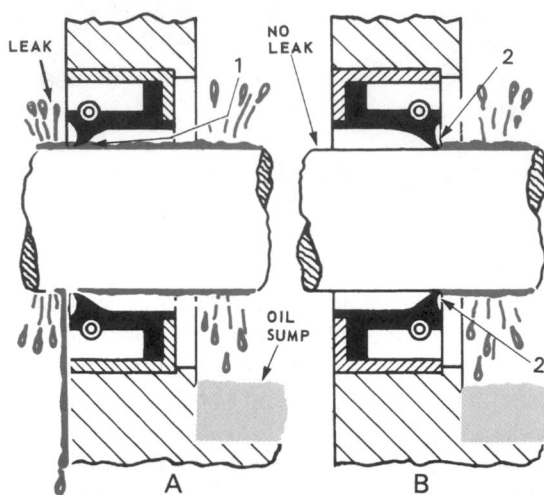

Figure 7-75. The seal lip must face the fluid! A—Seal has been installed backwards. Lip faces away from fluid. This permits fluid to force the seal lip from the shaft, causing leakage. B—Seal is correctly installed with the lip facing the fluid. Fluid pressure forces the seal against the shaft, preventing a leak.

Seals are often damaged through improper installation. The technician should be careful to use the correct **seal driver** or, if a driver is not available, treat the seal with care. The seal driver should be just a little smaller (about .020 in. or 0.51 mm) than the seal outside diameter when the seal will be driven below the surface. If the seal is to be driven flush (even with surface), the driver can be somewhat wider. In any case, the driver should contact the seal near the outer edge only. Never strike the inner portion of a seal. This might bend the flange inward and distort the sealing element, **Figure 7-76.**

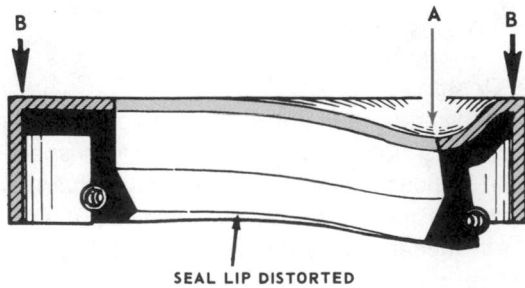

Figure 7-76. Damaged seal. This seal case was badly distorted by careless installation. A punch struck the case at A. All driving force should be applied at B. This seal would leak badly.

If a seal driver is not available, a section of pipe of the correct diameter can be used. Make sure the ends of the pipe are square. If a hammer is used to start a seal, follow it up with a drift punch. Be careful to strike the seal at different spots (near the outer edge) each time. If the seal begins to tip, strike the high side.

If a locating shoulder is used, drive the seal snugly against it. This is especially important if the seal inner edge has a rubber sealing compound designed to flatten against the shoulder.

When no shoulder is used, keep the seal square and stop at the specified depth. If you drive it in too far, you may ruin it while attempting to pull it back.

When driving a seal that must slip over a shaft, use care to see that the sealing lip is not nicked or abraded. If a plain shaft (no keyway, splines, or holes) is involved, check the shaft carefully for burrs and nicks.

If any are found, remove them by polishing (shoe shine motion) with crocus cloth (a very fine abrasive). Examine the shaft surface where the sealing lips will operate. It must be smooth at this point.

If the end of the shaft is chamfered (beveled), polish the chamfered area. If the chamfer is too steep (30° maximum), either reduce it or use a mounting bullet or thimble. See **Figure 7-77**. Once the shaft is chamfered and free of scratches, wipe it clean and apply a film of oil to the full length of the chamfer. Place a small amount of oil or soft grease on the seal lip and inner face. With the seal lip facing toward the fluid to be confined (counterbore with a thin coat of sealer), carefully slip the sealing lips over the chamfer and onto the shaft. Slide the seal along the shaft until it engages the counterbore. Using a suitable driver, seat the seal, **Figure 7-78**.

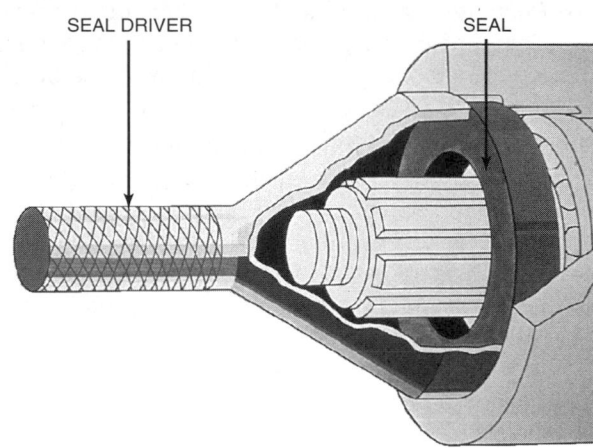

Figure 7-78. Installing a seal over a plain shaft. The seal will start over the chamfered shaft end without damage. The shaft must be smooth, clean, and oiled. (Federal Mogul)

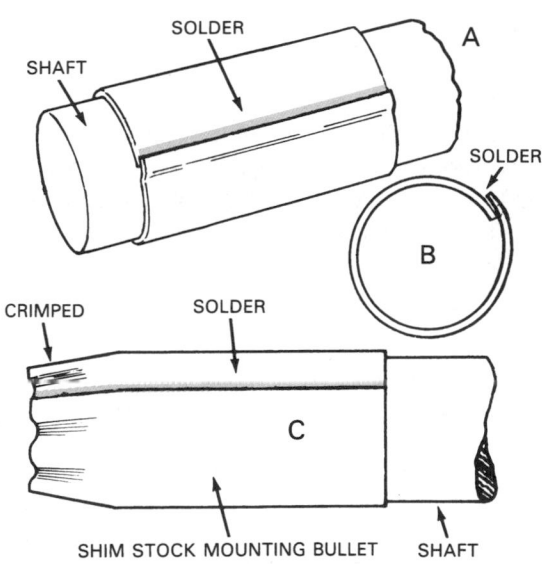

Figure 7-79. Shim stock mounting sleeve. A—The sleeve is formed and soldered. B—The edge is sanded smooth. C—The sleeve is installed and the leading edge is crimped. All edges must be smooth.

Wrap the stock tightly around the shaft (one wrap with a small lap) and trim the stock off. Tin the lap with a soldering iron. File the lapped edge after soldering. Then, smooth the lapped edge with abrasive cloth. Finally, bend the leading edge inward, **Figure 7-79C**.

Remember These Steps in Seal Installation
1. Clean seal counterbore, remove nicks and burrs, and if necessary, coat with a very thin layer of nonhardening sealer.
2. Inspect the shaft and polish burrs and scratches with crocus cloth. Pay particular attention to the area where the seal lip will operate.
3. Check the new seal for correct size and type.
4. Lube the sealing element and shaft.
5. If needed, install the mounting tool on the shaft.

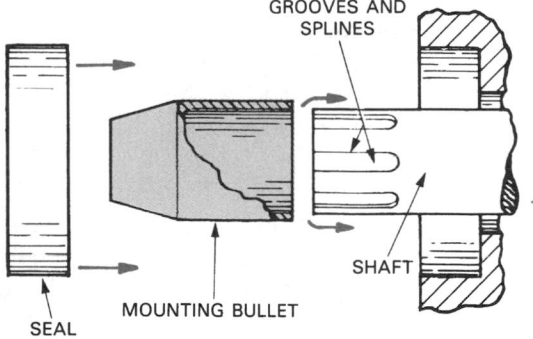

Figure 7-77. Installing a seal using a mounting bullet. The bullet, or sleeve, is placed over the shaft. The seal can then be installed without lip damage by the spline edges.

Mounting Sleeves

When driving a seal that must first slide over a keyway, drilled hole, splines, or square shaft end, a mounting sleeve, or bullet, should be used. This will prevent damage to the seal lip. **Figure 7-79** illustrates the proper setup. The outside diameter of the mounting sleeve should not be more than 1/32" (0.79 mm) larger than the shaft, or the seal lips will be spread excessively.

In the event no mounting tools are available, one can be quickly made using shim stock (thin brass sheets in various thicknesses).

6. Push the seal, lip edge toward fluid, up to counterbore.
7. Using a suitable driver, seat the seal. Make certain it is in the proper depth and is square with the bore.

Other Information on Seal Installation

The seal must be a drive or press fit in the counterbore. In other words, it must fit tightly. A seal that slides in easily will leak. When the housing has air vents to relieve pressure buildup, make sure they are open. If clogged, pressure within the housing will force the lubricant past the best of seals.

If the shaft is installed after the seal, observe the same precautions against seal damage. Cleanliness here, as in all automotive service operations, is important. If a new seal is improperly installed and must be removed, throw it away. Use another new seal.

Further specific instructions regarding gaskets, sealants, and seals will be given in chapters in which they apply.

O-Ring Seal Construction

O-ring seals are generally solid, round (doughnut shaped), and made from an elastic substance (synthetic rubber or plastic). They are used to create a seal between two parts, close off passageways, prevent the loss or transfer of fluids, and help retard the entry of dust and water. See **Figure 7-80.**

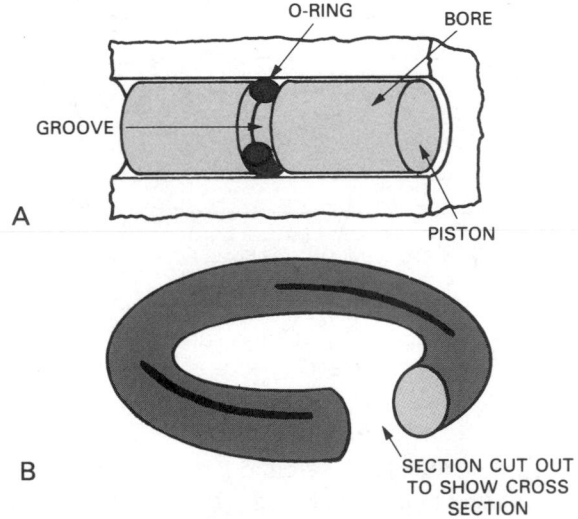

Figure 7-80. O-rings. A—Note how the O-ring is fitted into the groove in the piston. This allows piston movement while maintaining a seal. B—Typical O-ring construction. (Parker Seal)

O-Ring Operation

Because the O-ring is composed of a soft, pliable material, it seals when slightly squeezed between two surfaces. If the O-ring is also sealing under pressure, the pressure itself will aid in deformation (causing it to deform) of the ring, further making a final seal. O-rings can be used to seal both static (nonmoving) and dynamic (moving) parts. **Figure 7-81A** shows an O-ring correctly installed in a static

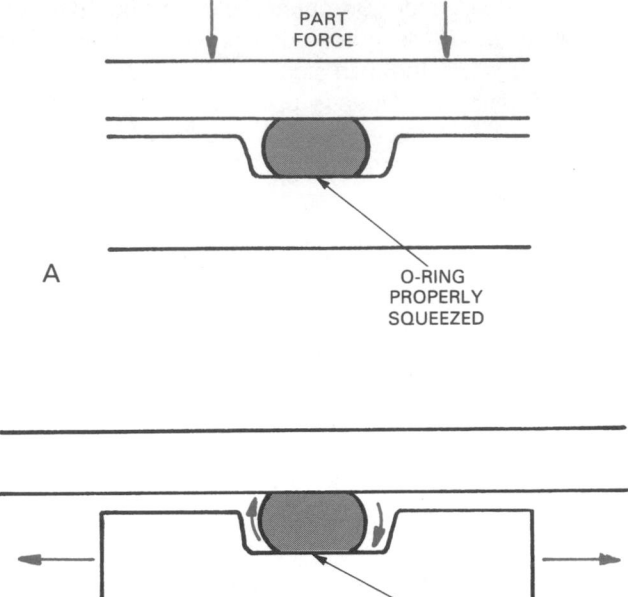

Figure 7-81. When an O-ring is installed, it is slightly squeezed. Note its oblong shape. The O-ring attempts to return to its round shape and thus maintains constant pressure to form a leakproof seal. A—Static seal. B—Dynamic seal. (Deere & Co.)

application. **Figure 7-81B** illustrates an O-ring sealing between moving parts.

O-Ring Installation Steps

1. Make sure the new O-ring is the correct size and that it is compatible with the fluid being sealed.
2. Thoroughly clean the area where the O-ring is to be installed.
3. Inspect the O-ring grooves or notches for burrs or nicks, which could damage the new ring. Dress any sharp areas with a fine abrasive stone. Again, thoroughly clean the area to remove any metal and stone particles.
4. Check the shaft or spool (if used) for sharp edges or nicks. Remove any damaged spots with a fine abrasive stone or cloth. Clean the area thoroughly.
5. Before installation, lubricate the O-ring with the same type of fluid used in the part or system.
6. Install the O-ring. Protect it from sharp edges and other parts. Do not stretch it more than necessary.
7. Be sure the parts are correctly aligned before mating to avoid damage to the O-ring.
8. Make a final check after the O-ring is installed to be sure there are no leaks and that the parts move correctly.

O-Ring Failure Diagnosis

Improper handling, installation, and application will reduce O-ring service life. **Figure 7-82** illustrates some

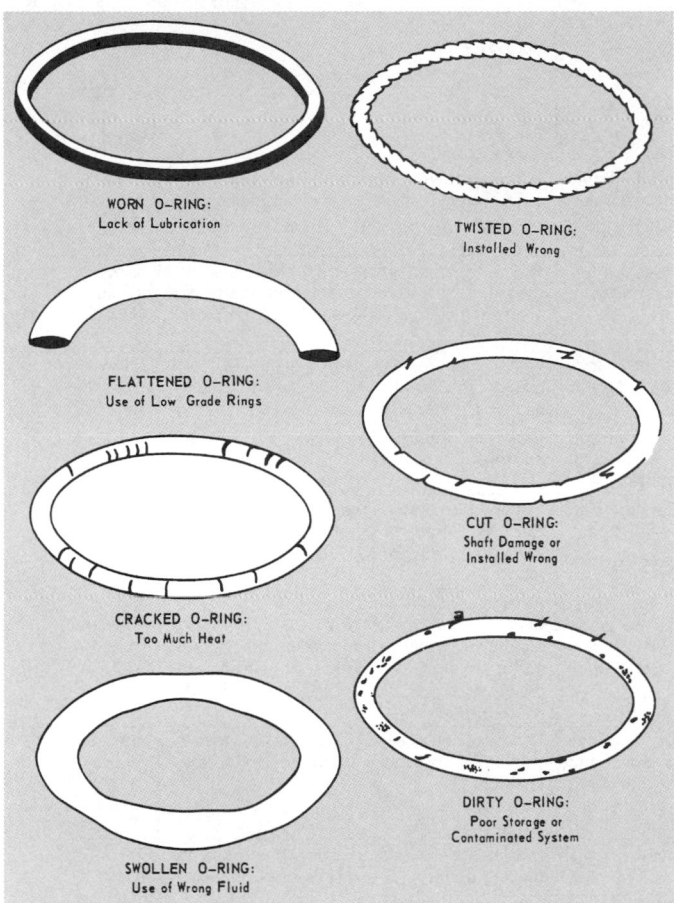

Figure 7-82. Some typical causes of O-ring failure. (Deere & Co.)

common O-ring failures and their causes. Be sure to follow manufacturer's recommendations when replacing or working with O-rings. When replacing O-rings that have failed in service, try to determine the reason behind the failure.

Adhesives and Sealants

The category of adhesives and sealants is a large one. Modern vehicles use many types of both. The section below explains their types and uses.

Adhesives

The modern automobile uses many types of *adhesives* to secure an array of parts. Adhesive uses include securing gaskets, weatherstripping, underhood fiberglass pads, body side molding, and inside rear view mirror bases (glued to the windshield). The adhesive material is generally a liquid or semi-liquid substance. It can be spread on (with its own dispenser or other suitable tool), brushed on, or sprayed on. When dry, most adhesives form a hard bond. Others remain somewhat pliable (flexible or rubbery). They can be removed with special removers or thinners. Follow the manufacturer's recommendations when using a specific adhesive.

Sealants

Sealant, or gasket sealer, is a liquid or semi-liquid material that is sprayed, brushed, or spread on the gasket surface. Various types, having different properties, are available. Some set up hard, and others remain pliable. Some can be used in place of a gasket, since they are able to form the gasket when placed between two mating surfaces and allowed to dry. Most sealants are highly resistant to oil, water, gas, grease, antifreeze, mild acid, and salt solutions. Resistance to heat and cold vary, but in general, most sealers are adequate for all applications other than on exhaust system components, where special high-temperature sealers must be used.

Form-in-Place Gaskets

Form-in-place gaskets are sealers that can be used in place of conventional gaskets. They can be very useful when an exact replacement gasket is not available. Some general rules for using form-in-place gaskets are:

1. The gasket surface should be clean. Wire brush all gasket surfaces to remove loose material. All oil and dirt should be removed, and blind holes should be inspected to ensure that they are free of old gasket material.
2. Inspect all stamped metal parts to ensure that the gasket-mounting surfaces are flat. Straighten if necessary.
3. Apply the gasket material in a continuous bead of approximately 1/10" (3 mm). The size of the bead should be even over the entire sealing surface. Too thin a bead will fail to seal properly, while too much sealer may clog a fluid passage.
4. Circle all bolt holes with the bead of sealant.
5. Do not allow the material to dry before installation. For best results, the parts should be assembled within 10 minutes and torqued in place within 15 minutes.
6. Remove all excess material with a rag before it dries.

The technician should be thoroughly familiar with sealants and their properties. The chart in **Figure 7-83** lists various sealants, properties, and recommended uses. Sealant manufacturers will be happy to provide the technician with specific recommendations for using their products.

The use of too much sealer is generally worse than using none at all. Excess sealer is squeezed out of the joint and can clog water, gas, and oil passages. A thin coat is ample. On some oil pan gaskets with corners that are difficult to seal, a small dab where the gaskets meet is permissible. In general, a nonhardening, flexible sealer will produce the desired results.

Some parts with extremely small holes or ports, such as carburetors and automatic transmission valve bodies, can be rendered useless if any sealant is squeezed into the openings. In cases such as this, do not use a sealant. In any specific application, be sure to follow the manufacturer's recommendations.

PRODUCT	TYPE OF APPLICATION	TEMP. RANGE (DEGREES F.) AND PRESSURE RANGE	USES	RESISTS	DRYS SETS SOLVENT
Form-A-Gasket® No. 1	Spreader Cap. spatula or mechanical spreader.	−65 to 400 5000 psi	Permanent assemblies, repair gaskets, fittings, uneven surfaces, thread connections, cracked batteries.	Water, steam, kerosene, gasoline, oil, grease, mild acid, alkali and salt solutions, aliphatic hydrocarbons, antifreeze mixtures.	Fast Hard Alcohol
Form-A-Gasket® No. 2	Spreader Cap. spatula or mechanical spreader.	−65 to 400 5000 psi	Semi-permanent reassembly work. Cover plates, threaded and hose connections.	Water, steam, kerosene, gasoline, oil, grease, mild acid, alkali and salt solutions, aliphatic hydrocarbons, antifreeze mixtures.	Slow Flexible Alcohol
Aviation Form-A-Gasket® No. 3	Brush or Gun	−65 to 400 5000 psi	Sealing of close fitting parts. Easy to apply on irregular surfaces.	Water, steam, kerosene, gasoline, oil, grease, mild acid, alkali or salt solutions, aliphatic hydrocarbons, antifreeze mixtures.	Slow Flexible Alcohol
Indian Head Gasket Shellac	Brush	−65 to 350 Variable	General assembly work and on gaskets of paper, felt, cardboard, rubber, and metal.	Gasoline, kerosene, greases, oils, water, antifreeze mixtures.	Slow Hard Alcohol
Pipe Joint Compound No. 51	Brushable, viscous liquid	−65 to 400 5000 psi	Threaded fittings, flanges. Can be applied over oil and grease film.	Hot and cold water, steam, illuminating gas, fuel oils, kerosene, lubricating oils, petroleum base hydraulic fluids, antifreeze mixtures.	Slow Flexible Alcohol
Super '300' Form-A-Gasket®	Brush or Gun	−65 to 425 5000 psi	Assembly work on hi-compression engines, diesel heads, cover plates, hi-speed turbine superchargers, automatic transmissions, gaskets.	Hi-detergent oils and lubricants, jet fuels, heat transfer oils, glycols 100%, mild salt solutions, water, steam, aliphatic hydrocarbons, diester, lubricants, antifreeze mixtures, petroleum base hydraulic fluids, aviation fuels.	Slow Flexible Alcohol
Stick-N-Seal®	Brush or Gun	−40 to 200 as an adhesive to 400° as a sealant Variable	Seal rubber to rubber, rubber to metal, sealing hydraulic and transmission oils, cork to metal.	Gasoline, grease, oils, aliphatic hydrocarbons, antifreeze mixtures. Glycols, alcohols.	Fast Flexible Methyl Ethyl Ketone and Toulene
Anti-Seize Compound	Stiff Brush or Spatula	−60 to 1000 —	Threaded connections, cable lubrication, manifolds, nuts and bolts, sliding metal surfaces especially where dissimilar metals meet. Prevents galling and seizure. Excellent on stainless steel.	Water, steam. Primarily designed as anti-binding and anti-corrosion compound.	Flexible Kerosene and light lubricating oil
Silicone Form-A-Gasket® Blue	Tube Cartridge Syringe	−80 to 600 5000 psi	Oil pan, valve covers, timing covers, oil pumps, transmission pans.	Regular and synthetic oil, antifreeze, grease, and transmission fluid.	Fast Flexible Gasket remover
Silicone Form-A-Gasket® Red	Tube Syringe	−80 to 650 5000 psi	Cross over manifolds, exhaust manifolds, hi-temp cam covers, hi-temp timing covers.	Regular and synthetic oil, antifreeze, grease, and transmission fluid.	Fast Flexible Gasket remover
Silicone Form-A-Gasket® Black	Syringe	−80 to 600 5000 psi	Water pumps, thermostat housings.	Regular and synthetic oil, antifreeze, grease, and transmission fluid.	Fast Flexible Gasket remover
Loctite® Master Gasket Flange Sealant	Syringe	−65 to 300 1900 psi	Overhead cam housings, cast metal timing and differential covers, compressors, and transmission assemblies.	Gasoline, gasohol, diesel fuel, regular and synthetic oils, grease, and transmission fluid.	Fast Flexible Gasket remover
Loctite® Quick Metal	Tube	Up to 300 3000 psi shear strength	Restores flywheel to pilot bearing fit. Restores wheel spindle to wheel bearing fit, etc.	Resistant to oils, cutting fluids, chlorinated solvents.	Fast Hard None (when set)
Loctite® Lock N' Seal	Tube Bottle	40 to 300	Starter and alternator mounts, flywheel and gear spline keys. Body and frame bolts. Vibration-prone assemblies. Protects threads from corrosion.	Oils, greases, fuels.	Fast Medium Solvent
Loctite® Super Bonder	Tube Bottle	Up to 175 5000 psi	General purpose. Bonds metals, alloys, plastics, vinyls, rubber, glass, etc.	Cold, mild vibration.	Fast Hard Super glue-type remover
Weatherstrip Adhesive	Tube	Up to 175	Door and windshield weatherstripping.	Freezing and high temperatures.	Fast Tough Solvent

Figure 7-83. Sealant and adhesive chart. (Permatex)

Tech Talk

When you begin a job that involves removing rusty fasteners, spray penetrating oil on the fasteners. Allow the penetrating oil to work as long as possible before trying to loosen the fasteners. Spray the fasteners when you start the repair, and remove other parts while you are waiting for the oil to work. If the vehicle is being kept overnight, spray the fasteners before going home. This will give the penetrating oil time to enter the threads and overcome much of the corrosion. If penetrating oil is given time to work, rusty bolts will often come off as if they were new. Be sure to use penetrating oil, since lubricating oils will not easily penetrate the rusted threads.

When doing a large job, put all the fasteners and small parts in old coffee cans that are labeled with the name of the component from which the fasteners and parts were taken. This will help you to find all of the needed parts when it is time to reassemble or install a particular component. If the plastic lid is still around, snap it over the can to keep out dirt and moisture, especially if the parts will not be reassembled for awhile. Do not use cardboard boxes to hold parts. They will lose their strength if soaked with oil and will fall apart if you try to move them.

Summary

Technicians must be concerned with fastener design, application, and torque. They must realize that the success or failure of the work depends upon the proper use of fasteners.

There are many types of fasteners: screws that thread into parts, bolts that pass through the parts and require nuts, studs that thread into parts, and nuts and sheet metal screws that cut their own threads.

Unified National Coarse series, Unified National Fine series, and Metric (SI) thread series are commonly used. Threaded fasteners are identified by material, thread pitch, diameter, length of thread, type, etc. Steel bolts and screws use radial markings on their heads to indicate material and tensile strength.

The removal of broken fasteners can cause difficulty unless done properly. Various methods are used. When threads in a hole are damaged beyond repair, the hole can be drilled and tapped to the next suitable oversize and a larger cap screw can be installed. The stripped threads can also be drilled to accept a patented coil wire insert. This requires special tools.

Snap rings, rivets, clevis pins, keys, and splines are nonthreaded fasteners. Self-locking nuts, various lock washers, safety wire, locking plates, and cotter pins are some of the methods of keeping fasteners tight.

To provide proper tension, fasteners should be torqued. Several types of torque wrenches are available for this purpose. When using a torque wrench, use high-pressure lubricant on the threads and under the head or under the nut area on fasteners. Be certain the fastener is correct for the application. Always follow the manufacturer's recommended torque and tightening sequence.

The selection, preparation, and installation of gaskets is important. Gaskets provide leakproof joints. They are made of paper, cork, rubber, steel, and copper. Different materials or combinations of materials are needed for specific applications.

Gaskets are of single- and multiple-layer construction. Many use steel or copper outer layers with a flexible center. Gaskets may have additional material around the sealing edges to increase unit loading at these points.

Used gaskets should be discarded. Beware of kinked multiple-layer gaskets. Where sealant use is recommended, use sparingly. When a gasket has failed, try to determine why, so you can correct the condition.

Oil seals are used to confine fluids, prevent the entry of foreign material, or to separate two fluids. Seals are generally constructed with a steel case, sealing element, and garter spring. Some specialized seals use fiber wicking or sections of synthetic rubber. Seals use both leather and synthetic rubber sealing elements. Many different seal lip designs are used.

When installing seals, the shaft must be smooth, the counterbore lightly coated with nonhardening sealer, and the seal driven to the proper depth. The seal lip should face toward the fluid to be confined. Protect the seal lip when installing the seal, and always use a suitable driver. Lubricate both the seal and the shaft before installing the seal. Cleanliness must be observed at all times.

O-rings are solid, pliable rings that have a round cross section. They are used to seal between parts and stop the entry of dust and water. They seal best when slightly compressed. Be sure to carefully follow installation instructions so the O-ring will not be damaged. Use care when handling. Never substitute or reuse O-rings.

The modern vehicle makes use of many different adhesives to secure parts. The adhesive material is usually a liquid or semi-liquid. When dry, adhesives can form a hard or pliable bond, depending on the chemicals used. Follow the manufacturer's recommendations when using or removing adhesives. Sealants of many kinds are available in both hardening and nonhardening types. Select the proper type for the job at hand.

Know These Terms

Fasteners	Major diameter
Machine screws	Minor diameter
Sheet metal screws	Thread pitch
Bolt	Thread class
Stud	Locking devices
Nuts	Keys
Screw extractor	Splines
Penetrating oil	Pins
Heli-Coil®	Locking plate
Keensert®	Safety wire
Tensile strength	Snap rings

Setscrews

Rivets

Torque

Tension

Elastic limit

Distortion

Tensile strength

Residual tension

Elasticity

Compression

Cold flow

Hooke's law

High-pressure lubricant

Torque specifications

Torque wrench

Tightening sequence

Run-down torque

Gasket

Compressibility

Unit loading

Mating surfaces

Sealant

Oil seal

Seal driver

Mounting sleeve

O-ring seals

Adhesives

Sealant

Form-in-place gaskets

Review Questions—Chapter 7

Do not write in this book. Write your answers on a separate sheet of paper.

1. A stud has threads on _____ end.
   (A) neither
   (B) one
   (C) each

2. Which of the following statements best describes a thread class 3 fit?
   (A) A tight fit.
   (B) An intermediate fit.
   (C) Generally used in automotive work.
   (D) Both B & C.

3. Which of the following statements best describes a thread class 2 fit?
   (A) A tight fit.
   (B) An intermediate fit.
   (C) Generally used automotive work fasteners.
   (D) Both B & C.

4. All of the following can cause screws, bolts, and nuts to loosen, EXCEPT:
   (A) corrosion.
   (B) vibration.
   (C) expansion.
   (D) contraction.

5. Internal and external are two types of _____.
   (A) palnuts
   (B) lock washers
   (C) cotter pins
   (D) Both A & C.

6. What is the size relationship of the head of a setscrew to the major diameter of the threads?
   (A) Smaller.
   (B) Larger.
   (C) The same size.
   (D) There is no head.

7. When one side of a part to be riveted is _____, pop rivets can be used.
   (A) inaccessible
   (B) thick
   (C) plastic
   (D) damaged

8. Torquing should be completed in _____ steps.
   (A) 2
   (B) 3
   (C) 4
   (D) None of the above.

9. Torque readings should be rechecked _____ times after the final torquing.
   (A) 2
   (B) 3
   (C) 4
   (D) None of the above.

10. Which of the following torque wrenches would you use to tighten a bolt to 50 foot-pounds?
    (A) 0-200 inch-pound.
    (B) 0-50 foot-pound.
    (C) 0-100 foot-pound.
    (D) 0-200 foot-pound.

11. All of the following statements about torquing fasteners is true, EXCEPT:
    (A) a popping sound indicates a sticking fastener.
    (B) break-away torque is the true fastener torque.
    (C) run-down torque should be added to the recommended torque.
    (D) increasing numbers on metric bolts indicate increasing tensile strength.

12. Unit loading is accomplished by the use of _____ at certain places in a gasket.
    (A) copper wires
    (B) grommets
    (C) rubber washers
    (D) All of the above.

13. Why should the technician try to determine the reason for gasket failure?

14. Some parts, such as _____, should be checked for dents where they meet the gasket and straightened if necessary.
    (A) valve covers
    (B) cylinder heads
    (C) engine blocks
    (D) intake manifolds

15. Which of the following is not part of a typical oil seal?
    (A) Outer casing.
    (B) Sealing element.
    (C) Locking fingers.
    (D) Garter spring.

16. When removing an oil seal, it is important not to damage the _____.
    (A) seal lip
    (B) seal housing
    (C) seal case
    (D) garter spring

17. What should be placed on the lip of a seal before installation?
    (A) Nonhardening sealer.
    (B) Hardening sealer.
    (C) Lubricant.
    (D) None of the above.

18. O-rings are usually made of _____.
    (A) copper
    (B) rubber
    (C) treated paper
    (D) cork
19. Nonhardening sealers remain _____.
    (A) flexible
    (B) liquid
    (C) brittle
    (D) None of the above.
20. Some sealants are used to make _____.
    (A) seals
    (B) gaskets
    (C) O-rings
    (D) All of the above.

ASE-Type Questions

1. The following are ways to remove broken screws or studs, EXCEPT:
   (A) grasp the broken section with pliers or a wrench.
   (B) cut a slot to allow the use of a screwdriver.
   (C) turn it in further to clear the threads.
   (D) weld a nut to the broken section.
2. Technician A says that a stripped hole can be repaired by installing a Heli-coil. Technician B says that a stripped hole can be repaired by installing the next larger size capscrew. Who is right?
   (A) A only.
   (B) B only.
   (C) Both A & B.
   (D) Neither A nor B.
3. Technician A says that three radial lines on the head of a bolt indicate that it has greater tensile strength than a bolt with six radial lines. Technician B says that Unified (customary) and Metric fasteners have coarse and fine thread series. Who is right?
   (A) A only.
   (B) B only.
   (C) Both A & B.
   (D) Neither A nor B.
4. Technician A says that all fasteners have threads. Technician B says that splines are a means of driving two parts. Who is right?
   (A) A only.
   (B) B only.
   (C) Both A & B.
   (D) Neither A nor B.
5. Technician A says that snap rings should never be reused. Technician B says that snap rings should not be reused if they are distorted or sprung out of shape. Who is right?
   (A) A only.
   (B) B only.
   (C) Both A & B.
   (D) Neither A nor B.
6. Technician A says that even though fasteners appear to be very strong, they will stretch when tightened. Technician B says that stretching a fastener too much will cause it to break. Who is right?
   (A) A only.
   (B) B only.
   (C) Both A & B.
   (D) Neither A nor B.
7. Technician A says to always push a torque wrench. Technician B says that once fasteners have been properly torqued, they will never need to be torqued again. Who is right?
   (A) A only.
   (B) B only.
   (C) Both A & B.
   (D) Neither A nor B.
8. Technician A says that a used gasket can be reinstalled if it is first soaked in water. Technician B says that a gasket that has shrunk can be used if it is first soaked in water. Who is right?
   (A) A only.
   (B) B only.
   (C) Both A & B.
   (D) Neither A nor B.
9. Technician A says that the lip of an oil seal should face the fluid to be confined. Technician B says that an oil seal should be installed with a special driver whenever possible. Who is right?
   (A) A only.
   (B) B only.
   (C) Both A & B.
   (D) Neither A nor B.
10. Technician A says that O-rings can be used on parts that move. Technician B says that O-rings can be used on parts that do not move. Who is right?
    (A) A only.
    (B) B only.
    (C) Both A & B.
    (D) Neither A nor B.

Suggested Activities

1. Obtain about 20 different nuts, bolts, and other threaded fasteners. List them according to the following specifications:
   a. Part Name
   b. Number
   c. Diameter
   d. Length
   e. Head Shape
   f. Wrench Size
2. Use a thread pitch gauge to measure the threaded fasteners used in Activity 1. Using the thread pitch readings and the information in Activity 1, determine whether the fasteners are:
   a. Coarse SAE thread sizes
   b. Fine SAE thread sizes
   c. Metric thread sizes
   d. Machine screw thread sizes
3. Observe the fasteners in various places on a vehicle and try to develop some general rules that determine

what fasteners are used for what purpose. Note any special fasteners and try to determine why they are used. Share your findings with the class.

4. Sketch a simple bolt and show what dimensions and other information are commonly used to describe a bolt.

5. Make a chart comparing the strength markings of SAE and metric bolts.

6. Take a sheet of paper and wad it into a ball. Pull it back out and lay it on the table. If you were to try to flatten it out, where would you place your hands (fastener) first? In what direction (sequence) would you move them? Try it. Demonstrate this procedure to your classmates and explain how it compares to the recommended tightening sequence?

7. Place two 1/4″ bolts (one with six radial lines on its head and the other with none) of equal length in a vise so that approximately 1/2″ of each bolt is secured by the jaws. Keep the bolts about 2″ apart. Run the vise up tightly. With a suitable torque wrench, turn each bolt until it snaps. Watch the scale carefully to determine torque at the moment of failure. Were the readings the same? If not, why? Does it take much effort to snap a 1/4″ bolt. Write a short report summarizing your findings.

8

Tubing and Hose

After studying this chapter, you will be able to:
- Identify different types of tubing, hose, and fittings.
- Select the correct type of tubing, hose, or fitting for the job.
- Properly install new tubing and hose.

Tubing and hose are used in many parts of the car. Brake systems, fuel delivery, vacuum-powered accessories, air conditioning, heating, transmission fluid cooling, engine cooling, power steering, suspension, lubrication, and instrumentation all utilize either tubing or hose. In some instances, both are used. Selecting and working with tubing is a part of most repair jobs. A well-trained technician should be thoroughly familiar with the different types, their application, and proper installation.

Tubing Material

Annealed (soft) copper, half-hard copper, steel, aluminum, plastic, and stainless steel are some of the materials used in the manufacturing of tubing. Although all of these are found in the automotive field, the most common types are steel and plastic.

Figure 8-1 shows the pressures that various types of tubing with different wall thickness will withstand. These are safe working pressures when a safety factor of five to one (material five times stronger than anticipated working pressure) is desired.

MATERIAL	O.D.	WALL THICKNESS	PRESSURE PSI
Polyethylene*	1/4 in.	.062	200
Nylon*	3/16 in.	.023	300
35 Aluminum		.018	500
5250 Aluminum		.018	1,000
Annealed Copper		.020	1,000
Half-hard Copper		.020	2,000
Double Wrap, Brazed Steel		.020	2,000
1010 Steel		.020	2,000
Annealed Stainless Steel		.020	3,000
4130 Steel		.018	5,000

* = at 70 deg. F.

Figure 8-1. Tubing pressure comparison chart. Note the variation in safe working pressure for each material.

The technician must know what material is used in the tubing. The technician must also have accurate knowledge of the pressures and temperatures produced by the system in which the tubing will be used. Keep in mind that both power steering and braking systems can develop pressures in excess of 1000 PSI (6,895 kPa).

Copper Tubing

Copper tubing resists rust, bends easily, and forms good joints. It can be used for vacuum lines, coolant and heater lines, lubrication lines, and for other low-pressure applications. Copper is more easily bent than steel, but is not as strong. In addition, it is subject to **work hardening** (material becoming hard and brittle from bending). Therefore, copper tubing should be protected from excessive vibration.

 Warning: Never use copper tubing on brake or power steering systems. These systems generate very high pressures. Never use copper tubing in fuel systems. Vibration and movement can weaken copper tubing, resulting in a leak and possibly a fire. Use only steel tubing in these systems.

Steel Tubing

Steel tubing is suitable for almost all automotive applications. When used in brake and fuel systems, the steel tubing should be of the double-wrapped, brazed, and tin-plated type. The **double wall construction** gives the tubing good strength and makes it easier to bend. The tin-plating protects it from corrosion.

Plastic Tubing

Polyethylene and nylon are two of the materials used in the construction of plastic tubing. Plastic tubing has the advantage of flexibility, resistance to corrosion, and work hardening. It will not withstand high pressures and excessive heat, however. It can be used for fuel, vacuum, and some lubrication lines. Special inserts are needed to attach plastic tubing to conventional tube fittings.

Handling Tubing

When removing tubing from a roll, place the roll in an upright position on a clean bench. Hold the free end of the tube with one hand while rotating the roll over the bench with the other. Never lay the roll flat and pull the tubing upward. This will cause the tubing to become twisted, **Figure 8-2.**

Avoid working (bending) the tubing more than necessary. Store tubing where no heavy tools or parts are liable to cause dents. Keep the open end of the tubing taped to prevent the entry of foreign material.

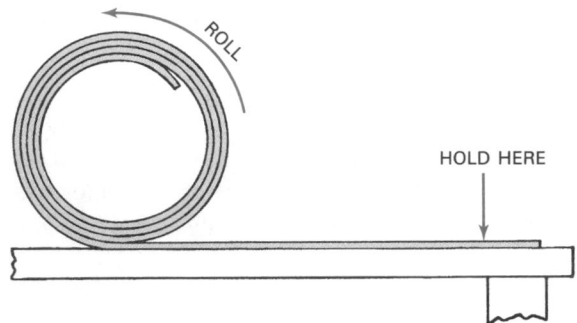

Figure 8-2. Always use the proper method of removing tubing from roll. Twisting can result if the tube is pulled from the roll.

Cutting Tubing

Tubing must be cut squarely, and all burrs must be removed, **Figure 8-3.** This is especially important when the ends are to be flared. Although a fine-tooth hacksaw will cut tubing, a **tube cutter,** which can produce a cleaner cut, is recommended.

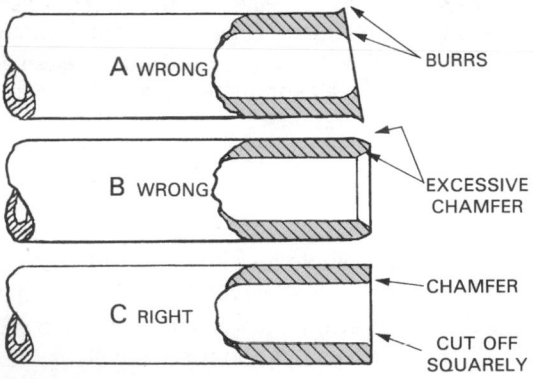

Figure 8-3. A—This tube was cut at an angle and heavily burred. B—This tube was cut squarely but reamed excessively. C—Good cut for metal tubing is square and reamed properly.

The cutter is placed around the tube. The cutting wheel is brought into firm contact and revolved around the tubing. After each complete revolution, the cutter is tightened. Do not overtighten. This process is repeated until the tubing is cut off, **Figure 8-4.**

Removing Burrs

After cutting, there will be a burred edge on the inside of the tubing. Remove the burr using a **reamer blade,**

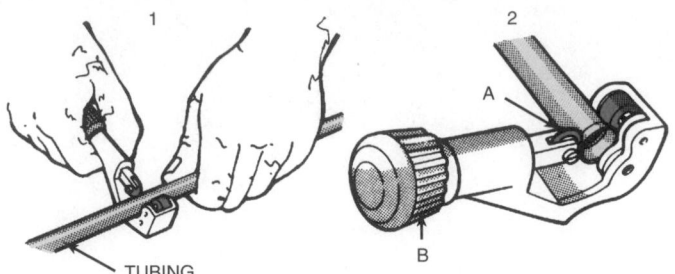

Figure 8-4. A tube cutter can make a cleaner cut than a hacksaw. Tighten the cutter wheel A by turning handle B. (Dodge)

which is usually on the cutter tool. Ream only long enough to remove the burr. Excessive reaming will ruin the end for flaring. When reaming, hold the end of the tubing downward so that the chips will fall free. See **Figure 8-5.**

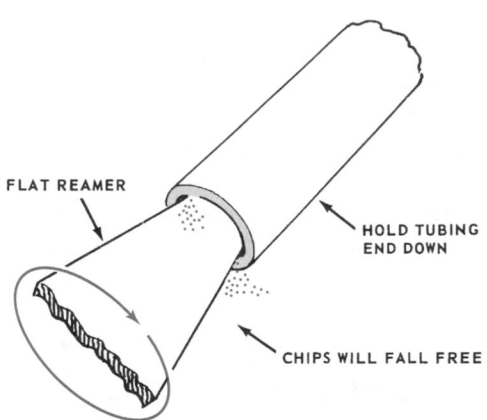

Figure 8-5. Remove burrs from metal tubing with a reamer, do not ream excessively.

Tubing Fittings and Connectors

Proper selection of fittings and connectors is important. The correct choice will speed up the job at hand. Flare, compression, and pipe fittings are available. Push-on fittings found on some vehicles are designed to be pushed into place. Many can only be removed with a special tool. There are a number of fittings of various shapes, designed to handle all types of installations. The technician should be familiar with the following basic designs and their use.

Flare Fitting

In the **flare fitting,** the end of the tubing is spread (flared) outward at an angle. The tube nut securely grasps both sides of the flare to produce a leakproof joint. The flare fitting can be of the **SAE** (Society of Automotive Engineers) type, **Figure 8-6,** or the **inverted** type, **Figure 8-7.** Tube nuts for flare (and compression) fittings are available in both standard and long lengths. Where the installation is subjected to heavy vibration, use the long nut. This will tend to support the tubing a greater distance from the actual connection.

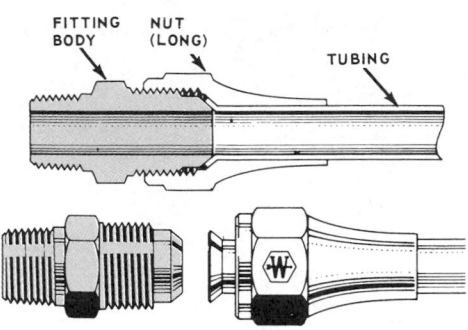

Figure 8-6. SAE 45° flare fitting. The nut threads over fitting body. (Weatherhead Co.)

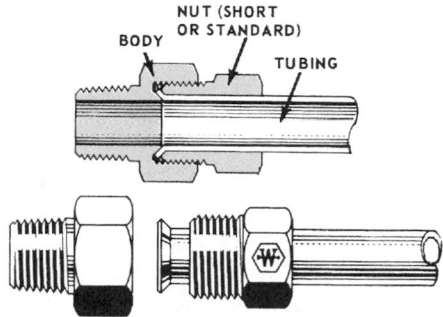

Figure 8-7. In the inverted 45° flare fitting, the nut threads into fitting body.

Figure 8-8 illustrates one type of flare connection. There are two flare angles, 37° and 45°. Be certain to determine the one needed before starting. Look at **Figure 8-9.** The flare may be a ***single-lap, double-lap,*** or ***I.S.O.*** (International Standards Organization) type. See **Figures 8-10** and **8-11.**

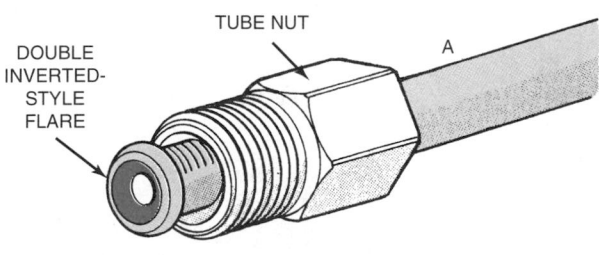

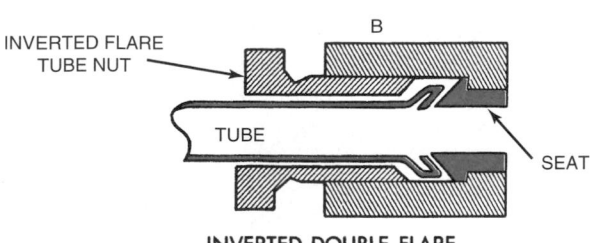

INVERTED DOUBLE FLARE

Figure 8-8. A—Inverted double flare connection. B—Notice how flare is pinched between fitting body and nut. (Chrysler)

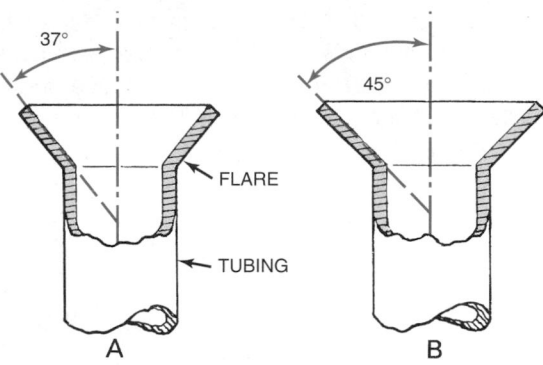

Figure 8-9. These are two typical flare angles. A—J.I.C. 37°. B—SAE 45°. Know the angle needed before starting your flare.

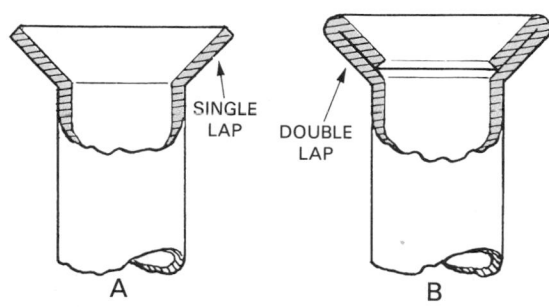

Figure 8-10 Automobiles use tubing with: A—Single-lap, and B—Double-lap flares. A good technician knows the difference and how to flare both.

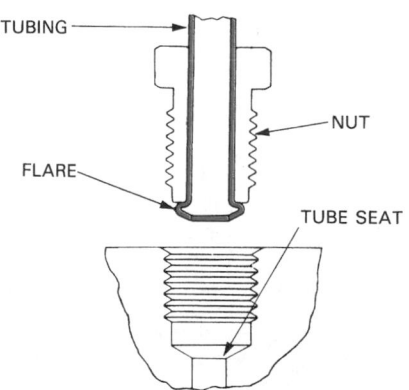

Figure 8-11. The I.S.O. flare is becoming popular with many car manufacturers. (Chevrolet)

 Caution: When flaring double-wrapped, brazed steel tubing, always use a double-lap flare or an I.S.O. flare. If a single lap is used with this type of tubing, it will split.

Flare fittings can be used on any type of tubing (copper, aluminum, steel) that will lend itself to flaring. Flared fittings ***must*** be used on high-pressure automotive applications such as brake and power steering systems.

Forming the Flare

Slide the nut, long or short depending on use, on the tubing. Flare the tubing making certain the flare is of the correct angle and width. The flare must be smooth and square with the centerline of the tubing. Careless cutting or improper use of the *flaring tool* will produce weak and uneven flares, which could leak. When a flare is made incorrectly, cut it off and form a new one. See **Figure 8-12.**

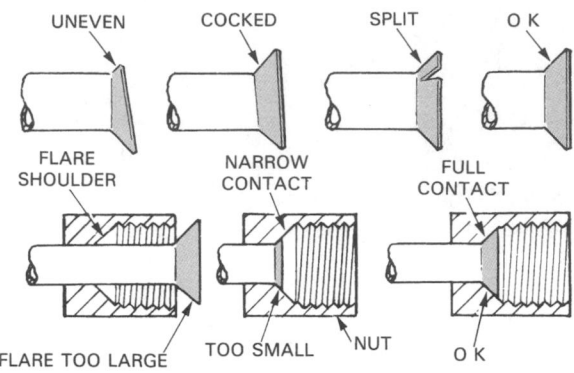

Figure 8-12.   All flares must be square with tube centerline and of correct size.

Forming a Double-Lap Flare

A double-flare should be used on brazed steel tubing, thin-wall tubing, and all tubing used in high-pressure applications. After cutting, reaming, and determining the proper flare angle, slide a fitting nut on the tubing and insert the tubing in a flaring tool. The flaring tool shown in **Figure 8-13** will produce either a single- or double-lap flare. Always follow the instructions provided by the tool's manufacturer.

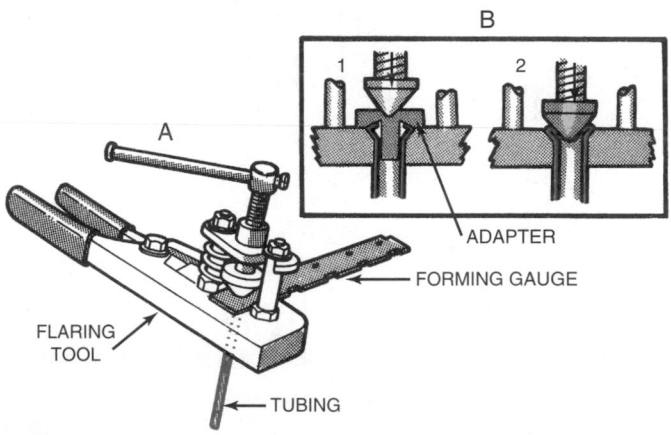

Figure 8-13.   A—One type of flaring tool. B—This tool will produce both single- and double-lap flares. (Dodge)

To use the flaring tool illustrated in **Figure 8-13,** arrange the gripping blocks so that the correct size tubing hole is directly beneath the flaring cone. Rotate the adapter plate until the correct size adapter is beneath the cone. Push the tubing through the gripper blocks until it strikes the adapter. Tighten the block securely so the tubing cannot be forced downward under flaring pressure, **Figure 8-14.**

Run the flaring cone down until it forces the adapter against the gripping block. This pushes the adapter to the end

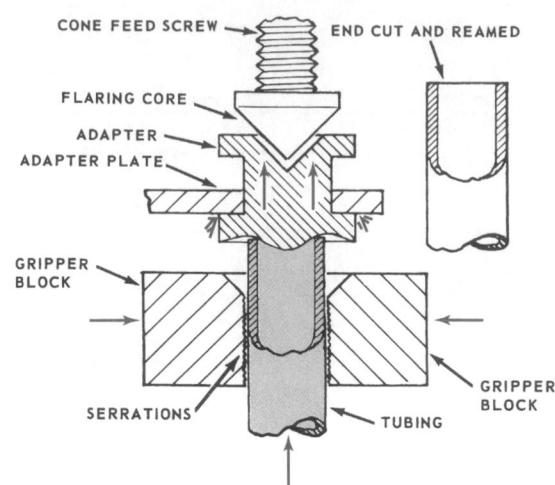

Figure 8-14.   To start a flare, first insert tubing. Push tubing in until adapter strikes adapter plate. Then, tighten gripper blocks.

of the tubing. This is the first step in doing a double-lap flare, **Figure 8-15.** Turn the flaring cone back. Swing the adapter out of the way, and run the cone tightly down into the belled tubing. This will form the finished flare, **Figure 8-16.**

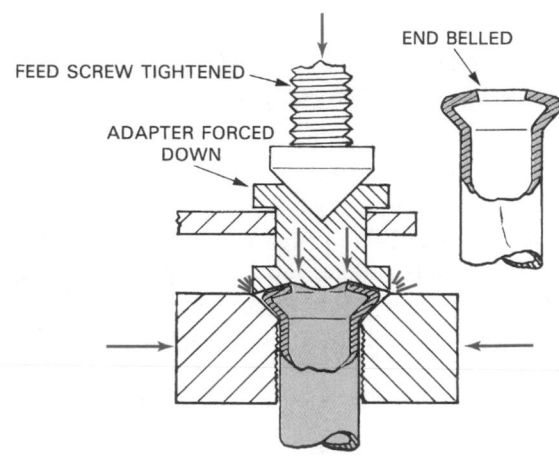

Figure 8-15.   Bell the end of the tube. Then tighten cone feed screw until adapter strikes gripper block.

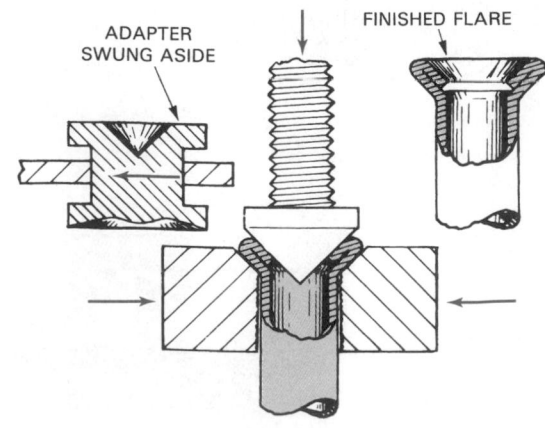

Figure 8-16.   This is a finished double-lap flare. Adapter is swung aside and cone forced into belled end.

Forming an I.S.O. Flare

The I.S.O. flare, also called a bubble flare, is produced with a tool similar to that used for making the double flare. The I.S.O. flare is made in just one step, however. After the tube is selected, cut, and deburred, it is secured in the flaring tool by tightening the two wing nuts. The tool is then clamped in a vise.

Once in the vise, the adapter, similar to the one shown in **Figure 8-17,** is forced down on the tube end. The adapter bends the end into the I.S.O. flare. When you are making any kind of tubing flare, be sure to follow the toolmaker's directions. Always slide the fitting nut on the tubing before flaring, **Figure 8-18.**

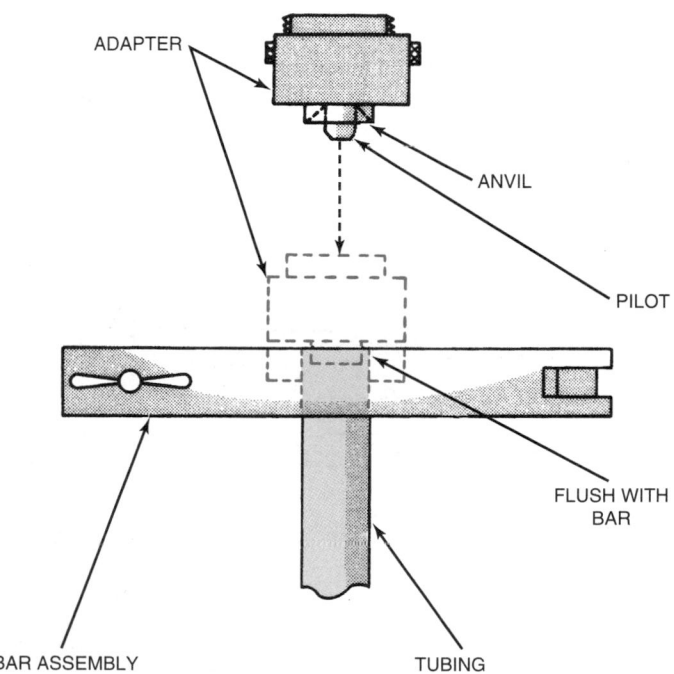

Figure 8-17. One type of I.S.O. flare producing tool. This will only make I.S.O. flares. Do not try to make a single- or double-lap flare with it, they are not interchangeable. (Dodge)

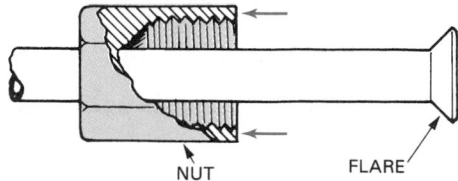

Figure 8-18. Always slide nut on tube before flaring.

Assembling Flare Fittings

Align the tubing with the fitting. Push the flare against the fitting seat and run the nut up finger tight. Using a flare-nut wrench, bring the nut up solidly. You will feel a firm metal-to-metal contact (flare securely pinched between nut and fitting body). At this point, give the nut an additional 1/6 turn.

Compression Fittings

A sleeve is used in **compression fittings,** either as a separate unit or as part of the nut. When the fitting and nut

are drawn together, the sleeve is compressed against the tubing, fitting, and nut. The separate sleeve-type compression fitting is pictured in **Figure 8-19.** The **double compression fitting,** using the nose of the nut as the sleeve, is shown in **Figure 8-20.** Compression fittings are used on low-pressure lines for vacuum, fuel, and lubrication. Since no flaring is required, connections are quick and easy to make.

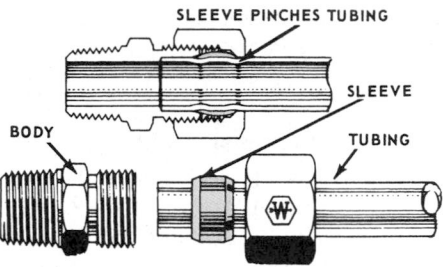

Figure 8-19. Study this separate sleeve compression fitting. Notice how upon tightening, sleeve pinches tubing.

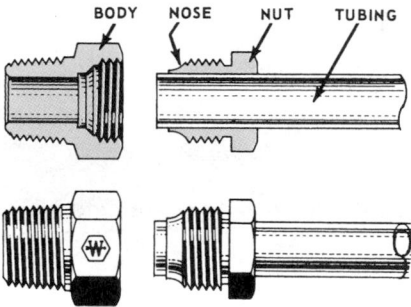

Figure 8-20. When this double compression fitting is tightened, the nose of nut is forced against the tubing.

 Caution: Do not use compression fittings on brake and power steering systems. The high pressures may cause them to leak or come apart.

Assembling Compression Fittings

Slide the nut and the sleeve on the tubing. When the tubing is aligned with the fitting, insert the tubing as far as it will go. While holding the tubing in, tighten the nut finger tight. Using a flare-nut wrench, tighten the nut until the sleeve just grasps the tubing. For 1/8", 3/16", and 1/4" tubing, give the nut an additional one and one-quarter turn. For 5/16" tubing, use one and three-quarter turns, and for all sizes 3/8" to 1", use two and one-quarter turns. While tightening, hold the tubing in the fitting. This tightening procedure applies *only* to new compression fittings. When assembling used fittings, bring the nut up firmly with no additional turns.

Plastic Tubing Compression Fittings

When rigid plastic tubing is used, a regular separate sleeve compression fitting will suffice. However, if the tubing is soft, a special insert is placed in the end so the sleeve will not crush the tube, **Figure 8-21.**

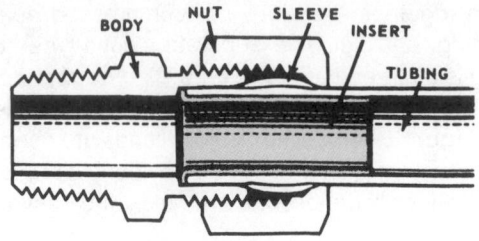

Figure 8-21. In a fitting for soft plastic tubing, the insert is needed to prevent sleeve from crushing tubing.

Other Specialized Compression Fittings

A compression fitting designed for resistance to extreme vibration is shown in **Figure 8-22.** Instead of the conventional metal sleeve, a composition sleeve material is used. This fitting is for low-pressure use. For some applications involving higher pressure, an Ermeto compression fitting is used. This fitting is designed to withstand high-pressure and can also be used with heavy, difficult-to-flare tubing.

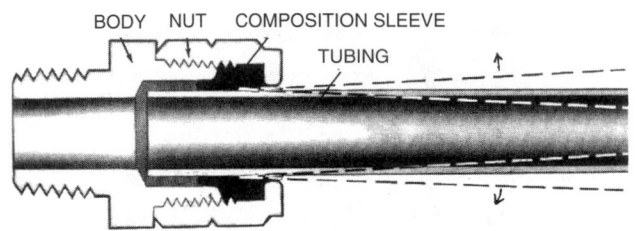

Figure 8-22. A composition sleeve in a flexible compression fitting allows heavy vibration without imposing an undue strain on tubing.

Pipe Fittings

The *pipe fitting* uses a tapered thread that produces leakproof joints. A development in pipe threads called the dryseal pipe thread produces leakproof joints without undue turning force. This is accomplished by a difference in the truncation (cutoff point) of the thread root and crest. As the fitting is drawn together, the root (bottom) and crest (top) of the threads come in contact before the flanks (sides). Final tightening causes metal-to-metal contact between root, crest, and flank. **Figure 8-23** shows a section of steel pipe joined to a hex nipple by using a coupling. Note the tapered threads.

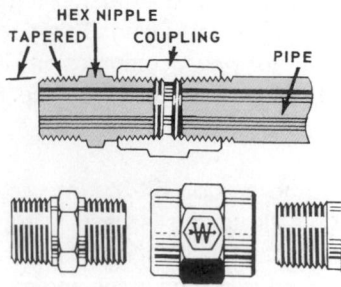

Figure 8-23. Study this pipe fitting. Note the tapered threads. (Weatherhead Co.)

Assembling Pipe Fittings

Clean the threads before installation. After firm hand tightening, give the fitting about three additional turns. This will lock the threads. Tightening beyond this point will be of no value and may split the fitting. Thread sealing compound (compatible with the system) should be used on critical applications. Use sparingly.

Push-On Fittings

Push-on fittings are pushed into place and held by a retaining or locking mechanism. Push-on fittings can be divided into two major classes: clip and spring.

Many push-on fittings are retained by clip ears, **Figure 8-24.** To disassemble the fitting, simply push the clip and pull the fitting apart. The spring lock clip, used on many fuel system and air conditioner lines, requires the use of a special tool. The removal processes for many push-on fittings are shown in **Figures 8-25** and **8-26.**

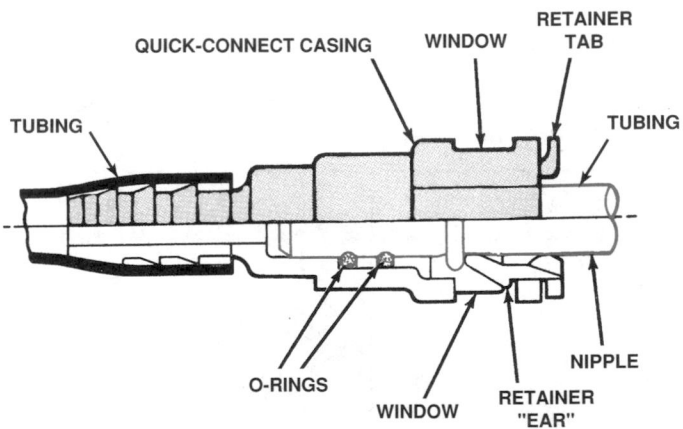

Figure 8-24. A cutaway of a plastic push-on fitting. Study the retainer tab and how it holds the tube in place.

> Caution: Remove all pressure from a system before removing a push-on fitting. This is especially important when dealing with fuel and air conditioner lines. Do not excessively bend or kink plastic fuel lines. This can cause a permanent restriction in the line.

T-, Pipe, Swivel, and O-Ring Fittings

A *T-fitting* is used where branch lines are necessary. The two common types are the branch-T and the run-T. Male and female types are available. Common pipe fittings are illustrated in **Figure 8-27.** Note that all connections are threaded. No flare or compression sleeves are needed. One end of a *swivel fitting* utilizes a swivel nut. This allows the fitting to move. These are available in straight connectors, elbows, and tees.

The *O-ring fitting* uses straight threads and depends on an O-ring to prevent leaks. In **Figure 8-28,** the elbow fitting can be positioned at any angle and held as the locknut is tightened. This crushes the O-ring and seals the fitting.

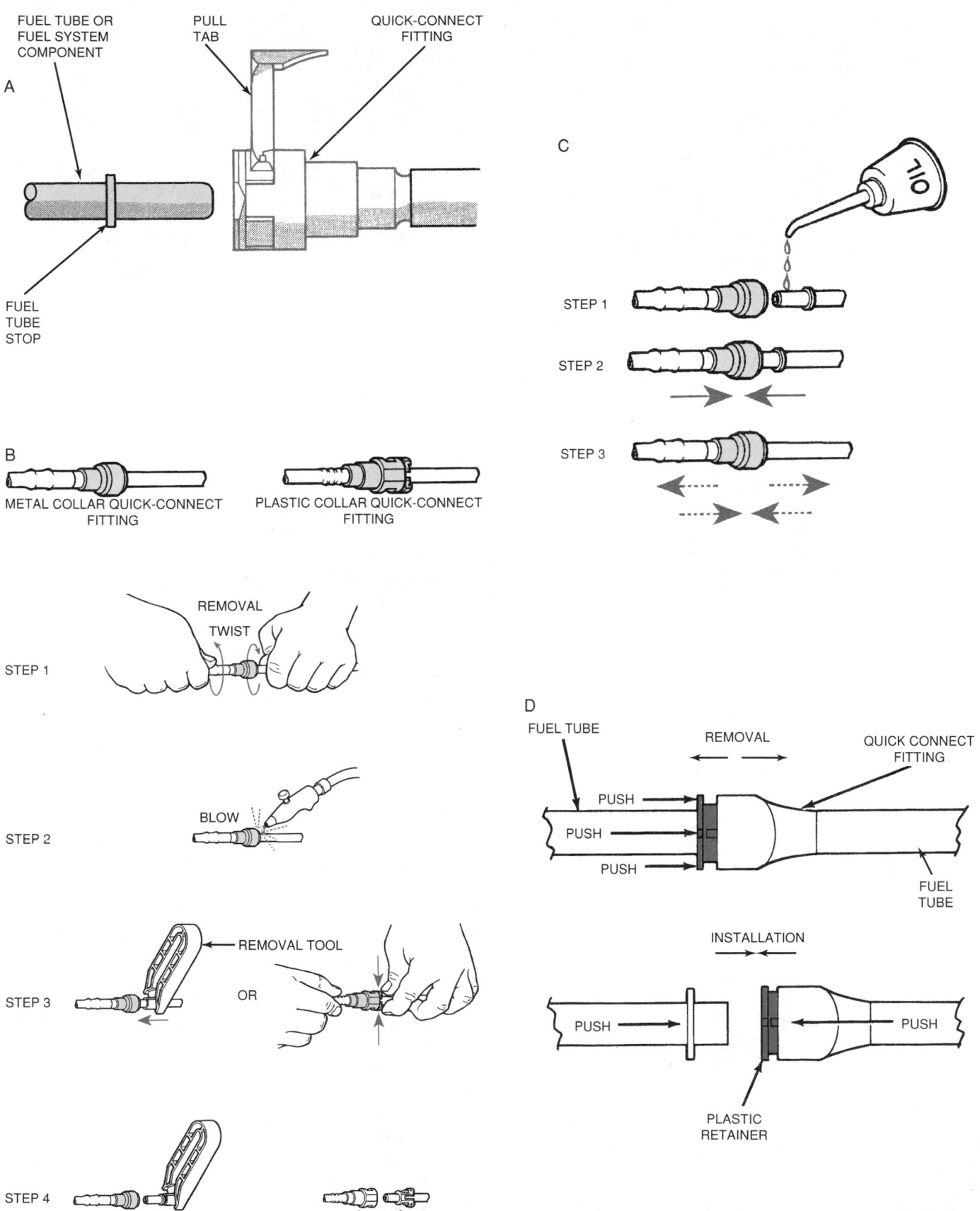

Figure 8-25. Several removal and installation procedures for push-on fittings. A—The plastic pull tab is removed to separate the line. B—The metal collar type requires a tool for removal, while the plastic collar unit may be disconnected by pressing the clips down with your fingers and pulling joint apart at the same time. C—Installation of the metal collar type requires a couple of drops of engine oil to ease installation. D—The plastic retainer ring fitting can be removed with a simple push of the retainer ring. (General Motors and Dodge)

A

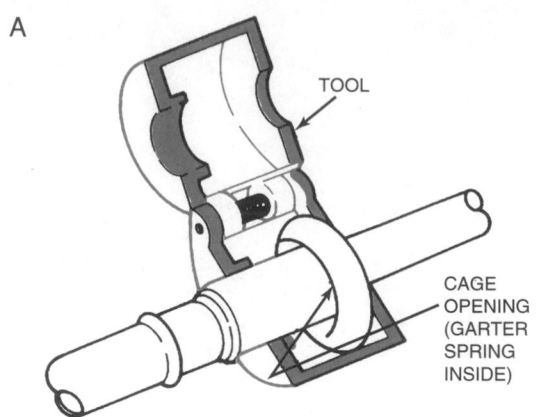

B

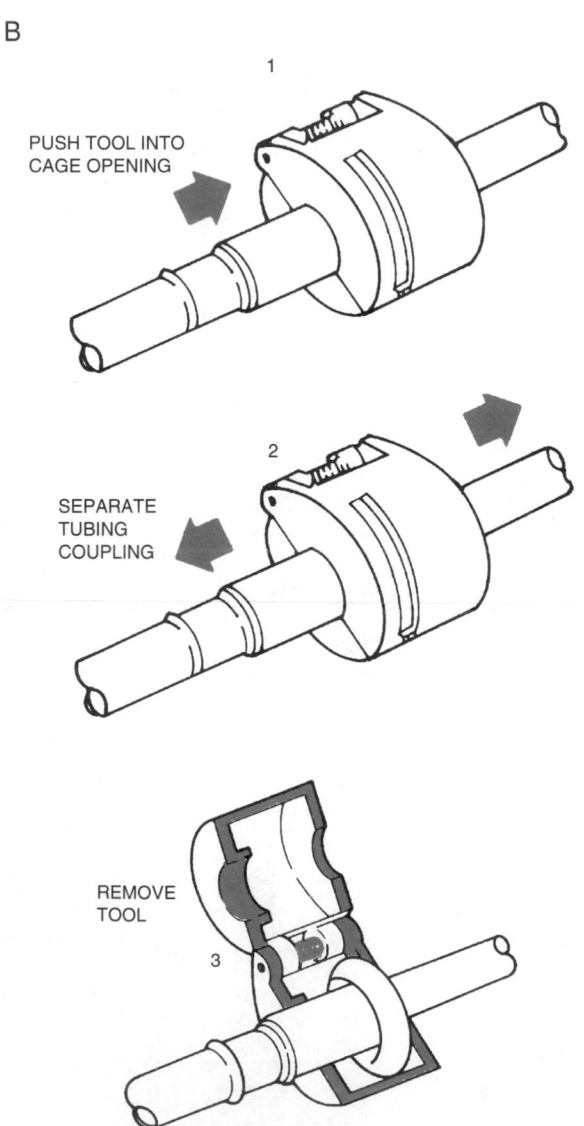

1

PUSH TOOL INTO
CAGE OPENING

2

SEPARATE
TUBING
COUPLING

REMOVE
TOOL

3

Figure 8-26. A—Spring lock coupling used on air conditioning lines can be separated with the use of a special tool which will release the garter spring when closed and pushed into the joint. B—1. Push tool into spring cage opening to release garter spring, 2. Pull tubing coupling apart, 3. Remove tool. Always discharge pressure from any system before disconnecting the coupling. (Kia Motors)

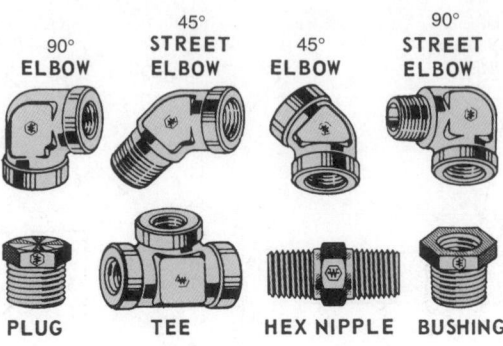

Figure 8-27. Several variations of pipe fittings.

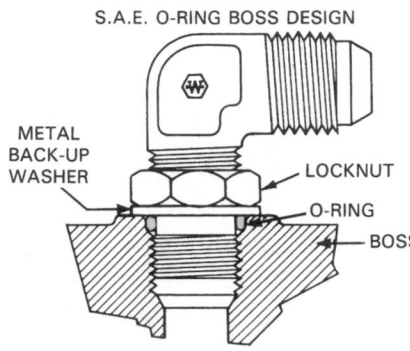

Figure 8-28. 90° O-ring adjustable elbow. The O-ring is crushed against the surface of the boss by the fitting

Connectors, Unions, and Elbows

Connectors are used to attach the tubing to a major vehicle unit, such as a carburetor, fuel injector, or fuel pump. Whenever a connector and tubing are assembled, a liquid sealer is used to coat the threads to ensure a good seal. Connectors can also be used to connect the threaded end of a pipe to a flare or compression fitting.

A **union** is designed to connect two or more sections of tubing. It can be disassembled without turning the tubing. The union often uses a compression fitting, which was dicussed earlier in this chapter. Compression union fittings are used with older and aftermarket mechanical fuel and oil pressure gauges. Due to advances in electric gauges, mechanical gauges are rarely used, which has all but eliminated the use of union fittings in modern vehicles.

When a line must leave the unit at an angle, 90°or 45° male or female **elbows** are used. Female refers to a fitting with internal threads. The male fitting has external threads. Elbows are normally used with flexible neoprene or braided steel hose. It is important to remember that anytime a fluid must pass through an elbow, the fluid pressure in the system changes. Also, elbows provide a natural point for corrosion to accumulate if they are used with engine coolant. For this reason, elbows are used as little as possible. Whenever an elbow must be installed, be sure to use an elbow with as minimal a bend as possible. It also must be made of material that is correct for the application.

Junction or Distribution Blocks

When several branch lines are served by a single feeder line, a **distribution block** can be used. One or more distribution blocks are often used with brake lines. They are used to minimize the amount of metal tubing in these systems. Like metal tubing, they must be secured to prevent damage and leaks. A distribution block is usually fitted with a mounting bracket, **Figure 8-29.**

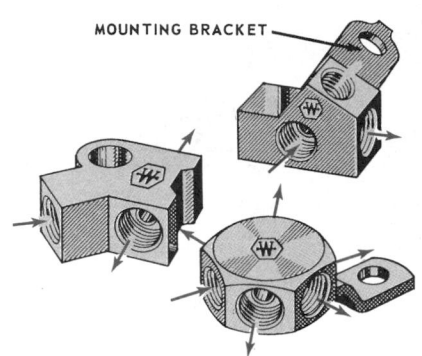

Figure 8-29. Typical distribution blocks. Always use a mounting bracket with any distribution block.

Shutoff and Drain Cocks

The **shutoff cock** is used to stop flow through a line. A **drain cock** is used to drain the contents of a system. Always install these fittings so that in the off position, the fluid flow is against the seat and not the threads. This prevents the threads, especially in radiator drain cocks, from becoming corroded and difficult to turn, **Figures 8-30** and **8-31.**

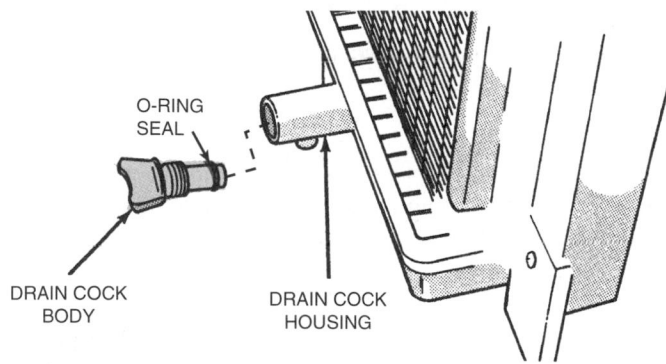

Figure 8-30. Plastic radiator drain cock and housing. (Chrysler)

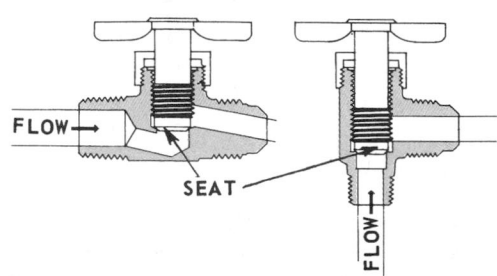

Figure 8-31. In these shutoff cocks, flow is against seat. Both shutoff cocks are in the closed position. (Weatherhead Co.)

Cleaning Tubing

Before installation, use compressed air to blow any chips or other foreign material out the tubing. Place the tub-

ing in a clean spot until ready to install. If there is any chance of dirt or grease being jammed into the tubing during installation, cover the ends with masking tape. The slightest amount of foreign material may ruin the job. Keep the tubing spotless.

Bending Tubing

Soft copper and small diameter thin-wall steel tubing can be bent by hand. Slip a **bending spring** over the tubing and then form the bend with your hands. When using a bending spring, make sure it is the correct size. Bend the tubing slightly more than needed. When it is bent to the desired shape, remove the spring, **Figure 8-32.**

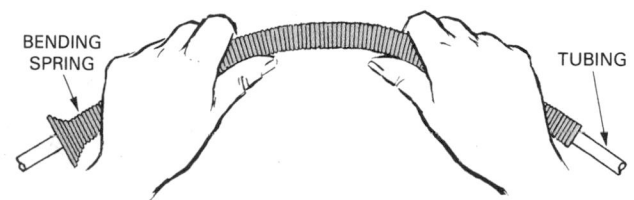

Figure 8-32. Use a spring tube bender to bend tubing. Do not use your bare hands to bend tubing.

Stiffer tubing may be handled with a lever-type bender. This tool will make uniform bends. It is often used on softer tubing when appearance is important. **Figure 8-33** shows tubing inserted in the tool. Note that the tool is marked in degrees to assist in controlling the amount of bend.

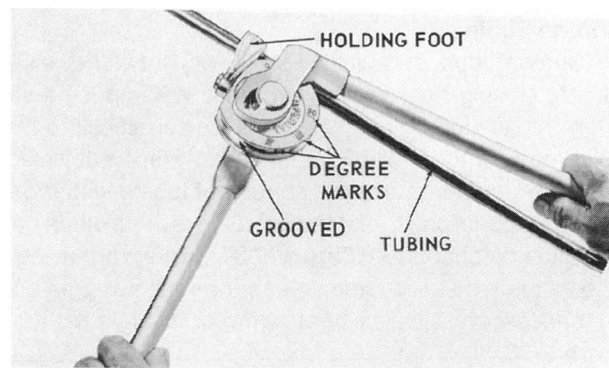

Figure 8-33. Tubing bent in a mechanical bender can be shaped to the desired angle by bending the tube to the degree mark on the tool.

It is often advisable to bend tubing prior to flaring. However, if the bend must be close to the flare, make the flare first so the bend will not interfere with the flaring tool. To facilitate assembly, never start the bend too close to the flare. Allow about twice the length of the nut, **Figure 8-34.**

 Caution: When bending tubing, be very careful to avoid kinks and flat spots. See Figure 8-35. Kinked or flattened tubing will restrict flow and lead to trouble. Always use a suitable bending device.

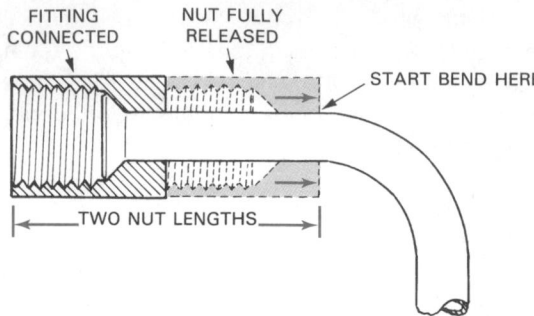

Figure 8-34. When flaring, allow enough space between fitting and bend so that nut will slide back as shown.

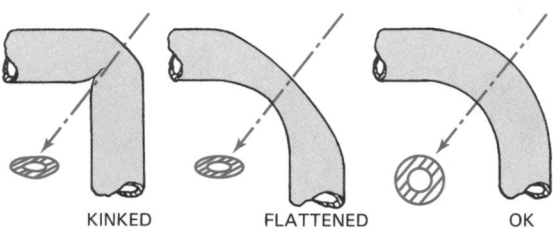

Figure 8-35. When bending, avoid kinking or flattening of tubing. If tubing kinks or flattens, cut it off and form a new flare.

Installing Tubing

Tubing must usually be bent in one or more directions to provide a proper fit. To ensure satisfactory service, a few important rules should be kept in mind prior to actual bending.

Running Tubing

Straight runs, especially if short, will not work well. The slightest shifting between the two units will impose a strain on the connections. Straight runs are also difficult to install and remove, **Figure 8-36.** Tubing can fail if subjected to excessive vibration. Secure long runs of tubing with **mounting clips.** Junction or distribution blocks and other heavy units must be supported, **Figure 8-37.** Never run tubing too close to the exhaust system. Keep it as far away as possible. If necessary, install a **heat baffle** or insulate the tubing, **Figure 8-38.**

Tubing Ends Should Align With Fittings

To prevent **cross-threading** (threads started and turned in a cocked position, ruining the threads), avoid leaks, and facilitate installation, make sure tubing ends are in line with the fitting. The tubing should *not* have to be forced into alignment. Fittings should start easily and turn several revolutions with finger pressure only. If fittings are hard to start, check for damaged threads, alignment, and size. Be careful not to cross-thread fittings. See **Figure 8-39.**

Assemble Both Ends Before Final Tightening

Connect the tubing long leg end first. Leave the fitting loose so that the other end can be moved enough to make the connection. Once both connections are made, tighten

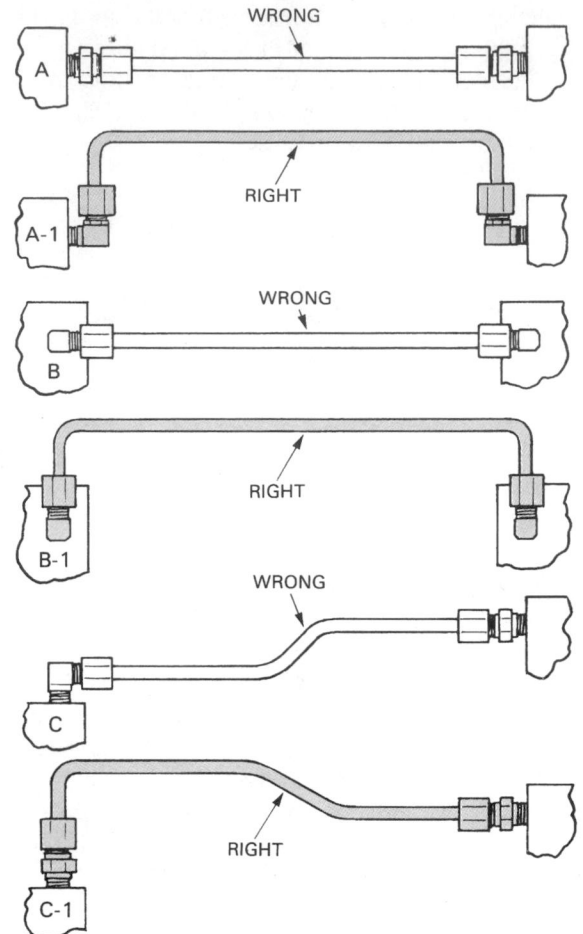

Figure 8-36. Avoid the straight runs in A, B, C, by installing tubing as shown in A-I, B-I, and C-1.

the fittings. Be careful when tightening, since many fittings are made of soft material and are easy to twist off. See **Figure 8-40.** If torque values are available, use them.

Hose

Numerous sections of hose are used on the modern automobile. Automotive type hose uses **rubber, Neoprene, Buna,** and other synthetic compounds in its construction. They are generally identified by use, pressure capacity, construction, and materials used. Hose will withstand vibration and normal flexing when properly installed.

The cooling, lubrication, fuel, vacuum, steering, and brake systems all utilize some flexible hose. The technician must know what replacement types are needed and the correct methods of installation.

Cooling System and Heater Hose

Cooling and heating system pressures are relatively low. Therefore, the hose used in both is of a **single-** or **double-ply** construction. Heavier hose is available for heavy-duty applications.

Radiator hose is available in straight, curved, molded (usually into a special shape), and flexible (designed to bend without collapsing) types. Radiator hoses often have a

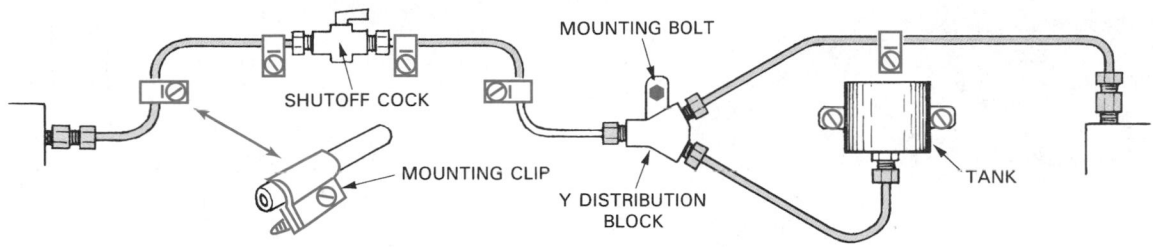

Figure 8-37. Long tubing runs and related units must be supported with mounting clips and bolts.

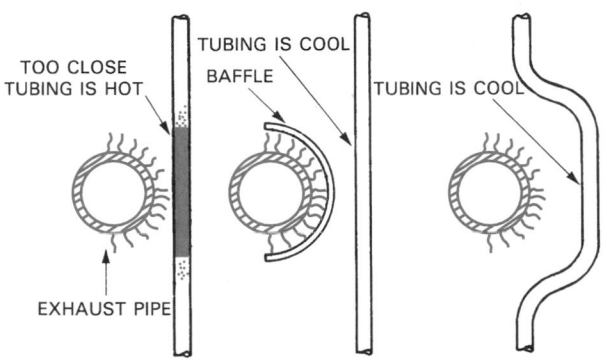

Figure 8-38. Protect tubing from hot surfaces by installing a heat baffle or rerouting.

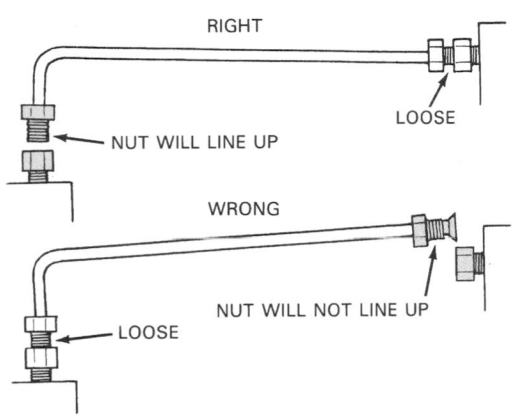

Figure 8-40. Assemble all tubing long leg end first. If short end is assembled first, the long end will be difficult to connect.

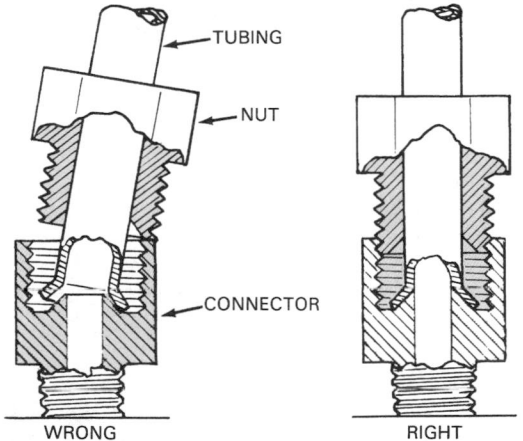

Figure 8-39. Proper fitting alignment is important. Nut on left would cross-thread. Never force a fitting into a thread.

built-in spiral of wire to prevent collapse due to the suction of the water pump.

Figure 8-41 illustrates the typical *molded radiator hose.* **Figure 8-42** shows the fabric ply and spiral wire construction of the *flexible radiator hose.*

Hose Clamps

In low-pressure hose installations, such as the heater and radiator, the hose is merely slid over the fitting. A spring or screw-type *hose clamp* is then installed. Use a small amount of sealer to ease installation and to provide extra protection against leaks. Locate the clamps so that they may be easily reached for tightening. Tighten securely.

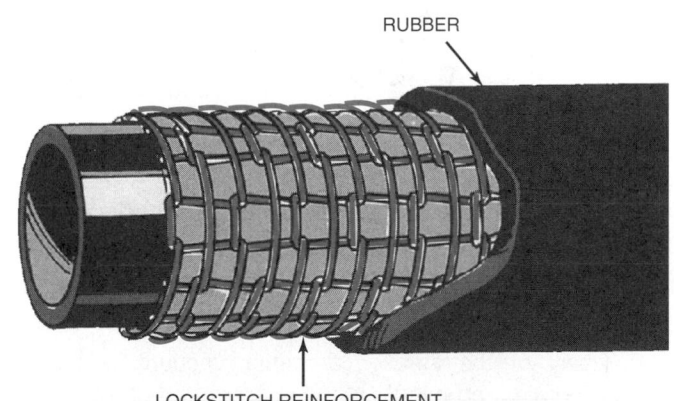

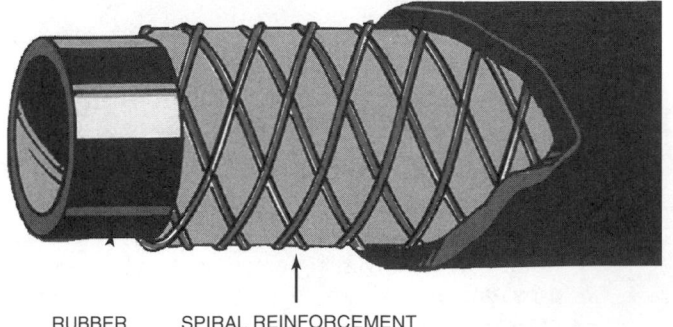

Figure 8-41. Sections of single ply, molded radiator hose. (Gates Rubber Co.)

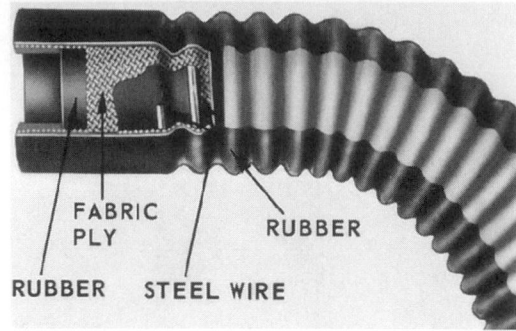

Figure 8-42. Cross section of flexible radiator hose. Note the built-in wire spiral.

If the hose fitting has a raised rib, make sure the clamp is installed on the fitting side of the rib. This will prevent the hose from working loose, **Figure 8-43. Figures 8-44** and **8-45** illustrate several methods of attaching a radiator hose using hose clamps. Some clamps must be discarded after use. If difficulty is experienced when attempting to remove an old hose, split the portion of the hose over the fittings as shown in **Figure 8-46.** In short runs, it is helpful to split the full length of the hose.

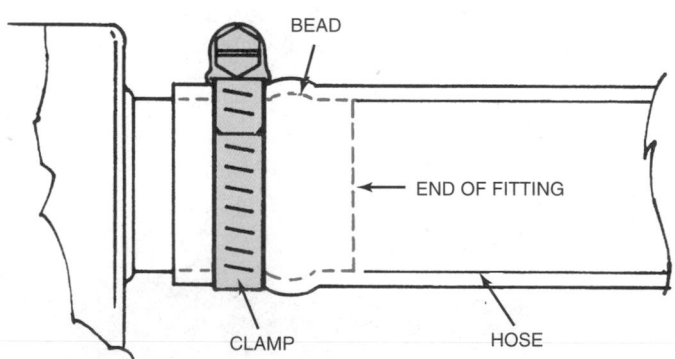

Figure 8-43. Always install hose clamps on the fitting side of the raised rib. (Gates Rubber Co.)

Nonreinforced Hose

Many of the smaller diameter vacuum, windshield washer, drain, and overflow hoses are made of rubber with no reinforcing.

Fuel System Hose

Fuel systems operate on both high- and low-pressures. Therefore, the correct type of fuel system hose must be used. Never use single-ply, synthetic hose in fuel injection systems. The high-pressure in these systems can cause a single-ply hose to rupture. See **Figure 8-47.** Never use hose that is not specifically designed to withstand fuel.

 Note: The modern fuel system is usually under pressure, even when the engine is off. System pressure must be released before any hoses, lines, or fittings are serviced. Figure 8-48 shows a typical pressure release arrangement.

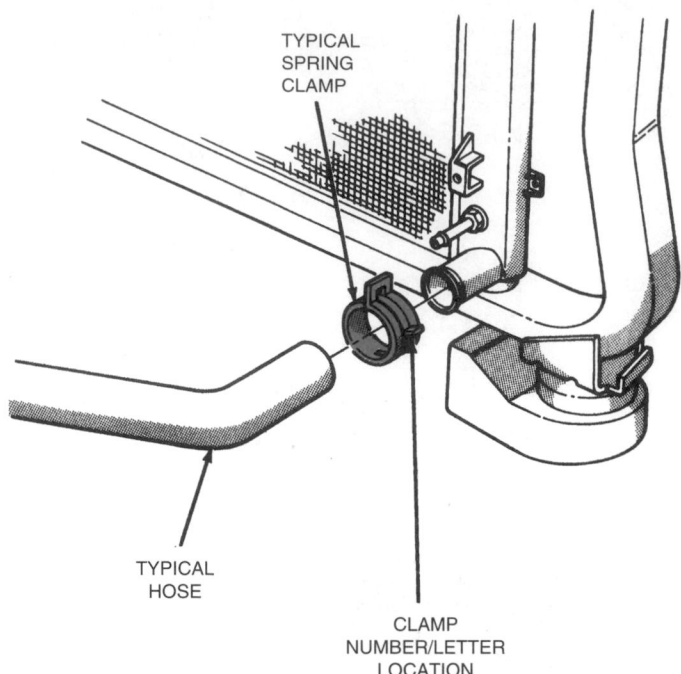

Figure 8-44. Spring hose clamps are used to connect radiator hoses on modern automobiles. (Chrysler)

Power Steering and Brake Hose

Power steering and brake systems create pressures exceeding 1000 PSI (6,895 kPa). The hose used must be of multiple-ply construction. Replacement hoses are readily available. See **Figure 8-49.**

 Caution: Do not make up hoses for power steering or brake systems. These systems generate high pressures and must have factory replacement hoses.

Lubrication Hose

Oil filter or oil cooler hoses can either be made up or purchased ready-made. Oil filter hoses utilize a synthetic rubber hose covered with a soft wire braid for pressure strength. Fabric ply lines are also used. The hose must be oil resistant.

Hose End Fittings

There are numerous types of end fittings. **Figure 8-50** illustrates a number of reusable (can be taken off and remounted on new hose) hose fittings. Notice they include pipe, 37° and 45° flare types. The reusable fittings shown in **Figure 8-50** are typical.

The following steps outline installation procedures for different types of hose ends. When assembling hose ends, always lubricate with water, soap, oil, brake fluid, air conditioning compressor oil, or other agent compatible with the system. Refer to the appropriate figures. Directions given for fittings in **Figure 8-51** are general.

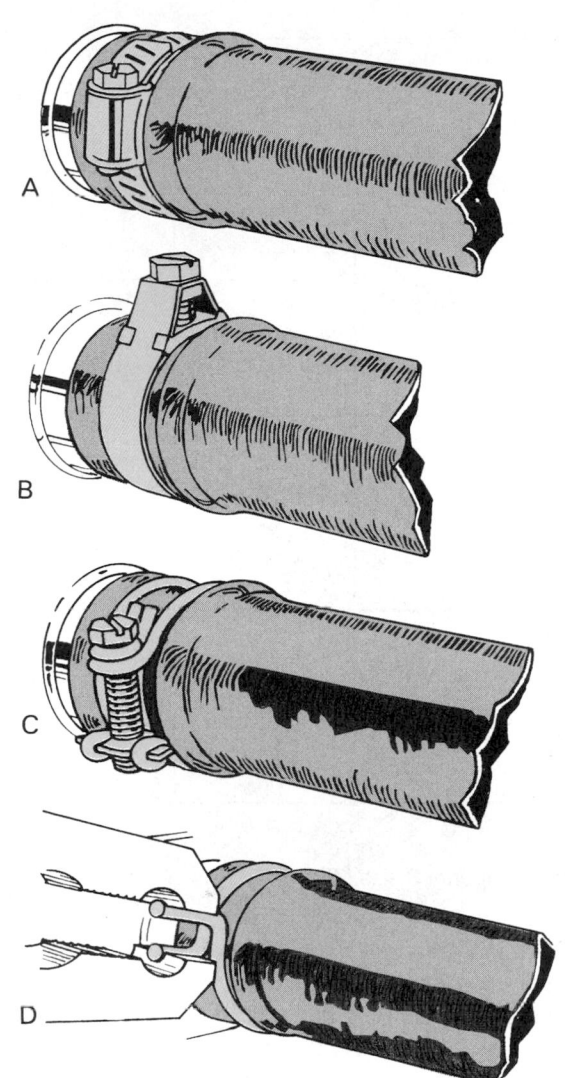

Figure 8-45. Hoses can be secured by the following:
A—Worm drive clamp. B—Screw-tower clamp. C—Twin-wire
clamp. D—Spring clamp. (Gates Rubber Co.)

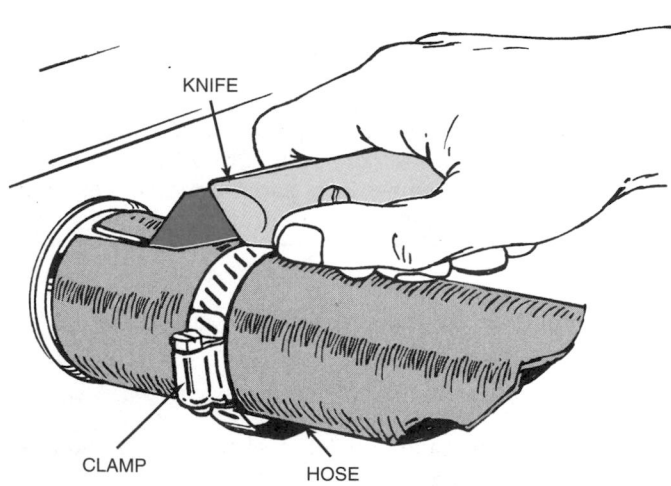

Figure 8-46. A knife can be used to cut away hose that is
difficult to remove. (Gates Rubber Co.)

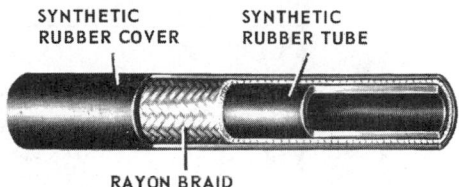

Figure 8-47. Fuel system hose construction. Fuel hose
sidewalls are relatively thick to prevent collapse under vacuum.
(Gates Rubber Co.)

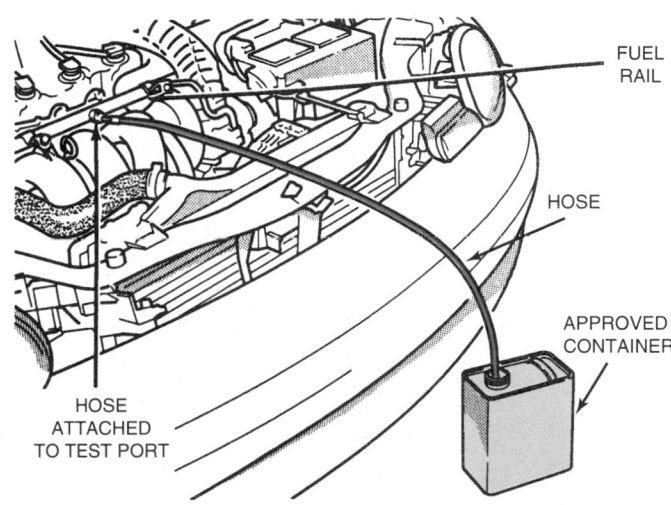

Figure 8-48. A typical fuel pressure release setup. Always
release fuel into an approved container. (Chrysler)

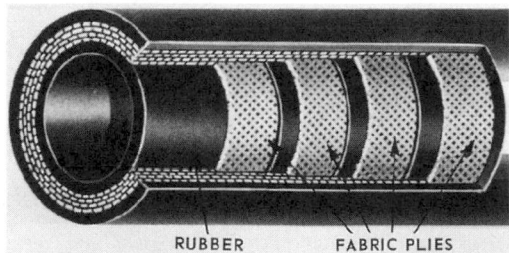

Figure 8-49. Multiple-ply, high-pressure hose. Keep in mind
that ply thickness, number of plies, material, and weave must
be considered in determining the working pressure.

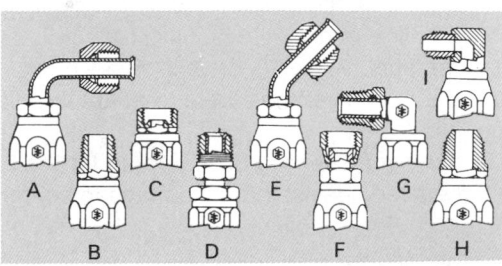

Figure 8-50. Reusable ends are used in many hose
applications. A—90° tube elbow. B—Male pipe. C—Inverted
flare, rigid. D—Inverted flare. E—45° tube elbow. F—Swivel.
G—90° elbow flare. H—37° J.I.C., rigid. I—90° elbow flare,
rigid. (Weatherhead Co.)

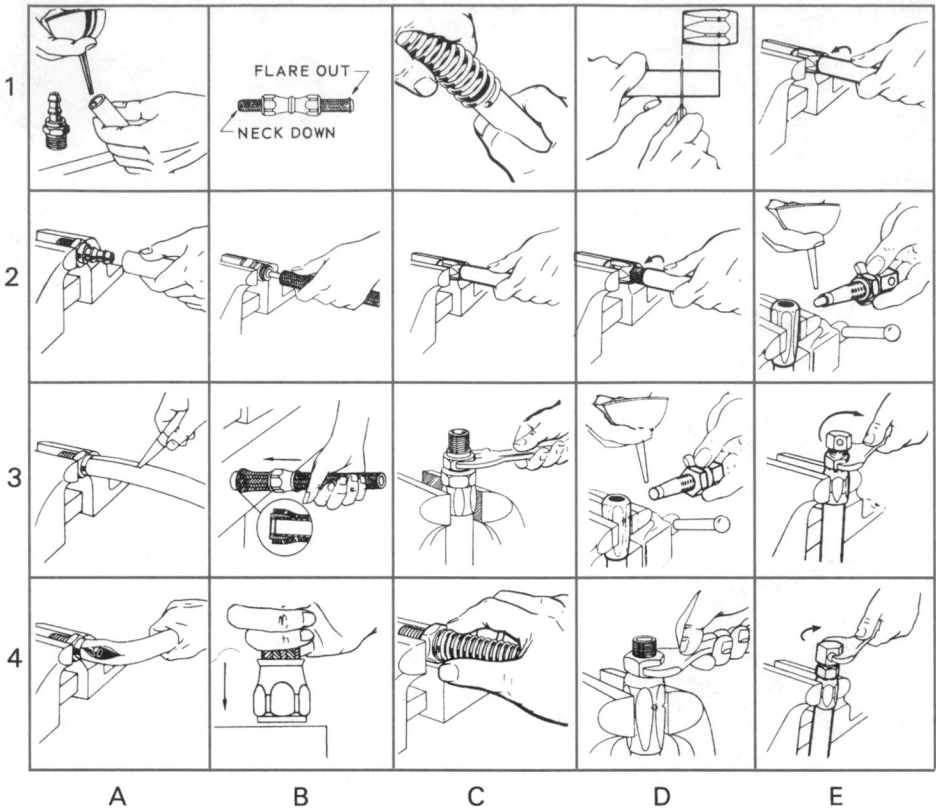

Figure 8-51. Study these general methods of attaching various hose ends. (Imperial Brass Mfg. Co.)

 Note: Do not use a lubricant that will attack the hose or contaminate the system.

A simple barb-type hose end installation is explained. Refer to **Figure 8-51A.**

1. Lubricate the hose and fitting.
2. Push the hose completely over the barbed end of the fitting.
3. If it is necessary to remove the hose end, cut the hose.

Figure 8-51B illustrates a compression fitting used for wire braid hose.

1. Neck down one end of the braid.
2. Flare the other end.
3. Install the nuts.
4. Install the hose over the nipple to adapt it to size, then remove it.
5. Place the insert over the hose and under the braid.
6. Push the hose against the flat surface to seat the insert fully.
7. Push the nuts over the insert.
8. Push the hose over the nipple.
9. Tighten the nuts.

Figure 8-51C shows a compression fitting on an air brake hose.

1. Slide the air brake hose spring over the hose.
2. Push the hose into the socket.
3. Thread the nipple into the socket, squeezing the hose between nipple and socket.
4. Snap the spring over the socket shoulder.

A different type of compression fitting is shown in **Figure 8-51D.**

1. Mark and *skive* the hose (remove outer layer of rubber down to first layer of cord).
2. Push the skived end into the socket.
3. Lubricate the nipple and hose.
4. Thread the nipple into the socket.

 Note: Be careful not to cut cord. Always follow the particular manufacturer's instructions. A skiving knife and mandrel set are shown in Figure 8-52.

In **Figure 8-51E,** another type of compression fitting is shown.

1. Push the hose into the socket.
2. Lubricate the mandrel (pilot to expand hose and assist in proper seating).
3. Thread in the nipple.
4. Seat the mandrel and then remove it.

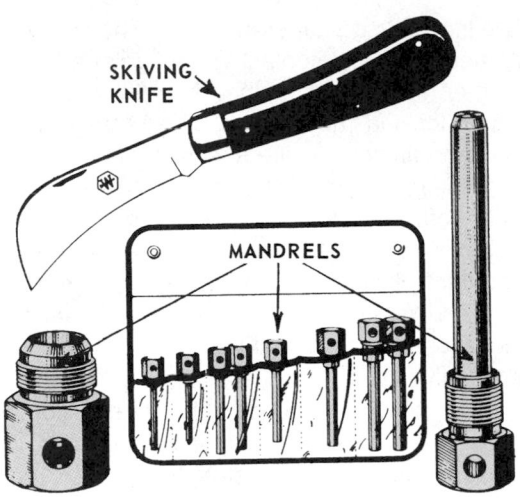

Figure 8-52. A skiving knife and mandrel set. These are essential tools for proper installation of certain types of hose ends.

Skived Hose

When instructions call for skiving a hose, be careful not to cut the cord. A fitting using a skived section is shown in **Figure 8-53.** Skive only that portion necessary. The skived portion should not extend out of the fitting.

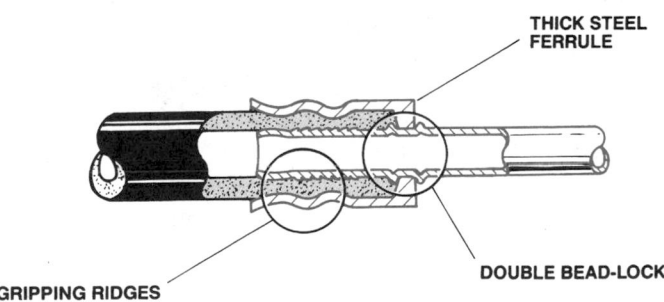

Figure 8-53. A permanent (not reusable) hose end. Note the skived section, which is placed under the steel ferrule. Also note the gripping ridges. (Moog)

Mounting Hoses

Avoid sharp or double bends and twisting, as this can cause premature failure. In determining how sharp a hose bend may be, figure that the radius of the bend should be at least five times the outside diameter of the hose. For example, a hose with an OD of 1/2″ (2.5 mm) should have a bend radius of 2 1/2″ (63.5 mm). This means if the hose were pulled around a circle, the circle would be at least 5″ (127 mm) in diameter. When making straight run connections, allow some slack to avoid stressing the hose from pressure, vibration, or part shifting.

Use flare-nut wrenches when tightening hose fittings. Always support one portion with one wrench while tightening with another to prevent twisting the hose. Tighten the swivel end last. **Figure 8-54** illustrates some typical hose installations. The methods shown in the left column are wrong. The correct methods are shown in the right column. Notice how single, smooth bends, without twisting, are made.

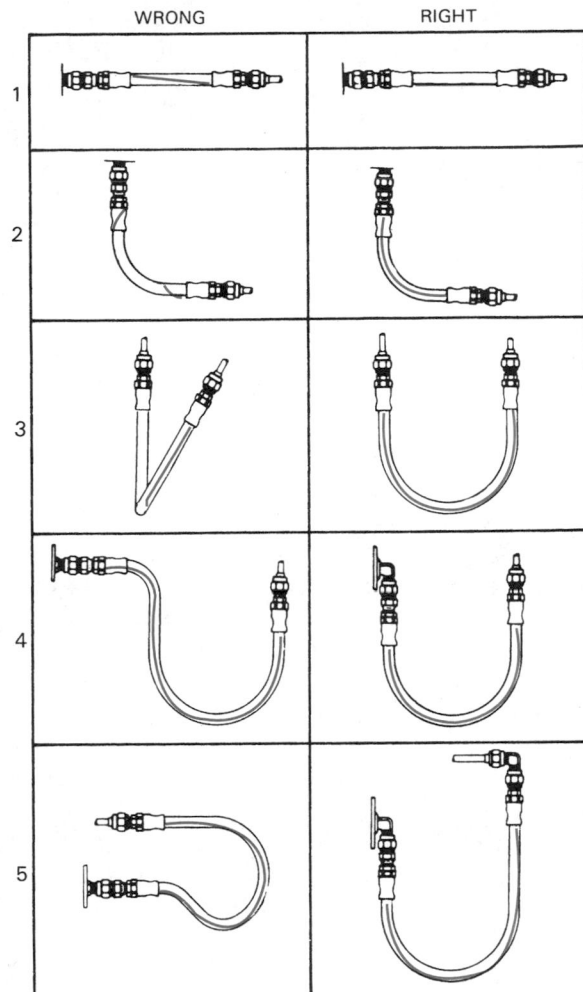

Figure 8-54. Study these incorrect and correct hose installations. Double bends and twisting must be avoided.

Some hoses are installed in the vehicle by the use of special locking devices attached to a flange made onto the vehicle body, **Figure 8-55.** These hoses should always be reinstalled on the correct flange opening, using the correct retaining device. Keep hoses away from the exhaust system. If the hose run is long, use clips to secure it in place. On off-highway vehicles, keep hoses and tubing well up within the frame to prevent snagging and shield them from flying rocks.

Hose Condition

Any hose that shows signs of cracking, undue softness, or swelling should be replaced. Hoses often deteriorate on the inside causing portions of the hose to break loose and producing partial or complete blockage. Check hoses carefully and if at all doubtful, replace them.

Storing Hose Supplies

Store hose in a cool spot, preferably in the original container. Avoid exposure to sunlight, fuel, lubricants, and chemical compounds. Do not place heavy objects on the hoses.

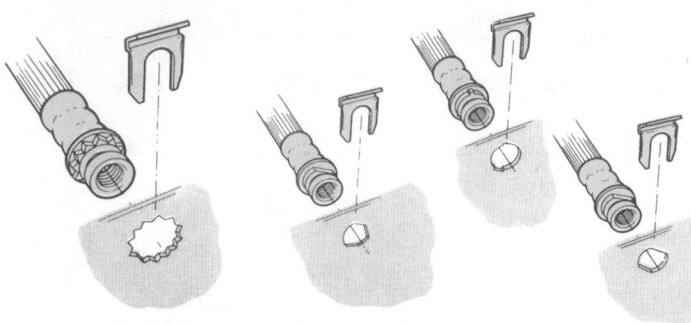

Figure 8-55. Various hose fitting mounting flange shapes. Always use a mounting clip when routing a hose through a flange. (Chevrolet)

Tech Talk

Flaring tubing is a simple task compared to other automotive jobs, such as reboring an engine or obtaining the proper mesh in a set of differential gears. Since flaring, like many other jobs, is relatively simple, students often tend to overlook its significance and concentrate on what they feel are the important jobs.

The experienced technician, who each day performs many so-called simple jobs, knows that the simple jobs are very important. Many major service jobs have failed due to careless or improper handling of the simple steps. Regarding the simple job, remember these facts:

- They must be done.
- They must be done correctly.
- Eventually, you will have to learn how to do them.

Keep this in mind as you study this and other texts. Read everything carefully and consider everything you read important. You will be glad you did.

Pipe fittings use a tapered thread. They produce a seal through metal-to-metal contact when tightened.

Push-on fittings are pushed into place and held by a retaining or locking mechanism. The removal process for some push-on fittings require special tools.

Connectors, unions, elbows, tees, O-ring, distribution blocks, shutoff, and drain cocks are the most commonly used fitting types.

When installing tubing, avoid straight runs. Support long runs and related parts. Protect from heat. Assemble both ends loosely before final tightening.

Automotive type hose uses rubber, Neoprene, Buna, and other synthetic compounds in its construction. Nonreinforced, single, and multiple-ply types are used.

Radiator hose is either straight, molded, or flexible. Vacuum wiper, overflow, windshield washer, and other applications often use nonreinforced hose. Fuel line hose must be resistant to gasoline and unless plastic is used, should have a reinforcing ply. Lubrication system hose must be reinforced and oil resistant. Power steering and brake hoses use multiple-ply construction. Do not make up these hoses, buy quality replacements.

Hose end fittings can be classed as permanent or reusable. Some hoses are attached with mounting clips. Barb-type fittings, where used, provide sufficient holding power. Threaded hose fittings can be of the flare, compression, or pipe type. Some low-pressure hoses are retained by spring or screw clamps.

Split old hoses (barb and clamp types) for easy removal. When installing hoses, avoid double bends, twisting, and sharp bends. Protect from heat, moving parts, and road damage.

Both hose and tubing must be clean before installation. Where sealant or lubrication is used, it must be compatible with the system involved. Support fittings with a wrench when tightening connections. Tighten swivel ends last. Use flare-nut wrenches. Always test the finished job for leaks or malfunctions. Protect stored tubing and hose from damage.

Summary

Copper, steel, aluminum, and plastic tubing are used in automotive work. Brake and steering systems must use double-wrapped, brazed steel tubing. Handle tubing carefully.

Tubing should be cut with a tube cutter. Bending should be done with either a spring or mechanical bender. Tubing ends must be square and all burrs removed.

Connections are made with either flared, compression, pipe, or push-on fittings. Flare fittings, 37° and 45° SAE, and inverted, must be formed with a flaring tool. Double-flare all double-wrapped steel tubing. Double-flare all high-pressure applications. Both standard and long nuts are available.

Compression, sleeve, and double compression fittings, are quick, easy, and suitable for fuel, lubrication, and vacuum lines. When tightening, be sure to hold tubing all the way in the fitting. Compression fittings on soft plastic tubing require a special insert.

Know These Terms

Work hardening	Swivel fitting
Double-wall construction	O-ring fitting
Tube cutter	Connectors
Reamer blade	Union
Flare fitting	Elbows
SAE	Distribution block
Inverted	Shutoff cock
Single lap	Drain cock
Double lap	Bending spring
I.S.O.	Mounting clips
Flaring tool	Heat baffle
Compression fittings	Cross-threading
Double compression fitting	Rubber
Pipe fitting	Neoprene
Push-on fitting	Buna
T-fitting	Single-ply

Double-ply   Hose clamp
Molded radiator hose   Skive
Flexible radiator hose

Review Questions—Chapter 8

Do not write in this book. Write your answers on a separate sheet of paper.

1. The more tubing is worked, the _____ it becomes.
   (A) softer
   (B) harder

2. Which of the following is the best method of cutting tubing?
   (A) Hacksaw.
   (B) File.
   (C) Tubing cutter.
   (D) Bolt cutter.

3. Always _____ double-wrapped steel tubing.
   (A) double-lap
   (B) single-lap
   (C) use a compression fitting on
   (D) Either A or C.

4. How many flaring steps does it take to make a double-lap flare?
   (A) 1.
   (B) 2.
   (C) 3.
   (D) 4.

5. How many flaring steps does it take to make an I.S.O. flare?
   (A) 1.
   (B) 2.
   (C) 3.
   (D) 4.

6. When assembling a used 5/16" compression, how many turns should the nut be tightened after the sleeve just grasps the tubing?
   (A) None.
   (B) One and one-quarter turns.
   (C) One and three-quarter turns.
   (D) Two and one-quarter turns.

7. After firm hand tightening, how many turns are necessary for pipe fittings?
   (A) 1.
   (B) 2.
   (C) 3.
   (D) 4.

8. Push-on tubing connectors can be removed with _____.
   (A) flare-nut wrenches
   (B) special tools
   (C) impact sockets
   (D) None of the above.

9. If you force fittings that start hard, you will _____ them.
   (A) thread
   (B) split
   (C) strip
   (D) Either B or C.

10. A union is designed to connect _____.
    (A) two sections of tubing
    (B) tubing and elbows
    (C) tubing and pipe threads inside of a part
    (D) All of the above.

11. What type of threads does an O-ring fitting use?
    (A) Straight.
    (B) Pipe.
    (C) Tapered.
    (D) All of the above, depending on design.

12. Which type of hose is a single layer type with no reinforcing?
    (A) Power steering hose.
    (B) Brake hose.
    (C) Fuel line hose.
    (D) Vacuum hose.

13. Removing the outer layer of rubber down to the first layer of cord is called _____.
    (A) necking
    (B) expanding
    (C) skiving
    (D) reducing

14. The radius of a hose bend should be at least _____ times the outside diameter of the hose.
    (A) 2
    (B) 3
    (C) 4
    (D) 5

15. Study the drawing of a tube installation on page 148. All fittings are missing. Can you name the correct fitting for each connection? A list is provided. Some are needed, some are not. Write down the number of each missing fitting and directly opposite it, write the name of the fitting you have chosen to use.

ASE-Type Questions

1. Technician A says that copper tubing should never be used on brake systems. Technician B says that copper tubing should never be used on power steering systems. Who is right?
   (A) A only.
   (B) B only.
   (C) Both A & B.
   (D) Neither A nor B.

2. Double-lap flares should be made whenever _____ system lines are replaced.
   (A) fuel
   (B) power steering
   (C) brake
   (D) Both B & C.

3. Technician A says that the tubing end should be held up when removing burrs. Technician B says that a reamer is the best tool for removing burrs. Who is right?
   (A) A only.
   (B) B only.
   (C) Both A & B.
   (D) Neither A nor B.

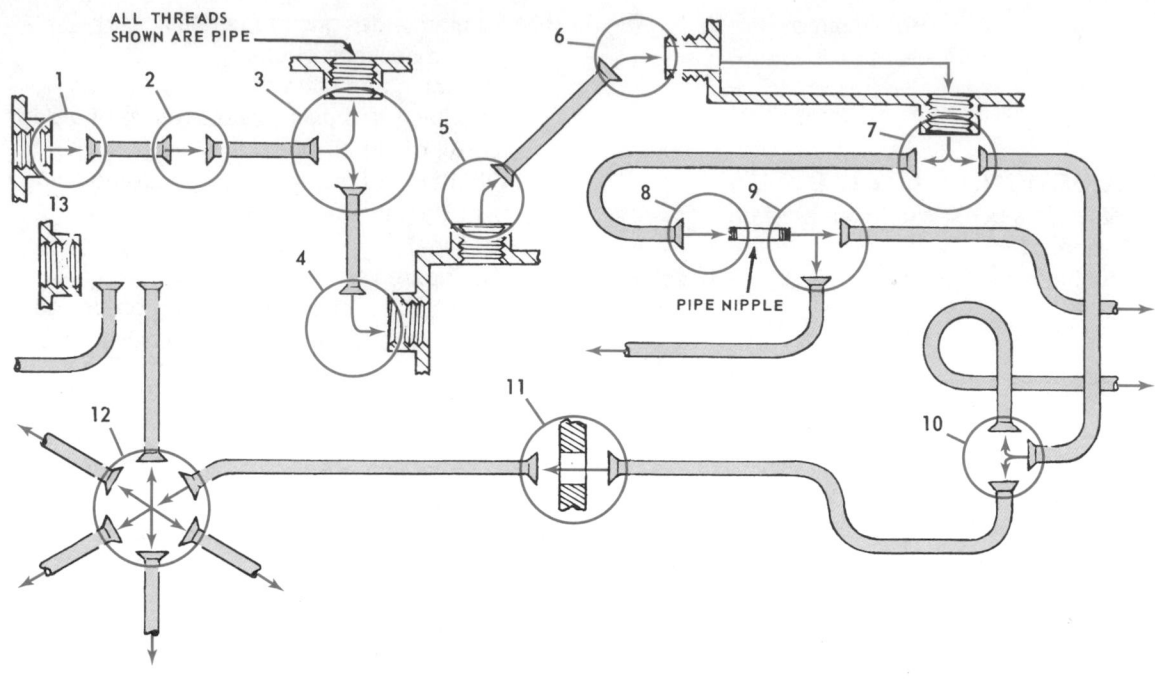

Male Run Tee.	Female Connector.	Female Double 90° Elbow.
Female 45° Elbow.	Union Cross.	45° Street Elbow.
Female Run Tee.	Female Branch Tee.	Pipe Coupling
Distribution Block.	Bulkhead Union.	Male 90° Elbow.
Male 45° Elbow.	Straight Union.	Male Branch Tee.
Male Connector.	Male Double 90° Elbow.	Union Tee.

4. Technician A says that a long nut will support tubing a greater distance from the actual connection than a short nut. Technician B says that straight runs of tubing should be made whenever possible. Who is right?
(A) A only.
(B) B only.
(C) Both A & B.
(D) Neither A nor B.

5. Technician A says that as long as the flare is the correct angle, it can be slightly cocked to one side. Technician B says that the nut should be placed on the tube before flaring. Who is right?
(A) A only.
(B) B only.
(C) Both A & B.
(D) Neither A nor B.

6. Tubing should be arranged to avoid all of the following, EXCEPT:
(A) exhaust system parts.
(B) moving parts.
(C) straight runs.
(D) the use of mounting clips.

7. Tubing fittings should be tightened with a

_____.
(A) pipe wrench
(B) flare-nut wrench
(C) crescent wrench
(D) box-end wrench

8. Technician A says that tubing bends that are close to the fitting should be made before the flaring operation. Technician B says that bends that are close to the fitting should start at least the distance of the fitting nut from the actual connection. Who is right?
(A) A only.
(B) B only.
(C) Both A & B.
(D) Neither A nor B.

9. Spring and screw clamps are used with

_____.
(A) power steering hoses
(B) heater hoses
(C) brake lines
(D) All of the above.

10. Technician A says that a hose that looks good on the outside will be good inside. Technician B says that hoses should be stored in a very warm area to drive out moisture. Who is right?
    (A) A only.
    (B) B only.
    (C) Both A & B.
    (D) Neither A nor B.

Suggested Activities

1. Practice bending tubing using various bending tools.
2. Inspect the diameter markings on various types of hoses and determine the most important diameter (inside or outside) for matching hoses to other vehicle parts.
3. Write a report on the different types of metals used in automotive tubing. Explain why different types of metal are used in brake systems, fuel lines, air conditioners, transmission cooler lines, and oil lines.
4. Cut off a piece of metal tubing using a hacksaw. Cut another piece using a tubing cutter. Is there a difference in the appearance? Which one made the best cut?
5. Try to make a tight 90° bend in a piece of metal tubing with your hands. Did the tubing remain round? Try it with both a spring and mechanical bender. Demonstrate proper bending techniques to your classmates.

Overview of an aluminum V-6 engine. This engine uses a wide variety of hoses, tubing, and wiring. (Honda)

9

Wire and Wiring

After studying this chapter, you will be able to:
- Identify different types of automotive wiring.
- Select the correct type of wiring for the job.
- Make basic wiring repairs.
- Read wiring diagrams.
- Perform basic circuit tests.

New wiring, when properly installed, is relatively trouble free. As the vehicle ages, the wires and connectors begin to deteriorate from exposure to heat, oil, gas, fumes, acid, moisture, dirt, salt, and vibration. Vehicles damaged by collision or fire often require extensive rewiring. All wiring used on vehicles can be divided into two major classes: primary wire and secondary wire. The use of printed circuits in modern vehicles is increasing and is replacing wire in many systems. A well-trained technician should be familiar with the various types of wire, wire sizes, and insulation. The technician should also be familiar with the various wire terminals, connections, and general installation procedures.

Primary Wire

Primary wire handles battery voltage. On modern vehicles it is usually 12 volts direct current. Older vehicles have 6 volt systems, some tractors and other agricultural machines have 8 volt systems, and some commercial vehicles have 24 volt systems. The primary wiring has sufficient insulation to prevent current loss at these voltages. All wiring circuits in the vehicle, with the exception of the ignition high-voltage circuit, are primary wires.

Primary Wire Construction

Primary wiring uses a stranded **conductor** made of soft copper. It is an excellent conductor, bends easily, and solders readily. Aluminum also is used to some extent. Stranded wires are made up of a number of small wires twisted together, instead of a single solid wire.

Most modern automotive wire **insulation** is made of plastic. Plastic is highly resistant to heat, cold, fumes, and aging. It strips (peels off) easily and offers excellent dielectric (nonconducting) properties. Primary wire insulation is designed to resist engine heat. The insulation on secondary wiring is much thicker than primary wire because of the high voltages used in the secondary system, **Figure 9-1.**

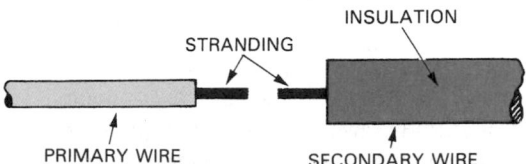

Figure 9-1. Compare the insulation on a primary and secondary wire. More insulation is required on secondary wires due to high voltage.

Wire Size

Every wire is assigned a number. The larger the number, the smaller the wire. This number applies to the size of the actual conductor and does not measure the thickness of the wire insulation. The **AWG** (American Wire Gage) is the commonly used standard for wire size. To find the gage of a solid wire, simply measure it with a micrometer. Then locate the measurement, or nearest size, on a wire gage chart. **Figure 9-2** shows a portion of an AWG chart. **Figure 9-3** shows a metric wire size conversion chart.

American Wire Gage	Wire Diameter In Inches	Cross-Sectional Area In Circular Mils
0000	.4600	211600
000	.40964	167800
00	.3648	133100
0	.32486	105500
1	.2893	83690
2	.25763	66370
3	.22942	52640
4	.20431	41740
5	.18194	33102
6	.16202	26250
8	.12849	16510
10	.10189	10380
12	.080808	6530
14	.064084	4107
16	.05082	2583
18	.040303	1624
20	.031961	1022
22	.025347	642.4
24	.0201	404.0
26	.01594	254.1
28	.012641	159.8
30	.010025	100.5

Figure 9-2. American Wire Gage chart (Not all sizes are shown). A technician can use this chart to find the proper gage of a wire if the wire diameter or the cross-sectional area is known.

METRIC WIRE SIZES (mm²)	AWG SIZES (AMERICAN WIRE GAUGE)
.22	24
.35	22
.5	20
.8	18
1.0	16
2.0	14
3.0	12
5.0	10
8.0	8
13.0	6
19.0	4
32.0	2

Figure 9-3. Note the relationship between AWG and metric wire sizes. (Chevrolet)

To find the gage of a stranded conductor, count the number of strands. With a micrometer, measure the diameter of one strand. Square this answer and multiply by the number of strands. This will give you the cross-sectional area of the conductor in circular mils, **Figure 9-2.** Locate this number (or the nearest one) on the chart. Move horizontally across the chart to the wire gage column to determine the gage. Special steel gauges are also available for quickly checking wire gage.

To avoid blown fuses, overheating, and possible fires, it is vital that the technician use a wire that can handle the current to be carried. Electrical load, line voltage, and wire length are the three important factors in determining correct wire gage or size.

Effect of Wire Size and Length

The electrical load on a wire is the sum of the individual loads of each unit serviced by that wire. As wire size increases, *resistance* decreases. Also, as wire length increases, resistance, as well as the resulting voltage drop increases. Resistance causes the conductor to heat. Excessive resistance can cause a wire to heat to the point where the insulation will melt and burn. To prevent high resistance and voltage drop, wire size must be increased as length is increased. With a given voltage and load, a 20 ft. long wire must use larger conductor than a 2 ft. long wire.

Selecting Correct Gage Wire

Most wire manufacturers furnish charts to assist the technician in proper gage selection, **Figure 9-4.** To use the chart shown, determine the total length of the wire needed. The wire lengths shown in the chart are for a single wire ground return. This means that a separate ground wire to the vehicle's battery is not needed, since the vehicle's frame or metal parts act as a return ground wire. If you are installing a two-wire circuit (one wire to a unit and another from the unit to ground), count the length of both wires.

Next compute the total electrical load of the circuit. Be certain to figure the load of all units in the circuit. If the load will fluctuate, use the peak load figure. The load may be figured in *amperes, watts,* or *candela* (the international term for candlepower). When the load is determined, look on the chart under the correct voltage column for the nearest listed load. Move across the chart horizontally to the nearest listed footage. This will give you the recommended gage.

Total Approx. Circuit Amperes 12V	Total Circuit Watts 12V	Total Candle Power 12V	Wire Gage (For Length in Feet)											
			3'	5'	7'	10'	15'	20'	25'	30'	40'	50'	75'	100'
1.0	12	6	18	18	18	18	18	18	18	18	18	18	18	18
1.5		10	18	18	18	18	18	18	18	18	18	18	18	18
2	24	16	18	18	18	18	18	18	18	18	18	18	16	16
3		24	18	18	18	18	18	18	18	18	18	18	14	14
4	48	30	18	18	18	18	18	18	18	18	16	16	12	12
5		40	18	18	18	18	18	18	18	18	16	14	12	12
6	72	50	18	18	18	18	18	18	16	16	16	14	12	10
7		60	18	18	18	18	18	18	16	16	14	14	10	10
8	96	70	18	18	18	18	18	16	16	16	14	12	10	10
10	120	80	18	18	18	18	16	16	16	14	12	12	10	10
11		90	18	18	18	18	16	16	14	14	12	12	10	8
12	144	100	18	18	18	18	16	16	14	14	12	12	10	8
15		120	18	18	18	18	14	14	12	12	12	10	8	8
18	216	140	18	18	16	16	14	14	12	12	10	10	8	8
20	240	160	18	18	16	16	14	14	12	10	10	10	8	6
22	264	180	18	18	16	16	12	12	10	10	10	8	6	6
24	288	200	18	18	16	16	12	12	10	10	10	8	6	6
30			18	16	16	14	10	10	10	10	10	6	4	4
40			18	16	14	12	10	10	8	8	6	6	4	2
50			16	14	12	12	10	10	8	8	6	6	2	2
100			12	12	10	10	6	6	4	4	4	2	1	1/0
150			10	10	8	8	4	4	2	2	2	1	2/0	2/0
200			10	8	8	6	4	4	2	2	1	1/0	4/0	4/0

Figure 9-4. Wire gage selection chart. Wire lengths shown are for a single wire ground return. (Belden Mfg. Co.)

Looking on the chart in **Figure 9-4,** if the vehicle has a 12V system, a computed electrical load of 20 amperes, and a wire length of 15 feet, you will find the recommended gage to be No. 14. For the same load and length in a 6V system, the recommended gage is 10. A 12V system uses a smaller gage wire than the 6V system used on very old cars. Using a larger gage than necessary will cause no particular harm unless the wire being replaced was originally designed to produce a specific resistance in the circuit.

Wiring Harness

A **wiring harness** is made up of various sections of system wiring with common wires (located in same area) either pulled through a loom (soft woven or plastic insulation tube), taped, or tied together. This speeds installation, makes a neat package, and secures the wire with a greatly reduced number of clamps or clips. **Figure 9-5** shows a typical wiring harness.

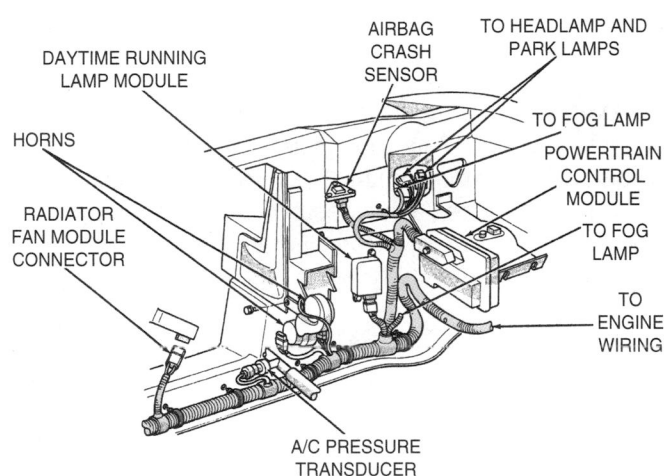

Figure 9-5. One type of automotive wiring harness. Note the use of looms and clips to secure the harness and fuse block. Also, note the plug-in type connectors.

Color Coding

All automotive wiring is **color coded** (each circuit is given a specific color or number of colors) to assist the technician in tracing various circuits. Manufacturers publish wiring diagrams that show all wires and color or colors of each. Wires can have a solid color or can be striped or banded. This makes it easier to identify and trace a wire.

After aging or exposure to dirt and oil, some wires are difficult to identify by color. In this case, trace the wire back to where it enters the harness. Then, cut away a small portion of the harness covering. This will expose a clean portion of the wire, so the color may be determined.

Wiring Diagrams

A **wiring diagram** is a drawing showing electrical units and the wires connecting them. Most diagrams also list the wire colors and terminal designations. Such a diagram is helpful when working on the wiring system. Wiring diagrams are available in various shop manuals and in some automotive reference books. **Figure 9-6** shows a typical wiring diagram.

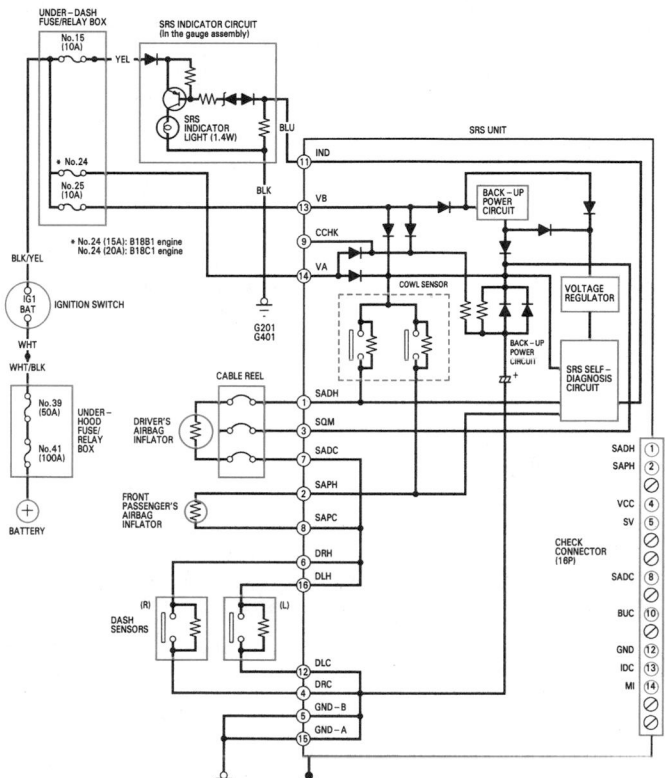

Figure 9-6. Note how each component is explained in an electrical service manual. Failure to use and understand these wiring diagrams can cause considerable electrical damage. (Honda)

Since the auto electrical system is becoming more complicated each year, many manufacturers break down the circuits into separate diagrams. This allows the technician to easily see the circuit's purpose and provides an overall diagram of the entire electrical system, **Figure 9-7.**

Electrical Wiring Symbols

There is a wide variation in the use of automotive electrical symbols. Some companies use their own drawings for some system components and standard symbols for others. The component's basic internal circuit is sometimes shown. In other diagrams, symbols are used for all components. **Figure 9-8** illustrates a number of typical symbols widely used in automotive electrical diagrams.

Primary Wire Terminals

Primary wire end **terminals** (connecting devices) are available in various shapes and sizes. Primary terminals may

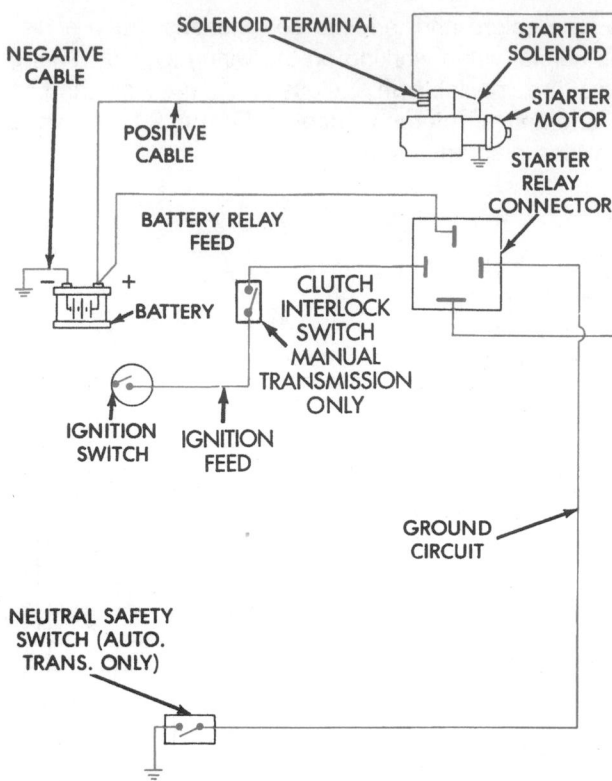

Figure 9-7. Wiring diagram for starter system. (Chrysler)

+	POSITIVE	(battery symbol)	BATTERY
−	NEGATIVE	(motor symbol)	MOTOR
(ground symbol)	GROUND	→)C100	CONNECTOR IDENTIFICATION
(fuse symbol)	FUSE	→	MALE CONNECTOR
(circuit breaker symbol)	CIRCUIT BREAKER	)—	FEMALE CONNECTOR
(capacitor symbol)	CAPACITOR	—⊃	DENOTES WIRE CONTINUES ELSEWHERE
(resistor symbol)	RESISTOR	⊢	WIRE GOES TO ONE OF TWO CIRCUITS
(rheostat symbol)	RHEOSTAT	⟨S100	SPLICE IDENTIFICATION
(coil symbol)	COIL	—○—	TERMINAL
(step up coil symbol)	STEP UP COIL	(condenser symbol)	CONDENSER
(wires crossing symbol)	WIRES CROSSING — NOT CONNECTED	(multiple connector symbol)	MULTIPLE CONNECTOR
(wires crossing symbol)	WIRES CROSSING — CONNECTED	(optional symbol)	OPTIONAL WIRING WITH WIRING WITHOUT
(closed switch symbol)	CLOSED SWITCH	88:88	DIGITAL READOUT
(open switch symbol)	OPEN SWITCH	(lamp symbol)	SINGLE FILAMENT LAMP
(transistor symbol)	TRANSISTOR	(lamp symbol)	DUAL FILAMENT LAMP
(pressure switch symbol)	PRESSURE SWITCH	(LED symbol)	L.E.D. — LIGHT EMITTING DIODE
(solenoid switch symbol)	SOLENOID SWITCH	(sensor symbol)	SENSOR
(diode symbol)	DIODE OR RECTIFIER	(fuel injector symbol)	FUEL INJECTOR

Figure 9-8. Study this chart of electrical symbols commonly used in automotive wiring diagrams. Learn these symbols; this is one of the marks of a well-trained technician. (Chrysler)

be classified as spade, lug, flag, roll, slide, blade, ring, and bullet types. They may either be solderable or solderless and are generally made of tin-plated copper. See **Figure 9-9.**

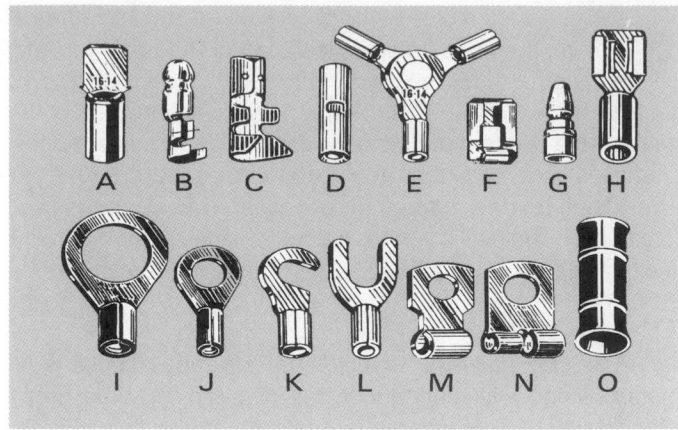

Figure 9-9. Common primary wire terminal types. A—Male slide. B—Bullet or snap-in. C—Female snap-on. D—Butt connector (must be crimped). E—Three-way connector. F—Female slide. G—Bullet. H—Female insulated slide. I—Lug. J—Ring. K—Hook. L—Spade. M—Roll. N—Flag. O—Female bullet connector. (Belden Mfg. Co.)

Plug-in Connectors

Modern vehicles use many *plug-in connectors,* sometimes called in-line connectors. Several plug-in connectors are shown in **Figure 9-10.** These connectors consist of a male and female connector which are plugged into each other. This simplifies removal and replacement, since there are no fasteners to loosen or tighten.

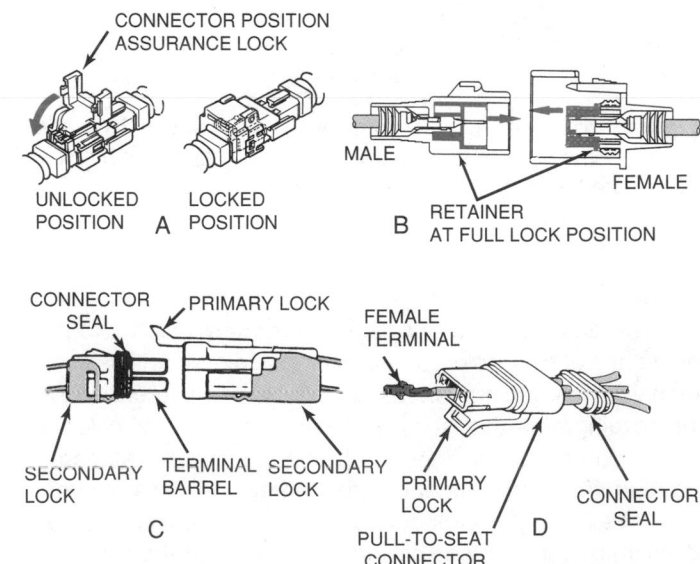

Figure 9-10. Several types of wire connectors. A—One type of airbag harness connector. It uses a connector position assurance (CPA) lock. This ensures that the connector is fully seated and will not vibrate or pull apart. B—Single wire connector shown with retainer in full lock position. Note the seals. C—Weather pack connector. D—Metri-pack connector. (Toyota and General Motors)

Many of these connectors are used to connect several wires at one junction. These are called multiple connectors or they are referred to by the number of wires in the connector, such as the three-wire or four-wire connector. It is almost impossible to plug the connectors in improperly, due to the connector's shape or the presence of special aligning lugs and slots in the connector. If a plug-in connector becomes damaged, it can be replaced with any one of the terminals shown in **Figure 9-9,** depending on the usage needed.

The plug-in connectors used with computer-controlled vehicles are often protected with *rubber grommets* that have as many as three sealing rings, **Figure 9-11.** This protects the connection from moisture and corrosion, since the voltages used in many computer-related components are very low. The slightest increase in resistance due to moisture and corrosion can affect computer operation. If a plug-in connector on a computer-controlled vehicle becomes damaged, a replacement connector from the manufacturer should be used.

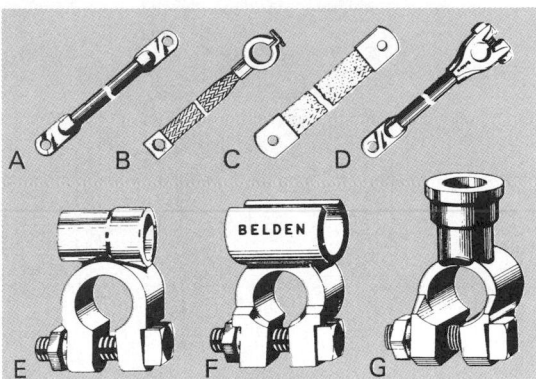

Figure 9-12. Typical battery cables and terminals. A—Solenoid-to-starter cable. B—Battery ground cable. C—Engine ground strap. D—Battery-to-solenoid cable. E—Closed barrel terminal. F—Open-split barrel terminal. G—Closed barrel terminal. Note that ground cables have no insulation and are of a woven construction. Regular insulated battery cable is also used for ground cables.

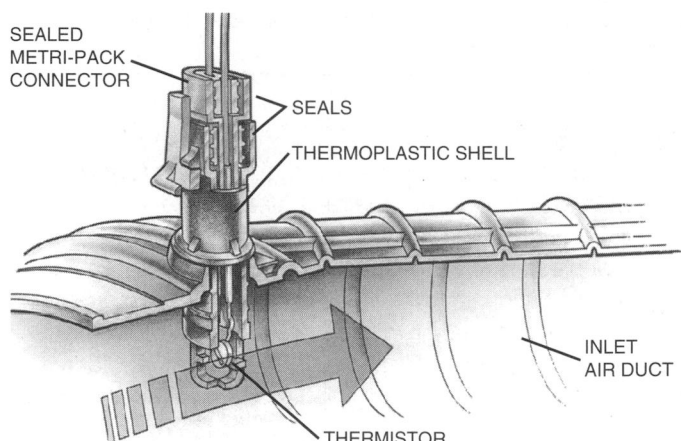

Figure 9-11. Cutaway view of one type of plug-in connector that uses rubber grommets for sealing the connection against dirt, water, etc. (Packard Electric)

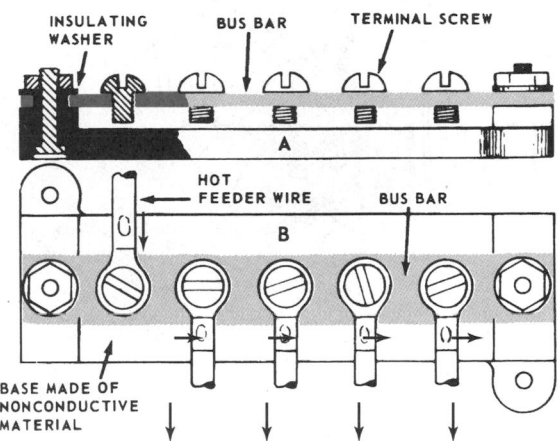

Figure 9-13. One type of terminal block. Notice how one hot wire is attached to bus bar, thus supplying current to other leads.

Battery Cable Terminals

New battery cables (with factory installed terminals) are generally used to replace a cable with a corroded, useless terminal. However, it is occasionally desirable to replace only the terminal. A number of different types are available, **Figure 9-12.**

Terminal Blocks

The *terminal block* is used to supply current to several circuits from one feeder source. The hot wire (wire connected to source of electricity) is attached to one terminal. This terminal is connected to all others by a bus bar (metal plate), **Figure 9-13.**

Junction Block

The *junction block* serves as a common connection point for a number of wires. It may be of the terminal

screw or the plug-in type. Unlike the terminal block, the junction block merely connects one wire to a corresponding wire on the other side. There is no common bus bar, **Figure 9-14.** Junction blocks are also known as power distribution centers.

Fuse Block

The *fuse block* is similar to the junction block except that a *fuse* is inserted between the connecting points. This protects each circuit against electrical overloads and groups a number of fuses in one location. **Figure 9-15A** illustrates a fuse block utilizing the compact miniature fuse. **Figure 9-15B** shows three different fuse elements.

Adding Fuses

When adding accessory units, such as fog lights, cellular telephones, and CD players, and no provision was

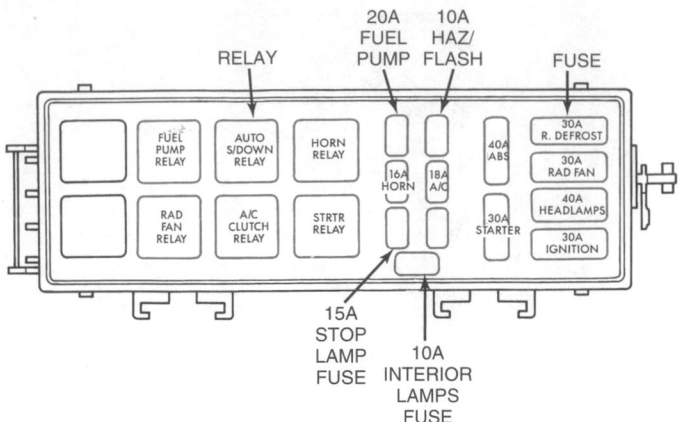

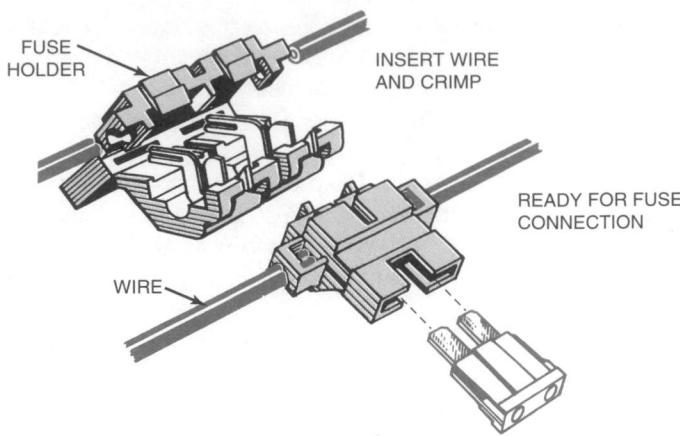

Figure 9-14 In modern automobiles, junction blocks contain fuses and relays to various vehicle systems. (Chrysler)

Figure 9-16. Installing an in-line fuse. Always try to fuse as close to the source as practical.

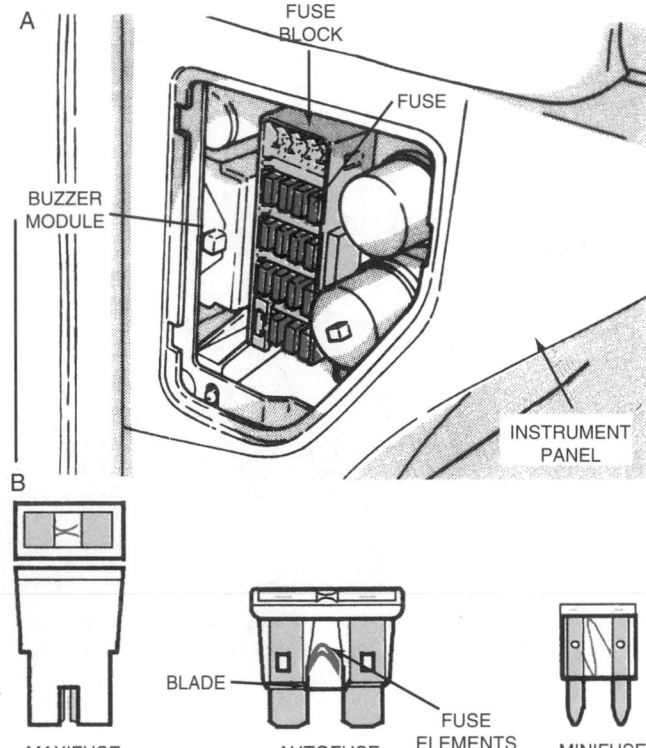

> **Caution: Never tap (connect) into an existing circuit to power an accessory. This could overload the system's fuse or circuit breaker and could cause damage to the system. Connect into a terminal block or install a battery cable with an auxiliary lead to power an accessory.**

Fusible Link

In some cases, a circuit is protected by a *fusible link.* A fusible link is a special wire that acts like a fuse. The wire is covered with Hypalon insulation. When the fusible link is subjected to an overload, it begins to heat up, causing the insulation to blister and smoke. If the overload is continued, the insulation will rupture and the fusible link will burn out, breaking the circuit. Follow the manufacturers recommended repair and replacement procedures carefully, **Figure 9-17.**

Figure 9-15. A—Fuse block incorporating a number of miniaturized fuses. B—Several different types of fuses used in the automobile. The maxifuse is usually found in junction blocks. Some maxifuses are a larger version of the autofuse. Autofuses and minifuses are typically found in the fuse block, but are sometimes used in junction blocks. (Dodge, Pontiac)

made for them in the original wiring, place a fuse in the circuit. Fuse as close as possible to the electrical source to reduce the possibility of a short between the fuse and source. A small fuse block or an *in-line fuse* can be installed. Be sure to inform the owner as to the location of the new fuse, **Figure 9-16.** If it is desired to have the accessory inoperative when the ignition key is *off,* it must be connected so that it can be turned off by the key switch circuit. Always follow the installation instructions for the accessory.

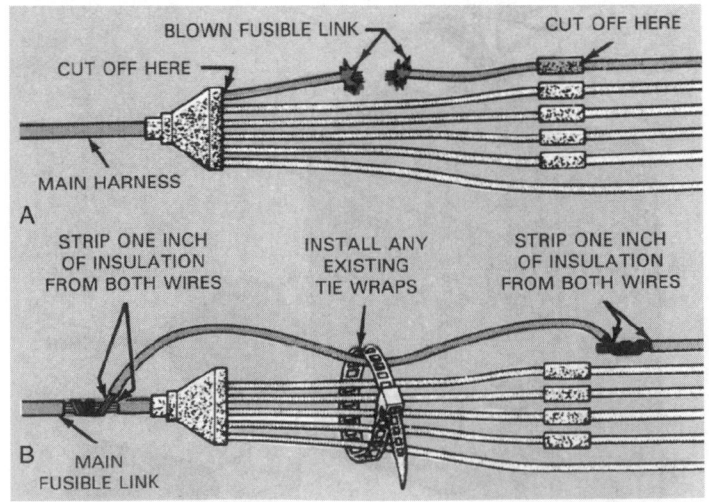

Figure 9-17. A fusible link helps prevent electrical system damage due to overloads, shorts, etc. A—Note how outer insulation has melted off the link. B—Repair requires cutting off the damaged area and installing a new fusible link section. Follow the manufacturer's repair procedures. (Chrysler)

Circuit Breaker

A *circuit breaker* feeds the current through a bimetallic strip, through a set of points, and on to the remainder of the circuit.

When amperage exceeds that for which the breaker is built, the bimetallic strip heats and bends to separate the points. When the strip cools, it will straighten out, closing the points and reestablishing the circuit. If the overload condition still exists, the strip will heat and reopen the points, **Figure 9-18**.

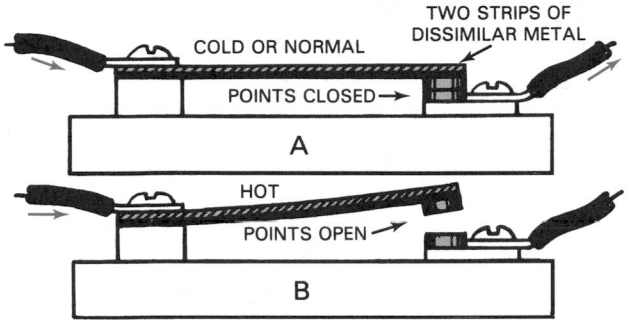

Figure 9-18. Operation of a simple circuit breaker. A—The breaker is carrying a normal system load. The contacts are closed, and the circuit is complete. B—The circuit breaker is overloaded, heating the bimetallic strip. The strip bends upward, separating the points and breaking the circuit.

The circuit breaker will open and close quite rapidly. This gives it an advantage over a fuse when used on a headlamp circuit. With the fuse, an overload will burn out the fuse and the headlights will go out until the fuse is replaced. This could cause an accident. The circuit breaker will cause the lights to flicker on and off rapidly but will still produce enough light to allow the driver to pull safely off the road. A defective circuit breaker should be replaced with one of the same construction and electrical load capacity. See **Figure 9-19**.

Joining Primary Terminals and Wires

After the wire gage is determined, select the connecting terminal. The terminal must be of proper size and type

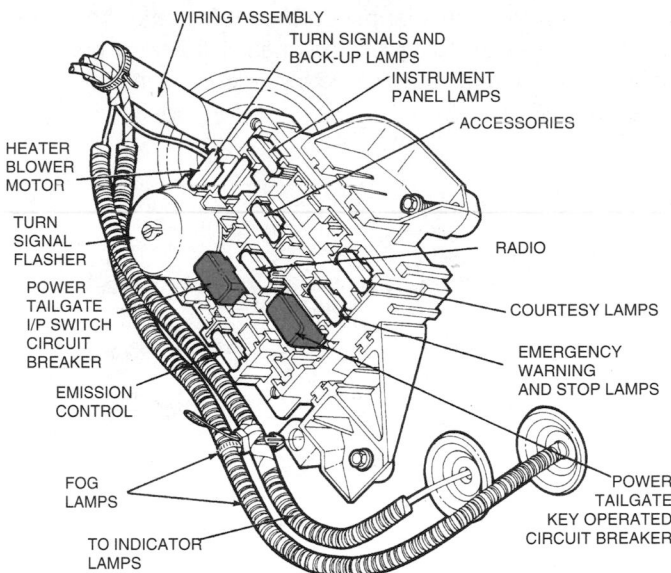

Figure 9-19. This fuse panel contains two power tailgate circuit breakers.

for the unit connecting post or prongs. It must have sufficient current capacity and should be heavy enough to prevent breakage through normal wire flexing and vibration. **Figure 9-20** shows some common errors in wire terminal selection.

Arrange terminals so they have clearance from metal parts that could ground or short them out. On critical applications or where heavy vibration is present, use a terminal such as the ring type that completely encircles the post. If the terminal retaining nut loosens, the wire will not fall off.

Terminals and wires may be connected by either *crimping* or *soldering* in place. Crimping is fast and forms a good connection. Soldering, if properly done, forms an excellent connection and is recommended in some cases. It is possible to both solder and crimp a connection. Solder forms an electrical path and is not depended on for strength.

Slide and bullet connectors are used where the wires must be separated at some future time. The appropriate slide or bullet terminals are crimped or soldered to the

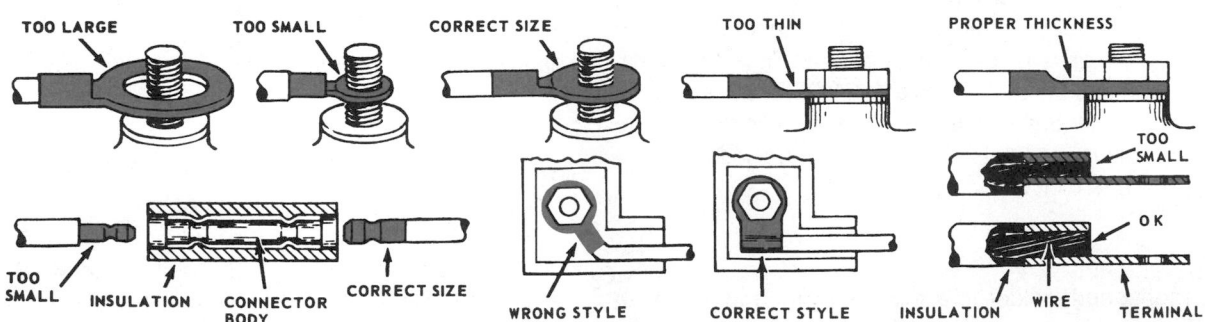

Figure 9-20. Common errors in terminal selection. Poor terminal selection can lead to problems. Select the correct terminal for the job.

wires. They are then snapped into the connector body, and the two halves are plugged together. If the wire ends are being joined permanently, soldering or butt connectors work very well, **Figure 9-21.** Aluminum wire requires crimped terminals.

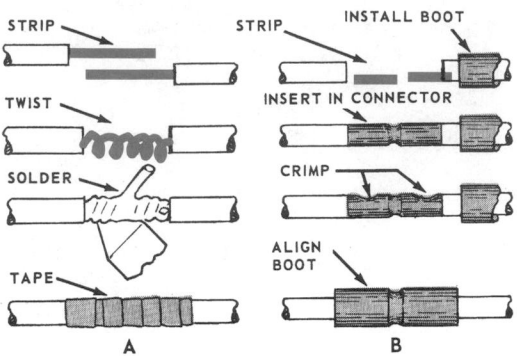

Figure 9-21. Wires can be joined by soldering (A) or using a crimp-type connector(B).

Crimping Terminals

A *crimping tool* is shown in **Figure 9-22.** It will cut and strip the wire as well as form a proper crimp. To use the crimping tool, first strip the insulation back for a distance equal to the length of the terminal barrel. Then push the wire into the barrel. While being held in, place the crimping tool over the spot to be crimped. Be sure to use the proper crimping edge. Squeeze the handles together to firmly crimp the terminal to the wire, **Figure 9-23.** Follow the tool manufacturer's instructions. Use the correct barrel size for the wire used.

 Caution: Never crimp a wire with the cutting edge of a pair of pliers. This would crimp the barrel but weaken it.

Soldering

Soldering can be defined as the act of joining two pieces of metal through the use of lead, tin, and other alloys. There is no actual fusion (melting together) involved. When the base metal is heated to the correct temperature, the solder dissolves a minute "skin" on the metal. Upon cooling, the solder and "skin" amalgamate (mix together), forming a tight bond. See **Figure 9-24.** The pieces to be soldered should fit together as closely as possible. The less solder separating the parts, the stronger the joint. A wire being soldered is pictured in **Figure 9-32.**

Solder

As mentioned, solder is a mixture of tin and lead with small amounts of zinc, copper, aluminum, and other substances. The percentage of lead to tin affects both the melting point (point at which solder becomes a full liquid) and the plastic range (temperature span from lowest point at

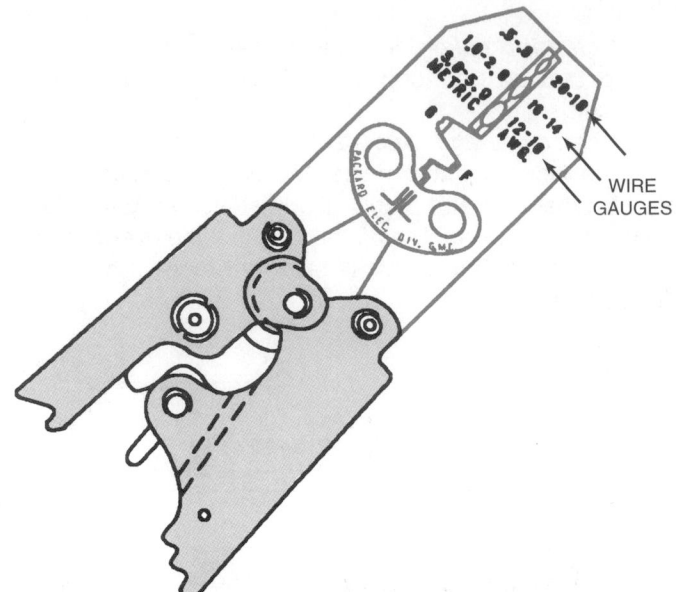

Figure 9-22. Hand-operated crimping tool. Note that the jaws provide both metric and AWG size information.

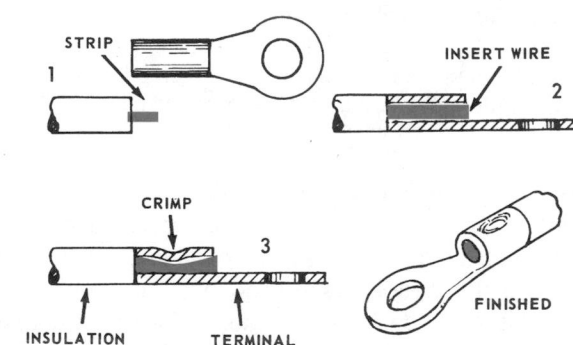

Figure 9-23. Crimping a terminal. Follow the tool manufacturer's instructions.

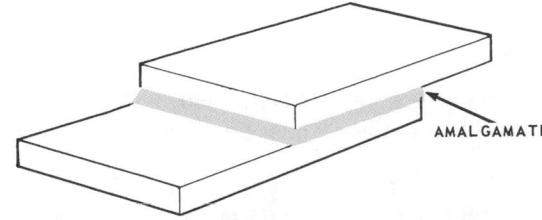

Figure 9-24. The solder and metal "skin" amalgamate upon cooling thus forming a tight bond.

which solder becomes mushy or plastic to the highest point just before plastic mixture liquefies).

You will note from **Figure 9-25** that pure lead melts at 621°F (328°C). Pure tin melts at 450°F (232°C). A mixture of about 63% tin to 37% lead will melt at 361°F (183°C). Study the chart in **Figure 9-25.** Temperature and plastic range are affected by alloying in different proportions. Commonly used solders are 40/60 (40% tin, 60% lead), 50/50, and 60/40. Flux core wire solder (wire solder with a hollow

TIN-LEAD FUSION DIAGRAM

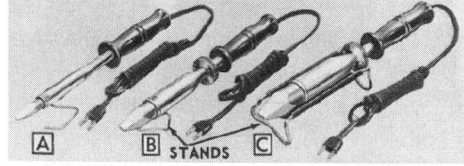

Figure 9-25. Tin-lead alloy plastic range and melting point chart. (Kester)

center filled with flux), solid wire solder, and solder ground into fine grains and mixed with flux, are used for general soldering.

Acid core solder is excellent for use on radiators and other applications where a corrosive and electrical conductive residue (flux remaining on work after soldering) is not harmful. However, *rosin core* solder or *resin core* solder must be used for all electrical work. The residue will not cause corrosion or conduct electricity. A special flux is required for soldering aluminum wires.

Soldering obviously heats the metal, which accelerates oxidization (surface of metal combining with oxygen in air). This leaves a thin film of oxide on the surface that tends to reject solder. It is the job of the flux to remove this oxide and prevent the reoccurrence during the soldering process.

Soldering Irons

The **soldering iron**, sometimes called a copper, should be of ample size for the job. An iron that is too small will require excessive time to heat the work and may never heat it properly. The proper size iron will bring the metal up to the correct soldering heat (around 525°-575°F or 274°-302°C) quickly and will produce a good solder joint. Electric irons are fast and efficient. A 35- to 100-watt size will handle most wire soldering jobs. See **Figure 9-26.** For electrical wiring, a *soldering gun* as shown in **Figure 9-27** is ideal. The tip reaches soldering heat in a matter of seconds.

Preparing to Solder

All traces of insulation, corrosion, and rust must be removed. Removing the insulation will usually expose

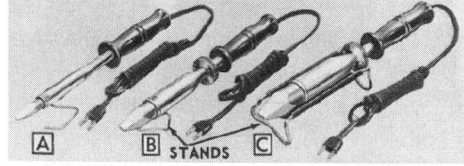

Figure 9-26. Handy size soldering irons. A—Light duty. B—Medium duty. C—Heavy duty. (Snap-On Tools)

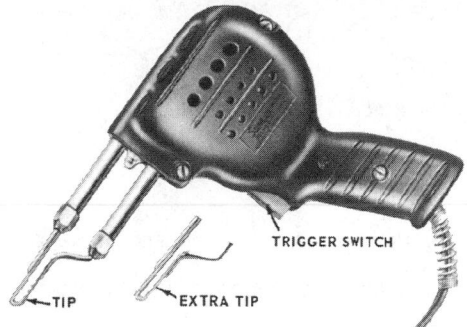

Figure 9-27. A soldering gun such as this works fast. (Snap-On Tools)

enough clean wire for soldering. Remember that good soldering requires clean, well-fitted surfaces. The soldering iron tip is made of copper. Through the solvent action of solder and prolonged heating, it will pit and corrode. An oxidized or corroded tip will not satisfactorily transfer heat from the iron to the work. It should be cleaned and tinned. Use a file and dress the tip down to the bare copper. File the surfaces smooth and flat. See **Figure 9-28.**

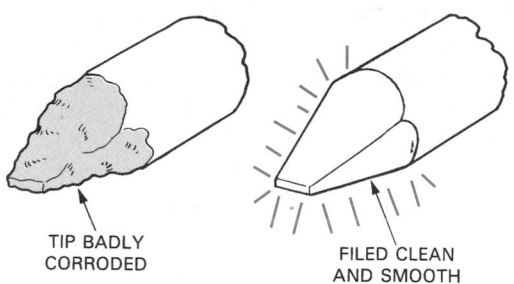

Figure 9-28. File soldering tip surfaces flat and smooth before tinning.

Plug in the iron. When the tip color begins to change to brown and light purple, dip the tip in and out of a can of soldering flux (rosin core). Quickly apply rosin core wire solder to all surfaces. If no paste flux is available, use rosin core wire solder. However, dipping the tip in flux provides a faster and better tinning job.

The iron must be at operating temperature to tin properly. When the iron is at the proper temperature, solder will melt quickly and flow freely. Never try to solder until the iron is properly tinned. See **Figure 9-29.** If a surplus of solder adheres to the tip during tinning, wipe off the excess with a rough textured cotton rag. Some shops use a block of sal ammoniac to aid in tinning. The hot iron is rubbed on the block as solder is applied.

Soldering Technique

The iron must be held so that the flat surface of the tip is in full contact with the work. This will permit a maximum transfer of heat. Look at **Figure 9-30.** Apply the wire solder at the edge of the iron where it contacts the work. This will release the flux where it will do the most good. Flowing sol-

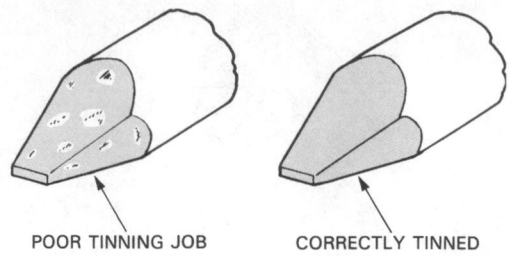

POOR TINNING JOB   CORRECTLY TINNED

Figure 9-29.   Tip must be properly tinned before soldering.

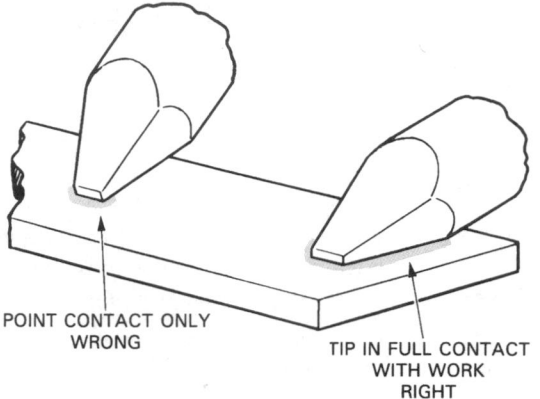

POINT CONTACT ONLY
WRONG

TIP IN FULL CONTACT
WITH WORK
RIGHT

Figure 9-30.   Hold the soldering tip flat against the workpiece.

der at this point will also provide a mechanical bond between the iron and the work. This will speed up heat transfer, **Figure 9-31.**

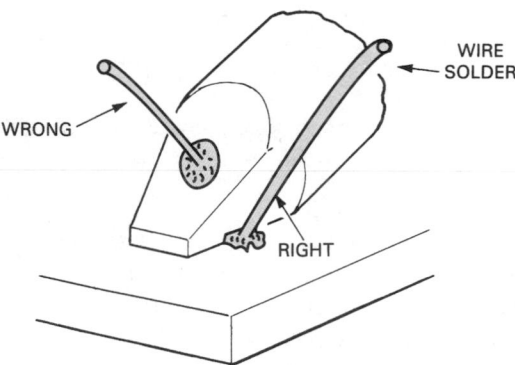

WRONG

WIRE
SOLDER

RIGHT

Figure 9-31.   Apply solder to the edge of the iron where it contacts the workpiece.

The workpiece to be joined should be heated so the solder is melted in the metals to be soldered together. When this is done, solder will flow readily and a good solder joint will result. If the solder melts slowly and is pasty looking, the work is *not* hot enough. This can result in a ***cold solder joint.*** If using a gas flame to heat the parts, be careful to avoid overheating.

Soldering Wire Splices

To solder wire splices, first make sure the wires are twisted together firmly. Apply the tip flat against the splice. Apply rosin core wire solder to the flat of the iron where it contacts the wire. As the wire heats, the solder will flow through the splice, **Figure 9-32.**

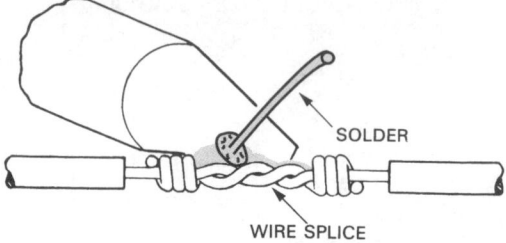

SOLDER

WIRE SPLICE

Figure 9-32.   Soldering a wire splice. Be sure to heat the wire, not the solder.

Soldering Terminals

Terminals do not have to be specially designed for soldering, but the lip-type terminal tang lends itself to soldering better than the closed or open barrel tang, **Figure 9-33.**

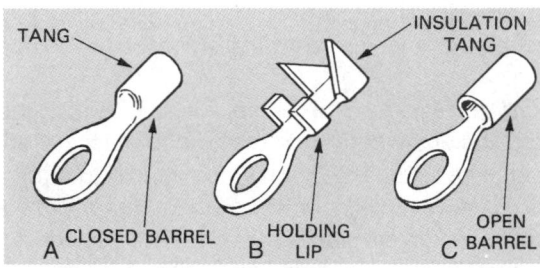

TANG   INSULATION
                                             TANG

A CLOSED BARREL   B HOLDING   C OPEN
                            LIP   BARREL

Figure 9-33.   Study these different terminal tangs. A—Closed barrel. B—Lip-type. C—Open barrel.

To solder the lip type, strip the wire back as shown in **Figure 9-34A.** Insert the wire as shown in **Figure 9-34B.** Crimp the wire holding lips, one after the other, tightly over the wire. Then, carefully fold the insulation tang around the insulated portion of the wire, **Figures 9-34C** and **9-34D.** Using rosin core wire solder, place a drop of solder on the holding lips. Hold the iron in contact with the drop until it flows into the lips and wire. Do not hold the iron in contact with the terminal any longer than necessary. This tends to melt the insulation.

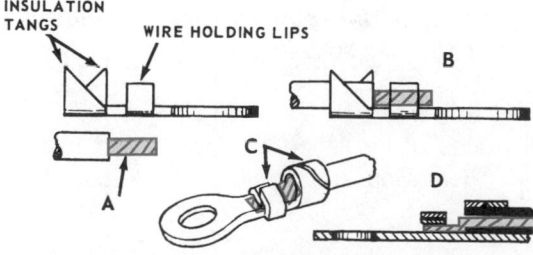

INSULATION
TANGS   WIRE HOLDING LIPS

                                              B

A   C   D

Figure 9-34.   The lip-type terminal design allows for easy soldering.

When soldering the open barrel type terminal, strip the wire as for crimping. Tin the exposed wire end (coat with a thin layer of solder) and insert the wire in the barrel. If both crimping and soldering the barrel connector is desired, crimp before soldering. While holding the exposed end upright, heat the socket with the iron. While heating, keep wire solder against socket end. When the solder melts, allow it to flow into the barrel. Hold the iron in place for a few seconds to allow the solder to bond to both the barrel and wire. See **Figure 9-35.** The closed barrel type terminal should be heated, and a small amount of solder should be allowed to flow into the hole. While keeping the barrel hot, press the tinned wire into the hole. Hold the iron in place for several seconds to ensure bonding.

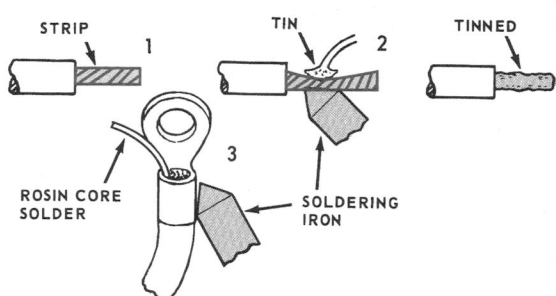

Figure 9-35. When soldering a barrel-type terminal, make sure the wire is tinned before installing. The terminal may be crimped along with soldering, but crimping should be done before soldering.

After Soldering

When joining two wires or terminals by soldering, be careful not to disturb them until the solder has set (cooled until it is solid). If they are moved while the solder is still in a pasty state, it can cause fracture lines that will result in a weak joint.

General Rules for Good Soldering

- Clean the area to be soldered.
- Make a good mechanical connection with the wires before soldering.
- Soldering iron must be of sufficient size and must be hot.
- Soldering iron tip must be tinned.
- Apply full surface of tip flat to work.
- Heat the wires to be joined until solder flows readily.
- Use the proper solder and flux for the job at hand.
- Apply enough solder to form a secure bond but do not waste.
- Do not move wires or connectors until solder sets.
- Place the hot iron in a stand or on a protective pad.
- Unplug electric iron as soon as you are finished.

Use **heat-shrink tubing** or tape to insulate soldered wires and noninsulated connectors. When an insulator boot is to cover the terminal tang or when attaching slide-type terminals that will be snapped back into a housing, always slide the boot, housing, etc., on the wire before soldering.

Installing Primary Wire

When installing primary wire, use the following guidelines. Make certain all terminals and posts are clean. Connect all terminals and tighten securely. Lock washers should be used on all screw and post connections. Slip insulator boots, where used, over exposed terminal tangs. Shove slide or bullet-type connectors together tightly and check to see that the connection is secure.

Keep all wiring away from the exhaust system, oily areas, and moving parts. Secure all wire with mounting clips or clamps. Fasten wire in enough spots to prevent excessive vibration and chafing.

Where the wire must pass through a hole in sheet metal, install a rubber grommet. When a wire must pass from the fender well or splash shield to the engine, leave enough slack to allow the engine to rock on the mounts without pulling the wire tight. If a number of primary wires travel in a common path, pull them through a loom (woven fiber or plastic conduit) or tape them together. See **Figure 9-36.**

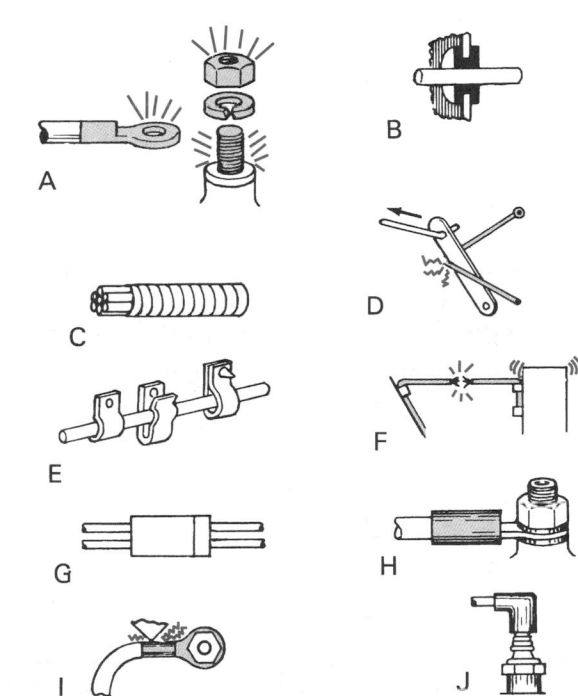

Figure 9-36. Wiring installation hints. A—Connections must be clean and bright. B—Use grommets to protect wire passing through thick metal. C—Tape common wires together. D—Avoid moving parts when locating wires. E—Support with suitable clamps. F—Allow some slack when wire runs to a unit that moves. G—Connectors must be pushed together tightly. H—Use boots on terminal tangs and select terminals heavy enough for job. I—Tighten terminals in a position away from metal—use boots also. J—Handle resistance plug wires by grasping the boots.

Secondary Wire

Secondary wire is used in the ignition system high voltage circuit—coil to distributor and distributor to spark plugs. Since voltages in secondary wire can exceed 50,000 volts, secondary wire has a heavy layer of insulation to protect against shorting to the engine block or another vehicle part. Insulation also limits **corona,** which is the loss of electrons to the surrounding air. Excessive corona could impart sufficient current into an adjacent wire to cause it to fire a plug. This is known as crossfiring.

Even with good insulation it is important to arrange spark plug leads so that leads to cylinders that fire consecutively are separated. Modern secondary wire uses a conductor, or core, made of carbon-impregnated string or fiberglass, and elastomer (plastic). The carbon impregnated string and elastomer type have a controlled resistance (between 4000 and 20,000 ohms per foot) in the secondary circuit to reduce radio interference.

> **Caution:** When working on the ignition system, handle resistance wires carefully. Sharp bending and pulling can separate the conductor, ruining the wire. When removing or installing such leads, grip the insulation boot, not the wire.

The secondary wires on older vehicles often had a metal core, usually copper. Copper core secondary wires are sometimes available as an aftermarket (nonfactory) item. *Resistance wire* should always be used on modern vehicles. They may be identified by such letters as IRS and TVRS stamped on the insulating material. Secondary wiring will be discussed in more detail in Chapter 18.

Secondary Wire Terminals

Figure 9-37 shows various secondary wire terminals and boots. The boots protect against moisture and dirt which can cause flashover (spark jumping to ground along outside of plug porcelain top). Ready-made sets often bond the boots to both the terminal and wire for added protection against flashover. When selecting plug end terminals, choose a shape that will snap on the plug without bending the wire sharply. The same applies to distributor terminals, also shown in **Figure 9-37.**

Joining Secondary Terminals and Wires

Although some plug end terminals have a sharp barb that is designed to penetrate the insulation and contact the wire (as well as providing holding power), it is good practice to strip the insulation enough to allow the wire to be bent around and laid against the outside of the insulation. This ensures a good electrical contact. See **Figure 9-38A.**

Some distributor end terminals have the barbs at the sides and end, **Figure 9-38B.** Wire stripping is not necessary if the barb is carefully inserted into the wire end. When attaching terminals to resistance-type plug wires, always use staples. The staple is pushed into the wire, ensuring a large contact area with the special conductor, **Figure 9-38C.**

Installing Secondary Wire

When installing secondary wires, avoid sharp bends. If the wires pass through a metal conduit (tube), the conduit should be securely grounded. Install or remove the plug wires by grasping the insulation boots and not the wire. Make sure that the terminals snap tightly on the plugs and the distributor ends are all the way in the housing towers. Follow the manufacturer's instructions in arranging the plug wires. If two leads going to cylinders that fire consecutively (one after the other) are together, there is a danger of crossfiring, especially as the wires age.

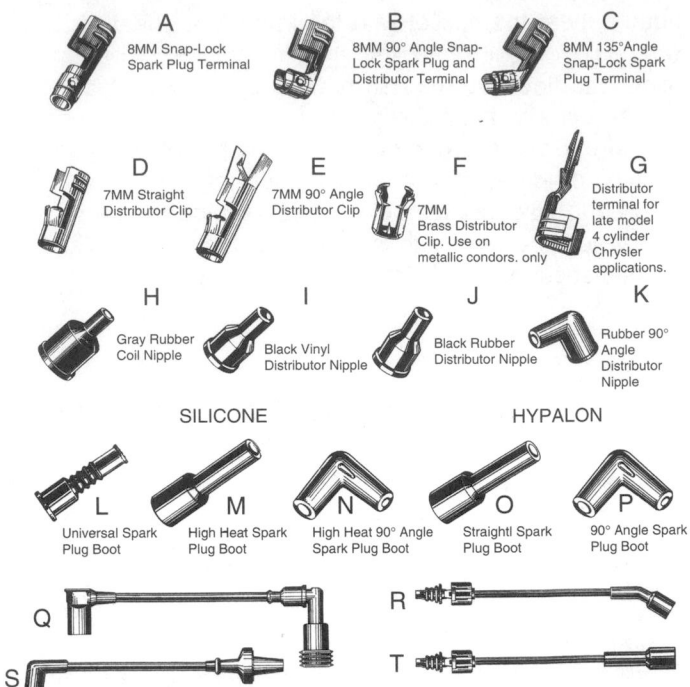

Figure 9-37. A-G—Spark plug wire terminals. H-P—Assortment of spark plug, coil, and distributor nipples (boots) for various applications. Q-T—Several replacement spark plug wire assemblies with boots and terminals attached. (Napa-Belden)

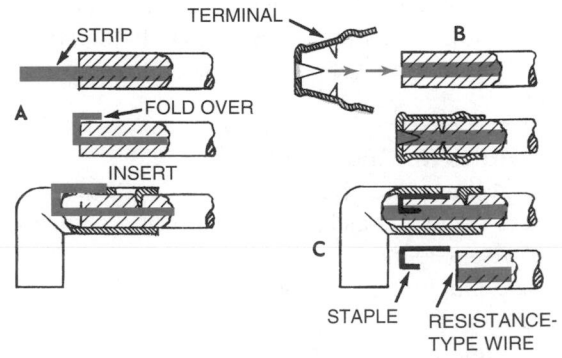

Figure 9-38. Attaching secondary wire terminals. A—Attaching a plug end terminal to a regular (nonresistance) spark plug wire. B—Attaching a distributor end terminal. C—Using a staple when attaching a terminal to resistance-type wire.

Printed Circuit

The *printed circuit* uses a nonconducting panel upon which the electrical components are affixed. The components are then connected by either thin conductor strips cemented to the panel or by a special electrically conductive material "printed" in the desired circuit patterns. This eliminates using a maze of wires to connect numerous small, complex components. Printed circuits permit a great number of individual circuits in a very small area. The modern auto uses printed circuits in such areas as engine and body control computers, audio accessories, and dash instrumentation. **Figure 9-39** illustrates the use of a printed circuit in a dash instrument cluster.

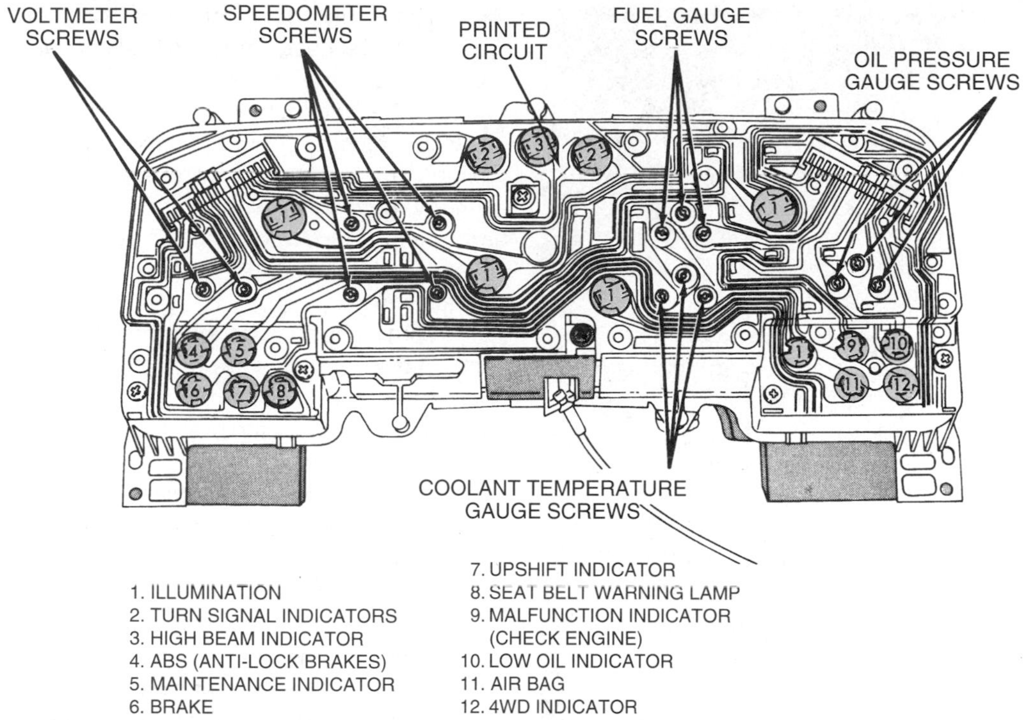

VOLTMETER SCREWS

SPEEDOMETER SCREWS

PRINTED CIRCUIT

FUEL GAUGE SCREWS

OIL PRESSURE GAUGE SCREWS

COOLANT TEMPERATURE GAUGE SCREWS

1. ILLUMINATION
2. TURN SIGNAL INDICATORS
3. HIGH BEAM INDICATOR
4. ABS (ANTI-LOCK BRAKES)
5. MAINTENANCE INDICATOR
6. BRAKE

7. UPSHIFT INDICATOR
8. SEAT BELT WARNING LAMP
9. MALFUNCTION INDICATOR (CHECK ENGINE)
10. LOW OIL INDICATOR
11. AIR BAG
12. 4WD INDICATOR

Figure 9-39. Rear view of a printed circuit instrument panel. (Dodge)

Troubleshooting Wiring

Many problems throughout the car can be traced to faulty wiring. Loose or corroded terminals; frayed, pinched, bare, or broken wires; and cracked, oil-soaked, or porous insulation are the most frequent causes.

 Caution: Do not pierce a wire to check a circuit. Piercing wires allows moisture and dirt to enter the wire, which can change the circuit's resistance. Doing this on a computer-controlled vehicle could cause major damage to the vehicle's computer.

Checking Wires and Connections

When troubleshooting a problem, visually check the wires, fuses, and connections carefully. Wires can separate with no break in the insulation (especially resistance-type secondary wire). A terminal may be tight and still be corroded. A fusible link may burn out at one end instead of in the center. Use a wiring diagram. A experienced technician is patient and thorough in any troubleshooting.

Wires and connections must occasionally be checked for resistance, *voltage drop, short circuits* or *near-short circuits.* These checks can be made with an *ohmmeter, voltmeter,* or *ammeter.* This will be discussed in the chapters where these tests pertain.

Checking for Continuity

A small *test light* (battery operated) may be used to test wires for internal breaks. Hold one prod against one end of the wire and place the other prod against the other end. If the test lamp burns, the wire is continuous or said to have *continuity.* This simple test light is also handy for

checking fuses, finding shorted field windings, and for tracing wires where there are no color codes. **Figure 9-40** illustrates several checks.

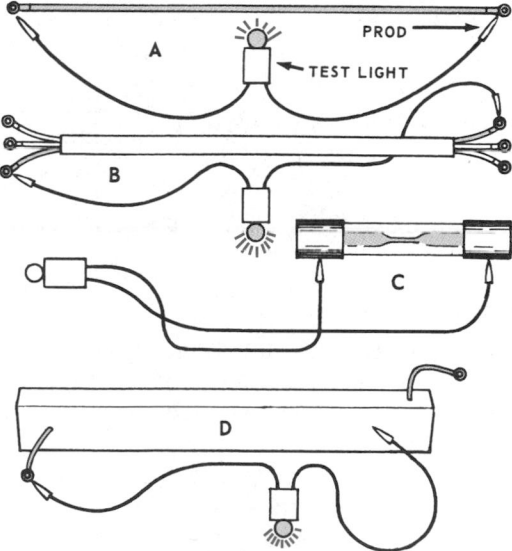

Figure 9-40. Some wiring checks using a simple test light. A—Prods on ends of wire. Lamp lights indicating wire is continuous. B—Prod held on the end of one wire and the other prod touched to various wire ends. When lamp lights, proper wire end is identified. C—Checking a fuse. Prods in place, lamp does not light. This indicates a faulty fuse. In this case, fuse will be burnt out at end instead of usual narrow center section. D—One prod touched to a wire end and the other prod to ground. If lamp lights, wire is shorted out.

Tech Talk

One of the most common vehicle electrical problems is bad grounds. Current must go through the vehicle's frame, body, or engine to return to the battery. If a ground is bad, the circuit will be open. Even slight resistance will often be enough to affect the performance of electrical units throughout the vehicle, especially on-board computer systems, which operate from very low voltages. Sometimes, a bad ground will ruin transmission or engine bearings, shift or brake cables, or other nonelectrical parts. This is because the electricity tries to return to the battery through these parts, causing them to overheat or transfer metal. The electricity may even try to ground through the engine cooling system, causing severe corrosion.

If any electrical problem is evident, start your troubleshooting process by checking the grounds for clean, tight connections. Often, someone has attached the negative battery cable to an exhaust manifold bolt. The heat from the exhaust gas causes a bad connection almost immediately. Make sure that there is a ground cable between the engine and body or between the body and the negative battery terminal. These grounds are often overlooked when a battery cable is changed. Ground cables between the engine and the body are sometimes pulled loose if one of the engine mounts breaks

Methods for checking for bad grounds are covered in later chapters. If you suspect that a bad ground exists between any part of the vehicle and the battery negative, you can run an extra ground wire. Simply connect a heavy gage wire (at least 8 or 10 gage) between the negative battery terminal and the body or between the body and an unpainted spot on the engine. An extra ground will not hurt any part of the electrical system.

Spade, lug, flag, roll, slide, ring, bullet, and push-on terminals are used on vehicle electrical systems. Terminal blocks allow one feeder wire to service a number of other wires. These can be of the screw, bullet, or slide type. Junction blocks provide a central connecting point for a number of wires. Fuse blocks give protection against circuit overloads. A wiring harness contains a number of wires either taped together or pulled through a loom. This keeps common wires neatly arranged and facilitates installation.

Wire ends may be joined by soldering or crimping. Be certain that terminals are of the correct style and size. They may be soldered or crimped to the wire. When crimping, use a suitable crimping tool. Solder is a mixture of lead and tin in varying amounts. Joints to be soldered must fit well. Solder has little strength if the parts are far apart. Wire solder, with flux-filled center core, is desirable.

Flux helps remove oxides and also prevents the formation of oxides while soldering. Be sure to use solder with rosin core only on electrical work. The joint to be soldered must be clean and dry. Lay the flat tip of the iron against the work and apply wire solder where the iron and work contact. Solder must run and tin freely. Do not move work while it is cooling.

Secondary wire (fiberglass, carbon impregnated thread, and elastomer stranding with very heavy insulation) is used on the ignition high tension circuit. Use staples when installing terminals on resistance-type secondary leads. Handle secondary resistance wire carefully.

When installing wires, keep away from heat, oily areas, and moving parts. Terminals must be clean and tight. Use clips to prevent chafing and excessive vibration. When adding accessories, fuse the circuit as close to the source as possible. Do not tap into an existing circuit to power an accessory. Printed circuits are increasingly used on modern vehicles.

Clean, tight connections, with proper size wire and good insulation, are imperative. When troubleshooting, always check connections and insulation. Replace cracked, spongy, or frayed wires. Many wiring checks can be made with a simple test light.

Summary

Primary wire (copper stranding, relatively thin insulation) is used for circuits handling battery voltage. Plastic is widely used for insulation. All automotive wire uses a stranded wire conductor.

The AWG (American Wire Gage) is determined by the cross-sectional area in circular mils. The larger the AWG number, the smaller the size. A micrometer or wire gauge can be used to determine wire size.

Automotive electrical systems are color coded. Use an accurate wiring diagram for troubleshooting or replacing wires. Electrical load, line voltage, and wire length must be taken into consideration when choosing wire gage. A wire gage chart will assist in making the right selection. Remember that undersize wires increase resistance, reduce unit efficiency, and can overheat or burn. On two-wire circuits (one wire for ground) count the length of both wires.

Know These Terms

Primary wire	Terminal block
Conductor	Junction block
Insulation	Fuse block
AWG	Fuse
Resistance	In-line fuse
Amperes	Fusible link
Watts	Circuit breaker
Candela	Crimping
Wiring harness	Soldering
Color coded	Crimping tool
Wiring diagram	Acid core
Terminals	Rosin core
Plug-in connectors	Resin core
Rubber grommets	Soldering iron

Soldering gun
Cold solder
Heat-shrink tubing
Secondary wire
Corona
Resistance wire
Printed circuit
Voltage drop

Short circuits
Near-short circuits
Ohmmeter
Voltmeter
Ammeter
Test light
Continuity

Review Questions—Chapter 9

Do not write in this book. Write your answers on a separate sheet of paper.

1. Most primary wire used in automobiles is made of _____.
   (A) solid copper
   (B) solid aluminum
   (C) stranded copper
   (D) stranded aluminum

2. No. 16 wire is smaller than No. ___ wire.
   (A) 14
   (B) 18
   (C) 20
   (D) depends on the insulation thickness

3. The higher the system voltage, the _____ the wiring gage can be.
   (A) smaller
   (B) larger
   (C) longer
   (D) None of the above.

4. Automotive wiring is _____ coded.
   (A) size
   (B) color
   (C) length
   (D) number

5. The _____ protects a circuit from an overload.
   (A) wire size
   (B) wire length
   (C) wire material
   (D) fuse

6. Which of the following wire arrangements requires the largest wire gage?
   (A) 20 foot long wire, 12 volt system
   (B) 20 foot long wire, 6 volt system
   (C) 6 foot long wire, 12 volt system
   (D) 6 foot long wire, 6 volt system

7. When soldering electrical work, _____ flux should be used.
   (A) acid
   (B) rosin
   (C) aluminum
   (D) organic

8. When applying wire solder, touch the wire to the _____.
   (A) top of the iron
   (B) work away from the iron
   (C) iron where it contacts the work
   (D) side of the iron

9. The conductor of most modern secondary wire is made of _____.
   (A) copper
   (B) aluminum
   (C) carbon impregnated string
   (D) plastic

10. Match the electrical symbols in the left-hand column by placing the letter of the description in the right-hand column beside the number of the matching symbol.

1. _____

2. _____

3. _____

4. _____

5. _____

6. _____

7. _____

8. _____

9. _____

10. _____

11. _____

12. _____

13. _____

14. _____

15. _____

A. Resistor.

B. Circuit Breaker.

C. Wires Crossing   Not Connected.

D. Fuse.

E. Diode or Rectifier.

F. Wires Crossing - Connected.

G. Positive.

H. Terminal.

I. Open Switch.

J. Rheostat.

K. Transistor.

L. Battery.

M. Negative.

N. Condenser.

O. Ground.

ASE-Type Questions

1. The most commonly used insulation material in modern vehicles is _____.
   (A) rubber
   (B) aluminum
   (C) plastic
   (D) treated paper

2. Technician A says that the larger the wire number, the thicker the wire. Technician B says that cross-sectional area in square mils determines the wire size. Who is right?
   (A) A only.
   (B) B only.
   (C) Both A & B.
   (D) Neither A nor B.

3. All of the following are considerations when selecting the correct wire gage for a circuit, EXCEPT:
   (A) wire length.
   (B) wire thickness.
   (C) wire insulation.
   (D) electrical load.

4. Technician A says that an undersize wire will overheat. Technician B says that an undersize wire will increase electrical resistance in the circuit. Who is right?
   (A) A only.
   (B) B only.
   (C) Both A & B.
   (D) Neither A nor B.

5. A number of common wires, taped together, with leads leaving at various spots, is referred to as a wiring _____.
   (A) set
   (B) harness
   (C) package
   (D) herd

6. Technician A says that soldering involves fusion. Technician B says that the wires should have a good mechanical connection before soldering. Who is right?
   (A) A only.
   (B) B only.
   (C) Both A & B.
   (D) Neither A nor B.

7. Flux is used in soldering to _____.
   (A) clean the metal
   (B) prevent overheating of metal
   (C) cement parts together
   (D) prevent rusting

8. Technician A says that resistance-type spark plug wires are used to provide a hotter spark. Technician B says that resistor spark plug wires are easily damaged by sharp bends. Who is right?
   (A) A only.
   (B) B only.
   (C) Both A & B.
   (D) Neither A nor B.

9. Technician A says that using copper secondary wire may cause radio interference. Technician B says that when plug leads pass through a metal conduit, the conduit should be grounded. Who is right?
   (A) A only.
   (B) B only.
   (C) Both A & B.
   (D) Neither A nor B.

10. All of the following statements about wires are true, EXCEPT:
    (A) spark plug wires can crossfire if wires are too close together when they serve cylinders that fire consecutively.
    (B) as long as the insulation is all right, a wire can be considered OK.
    (C) a frayed wire can cause a short circuit.
    (D) a corroded connection will increase resistance to electrical flow.

Suggested Activities

1. Using the primary wire size selection chart in **Figure 9-4,** determine the correct size wire for the following:
   A. Load—100 candela; Wire length—11 feet; Voltage—12 volts.
   B. Load—50 amperes; Wire length—20 feet; Voltage—12 volts.
   C. Load—72 watts; Wire length—15 feet; Voltage—12 volts.

2. Use a schematic to trace out a simple wiring circuit, such as tail and stoplights, or the horn. List the switches and relays used in the circuit.

3. Compare wire sizes as used on a modern vehicle. Note variations in wire sizes and determine why different sizes must be used. Write a short report summarizing your findings.

4. Check several electrical connectors on a vehicle, under the hood, in the passenger compartment, and under the chassis. Explain why certain ones are sealed, while others are not.

5. Obtain spark plug firing orders for various engines. Demonstrate how to rewire an engine using the firing order. Also demonstrate how to rewire an engine when the firing order is not available.

10

Friction and Antifriction Bearings

After studying this chapter, you will be able to:
- Compare the differences between friction and antifriction bearings.
- Explain the application of different bearing designs.
- Properly install friction bearings.
- Diagnose common reasons for bearing failures.
- List the different kinds of antifriction bearings.
- Explain the advantages of each type of antifriction bearing.
- Describe service procedures for antifriction bearings.

This chapter will cover the design, construction, application, and service of the bearings used in automobiles and light trucks. Common reasons for bearing failure will also be presented. Bearings are critical to the operation of many vehicle components. Study this chapter carefully.

Major Classes of Bearings

Bearings can be grouped into two major classifications: friction bearings and antifriction bearings. The contact area of the *friction bearing* slides against the portion of a shaft designed to accept the bearing, usually called the bearing journal. The *antifriction bearing* utilizes ball or roller elements that roll against the contact area. This reduces but does not eliminate friction. See **Figure 10-1**.

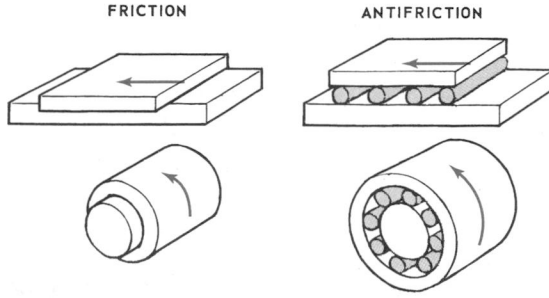

Figure 10-1. Friction bearing uses a sliding contact while antifriction bearing utilizes a rolling contact.

Both types are used in automobiles and trucks. Major use of the friction bearing is confined to the engine and transmission, **Figure 10-2**. The camshaft, crankshaft, and

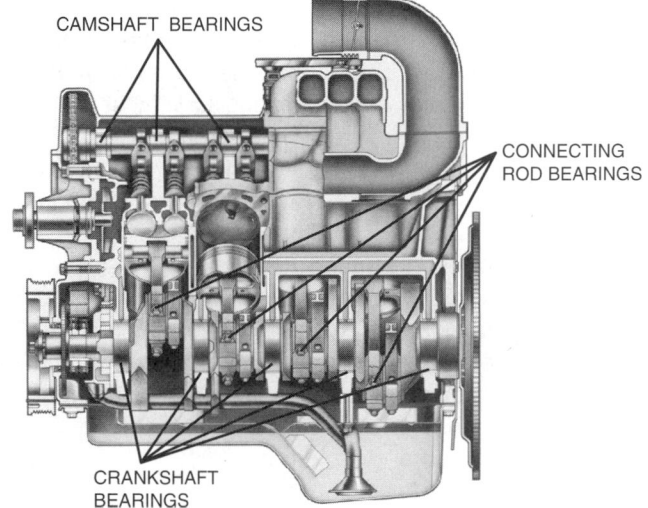

Figure 10-2. Automobile engine makes use of a great many friction bearings. How many are you able to find and identify? (Ford)

connecting rods of vehicle engines all use friction-type bearings. Friction bearings used in transmissions and transfer cases are often called *bushings.* The antifriction bearing is used in some transmissions, transfer cases, and in various places in the drive line, wheels steering system, and belt-driven engine accessories. Antifriction bearing application in engines is largely confined to small, high speed engines used for motorcycles, outboard motors, and chain saws. Checking bearing clearance, determining bearing size requirements, prestart lubrication, bearing installation, and torquing will be discussed in detail in the chapters on engine overhaul.

Bearing Load

There are two major loads placed on any bearing used with a rotating shaft. *Radial loads* occur at right angles to the axis of the bearing. An example would be the sideways load placed on a connecting rod bearing as the piston pushes the rod to turn the crankshaft. *Thrust loads* are placed parallel to the axis. An example would be the outer pull on a wheel bearing when the vehicle is turned. See **Figure 10-3**.

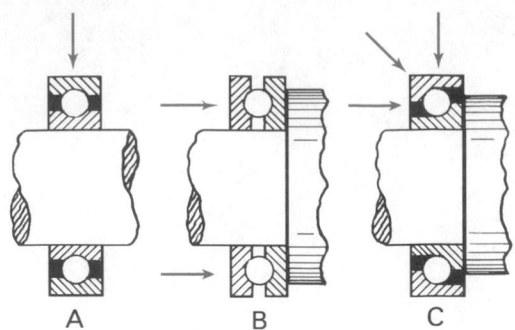

Figure 10-3. Loading designs. A—Radial. B—Thrust. C—Combination radial and thrust. Arrows in color indicate direction of load.

Friction Bearings

Engine connecting rods, crankshafts, and camshafts use a type of friction bearing called a *precision insert bearing.* The precision insert bearing is light and strong. However, it does demand care in handling and installation. Precision insert bearings are made in one- and two-piece designs and in a wide range of sizes. Crankshaft and connecting rod inserts are usually two-piece design.

A precision insert bearing has one or more layers of lead, tin, copper, aluminum, or alloys of these metals commonly referred to as babbitt metal. These layers are bonded to a steel core, sometimes called a back. **Figure 10-4** shows the layers of soft metal on a common insert bearing. Note that this bearing is composed of layers of lead-copper alloy, copper, tin-lead alloy, and pure tin.

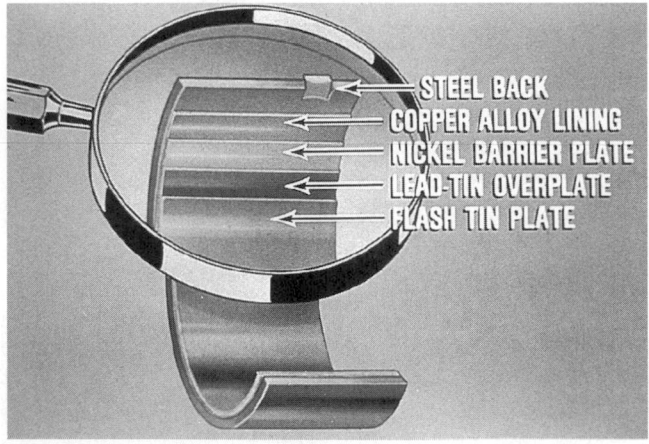

STEEL BACK
COPPER ALLOY LINING
NICKEL BARRIER PLATE
LEAD-TIN OVERPLATE
FLASH TIN PLATE

Figure 10-4. Note the five layers (counting steel back) of this insert bearing. (Federal-Mogul)

Camshaft Bearings

The camshaft bearing is constructed like the connecting rod and crankshaft inserts. However, they are a one-piece design. The camshaft bearing must be *pressed* into place. In addition to the standard sizes, they are available in large undersizes to permit line boring. Line boring is done by attaching a cutter to a long, rigid steel bar. The bar is passed through the bearings, boring them in line with each other. The bearing material is affixed to steel strip stock. The stock is rolled into a full circle with either a butt or butt and clinch joint. The bearing material is usually babbitt, **Figure 10-5.**

Bushings

Bushings are full-round bearings, usually made of solid bearing bronze, which is a mixture of copper, lead, tin, and zinc. Some applications use rubber or steel back precision bushings. The bushing is pressed into place and either bored, reamed, or honed to size. Bushings are used where it would be impractical to use two-piece bearings, or where the fit does not have to be as precise. See **Figure 10-6.** Steel and rubber suspension system bushings will be covered in the suspension and steering chapters.

Friction Bearing Inspection

A properly selected and installed bearing, under normal operating conditions, will last in excess of 50,000 miles (80,000 km), and usually over 100,000 miles (160,000 km).

There are many things or combinations of things that will cause premature failure. It is important that the technician be familiar with the most significant ones and the effects they have on the bearing insert. Bearing failure is generally preceded by a lowering of oil pressure due to increased clearance. As bearing clearance increases, engine oil consumption will rise from excessive oil throw off. Eventually, the bearings will start to knock. Whenever an engine is torn down, bearings should always be cleaned and carefully inspected. The cause of bearing failure will often be apparent in a close study of a damaged bearing.

Dirt—Number One Cause of Bearing Failure

Field and laboratory studies have shown that *dirt* is the most frequent cause of bearing failure. See **Figure 10-7.** The word dirt is used to describe foreign particle damage to moving parts. This can include sand, cast iron and steel chips, pieces of bronze, grinding stone grit, and other materials. Normal engine wear will produce fine particles worn from the various moving parts. Most of these are normally removed by the oil filtration system. Abnormal engine wear will produce large bits of dirt that will greatly accelerate the wear process. Dirt is a bearing's worst enemy. Get it out of the unit and use every precaution to keep it out. Study the bearings shown in **Figure 10-8.** Each was damaged by dirt.

Dirt from Reconditioning and Cleaning

Valve grinding, cylinder boring and honing, and shaft grinding deposit metal and other abrasive particles. These must be removed from a reconditioned part by thorough cleaning. Machined particles are sometimes present in new engines. This is due to poor cleaning.

A sloppy job of cleaning often loosens carbon and other deposits but fails to completely remove them. Final rinsing in dirty solvents often contaminates parts. Once the engine is assembled and put into operation, the washing and cleaning action of the oil will cause these deposits to reach the bearings. Oil filters will not protect the bearings if the engine is very dirty. The filter will become completely clogged very quickly, forcing the bypass open. This channels dirt directly into the bearings.

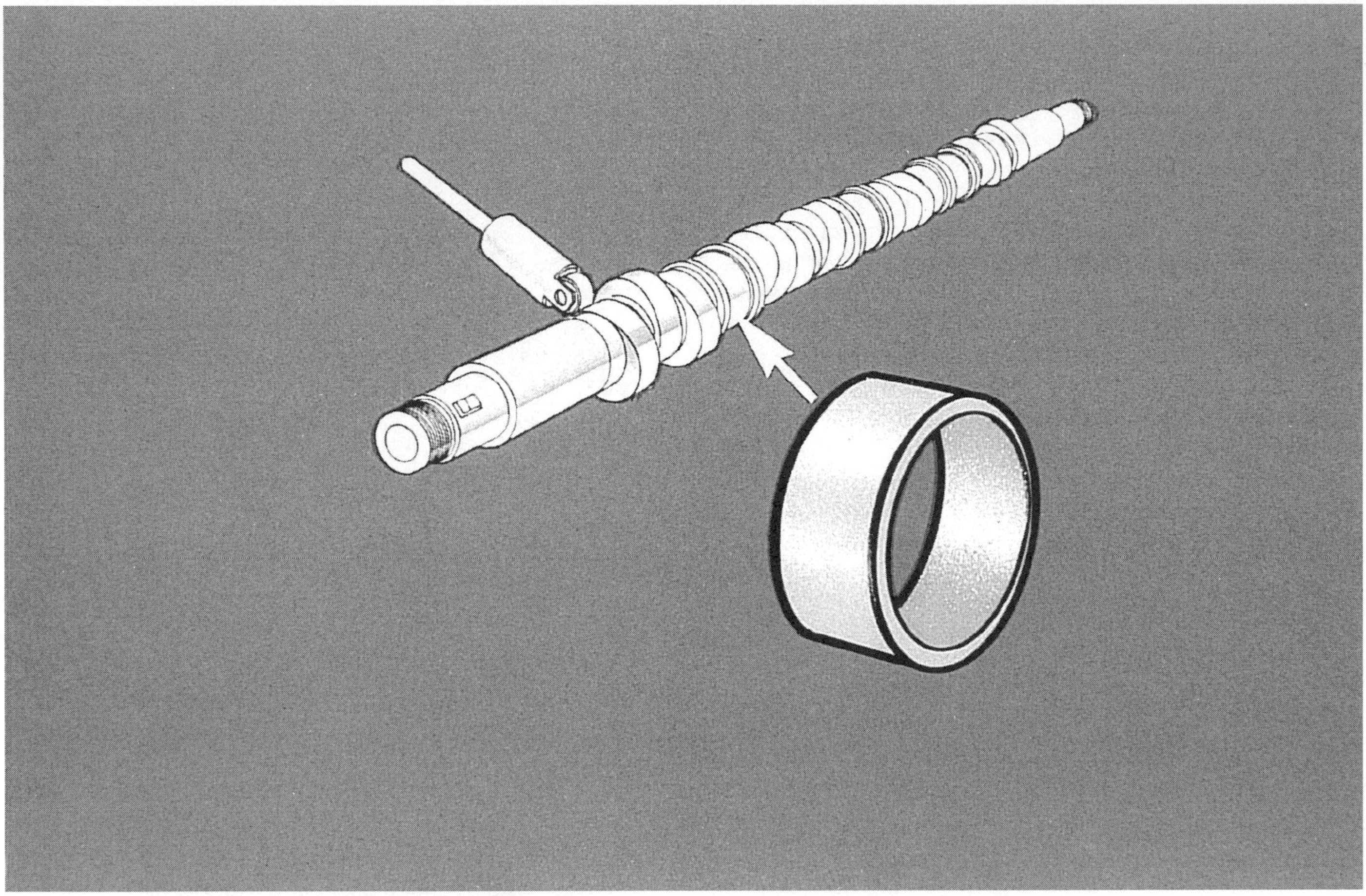

Figure 10-5. A typical camshaft insert bearing. (Federal-Mogul)

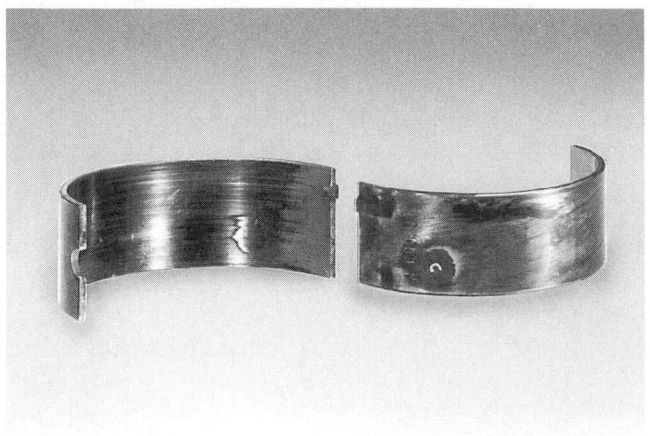

Figure 10-6. Typical metal bushings. These are steel backed precision type. (AE Clevite)

CAUSES OF BEARING FAILURE	
Dirt	42.90%
Insufficient Lubrication	15.30%
Misassembly	13.40%
Misalignment	9.80%
Overloading	8.70%
Corrosion	4.50%
Indeterminate and Other Causes	5.40%

Figure 10-7. Causes of bearing failure and the percentage of occurrence. Note that dirt far exceeds the others.

Figure 10-8. Dirt ruins bearings fast! Study these bearings; they were damaged by dirt. (AE Clevite)

Dirt from External Sources

The engine may be contaminated by working under dusty conditions or by careless handling of parts. Keep clean parts covered until ready for installation. Work in a clean area, protected from wind-borne dust. When not working on a part, even for a few minutes, cover it. Keep hands and tools (especially sockets) free of dirt when assembling parts. Avoid the use of blowguns, sandblasters, or steam cleaners near open engines or other sensitive units. Once the engine is assembled and placed in service, dirt can still enter. The most common entrances for dirt are through the air cleaner, breather system, fuel system, cooling system, dipstick, vacuum lines, and lubrication system.

Cover carburetors and throttle openings when the air cleaner is removed. Keep air cleaners clean and properly serviced. Clean and properly service crankcase breather systems. Maintain a clean filter in the fuel system. Check for coolant leaks into the cylinders (ethylene glycol antifreeze forms a gummy residue in bearings and will cause serious problems). Never lay a dipstick on a dirty surface. Wipe both stick and area around stick entry hole before returning. When changing oil filters, wipe contact area thoroughly. Keep bulk oil tanks clean. Oil filler cans and spouts should be cleaned and stored to prevent contamination. When removing drain plugs, clean them thoroughly before replacing. Check filler tube for dirt before adding oil. See **Figure 10-8.**

Bearing Lubrication Failure

Low oil pressure caused by worn bearings, faulty pump, clogged pickup screen, or an insufficient oil supply will cause rapid failure. Dry starts (engine overhauled and started without initially charging the oil system) can cause damage that will cut down the life expectancy of the bearings. Loss of oil through damage to the pan, broken pump or line, leaking gasket, poorly installed oil filter, or failure to replace plug after draining will cause sudden failure, **Figure 10-9.**

Figure 10-9. These aluminum bearings were ruined from lack of lubrication. (Federal-Mogul)

Bearing Failure from Improper Assembly

Dirt on the insert back, insufficient clearance, reversing caps, placing a lower insert in the upper position, bowed (warped) crankcase, and bent crankshaft or rods will cause bearing failure. **Figures 10-10** through **10-16** illustrate the results.

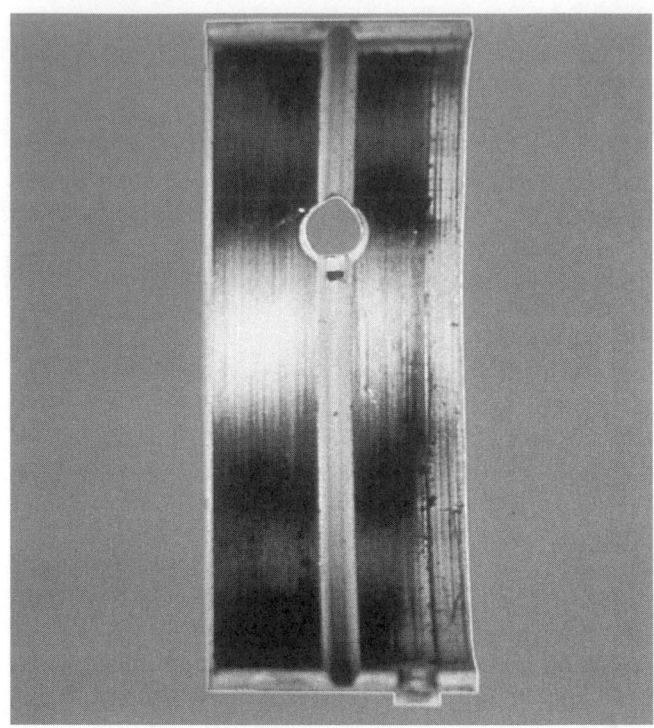

Figure 10-10. Bearing damage caused from a tapered housing bore. (Federal-Mogul)

Figure 10-11. Nicked and dented cap bore will transfer marks to back of insert, thus causing localized high pressure areas.

Operational Faults

Lugging (pulling hard at low engine RPM), detonation (rapid burning of fuel charge caused by a secondary flame front), preignition (fuel charge firing before plug fires), prolonged slow idling, and excessive RPM will all place the bearings under a heavy load. This can easily lead to premature failure. When bearing condition indicates such problems, the vehicle driver should be informed of the cause to prevent a reoccurrence. See **Figures 10-17** through **10-20.**

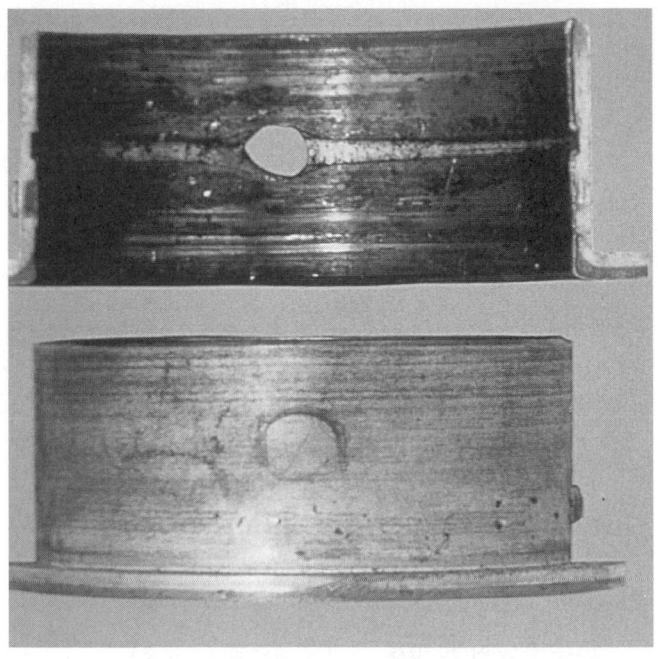

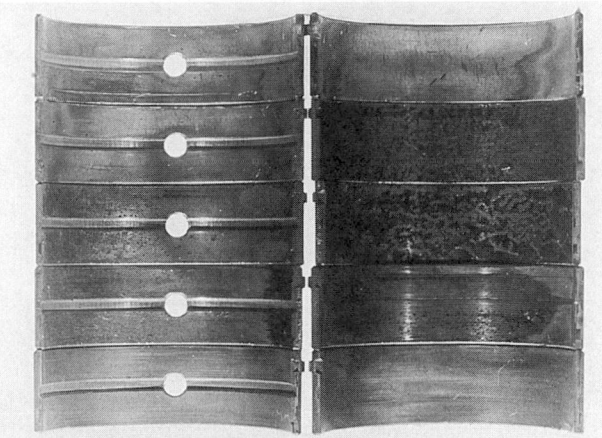

Figure 10-14. A bent crankshaft ruined this set of main bearings. (AE Clevite)

Figure 10-12. Upper insert, with oil hole, was installed in bottom position. Lower insert (see oil passageway impression on back) blocked flow of oil to bearing. (Federal-Mogul)

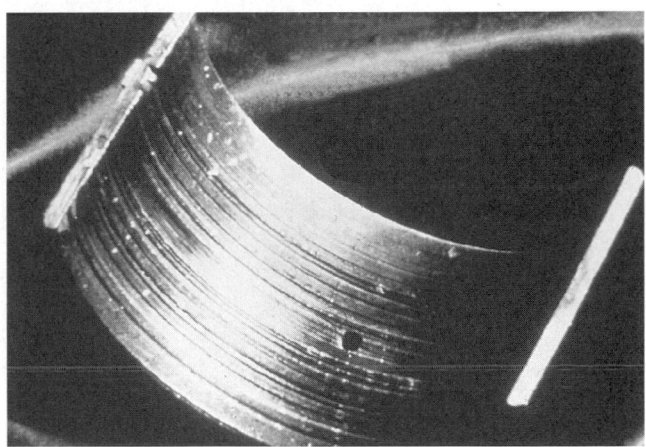

Figure 10-15. A rough and scored journal caused this bearing to fail. (Federal-Mogul)

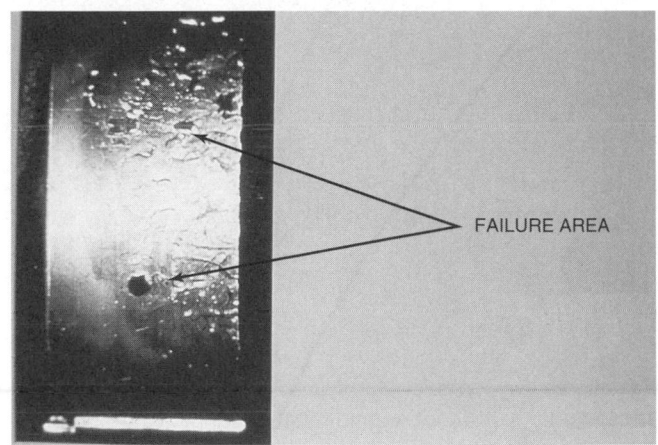

FAILURE AREA

Figure 10-13. A misaligned connecting rod placed one side of this insert under pressure. Note failure area. (Federal-Mogul)

DIRT BEHIND CAP RUINED THIS AREA

Figure 10-16. A particle of dirt between insert and bore caused a high pressure area that damaged this bearing.

Friction Bearing Installation

Precision insert bearings are what the name implies: precision units which should be handled with utmost care. Do not mix halves. Protect them from dirt and physical damage. Keep your fingers off the bearing surfaces; this can cause corrosion. When installing, never force or pound the insert into place. Use the proper installation tools. Make certain the bore and insert is spotless and locating lugs are in place. After installing, coat bearing surface with clean engine oil. Never file an insert. Always check for proper clearance.

Insert and Housing Bore

The block can become distorted through the effects of heating and cooling. This will throw the camshaft and crankshaft bearing bores out of alignment. This will force the camshaft and crankshaft out of alignment, creating heavy bearing loading and uneven stressing. See **Figure 10-21.**

Figure 10-17. Excessive idling will produce bearings like this. (Federal-Mogul)

Figure 10-18. Riding clutch (holding foot on the clutch all the time) places main bearing thrust flange under prolonged loading. Note the ruined thrust surface. (Federal-Mogul)

Figure 10-19. Antifreeze leaking into an engine will contaminate bearings. Note gummy deposits on these inserts. Deposits can build up and eliminate oil clearance, with disastrous results. (Federal-Mogul)

Figure 10-20. A set of engine main bearings. Note thrust flanges on both sides of center main. (Federal-Mogul)

The heavy stresses within the engine can cause the housing bores to elongate. If an insert is installed in such a bore, it will conform to the bore elongation, creating an egg-shaped bearing surface. Clearance in one direction will be excessive while clearance in the other will be insufficient, causing extreme friction and wear. Such bores must be reconditioned or the part replaced, **Figure 10-22.**

The housing bores, insert backs, and parting surfaces must be free of nicks, burrs, or foreign materials. If an insert is prevented from making perfect contact, pressure spots, misalignment, and overheating will result. Always carefully check the housing bores and insert backs to make certain they are smooth and clean. Do not oil these surfaces.

Bearing Oil Grooves and Holes

The insert often has *oil holes* and *oil grooves* to permit oil to enter freely. Holes are used to allow oil passage to other areas. Annular, thumbnail, and distribution or spreader grooves are often incorporated. Not all inserts are drilled or grooved, **Figure 10-23.**

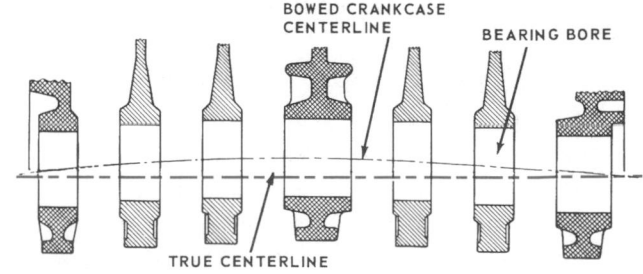

Figure 10-21. A bowed crankshaft will shift main bearing bores out of alignment with their true centerline.

Bearing Journals

The section of a shaft that contacts the bearing surface is called a *journal.* It must be round, smooth, and straight.

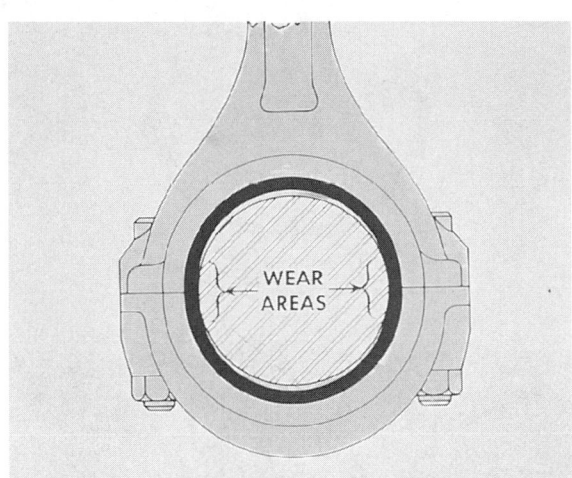

Figure 10-22. Elongated rod bearing bore. Note excessive clearance at top and bottom while zero clearance exists at sides. Insert life would be short. (AE Clevite)

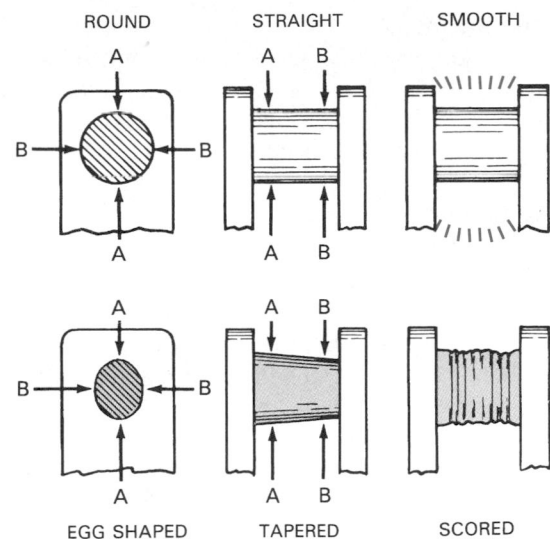

Figure 10-24. Bearing journals must be round, straight, and smooth.

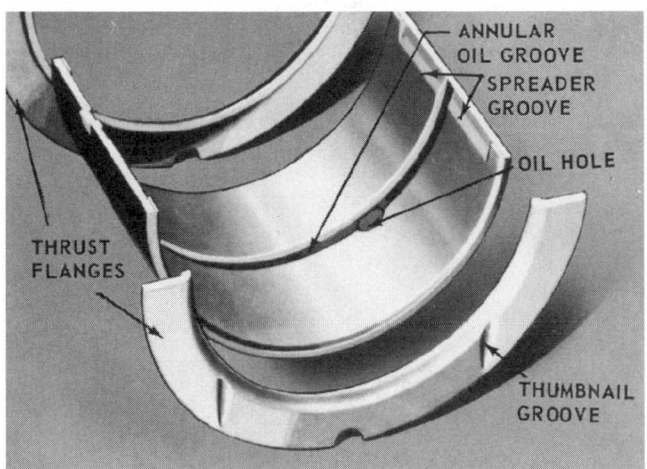

Figure 10-23. Typical bearing inset oil grooves. This particular main bearing uses separate thrust flanges. (AE Clevite)

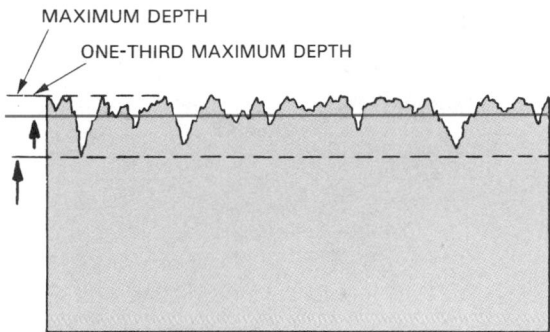

Figure 10-25. Determining surface finish in microinches.

allow oil to enter the thrust surfaces. Some thrust flanges are not part of the bearings, but are inserted as separate pieces, **Figure 10-26.**

Nicks and scratches will ruin the bearing material, **Figure 10-24.** Manufacturers have established a minimum surface finish of 16 microinches or smoother. The microinch (one millionth or 0.000001 of an inch) is used as a measurement of surface finish. To measure a surface finish in microinches, tests are made to determine the depths of all grooves or scratches, from which the average depth is calculated. This is usually about one-third of the maximum depth. In **Figure 10-25,** you will note that the red line indicates one-third the maximum depth. If the maximum depth is 90 microinches, the finish would be 30 microinches.

Thrust Flange

Whenever an insert bearing must control thrust forces (pressure parallel to shaft centerline), a **_thrust flange_** is incorporated on one or both sides of the bearing. The thrust faces are lined with bearing material. Thumbnail oil grooves

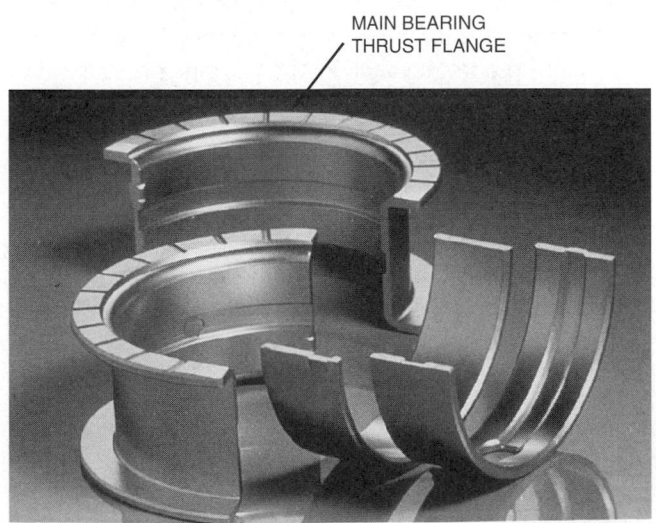

Figure 10-26. Crankshaft main bearing with thrust flanges. (Federal-Mogul)

Installing the Insert

To provide adequate support, heat transfer, and alignment, it is essential that the insert contact the housing or cap properly. Inserts are manufactured to produce proper fit by using *bearing spread* and *bearing crush.*

Bearing Spread

The insert diameter across the parting edges is slightly larger (.005″-030″ or 0.13-0.76 mm) than the bore. This makes it necessary to force or snap the insert into the bore by applying thumb pressure to the parting edges. Spread also helps hold the bearing in place during assembly, **Figure 10-27.**

 Caution: Do not force the insert into place by pressing on the center. This could warp the insert.

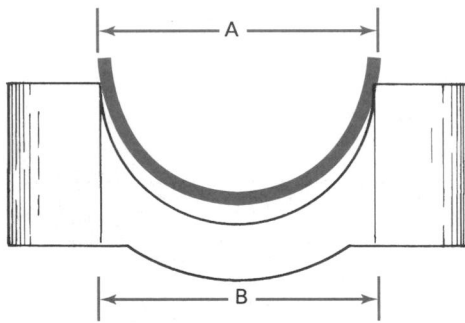

Figure 10-27. Positive bearing spread. Note that diameter A across parting surface is slightly larger than bore diameter B.

Bearing Crush

The insert is also designed so that after it is snapped into place, the parting edges will protrude a slight amount above the bore parting edge. In effect, each insert half is slightly larger than a full half circle. Refer to **Figure 10-28.** When the bearing is bolted together, the crush area touches first. As tightening progresses, the crush area is forced beneath the bore parting edges. This creates a tight insert-to-bore contact through radial pressure. Look at **Figure 10-28.**

 Caution: Never file bearing caps or crush. Doing so will ruin the bearing. The insert must not turn.

Inserts have locating lugs (sometimes called tangs) or dowels to prevent the insert from turning. When installing inserts, be certain the lugs are properly aligned with the slots in the housing. Dowels, when used, must enter their holes. See **Figure 10-29.**

Align Housing Bore Halves

Even though the bore and insert are clean and the insert spread and crush are correct, the bearing will still be ruined if the upper and lower (in case of split bearings) bore halves are not properly aligned. It is possible to reverse

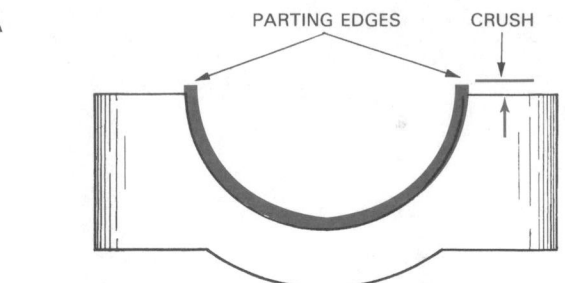

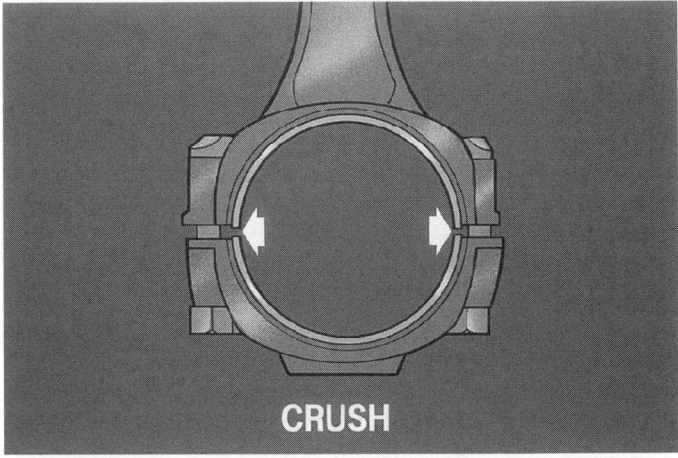

Figure 10-28. A—Bearing crush. Note that both insert parting edges (exaggerated for emphasis) protrude slightly above cap. B—When rod and cap are drawn together in bearing crush, radial pressure is produced, forcing insert tightly against bore. (Federal-Mogul)

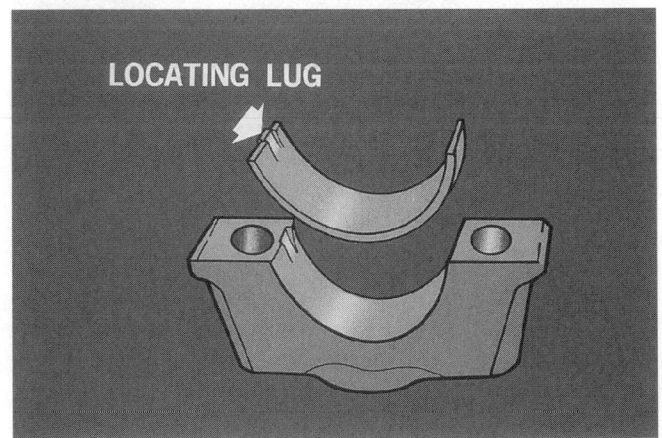

Figure 10-29. Locating lugs and dowels keep the insert from turning. (Federal-Mogul)

some bearing caps (lower halves). This will shift the upper and lower bores out of alignment. When disassembling bearing caps, always mark the upper and lower halves before removal. Use numbers so that you replace the cap in its original position. See **Figure 10-30.** Used inserts should always be saved for study. If they appear usable, or you cannot obtain replacements, mark them on the back with a fine scribe. If you are sure that they will be replaced, mark them on the bearing surface.

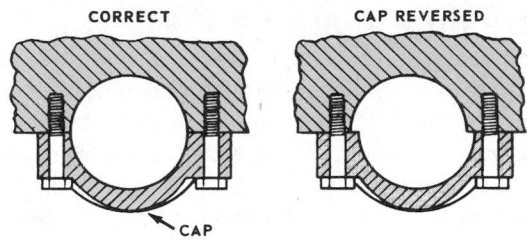

Figure 10-30. Reversing bearing caps will shift upper and lower bore halves out of alignment.

Do Not Mix Bearing Halves

Insert halves are made in matched pairs, but they are not identical. It is important that they are not mixed. If one of the insert halves is drilled and the other is not, be certain to place the drilled half in the drilled bore. When installing full-round inserts, such as the camshaft bearings, make sure the oil holes are aligned. Neglecting to do this may result in a blocked oil hole, which will cause immediate bearing failure. Look at **Figure 10-31.** Many split bearings are manufactured with both halves drilled to prevent improper assembly.

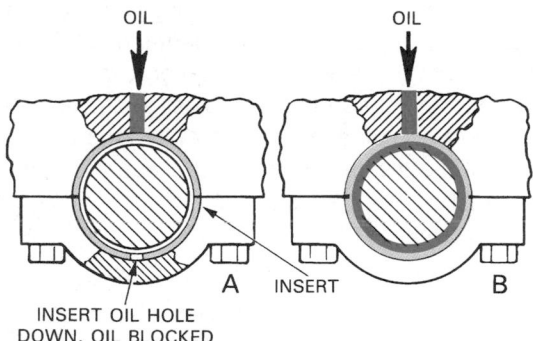

Figure 10-31. Align insert oil with oil passage. A—Insert oil hole has been placed down, cutting off oil supply. B—Insert oil hole aligned with passageway. Proper lubrication will result.

Wrench Side Pressure

Thick wrenches and sockets can create enough pressure against the cap to shift it out of alignment. Use the correct size wrench or socket. Tighten by alternating from one bolt or nut to the other. When cap is just snug, tap lightly with a plastic hammer to assist cap alignment. Using a torque wrench, torque the fasteners to the recommended value. Study **Figure 10-32.**

Bearing Oil Clearance

The precision insert bearing must have enough clearance to allow oil to penetrate and form a lubricating film. The clearance must provide proper flow through the bearing to aid in cooling and passage to other critical areas needing lubrication.

Too much clearance will allow so much oil flow that it can lower oil pressure. It can also cause excessive throw off (oil running from bearings thrown off the crankshaft at high velocity). This can flood the cylinder walls with oil

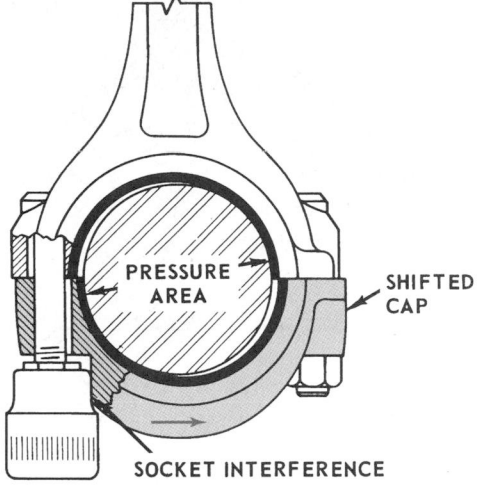

Figure 10-32. Thick wall socket has exerted side pressure, thus shifting cap to one side.

beyond the capacity of the piston rings to control. Excessive clearance will also allow movement between parts sufficient enough to literally pound the bearing. The chart in **Figure 10-33** shows average minimum clearances for engine bearings of different sizes and types. The chart is intended to indicate average clearances only, and should not be used when engine manufacturers' recommendations are available.

RECOMMENDED OIL CLEARANCES FOR ENGINE BEARINGS

SHAFT-SIZE	SB (High Lead or tin base)	CA (Copper Alloy)	AP & CP (Over plated bearing)	AT (Aluminum Alloy)
2 —2¼	.0010	.0020	.0010	.0025
2¹³/₁₆ —3½	.0015	.0025	.0015	.0030
3⁹/₁₆ —4½	.0020	.0030	.0020	.0037

NOTE: Chart above indicates minium diametral clearances. For maximum permissible clearance, add .001"

Figure 10-33. Typical average minimum clearances for engine bearings. (Federal-Mogul)

Checking Bearing Clearance

Approximate clearance of engine bearings can be determined by attaching an engine prelubricator (air pressure operated oil tank). Observe the amount of oil dripping from the bearings. This is often done after the pan is removed, but before disconnecting any bearings. It gives the technician an approximate idea of bearing condition. The prelubricator is used again after engine assembly to charge the lubrication system with oil. At the same time, it provides a final visual check on bearing clearances.

One of the most common methods of obtaining precise clearance measurements is a special plastic wire (trade name Plastigage®). A section is placed either on the journal or on the insert. The bearing is tightened, then removed. The plastic will be flattened. By using a paper gauge supplied with the wire, the width of the wire can be accurately related to clearance in thousandths of an inch, **Figure 10-34.** Complete instruction on the use of the pre-

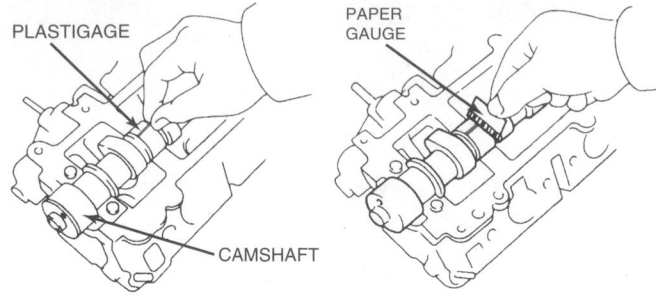

Figure 10-34. Checking bearing clearance with Plastigage. (Toyota)

lubricator and Plastigage will be given in the chapters on engine overhaul.

Undersize Bearings

To compensate for wear, inserts are available in a series of undersizes. If journal wear is slight, the recommended clearance can often be obtained through the use of inserts .001″ or .002″ (0.025 or 0.05 mm) undersize. The shaft must be carefully measured and the largest diameter compared to the original size to determine the correct undersize.

Inserts are available in .010″, .020″, .030″ (0.25, 0.51, 0.76 mm) undersize. When journal wear is severe or when journals are scored or egg shaped, the shaft is ground to fit one of the bearing undersizes. This brings the bearing-to-journal clearance up to acceptable standards. Occasionally semifinished (greatly undersize) inserts are bored out to a specified size.

Antifriction Bearings

The antifriction bearing utilizes *rolling elements* (balls or rollers) to reduce friction through rolling contact. In most applications, the rollers or balls are placed between inner and outer rings, usually called *races.* The rolling elements are separated by a *cage* or separator, generally made of stamped steel. The cage prevents the elements from bunching and sliding against each other. In the case of separable (can be taken apart) bearings, the cage prevents the loss of the elements. The balls or rollers, as well as the inner and outer races, are hardened and ground to assure proper contact and clearance.

Antifriction bearings are used in many places in modern vehicles. They can be divided into four types: *ball bearings, roller bearings, needle bearings,* and *self-aligning bearings.* Each type has certain applications it serves best. For instance, the ball bearing produces the least amount of friction, but does not have the load carrying ability of the roller. All three types are used in automotive construction. **Figure 10-35** illustrates the three types.

There are many variations of the three basic types. Some of the more common variations are the deep groove ball, angular contact ball, straight roller, spherical roller, tapered roller, multiple row, and self-aligning. Each different design attempts to meet a specific demand. The installation may call for light or heavy loads, high or low speeds, radial, thrust, or a combination loading. Most antifriction bearings must handle a combination of both radial and thrust loads.

You will note that several of the bearings shown will sustain thrust in one direction only. Thrust in the opposite direction would force the races apart. By using two or more

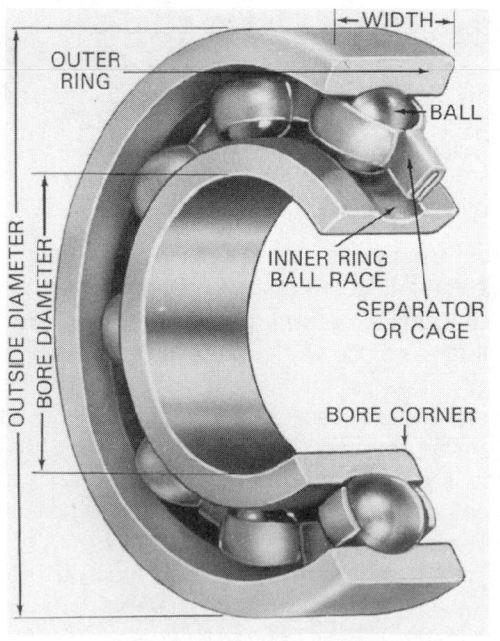
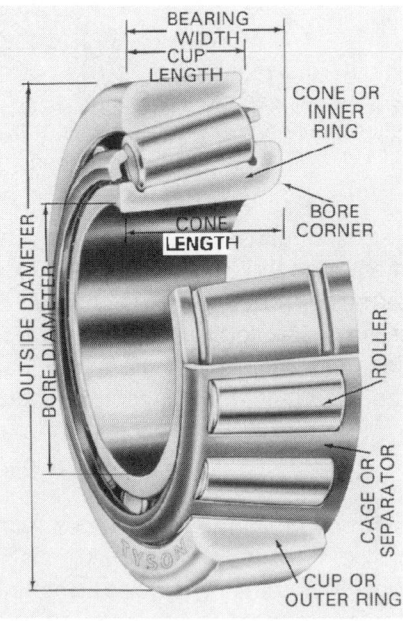
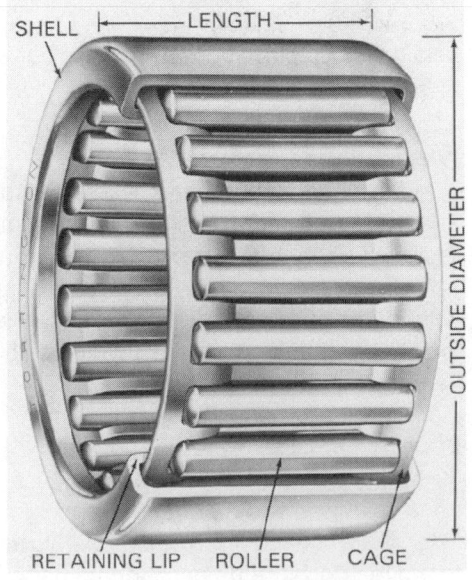

Figure 10-35. Three types of antifriction bearings. A—Typical ball bearing construction. Note how cage keeps balls evenly spaced. (Nice) B—Roller bearing. This bearing uses tapered roller design. Outer race is separate. (SKF) C—Caged needle bearing. Rollers in this bearing operate against outer shell and in direct contact with hardened, ground shaft surface. (Torrington)

bearings, facing in opposite directions, thrust in either direction can be handled. See **Figure 10-36.** They can also be designed to provide for thrust loads in both directions. The bearings shown in **Figures 10-37** and **10-38** are designed to handle thrust forces. Understanding the problems involved and the type of bearing needed will help the technician to properly service bearings.

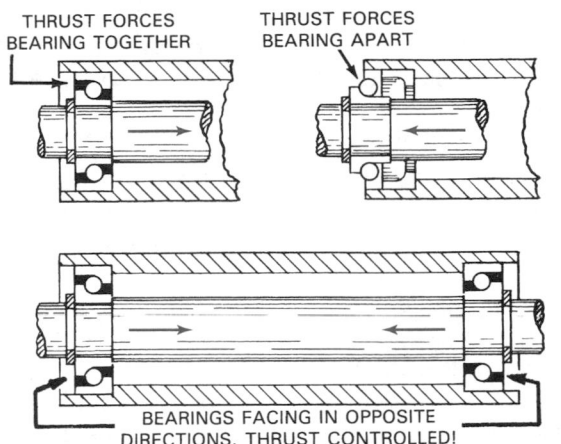

Figure 10-36. By using two bearings, thrust in either direction is controlled. Arrows indicate thrust direction.

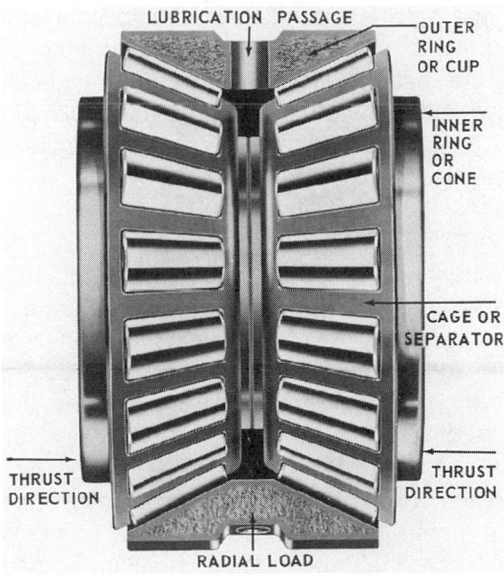

Figure 10-37. Double row, tapered roller bearing. The outer race is one piece, the inner races are separate. (Timken)

Ball Bearings

The deep groove ball bearing will handle heavy radial and moderate thrust loads. Neither the inner or outer race is separable, **Figure 10-39.** The angular contact ball bearing will handle heavy thrust and radial loads. The balls are contained within a cage. Both inner and outer races are separable, **Figure 10-40.**

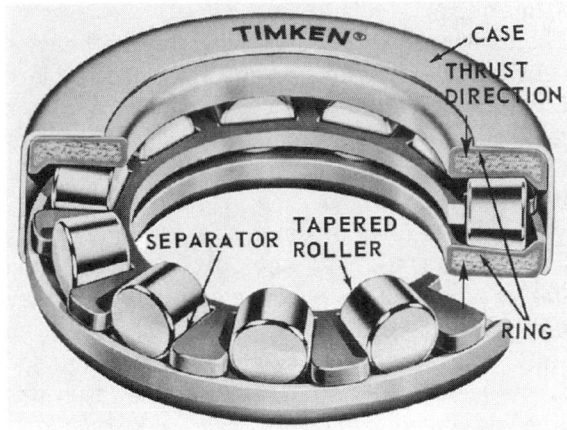

Figure 10-38. A—Tapered roller thrust bearing. Study the case and roller layout. (Timken)

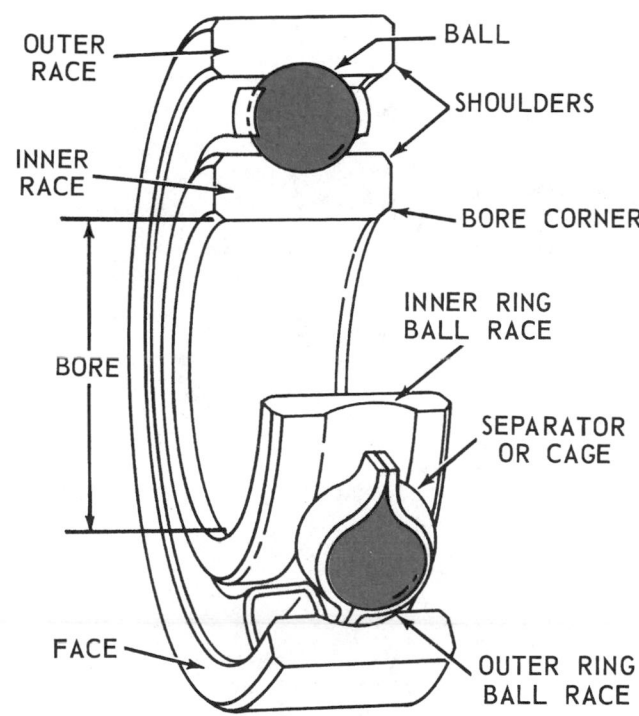

Figure 10-39. Cutaway of a ball bearing assembly. (Deere & Co.)

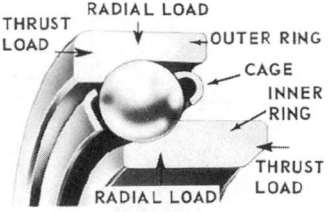

Figure 10-40. Angular contact ball bearing. This type is often used as car front wheel bearings.

Roller Bearings

The straight roller is designed to handle heavy radial loads. Most straight roller designs will handle little or no thrust, **Figure 10-41.** The rollers in the spherical roller bearing are of a curved or spherical shape. It will handle heavy radial loads and moderate thrust loads and is self-aligning to a degree, **Figure 10-42.** The tapered roller is the most widely used of the roller bearings as it will carry both heavy thrust and radial loads. The apex of the angles formed by both the rollers and raceways, if extended, would meet on a common axis. This allows the roller to follow the tapered raceways with no bind or skidding. The rollers are secured to the cone with a steel cage. The cone raceway is indented to form a lip that keeps the rollers centered. The cup is then separable. Look at **Figure 10-43.**

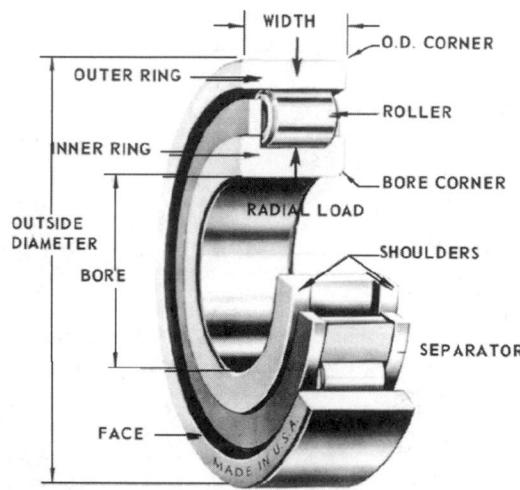

Figure 10-41. Straight roller bearing designed for radial load only. (AFBMA)

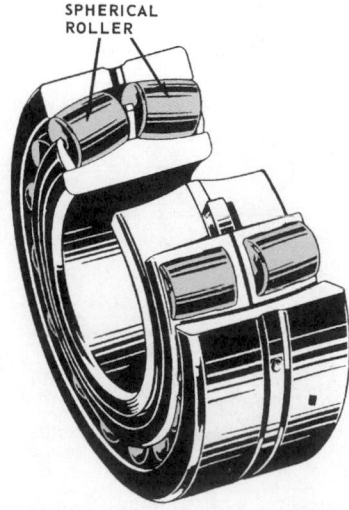

Figure 10-42. Spherical roller bearing. Note "barrel" shape of rollers. (SKF)

Needle Bearing

Needle bearings (long, thin rollers) often use only an outer shell. In some needle roller applications, the bore and shaft are hardened, then ground and placed in direct contact with the rollers. A variation of the needle bearing is the Torrington bearing. They are often used in place of thrust washers where the axial loads would quickly wear out a washer. Torrington bearings consist of a set of needle bearings which rotate around a central opening. The bearing slips over a shaft and is held in place by the parts which it separates. A Torrington bearing is shown in **Figure 10-44.**

Self-Aligning Bearings

A self-aligning bearing is used when there is a possibility or a desirability of either housing or shaft misalignment during operation. This bearing will allow a degree of tilt without distorting the bearing elements. Both internal and external self-aligning bearings are shown in **Figure 10-45.**

Bearing Identification

All bearings are marked with a part number for ease of replacement. The number is usually on the face of the races. If necessary, replacement bearing size can be checked by careful measurement.

Bearing Seals

Bearings can be sealed on one or both sides. Sealing on one side is often used to help confine lubricant and to prevent the entry of dirt. When both sides are sealed, the bearing is prelubricated (lubricated during assembly) and the technician cannot add lubricant during service. These bearings are sometimes called **sealed bearings.** See **Figure 10-46.**

Removing Bearings

The best way to remove a bearing is with mechanical or hydraulic pushing or pulling tools. They exert a constant, heavy force, **Figure 10-47.** A suitable hammer (brass, lead, or plastic) and soft steel drifts, sleeves, and cup drivers can be used when pullers are not available or where their use is impossible or undesired.

Any attempt to pull or install a bearing by exerting force on the free (not tight) race may chip the balls or rollers. The race itself could crack and fly apart. There are some instances that require force on either the free race or rolling elements. Whenever possible, exert the force on the tight race only.

Figure 10-48 shows both the correct and incorrect way of applying pulling force. Note that in A, the supporting puller plate rests on the free outer race. In B, the plate supports the inner race only, thus avoiding damage to the outer race and rolling elements.

 Note: Prior to pulling bearings, clean the surrounding area to prevent contamination. When a separable bearing is removed, keep the parts together. Do not mix used bearing elements for any reason.

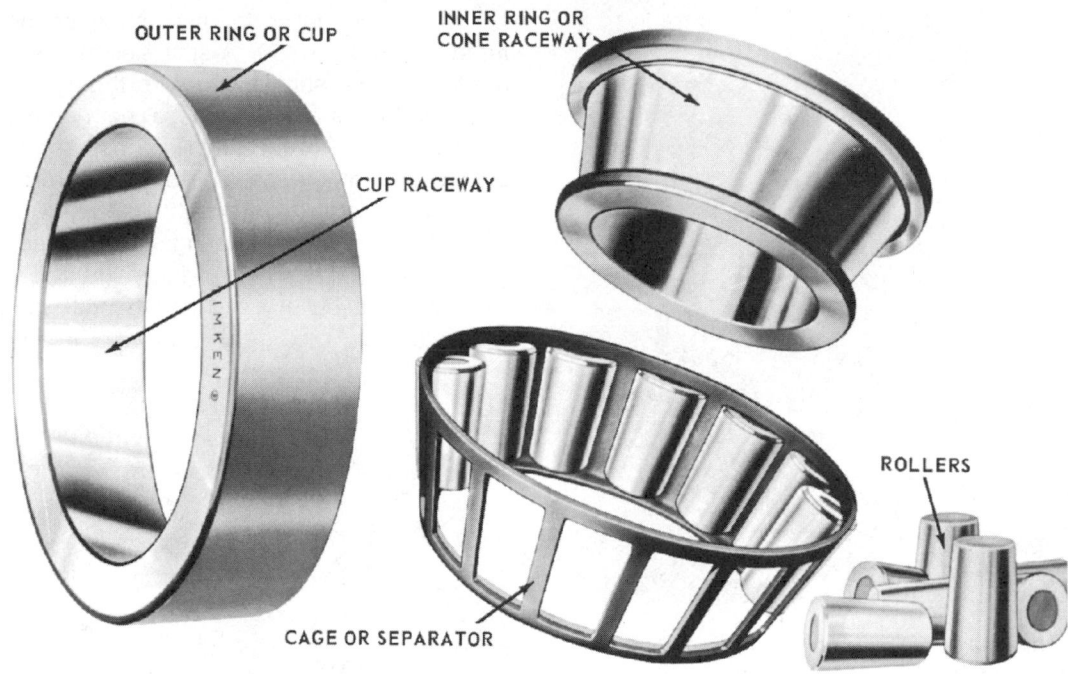

Figure 10-43. Tapered roller bearing parts. Once assembled, this particular bearing will have a separable outer race but rollers, cage, and inner race will be one unit.

Figure 10-44. Needle thrust bearing. Note how two-piece case also acts as needle separator. (Torrington)

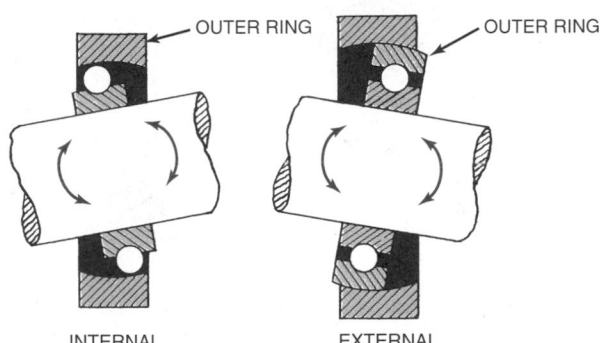

Figure 10-45. Internal and external self-aligning bearings. Note how the shaft is free to tilt. The external design will handle heavier loads as ball has a wider contact area with the outer race.

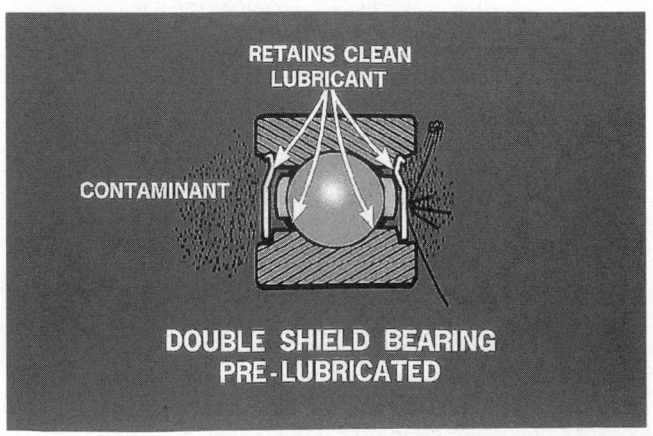

Figure 10-46. Bearing seal construction. (Federal-Mogul)

When Inner Race or Bearing Cannot Be Grasped

Occasionally, the bearing inner race is pressed against a shoulder that is as wide or wider than the race. In the case of the tapered roller bearing, a special segmented (made in parts) adapter race can be used. It applies the pulling force to the ends of the rollers while forcing them against the cone. This allows the bearing to be removed without damage, **Figure 10-49.**

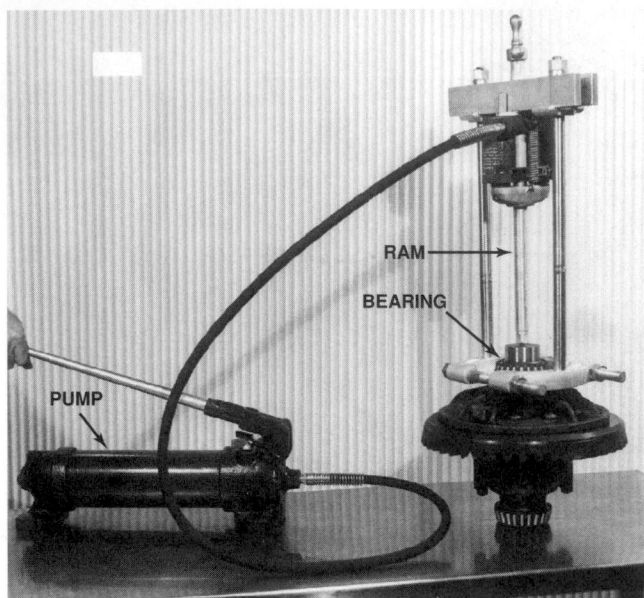

Figure 10-47. This technician is removing a differential carrier bearing with a hydraulic puller. (Timken)

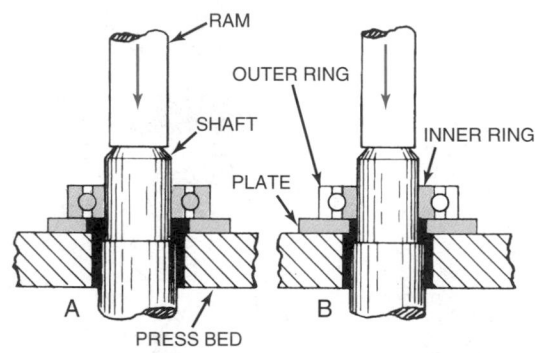

Figure 10-48. Pulling setups. A—Wrong as force is applied through free outer race and rolling elements. B—Correct. Force is through tight race only.

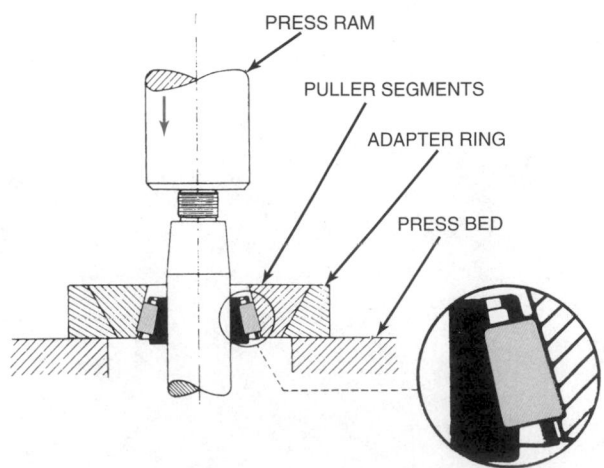

Figure 10-49. Pulling bearing by applying pressure through rollers. Magnified portion at lower right shows how end of roller is grasped by puller segments. (Timken)

A special puller for axle shaft bearing work is pictured in **Figure 10-50.** A split sleeve with pulling races is used. The axle shaft passes up through a section of tubing. The puller sleeve grasps both bearing and tubing. The top section of the tubing is fastened to a heavy plate on the bed of the press. As pressure is applied to the shaft end, it is forced through the tube to pull the bearing. Note that the entire bearing is shrouded or shielded to protect the operator from flying parts if the bearing should explode. This puller will remove both tapered roller and ball bearings.

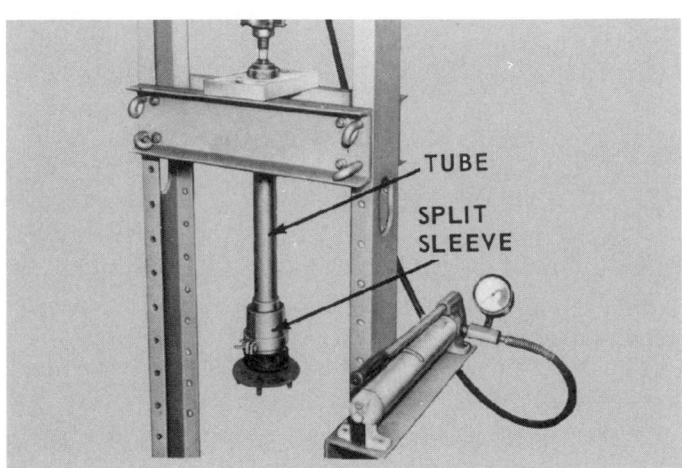

Figure 10-50. Removing axle shaft bearing with special puller.

Sometimes, a retaining plate or dust shield is so close to or surrounding the bearing that it is impossible to grasp. In these cases, you must grind away a portion of the inner race (protect shaft with a metal sleeve). Cut out the cage and remove the elements. The outer race can then be removed, exposing the inner race for grasping. Unhardened retaining rings are sometimes used to hold bearings in place. They are best removed by notching with a sharp chisel. This will loosen them enough for easy removal. See **Figure 10-51.**

Inner bearing races can also be removed by partial grinding or by cutting with an acetylene torch. Wrap the shaft on both sides of the bearing with wet cloths to prevent heating. Cut only partially. The race is then squeezed tightly in a vise and struck with a hammer where indicated by the arrows in **Figure 10-52.** This will crack the race and allow it to be pulled.

STOP **Warning: Bearing materials are extremely brittle, and may fly apart with great force when broken. Wear safety goggles when striking bearing parts. Keep other personnel away from work area. Always pull bearings whenever possible. Avoid grinding and cutting with a torch, unless absolutely necessary. Whenever possible, shield the bearing.**

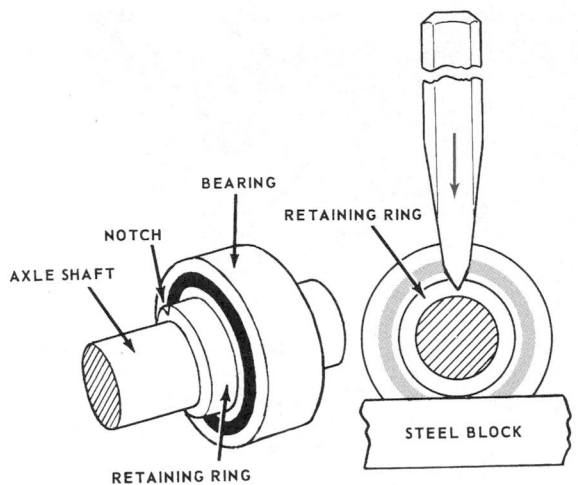

Figure 10-51. Removing bearing retaining race by notching with a chisel.

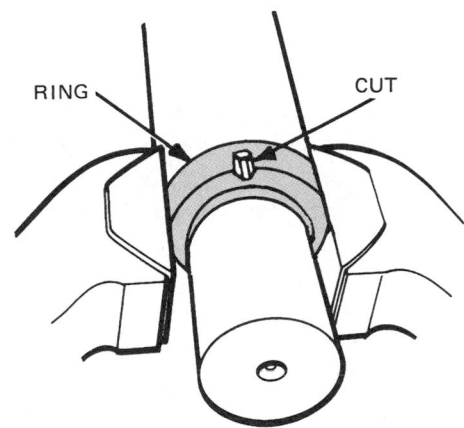

Figure 10-52. Bearing inner race partially cut and then squeezed in a vise. Strike with a hammer where indicated by arrows. (Federal-Mogul)

General Rules for Antifriction Bearing Removal
• Exert force on the tight race when possible.
• Use pullers of the correct size and shape.
• Mount puller to exert force in a line parallel to the bearing axis.
• Use unhardened, mild steel drifts and sleeves.
• Never strike the outer or free race.
• Do not damage the shaft or housing.
• If it is necessary to hammer a shaft, use a brass, lead, or plastic hammer.
• Keep all bearing parts together.

Antifriction Bearing Service

When the bearing is removed, wipe off all surplus grease or oil. Soak in a nonflammable cleaning solvent. A cleaning tank with tray and solvent hose is ideal. If none is available, a clean bucket will suffice, **Figure 10-53.** Never use gasoline, kerosene, or other volatile fluids for cleaning. They are rough on hands and will ignite readily. Do not use carbon tetrachloride as it produces poisonous fumes.

Figure 10-53. Tray full of bearings being placed in solvent.

While the bearings are soaking, brush each in turn with a nylon bristle brush and blow out the worst of the grease. Continue soaking and brushing until the bearing looks clean. Blow the bearing out again. If any sign of grease is visible, soak, brush, and blow out once more.

 Warning: Never spin a bearing with air pressure. Not only will it damage the bearings, it can also be dangerous. When the outer race of a separable bearing is removed, only the sheet metal cage holds the rolling elements to the center race. If the cage and rollers are spun, the tremendous centrifugal force generated can cause the elements to fly outward with violent force.

When the bearing is clean, rinse in a container of clean solvent and blow dry. Look at **Figure 10-54.** Once the bearings are dry, take them to a clean work area. It is a good idea to reserve an area that will be free of dust, dirt, and moisture. **Figure 10-55** pictures an ideal work section.

Note: Use clean, dry air. Most air compressor systems are equipped with a filter and moisture trap. Service them often. Directing a stream of air into a white cloth will show if dirt, moisture, or oil is present.

Sealed Bearing Service

When a bearing is factory-packed and completely sealed on both sides, it must not be washed. Since there is no satisfactory way to relubricate it, washing will dilute the lubricant and lead to early failure. Wipe off the outside with a clean, dry cloth.

Antifriction Bearing Inspection

Prior to discussing checking procedures, it is wise to familiarize yourself with some of the most common bearing defects. As is the case with friction bearings, dirt is the

Figure 10-54. Using clean, dry air, blow bearing dry. Do not allow bearing to spin. (Federal-Mogul)

Figure 10-56. Holding bearing for inspection. Hold the inner race with one hand while rotating the outer race with the other. (Federal-Mogul)

Figure 10-55. An ideal bearing work area is clean and dry. (Bower)

number one enemy of antifriction bearings. It will cause scratching, pitting, and rapid wear. Other common defects include corrosion, spalling, brinelling, overheating, physical damage, electrical pitting, and damaged seals.

When inspecting nonseparable bearings, place the fingers of one hand through the center race, **Figure 10-56.** Rotate the outer race with the other. The bearing should revolve smoothly with no catching or roughness. If either condition is present, rinse and blow dry again. If the symptoms still persist, discard the bearing. Also check for signs of overheating and wear on the outer surfaces of both races. A bearing that has been loose in the bore or on the shaft will have highly polished areas showing.

If the bearing can be separated, carefully inspect the raceways and rolling elements. They should be absolutely

smooth and free of heat discoloration. Inspect each ball or roller since only one or two may be damaged. If the bearing passes the visual check, place the elements together. While forcing them together, rotate the bearing. The operation should be smooth.

When revolving bearings, do so a number of times. A single damaged ball or roller may not "catch" the first few times around. When checking thrust bearings, place one side on a solid surface. Press down on the other with the heel of your hand and rotate while maintaining pressure. Keep hands clean, dry and away from raceways and rolling elements. See **Figure 10-56.** Do not assume looseness is a sign of wear. A new bearing often feels loose before installation. When either raceways or rolling elements are worn enough to produce looseness, it will be evident by examining the surfaces. One or more of the following conditions will be visible.

Dirt and Corrosion Damage

If the dirt is very fine, it will have a lapping effect (removal of surface metal through fine abrasive action) that will leave the rolling elements and raceways with a dull, matte (nonreflecting) finish. Larger dirt particles will produce scratches and pits. The entry of moisture (often from air hose), wrong or contaminated lubricant, or storage near corrosive vapors can produce corrosion in the bearing. A bearing remaining static (not being rotated) for an extended time often corrodes, **Figure 10-57.**

Spalling

Foreign particles, overloading, and normal wear over an extended period can lead to **spalling.** Spalling starts when tiny areas fracture and flake off. These small flakes are carried around in the bearing causing more flaking. Advanced flaking or spalling will produce large craters, **Figure 10-58.**

Figure 10-57.   A badly corroded bearing race. (Federal-Mogul)

Figure 10-59.   Brinelled needle bearing shell.

Figure 10-58.   A badly spalled inner race. (AFBMA)

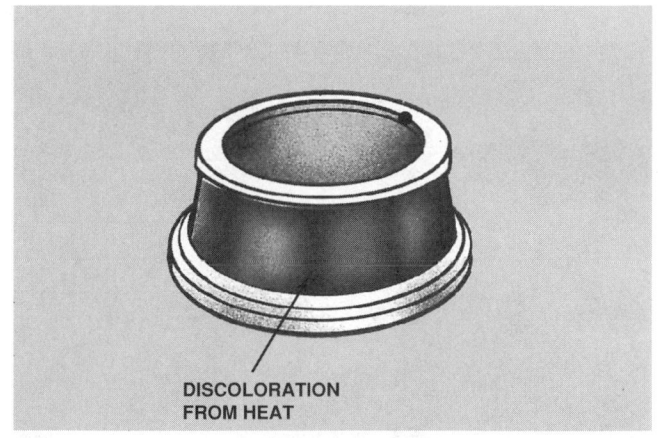

Figure 10-60.   An overheated bearing. Note the discoloration on the bearing. (Federal-Mogul)

Brinelling

Brinelling is the term used to describe a series of dents or grooves worn in one or both races. The grooves run across the raceway and are usually spaced at regular intervals. Once brinelling starts (often from inadequate lubrication) a fine reddish iron oxide powder is formed. As the powder is carried around, it increases the wear rate. **Figure 10-59** shows a badly brinelled outer shell.

Overheating

Overheating will break down the physical properties of the bearing and cause rapid failure. Inadequate or improper lubrication and poor adjustment are the principal causes. The bearing races and rolling elements which have been overheated will have a blue or brownish-blue discoloration. See **Figure 10-60.**

Physical Damage

One or both races may be cracked. Improper removal or assembly techniques and wrong bore or shaft size are common causes. Look at **Figure 10-61.** Improper removal and assembly procedures will often result in a dented or broken cage. Pieces of dirt and metal chips will also cause cage breakage. Refer to **Figure 10-62.** As with a broken cage, careless assembly often produces dented shields. This could also damage the cage as well as cause binding and lubricant loss. See **Figure 10-63.**

Electrical Pitting

Electric motor or generator bearings are sometimes pitted by the passage of current (from an internal short or from static electricity) through the bearing. The minute arcing produces numerous tiny pits. Engine and transmission bearings are also frequently pitted when the engine-to-body ground straps are removed or broken. **Figure 10-64** illustrates the effect of *electrical pitting,* dirt, corrosion, and poor lubrication on rollers.

Replace the Entire Bearing

If any part of a bearing, outer or inner race, or rolling elements are damaged, discard the *entire* bearing. Never replace part of a bearing. Before discarding, write down the part number. It is a good idea to wire the parts together and keep for comparison with the replacement bearing. Mark the bearing as defective.

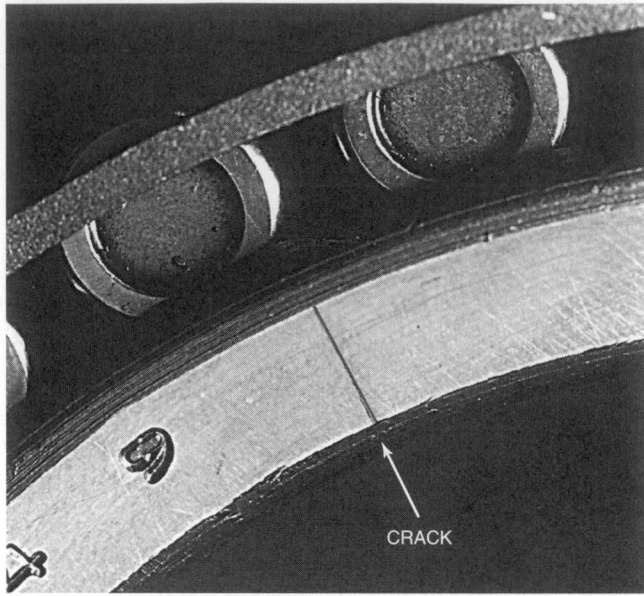

Figure 10-61. Cracked inner bearing race. (CR Industries)

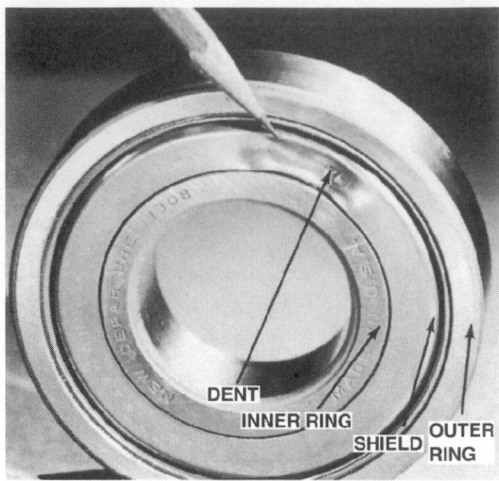

Figure 10-63. Badly dented bearing shield or seal. (New Departure)

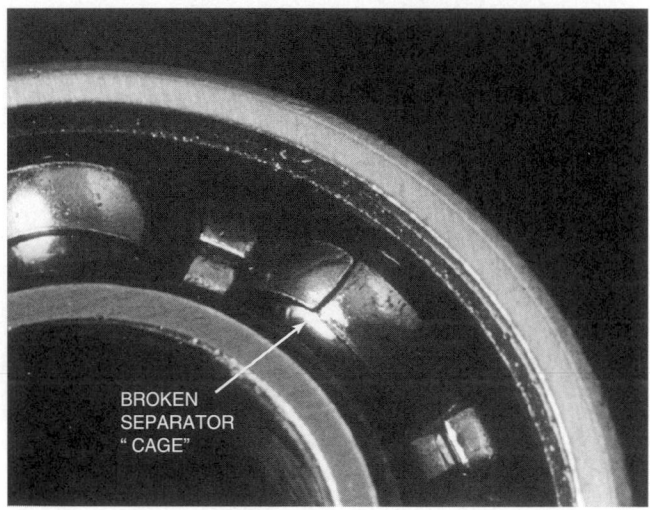

Figure 10-62. Broken bearing cage. (CR Industries)

Figure 10-64. Roller damage. A—Corrosion. B—Electrical pitting. C—Poor lubrication and dirt. (SKF)

Bearing Lubrication

If the bearing will be placed into service at once, it may be oiled or may be packed with grease, depending upon the application. Cover with a clean cloth until ready to install. If it will be stored for a few days, coat with oil and place in a clean box or container.

If the bearing will be stored for an extended period, coat with light grease. Wrap in oilproof paper and place in a clean box. Be sure to identify the bearings to prevent opening a number of them when looking for a specific one. When coating bearings for storage, immediately following inspection, coat with the desired lubricant to prevent the formation of rust. Rotate to ensure proper penetration and coverage, **Figure 10-65.**

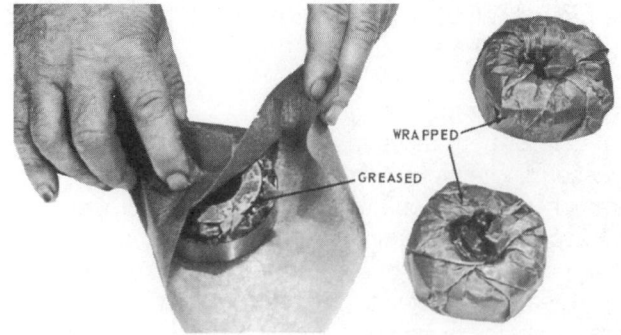

Figure 10-65. Bearings greased and wrapped for extended storage.

Packing Bearings with Grease

When a bearing calls for grease (there are specific recommendations for every type of bearing), use a ***bearing packer.*** If no packer is available, place some grease on the palm of one hand. Your hands must be clean and dry. With the other, press the edge of the bearing into the grease (near edge). Repeat this until grease flows out the top. Move around to different sections until the bearing is fully packed. Separable races should be coated also. See **Figure 10-66.** All grease and oil in the shop should be kept in clean containers and kept tightly covered when not in use. When opening, wipe dirt off lid and avoid dusty areas. An open can of grease near a grinder or cutting torch is an open invitation to disaster. If any oil or grease seals are related to the job at hand, inspect them. If necessary, replace the seals at this time. In some instances, seals must be installed after the bearings.

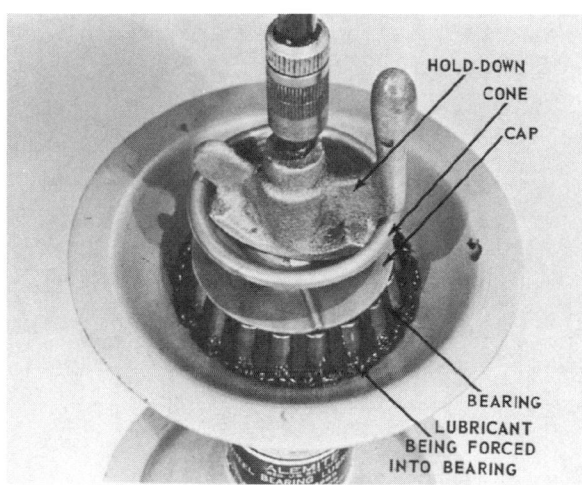

Figure 10-66.   A bearing packer is fast and efficient. (Timken)

Bearing Installation

Bearings are often similar (but not exact) in type and size. Before attempting installation, make certain you are installing the correct one. Be especially careful with new replacement bearings. Check numbers and measurements. Bearing installation calls for care and intelligent use of tools. Many otherwise good jobs have been ruined by careless installation.

Clean and Inspect Bores and Shafts

Clean bearing housing bores and shafts thoroughly. Remove any nicks or burrs with a fine file. Be careful not to file a flat spot. Following filing, polish with very fine emery or crocus cloth. On a shaft where the inner race is designed to walk (creeping movement around shaft), inspect carefully. Polish if necessary. If the counterbores or press-fit shaft areas are worn from race slippage, do not center punch or knurl (crosshatch pattern pressed into metal) as an attempt to increase size. Such procedures will only result in failure

as the bearing, under load, will quickly flatten these raised areas. The area should be built up by metallizing (spraying molten metal onto shaft) and then ground to the correct size. Watch for dirt in threads, splines, and other areas. Look at **Figure 10-67.** A sprung shaft or bent housing will cause the bearing to operate in a distorted position, greatly shortening its life. For those jobs in which the bearing failed in a short time, despite proper installation, lubrication, and adjustment, always check shaft and housing for any warpage or other misalignment. The use of a thin film of oil or micronized (finely powdered) graphite will ease installation, prevent corrosion around race contact area, and facilitate future removal. See **Figure 10-68.**

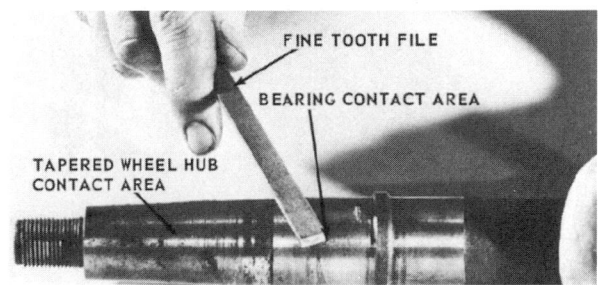

Figure 10-67.   Removing burrs from axle shaft bearing area with a fine tooth file.

Figure 10-68.   Use lubricant to facilitate assembly.

After determining correct installation position (do not press on backwards or fail to position any retainers or snap races that must go on first), start the bearing or race with your fingers. Attach puller or set up in press and force bearing into place. Make certain it goes on squarely and to the full distance required. Apply pressure, whenever possible, on the tight race. As in pulling, observe safety precautions.

If pressing tools are not available, simple driving tools will handle many installation jobs in a satisfactory manner. Brass tools tend to mushroom and chip, which can contaminate the bearings. Use soft steel tools. Make sure they are clean and in good condition. Strike the tight race only.

Using Heat and Cold

In difficult assembly jobs, primarily large bearings, place the outer race in dry ice or in a deep freeze. This will reduce the diameter and help installation. Inner races can be heated in clean oil or a special electric oven. Use a thermometer. Never heat bearings with a torch, or allow the bearing temperature to exceed 275°F (135°C). Follow manufacturers' instructions. See **Figures 10-69** and **10-70**.

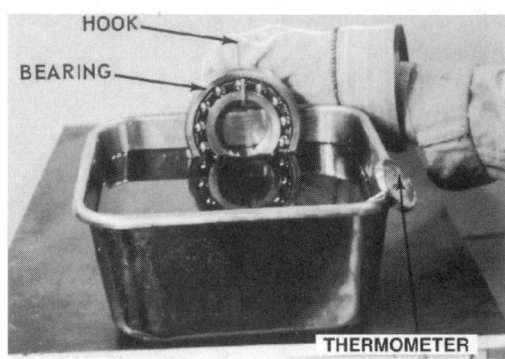

Figure 10-69. Heating a bearing in oil. Hook keeps bearing from touching bottom of container.

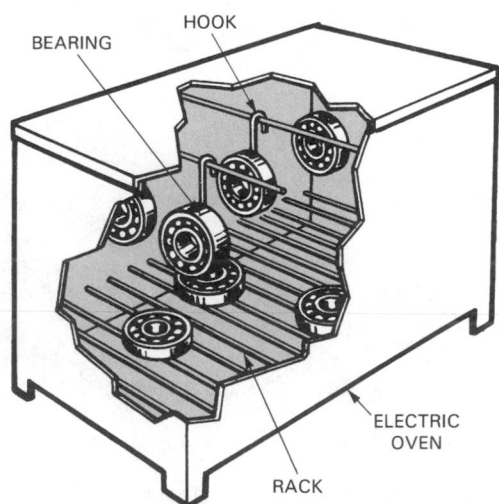

Figure 10-70. One type of electric bearing oven. Note that bearings are placed on racks or suspended with hooks. Do not put them in direct contact with heat source. Follow manufacturers' instructions when operating. (Federal-Mogul)

Bearing Adjustment

Some bearings require adjustment after installation. Proper adjustment depends on the application. Some require a specific amount of free play. Others require preloading (placing bearing under pressure so that when a driving force is applied to parts, they will not spring out of alignment). As the various service operations are described throughout the text, general bearing measurement and adjustment recommendations will be given.

General Rules for Antifriction Bearing Installation

- Clean all contact surfaces and remove any burrs and nicks.
- Install all parts that precede bearing.
- Lubricate for easy installation.
- If heat is required, do not exceed 275°F (135°C).
- Start bearing squarely.
- Align tools so that bearing will be forced on squarely.
- Use only soft steel driving tools.
- Whenever possible, avoid applying pressure through balls or rollers.
- If a vise is needed, use protective jaw covers.
- Driving tools must have smooth, square cut ends.
- Do not mar shaft or bore surfaces.
- Use safety precautions.
- Press on the full distance required.

Figure 10-71 illustrates a few do's and don'ts regarding bearing assembly.

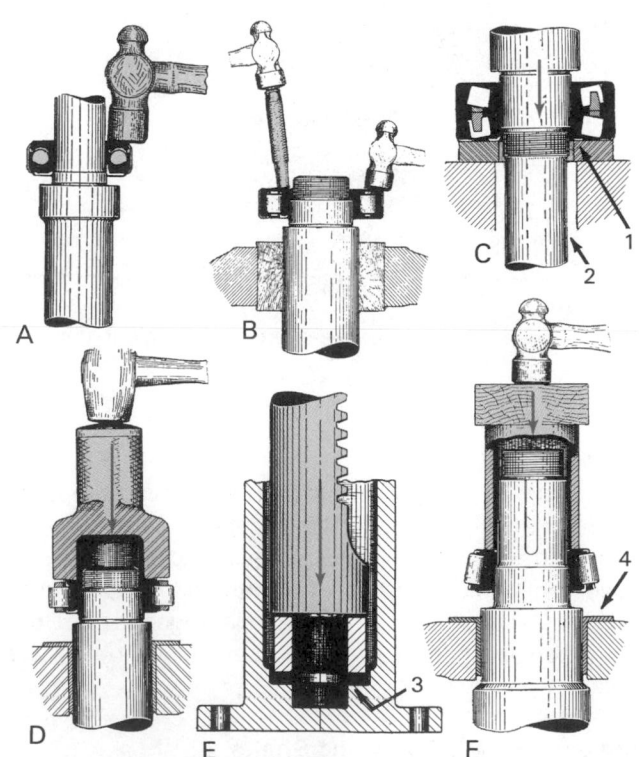

Figure 10-71. Bearing installation hints. A—Do not strike bearing with a hammer. B—Do not use wide punches on bearings. C—Do apply force to tight race (1) and have clearance (2) for shaft. D—Use driver with smooth, square cut ends that strike tight race. E—Clean bearing race recess (3) and force race to full depth. F—Block placed on open pipe driver allows driving force to be centralized. Use protective vise jaw covers (4). (AFBMA)

Tech Talk

A common mistake when dealing with bearings (or any moving parts) is to assume that penetrating oils or silicone sprays make good lubricants. Even some experienced technicians believe that these products can take the place of the specified lubricants. While these compounds are excellent when used to loosen bolts or drive out water, they have no lubrication value. A bearing assembled with one of these compounds instead of the proper lubricant will be destroyed in a few minutes of operation.

When lubricating bearings, or any moving parts, make sure that you use the correct lubricant. Also, do not wrap bearings in newspaper. Although newspaper appears clean, it is full of fine paper particles that will flake off and enter the bearing. In addition, newspaper will absorb some of the additives in the lubricant, reducing the amount of lubrication available to the bearing. Always wrap clean, lubricated bearings in slick paper.

Summary

Bearings can be classified as friction or antifriction. The friction bearing operates with sliding friction. Camshaft bearings are of the full-round type, usually babbitt lined. Bushings are usually bronze or bronze-faced steel, and are bored, reamed, or honed to size.

The friction bearing contact area slides against the bearing journal surface. Friction is reduced to acceptable limits by a film of oil. Most modern bearings are of the precision insert type. They can be of the full-round or split-halves type. They utilize steel backs that can be faced with lead-tin babbitt, copper alloys, or aluminum alloy. End thrust is controlled by incorporating thrust flanges on one or more bearings.

Low oil pressure, excessive oil consumption, and knocking are danger signals that indicate excessive bearing wear. Bearing failures are usually caused by dirt. Dirt enters the engine from normal wear, poor cleaning and reassembly, or improper storage conditions. Inadequate lubrication, improper assembly, and improper driving habits also cause bearing failures.

Journals must be round, straight, and smooth. Handle bearings carefully. The insert must closely contact the housing bore. Bearing spread, crush, and cleanliness assure a proper fit. Never file bearing inserts or caps. Locating lugs should be in the proper slots. Bearing back and bore must be clean and free of nicks or foreign material. Never reverse or mix bearing caps. Tighten properly using a torque wrench. Check bores for alignment.

Oil grooves and holes are vital. They must be located properly when installing inserts. Bearing clearance is critical. Worn or reground journals must be fitted with undersize bearings. Semifinished inserts may be bored to a specified size. Bearing clearance is best checked with plastic wire (Plastigage).

The antifriction bearing utilizes ball or roller elements that roll against the contact area. Antifriction bearings can be divided into three basic types: ball, roller, and needle. The ball and roller bearings usually consist of an inner and outer race with the rolling elements placed between them and positioned with a cage or separator. The needle bearing can use an outer shell, or can be placed in direct contact with a hardened and ground bore and shaft. Bearings are designed to carry either straight thrust, radial, or combination loads.

The deep groove ball, angular contact ball, straight, spherical, and tapered roller, needle bearing, and self-aligning bearings are the common variations. Bearings are marked with a part number. Bearings are often sealed on one or both sides. Never wash bearings sealed on both sides.

Hydraulic and mechanical pulling or striking tools can be used to remove bearings. If available, hydraulic and mechanical pullers are recommended. Pull bearings, whenever possible, by the tight race. Special tools are available for pulling by exerting pressure through the balls or rollers. Avoid the use of heat. Do not mar bore or shaft surfaces. Keep all bearing parts together.

Clean bearings in solvent. Blow dry. Rinse in fresh solvent and blow dry again. Do not spin the bearing. Inspect the cleaned bearing. If satisfactory, oil or pack with grease at once. A bearing packer is handy for greasing. Keep covered until ready to install. Rejected bearings may be kept for size comparison with replacements, but mark them as rejects. Never replace one part of a bearing. Replace defective grease or oil seals. Clean bore and shaft. Remove burrs and install any parts that must precede bearing.

Lubricate bearing seat area. Position bearing correctly and start by hand. Pull, press, or drive bearing fully into place, keeping square at all times. Do not damage shaft or bore. Installation tools must be spotlessly clean. In difficult assembly jobs, the use of both heat and cold will ease installation. If necessary, carefully adjust bearing.

Know These Terms

Friction bearing	Rolling elements
Antifriction bearing	Races
Bushings	Cage
Radial loads	Ball bearings
Thrust loads	Roller bearings
Precision insert bearing	Needle bearings
Dirt	Self-aligning bearings
Oil holes	Sealed bearings
Oil grooves	Spalling
Journal	Brinelling
Thrust flange	Overheating
Bearing spread	Electrical pitting
Bearing crush	Bearing packer

Review Questions—Chapter 10

Do not write in this book. Write your answers on a separate sheet of paper.

1. All of the following can cause rapid friction bearing wear, EXCEPT:
   (A) detonation.
   (B) low RPM.
   (C) lugging.
   (D) preignition.

2. Fingerprints on insert bearing surfaces can cause _____.
   (A) warping
   (B) spalling
   (C) brinelling
   (D) corrosion

3. To keep the insert from turning, all of the following are used, EXCEPT:
   (A) lugs.
   (B) keys.
   (C) tangs.
   (D) dowels.

4. A bearing cap can be shifted out of alignment by using a _____ wrench.
   (A) thick
   (B) socket
   (C) 12-point
   (D) All of the above.

5. When journals are worn or reground, _____ bearing inserts are required.
   (A) standard
   (B) oversize
   (C) undersize
   (D) None of the above.

6. Needle bearings make use of long, thin _____.
   (A) races
   (B) housings
   (C) rollers
   (D) Both A & C.

7. Which type of roller bearing can handle heavy radial and axial loads?
   (A) Straight roller.
   (B) Curved roller.
   (C) Tapered roller.
   (D) Needle.

8. Describe how a bearing should be stored for later use.

9. All striking type bearing pulling tools should be made of _____.
   (A) soft steel
   (B) brass
   (C) hardened steel
   (D) wood

10. A bearing showing some looseness _____.
    (A) should always be rejected
    (B) should be repacked with heavier grease
    (C) may be good
    (D) Both B & C.

11. When a separable bearing is being inspected, every _____ should be checked.
    (A) race
    (B) seal
    (C) ball or roller
    (D) All of the above.

12. What is the maximum temperature to which a bearing can be heated?
    (A) 212°F (100°C).
    (B) 275°F (135°C).
    (C) 350°F (177°C).
    (D) 400°F (204°C).

13. List five general rules for antifriction bearing removal.

14. List five general rules for antifriction bearing installation.

15. Look at the bearings on page 189. Name each bearing.

ASE-Type Questions

1. All of the following statements apply to insert type friction bearings, EXCEPT:
   (A) insert bearings rely on sliding friction to reduce wear.
   (B) most insert bearings consist of steel bonded to a soft metal core.
   (C) most insert bearings must be snapped into place.
   (D) lugs hold the insert bearing in place.

2. All of the following will cause early bearing failure, EXCEPT:
   (A) reversing insert caps.
   (B) prelubrication.
   (C) bent crankshaft.
   (D) dirt on the insert back.

3. Technician A says that oil filters will always catch all foreign particles in the engine. Technician B says that dirt can enter the engine through a vacuum leak. Who is right?
   (A) A only.
   (B) B only.
   (C) Both A & B.
   (D) Neither A nor B.

4. Technician A says that thrust flanges are used to control movement of the bearing in its housing. Technician B says that one should not force a bearing insert into place by pressing on the center. Who is right?
   (A) A only.
   (B) B only.
   (C) Both A & B.
   (D) Neither A nor B.

5. Technician A says that bearing spread helps to hold the bearing in place during assembly. Technician B says that the crush area creates a tight insert-to-bore contact. Who is right?
   (A) A only.
   (B) B only.
   (C) Both A & B.
   (D) Neither A nor B.

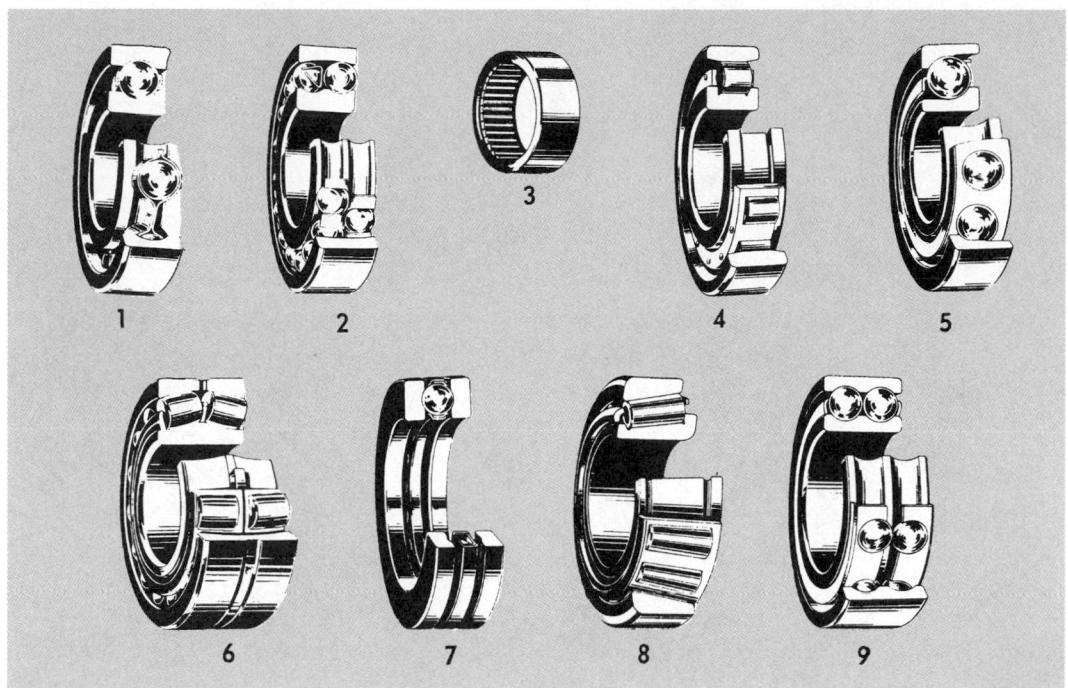

6. Technician A says that a few nicks in the insert housing bore are not harmful. Technician B says that reversing or mixing bearing caps will cause the bores to become misaligned. Who is right?
   (A) A only.
   (B) B only.
   (C) Both A & B.
   (D) Neither A nor B.

7. Never _____ a bearing sealed on both sides.
   (A) grease
   (B) wash
   (C) spin
   (D) Both A & B.

8. Technician A says that hydraulic or mechanical pullers are superior to striking tools for bearing removal and installation. Technician B says that you should always apply pulling force to the free race. Who is right?
   (A) A only.
   (B) B only.
   (C) Both A & B.
   (D) Neither A nor B.

9. Technician A says that bearings, under pulling pressure, can fly apart with great force. Technician B says that if a bearing is started in a "cocked" position, it will line up under pressure. Who is right?
   (A) A only.
   (B) B only.
   (C) Both A & B.
   (D) Neither A nor B.

10. All of the following statements about servicing antifriction bearings are true, EXCEPT:
    (A) bearing parts should never be mixed.
    (B) when blowing dry, never spin a bearing.
    (C) it is always safer to pull a bearing from its housing or shaft.
    (D) since bearings are hardened, a small amount of dirt will not hurt them.

Suggested Activities

1. Check the clearance of various engine bearings using Plastigage. Compare your measurements to the manufacturer's specifications. Make a chart showing the manufacturer's specifications, the actual clearance, and the difference between these two values.

2. Mike a used crankshaft (both main and rod journals). Using manufacturer's specifications, determine the amount of wear. Would the shaft accept a standard undersize bearing? Check the journals for nicks and scoring.

3. Secure a number of damaged friction and antifriction bearings. Clean and inspect each one. Identify the cause of rejection. Write a report summarizing your findings.

Precision insert bearings help prevent wear of critical engine parts. (AE Clevite)

11

Engine Mechanical Troubleshooting

After studying this chapter, you will be able to:
- Summarize preliminary test steps.
- Perform a compression test.
- Use a cylinder leakage detector.
- Perform a vacuum test.
- Check engine oil pressure.
- Diagnose engine mechanical problems.

This chapter is concerned with engine mechanical troubleshooting. Mechanical troubleshooting involves checking the overall condition of the engine. Checks and measurements of specific internal engine parts are covered in the next few chapters. Other chapters deal with the diagnosis and repair of engine related systems, such as fuel, ignition, emissions, exhaust, and cooling systems.

Steps to Diagnosing Engine Problems

The following sections outline the procedures for isolating the causes of engine problems. These procedures help the technician determine which engine component is defective.

Work Logically

Always proceed logically when attempting to locate engine problems. This is true even when the problem seems obvious. For example, a locked up engine may seem to require a complete engine teardown, when the actual problem is that someone used a flywheel bolt that was too long, jamming the flywheel to the engine block. Jumping to an immediate conclusion or replacing the first component that comes to mind will almost never solve the problem. To properly diagnose an engine problem, concentrate on the probable sources of the problem and make simple checks first. Proceeding logically and testing everything before replacing anything will pay big dividends in the long run.

Preliminary Checks

Before checking engine mechanical condition, several important nonengine systems must be checked, depending on the exact engine complaint. These checks may uncover a problem cause that is unrelated to the engine's mechanical

condition. The units involved in these *preliminary checks,* if faulty, can produce a variety of apparent faults in other related systems. Failure to make these preliminary checks can lead the technician to disassemble an engine for no reason.

 Note: These procedures are covered in later chapters.

Solicit the Owner's Comments

The most important preliminary check is to find out the exact nature of the problem. Before starting diagnostic procedures, ask the vehicle owner or driver to describe the problem. The owner's comments and answers to specific questions can provide valuable clues. It may also be helpful to take a short test-drive to experience the problem first-hand.

Try to relate the driver's comments to a specific problem, such as hard starting, poor acceleration, or missing. Then determine under what conditions the problem occurs: vehicle speed; transmission gear; engine temperature; weather conditions; whether the problems occur occasionally or all the time; recent changes, such as other work done on the vehicle, new parts, or a different fuel; and related sounds, such as backfire, howl, grind, or whistle. A set of prepared questions may be used to make sure all important areas are discussed.

Make Preliminary Checks

The following checks of nonengine systems may reveal the problem without further testing. In some cases, it may be logical to skip certain checks, depending on the nature of the problem.

- Ignition System—Check the condition of the spark plugs, wires, coil rotor, distributor cap, primary wiring, and other ignition-related components.
- Fuel System—Check the condition of the fuel injection system or carburetor, the air and fuel filters, and the fuel lines.
- Computer Control System—Retrieve any on-board computer trouble codes, and track down any computer-related defects.

- Emission Control Systems—Check the operation of the PCV and EGR valves, smog pump, thermostatic air cleaner, evaporative emission controls, and other emission components. Correct and recheck operation.
- Battery and Electrical System—Check battery voltage and perform a capacity test. Check the starter, battery, coil, and alternator leads for good connections. Check starter and alternator/regulator operation.
- Oil and Coolant Levels—Check the dipstick for the amount and condition of engine oil. Check the radiator coolant level. Check for signs of oil in the radiator or coolant in the engine oil.
- Fasteners—Tighten the intake manifold and throttle body fasteners. If needed, torque the head bolts.
- Fittings—Check and tighten fuel line and vacuum fittings.

Check the Engine's Mechanical Condition

If the checks listed above do not pinpoint the problem, check the mechanical condition of the engine. Directions for conducting a compression test, a cylinder leakage test, a vacuum test, and an oil pressure test are presented in the following sections.

The technician should check compression in all cylinders. Checking one or two cylinders where the plugs are easy to remove is not sufficient. If the compression (or cylinder leakage) test indicates a doubtful condition, be sure to inform the owner of the need for internal repairs. If the engine fails in the compression test, run a cylinder leakage test to determine just where the trouble lies.

Performing a Compression Test

Before performing a **compression test,** operate the engine until normal operating temperature is reached. To perform the compression test, proceed as follows:

1. Remove the spark plugs (this is covered in more detail in Chapter 18) and the air cleaner.
2. Block the throttle valve in the wide open position. The choke must also be fully opened if the vehicle has a carburetor.
3. Make sure that the battery is fully charged. Ground the distributor end of the coil secondary wire.
4. Attach a remote starter control. If the key switch will be damaged by remote cranking when in the lock or off position, turn the key to the on position.
5. Insert a compression gauge tightly in the spark plug hole, or port.
6. Crank the engine until the gauge shows no further rise in pressure. This will require at least 4 or 5 compression strokes. See **Figure 11-1.**

On a cylinder with good compression, the first compression stroke will force the gauge indicator needle a considerable distance up the scale. Succeeding strokes will raise it more until the highest level is shown. Record the highest reading for each cylinder. For engines having plug holes that are difficult to reach, a compression gauge having an offset tip or a flex hose is useful. Look at **Figure 11-2.**

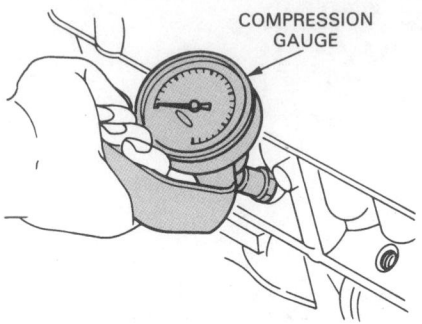

Figure 11-1. A compression gauge can be used to check gasoline engine mechanical condition (valves, rings). (Nissan)

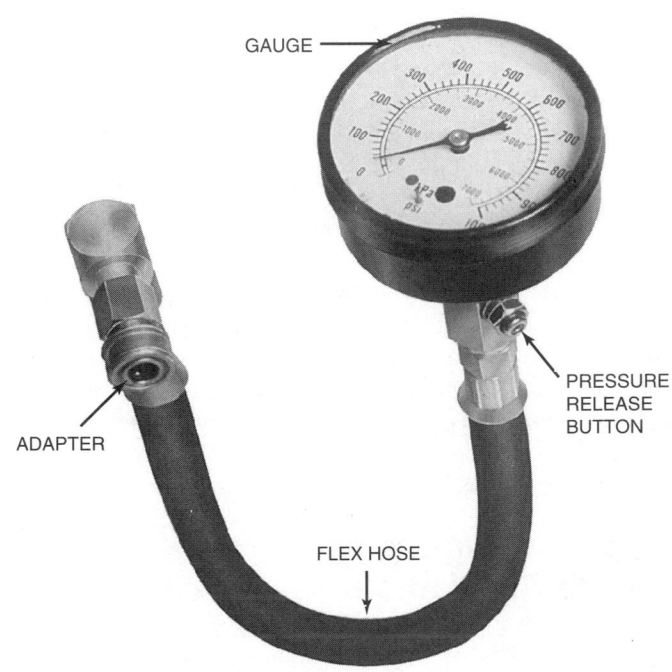

Figure 11-2. One type of engine compression text gauge. This unit may be used on both gasoline and diesel engines. Note the flex hose, which allows easier access to spark plug holes and injector holes. (Lisle Tools)

When checking compression on diesel engines, remember that compression levels will be considerably higher than those produced in a gasoline engine. Note that the gauge in **Figure 11-3** is not hand-held, but is securely attached. In some setups, the gauge adapter is bolted in place. In other applications, the gauge is threaded into a glow plug opening. Follow the manufacturer's recommendations.

Interpreting Compression Readings

Examine the readings for all cylinders. Generally, the lowest cylinder should not read more than 10%-15% below the highest cylinder. This figure depends on engine design, compression ratio, etc. Some manufacturers' specifications permit greater variation. Variations between cylinders will have a more adverse effect upon engine performance than overall readings that are even but slightly below specifications.

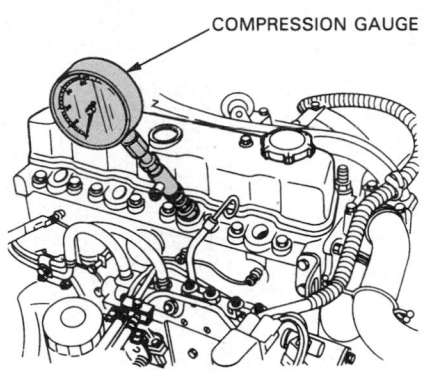

COMPRESSION GAUGE

Figure 11-3. This diesel engine compression gauge is firmly attached to provide a positive leakproof seal. (Nissan)

Low Compression Readings

When taking compression readings, watch the action of the gauge needle. When the needle raises a small amount on the first stroke and only a little more on succeeding strokes, one of the valves is probably not sealing because it is burned, warped, or sticking.

A low buildup on the first stroke with a gradual buildup on succeeding strokes until the needle reaches a moderate reading can mean worn, stuck, or scored rings. If two adjacent cylinders are low, a blown head gasket or warped head-to-block surface could be responsible.

To help pinpoint the cause of low compression, add one tablespoon of heavy engine oil (30W minimum) to the gasoline engine cylinder with a low reading.

Caution: Diesel engines have very high compression. When at top dead center, there is a minimum of space between the piston and cylinder head. An excess amount of oil can cause serious engine damage because the oil will not compress. Some diesel makers forbid the use of any oil. Oil should only be used in a diesel engine when recommended by the manufacturer.

After adding the oil, reattach the compression gauge. Crank the engine for a few extra compression strokes and watch the gauge. If the compression goes up a noticeable amount, worn rings are indicated. If the addition of the oil produces no significant rise, valve trouble, a broken piston, or a blown gasket is probably causing the low reading.

Sometimes, sticking valves or rings may free up if special oil treatments are added to the crankcase and the engine operated for a period of time to free the valves or rings. In the past, many treatment products could be poured through the carburetor with the engine running. However, modern vehicles equipped with a catalytic converter should never have any kind of cleaner or oil treatment poured through the carburetor or the throttle body on fuel injection engines.

High Compression Readings

If the *compression pressure* exceeds specifications, the engine may have been modified to increase the compression. There could also be a buildup of carbon on the head of the piston and on the combustion chamber walls. If carbon buildup is causing pinging that cannot be stopped by retarding the timing or by switching to a higher octane gasoline, the engine should be disassembled and the carbon should be removed.

Another sign of excessive carbon is "dieseling" (engine continues to run after ignition is turned off). Dieseling action can be caused by glowing bits of carbon in the combustion chambers. Hard or slow cranking can also indicate excessive compression from carbon buildup.

Using a Cylinder Leakage Detector

When a cylinder produces a low compression reading, it is often helpful to perform a cylinder leakage test. Unlike a compression gauge, the *cylinder leakage detector* can be used to pinpoint the exact cause of the problem. The leakage detector is inserted in the spark plug hole. The piston is then brought up to dead center on the compression stroke, and compressed air is admitted to the cylinder. Once the combustion chamber is pressurized, a special gauge will read the percentage of leakage. Refer to **Figure 11-4.** Leakage exceeding 20% is considered excessive.

While the air pressure is retained in the cylinder, listen for the hiss of escaping air. A leak by the intake valve will be audible in the throttle body or carburetor. A leak by the exhaust valve can be heard at the tail pipe. Leakage past the rings will be audible when the oil filler cap is removed or at the PCV (positive crankcase ventilation) connection. If air

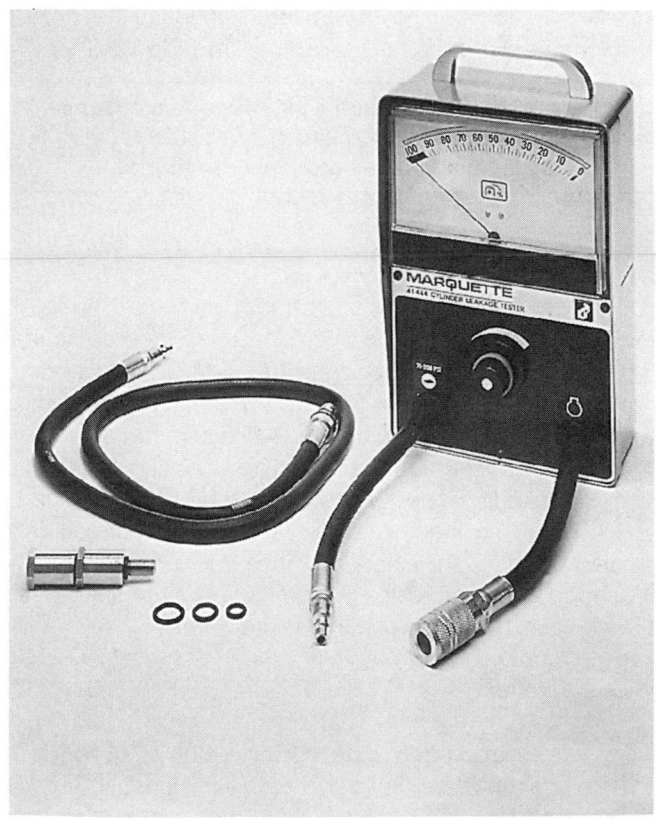

Figure 11-4. One type of cylinder leakage test tool. (Marquette)

is passing through a blown gasket to an adjacent cylinder, the noise will be evident at the plug hole of the cylinder into which the air is leaking. Cracks in the block or gasket leakage into the cooling system may be detected by a stream of bubbles in the radiator.

Using a Vacuum Gauge

A *vacuum gauge* is a useful diagnostic tool. It can be used to detect vacuum leaks, sticking valves, worn rings, clogged exhaust, and incorrect valve or ignition timing. Great care, however, must be used in interpreting the readings and actions of the gauge indicator needle. In many instances, the readings will point to several possible problems. Further checking will be required to isolate the exact cause.

Vacuum gauges are calibrated in inches of mercury, which is a common way to express vacuum, or negative pressure. Mercury is usually abbreviated as its chemical symbol, Hg. The vacuum gauge reads the difference in pressure between the air in the intake manifold and the outside air. The vacuum reading for a given engine can be affected by fuel system adjustment and condition, ignition timing, valve timing, valve and valve guide condition, cylinder wear, piston and ring condition, vacuum leaks, PCV condition, exhaust restrictions, and spark plug adjustment.

Attaching a Vacuum Gauge

When possible, connect the vacuum gauge to the intake manifold. Some manifolds incorporate a plug that may be removed so that a vacuum line adapter can be installed. If no opening is provided, connect the hose to another vacuum-operated unit fitting. See **Figure 11-5.**

 Note: If the distributor has a vacuum advance unit, do not remove it to connect the vacuum gauge. Find some other vacuum fitting.

Cranking Vacuum Test

When performing the *cranking vacuum test,* the engine must be at normal operating temperature. Connect the vacuum gauge as shown in **Figure 11-5.** Make sure the throttle valve is fully closed. Ground the coil high-tension wire or unplug the ignition module if recommended. Crank the engine and average the readings. Cranking speed must be up to specifications.

A relatively steady (some pulsation is normal), high vacuum reading indicates an absence of vacuum leaks and good ring and valve action. A low but fairly steady reading can mean vacuum leaks, worn intake valve guides, poor compression, improper valve timing, and other problems.

An erratic (uneven) reading can point to burned or sticky valves, a damaged piston, or a blown gasket. If the cranking vacuum test indicates problems, conduct a cylinder leakage test. If cylinder leakage test equipment is not available, conduct a compression test.

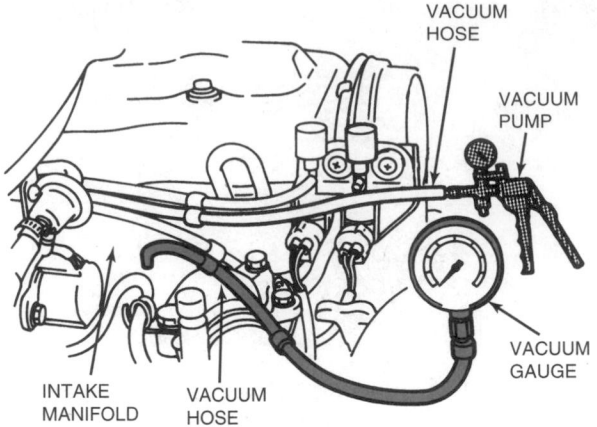

Figure 11-5. A vacuum gauge connected to the intake manifold. Note the vacuum pump, which is used to supply a vacuum to certain parts during some vacuum tests. Follow the manufacturer's recommendations for accurate readings. (Geo)

Vacuum Test with Engine Running

Bring the engine to normal operating temperature and connect the vacuum gauge to the intake manifold. Run the engine at the specified idle speed.

The vacuum gauge should read between 15 and 22 inches Hg., depending upon the engine and the altitude at which the test is performed. As altitude increases, vacuum readings will decrease. Therefore, subtract one inch Hg. from the specified reading for every 1000 feet of elevation above sea level. The reading should be steady. High-performance engines with considerable valve overlap tend to produce a lower, more erratic vacuum reading, especially at idle.

 Caution: If the engine is equipped with a turbocharger, do not run the engine at a speed high enough to cause the turbocharger to begin boosting manifold pressure. This positive pressure will be transmitted to the vacuum gauge, ruining it.

Interpreting Vacuum Gauge Readings

Observing the vacuum gauge reading while the engine is idling will help pinpoint trouble areas. Remember, however, that many vacuum gauge readings can be caused by more than one problem. Always conduct all other appropriate tests before arriving at a final diagnostic decision.

Figure 11-6 shows a number of vacuum gauge readings. Note that the gauge area from 15 to 22 in. Hg. is marked in color. This is the normal range for most vehicles. Check manufacturer's specifications for exact readings.

The typical problems listed on the next page are numbered 1 through 16. These numbers correspond to numbers in **Figure 11-6.** Study the gauge readings and then read the corresponding descriptions.

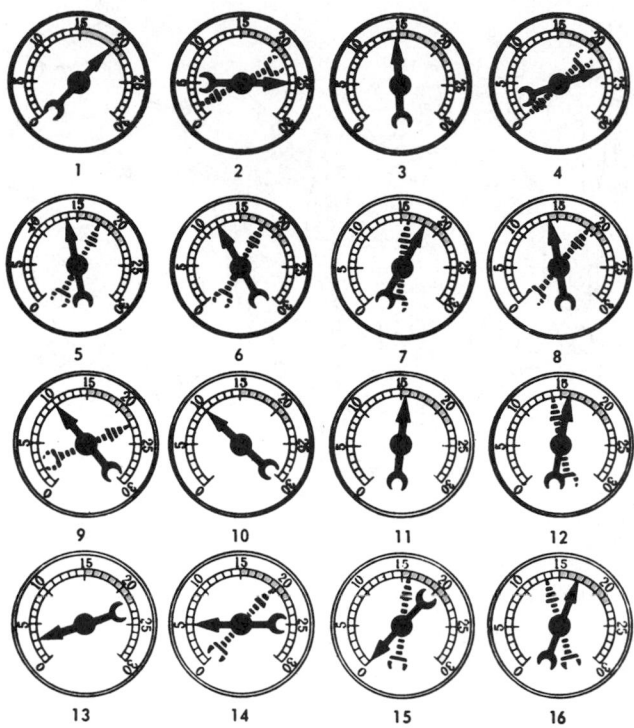

Figure 11-6. Typical vacuum gauge readings. (Nissan)

1. Needle between 15 and 22 in. and holding steady as engine idles: *Normal reading.*
2. When the throttle is rapidly opened and closed, (dotted needle) needle will drop to a low (but not zero) reading. When the throttle is suddenly released, the needle will snap back up to a higher-than-normal figure: *Normal reading during rapid acceleration and deceleration.*
3. Needle will register as low as 15 in., but it will be relatively steady at engine idle: *Normal for high lift cam with large overlap.*
4. When the engine is accelerated (dotted needle) the needle drops to 0 in. Hg. Upon deceleration, needle will snap back to a higher-than-normal reading for a very brief time: *Worn rings or diluted oil.*
5. The needle (dotted) remains steady at a normal vacuum as the engine idles, but it occasionally makes a sharp, fast movement down and back about 4 in. Hg.: *One or more valves may be sticking.*
6. A regular, evenly spaced drop of the needle at idle: *One or more burned or warped valves, or insufficient tappet clearance.*
7. A small but regular vacuum drop at idle: *One or more valves are not seating.*
8. The needle oscillates (swings back and forth) over about a 4 in. Hg. range at idle speed. As engine speed is increased, the needle becomes steady: *Worn valve guides.*
9. Reading at idle is relatively steady, but the needle oscillation becomes more pronounced as engine rpm is increased: *Weak valve springs.*
10. A steady but low reading at idle: *Late valve timing.*
11. A steady but low reading at idle: *Retarded ignition timing.*

12. Regular, small pulsation of the needle at idle: *Spark plug gaps too small or the ignition primary system is not producing enough voltage.*
13. A low, steady reading: *Intake manifold or throttle mounting flange gasket leak.*
14. A regular drop of four to eight inches: *Blown head gasket or warped head-to-block surface.*
15. When the engine is first started and is idled, the reading is normal, but as the engine rpm is increased, the needle will slowly drop to a low reading, sometimes as low as 0 in. Hg.: *Exhaust back pressure caused by a clogged muffler or kinked tail pipe.*

 Note: Excessive exhaust clogging may cause the needle to drop to a low reading at idle.

16. The needle moves slowly back and forth: *Improper fuel mixture.*

 Note: Improper fuel mixture may be caused by problems in the fuel injection or computer control system or by a maladjusted or defective carburetor.

These examples are typical. The information, if used with care, should be helpful in locating trouble on actual jobs.

Checking Oil Pressure

Oil pressure is critical to the operation of the engine. It prevents premature engine wear by delivering oil to pressure points. It also fills the hydraulic lifters or hydraulic lash adjusters, allowing them to properly operate the valves. An early sign of low oil pressure is often noisy valves. If an engine is operated for any time without oil pressure, it will be destroyed.

Before testing oil pressure, make sure that the engine oil level and the engine idle speed are satisfactory. If these are OK, obtain an oil pressure gauge of the proper range, such as the one shown in **Figure 11-7.** Most engine lubrication systems develop no more than 80 PSI (552 kPa), so a 0-100 PSI (689.5 kPa) gauge will be satisfactory for most oil pressure testing.

 Note: If the oil pressure specifications are given in kilopascals (kPa) and your gauge reads only pounds per square inch (PSI), multiply the PSI reading by 6.895 to obtain the kPa figure.

Next, locate the engine *oil pressure sender.* This is the device that sends the pressure signal to the dashboard indicator. It is often located near the oil filter or on the side of the engine block. Carefully remove the sender and install the gauge using the proper threaded adapter. Use of an incorrect adapter will cause oil to spray when the engine is started.

Start the engine and observe the oil pressure. Compare the pressure readings to the specifications for the particular engine. As a general rule, pressure should be at least 20 PSI (138 kPa) at idle on a warm engine. Oil pressure should increase as engine speed is increased.

If oil pressure is low, the oil pump could be defective, the pressure regulator could be stuck open, or there could be internal leaks in the engine oiling system. In addition, the oil pickup system could be clogged or leaking air or the oil could be too thin. If oil pressure is too high, the pressure regulator could be stuck or the oil could be too heavy.

Engine and Engine System Problem Diagnosis Charts

The following charts list major problems, possible causes, and suggested corrections. Some problems have more than one cause. In such cases, each cause must be properly identified and applicable corrections must be made. Coverage is given to the identification and correction of common engine and accessory noise problems. Note that in many cases, the actual problem is not in the engine mechanical system. Frequently, a problem can be solved with a simple adjustment. Other chapters cover non-mechanical engine problems in more detail.

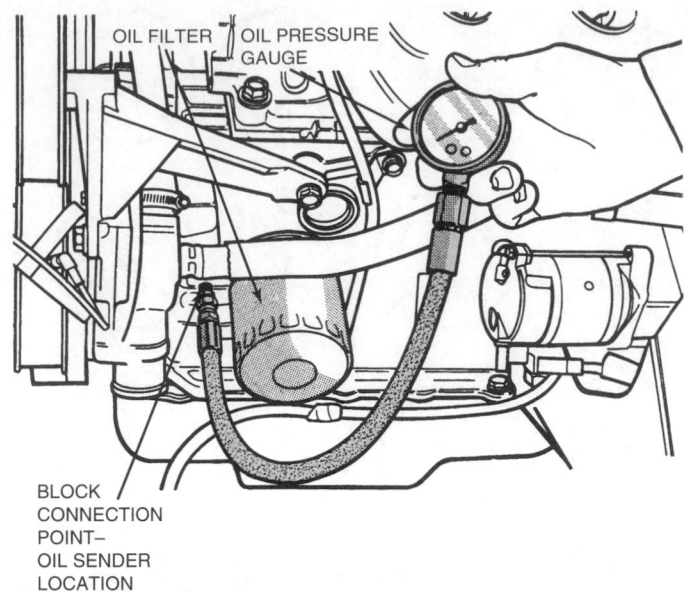

Figure 11-7. Oil pressure gauge. (Chrysler)

Engine and Engine System Problem Diagnosis Charts

Problem: Low Compression

Possible Cause	Correction
1. Worn or stuck piston rings.	1. Replace rings, clean piston oil drain holes.
2. Broken rings or pistons.	2. Replace rings and pistons.
3. Bent connecting rod.	3. Replace rod(s).
4. Incorrect connecting rods or pistons.	4. Install new rods or pistons.
5. Blown head gasket.	5. Replace gasket, check for warped head/block.
6. Cracked head or block.	6. Replace head or block.
7. Valves burned or stuck, eccentric (out-of-round) seats.	7. Replace valves, repair seats.
8. Broken timing chain or belt.	8. Replace chain/belt.
9. Broken camshaft.	9. Replace camshaft.
10. Incorrect valve timing.	10. Retime valve train.
11. Valves set too tight.	11. Adjust valves.

Problem: Low Oil Pressure

Possible Cause	Correction
1. Low oil level.	1. Add oil.
2. Improper oil viscosity.	2. Use proper viscosity oil.
3. Oil diluted.	3. Change oil, check for cause of dilution.
4. Camshaft, main, or connecting rod bearings worn.	4. Install new bearings.
5. Crankshaft or camshaft journals worn.	5. Grind journals.
6. Oil pump worn.	6. Replace or rebuild oil pump.
7. Pressure relief valve spring weak.	7. Replace spring or add washers.
8. Oil pump intake clogged.	8. Clean screen and pipe; tighten connection.
9. Hole in oil pickup pipe.	9. Replace pipe.
10. Oil line connection leak.	10. Tighten connection.
11. Defective gauge (direct pressure type).	11. Replace gauge.
12. Defective sender or gauge (electric type).	12. Replace sender or gauge.
13. Plugged oil filter.	13. Replace filter and oil.
14. Improperly installed bypass oil filter.	14. Install correctly.
15. Low idle speed.	15. Set speed to specs.
16. Oil galleys clogged.	16. Clean out or replace block.
17. Loose or missing oil galley plugs.	17. Tighten and/or install plugs.

Problem: Excessive Oil Pressure

Possible Cause
1. Oil too viscous (heavy).
2. Pressure relief valve spring under too much tension.
3. Pressure relief valve stuck.
4. Main oil line from pump clogged.
5. Defective gauge (direct pressure type).
6. Defective sender or gauge (electric type).

Correction
1. Change to lighter oil.
2. Reduce spring pressure.
3. Clean valve.
4. Clean line.
5. Replace gauge.
6. Replace sender or gauge.

Problem: Engine Oil Contamination

Possible Cause
1. Blowby caused by worn piston rings.
2. Blowby—excessive piston or cylinder wear.
3. Coolant entering oil—cracked block or head.
4. Coolant entering oil—blown head gasket.

5. Fuel entering oil—excessive choking (carburetor only).
6. Fuel entering oil—float level too high (carburetor only).
7. Fuel entering oil—float valve leaks (carburetor only).
8. Fuel entering oil—fuel pump diaphragm cracked.
9. Water entering oil—crankcase condensation.
10. Rapid formation of sludge.

Correction
1. Install new rings.
2. Rebore and install new pistons.
3. Seal leak or replace part. Drain oil, flush, and refill.
4. Replace gasket. Check head and block surface for warpage. Drain oil, flush, and refill.
5. Adjust choke.
6. Adjust float level.
7. Replace float valve needle and seat.
8. Replace diaphragm or pump.
9. Clean or replace PCV valve.
10. Clean or replace PCV valve; use detergent oil; raise engine operating temperature if too cold; check for missing thermostat, short trip driving.

Problem: No Oil Pressure

Possible Cause
1. Oil level too low.
2. Oil pump inoperative.
3. Defective gauge (direct pressure type).
4. Defective sender or gauge (electric).
5. Wire between sender and gauge disconnected.
6. Pump intake screen or tube clogged.
7. Pressure relief valve stuck.
8. Line to sender or gauge clogged.

Correction
1. Add oil.
2. Repair or replace pump, check pump drive mechanism.
3. Replace gauge.
4. Replace sender or gauge.
5. Connect wire.
6. Clean screen and tube.
7. Clean relief valve, check for free operation.
8. Clean line.

Problem: Excessive Oil Consumption

Possible Cause
1. Oil too light.
2. Oil diluted.
3. Oil level too high.
4. Worn or clogged rings.
5. Excessive piston and cylinder wear.
6. Worn valve guides.
7. Worn valve stems.
8. Excessive speed.
9. Cylinder torque distortion.
10. Worn bearings—excess oil throw-off.
11. Clogged PCV system.
12. Excessive oil pressure.
13. Engine running too hot.
14. Rear main seal leak.
15. Crankshaft front seal leak.
16. Pan gasket leak.
17. Valve cover gasket leak.
18. Timing gear cover leak.
19. Fuel pump mounting flange loose.
20. Oil filter cover leak.

Correction
1. Install heavier oil.
2. Change oil, refer to engine oil contamination chart.
3. Lower oil level.
4. Install new rings.
5. Rebore and install new pistons.
6. Replace guides or ream to next oversize stem.
7. Replace valves.
8. Advise driver to reduce speed.
9. Torque head fasteners correctly.
10. Replace bearings.
11. Clean PCV system.
12. Reduce pressure.
13. Reduce operating temperature.
14. Replace seal.
15. Replace seal.
16. Replace gasket or tighten fasteners.
17. Tighten fasteners or replace gasket.
18. Tighten fasteners or replace gasket.
19. Tighten fasteners.
20. Tighten cover or replace gasket.

Possible Cause (cont.)

21. External line leak.
22. Oil pan drain plug leak.
23. Oil gallery plug loose.
24. Oil gauge or sender leak.
25. Rear camshaft plug leak.
26. Wrong oil ring design.
27. Rings installed wrong.
28. Glazed cylinder walls—rings will not seat.
29. External leaks.
30. Piston(s) improperly installed.
31. Improper reading of dipstick.

32. Damaged turbocharger seals.
33. Loose or broken turbocharger oil feed line(s).
34. Leaking oil cooler.

Correction (cont.)

21. Repair or replace line.
22. Tighten or replace gasket.
23. Tighten plug.
24. Tighten or replace.
25. Replace plug.
26. Install correct rings.
27. Install correctly.
28. Hone walls; install new rings.
29. Locate and repair.
30. Install correctly.
31. Check with vehicle on level surface; allow sufficient drain-down time; check for possible incorrect dipstick.
32. Replace seals.
33. Tighten or replace as necessary.
34. Repair or replace.

Problem: Backfiring in Intake Manifold

Possible Cause

1. Intake valve not properly seating.

2. Lean mixture.

3. Cross-firing.
4. Plug wires installed wrong.
5. Carbon tracking in distributor cap.
6. Choke not closing fully (carburetor only).
7. Incorrect ignition timing.
8. Incorrect valve timing.

Correction

1. Check for broken spring, valve clearance, sticking, seat condition.
2. Adjust mixture when possible; check fuel injection and computer control system for cause of lean mixture.
3. Arrange plug wires or install new wires, if needed.
4. Connect wires to proper plugs.
5. Replace cap and rotor.
6. Adjust choke.
7. Set timing to specifications.
8. Check for jumped timing chain or belt, reset valve timing to specifications.

Problem: Backfiring in Exhaust System

Possible Cause

1. Turning key off and on while car is in motion.
2. Coil-to-distributor cap secondary wire or coil shorting.
3. Current flow interruption in primary circuit.

4. Incorrect valve timing.
5. Air injection system anti-backfire or diverter valve inoperative.

Correction

1. Advise driver to avoid this practice.
2. Check wire and coil.
3. Check circuit for loose connections and intermittent shorts; check points and condenser where used; check reluctor air gap where adjustable.
4. Correct valve timing.
5. Replace valve.

Problem: Starter Will Not Crank Engine (Electrical System OK)

Possible Cause

1. Defective starter armature or drive.
2. Starter drive pinion jammed into flywheel teeth.

3. Engine crankshaft and/or bearings seized.
4. Engine bearings too tight.
5. Piston-to-cylinder wall clearance too small.
6. Water pump frozen.
7. Insufficient piston ring clearance.
8. Hydrostatic lock (water in combustion chamber).
9. Flywheel or vibration damper bolt too long, contacting engine block.

Correction

1. Rebuild or replace starter.
2. Remove starter. Install new pinion and replace starter ring gear if needed.
3. Grind shaft and replace bearings.
4. Install correct bearings.
5. Fit pistons correctly.
6. Thaw, install antifreeze in cooling system.
7. Install correct rings.
8. Remove water. Repair leak.
9. Replace with correct bolt.

Engine Noise Diagnosis

The noises that can be produced by the engine and engine accessory systems are numerous. Whines, squeals, knocks, rattles, and many other sounds can come from the engine. They can be loud or soft, sharp or indistinct, metallic or nonmetallic. Accurate diagnosis of engine noises takes a great deal of practice, and even the experienced technician can be puzzled. Whenever possible, listen to engine noises while attempting to pinpoint the cause. The use of a technician's stethoscope is very helpful in identifying the source of noises. When the engine is torn down, check to see how accurate your diagnosis was.

Be careful when making a diagnosis based on sounds. Do not recommend an engine teardown unless you are positive that the noise is caused by internal engine parts. Remember that a great number of noises can be made by other vehicle parts, such as the water pump, fan, alternator, and air conditioning compressor. These components can be quickly checked by disconnecting their drive belt(s). The belts themselves can be the source of squeaks and ticking noises. Other noises can come from the flywheel, torque converter, or other parts of the driveline. Broken engine mounts can cause heavy metallic noises and can cause the fan or pulleys to contact stationary vehicle parts. Exhaust pipes, mufflers, and tail pipes can cause various thumps, clangs, and rattles. Exhaust leaks are often the source of ticking noises during acceleration that can be mistaken for valve train noises.

Problem: Noisy Valve Train

Sound Identification: Noisy valves may be identified by either a regular or irregular, sharp clicking or tapping sound. If excessive tappet clearance exists, the clicking will be very regular and the frequency will increase with engine rpm. Sticking valves and faulty lifters will cause intermittent clicking of varying intensity.

Possible Cause	Correction
1. Insufficient lubrication.	1. Provide ample lubrication.
2. Insufficient stem-to-guide clearance.	2. Ream guides to correct size.
3. Warped valve stem.	3. Replace valve.
4. Carboned stem and guide.	4. Clean stem and guide. Replace both if excessive wear is present.
5. Broken valve spring.	5. Replace spring.
6. Weak, corroded, or incorrect spring.	6. Replace with correct spring.
7. Sticking hydraulic lifters.	7. Clean or replace lifters.
8. Improper valve train clearance.	8. Set clearance as specified.
9. Valve seat not concentric with guide or stem.	9. Regrind valve and/or seat.
10. Sticking rocker arm.	10. Clean or replace.
11. Valve lifter loose in bore or chipped.	11. Replace lifter.
12. Valve spring installed incorrectly .	12. Reverse spring position.
13. Excessively low or high oil level in pan.	13. Bring oil level to correct height.
14. Loose or broken rocker arm.	14. Tighten or replace arm.
15. Loose or broken valve seat.	15. Replace insert and stake as recommended.

Problem: Crankshaft Bearing and Flywheel Knocks

Sound Identification: Dull, heavy pound or thud - especially noticeable during periods of heavy engine loading. Frequency is related to crankshaft rpm. The loose bearing may generally be isolated by shorting spark plugs. When the plugs in line with the bearing are shorted, the sound will change. If all the main bearings are quite loose, a great deal more noise will be evident and the frequency will increase. When excessive end play causes knocking, holding in the clutch will usually alter the sound. To test for a loose flywheel, turn off the key and just before the engine stops, turn the key on again. If the flywheel is loose, a distinct knock will occur when the key is turned on.

Possible Cause	Correction
1. Shaft worn.	1. Regrind or replace shaft.
2. Bearing worn.	2. Replace bearing.
3. Thin oil.	3. Change to correct viscosity.
4. Low oil pressure.	4. Correct as required.
5. Excessive end play.	5. Correct end play.
6. Sprung crankshaft.	6. Straighten or replace crankshaft.
7. Loose flywheel.	7. Tighten flywheel fasteners.

Problem: Connecting Rod Knock

Sound Identification: The connecting rod knock is usually more evident when the engine is floating (not accelerating or holding back on compression) at speed around 30 mph (48 km/h) in direct drive. The knock, a regular light metallic rap, can either be eliminated or greatly subdued by shorting out the cylinder concerned.

Possible Cause	Correction
1. Crankshaft rod journal worn.	1. Grind journal or replace shaft.
2. Connecting rod bearings worn.	2. Install new bearings.
3. Oil diluted.	3. Change to correct viscosity.
4. Low oil pressure.	4. Correct as required.
5. Bent or twisted rod.	5. Straighten rod. Replace insert bearing. Replace rod if bend or twist is excessive.

--- Problem: Piston Slap ---

Sound Identification: Piston slap is caused by the piston tipping from side to side in the cylinder. This tipping produces sounds that can range from a regular clicking to a very distinct hollow clatter, depending on the severity of wear. Piston slap will be more noticeable when the engine is cold. In mild cases, it may actually disappear after the engine is warmed up. The noise may also disappear if the plug wire on the affected cylinder is removed and the vehicle driven. Adding a tablespoon of heavy oil to each cylinder should temporarily quiet the noise. Do not add oil to a diesel engine.

Possible Cause
1. Cylinder worn.
2. Pistons badly worn.
3. Pistons mildly worn.
4. Piston pin fitted too tight.
5. Insufficient lubrication.

Correction
1. Rebore and fit oversize pistons.
2. Rebore and fit oversize pistons.
3. May be expanded by knurling, peening, etc.
4. Fit pins as specified.
5. Correct as required.

--- Problem: Loose Piston Pins ---

Sound Identification: Loose pins will cause a sharp, double-knock, especially at idle speeds. If only one pin is loose, the knocking will become more distinct when the spark plug in the affected cylinder is shorted. If all pins are loose, shorting one plug will not alter the sounds.

Possible Cause
1. Piston pin worn.
2. Piston pin hole worn.
3. Connecting rod bushing worn.
4. Insufficient lubrication.
5. Piston pin locks missing.
6. Piston pin lock loose.

Correction
1. Fit new pins of correct size.
2. Fit oversize pin.
3. Replace bushing or fit oversize pin.
4. Correct as required.
5. Install locks.
6. Tighten lock.

--- Problem: Timing Gear, Chain, and Belt Noise ---

Sound Identification: Timing gears, chains, and belts can produce noises varying from a high-pitched howl (fitted too tight) to a low-level chatter or growl (badly worn). The timing chain or belt can slap against the cover, producing a thumping or scraping sound. A missing chain tooth will cause a regular and distinct knock. A tight belt can also produce a whirring sound.

Possible Cause
1. Worn chain.
2. Worn sprockets.
3. Loose gear or sprocket.
4. Excessive end play.
5. Gear misalignment.
6. Worn gear.
7. Excessive front camshaft or crankshaft bearing clearance.
8. Gear tooth missing.
9. Worn belt.
10. Worn or defective belt adjuster.

Correction
1. Replace chain and sprockets.
2. Replace chain and sprockets.
3. Replace gear.
4. Correct as needed.
5. Align properly.
6. Replace both camshaft and crankshaft gear.
7. Replace bearings.
8. Replace both gears.
9. Replace belt.
10. Replace adjuster.

--- Problem: Combustion Knocks ---

Sound Identification: Combustion knocks can be divided into two classes: preignition and detonation. Preignition occurs when the fuel-air mixture ignites before the spark plug fires. Detonation occurs when an extra flame front is produced in the combustion chamber, creating an explosion of the fuel charge before it can finish burning evenly. The result is the same: a sharp metallic pinging sound. This pinging is most noticeable during acceleration.

--- Problem: Preignition ---

Possible Cause
1. Overheated engine.
2. Glowing pieces of carbon.
3. Spark plugs overheating.
4. Sharp valve edges.
5. Glowing exhaust valve.

Correction
1. Check cooling system.
2. Remove carbon.
3. Change to cooler plugs, check plug tightness.
4. Install valves with full margin.
5. Check for proper tappet clearance, sticking, air leaks, etc.

--- Problem: Detonation ---

Possible Cause
1. Ignition timing advanced.
2. Engine temperature too high.
3. Carbon buildup raising compression ratio.
4. Low octane fuel.
5. Exhaust heat control valve stuck, or vacuum line improperly connected.
6. Block or head shaved to increase compression.
7. EGR valve disconnected.
8. Thermostatic air cleaner valve stuck in cold position.

Correction
1. Retard timing.
2. Check cooling system.
3. Remove carbon.
4. Switch to high octane fuel.
5. Free valve; check vacuum line connections.
6. Use thicker gasket, change head.
7. Reconnect EGR and check operation.
8. Repair as needed.

--- Problem: Fuel Pump Noise (Mechanical Fuel Pump) ---

Possible Cause
1. Pump-to-block fasteners loose.
2. Rocker arm or eccentric worn.
3. Rocker arm spring weak or broken.
4. Pushrod or bore worn.

Correction
1. Tighten fasteners.
2. Replace.
3. Replace rocker arm spring.
4. Replace pushrod; check for bore wear.

Tech Talk

Some of the most overlooked tools in your possession are the cheapest: a pencil and paper. Why is it important to have a pencil and paper in your toolbox? To write down the readings that you get when using your expensive measuring tools. Do not try to remember readings. In addition, writing the readings down gives you a record if the owner wants to see what is wrong with his or her vehicle.

Summary

Always proceed logically when attempting to locate engine problems. Before starting, ask the vehicle owner or driver for any comments regarding engine performance and make necessary preliminary checks of nonengine systems.

The technician should check compression in all cylinders. Variations between cylinders will have more effect on engine performance than low overall readings. Possible causes of low compression are defects in the valves, rings, pistons, head, block, or head gasket. Excessively high compression is usually caused by carbon buildup in the cylinder head.

When a cylinder produces a low reading, the cylinder leakage detector can pinpoint the exact problem.

A vacuum gauge can be used to detect vacuum leaks, sticking valves, worn rings, clogged exhaust, and incorrect valve or ignition timing. Vacuum gauge readings may be due to several possible problems, and further checking will be required to isolate the exact problem.

Proper oil pressure prevents premature engine wear by delivering oil to pressure points. Oil also fills the hydraulic lifters or hydraulic lash adjusters. If an engine is operated for any time without oil pressure, it will be destroyed. The oil pressure gauge will allow the technician to determine whether the engine has an oil pressure problem. Oil pressure problems can be caused by a low oil level, a worn oil pump, a clogged oil filter or intake strainer, or internal pressure leaks.

Know These Terms

Preliminary checks
Compression test
Compression pressure
Cylinder leakage detector
Vacuum gauge
Cranking vacuum text
Oil pressure sender

Review Questions—Chapter 11

Do not write in this book. Write your answers on a separate sheet of paper.

1. When taking a compression reading, the technician should crank the engine through at least _____ compression strokes.
   (A) 2
   (B) 3
   (C) 4
   (D) 6

2. Excessive compression pressure could indicate a buildup of carbon in the ____.
   (A) combustion chamber
   (B) oil galleries
   (C) ring groves
   (D) oil pickup tube

3. A steady vacuum gauge reading of 12 inches at idle could indicate _____.
   (A) normal engine operation
   (B) a burned valve
   (C) an over-rich mixture
   (D) late valve timing

4. Installing a high-lift cam with more valve overlap would have what effect on the engine vacuum at idle?
   (A) Vacuum would be lower but steadier.
   (B) Vacuum would be higher and steadier.
   (C) Vacuum would be lower and more erratic.
   (D) Vacuum would be higher and more erratic.

5. The technician should subtract one inch of vacuum from vacuum specifications for every _____ feet of elevation above sea level.
   (A) 500
   (B) 1000
   (C) 2000
   (D) 10,000

6. If an engine comes into the shop with low oil pressure, what is the first thing that the technician should check?
   (A) Oil pump condition.
   (B) Pickup screen condition.
   (C) Engine idle speed.
   (D) Engine oil level.

7. List five possible causes of low cylinder compression.

8. List four engine defects that can be located with a vacuum gauge.

9. List four possible causes of low oil pressure.

10. Which of the following could cause high oil pressure?
    (A) Internal oil passage leaks.
    (B) Plugged oil filter.
    (C) Low oil level.
    (D) Stuck pressure regulator valve.

ASE-Type Questions

1. Technician A says that owner comments or answers to questions will usually mislead the technician. Technician B says the fuel and ignition systems should be eliminated as sources of problems before checking the engine mechanical system. Who is right?
   (A) A only.
   (B) B only.
   (C) Both A & B.
   (D) Neither A nor B.

2. The compression test and/or cylinder leakage test can be used to determine all of the following engine problems, EXCEPT:
   (A) defective oil pump.
   (B) burned valve.
   (C) worn rings.
   (D) blown head gasket.

3. Technician A says that it is more important for compression readings to be the same in all cylinders than for all cylinders to be up to the specified pressure. Technician B says that adding oil to the cylinder will raise the compression reading somewhat if the valves are burned. Who is right?
   (A) A only.
   (B) B only.
   (C) Both A & B.
   (D) Neither A nor B.

4. When two adjacent cylinders give similar but low compression readings, what is the most likely cause?
   (A) Sticking valves.
   (B) Burned valves.
   (C) Worn rings.
   (D) Blown head gasket.

5. When testing compression on a diesel engine, adding a large amount of oil to a cylinder will _____.
   (A) damage the engine.
   (B) help the engine crank over faster.
   (C) give a more accurate gauge reading.
   (D) produce a low reading.

6. Technician A says that preignition occurs when an extra flame front is produced in the combustion chamber. Technician B says that detonation occurs when the fuel-air mixture ignites before the spark plug fires. Who is right?
   (A) A only.
   (B) B only.
   (C) Both A & B.
   (D) Neither A nor B.

7. Coolant in the engine oil could be caused by all of the following, EXCEPT:
   (A) cracked head.
   (B) blown head gasket.
   (C) ruptured fuel pump diaphragm.
   (D) cracked engine block.

8. Technician A says that the hydraulic lifters are kept filled by engine oil pressure. Technician B says that low oil pressure could cause the valves to be noisy. Who is right?
   (A) A only.
   (B) B only.
   (C) Both A & B.
   (D) Neither A nor B.

9. Which of the following noises is greatly reduced when the spark plug wire is removed?
   (A) Connecting rod knock.
   (B) Valve tapping.
   (C) Piston slap.
   (D) Both A & C.

10. Technician A says that belt-driven accessories can cause noises that may be mistaken for internal engine noises. Technician B says that many exhaust system problems can be mistaken for internal engine problems. Who is right?
    (A) A only.
    (B) B only.
    (C) Both A & B.
    (D) Neither A nor B.

Suggested Activities

1. Perform a compression test. Write down the readings for each cylinder. Calculate the percentage difference between the highest reading and the lowest reading.

2. Check and record engine oil pressure at various engine speeds.

3. Convert pressure gauge readings from psi to kPa or from kPa to psi.

4. Use a vacuum gauge to diagnose engine problems. Write down the readings at various engine speeds. Discuss the readings from the above tests with other members of your class and decide what they indicate about engine condition.

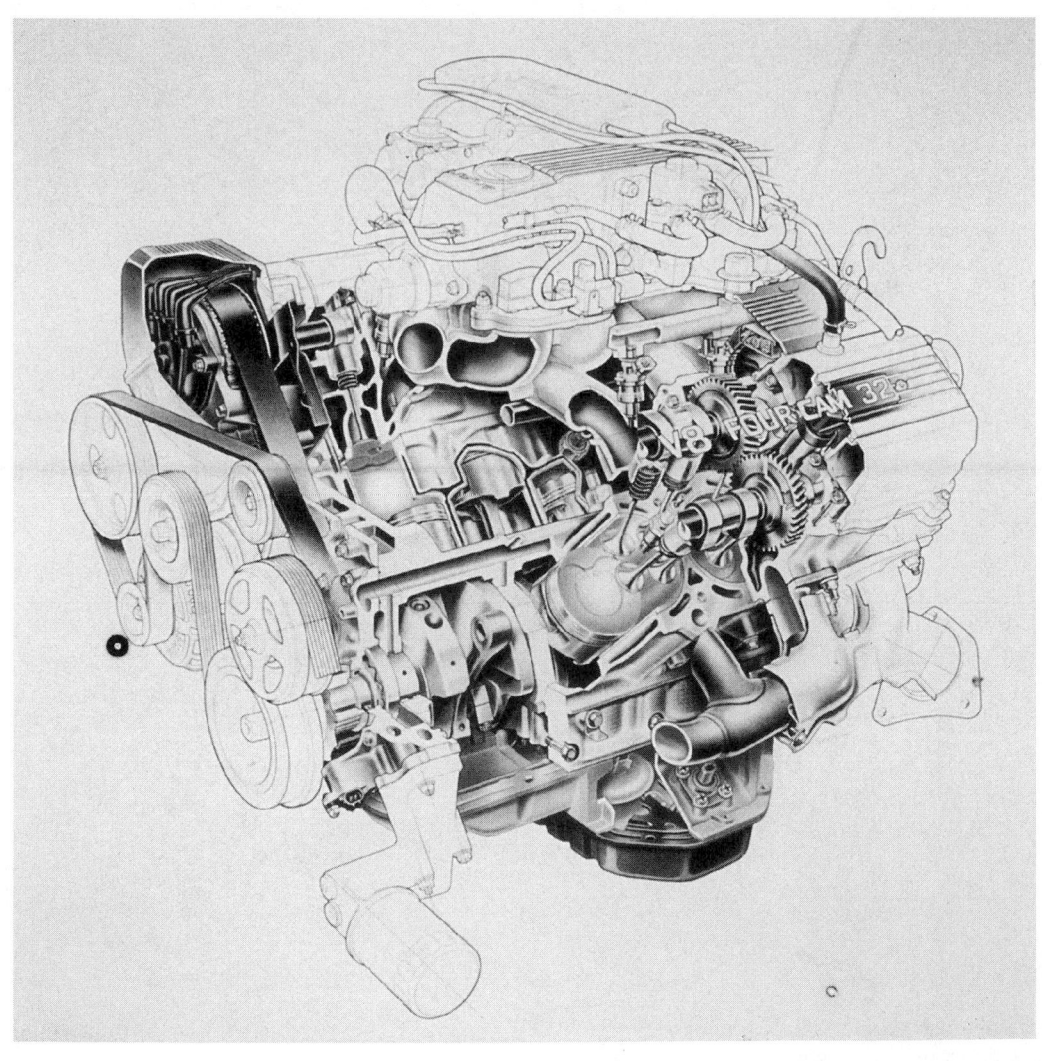

Cutaway of a four-cam, 32-valve, V8 engine. This engine produces 260 hp at 5300 rpm. (Lexus)

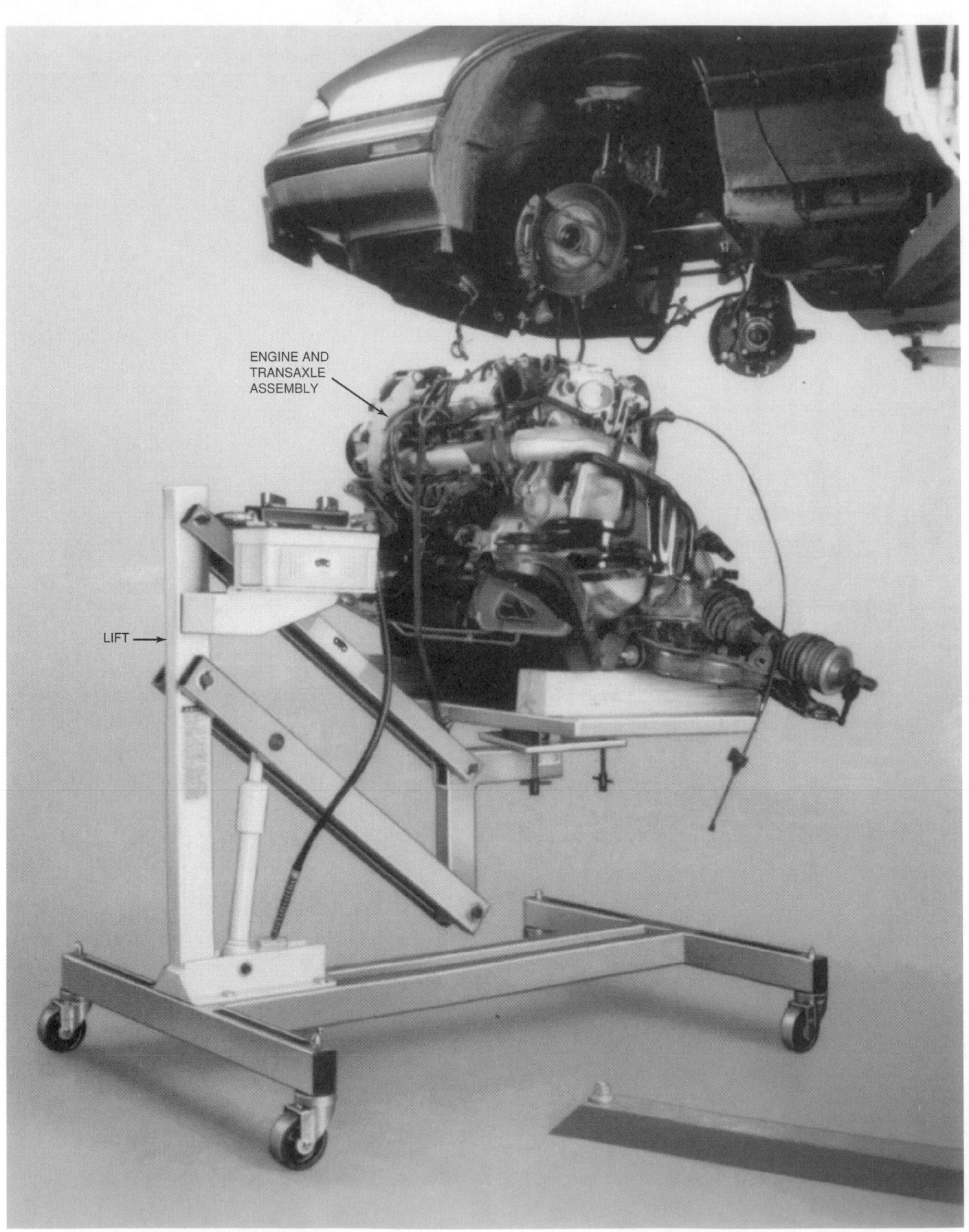

ENGINE AND
TRANSAXLE
ASSEMBLY

LIFT

This power train lift was used to remove the engine and transaxle assembly from beneath the vehicle. Refer to the manufacturer's manual for proper removal procedures. (OTC)

12

Engine Removal, Disassembly, and Inspection

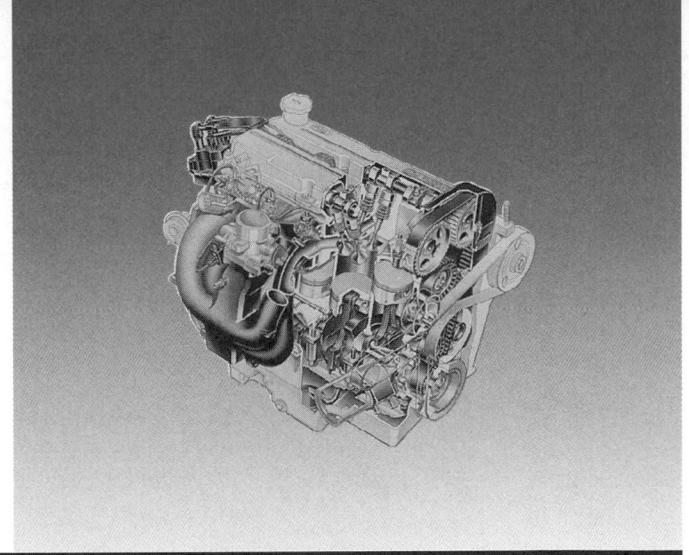

After studying this chapter, you will be able to:
- Describe general procedures for removing an engine from a car.
- Explain the use of engine removal equipment.
- List safety rules that apply to engine removal.
- Describe general procedures for disassembling an engine.
- Explain how to make visual checks of major engine parts.

This chapter explains how to remove, disassemble, and check the internal parts of a typical internal combustion engine used in modern vehicles. These procedures apply to any piston engine built within the last 50 years. The major differences occur not in internal engine design, but in the removal methods between front- and rear-wheel drive vehicles. Other differences are between the overhead camshaft and pushrod type of valve mechanisms, and the increasing use of aluminum for blocks and cylinder heads.

General Removal Procedures

There are many ways that an engine can be removed from a car. When removing an engine, you must consider whether the vehicle is front- or rear-wheel drive, placement of the engine in the vehicle, frame and body clearance, accessory equipment, and the type of transmission or transaxle. Manufacturers' shop manuals will be helpful in determining exact steps for specific engines.

On most rear-wheel drive vehicles and some front-wheel drive vehicles, the engine is pulled upward out of the engine compartment. A different procedure is required when the engine must be removed from beneath the vehicle. See **Figure 12-1.**

Some installations allow the removal of the engine with the transmission or transaxle attached. Others require it to be separated and the engine pulled by itself.

Support the Transmission or Transaxle

If the engine alone is to be pulled, be certain to provide proper support for the transmission or transaxle. The drive plate (provides drive from crankshaft to torque converter) will not support a load. If the transmission or transaxle is not properly supported, serious damage can be done. An

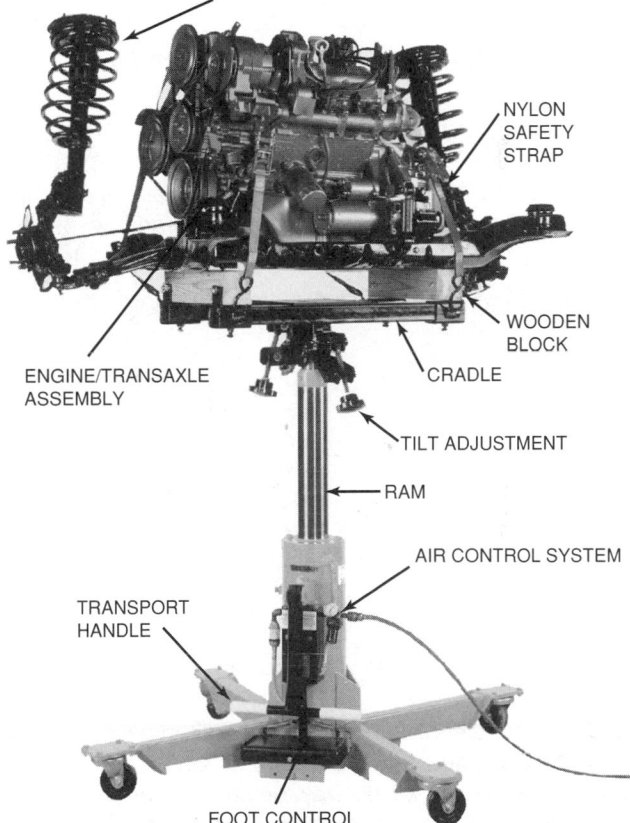

Figure 12-1. Engine, transaxle, and front suspension that have been removed from under a vehicle. Note the nylon safety straps that secure the assembly to the lift. Follow the manufacturer's recommendations. (Meyer Hydraulics)

adjustable stand or a special frame cross member support may be used.

Protect the Vehicle

Before removing the engine, cover the vehicle's fenders with *protective pads.* If the hood hinge attaching points are adjustable, scribe around the hinges with a sharp pointed tool. The scribe lines will speed up hood alignment when replacing the hood. Look at **Figure 12-2.** Remove hinge fasteners. Lift off hood and store it upright in a protected area. Replace all fasteners in their original holes so they will not be lost.

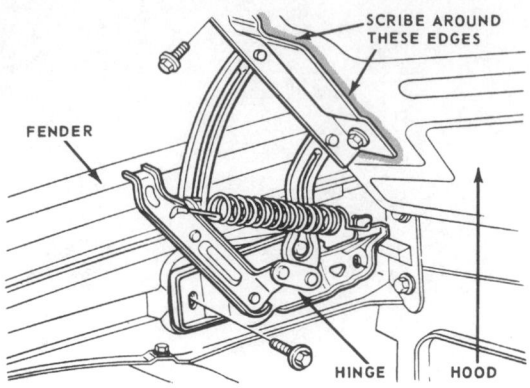

Figure 12-2. Scribing around edges of hood hinge attaching plate will make hood alignment easy during reassembly. (Chevrolet)

Disconnect All Attached Wiring, Tubing, Hoses, and Controls

Remove the battery and battery cables. Disconnect the coil primary lead, starter and alternator wires, oil pressure and temperature indicator wires, engine ground strap, and any other accessory wires. As the parts and wires are removed, they should be marked with masking tape for correct installation, **Figure 12-3.**

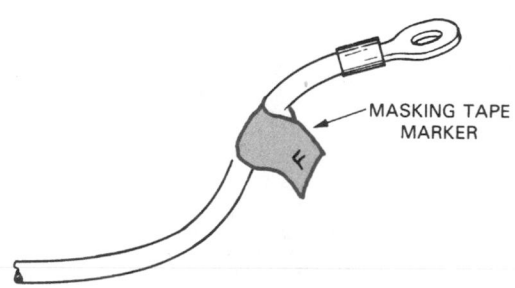

Figure 12-3. Marking wires with tape will facilitate installation.

Caution: Avoid part damage. When pulling tubing and hose out of the way, be careful not to kink or damage them. Cover the ends of hose and tubing with tape to prevent the entry of dirt.

Disconnect the fuel and emissions lines, vacuum lines, oil pressure gauge line (if used), and any other lines attached to the engine. Remove the air cleaner and cover the throttle body or carburetor with a plastic bag.

STOP Warning: In most fuel injection systems, fuel pressure must be released before disconnecting the fuel lines. Failure to release pressure can result in serious injury.

Disconnect throttle body or carburetor linkage and transmission and transaxle throttle valve cable where used. Disconnect the exhaust pipe at the exhaust manifold. Disconnect the clutch linkage, speedometer cable, and transmission or transaxle control rods and cables if they will be pulled with the engine.

Note: Once a wire, control rod, or other part has been removed, put the fasteners back into place. This will speed up reassembly and avoid improper placing of fasteners.

Drain the oil from the engine and remove the oil filter. Drain the cooling system. Remove the radiator hoses. On vehicles with an automatic transmission or transaxle, remove the fluid cooler lines. Plug the lines to prevent the entry of dirt. Remove the radiator. Handle the radiator carefully and protect it during storage. Disconnect the propeller shaft or drive axles and wire them out of the way.

Remove the starter and alternator, if necessary. The power steering pump, air conditioning compressor, or smog pump may be moved to one side or removed.

Note: It may be necessary to discharge the air conditioning system before removing the engine. Refer to Chapter 40 for more information on air conditioning system service.

Loosen, but do not remove, the engine mounting (motor mount) bolts. Make a thorough final check to make certain all necessary items have been removed before attempting to remove the engine.

Attach a Lifting Device

Attach the puller *cable, strap,* or *bar* to a suitable spot on the engine. Eyebolts may be used or cylinder head cap screws may be removed, placed through the puller brackets, and reinstalled. Some engines have specific *attachment points.* Consult the correct vehicle manual. Regardless of the attachment point, make certain that the eyebolt, cap screw, or bolt is threaded into the hole a distance of at least one and one-half times its diameter. This will ensure proper holding strength. See **Figure 12-4.**

Puller Bracket Must Be Snug against the Engine

Occasionally, the head or heads have been removed from the block before engine removal. Never use the head

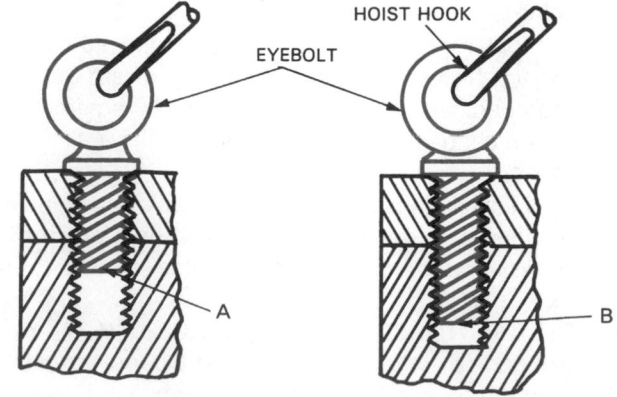

Figure 12-4. Puller fastener must have ample thread. A—Eyebolt threads a very short distance into hole and will very likely rip out under pulling pressure. B—By using a longer eyebolt, ample thread is assured.

cap screws or studs to attach the puller brackets unless they are shimmed to force the bracket against the block. Failure to do this will place a heavy side pull on the fastener, causing it to fail. This principle also applies to any fastener that is too long, **Figure 12-5.** When attaching puller brackets, select fasteners of sufficient strength. Thread them into areas that will withstand the pressure of lifting.

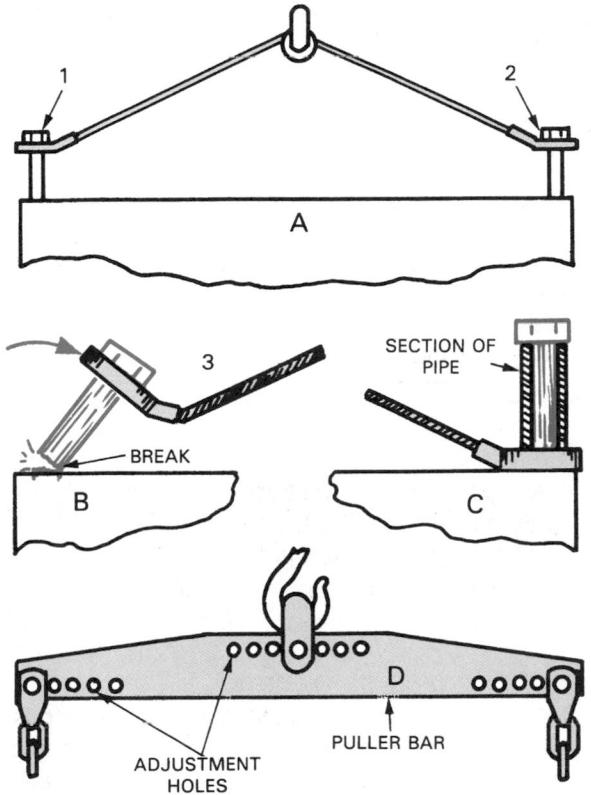

Figure 12-5. A—Puller brackets have slid up cap screws. B—When the hoist exerts a force on the puller cable, the puller bracket will force the cap screw sideways, causing it to break or bend. C—The bracket is held against the block by a short section of pipe to prevent cap screw damage. D—Typical puller bar. Note the adjustment holes.

Select the Proper Balance Point

Attach the puller at the appropriate *balance point,* so that the weight of the engine, or engine and transmission, will be balanced at the angle desired. Failure to do this will cause tipping that could damage parts and make removal difficult. Look at **Figure 12-6.**

Pull Point Must Not Slip

Make certain that the *pull point* (point of attachment on puller) cannot slip under pressure. **Figure 12-7** shows what can happen when a chain hook is placed on a plain cable pulling strap. Look at the puller strap in **Figure 12-8.** It allows the pull point to be moved along the length of the cable. However, under pressure, the hoist bracket will bind against the cable, thus preventing slippage.

Position the Lift

After the pulling device is firmly attached, move the lift into a position that will raise the engine without causing any

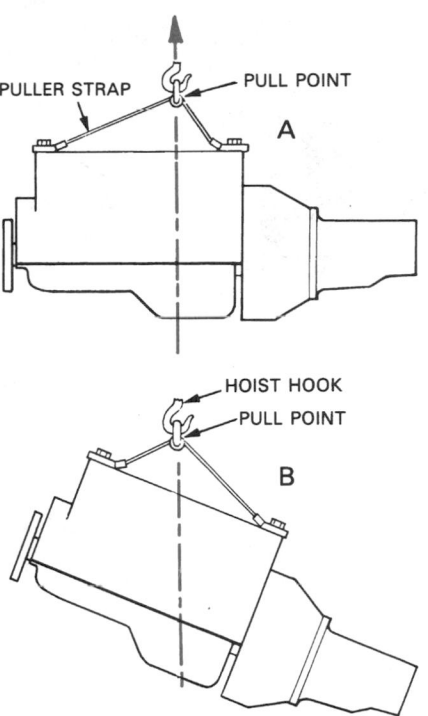

Figure 12-6. A—The engine can be lifted in a level position by arranging the pull point properly. B—The lifting angle is altered by moving the pull point toward the front of the engine. Any number of angles are possible.

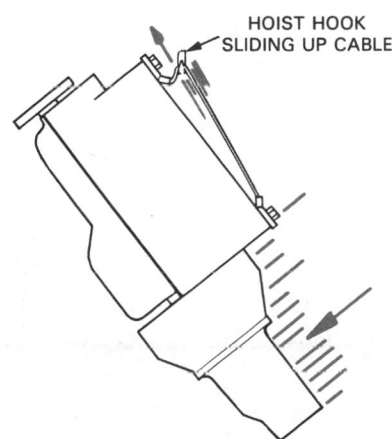

Figure 12-7. This engine was being lifted by placing a hoist hook around a plain cable puller strap. The rear of the engine tipped down, and the hoist hook slid to the front end of the cable. The rear of the engine is now falling downward with dangerous force. Make certain that the pull point cannot slip.

undesirable side or fore-and-aft pressures. Insert the lift hook into the puller. Place a light lifting strain on the engine. Finish removing the engine mounting bolts.

Lift the Engine

Start raising the engine while checking for proper clearance. Be careful of the *lifting angle.* If the engine assumes the wrong balance angle, lower it back into position and change either the pull point on the puller or the location of the puller brackets.

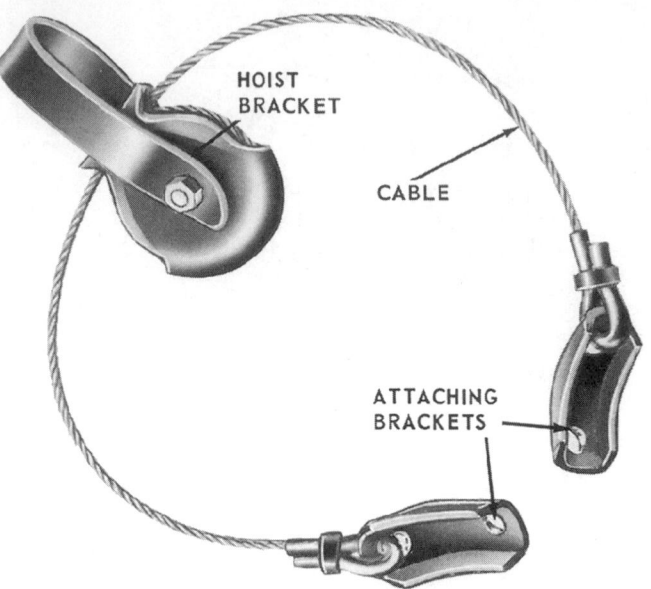

Figure 12-8. Cable-type engine pulling strap. Hoist bracket attaching point is adjustable but will bind under lifting pressure to prevent pull point change. (Snap-on Tools)

As the engine begins to rise, pull it forward until it is free of the transmission or transaxle (if the transmission or transaxle will be left in the vehicle). As lifting progresses, make sure that the flywheel ring gear or drive plate (automatic transmission or transaxle) does not hang up. Also watch carefully for any wires or hoses that you may have forgotten to remove.

If removing the transmission with the engine on a rear-wheel drive vehicle, the unit will often have to assume a relatively steep angle to clear. See **Figure 12-9.**

As the pulling continues, give the engine an occasional gentle rocking motion. This will ascertain that it is free. If the engine stops moving at one point and continues at another, stop and check for an obstruction. Continue raising while guiding the engine with the hands and by altering lift position.

Raise the engine to a height sufficient to clear the car. Remove engine and immediately lower it until it is just above the floor. Move the engine to the cleaning area and steam clean. Remove the transmission or transaxle, if attached.

Safety Rules for Pulling

* Attach a lift strap or bar at the correct balance point.
* Lift strap fasteners must have ample thread and strap brackets should be in contact with the engine, not with the end of a long cap screw or stud.
* Watch your hands and keep clear of the engine at all times.
* Lower the engine as soon as it has been removed.
* Do not use a rope as an engine sling.
* Do not depend on a knot in a chain. Bolt it together.
* If a chain is used as a strap, use heavy, wide washers under the head of the fastener to prevent the fastener head from pulling through the link.
* Make sure the pulling point cannot slip.

Place the Engine on a Stand

The engine should be placed on an **engine stand.** This allows the technician to easily reach all parts of the engine and to turn the engine when necessary to reach the bottom components. See **Figure 12-10.**

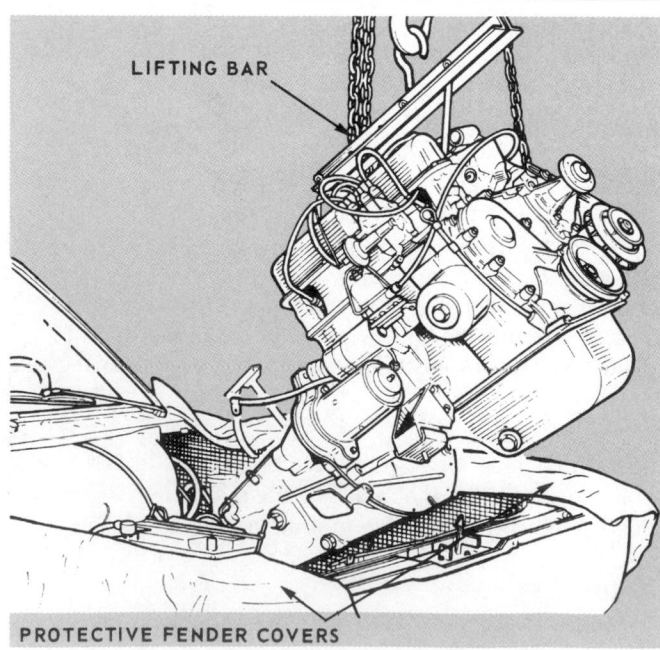

Figure 12-9. Using a chain hoist unit to pull an engine. Be very careful. (Honda)

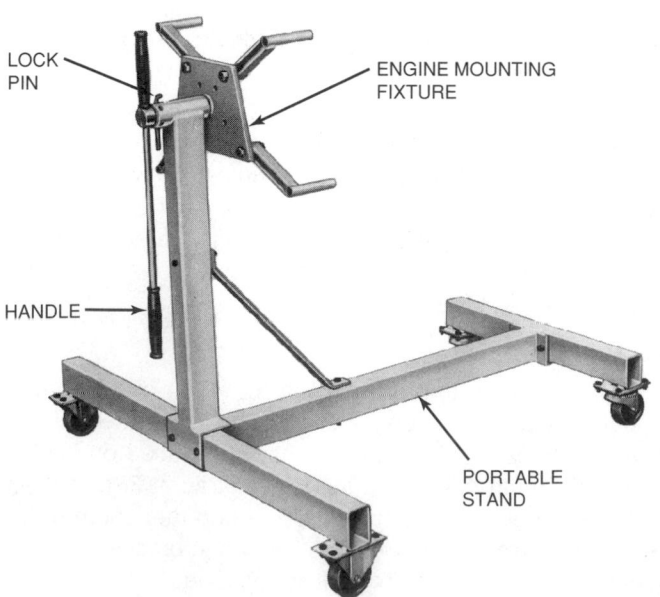

Figure 12-10. One particular type of portable engine repair stand. (Snap-on Tools)

Engine Disassembly and Inspection

The following sections cover engine disassembly and the visual inspections used to check for obvious engine damage. Other chapters will cover further disassembly and making detailed measurements with the appropriate measuring tools.

Cylinder Head Removal

Never remove a cylinder head until the engine has cooled. Removal while hot can cause the head to warp upon cooling. In hot weather, it may take as long as 6 hours for an engine to cool down completely. Begin by removing the intake and exhaust manifolds (when necessary), spark plugs, wires, rocker arm cover, and any accessory units attached to the head.

Remove the Rocker Arm Assembly

On most engines, it will be necessary to remove the rocker arms (and camshaft if the engine is an overhead cam model) to gain access to the head cap screws, or head bolts.

 Note: If the engine uses an overhead camshaft, consult the manufacturer's service manual for information on removing the camshaft and timing belt or chain before proceeding.

On engines using a rocker arm shaft, remove the rocker arm assembly by starting at one end. Loosen each support bracket bolt a couple of turns. Repeat this step until the assembly is free. If each bracket bolt is completely removed before moving to the next, the last bracket could be damaged. Valve spring pressure could push the free portion of the shaft upward. See **Figure 12-11.**

On engines using ball stud-type rocker arms, loosen each ball nut until the rocker arm can be swiveled sideways to clear the push rod. Look at **Figure 12-12.** In cases where rocker arm shaft support brackets are an integral part of the

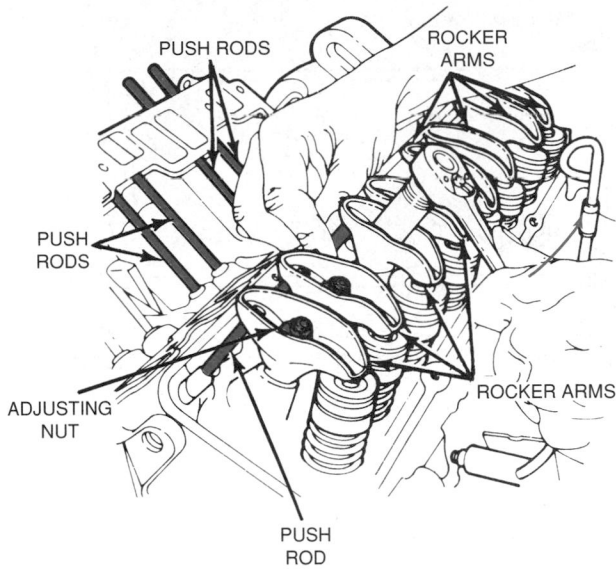

Figure 12-12. Loosen the adjusting nut so the rocker arm will move, allowing push rod removal. (Chevrolet)

head, the head may be pulled before sliding the rocker shaft out of the brackets.

Remove the Push Rods

If push rods are used, remove and place each push rod in a marked holder so it can be replaced in its original position. See **Figure 12-13.** Skip this step if the engine does not use push rods.

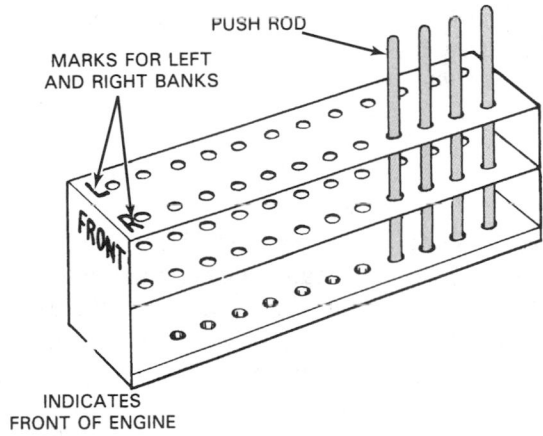

Figure 12-13. Keep the individual push rods in order by placing them in a marked holder.

Loosen the Cylinder Head Fasteners

Using the recommended tightening sequence, reverse the order and crack (just break loose) each head cap screw. Once all have been loosened, they may be removed. If length varies or if a cap screw is drilled or machined for oil passage, note the correct location. See **Figure 12-14.**

If the cylinder head is stuck, use pry bars or a screwdriver to loosen it. Be careful not to damage the head. Do not force a tapered object between head and block mating surfaces. The slightest nick or dent may cause serious damage. When the head is loose, remove it, as in **Figure 12-15.**

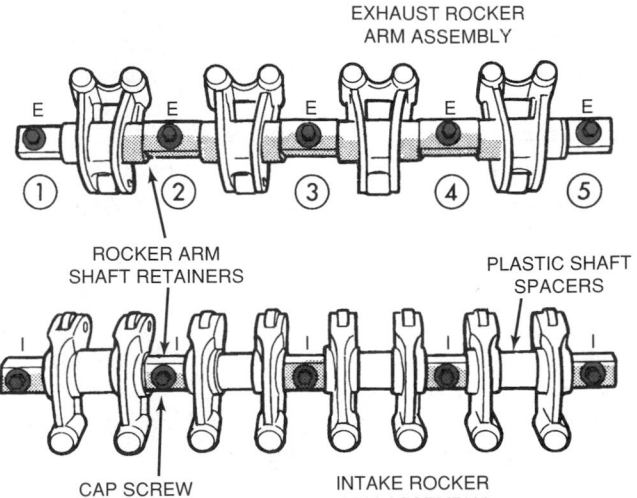

Figure 12-11. The proper sequence must be used when unbolting the rocker arm assembly. Keep all parts in order. (Chrysler)

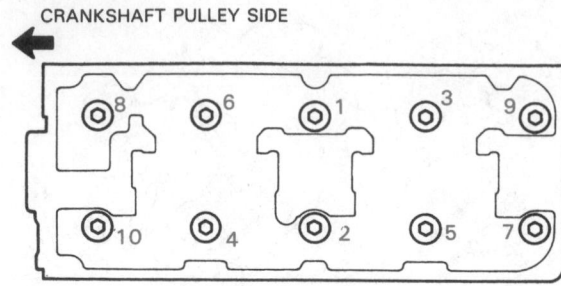

Figure 12-14. "Crack" the cylinder head bolts one at a time. Remove them in the reverse order of tightening. (Chrysler)

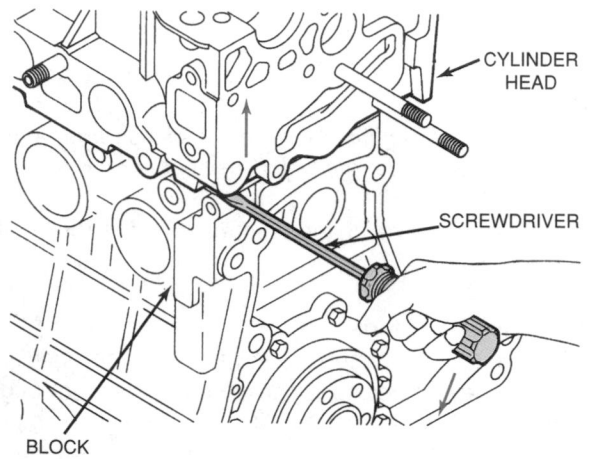

Figure 12-15. A—Using a large screwdriver to loosen the cylinder head. Be careful not to damage the head and block mating surfaces. B—Using lift brackets to aid in removing the cylinder head from the block. (Geo, GM)

Place the Cylinder Head in a Holding Fixture

Following cylinder head removal, place the head in a suitable repair stand. The next chapter will explain how to disassemble and check the head and its components.

Crankshaft Removal

Before beginning crankshaft removal, turn the engine over and remove the oil pan. Then, pull the vibration damper. Remove the front cover and then the chain, gear, or belt. Next, mark the connecting rod caps for reassembly and remove them. Push each piston and rod towards the top of the cylinder to provide clearance for the crankshaft journals. When necessary, remove the oil pump, oil lines, and front engine plate.

> **Note: On many engines, the oil pump, vibration damper, timing cover, and timing gears or sprockets must be removed before the crankshaft can be removed. Removal procedures for these components are covered in the following sections.**

Mark the Bearing Caps before Removal

Before removing the main bearing caps or cap, mark each cap and the crankcase web with a prick punch or a number stamp. Place the cap and web marks on the same side of the engine. Never mark on the top of the cap. Use a heavy section near one side to prevent distortion, **Figure 12-16.** One particular engine incorporates the use of a one-piece main bearing cap, which has the five individual insert areas machined out. This is shown in **Figure 12-17.**

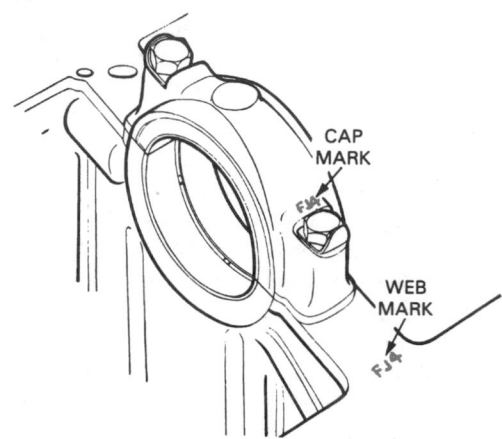

Figure 12-16. Mark the bearing caps before they are removed. They must be reassembled in the proper position and direction. (Chrysler)

Remove the Main Bearing Cap

Remove locking devices, if used, and crack each cap bolt loose. Remove all cap screws while watching for variations in diameter and length. If main bearing cap cross bolts are used, remove them before the cap bolts. Do not misplace the cross bolt crankshaft-to-cap spacers, if used. Keep all bolts and spacers in proper order. Carefully pry the caps free while lightly tapping with a plastic or rawhide hammer. Never pound on the caps or use a pry bar between the crank journal and the cap bore. The caps can be easily damaged. Some caps are designed to accept a special puller.

Lift the Crankshaft from the Crankcase

Lift the crankshaft straight up, being careful to avoid any damage to the journal or thrust surfaces. If the crank is too heavy to handle by hand, get help from an assistant or use a sling and lift.

Study the bearing inserts to determine whether they have been worn or damaged. A close look at the bearing inserts will reveal the exact nature of any block, crankshaft, or connecting rod misalignment, as well as many other engine problems. Servicing the crankshaft and bearings is covered in more detail in Chapter 15.

Camshaft Timing Mechanism Removal

The camshaft timing gears, chain, or belt must be removed by following the set of steps on page 211. In many

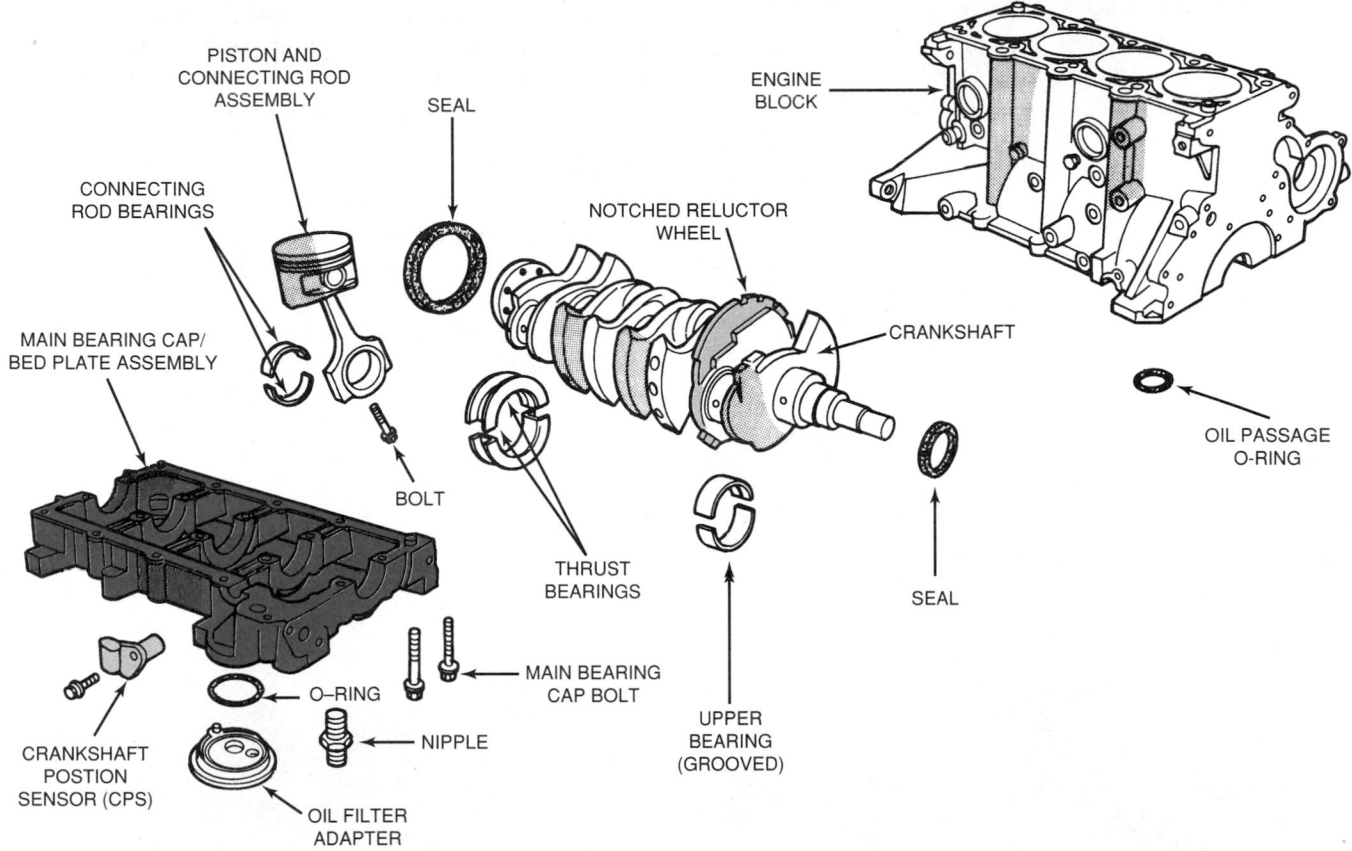

Figure 12-17.   This engine incorporates a one-piece main bearing cap and bed plate assembly, which houses machined insert bores. Note that the crankshaft has an integral reluctor wheel used with distributorless ignition. The crankshaft sensor and a camshaft sensor signal the electronic control unit. (Chrysler)

cases, these parts must be removed before the crankshaft can be removed. Timing mechanism service is covered in detail in Chapter 16.

Remove the Vibration Damper

Begin by removing any bolt-on pulleys attached to the vibration damper, or harmonic balancer. Next, remove the retaining cap screw in the end of the crankshaft, if used. If a retaining screw was used, the damper may now slide off the crankshaft. If the damper must be pulled off, attach a suitable puller to the damper hub (do not pull on the outer rim) and withdraw the damper. See **Figure 12-18.**

 Caution: Be careful not to damage the crankshaft threads. If the puller screw is not large enough to avoid entering the threaded hole, place a cap over the end of the crankshaft.

Remove the Timing Cover

Remove the cap screws holding the timing gear, chain, or belt cover. Watch for variations in cap screw lengths. Then remove the cover to expose the timing gears and the belt or chain.

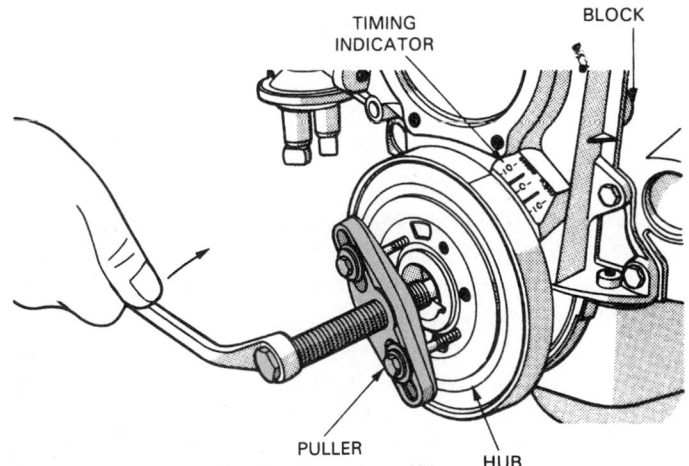

Figure 12-18.   Using a puller to remove the vibration damper from the crankshaft. The pulling force is applied to the center hub. (Dodge)

Check for Timing Gear Wear

Visually inspect both camshaft and crankshaft gears or sprockets and the timing chain or belt, if used. Worn, chipped, or galled parts must be replaced.

Remove the Timing Gear Assembly

When a timing chain is used, the timing gears and the chain can generally be removed as an assembly after the attaching bolts are removed, **Figure 12-19.** When timing belts are used, the belts can be removed first, and then the timing gears can be removed. If the engine uses two timing gears with no chain or belt, each gear can usually be removed without removing the other.

 Note: When it is necessary to replace any of the camshaft timing parts, both the gears and the timing chain or belt should be replaced.

Figure 12-19. This timing chain uses a bolt-on camshaft gear and a pressed-on crankshaft gear. (Chrysler)

Remove the Camshaft

Some camshaft gears are bolted in place and are simple to remove. Others, however, are force fit on the camshaft and are best pressed off. Turn the cam gear so that the thrust plate (when used) retaining cap screws are accessible. Remove the cap screws. After the retainers are removed, pull the camshaft from the engine, being careful to avoid damage to the camshaft bearings.

 Note: Before the camshaft can be pulled, the distributor or oil pump, (depending on which one has a gear which engages a gear on the camshaft), fuel pump, and valve lifters must be removed.

Piston Removal

With the crankshaft removed, the pistons can be pushed out of the engine block. However, most engines have developed a *ring ridge* at the top of the block. The ring ridge is formed as the piston rings wear the top of the cylinder. The top ring does not reach the very top of the cylinder, so the top of the cylinder remains at its original diameter. Since the ring has expanded to fit the worn part of the cylinder, pushing the piston out before removing the ring ridge will cause the rings to strike the ridge and break either the rings, the piston lands, or both. This ring ridge must be removed.

Remove the Ring Ridge

Before attempting to remove the ring ridge, run the piston down in the cylinder. Wipe the cylinder and block surfaces with an oily rag and insert a suitable *ridge reamer.* One type is pictured in **Figure 12-20.** Note the guide foot roller beneath the cutter to prevent undercutting the cylinder.

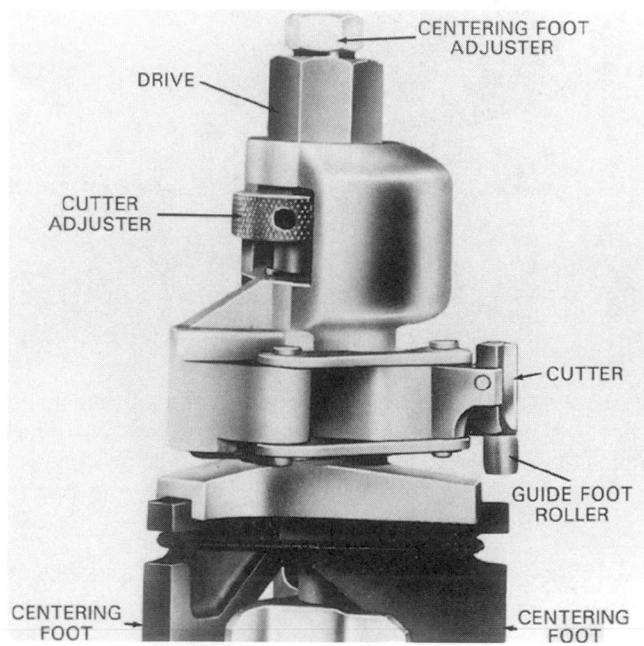

Figure 12-20. One type of cylinder ring ridge reamer. The reamer is supported by expanding "centering feet" out against the cylinder wall. The guide foot roller aids in obtaining smooth operation.

The ridge reamer should be expanded tightly in the cylinder. If it is the type shown in **Figure 12-21,** a downward pressure should be exerted to keep the guide finger lips against the block surface. Turn the tool with smooth strokes. After each revolution, adjust the pressure to keep the cutter tight against the cylinder. This will help prevent the cutter from catching and making chatter marks. For cylinders that terminate in a tapered block surface, use a ridge reamer supported and aligned by the cylinder walls. Stop cutting when the ridge has been removed. Be very careful to avoid cutting below the ridge and into the cylinder. The ridge area should blend smoothly into the cylinder proper, **Figure 12-22.**

Inspect the Cylinders

Following piston removal, wipe out the cylinders. Using a bright light, carefully inspect each cylinder for cracks and score marks. Minor scoring and heavy scratches will require

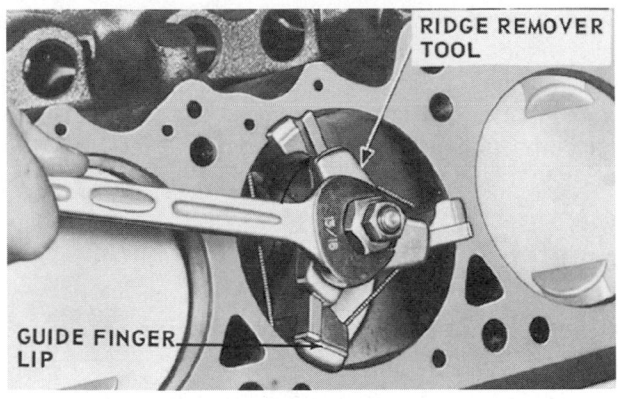

Figure 12-21. Removing the cylinder ring ridge. The reamer is supported with lips on the top of the guide fingers. (Chrysler)

reboring to a suitable oversize. If the cylinder is smooth and wear is within limits, new rings will function correctly after the cylinder walls are properly prepared. Measuring cylinder wear limits and cylinder repair are covered in Chapter 14. Heavy scoring (that a maximum size rebore will not clean up) will require the installation of a sleeve or the replacement of the block. A crack in the cylinder, or anywhere else on the block, usually means that the block must be replaced. Depending on its location and severity, a cracked block may be saved by installing a sleeve or by careful welding.

Remove the Piston Rings

If the rings will not be reused, they can be expanded over the piston lands and removed. Special tools are available to remove the old rings and install new rings. Be sure to carefully remove all dirt and carbon from the ring lands after the rings are removed.

Remove the Piston Pins

Before removing a piston pin, make certain the piston is marked so that it may be reassembled to the same rod in the same position. Prick punch marks will suffice if no factory identification has been provided. Exact removal procedures are covered in Chapter 14.

Oil Pump Removal

When the oil pump drive shaft contains a drive gear that also turns the distributor, the ignition timing will be thrown off when the pump and gear are pulled. If the engine will not be completely disassembled, turn the crankshaft until the number one piston is near the top of the firing stroke. Stop when the timing pointer is aligned with the proper ignition timing mark on the engine front pulley or damper. (See Chapter 18 on ignition for details on timing and installing a distributor.) At this point, the distributor rotor should be pointing to the number one cylinder wire tower. Mark the distributor body with chalk directly in line with the rotor. Then remove the oil pump. If the oil pump is driven by a slot in the distributor shaft or driven by a gear that does not connect to the distributor shaft, the ignition timing will not be affected when the pump is removed.

If in doubt as to what effect the pump removal has on ignition timing, remove the distributor cap and bring the number one piston into position as outlined. Mark the rotor position, pull the pump, and try to turn the distributor rotor. If the pump drives the distributor, the rotor will turn freely. If the distributor drives the pump or is driven by a separate gear, the rotor will not turn.

Disassemble the Oil Pump

After removing the pump cover, but before pulling either the rotors or gears, lightly mark them with a sharp scribe. Then when reassembled, the same ends of the rotors or gears can be positioned to face the cover plate. Both units should mesh with each other in the same position. Pump disassembly and inspection procedures are covered in more detail in Chapter 14.

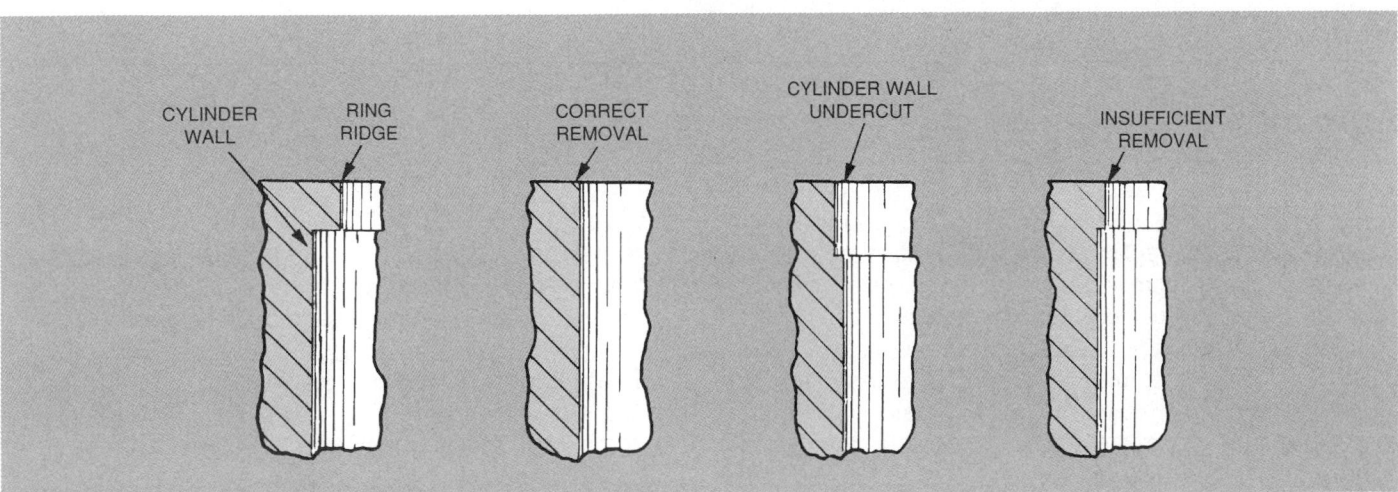

Figure 12-22. The ring ridge should be removed until the ridge area is cut just flush with the cylinder wall.

Tech Talk

Big factories make money by doing something called production planning. They figure out how to make the most of their materials and time by carefully planning when to do certain jobs, when to send out for more parts, and when to send some work out to be done by other companies. This allows the factory to make its finished product with as little downtime (time spent doing nothing) as possible and to make the most of its time, parts, and employees.

Production planning can also be used by the automotive technician. Think of a big repair job, such as overhauling an engine. You do not want to be sitting around a half-assembled engine waiting for parts to be delivered or the heads to come back from the machine shop.

Try to schedule part delivery and outside services. For example, as you tear down the engine, find out exactly what parts and outside services you will need to make a complete repair. You can then order the parts and send the components that need machining to the machine shop. While you are waiting for the parts and machining, you can clean the internal engine parts, hone the cylinders, and make other repairs. When the new parts and machined components are delivered, you will be ready to put the engine back together.

Compare this process with cleaning the internal parts, honing the cylinders, preparing to put the engine back together, and then ordering parts. You will be in for a long wait, sitting around and watching dust settle on your clean engine parts.

Before beginning any job, take a few minutes to decide how it can be done most efficiently. Pay particular attention to one of the most common problem areas: not ordering all the needed parts and services. These few minutes spent ordering parts and services will save you hours later. Production planning will pay big dividends in time saved, but only if you do it.

Summary

Before removing an engine, determine if the transmission or transaxle will be pulled with the engine. Cover the fenders. Scribe the hinges and remove the hood. Drain the coolant, remove the radiator hose, and remove the radiator. If desired, drain the engine oil and the transmission fluid. Disconnect all wiring, tubing, hose, and controls attached to engine and, if necessary, to transmission or transaxle. Attach puller strap securely to properly balance the assembly. Pull the engine slowly, checking to make certain all parts are free. When the engine is high enough to clear the vehicle, remove and lower it. Steam clean the engine and place it in a repair stand. Be very careful. Stay out from under the engine at all times.

Begin engine disassembly by removing the cylinder head or heads. Next, remove the oil pan, crankshaft, timing cover, camshaft timing mechanism, and camshaft. Then, remove the cylinder ridge and remove the pistons. Remove the oil pump, noting whether or not timing is affected. Check all parts for obvious wear.

Know These Terms

Adjustable stand	Balance point
Protective pads	Pull point
Cable	Lifting angle
Strap	Engine stand
Bar	Ring ridge
Attachment points	Ridge reamer

Review Questions—Chapter 12

Do not write in this book. Write your answers on a separate sheet of paper.

1. Engines must always be pulled with the _____.
   (A) transmission and transaxle attached
   (B) transmission and transaxle removed
   (C) Either A or B, depending on the application.
   (D) Neither A nor B.
2. If adjustable, _____ around hood hinges before removal.
3. Whenever practical, always _____ fasteners after a part is removed.
4. _____ wire ends after removal to facilitate reassembly.
5. Engine angle during lifting should be _____.
   (A) level
   (B) back tipped down
   (C) front tipped down
   (D) Depends on situation.
6. A gentle _____ motion will help to determine if engine is clear during pulling.
7. Lift strap or bar brackets should be attached to the _____.
   (A) head cap screws
   (B) intake manifold
   (C) exhaust manifold
   (D) Depends on situation.
8. When pulling tubing free of engine, be careful to avoid _____.
9. List eight safety rules for engine pulling.
10. Name three defects to look for in an engine cylinder.

ASE-Type Questions

1. As soon as the engine assembly clears the vehicle, it should be _____.
   (A) lowered to just above the floor
   (B) steam cleaned
   (C) moved to the bench
   (D) disassembled
2. Technician A says that the cylinder head should always be removed before it has time to cool. Technician B

says that, on most engines, it is not necessary to remove the overhead camshaft to head cap screws. Who is right?

(A) A only.
(B) B only.
(C) Both A & B.
(D) Neither A nor B.

3. Which of the following is not removed to remove an overhead-valve cylinder head?

(A) Rocker arm cover.
(B) Push rods.
(C) Camshaft.
(D) Head cap screws.

4. Technician A says that the cylinder head cap screws may be of different lengths. Technician B says that head cap screws may be drilled for oil passages. Who is right?

(A) A only.
(B) B only.
(C) Both A & B.
(D) Neither A nor B.

5. If improperly used, a vibration damper puller can damage the _____.

(A) damper
(B) crankshaft threads
(C) timing cover
(D) Both A & B.

6. When it is necessary to replace a timing chain, what else should be replaced?

(A) Camshaft sprocket.
(B) Crankshaft sprocket.
(C) Both A & B.
(D) Neither A nor B.

7. Technician A says that piston rings should be removed with a special tool. Technician B says that carbon deposits in the ring lands should be left in place to assist the seating of new rings. Who is right?

(A) A only.
(B) B only.
(C) Both A & B.
(D) Neither A nor B.

8. Removing the ring ridge will prevent damage to all of the following, EXCEPT:

(A) rings.
(B) piston ring lands.
(C) engine block.
(D) None of the above.

9. Which of the following oil pump drive designs will allow the ignition timing to be disturbed when the oil pump is removed?

(A) Oil pump driven by slot in distributor shaft.
(B) Oil pump driven by gear on crankshaft.
(C) Oil pump gear drives distributor.
(D) Oil pump directly driven by engine timing belt.

10. Technician A says that on many vehicles, the oil pump is driven by the distributor. Technician B says that on many vehicles, the distributor is driven by the oil pump. Who is right?

(A) A only.
(B) B only.
(C) Both A & B.
(D) Neither A nor B.

Suggested Activities

1. Tear down an engine and list all the parts needed to overhaul the engine.

2. Calculate the cost of overhauling the above engine by the following process:

   a. Using a flat rate manual, find the prices of the needed parts.

   b. Using a flat rate manual, find the labor times for replacing needed parts and other labor needed to overhaul the engine.

   c. Total the labor times and multiply them by the average labor rate for your area.

   d. Add the total cost of parts to the total labor.

   e. Add other charges, such as supplies (rags, cleaners, and oil absorbent) and outside services (machine shop work) for a grand total of what it would cost to overhaul the engine.

3. Discuss your price calculation with the other members of your class. Ask if there is anything that you missed. Determine whether the cost of an overhaul would be greater or less than the cost of a replacement engine. Also, decide what a fair profit on this job would be.

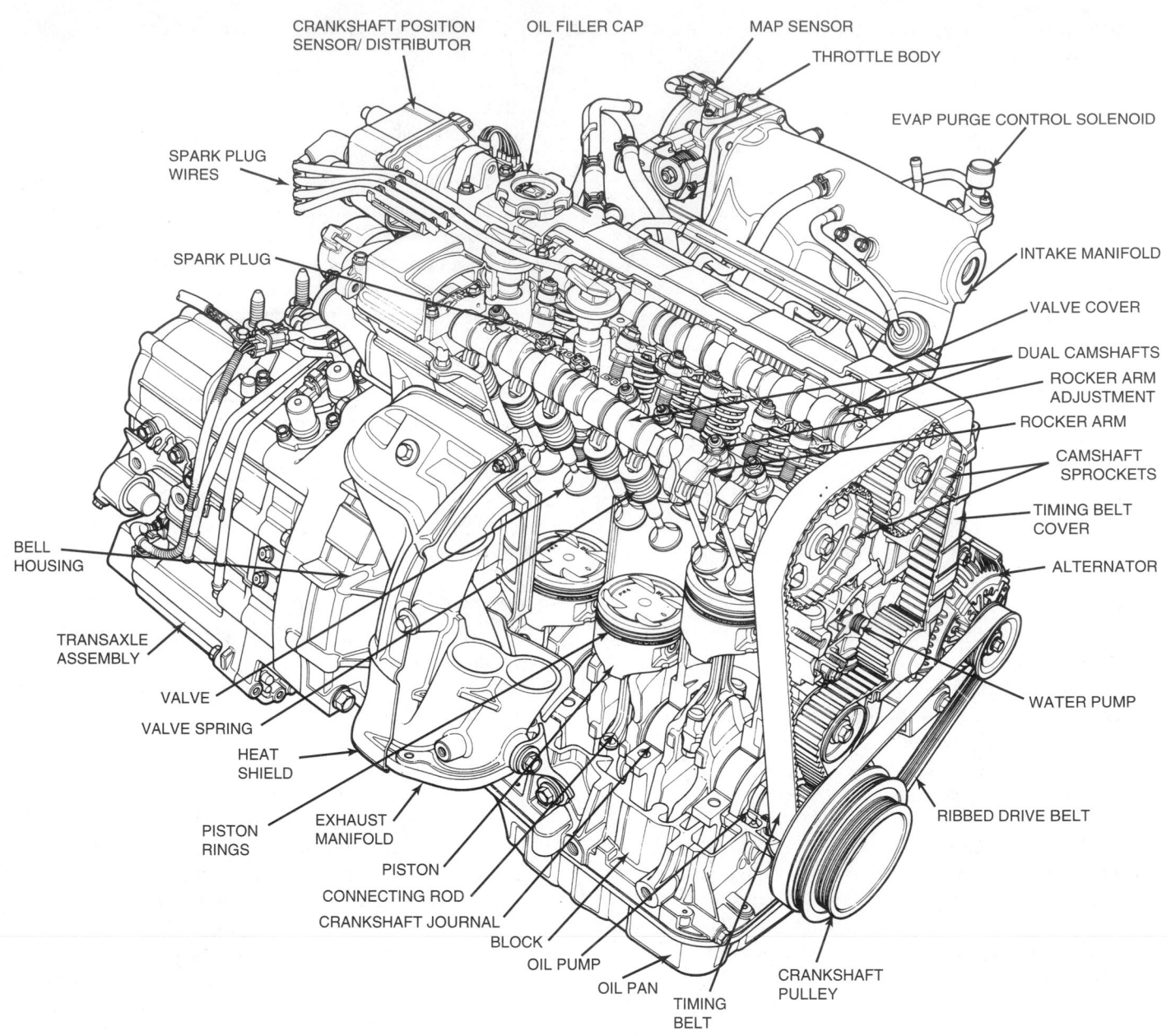

CRANKSHAFT POSITION SENSOR/ DISTRIBUTOR

OIL FILLER CAP

MAP SENSOR

THROTTLE BODY

EVAP PURGE CONTROL SOLENOID

SPARK PLUG WIRES

SPARK PLUG

INTAKE MANIFOLD

VALVE COVER

DUAL CAMSHAFTS

ROCKER ARM ADJUSTMENT

ROCKER ARM

CAMSHAFT SPROCKETS

TIMING BELT COVER

ALTERNATOR

BELL HOUSING

TRANSAXLE ASSEMBLY

VALVE

VALVE SPRING

HEAT SHIELD

PISTON RINGS

EXHAUST MANIFOLD

PISTON

CONNECTING ROD

CRANKSHAFT JOURNAL

BLOCK

OIL PUMP

OIL PAN

TIMING BELT

CRANKSHAFT PULLEY

WATER PUMP

RIBBED DRIVE BELT

Cutaway of a 1.8-liter, 16-valve, dual overhead cam, four-cylinder engine. Note the position of the valve train components. (Honda)

13

Cylinder Head and Valve Service

After studying this chapter, you will be able to:
- Properly disassemble a cylinder head.
- Inspect the cylinder head and valve train for signs of trouble.
- Properly grind valve seats and valves.
- Test valve springs.
- Service valve guides.
- Reassemble and install a cylinder head.

This chapter covers cylinder head and valve service. Although some of these service procedures can be performed without removing the head from the engine, you should thoroughly study Chapter 12, Engine Removal, Disassembly, and Inspection, before beginning this chapter. Study this chapter carefully and practice the various repair procedures-especially valve and valve seat resurfacing. Valve and cylinder head work are critical to obtaining maximum engine life and performance.

Cylinder Head Disassembly and Inspection

You will remember from Chapter 12 that the cylinder head should be placed in a suitable repair stand before beginning disassembly. Compress the *valve springs* and remove the *split keepers, spring,* and *spring retainer* assembly. A typical *valve spring compressor* is shown in **Figure 13-1A.** This compressor uses a clamping action to compress the spring and retainer so the keepers may be removed. Another type of spring compressor, shown in **Figure 13-1B,** can also be used to compress springs while the head is on the engine. It is attached to the head and uses a lever action to compress the springs.

Another method of removing the valves is to place a socket over the valve as shown in **Figure 13-2.** When the socket is struck with a hammer, the spring will be compressed and the shock of the hammer blow will cause the retainers to pop out. As the valves are removed, place them in a *rack* so they can be replaced in their original guides. Use a rack similar to that shown in **Figure 13-3.** Determine which cylinder head parts can be reconditioned and which must be discarded. Discard all burned, cracked, or warped valves. Also discard any broken or worn springs, keepers, and related parts.

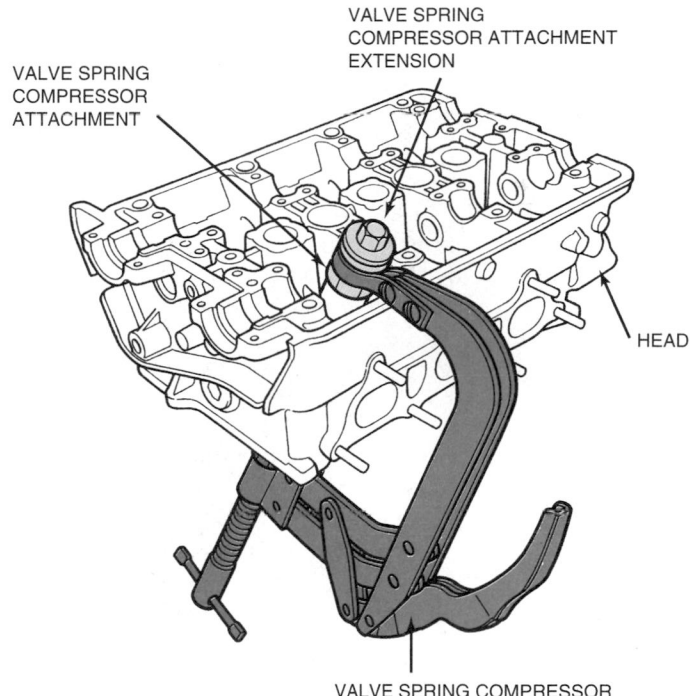

A

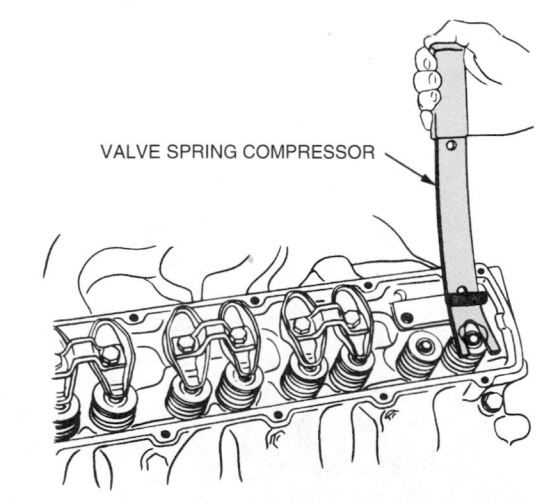

B

Figure 13-1. A—Compressing valve springs with a valve spring compressor. B—Another type of valve spring compressor. This one is particularly handy for removing a spring with the head on the engine. (Acura)

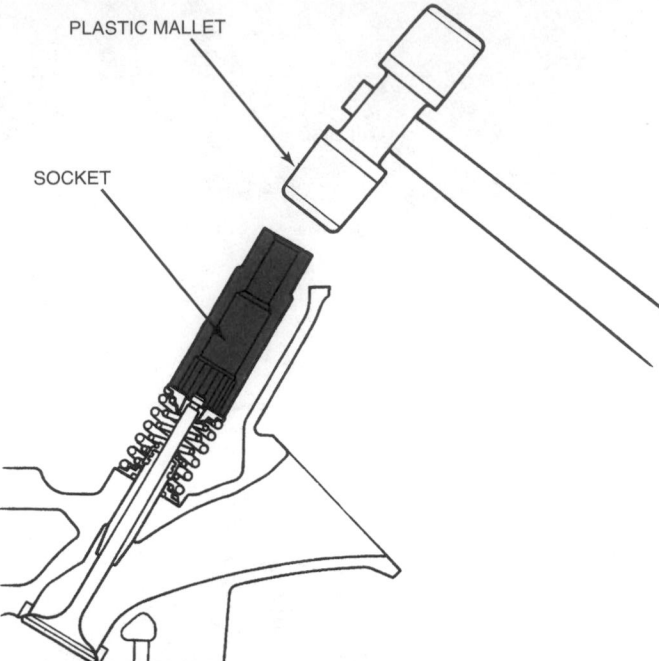

Figure 13-2. A plastic mallet and a socket can be used to loosen keepers before using the valve spring compressor. (Acura)

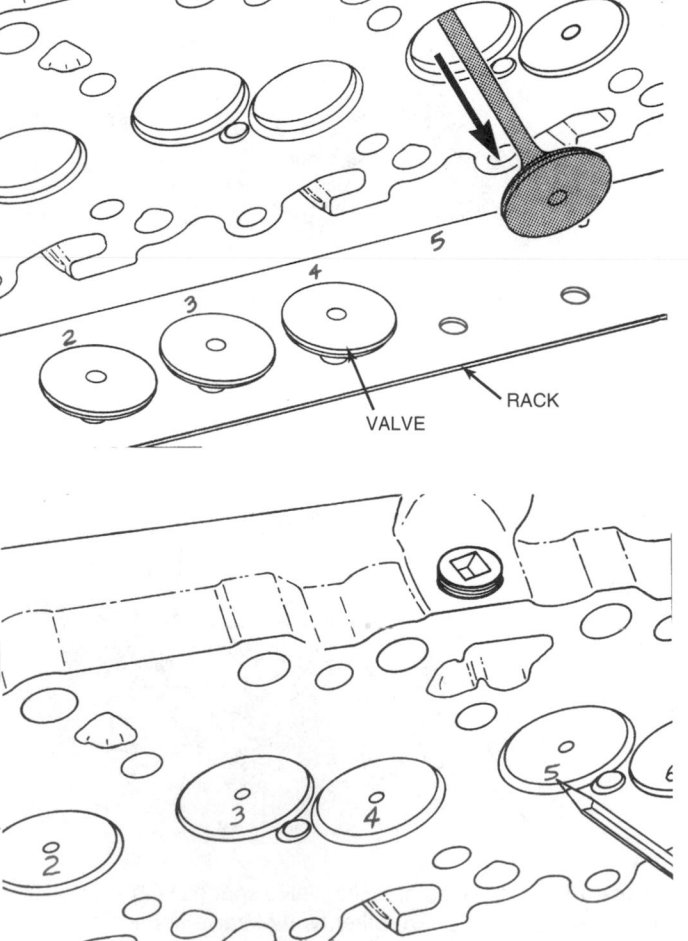

Figure 13-3. Place valves in a rack and number them in proper order during removal and installation. (Dodge)

Cleaning the Cylinder Head

Begin cleaning the head by using a wire brush to remove any carbon from the combustion chambers and valve ports, **Figure 13-4.** Clean the head-to-block surface with a scraper. Be careful not to scratch the surface. If the cylinder head coolant passages are badly clogged, give the head an additional cleaning in a hot tank. Do not hot tank an aluminum head.

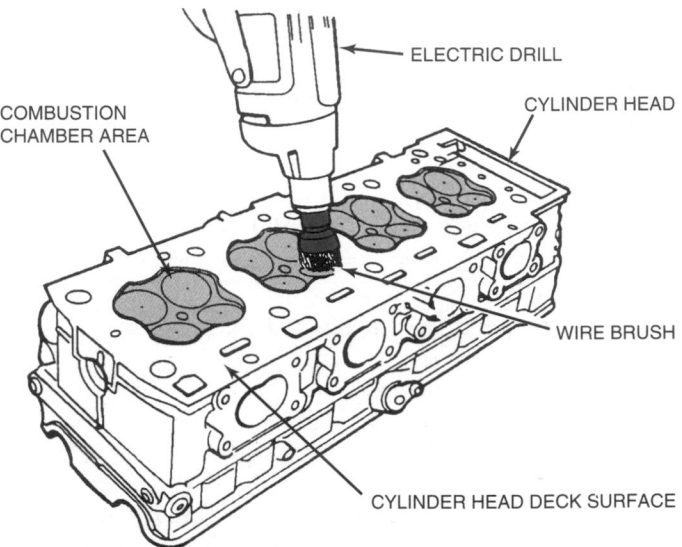

Figure 13-4. Removing carbon from cylinder head combustion chamber and ports using a wire brush. Wear safety goggles! (Chevrolet)

A spring-type *valve guide cleaner* can be used to remove the carbon in each guide. Look at **Figure 13-5.** Follow the valve guide cleaner with a valve guide bristle brush to remove all loosened carbon, **Figure 13-6.** Blow all dust and carbon from the combustion chambers, ports, and guides. Push a cloth moistened with solvent through all the valve guides to remove any remaining foreign material. The stem clearance check will not be accurate if any foreign material is left in the guide. When the valve seat grinding pilot is inserted, it will be tipped and throw the seat out of alignment.

Checking Cylinder Head for Cracks and Warpage

Check the head for obvious cracks (Chapter 14 contains information on other methods of crack detection and repair). Head surface must also be free of nicks and scratches. To ensure the close fit necessary between the head and block, the head should be checked for warpage. The use of a straightedge for checking cylinder head surface distortion is shown in **Figure 13-7.**

Place the straightedge across the head as shown. Sight along the edge to detect any warpage. If necessary, slide a feeler gauge between the straightedge and the head to determine the amount of distortion. Some warpage, around .003″ (0.08 mm) in any 6″ span (152.4 mm) or .006″ (0.15 mm) overall, is permissible. Distortion beyond this point should be corrected by grinding or milling a small

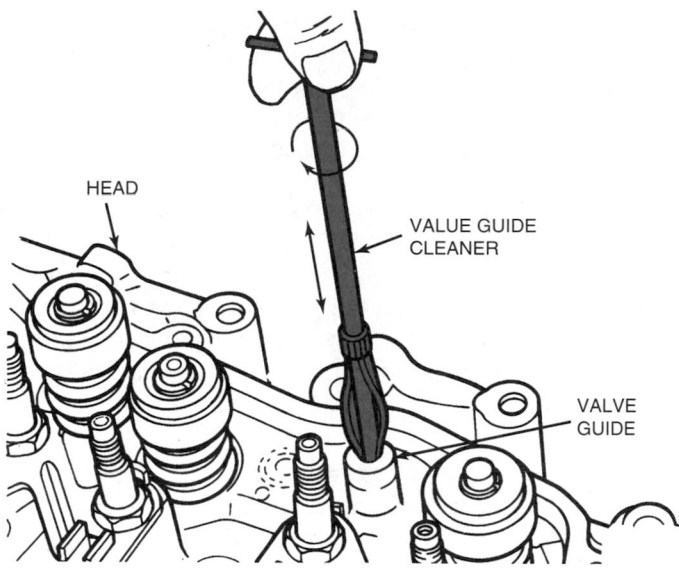

Figure 13-5. Using a spring blade valve guide cleaner to remove carbon from a valve guide. (Buick)

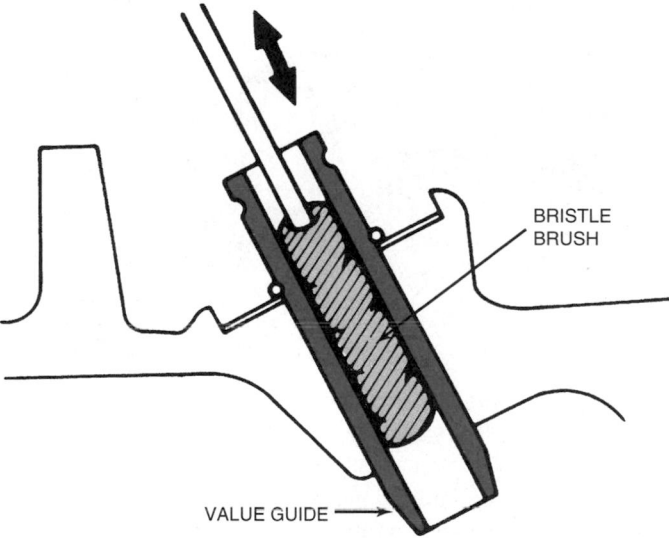

Figure 13-6. Use a brush to remove loosened carbon from a valve guide. (Toyota)

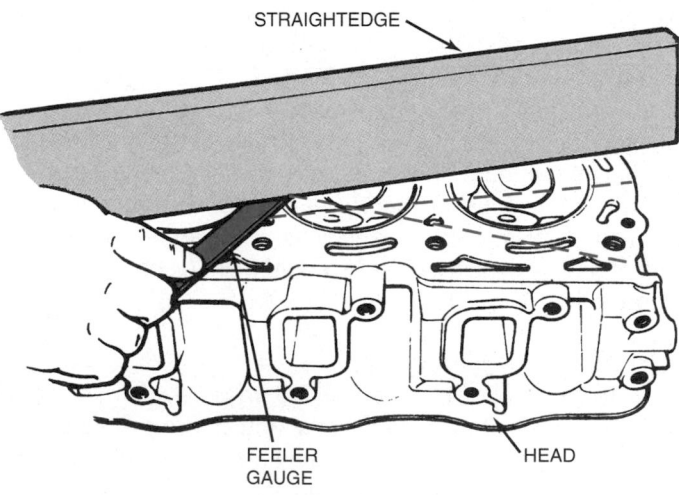

Figure 13-7. Use a straightedge and feeler gauge to check a cylinder head surface for warpage. (Suzuki)

amount from the surface. See manufacturer's specifications for the maximum amount permissible to be removed.

Removal of metal from the head or block will raise the compression ratio in most engines by reducing the size of the combustion chamber. It will also change the effective length from the lifters to the rocker arms. On an overhead camshaft engine, the timing chain length will be altered. Special head gaskets, which are thicker than standard, are available to maintain compression and working dimensions when metal has been removed from either the head or block.

Valve Reconditioning

Inspect each valve for signs of **burning, pitting,** and heavy **carbon deposits.** Burned or pitted valves can be caused by valves sticking in guides, insufficient tappet clearance, weak springs, clogged coolant passages, a warped valve stem, and improper ignition or valve timing. See **Figure 13-8.**

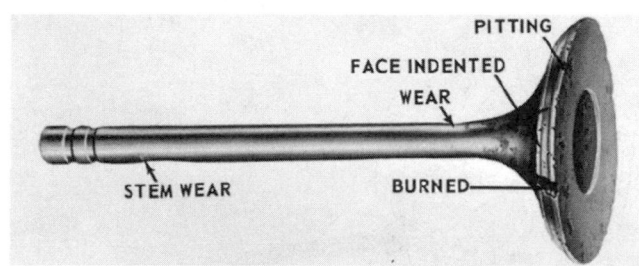

Figure 13-8. A burned valve indicates cylinder head or valve train problems. (Albertson-Sioux)

Heavy carbon deposits, especially under the head of the intake valve, indicate worn valve guides, damaged seals, worn rocker arm bushings, clogged oil drain holes in the head, or rocker arm shaft oil holes facing the wrong direction. Look at **Figure 13-9.** Discard all burned, cracked, or warped valves. The grinding necessary to clean them up will leave insufficient valve margin, **Figure 13-10.** Using a power wire wheel, brush all traces of carbon from the valve head and stem. Following wire brushing, rinse the valve in solvent and blow dry, **Figure 13-11.** Place the valve back in the rack so that it may be reinstalled in the original guide.

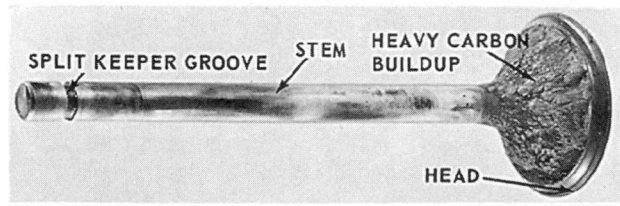

Figure 13-9. Heavy carbon deposits under the valve heads indicate excess oil consumption through the valve guides. (AE Clevite)

Valve Grinding

A typical **valve grinder** is shown in **Figure 13-12.** Study the names of the parts. Note the provisions for setting

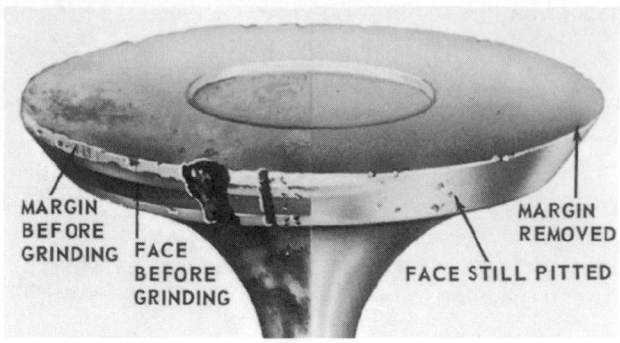

Figure 13-10. The amount of grinding required to clean up a valve in this condition will remove the margin and render the valve useless.

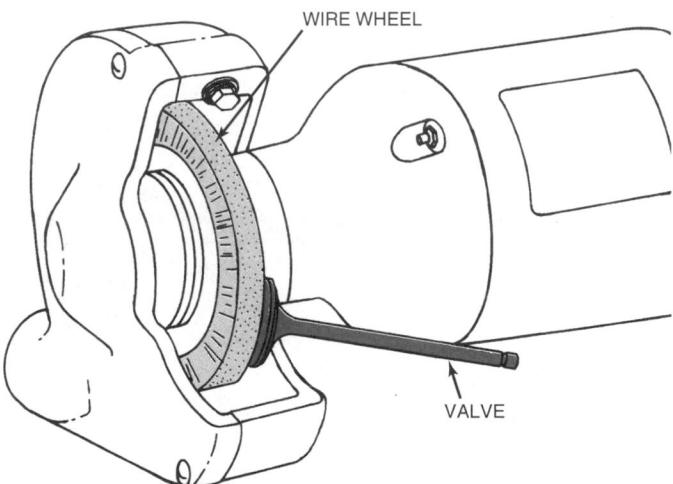

Figure 13-11. Using a wire wheel to clean carbon from a valve. Valves must be free of carbon and gum before reconditioning can begin. The safety guard is removed for illustration purposes. (Dodge)

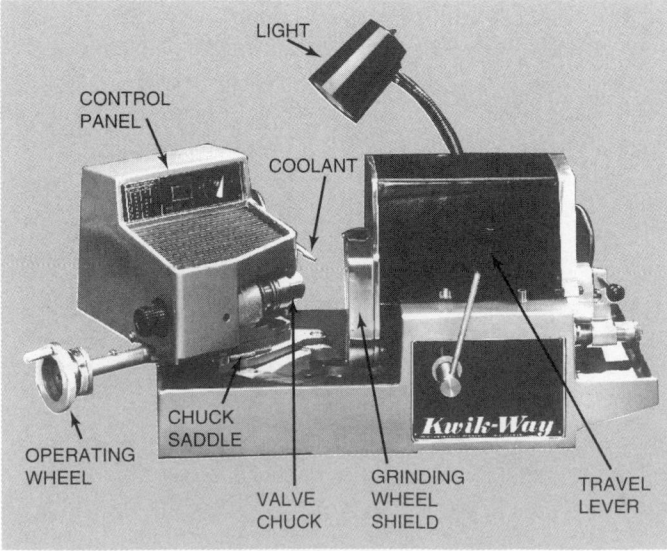

Figure 13-12. A typical valve grinding machine. Learn the name of each part. (Kwik-Way)

the valve cutting angles and cooling the valve as it is ground. A valve grinder will perform a job in direct relation to the condition of the *cutting stones.* The cutting stones must be trued up or *dressed* to the correct angle and kept in that condition. A properly dressed stone will work better and faster.

Put the diamond-tipped *dressing tool* into position and tighten it securely. Start the machine and advance stone *slowly* toward the diamond. When the diamond just touches the stone, turn on the coolant, **Figure 13-13.** Move the diamond back and forth slowly across the stone until the stone is smooth, clean, and true. Several very fine cuts may be required.

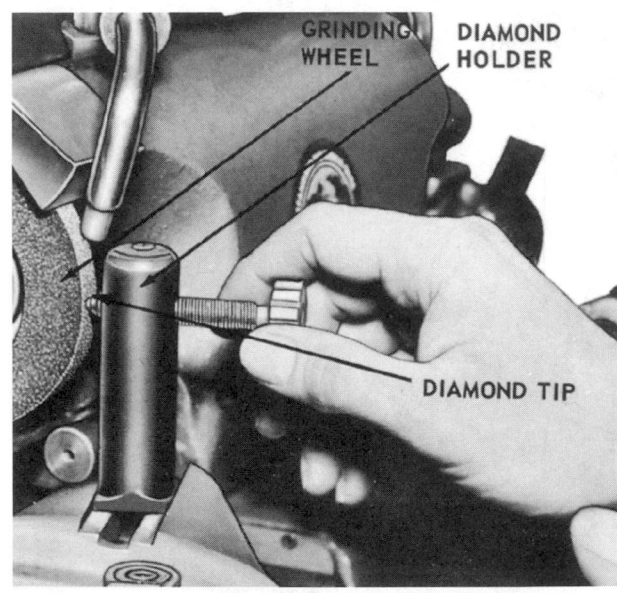

Figure 13-13. Dress the grinding wheel with a diamond dresser before grinding valves.

After dressing the cutting stones, loosen the chuck swivel nut and swing the chuck to the desired angle. Carefully adjust the chuck aligning edge to the desired angle marking. Lock the swivel and recheck the angle setting, **Figure 13-14.** Place the valve in the chuck. Various gripping devices are used, so follow manufacturer's recommendations. Make sure that an excessive amount of the valve stem does not protrude. This can cause chatter (valve vibrating during grinding), **Figure 13-15.** Close the chuck tightly. Turn on the machine and watch the valve rotate. If a noticeable amount of wobble or *runout* is present, stop the chuck and reposition the valve. If excessive runout is still present, a warped stem is indicated. If warped to the point that grinding will leave insufficient margin, discard the valve, **Figure 13-16.**

Grinding the Valve Face

Determine the correct *valve face angle.* On some engines, both intake and exhaust angles are the same. On others, they are different. Common angles are 30° and 45°. To provide fast initial seating, it is often recommended practice to grind the 30° valve to 29° and the 45° to 44°. This

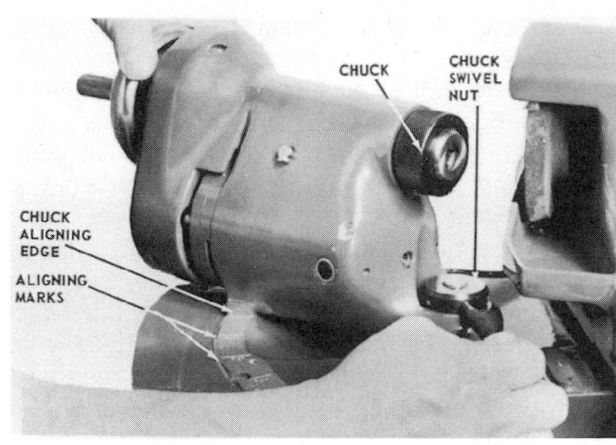

Figure 13-14. Setting the valve chuck to the desired angle. Use care when working with valve grinding equipment.

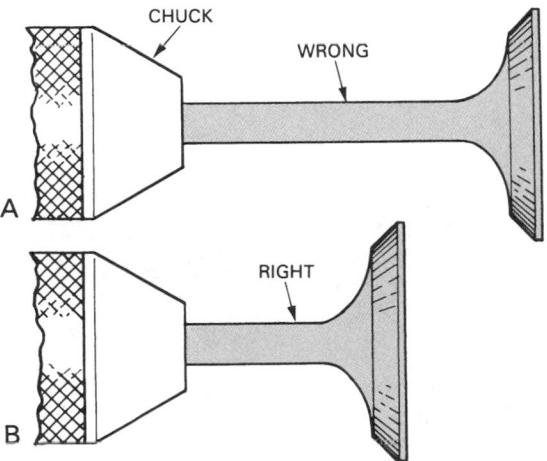

Figure 13-15. A—Valve protruding too far out of the chuck will chatter. B—Valve depth is correct.

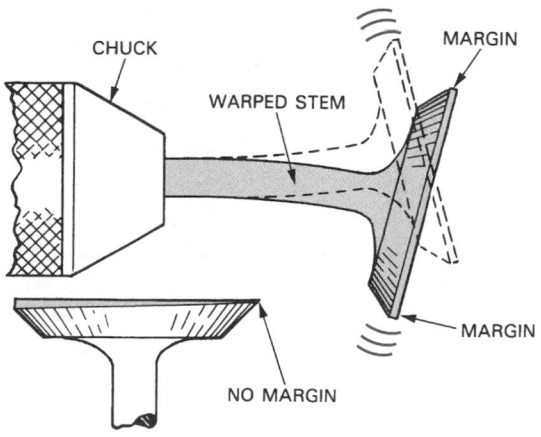

Figure 13-16. Excessive valve wobble will cause valve margin to be removed on one edge.

provides an *interference angle* that produces a hairline contact between the valve face and the top of the valve seat. Some manufacturers feel that due to valve design and material, the interference will allow the valve to form a perfect fit when heated, **Figure 13-17.**

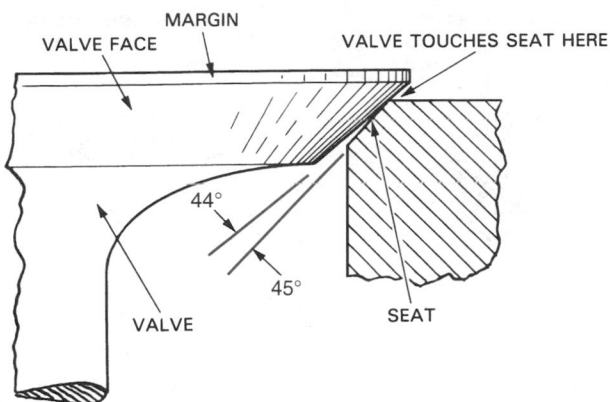

Figure 13-17. Interference angle. Note the 1° difference in angles and how the valve face contacts the top edge of the seat. One manufacturer recommends a 2° difference.

Move the chuck until the valve is in front of but not touching the stone. Turn on the valve grinding machine and engage the chuck drive to spin the valve. Turn on the coolant and direct the stream toward the valve. The valve face and stone should be parallel if you have selected the proper angle. See **Figures 13-18** and **13-19.** If parallel, make sure valve is turning and slowly advance the stone until it just starts to cut. Move the valve face back and forth across the stone. Never run the valve off the stone, **Figure 13-20.**

 Caution: Some valves use a special coating, such as nickel-chrome, on the face area. Only a limited amount of this coating can be removed.

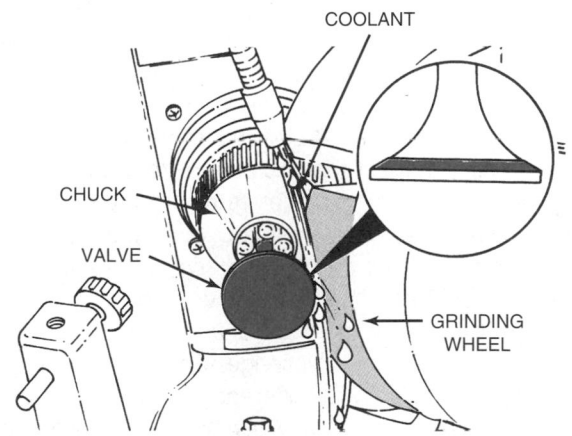

Figure 13-18. Grinding a valve face. Proceed slowly and grind a little at a time. (Cummins Engine Co.)

If your machine has a micrometer feed, set it to zero at the point where the stone just starts to cut. Advance the stone against the valve around .001″ to .002″ (0.025 to 0.05 mm) at a time. Watch the valve face carefully. As soon as all dark spots disappear, center the valve face on the stone. Allow the stone to run a few seconds without advancing it. Then, carefully back the stone away from the valve.

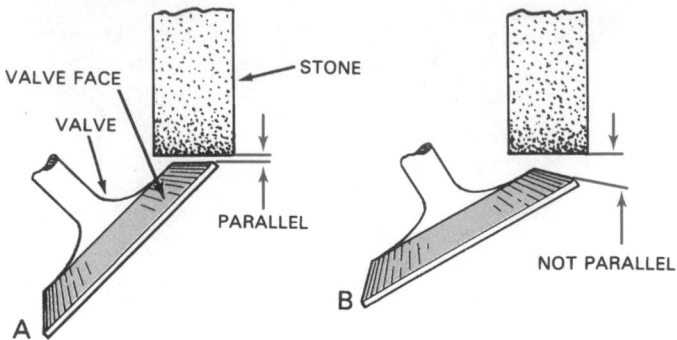

Figure 13-19. If the chuck is set at the proper angle, the valve face and stone will be parallel. A—Correct angle setting. B—Wrong angle adjustment.

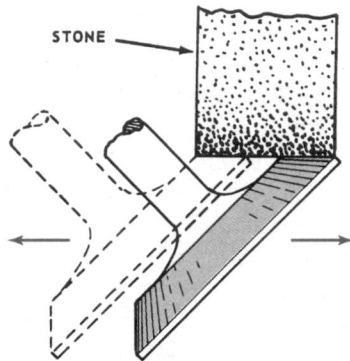

Figure 13-20. When grinding, move the valve back and forth while keeping the valve face in full contact with the stone.

Disengage the chuck drive and rotate the valve by hand while examining closely for any remaining pits or burns. The valve face should be bright, smooth, and free of *all* defects. The margin should be ample (1/32″ or 0.03 mm or more). If the valve is not cleaned up, repeat the process. When finished, inspect the micrometer feed dial and mark down the amount of material removed from the valve. Return the valve to the rack. If you have marked down the amount removed from each valve face, it is recommended that you remove a comparable amount from the stem.

Grind the remaining valves using the same procedure. Do not forget to change angles if intake and exhaust face angles are different. When using a valve grinder, proceed slowly. Many beginners inadvertently turn the feed wheel the wrong way or too fast and jam the stone against the valve. If the cut is suddenly too heavy, do not panic and crank the wheel. You may turn it the wrong way. Shut the machine off and when it has stopped, move the stone away.

Grinding Valve Stem Ends

The *valve stem* end should always be trued up and smoothed by grinding. This will help maintain original tappet clearance. Never remove an excessive amount (up to about .010″ or 0.25 mm), as the surface hardening is not deep on some valves. If the valve stem is ground below the hardening, rapid wear will result.

Dress the side of the wheel used for stem grinding. Chuck the valve in the V-block holder. Run it in until it just touches the stone. If so equipped, set the micrometer feed dial to zero. Back off the valve and start the wheel. As with valve face grinding, direct a good stream of coolant on the portion of the valve being ground. Advance the stem against the wheel. Continue advancing with light cuts until the micrometer dial indicates that you have removed the same amount as was taken from the face. If the machine has no micrometer feed, remove enough to produce a smooth square end. The operator in **Figure 13-21** is grinding a valve stem end. Notice how the stone feed lever is grasped. Once the stone is close to the valve, hold it as shown. This method will permit smoother and more accurate adjustments.

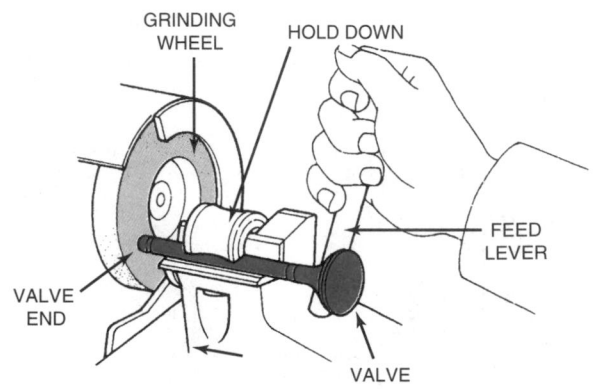

Figure 13-21. Truing a valve stem end. Note the position of the operator's hand. (Lexus)

🛑 **Warning: Some exhaust valve stems are partially filled with metallic sodium which aids in valve cooling. Sodium is extremely toxic and reacts violently with any form of water, even the moisture in the air. Never cut, drill, melt, or burn a *sodium-filled valve*. When the valve is worn out, dispose of it properly. Always follow manufacturer's recommendations for proper disposal.**

When using a plain V-block in which the valve must be hand held, make certain the block is close to the wheel. This will prevent the valve stem from catching and pulling the valve between block and wheel. Position the valve stem in the block. Hold down firmly and advance stem against the wheel. If some of the *chamfer* on the valve stem end has been removed through wear and refacing, the chamfer may be renewed by grinding. Place the valve in the V-block. Set the holder at 45° and adjust the stop to grind about a 1/32″ (0.80 mm) chamfer, **Figure 13-22.**

Inspect Each Valve

Perform a final inspection of each valve. Each valve must be smooth and free of all pits, scratches, and burns. There must be ample margin remaining to prevent burning. Valve stem wear must not be excessive. The stem should be free of nicks and scratches that could cause eventual breakage or sticking. Keeper grooves must be undam-

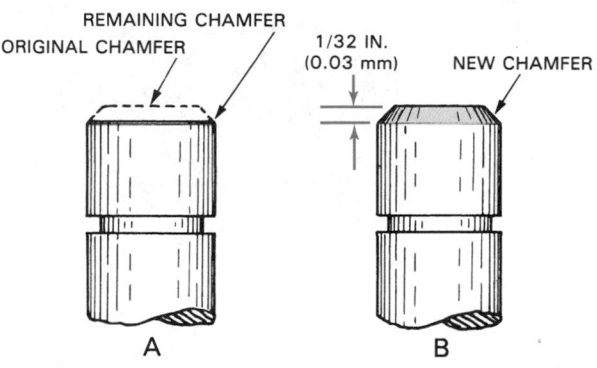

Figure 13-22. A—The chamfer on this valve stem end has worn off. B—Same end after renewing chamfer.

aged. Valve stem ends must be smooth, squared, and lightly chamfered. Check manufacturer's specifications. **Figure 13-23** illustrates two valves, one is acceptable, the other is not. Following the final inspection, each valve must be thoroughly washed and blown dry. Place in a clean rack and cover until ready to use.

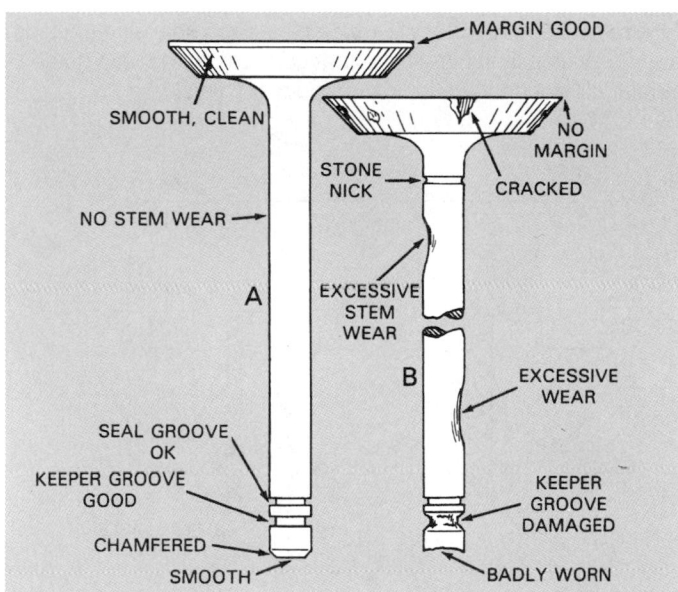

Figure 13-23. A—This valve is acceptable. B—This valve is not acceptable. Note the characteristics of each.

Cylinder Head Reconditioning

The following sections explain the steps in servicing the cylinder head. Pay particular attention to the sections on checking valve guide clearance and refinishing the valve seats. These operations have a great effect on head durability.

Valve Guides

When deciding whether or not to use the old valve guides, you are not concerned about too little clearance unless new valves with oversize stems are being installed. However, excessive clearance will often be present. This will promote oil consumption, poor seating, and possible valve breakage, **Figure 13-24.**

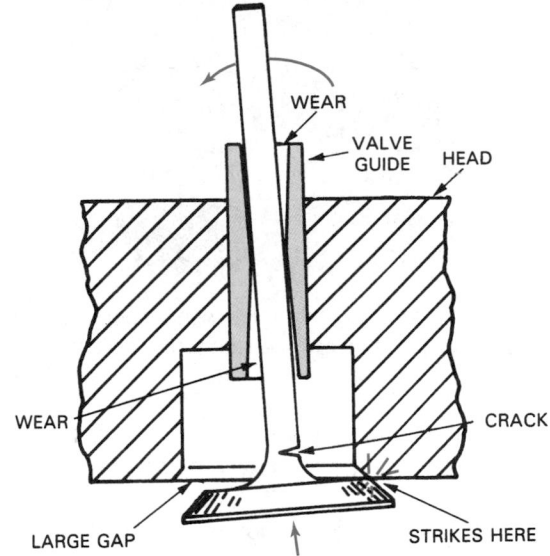

Figure 13-24. Excessive valve guide wear will cause trouble and can ruin an otherwise good valve job.

Two methods are commonly used to check for excessive **valve stem clearance.** In one method, a small hole gauge is carefully fitted to the largest valve guide diameter (do not measure exhaust guide counterbores). It is then read directly or removed and measured with an outside micrometer, **Figure 13-25.** The valve stem is then miked at a corresponding wear area. The difference can be computed to determine stem clearance.

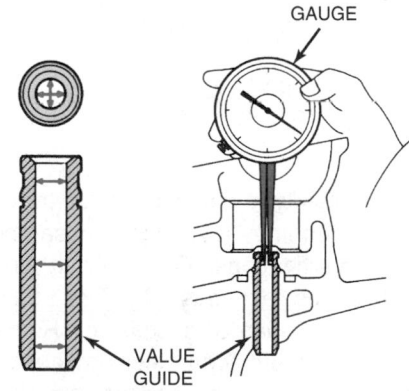

Figure 13-25. Measuring valve guide inside diameter using a hole gauge. Note the depth at which the measurement is obtained. (Lexus)

Another method is to drop the valve into position with the head just free of the seat. It can be held in this position by a special tool or by slipping a piece of rubber tubing over the valve stem as shown in **Figure 13-26.** A dial indicator is then clamped to the head. The indicator stem is placed against the valve margin. Without raising the valve, move it back and forth against the stem. Watch the indicator to determine the travel. Remember that the reading will not be the actual clearance because the measuring point is above

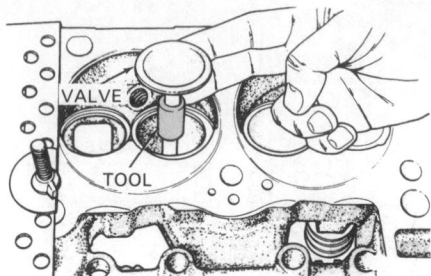

Figure 13-26. Positioning the valve with a special tool prior to checking stem-to-guide clearance with a dial indicator. (Dodge)

the guide. The extra length will magnify the reading. Follow the manufacturer's recommendations for maximum allowable movement, **Figure 13-27.** Some valve seat grinder pilots can be used if a hole gauge is not available.

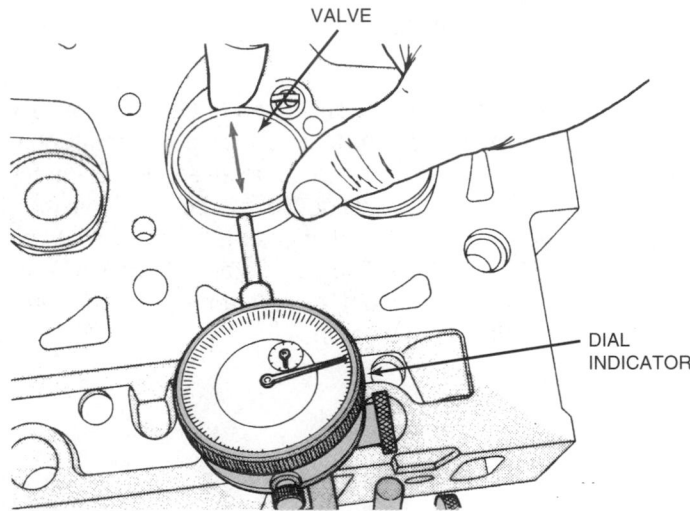

Figure 13-27. Checking valve stem play to determine stem-to-guide clearance. (Chrysler)

Engine design, type of oil seal, and amount of lubrication all determine acceptable clearance. Follow manufacturer's specifications. Generally, when the actual valve stem clearance exceeds .005″ to .006″ (0.13 to 0.15 mm), it is considered excessive. Remember that both the guide and stem wear less in the center. Even though a stem-to-guide clearance at the center is correct, the clearance at the ends may be excessive and cause tipping, **Figure 13-28.** Some valve guides are removable. When an excessive stem-to-guide clearance is present, the valve guides may be replaced. Integral guides cannot be removed, **Figure 13-29.** When worn, they can be reamed to an oversize and new valves with oversize stems can be installed. See **Figure 13-30.**

Replacing Valve Guides

Removable **valve guides** may either be driven or pressed out. The punch should have a pilot section extending into the guide. The pilot should be a few thousandths

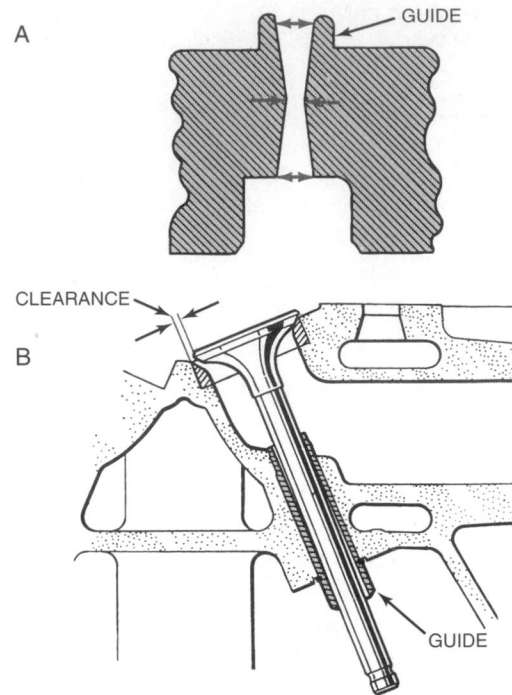

Figure 13-28. A—Stem-to-guide clearance near end of guide must be within limits. B—Note that correct clearance in guide center will not prevent tipping. (Jaguar & Chrysler)

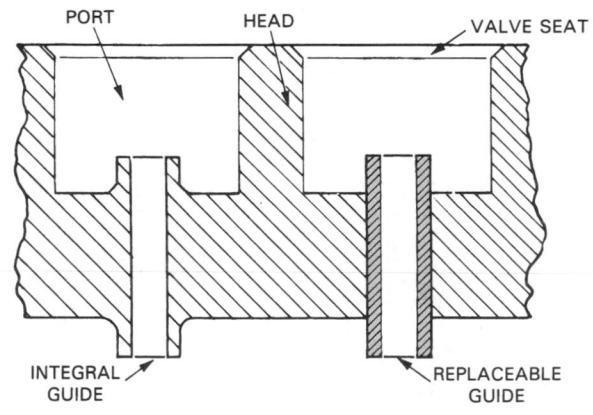

Figure 13-29. Integral and replaceable valve guides.

smaller than the guide hole to prevent binding. This is due to guide hole diameter reduction when using the punch for installation. The main body of the punch should be slightly smaller than the guide so it will follow the guide through the hole. The contact edge should be smooth and square with the punch centerline.

Before driving out the guides, make a note of the distance from the surface of the head to the face of the guide. Also note the shape of the end that extends into the combustion chamber. Distinguish between exhaust guide shapes and intake guide shapes. This is to get the correct guides for each valve separated. Also, the proper end can be distinguished so the guides can be driven to the correct depth. Look at **Figure 13-30.** Place the punch in the guide. While holding the punch in firm contact with the guide, drive

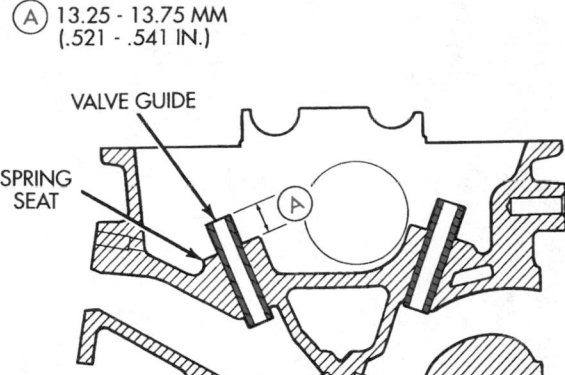

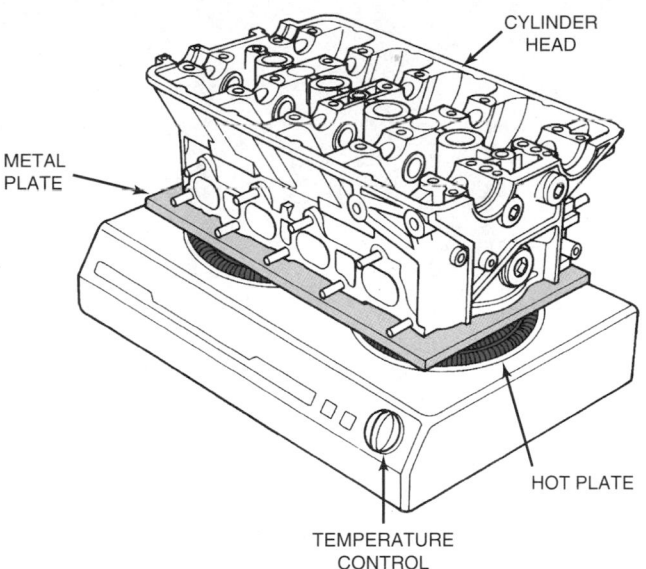

Figure 13-30. Guide depth in this engine is measured from the valve spring seat surface. (Chrysler)

Figure 13-32. Some heads can be heated to assist in removing and installing valve guides. (Acura)

the guide from the hole. Refer to **Figure 13-31.** Guides are brittle and may crack if the punch is loosely held. Some heads must be heated before attempting to remove the guides, **Figure 13-32.**

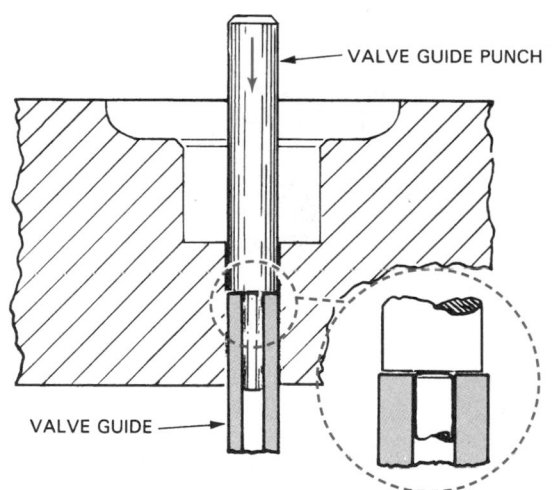

Figure 13-31. One form of a valve guide punch. Use a punch mark on tool to determine when guide has been driven to the proper depth.

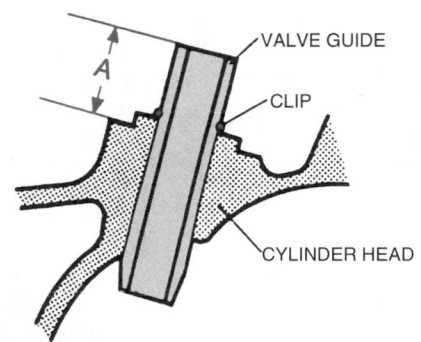

Figure 13-33. This valve guide has been installed to the proper depth. (Mazda)

Installing Guides

Before installing guides, make sure guide holes are spotlessly clean. If a refrigerator or freezer is handy, the guides may be placed in the freezer compartment long enough to thoroughly chill them. Dry ice or liquid nitrogen may also be used. The resultant reduction in diameter will aid in their installation. Give the guide and hole a thin coat of hypoid lubricant (Lubriplate or similar type). Insert the proper end of the guide into the correct guide hole. Drive the guide to the specified depth; do not drive it past the required depth. As in **Figure 13-33,** a mark may be used to provide a means of measuring valve guide height from a given surface. Some guide installation tools have a stop that will contact the head surface when the guide is at the correct height.

Reaming Guides after Installation

Some guides are factory reamed and do not require additional reaming following installation. If the guides must be reamed, use a *valve guide reamer* of the exact size. Start the reamer carefully and turn it clockwise both while entering and leaving the guide. Ream dry, while being careful to avoid any side pressure on the tool. Allow the pilot portion of the reamer to guide it through. A properly reamed guide will provide approximately .002″ (0.05 mm) guide clearance, **Figure 13-34.** Consult the manufacturer's specifications for each vehicle.

Servicing Integral Guides

When the guide is cast as part of the head, it is necessary to determine the extent of the wear. If wear is excessive, select a new valve with a suitable oversize stem. Stem oversizes generally are available in .003″, .015″, and .030″ (0.08, 0.38, and 0.76 mm). Ream the worn guide to fit the valve stem. As with removable guides, use a sharp reamer of the correct size. Following reaming, wash the guides and blow them dry.

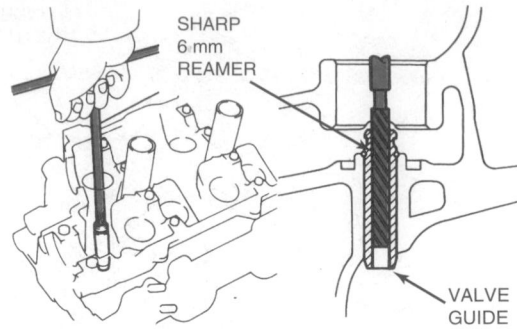

Figure 13-34. Reaming a valve guide. Note the close tolerances between valve guide and valve stem. (Lexus)

Preparing Valve Guide for Oil Seal

Some guides are designed to accept special *oil seals,* others are not. **Figure 13-35** shows one type of guide seal. The guide illustrated is already machined to fit the Teflon seal. Both integral and removable guides may be prepared for this seal. To install this particular seal, the valve stem end is covered with a protective plastic cap. The seal is then pressed over the end and down the stem, **Figure 13-36.** The seal is forced over the machined section of the guide as far as possible with the fingers. A special tool is used to complete the seating in some cases by grasping the seal and forcing it fully down, **Figure 13-37.**

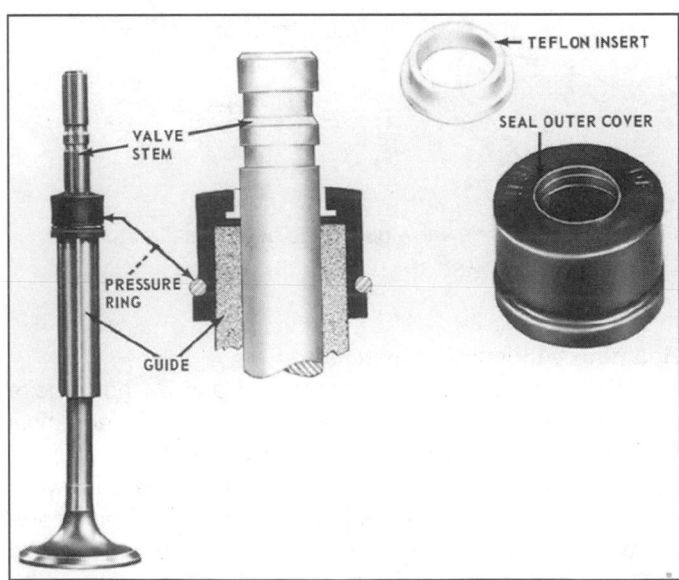

Figure 13-35. Teflon valve guide oil seal.

Oil control through the guides in overhead valve engines is critical. Great quantities of oil are pumped to the rocker arms for lubrication. A considerable amount finds its way to the valve stem ends. The combined forces of gravity, inertia, and vacuum attempt to draw the oil down through the guides. See **Figure 13-38.** Although oil is somewhat more likely to pass through the intake guide due to the strong vacuum in the cylinders during the intake stroke, the exhaust valve is also subjected to a mild vacuum. This vacuum is caused by the exhaust gases rushing over the head of the guide.

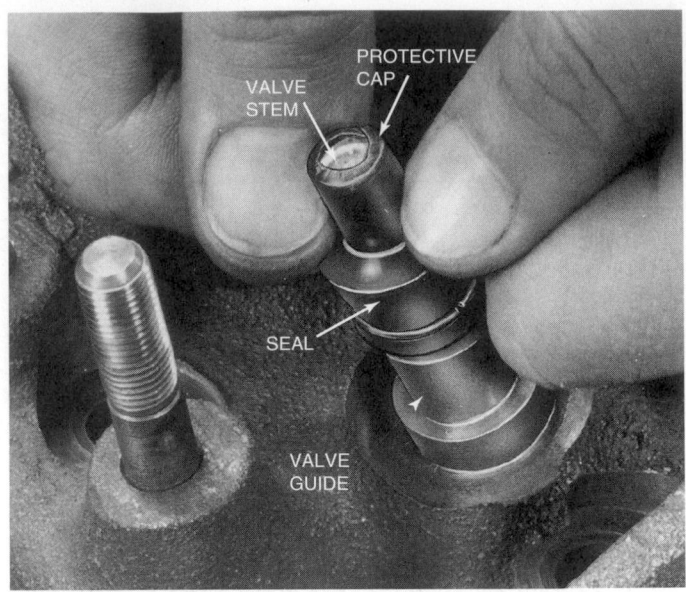

Figure 13-36. Pressing seal over protective cap on valve stem end. (Perfect Circle)

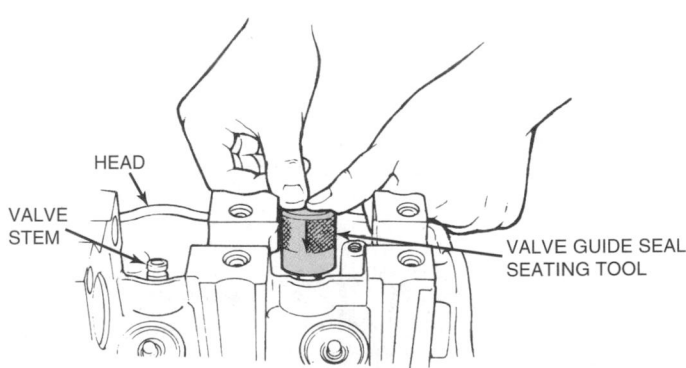

Figure 13-37. Seating valve guide seal using a special tool. (Chevrolet)

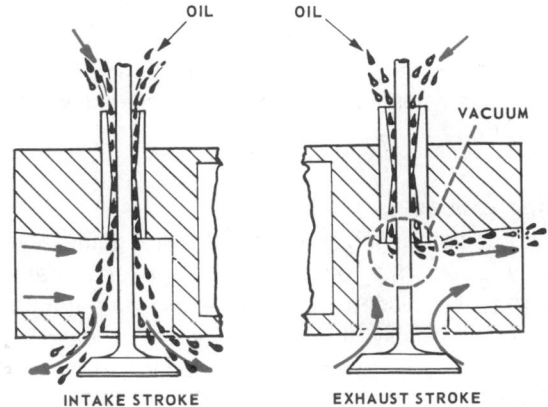

Figure 13-38. Both intake and exhaust guides will pass oil.

In addition to the special guide seal shown, protective shields, umbrella seals, and neoprene rings are often used on the valve stem ends to prevent oil from flowing down the stem to the guide. Valve guides are often cut at an angle to prevent oil from puddling on the top. When installing the valve assembly, be careful to avoid damage to the seals. Occasionally, only the intake valves are protected with guide seals, tapered guide heads, and stem end shields. Make sure they are correctly installed, **Figure 13-39.**

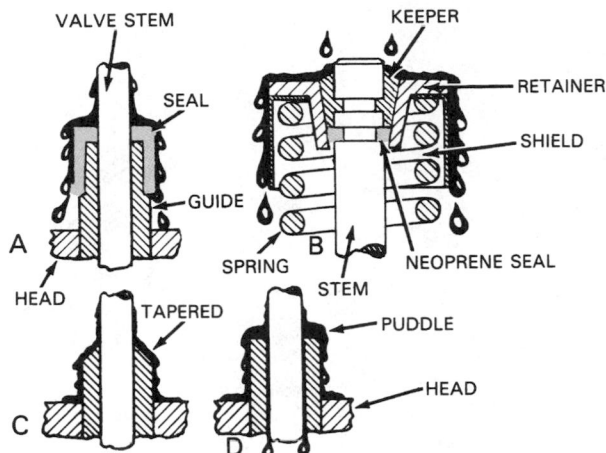

Figure 13-39. Devices used to prevent oil consumption through the valve guides. A—Guide seal. B—Neoprene seal and shield. C—Tapered guide top. D—Note how square cut guide allows oil to puddle and run through the guide.

Valve Seats

Inspect each *valve seat* for signs of excessive burning or cracking. If the seat is an insert type and shows any signs of damage, it must be removed and replaced with a new ring. *Valve seat inserts* are steel rings pressed into the head. These inserts are often used on aluminum heads. If an integral valve seat is damaged, it must be cut out and a replacement insert must be installed. In some cases, replacement inserts cannot be used and the head must be replaced. Typical seat damage includes looseness, burning, or cracking.

Servicing Valve Seat Insert

A special chisel or mechanical puller may be used to remove valve seats. When removing, be careful not to damage the seat recess. Refer to **Figure 13-40.** Make certain you have the correct size insert. Outside diameter (called OD), depth, and inside diameter (called ID) should match that of the insert being replaced.

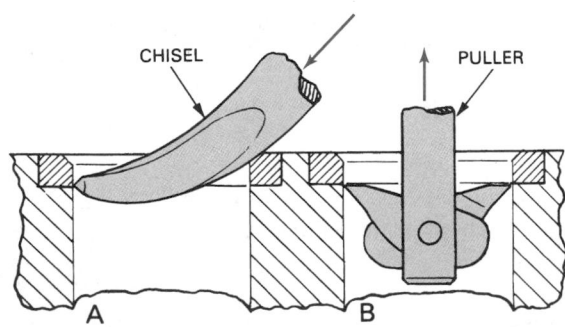

Figure 13-40. Removing valve seat inserts. A—Special chisel. B—Mechanical puller.

If the original inserts were cast iron, cast iron replacements can be used. If a hard valve seat insert is removed, replace with a similar type. Hard seat inserts are usually made of special heat resistant steel such as Stellite. The recess must be clean and free of nicks and dents. Place a special driver pilot in the valve guide. Install a driving head on the driver. The head should be just a little smaller than the insert OD.

The insert's outside diameter will be one or two thousandths larger than the recess. This will produce an interference fit to assist in securing the insert. It will also produce good heat transfer from the insert to the head. If the inserts have been chilled in dry ice or in the freezer, remove and install them one at a time. If all inserts are removed, they will warm up before installation. Freezing will reduce the OD and assist installation. Lay the insert, beveled edge down, over the recess in the head. Slide the driver over the pilot and start the insert with several firm blows. As the insert nears the bottom, reduce the strength of the hammer blows. Do not continue to pound the insert after it is fully seated. **Figure 13-41** shows a cross section of a typical insert driver set up for work.

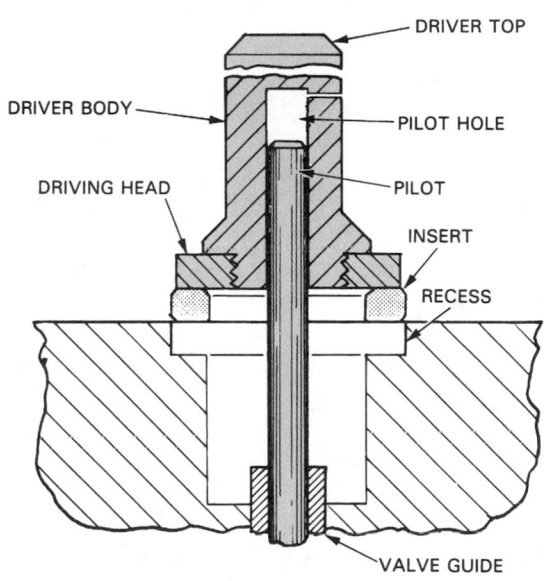

Figure 13-41. Installing valve seat insert with a special pilot driver combination.

Peening or Swaging Insert

The head metal around the outside of the valve seat insert may be either *peened* (upsetting head metal around the insert outside diameter to hold it in place) or *swaged* (upset by a rolling or rubbing action). All hard inserts and inserts set in an aluminum head must be peened or swaged. The insert will have a small chamfer on the upper OD into which the head metal is forced.

For peening, a pilot is placed in the valve guide and a special peening tool body is dropped over the pilot. The peen is adjusted so that it contacts the head metal along the edge of the insert. By turning and hammering the peening tool, the metal will be upset (bulged). Soft cast iron inserts have the same coefficient of expansion as cast iron head metal. If cast iron inserts are properly fitted, they will not have to be peened. Many technicians peen all types of inserts to provide an extra measure of safety. Other tools apply a rolling pressure to swage the metal into the chamfer, **Figure 13-42.**

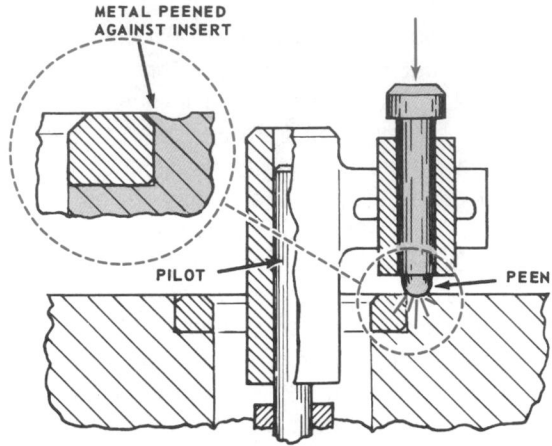

Figure 13-42.   Using a special tool to peen the metal around insert edge. Note how metal is forced against insert.

Cutting Insert Seat Recess

Where no insert is used and the integral seat is damaged beyond repair, a recess may be cut and an insert seat can be installed. In cases where an insert is used but is loose, a recess may be cut for an insert of slightly larger outside diameter. If the guide is in good shape, select a pilot that fits the guide as recommended by the tool manufacturer. Choose a cutter of the correct size and install.

Fit the guide to the pilot assembly and drop the tool body over the pilot. All alignment screws must be loose. Place the anchor bolt slot over a convenient head bolt hole and install the anchor bolt. Align the tool body with the pilot by shaking the tool slightly. Lock the anchor bolt and alignment screws securely. The cutter should revolve with finger pressure when all screws are secured. If binding is present, loosen the alignment screws, readjust, and retighten. The object is to have the tool body and drive mechanism secure without binding the pilot and cutter assembly. **Figure 13-43** shows two types of insert recess tools.

With the cutter just touching the work, place the insert ring on the stop block. Run the stop collar down until it touches the ring. Lock the feed screw to the cutter sleeve and remove the ring. The tool will then cut to the exact depth of the ring. Make certain all alignment screws are tight. Use either a ratchet handle or a power drive mechanism to rotate the cutter.

With the cutter just clearing the work, start the cutter. Feed the cutter into the work by turning the knurled stop collar. Do not force the cutter. Give the stop collar several turns, and then feed the cutter down lightly. Repeat this process until the stop collar engages the stop block. At this point, give the tool a few additional turns to produce a smooth seat for the insert. Turn the cutter out. **Figure 13-43**

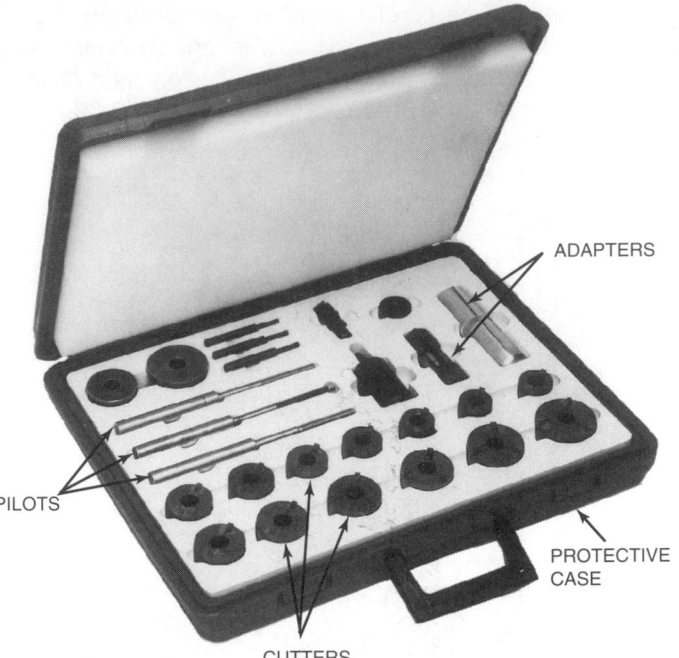

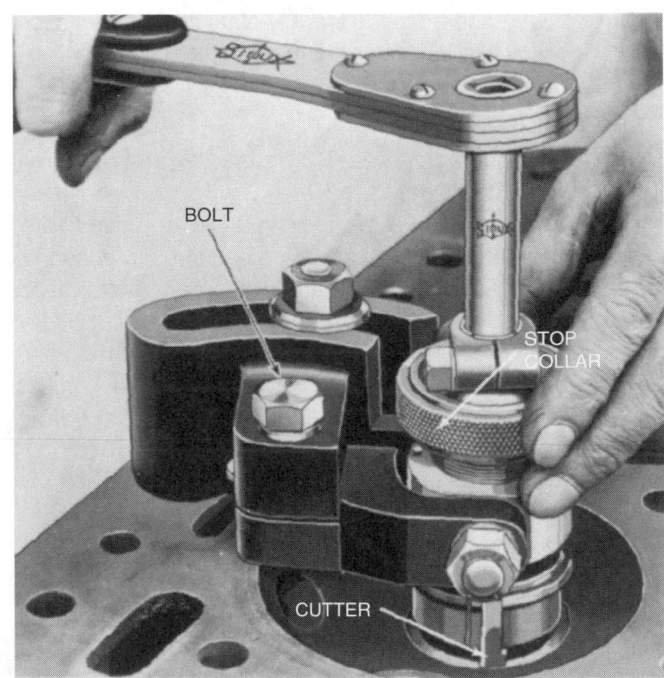

Figure 13-43.   A—A set of valve seat recess cutters with various pilots and adapters stored in a protective carrying case. Avoid dropping these cutters. They can be easily damaged. B—A different style of cutter being used to cut a new insert recess. Follow the toolmaker's operating instructions. (Lisle Tools and Sioux Tools)

shows the technician moving the cutter into the work by turning the stop collar. **Figure 13-44** illustrates a power-driven cutter tool.

Valve Seat Service

After all valve guide and insert work is complete, the valve seats are ready to be *refaced.* The seat must be free

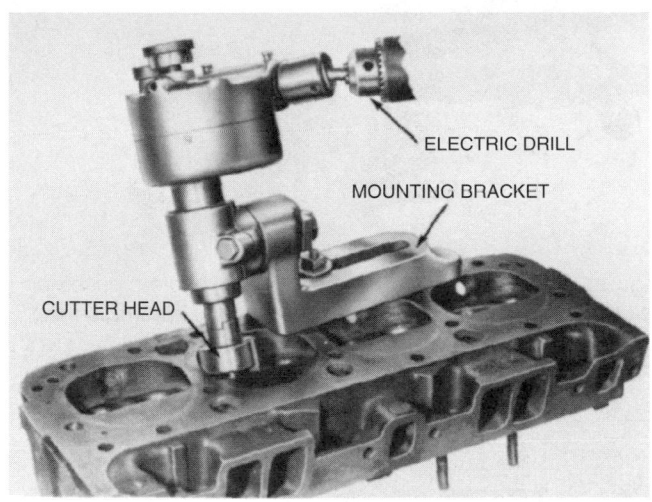

Figure 13-44. Using a power-driven valve seat recess cutter. (Kwik-Way)

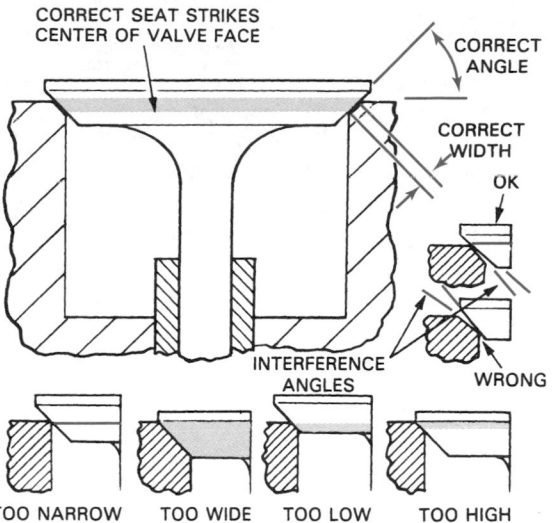

Figure 13-45. Correct and incorrect valve seats. Note the interference angles.

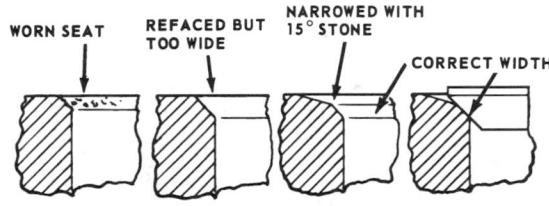

Figure 13-46. Narrowing valve seat width after refacing. A 30° stone is occasionally used to narrow 45° seats. Sometimes a flat stone is required.

of carbon, oil, and dirt. The cutting device will quickly fill with debris if the seat is not clean, ruining the cutting action. The valve guides must be clean to allow the pilot to properly align with the guide hole. Valve seat refacing can be done using grinding stones or hardened cutters.

The valve seat must be cut at the correct angle and be clean, smooth, and free of cracks, nicks, and pits. It must be of the correct width and engage the face of the valve near its central portion. Common seat angles are 30° and 45°. Where an interference fit is desired, the interference angle may be ground on either the seat or the valve. Follow manufacturer's specifications.

Seat width varies with each manufacturer but will average around 1/16" (1.58 mm) for both intake and exhaust seats. A seat that is too narrow will pound out of shape easily. It will also fail to dissipate enough heat from the valve face. A seat that is too wide will tend to collect carbon, eventually preventing a good seal. This can lead to valve overheating and burning. See **Figure 13-45.**

When refacing a seat, the removal of stock will widen the seat beyond original specifications. It must be narrowed by removing metal from the seat's upper portion. Look at **Figure 13-46.** In cases where the valve port walls narrow or are uneven, metal will have to be removed from the bottom of the seat. If the walls are smooth and of constant diameter, only a very light cut with a 60°-70° stone should be taken. If inserts are used, the bottom cut is not necessary, **Figure 13-47.** The light bottom cut will produce a seat that is the same width at all spots.

Preparing to Grind Valve Seats

The following sections explain how to use grinding stones to reface valve seats. The information concerning grinding stone selection and preparation should be carefully followed. Many heads have been ruined by the use of a worn stone or a stone of the wrong angle.

Seat stones are available in various widths. Coarse-textured roughing stones are used for the initial, or roughing, cut on steel seats. The fine textured finishing stone is used

for the last cut on steel seats. The cast iron block or head requires only the use of the finishing stone. Special stones are available for grinding Stellite and other hard seat inserts. The stone must be a little wider than the finished seat in order to prevent counterboring. It must not be so wide as to strike other parts of the combustion chamber. **Figure 13-48** illustrates how various stone widths affect the job.

Select a cutting stone with the correct angle for the job. This will save time in dressing and will prolong the life of the stone. Many stones are constructed so that an angle may be ground on both ends, **Figure 13-49.** After selecting a cutting stone of the correct size and texture, screw it snugly onto the stone holder or sleeve. Place the stone sleeve on the dressing stand pilot. Adjust the diamond holder to the correct angle and lock all adjustments. Back the diamond away from the stone. Engage the stone drive motor and run the diamond tip fully across the stone's face. Use care when dressing the stone to see that the cuts are not too heavy. Take light cuts on the stone until the angle is correct and the full stone face is clean and true. The full stone angle must also be dressed to prevent injury to the diamond. **Figure 13-50** illustrates the effects of both an initial heavy cut and failure to dress the full width.

There are basically two types of stone pilots in use. One is the adjustable type that is slipped into the guide and

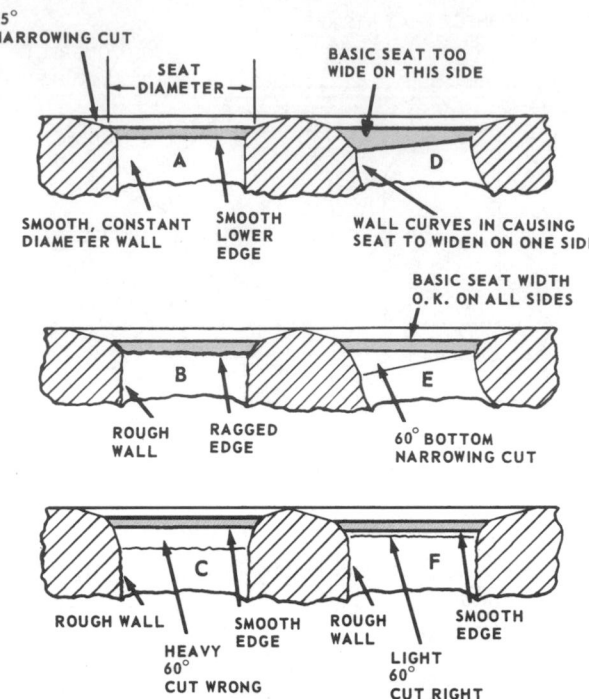

Figure 13-47.   Narrowing valve seat. A—15° cut from top makes a good seat when port walls are smooth and of constant diameter. B—Rough wall leaves a ragged lower edge on seat. C—Heavy bottom cut produces smooth lower seat edge, but widens seat diameter. D—Curved port walls produce an uneven seat width. E—Bottom cut produces an even width. F—Very light bottom cut smoothes seat edge without appreciable increase in seat diameter.

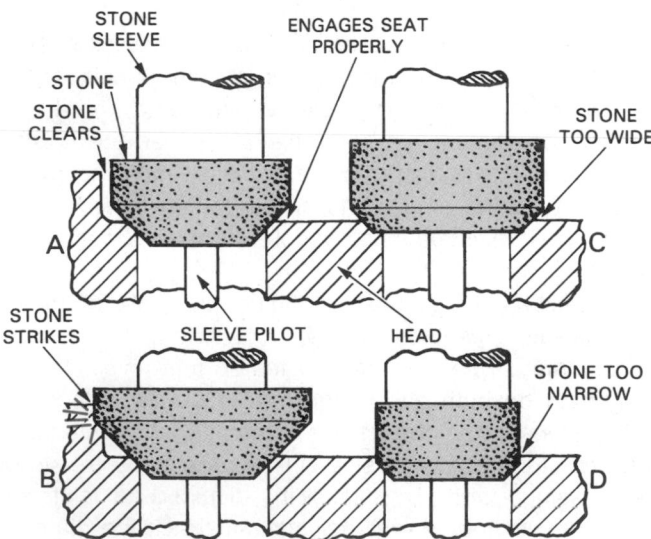

Figure 13-48.   Stone must be of correct width. A—Stone OK. B—Too wide. C—Too wide, makes a horizontal step at bottom of seat. D—Too narrow, makes a vertical step at top of seat.

then expanded. The other is of tapered construction that is secured through friction between the guide and a tapered section. Make sure that the guide is clean, regardless of the type used. Wipe off the pilot with a clean, lightly-oiled rag, and insert the pilot. The pilot must be rigid. See **Figure 13-51.** Mount the correct seat angle stone on one sleeve

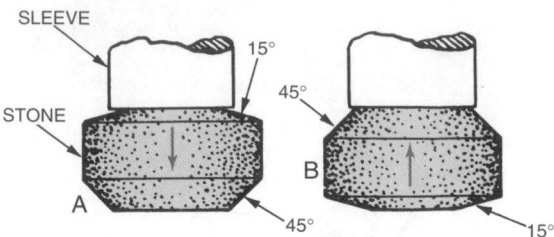

Figure 13-49.   Some stones can have an angle dressed on both ends. A—Stone with 45° angle down. B—Same stone, reversed with 15° angle down.

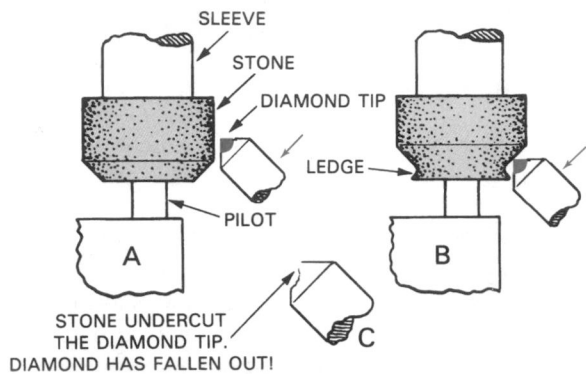

Figure 13-50.   Do not ruin the diamond. A—Heavy cut will strike steel below diamond. B—Failure to dress full width leaves a ledge that can strike steel beneath diamond. C—When steel beneath diamond is undercut, diamond tip will fall out.

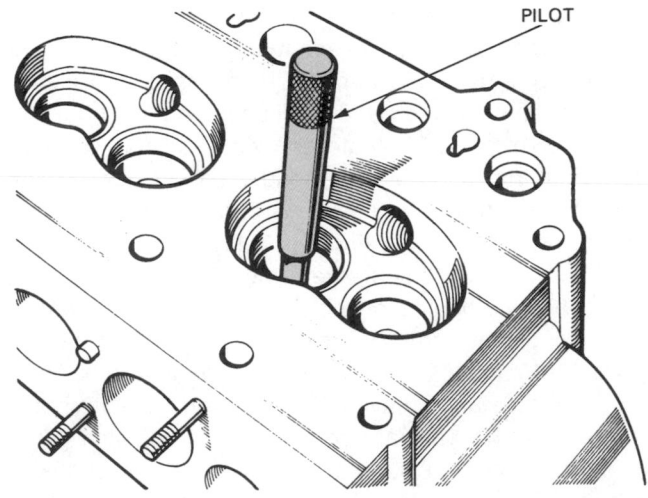

Figure 13-51.   Valve seat stone sleeve pilot in place in valve guide. Pilot must be tight. (British-Leyland)

and the 15° and 70° stones on two other sleeves. This will allow you to grind and narrow the seat without removing and changing stones. Once the pilot is inserted, finish the complete seat operation before moving to the next one.

Grinding the Valve Seat

Once the stone is dressed and clean, place the sleeve on the pilot, **Figure 13-52.** The stone should contact the seat. Insert the motor drive head into the sleeve. Tilt the motor up, down, and sideways to feel for a non-binding,

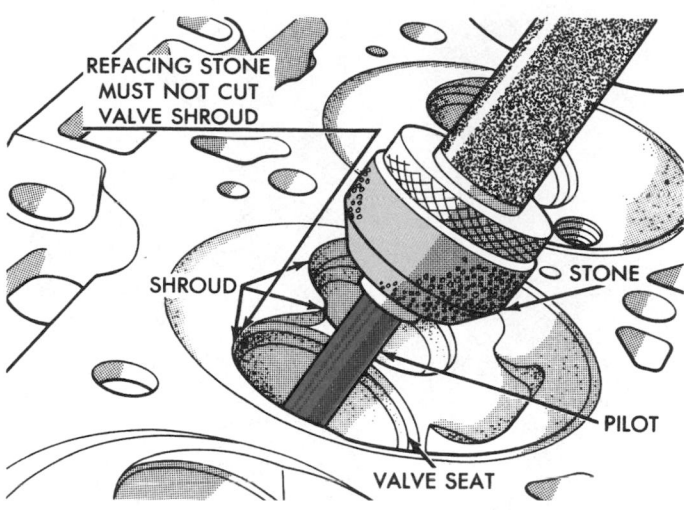

Figure 13-52. Refacing (grinding) a valve seat. Wear safety glasses. (Dodge)

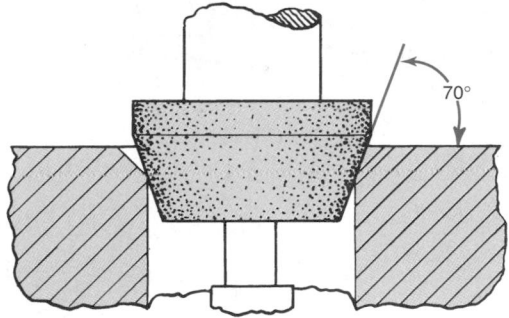

Figure 13-53. Taking a light cut on bottom of seat with a 60°-70° stone.

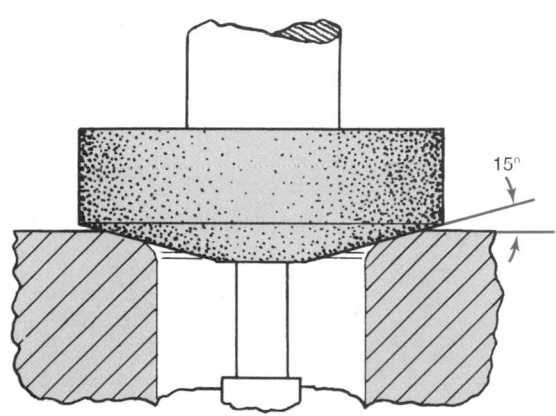

Figure 13-54. Narrowing seat to specified width by removing metal from top with a 15° stone.

central position. While supporting the motor, engage the switch. Allow stone to grind for a few seconds. Then, stop and remove motor. Raise the sleeve and examine the seat. Repeat this procedure until the seat is smooth, clean, and free of burns and pits.

 Caution: Remove only enough stock to clean seat. If integral seat is hardened, excessive grinding can cut through the hardened area. Check manufacturer's specifications.

On hard inserts, dress the stone several times for each seat. Never continue grinding when the stone surface needs dressing. If using a roughing stone, stop when the seat is cleaned up. Switch to a finishing stone and polish the seat. The finished seat will be only as accurate as the stone.

Using a 60°-70° stone, grind until the 60°-70° angle touches the basic 30°-45° seat surface all the way around. This 60°-70° stone cuts very quickly. Do not apply down pressure and cut for only about two seconds before checking, **Figure 13-53.** With the 15°-30° stone, (see manufacturer's specifications) remove stock until the seat is down to the specified width. See **Figure 13-54.** A small measuring tool will assist in a careful measurement of seat width. A trick often used for seat grinding is to mark the seat (after grinding basic angle) with a series of soft pencil marks across the width. When removing stock from above and below the seat, the pencil marks will clearly show what is left of the base seat angle, **Figure 13-55.**

Using Valve Seat Reamers

Valve seat reamers, sometimes called seat cutters, are replacing grinding stones in many shops. The seat reamer consists of a cutting head with several blades attached. The cutter blades resemble small files. Cutting heads are available in all of the common valve seat angles, as well as extra wide and narrow versions for narrowing and positioning the seat.

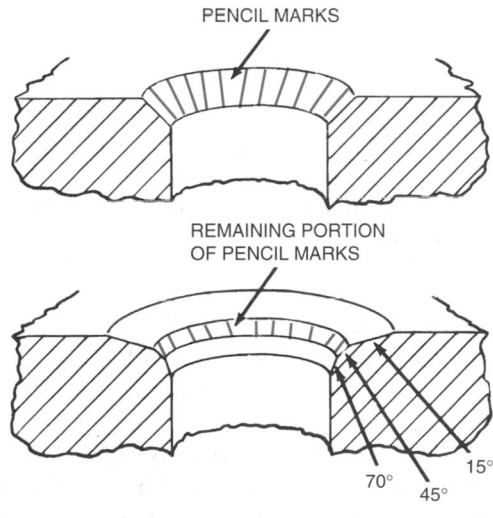

Figure 13-55. Using pencil marks to determine width of basic 30° or 45° seat.

The advantage of the valve seat reamer is that it is hand-operated. The reamer teeth do not require dressing and are replaced when the blades become dull. A typical valve seat cutter is shown in **Figure 13-56.** A pilot shaft must be installed in the valve guide in the same way as when using a grinding stone. The reamer must always be turned in the proper direction, usually clockwise. The finished cut is checked in the same way as with a grinding stone.

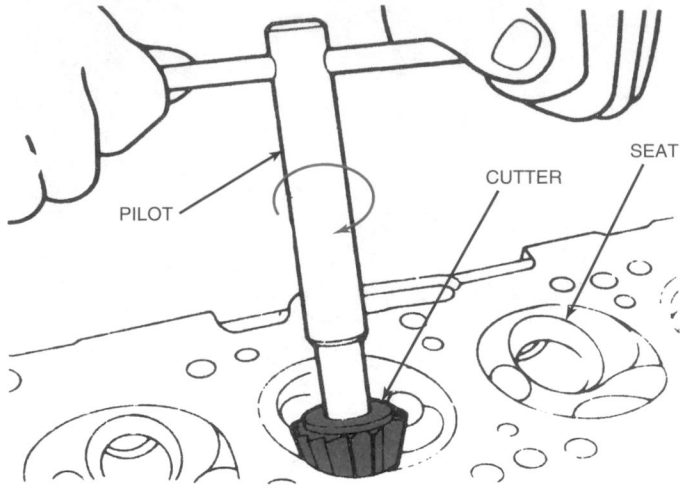

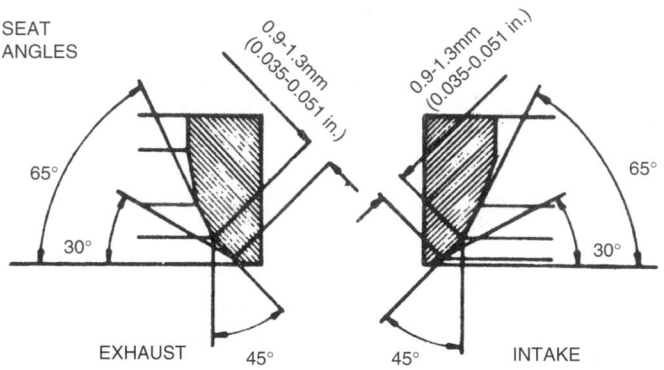

Figure 13-56. A valve seat cutter is used to clean and true seat. Always check the valve guide for wear before cutting the seat. (Hyundai)

 Note: Valve seat reamers cannot be used on some hardened valve seats. Check the appropriate service manual and use a grinding stone where indicated.

Testing Valve Seats

To test a valve seat for *concentricity* (true roundness), place a special valve seat dial indicator on the pilot. Adjust the indicator bar so that it contacts the center of the valve seat. The dial needle should travel about a half turn when the bar length is correct. Set the dial to zero. Hold the upper dial section and slowly turn the bottom section around so the bar travels completely around the seat. The dial needle will indicate any runout. The entire seat should be within .002″ (0.05 mm). If runout exceeds .002″ (0.05 mm), check the setup carefully and try again. If runout is still excessive, regrind the seat, **Figure 13-57.**

Lapping Valves

Valve *lapping* consists of turning the valve against the seat using lapping compound, which is a fine abrasive powder. Lapping was often performed in the past, sometimes as a substitute for grinding the valves and seats.

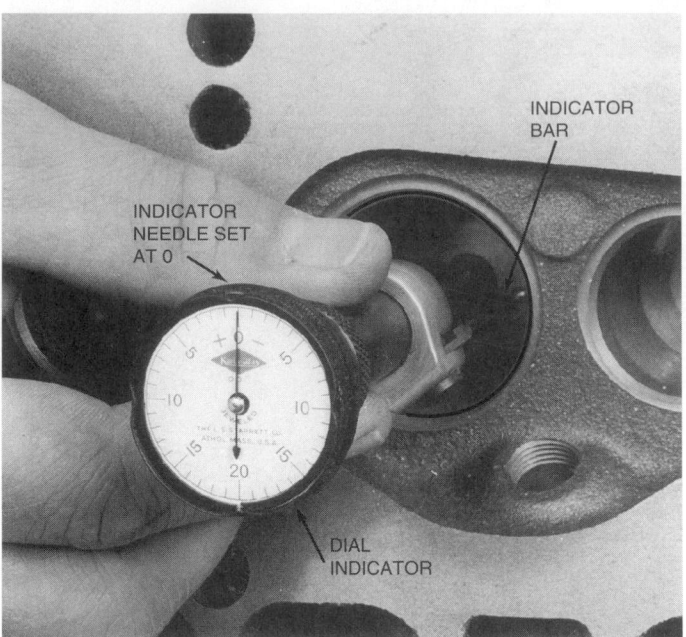

Figure 13-57. Checking valve seat concentricity with a dial indicator. (Kwik-Way)

Today, lapping is sometimes performed to make a final fit between the valve and seat. Some technicians feel that it produces a more accurate seal between valve and seat, while others contend that it is of no value. Many manufacturers say that when modern valve grinding equipment is properly used, lapping is not necessary. Lapping when an interference fit is desired can actually damage the seal.

Final Check of Seat and Valve Face

Before checking by placing valves in the guides, the head and the guides should be thoroughly washed, flushed, and blown dry. Rub a very thin film of *Prussian blue* on the valve face. Place the valve in position. While pressing in the center of the valve, rotate the valve about one-quarter turn in either direction and then back to the point of beginning. Remove the valve and examine the seat. It should be marked with blue around its entire circumference. The seat should mark the valve face near the center. Pencil marks about 1/4″ (6.35 mm) apart around the valve face will also provide a check, **Figure 13-58.** Turning the valve should wipe out all marks.

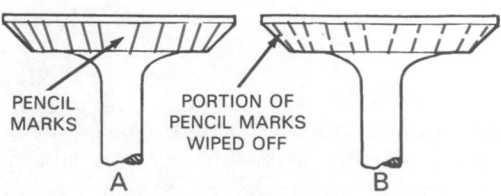

Figure 13-58. Pencil marks on valve face will determine valve face-to-seat accuracy. A—Marks applied. B—Portion of marks wiped off by placing valve in seat and giving it one-quarter turn.

Replacing Rocker Arm Studs

If the cylinder head uses individual **rocker arm studs,** check them for signs of damage or looseness. If a replacement is necessary due to breakage, a standard size replacement will suffice. If the stud is loose, the hole will have to be reamed to one of several available oversizes. Most rocker arm studs are pressed in, however, some heads use screw-in studs.

To remove the stud, place the pulling sleeve over the stud. Tighten the nut against the sleeve and turn the nut to pull the stud, **Figure 13-59.** If the stud is broken off at the boss, drill and remove with a stud extractor. If an oversize stud is required, ream the hole with a special reamer of the correct size. If a larger oversize stud is needed, ream the hole in two steps. Use the smaller oversize reamer first, then finish with the desired size. See **Figure 13-60.** Thread the replacement stud in the driver. Coat the plain end with hypoid lubricant or Lubriplate. Place the stud over the hole and drive it down until the driver body touches the stud boss. This will be the correct depth. Remove driver tool, **Figure 13-61.**

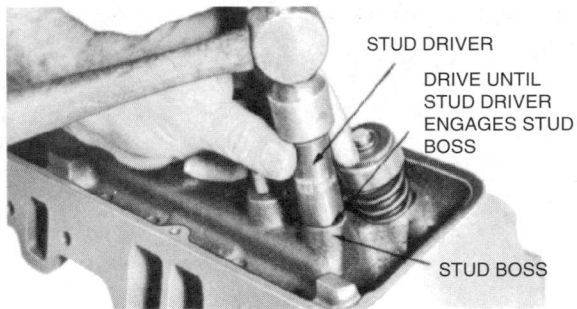

Figure 13-61. Driving a rocker arm stud into place.

Valve Springs

Valve springs should be soaked in solvent, brushed, and thoroughly rinsed. Never clean painted springs in strong cleaners. This will remove the paint and other coatings that prevent rust. Power wire wheels will also remove this protective coating, shortening spring life. After extended service, valve springs tend to lose tension. Since correct **spring tension** is important to proper valve action, each spring must be tested to make certain it meets minimum requirements. Manufacturers provide specifications listing the amount of pressure, in pounds or kilograms, that a given spring should exert when compressed to a specific length. The spring is placed in an appropriate measuring device and compressed to the specified length. The pressure is then determined, **Figure 13-62.**

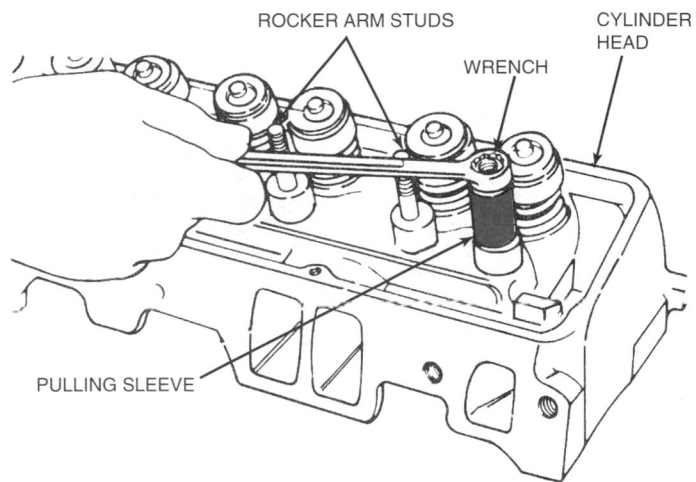

Figure 13-59. Pulling a rocker arm stud. (Chevrolet)

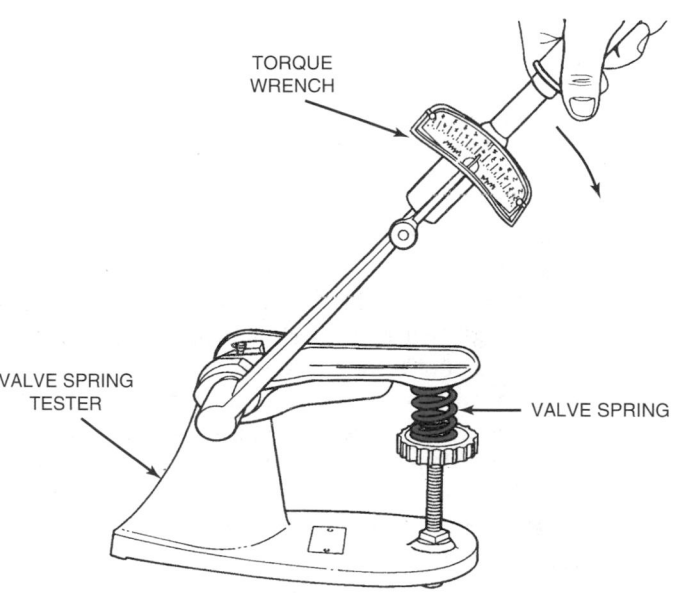

Figure 13-62. Testing valve spring tension. Spring is placed on base. When lever is pulled down, pointer pad compresses the spring to the specified distance on scale. Tension is then read on dial. (Chrysler)

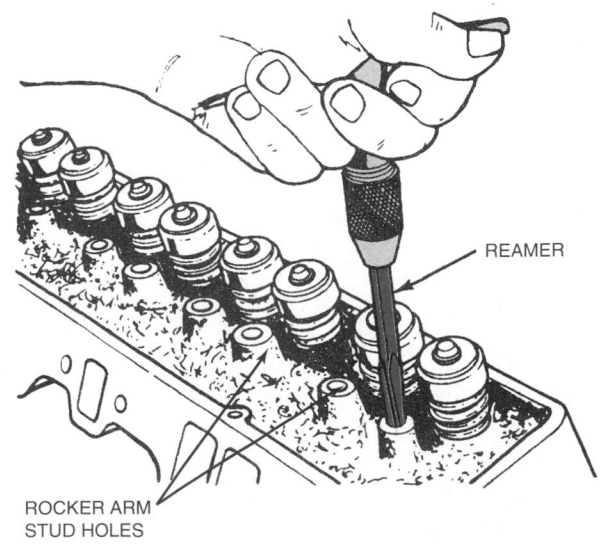

Figure 13-60. Reaming a rocker arm stud hole. Ream in steps if installing an oversize stud. (GMC)

Place the spring on a flat surface. Slide a combination square up to the spring (do not tip spring). Using the scale on the blade, measure the **spring free length** (length when spring is not under pressure). It should meet the manufacturer's specifications. Check the spring for *squareness* by carefully sighting the spring between its edge and the blade. Give the spring a partial turn and check again. Place the spring on its opposite end and check again. The spring should be parallel to the blade in all cases. If both sightings indicate that the spring is parallel (not more than 1/16″ (1.59 mm) difference between top and bottom), you can assume that the spring is square, **Figure 13-63.**

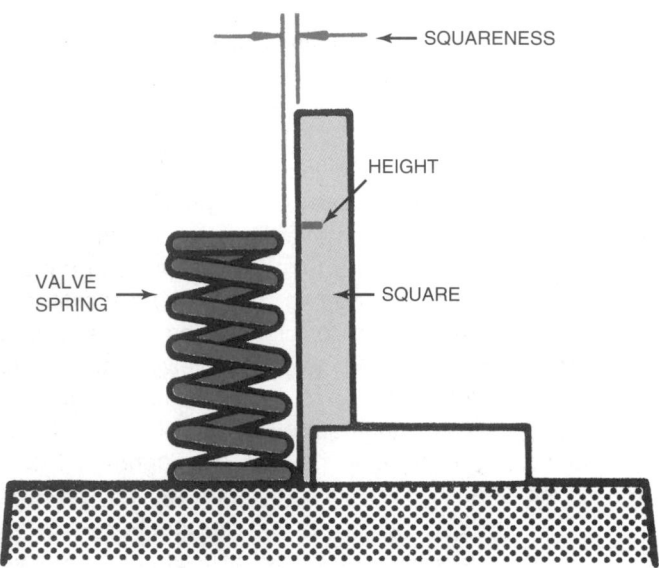

Figure 13-63. Checking spring free length and squareness. (Suzuki)

 Note: While inspecting the valve springs, check for any signs of rust, corrosive etching, scratches, and nicks.

Discard springs that fail to meet specified compressed pressure, free length, squareness, or that show other problems. A weak spring will cause valve float (valve closing so slowly that the camshaft lobe starts to open it again before it has fully seated). Valves may start sticking in the guides, causing heavy tappet noise, missing, burning, and breakage. Remember that using poor valve springs can be expensive. New springs are inexpensive and will certainly raise the level of reliability and performance. Inspect *damper springs* (used inside regular spring to reduce spring vibration) and damper clips if used. Discard any that are worn or fail to meet specifications.

Cylinder Head Assembly

With the cylinder head back in a suitable fixture and spotlessly clean, oil the valve guides. Select the proper valve, oil the stem, and insert the valve into the guide. Each valve should be installed in the port that it was removed from. On engines that do not have provisions for adjusting rocker arm-to-push rod clearance, the height of the valve stem from the head should be checked. The amount of metal removed from the valve face and seat might allow the stem to protrude farther. If this happens, the rocker arm will

be tipped down on the push rod side, forcing the hydraulic lifter plunger near the bottom of its travel. Malfunctions can result if provisions are not built into the lifter to adjust to this change. If the stem height is excessive, the valve must be removed and the stem end ground down the proper amount. Check all valves, **Figure 13-64.**

While holding the valve in place, install stem-to-guide oil seal if used. If required, place steel washer around guide and in contact with head. Check springs for a closed coil end (one end of spring may have coils spaced closer together). Place closed end toward the head, over the stem, and in contact with the head, **Figure 13-65.** On some engines, there are differences between intake and exhaust springs and retainers. Be careful to assemble them in the proper locations. If dual coils or a damper spring are used, space coil ends per manufacturer's instructions, usually about 180° apart.

Install a shield or an umbrella seal and retainer over the spring. Using a spring compressor, compress the spring just far enough to expose the stem oil seal groove. Slip the

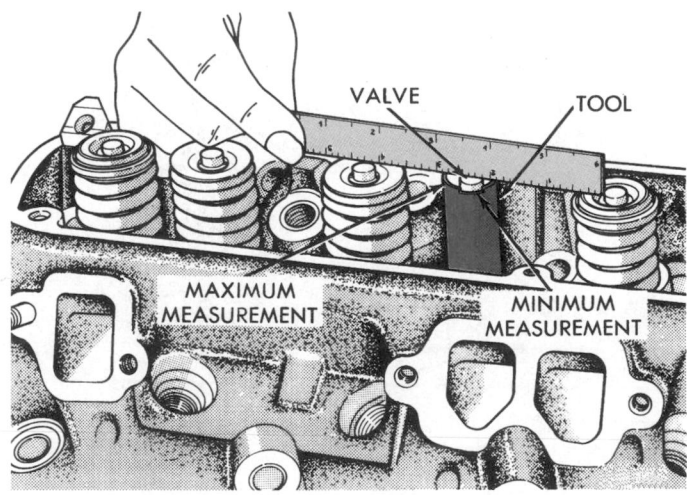

Figure 13-64. Checking valve stem height. Incorrect valve stem height can cause serious problems. (Chrysler)

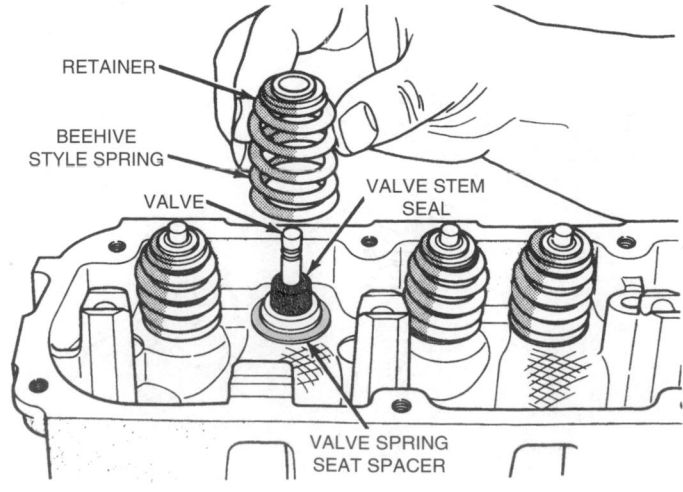

Figure 13-65. Guide seal installed. Spring and retainer being placed in position. (Chrysler)

seal into the groove. Make sure it is positioned properly and is not twisted. Insert the split keepers, or locks, and slowly release the spring. As the spring rises, guide the retainer so it is centered around the keepers. When fully released, check keepers to make certain they are fully engaged. See **Figure 13-66.**

> **STOP** **Warning: If keepers are not locked into position, they can slip and fly out with dangerous force. Stay to one side of the valve and spring assembly. Always wear safety goggles when compressing springs.**

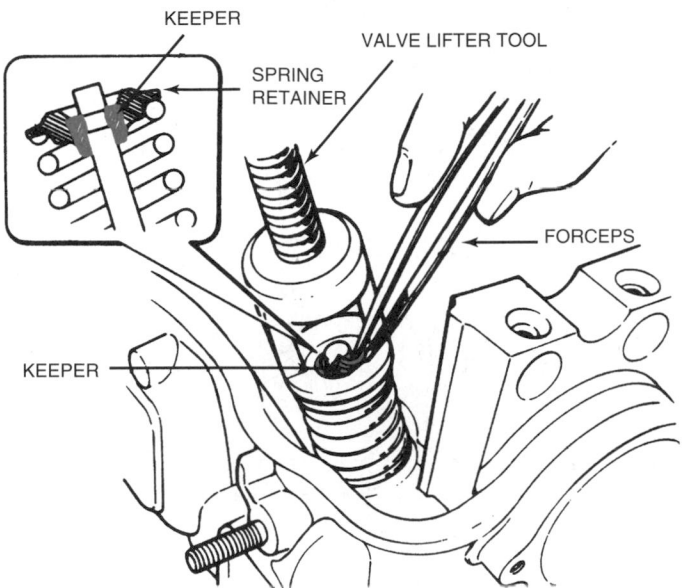

Figure 13-66. Compressing valve spring and installing split valve keepers. (Suzuki)

Figure 13-67 shows a typical valve stem assembly. Note the stem seal. When a stem seal is employed, it can be tested with a vacuum pump and a small vacuum cup

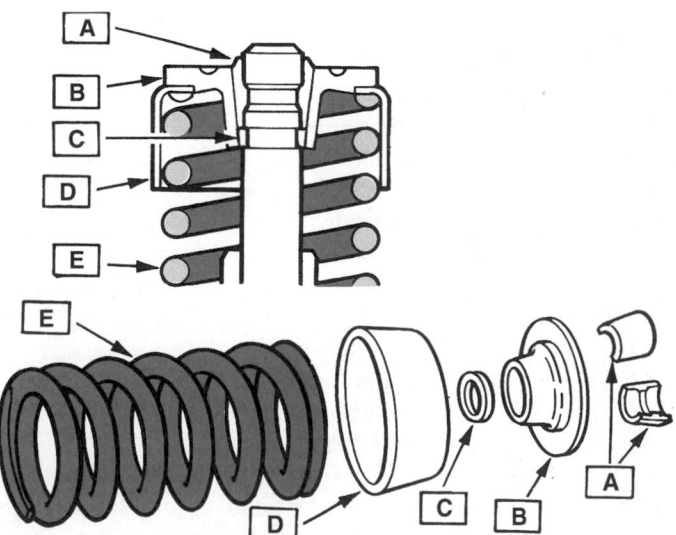

Figure 13-67. Typical valve spring assembly. A—Keepers (locks). B—Retainer (cap). C—Seal. D—Shield. E—Valve spring. (Buick)

adapter. Place the vacuum cup over the retainer and squeeze the vacuum pump. When the pump is released, the reading on the gauge should hold steady, indicating an airtight seal. See **Figure 13-68.**

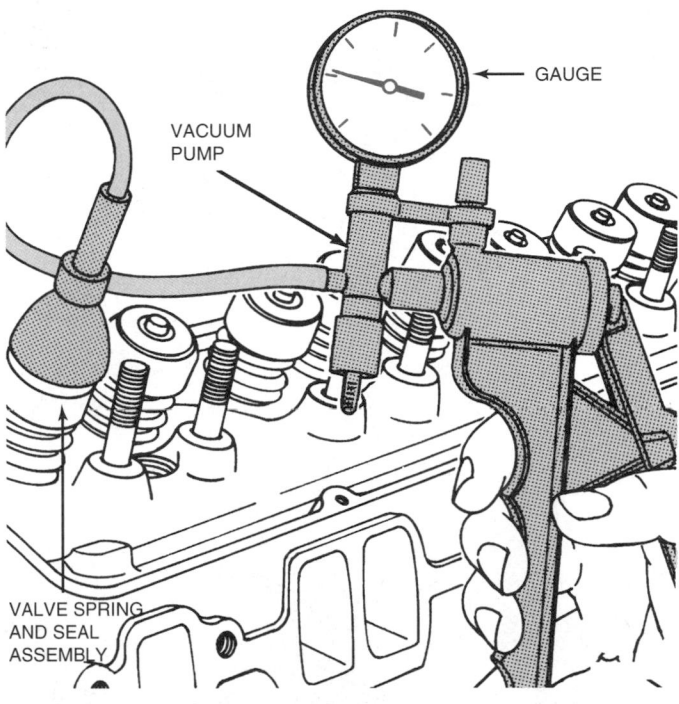

Figure 13-68. Using a hand-operated vacuum pump to check a valve stem seal for leakage. If the seal leaks, the gauge needle will slowly drop. (General Motors)

Checking Installed Height of Valve Spring

As with the valve stem end, removal of stock from valve face and seat will allow the keeper grooves to protrude higher above the head. This will increase the installed height of the spring and reduce spring tension. Using manufacturer's specifications, measure the ***installed height*** of each spring, **Figure 13-69.**

If the height is excessive, it must be corrected by removing the spring and placing a special steel washer or insert between the spring and the head. These washers are

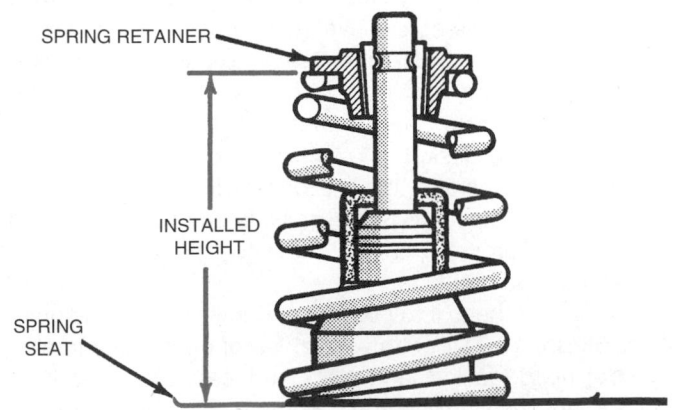

Figure 13-69. Checking valve spring installed height as measured from the spring seat to the bottom of the spring retainer. (Chrysler)

available in different thicknesses. Do not install washers that are too thick, as the spring pressure can be increased to the point of causing rapid lifter and camshaft wear. **Figure 13-70** illustrates one type of washer used to compensate for excessive stem length.

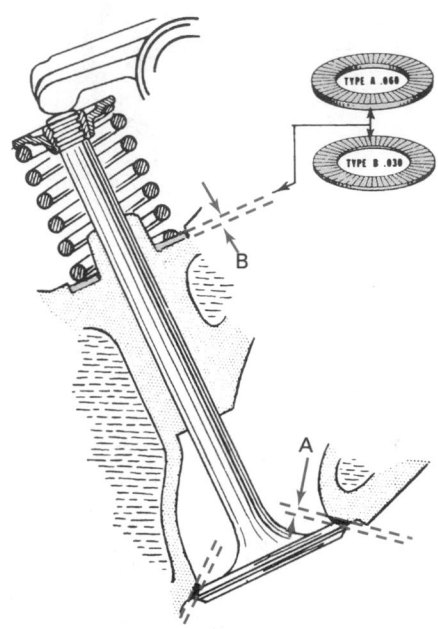

Figure 13-70. Correcting excessive valve spring installed height by adding a washer between head and spring end. A—Amount of metal removed by grinding valve and seat. B—Washer thickness comparable to A. (Dodge)

Installing Cylinder Head

When the ball joint rocker arms are used, the rocker arms may be attached loosely to the studs and left in position while the head is installed. However, the rocker shaft and arm assembly is generally installed after the head is in position and has been torqued. The block must be within acceptable distortion measurements. The surface must be absolutely clean and free of nicks and dents. All head bolt holes should be clean.

If the block does not have built-in **guide pins,** you can make some out of old cylinder head bolts. Cut off the heads of the bolts and file screwdriver slots in the tops. Taper the cut end of each so it will enter the head easily. Screw them into the block, one near each end. Place the cylinder head gasket on the block. Check that the right side is up and the front end of the gasket is at the front of the engine. Also check to make certain that the gasket fits properly and all passages are exposed. Some gaskets come with a special coating that provides a seal as soon as the engine is warmed up the first time.

Place the head into position and lower it over the guide pins. **Figure 13-71** illustrates the use of dowel pins to align cylinder head, gasket, and block surfaces. Clean the head bolt threads with a wire brush. Some manufacturers recommend replacing the head bolts, so check the manual. Coat the head bolt threads with a suitable thread compound. The

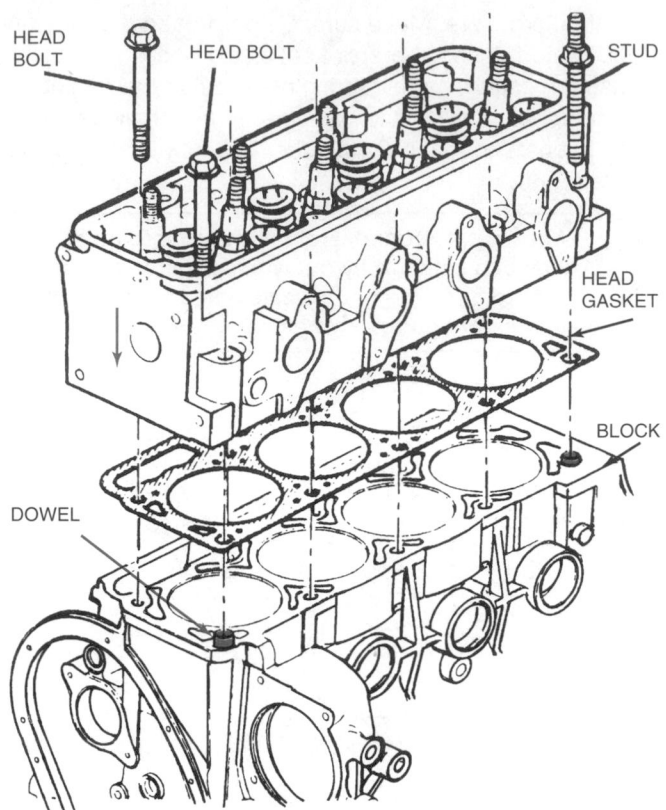

Figure 13-71. Lowering cylinder head into position. Note the permanent short guide pins. (General Motors)

compound should have the necessary sealing properties, especially when the bolts thread into a hole that enters a water jacket or oil gallery. Insert the bolts in their proper locations. Watch for different lengths. If one of the bolts is designed to pass oil from the block through the head to the rocker assembly, be certain it is placed in the correct spot. Tighten all bolts until they just engage the head. Remove the guide pins and install bolts in these holes.

Torque the Head Bolts

Using a torque wrench and following the recommended **torquing sequence,** bring all bolts up to one-third torque, then to two-thirds torque, and finally to full torque. Go over them again to make sure none have been missed. Remember that proper torque is a *must.* Excessive or uneven tightening will distort cylinders, valve guides, and valve seats, **Figure 13-72.** Follow manufacturer's recommendations. Chapter 16 will cover rocker arms, push rods, and valve adjustment.

Torque-Plus-Angle Tightening

The cylinder head specifications on many modern engines call for a special bolt tightening method. This method is often used to torque aluminum heads on cast iron blocks. Begin by torquing the heads to a relatively low torque, as given in the manufacturer's specifications. Then, tighten the bolt an additional fraction of a turn (usually 90° or 1/4 turn). Special angle gauges are available to accurately

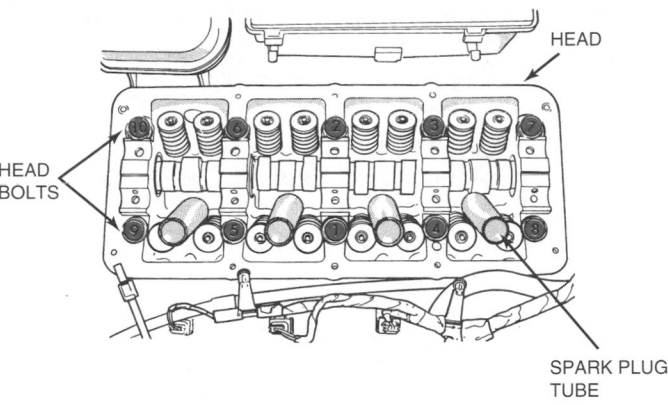

Figure 13-72. Torque head bolts in sequence recommended by engine manufacturer. (Plymouth)

measure the fraction of a turn needed. Each bolt is tightened one time only. Manufacturers claim that this method is more accurate, since it stretches the bolt the exact amount needed to allow for the different expansion rates of cast iron and aluminum. Always check the manufacturer's specifications, and never substitute traditional torquing methods for the torque-plus-angle method.

> **Caution: Many head bolts are designed to be used one time only. Do not reuse these fasteners, as they are permanently stretched and will not properly seal, even if torqued correctly.**

Servicing Valve Springs with Head on Engine

It is possible to service valve springs, retainers, and seals with the head on the engine. Bring the piston to Top

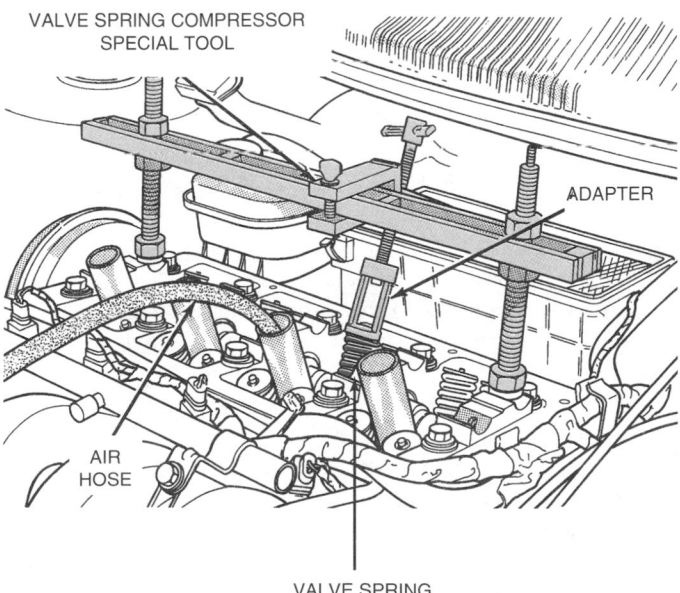

Figure 13-73. This valve spring compressor can be used to remove springs with the head installed on the block. Maintain air pressure to the cylinder so the valve cannot drop inside the engine. (Chrysler)

Dead Center (TDC) on the compression stroke (both valves closed) and remove the rocker arms for that cylinder. Remove the spark plug and insert an air hose adapter. Apply full air pressure to the cylinder. With the rocker arm out of the way, the spring may be compressed and the keepers removed. A new spring or valve guide seal may be installed. Keep air pressure to the cylinder until the valve spring is replaced and the keepers installed, **Figure 13-73.**

Tech Talk

Did you ever duck into a fast-food place, order a cheeseburger, and get a fish sandwich instead? When you sent it back, did you get a hamburger instead of a cheeseburger? Annoying, wasn't it? Chances are you avoid that place now. The restaurants that you go to regularly are not like that. You get what you want the first time. That is why you go back.

The automotive service business works the same way. Your customers will come back if they get what they want. Customers expect something for their money—service. Service consists of giving them what they asked for. There are so many places that do not give good service that a place that does is almost guaranteed success.

A person who wants to get a vehicle fixed is not very different from a person who wants a cheeseburger. Always do your best possible work to guarantee your success.

Summary

When disassembling a cylinder head, keep all valves, springs, keepers, and retainers in order so that they may be replaced in the same location. The head, valves, guides, and other parts must be thoroughly cleaned. Do not scratch the head surface. Using an accurate straightedge, check the cylinder head for warpage. Reface all valves and reject any that will not clean up or have insufficient margin. An interference angle may be used in some engines. Dress all cutting stones. Smooth and chamfer valve stem ends. Stems must not be worn beyond limits.

Be sure to check valve stem-to-guide clearance. If clearance is excessive, replace the guides or ream for an oversize stem. When replacing valve guides, be certain to get the proper guide right side up and in the correct hole. Drive the guide in the specified distance. Some guides require reaming after installation. Seals are often used on the guides and on the stems of both intake and exhaust valves to prevent excessive oil consumption.

A cracked or burned valve seat can be repaired by installing a valve seat insert. Grind the valve seat at the correct angle until it is cleaned up. Narrow the seat to the specified width by using a 15°-30° stone on the top and in some cases, a 60°-70° stone on the bottom. Keep all cutting stones properly dressed and remove no more metal than is necessary. Test the valve seat for concentricity.

Replace any broken, loose, or damaged rocker arm studs. If loose, ream and install an oversize stud. Check valve springs for squareness, tension, rust, or nicks. Replace any that show the slightest defect. Lubricate and install the valves. Check the stem height above the head. Install the springs with the closed coil end against the head. Check the installed spring height. Add an insert between the spring and the head, if needed. Check the stem seal with a suction cup.

The block surface must be clean and accurate. Place the head gasket right side up and correct end forward on block. Using guide pins, lower head into position. Head bolts and holes in block must be clean and coated with thread compound. Torque head to manufacturer's specifications.

Know These Terms

Valve springs	Valve guides
Split keepers	Valve guide reamer
Spring	Oil seals
Spring retainer	Valve seat
Valve spring compressor	Valve seat inserts
Rack	Peened
Valve guide cleaner	Swaged
Burning	Refaced
Pitting	Valve seat reamers
Carbon deposits	Concentricity
Valve grinder	Lapping
Cutting stones	Prussian blue
Dressed	Rocker arm studs
Dressing tool	Spring tension
Runout	Spring free length
Valve face angle	Squareness
Interference angle	Damper springs
Sodium-filled valve	Installed height
Chamfer	Guide pins
Valve stem clearance	Torquing sequence

Review Questions—Chapter 13

Do not write in this book. Write your answers on a separate sheet of paper.

1. What is normally done to correct cylinder head warpage?
2. Valve grinding stones are dressed with:
   (A) a file.
   (B) another stone.
   (C) a diamond.
   (D) a hardened steel rod.
3. When the valve is ground at a slightly different angle (about 1° than the seat, a(n) _____ fit is produced.
4. To control stem height above the head, it is necessary to grind the _____ end.
5. Where excessive valve stem-to-guide clearance is present, it may be corrected by _____ guides or by _____ for an _____ valve stem.

6. Valve seat runout should be kept within approximately:
   (A) .002″ (0.05 mm).
   (B) .006″ (0.15 mm).
   (C) .020″ (0.51 mm).
   (D) .0003″ (0.0762 mm).
7. The valve seat should engage the valve face near the _____.
8. Valve springs should be tested for _____ and _____.
9. To facilitate accurate head, gasket, and block alignment, _____ should be used when installing the head.
10. Valve springs and seals can be replaced with the head on the engine by:
    (A) applying air pressure to the cylinder.
    (B) bringing the piston in the affected cylinder to Top Dead Center on the compression stroke.
    (C) bringing the piston in the affected cylinder to Bottom Dead Center.
    (D) Both A & B.

ASE-Type Questions

1. Technician A says that valves should be closely inspected to determine what caused them to fail. Technician B says that the cylinder head should be checked for warpage before reassembly. Who is right?
   (A) A only.
   (B) B only.
   (C) Both A & B.
   (D) Neither A nor B.
2. It is necessary to keep all cylinder head parts in order because:
   (A) they may be lost.
   (B) they can be kept in a smaller area.
   (C) it is important that they be returned to their original positions.
   (D) it is just a good habit.
3. The most important reason to keep wheels dressed is:
   (A) they cut faster.
   (B) they will produce accurate angles.
   (C) they wear longer.
   (D) they look better.
4. When grinding the valve face:
   (A) keep the valve in the center of the stone.
   (B) move the valve back and forth—staying on the stone.
   (C) move the valve back and forth—off both sides of the stone.
   (D) keep the valve on the right-hand side of the stone.
5. What tool would be used with a hole gauge when checking valve stem-to-guide clearance?
   (A) Micrometer.
   (B) Dial indicator.
   (C) Feeler gauge.
   (D) Caliper.

6. Technician A says that a cracked intake valve seal will cause excessive oil consumption. Technician B says that excessive exhaust valve-to-guide clearance will cause excessive oil consumption. Who is right?
   (A) A only.
   (B) B only.
   (C) Both A & B.
   (D) Neither A nor B.

7. A valve seat that is too wide will:
   (A) pack with carbon and start to leak and burn.
   (B) run too cold.
   (C) break the valve stem.
   (D) be loose.

8. Technician A says that the valve seat must be concentric with the guide hole. Technician B says that a dressed valve seat stone can grind approximately twelve seats before it must be dressed again. Who is right?
   (A) A only.
   (B) B only.
   (C) Both A & B.
   (D) Neither A nor B.

9. Excessive valve spring installed height can cause:
   (A) heavy spring tension.
   (B) valve float.
   (C) slow valve timing.
   (D) seal damage.

10. Technician A says that all valves, lifters, push rods, rocker arms, and other parts should always be installed in the spot from which removed. Technician B says that gasket cement must always be applied to the head gasket. Who is right?
    (A) A only.
    (B) B only.
    (C) Both A & B.
    (D) Neither A nor B.

Suggested Activities

1. Disassemble a cylinder head and determine the repairs needed. Prepare a list of all needed parts and services (seat reconditioning, guide reaming, surface machining).
2. Using a flat rate manual, calculate the parts and labor needed to restore the head to service.
3. Discuss your price calculation with other members of your class. Ask if there is anything that you missed. What would be a fair profit on this job?
4. Determine which parts of the cylinder head overhaul process can be done in your shop and make a list of the jobs to be done by an outside machine shop. Write a short report outlining how you will handle having the outside work performed.

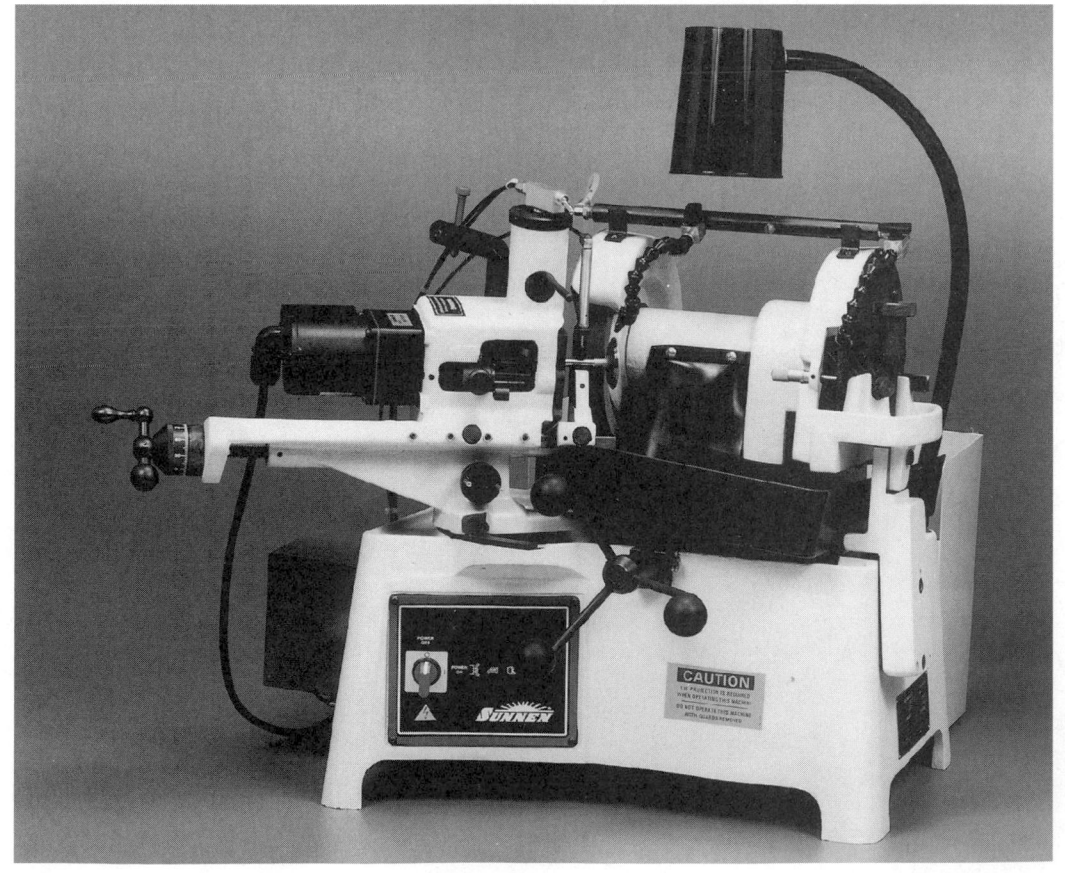

In many instances, a valve grinding machine can be used to recondition valves. Make sure that all guards are in place when using this tool. (Sunnen)

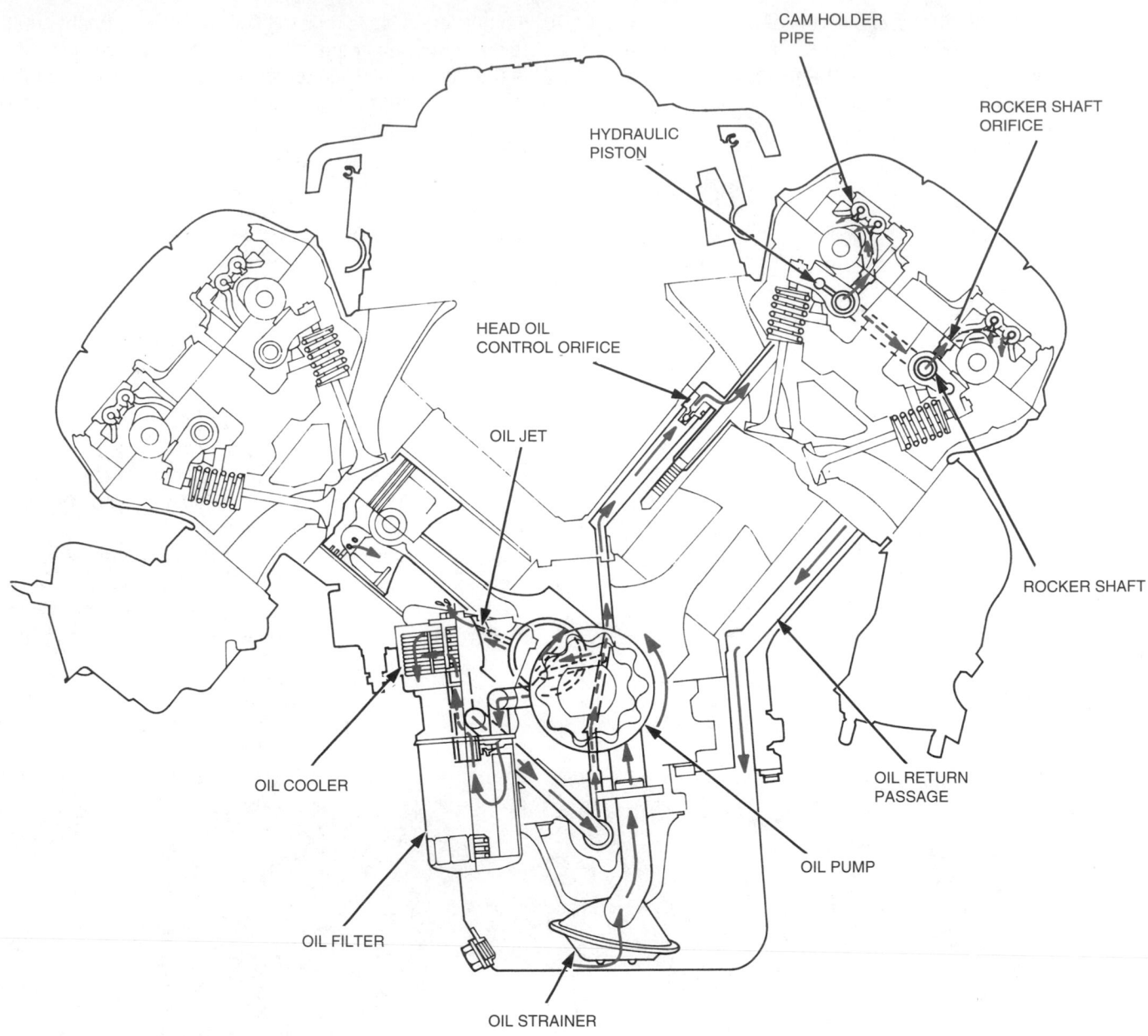

Cross section of a V-6 engine showing the flow of engine oil. Note the location of the oil strainer, the oil pump, and the oil filter. (Honda)

14

Engine Block and Lubrication System Service

After studying this chapter, you will be able to:
- Check the condition of a cylinder block.
- Check for a cracked cylinder block.
- Measure cylinder wear.
- Hone a cylinder wall.
- Describe cylinder reboring.
- Service connecting rods.
- Service automotive pistons.
- Properly install piston rings.
- Correctly install a piston and rod assembly in its cylinder.
- Measure bearing clearance with Plastigage.
- Service engine oil pumps.

This chapter covers engine block and lubrication system service and repair. Block reconditioning, ring ridge removal, boring, honing, cylinder sleeve repair, piston service, and connecting rod service are discussed. The installation and service procedures for various types of engine oil pumps are also covered.

Engine Block Service

The *engine block* is the foundation on which all of the other engine parts are assembled. Part alignment and wear demand that the block be free of *distortion* and cracks. In preparing to check the cylinder block for warpage or distortion, the first steps are dismantling and thorough cleaning. All parts should be cleaned down to the bare metal. This will allow close inspection and accurate measurement.

During block reconditioning, it is imperative that all *oil galleries* be cleaned. This is best done by removing the gallery end plugs before cleaning the block in a hot tank solution. Do not hot tank an aluminum block. All passageways should be cleaned out with a stiff wire brush, rinsed, and blown dry. The cooling system must be free of rust and scale. Any dirt, sludge, or particles left in the distribution passages could be circulated and cause immediate and severe wear. Replace and tighten all end plugs.

Replace all defective *freeze plugs.* Refer to Chapter 22 on cooling system service for procedures to replace the freeze plugs. The main bearing bores and camshaft should be checked for alignment. These procedures are covered in Chapters 15 and 16. Inspect all threaded holes for evidence of dirt, rust, scale, and stripped or galled threads. Thread repair was discussed in Chapter 7.

Checking Block for Distortion and Cracks

Check the cylinder block for warpage with a steel straightedge and feeler gauge as shown in **Figure 14-1.**

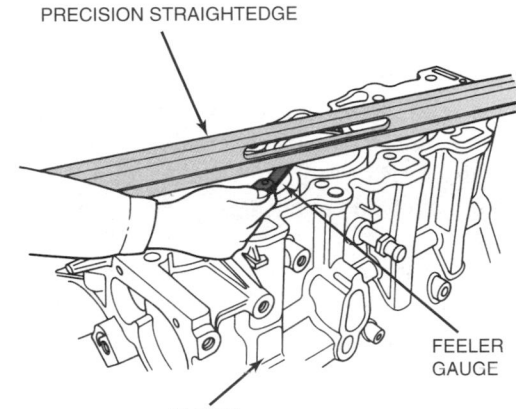

Figure 14-1. A—Straightedge measuring placement diagram. B—Straightedge and feeler gauge used to measure warpage (distortion of block). Note the limits allowed for this particular engine block. (Acura)

The surfaces should be true and flat within manufacturer's specifications (about .003″ or 0.08 mm in any 6″ span or 152 mm). If the distortion is not within these limits, the block will require *resurfacing.* See **Figure 14-2.** A minimum amount of metal should be removed. Removing an excessive amount can change the compression ratio, lifter-to-rocker arm distance, and piston-to-valve clearance. Special head gaskets are available to compensate for removal of excessive head or block metal.

Checking for Cracks

The cylinder block is the engine part that most commonly develops cracks. *Block cracks* can be caused by general engine overheating, localized overheating due to clogged cooling passages, lack of antifreeze in the cooling system during below freezing weather, and mechanical damage from a foreign object in a cylinder. During reconditioning, the block should be thoroughly cleaned and visually inspected for signs of cracking. Pay particular attention to the cylinder walls, lifter galleys, block water jackets, and the main bearing saddles.

Figure 14-2. Resurfacing block in grinder. Remove only a minimum amount of metal. (Winona Van Norman)

It is also wise to check for cracks that cannot be seen by the naked eye, especially if the engine is known to have been subjected to freezing, severe overheating, or mechanical damage. Many other parts of the automobile, such as transmission cases, gears, axles, steering gears, and wheel spindles, can crack during service. Any part can develop one of three main types of cracks:

• Cracks that are plainly visible to the eye.
• Cracks that are so fine they are invisible without detection equipment.
• Internal cracks that do not reach the surface.

A part may develop one, two, or all three types of cracks during service. Locating and repairing one cracked area does not mean that you have located all of the cracks in a part, especially in a large part such as an engine block.

Crack Detection Methods

There are a number of techniques used to check for the presence of cracking, including *X-ray, magnetic, fluorescent, dye penetrants,* and combinations of these techniques. The X-ray technique requires expensive equipment and is only used in large specialty shops. The following crack detection methods can also be used to find cracks in cylinder heads, connecting rods, and crankshafts.

Magnetic Field with Iron Powder

A powerful permanent magnet or an electromagnet is placed across a suspected area. The metal under the magnet's feet becomes heavily magnetized. A fine iron powder is then dusted over the area. A crack will interrupt or break the magnetic field enough to cause the iron powder to collect along the crack. Because this process works best when the crack is at right angles to the magnetic field, the magnet should be moved into different positions. This process works only on cracked parts made of iron or other ferrous (iron containing) metals, such as steel. Parts made of alu-

minum or other nonferrous material cannot be checked by this method. **Figure 14-3** illustrates the use of a powerful permanent magnet. Note the crack that has been exposed by iron powder collecting along the entire length. The poles of the magnet are at right angles to the crack.

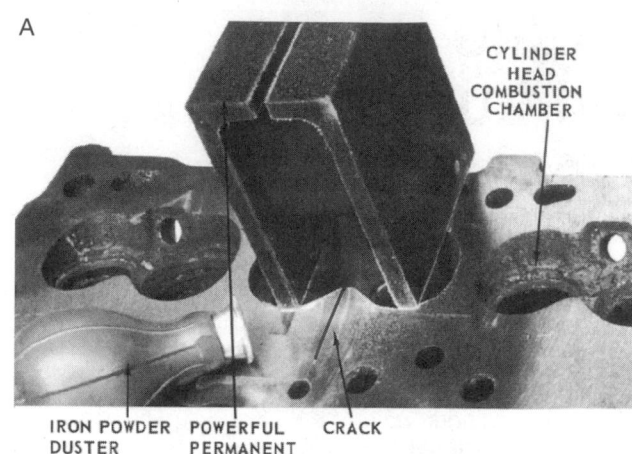

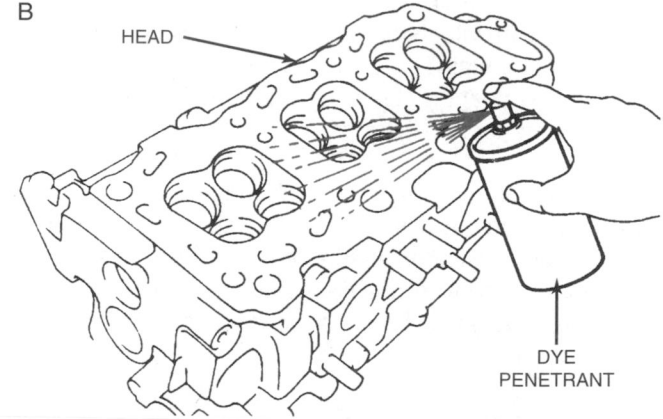

Figure 14-3. A—A crack in this cylinder head is exposed by using a powerful magnet and iron powder. B—A cylinder head being sprayed with a dye penetrant to help show possible cracking. Follow the manufacturer's recommendations. (Storm-Vulcan, Toyota)

> **Note:** If in doubt as to whether or not a part contains iron, apply a magnet to the part. If the magnet sticks, the part contains iron and can be checked magnetically.

Magnetic Field with Fluorescent Ferromagnetic Particles

Ferromagnetic particles require a strong magnetic field to be set up in the part. This method will work only on ferrous metals. A special solution that contains the fluorescent particles is sprayed on the area to be tested. As with iron powder, the ferromagnetic particles are attracted to and held along the crack line. When exposed to a black light, the particles packed along the crack line will glow white while the remainder of the part will remain blue-black.

Crack Detection Using Fluorescent and Dye Penetrants

Crack detection using penetrants involves coating a part with a special fluorescent chemical or dye that can readily enter even the smallest cracks. If a crack is present, it is brought out by a fluorescent light or by the use of a special developer. These penetrant methods will work on both ferrous and nonferrous materials.

Penetrants are ideal for use on aluminum blocks or cylinder heads. The area to be checked is first cleaned with a special cleaner. See **Figure 14-4A.** Then, the penetrant is sprayed over the area, **Figure 14-4B.** A small amount of cleaner is sprayed on the gear, and the excess penetrant is wiped off with a clean cloth, **Figure 14-4C.** The part is then sprayed with a developing solution. The developer will draw the penetrant to the surface of any cracks, **Figure 14-4D.** The gear is examined under a lamp that emits black light. If any cracks are present, the developed fluorescent penetrant will glow visibly, **Figure 14-4E.** Dye penetrant will show as a bright line against a whitish background when exposed to a developer.

Crack Repair

Ideally, a cracked part should be discarded. However, if it is necessary to salvage a part, cylinder head or block cracks can be repaired by either brazing, welding, or *pinning.* The use of threaded pins is quite popular because no heat is required, eliminating any chance of warpage. If the pins are to be effective, they must reach slightly past the ends of the crack. If they do not reach the ends, the crack may continue to lengthen. Further cracking can generally be halted by drilling a hole at the end of the crack.

To use special threaded taper pins designed for crack repair, start by drilling and tapping a hole that centers on the crack line just beyond the end of the crack. Thread the correct size pin (pin may be coated with a special heatproof sealant, if desired) into the hole. When tight, use a sharp chisel to notch the pin about 1/8″ (0.125 mm) above the casting and twist off any excess material. In some cases, a hacksaw may be used to cut the pin. Drill and tap for the next pin so the hole just cuts through the threads of the first pin. Install the plug, notch it, and twist off any excess material. Repeat this process until the full length of the crack is pinned. Remember that each pin must cut partially into the preceding pin for the repair to be effective. See **Figure 14-5.** If steel pins are used, they should be lightly peened. Grind the pins nearly flush and finish with a clean, sharp mill file. If the area cannot be filed, grind the pins flush.

Cylinder Service

High-mileage engine cylinders may be out-of-round and tapered to the extent that machining is required. Before pulling the pistons, the cylinder *ring ridge* must be removed. This will prevent the rings from striking the ridge and breaking either the rings, piston lands, or both. This is covered in detail in Chapter 12. The cylinder must be inspected for cracks and scoring. Measure the cylinder diameter and the amount of taper, out-of-roundness, and wear.

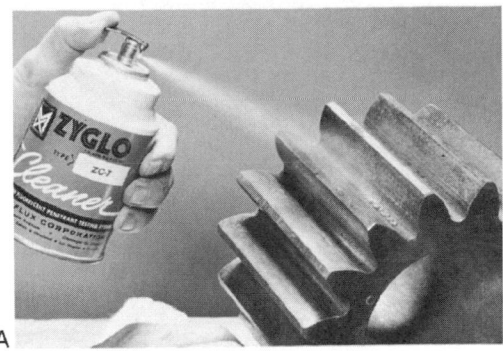
A

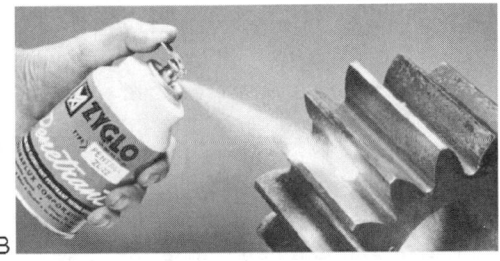
B

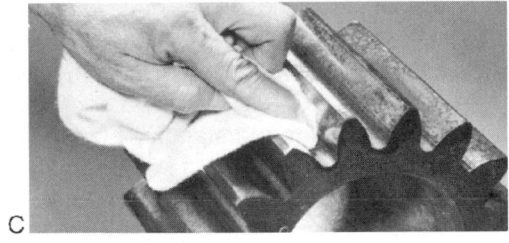
C

D

E

Figure 14-4. Make sure that any part to be tested is clean prior to application of fluorescent penetrant. A—Cleaning section of a large gear before fluorescent penetrant is applied. B—Apply the fluorescent penetrant. C—Remove any excess penetrant. D—Apply the developer solution. E—The crack will show when the part is examined under a black light. (Magnaflux)

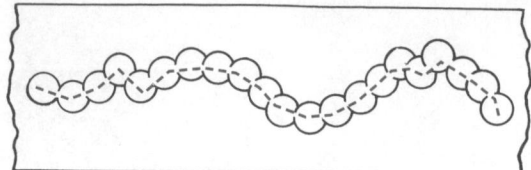

Figure 14-5. Cracks can be repaired by pinning. Each pin should slightly overlap the preceding pin. A broken line indicates a crack.

Inspecting the Cylinder

Following piston removal, wipe out the cylinders. Using a bright light, carefully inspect each cylinder for cracks and scoring. If the cylinder is smooth and wear is within limits, new rings will function properly following deglazing. Minor scoring and heavy scratches will require reboring to a suitable oversize. Heavy scoring or cracking, depending on its location and severity, may require the installation of a cylinder sleeve.

Before any other measurements and repairs are performed, the **cylinder diameter** must be determined. This measurement will form the basis upon which new rings are ordered and rebore sizes figured. Carefully measure each cylinder at the bottom using an inside micrometer. Write down these measurements; as they will help in determining the original factory cylinder diameter. If your measurements are not more than .009″ (0.23 mm) larger than factory specifications, the cylinders are standard size. If your measurements are .010″ to .019″ (0.25 to 0.48 mm) larger than specs, the engine has already been rebored to .010″ (0.25 mm) oversize. If the measurements are .020″ to .029″ (0.51-0.74 mm) larger than specs, the cylinders have been rebored to .020″ (0.51 mm) oversize, etc.

For example, assume that your measurements show a cylinder diameter of 3.924″ (97.66 mm) and the specifications list 3.910″ (99.31 mm) as standard. The cylinder measurements are .014″ (0.35 mm) larger than standard. This indicates that the engine was bored .010″ (0.25 mm) oversize. The additional .004″ (0.10 mm) would be wear in the lower area. See **Figure 14-6.** Occasionally, the factory will bore the cylinders oversize in order to salvage an otherwise sound block. When this is done, various markings are used to indicate such a condition. A factory rebored engine will generally have the amount of oversize stamped on the head of the pistons. Replacement pistons, usually a few ten thousandths different in diameter, are individually fitted. Both the cylinder and piston will have size marks stamped on them so that the piston may be returned to the cylinder to which it was fitted.

Checking Cylinder for Wear

Cylinder wear is usually heaviest in the upper portion of the cylinder. This is due to the pressure of the rings, intense heat, poor lubrication, combustion pressure, and abrasive material introduced to the combustion area through the air inlet system. The unworn area above the ring travel is referred to as the ring ridge. The bottom of the cylinder generally shows little wear. The cylinder bottom is usually

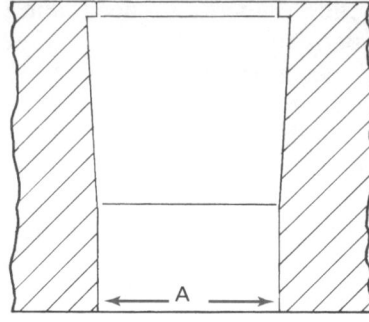

A = 3.924
STANDARD = 3.910
DIFFERENCE = .014
OVERSIZE = .010 + .004 WEAR AT A

Figure 14-6. Compare measurement A with the manufacturer specifications to determine cylinder oversize.

free of ring wear because it is lubricated better and is subjected to less piston thrust pressure than the upper portion. Wear in the upper portion of the cylinder above normal ring travel is also minor.

From **Figure 14-7,** you will note that the heaviest cylinder wear is at the top of the ring travel. The heavy wear area extends downward about 3/4″ to 1″ (19.05 to 25.4 mm). Below this, there is a steady reduction in wear. This condition is known as *taper.* Another ridge often exists at the bottom of the ring travel. However, it is much less pronounced.

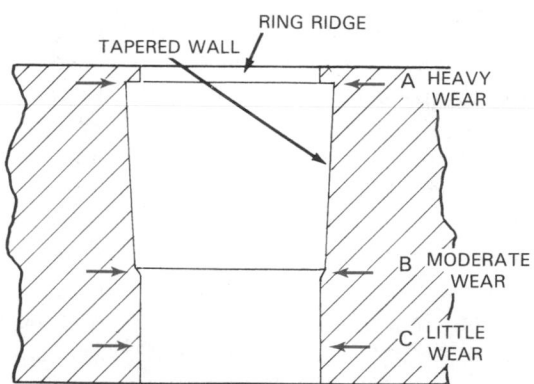

Figure 14-7. Study this cylinder wear pattern. Diameter through A (top of ring travel), minus B (bottom of ring travel), indicates the amount of taper. Note the sharp edge formed by upper ring ridge while the ridge at bottom of ring travel is much less pronounced.

The cylinder may have an oval shape and is considered to be worn *out-of-round.* The greatest wear will be at right angles to the engine or crankshaft centerline. Out-of-roundness is primarily caused by the side thrust forces generated during the compression and firing strokes. Since the crankshaft connecting rod journal is offset to the line of piston travel, the piston attempts to move sideways in addition to up and down. See **Figure 14-8.**

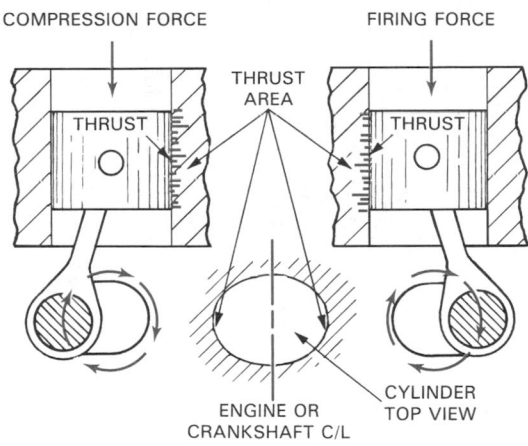

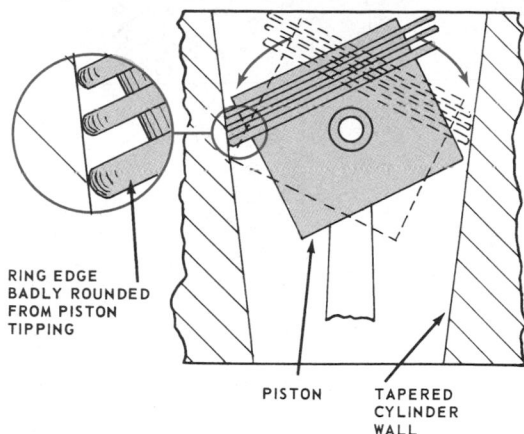

Figure 14-8.   Thrust forces can wear a cylinder out-of-round at right angles to the engine centerline.

Figure 14-10.   A piston that is loose in the bore will allow tipping to occur (exaggerated in drawing). This will produce rounded ring edges, thus destroying their efficiency.

Measuring Cylinder Taper and Out-of-Roundness

It is important that each cylinder be checked for taper and out-of-roundness. Rings must follow the cylinder wall if they are to function properly. As taper increases, ring efficiency decreases. **Ring float** and **tipping** will destroy the seal and can cause rings to break or scuff the cylinder wall. When taper is excessive, the rings are compressed at the bottom of their travel. As the piston enters the enlarged upper cylinder area, the piston will tip back and forth. This causes both the upper and lower ring edges to round off. As the piston travels to the wider cylinder top at high RPM, it can begin to literally float at the top of the cylinder before the rings have a chance to expand outward. See **Figure 14-9.** Sealing efficiency is lost and **scuffing** can occur, **Figure 14-10.** In addition to tipping, the piston will be slammed from one side of the cylinder to the other as the crankshaft rod journal passes over TDC (top dead center). This produces a noise called **piston slap.** In addition to ring damage, the piston can fatigue and literally disintegrate.

A quick and accurate method of measuring taper and out-of-roundness is to use a cylinder dial gauge. Slide the gauge near the bottom of the bore and zero the indicator. While keeping the guide feet in firm contact with the wall,

slowly pull the indicator up through the cylinder. Slide the gauge up and down in several different sections and note the total indicator reading. This will determine the amount of taper.

Slide the gauge into the bore so that the indicator stem is located in the area of ring wear. While holding the guide feet in firm contact, slide the gauge around in the bore. The indicator reading will show maximum out-of-roundness. Write down the readings for each cylinder, **Figure 14-11.** Another method is to measure the bore with an inside micrometer, **Figure 14-12.** To do this, make two measurements near the bottom of the cylinder, one parallel to the engine centerline and the other at a right angle to the cylinder. Make two similar measurements at the spot of greatest wear at the top of the cylinder. See **Figure 14-13.** Write all of the measurements down.

 Note: This is a critical step. Be sure to make accurate readings.

The various readings may be listed as shown in **Figure 14-14** to facilitate taper and out-of-roundness computations. Be certain to indicate the number of each cylinder concerned. If the cylinder is not scored, cracked, or scuffed, taper up to a maximum of .012″ (0.30 mm) is usually permissible. Taper beyond this point will prevent the new rings from working properly. Excessively tapered cylinders must be rebored. Cylinder out-of-roundness should not exceed .005″ (0.13 mm). The rings cannot conform to the cylinder wall beyond this point, resulting in heavy oil consumption, **Figure 14-15.** Some manufacturers specify even less than a maximum of .005″ (0.13 mm) due to differences in engine design and application. Always follow the manufacturer's specifications.

Cylinder Reconditioning

A shiny, glazed cylinder wall surface will cause the time for ring break-in to become excessive. In some cases, the rings may never seat properly. Cylinders with minor

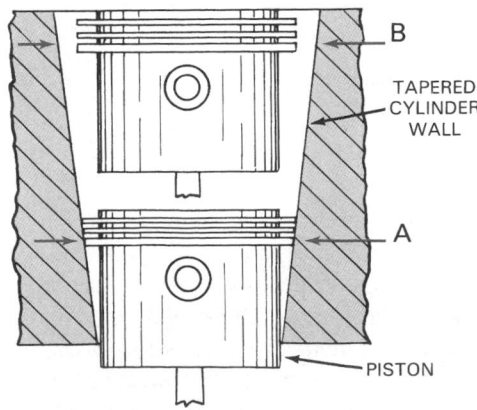

Figure 14-9.   Excessive cylinder taper can cause ring float. Note how the rings contact the cylinder wall at A, but before they can expand outward at B, the piston starts down again.

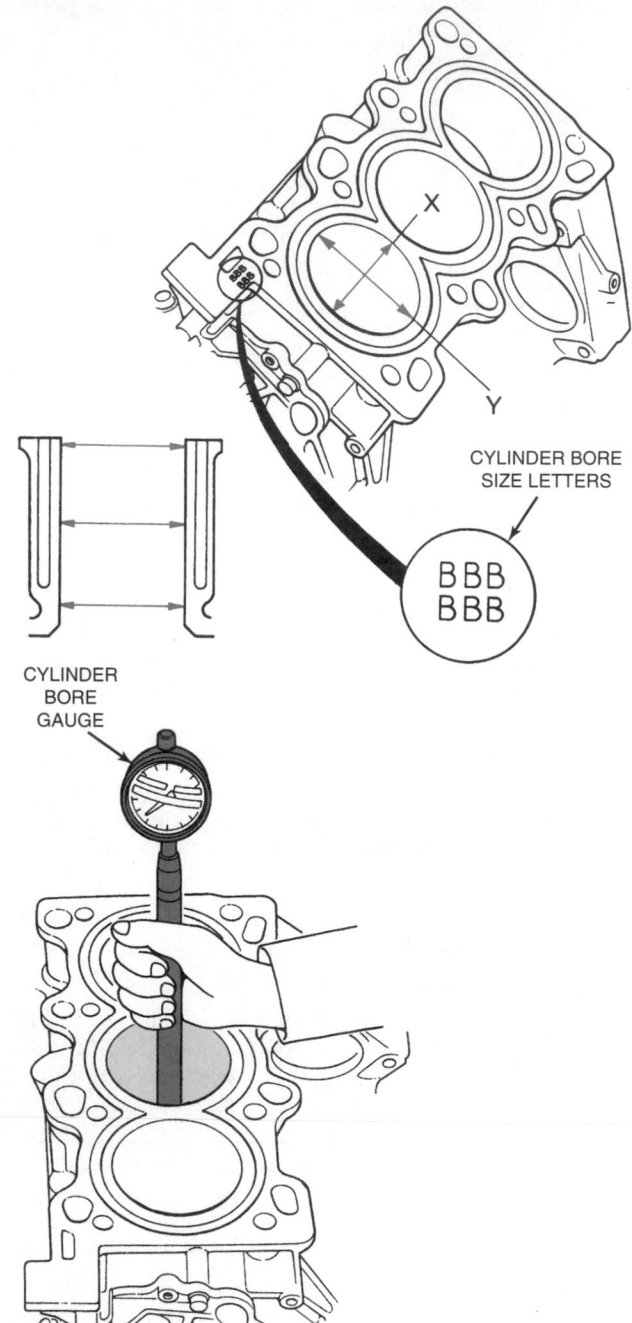

CYLINDER BORE
SIZE LETTERS

BBB
BBB

CYLINDER
BORE
GAUGE

Figure 14-11. Using a dial indicator cylinder bore gauge to check for cylinder taper and out-of-roundness. Note the recommended measuring areas ("X" and "Y") and the three measuring levels. (Acura)

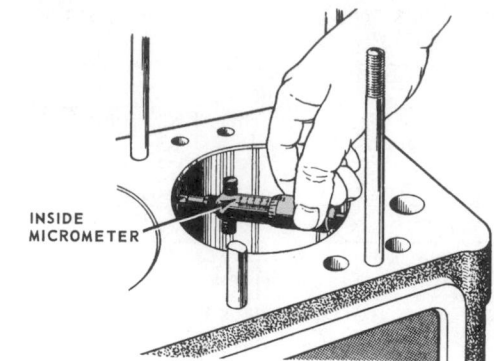

INSIDE
MICROMETER

Figure 14-12. Checking cylinder diameter with an inside micrometer.

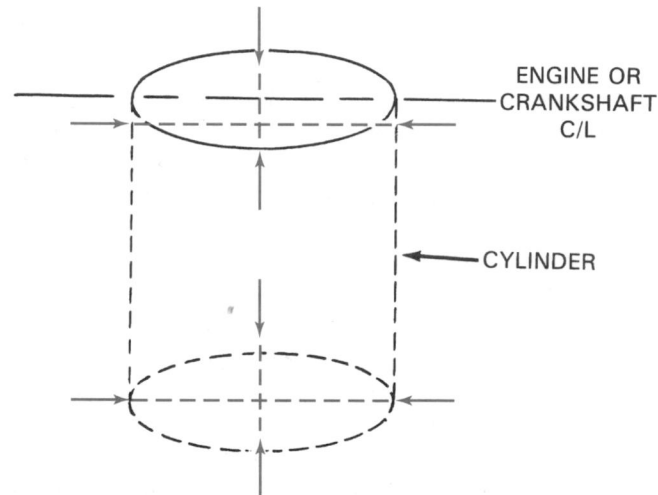

ENGINE OR
CRANKSHAFT
C/L

CYLINDER

Figure 14-13. Measure each cylinder at these points.

CYLINDER NUMBER	1	2	3
TOP R/A	3.885		
TOP C/L	3.880		
OUT-OF-ROUND	.005		
TOP R/A	3.885		
BOT. R/A	3.8765		
TAPER	.0085		
BOT. R/A	3.8765		
STANDARD	3.875		
OVERSIZE	.0015		

(R/A = MEASUREMENT AT RIGHT ANGLES TO
        ENGINE CENTERLINE)
(C/L = MEASUREMENT ALONG ENGINE
        CENTERLINE)

Figure 14-14. Cylinder measurements may be listed in this manner to facilitate taper, out-of-roundness, and oversize computations.

taper and out-of-roundness can be deglazed using a spring-loaded hone or an abrasive-tipped wire deglazer. Excessively worn cylinders or cylinders that are scored may need to be honed or bored, followed by a final honing to impart the correct microinch finish.

New rings have minute tool thread marks around the ring-to-cylinder edge. The cylinder wall should also have minute scratches imparted by the hone. As the new rings travel up and down, both the cylinder wall and the rings will

wear a tiny amount. High spots on the rings will tend to wear off, allowing the low spots to contact the wall. The correct cylinder wall microinch finish will allow the rings to seat at about the same time the cylinder wall returns to its glazed condition. Finishing stones with grit sizes of 180 and 220 will produce finishes of around 20-30 and 15-25 microinches (millionths of an inch) respectively. Equipment for checking in microinches is not available in most shops, however. A finish that is too rough will wear the rings excessively.

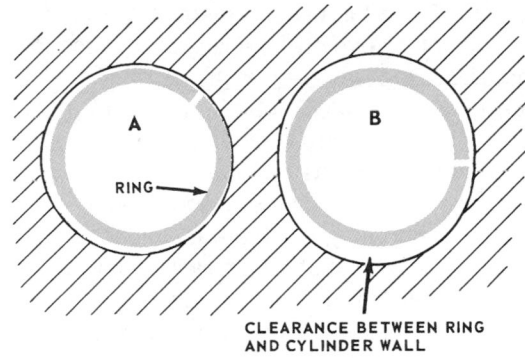

Figure 14-15.   Rings cannot conform to cylinders exceeding .005″ or 0.013 mm out-of-roundness. A—A good cylinder is round. B—Note the poor ring fit in an out-of-round cylinder.

A finish that is too smooth can prolong or even prevent seating. Properly seated rings will retain some thread marks for thousands of miles. The microinch finish for any given stone can be controlled by varying the pressure of the stones against the wall. A light pressure will produce a finer finish. Heavy pressure will cause the abrasive particles to cut deeply, producing a rougher surface. Light to medium pressure is recommended.

Deglazing Cylinder Walls

Although discouraged by a few manufacturers, *deglazing* is commonly accepted as good practice if:

* Cylinder honing is not excessive.
* The correct microinch surface is imparted.
* The cylinders are thoroughly cleaned after honing.

Deglazing hones are available in a variety of sizes, **Figure 14-16.** Cover the crankshaft with rags and swab honing oil on the walls. Using a suitable drill for power, insert the hone and start it spinning. Move the hone up and down in the cylinder. Do not let stones protrude more than 1/2″ (12.7 mm) on the top or bottom. Move the hone rapidly enough to produce a crosshatch finish similar to that shown

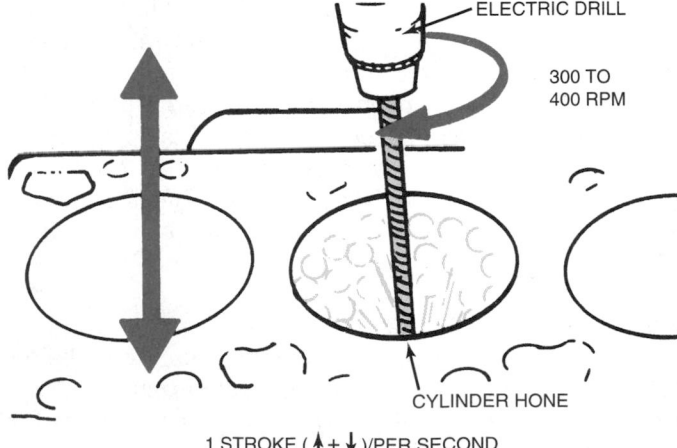

Figure 14-16.   Honing a cylinder bore with an abrasive-tipped brush. (Dodge)

in **Figure 14-17.** Note that the cross lines form an included angle of about 50°-60°. Do not be concerned about an exact angle. An angle from 20°-60° is usually acceptable. Make about twelve complete strokes with the hone. Wipe the bore and inspect the walls. If a hone pattern is visible over most of the ring travel area, consider the cylinder finished. If the pattern is not visible, repeat the deglazing procedure and check the walls again.

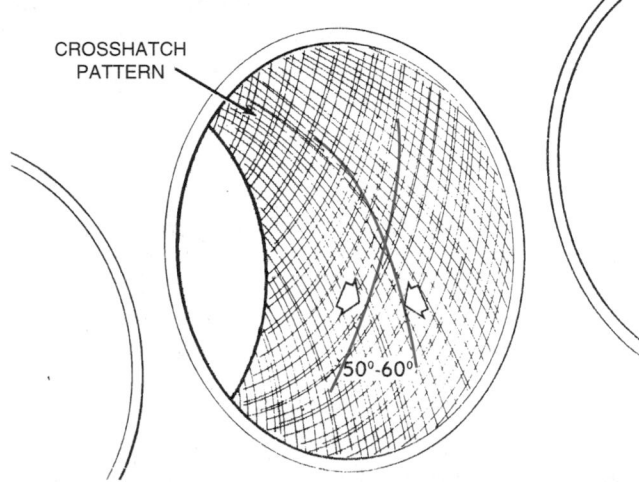

Figure 14-17.   A spring-loaded hone was used to create this desirable crosshatch pattern. (Chrysler)

Honing Cylinders

When cylinder wear has almost reached maximum acceptable taper and out-of-roundness, an adjustable rigid hone should be used, **Figure 14-18.** This type of hone will

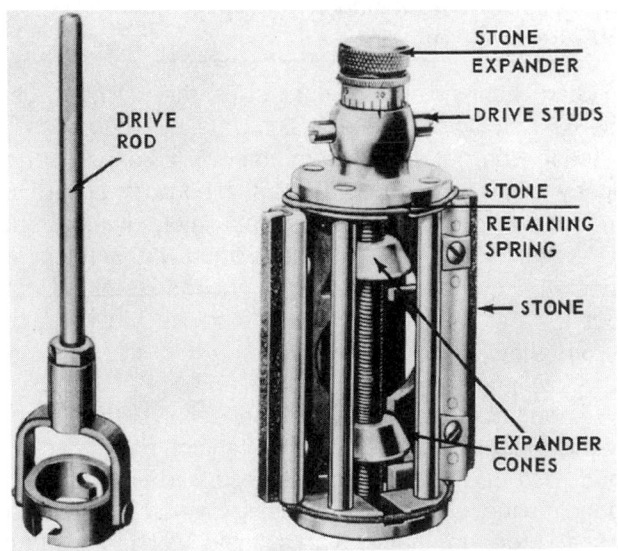

Figure 14-18.   One particular type of adjustable, rigid hone. The stone expander is calibrated so that the depth of the cut can be adjusted. The expander cones force the stones against the cylinder wall when the expander knob is turned. The hone is generally driven with a 1/2″ or 3/4″ drill. Never start the hone when it is out of the cylinder or pull it completely out of the cylinder while it is turning.

not flex to fit the wall taper and will help to remove both taper and out-of-roundness. Ideally, all **honing** operations should take place with the crankshaft removed from the block. If this is not possible, cover the crankshaft.

Apply honing oil and insert the hone in the bottom of the bore. Using 180 or 220 grit stones, adjust the stones outward until firm contact with the cylinder wall is obtained. Before starting the hone, push it down to the bottom of the cylinder. Note the exact position on the hone assembly in the cylinder. This will assist in determining when the proper depth has been reached. **Figure 14-19** illustrates the honing sequence. Drive the hone with a 1/2″ or 3/4″ drill.

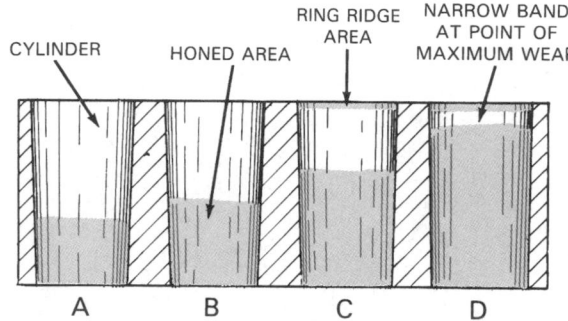

Figure 14-19. Note this hone pattern sequence. The hone was started in the bottom of the cylinder (A). As honing progresses, the crosshatch pattern covers more and more of the bore (B, C, D).

 Warning: This type of hone requires considerable torque to start. Grasp the drill handles tightly. Keep your clothing away from the spinning hone. Never pull the hone out of the cylinder while it is spinning. The hone parts are rotating at high speeds and can fly apart with great force.

Start honing at the bottom of the cylinder using short up and down strokes. Since the cylinder walls are the least worn at the bottom, they will keep the hone properly aligned. Keep adjusting the hone to ensure firm stone-to-wall contact. After approximately twenty short, fast strokes, loosen the stones, withdraw the hone, and inspect the cylinder. As soon as the hone marks cover about 70% of the cylinder's length, move the hone over the full length of the cylinder.

Allow the stones to protrude about 1/2″ (12.7 mm) above and below the cylinder. Do not strike the crankshaft if it was left in the block. Try for a crosshatch pattern as mentioned. Use of the rigid hone as described will necessitate expanding the old pistons or using oversize pistons and rings in order to maintain a suitable working clearance between the piston and cylinder. This will be discussed later in this chapter.

Reboring Cylinders

When cylinders have exceeded wear limits or when heavy scoring is present, they should be rebored to a suitable **oversize.** Ideally, all cylinders should be bored to the

same size. After careful measurement of all cylinders, compute the amount of oversize necessary to recondition the worst one. **Reboring** is done in multiples of .010″ (0.25 mm). Oversizes of .010″, .020″, .030″, and .040″ (0.25, 0.51, 0.76, and 1.01 mm) are most commonly used.

Do not try to rebore the cylinders with an oversize that is just barely larger than the poorest cylinder. Small variations in boring bar centering may leave areas untouched. However, using the smallest practical oversize will permit correction for wear in the future. Do not use excessive oversizes unless raising engine displacement for performance is desired.

 Note: Some aluminum blocks use cast iron sleeves that are relatively thin. On these engines, it is especially important to remove a minimum amount of metal.

There are numerous types of **boring bars,** ranging from fairly portable to massive production-type units. Always follow the manufacturer's directions when using this equipment. The block face should be draw filed by laying a large, flat file across the top of the block (cylinder deck) and pulling it toward you. This will remove any burrs and high spots. Center the bar carefully in the cylinder. Because the bottom is the least worn, it is advisable to center in this area. Following centering, the bar should be firmly clamped to the block. The cutter must be kept sharp. It should be carefully set to cut a hole that will be .0025″ (0.064 mm) smaller than the finished size. This allows for final cylinder honing to remove boring tool marks and fractured metal, and to impart the correct microinch finish.

 Note: While some boring bar manufacturers insist that no further finishing is needed after boring, it is a good precaution to hone the cylinder after boring. Boring the cylinder will sometimes leave the cylinder finish too rough for proper ring and cylinder operation and durability.

The boring cut will heat up the cylinder. There is a chance that the cylinder will be distorted upon cooling if the adjacent cylinder is bored next. Always bore alternate cylinders. This will allow each cylinder to cool before boring the one next to it. Back off the cutter before withdrawing it from the finished cylinder. The sharp edge at the top of the cylinder must be chamfered by hand-feeding the bar. Remember that accurate centering, firm clamping, sharp tools, and exact cutter settings are essential. Mike each bore for size and use a cylinder dial gauge to check for taper or out-of-roundness. A typical boring bar is shown in **Figure 14-20.**

Honing Following Boring

Use a hone with 180 or 220 grit stones. Hone the full length of the bore to produce a correct crosshatch finish. Hone the cylinder until the new piston is correctly fitted. If the desired .0025″ (0.064 mm) of material was removed following boring, a satisfactory base metal (final finish that is produced in solid, unfractured block metal) finish will result.

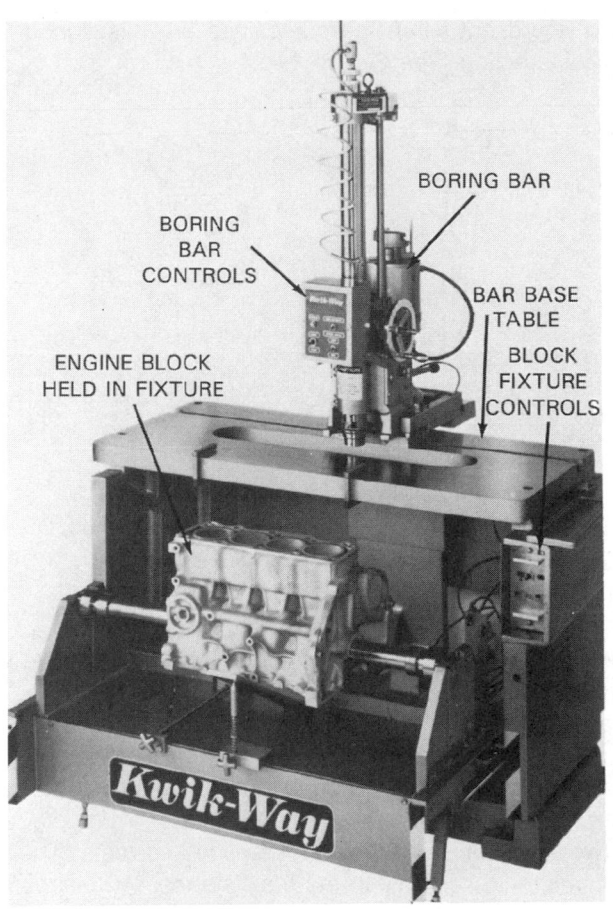

Figure 14-20. Note that this boring bar is not directly attached to block.

Installing a Cylinder Sleeve

A badly scored or cracked cylinder can often be salvaged by cutting the block to accept a **cylinder sleeve.** After the sleeve is installed, it is bored and honed to size. Maximum bar cuts should be around .050″ (1.27 mm). Take several cuts. Use a light finishing cut when nearing the proper size. Follow specifications for sleeve-to-block fit. **Figure 14-21** shows a sleeve being forced into place.

Cleaning Cylinders Following Honing

A thorough cleaning following honing is of vital importance. Do not use gasoline, kerosene, cleaning solvent, or oil. Use hot, soapy water and a stiff bristle brush. Scrub the cylinders and rinse twice with a hot, clear water rinse. This procedure will remove excess honing oil and minute, abrasive metal particles. Immediately wipe the cylinders dry and swab them with clean engine oil. If the crankshaft was left in place, it must be cleaned, dried, and the journals must be oiled. Check the crankcase area under the cylinders carefully. Despite a fine job of cylinder reconditioning, the whole job may be destroyed if cleaning is not thorough. **Figure 14-22** shows a technician drying the cylinders following the final hot water rinse.

Connecting Rod Service

Before removing any rods, check to see that all rods are marked and that both upper and lower bearing halves

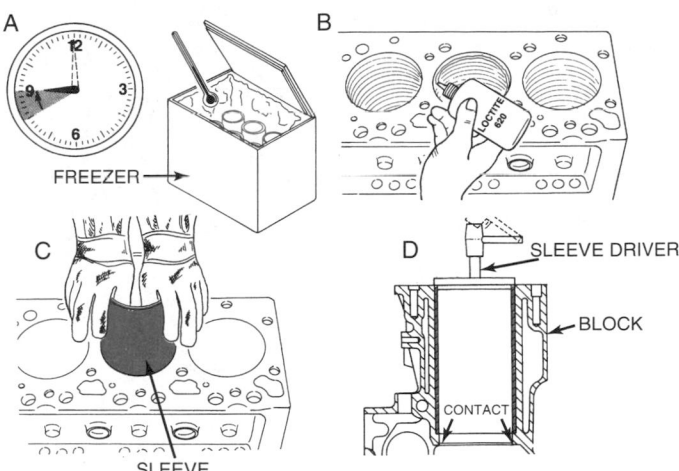

Figure 14-21. A—Cooling sleeves to 10°F (-12°C) or below for one hour in a freezer. B—Applying Loctite 620 to bore to be sleeved. C—Pushing the sleeve into the bore as far as possible by hand. Wear gloves. D—Drive the sleeve into its bore until it contacts the step at the bottom of the bore. (Dodge)

Figure 14-22. Cylinders must be thoroughly cleaned following honing. Continue wiping with a white rag until it comes out clean. Remove any tape from holes that were covered during honing. (Dodge)

are marked with the same number. They should be marked in order starting with the number one cylinder. Note the relationship between the numbers and the block so the rods can be installed without reversing them. If the rods are not numbered or if one or more rods show the wrong number, renumber them in the proper order. See **Figure 14-23.**

 Note: Correct numbering of all rods is important. The rod and piston must be in the correct relationship to each other and replaced in the proper cylinder with the marks facing in the original direction.

Rotate the crankshaft to bring the rod journal near bottom dead center (BDC). Remove the rod cap. If working on an older model car in which shims are used, remove the shims and mark the position on the rod. Install protectors

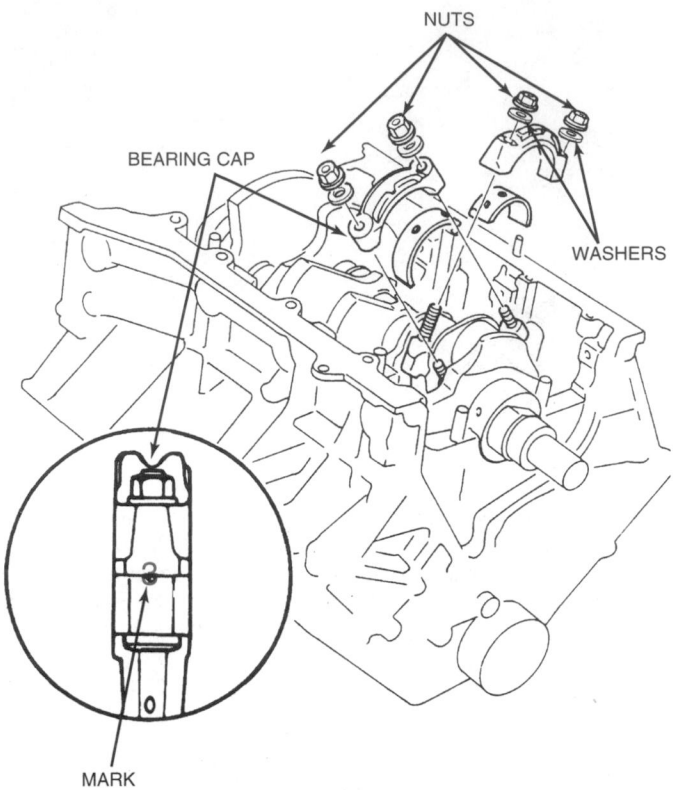

Figure 14-23. Check the connecting rods for correct identification numbering or marks. (Honda)

over the rod bolts to prevent them from nicking the journal. If using a driving and installing tool, drive the rod and piston up out of the cylinder. If a driver is not available, a clean hammer handle can be used to tap the rod. Following the removal of the piston assemblies from the engine, remove the rings and soak each piston and rod assembly in a good carbon removing solvent. Rinse and dry the piston and rod assemblies and place them in a clean work area.

 Caution: The ring ridge must be removed before pulling pistons. This will prevent the piston rings from catching on the ridge and possibly breaking the piston lands.

When pistons must be removed for ring work, the rods usually need reconditioning, too. Modern high RPM and high horsepower engines impose tremendous loads on the rods. In order to reduce reciprocating weight, the rods are made as light as feasible. This reduction in weight, while beneficial, does tend to allow distortion of the large end bearing bore. It can also allow the rod to twist and bend. High RPM, heavy loads, centrifugal and inertia forces, and the effects of heating and cooling are primarily responsible. Connecting rods should always be checked for twist, bend, and bearing bore distortion.

Connecting Rod Twist and Bend

Rods can have *twist* and/or *bend.* Twisting is a condition in which the centerlines of the upper and lower rod bearing bores are out of alignment in a horizontal plane.

Bend is present when the centerlines are misaligned in a vertical direction. See **Figure 14-24.**

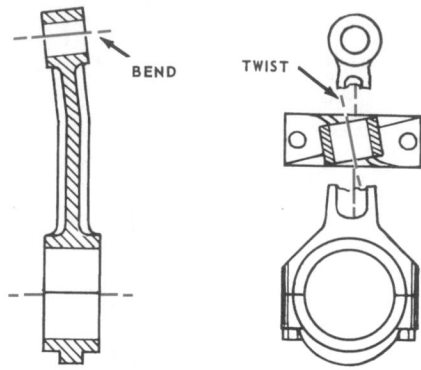

Figure 14-24. Bend and twist or a combination of both can be present in a connecting rod.

Note the wear pattern on the piston in **Figure 14-25.** The top right side of the piston is worn. A diagonal wear pattern extends down to the lower left portion of the skirt. This wear is caused by a misaligned rod. There are a number of rod alignment tools available. All have one thing in common—they must be used with skill and care. One such tool is shown in **Figure 14-26.** Note that the piston pin rests on two steel V's. The two V's are spaced correctly. The piston pin is held securely to the V's. The test rod blades and lower bearing bore are brought together in two positions. Bringing the test rod blade against the side of the tool shows the amount of bend and twist.

Removing Bend or Twist

A bent or twisted rod should normally be discarded. However, if it is necessary to remove a bend or twist, it is an

Figure 14-25. This piston wear pattern was caused by a misaligned rod.

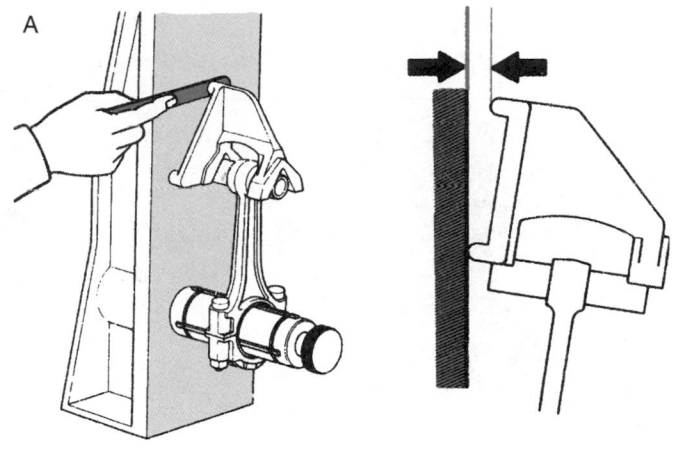

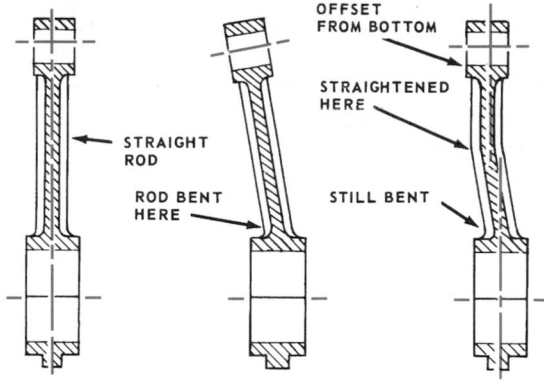

Figure 14-27. A rod can be accidentally offset by straightening in an area other than the bent area.

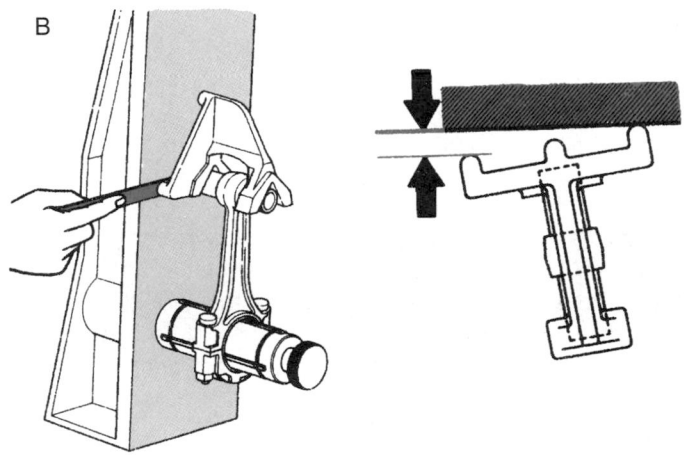

Figure 14-26. Tool for checking connecting rod. A—Checking for rod bend. B—Checking for rod twist. (Toyota)

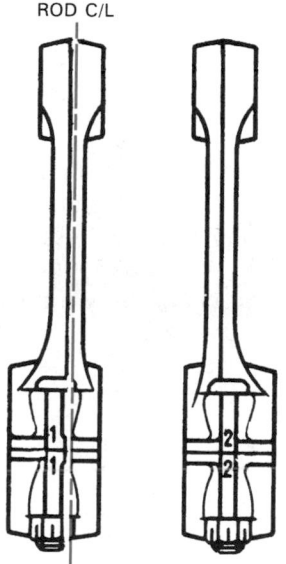

Figure 14-28. A pair of regular offset connecting rods. Note the numbering on the rods. (Fiat)

operation that requires care. One method employs a hand bending bar. The large end of the rod is clamped in a smooth vise and the bar is inserted into the hollow piston pin. The bar is lifted or lowered to correct bend or pulled sideways to correct twist. By using anvils in different positions in a hydraulic rod straightening press, both bend and twist can be removed.

When trying to straighten a bent rod, it is possible to offset the rod by moving the upper bearing bore to one side in relation to the lower bore. This is caused by bending an area other than that causing the original bend. See **Figure 14-27.** Do not confuse this condition with a regular offset connecting rod. Rods are occasionally offset to provide proper alignment between the cylinder and crank journal. Some normally offset rods are pictured in **Figure 14-28.** Notice how the web centerline (C/L) intersects the lower bore to one side. Also note how the offset on each rod faces different sides.

Checking Connecting Rod Large End Bore

The connecting rod *large end bearing bore* should be checked for roundness, bore size, straightness, and surface condition, **Figure 14-29.** Checking and reconditioning the upper connecting rod bore and bushings is covered in this chapter in the section on piston and piston pin service. After

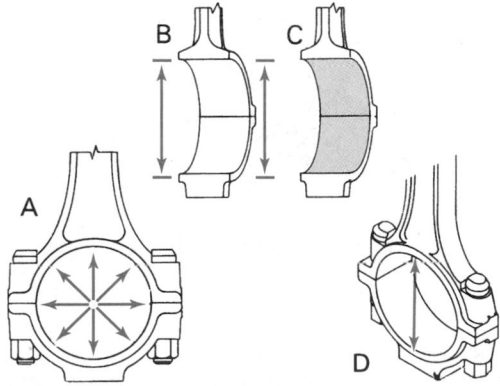

Figure 14-29. Important connecting rod large end bore checks. A—Out-of-roundness. B—Straightness. C—Surface condition. D—Bore size.

the cap is aligned and torqued to the rod, the connecting rod large end bore should be checked for out-of-roundness by either measuring with a telescoping gauge and micrometer or using an out-of-roundness gauge as shown in **Figure 14-30.**

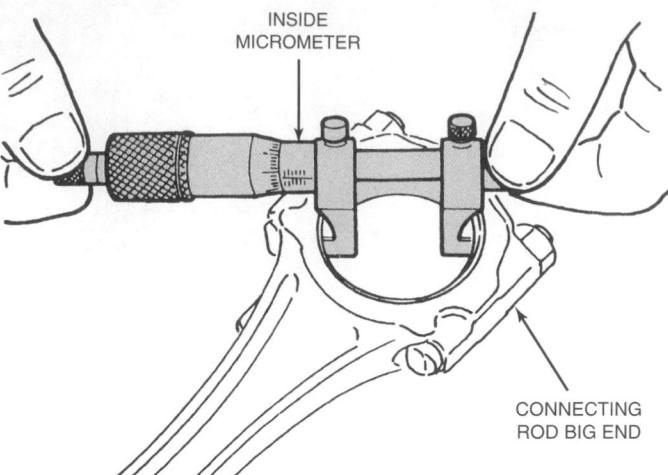

Figure 14-30. Connecting rod large end bore out-of-roundness can be quickly determined with an inside micrometer. (Nissan)

The rod bore should be checked in several positions to give an accurate reading. Out-of-roundness should not exceed .001" (0.025 mm). If the crankshaft journal is at its maximum out-of-round limits, the bore out-of-roundness should be less than .001" (0.025 mm). As a general rule, bore elongation direction will vary from vertical to around 30° from vertical, **Figure 14-31.**

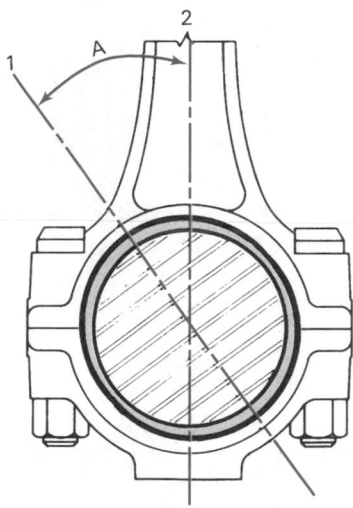

Figure 14-31. Connecting rod bore elongations will generally be in area A between centerlines 1 and 2.

Correcting Out-of-Roundness

After determining the amount of out-of-roundness, half of the amount of material required for correction is removed from the upper bore and half is removed from the lower bore using a special grinder. Following stock removal, the cap is assembled to the rod and properly torqued. Note how the jig in **Figure 14-32** holds both upper and lower bore halves in alignment. This also removes any twisting strain applied by torquing.

The rod bores in **Figure 14-33** are being honed to size. Note the support arms. When honing, direct a stream

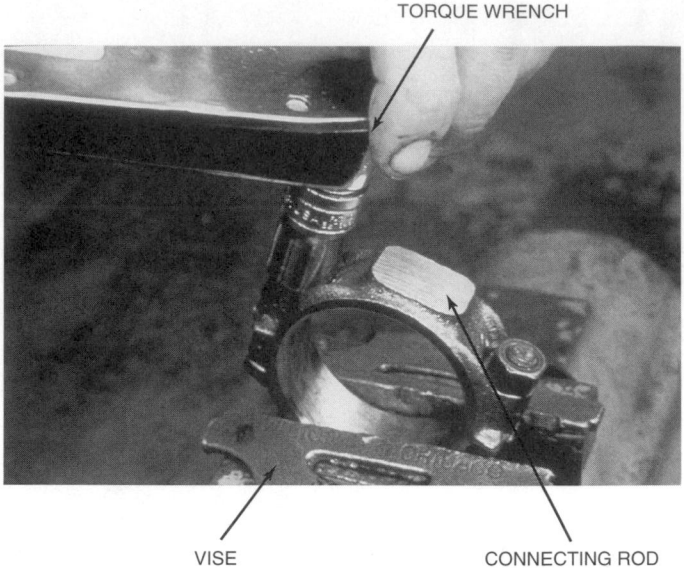

Figure 14-32. Holding connecting rod halves in a vise with protective jaw covers. Clamping the rod halves helps relieve strain on the rod when torquing. (Federal-Mogul)

of honing oil so that an ample amount will enter the bore. Move the rods back and forth over the stones, being careful to avoid exerting any side pressure that would cause the rods to tip. Keep the stones snug in the bores to reduce chatter. The stones must be of the correct grit size to produce a 30-40 microinch finish and kept dressed to ensure straight, smooth bores.

Figure 14-33. Honing the connecting rod large end bores back to factory specifications.

After the initial removal of rough stock with the hone, check the bore size often to avoid honing oversize. **Figure 14-34** illustrates the use of a special precision gauge to determine bore diameter. With careful work, it will be possible to bring the bore back to the original size and limit out-of-roundness to the generally recommended .0003" (0.0076 mm). The rod should always be carefully checked for bend and twist after reconditioning either the wrist pin or large end bore.

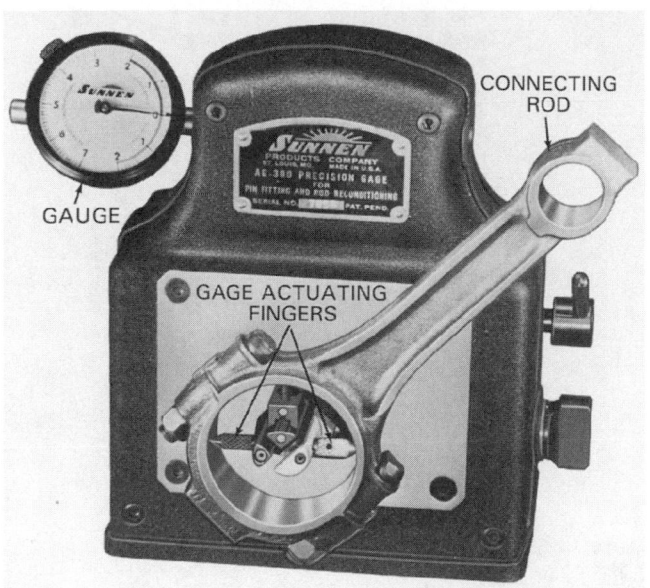

Figure 14-34. One type of precision gauge used to check connecting rod bore for out-of-roundness and to determine pin fit. (Sunnen)

Piston Service

All **pistons** must be of the correct type, weight, and size. They must be free of cracks, scoring, burning, and damaged ring grooves. They must be properly fitted to the cylinders, rings, and piston pins. If the cylinders have been rebored, the original pistons must be discarded and new pistons of the proper oversize obtained.

Inspect Pistons

After cleaning and drying, clamp the connecting rod lightly in a vise with the piston skirt just clearing the jaws. Clean any remaining carbon from the **ring grooves.** Be careful to avoid cutting any metal from either the side or the bottom of the grooves. **Figure 14-35** illustrates one type of **ring groove cleaner.** Check each piston and reject pistons that show any signs of cracking, scuffing, scoring, burning, or corrosion. Pay particular attention to the piston pin bosses and skirt. The piston cutaway in **Figure 14-36** shows cracks in both pin bosses. Also note damaged snap ring grooves.

 Caution: Any cracking, no matter how small, means the piston should be discarded. Do not attempt to repair a cracked piston.

Installation with insufficient clearance caused the heavy scoring on the thrust side of the piston shown in **Figure 14-37.** Scuffing is caused by metal-to-metal contact. Excessive heat will build up and particles will be torn from one surface and deposited on another. Scuffing and scoring are closely related. Scuffed areas will generally be discolored by the effects of the heat generated. Burning is sometimes severe, as pictured in **Figure 14-38.** When pistons show signs of corrosion, look carefully for possible coolant leaks such as a cracked head or cylinder, warped head or block, damaged gasket, or other problems. The piston illustrated in **Figure 14-39** was badly corroded by coolant.

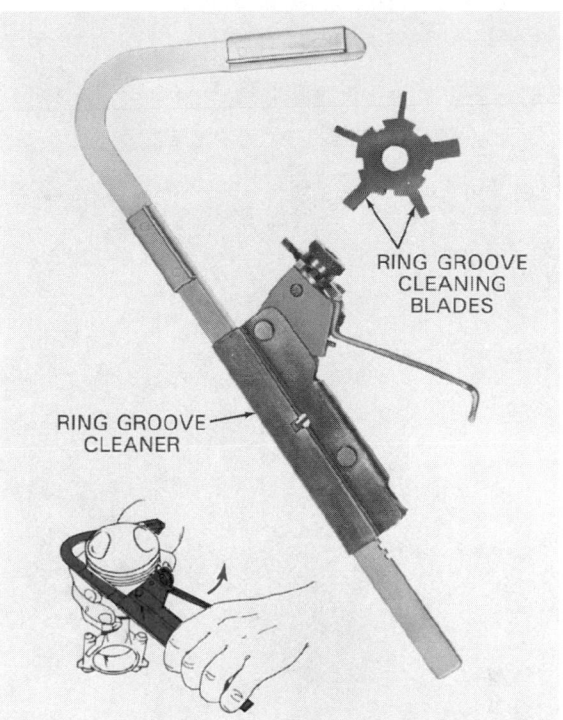

Figure 14-35. Cleaning piston ring grooves with one type of hand held tool. Note different blade sizes. (Lisle Tool)

Figure 14-36. Note the cracked pin bosses and damaged snap ring grooves. (Sunnen)

Examine all ring grooves for burrs, dented edges, and side wear. Pay particular attention to the top compression ring groove. It is the one most subject to wear, **Figure 14-40.** Groove width can be checked by sliding a new ring into the groove and using a feeler gauge to determine clearance. Check clearance at several spots around the groove. Special gauges are also available for a quick check of groove wear. The gauge shown in **Figure 14-41** has several lips that are .006″ (0.15 mm) larger than the standard grooves for which they are designed. If the lip will enter the groove, clearance is excessive and the groove needs to be reconditioned.

Figure 14-37. Insufficient clearance caused heavy scoring and scuffing on this piston.

Figure 14-38. Preignition burned a hole through the head of this piston. (Perfect Circle)

The ring groove can be reconditioned by cutting the groove wider and installing a steel *ring groove spacer* on the top edge. Hand-driven tools are usually available. See **Figure 14-42.** One popular method of affixing the steel spacer is shown in **Figure 14-43. Figure 14-44** shows how failure to repair a top ring groove caused excessive ring play that ruined the piston.

Resizing Pistons

If the old pistons are to be used on reconditioned cylinders, they should be *resized* to provide proper fit in the cylinders. Normal cylinder and piston wear may leave the pistons loose enough in the cylinders to cause tipping. Tipping will round the ring faces, rendering them useless. This looseness will also cause piston slap.

One way to resize pistons is to have the thrust areas of the skirts *knurled.* Special knurling equipment is avail-

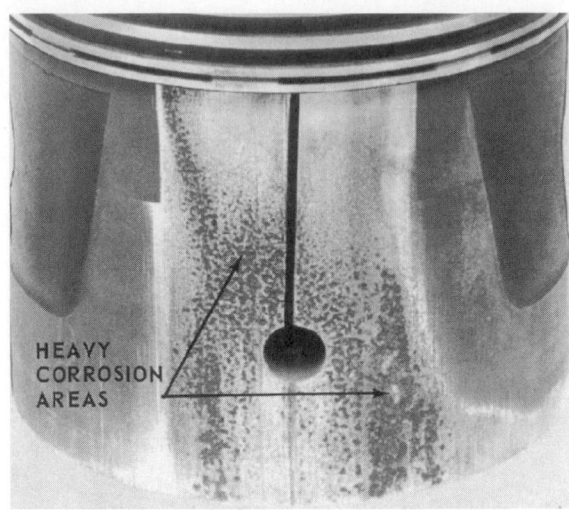

Figure 14-39. Coolant leakage caused the corrosion on the skirt of this piston.

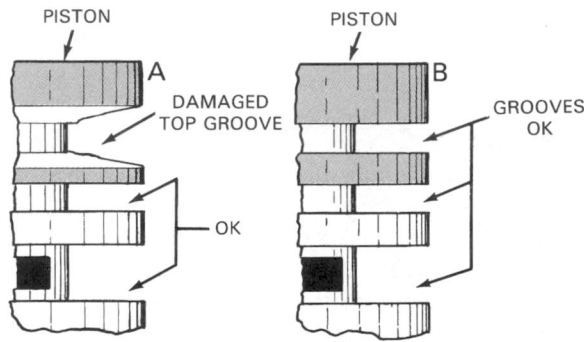

Figure 14-40. Compare these two ring grooves. A—Badly damaged top ring groove. B—Normal groove.

Figure 14-41. Checking ring groove width with a special gauge. (Perfect Circle)

able for this purpose. This equipment creates a series of narrow dents in the piston's outer surface. The piston metal around the dents forms a raised area that increases piston diameter. See **Figure 14-45.** Instructions supplied by the manufacturer of the knurling equipment should be followed carefully. The knurled grooves retain oil for lubrication and act as traps for minute metal particles that would otherwise cause scoring. Other resizing techniques are also used, such as shot-peening or cold-expanding followed by heating and quenching, or installing spring skirt expanders.

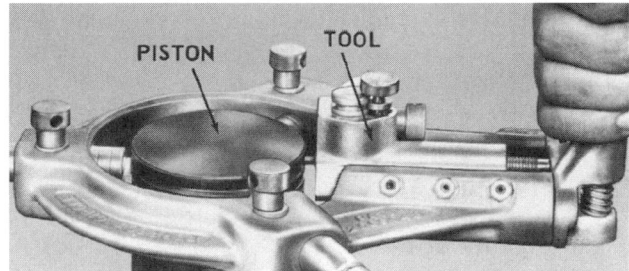

Figure 14-42. Reconditioning top ring groove with a hand operated tool.

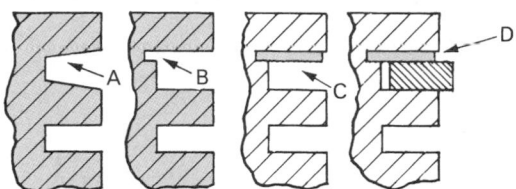

Figure 14-43. Steps in repairing a worn top ring groove. A—Worn groove. B—The groove is widened and a spacer section notched. C—Spacer is installed. D—Ring will now fit as specified.

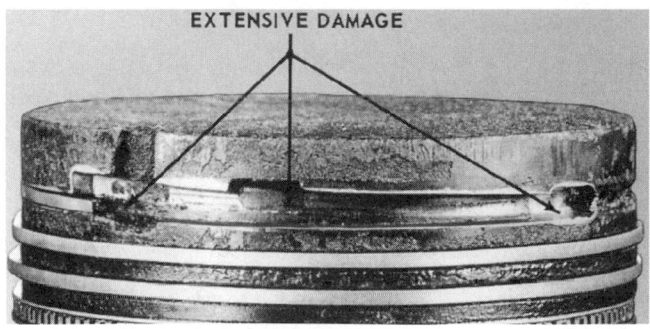

Figure 14-44. Excessive ring groove wear ruined this piston.

Figure 14-45. Complete knurl pattern on piston skirt.

Fitting Pistons

New or resized pistons must be checked for proper clearance, or *fit,* in the cylinder. New pistons require that the cylinder bore be honed until the piston clearance is correct. In the case of resized pistons, the knurled area can be wire brushed to produce a desired fit. An oiled, long feeler gauge strip is placed in the bore. The piston is inverted and shoved down into the bore so that the skirt thrust surface bears against the strip. A spring scale is attached to the feeler gauge strip and the strip is withdrawn. The manufacturer's specifications will indicate the correct pull in pounds or kilograms for specific feeler gauge thickness. See **Figure 14-46.** In worn cylinders, the check should be made near the bottom.

Piston-to-cylinder clearance may also be determined by careful measurement of both piston and cylinder. Measure the piston at both top and bottom of the skirt across the thrust surfaces. Some manufacturers specify an exact location for piston measurement. Measurements should be taken when metal is at room temperature, 60° to 70°F (16° to 21°C). Once a piston is properly fitted, it should be marked for the cylinder concerned. Clearances with .001″ to .0015″ (0.025 to 0.038 mm) are about average.

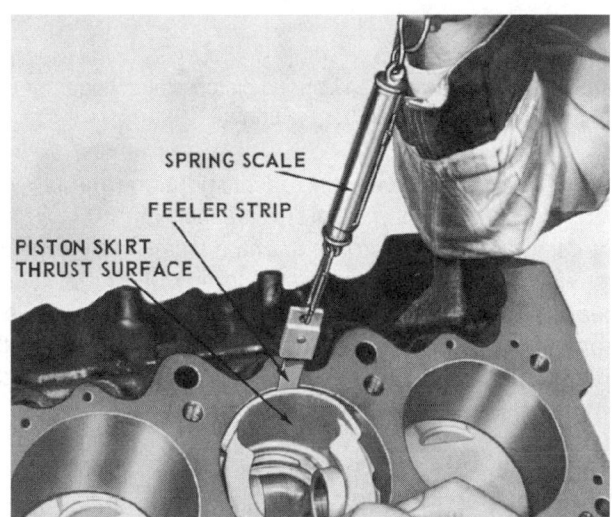

Figure 14-46. Checking piston-to-cylinder clearance with a feeler strip and spring scale. (Plymouth)

Piston Pins

Most **piston pins** are designed to oscillate in the connecting rod, in the piston, or in both. Piston pins are sometimes called wrist pins. **Figure 14-47** illustrates five pin arrangements. **Piston pin fit** (clearance between pin and bearing surface) is important. A pin must have ample clearance for oil, yet it must not have looseness that will result in pin knock and ultimately pin failure. The bearing surfaces must be round, smooth, straight, and in perfect alignment, **Figure 14-47.**

Clamp the connecting rod lightly in a vise. Attempt to rock the piston on the pin. Any discernible movement between pin and piston or pin and rod is cause for pin

PIN TYPE & DESCRIPTION   CUTAWAY VIEW

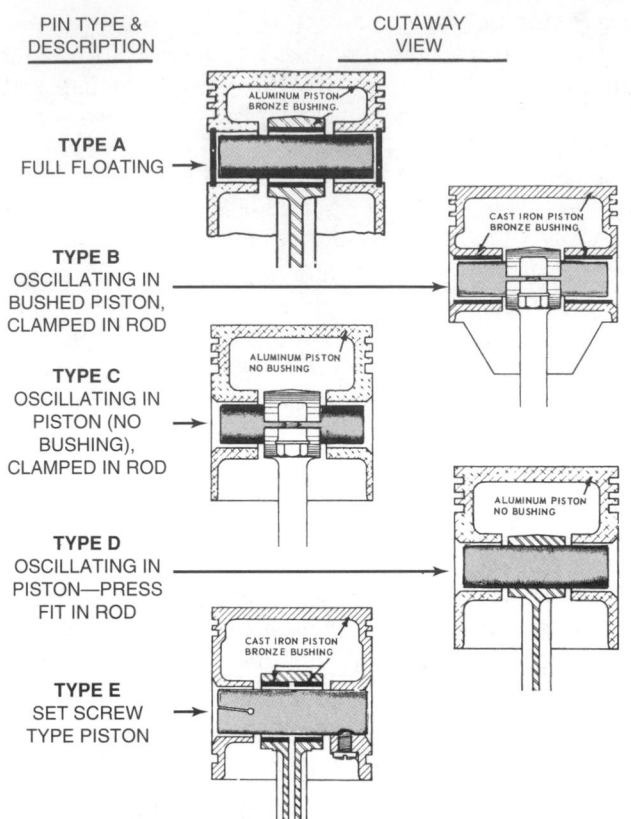

TYPE A
FULL FLOATING

TYPE B
OSCILLATING IN BUSHED PISTON, CLAMPED IN ROD

TYPE C
OSCILLATING IN PISTON (NO BUSHING), CLAMPED IN ROD

TYPE D
OSCILLATING IN PISTON—PRESS FIT IN ROD

TYPE E
SET SCREW TYPE PISTON

Figure 14-47. Study these various piston pin arrangements. Type D is currently in wide use. (Sunnen)

rejection. Do not confuse the rod sliding along the pin with up-and-down movement. Careful measurement of pin and boss using a vernier micrometer and a small hole gauge will determine exact clearance. See **Figure 14-48.** If wear is excessive, it will be necessary to install an oversize pin, and in some instances, new bushings. If the pin is bushed in the rod or piston and the bushing shows only minor wear, the old bushings may be honed to fit the oversize pin.

Piston Pin Removal

Before removing the piston pin, make certain the piston is marked so that it may be reassembled in the same position to the same rod. Prick punch marks will suffice if no

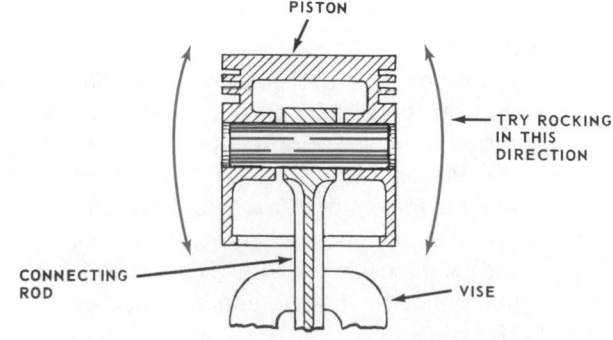

Figure 14-48. There should be no discernible movement between the piston or connecting rod and piston pin.

factory identification has been provided. **Figure 14-49** illustrates one type of factory identification. If the pin is clamped to the rod, remove the clamp screw and tap the pin out. If the piston pin is the floating type, remove the end locks (snap rings) and tap the pin free. Do not mar the piston pin bearing area. Use care in removing the end locks so as not to distort them. Most engines currently use a pin that oscillates in the piston and is a press fit in the rod. With this type, use a press or puller arrangement to remove the pin, **Figure 14-50.**

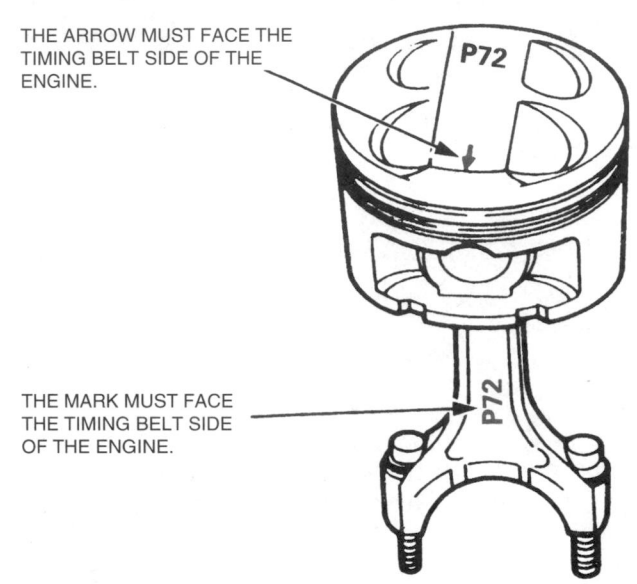

THE ARROW MUST FACE THE TIMING BELT SIDE OF THE ENGINE.

THE MARK MUST FACE THE TIMING BELT SIDE OF THE ENGINE.

Figure 14-49. Factory identification marks are used to ensure correct relationship between piston, connecting rod, and block for one specific engine. (Honda)

Fitting Piston Pins

Since piston-to-pin clearances are extremely small (.0002″-.0005″ or 0.005-0.0127 mm typical in aluminum pistons), pin fitting is an exacting job. Modern honing and boring machines will do such highly accurate work that a pin will slide freely through the piston with as little as .0001″ (0.0025 mm) clearance. Even though the pin feels free, this space would not provide sufficient oil clearance. The pin would probably seize in the piston. **Figure 14-51** shows a piston in which the pin had started to seize. Note the seizure marks in the bosses and on the pin. Seizure can literally demolish the piston.

Pin clearance in bushed rods is somewhat greater, averaging around .0005″ (0.0127 mm). In pressure-fed rod bushings, the clearance is about .001″ (0.025 mm). The pin in **Figure 14-52** had insufficient clearance. The rod oscillated around and seized in the bushing. Proper pin clearances depend on pin diameter, method of attachment, type of piston material, piston operating temperature, and the use of a bushing in the rod. Many pin fitting machines are equipped with highly accurate measuring devices that will control pin clearance within a few ten-thousandths of an inch. The pin may also be measured with a vernier micrometer. There

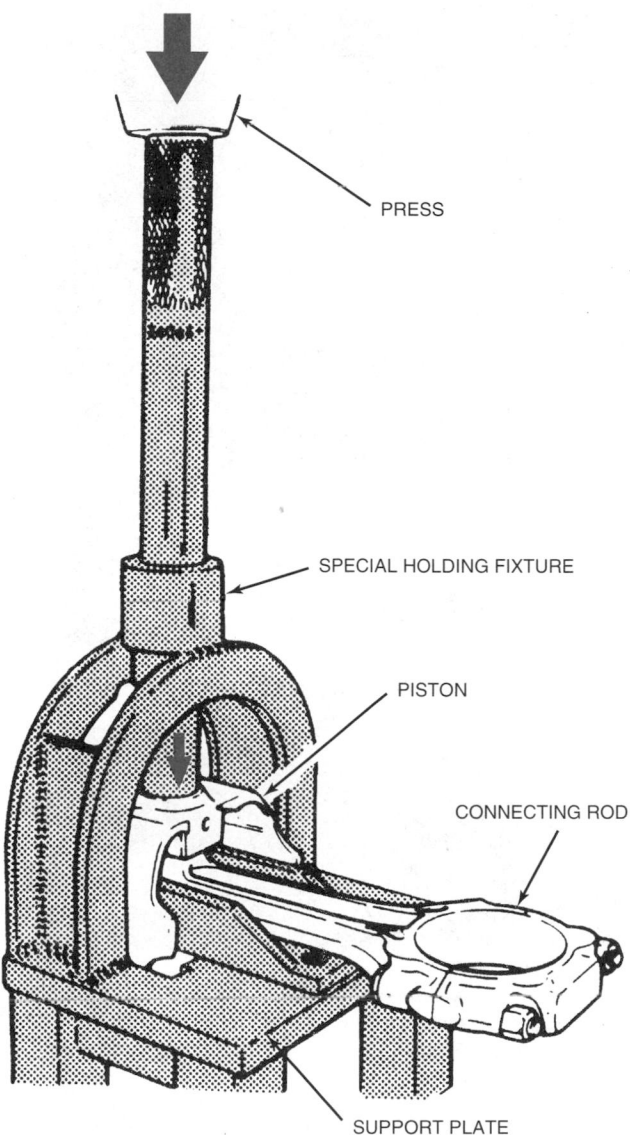

Figure 14-50. Using a hydraulic press and a special holding fixture to force out the connecting rod wrist pin. Note how the piston and rod assembly are carefully held on the support plate. Wear safety glasses and use care. (Chevrolet)

Figure 14-51. Insufficient pin clearance caused this pin to seize. Note the scoring.

Figure 14-52. Piston pin seized in the rod bushing causing the rod to oscillate on the bushing.

is no ideal average that will work well on all engines. Consult and carefully follow the manufacturer's specifications. **Figure 14-53** demonstrates the difference between a reamed finish and a honed or diamond-bored finish. Bearing bore diameter should be checked with a small hole gauge and vernier micrometer. If the measurements are done carefully, accurate clearances can be determined.

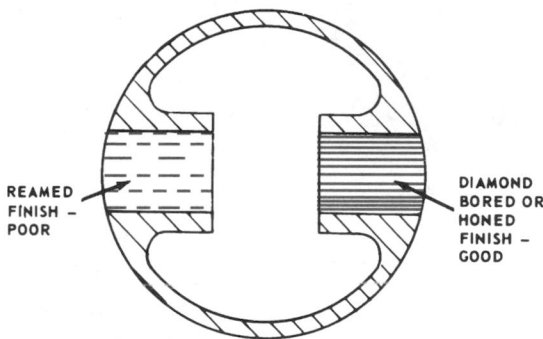

Figure 14-53. Do not use a reamer for a final pin fit. Such a surface will allow high initial wear. Fit pins by actual measured clearances and never by thumb or palm push fits.

Bushing Installation and Fitting

Although rarely used in the pistons (cast iron pistons used bushings), **bushings** are still used in the upper connecting rod bore, or eye, when the rod is designed to oscillate on the pin. If the bushing is in good condition but has excessive clearance, it may be honed or bored to fit an oversize pin. In cases where the bushing is beyond repair, it must be driven out and a new bushing pressed into place.

Following bushing removal, clean the rod bore and cut a small chamfer on one side. Line up the oil hole and press the bushing into place. The bushing must start straight and remain straight until fully seated. A press should be used to seat the bushing. Lacking a press, a vise with parallel, smooth jaws may be used. Avoid driving as it tends to upset (expand) the driven end and bulge the center, **Figure 14-54.**

It is advisable to **burnish** the bushing. This procedure expands the bushing tightly into the rod bore, preventing it from loosening and turning. Burnishing will help the bushing conduct heat and withstand shock loads without opening up. See **Figure 14-55.**

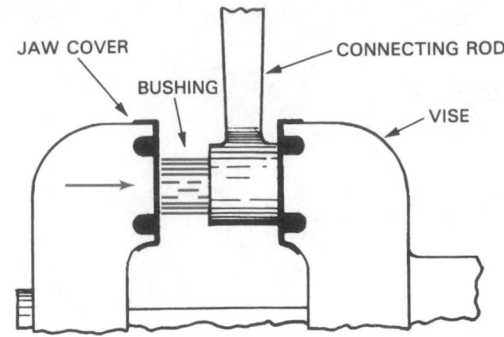

Figure 14-54. Use a vise to seat a bushing. Note the use of protective jaw covers.

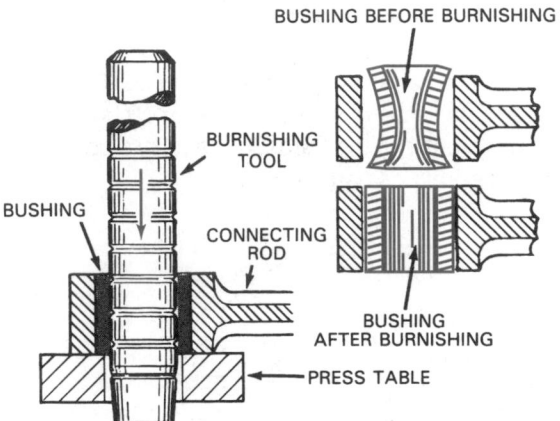

Figure 14-55. Burnishing a bushing. Note how burnishing tool forces loose bushing tightly against the rod eye.

Special tools are used to burnish the bushing. Most tools operate by tightening a screw that causes the tool to expand the bushing. When burnishing, support the bushing so that it is not forced from its proper location. If two bushings are used in the same bore, install one and burnish it before installing the other. This will permit burnishing the second bushing without dislocating the first. Bore or hone the bushing to the specified clearance. Check oil hole alignment. If a great deal of bushing material must be removed, a reamer may be used to bring the bushing within a few thousandths of finished size.

General Boring and Honing Precautions

To do good work, the technician must thoroughly understand the boring or honing machine. You can learn how to operate it through practice on scrap rods and pistons until you are thoroughly competent. Despite the built-in accuracy of the machine, the operator usually must build experience before first-class work can be performed. A typical honing machine is pictured in **Figure 14-56.**

Honing stones loose in the bearing or looseness in a boring setup will produce oblong holes. This will provide spot contact resulting in rapid wear and failure, **Figure 14-57.** Worn stones will produce tapered holes if not properly dressed. Reversing the rod or piston on the hone will not remove the taper but will produce a double taper. Wobbling

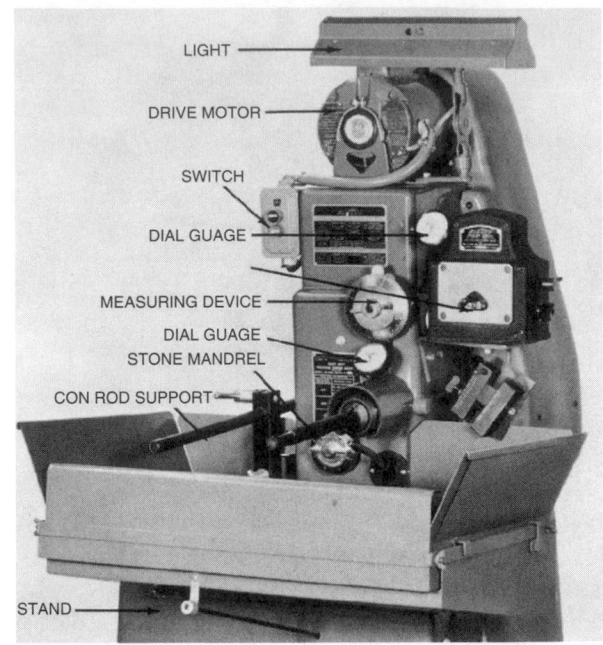

Figure 14-56. Typical honing machine. (Sunnen)

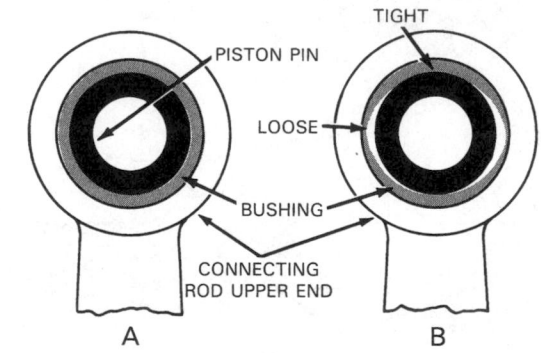

Figure 14-57. A—Hone bushings accurately. B—A loose honing or boring setup will produce an oblong hole.

the rod will also produce a tapered hole. See **Figure 14-58.** Unless an accurate centering cone is used, boring or honing one pin boss and then the other can cause misalignment between boss pinholes. Look at **Figure 14-59.**

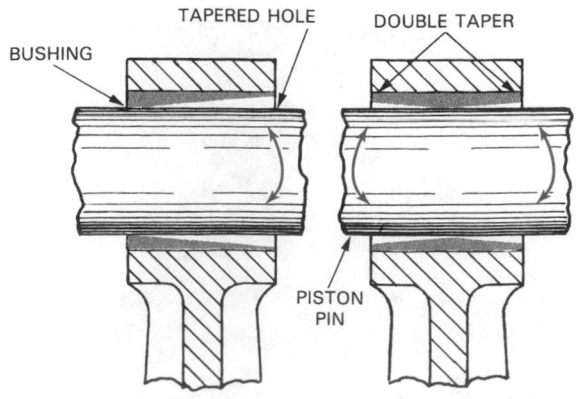

Figure 14-58. Pinholes must be straight. Tapered holes are not satisfactory.

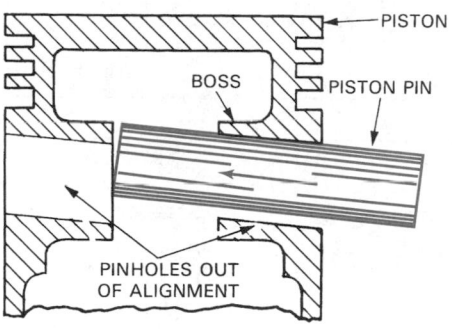

Figure 14-59.   Pinholes out of alignment.

Hole misalignment will be noticed when sliding the pin through one hole into the other. If the pin clicks or catches before entering the second hole, misalignment is present. If both boss pinholes are of the correct size, any appreciable misalignment will stop the pin from entering. Sharp cutters and properly dressed stones of the correct grit size will leave an extremely smooth finish. Loose or dull cutters and rough or glazed stones will leave a rough finish that will not wear properly.

Figure 14-60 shows a technician honing a connecting rod bushing to size. Note the support rod for the large end. Also note the method of holding the bushed end to prevent side pressure that would cause misalignment, bell mouthing, or taper. Remember that pin fits must be accurate. A free pin does not always indicate adequate clearance. Clearances vary, so consult the manufacturer's specifications.

When a pin is fitted, keep it with the piston and rod to which it was fitted. When fitting pins that are locked with a screw to one piston boss, do not fail to provide the specified fit on the free end. Cam ground pistons, which are ground to an oval shape, cause the bosses to travel on the pin. If

one end is locked and the other is too tight, extensive piston damage may result, **Figure 14-61.**

In **Figure 14-62,** insufficient pin clearance in the rod ruined the piston (pin locked to one boss type). If oversize pins have been fitted to the piston, it will be necessary to hone the connecting rod to provide the specified interference fit. This fit must hold the pin tightly to prevent end movement that would ruin the cylinder wall. When new pistons with standard pins are being fitted to an old rod, check to see if the rod bore has been enlarged for an oversize pin. If so, the piston must be refitted to a correct oversize pin or the rod must be discarded.

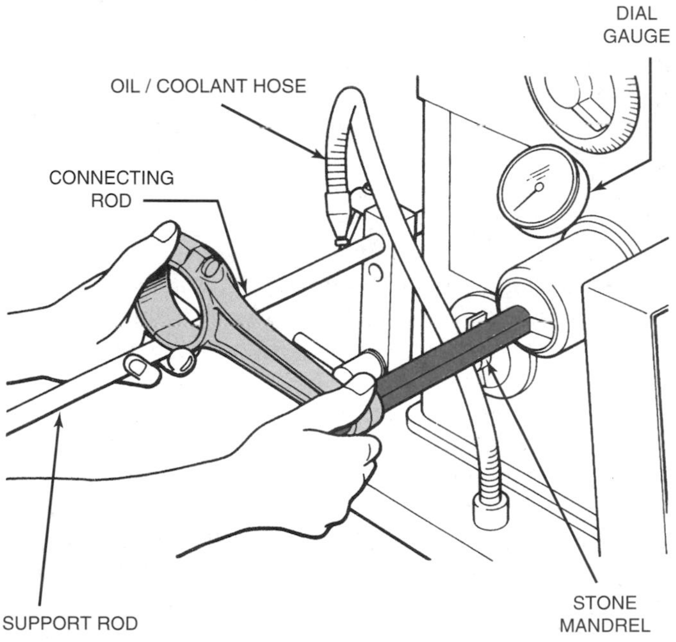

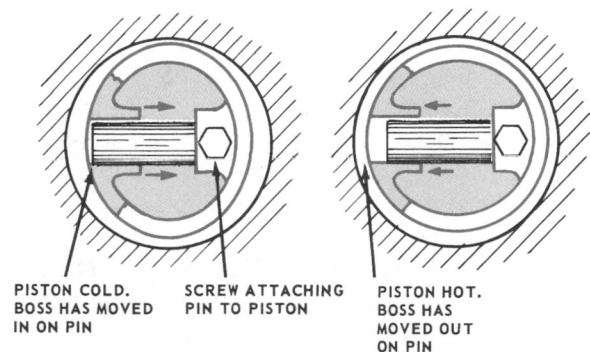

Figure 14-61.   When a cam ground piston is heated up, the free end boss moves outward on pin.

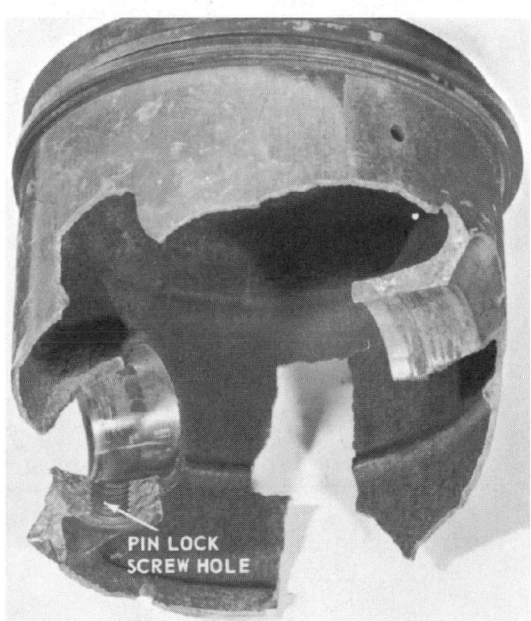

Figure 14-62.   Insufficient clearance between the pin and rod caused this pin to seize in the rod. As the pin was locked to one piston boss, this piston suffered extensive damage.

Assembling Connecting Rod and Piston

Clean pistons, pins, and rods twice with a round bristle brush and hot, soapy water and rinse thoroughly. Pay special attention to pinholes and hollow pins, locking lip recesses, bolt holes, and other areas where grit may be trapped.

Figure 14-60.   Honing a connecting rod bushing to size. Note how rod is held to prevent tipping. (Toyota)

Caution: When torquing rod caps out of the engine, pressing piston pins into the rod upper bore, or grasping rods in a vise, use extreme care to avoid bending or twisting the rods.

All parts must be clean and dry, checked for proper clearance, and thoroughly lubricated. While holding the piston and rod in the correct relationship to each other, pass the pin through the units. If an interference fit in the rod is used, a press or puller is required, **Figure 14-63.** Some shops apply controlled heat to the rod bore to ease pin installation and prevent galling. If the pin is a press fit in the rod or held to the rod with a clamp setup, the pin must be carefully centered so that rod side movement will not cause the pin to strike the cylinder wall. See **Figure 14-64.** The interference fit between the pin and rod can be checked by measuring the torque required to pass the pin through the rod. Be sure to check the manufacturer's specifications.

On the floating pin installation, make certain the end locks are not distorted or weak. Check to see that they are fully seated in their grooves. Install the open end toward the bottom of the piston. This will tend to cause them to expand into the grooves during the shock period imposed during the firing stroke. Loose pin locks can actually cut through the boss from the inertia force. When removing or installing locks, spring them only as far as necessary. If the lock breaks and moves out of its groove, the cylinder, piston, or both can be damaged.

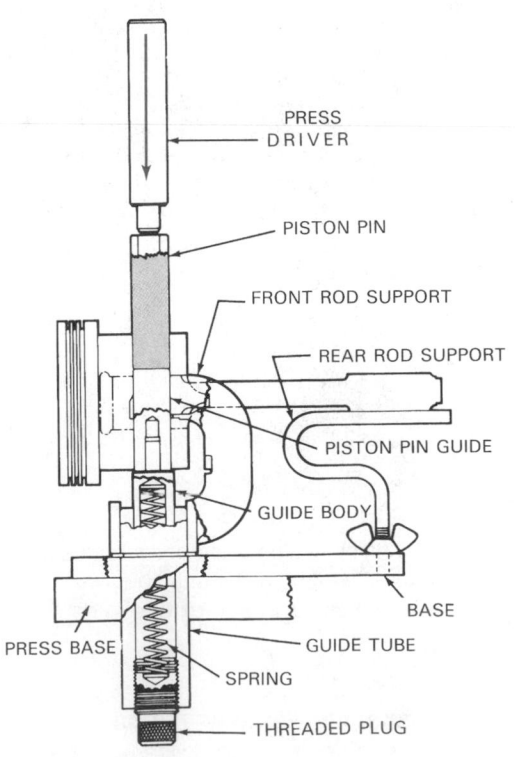

Figure 14-63. Using a press to properly install a piston pin. The pin is press fit in the connecting rod. (Chevrolet)

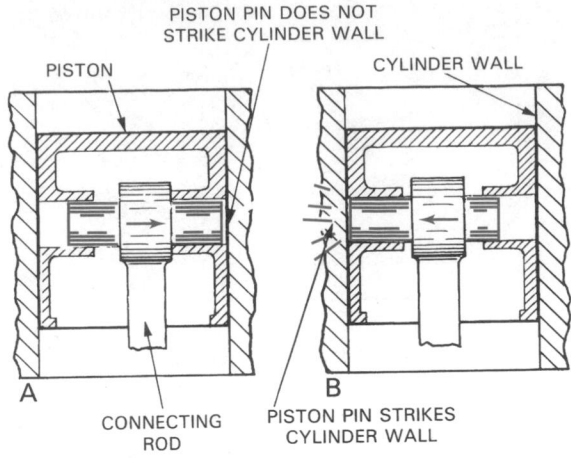

Figure 14-64. A—When the piston pin is centered in the rod, rod side movement will not cause the pin to strike the cylinder wall. B—An offset pin will cause trouble.

Ring Service

The two basic ring types, **compression rings** and **oil control rings,** are available in a multitude of designs. The use of **chrome** on the cylinder wall contact edge of one or more rings in a set lengthens the service life and reduces the chance of scuffing. Special break-in coatings, such as phosphate and ferrous oxide, are often applied. Compression rings are usually of the torsional twist type, taper face type, or a combination of the two. Oil control rings can be constructed of one or more pieces using either a hump-type expander, a circumferential coil expander, or a circumferential spacer expander. See **Figure 14-65.**

Replacement rings are available in sets designed for either a rebored or a worn cylinder. The set for installation in a rebored cylinder is commonly referred to as a factory or rebore set while rings for a worn cylinder is called an engineered or oil control set. Mild taper (up to .005″ or 0.13 mm) can usually be handled well by a rebore set. The oil control set is of a somewhat different design with stiffer expander springs to force the rings to follow tapered walls. The oil control set can be used in cylinders with severe taper, but will produce more drag and wear. See **Figure 14-65.** Specify cylinder diameter (standard, .010″, .020″, etc. oversize) when ordering ring sets.

Checking Ring Groove Clearance

When rings are installed in a cylinder, a certain amount of clearance, or **ring gap,** must exist between the ends. As the rings heat up, they expand. If the ends touch and expansion continues, scuffing, scoring, and damage will occur. It is advisable to allow a minimum of .003″ to .004″ (0.08 to 0.10 mm) gap for each inch (25.4 mm) of cylinder diameter. For example, a 3″ (76.2 mm) cylinder would require a gap of .009″ to .012″ (0.23 to 0.30 mm). Start the ring by hand. Then use a piston to push it to the bottom of the ring travel. This will square the ring with the bore. Use a feeler gauge to check compression rings for proper gap, **Figure 14-66.**

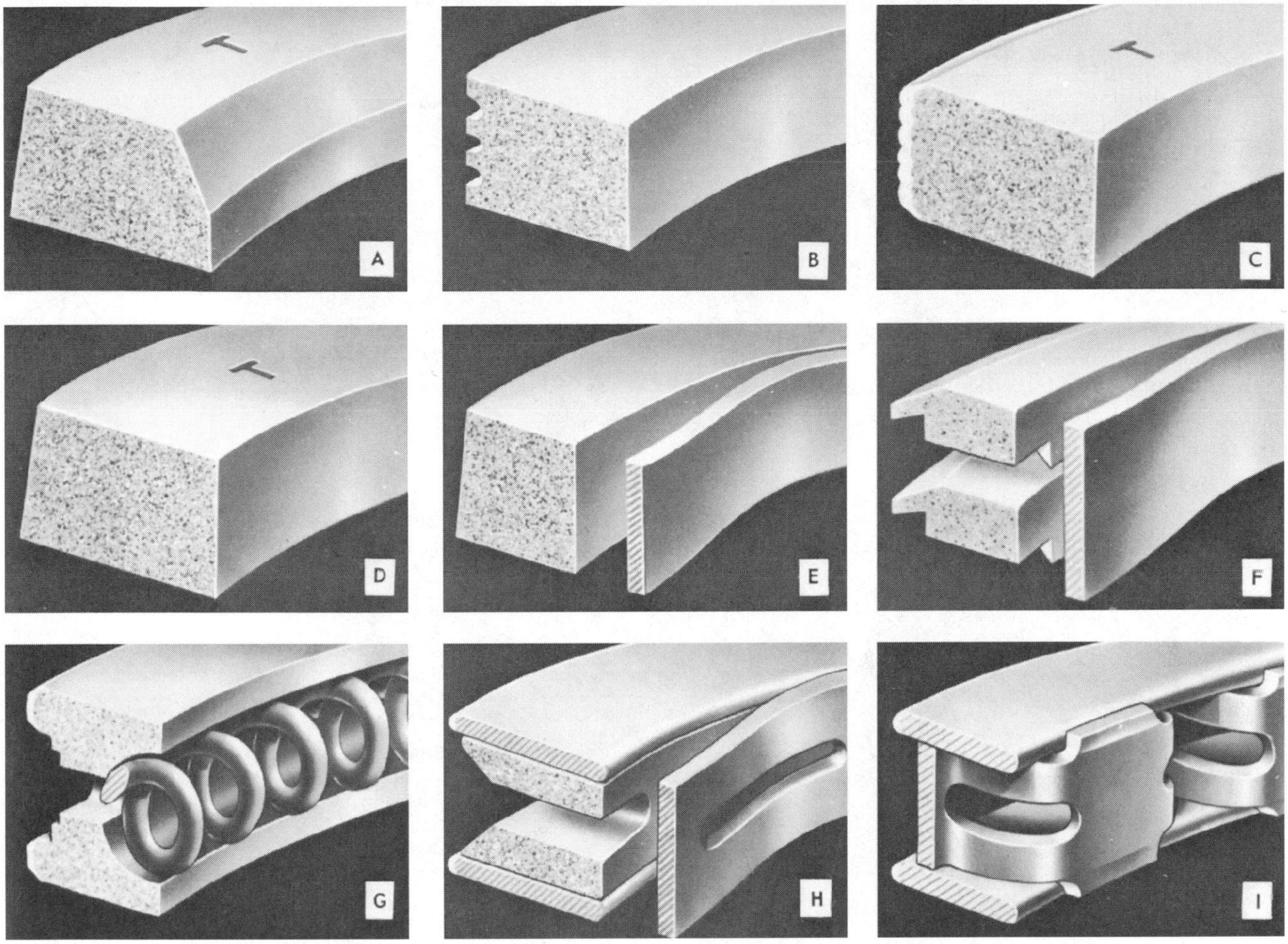

Figure 14-65. Learn these ring types. A—Combination torsional twist and taper face. B—Plain grooved face. C—Plain chrome face. D—Taper face. E—Taper face with hump-type expander. Rings F through I are oil control rings. F—Twin scraper, hump-type expander. G—Chromed twin scraper with circumferential coil expander. H—Cast iron spacer, two chrome side rails, hump expander. I—Two chrome side rails, circumferential expander-spacer. (Sealed Power)

A gap of up to .008″ per inch (0.20 mm per 25.4 mm) of bore diameter is acceptable. Anything above this would indicate a wrong size ring set. If the gap is a few thousandths small, it may be widened by clamping a small, fine tooth mill file in the vise and rubbing the ends of the ring across the file surface. Hold the ring near the ends and be very careful. Remove the ring from the cylinder by pulling upward on the ring directly opposite the gap. If the side of the ring near the gap is lifted, the ring can be distorted or broken.

Checking Groove Depth and Side Clearance

Rings are made for a variety of *groove depths.* The ring must not touch the bottom of the groove when installed in the cylinder. A gauge may be used to check the oil ring groove depth, **Figure 14-67.** The groove should not be too deep because certain types of expanders push outward from the groove bottom. Excessive groove depth will reduce expander pressure. Shallow grooves can be deepened in some cases if the correct rings are not available. Some manufacturers supply shims to reduce excessive depth.

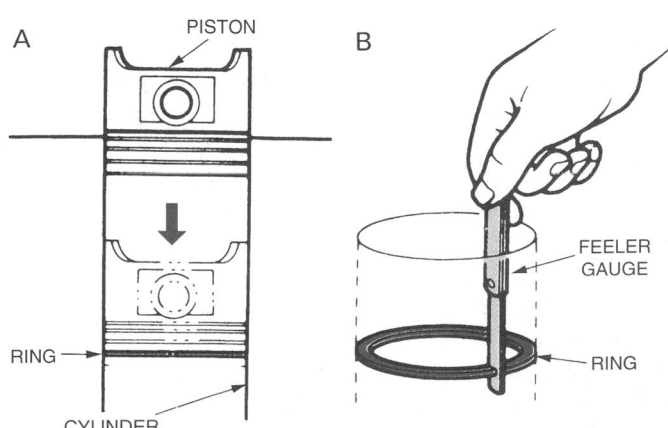

Figure 14-66. To measure ring gap, A—Use a piston to seat ring squarely at bottom of ring travel in cylinder. B—Measure the ring gap with a feeler gauge. (Mazda)

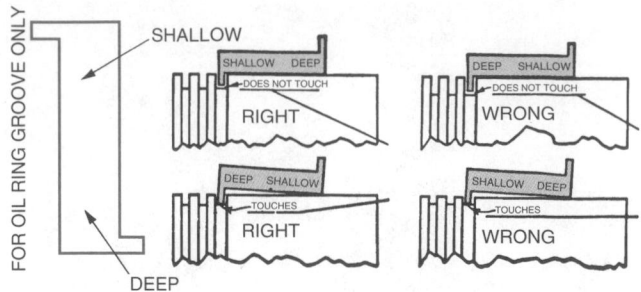

Figure 14-67. When a gauge such as this is enclosed with the ring set, be sure to use it. The shallow tip should not touch. The deep tip should touch. If the deep tip does not touch or if the shallow tip does, the ring set is wrong for the piston in question. (Hastings)

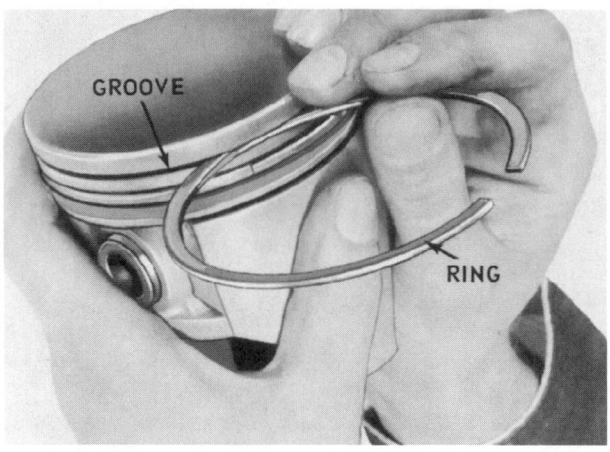

Figure 14-68. Roll the ring completely around the groove to check for binding.

Rings should be rolled around in their respective grooves to check for binding. See **Figure 14-68.** Check *ring side clearance* by inserting the ring into the groove and passing a feeler gauge between the ring and groove side. Check clearance in several spots around the groove. Clearance should not exceed .006″ (0.15 mm) or be less than .0015″ (0.038 mm) for top rings. See **Figure 14-69.** Some multiple piece oil rings are designed so that the expander-spacer forces the rails not only against the cylinder walls but against the ring groove sides as well.

Installing Rings

Grasp the connecting rod in a clean vise. All ring grooves must be clean. Make certain oil ring groove drain holes are open. Starting with the bottom oil ring, install each ring according to the directions supplied by the ring's manufacturer. Multiple piece oil ring side rails must be spiraled over the piston. This is shown in **Figure 14-70.** Do not try to expand them. Note that the ends of the flexible spacer in **Figure 14-70A** must be butted together. Do not let them overlap. Butted ends must be located over a solid portion of the groove bottom. Some grooves have little solid area. Special shims are available to prevent the spacer ends from bending inward through the groove.

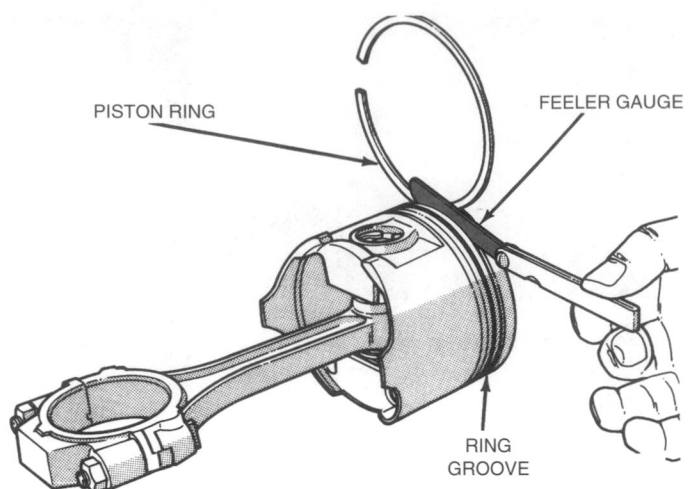

Figure 14-69. Using a feeler gauge to check ring side clearance in its groove. (Dodge)

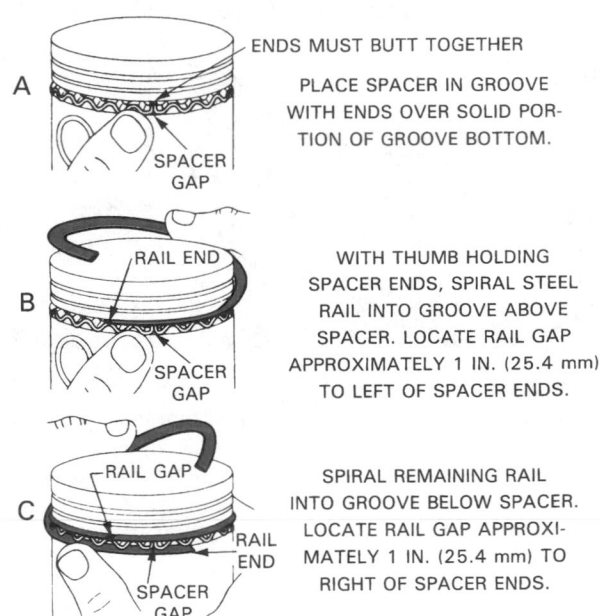

Figure 14-70. Oil ring side rails must be spiraled into place. Do not cut off the ends of the expander spacer.

When spiraling rails into position, **Figures 14-70B** and **14-70C,** be careful to avoid scoring the piston with the sharp rail end. The end can be slid over a piece of stiff feeler stock to prevent piston damage. After both rails are installed, check the spacer ends to make sure they are not overlapped. Use a good quality *ring expander* to install the remaining rings. Do not expand any ring more than necessary. See **Figure 14-71.**

Be careful to install the rings with the side up as recommended. Many rings are marked with the word *top.* This is to remind the technician to face that side of the ring toward the top of the piston. If no markings are present and no illustrations are provided, a study of the ring's profile will usually determine the top side. Study the typical ring profiles in **Figure 14-72.** Do not forget to install expanders for compression rings when so equipped. On multiple piece

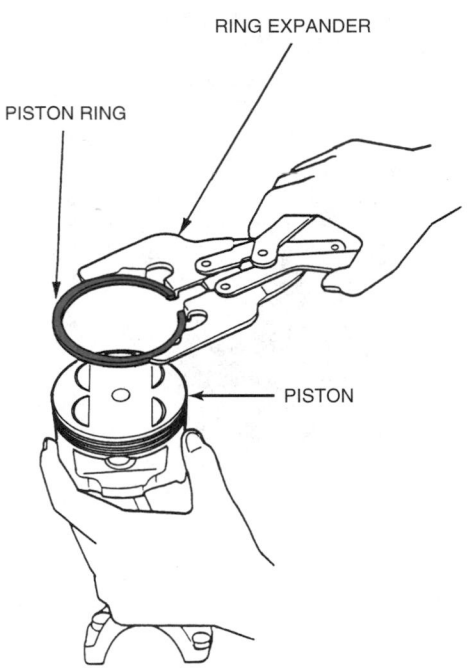

Figure 14-71. Use a good quality ring expander to install rings. (Honda)

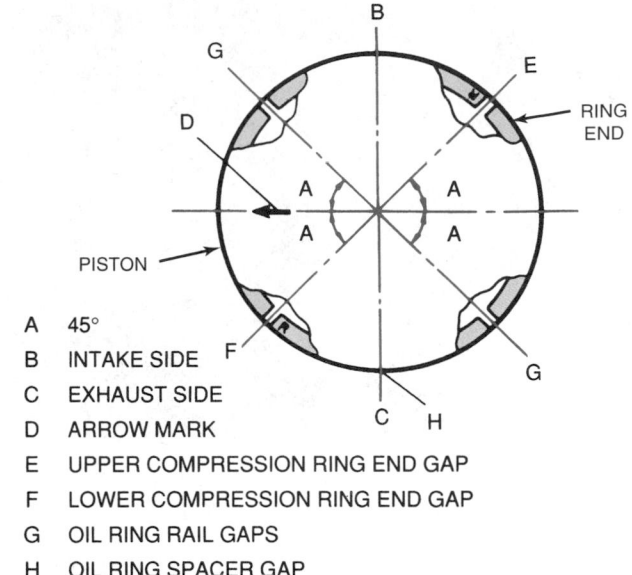

A   45°
B   INTAKE SIDE
C   EXHAUST SIDE
D   ARROW MARK
E   UPPER COMPRESSION RING END GAP
F   LOWER COMPRESSION RING END GAP
G   OIL RING RAIL GAPS
H   OIL RING SPACER GAP

Figure 14-73. Ring gap spacing for one particular engine. (General Motors)

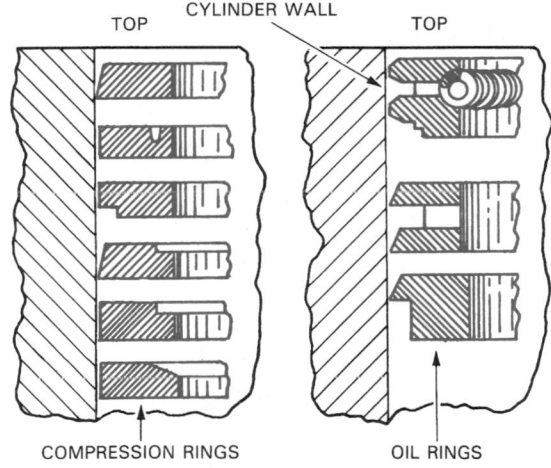

Figure 14-72. Rings of this general shape are usually installed as shown.

rings, follow manufacturer's recommendations. Although rings tend to float (move around in their grooves), it is a good idea to space the ring gaps around the piston so that they are not in alignment. See **Figure 14-73.**

Installing Rod and Piston Assembly

Give the rod and piston assembly a final check. Check that the piston pin is centered and secure and the piston and rod are correctly assembled in relation to each other. Check that the rings are properly installed and that oil holes, where used, are open. See **Figure 14-74.** Squirt a heavy coat of clean engine oil over the rings and piston. Apply plenty to the pin and work the rod back and forth to ensure oil enters the pin bushing. Hands and work area must be clean. See **Figure 14-75.** Grasp the rod in a vise. Ensure

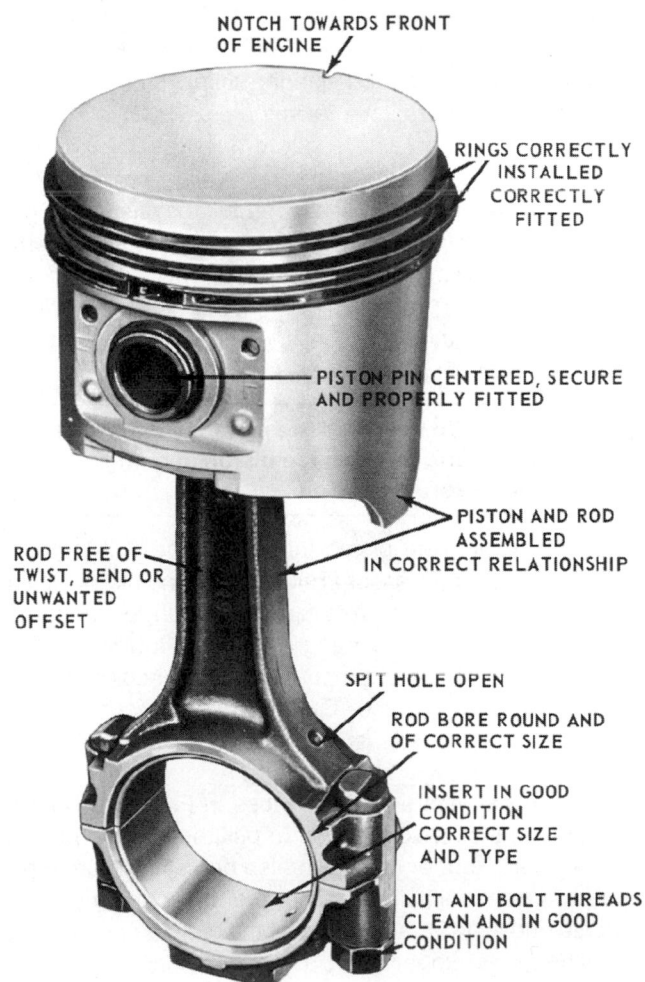

Figure 14-74. Give each rod and piston assembly a final check before installing in the engine. (Plymouth)

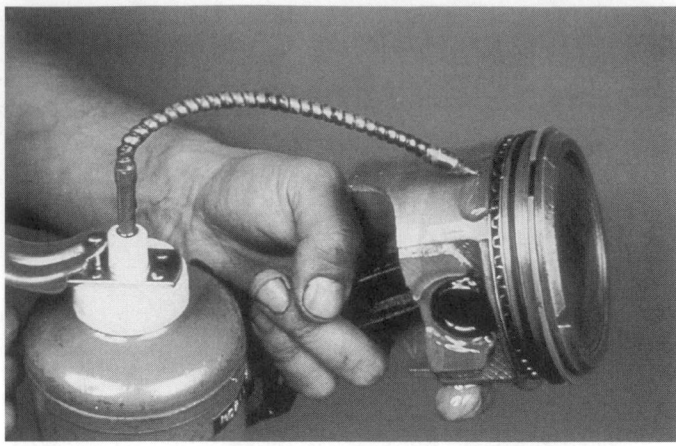

Figure 14-75. The cylinder, piston, rings, pin, and rod bearings must be heavily oiled. (Federal-Mogul)

that the *ring compressor* is clean and lightly lubricated. Then slide the ring compressor down over the rings until the lower tightening band is below the lowest ring. Tighten the compressor securely.

 Note: Tap lightly around the outside of the compressor using the tightening wrench. Then, retighten. This will ensure the rings are fully compressed.

Snap in the upper rod bearing insert and lubricate it. Install the journal protectors. Turn the crankshaft so that the connecting rod journal is at bottom dead center. Slide the exposed piston skirt into the cylinder while keeping the rod aligned with the journal. Make certain the piston identification marks face the correct direction. Using a hammer handle, tap the piston through the compressor and into the cylinder. The piston should enter with light tapping. If the piston catches on the way in, a ring is probably hung up on the cylinder block surface.

 Caution: Do not force the piston into the cylinder. Remove and reinstall the piston and ring compressor.

While tapping the piston into the cylinder, it is important to keep the compressor firmly against the block. Failure to do this may allow it to ride up far enough for an oil ring side rail to pop out and hang up. See **Figure 14-76.** A slightly different shaped compressor is required for a block with a slanted top surface. Guide the rod bearing around the journal as the piston is tapped or pulled down through the cylinder.

Journal protectors such as those in **Figure 14-77** provide a handle that is very handy to pull the rod into position on the journal. Rubber hose can also be used if journal protectors are not available. Snap in the lower bearing insert. Lubricate and install the cap so that the cap number is on the same side as the upper mark. Tighten the cap bolts or nuts until the cap is snug. If the journal serves a single rod, turn the crankshaft a couple of revolutions to allow the rod to center before the final bearing tightening. If two rods operate on the same journal, install both rods and then revolve the shaft.

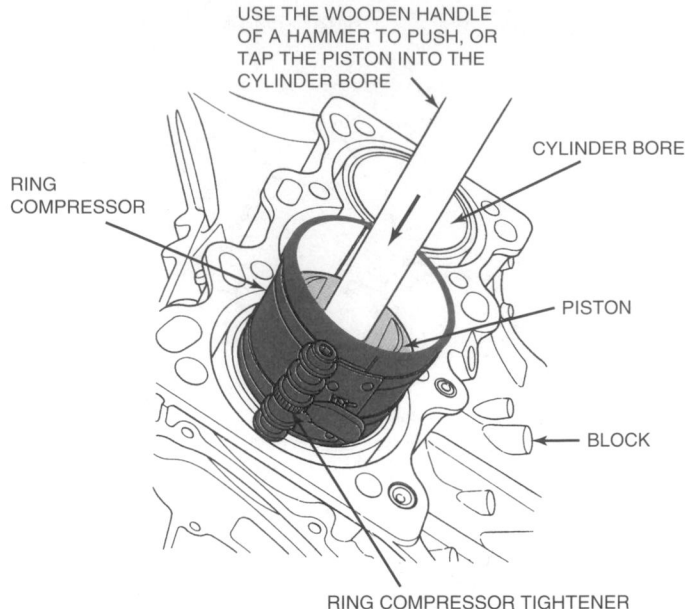

Figure 14-76. Installing a piston with a ring compressor. Maintain a downward pressure on the ring compressor to prevent the rings from expanding out between the compressor and the bore before they enter the cylinder bore. (Acura)

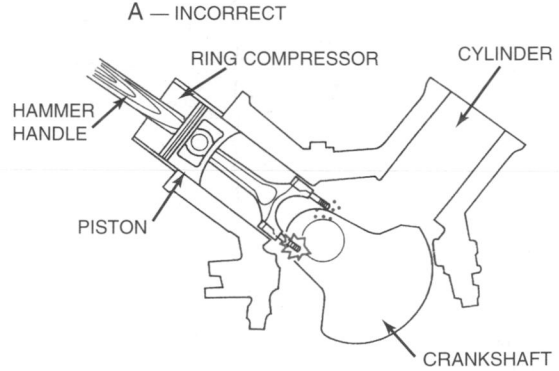

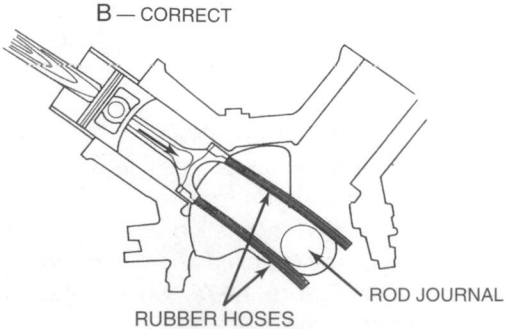

Figure 14-77. Pulling a connecting rod into contact with the crankshaft. A—Incorrect. The bolts hit the crank journal. B—Correct. The rubber hoses guide the bolts past the journal, preventing bearing surface damage. (Acura)

Checking Connecting Rod Clearances

After the cap is installed, the rod *bearing clearance* must be checked. Rotate the crankshaft to BDC if you are sure that the journal is round. If the journal is out-of-round, rotate downward just far enough to remove the cap. This will allow a bearing clearance check more in line with the widest journal diameter. Remove the cap and wipe all oil from the journal and insert. Place a strip of *Plastigage* across the insert about 1/4″ (6.35 mm) off center. Install the cap and torque it to specs. It is important to make certain the upper rod bearing is held against the top of the journal while torquing. This will prevent the lower cap from drawing the rod and piston assembly downward, thus flattening the Plastigage and giving a false reading.

Without turning the crankshaft, remove the cap and check the width of the flattened Plastigage. See **Figure 14-78.** An even width of flattened Plastigage indicates a straight journal. Remove the Plastigage, lubricate the insert and install cap and torque. Following manufacturer's specifications (.004″ to .010″ or 0.102 to 0.254 mm average), check the connecting rod *side clearance.* Use a suitable feeler gauge or dial indicator. See **Figure 14-79.** Retorque all rods. Palnuts, if used, should be installed. Turn the crankshaft to make sure all parts are clear and that excessive drag is not present.

Oil Pumps

There are two main types of oil pumps, the *rotor pump* and the *gear pump.* A typical rotor-type oil pump is pictured in **Figure 14-80.** Note that the pump contains an oil *pressure relief valve.* Check the end clearance of both inner and outer *pump rotors* by placing a straightedge across the pump body and passing a suitable feeler gauge (.004″ or 0.10 mm con-

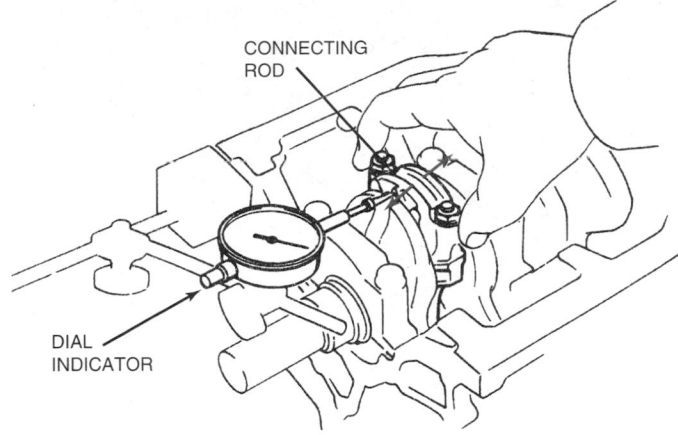

Figure 14-79. Checking connecting rod side play (clearance) with a dial indicator. (Toyota)

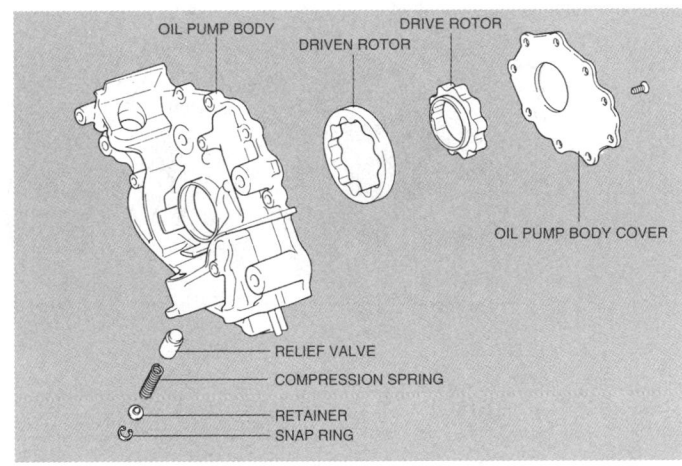

Figure 14-80. A rotor oil pump. This pump is driven by the engine crankshaft. (Toyota)

sidered maximum) between the straightedge and rotor surfaces, **Figure 14-81.** The type of gasket, if any, between the pump body and cover must be considered when checking end clearance. The pump type shown in **Figure 14-82** does not use a gasket or an O-ring seal. The measured clearance between the rotors and the body is actual end clearance. If a thin gasket is used, the thickness of the compressed gasket must be added to the feeler gauge reading.

When the end clearance is excessive, determine if the wear is in the pump body or in the rotors. Measure the length of both the inner and outer rotors. Use manufacturers' wear limit specifications. See **Figures 14-83** and **14-84.** Use a feeler gauge to check the clearance between the outer rotor and pump body (.012″ or 0.30 mm considered maximum). See **Figure 14-85.** Then check the tip clearance between inner and outer rotors (.010″ or 0.25 mm considered maximum). See **Figure 14-86.** Place a straightedge on the cover and use a feeler gauge to determine cover wear (.0015″ or 0.038 mm considered maximum). See **Figure 14-87.**

The inner rotor shaft-to-body bearing clearance should also be checked (.001″-.003″ or 0.025-0.08 mm average range). This can best be done by carefully measuring the

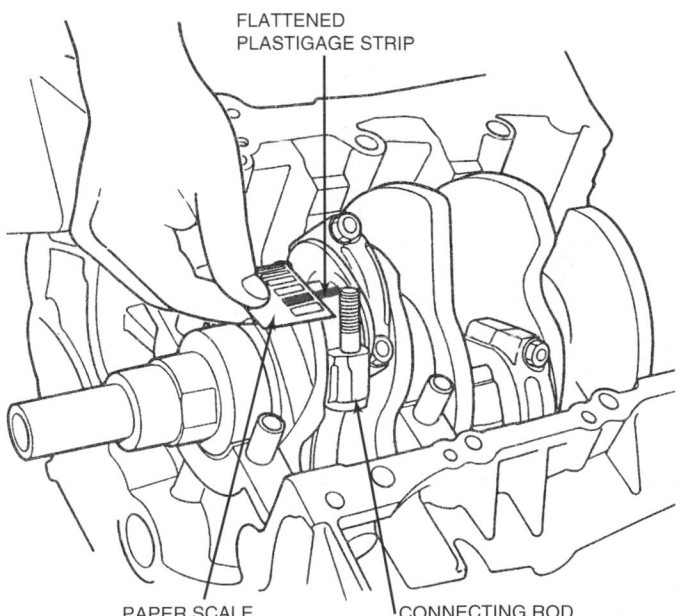

Figure 14-78. Checking the width of flattened Plastigage with a paper scale. This engine has a new rod bearing-to-crankshaft journal oil clearance of 0.0009″-0.0018″ (0.022-0.046 mm) and a service limit of 0.002″ (0.05 mm). (Acura)

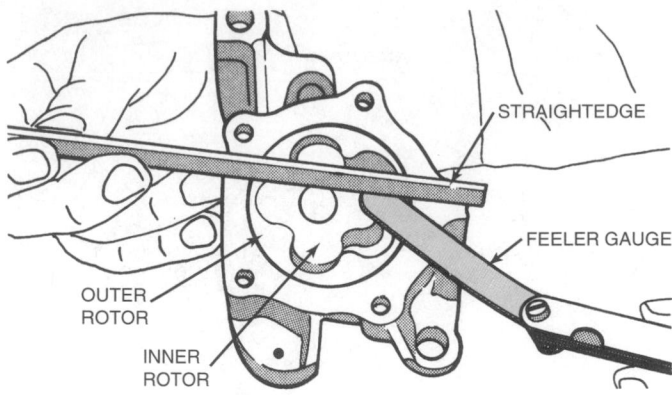

Figure 14-81. Checking oil pump rotor end clearance. (Chrysler)

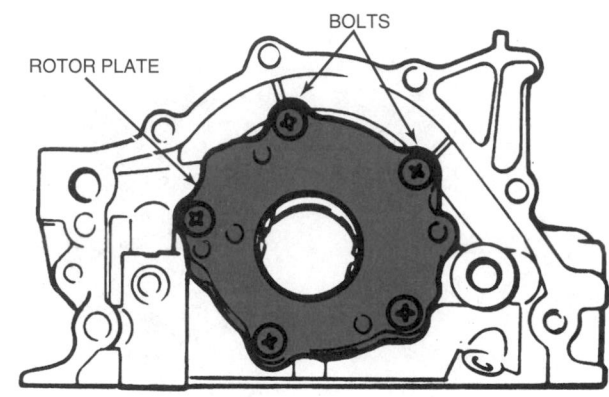

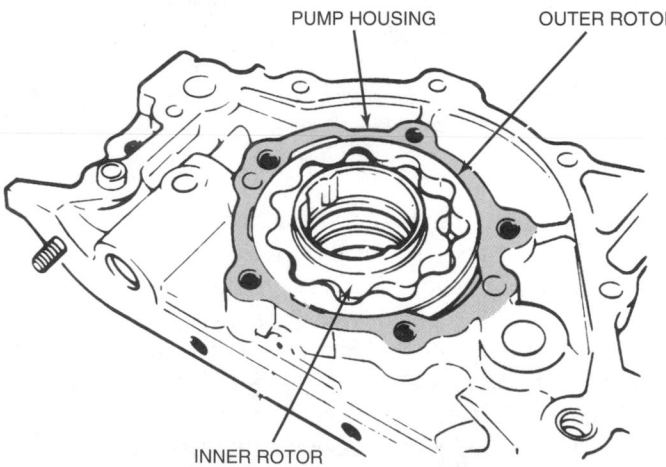

Figure 14-82. This rotor-type oil pump does not use a gasket or an O-ring between the rotor end plate and the housing. (Geo)

shaft and the bearing hole. Inspect the rotors and shaft for scoring, galling, and chipping. Check pump body for cracks.

> ⚠ **Note: Always replace rotors as a pair. Never replace one rotor. Remember that in order to function properly, the rotor pump working clearances between the inner and outer rotor, between the outer rotor and pump body, and between the rotor ends and the pump cover must be within specified limits.**

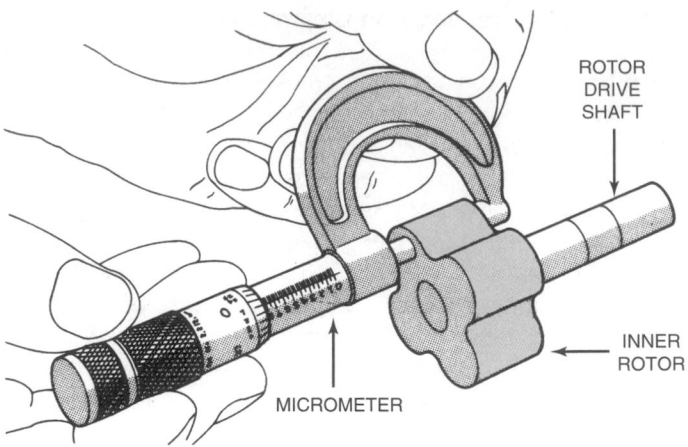

Figure 14-83. Using a micrometer to measure the inner rotor length. This rotor will require replacement if it measures .825" (20.9 mm) or less. (Chrysler)

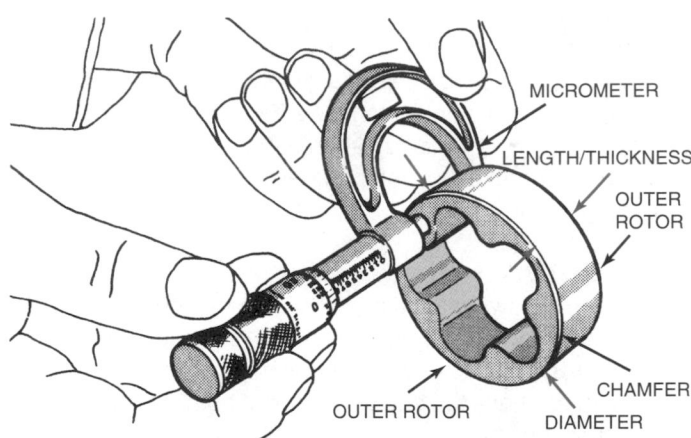

Figure 14-84. Measuring the outer pump rotor length with a micrometer. (Chrysler)

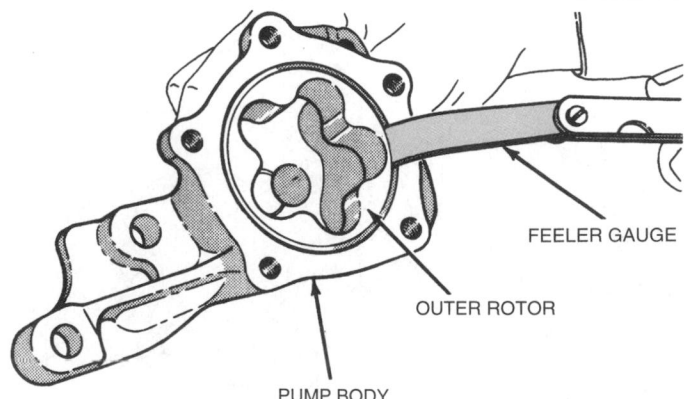

Figure 14-85. Measuring rotor-to-pump body clearance. If this particular pump wear exceeds .014" (0.356 mm), the pump assembly must be replaced. (Chrysler)

Checking Gear-Type Oil Pump

Study the disassembled gear-type oil pump in **Figure 14-88.** This pump also incorporates a pressure relief valve. Use a straightedge and feeler gauge to check the end clearance between the gears and pump body (.004" or 0.10 mm maximum). Remember to factor in gasket effect on clear-

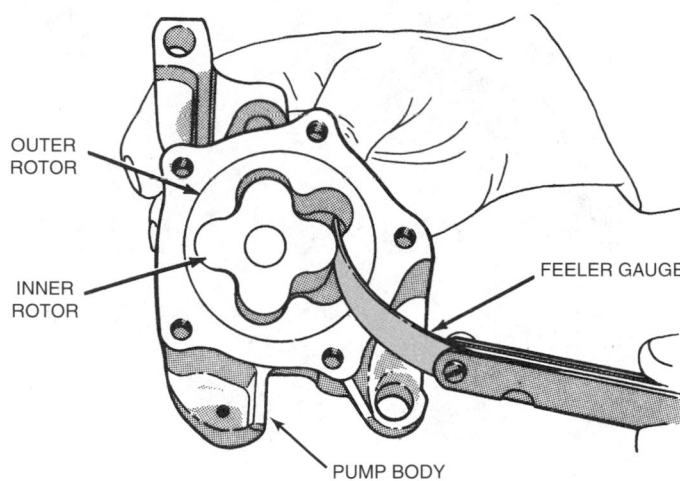

Figure 14-86. Measuring the clearance between rotor high points. (Chrysler)

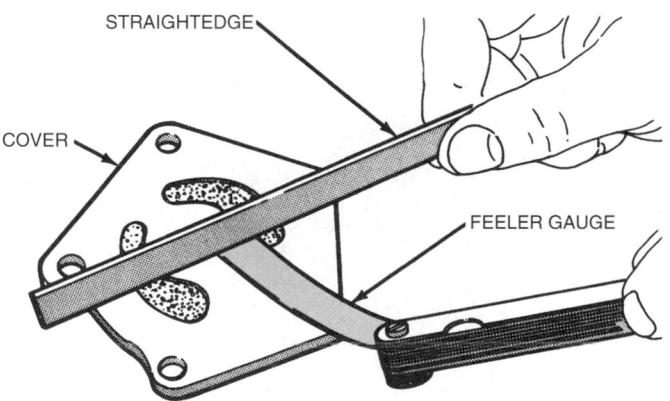

Figure 14-87. Checking the pump cover for wear. (Dodge)

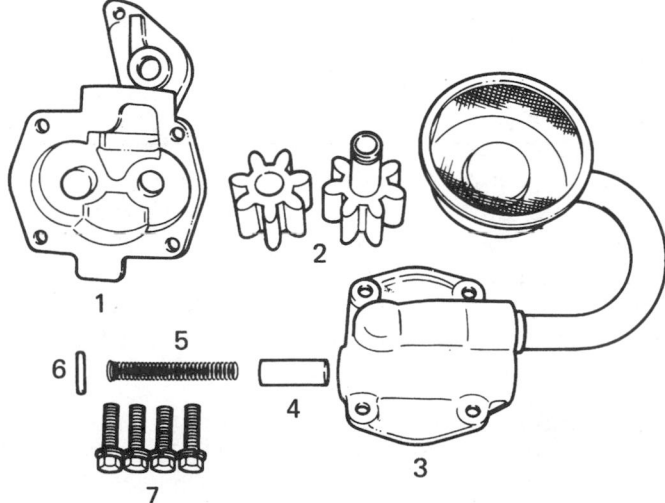

Figure 14-88. A disassembled view of a gear-type oil pump. 1—Pump body. 2—Gears. 3—Cover/pickup assembly. 4—Relief valve. 5—Relief valve spring. 6—Retaining pin. 7—Cover bolts. (Buick)

ance when used. Check clearance between gear teeth and pump body. **Figure 14-89** illustrates pump gear end clearance being checked with a straightedge and feeler gauge. A narrow feeler gauge or a dial indicator can be used to check the backlash between the two gears (.015″ or 0.38 mm maximum). Drive shaft to shaft bearing clearance should not exceed .003″ (0.08 mm).

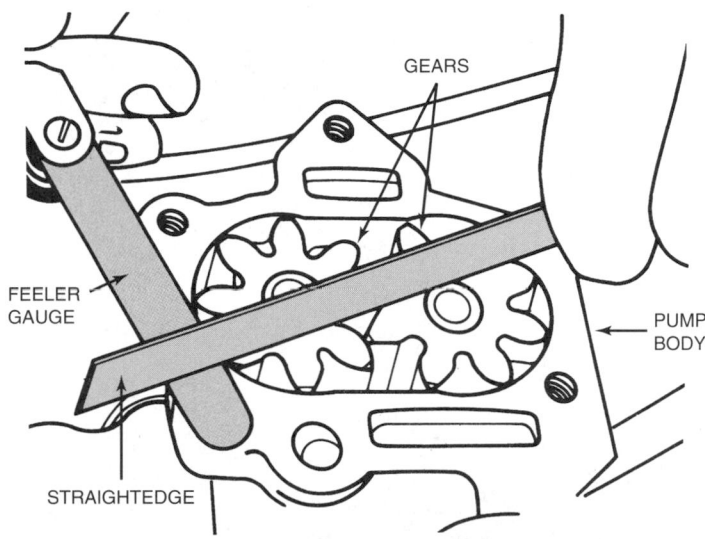

Figure 14-89. Measuring oil pump end clearance. No gasket is used during measuring on this pump. Some pumps will require a gasket to be in position when checking the clearance. (Buick)

Use a feeler gauge to check the clearance between the gear teeth (use tip of tooth) and the pump body. See **Figure 14-90.** Check the backlash between the gear teeth with a feeler gauge. It will generally measure between .002″ to .008″ (0.05 to 0.20 mm). If backlash is not within recommended limits, replace both gears as a pair, **Figure 14-91.** Check the pump cover for flatness using a straightedge and feeler gauge as shown in **Figure 14-92.** A wear depth of .002″ (0.05 mm) is generally the maximum allowable. If the cover is not within this specification, it can be sanded down on the face with 400 grit or finer sandpaper on a flat surface. Always follow manufacturer's recommendations.

After sanding the cover, polish the surface with crocus cloth to remove scratches and clean it thoroughly. Other gear pump checkpoints include gear tooth wear, scoring, and chipping. Check the pump body and cover for cracks. Also, clean and check the relief valve. End clearance between the gears and the cover plate can be checked by placing a strip of Plastigage across the face of the gears and bolting the cover in place. Without turning the gears, remove the cover and check the flattened Plastigage. See **Figure 14-93.** Another type of gear oil pump is pictured in **Figure 14-94.** You will note that it uses an internal gear driven by an external gear. This particular pump mounts directly to the engine and is driven by the crankshaft.

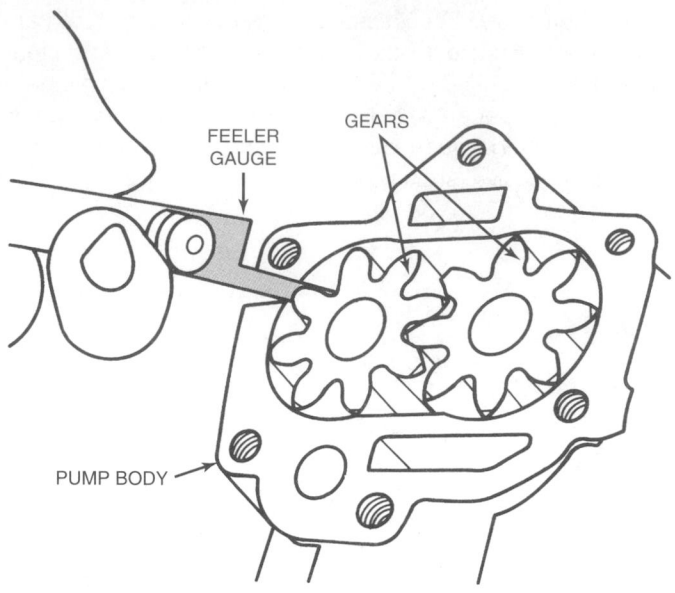

Figure 14-90. Measuring gear tooth-to-pump body clearance. (Buick)

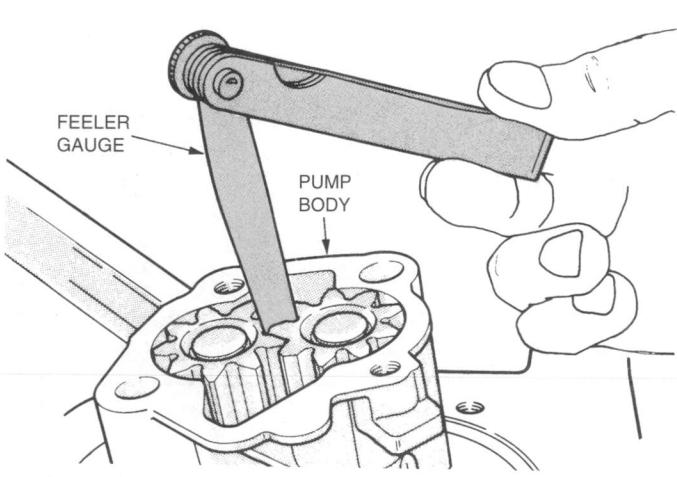

Figure 14-91. Using a feeler gauge to check gear pump tooth backlash. Excessive lash (clearance) will lower the pump output pressure. (Chrysler)

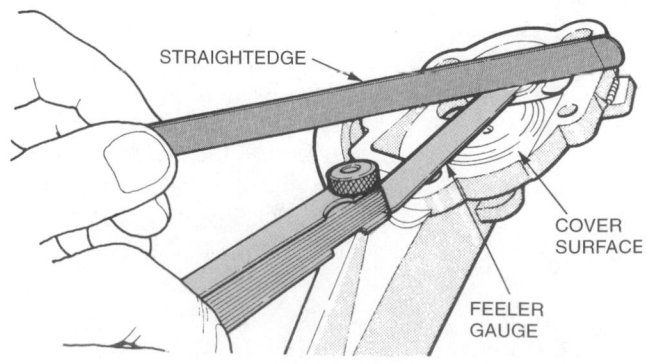

Figure 14-92. Using a steel straightedge and a proper size feeler gauge to check the oil pump cover for flatness. (Chrysler)

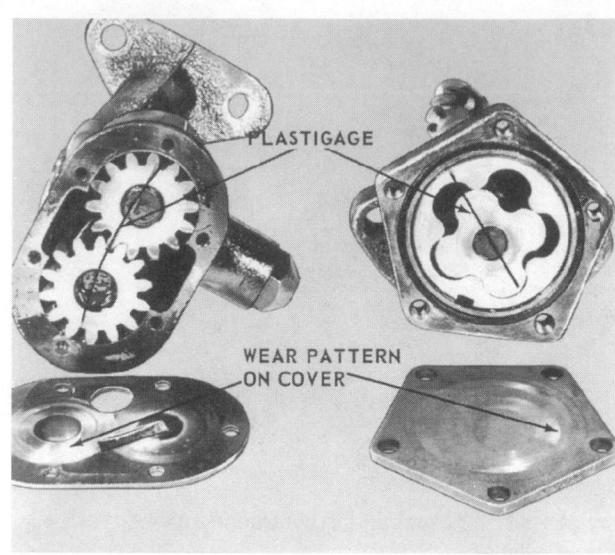

Figure 14-93. Using Plastigage to check clearance between gear or rotor units and their respective covers. (Perfect Circle)

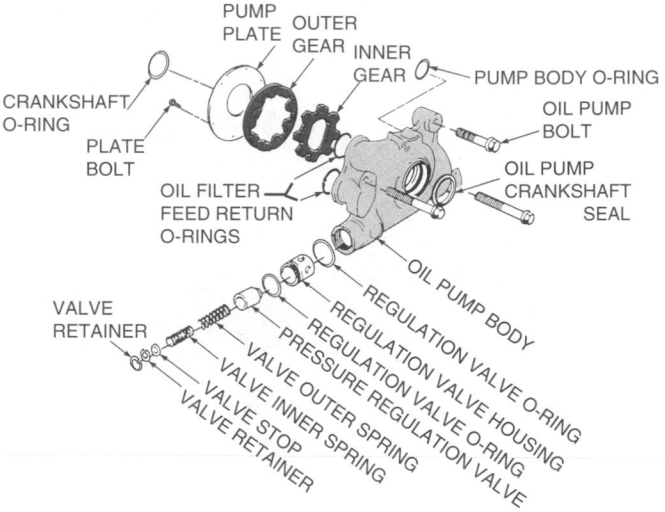

Figure 14-94. An oil pump using internal (driving) and external (driven) gear arrangement. The driving gear is rotated by the engine crankshaft. (GM)

Pump Assembly

All pump parts must be spotlessly clean. Lubricate shafts and gear or rotor. Install parts, gaskets, and tighten all fasteners. Before putting the pump into position, fill the gear or rotor cavities with engine oil. Some manufacturers recommend packing the pump with petroleum jelly (never chassis lube) to make sure it primes. If a drive gear shaft was pinned, make certain a new pin is in place and properly peened. The pump drive shaft should turn freely.

Pump Installation

Install the pump carefully. If ignition timing is affected, it will have to be reset. This is covered in Chapter 18. Clean and attach any external lines. Check pickup tube and screen positioning. Make certain the pump is firmly attached. Also check that any gaskets or seal rings are in good condition and properly positioned. See **Figure 14-95.**

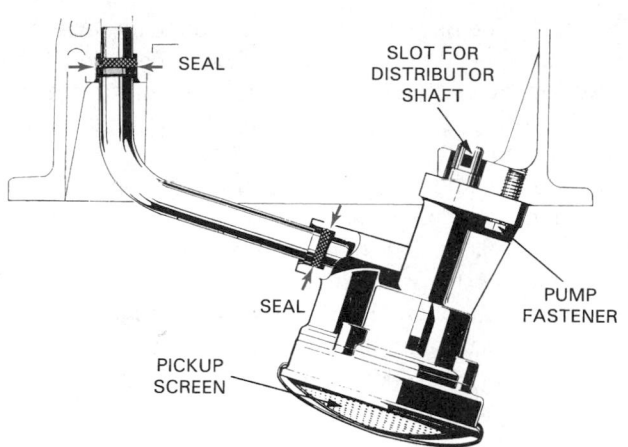

Figure 14-95.   Be careful when installing an oil pump. Make certain that all fittings, fasteners, seals, and gaskets are in good condition and properly located. If adjustable, check the pump pickup height. (Volvo)

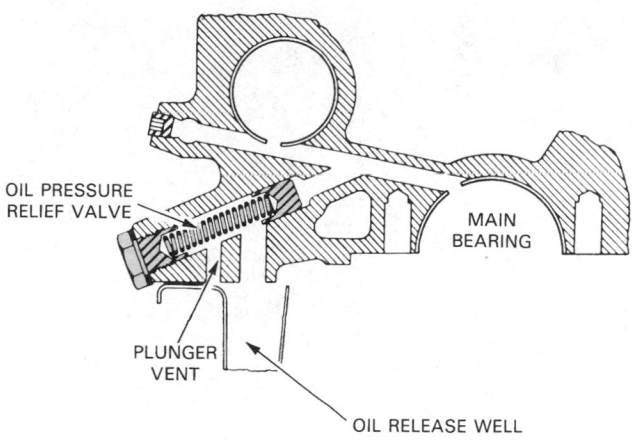

Figure 14-96.   A pressure relief valve built into the block. (Clevite)

Note: Before starting an engine following reconditioning, the lubrication system should be charged, or *primed,* with oil under pressure. The pressurizing procedure is described in Chapter 17 on engine assembly and installation. This will assist the pump in priming itself (drawing a vacuum and pulling oil from sump).

A pressure relief valve is incorporated in the lubrication system to limit maximum pressures. The valve may be part of the pump or can be built into the block. See **Figure 14-96.** The pressure relief valve should be disassembled, cleaned, and checked. Check the spring for free length (the length of the spring when not under pressure). If specified, check pressure when compressed to a specified length. Inspect the fit of the plunger valve in the bore. The plunger and bore must be free of scoring. Crocus cloth may be used to remove carbon and minor scratches from both bore and plunger. The idea is to clean and smooth the valve and bore while removing very little metal. Afterwards, thoroughly rinse, dry, lubricate, and assemble the valve. See **Figure 14-97.**

Note: Relief valve pressure control will be altered by any change in spring length, either by stretching or by adding or subtracting shims. Never stretch the spring. If it does not meet specifications, replace it.

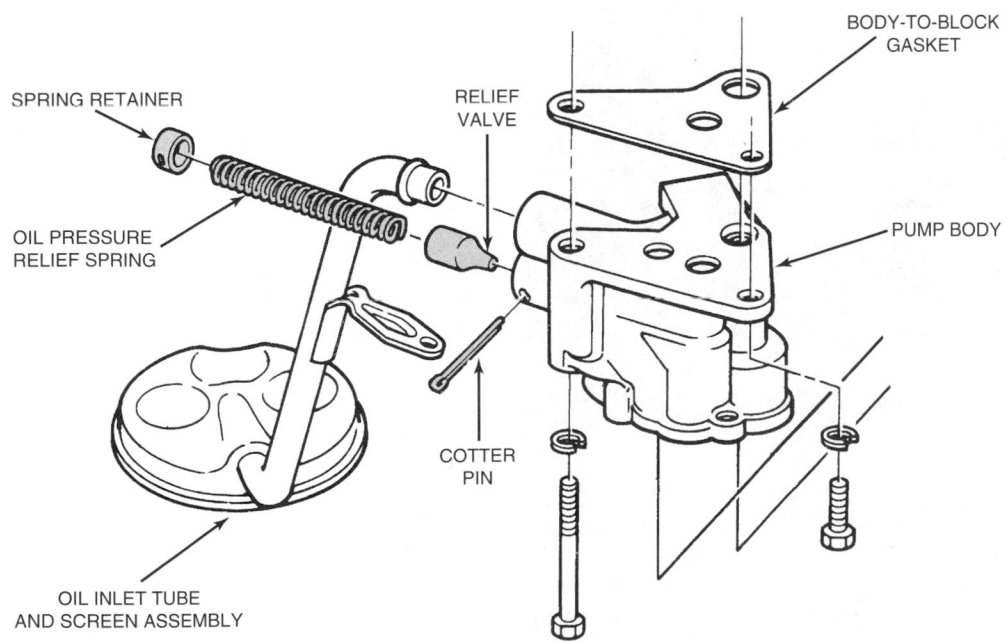

Figure 14-97.   Oil pump oil pressure relief valve parts. Parts and bore must be clean. Assemble in proper order. (Chrysler)

Tech Talk

After boring engine cylinders oversize, you will probably want to know the new engine displacement. To find the displacement of each cylinder, find the area of the cylinder by squaring the bore (multiplying the bore by itself [D^2]) and then multiplying that figure by 0.7854. This gives you the area of the cylinder. Multiply the area of the cylinder by the piston stroke, or travel from TDC to BDC. Multiply this answer by the number of cylinders to get the total engine displacement in cubic inches. The formula is stated below:

Total Displacement = D^2 × 0.7854 × Stroke × Number of Cylinders

For example, you want to find the displacement of a Chrysler 318 cubic inch (5.2 liter) V-8 engine that has been bored .030" over. Start by adding .030" to the original bore (3.91") to get a new bore of 3.94". The stroke is 3.31", so you can use the formula:

Total Displacement = D^2 × 0.7854 × Stroke × Number of Cylinders =
3.94^2 × 3.31 × 8 =
15.52 × 3.31 × 8 = 322.77 cu. in.

This makes the "318" (5.2 liter) engine into a "323" (5.4 liter) engine.

When the displacement is increased, the compression ratio is also increased. The formula for finding the exact increase in compression involves a complex series of measurements. However, a simple way to determine the approximate increase in compression is to add 2% to the compression ratio for each .030 inch increase in bore size. To make the calculation, simply add the extra percentage to 100%, which was the original compression ratio, then multiply the new percentage by the original compression. If you show the percentages as decimals (2% would be .02), the formula looks like this:

New Compression Percentage = .02 × each .030 inch bore increase + 1.00

New Compression Ratio = New Compression Percentage × Original Compression Ratio

For instance, if the 318 above had a compression ratio of 9.5 to 1, multiply 9.5 by 102%, or 1.02. This gives an approximate new compression ratio of 9.69 to 1, which can be rounded off to 9.7 to 1. If the bore had been increased by .060, the new compression ratio would be 9.5 × 1.04, which gives a new compression ratio of 9.88 to 1.

Summary

The block must be thoroughly cleaned and checked for warpage and cracks. Check camshaft and crankshaft bore sizes and alignment and measure all cylinders for size, taper, and out-of-roundness. Check each cylinder for scoring, scuffing, and cracks. A block crack can be detected by using a magnetic technique involving iron powder or fluorescent particles or by using a fluorescent or dye penetrant.

Cracks in engine blocks and heads can often be repaired by pinning. Use only tapered, threaded pins. The pins should overlap slightly and must run the full length of the crack.

Cylinder taper up to .012" (0.30 mm) and out-of-roundness not exceeding .005" (0.13 mm) should be considered maximum. Any cylinder wear beyond this point will require reboring. Cylinders should be deglazed to assist ring break-in. Cylinders should be honed with 180 or 220 grit stones to produce a 20 to 30 microinch finish. When reboring, rebore to the nearest standard oversize. Cylinders should be carefully cleaned with hot soapy water and rinsed with clear, hot water. Dry and oil at once.

Each connecting rod should be numbered on the upper and lower halves on the same side. The cylinder ring ridge must be removed before pulling the piston and rod assembly. Use rod bolt protectors to prevent damage to the crankshaft journals. Each rod must be checked for twist and bend. The large end bore must be round, straight, and smooth and of the correct size. Rods not meeting specifications must be replaced or reconditioned.

Clean pistons by soaking, then scraping. Do not use a wire brush. Use a suitable ring groove cleaner to remove carbon from the ring grooves. Oil drain holes must be clean and open. Check each piston for wear, scoring, scuffing, and cracks. A worn ring groove can be repaired by cutting it wider and installing a steel spacer. Pistons may be resized by various methods, including knurling, cold expanding, and shot peening.

Proper piston-to-cylinder fit is important. The use of a feeler gauge strip and spring scale is used to check for correct clearance. When measuring pistons, measure across the skirt at right angles to the pin. If replacing one or more pistons, pistons used for replacement should weigh the same as the others in the engine. Piston tops are generally marked so that they may be correctly installed. On some engines, pistons are not interchangeable from one cylinder bank to the other.

Before removing piston pins, determine correct relationship between the piston and rod so that they are assembled together correctly. Piston pins are retained by snap ring locks, are bolted to the piston or rod, or press-fitted to the rod. New bushings should be burnished before honing to secure them properly. Never fit pins by feel or by using a reamer. A proper fit must be determined by careful measurement. Pinholes must be straight, smooth, round, and in perfect alignment. Oversize pins should be used to remove excessive clearance from a piston and rod assembly. Honing or diamond boring are recommended. Accurate work when fitting pins is a must.

Following reconditioning, clean piston and rod assemblies in hot, soapy water and rinse, dry, and oil. Install the snap ring end locks with the open ends down. The snap ring lock fits tight in the groove. When the pin is affixed to the rod, center it carefully to prevent scoring the cylinder walls. When handling rods, do not subject them to any twisting or bending forces.

Ring sets are available in rebore (accurate cylinder) and oil control (worn cylinder) types. Rings must be of the correct size and width compatible with the cylinder. Check each ring for proper end gap, groove clearance, and groove depth. Install rings as recommended by the manufacturer. Use a ring expander if needed. Space ring gaps around the piston.

Lubricate piston pin, rings, piston, cylinder, and upper rod insert prior to installing each rod and piston assembly. Use a ring compressor and tap the piston into the cylinder. Check for proper bearing clearance, lubricate, and torque rod caps. Check for rod bearing and side clearance on the crankshaft journal.

Know These Terms

Engine block	Scuffing
Distortion	Compression rings
Oil galleries	Oil control rings
Freeze plugs	Chrome
Resurfacing	Ring gap
Block cracks	Groove depth
X-ray	Ring side clearance
Magnetic	Ring expander
Fluorescent	Piston slap
Dye penetrants	Deglazing
Pinning	Honing
Pistons	Oversize
Ring grooves	Reboring
Ring groove cleaner	Boring bars
Ring groove spacer	Cylinder sleeve
Resized	Twist
Knurled	Bend
Fit	Large end bearing bore
Piston pins	Ring compressor
Piston pin fit	Bearing clearance
Bushing	Plastigage
Burnish	Side clearance
Ring ridge	Rotor pump
Cylinder diameter	Gear pump
Taper	Pressure relief valve
Out-of round	Pump rotors
Ring float	Primed
Tipping	

Review Questions—Chapter 14

Do not write in this book. Write your answers on a separate sheet of paper.

1. If the ring ridge is not removed _____.
   (A) the rings will not seat properly
   (B) the cylinder walls will be distorted
   (C) the top ring and piston can be broken
   (D) the piston will be hard to install
2. Cylinder wear is greatest at _____.
   (A) the bottom of the ring travel
   (B) the center of the ring travel
   (C) the top of the ring travel
3. When honing worn cylinders, always_____.
   (A) hone at the top
   (B) hone at the bottom
   (C) start honing at bottom then work up the cylinder
   (D) start honing at top then work down into the cylinder

4. Before removing connecting rods, check for proper _____ on both upper and lower bore halves.
5. The crankshaft journal can be damaged by the _____ when removing or installing pistons and rods with the crankshaft installed.
   (A) ring ridge
   (B) bearing crush
   (C) bearing cap
   (D) rod bolts
6. Connecting rod large end bore elongation is corrected by _____.
   (A) honing to a suitable oversize
   (B) reducing diameter by removing stock from the parting surfaces and then honing to standard
   (C) knurling
   (D) building up with arc welding then boring to standard
7. If the crankshaft journal is .0015" (0.0381 mm) out-of-round and the rod bore is .002" (0.05 mm) out-of-round and the bearing is fitted so that the minimum clearance is .002" (0.05 mm), what would the maximum clearance be?
8. Heavy score marks on pistons require:
   (A) scrapping the pistons.
   (B) filing to remove marks.
   (C) knurling.
9. Pistons are often fitted to the cylinders by using a _____ and a spring scale.
10. A typical pin fit in an aluminum piston would have the following clearance:
    (A) .002" to .004" (0.05 to 0.10 mm).
    (B) .0002" to .0005" (0.0051 to 0.0127 mm).
    (C) .020" to .0205" (0.51 to 0.5207 mm).
    (D) .006" to .010" (0.15 to 0.25 mm).
11. Pinholes are best reconditioned by careful reaming. True or False?
12. After installing a pin bushing, but before fitting, it should be _____.
13. Piston pinholes must be _____ and of the correct diameter.
    (A) round
    (B) straight
    (C) smooth
    (D) All of the above.
14. The clearance between the ends of the ring when installed in the cylinder is referred to as _____.
15. Normally, .020" (0.51 mm) oversize rings will function in cylinders _____.
    (A) standard to .020" (0.51 mm) over
    (B) .010" to .030" (0.25 to 0.76 mm) over
    (C) .020" (0.51 mm) over
    (D) .020" to .040" (0.51 to 1.01 mm) over
16. Taper face rings should be installed so that the widest edge faces _____.
17. Rings should be checked for _____ gap, side _____, and proper size.
18. It is necessary to use a ring _____ to install the piston and rod assemblies.

19. Most oversize pistons will have the amount of oversize stamped on the _____ of the piston.
20. Connecting rod bearing to crankshaft journal clearance is best determined by using _____.

ASE-Type Questions

1. Cylinder block and cylinder head mating surfaces are _____.
   (A) never warped
   (B) seldom warped
   (C) often warped
   (D) always warped
2. Technician A says that the ring ridge should not be completely removed. Technician B says that, when removing the ring ridge, one should undercut into the cylinder wall. Who is right?
   (A) A only.
   (B) B only.
   (C) Both A & B.
   (D) Neither A nor B.
3. All of the following statements about cylinder wall taper are true, EXCEPT:
   (A) taper is the difference between the diameter at the top of the cylinder and the diameter at the bottom of the ring travel.
   (B) the ring ridge is still at the original (factory) diameter of the cylinder.
   (C) if the taper is more than .006″ (0.15 mm), the cylinder must be rebored.
   (D) the cylinder wears more at the top than the bottom.
4. Technician A says that cylinders must be deglazed or honed before installing new piston rings. Technician B says that cylinders should not be honed following reboring. Who is right?
   (A) A only.
   (B) B only.
   (C) Both A & B.
   (D) Neither A nor B.
5. Technician A says that worn cylinders must be honed until all of the glazed surface is removed. Technician B says that a reconditioned cylinder should be cleaned first by wiping with an oily rag. Who is right?
   (A) A only.
   (B) B only.
   (C) Both A & B.
   (D) Neither A nor B.
6. Technician A says that rods can become bent or twisted in normal service. Technician B says that rod bend and rod twist are best removed by heating. Who is right?
   (A) A only.
   (B) B only.
   (C) Both A & B.
   (D) Neither A nor B.

7. All of the following statements about worn pistons are true, EXCEPT:
   (A) worn piston pin bores in the rod or piston can be restored by knurling to expand the pin.
   (B) cracked pistons should be discarded.
   (C) slightly worn pistons can be resized.
   (D) proper oversize pistons must be used with a rebored cylinder.
8. Technician A says that the ends of the oil ring expanders must be lapped over each other. Technician B says that the gaps on all rings must be in a straight line. Who is right?
   (A) A only.
   (B) B only.
   (C) Both A & B.
   (D) Neither A nor B.
9. Technician A says that the lower piston ring groove contains the compression ring. Technician B says that the oil rings should be installed first. Who is right?
   (A) A only.
   (B) B only.
   (C) Both A & B.
   (D) Neither A nor B.
10. Technician A says that pistons are always interchangeable from one bank of a V-type engine to the other. Technician B says that pistons are always interchangeable between cylinders on any one bank. Who is right?
    (A) A only.
    (B) B only.
    (C) Both A & B.
    (D) Neither A nor B.

Suggested Activities

1. Obtain a used engine block and measure all of the cylinders for wear. Be sure to record your measurements.
2. Using a flat rate manual, calculate the labor time to bore one cylinder oversize. Discuss your price calculation with the members of your class.
3. Using a block that must be bored, set up the boring bar, make the cut(s), and take final measurements. Record your answers and calculate the new displacement of the engine.

15

Crankshaft Service

After studying this chapter, you will be able to:
- Remove and install a crankshaft.
- Check crankshaft and main bearing bores for problems.
- Install new main bearing inserts and rear seal.
- Measure main bearing clearance and crankshaft end play.

This chapter covers crankshaft, bearing, and seal service. Crankshaft removal, inspection, and repair procedures are presented in detail. Measuring bearing clearances and crankshaft end play is covered. Information on main bearing oil seal service is also included.

Removing the Crankshaft

The first step in removing a crankshaft is to remove the oil pan from the engine. Then, pull the vibration damper. Remove the front cover and then remove the timing belt or chain and the timing gears. Next, remove the piston and rod assemblies. When necessary, remove the oil pump, oil lines, and front engine plate. (See Chapter 16 for more information on camshaft, gear, and chain or belt service.)

Mark Caps before Removal

Before removing the main bearing caps, mark each cap and the corresponding crankcase web with a prick punch or a number stamp. Place the cap and web marks on the same side of the engine. Never mark on the top of the cap. Use a heavy section near one side to prevent distortion. One particular engine incorporates the use of a one-piece main bearing cap that has the five individual insert areas machined out. This is shown in **Figure 15-1.**

Main Bearing Cap Removal

To remove the main bearing caps, remove any locking devices and crack each cap bolt loose. Remove all cap screws while watching for variations in diameter and length. If main bearing cap cross bolts are used, remove them *before* removing the cap bolts. Do not misplace the cross bolt crankshaft-to-cap spacers. Keep them in the proper order, **Figure 15-2.** After all bolts are removed, carefully pry the caps free. Light tapping with a plastic or rawhide hammer will help. Some caps must be removed with a special puller.

Caution: Never pound on the caps or use a pry bar between the crank journal and the cap bore. The caps may look sturdy, but they can be damaged easily.

Lifting the Crankshaft from the Crankcase

After removing the bearing caps, lift the crankshaft straight up, being careful to avoid damage to journal or thrust surfaces. If the crank is too heavy to handle by hand, use a sling and lift. **Figure 15-3** shows a crankshaft being lifted from a crankcase.

Note

The maximum acceptable limit figures given in this chapter for bore alignment, bore out-of-roundness, shaft alignment, journal taper, and journal out-of-roundness are fairly small. Some manufacturers' specifications will call for even smaller limits. Some sources allow more. The technician must use a great deal of discretion when deciding what the acceptable limits are for the engine at hand. If the car is old and of little value, or if the owner only wants to "get by" for a short while, some technicians feel these limits can be extended. Type of engine, use, and driving needs of the owner are also important factors.

Always give the owner an accurate appraisal of the engine's condition and explain just what is needed for a proper repair. Carefully explain how service life is shortened, how engine efficiency is lowered, and how part failure can occur if limits are overextended.

Many shops refuse to do any work that is not up to high standards. Others will perform the work, but only after a written agreement with the customer in which the hazards are set forth. No guarantee is given.

Check Main Bearing Bores

After removing the crankshaft, remove all the bearing inserts and mark them for study. Clean the web, cap bore, and parting surfaces. Reinstall and torque all bearing caps. Using an inside micrometer, carefully check the bores for distortion (out-of-roundness). Distortion greater than approximately .0015″ (0.0381 mm) will require correction in one of two ways. In the first correction method, undersize,

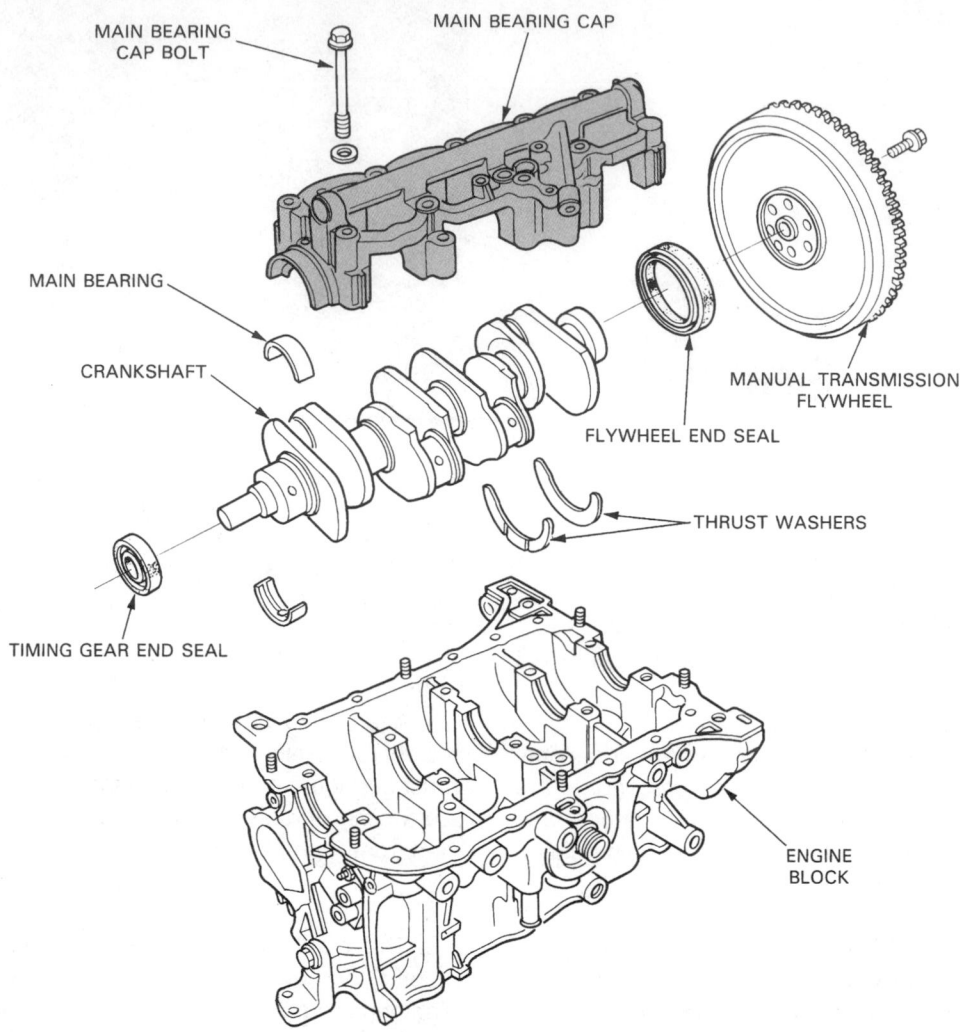

MAIN BEARING CAP BOLT

MAIN BEARING CAP

MAIN BEARING

CRANKSHAFT

TIMING GEAR END SEAL

MANUAL TRANSMISSION FLYWHEEL

FLYWHEEL END SEAL

THRUST WASHERS

ENGINE BLOCK

Figure 15-1.   This engine uses a one-piece main bearing cap. It houses machined areas for individual inserts. (Honda)

semifinished inserts can be installed and align bored. In the second method, material can be ground from the cap parting edges. The caps are then replaced, torqued, and align bored to their original specifications. The latter technique is preferred because it allows standard size precision inserts to be used. Any future work on the crankshaft bearings will also be facilitated.

If the individual main bearing bores are acceptable, they must then be checked for alignment. A study of the bearing inserts will indicate bore misalignment. Wiping wear of the bearing insert surfaces will usually be more evident at the center mains and will diminish toward both ends of the crank.

An aligning bar that is about .001" (0.025 mm) smaller than bore specifications may be placed in the main bores. The parting surfaces and bores must be clean, and the caps must be torqued. The bar should turn by hand using a bar or wrench with a handle of 12" (304.8 mm) or less in length. If you cannot turn the bar, the bores are out of alignment. Make sure no caps were reversed. Alignment can also be checked by placing an accurate straightedge across the bores. Keep the straightedge parallel to the

bore centerline. Check in several different positions. If a .0015" (0.0381 mm) feeler can be inserted between the straightedge and any bore, alignment must be corrected. Removal of material from the cap parting surfaces and align boring is the preferred method of correction. Remember, proper clearance between the inserts and journals requires round bores that are in proper alignment.

Cleaning the Crankshaft

Before performing any service, the crankshaft must be thoroughly cleaned. Use a rifle brush to clean the oil channels, **Figure 15-4.** Flush all passages and blow them dry with air. Lightly oil all journal surfaces immediately after drying.

Check Main and Rod Journals for Finish and Accuracy

Place the crankshaft on a pair of smooth, clean, oiled V-blocks. If the blocks are not absolutely smooth, cover the V's with thin, hard paper. Turn the shaft slowly and visually check each journal for signs of scratching, ridging, scoring, or nicks. You will often note a dark line around the journal.

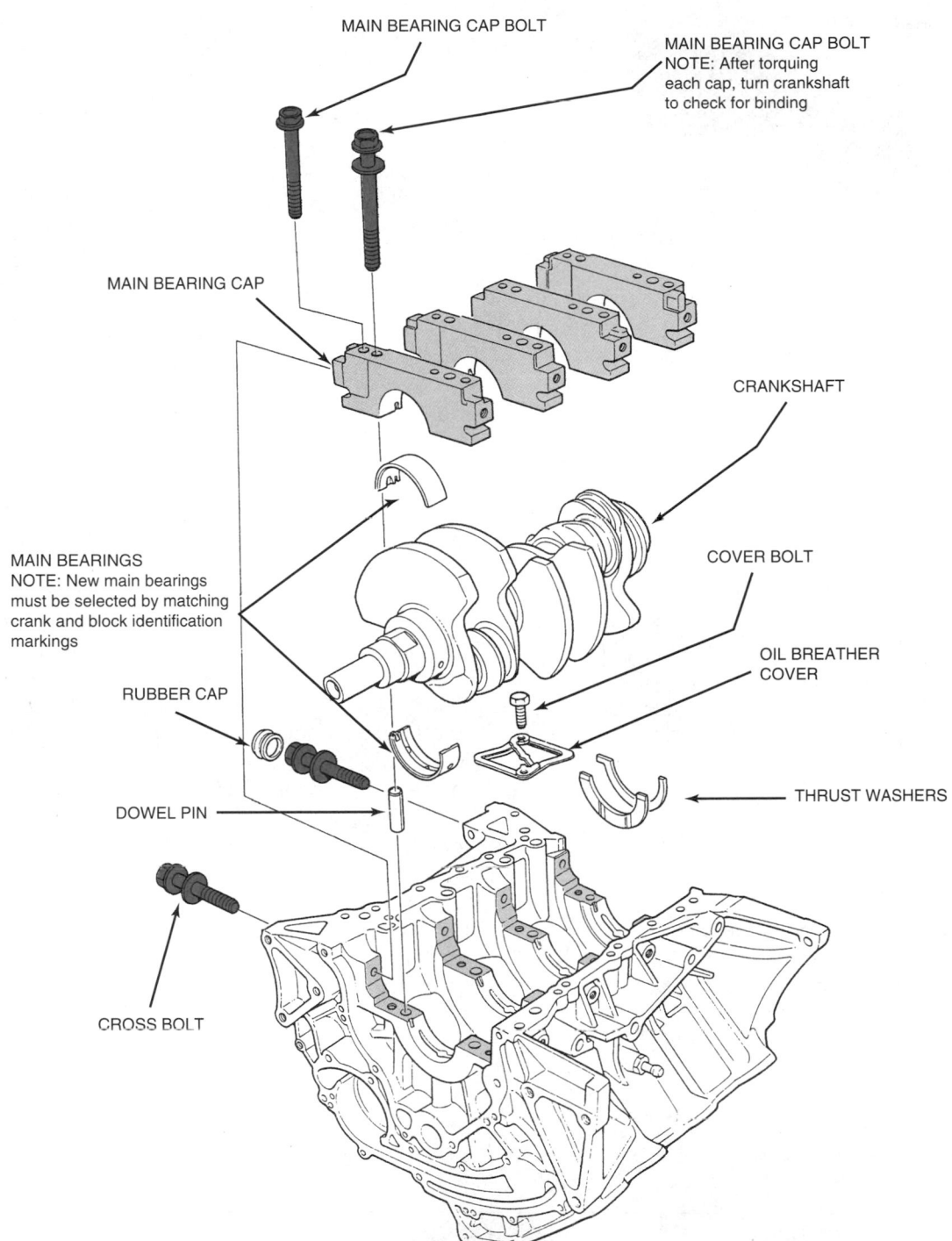

MAIN BEARING CAP BOLT

MAIN BEARING CAP BOLT
NOTE: After torquing
each cap, turn crankshaft
to check for binding

MAIN BEARING CAP

CRANKSHAFT

MAIN BEARINGS
NOTE: New main bearings
must be selected by matching
crank and block identification
markings

COVER BOLT

RUBBER CAP

OIL BREATHER
COVER

DOWEL PIN

THRUST WASHERS

CROSS BOLT

Figure 15-2. Note the use of main bearing cross bolts in this engine. (Honda)

This is caused by the oil groove in the insert and is not harmful unless it protrudes more than .0003-.0004″ (0.0076-0.0102 mm) from the surface of the journal. This dark line should be polished with crocus cloth (extremely fine abrasive) to remove any accumulated carbon or gum.

Crocus cloth can also be used to remove any small burrs caused by tiny nicks or scratches. Pull the cloth around the journal in a "shoe shine" motion. By keeping the cloth pulled around half of the journal, the polishing will not produce flat spots.

All journals must be absolutely smooth. Any roughness, ridging, or scoring must be ground smooth. The shaft in **Figure 15-5** is badly scored.

If the journal surfaces are in good shape, they must then be checked for *out-of-roundness, taper,* and *wear.* Measurements should be taken near one end of the journal in several spots around the diameter. Be careful to keep off the corner fillet radius. Write down each measurement. Repeat this process near the other end of the journal, **Figure 15-6.**

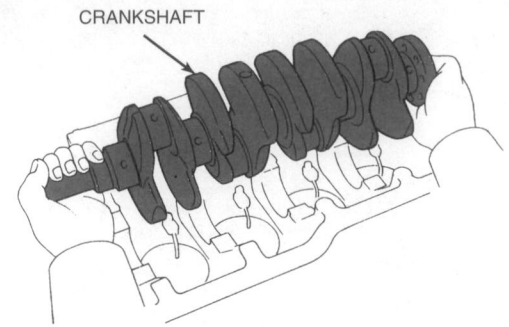

Figure 15-3. Removing a crankshaft by hand. Be careful! If the crankshaft is too heavy, use a lift and a sling. (Toyota)

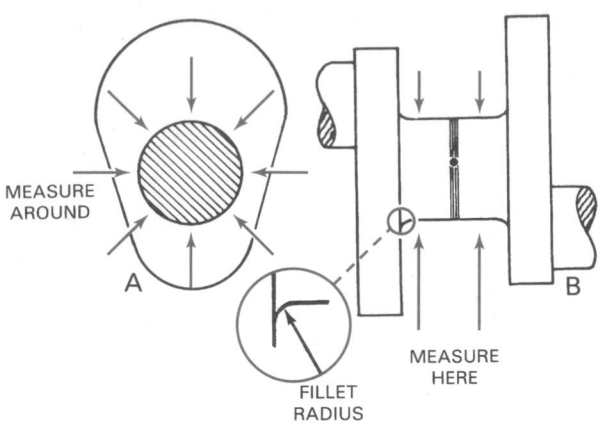

Figure 15-6. A—End cross-sectional view of a journal. B—Side view of a journal. Make measurements as indicated.

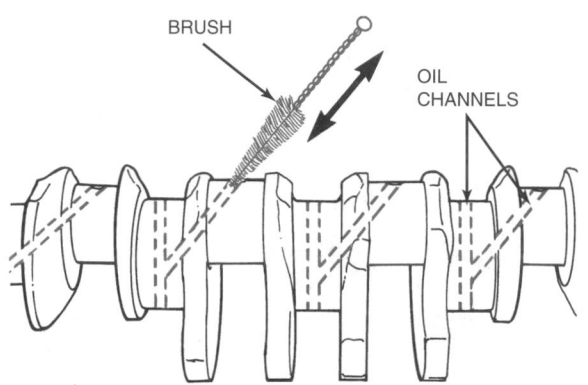

Figure 15-4. Using a rifle-type brush to clean out the oil channel in a crankshaft. (Cummins Engine Co.)

Out-of-Roundness, Taper, and Undersize

The measurements performed in **Figure 15-6** will determine three important points: out-of-roundness, taper, and undersize.

Out-of-roundness will be computed by figuring the difference in diameter measurements at various points. Out-of-roundness must not exceed .001″ (0.025 mm). **Figure 15-7** illustrates three journals—one within limits (would accept a standard size insert), one requiring grinding, and one within limits but worn .001″ (0.025 mm) undersize.

You will note that the journal in **Figure 15-7A** is only .0003″ (0.0076 mm) out-of-round and has worn a mere .0001″ (0.025 mm). Providing the taper is within limits, this journal will be satisfactory. If a new insert is required (it pays to use new inserts), a standard size is required.

In **Figure 15-7B,** the journal is .003″ (0.08 mm) out-of-round and has worn a maximum of .001″ (0.025 mm). This journal is unfit for service and should be reground.

In **Figure 15-7C,** the journal is only .0002″ (0.0058 mm) out-of-round, but has worn an even .001″ (0.025 mm). If the taper is satisfactory, this journal can still be used but will require a .001″ (0.025 mm) *undersize* insert.

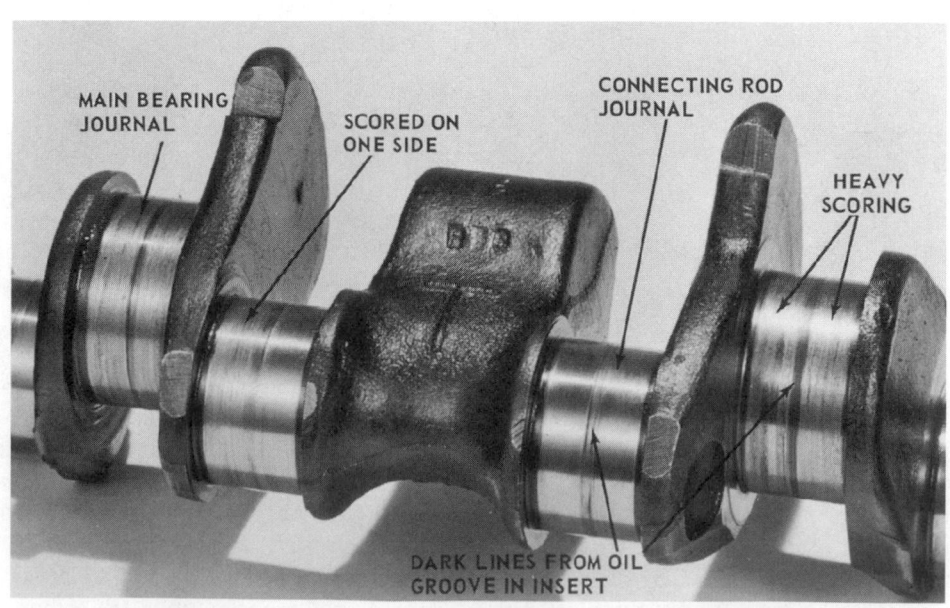

Figure 15-5. The journals on this crankshaft are badly scored. The shaft must be reground. (Clevite)

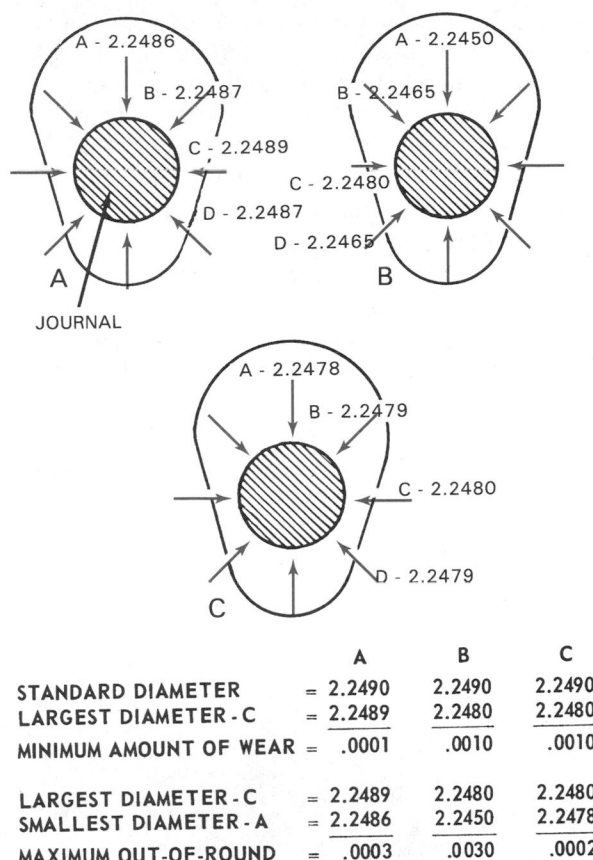

Figure 15-7. End cross-sectional view of three journals. A—Acceptable for a standard insert. B—Must be reground. C—Acceptable, but requires a .001″ (0.025 mm) undersize insert.

	A	B	C
STANDARD DIAMETER	= 2.2490	2.2490	2.2490
LARGEST DIAMETER - C	= 2.2489	2.2480	2.2480
MINIMUM AMOUNT OF WEAR	= .0001	.0010	.0010
LARGEST DIAMETER - C	= 2.2489	2.2480	2.2480
SMALLEST DIAMETER - A	= 2.2486	2.2450	2.2478
MAXIMUM OUT-OF-ROUND	= .0003	.0030	.0002

Selecting Correct Undersize Insert

When journal wear is minor and the journal out-of-roundness and taper are within limits, the proper oil clearance can often be maintained by installing .001″ or .002″ (0.025 or 0.05 mm) undersize inserts. When determining the correct undersize, always use the largest journal measurement. If the smallest measurement or an average of all measurements, is used, there could be insufficient oil clearance and the bearings will quickly fail. If the largest measurement indicates the journal has worn .0005″ (0.0127 mm) below standard, no undersize is required. For wear from .001″ to .0019″ (0.025 to 0.0482 mm), a .001″ (0.025 mm) undersize is needed. For wear from .002″ to .003″ (0.050 to 0.08 mm), a .002″ (0.050 mm) undersize will suffice. For wear much above .003″ (0.080 mm) a .002″ (0.050 mm) undersize will not bring the oil clearance within limits. An average oil clearance would be about .001″ (0.025 mm) for each inch (25.4 mm) of journal diameter in pressure lubricated systems. Bearing material, engine design, and RPM all affect the amount of clearance required, so *always* check the manufacturer's specs.

Taper

By computing the difference in diameter readings between both ends of the journal, the amount of taper can be determined. Taper should not exceed .001″ (0.025 mm). In **Figure 15-8A,** the journal taper is .0002″ (0.0051 mm) and thus is acceptable. The journal in **Figure 15-8B** shows a taper of .003″ (0.08 mm) and therefore must be reground.

Connecting rod journals tend to wear more out-of-round and tapered than the main bearing journals. This is basically due to the fluctuating load that places certain areas of the journal under heavy, sudden stresses. Rod twist and bend exert uneven edge loading, which tends to taper the journal.

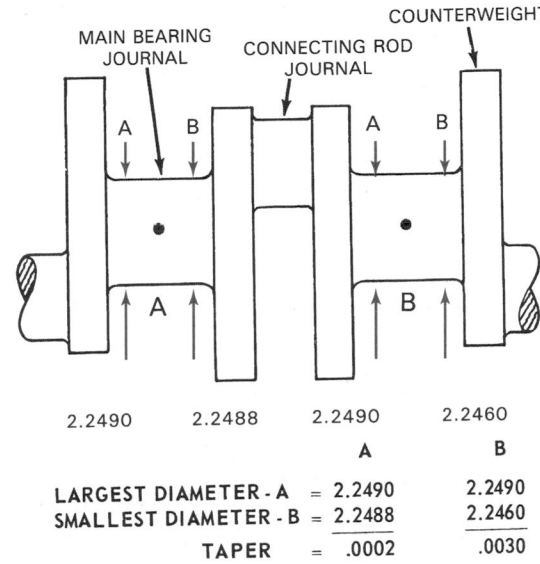

LARGEST DIAMETER - A	= 2.2490	2.2490
SMALLEST DIAMETER - B	= 2.2488	2.2460
TAPER	= .0002	.0030

Figure 15-8. Journal A has only .0002″ (0.0051 mm) taper and is acceptable. Journal B shows a taper of .003″ (0.08 mm) and must be reground.

Crankshaft Alignment

Even though the journals are smooth and within limits, bearing life will be greatly shortened if the crankshaft is out of alignment.

Check the shaft by placing both end journals on a set of V-blocks, **Figure 15-9A.** Adjust a dial indicator to the center or intermediate mains. Turn the shaft and record the amount of runout. Check each main journal. To record the end journals, move a V-block in to the intermediate main.

On long shafts, it may be necessary to support the shaft at the intermediate journals to prevent sag. *Average maximum misalignment (consult manufacturer's specs) should be held to .001″ (0.025 mm) between journals and .002″ (0.050 mm) overall.* Remember that any journal out-of-roundness must be taken into consideration, as it will affect the indicator reading.

If the crankshaft is only slightly out of alignment, it may be possible to straighten it. This can be done by either cold bending or bending with pressure and heat. In some cases, the application of heat alone will cause the crankshaft to straighten. In general, forged steel crankshafts will allow a greater degree of straightening than the cast iron or nodular iron types. **Figure 15-9B,** illustrates one type of straightening tool.

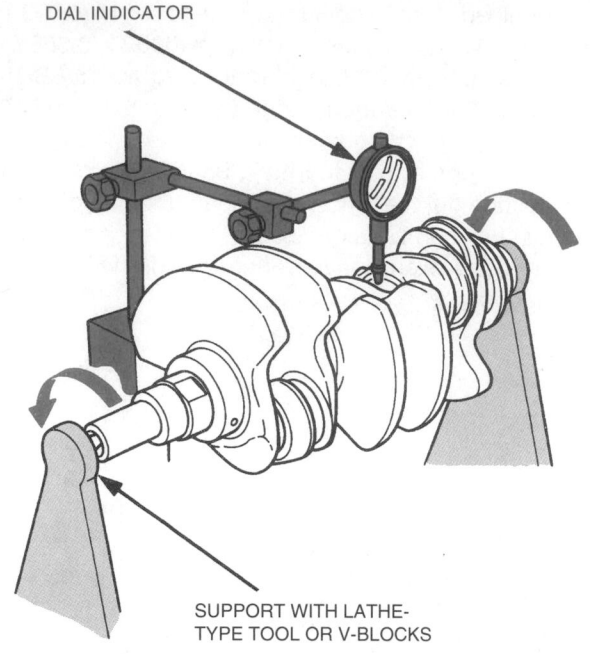

DIAL INDICATOR

SUPPORT WITH LATHE-
TYPE TOOL OR V-BLOCKS

A

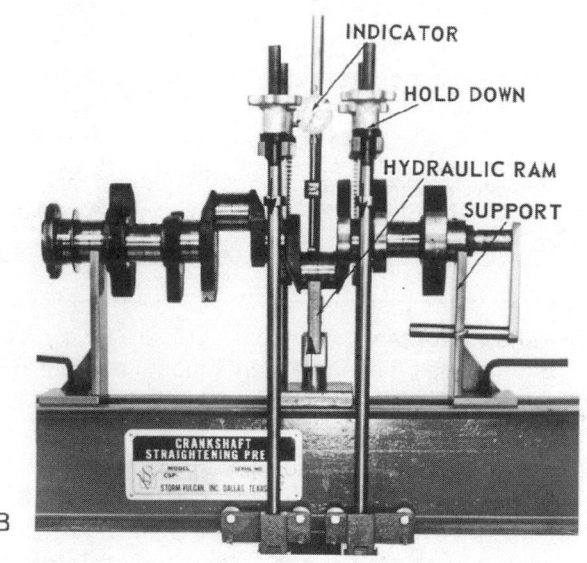

INDICATOR

HOLD DOWN

HYDRAULIC RAM

SUPPORT

B

Figure 15-9. A—Using a dial indicator and V-blocks to check crankshaft alignment or straightness. B—Straightening a crankshaft in a special press. (Honda, Clevite)

Regrinding a Crankshaft

Crankshaft regrinding is a specialty operation. Most auto shops do not have the necessary heavy equipment. They send, or "farm out," such jobs as crankshaft and camshaft grinding, reboring, align boring, and shaft straightening to machine shops.

Crankshaft grinding requires accurate machinery and a skilled operator. Tolerances must be held to close limits and finishes must be extremely smooth (16 micro inch or

smoother). The shaft is cleaned, checked for alignment, and if necessary, straightened. It is then set up in the grinder, and the journals are ground to a suitable undersize.

The journal showing the most wear is miked. The amount of material to be removed to "clean it up" is determined. Material may be removed in multiples of .010″ (0.25 mm). All other related journals are then ground to the same undersize. **Figure 15-10** shows a crankshaft set up for grinding. Note the graduated cross slides for offsetting shafts the proper amount.

The amount of material that can be safely removed from the journals depends on a number of considerations. Shaft material, size, engine HP, RPM, and operating conditions all enter into the picture. Grinding to .010″, .020″, or .030″ (0.25, 0.51, 0.75 mm) undersize is commonly done. Some shafts will stand .040″ (1.01 mm) or more. The machine operator must maintain the same fillet radius at each corner of the journal.

CHUCK   GRINDING WHEEL   CRANKSHAFT

Figure 15-10. Regrinding a crankshaft. (Federal-Mogul)

Crankshaft Welding, Spraying, and Plating

If one journal is damaged so badly that excessive undersize would result from grinding, the journal can be built up by spraying it with molten steel or by welding continuous arc weld beads around it, **Figure 15-11.** Regardless of the method employed, the journal is built up above its original diameter and then ground to the desired size. Journals can also be built up a certain amount by electroplating with hard chromium.

Polishing the Journals

A properly ground shaft may look smooth, but in reality, the surface has thousands of tiny, sharp edges. Following grinding, the journals should be for **polished** to remove these abrasive edges. Each fillet radius and shaft thrust surface should also be polished. A good polishing operation will produce an extremely smooth surface—7 micro inches or smoother (a 16 micro-inch finish is satisfactory). The operator in **Figure 15-12** is polishing a crankshaft.

Figure 15-11. This damaged journal has been built up by arc welding. The journal will be ground to the proper size. (Storm-Vulcan)

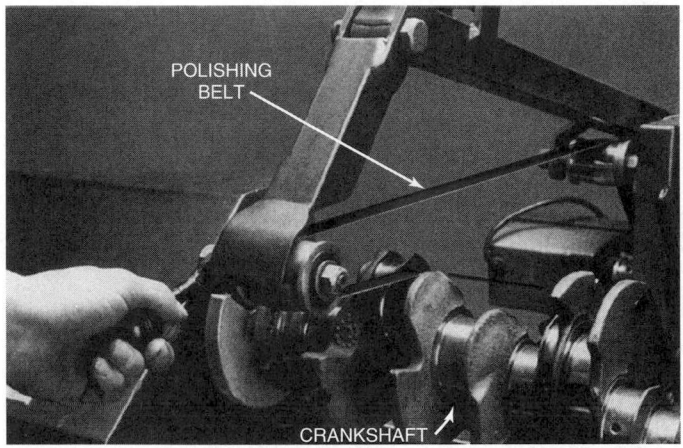

Figure 15-12. This technician is polishing the crankshaft journals. Wear safety glasses. (Dana Corp.)

Checking the Crankshaft for Cracking

It is good practice to visually inspect the crankshaft for signs of cracking. Many shops use a special penetrating dye or a magnetic process to check for cracking. (See Chapter 14 for more information on crack detection.)

Cleaning and Storage

After grinding and polishing, the crankshaft should be thoroughly cleaned and oiled. It should then be covered until it is ready to use. If the shaft is to be stored for some time, stand it on end or support it in several spots. If the shaft is allowed to sag during storage, it can take on a permanent set (bend), throwing it out of alignment.

Main Bearing Insert Installation

Bearing inserts must be of the correct size, design, and material. The block, oil galleries, and bearing bores must be spotlessly clean. **Figure 15-13** illustrates a set of typical main bearing inserts for use in a V-6 engine. Note that only the upper halves are drilled for oil entry.

On some crankshafts, all mains are of the same size. Other shafts are designed so that the front main is the

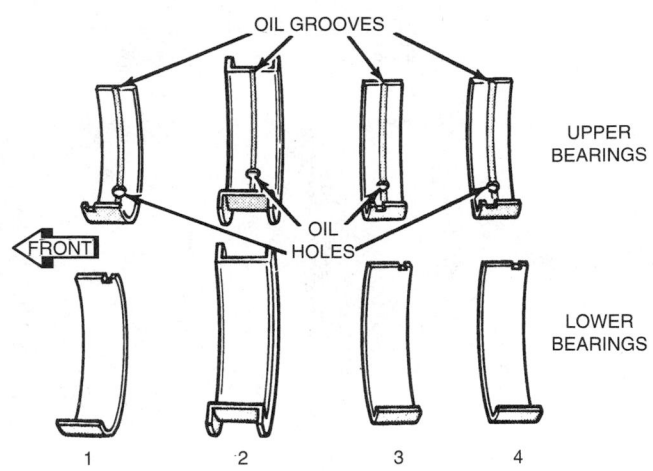

Figure 15-13. A set of main bearing inserts. Note that only the upper halves are drilled for oil entry. (Chrysler)

smallest, with a gradual increase in size from front to back. If an engine uses the latter type, the inserts are not interchangeable. Look at **Figure 15-14.**

Working on one bearing at a time, install the proper inserts. Bearing bores and insert backs must be clean and dry. The inserts should snap into place. The *locating lugs* should fit the recesses properly, and the correct amount of crush should be evident. The bearing half that is drilled for oil entry must be placed in the upper, or crankcase, bore. Check each insert to be sure the oil hole aligns with the oil passageway. Some front main inserts are designed to

MAIN JOURNAL CODE LOCATIONS (NUMBERS OR BARS)

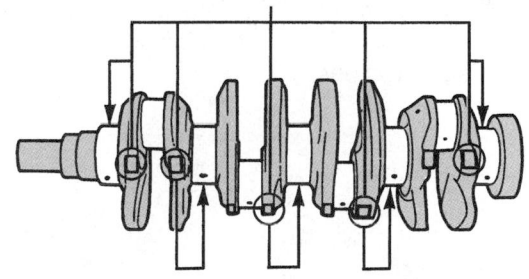

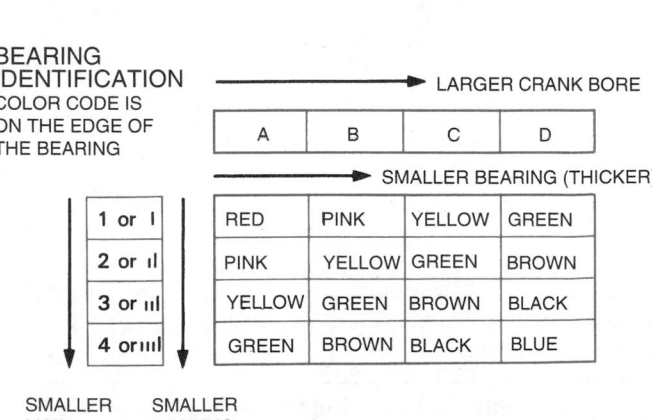

Figure 15-14. Crankshaft and bearing identification color code and size chart. (Honda)

facilitate timing chain lubrication. In such cases, make certain they are properly located. See **Figure 15-15**.

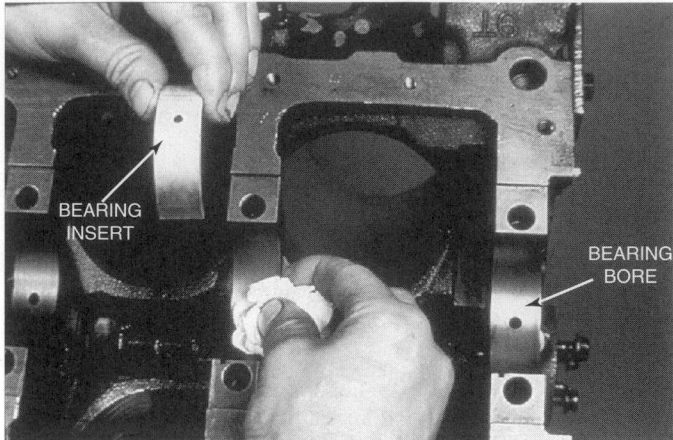

Figure 15-15. Installing an upper main bearing insert. (Federal-Mogul)

Checking Bearing Clearance

Wipe a thin film of clean engine oil over the surface of all upper inserts. The rear main oil seal is left out at this time. It tends to hold the shaft away from the bearing surface when checking clearance. Carefully lower the crankshaft into position. Be careful to avoid damage to the thrust bearing flange surfaces. Rotate the shaft several times to seat the journals.

Using a clean cloth, wipe off the exposed surface of each journal. Place a length of Plastigage® across each journal, about 1/4″ (6.35 mm) from top center. The Plastigage should span the width of the insert. Do not place it across an oil hole, **Figure 15-16**. Then install the caps and torque them to specifications.

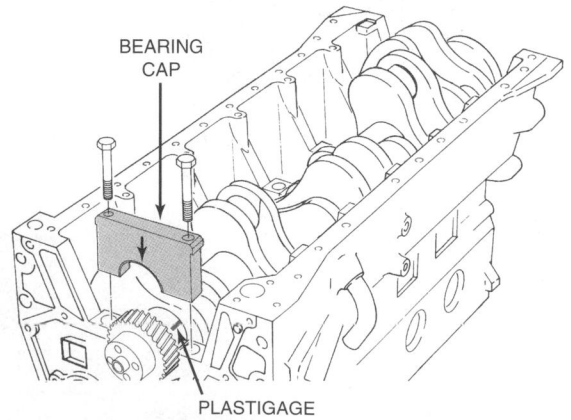

Figure 15-16. Placing Plastigage on a journal. It is placed slightly to one side of top center. (Cummins Engine Co.)

 Caution: Do not rotate the shaft until you are finished with the clearance check, as the Plastigage will be smeared.

Remove each cap. Check the width of the Plastigage with the paper scale. Slide the scale over the flattened

Plastigage until you find the marked band that is closest to the width of the Plastigage. The number on the band will indicate the bearing clearance in thousandths of an inch. All bearings should show specified clearance, **Figure 15-17**.

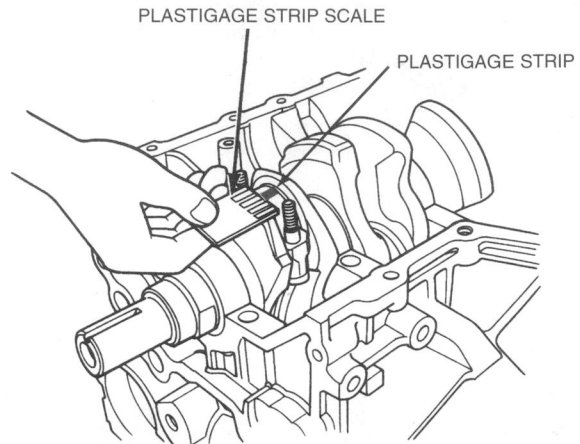

Figure 15-17. Checking a flattened Plastigage to determine clearance. (Honda)

If there is a variation in the width of the flattened Plastigage (from one side of the journal to the other), taper is present. The difference between the widest and narrowest section would determine the amount of taper. After determining clearance and taper, wipe off the Plastigage and remove the shaft.

Rear Main Bearing Oil Seals

There are two common materials used for main bearing oil seals: *graphite impregnated wick* and *synthetic rubber.*

Proper Oil Seal Installation Is Important

A number of different designs are used to seal the rear main bearing against the passage of oil. Regardless of design, this is one operation that must be done with care. Far too often, this job is done in a haphazard manner. Basically, oil can find its way into the flywheel housing by passing along the shaft, through the rear main parting surfaces, along the rear main cap edges (in some applications), and in one design, through the crankshaft flywheel flange bolt holes. When installing the seal, give some thought to the basic setup and just how it prevents oil leakage.

Wick Seals

If properly installed, the for *wick seal* will do a good job of preventing oil leakage. It is good practice to soak the seal in engine oil for 30 minutes before installation. Clean out the seal groove in the cap and crankcase bore. Lay one section of wicking over the groove in the upper bore. Starting in the center, press the seal fully into the groove. Work up each side by pressing *in* and *down* to bottom the seal. When almost seated (an equal amount should protrude above each parting surface), place an installing tool against the seal and tap the seal into place. Refer to **Figure 15-18**.

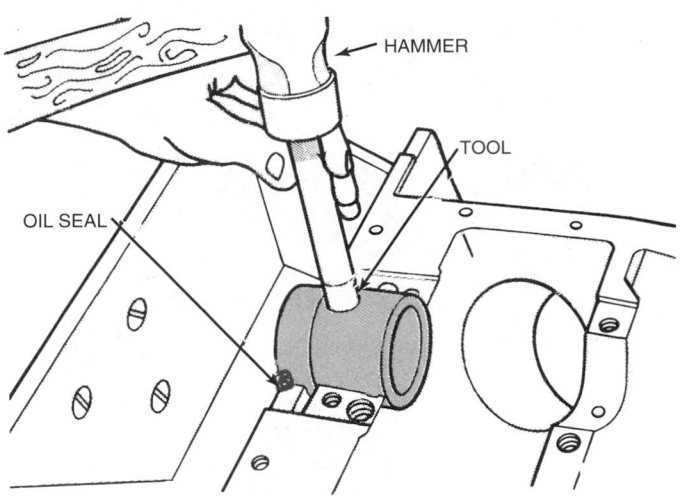

Figure 15-18. Using a special installing tool to seat a rear main upper oil seal. (Dodge)

If an installing tool is not available, a smooth, round bar or a large socket may be used.

When the seal is fully seated, keep the installing tool in place. Using a sharp knife or razor blade, cut off the protruding seal ends flush with the parting surfaces. Make certain no loose ends of seal material are left that could jam between the parting edges and prevent the cap from seating. See **Figure 15-19.**

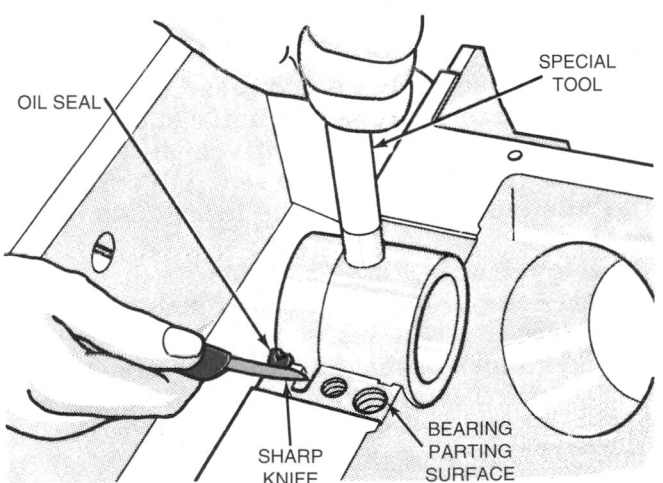

Figure 15-19. Trimming seal ends flush with the parting surface. The soft bumper protects the knife edge as it passes through the seal. (Dodge)

Install the seal wicking in the cap. Seat the seal in the center of the cap and work the seal down and in toward the bottom, **Figure 15-20.** When the seal is fully seated, hold the installing tool against the seal opposite the parting edge and trim the seal flush.

Synthetic Seals

Instead of the wick-type seal just discussed, a number of engines employ synthetic (neoprene) main bearing seals. **Figure 15-21** illustrates the procedure for removing a ***split-type (two piece) synthetic rear main bearing seal.***

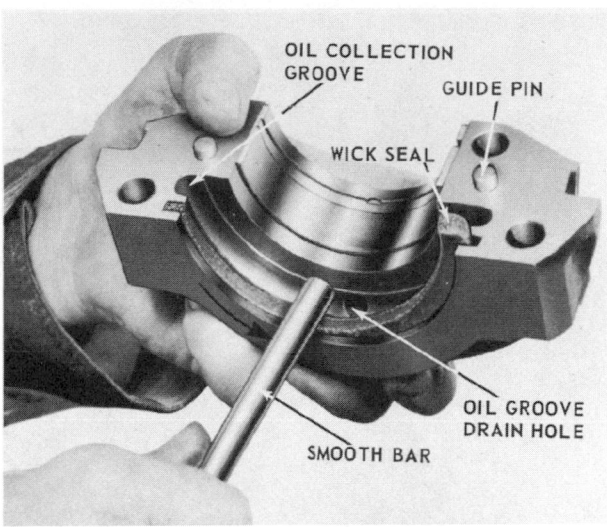

Figure 15-20. Seating a cap seal using a smooth bar. The collection groove catches oil thrown off by the slinger. Oil flows back into the pan through the collection groove drain hole. Always make certain it is open. (GMC)

Carefully install the split seal according to the manufacturer's instructions. Use engine oil on the seal lips and apply sealer where needed. The rear main cap used in the setup shown in **Figure 15-22** utilizes side seals and cap screw plugs to prevent leakage. These must be carefully installed also.

With parting edges clean, apply a thin layer of sealer on the cap. Some technicians coat only the last portion past the oil slinger. Some synthetic seals have a special glue on their ends. In these cases, be careful to avoid getting oil or sealer on the ends. Do not get sealer on the journal. Be sure the coating on the parting surface is not so heavy that it will squeeze out onto the journal.

Other engines utilize a one-piece (continuous) rear main bearing seal. Remove the seal carefully, **Figure 15-23.** Clean the recess. Coat the seal as needed. Using a seal guide to prevent seal damage, **Figure 15-24,** drive the seal into place. Make certain that the seal lip faces inward and that the shaft seal contact area is smooth. The use of a special seal driver is recommended. See **Figure 15-25.**

Installing the Crankshaft

Before installing the crankshaft, wipe a heavy film of oil on all bearing surfaces. Lower the crankshaft into place. Place caps in position. Do not reverse them. Insert the cap bolts and tighten them snugly. However, leave the thrust bearing cap loose. Tap the caps lightly with a plastic mallet to assist in alignment. Torque all caps except the one used for the thrust bearing.

Pry the shaft forward against the lower thrust flange. While holding the shaft forward, pry the cap back to force the cap thrust flange against the shaft thrust surface. Maintain forward pressure on shaft and torque the cap. This will ensure an even contact between crank and thrust bearing flanges, **Figure 15-26.**

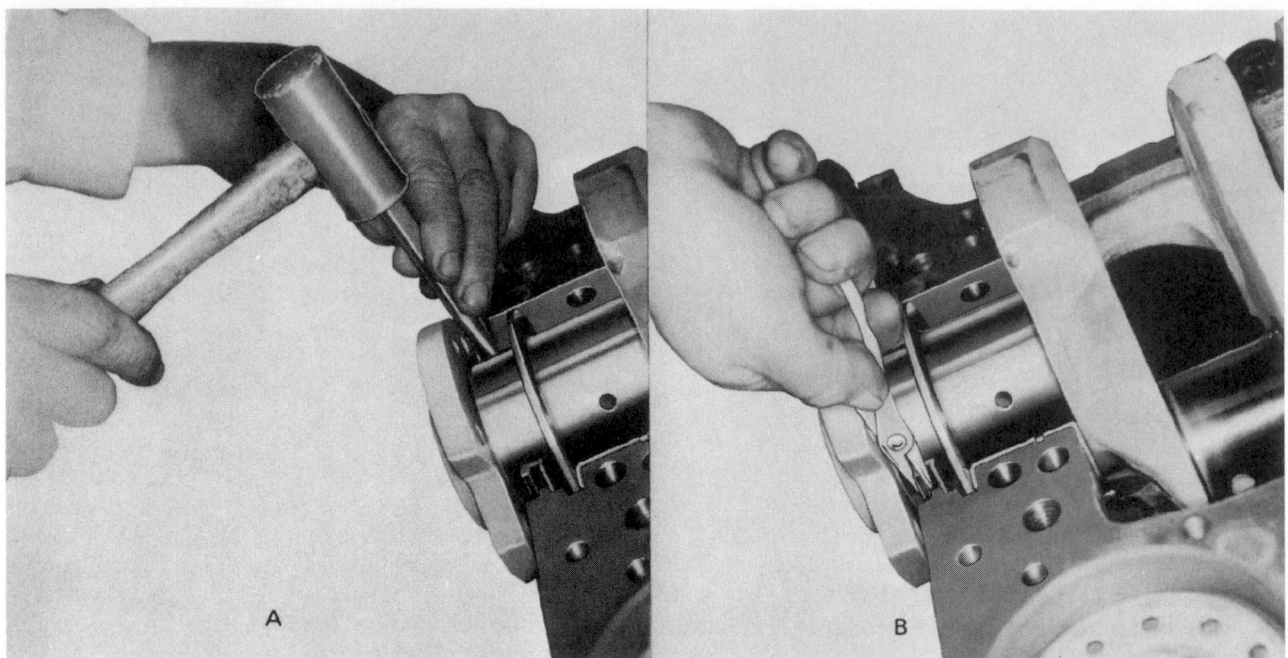

Figure 15-21. Removing a synthetic upper rear main bearing seal. A—One end of the seal is tapped down with a punch until the opposite end protrudes far enough to grasp it with pliers. B—The seal is then pulled from the groove. (Chevrolet)

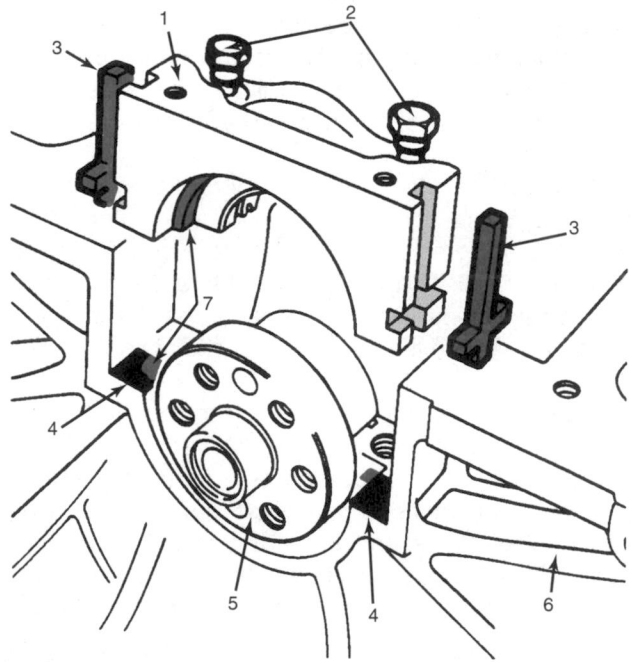

Figure 15-22. Setup using a synthetic, two-piece rear main bearing seal. 1—Bearing cap. 2—Cap bolts. 3—Cross side seal. 4—Sealer. 5—Crankshaft. 6—Block. 7—Seal. (Land Rover)

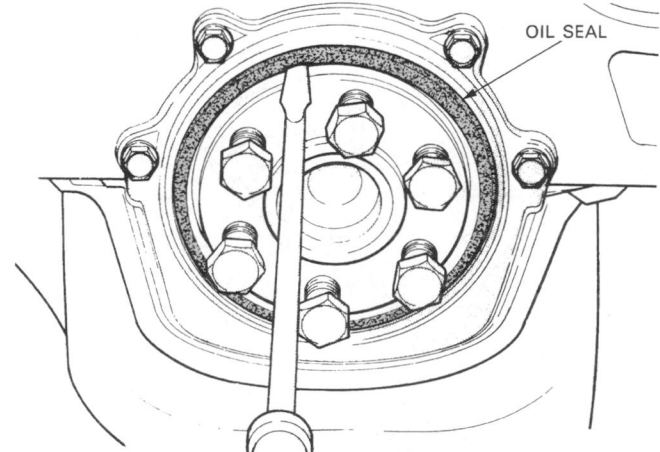

Figure 15-23. Removing a continuous (one piece) synthetic rear main bearing oil seal. Do not scratch or nick the seal lip contact surface. (Chrysler)

Checking Crankshaft End Play

A dial indicator or a feeler gauge can be used to check for *crankshaft end play,* **Figure 15-27.** If a feeler gauge is used, force the shaft to its limit of travel in one direction. Slip the feeler gauge between the insert thrust flange and the crank thrust face on the free side. This will let you determine clearance.

Crankshaft end play should be checked against the manufacturer's specifications, but generally ranges from .004″ to .008″ (0.10 to 0.20 mm). Do not jam the feeler blade into the clearance area because the thrust bearing flange could be marred.

Most engines have thrust flanges built into one of the main bearings, and the entire bearing must be changed to adjust end play. Some engines have separate thrust shims (washers), as shown in **Figure 15-1.** Other engines use a thrust plate that allows end play to be adjusted by adding or removing shims. This setup is used on the front of the shaft, **Figure 15-28.**

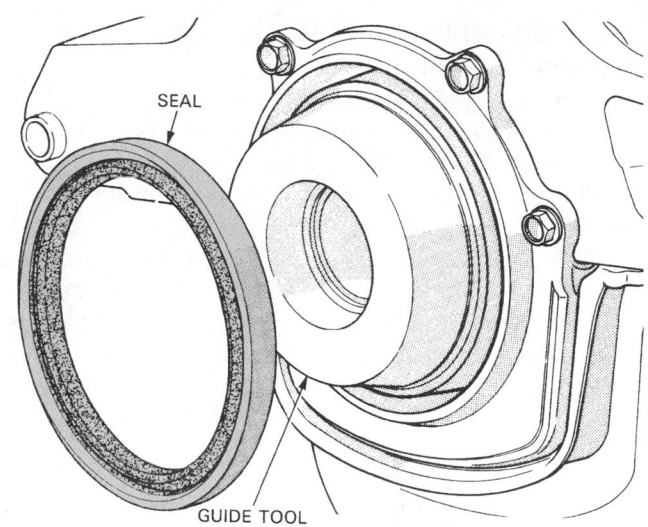

Figure 15-24.   When installing a one-piece rear main bearing seal, use a properly designed seal installation guide tool to prevent seal damage. Use oil on the seal lip and crank seal contact surface. Coat the seal outer diameter with recommended sealer. The guide must be clean and lightly oiled. (Chrysler)

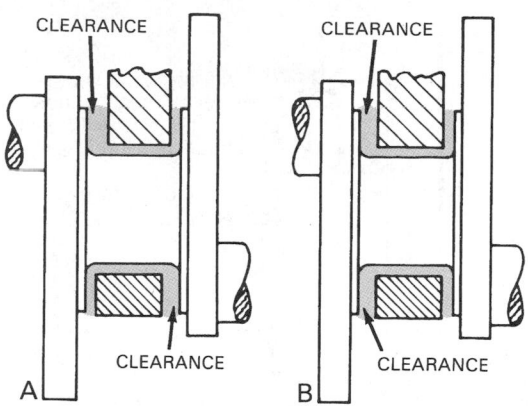

Figure 15-26.   Upper and lower insert thrust flanges must be aligned with the crankshaft thrust surface. A—This shaft would have *no end play* due to misaligned flanges. B—The shaft would have correct end play because flange alignment is acceptable.

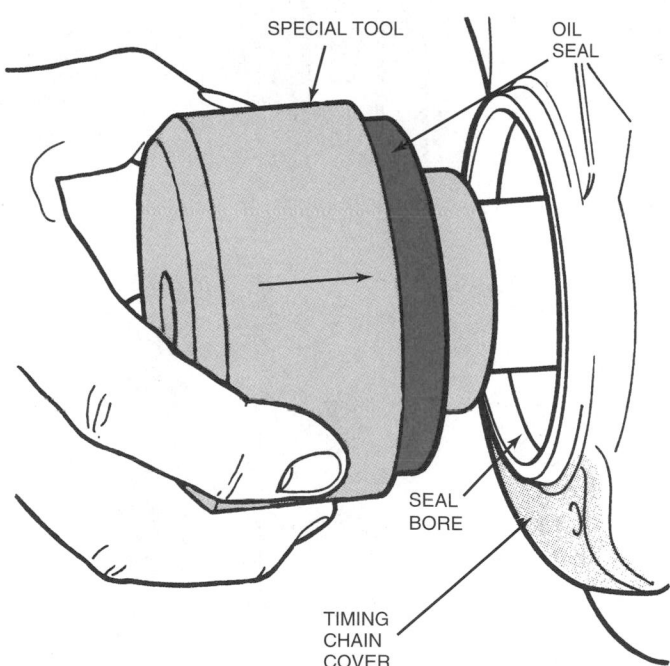

Figure 15-25.   One type of seal driver used for installing one-piece rear main bearing oil seals. (Dodge)

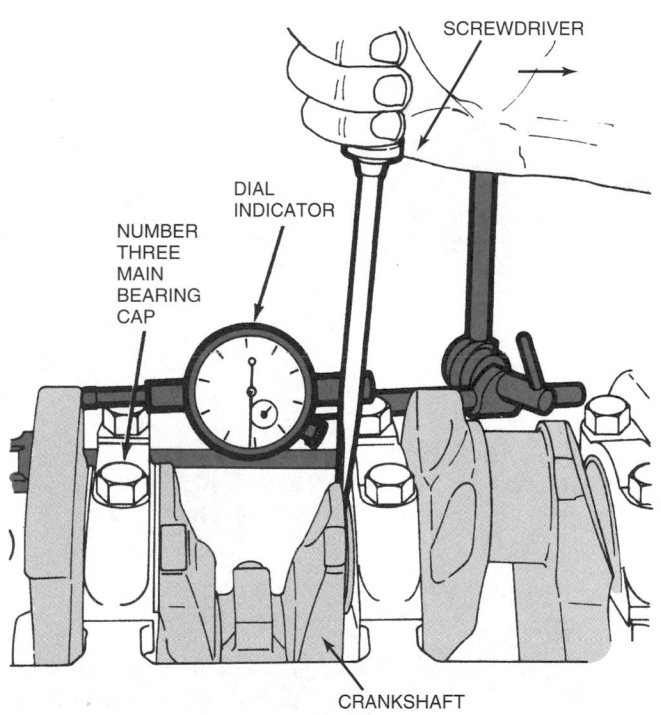

Figure 15-27.   Checking crankshaft end play with a dial indicator. (Jeep)

Measuring Crankshaft Main Journals—Engine in Car

At times, it may be desirable to install new main bearings without removing the engine from the car. To select the proper replacements, it is necessary to measure each journal.

There are several different types and styles of measuring devices available. One is a gauge that allows the shaft to be measured without rolling out the upper insert. To use this gauge, the journal and gauge contact pads are wiped clean. The central plunger is locked down, and the gauge is placed against the shaft. The plunger is then released. When the plunger is in full contact with the shaft, the plunger is locked with the thumbscrew. A regular outside micrometer is used to measure across the length of the plunger. This distance is the radius (one-half diameter) of the shaft. It must be doubled to determine shaft diameter. As with all precision measuring tools, this gauge must be used with extreme care, **Figure 15-29.**

Another gauge consists of an outside micrometer with special caliper-type jaws. It requires that the upper

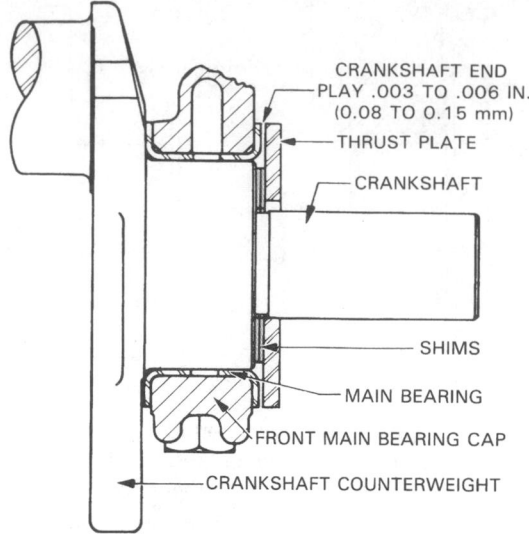

Figure 15-28.   Shims can be used to adjust end play in this shaft.

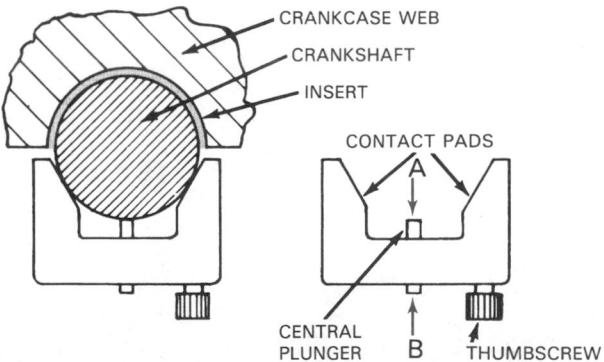

Figure 15-29.   Crankshaft main journal gauge. Measure distance A-B and *double* it. Note that the gauge is placed against the journal and that insert may be left in place.

insert be rolled out to allow room for jaw entrance. Look at **Figure 15-30.**

Whatever type of measuring tool is used, use care as it is easy to make a poor reading. Rotate the shaft so that you can take measurements at several points.

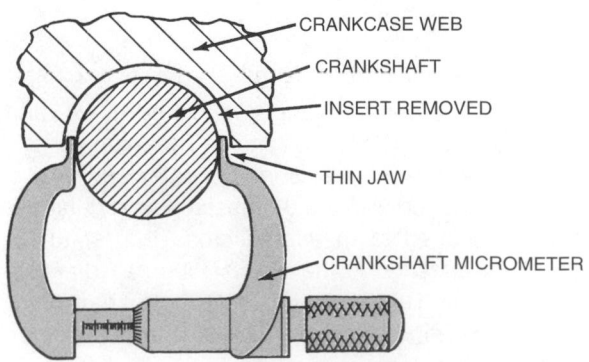

Figure 15-30.   Special crankshaft micrometer. Thin jaws will enter between the journal and bore after the insert is removed.

Removing Crankshaft Main Bearing Upper Inserts—Engine in Car

On many engines, it is possible to remove and replace the upper main bearing inserts with the engine in the car. Loosen the front and rear caps but do not remove them. This will assist in the removal of the intermediate bearing inserts. Remove the intermediate caps. Insert a suitable removal plug into the journal oil hole. The flat section of the plug must be a little narrower and thinner than the insert to prevent binding in the bore. It should contact the insert end squarely, **Figure 15-31.** In an emergency, a plug can be made from a cotter pin, **Figure 15-32.**

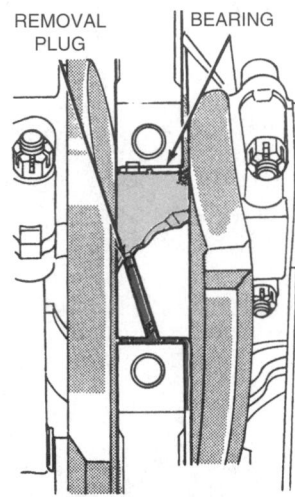

Figure 15-31.   Typical insert removal plug. (Dodge)

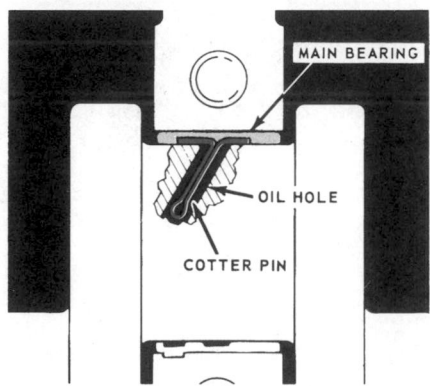

Figure 15-32.   A cotter pin can be used as a removal plug.

Rotate the shaft to bring the flat section of the plug against the insert end *opposite* the locating lug. Make sure it will clear the bore. Slowly rotate the shaft and the insert will be forced around and out of the upper bore, **Figure 15-33.**

Rolling in a New Bearing Insert—Engine in Car

Before installing a new insert, the upper bore and crank journal should be thoroughly cleaned. Do not leave any loose threads of cloth in the bore. Lubricate the journal and the new insert. Place the insert against the journal, plain end toward the bore locating lug recess. Slip the insert

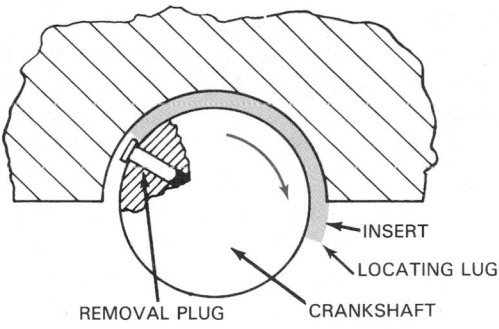

Figure 15-33. As the shaft is rotated, the removal plug will force out the insert.

into the bore as far as possible. Place the removal plug in the journal's oil hole and rotate it against the locating lug end of the insert. Continue rotation until the insert is properly seated. Make certain that the insert locating lug engages the lug recess in the bore. See **Figure 15-34.**

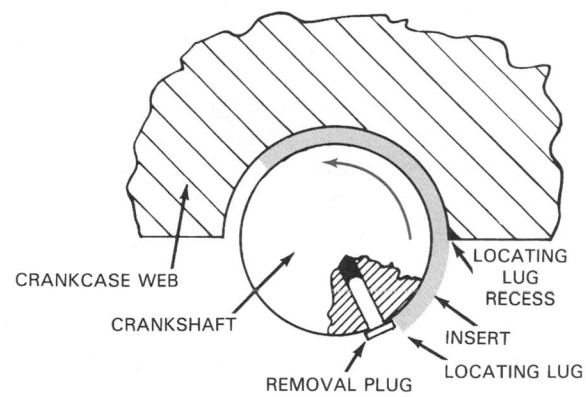

Figure 15-34. Rolling a new insert into position.

Snap the lower insert into the cap. Lubricate the insert and install the cap. Install the cap bolts and tighten them snugly. Back them off a few thousandths and remove the front and rear main inserts. When installing the rear main upper insert, make sure the oil seal does not rotate out of position. When all inserts are in, torque all caps but the one with the thrust bearing. Align the upper and lower flanges with the crank thrust surface and torque the cap. Bearing clearance should be checked with a Plastigage.

Checking Main Bearing Clearance—Engine in Car

Working on *one* bearing at a time, remove the cap. Wipe the journal and the cap insert clean. With an extension jack, apply upward pressure to the crankshaft adjacent to the journal being checked. This will keep the shaft in contact with the upper insert so that the Plastigage will provide a true reading. If the shaft is allowed to sag downward, the Plastigage material will be flattened when the cap is torqued, giving a false reading.

Place a strip of Plastigage across the lower insert, install the cap, and torque the cap bolts to specifications. Finally, remove the cap and determine clearance by measuring the flattened Plastigage.

Installing a Rear Main Bearing Oil Seal—Engine in Car

Some engines are designed so that the rear main oil seal can be replaced without removing the crankshaft. Replacing these seals is often tricky and requires care.

Remove the cap. Pry out the old seal and clean the groove. If a synthetic rubber seal is used, install it in the cap at this time. Using a clean brass drift punch, tap on the end of the upper seal (it may help to rotate the shaft also) to push the other end out. As soon as the end is clear, grasp it with pliers and pull the seal from the bore. If difficulty is encountered when removing a wick-type seal, it will help to drop the shaft a few thousandths of an inch. A corkscrew-type attachment can be screwed into the end of the wick to help pull it out to a point where pliers can be used. Use care not to nick the journal seal surface.

Lubricate the new upper rubber seal and insert it into the groove. To seat the seal, push it into the groove while rotating the crankshaft in same direction.

In cases where a wick seal or packing is used, remove it as previously described. To insert the new upper wick seal, attach a soft wire to one end of the wick, **Figure 15-35.** Using the cap, preform the wick by installing it in the cap groove. Do not cut off the ends. Remove the wick from the cap and lubricate the wick thoroughly. Pass the wire through and around the upper groove. Force the end of the wick into the groove. Tuck all fibers in and pull on the wire. Wiggle the wick where it enters the groove, making sure the wick does not bulge out and hang up. Pull the wick through the groove until an equal amount protrudes from each side. Rotating the crankshaft will help. Cut the wick off flush with the parting surface. To prevent nicking the journal surface, a thin piece of shim stock can be slid between the end of the wick and the journal.

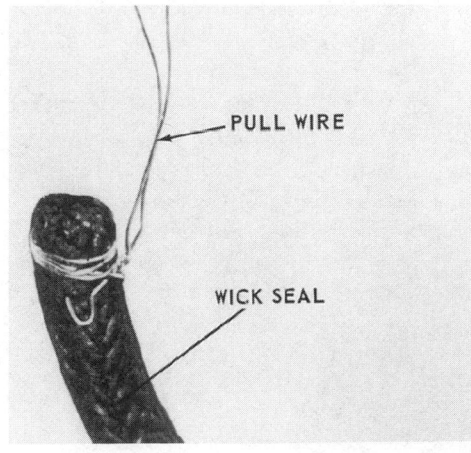

Figure 15-35. A pull wire is attached to a wick-type upper seal.

Checklist for Crankshaft and Bearing Service

The answer to all of the following questions should be yes.

- Were the crankshaft journals within all specifications for size, out-of-roundness, and taper? If not, were they reconditioned to meet specifications?
- If applicable, was the crankshaft stored properly?
- Were all parts thoroughly cleaned before reassembly?
- Were the bearing inserts correct as to spread and crush?
- Were the oil holes and aligning lugs properly installed?
- Were bearing clearances checked with Plastigage and within specifications?
- Were the bearing caps placed in their original positions?
- Were all bearing cap alignment marks in their original positions?
- Were the bearing caps properly torqued?
- Was crankshaft end play checked? If it was not within specifications, was it corrected?
- Were seals installed properly?

Tech Talk

If your state has a lottery, or if there is a race-track nearby, you might think that placing a small bet or two is a good way to have fun and maybe win a few bucks. However, gambling when you overhaul an engine is neither fun nor profitable. You might get away with putting in a new set of rod and main bearings without miking the crankshaft. You might even get away with it several times. But sooner or later, your luck will run out and the problems encountered will make up for the times you got away with second-rate work.

Never take chances when overhauling an engine. Check anything that needs checking and even some things that do not. In many cases, checking a part that does not normally require checking will reveal a problem that you did not know existed. For example, after you check the crankshaft journals, take a look at the keyway that holds the timing gear on the crankshaft. Keyways do not become loose and sloppy very often, but it happens often enough to be worth checking.

By checking everything carefully, you can put the vehicle back together with confidence that everything is as it should be. In this way, it is a bet that you are sure to win.

Summary

Mark bearing caps before removal. Remove the caps by lightly tapping and prying. Remove the crankshaft carefully and place it where the journals will not be damaged. With caps in place and torqued, check the main bearing bores for distortion and alignment. Bore out-of-roundness and misalignment can be corrected by align boring.

Clean the crankshaft thoroughly and oil it lightly. Check the finish and accuracy of all journals. Journals must be smooth and free of excessive taper, out-of-roundness, and overall wear. Check crankshaft alignment with V-blocks and a dial indicator. Runout should not exceed specifications.

Crankshafts can often be straightened by bending or through the use of heat. Out-of-roundness, taper, and wear can be corrected by grinding. After grinding, all journals and fillets should be polished to produce a surface finish of 16 micro inches or smoother. Severely damaged journals must be built up prior to grinding. Undersizing journals in excess of .030″ (0.76 mm) is questionable. Store the crankshaft on end or support it properly to prevent bending.

Bearing inserts must have proper spread and crush. They must be cleaned and oiled. The inserts must be of the exact size required, and they must be snapped into clean bores. Be sure that oil holes are aligned and that the locating lugs are in the recesses. Check bearing clearance with Plastigage. If the engine is in the car, push up on the crankshaft before checking clearance.

Rear main oil seals must be carefully installed. Use a thin coating of gasket cement between the cap and block parting surfaces.

When installing main bearing caps, align the thrust bearing upper and lower halves with the crankshaft thrust surface. Torque all caps. Marks on corresponding caps and crank webs must align. Check crankshaft end play. When measuring main journals with the engine in the car, use a special gauge or an outside micrometer with caliper-type jaws.

To remove and install upper main inserts with the engine in the car, use special removal plugs. Rear main seal upper halves can often be installed with the crankshaft in place by pulling or forcing the seal around in the groove.

Know These Terms

Out-of-roundness	Graphite impregnated wick
Taper	Synthetic rubber
Wear	Wick seal
Undersize	Split-type synthetic rear
Crankshaft regrinding	main bearing seal
Polished	Crankshaft end play
Locating lugs	

Review Questions—Chapter 15

Do not write in this book. Write your answers on a separate sheet of paper.

1. Prior to removal, main bearing caps should be _____.
   - (A) carefully studied
   - (B) tapped lightly with a rawhide hammer
   - (C) marked
   - (D) thoroughly washed

2. Bearing bores should not show out-of-roundness in excess of:
   - (A) .0001″ (0.0025 mm)
   - (B) .0015″ (0.0381 mm)
   - (C) .007″ (0.18 mm)
   - (D) .015″ (0.38 mm)

3. For an acceptable journal finish, the micro inch finish should be _____.
   - (A) 100 micro inches
   - (B) 1 micro inch
   - (C) 16 micro inches
   - (D) 160 micro inches

4. In measuring a journal in four places on end A, you have readings of 2.8950, 2.8960, 2.8980, 2.8960. On end B, the readings are 2.8935, 2.8945, 2.8960, 2.8945. The standard for the journal is 2.900. List the correct figures for:
   - (A) Maximum wear reading. _____
   - (B) Minimum wear. _____
   - (C) Maximum taper. _____
   - (D) Out-of-roundness. _____

5. Should the journal in question 6 be ground? Explain your answer.

6. Could an undersize bearing be used with the journal in question 6 without grinding? Explain your answer.

7. If damaged journals are too far gone to be reground, they can often be saved by _____ and then _____.

8. Small nicks can be smoothed down to the shaft surface with _____ cloth.

9. For storage, the crankshaft should be _____.
   - (A) stood on end
   - (B) oiled
   - (C) covered
   - (D) All of the above.

10. Bearing clearance is best checked with _____.

11. List three ways oil can leak into the flywheel housing from the rear main bearing.

12. Name two materials often used for rear main bearing seals.

13. When installing the wick seal _____.
   - (A) trim the ends flush with the parting surface
   - (B) let the excess protrude
   - (C) lay the excess across the parting surface
   - (D) drive the excess down into the groove

14. Some rear shaft seals are constructed so that oil resistant _____ must be applied to the cap screw threads.

15. How are bearing inserts installed with the crankshaft in the car?

State the maximum clearances for the following:

16. Bearing bore misalignment _____.
17. Crankshaft overall alignment _____.
18. Journal out-of-round _____.
19. Journal taper _____.
20. Journal oil groove protrusion _____.

ASE-Type Questions

1. Technician A says that bearing caps may be pounded on heavily during removal. Technician B says that bearing caps can be removed by light tapping and prying. Who is right?
   - (A) A only.
   - (B) B only.
   - (C) Both A & B.
   - (D) Neither A nor B.

2. If the main bearing bores are out of alignment, the bearing inserts at _____ journal(s) will show the most wear.
   - (A) the center
   - (B) the end
   - (C) every other
   - (D) All journals will be worn equally.

3. Each of the following methods cannot be used to correct main bearing bores that are out of alignment EXCEPT:
   - (A) align boring.
   - (B) crankshaft grinding.
   - (C) crocus cloth.
   - (D) installing new standard size bearings.

4. The following crankshaft journal conditions require that the shaft be ground EXCEPT:
   - (A) scoring.
   - (B) dark lines.
   - (C) scratching.
   - (D) roughness.

5. Technician A says to use the largest crankshaft journal measurement when selecting an undersize bearing insert. Technician B says to use the smallest journal measurement when selecting undersize bearing inserts. Who is right?
   - (A) A only.
   - (B) B only.
   - (C) Both A & B.
   - (D) Neither A nor B.

6. Technician A says that all insert sets have both upper and lower shells drilled for oil entry. Technician B says that upper and lower insert thrust flanges automatically align when the cap is torqued. Who is right?
   - (A) A only.
   - (B) B only.
   - (C) Both A & B.
   - (D) Neither A nor B.

7. Which of the following is used to check crankshaft end play?
   (A) Dial indicator.
   (B) Feeler gauge.
   (C) Plastigage.
   (D) Both A & B.

8. When the engine is in the car, the upper inserts can best be removed by _____.
   (A) blowing them out with air pressure
   (B) driving them out with a punch
   (C) rolling them out with a removal plug
   (D) pulling them out with a wire

9. Technician A says that main bearing journals can be measured with the crankshaft in the engine. Technician B says that bearing crush should be filed off before installing new bearings. Who is right?
   (A) A only.
   (B) B only.
   (C) Both A & B.
   (D) Neither A nor B.

10. The crankshaft does not have to be removed to perform any of the following, EXCEPT:
    (A) checking journal wear.
    (B) replacing main bearings.
    (C) changing a one-piece seal.
    (D) changing a two-piece seal.

Suggested Activities

1. Mike all of the journals on a crankshaft and write down your readings. Using the readings, decide whether the journals require turning, if oversize bearing inserts can be used, or if the crankshaft must be replaced. List all needed work, including the number of rod and main bearing journals that require turning.

2. Using a flat rate manual, calculate the parts and labor needed to repair the crankshaft to service.

3. Discuss your price calculation with your class. Ask if there is anything that you missed. Determine whether the cost of repairing the crankshaft will be greater than the cost of a replacement crankshaft.

16

Camshaft and Valve Train Service

After studying this chapter, you will be able to:
- Remove, check, and install a block-mounted camshaft.
- Remove, check, and install a cylinder-head-mounted camshaft.
- Remove and install camshaft bearings.
- Properly remove and install a vibration damper.
- Measure timing gear and chain wear.
- Remove and install camshaft gears and sprockets.
- Inspect a camshaft and its drive mechanism for problems.
- Service a front cover oil seal.
- Remove and install a timing belt.
- Service camshaft bearings.
- Test and service mechanical lifters.
- Test and service hydraulic lifters.

This chapter covers servicing the engine camshaft, the camshaft drive mechanism, and other associated valve train parts. In addition to the camshaft, valve train parts include valve lifters, pushrods, and rocker arms. The information presented in this chapter is applicable to both cam-in-block engines and overhead cam engines. Any difference in service between the two types is called out in the text.

Servicing the Camshaft Drive Components

The camshaft is driven from the *crankshaft* by one of three methods: two mating gears, a timing chain and sprockets, or a timing belt and sprockets. This section covers the service of the timing gears, chains, belts, and sprockets. Despite the relatively long service life of the parts concerned, it is an extremely poor practice to neglect these areas.

Worn gears, chains, belts, and sprockets will alter *valve timing* and may cause damaging camshaft **torsional vibration**. Engine overheating, accelerated wear, and sluggish operation can result. Wear will make accurate valve lash settings impossible. With advanced wear, objectionable noise will appear. Extreme wear will cause the valve to hit the top of the piston, **Figure 16-1.** Therefore, gears, chains, belts, and sprockets should receive careful attention. The following sections explain how to gain access to these parts and how to service them.

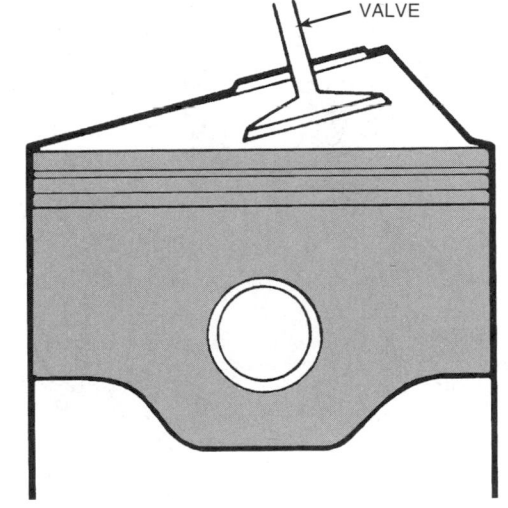

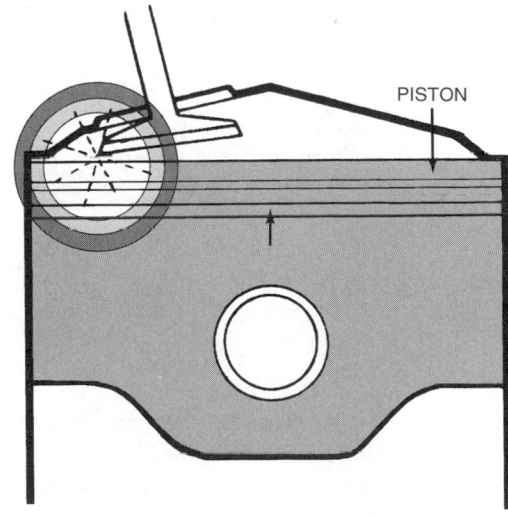

Figure 16-1. Engines with timing belts can be classified as (A) free running or (B) interference, depending on what happens if the piston and valve synchronization is lost due to a broken or damaged timing belt. Note piston-to-valve contact in B. This can cause severe engine damage.

Removing the Vibration Damper

The first step in servicing the camshaft drive components is to remove the *vibration damper,* or *harmonic balancer.* To remove the vibration damper, remove the retaining cap screw in the end of the crankshaft, if used. Remove any bolt-on pulleys. Attach a suitable puller to the damper *hub* (do not pull on the outer rim) and withdraw the damper, **Figure 16-2A.**

When tightening the puller screw against the hollow end of the crankshaft, be careful not to damage the crankshaft threads. If the threaded hole in the crankshaft is larger than the puller screw, place a cap over the end of the crankshaft, **Figure 16-2B.** Never allow the puller screw to enter the threaded hole in the crankshaft.

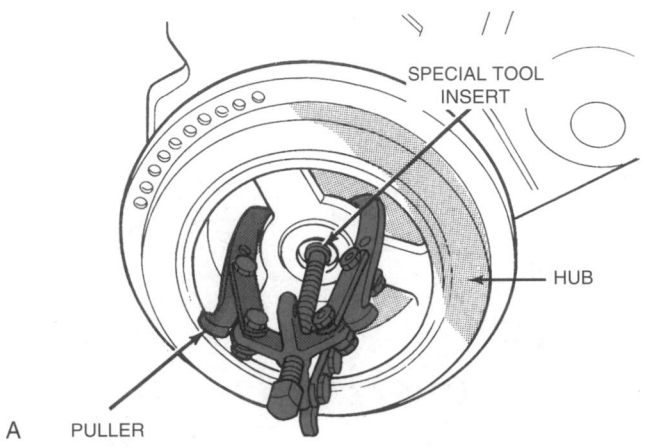

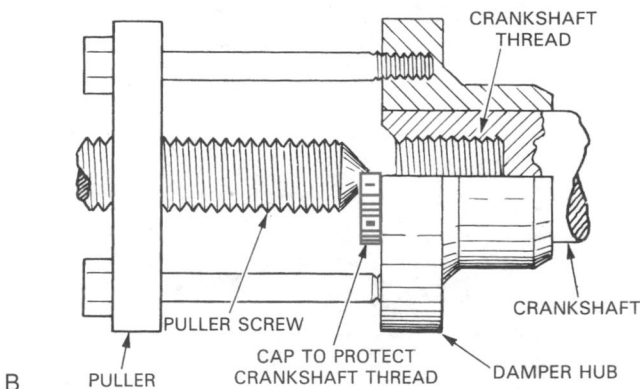

Figure 16-2. Pulling a vibration damper. A—The pulling force is applied to the center of the hub. B—If necessary, a plug can be used to protect the crankshaft threads.

Removing the Front Cover

To remove the **front cover,** remove the screws that hold the cover to the engine block or the oil pan. Watch for variations in cap screw lengths. If possible, leave the water pump in place. Once the cap screws have been removed, gently pry on the cover to break the gasket seal. Then, pull the cover away from the engine.

Servicing the Timing Gears

The following procedure applies to engines using two **gears** to drive the camshaft. Visually inspect both camshaft and crankshaft gears. If any teeth are obviously worn, chipped, or galled, replace both gears. If the gears appear to be in good condition, check the **backlash** (distance one gear will rotate without moving the other gear). Backlash can be checked with a dial indicator or with a feeler gauge.

Always consult the manufacturer's service manual for exact procedures. Typical gear checking procedures are shown in **Figures 16-3** and **16-4.**

> **Caution:** If any one of the camshaft drive parts requires replacement, all of the parts should be replaced. A worn gear or chain will not engage the new parts perfectly and will cause premature wear.

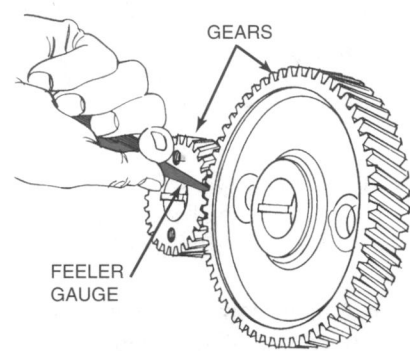

Figure 16-3. Feeler gauge being used to check backlash between the gear teeth. Check backlash in several different spots. (Sealed Power)

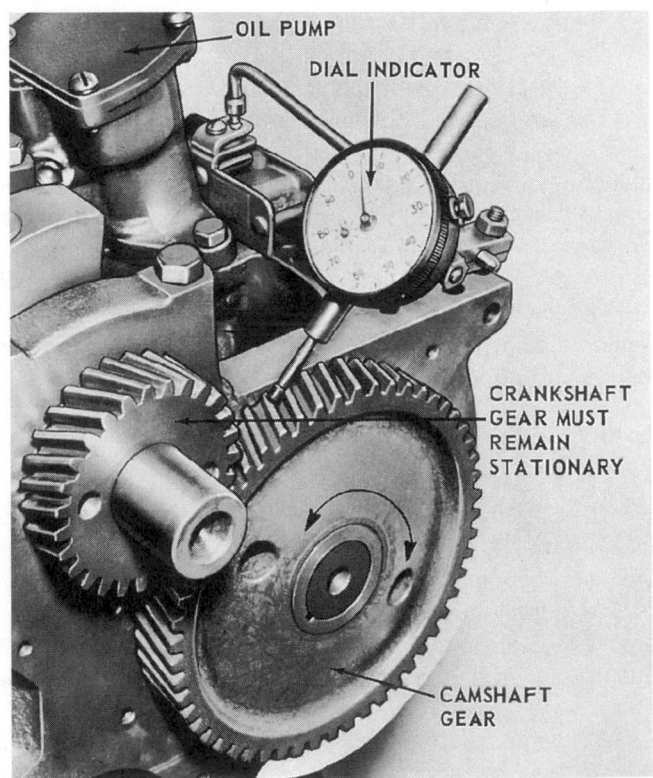

Figure 16-4. Checking gear backlash with a dial indicator. Make certain that the indicator stem parallels the direction of tooth movement. (GMC)

Removing the Camshaft Gear

Some camshaft gears are bolted in place and removal is simple. Others, however, are force fit on the camshaft and must be pressed off. Before removing the camshaft gear, the camshaft must often be removed from the engine. To remove the camshaft, turn the cam gear so that the *thrust plate* (when used) retaining capscrews are accessible and remove the capscrews, **Figure 16-5.**

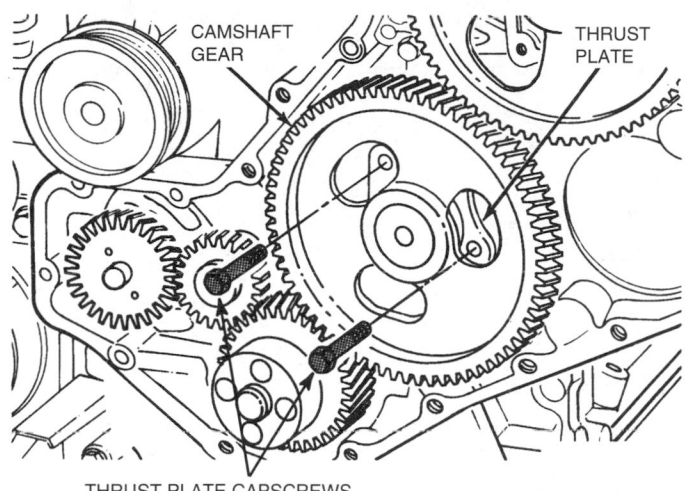

Figure 16-5.   Removing camshaft thrust plate capscrews.

Before the camshaft can be pulled, the distributor or oil pump (depending on which one has a gear), fuel pump, and valve lifters must be removed. Mushroom-type lifters that must be removed from below should be pulled up and secured with clamps to hold them out of the way. Then, pull the camshaft from the engine. Pull the camshaft straight out to avoid damaging the camshaft bearings. After removing the camshaft, the gear can be pressed from the shaft. The camshaft must be held so it will not drop and be damaged.

Installing a New Camshaft Gear

Before installing a new camshaft gear, clean the gear engagement area thoroughly and lubricate it lightly. Slide a new spacer and thrust plate into place. Be sure to face them in the correct direction. Install a new *Woodruff key.* Set up the camshaft in a press (support the shaft under the front bearing journal edge) and press the timing gear on all the way. Remember to apply pressure to the steel hub only.

 Note: Camshaft alignment and condition checks will be discussed later in this chapter. These checks should be done before installing the camshaft.

Checking End Play at Thrust Plate

After the camshaft gear is pressed on, use a feeler gauge or dial indicator to check clearance (end play) between the thrust plate and the face of the camshaft journal. See **Figure 16-6.**

Removing and Replacing Crankshaft Timing Gear

If the crankshaft gear is to be replaced, remove it before installing the camshaft gear. If there are no threaded

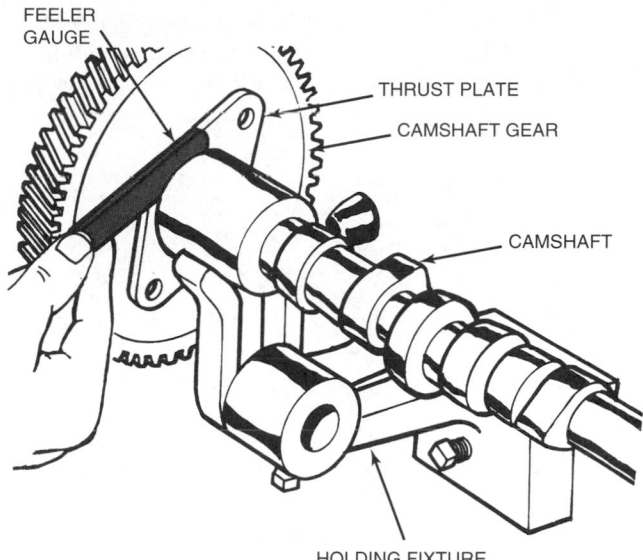

Figure 16-6.   This technician is using a feeler gauge to check end clearance.

holes in the gear for puller bolts, use a puller setup that is similar to the one shown in **Figure 16-7.** Be careful not to damage the gear teeth during pulling.

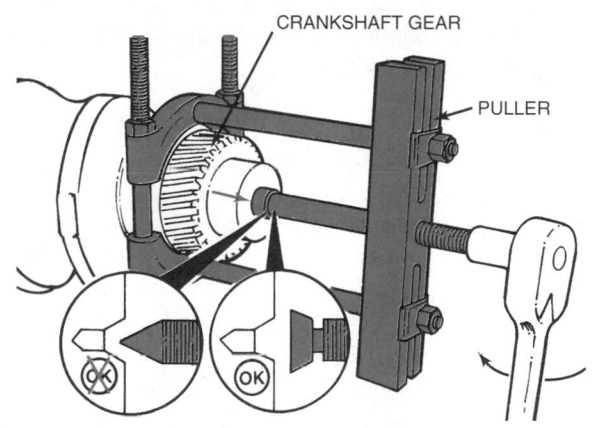

Figure 16-7.   Crankshaft gear being removed with a puller. Wear safety glasses. (Dodge)

To replace the gear, clean and lubricate the end of the crankshaft. Make certain that the Woodruff keys are in place. The forward key often has a tapered end to facilitate alignment of the crankshaft gear and damper. Make sure it faces forward.

 Note: Reinstall the crankshaft gear before the camshaft and gear are installed.

Install the crankshaft gear with the timing mark facing outward. Drive the gear fully into place with a suitable sleeve and a heavy hammer. Do not mar the gear's teeth.

Installing Camshaft and Gear

Before installing the camshaft, turn the crankshaft so the timing mark faces the center of the front cam bearing.

Lubricate the cam bearing journals and lobes. Slide the camshaft carefully into position, making certain the camshaft gear timing mark is aligned with the crank gear mark, **Figure 16-8.**

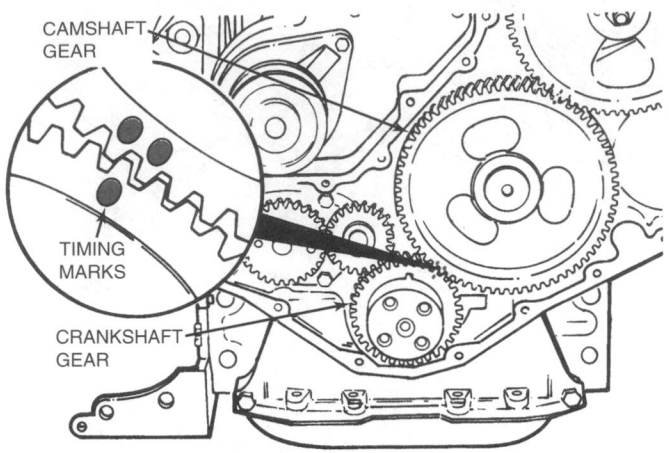

Figure 16-8. Correctly aligned timing marks on this particular gearset. (Dodge)

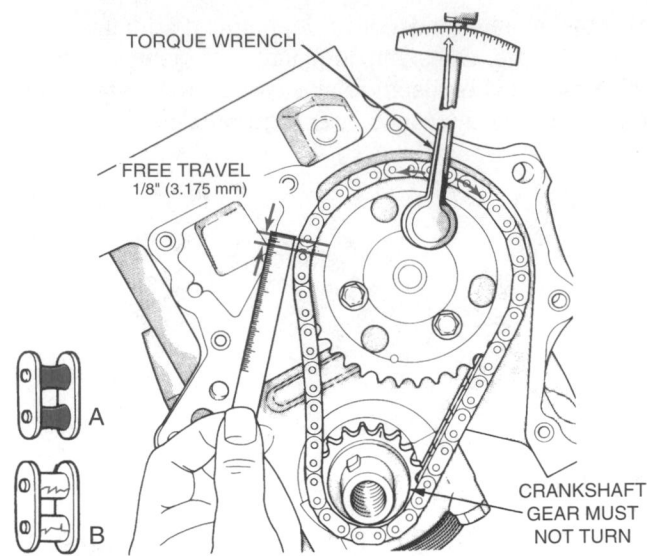

Figure 16-9. Checking timing chain wear by measuring sprocket free travel. A—Wear on link. B—Link cracked. (Dodge, Nissan)

Install the thrust plate cap screws (use new locks) and torque them to specifications. Check for correct backlash and runout and then lube the gears thoroughly. The gears must be properly aligned with each other (tooth engagement across full gear width).

Servicing Timing Chain and Sprocket

The following section explains how to service the *timing chain* and *sprocket* assembly. This arrangement is the most common type of camshaft drive used on engines without overhead camshafts. It is also used on some overhead cam engines.

Checking Chain for Wear

To check a timing chain for wear, place a steel rule against the block as shown in **Figure 16-9.** Turn the camshaft sprocket clockwise as far as it will go (crankshaft must not turn). Align one of the chain link pins with a mark on the rule. Without moving the rule or the crankshaft, turn the gear counterclockwise as far as possible. Note the distance the link pin has moved and check this distance against manufacturer's specifications.

Another technique for checking timing chain wear involves turning the crankshaft so that all *slack* is taken up on one side. Carefully measure from the tightened chain surface (about midpoint) to a reference point on the block. Rotate the crankshaft in the opposite direction to produce all possible slack on the same side. Pull the slack chain outward toward the reference point as far as possible. While holding the chain out, measure from the surface to the reference point. The difference in the two measurements should, in general, not exceed 1/2" (12.7 mm), **Figure 16-10.** A new chain on new sprockets will have about 1/4" (6.35 mm) of slack. Note that there are also special spring-loaded timing chains that have no slack.

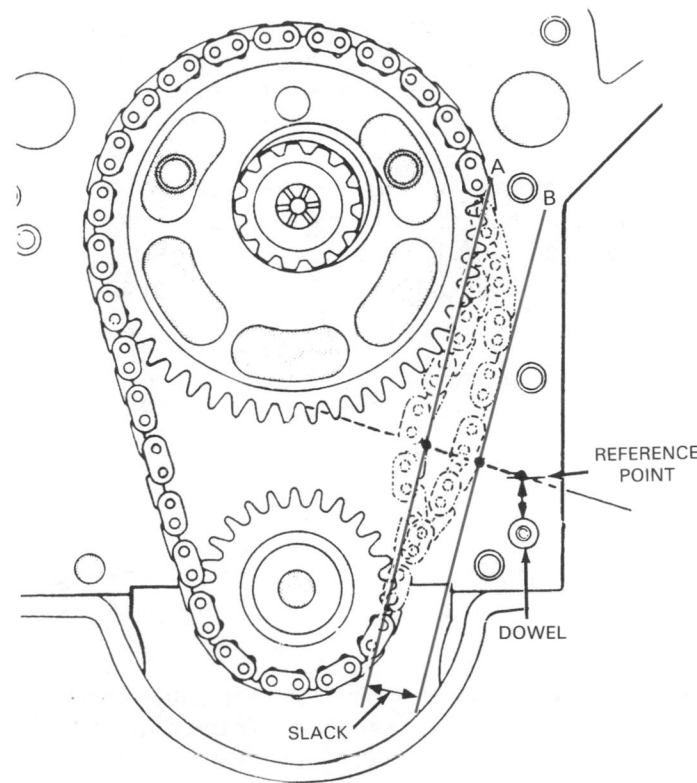

Figure 16-10. Timing chain wear can be checked by measuring slack. The distance between lines "A" and "B" represents the amount of slack in the chain. (Chrysler)

Long Chains for Overhead Camshafts

Some overhead camshaft engines use long timing chains or timing belts. Slack is controlled by idler sprockets, rubbing blocks, or spring-loaded tensioning devices.

Removing Timing Chain

Crank the engine until the timing marks on both sprockets face each other and are aligned with a line between the center of the crankshaft and camshaft. To facilitate sprocket and chain installation, do not rotate the crankshaft until the chain and sprockets are replaced. Look at **Figure 16-11.**

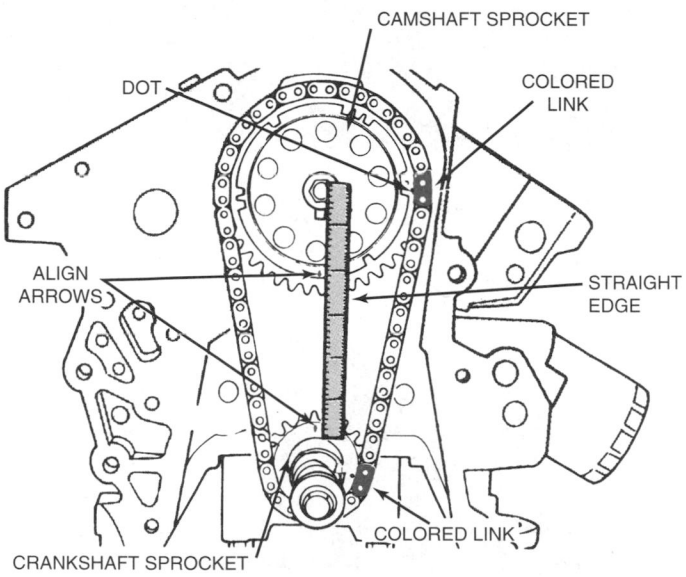

Figure 16-11. Align timing marks with crankshaft and camshaft centers using a straight edge before removal. (Chrysler)

Remove the camshaft sprocket-to-camshaft cap screws. These cap screws are often used to retain a fuel pump eccentric and, in some cases, a distributor drive gear.

Work both sprockets forward until the camshaft sprocket is clear of the shaft end. Two large screwdrivers can generally be used for this purpose. In some cases, a puller must be used to remove the sprockets. On some installations, the cam sprocket will clear without removing the crank sprocket. After removing the camshaft sprocket, remove the crankshaft sprocket from the crankshaft.

Inspecting Sprockets

After removal, carefully inspect both sprockets for signs of wear or chipping. The slightest indication of wear is cause for rejection. Look for shallow chain imprints on the sprocket teeth, **Figure 16-12.** If a thrust plate is used, check it for signs of excessive wear and replace it if necessary.

New Sprockets are Good Investments

When installing a new timing chain, the best practice is to use new sprockets. Worn sprockets will increase the wear rate on the new chain. Used sprockets will also wear faster when a new chain is installed.

Installing Chain and Sprocket

If the camshaft sprocket can be installed without disturbing the crank sprocket, drive the crank sprocket fully into place, **Figure 16-13.**

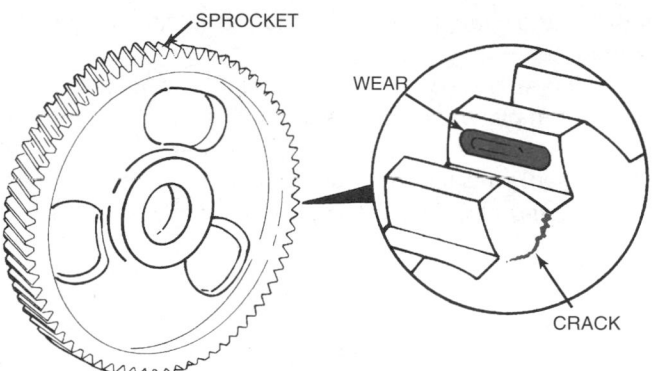

Figure 16-12. Sprocket teeth show wear and cracking. This sprocket *must* be replaced. (Dodge)

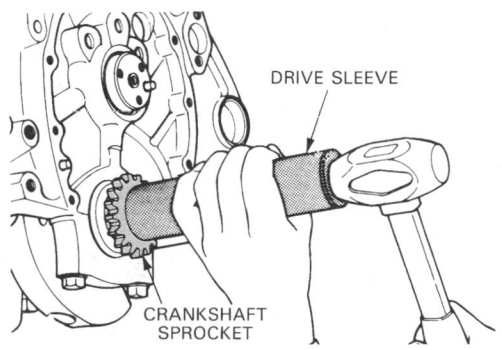

Figure 16-13. Driving crankshaft sprocket into place. (Chevrolet)

When both sprockets must be installed together, align the timing marks and place the chain around the sprockets. With the timing marks facing away from the engine, slip the crankshaft sprocket onto the crank until the cam sprocket touches the camshaft. At this point, make certain the timing marks are together and in line with the center of the crankshaft and the camshaft. Refer to **Figure 16-14.** If not, rotate the crankshaft and camshaft as needed to obtain proper alignment. Use the attaching cap screws to pull the cam sprocket into place. Do not hammer the cam sprocket on,

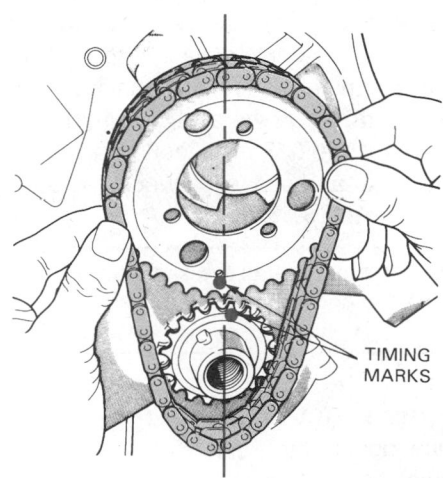

Figure 16-14. Installing chain and camshaft sprocket. Timing marks are together and aligned with the shaft centers. (Chrysler)

as the rear oil seal plug (Welch plug, core hole plug) could be loosened.

Make sure the fuel pump eccentric or distributor drive, if used, is in place. Torque the cap screws. Make a final timing mark alignment check. Install the crankshaft oil slinger (when used) and check sprocket runout, chain slack, and camshaft end play. Look at **Figure 16-15**.

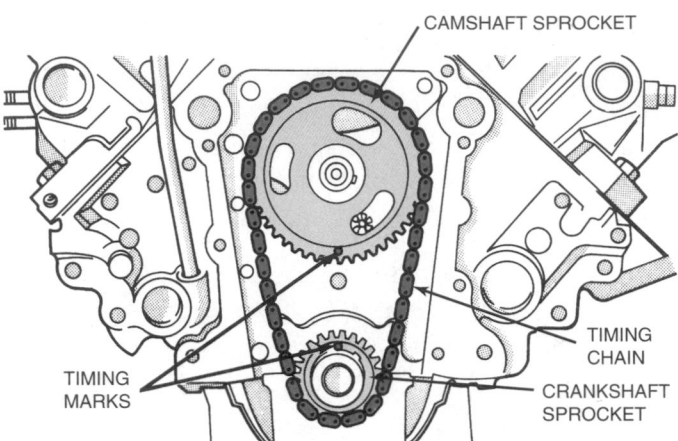

Fig: 16-15. Timing chain and sprockets installed. Note how timing marks align. (Plymouth)

Removing and Replacing Front Cover Oil Seal

Either drive or pull out the **crankshaft front oil seal**. When driving a seal out, support the cover so that it is not sprung or cracked. **Figure 16-16** illustrates the use of a special seal puller.

In **Figure 16-16A,** the puller blocks have been expanded outward to grasp the retainer lip. A removal sleeve is then placed over the puller screw, **Figure 16-16B**. The puller screw is held stationary and the draw nut is tightened to pull the seal out.

Before installing a new seal, clean the cover thoroughly. Coat the OD of the new seal with sealer and start it into the seal recess. Install the puller and plate, **Figure 16-17A**. While holding the puller screw stationary, turn the draw nut to force the seal into place, **Figure 16-17B**.

Remove the installing tool and check the seal to make sure it is fully seated. On the seal shown in **Figures 16-16** and **16-17,** a .001″ (0.025 mm) feeler gauge should not fit between the cover and seal edge when the seal is properly seated. See **Figure 16-18**.

 Note: Always install the seals so that the seal lip faces the engine.

Installing the Front Cover

Before installing the front cover, cement a new cover gasket into position. If dowel pins are used to properly locate the cover, it may be bolted into place. See **Figure 16-19**.

If the cover is not positioned with dowel pins, it is imperative that a suitable **centering sleeve** be used. The centering sleeve will align the cover crankshaft seal with

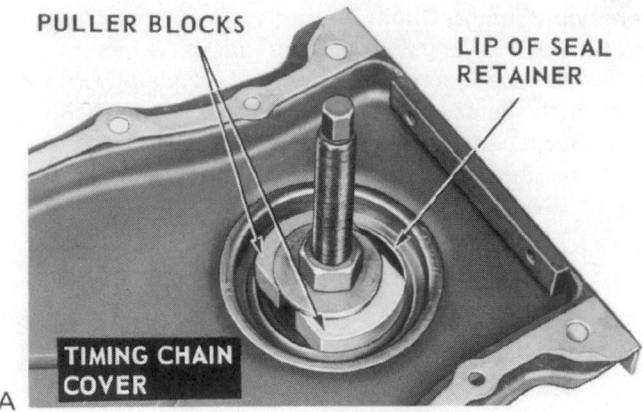

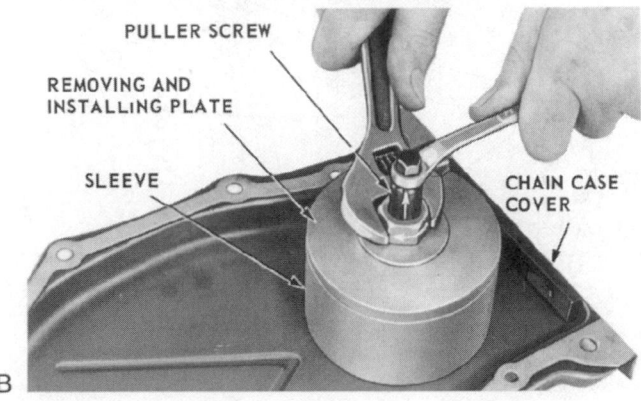

Figure 16-16. A—Puller blocks expanded to grasp seal retainer lip. B—Pulling chain cover oil seal. (Chrysler)

the crankshaft. If the sleeve is not used, the seal may be off-center, causing it to leak. Slide the sleeve over the crankshaft, **Figure 16-20.** Lubricate the sleeve. Slide the seal over the sleeve and force the cover against the block. Start all screws with finger pressure. With the sleeve in place, tighten screws properly. Finally withdraw the sleeve, leaving the seal centered perfectly around the crankshaft.

Installing the Vibration Damper

Before installing the vibration damper, lubricate the seal surface of the damper. Make sure it is absolutely smooth to prevent seal failure. Install the damper (do not forget the Woodruff key) with a puller or by driving it into place. Make sure the damper is seated fully, **Figure 16-21**.

Some vibration dampers can be damaged by driving unless a special driver that supports the outer rim section is used, **Figure 16-22**. Install the pulley and, if used, the crankshaft end cap screw.

Chain and Gear Lubrication

Always check the timing chain or gear **oil nozzles** to make certain they are open. If feeder troughs are used, they must be clean and properly located. Improper lubrication will cause both the gears and the chain to quickly fail. When a front cover is removed and the chain or gears are badly worn and dry looking, check out the lubrication system thoroughly. Note the timing gear oil nozzle in **Figure 16-23**.

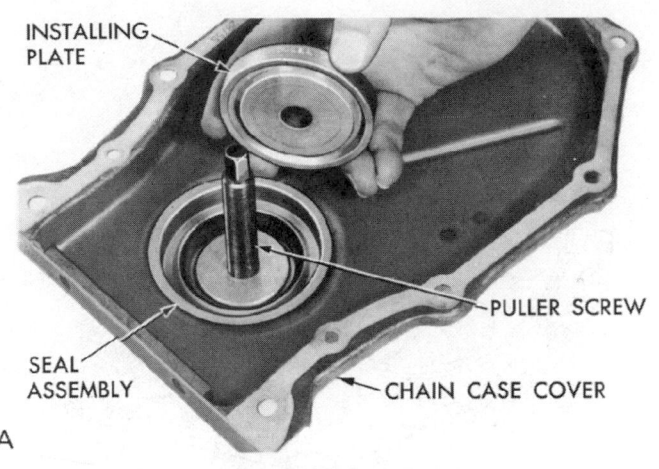

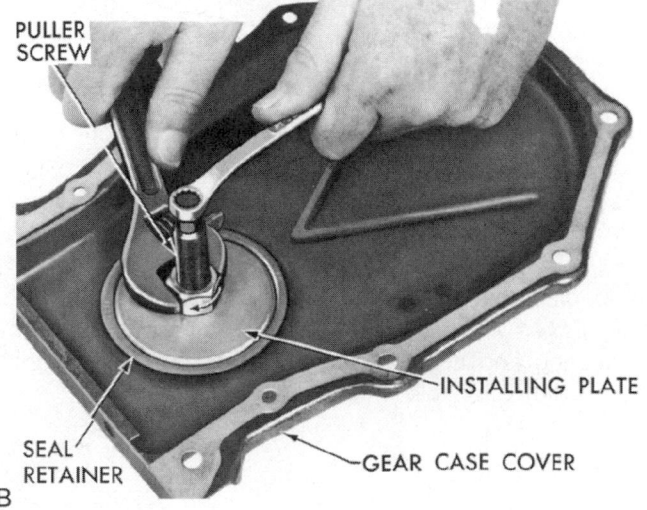

Figure 16-17.   A—Setting up the puller for seal installation. B—Pulling the seal into place. (Chrysler)

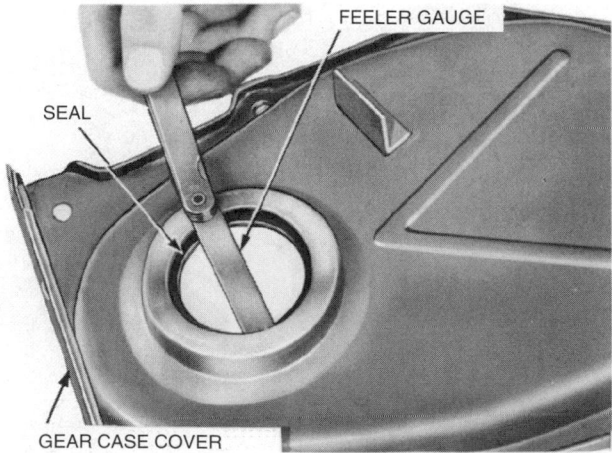

Figure 16-18.   Checking the oil seal for proper seating depth. (Chrysler)

Other Timing Chain Marks

Some manufacturers specify a certain number of links or pins between timing marks. Some timing chains have colored links that must be aligned with the timing marks, **Figure 16-24.**

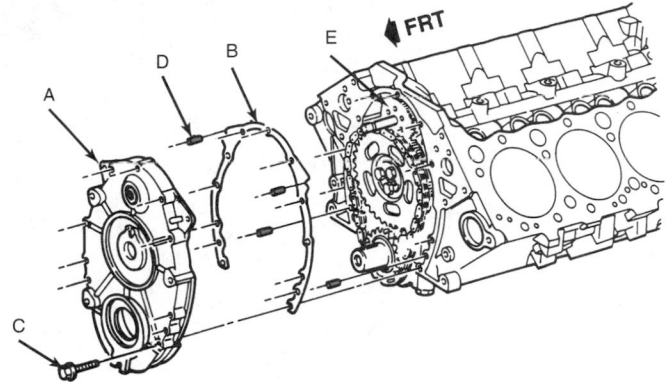

Figure 16-19.   Dowel pins used to align cover, centering seal on crankshaft. A—Front cover. B—Cover gasket. C—Cover bolt. D—Dowel pin. E—Water pump drive gear and shaft. (Chevrolet)

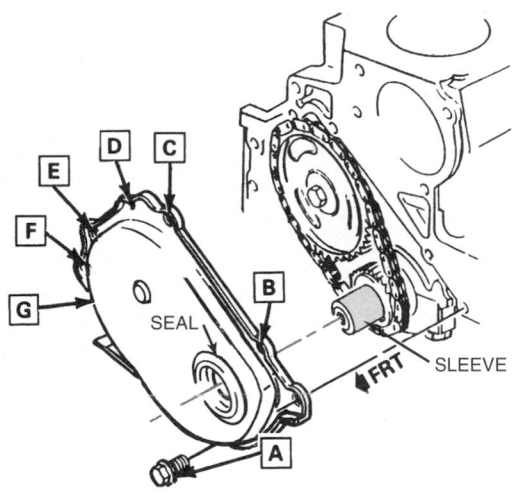

Figure 16-20.   Using centering sleeve to align oil seal on crankshaft. Tighten cover and bolts in sequence (A-G) with the sleeve in place. (Buick)

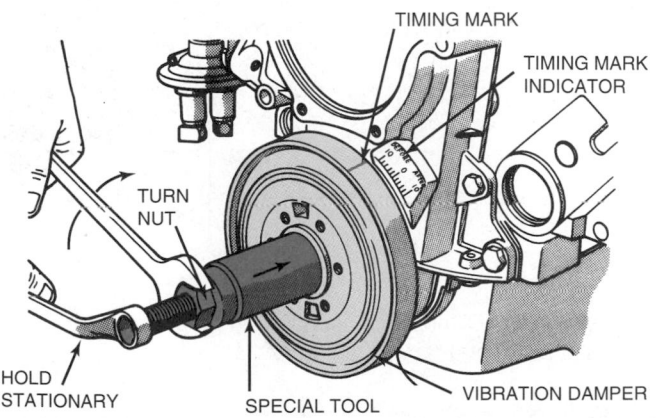

Figure 16-21.   This technician is installing and seating the vibration damper with a special tool. (Dodge)

Handle Gears and Sprockets with Care

Both gears and sprockets can be damaged by careless handling. Never hammer on them except with a proper driver.

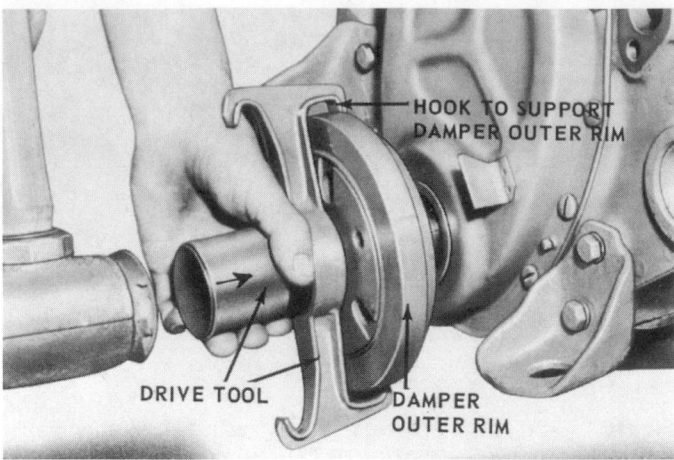

Figure 16-22. This driver is designed to support the damper's outer rim, protecting the damper during installation. (GMC)

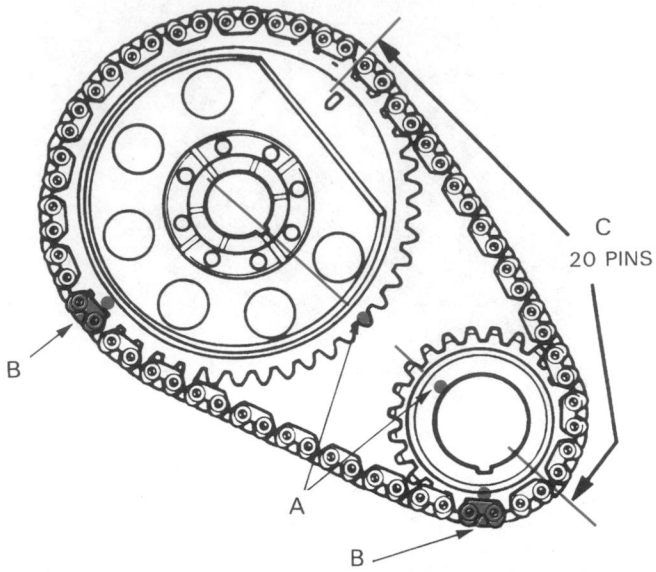

Figure 16-24. Three methods of timing the camshaft. A—Marks together and aligned with shaft centers. B—Colored links aligned with sprocket marks. C—Specific number of pins or links between marks. (Jeep)

pump, oil pump, and accessory shaft. The belt itself is generally driven with aluminum or sintered iron (metal formed by heating and compressing powdered iron and graphite into a solid) sprockets. See **Figure 16-25.**

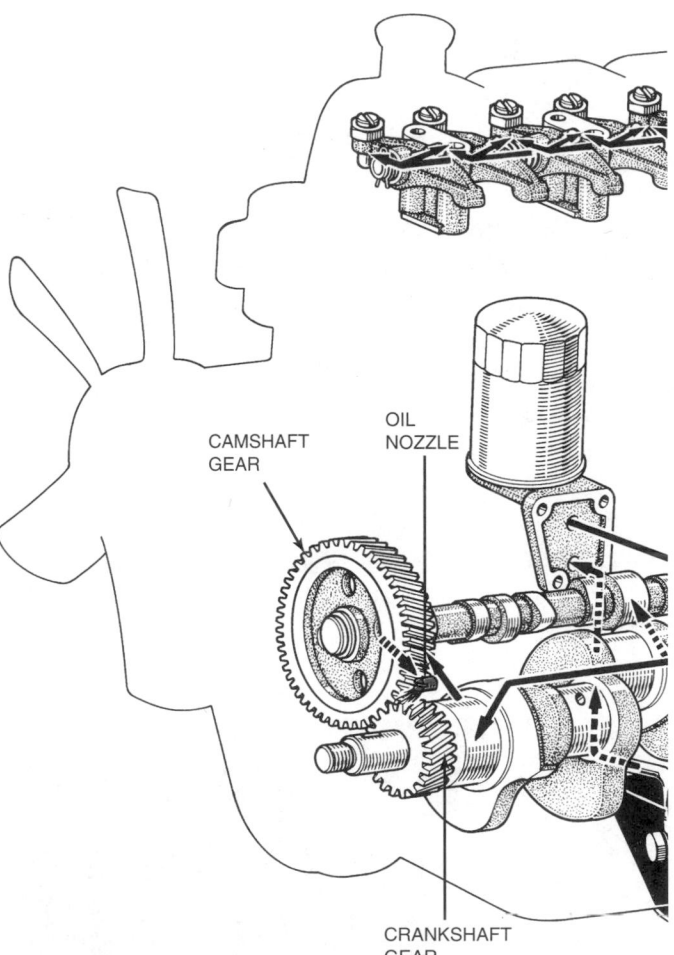

Figure 16-23. Oil nozzle must be open for proper gear lubrication. (Toyota)

Make sure the driver is only used on the center hub. Avoid nicking or scratching the teeth. Keep gears and sprockets clean and lubricate them thoroughly upon assembly.

Servicing the Timing Belt and Sprocket

Some engines are equipped with a ribbed, fiberglass-reinforced rubber **timing belt** to drive the camshaft, fuel

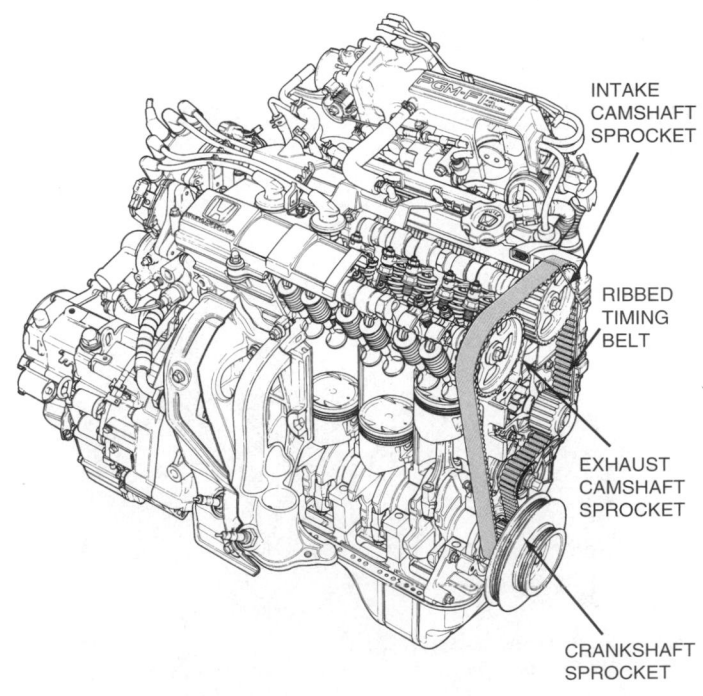

Figure 16-25. This four-cylinder, dual-overhead camshaft, 16-valve engine uses a ribbed timing belt. Note that one camshaft operates all intake valves and one camshaft operates all exhaust valves. (Honda)

Removing the Timing Belt

The following is a basic procedure for timing belt removal. Follow the manufacturer's recommendations for the engine at hand.

1. Remove the water pump, air pump, and other belts.
2. Remove the pulley(s).
3. Remove the timing belt cover.
4. Line up the timing marks.
5. Loosen the belt tensioner.
6. Remove the timing belt.

Belt Inspection and Precautions

If a timing belt is to be reused, examine it thoroughly for damage. When examining the belt, do not twist or bend it into a curved diameter of 1″ (25 mm) or less. Also, do not turn it inside out. Carelessly handling the timing belt can cause core damage. Keep the belt away from oil, chemicals, direct sunlight, and excessive heat.

Check the belt for the following problems:

- Hardened surface rubber.
- Cracked back rubber.
- Cracked or peeling canvas.
- Badly worn teeth.
- Cracked tooth bottom.
- Missing teeth.
- Worn or cracked belt sides.
- Oil or water saturation.

If one or more of the listed conditions are present, replace the belt with a new one of the same quality. Some belt conditions are pictured in **Figure 16-26.**

Inspecting, Removing, and Installing the Sprockets

After the belt has been examined, check all sprockets for looseness, tooth wear, burrs, or cracks. If any damage is found, replace the sprocket.

Sprockets are generally pressed and/or bolted onto the camshaft, crankshaft, and accessory shaft. When removal is necessary, follow the manufacturer's recommendations. **Figure 16-27** shows a particular crankshaft sprocket being removed with a special puller.

When installing sprockets, make sure they are not turned around (front to back). Install all keys (where used) and line up all timing marks. Replace sprocket fasteners and torque them to specifications.

Installing the Belt

The following is a basic belt installation procedure. Line up all sprocket timing marks and install the belt, **Figure 16-28.** Be sure the belt is routed correctly. Note that many belt drives have more than one timing mark. Extra timing marks are needed for dual overhead camshafts and timing-belt-driven distributors.

Remove all spark plugs and revolve the crankshaft to TDC (top dead center) in the direction of normal travel. Turning the crankshaft backwards can cause the belt to skip teeth and alter the timing. Place the belt tensioner tool horizontally on the tensioner hex and loosen the tensioner locknut. Rotate the crankshaft through two full revolutions from TDC. Secure the locknut on the tensioner while keeping the belt tensioning tool in position. See **Figure 16-29.**

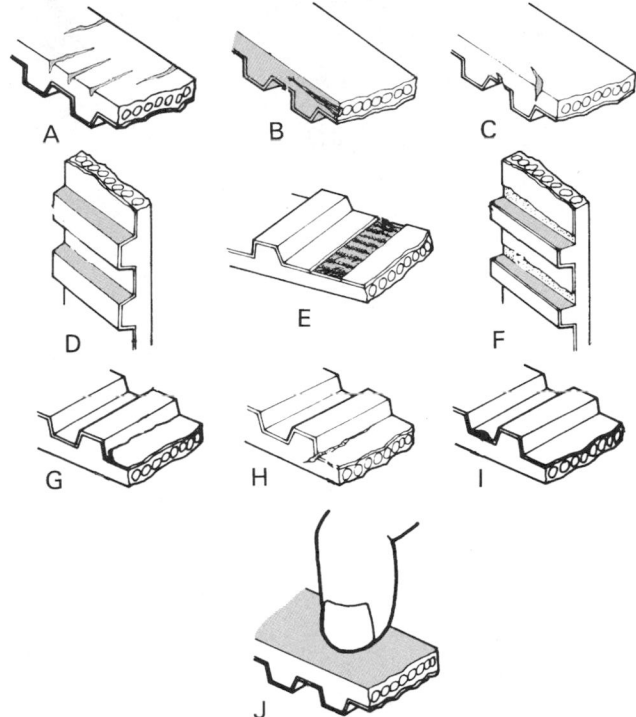

Figure 16-26.   Some common timing belt problems. If any are present, discard the belt. A—Cracked belt back surface rubber. B—Side wear. C—Edge cracking. D—Flank on teeth worn (load side). E—Missing tooth. Reinforcing belts exposed. F—Extreme flank wear. Canvas worn. Rubber exposed. G—Cracked and separated canvas. H—Cracked canvas. I—Canvas separating from rubber. J—Back surface rubber hardened. Even firm pressure with fingernail will not leave marks. (Chrysler)

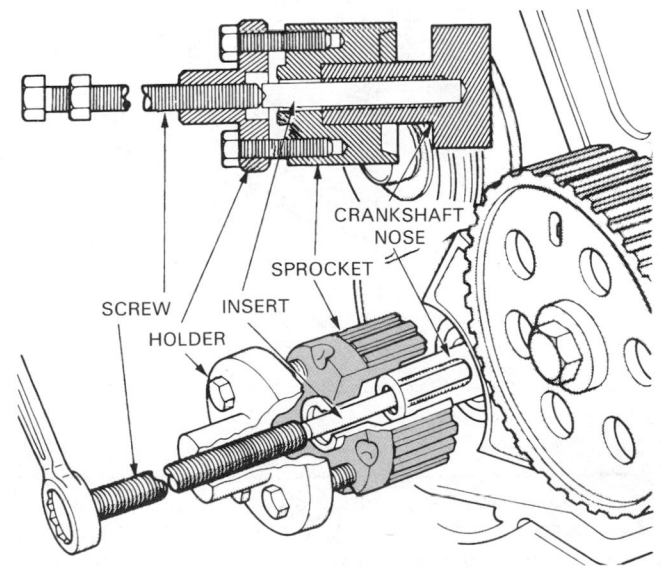

Figure 16-27.   The crankshaft sprocket is removed from the crankshaft nose using a special puller. (Chrysler)

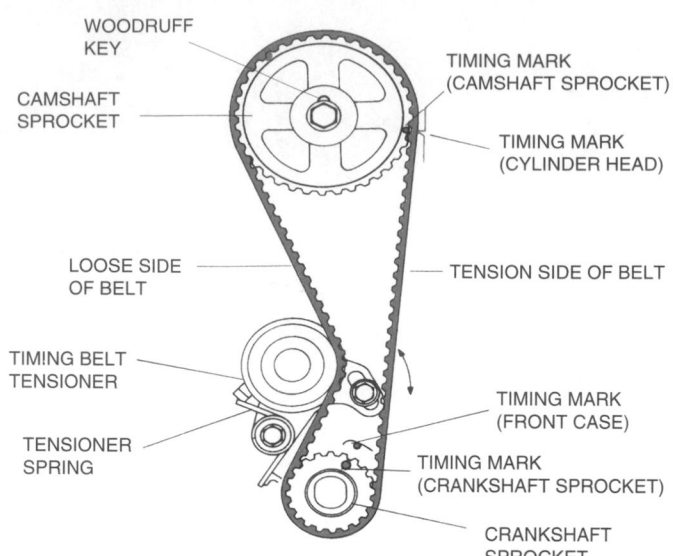

Figure 16-28. Sprockets and belt correctly assembled with timing marks aligned. Note the spring-loaded belt tensioner. (Hyundai)

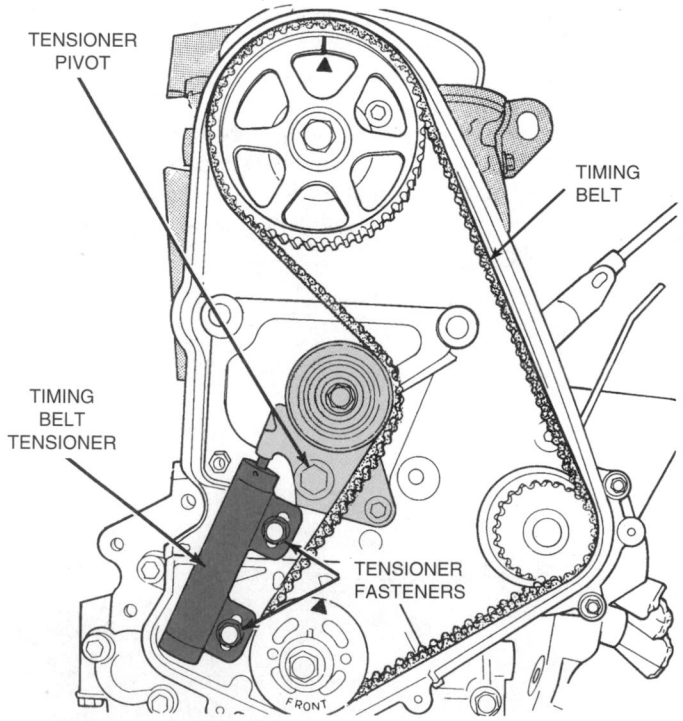

Figure 16-29. Timing belt tension is kept properly adjusted with a belt tensioner. Some of these tensioners may contain silicone oil. Always check for signs of leakage. (Chrysler)

> **Caution:** If a whirring sound is heard after you start the engine, stop the engine. This sound indicates that the belt is too tight. This condition will greatly reduce the belt's service life.

Checking the Camshaft

This section explains how to service the *camshaft.* Camshaft service is similar for all engines, no matter where the cam is placed or how it is driven.

Checking Journal-to-Bearing Clearance

Worn *camshaft bearings* can seriously lower oil pressure and produce excessive throw off, increasing oil consumption. Other vital engine bearings may be starved, and deposits (carbon) in the combustion chambers can build to dangerous levels.

Camshaft-journal-to-bearing clearance can be checked in several ways. Feeler (narrow blade) gages of varying thickness can be inserted between the camshaft journal and the bearing until the clearance is determined. Do not force the gage and damage the bearing surface. Maximum clearance will be around .005″-.006″ (0.13-0.16 mm).

Plastigage may also be used to check clearance. Place the Plastigage on the camshaft bearing journal, install the bearing cap, and torque the cap bolts to specifications. Remove the bearing cap carefully and measure the Plastigage. Do not rotate the camshaft with the bearing cap in place. A false reading will result. See **Figure 16-30.**

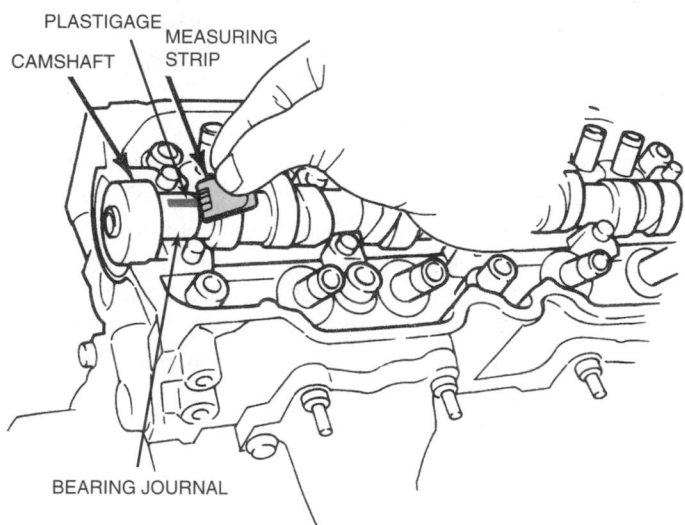

Figure 16-30. Checking camshaft journal bearing clearance with Plastigage. (Geo)

A dial indicator can be set up so that clearance (movement) will be indicated when the camshaft is forced up and down (right angles to bore).

A small hole gage (camshaft removed) can be used to measure the bearing inside diameter (ID). By subtracting the diameter of the journal from the bearing ID, an accurate indication of clearance will be given. Check the bearings for signs of wiping, imbedded dirt, and scoring.

Inspecting the Camshaft

Clean, rinse, blow dry, and lightly oil the camshaft. Mike each journal in several spots to determine the amount of wear and the extent of out-of-roundness. Overall wear exceeding .0015″ per inch (0.038 mm per 25.4 mm) of journal diameter or out-of-roundness beyond .001″ (0.025 mm) will require regrinding and the use of undersize inserts. Journals must be smooth.

Check camshaft journal alignment with V-blocks and a dial indicator. Check specs for maximum runout (varies from .002″ to .005″ [0.05 to 0.13 mm], depending on design). Refer to **Figure 16-31**.

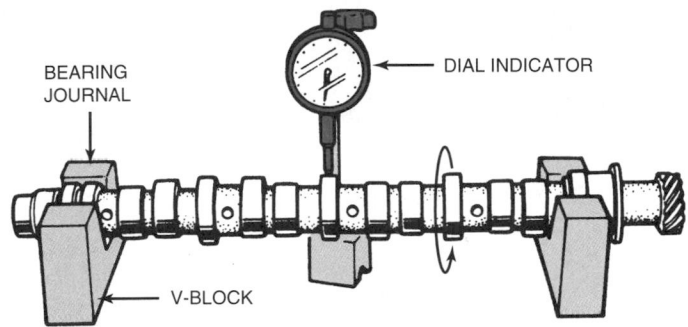

Figure 16-31. Checking camshaft runout. Mount the camshaft in V-blocks and measure runout with a dial indicator. This cam shaft has a runout limit of 0.0039″ (0.010 mm). (Suzuki)

Inspect each *cam lobe* for signs of galling, chipping, or excessive wear, which can reduce valve lift and damage lifters. The wear pattern will usually vary in width, being somewhat narrower on the base circle and widening toward the nose of the cam. The pattern may be somewhat off-center, **Figure 16-32**.

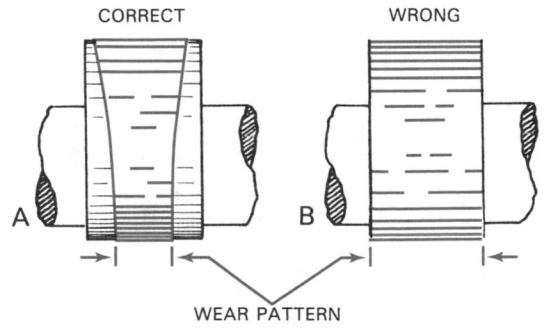

Figure 16-32. Usual cam lobe wear pattern. A—Correct. B—Incorrect.

The wear pattern should not show across the full width of the lobe. The majority of camshafts are ground so that the cam lobe surface is slightly tapered. By grinding the bottom of the lifter with a slight crown and placing it slightly off-center in relation to the cam, the lifters will tend to rotate. Also, the loading (pressure) area will not extend to the edge of the lobe, where it could cause damage, **Figure 16-33**.

When lifter bottoms are reground, the original crown should be retained. If the bottoms are ground flat, edge loading will result and both cam and lifter wear will be greatly accelerated, **Figure 16-34**.

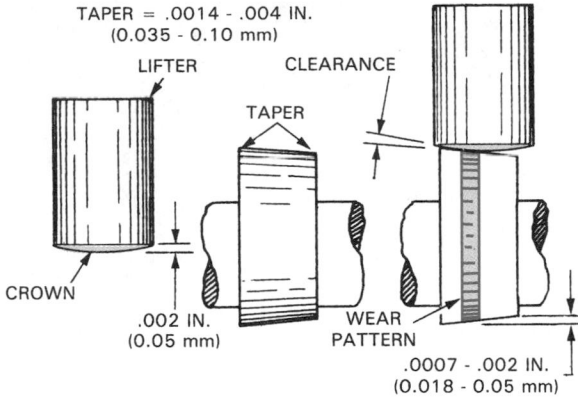

Figure 16-33. Cams are often ground with a taper. The lifter base is crowned.

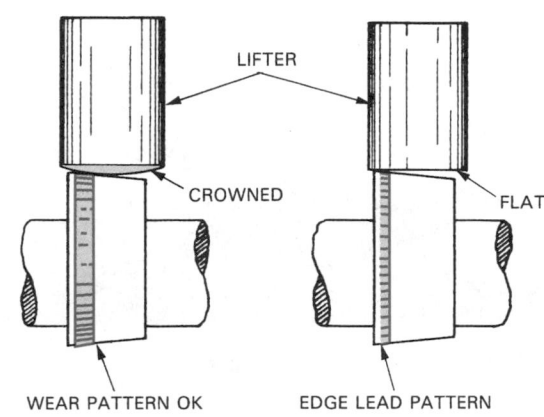

Figure 16-34. If lifter base is reground, the crown should be retained. A flat base will cause damage from edge loading.

Camshaft Welding and Regrinding

A chipped or badly worn cam can be built up by welding and then reground to original specifications. Camshaft availability and replacement cost will determine the feasibility of this procedure. Study **Figure 16-35**.

A camshaft showing reasonable wear on either the journals or cams can often be repaired by grinding. As with crankshaft grinding, camshaft grinding equipment must be highly accurate and the operator must be fully experienced, **Figure 16-36**. After grinding, undersize inserts are required.

Camshafts are generally surface hardened to a depth of at least .040″ (1.01 mm). When regrinding, the journals are customarily ground either .010 or .020″ (0.25 or 0.51 mm) undersize. The new inserts are then align bored to produce the proper bearing clearance of from .001 to .003″ (0.025 to 0.08 mm). To provide proper break in and longer wear, many regrinders cover the cam lobes (never the journals) with a special phosphate coating.

Installing New Camshaft Bearings

Some engines, especially those with overhead cams, use two-piece camshaft bearings. The camshaft bearing caps are removed to allow access to the camshaft. The bearings are replaced much like crankshaft main bearings. See **Figure 16-37**.

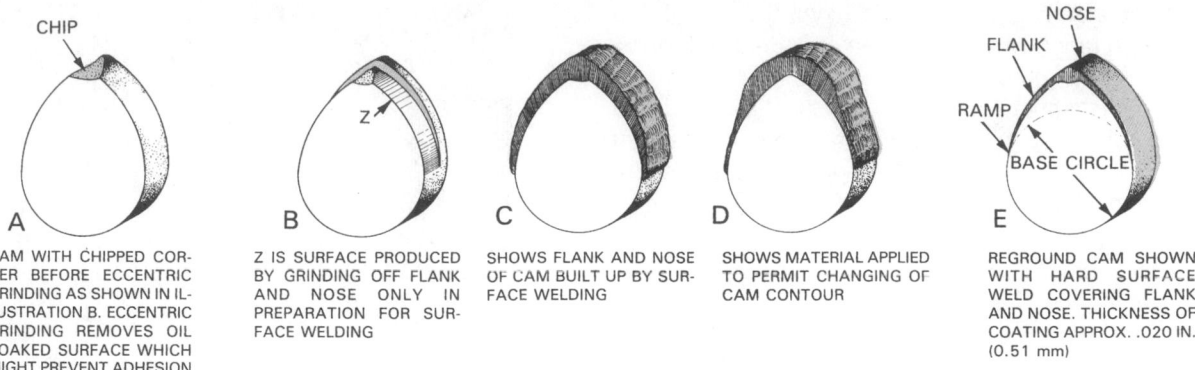

A — CAM WITH CHIPPED COR-NER BEFORE ECCENTRIC GRINDING AS SHOWN IN IL-LUSTRATION B. ECCENTRIC GRINDING REMOVES OIL SOAKED SURFACE WHICH MIGHT PREVENT ADHESION OF WELDING MATERIAL

B — Z IS SURFACE PRODUCED BY GRINDING OFF FLANK AND NOSE ONLY IN PREPARATION FOR SUR-FACE WELDING

C — SHOWS FLANK AND NOSE OF CAM BUILT UP BY SUR-FACE WELDING

D — SHOWS MATERIAL APPLIED TO PERMIT CHANGING OF CAM CONTOUR

E — REGROUND CAM SHOWN WITH HARD SURFACE WELD COVERING FLANK AND NOSE. THICKNESS OF COATING APPROX. .020 IN. (0.51 mm)

Figure 16-35.   Chipped cam lobe repaired by welding and grinding. (Van Norman)

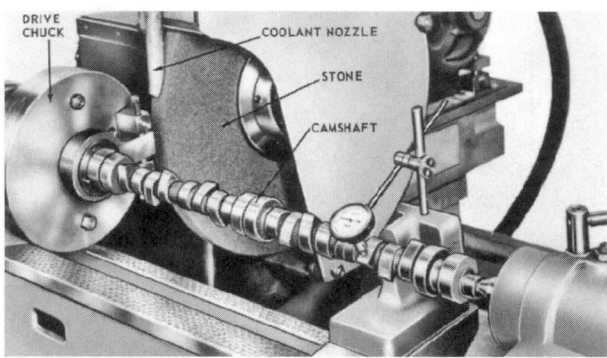

Figure 16-36.   Regrinding a camshaft.

With one-piece bearing inserts, the old inserts are either driven or pulled out. The bore may be slightly chamfered on the front side so that material will not be shaved from the new bearing as it is forced into place. Look at **Figure 16-38.** Clean the bores and oil the delivery holes. Then check the bores for size and alignment.

There are a number of camshaft bearing removal and installation tools. In one type, the proper size mandrel is selected and fitted to a drive bar, **Figure 16-39.** The drive bar is passed through the bores until the mandrel is positioned properly. The insert is oiled and slipped on the mandrel. Rotate the bar until the mandrel expands snugly inside the insert. Align the oil hole in the bearing with the oil hole in the bore and start the bearing by hand, **Figure 16-40.**

At this point, rotate the bar one-eighth turn counter-clockwise, **Figure 16-41.** This will reduce the mandrel diameter about .004″ (0.10 mm) to allow the bearing ID to reduce as it is driven into place. Using a hammer, drive the bearing into the bore, **Figure 16-42.** Stop driving when the drive face of the mandrel is flush with the bore, **Figure 16-43.** Remove the bar. Check to make certain the oil hole in the bearing is correctly aligned with the oil hole in the block, **Figure 16-44.**

When installing cam bearings, be sure they are started properly. The oil holes must be aligned, and material must not shave as the bearing enters. If the bearing is cocked, it will be distorted. It can even become loose enough to rotate in the bore, cutting off the oil supply.

If the front bearing is specially designed to provide lubrication for the timing chain or gears, make sure the cor-

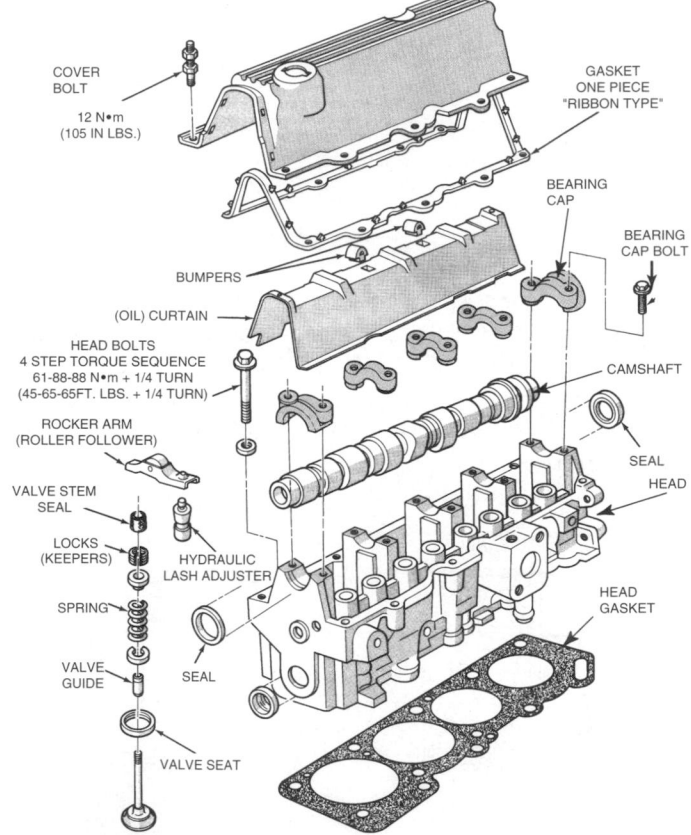

Figure 16-37.   One four-cylinder engine using two-piece camshaft bearings. Cylinder head houses integral bottom half of the bearings. Removable bearing caps make up the top half. Note the use of roller rocker arms. (Chrysler)

rect end of the bearing faces forward and that it is installed to the proper depth. If the bearing shells are chamfered on one end, start them so the chamfer enters the bore first. When possible, install the split seam toward the top of the engine (away from the high load area). If the original inserts were staked in place (a portion of shell dented into a recess with a punch), the new inserts should also be staked to prevent the insert from turning.

After align boring, clean and lubricate the bearings. Oil and carefully install the camshaft, **Figure 16-45.** The edges of the cam lobes and gear teeth can easily damage the soft babbitt bearing lining. Use extreme care.

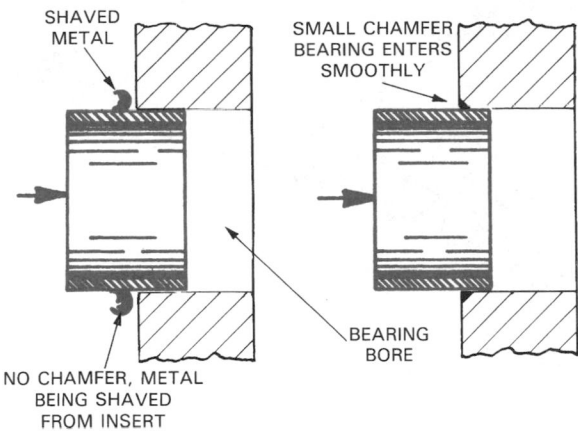

Figure 16-38.   Chamfer bearing bore on front side. A *small* chamfer is ample.

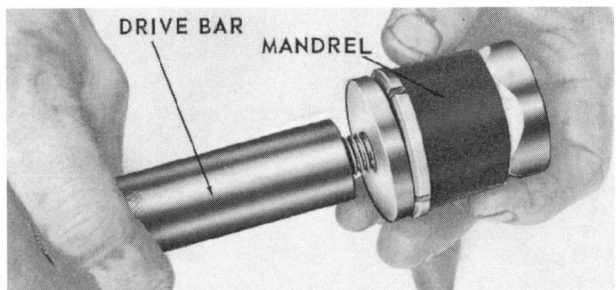

Figure 16-39.   Fitting a proper mandrel to a drive bar. (Dura-Bond)

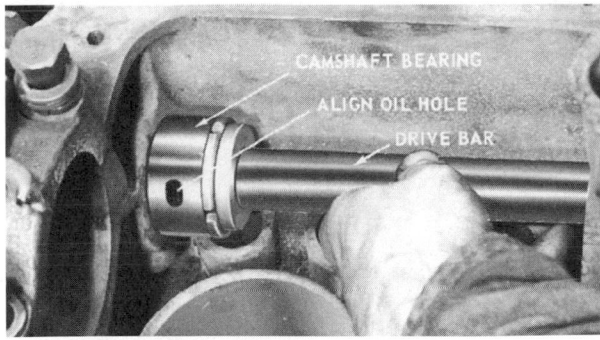

Figure 16-40.   The bearing is installed on a mandrel and oiled, the oil holes are aligned, and the bearing is started into bore by hand.

Camshaft Rear Bearing Core Plug or Oil Seal Plug

When replacing the camshaft rear bearing oil seal plug (often called Welch plug or core hole plug), clean out the plug counterbore. Coat both the OD of the new plug and the counterbore sides with sealer. Drive the plug in squarely. Do not drive the plug below recommended depth. In some cases, a stop ledge is provided. Use a suitable driver that contacts the plug outer edge.

In some designs, striking the plug in the center (after fully seating it with a driver) will cause it to expand tightly against the walls of the counterbore. This type of plug is crowned. Be sure to install it with the crown facing outward,

Figure 16-41.   Rotate the drive bar 1/8 turn counterclockwise. This will loosen the mandrel in the camshaft bearing to allow the bearing ID to decrease when the bearing is driven into place.

Figure 16-42.   Driving a camshaft bearing into position with a drive bar and a proper mandrel. (Federal-Mogul)

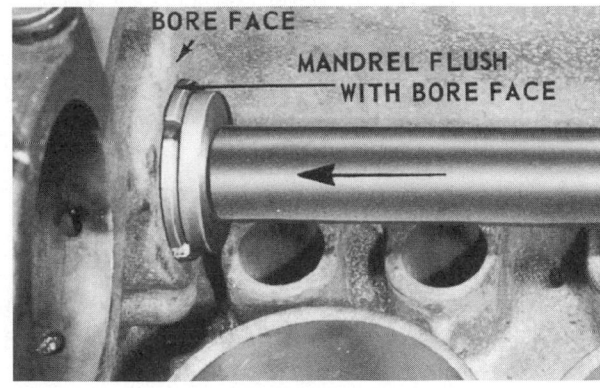

Figure 16-43.   Drive the bearing in until the mandrel is flush with the bearing bore face. (Dura-Bond)

Figure 16-46. As with all plug installations, make sure you have a strong, permanent seal. If a leak develops after engine installation, the repair can be very expensive.

Figure 16-47 illustrates a camshaft and thrust plate for a V-10 engine. **Figure 16-48** illustrates a camshaft, chain sprocket, and thrust plate. Note the oil pump drive gear. **Figure 16-49** illustrates one particular chain-driven camshaft arrangement for a four-cylinder engine.

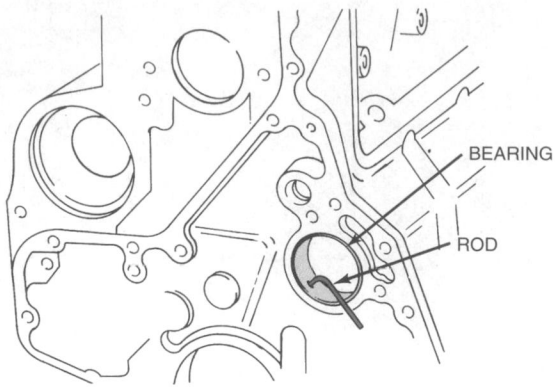

Figure 16-44. Checking camshaft bearing oil hole alignment after bearing installation. This engine calls for a 0.128″ (3.2 mm) diameter rod to check for proper clearance. Rod must pass through bearing hole and into oil hole. (Dodge)

Figure 16-45. Be careful not to damage bearing surfaces when installing the camshaft. If required, lubricate the camshaft before installation. (Federal-Mogul)

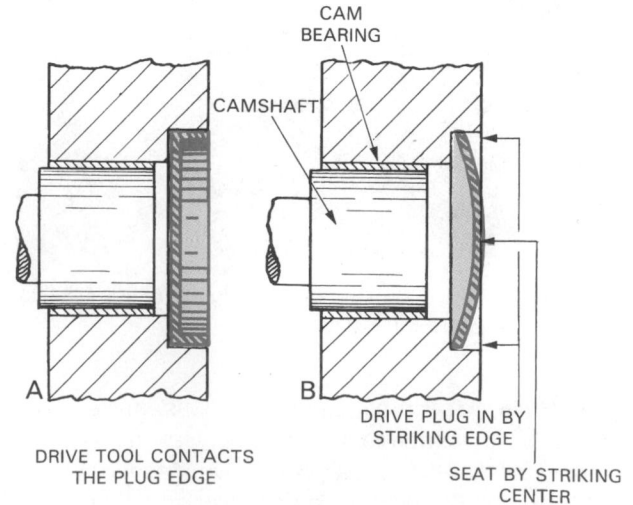

Figure 16-46. Typical camshaft rear journal oil seal plugs. A—Driven in on edge. B—Driven in on edge and seated with blow in center.

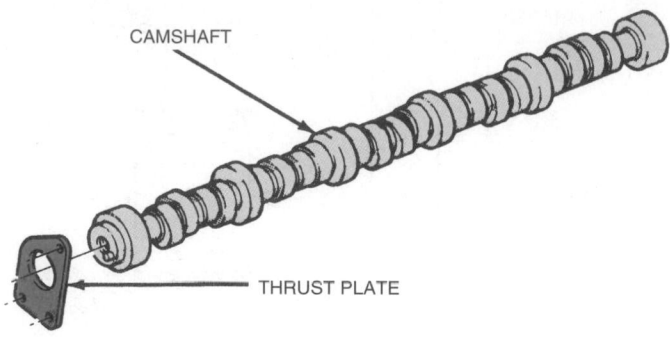

Figure 16-47. Typical camshaft and thrust plate. (Chrysler)

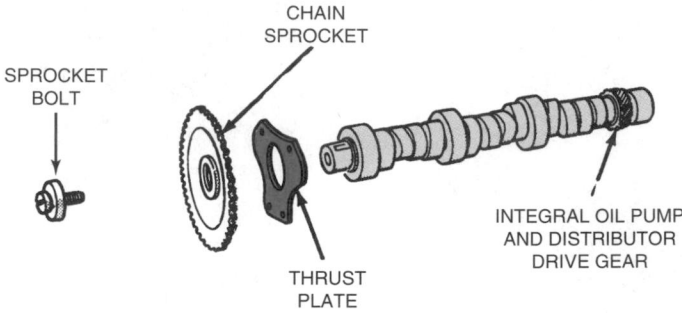

Figure 16-48. A chain-driven camshaft for a V-6 engine. Note the oil pump and distributor drive gear. (Dodge)

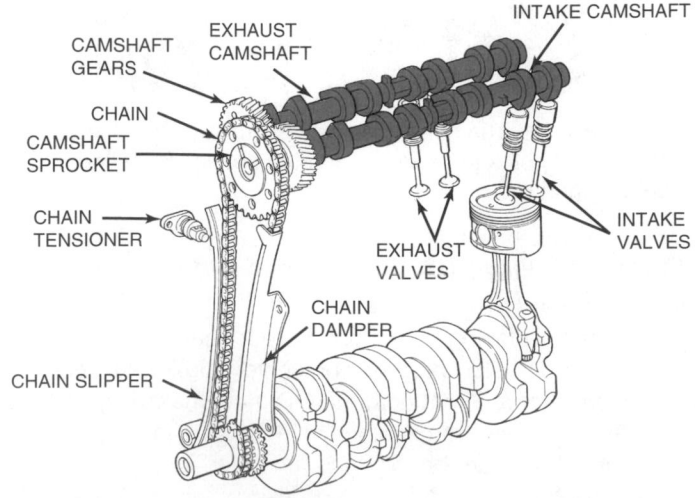

Figure 16-49. One type of dual overhead camshaft arrangement. Intake cam is driven by a chain, and the exhaust cam is gear driven by the intake camshaft. Note that no rocker arms are used. (Toyota)

Camshaft Drive Thrust Direction

During operation, some camshafts tend to exert a **thrust** toward the rear of the engine. This type of shaft does not utilize a bolt-on thrust flange. Camshafts that exert a forward thrust must obviously be restrained. This is the job of the front thrust washer. In addition, some engines use a small spring located between the camshaft gears and the front cover to place a rearward pressure on the gear.

Checking Cam Lobe Lift

When the cam lobes wear, they may not raise the lifters to the specified height. This, in turn, reduces the valve opening, or lift, distance. Refer to **Figure 16-50.** With the cam out of the engine, **cam lobe lift** can be checked with V-blocks and a dial indicator.

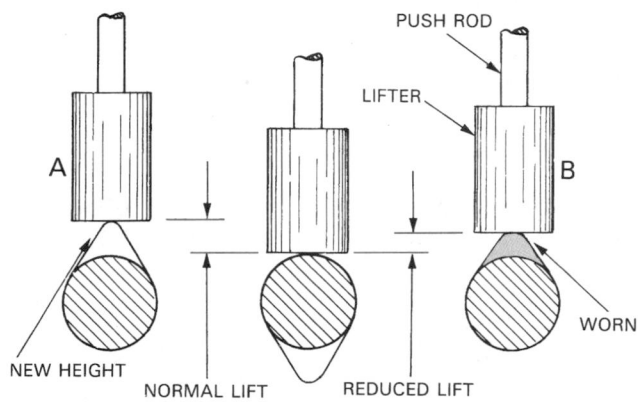

Figure 16-50.   Cam wear lowers lift. A—No wear on cam, normal lift. B—Worn cam, reduced lift.

If the cam is installed in the engine, the procedure for measuring lift depends on the engine type. In an overhead cam engine, lift can be checked by mounting a dial indicator as shown in **Figure 16-51A.** Turn the crankshaft until the dial indicator stem is riding on the cam base circle (lowest indicator reading). At this point, zero the indicator and slowly turn the crankshaft until the lifter rests on the cam nose. Record the highest reading on the indicator as the nose passes under the lifter. The total indicator reading (TIR) will be the amount of lift. Check specifications for maximum lobe lift wear.

If the cam is in pushrod engine, lift can be checked by mounting a dial indicator as shown in **Figure 16-51B.** Hold the push rod down and turn the crankshaft until the lifter is riding on the cam base circle. At this point, zero the indicator and turn the crankshaft until the lifter rests on the cam nose. Do this slowly, so that you can record the highest reading on the indicator as the nose passes under the lifter. As with the overhead cam engine, total indicator reading will indicate the amount of lift.

Lifter Service

Worn or sticking **lifters** can cause missing or noises and will contribute to the wear of the other engine parts. Therefore, they should be carefully checked.

Valve lifters can be divided into two main types: mechanical lifters and hydraulic lifters. The hydraulic lifter is by far the most common. The hydraulic valve lifters used on overhead camshaft engines are sometimes called **valve lash adjusters.** The basic lifter operating principles remain the same, however.

The portion of the lifter body that protrudes below the guide bore is often coated with gum and varnish. This makes removal difficult unless a special tool is used to grasp the lifter. The tool is engaged and the lifter pulled upward with a twisting motion, **Figure 16-52.**

Servicing Mechanical Lifters

Mechanical lifters, or tappets, are found on some high-performance engines and some older vehicles. They are simple in construction and operation. Begin the inspection process by cleaning the lifter. Inspect the push rod socket for signs of wear or galling. The lifter-to-camshaft surface should be smooth and free of cam wear, grooving, chipping, and galling. Lifters showing heavy camshaft wear or worn sockets should be replaced. If the wear is minor, the tappet may be resurfaced on the valve grinding machine. Lifter wear patterns are shown in **Figure 16-53.** Tappet adjusting screws, such as shown in **Figure 16-54,** are found on older vehicles and off-road equipment using flathead or F-head engines. They may also be resurfaced providing the valve stem surface has not worn below the hardened portion.

Grinding Mechanical Lifters

Before grinding a mechanical lifter, dress the grinding wheel surface. Secure the lifter in the V-block holder. While applying a stream of coolant to the lifter end, advance the lifter against the stone. Cuts should not exceed .002″ (0.05 mm). Move the lifter back and forth over the stone surface. Do not remove more stock than is absolutely necessary. At the end of the last cut, continue to move the lifter back and forth until the cutting action stops. This will produce a smooth finish. If both ends of the lifter are adaptable to grinding, reverse the lifter and repeat the process, **Figure 16-55.**

When lifter wear is pronounced or galling and chipping are present, check the cam lobes carefully as they may also be damaged. Oversize lifters may be used to correct lifter-to-bore clearance. When clearance exceeds .005″-.006″ (0.13-0.15 mm), replacement is necessary. The bores should be reamed to the exact oversize needed.

Servicing Hydraulic Lifters

Unlike mechanical lifters, hydraulic lifters contain internal parts. These lifters must be disassembled for cleaning and inspection.

Keep Lifters in Order

Each lifter should be placed in a marked holder so that it may be returned to the guide bore from which it was removed. A block of wood with two rows of holes, each row representing one bank of lifters, will do.

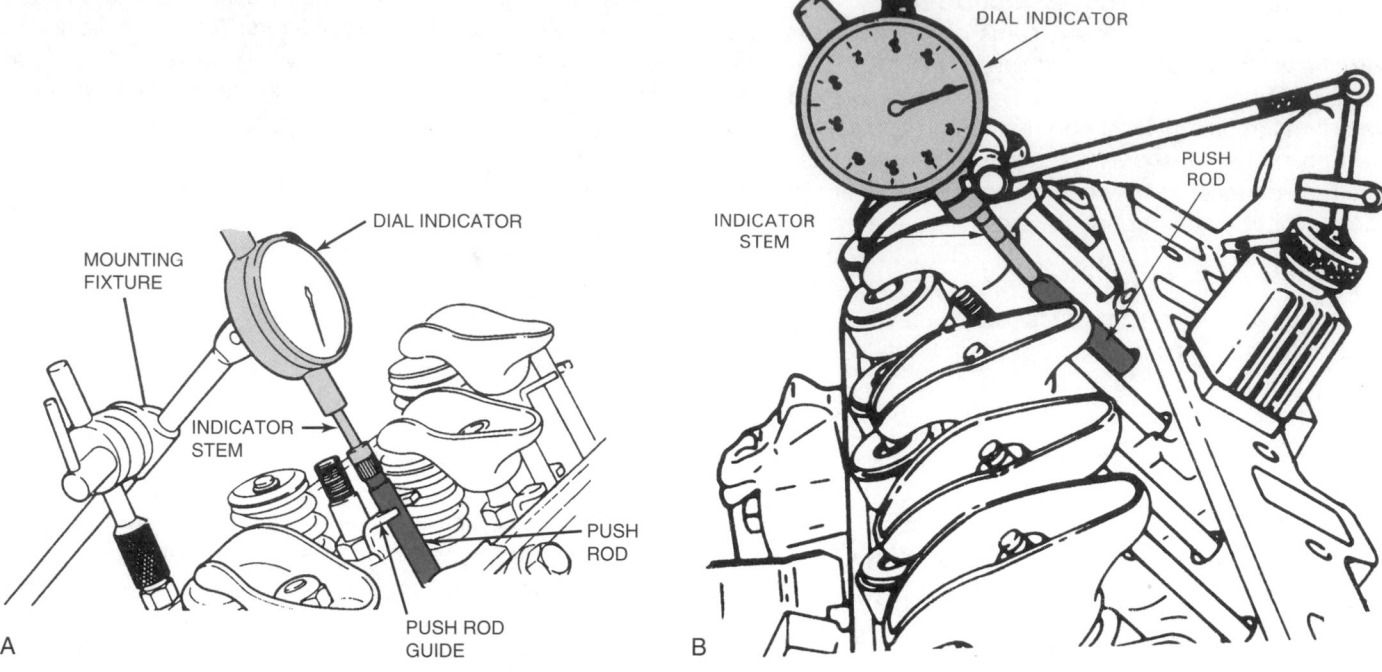

Figure 16-51. Camshaft lobe lift can be measured with a dial indicator. A—Checking lift on overhead cam engine. B—Checking lift on a pushrod engine. The indicator stem and push rod must be parallel to obtain the correct measurement. (Pontiac)

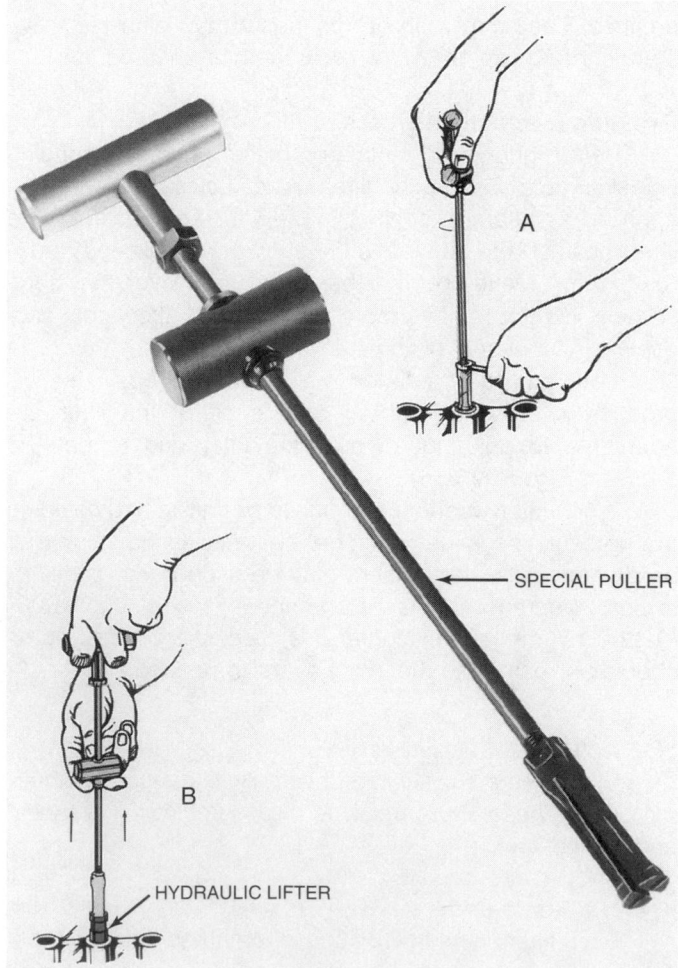

Figure 16-52. Using a special puller to remove a hydraulic lifter. (GMC)

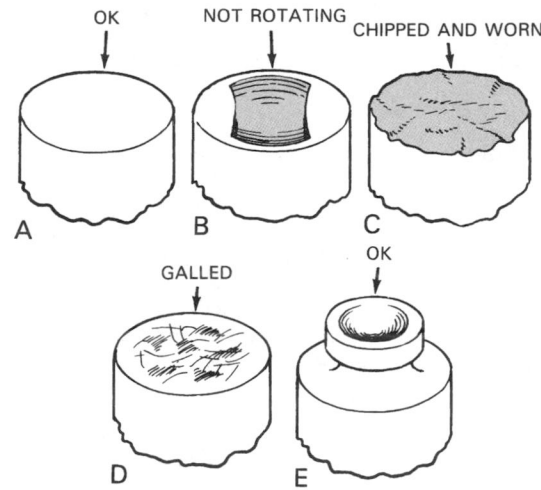

Figure 16-53. Lifter wear patterns. A, B, C, D—Camshaft end of lifter. E—Push rod end of lifter.

Disassembling a Lifter

To disassemble a lifter, place the lifter body right side up on a clean board. Using a push rod, depress the plunger and snap out the retaining ring, **Figure 16-56.** Then, release pressure on the plunger and guide it out of the lifter body. If the plunger sticks, and it often will, it can be removed with a tool designed for this purpose.

Keep Lifter Parts Together

Lifter parts are made to extremely close tolerances (.0001″ or 0.00254 mm). During original assembly, the plunger is selectively fitted to the body by trying several

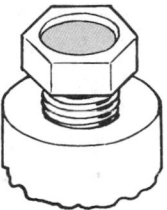

Figure 16-54.   Tappet adjusting screw.

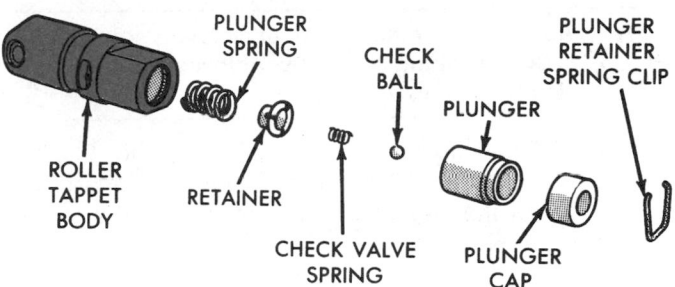

Figure 16-57.   Typical hydraulic lifter.

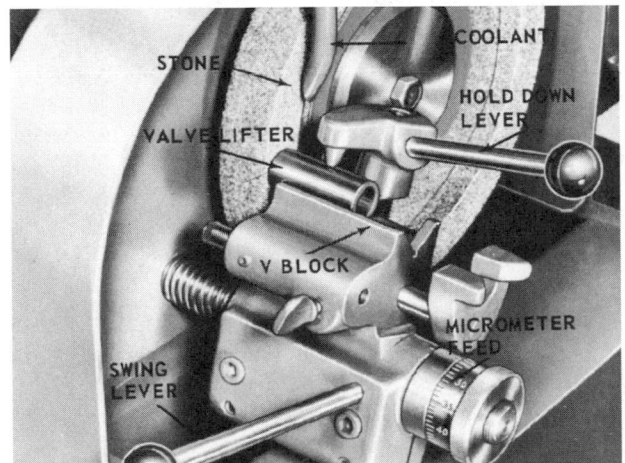

Figure 16-55.   Resurfacing the end of a solid valve lifter. (Van Norman)

Cleaning Lifters

A special cleaning station, such as the one shown in **Figure 16-58,** is desirable. Note the trays used to keep the lifter parts together. The tray on the left contains a special cleaning solvent designed to dissolve gum and varnish. The central tray contains clean solvent for rinsing. The small tray contains clean solvent for a final rinse.

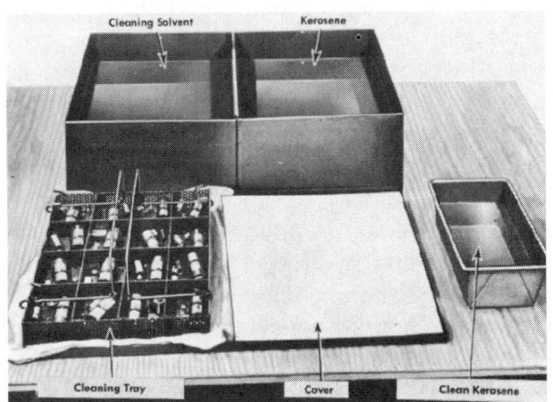

Figure 16-58.   A good setup for cleaning hydraulic valve lifters.

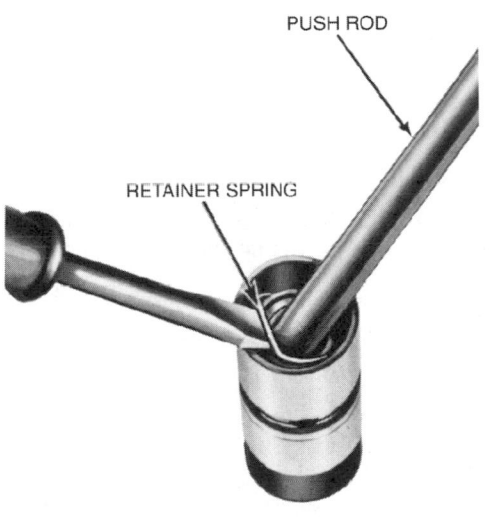

Figure 16-56.   Removing the lifter plunger retaining ring. (Chevrolet)

Due to the close working tolerances, lifters must be thoroughly cleaned and assembled in a spotless condition. The slightest trace of grit, dust, or lint will cause faulty operation.

After all lifters are dismantled, rinse each group of parts in clean solvent. Do not use the solvent in the trays. This first rinse is merely to remove most of the oil and sludge, so the useful life of the special cleaning solvent will be prolonged.

Soak in Solvent

Following the initial rinse, place the tray with compartments into the cleaning solvent. Lay plungers and lifter bodies on their sides so the solvent will enter. Allow them to soak for about one hour. Exact soaking time will depend on the type of solvent used, the condition of the solvent, and the condition of the lifters.

plungers until one fits perfectly. Therefore, the plunger and lifter body are not interchangeable and must be kept together. **Figure 16-57** shows a disassembled lifter. The check valve retainer, spring, and valve are still in place on the plunger. As each lifter is disassembled, place its parts in a marked tray.

Warning: Keep hands out of cleaning solvent and avoid splashing. Use rubber gloves when cleaning lifters.

When the soak cycle is completed, elevate the tray. After tipping it from side to side to empty the parts of solvent, suspend the tray over the solution until the excess solvent has dripped off.

Rinse in Solvent

When thoroughly drained, place tray in the pan of initial rinse solvent. Agitate the tray several times by lifting and lowering. Remove the tray from the rinse solvent and allow it to drain. This rinse will remove the cleaning solvent and a great deal of the loosened deposits.

Wipe all lifter surfaces with a clean, lint-free cloth. Use a firm wiping action to remove all remaining gum. A soft brush should be used for the inside of lifter and plunger bodies. When all lifters have been cleaned, place the tray in the center container of solvent. Agitate the tray, remove it from the solvent, and allow it to drain. Finally, blow all parts dry.

Inspecting Lifter Parts

Start with the lifter plunger. Use a magnifying glass to inspect the plunger check valve seat for nicks, scratches, and wear. Inspect the outer plunger body for signs of galling. Any scratches on either the check seat or plunger body that can be felt with the fingernail are cause for rejection. Ignore the slight edge that may occur where the plunger extends beyond the inner working surface of the lifter body. However, if this edge is quite sharp, the plunger must be considered defective.

Check the lifter body inner and outer surfaces. They must be smooth and free of scoring. The lifter-to-cam-lobe surface must also be smooth and free of galling, chipping, and excessive wear. A round wear pattern (lifter was rotating) or a square wear pattern (lifter not rotating) is acceptable as long as the pattern is smooth and free of excessive wear.

The outer portion of the lifter body that contacts the lifter guide bore will usually show a distinct wear pattern caused by cam lobe side thrust. It, too, can be considered acceptable unless scoring or pronounced wear is evident. If the push rod seat is scored or badly worn, it must be replaced.

Examine the check ball with the magnifying glass. Any nicks, dents, or scratches will render it useless. The ball retainer will show a bright spot where it contacts the check ball. This is normal. A pounded area or any cracks will be cause for rejection.

Inspect both plunger and check valve springs for signs of distortion or other damage. Replace them if necessary. Discard any retainer rings that are bent out of shape.

Replacing Parts

Some shops replace internal lifter parts when required. Based on the argument that the cost of new lifters is small compared to that of the possible comeback from premature lifter failure, many shops discard the entire assembly when any part shows damage. When there is considerable mileage on an engine, most shops will automatically discard lifters in favor of new ones. Disassembly, cleaning, inspection, reassembly, and testing take time. If the cost of this labor is deducted from the price of new lifters and the increased reliability factor is taken into account, there is much to be said for replacement.

Inspect and Assemble One Lifter at a Time

After all the parts of one lifter have been inspected and, where required, replaced, each part should be rinsed in the central tray of solvent, blown dry, and thoroughly rinsed in the small pan of solvent. As each part is assembled, it must be put through this sequence. The parts for one entire lifter should be inspected and assembled before going on to the next.

Assembling Lifters

To assemble a lifter, proceed as follows:

1. With the plunger held vertically, the push rod seat in position, and the check valve seat up, place the check ball or check disc on the seat.
2. Position the check valve spring over the valve.
3. Place the valve retainer over the spring and snap it down into the plunger recess.
4. Place the plunger spring over the ball retainer and lower the lifter body down over the plunger.
5. Turn the lifter body right side up.
6. Depress the push rod seat and install the retainer ring.
7. Wrap the assembly in clean, slick paper and proceed to the next lifter.

 Note: All lifter parts should be assembled wet with rinse solvent. Do not wipe or blow dry.

Figure 16-59 shows a cross-section of a typical hydraulic lifter assembly. Note the position of all parts.

Checking Leakdown Rate

Each lifter must possess the correct leakdown rate characteristic. **Leakdown rate** is the length of time it takes for a specified weight to move the plunger (lifter filled with test fluid) from the top to the bottom. This is usually a specified distance.

If a test tool similar to that shown in **Figure 16-60** is available, test the leakdown rate as follows:

1. Raise the weight arm and ram.
2. Place the lifter in the special sleeve inside the test cup. The cup must have sufficient clean test fluid to completely cover the lifter.
3. Lower the ram against the push rod seat.
4. Swing the weight arm down on the ram and depress lifter plunger.
5. Work the weight arm up and down to completely fill the lifter with fluid. After a number of strokes, you will notice

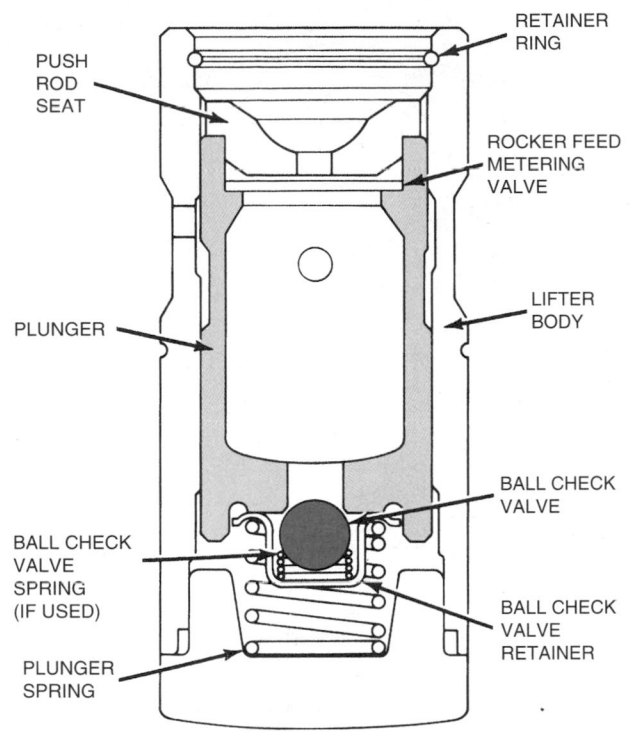

Figure 16-59. Cutaway of a hydraulic lifter utilizing a ball check valve.

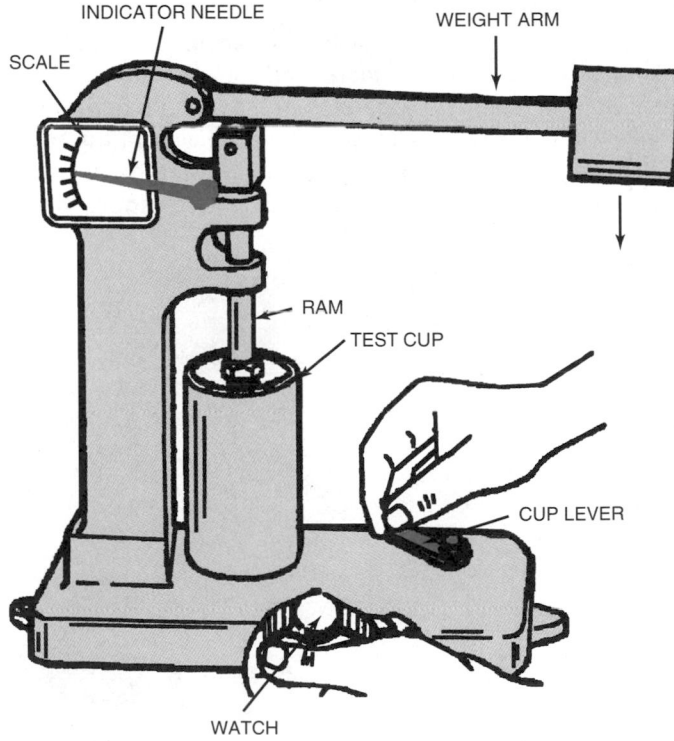

Figure 16-60. Testing hydraulic lifter leakdown rate. (Chevrolet)

a firm resistance on the compression stroke. Give the arm 8 or 10 additional fast pumps to make certain that all air is expelled.

6. Raise the weight arm and allow the plunger to rise against the stop ring.

7. Place the weight on the ram.
8. Using a watch with a second hand, observe the time the instant the indicator needle begins to move.
9. Give the cup lever a complete turn every two seconds while the plunger is being depressed.
10. When the indicator needle has traveled the prescribed distance, check to see how many seconds have elapsed. See manufacturers' specifications for the acceptable leakdown rate.

Another leakdown tester is shown in **Figure 16-61.** To use this tester, remove the push rod seat and submerge the lifter in clean solvent. Depress the check valve with a clean, soft rod. This will allow the bottom area to fill. When completely filled, remove the lifter and reinstall the push rod seat. Engage the test pliers as shown and squeeze the handles. The plunger should slowly move downward. If travel is rapid, disassemble, clean, check, and reassemble the lifter. Make sure the lifter is completely filled with solvent before testing.

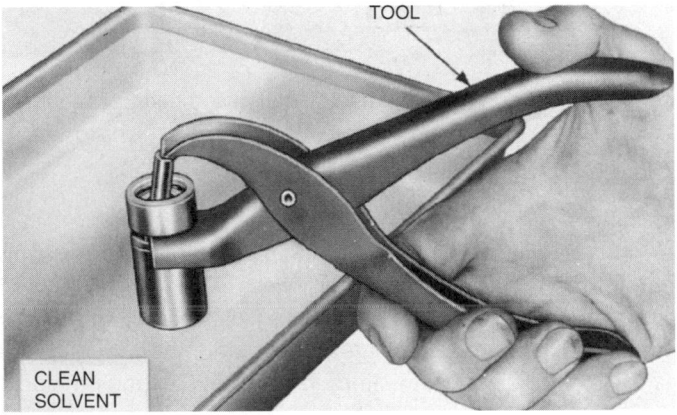

Figure 16-61. Testing leakdown rate with special test pliers. (Dodge)

Installing Lifters

Before installation, fill the lifters with engine oil. Begin by removing the push rod seat and draining out the solvent. Fill the plunger body with clean oil. Jiggle the check valve open to allow oil to fill the lower compartment. When this compartment is full, fill the plunger body and replace the push rod seat. Lubricate the outside of the lifter body and the lifter guide bore. Rub a small amount of Lubriplate or rear axle lubricant on both the cam lobe and the push rod ends of the lifter. Install the lifter in the hole from which it was removed.

When lifters have been installed without filling them with oil, the engine RPM should not exceed a fast idle until all lifters are pumped up (filled with oil).

Overhead Camshaft Hydraulic Lifters

Some engines with overhead camshafts use hydraulic lifters. The lifters can be incorporated into the overhead valve assembly as shown in **Figure 16-62.** The hydraulic adjusting mechanism is located between the camshaft lobe and the valve stem.

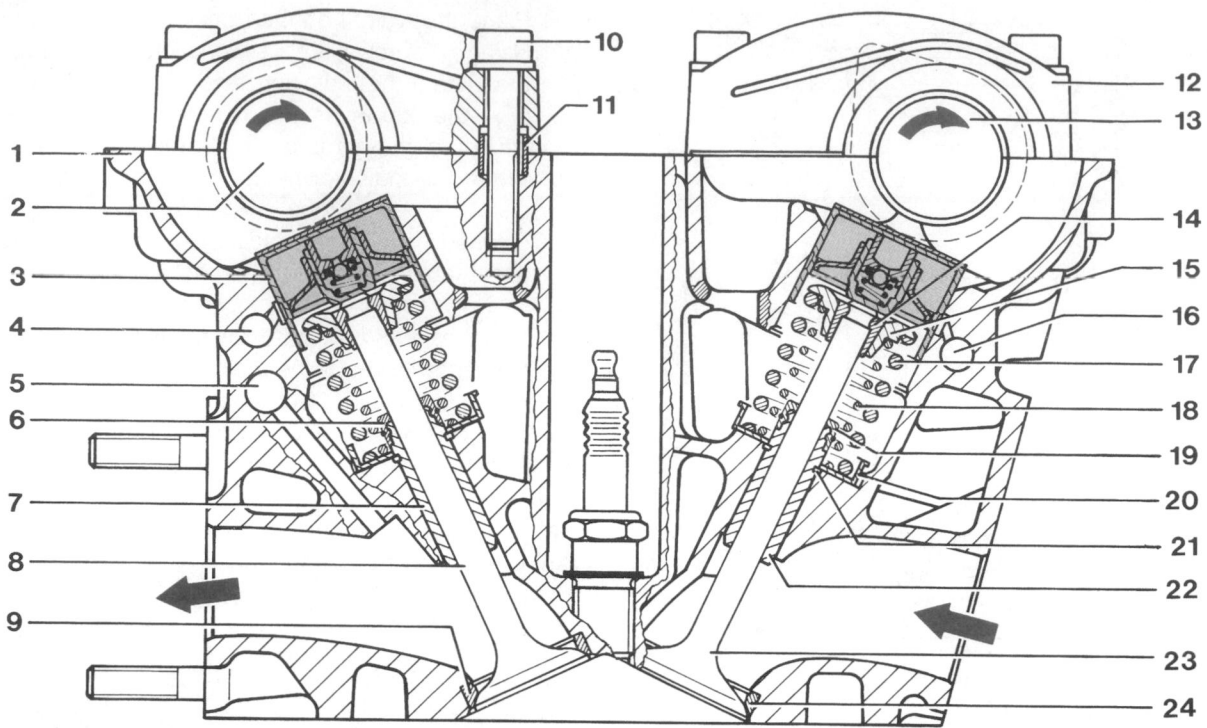

Figure 16-62. An overhead camshaft assembly that uses hydraulic valve lifters. (Mercedes-Benz)

Another type of lifter, sometimes called a lash adjuster, is shown in **Figure 16-63**. This type incorporates a rocker arm that is directly acted on by the overhead camshaft. One side of the rocker arm opens the valve. The lash adjuster is installed on the opposite side and adjusts the clearance as the engine operates. The internal operation of both of these lifter types is identical to lifters installed in the engine block.

Roller Lifters

Many late-model engines are equipped with roller lifters, which help reduce friction and lessen camshaft and lifter wear. A roller lifter operates in the same manner as a conventional hydraulic lifter with the exception of the roller, which engages the camshaft lobe. Instead of a sliding action, the lifter rolls on the cam surface. See **Figure 16-64**.

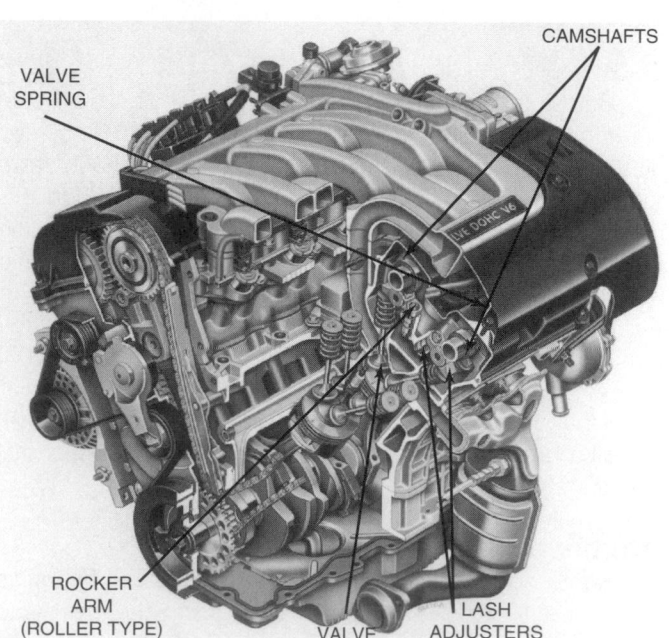

Figure 16-63. Cutaway view of a V-6 gasoline engine that incorporates lash adjusters. Note the four valves per cylinder. (Ford)

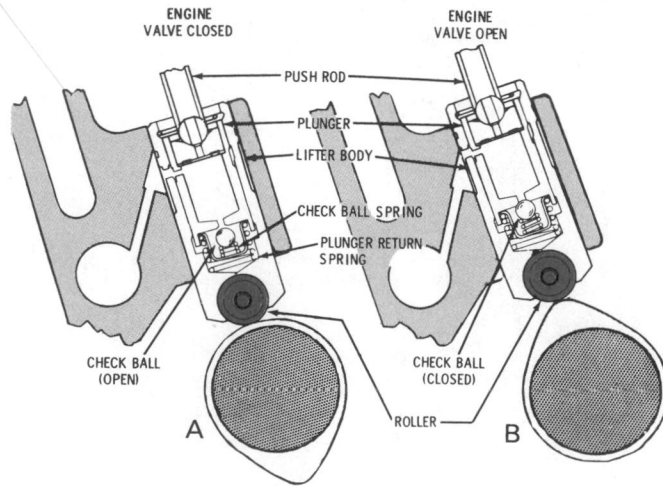

Figure 16-64. Cross section of a hydraulic roller lifter. A—Valve in the closed position. B—Valve open. (Buick)

Servicing Roller Lifters

When removing roller lifters, be sure to keep them in proper order. If any part of the lifter needs replacing, discard the entire unit and replace it with a new lifter assembly. Roller lifters are serviced in the same manner as the non-roller type.

Inspecting Roller Lifters

After the lifter has been disassembled and thoroughly cleaned, check all components for scoring, pitting, galling, varnish buildup, and evidence of other problems. Examine the roller closely. It should be free of pits and roughness, and it must rotate smoothly.

If pitting or roughness is present on the roller, check the corresponding camshaft lobe for damage. If the same condition exists on the camshaft, the shaft must be replaced. If the camshaft is undamaged, just replace the lifter assembly.

Servicing Rocker Arm and Shaft

Clean each *rocker arm shaft.* Pay special attention to the hollow center. Examine the shaft for signs of wear and scoring. Replace it if necessary. Check the condition of the rocker-arm-to-shaft bearing surface. If bushings are used, wear can be corrected by installing a new bushing and honing it to size. Excessive rocker-arm-to-shaft clearance will permit a heavy flow of oil that can flood valve stems and increase oil consumption.

Grinding the Rocker Arm

The rocker arm valve stem end should be ground to a smooth, even curve. Using a valve grinder, mount the rocker arm so the end is parallel to the stone. Adjust the swivel attachment in such a way that the rocker arm end curve will be maintained. Dress the wheel. With one hand operating the swivel arm and the other holding the rocker arm against the stone, wet grind the rocker arm until the surface is clean and true. Remove no more stock than necessary, **Figure 16-65.**

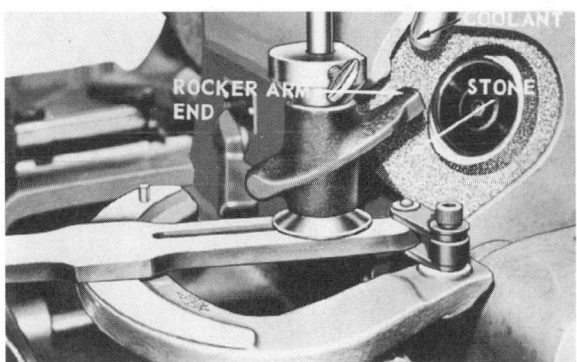

Figure 16-65. Grinding rocker arm end. Remove no more stock than absolutely necessary. (Albertson-Sioux)

Check the push rod end of the rocker arm. On non-adjustable versions, there will be a swivel pocket in the end. This pocket must be smooth and free from galling. When an adjusting screw is provided, check the ball, **Figure 16-66.**

Inspecting Push Rods

Push rods should be straight and both ends must be smooth. If the push rod is designed to carry oil, be certain to clean the inside and blow it dry.

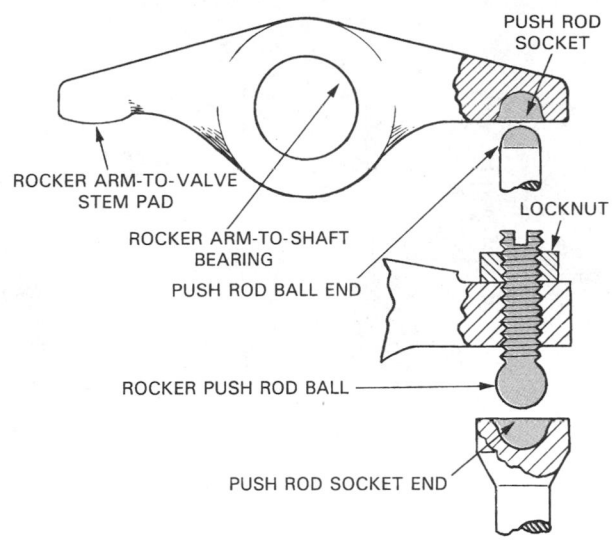

Figure 16-66. Check rocker arm socket and ball. These must be smooth and free of excessive wear.

Rod straightness can be checked with V-blocks and a dial indicator. Maximum allowable runout will vary. See specifications and **Figure 16-67.**

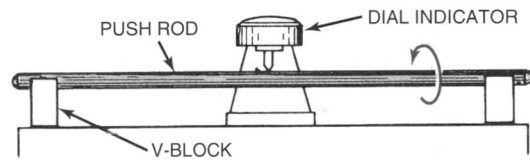

Figure 16-67. Checking push rod straightness with V-blocks and a dial indicator.

Assembling and Installing Rocker Arms and Shaft

After cleaning and inspection, the rocker arms, spacers, springs, and related parts should be lubricated and assembled on the shaft. Be very careful to install the arms in the correct locations and in the right direction. The arms must also be correctly placed in relation to the front of the shaft. **Figure 16-68** shows the installation of rocker arms on a shaft that bolts to the head. The assembled rocker arms and springs are shown in **Figure 16-69.**

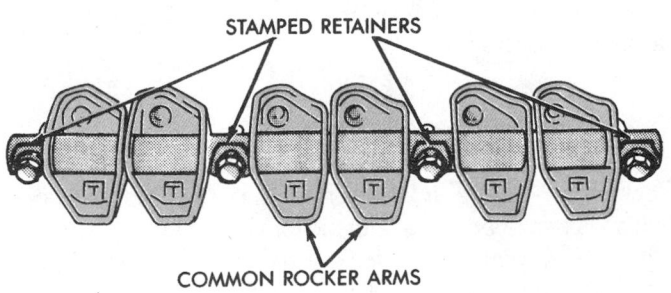

Figure 16-68. Properly installed rocker arms. The shaft is bolted to the integral supports, which are cast with the head. (Chrysler)

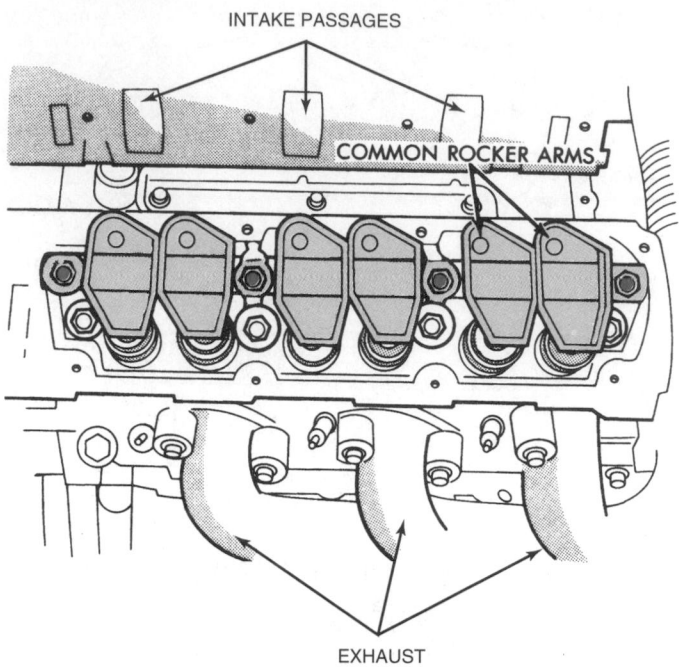

Figure 16-69. A rocker arm assembly bolted to the cylinder head. Torque the fasteners down slowly, starting in the center. Allow 20-30 minutes for the lifters to bleed down before starting the engine. (Dodge)

Two different rocker arm assembly designs are pictured in **Figures 16-70** and **16-71**. Note the flat on the front end of the rocker shaft in **Figure 16-71**.

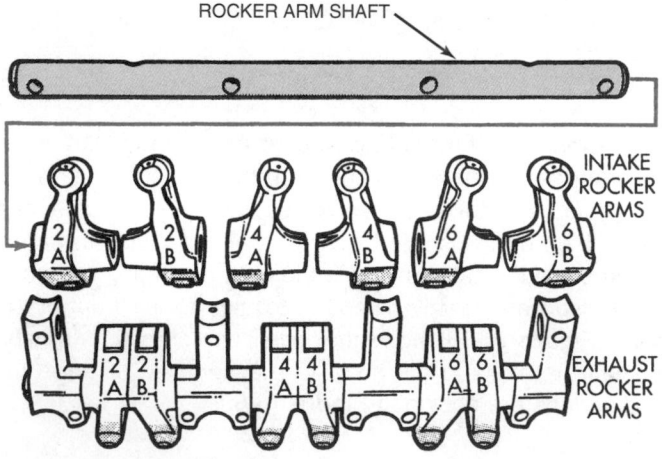

Figure 16-70. One particular style of roller rocker arm assembly. (Chrysler)

Positioning the Rocker Arm Shaft

The hollow rocker shaft carries a supply of oil to the rockers. Therefore, it is important that the support bracket, which is designed to transfer oil from the cylinder head to the shaft, is properly located. **Figures 16-72** and **16-73** show two methods of carrying oil through the support brackets.

To ensure that the oil supply opening in the shaft indexes with the correct bracket, make sure that the marked

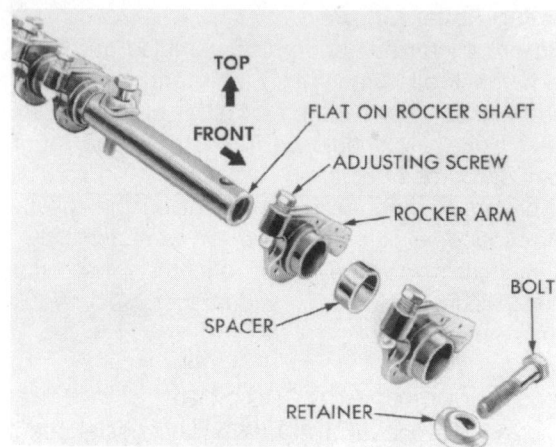

Figure 16-71. Another style rocker arm assembly. Note the use of spacers between the rockers.

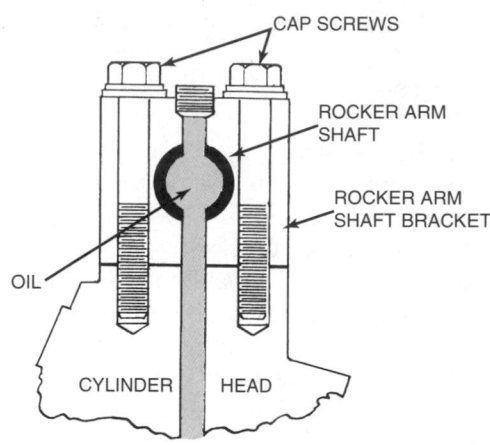

Figure 16-72. One method of furnishing engine oil to the rocker arm shaft via the support bracket.

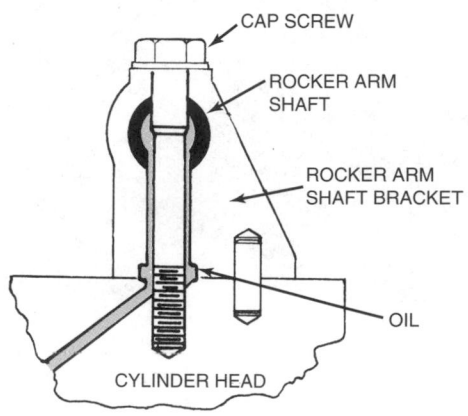

Figure 16-73. Supplying oil to the rocker arm shaft by way of the support bracket.

end (flat or notch) faces the specified end of the engine. The notch or flat must also be positioned (up, down, to the side) as recommended. **Figure 16-74** illustrates the marked ends and the various positions for these particular assemblies.

The individual rocker oil passages are generally positioned so they face the head. This provides positive

Figure 16-74. Rocker arm shaft positioning marks.

lubrication for the heavily stressed lower rocker bearing area. It also permits less oil flow because of the reduced clearance between the rocker and the bottom of the shaft. If the oil passages were turned upward, an excessive amount of oil would be passed. This would over-lubricate the valves, resulting in heavy oil consumption. **Figure 16-75** illustrates the usual positioning of these oil passages. Note that less clearance exists between shaft and the rocker arm at the bottom than at the top.

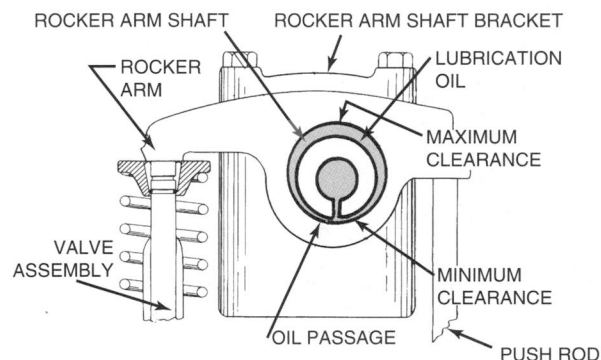

Figure 16-75. Rocker arm oil passages in shaft generally face toward the head.

The individual ball stud rocker arms are lubricated by a metered flow of oil delivered through hollow push rods. Shaft-mounted rocker arms are drilled in various ways to facilitate the flow of oil to both valve stem and push rod ends. See **Figure 16-76.**

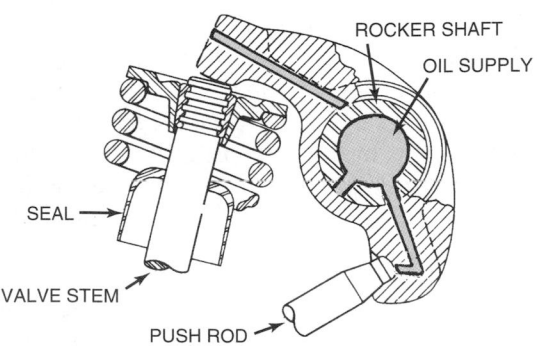

Figure 16-76. Rocker arm drilled for oil.

Installing the Rocker Arm Assembly

On some engines, the push rods are installed before the rocker assembly. On others, the rocker assembly is installed first. The push rods are placed in the lifters, and the valve springs are compressed. This tips the rocker high enough to place the push rod under the rocker ball end. A small amount of Lubriplate or other suitable lubricant should be applied to each end of the push rod before installation.

Tighten Rocker Shaft Brackets Evenly and Slowly

Lubricate the bracket cap screws and tighten them finger-tight. Give each bracket bolt a couple of turns. Proceed slowly. If the hydraulic lifters are filled with oil and the shaft assembly is drawn rapidly against the head, bent push rods, bulged lifters, warped valve stems, and sprung rockers can result. By drawing the assembly down slowly, the lifters will have time to leak down without undue strain on the various parts.

If used, the rocker adjusting screws should be backed off before tightening the assembly. This also applies to conventional lifter setups. When the brackets are snugged against the head, torque them to specifications, **Figure 16-77.** If an oil overflow line is incorporated in the rocker assembly, make sure it is installed properly.

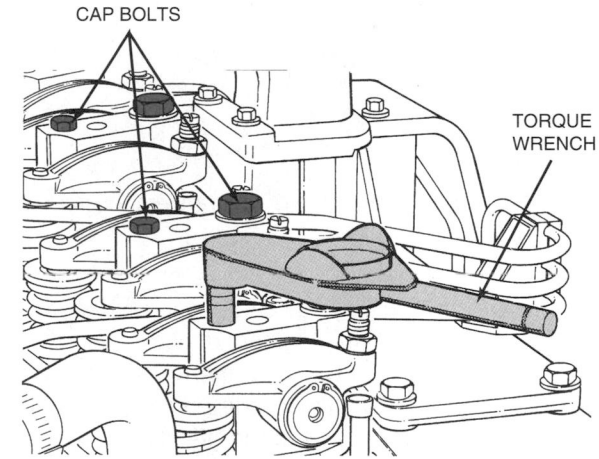

Figure 16-77. Torquing the rocker arm shaft retaining cap bolts.

Adjusting Valve Lash (Hydraulic Lifters)

Hydraulic lifters are used primarily to eliminate the need for *lash,* or clearance, between the end of the valve stem and the rocker arm. When the parts heat up and elongate, the lifter will leak down. Any shortening will cause the lifter to pump up. In this way, "zero" clearance is constantly maintained. Once set, the hydraulic lifter does not require further adjustment.

Some engines have no provision for valve lash adjustment on the rocker arms. Valve stem length above the head, head gasket thickness, and push rod and rocker wear all become critical on an installation of this type. However, push rods are available in different lengths to compensate for small changes needed.

The object in adjusting hydraulic lifters is to place the lifter plunger somewhere near the center of its stroke. This will allow changes in both directions. If the plunger is forced to the bottom, it will act as a solid lifter. If allowed to remain at the top, it cannot compensate for wear and temperature contractions.

Lifter Must Be on Cam Lobe Base Circle

Rotate the engine until the cam lobe nose faces directly away from the lifter. The lifter will then rest on the base circle. See **Figure 16-78.**

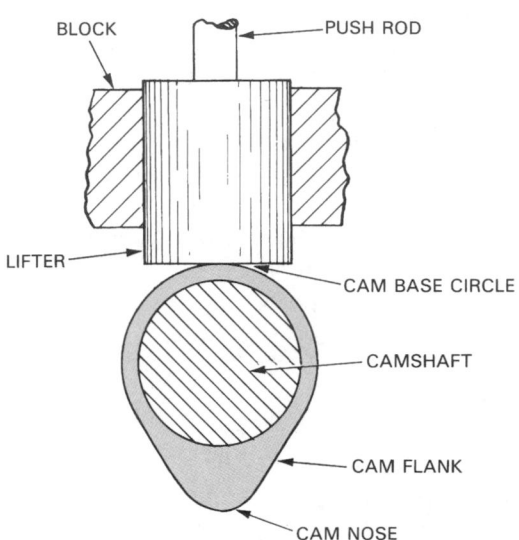

Figure 16-78.   To set valve lash or clearance, the lifter must rest on the cam base circle.

There are several ways of determining when the lobe is in this position. On some engines, such as the overhead camshaft type, the lobe is visible. If the engine is in the car and the ignition is properly timed, the engine can be slowly turned over until the plug lead to the affected cylinder fires. At this instant, both valves are closed and the lobes are in the proper position for lash setting.

Slowly crank the engine until a particular valve is fully opened. Then give the crankshaft exactly one full turn (mark damper with chalk). The cam lobe will be turned one-half revolution, placing the lobe nose opposite the lifter.

When a piston is brought to TDC (top dead center) on the compression stroke (both valves closed), the lobes will be in the correct position for that cylinder.

Another technique involves using chalk marks to divide the damper into two 180° sections (four cylinder), three 120° sections (six cylinder), or four 90° sections (V-8). One of the marks is on the timing notch, and the others are related in degrees to this mark. By cranking the engine until the marks index with the timing pointer, it is possible to set certain valves and reduce the amount of cranking required.

Lifter Plunger Must Be at the Top of Travel

The rocker arm adjustment should be loosened so the lifter plunger travels to the top of its stroke. At this point, the push rod can be "jiggled" sideways and up and down. See **Figure 16-79.**

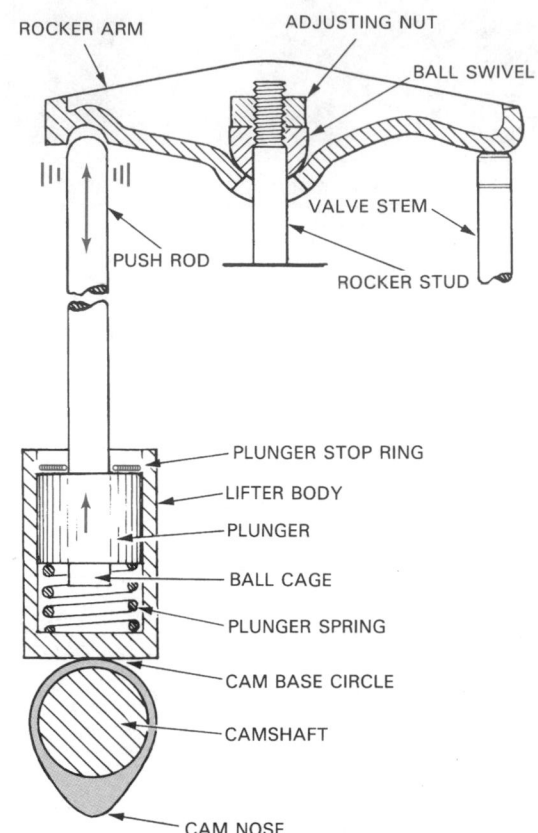

Figure 16-79.   The hydraulic lifter plunger is against the stop ring, and the rocker arm is backed off until push rod shake is evident.

Grasp the push rod concerned with the thumb and forefingers. While gently shaking the push rod sideways, slowly tighten the rocker arm adjustment. As the rocker arm push rod end moves downward, the amount of shake will be reduced. Stop at the instant all play or shake is gone. At this point, no lash is present between valve stem and rocker or rocker and push rod.

Following manufacturer's specs, give the rocker arm adjustment an additional number of turns (typically 1 1/2 turns). This will force the plunger down to the midpoint of its stroke. Repeat this process on all rockers. **Figure 16-80** shows a technician shaking the push rod while drawing the rocker downward until all clearance is gone. Where adjustment is not provided, compress the lifter and check push-rod-to-rocker clearance against specifications. If necessary, install a longer or shorter push rod to correct clearance.

Adjusting Valve Lash (Mechanical Lifters)

A certain amount of lash, or clearance, between the valve stem and the rocker arm is a must when mechanical lifters are employed. The exact amount will vary from engine to engine, depending on the use, design, and construction. Always use the amount specified by the manufacturer.

Excessive clearance will cause noisy operation, late valve opening, early valve closing, lowered valve lift, excessive wear, and possible valve breakage. Insufficient clearance will cause early opening, higher lift, late closing, and valve burning.

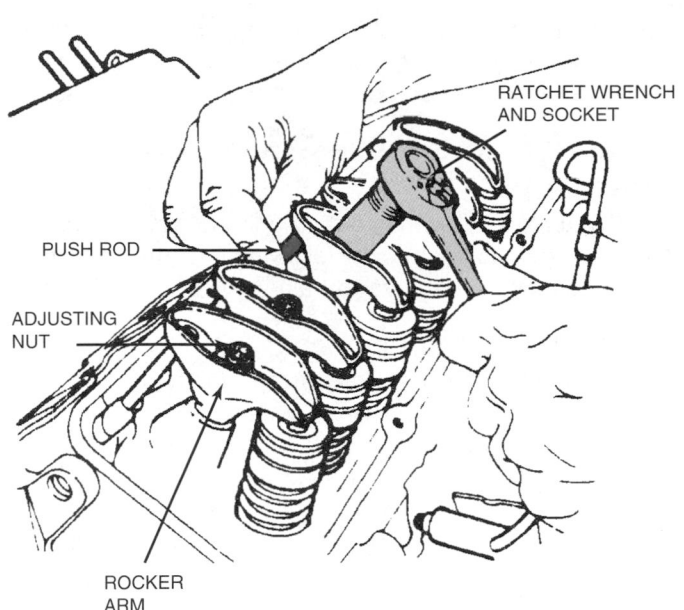

Figure 16-80. This technician is removing push rod shake prior to final adjustment of hydraulic lifters. (Chevrolet)

As with the hydraulic lifter, the mechanical lifter must rest on the cam base circle during adjustment. The rocker arm is carefully adjusted so that the correct clearance exists between valve stem and rocker arm.

A feeler gauge of the exact thickness or a stepped *go/no go* blade (go = .001″ [0.025 mm] below specs. no go = .001″ [0.025 mm] above specs) should pass between rocker and valve stem (hold push rod end down) with a slight drag, **Figure 16-81. Figure 16-82** illustrates valve clearance being checked with a dial indicator. This device gives highly accurate settings.

Cold and Hot Clearance Settings (Mechanical Lifters)

When an engine is reassembled, an initial, or cold, setting of the valve clearance is necessary. For a final hot clearance setting, the engine must be up to normal operating temperature (oil and water temperature). This will require about thirty minutes of engine operation. The procedure for setting hot clearance of mechanical lifters is identical to the procedure for setting cold clearance.

 Note: Accurate valve clearance is important. Make certain the engine is hot and the clearance settings are exact. Follow the manufacturer's suggested adjustment procedures and clearances.

Rocker Arm Adjusting Screws

Some rocker arm adjusting screws are self-locking. A specified amount of torque must be applied to move them. If the "breakaway" torque is below accepted limits, change the screw or the nut.

If a locknut adjusting screw is used, loosen the nut and adjust the screw. While holding the screw, firmly tighten the nut. After tightening, recheck clearance, **Figure 16-83.**

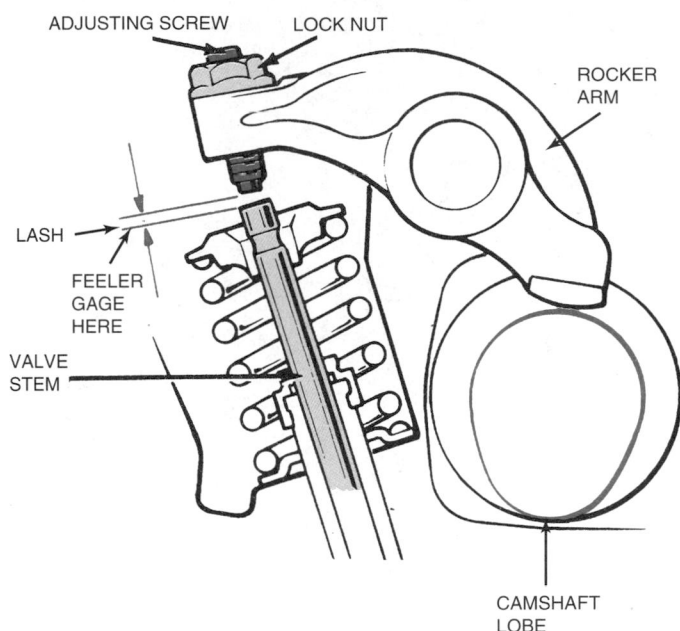

Figure 16-81. Valve clearance adjustment with the rocker arm resting on the camshaft base circle. The locknut is loosened, and the adjusting screw is turned in or out until the correct clearance (lash) is obtained. The locknut is then retightened to the proper torque. (GM)

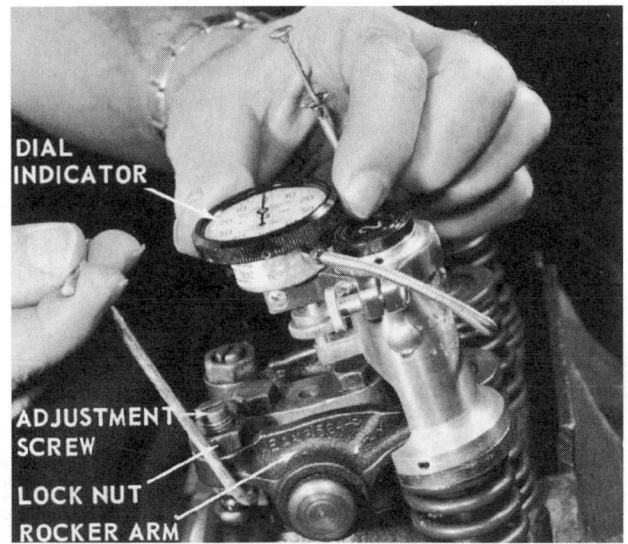

Figure 16-82. Using a special dial indicator setup to check tappet clearance. Adjustment screws have locknuts. (P and G Co.)

Direct Acting Overhead Camshaft Adjustments

In some overhead camshaft engines, the cam lobes act directly on the valves through a cam follower. No rocker arms are needed. **Figure 16-84** shows an engine with such an arrangement.

Valve clearance is set by an *adjusting disc* that is located on the top of the follower, **Figure 16-85,** or between the follower and the valve stem. Various disc thicknesses are available to alter clearance as needed.

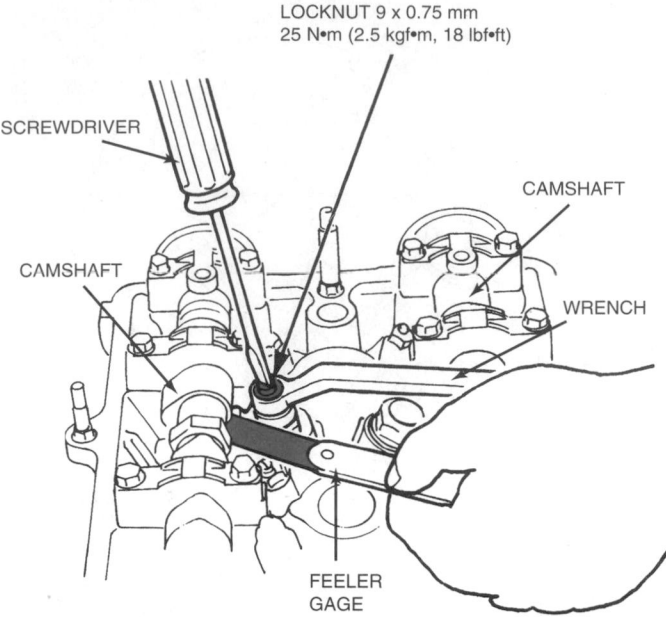

Figure 16-83. Adjusting valve clearance. Loosen the locknut and turn the adjusting screw until the feeler gage just slides back and forth with a slight drag. Retighten the locknut and double-check clearance. Readjust if necessary. (Acura)

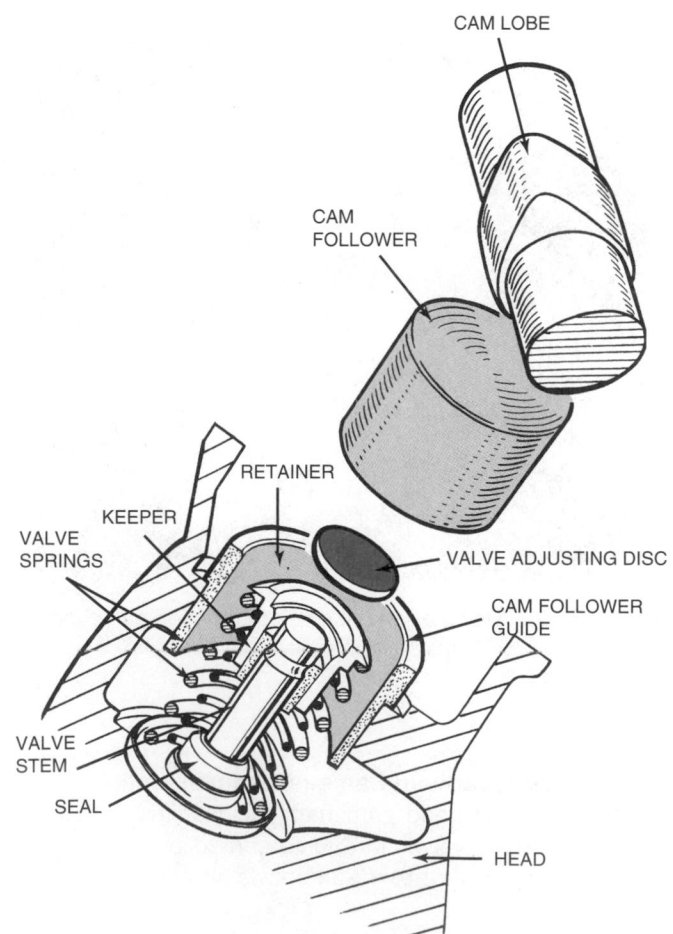

Figure 16-84. A direct-acting overhead camshaft setup. Note the valve adjusting shim (disk), which is placed between the cam follower and the valve stem. (Jaguar)

Another setup uses a tapered adjusting screw to set clearance. The taper produces a wedging effect that alters clearance when the screw is turned. See **Figure 16-86.**

Camshaft and Valve Train Service Check List

If you have performed a thorough job, you will be able to answer "yes" to each of the following important questions relating to camshaft and valve train service.

Camshaft Drive Components

- Are the timing gear teeth smooth and sound?
- Is the timing gear backlash correct?
- Is gear runout within limits?
- Is camshaft end play as specified?
- Are the timing marks properly aligned?
- Are the chain (or belt) sprockets in good condition?
- Is chain (or belt) slack within limits?
- Is sprocket runout acceptable?
- Are the chain (or belt) and sprockets meshed so the timing marks align properly?
- If rubbing blocks or tensioners are used, are they in good condition and properly placed and adjusted?
- Were all Woodruff keys replaced?
- Is the chain or gear oiling nozzle clean?
- Are camshaft journals smooth, round, and within maximum wear limits?
- Is the camshaft runout within limits?
- Are the cam lobes in good condition and is lift as specified?
- Are the cam bearings good and do they provide correct clearance?
- Are the cam bearings oil holes aligned?
- Are the cam bearings secure in the bore and were they pressed in the proper distance?
- Is the distributor-oil pump drive gear in good condition?
- If a thrust plate is used, is it securely bolted into place and is wear within limits?
- Have camshaft gears and sprocket cap screws been torqued?
- If detachable, is the fuel pump eccentric and distributor drive gear secured in place?
- Is the rear camshaft bearing oil seal plug sealed and tightly installed?
- Is the crankshaft oil slinger correctly in place?
- Was a new oil seal installed in the gear or chain cover with the lip facing the engine?
- Was the chain cover oil seal properly centered in relation to the crankshaft before tightening the cover?
- Is the damper installed securely and to the proper depth?
- Is the damper seal lip contact surface smooth and oiled?
- If a damper retaining cap screw is used, is it in place and torqued properly?
- Was the damper carefully installed so it was not damaged?
- Were all gears, chains, journals, and cams thoroughly lubricated before assembly?

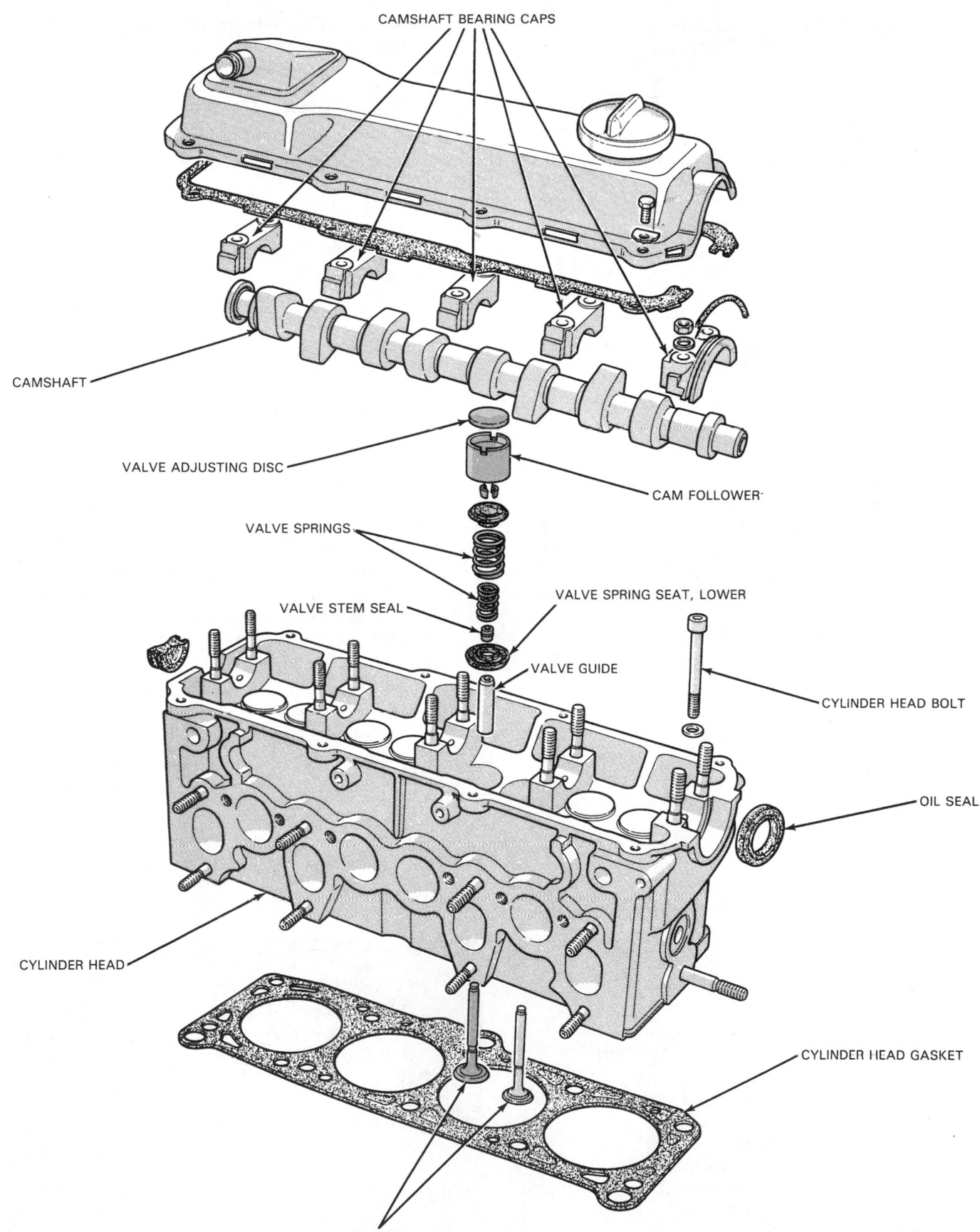

CAMSHAFT BEARING CAPS

CAMSHAFT

VALVE ADJUSTING DISC

CAM FOLLOWER

VALVE SPRINGS

VALVE STEM SEAL

VALVE SPRING SEAT, LOWER

VALVE GUIDE

CYLINDER HEAD BOLT

OIL SEAL

CYLINDER HEAD

CYLINDER HEAD GASKET

VALVES

Figure 16-85. One direct-acting, overhead camshaft setup. The cam lobe acts directly (no rocker arm) on the valve stem via cam follower. Proper clearance is set by selecting the correct thickness valve adjusting disk. (Plymouth)

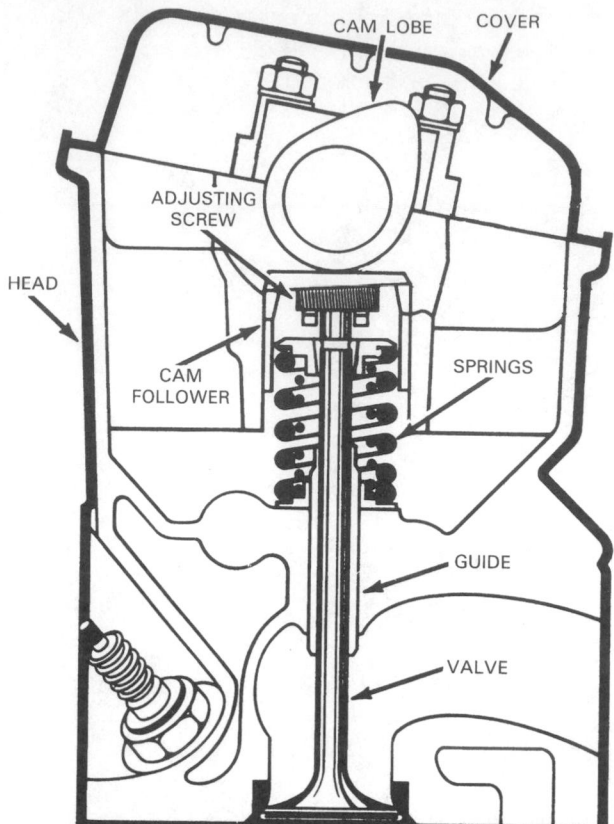

Figure 16-86. The valve clearance for this overhead camshaft engine is adjusted by turning a tapered adjusting screw. This will increase or decrease the distance between the cam lobe and the follower. (Chrysler)

Rocker Arms
- Is the end contacting the valve stem smooth and accurately ground?
- Are the oil holes open?
- Is the rocker shaft or ball stud bearing surface smooth and within wear limits?
- Is the push rod ball or socket end smooth and free of wear?
- Is the rocker correctly installed and does it contact the valve properly?
- Is the rocker clean?

Rocker Shaft and Ball Studs
- Is the rocker shaft clean inside and out?
- Are the rocker arm bearing areas smooth and within limits?
- Is the correct end of the shaft forward?
- Do the rocker arm oil holes face in the correct direction?
- Are the shaft brackets in the correct location, torqued, and free of cracks?
- Is ample oil reaching the assembly?
- If an overflow pipe is used, is it correctly located?
- Are the ball studs tight in the head?
- Are the ball stud adjusting nut threads in good shape?
- Are the ball stud nuts within breakaway specifications?

- Are the self-locking rocker arm valve clearance adjusting screws within breakaway specifications?

Push Rods
- Are the rods straight?
- Are rod ends smooth and free of excessive wear?
- If the rods carry oil, is the hollow section thoroughly clean?
- Is the correct end up?
- Are both ends in proper contact?
- If no clearance adjustment is provided, are the rods the correct length?

Lifters
- Have the mechanical lifters been trued on the grinder?
- Are ends and sides smooth and free of wear and galling?
- Is the lifter-to-lifter-bore clearance correct?
- Are the hydraulic lifters immaculately clean and in good condition?
- Have the hydraulic lifters been checked for leakdown?

Valve Lash
- If mechanical lifters are used, is the valve stem-to-rocker-arm clearance as specified?
- Was the clearance rechecked after thorough engine warm-up and head retorquing?
- Was the lifter on the base circle when the clearance was set?
- Are all adjustment screws and locknuts tight?
- If hydraulic lifters are used, were they set so that the plungers are near the center of their travel?

General
- When possible, were all parts replaced in the location from which they were removed?
- Were all parts thoroughly cleaned?
- Were all parts properly lubricated before assembly?

Tech Talk

Many technicians spend a lot of time and effort replacing a camshaft and lifters. They thoroughly clean everything, press in new cam bearings, carefully install the new cam and lifters, and then ruin the whole job by not lubing the cam lobes. When the engine first starts with a new camshaft, it takes a few minutes for the oil to reach the cam lobes. If the lobes are dry, the new camshaft can be destroyed in five minutes.

Never install a camshaft (or any engine part) without plenty of lubrication. Use a general-purpose heavy lube or the special camshaft lube that is supplied with many new camshafts. It is far better to over lubricate a camshaft than to take a chance on under lubricating.

Summary

Camshaft and valve train conditions are of critical importance to proper engine performance. Pull and install the vibration damper by exerting pressure on the hub portion. Do not damage the crankshaft end threads.

Timing gear teeth must be smooth. Gear runout and backlash must be within limits. Some camshaft timing gears are bolted on; others are pressed on. When replacing a gear or a sprocket, it is good practice to replace the mating gear or sprocket.

When replacing a timing belt, check sprockets for possible damage. Remove and install the camshaft carefully to avoid damage to the bearing surfaces.

When pressing a new timing gear into place, apply pressure to the hub only. Check camshaft end play at the thrust plate with a feeler gauge. A dial indicator can also be used. Install the crankshaft gear before the camshaft gear. Make certain that the gear timing marks face outward and that they are aligned properly.

Never pound on gears, chains, belts, camshafts, or sprockets. When replacing a timing chain, install new sprockets. Check sprocket runout and chain slack. The chain and sprockets must mesh to properly align the timing marks. Some timing instructions call for sprocket marks to face each other on a line between crank and camshaft centers. Some call for colored links to align with the marks. Others give a specific number of links or pins between marks.

Slack in long chains is often controlled with rubbing blocks and tensioning devices.

Place the chain around the sprockets and install them as a unit. Replace all Woodruff keys. Then, install gears, sprockets, or vibration damper. Never force a camshaft back into the engine, as it may loosen the rear bearing core hole plug.

Always install a new chain or gear cover oil seal with its lip facing the engine. Center the seal to the crankshaft before tightening the cover screws. The vibration damper seal contact area must be smooth. Lubricate all gears, chains, and bearings before installation. Never lubricate a timing belt.

Camshaft bearing clearance must be checked. Replace bearings if necessary. Align oil holes when installing. Check camshaft bearing journals, distributor drive gear, fuel pump eccentric cam, and cam lift.

True up mechanical lifters on a valve grinder. Disassemble, clean, inspect, and reassemble hydraulic lifters. When assembling, the parts must be *clean*. Lubricate and install the lifters. Lubricate and install the rocker arms on the shaft. Make certain that the shaft has its correct end forward and that rocker oil holes face the head (usual). Tighten the shaft brackets slowly and evenly. This will allow the hydraulic lifters to leak down. Rocker arm valve clearance adjustment screws should be backed off. Use a torque wrench for final tightening. The ends of the lifters, push rods, and rocker arms should be lightly coated with lubricant.

When an adjustment is provided, center the lifter plunger. With mechanical lifters, adjust valve-stem-to-rocker-arm clearance. In both cases, the lifter must be on the cam base circle. When the engine is thoroughly warm, the head should be retorqued and the valve clearance should be reset.

Know These Terms

Crankshaft	Oil nozzles
Valve timing	Timing belt
Torsional vibration	Camshaft
Vibration damper	Camshaft bearings
Harmonic balancer	Cam lobe
Front cover	Thrust
Gears	Cam lobe lift
Backlash	Lifters
Thrust plate	Valve lash adjusters
Woodruff key	Leakdown rate
Timing chain	Rocker arm shaft
Sprocket	Push rods
Slack	Lash
Crankshaft front oil seal	Adjusting disc
Centering sleeve	

Review Questions—Chapter 16

Do not write in this book. Write your answers on a separate sheet of paper.

1. Worn camshaft bearings can cause _____.
   (A) excessive shaft end play
   (B) excessive oil consumption
   (C) crankshaft failure
   (D) loose vibration damper

2. Worn timing gears, sprockets, or chains will _____.
   (A) alter valve timing
   (B) cause crankcase fumes
   (C) increase oil consumption
   (D) reduce engine oil pressure

3. Gear backlash can be checked with a _____ or a _____.

4. When installing a bolt-on timing gear or sprocket, it is best to _____.
   (A) drive the gear tightly against the camshaft
   (B) start the gear evenly and use the cap screws to pull it on
   (C) tighten the cap screws a little, drive the gear on a small amount, tighten the cap screws again, and drive the gear on until it is fully seated
   (D) None of the above.

5. When installing a gear-driven camshaft, the timing marks should _____.
   (A) face in opposite directions
   (B) be placed 90° apart
   (C) face each other in perfect alignment
   (D) both be in the down position

6. Describe two methods of checking for excessive chain slack.

7. When replacing a timing chain, it is good practice to also replace _____.
   (A) the camshaft
   (B) the camshaft sprocket
   (C) both sprockets
   (D) the oil slinger

8. Before installing the chain or gear cover, you should _____.
   (A) replace the oil seal
   (B) replace the oil seal if worn
   (C) soak the old seal to make it pliable
   (D) tighten the old seal to prevent leakage

9. To ensure proper lubrication, all oiling devices must be _____ and properly _____.

10. Most camshaft lobes are _____.
    (A) ground with a slight taper
    (B) ground with a slight crown
    (C) ground flat
    (D) ground slightly concave

11. Typical camshaft journal to bearing clearance should be about _____.
    (A) .0025″ (0.7-0.8 mm)
    (B) .005″ (0.13-0.15 mm)
    (C) .010″ (0.26-0.30 mm)
    (D) .020″ (0.52-0.60 mm)

12. Camshaft journal out-of-roundness should not exceed _____.
    (A) .0001″ (0.0025 mm)
    (B) .1115″ (2.832 mm)
    (C) .001″ (0.025 mm)
    (D) .010″ (0.25 mm)

13. Camshaft journal runout is best checked with _____ and a _____.

14. Overall journal wear per inch (25.4 mm) of shaft diameter should not exceed _____.
    (A) 0.100″ (2.54 mm)
    (B) 0.0015″ (0.038 mm)
    (C) 0.008″ (0.20 mm)
    (D) 0.0001″ (0.0025 mm)

15. Prior to installing new cam bearings, the leading edge of the bearing bore should be slightly _____.

16. Camshaft bearing _____ must be accurately aligned with those in the bore.

17. List eight types of damage to look for when inspecting a timing belt.

18. After cleaning and reassembly, hydraulic lifters should be tested for _____.

19. Rocker shaft and rocker arm oil holes usually face _____.
    (A) away from the head
    (B) toward the head
    (C) sideways
    (D) Both A and C.

20. Excessive valve clearance will _____.
    (A) increase horsepower
    (B) cause early valve opening
    (C) prolong the life of the valve
    (D) cause late valve opening and a lower lift

ASE-Type Questions

1. Technician A says that a pressed-on vibration damper can be removed by grasping its outer rim with a puller. Technician B says that on an engine using a gear drive, installing new gears will automatically provide correct backlash. Who is right?
   (A) A only.
   (B) B only.
   (C) Both A & B.
   (D) Neither A nor B.

2. Technician A says that some pressed-on camshaft timing gears can be replaced with the camshaft in the engine. Technician B says that timing chains with excess slack should be replaced. Who is right?
   (A) A only.
   (B) B only.
   (C) Both A & B.
   (D) Neither A nor B.

3. Slack in long timing chains is often controlled through the use of all of the following, EXCEPT:
   (A) idler sprockets.
   (B) jam nuts.
   (C) rubbing blocks.
   (D) spring-loaded tensioning devices.

4. Technician A says that a special centering sleeve should be used if the timing gear cover is not aligned to the block with dowel pins. Technician B says that the front cover oil seal lip should face the engine. Who is right?
   (A) A only.
   (B) B only.
   (C) Both A & B.
   (D) Neither A nor B.

5. Technician A says that a camshaft wear pattern should cover the complete width of the lobe. Technician B says that new lifters should always be used with a new camshaft. Who is right?
   (A) A only.
   (B) B only.
   (C) Both A & B.
   (D) Neither A nor B.

6. Timing belts can be used to drive all of the following, EXCEPT:
   (A) power steering pumps.
   (B) water pumps.
   (C) distributors.
   (D) oil pumps.

7. Technician A says that all valves, lifters, push rods, rockers, and other parts should always be installed in the spot from which they were removed. Technician B says that once the push rods are installed, the rocker arm brackets should be tightened down by starting on one end and fully tightening the first bolt. Who is right?
   (A) A only.
   (B) B only.
   (C) Both A & B.
   (D) Neither A nor B.

8. Technician A says that the rocker arm end that contacts the valve should be ground smooth and flat. Technician B says that hydraulic lifter parts are accurately made and can be interchanged between lifters. Who is right?
   (A) A only.
   (B) B only.
   (C) Both A & B.
   (D) Neither A nor B.

9. Technician A says that hydraulic lifter plungers should be about in the center of their travel when properly installed and adjusted. Technician B says that the valve lifter should be on the high point of the cam to adjust valve clearance. Who is right?
   (A) A only.
   (B) B only.
   (C) Both A & B.
   (D) Neither A nor B.

10. All of the following statements about roller lifters are true, EXCEPT:
    (A) they are being used more in late-model engines.
    (B) they reduce cam lobe life.
    (C) they perform the same basic function as conventional lifters.
    (D) they reduce friction.

Suggested Activities

1. Obtain a used camshaft and measure the lift of the lobes. Be sure to identify the intake and exhaust lobes before measuring. Record your measurements. How does the lift compare with the factory specifications?
2. Check several lifters for wear on the body and the contact face. Record your findings.
3. Determine whether the camshaft and lifters checked above should be replaced. Present your findings to your classmates.
4. Count the teeth on a camshaft and crankshaft gear. Explain why the cam gear has twice as many teeth as the crank gear.

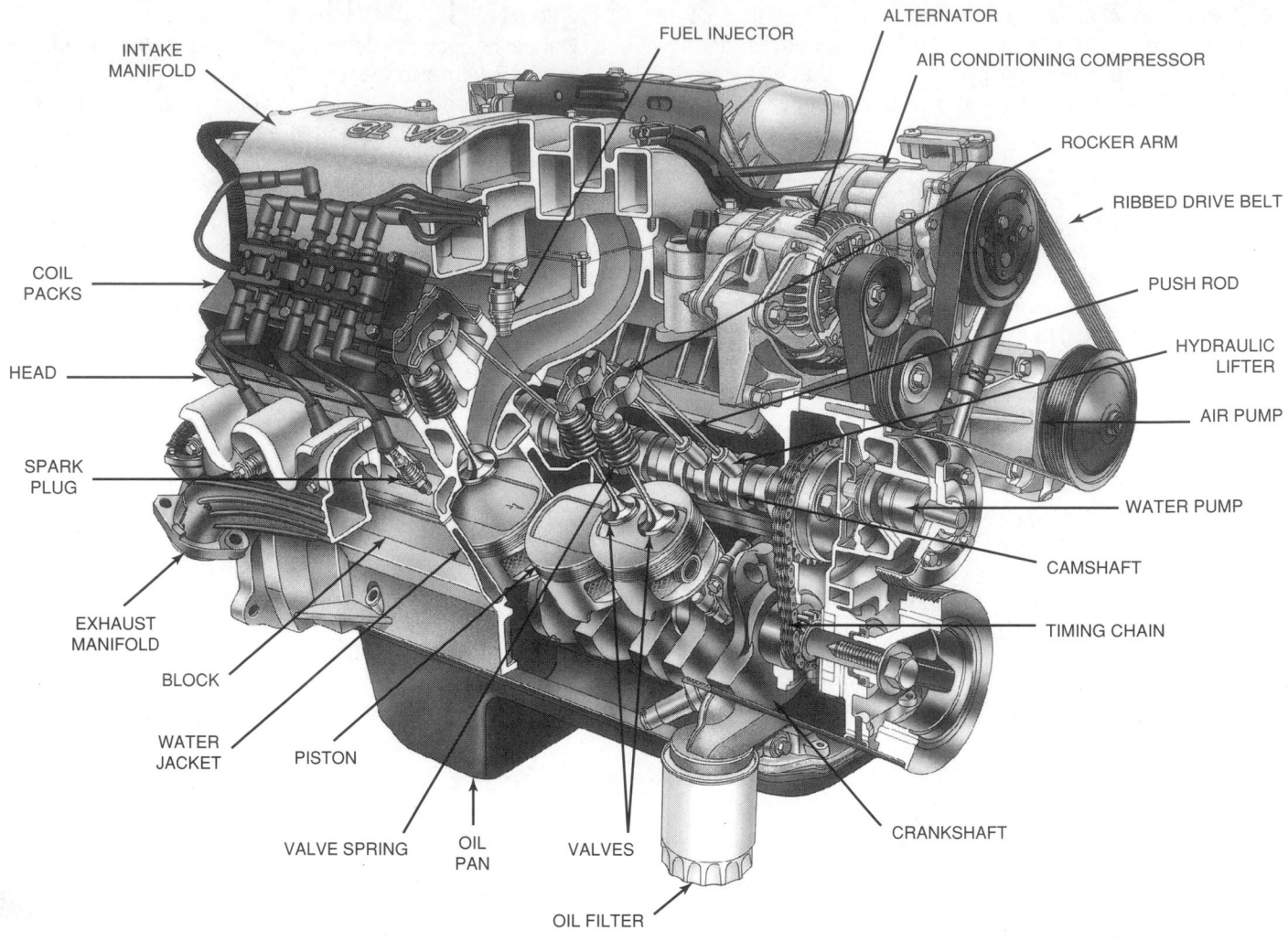

INTAKE MANIFOLD

FUEL INJECTOR

ALTERNATOR

AIR CONDITIONING COMPRESSOR

ROCKER ARM

RIBBED DRIVE BELT

COIL PACKS

PUSH ROD

HYDRAULIC LIFTER

HEAD

AIR PUMP

SPARK PLUG

WATER PUMP

CAMSHAFT

EXHAUST MANIFOLD

TIMING CHAIN

BLOCK

WATER JACKET

PISTON

VALVE SPRING

OIL PAN

VALVES

CRANKSHAFT

OIL FILTER

Cutaway of a late-model V-10 engine. Study the location of the various components. (Dodge)

17

Engine Assembly, Installation, and Break-In

After studying this chapter, you will be able to:
- Summarize a typical sequence for assembling an engine.
- Describe how to install an engine in a car.
- Pressurize the engine lubrication system with oil.
- Make final checks before starting the engine.
- Operate an engine properly for safe break-in.

No single method of reassembling engine components is right every time. Technician preference, engine design, and part availability all help determine the order of assembly for any given engine.

This chapter gives a general overview for engine reassembly and installation. The following sequence of assembly is typical for most engines and may be used as a general guide. It is important, however, for the technician to study the construction of each specific engine and the manufacturer's shop manual, if available. This advance planning will help the technician to anticipate and prevent any problems caused by assembling the parts in the wrong sequence.

For example, assume you are working on an engine with a mechanical fuel pump. If you installed the fuel pump and then tried to install the camshaft, you would find that the fuel pump arm contacts the camshaft journals, preventing you from installing the camshaft. You will have to remove the fuel pump to install the camshaft.

Or, assume that you are working on an overhead cam engine and that you have installed the camshaft before installing the head on the block. On some engines, you would be forced to remove the camshaft to install the head bolts.

In both examples, as a result of your failure to study the engine construction and to "think ahead," you would have to waste valuable time removing parts to permit the installation of others.

Typical Engine Assembly Sequence

The *sequence of assembly* described in this chapter covers major units. It is assumed that subassemblies such as valves, springs, bearings, and rings have been correctly installed. It is further assumed that all parts have been cleaned, checked, lubricated, and replaced or repaired as needed. Any particular step in this sequence may be reviewed in detail by referring to the chapter covering the operation or part concerned. If additional information is needed, consult the appropriate service manual.

To assemble an engine, mount the engine block in a suitable stand and install the following components:

1. Oil gallery and core hole plugs.
2. Crankshaft.
3. Camshaft. (If the camshaft timing gear is pressed on, make sure it is installed before installing the camshaft.)
4. Timing gears, timing chain, and sprockets. (Make sure the timing marks are aligned properly.) On overhead camshaft designs, timing chain, gear, or belt installation must be delayed until the cylinder head is installed.
5. Piston and rod assemblies.
6. Oil pump, oil pickup, and connecting lines.
7. Front cover.
8. Vibration damper and pulleys.
9. Oil pan.
10. Cylinder head(s).
11. Water pump.
12. Valve lifters, push rods, and rocker arm assemblies. (Set valve clearance at this time.)
13. Intake manifold.
14. Exhaust manifold(s).
15. Distributor (make certain timing is correct), plugs, coil, and secondary wires.
16. Fuel pump, fuel injectors or carburetor, and fuel and vacuum lines.
17. Wiring connectors, alternator, starter, and temperature and oil pressure senders.
18. Drive belts.
19. Flywheel. (On standard transmission models, the clutch disc, pressure plate, and clutch or flywheel housing can be installed at this time.)
20. Transmission or transaxle. (In some cases, it is desirable to attach the transmission or transaxle to the engine and install them together; in other cases, the engine must be installed alone.)

Do Not Hurry!

Technicians often become anxious as the time to start the engine draws near. This is natural because your knowledge, care, and skill will receive a crucial test when the engine is started.

It is at this point that many fine overhaul jobs are ruined by carelessness brought about by hurrying. Work energetically, but work carefully. Think and avoid a "last minute rush!"

Cover Engines when Not Working on Them

When not actively working on an engine, it is advisable to cover it with a protective cloth. When the heads and the intake manifold are installed, install the spark plugs and cap off the manifold to prevent the entry of dirt or small parts.

Engine Installation

Proper engine installation is just as important as proper assembly. Not only can the rebuilt engine be ruined by careless installation, but other parts of the vehicle can be damaged.

Attach Lift Equipment

Begin installation by attaching a **lift strap** or fixture to the engine. Study Chapter 12 for recommendations on attaching lift devices. Pay particular attention to the safety rules for engine removal. They also apply to installation. It is usually easiest and safest to attach the lifting equipment in the same way that it was attached during removal.

Place **protective pads** on the fenders. Raise the engine with a suitable **hoist,** being careful to balance the engine at the angle desired. Look at **Figure 17-1.**

Installation—Transmission or Transaxle in Car

To install an engine when the transmission or transaxle is in the vehicle, guide the engine into the engine compartment. When engine crankshaft and transmission/transaxle input shaft centerlines are at the same level and parallel with each other, move the engine back to engage the transmission or transaxle. For manual shift vehicles, make sure the input shaft passes through the throwout bearing, through the clutch disc, and into the crankshaft pilot bearing. See Chapter 29 on clutch service for full details. For automatics, start the converter pilot into the crankshaft. Be careful not to bend the relatively light flex-type flywheel or drive plate. Remove the converter restraining strap.

Install the fasteners that secure the clutch or converter housing to the engine. On automatics, install fasteners that secure the converter to the flywheel. Torque the engine mount bolts.

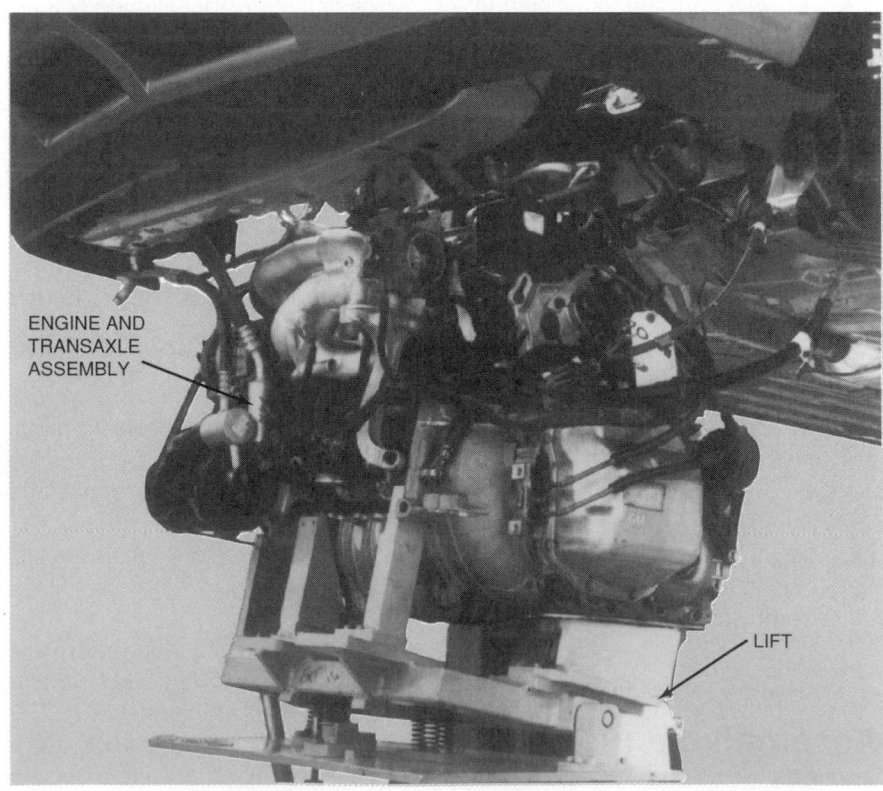

ENGINE AND TRANSAXLE ASSEMBLY

LIFT

Figure 17-1.   Use great care when removing or installing an engine. Make certain that the hoist or lift is securely attached. Always correctly support the vehicle to prevent tipping or falling as weight is added or removed. (Oldsmobile)

Installation—Transmission or Transaxle on Bench

To install an engine when the transmission or transaxle is out of the vehicle, guide the engine into place on the front mounts. Install the mount bolts loosely. Use a strap to support the rear of the engine. Then, remove the engine lift or hoist.

Raise the car and install the transmission or transaxle. Attach the engine rear mount cross member and tighten the engine mounts. Remove the support strap and torque all mount bolts to factory specifications.

Installation—Transmission or Transaxle on Engine

Installing an engine with the transmission or transaxle attached requires care and skillful maneuvering. On a rear-wheel drive vehicle, the engine and transmission form a long unit. The engine will usually have to be tipped at a steep angle (up to 45°) and guided into place. Position the transmission with a jack, using a wood block to prevent damage to the transmission pan. Install the rear support cross member and attach to the engine rear mount. Install and torque all mount bolts. Remove the jack and install the drive shaft.

On a front-drive vehicle, the extra size and weight of the transaxle make maneuvering the assembly more difficult. Begin by guiding the engine and transaxle into place in the engine compartment. Install the lower engine and transaxle mounts, and then position and install all side and upper mounts. Finally, install both CV axle shafts.

Use Care

When installing the engine, lower it slowly and carefully. Avoid damage to the car body or to underhood accessories. As the lowering progresses, make sure the engine is not catching on some part of the vehicle. Gentle shaking, pressure with a pry bar, and careful use of a jack are all helpful in engine positioning. If difficulty is encountered, do not try to force the engine into place. Find out what is causing the trouble and remedy it. Make sure the mounts are properly assembled and torqued. **Figure 17-2** shows how engine mounts are used on a front-wheel drive vehicle with a transverse-mounted (sideways) engine.

Connect All Wiring, Hose, Tubing, and Linkage

Connect all fuel and vacuum lines. Attach the radiator hoses, air conditioning lines, and oil cooler lines, if used. Reconnect exhaust system pipes. Make sure that the ignition switch is turned to the off position and then reconnect all wiring—battery cables last. However, do not install the battery at this time. Attach transmission or transaxle shift linkage and throttle linkage or wiring. Connect power steering and air conditioning lines. Refer to the chapter on air conditioning for recharging procedures. Check each unit to make sure it is properly connected.

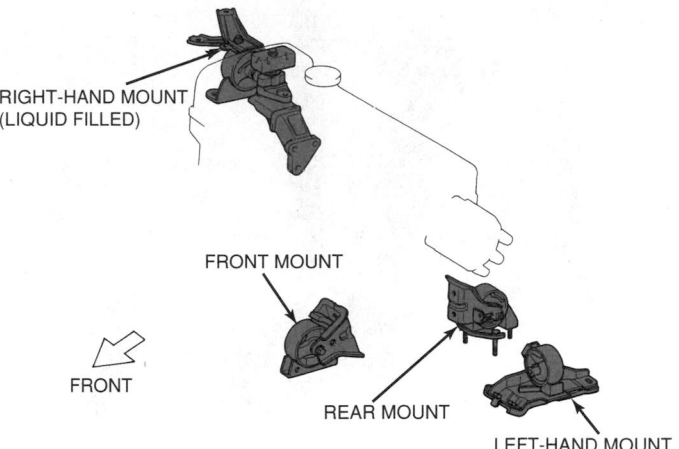

Figure 17-2. A four-point engine/transaxle mount setup. Note that the right-hand mount is liquid filled. This helps to reduce engine noise and vibration. (Toyota)

Marking Pays Off

As mentioned in the chapter on engine removal, all wires, lines, and hoses should be clearly marked so they may be reinstalled in a minimum amount of time. If you marked the various items properly when they were removed, you will now appreciate the importance of careful marking.

An Overhauled Engine Needs Instant Lubrication

When an overhauled engine is started, it is vitally important that all moving parts receive adequate lubrication. Even though all parts may have been thoroughly lubricated during assembly, most of this oil will have drained off into the pan. The oil galleries are dry, the filter is dry, and the tappets (hydraulic) will need additional oil.

Upon starting, the oil pump must prime itself. It must then force oil throughout the system, filling the galleries, filter, and other areas before supplying oil to the bearings. This takes time. Do not be fooled by the oil pressure gauge registering immediate pressure. This could be caused by air in the lines.

During this critical period of time, the engine is operating without proper lubrication. New parts are closely fitted and areas such as cylinder, ring, and piston surfaces will quickly heat up and cause *scoring* and *scuffing*. Bearings and journals can also be damaged by the lack of oil upon starting (dry start). This can be prevented by *pressurizing the lubrication system* before starting the engine.

Pressurizing the Engine Lubrication System

The lubrication system may be pressurized by using a special tank and hose setup, **Figure 17-3.** The tank is

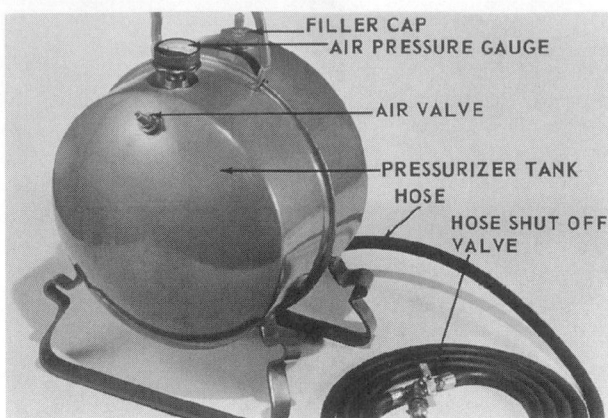

Figure 17-3. Typical lubrication system pressurizer. (Clevite)

filled to the indicated level with the same kind of oil that will be used in the engine. Air pressure up to the normal system pressure (around 40 lb. psi or 276 kPa) is then admitted to the tank. Watch the gauge to avoid excess pressure.

The hose fitting is attached to some external entry point into the lubrication system, such as the oil sender hole. The valve is opened and oil under pressure flows through the system. This primes the oil pump and fills the galleries, filter, lifters, and bearings. This ensures prompt lubrication upon starting. Rotate the engine several times while pressurizing, **Figure 17-4.**

Pressurizer as a Bearing Leak Detector

The **pressurizer** (often referred to as a bearing leak detector) can also be used to check bearing clearance. Some technicians prefer to pressurize the lubrication system before installing the oil pan. This technique permits watching the leakage rate at the ends of the bearings. The oil should pass through each bearing and fall in a series of individual drops. A steady stream indicates excessive clearance. When a steady stream is found, turn the crankshaft one-half revolution in case registration (alignment) of the oil holes is responsible. A rate of fewer than 20-25 drops per minute indicates insufficient clearance, **Figure 17-5.**

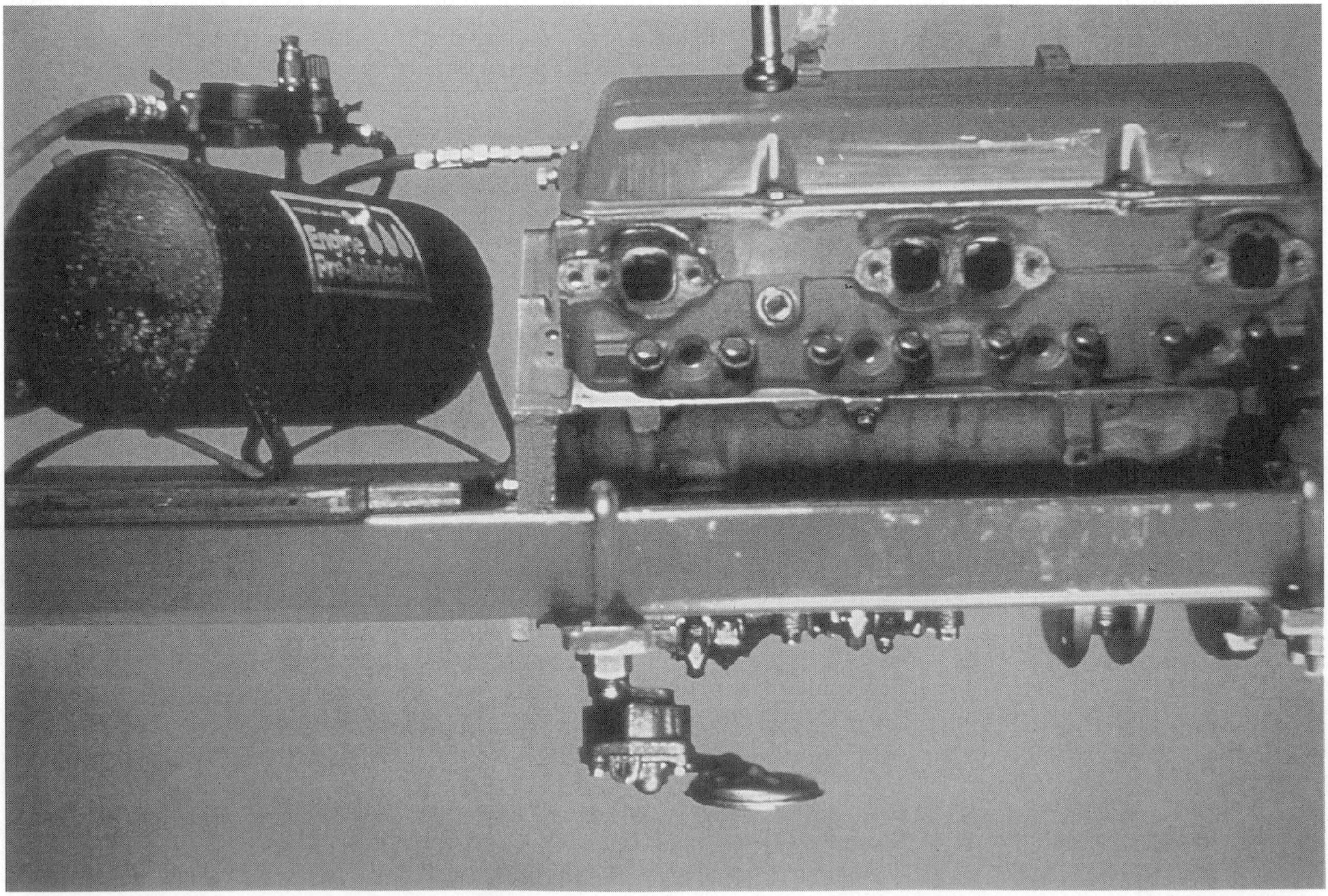

Figure 17-4. Preparing to pressurize the lubrication system with a pressurizer. (Federal-Mogul)

Figure 17-5. The amount of engine oil passing by the bearings will provide some indication as to the bearing clearances. (Federal-Mogul)

An engine that has been in storage for a length of time should be pressurized upon installation, even though it may have been pressurized upon completion of the overhaul.

Fill with Oil

Bring the oil level in the pan up to the full mark. Do not over fill. Use a top-quality oil of the type and viscosity recommended by the manufacturer. Prestart pressurizing eliminates the need to add additional oil to fill the filter.

Fill the Cooling System

Fill the radiator to the full mark (do not overfill) with factory-recommended mixture of clean water and antifreeze. This will provide water pump seal lubrication, resistance to leaks, protection from rust and corrosion, and protection for freezing and overheating.

 Caution: Do not use water alone in the cooling system. Many car makers insist on the use of antifreeze. Failure to add antifreeze could damage the engine and void the manufacturer's warranty.

Check the Fuel Tank

Check the fuel level, and if needed, add fuel to the tank. If the vehicle has been in storage for an extended period of time, it is a good idea to drain the tank and refill it with fresh fuel. If the tank is to be drained, refer to Chapter 19 on fuel systems for necessary safety precautions.

Check the Battery

If possible, check the battery electrolyte level and add distilled water to bring the electrolyte up to the proper level. The battery should be in good condition and fully charged. Install the battery and connect the battery cables.

Double-Check before Starting

Before starting the engine, double-check the following items:

- Engine oil level.
- Coolant level in the radiator.
- Spark plug wire installation order.
- Point gap or reluctor-to-armature air gap, if applicable.
- Ignition timing.
- Valve clearance.
- Automatic choke adjustment, if applicable.
- Transmission shifter position.

Remove tools, extension cords, and wiping cloths from the engine compartment. Have a fire extinguisher ready in case of emergency.

Starting the Engine

A properly overhauled engine should start readily. Fuel injection systems and carburetors on cars equipped with electric pumps will fill if the ignition switch is turned on for about 60 seconds without cranking.

Vehicles with mechanical fuel pumps may have to be cranked for a short time to allow the fuel pump to fill the carburetor. Some technicians fill the carburetor with a gravity feed can or use an electric pump to force gas from a container into the carburetor. This helps eliminate excessive cranking.

If the vehicle has a carburetor, make certain that the automatic choke has closed the choke valve. Do not place the palm of your hand over the carburetor air horn to choke the engine while cranking. A backfire through the carburetor could inflict a serious burn.

If the engine cranks slowly because of an old battery, a booster battery may be used to facilitate starting. Hook the booster in parallel to the car battery—positive to positive and negative to negative. Never hook a booster battery in series. A series hookup doubles battery voltage and can cause extensive damage to the electrical system. See Chapter 26 on battery service for details on the use of booster batteries.

Proper Break-In Is Important

Modern design, materials, machinery, and repair procedures make it possible to assemble an engine with highly accurate clearances and controlled finishes. This has eliminated the long, old-fashioned **break-in period.** Despite the fact that break-in is simplified, proper break-in is still of major importance. The first hour or so of engine operation is extremely critical. Lubrication, RPM, temperature, and loading are all vital. If these are correct, they will produce proper wearing in of the rings, cylinder walls, and bearings until mating parts are smooth enough to provide proper sealing and to reduce friction to a normal level.

Failure to follow accepted break-in rules may result in extensive engine damage from scuffing and scoring. The amount of damage is often hard to determine immediately, but the engine may fail in service thousands of miles sooner than would be normally expected.

Run Engine at Fast Idle until Normal Temperature Is Reached

When the engine is first started, the choke (on older vehicles) or the electronic control system (on newer vehicles) will cause the idle speed to be higher than normal. This is desirable to ensure an oil pressure and throw-off sufficient to adequately lubricate the cylinder walls. Operate the engine at this speed until normal operating temperature is reached (usually 15 to 20 minutes). If the cold idle is not approximately 1200 rpm, raise the idle by some means until the engine is warm.

If for some reason it was not possible to pressurize the lubrication system before starting the engine, a few squirts of engine oil should be directed into the carburetor air horn during the first minute or two of operation. This will provide cylinder lubrication until bearing throw-off and "spit hole" lubrication take over. Follow the manufacturer's recommendations.

Check oil pressure and coolant temperature occasionally during the warm-up. Also check coolant level, as there may have been air in the system when filling. Inspect for any signs of fuel, oil, or coolant leakage.

Adequate Ventilation

Never operate on engine in an enclosed area. Open plenty of windows and doors. If special *exhaust disposal lines* are available, run the exhaust into these lines. If the weather permits, run the engine outside.

Remember that exhaust gases contain *carbon monoxide*. Carbon monoxide is a deadly poison and is cumulative. If you are exposed to exhaust fumes every day, even in relatively small amounts, it will build up in your system until you become physically ill. Avoid all possible exposure to exhaust fumes.

Make Final Adjustments

When normal temperature is reached, turn the engine off. *Retorque* the head and manifold bolts, and give the valve clearance a final adjustment if required. See **Figure 17-6.** If setting mechanical lifter clearance, use the hot setting recommendations. Start and run the engine long enough to check the ignition timing and idle speed if they are not controlled by the computer.

Road Test and Break-In Run

Drive the vehicle to a spot where you can safely reach a speed of 50 mph (80 km/h). Accelerate rapidly up to about 50 mph (80 km/h). Immediately let up on the accelerator and allow the car to coast down to around 30 mph (48 km/h). Drive the vehicle at 30 mph (48 km/h) for a block or so and again accelerate rapidly up to 50 mph (80 km/h). Once again, coast back to 30 mph (48 km/h). Accelerate and coast fifteen to twenty times. When slowing down, watch for cars behind you.

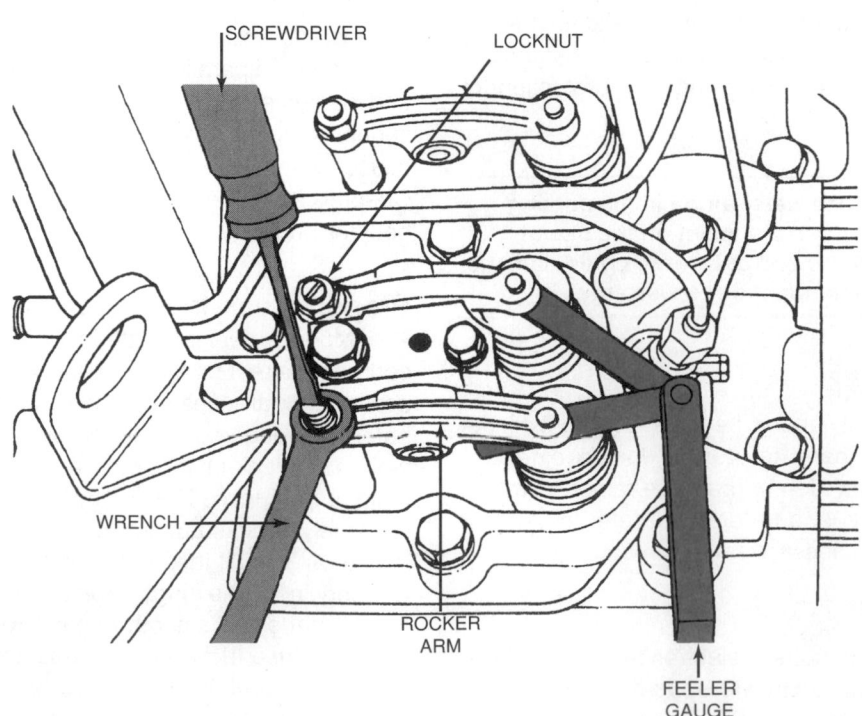

Figure 17-6. After the initial break-in, it is a good idea to recheck valve clearances on engines that do not use self-adjusting valve trains. Be sure to follow the manufacturer's recommendations. (Cummins)

The object of the acceleration is to increase ring loading against the cylinder walls, speeding up break-in. During the coast period, heavy vacuum in the cylinders will draw additional oil up around the rings.

Devote as much time as practical to the break-in run. The fifteen to twenty acceleration-coast cycles mentioned are minimum requirements. Observe oil pressure, temperature, steering, braking, engine performance, and shifting during the run. When back at the shop, check again for any possible leakage.

Dynamometer Break-In

If possible, mount the engine or vehicle to a **dynamometer** for break-in. The dynamometer allows the technician to make a road test in the shop. See **Figure 17-7.**

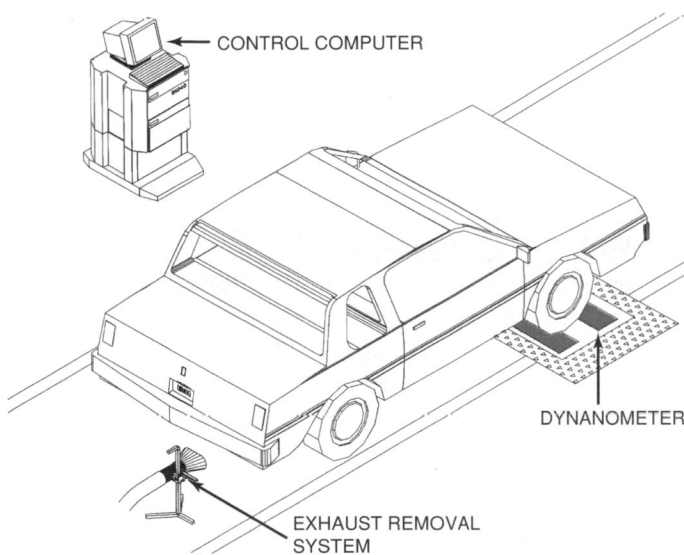

Figure 17-7. A front-wheel drive vehicle having a newly rebuilt engine broken in on a dynamometer. (Clayton Mfg.)

Deliver the Vehicle to the Owner

After the initial break-in, final checks, and vehicle cleanup, the car is ready for delivery.

 Note: Be sure that the owner is told to avoid sustained high-speed driving and heavy loads during the first 200 to 300 miles (320 to 480 km). Also inform the owner that oil consumption may be noticeable until the rings are seated.

Ask the owner to bring the car in at the end of the first 500 miles (800 km) for an oil change and a checkup. During break-in, metal particles will be dislodged and enter the oil. Changing the oil and the filter at the end of the first 500 miles (800 km) eliminates the possibility of engine damage caused by the prolonged use of contaminated oil. At the time of the oil change, be sure to check for leaks. Also, ask the owner how the car has been performing.

Ring Seating Takes Time

The overhauled engine may continue to burn oil for a short period of time. Oil consumption should drop to an acceptable level by the end of 2500 miles (4 000 km) or around 65 hours of operation. Remember that the normal amount of oil consumption varies with engine condition, design, vehicle use, operating conditions, and driving habits. A general rule of thumb is to consider excessive oil consumption a condition in which a quart of oil is consumed in less than 700 miles (1 120 km). One quart per 1500 miles (2 400 km) may be considered good oil mileage. These are approximations and are for normal driving.

The Engine Needs Help

While an engine may be in good mechanical condition, the ignition, fuel, and cooling systems must be functioning properly or engine performance will be substandard.

Protect your work and your reputation by encouraging the owner to have essential work performed in these areas. Point out why the work is important and what can be expected if the work is not done. It is a good idea to put the suggestions in writing, so the owner will not later say, "I certainly wish that the technician would have told me this work was needed."

Tech Talk

Unlike gardens, engines do not need dirt. Dirt in an overhauled engine will cause scuffed pistons, worn bearings, clogged ports, sticking and collapsed lifters, and many other problems. This can create an instant comeback.

Much of the dirt that enters the engine during an overhaul is the result of carelessness. This is especially true if you lay engine parts around the shop where dust, grinding grit, welding smoke, and other contaminants can get to them. The undersides of parts can pick up dirt and metal filings from work benches. To keep dirt out of the engine, make sure that you do the following:

1. Thoroughly clean each part before and after working on it.
2. Cover all parts that will not be assembled immediately.
3. Carefully inspect all parts before installing them.

When working on all automotive assemblies, think clean!

Summary

Engine component order of assembly varies. Study the engine construction and "think ahead." Do not rush the assembly work. Proceed carefully. Follow safety rules when installing the engine. If a manufacturer's shop manual is available, use it for assistance. Lower the engine into place slowly and avoid damage to car or accessory units.

Attach all wiring, hose, and tubing. Connect transmission, clutch, and accelerator linkage. Torque engine mounts and adjust belts.

Pressurize the lubrication system before starting the engine. Bring the oil level up to the full mark. Fill the radiator and check the battery. Clear away tools, cords, and cloths. Have a fire extinguisher ready. Never use your hand for a choke.

Upon starting, run the engine at about 1200 RPM until normal operating temperature is reached. Check for leaks while the engine is running. Also check oil pressure and coolant temperature. Shut off the engine and retorque the heads and manifolds. Drive the car up to 50 mph (80 km/h) and then coast to 30 mph (48 km/h). Repeat this procedure fifteen to twenty times. If desired, the engine may be run in on a dynamometer. Instruct the owner as to importance of proper operation during the first 200 miles (240 km), a 500-mile (800 km) oil change, and taking care of any needed adjustments or repairs in the cooling, fuel, and ignition systems.

Know These Terms

Sequence of assembly	Pressurizer
Lift strap	Break-in period
Protective pads	Exhaust disposal lines
Hoist	Carbon monoxide
Scoring	Retorque
Scuffing	Dynamometer

Review Questions—Chapter 17

Do not write in this book. Write your answers on a separate sheet of paper.

1. List eight things which should be double-checked before attempting to start an overhauled engine.
2. When installing the engine, the transmission should be _____.
   (A) on the engine
   (B) in the car
   (C) on the bench
   (D) varies with different makes and models
3. When hooking up a booster battery, connect _____.
   (A) positive to positive and negative to negative
   (B) positive to negative and negative to positive
   (C) positive and negative both to car battery positive
   (D) positive and negative both to car battery negative
4. Name four things that should be checked during the initial warm-up period.
5. Tell the vehicle driver to avoid sustained high-speed driving and heavy loads during the first _____ miles of operation.
   (A) 50 (80 km)
   (B) 100-200 (160-320 km)
   (C) 200-300 (320-480 km)
   (D) 500-1000 (800-1 600 km)

6. Name five things that should be done after the initial warm-up.
7. Excessive oil consumption means that the engine consumes a quart of oil in less than _____.
   (A) 700 miles (1 120 km)
   (B) 1500 miles (2 400 km)
   (C) 3000 miles (4 800 km)
   (D) 6000 miles (9 600 km)
8. Brief, rapid acceleration followed by coasting will help to _____ on a new engine.
   (A) lube the camshaft lobes
   (B) wear in the rod bearings
   (C) seat the rings
   (D) seat the valves
9. Break-in can also be performed with the engine mounted on a _____.
10. The first oil change on the overhauled engine should occur at _____.
    (A) 500 miles (800 km)
    (B) 1000 miles (1 600 km)
    (C) 2500 miles (4 000 km)
    (D) 7500 miles (12 000 km)

ASE-Type Questions

1. Technician A says that there is an exact order of assembly that applies to all engines. Technician B says that anticipating problems will slow both engine assembly and engine installation. Who is right?
   (A) A only.
   (B) B only.
   (C) Both A & B.
   (D) Neither A nor B.
2. The lubrication system should be pressurized before starting the engine to prevent immediate engine _____.
   (A) wear
   (B) noise
   (C) overheating
   (D) Both A & B.
3. Technician A says that pressurizing the lubrication system will protect against engine damage and can be used to check for excessive bearing leakage. Technician B says that the oil placed on parts during assembly will provide adequate lubrication when the engine is first started. Who is right?
   (A) A only.
   (B) B only.
   (C) Both A & B.
   (D) Neither A nor B.
4. If oil pressure is excessive (too high) on a rebuilt engine, which of the following is the most likely cause?
   (A) Loose main bearings.
   (B) Loose rod bearings.
   (C) Excessive hydraulic lifter leakdown.
   (D) Stuck oil pressure regulator.

5. Technician A says that clean water is all that is needed to fill the cooling system. Technician B says that placing a hose in the radiator and allowing the hose to run while the engine is warmed up will help the rings seat. Who is right?
(A) A only.
(B) B only.
(C) Both A & B.
(D) Neither A nor B.

6. When the engine is first started, it should be operated at _____ until normal operating temperature is reached.
(A) normal idle
(B) fast idle
(C) 3000 RPM
(D) varying speeds

7. A newly rebuilt engine should be road tested for _____.
(A) 5 to 10 acceleration-coast cycles
(B) 15 to 20 minutes minimum
(C) 20 to 30 minutes maximum
(D) 15 to 20 acceleration-coast cycles

8. During the road test, you should accelerate to a speed no faster than _____.
(A) 30 mph (48 km/h)
(B) 50 mph (80 km/h)
(C) 65 mph (104 km/h)
(D) 55 mph (88 km/h)

9. Engine _____ may be noticeable until the rings are seated.
(A) noise
(B) oil consumption
(C) leakage
(D) sluggishness

10. A rebuilt engine burns one quart of oil in the first 500 miles (800 km) of operation. Technician A says that the cause could be rings that have not yet seated. Technician B says that the vehicle must be driven further to determine whether oil consumption is excessive. Who is right?
(A) A only.
(B) B only.
(C) Both A & B.
(D) Neither A nor B.

Suggested Activities

1. Using a factory service manual as a reference, write step-by-step instructions for reassembling a particular engine.

2. Locate the engine mounts on various vehicles and make sketches of mount locations.

3. Using the shop engine hoist and a junk engine, determine how to attach the lifting fixtures to keep the engine:
    level.
    tilted toward the rear.
    tilted toward the front.
    tilted to the right or left side.
After deciding where to make the attachments, lift the engine a few inches from the floor and determine whether your calculations are correct.

 Caution: Engines are heavy. Your instructor should supervise this activity.

4. Identify all the connections (electrical, fuel, and vacuum lines, brackets, control cables, and linkages) that must be made when reinstalling an engine in a vehicle.

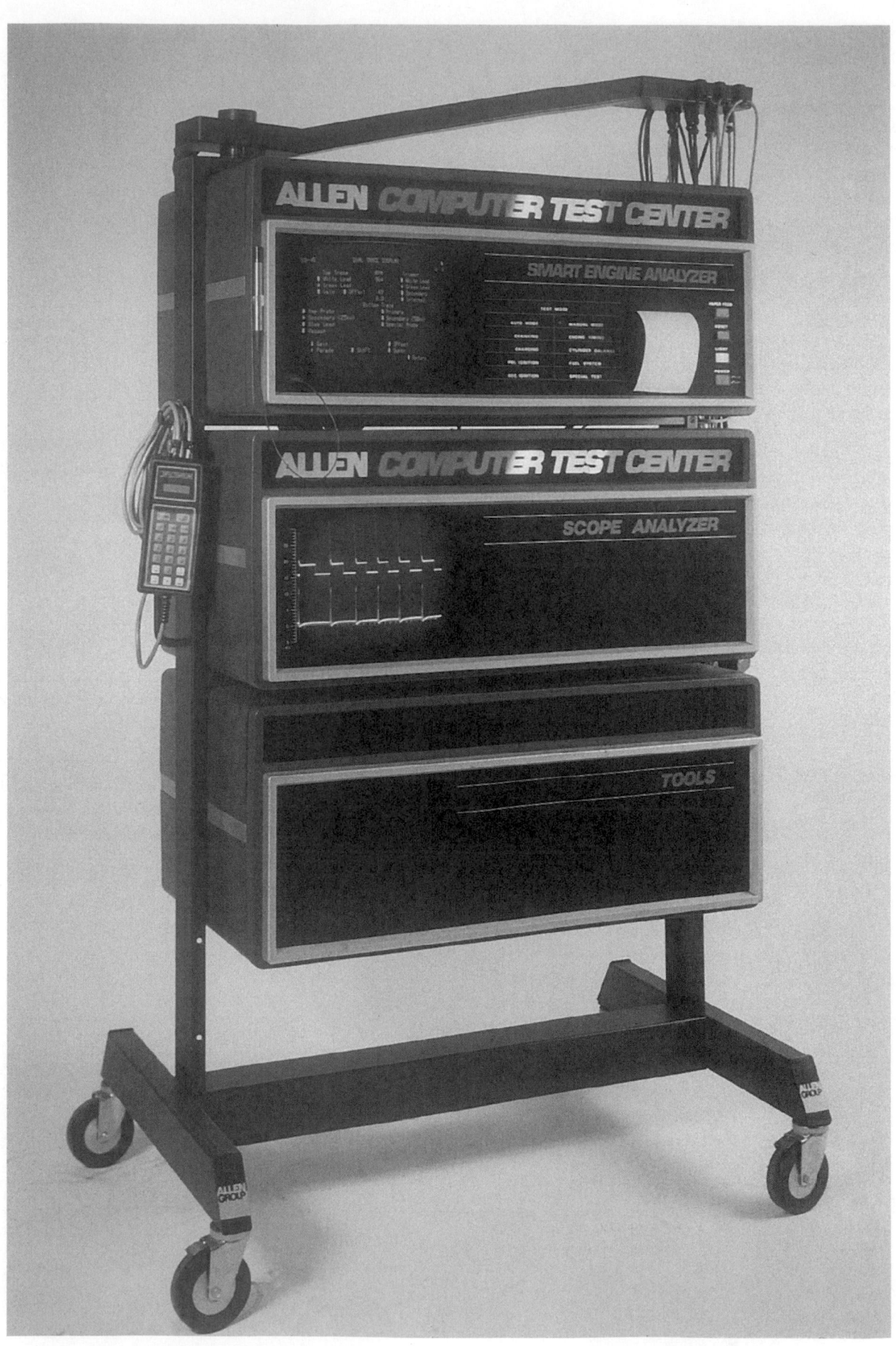

An engine analyzer, such as the one shown above, is often used when diagnosing ignition system problems. (Automotive Diagnostics)

18

Ignition System Service

After studying this chapter, you will be able to:
- Inspect, test, and repair electronic ignition systems.
- Explain the difference between electronic ignition systems and computerized ignition systems.
- Inspect, test, and repair contact point ignition systems.
- Describe the purpose of firing order information.
- Remove, test, and replace a distributor assembly.
- Adjust ignition timing.
- Clean, inspect, test, and replace spark plugs.
- Explain the use of an ignition oscilloscope.

All ignition systems, whether they are controlled by an electronic ignition module, the engine computer, or a mechanically operated set of contact points, have the same function: to change battery voltage into high voltage capable of jumping the spark plug gap and to distribute this voltage to the right plug at the right time. This chapter will cover the diagnosis and service of engine ignition systems. In some cases, you will be referred to other chapters that cover certain aspects of the ignition system in more detail. Refer to Chapter 20 for additional information on diesel ignition. Glow plugs, grid heaters, etc., will be discussed.

Ignition System Problem Diagnosis

The first step in ignition system problem diagnosis is to visually inspect the ignition components. Study the primary wires for signs of cracking, burning, and corrosion. All connections must be clean and tight. If the resistance in the *primary circuit* is excessive, the primary voltage may be reduced to a level that can seriously affect the *secondary circuit* available voltage. Check the coil and distributor cap for signs of flashover, burning, and corrosion. Coil polarity must be correct. Examine the secondary wires for evidence of swelling and deterioration. Wire ends should have good boots and must be inserted fully into the correct towers.

Troubleshooting a No-Start Condition: Spark Test

Caution: Electronic and computerized ignition systems produce between 30,000 and more than 100,000 volts. To reduce the risk of shock, always wear rubber gloves or use insulated pliers when performing spark tests on these systems.

If the engine will crank but not start, a spark test can be used to pinpoint the source of the problem. To perform this test, remove the coil secondary wire from the distributor cap. Hold the wire approximately 1/4″ (6.350 mm) from the engine block (or another appropriate ground) and crank the engine. As the engine is cranked, an arc should jump between the wire and ground, **Figure 18-1.** If this does not

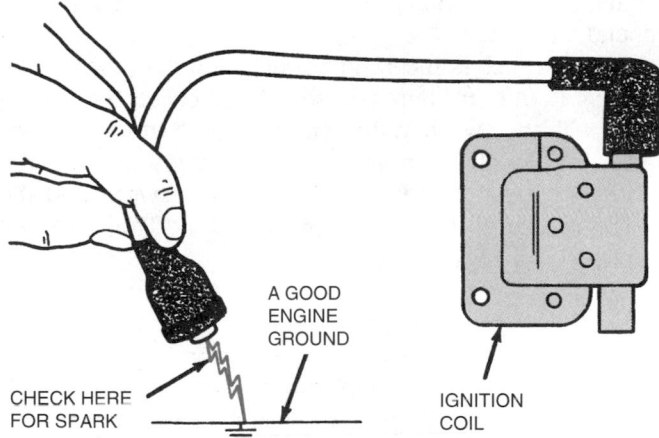

Figure 18-1. When performing a spark test, hold the secondary wire approximately 1/4″ from an appropriate ground. (Chrysler)

occur, check the primary side of the ignition system. Components that may be at fault include the coil, ignition switch, electronic control unit, points and condenser (if used), and the ignition resistor. Methods for testing these items will be covered later in this chapter. If a spark is produced at the coil secondary wire, reconnect the wire and remove a secondary wire from a spark plug. Again, hold the wire 1/4″ (6.350 mm) from the engine block and crank the engine. If there is no spark between the wire and ground, check the spark plug wire, distributor, and rotor. If a spark is produced, study the spark plugs for signs of fouling and other abnormalities. Remember, a no-start condition can be caused by a fuel system problem.

The ignition system can also be checked by attaching an oscilloscope and checking for a secondary pattern as the engine is cranked. Some manufacturers recommend this method instead of checking for a spark by removing secondary wires.

Testing, Replacing, and Adjusting Ignition System Components

When an individual part of the ignition system is suspected of being faulty, it should be inspected, tested, adjusted, repaired, or replaced. Always recheck the system following any adjustment or replacement to make certain the repaired circuit meets specifications.

Ignition switch

The *ignition switch* can fail to deliver battery voltage to the ignition system during cranking or when it is in the on position. If the engine starts but immediately dies when the ignition switch is returned to the on position, the run terminal is defective. If the engine will not crank or cranks but will not start, the start terminal may be defective.

Ignition switches rarely fail, so check all other possibilities before suspecting a bad switch. To check the ignition switch, touch the probe of a non-powered test light to the battery terminal of the switch. If the light illuminates, the ignition switch is receiving power. If the light does not illuminate, check the wiring between the positive battery terminal and the switch.

If the switch is receiving power, touch the probe of the test light to the "on" terminal (sometimes called the *ign* terminal) with the switch in the "on" position. If the light illuminates, the switch is delivering current to the ignition wire and the problem is in wiring between the switch and the ignition system or in the system itself. If the light does not illuminate, the switch is defective.

Next, touch the test light probe to the start terminal of the switch as you attempt to crank the engine. If the light illuminates, the switch is good. The problem is farther along in the wiring or in the starting or ignition systems. If the light does not illuminate, the problem is in the switch itself.

Ignition Resistor

The *ignition resistor,* where used, must offer a specified amount of resistance to the battery-to-coil circuit. An ignition resistor can be a calibrated resistance wire built into the wire harness or a separate ballast resistor.

 Note: Many modern electronic ignition systems operate on full battery voltage at all times. Consult the proper service manual for exact input voltage specifications.

Since an ignition resistor reduces the amount of electricity in the circuit, the simplest way to check a resistor is to determine whether the voltage at the resistor is less than battery voltage. Disconnect the battery wire at the coil and attach a voltmeter (measures system voltage). With the ignition switch in the on position, voltage should be about 9 volts, assuming the battery is at 12 volts or higher. If the reading exceeds 9 volts, or if there is no voltage at the wire, replace the resistance wire or ballast resistor. Be careful to

install a correct service replacement. Recheck voltage after the replacement is installed.

An *ohmmeter* (measures resistance in ohms) is being used to check the resistance imparted by the ballast resistor in **Figure 18-2.** Check the reading against manufacturer's specifications. The ohmmeter can also be used to check the resistance wire type. Do not make a test hookup that will connect the resistor directly across the battery because this will burn out and destroy the resistor.

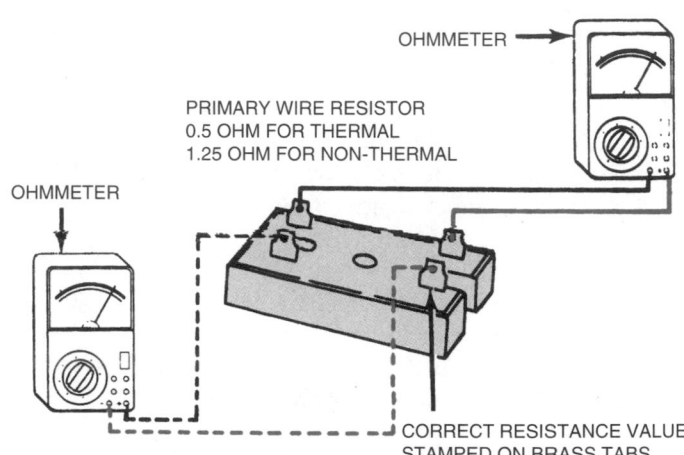

Figure 18-2. Testing a ballast resistor with an ohmmeter. (Sun Electric Corp.)

Testing the Ignition Coil

The *ignition coil* should be checked for available voltage. This test should be performed after the coil has reached operating temperature. Other checks include testing both primary and secondary circuit resistance and current draw during idle and when the engine is stopped.

These tests usually expose any internal shorts, grounds, opens, insulation breakdown, and loose or corroded connections. Use reliable test equipment and follow the manufacturer's instructions.

Figure 18-3 shows a coil being tested for both primary and secondary circuit resistance. The ohmmeter readings should be compared against the manufacturer's specifications to determine whether the coil is good. As a general rule, a coil should read about 1.5 ohms across the primary terminals and about 8000 to 9000 ohms across the secondary (center) tower and either primary terminal. There should be a very high resistance (at least 500,000 ohms) between any terminal and the coil housing.

Figure 18-4 illustrates the use of an ohmmeter to check resistance in both an electronic ignition system coil and a pickup coil. The parts being tested are:

- A—GM HEI V-8 distributor cap and coil combination.
- B—GM four- and six-cylinder separate coil.
- C—GM HEI system pickup coil.

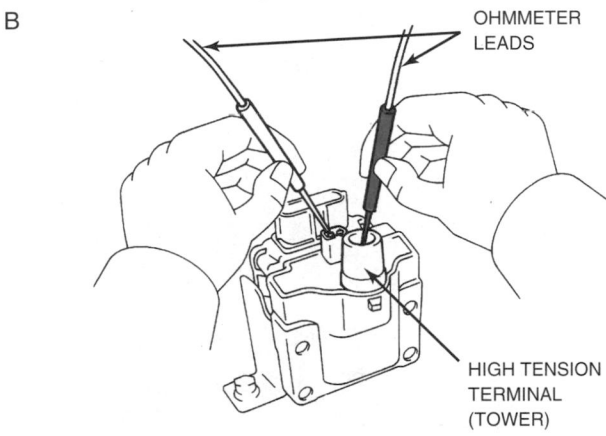

A

POSITIVE AND
NEGATIVE
TERMINALS

COIL

B

OHMMETER
LEADS

HIGH TENSION
TERMINAL
(TOWER)

Figure 18-3. Coil secondary and primary resistance test points. A—Primary test connections. B—Secondary coil resistance connections. (Toyota)

Test point resistance indicators are: 1—Primary resistance (0-1 ohm). 2—Secondary resistance (high scale). If both readings are infinite, replace the coil. 3—Primary resistance (0-1 ohm). 4—Secondary resistance (replace coil if less than 6000 or more than 30,000 ohms). 5—Replace coil if resistance is less than infinite. 6—Replace pickup coil if resistance is less than infinite. 7—Should read between 500-1500 ohms for this pickup coil.

These values are for this particular system. Values for other systems will vary, depending upon design. Always use specifications that pertain to the exact unit being tested.

Remember that the coil is a vital part of the ignition system. When not in excellent condition, it should be replaced. **Figure 18-5** shows two types of coils.

Check the Coil Tower for Corrosion and Flashover

Pull the high tension lead from the coil tower. Using a light, check the tower for signs of corrosion and burning. If corroded, clean the tower with a round bristle brush or sandpaper on a pencil. After cleaning, blow the tower out with air.

Examine the tower for any sign of *flashover* (high voltage leaving its intended circuit or path and leaping down, around, or across the tower and directly to ground). Flashover can be caused by moisture or dirt on the tower surface, by a corroded tower, or by failing to push the high tension wire fully into the tower.

Continued flashover burns the surface of the tower material, forming a path of carbon tracks. This path makes flashover even easier, and the tower may be severely damaged. Note the carbon tracks (path) left by flashover on the coil tower in **Figure 18-6.** When flashover has cracked the tower or has left a burned path, replace the coil. When replacing a coil damaged by flashover, replace the old

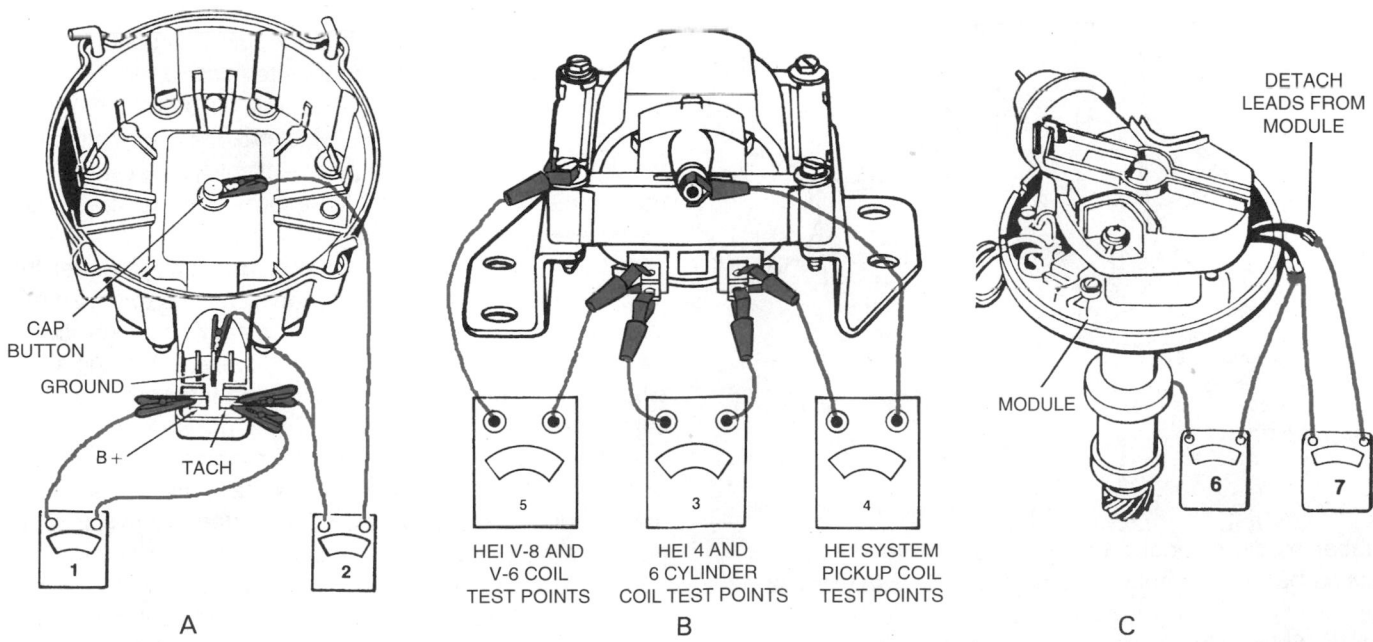

CAP
BUTTON

GROUND

B+   TACH

1   2

A

HEI V-8 AND
V-6 COIL
TEST POINTS

HEI 4 AND
6 CYLINDER
COIL TEST POINTS

HEI SYSTEM
PICKUP COIL
TEST POINTS

5   3   4

B

DETACH
LEADS FROM
MODULE

MODULE

6   7

C

Figure 18-4. Using an ohmmeter to check for specified resistance values. (Champion)

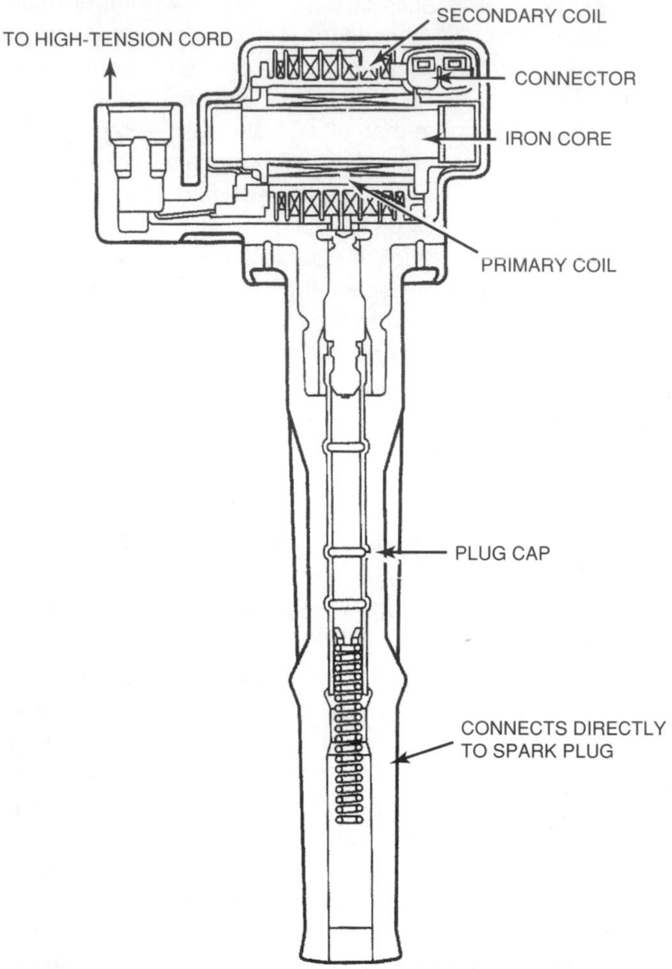

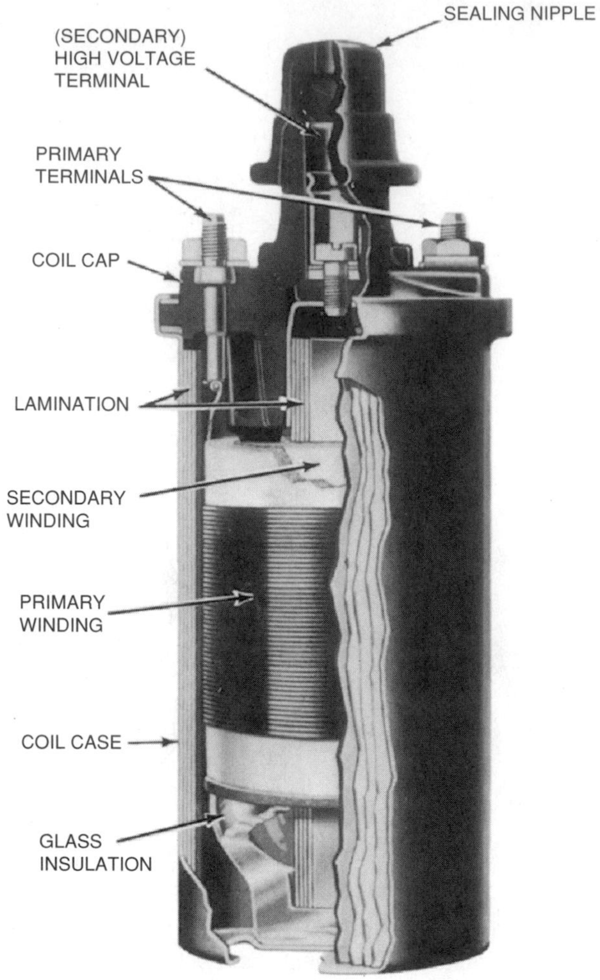

Figure 18-5. Cutaways illustrating two different ignition coils. (Chevrolet, Toyota)

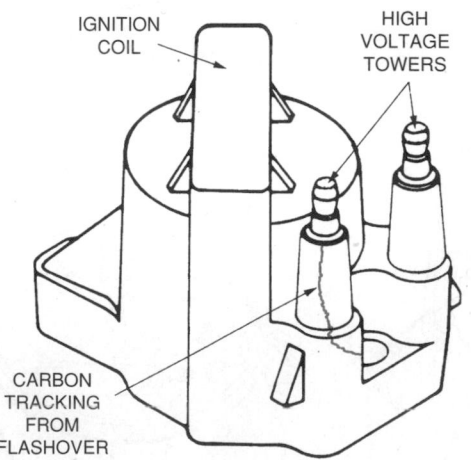

Figure 18-6. Flashover has ruined this coil. Note the carbon tracking path. (GM)

rubber nipple or boot on the high-tension lead. It probably has carbon tracks that will cause flashover with the new coil.

Prevent flashover by having a clean, tight tower wire connection, by having a good boot in place, and by keeping the tower and coil top free of dirt and moisture.

Coil Polarity Must Be Correct

The coil must be connected into the primary circuit so that the coil polarity marks (+ or -) correspond to those of the battery. If the negative battery post is grounded, which is common practice, the negative terminal on the coil must be grounded. The coil negative will be grounded through the ignition module of an electronic ignition system or through the contact points on a point-type system. Connecting the coil in this way will ensure that the spark plug's center electrode has negative polarity.

The center electrode of the plug is always hotter than the side electrode. Since it takes less voltage to cause electrons to move from a hot surface to a cold surface, current flow must be from the hot center electrode to the cooler side electrode. By giving the center electrode negative polarity, current flow will be as desired. See **Figure 18-7.**

If the coil is connected so that the plug's center electrode is positive, up to 40% more voltage will be required to fire the plug. This can cause hard starting, missing, and poor overall performance. Always check for correct coil polarity. The easiest way to check coil polarity is to visually observe the coil connections. Many late-model vehicles will have molded plastic connectors that cannot be reversed, **Figure 18-8.** When a vehicle with reversed coil connections

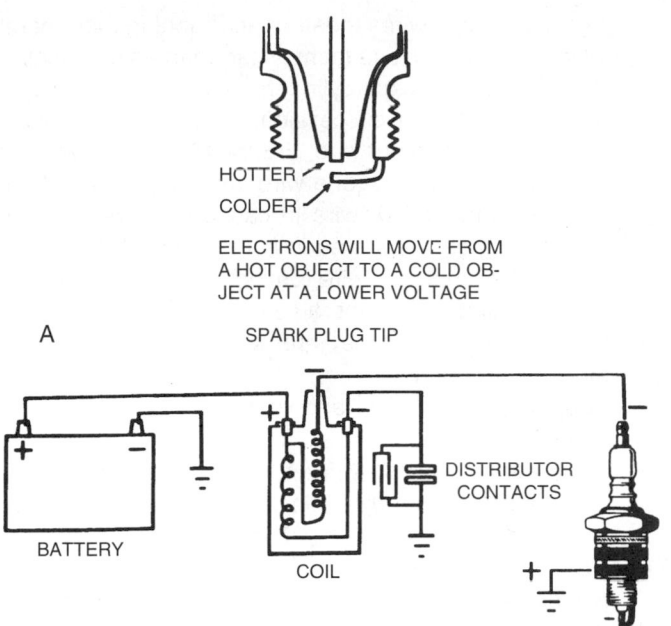

HOTTER

COLDER

ELECTRONS WILL MOVE FROM
A HOT OBJECT TO A COLD OB-
JECT AT A LOWER VOLTAGE

A   SPARK PLUG TIP

DISTRIBUTOR
CONTACTS

BATTERY

COIL

THE PRIMARY TERMINALS OF THE COIL SHOULD BE CONNECTED
SO THAT THE POLARITY MARKINGS CORRESPOND TO THE POLARITY
OF THE BATTERY

CORRECT SPARK PLUG POLARITY WILL RESULT IF THE COIL IS
PROPERLY CONNECTED

B   CORRECT COIL CONNECTIONS

Figure 18-7. The coil must be connected to impart a negative polarity to the spark plug's center electrode. (Ignition Mfg.'s. Institute)

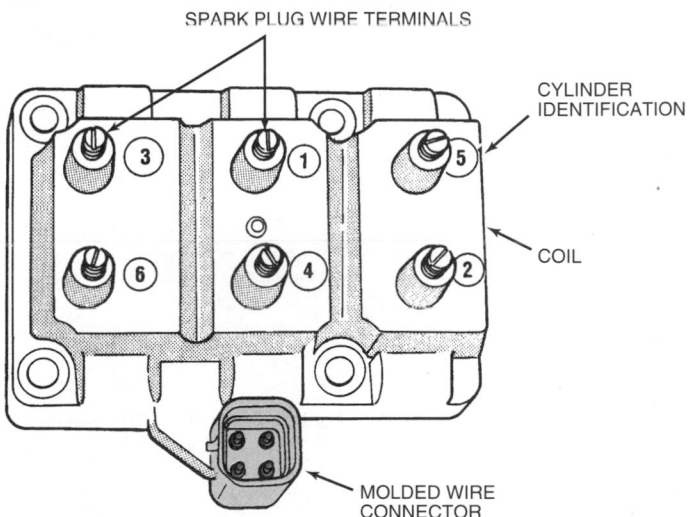

SPARK PLUG WIRE TERMINALS

CYLINDER
IDENTIFICATION

COIL

MOLDED WIRE
CONNECTOR

Figure 18-8. A coil pack that uses molded plastic connectors for the wiring. Note the cylinder identification number by each spark plug wire tower. (Chrysler)

is connected to an oscilloscope, the waveform will be upside down. Oscilloscope patterns are discussed later in this chapter.

Checking Secondary Wires

Many cars utilize special *resistance-type secondary wiring.* In the event of ignition trouble, it is often wise to

check each wire with an ohmmeter to determine if the resistance is within specified limits. This test will also show if there are breaks in the conductor or poor conductor-to-terminal connections, **Figure 18-9.**

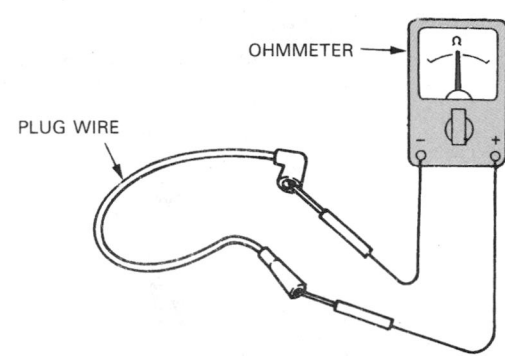

OHMMETER

PLUG WIRE

Figure 18-9. Checking a plug wire resistance with an ohmmeter. (Chrysler)

Replace wires that are not within specifications. Use wires with specified resistance. Secondary wires can be made up as needed or secured as a factory set. Special gripping tools are available to aid in the removal of old wires and boots, **Figure 18-10.**

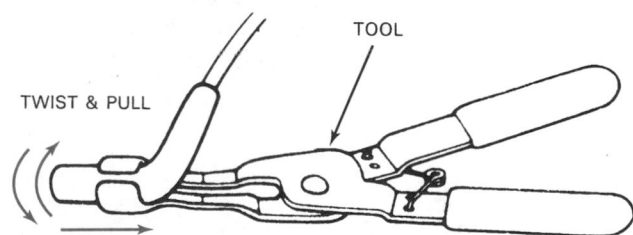

TOOL

TWIST & PULL

Figure 18-10. A special tool should be used to avoid damaging the boot or wire during removal from the spark plug. (Ford)

Remove one old wire at a time and replace it with a new one. Use new boots. Make sure the wire is snapped firmly on the plug and is fully seated in the distributor tower. Repeat this procedure until the entire set is replaced.

Remember that resistance wire is easily damaged. Grasp the boot (not the wire) and twist it one-half turn to break the seal. Then, pull the boot from the plug or tower. Never kink or jerk resistance wires. Avoid piercing insulation with test probes.

 Caution: Some plug wires have distributor cap electrodes that are permanently attached to the wire. These wires cannot be pulled until the positive locking terminal electrode is compressed from inside the cap. Figure 18-11 shows how the terminal is compressed to remove the wire.

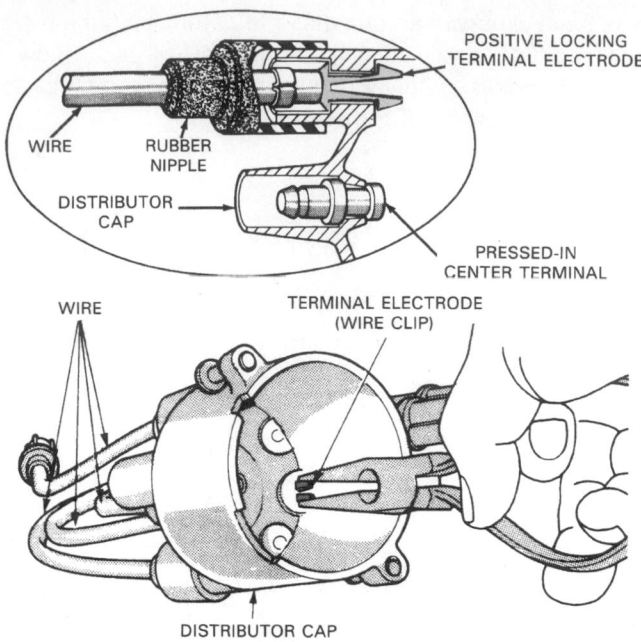

Figure 18-11. This locking terminal electrode must be squeezed together so that the plug wire terminal can be pulled out of the cap. (Chrysler)

Arrange Wires to Prevent Problems

Arrange wires in the holders as recommended by the manufacturer. See **Figure 18-12.** Coat the inside of the plug boots with silicone compound if so suggested. If no directions are available, keep the following points in mind:

- Avoid bunching wires together and running them parallel to each other. Keep them as far apart as practical.
- Where two adjacent cylinders (plugs) on the same bank (side) fire in succession, keep their plug wires separated by another wire, **Figure 18-13.** This will help prevent *cross firing* (one wire imparting enough voltage into an adjacent wire to cause it to fire its plug). Cross firing can cause serious mechanical damage to the engine. Improper wire routing can also cause short circuiting and significant radio interference.
- Route wires so that they are not pinched or frayed by other engine parts.
- Support wires properly and keep them away from heat and oil.
- Make certain that all wire ends are clean and firmly in place. All boots and wires must be in excellent condition.

Firing Order

When replacing plug wires, be sure to maintain the correct *firing order.* This is the numerical order in which cylinders fire the fuel charge, starting with the number one cylinder.

Place the number one plug wire in the number one distributor tower. Insert the remaining wires in their correct firing order, going around the cap in the direction that the distributor rotor turns. Pass the wires through any wire supports and connect them to the correct plugs.

On inline engines, the front cylinder (nearest timing chain cover) is the number one cylinder. On V-type engines, the number one cylinder will be at the front (timing chain end), but it can be either on the left or right bank. Usually

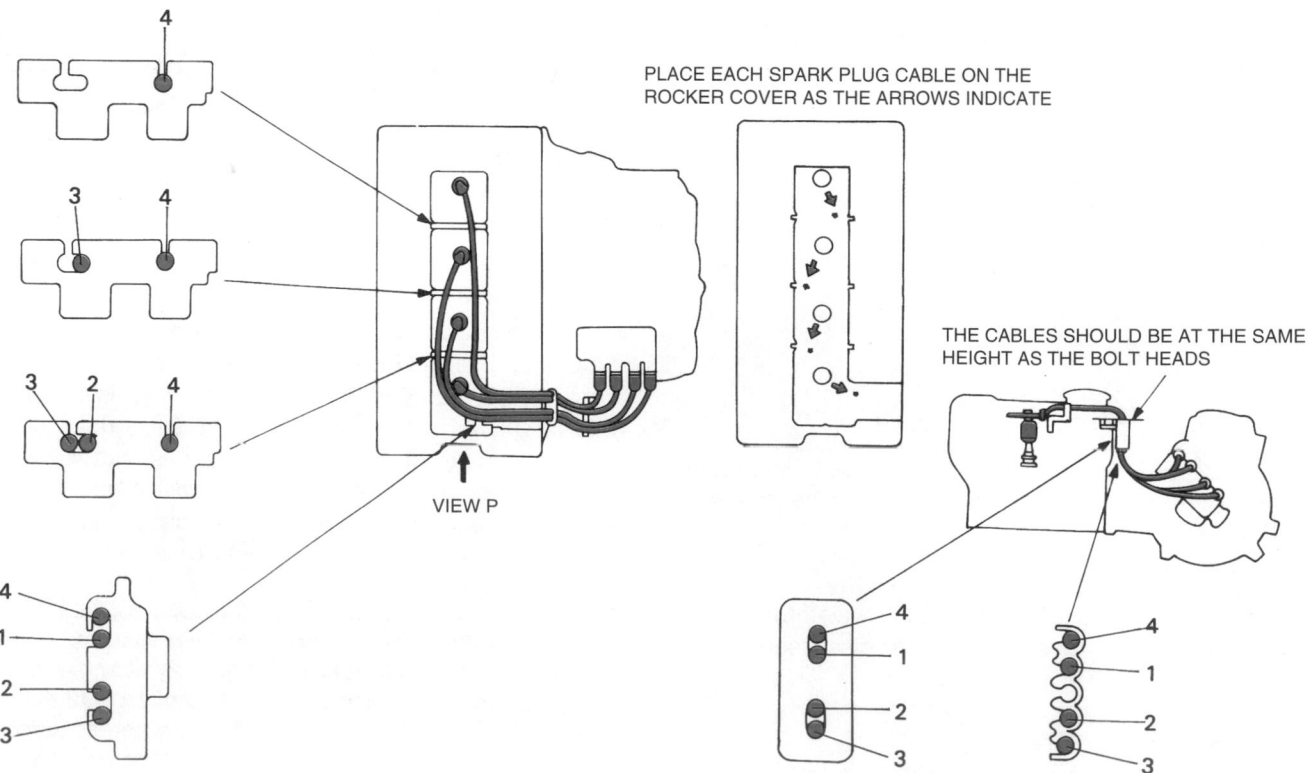

Figure 18-12. Spark plug wires must be routed through the holders properly. (Hyundai)

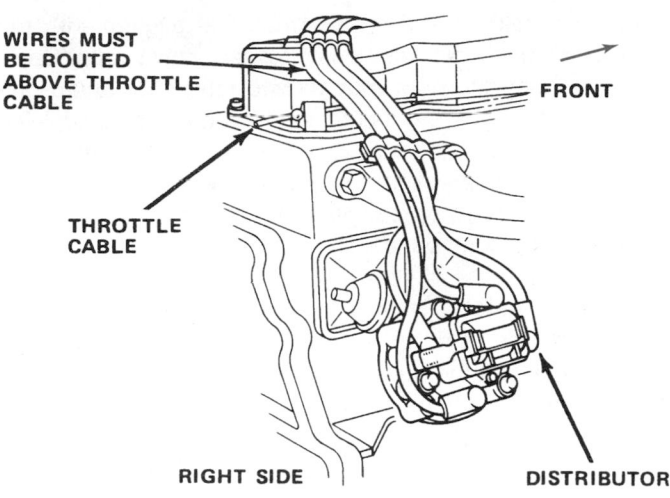

Figure 18-13. To avoid cross firing, radio interference, grounding, and damage, arrange the spark plug wires as specified by the manufacturer. (Chrysler)

the bank that extends farthest toward the front contains the number one cylinder. Always check the manufacturer's specifications.

How to Find the Number One Wire Tower on a Distributor Cap

To find the number one wire tower on the *distributor cap* when the manufacturer's shop manual is not available, remove the distributor cap and the spark plugs. Crank the engine until the number one piston is coming up on the compression stroke. Bump the engine over in small steps until the ignition timing mark is aligned with the pointer. Mark the outside of the distributor housing with chalk directly in line with the front of the rotor tip. Line up the distributor cap and snap it into place, making certain that the aligning tang is in place. Because the engine is now positioned to fire the number one cylinder, the rotor (chalk mark) will be aligned with the number one tower.

Distributor Cap Inspection

Pull each wire (one at a time) from the distributor cap wire towers. Inspect the towers for signs of corrosion, burning, or flashover. Mild corrosion may be removed with a special wire brush or with sandpaper. Replace the cap if flashover has been present.

When reinstalling the wires, make sure the terminals are clean and are shoved into the towers to the full depth. If the distributor cap has been replaced, use new boots when reinstalling the wires.

Remove the distributor cap by unsnapping the spring arms, removing the attaching screws, or using a screwdriver to press down and turn the latch arms, **Figure 18-14.** Inspect inside of distributor cap for signs of flashover. Check the cap for cracking and check the central carbon button or rotor contact for burning or cracking, **Figures 18-15** and **18-16.** If terminal posts are burned or grooved, replace the cap. Mild scaling, caused by sparks leaping from rotor tip to terminal post, can be scratched off with a

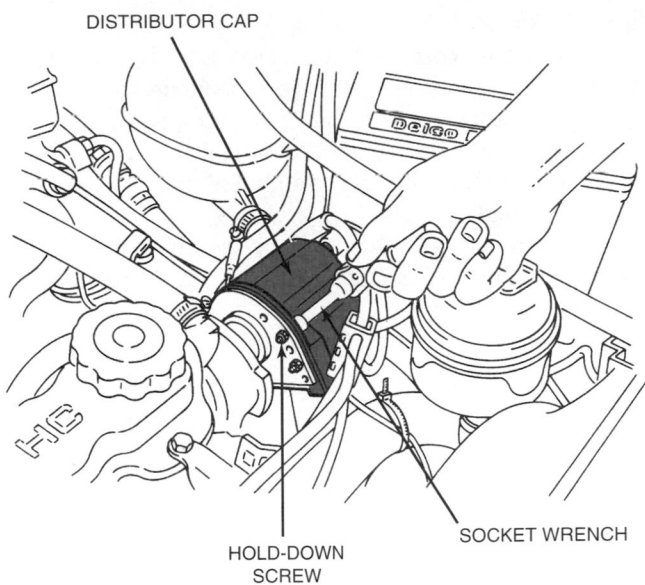

Figure 18-14. This technician is removing the distributor cap hold-down screws with a socket wrench. Some caps are secured with spring clips or spring-loaded latch arms. (Geo)

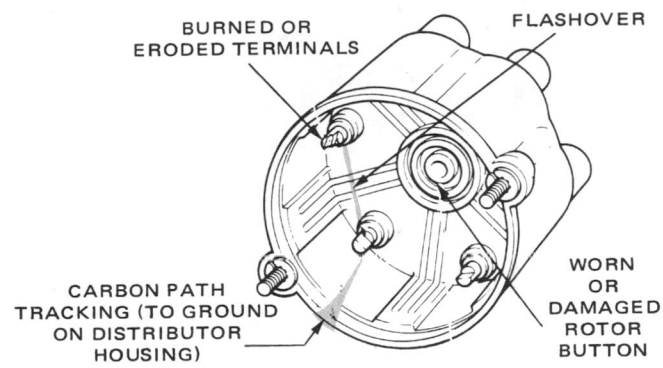

Figure 18-15. Cap cracks, broken towers, or carbon tracking from flashover can cause serious ignition troubles. (Jeep)

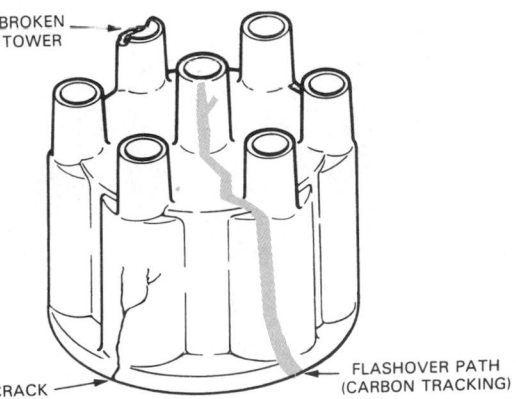

Figure 18-16. This carbon tracking was caused by flashover from the distributor central coil terminal traveling down one side of the cap to ground on distributor housing. Note other cap damage. (Jeep)

sharp knife. When replacing the cap, it is wise to replace the rotor. Make sure that the rotor is in place and the cap is properly aligned with distributor housing.

Testing a Rotor

Inspect the *rotor* for excessive burning on the tip. Check the contact spring and the resistance rod (if used). **Figure 18-17** shows a rotor that is in good condition. **Figure 18-18** shows the same type of rotor with the tip completely burned off. Whenever the distributor cap is replaced, replace the rotor.

Some rotors are removed by grasping and pulling straight up. Other rotors are attached with screws. When

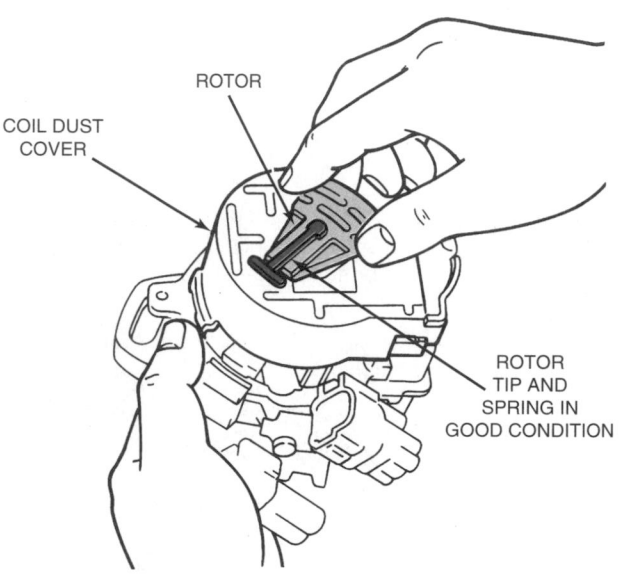

Figure 18-17. Check the rotor for burning, cracking, a broken spring, etc. (Geo)

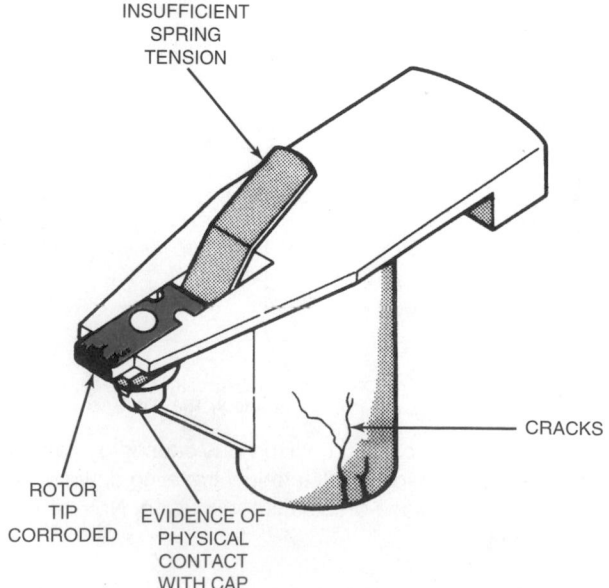

Figure 18-18. The tip has been burned off this rotor. Note other damage. This rotor must be replaced. (Chrysler)

installing a rotor, make certain that it is aligned with the distributor shaft and that it is pressed down fully. Carelessly installing the rotor may damage the rotor and/or the distributor cap. Some manufacturers recommend applying a silicone grease compound to the end of the rotor tip. This helps to suppress radio interference. Apply silicone to the rotor tip only when specified by manufacturer. Use the recommended compound.

Electronic Ignition Distributor Service

Electronic ignition systems use several methods to produce and time the output of the coil. Most electronic systems use a distributor-mounted trigger mechanism, usually a *magnetic pickup coil* or a *Hall effect pickup coil.* Some systems use an optical, or photoelectric, sensor in the distributor, while other systems use a *crankshaft position sensor* mounted in the engine block. All electronic systems have an ignition control unit to interpret the signal from the triggering mechanism and to operate the ignition coil.

There is usually no periodic service needed on the electronic ignition system except for replacing the spark plugs and rotor and checking ignition timing. Although the components of the electronic ignition distributor are much more reliable and trouble free than the older contact point systems, problems can still develop. Checking these problems can be more complicated than on the older systems and may require the use of special equipment.

If a malfunction occurs in an electronic ignition system, all the components should be visually inspected for damage. Remember that the secondary system (cap, rotor, wires, plugs) can develop the same problems as older systems. Study the wires for breaks and worn insulation, and carefully check all connectors for corrosion. The trigger wheel in magnetic and Hall effect pickup assemblies should be checked for broken teeth (blades), **Figure 18-19.** If the system uses a remotely located crankshaft position sensor, such as the one in **Figure 18-20,** it can often be checked with an ohmmeter. Pickup coils should be inspected for external damage. On some systems, the air gap between the trigger wheel and the pickup coil can be adjusted. If an optical distributor system is used, make sure that the slots in the rotor disk are unobstructed.

Methods for checking magnetic pickups, Hall effect pickups, and optical sensors vary from manufacturer to manufacturer. Always consult an appropriate service manual before testing these units. An ohmmeter can be used to check the condition of some Hall effect pickups and magnetic pickup coils. If the pickup's resistance is not within the manufacturer's specifications, the unit must be replaced.

Many electronic distributors also have additional functions. The distributor body may contain an additional pickup for a speed sensor that is used in conjunction with the engine computer or cruise control. Make sure you are checking the correct pickup.

Many of the components of an electronic ignition distributor can be replaced without removing the distributor from the engine. Always refer to the manufacturer's instructions before replacing any part.

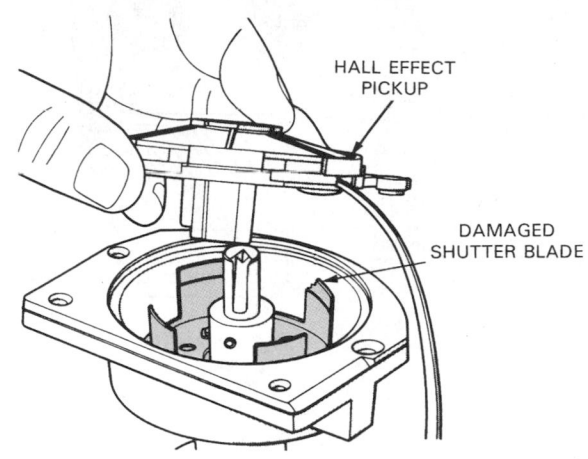

Figure 18-19. Crankshaft position sensors should be inspected for damage. Note the broken shutter blade on this Hall effect assembly. (Chrysler)

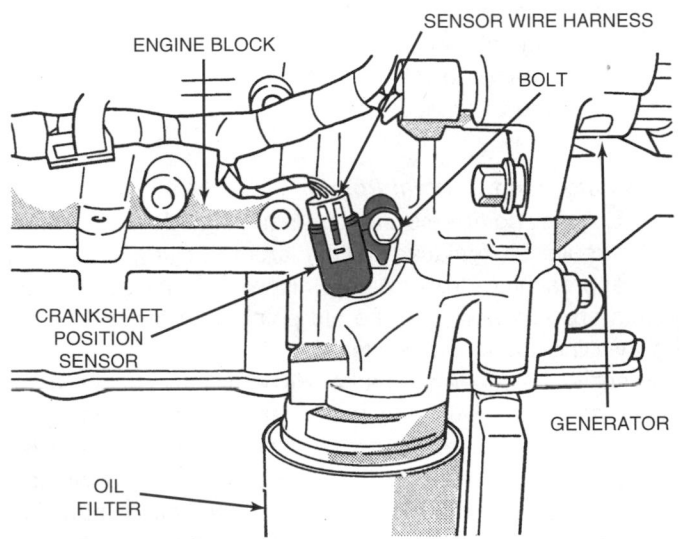

Figure 18-20. A remotely located crankshaft position sensor. (Dodge)

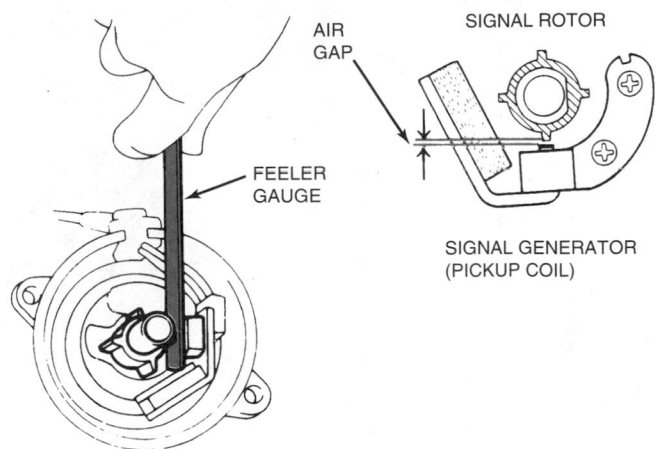

Figure 18-21. Adjusting the air gap on one particular electronic ignition distributor. Note the use of the brass (nonmagnetic) feeler gauge. (Toyota)

Adjusting the Air Gap

On some electronic ignition distributors, it is possible to adjust the *air gap* between the trigger wheel and the magnetic pickup. This is done using a non-magnetic (usually brass) feeler gauge. If a steel feeler gauge is used, the magnet in the pickup will attract the gauge, resulting in drag and a false reading.

To adjust the air gap, loosen the screw holding the pickup coil to the distributor base plate. Then, bump the engine until one tooth of the trigger wheel is directly across from the pickup coil. Using the correct thickness brass feeler gauge, move the pickup assembly until a light drag is felt on the gauge, **Figure 18-21.** Tighten the pickup screw and recheck the clearance. Finally, crank the engine and recheck the clearance on several teeth.

Electronic Ignition Control Module Service

Many electronic ignition *control modules* can be tested with a voltmeter or an ohmmeter. Some ignition con-

trol modules must be checked with special equipment, while others can only be checked by substituting a known good unit. Testing procedures vary from manufacturer to manufacturer. Always consult an appropriate service manual before testing the module. Improper equipment or incorrect connections can destroy the unit. Always make certain that the module is mounted tightly. A tight connection helps the ignition module dissipate heat, which can cause serious damage to the unit's internal components.

To aid in locating intermittent problems, many technicians heat the ignition control module as the engine operates. This can be done with a heat lamp or a heat gun. Heat the unit only until it reaches its normal operating temperature. Excessive heat can destroy the ignition module's internal components. In some cases, tapping on the module with a screwdriver handle as the engine operates can reveal a problem. If the engine begins running roughly as the module is tapped, a loose internal connection could be causing a problem.

Distributorless Ignition System Service

The engines in some late-model vehicles do not have a distributor. Instead, the ***distributorless ignition system*** (DIS) contains two or more coils. These coils are triggered by one or two position sensors installed on the engine. **Figure 18-22** shows a common distributorless ignition system. Since there is no distributor shaft, rotor, or cap, service of these systems is limited to replacing the spark plugs and checking the secondary wires for damage. System troubleshooting requires special equipment.

Contact Point Service

The ***contact points*** used on older vehicles should be replaced whenever the ignition system is serviced. This is especially true if the points are burned or badly pitted, **Figure 18-23,** or if the movable contact arm rubbing block is worn. A defective condenser or a condenser of the improper capacity can cause heavy point arcing or excessive metal transfer, **Figure 18-24.** Metal transfer can also be caused

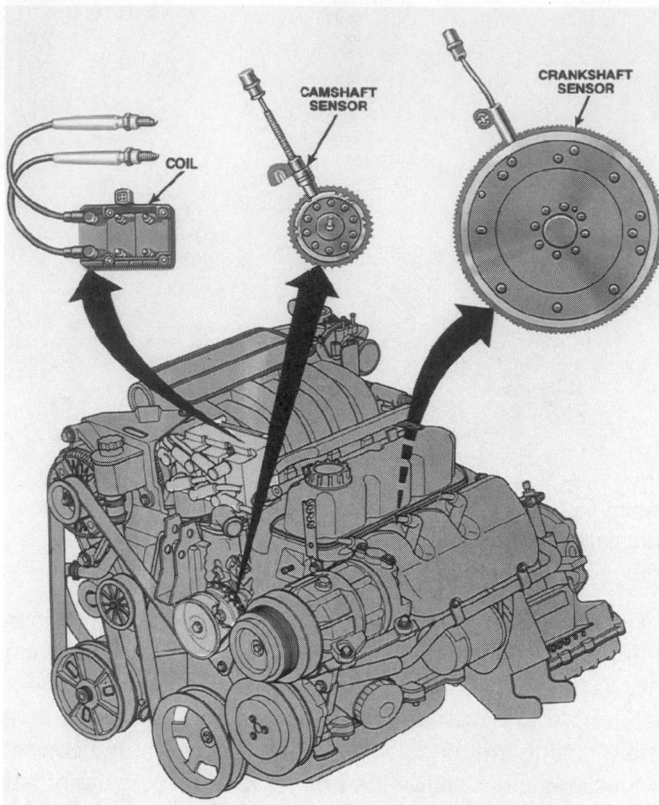

Figure 18-22. Components of one distributorless ignition system. This system uses various sensors to trigger the ignition coils. (Chrysler)

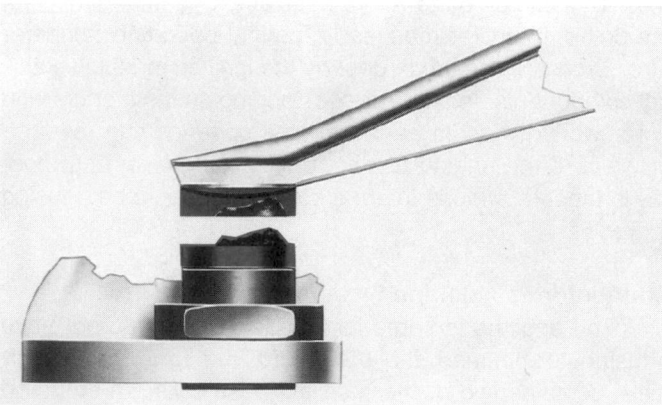

Figure 18-23. A point set with badly burned and pitted contact points. These must be replaced. (Chrysler)

by high-speed operation, incorrect dwell angle, or a high voltage regulator setting. Rapid rubbing block wear can be caused by a rough cam surface, excessive spring pressure, or a lack of lubricant.

Contact Point Removal

Before removing the old points, block any hole in the contact mounting plate (usually called the breaker plate) that is large enough to allow a small screw or washer to drop through. Note the location and positioning of the

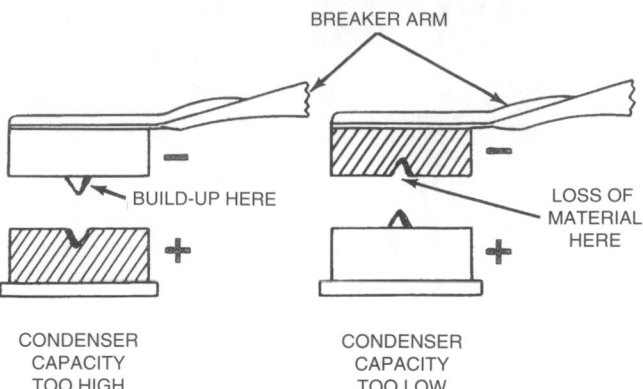

Figure 18-24. A point set with excessive metal transfer and build-up caused by a defective condenser. (Deere & Co.)

primary lead wire and condenser terminals before removing the old points. Then remove the old points. Clean the point mounting area and install new points. It may not be necessary to completely remove the attaching screws to remove the points. Many points will slide out of the breaker plate when the screws are loosened.

Servicing Used Contact Points

Contact point sets seldom last beyond 15,000 miles and should be replaced if they are removed when they are approaching this mileage. However, if replacement points are not available, the old points can be cleaned by lightly filing them with a clean, fine cut point file. Do not attempt to file away all marks. Never file the points at an angle or in any way alter the shape of the contact surfaces. Do not use emery cloth or sandpaper to clean the points. When finished filing, pull a clean piece of smooth paper through the points to remove any metal particles. Dampening the paper with a suitable cleaner will help remove traces of oil.

Contact Point Installation and Setting

Install the points in reverse order of removal. Point gap (the space between each point when fully opened by the cam lobe) is critical. When the gap is too small, the points will arc and burn. Excessive gap will reduce the dwell angle (amount of time during which the points are closed) and cause missing at high speed. To adjust the points, turn the distributor cam until the contact arm rubbing block is on the highest tip of one of the lobes. Look at **Figure 18-25.** Loosen the attaching screw A, **Figure 18-26,** just enough to allow the contact support plate to be moved by turning screw B. Turn screw B as required to open the points to the specified gap. This gap may be initially set with a feeler gauge.

 Note: Used points cannot be set accurately with a feeler gauge. The gauge will measure between the high spots. The actual opening distance can be much greater, Figure 18-27. Always check dwell as explained later in this chapter.

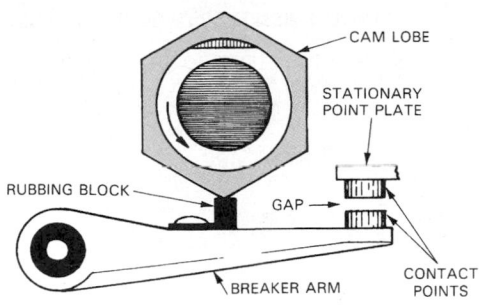

Figure 18-25. Turn the distributor cam until the contact arm rubbing block bears against the highest portion of the cam lobe.

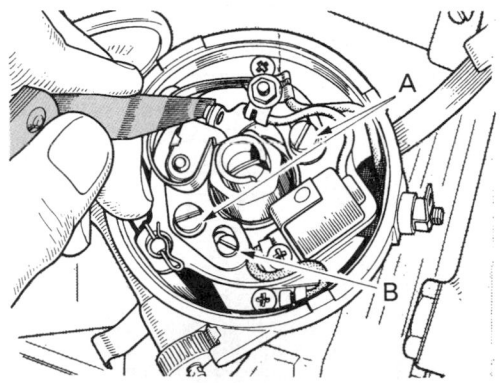

Figure 18-26. Checking initial (new points) contact point gap setting with a feeler gauge. If the points have been in service, a feeler gauge will not provide the necessary accuracy. To adjust, loosen screws at A and turn screw B as required. (Jaguar)

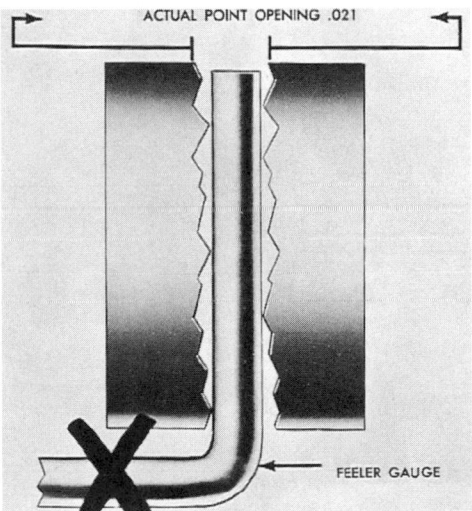

Figure 18-27. Gapping used points with a feeler gauge will give false settings. Note how a .016″ (0.41 mm) feeler is snug, but the actual opening is .021″ (0.53 mm).

Ignition Condenser

A defective **condenser** can cause point damage and low firing voltage. In some cases, it may cause a no-start condition. The condenser is usually changed with the points. If the condenser is not to be changed, it should be checked for capacity, resistance, and leakage. A new condenser should also be checked before installation.

Lubricate Distributor Cam

When new points are installed, the distributor cam should be cleaned and given a thin coat of high-temperature grease. Do not use engine oil or low-temperature grease. They will be thrown outward into the points. Some point sets include cam lubricant in a small capsule.

Setting Dwell Angle

If the distributor is off the car and a distributor tester is available, it can be used to set up the distributor. Set specified **dwell** (use dwell meter) by carefully adjusting the points.

If the distributor is on the engine, attach a dwell meter. Always follow the test instrument manufacturer's directions. While idling the engine, check the dwell. Adjust point gap as required. The points in **Figure 18-28** are adjusted by turning the adjusting screw as the engine idles, while most others require that the distributor cap be removed to make the adjustment. If point adjustment fails to give the specified dwell, the distributor cam may be worn or the point set may be incorrect for the engine.

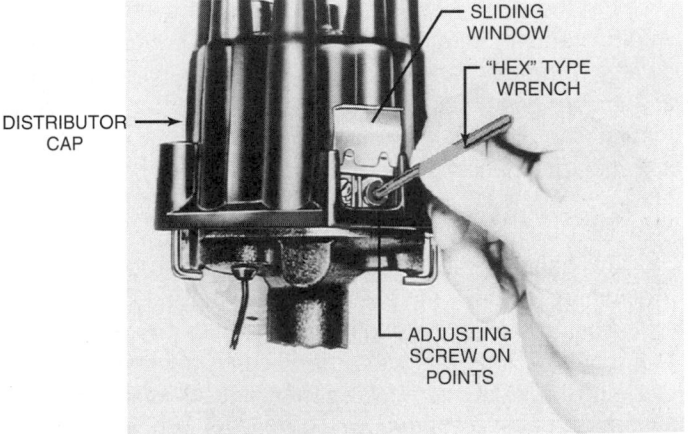

Figure 18-28. Technician adjusting a point set by placing a hex wrench through a sliding window in the distributor cap. Be careful when performing this procedure. Keep your hands, tools, and clothes away from moving engine belts, pulleys, fans, etc. (General Motors)

Run the engine up to around 1500 RPM. The dwell should not vary more than 3 to 6 degrees. Variations in excess of this indicate a worn breaker plate or a faulty distributor shaft. **Figure 18-29** illustrates how a tach-dwell (combination tachometer and dwell meter) is set up to check dwell.

Dwell on Electronic Ignition Systems

The dwell period is controlled electronically in the electronic ignition system, and no adjustment can be made. On many electronic systems, dwell is automatically increased as engine RPM rises and decreases with a speed reduction. This provides the required spark intensity without overheating the coil.

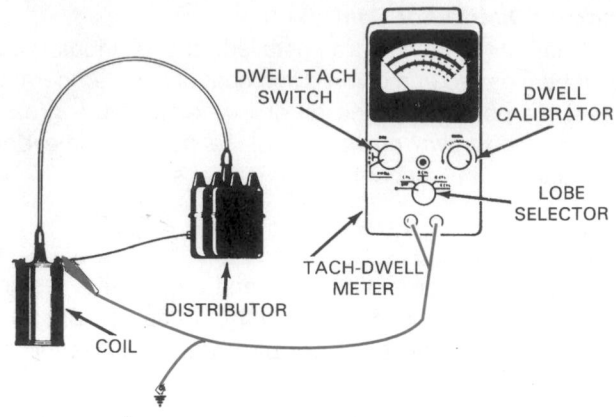

Figure 18-29. Checking dwell angle with a tach-dwell meter. The diagram shows *negative* ground connections. Reverse the leads for positive ground. (Sun Electric)

Setting Ignition Timing

On many modern vehicles, the *timing* is determined by a crankshaft position sensor and timing is not adjustable. However, it is still possible to check and, if needed, adjust the timing on most engines.

On the old contact point type ignition systems, timing would gradually retard as the points wore, increasing the dwell. On modern engines with electronic ignitions, the initial timing does not vary unless the distributor body is moved, the distributor shaft bushings become worn, or the advance mechanisms fail.

Performing Preliminary Steps

To begin setting timing, perform any recommended preliminary steps. These steps are usually listed on the emissions sticker in the engine compartment, **Figure 18-30.** This could include removing the vacuum advance line and plugging the vacuum fitting, disconnecting the ignition module from the engine computer, or placing the engine computer in the "test" mode. The engine should be warmed up and off at this time. Next, loosen the distributor clamp bolts just enough to allow the distributor to be turned without undue force. Look at **Figure 18-31.**

Attach a power (stroboscopic) *timing light* and *tachometer* as directed by the manufacturer, **Figure 18-32.** The ideal timing light will have provisions for measuring advance (in degrees) and engine speed. If the engine has provisions for a magnetic probe, **Figure 18-33,** the "monolithic" (electronic timing) light may be used. Use either a jumper wire from the plug to the plug wire or use an inductive-type pickup, **Figure 18-34.** Under no circumstances should the plug wires be pierced with a probe.

Clean off the timing scale and index mark. Paint or chalk the index mark to make it more legible. See **Figure 18-35.** Some engines have a pointer on the block with the scale stamped on the vibration damper. The front-wheel drive setup pictured in **Figure 18-36** uses a scale stamped on the flywheel. It is visible through an access hole in the bell housing. Note the timing pointer.

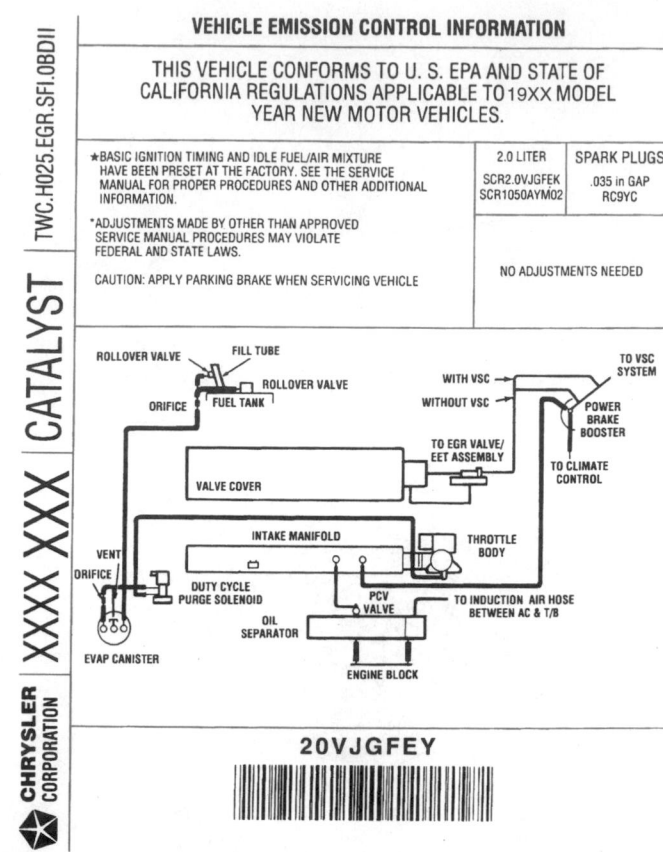

Figure 18-30. One particular vehicle emission control information (VECI) label. If the label is missing, obtain a replacement and follow the recommended procedures and adjustments. (Chrysler)

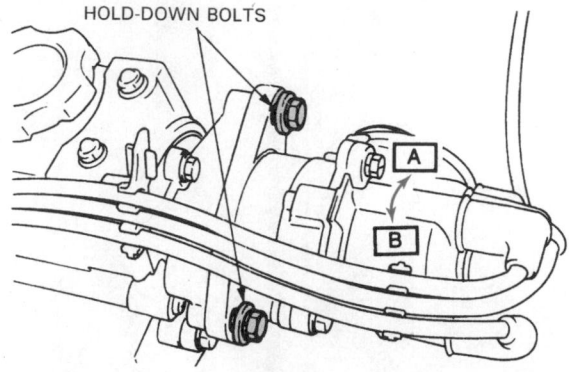

Figure 18-31. Distributor assembly with two hold-down bolts. Turning the distributor toward "A" will advance the timing. The hold-down bolts must be torqued to specifications after timing is adjusted. (Geo)

Checking Timing

Check the underhood area to make certain all wires and tools are free of the fan and exhaust system. Then, start the engine. Operate the engine at idle to avoid bringing the centrifugal advance into play. Direct the power timing light beam on the timing marks.

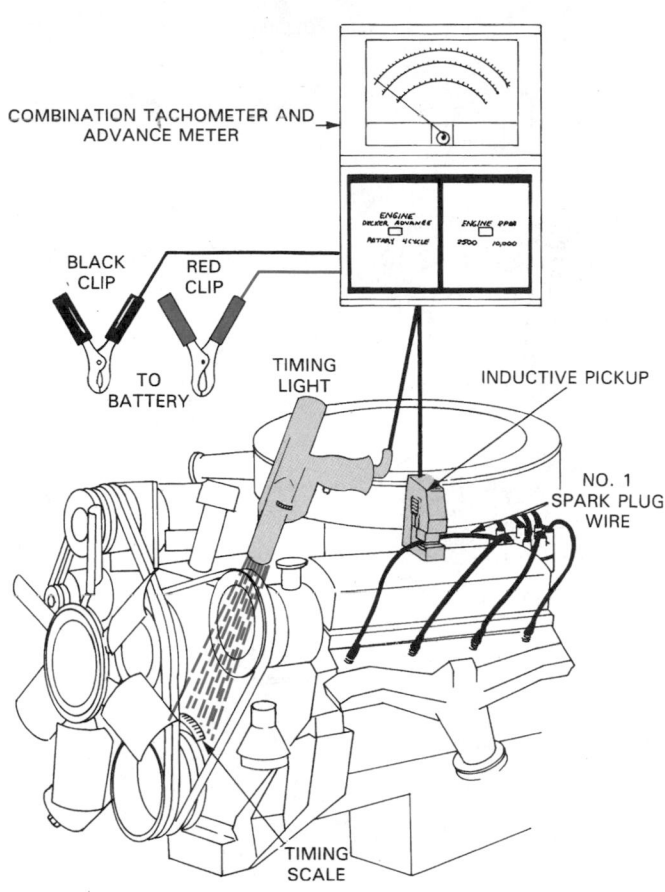

Figure 18-32. Using a timing light to set ignition timing. Note the use of the inductive pickup. The battery is not shown. (Snap-On)

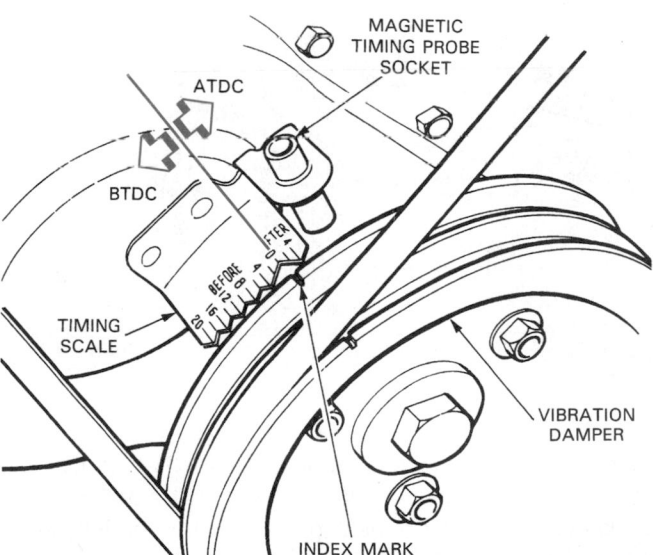

Figure 18-33. Clean the timing scale and chalk or paint the index mark for easy visibility. This setup has a magnetic timing probe socket to allow the use of electronic timing equipment. (Chrysler)

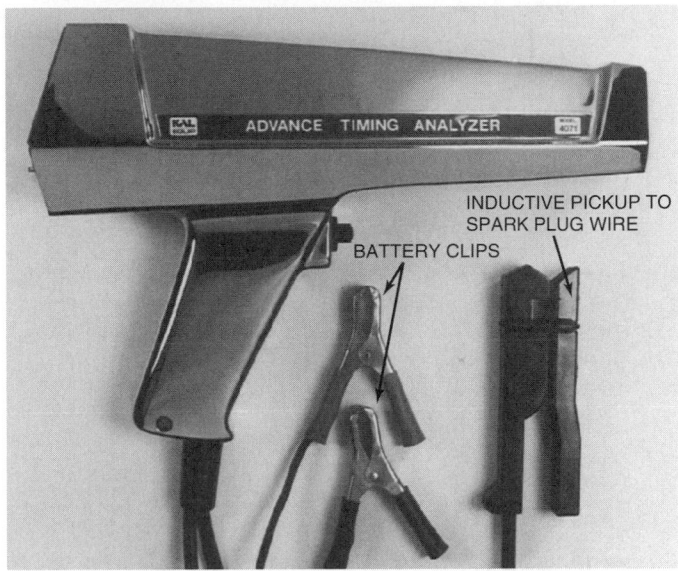

Figure 18-34. An inductive-type pickup timing light with battery clips and a spark plug wire clamp that does not pierce the wire insulation. (Ken Tool)

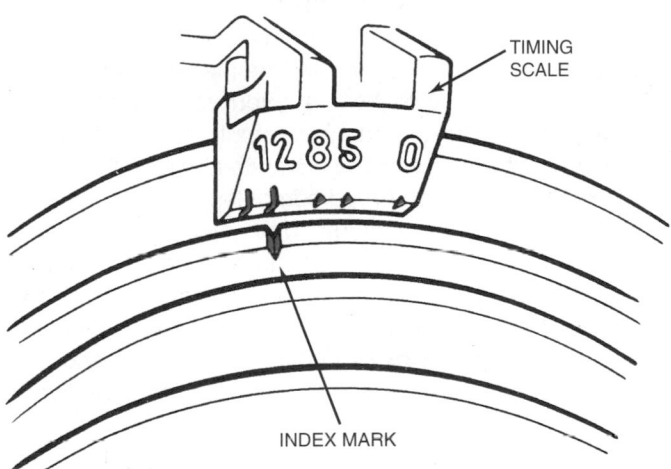

Figure 18-35. Placing paint or chalk on the timing marks to make them more legible. (Toyota)

 Warning: Do not stand in line with fan. Keep wires and fingers away from the moving fan and belts.

Turn the distributor as required to bring the painted mark in line with the scale or pointer. When the mark is exactly in line, tighten distributor clamp. After tightening, recheck timing to make sure the mark is still aligned.

 Note: On vehicles with contact point ignition systems, point gap or dwell must be set before timing. Changing the gap will alter the timing.

Replace vacuum hoses and other connectors as necessary. The operation of the spark advance devices can now be checked.

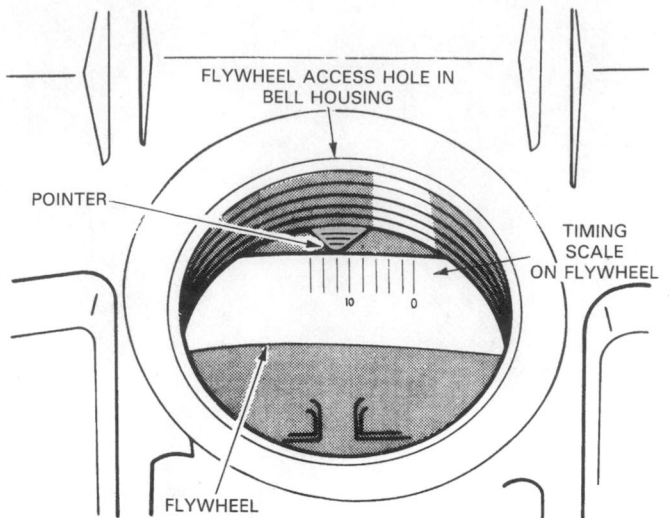

Figure 18-36. Timing marks as used on one front-wheel drive car. The marks are visible through an access hole in the bell housing. (Plymouth)

Spark Advance Mechanisms

To provide the proper spark advance or retard to fit all speeds, throttle openings, and engine loading, older distributors are equipped with both a *vacuum advance* and a *centrifugal advance.* Modern distributors have no spark advance control units, and the advance and retard functions are controlled by the on-board computer.

Figure 18-37 illustrates one type of centrifugal advance. A vacuum advance unit is also shown. A typical single-diaphragm vacuum advance mechanism is pictured in **Figure 18-38.** Note how the diaphragm lever actuates the movable magnetic pickup plate. The vacuum and centrifugal units may stick, wear out, or become defective in other ways.

Testing Centrifugal Advance

If the distributor is on the car, disconnect the vacuum line to the vacuum advance. Run the engine slowly from an idle up to around 4000 RPM. Use a timing light to watch the timing mark. It should advance smoothly against the direction of engine rotation. If the action is jerky, stop the engine. Remove distributor cap and twist the rotor in the direction of rotation. When the rotor is released, it should snap back to the original position. A slow return indicates a gummy or corroded advance unit. Clean and oil the unit. A loose rattle-type condition indicates broken or stretched return springs. Replace parts as needed. The centrifugal advance should then be rechecked on the engine or with a distributor tester.

Testing Vacuum Advance

With the distributor installed on the engine, disconnect the vacuum advance line. Connect a power timing light. Start engine and run it at a steady 1200 RPM. Note the position of the timing mark in relation to the pointer. Connect vacuum advance line. When line is connected, the timing mark should immediately advance against the direction of engine

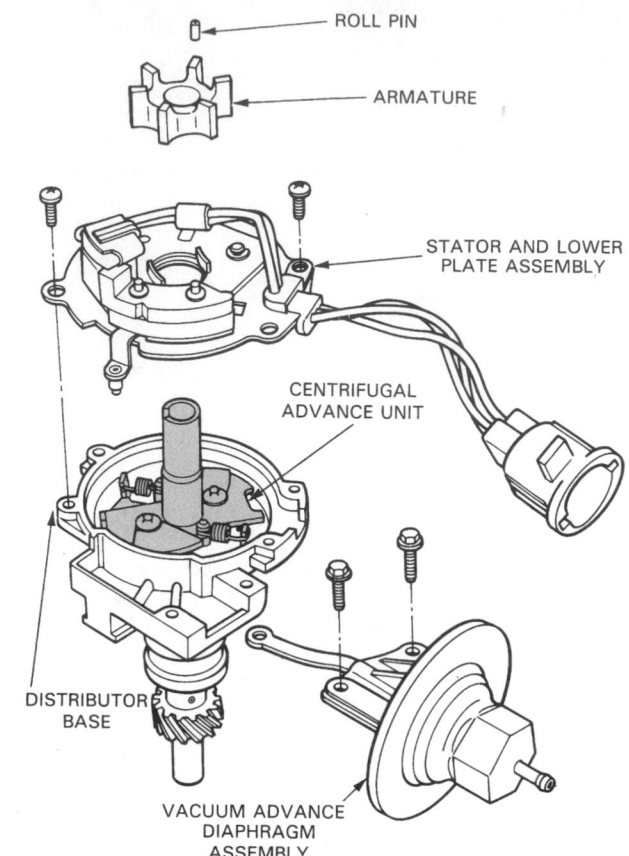

Figure 18-37. One type of centrifugal advance assembly. (Ford)

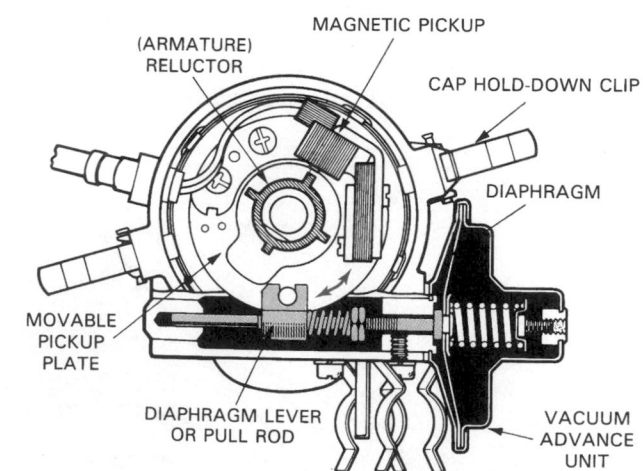

Figure 18-38. Cutaway showing the construction of a single diaphragm vacuum advance unit. (Toyota)

rotation. If the mark does not move, ensure that the vacuum line connection is receiving vacuum. If it is, the problem is in the distributor, usually a leaking vacuum unit or, less commonly, a sticking breaker plate.

To pinpoint the problem, either apply vacuum to the vacuum advance with a hand-held vacuum pump or remove the distributor and test it on a distributor machine. A hand-operated vacuum pump can be used to apply a controlled vacuum. See **Figure 18-39.** When applying vacuum, check

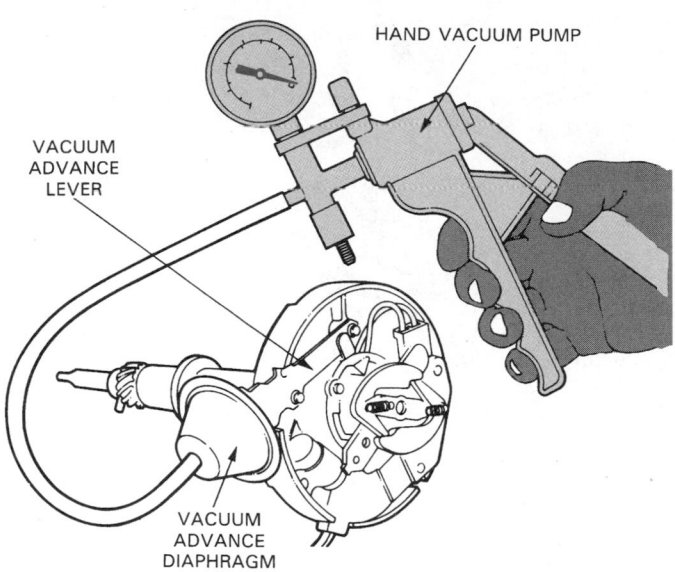

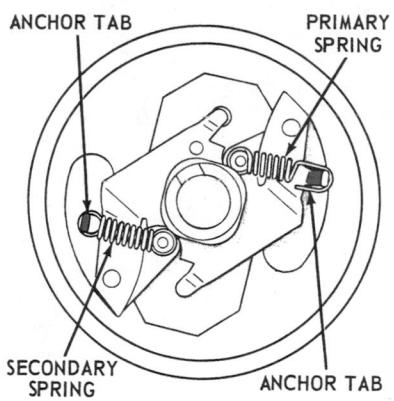

Figure 18-40. Typical distributor centrifugal advance unit. Note the spring anchor tabs. These may be bent to vary spring tension as needed to adjust advance characteristics. (Toyota)

Figure 18-39. Using a hand-operated vacuum pump to test distributor vacuum advance operation. (GM)

vacuum advance operation for function and smoothness. The vacuum advance diaphragm should hold in position until vacuum is released. If any sign of leakage is observed, replace the unit. The distributor tester can also check the distributor for dwell, point bounce, bent shaft, worn bushings, worn cam, and vacuum and centrifugal advance action.

Test Tools for Checking Distributor on Car

Test tools are available for checking the degree of advance provided by the vacuum and centrifugal units. If checks indicate repairs are needed, the distributor should be removed, repaired, and checked on a distributor tester.

Adjusting Centrifugal Advance Unit

The centrifugal advance unit should be clean and lightly oiled. Some units provide adjustable (bendable) spring anchor tabs or posts to vary spring tension. This lets you bring the advance curve (relation between the degree of advance and engine RPM plotted from idle to high RPM) within specifications. Other units require spring alteration or replacement. On some distributors, the weights can be altered to change the advance curve, but this must be done carefully.

Figure 18-40 illustrates a typical centrifugal advance mechanism. Note the anchor tabs. When adjustment or spring replacement has been completed, the unit must be tested for proper operation. Follow the manufacturer's specifications.

Adjusting Vacuum Advance Unit

Most vacuum advance units are nonadjustable and must be replaced. Older distributors are provided with spacer washers that may be added or removed to vary the spring tension. Following adjustment (on either vacuum or centrifugal advance unit), the distributor must be carefully checked against specifications on an accurate distributor test machine.

Computerized Ignition Service

Some vehicles are equipped with a computer that controls specific ignition system functions. ***Computerized ignition systems*** often contain many of the same components found in electronic ignition systems. The fundamental difference between electronic ignition and computerized ignition is the way that each system advances the ignition timing. Electronic ignition systems use traditional centrifugal and vacuum advance systems. Computerized systems use sensors to monitor various operating conditions. The computer constantly adjusts the timing in response to these conditions, **Figure 18-41.**

Many computerized ignition systems have self diagnostic capabilities. When a malfunction occurs, the computer stores a trouble code in its memory and activates a warning light on the vehicle's dash. The automotive technician can retrieve the trouble code by performing a specific test sequence or by using a special scan tool. The trouble code will indicate which circuit or component the technician can use as a starting point for diagnosis.

Computer-operated ignition systems can be damaged by using the wrong test equipment or grounding the incorrect terminals. Proper connections are imperative. Follow all the manufacturer's service instructions carefully. Always turn the ignition switch off when connecting or disconnecting electronic components in computerized ignition systems. For more information about computerized control systems, sensors, and trouble codes, see Chapter 25.

Overhauling Distributors

Distributors must be overhauled when the bushing, shaft, gear, or cam wear becomes excessive, or when the advance mechanisms fail to function correctly. Note the areas of the typical distributor in **Figure 18-42** that could require overhaul. Some newer distributors are nonrepairable and are replaced as a unit.

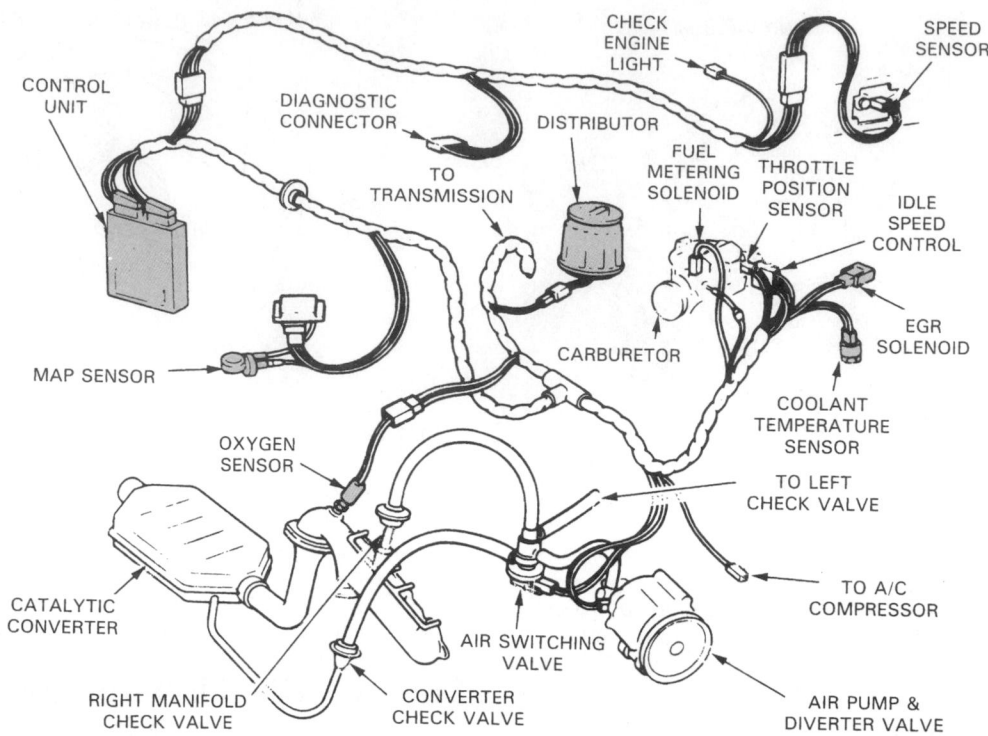

CONTROL UNIT

DIAGNOSTIC CONNECTOR

TO TRANSMISSION

CHECK ENGINE LIGHT

DISTRIBUTOR

FUEL METERING SOLENOID

SPEED SENSOR

THROTTLE POSITION SENSOR

IDLE SPEED CONTROL

EGR SOLENOID

CARBURETOR

COOLANT TEMPERATURE SENSOR

TO LEFT CHECK VALVE

TO A/C COMPRESSOR

MAP SENSOR

OXYGEN SENSOR

CATALYTIC CONVERTER

RIGHT MANIFOLD CHECK VALVE

CONVERTER CHECK VALVE

AIR SWITCHING VALVE

AIR PUMP & DIVERTER VALVE

Figure 18-41. Schematic of a computer controlled ignition system. Note the various sensors used to monitor engine operating conditions. (Sun Electric)

Removing the Distributor

Before removing the distributor from the engine, mark the relative position of the distributor housing and rotor to the engine. Then, remove the electrical connections and the hold-down bolt and pull the distributor from the engine. If the distributor housing sticks in the engine, a light tap with a plastic hammer will usually free it.

Disassembling the Distributor

Before removing the gear from the shaft, measure from the top of the gear to some reference point on the distributor housing (where used) and pull shaft. See **Figure 18-43.** Where applicable, replace both upper and lower bushings if worn. Ream and burnish if required, **Figure 18-44.**

Replace the vacuum advance diaphragm unit if it is faulty. Clean and oil the centrifugal advance. Replace rusty or stretched advance springs. Clean, examine, and oil the movable breaker bushing or bearings as required. Replace the shaft if it is worn, rough, or bent. Check the housing for cracks or other damage. Check the drive gear for chipping or wear.

Assembling the Distributor

Assemble the distributor and check both shaft side and end play. Make sure the pin is through the gear. If the pin is of the solid (not roll pin) type, check that it is securely peened. Lubricate as required. Install various components. After assembly, check out the distributor on a distributor tester.

Installing the Distributor (Engine Undisturbed)

If the distributor was marked to indicate the position of the rotor and also scribed to show housing-to-engine relationship, installation is simple. Align the rotor with the chalk or scribe mark. See **Figure 18-45.**

Align the housing-to-engine block scribe lines. Push the distributor into place. As the distributor is moved down, you will notice that the rotor will turn a small amount as the distributor gear meshes. Pull the distributor up far enough to disengage the gear, move the rotor back far enough to compensate for the turning and press down again. When the housing flange is flush against the block, the housing-to-engine and rotor housing scribe lines should all be aligned. Lock distributor into place.

 Caution: If the distributor will not bottom, do not attempt to force it down by using the hold-down clamp to draw it in. The distributor shaft is probably not aligned with the oil pump shaft slot or tang. Push the distributor downward by hand while cranking the engine. When the two shafts are aligned, the distributor will drop into place.

Installing the Distributor (Engine Disturbed)

If the engine was cranked following distributor removal, crank the engine until the number one piston is starting up on the compression stroke. Turn engine over until the timing marks are aligned. The engine is now ready to fire the number one cylinder. Align the housing-to-engine scribe marks. Turn the rotor to face the number one cap tower. Press the

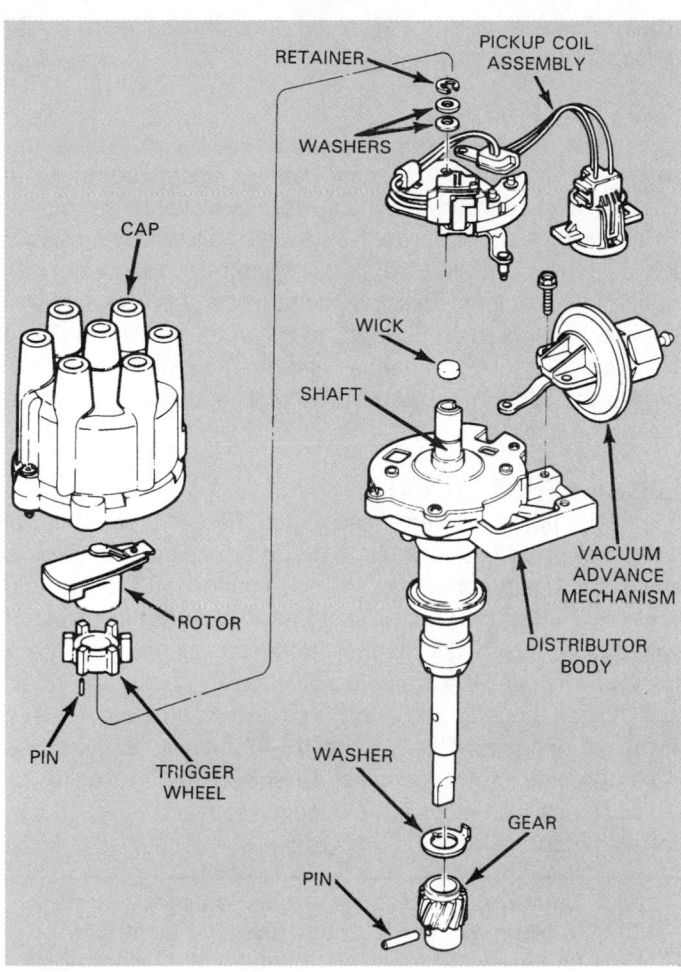

Figure 18-42. Typical electronic ignition distributor. Note the areas that would need replacement if worn, bent, or corroded. (Chrysler)

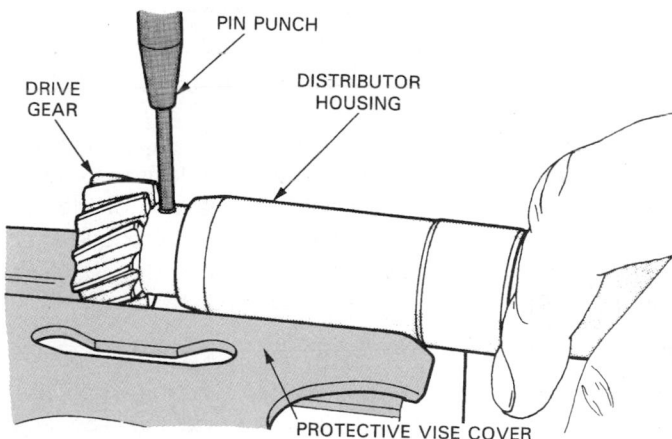

Figure 18-43. Support the gear and shaft when removing or installing the retaining pin. (Plymouth)

rotor into place. Pull up and adjust for rotor movement. When correct, distributor will be fully bottomed. The points (if used) will just be opening, and the rotor will point at number one cap tower.

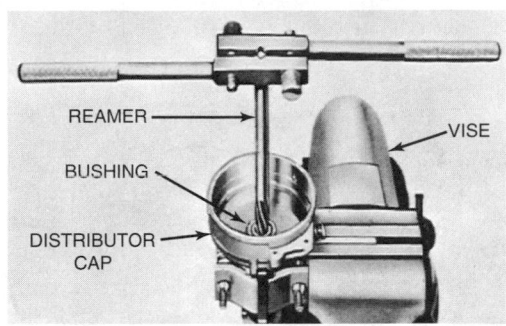

Figure 18-44. Reaming a new distributor shaft upper bushing.

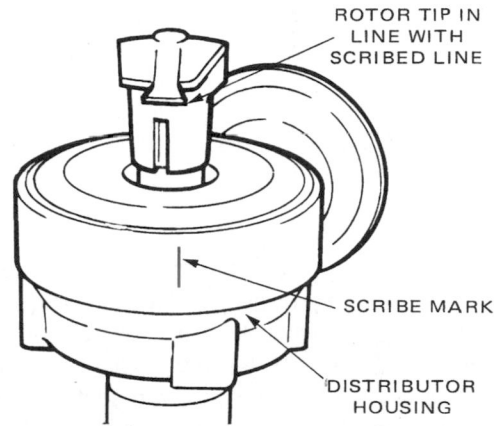

Figure 18-45. Align the rotor tip with the scribe mark on the distributor housing. (Chrysler)

When the distributor is driven by the oil pump, it is necessary to align the pump gear as specified before inserting the distributor. If no specifications are available, bring the engine into position to fire the number one cylinder (see preceding paragraph). The distributor may then be meshed with the slot in the oil pump gear or shaft. **Figure 18-46** illustrates the recommended positioning for one type of oil pump gear setup. When the gear is in this position, the distributor may be inserted.

Timing the Distributor

The distributor initial setting (timing mark aligned with the pointer or scale and the rotor facing the number one plug wire tower) will suffice for starting the engine. Try for a slightly retarded setting (spark occurs later than specified) to prevent "kicking back" (engine attempting to rotate backwards due to plug being fired too early), which can damage the starter mechanism. After starting the engine, set the timing as explained earlier in this chapter.

Servicing Spark Plugs

Almost everyone knows what *spark plugs* are, but their familiarity often leads to problems. It is not enough to remove the old plugs and install new ones. The following section explains the proper selection and service of spark plugs.

Figure 18-46. On this engine, the oil pump gear slot is aligned with the centerline of the crankshaft (number one piston on compression stroke, ignition timing marks aligned). If this gear has not been removed, it is only necessary to mesh the distributor shaft tang with the gear slot. Note how the slot is offset.

Spark Plug Service Life

Spark plug service life varies a great deal, depending on such factors as engine design, type of ignition system (contact point or electronic), type of service, driver habits, and type of fuel. Older vehicles with contact point ignitions and operating on leaded gas required that the plugs be cleaned and inspected every 10,000 to 15,000 miles (16,000 to 24,000 km). In extreme cases, some plugs required replacement at 5000 miles (8,000 km). Plugs in newer vehicles with electronic ignition systems may last beyond the often-recommended replacement interval of between 15,000 to 30,000 miles (24,000 to 48,000 km). Some of the newest vehicles are intended to travel over 100,000 miles (160,000 km) on one set of spark plugs.

In deciding whether to clean and reinstall or replace the plugs, the modern technician should weigh the cost of services for cleaning, filing, and gapping in light of the remaining useful life. Unless the plugs are in almost perfect condition, it usually pays to replace them.

Removing Spark Plugs

Pull the plug boot and wire assemblies carefully. Direct a stream of compressed air around the base of each plug to blow out any foreign material.

 Caution: Do not remove the spark plugs from a hot aluminum cylinder head. Damage to the head will result if it is not allowed to cool before spark plug removal.

Using a plug socket (rubber lined), remove the plugs. Make sure that the gaskets (where used) are also removed. Keep plugs in order so that any peculiar plug conditions can be related to the cylinder concerned.

Examining Spark Plugs

A careful study of the spark plugs is helpful in determining engine condition, plug heat range selection, and trouble resulting from operational conditions, **Figure 18-47** illustrates typical spark plug conditions.

Spark Plug Problems

Study **Figure 18-48.** Note that in A, the plug fires normally. In B, a dirty insulator caused flashover. In C, a cracked insulator allowed the current to travel to ground. In D, conductive deposits on the insulator allowed the current to travel to ground. In E, excessive gap raised required voltage above that available. In F, conductive deposits between the electrodes allowed current to travel to ground. In G, an overheated insulator nose fired the fuel charge (preignition) before the voltage could build up high enough to force the current to jump the gap.

Cleaning Spark Plugs

If the plugs will be reused, place them in a container of clean solvent. Clean the plugs with a bristle brush and blow them dry. Make certain all oil is removed with solvent and that the plug is blown dry. Dampness around the insulator will cause the blast cleaner abrasive material to pack instead of clean. If a spark plug cleaning machine is available, install the plug and apply a stream of abrasive to clean away all deposits. See **Figure 18-49.** While applying the abrasive blast, rock the plug as shown in **Figure 18-50.** This will assist in thorough cleaning. Repeat this procedure for all plugs.

 Note: Apply the abrasive blast only long enough to clean the insulator and shell. If cleaning is continued beyond this point, the side electrode and insulator may be badly worn.

Blow each plug free of all abrasive. If a plug contaminated with abrasive is placed in the engine, the abrasive will work its way out and cause serious wear and scoring. Next, use a hand wire brush to remove all carbon from the plug threads. Check the threads in the head. If they are carboned, rusty, or stripped, run a special spark plug tap through the holes.

As a final step to restore used spark plugs, file both plug electrodes. File the end of the inner electrode and the inside of the side electrode flat. File the end of the side electrode square to remove all deposits and produce sharp edges that will improve plug performance. Look at **Figure 18-51.**

Gapping Plugs

Whether the plugs are new or used, the **spark gap** should be checked. To adjust gap, bend the side electrode until the proper gap is set between the electrode surfaces. Gaps vary widely, so always check and follow the manufacturer's specifications for the plug and engine. Check for correct gap by using a special plug gauge. Note **Figure 18-52.**

 Caution: Bend only the side electrode. If any attempt is made to bend the center electrode, the insulator will be cracked. Refer to Figure 18-53.

TYPICAL SPARK PLUG CONDITIONS

NORMAL PLUG APPEARANCE

A spark plug operating in a sound engine and at the correct temperature will have some deposits. The color of these deposits should range from tan to gray. The electrode gap will show growth of about .001 in. (0.025 mm) per 1000 miles (1600 km), but there should be no evidence of burning.

FUEL FOULING

Fuel fouling (dry, fluffy, black carbon deposits) can be caused by plugs that are too cold for the engine, a high fuel level in the carburetor, a stuck heat riser, a clogged air cleaner, or excessive choking. If only one or two plugs show evidence of fuel fouling, inspect the plug wires for those cylinders. Sticking valves can also cause fuel fouling.

OIL FOULING

Oil fouling (wet, black deposits) is caused by an excessive amount of oil reaching the cylinders. Check for worn rings, valve guides, or valve seals. A ruptured vacuum pump diaphragm can also cause oil fouling. Switching to a hotter spark plug may temporarily relieve the symptoms, but will not correct the problem.

SPLASHED FOULING

Splashed fouling (plugs coated with splashes of deposits) can occur when new plugs are installed in an engine with heavy piston and combustion chamber deposits. The new plugs restore regular firing impulses and raise the operating temperature. As this occurs, accumulated engine deposits flake off and stick to the hot plug insulator.

GAP BRIDGING

Gap bridging (carbon-lead deposit connecting the center and ground electrodes) is not often encountered in automotive engines. Prolonged low speed operation followed by a sudden burst of high speed operation can form gap bridging. It can also be caused by excessive fuel additives.

MECHANICAL DAMAGE

Mechanical damage can be caused by a foreign object in the combustion chamber. When a plug shows evidence of mechanical damage, all cylinders should be inspected. Valve overlap may allow small objects to travel from one cylinder to another.

OVERHEATING

Overheating (dull, white insulator and eroded electrodes) can occur when the spark plugs are too hot for the engine. Cooling system problems, advanced ignition timing, detonation, sticking valves, and excessive high speed driving can also cause spark plug overheating.

PREIGNITION

Preignition (fuel charge ignited by an overheated plug, piece of glowing carbon, or hot valve edge before the spark plug fires) will cause extensive plug damage. When plugs show evidence of preignition, check the heat range of the plugs, the condition of the plug wires, and the condition of the cooling system. The engine should be checked for physical damage because it has been subjected to excessive combustion chamber pressure.

DETONATION

Detonation can cause the insulator nose on a spark plug to crack and chip away. The explosion that occurs during heavy detonation creates extreme pressure in the cylinder. Detonation can be caused by an excessively lean fuel mixture, low octane fuel, advanced ignition timing, or extremely high engine temperatures.

HIGH SPEED GLAZING

High speed glazing (hard, shiny, yellowish-tan, electrically conductive deposits) can be caused by a sudden increase in plug temperature during hard acceleration or loading. This condition often causes misfiring at speeds above 50 mph (81 km/h). If high speed glazing reoccurs, cooler plugs should be used.

ASH FOULING

Ash fouling (heavy white and yellowish deposits) is caused by the buildup of combustion deposits. The deposits may be caused by burning oil or fuel additives. Although ash fouling is not conductive, excessive deposits can cause spark plugs to misfire.

WORN OUT

Extended use will cause the spark plug's center electrode to erode. When the electrode is too worn to be filed flat, the plug must be replaced. Typical symptoms of worn spark plugs include a drop in fuel economy and poor engine performance.

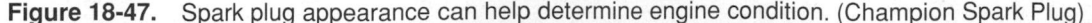

Figure 18-47.   Spark plug appearance can help determine engine condition. (Champion Spark Plug)

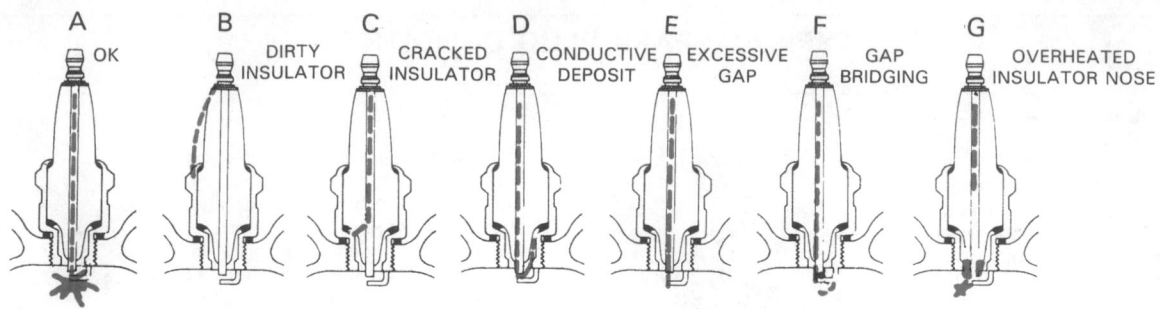

Figure 18-48. Typical spark plug problems.

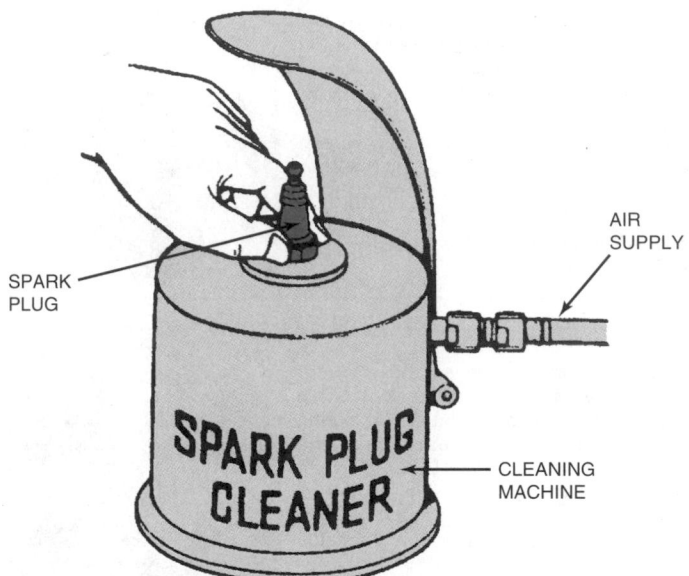

Figure 18-49. Spark plug cleaning machine. This machine uses water, air pressure, and a special microbead cleaning compound. (Toyota)

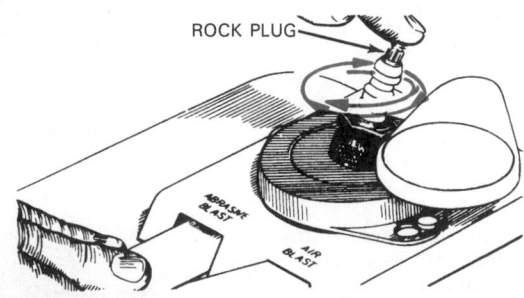

Figure 18-50. Rock the spark plug while applying the cleaning blast. This will expose all areas to the abrasive compound.

Testing Plugs for Firing Efficiency

If the cleaning machine has a provision for testing plug firing efficiency, use it to test each cleaned plug. Discard those with a weak or intermittent spark. Follow the machine manufacturer's test instructions. After testing, give the plugs a final rinse in clean solvent and blow them dry to completely remove all abrasive.

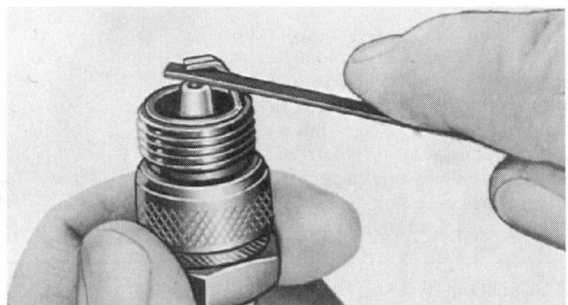

Figure 18-51. File both electrodes to remove deposits and to produce square edges.

Installing Plugs

When reusing plugs that have been cleaned and gapped, use new gaskets (where used) if possible. Wipe the plug gasket seat in the head. Insert the plug gasket in place where required (make sure only one gasket is in place). Tighten the plug until it is snug. Use a torque wrench to bring it up to specified torque. Be careful to avoid placing side pressure on the wrench. This could tip the socket and crack the plug insulator.

If no torque specifications are available, a good rule of thumb for a plug with a new gasket is to tighten the plug until it is snug (finger tight). Then, give it another one-quarter turn. For tapered seat plugs, tighten until snug and then give them another one-sixteenth turn.

> **Caution: Overtightening plugs can change the gap and cause thread damage to the plug or block.**
> **Low torque will cause the plug to overheat and possibly cause preignition. Leakage and loosening can also result.**

After installing the plugs, wipe the insulators clean and attach the plug wires. Be careful to maintain the correct firing order.

Plug Heat Range, Size, Reach, and Type

When selecting new plugs, choose plugs having the specified *heat range.* A plug that is too cold will soon foul out with heavy deposits. A plug that is too hot will suffer from burning and preignition.

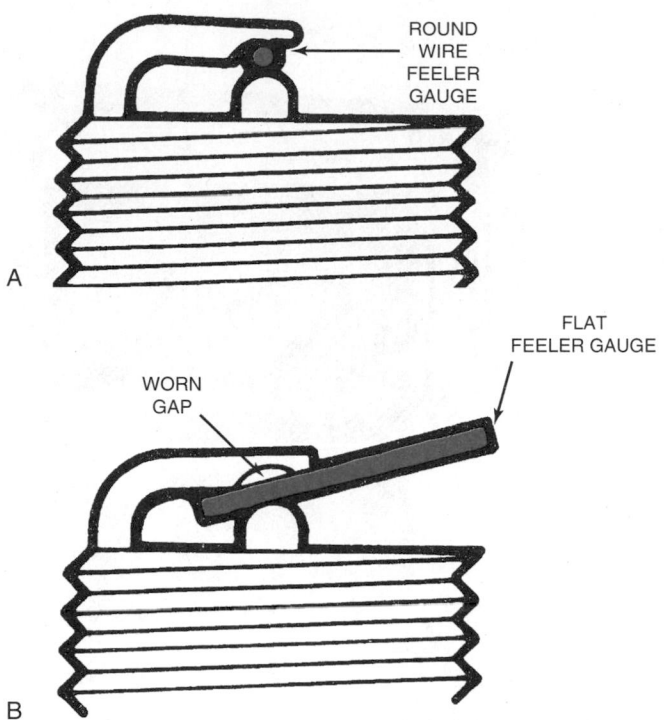

Figure 18-52. When adjusting gap, bend the side electrode only.

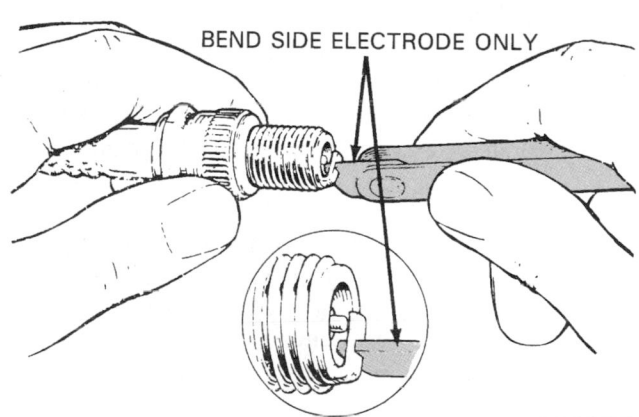

Figure 18-53. A—Using a wire feeler gauge to adjust spark plug electrode gap. Set the gap to the manufacturer's specifications. B—Note how the flat gauge does not properly measure the worn gap. (AC-Delco)

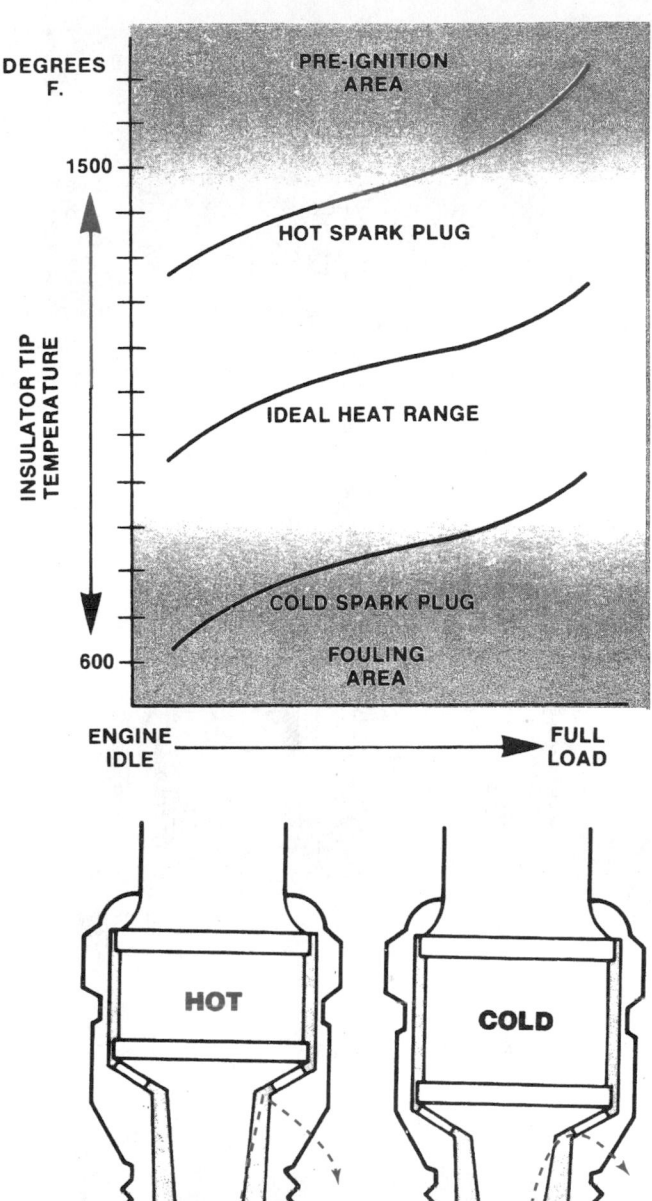

Figure 18-54. Spark plug heat range is controlled by the length of the insulator exposed to the heat of combustion. The hot plug takes longer to dissipate the combustion heat. (AC-Delco)

Notice that the plugs in **Figure 18-54,** although of the same size and reach, have different heat ranges. The heat range is controlled by the length of the insulator from the tip to the sealing ring. The longer the insulator, the hotter the plug.

Size (18 mm, 14 mm, 10 mm) is determined by the diameter of the threaded section. **Reach** is determined by the length of the threaded section. Excessive reach can cause preignition, poor fuel charge ignition, difficult plug removal, and mechanical damage from striking a piston or valve.

Type indicates resistor, nonresistor, projected core nose, single ground electrode, or multiple ground electrode. See **Figure 18-55.**

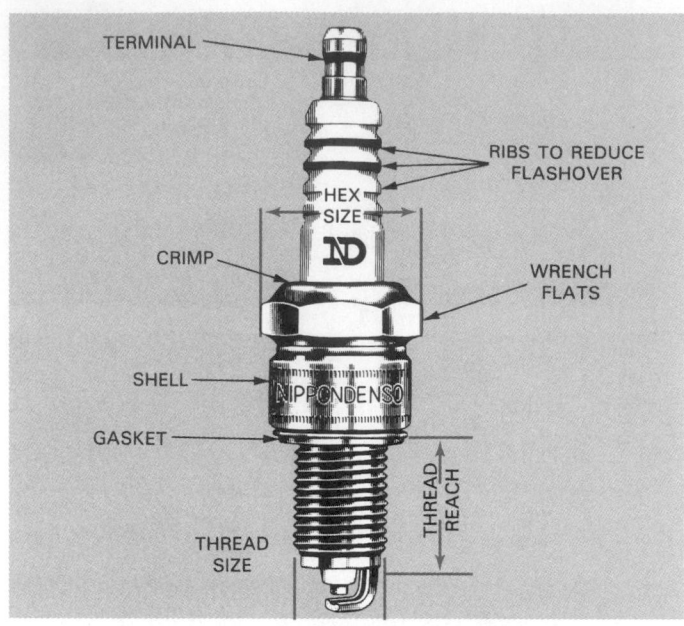

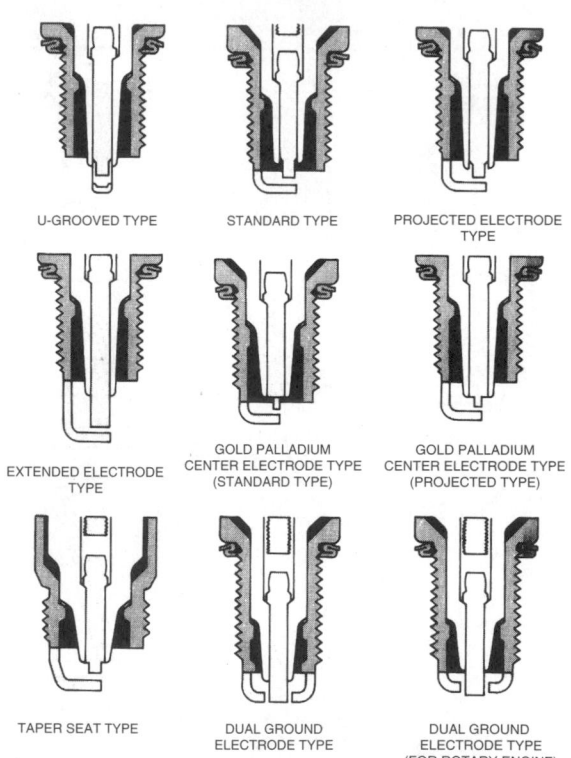

Figure 18-55. Spark plug terminology. Note the various types of plugs offered by this manufacturer. (Nippondenso)

Checking the Ignition System with an Oscilloscope

The *oscilloscope* produces a visual pattern, or waveform, on a screen (much like a TV set). See **Figure 18-56.** When attached to the vehicle's ignition system, the oscilloscope will produce a visual record of what is happening in the system. The oscilloscope is often used to diagnose problems in both the primary and secondary sides of the ignition system. Properly used, it will provide fast and accurate information on all parts of the ignition system components.

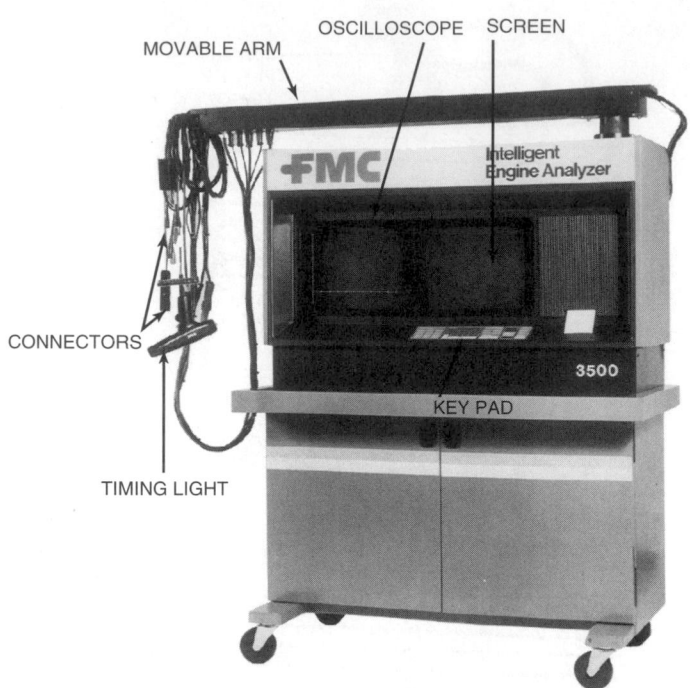

Figure 18-56. One type of engine testing unit with a built-in oscilloscope, computer and screen, and various engine connectors. Note the movable arm, which swings out toward the engine. (FMC)

Secondary Pattern

An ignition system in good order will create a normal waveform on the oscilloscope screen. **Figure 18-57** shows the normal secondary pattern for an ignition system. Point type and electronic systems produce similar patterns.

Pattern-Firing Section

Refer to **Figure 18-57.** At point A, the power transistor shuts off (electronic ignition) or the points open (conventional ignition). Primary current stops flowing in the coil, creating a secondary voltage that fires the plug (firing line). The amount of voltage required is indicated by the height of the firing line at B.

As soon as the plug fires, required voltage drops to C, where it remains fairly constant (with the spark still jumping the plug gap) to point D.

Pattern-Intermediate Section

The spark goes out at D in **Figure 18-57.** Starting at D, unused energy bounces between the coil and the electronic module or condenser and is dissipated (used up) in a series of gradually reduced oscillations until point E is reached.

Pattern-Dwell Section

At E, the power transistor turns on (electronic ignition) or the points close (conventional ignition). Primary current begins flowing through the coil, producing a series of small oscillations. Power flows through the coil from E to F. This is called the dwell period.

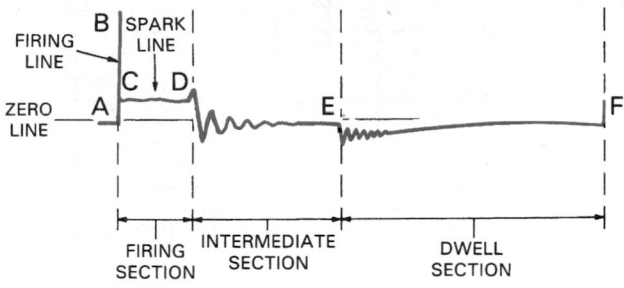

Figure 18-57.   Normal (system OK) oscilloscope pattern.

Pattern Presentations

By means of adjustments, it is possible to view the pattern as produced by a single cylinder, **Figure 18-58;** as cylinder patterns superimposed on each other, **Figure 18-59;** or as all cylinders displayed on the screen at once but as separate patterns (parade), **Figure 18-60.** A raster pattern displays the individual patterns formed by each cylinder. They are arranged in firing sequence, one above the other. This allows easy comparison for uniformity. **Figure 18-61** shows a secondary raster pattern.

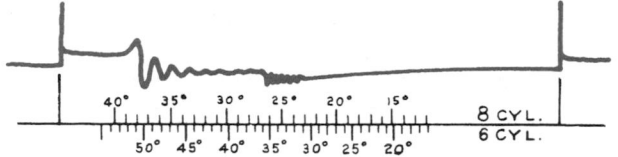

Figure 18-58.   Single cylinder oscilloscope pattern presentation.

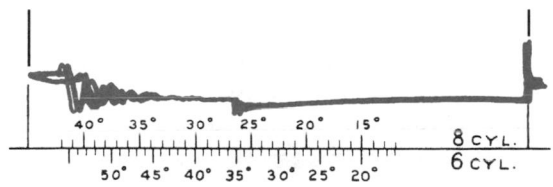

Figure 18-59.   Superimposed oscilloscope pattern presentation.

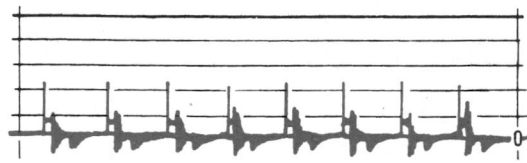

Figure 18-60.   Oscilloscope parade pattern.

Primary Pattern

The primary pattern resembles the secondary pattern, except for the extra oscillations in the firing section and the absence of oscillations at the beginning of the dwell section. Compare the primary pattern at the top of **Figure 18-62** to the secondary pattern in **Figure 18-59.**

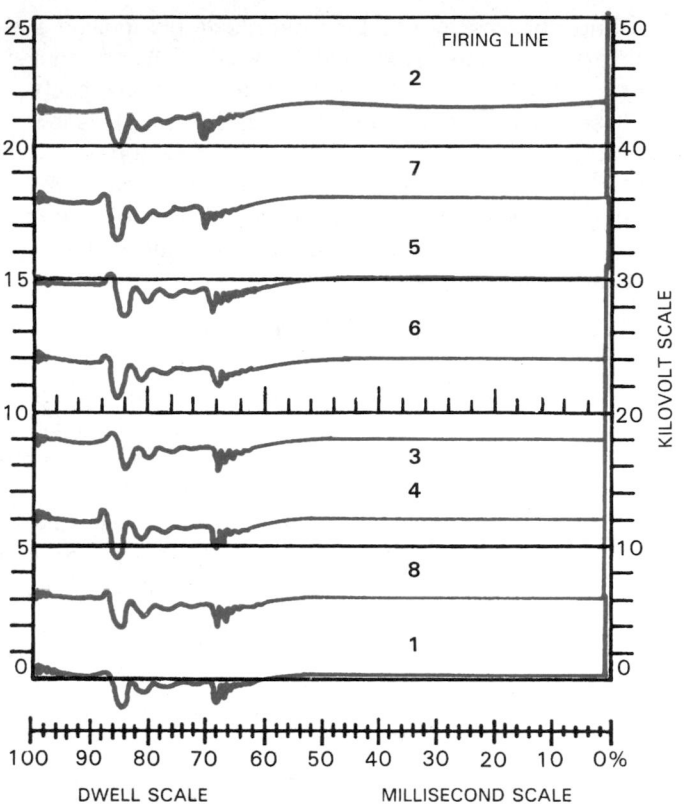

Figure 18-61.   Oscilloscope raster pattern. Cylinder patterns are displayed in the order of firing. (Sun Electric)

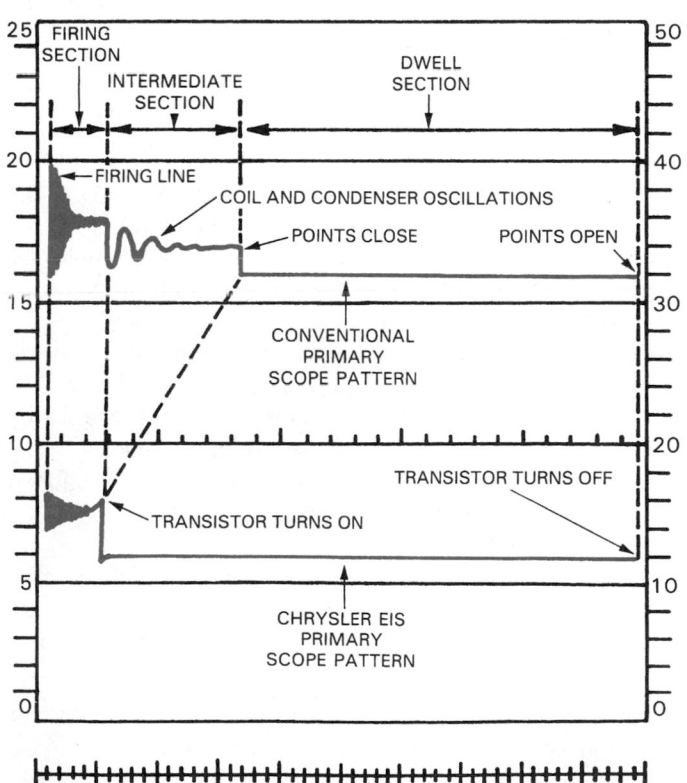

Figure 18-62.   Comparison between a conventional contact point ignition system pattern and the pattern formed by the Chrysler EIS (Electronic Ignition System). Note the intermediate section comparison. (Sun Electric)

The patterns formed by most electronic ignition systems are similar to those formed by conventional contact point systems. However, some electronic systems, such as the Chrysler Electronic Ignition System (EIS), show a marked difference. Note that in **Figure 18-62** (primary pattern), the EIS system has no intermediate section. When using an oscilloscope, be certain to follow the manufacturer's directions and pattern evaluation specifications for the exact system at hand.

Typical Oscilloscope Patterns and Their Meanings

Anything that does not look like the normal pattern is evidence of an ignition system problem. Pattern irregularities provide clues as to what unit or units in the system are faulty and to what extent.

Accurate analysis of the various pattern irregularities requires that the technician be familiar with the machine in use. The technician must also be experienced in interpreting the patterns themselves. To become thoroughly skilled in the use of an oscilloscope as a diagnostic tool, be sure to practice whenever possible. Once the tool is understood and pattern irregularity meaning is clear, the technician will find this a very fast and efficient aid.

Figure 18-63 illustrates seven different patterns. Note that each has specific irregularities that have a certain significance:

A—Normal pattern, firing voltages uniform but too high. Could be caused by worn electrodes, lean fuel mixture, or improperly gapped plugs.

B—Pattern normal but inverted. Caused by wrong coil polarity.

C—Normal pattern but firing voltages are uneven. Could be caused by defective plug wires, defective plugs, a fuel mixture imbalance, or a worn distributor cap.

D—High resistance affecting all cylinders. Could be caused by high resistance in the coil tower, coil wire, or rotor.

E—One plug line is much higher than the others. This is caused by a defective plug wire.

F—Irregular point opening pattern. Could be caused by burned or dirty points or a condenser defect.

G—Irregular point closing pattern. Point bounce caused by a weak contact arm spring.

These seven patterns represent only a few of the possible pattern irregularities. The manual supplied by the manufacturer of the equipment in your shop should be studied carefully.

Electronic Ignition Spark Waveform Patterns

The electronic ignition system provides a rapid and intense current buildup in the coil. It also produces less voltage fluctuation (oscillation) following plug firing. See A and B in **Figure 18-64**. At higher engine speeds, the conventional system available voltage drops considerably. The electronic system available voltage remains high. See C and D in **Figure 18-64**.

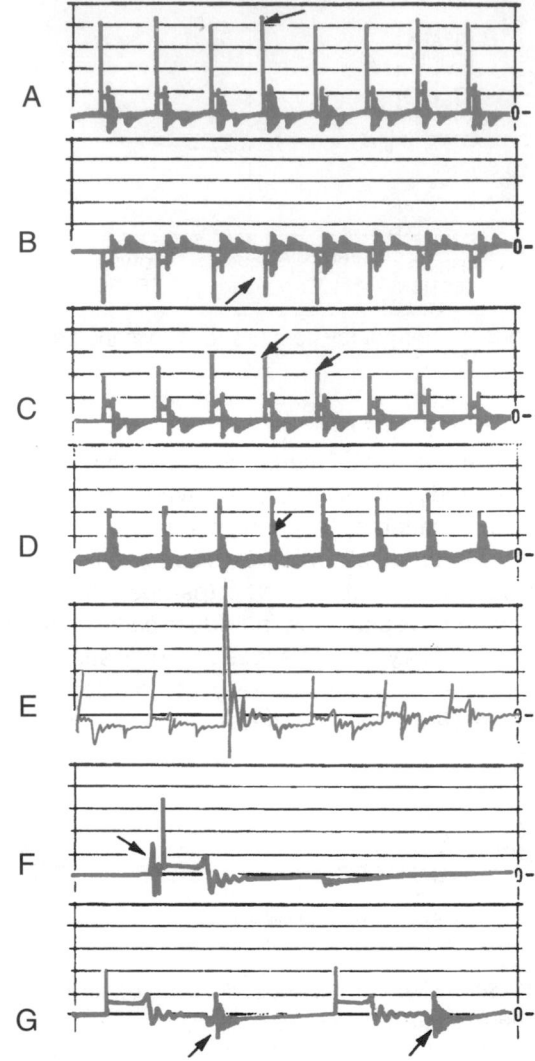

Figure 18-63. Several pattern irregularities and their meanings. A—Firing voltage too high in all cylinders. B—Inverted pattern. Wrong coil polarity. C—Firing voltages uneven. D—High resistance in all cylinders. E—One plug line is much higher than the others. This is caused by a defective plug wire. F—Faulty point opening. G—Faulty point closing.

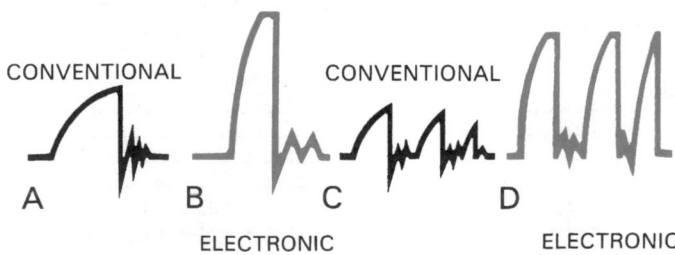

Figure 18-64. Spark waveform patterns as produced by conventional and electronic ignition systems. Note the differences and similarities. (Ford)

Special adapters are available to allow a distributorless ignition system to be checked with an oscilloscope. The distributorless system can be diagnosed in the same way as an electronic system with a distributor.

Tech Talk

Electronic and computer-controlled ignition systems produce extremely high voltages. It is vital to route the spark plug wires away from any other part of the vehicle. Often, the spark will jump through plastic parts, especially if they are damp. After a while, a carbon track is built up through the plastic part, causing a mysterious miss. These high voltages also make it doubly important to check the nonelectronic components. It is common for high secondary voltages to punch through rotors and distributor caps on late-model vehicles.

When checking any ignition system for a hard starting condition, do not forget to check the voltage available at the coil during cranking.

Before removing a distributor, make sure that you line up the rotor with a spot on the distributor body. In many cases, you can stick a cotter pin on the distributor body directly under the rotor before pulling the distributor. This will locate the rotor when you are ready to reinstall the distributor.

The timing can be set on most engines. A stroboscopic timing light is used to set ignition timing. Distributor vacuum and centrifugal advance units should be tested for correct operation. Many automobiles use a computer to control ignition timing. A few computer-controlled ignition systems do not have a distributor.

A distributor tester does an accurate job of checking shaft, cam, dwell, point bounce, and advance units. Some worn distributors can be overhauled. When installing a distributor, make certain that the timing is correct, the oil pump shaft is engaged, and the distributor is locked into position.

Clean around spark plugs before removing them. Examine the plugs for abnormal wear and deposits. Replace them when necessary. An oscilloscope can be used for quick and accurate ignition system diagnosis. Use the oscilloscope as recommended by the manufacturer.

Summary

The first step in ignition system problem diagnosis is to visually inspect all system components. Primary wiring must be in good condition. A quick check for spark will quickly isolate the problem to the ignition system. Check the coil and distributor cap for flashover, burning, or corrosion. Coil polarity must be correct. Secondary wiring must be in good condition. All terminals should be properly connected. Wire ends should have good boots and should be fully inserted into the correct towers.

Problems in the primary circuit may be caused by the ignition switch, resistor, or coil. The distributor, rotor, and spark plug wires can cause trouble in the secondary circuit. Handle plug wires carefully. Pull on the boot or terminal rubber jacket. Avoid sharp bends. Plug wires should have specified resistance. Arrange them to prevent cross firing.

Firing order always starts with the number one cylinder and proceeds as specified by the manufacturer. Change secondary wires one at a time or mark all wires before removal. Always use new boots. Most electronic distributor pickup units can be tested with an ohmmeter. If a component's resistance is not within specifications, it must be replaced. Electronic ignition control modules are usually tested with a voltmeter or an ohmmeter. Some units require the use of special testing equipment. Some technicians heat the ignition control module to help locate intermittent problems.

Contact points must be properly cleaned and gapped. The distributor cam should be lubricated if recommended by the manufacturer. A dwell meter should be used to set the cam angle (dwell). Dwell adjustments are not necessary in electronic ignition systems.

Know These Terms

Primary circuit	Distributorless ignition
Secondary circuit	system
Ignition switch	Contact points
Ignition resistor	Condenser
Ohmmeter	Dwell
Ignition coil	Timing
Flashover	Timing light
Resistance-type secondary	Tachometer
wiring	Vacuum advance
Cross firing	Centrifugal advance
Firing order	Computerized ignition
Distributor cap	systems
Rotor	Spark plugs
Electronic ignition systems	Spark gap
Magnetic pickup coil	Heat range
Hall effect pickup coil	Size
Crankshaft position sensor	Reach
Air gap	Type
Control modules	Oscilloscope

Review Questions—Chapter 18

Do not write in this book. Write your answers on a separate sheet of paper.

1. Excessive circuit resistance lowers _____.
   (A) voltage
   (B) temperature
   (C) firing strength
   (D) Both A & C.

2. Firing order means _____.
   (A) the order in which cylinders fire
   (B) that a piston is at top dead center on the firing stroke
   (C) the direction the distributor turns
   (D) the point at which the timing marks line up

3. Which type of ignition system contains a condenser?
   (A) Contact point.
   (B) Electronic with pickup coil.
   (C) Electronic with Hall effect switch.
   (D) Computer controlled.

4. Computerized ignition systems eliminate the need for _____ and _____ advance systems.

5. The distributor centrifugal advance unit is adjusted by altering the _____.
   (A) return spring pressure
   (B) weight size
   (C) shaft speed
   (D) All of the above, depending on the manufacturer.

6. When timing the engine with a stroboscopic light, it is often necessary to disconnect the distributor _____.
   (A) vacuum lines
   (B) electrical connector
   (C) coil wire
   (D) Both A & B.

7. Electronic ignition systems are equipped with _____.
   (A) self-test connectors
   (B) electronic control modules
   (C) condensers
   (D) temperature sensors

8. Spark plugs in modern engines may operate for as much as _____ before requiring replacement.
   (A) 5000 miles (8000 km)
   (B) 20,000 miles (32,000 km)
   (C) 100,000 miles (160,000 km)
   (D) 250,000 miles (400,000 km)

MATCHING

Plug Color	Probable Condition
9. tan or gray	(A) oil fouling
10. dry black	(B) overheating
11. wet black	(C) detonation
12. dull white	(D) normal used plug
13. shiny yellow	(E) fuel fouled
	(F) high-speed glazing

14. When gapping plugs, bend the _____ electrode only.

15. Name the factors to be considered when selecting a new set of plugs for any engine.

ASE-Type Questions

1. A defective ignition switch can cause _____.
   (A) a no-start condition
   (B) missing at high speeds
   (C) spark plug damage
   (D) Both A & B.

2. Technician A says that a spark test can be used to help pinpoint ignition system problems. Technician B says that the spark plug center electrode must have a negative polarity. Who is right?
   (A) A only.
   (B) B only.
   (C) Both A & B.
   (D) Neither A nor B.

3. Secondary wire towers should be checked for all of the following, EXCEPT:
   (A) corrosion.
   (B) cracks.
   (C) carbon tracks.
   (D) discoloration.

4. Reversed coil polarity can be easily detected on the oscilloscope because the waveform will appear _____.
   (A) normal but backward
   (B) right side up but with broken lines
   (C) normal but upside down
   (D) on the primary pattern only

5. Technician A says that plug wires can have excessive resistance. Technician B says that crossover can occur when any two spark plug wires run too close together. Who is right?
   (A) A only.
   (B) B only.
   (C) Both A & B.
   (D) Neither A nor B.

6. Technician A says that point gap affects dwell. Technician B says that dwell affects spark timing. Who is right?
   (A) A only.
   (B) B only.
   (C) Both A & B.
   (D) Neither A nor B.

7. Computerized ignition systems are equipped with _____ that monitor various engine operating conditions.
   (A) self-test connectors
   (B) sensors
   (C) triggering devices
   (D) output devices

8. Technician A says that an oscilloscope can be used to spot a defective plug wire. Technician B says that an oscilloscope can be used to spot a defective distributor cap. Who is right?
   (A) A only.
   (B) B only.
   (C) Both A & B.
   (D) Neither A nor B.

9. What section is missing from some electronic ignition oscilloscope patterns?
   (A) Firing.
   (B) Intermediate.
   (C) Dwell.
   (D) All of the above, depending on manufacturer.

10. All of the following statements about oscilloscopes are true, EXCEPT:
    (A) oscilloscopes produce a visual record of what is happening in the ignition system.
    (B) anything that does not look like the standard pattern indicates a problem.
    (C) using the oscilloscope is quicker than using an ohmmeter or removing the plugs.
    (D) the oscilloscope can diagnose problems in the secondary ignition system only.

Suggested Activities

1. Draw a schematic of an ignition system. Show the secondary and primary systems. Show how high voltage is developed in the system.
2. On a sheet of graph paper, draw the following oscilloscope patterns:
   Secondary pattern—electronic ignition system.
   Secondary pattern—point-type ignition system.
   Primary pattern—electronic ignition system.
   Primary pattern—point-type ignition system.
3. Using the information in this chapter as a reference, demonstrate how to perform a spark test.
4. Examine one or more ignition systems and determine which of the following classes it fits into:
   Point-type.
   Electronic with vacuum and centrifugal advance mechanism.
   Computer controlled.
   Distributorless.
5. Visually inspect the secondary ignition components for signs of arcing and flashover. Discuss your findings with your instructor or the other members of your class.

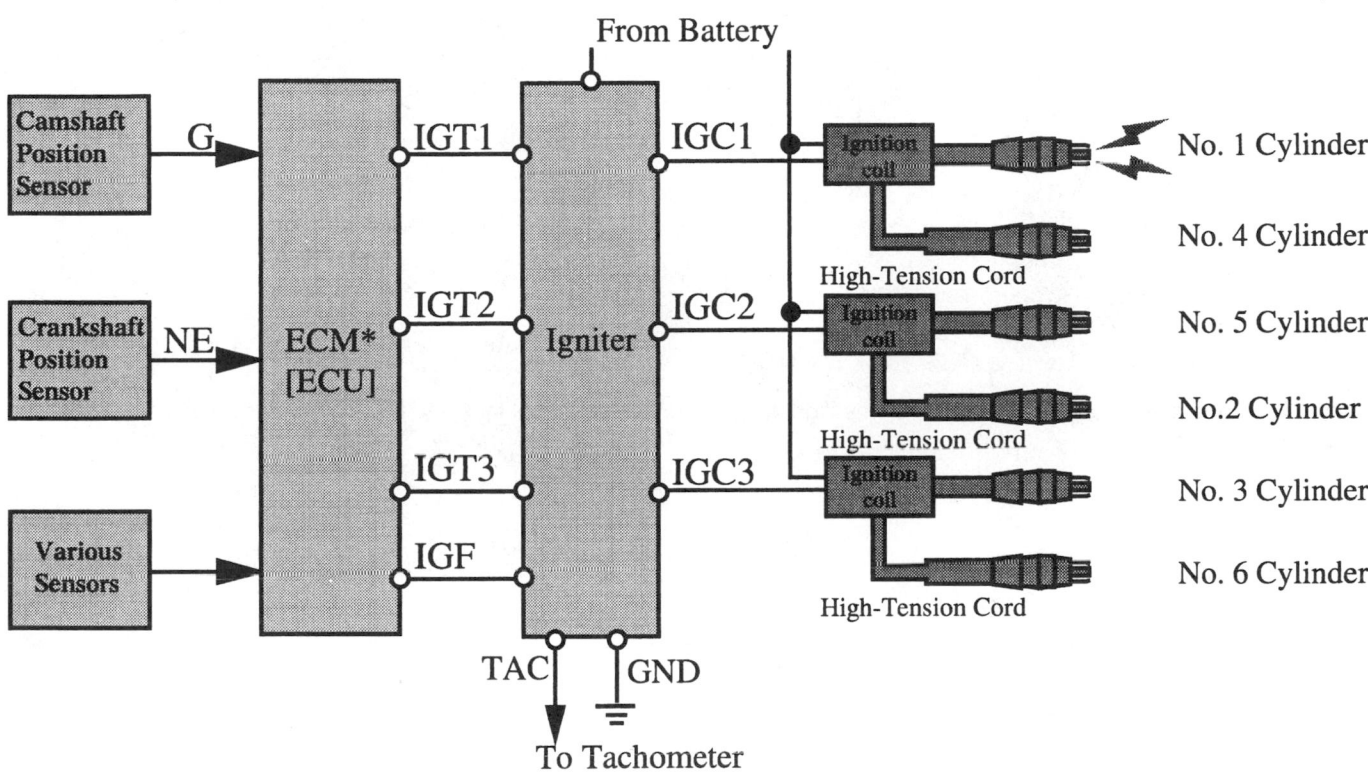

*: ECM (Engine Control Module)

Schematic of a distributorless ignition system. Note that each ignition coil serves two cylinders. (Toyota)

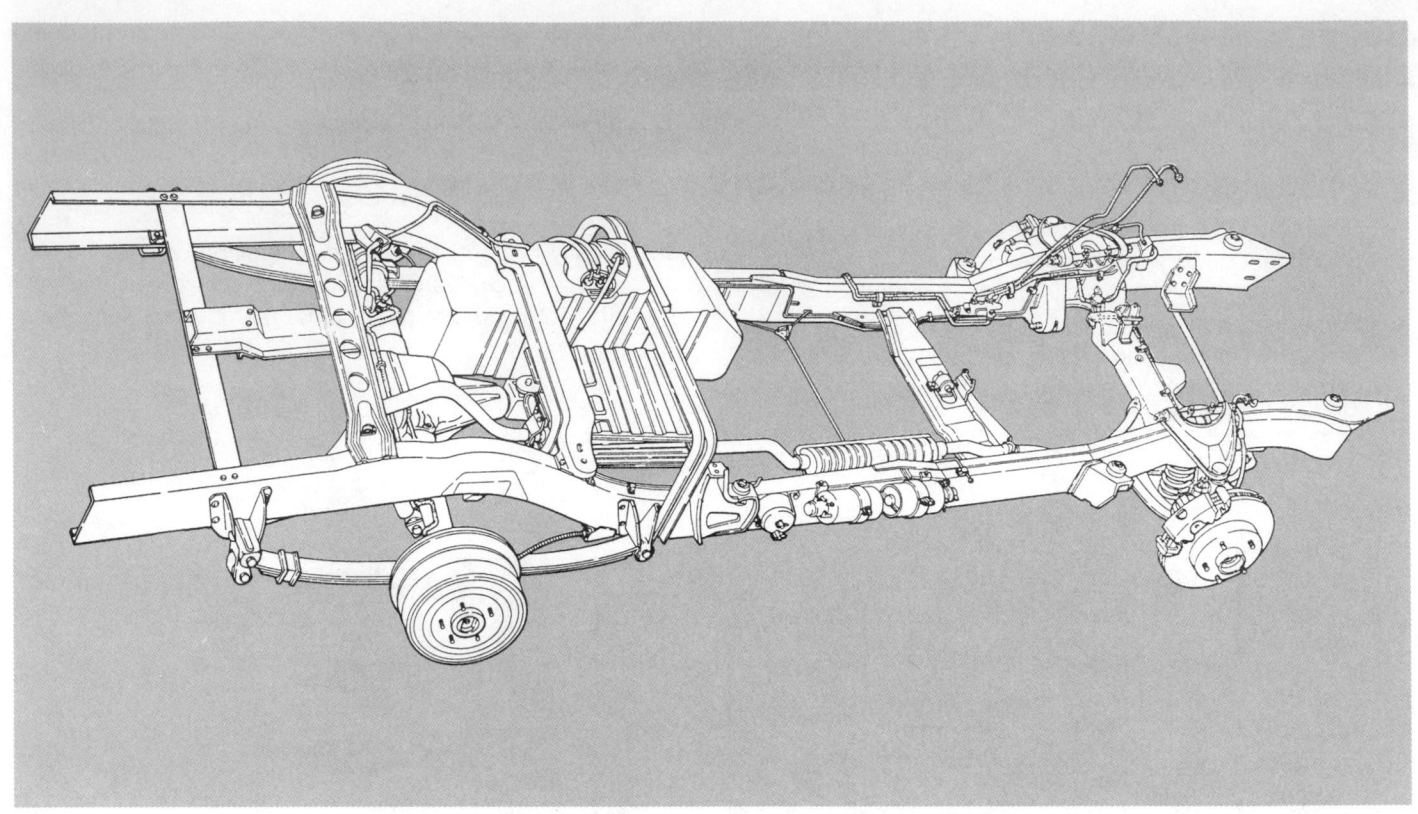

Frame and frame components used on a two-wheel drive truck. Note that the fuel tank and fuel lines are located inside the frame rails for safety. (Dodge)

19

Fuel Delivery

After studying this chapter, you will be able to:
- Describe the cleaning, removal, repair, and replacement of fuel tanks.
- Clean, repair, and install fuel lines.
- Test, remove, repair, and replace mechanical fuel pumps.
- Test, remove, repair, and replace electric fuel pumps.
- Service fuel filters.
- Explain vapor lock.
- List the safety rules involved in fuel delivery system service.

This chapter will cover the operation and service of fuel system components including the fuel tank, fuel line, fuel pump, and filter. This will prepare you for the upcoming chapters on fuel injection and carburetors. Most of the material in this chapter applies to both fuel injected and carbureted vehicles.

Fuel Tanks

Fuel tanks are designed to safely carry enough fuel to allow the vehicle to travel as many miles as possible before refueling is necessary. At the same time, the tank is not so large that it overloads the vehicle when completely filled. A typical fuel tank, along with other fuel system components, is shown in **Figure 19-1**. Most fuel tanks are made of steel. Fuel tanks on some late-model vehicles are made of nylon or **plastic,** such as polyethylene. The fuel tank is attached to the vehicle with straps. Insulation is placed between the tank and the body to reduce noise transfer. Internal baffles in the tank reduce fuel sloshing.

Fuel Tank Service

Before starting work on any part of the fuel system, relieve the residual fuel system pressure using the procedure recommended by the vehicle's manufacturer. Remove the negative battery cable terminal. This should be done before starting work on any part of the fuel system.

Relieve Pressure

Fuel injection systems can maintain considerable pressure for some time after the engine is stopped. A special pressure relief valve is sometimes provided to relieve system

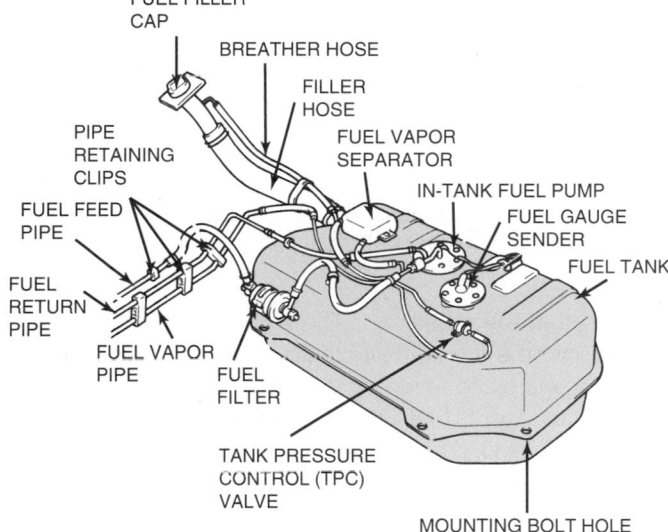

Figure 19-1. A molded steel fuel tank with its various lines and fittings. This tank is secured to the vehicle with five bolts. (Geo)

pressure. If so equipped, use this valve following manufacturer's directions. One procedure is shown in **Figure 19-2**. Where no mechanical provision is made for pressure relief, it may be possible to disconnect the fuel pump electrical connector and operate the engine until is stops from lack of fuel. Consult the vehicle's service manual for the proper relief procedure. Loosen all connections slowly and use an absorbent cloth or an approved container to catch any spillage.

 Note: Properly dispose of gasoline soaked rags.

Draining the Tank

The fuel tank will be much easier to handle if it is empty. If the tank is not close to empty (less than 1/8 full), drain the fuel tank. This can usually be done by **siphoning.** A handy siphoning device can be created from a length of 3/8″ inside diameter (ID) hose. A tapered slit is cut about 18″ (457 mm) from one end of the hose and a pipe nipple

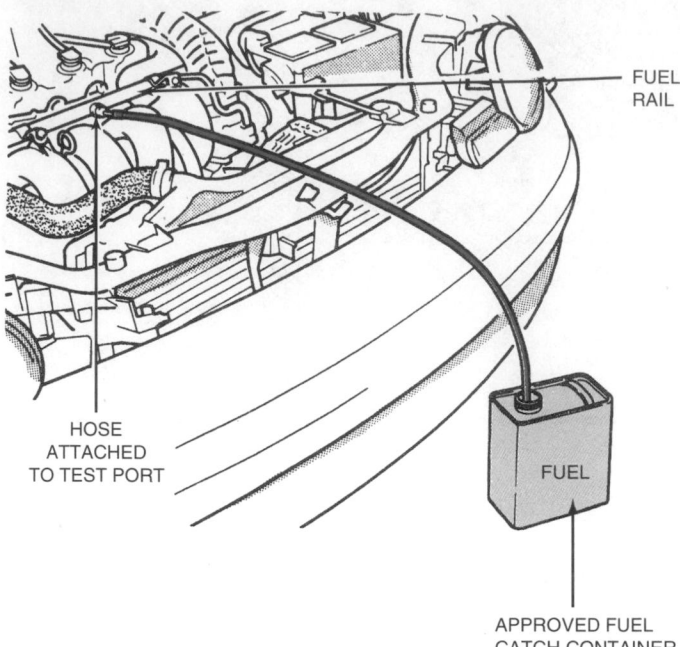

FUEL
RAIL

HOSE
ATTACHED
TO TEST PORT

FUEL

APPROVED FUEL
CATCH CONTAINER

Figure 19-2. Using an approved fuel container to catch fuel during the pressure release procedure. Always relieve fuel pressure before working on the system.

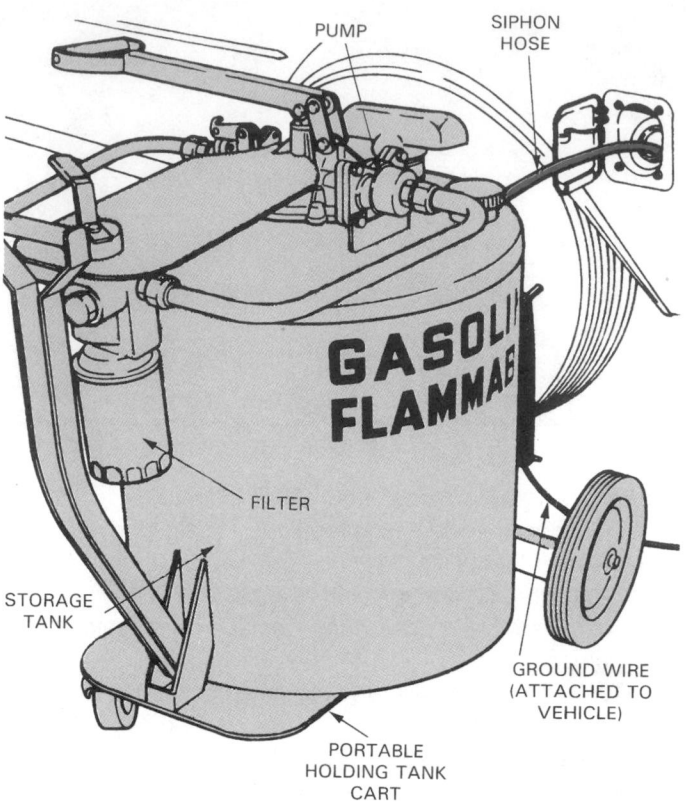

PUMP

SIPHON
HOSE

GASOLIN
FLAMMAB

FILTER

STORAGE
TANK

GROUND WIRE
(ATTACHED TO
VEHICLE)

PORTABLE
HOLDING TANK
CART

Figure 19-3. Portable fuel storage tank. This unit can drain and then refill the tank. Note ground wire. (Chrysler)

is installed in the other end. The nipple end of the hose is inserted into the tank until it strikes the bottom. The slit end of the hose is placed below the level of the fuel tank. An air blow gun is inserted into the slit and a short blast of air is applied. This will create a vacuum that will start the fuel flowing through the siphon.

Another method of siphoning is to use two separate lengths of hose. Insert one end of each hose into the fuel tank. Place a clean rag into the filler neck to form a seal around the two pieces of hose. Cover any external vents with masking tape. Blowing air into one hose will create pressure in the tank and siphoning will be started in the other hose. *Never* start a siphon by sucking on the hose.

The two siphoning techniques just mentioned should be used only when no commercial siphoning tool is available. They must be used very carefully to reduce the danger of fire. Whenever possible, a tool such as the one shown in **Figure 19-3** should be used. This tool is equipped with a fuel pump, filter, and storage tank. Some fuel tanks are equipped with a baffle that makes siphoning impossible. Others tanks contain check valves which could be damaged by conventional siphoning. Some fuel tanks are equipped with a drain plug. Check the vehicle's service manual for the proper fuel removal method.

STOP **Warning: Be careful of fire when working with gasoline or diesel fuel. Do not smoke while working on any part of the fuel system. Place gasoline or diesel fuel in a closed, properly designed container. Avoid getting fuel on your clothing. Most tanks usually contain some fuel even after siphoning. The weight of the fuel and the physical dimensions of the tank can make it awkward to handle. Get someone to help you before you begin removing the tank from the vehicle.**

Tank Removal

Raise the vehicle and disconnect the fuel lines. Cover all fuel line ends with masking tape. Disconnect the filler pipe and any external vents. Also remove the *fuel gauge sender* wires and fuel pump wires if the fuel pump is installed in the tank. Removal of other components may also be necessary on some vehicles. With the help of an assistant, remove the tank support straps and lower the tank.

Note: The fuel tanks of most late-model vehicles are sealed from the outside air. Some tank vent tubes are routed through a filter or carbon canister, which is part of the emissions control system. The carbon canister stores any excess fuel vapors until they can be burned in the engine. All tank vents should be carefully noted and reinstalled in their original positions.

Remove the *lock ring* which holds the fuel gauge sender assembly and remove the assembly from the tank, **Figure 19-4.** Use care to avoid bending the float arm or the pickup pipe. Some fuel pumps are part of the fuel gauge sender assembly, **Figure 19-5.** If the fuel pump is installed in the tank, it will be removed along with the sender. With the help of an assistant, tilt the tank and drain out any remaining fuel into an approved container.

STOP **Warning: Do not leave open containers of fuel in the shop. Vapors can travel a great distance and can ignite if they come into contact with the slightest spark.**

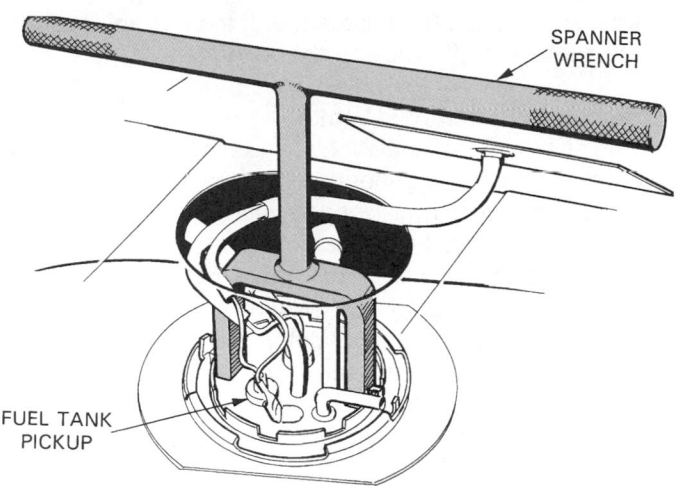

SPANNER WRENCH

FUEL TANK PICKUP

Figure 19-4.   Use a special spanner tool to remove the fuel tank pickup unit. Always disconnect the battery before working on any part of the fuel system. (Volvo)

Cleaning the Fuel Tank

Begin by inspecting the tank interior. A fuel tank that is contaminated with excessive quantities of water or foreign material should be cleaned. The contaminants will enter the rest of the fuel system and can cause serious problems if not removed. Replace the tank if the interior is corroded or if any of the baffles are broken. Proceed with cleaning if the tank is not corroded or damaged internally. Place a quart of clean, nonflammable solvent in the tank. You may have to add more or less depending on the size of the tank. Do not use gasoline to clean a fuel tank. While holding a clean rag over the filler neck and sender hole, tilt the tank vigorously to move the solvent around. Drain the tank and repeat the process. Blow the tank dry with compressed air and inspect for any remaining contaminants. Stubborn dirt may require cleaning the tank interior with steam. Clean the pickup pipe and filter screen by directing a gentle blast of air down through the pickup pipe. If the pickup pipe is connected to an in-tank fuel pump, remove the pump before cleaning. Replace the pickup filter screen if badly clogged.

> **STOP** **Warning: An empty or partially empty fuel tank will contain vapors. If ignited, these vapors will produce a violent explosion. Do not clean or work on the tank anywhere near a flame or source of sparks.**

Installing the Fuel Tank

Before reinstalling the tank, replace the sender or sender-pump unit if needed. Use a new gasket whenever the sending unit is removed. Make sure the tank insulation strips are in place. With the help of an assistant, carefully raise the tank into position and attach the tank retaining straps. If the tank uses an airtight, or **nonvented,** cap, make certain that the vent tube is open. Torque the tank strap bolts, do not overtighten. Install the fuel lines and other components as needed and reconnect all wiring. Reconnect the battery as the final step. Do not refill the tank until it is completely installed.

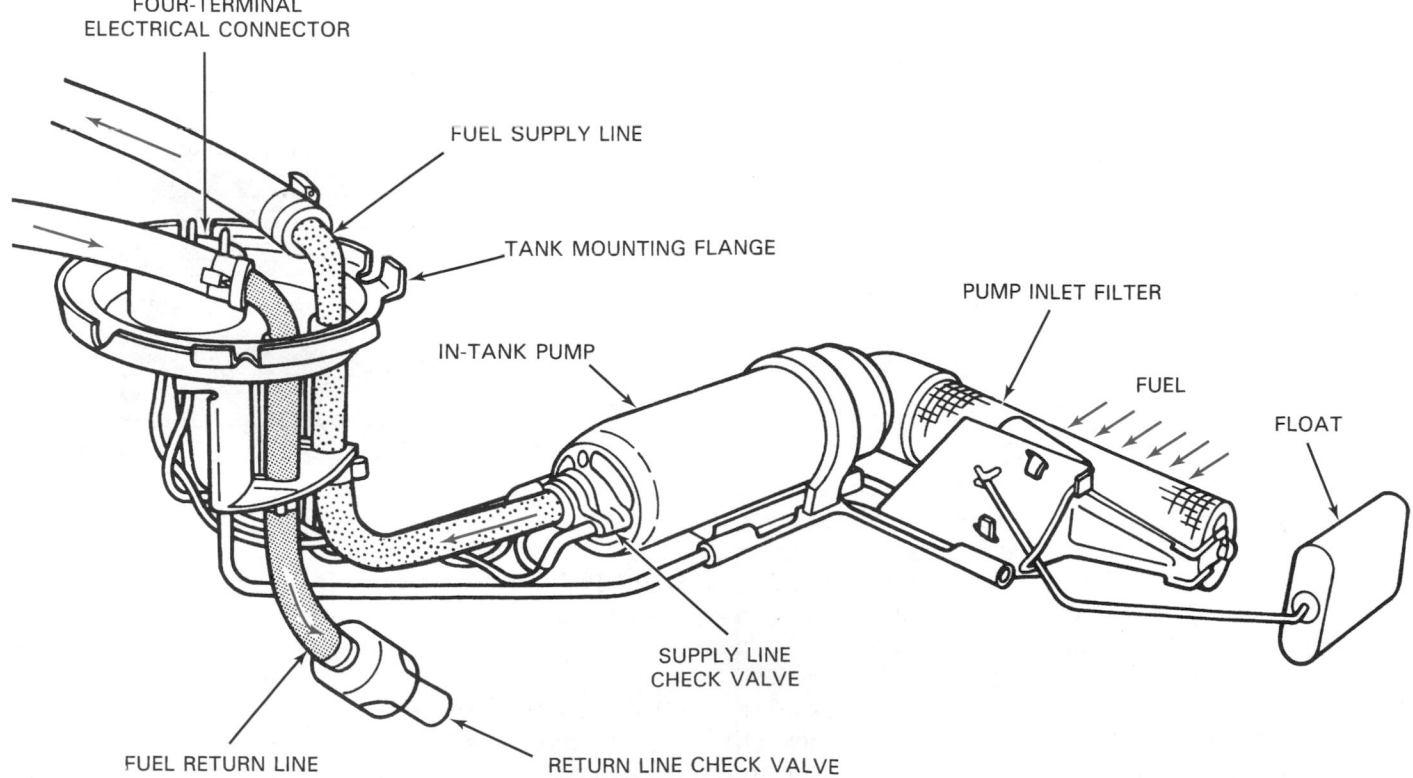

FOUR-TERMINAL ELECTRICAL CONNECTOR

FUEL SUPPLY LINE

TANK MOUNTING FLANGE

IN-TANK PUMP

PUMP INLET FILTER

FUEL

FLOAT

SUPPLY LINE CHECK VALVE

FUEL RETURN LINE

RETURN LINE CHECK VALVE

Figure 19-5.   Some vehicles have the fuel tank pickup pipe, filter, float, and return pipe combined in one unit. Note the fuel return line. (Chrysler)

Tank Repair

Note: The foregoing techniques for fuel tank repair apply only to automobile fuel tanks. Heavy steel tanks, high pressure containers, grease, and oil drums require additional safeguards and different techniques.

A leaking fuel tank should be replaced in most situations. However, a metal fuel tank may be repaired by soldering or brazing *if* adequate safeguards are taken. The fuel tank should be thoroughly steam cleaned inside and out. Following cleaning, the tank should be filled with an nonexplosive gas such as carbon dioxide or nitrogen, or an *inert* gas or completely filled with water as illustrated in **Figure 19-6.**

Warning: Use the utmost care in all tank cleaning and repair procedures. Fuel tanks can become lethal bombs capable of instantly killing anyone nearby. Have a fire extinguisher handy and keep other persons away from the operation.

An older method used to repair fuel tanks was to initially clean the tank and then to place a quart of carbon tetrachloride in the tank. However, this procedure is not recommended even if carbon tetrachloride is available. Carbon tetrachloride fumes are *toxic* and will displace the oxygen in an enclosed space. There is also some evidence that carbon tetrachloride can cause cancer.

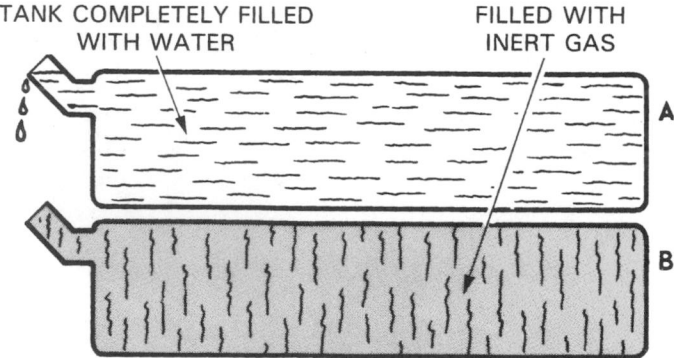

TANK COMPLETELY FILLED WITH WATER   FILLED WITH INERT GAS

A

B

Figure 19-6. Solder or braze fuel tanks only after thorough steam cleaning and preparing the tank as shown in either A or B.

Cold Patching

There are various epoxy sealants and special patching cloth that can be used to repair both metal and plastic tanks. **Cold patching** works very well for some leak repairs if done properly. Follow the manufacturer's recommendations. Test all tank repairs by covering with a wet soap lather. Place an air hose in the tank and apply air. A mild pressure can be applied to the tank by holding a rag around the hose where it enters the tank. If the repair is sound, air bubbles will not appear. Afterwards, blow the tank dry and install. Regardless of the type of repair chosen, work carefully. Remember that fuel tank integrity is vitally important.

Even a small leak can cause a fire. If there is any doubt as to the success of the repair, *replace* the tank.

Expanded (Bulged) Fuel Tank

In the modern sealed fuel system, considerable in-tank pressure can be generated by such items as a defective fuel cap, pinched or clogged vapor lines, or a plugged vapor canister filter. Fuel tanks can become expanded, or *bulged,* from excessive in-tank pressure. This can cause tank damage and fuel leaks. Whenever a bulged tank is encountered, replace it and determine the cause. Make certain that the excess pressure condition is no longer present following repairs. In many systems, the pressure relief valve in the filler cap should open at around 1 1/2 to 2 psi (10 to 17 kPa).

Removing a Dent in the Fuel Tank

Occasionally, the bottom of a fuel tank is shoved inward by striking an object. If none of the internal baffles are damaged, the tank can often be straightened by filling the tank with water. Remove the tank from the car, plug the vent tube, and place a nonvented cap on the filler neck. Remove the in-tank fuel pump if used. Apply air through the pickup tube. The air will exert pressure on the water and will usually cause the dented area to bulge outward. Be sure to apply only enough air pressure to pop the dent out. See **Figure 19-7.**

Caution: Always fill the tank with water before applying air pressure. The use of air alone can cause the tank to rupture and fly apart with great force.

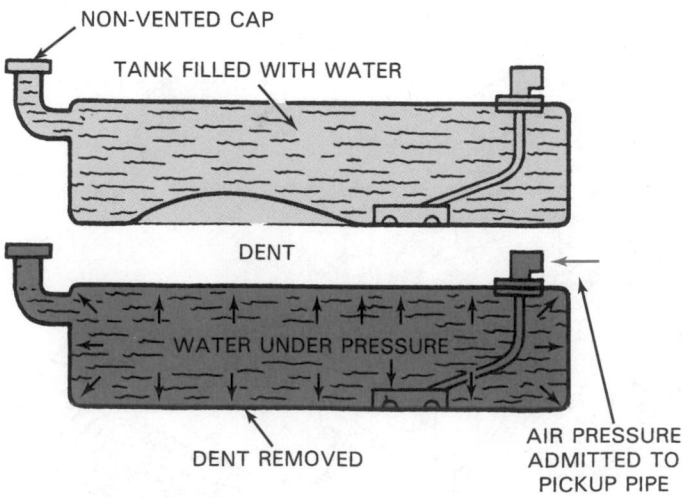

NON-VENTED CAP

TANK FILLED WITH WATER

DENT

WATER UNDER PRESSURE

DENT REMOVED

AIR PRESSURE ADMITTED TO PICKUP PIPE

Figure 19-7. Remove a dent in a fuel tank by filling it with water and applying low air pressure.

Fuel Line Service

The *fuel lines* are normally trouble free, but may collect water and dirt from the tank. In other cases, external damage, corrosion, or vibration may restrict fuel flow or cause the lines to leak. The section below explains how to service fuel lines. **Figure 19-8** illustrates a typical fuel line arrangement.

Cleaning Fuel Lines

Water or dirt in the fuel lines can contaminate the fuel system and can cause serious damage. Disconnect the fuel line at the tank and at the fuel pump. Some electric fuel pumps are in the tank. In these cases, disconnect the line from the carburetor, injection fittings, or filter as applicable. If the vehicle is equipped with plastic fuel lines, take care not to kink the lines, as this can cause a permanent restriction. Remove any in-line filter before applying pressure. Replace with a new filter. Next, direct an air blast from the fuel pump and toward the gas tank until clean. Always blow in the direction opposite of fuel flow. If the line remains restricted, check for a dented or kinked spot.

Repairing Damaged Fuel Line

Other than the rubber flex hose used on some carbureted systems, the fuel lines rarely need repair. If a metal fuel line is dented, severed, or corroded, the damaged section can be removed and replaced with a new section of tubing. Make sure joining connections are tight. Refer to Chapter 8 on tubing and hose for full instructions. Plastic fuel lines are not repairable and must be replaced as an assembly if they are kinked or damaged.

Fuel Pump Service

The *fuel pump* is vital to the proper operation of the vehicle. Without the fuel pump, the other components of the fuel system are useless. The following sections explain how to service mechanical and electric fuel pumps. The fuel pump should be checked for leaks, output pressure, flow volume, and inlet vacuum when driveability or fuel system problems exist or as part of a thorough tune-up.

Mechanical Fuel Pump Repair

The following section briefly explains how to test, remove, install, and rebuild a *mechanical fuel pump.* Before testing the pump, make sure there is fuel in the tank. Inspect the fuel and vent lines for kinks, dents, and leaks. Tighten the pump diaphragm, filter bowl and pulsator cover, and mounting screws. Clean or replace the fuel filter. There are two tests that must be done to properly evaluate fuel pump pressure. The first is a test of pump *fluid pressure;* the second is a test of pump *static pressure* (not supplying fuel to carburetor, hence no fuel flow pressure).

Pump Fluid Pressure Test

Disconnect the fuel line at the carburetor or recommended point and install a suitable fuel pressure gauge. The gauge illustrated in **Figure 19-9** can handle both pressure and volume tests. Regardless of the type used, the gauge should be held at or near the carburetor level, but not more than 6″ (152 mm) above or below to prevent false readings. If using a pressure gauge similar to that in **Figure 19-9,** place the flow volume hose in a container and pinch off the hose before starting the engine. Some manufacturers specify that pump pressure is to be tested at normal operating speed, while others at cranking speed.

With the engine cranking or running, open the hose shutoff and draw about 4 ounces (118 ml) of fuel. This will vent the pump and remove any trapped air that could cause a false reading. Stop the engine and dispose of the fuel in the container. When empty, replace the volume hose and

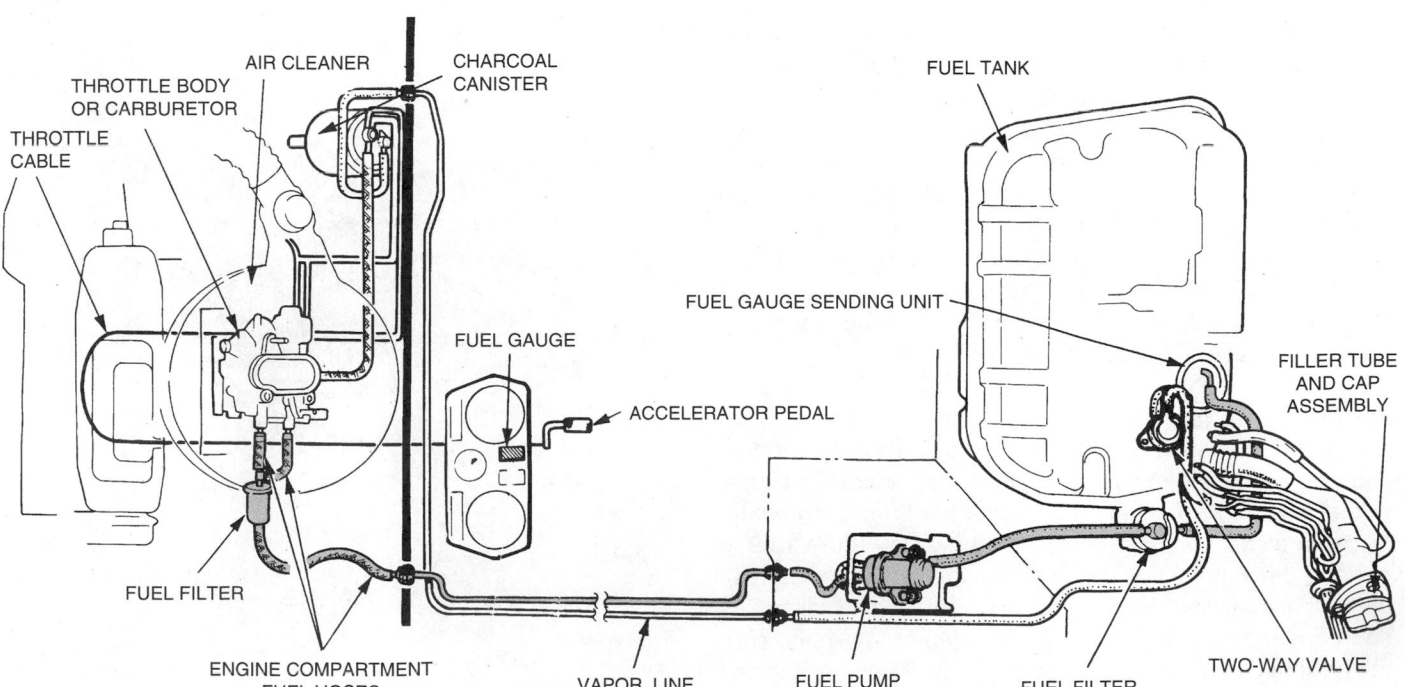

Figure 19-8. Study this fuel line setup from the fuel tank to the carburetor. Learn the name of each part. (Honda)

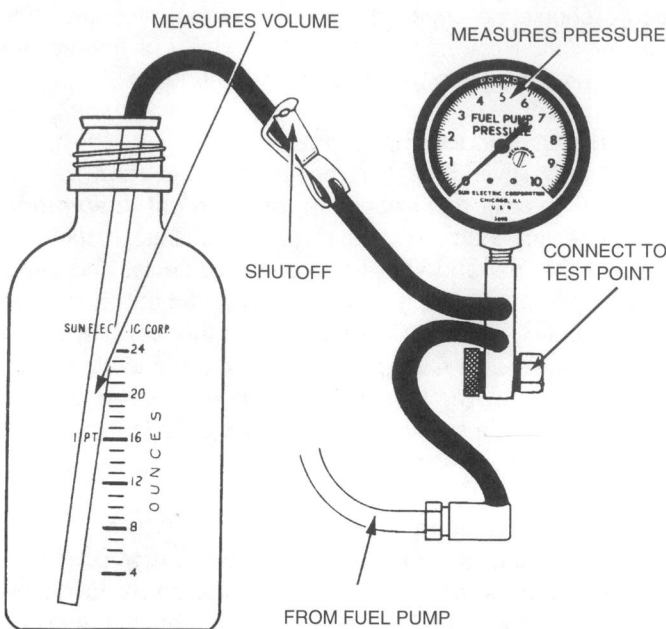

Figure 19-9. This gauge setup can be used to check fuel pump pressure and volume. (Sun Electric)

start the engine. While cranking or idling, note the pressure on the gauge. Average fuel pressure should be from 4 to 6 psi (28 to 41 kPa) and should stay relatively constant.

Stop the engine and watch the gauge to check pump static pressure. The fuel pressure should either remain constant or fall slowly. A rapid loss of pressure indicates a leaky fitting, a faulty pump outlet valve, or a leaky carburetor float valve. A different gauge setup can be used to check pump static pressure, **Figure 19-10.** Note that the pressure gauge is attached directly to the end of the pressure line. The engine is operated on the fuel remaining in the fuel bowl.

When taking pressure tests on a fuel pump equipped with a vapor return line, it is important that the line be pinched off. Look at **Figure 19-11.** An open valve will result in a false pressure reading. Start the engine and remove the return line at the valve. Hold a container under the valve outlet to catch any fuel being discharged. A fuel discharge rate of about 2 1/2 ounces (74 ml) per minute is normal and indicates that the valve is closed. Fuel discharge in appreciable amounts indicates the vapor valve is either open from heat or is stuck open. In the case of heat, cool the pump with wet rags. If it is stuck, clean or replace.

Pump Volume Test

After evaluating pump pressure, a *pump volume* test must be performed to make certain that an adequate supply of fuel is actually reaching the throttle body, injection pump, or carburetor. Use the gauge setup shown in **Figure 19-9** to perform the volume test. Noting the exact time (in seconds), open the fuel flow line shutoff with the engine idling. As soon as there is about 4 ounces (118 ml) of fuel in the container, firmly push the tube into the fuel. Watch for bubbles in the fuel that would indicate an air leak in the intake line. As soon as approximately 16 ounces (473 ml) has been drawn, note the time in seconds and close the flow shutoff

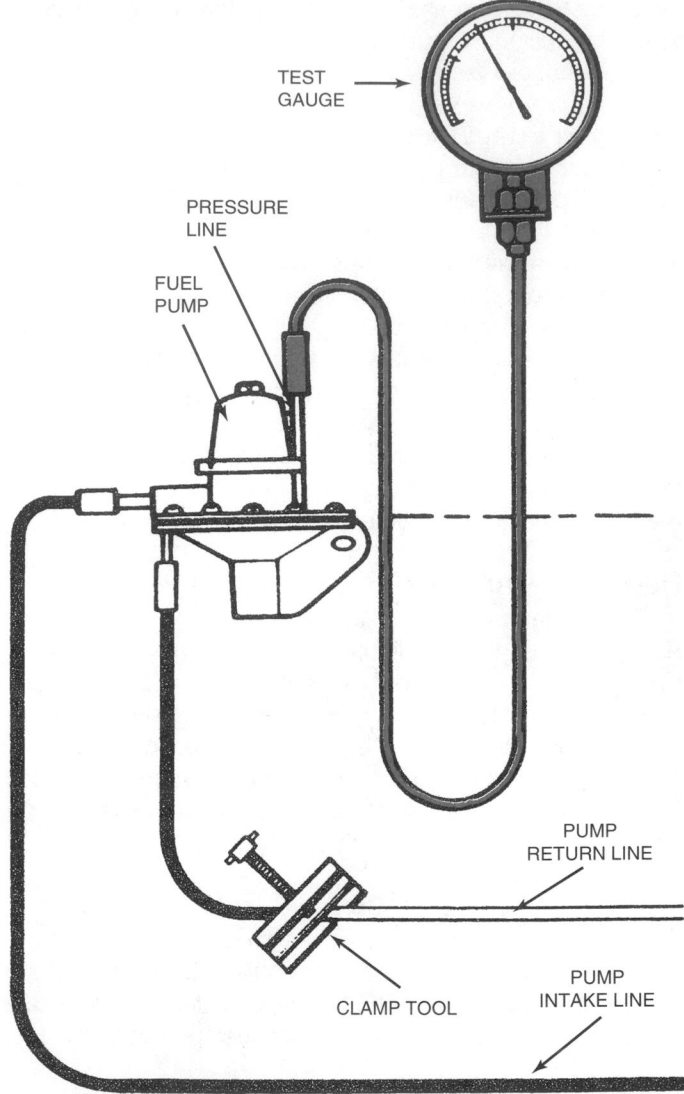

Figure 19-10. Checking pump static pressure.

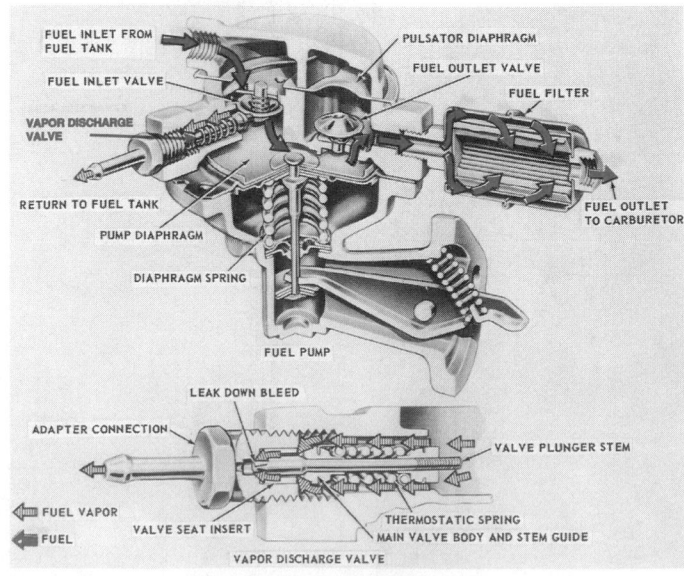

Figure 19-11. This fuel pump has a vapor discharge valve. Note how fuel vapor passes through the valve. (Lincoln)

and stop the engine. Manufacturer's specifications will generally call for a flow equivalent of one quart in one minute at 500 RPM. See **Figure 19-12.**

> **Caution: Use extreme care when conducting both pressure and volume tests. A fuel pump can spray fuel a long distance. Make certain all connections are tight and that the volume hose is in the container. Container should be made of clear plastic.**

A

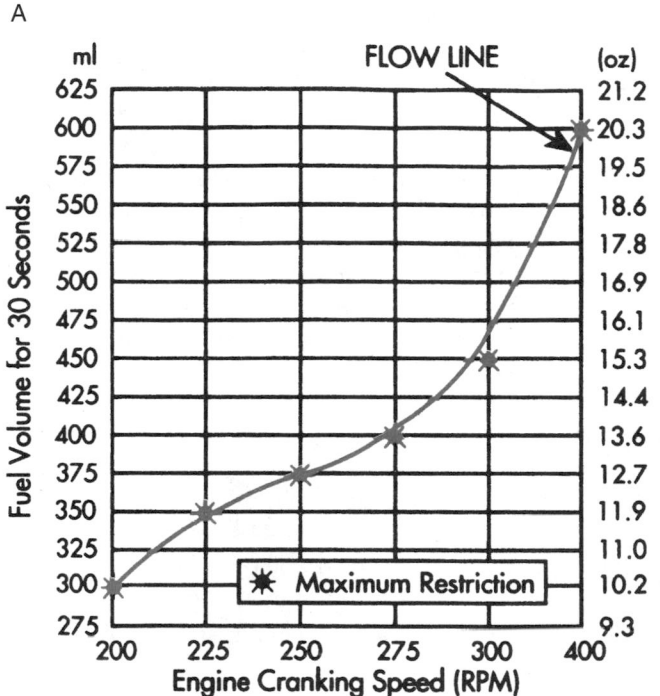

B

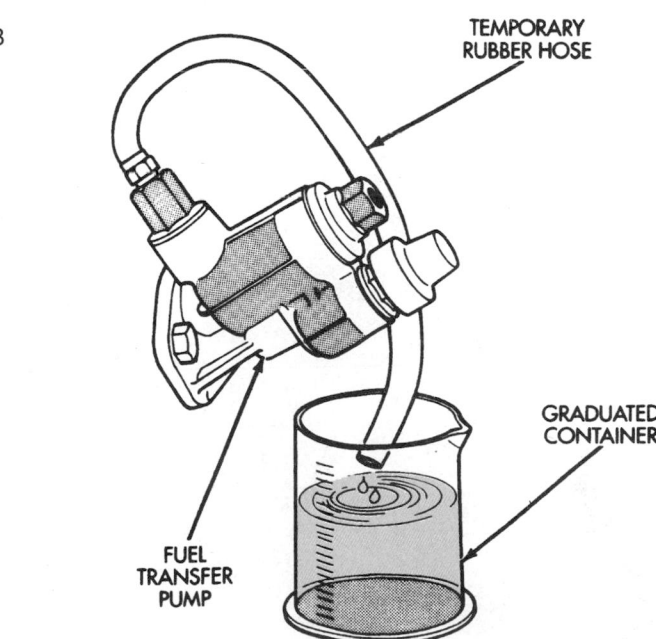

Figure 19-12. Checking fuel pump volume on one type of diesel engine. A—Fuel volume versus engine cranking speed graph. B—Fuel pump volume being measured in a graduated container. (Dodge)

Pump Inlet Vacuum Test

When volume or pressure does not meet specifications, the pump *inlet vacuum* should be determined before condemning the fuel pump. If the suction line (line from the tank pickup tube to the pump) is restricted or leaking air, the pump cannot be expected to perform as required. Disconnect the inlet fuel line from the pump. If gas drips from the open fuel line, cap it off. Attach the vacuum gauge to the inlet fitting or the pump inlet flex line. Disconnect the output fuel line from the pump at the carburetor. Attach a hose to the carburetor line end and place it in a container to catch the fuel.

Start the engine and allow it to idle until the gauge reads a vacuum. In general, a minimum vacuum reading of 10″ (34 kPa) should be obtained. When the engine is stopped, the reading should hold steady. A reading of 10″ (34 kPa) or more indicates the pump valves, diaphragm, flex line, and bowl gasket (where used) are airtight. See **Figure 19-13.** If the reading is below specs or if the vacuum falls off rapidly when engine is stopped, a leak in the flex line or a leak between the pump and the carburetor is indicated. If a flex line is used, remove the line and attach the gauge directly to the pump inlet fitting. If the low vacuum reading or fall off continues, the pump is defective. If the vacuum reading is now normal, the flex line is leaking. When the vacuum test indicates that the pump and flex line are not leaking, test the entire inlet system by removing the line at the fuel tank and attaching the vacuum gauge at this point. Connect the flex line to the fuel line and operate the engine. If the vacuum reading drops below specifications, or if it falls off rapidly, an air leak in the inlet system is indicated.

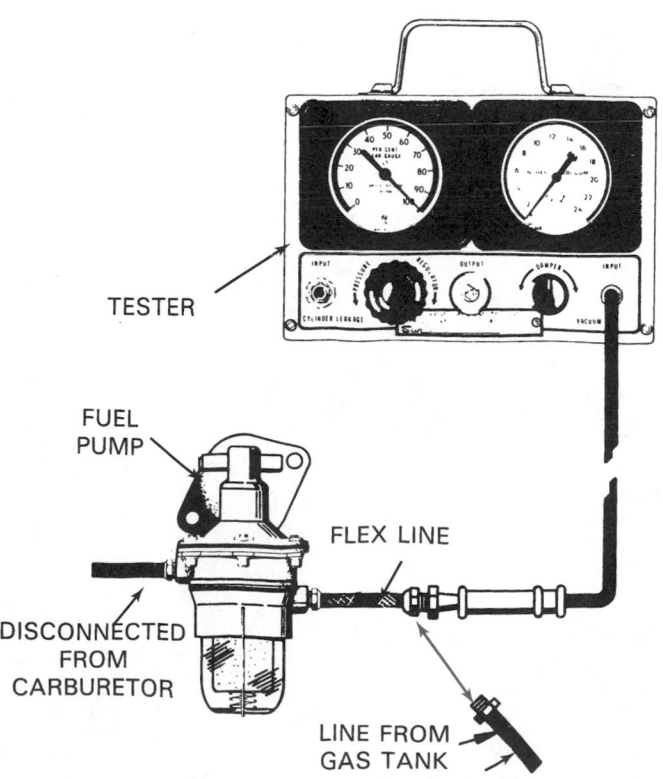

Figure 19-13. Use this gauge to check a fuel pump for vacuum leaks. (Sun Electric)

Pump Removal

Clean all dirt and any oil from around the pump line connections and mounting flange. Remove the fuel and vapor lines, then the pump fasteners. Cover the line ends and stuff a clean rag into the engine pump rocker arm opening. If a push rod is used, it should be removed for cleaning and inspection. Brush the outside of the pump with solvent and rinse off. When ordering a new fuel pump, give the vehicle make, year, model, and engine size. If possible, provide the pump number. See **Figure 19-14.** Lubricate the rocker arm on the new pump before installation.

Pump Installation

Scrape away the old mounting gasket and install the pump with a new mounting gasket coated with gasket cement. Check location of cam or push rod and install pump

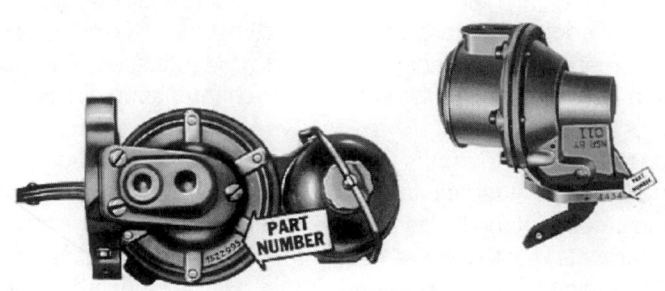

Figure 19-14. When ordering a new pump, be sure to give as much information as possible. Get the pump's part number, if possible. (AC)

to make correct contact. Make certain that the rocker arm rubbing pad (contact surface) bears against the eccentric cam or push rod where used. **Figure 19-15** illustrates one type of rocker arm pad-to-eccentric contact arrangement. Mounting the rocker rubbing pad to one side of the eccentric cam or off of the push rod can cause pump breakage and possible engine damage. Push the pump inward until the pump is against the mounting pad. Install all pump retaining fasteners and torque to specifications. See **Figure 19-16.** Never force the pump to the engine by using the fasteners to pull it in.

Attach the fuel lines or hoses. Any rubber hose used must be in good condition. Carefully align and hand thread the fittings for at least two turns to prevent cross threading. Hold the pump and/or the filter fitting with one wrench while tightening the flare nut with the other. See **Figure 19-17.** When using push-on type fittings, make certain that the tube and the fitting inside is clean. Align the fitting and tube and push the fitting on the tube. Be certain to replace the retaining clip if removed. Several different types of push-on fittings are illustrated in **Figure 19-18.** Start the engine and check for leaks. Test pump pressure and volume to ensure that there are no other problems.

Rebuilding Older Mechanical Fuel Pumps

Today, most mechanical fuel pumps are simply replaced. However, some older pumps can be rebuilt. Disassembly procedures will vary somewhat depending on the pump design. Begin by scribing a line on the pump so that the parts may be reassembled in their correct relationship. Remove the valve body cover, noting the relationship of the

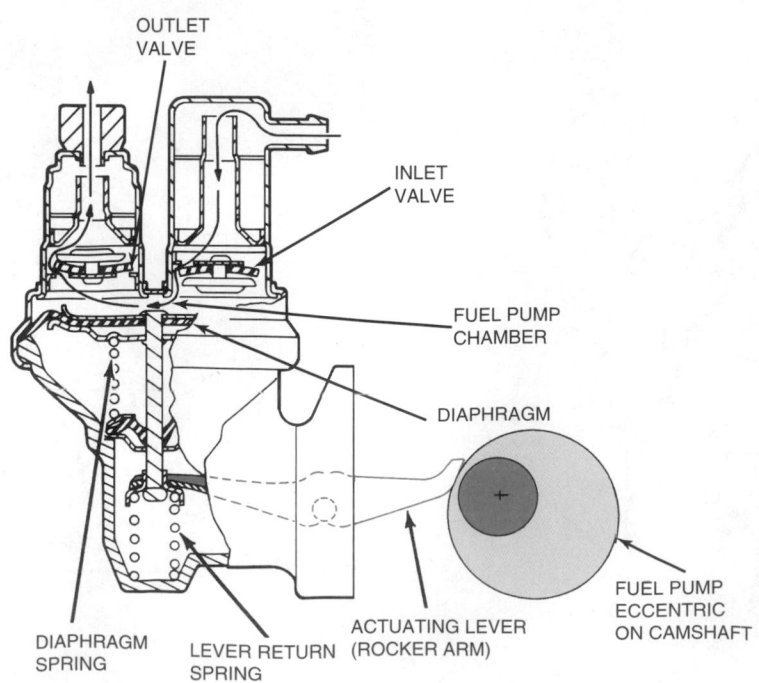

Figure 19-15. A fuel pump illustrating one rocker arm (actuating lever) to fuel pump eccentric on the camshaft. There are a number of different styles. (Jeep)

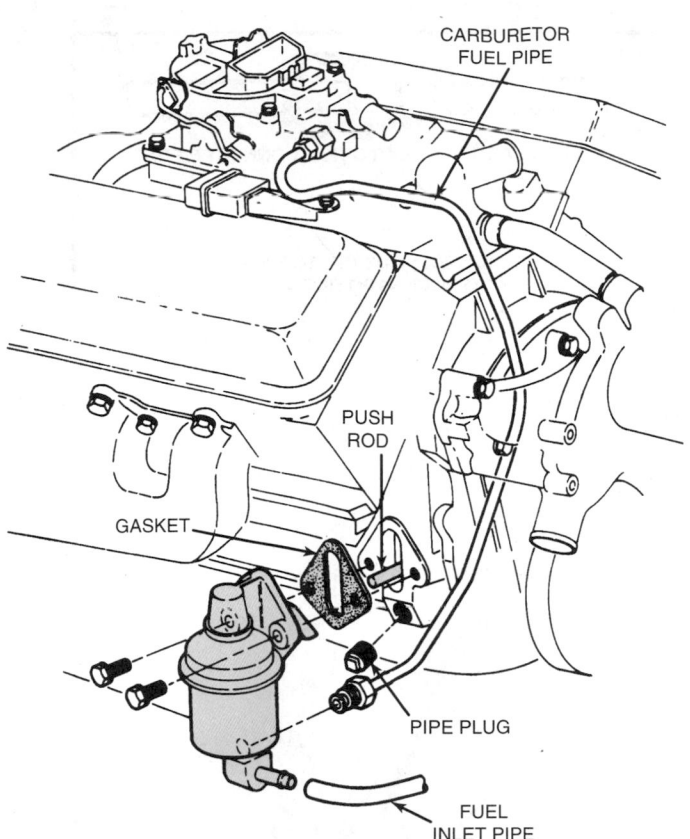

Figure 19-16. When installing a fuel pump, make certain rocker arm contacts cam or as in this case the push rod, correctly. Do not use fasteners to force pump into place. (AC)

diaphragm to the valve body. Then remove the valve body-to-pump body screws. Remove the stake marks (places where the metal is dented) from valve assemblies and pry the valves out of the pump body. Note the location and position, either up or down, of each valve so that the new valves may be reinstalled correctly. Remove the rocker arm pin and pull the rocker arm and link assembly from the pump body. Note the relative position of the link and rocker arm assembly. Pull the diaphragm rod arm seal and seal retainer. A cutaway view of a mechanical fuel pump is shown in **Figure 19-19.**

Soak all metal parts of the pump in carburetor cleaner for no more than 15 minutes. After rinsing and blow drying, lay out the parts on a clean surface. Check all parts for nicks, excessive wear, cracks, and warpage. Open the repair kit and lay out all parts. Assemble the pump using all of the new parts in the correct relationship to each other. If the pump contains a filter, it must be cleaned or replaced. Realign scribe marks and start all fasteners. Tighten all screws until they just start to tighten against the lock washers.

Electric Fuel Pumps

There are four types of **electric fuel pumps** including **diaphragm, bellows, impeller,** and **roller-vane** types. Accurate pressure and volume tests depend upon a properly charged battery and a mechanically sound pump motor or solenoid. The impeller type pump shown in **Figure 19-20** is placed inside the gas tank. Other electric pumps are installed on the engine or on the frame under the vehicle, **Figure 19-21.**

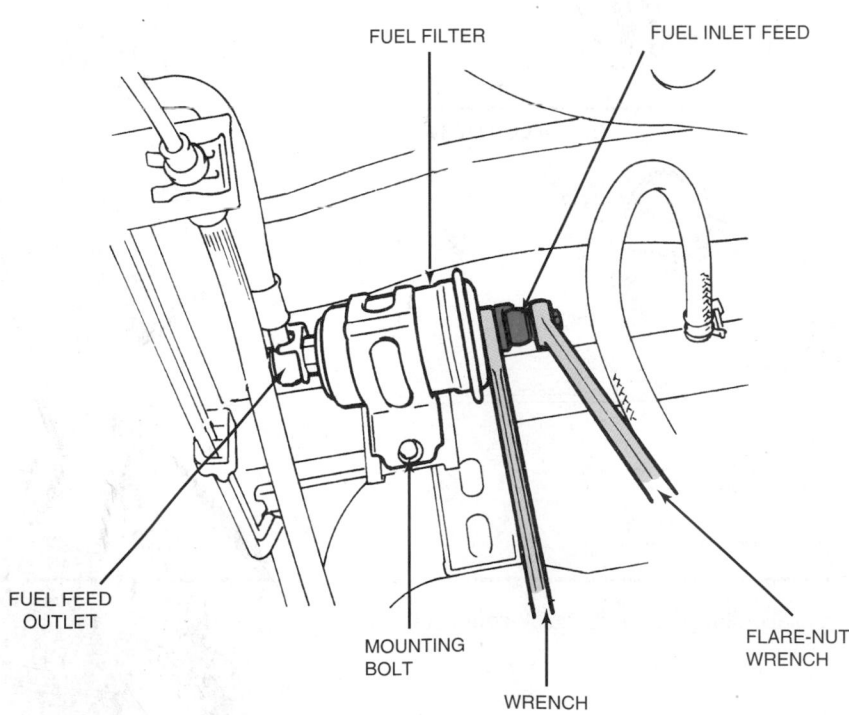

Figure 19-17. Tighten fittings securely. Do not cross thread. Note how the technician is holding the filter fitting while tightening the flare nut. (Geo)

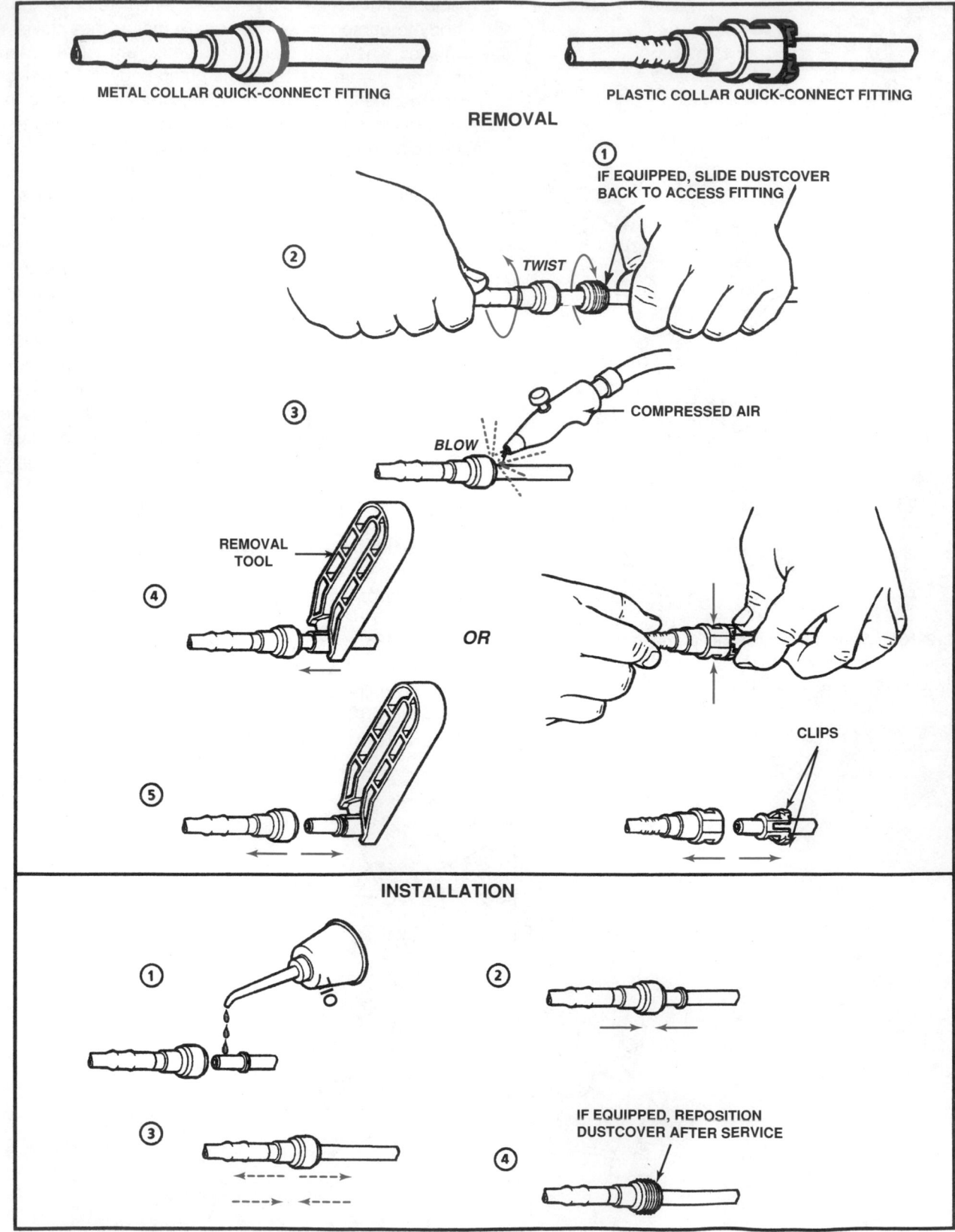

METAL COLLAR QUICK-CONNECT FITTING

PLASTIC COLLAR QUICK-CONNECT FITTING

REMOVAL

① IF EQUIPPED, SLIDE DUSTCOVER BACK TO ACCESS FITTING

② *TWIST*

③ *BLOW*   COMPRESSED AIR

④ REMOVAL TOOL

OR

⑤   CLIPS

INSTALLATION

①

②

③

④ IF EQUIPPED, REPOSITION DUSTCOVER AFTER SERVICE

Figure 19-18   Removal and installation techniques for quick-connect fittings.

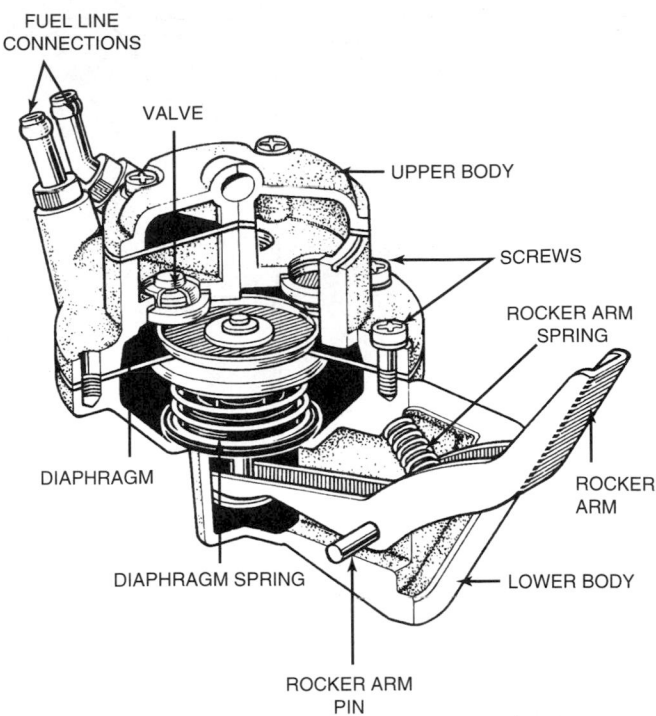

Figure 19-19. Look at this serviceable fuel pump. Although most mechanical fuel pumps are now simply replaced, learn the name of each part. (Toyota)

Troubleshooting Electric Fuel Pumps

Make sure that electric power is reaching the pump before condemning it. Many pumps are operated by a **fuel pump relay.** Check the relay by bypassing it to determine whether the pump operates. If the pump begins working, the relay is defective. Also check the pump fuse and all wires for good connections. **Figure 19-22** shows a pump relay and fuse. Another often overlooked area is the fuel pump ground. Many electric fuel pumps are grounded through the mounting bracket. Check the bracket mounting screws or ground circuit for tightness.

Testing Electric Fuel Pumps

The procedure for checking an electric fuel pump is generally similar to that for checking a mechanical fuel pump. Since pump pressures are higher than with mechanical pumps, the pressure gauge should be designed to read higher pressures. Refer to **Figure 19-23.** Since pressures are so much higher, the volume is assumed to be sufficient if the pressure is correct. When stopped, there is no residual line pressure. Do not run electric pumps without fuel. When performing electrical checks, follow the manufacturer's procedures to avoid damage to parts and to obtain correct test readings.

If a fuel pump appears to be stuck, try lightly tapping it with a wrench or a small hammer (do not pound, a light tap is all that is needed). If the pump begins working, replace it. The pump was stuck and will probably stick again.

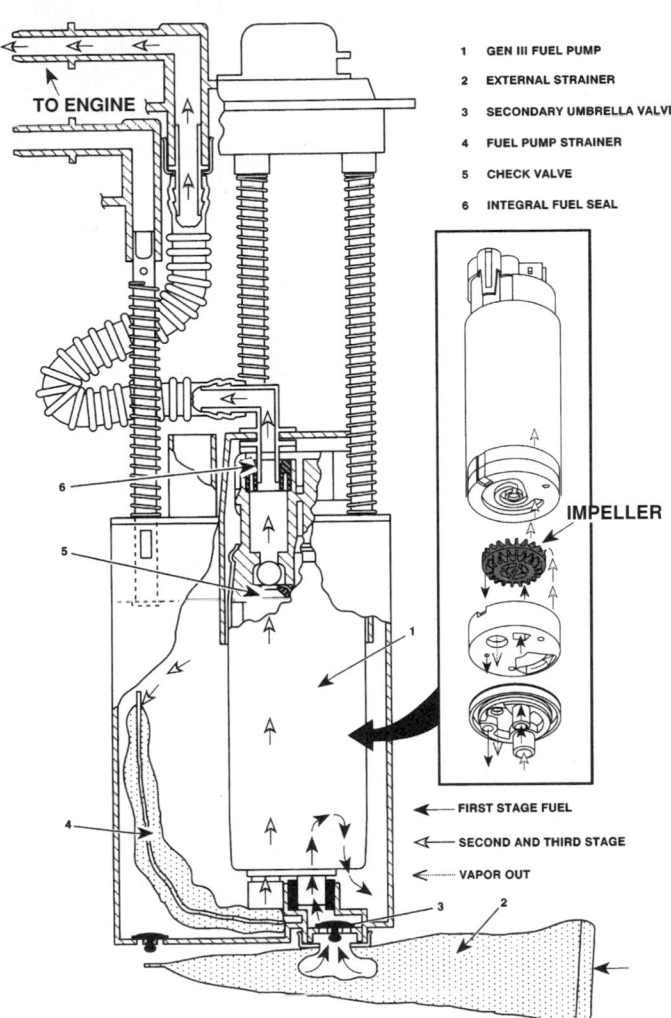

Figure 19-20. A cutaway view of an impeller-type electric fuel pump and related parts. Handle these units carefully to prevent damage. (Cadillac)

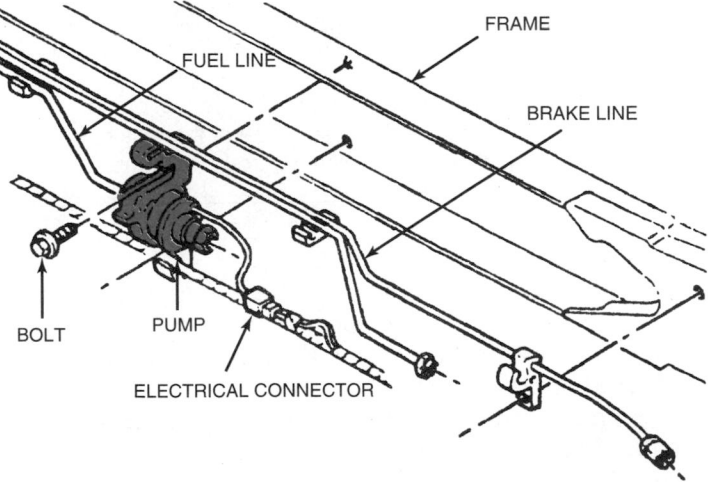

Figure 19-21. This electric fuel pump is mounted on the inside of the vehicle's frame.

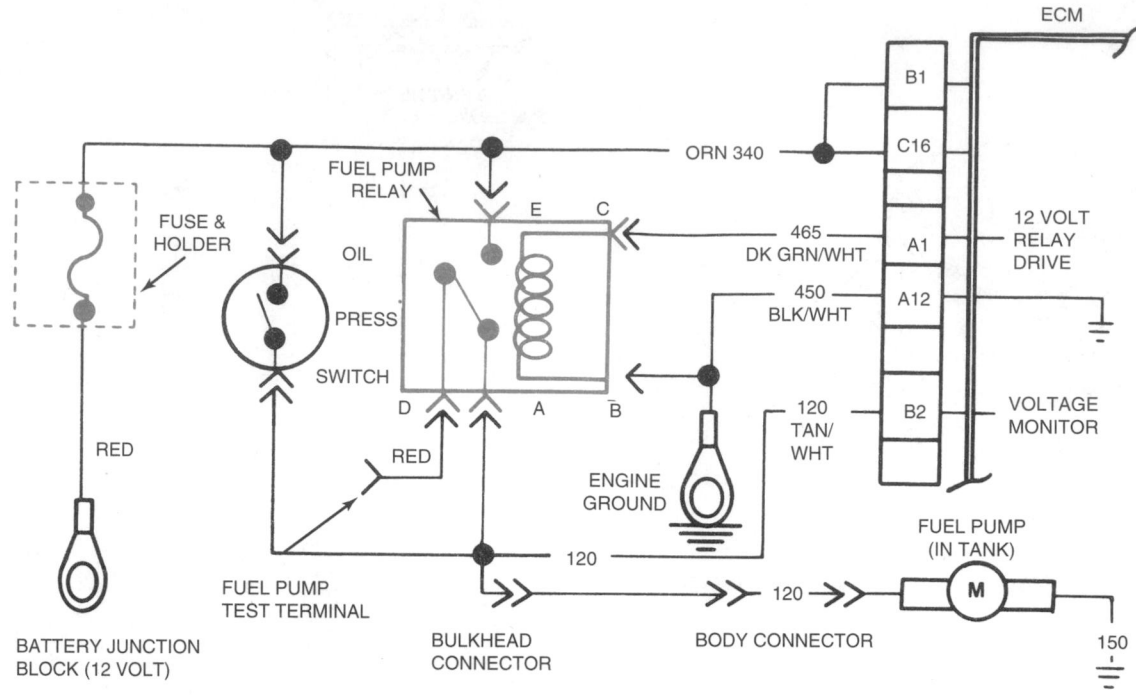

Figure 19-22. An electric fuel pump circuit schematic. Note the fuse and fuel pump relay. This system is controlled by the electronic control module. (AC-Delco)

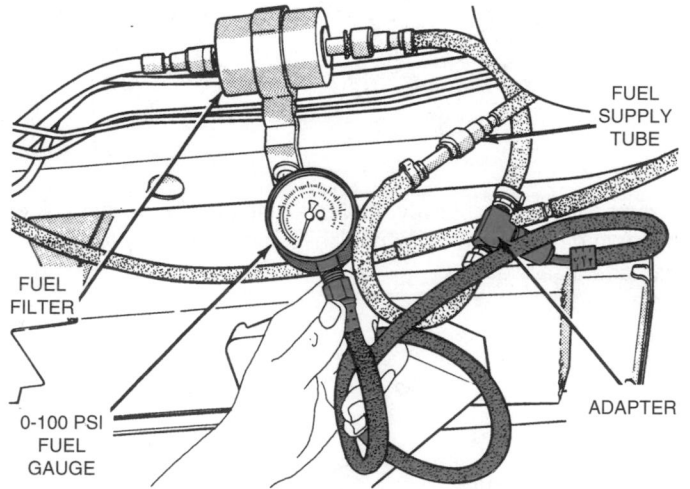

Figure 19-23. This technician is obtaining a fuel pump pressure reading with a fuel pressure gauge that has been attached to the fuel supply line coming from the pump.

Electric Fuel Pump Service

Most electric fuel pumps are replaced as a unit, and no service is possible. A few pumps can be at least partially serviced. The manufacturer's service manual should be checked before discarding the pump.

Before replacing any electric pump, disconnect the battery cable. To replace an inline pump, bleed off all pressure and disconnect the fuel and electric lines. To replace an in-tank pump, remove the lock ring holding the pump assembly to the tank. Replacement is the reverse of removal.

Electric Fuel Pump Inertia Switch

Some vehicles use an *inertia switch* to turn off the electric fuel pump during an accident. In a typical inertia switch, a steel ball is held in place by a magnet. See **Figure 19-24.** On impact, the ball breaks away, rolls up a ramp, and strikes a target plate. The target plate opens an electrical switch which turns the fuel pump off. The electrical switch must be manually reset before restarting the vehicle. A digital volt/ohm meter can be used to test the electric fuel pump inertia switch. If the voltage reading across the electrical contacts exceeds 0.3 volts when the circuit is energized, the switch must be replaced.

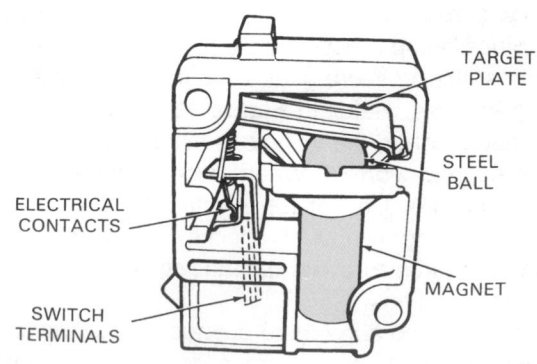

Figure 19-24. Cutaway view of an inertia switch. Caution: If you see or smell fuel, do not reset the switch until the fuel leak is corrected. (Ford)

Fuel Filter Service

Filters play an important part in maintaining a properly running engine. Clean or change at recommended intervals or as needed. Most modern *fuel filters* are intended to be thrown away instead of being cleaned and reinstalled. Some utilize an internal *paper* element that may be changed. Others require disposal of the entire unit, **Figures 19-25** and **19-26.**

The bowl-type filter pictured in **Figure 19-26** is found on older vehicles and some off-road equipment. The paper element shown should be discarded when clogged. Other element types, such as the *screen, porous bronze, cuno,* and *ceramic,* can be cleaned and blown dry. Some carburetor designs incorporate a filter in the fuel inlet, as shown in **Figure 19-27.**

Many diesel fuel systems utilize a filter that not only removes rust and dirt particles, but also contains a *water trap* that protects against the entry of water which can cause serious damage if it gets into the injector pump. One

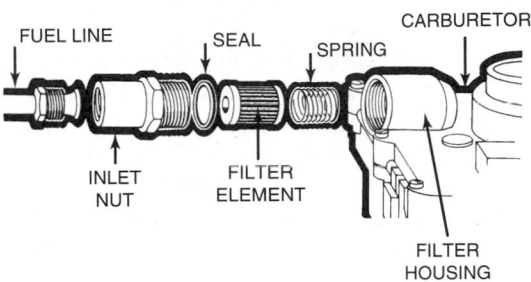

Figure 19-27.   One type of carburetor inlet fuel filter. (Fram)

such filter is pictured in **Figure 19-28.** This particular filter incorporates a *water sensor* to actuate a dash light when water is present and has a provision for draining off any water which may accumulate. When apparent fuel pump troubles occur, check filters to make certain they are clean. Some require presoaking to remove filter particles, which can clog injectors. Always check for leaks after servicing a fuel filter.

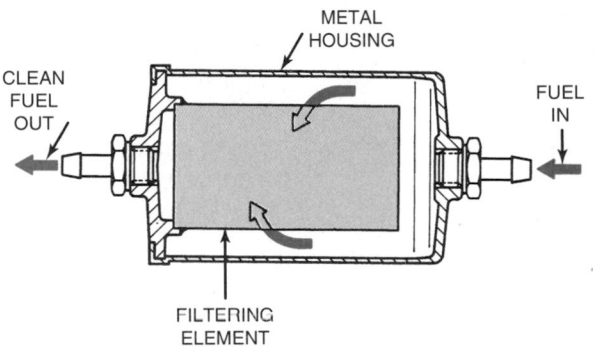

Figure 19-25.   A cross section of a gasoline filter. The entire filter assembly must be discarded when clogged. Be sure to install the new filter with the flow arrows pointing in the right direction. (Mercedes-Benz)

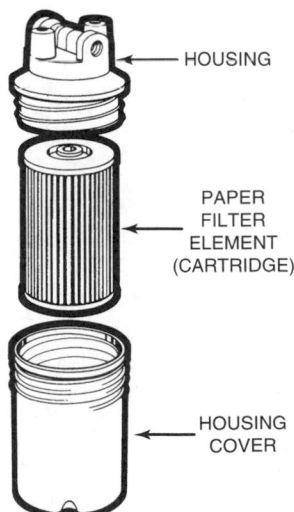

Figure 19-26.   Exploded view of a gasoline filter that uses a disposable paper element. On this filter assembly, the housing cover is unscrewed to expose the filter. Always check for leaks after replacing the element. (Fram)

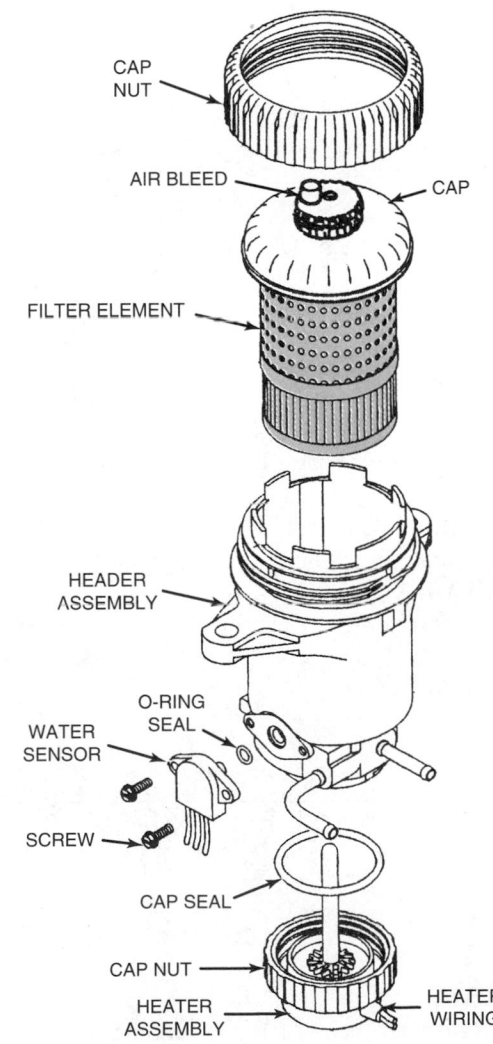

Figure 19-28.   Exploded view of a diesel fuel filter assembly. This setup uses a water sensor, which triggers a dash light to warn the driver of water in the fuel. Note the fuel heater, which is used to help thin cold fuel. The heater also helps prevent wax buildup, which can clog the filter. (GM)

Vapor Lock

Vapor lock is a condition in which the lines or pump becomes heated to the point that the fuel inside begins to vaporize. This vaporization causes the formation of tiny air bubbles. If enough air bubbles are formed, fuel flow to the carburetor can be reduced, or stopped in some cases. Some causes of vapor lock include routing fuel lines too close to the exhaust manifold, excessive looping and bending of the fuel line, or failure to reinstall a heat shield.

When vapor lock occurs, it can be temporarily cured by stopping the engine and placing cold wet rags on the lines and pump. As soon as the fuel cools, the vapor condenses and the car should start. To correct the situation, determine the cause for the vapor lock condition and make any necessary repairs. Sometimes, gasoline manufacturers will increase the **volatility** (able to vaporize) of gasoline during cold weather. During a sudden hot spell or if the vehicle is driven through a hot area, the gasoline can vapor lock even if the fuel lines are correctly mounted. This can sometimes be cured by using high octane gasoline, which has a lower volatility.

Tech Talk

In the past, automotive components such as fuel pumps, water pumps, alternators, and carburetors were always rebuilt when they began causing problems. Today, however, it is sometimes cheaper and easier to replace components than to rebuild them. Major components that are commonly replaced instead of being rebuilt include alternators, starters, water and fuel pumps, carburetors, fuel injectors, air conditioner compressors, and power steering pumps. Sometimes, complete engines and transmissions are replaced instead of being rebuilt.

Nevertheless, it is still possible to repair some defective major components by replacing a few simple parts. Many alternators, for instance, can be restored to service by replacing the bearings and brushes. It is still common to rebuild brake system wheel cylinders. Carburetors can often be rebuilt successfully.

Some units used on modern vehicles, such as master cylinders and water pumps, should not be rebuilt unless a new part is not available. A good rule of thumb that will save time in the long run is to rebuild a component once only. If it begins to give you trouble again, replace it.

Summary

Fuel tanks are constructed of treated steel or plastic. Use a special siphoning device to remove fuel from tank and store in an approved container. Try to siphon as much fuel as possible from the tank prior to removal. Metal fuel tanks can sometimes be repaired by soldering, brazing, or cold patching. Remember that fuel tanks can explode with great force.

Fuel lines can be cleaned by forcing air through them. Use the proper size and type replacement tubing or hose. Route fuel lines away from hot areas or use heat baffles. Attach all fuel lines securely and avoid cross threading.

Fuel pumps are either mechanically or electrically operated. Some electric fuel pumps are located in the tank. Test fuel pumps for pressure, flow volume, and inlet vacuum. Use the proper tools and take care to prevent a fire from spraying or leaking fuel. When replacing a pump, obtain as much information as possible to select the correct pump. Support all fittings while tightening the flare nut.

Keep all fuel filters clean. Service the filter or replace if of the disposable type. Vapor lock can slow or completely stop delivery of fuel to the engine. Protect fuel lines from heat to minimize the chance for vapor lock.

Know These Terms

Fuel tanks	Electric fuel pump
Plastic	Diaphragm
Siphoning	Bellows
Fuel gauge sender	Impeller
Carbon canister	Roller-vane
Lock ring	Fuel pump relay
Nonvented	Inertia switch
Inert	Fuel filters
Toxic	Paper
Cold patching	Screen
Bulged	Porous bronze
Fuel lines	Cuno
Fuel pump	Ceramic
Mechanical fuel pump	Water trap
Fluid pressure	Water sensor
Static pressure	Vapor lock
Pump volume	Volatility
Inlet vacuum	

Review Questions—Chapter 19

Do not write in this book. Write your answers on a separate sheet of paper.

1. What is the most important thing to remember about removing and repairing a fuel tank?
   (A) Some tanks are sealed.
   (B) Most tanks are held by straps.
   (C) Gasoline is extremely dangerous.
   (D) Tanks have electrical connections.

2. If the inside walls of a fuel tank are rusted, the tank should be _____.
   (A) discarded
   (B) soldered
   (C) steam cleaned
   (D) blown out with air

3. When cleaning a fuel line, blow from the _____ and towards the _____.

4. Fuel pumps should always be tested for _____ and _____.

5. Before disassembly, the fuel pump halves should be _____ to ensure correct _____.
6. When installing the fuel pump, be sure that the _____ contact surface bears against the cam or eccentric.
7. Inertia switches will turn off the electric fuel pump under what conditions?
   (A) High fuel system pressure.
   (B) Low fuel system pressure.
   (C) An accident.
   (D) All of the above.
8. Explain what causes vapor lock.
9. Diesel fuel systems often employ a special sensor to alert the driver that there is _____ in the fuel system.
10. When removing fuel supply lines from fuel injected cars, relieve the residual pressure in the _____.
   (A) fuel tank
   (B) fuel lines
   (C) intake manifold
   (D) cooling system

ASE-Type Questions
1. Volatility is the ability of gasoline to _____.
   (A) burn
   (B) vaporize
   (C) condense
   (D) absorb water
2. Fuel tanks are usually attached to the vehicle with _____.
   (A) metal straps
   (B) bolts or threaded studs
   (C) an interference fit between the frame and body
   (D) spot welds or rivets
3. Brazing or soldering a fuel tank is _____.
   (A) somewhat safe
   (B) slightly hazardous
   (C) extremely dangerous
   (D) completely safe
4. Technician A says that it is OK to begin siphoning by sucking on the outlet hose. Technician B says that it is OK to begin siphoning by blowing into a hose in the filler opening. Who is right?
   (A) A only.
   (B) B only.
   (C) Both A & B.
   (D) Neither A nor B.
5. If the fuel pump has a vapor return line, what must be done before testing?
   (A) Remove the pump from the engine.
   (B) Pinch off the vapor return line.
   (C) Drain the fuel tank.
   (D) Disconnect the inlet line from the pump.

6. Electric fuel pumps can be mounted _____.
   (A) on the engine
   (B) in the fuel tank
   (C) on the vehicle frame
   (D) All of the above.
7. Technician A says that all fuel pumps may be rebuilt. Technician B says that the pump fasteners should never be tightened to force the fuel pump into place. Who is right?
   (A) A only.
   (B) B only.
   (C) Both A & B.
   (D) Neither A nor B.
8. When fuel pump trouble is suspected, all of the following should be checked before condemning the pump, EXCEPT:
   (A) fuel tank vent.
   (B) fuel lines.
   (C) fuel filters.
   (D) fuel octane.
9. Technician A says that carbon tetrachloride fumes can be deadly. Technician B says that a fuel tank can be filled with water to prevent an explosion. Who is right?
   (A) A only.
   (B) B only.
   (C) Both A & B.
   (D) Neither A nor B.
10. Technician A says that some push-on fittings must be removed with a special tool. Technician B says that push-on fittings should always be tightened with a low reading torque wrench. Who is right?
   (A) A only.
   (B) B only.
   (C) Both A & B.
   (D) Neither A nor B.

Suggested Activities
1. Draw a schematic of fuel flow from the fuel tank to the engine on a carbureted engine. Include all filters, pumps, and lines.
2. Check fuel pump pressure on a vehicle selected by your instructor and write down your readings.
3. Discuss the fuel pump pressure readings obtained in Activity 2 with your classmates. What do the readings reveal about the condition of the fuel pump?
4. Write step-by-step instructions for checking mechanical fuel pumps and electric fuel pumps.
5. Inspect a fuel filter for clogging. Discuss your findings with your instructor or the class.

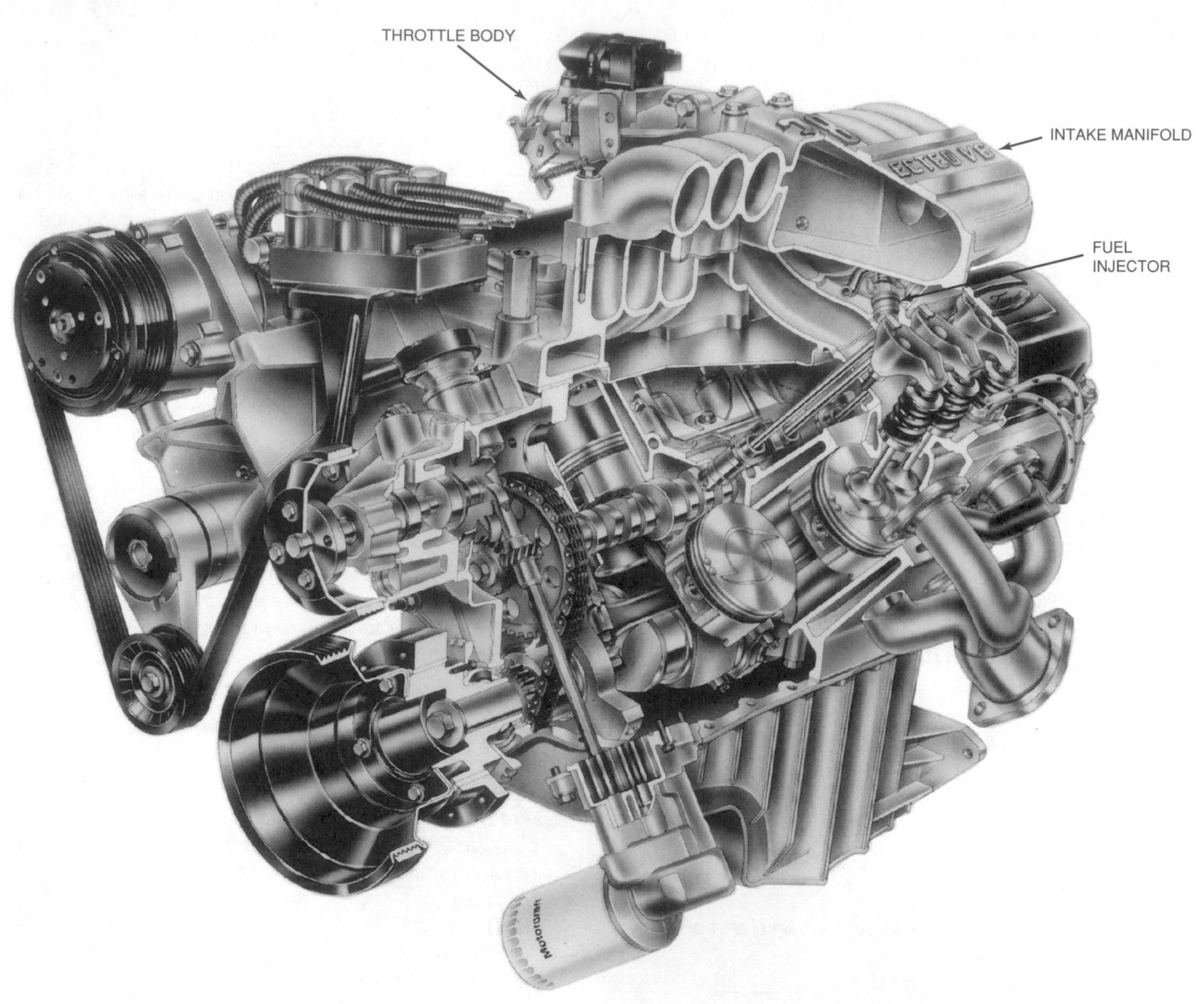

THROTTLE BODY

INTAKE MANIFOLD

FUEL INJECTOR

Cutaway of a 3.8-liter V-6 engine. This engine is equipped with a sequential, multiport fuel injection system. (Ford)

20

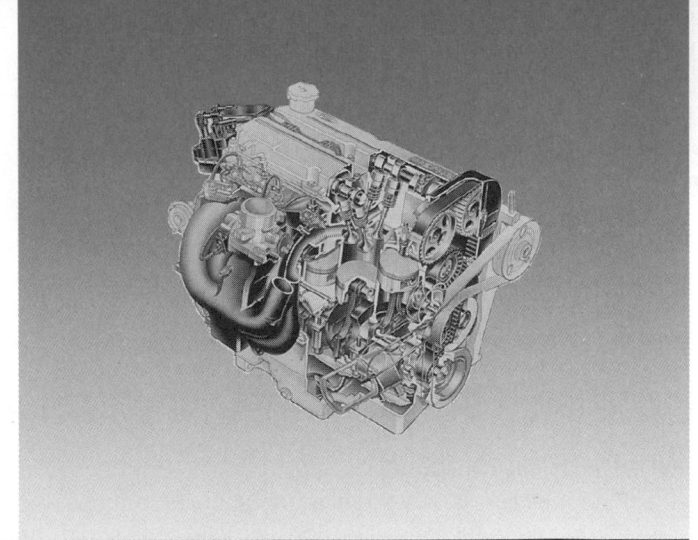

Fuel Injection

After studying this chapter, you will be able to:
- Explain mechanical fuel injection construction, operation, and service.
- Describe the construction, operation, and service of pulsed and continuous electronic fuel injection.
- Explain diesel injection construction, operation, and service.
- Describe the construction, operation, and service of turbochargers.
- Service different types of air cleaners.
- Perform a fuel mileage test.

This chapter will cover gasoline and diesel fuel injection system service. *Fuel injection* is the process of precisely spraying fuel into the intake manifold or combustion chamber. Fuel injection allows for precise fuel mixtures by closely controlling injector operation. Fuel injection systems can compensate for many of the conditions which can affect carburetors, such as air pressure, temperature, humidity, and even road grades and turns. Fuel injection has become much more common in gasoline engines in the last few years. Diesel engines have always used fuel injection. Every car and light truck currently sold in the United States is fuel injected.

Fuel Injection Service Precautions

Remember that the fuel lines in a fuel injection system may be under pressure and that fuels are always flammable. Become familiar with the precautions below before reading further in this chapter. Other cautions will be given as they are needed.

- Disconnect the battery ground cable before working on the fuel lines or any part of the fuel injection system.
- Carefully bleed off line pressure by the method approved by the vehicle's manufacturer.
- Cover any fittings or bleeders with a clean cloth to catch any pressurized fuel that might come out.
- Clean up any fuel spills immediately. Remember that gasoline and diesel fuel are extremely flammable and explosive. Dispose of fuel-soaked cloth properly. Do

not allow any sources of ignition near the fuel system or spilled gasoline.

Why Fuel Injection Is Needed

Many persons wonder why fuel injection is necessary, since carburetors (covered in Chapter 21) have had a long and successful career and, until relatively recently, they were the only way to deliver fuel to a gasoline engine. To explain why fuel injection has replaced the carburetor, it is necessary to understand three things.

- To burn, fuel must be broken up into small droplets, or atomized, and thoroughly mixed with the air, or vaporized.
- Air and fuel must be mixed in the proper proportions, or *air-fuel ratios,* to provide proper burning under various engine operating conditions. Improper burning wastes fuel, reduces power, and increases emissions.
- Modern vehicles must have the air-fuel ratio closely controlled to meet government mandated emissions and fuel economy laws.

Carburetors often cannot supply an ideal air-fuel mixture. Since the main circuits in a carburetor depend on air pressure differences to operate, they are affected by atmospheric pressure, engine tune, and many other factors. Also, the carburetor is slow to respond to changes in air pressure, temperature, and throttle opening. Many additional systems are used to assist the basic carburetor circuits in decreasing fuel consumption and exhaust emissions. These systems also solve driveability, starting, and performance problems by controlling the carburetor mixture.

In the past, the simplicity and lower cost of the carburetor held back the development of fuel injection. Early attempts at fuel injection systems did not increase power or mileage, were expensive to manufacture and service, and were prone to problems from small amounts of dirt and water which would not affect a carburetor. Two factors caused fuel injection to displace the carburetor:

- Carburetor mixtures could not be controlled precisely in order to meet increased standards for emissions and mileage.

• Increased use of electronics allowed fuel injection systems to be precisely controlled.

Fuel injection can maintain precise control of the fuel mixture. This permits better gas mileage and lowered exhaust emission levels. Modern manufacturing methods and improved fuel filtering have made fuel injection much more effective.

What Is Fuel Injection?

Fuel injection is a system which supplies a measured quantity of fuel into the valve port, or intake manifold, on gasoline engines and into the cylinder on diesel engines. This process always involves one or more *fuel injectors.* The injection process breaks into very small particles, or *atomizes,* the fuel. It then *vaporizes,* or mixes it with the air moving into the cylinder. This allows the engine to maintain a *stoichiometric* air-fuel mix of 14.7 to 1 in the cylinder. This air-fuel ratio will give optimum engine performance while maintaining low exhaust emissions.

Figure 20-1 shows a typical gasoline injection system where fuel is injected into the intake valve port area. **Figure 20-2** shows a diesel injection system where fuel is injected directly into the combustion chamber. Fuel injection systems can be divided into two main groups, electronic and mechanical. Modern gasoline engines use *electronic*

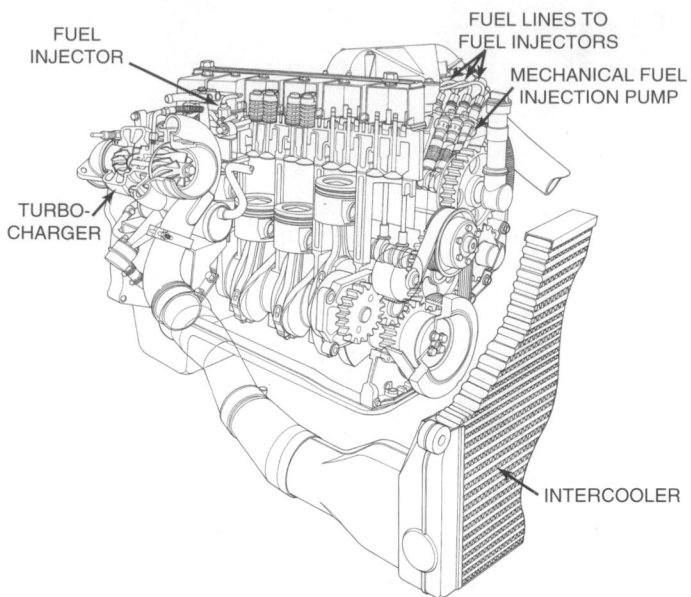

Figure 20-2. Cutaway of an inline, six-cylinder diesel engine that incorporates a mechanical fuel injection system. The fuel injection pump can produce fuel pressures of 17,405 psi (120,000 kPa) to the fuel injectors. (Dodge)

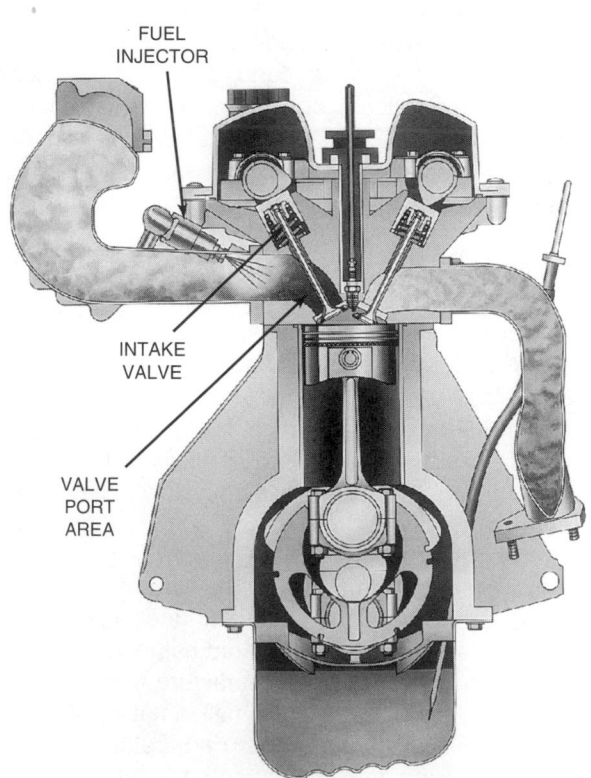

Figure 20-1. Gasoline engine incorporating fuel injection. The fuel injector is spraying fuel into the intake valve port area. The fuel is drawn into the cylinder with air during the intake stroke. (Saturn)

fuel injection systems. *Mechanical fuel injection* is used on diesel engines and a few older gasoline engines.

Electronic Fuel Injection

The electronic fuel injection system relies on an electric fuel pump to provide the fuel system pressure. While there are numerous electronic fuel injection systems, they can be classified under two basic types:

• *Pulsed injection.* Air/fuel ratio is controlled by varying the length of time that the injector is open.
• *Continuous injection.* The injector is always open and the air-fuel ratio is controlled by varying the fuel pressure at the injector.

Pulsed Injection Systems

Injectors used on the pulsed injection system always contain an internal electrical solenoid. The injector valves are opened for a very brief period of time, usually thousandths of a second. The injectors are held closed during the remainder of the time. Most pulse injection systems are designed so that the injector opening is timed with the operation of the ignition system. The more often the ignition system fires the plugs, the more often the injectors are opened. This matches fuel flow to engine speed.

On pulse fuel injection systems, the length of time that the injector is open is changed by varying the length of the pulse or electrical signal from the engine control module. The control module bases its signal to the injector on inputs from various engine and drive train sensors. The functions of the more common fuel injection related sensors are discussed in more detail later in this chapter.

Throttle Body Injector Systems

Some engines use a throttle body assembly containing one or two fuel injectors. The throttle body is mounted on the intake manifold, usually in the same position formerly occupied by the carburetor. These systems are referred to by various names, including **throttle body injection** (TBI), **single-point injection,** or **central fuel injection** (CFI). These systems inject fuel ahead of the throttle valve. A typical single unit injector is shown in **Figure 20-3.**

Multiport Injection Systems

Most of the latest injection systems use one injector per cylinder. Each injector is located inside the intake manifold or in the cylinder head, close to the intake valve. This system is referred to as **multiport injection** system. Other names used for the multiport system can include **multipoint injection, sequential fuel injection,** and **port fuel injection.** A typical multiport injector rail assembly is shown in **Figure 20-4.**

These systems are usually timed to open each injector just before the associated intake valve opens. A version of the multiport injector system uses one central fuel injector with lines connecting it to outlet nozzles at each intake passage. This system combines the simplicity of the single injector with the more precise fuel control of the multiport system, **Figure 20-5.**

Fuel Injection System Components

The typical modern fuel injection system can be broken into four basic parts: **air induction system, fuel delivery system, electronic control module,** and **electronic sensors.** These parts work together to deliver the right amount of fuel to the engine at the right time.

Air Induction System

The air induction system consists of an **air cleaner assembly, throttle body,** and **intake manifold.** The air

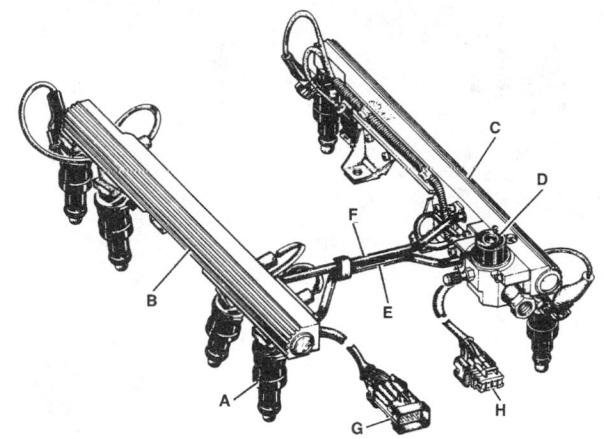

A MPFI INJECTOR ASSEMBLY	E FUEL RETURN TUBE
B FRONT FUEL RAIL ASSEMBLY	F FUEL CROSSOVER TUBE
C REAR FUEL RAIL ASSEMBLY	G FRONT WIRING (RAIL) ASSEMBLY
D PRESSURE REGULATOR AND BASE ASSEMBLY	H REAR WIRING (RAIL) ASSEMBLY

Figure 20-4. A multiport fuel injection (MPFI) setup. Study the various parts and their locations. (Cadillac)

induction system may have a thermostatic air cleaner, covered in detail in Chapter 24. The throttle body section contains the **throttle valve** and idle air control motor or air bypass solenoid. Each controls the amount of air entering the intake manifold. On central fuel injection systems, the throttle body also contains the fuel injection components. The intake manifold forms a closed passageway between the throttle body and the cylinder head. A typical intake manifold and throttle body is pictured in **Figure 20-6.**

Fuel Delivery System

The fuel delivery system provides the fuel which mixes with the air. Pressure is provided by an electric fuel pump, which was covered in Chapter 19. Most systems use only one pump. However, some systems use two pumps, a low-pressure fuel pump that delivers fuel to another pump which in turn develops the pressure needed at the injectors.

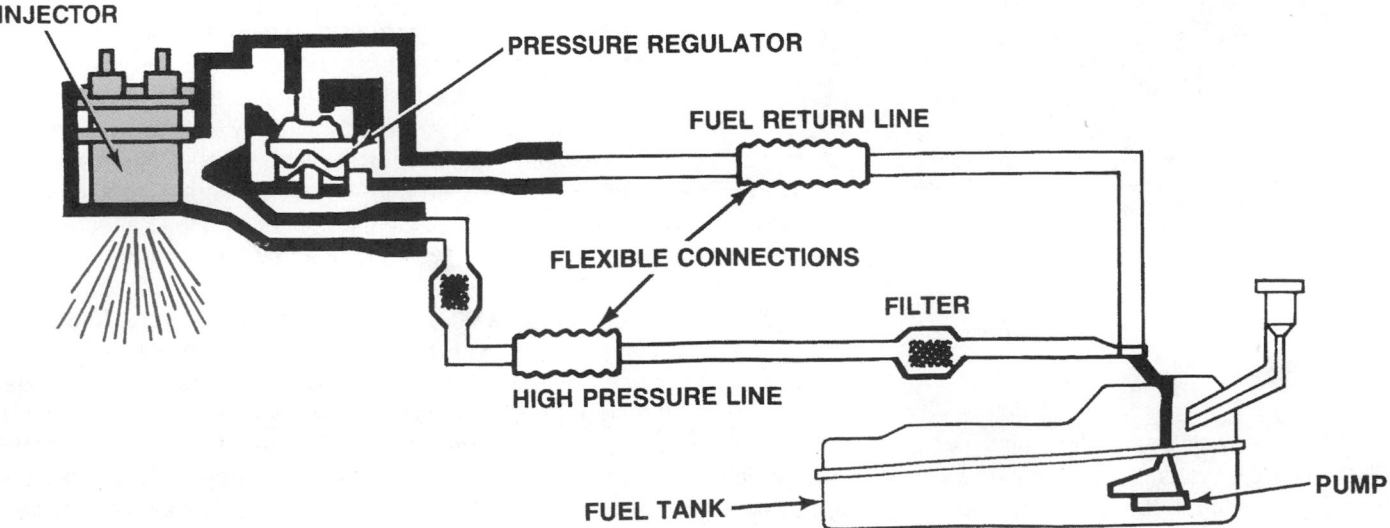

Figure 20-3. A typical single injector mounted in a throttle body fuel injection system. (Champion)

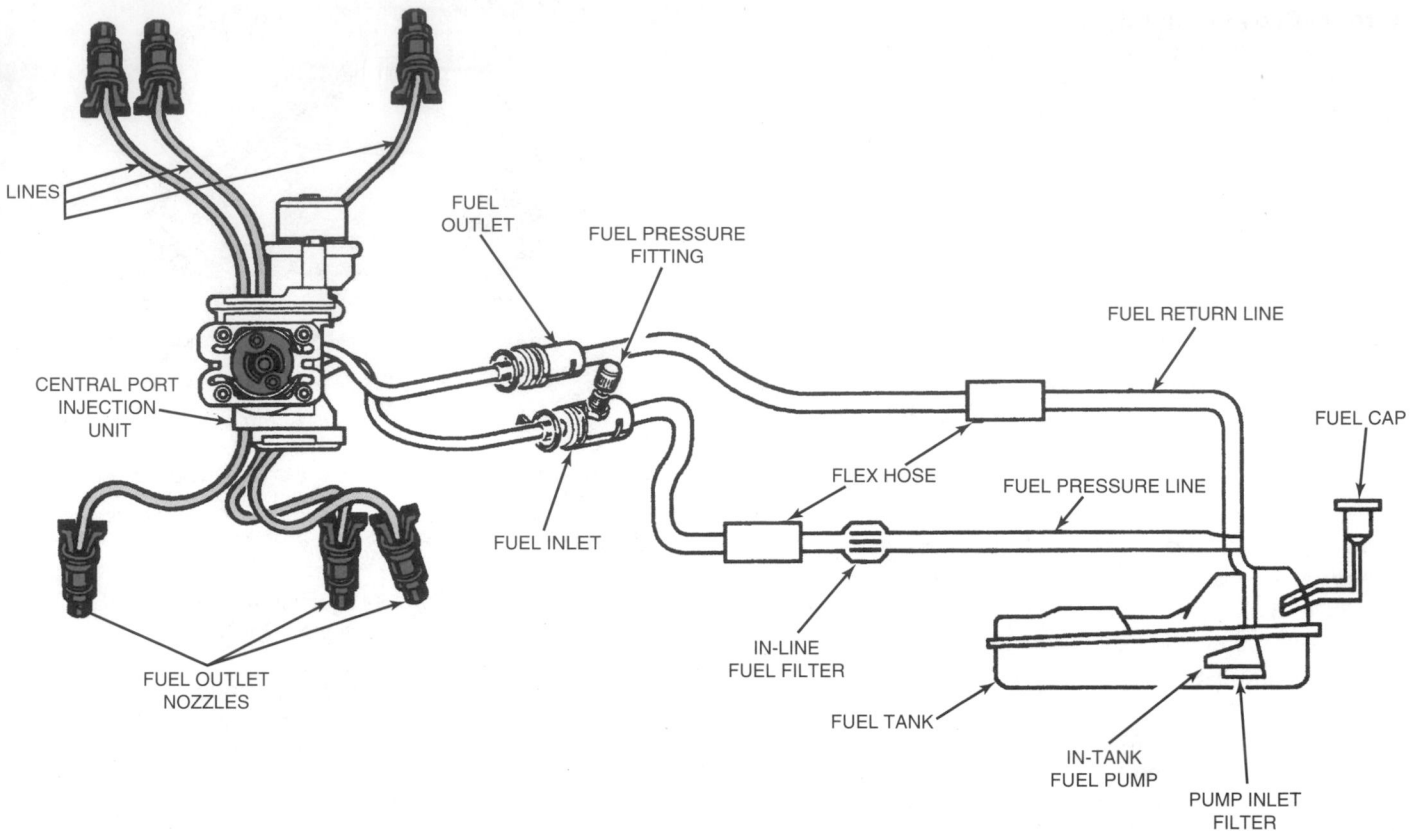

Figure 20-5. Central port fuel injection (CPI) with lines leading to the fuel outlet nozzles. (General Motors)

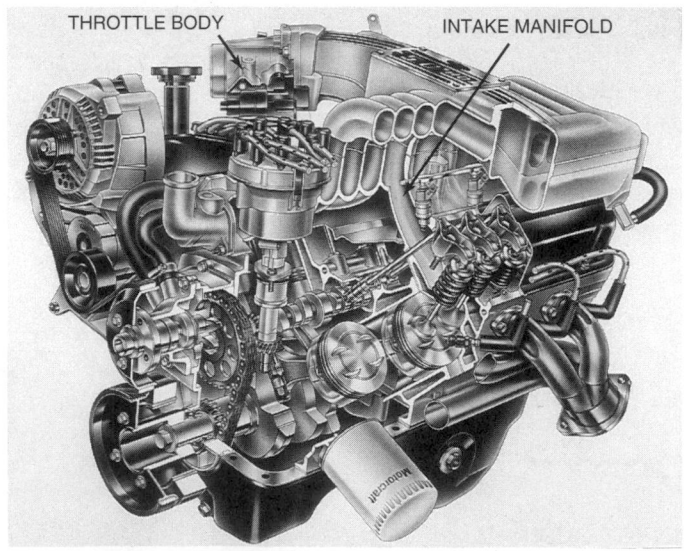

Figure 20-6. A cutaway of a 5.0 liter V-8 engine showing the throttle body and the intake manifold. The air cleaner is not shown. Study the various parts. (Ford)

The fuel delivery system also contains at least one *filter.* Diesel systems also have a *water trap* which removes water from the fuel. A fuel delivery system using a single, in-tank pump is shown in **Figure 20-7.** The in-tank electric pump forces fuel from the tank, through a filter and into the fuel rail. The fuel tank and lines on most newer fuel injected cars are made of plastic. This is to eliminate injector clogging from corroded metal.

Fuel Injection Pressure Regulators

Pressure in some central fuel injection systems is as low as 7 psi (55 kPa), while some multiport systems can reach 60 psi (380 kPa). Injection system pressure is controlled by a *pressure regulator.* The regulator controls fuel pressure by bleeding excess fuel back into the inlet line or fuel tank. The pressure regulators used on most central fuel injection systems are operated by spring pressure.

Pressure regulators on multiport fuel injection systems are vacuum-controlled and are usually connected by a hose to the intake manifold. Changes in engine load affect *intake manifold vacuum,* which is used by the pressure regulator to control fuel pressure. Typical pressure regulators are shown in **Figure 20-8.** In the regulator in **Figure 20-8C,** the spring is assisted by manifold vacuum. High vacuum caused by low engine load allows fuel pressure to unseat the spring easily, keeping fuel pressures low. Low vacuum caused by high engine loads allows the spring to apply pressure to the fuel return valve to keep the fuel pressure high. Note that pressure is controlled by a spring on the regulator in **Figure 20-9.**

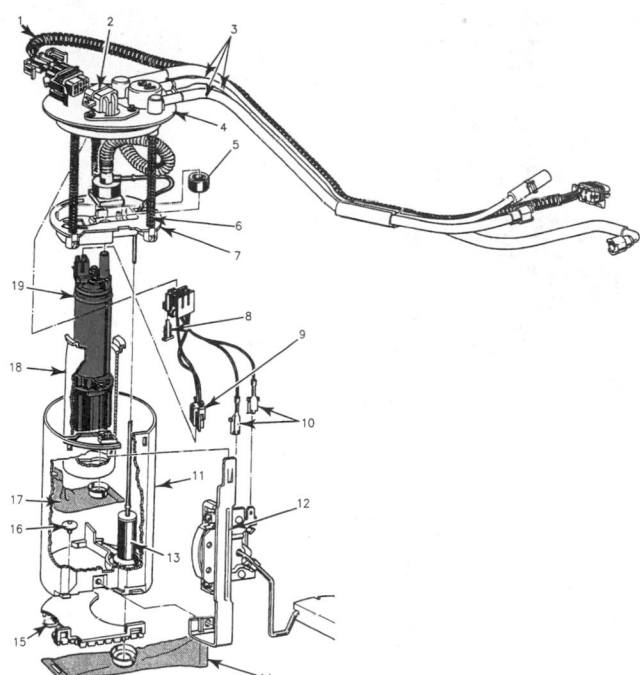

Figure 20-7. A roller-vane, in-tank, electronic fuel pump assembly. 1—Wiring harness. 2—Wiring connector. 3—Fuel pipes. 4—Fuel sender cover assembly. 5—Fuel pump seal/dampener. 6—Fuel pump reservoir support assembly. 7—Fuel pump reservoir retainer. 8—Connector position assurance pin. 9—Fuel pump harness assembly. 10—Fuel level sender harness assembly. 11—Fuel pump fuel reservoir. 12—Fuel level sensor assembly. 13—Pump assembly. 14—Fuel sender strainer. 15—Fuel sender bumper pad. 16—Valve (secondary umbrella valve)-fuel pump reservoir inlet check. 17—Pump fuel strainer. 18—Fuel pump baffle. 19—Roller vane pump assembly. (Chevrolet)

Fuel Injectors

The fuel injectors receive fuel from the pump or pumps and pressure regulator and spray it into the intake manifold. Injectors can be part of a central fuel system setup, **Figure 20-10,** or installed in the intake manifold and connected to the fuel system through a **fuel rail, Figure 20-11.** The rail is a rigid piece of steel tubing that feeds fuel to the injectors. Some systems use flexible hoses to connect the injector to the fuel rail.

One type of electronic injector is illustrated in **Figure 20-12.** Fuel passes from the fuel rail to the injector via the flex hose A. Filter B is built into the injector. The fuel moves down through the injector until stopped at the **nozzle** (injector outlet) by the **sealing needle** F. When the injector is energized by the control module, the **solenoid winding** C forms a strong magnetic field that attracts the sealing needle armature E and draws it upward against **spring pressure** D. In this injector, the sealing needle F is lifted about .006″ (0.15 mm), allowing fuel to spray out. When de-energized, spring pressure forces the needle closed. The length of time that the injector remains open, often called **pulse width,** is very short and is usually measured in thousandths of a second.

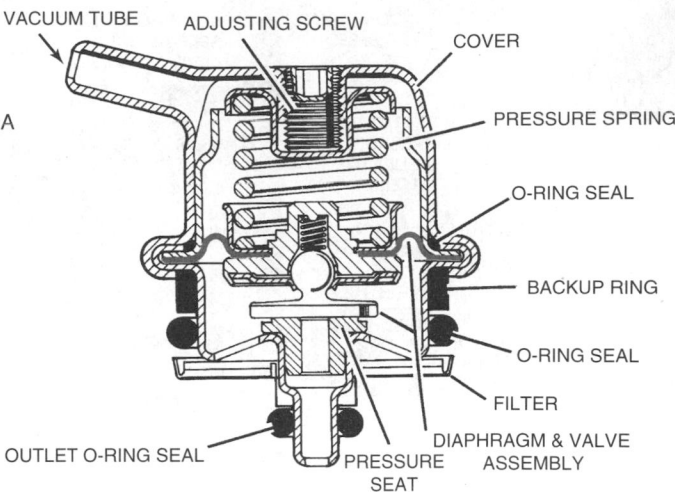

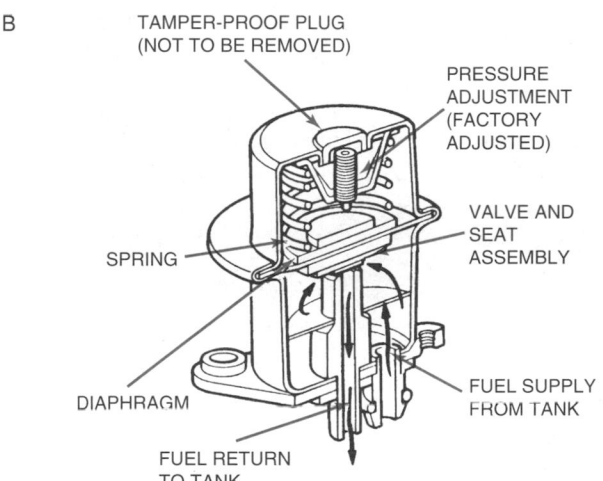

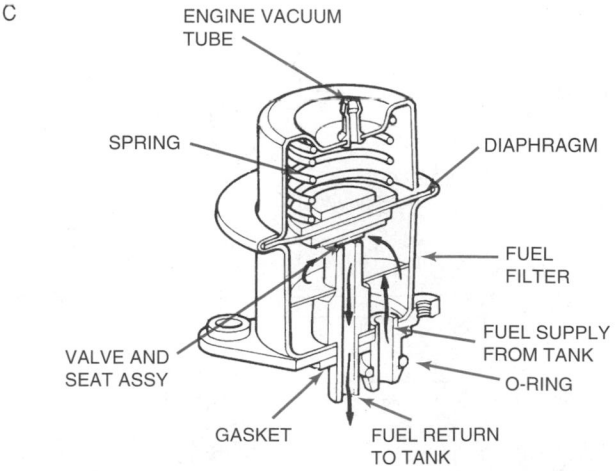

Figure 20-8. Several typical fuel pressure regulators. All three contain a diaphragm. A and C have fuel pressure on one side and engine vacuum on the other. B uses fuel pressure one side and a preset factory spring pressure on the other. Study the construction. (Champion and General Motors)

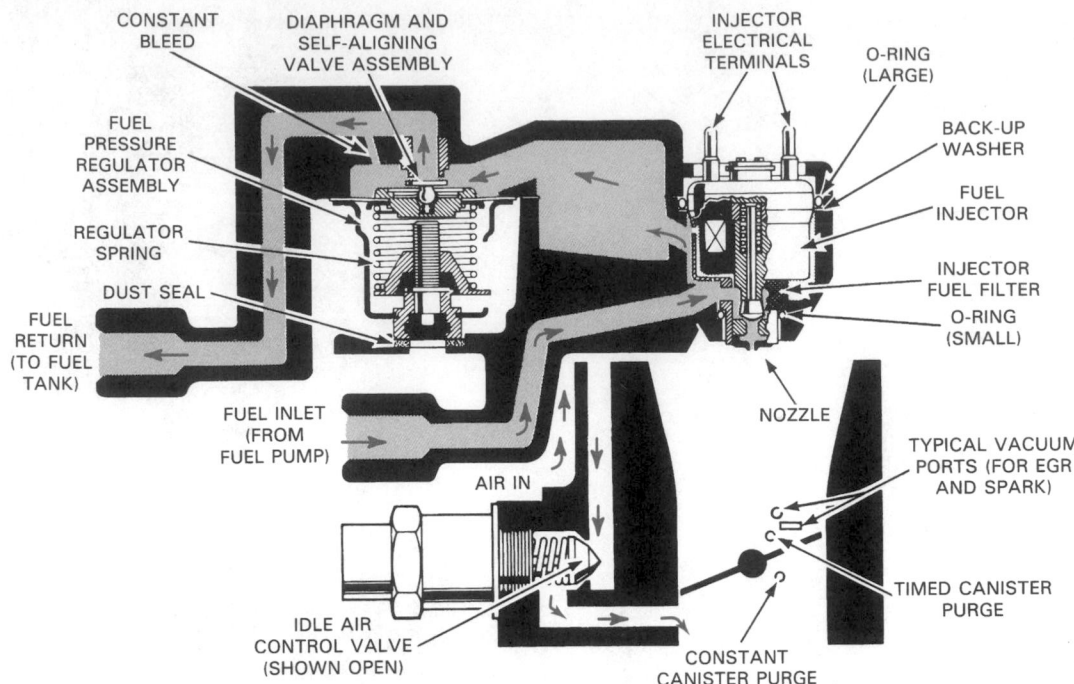

Figure 20-9. One form of fuel pressure regulator. This one maintains a constant 11 PSI pressure. (Buick)

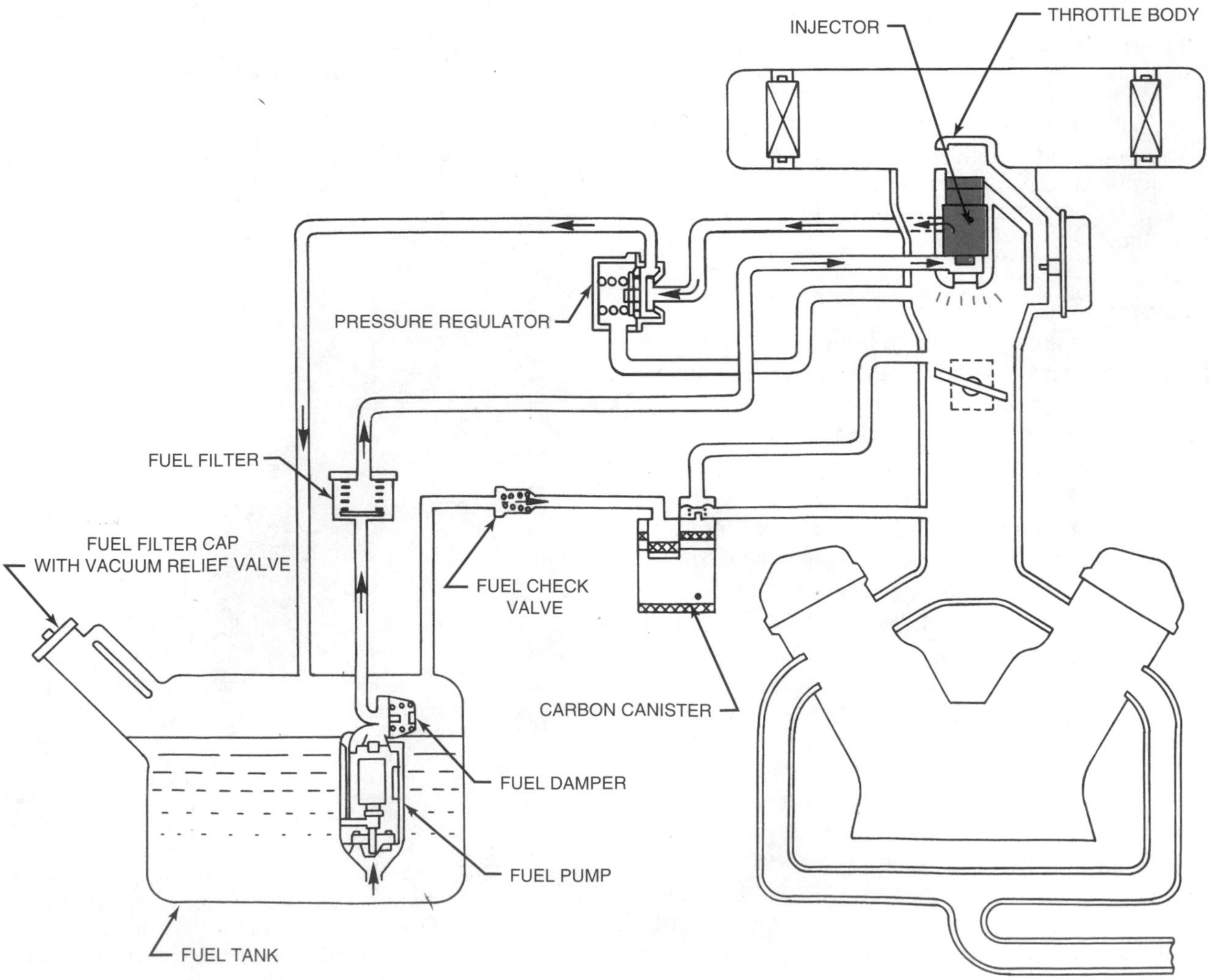

Figure 20-10. Study the components of this central port fuel injection (CPI) system. (Nissan)

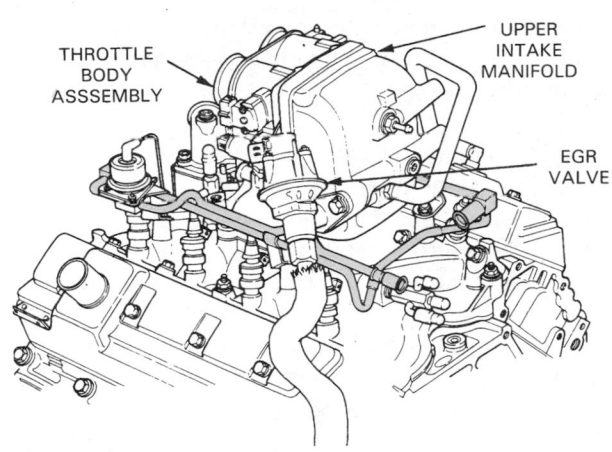 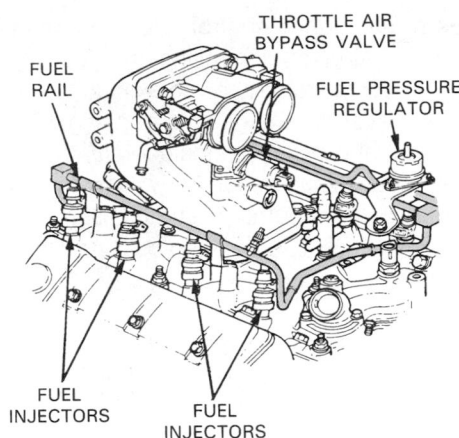

Figure 20-11.   Fuel rail as used on one fuel delivery system. Note how injectors are connected directly to the fuel rail. Others are attached using a flexible hose. (Ford)

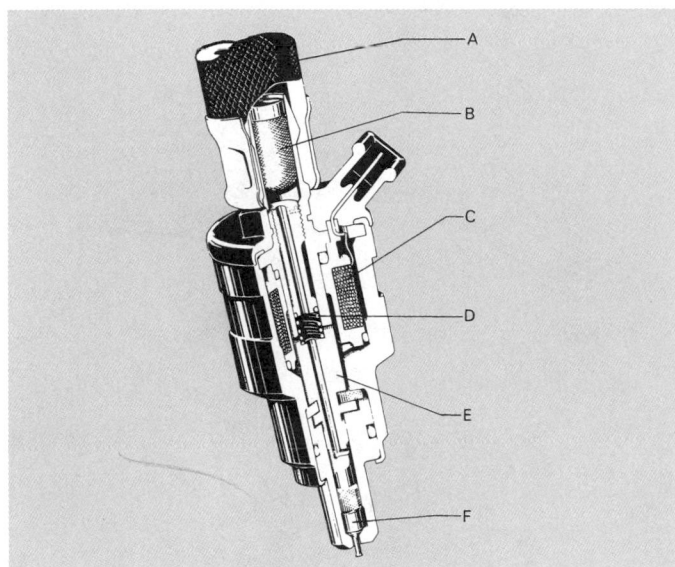

Figure 20-12.   Electrically operated fuel injector. A—Flex hose. B—Filter. C—Winding. D—Needle return spring. E—Needle armature. F—Sealing needle. (Volvo)

Cold Start Aids

In addition to the sensors described, the system can incorporate other units for special functions, such as cold starts. Some systems use a **cold start valve** to add extra fuel to the intake manifold when starting a cold engine. The cold start valve is an extra injector which supplies additional fuel into the intake manifold for a temperature-controlled period of time. The amount of fuel injected is controlled by a thermal switch which regulates the amount of time that the valve is energized, depending on the engine temperature. The valve will be energized for the maximum amount of time when engine temperature is below -5°F (-21°C). As engine temperature increases, the amount of time that the valve is energized will decrease until an engine temperature of 95°F (35°C) is reached. Above this point, the cold start valve will not be energized.

During a cold startup on some systems, an **auxiliary air regulator** admits additional air into the intake manifold to increase idle speed. The auxiliary air regulator is controlled by a thermostatic switch located in the engine water jacket. At a coolant temperature of -13°F (-25°C), the thermostatic switch allows maximum airflow through the air regulator. As the coolant warms up, the air regulator flow is gradually decreased. When the temperature reaches 140°F (60°C), airflow is completely shut off.

On some vehicles with electronic fuel injection, the pulse width is increased to richen the mixture and the idle speed control increases idle. When a normal engine temperature is reached, the computer decreases pulse width and idle speed.

Electronic Control Module

An electronic control module, or ECM, is a solid-state preprogrammed computer, **Figure 20-13.** The module size and complexity can vary depending upon the vehicle. The control module is usually located inside of the car or in the engine compartment and is connected to the wiring system by means of a sealed wiring harness plug.

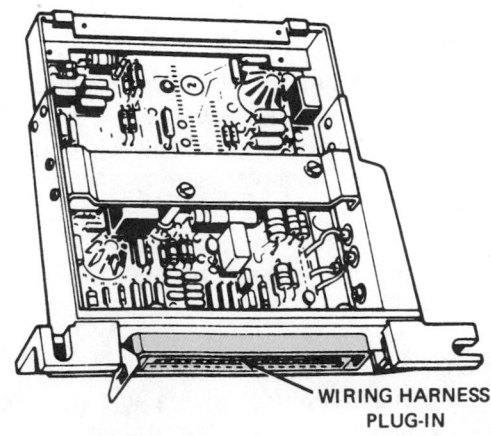

Figure 20-13.   One type of electronic control module. These are precision units not usually serviced in the field (shop) but exchanged for a good unit.

Modern electronic control modules monitor engine systems in addition to controlling the fuel injectors. The electronic control module receives signals from a number of sensors whenever the engine is running, **Figure 20-14.** From this input, the control module evaluates engine needs and makes adjustments accordingly. Some control modules also energize the fuel pump or pumps. Sometimes an electronic control module is referred to as a **powertrain control module,** or PCM.

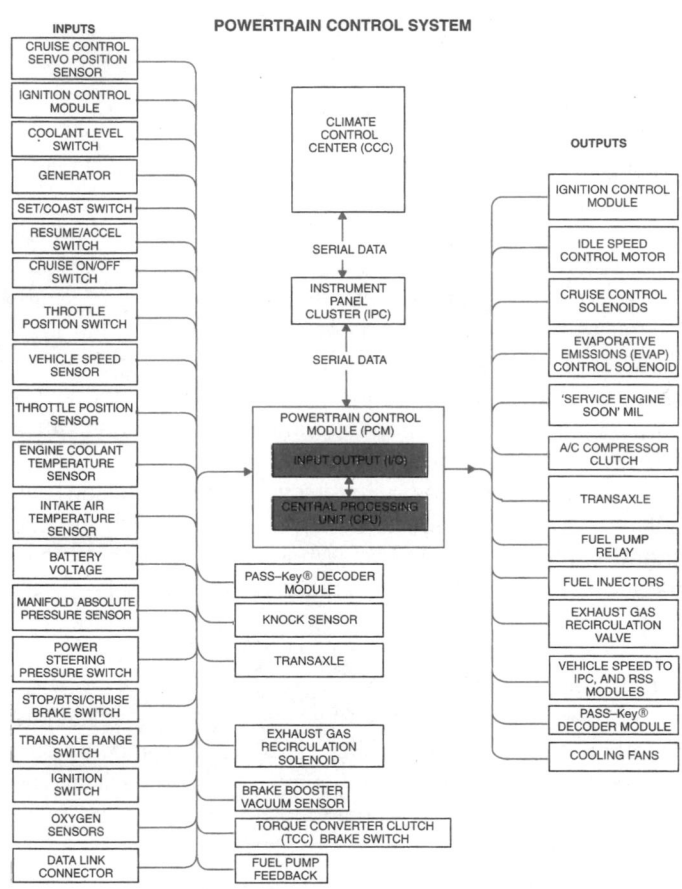

Figure 20-14. A diagram showing inputs from the sensors to the electronic control module (ECM) and outputs from the ECM to various components. (Cadillac)

Electronic Sensors

The electronic **sensors** allow the electronic control module to monitor various engine functions. The number and types of sensors can vary with each vehicle. **Figure 20-14** illustrates some of the sensors used by one system. Note that the information from the sensors enters the control module where it is processed into commands to the various engine systems. Some common sensors are described in the following sections.

Oxygen Sensor

The **oxygen sensor** monitors the amount of oxygen in the engine's exhaust gases. As the oxygen content in the exhaust gases changes, the voltage signal produced by the sensor also changes. The electronic control module uses signals from the oxygen sensor to control the air-fuel mixture. The oxygen sensor is generally mounted in the exhaust manifold.

Engine Speed Sensor

The **engine speed sensor** monitors engine RPM. This information is utilized by the control module along with other sensor input to help determine injector pulse timing and pulse width. Some speed sensors are mounted in the distributor, where they obtain a signal from the rotating distributor shaft. In some cases, the ignition coil or Hall-effect switch provides the signal to the electronic control module. In other systems, the speed sensor is mounted so that it can monitor crankshaft and/or camshaft rotation. These sensors also indicate the position of the crankshaft and camshaft so that the control module can open the injector just before the intake valve opens. See **Figure 20-15.**

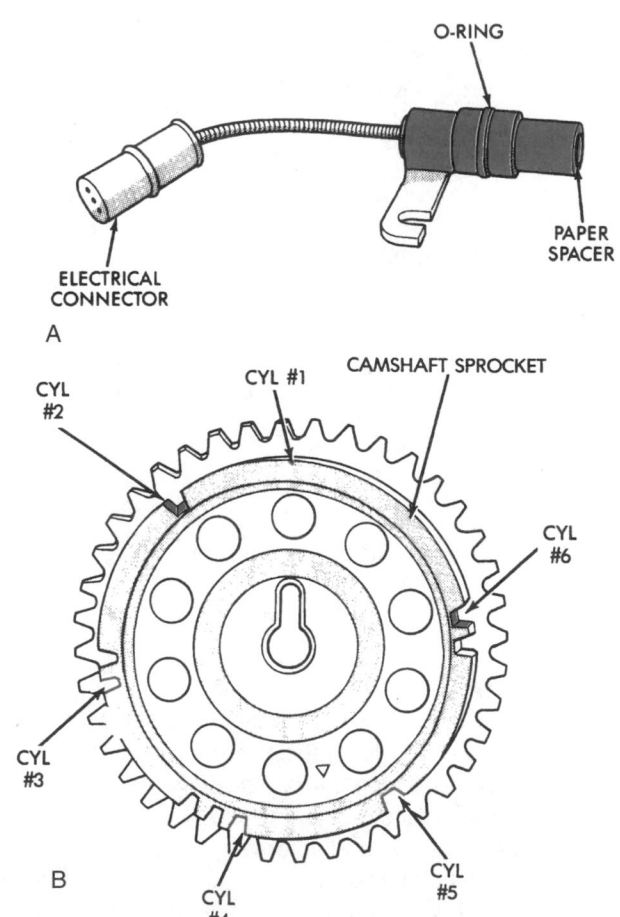

Figure 20-15. A camshaft position sensor. A—Position sensor. B—Notched camshaft sprocket. As the notches in the sprocket pass by the position sensor, electrical pulses are generated and sent to the electronic control module. The voltage produced by this sensor and sprocket ranges from approximately 0.3 volts to 5.0 volts, depending on the speed of camshaft rotation. When an oscilloscope is used in testing, it will produce square waveform patterns for each timing series. Handle these sensors with care.

Throttle Position Sensor

Throttle position is relayed to the control module by the **throttle position sensor.** Throttle position sensors can be either resistance types or transducers. Resistance sensors contain variable resistance modules that send a varying signal to the control module, depending on throttle position, **Figure 20-16.** Transducers vary the input signal by creating a magnetic field which is then modified by movement of a metal rod attached to the throttle linkage. Throttle position sensors are installed on the throttle body and are sometimes referred to by the initials TPS.

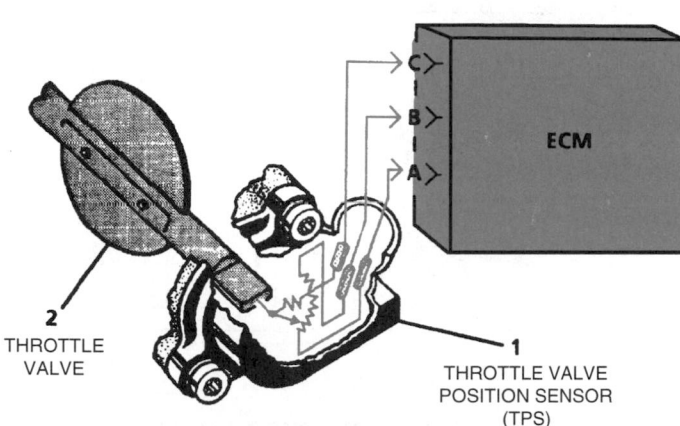

THROTTLE VALVE
2
1
THROTTLE VALVE POSITION SENSOR (TPS)

Figure 20-16. A resistance type throttle position sensor (TPS). An internal potentiometer (variable resistor), will change its resistance (voltage drop or increase) in relation to the throttle position. Voltage then travels to the electronic control module for processing. (General Motors)

Manifold Vacuum and Atmospheric Pressure Sensor

Engine load is transmitted to the control module by means of an intake **manifold vacuum sensor.** The sensor shown in **Figure 20-17** converts manifold vacuum into a small electrical signal. This input allows the control module to increase fuel supply when the engine is under load and needs a rich mixture, and decrease fuel supply when engine load is light.

Many injection systems also have a sensor to measure the outside air pressure, usually called atmospheric pressure. Atmospheric pressure is compared with manifold vacuum by the control module to more closely monitor engine load. The input of this sensor is important when the vehicle is driven to higher and lower altitudes. This sensor is sometimes combined with the manifold vacuum sensor into a single unit, called a **manifold absolute pressure sensor** or MAP sensor, **Figure 20-18.**

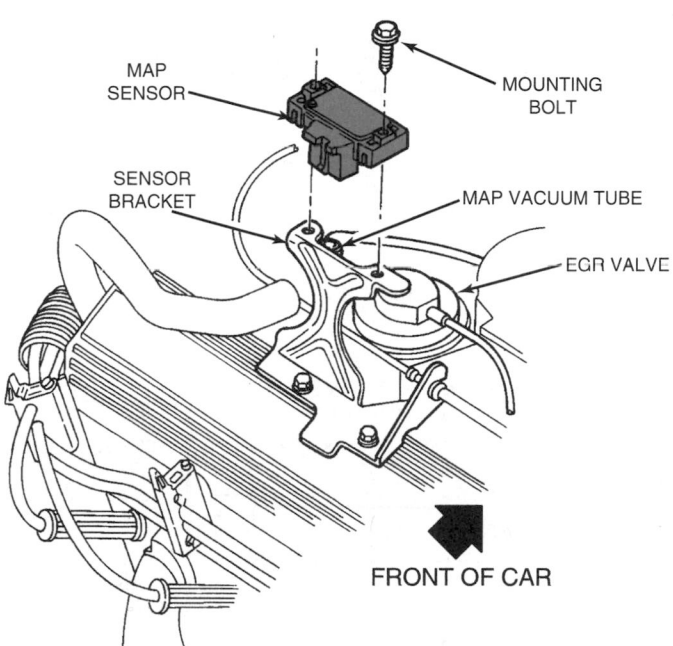

MAP SENSOR
MOUNTING BOLT
SENSOR BRACKET
MAP VACUUM TUBE
EGR VALVE
FRONT OF CAR

Figure 20-18. One particular atmospheric pressure sensor (also called a barometric pressure sensor). It measures changes in the intake manifold pressure in relationship to the engine load and speed (RPM) changes. (Cadillac)

Temperature Sensor

Since cold fuel has a tendency to condense, temperature has a great effect on the operation of the injection system. Cold engines must have a richer mixture if they are

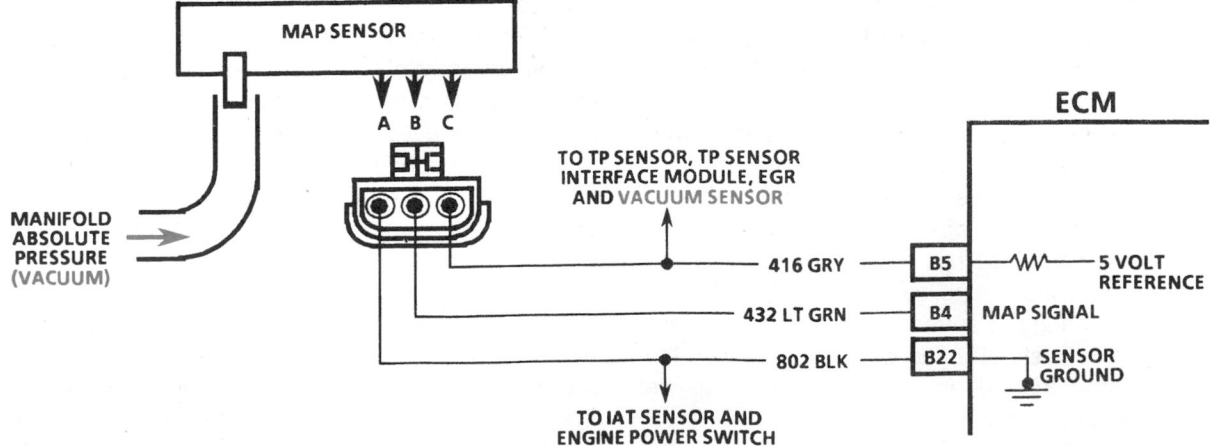

Figure 20-17. One type of manifold vacuum sensor unit. (General Motors)

to run properly. Every injection system has a **temperature sensor** to measure engine coolant temperature. Many injection systems have an additional sensor to measure the temperature of the incoming air. A typical temperature sensor is shown in **Figure 20-19.**

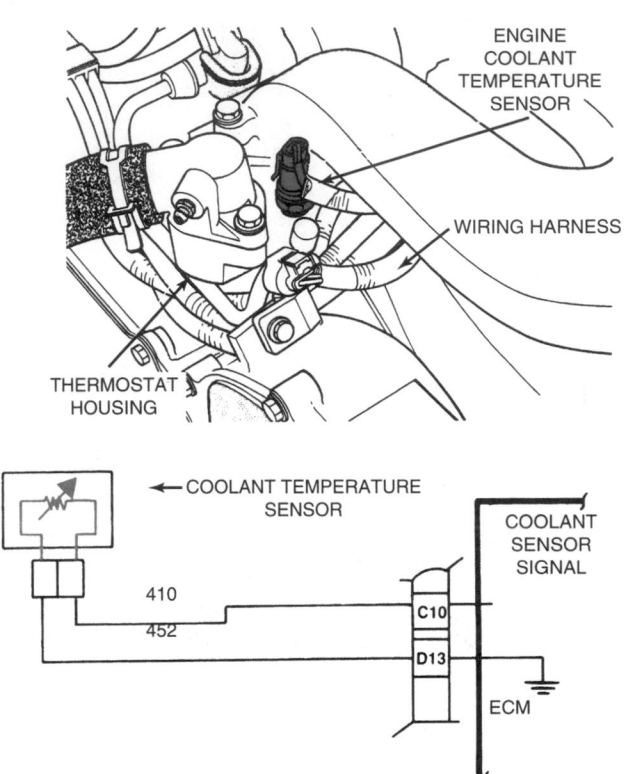

Figure 20-19. An engine coolant temperature sensor unit. (AC-Delco and Chrysler)

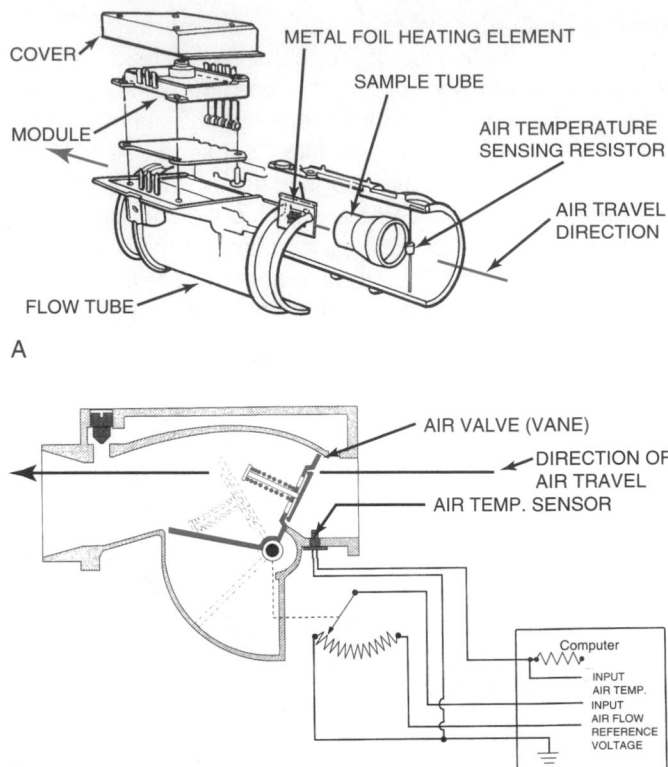

Figure 20-20. A—One type of heated element (film) in a ceramic-based mass airflow sensor. If defective, this unit may cause a no-start or stall after start-up problem. B—An air valve (also called a vane) type mass airflow sensor with wiring schematic. (Champion and OTC tools)

Mass Airflow Sensor

Some fuel injection systems have a **mass airflow sensor.** This precisely monitors the amount of air entering the engine. The control module takes this input and compares it with engine RPM and manifold vacuum to determine the amount of fuel to inject. There are two types of airflow sensors, the heated wire, **Figure 20-20A,** and the air valve, **Figure 20-20B.**

The heated wire type uses a heated resistance wire which extends into the incoming air stream. As the wire heats up, its resistance increases, and the amount of current which flows through the wire decreases. When more airflow enters the sensor, it carries away heat, reducing the wire's resistance and increasing current flow. The control module reads this change in current as changes in airflow. The air valve type consists of a flap which extends into the incoming air stream. Changes in air movement cause the flap to move, which moves the contacts in an electrical resistance module. Changes in current flow through the resistance module are read by the control module as changes in airflow. The complete electronic fuel injection system for a common vehicle is shown in **Figure 20-21.** This is a schematic showing the overall system that contains sensors, controls, and other components similar to those just discussed. Study **Figure 20-21** until you are thoroughly familiar with the various units and the part they play in the overall operation.

Speed Density

Some vehicles use a combination of the sensors described earlier to determine airflow, which eliminates the need for an airflow sensor. This method is referred to as **speed density.** The electronic control module receives information from these sensors and controls the injectors based on a *calculated* airflow. This method is used primarily on throttle body injected systems and some multiport systems. As electronic control modules become more powerful, use of this method will increase.

Continuous Fuel Injection System

On the continuous injection system, the injectors are always open. These systems contain a mechanically-operated pressure control valve that varies the fuel pressure to match the air flow. On later versions of these systems, the fuel pressure is modified by an electronic control system, which bases its pressure decisions on inputs from various sensors. A modern system is shown in **Figure 20-22.**

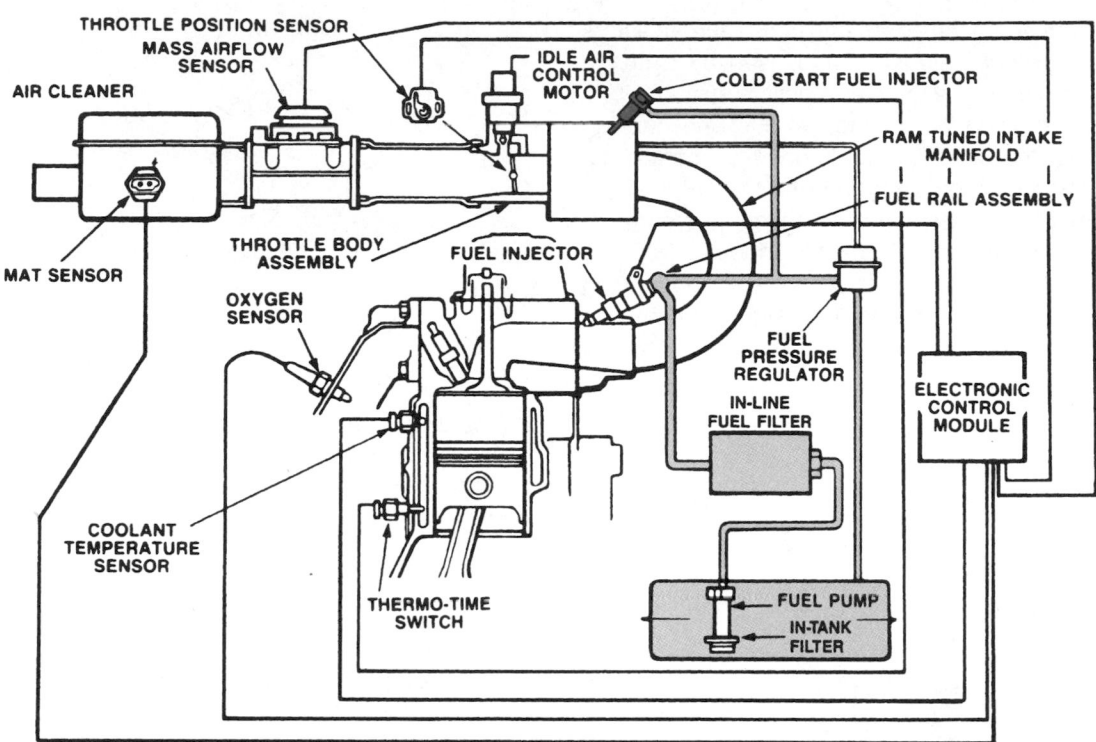

Figure 20-21. A complete electronic multiport fuel injection system for one particular vehicle. Note the cold start injector, which is used to supply a richer fuel mixture to all of the cylinders simultaneously during cold starting. (AC-Delco)

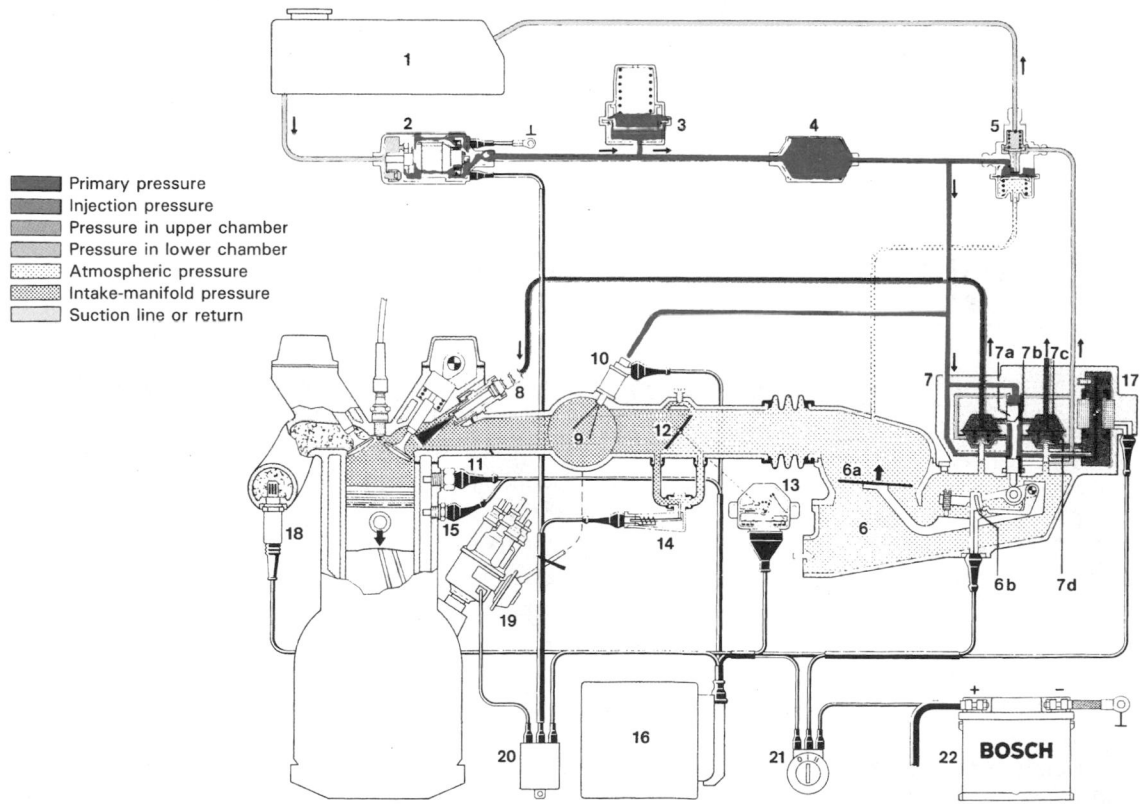

Figure 20-22. Schematic diagram of a continuous fuel injection system. 1—Fuel tank. 2—Fuel pump. 3—Fuel accumulator. 4—Fuel filter. 5—Primary pressure regulator. 6—Airflow sensor. 6A—Sensor plate. 6 B—Potentiometer. 7—Fuel distributor. 7A—Control plunger. 7B—Control edge. 7C—Upper chamber. 7D—Lower chamber. 8—Fuel injection valve. 9—Intake manifold. 10—Cold start valve (injector). 11—Thermal time switch. 12—Throttle valve. 13—Throttle valve switch. 14—Auxiliary air device. 15—Engine temperature sensor. 16—Electronic control module. 17—Electro-hydraulic pressure actuator. 18—Oxygen sensor. 19—Distributor. 20—Control relay. 21—Ignition switch. 22—Battery. (Bosch)

In most continuous injection systems, the injectors have a *valve* or *check ball* which is closed by a spring when there is no pressure in the injection system. This keeps fuel from dripping out of the nozzles and causing hard starting when hot. The injector is opened at minimum fuel pressure. The injectors in **Figure 20-23** open at 47 psi (324 kPa). As long as the engine is operating, pressure will exceed this amount and fuel will flow continuously from the injector nozzles. The amount of fuel will vary depending upon system pressure. The injector is designed to atomize fuel properly at any pressure or flow rate.

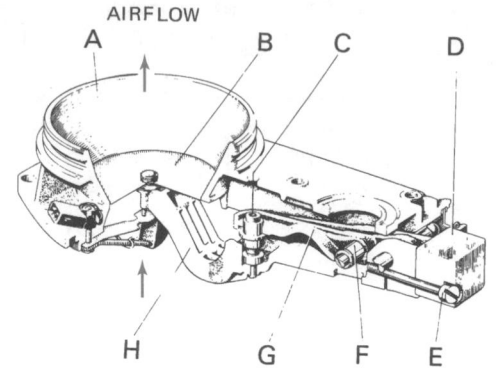

Figure 20-24. Airflow sensor assembly. A—Air venturi. B—Airflow sensor plate. C—CO adjustment screw. D—Balance weight. E—Lock screw. F—Pivot shaft. G—Adjustment arm. H—Lever. (Volvo)

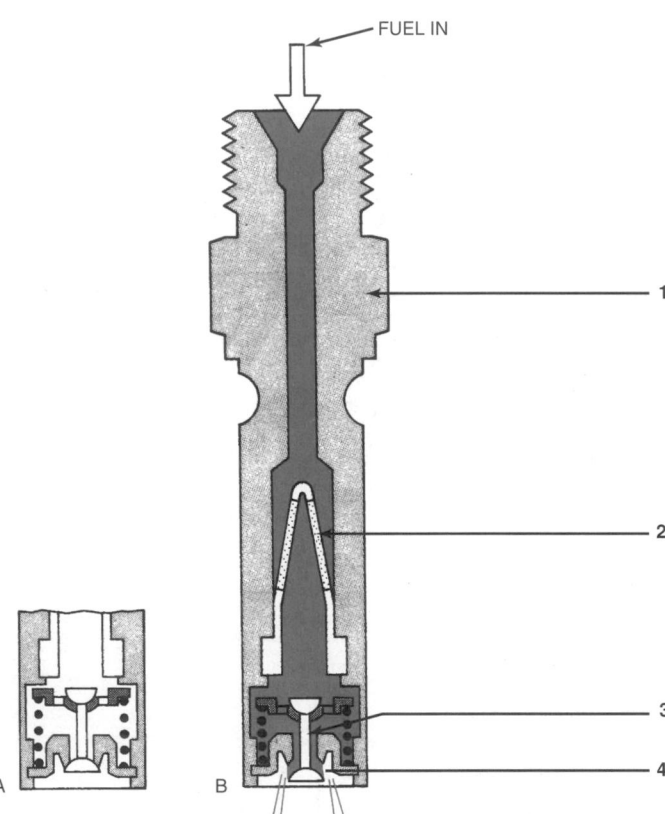

Figure 20-23. A continuous fuel injection system injector cutaway. A—Not operating. B—During injection. 1—Housing. 2—Filter. 3—Needle valve. 4—Needle valve seat. (Bosch)

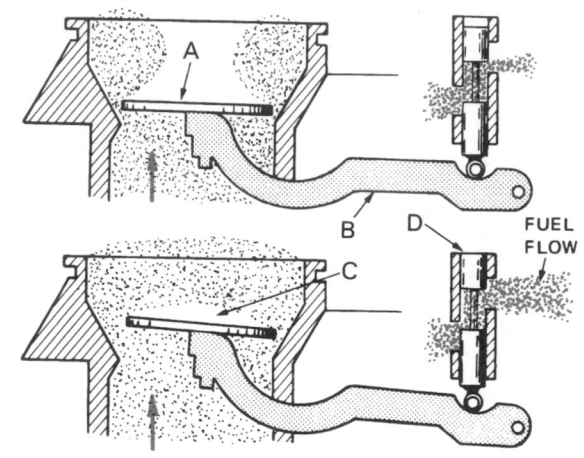

Figure 20-25. Airflow sensor operation: Top. Part load operation. Bottom. Full load operation. A—Sensor down. B—Lever arm. C—Sensor up. D—Fuel valve open.

Fuel Flow Control

Air passing into the intake manifold flows through a *mechanical airflow sensor,* **Figure 20-24.** The sensor utilizes a hinged lever H that pivots on pivot rod F. An airflow sensor plate B affixed to one end of the lever rides up and down in the center of the air venturi A. A balance weight D is used to balance the lever and plate assembly, which allows the sensor plate B to float in the venturi.

During part load operation, **Figure 20-25A,** the airflow has forced the sensor plate A to rise a small amount. Note that the fuel distributor control valve installed in the distributor block has been raised somewhat by the lever B. The airflow sensor controls the fuel distributor valve. As the engine is accelerated, more and more air flows through the venturi raising the sensor plate higher and higher.

Finally, at full load, **Figure 20-25B,** the sensor plate is raised to its highest position C. The lever has moved the fuel distributor control valve to the wide open position D, permitting maximum fuel flow to the injectors. In order to provide a constant pressure drop through the fuel distributor metering slots, a pressure regulating valve is used for each injector outlet. The valves are built into the fuel distributor housing. The constant pressure drop is needed to keep the amount of fuel injected directly proportional to the size of the metering slot opening.

Complete Air-Fuel Control Unit

Figure 20-26 pictures the complete air-fuel control unit, consisting of the airflow sensor, fuel distributor, pressure regulator valve, and related parts. Note that there is pressure in the control chamber F above the control plunger G. This controlled pressure (around 52.2 psi or 360 kPa) is needed to dampen sensor plate lever B movement so that, upon sudden acceleration, the sensor plate is not raised beyond the point that the airflow will be maintained.

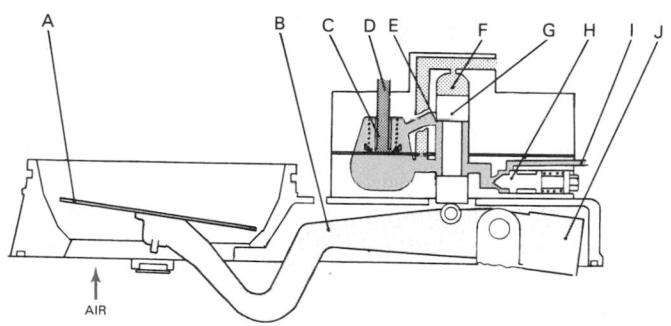

Figure 20-26. Complete air-fuel control unit. A—Airflow sensor plate. B—Sensor plate lever. C—Pressure regulating valve. D—To injector. E—Control plunger head. F—Control pressure. G—Control plunger. H—Line pressure regulator. I—Fuel inlet from tank. J—Balance weights. (Volvo)

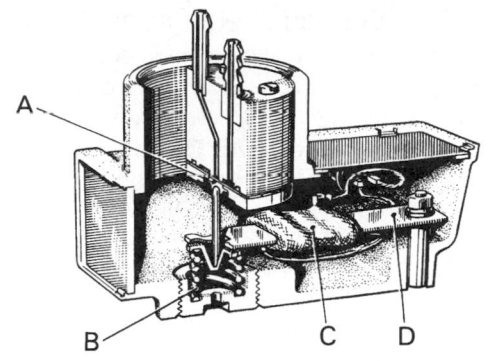

Figure 20-27. Control pressure regulator. A—Diaphragm valve. B—Spring. C—Coil. D—Bimetallic spring.

Control Pressure Regulator

The control pressure regulator maintains a steady pressure of 52.2 psi (360 kPa) in chamber F above the control plunger G in **Figure 20-26** when the engine is at normal operating temperature. In **Figure 20-27,** the heating coil C causes bimetallic spring D to alter pressure on spring B, which changes spring pressure on the diaphragm valve.

This causes a lowering of control pressure which will allow the sensor plate lever to shove the control plunger farther up. This allows extra fuel to flow through the metering slots. As the engine warms, normal fuel pressure is resumed. A schematic of the entire continuous fuel injection system is illustrated in **Figure 20-28.** Study all of the parts and relate their individual functions to that of the overall system.

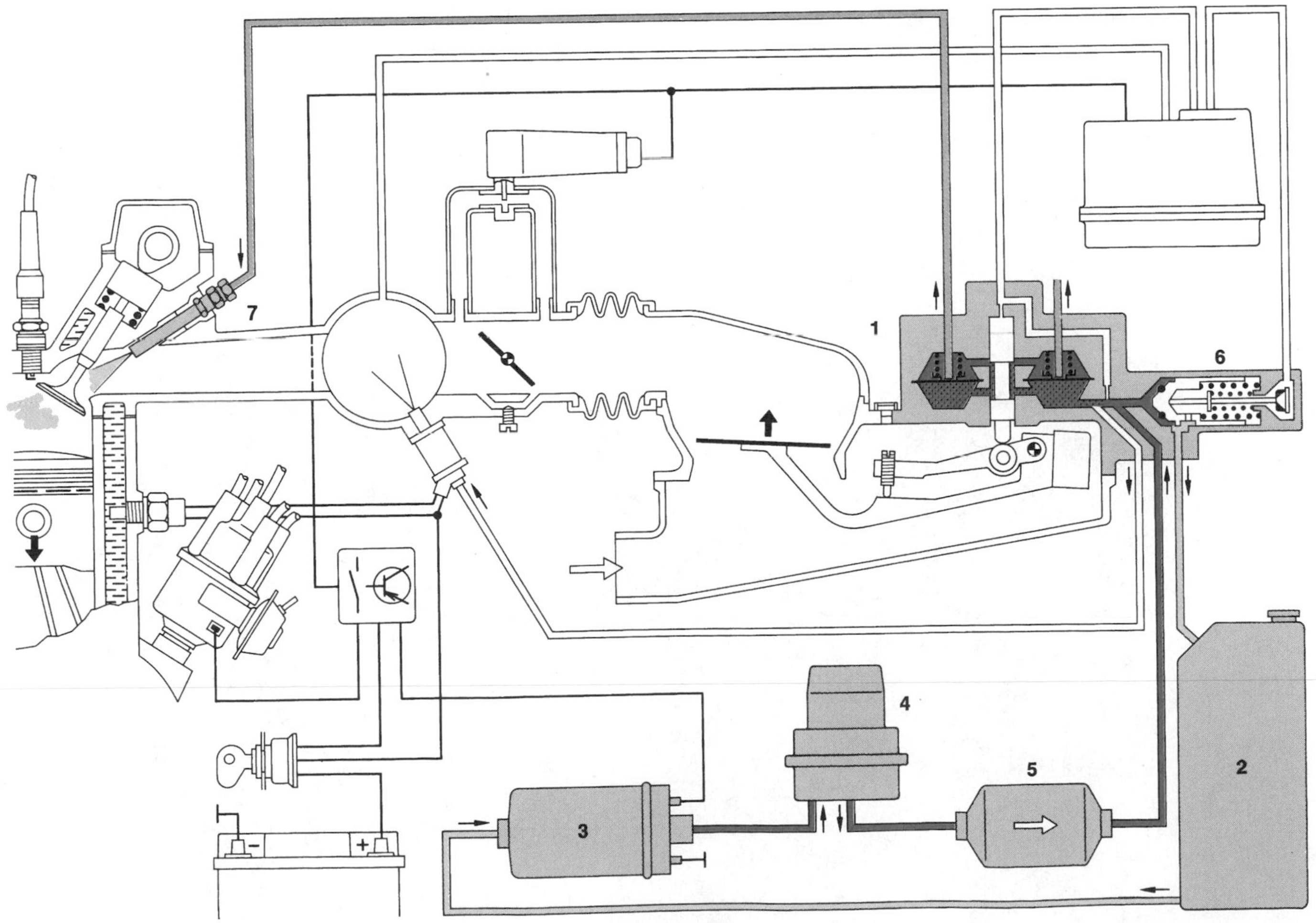

Figure 20-28. A schematic of a continuous fuel injection system. 1—Mixture control unit. 2—Fuel tank. 3—Electric fuel pump. 4—Fuel accumulator. 5—Fuel filter. 6—Fuel pressure regulator. 7—Fuel injection nozzle (valve). (Bosch)

Fuel Injection Service Precautions

When testing or servicing a fuel injection system, certain precautions are necessary. Always double-check the vehicle's service manual for any recommended cautions for the exact system being serviced. The following precautions apply to all electronic fuel injection systems:

- Turn off the ignition switch before connecting or disconnecting electronic control module.
- Do not apply voltage to or ground the electronic control module circuits unless it is specifically called for in the service manual.
- Do not expose an electronic control module to excessive heat such as found in some paint drying ovens.
- Before removing any battery cable connections or fuses, turn the ignition switch off.
- Disconnect the battery before working on the fuel system.
- Maintain extreme cleanliness on all fuel line work as the slightest bit of dirt can jam some injectors.
- Use only high quality, properly designed replacement lines and hoses for the fuel delivery system. Torque all fittings as directed.
- Upon completion of service, always check for fuel leaks.
- Use test equipment specifically designed for the job at hand.

Remember that modern fuel injection systems are part of the vehicle's emission controls and that proper functioning is dependent upon overall system soundness. Never attempt any service procedure unless you have had the proper training. You must also have the recommended test equipment and a service manual for the vehicle at hand. Improper service procedures can cause extensive and expensive system damage. A schematic of a complete electronically controlled fuel injection system is illustrated in **Figures 20-29** and **20-30**.

Electronic Fuel Injection System Service

To properly diagnose, test, and service a fuel injection system, you should have the proper tools and test instruments. You also should have, and use, test and service specifications for the specific system.

 Warning: Before loosening any fuel injection fuel lines, always remove the pressure from the lines.

System Diagnosis

When a vehicle is experiencing possible fuel system problems, always give the complete system an initial inspection before beginning diagnostic tests. Question the vehicle's owner regarding the problem. Ask the owner when the problem occurs, how it sounds, and how it affects engine performance. Road test the vehicle to confirm the

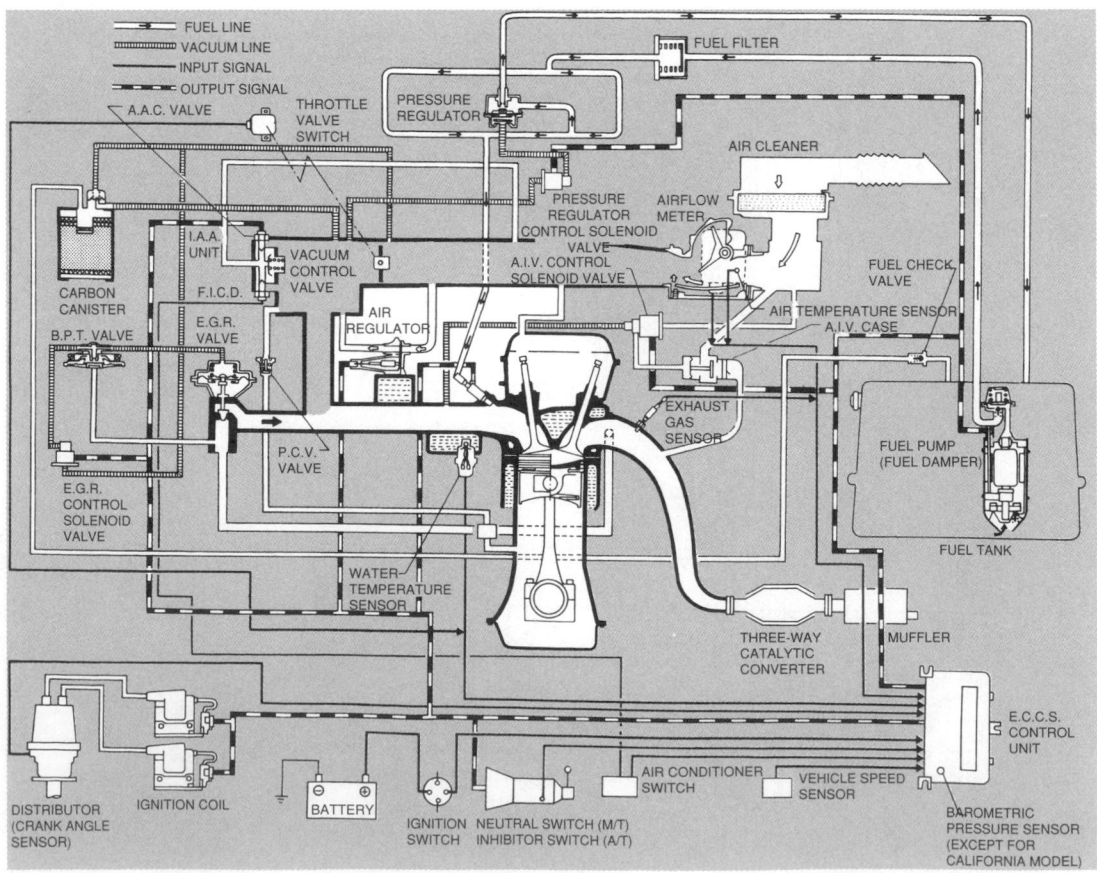

Figure 20-29. Part and layout schematic for an electronically controlled fuel injection system. Study the various parts and relationships to each other. (Nissan)

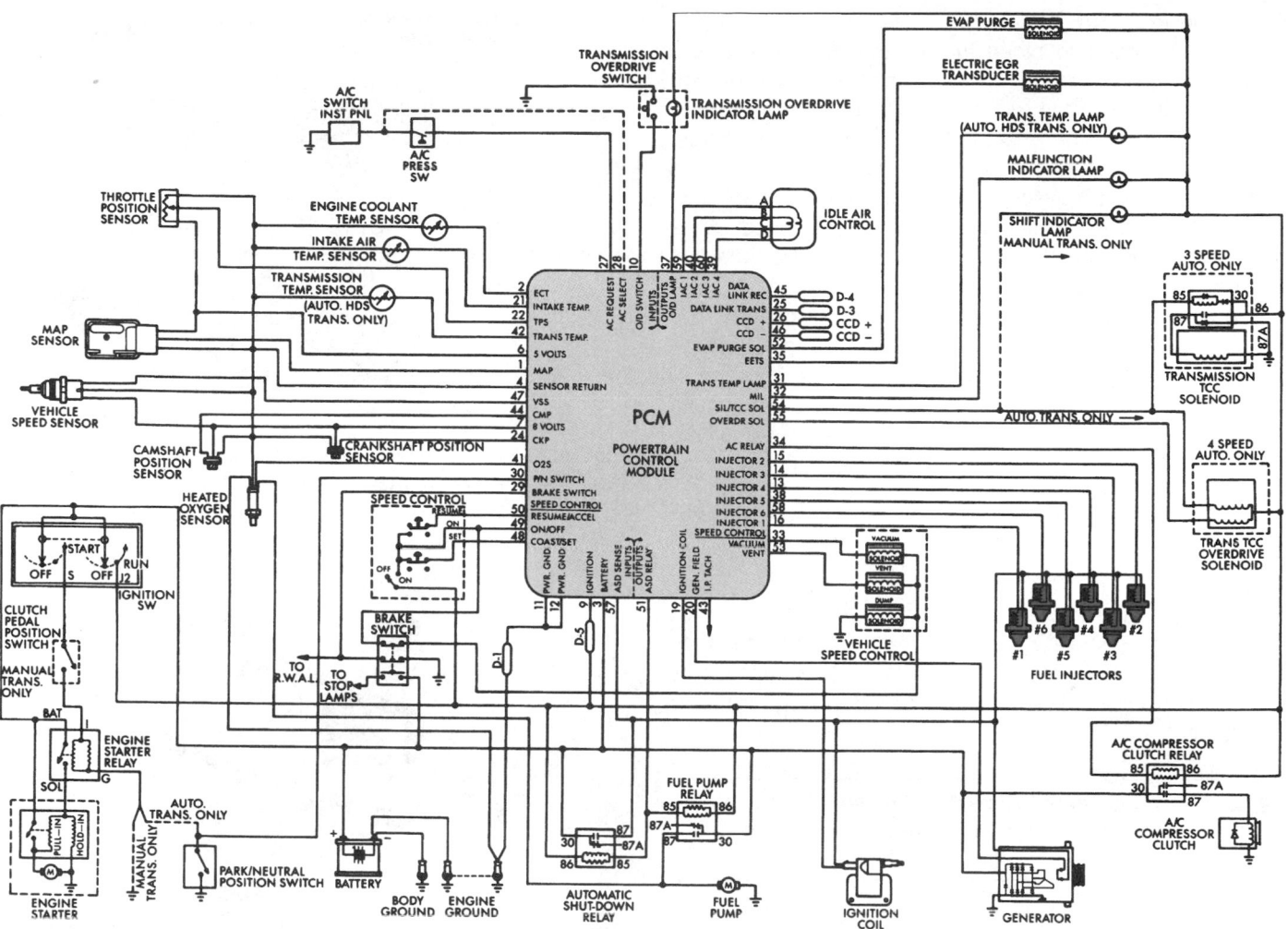

Figure 20-30. An electrical schematic for one particular electronic fuel injection system. This system is used on a V-6 engine. (Chrysler)

problem. Also, before blaming the fuel injection system, check whether or not some other vehicle component located in the ignition, electrical, engine mechanical, exhaust, or emission systems is causing the problem. Symptoms of fuel injection problems are similar to many of those experienced in a carbureted vehicle. The causes and corrections are different. Some typical injection system problems would be:

- Engine will not start.
- Engine starts, but stalls.
- Engine starts hard (must be cranked excessively).
- Engine idles rough.
- Engine stays on fast idle.
- No fast idle.
- Engine hesitates on acceleration.
- Engine cuts out or misfires at all speeds.
- Engine performs poorly at high speed.
- Excessive fuel consumption.
- Poor low speed operation.
- Engine backfires.
- Loss of power.
- Engine surges (fast-slow-fast).
- Engine emits black smoke.

An initial inspection will often pinpoint the problem. A thorough inspection can help you avoid wasting time performing unnecessary tests. The experienced technician will check all of the following before performing diagnostic tests:

- Check all fuel lines for tight fittings, cracks, pinched, or collapsed sections.
- Check all vacuum lines for poor connections, improper connections, kinks, or leaks.
- Check wiring for tight connectors, improper connections, shorting, frayed, pinched, or broken wires, or a blown fuse.
- Inspect any mechanical linkage for freedom of operation and correct adjustment.
- Check air intake and air cleaner for clogging or obstructions.
- Retrieve any computer diagnostic codes (see Chapter 25).
- Check the level, type, and octane rating of fuel being used.
- Inspect related emission controls for possible malfunction.
- Check exhaust system for kinks or clogging.

Removing Pressure

It is important to bleed fuel system pressure before working on the fuel system. Some manufacturers recommend disconnecting the fuel pump and running the engine until it stops. After the engine stops, crank it a few times. Disconnect the battery ground cable. The fuel lines should then be cracked (barely loosened) to check for any possible pressure. Some fuel injection systems are equipped with a *schrader valve.* This valve is usually mounted on the fuel rail and can be used to bleed system pressure.

Another pressure relief method is to disconnect the battery, and then slowly *crack* or loosen a fitting to release pressure. When cracking a fuel fitting or using a schrader valve, cover the area with a shop cloth to catch and contain any fuel that may spray out. Immediately dispose of the fuel-soaked cloth. Wear protective goggles and keep an approved fire extinguisher handy.

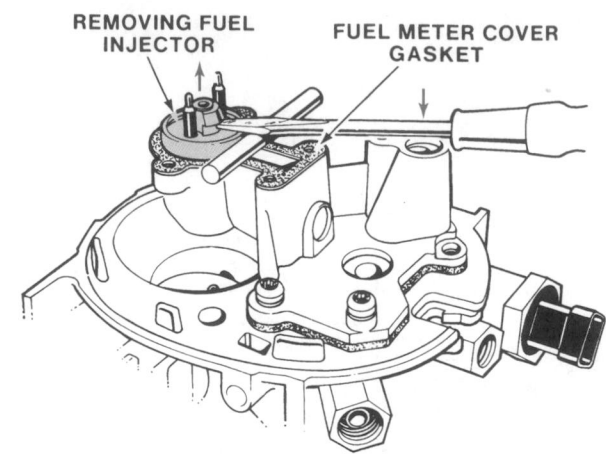

Figure 20-31. Removing fuel injector from a throttle body. Use care to avoid damaging the unit. (Chevrolet)

Fuel Injector Service

The following section explains how to properly check injectors in the vehicle and how to remove, test, and clean injectors. Also discussed are methods of removing central fuel injection throttle bodies and injection system pressure regulators.

 Warning: Do not allow gasoline spills to remain on the engine or floor. Clean up gasoline spills immediately.

Testing Injectors on the Vehicle

The easiest way to check injectors is to place a screwdriver or a long rod on the injector as the engine operates. If you hear a clicking sound, the injector is operating. No click means that the injector is defective, or the control system is not energizing it. On central fuel injection systems, the spray can be observed as the engine operates. To make the spray pattern more visible, connect a timing light to the engine, and point it at the injector as the engine runs. The light will illuminate the spray every time the spark plug fires.

Removing Fuel Injectors

Always remove injectors using procedures recommended by the vehicle's service manual. It may be necessary to remove the intake manifold or plenum to gain access to multiport injectors. Also remove the injector electrical connectors. Be sure to remove any brackets holding the fuel rail to the engine. Then remove the fuel rail and injector assembly by pulling the rail straight up so that the injectors come out of the intake ports. Do not bend or flex the fuel system tubing, since most fuel injector tubing has an internal coating which can flake off if the tubing is bent or flexed. **Figure 20-31** shows one method used to remove an injector from a central fuel injection throttle body. **Figure 20-32** shows removal of a multiport fuel injector fuel rail.

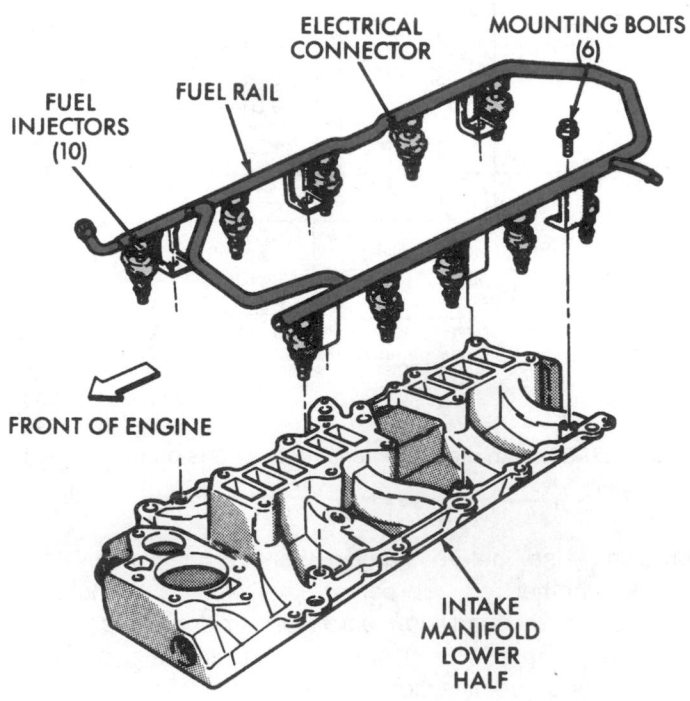

Figure 20-32. Removal of a fuel rail from a V-10 engine intake manifold. Be sure to cover or plug injector holes to prevent the entry of dirt, small parts, etc. (Dodge)

Cleaning Fuel Injectors—On or Off the Engine

The openings inside the fuel injectors are extremely small and may become plugged by small amounts of dirt or gasoline deposits. This can result in many driveability problems. Do not immerse the injector in solvent of any kind. The injector is electrically operated and solvent can damage the solenoid windings, as well as any internal O-rings or seals. The best way to clean the injection system is by using a special injector cleaner device, which is part of the kit shown in **Figure 20-33.** Some manufacturers recommend that certain types of injectors should not be cleaned. Follow the manufacturer's cleaning instructions. In many cases injectors cannot be successfully cleaned and must be replaced.

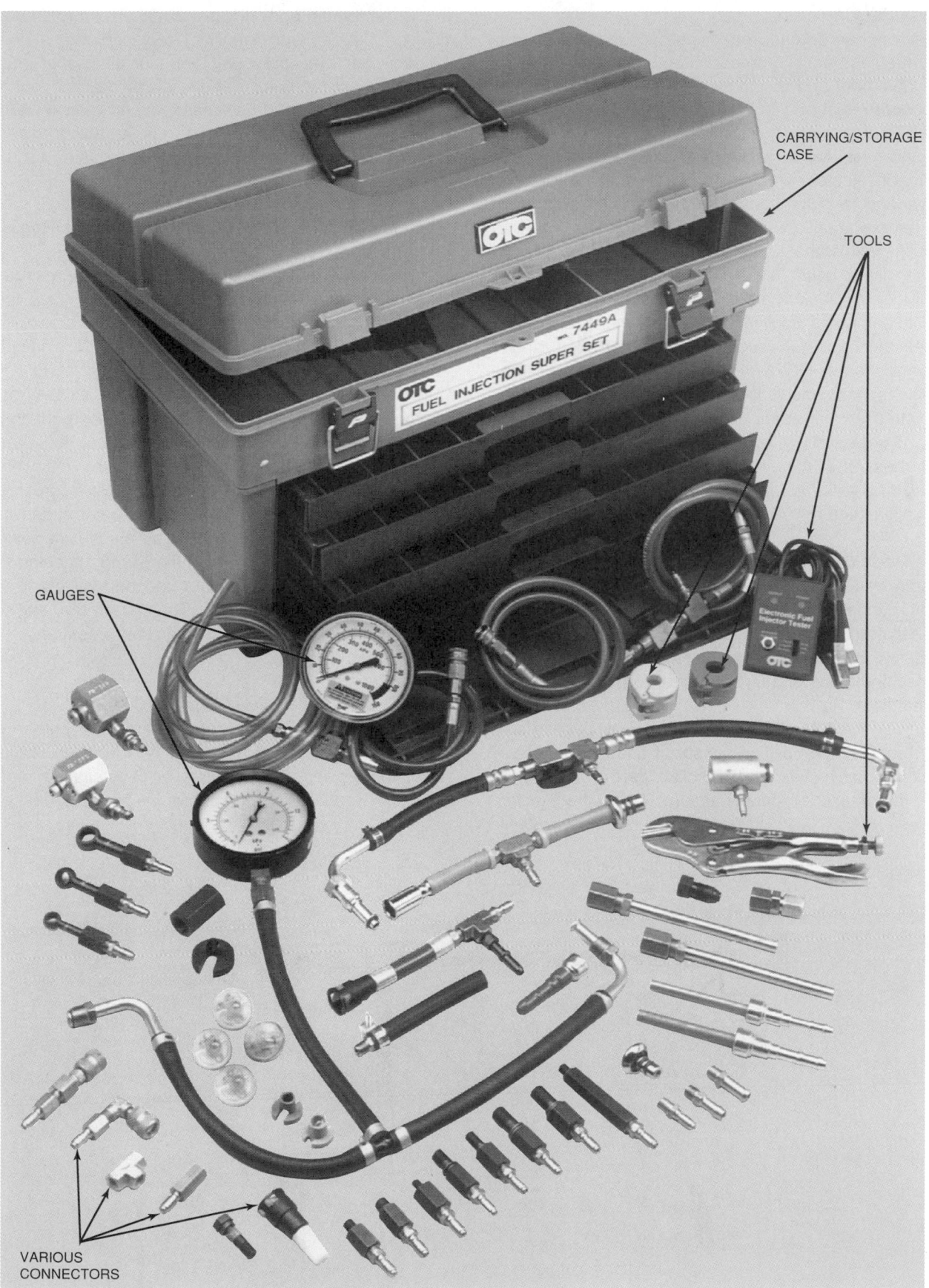

Figure 20-33. A fuel injection/injector system cleaning set with all the necessary connectors, gauges, etc. Follow the tool manufacturer's operational instructions for cleaning. (OTC Tools)

Checking Fuel Injectors

Injectors can be checked for proper functioning, spray pattern, fuel output, and freedom from leakage. Use the proper equipment and recommended test procedures. One test procedure is shown in **Figure 20-34.** Fuel injectors are replaced as a unit. If the injector is defective, replace it with a new one. Make certain that you have the correct replacement injector. If you plan on reusing any injector, put it in a secure place so that the tip cannot be damaged before reinstallation. Before installing injectors, lubricate any O-rings with transmission fluid or clean motor oil.

Carefully reinstall the injector into the intake ports. When all of the injectors are properly installed, reinstall the fuel rail assembly, if applicable, injector electrical connectors, pressure regulator vacuum, fuel supply hose, and all other components. Reconnect the battery negative cable and make a final check to ensure all fittings, fuel lines, ground straps, and wiring harnesses are correctly reinstalled. Turn the ignition on and allow the fuel pump to fill the fuel lines. Start the vehicle and check the fuel system for leaks. If no leaks are found, check fuel system pressure and general injector system operation.

Throttle Body Overhaul

Begin by removing the air cleaner or intake ducts, all electrical connections, and vacuum lines at the throttle body. Then remove the throttle linkage or cable, automatic transmission linkage, and fuel lines. Remove the throttle body attaching bolts, and remove the throttle body from the intake manifold.

Remove the idle air control motor or air bypass solenoid and the throttle position sensor, if used. If necessary, the throttle body halves can be split. Then remove all old gaskets, the pressure regulator assembly, and the injector if it is in the throttle body, **Figure 20-35.** The throttle body can now be cleaned and rebuilt or replaced with a new part. Closely check the pressure regulator for proper operation. Obtain a new regulator if there is any doubt about the old one. Obtain new parts as needed and closely follow the manufacturer's instructions to rebuild the throttle body. Reinstall by reversing the removal process and make any necessary adjustments.

Replacing Multiport Fuel Injection Pressure Regulator

Pressure regulators are installed on the fuel rail of multiport systems, as in **Figure 20-36.** Most pressure regulators are nonadjustable and are replaced when they are unable to properly control the fuel system pressure. If an adjustable pressure regulator cannot be successfully adjusted, it should be replaced.

Begin by removing the air cleaner, hoses, or other components which obstruct access to the regulator. Then remove the vacuum line to the regulator if it has one. Remove the fittings and fasteners that hold the pressure regulator to the fuel rail. Remove the pressure regulator from the rail. See **Figure 20-37.** Install all needed gaskets and seals on the new regulator and place it in position on the fuel rail. Install the fuel line fittings and attaching screws. Replace the regulator vacuum line and all other components which were removed. Then start the engine and check for leaks and proper fuel system pressure.

Mechanical Fuel Injection

Mechanical fuel injection systems are primarily used on diesel engines, but may also be found on some older gasoline engines. The next section details the operating principles and service methods of mechanical fuel injection.

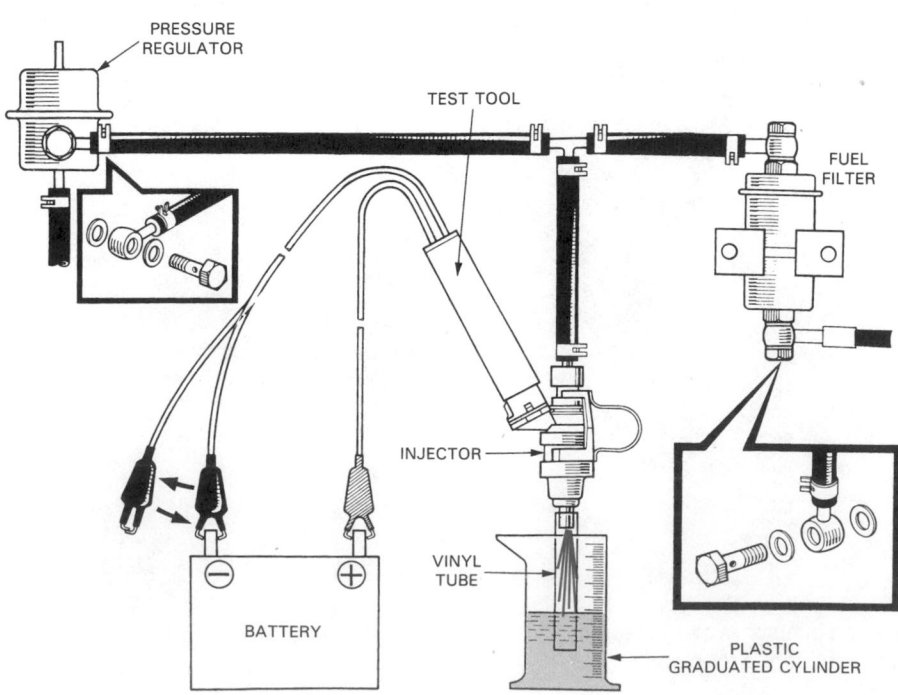

Figure 20-34.   Testing fuel injector flow rate. Note vinyl tube around injector to restrict fuel spray to plastic cylinder. (Toyota)

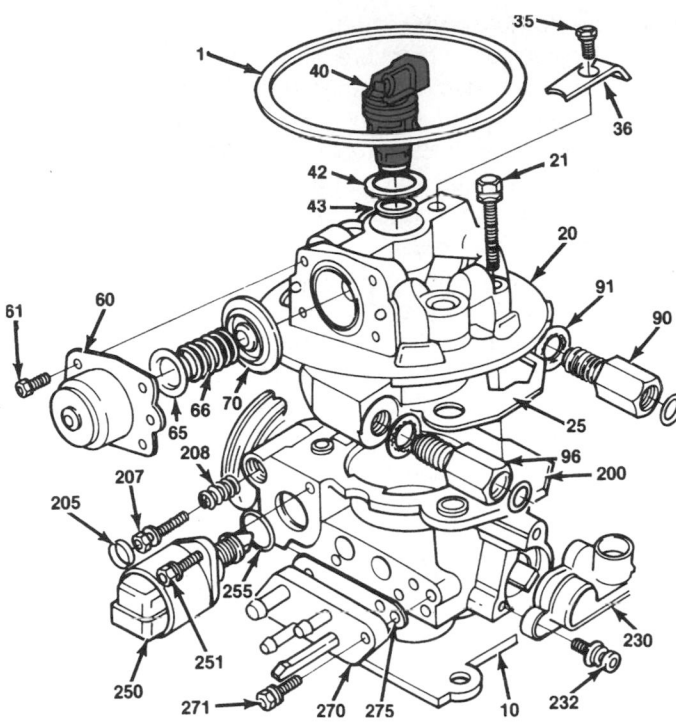

Figure 20-35. An exploded view of a single injector throttle body arrangement. 1—Air filter gasket. 10—Gasket flange. 20—Fuel meter assembly. 21—Screw and washer assembly-Fuel meter body attaching. 25—Fuel meter body-to-throttle body gasket. 35—Injector retainer screw. 36—Injector retainer. 40—Fuel injector. 42—Fuel injector upper O-ring. 43—Fuel injector lower O-ring. 60—Pressure regulator cover assembly. 61—Pressure regulator attaching screw. 65—Spring seat. 66—Pressure regulator spring. 70—Pressure regulator diaphragm assembly. 90—Fuel inlet nut. 91—Fuel nut seal. 96—Fuel outlet nut. 200—Throttle body assembly. 205—Idle stop screw plug. 207—Idle stop screw and washer assembly. 208—Idle stop screw spring. 230—Throttle position sensor (TPS). 232—TPS attaching screw and washer assembly. 250—Idle air control valve (IACV). 251—IACV attaching screw. 255—IACV O-ring. 270—Tube module assembly. 271—Manifold attaching screw. 275—Manifold tube gasket. (AC-Delco)

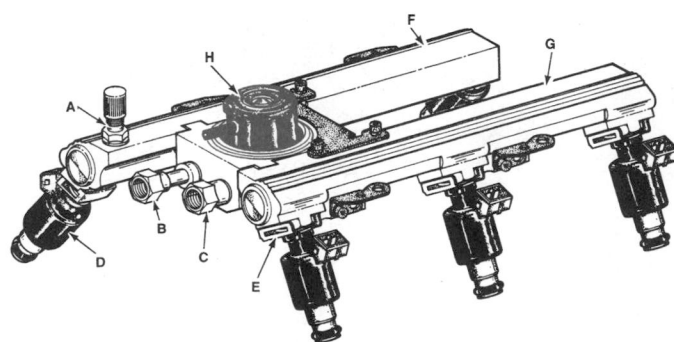

A	FUEL PRESSURE CONNECTION ASSEMBLY	E	INJECTOR RETAINER CLIP
B	FUEL INLET FITTING	F	L/H FUEL RAIL & PLUG ASSEMBLY
C	FUEL OUTLET FITTING	G	R/H FUEL RAIL & PLUG ASSEMBLY
D	MPFI MULTEC INJECTOR ASSEMBLY	H	PRESSURE REGULATOR ASSEMBLY

Figure 20-36. A multiport fuel injector pressure regulator as mounted by one manufacturer. This particular regulator is serviced as a complete assembly. No repair is possible. (AC-Delco)

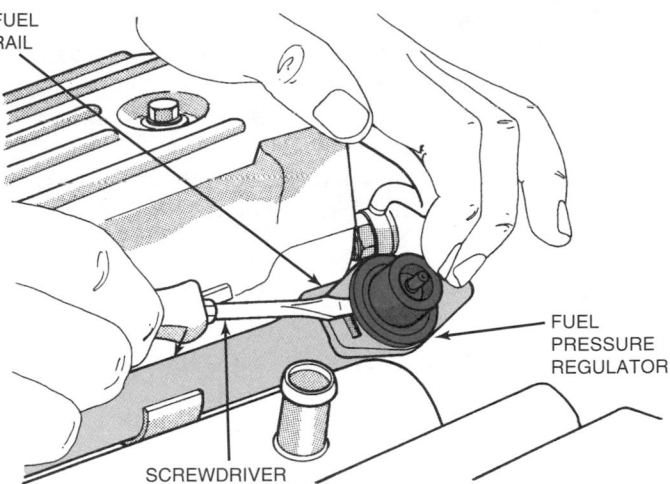

Figure 20-37. A fuel pressure regulator being carefully removed from the fuel rail. Be sure to relieve fuel pressure first. (Chrysler)

Mechanical Gasoline Fuel Injection

Mechanical gasoline fuel injection systems are found on some older imported vehicles. The mechanical gasoline injection system uses an engine-driven injection pump. An electric fuel pump forces gasoline from the tank through fine filters and on to the mechanical injection pump. Through a series of pistons and cams, the injection pump compresses a measured quantity of fuel and delivers it to a specific injector. The fuel charge, under pressure from the pump, pushes the spring-loaded injector needle off its seat. Fuel is forced through the injector nozzle, becoming atomized as shown in **Figure 20-38.**

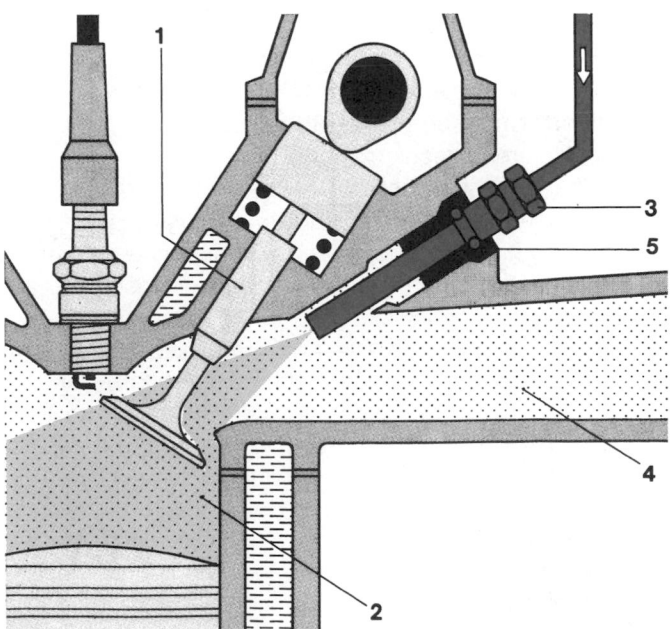

Figure 20-38. Mechanical fuel injector nozzle 3 spraying fuel past the intake valve 1 and into the combustion chamber 2. Note how the nozzle is mounted in the intake manifold 4 and protected with a heat-isolation mount. (Bosch)

The injection pump meters the amount of fuel needed in accordance with throttle valve positioning. To meet varying conditions, such as cold starting or high altitude operation, the positioning of the injection pump control rod is automatically altered to compensate for the immediate fuel demand. A typical mechanical fuel injection system is shown in **Figure 20-39**. This system uses a four-piston pump.

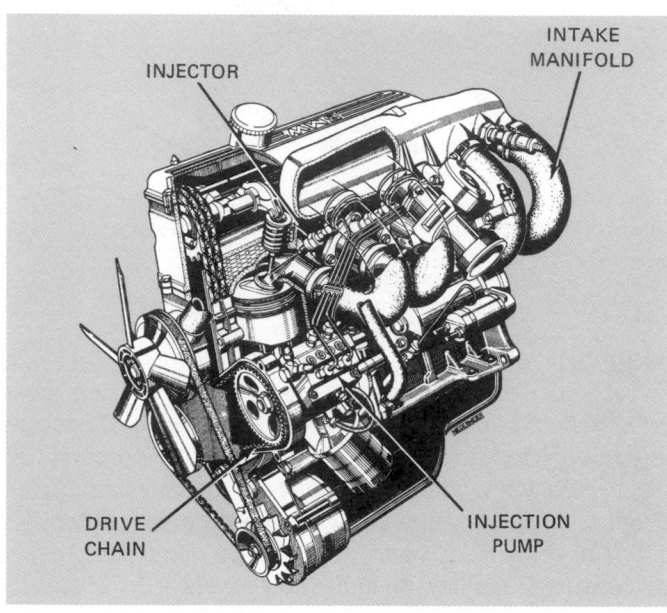

Figure 20-39. Mechanical fuel injection system. Each cylinder, at the exact time needed, has a metered amount of fuel injected into the intake port area. (BMW)

Mechanical Fuel Injection Service

Unlike electronic fuel injection systems, mechanical fuel injection systems have many adjustment points. Adjustments must be precise to ensure correct operation. A manufacturer's repair manual covering the exact system at hand must be used. Closely follow instructions and recommended clearances, adjustments, and pressures. Use the proper service tools and test equipment. Some of the more common service adjustments, inspections, and repairs follow.

Fuel cleanliness is critical on all injection systems. Injector pump internal parts are fitted to extremely close tolerances, sometimes as close as 0.0001″ (.002 mm), and any foreign particles can cause problems. Clean or replace all filters and water traps as recommended. All fuel lines used between the injection pump and injectors are under high pressure. Check the condition of all hose and tubing; look closely for leaks, loose fittings or clamps, worn or abraded sections, or hoses routed close to moving parts or heat sources. Replace any defective parts and reposition hoses to ensure that no further damage occurs. Use replacement parts of the correct size and material. Test the system for leaks after repairs.

Injection Pump Service

Injection pump pressure and volume output may be checked. Check electrical connections for looseness and/or corrosion. If pump seems noisy, check the pump mountings for interference with other objects. Make certain all hoses are in good condition and that clamps and fittings are tight. Other injection pump checks can be made according to the proper service manual.

Pump overhaul or any service of internal components should be handled by a shop with specialized equipment. Proper injector pump overhaul requires the use of a test stand and appropriate tools. Clearances are precise and require absolute cleanliness and care. Do not attempt pump overhaul unless the proper tools and specifications are available. When removing or installing the pump, pay particular attention to spacers, adjustment washers, and index marks.

Throttle Linkage Adjustments

The linkage should move freely without binding or interference with other parts. When adjustment is necessary, it must be done exactly as specified by the manufacturer, especially those between the throttle valve and injection pump. When needed, use recommended adjustment tools. Lubricate as needed and double check to ensure that all adjustments are correct. **Figure 20-40** shows the typical detailed linkage adjustment specifications needed for one section of the linkage system.

Fuel Mixture Adjustment

Adjusting devices are used to provide proper idle, part load, and full load fuel mixture, **Figure 20-41**. When adjusting the engine idle, make certain that the RPM is correct

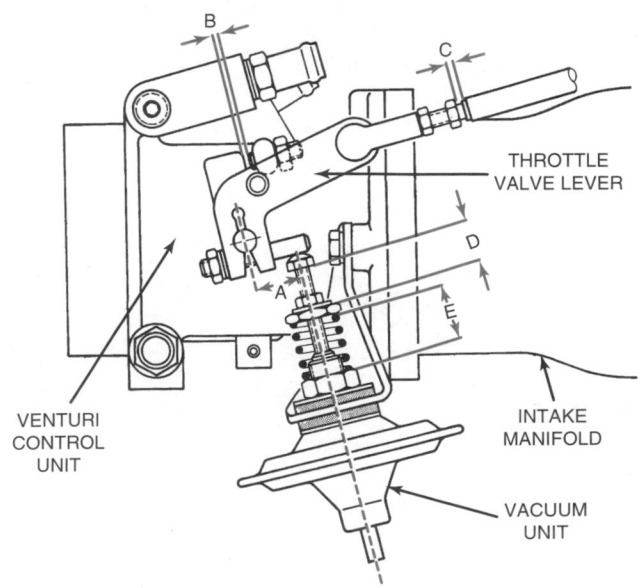

Figure 20-40. Mechanical fuel injection linkage adjustment must be precise. Follow manufacturer's instructions. A—Shaft distance. B—Throttle valve opening. C—Idle travel of sliding rod. D—Length of thrust bolt. E—Spring height. (Mercedes-Benz)

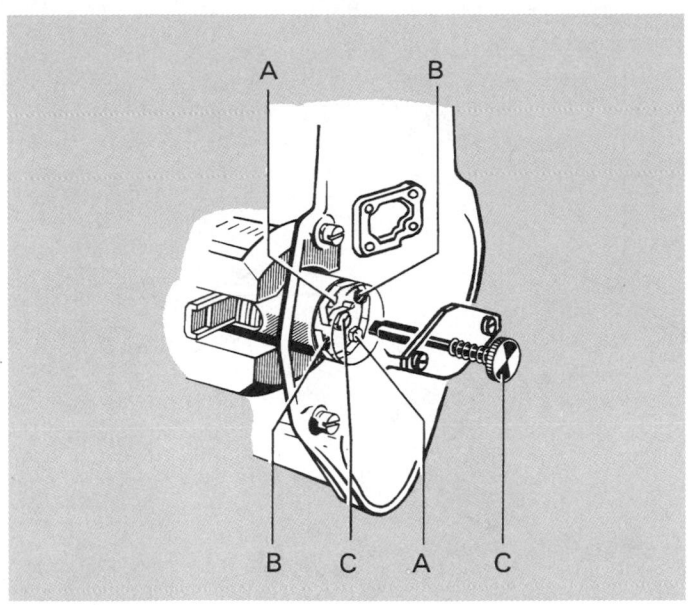

Figure 20-41. One type of idle adjustment for a gasoline fuel injection system. A—Top part load adjusting screw. B—Bottom part load adjusting screw. C—Idle speed adjusting screw.

and that the specified emission values are met. Some systems have two idle adjusting screws, one on the injector pump and an idle air speed screw in the intake manifold. They are used in conjunction with each other to secure the proper air-fuel mix. **Figure 20-41** shows one setup used on the injector pump. Partial and full load adjustments are best made on a chassis dynamometer, but if one is not available, road testing will suffice. Follow the manufacturer's directions and make any adjustment in small amounts.

Other Checks and Adjustments

The injector valves can be tested for leakage, proper opening pressure, and spray pattern shape. Use an injector test unit and replace any faulty valves. When installing injectors, use new seal rings and torque to specifications. Depending upon the particular injection system, there can be other related control units in the system such as a starting valve, thermoswitch, etc. Check for proper system operation and adjust, repair, or replace as needed.

Diesel Fuel Injection

Diesel engines have always had fuel injection systems. Heat caused by the high compression ratios is the ignition source for the diesel fuel. The fuel cannot be compressed along with the air inside the diesel engine cylinder or it would ignite before the piston reaches the top of its compression stroke. Therefore, the diesel engine injection system differs from the mechanical gasoline fuel injection in these respects:

*   Diesel fuel is injected directly into the cylinder combustion area.
*   Injection must be timed to occur at the top of the compression stroke.
*   Fuel must be injected into the combustion chamber area at the height of compression. This requires tremendous pressure.

To overcome compression pressure, diesel injection systems pressurize the fuel from several hundred to several thousand psi. Diesel engines pollute less than gasoline engines. The basic injection system is not controlled by an on-board engine computer. However, the glow plug system is often computer controlled. The typical diesel injection system uses an engine-driven (by chain, belt, or direct connection) *injector pump.* An overall view of a diesel fuel injection system is shown in **Figure 20-42**. **Figure 20-43** is a schematic showing the component layout of a typical diesel injection system.

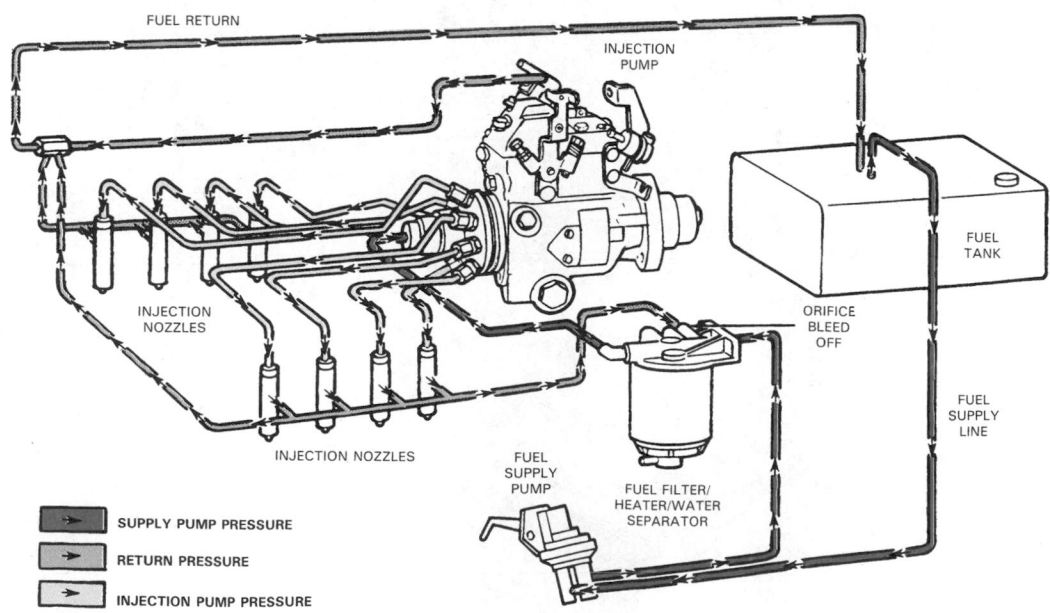

Figure 20-42. Schematic of one type of diesel fuel injection system. This system uses a rotary injection pump. (Ford)

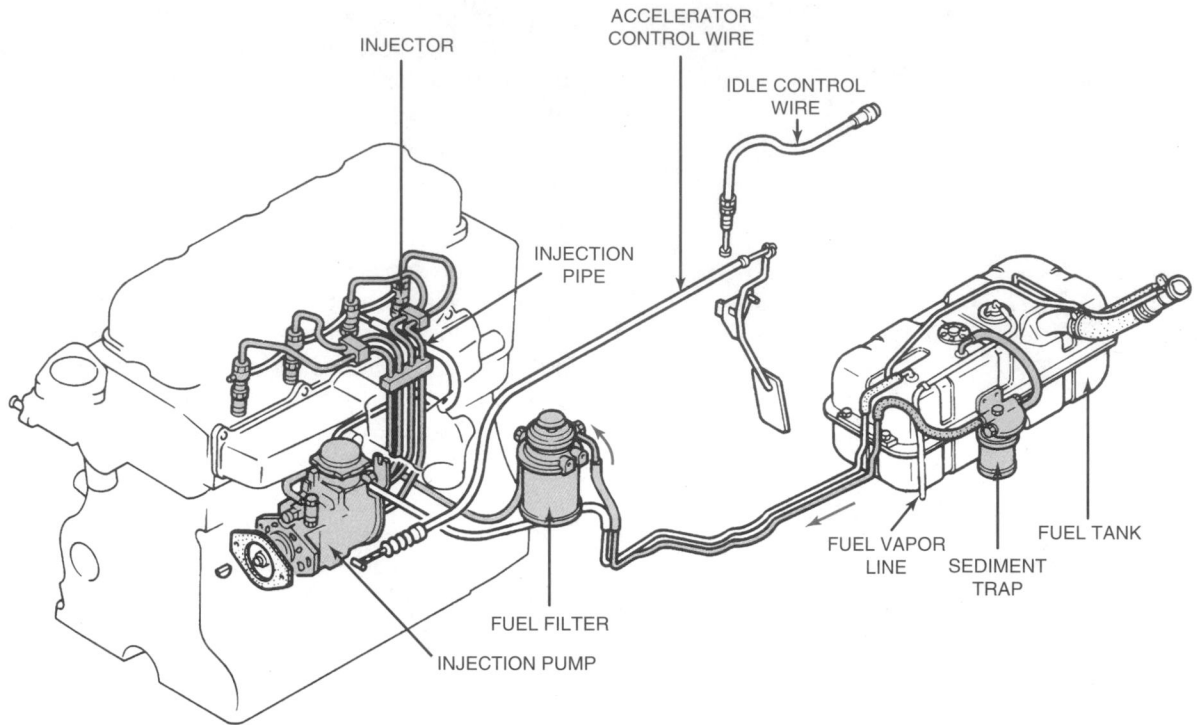

INJECTOR

ACCELERATOR
CONTROL WIRE

IDLE CONTROL
WIRE

INJECTION
PIPE

FUEL VAPOR
LINE

FUEL TANK

SEDIMENT
TRAP

FUEL FILTER

INJECTION PUMP

Figure 20-43. Study this four-cylinder diesel engine fuel system. (Mazda)

A cutaway view of a four-cylinder automotive diesel engine is pictured in **Figure 20-44**. Note that the fuel injection pump is driven by a cogged belt. A V-8 diesel engine is shown in **Figure 20-45**. A cross-sectional view of a fuel injector in place in the cylinder head is illustrated in **Figure 20-46**.

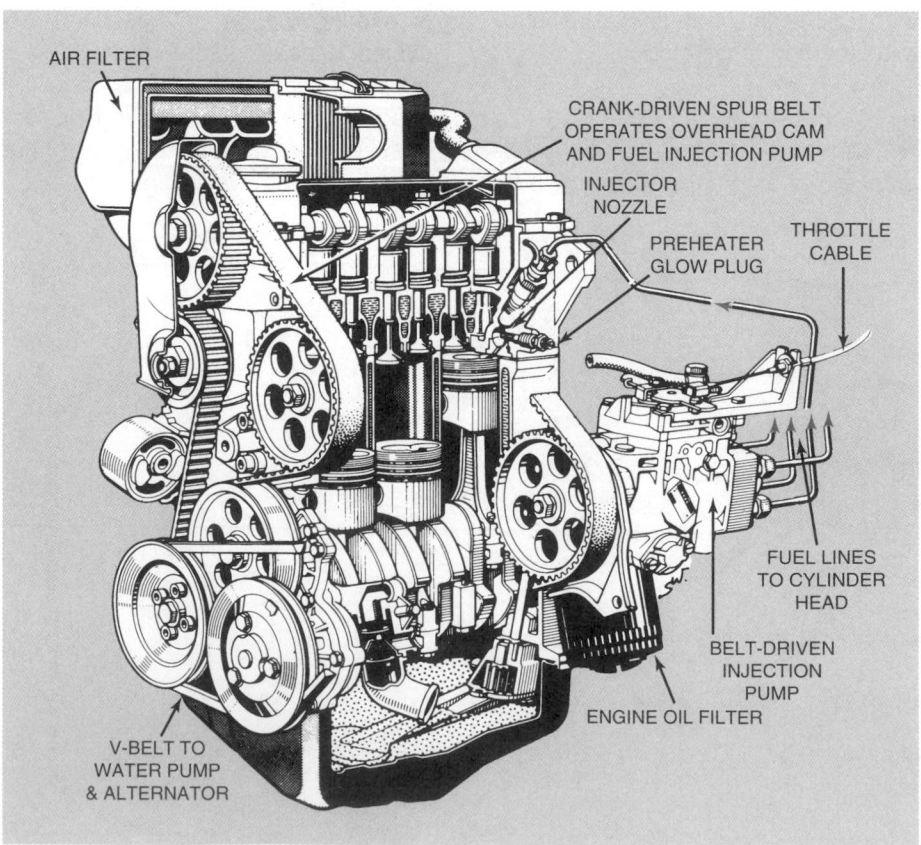

AIR FILTER

CRANK-DRIVEN SPUR BELT
OPERATES OVERHEAD CAM
AND FUEL INJECTION PUMP

INJECTOR
NOZZLE

PREHEATER
GLOW PLUG

THROTTLE
CABLE

FUEL LINES
TO CYLINDER
HEAD

BELT-DRIVEN
INJECTION
PUMP

ENGINE OIL FILTER

V-BELT TO
WATER PUMP
& ALTERNATOR

Figure 20-44. A four-cylinder, 1.5-liter, diesel engine. This engine develops 48 (SAE Net) hp at 5000 RPM. (Volkswagen)

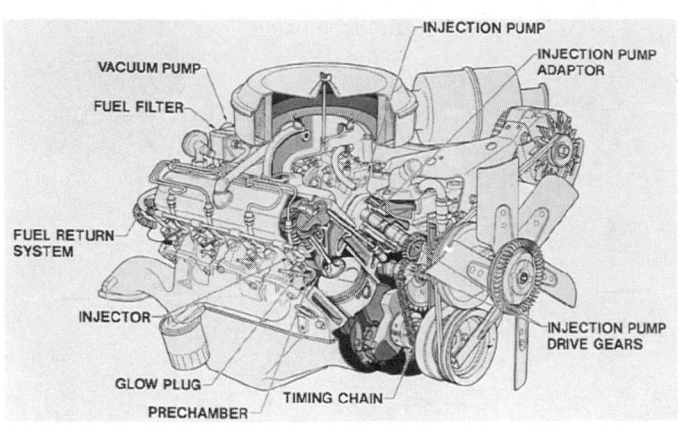

Figure 20-45. An eight-cylinder diesel engine of 350 cu. in. displacement. This engine develops 120 hp at 3600 RPM. Speed is limited to 4000 RPM. Compression ratio is 22.3 to 1. (GM)

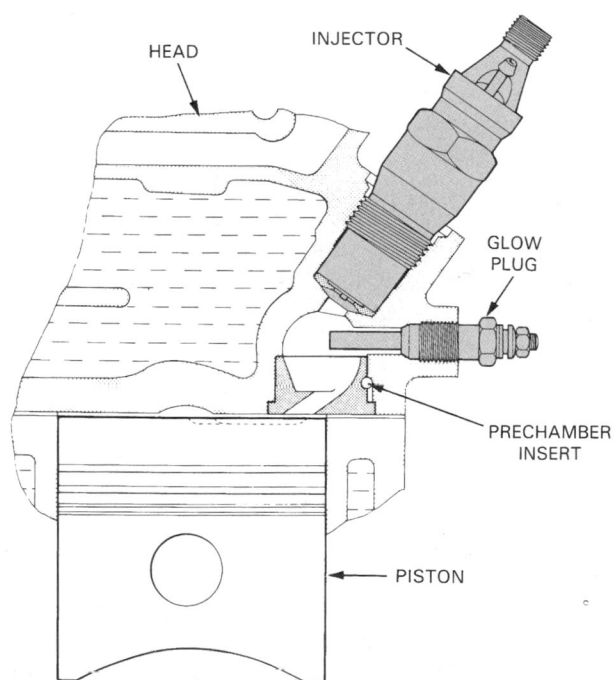

Figure 20-46. Diesel injector and glow plug arrangement. (Champion)

Diesel Injection System Service

Begin by obtaining a service manual which covers the exact diesel engine to be serviced. Diesel injection system tests and adjustments must be precise to ensure correct operation. Closely follow the recommended service procedures, clearances, adjustments, and pressures. Use the proper service tools and test equipment. Some of the more common service adjustments, inspections, and repairs follow.

 Note: Diesel fuel cleanliness is critical. Injector pump internal parts are fitted to extremely close tolerances and any contamination from dirt or water can cause driveability problems. Clean or replace all filters and water traps as recommended.

Stopping a Runaway Diesel Engine

It is possible for a diesel engine to continue running even after the key is turned off. This is called a **runaway diesel engine,** and can result from wiring problems, vacuum leaks, incorrect vacuum connections, damaged vacuum control unit, defective vacuum pump, or a fuel solenoid not returning the fuel valve to the closed position. The correct method of stopping a runaway engine varies with the injection system. Many injection systems will stop if the wire to the fuel solenoid is disconnected. If the engine still continues to run, interrupt the flow of fuel from the tank to the injection pump by disconnecting the wire to the supply pump.

Diesel Injector Service

To replace diesel fuel injectors, release the fuel pressure by cracking a fuel line. Then loosen and remove the fuel line fitting from the injector to be replaced. If the injector has a return line, remove it also. Pull the lines away from the injector, being careful not to bend or kink the tubing. Loosen and unscrew threaded injectors, and pull press-in injectors. Thread or press the new injector in the head. Be careful not to damage the sealing washer during installation and line up any alignment marks on a press-in injector before pushing it to its fully-installed position. Use new gaskets as needed and tighten all fasteners to specified torque. On injectors such as shown in **Figure 20-47**,

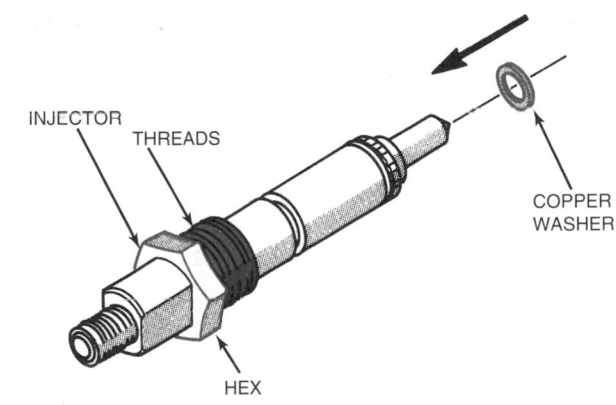

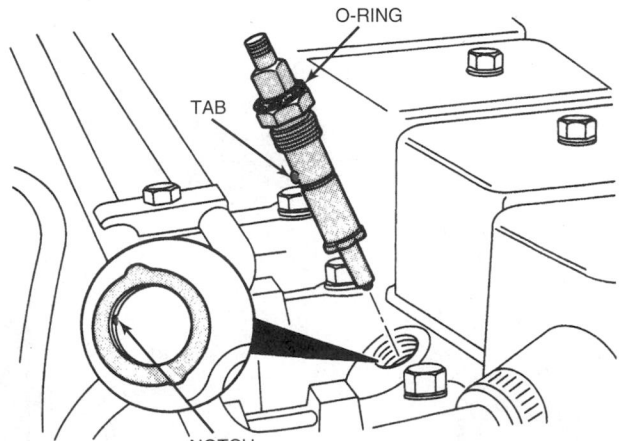

Figure 20-47. A diesel fuel injector which uses a copper sealing washer and threads into place. Use a wrench on the hex top to tighten. Notice the alignment tab and notch. (Dodge)

place a wrench on the hex nut when tightening. Install fuel line fittings and torque. Purge the injectors when necessary, following the instructions given later in this chapter. Check for leaks following engine startup.

Testing Injectors

The injectors, if dirty, damaged, or sticking, can cause rough running, loss of power, knocking, and smoking. The proper tools must be used to disassemble and test diesel injectors. Diesel injectors should be tested for leaks, opening pressure, spray pressure, chatter, spray jet shape, and leakage. An exploded view of a diesel injector is shown in **Figure 20-48**. Use the recommended disassembly techniques. When disassembling system lines and parts, remember to always cap lines, nozzles, and pump fittings to prevent the entry of dirt. Always wipe fittings before reassembly with a clean, lint-free cloth.

Keep all parts of each injector nozzle together as they are carefully matched. Do not mix injector parts. Clean thoroughly in a sonic bath or other suitable cleaner. **Figure 20-49** illustrates the use of a special cleaning tray designed to keep the parts of each injector separate. The tray is lowered into the cleaning bath. When thoroughly clean, reassemble as recommended. For manual cleaning, use a wooden stick or soft brass brush to prevent damaging nozzle parts.

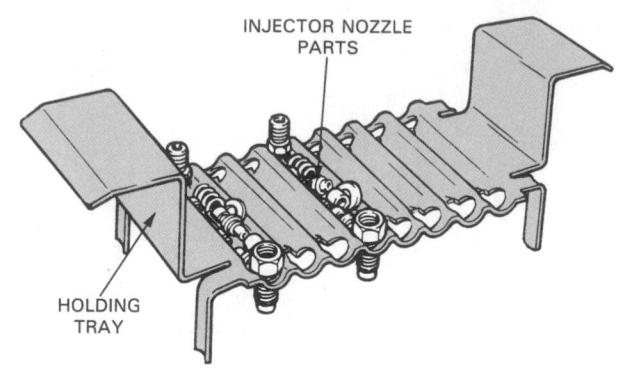

Figure 20-49. This handy cleaning tray keeps parts of each injector separate. Never mix parts. (Chevrolet)

When testing injectors, use a special test liquid instead of diesel fuel. The test liquid will minimize skin problems and is stable in relation to corrosion inhibition. Use the proper test equipment. It is advisable to shroud the injector nozzle with a clear, protective plastic shield. The use of such a shroud is pictured in **Figure 20-50**. Spray pattern should meet manufacturer's recommendations. Injectors should also be checked for nozzle tightness. Using a test stand, build pressure in injector (nozzle tip dry) to slightly below the actual opening pressure (around 150 psi or 1034 kPa). Hold for the recommended time, usually a few seconds, and check the nozzle tip. One manufacturer's acceptable indicators are pictured in **Figure 20-51**.

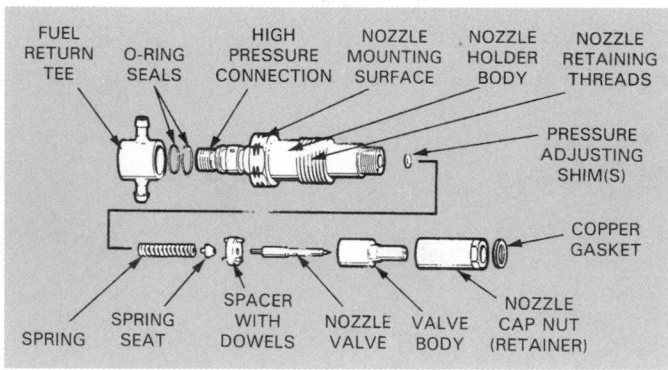

Figure 20-48. Exploded view of a diesel injector and holder assembly. (International/Navistar)

Warning: Do not point an injection nozzle toward your body when conducting tests. Use a clear protective shroud around injector nozzle. Never place your hands in front of the nozzle. When spraying, the fuel leaves the nozzle with tremendous force. It can literally drill through flesh, creating a severe injury with a possibility of blood poisoning. Use care also when working on injection pump or injector line fittings. Wear protective goggles. Crack each fitting to bleed pressure.

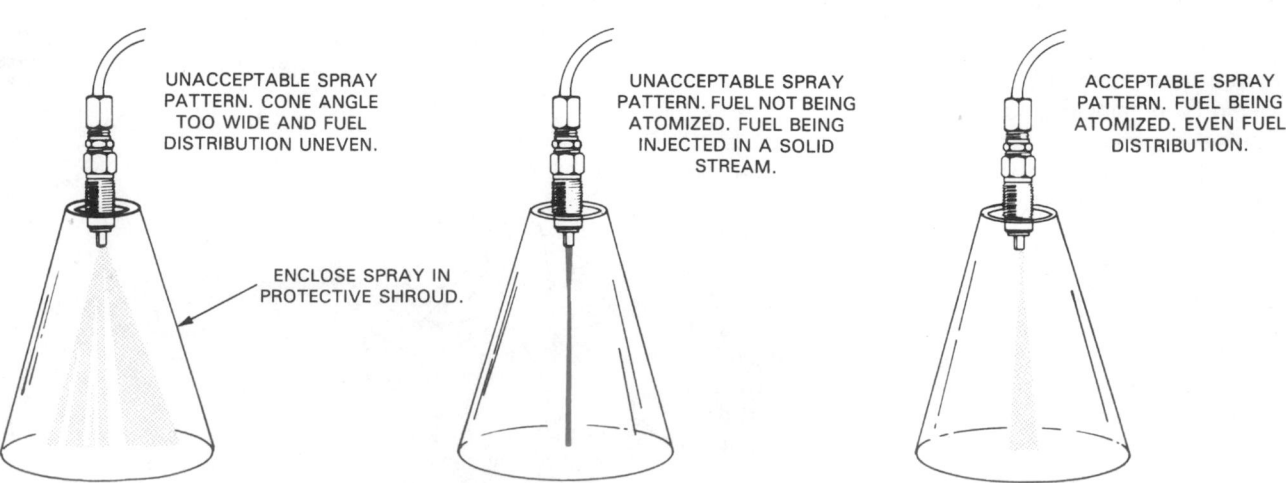

Figure 20-50. Testing diesel injector nozzle spray pattern. Note the use of a protective shroud. (Cadillac)

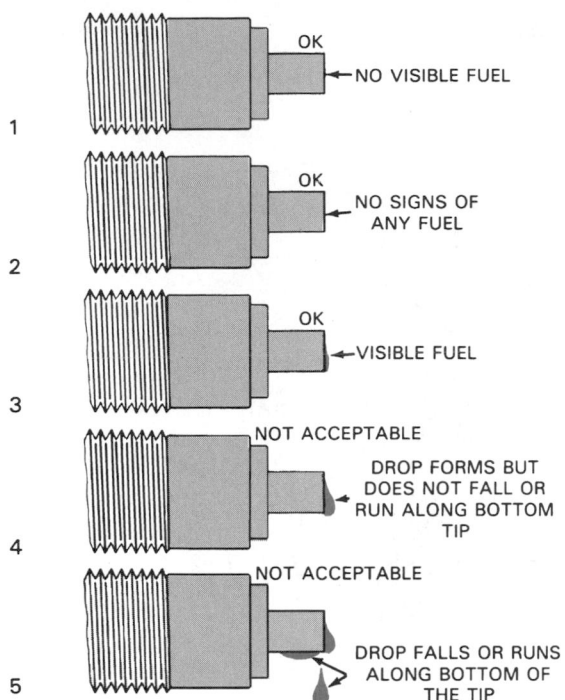

1 — OK ← NO VISIBLE FUEL

2 — OK ← NO SIGNS OF ANY FUEL

3 — OK ← VISIBLE FUEL

4 — NOT ACCEPTABLE — DROP FORMS BUT DOES NOT FALL OR RUN ALONG BOTTOM TIP

5 — NOT ACCEPTABLE — DROP FALLS OR RUNS ALONG BOTTOM OF THE TIP

Figure 20-51. Checking injector nozzle for tightness (sealing ability). After maintaining recommended pressure for a few seconds, nozzle should not show signs of excessive leakage, as in 4 and 5. (Oldsmobile)

Injector Pump Service

Injection pump problems can cause heavy exhaust smoking, surging, rough running, and noise. Binding or improperly adjusted linkage can affect idle speed range. In some instances, the injection pump timing can be off, resulting in very noisy engine operation. Some pumps are timed mechanically by the position of the drive gears. Others must be timed with a luminosity meter. As with the injectors, proper injection pump test tools are essential. Special training in injection pump repair is required. Great care and cleanliness is absolutely necessary. Many shops specialize in pump rebuilding and testing. Do not attempt to make internal repairs to a diesel injection pump without the proper tools and training. Accurate control linkage adjustments are of vital importance. Follow the manufacturer's recommendations.

An in-line injection pump is illustrated in **Figure 20-52**. This pump serves each injector by a separate cylinder-plunger-cam arrangement. A distributor type pump is shown in **Figure 20-53**. Note that a single set of pump plungers generates the required pressure. Fuel is fed from the pump to a fuel distributor rotor. As the rotor revolves, it distributes fuel to the various outlets as required.

Purging the Injection System

In many cases, air in the diesel injection system will cause the engine to misfire or fail to start. This air must be

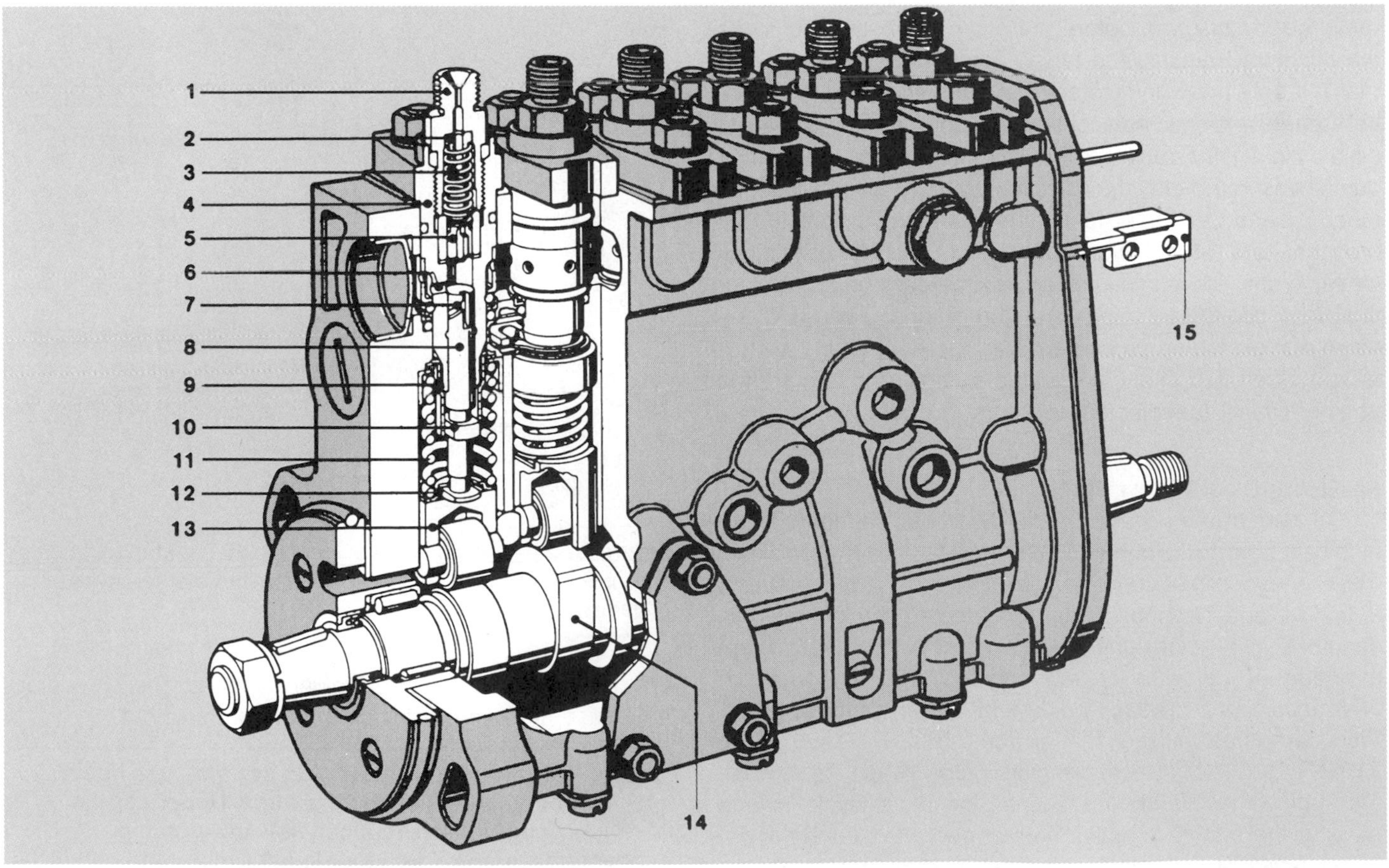

Figure 20-52. One type of in-line fuel injection pump. 1—Delivery valve holder. 2—Filler piece. 3—Delivery valve spring. 4—Pump barrel. 5—Delivery valve. 6—Inlet and spill port. 7—Helix. 8—Pump plunger. 9—Control sleeve. 10—Plunger control arm. 11—Plunger return spring. 12—Spring seat. 13—Roller tappet. 14—Cam. 15—Control rod. (Bosch)

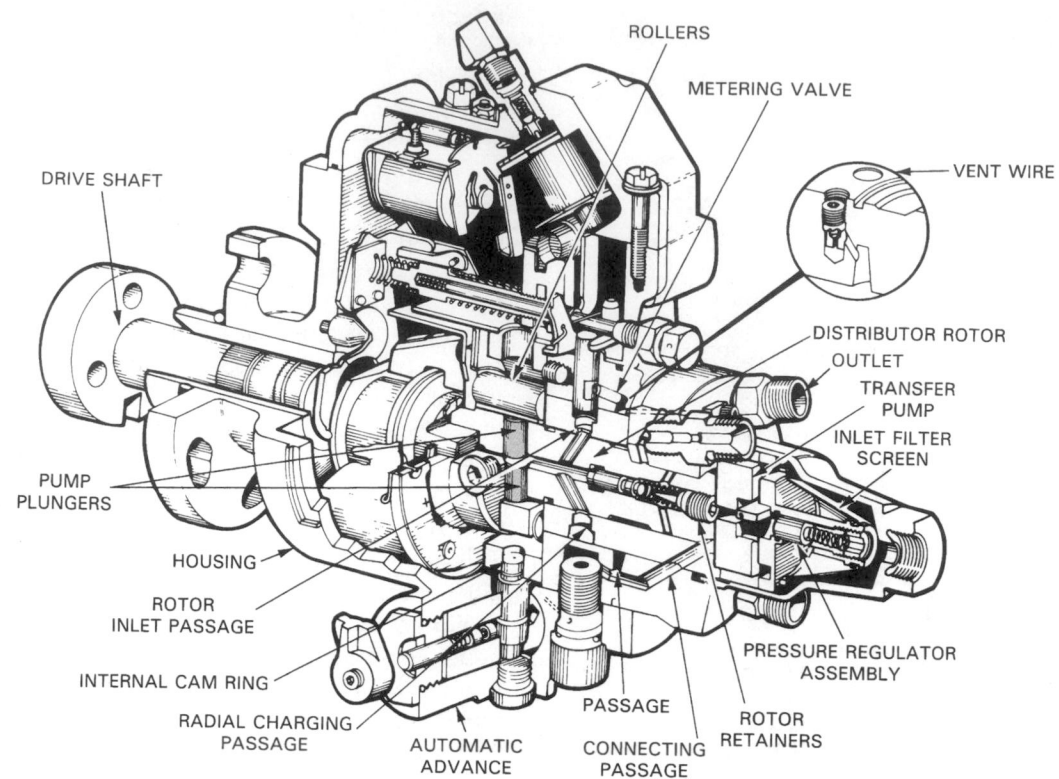

DRIVE SHAFT

ROLLERS

METERING VALVE

VENT WIRE

DISTRIBUTOR ROTOR
OUTLET
TRANSFER
PUMP
INLET FILTER
SCREEN

PUMP
PLUNGERS

HOUSING

ROTOR
INLET PASSAGE

INTERNAL CAM RING

RADIAL CHARGING
PASSAGE

AUTOMATIC
ADVANCE

PASSAGE

CONNECTING
PASSAGE

ROTOR
RETAINERS

PRESSURE REGULATOR
ASSEMBLY

Figure 20-53. Rotary type diesel injection pump. Note double pump plungers. As rotor turns, it passes fuel to various injectors. (Ford)

removed, or **purged,** before the engine will start. To purge the injectors, reinstall the tubing fittings but do not tighten them. If only a few injectors were removed, the engine can be started and the replacement injectors will be purged of air as the engine runs. If all of the injectors or the injector pump was removed, the injection system will contain too much air and the pump will not be able to develop sufficient pressure to start the engine. With all of the injector fittings loose, crank the engine for approximately one minute, or until fuel begins squirting from the fittings. Following the usual diesel starting procedure, start the engine and allow it to run briefly. Tighten the tubing fittings and restart the engine. Check the injector system for proper operation.

Servicing Diesel Glow Plugs

When the engine is cold, compression heat is not high enough to properly ignite the fuel charge. Diesel engines use **glow plugs** for cold starting. A glow plug is a low-voltage heating element located in the combustion chamber. When the ignition is turned on, (engine coolant temperature below a certain point), the glow plugs are energized and can reach peak heat in just a few seconds. Plug temperature can range from 1832°F (1000°C) to 2192°F (1200°C). Once the glow plugs reach peak heat, the engine may be started. Some glow plugs cycle on and off until the engine reaches normal operating temperature. Three types of glow plugs are illustrated in **Figure 20-54.**

A glow plug wiring harness A, and wiring circuit B, are shown in **Figure 20-55.** Never bypass the power relay to

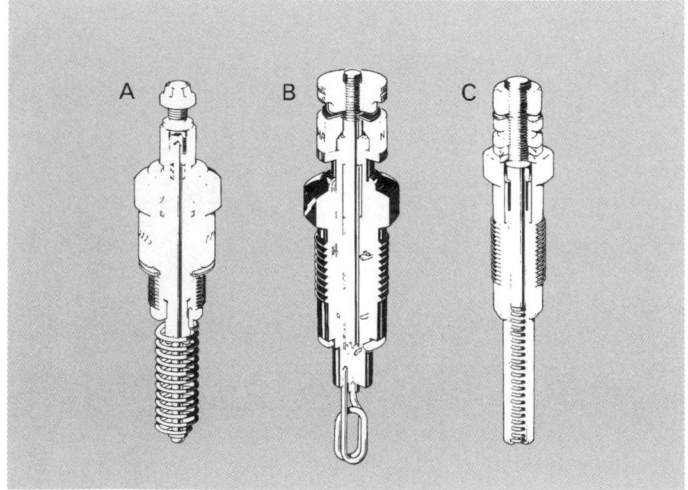

Figure 20-54. Three types of glow plugs. A—Manifold heater type. B—Open element type. C—Sheathed element type. (Champion)

the glow plugs. A constant power supply to the glow plugs will cause them to quickly overheat and burn out.

 Warning: Some glow plug systems use heavy, uninsulated connecting wires. Under certain conditions, current can flow through the connecting resistor wires for almost two minutes after the control light goes out. The wires can become very hot. Keep hands and arms away.

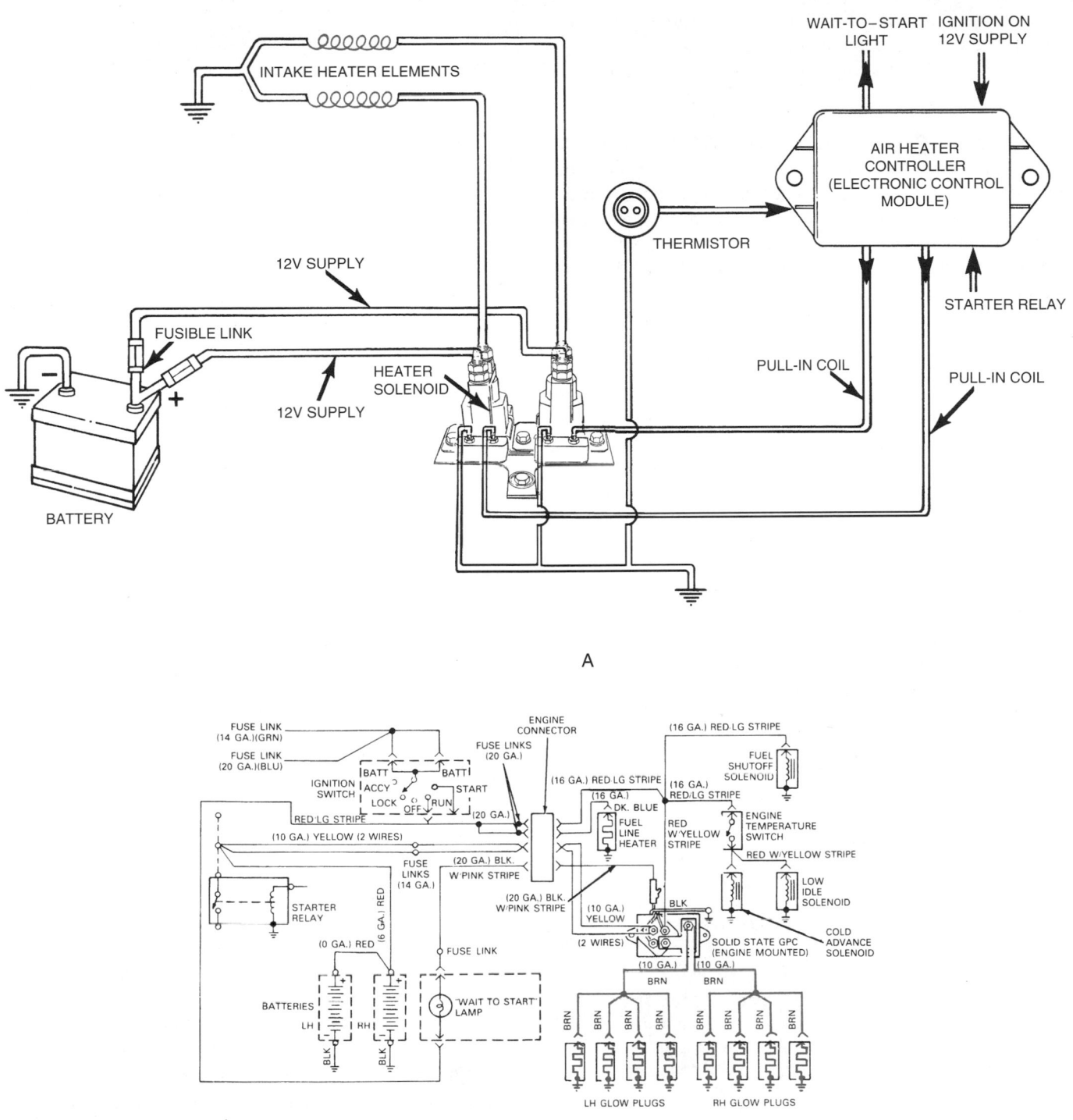

Figure 20-55. A—Schematic illustrating a grid type intake air heating system as used with one type of diesel engine starting system. B—Glow plug electrical circuit. Note that this system is for a four-stroke cycle, V-8, diesel engine. (International/Navistar)

Defective glow plugs or glow plug system problems can cause cold start problems. To isolate a defective glow plug, check the glow plug with an ohmmeter. If the reading is infinity or zero, the plug has probably burned out. Test the glow plug system with the engine cold. Turn the ignition key to the on position and place a test light on each glow plug terminal. If the light does not come on, the system is not sending current to the glow plugs. Check for defective current relays or other components of the control system.

Diesel Service Precautions

Diesel systems can vary widely in some respects. Be certain you understand the system at hand and that you have the proper tools and specifications. Never steam clean or wash injection pumps with the engine running or when the pump is warm. Pump parts are very closely fitted. A sudden temperature change can warp the unit and cause part binding.

Superchargers and Turbochargers

A *supercharger* is a belt-, chain-, or gear-driven pump that forces a dense mixture of air and fuel into the cylinders. By compressing the air-fuel mixture, the supercharger increases the engine's effective compression ratio, resulting in a higher engine power output. See **Figure 20-56**. *Turbochargers* are superchargers that are driven by the force of the engine exhaust. They literally ram the air into the cylinders by raising the pressure of the air in the intake manifold. **Figure 20-57** is a schematic showing the principle of a turbocharger. Many superchargers and turbochargers have an air or liquid *intercooler* installed between the charger output and the engine. The intercooler cools the pressurized air mixture. This reduces engine knocking and improves driveability and performance.

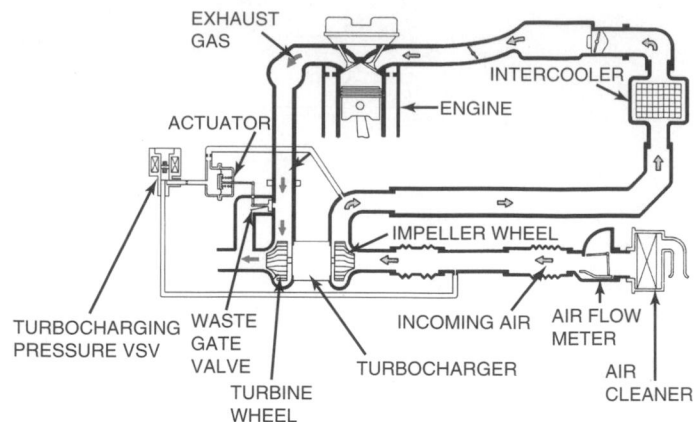

Figure 20-57. Schematic illustrating an exhaust-driven turbocharger. Note the use of an intercooler to drop the mixture temperature. Study the flow of the intake air and the exhaust gas. (Toyota)

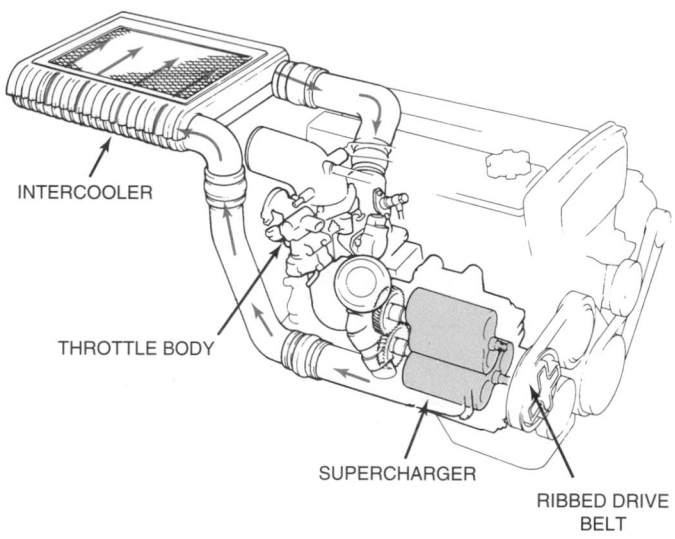

Figure 20-56. One type of supercharger system. The aluminum rotors are turned by a ribbed drive belt, which is connected to the engine's crankshaft. Note the part relationships. This supercharger has an RPM range of approximately 10,000-15,000 RPM. (Toyota)

Superchargers

The supercharger responds immediately when the accelerator is pressed. Boost pressure that is unused by the engine is routed through a *by-pass valve* and back into the supercharger. The by-pass valve is operated by a mechanical linkage or manifold vacuum. The supercharger is generally located between the carburetor or fuel injection system and the intake manifold or intercooler.

Supercharger Service

Supercharger service consists of making sure that the unit is clean, well oiled, and in proper condition. All hoses,

clamps, fittings, and drive mechanisms must be in good condition. The air cleaner element should be checked for restrictions. Small vacuum leaks on the intake side of the supercharger will allow dust to enter the system. Excess dust can prematurely destroy the supercharger. Some superchargers are lubricated by the engine's oil system, in others, the oil is self-contained in the supercharger. Both standard and synthetic oils can be used in an engine with a supercharger. Defective supercharger units usually need to be replaced. Rebuilding is generally performed by the manufacturer.

Turbochargers

Turbochargers use exhaust gas pressure which already exists, and can be thought of as a way to tap into free power. Turbochargers are slightly slower to respond to throttle opening than superchargers, since the turbine must reach very high RPM before it can begin pumping extra air into the engine. To keep the turbocharger from developing too much pressure in the intake manifold, a *waste gate* is installed in the exhaust passages. The waste gate is operated by a diaphragm connected to the intake manifold through a hose. When the turbocharger overpressurizes the intake manifold, this pressure is transmitted to the diaphragm, which opens the waste gate. When the waste gate opens, exhaust gases bypass the turbocharger, causing it to slow down and reduce manifold pressure. Turbocharger bearings are lubricated by pressurized oil from the engine lubricating system.

Although turbochargers can spin at great speed, over 100,000 RPM, they generally require little service during their normal life. All gaskets must seal, fasteners must be properly torqued, and the oil supply system open and functioning. Auxiliary controls such as the waste gate must operate correctly. The most common turbocharger problem is oil seal failure, resulting in lubricating oil being pumped into the exhaust system. This results in excessive oil smoke from the exhaust.

When removing the unit from the engine, clean before removal and cover any openings into the engine. Use extreme care during handling and repair to avoid the slightest nicking or bending of any part of the turbine or compressor blades. Blade damage would seriously reduce the unit's life. In some cases, it could cause the unit to literally destroy itself.

Inspect the turbine and compressor for nicks, bends, cracks, or clogs. Unit should spin freely and quietly. Check axial end play with a dial indicator. Inspect the boost control or by-pass valve for proper operation. Follow all manufacturer's recommendations. If the turbocharger is damaged, it is usually easier to replace the entire assembly rather than attempting to rebuild it.

Air Cleaner Service

All modern cars and light trucks use paper *air cleaner elements.* These elements can be round (radial airflow), as in **Figure 20-58**, or flat (linear airflow), as shown in **Figure 20-59**. A few older vehicles and some large trucks use an oil-wetted polyurethane element. The paper air cleaner element should be replaced at specified intervals. It is important that great care be exercised when removing the element. Do not let dirt fall into the carburetor or intake area. When practical, it is advisable to remove the air cleaner as a unit. When the filter is removed, cover the carburetor or fuel injection induction port with a clean cloth.

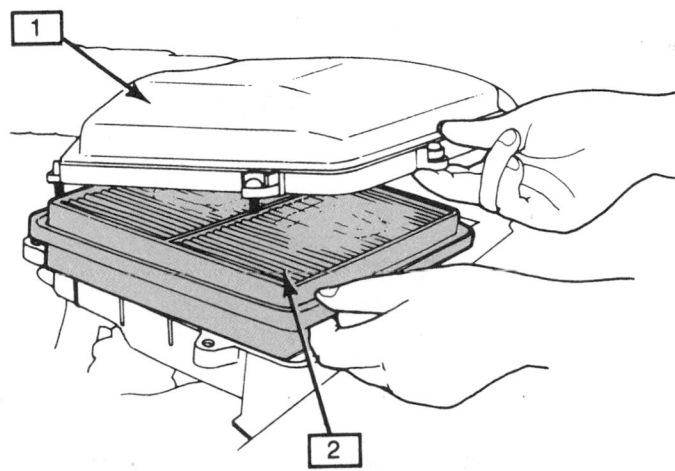

Figure 20-59. Linear flow air filter element (2), being removed from its housing (1). Some are marked to indicate "up" or "airflow" direction. Be sure to install filter correctly. (Geo)

The flat air filter element is designed for use in a remotely mounted air cleaner housing. Transverse engines and styling changes that limit clearance under the hood have made it necessary to relocate the air cleaner assembly on some vehicles. Although the filter element can be cleaned, replacement is generally suggested.

If it is not excessively dirty or oil soaked, the air cleaner element can be cleaned by directing a stream of compressed air through the element in a direction opposite to regular airflow. See **Figure 20-60**. The paper element

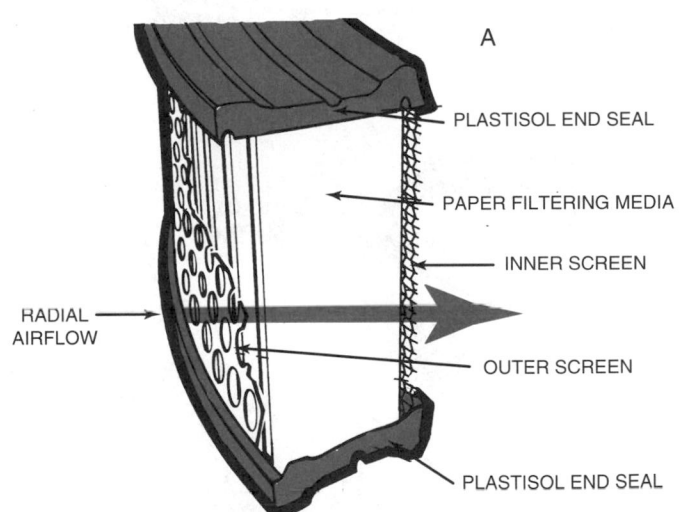

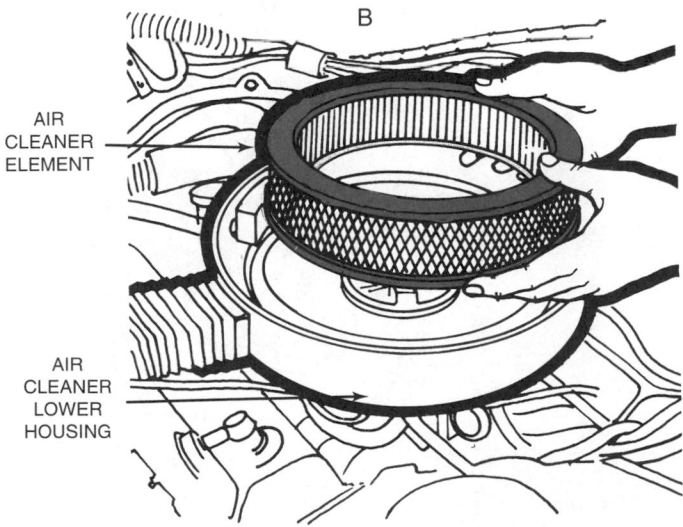

Figure 20-58. A round, radial-airflow air cleaner element. A—Cutaway of a paper element. B—This technician is replacing a dirty air cleaner element with a new one. (Fram)

Figure 20-60. Cleaning a paper filter element by blowing air through it from inside. Use a relatively soft stream of air and keep nozzle well back from filter surface. Wear safety glasses. (Chrysler)

also may be cleaned by lightly tapping it on a flat surface. This will dislodge much of the dirt. Some dry type filters can be washed in water and mild detergent. This will usually be indicated on the filter itself or on an air cleaner housing decal. Refer to **Figure 20-61**. Dry before using. Do not use excessive heat.

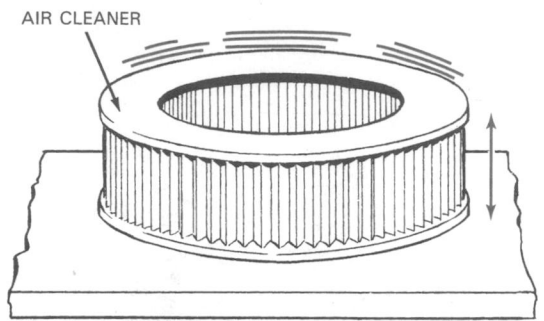

AIR CLEANER

Figure 20-61. Cleaning a paper filter element by tapping on a flat surface. Do not tap on one edge; strike with the entire seal surface.

Before replacing a paper air filter element, check the element against a light source, such as a drop light, to make sure there are no ruptured spots. Check top and bottom gasket surfaces for injury. Install right side up where indicated. The element shown in **Figure 20-62** was badly damaged from careless handling. A polyurethane element from an older vehicle can be cleaned and reused. First, remove it from the support screen. Wash it thoroughly in a nonflammable solvent. Remove the excess solvent by gently squeezing the element. Never twist, shake, slap, or wring because this may tear the element. Next, check the element for tears or other damage. If it is OK, place it in clean, light engine oil. Squeeze excess from the element and replace element on screen support. Make sure the element is placed on the support to form a sound seal for both top and bottom contact edge.

Figure 20-62. Physical damage rendered this element unfit for further service. (Perfect Circle)

When servicing both the paper and polyurethane element filters, be sure to clean the filter body and cover before replacing element. Make certain the carburetor-to-cleaner body gasket is in good shape and is in place. Tighten the cover nuts securely. See **Figure 20-63**. When replacing the cleaner body, be sure it faces in the correct direction. If a tang or a locating lug is present, see that the tang or lug engages properly.

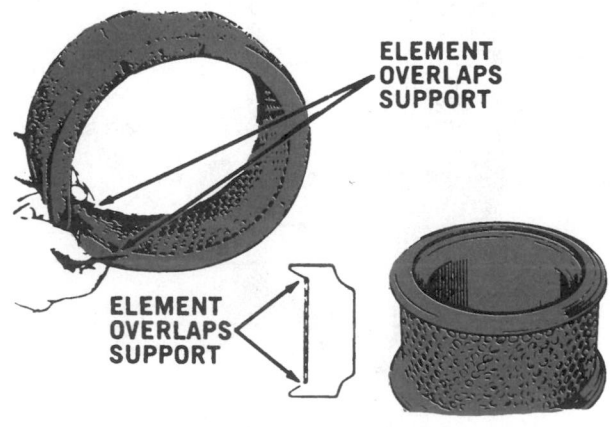

ELEMENT OVERLAPS SUPPORT

ELEMENT OVERLAPS SUPPORT

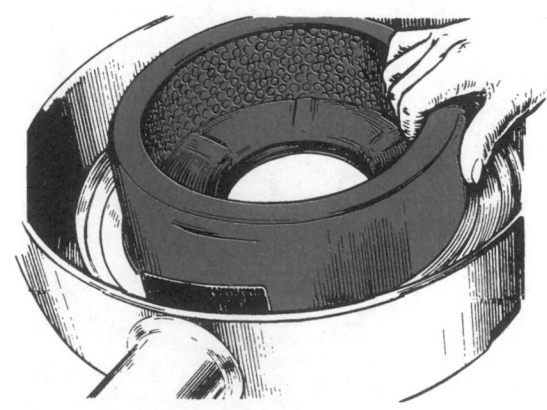

Figure 20-63. Cleaning procedure for a polyurethane type filter element. Soak in solvent and squeeze as dry as possible. Soak in clean oil and squeeze out excess. Install element on support screen. Install in cleaner body.

Fuel Mileage Check

Many owners complain about poor *fuel mileage* without considering the factors that contribute to poor mileage. Explain that mileage figures obtained in economy runs or on a long trip give false indications of the mileage to be expected from normal day-to-day driving. When there is a lot of stop-and-go driving, cold starting, or idling, fuel mileage suffers. Always inform the owner about the gas robbing effect of rapid acceleration, prolonged idling, excessive speed, stop-and-go driving, low tire pressure, engine out of tune, and clogged air cleaners.

By using a measured amount of gas and driving the car at a normal cruising speed over a level stretch, it is possible to come up with an accurate mile-per-gallon figure for average cruising speeds. Make the test in two directions on a selected strip to allow for any wind or downgrade. **Figure 20-64** illustrates the use of a flow-meter to determine approximate miles-per-gallon. This particular setup is part of a testing stand that will allow a number of engine tests to be made in the shop. The car's rear wheels are placed on rollers.

Figure 20-64. Using a flow-meter to determine approximate gas mileage. This setup is used inside the shop on a special test machine. (Bear)

Tech Talk

Before getting too involved when diagnosing a suspected fuel injection system problem such as a rough idle, check for vacuum leaks. The most common cause of rough idle, surging, and poor acceleration is a vacuum leak. Typical causes of vacuum leaks are disconnected or cracked hoses. If the hose connects to a vacuum-operated component, the device may not operate.

To check a vacuum leak, begin with the vacuum hoses. Start by carefully checking for splits and cracks. Unplug each hose with the engine running, plug the end of the hose, and see if the idle improves. If the idle does improve, check the part that is operated by that hose for a defect. If all hoses and vacuum-operated accessories check out, check the intake manifold bolts and throttle body fasteners. Also closely check the EGR valve, as it often sticks partially open.

If nothing is found, squirt light oil around suspected gaskets and then race the engine. If the exhaust smokes, the oil is being drawn into the engine through the leak. If all gaskets and hoses check out good, check for a cracked manifold or head.

Summary

Fuel injection is becoming more widely used because it provides reduced emission levels and better gas mileage. The two basic types of gasoline fuel injection are electronic and mechanical. The electronic system uses an electric fuel pump to produce the needed pressure. The mechanical systems use an engine-driven injector pump. Two kinds of electronic fuel injection systems are the pulsed and continuous flow systems. Be careful to bleed fuel lines before performing any service work. Injector pumps require special tools and clean working conditions.

The basic pulse system consists of four parts: air induction, fuel delivery, electronic control module, and the electronic sensors. Pulse injectors are opened electrically while injectors in the continuous system are always open. Diesel engine injection systems use high injector pressures and inject the fuel directly into the combustion chamber. When working on injectors or pumps, use extreme care. Injector or line spray can be lethal. Keep diesel fuel systems free of water.

Superchargers are driven by belts, gears, or chains. Turbochargers use exhaust gases to spin a turbine which drives a compressor. The compressor boosts air pressure in the intake manifold. Use care to avoid denting or nicking the turbine or compressor vanes. Vane damage could cause a destructive unbalanced condition.

Change replaceable air cleaner elements at recommended intervals and service others as required. When using compressed air to clean a filter element, use care to avoid damaging the element. Accurate fuel mileage estimates require careful testing. Inform the vehicle's owner that fuel mileage can be greatly improved by good driving habits and proper maintenance.

Know These Terms

Fuel injection	Solenoid winding
Air-fuel ratios	Spring pressure
Fuel injectors	Pulse width
Atomize	Cold start valve
Vaporize	Auxiliary air regulator
Stoichiometric	Powertrain control module
Electronic fuel injection	Sensors
Mechanical fuel injection	Oxygen sensor
Pulsed injection	Engine speed sensor
Continuous injection	Throttle position sensor
Throttle body injection	Manifold vacuum sensor
Single-point injection	Manifold absolute pressure
Central fuel injection	sensor
Multiport injection	Temperature sensor
Multi-point injection	Mass airflow sensor
Sequential fuel injection	Schrader valve
Port fuel injection	Speed density
Air induction system	Valve
Fuel delivery system	Check ball
Electronic control module	Mechanical airflow sensor
Electronic sensors	Injector pump
Air cleaner assembly	Runaway diesel engine
Throttle body	Purged
Intake manifold	Glow plugs
Throttle valve	Supercharger
Filter	Turbocharger
Water trap	Intercooler
Pressure regulator	By-pass valve
Intake manifold vacuum	Waste gate
Fuel rail	Air cleaner elements
Nozzle	Fuel mileage
Sealing needle	

Review Questions—Chapter 20

Do not write in this book. Write your answers on a separate sheet of paper

1. Continuous and pulsed are the two classifications of _____ injection systems.
   (A) mechanical diesel
   (B) electronic diesel
   (C) mechanical gasoline
   (D) electronic gasoline

2. Injectors in the continuous systems are opened by _____.
   (A) electric solenoids
   (B) fuel pressure
   (C) air pressure
   (D) spring pressure

3. In the continuous flow system, basic air-fuel ratio control is provided by a_____ sensor.
   (A) pressure
   (B) engine speed
   (C) manifold vacuum
   (D) airflow

4. Bleeding is used to remove _____ from the fuel injector lines.
   (A) fuel
   (B) pressure
   (C) air
   (D) water and dirt

5. The speed sensor in the pulsed system is mounted so that it can monitor the rotation of the _____.
   (A) crankshaft
   (B) camshaft
   (C) distributor shaft
   (D) All of the above.

6. List the four basic parts of the pulsed fuel injection system.

7. Fuel injectors can be cleaned by using _____.
   (A) a special tool and cleaning solvent
   (B) carburetor spray cleaner
   (C) kerosene
   (D) parts solvent

8. The continuous flow injector is opened by _____.
   (A) an electric solenoid
   (B) spring pressure
   (C) fuel pressure
   (D) Intake manifold vacuum

9. Superchargers can be driven by _____.
   (A) belts
   (B) gears
   (C) chains
   (D) All of the above.

10. Turbochargers boost the pressure in the _____.
    (A) intake manifold
    (B) exhaust manifold
    (C) cylinder head
    (D) Both A & C.

11. The turbocharger waste gate reduces manifold pressure by _____.
    (A) bleeding intake pressure into the exhaust system
    (B) allowing the exhaust gases to bypass the turbocharger
    (C) allowing the exhaust gases to enter the intake manifold
    (D) bleeding intake pressure into the air cleaner housing ahead of the throttle

12. Paper air filter elements can be cleaned by any of the following methods, EXCEPT:
    (A) hot water and mild detergent.
    (B) tapping on a flat surface.
    (C) blowing out with air pressure.
    (D) All of the above.

13. Name four driver habits that can cause poor fuel mileage.

14. Name two vehicle problems that can cause poor fuel mileage.
15. When working on fuel systems, always keep an approved _____ handy.

ASE-Type Questions

1. Technician A says that mechanical gasoline injection systems inject the fuel directly into the combustion chamber. Technician B says that diesel engine injection systems do not need an electronic control system. Who is right?
   (A) A only.
   (B) B only.
   (C) Both A & B.
   (D) Neither A nor B.

2. Purging is used to remove _____ from the fuel injector lines.
   (A) fuel
   (B) pressure
   (C) air
   (D) water and dirt

3. Technician A says that electronic injection systems use an electric fuel pump to produce the needed injector pressure. Technician B says that mechanical injection system injectors are opened by fuel pressure. Who is right?
   (A) A only.
   (B) B only.
   (C) Both A & B.
   (D) Neither A nor B.

4. All of the following statements about intake manifold vacuum are true, EXCEPT:
   (A) high engine load causes low vacuum.
   (B) vacuum increases when engine load increases.
   (C) low engine load causes high vacuum.
   (D) vacuum is proportional to engine load.

5. Technician A says that all gasoline injection systems use higher pressures than diesel injection systems. Technician B says that some gasoline injection systems use higher pressures than diesel injection systems. Who is right?
   (A) A only.
   (B) B only.
   (C) Both A & B.
   (D) Neither A nor B.

6. Technician A says that when testing a diesel injector spray pattern, use a protective shroud around the fuel discharge. Technician B says to use a good grade of diesel fuel for all diesel injector testing. Who is right?
   (A) A only.
   (B) B only.
   (C) Both A & B.
   (D) Neither A nor B.

7. All of the following statements about diesel injectors are true, EXCEPT:
   (A) the discharge from a diesel injector can penetrate deeply into human flesh.
   (B) diesel injectors inject fuel directly into the cylinder.
   (C) diesel injectors are opened electrically.
   (D) diesel injectors are closed by spring pressure.

8. Glow plugs are used to _____.
   (A) open the injectors
   (B) heat the injectors
   (C) assist in cold starting
   (D) assist in hot starting

9. Turbochargers are driven by _____.
   (A) intake airflow
   (B) a small electric motor
   (C) exhaust gases
   (D) a V-belt

10. Technician A says that turbochargers speed can exceed 100,000 RPM. Technician B says that turbocharger bearings are pressure lubricated from the engine oiling system. Who is right?
    (A) A only.
    (B) B only.
    (C) Both A & B.
    (D) Neither A nor B.

Suggested Activities

1. Locate fuel injection components on a vehicle. Draw a schematic diagram of the system. Add arrows to show fuel flow.
2. Referring to the above activity, determine whether the fuel injection system was a central or multi-point system. Make a chart showing the differences between central and multi-point fuel injection systems.
3. Using a factory service manual, create a troubleshooting chart for a common fuel injection system problem, such as hesitation, missing, or no-start.

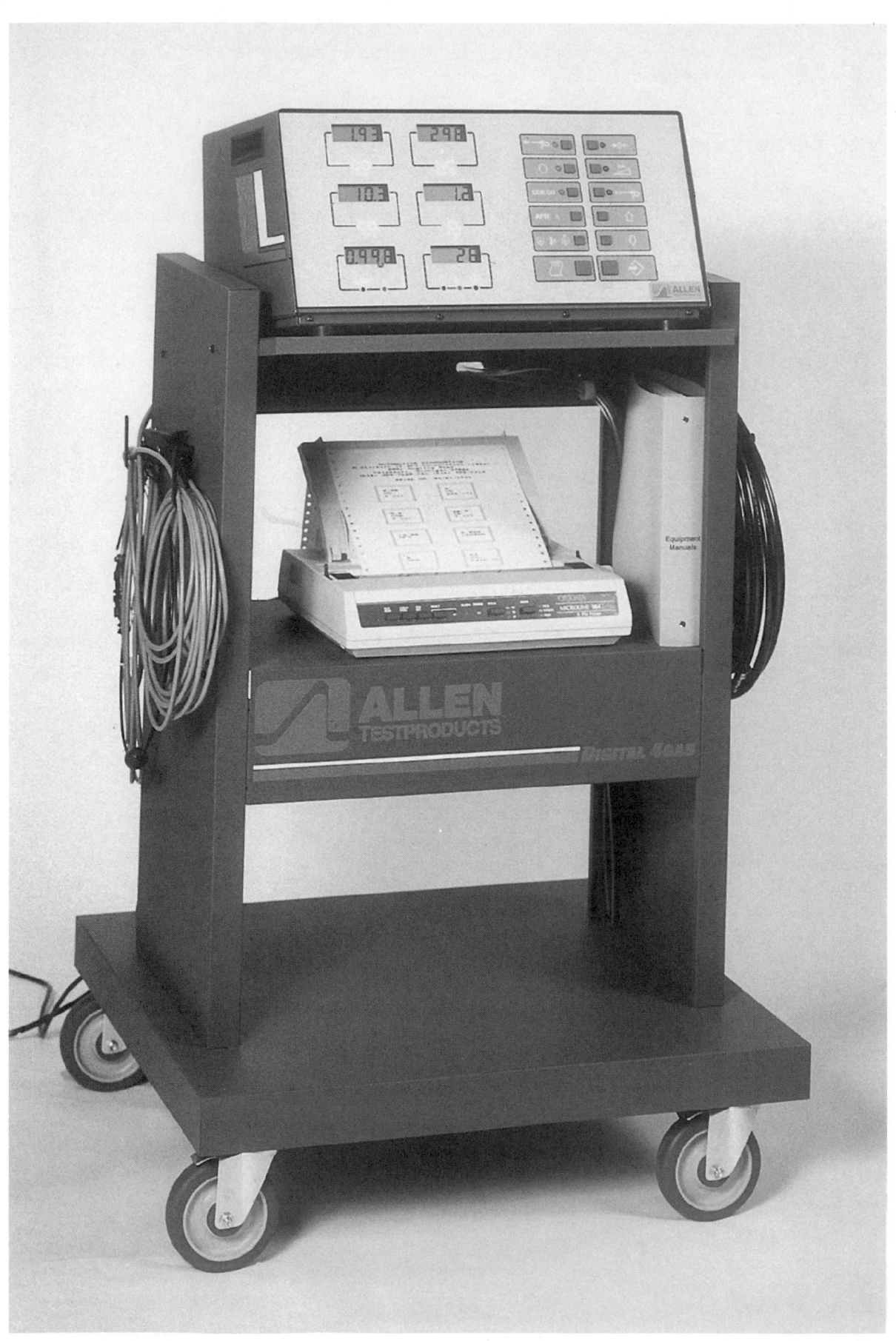

An exhaust gas analyzer, such as the digital four gas analyzer shown above, is frequently used to adjust the idle mixture on emission controlled carburetors. (Allen Test Products)

21

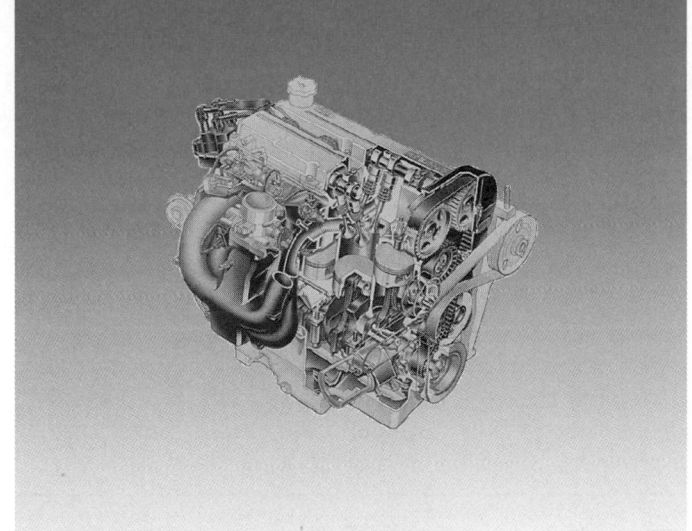

Carburetor Service

After studying this chapter, you will be able to:
- Detect intake manifold air leakage.
- Adjust carburetor idle speed and idle mixture.
- Adjust a manual and automatic choke.
- Adjust throttle linkage.
- Service a manifold heat control valve.
- Adjust a fuel bowl vent.
- Set float level and float drop.
- Adjust an accelerator pump.
- Disassemble, clean, inspect, and reassemble a carburetor.

Although they are no longer installed on late model vehicles, there are still millions of carburetors in use. This chapter covers the adjustment, disassembly, and repair of carburetors. Carburetor service should be done carefully since gasoline is extremely dangerous and carburetors are precision devices, which are easily damaged.

 Warning: Carburetor testing, inspecting, and repair involves the possibility of fire or explosion from spilled gasoline. Dispose of spilled gasoline and gasoline-soaked rags properly. Do not allow flames, sparks, or smoking materials anywhere near the fuel system when it is being serviced.

Carburetor Functions

There are many sizes and types of carburetors. However, all carburetors have the same basic function. Carburetors atomize gasoline, mix it with air, and deliver the mixture to the engine. The typical carburetor is a soft metal casting with internal passages for fuel and air flow. Various valves, springs, vacuum diaphragms, linkages, gaskets, and seals are also used. Sensors and control devices are installed on modern carburetors for use with electronic engine control systems.

All carburetors have six basic systems:

- The *float system* controls the level of fuel in the carburetor bowl.
- The *main metering system* uses *venturi* vacuum (vacuum developed in the carburetor throat) to pull fuel from the bowl at cruising speeds.

- The *idle* and *off-idle systems* use intake manifold vacuum to pull fuel from the bowl at idle and low speeds.
- The *power system* delivers extra fuel when the engine is under heavy load.
- The *accelerator pump* supplies extra fuel into the air horn when the throttle is opened.
- The *choke system* enriches the air-fuel mixture when the engine is cold.

Other related systems are used on some carburetors and not others. Carburetor systems are operated by manifold and venturi vacuum, gravity, calibrated springs, and mechanical linkage. Newer carburetors use motors or solenoids to control idle speed and mixture. These devices are operated by the engine control module. New carburetors also contain input sensors.

Carburetor Service

The carburetor is a complex device requiring special service procedures. However, it can be adjusted and repaired as long as careful attention is paid. The following sections detail the general procedures for servicing carburetors.

Pre-Service Checks

Before performing carburetor diagnosis and service, make sure that all related systems are functioning properly. What appears to be a carburetor problem quite often turns out to be a problem in another engine system. Inspect all related emission control systems such as exhaust gas recirculation (EGR), positive crankcase ventilation (PCV), computer sensors, and electrical connections. Spark plugs must be in good condition, clean, and correctly gapped. Check ignition timing and ignition secondary wiring. Engine compression should be up to specifications in all cylinders. Fuel delivery system must be functioning properly. The air cleaner must be clean. Check the action of any intake air heat control devices.

Vacuum leaks are a common source of idle and low speed problems, especially rough idle, surging, and hesitation. Check for possible vacuum leaks around the intake manifold, carburetor mounting gasket, and vacuum hose connections. When an intake manifold leak is suspected, torque the manifold fasteners. Check for a leak by squirting oil along the gasket edge and other areas where a leak could occur. If a leak exists, the idle speed and vacuum readings will change. See **Figure 21-1.** These checks along with any others related to the specific vehicle will pay off in time saved. They will often prevent expensive repairs that were not needed and that would fail to correct the problem. Unless the trouble is definitely known to be in the carburetor, always check these other areas before starting extensive repairs, adjustments, and replacement.

 Caution: Avoid dropping anything into the carburetor when the air cleaner is off.

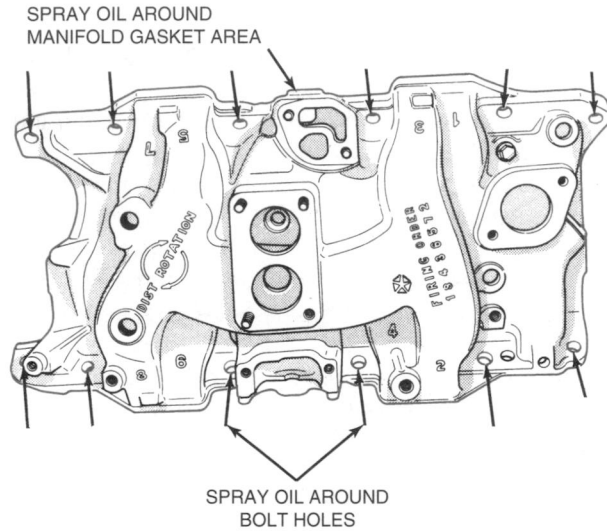

Figure 21-1. Spray oil around the intake manifold gasket and bolt areas to check for any vacuum leaks. (Chrysler)

Carburetor Adjustments

Many adjustments can be made with the carburetor on the engine. Other adjustments require carburetor removal and partial or complete disassembly. All carburetor adjustments can affect emissions. Most newer carburetors do not have any provisions for idle mixture adjustment. On other new vehicles, the engine control module will compensate for any adjustment to the fuel mixture, canceling out any attempt to readjust the carburetor. Since there are a number of different manufacturers and countless models of carburetors, the following procedures will be general and applicable to the adjustment of a typical carburetor. Since carburetor designs vary, the technician should consult a manual covering the specific carburetor to be adjusted or repaired.

 Warning: Use extreme caution when the engine is operating. Do not stand directly in line with the fan. Do not place your hands near the pulleys, belts, or fan. Do not wear loose clothing. If you have long hair, tie it back or wear it under a hat. Keep face and hands away from the carburetor when the engine is running. A backfire through the carburetor can produce a serious burn.

Fast Idle Speed Adjustment

A *fast idle* setting is necessary to keep the engine from stalling when it is cold. Bring the engine to normal operating temperature. Shut off the engine and connect a tachometer. Open the throttle and adjust the fast idle cam so that the *fast idle adjusting screw* contacts the recommended step or index mark.

Some specifications call for the automatic transmission to be in drive. If this is the case and if the car is equipped with a vacuum emergency brake release, disconnect it and attach a vacuum gauge to the vacuum line at the brake release diaphragm or vacuum cylinder. Failure to do this can cause the brake to release, thus allowing the car to lunge forward. It is also advisable to block the wheels. Start the car and turn the fast idle adjusting screw in or out to bring the engine RPM to specifications. Specifications usually average about 750 RPM when the screw is resting in the first or lowest step on the cam. See **Figure 21-2.**

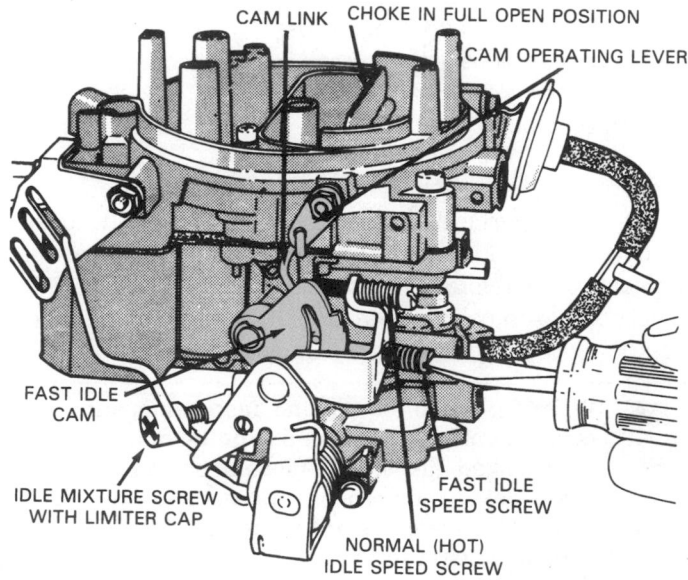

Figure 21-2. Note the position of the fast idle adjusting screw, fast idle cam, and cam operating lever and link. (Chrysler)

Adjusting Fast Idle Cam Linkage

Because the *fast idle cam* position is determined by the degree of choke valve opening, it is important that the relationship be accurate. With the engine stopped, hold the throttle open and close the choke valve. Some carburetors require the choke to be open a measured distance. Allow the throttle lever to return to the idle position. Note where the fast idle screw contacts the fast idle cam. Specifications call for the contact to be on a certain step or in line with an index mark. If the contact is off, align the index mark with the fast idle screw and bend the control rod as needed to produce the specified choke valve closure, **Figure 21-3.** If any adjustment was necessary, the fast idle RPM setting should also be reset.

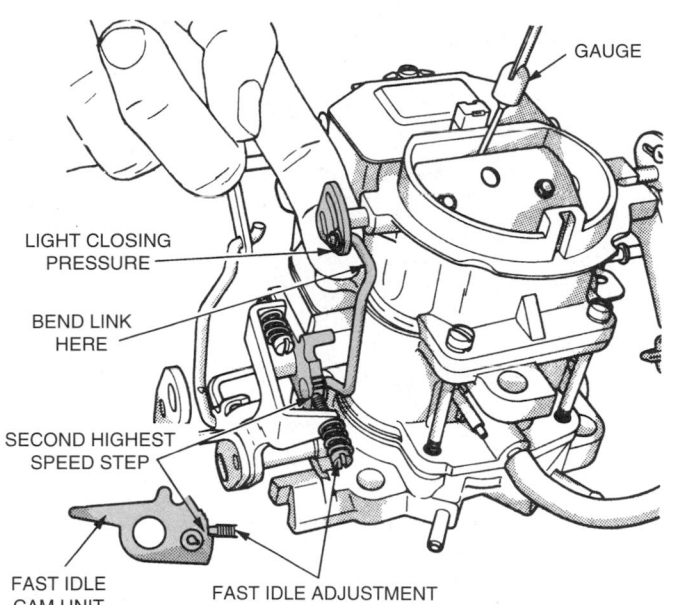

Figure 21-3. Checking fast idle cam adjustment. Note how the fast idle adjustment screw contacts the fast idle cam. (Chrysler)

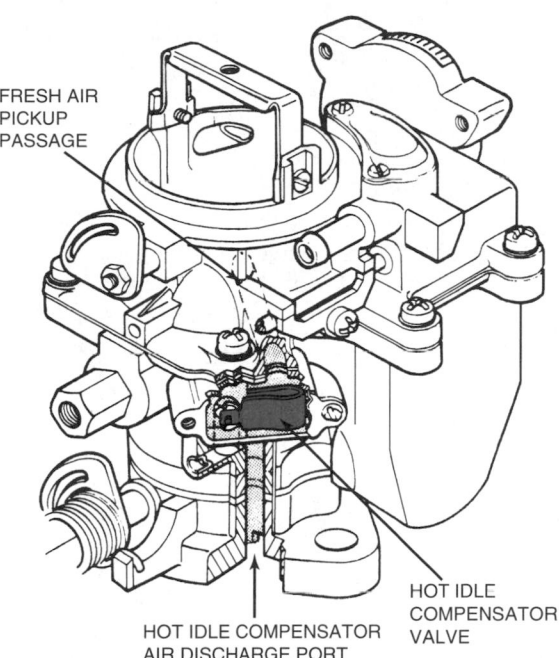

Figure 21-4. One particular hot idle compensator valve arrangement. (Ford)

Hot Idle Speed Adjustment

The *hot idle* adjustment is made when the engine is at normal operating temperature. Check specifications to determine if the automatic transmission or transaxle should be in drive or neutral. If it is to be in drive, set the hand brake and block the wheels. If a vacuum emergency brake release is used, disconnect vacuum line at diaphragm and insert a vacuum gauge. Attach a tachometer to monitor engine speed.

> **Note: Refer to the section on idle speed-up devices if the engine has an idle speed-up or anti-dieseling solenoid.**

Check to see if the air conditioning compressor should be turned on. Some specifications require that the headlights be turned on to load the alternator. Remove the air cleaner and plug any vacuum lines. Check the choke to make sure it is fully open. The secondary throttle valves (when used) must be fully closed at idle. If a hot idle compensator is used, it must be held closed. See **Figure 21-4.** To prevent permanent damage to the compensator valve, press on the valve end and not on the bimetallic strip. Adjust the idle speed screw to produce the specified RPM.

On older carburetors, after making the hot idle speed adjustment, readjust the idle mixture. Idle mixture adjustments are covered in the next section. In some carburetors, a single idle speed adjustment screw is used. If this is the case, adjust for slow (hot) idle with the screw contacting the lowest part of the fast idle cam. The fast idle speed will be automatically adjusted as the choke pulls the cam upward. See **Figure 21-5.**

Idle Control Devices

Idle speed control solenoids or *motors* are used to change the engine idle speed when the idle load changes. This can occur when the air conditioner is turned on or when the automatic transmission is placed in gear. Other idle control devices are used to hold the throttle open when decelerating to reduce exhaust emissions. Some idle speed control solenoids can be adjusted. Adjustment procedures are similar to those for idle speed screws. Refer to **Figure 21-6.** The solenoid can be checked by turning the ignition switch to the on position without starting the engine. The solenoid should extend when the throttle plate is slightly opened. If the solenoid is an air conditioner speed-up solenoid, it should extend when the air conditioner compressor turns on. On many late model engines, no solenoid adjustments are possible.

Anti-Dieseling Solenoids

Anti-dieseling solenoids are used to set the hot idle on some engines. When the engine is turned off, the solenoid de-energizes, closing the throttle completely. This prevents engine dieseling or run-on caused by hotter combustion chamber temperatures in emission-controlled vehicles. Refer to **Figure 21-7.** The anti-dieseling solenoid can be checked by turning the engine off while observing the throttle shaft. The throttle should close completely when the ignition is switched off. If the throttle does not close completely, the solenoid is defective or the idle speed has been set with the carburetor idle screw. If the engine idle speed is too low, check to see if the solenoid extends when the ignition switch is turned on. If the solenoid is working, it can be adjusted to obtain the proper idle speed. Adjustment procedures are similar to those for idle speed screws.

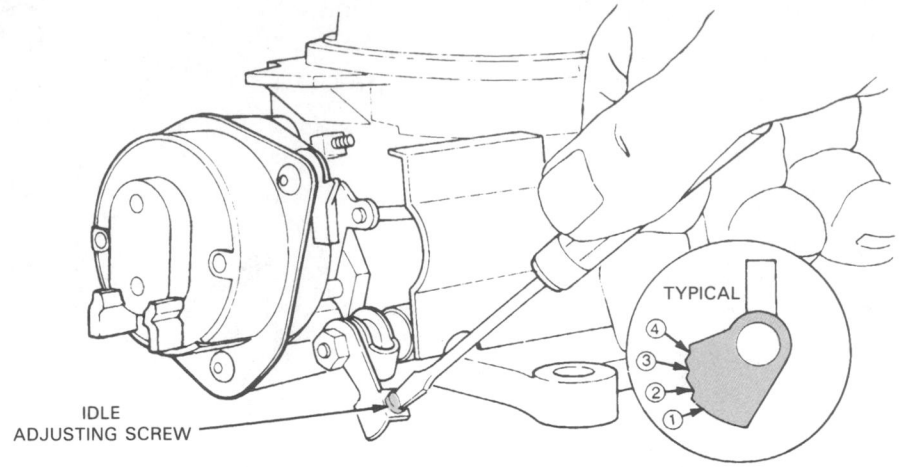

Figure 21-5. Idle RPM adjustment. Note the four different cam steps. Each step will change the speed setting. (Ford)

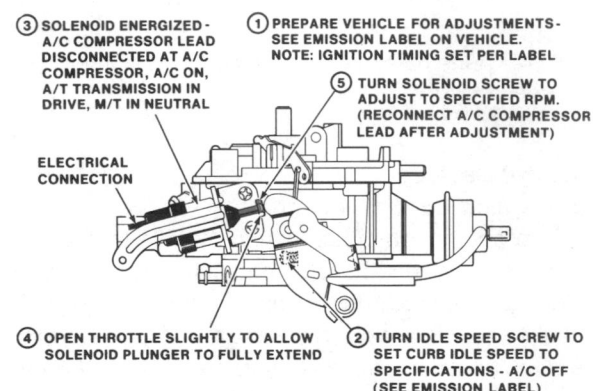

③ SOLENOID ENERGIZED - A/C COMPRESSOR LEAD DISCONNECTED AT A/C COMPRESSOR, A/C ON, A/T TRANSMISSION IN DRIVE, M/T IN NEUTRAL

① PREPARE VEHICLE FOR ADJUSTMENTS - SEE EMISSION LABEL ON VEHICLE. NOTE: IGNITION TIMING SET PER LABEL

⑤ TURN SOLENOID SCREW TO ADJUST TO SPECIFIED RPM. (RECONNECT A/C COMPRESSOR LEAD AFTER ADJUSTMENT)

ELECTRICAL CONNECTION

④ OPEN THROTTLE SLIGHTLY TO ALLOW SOLENOID PLUNGER TO FULLY EXTEND

② TURN IDLE SPEED SCREW TO SET CURB IDLE SPEED TO SPECIFICATIONS - A/C OFF (SEE EMISSION LABEL)

Figure 21-6. An idle speed solenoid. This unit is adjusted by turning the plunger. (General Motors)

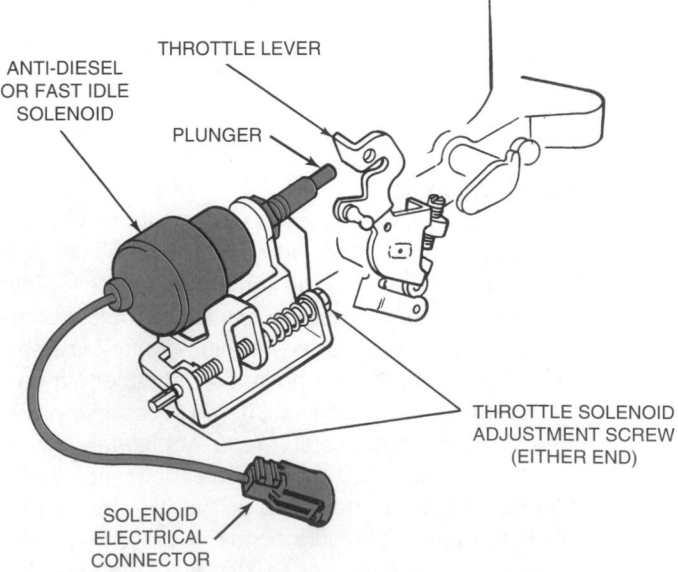

ANTI-DIESEL OR FAST IDLE SOLENOID

THROTTLE LEVER

PLUNGER

THROTTLE SOLENOID ADJUSTMENT SCREW (EITHER END)

SOLENOID ELECTRICAL CONNECTOR

Figure 21-7. Anti-dieseling solenoid as used by one manufacturer. Note its adjustable mounts. (Motorcraft)

Anti-Stall Dashpot

The **anti-stall dashpot** prevents engine stalling when the throttle must be closed suddenly at low speeds. The dashpot creates a gradually reduced resistance to throttle closing. When the dashpot is actuated, it should move slowly and with resistance. If it fails to do this, repair or replace as required.

To adjust, move the throttle to the fully closed position. Make sure the fast idle cam is not holding the throttle partially open. While holding throttle in the full-closed position, push the dashpot plunger rod away from the throttle contact area as far as possible. Measure the distance between the plunger and the throttle contact. Adjust the dashpot (or dashpot plunger in some cases) to provide specified clearance. See **Figure 21-8.**

Adjusting Idle Mixture

The **idle mixture** can be adjusted to vary the air-fuel ratio at idle. However, all carburetors produced after 1968 have some provision for reducing the amount that the mixture can be enriched. Many modern carburetors cannot be adjusted without removing the carburetor and drilling or breaking away parts of the carburetor throttle body or plate, or by removing special sealing plugs. On other carburetors, the mixture is controlled by a **mixture control solenoid,** and no provision is available for adjusting the idle mixture.

 Note: Adjusting carburetor idle mixture settings must be done according to manufacturer's procedures and specifications. Failure to do so is a violation of federal and state emission control laws.

Idle Mixture Adjustment Procedures

The following adjustment procedures are general in nature and apply to vehicles built before 1968. They can be made with a vacuum gauge and tachometer and are used to obtain the highest, smoothest idle. Ensure that the

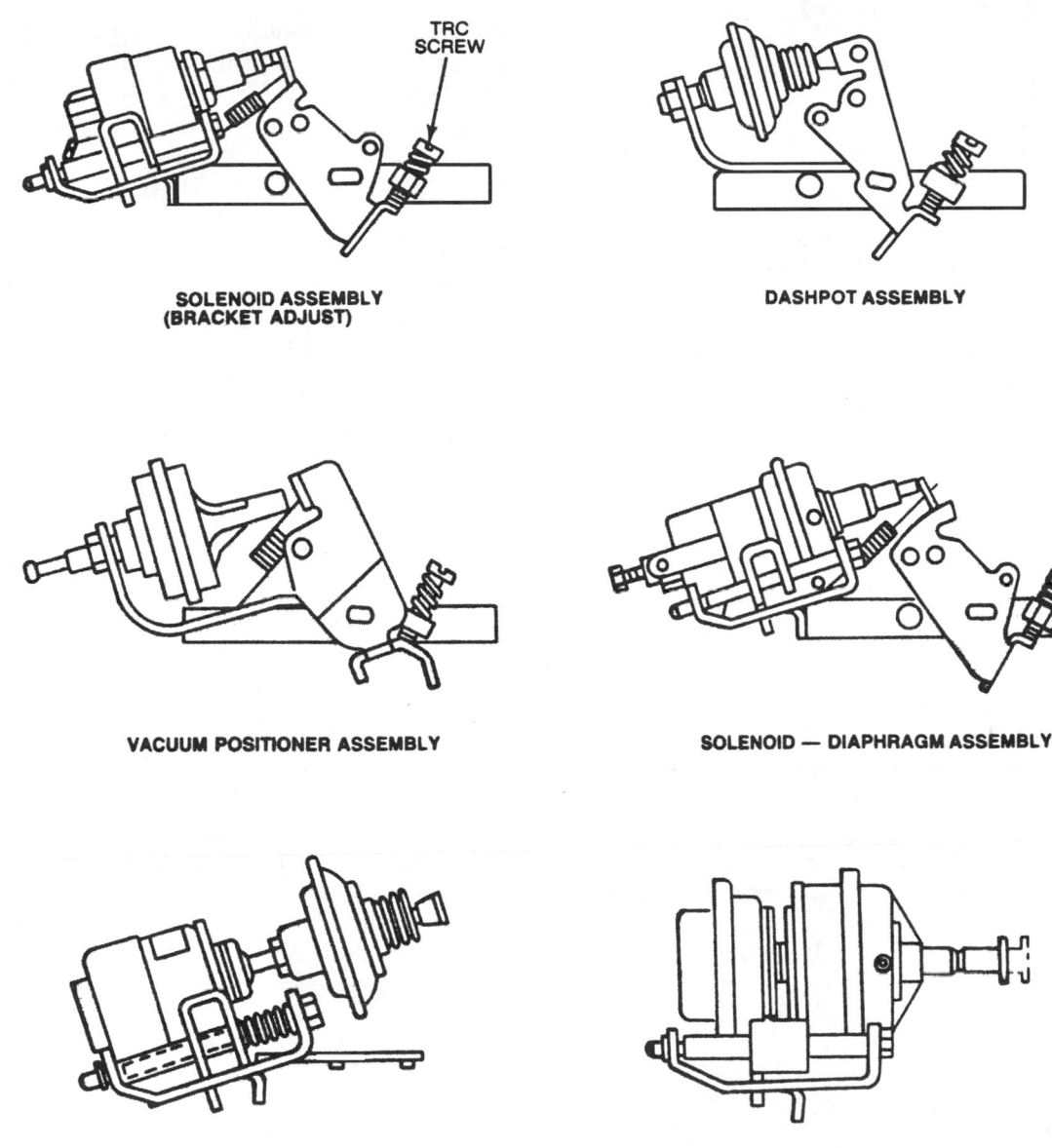

SOLENOID ASSEMBLY (BRACKET ADJUST)

DASHPOT ASSEMBLY

VACUUM POSITIONER ASSEMBLY

SOLENOID — DIAPHRAGM ASSEMBLY

SOLENOID — DASHPOT ASSEMBLY

DASHPOT AND CONTROL ASSEMBLY

Figure 21-8. An assortment of anti-stall dashpots. They can be vacuum, spring, or electrically operated to prevent engine stalling. (Ford)

engine is fully warmed up. Then install a vacuum gauge and tachometer on the engine.

Turn each *idle mixture screw* inward until it is lightly seated. Never seat mixture screws tightly as this will groove the tip and prevent a smooth idle. Back each screw out about two turns. Start the engine and adjust each screw in or out to produce the highest RPM and vacuum reading. If the engine begins to miss, this is due to a lean mixture. If the engine begins to run roughly, or *roll,* this indicates a rich mixture. If the idle speed has changed following the mixture adjustment, reset with the idle speed screw. Repeat the process of adjusting the mixture and setting the idle speed until the vacuum gauge shows the highest reading when the idle speed is as specified. Carefully count the turns to ensure that both screws are turned out an equal amount. Screws should

be adjusted to be within one-quarter to one-half turn of each other. See **Figure 21-9.**

Adjusting Idle Mixture on Emission Controlled Carburetors

Idle adjustments on vehicles made after the beginning of the 1968 model year are subject to federal law and, in some areas, state law. Always check the emissions label in the engine compartment and follow the procedures and specifications given on this label. The three most common methods to adjust mixture on late model vehicles are the *idle drop method,* the *propane enrichment method,* and the *exhaust gas analyzer method.*

Vehicles made after the 1968 model year have some form of *limiter cap* or *seal plug.* Some idle limiter caps allow a small amount of mixture screw adjustment while

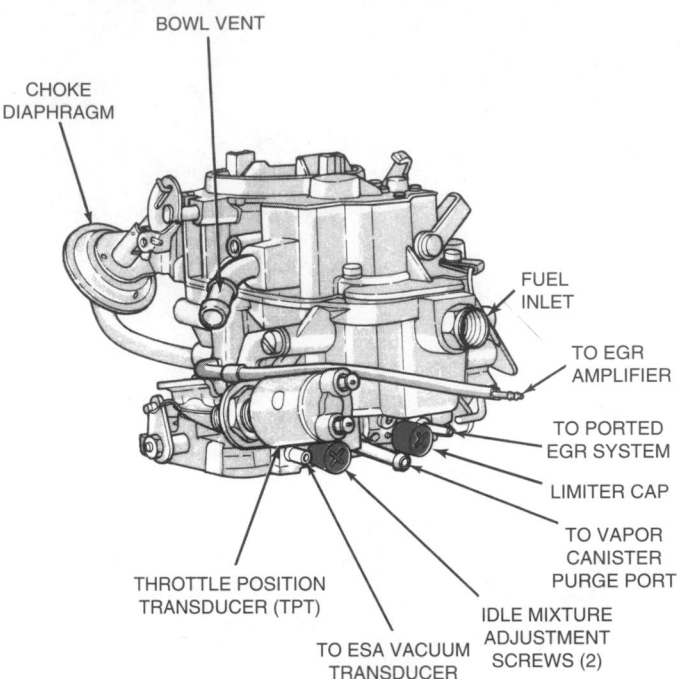

Figure 21-9. Idle mixture adjustment screws covered with limiter caps on one particular carburetor. The limiter caps must be removed to allow for adjustment. They should then be reinstalled. (Plymouth)

others prevent any adjustment. Some idle mixture screws are recessed into the body of the carburetor and covered with a plug. The plug must be removed to access the idle mixture screws, **Figure 21-10.** Most plastic limiter caps can be removed with the carburetor installed, while most plugs can only be removed after the carburetor is removed from the engine.

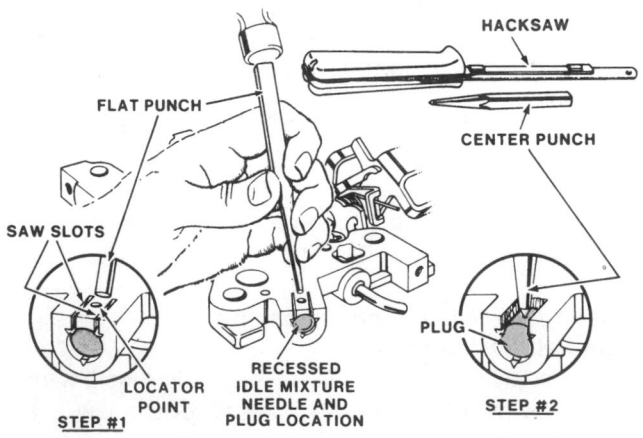

Figure 21-10. Procedure involved in removing one type of idle mixture screw limiter plug. Avoid heavy hammering. (Chevrolet)

On most late model vehicles, the control module adjusts the air-fuel ratio through a mixture control solenoid installed in the carburetor. In addition, the catalytic converter on newer vehicles will attempt to clean up a rich mixture. Therefore, incorrect air-fuel ratios will not show up as

prominently as on engines without converters. A defective or missing converter will make a properly running engine seem much richer than it really is. For this reason, always check the service literature for the exact procedures and for proper specifications for the year and make of vehicle before beginning carburetor adjustments.

Idle Drop Method

This adjustment procedure applies to some older engines only and can be made using only a vacuum gauge and tachometer. Begin by removing the restrictor caps from the idle mixture screws and adjusting the mixture to obtain the highest, smoothest idle at the RPM listed on the emissions label. Then turn the mixture screws in until the idle speed drops the amount listed on the emissions label, usually between 50 and 100 RPM. Readjust as needed to obtain the smoothest idle at the specific RPM. Then reinstall the restrictor caps or color-coded replacement caps.

Propane Enrichment Method

Idle mixture adjustments on some carburetors require the use of a propane enrichment device. The propane enters the carburetor through a tube attached to the air cleaner or intake manifold fitting and creates a rich fuel mixture, **Figure 21-11.**

 Warning: Propane can be dangerous. Follow all service procedures carefully.

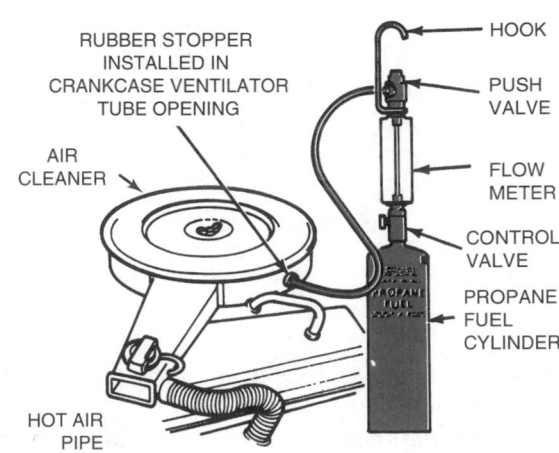

Figure 21-11. A propane idle enrichment mixture setup. Be extremely careful while using propane gas. (AC Delco)

Begin by attaching the propane enrichment device to the air cleaner or intake manifold as indicated. Also attach a tachometer and remove the restrictor caps from the idle mixture screws. Start the engine and adjust the propane valve opening according to instructions. With the propane valve open, adjust the mixture screws to obtain the highest, smoothest idle at the RPM listed on the emissions label. Readjust both mixture and idle speed screws as needed to obtain the smoothest idle at the specific RPM. Then close the propane valve. The idle speed should drop by the amount listed on the emissions label. If the idle drops properly, reinstall the restrictor caps, or color-coded replacement caps if required by law.

Exhaust Gas Analyzer Method

Using an exhaust gas analyzer is the only sure method of determining the air-fuel ratio. There are several brands of exhaust gas analyzers, therefore, the following information is a general guide only. Always follow the equipment and vehicle manufacturer's instructions exactly.

> **Note: The exhaust gas analyzer can be used to check air-fuel ratios at any engine speed. Consult the analyzer instruction manual for exact testing procedures. This is covered in more detail in Chapter 25.**

Begin by starting and calibrating the exhaust gas analyzer. Then start the engine and run it long enough to warm to normal operating temperature. Place the analyzer probe in the vehicle tailpipe, and allow the engine to idle as analyzer readings stabilize. Note the air-fuel ratio and compare it with specifications for the engine. If possible, turn the idle mixture adjustment screws to obtain the proper readings. On newer carburetors, the idle mixture cannot be easily adjusted. The carburetor may require rebuilding if the readings cannot be corrected. After the idle mixture has been properly adjusted, replace the limiter caps or plugs with new ones. A typical four gas exhaust analyzer is shown in **Figure 21-12.**

Choke Service

All modern carburetors are equipped with **automatic chokes,** which open and close depending on engine temperature. This is accomplished through the use of a **thermostatic spring,** sometimes called a bimetal spring. Chokes are usually located on the carburetor, as shown in **Figure 21-13.** Most newer chokes are heated by a **electric heating element** located on the housing. This heating element is energized by the alternator output terminal through a special temperature relay or by the control module. The choke system shown in **Figure 21-14** places the thermostatic spring directly over the hot exhaust crossover passage instead of on the carburetor. This choke positioning is called a **divorced choke.** A few older vehicles have **manual chokes** that are operated by the vehicle driver. The following sections cover the adjustment and service of chokes.

Checking Choke Operation

The simplest way to check choke operation is to observe the choke when the engine is cold. When the throttle is moved slightly, the choke should snap closed. When the engine is started, the choke should open slightly. As the engine warms up, the choke should gradually open until it opens completely on a thoroughly warmed-up engine. If the choke does not perform as expected, check for maladjustment, binding or dirty linkage, or a defective thermostatic coil. On electric chokes, check for current to the heating element. Check the element with an ohmmeter to ensure that

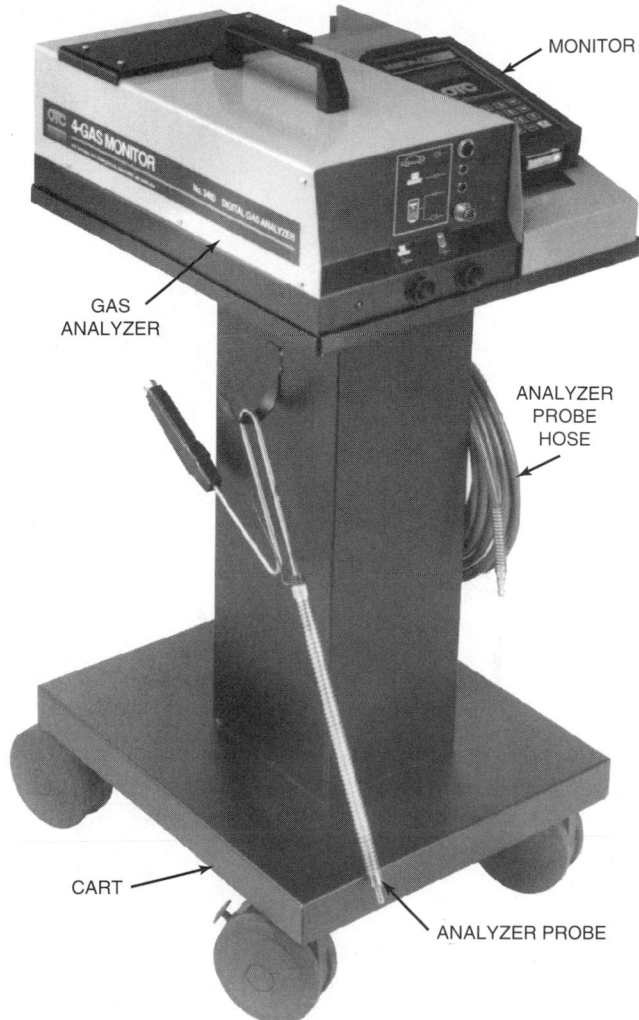

Figure 21-12. A four gas analyzer, monitor, analyzer probe, and hose. Note that they are on a cart which allows it to be rolled up to a vehicle. Follow all operating instructions. (OTC Tools)

the element has not burned out. Also check the operation and adjustment of the vacuum break.

Adjusting Automatic Choke

The automatic choke is operated by tension of an bimetallic spring. The spring coils and uncoils as engine temperature changes. The amount of thermostatic spring tension is determined by the positioning of the choke housing and cover index marks. Many chokes are not adjustable, or can only be adjusted by drilling out rivets holding the housing and replacing them with screws. If the choke has no provision for adjustment and is defective, it must be replaced. If the choke can be adjusted, align the marks as recommended by the manufacturer. This initial setting, although usually very close, may require a slight adjustment after testing the choke operation. The choke in **Figure 21-15** is adjusted one notch lean.

Some covers are marked to indicate the direction in which to turn for a lean or rich setting. Hard starting, sputtering, spitting, and coughing during warm-up may indicate

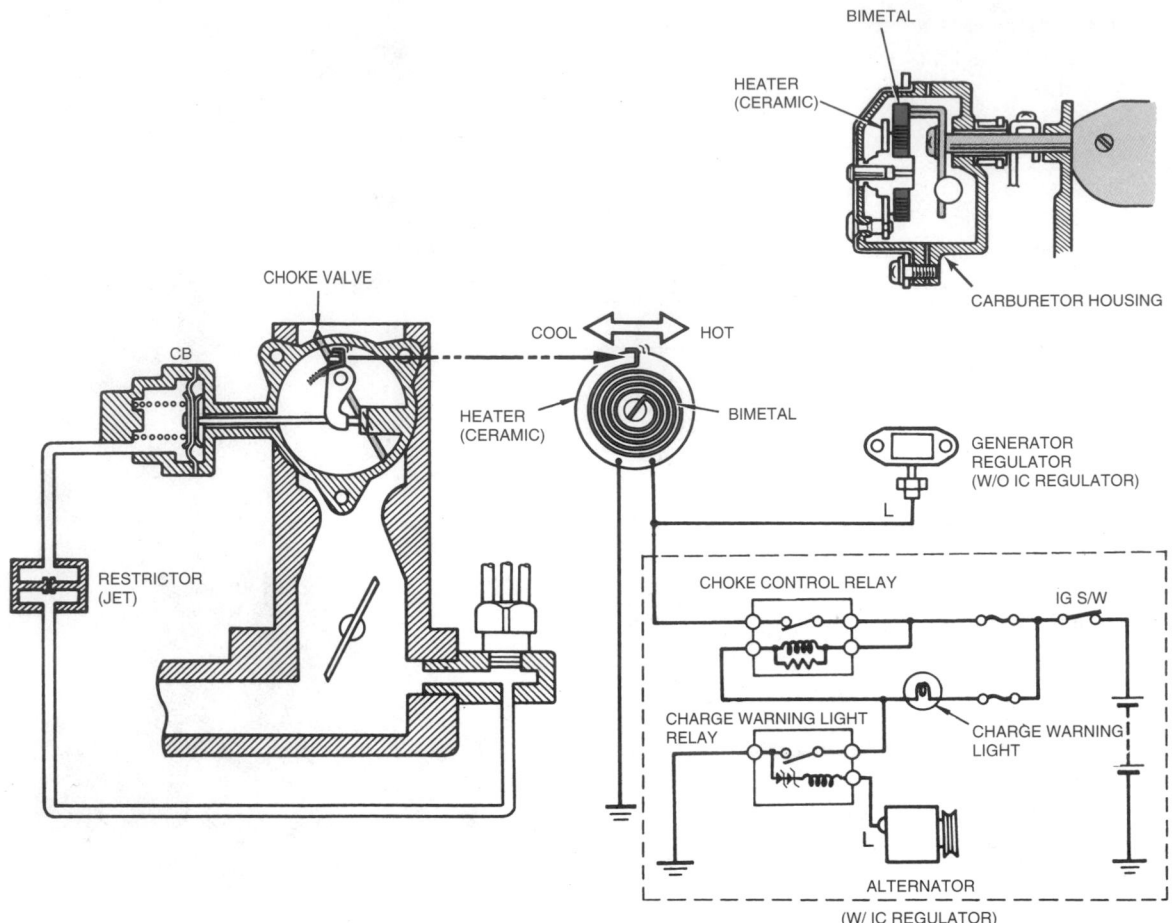

Figure 21-13.   A bimetal (bimetallic) thermostatic spring choke arrangement which mounts directly to the carburetor housing. This particular one is heated electronically. (Toyota)

the need of a richer setting. Engine loping and black smoke from the exhaust indicate the need for a leaner setting. Remember the choke valve should be closed with the engine cold and wide open with the engine hot (normal operating temperature). The divorced choke is adjusted by loosening a locknut and turning with a screwdriver until the index mark is aligned as desired. Other divorced chokes are adjusted by bending the linkage rod which connects it to the choke shaft.

Cleaning Automatic Choke

Occasionally chokes require cleaning, especially those which are heated by air passing through the choke housing. To clean the choke, remove the air cleaner and note the position of the thermostatic spring housing index mark in relation to the choke housing marks. Then remove the choke cover, thermostatic spring, and related parts. If the cover is secured with rivets, they may be drilled out, **Figure 21-16.**

Clean all metallic parts in recommended cleaner and blow dry. Do not wash electrical parts. Be careful not to distort the thermostatic spring. While moving the choke valve, apply a few drops of clean carbon solvent to the choke shaft bearings and the external linkage. If the linkage is dirty, use a small brush to remove the dirt. Reassemble all choke

parts and use a new cover gasket. Make certain the thermostatic spring is positioned correctly and that it engages the choke shaft lever. Align the housing and cover index marks and tighten cover fasteners securely.

Manual Choke Adjustment

A few older vehicles are equipped with manual chokes. The manual choke is operated by the driver. Manual chokes are also available as aftermarket items to replace an automatic choke that has failed when replacement parts cannot be located. To check the operation of a manual choke, remove the air cleaner. Then pull the choke knob out as far as it will go while stepping on the accelerator pedal. The choke plate should close completely. Then push the choke knob completely in. The choke valve should be completely open. If necessary, adjust the choke by loosening the swivel mounted on the choke shaft.

Adjusting Choke Vacuum Break

The choke valve must be completely closed to start a cold engine. As soon as the engine starts, however, the choke must be opened slightly to allow some air to enter the engine. The choke valve is slightly offset so that the incoming air pressure will try to open the choke. However, the pressure of the thermostatic spring attempts to close the

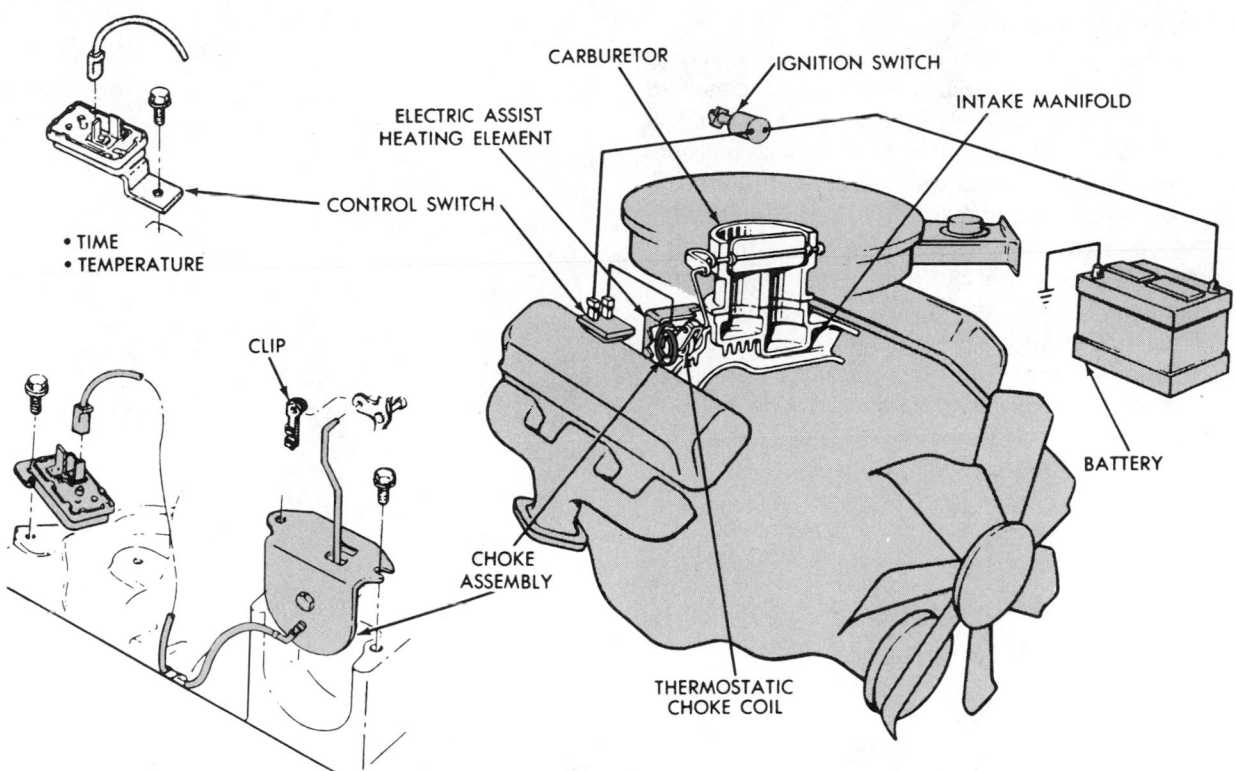

Figure 21-14. A divorced choke system. Note that the thermostatic choke coil spring is placed in a well located in the intake manifold. (Colt Industries)

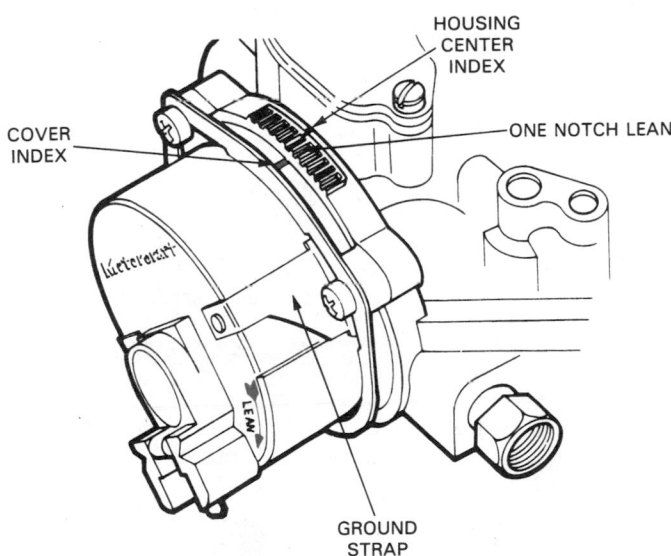

Figure 21-15. This particular application specifies an initial setting one notch (index mark) on the lean side. On some electric chokes, a ground circuit is completed via a metal plate placed at the back of the choke cover. On these, a gasket is not used between the cover and the housing because it would break the circuit. (Ford)

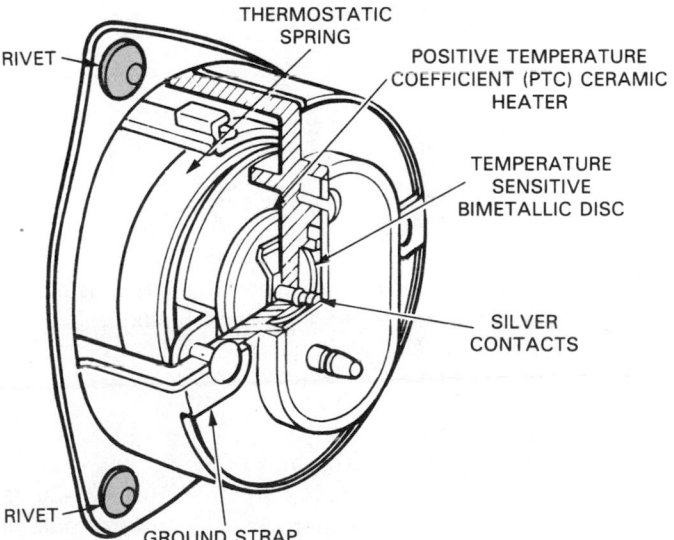

Figure 21-16. This choke cover is secured with rivets. Remove the cover by drilling out the rivets. Note the electric heating unit. (Ford)

choke. To offset the choke spring when the engine is first started, a **vacuum break** device is used.

The vaccum break uses the intake manifold vacuum that develops as soon as the engine starts to pull the choke slightly open. This device is also referred to as a choke kick, or unloader. Older chokes were opened by an internal vacuum break piston. Newer carburetors use a choke that has a vacuum-operated diaphragm. Proper operation of the vacuum break requires an accurate relationship between the position of the vacuum piston or diaphragm and the choke valve. Adjustment is provided so that a proper setting may be made.

Setting Piston-Type Vacuum Break

Remove the thermostatic spring cover and spring. Block the throttle half open. Move the vacuum piston to the specified position by using a wire gauge as shown in **Figure 21-17.** While the piston is held in this position, apply light pressure on the choke valve (in the closing direction) to eliminate linkage slack. Slip a gauge between the edge of the choke valve and the air horn. The gauge should enter with a very light drag. If the gauge indicates improper clearance between the valve and the air horn wall, adjust as directed. **Figure 21-18** shows the procedure. The choke break is set with an adjusting nut on this particular carburetor. Other methods of adjustment include bending the linkage or loosening and repositioning the choke shaft lever on the shaft. See **Figure 21-19.**

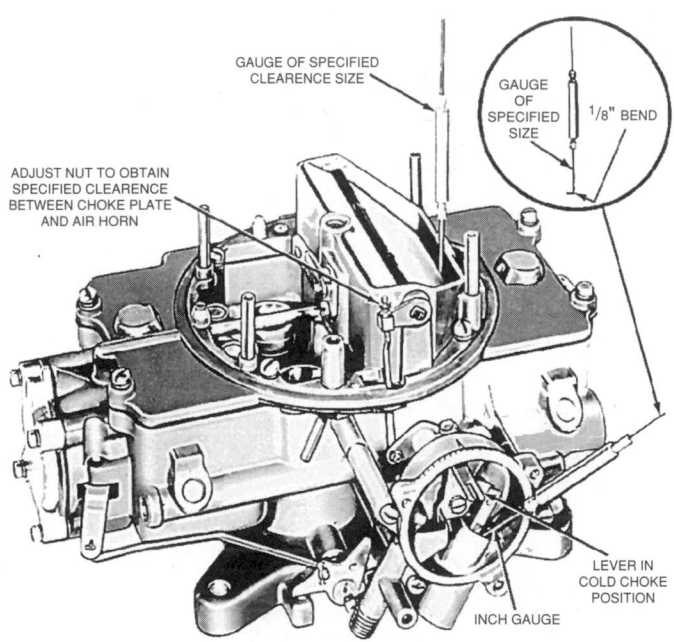

Figure 21-17. Obtaining the correct choke break adjustment with the proper size wire gauges. For top performance, it is essential that all carburetor adjustments be made as carefully and as accurately as possible. (Ford)

Setting Diaphragm-Type Vacuum Break

The vacuum break diaphragm in **Figure 21-20** is adjusted by forcing the diaphragm rod inward until it reaches the bottom of its travel. While holding it in this position, the clearance between the choke valve and air horn wall is measured. Adjustment is done by bending the linkage rod. The divorced choke shown in **Figure 21-21** also uses a vacuum diaphragm choke break. This break is also adjusted by bending the choke rod.

Setting Wide-Open Throttle Break or Unloader Adjustment

The wide-open break linkage opens the choke plate slightly when the throttle valve is opened completely. This linkage is used to help clear a flooded engine. Adjust by moving the throttle to the wide-open position until the

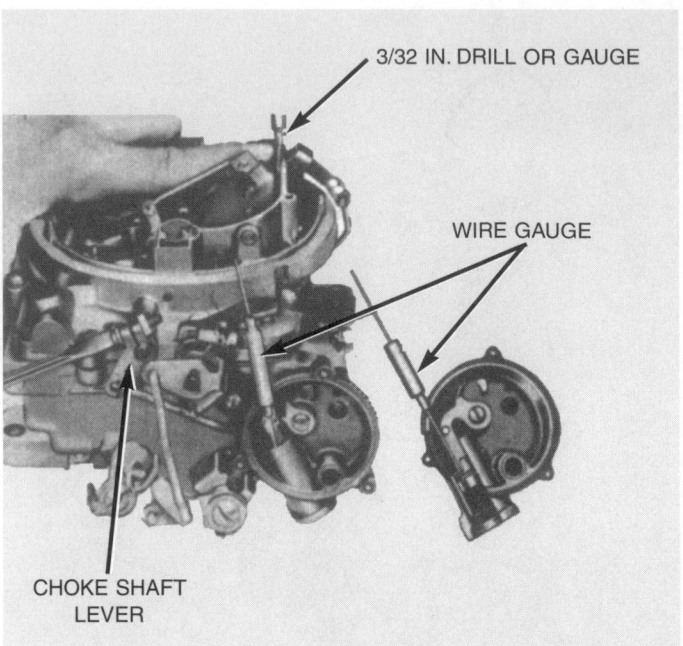

Figure 21-18. On this carburetor, choke vacuum break setting is adjusted by loosening and repositioning choke shaft lever. Note how choke piston (cutaway inset) is positioned with wire gauge.

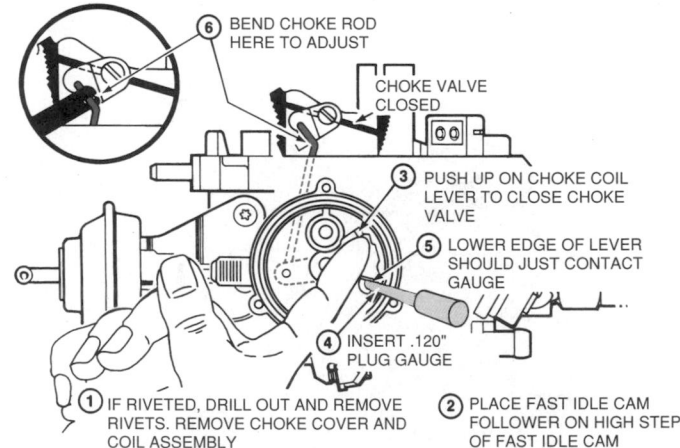

Figure 21-19. Adjusting the choke coil lever by bending the linkage rod. Note the plug gauge used to obtain the proper setting. (General Motors)

throttle lever tang strikes the fast idle cam, causing the choke valve to be partially opened. While holding the throttle in the wide-open position, check the clearance between the choke valve and the air horn wall. Bend the tang to secure correct opening. Do not bend the link as this will upset the fast idle cam adjustment. See **Figure 21-22.**

Accelerator Pump Checks and Adjustment

The **accelerator pump** supplies extra fuel to the carburetor air horn to prevent flat spots when accelerating. Accelerator pumps can be the plunger type, **Figure 21-23,** or the diaphragm pump type. To check accelerator pump operation, remove the air cleaner and open the throttle

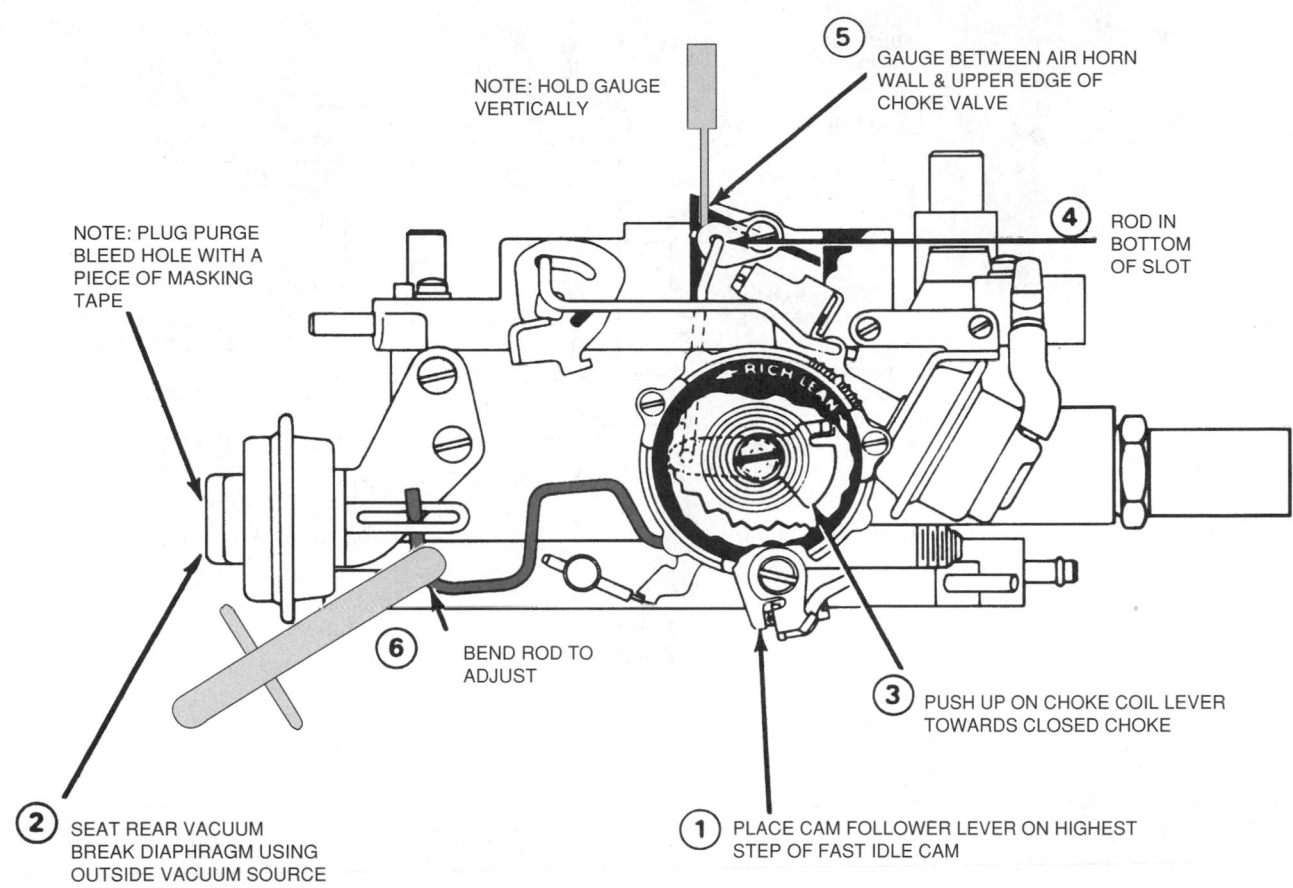

NOTE: HOLD GAUGE VERTICALLY

⑤ GAUGE BETWEEN AIR HORN WALL & UPPER EDGE OF CHOKE VALVE

④ ROD IN BOTTOM OF SLOT

NOTE: PLUG PURGE BLEED HOLE WITH A PIECE OF MASKING TAPE

⑥ BEND ROD TO ADJUST

③ PUSH UP ON CHOKE COIL LEVER TOWARDS CLOSED CHOKE

② SEAT REAR VACUUM BREAK DIAPHRAGM USING OUTSIDE VACUUM SOURCE

① PLACE CAM FOLLOWER LEVER ON HIGHEST STEP OF FAST IDLE CAM

Figure 21-20. Setting a diaphragm type vacuum break on a four-barrel carburetor. (AC-Delco)

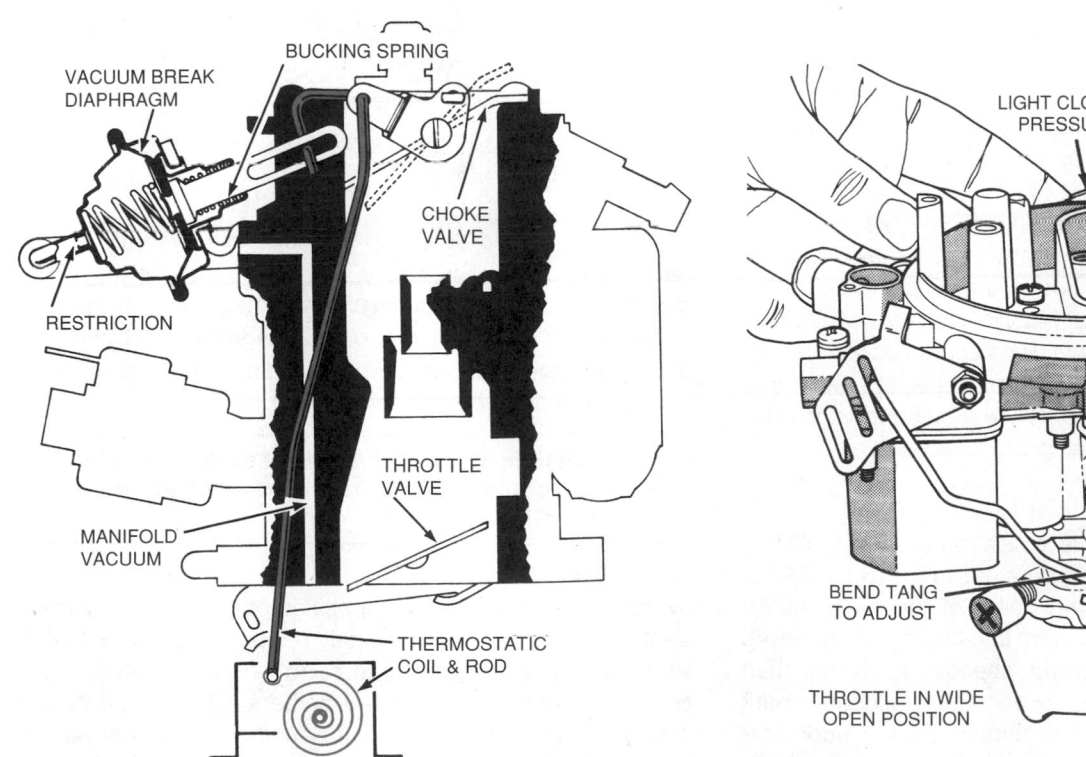

VACUUM BREAK DIAPHRAGM

BUCKING SPRING

CHOKE VALVE

RESTRICTION

THROTTLE VALVE

MANIFOLD VACUUM

THERMOSTATIC COIL & ROD

LIGHT CLOSING PRESSURE

GAUGE

BEND TANG TO ADJUST

THROTTLE IN WIDE OPEN POSITION

Figure 21-21. A vacuum break arrangement as used with one particular divorced choke setup. (General Motors)

Figure 21-22. Setting the wide-open throttle break (unloader) adjustment. Bend the unloader tang until the correct adjustment is obtained. (Chrysler)

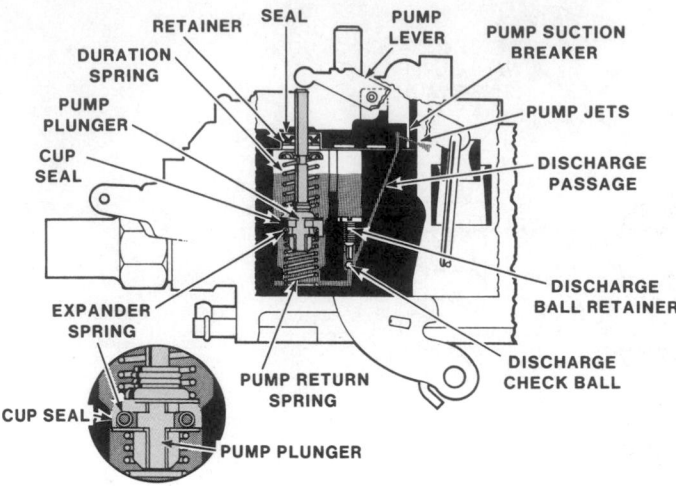

Figure 21-23. A cutaway of a plunger type accelerator pump. (Buick)

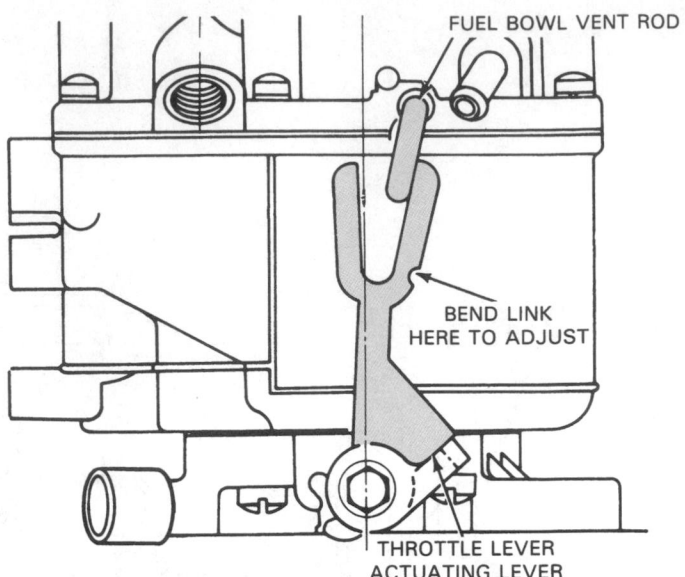

Figure 21-24. Note the adjustments on this fuel bowl vent actuating linkage. (Ford)

quickly. Observe the pump discharge nozzle in the air horn. Depending on the pump nozzle design, one or two streams of gas should be evident. The fine gas stream should be strong and should last for a short time even after the throttle reaches full open. If little or no gas output is observed, the accelerator pump piston or diaphragm could be cracked or worn. Check valves can be stuck open by dirt or the discharge nozzle feed system could be clogged. Clean and repair as needed.

Accelerator Pump Adjustment

Most late-model accelerator pumps are not adjustable. To adjust the accelerator pump on an older carburetor, close the throttle and check the position of the accelerator pump linkage in relation to a specified portion of the carburetor. Bend the link or lever as required. By placing the rod in different holes, the pump stroke and amount of gasoline delivered to the air horn can be varied.

Fuel Bowl Vent Adjustment

To allow the gasoline in the bowl to be drawn into the engine, carburetors have a *bowl vent.* Older carburetors are vented to the atmosphere. Modern closed fuel systems vent to the air horn or to the emission control vapor storage canister. The vent can be checked for proper operation and adjusted as necessary. **Figure 21-24** shows the vent actuating setup on one carburetor.

Checking and Setting Float Level

The *float level* setting is critical since it establishes the height of the fuel in the carburetor bowl, **Figure 21-25.** This has a direct effect on the ability of the main metering system to pull gasoline from the bowl and therefore on the air-fuel ratio at cruising speeds. A higher than specified fuel level will result in poor gas mileage, spark plug fouling, crankcase dilution, and all-around poor performance. A low fuel level will cause backfiring, bucking, and loss of power.

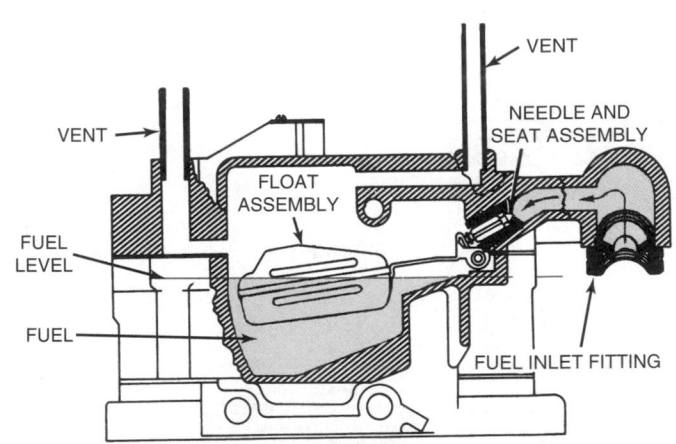

Figure 21-25. The float level determines the height of the fuel in the bowl. (Plymouth)

Checking and adjusting the float level with the carburetor disassembled is called *dry level.* Dry float level is checked by either measuring from some portion of the float to the cover, or by using a gauge. **Figure 21-26** shows a gauge designed for the purpose. Adjust the float level by carefully bending the float arm.

 Caution: The carburetor float system is delicate and can be severely damaged by improper handling.

A *float drop* setting may be checked with a gauge or by measuring between two specified points. Adjust by careful bending of the float stop tab or lip. See **Figure 21-27.** When adjusting, be careful to bend where indicated. Make certain the float is not twisted or bent sideways. If it is, it may hang up on the bowl walls. Another method of adjusting the float level on some carburetors is to move an adjustable inlet or float needle seat.

Figure 21-26. One particular dry float level adjustment using a float level gauge. The carburetor has been partly disassembled to provide access to the float and chamber. (Ford)

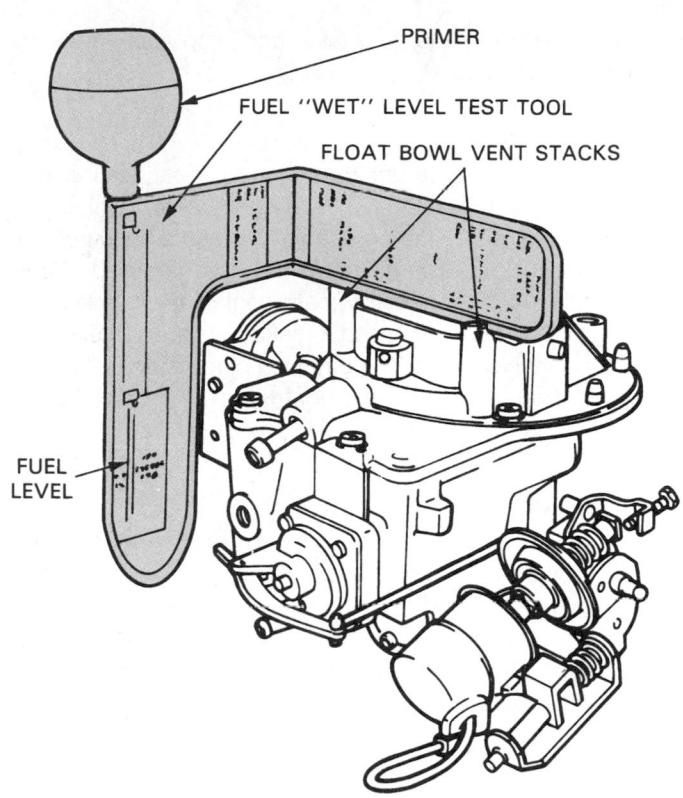

Figure 21-28. Using a special gauge to check fuel level wet setting. This tool has a hollow tube that is inserted into one of the float bowl vent stacks. Priming will cause fuel to seek its level on the gauge scale. Use as directed. (Ford)

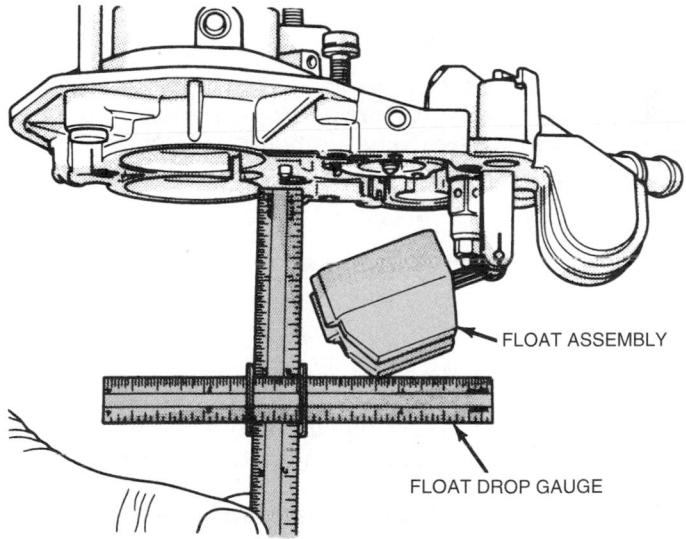

Figure 21-27. Measuring float drop. Be careful in handling the unit to prevent springing or bending the float. (Chrysler)

Checking Actual or Wet Fuel Level

The float level and drop settings provide a basic dry setting. It is often necessary to check the actual level, or *wet level,* of the fuel in the bowl. This can be done by running the engine until warm, stopping and measuring the distance from a specified point to the fuel level. **Figure 21-28** shows the use of a special test gauge to check wet float level. This tool has a tube that is inserted into a float bowl vent stack. When fuel is siphoned from the bowl by squeezing the primer, fuel will reach a level in the sight tube. A scale shows the correct height.

Another method utilizes a sight plug in the end of the bowl. The plug is removed and the fuel level determined by the relationship between the fuel level height and the bottom of the hole. The float must be readjusted to provide the exact fuel level required. When checking, the car must be level, engine at normal operating temperature, fuel pump pressure normal, and the inlet needle must not be leaking.

Adjusting Wet Fuel Level

Where an adjustable needle seat is used, the float wet adjustment is easy. Warm up the engine, then turn it off. Remove the sight plug and check the fuel level. If the fuel level is too low, hold the adjusting nut and loosen the lockscrew.

 Warning: Do not loosen the lockscrew or open the sight plug when the engine is running.

Turn the nut out (counterclockwise) to raise the fuel level. Tighten the lockscrew and replace the sight plug. Start the engine and run it for a minute. Stop the engine and remove the sight plug and recheck. Repeat until the fuel level is exact. If the fuel level is too high, lower below the specified level and then raise it to the height required. The fuel bowl inlet *needle and seat* (the control valve assembly for fuel entering the bowl) will eventually wear and start to leak. Replace the needle and seat as a matched set.

Be sure to readjust the float level and drop after replacing the needle and seat.

Checking the Float

The float must be *airtight,* that is, no gasoline can enter the float. Occasionally a float will leak, which will cause it to sink and become useless. Shake a hollow metal float to test for gasoline inside. If there is gas in the float, replace it. Most solid plastic floats cannot be checked for leakage and must be replaced if leakage is suspected. One method of checking a solid float is to place it on a flat surface and observe whether the float is pulled off balance by the metal hinge. If it is, the float is probably OK.

Variable Venturi Opening Check

Some carburetors employ a *variable venturi valve* that alters the size of the venturi opening to meet various engine speed and load conditions. There are many checks to be made to a variable venturi carburetor, so the factory service manual should be consulted. A common check and adjustment concerns the maximum venturi valve opening at the wide open throttle position.

Mixture Control Solenoids

A number of carburetors utilize a mixture control solenoid. The mixture control solenoid is operated by the engine control module. Energizing the solenoid causes a valve to open and close. This valve can control the flow of gasoline or air, depending on the type of carburetor and engine control system. The operation and service of the mixture control solenoid is covered in more detail in Chapter 25.

Throttle Position Sensors

Many late model carburetors have a throttle position sensor, or TPS, installed on the throttle shaft or operated by the accelerator pump linkage. This sensor sends an electrical input signal to the engine control module. The control module reads this input as the amount that the throttle is opened. This helps the control module to decide which output commands to send to various output devices. The operation and service of throttle position sensors is covered in more detail in Chapter 25.

Altitude Compensator Adjustment

Carburetors intended for use at high elevations are sometimes equipped with an *altitude compensating device.* High elevations provide less oxygen per unit of air, as well as less atmospheric pressure. By adding additional amounts of air, the correct air-fuel ratio can be maintained. The altitude compensator makes use of an *aneroid,* which is a sealed bellows under a partial vacuum. The aneroid expands with a drop in barometric pressure and contracts with a pressure increase. As the altitude increases, the aneroid capsule expands and forces open an air valve in the carburetor. The air valve admits additional air to the fuel

mixture. The altitude compensator must be set as specified by the manufacturer, as in **Figure 21-29.**

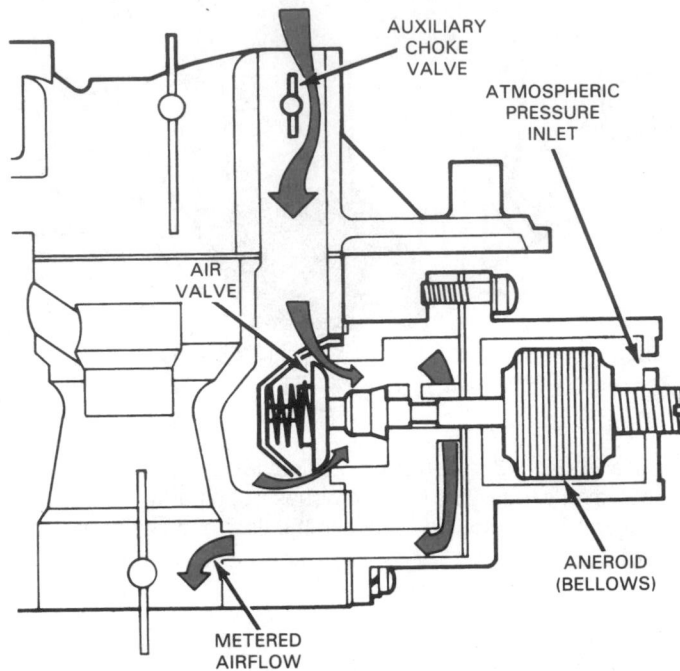

Figure 21-29. Cutaway showing an aneroid-operated altitude compensating system. As elevation increases, the aneroid expands, opening the air valve and admitting extra air to the air-fuel mixture. (Chrysler)

Other Carburetor Adjustments

Other carburetor adjustments are needed on some carburetors in addition to those covered. These include secondary throttle opening point, secondary throttle choke lockout, power valve opening, and metering rod position. To ensure complete and accurate work, always use a service manual covering the exact carburetor being serviced.

 Note: When making adjustments on computer-controlled carburetors, it is sometimes helpful to use a diagnostic scan tool, if available, so that you can monitor the actual amount of adjustment.

Carburetor Overhaul

Reasons to remove and overhaul the carburetor include buildup of gum and varnish, excessive dirt and water in the carburetor, leaky gaskets, and failure of mechanical parts such as the accelerator pump, needle and seat, vacuum diaphragms, and linkage or throttle valve shafts.

Carburetor Removal and Overhaul

Remove the carburetor fuel lines, vacuum lines, electrical connectors, and throttle linkage. Then remove the bolts holding the carburetor to the intake manifold and lift the carburetor from the intake manifold. Remove any old gasket material from the intake opening and plug it with a clean cloth. Begin disassembly by attaching repair legs to the carburetor to prevent damage to the throttle plates or valves. See **Figure 21-30.** Use a sharp scribe to mark parts before disassembly. If jets are to be removed, mark jet and adjacent area.

Carefully disassemble the carburetor and soak all metal parts in clean carburetor cleaner. Do not soak electrical parts, power valve, accelerator pump plunger, anti-stall dashpot, diaphragm units, fuel enrichment valve, plastic float, or any other parts made of rubber, leather, fabric, or fiber. Wipe parts not soaked in cleaner with a clean cloth. Soak the metal parts no longer than fifteen minutes, as the cleaner will begin to remove needed coatings. Remove the parts, rinse as directed, and blow dry. Blow out all passageways. Never use a wire or drill to probe into jets, air bleeds, or other passages. To prevent damage, use the air blast only. Do not direct air blast into any diaphragm units. Inspect all parts for cracks. Check all parting surfaces for nicks and burrs. Examine choke and throttle shafts and bearings for excessive looseness or out-of-roundness. Check idle mixture screws and float needle and seat, and replace if grooved or worn. Test the float for leakage. Check float arm-to-needle surface for roughness or grooving.

Replace all defective parts, stripped fasteners, and distorted springs, and discard all other old parts that will be replaced by those in the repair kit. The carburetor part number is needed in order to obtain a carburetor overhaul kit and all other needed parts. This number is either stamped on the carburetor housing or on a metal label attached to the carburetor. Most carburetor overhaul kits contain all needed gaskets, plus a new needle and seat, accelerator pump, and minor hardware parts such as clips and plugs. A simple float adjusting gauge will also be included. While overhauling a computer-controlled carburetor, you might want to replace the throttle position sensor and mixture control solenoids. These parts are usually located inside the bowl of most computer-controlled carburetors, making replacement after an overhaul difficult.

 Note: Be sure that the overhaul kit is the correct one for the carburetor that you are servicing. Always use new gaskets when overhauling a carburetor.

Carburetor Assembly

Refer to the proper service manual, or use the exploded view of the carburetor that is included in the overhaul kit to ensure that the carburetor is properly reassembled. An exploded view of a typical two-barrel carburetor employing an electrically operated mixture control solenoid is pictured in **Figure 21-31.**

Reassemble the carburetor in a clean area using clean tools. Do not use gasket cement unless directed to do so by manufacturer's instructions. Assemble carefully and avoid the use of excessive force. Use tools designed for the job, **Figure 21-32.** Tighten all fasteners securely. If torque specifications are given, use them. Perform all required adjustment checks, including float level and drop, accelerator pump stroke, and initial idle speed and mixture settings, if possible. Fill the fuel bowl and check accelerator pump operation.

Carburetor Installation

Clean the mounting area on the intake manifold. Use a new mounting gasket and reinstall the heat spacers, if used. Torque the carburetor fasteners and attach fuel and vacuum lines, electrical connectors, and all linkage. Start the engine and check for leaks, choke operation, and idle speed. Perform all required adjustments. Road test for performance.

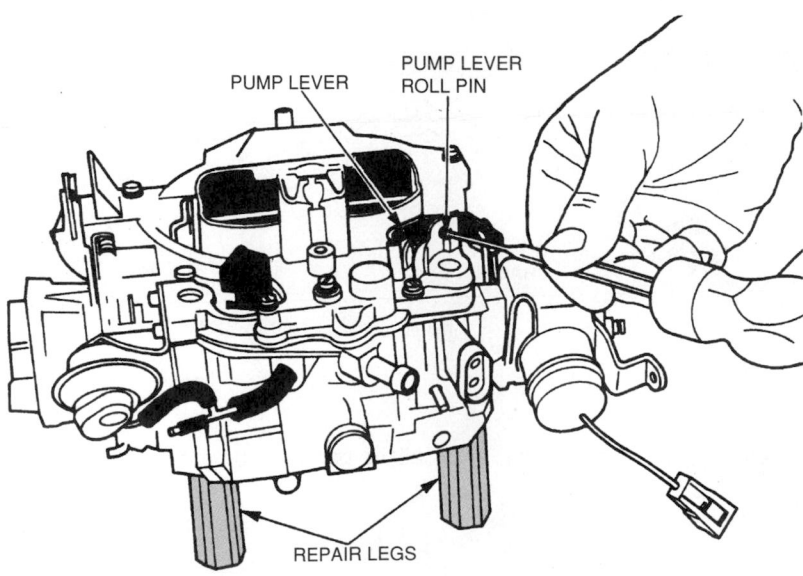

PUMP LEVER

PUMP LEVER ROLL PIN

REPAIR LEGS

Figure 21-30. A carburetor mounted on repair legs greatly facilitates overhaul and prevents damage to the throttle plates. (Cadillac)

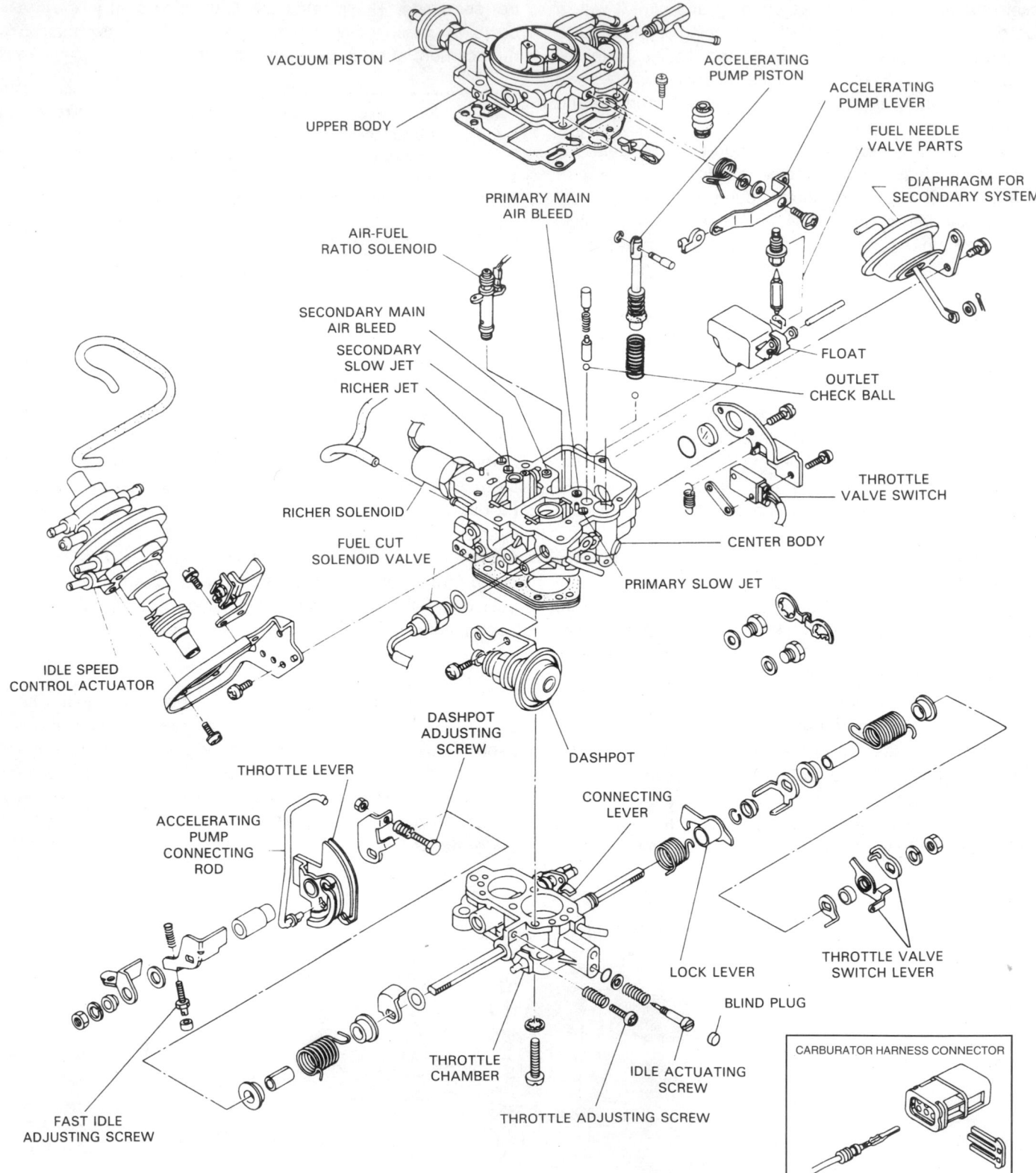

VACUUM PISTON

UPPER BODY

ACCELERATING PUMP PISTON

ACCELERATING PUMP LEVER

FUEL NEEDLE VALVE PARTS

DIAPHRAGM FOR SECONDARY SYSTEM

PRIMARY MAIN AIR BLEED

AIR-FUEL RATIO SOLENOID

SECONDARY MAIN AIR BLEED

SECONDARY SLOW JET

RICHER JET

FLOAT

OUTLET CHECK BALL

THROTTLE VALVE SWITCH

RICHER SOLENOID

FUEL CUT SOLENOID VALVE

CENTER BODY

PRIMARY SLOW JET

IDLE SPEED CONTROL ACTUATOR

DASHPOT ADJUSTING SCREW

THROTTLE LEVER

DASHPOT

CONNECTING LEVER

ACCELERATING PUMP CONNECTING ROD

LOCK LEVER

THROTTLE VALVE SWITCH LEVER

BLIND PLUG

THROTTLE CHAMBER

IDLE ACTUATING SCREW

FAST IDLE ADJUSTING SCREW

THROTTLE ADJUSTING SCREW

CARBURATOR HARNESS CONNECTOR

Figure 21-31. Exploded view of a two-barrel carburetor. Study all the parts and note their relationship to the overall assembly. (Nissan)

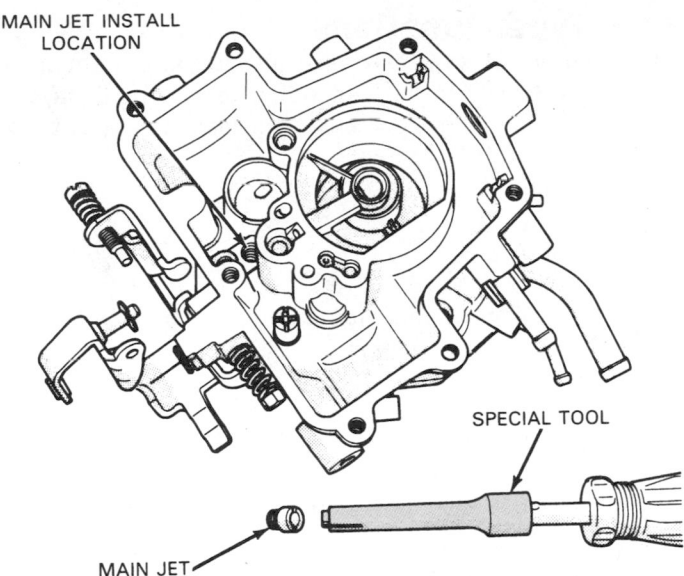

MAIN JET INSTALL LOCATION

SPECIAL TOOL

MAIN JET

Figure 21-32. Special tools, such as this jet wrench, will greatly assist in carburetor repair and will prevent part damage. (Chrysler)

Tech Talk

A technician's work is never done. Even though you may find yourself without a vehicle to service, there is still plenty of work around you that must be completed. Look around your work area and throw away any old parts, boxes, paper, shop rags, and any accumulated trash. Sweep the floors of any dirt and follow this with a good scrubbing with detergent and water. Clean your tools and toolbox and fix any tools that can be repaired. You can help your fellow technicians with a problem car or other work that they are performing. Not only does this build goodwill with the customer (the vehicle is finished sooner), the technician you helped will be more inclined to help you when you need it.

Summary

Before diagnosing a carburetor as faulty, check other items such as ignition and emission system problems and vacuum leaks. There are many different carburetor adjustments depending upon the model. Always use a good service manual that deals with the exact carburetor you are working on.

Basic idle speed adjustments are the fast idle and slow idle settings. Use a tachometer to set speeds as recommended. Idle mixture setting is very important to smooth operation and exhaust emission levels. Set all carburetor adjustments carefully. Replace idle screw limiter devices and test for proper emission levels.

Chokes are usually fully electric, hot air operated, or a combination of both. Some chokes have covers that are held on with rivets, while others use screws. Check the choke for proper operation. If service is required, disassemble, clean, assemble, and carefully reset. Be sure to check the operation of the choke break. Set anti-stall dashpot, idle speedup, and anti-dieseling devices to proper specifications. Check operation. Accelerator pumps use either a piston or a diaphragm to furnish extra fuel for acceleration. Check for proper operation and set as specified.

Float level is important to proper carburetor operation. Floats may be checked for float drop and float level. Use the proper gauge if required, or in some cases, an accurate rule. These are referred to as dry settings. The fuel level in the bowl is a function of float level. The wet fuel level may be checked on some carburetors that list a wet (measuring actual fuel level in bowl) setting. Any wet settings can be taken through a removable plug on some carburetors. Others allow bowl access through vent stacks or a removable cover. Be careful of fire when checking wet level.

Scribe vital parts before carburetor disassembly to aid in proper reassembly. Wash all metallic parts in proper solvent, rinse, and blow dry. Many carburetor parts cannot be washed. Inspect all parts for wear, breakage, and binding and replace any defective parts. Assemble the carburetor carefully. Work with clean parts in a clean area with clean tools. Check and adjust all settings as specified. Reinstall the carburetor using the proper gaskets and insulators. Torque all fasteners and secure all lines and hoses.

Know These Terms

Float system
Main metering system
Venturi
Idle system
Off-idle system
Power system
Accelerator pump
Choke system
Fast idle
Fast idle adjusting screw
Fast idle cam
Hot idle
Idle speed control solenoids
Anti-dieseling solenoid
Anti-stall dashpot
Idle mixture
Mixture control solenoid
Idle mixture screw
Idle drop method
Propane enrichment method
Exhaust gas analyzer
   method
Limiter cap
Seal plug
Automatic chokes
Thermostatic spring
Electric heating element
Divorced choke
Manual chokes
Vacuum break
Accelerator pump
Bowl vent
Float level
Dry level
Float drop
Wet level
Needle and seat
Airtight
Variable Venturi valve
Altitude compensation
   device
Aneroid

Review Questions—Chapter 21

Do not write in this book. Write your answers on a separate sheet of paper.

1. On some vehicles, hot idle speed is set by adjusting one of the following, EXCEPT:
   (A) idle speed screw.
   (B) combination hot and fast idle speed screw.
   (C) anti-dieseling solenoid.
   (D) throttle position sensor.
2. Intake manifold air leaks can often be found by squirting _____ along the gasket edge.
3. Automatic chokes can be opened by _____.
   (A) hot air
   (B) electric heat
   (C) hot air with electric assist
   (D) All of the above.
4. Why it is important that limiter caps be replaced following service?
   (A) Emission laws require it.
   (B) It prevents unauthorized tampering.
   (C) Without the caps, the mixture screws will vibrate loose.
   (D) Both A & B.
5. List four carburetor parts that should not be soaked in carburetor cleaner.
6. The idle mixture screw does which of the following?
   (A) Opens or closes the throttle.
   (B) Determines the amount of air-fuel mixture that reaches cylinder during idling.
   (C) Governs the choke valve tension.
   (D) Must contact the fast idle cam.
7. When the engine is cold, the automatic choke valve should be _____.
8. Choke vacuum break means _____.
   (A) partial opening of the choke valve by a piston or diaphragm when the engine is started
   (B) full closing of choke by vacuum means
   (C) that when the choke opens a certain distance, vacuum in the air horn is broken
   (D) using vacuum to slow down opening of choke
9. Look into the air horn while working the throttle linkage. This is a description of how to perform a quick check on the _____.
   (A) idle speed screw
   (B) accelerator pump
   (C) choke thermostat
   (D) altitude compensator
10. Fuel level in the bowl is best adjusted by _____.
    (A) adjusting the fuel pump pressure
    (B) changing the bowl fuel inlet needle
    (C) altering the main jet size
    (D) bending the float needle contact arm

ASE-Type Questions

1. Technician A says that most engine problems can be traced directly to the carburetor. Technician B says a problem in the ignition could be mistaken for a carburetor problem. Who is right?
   (A) A only.
   (B) B only.
   (C) Both A & B.
   (D) Neither A nor B.
2. Fast idle adjustments are performed with a _____ engine.
   (A) cold
   (B) hot
   (C) warmed up
   (D) any temperature
3. Technician A says that on any vehicle made after 1968, the idle mixture screws are sealed and cannot be adjusted. Technician B says that any vehicle can be adjusted by adjusting the mixture screws to obtain the highest vacuum and RPM. Who is right?
   (A) A only.
   (B) B only.
   (C) Both A & B.
   (D) Neither A nor B.
4. The best equipment for adjusting the idle mixture is _____.
   (A) a vacuum gauge
   (B) a vacuum gauge and tachometer
   (C) a propane enrichment device
   (D) an exhaust gas analyzer
5. All of the following statements about the aneroid bellows in an altitude compensating device are true, EXCEPT:
   (A) the bellows is sealed.
   (B) the bellows can be adjusted.
   (C) the bellows is energized by the engine control module.
   (D) the bellows operates an air valve in the carburetor.
6. Technician A says that carburetor castings should be blown out with compressed air to ensure that all passages are clear. Technician B says that vacuum diaphragms should be blown out to make certain all oil is removed. Who is right?
   (A) A only.
   (B) B only.
   (C) Both A & B.
   (D) Neither A nor B.
7. Technician A says that you should always begin adjusting the idle mixture by seating the idle mixture screws very firmly against their seats and then back off about 1 1/4 turn. Technician B says that adjusting the idle mixture can change the idle RPM. Who is right?
   (A) A only.
   (B) B only.
   (C) Both A & B.
   (D) Neither A nor B.

8. The automatic choke is adjusted by altering the tension on the _____.
   - (A) thermostatic spring
   - (B) choke plate
   - (C) choke housing
   - (D) connecting linkage

9. Technician A says that the best time to replace the throttle position sensor and mixture control solenoids is during a carburetor overhaul. Technician B says that the carburetor's part number is usually needed to order the correct overhaul kit. Who is right?
   - (A) A only.
   - (B) B only.
   - (C) Both A & B.
   - (D) Neither A nor B.

10. The best method to use for cleaning carburetor jets is to _____.
    - (A) run a drill through the jet
    - (B) run a soft wire through the jet
    - (C) blow out with an air blast
    - (D) run a wire through and then blow out

Suggested Activities

1. Obtain a carburetor and examine it. Make a sketch of it and note the location of each possible adjustment. If possible, obtain a service manual for the vehicle the carburetor is used on and identify the function of each adjustment.

2. Tear down a scrap carburetor and identify each part and its relation to the overall function of the carburetor.

3. Remove the air cleaner from the carburetor used on a computer-controlled vehicle. Turn on the ignition and note any obvious functions. In a well ventilated area, start the vehicle and allow it to reach normal operating temperature. Note any observations as to carburetor function. Write a short report of your observations.

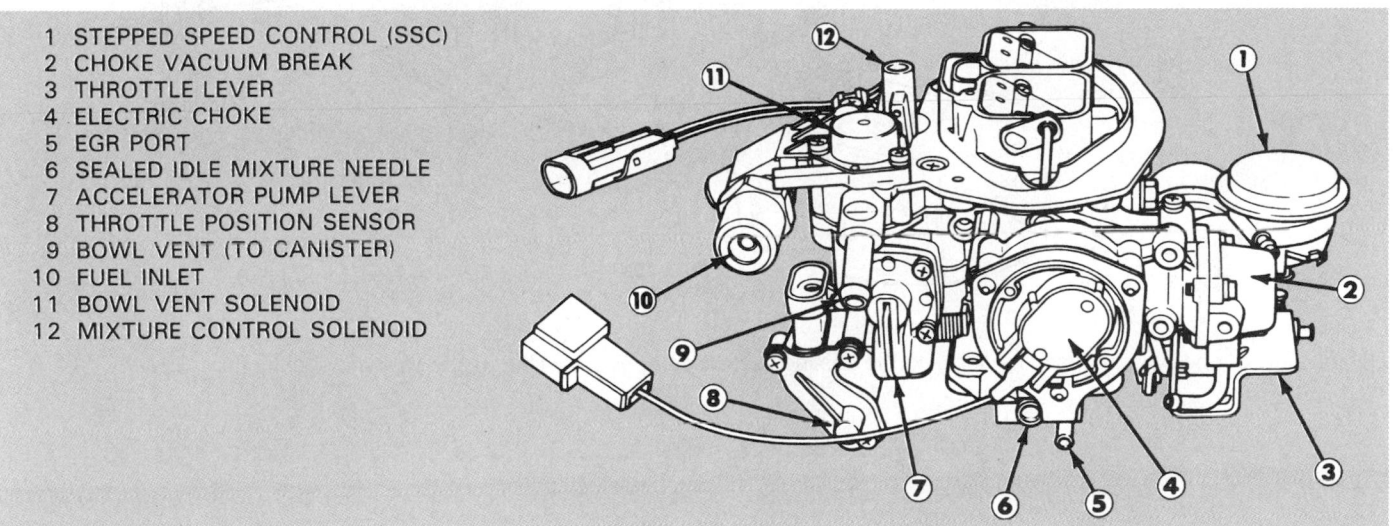

```
 1  STEPPED SPEED CONTROL (SSC)
 2  CHOKE VACUUM BREAK
 3  THROTTLE LEVER
 4  ELECTRIC CHOKE
 5  EGR PORT
 6  SEALED IDLE MIXTURE NEEDLE
 7  ACCELERATOR PUMP LEVER
 8  THROTTLE POSITION SENSOR
 9  BOWL VENT (TO CANISTER)
10  FUEL INLET
11  BOWL VENT SOLENOID
12  MIXTURE CONTROL SOLENOID
```

Typical two-barrel carburetor. Study the location of the various parts. (GM)

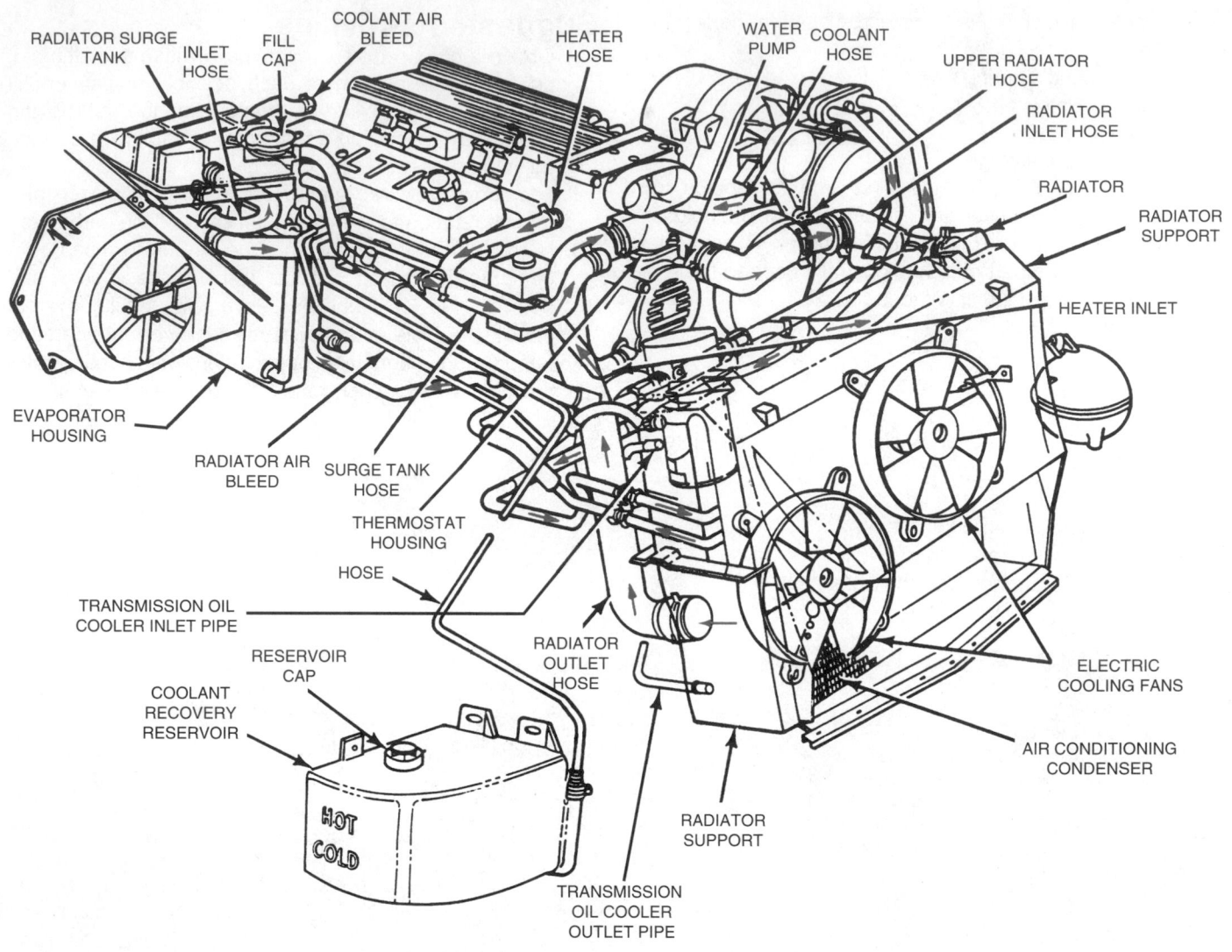

RADIATOR SURGE TANK

INLET HOSE

FILL CAP

COOLANT AIR BLEED

HEATER HOSE

WATER PUMP

COOLANT HOSE

UPPER RADIATOR HOSE

RADIATOR INLET HOSE

RADIATOR

RADIATOR SUPPORT

HEATER INLET

EVAPORATOR HOUSING

RADIATOR AIR BLEED

SURGE TANK HOSE

THERMOSTAT HOUSING

HOSE

TRANSMISSION OIL COOLER INLET PIPE

RESERVOIR CAP

COOLANT RECOVERY RESERVOIR

HOT COLD

RADIATOR OUTLET HOSE

ELECTRIC COOLING FANS

AIR CONDITIONING CONDENSER

RADIATOR SUPPORT

TRANSMISSION OIL COOLER OUTLET PIPE

Overall view of one particular engine showing the cooling system components. The arrows indicate coolant flow. (GM)

428

22

Cooling System Service

After studying this chapter, you will be able to:
- Explain the role of antifreeze in an engine cooling system.
- Properly clean a cooling system.
- Detect leaks in a cooling system.
- Test a radiator pressure cap.
- List the safety rules dealing with cooling systems.
- Inspect and replace cooling system hoses.
- Inspect, replace, and adjust drive belts.
- Test and replace a thermostat.
- Inspect, repair, and replace a coolant pump.

This chapter will cover the service requirements of modern cooling systems, including diagnosis, coolant replacement, system flushing, and repair operations. Although most of the information in this chapter covers liquid-cooled systems, air-cooled systems are also discussed.

 Caution: Use care when working on vehicles equipped with airbags. Some sensors are located near the radiator.

The Need for a Cooling System

Automobile engines generate a great deal of heat. About one-third of the heat energy developed by the fuel burning in the cylinders is converted into power to drive the automobile. Another third is wasted and goes out the exhaust unused. The remaining third is absorbed by the metal of the engine and must be disposed of by the cooling system to prevent overheating.

Figure 22-1 shows the approximate temperatures of the various engine parts during operation. When properly designed and maintained, automobile cooling systems are good at keeping these temperatures within the normal range. However, the failure or malfunction of one or more cooling system components can lead to serious overheating. Under certain conditions, cooling system problems can also cause overcooling.

Cooling System Service

Modern cooling systems are relatively trouble free. However, they can develop problems, especially if they are neglected. Routine checks and periodic coolant replacement will usually reveal cooling system problems before they reach the serious stage. It is important for the technician to become familiar with problems associated with the cooling system. The technician must know which units are responsible for specific problems, how they can be checked, and if faulty, how they are repaired. See **Figure 22-2.**

Dealing with an Overheated Engine

If the engine is greatly *overheated* (steam is spurting from the overflow), shut it down at once. If an engine is moderately overheated, it is best to run the engine at high idle for a minute or two before shutting it down. Flow of the coolant helps to carry excess heat from the cylinders and valves, and there is less possibility of cylinder distortion and warped valves.

Never run cold water into the radiator of an overheated engine. Raise the hood and allow the engine to cool down until the coolant is no longer boiling. This will take at least thirty minutes. Then, start the engine. While running the engine at a fast idle, slowly add water to the radiator. The pump will mix the hot coolant and the cold water. Run the engine until the temperature is normal. Then, recheck the radiator coolant level. Finally, find out what caused the engine to overheat and correct the problem. Problem diagnosis and correction is covered later in this chapter.

Antifreeze

In all areas where temperatures may drop below freezing (32°F [0°C]), it is necessary to keep *antifreeze* in the cooling system to prevent engine damage. In addition, an antifreeze-water mixture is better than plain water at transferring heat in hot weather. The proper antifreeze-water mixture has a boiling point that is approximately 11°F (6°C) higher than plain water. Modern antifreeze contains *rust inhibitors,* which prevent damage to the engine, radiator, and heater core, and small amounts of *water soluble oils,* which lubricate the coolant pump seals and heater shut-off valves.

Ethylene Glycol Antifreeze

In the past, many liquids were used as antifreeze, including kerosene, denatured ethyl alcohol, and methanol

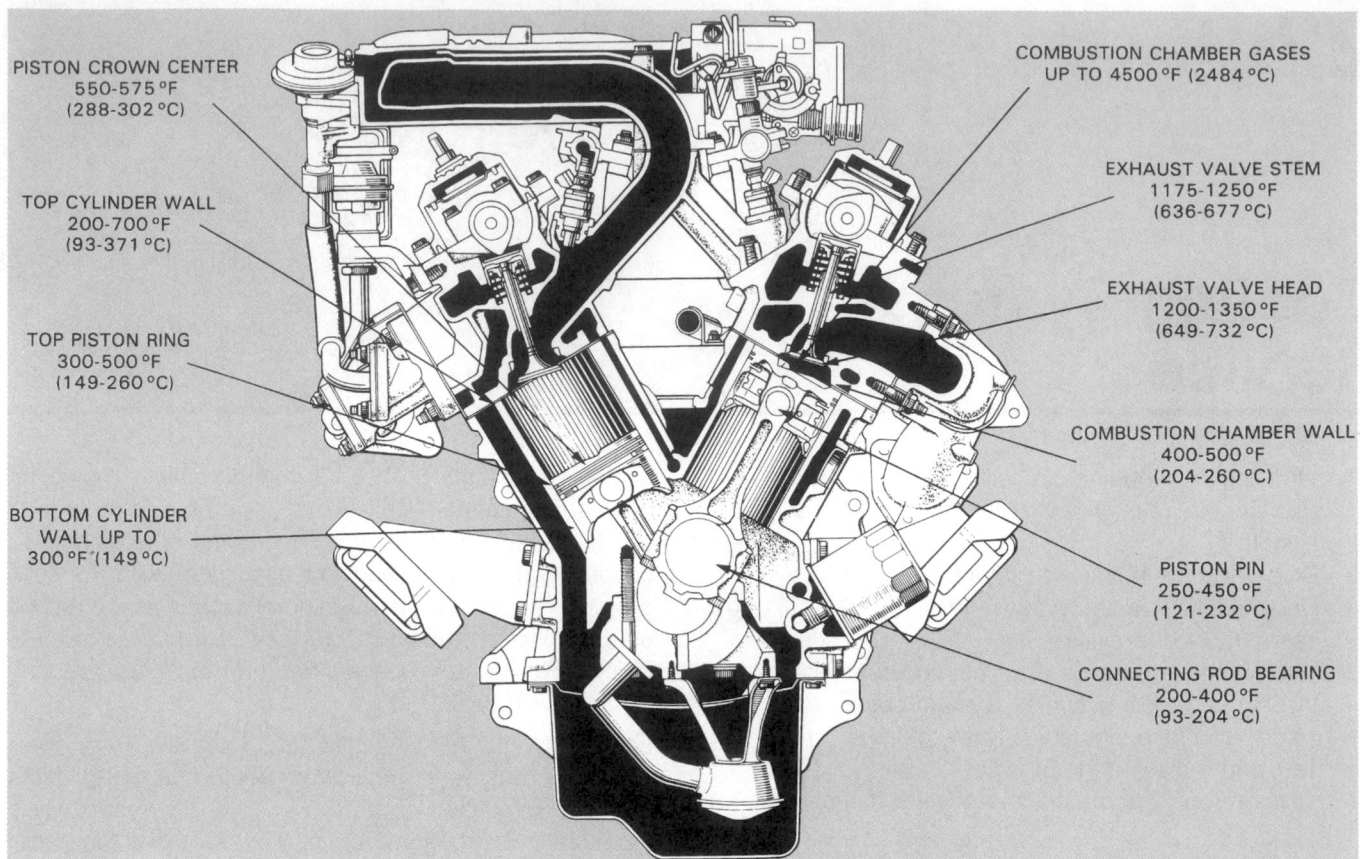

PISTON CROWN CENTER
550-575°F
(288-302°C)

TOP CYLINDER WALL
200-700°F
(93-371°C)

TOP PISTON RING
300-500°F
(149-260°C)

BOTTOM CYLINDER
WALL UP TO
300°F (149°C)

COMBUSTION CHAMBER GASES
UP TO 4500°F (2484°C)

EXHAUST VALVE STEM
1175-1250°F
(636-677°C)

EXHAUST VALVE HEAD
1200-1350°F
(649-732°C)

COMBUSTION CHAMBER WALL
400-500°F
(204-260°C)

PISTON PIN
250-450°F
(121-232°C)

CONNECTING ROD BEARING
200-400°F
(93-204°C)

Figure 22-1. Approximate temperatures of various engine components and areas. Temperatures vary depending upon engine design and application. (Dodge)

(wood alcohol). Today, most antifreeze solutions are composed of *ethylene glycol.*

Ethylene glycol has several advantages over older types of antifreeze. Ethylene glycol is not a fire hazard, and it does not harm paint finishes. It does not readily evaporate at normal system temperatures, and it can be used with high-temperature thermostats. Additionally, it can be left in the cooling system all year without causing problems.

 Warning: Ethylene glycol antifreeze is poisonous and must not be taken internally. Keep antifreeze away from children and animals. Never put beverages or drinking water in empty antifreeze containers. A type of safety antifreeze, which is made with propylene glycol, is now available. However, it is still toxic to some extent, especially after it has been used in the cooling system. Some manufacturers do not recommend propylene glycol antifreeze.

All vehicle manufacturers recommend keeping at least a 50-50 mixture of water and antifreeze in the cooling system at all times. The correct amount of antifreeze to use is determined by the capacity of the cooling system. For example, a 20 quart cooling system should have 10 quarts of antifreeze and 10 quarts of water. Never try to economize by adding just enough antifreeze to get by. Modern engines and cooling systems contain cast iron, aluminum, steel, brass, copper, and various types of solder. These dissimilar

metals can cause *electrolysis* (creation of an electric current) in the system, with resulting damage to the metals. Ethylene glycol antifreeze must be used to keep this metal interaction from destroying the engine.

Always use clean water to top off the antifreeze solution. In most areas, tap water is acceptable for use in cooling systems. However, the water supply in some localities has high concentrations of lime and other minerals. Water containing these minerals is known as *hard water.* Hard water can cause hard layers of chemicals to build up in the cooling system, reducing the transfer of heat from the metal to the coolant. If your area has this type of water, use another source of water, such as bottled distilled water.

Useful Life of Antifreeze

The cooling systems of most new cars are filled with a mixture of etylene glycol antifreeze, rust inhibitors, pump lubricant, and clean water. Unless excessive coolant is lost for some reason, the coolant can be left in the system for the time period recommended by the manufacturer. This time period will vary, but is usually about 24 months. Following the first change period, many vehicle makers insist on the use of permanent-type antifreeze year round. Failure to comply to the manufacturer's recommendations may void the vehicle's warranty. It is suggested that the recommendations of the manufacturer be followed regarding the type of antifreeze and length of use.

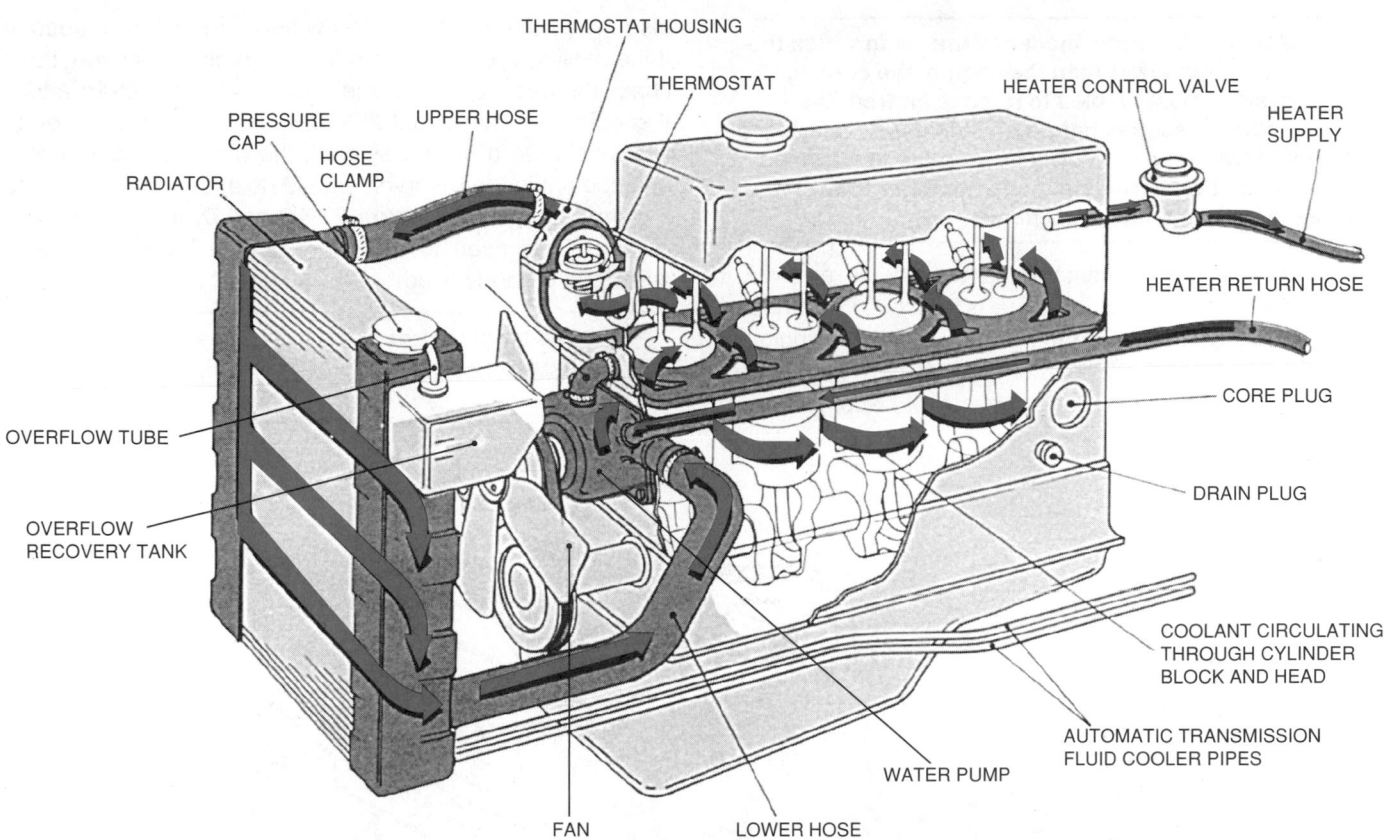

Figure 22-2. Potential cooling and/or heating system problem areas. (Gates Rubber)

Checking Antifreeze

To test the coolant protection level at operating temperature, use a special antifreeze **hydrometer.** Most antifreeze hydrometers have some form of temperature correction, so they can be used with hot or cold coolant. Draw the coolant in and out of the hydrometer several times to bring hydrometer temperature up to coolant temperature. When using the test unit, follow manufacturer's instructions. See **Figure 22-3.**

 Note: A battery hydrometer cannot be used to check antifreeze.

Draining and Refilling the System

Set the heater control to the maximum heat position and loosen the radiator cap to prevent pressure buildup. Operate the engine until it reaches normal operating temperature. Then, shut off the engine. Cover the radiator cap with a thick rag and remove the cap carefully. Open the radiator drain cock and remove the drain plugs from the engine block.

If the coolant is rusty, or if the interior of the radiator appears to be dirty, the system should be cleaned using a chemical cleaner before the new antifreeze is installed. The cleaning procedure is discussed later in this chapter. If the system is clean, flush it out with clean water.

After cleaning, tighten the radiator and heater hose clamps, and look carefully for signs (rust streaks, discol-

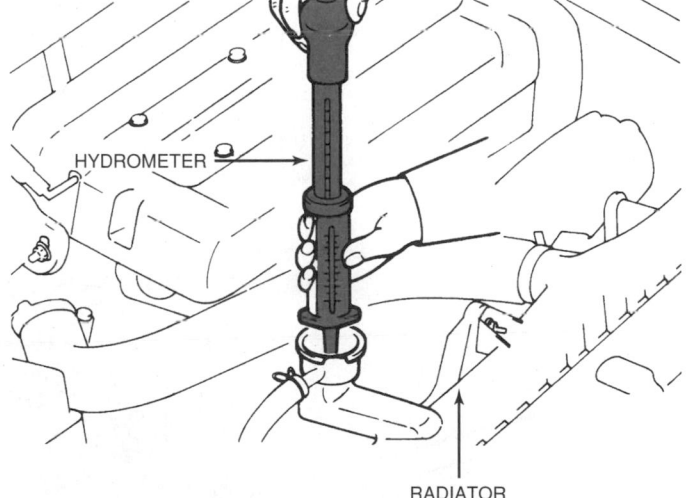

Figure 22-3. One type of antifreeze hydrometer being used to check the concentration (percentage) of antifreeze in the system. (Hyundai)

oration from antifreeze, dampness) of coolant leakage. Repair leaks as necessary. Close the drain cock and reinstall the block drains.

Shake the container of antifreeze to mix it well and add the required amount to the radiator. Add water until the level is about 2″ (50.8 mm) below the filler neck. This will allow for expansion when the engine is restarted.

Caution: On some modern vehicles in which the radiator is lower than the engine, the cooling system must be bled to remove air from the engine cooling passages before the engine is restarted. This type of system can usually be identified by a small bleed valve on the thermostat housing. Refer to the service manual for exact procedures.

After refilling the radiator, start the engine and run it until normal operating temperature is reached. The heater control should be set to maximum heat. When the engine is warm, the thermostat will open and release any air trapped in the system. Running the engine until it becomes warm also mixes the antifreeze and water. Add water as needed. If the cooling system is open (no reservoir or recovery tank), check the coolant level in the radiator, **Figure 22-4A** and **B**. It should be within about 2″ (50.8 mm) of the bottom of the filler neck. On a closed system, the radiator should be full and coolant in the reservoir should be at the correct level for a warm engine. See **Figure 22-4C** and **D**. If the level in the reservoir has risen to the warm engine level, the cooling system is properly filled.

STOP   Warning: Do not remove the pressure cap from a closed system to check the coolant level.

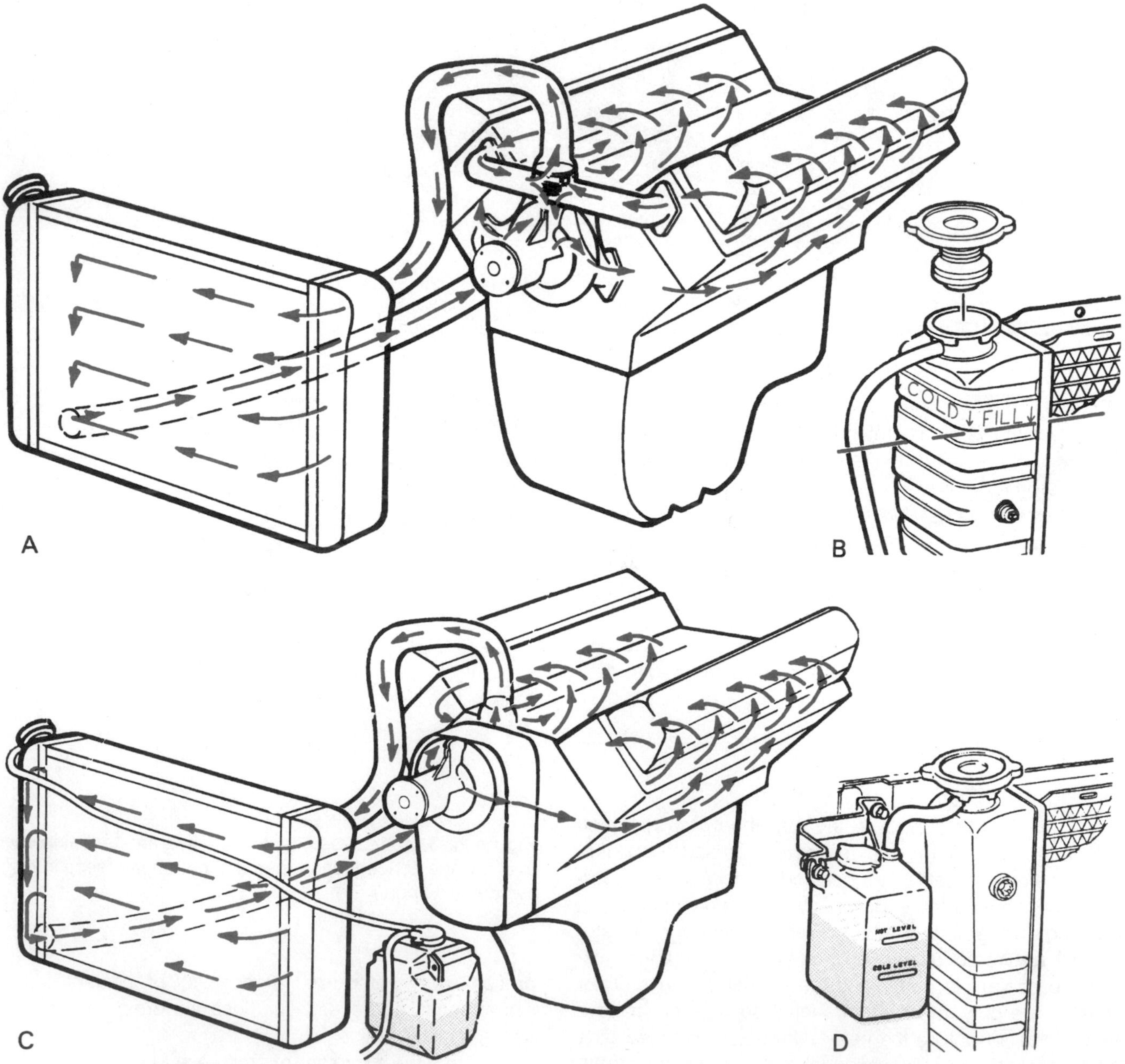

Figure 22-4. Typical cooling systems. A—Coolant flow in an open system. B—Cold fill level for an open system. Note the marks on the side tank. C—Coolant flow in a closed system. D—Hot and cold fill level marks on a closed system coolant reservoir. With a closed system, the coolant level in the reservoir falls with engine cooling and rises with engine heating. The radiator is always completely full. (Cadillac and Ford)

Routine System Cleaning

Mild rust and scale buildup in the cooling system can usually be corrected by cleaning the system with a chemical *cooling system cleaner.* When the vehicle uses an aluminum engine, cylinder head, or radiator, use a cleaner that is harmless to aluminum. Avoid splashing cleaner on the paint finish. Carefully follow the instructions supplied by the manufacturer of the cleaning product. Some cleaners are of a one-step type, while others require two or more separate operations.

System Cleaning Procedures

Drain the old antifreeze solution from the system. Close all drains. Fill system with clean water, reinstall the radiator cap, and run the engine until normal operating temperature is attained. Add cleaner to the system and start the engine. Set the heater control to maximum heat, allowing coolant and cleaner to circulate through the heater lines and core. After allowing the cleaner to circulate for the recommended period of time, stop the engine and drain the system again. Remove radiator cap while draining. Do not let solution of water and cleaner boil. If the vehicle is outside and the weather is very cold, be careful of slush ice forming in the radiator.

 Warning: Use extreme caution when removing system pressure caps when coolant is hot.

Neutralizing and Flushing

If an acid type cleaner is used, it must be neutralized. A *neutralizer* reacts with any of the cleaning chemical left in the cooling system, transforming it into a harmless substance. Failure to neutralize and flush properly may leave acids, which will attack the system and destroy the protective properties of the inhibitors and the antifreeze. Pour the neutralizer into the system, run the engine for the specified length of time, and drain.

Refilling with Antifreeze and Water

Using a coolant mixture of around 50% ethylene glycol antifreeze and 50% clean, soft water, refill the system. Run the engine until normal temperature is reached and add coolant as needed.

Heavy-Duty System Cleaning

Long periods of neglect often result in a cooling system that is literally choked with rust and scale. This can often be detected by feeling the radiator on a moderately warm engine. Cold spots on the radiator surface are evidence of clogged tubes. Ultimately, the radiator tubes are blocked enough to cause the coolant in the system to boil. The boiling action breaks loose large quantities of scale that may plug the radiator completely. See **Figure 22-5**. Correction requires *reverse flushing.*

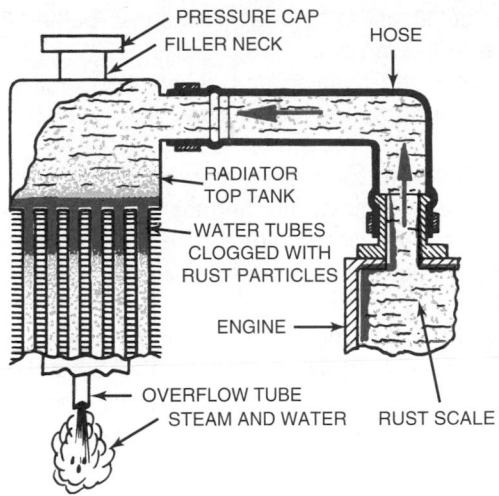

Figure 22-5. Note how rust particles have completely clogged the water tubes in this radiator.

Radiator Reverse Flushing

Reverse flushing forces water through the system in a direction opposite to that of normal flow. This facilitates the removal of particles jammed into openings. Severe radiator clogging may require removal and boiling in a hot tank. This will be described later in this chapter.

To begin reverse flushing, remove the upper and lower radiator hoses. Disconnect the heater hoses. Attach the flushing gun to the lower radiator outlet and a lead-away hose to the top radiator outlet. Replace the radiator cap. See **Figure 22-6**.

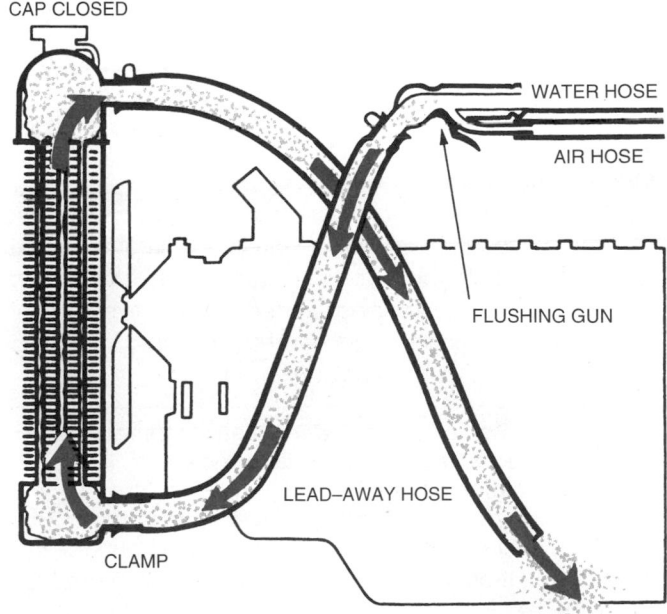

Figure 22-6. Setup for reverse flushing a radiator. (Harrison Radiator)

Run a stream of water through the radiator and periodically admit blasts of air to agitate and loosen particles so that they can be flushed out. Do not exceed a maximum air pressure of 20 psi (138 kPa). Pressures higher than this may rupture the radiator.

Continue the flushing and air blasting until the water that flows out of the radiator is clear.

Reverse Flushing the Engine Block

Be sure to remove the thermostat before flushing the block. Some vehicles require the removal of the coolant pump and heater hoses, as pressure flushing can damage the seal.

Attach the flushing gun to the top water outlet in the block. Attach a lead-away hose to the bottom outlet (if needed). Reverse flush the block using the procedure described for the radiator. See **Figure 22-7**. After flushing, reattach all hoses securely. Fill the system with water and add antifreeze or inhibitor as needed. Finally, test the system for leaks.

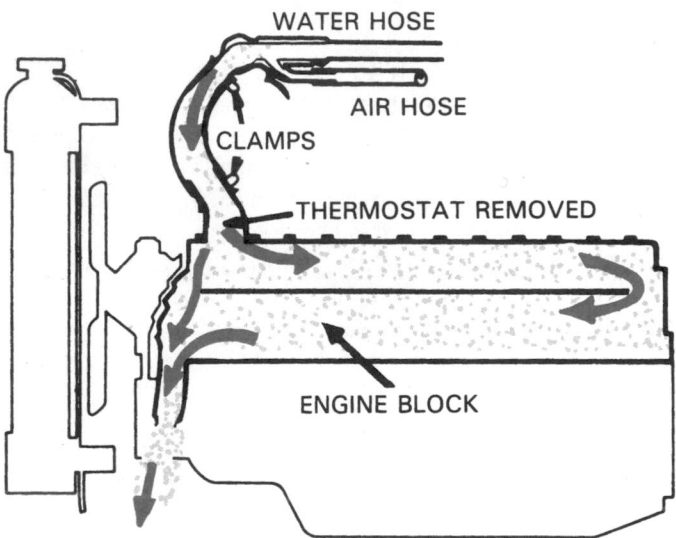

Figure 22-7. Reverse flushing an engine.

Reverse Flushing the Heater Core

After determining the direction of coolant flow, remove the heater hoses from the engine block. Be sure to remove the heater shut-off valve (if used) from the heater system before beginning the flushing procedure. To reverse flush the heater core, follow the procedures presented in the section on reverse flushing a radiator.

 Note: Some heater systems cannot be reverse flushed. Check the manufacturer's recommendations.

After flushing, reconnect the heater hoses and reinstall the heater shut-off valve. Refill the cooling system and test it for leaks.

Finding Leaks in the Cooling System

Cooling system leaks can develop over time. Leaks can be caused by corrosion, vibration, or the gradual loosening of system fittings. Sometimes, cleaning may open tiny cracks or other openings that have been sealed with rust. Removal of the rust allows leakage to start.

Coolant external leakage can cause engine overheating and damage to the pistons, valves, and cylinder head. If coolant containing ethylene glycol leaks into the cylinders, it may plug the rings and cause hard starting, excessive oil consumption, piston corrosion, and bearing failure. Combustion gas leakage into the cooling system can cause severe cooling system corrosion. Any time the cooling system loses water and an obvious leak cannot be found, the system should be pressure tested or tested with special chemicals or a black light, **Figure 22-8**.

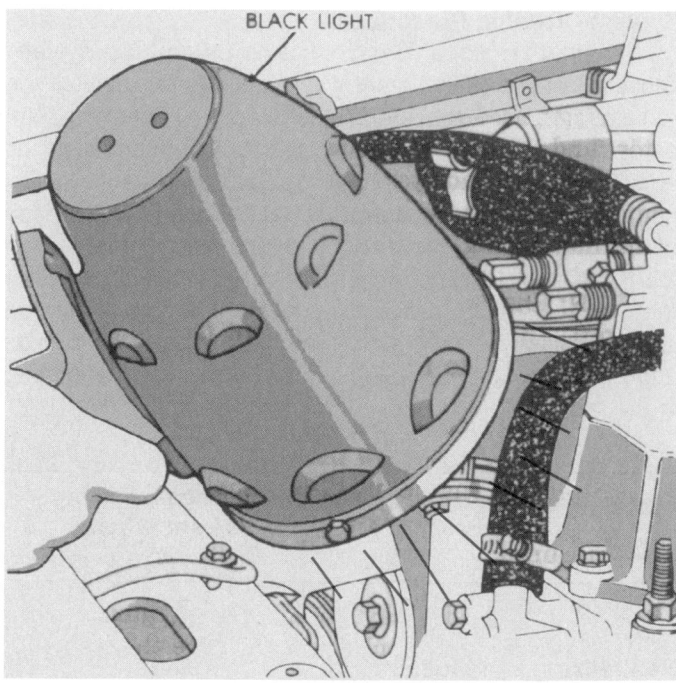

Figure 22-8. Using a black light to detect coolant leaks. Add the proper dye, warm the engine (use pressure tester on cold engine), and direct the light at the suspected leak area. (Dodge)

Pressure Testing the Cooling System

Fill the radiator to within 1/2″ (12.7 mm) of the filler neck. Attach the **pressure tester** to the filler neck. Build up pressure in the system carefully. Do not exceed the pressure for which the system is designed. Check the pressure marking on the radiator cap or obtain information from the manufacturer's manual. See **Figure 22-9**.

When the system is pressurized, watch the gauge. If the pressure holds steady, the system is probably all right. If the pressure drops, check all areas for leaks. Look carefully for leaks. Even dampness indicates enough loss of coolant to cause trouble. If leaks cannot be found, check the tester filler neck connection to make certain it is not leaking.

Remove the tester. Replace the radiator cap and run the engine until normal temperature is reached. Remove the cap, attach the pressure pump, and once again pressurize the system. Recheck the system for leaks.

Occasionally you will find that a system leaks only when cold or when hot. By checking the system before and after engine warm-up, both types of leaks will be exposed.

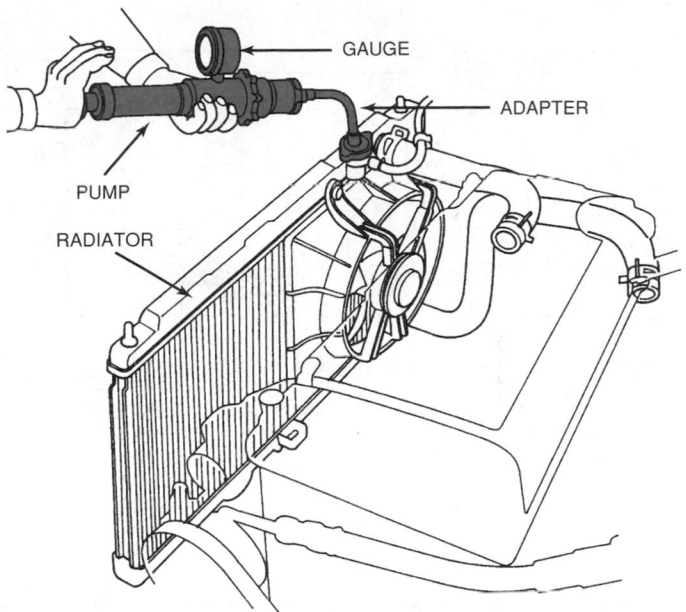

Figure 22-9. Pressurizing pump attached to a radiator. Pressure is being built up in the system to check for possible leaks. (Honda)

When finished with the pressure test, adjust coolant to the proper level in the radiator.

Checking for Internal Leaks with a Pressure Gauge

If the system loses coolant and no external source is found, check for internal leakage. Apply 6 to 8 psi (41-55 kPa) of pressure to the system. Run the engine at a slow speed and watch the pressure pump gauge. Pressure buildup indicates a combustion leak—a cracked head, blown gasket, etc.

 Warning: Do not allow pressure to build up beyond pressure cap rating.

To determine which bank on a V-type engine is leaking, disconnect all the spark plug wires on one bank and run the engine. If the pressure buildup stops, the leak is in that bank. If not, the leak is in the firing bank. Repeat the test on both banks.

Checking for Internal Leaks with Test Chemicals

By drawing air from the top of the radiator through a special test chemical, it is possible to detect combustion leaks. The test chemical will change color if combustion gases are present in the cooling system.

On V-type engines, operate the engine on one bank and test the system for leakage. Then, repeat the test while operating the engine on the other bank. In this way, you can determine if one or both banks are leaking. **Figure 22-10** illustrates a leak detector tool.

Other Checks for Internal Leaks

Another method of checking for internal leaks requires no special tools. Drain the system down to the level of the

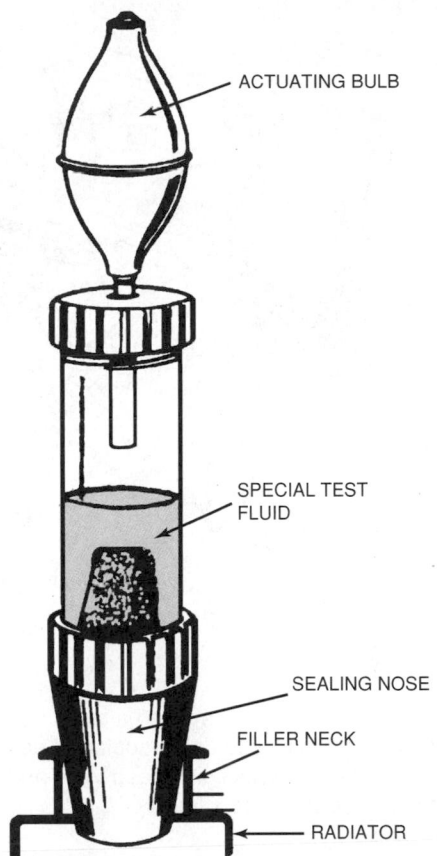

Figure 22-10. Combustion leak detector. Note the special fluid. (P and G Mfg. Co.)

engine outlet hose. Then, remove the hose. If necessary, add coolant to bring the level up to the hose fitting neck. Disconnect the coolant pump drive belt. Start engine and accelerate rapidly several times. Watch for bubbles or for a surge in the water level, either one of which indicates a combustion leak.

Pull the engine oil dipstick. Tiny water droplets in the oil clinging to the stick indicate internal leakage. Oil in the radiator may indicate a combustion leak or a leak in the transmission oil cooler. When draining the oil, always watch for water contamination.

Water or steam discharge from the tail pipe when the engine is operating at a normal temperature can mean internal leakage. Water discharge is normal during warm-up. Another way to check for leakage is to use a black light and dye, **Figure 22-11**.

Servicing Internal Leaks

External and internal leaks should be repaired immediately, or they may cause severe engine damage. Sealing compounds should not be poured into the radiator to stop leaks. These sealers can plug up coolant passages and will not stop major leaks.

If internal engine leaks are discovered, the oil should be drained. If ethylene glycol was being used as an antifreeze, the lubrication system must be thoroughly flushed. A special flushing agent is required to dissolve the gummy residue deposited by the antifreeze. In cases of

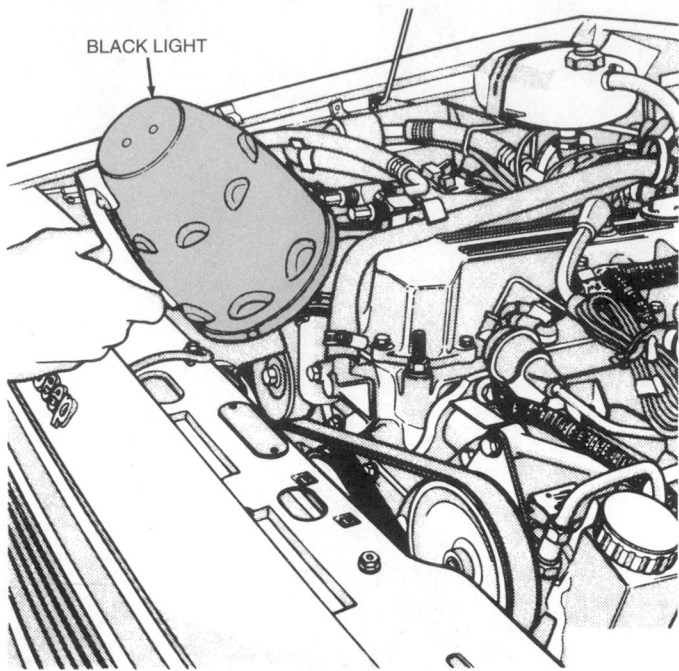

Figure 22-11. This technician is using a black light to check for coolant leaks. Dye is placed in the coolant. Leaking coolant will be illuminated by the black light. Keep tools and hands away from the fan, pulleys, etc. (Jeep)

severe contamination, proper cleaning may require that the engine be disassembled.

Radiator Pressure Caps

Pressurizing the cooling system raises the boiling point of the coolant mixture. This allows the engine to operate at higher temperatures without causing the coolant to boil. Hotter temperatures increase combustion efficiency, resulting in more power, better mileage, and lower emissions. Cooling systems are pressurized by using a radiator *pressure cap.* The pressure cap contains a spring that will not allow pressure to escape from the system until a certain pressure setting is reached.

The boiling point of the coolant is raised about 3°F (1.6°C) for each pound of pressure added. If pressure buildup permitted by the radiator cap is 15 psi, the boiling point of the coolant under pressure will be increased by 45°F (15 x 3°F). At sea level, water boils at 212°F (100°C). Adding 45°F to 212°F gives us 257°F, the temperature at which radiator coolant will boil when placed under 15 psi of pressure. To maintain specified pressure, the cap pressure valve spring and seal surface must be in good condition, **Figure 22-12.**

Pressure Cap Testing

Cap operation can be checked by using a pressure tester, **Figure 22-13.** The cap should retain a pressure within 1 1/2 psi (10 kPa) of its specified pressure rating. If

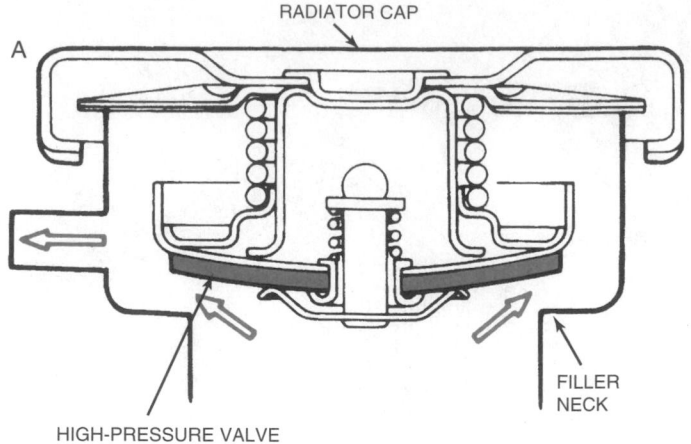

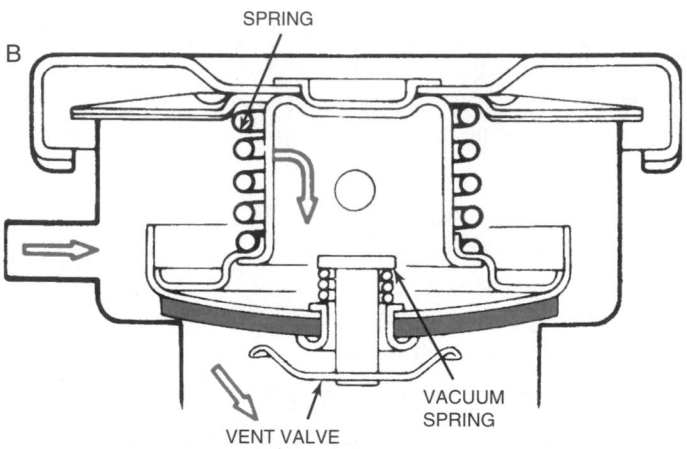

Figure 22-12. Parts of the radiator cap. A—The pressure valve is forced off its seat when the specified psi is reached. B—The vacuum valve is lowered, allowing atmosphere pressure into the radiator and preventing its collapse. (Hyundai)

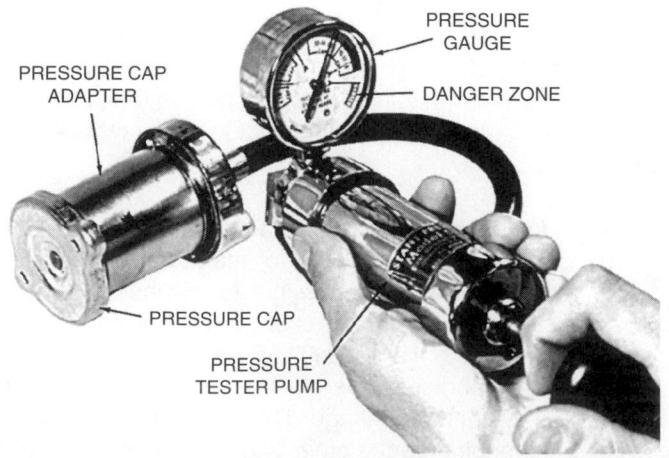

Figure 22-13. Using a pressure tester to check radiator pressure cap function. This particular tester can be used for checking both the radiator and the pressure cap. Note the "danger zone" on the gauge. *Never* raise pressure to this level! (Stant)

the cap fails to pass the test, replace it with a new cap of the correct pressure rating. Do not use a non-pressure cap on a pressurized system. Do not use a cap designed for an open system (no coolant reservoir) on a closed system (coolant recovery reservoir).

STOP **Warning: Removing a pressure cap from a hot radiator can be very dangerous. Sudden release of the pressure may cause the water to turn to steam and literally "explode" into the face of the person removing the cap.**

Always place a protective rag over the cap during removal. Stand to one side. Open the cap to the safety stop and wait for steam pressure to subside. The cap may then be safely removed.

Inspecting the Radiator Filler Neck

Check the condition of the inside sealing seat (surface that contacts the cap) in the filler neck. It must be smooth and clean. Moderate roughness can be removed with a special reaming tool. Cam edges must be true and the overflow tube must be clean and free of dents. A pressure cap cannot function properly unless the filler neck is in good condition. See **Figure 22-14**.

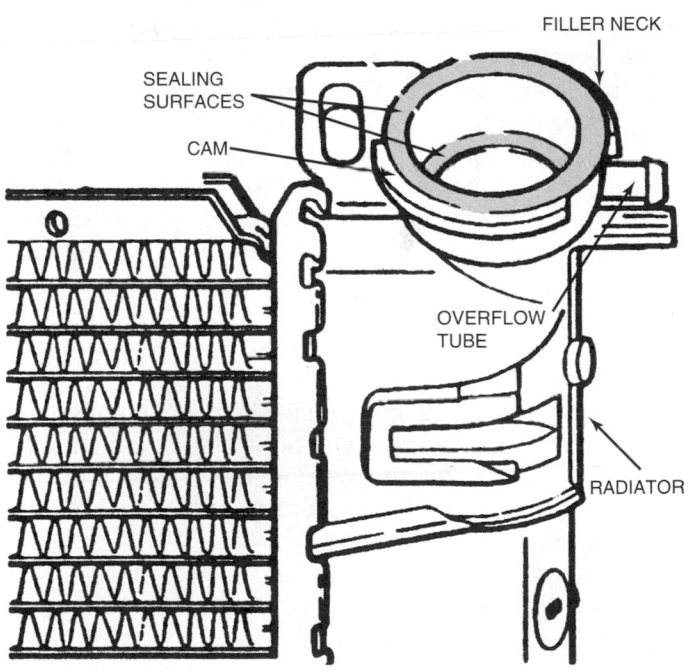

Figure 22-14.   Inspect the radiator filler neck for signs of damage. Note the dent in the overflow tube. (Ford)

Hose Inspection

The **coolant hoses** have a simple job—directing water between the engine, radiator, and heater core. Nevertheless, a hose failure can be catastrophic. Visually check all hoses for signs of deterioration. Squeeze each hose. A hose should not be hard and brittle or soft and swollen. See **Figure 22-15** and **22-16**. Bend heater hoses to check for

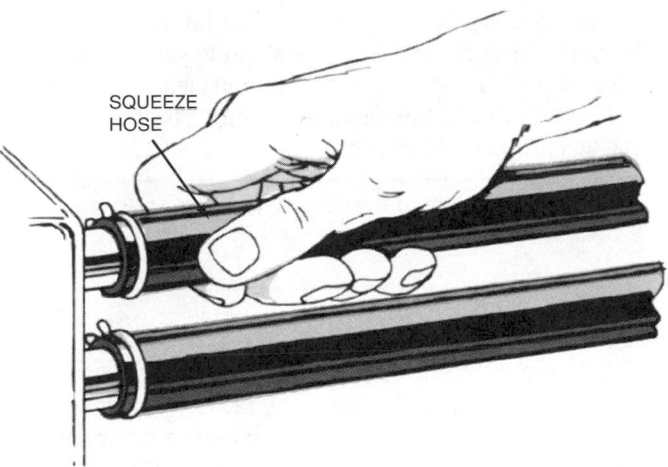

Figure 22-15.   Squeeze the hoses to check for hardness or for swelling and softness. (Gates Rubber)

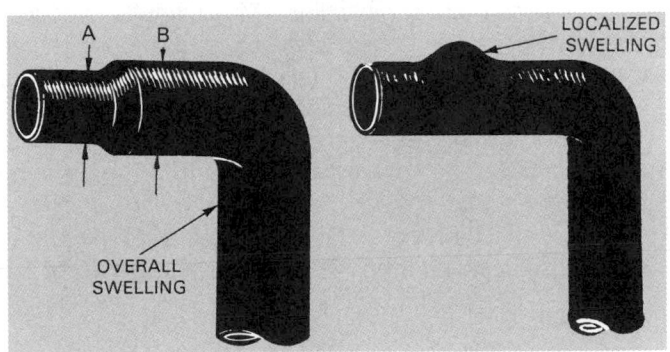

Figure 22-16.   Overall and localized swelling of a radiator hose. Note dimensions. A—Normal diameter. B—Swollen diameter. A hose with any abnormal swelling should be replaced. (Toyota)

surface cracking, abnormal swelling, and hardness. If any show signs of deterioration, they should be replaced. The radiator hose in **Figure 22-17** has deteriorated badly.

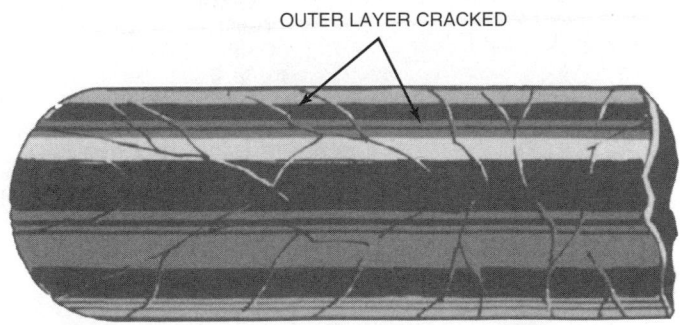

Figure 22-17.   This hose should have been replaced long before reaching this advanced state of deterioration. (Gates Rubber)

Pay careful attention to the bottom radiator hose. It is subject to pump suction whenever the engine is running. If the bottom hose is soft, it will collapse and cut off the coolant circulation. If the bottom hose is loose or cracked, it can admit air into the system. Aeration (air bubbles in system) can cause rust to form faster than normal. When a hose rots on the inside, the rubber particles may break off and be carried into the radiator. Once in the radiator, the particles can cause clogging.

 Note: If there is the slightest doubt as to the condition of a hose, replace it.

Hose Replacement

Use replacement hose of the correct inside diameter. Do not use a rigid hose between the radiator and the engine because the normal movement of the engine can cause the radiator hose fittings to crack loose and leak. Relatively soft, molded hose is satisfactory for this purpose. Flexible accordion-type hose can also be used. More information on hoses is available in Chapter 8.

If the hose originally installed by the manufacturer contains a spiral wire inside to prevent it from collapsing, make certain the same type of hose is used for replacement. If the spiral wire is badly rusted, replace it.

When installing a new hose, clean the metal hose fitting and coat the fitting with a thin layer of nonhardening gasket cement. Do not coat the inside of the hose, as gasket cement may be scraped off into the system. The proper method for cementing a hose is shown in **Figure 22-18**.

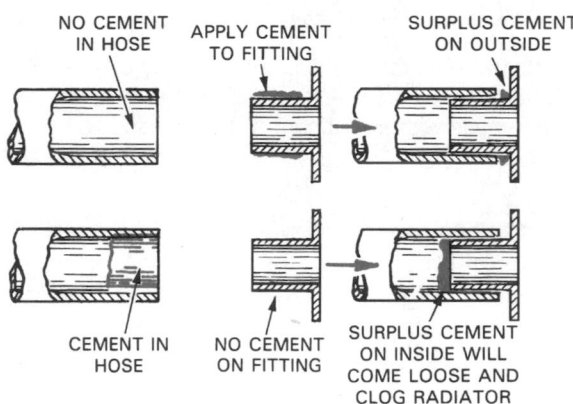

Figure 22-18. Coat the hose fitting, not the hose.

Make certain the hose ends pass over the raised sections of the fittings far enough to position the clamps properly. Before securing the clamps, make certain that any factory alignment marks used on the hoses and radiator are lined up, **Figure 22-19**.

If the hose must bend, use either a specially shaped molded hose or a flexible hose. **Figure 22-20** illustrates hose replacement steps.

Drive Belt Inspection

Flexible **drive belts** drive the coolant pump, as well as the alternator, power steering pump, air injection pump, and air conditioning compressor. Most belts consist of a woven fiberglass core that is surrounded by rubber. Traditional V-belts are still used on many engines. In some systems, sev-

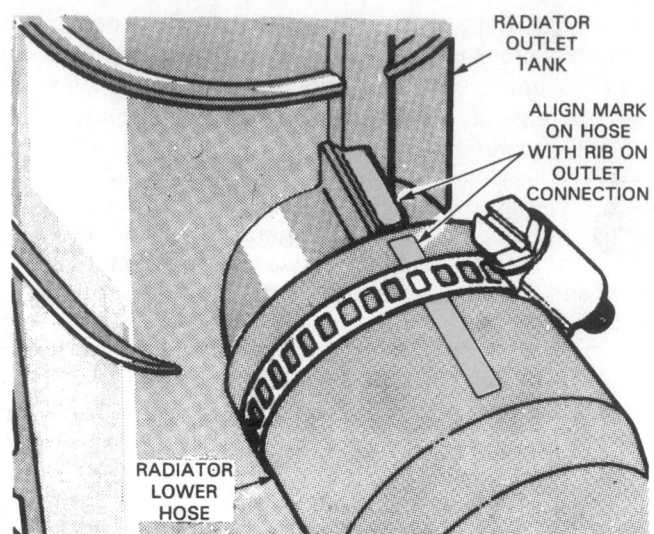

Figure 22-19. This illustrates the proper alignment of the lower radiator hose to the outlet tank. A twist in the hose (not aligned) would place a strain on the tank that could cause the tank to crack or break prematurely. (Ford)

eral belts are used, each one driving a different accessory unit. In other systems, the belts are arranged so that the air conditioner and alternator belts will both drive the coolant pump. Some vehicles use a flat, ribbed belt to drive one or more accessory units. Many late-model vehicles are equipped with a single belt that drives all accessories.

To check a belt, grasp it and roll it around so that the bottom and one side are clearly visible. Look for signs of cracking, oil soaking, glazing, splitting, and fraying. Replace belts showing these signs and belts that are older than four years, **Figure 22-21**. Modern belts may look OK, but they often fail suddenly from aging. Broken belts can be both inconvenient and dangerous.

Belt Replacement

Disconnect the battery ground clamp before removing the belt. Slack off the alternator, power steering pump and any other units; then remove the belt. Make sure the replacement belt is of the correct width, length, and construction.

Clean oil and grease from the pulley surfaces and install the new belt. If the belt has a directional arrow, install the belt so the arrow faces in the direction of belt travel. Adjust belt tension. When matched belts are being replaced, make sure new belts of exactly the same length are used. Do not force a belt over the pulley edges with a screwdriver or pry bar.

Adjusting Belt Tension

There are several methods that can be used to adjust **belt tension**—the amount that the belt is tightened. One method involves pushing the belt inward and measuring the amount of deflection under a certain pressure. See **Figure 22-22**. Keep in mind that the specifications will vary with different engines. Always follow the manufacturer's directions.

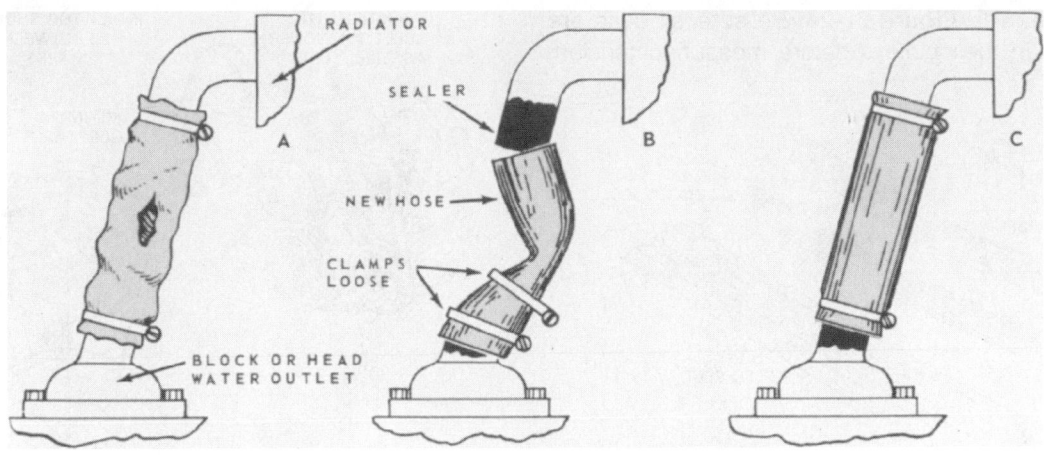

Figure 22-20. Typical steps in water hose service. A—Inspect and remove the old hose if needed. B—Coat the fittings with sealer. Place the clamps loosely on the hose. Crimp the hose to install. C—Center the hose on the fittings and tighten the clamps.

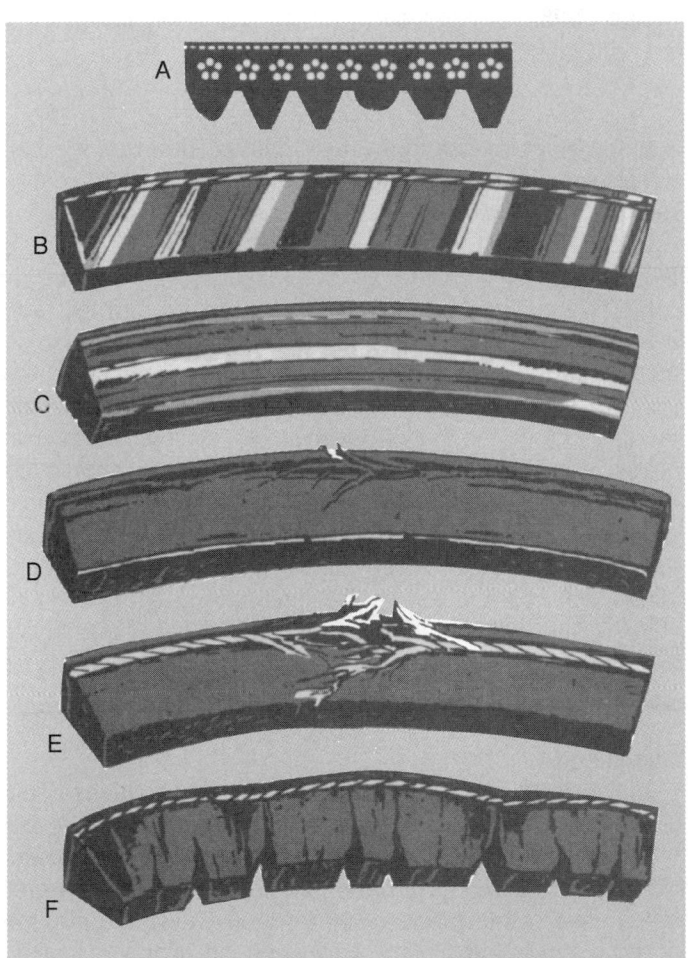

Figure 22-21. Drive belt wear signs. Replace the belt if wear is evident. A—Bottom cracked. B—Bottom cracked. C—Broken fabric. D—Top cover fabric torn. E—Burned from slipping. F—Gouged edge. (Gates Rubber)

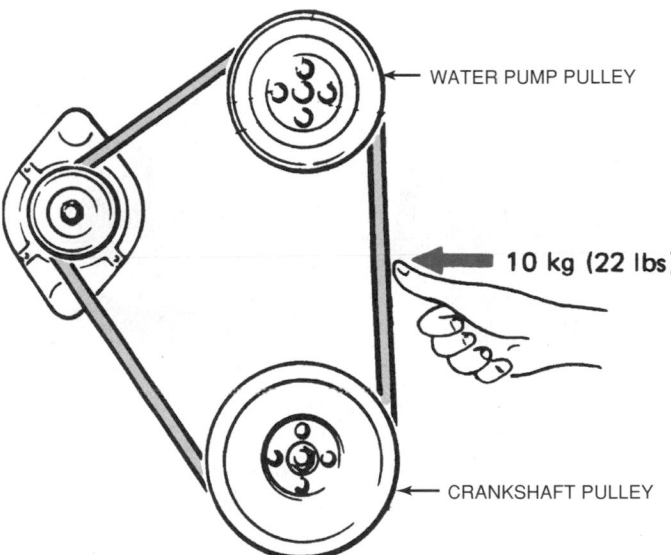

Figure 22-22. Checking belt tension by measuring the amount of belt deflection under a specific amount of pressure. (Suzuki)

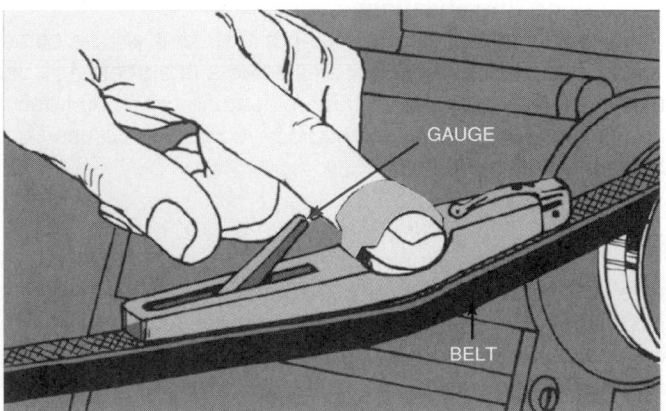

Figure 22-23. Checking belt tension with a tension gauge. (Gates Rubber)

Another way to check belt tension is to utilize a special belt strand tension gauge. The gauge deflects the belt and indicates belt tension on a gauge, **Figure 22-23**. This gauge can be used to check both the conventional, cogged V-belts and ribbed belts. See **Figure 22-24**. Be sure all belts are properly seated in their pulleys before measuring tension, **Figure 22-25**.

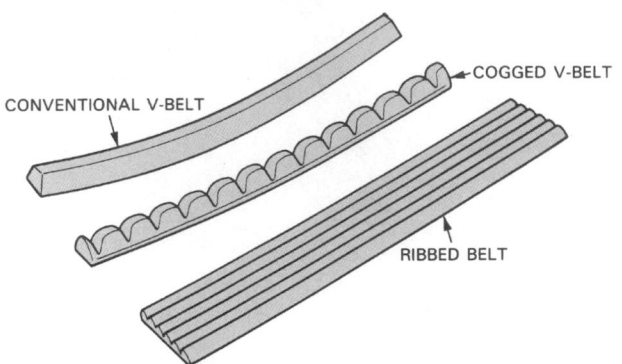

Figure 22-24. Three common types of drive belts. Each serves a specific purpose. (Ford)

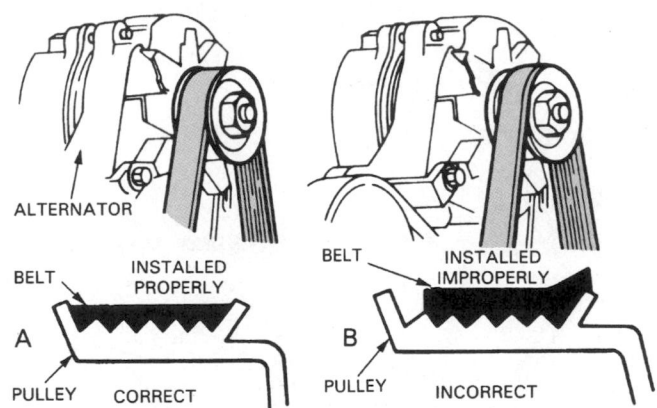

Figure 22-25. A—Ribbed belt is properly seated. B—The belt has been installed on the pulley incorrectly. This belt will give a false tension reading. (Ford)

Belt tension can also be determined by measuring how much torque must be applied to the alternator pulley, power steering pump pulley, or other accessory pulley before it begins to slip on the belt. On many late-model vehicles, an automatic belt tensioner is used to maintain proper tension, **Figure 22-26**.

Tensioning Specifications

Specifications for tensioning a new belt will be somewhat different from those for tensioning a used belt. Any belt that has been tensioned and placed in operation for a period of 10 or 15 minutes should be considered a used belt for purposes of retensioning.

Proper Belt Tensioning Is Important

A properly tensioned belt will run quietly and will provide maximum service life. Power steering pump action, alternator output, and compressor and coolant pump efficiency will be maintained. A loose belt will squeal, flap, and reduce the efficiency of the unit being driven. Belt life will be greatly reduced.

A belt that is too tight will place the alternator, coolant pump, or other unit bearings under a heavy strain and will

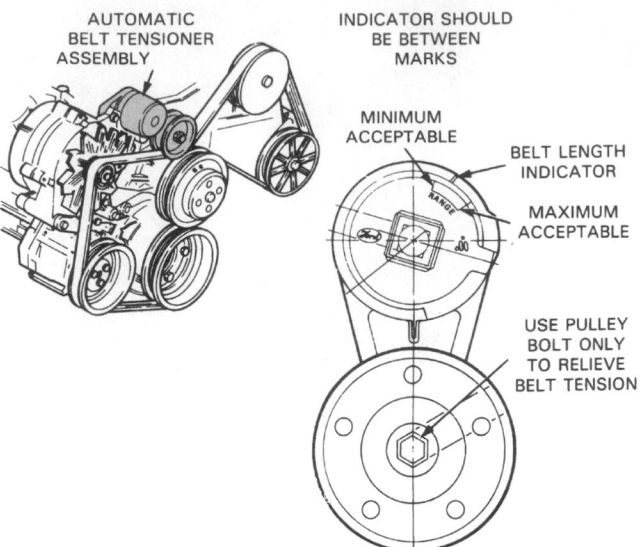

Figure 22-26. Spring-loaded belt tensioner. Note the acceptable belt length indicator. (Ford)

cause premature bearing wear. Constant strain on the belt will also cause belt breakage. Always tension belts carefully. Use the manufacturer's specifications.

Fan Service

The function of the fan is to draw air through the radiator whenever the vehicle is not moving fast enough to push air through. In some cases, the fan is installed on the front of the coolant pump shaft and driven by the pump belt. In other cases, the fan is driven by an electric motor. Fan blade assemblies are carefully balanced and should be replaced whenever blades are bent or cracked. Do not weld or braze fan blades. Never attempt to straighten fan blades that are badly bent. When installing a fan, use a spacer where required and torque the fasteners to specifications. Never stand in line with a revolving fan. Keep your fingers away from the blades. Remove the battery ground clamp before working on a fan.

Servicing Fluid Clutch Fans

The *fluid clutch fan* is a sealed drive clutch assembly filled with silicone. The two sides of the clutch separate the fan blades from the fan pulley. As engine speed increases, the torque required to turn the fan also increases. At a predetermined speed (about 2500 to 3200 RPM), the silicone driving fluid in the clutch allows enough slippage to limit maximum fan blade RPM. See **Figure 22-27**.

Some models of fluid clutch fans use either a bimetallic strip or a bimetallic spring that senses radiator temperature. The bimetallic spring operates a valve that can be designed either to start the fan turning when the temperature indicates the need or to alter the maximum RPM in accordance with cooling needs.

Checking Fluid Clutch Fan Operation

The fluid clutch fan unit is sealed. When it is defective, it should be replaced. Silicone oil leaking from the unit, a

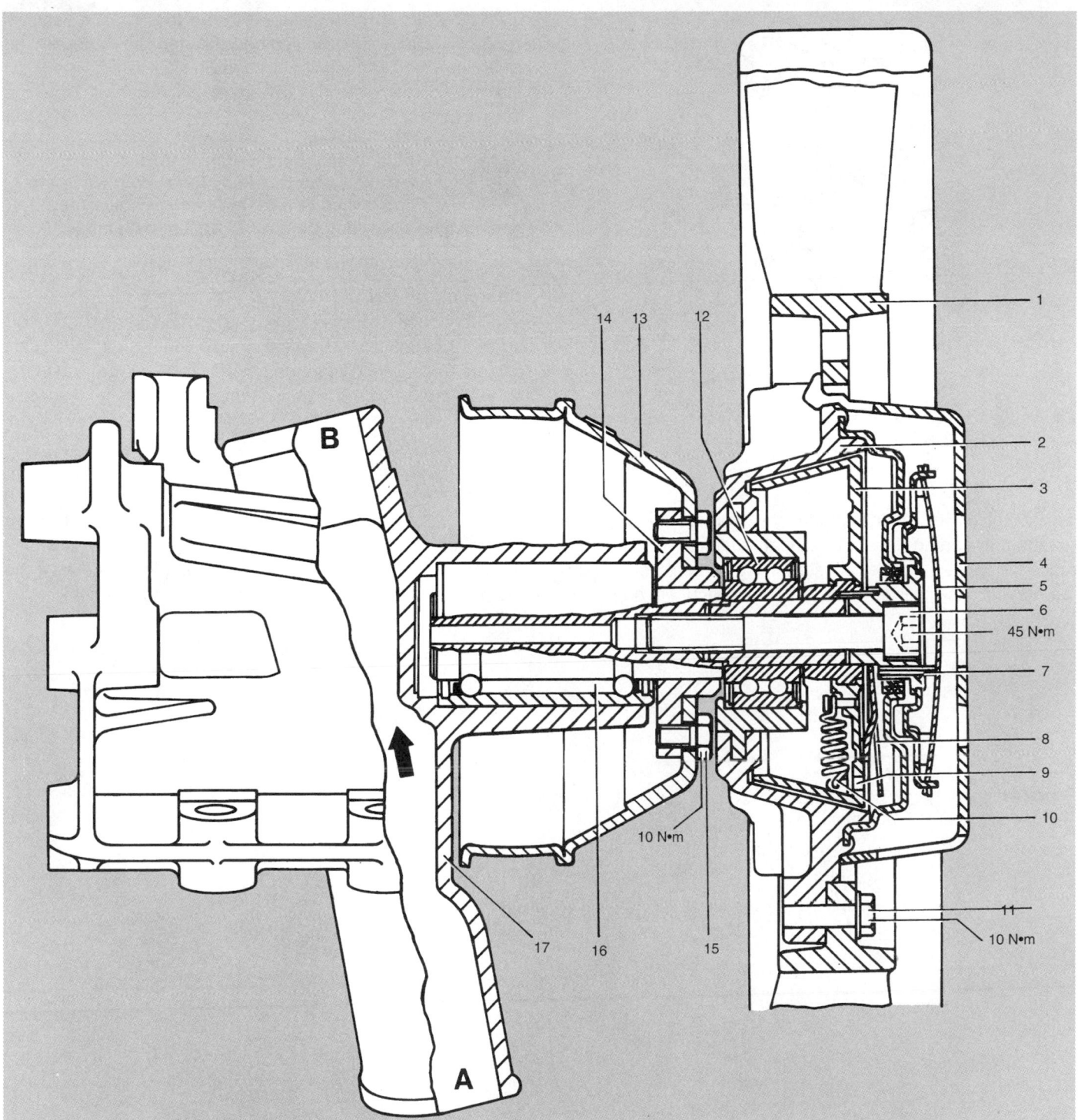

Figure 22-27. Cutaway of a fluid drive fan unit. 1—Fan. 2—Clutch body. 3—Driving disc. 4—Cover. 5—Bimetallic strips. 6—Bolt. 7—Control pin. 8—Spring plate. 9—Transition bore. 10—Tension spring. 11—Bolt. 12—Double-row ball bearing. 13—Pulley. 14—Hub. 15—Bolt. 16—Bearing body with shaft. 17—Visco-fan clutch carrier. A—From radiator. B—To thermostat. (Mercedes-Benz)

broken or stuck spring, or a faulty valve can render the unit inoperative. The unit illustrated in **Figure 22-28** can be checked by running the engine until normal operating temperature is reached. When the engine is stopped, the fan should revolve no more than 1/2 turn. If the fan continues to turn, the fluid clutch unit is defective and should be replaced.

Servicing Electric Fans

Most late-model vehicles use a cooling fan driven by an electric motor instead of the conventional belt-driven unit. One type of *electric fan assembly* is pictured in **Figure 22-29**. The fan motor is turned on and off by a temperature-sensitive *thermoswitch*. The thermoswitch can be mounted in the radiator tank, heater hose, or

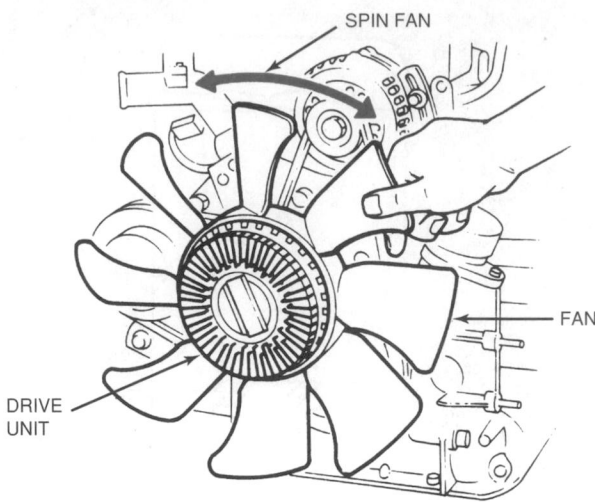

Figure 22-28. Checking the fan fluid drive unit. Always remove the battery cable before servicing an electric fan. (Mazda)

engine block or head. When the coolant temperature reaches a certain level, electrical contacts in the thermoswitch close and the fan starts. When the coolant temperature drops sufficiently, the thermoswitch will open and break the circuit. This causes the fan to stop. On vehicles equipped with air conditioning, the fan is generally on whenever the air conditioning compressor is activated. On the newest vehicles, the on-board computer controls the fan motor.

> **STOP** **Warning: If the coolant temperature is hot enough, the fan can come on at any time, even when the ignition switch is *off*. Always disconnect the battery before working on or near the fan assembly.**

Checking Electric Fan Operation

To check fan operation, the engine should be thoroughly heated up. The fan should come on when the coolant temperature reaches a certain value, as given in the appropriate service manual. Remember that most electric fans will also be on whenever the air conditioner is on, regardless of engine temperature. If the fan does not come on when it is supposed to, check for a defective or disconnected thermoswitch, a blown fuse, or a defective fan motor. One way to further isolate the problem is to remove the battery negative cable and use jumper wires to energize the fan motor. If the motor will not turn, it is defective. If the motor operates, the problem is in the control system.

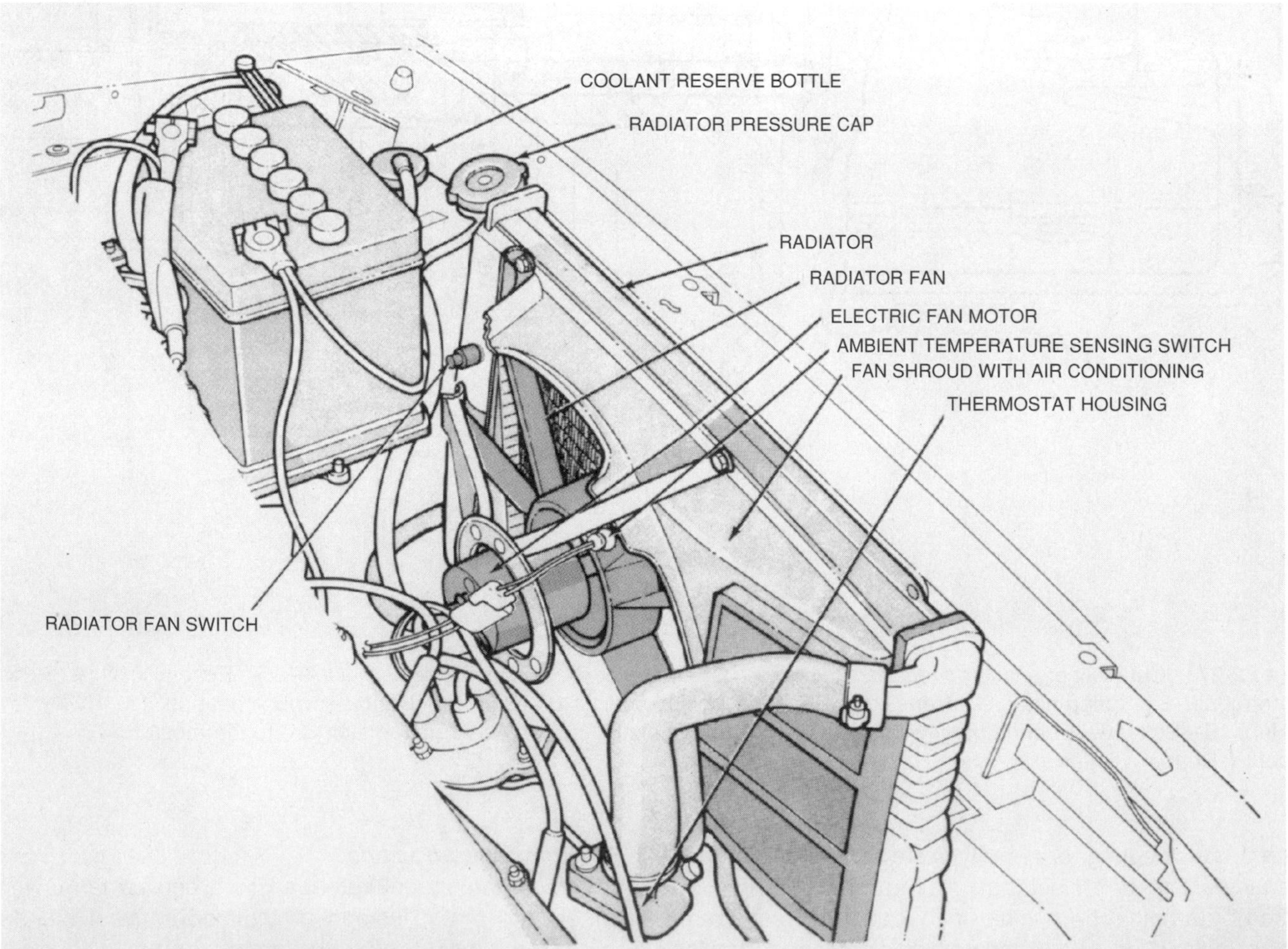

Figure 22-29. One type of electrically driven fan assembly. This unit uses a five-bladed plastic fan. The fan motor only runs when the coolant temperature reaches 193°-207°F (89°-97°C) or when the air conditioning is on. (Chrysler)

As with belt-driven fans, do not attempt to solder, weld, or glue the fan hub or blades together if they are cracked, broken, or damaged. If the motor is defective, it should be replaced with a unit specifically designed for the vehicle. Always follow the manufacturer's recommendations. A motor, fan, and fan retainer clip are shown in **Figure 22-30**.

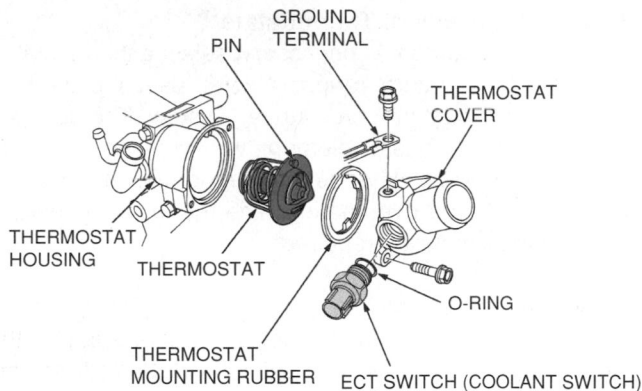

Figure 22-31. Thermostat setup. Note the coolant temperature sensor, which monitors coolant temperature and sends an electrical signal to the electronic control unit. (Honda)

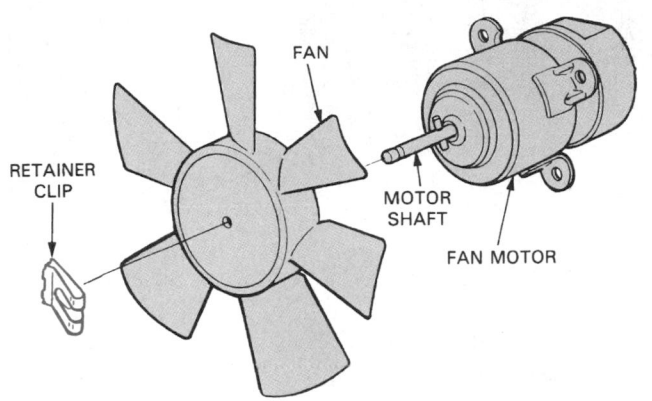

Figure 22-30. One type of plastic fan and electric fan motor. Note the retainer clip that secures the fan to the motor shaft. (Ford)

Thermostat Service

The **thermostat** is used to prevent coolant circulation when the engine is cold. This allows the engine to warm up quickly. Thermostats in older vehicles were often set to open at temperatures as low as 160°F (70°C). Modern vehicles, however, depend on higher coolant temperatures to help control emissions, and thermostats may not begin to open until coolant temperatures reach as high as 210°F (99°C).

Thermostats can cause overheating by either failing to open or by not opening far enough. The result can be a cracked or warped block or head, blown head gaskets, extra carbon formation, detonation, burned valves, or damaged bearings. Overcooling (engine running too cool) can result from a thermostat sticking in the open position. Damage can include crankcase sludging, poor fuel vaporization, sluggish performance, poor gas mileage, and oil dilution.

Checking Thermostats

When a defective thermostat is suspected, drain the system (save the coolant if it is clean) until the coolant level is below the thermostat housing. Remove the housing or the housing cap. Remove and rinse the thermostat. In **Figure 22-31**, the housing is off and the thermostat is removed.

Inspect the thermostat valve. It should be closed snugly. Hold it against the light to determine how well the valve contacts the seat. A spot or two of light showing is not cause for rejection. If light shows all around the valve, discard the thermostat.

To check opening temperature, suspend the thermostat with the pellet facing downward in a container of water. The thermostat must be completely submerged and must not touch the container sides or bottom.

Suspend an accurate thermometer (it must not touch container sides or bottom) in the water. Place the container over a source of heat and gradually raise the temperature of the water. Stir the water gently as the temperature increases. See **Figure 22-32**.

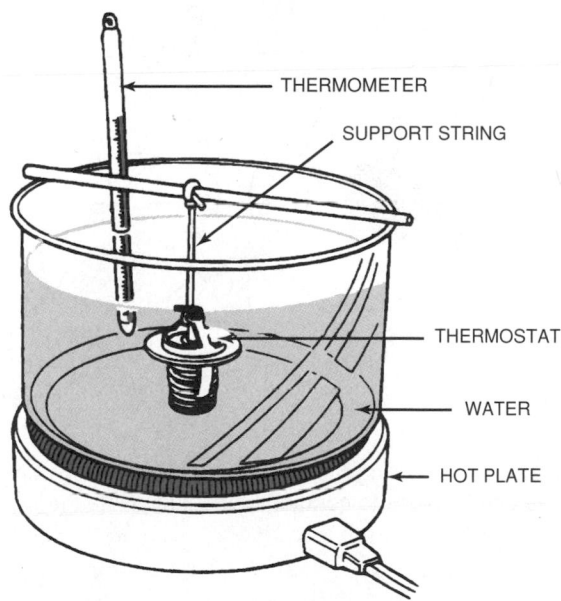

Figure 22-32. Checking thermostat opening temperature. Note that both the thermometer and the thermostat are kept free of container sides and bottom. (Honda)

Watch the thermostat closely. As the thermostat begins to open, note the water temperature. It should be within 5° to 10°F (3° to 6°C) of the temperature rating stamped on the thermostat.

Continue heating the water until the valve is fully opened and note the water temperature. In general, the thermostat should be wide open at a temperature around 20° to 24°F (11° to 13°C) above opening temperature. Discard a thermostat that does not meet specifications. Do not try to repair a thermostat.

Selecting Replacement Thermostats

When replacement is necessary, select a thermostat of the correct temperature range. Always use a pellet-type thermostatic element in a pressurized system. The obsolete bellows-type thermostatic element will work only in non-pressurized systems. Never leave the thermostat out of the engine to try to cure overheating. The thermostat is essential. Use one or more as required.

Thermostat Installation

Clean out the thermostat pocket and housing. If the system is rusty, it should be cleaned and flushed. Always install the thermostat so that the thermostatic element will be in contact with the coolant in the engine block. See **Figure 22-33**. If you cannot determine which way is correct, refer to the manufacturer's service literature. Reversing the thermostat so the pellet faces away from the engine will cause serious overheating. As the coolant in the block heats up, it cannot contact the pellet. The coolant in the engine may begin to boil before the thermostat can open enough to allow sufficient flow through the radiator.

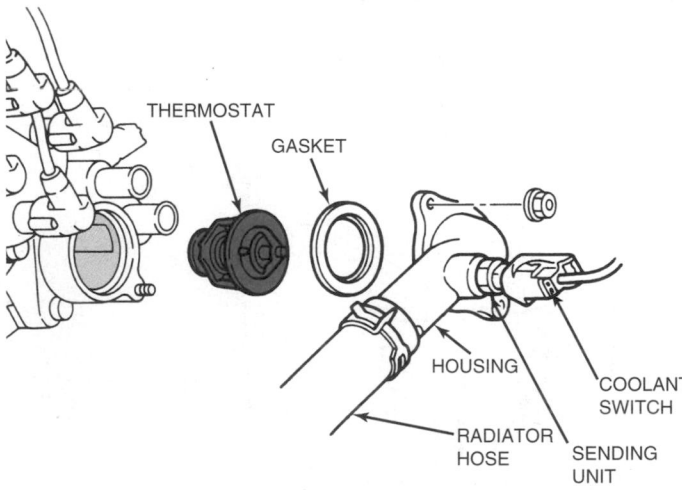

Figure 22-33. Installing a thermostat. The actuating pellet faces the engine block to contact the coolant. Note the temperature sender. (Geo)

When reinstalling the thermostat housing, be sure to use a new gasket, O-ring, or RTV sealer. Follow the manufacturer's recommendations. Torque the housing fasteners to specifications.

Radiator Removal and Repair

Before removing the radiator, drain the cooling system. Then, remove hoses and oil cooler lines (where used). Remove the fan if necessary. Remove the radiator support fasteners and carefully remove the radiator. Do not dent the cooling fins or tubes.

If the radiator contains a transmission oil cooler, plug the entry holes so that foreign matter cannot enter. Also plug the lines from the transmission. Place the radiator in a spot where it will be protected from physical damage. A typical cross-flow radiator is shown in **Figure 22-34**.

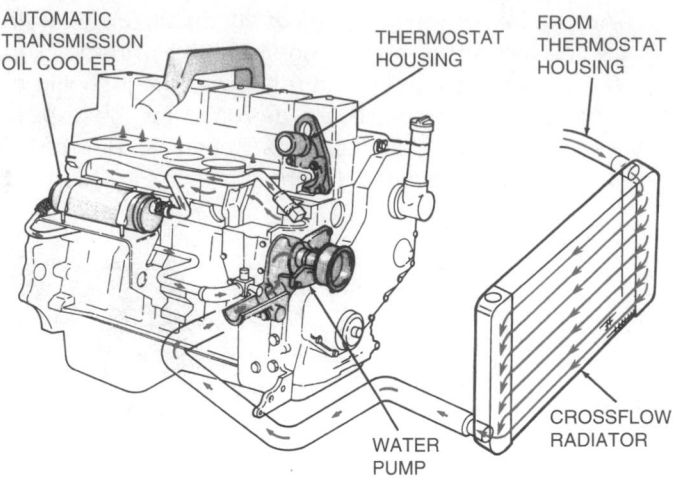

Figure 22-34. Coolant flow in a cross-flow radiator. (Dodge)

Flow Testing a Radiator

To determine the extent of radiator clogging (if any), it may be **flow tested.** Testing can be done either on or off the vehicle. Flow testing consists of pumping water through the radiator and measuring the flow in gallons (liters) per minute. Flow rate specifications are supplied by equipment manufacturers.

The technician in **Figure 22-35** is flow testing a radiator to make certain it will allow proper circulation.

Figure 22-35. Flow testing a radiator to determine the extent of clogging. (Inland)

Off-Vehicle Radiator Cleaning

The radiator is placed in a special hot cleaning tank and is boiled until all scale and rust is loosened. The radiator is then removed and thoroughly flushed. Use care with aluminum radiators. Some radiators have the tanks held in place with tabs that are an integral part of the tank plate. Gaskets are used to seal in the coolant. See **Figure 22-36**.

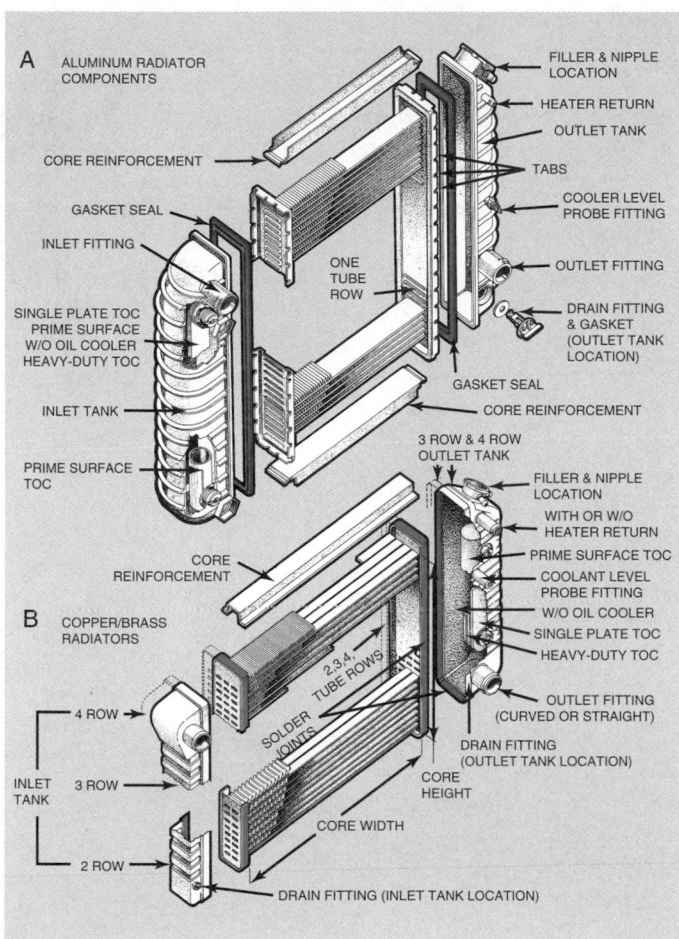

Figure 22-36. This radiator makes use of gaskets to seal the upper and lower tanks, preventing coolant leaks. (Harrison Radiator)

Figure 22-37. Placing a radiator in a hot cleaning tank.

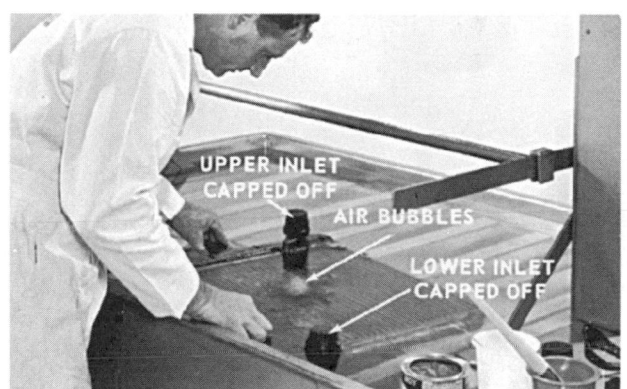

Figure 22-38. Testing a radiator for leaks. Note how air bubbles pinpoint leakage.

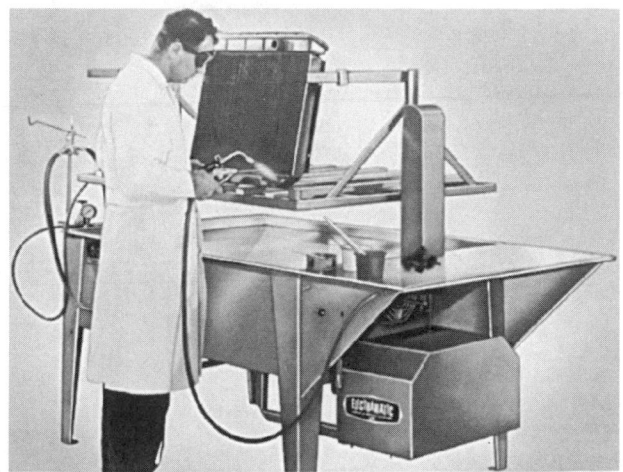

Figure 22-39. Radiator repair stand. (Inland)

If this type of radiator is to be placed in a hot cleaning tank, it should be disassembled to prevent damage to the gaskets. Other radiators have tanks that are made from plastic. Do not place plastic units in the hot cleaning tank. Instead, disassemble the radiator and clean only the metal parts in the tank. The cleaning solution must be compatible with the metal, **Figure 22-37**. Instructions supplied by the manufacturer of the cleaning solution should be carefully followed.

Off-Vehicle Radiator Leak Testing

To test a radiator for leaks, the hose connections are capped off and an air source is attached to the filler neck, **Figure 22-38**. The radiator is then lowered into a tank of clear water and air pressure (not to exceed pressure cap rating) is applied. Leaks are easily seen as bubbles. Mark the leaks for repair.

Radiator Repair

Leaks may be repaired by careful soldering (brass and copper radiators) and, in some radiators, by replacing gaskets. A handy repair stand is shown in **Figure 22-39**. Note the use of a torch. Special repair materials are available for use on aluminum radiators.

Regardless of the material used in radiator construction, any area to be repaired must be thoroughly cleaned. Always test for leaks after repairing a radiator.

Coolant Pump Service

The **coolant pump** circulates the coolant through the engine and radiator. The pump illustrated in **Figure 22-40** utilizes the block or the engine front cover to form a housing around the **impeller** (pumping unit). Other construction methods place the pump away from the block and connect it to the block by cast passages or hoses. An exploded view of a self-contained coolant pump (does not need a special recess in block to function) is shown in **Figure 22-41**. Most pumps are driven by a belt from the engine crankshaft.

Pump Inspection

The most common coolant pump problems are worn bearings and leaking seals. In a few cases, the impeller blades will be worn down by corrosion or broken by debris in the cooling system. Begin coolant pump inspection by checking the pump for signs of coolant leakage at the seal drain hole and gasket area. Also, check the housing for cracks.

Loosen the drive belt to remove pressure from the pump bearings. Grasp the hub and attempt to move the

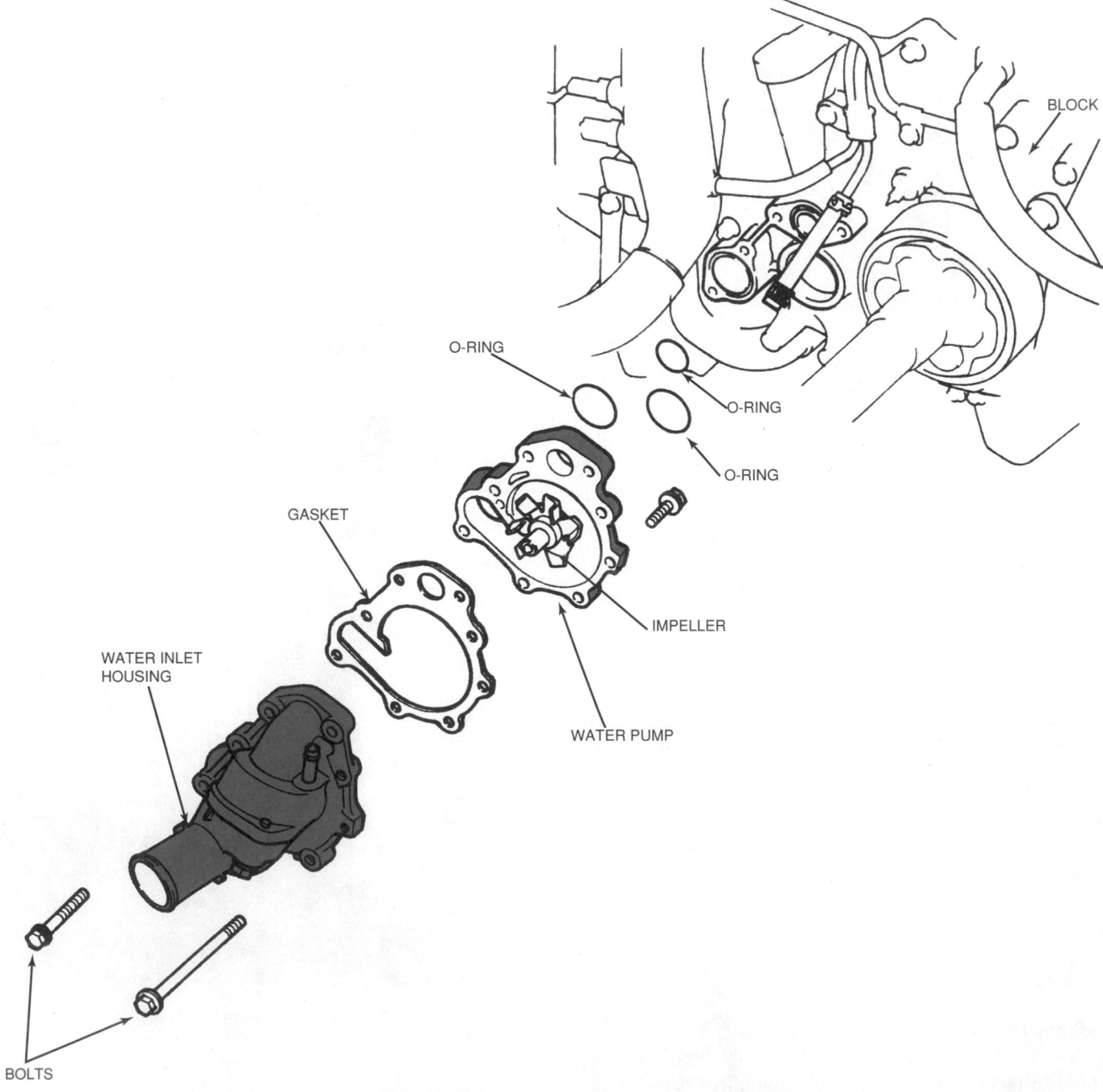

Figure 22-40. Exploded view of a self-contained water pump. Note the O-rings, which are used to seal the pump-to-block connections. New O-rings are generally used if the pump is removed for service or replacement. (Toyota)

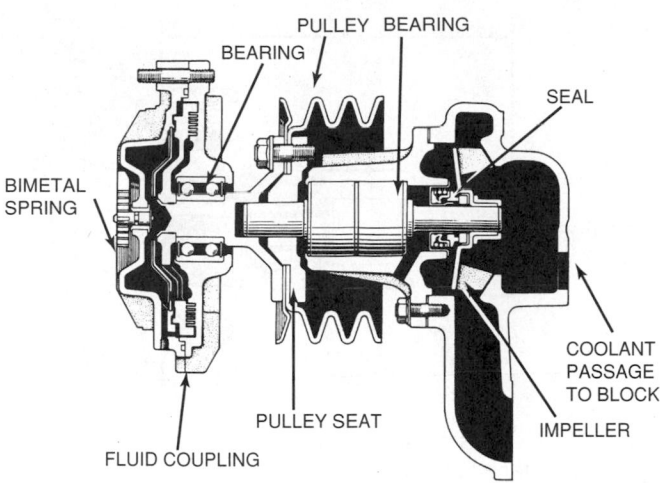

Figure 22-41. Self-contained coolant pump. Note the part names. (Toyota)

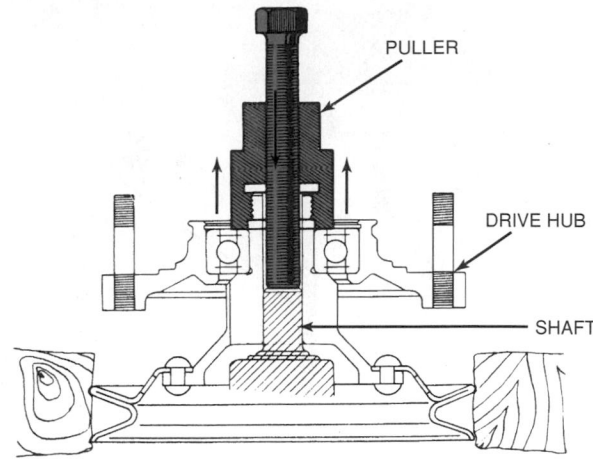

Figure 22-42. Removing the water pump drive hub with a special puller. A press can also be used to perform this job. (Toyota)

shaft up and down. Little or no play should be present. In many cases, the pump bearings will be so worn that they will have play even with the belt tightened. Next, spin the shaft to detect any bearing roughness. To inspect the internal components, the pump must be removed.

Pump Removal

Begin by draining the cooling system. Remove any brackets or other components blocking access to the pump and remove the fan if necessary. Remove any hoses connected to the pump and remove the drive belt. Remove the pulley if necessary. Remove the fasteners holding the pump to the engine and remove the pump.

Pump Disassembly

Some pumps can be disassembled and repaired, while others must be replaced as a unit. Check to see if repair parts are available before disassembling the pump. If the pump can be disassembled and repaired, measure the distance from the hub to the housing. Also determine the clearance between the impeller and housing. Write this information down, so the pump can be reassembled with correct tolerances.

Remove the pump cover plate (where used), fan, and drive pulley. Pull or press off the drive shaft hub, **Figure 22-42**. If the drive shaft, bearing, and impeller assembly must be pressed out, support the pump housing on blocks to prevent damage. Apply pressure to the bearing outer race, not to the shaft. Pressure on the shaft will damage the bearings. If necessary, press the impeller from the shaft. Work carefully. Plastic, thin stamped metal, or cast impellers may be broken from the shaft by hammering. Clean all parts. If the bearings will be reused, do not clean them in solvent. This would dilute the grease and probably cause bearing failure.

Pump Reassembly

Install a new seal assembly. Before driving it into place, coat the edge of the seal cup with gasket cement.

Seat the seal in the seal cup recess. A special tool should be used. See **Figure 22-43**. If necessary, press the shaft and bearing assembly in to the specified depth.

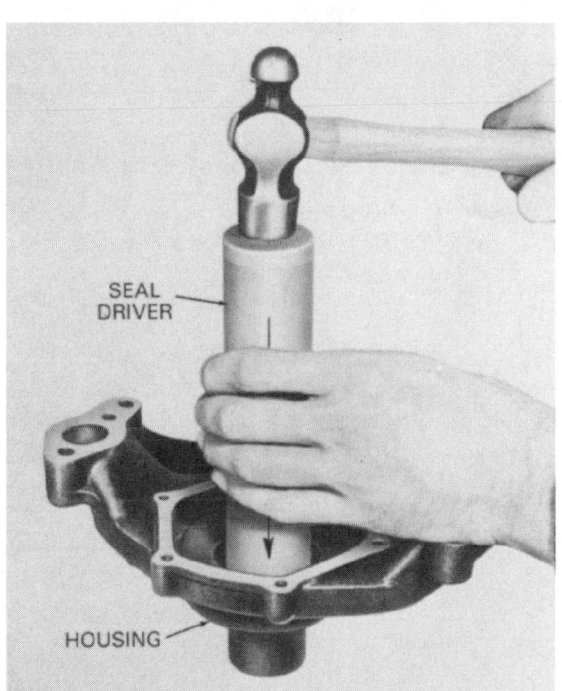

Figure 22-43. Driving coolant pump seal into place.

Next, press the impeller on the shaft, **Figure 22-44**. The impeller seal contact surface must be smooth. Press the impeller on until the specified clearance exists. See **Figure 22-45**. A feeler gauge should be used to check impeller-to-housing clearance. Force the drive hub the correct distance up the shaft. **Figure 22-46** shows typical dimensions for the hub and impeller.

Replace the pump cover (where used). Use gasket cement and a new gasket. An assembled pump is shown in **Figure 22-47**. Note the critical positioning of the parts in

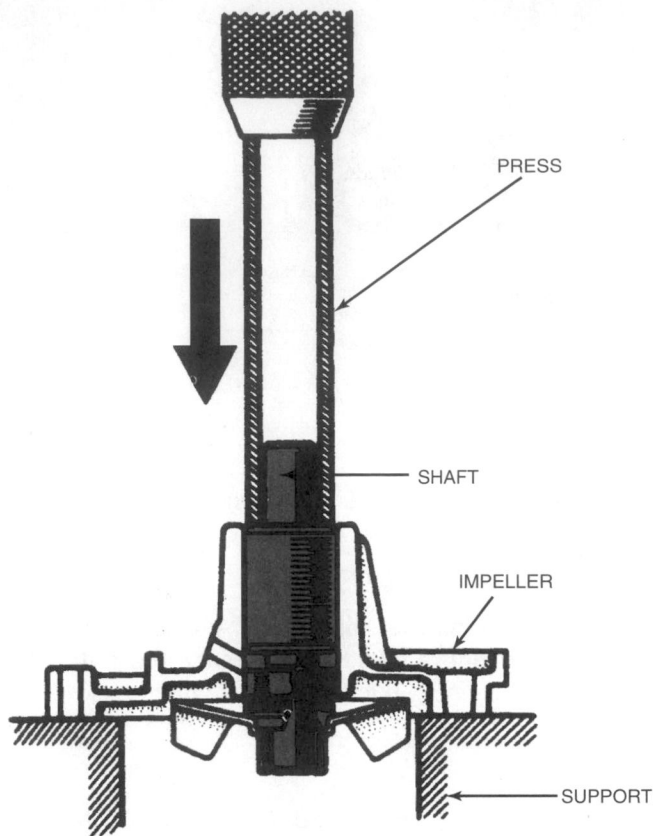

Figure 22-44. A press being used to force the water pump shaft into the impeller. Wear safety glasses. (Toyota)

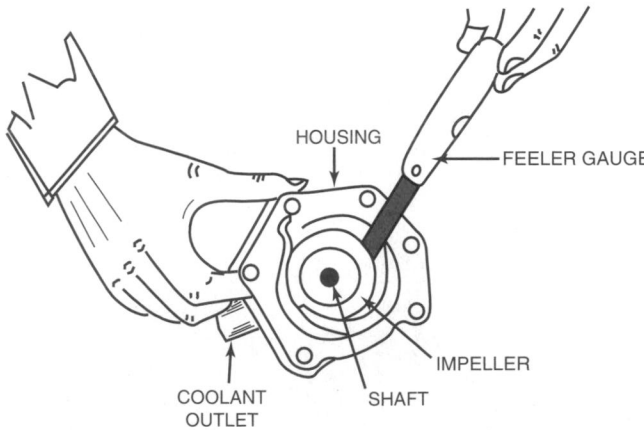

Figure 22-45. This technician is using the proper size feeler gauge to check to impeller-to-housing clearance on this water pump after assembly.

relation to each other. Part positioning specifications vary. Make certain you have the correct specifications.

Pump Installation

Use a new gasket or gaskets, O-rings, or RTV silicone sealer as required. Install the fasteners and tighten them evenly to the correct torque. Pumps are easily cracked by careless tightening. Install the hose, pulley, spacers, fan, fan belt, and related components. Then, tension the belt.

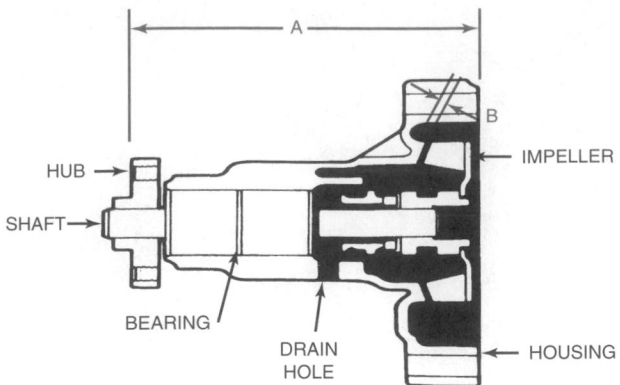

Figure 22-46. Assembled pump. A—Required distance from the hub front face to the pump rear face. B—Required clearance between the impeller blades and the housing. (Hyundai)

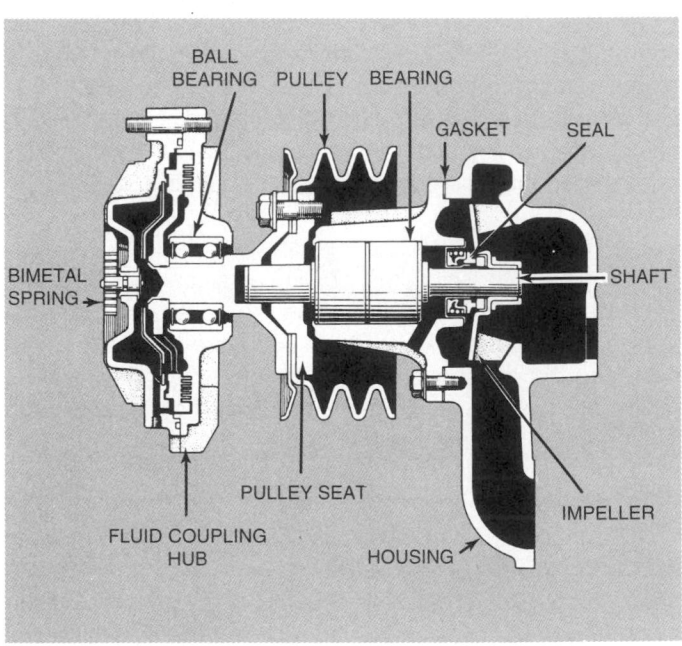

Figure 22-47. Cross section of a typical water pump.

Sight across the pulleys to make certain the drive hub is positioned to bring the pump pulley in line with the crankshaft drive pulley and any other pulley concerned. Pulley misalignment will cause rapid belt wear. Refill the cooling system with antifreeze and water according to the directions given earlier in this chapter.

Freeze Plug Repair

Freeze plugs, sometimes called core plugs, are installed to plug up holes left in the engine block and head after casting. Even though these plugs are called freeze plugs, they will not protect the block from freeze damage. Leaking core plugs should always be replaced.

Drive a sharp-nosed pry bar through the center of the freeze hole plug. By prying sideways, the plug should pop out. Another technique involves drilling a small hole in the center of the plug. Punching or drilling near an edge can damage the plug seat ledge in the block. A hook-shaped rod is then inserted in the hole, and the other end of the rod is attached to a slide hammer puller. A few taps should pull the plug out.

Clean the seating area of the plug hole thoroughly. Coat both the plug and the hole seat with nonhardening sealer and drive the plug into place. Special tools can be used to seat both cup and expansion-type core plugs, **Figure 22-48**.

Where driving space is limited, special plugs can be used. These plugs are pulled into place and retained by a screw fastener. Another type is made of rubber with a central nut and bolt arrangement. After the plug is put into place, the bolt and nut are tightened, expanding the rubber against the walls of the block.

Air-Cooled Systems

A few modern vehicles use *air-cooled engines.* On air-cooled engines, be sure to check blower fan belt condition and tension. Clean all finned surfaces and make certain that all air ducts are free of debris. Check the condition of the duct airflow control valves and thermostat where used.

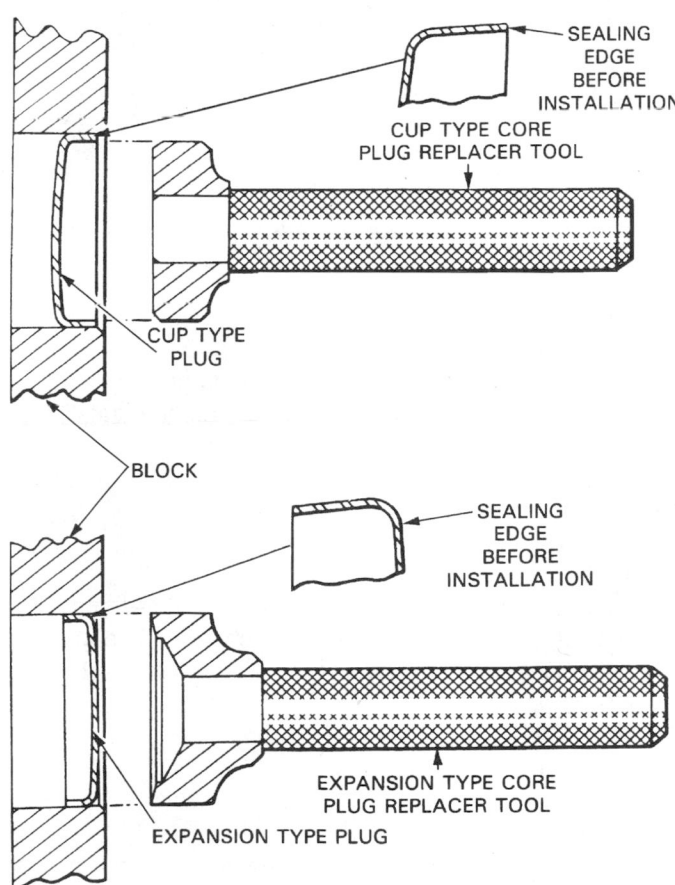

Figure 22-48. Typical core plug installation tools. These are not interchangeable. If the wrong tool or core plug is used, a damaging leak or plug "blow out" could occur. (Ford)

Tech Talk

One of the most common mistakes that beginning technicians make is to over tighten drive belts. Over-tightening a belt can ruin bearings in the alternator, water pump, air conditioner compressor, power steering pump, or air injection pump. Many times this is done to cure a noisy belt. Usually when a belt starts squealing, it is glazed (shiny) and should be replaced. If an almost new belt begins to act up, check for a grooved pulley. Grooved pulleys are especially common on alternators and air conditioner compressors.

Always use a belt tension gauge if one is available. If a gauge is not available, tighten the belt so that there is about 1/4" of deflection when you lightly press on the belt between the pulleys. Another way to check a belt used to drive the alternator is to try turning the alternator fan by hand. If you can turn the fan the belt is too loose. Tighten the belt to until it is just past the point where you can no longer turn the fan.

Summary

When working properly, the cooling system is quite efficient. The technician should understand the function of all parts in the system.

The only antifreeze that should be used in modern cooling systems is ethylene glycol. Inhibitors should be used to prevent rust and corrosion. Antifreeze solutions include inhibitors and coolant pump seal lubricant. A special hydrometer may be used to check the strength of the system antifreeze solution.

Always use clean, soft water when filling cooling system. Drain and flush system before filling with fresh water and antifreeze. Tighten hose clamps and check for leaks.

Moderately contaminated systems may be cleaned by using chemical cleaners, running the engine, and draining. Heavy rusting or scaling requires the use of stronger chemicals and reverse flushing of the radiator and block. In severe cases of radiator clogging, the radiator must be removed and cleaned in a hot tank. In some instances, partial dismantling is required.

Pressure test the system to detect external leaks. Do not exceed the pressure stamped on the pressure cap. Check the system while cold and hot. A special tool and fluid can be used to detect combustion leaks in cooling system.

The pressure cap should be tested. Inspect the radiator filler neck cap seat and locking cams. The overflow tube must be open. Use great care when removing a pressure cap while the engine is hot. Never add water to an overheated engine. Allow the engine to cool somewhat. Then, start the engine, run it at fast idle, and add water slowly.

Check hose condition. Look for hardening, cracking, swelling, and softening. Tighten the hose clamps. Use nonhardening cement on hose fittings when replacing a hose. Use hose of the correct shape and size. Avoid forcing bends in hose unless of the flexible type.

Check the drive belts for proper condition. Cracked, frayed, split, glazed, or oil-soaked belts should be replaced. Set belt tension to specifications by using the belt deflection method or the belt strand tension gauge.

Never try to straighten, weld, or glue damaged fan blades. Fluid clutch fans must generally be serviced as a unit, although some models permit the replacement of a bimetallic spring or bimetallic strip and operating piston. Fans driven by electric motors are used on some installations. They are controlled by coolant temperature sensors. Motors are generally not serviceable and should be replaced when defective.

Always remove the ground clamp from the battery before working on a coolant pump, fan, radiator, hoses, or belts. Test thermostats for condition and for initial opening and full opening temperature points. Never use a bellows thermostat in a pressurized system. The pressurized system requires a pellet thermostat. Install thermostats with the thermostatic unit facing the engine so that the unit will be contacted by the coolant in the block.

Radiators can be flow tested to determine extent of clogging. In some instances, the radiator must be removed from the vehicle for cleaning, testing, and repair. Some coolant pumps can be rebuilt. When rebuilding, assemble so that part positioning is correct. Use care when installing new freeze plugs.

Know These Terms

Overheated	Coolant hoses
Antifreeze	Drive belts
Rust inhibitors	Belt tension
Water soluble oils	Fluid clutch fan
Ethylene glycol	Electric fan assembly
Electrolysis	Thermoswitch
Hard water	Thermostat
Hydrometer	Flow tested
Cooling system cleaner	Coolant pump
Neutralizer	Impeller
Reverse flushing	Freeze plugs
Pressure tester	Air-cooled engines
Pressure cap	

Review Questions—Chapter 22

Do not write in this book. Write your answers on a separate sheet of paper.

1. Ethylene glycol antifreeze contains _____.
   (A) rust inhibitors
   (B) stop leak
   (C) Methanol
   (D) Ethanol
2. Thermostat temperature ratings on new vehicles can be as high as _____.
   (A) 160°F (71°C)
   (B) 180°F (82°C)
   (C) 190°F (88°C)
   (D) 210°F (99°C)
3. When reverse flushing, the thermostat should be _____.
   (A) in place
   (B) removed
   (C) installed upside down
   (D) wired to prevent opening
4. During the cooling system cleaning process, the heater control should be set to the _____ position.
5. When pressure testing the cooling system, limit the maximum pressure to that stamped on the _____.
6. Name three hose conditions that call for hose replacement.
7. List three drive belt conditions that call for belt replacement.
8. Before working on fans, coolant pumps, or V-belts, always disconnect the _____.
9. The extent of radiator clogging can best be checked by _____.
   (A) reverse flushing
   (B) looking in the filler neck
   (C) draining and checking coolant color
   (D) flow testing
10. List three possible coolant pump problems.

ASE-Type Questions

1. Cooling systems must be protected from rust and corrosion by using _____.
   (A) clean, soft water
   (B) inhibitors
   (C) alcohol antifreeze
   (D) a 15 psi (103 kPa) pressure cap
2. Ethylene glycol is _____.
   (A) poisonous
   (B) a fire hazard
   (C) harmful to paint finishes
   (D) wood alcohol
3. On some modern vehicles, the cooling passages in the engine block must be _____ to properly install new antifreeze.
   (A) cold
   (B) hot
   (C) bled
   (D) Both A & C.
4. Technician A says that it is best to reverse flush the radiator and block separately. Technician B says that one should always reverse flush the vehicle heater. Who is right?
   (A) A only.
   (B) B only.
   (C) Both A & B.
   (D) Neither A nor B.
5. Technician A says that combustion leaks can be detected only by removing the cylinder heads for a visual inspection. Technician B says that ethylene glycol leaking into the cylinders can clog rings, bearings,

and other parts. Who is right?
(A) A only.
(B) B only.
(C) Both A & B.
(D) Neither A nor B.
6. Completely removing a pressure cap when an engine is hot can cause a _____.
(A) cracked block
(B) warped valve
(C) sudden, violent flash of steam
(D) bulged radiator
7. Technician A says that thermostats should be installed with the thermostatic element contacting the coolant in the engine. Technician B says that leaving the thermostat out of the engine is a good way to cure overheating. Who is right?
(A) A only.
(B) B only.
(C) Both A & B.
(D) Neither A nor B.
8. All of the following statements about coolant pumps are true, EXCEPT:
(A) all pumps can be replaced.
(B) all pumps contain an impeller.
(C) all pumps can be repaired.
(D) all pumps contain bearings and seals.
9. Core plugs can be sources of _____.
(A) leaks
(B) overheating
(C) corrosion
(D) Both A & C.
10. Air cooled engines use all of the following parts, EXCEPT:
(A) drive belt.
(B) cooling fan.
(C) core plugs.
(D) cooling fins.

Suggested Activities

1. Find the lowest outside temperature that occurs in your area. Use an antifreeze chart to determine the ratio of antifreeze and water that will protect against freezing. Then find the cooling system capacity of your vehicle in quarts. Determine how many quarts of antifreeze are needed to protect your cooling system.
2. Obtain a cooling system pressure tester, properly install it on the radiator filler neck, and pressurize the cooling system to the pressure listed on the radiator cap. Wait about 5 minutes and then answer the following questions.

 Caution: Allow the engine to cool off before removing the radiator cap.

Has the pressure dropped?
Are there any cooling system leaks?
What was done to correct them?
3. Obtain a cooling system pressure tester and properly install it on the radiator cap. Pressurize it to the listed pressure. Wait about 5 minutes and then answer the following questions.

 Caution: Allow the engine to cool off before removing the radiator cap.

Has the pressure dropped?
What do you think is the cause?
4. Obtain an antifreeze tester and test the antifreeze in your vehicle or one assigned by your instructor. Discuss whether the vehicle has sufficient freezing and corrosion protection.
5. Check belt tension using a tension gauge. Adjust the belt(s) if necessary. While adjusting, check belt condition. If any belts are glazed, frayed, or oil soaked, consult your instructor.

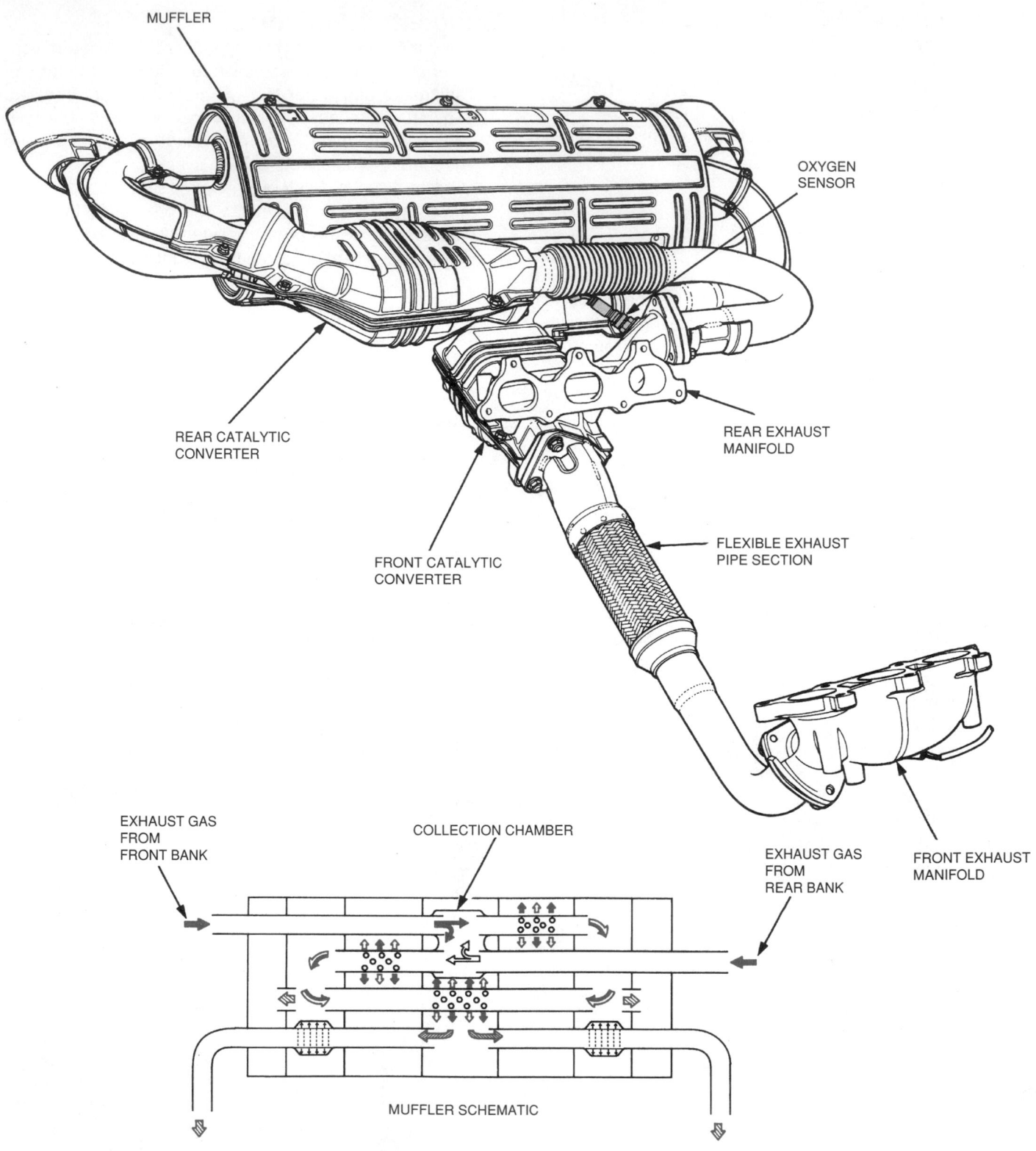

MUFFLER

OXYGEN
SENSOR

REAR CATALYTIC
CONVERTER

REAR EXHAUST
MANIFOLD

FRONT CATALYTIC
CONVERTER

FLEXIBLE EXHAUST
PIPE SECTION

EXHAUST GAS
FROM
FRONT BANK

COLLECTION CHAMBER

EXHAUST GAS
FROM
REAR BANK

FRONT EXHAUST
MANIFOLD

MUFFLER SCHEMATIC

This exhaust system is used with a six-cylinder engine. Note the oxygen sensor and the flexible exhaust pipe section. Follow the exhaust flow through the muffler schematic. (Honda)

452

23

Exhaust System Service

After studying this chapter, you will be able to:
- Explain heat control valve operation, service, and repair.
- Describe exhaust manifold removal and installation.
- Summarize muffler design and operation.
- Remove and install a muffler.
- Describe exhaust and tailpipe removal and installation.
- Use special exhaust system service tools.

This chapter will cover the service of exhaust system parts, including the exhaust manifolds, heat control devices, exhaust pipes, mufflers, and resonators.

Exhaust System Service

The exhaust system removes the spent exhaust gases from the engine. The exhaust system must do this while keeping noise levels to a minimum and preventing the entrance of poisonous gases into the passenger compartment. Other devices are placed on the exhaust system to assist in heating the fuel mixture and reducing emissions. In most cases, service is limited to replacing parts and ensuring that the system is not leaking.

 Warning: The exhaust system parts can become extremely hot. Allow exhaust parts to cool off completely before servicing.

Exhaust Manifold

As the burned gases leave the engine cylinders, they pass into the *exhaust manifold.* The manifold is usually made of cast iron or stainless steel and is attached to the cylinder head with a series of fasteners. It is designed to route the exhaust gases with a minimum of sharp bends. Once affixed to the engine, periodic service (other than lubrication of the exhaust manifold heat control valve) is usually not required.

To remove the manifold, disconnect the exhaust pipe flange and any braces or tubing that may be connected to the manifold. Then, remove the manifold fasteners. If the fasteners are stuck, apply penetrating oil and allow it to soak for 15 to 20 minutes before attempting to loosen the fasteners.

When installing a manifold, all mounting surfaces must be clean. Use a file to remove burrs and bits of hardened gasket material. Install new gaskets where needed. Torque fasteners in proper sequence. If the new manifold-to-head gaskets are made of a composition material (not steel), the fasteners should be retorqued after the engine has been operated. This will bring fastener torque back up to compensate for the torque lost due to the gasket flattening out after heating.

Use fastener locks when required to prevent the fasteners (especially end ones) from loosening. Connect the exhaust pipe (use new gasket) and hook up the parts originally attached to the manifold.

Figure 23-1 illustrates a typical exhaust manifold. Note that in this particular case, the intake manifold is connected to the exhaust manifold by a metal tube. The tube provides exhaust gases for EGR (exhaust gas recirculation) valve operation. Exhaust manifolds for V-type engines use similar construction.

Heat Control Valve

To provide heat to help vaporize the fuel charge during engine warm-up, a *heat control valve,* or *heat riser,* may be installed in the exhaust manifold. It may also be installed between the exhaust manifold and the exhaust pipe. When the valve is used on an older engine, it is actuated by a bimetallic spring. In newer vehicles, the heat riser is operated by a *vacuum motor* (diaphragm unit). The vacuum-operated heat control valve is often called an *early fuel evaporation device* (EFE device).

Figure 23-2 shows heat control valve action. With the engine hot, **Figure 23-2A**, exhaust gases flow directly into the exhaust system. In **Figure 23-2B**, the hot gases are directed to the floor of the intake manifold. As the spring heats up, it uncoils gradually to change the valve from fully closed to fully opened.

The manifold heat control valve shown in **Figures 23-2A** and **23-2B** is incorporated in the exhaust manifold. In **Figure 23-2C**, the heat control valve is shown between the exhaust manifold and the exhaust pipe. This is a popular arrangement on V-type engines.

On a typical V-type engine, only one exhaust manifold is fitted with a heat control valve. When it closes, the hot

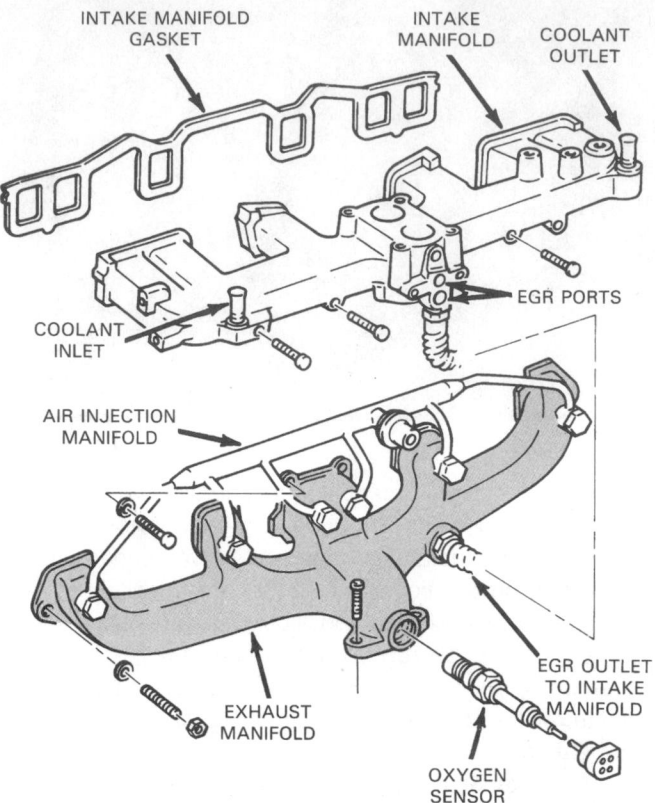

Figure 23-1. Typical exhaust manifold as used on an inline engine. (Chrysler)

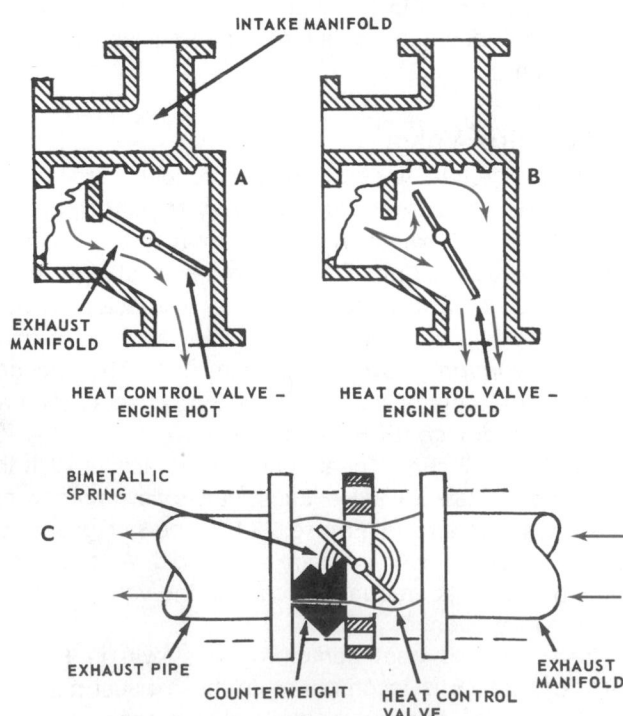

Figure 23-2. Two types of heat control valves. A—An inline engine in the hot engine position. B—The valve has moved to the cold engine position. C—Typical V-type engine heat control valve.

gases are forced to travel up through the heat riser and to the other exhaust manifold. They are then discharged into the exhaust system, **Figure 23-3**. As the gases pass through the intake manifold, the area beneath the carburetor or throttle body is heated, thus aiding fuel vaporization during cold engine operation.

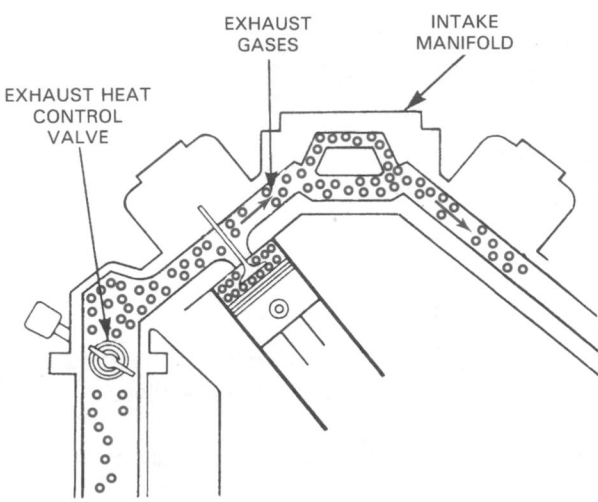

Figure 23-3. The exhaust heat control valve action directs exhaust gases to the intake manifold to aid cold engine operation by warming the fuel mixture. (Chevrolet)

Vacuum-operated heat valves are pictured in **Figures 23-4** and **23-5**. In each of these setups, a thermal vacuum switch is used to apply enough engine vacuum to match engine temperature. When the engine is cold, full vacuum is

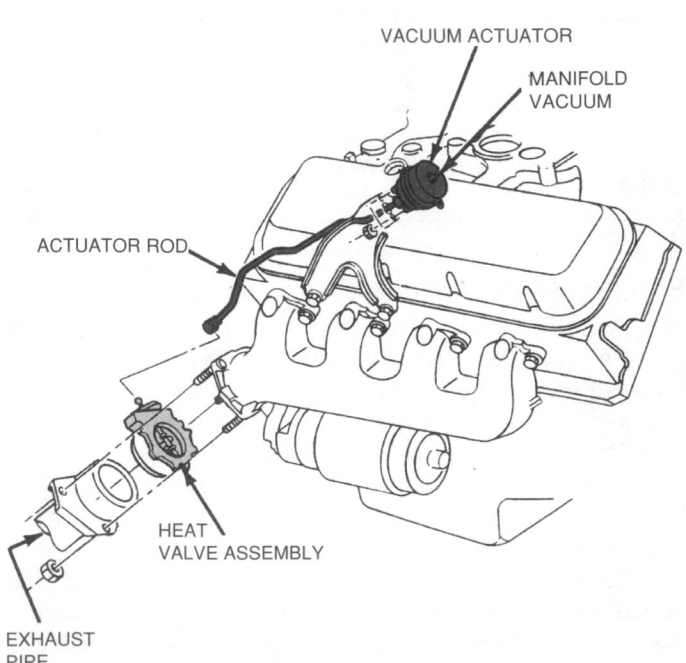

Figure 23-4. Vacuum-operated exhaust heat control valve assembly. (AC-Delco)

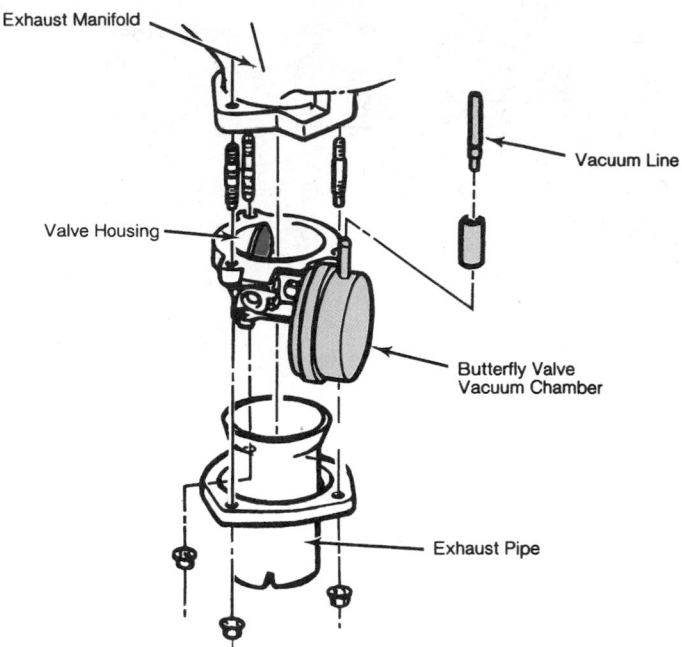

Figure 23-5.   A vacuum-controlled exhaust heat control valve. (Sun Electric Corp.)

The counterweight should move, indicating that the shaft is free. To double check, allow the manifold to cool off thoroughly and then try to move the weight by hand to make sure the valve has full travel.

Vacuum-operated heat control valves can be checked by removing the vacuum line when the engine is cold. If the spring does not return the valve to the open position when vacuum is removed, the valve is stuck, the linkage is binding or disconnected, or the diaphragm is leaking.

If the heat control valve is stuck, allow the manifold to cool off and apply several drops of penetrating oil to both ends of the shaft where it passes through the manifold. Work the valve back and forth until it is free. Add more penetrating oil as needed. When the valve is stuck so tight that it cannot be moved by hand, tap the ends of the shaft after applying the penetrating oil. After the valve is free, lubricate the shaft with a special heat-resistant graphite mixture or leave it dry and clean. Never use engine oil, as it will burn and form more carbon.

Caution: Do not use carburetor cleaner or oil in or on a vacuum motor assembly.

applied and the valve is pulled closed. As the engine warms, the vacuum signal weakens. When the engine reaches operating temperature, no vacuum is applied and the valve is held open by spring pressure.

The heat control valve will often stick due to an accumulation of carbon. When stuck in the open position, slow warmup, carburetor icing and stalling, flat spots during acceleration, and crankcase dilution may occur. If the valve sticks closed, overheating, detonation, burned valves, and a warped manifold may result. It is important to have the heat control valve free in its bushings. The thermostatic spring should not be distorted.

To check an older spring-operated heat control valve, accelerate the engine quickly while watching the heat valve.

Exhaust System

The exhaust gas travels from the exhaust manifold into pipes that carry it to the other parts of the exhaust system. Exhaust systems may be of the single type, **Figure 23-6**, or the dual type, **Figure 23-7**. The exhaust sound is silenced and routed to either the end or the side of the vehicle, where it is discharged into the atmosphere. The parts of the exhaust system are discussed below.

Mufflers

Mufflers are designed to reduce, or muffle, the sound of the exhaust system. They should silence the exhaust effectively while providing freedom from objectionable **back pressure.** Back pressure occurs when the exhaust gases

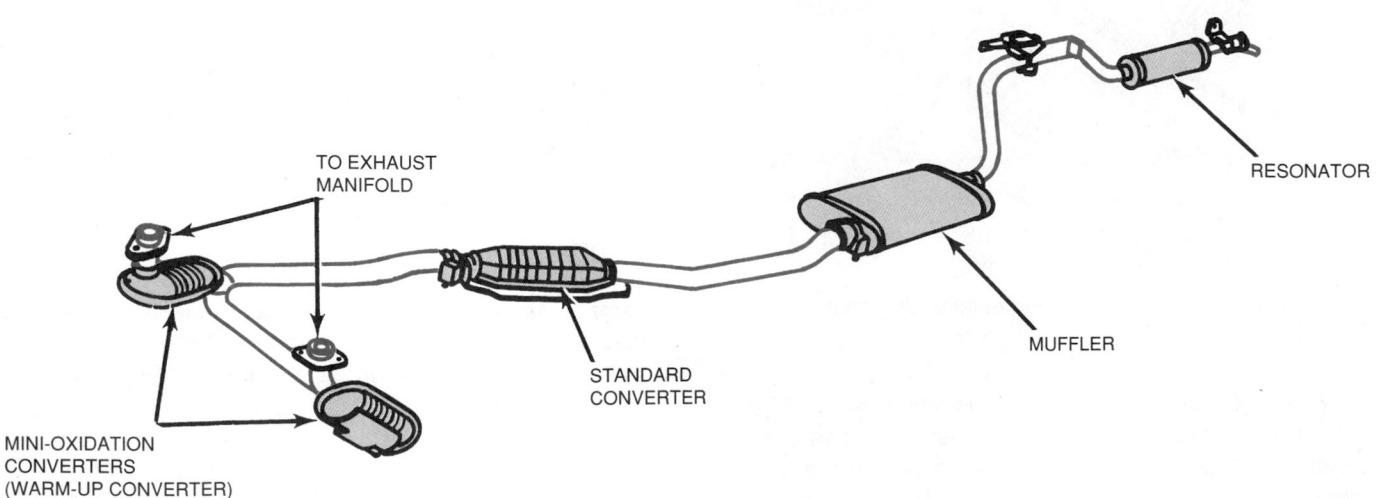

Figure 23-6.   A single exhaust system setup used by one manufacturer. (Sun Electric Corp.)

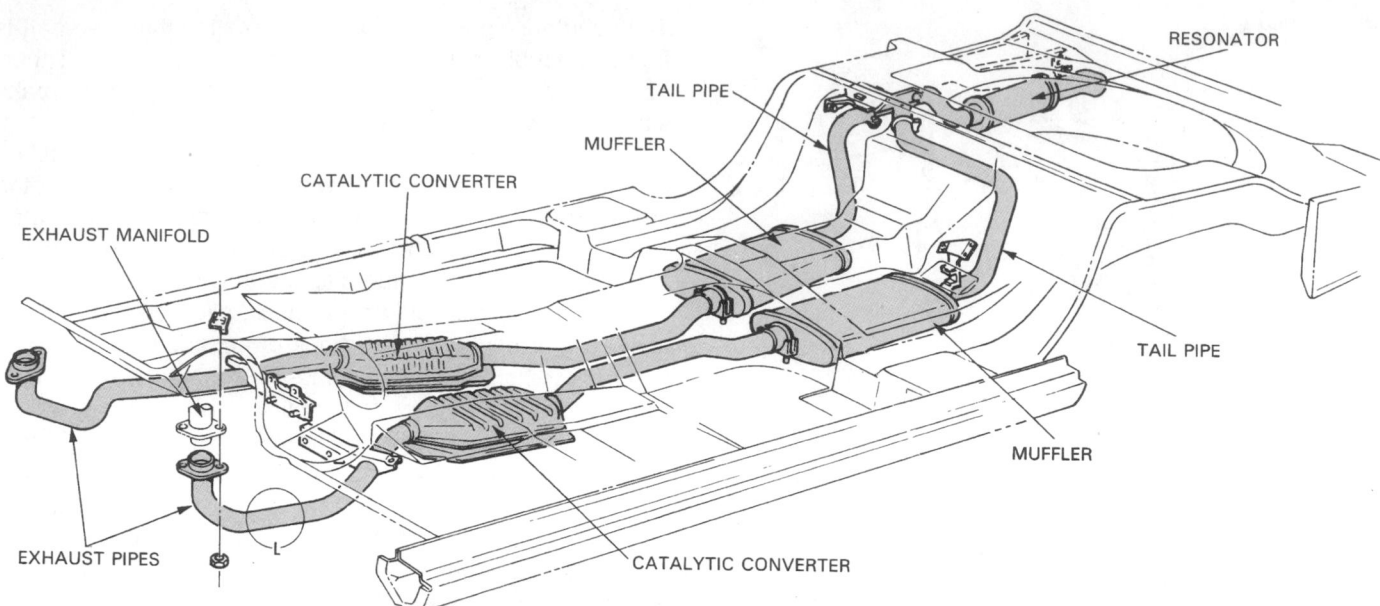

Figure 23-7. Typical dual exhaust system. Note the catalytic converters. (Chrysler)

cannot pass through the muffler fast enough and thus build up pressure that reduces the ability of the engine piston to push exhaust gases out of the cylinder. Mufflers are generally one of three basic designs: baffled reverse-flow muffler, straight-through muffler, and chambered-pipe muffler.

A ***baffled reverse-flow muffler*** is pictured in **Figure 23-8**. This particular muffler is of double-wall construction and is coated for increased service life. Gas flow is reversed within the muffler to allow exhaust pulsations to cancel each other, reducing noise. The baffles further absorb noise.

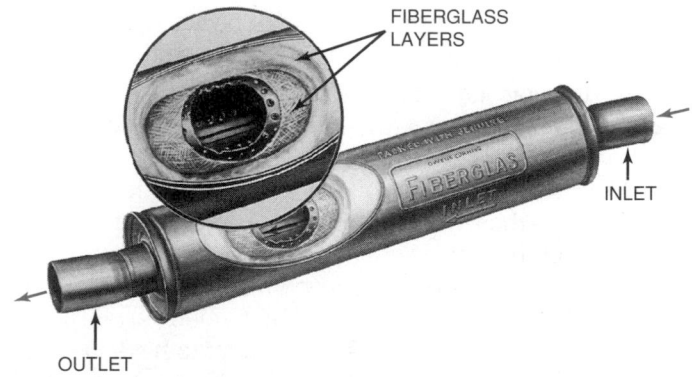

Figure 23-9. Straight-through muffler design. Note the layers of fiberglass. (McCord)

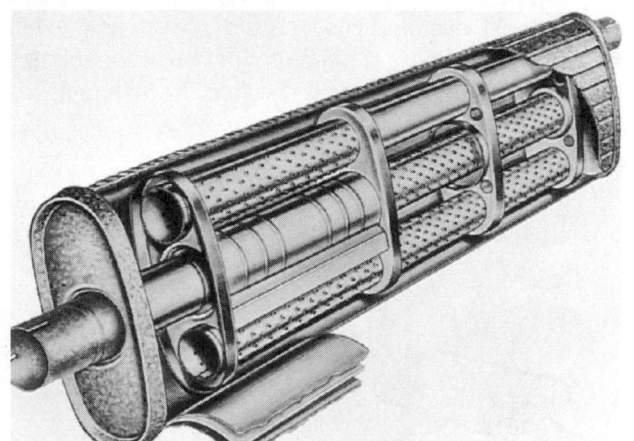

Figure 23-8. Cutaway of a baffled reverse-flow muffler. (McCord)

The ***straight-through muffler*** is illustrated in **Figure 23-9**. As the name implies, the exhaust gas flows straight through this type of muffler. The single perforated pipe is surrounded with two layers of Fiberglass to effectively absorb and dampen the sound.

The ***chambered-pipe muffler,*** a variation on the reverse-flow design, uses different sizes of pipe to reduce noise. This design, **Figure 23-10**, controls exhaust sound with a minimum of bulk, but it is not as quiet as the baffled reverse-flow muffler.

Mufflers may be constructed of ceramic-coated steel, aluminized (coated with aluminum) steel, or stainless steel (partially or completely) to ensure long life.

Resonators

In addition to a muffler, some installations have a ***resonator*** to further dampen the exhaust pulsations. The resonator is a small version of the muffler and is always installed after the muffler in the exhaust system.

Catalytic Converter

The ***catalytic converter*** lowers hydrocarbons (HC) and carbon monoxide (CO). Catalytic converters are discussed in Chapter 24.

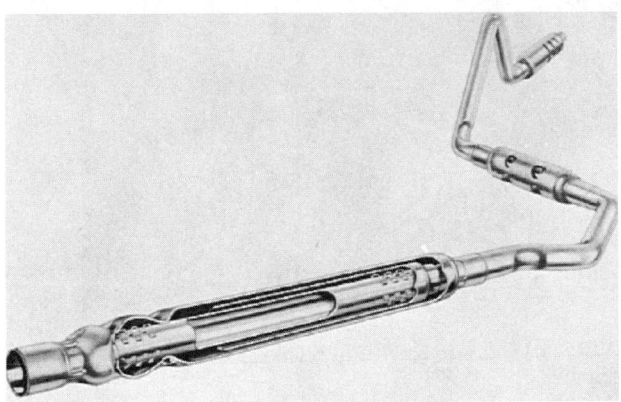

Figure 23-10.   Chambered-pipe muffler.

Pipes

The pipes connecting the engine to the muffler (and converter) and the muffler to the resonator are called **exhaust pipes.** The first pipe on a V-type engine, which connects the two exhaust manifolds to a single pipe, is called the **Y-pipe.** The last pipe in the system, which allows the exhaust gases to exit to the atmosphere, is called the **tailpipe.** Exhaust pipes and tailpipes may be aluminized steel and may use single- or double-wrap construction. The double wrap is more effective in reducing exhaust noise resulting from system pulsations.

Clamps and Support Brackets

The various parts of the exhaust system must be properly joined and supported. **Joint clamps** and **support brackets** of many types are used. **Figure 23-11** shows a random sampling. Always use clamps of the proper size to ensure a good joint. Check support bracket flexible straps for breakage and replace them as needed.

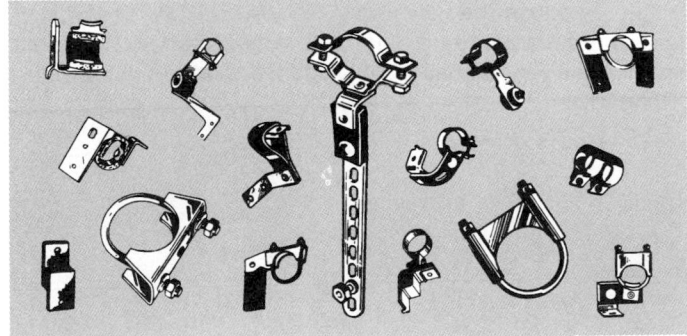

Figure 23-11.   Typical clamp and support brackets. (McCord)

Exhaust System Tools

Exhaust system service is highly competitive. To show a profit, the work must be done swiftly. To accomplish this, it is essential that proper tools be used. The power chisel, with suitable cutter heads, is useful for cutting welded mufflers free and for removing tailpipes and exhaust pipes, **Figure 23-12.** Note the assortment of cutting heads with the

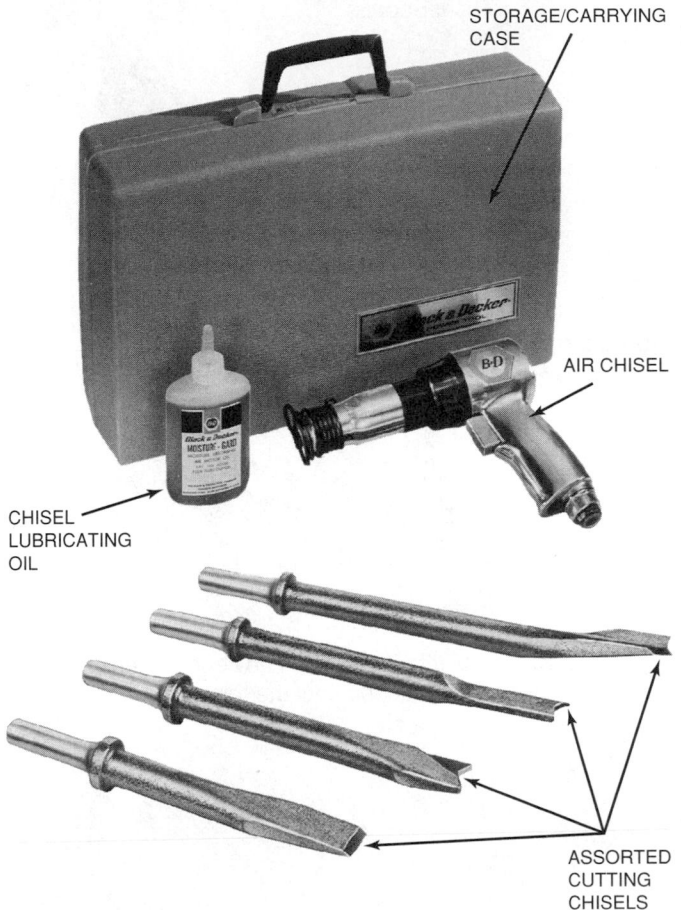

Figure 23-12.   Power chisel with assorted cutting heads. (Black and Decker, Walker)

chisel. A hand pipe cutter, illustrated in **Figure 23-13**, can also be very helpful.

Often, pipes must be expanded to provide a proper joint fit. This is done easily with a **pipe expander.** See **Figure 23-14.** The pipe end is often crimped or otherwise distorted. It can be readily brought back to a round shape by using a **straightening cone,** **Figure 23-15.** A chain wrench provides a way of both pulling and twisting a pipe to free the joint or provide proper alignment. See **Figure 23-16.**

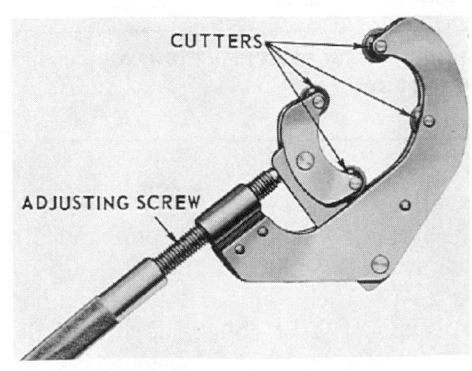

Figure 23-13.   Hand-operated pipe cutter. (Walker)

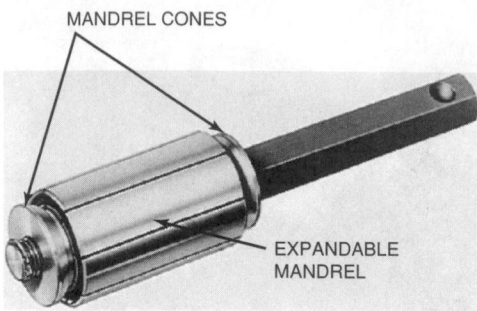

Figure 23-14.   Pipe expanding tool.

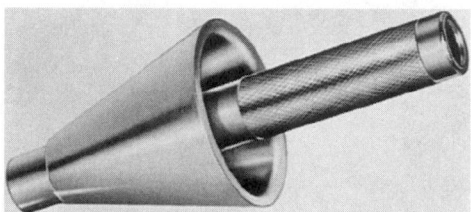

Figure 23-15.   Straightening cone. The cone is placed in the deformed pipe end and tapped until the pipe is round.

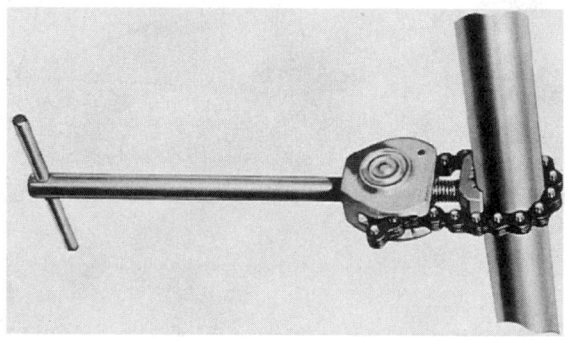

Figure 23-16.   The chain wrench provides a good grip on the pipe to facilitate removal or alignment. (Walker)

Exhaust System Service

To perform any exhaust system repair, begin by raising the vehicle. It is very difficult to change exhaust system parts without the clearance provided by raising the vehicle. A frame contact hoist works well for exhaust system service because it allows the rear axle to hang down, providing ample room for part removal.

 Warning: Wear eye protection when servicing an exhaust system.

Part Removal

After raising the vehicle, apply penetrating oil to the pipe bracket fasteners and to the muffler outlet joint clamp. See **Figure 23-17**. Then, remove the clamps and bracket fasteners. An impact wrench speeds up this job. See **Figure 23-18**. Apply penetrating oil and tap the outlet joint. Apply

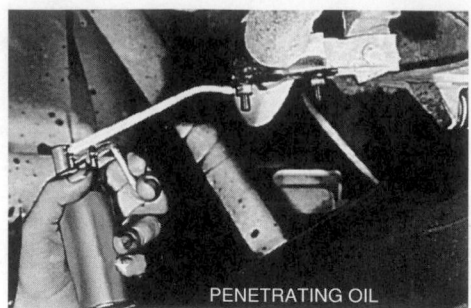

Figure 23-17.   Use penetrating oil to facilitate fastener removal.

Figure 23-18.   Removing muffler clamp nuts with a power wrench.

heat if needed. Pull the pipe free with a chain wrench, **Figure 23-19**. If any pipe is to be reinstalled, use care during removal. If the pipe remains stuck, cut it off just clear of the muffler or pipe outlet nipple. Look at **Figure 23-20**. Then, use a power chisel and split the section of the pipe remaining in the nipple. Finally, remove the split section with pliers.

 Note: Some exhaust parts are welded together. In such cases, cut off the pipe where necessary to engage the new parts, Figure 23-21. After cutting, straighten the pipe end. The replacement part will have a connection nipple that will engage the existing pipe.

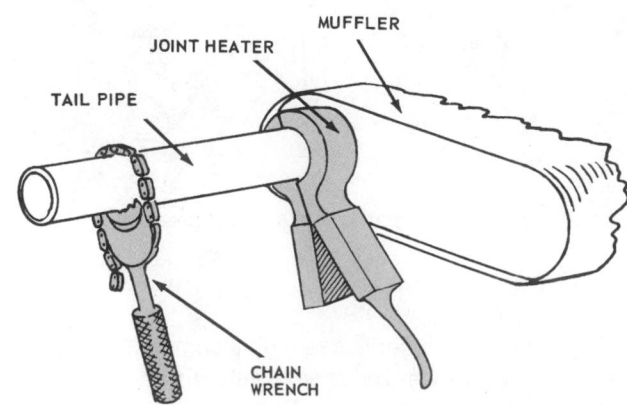

Figure 23-19.   Using heat and a chain wrench to free a tailpipe from a muffler.

Figure 23-20. Cutting a tailpipe with a hand pipe cutter.

Figure 23-21. Cutting a muffler from an exhaust pipe using a power chisel.

Part Cleaning

Use coarse emery cloth to clean the inside or outside of the nipples that will be reused. If a nipple is distorted, use the pipe end straightening tool to restore it to a perfectly round state.

Obtain and Check New Parts

To ensure that you get the correct exhaust system parts, order new parts by vehicle model and engine size. Always use mufflers and pipes designed for the vehicle at hand. Do not use undersize pipes or mufflers.

Some shops are equipped with pipe benders that can create any exhaust pipe configuration from straight pipe stock. When making pipes on a bender, always follow the manufacturer's instructions. Accuracy is extremely important when making pipes.

Exhaust System Sealer

Before reassembly, apply a liberal coating of exhaust system sealer to the section of the tailpipe that will be in contact with the muffler or converter nipple. Refer to **Figure 23-22**. Use exhaust sealer on all exhaust system joints. It makes the joints slide together easily, assists in alignment, and prevents dangerous exhaust leaks.

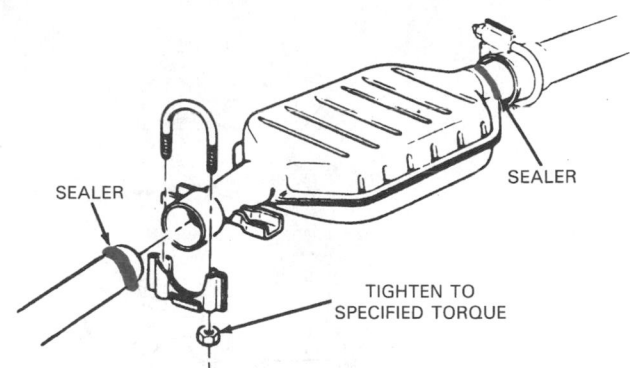

Figure 23-22. Exhaust system sealer helps eliminate leaking joints. Use proper sealer. (Chevrolet)

Some makers have designed special joints that are first assembled and then sealed. On setups requiring this technique, you must inject a special sealer into an annular ring, or bead, formed in the pipe. After injecting the sealant, idle the engine for about ten minutes to harden the compound. **Figure 23-23** illustrates this procedure.

Assembling Parts

Slide the pipes and nipples together. Make certain that the depth is correct, **Figure 23-24**. Slide the clamp into position, **Figure 23-25**, and tighten the clamps lightly. Make sure the pipes, catalytic converter, muffler, and resonator are installed in the correct position and in the proper direction. See **Figure 23-26**. Finally, secure all connections, **Figure 23-27**.

Setting Pipe Depth in the Nipple

When inserting one pipe into another, insert the pipes so that they engage to the proper depth. If the pipe enters too deeply, it can cause back pressure. Insufficient contact will not allow proper clamping and may permit leakage or pipe separation.

Installing Joint Clamp

Install the clamp so it is about 1/8" (3.18 mm) from the nipple end (or pipe end when pipe slips over nipple). Look at **Figure 23-28**. After aligning all mufflers, resonators, and pipes, tighten the clamps and brackets.

 Note: Do not tighten the clamp to the point that the joint starts to collapse.

Checking Exhaust System Alignment

Exhaust system alignment is critical. It affects the clearances between various parts of the vehicle and the exhaust system. Make a careful check of the entire system to make certain that all parts have sufficient operating clearance. Pay particular attention to the area where the tail pipe crosses over the rear axle. Make sure that the pipe will

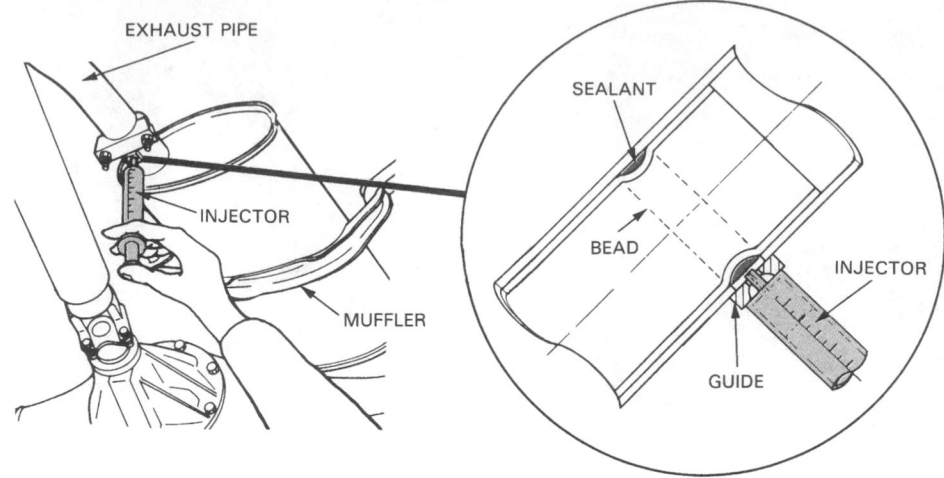

Figure 23-23.   This exhaust system joint is designed to be assembled, tightened, and then sealed by injecting sealer into an annular groove. (Nissan)

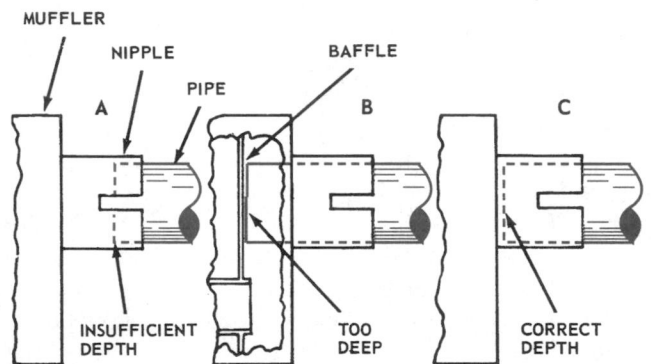

Figure 23-24.   A and B—Wrong. C—Pipe must enter the muffler nipple to the correct depth.

Figure 23-25.   A new muffler installed on an exhaust pipe.

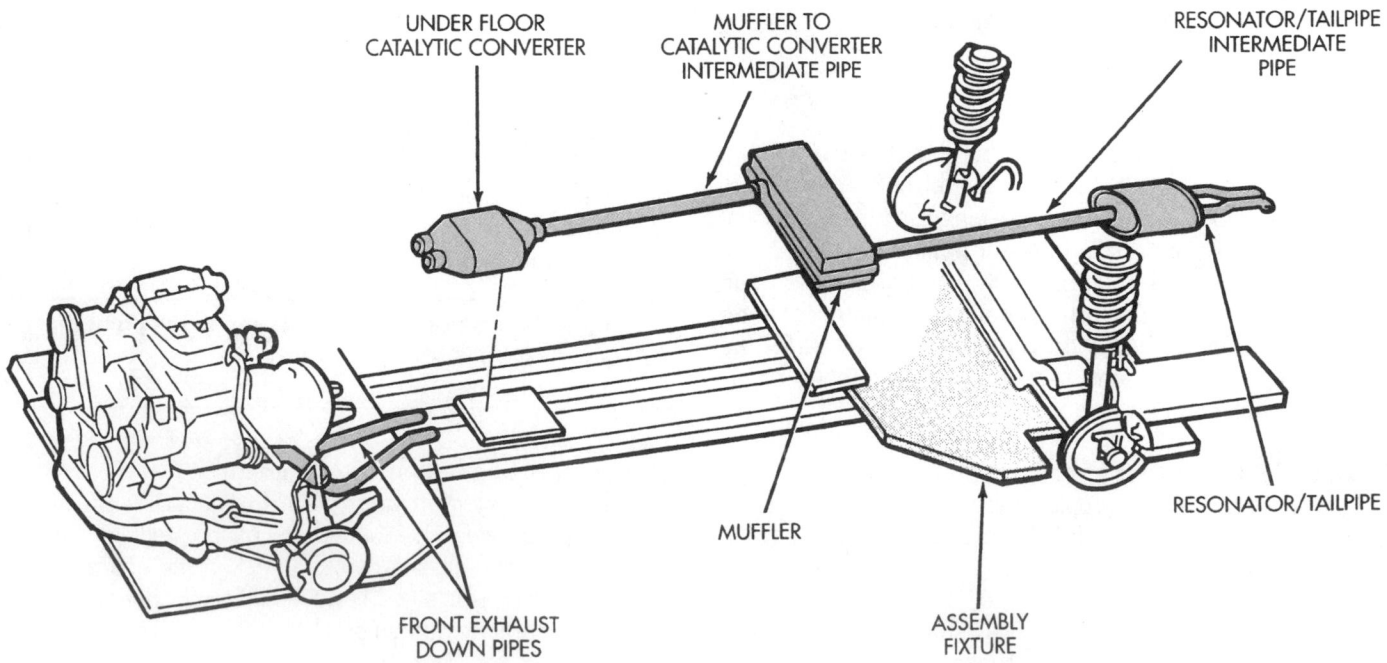

Figure 23-26.   Pipes, converter, muffler, and resonator are correctly aligned.

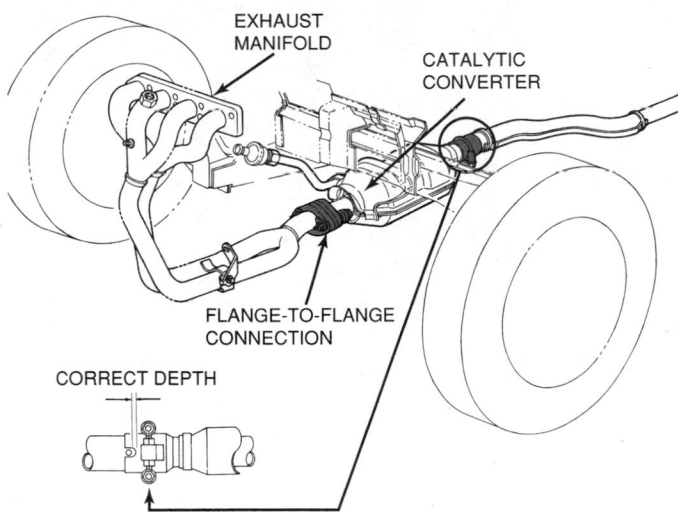

Figure 23-27. Several commonly used exhaust pipe connection types. Note the correct pipe-to-nipple engagement depth for this particular system.

clear the springs, shocks, and axle when the springs bottom under a heavy load or when hitting bumps. The pipes must also clear the propeller shaft, brake lines, and gas lines.

Checking System for Leaks

As a final step, always operate the engine and check each joint for signs of exhaust leakage. See **Figure 23-29**. The system must be airtight to prevent the escape of exhaust gases. If a leak is found, repair the joint.

STOP Warning: Exhaust gases contain carbon monoxide (a deadly poison) and, therefore, must not escape under the vehicle. They could flow into the vehicle's passenger compartment, causing serious injury or death.

Figure 23-30 shows some important considerations for exhaust system service: A—Use penetrating oil. B—Tighten clamps securely, but not excessively. C—Slitting the joint makes pipe or muffler removal easy. D—Cut off the exhaust pipe when it is part of the muffler. E—Clean all connections and use sealer. F—Use a new exhaust pipe-to-manifold gasket when this joint is disconnected. G—The muffler inlet must fit the exhaust pipe. H—The muffler outlet must fit the tailpipe.

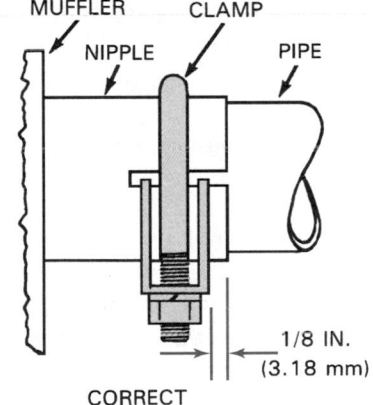
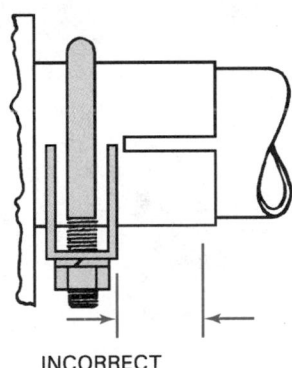

Figure 23-28. The retaining clamp should be positioned about 1/8" (3.18 mm) from the end of the nipple or pipe.

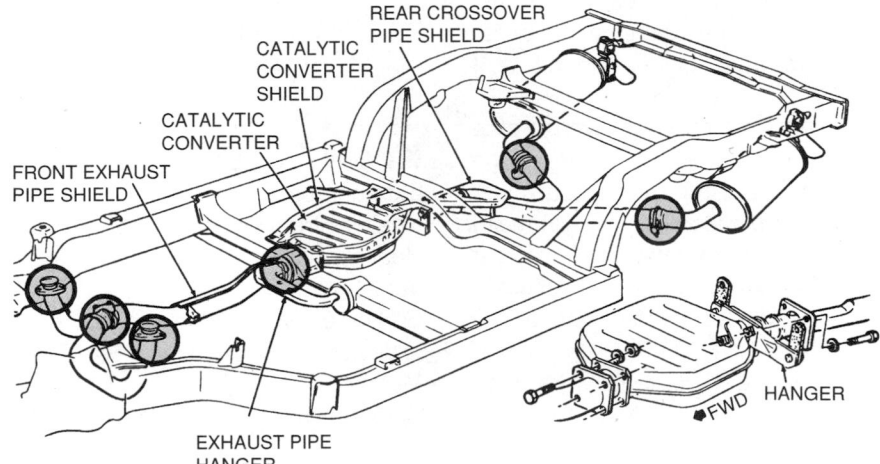

Figure 23-29. Check connections (circled areas) for leaks. (Chevrolet)

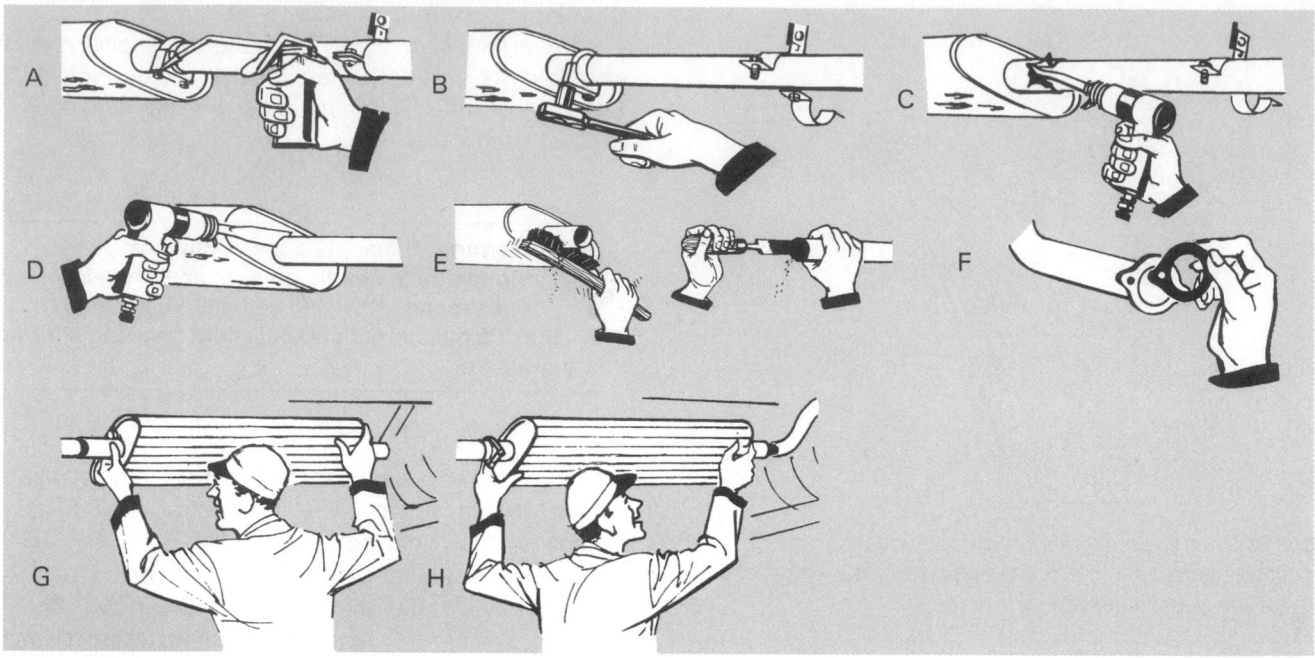

Figure 23-30. Important considerations in exhaust system service. (A. P. Parts)

Summary

Upon leaving the cylinder head, the exhaust gases enter the exhaust manifold. Use penetrating oil to help loosen the exhaust manifold fasteners. When installing an exhaust manifold, clean the mounting surfaces. Use a gasket where needed and torque the fasteners to specifications. Retorque the fasteners after engine operation if required.

The exhaust manifold heat control valve diverts some of the exhaust gases to warm the incoming fuel-air mixture during engine warm-up. Heat control valves on older engines are operated by a thermostatic spring, while those on late-model engines are vacuum operated. The exhaust pipe carries the exhaust gases from the exhaust manifold to the converter and/or muffler. Exhaust systems are of the single or dual type.

Mufflers are generally of the reverse-flow, straight-through, or chambered-pipe design. Mufflers are often ceramic or aluminum coated to increase service life. Some are made of stainless steel. Occasionally, the entire system may be stainless.

Proper tools speed up exhaust system work. Some of the handy tools are the power chisel, hand pipe cutter, joint heater, pipe expander, straightening cone, chain wrench, and power wrench.

Remember:

- Pipe clamps must be of the correct size and design.
- A frame contact hoist is handy for exhaust system work.
- Use penetrating oil on clamp and bracket fasteners.
- Clean all joints thoroughly.
- Use exhaust system sealer on pipe-muffler joints.
- Pipe depth in the nipple must be correct.
- Position clamps properly.
- Cut exhaust pipe when it is an integral part of the muffler.
- Align the exhaust system for proper clearance.
- Check for leaks when the job is complete.
- Use mufflers and pipes of the correct size and design for the specific vehicle.

Know These Terms

Exhaust manifold	Chambered-pipe muffler
Heat control valve	Resonator
Heat riser	Catalytic converter
Vacuum motor	Exhaust pipes
Early fuel evaporation device	Y-pipe
Mufflers	Tailpipe
Back pressure	Joint clamps
Baffled reverse-flow muffler	Support brackets
	Pipe expander
Straight-through muffler	Straightening cone
	Exhaust system alignment

Review Questions—Chapter 23

Do not write in this book. Write your answers on a separate sheet of paper.

1. List the five major parts of a typical exhaust system.
2. Exhaust systems are of the _____ or dual type.
3. List the three basic muffler designs.
4. If exhaust system parts are not to be saved, the quickest way of freeing a stuck joint is to _____ the joint with a _____.
5. If a pipe end is crimped or kinked, it can be brought back to form by using a_____.
6. Some pipes can be formed into the needed shape by using what special tool?
7. To provide additional insurance against leaks, it is wise to coat each joint with _____.
8. When installing a clamp on a joint, allow about _____ between the clamp and the end of the pipe (or nipple) that it surrounds.
9. An exhaust system must be properly _____ in order to prevent noises and damage.
10. What is the last step in any exhaust system repair?

ASE-Type Questions

1. Each of the following are accomplished by the exhaust system EXCEPT:
   (A) reduced noise.
   (B) provide freedom from excessive back pressure.
   (C) prevent poisonous gases from entering the passenger compartment.
   (D) decrease exhaust emissions.
2. Technician A says that composition exhaust manifold gaskets should be retorqued after the first engine warm-up. Technician B says that if exhaust manifold fasteners are properly tightened, locking devices are never needed. Who is right?
   (A) A only.
   (B) B only.
   (C) Both A & B.
   (D) Neither A nor B.
3. The manifold heat control valve _____.
   (A) warms the gasoline coming to the carburetor or fuel injectors
   (B) warms the fuel charge in the intake manifold
   (C) warms the air before it enters the carburetor or fuel injectors
   (D) warms both air and gasoline before it enters the carburetor or fuel injectors
4. All of the following are types of exhaust system mufflers EXCEPT:
   (A) baffled reverse-flow.
   (B) straight-through.
   (C) straight reverse-flow.
   (D) chambered pipe.
5. Technician A says that a power chisel can be used to remove exhaust system parts that are not to be reused.

Technician B says that heat can be used to free exhaust system parts. Who is right?
   (A) A only.
   (B) B only.
   (C) Both A & B.
   (D) Neither A nor B.
6. An exhaust part must be cleaned. Technician A says to use coarse emery cloth. Technician B says to use crocus cloth. Who is right?
   (A) A only.
   (B) B only.
   (C) Both A & B.
   (D) Neither A nor B.
7. Exhaust system sealer should be _____.
   (A) liberally coated on the sections to be joined
   (B) used only when needed
   (C) never be used
   (D) mixed with a catalyst before using
8. When inserting a tailpipe or exhaust pipe into or over a muffler nipple, the pipe should be shoved in or over _____.
   (A) one third of the way
   (B) halfway
   (C) the full nipple depth
   (D) Any of the above.
9. Technician A says that the diameter of the exhaust pipe, tail pipe, or muffler in not important as long as they fit. Technician B says that the exhaust system should be aligned before the final tightening of exhaust system clamps and brackets. Who is right?
   (A) A only.
   (B) B only.
   (C) Both A & B.
   (D) Neither A nor B.
10. All of the following statements about exhaust system leaks are true, EXCEPT:
    (A) leaks under the vehicle cannot enter the passenger compartment.
    (B) after completing any work on the exhaust system, the system should be checked for leaks.
    (C) reusing old gaskets can cause leaks.
    (D) failure to tighten joint clamps can cause leaks.

Suggested Activities

1. Compare the sizes of reverse-flow and straight-through mufflers. Figure out the reason for any differences in size.
2. Check the exhaust system components on a specific vehicle for damage. Make a sketch of the system and label any defects that you found. Determine whether the defective parts can be fixed or if new parts are required.
3. Use a vacuum gauge to check for excessive exhaust back pressure. Discuss your findings with your instructor or class.

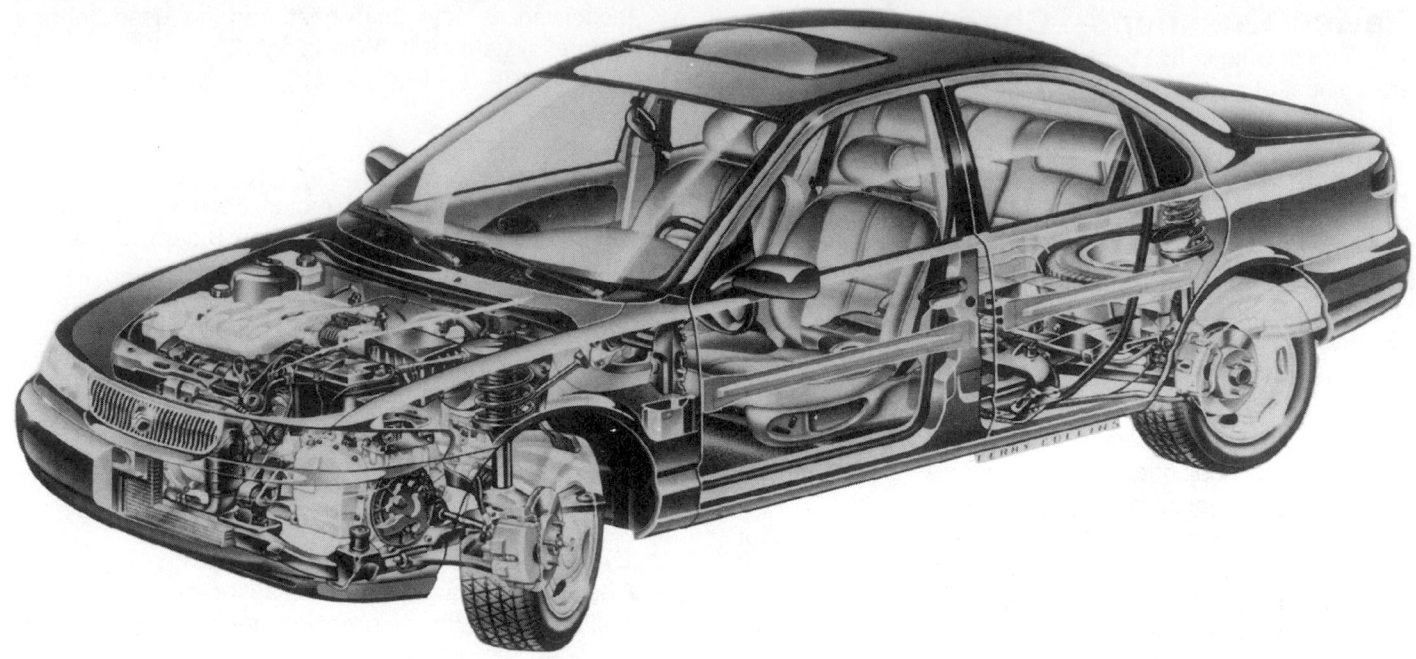

Phantom view of a late-model, front-wheel drive automobile. To meet federal emissions standards, manufacturers equip their vehicles with a variety of emission control devices. (Ford)

24

Emission System Service

After studying this chapter, you will be able to:
- Describe internal engine modifications for reduced emissions.
- Describe fuel system modifications for reduced emissions.
- Describe thermostatic air cleaner operation, service, and repair.
- Explain early fuel evaporation system operation, service, and repair.
- Explain exhaust gas recirculation system operation, service, and repair.
- Explain catalytic converter construction and operation.
- Remove, install, and service a catalytic converter.
- Describe air injection system operation, service, and repair.
- Explain positive crankcase ventilation system operation, service, and repair.
- Explain evaporative control system operation, service, and repair.
- Diagnose exhaust system and emission control problems.

This chapter will cover the emission control systems installed on most vehicles. Because of the interaction of modern emission controls with other engine systems, the reader will be directed to other chapters for additional information about certain systems. The reader should pay particular attention to references to Chapter 25, since almost all emission devices are now controlled through the engine control module.

Emission Control System Service

Incomplete burning of the engine fuel causes the formation of **hydrocarbons** (HC) and **carbon monoxide** (CO). Excessive combustion chamber temperatures can cause the production of **oxides of nitrogen** (NO_x). Unburned gasoline from the fuel system is responsible for large amounts of HC. This combination of HC, CO, and NO_x, if released into the atmosphere, could cause serious air pollution problems. To reduce the level of pollution from vehicle emissions, a number of emission controls have been developed. They can be divided into three basic classifications:

- Engine modifications and engine controls.
- External cleaning systems.
- Fuel vapor controls.

Engine modifications and **engine controls** are designed to allow the fuel charge to burn more completely within the combustion chamber and to ensure that the gases leaving the chamber are as environmentally safe as possible. Engine modifications include the basic design of internal engine parts such as combustion chamber shape, camshaft lift and duration, and intake manifold design.

Control systems are also used to alter ignition timing, fuel mixture, and combustion chamber temperature. **External cleaning systems** are used to assure continued burning of the exhaust between the combustion chamber and the tailpipe. These control systems include the air injection system and the catalytic converter. The **fuel vapor controls** are designed to prevent the escape of gasoline vapor from the tank filler cap, tank, carburetor, and other vehicle components. These are a common source of unburned hydrocarbons. This system also controls engine crankcase fumes caused by unburned fuel leaking past the piston rings.

Internal Engine Modifications and Controls

This classification contains two major subdivisions, internal modifications to the engine, and external controls placed on the fuel and ignition systems. In modern vehicles, engine internal parts are designed to balance the needs of performance, emissions, and driveability.

Combustion Chamber Shapes

The combustion chamber in a modern cylinder head is designed to reduce the amount of hydrocarbons in the exhaust. Older head designs had complex combustion chamber shapes with areas that would almost touch the piston head when it was at the top of the cylinder. This design mixed the air and fuel more thoroughly, which produced more power with less detonation. However, this design would cause unburned fuel to condense and cling to the sides of the combustion chamber.

Combustion chambers in newer heads have simple shapes and as small a surface area as possible to reduce fuel condensation. They also have a larger volume to lower the compression ratio, which is discussed later in this section. The combustion chamber area at the top of piston travel is reduced, which minimizes the opportunity for fuel to become trapped.

Camshaft Designs

A camshaft with a large amount of overlap will give the engine good high speed performance. However, this overlap will cause the incoming air-fuel mixture to be diluted by exhaust gases at idle and low speeds. On older engines, this dilution was overcome by rich idle mixtures. Modern camshafts have less overlap (the time when both the intake and exhaust valves are open) than older camshaft designs. Since it is no longer desirable to have rich idle mixtures, overlap was reduced to prevent exhaust dilution and a rough idle. These milder camshafts reduce engine power to increase smoothness.

Hotter Thermostats

Cooling system thermostats used on modern engines do not begin to open until the coolant temperature has reached at least 190°-200°F (88°-93.5°C). Thermostats used on older vehicles would usually open at 160°-180°F (71°-82°C). The modern engine cooling system warms up quickly and operates at higher temperatures. This keeps the combustion chamber at higher temperatures for the majority of the time that the engine is operating. Higher temperatures reduce gasoline condensation on the combustion chamber surfaces and cylinder walls which lowers the level of hydrocarbons (HC).

Lower Compression

Lower compression ratios allow the use of lower octane unleaded gasoline in modern engines without detonating or dieseling. Since lower compression also lowers the temperature of the combustion process, the oxygen and nitrogen are less likely to combine into oxides of nitrogen (NO_x). In addition, the lower compression allows the engine to operate on unleaded gas, which must be used if the vehicle has a catalytic converter. Note that these internal engine designs can only be serviced by changing the engine parts. In most cases, replacing these components with a design not specified by the manufacturer is illegal. Engine part replacement was covered in earlier chapters.

Fuel System Controls

Most fuel system controls involve producing a leaner air-fuel ratio than previously used. This leaner ratio reduces carbon monoxide and hydrocarbon emissions.

Carburetors

The carburetor on most newer vehicles try to maintain a stoichiometric air-fuel ratio, which is as close to 14.7 to 1 as possible. This is the ideal ratio for mileage and emissions, but not necessarily for power and driveability. Newer carburetors have smaller main jets, reduced accelerator pump output, and power valve springs which do not allow the power valve to open until the engine is under very heavy loads. The idle mixture screws are sealed to prevent readjustment. See **Figure 24-1.**

Modern carburetors are controlled by the engine control module through a mixture control solenoid installed in the carburetor, **Figure 24-2.** When the engine is warming up or when wide open throttle operation is necessary, the

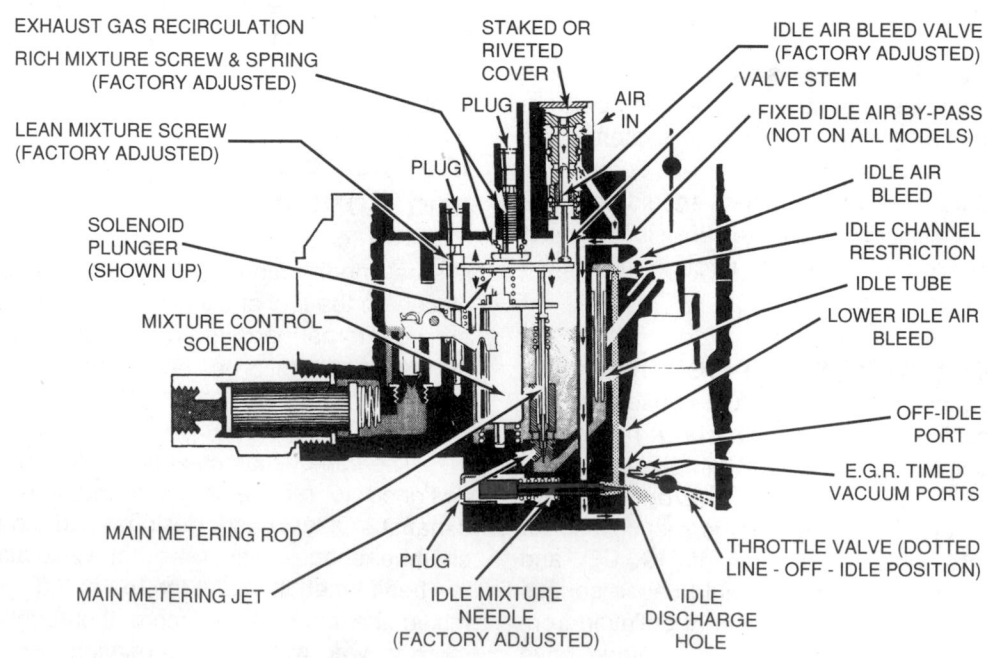

Figure 24-1. Typical carburetor cross-sectional view depicting an idle mixture needle (screw) and tamper resistant plug. (Buick)

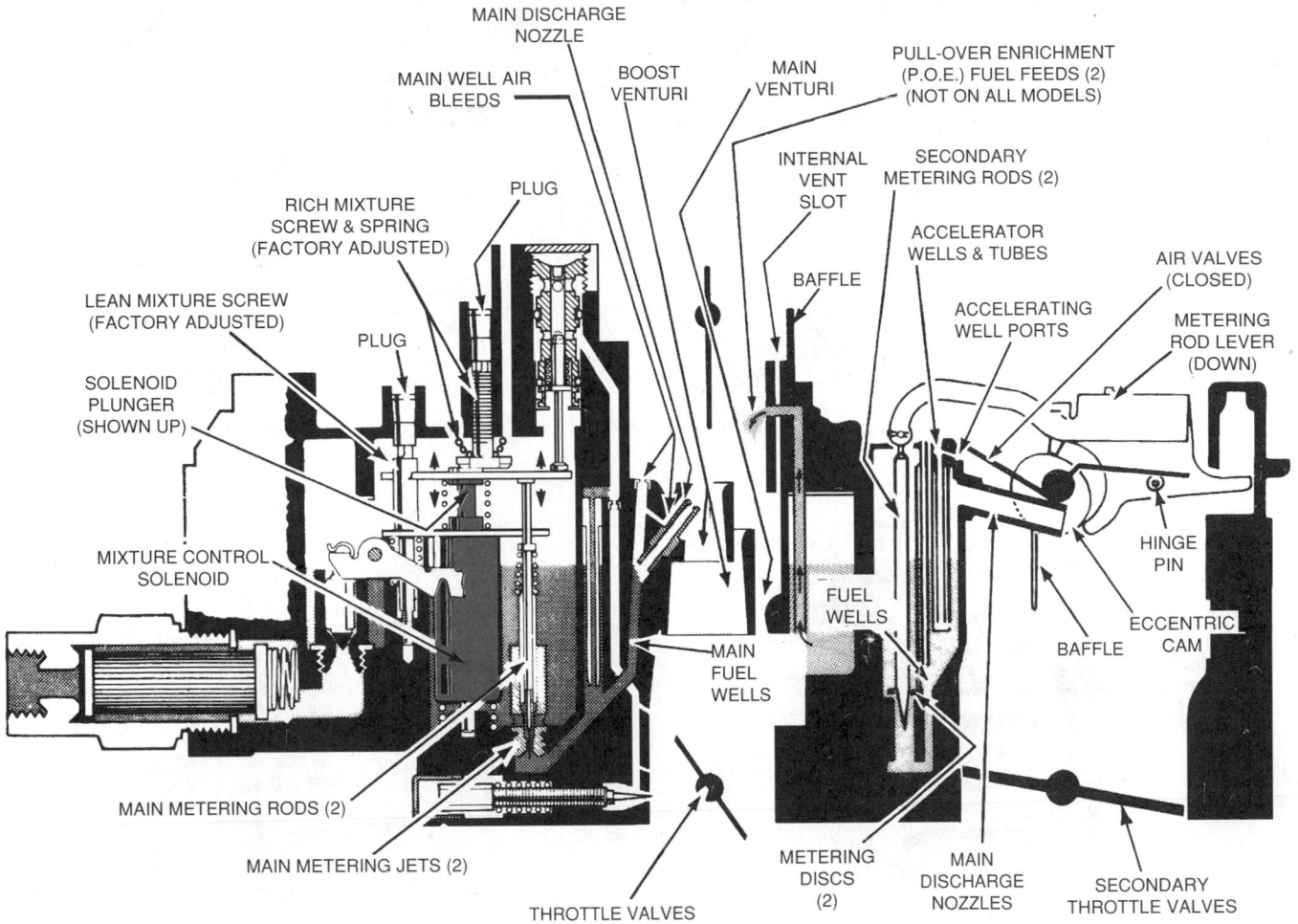

MAIN DISCHARGE NOZZLE

MAIN WELL AIR BLEEDS

BOOST VENTURI

MAIN VENTURI

PULL-OVER ENRICHMENT (P.O.E.) FUEL FEEDS (2) (NOT ON ALL MODELS)

RICH MIXTURE SCREW & SPRING (FACTORY ADJUSTED)

PLUG

INTERNAL VENT SLOT

SECONDARY METERING RODS (2)

ACCELERATOR WELLS & TUBES

AIR VALVES (CLOSED)

LEAN MIXTURE SCREW (FACTORY ADJUSTED)

PLUG

BAFFLE

ACCELERATING WELL PORTS

METERING ROD LEVER (DOWN)

SOLENOID PLUNGER (SHOWN UP)

HINGE PIN

MIXTURE CONTROL SOLENOID

FUEL WELLS

ECCENTRIC CAM

MAIN FUEL WELLS

BAFFLE

MAIN METERING RODS (2)

MAIN METERING JETS (2)

THROTTLE VALVES

METERING DISCS (2)

MAIN DISCHARGE NOZZLES

SECONDARY THROTTLE VALVES

Figure 24-2.   Cross-sectional view of a four-barrel carburetor which uses a mixture control solenoid. The wiring to the engine control module is not shown. (Buick)

air-fuel ratio may be richened by the choke, accelerator pump, or power valve. Rich air-fuel mixtures are used as little as possible. Other ways in which the carburetor has been modified to produce lower emissions are faster opening chokes and more precise control of idle speeds. These devices are covered in more detail in Chapter 21. More precise control of air-fuel ratios has been achieved through the use of computer-controlled electronic fuel injection. Fuel injection, which was covered in Chapter 20, has replaced the carburetor on all late model engines.

Heating the Air-Fuel Mixture

To allow a cold engine to run properly with lean mixtures, the incoming air must be heated to prevent any fuel condensation in the intake manifold. Heating the incoming air allows the choke to open sooner, which reduces hydrocarbon (HC) emissions. These devices also help to prevent *carburetor icing.* Carburetor icing occurs when the lower air pressure in the carburetor venturi causes water vapor to freeze in the carburetor throat. This ice formation can cause the engine to run roughly or stall in cold, damp weather.

Thermostatic Air Cleaner

The *thermostatic air cleaner* is one of the devices used to heat the incoming air, **Figure 24-3.** It employs a valve in the air inlet section. When the valve is closed, cooler ambient air is drawn in. When the valve is fully opened, heated air (usually drawn from a shroud around the exhaust manifold) is admitted and the cooler air excluded. At positions in between, a blend of both heated and cooler air is admitted. This permits smooth engine operation while allowing the use of relatively lean fuel mixtures.

The modern air control door is actuated by a vacuum motor, **Figure 24-4.** When the engine is started cold, the thermal sensor bleed valve is closed and full vacuum is applied to the vacuum motor. This pulls the diaphragm up against spring pressure and fully opens the air valve to allow heated air to enter. The cold engine start position is shown in **Figure 24-4A.** When the thermal sensor warms, it opens the air bleed. This stops vacuum to the vacuum motor, allowing the spring to force the diaphragm down and close the valve, **Figure 24-4B.** A cutaway view of the entire thermostatically controlled air cleaner assembly is illustrated in **Figure 24-5.** Study the parts and arrangements.

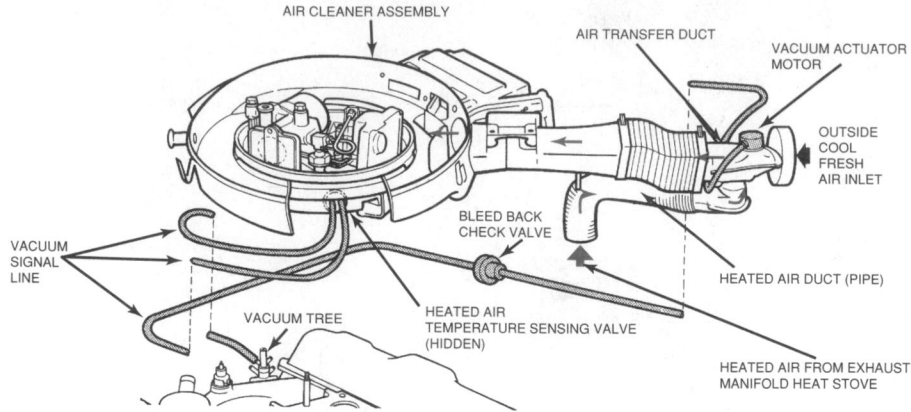

Figure 24-3. A thermostatically controlled air cleaner assembly. The air cleaner housing cover has been removed. Follow the heat arrows. (Chrysler)

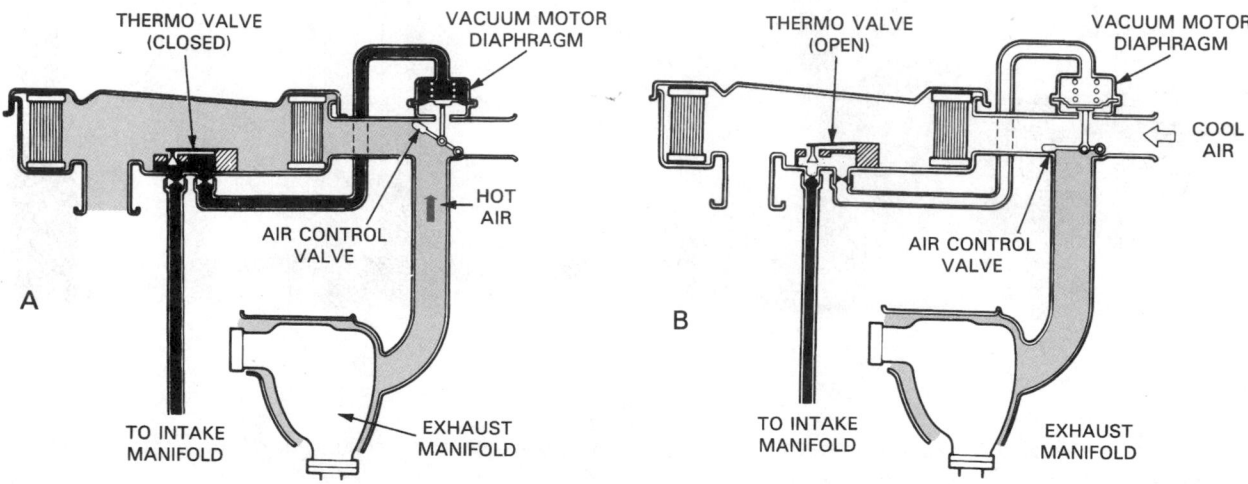

Figure 24-4. Vacuum motor control of thermostatically controlled air cleaner. A—Cold engine, valve open. B—Engine at normal operating temperature, valve closed. (Toyota)

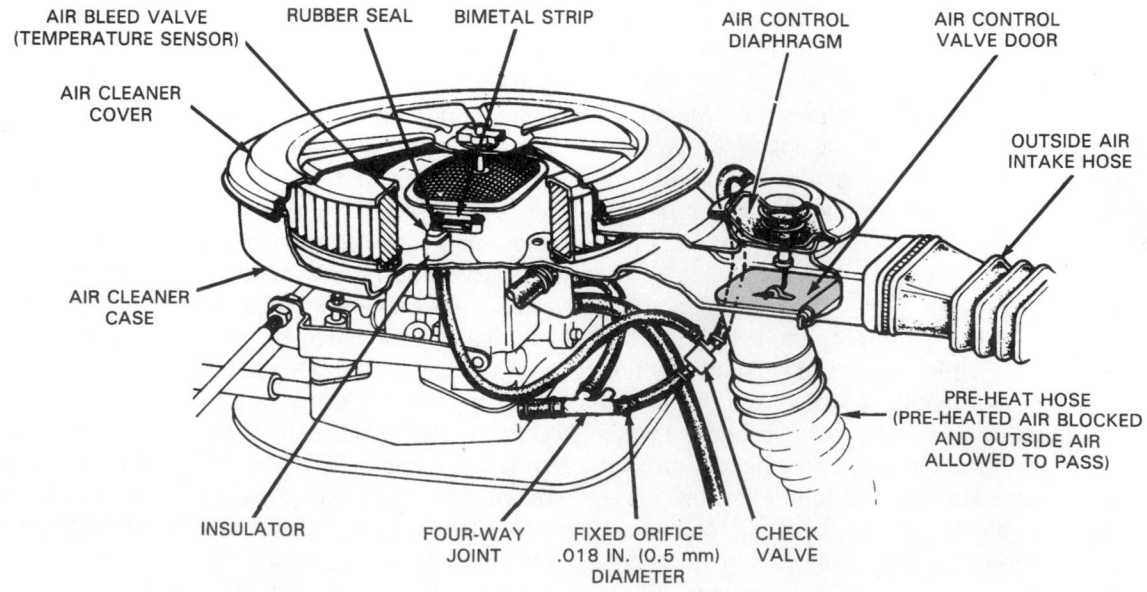

Figure 24-5. Cutaway view of a thermostatically controlled air cleaner system. (Honda)

Thermostatic Air Cleaner Service

Make certain that system hoses are in good condition, properly connected, and free of kinks. Following the manufacturer's specifications, make certain that the valve starts to open and goes to the full open position at the correct temperature. Check the vacuum bleed sensor operation as well as air motor operation. **Figure 24-6** illustrates the use of a hand vacuum pump to test the air motor vacuum diaphragm. Check for vacuum leakdown, starting door lift vacuum, and full open vacuum measurement.

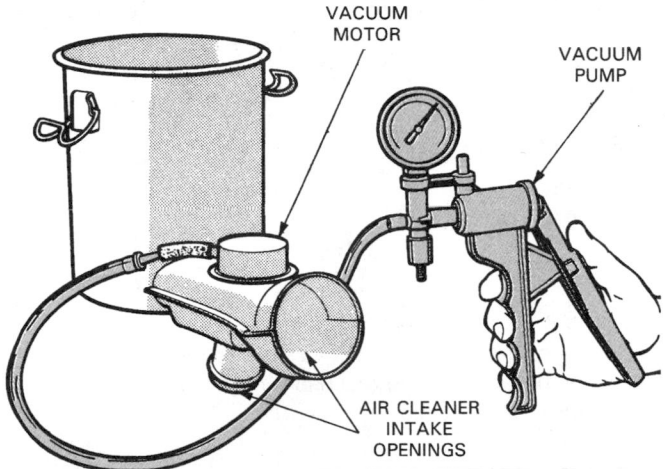

Figure 24-6. Testing thermostatic air cleaner vacuum motor operation. (Chrysler)

Early Fuel Evaporation System

The **early fuel evaporation** (EFE) system warms the incoming air by transmitting exhaust heat to the exhaust crossover under the intake manifold. A vacuum-operated valve provides this enriched flow of hot gases during cold engine operation. This improves engine performance and reduces emissions. A thermal vacuum switch controls the EFE valve. When the coolant temperature reaches a certain point, the vacuum switch triggers the EFE valve, which diverts the gases through the manifold and on to the exhaust pipe. See **Figure 24-7.** When servicing, check the operation of the thermal vacuum switch, EFE valve, and hose connections. For full details on the operation of the EFE system, see the heat control valve section in Chapter 23.

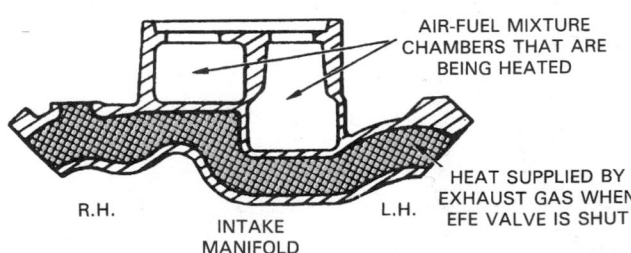

Figure 24-7. An early fuel evaporation system heated the intake manifold during cold engine operation. (Pontiac)

Spark Timing Controls

A number of systems have been developed to adjust ignition spark timing to meet most engine conditions. Most of these systems retard the operation of the vacuum advance unit, when used, or use the engine computer to modify the timing. Older vehicles may have a **vacuum advance restrictor** attached between the vacuum advance unit and the intake manifold. On these systems, the advance unit is connected to manifold vacuum through a ported vacuum opening on the carburetor. The ported vacuum connection ensures that no vacuum reaches the advance unit at idle speeds. A vacuum restrictor is inserted into the vacuum line. When the throttle is opened, ported vacuum is forced to pass through the restrictor. The restrictor prevents full vacuum from reaching the advance unit for as much as 30 seconds after the throttle is opened. This lowers hydrocarbon emissions while giving good fuel mileage.

On some older vehicles, a solenoid-operated valve is installed in the vacuum line from the manifold to the advance unit. These valves are energized by electrical switches on the transmission or speedometer. This valve will not allow the vacuum advance to receive full vacuum until the vehicle is in high gear or has reached a certain speed. Some systems override the control system when the engine or outside air temperature is below a certain point. A temperature override switch opens, which deenergizes the solenoid and provides full vacuum advance until the engine warms up.

Since the introduction of electronic engine controls, ignition timing is precisely controlled by the engine control module. These systems use a number of engine sensors along with electronic spark control to provide constant timing control. This permits smooth engine operation while using lean fuel mixtures. Service on these systems usually involves checking that the spark retard system is operating properly. Service is confined to replacing defective parts and rechecking initial timing. For details on ignition system service, refer to Chapter 18.

Exhaust Gas Recirculation

When the temperature of the burning fuel mixture exceeds around 2,500°F (1,372°C), nitrogen in the air tends to chemically combine with oxygen. This forms oxides of nitrogen, usually called NO_x. By recirculating a portion of the burned exhaust gas back into the intake manifold, the peak flame temperature in the cylinders is lowered. This provides a significant reduction in the amount of NO_x produced.

The amount of exhaust gas fed into the intake manifold is automatically controlled by the **exhaust gas recirculation** (EGR) valve. The EGR valve is opened when the engine is under light and moderate loads. During idle and wide open throttle conditions, the EGR valve remains closed. EGR valves are operated by engine vacuum, electrical signals, or a combination of both.

Testing the EGR Valve

When possible, depress the EGR diaphragm with the tips of your fingers. If the engine was idling smoothly, it should immediately lose about 200 RPM and show signs of roughness. If this happens, the EGR valve is all right so far. If no loss in RPM is evident and if engine operation is smooth, the passage between the EGR valve and the intake manifold may be plugged. Remove and clean the EGR valve and passageway.

 Warning: The EGR valve can become very hot. Exercise care to avoid burns on your hands and fingers.

If no loss in RPM is evident and the engine idle is rough, the valve may be admitting exhaust gases all the time. This indicates a faulty valve or improper hose routing. Place a T fitting in the vacuum signal line and attach a vacuum gauge. Increase engine RPM and note the vacuum reading when the diaphragm starts to move. Valve opening should fall within specified limits.

Ported EGR Valve

The simplest type of EGR valve is operated by *ported vacuum* from the carburetor. A vacuum port above the closed throttle plate cannot receive vacuum at idle, but can receive vacuum as soon as the throttle is opened slightly. A spring-loaded diaphragm is used to keep the valve closed. In **Figure 24-8A,** vacuum is low and the spring keeps the valve closed. In **Figure 24-8B,** increased vacuum has pulled the valve upward to pass burned exhaust gases back into the intake manifold. Under heavy loads, the manifold vacuum drops off and the spring closes the valve. To test the valve, accelerate the engine while observing the EGR valve stem. If the stem does not move, the valve is stuck, or the diaphragm is leaking, or not receiving vacuum.

EGR Coolant Temperature Override Switch

A coolant temperature controlled *vacuum override switch* is used on some models. The EGR vacuum hose from the carburetor port is connected to one side of the

switch. The other side goes to the EGR valve. When engine temperature is below a specified point, the switch cuts off vacuum to the EGR to improve cold engine operation. See **Figure 24-9.**

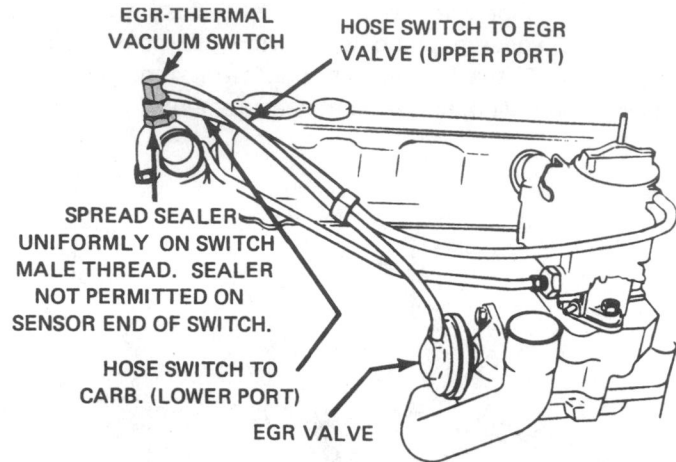

Figure 24-9. EGR coolant temperature override switch (thermal vacuum switch) will cut off the vacuum signal to the EGR valve until the engine reaches normal operating temperature. (Oldsmobile)

To test the switch, remove the vacuum line from the EGR valve or from the transducer if not of the integral type. With the engine cold, connect a vacuum gauge to the line and run the engine at 1500 RPM. No vacuum should be indicated. Replace the switch if vacuum is present. Operate the engine at 1500 RPM until the coolant temperature reaches the specified level. Vacuum should register on gauge. If there is no vacuum, replace the switch.

Positive Back Pressure Transducer Valve

Some EGR valves use an exhaust *back pressure transducer valve* (BPV) to modulate the amount of vacuum operating on the EGR valve diaphragm. The BPV is a

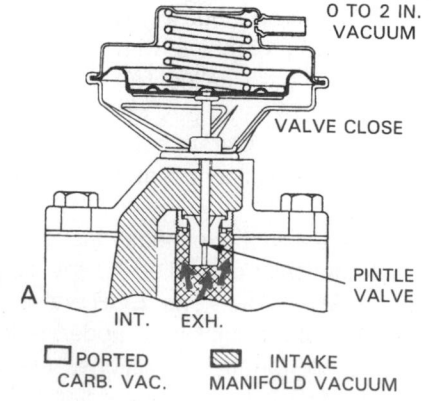 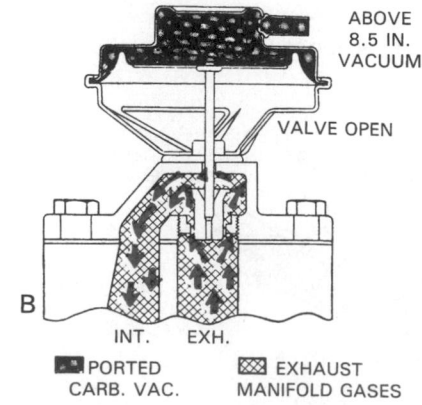

Figure 24-8. Ported EGR valve action. A—Low vacuum signal, valve is closed. B—High vacuum signal, diaphragm opens valve. (Oldsmobile)

device that utilizes power from one source to provide control of power or action. The transducer is incorporated into the EGR valve. In **Figure 24-10A,** exhaust gas cannot flow to the intake manifold, but can create a pressure on the transducer diaphragm. Pressure is low and the spring control valve remains open. This allows air to flow through the bleed holes in the diaphragm plate, past the diaphragm, and through the spring control valve. This weakens the vacuum in the vacuum chamber and the main diaphragm will not draw the exhaust gas recirculation valve open.

In **Figure 24-10B,** exhaust back pressure has built up, pushing the transducer diaphragm upward. This closes the control valve and stops air flow into the vacuum chamber. As a vacuum is no longer weakened by bleed air, the main diaphragm rises and opens the valve. This permits flow of gases to the intake manifold. An EGR valve with a back pressure transducer valve will not open if test vacuum is applied with the engine off. If the EGR does open, replace the valve.

Negative Back Pressure Valve

A *negative back pressure valve* controlled EGR system is pictured in **Figure 24-11.** You will note that in this setup, the bleed valve spring is located below the diaphragm. In this position, the spring holds the diaphragm against the air bleed hole, keeping it closed. As soon as engine vacuum is applied to the EGR valve, the diaphragm will be forced upward, opening the valve. It then passes a metered quantity of exhaust into the intake manifold. With negative exhaust back pressure, the central diaphragm area is pulled down against the small spring. The bleed hole

is then exposed, lowering the effect of engine vacuum. This causes the heavy top spring to force the main diaphragm downward, closing the valve. An EGR valve with a negative back pressure valve will open if test vacuum is applied with the engine off. If the EGR does not open, replace the valve.

Integrated Electronic EGR Valve

Vacuum flow to the *integrated electronic EGR valve* is controlled by the engine control module (ECM). The control sends an electrical signal to a voltage regulator in the EGR valve. This regulator controls current to a solenoid which in turn controls vacuum to the ERG diaphragm. The ECM controls EGR flow using a modulated signal (modified pulse width) based on air flow, throttle position, and engine speed. A pintle position sensor is also used. As EGR flow increases, the position sensor's output increases. See **Figure 24-12.** Test procedures are covered in Chapter 25.

Digital EGR Valve

The *digital EGR valve* functions without engine vacuum. EGR flow passes through three orifices, which are opened and closed by electric solenoids. The solenoids are operated by the engine control module. When the solenoids are energized, the armature rises and the pintle is lifted from its seat. The computer uses input signals from the throttle position sensor (TPS), coolant temperature sensor, and the mass airflow sensor (MAF) to calculate the proper orifice openings. This valve usually operates above idle and during warm engine operating conditions. A digital EGR valve is shown in **Figure 24-13.** Test procedures are covered in Chapter 25.

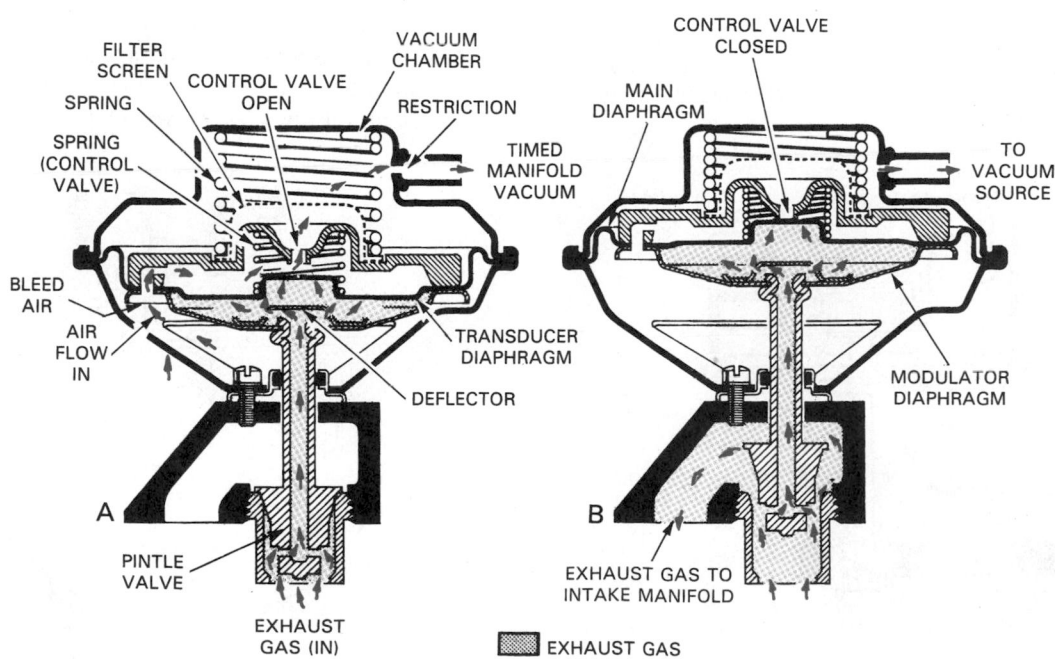

Figure 24-10. Internally modulated EGR valve. A—When the control valve is open, the EGR valve is closed. B—Exhaust back pressure closes control valve, causing the EGR valve to open. (Chevrolet)

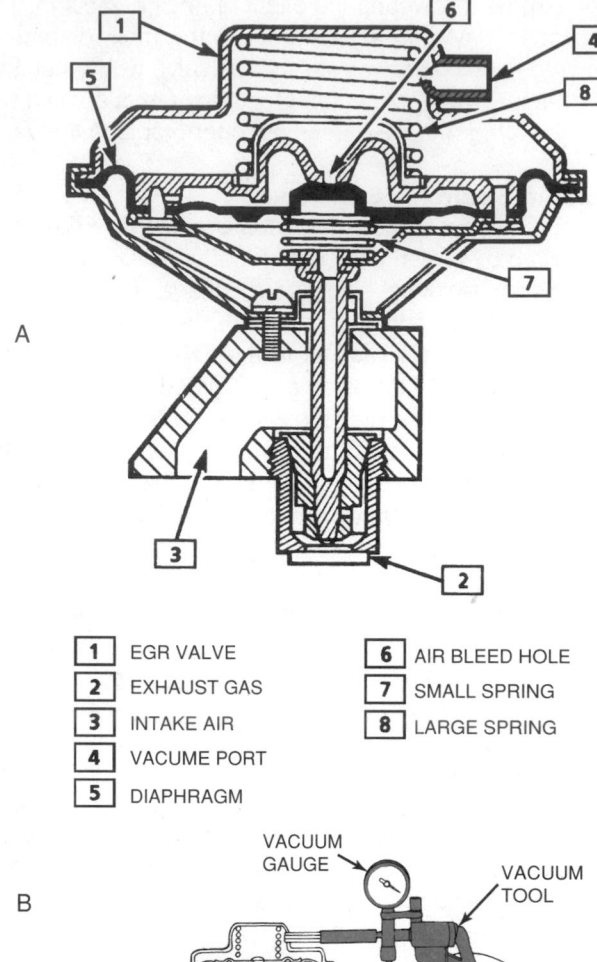

1	EGR VALVE	**6**	AIR BLEED HOLE
2	EXHAUST GAS	**7**	SMALL SPRING
3	INTAKE AIR	**8**	LARGE SPRING
4	VACUME PORT		
5	DIAPHRAGM		

Figure 24-11. A—cross-sectional view of a negative backpressure EGR valve. B—EGR valve with a vacuum pump tool installed onto the vacuum port to check valve for proper operation. (Chevrolet and Hyundai)

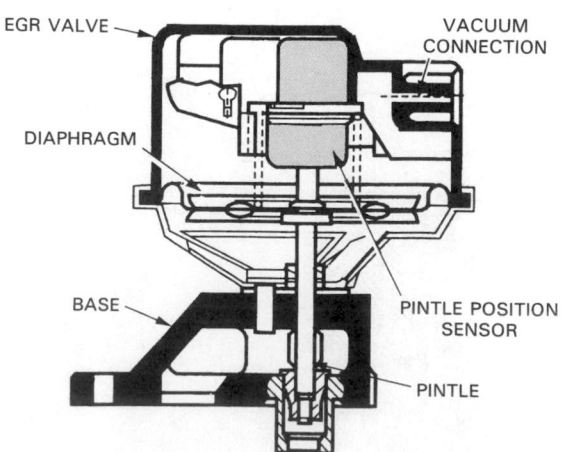

Figure 24-12. Study this cutaway view of an integrated electronic EGR valve. Note the pintle position sensor. (Sun Electric)

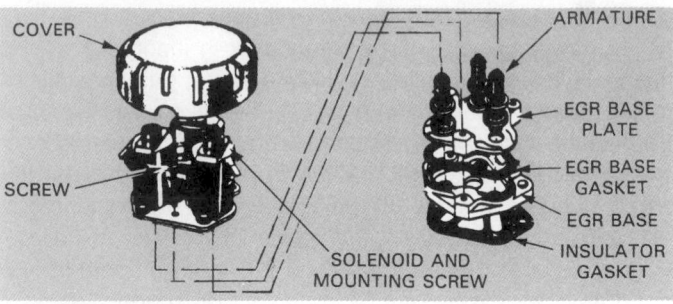

Figure 24-13. Exploded view of a digital EGR valve. Follow manufacturer's recommendations when servicing this unit. (Sun Electric)

> **Caution: Never disconnect or render the EGR valve inoperative on a permanent basis. To do so is a violation of federal and state law and will cause emission levels to rise. In addition, many engines will run hotter and in some cases, detonate to the point of serious engine damage (burned valves and pistons).**

Cleaning the EGR Valve

Some EGR valves may be disassembled for cleaning. On those that are not, the open end of the pintle valve may be tapped lightly with a plastic hammer to break loose any carbon accumulation. A brush may also be used to assist cleaning. Do not sandblast an EGR valve.

> **Caution: Never soak or wash an EGR valve in cleaning solvent. This could seriously damage the diaphragm.**

One type of serviceable EGR valve is shown in **Figure 24-14.** This type of valve should be cleaned approximately once every three years or 30,000 miles (48,000 km). General steps in disassembly and cleaning are given in **Figure 24-15.** Clean off any gasket material and check for the two

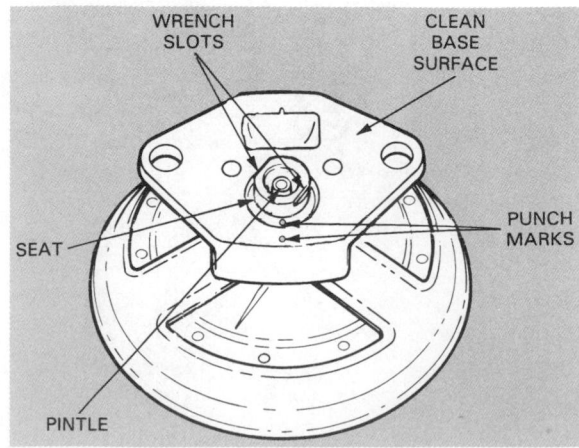

Figure 24-14. Before disassembling this serviceable EGR valve, make certain there are punch marks and that they are aligned. (Buick)

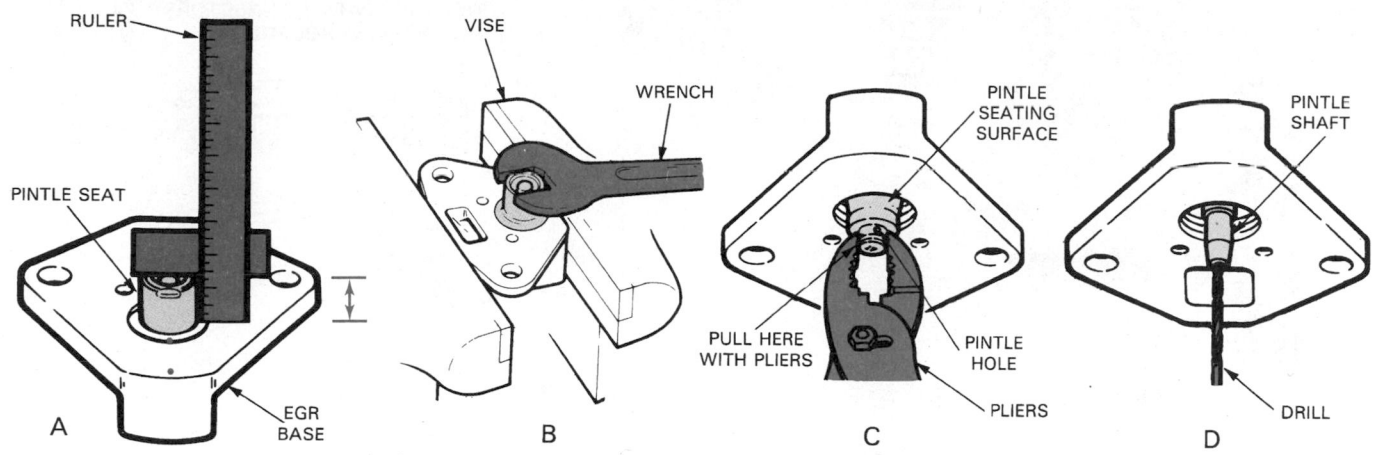

Figure 24-15. Steps involved in disassembly of this EGR valve. A—Check height of pintle seat shoulder-to-base. B—Remove pintle seat. C—Pull pintle from shaft. D—Clean carbon from hollow shaft with appropriate drill bit. (Buick)

punch marks. These marks will ensure proper alignment upon reassembly. Measure the distance from the base to the shoulder as shown in **Figure 24-15A.** Note this distance because it must be established again during reassembly. Remove the seat by fitting a wrench on the seat, **Figure 24-15B.** A small amount of penetrating oil on the threads will ease removal. Do not allow penetrating oil to foul the diaphragm.

After the pintle seat is removed, with the valve in an upright position, grasp the pintle (not on sealing surface) and pull it downward, **Figure 24-15C.** Using the specified size drill bit, turn the drill bit clockwise up into the shaft. Go in a short distance (about an inch) and withdraw to clear the drill bit of carbon. Continue until the drill passes through the shaft hole. Tap the base to jar out any loose particles, **Figure 24-15D.** Also, brush and shake the valve. If compressed air is used, do not direct air into the shaft opening. Reinstall the pintle on the shaft and force it down until it snaps into place. Reinstall the base and thread in to their original height making sure the punch marks are aligned. Restake the seat using a prick punch. Using a new gasket, reinstall the EGR valve. If cleaning does not restore proper EGR operation, replace the valve.

Closed Loop Emission Control Systems

Closed loop systems use an **oxygen sensor** in the exhaust stream to constantly monitor the amount of oxygen in the exhaust. One type is shown in **Figure 24-16.** As the oxygen sensor responds to changes in oxygen levels, which coincide with emission levels, it sends an electrical signal to an electronic control module. The control module receives constant electronic signals from the oxygen sensor.

Based on the information from the oxygen sensor and other sensors (engine temperature, vehicle speed, engine RPM, atmospheric pressure), the control module makes constant changes in the air-fuel mixture, engine timing, EGR, and other functions. This highly efficient system, in

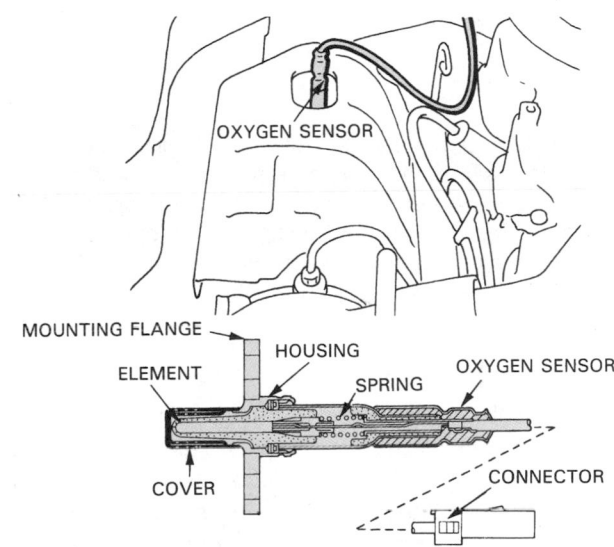

Figure 24-16. This oxygen sensor assembly mounts in the exhaust stream and provides constant monitoring of exhaust oxygen levels. (Chrysler)

effect, constantly monitors its own exhaust, then makes the adjustments necessary to maintain the lowest possible emission levels. Study the closed loop system pictured in **Figure 24-17.** Note the various sensors and how they relate to the overall system. The closed loop control system is covered in detail in Chapter 25.

Emission Control Wiring

Some electrical units in the emission control system operate at very low levels of current and/or voltage. For example, the oxygen sensor can operate on voltage as low as 500μV (microvolt—one millionth of a volt) and amperage as low as 250μA (microampere—one millionth of an ampere). As a result, all connections must be clean, tight, and sealed from the atmosphere when needed. When

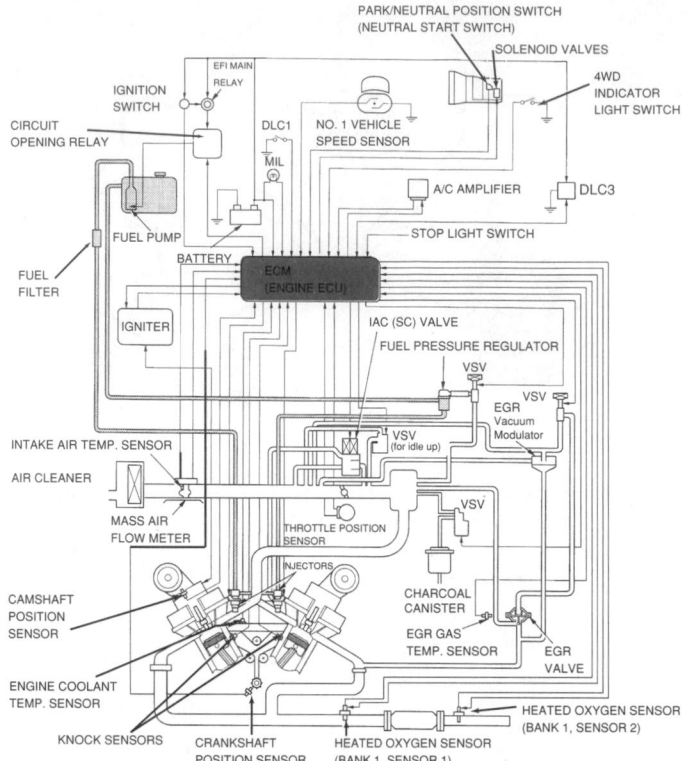

Figure 24-17. One particular closed loop emission control system. Signals from the heated oxygen sensors and other units cause the electronic control unit (ECU) to adjust the air-fuel ratio, EGR action, ignition timing, etc., to help provide the lowest possible engine emission levels. Study the various circuits and components. (Toyota)

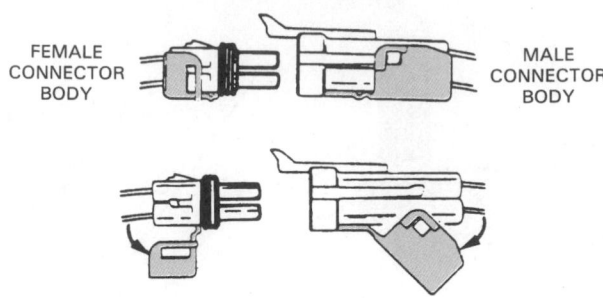

WEATHER PACK CONNECTORS REPAIR PROCEDURE

1. OPEN SECONDARY LOCK HINGE ON CONNECTOR.

2. REMOVE TERMINALS USING SPECIAL TOOL.

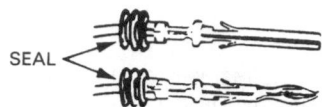

3. CUT WIRE IMMEDIATELY BEHIND CABLE SEAL.

4. SLIP NEW CABLE SEAL ONTO WIRE (IN DIRECTION SHOWN) AND STRIP 2 in. (5.00 mm) OF INSULATION FROM WIRE. POSITION CABLE SEAL AS SHOWN.

Figure 24-18. Repair procedure for one type of special wire connector designed to hold terminals in tight contact and to shield them from underhood environment. (Oldsmobile)

removing, replacing, or repairing wiring harness connectors, use care to avoid bending. When repairing, use recommended procedures and materials to ensure a proper connection. Solder any and all splices. **Figure 24-18** shows the recommended repair procedure for one specific connector.

External Engine Controls

Common external engine controls are the air injection system and catalytic converter. Unlike the earlier systems discussed, which reduce the amount of harmful gases produced by the engine, these devices clean up the exhaust gases after they leave the engine.

Air Injection System

The *air injection system* attacks the emissions problem by continuing the combustion process outside the cylinder. This is accomplished by a belt-driven air pump which is also known as an *air injection reactor (AIR), thermactor, air guard,* or *smog pump.* The system uses a system of tubes or passages to route a stream of fresh air into the exhaust just as it passes out the exhaust valve.

The system provides extra oxygen which causes further burning of the exhaust gases. This additional burning reduces the amount of hydrocarbons and changes a sizable

portion of the carbon monoxide (poisonous gas) into ***carbon dioxide*** (nonpoisonous gas). A schematic of one specific system is shown in **Figure 24-19.** Study the flow of air from the air cleaner to the exhaust valve port. Note that during deceleration, a controlled amount of air is fed into the intake manifold to lean out the rich mixture that tends to form during deceleration. This helps prevent backfiring.

Air Injection System Air Pump

The *air pump* is a positive displacement vane pump. A belt drives the pump rotor, causing the vanes to rotate in the housing. Carbon shoes and springs in the rotor keep the vanes aligned and permit a sliding movement between the vanes and rotor. The vanes pass very close to the housing to limit air leakage. As the vanes rotate, each one in turn passes the intake chamber where a charge of air is drawn in, **Figure 24-20.** The vane that follows forces this air charge around into the compression chamber where the air volume is reduced. This places it under pressure. The pressurized air is then discharged through the exhaust chamber. The intake and exhaust chambers are separated by the stripper (section of housing).

Pump maximum pressure is controlled by a pressure relief valve, which is located either in the pump housing or

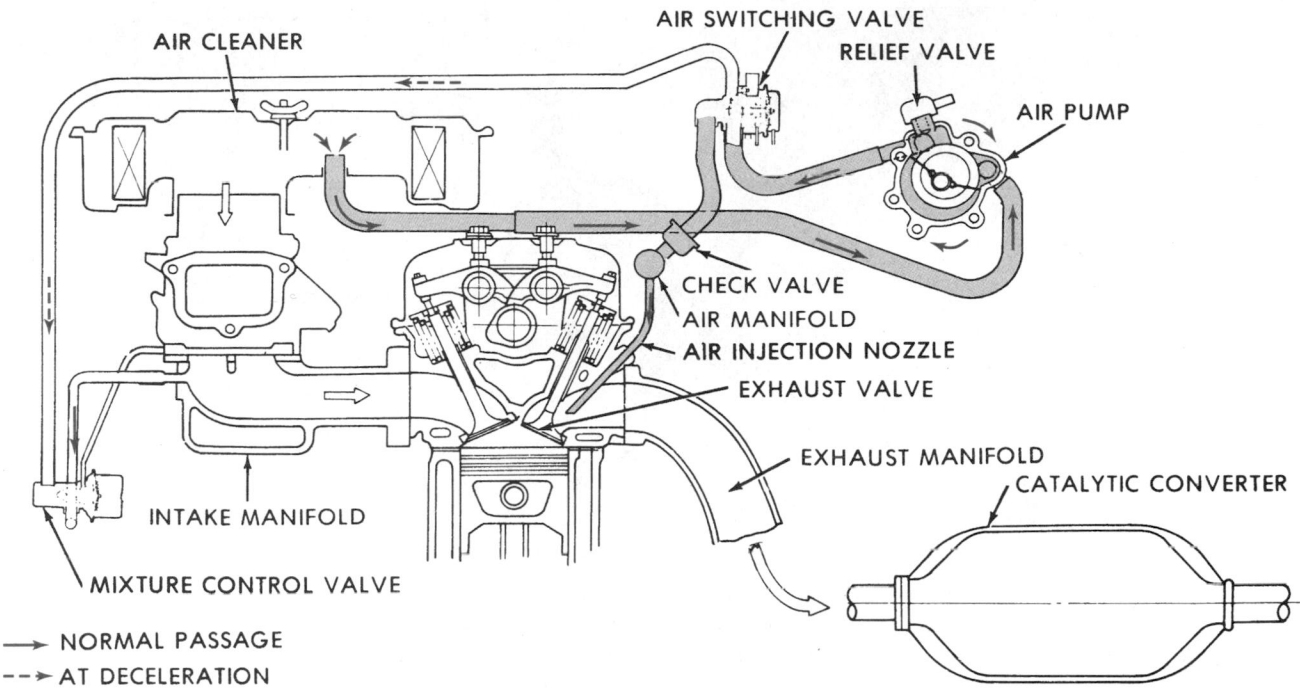

AIR CLEANER

AIR SWITCHING VALVE
RELIEF VALVE

AIR PUMP

CHECK VALVE
AIR MANIFOLD
AIR INJECTION NOZZLE
EXHAUST VALVE

EXHAUST MANIFOLD
CATALYTIC CONVERTER

INTAKE MANIFOLD

MIXTURE CONTROL VALVE

→ NORMAL PASSAGE
--→ AT DECELERATION

Figure 24-19. Schematic showing a typical air injection system. The air switching valve prevents backfires. (Chevrolet)

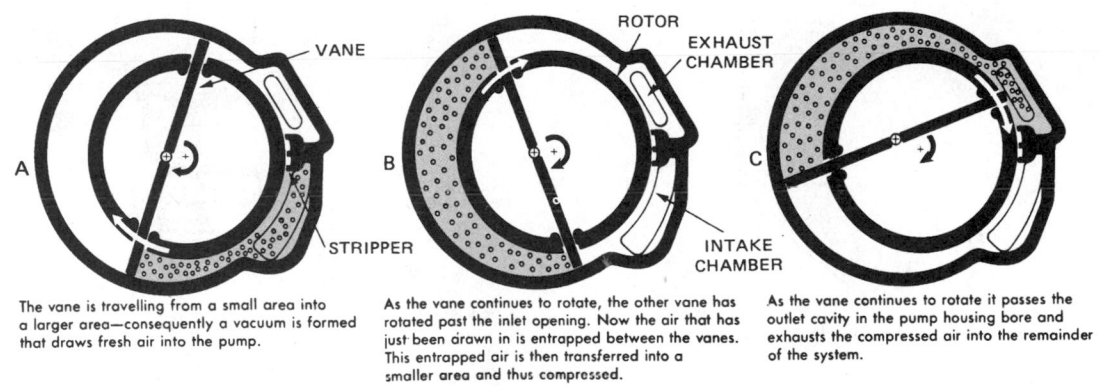

VANE

ROTOR
EXHAUST
CHAMBER

A

STRIPPER

B

INTAKE
CHAMBER

C

The vane is travelling from a small area into a larger area—consequently a vacuum is formed that draws fresh air into the pump.

As the vane continues to rotate, the other vane has rotated past the inlet opening. Now the air that has just been drawn in is entrapped between the vanes. This entrapped air is then transferred into a smaller area and thus compressed.

As the vane continues to rotate it passes the outlet cavity in the pump housing bore and exhausts the compressed air into the remainder of the system.

Figure 24-20. Air pump operation. Note how vanes function. A—Drawing in air. B—Moving air around. C—Compressing and exhaust air.

as part of the diverter valve. See **Figure 24-21.** Metering grooves in the housing wall (in both intake and exhaust chambers) quiet pump operation by providing a smoother transition from intake through exhaust. **Figure 24-22** shows an exploded view of an air pump.

Air Distribution

The pump intake air is filtered either by drawing it from the air cleaner, through a special filter, **Figure 24-23,** or by using a centrifugal filter. Centrifugal filter operation is pictured in **Figure 24-24.** The air flows from the pump through the diverter valve (discussed below), through a hose, and on to a ***check valve.*** See **Figure 24-25.** The check valve is forced off its seat by pump air pressure, thus allowing the air to enter the distribution manifold. If the pump or drive belt fails, or if exhaust pressure exceeds pump pressure,

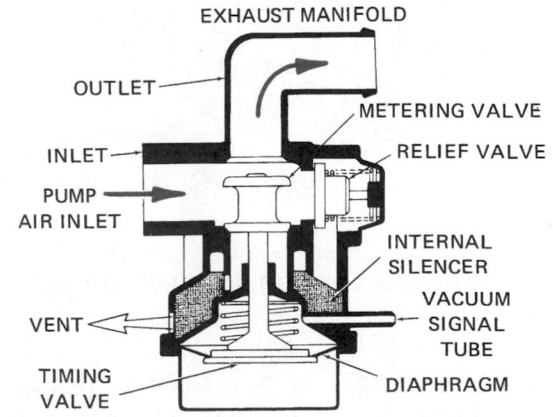

EXHAUST MANIFOLD

OUTLET

METERING VALVE

INLET

RELIEF VALVE

PUMP
AIR INLET

INTERNAL
SILENCER

VACUUM
SIGNAL
TUBE

VENT

TIMING
VALVE

DIAPHRAGM

Figure 24-21. Typical diverter valve, which is also called an anti-backfire valve. (Cadillac)

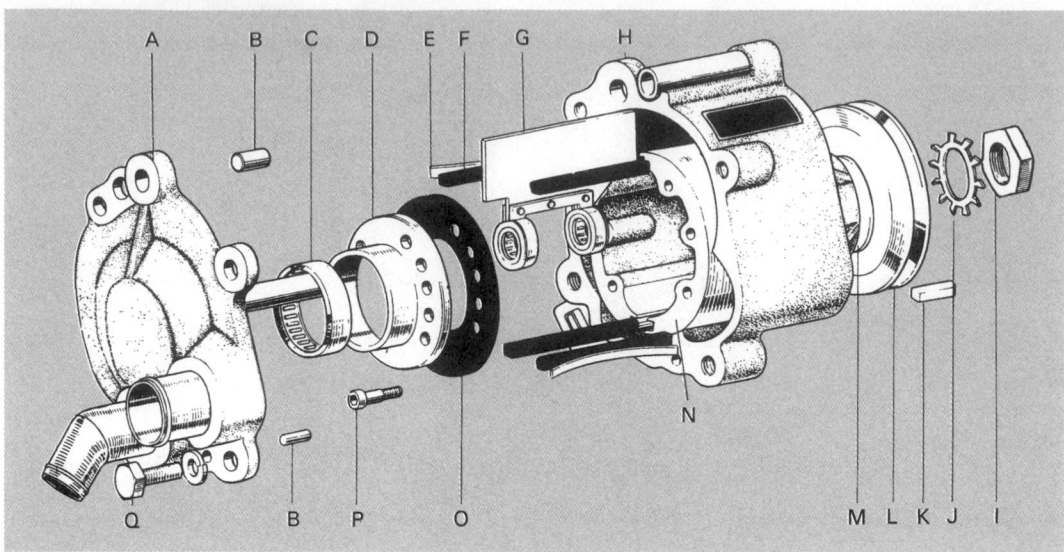

Figure 24-22. Exploded view of one type of air injection system pump. A—End cover. B—Dowel. C—Bearing. D—Rotor ring. E—Shoe spring. F—Carbon shoe. G—Vane. H—Housing. I—Lock nut. J—Lock washer. K—Key. L—Pulley. M—Pulley plate. N—Rotor. O—Rear seal. P—Rotor ring screw. Q—Cover bolt. (Toyota)

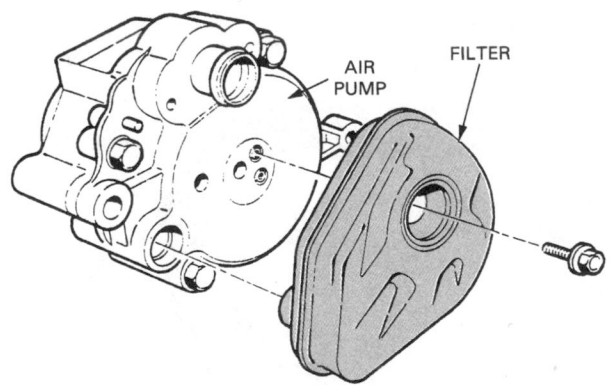

Figure 24-23. Air injection system pump filter. (Ford)

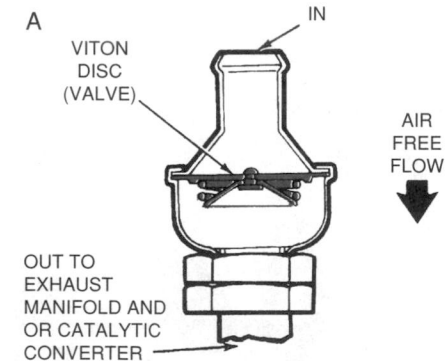

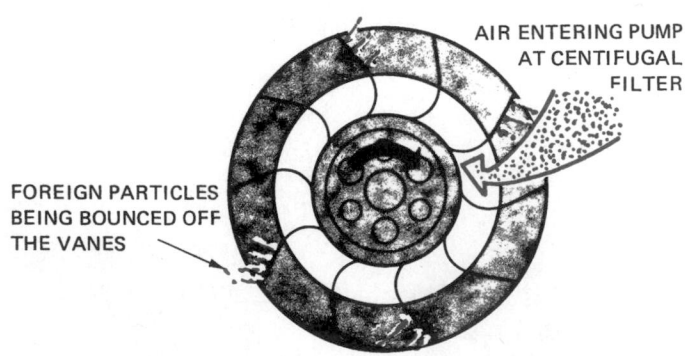

Figure 24-24. Centrifugal air filter spins at high speed and throws foreign particles outward by means of whirling vanes. (Chevrolet)

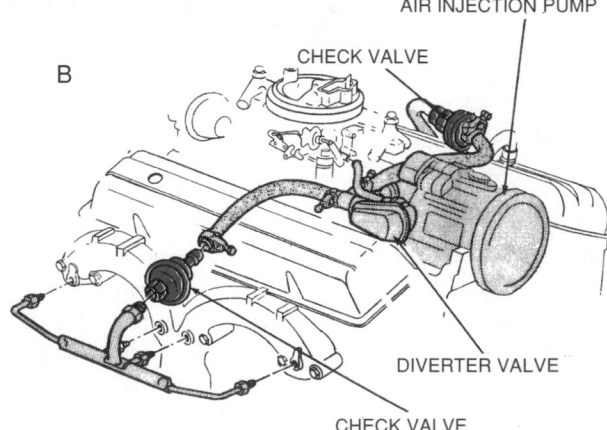

Figure 24-25. A—Air check valve cutaway. B—Overall air injection reaction (AIR) system with a check valve. (General Motors and Ford)

the check valve returns to its seat. This prevents the exhaust gases from flowing through the hose to the pump.

From the check valve, the air enters the distribution manifold. From the manifold, the air flows through the air injection tubes. It then enters the exhaust gas near the exhaust valve. Extra oxygen provided by this system combines with and burns any excess hydrocarbons which escaped the combustion chamber. This reduces the hydrocarbon emission levels. **Figure 24-26** shows one type of air injection arrangement used on a V-8 engine.

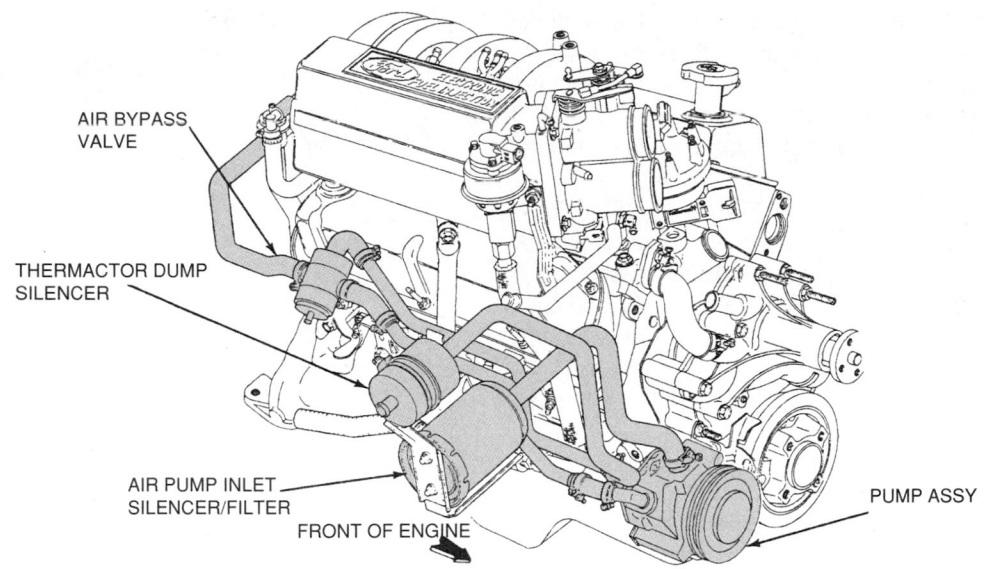

Figure 24-26.   Air injection arrangement on an electronic fuel injected V-8 engine. Note the air pump inlet silencer/filter unit. (Ford)

Diverter Valve Operation

When the throttle valve is closed quickly, gasoline will continue to flow momentarily. Since little or no air is entering the engine during this period, the excess gasoline will produce a rich mixture. It will leave a considerable amount of unburned gas following the power stroke. When this unburned gas enters the exhaust manifold and meets the injected stream of oxygen, it will begin to burn again with explosive force, causing a backfire.

The *diverter valve* is designed to momentarily divert the air stream from the diverter valve to the injection nozzles. It does this by means of a vacuum diaphragm or electrically controlled metering valve. See **Figure 24-27.** The electrically controlled valves have three operating modes. In the cold mode, the switching solenoid valve is energized, which opens the port valve and allows flow to the exhaust ports. The switching solenoid is de-energized and the bypass solenoid is energized in the warm mode. This

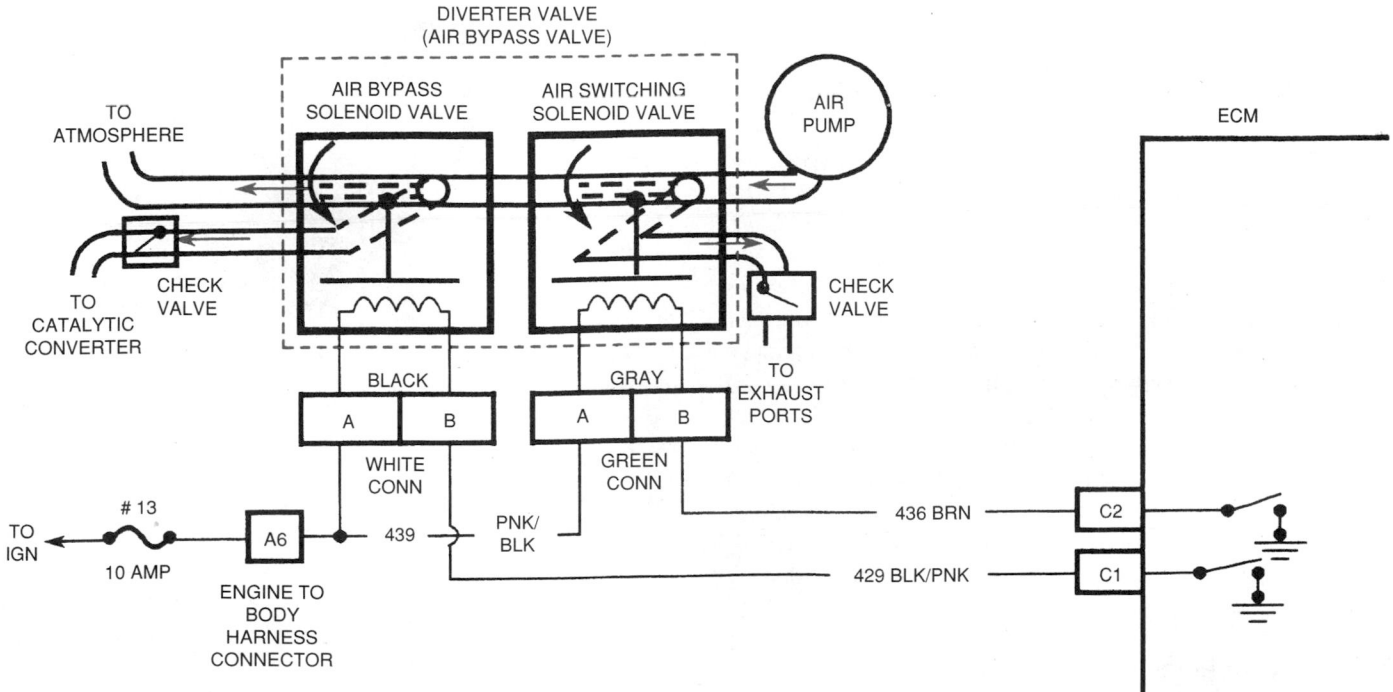

Figure 24-27.   Schematic illustrating a diverter (air bypass) valve which is operated with electric solenoids that are controlled by the ECM. (Chevrolet)

closes the port valve and keeps the converter valve seated, forcing air into the catalytic converter. Both solenoids are deenergized in the divert mode. This action opens the converter valve, permitting the air to take the path of least resistance, which is out of the diver/relief tube to the atmosphere, **Figure 24-27.**

Diverter valve action is shown in **Figure 24-28.** In **Figure 24-28A,** airflow is passing through the diverter valve and on to the air injectors. When the throttle is suddenly released, heavy intake manifold vacuum is applied to the metering valve control diaphragm. The diaphragm is drawn downward, forcing the metering valve to block off passage to the air injection manifold. This downward movement opens up the diverter passage and pump air is momentarily discharged into the atmosphere. See **Figure 24-28B.**

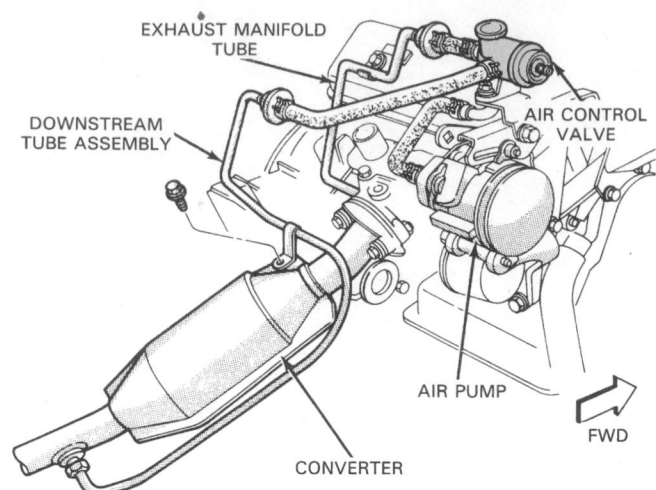

Figure 24-29. Air control valve on this setup directs pump air to the exhaust manifold when the engine is cold and to the exhaust pipe through the downstream tube when hot. (Chrysler)

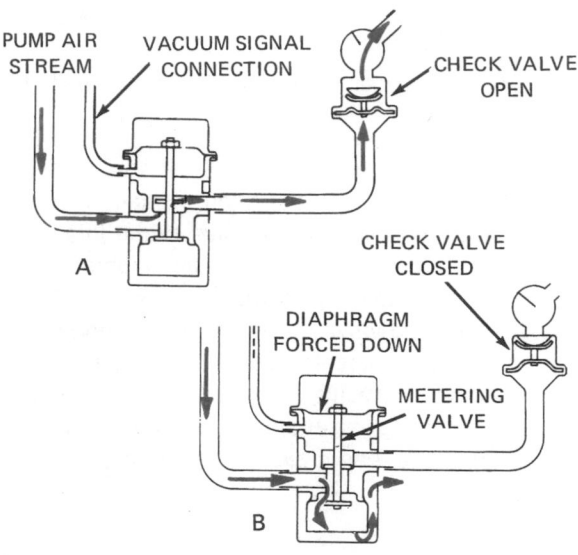

Figure 24-28. Diverter valve action. A—Valve in normal position. B—During deceleration, air is diverted into atmosphere. (Toyota)

Air Control Valve Operation

Some air injection systems use an **air control valve** which can be made as an integral, combination unit or as separate valves, each performing a specific function. The air control valve can be used to perform the normal diverter valve functions. It can also be used for channeling pump air to the intake manifold, exhaust manifold, or to the catalytic converter, as determined by system needs. **Figure 24-29** shows one air control valve that, during engine warm-up, channels pump air to the exhaust port area. Then, when normal operating temperature is reached, it diverts the air to the catalytic converter. A cross-sectional view of another type air control combination valve is pictured in **Figure 24-30.** Study the valve's construction and note the various air channels.

Pulse Type Air Pump System

One air injection system utilizes the pulse effect of the engine exhaust to pull air into the exhaust manifold. Small pulses or gulps of air are drawn in through the check

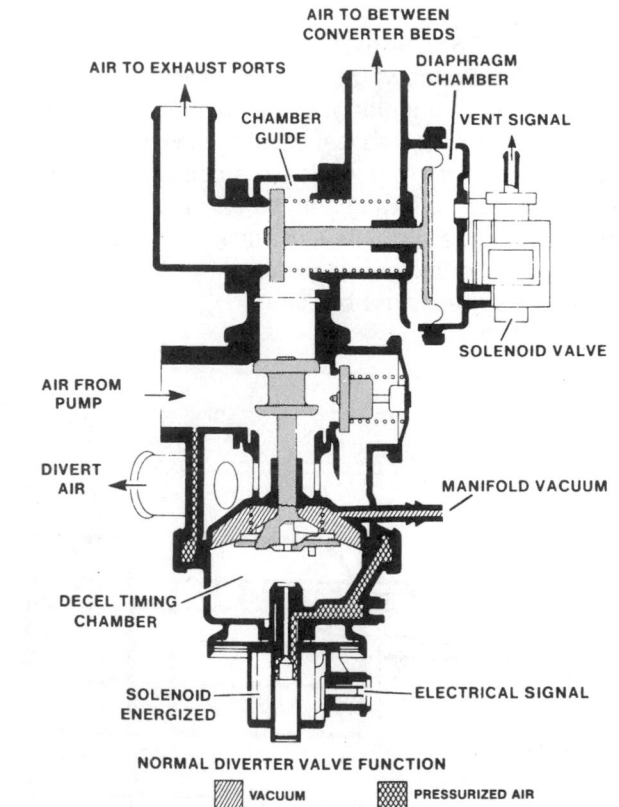

Figure 24-30. This air control valve is in divert mode. It is controlled both by vacuum and electrical signals. Note the exhaust port and converter air outlets. (Chevrolet)

valves. See **Figure 24-31.** This system is called the **pulse air injection system.** Another adaptation of the pulse principle is illustrated in **Figure 24-32.** The crankcase area of the number three engine cylinder is baffled so that the reciprocating action of the piston causes pressure pulsations. These pulsations cause the diaphragm in the pulse air feeder to move up and down. This action pulls air in from

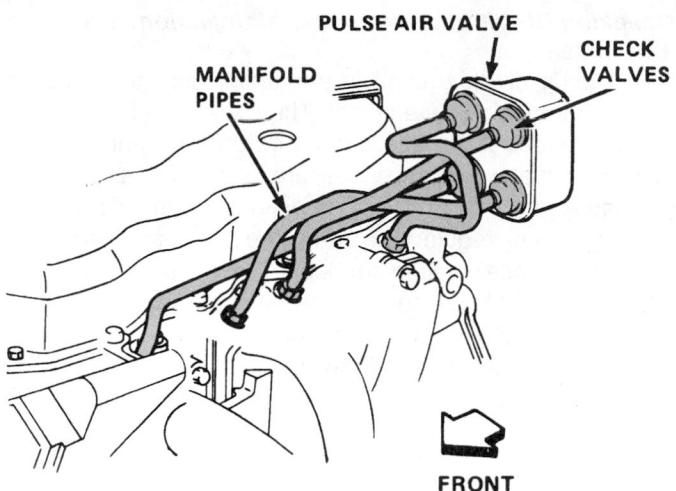

Figure 24-31. Air injection system using the pulse principle. Pulses in exhaust pull air in through check valves in small gulps. (GMC)

the air cleaner and then forces it out and on to the converter area. Study the system construction. Note the oil drain line that allows any oil collected in the pulse air feeder to return to the pan sump.

Air Injection System Service

The injection system is relatively trouble free and will require little service during its life. The air pump has sealed bearings, so periodic maintenance is not required. Valves and other parts are designed to be maintenance free. Some maintenance and checking procedures are given below.

Note: The engine should be brought to operating temperature before conducting air injection system tests.

Air Cleaner and Drive Belt Service

When the air pump intake is by way of the carburetor air cleaner, normal cleaner maintenance schedules should be followed. When a separate filter is used, replace the filter at recommended intervals. If the vehicle is operated in severe conditions, change it more often. When installing a new filter, wipe off filter body and air horn assembly.

Drive belt tension is important and should be as specified. A loose belt will reduce pump efficiency. A tight belt will cause premature wear of the pump bearings. When adjusting the belt, avoid prying on the pump housing. Pull on the pump with your hand only or use a built-in adjustment slot or pin where provided. Use a gauge to tension the belt properly.

Checking Pump Operation

To check the pump for operation, remove the outlet hose at the pump and start the engine. A discharge of air at the pump outlet should be evident. A special low pressure gauge may be used to check pump pressure. Pressure will be about 1 psi (6.9 kPa). If the pump is not producing sufficient pressure, check the air filter for clogging. When difficulty is experienced with the pump relief valve, remove the pump and install a new valve. If a pump seems noisy, remove the drive belt and retest. Keep in mind that air pumps are not completely silent even when in perfect condition.

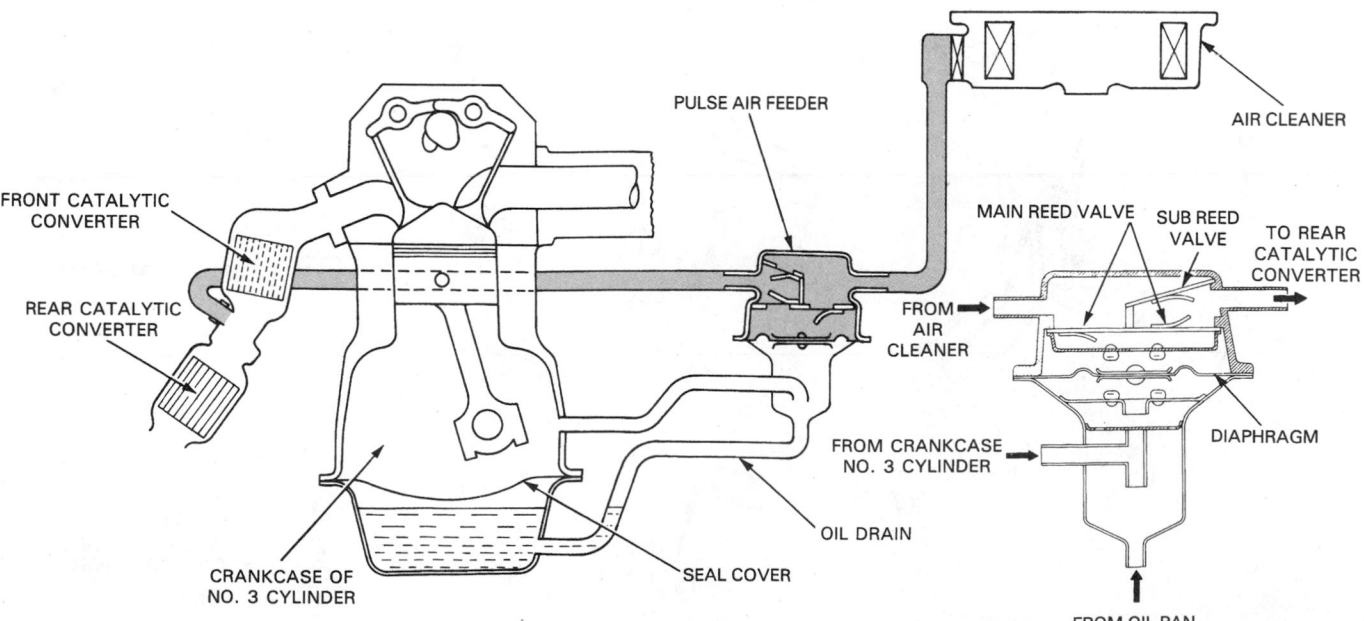

Figure 24-32. Another system using the pulse principle. In this case, pulses are formed in the number three cylinder crankcase area. Piston movement in this baffled area causes pulse in crankcase pressure that operates pulse air feeder. Feeder, much like action of fuel pump, pumps air from cleaner into exhaust stream. (Chrysler)

Testing the Check and Diverter Valves

Remove the hose from the valve. Start the engine and operate at 1500 RPM. There should be no sign of exhaust leakage. The valve may flutter when the engine is idled, this condition is normal. With the engine off, use a thin instrument to press against the valve plate. It should open readily and return to its original position when released. Check both valves on V-type engines. Replace as needed. Check lines (especially vacuum signal line) for kinks, pinches, or leaks. Remove the vacuum signal line at the diverter valve. A vacuum signal must be present with the engine running. With the engine running at idle, no air should be diverted. When the throttle is opened up and then quickly released, a sudden gust of air should be discharged into the atmosphere. If the diverter valve is defective, replace it.

> **Caution: Do not try to clean diverter valves or check valves by using compressed air. This can ruin the valve. If dirty, flush the valve with solvent and shake dry.**

Checking Distribution Manifold, Air Injection Tubes and Hoses

The distribution manifold and air injection tubes do not require periodic maintenance. They are usually made of stainless steel. If the injection tubes become burned, they may be replaced. If the tubes are clogged, they may be cleaned with a wire brush. If the distribution manifold needs cleaning, use regular cleaning methods and solvents. Check the hose system for loose connections, kinks, or other damage. Hoses should also be checked for leaks and possible restrictions. Repair or replace as needed. Typical hose routing is pictured in **Figures 24-33.** Soapy water may be placed on the hose or hose connections. An air leak will cause bubbles to form.

Catalytic Converter

To further reduce exhaust emissions, a great number of vehicles are equipped with a *catalytic converter.* The catalytic converter contain substances called *catalysts* that

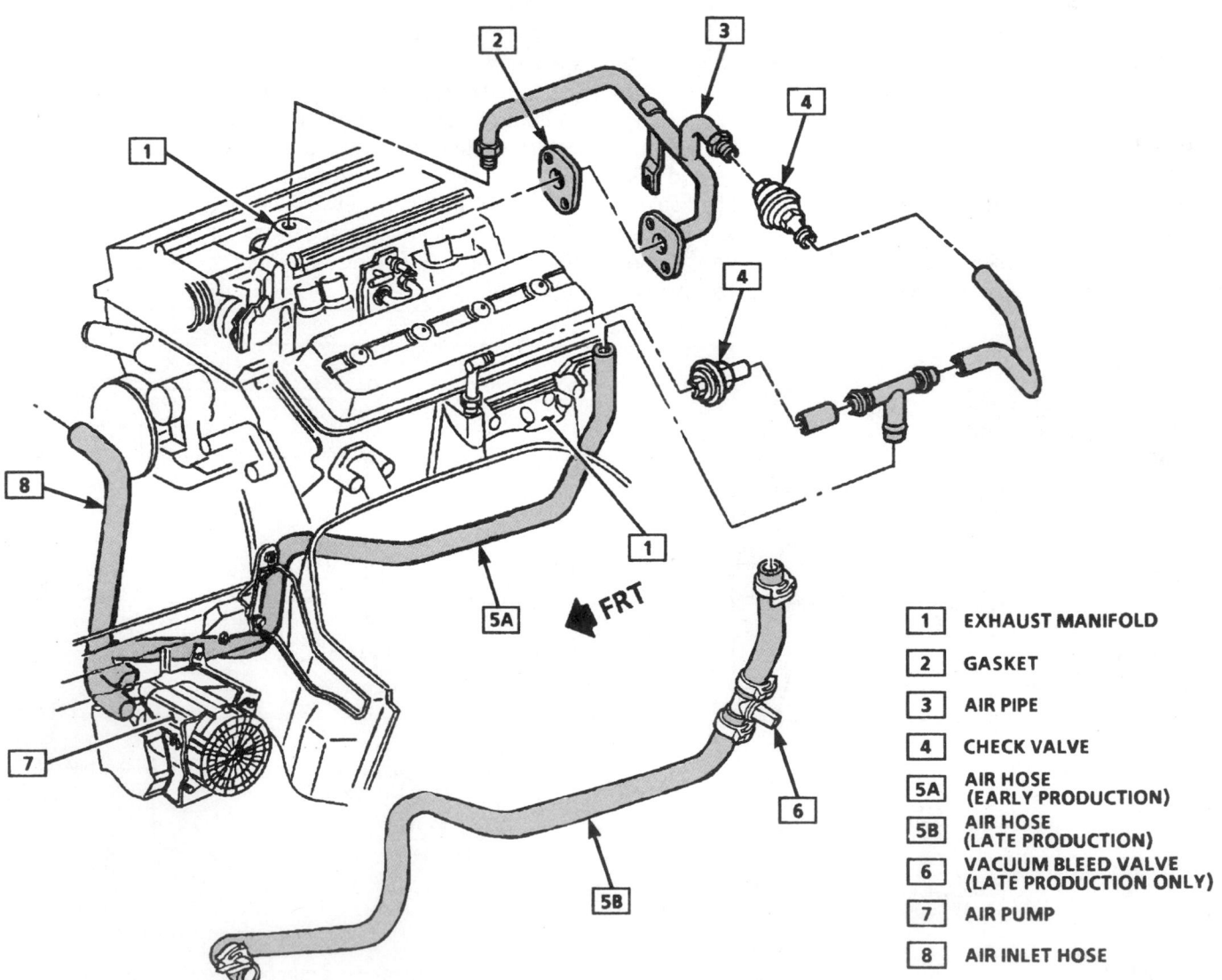

1	EXHAUST MANIFOLD
2	GASKET
3	AIR PIPE
4	CHECK VALVE
5A	AIR HOSE (EARLY PRODUCTION)
5B	AIR HOSE (LATE PRODUCTION)
6	VACUUM BLEED VALVE (LATE PRODUCTION ONLY)
7	AIR PUMP
8	AIR INLET HOSE

Figure 24-33. One AIR system showing hose and tube routing. This system uses an electric air pump which is turned on and off by the electronic control module (ECM) which is not shown. (Chevrolet)

cause chemical changes in other substances without themselves being changed. The catalysts are usually the elements **platinum** and **palladium,** which convert hydrocarbons (HC) and carbon monoxide (CO) into carbon dioxide (CO_2) and water (H_2O). Oxides of nitrogen (NO_x) are also lowered in converters containing the element **rhodium** as one of the catalyst agents.

Some vehicles use a single converter while others employ a smaller unit close to the exhaust manifold, **Figure 24-34.** This unit starts the reaction and heats up the exhaust. A larger downstream converter continues and completes the burning and reduction process. This type is referred to as a two-stage converter. Air may also be injected into the exhaust between the two converters or into the converter itself. See **Figures 24-35** and **24-36.**

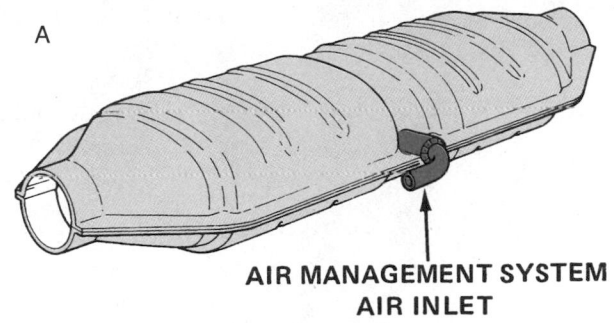

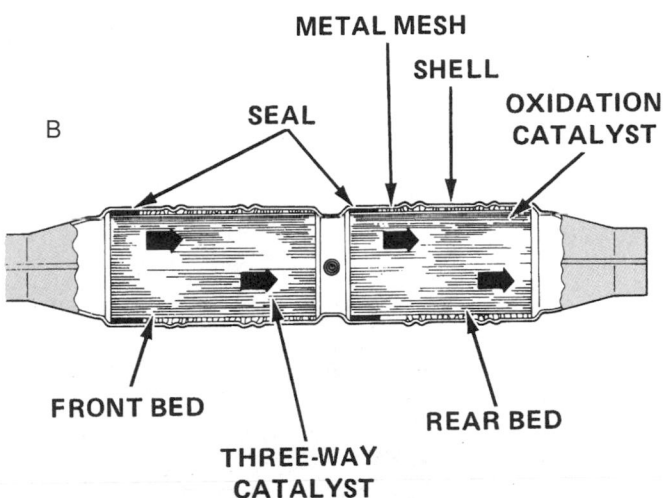

Figure 24-36. As the exhaust gases pass through the converter catalyst sections, the sudden increase in temperature changes the hydrocarbons and carbon monoxide into water and carbon dioxide. A—Air entering the mixing chamber provides additional air for the oxidizing (burning) process. B—This converter uses two separate catalyst beds that are separated by the mixing chamber. (Pontiac)

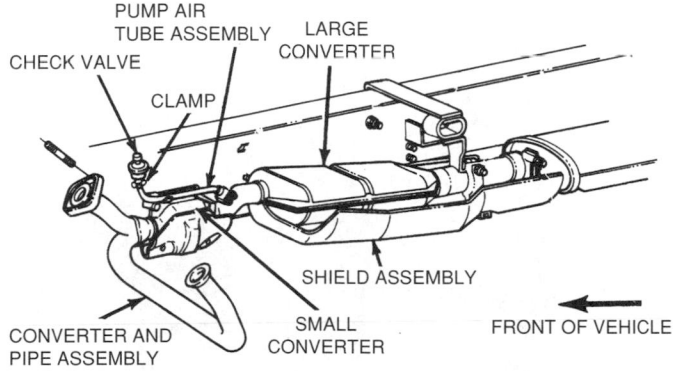

Figure 24-34. Dual converter setup. Note small converter close to exhaust manifold connecting pipes. Pump air is fed into exhaust pipe connecting small and large converters. (Ford)

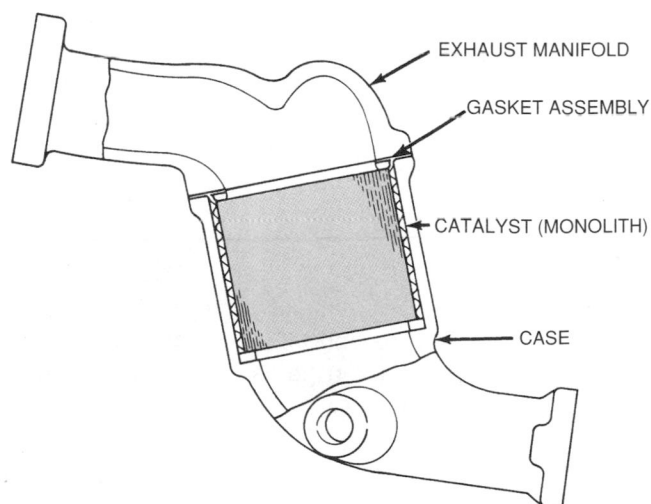

Figure 24-35. This Mini-type converter is mounted near end of exhaust manifold. A larger converter will be used further downstream. (Chrysler)

Converter Construction

A catalytic converter basically consists of a stainless steel shell, a catalyst coated core, and exterior insulation and shielding. Stainless steel is used because converter temperatures can exceed 1,600°F (861°C). This high heat

level also requires the use of insulation and shielding to protect the underside of the vehicle and the ground beneath it.

The converter core is made in one of two ways. One technique employs a great number of porous **ceramic pellets,** or beads, about an eighth of an inch in diameter. The pellets are thinly coated with a mixture of aluminum oxide, followed by a coating of platinum (70%) and palladium (30%). The coated pellets are placed in a perforated container located inside the converter shell, **Figure 24-37. Figure 24-38** illustrates a typical dual bed (layer), pellet type catalytic converter. The other method of construction uses a single **honeycomb ceramic core** coated with aluminum oxide. The aluminum oxide is further coated with a platinum and palladium mixture. The core is separated and supported by a corrugated wire mesh. This assembly is then secured in the converter shell. See **Figure 24-39.** Some converters also have a separate section containing rhodium in addition to the regular platinum and palladium.

How a Catalytic Converter Works

A catalyst is a substance (platinum, palladium, or rhodium in this case) that will cause an increase in the rate of a chemical reaction. Yet, it will not be consumed

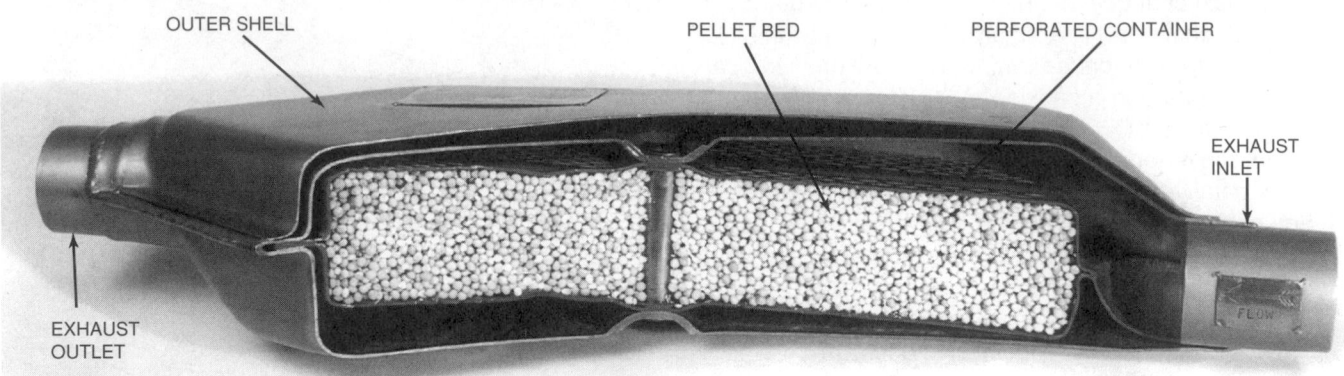

Figure 24-37. A cutaway of a single bed, pellet type, catalytic converter. (Automotive Products, Inc.)

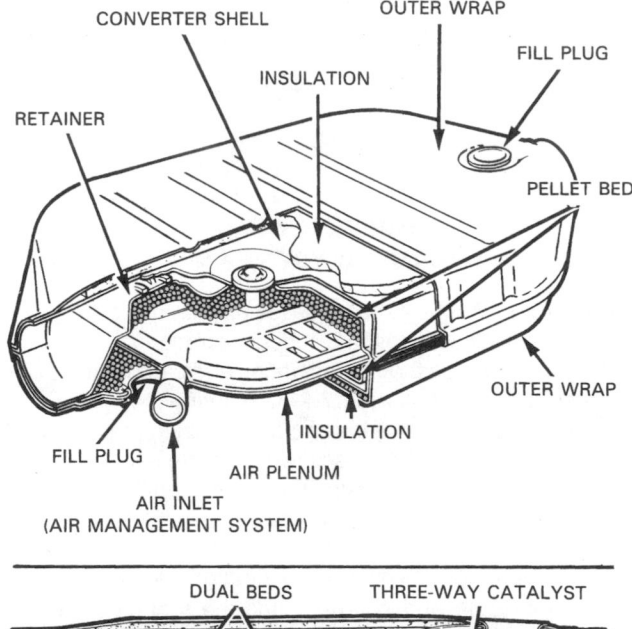

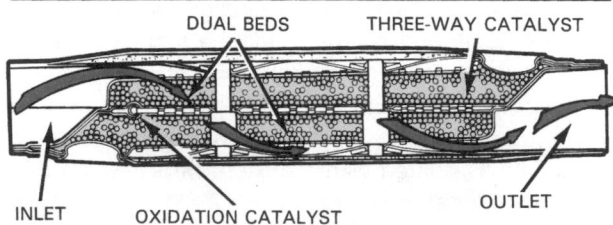

Figure 24-38. Catalytic converter using a dual bed, pellet type catalyst. Study exhaust flow. (Cadillac)

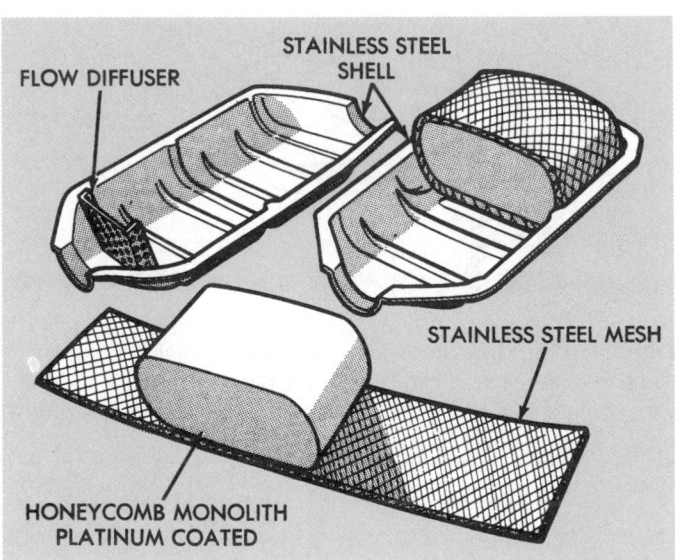

Figure 24-39. This catalytic converter uses a honeycomb monolith type catalyst. (Chrysler)

or permanently altered by the reaction. The converter is inserted into the exhaust system between the exhaust manifold and muffler. As hot exhaust gases pass through the converter, they come into contact with the catalyst coating on the ceramic pellets or ceramic core, depending on construction. The catalyst causes a chemical reaction which changes the hydrocarbons and carbon monoxide into harmless water vapor and carbon dioxide. Converters containing rhodium also reduce the amount of oxides of nitrogen, bonding the oxygen to carbon to form carbon dioxide and allowing the nitrogen to return to its normal state, uncombined with any other element.

Unleaded Fuel

Even if leaded gas is available in your area, it should never be used in a vehicle equipped with a catalytic converter. Using leaded gas will cause a coating to form over the catalytic surfaces and can render the catalyst inert. A lead-damaged converter can soon clog, resulting in excessive exhaust system back pressure, engine damage, poor performance, and a decrease in gas mileage. Converter equipped vehicles have a small filler neck that requires the use of a special unleaded fuel dispensing nozzle. This is illustrated in **Figure 24-40.**

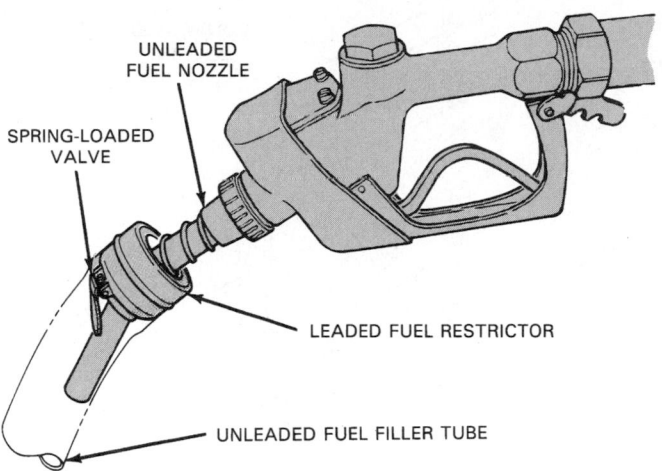

UNLEADED
FUEL NOZZLE

SPRING-LOADED
VALVE

LEADED FUEL RESTRICTOR

UNLEADED FUEL FILLER TUBE

Figure 24-40. To prevent accidental use of leaded fuel in converter equipped vehicles, fuel tank filler opening is equipped with a restrictor. All unleaded fuel pumps will have a special, small size nozzle that will pass through restrictor. (Plymouth)

Other Converter Cautions

Catalytic converters can overheat from a rich mixture. Allowing unburned fuel to enter the converter can cause serious overheating, resulting in a ruined converter, melted floor insulation, fires, and other problems. Causes of a rich mixture include:

- A long-term engine miss due to fouled plugs, loose or defective wires, or a cracked distributor cap.
- Excessive use of the carburetor choke.
- Using carburetor cleaner with the engine running.
- Shorting out plugs during engine testing.
- Excessive cranking tests with the ignition disabled.

Converters can also be damaged by backfiring in the exhaust system. Locate and fix all sources of backfiring, such as crossed wires, sticking or burned valves, carbon tracked distributor cap, or defective diverter valve. Do not operate the engine until it runs out of fuel as this can cause backfiring.

Converter Service

Theoretically, a catalytic converter could last the life of the vehicle since the catalyst is not consumed. Converters are designed to last for a minimum of 50,000 miles (80 000 km), and usually last much longer. This is provided the catalyst is not exposed to lead, overly rich mixtures, or other damage. Initial converter failure can be difficult for the driver to detect. Engine performance is sometimes not affected until the converter becomes clogged. To test converter efficiency, measure the exhaust gas temperature or use an exhaust gas analyzer as explained later in this chapter.

Some converters that are damaged on the bottom may have that area cut away and replaced. A special kit is offered by some manufacturers for this purpose. See **Figure 24-41.** Always be certain that all heat shielding is in good condition and in their proper place. Never spray undercoating on any part of the exhaust system or any portion of the heat shielding. In the event of failure, the pellet type catalytic converter permits removal of the old pellets and insertion of new ones. A special vibrator and vacuum tools are needed. Other types of catalytic converters require total replacement. If the converter is replaced, turn the old converter in to be recycled, do not discard it as scrap.

Converter Pellet Replacement

The pellet type converter has a plug in one end on the bottom. Prior to removal, install a special vacuum pump on the end of the tail pipe, **Figure 24-42.** While the vacuum pump is operating, remove the pellet access plug from the converter bottom. Attach a special vibrator tool to the pellet access hole and shut off the vacuum pump. See **Figure 24-43.** Apply air to the vibrator tool and allow it to run for about ten minutes or until all pellets are removed.

When all of the pellets are removed, empty the vibrator. Install the refill can on the vibrator. Apply shop air (80 psi or 552 kPa minimum) to both the vibrator tool and vacuum pump to draw the pellets into the converter. When the converter is full, remove the vibrator, but leave the vacuum pump running. Cap the pellet access hole with a special plug kit shown in **Figure 24-44** and remove the vacuum

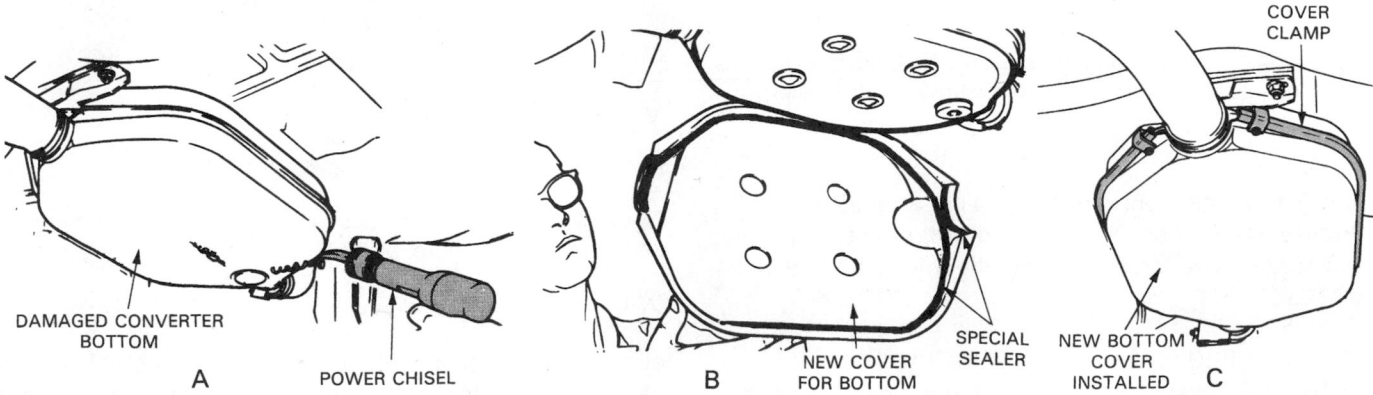

DAMAGED CONVERTER BOTTOM

A   POWER CHISEL

B   NEW COVER FOR BOTTOM   SPECIAL SEALER

COVER CLAMP

NEW BOTTOM COVER INSTALLED   C

Figure 24-41. Replacing a damaged converter bottom shell. A—Removing old bottom using a power chisel. B—Applying sealer to new, replacement bottom. C—Attaching new bottom with special cover clamps. (Pontiac)

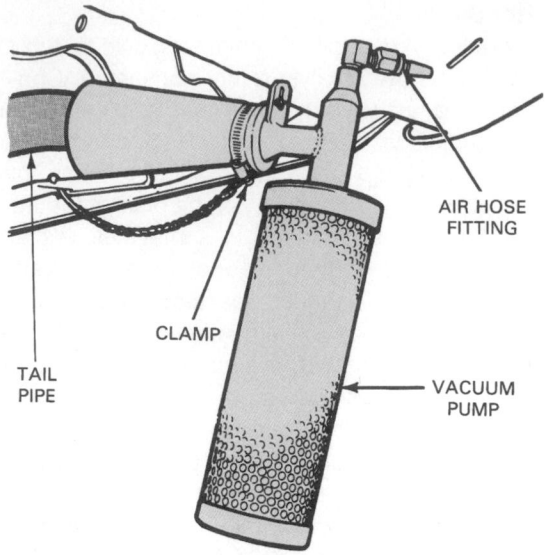

Figure 24-42. A special vacuum pump is used on end of tail pipe as an aid in catalyst pellet replacement. (Chrysler)

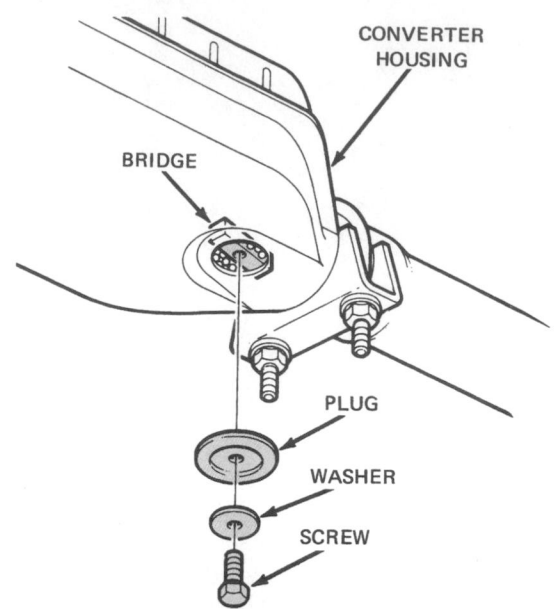

Figure 24-44. Pellets are removed and inserted through this access hole. Shown is a special replacement plug to cap hole following pellet replacement.

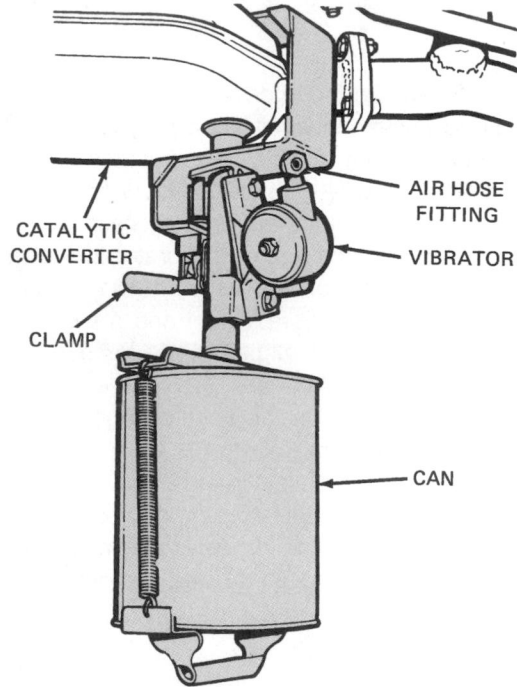

Figure 24-43. Special vibrator tool used to remove and replace pellets in one form of catalytic converter. (Chrysler)

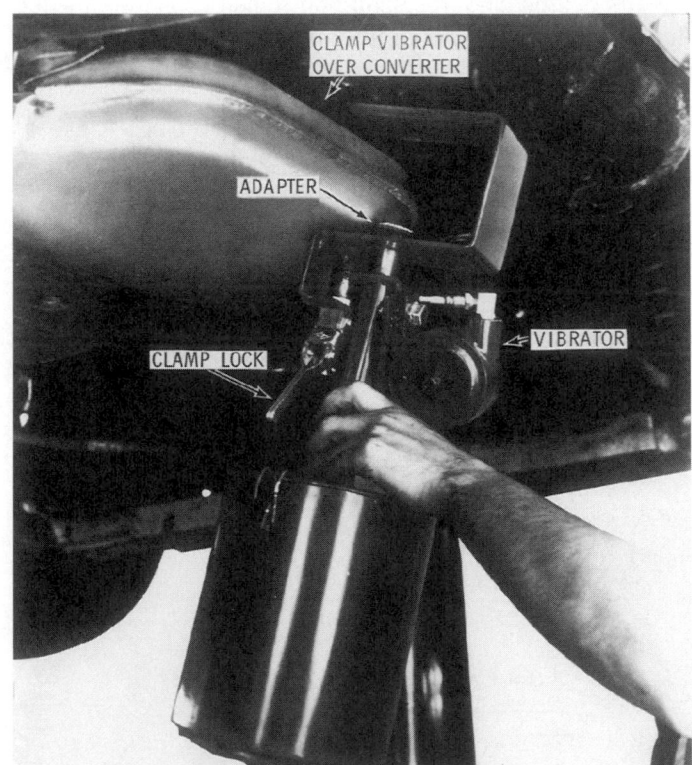

Figure 24-45. A pellet type catalytic converter vibrator tool being installed. (General Motors)

pump. The vibrator tool is pictured in place on the converter in **Figure 24-45.** If any pellets are drawn from the tail pipe, it indicates converter failure and the whole unit must be replaced.

Diesel Engine Catalytic Converters

Several diesel engine manufacturers use an oxidizing-type catalytic converter. This emission control unit is placed in the exhaust system to aid in reducing diesel smoke particulates (tiny particles). The oxidizing converter functions at a normal exhaust system temperature. The oxidation of particles inside the converter does not cause a chemical reaction that raises the temperature. These units are not serviceable. If found to be defective, they must be replaced with the correct type.

Vapor Control Devices

One of the most obvious and easily controlled emission sources is the evaporation of unburned fuel from the gas tank, fuel supply system, and engine crankcase. Controls to reduce the emission of vapors are explained below.

Positive Crankcase Ventilation System Operation

Positive crankcase ventilation utilizes engine vacuum to draw the crankcase fumes back into the cylinders for burning. This system is commonly referred to by the initials *PCV.* The PCV system is one of the oldest emission controls. A malfunctioning PCV system can produce serious engine problems such as rough idle, oil loss, blown engine gaskets, and increased emissions.

Servicing the Positive Crankcase Ventilation System

Proper PCV valve operation is shown in **Figure 24-46.** The PCV system operation should be checked at every oil change. To check system operation, remove the PCV valve from the engine and shake it vigorously. A valve that is not stuck will rattle when shaken. Another way to check is to use a suitable gauge to determine whether air is flowing through the crankcase. Use as recommended by the manufacturer. Manufacturers' recommendations for cleaning or changing the PCV valve range from once each year or 12,000 miles (19 200 km), whichever comes first, to over 100,000 miles (160 000 km). More frequent cleaning or replacement may be required if the engine is badly worn or if it is operating under severe conditions.

To service a PCV system, remove the connecting hose or pipe and the control valve, **Figure 24-47.** Rinse out the PCV system connecting hoses. If the valve can be disassembled for cleaning, carefully take it apart. Sealed valves can often be cleaned by soaking in carburetor cleaner, rinsing, and blowing dry. Some valves contain internal parts that can be ruined by solvents and must be replaced if stuck. Follow the manufacturer's recommendations.

 Caution: Do not interchange PCV valves. PCV valves are matched for the vacuum and flow needs of each engine. Always use a valve designed for the engine being serviced.

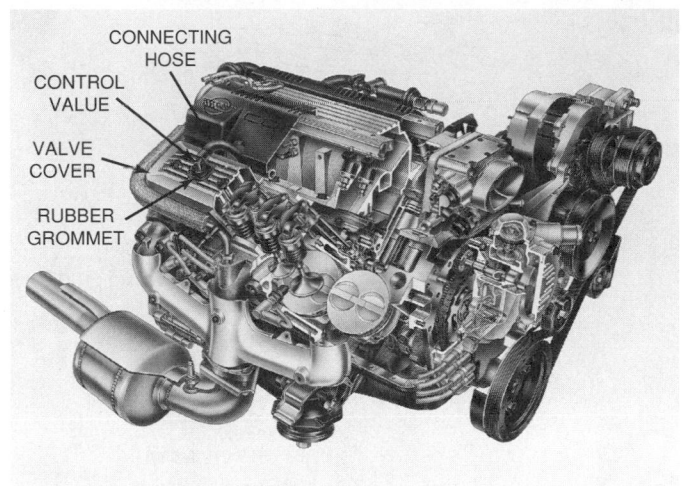

Figure 24-47. Remove hose and control valve to service PCV system. (Chevrolet)

If system is the older open type, rinse and reoil the breather cap. Some caps utilize a dry-type filter element which should not be washed or oiled. Replace a dry filter at recommended intervals or when clogged. On a closed system, clean the hose from the breather or other opening to the air cleaner. If a special mesh is used in the air cleaner for filtering the incoming air to the crankcase, wash and reoil or replace as recommended. A modern closed PCV system is illustrated in **Figure 24-48.** Reinstall the valve so it faces the correct direction. Check for directional marks on the valve. Connect all hoses (make certain that the hoses are open). Start the engine and bring it to operating temperature before checking operation.

 Caution: Do not install a closed-type breather cap on an open PCV system. Internal engine corrosion and heavy sludging will soon follow.

Evaporation Control System

While there are some design variations, most *evaporation control systems* (ECS) use a fuel tank that is not vented to the atmosphere. A pressure-vacuum filler cap, a

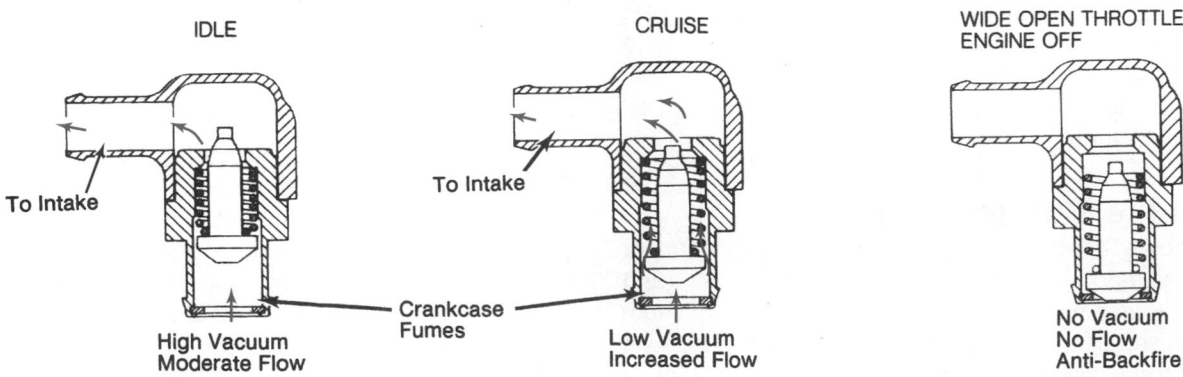

Figure 24-46. Operation of a positive crankcase ventilation (PCV) valve during engine idle, cruise, and wide open throttle. (Sun Electric Corporation)

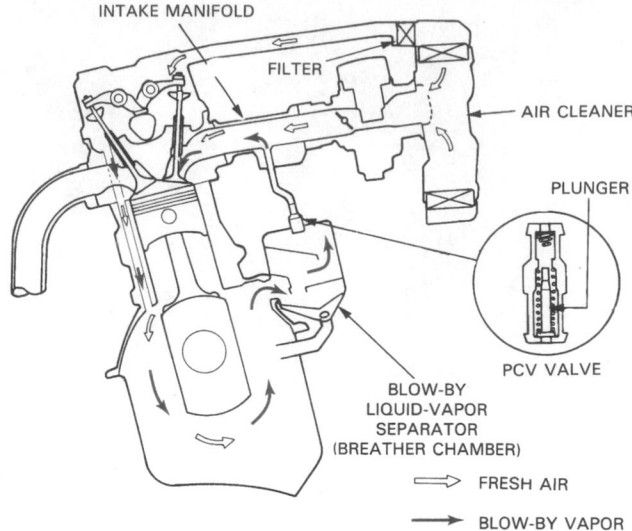

Figure 24-48. Typical, modern *closed* PCV system. Note how PCV valve allows vacuum from intake manifold to draw fresh air through the air filter and into the engine crankcase. This effectively removes harmful blow-by gases from crankcase where they enter intake air for burning in combustion chamber. Note use of liquid-vapor separator to prevent engine oil from being drawn into intake manifold. (Honda)

liquid-vapor separator, a vent line, charcoal canister, and an excess fuel and vapor return line to the tank are also used. Some systems contain a roll-over valve.

The system shown in **Figure 24-49** takes fuel vapors from the tank and carburetor float bowl (when used) and passes them into the charcoal canister. The canister absorbs the vapors, preventing them from entering the atmosphere. When the engine is started, intake manifold vacuum draws the vapors from the canister through the purge line into the intake system. The vapors are then burned in the engine. Note the use of the roll-over valve in the evaporation control system diagram shown in **Figure 24-50.** This valve prevents fuel leakage in the event the vehicle is rolled over.

Airflow through typical two and three tube canister systems is shown in **Figure 24-51.** Study the air flow. Note the air filter in the bottom of each unit. Some canisters have a closed bottom and admit purge air through a tube attached to the interior of the air cleaner, as in **Figure 24-51B.** Service the evaporation control system as indicated by the manufacturer, paying special attention to time and mileage recommendations. The filter located in the carbon canister requires periodic cleaning or replacement as recommended by the manufacturer.

Preventive Maintenance

A properly operating emission control system cannot successfully reduce hydrocarbon, carbon monoxide, and oxides of nitrogen unless the engine is properly maintained. On modern vehicles, emission maintenance usually consists of replacing the spark plugs and filters at certain time or mileage intervals and checking the operation of all emission related engine and drive train components.

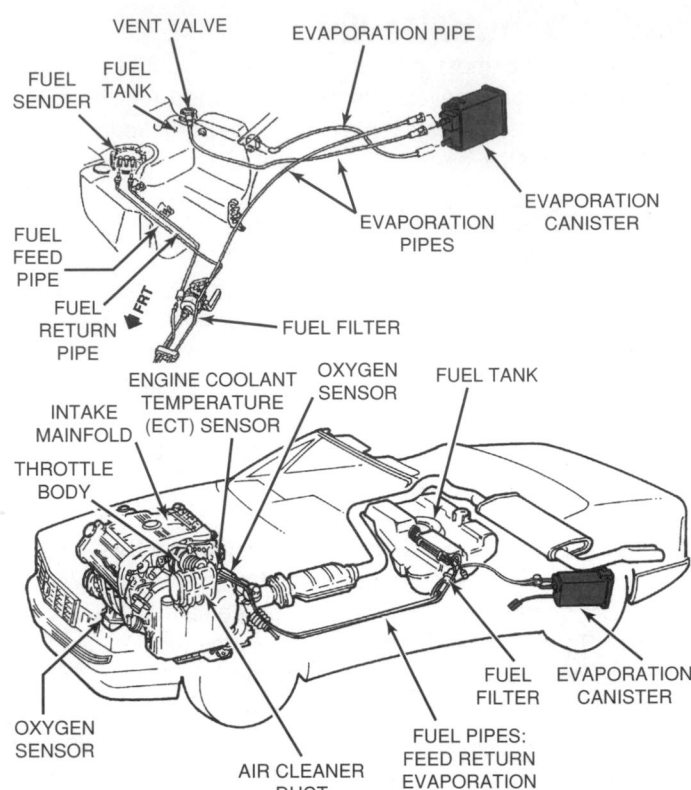

Figure 24-49. One particular evaporation control system layout and the various components. These systems will vary from manufacturer to manufacturer. (Cadillac)

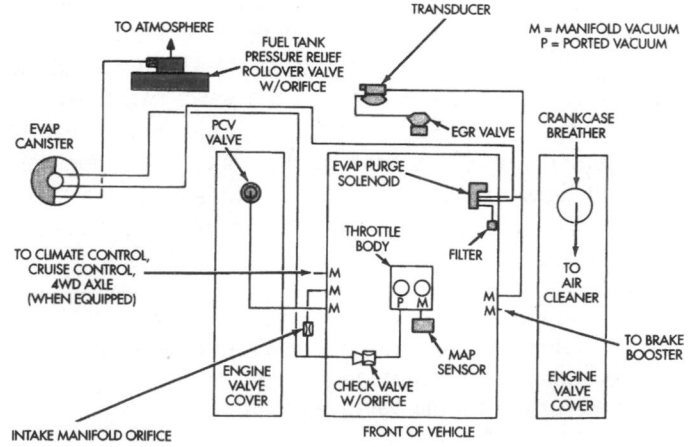

Figure 24-50. A roll-over check valve as used in one evaporative control system. (Dodge)

Checking Emissions Levels

An *exhaust gas analyzer* is used to determine the engine air-fuel ratio and is the only sure method of verifying the overall operation of the emission system. There are several brands of exhaust gas analyzers available. Some analyzers are extremely simple and will only measure carbon monoxide (CO). Other analyzers are extremely sophisticated and will measure four different gases: carbon monoxide (CO), unburned hydrocarbons (HC), oxides of nitrogen (NO_x), and free oxygen (O_2). Therefore, the following information is a general guide only. Always follow the equipment

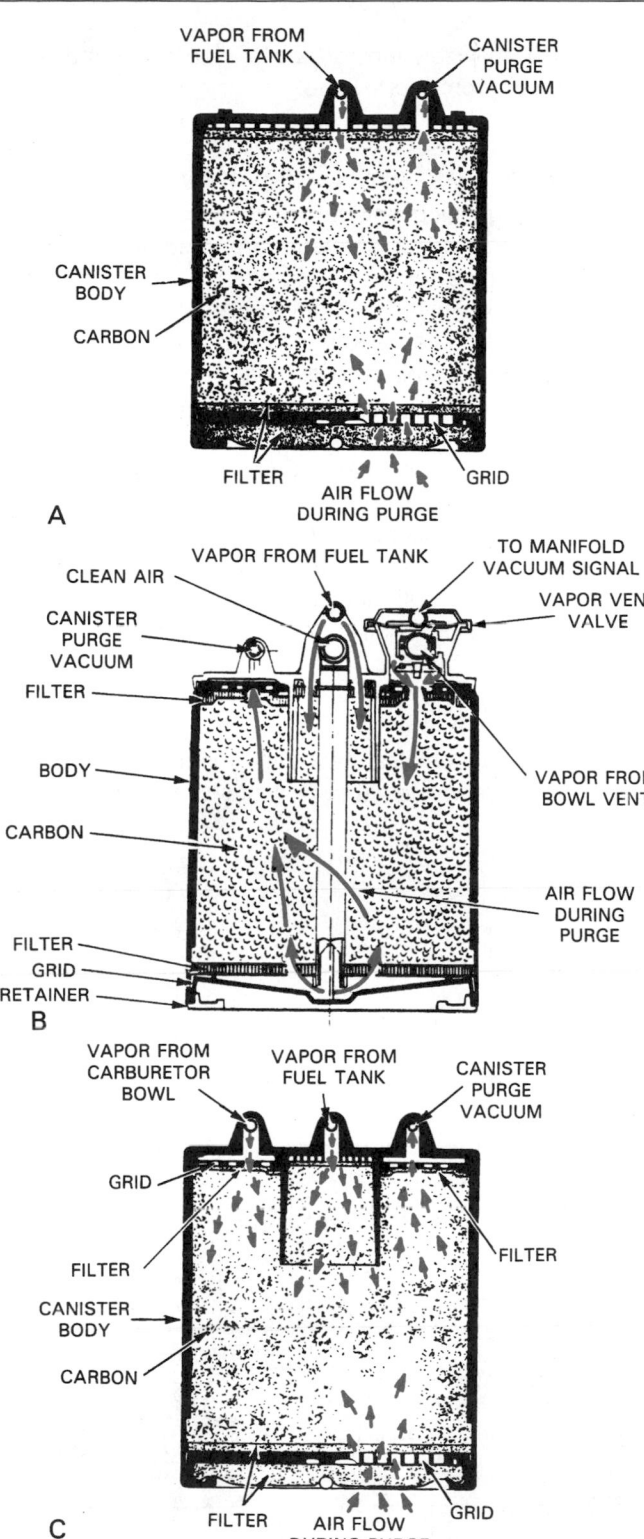

VAPOR FROM
FUEL TANK

CANISTER
PURGE
VACUUM

CANISTER
BODY

CARBON

FILTER

AIR FLOW
DURING PURGE

GRID

A

CLEAN AIR

VAPOR FROM FUEL TANK

TO MANIFOLD
VACUUM SIGNAL

VAPOR VENT
VALVE

CANISTER
PURGE
VACUUM

FILTER

BODY

CARBON

VAPOR FROM
BOWL VENT

FILTER
GRID
RETAINER

AIR FLOW
DURING
PURGE

B

VAPOR FROM
CARBURETOR
BOWL

VAPOR FROM
FUEL TANK

CANISTER
PURGE
VACUUM

GRID

FILTER

CANISTER
BODY

CARBON

FILTER

FILTER

AIR FLOW
DURING PURGE

GRID

C

Figure 24-51. Three types of emission system vapor canisters. A—Two tube, open bottom. B—Three tube, closed bottom. C—Three tube, open bottom. (Pontiac)

and vehicle manufacturers' instructions exactly. First, start and calibrate the exhaust gas analyzer. Start the engine and run it long enough to warm to normal operating temperature. Place the analyzer probe in the vehicle tailpipe and allow the engine to idle while the analyzer readings stabilize. **Figure 24-52** shows one type of exhaust gas analyzer.

 Note: Some areas mandate that certain procedures be used when testing exhaust emissions. You should be aware of and use these procedures along with those recommended by the manufacturer.

OPERATING
INSTRUCTIONS

CONTROL HEAD

PRINT-OUT SLOT

STAINLESS
STEEL PROPE
WITH CORD

REGULATOR

TANK OF
CALIBRATION
GAS

ROLL STAND

Figure 24-52. One type of exhaust gas analyzer. The stainless steel probe is placed in the tailpipe to obtain a reading. Follow equipment manufacturer's operating instructions. (Bear Service Equipment)

Note the air-fuel ratio and compare it with specifications for the engine. On carburetor equipped engines, adjust the idle mixture screws (if possible), as explained in Chapter 21. If the idle is not correct, check for problems in the carburetor, fuel injection system, ignition or compression systems, or emission controls. Once the vehicle air-fuel ratio at idle is correct, allow the exhaust gas analyzer's readings to stabilize.

On vehicles with a carburetor, briefly open the throttle, then allow it to return to idle. Observe the exhaust gas analyzer. The mixture should briefly become much richer, then return to the original settings. This will confirm that the carburetor accelerator pump is working properly. Check emissions levels as necessary at different engine speeds. If the readings are not correct, check for problems in the fuel or ignition systems or in the emission control systems.

If the vehicle is equipped with a computer control system and oxygen sensor, the following checks can be made. Start by creating a rich mixture; this can be done by partially closing the choke plate on a carbureted engine, or briefly throttling (restricting) the air flow into a fuel injected engine. The throttle plate should remain closed; restrict the air flow just enough to create a rich mixture, but do not stall the engine. Do not spray gasoline or carburetor cleaner into the intake to enrich the mixture, as this will overload the oxygen sensor.

When the air flow is restricted, the exhaust gas analyzer should show a momentary rich mixture. Then the engine will begin to lean out as the engine control module compensates for the rich mixture signal from the oxygen sensor. When this check is complete, remove the air flow restriction and operate the engine at high idle for one minute to clear any extra gasoline out of the intake passages. Then allow the exhaust gas analyzer readings to stabilize. Next, create a lean mixture by removing the PCV hose or another vacuum hose. The exhaust gas analyzer should show a momentary lean mixture, then begin to move to the rich position as the control module begins to compensate for the lean signal from the oxygen sensor. When the test is complete, reconnect the hose.

If the exhaust gas analyzer readings indicate that the computer control system is reading the changes in air-fuel ratio and is changing fuel system settings to compensate, the system is in good condition. If the system does not appear to be reacting to air-fuel ratio changes, refer to the vehicle manufacturer's troubleshooting procedures to determine the cause. After completing all needed tests with the exhaust gas analyzer, turn off the engine and remove the analyzer probe from the tailpipe.

Emission System Overview

When diagnosing engine or emission problems, keep in mind that many of the systems are interrelated. A properly running engine requires a careful balancing of all systems. A failure or misadjustment in one system can affect the operation of other systems. Proper emission control diagnosis is impossible unless the engine is in sound mechanical condition and is properly tuned. Always check these areas first.

Use care in diagnosing. Work carefully and follow manufacturer's specifications. Always test vehicle emission levels for compliance with established standards. If diagnostic connectors are employed on the vehicle, use them. Use proper test equipment. **Figure 24-53** shows the various emission control devices as employed by one manufacturer.

Emission Label

All modern vehicles have an underhood *emission information label.* This label provides the technician with

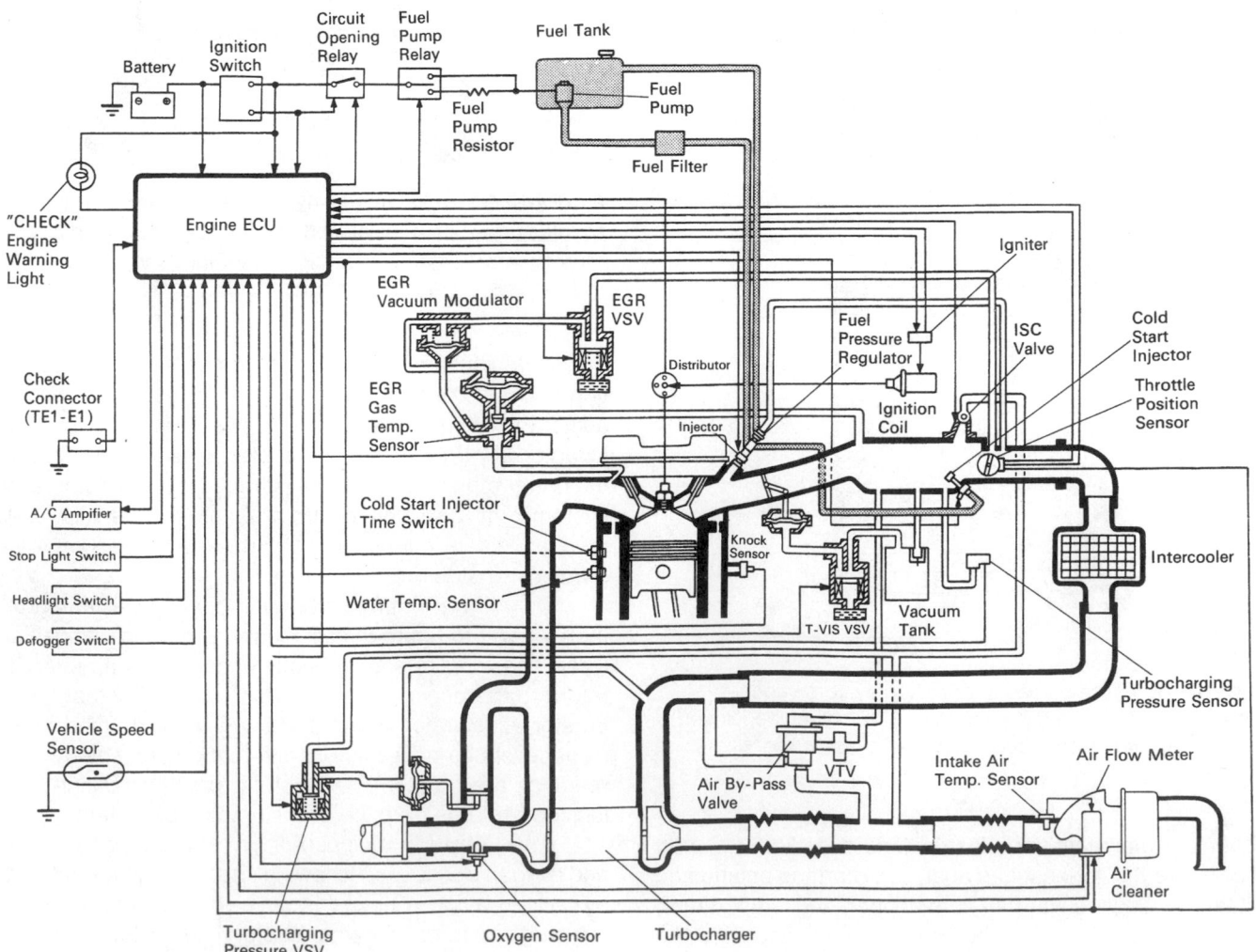

Figure 24-53. Various emission control devices and their locations as used by one manufacturer. (Toyota)

important emission control system specifications for that exact vehicle. Many labels also give specific instructions for setting ignition timing and fuel mixtures as well as correct spark plug and filter part numbers and other service information. Always use and follow the information provided to be certain the vehicle complies with emission standards. A typical emission label is pictured in **Figure 24-54.** Remember that the label is intended for use only with the vehicle on which it is attached. Never remove the label.

Additional Precautions

In addition to the notes and service precautions already discussed, remember the following precautions:

- Do not use an impact wrench to remove or install thermo sensors or thermo switches.
- Never drop vital electrical units such as thermal relays, sensors, etc., on a hard surface. If they are dropped, replace them.
- When separating electrical connectors, apply pressure to the connector body and not to the wires.
- Do not pierce wire insulation.
- Do not bend connector terminals through the careless use of test probes.
- To remove a vacuum line, pull on the end. Never pull in the center of the hose.
- Do not force vacuum hoses over connectors that are too large. This can cause splitting. When using a vacuum gauge, make certain connector does not fit too tightly. This can stretch the hose. When the hose is returned to its own connection, it will leak.
- Never steam clean an engine without first protecting the carburetor, distributor, air pump, EGR vacuum modulator, air filter, etc. Never apply steam directly to any electrical units.
- When possible, always disconnect the battery before testing or making electrical repairs.

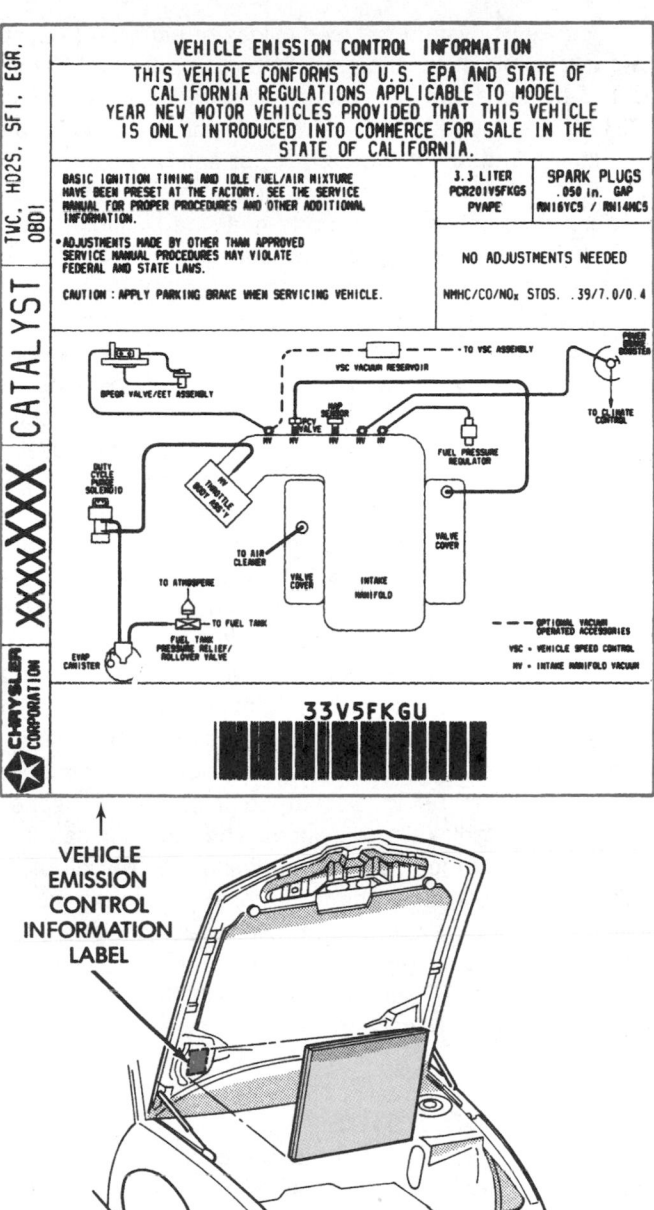

Figure 24-54. A typical, underhood emission control label. Remember to use the information on these labels as they give very specific information for vehicle they are placed on. Do not use this information for any other vehicle, even one of same year and model. Labels will vary depending upon vehicle destination, engine size and type, transmission, fuel system, etc. (Chrysler)

Tech Talk

Several years ago, it was popular to disconnect emission controls. It did not help much, but it was the "in" thing to do. In fact, before emission control laws were tightened, it was possible to advertise that you were in the business of removing emission controls.

Today, however, emission controls are an integral part of the operating system and are controlled by the on-board computer. Taking off the emission controls is not only illegal, but it is usually impossible. No one with any sense would want to anyway. Thanks to the precise control of all engine systems by the computer, new vehicles run smoother, have more power, and get better gas mileage.

What today's technician must learn is not how to bypass emission controls, but how to work on and with them to restore the vehicle to peak performance.

Summary

To reduce emission of hydrocarbons and carbon monoxide, vehicles are equipped with emission controls. Many emissions-related modifications are made to the engine, ignition system, and fuel system. Modern vehicles use leaner fuel mixtures than in the past. Intake air may be heated by a thermostatic air cleaner or early fuel evaporation system.

The EGR system reduces oxides of nitrogen (NO_x) by lowering combustion chamber flame temperature. Various control systems are used to modify the operation of the EGR valve. Closed loop systems monitor the exhaust and alter timing and fuel mixtures to lower emissions.

The air injection system forces fresh air into the exhaust gases in the valve ports near the exhaust valves. This air causes the gases to continue burning, which reduces the hydrocarbon level and changes much of the carbon monoxide into carbon dioxide. The air injection system uses an air pump. The air is filtered with a special filter or is drawn in through the air cleaner. The air is directed into the valve ports by a distribution manifold and injection tubes. A check valve prevents exhaust gases from traveling into the air injection system. A diverter valve is used to prevent backfiring upon sudden closing of the carburetor throttle valve. Catalytic converters are also used in the exhaust system to further lower emissions. They cause a chemical reaction in the exhaust gases, changing then to harmless gases.

To reduce gasoline vapors, all engines are equipped with PCV (Positive Crankcase Ventilation) systems. The PCV system draws the crankcase fumes into the cylinders for burning. The evaporative control system prevents gasoline vapors from being discharged into the atmosphere from the fuel tank or fuel system. The exhaust gas analyzer is the only method of determining whether all of the emission controls are operating properly. In order for the emission control system to function as designed, the engine must be in proper tune and in sound mechanical condition. Emission labels are affixed to the engine compartment of all vehicles to provide emissions-related information.

Know These Terms

Hydrocarbons (HC)
Carbon monoxide (CO)
Oxides of nitrogen (NO_x)
Engine modifications
Engine controls
External cleaning systems
Fuel vapor controls
Carburetor icing
Thermostatic air cleaner
Early fuel evaporation
Vacuum advance restrictor
Exhaust gas recirculation
Ported vacuum
Vacuum override switch
Back pressure transducer
  valve
Negative back pressure
  valve
Integrated electronic EGR
  valve
Digital EGR valve
Closed loop systems
Oxygen sensor

Air injection system
Air injection reactor (AIR)
Thermactor
Air guard
Smog pump
Carbon dioxide (CO_2)
Air pump
Check valve
Diverter valve
Air control valve
Pulse air injection system
Catalytic converter
Catalysts
Platinum
Palladium
Rhodium
Ceramic pellets
Honeycomb ceramic core
Positive crankcase
  ventilation (PCV)
Evaporation control systems
Exhaust gas analyzer
Emissions information label

Review Questions—Chapter 24

Do not write in this book. Write your answers on a separate sheet of paper.

1. Name the three major automotive pollutants (write out in full).

2. Emission controls such as leaner carburetors and EGR valves are considered _____.
   (A) engine modifications and controls
   (B) external cleaning systems
   (C) fuel vapor controls
   (D) All of the above.

3. The EGR valve is operated by _____.
   (A) intake manifold vacuum
   (B) electric solenoids
   (C) exhaust back pressure
   (D) Both A & B

4. In the Air Injector Reactor (AIR) system, the diverter valve is used to prevent _____.
   (A) NO_x formation
   (B) backfiring
   (C) knocking
   (D) dieseling

5. The purpose of the air injection emission control system is to provide extra _____ to help combust unburned hydrocarbons.
   (A) air
   (B) heat
   (C) exhaust gases
   (D) turbulence

6. Air injector pump pressure will be about _____.
   (A) 1 psi (6.9 kPa)
   (B) 2 psi (13.8 kPa)
   (C) 3 psi (20.7 kPa)
   (D) 4 psi (27.6 kPa)

7. Why must catalytic converters have heat shielding?

8. The oxygen sensor is mounted in the _____.
   (A) air horn
   (B) intake manifold
   (C) exhaust system
   (D) radiator

9. A common cause of catalytic converter overheating is a _____.
   (A) lean mixture
   (B) rich mixture
   (C) backfire
   (D) vacuum leak

10. Technician A says that the simplest exhaust gas analyzer will measure HC levels. Technician B says that newer exhaust gas analyzers can measure O_2 levels. Who is right?
    (A) A only.
    (B) B only.
    (C) Both A & B.
    (D) Neither A nor B.

ASE-Type Questions

1. Heating the incoming air reduces the chances of
_____.
   (A) NO$_x$ formation
   (B) carburetor icing
   (C) rich idle mixtures
   (D) knocking

2. Technician A says that the air injector reactor pump can be rebuilt. Technician B says that a check valve prevents pump air from entering the exhaust manifold. Who is right?
   (A) A only.
   (B) B only.
   (C) Both A & B.
   (D) Neither A nor B.

3. The PCV system draws fumes from the _____ back into the cylinders for burning.
   (A) exhaust manifold
   (B) crankcase
   (C) intake manifold
   (D) carbon canister

4. Technician A says that the catalyst in some converters can be replaced. Technician B says that the air pump output is sometimes directed to the catalytic converter. Who is right?
   (A) A only.
   (B) B only.
   (C) Both A & B.
   (D) Neither A nor B.

5. All of the following statements about the air control valve are true, EXCEPT:
   (A) the air control valve can perform functions of a diverter valve.
   (B) the valve can channel pump output air to the exhaust manifold.
   (C) the valve can channel pump output air to the EGR valve.
   (D) the valve channels air output according to engine temperature.

6. A clogged converter can cause _____.
   (A) engine damage
   (B) poor performance
   (C) low gas mileage
   (D) All of the above.

7. The carbon canister holds all of the following, EXCEPT:
   (A) unburned hydrocarbons.
   (B) oxides of nitrogen.
   (C) evaporated fuel.
   (D) raw gasoline.

8. Technician A says that all PCV valves can be disassembled and cleaned. Technician B says that all PCV valves can be soaked in solvent to clean them. Who is right?
   (A) A only.
   (B) B only.
   (C) Both A & B.
   (D) Neither A nor B.

9. Technician A says that when a thermal sensor or thermal switch receives a sharp jolt by dropping on a hard surface, it should be replaced. Technician B says that when a thermal sensor or thermal switch receives a sharp jolt, it should be carefully inspected before installation. Who is right?
   (A) A only.
   (B) B only.
   (C) Both A & B.
   (D) Neither A nor B.

10. All of the following are common ways for unburned hydrocarbons to exit the vehicle, EXCEPT:
    (A) filler cap.
    (B) carburetor.
    (C) crankcase.
    (D) exhaust pipe.

Suggested Activities

1. Inspect a vehicle and locate the emissions systems components. List all components and give their function. Determine whether the vehicle has any internal emission controls, such as engine modifications.

2. Locate an emissions label on a late-model vehicle. Identify and study the instructions for setting timing or idle. Explain to your classmates what the information means.

3. Obtain a copy of the latest Environmental Protection Agency (EPA) publications on air pollution, fuel mileage, and oxygenated gasoline. The EPA's phone number is listed in your local telephone book. Review the materials and write a short report summarizing them.

4. Check the operation of a vehicle's thermostatic air cleaner by following the instructions given in the appropriate service manual.

Cutaway of a late-model automobile. Computers are used to control and monitor many systems in this vehicle. (Cadillac)

25

Computer System Service

After studying this chapter, you will be able to:
- Explain engine computer control system operation.
- Define control loops.
- Explain the function and operation of input sensors.
- Explain the function and operation of output actuators.
- Access computer control system self-diagnostic systems.
- Troubleshoot electronic control system problems.
- Troubleshoot and service sensors, actuators, and electronic control units.

The computer control systems found in modern vehicles are networks of miniaturized solid state electronic components. The untrained technician cannot service vehicles equipped with these systems based on mechanical aptitude alone. The most important tool for troubleshooting and servicing computer control systems is a thorough understanding of how they operate.

This chapter will provide the general theory necessary to tackle computer control system problems. It covers the operation, diagnosis, and service of the most common computer control system components. Some of the typical computer control system components used in modern vehicles are illustrated in **Figure 25-1.**

 Note: This chapter is designed to be used as a supplement to the manufacturer's service manual when troubleshooting and servicing computer systems. It is not intended to replace the service manual. Computer control systems vary from manufacturer to manufacturer. Always consult the appropriate manual before attempting to service a computer system. Incorrect testing procedures can destroy delicate computer system components.

The Need for Computers

The use of computers in the automotive industry was prompted by governmental regulations requiring manufacturers to build fuel efficient vehicles that produced fewer exhaust emissions. Computerized engine control systems offered accurate and instantaneous control over the fuel, ignition, and emission systems. These control systems provided better gas mileage, lower exhaust emissions, and smoother operation than their mechanical predecessors. Most components in a computerized system are not subject to physical wear and, therefore, do not require periodic replacement or adjustment.

In addition to precisely controlling engine operating conditions, computers are used to govern various systems in today's automobiles and light trucks, including the brake system, the occupant restraint (air bag) system, and the suspension system.

Computer Control System Components

In order to control operating conditions within an engine, the computer control system must be able to monitor and alter these conditions, **Figure 25-2.** To accomplish this, computer control systems use the following classes of components:

- **Sensors**—Convert physical conditions to electrical input signals.
- **Electronic control unit**—Processes input signals and supplies output data.
- **Output actuators**—Convert output signals into physical actions.

Computer Control System Stages

Computer control systems can be broken down into three stages of operation:

- Input stage.
- Processing stage.
- Output stage.

Figure 25-3 shows these three stages. Note that these three stages correspond to the three classes of computer control system components. These stages are repeated thousands of times each second during computer control system operation.

Input Stage

The **input stage** is the first step in the computer control process. During this stage, input sensors monitor various engine and vehicle operating conditions, as well as outside (ambient) air conditions. They then produce

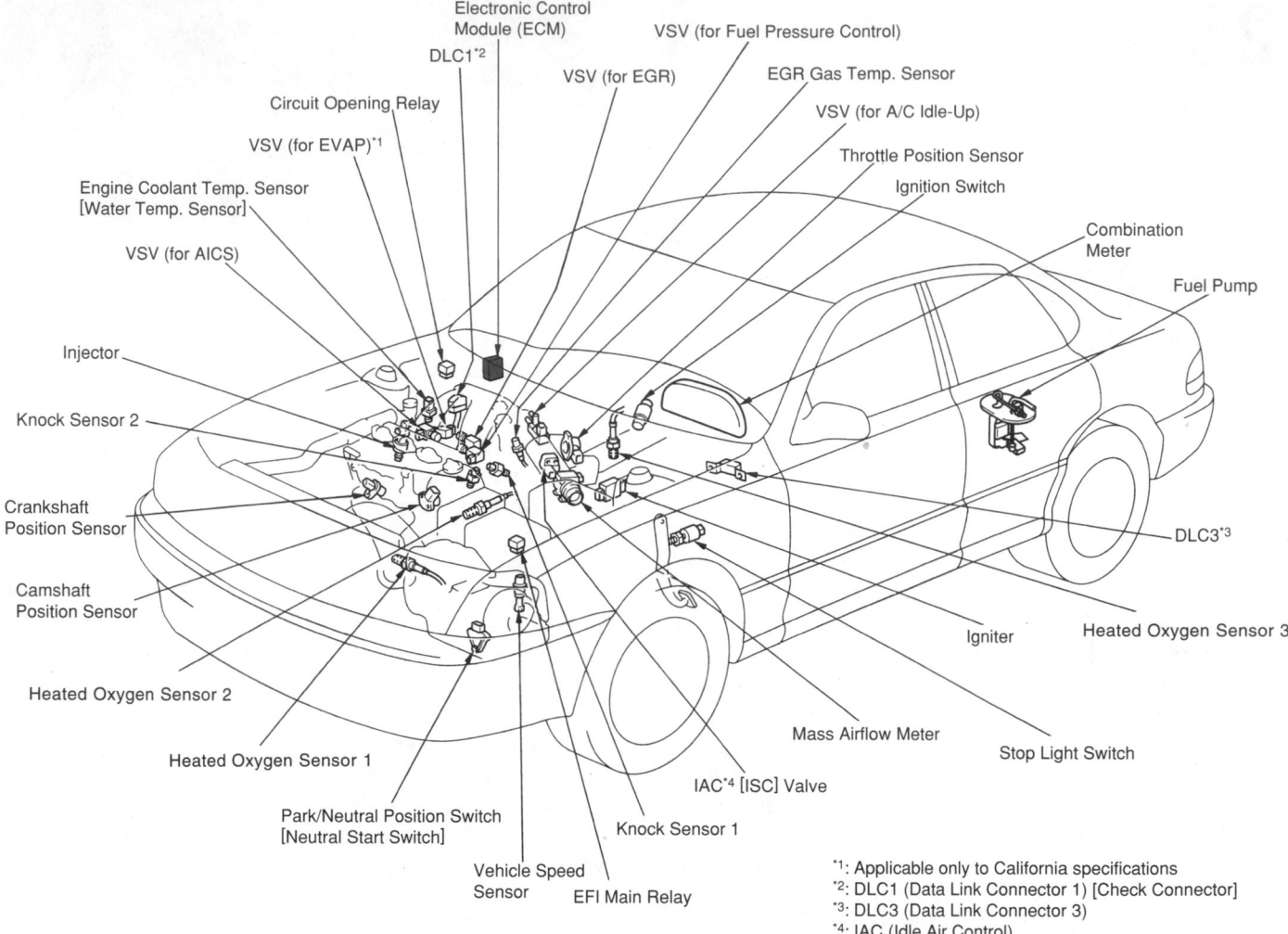

Figure 25-1. Modern computer control systems use several common components. Note the location of the various parts. (Toyota)

electrical signals representing these conditions. These electrical signals are then sent to the electronic control unit. Note that some inputs, such as alternator output voltage, are already electrical signals and, therefore, do not require a sensor.

Processing Stage

During the *processing stage,* the electronic control unit, or ECU, analyzes the input signals from the sensors. It uses this input information to decide if an adjustment needs to be made in the monitored operating system. If an adjustment is required, the decision of how it will be made occurs in the processing stage.

Output Stage

During the *output stage,* the computer carries out the decisions made in the processing stage. Electrical signals representing these decisions are sent to output devices called output actuators. The output actuators make physical adjustments to change engine operating conditions.

Control Loop Operation

The process by which the computer control system receives inputs from the sensors, processes these inputs,

and sends output signals, is called the *control loop.* The system can be in one of two loop modes: *closed loop* or *open loop.* When the system is operating in the closed loop state, **Figure 25-4A,** the inputs, processing, and outputs combine to form a complete circle, or loop. If this cycle is broken, the system goes into the open loop state. When in open loop, the computer does not control operating conditions within a vehicle. Instead, the vehicle operates on pre-set basic settings, **Figure 25-4B.** Most computer systems will operate in closed loop mode except when engine coolant or exhaust gas temperatures are low or when a system component is defective.

Computerized Engine Control Components

Sensors, output actuators, and control units are used to govern many systems in a vehicle. For clarity, however, the following sections on the operation, troubleshooting, and service of computer system components will emphasize the actuators, sensors, and control units that affect engine operating conditions. Air bag systems, anti-lock brake systems, and computerized suspension systems will be covered in detail in other chapters.

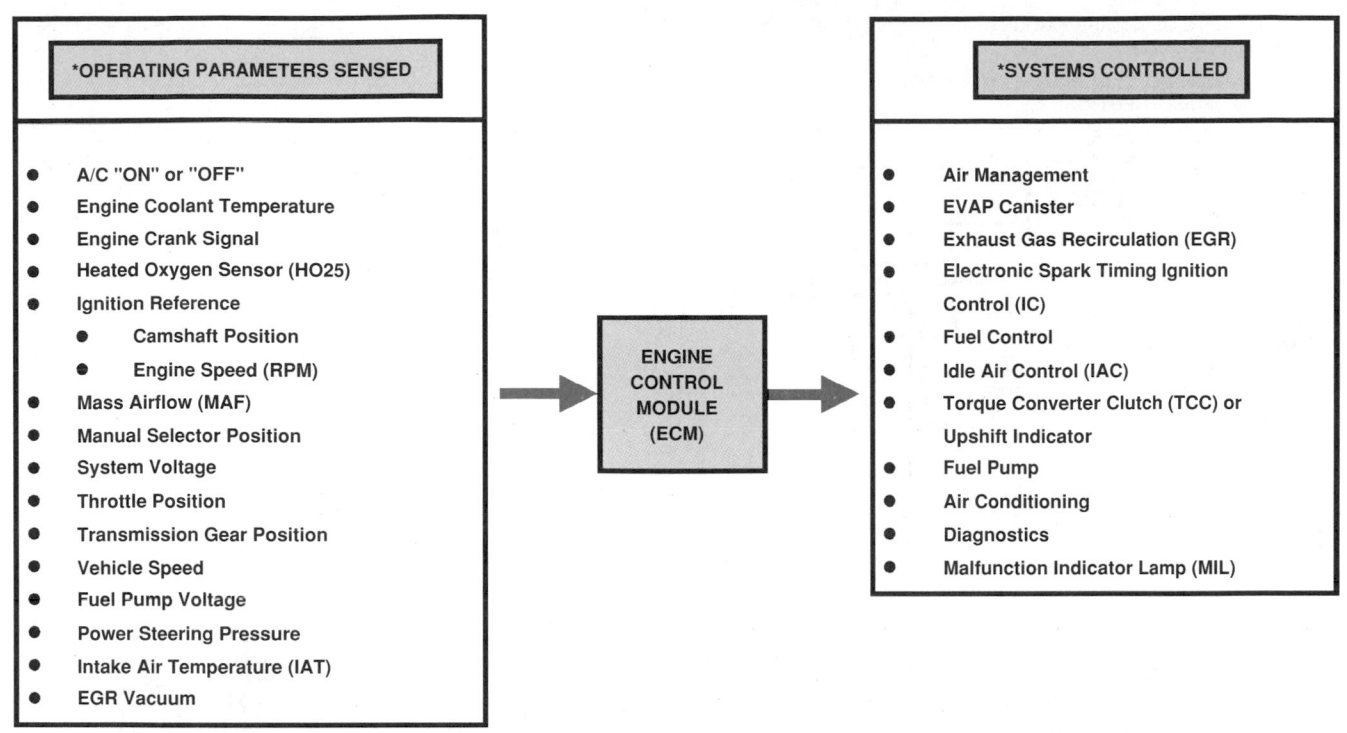

Figure 25-2. Computer systems monitor and control many systems throughout the automobile. The electronic control unit analyzes signals that represent operating parameters and adjusts operating systems based on these signals. (Geo)

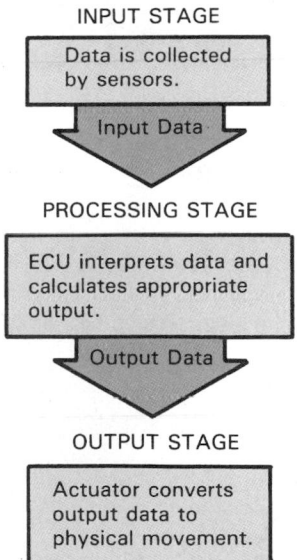

Figure 25-3. Computer control system operation occurs in specific stages. These stages are repeated constantly during system operation.

Sensors

Sensors are used to monitor various operating conditions throughout the engine and vehicle. Many technicians refer to sensors as transducers. A transducer can be defined as a device that converts an input to an output of a different form. Sensors convert physical conditions into electrical signals. The electronic control unit uses sensor signals to analyze operating conditions.

Signal-Producing Sensors

In response to specific operating conditions, some sensors generate a voltage signal, **Figure 25-5.** This signal is sent to the electronic control unit for processing. Typical *signal-producing sensors* include:

*   Oxygen sensors.
*   Engine speed and position sensors.
*   Detonation sensors.

Oxygen Sensor

The *oxygen sensor* (O_2 sensor) is one of the most important sensors in the computer control system, **Figure 25-6.** It is used to monitor the amount of oxygen in the engine's exhaust gas and is usually located in the exhaust manifold or near the catalytic converter.

Most oxygen sensors operate like a small, variable battery. Differences in oxygen content between the sensor's inner and outer surfaces cause an internal chemical reaction that generates a small voltage signal that is transmitted to the electronic control unit. As the oxygen content of the exhaust gas changes, the sensor's voltage signal also changes. The electronic control unit uses information from the oxygen sensor to monitor and control the engine's air-fuel ratio. A faulty oxygen sensor can cause an excessively rich or lean fuel mixture.

Many computer control systems rely on the oxygen sensor to determine whether the system is in open or closed loop operation. If the sensor's temperature is below approximately 600°F (315°C), it will not produce a signal

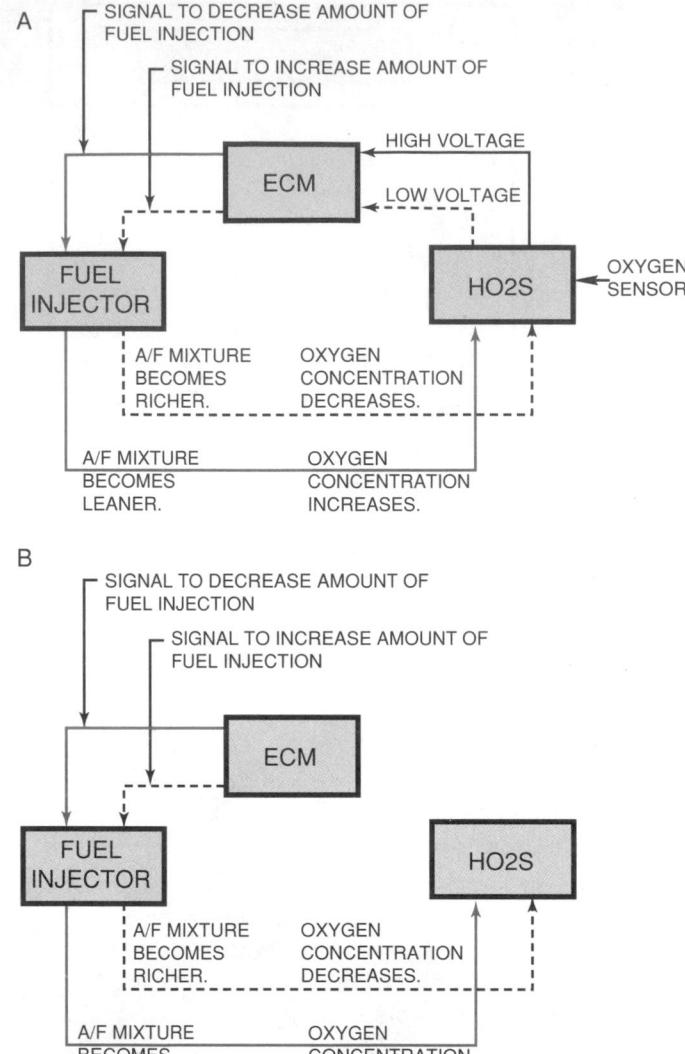

A

SIGNAL TO DECREASE AMOUNT OF
FUEL INJECTION

SIGNAL TO INCREASE AMOUNT OF
FUEL INJECTION

HIGH VOLTAGE

ECM

LOW VOLTAGE

FUEL
INJECTOR

HO2S

OXYGEN
SENSOR

A/F MIXTURE
BECOMES
RICHER.

OXYGEN
CONCENTRATION
DECREASES.

A/F MIXTURE
BECOMES
LEANER.

OXYGEN
CONCENTRATION
INCREASES.

B

SIGNAL TO DECREASE AMOUNT OF
FUEL INJECTION

SIGNAL TO INCREASE AMOUNT OF
FUEL INJECTION

ECM

FUEL
INJECTOR

HO2S

A/F MIXTURE
BECOMES
RICHER.

OXYGEN
CONCENTRATION
DECREASES.

A/F MIXTURE
BECOMES
LEANER.

OXYGEN
CONCENTRATION
INCREASES.

Figure 25-4. A—When the computer control system is operating in the closed loop state, the ECU receives signals from the sensor. B—If the sensor does not produce a signal, the ECU cannot control operating conditions. (Geo)

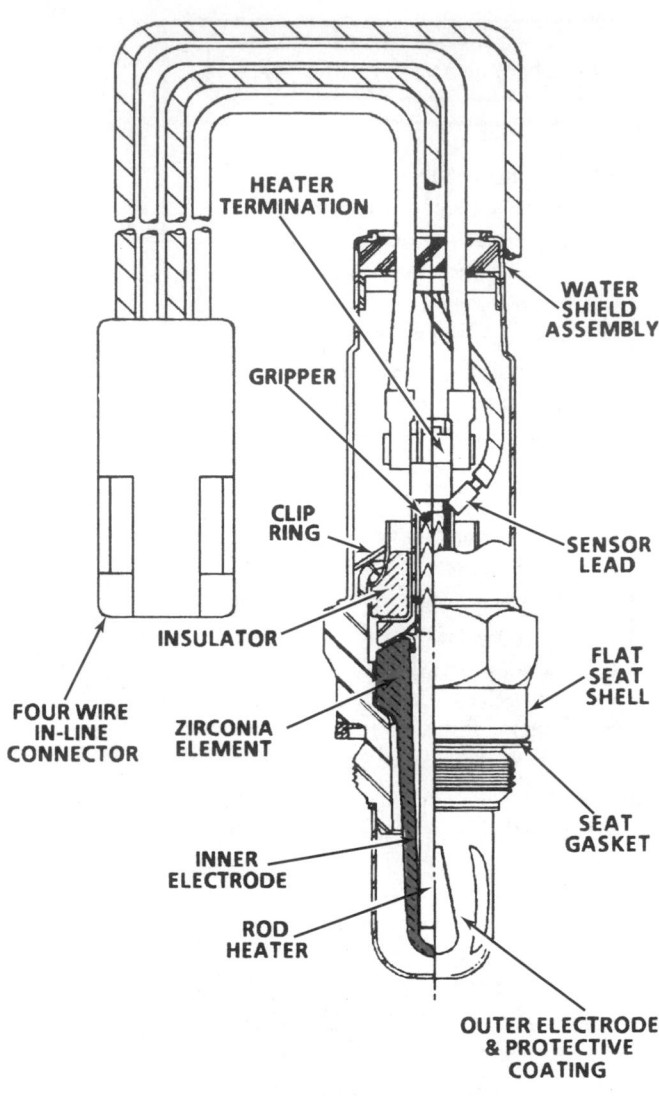

Figure 25-6. Cutaway view of one particular heated oxygen sensor. This sensor must be heated to 600°F (315°C) before it will produce a voltage signal. The voltage signals from this sensor are sent to the electronic control unit (ECU). (GM)

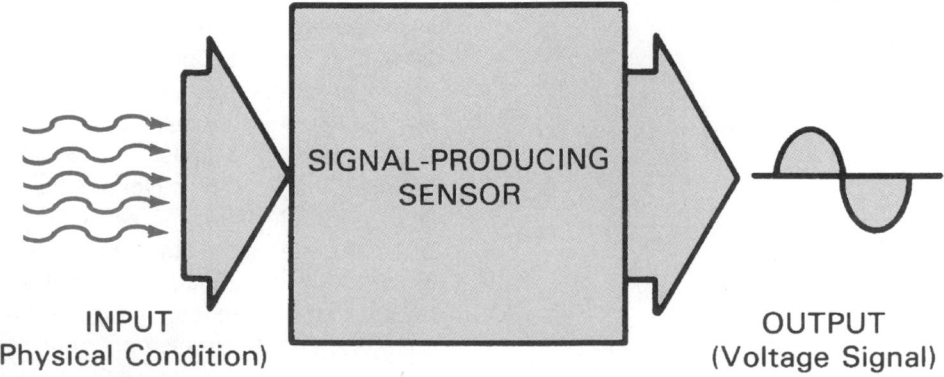

INPUT
(Physical Condition)

SIGNAL-PRODUCING
SENSOR

OUTPUT
(Voltage Signal)

Figure 25-5. Signal-producing sensors generate a small voltage signal that varies as operating conditions change.

and the system will remain in an open loop state. Once the sensor reaches the correct operating temperature, it will send a signal to the computer and the system will begin closed loop operation.

Engine Speed and Position Sensors

Engine speed sensors provide the electronic control unit with information about engine speed (RPM) and piston position. The computer uses this information to calculate ignition timing and fuel injection timing. These sensors monitor crankshaft or distributor shaft rotation, **Figures 25-7** and **25-8**. A magnetic field, which is produced by the rotation of the crankshaft (or distributor shaft), creates a voltage signal in the sensor. The strength of this signal varies in relation to the speed of shaft rotation. A camshaft position sensor works on the same principles as the crankshaft sensor, but it monitors camshaft rotation. On many systems, the engine speed signal is obtained from the ignition control module, which was discussed in Chapter 18.

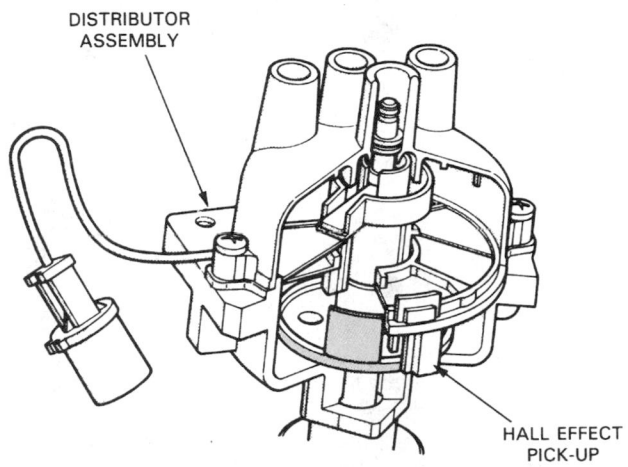

Figure 25-7. This engine speed sensor monitors distributor shaft rotation. As shaft turns, voltage is produced in the sensor. (Chrysler)

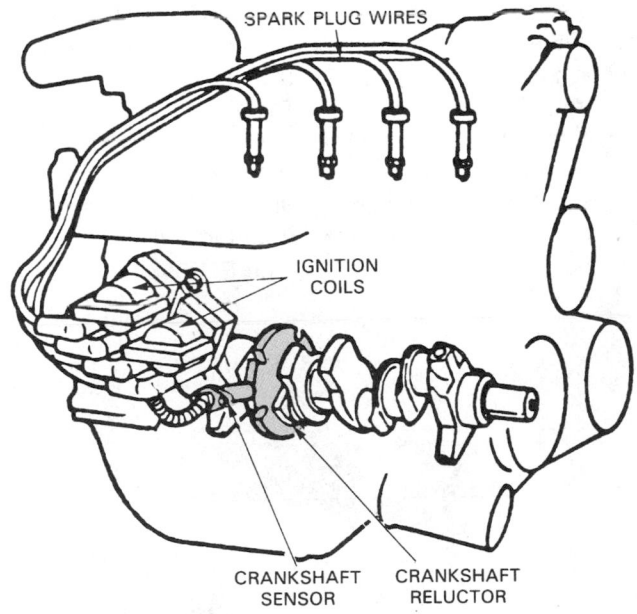

Figure 25-8. This engine speed sensor monitors the rotation of the crankshaft. Note that the sensor is mounted to the engine block and the reluctor is attached to the crankshaft. (Chevrolet)

The **engine position sensor** is similar in operation to the engine speed sensor. A magnetic field is produced by the rotation of the crankshaft or camshaft. This magnetic field creates a voltage signal that is used to tell the computer the exact position of the crankshaft and, therefore, of the piston. The computer uses this signal to more precisely control spark timing.

Detonation Sensors

A **detonation sensor,** or **knock sensor,** is used to alert the electronic control unit or knock sensor module of engine pinging and knocking. It converts abnormal engine vibrations into electrical signals. Upon receiving signals from the detonation sensor, the electronic control unit can retard the ignition timing to correct the condition. A detonation sensor is shown in **Figure 25-9**.

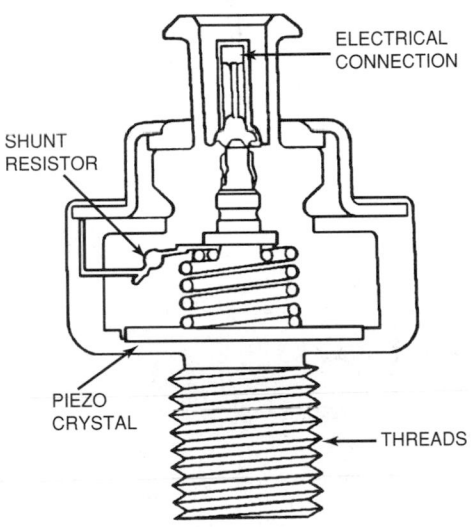

Figure 25-9. The detonation (knock) sensor converts engine pinging and knocking into electrical signals. This sensor mounts in the engine block. (Buick)

Signal-Modifying Sensors

Signal-modifying sensors do not have the ability to produce a voltage signal and must rely on a **reference voltage** supplied by the electronic control unit. The reference voltage, which is usually 5 volts, is modified by the sensor and sent back to the computer, **Figure 25-10**. The control unit analyzes the changes in reference voltage and makes adjustments accordingly. Most signal-modifying sensors change the reference voltage by varying their resistance in response to changes in engine operating conditions. As the resistance of the sensor changes, the output voltage of the sensor circuit changes. Typical signal-modifying sensors include:

- Coolant temperature sensors.
- Manifold air temperature sensors.
- Throttle position sensors.
- Manifold absolute pressure sensor.
- Airflow sensors.

Coolant Temperature Sensor

As its name implies, the **coolant temperature sensor** monitors the temperature of the engine coolant. The tip of

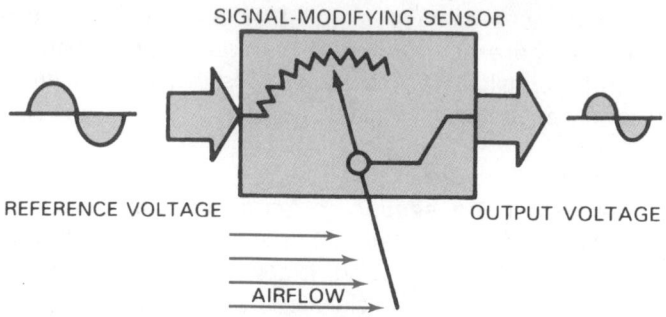

Figure 25-10. Typical signal-modifying sensor. This particular sensor varies its resistance as airflow changes.

this sensor is exposed to the engine coolant. The sensor varies its internal resistance as the temperature of the coolant changes. The electronic control unit uses the output signal from the coolant temperature sensor circuit to calculate the appropriate air-fuel mixture for cold or warm operating conditions. **Figure 25-11** illustrates a typical coolant temperature sensor.

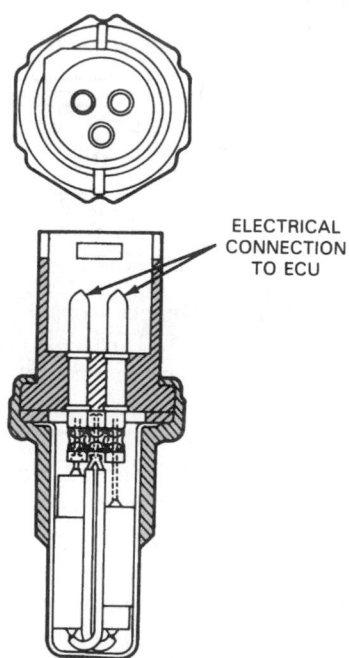

Figure 25-11. Typical coolant temperature sensor. This sensor is generally mounted near the thermostat housing. (Ford)

Some older computer control systems rely on input from the coolant temperature sensor to determine whether the control loop should be open or closed. If the sensor's temperature is below a certain value, usually about 180°F (82°C), the system will stay in the open loop state. Once the coolant reaches normal operating temperature, the system will begin operating in the closed loop state.

Manifold Air Temperature Sensor

The **manifold air temperature (MAT) sensor** measures the temperature of the air entering the intake mani-

fold, **Figure 25-12.** As intake air temperature changes, the internal resistance of the sensor changes. This change in resistance varies the voltage signal that the sensor returns to the electronic control unit. The computer uses the output signal from the MAT sensor circuit to help determine the optimal air-fuel mixture. As intake air gets warmer, less fuel is needed to operate the engine efficiently.

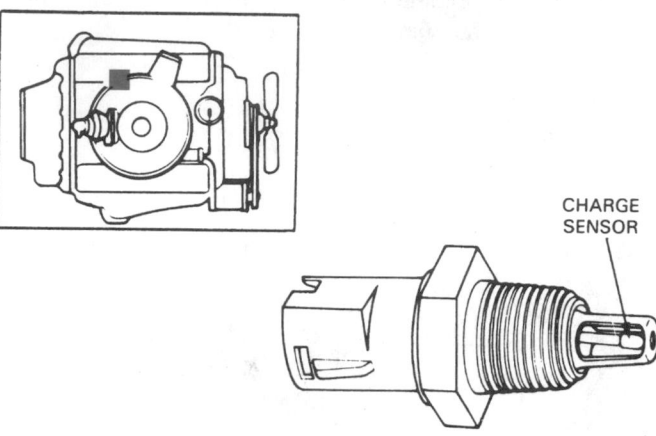

Figure 25-12. Manifold air temperature sensor monitors the temperature of air entering the intake manifold. This sensor is commonly mounted in the air cleaner housing near the throttle body or intake manifold. (Chrysler)

Throttle Position Sensor

The **throttle position sensor (TPS)** is one of the only computer control components that is mechanical in nature. The TPS monitors the position of the throttle valve. The sensor changes its resistance in relation to the position of the throttle shaft. When the throttle is closed, the output signal from the TPS circuit is low. The TPS circuit output voltage rises proportionally as the throttle is opened. A typical throttle position sensor is illustrated in **Figure 25-13**. The computer uses the signals from the TPS circuit to control ignition timing, fuel delivery, and EGR valve position.

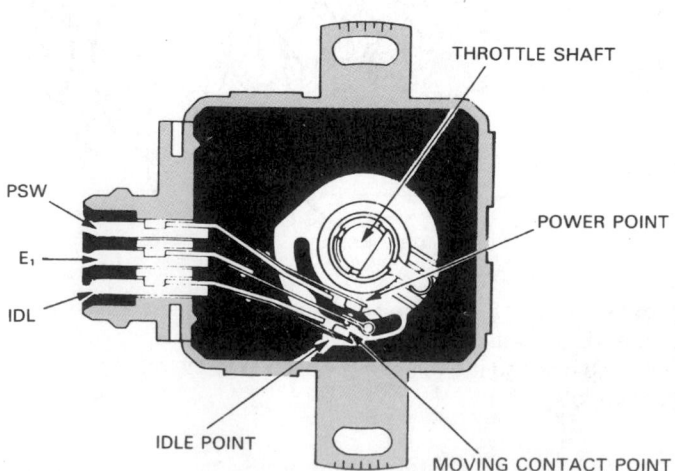

Figure 25-13. Cutaway view of a throttle position sensor. As the throttle shaft moves, the resistance of the sensor changes.

Manifold Absolute Pressure Sensor

The *manifold absolute pressure (MAP) sensor* monitors changes in the engine's intake manifold pressure, **Figure 25-14.** As the manifold pressure changes, the sensor's internal resistance varies. The computer uses the output signal from the MAP sensor circuit to help calculate the correct amount of fuel entering the engine.

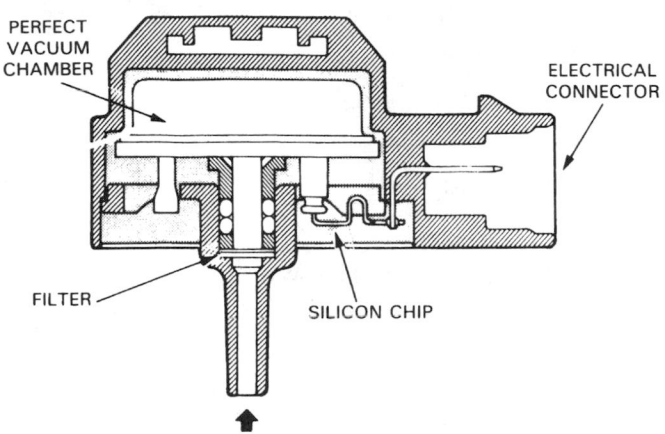

Figure 25-14.   Cutaway view of a manifold absolute pressure sensor. Note the hookup for a vacuum hose and an electrical connector. (Toyota)

Airflow Sensors

Airflow sensors monitor the amount of air entering a vehicle's throttle body or carburetor. There are two basic kinds of airflow sensors: the flap sensor and the heated wire sensor, sometimes called the mass airflow sensor. The flap sensor utilizes a pivoting flap, which is connected to a variable resistor, **Figure 25-15.** As the amount of air flowing through the sensor varies, the flap moves and the resistance of the sensor changes. This change in resistance alters the reference voltage. The output from the flap airflow sensor circuit is used to help calculate the proper air-fuel mixture.

The heated wire air flow sensor, like a flap airflow sensor, is used to measure the volume of air entering the engine, **Figure 25-16.** This sensor, however, has the ability to compensate for changes in air temperature and atmospheric pressure. Therefore, the need for an air temperature sensor and a barometric pressure sensor is eliminated in systems using a heated wire airflow sensor.

A heated wire airflow sensor uses a wire screen located in the airflow path to monitor the amount of air entering the intake manifold. The screen is heated by a reference voltage, which is supplied by the electronic control unit. As air flows through the screen, the temperature of the screen is reduced. As the temperature drops, the computer increases the reference voltage to maintain a constant temperature at the screen. The computer analyzes reference voltage changes and calculates the rate of airflow. The computer then adjusts the air-fuel ratio to compensate for changes in airflow.

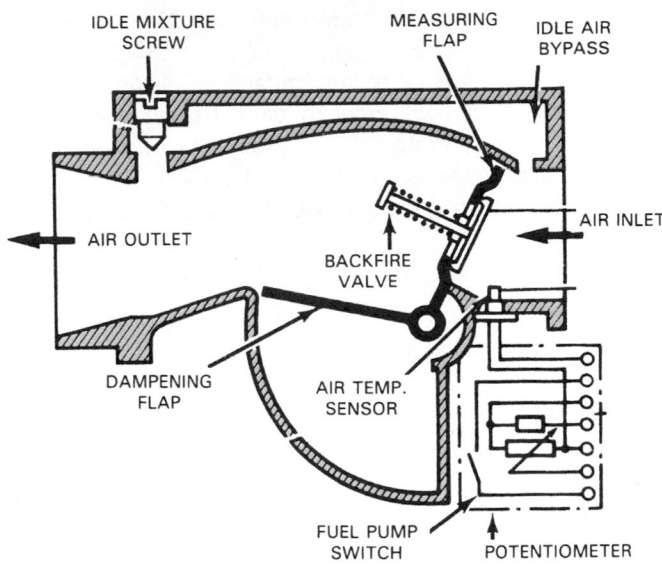

Figure 25-15.   Cutaway view of a flap airflow sensor assembly. Note the air temperature sensor and the idle air bypass. (Bosch)

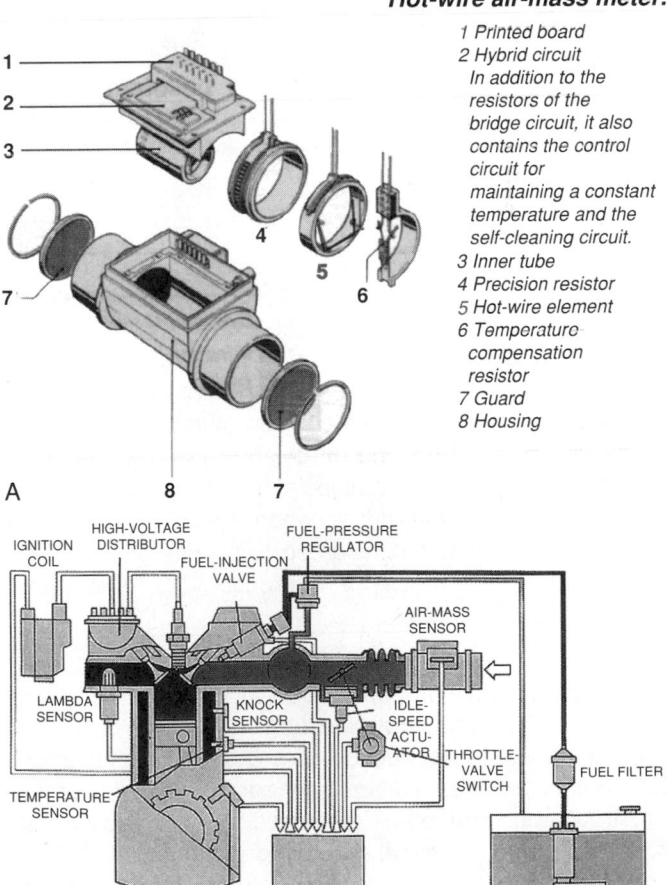

Hot-wire air-mass meter.

1 Printed board
2 Hybrid circuit
  In addition to the resistors of the bridge circuit, it also contains the control circuit for maintaining a constant temperature and the self-cleaning circuit.
3 Inner tube
4 Precision resistor
5 Hot-wire element
6 Temperature compensation resistor
7 Guard
8 Housing

Figure 25-16.   A heated wire airflow sensor. A—Exploded view of the sensor assembly. B—Overall system schematic.

The airflow sensor is shown in **Figure 25-17** measures the airflow volume by detecting the vibration of a thin metal-foil mirror. Mirror vibrations are caused by air generating a Karman vortex. A light emitting diode (LED) and a light receptor (photo transistor) are positioned opposite the mirror and optically sense vibrations. The ECU uses signals from this sensor to calculate injection volume and ignition advance angle.

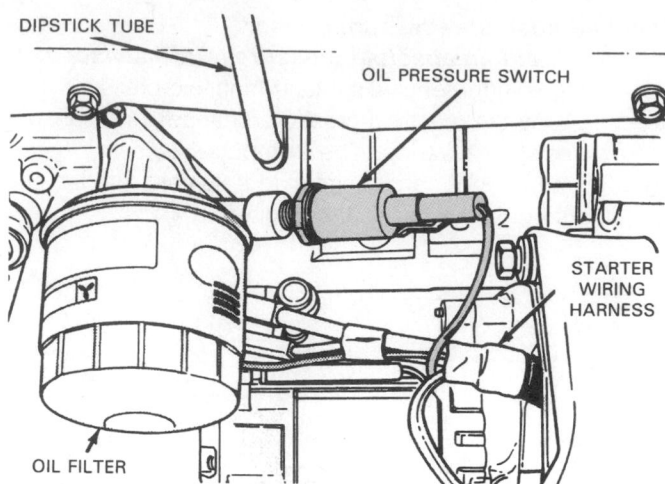

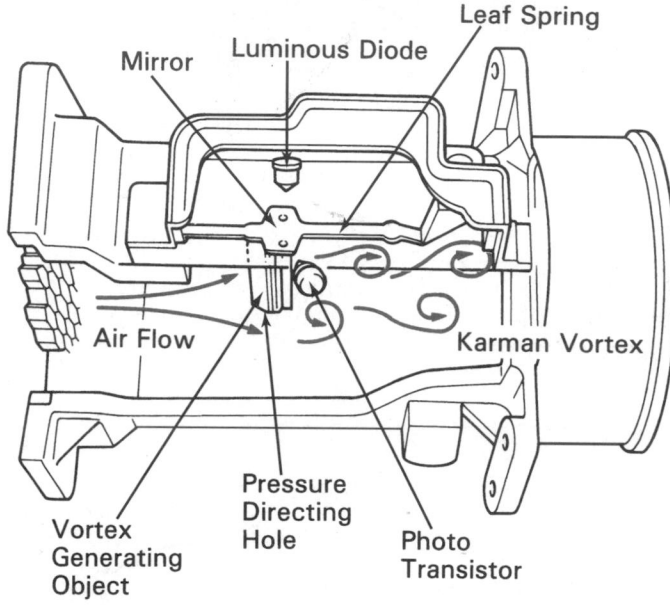

Figure 25-17. Cutaway of a volume airflow sensor assembly. Note the Karman vortex, which exerts pressure on the mirror, causing vibration. (Lexus)

Switching Sensors

Computer control systems use *switching sensors* to monitor some engine and vehicle operating conditions. These sensors simply turn on and off in response to specific situations. Some sensors use an internal pressure-sensing element, **Figure 25-18.** Many switching sensors are physically switched on and off by moving parts within the monitored circuit. An example is a transmission position switch moved by the driver when gears are changed. Switching sensors are considered to be passive transducers because they modify a reference voltage that they receive from the computer.

Electronic Control Unit Operation

The *electronic control unit*, or *ECU,* is a very complex device. It is housed in a box-like casing and is constructed from a number of integrated circuits, printed circuit boards, and other electronic components. **Figure 25-19** illustrates a typical electronic control unit.

It is not necessary to know how the internal components of the ECU work. It is helpful, however, to understand the basic operation of the unit in order to effectively troubleshoot a computer control system. The ECU can be divided into five basic sections:

Figure 25-18. An oil pressure switch is a typical switching sensor. When pressure drops below a certain point, this sensor switches on to alert the ECU of the condition. (Chrysler)

- Input.
- Memory.
- Arithmetic/logic.
- Control.
- Output.

Each section performs a specific function within the unit. See **Figure 25-20.**

Input Section

The *input section* of the electronic control unit allows sensors to communicate with the other sections in the unit. Input signals often reach the ECU in a form that it cannot process. The input section converts sensor signals to a form that the computer can use.

Memory Section

The electronic control unit's *memory section* stores data until it is needed for processing operations. The three types of memory commonly used in modern computer systems include:

- Read only memory (ROM).
- Programmable read only memory (PROM).
- Random access memory (RAM).

Each memory type performs a specific function in the computer's memory system.

ROM

ROM (read only memory) is used to store the computer's operating instructions (programs). It also stores general information that tells the computer how various components should perform under specific operating conditions. As its name implies, data in ROM can only be read. The information in ROM can never be modified. The contents in ROM will not be lost if power to the computer is disconnected. The data stored in ROM is universal, and therefore, a manufacturer

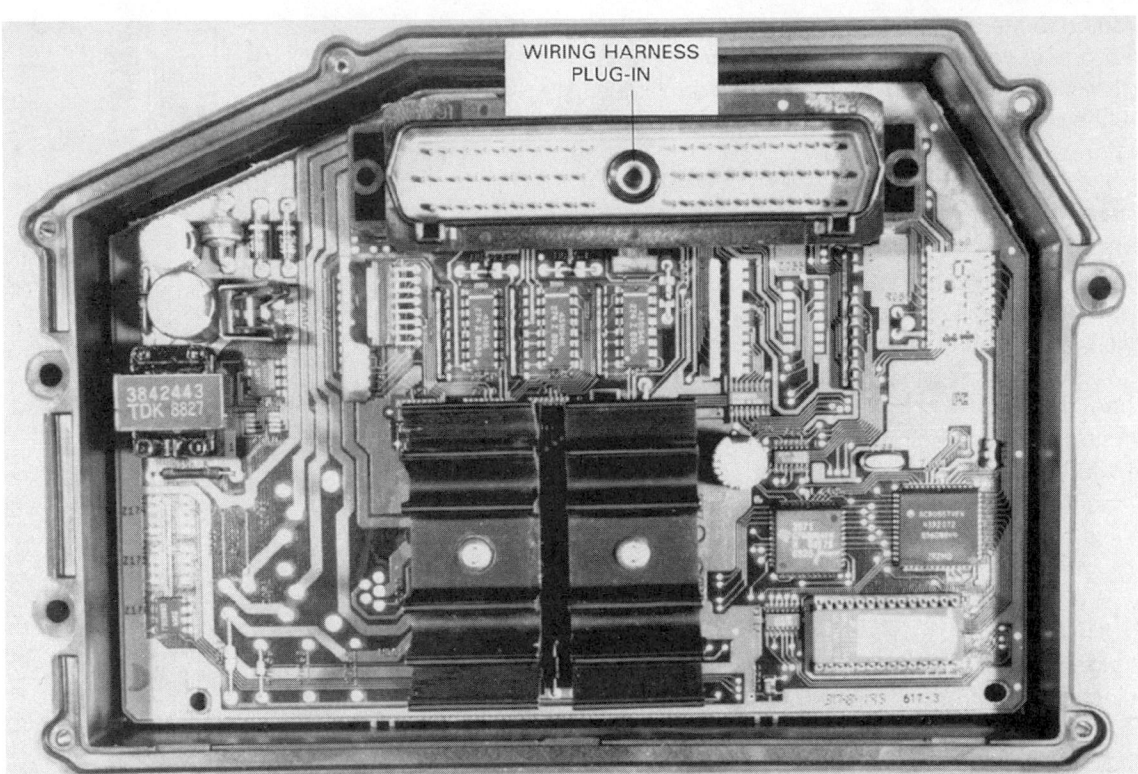

Figure 25-19.   View of electronic components inside one type of electronic control unit. Electronic control units cannot be serviced in the field. (Chrysler)

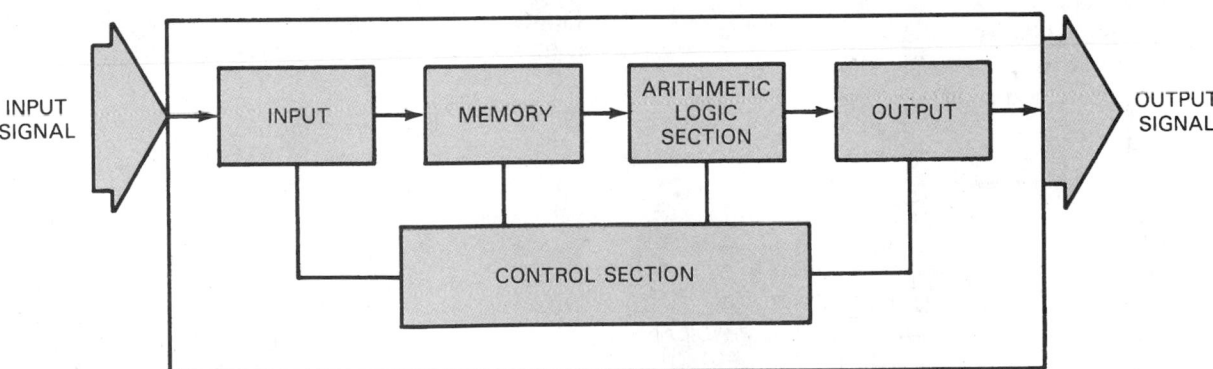

Figure 25-20.   The electronic control unit can be divided into five sections. Each section performs a specific function within the unit.

can use the same ROM memory for an entire product line. The electronic control unit compares data stored in ROM to input information from the sensors. If the result of the comparison is not within acceptable parameters, the ECU will take action to change operating conditions.

PROM

PROM, like ROM, contains permanent information about how components should perform under various operating conditions. The information in PROM, however, is much more specific than the data stored in ROM. The information in PROM depends on a vehicle's options. For example, a vehicle with an automatic transmission would have a different PROM than an identical vehicle with a standard transmission. The PROM is the only part of the electronic control unit that can be serviced in the field.

RAM

RAM (random access memory) is used as a temporary storage place for data from the sensors. The electronic control unit uses the information stored in RAM to analyze specific operating conditions. RAM is also used to store trouble codes when abnormal operating conditions occur. Trouble codes will be covered in detail later in this chapter. RAM is considered to be a volatile memory because its contents will be lost if battery voltage is disconnected from the computer.

Arithmetic/Logic Section

The **arithmetic/logic section** of the electronic control unit analyzes input information and calculates output data. In addition to making mathematical calculations, the arithmetic/logic section uses logic to make output decisions. For example, when the ECU receives input from the oxygen sensor, it is routed to the arithmetic/logic section, where it is compared to a preset value stored in the computer's memory. The arithmetic/logic section determines if the value received from the sensor is greater than, less than, or equal to the value stored in the ECU's memory.

Control Section

The **control section** governs all of the other sections in the computer. For example, the control section can instruct the arithmetic/logic section to compare the input from a specific sensor to the ideal value stored in ROM.

Output Section

The function of the electronic control unit's **output section** is similar to the function of the input section. This section converts the computer's output signal to a form that an output device can use to produce an appropriate control function.

Output Actuators

Output actuators convert the electrical output signals sent by the electronic control unit into physical movements, **Figure 25-21.** The ECU uses the output actuators to make physical adjustments that change operating conditions. Commonly used actuators include:

- Fuel injectors.
- Idle speed motors.
- Mixture control solenoids.
- Electric fan relays.
- Ignition modules and coils.

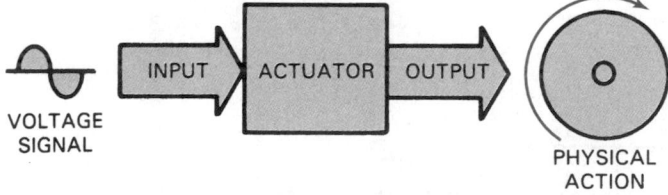

Figure 25-21. Actuators convert output signals from the electronic control unit into physical actions. Most actuators are motors, solenoids, or relays.

Fuel Injectors

A **fuel injector** is an actuator that meters the amount of fuel injected into the throttle body or cylinders, **Figure 25-22.** When the computer energizes the injector, a sealing needle is lifted from its seat, allowing fuel to spray out. When the computer signal stops, spring pressure will force the needle valve closed. Fuel injector operation is explained in detail in Chapter 22.

Idle Speed Motors and Solenoids

The computer uses the **idle speed motor** to increase idle speed when the engine is under a heavy load. This actuator increases idle speed by moving the throttle lever. A load, such as an air conditioning com-

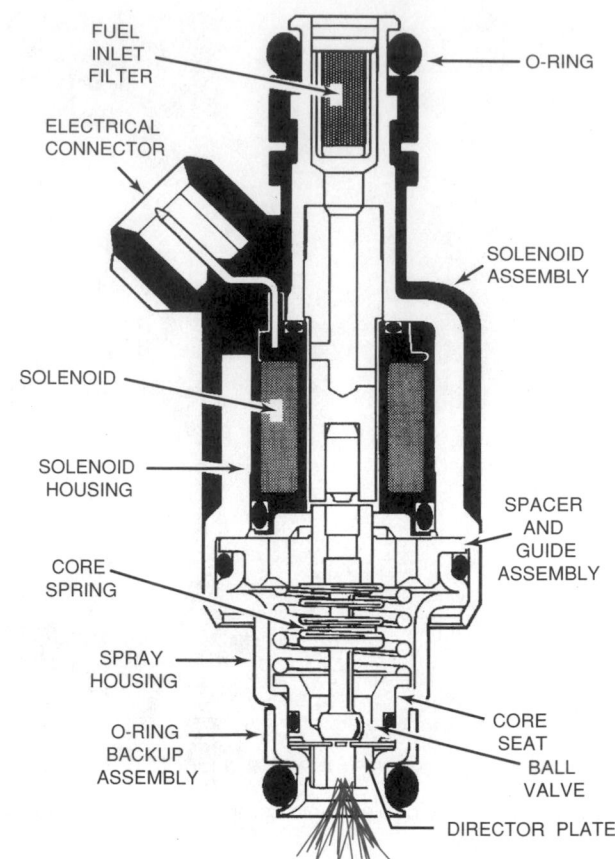

Figure 25-22. Cross section of an electronic fuel injector used with port fuel injection. When the injector is energized, the coil opens the ball valve, allowing fuel to flow past the director plate to the nozzle. (Cadillac)

pressor, can cause the engine to stall if the idle speed sensor is not working properly. A typical idle speed motor is illustrated in **Figure 25-23.**

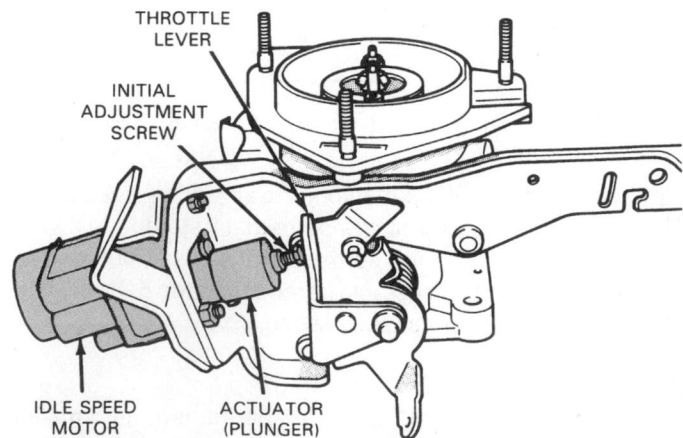

Figure 25-23. Idle speed motor assembly. Note that the actuator just touches the throttle lever when in the retracted position. (Jeep)

Idle speed solenoids are similar to the idle devices covered in Chapter 22. The major difference is that they are operated by the ECU. These were explained in more detail in Chapter 22. Air bypass solenoids control idle speed by increasing or decreasing airflow through an opening that bypasses the throttle valve.

Mixture Control Solenoid

The **mixture control solenoid** is only used on engines equipped with carburetors. When this actuator is energized, the solenoid moves the carburetor's metering rod in and out of the metering jet. The mixture control solenoid is typically cycled on and off several times a second. A mixture control solenoid is shown in **Figure 25-24.**

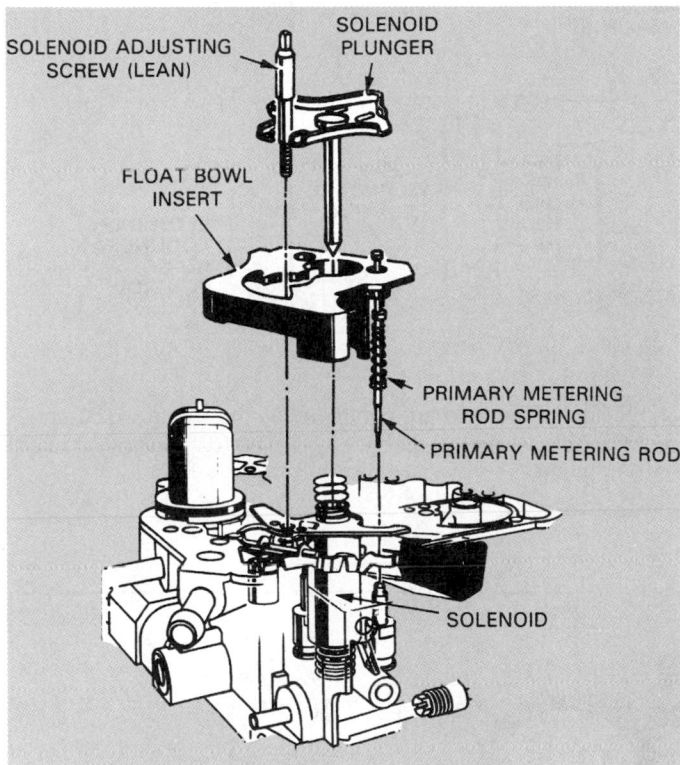

Figure 25-24. Exploded view of a carburetor mixture-control solenoid unit. (Chevrolet)

Electric Fan Relay

When engine coolant reaches a certain temperature, usually around the boiling point of pure water at sea level (approximately 212°F or 100°C), the computer energizes the **electric fan relay.** This relay activates the electric fan motor(s). Some fan relays are automatically activated each time the air conditioner is switched on. The wiring schematic for a specific fan relay circuit is shown in **Figure 25-25.**

Ignition Modules and Coils

Although the purpose of the **ignition module** and **coil** is to produce the high-tension spark, they are controlled by the ECU, and are therefore, output actuators. Some computer control systems interface with the ignition module and control spark timing through it. Other computers operate the coil directly, controlling its firing to time the

spark. Ignition modules and coils were covered in detail in Chapter 18.

Troubleshooting — A Logical Approach

A thorough understanding of basic computer control system operation is necessary to effectively troubleshoot computer control systems. A logical approach must be taken when attempting to locate a problem. There are many sophisticated procedures involved in testing computer control systems. It is not within the scope of this text to explain every possible testing method. Therefore, a general overview of the most common testing procedures is presented in the following sections. They are designed to provide the background information necessary to effectively use the diagnostic resources available when servicing computerized control systems.

Even trained technicians cannot expect to learn enough about these complex systems to solve problems on their own. Today's automotive technicians must rely on the information found in manuals, diagnostic charts, and other service publications when troubleshooting computer control systems.

Using Self-Diagnostic Systems

Although computer control systems precisely control various operating conditions in modern vehicles, they are often very difficult to service. To aid the technician in troubleshooting the computer system, manufacturers have designed **self-diagnostic systems** into their products. These systems continuously monitor the operation of the sensors, the actuators, and the ECU. If an abnormal condition is detected, a warning signal is placed in the electronic control unit's memory. If the defect is serious enough, the system will also place itself into the **disabled mode,** or **limp-in mode.** In this mode, it operates on the same preset values used in open loop mode until repairs are made. The system will also illuminate a **warning light,** usually labeled "check engine" or "service engine soon," on the vehicle's dashboard. The warning light alerts the driver to the fact that the vehicle requires service.

Self-diagnostic capabilities have been a tremendous help to the automotive technician. It is very important to be able to use these features effectively.

Trouble Codes

When the electronic control unit's self-diagnostic system detects an abnormal operating condition, it places a warning signal into the unit's memory. These signals are called **trouble codes.** Whenever a trouble code is stored in memory, the warning light is activated on the vehicle's dashboard, **Figure 25-26.**

Activating Self-Diagnostic Systems

If the warning light remains on when the engine is running, the technician can assume that there is at least one trouble code stored in the electronic control unit's memory. In order to retrieve stored trouble codes, the technician must prompt the ECU's self-diagnostic system to release

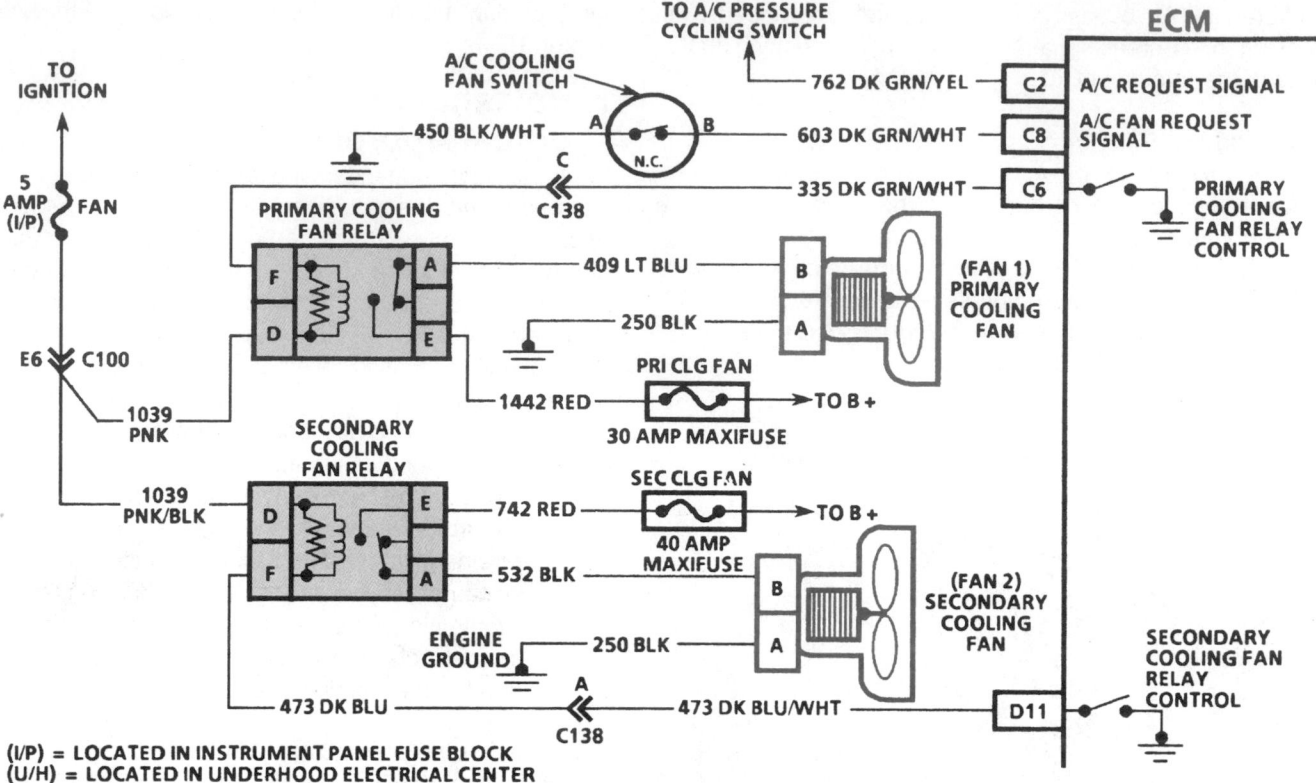

Figure 25-25. A schematic diagram of a dual electric cooling fan control circuit. The fans are controlled by the electronic control module. The ECM uses information from various sensors to determine when to operate one or both fans. The first (primary) fan will come on when the engine coolant temperature is greater than 226°F (108°C). (GM)

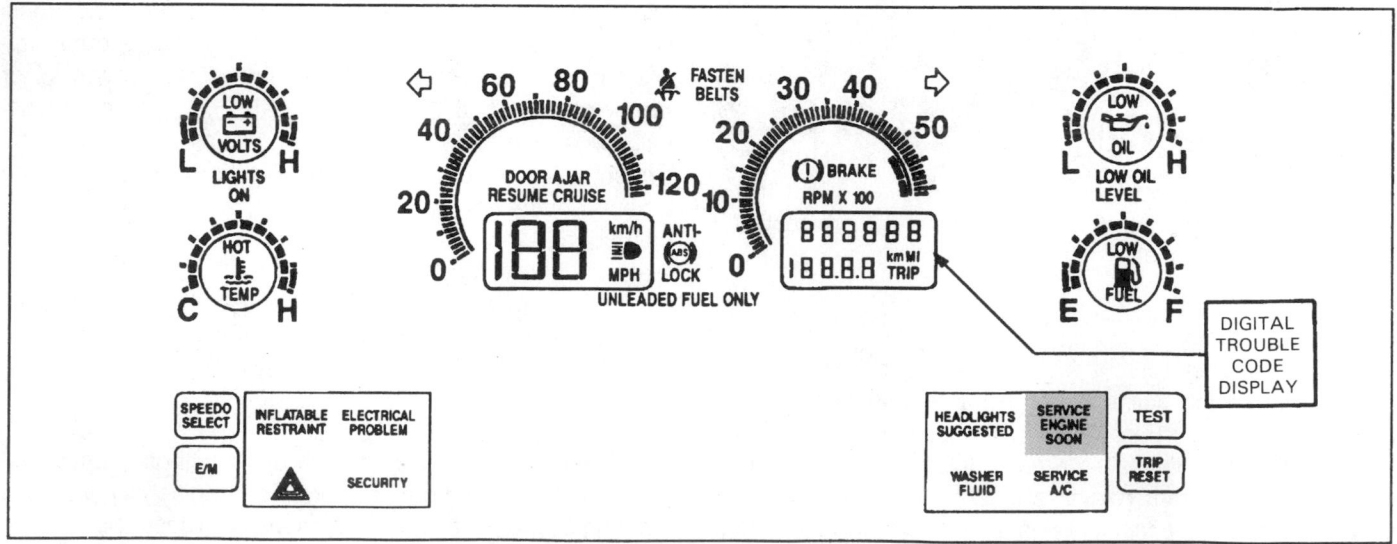

Figure 25-26. The check engine or service engine soon light is often used to alert the driver to a problem in the computer control system. The light will remain on if there is a trouble code stored in the computer's memory. Note that trouble codes in this system are digitally displayed on the vehicle's dashboard. (Buick)

them from memory. Methods for extracting trouble codes vary. Some systems simply require connecting test leads across individual pins of a diagnostic link. Others require the use of special testing equipment. The most common methods of retrieving trouble codes from the computer's memory include the following:

- Switching a control mode selector on the side of the electronic control unit.
- Turning the ignition switch on and off several times in a specified time.
- Connecting a voltmeter to one or more terminals of the diagnostic test link.

- Grounding one of the terminals on the diagnostic test link.
- Connecting two specific diagnostic test link terminals.

These are only a few examples of the possible methods for retrieving trouble codes. Before attempting to access the self-diagnostic system of any vehicle, always consult an appropriate service manual to determine which method is correct for the vehicle at hand. The wrong test hookup or grounding incorrect terminals can destroy fragile computer system components.

Diagnostic Link

Many vehicles are equipped with a special **diagnostic link,** which is used to check the computer control system at the factory. These multi-pin terminals also serve as connecting points for test equipment in the field. The diagnostic link can be located in various places on the vehicle, **Figure 25-27.** Common locations include the following:

- Under the glove compartment.
- Under the steering column.
- In the engine compartment (on fire wall or wheel well).

Some manufacturers refer to the diagnostic link as an assembly line diagnostic link (ALDL) or as a self-test connector.

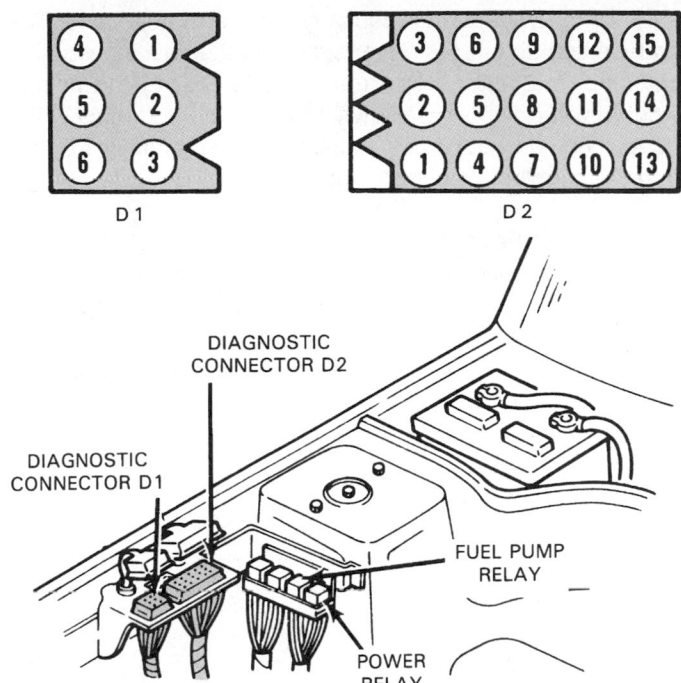

Figure 25-27. One type of diagnostic link located on a wheel well. This vehicle is equipped with two separate diagnostic connectors. Note the caps that protect the connectors when they are not being used. (Chrysler)

Reading Trouble Codes

Once the self-diagnostic system has been activated, the computer will release the stored trouble codes. The codes can be displayed in several ways. Always refer to the service manual for information on how to read trouble codes for the system at hand. Some typical ways that these codes are displayed include:

- Counting flashing warning light.
- Counting meter needle sweeps.
- Observing digital dash readout.

Flashing Warning Light

A flashing warning light is one of the most common methods used to display trouble codes. The technician simply counts the flashes produced by a warning light (check

engine or service engine soon) in the vehicle's dashboard. The number of flashes represents the trouble code stored in memory. For example, if the trouble code is 3, the light will flash three consecutive times. If there is more than one code in memory, there will be a 2.5 second pause before the second code is displayed. Some systems are set up to display two digit trouble codes. In these systems, the light flashes the first digit, pauses for 1.5 seconds, and then flashes the second digit. Again, when more than one code is stored in memory, there will be a 2.5 second pause between codes. A two digit trouble code is illustrated in **Figure 25-28.**

Analog Meter Sweeps

Some systems require the use of an analog voltmeter to retrieve trouble codes. The meter's needle moves

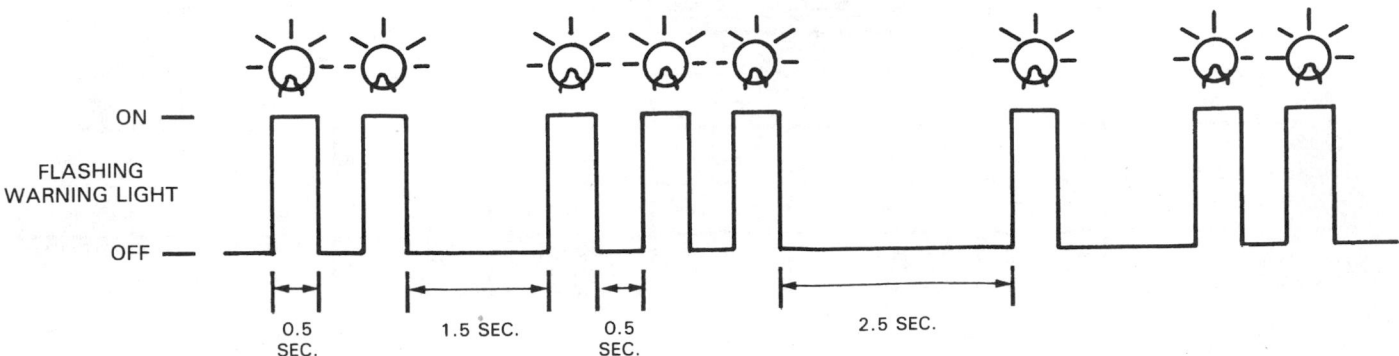

Figure 25-28. Trouble codes are often displayed with flashing warning lights. Note the 1.5 second pause between digits of two digit codes and the 2.5 second pause between individual codes. Trouble codes 23 and 12 are represented here.

sharply, or "sweeps," for each digit of the trouble code. The code is counted in a manner similar to the flashing warning light. For example, if the trouble code is five, the needle would sweep five consecutive times. If the code is 12, the needle would sweep once, pause for approximately 1.5 seconds, and sweep two more times.

Digital Dash Readout

Some highly technical self-diagnostic systems display trouble codes directly onto a screen mounted in the vehicle's instrument panel. See **Figure 25-29.** This method eliminates the possibility of error from misinterpreting flashing codes or analog meter sweeps. Most digital display systems are activated by simply pressing designated instrument controls simultaneously until an audible signal is detected. In addition to the ability to troubleshoot the entire computer control system, many digital self-diagnostic systems can perform specialized tests. For example, most of these systems have the ability to measure and record the voltage signals sent by individual sensors.

Using Trouble Code Charts

Once the trouble codes have been obtained, the technician must compare the code numbers to a **trouble code chart.** The trouble code chart contains information about the meaning of each trouble code. This information can be used as a starting point in the troubleshooting process. Most trouble codes simply identify the circuit in which a problem is detected. For example, in some systems the trouble code 21 represents a malfunction in the oxygen sensor circuit, **Figure 25-30.**

Scan Tools

Diagnostic **scan tools** are often used to retrieve trouble codes, **Figure 25-31.** Most scan tools convert the codes directly into a digital display. Scan tools do not have the ability to pinpoint problems within a circuit. Many scan tools, however, have the capability to record the signal values that the electronic control unit receives from the sensors. This eliminates the need to check each sensor individually.

Diagnostic Analyzers

Modern **diagnostic analyzers** can be used to troubleshoot computer control systems. Most analyzers connect directly to the vehicle's diagnostic link. The analyzer uses information from the sensors and the electronic control unit to determine if the system is operating properly. Many analyzers have the ability to supply the technician with troubleshooting and repair instructions based on these values. Some systems are so sophisticated that they can communicate with a mainframe computer at a remote location. One type of diagnostic analyzer is illustrated in **Figure 25-32.**

Using Diagnostic Information

As mentioned, trouble codes indicate the circuit or area that is operating improperly. Most codes, however, do not pinpoint the exact cause of the problem. The trouble could be a shorted wire, a loose connection, a faulty sensor, actuator, or control unit. Once a trouble code has been obtained, it is often necessary for the technician to perform a series of specialized tests to locate the faulty component(s) within a circuit. These procedures are often referred to as pinpoint tests.

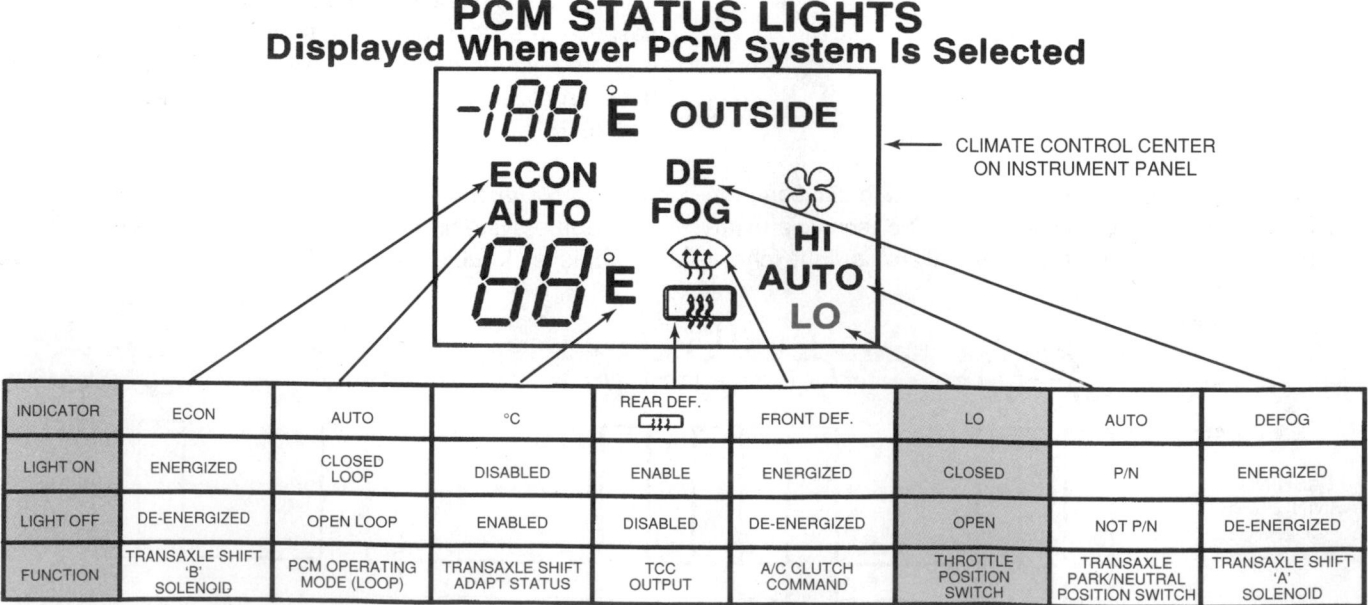

INDICATOR	ECON	AUTO	°C	REAR DEF.	FRONT DEF.	LO	AUTO	DEFOG
LIGHT ON	ENERGIZED	CLOSED LOOP	DISABLED	ENABLE	ENERGIZED	CLOSED	P/N	ENERGIZED
LIGHT OFF	DE-ENERGIZED	OPEN LOOP	ENABLED	DISABLED	DE-ENERGIZED	OPEN	NOT P/N	DE-ENERGIZED
FUNCTION	TRANSAXLE SHIFT 'B' SOLENOID	PCM OPERATING MODE (LOOP)	TRANSAXLE SHIFT ADAPT STATUS	TCC OUTPUT	A/C CLUTCH COMMAND	THROTTLE POSITION SWITCH	TRANSAXLE PARK/NEUTRAL POSITION SWITCH	TRANSAXLE SHIFT 'A' SOLENOID

Figure 25-29. Instrument panel powertrain control module status lights are displayed. The status of the throttle position switch is indicated by the "lo" fan symbol on the CCC. If the "lo" fan symbol is on, it indicates a closed throttle position switch. If the "lo" fan symbol is off, the throttle position switch is open. Notice the various functions and their symbols.

Code No.	Item	Diagnosis	Trouble Area	"CHECK ENGINE" Lamp
12	RPM Signal	No "Ne" or "G" signal to ECU within 2 seconds after the engine has been cranked.	• Distributor circuit • Distributor • Starter signal circuit • ECU	ON
13	RPM Signal	No "Ne" signal to ECU when the engine speed is above 1000 rpm.	• Distributor circuit • Distributor • ECU	ON
14	Ignition Signal	No "IGf" signal to ECU 8 ~ 11 times in succession.	• Igniter and ignition coil circuit • Igniter and ignition coil • ECU	ON
21	Oxygen Sensor Signal	During air-fuel ratio feedback correction, voltage output from the oxygen sensor does not exceed a set value on the lean side and the rich side continuously for a certain period.	• Oxygen sensor circuit • Oxygen sensor	ON
	Oxygen Sensor Heater Signal	Open or short circuit in oxygen sensor heater signal (HT).	• Oxygen sensor heater circuit • Oxygen sensor heater • ECU	
22	Water Temp. Sensor Signal	Open or short circuit in water temp. sensor signal (THW).	• Water temp. sensor circuit • Water temp. sensor • ECU	ON
24	Intake Air Temp. Sensor Signal	Open or short circuit in intake air temp. sensor signal (THA).	• Intake air temp. sensor circuit • Intake air temp. sensor • ECU	ON*
25	Air-fuel Ratio Lean Malfunction	(1)* When air-fuel ratio feedback correction value or adaptive control value continues at the upper (lean) or lower (rich) limit renewed for a certain period of time. (2)* When air-fuel ratio feedback correction value or adaptive control value feedback frequency is abnormally high during feedback condition. (3) Open or short circuit in oxygen sensor signal.	• Injector ciucuit • Injector • Fuel line pressure • Ignition system • Oxygen sensor circuit • Oxygen sensor • Air flow meter • Water temp. sensor • ECU	ON*
26	Air-fuel Ratio Rich Malfunction		• Injector circuit • Injector • Fuel line pressure • Cold start injector • Air flow meter • Water temp. sensor • ECU	ON*
31	Airflow Meter Signal	Open circuit in V_C signal or short circuit between V_C and E_2 when idle contacts are closed.	• Airflow meter circuit • Airflow meter • ECU	ON
32	Airflow Meter Signal	Open circuit in E_2 or short circuit between V_C and V_S.	• Airflow meter circuit • Airflow meter • ECU	ON
34	Turbocharging Pressure Signal	Excessive turbocharging pressure.	• Turbocharger • Turbocharging pressure sensor circuit • Turbocharging pressure sensor • ECU	ON
35	Turbocharging Pressure Sensor Signal	Open or short circuit in turbocharging pressure sensor signal (PIM).	• Turbocharging pressure sensor circuit • Turbocharging pressure sensor • ECU	OFF

*Applicable only to California specification vehicles.

Figure 25-30. Once trouble codes have been extracted, the technician can use a trouble code chart to determine what the codes represent. Codes usually indicate circuit malfunctions and do not pinpoint specific problems. (Toyota)

Typical Test Equipment

Although some systems require specialized testing equipment, many components can be checked using traditional test instruments, including a high-impedance multimeter, a tachometer, a vacuum pump and gauge, and a timing light.

In the following sections, common methods for testing computer control system components will be covered. Although these tests are not typical for all computer systems, they are designed to provide a general overview of routine testing procedures. Always consult an appropriate owner's manual before attempting to troubleshoot any computer system component.

Visual Inspection

The first step in pinpointing a computer control system problem is to visually inspect the suspected circuits and all related components. Most computer system problems are

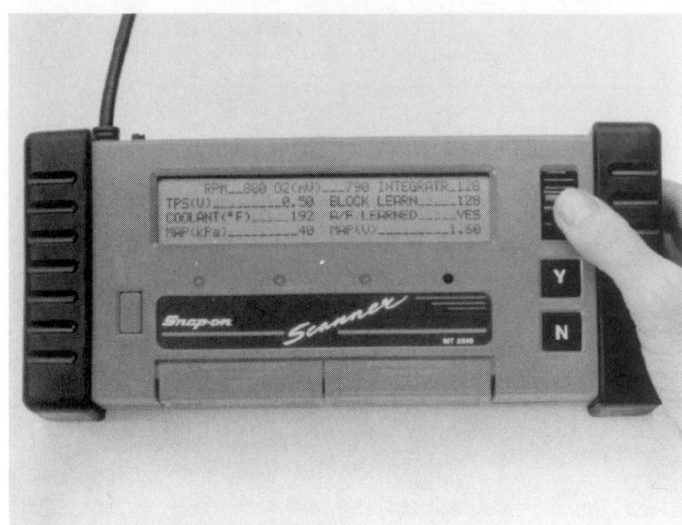

Figure 25-31. Many manufacturers recommend the use of scan tools to record signals from individual computer control system components. Always follow instructions when connecting any testing device in electronic systems. (OTC, Snap-on Tools Co.)

caused by loose connections, leaking vacuum hoses, or physical damage. Check electrical terminals for signs of oxidation and misalignment. Wiggling a connector may help locate an open circuit or an area of high resistance. Wiring problems should always be suspected when an open circuit or a faulty sensor is indicated by trouble codes. Check vacuum hoses for cracks and restrictions. Examine hoses for proper connections. Improper hose routing can upset the operation of a computer controlled system.

Testing Circuit Wiring

Circuit wiring can be checked with a standard ohmmeter. To test a suspected wire, disconnect the wire at both ends of the circuit and measure its resistance with the meter. If the ends of the wire are far apart, the measurement can be taken by attaching one end of the wire to ground. Attach one meter lead to the ungrounded end of the wire and the other lead to a common ground. If the resistance measured in either of these tests is greater than 5 ohms, the wiring should be repaired, **Figure 25-33.**

The ohmmeter can also be used to check for a short circuit. Connect the ohmmeter to one end of the wire in question and the other lead to a good ground. If the resistance is less than several hundred thousand ohms, the wire may be shorting to ground.

Servicing Electronic Engine Control System Components

The following sections explain how to service common electronic engine control system components. Included are testing and replacement procedures. Note that these procedures are general and may not apply to all systems. To prevent damage to the computer control system, always consult the manufacturers' manual for exact procedures.

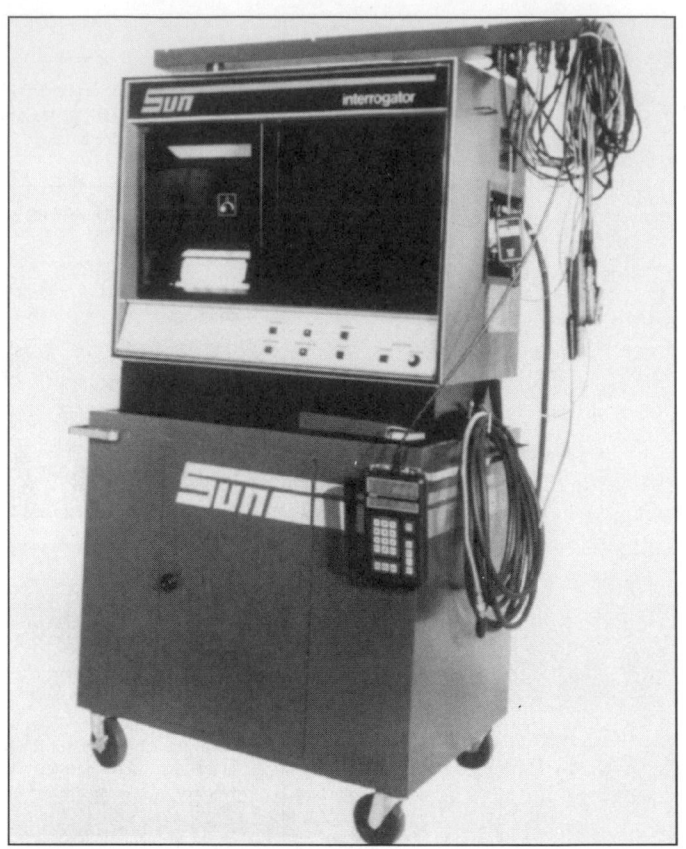

Figure 25-32. Diagnostic analyzers have the ability to communicate with the electronic control unit and to interpret data from the sensors. This particular model provides the technician with a printout of its findings. (Sun)

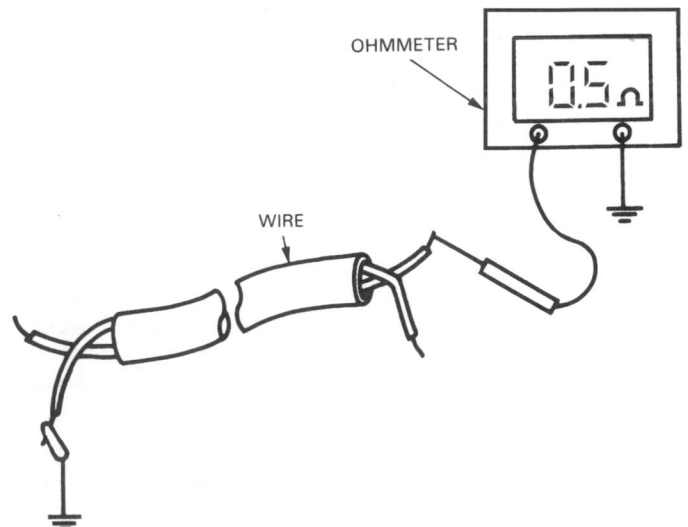

Figure 25-33. Checking wire condition with an ohmmeter. Make sure the wire is disconnected from the power source before connecting the meter.

Sensor Service

Sensor service usually consists of testing the suspected components and replacing them if they are faulty. An ohmmeter is often required to check the operation of signal-modifying sensors. The meter is used to verify the sensor's internal resistance. A voltmeter is usually used to test the output of signal producing sensors. All measured values should be compared with service manual specifications. Some systems require a special scan tool to extract voltage and resistance values from the sensors.

 Caution: Do not conduct tests on electronic and computerized components without consulting the appropriate service manual. Improper testing methods can destroy a sensor.

Oxygen Sensor Service

The oxygen sensor has the ability to produce a small voltage signal, which is used by the electronic control unit to calculate the oxygen content in the exhaust gas. When there is a high oxygen content in the exhaust gas (lean mixture), the oxygen sensor generates a low signal of approximately 0.10 volt. When the oxygen content is low (rich mixture), the sensor generates approximately 1.0 volt. Many manufacturers require a scan tool to measure oxygen sensor output. Some oxygen sensors can be checked using a digital voltmeter.

There are two common causes of oxygen sensor failure. The first is age. Under normal operating conditions, an oxygen sensor can be expected to last approximately 70,000 miles. The second and most common cause of oxygen sensor failure is contamination. Carbon, lead, silica, and oil can all contaminate an oxygen sensor. The buildup of these substances will eventually cause sensor failure.

If a vehicle experiences multiple oxygen sensor failures, check for sensor contamination, **Figure 25-34.** Carbon leaves a black, fluffy coating. Silica contamination appears in the form of a white powder. Engine oil usually leaves a brown residue on the oxygen sensor. The cause of the contamination should be eliminated before replacing the sensor.

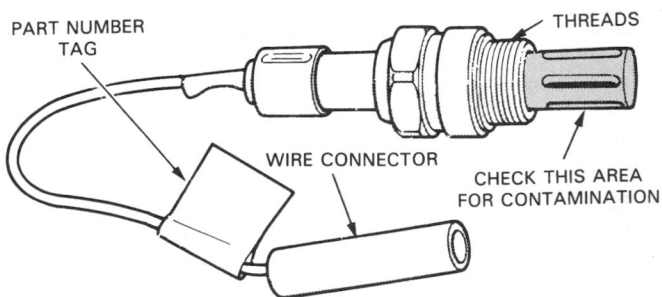

Figure 25-34. Check the oxygen sensor for signs of contamination. A buildup of silica, carbon, lead, or oil can cause failure. (Chrysler)

 Caution: The oxygen sensor is a very delicate device and should never be tested with an ohmmeter.

Engine Speed Sensor Service

When operating properly, the engine speed sensor generates a small voltage signal that is proportional to the speed of the engine. If the sensor is faulty, the correct voltage will not be produced. A defective engine speed sensor can cause problems with the ignition system and prevent the engine from running, **Figure 25-35.** A voltage check is commonly recommended for the engine speed sensor. As the engine is cranked, a small voltage should be produced in the sensor. If the voltage is not within the manufacturer's specifications, the sensor must be replaced. Many manufacturers recommend checking the resistance of the sensor coil. The resistance should be within specifications.

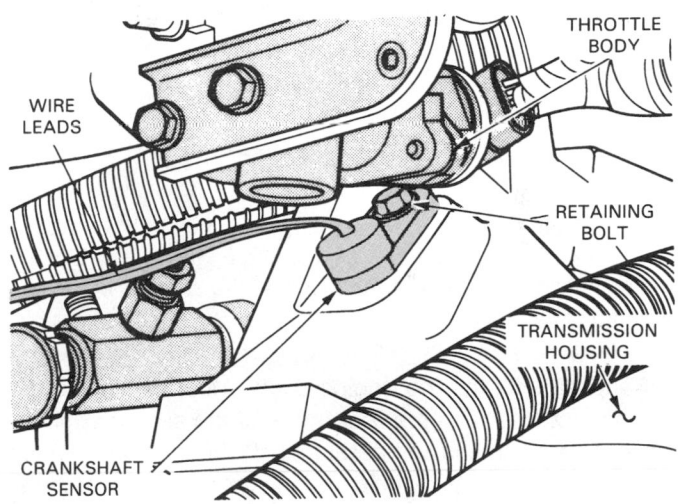

Figure 25-35. This engine speed sensor mounts directly to the block and monitors crankshaft rotation. Make sure the retaining bolt is tight and the wire leads are intact. (Chrysler)

Detonation Sensor Service

The detonation sensor converts abnormal engine vibrations into electrical signals. A faulty detonation sensor can adversely affect engine performance and fuel economy. If a trouble code indicates a problem in the detonation sensor circuit, the sensor can be easily checked with a variable timing light. Connect the timing light as recommended and run the engine at a fast idle. Lightly tap the intake manifold or the engine block near the sensor and watch the ignition timing, **Figure 25-36.** If the sensor is working correctly, it should retard the timing to compensate for the knock. The amount of change in timing should be proportional to the strength of the tapping. The maximum amount of timing change should be approximately 10 degrees. As an alternate method, some manufacturers recommend the use of a voltmeter or an ohmmeter to check the sensor. If the sensor does not produce the required readings, it must be replaced.

Coolant Temperature Sensor Service

The coolant temperature sensor varies its internal resistance as the operating temperature of the engine changes. The resistance is usually low when the engine is

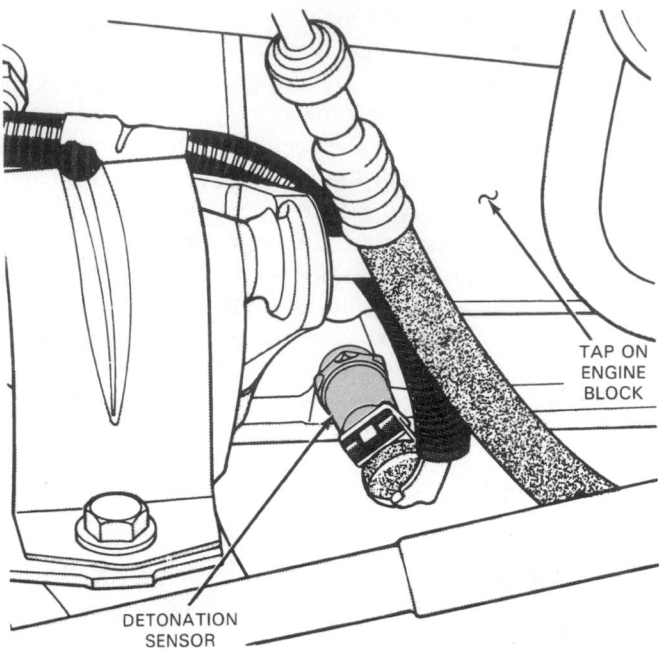

TAP ON
ENGINE
BLOCK

DETONATION
SENSOR

Figure 25-36. Detonation sensor operation can be checked by observing ignition timing while tapping on the engine block. Timing change should be proportional to the strength of the tapping. (Jeep)

hot and it climbs as the engine cools. Most manufacturers recommend checking the resistance of the sensor at different engine operating temperatures. If the resistance does not change or is not within recommended specifications, check the wiring for shorts or open circuits before condemning the sensor, **Figure 25-37.**

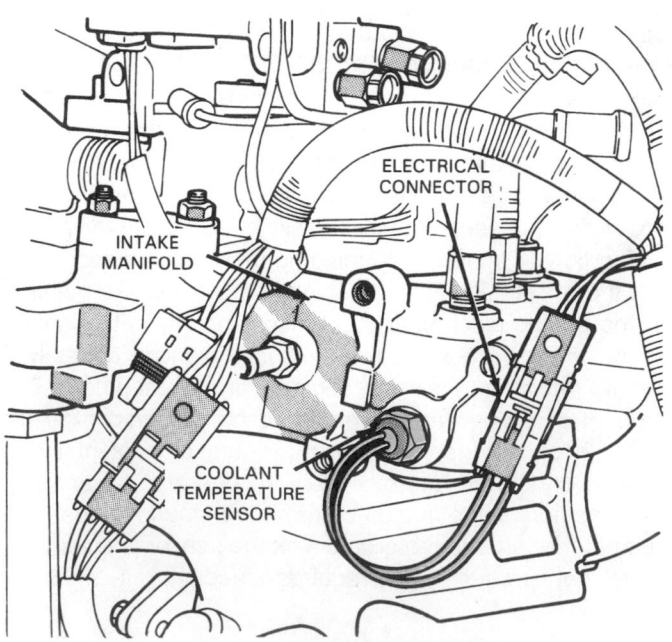

ELECTRICAL
CONNECTOR

INTAKE
MANIFOLD

COOLANT
TEMPERATURE
SENSOR

Figure 25-37. This coolant temperature sensor is mounted in intake manifold coolant passage area. Disconnect the wires at the electrical connector to check the sensor's resistance. (Jeep)

 Warning: Always depressurize the cooling system before removing the coolant temperature sensor.

Manifold Air Temperature Sensor Service

The manifold air temperature sensor is similar to the coolant temperature sensor. Usually, the resistance of the sensor is checked with a scan tool or an ohmmeter. Always follow the manufacturer's instructions when testing. A faulty air temperature can cause an excessively lean or rich fuel mixture.

Throttle Position Sensor Service

The throttle position sensor (TPS) changes its output signal in relation to the position of the throttle valve. The signal can range from 0.5 volts at idle to approximately 5 volts at wide open throttle. Many manufacturers recommend checking the TPS with a scan tool. Many of these tools are capable of displaying the signal voltage and the percentage of throttle opening. A voltmeter or an ohmmeter is sometimes recommended to check the operation of the TPS. A common test performed on a TPS involves slowly opening the throttle while monitoring changes in the output voltage. The voltage should rise smoothly and continuously in relation to the rate of throttle movement. If the voltage readout is erratic, the TPS must be replaced, **Figure 25-38.**

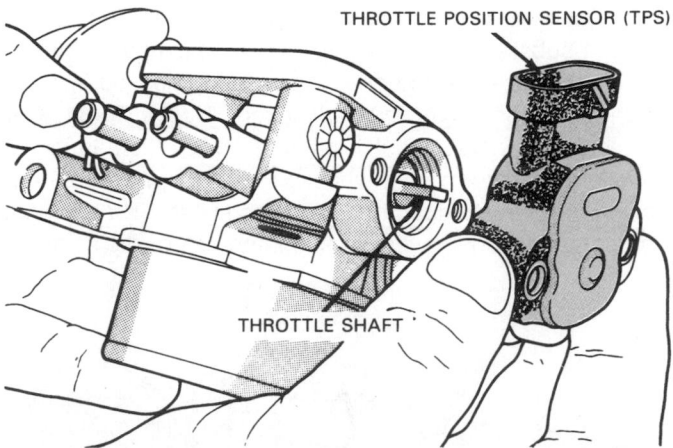

THROTTLE POSITION SENSOR (TPS)

THROTTLE SHAFT

Figure 25-38. If the resistance of the throttle position sensor is not within specifications, the unit must be replaced. This sensor was held in place with screws. Some throttle position sensors are equipped with tamper-resistant caps that must be removed before the sensor can be replaced. (Chrysler)

Manifold Absolute Pressure Sensor Service

The manifold absolute pressure sensor (MAP) responds to changes in manifold pressure (vacuum). An external vacuum source is often required when checking a MAP sensor. The sensor circuit's output voltage is usually checked while applying a specified amount of vacuum to the sensor. If the voltage at the recommended vacuum readings does not agree with the manufacturer's specifications, the sensor must be replaced. Always check vacuum hose connections when a faulty MAP sensor is suspected, **Figure 25-39.** Some manufacturers recommend taking resistance readings while applying vacuum to the sensor. A scan tool can also be used to check the manifold absolute pressure sensor. Using the scan tool usually eliminates the need for an external vacuum source. Always follow the manufacturer's recommendations when using a scan tool.

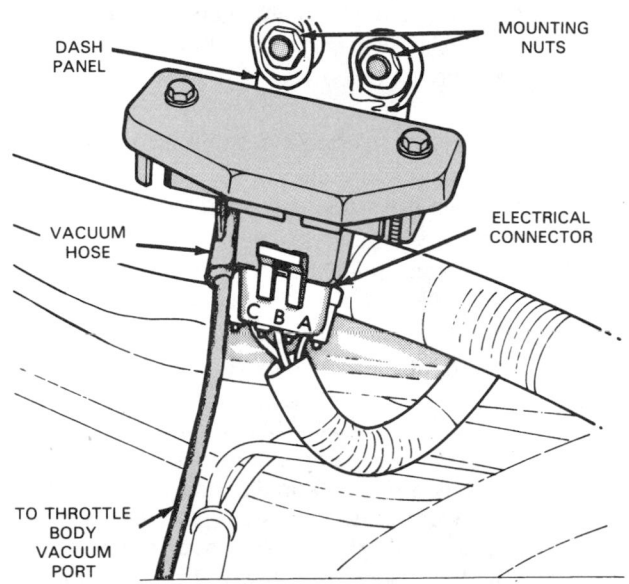

Figure 25-39.   One type of manifold absolute pressure (MAP) sensor. Note the vacuum hose that connects the sensor to the throttle body vacuum port. (Chrysler)

Airflow Sensor Service

Most airflow sensors vary their resistance in relation to the amount of air entering the engine. The resistance of some units can be checked with an ohmmeter and compared to the manufacturer's specifications. Some manufacturers recommend checking the sensor circuit output voltage using a digital voltmeter. Always check areas around the sensor for possible air leaks. An air leak around the sensor can cause false readings. Some airflow sensors must be tested with a scan tool. If a flap airflow sensor is used, make sure that the flap is pivoting freely. When checking a mass airflow sensor, make sure that the wire screen is free from obstructions that could restrict airflow, **Figure 25-40.**

Switching Sensor Service

Switching sensors are usually checked with an ohmmeter. If a switching sensor can be manually operated, it should be opened and closed while checking the component's resistance. These sensors should have high resistance when open and no resistance when closed. Switching sensors that use pressure sensitive elements are usually tested by checking resistance readings under specified operating conditions.

Checking Reference Voltage

Signal-modifying sensors will not operate properly if they are not receiving an acceptable reference voltage from

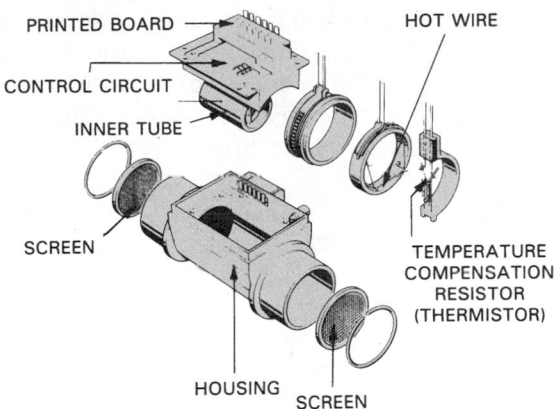

Figure 25-40.   Exploded view of a mass airflow sensor. Check the screens for obstructions that could limit airflow. (Bosch)

the electronic control unit. When testing signal modifying sensors, some manufacturers recommend that the reference voltage be verified.

To check reference voltage, connect a voltmeter to the sensor's input lead, **Figure 25-41.** The voltage reading should equal the value recommended by the manufacturer. A low voltage reading can be caused by an area of high resistance, such as an open circuit or a corroded connector. If wiring proves to be adequate, a faulty ECU could be the problem. Always consult the service manual for recommended procedures before attempting to measure the reference voltage.

Output Actuator Service

Defective output actuators can also cause problems in a computer control system. If an actuator is not operating

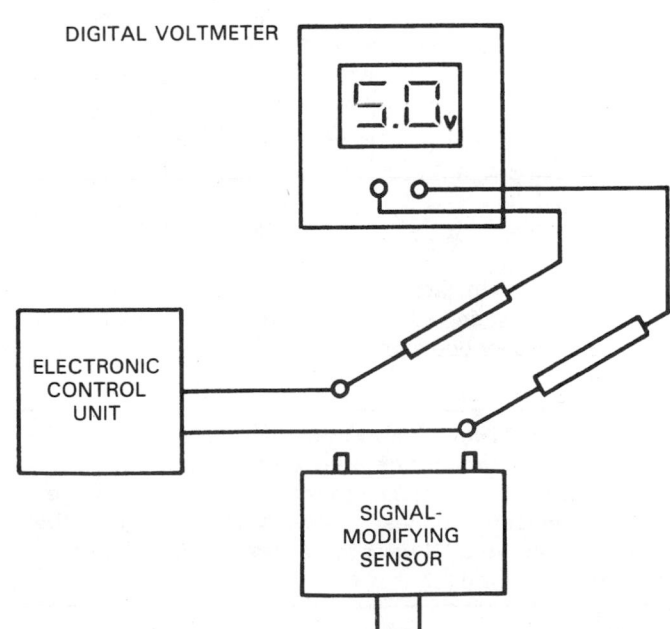

Figure 25-41.   Reference voltage can be checked with a traditional voltmeter. Make sure sensor wiring is in good condition.

correctly, the computer cannot control the system properly. Therefore, when a trouble code points to a specific circuit, it is important to verify the operation of the actuators in the circuit. Because actuators are either relays, motors, or solenoids, most actuator tests are fairly standard. Unlike sensors, most output actuators are operated by battery voltage and can often be checked by attempting to actuate them with a 12-volt power source.

Output Cycling Tests

Some systems with self-diagnostic capabilities have the ability to cycle the computer's output signals on and off. These signals trigger the actuators. Because actuators convert electrical signals into physical movements, most can be seen or heard when cycled on and off.

Standard Actuator Tests

Many systems still require individual actuator tests to verify proper operation. Most units can be checked by measuring their internal resistance with an ohmmeter. If the value measured does not fall within the range specified by the manufacturer, the unit must be replaced, **Figure 25-42.**

Some manufacturers recommend using jumper wires to apply an external voltage source (often battery voltage) to the actuator. If the component functions, you can assume that it is working properly.

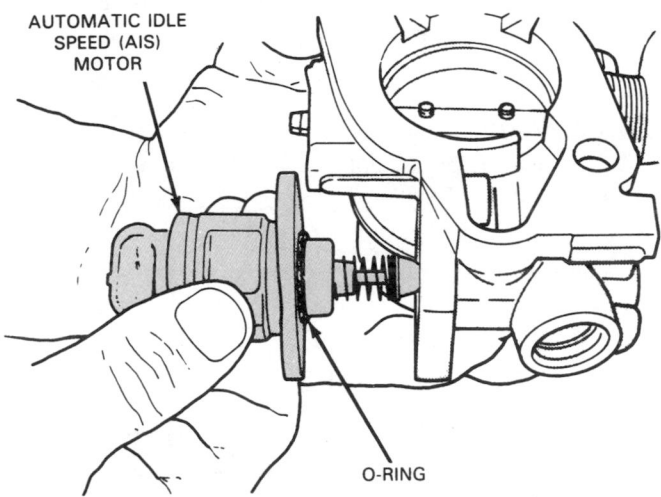

Figure 25-42. If the actuator does not respond when energized, it must be replaced. This idle speed motor is being checked for proper operation. (Chrysler)

 Note: Always follow manufacturer's recommendations when testing actuators. Improper testing methods or excessive voltage can severely damage these units. Always disconnect the actuator from the ECU prior to performing any testing procedures.

Electronic Control Unit Troubleshooting

The electronic control unit is one of the most dependable components on modern vehicles. Therefore, all other potential trouble spots should be tested before condemning the ECU. Always check the sensors and actuators before attempting to troubleshoot the electronic control unit. Check the wiring to the control unit for shorts and opens. To check for proper connections, unplug and reconnect all connectors going into the ECU.

Most manufacturers require the use of special testing equipment to verify ECU operation. Some units, however, can be tested with ordinary voltmeters and ohmmeters. Some self-diagnostic systems have the ability to locate ECU problems and to place appropriate trouble codes in memory.

Many technicians still depend on the process of elimination when servicing computer control systems. If all other system components are working properly, they assume that the electronic control module is causing the problem. This method is not recommended and should only be used as a last resort.

The electronic control module is a very delicate and expensive component. Always follow manufacturer's recommendations when testing and servicing these units.

Caution: Most electronic control units are sensitive to electrostatic discharge. The static electricity generated by sliding across a seat can destroy an ECU or a PROM chip. To reduce the risk of damage due to static electricity, always touch a good ground before handling the ECU or related electronic components. A grounding strap can also be worn to protect sensitive electronic parts. See Figure 25-43.

Electronic Control Unit Service

The electronic control unit, like most sensors, is not serviceable as a unit. When an ECU is found to be defective, it must be replaced. The computer's programmable read only memory chip (PROM), however, is removable and is usually reused when a new electronic control unit is installed. When removing the ECU from a vehicle, always turn the ignition key off. As an added precaution, the battery should be disconnected. The computer can be removed from a vehicle by simply disconnecting all wires from the unit and unbolting it from its mounting brackets.

When changing an ECU, always replace it with an identical unit. Manufacturers produce many different types of electronic control units. Always record the faulty unit's identification number. The year and model of the vehicle you are working on may not provide the information required to obtain an exact replacement.

Replacing a PROM Chip

When replacing an electronic control unit, the original PROM chip is often installed in the new unit. This is because the information stored in PROM is specific to the vehicle being repaired.

A special tool should always be used when handling a PROM chip. Never touch a PROM chip directly. Oil from hands and fingers can have an adverse effect on the operation of the chip. Before removing the chip, note its position.

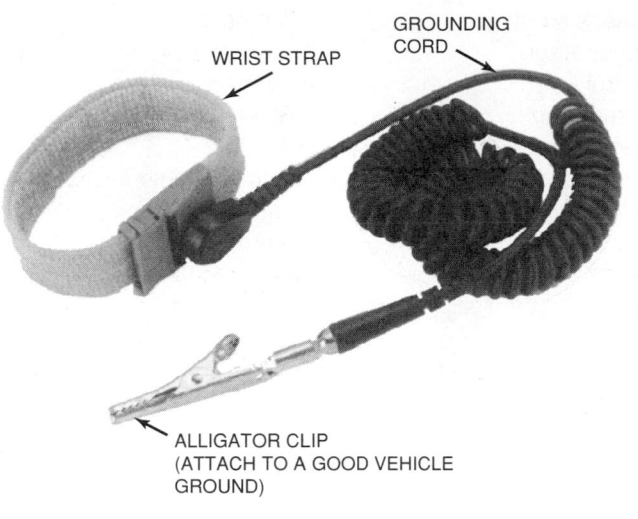

WRIST STRAP

GROUNDING CORD

ALLIGATOR CLIP
(ATTACH TO A GOOD VEHICLE GROUND)

A

NOTICE

CONTENTS SENSITIVE TO STATIC ELECTRICITY

HANDLE IN ACCORDANCE WITH STATIC CONTROL PROCEDURES GM9107P and GM9108P, OR GM DIVISIONAL SERVICE MANUALS.

B

Figure 25-43. Always touch a good ground or put on an approved grounding strap before handling components that are sensitive to static electricity. A—Anti-static wrist strap. B—Some units are labeled with a warning similar to the one shown. (OTC, Pontiac)

Many manufacturers mark the PROM to ensure proper installation. Gently pull the PROM chip from its socket.

Before installing a PROM into a new unit, make sure it is positioned correctly. If the PROM is installed incorrectly, it will be destroyed. See **Figure 25-44.**

To install a PROM, simply press it into the correct socket in the ECU. A blunt, nonmetallic object should be used to avoid touching the chip. Gently press on the corners of the PROM to make sure it is seated properly.

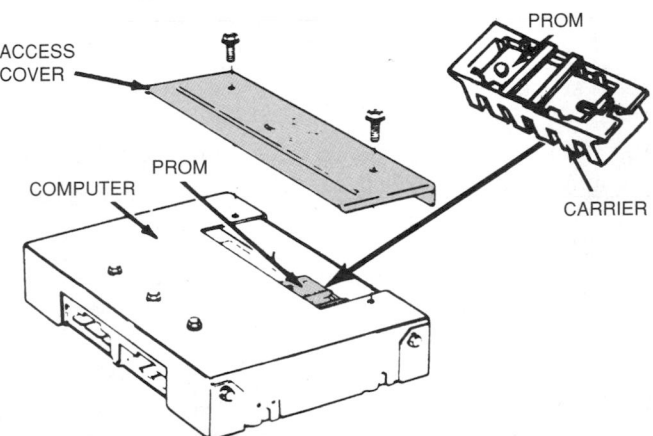

ACCESS COVER

PROM

COMPUTER

PROM

CARRIER

Figure 25-44. The PROM chip can be moved from one computer to another. Never touch the PROM with bare hands. Note that this PROM chip is mounted in a special carrier. Always use the correct PROM removal tool.

Tech Talk

About 30 years ago, the only electronic part on an automobile was the radio. The first electronic ignition systems and electronic voltage regulators were introduced in the mid 1960s and did not become common until almost ten years later. Technicians who could understand point-type ignition systems and five or six circuits in the carburetor were considered current. A technician in those days could keep up with things by keeping his eyes open and gaining some trial-and-error experience as newer cars came into the shop.

Of course, all of this has changed. The modern technician must understand electronic ignitions, fuel injection, emission controls, on-board computers, and all sorts of government rules and regulations. Just keeping up from year to year takes considerable reading and study.

So what does this mean to you, the future technician? For starters, trial-and-error learning is out. One error on a computer-controlled system will destroy several hundred dollars worth of computer equipment.

The only way to troubleshoot and repair the new systems properly and efficiently is to get your hands on every bit of new information you can and study it thoroughly. Now is the time to begin collecting information about modern vehicles and taking time to read about the latest developments.

Summary

Computerized engine control systems offer accurate and instantaneous control over the fuel, ignition, and emission systems. These systems are much more dependable than their mechanical predecessors.

There are several common components in all computer control systems, including sensors, an electronic control unit, and actuators.

Computer control system operation can be divided into three stages: the input stage, the processing stage, and the output stage. During the input stage, sensors send signals to the electronic control unit. During the processing stage, the ECU analyzes these signals and decides if any adjustments are required. If necessary, engine operating conditions are adjusted during the output stage.

Sensors are devices that convert physical conditions into electrical signals. Some sensors generate their own voltage signals. Other sensors modify a reference voltage that is supplied by the electronic control unit.

The electronic control unit is a complex device constructed of integrated circuits, printed circuit boards, and miscellaneous other electronic components. It is not necessary to know how these components work. However, it is helpful to understand the basic operations of the ECU when trying to locate trouble in computer controlled systems. The ECU can be divided into five sections: the input section, memory section, arithmetic/logic section, control section, and the output section.

Actuators are devices that convert electrical output signals into physical movements. Most actuators can be classified as motors, solenoids, or relays.

A logical approach must be taken when troubleshooting a computer controlled system. Today's automotive technician must rely on information found in service manuals, diagnostic charts, and other service publications when trying to locate problems.

Most computer control systems have self-diagnostic capabilities. These systems continuously monitor the operation of the sensors, the ECU, and the actuators. A trouble code is placed in the computer's memory if an abnormal operating condition is detected. Trouble codes can be accessed in several ways. Always consult the appropriate service manual for the proper method.

Although self-diagnostic systems can locate a malfunctioning circuit, they do not pinpoint the source of the problem. Therefore, specific tests, called pinpoint tests, are often required to locate the exact cause of a problem.

Sensors and actuators can usually be tested with standard equipment. Some manufacturers, however, require the use of specialized diagnostic tools to troubleshoot individual components. Never conduct tests on electronic or computerized components without consulting the appropriate service manual.

Know These Terms

Sensors
Electronic control unit
Output actuator
Input stage
Processing stage
Output stage
Control loop
Closed loop
Open loop
Signal-producing sensor
Oxygen sensors
Engine speed sensor
Engine position sensor
Detonation sensor
Knock sensor
Signal-modifying sensor
Reference voltage
Coolant temperature sensor
Manifold air temperature (MAT) sensor
Throttle position sensor (TPS)
Manifold absolute pressure (MAP) sensor
Airflow sensor
Switching sensor
Electronic control unit (ECU)
Input section
Memory section
ROM
PROM
RAM
Arithmetic/logic section
Control section
Output section
Output actuators
Fuel injector
Idle speed motor
Mixture control solenoid
Electric fan relay
Ignition module
Coil
Self-diagnostic systems
Disabled mode
Limp-in mode
Warning light
Trouble codes
Diagnostic link
Trouble code chart
Scan tools
Diagnostic analyzer

Review Questions—Chapter 25

Do not write in this book. Write your answers on a separate sheet of paper.

Match the components on the left with the stage of operation on the right.

1. ECU.
2. Ignition coil.
3. Alternator voltage.
4. Fuel injector.
5. Mixture solenoid.
6. Electric fan relay.
7. Oxygen sensor.

(A) Input.
(B) Processing.
(C) Output.

8. If the engine coolant or oxygen sensor is at 100°F (38°C), the computer control system will be in _____ loop mode.
9. A sensor that generates its own voltage signal is called a _____.
10. The three types of memory commonly used in an automotive computer system include _____, _____, and _____.
11. Actuators convert electrical signals into _____.
12. To assist the technician when troubleshooting computer controlled systems, many manufacturers have designed _____-_____ capabilities into their systems.
13. The _____ can be used as a connecting point for various control system test equipment.
14. Since most actuators can be classified as motors, relays, or solenoids, they can be tested by applying an external _____ to the appropriate input terminals.

15. The last component to be tested in the computer control system should be the _____.

ASE-Type Questions

1. Technician A says that the use of computers in the automotive industry was prompted by governmental regulations requiring better mileage. Technician B says that the use of computers in the automotive industry was prompted by governmental regulations requiring fewer emissions. Who is right?
   (A) A only.
   (B) B only.
   (C) Both A & B.
   (D) Neither A nor B.

2. An oxygen sensor monitors the oxygen content in the _____.
   (A) incoming air
   (B) exhaust gases
   (C) crankcase vapors
   (D) All of the above, depending on where it is placed.

3. Technician A says that a flap airflow sensor eliminates the need for a barometric pressure sensor. Technician B says that a heated wire airflow sensor can compensate for changes in air temperature and atmospheric pressure. Who is right?
   (A) A only.
   (B) B only.
   (C) Both A & B.
   (D) Neither A nor B.

4. If a severe problem occurs in a computer controlled system, the system may respond by _____.
   (A) forcing the engine into open loop operation
   (B) placing a trouble code into the systems memory
   (C) illuminating a warning light on the vehicle dashboard
   (D) All of the above.

5. Technician A says that a flashing warning light is often used to display trouble codes. Technician B says that an oxygen sensor can be tested with an ohmmeter. Who is right?
   (A) A only.
   (B) B only.
   (C) Both A & B.
   (D) Neither A nor B.

6. Output cycling tests perform which the following operations?
   (A) Measure the output of various sensors.
   (B) Verify the operation of the self-diagnostic system.
   (C) Switch ECU output signals on and off to verify operation of actuators.
   (D) All of the above.

7. Technician A says that if the electronic control unit is faulty, it must be replaced. Technician B says that a defective oxygen sensor can be cleaned and reinstalled. Who is right?
   (A) A only.
   (B) B only.
   (C) Both A & B.
   (D) Neither A nor B.

8. The only part of the electronic control unit that can be serviced is the _____.
   (A) internal printed circuit board.
   (B) arithmetic/logic section.
   (C) PROM chip.
   (D) All of the above.

9. A diagnostic trouble code indicates that the oxygen sensor is reading a rich exhaust. Technician A says that the problem could be a defective sensor. Technician B says that the rich exhaust could be a result of a defect in the engine. Who is right?
   (A) A only.
   (B) B only.
   (C) Both A & B.
   (D) Neither A nor B.

10. The ECU activates the vehicle's check engine light, however, no codes are stored. Technician A says this is a result of an intermittent sensor failure. Technician B says that this indicates that the ECU is defective. Who is right?
    (A) A only.
    (B) B only.
    (C) Both A & B.
    (D) Neither A nor B.

Suggested Activities

1. Using factory service manuals, locate the computer diagnostic test connectors on several different makes of vehicle. Make a chart comparing the connector locations by manufacturer and the type of equipment needed to access the trouble codes. Sketch the shapes of the connectors and show which terminals must be connected to put the computer into the diagnostic mode.

2. Obtain a vehicle with an on-board computer and retrieve trouble codes. Use the procedure outlined in the service manual. If your instructor okays it, create trouble codes by disconnecting a computer sensor or an output device and briefly running the engine. What codes were found? What do the codes indicate?

3. Based on the above activities, consult the appropriate factory service manual to determine the next steps to be taken to isolate a computer problem.

4. Determine the effect on the computer system of disconnecting a non-computer device. For instance, what happens to the fuel mixture when the air injector (smog) pump belt is removed? What happens to the timing advance if a vacuum leak develops on an engine with MAP sensor? What happens to the computer open and closed loop cycle if the cooling system thermostat is removed? Discuss you findings with the other members of the class and try to figure out how one system affects another.

Can you locate the alternator and the starter on this 5.7-liter V-8 engine? (Buick)

26

Charging and Starting System Service

After studying this chapter, you will be able to:
* Install, test, and service a battery.
* Use jumper cables correctly.
* Test, service, and repair a charging system.
* Service an alternator and a voltage regulator.
* Test, service, and repair a starting system.
* Service a starter and starter solenoid.

This chapter covers the service of the starting and charging systems, including the battery, starter, starter solenoid, alternator, voltage regulator, and associated cables and wiring. Effective operation of a vehicle's electrical system depends on a good battery, a charging system that can keep the battery charged, and a starting system that can properly utilize the battery power.

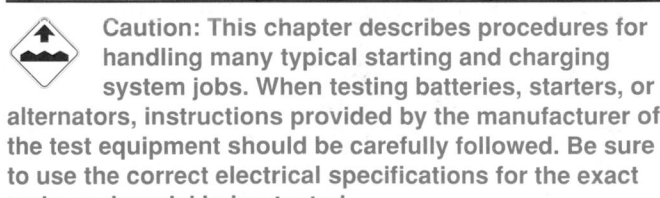 **Caution: This chapter describes procedures for handling many typical starting and charging system jobs. When testing batteries, starters, or alternators, instructions provided by the manufacturer of the test equipment should be carefully followed. Be sure to use the correct electrical specifications for the exact make and model being tested.**

Battery Service

The effectiveness of the starting system depends on the vehicle **battery.** The battery plays a key roll in the overall functioning of the electrical system. To ensure reliability and extend useful service life, the battery should receive periodic inspection and maintenance. The level of **electrolyte** (the liquid in each battery cell) must be correct. The battery must be fully charged. The posts must be clean. Battery cables and terminals must be in good condition and firmly attached. The charging system should also be functioning correctly to recharge the battery during operation.

Visual Inspection

A visual inspection will help to determine which battery maintenance services are needed. Typical needs include cleaning the cable terminals, battery posts, and battery top; adding distilled water to the cells (not needed with maintenance-free battery); tightening the battery hold-down;

charging the battery; or replacing the battery. A 12-volt side terminal battery is shown in **Figure 26-1.**

Batteries Can Be Dangerous

Battery service involves two dangerous substances: corrosive electrolyte and explosive gases. Battery electrolyte contains about 38% **sulfuric acid** and can cause serious skin and eye burns. If the electrolyte contacts your skin, flush the area with large quantities of cold water. If it contacts your eyes, flush them with cold water and then consult a physician. Battery acid on the vehicle or on clothing should be flushed with cold water. Follow with a mixture of baking soda and water to neutralize the acid.

In most cases, battery electrolyte is premixed and does not require mixing by the technician. If it is ever necessary to mix sulfuric acid and water to make an electrolyte mixture, pour the acid into the water. Do not pour water into the acid. Add acid slowly and stir constantly with a clean stick.

Battery charging creates a mixture of hydrogen and oxygen gases, which is extremely flammable. The slightest source of ignition can ignite the mixture, causing it to burn with explosive force. This could rupture the battery case and throw acid over a wide area Never strike a spark, light a match, or bring other open flames near a battery.

The following safety rules should be observed at all times:

* When handling battery electrolyte, wear goggles and rubber gloves.
* Use a properly fitted lift strap to move batteries.
* When a battery is removed from the vehicle, place it where it will not be knocked over, dropped, or exposed to sparks or flame.
* Store battery acid or dry-charge battery electrolyte where the containers will not be broken.

Dealing with Corrosion

The hydrogen gas produced by battery charging is highly corrosive. The hydrogen eventually attacks the terminals. This causes corrosion. Unless the corrosion is removed, the terminals will be eaten away. Corrosion also causes high resistance between the battery terminals and

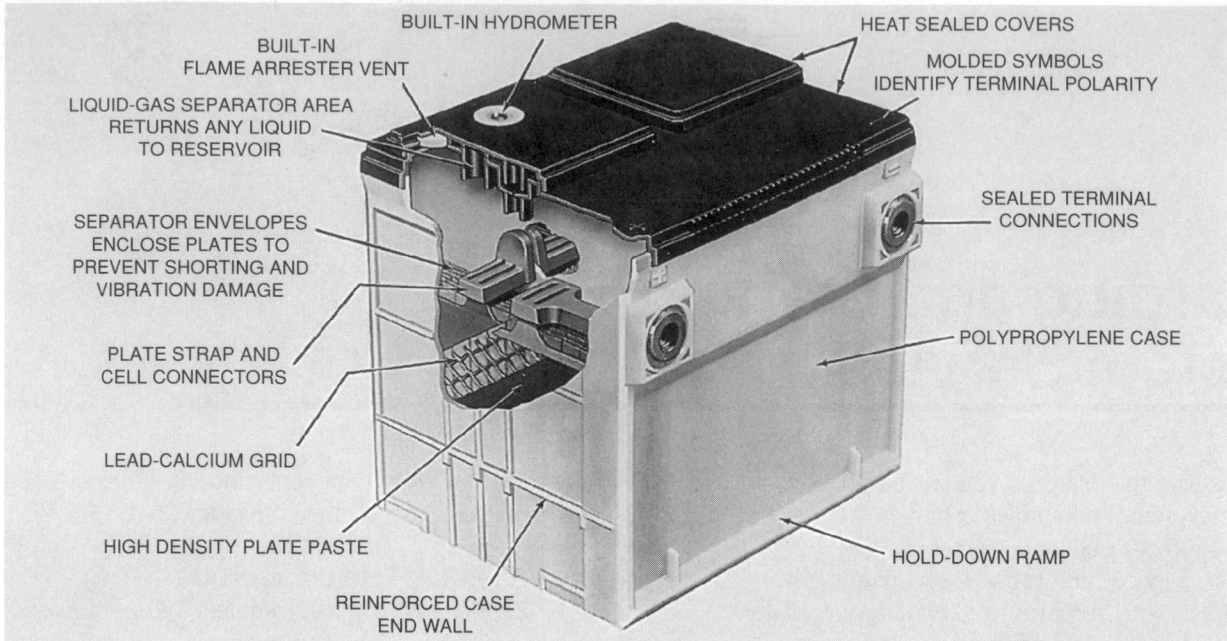

Figure 26-1. A typical 12-volt side terminal battery. Note the sealed construction and the use of a built-in hydrometer. (General Motors)

battery posts, making electrical flow difficult. A dirty battery top will attract electrolyte and become conductive, allowing a small but steady flow of current from one post to the other. Such a condition will cause slow discharge of the battery.

Use a wire brush to clean away the bulk of the corrosion. Remove the battery cable terminals. Plug the cap vent holes (if used) with toothpicks or masking tape. Brush a solution of baking soda and water over the terminals, posts, and battery top. Do not allow the baking soda mixture to enter the battery cells, **Figure 26-2.**

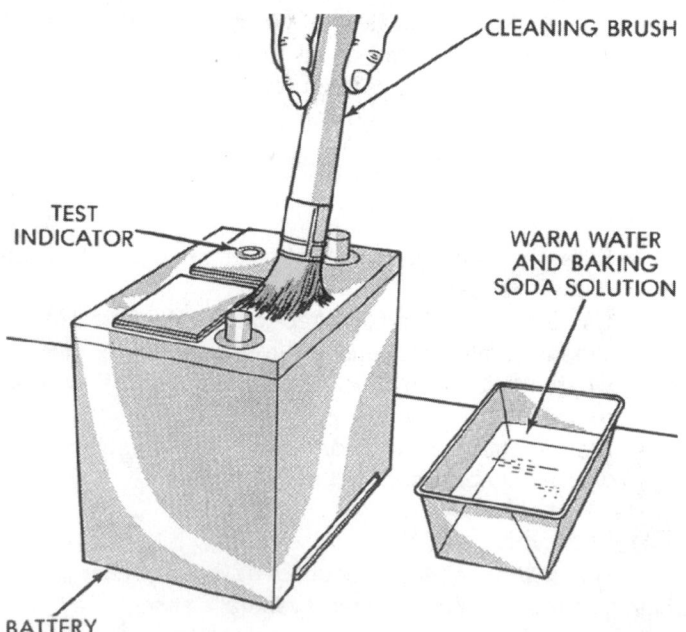

Figure 26-2. A solution of baking soda and water can be used to clean corrosion from a battery. Do not allow the solution to enter the battery cells. (Chrysler)

Let the solution stand until the foaming action stops. Apply fresh solution to areas needing it. Then, rinse thoroughly with clean water. Wipe the posts and terminals dry. Brighten the posts and the inside of the terminals with sandpaper or a steel brush. Coat them with nonmetallic grease. Install the terminals and tighten them securely. Install a protective terminal boot. Finally, remove the plugs from the cap vents.

Battery Hold-Down Should Be Snug

The battery hold-down device should be tight enough to hold the battery securely, but not tight enough to place excessive pressure on the case. Undue hold-down pressure can cause case failure.

Replace badly eroded hold-downs. Coat bolts and nuts with grease to protect against corrosion. Several efficient spray products that prevent corrosion are also available.

Check Electrolyte Level

On batteries with filler caps, check the electrolyte level in each cell. Most batteries have a correct level indicator (slot, notch, lip). Add water to bring the electrolyte up to the mark. If no mark is used, raise the level to 3/8″ (9.53 mm) above the top of the separators. To prevent electrolyte leakage caused by expansion pressure, avoid overfilling. When a battery uses an excessive amount of water, check the system for overcharging. Prolonged overcharging will reduce battery life.

Use Distilled Water

Although some tap water may be satisfactory for filling a battery, it is best to use distilled water. Tap water in many areas has a high mineral content. It will prove injurious to batteries. Keep distilled battery water in a clearly marked container.

Checking Battery Condition

The condition of a given battery is determined by the state of charge, the temperature, and the mechanical condition of the plates, separators, and connectors. Although it is difficult to determine the exact amount of useful life remaining in any battery, several tests will give an indication of its ability to perform satisfactorily for a period of time.

Cold weather reduces the efficiency of batteries. **Figure 26-3** illustrates how battery capacity (amount of electricity that can be drawn from a fully charged battery in a specified length of time) is reduced in cold temperatures. A battery that cranks a vehicle during moderate weather may crank slowly or fail completely during the first cold snap.

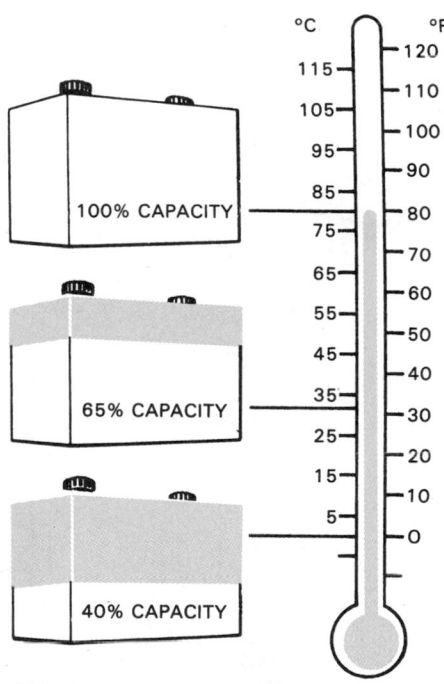

Figure 26-3. Battery capacity is greatly reduced by cold weather. Capacities at indicated temperatures are for sound, fully charged batteries. (Gulf Oil)

There are two kinds of tests that can be given to modern batteries: a specific gravity test and an electrical load test. The specific gravity test can only be performed on batteries with removable filler caps. The load test can be performed on any type of battery. If tests indicate a borderline condition, discard the battery. The little additional use that can be squeezed out by leaving the battery in service will be offset by the cost of charging, the possibility of a failure in the field, and the cost of a service call.

> **Note: If a battery is frozen, it cannot be tested. Only badly discharged batteries will freeze. In addition, freezing generally damages the battery plates. Therefore, frozen batteries should be replaced. If a frozen battery is not replaced, it must be thawed and recharged before testing.**

Checking Open-Circuit Voltage before Testing

The *open-circuit voltage test* (no load on the battery) is performed with a voltmeter. The battery cables must be disconnected for this test. Always remove the negative cable first. If the battery was recently charged, boosted, or load tested, allow it to stabilize for 15 minutes before starting the test. Connect the meter leads to the battery terminals. Make sure the positive meter lead is connected to the positive battery terminal and the negative lead is connected to the negative terminal. The voltage reading across the terminals will indicate the *percentage of charge* in the battery. See **Figure 26-4**. Open-circuit voltage should be approximately 12.6 volts. Note the relationship between open-circuit voltage and the percentage of charge.

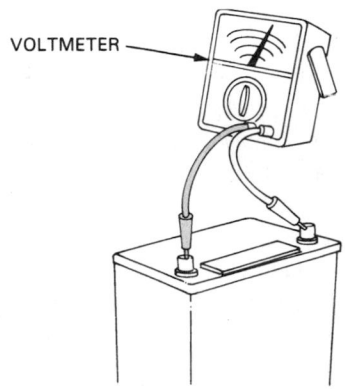

BATTERY OPEN CIRCUIT VOLTAGE	
Open Circuit Volts	**Percent Charge**
11.7 volts or less	0%
12.0	25%
12.2	50%
12.4	75%
12.6 or more	100%

Figure 26-4. Checking open-circuit voltage with a voltmeter. Follow the test instrument operating instructions carefully. (Dodge)

> **STOP** **Warning: A charging battery or a recently charged battery will have a great deal of hydrogen and oxygen gas in its cells. A spark from the voltmeter prods could ignite it.**

If open circuit voltage is below specifications, the battery must be charged before further testing can be done.

Specific Gravity Test

The *specific gravity* of the electrolyte in a battery provides an indication of battery charge and cell condition. A fully charged battery will have a specific gravity from 1.230-1.280. Specific gravity is a comparison between the weight of electrolyte and the weight of water, which has a specific gravity of 1. The electrolyte of a charged battery, therefore, is 1.230 to 1.280 times heavier than the same amount of water.

As the battery becomes discharged, the sulfuric acid combines with the plate material. This leaves a lower percentage of acid in the electrolyte. Since the sulfuric acid is heavier than water, the reduction in acid content will reduce the electrolyte's specific gravity. By measuring the specific gravity of a sample of the electrolyte with a **hydrometer,** the state of charge can be determined.

Check Specific Gravity with a Hydrometer

Note: A specific gravity test is possible only when the battery has removable fill caps. If the electrolyte level is so low that it is impossible to draw a sufficient amount into the hydrometer, add water and either charge the battery or check the charge after a reasonable amount of vehicle usage. Never add water just before checking specific gravity.

If the battery was just charged, crank the engine for several seconds to reduce the **surface charge** (electrolyte at the top of the battery temporarily having a higher-than-average charge). Hold the hydrometer in a vertical position and draw in enough electrolyte to suspend the float. Then, squirt the electrolyte out. Repeat this sequence several times to bring the float temperature to that of the electrolyte. The float should not touch either the bottom or top of the float barrel. Allow the gas bubbles to rise to the surface and any sediment to sink to the bottom before taking a reading. See **Figure 26-5.**

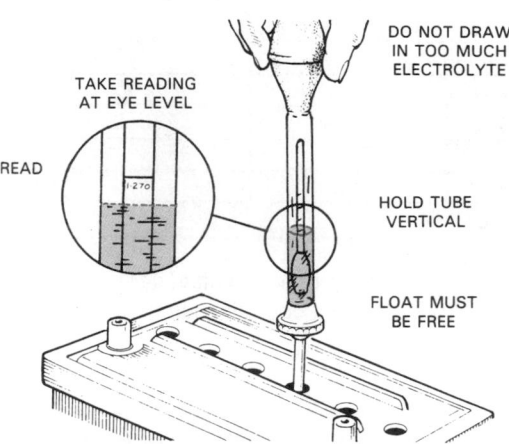

Figure 26-5. Draw electrolyte into the hydrometer until the float is suspended free of both top and bottom of glass barrel. Read the hydrometer at eye level. (British Leyland)

The higher the specific gravity, the higher the float will ride out of the electrolyte. Hold the hydrometer at eye level. Note the scale reading at the exact point the float scale emerges from the electrolyte. This reading will have to be corrected by relating it to the standard 80°F (26.7°C) test temperature.

The chart in **Figure 26-6** shows the relationship between electrolyte specific gravity and state of charge. Specific gravity for a fully charged battery will vary slightly from battery to battery.

State of Charge*	Specific Gravities as Used in Cold and Temperate Climates		Specific Gravity as Used in Tropical Climates
Fully Charged	1.280	1.260	1.225
75% Charged	1.230	1.215	1.180
50% Charged	1.180	1.170	1.135
25% Charged	1.130	1.120	1.090
Discharged	1.080	1.070	1.045

*State of charge as indicated by specific gravity when discharged at 20 hour rate.

The above are more or less typical specific gravity ranges. Gravity ranges will vary somewhat, depending on battery construction and ratio of electrolyte volume to active material.

Figure 26-6. Relationship between specific gravity and battery state of charge. (AABM)

Correcting Float Reading for Temperature

Note the temperature of the electrolyte and add .004 for each 10°F (5.55°C) above 80°F (26.7°C) or subtract .004 for each 10°F (5.55°C) below 80°F (26.7°C). This requires the use of a hydrometer with a built-in thermometer, **Figure 26-7.** For example, assume that the specific gravity reading is 1.125 and the electrolyte temperature is 110°F (43.4°C). Since the temperature is 30°F (16.6°C) above the standard temperature, the technician must add .012 (3 × .004) to the original reading to get a corrected specific gravity reading of 1.137.

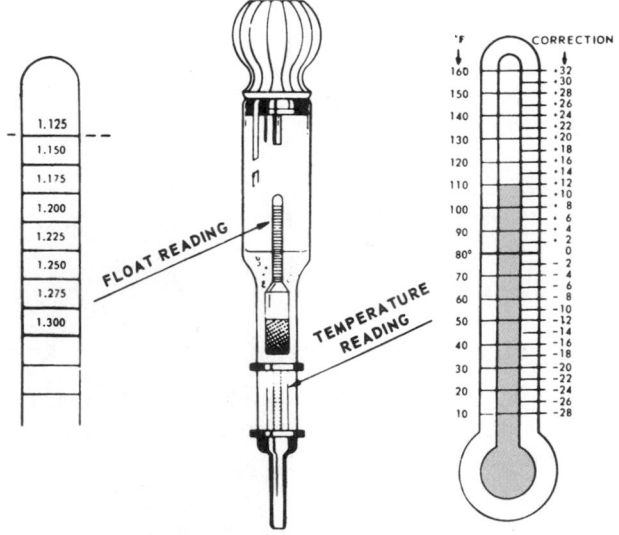

Figure 26-7. Temperature correcting hydrometer float reading. (Ignition Mfg's. Inst.)

Interpreting Hydrometer Readings

When a hydrometer reading indicates that the battery is less than 75% charged (1.215-1.260), it should be recharged. Attempt to determine the reason for the low state of charge. Possible problems include a defective alternator or regulator, excessive electrical loads, or a battery defect.

A difference of more than 25 points (.025) between individual cell readings indicates that the battery is starting to fail due to internal shorts, plate deterioration, or loss of acid. If the highest cell specific gravity is below 1.190, charge the battery and then retest it. Perform the capacity (load) test for a more accurate picture of battery condition.

Built-in Hydrometer

Many batteries are sealed and have a built-in hydrometer. Refer to **Figure 26-8.** Battery state of charge is indicated by the color of the built-in hydrometer, or "eye" indicator. When the battery is charged, the indicator will show as a darkened area with a bright green (or other color on some batteries) dot in the center. A sound but discharged battery is indicated by a darkened indicator with no center dot. A battery that generally needs replacing will be indicated by a bright (clear) indicator with no dot.

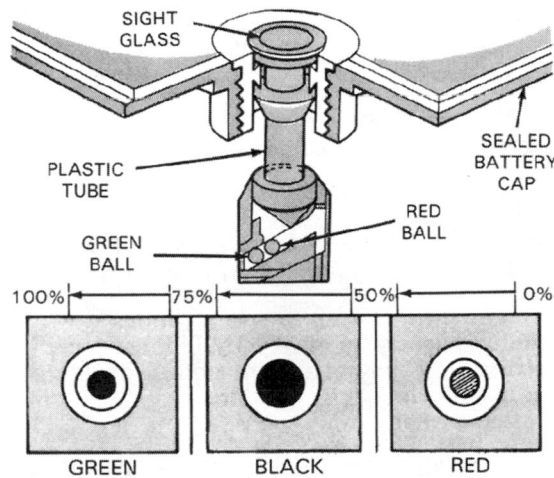

Figure 26-8. A battery indicator "eye" (built-in hydrometer) provides a fast check on battery condition. (Chrysler)

Electrical Load Test

Open-circuit voltage and specific gravity readings provide a general indication of battery condition. However, a more accurate appraisal may be made by making an **electrical load test.**

 Note: Do not attempt the electrical load test if either the open-circuit voltage or the specific gravity readings indicate that the battery is discharged. Recharge the battery before testing.

Attach the electrical load tester as directed by the manufacturer. Connect the positive leads to the battery positive post. Connect the negative leads to the negative post. All electrical load testers have a device used to place an adjustable electrical load on the battery. Therefore, the tester should be switched off to prevent sparking when attaching the leads. If necessary, also attach a voltmeter to the battery.

 Note: Many newer battery testers will automatically go through the battery testing procedure once the tester cables are attached. Follow the tester manufacturer's directions carefully.

If the battery was just charged, crank the engine for about 15 seconds or use the tester to apply a load of approximately 300 amps on the battery to reduce the surface charge. Then wait for about 15 seconds to allow the battery electrolyte to stabilize.

Next, apply the load specified on the battery label, usually as the "test load." Wait for 15 seconds and then read the battery voltage. Immediately remove the electrical load. At a battery temperature of 70°F (21°C), the battery voltage should not drop below 9.6 volts. If the battery temperature is lower, the voltage will also be lower on a good battery. As a general rule, voltage can be at 9.1 volts at 32°F (0°C) and 8.5 volts at 0°F (–17.8°C) for a good battery. Check the manufacturer's specifications for exact temperature and voltage relationships. Battery temperature can be estimated by determining the temperature that the battery has been exposed to for the preceding three hours.

If the battery voltage was at or above the minimum during the load test, the battery is good. If the voltage is below the minimum specification, the battery should be replaced.

Battery Charging

Batteries in sound mechanical condition can be brought up to full charge with a **battery charger.** The battery charger is used to pass a metered amount of DC (direct current) electricity through the battery. Fast charging or slow charging may be used. As the charging rate is increased, the time necessary to completely recharge the battery is reduced.

Slow Charging

Slow charging passes a relatively small amount of current, usually around 5 to 7 amps, through the battery for a fairly long period (14-16 hours or longer).

Slow charging is preferred to fast charging if time is available. Heavily sulphated batteries (plate active materials changed to lead sulphate, which resists essential chemical reactions) can overheat during fast charging. Because battery cell condition is not always known, slow charging minimizes the risk of possible damage caused by charging. However, a sound battery will not be damaged by proper fast charging.

Begin by cleaning the battery and filling it to the recommended level (if it has filler caps). Replace the caps where used. If the battery will remain in the vehicle, disconnect the cables to prevent damage to electronic components.

Attach the positive charger lead to the positive battery post. Connect the negative lead to the negative post. Switch the charger to either 6 or 12 volts as needed. Set the rate of charge to the lowest possible setting that will recharge the battery in the time allowed. The battery will generally be fully charged within 12-16 hours, although a sulphated battery may require longer. Leave the battery on the charger until the specific gravity or no-load voltage test indicates that it is fully charged.

Watch the battery temperature during charging. If the temperature exceeds 125°F (51.7°C), lower the charge rate. Temperatures in excess of 125°F (51.7°C) will cause serious battery damage. Be certain to remove the battery when charged. Overcharging is harmful.

Fast Charging

Fast charging sends a relatively high initial current, usually about 50 to 60 amps, through the battery. This will charge most batteries in a reasonably short time (one to two hours).

Before fast charging, clean the battery and add water if necessary. Disconnect the battery cables to protect electronic devices. Then, attach the fast charger positive lead to battery positive post and the negative lead to negative post. Set the current control as directed. Switch the charger to either 6 or 12 volts as needed and turn it on. As the battery charge begins to rise, many chargers will automatically reduce the charging rate. Watch battery temperature. If it reaches 125°F (51.7°C), lower the rate at once.

If the specific gravity or no-load voltage tests do not show a considerable increase within an hour, try slow charging the battery.

Trickle Charging

Wet batteries (batteries containing electrolyte) that must be kept for any length of time are often placed on a *trickle charger.* The trickle charger passes a very low current, often less than one ampere, through the batteries. Despite the small current, batteries can be damaged from trickle charging. Many shops shut off the trickle charger during the night to help prevent overcharging.

Battery Storage

If a wet battery is not to be trickle charged, it should be stored in a cool, dry area. A battery stored at 0°F (−17.8 °C) will retain a charge for nearly a year, while the same battery stored at 125°F (51.7°C) will lose its charge within a month.

Dry-charged batteries (batteries with plates charged but contain no electrolyte) must be stored in a cool, dry area with as even a temperature as possible. Although the dry-charged battery will retain its charge over a long period of time, it is wise to activate the battery by the end of the third year of storage.

Activating a Dry-Charged Battery

Most modern automotive batteries are wet, but the technician may encounter some dry-charged batteries. These batteries are used in farm equipment, lawn equipment, and motorcycles. Proper activation (preparing battery for service) steps should be followed.

When activating a dry-charged battery, observe the following instructions. Take the time needed to do the job right. This will prevent unnecessary comebacks and complaints.

Remove the cell caps and the cell cap vent plugs. Using a glass or plastic funnel, add the specified electrolyte to each cell until the separators are just covered (this allows room for expansion during charging). To prevent a chemical reaction, never use a metal funnel when adding electrolyte.

After filling, replace the caps. Place the battery on the charger and apply a moderate charge to the battery, depending on the instructions supplied with the battery. If excessive gassing occurs, lower the charge rate. Continue charging the battery until the specific gravity reaches at least 1.240 and the electrolyte temperature is 80°F (26.5°C) or above. It is important that both specific gravity and temperature reach the levels indicated.

After charging, add electrolyte (not just water) to bring the level up to the mark. If using a disposable electrolyte container, wash it out with water and discard. Finally, install the battery properly. (See Battery Removal and Installation.) See **Figure 26-9.**

Battery Selection

Never replace an original equipment battery with one that has less electrical capacity. When additional electrical devices have been added to a vehicle, or if the vehicle is operated at low speeds or stopped and started frequently, select a battery of greater capacity.

Battery Groups

Battery manufacturers divide their products into *battery groups* based on three criteria:

*   *Size:* Size is the physical dimensions of the battery. Size varies greatly due to the variety of vehicle types and sizes on the road.
*   *Voltage:* Although every vehicle made today uses a 12-volt battery, some older vehicles had 6-volt systems. Some modern agricultural and construction equipment and many large trucks have 24-volt systems.
*   *Terminal type:* All vehicles and light trucks have either top or side terminals. Some off-road and marine electrical systems use threaded studs as terminals, often with wing nuts as fasteners.

If a larger battery (physical size) is desired, be certain that the battery hold-down will fit properly. Be especially careful if the battery is installed near moving parts. Also check vertical height of the battery in case the hood is relatively close to the battery when closed.

Battery Ratings

A battery's electrical size has almost no relationship to its physical size. Often, a small battery will have a higher cranking amp rating than a large battery. This is due to variations in battery materials and construction standards. The ratings below are the latest *battery rating* measurements:

*   *Cold cranking amps (CCA):* The maximum amount of current that flows for 30 seconds at 7.2 volts with the battery temperature at 0°F (−17.8°C). This measurement indicates how much current the battery can produce when cold and is the standard measurement for modern batteries.

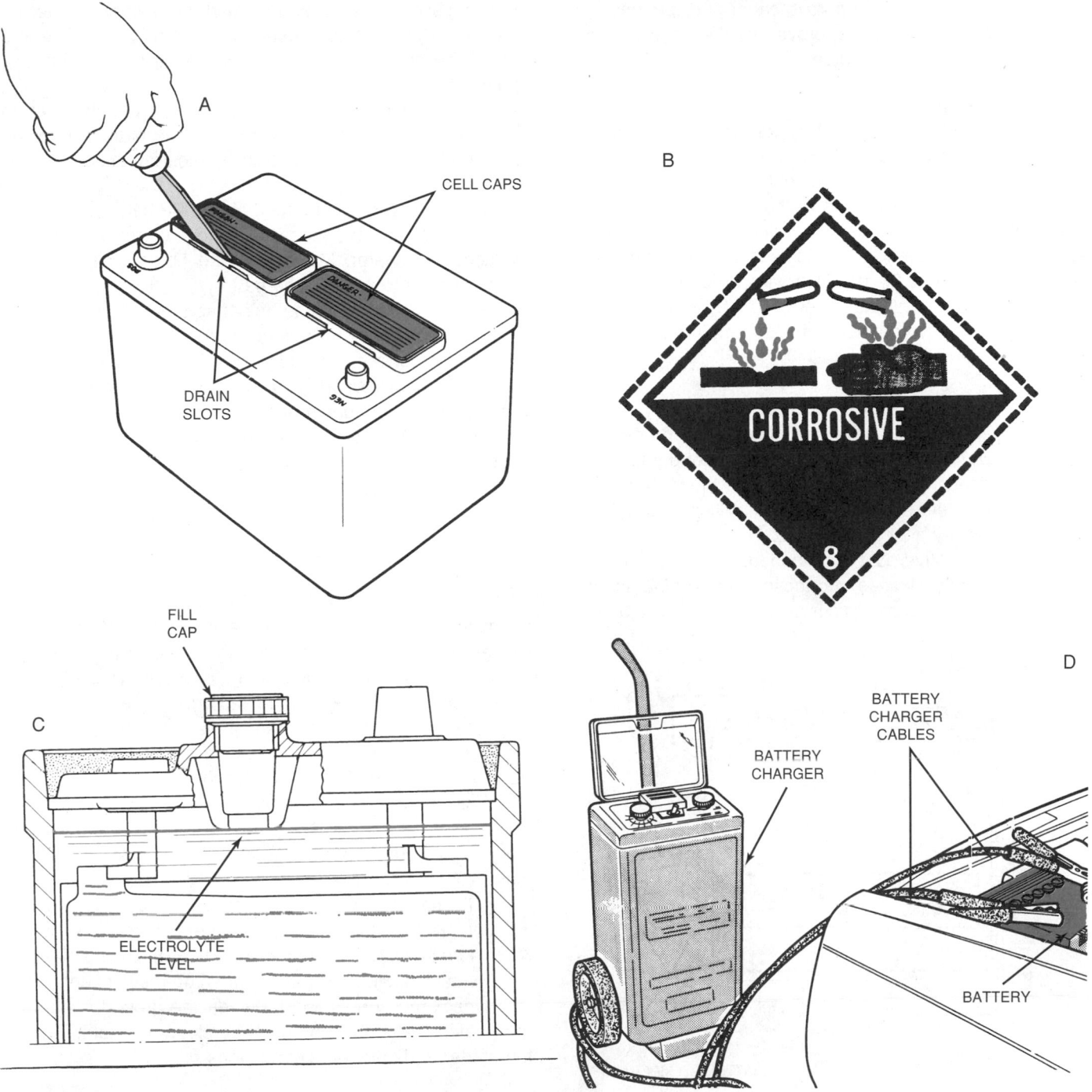

Figure 26-9. Some steps in activating a dry-charged battery. A—Remove the cell caps. B—Add specified electrolyte. C—Fill to proper level. D—Charge. Follow the manufacturer's recommendations. (Chrysler, Ford)

- **Cranking amps (CA):** The maximum amount of current that flows for 30 seconds at 7.2 volts with the battery temperature at 32°F (0°C). This measurement may also be called hot cranking amps (HCA), or marine cranking amps (MCA).
- **Reserve capacity (RC):** The number of minutes that the battery can produce 25 amps at 10.5 volts with battery temperature at 80°F (26.5°C). Reserve capac-

ity indicates how long the battery can operate the vehicle electrical system in the event of a charging system failure.

Battery Additives

It is recommended that nothing but pure water be added to a battery. Do not add acid unless the battery has been overturned or the electrolyte has leaked out. The use of additives to supposedly improve capacity or prolong battery life, unless specifically approved by the battery manufacturer, can void the guarantee.

Battery Temperature Sensor

Some vehicles use a *battery temperature sensor* to help control battery overcharging. See **Figure 26-10.** Temperature data from this sensor is sent to the powertrain control module (PCM), which controls the battery charging rate. Excessive overcharging will shorten the battery's useful life. Most temperature sensors are tested using an ohmmeter. The sensor in **Figure 26-10** will provide an ohmmeter reading of 9000-11,000 ohms at 75-80°F (23.9°-26.7°C). If not, the sensor must be replaced. Follow the manufacturer's recommendations for proper testing.

Battery Removal and Installation

Battery removal is relatively simple, but precautions must be taken to ensure that the vehicle is not damaged by acid or electrical shorts. Begin by covering the fender with a protective pad. Before removing the battery cable terminals, note which battery post is grounded. On almost all modern vehicles, the negative post is grounded.

Put on safety glasses and loosen the terminal fasteners. If the terminals are difficult to remove, use a battery

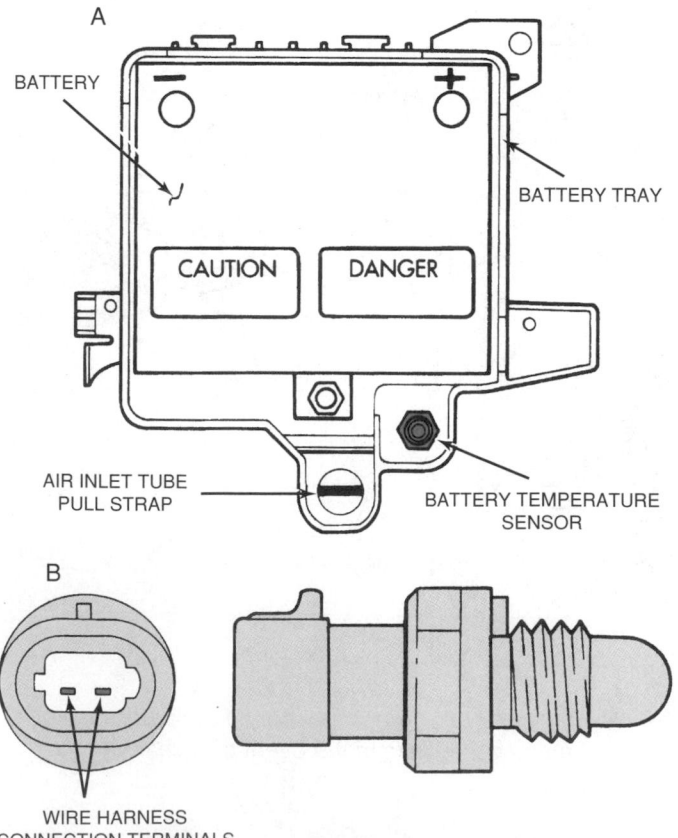

Figure 26-10. Battery temperature sensor. A—Location of the battery temperature sensor on the battery tray. B—The sensor has been removed for testing. The ohmmeter leads are connected to the two wire harness terminals on the sensor.

terminal puller. Never pound or twist the post or side terminals in an attempt to loosen them. Always remove the ground terminal first, and when installing the battery, replace it last.

Remove the hold-down plate. Using a battery lift strap or an approved removal tool, remove the battery from the vehicle. Make sure the lift strap is securely attached. See **Figure 26-11.**

Before installing a battery, check the battery holder for signs of corrosion. If necessary, remove corrosion with baking soda and water. Make sure the holder is structurally sound enough to support the battery.

Place the battery in the holder so that the terminals are properly positioned with respect to the cables. Replace the battery hold-down if it is badly corroded. If the hold-down is corroded but still usable, clean it with baking soda and water. Dry the hold-down and paint it with acid-proof paint. Finally, install the hold-down. Do not overtighten. Clean the battery terminals until bright and coat them with nonmetallic grease.

Battery Polarity Must Be Correct

Before attaching the battery terminals, make certain that the correct *polarity* (direction of current flow) will be maintained. If the polarity is reversed by accidentally reversing the terminals, the diodes in the alternator and the transistors in the radio, ignition system, or electronic control unit will be ruined when the engine is started.

The positive post is wider in diameter than the negative post. The positive post may be painted red and may have a (+), P, or POS stamped on the top.

The negative post may be painted black and may be marked with (–), N, or NEG on the top. If in doubt as to whether to ground the positive or negative post, refer to the manufacturer's manual.

If the battery has filler caps, attach the terminals so they will not prevent cap removal. Tighten the caps securely. Make sure that the cables are in good condition and that they have enough slack to prevent a strain on the connections.

Check the connection between the ground cable and the frame. The connection must be clean and tight. Tighten the starter and solenoid connections.

Battery Drains

Two things can cause the battery to discharge over a period of time: shorts and parasitic loads.

Shorts are unwanted electrical connections. They drain battery power by allowing a constant flow of current through the battery. Typical sources of shorts are frayed or pinched wires; internal defects in switches, solenoids, or motors; and stuck relays. Another type of short is an internal short between the positive and negative plates of the battery. Shorts can run down a battery overnight and must be found and corrected.

Parasitic loads are electronic components that place a small, continuous drain on the battery after the ignition is turned off. The current drain from these loads is extremely

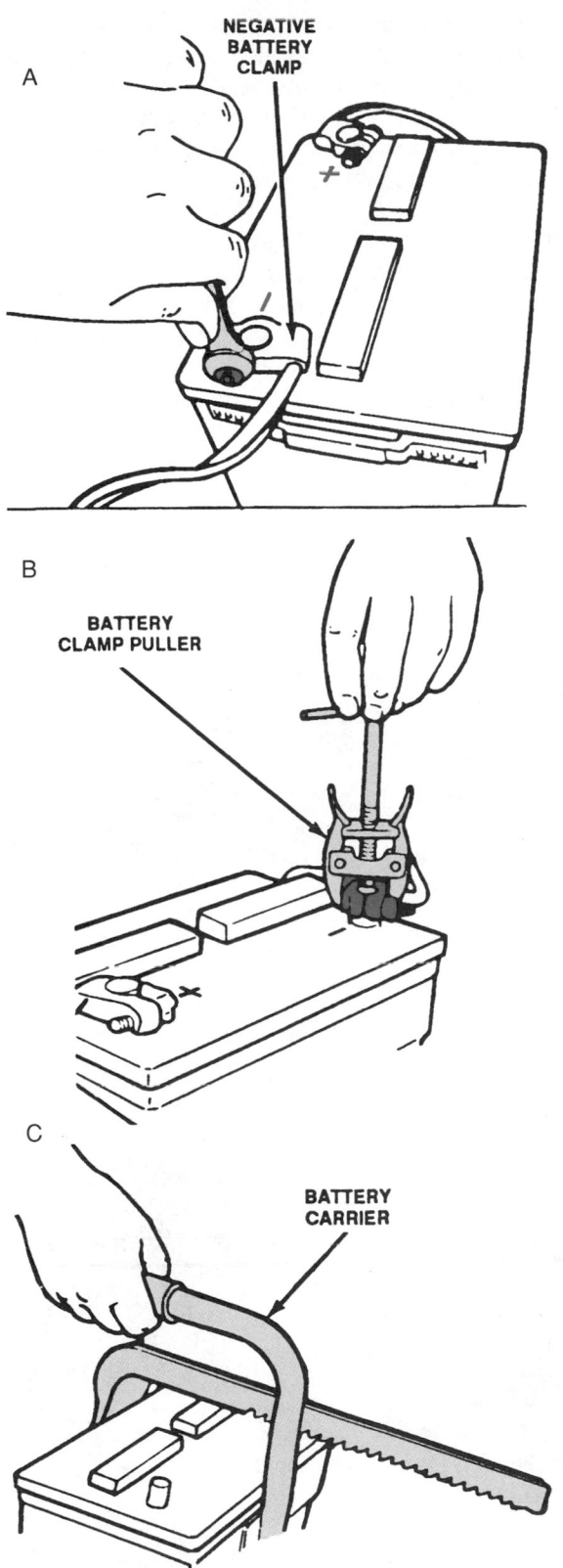

Figure 26-11. Steps in battery removal. A—Remove the battery cable terminals, ground cable first. B—Use a puller if the terminal is stuck. C—Attach a battery carrier. (Ford)

small and, therefore, does not discharge the battery, **Figure 26-12A.** Nevertheless, parasitic loads must be taken into account when testing for excessive battery drain, **Figure 26-12B.**

Component	Typical Parasitic	Maximum Parasitic
BCM	3.6	12.4
ECM	5.6	10.0
Radio	3.0	6.0
Regulator	1.4	2.0
ELC	2.0	3.3
CPS	1.6	2.7
Illuminated Entry	1.0	1.0
Theft	0.4	1.0
Auto Door Locks	1.0	1.0
Chime	1.0	1.0
HVAC Power Mod.	1.0	1.0

A

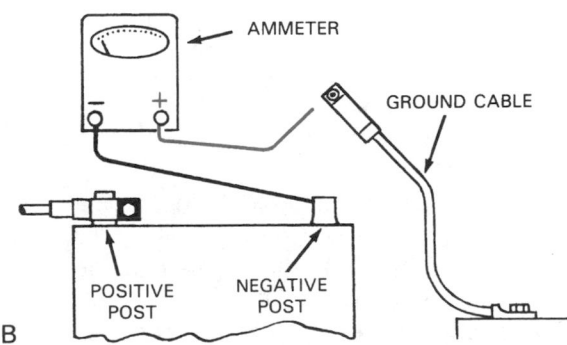

B

Figure 26-12. A—Current drain caused by parasitic loads is measured in milliamps (mA). B—An ammeter is used to check for excessive current drain at battery. A small amount of current flow is considered normal.

Jump Starting with a Booster Battery

When a battery has become discharged to the point it will not crank the engine, the engine can be *jump started* with a *booster battery.* A booster battery is an additional, properly charged battery of the same voltage as the discharged battery. It is connected to the vehicle's discharged battery with two *jumper cables.*

Follow These Safety Precautions

When performed correctly, jump starting is safe. However, ignoring safety precautions can cause the battery to explode, causing serious injury and vehicle damage. Batteries (even discharged) contain hydrogen gas that, if ignited, will explode, scattering battery parts and acid in all directions. Follow these safety precautions:

- Make certain vehicles are not touching each other.
- Wear protective glasses, avoid contact with battery electrolyte, and do not lean over the battery when making connections.
- In very cold weather, check for frozen electrolyte or no visible signs of electrolyte. If either condition exists,

warm the battery until it reaches a temperature of at least 40°F (4.4°C) before attaching the booster. This will prevent battery rupture or explosion.

- Keep open flames or sparks away from the battery.
- The last jumper cable connection should be the negative cable to the engine block of the vehicle with the dead battery, not to the negative battery terminal. This will reduce the chance of a spark igniting the hydrogen gas buildup.
- Remove metal watchbands, rings, and other jewelry when working on or around batteries. Use proper tools.
- If electrolyte (sulfuric acid) is splashed on you or the vehicle, flush it immediately with water. A solution of baking soda and water can be poured on clothing to neutralize the acid.
- When using a portable starting unit, do not exceed 16 volts to prevent starter, battery, or other electrical system damage.

Jump Starting—Sequence of Operations

When using jumper cables, it is important to connect them in the proper sequence. Turn off all switches on both vehicles. Make certain the vehicles are not touching. Then, proceed as follows:

1. Connect one jumper clamp to the booster positive terminal.
2. Connect the other end of the same cable to the dead battery positive terminal.
3. Connect one end of the other jumper cable to the booster negative terminal.
4. Clamp the other end of the same cable to the disabled vehicle's engine or frame.
5. Start the engine in the booster vehicle. Run the booster vehicle for a few minutes.
6. Start the disabled vehicle.
7. With both vehicles running, disconnect the jumper cables in exact reverse order: negative jumper from the vehicle engine, negative jumper from the booster negative, positive jumper from the discharged battery, and positive jumper from the booster. Never let the clamp ends touch during operation.

 Caution: Always turn the ignition switch off when working with jumper cables. Failure to do so can damage on-board computers and other electronic parts. Cellular telephones can also be damaged during jump starting operations. If necessary, disconnect the phone's power lead by unplugging it from the cigarette lighter or removing the power lead fuse. Check with the phone manufacturer for specific instructions.

Charging System Service

All modern vehicles use a charging system that contains an *alternator* and a *voltage regulator*. The charging system keeps the battery charged and supplies the electrical needs of various units during engine operation. The function and service of the alternator and regulator are covered in this section.

Periodic servicing, such as drive belt tensioning and lubrication, will usually be all that is required for thousands of miles. Many late-model alternators use sealed bearings, which eliminate the need for periodic lubrication. In many cases, replacement parts are not available and the entire unit must be replaced if defective.

Charging System Problems

Normal wear, part failure, and service-incurred damage may result in charging system malfunction. Many problems in the charging system start out as minor problems and gradually become worse. Problems in the charging system may produce one or more of the symptoms detailed below. See **Figures 26-13** and **26-14.**

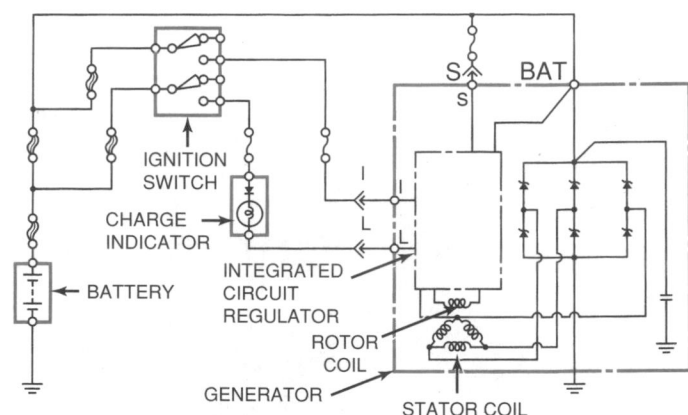

Figure 26-13. Typical charging circuit. (Geo)

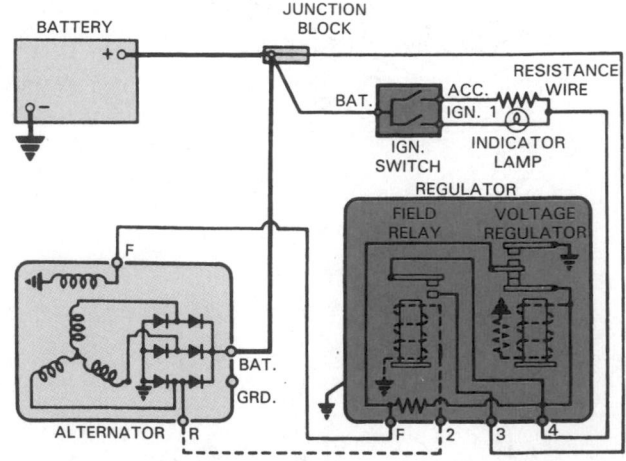

Figure 26-14. Typical charging circuit schematic for an electro-mechanical system.

Overcharging

Short light bulb life and the frequent need of battery water are two common indications that the system is *overcharging*. If the vehicle uses an ammeter, it will indicate a high charging rate with a charged battery.

Undercharging or No Charging

Slow cranking, dim headlights, and very infrequent need of battery water indicates battery *undercharging*. If used, the vehicle ammeter will indicate a low charging rate with an undercharged battery. The charge indicator light may be on or flicker when the engine is running.

Noisy Alternator

A light whining noise from the alternator is normal. A loud whine at idle speed can indicate a faulty diode or stator. Diode and stator defects can also cause noise in the AM band of the radio. Belt squeal can be caused by a loose or glazed belt. Dry or worn bearings can cause roaring or squealing noises. A loose pulley can cause clicking or rattling noises.

Ammeter or Indicator Light Problems

If the ammeter needle does not move in either direction when the engine is started and operated, the ammeter is defective. If the charge indicator does not light when the key is on, the bulb is burned out or the regulator is disconnected or defective. If the light is on at any time the engine is running, the regulator is defective or idle speed is very low. If the light is on when the key is off, the vehicle wiring is shorted.

A Quick Initial Check Can Save Time and Trouble

Before making any tests or replacing parts, give the system a quick initial inspection. Such a check will often turn up the source of the trouble. Check the drive belt condition and tension. Inspect all connections for tightness and signs of overheating. Examine wires for signs of burning or fraying. Check the regulator and alternator for evidence of physical damage.

A Sound Battery Is a Must

A worn out or badly sulphated battery will produce numerous problems that cannot be corrected until the battery is replaced. Always check battery condition as explained earlier in this chapter before condemning the charging system. A fully charged battery is a must for conducting accurate systems tests.

Units That May Cause Charging Problems

Charging system malfunctions can be traced to either the battery, alternator, regulator, ammeter, indicator lights, or wiring. Troubles may involve one unit or, in some cases, all units. Never replace a defective unit without determining what caused the failure. If the failure was brought on by some other unit or units, they, too, must be repaired or replaced or the new unit will fail.

Alternator Service Precautions

There are a number of important precautions that are vital when working on the alternator charging system. Failure to observe these rules can result in serious system damage. Learn and observe all the following rules:

- When installing the battery, make sure that the correct terminal is grounded.
- When using a booster battery or charger, connect it in parallel—positive to positive and negative to negative.
- Disconnect battery cables when charging the battery.
- When soldering a diode lead, take precautions to protect the rectifier from overheating.
- Never operate the alternator with an open circuit (output lead or battery terminal disconnected). This will allow the alternator to build up very high voltage that can damage diodes and can be very dangerous to anyone touching the alternator battery terminal.
- Do not ground the alternator field circuit, except for brief testing.
- To prevent accidental shorts, remove the battery ground lead before removing any system wires or connecting test equipment other than a voltmeter.
- When adjusting an electro-mechanical regulator, use an insulated tool to prevent accidental grounding.
- Do not ground the alternator output terminal or any regulator terminals.
- Make sure the ignition switch is off before removing or installing a regulator cover.
- Disconnect the connector plug from the regulator before removing the mount screws. Pulling the connector from an ungrounded regulator can ruin it.
- Use the correct alternator and regulator for the vehicle.
- Alternator testing procedures vary. Always follow the manufacturer's recommendations for the vehicle at hand.

Making Alternator Visual Checks

Give the alternator system a quick check for wire condition, terminal tightness, and drive belt tension. Check the battery for condition and state of charge. Charge or replace the battery if necessary. Clean and tighten the battery cable terminals.

Checking Alternator Output

Two electrical properties must be checked to determine whether the charging system is operating properly. These are output *amperage* and *voltage.* If the alternator and regulator are doing their jobs, both of these will be within specifications. To make this test, connect a voltmeter across the battery terminals and connect an ammeter to the output terminal of the alternator. If you are using a charging system tester, follow the manufacturer's instructions.

Once all connections have been made, start the engine and run it at fast idle. Observe the ammeter and voltmeter. Amperage should be within specifications, and voltage should be between 12.5 and 14.5 volts, depending on the voltage regulator setting and state of battery charge. Be sure to check the manufacturer's specifications before deciding on the condition of the charging system.

If the amperage and voltage are within specifications, disconnect the tester. If the readings are incorrect, the problem must be isolated to either the alternator or regulator. To make this test, stop the engine and locate the voltage regulator and field lead.

If the vehicle has an external alternator, disconnect the field lead and run a jumper wire with an on-off switch from the alternator field terminal to the battery positive terminal.

Make sure the switch is set to the off position. Then, restart the engine. Throw the switch to the on position and recheck the charging system output. If the alternator starts charging with the regulator bypassed, the regulator or its associated wiring is defective. If the alternator still does not charge, it is defective. Throw the jumper wire switch to off, stop the engine, and remove the jumper wire.

 Caution: Make this check quickly (a few seconds maximum), as the unregulated alternator can produce enough voltage to damage the vehicle's electrical and electronic equipment.

If the regulator is built into the alternator, follow manufacturer's instructions to bypass the regulator. Some alternators, such as the one shown in **Figure 26-15,** allow the regulator to be bypassed by inserting a screwdriver in a hole in the rear of the alternator.

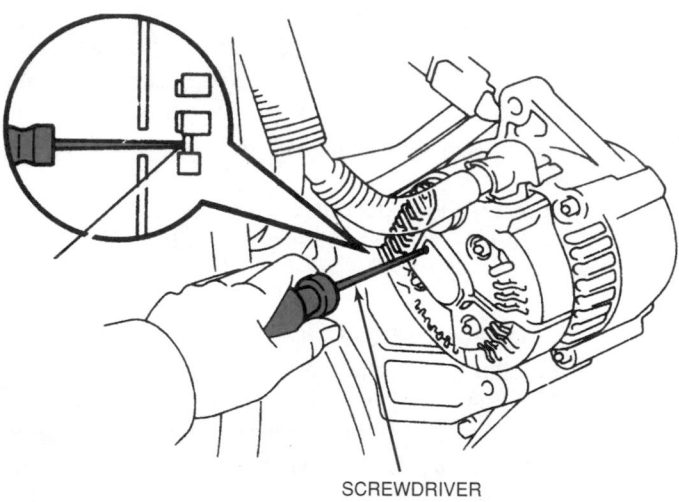

SCREWDRIVER

Figure 26-15. An alternator regulator being bypassed by inserting a screwdriver in the back of the alternator. (Toyota)

Voltage Regulator Service

If the problem has been isolated to the voltage regulator, it can be serviced or replaced. Most *electronic regulators* are not serviceable and must be replaced. Some regulators are part of a non-serviceable alternator assembly. If this type of regulator is faulty, the entire alternator must be replaced. *Electro-mechanical regulators* can be serviced, but many technicians prefer to replace them with new units.

 Caution: When testing or adjusting alternator voltage regulators, observe all the cautions regarding alternator system service.

Electronic Voltage Regulator Service

Many vehicles are equipped with electronic voltage regulators. These units regulate the alternator's output using transistors, diodes, resistors, and capacitors, **Figure 26-16.** Although electronic voltage regulators handle heavy loads and provide excellent service, they can still malfunction under certain conditions. The bypass test described above is the simplest way to check the regulator for proper operation.

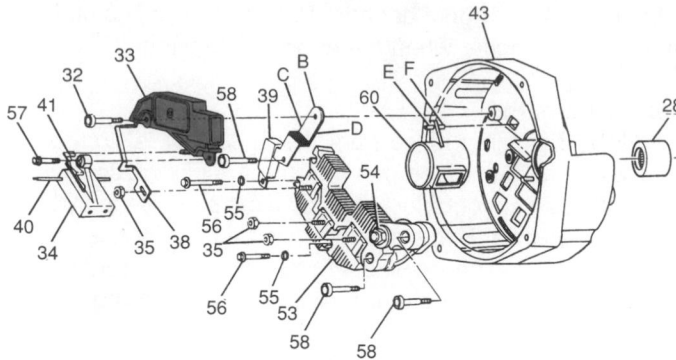

Figure 26-16. An exploded view of an alternator slip ring end frame and components. Note the electronic voltage regulator. This unit is not adjustable and must be replaced if defective. B—Capacitor strap. C—Metal side. D—Insulated side. E—Plastic retaining pin. F—Dust shield retaining clip. 28—Rotor slip ring end frame bearing. 32—Regulator attaching screw. 33—Alternator voltage regulator. 34—Brush holder. 35—Stator lead attaching nut. 38—Regulator connector strap. 39—Capacitor. 40—Brush retaining pin. 41—Brush. 43—Slip ring end frame. 53—Rectifier bridge. 54—Battery terminal nut. 55—Rectifier bridge washer. 56—Rectifier bridge bolt. 57—Brush holder screw. 58—Capacitor/rectifier bridge screw. 60—Dust shield. (GM)

Most electronic voltage regulators cannot be repaired. If they are faulty, they must be replaced. Replacement is simple when the regulator is installed on the engine firewall or inner fender. Simply remove the battery negative cable, the regulator wiring, and the attaching bolts. To install a new regulator, reverse the removal process. If the regulator is installed in the alternator, the alternator must be disassembled. Alternator disassembly is explained later in this chapter. A few regulators are installed on the back of the alternator and can be replaced without disassembling the alternator.

Electro-Mechanical Voltage Regulator Service

Many older vehicles are equipped with electro-mechanical voltage regulators. These units use electric coils and contact points to regulate alternator output. Electro-mechanical regulators are not as reliable as electronic regulators and require periodic adjustment. Always refer to an appropriate service manual before servicing these regulators. Testing procedures and adjustment specifications can vary from manufacturer to manufacturer. Many electro-mechanical voltage regulators have a radio suppression capacitor. Although this capacitor seldom fails, it should be unplugged before testing the regulator.

Most electro-mechanical voltage regulators can be replaced by unplugging the regulator wiring plug and removing the fasteners. Install the new regulator, install and tighten the fasteners, and plug the wire connector into the regulator.

Charge Indicator Light

If the indicator lamp fails to light when the ignition key is turned on (engine stopped), check for a burned out bulb; corrosion or looseness in the lamp socket; and loose, corroded, or open connections in the circuit. If the indicator light stays on when the ignition key is turned off, check for a shorted positive diode in the alternator.

When the engine is idling, the indicator light should go out. If it continues to burn, check for slow idle speed. If this does not correct the problem, check the alternator drive belt adjustment, field relay operation, and alternator output. Conduct other system tests as required to pinpoint the bad unit or units.

Computerized Charging System

In many vehicles, an on-board computer controls the current to the alternator's field terminal. This arrangement eliminates the need for a voltage regulator. Most computerized charging systems have self-diagnostic capabilities. When the computer detects a malfunction in the charging system, it stores a trouble code in its memory and activates the check engine light. A typical computerized charging system is illustrated in **Figure 26-17.** For more information on trouble codes and computerized systems, see Chapter 25.

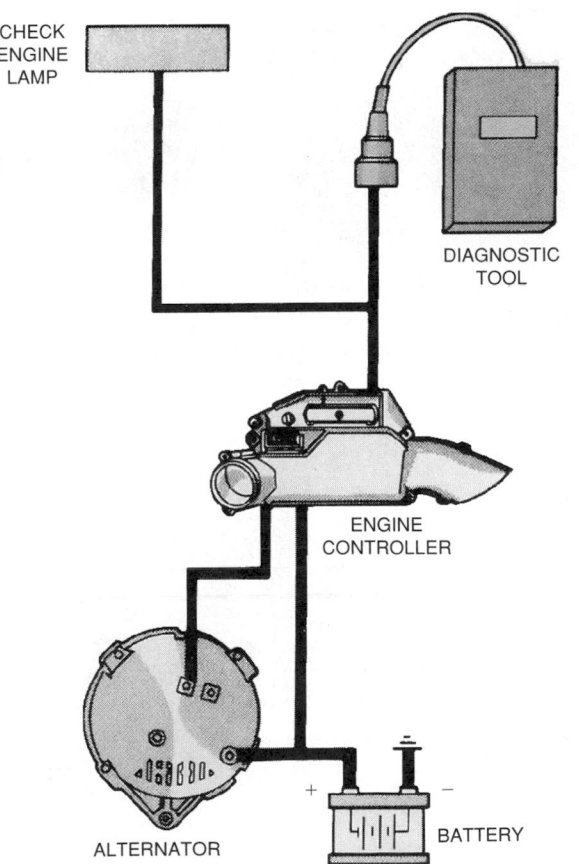

Figure 26-17. Typical computerized charging system. Note hookup for diagnostic tool. (Chevrolet)

Check Alternator Charging Circuit for Excessive Resistance

The charging system cannot function properly when excessive electrical **resistance** is present. When system malfunctions are evident and the quick check does not reveal the exact cause, check the system resistance before

conducting more exhaustive tests. When high resistance is found, replace the wire or clean and tighten connections.

Field Circuit Resistance Test

Connect test instrument as instructed by the manufacturer. For the setup shown in **Figure 26-18,** disconnect the slip-on connector from one end of the ballast resistor. Turn on the ignition switch (accessories off, doors and trunk closed) and read the voltmeter. A reading in excess of 0.55 volt indicates high resistance.

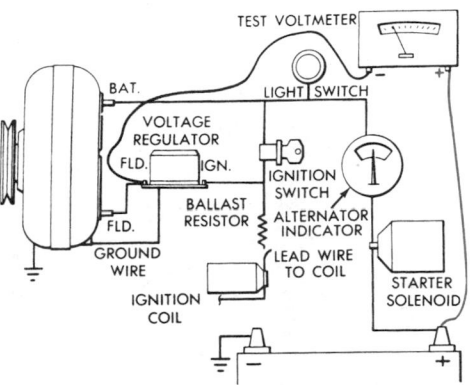

Figure 26-18. Testing alternator field circuit resistance. (Dodge)

If excessive resistance is present, start moving the negative voltmeter lead along the circuit. Check resistance at each connection. Move the wire and apply a small twisting force to each terminal while watching the meter. When a quick voltage drop is found, clean and tighten the connection.

Alternator-to-Battery Positive Terminal Resistance Test

One alternator-to-battery positive terminal resistance test hookup is illustrated in **Figure 26-19.** For this setup, turn off all accessories. Close the battery post adapter switch and start the engine. When started, open the switch.

Bring engine speed up to 2000 RPM. Produce an ammeter reading of 20 amps by adjusting the field rheostat. With engine at 2000 RPM and the ammeter reading 20 amps, the voltmeter reading should not exceed 0.3 volts.

Alternator-to-Battery Ground Terminal Resistance Test

An alternator-to-battery ground terminal resistance test hookup shown in **Figure 26-20.** When performing this test, turn off all accessories. Close the battery adapter switch and start the engine. Open the adapter switch and bring engine speed to 2000 RPM. Adjust the ammeter reading to 20 amps by moving the field rheostat. The voltage reading should not exceed 0.1 volt.

Alternator Disassembly and Overhaul

Most alternators can be easily disassembled, and faulty parts can be replaced. In a few designs, however, the alternator must be serviced as a unit and no replacement parts are available.

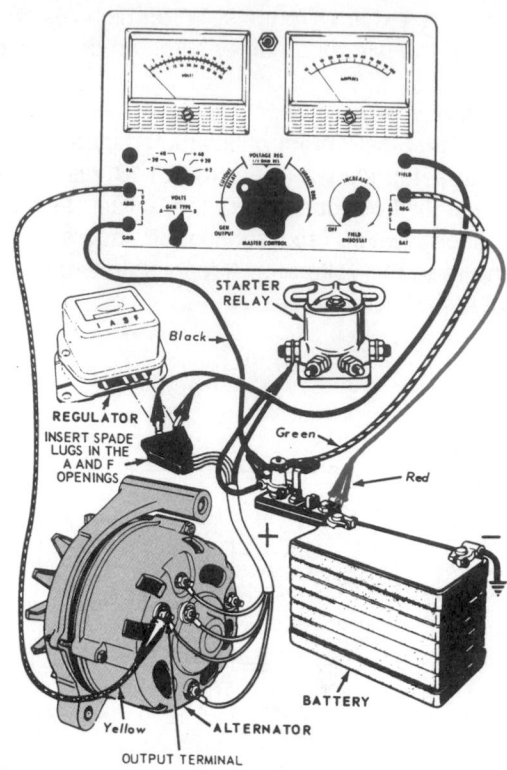

Figure 26-19. Alternator-to-battery positive terminal resistance test. (Lincoln)

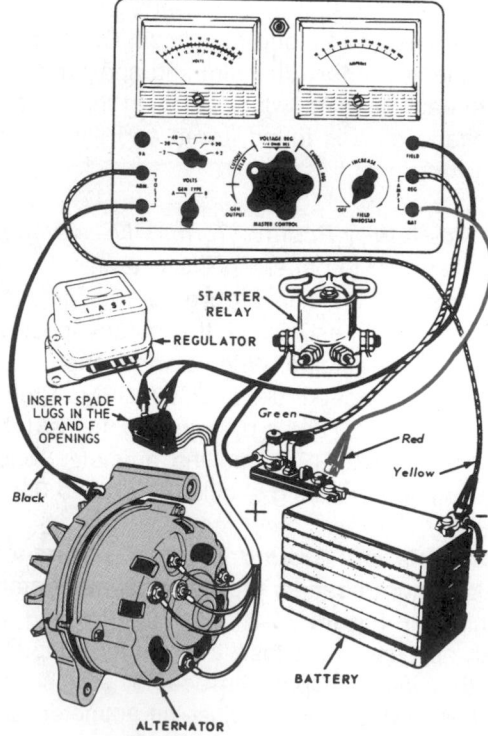

Figure 26-20. Alternator-to-battery ground terminal resistance test.

Alternator Disassembly

Specific disassembly varies with the design of the alternator. The following steps are typical for many alternators.

1. Remove the pulley nut.
2. Using a suitable puller, remove the pulley.
3. Mark the units with a scriber before disassembly.
4. Remove the through-bolts.
5. Pry the slip ring end frame and drive end frame apart. Separate the units. On some models, the brush assembly must be removed before dismantling the alternator. See **Figure 26-21.**
6. When needed, use pullers to remove end plates and bearings.
7. Remove stator and diode frames and voltage regulator if used. A cutaway view of a typical alternator is shown in **Figure 26-22.**

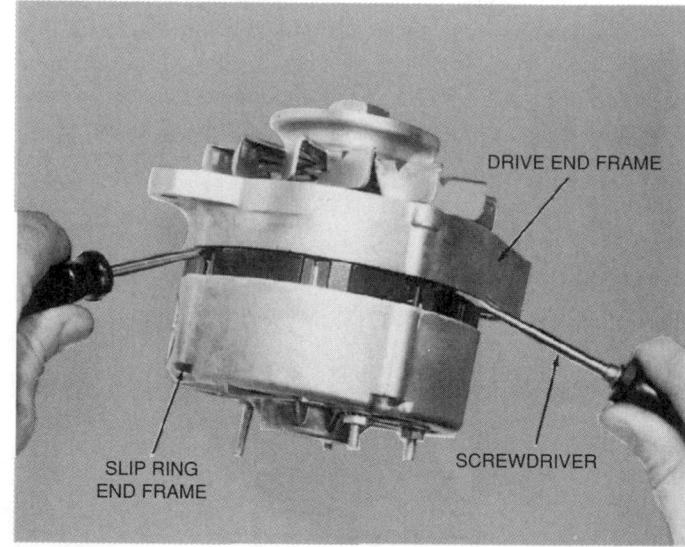

Figure 26-21. Separating the alternator drive and slip ring end frames. (Chrysler)

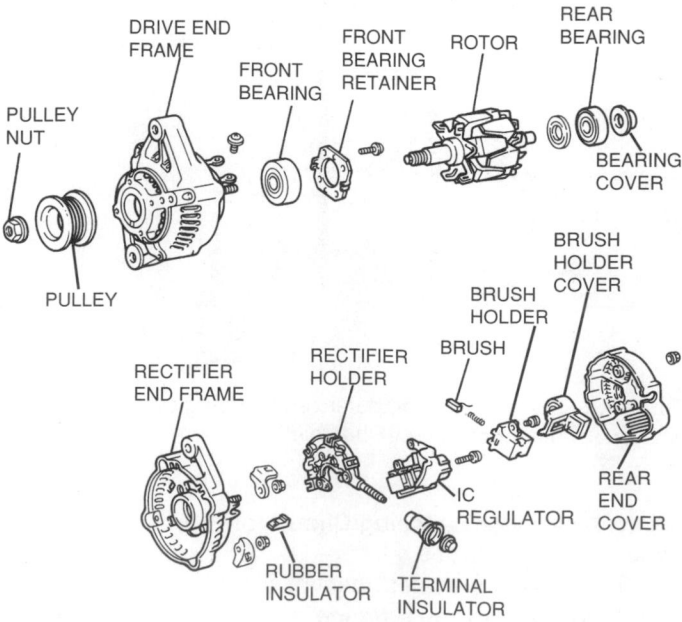

Figure 26-22. Typical alternator construction. (Geo)

Clean all parts except the rotor, stator, slip ring, and brush assemblies in solvent. Wipe with a clean cloth. If the bearings are of the sealed type, do not place them in solvent. Where applicable, clean and inspect the bearings. If the bearings are the sealed type, inspect them for wear, roughness, and loss or hardening of lubricant. Pack the bearings with high-temperature bearing grease where required.

Check Brushes

The **brushes** should be checked for proper length and replaced if they show any wear. During an overhaul, it is good practice to replace the brushes regardless of how much wear they show. Also check the brush springs. Brushes must be absolutely free of oil or grease. If the brushes come in contact with grease during alternator disassembly, clean them at once.

Test Rotor Windings for Opens, Grounds, and Shorts

Use an ohmmeter to check the rotor for grounds, opens, and shorts. To check for grounds, place one ohmmeter lead on one slip ring and the other lead on the shaft, core, or rotor. See **Figure 26-23**. If the ohmmeter gives a low reading, the windings are grounded. A test lamp may also be used for this test. The lamp will light if a ground is present.

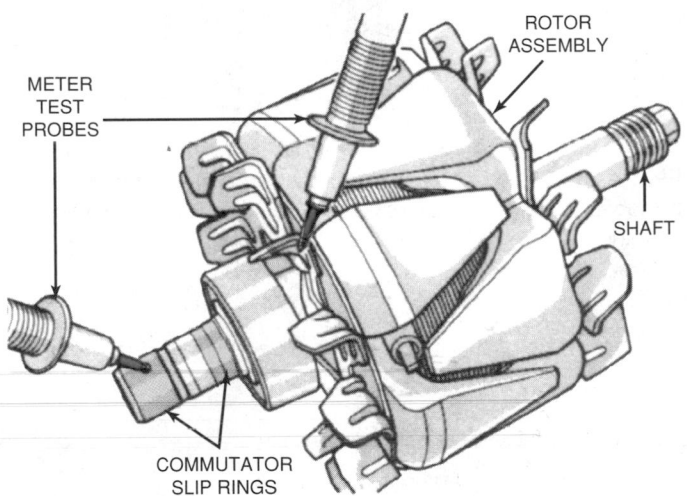

Figure 26-23.   Testing an alternator field circuit for a ground with an ohmmeter.

To test for opens, **Figure 26-24,** place one ohmmeter lead on each slip ring. If the windings are open, a high (infinite) reading will occur. If a test lamp is used, the lamp will not light if the windings are open. To check for shorts, attach an ohmmeter lead to each slip ring, **Figure 26-24.** Check the ohmmeter reading against specifications. If the reading is below specifications, the windings are shorted. When using a test light, never place the prods on the portion of the slip ring contacted by the brush or on the portion of the rotor shaft contacted by the bearing. To do so could pit the surface from arcing.

The slip rings must be smooth and round. If they are dirty, they should be cleaned by turning the rotor while hold-

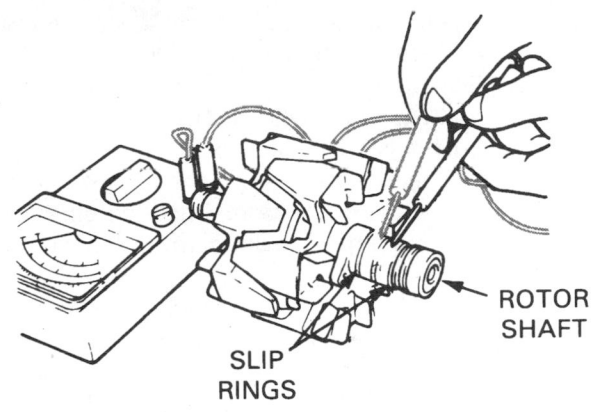

Figure 26-24.   Testing an alternator rotor for shorts and opens. (Plymouth)

ing 400 grain polishing cloth against the slip rings. Do not use emery cloth.

If the rings are scored or out-of-round, they can be turned down until true. Remove as little material as possible. Polish with 400 grain polishing cloth. See **Figure 26-25.** Check the rotor shaft bearing areas for signs of wear, scoring, and other problems.

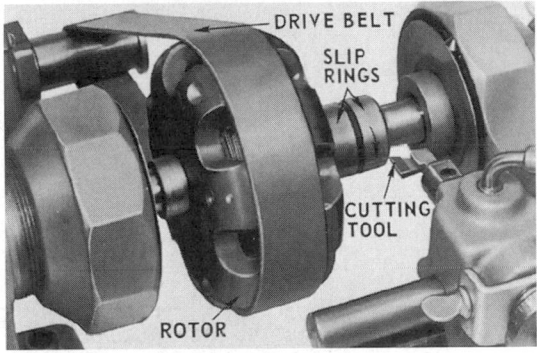

Figure 26-25.   Turning the slip rings on an alternator rotor. (Trucut)

Check Diodes

Quite often, the **diodes** are responsible for charging system problems. Carelessness in battery charging, improper use of booster batteries, and inexperienced servicing can quickly ruin the diodes. When the alternator is found defective, always test the diodes.

Testing Diodes

Some alternators require disassembly in order to test the diodes. Others do not. Follow manufacturer's instructions. Diodes may be tested by using a special diode tester, by using an ohmmeter, or by using a 12-volt test lamp. Do not use a 120-volt test lamp. If a 12-volt test lamp is selected, use a No. 67 bulb. Both the ohmmeter and the test lamp methods require disconnecting the diode leads.

When a test lamp is used, one prod should be placed on the rectifier lead and the other on the outer case or heat sink. Make sure the connections are good. Reverse the prods. If the diode is good, the lamp will light with the prods in one position but will not light in the other. An open diode will fail to light the lamp in either direction. A shorted diode will light the lamp in both directions.

The ohmmeter is used much like the test lamp. Place one test prod on the diode case. Place the other test prod on the diode lead. Again, make sure the connections are good.

If the diode is good, a high reading will be given with the test prods in one position and a low reading will be given when the prods are reversed. An open diode will give high readings in both positions. A shorted diode will give low readings in both directions.

Prod tips must be sharp. Make certain they penetrate any varnish coating present on the terminals. Be sure to test all diodes. Positive diodes will test the same as negative diodes, but the lamp will light in the opposite prod position. See **Figure 26-26.**

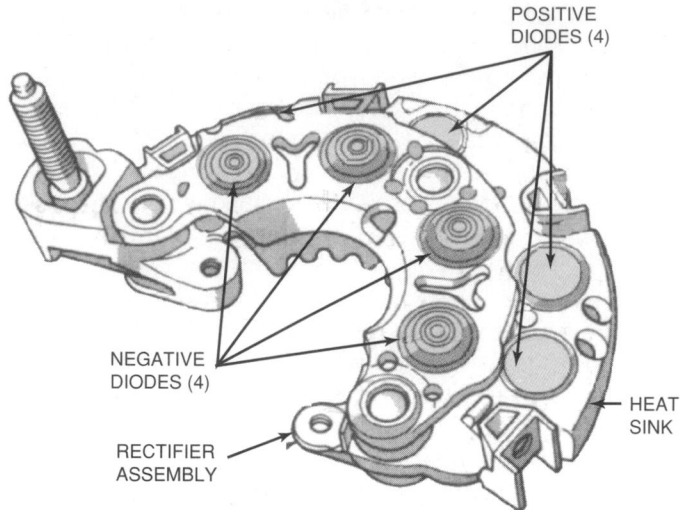

Figure 26-27. These diodes have been pressed into the heat sink.

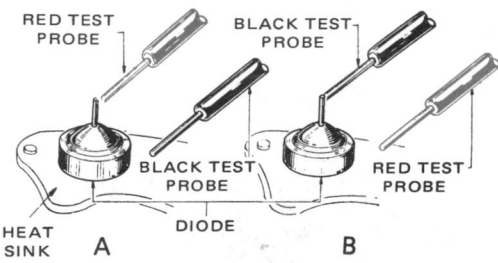

Figure 26-26. Testing a diode. A—First test. B—Second test. Note that the leads are reversed in B. The test light should come on in one test and go out in the other if the diode is good. (Nissan)

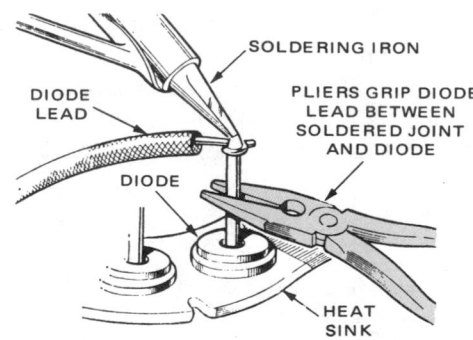

Figure 26-28. Using pliers as a heat dam, or heat sink, to protect a diode from excessive heat during soldering. (British Leyland)

 Note: Be sure to test the radio suppression capacitor, when used. A faulty capacitor is often the cause when the diodes test open or shorted.

Removing and Replacing Diodes

Never pound on a diode in an attempt to remove or replace it. Use a press and suitable tools. **Figure 26-27** shows diodes that have been pressed into place in the heat sink. The pressing tool must bear against the outer edge of the diode case. Follow the manufacturer's recommendations for diode removal and installation.

When soldering diode leads, always grip the lead between the diode and the soldered area with a pair of pliers. The pliers will protect the diode from excessive heat. See **Figure 26-28.**

Some alternators use three diodes (sometimes called a "diode trio") in combination with the internal voltage regulator. These diodes are separate from the output diodes. They are enclosed as a group and in a dielectric (nonconducting) material. These must be serviced as a unit. See **Figure 26-29.**

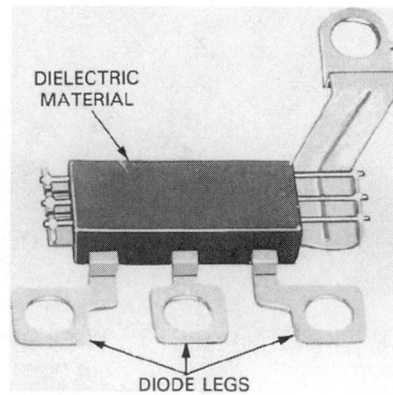

Figure 26-29. A typical diode "trio." Three diodes are held within a molded dielectric material. (Deere & Co.)

Test Stator Windings for Opens, Grounds, and Shorts

To check the stator windings for grounds, connect an ohmmeter or test lamp as shown in **Figure 26-30A.** This one connection will check all three legs of the windings. The lamp should not light. The ohmmeter will show a high reading. If the light comes on, or if the ohmmeter shows a low reading, the circuit is grounded.

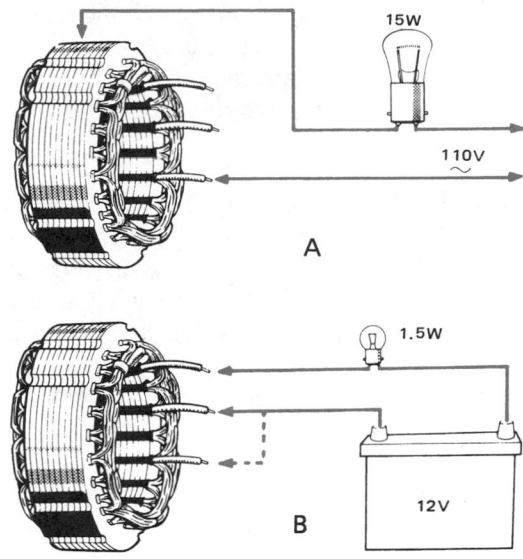

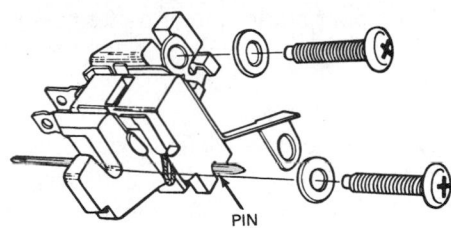

Figure 26-31. A pin holds the brushes in a holder for easy assembly. (Pontiac)

Figure 26-30. Testing stator windings. A—Testing for grounds. B—Testing for opens. (British Leyland)

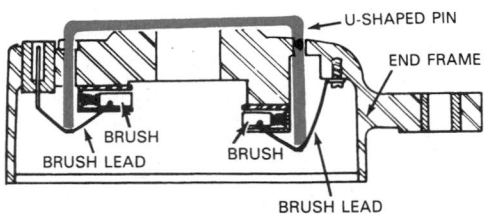

Figure 26-32. A stiff, U-shaped pin keeps these brushes retracted to allow installation of the rotor. (Motorcraft)

To test for opens, connect a test lamp as shown in **Figure 26-30B.** The lamp should light. An ohmmeter should show specified resistance. If the lamp does not light, or if the ohmmeter shows an infinite resistance, the windings are open.

The check for winding shorts is sometimes difficult and requires more test equipment. Visually inspect the windings for signs of overheating. When the alternator does not produce its specified output and all other electrical checks are OK, you may assume that the stator windings are shorted.

Test Capacitor

The capacitor can be tested by disconnecting it and placing an ohmmeter across the leads. An infinite reading indicates good condition. A low reading indicates a defective condenser. To test condenser capacity in microfarads, use a condenser tester.

Alternator Reassembly

Where specified by the manufacturer, bearings must be packed with grease. Assemble the alternator in the reverse order of disassembly. Work carefully. When parts are a press fit, use a press. Align scribe marks. Torque the pulley retaining nut. Never clamp the rotor to hold it while torquing the pulley nut. To do so may deform the rotor. Clamp the pulley.

Some alternator brush assembly designs permit the use of a pin to hold the brushes in the holder during assembly. Some require hooking the brush leads over a section of the brush holder for installation. Another type uses simple brush holders that permit installation after the alternator is assembled.

If a brush holder pin is used, or if the leads are hooked, remove the pin or straighten the leads after assembly. See **Figures 26-31** and **26-32.** Make sure all parts are correctly located. Spin the rotor to check for free operation.

When assembling the alternator to the engine, adjust belt tension by prying on the heavy drive end frame edge. Never pry against the center or at the slip ring frame end. Connect all leads to the alternator. Connect the battery leads. Start the engine and test the alternator.

Starting System Service

The starting system consists of the battery, starter motor, solenoid, ignition switch, neutral safety switch, and related wiring, **Figure 26-33.** Often, determining which part is at fault when the engine will not crank is more difficult than replacing the defective parts.

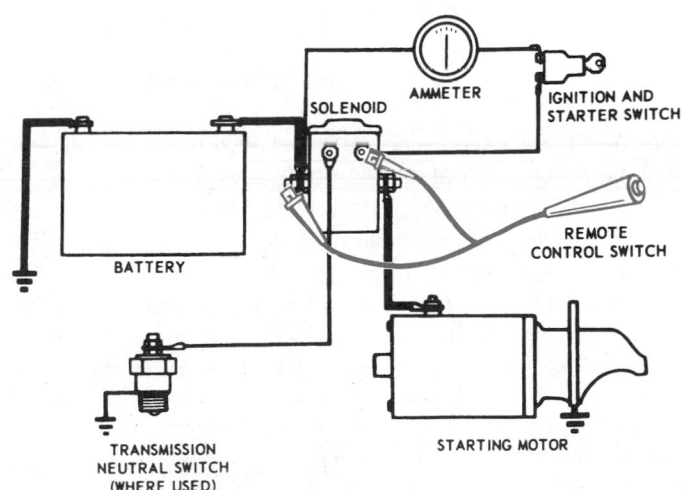

Figure 26-33. Component parts of starting system or circuit. Note remote starting (control) switch. (Ignition Mfg's Inst.)

Always Check the Battery First

Many complaints of poor starter performance are traced to a discharged or defective battery. Give the battery a thorough check, as explained earlier in this chapter.

Remember that proper starter motor performance demands a charged, sound battery.

Checking Starter Circuit

Give the starter circuit wiring a quick visual check. Remove and clean corroded battery terminals. Clean and tighten other loose, burned, or corroded connections. Look for frayed, broken, or shorted wires.

After the visual check of the starter circuit, test the circuit for excessive resistance. Use an accurate low-reading voltmeter.

Make the voltmeter connections as illustrated in **Figure 26-34.** Remove the ignition coil high-tension lead from the distributor. Ground it or ground the primary distributor terminal of the coil. The technique used must be compatible with the type of ignition system.

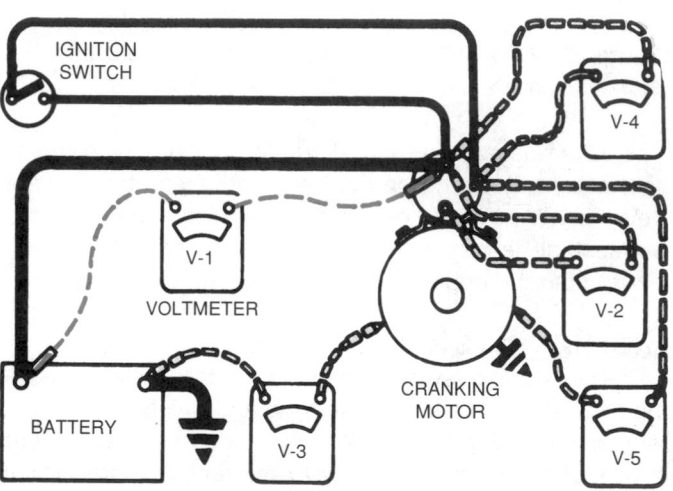

Figure 26-34. Voltmeter connections for checking starting circuit resistance. (Oldsmobile)

Crank the engine with the voltmeter leads connected across the battery positive post and the battery terminal of the **starter solenoid** —V-1 connection, **Figure 26-34.** The voltage reading (drop) should not exceed 0.2 volt.

Make voltmeter V-2 connections across the battery terminal and the motor terminal of the solenoid. Crank the engine. The drop should not exceed 0.2 volt.

Place the voltmeter leads in the V-3 position across the battery negative post and the starter motor frame. Crank the engine. The voltage drop should not exceed 0.2 volt.

> **Caution: Do not operate the starter motor for extended periods as it will be damaged from overheating. Operate it for a maximum of 20 or 30 seconds. Then, allow it to cool for at least two minutes before resuming cranking.**

The V-4 position (across battery terminal and switch terminal on solenoid), **Figure 26-34,** is used to detect excessive voltage drop in the solenoid circuit. Voltage drop (engine cranking) should not exceed 2.5 volts.

The V-5 connection (across switch terminal of the solenoid and starter frame) will measure the voltage available at

the switch terminal. If voltage at the switch meets specifications and the solenoid does not pull in, remove the starter for further testing. The voltage drops used here are averages. Always use the manufacturer's specifications for the vehicle at hand.

Solenoids, Relays, and Switches

In the event of starter circuit difficulties, do not overlook the ignition switch and starter solenoid. These units will occasionally fail. Check each one for correct operation. This can be done by bypassing a switch with a jumper wire or by replacing a suspected relay or solenoid with one that is known to be good. If the solenoid clicks when energized but the starter does not operate, the problem is in the starter or the internal solenoid contacts. On some vehicles, if the starter turns but does not engage the flywheel, the solenoid may be failing to engage the starter drive mechanism.

All vehicles with automatic transmissions have a safety lockout switch, which is usually called the **neutral safety switch.** This switch will not allow the ignition switch to energize the starter solenoid unless the transmission is in park or neutral. Late-model vehicles with manual transmissions have a safety switch installed on the clutch linkage. This switch will prevent starting unless the clutch pedal is depressed.

Safety switches can fail or move out of adjustment. Check the correct service manual for exact testing, adjustment, and replacement procedures. A typical test procedure for a clutch safety switch is shown in **Figure 26-35.**

Starter Load Test

The starter **load test** will indicate the current draw in amperes during cranking. It will provide an indication of starter motor condition. Excessive engine friction will also be disclosed by this test. Excessive engine friction can be caused by new engine parts that are (rings, bearings, or pistons) fitted too tight. If a good starter draws a high current but will not crank an engine that has been in service (used), there is probably severe internal engine damage. If the starter will not engage the flywheel, the starter drive is defective or the flywheel teeth are stripped.

Instruments for the load test may be connected as illustrated in **Figure 26-36.** A remote control starter switch is shown in place. The technician can use this switch to energize the starter without getting into the vehicle to operate the regular starter switch. The method of attaching this remote starter varies according to circuit design.

Ground the coil secondary lead, the coil distributor lead, or the ignition control module to prevent the engine from starting. While cranking the engine, note the exact voltmeter and ammeter readings. Compare the readings with the manufacturer's specifications.

Starter No-Load Test

The starter **no-load test** is done by allowing the starter to spin freely while readings are taken. Disconnect the battery ground strap and remove the starter from the engine. With the test connections pictured in **Figure 26-37,** adjust

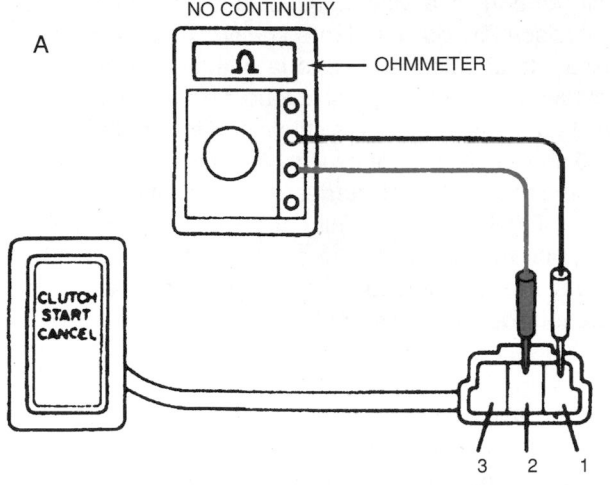

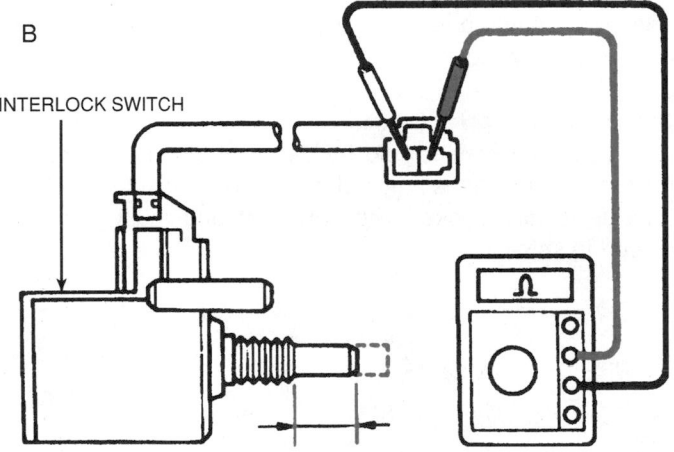

Figure 26-35. Testing procedure for a clutch safety switch.

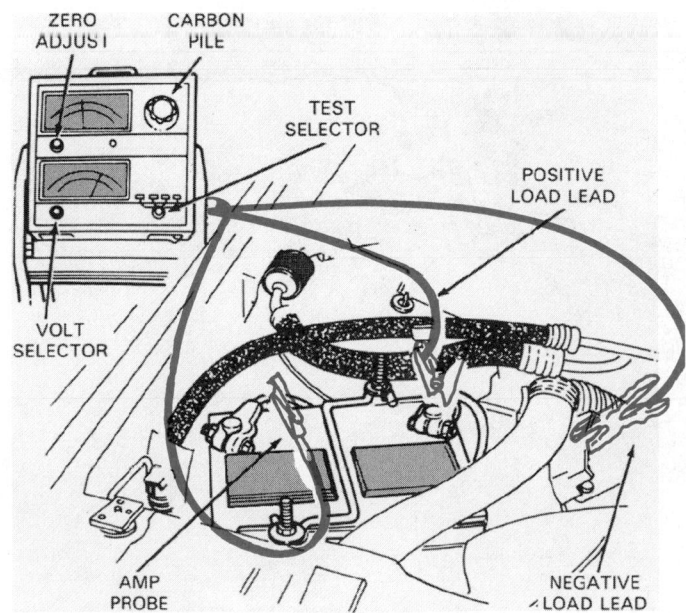

Figure 26-36. Starter load test connections.

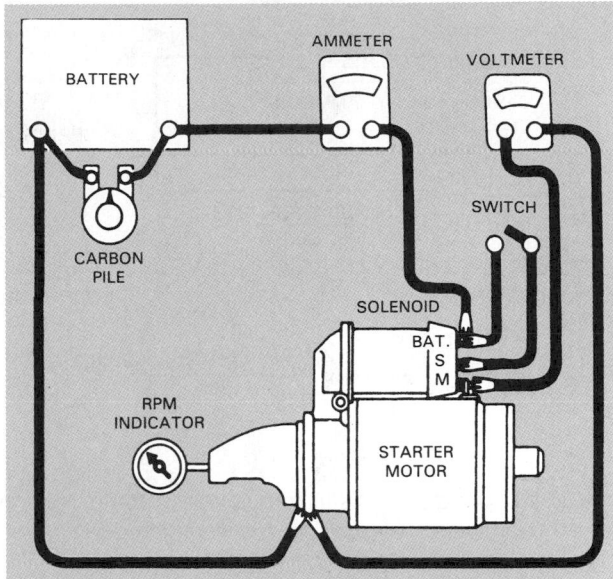

Figure 26-37. One starter no-load test hookup.

the load control (rheostat) to the extreme clockwise setting. This will prevent any current flow through the ammeter.

Hook up the starter as shown. While the starter is operating, note the exact voltmeter reading. Disconnect the starter and back off the load control until the voltmeter reading corresponds to that noted during starter no-load operation. At this point, the ammeter reading will indicate the no-load current draw.

Secure the starter before making no-load connections. Violent starting torque and extreme no-load RPM can make the starter dangerous.

A tachometer can also be attached to the starter to check no-load RPM. Check current draw and RPM against specifications. Some manufacturers give test specifications for no load operation that require a specific voltage to be applied to the starter. Current draw at this exact voltage must be measured.

Stall Torque (Locked Armature) Test

The **stall torque** test will indicate both starter torque and current draw at a specified voltage. A typical test setup is illustrated in **Figure 26-38.**

To conduct the test, the starter is attached to a test stand and the pinion is secured by a special brake or torque arm. The switch is closed and the carbon pile rheostat is adjusted to apply the specified voltage to the starter. Current draw will be indicated on the ammeter.

Torque, in foot-pounds, will show on the scale. Make this test as quickly as possible to avoid overheating the starter.

The stall torque and no-load tests will bring to light such problems as a dragging armature, shorted or open windings, frozen bearings, dirty commutator, and poor connections. If the starter fails to meet specifications, it must be dismantled and thoroughly checked.

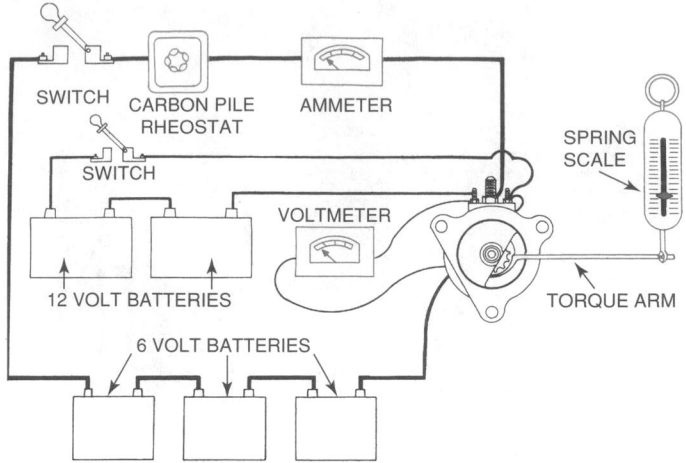

Figure 26-38. One type of stall torque testing setup. Note the torque arm and the spring scale for measuring torque.

Starter Disassembly

Unlike other vehicle electrical units, most starters can be disassembled and repaired. In most cases, however, it is less expensive and quicker to replace the entire starter. Disassemble the starter carefully. Note the location of all parts. Scribe a line on the pinion housing, frame, and end plate to assist in correct alignment during reassembly (starters are generally equipped with a locating dowel to guarantee

proper alignment). If a vise is used to support the starter during disassembly, do not clamp tightly. In some cases, it is necessary to unsolder a lead to facilitate part removal.

A cutaway view of a typical solenoid-actuated, overrunning-clutch, drive-type starter is shown in **Figure 26-39. Figure 26-40** shows an exploded view of a starter assembly.

A somewhat different starter drive actuating setup is pictured in **Figure 26-41.** This arrangement employs a movable pole shoe that is connected to the starter drive. When the starter is energized, magnetic action causes the pole shoe to slide sideways, thus engaging the starter drive pinion.

Cleaning the Starter

Clean all parts (except armature, field coil, commutator, and when used, overrunning clutch drive) in solvent. A rag that is slightly dampened with clean solvent may be used to wipe off the armature, the field coils, and the outside of the overrunning clutch unit if they are oily. If no oil is present on these parts, use a soft brush, mild air pressure, or a clean, dry rag.

Cleaning the Starter Drive

Starter drives should be carefully cleaned. A Bendix drive may be cleaned in solvent. The overrunning clutch drive is factory packed with lubricant and must never be placed in solvent.

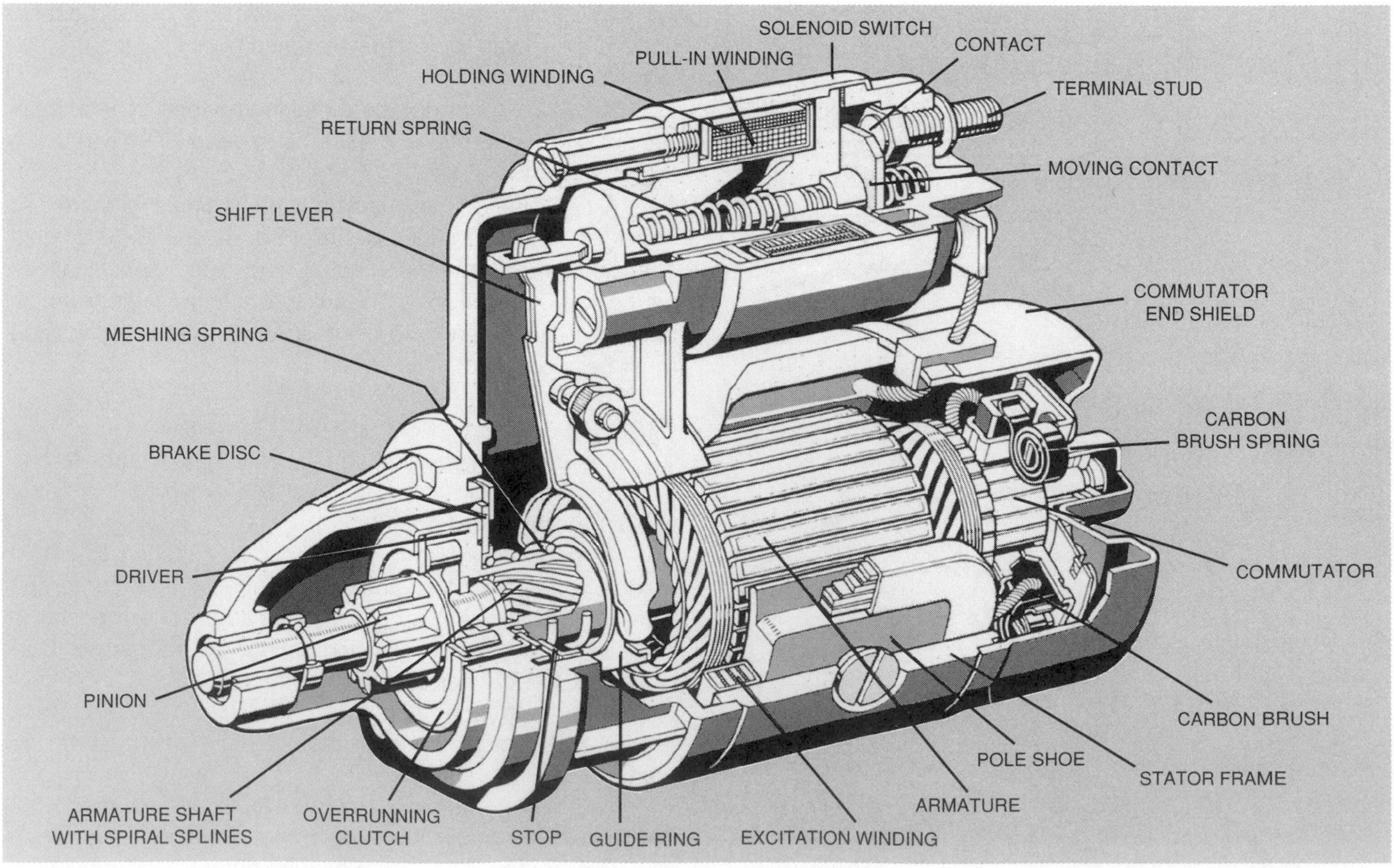

Figure 26-39. Typical starter employing a solenoid-engaged overrunning clutch drive. The solenoid also actuates the starter motor. (Bosch)

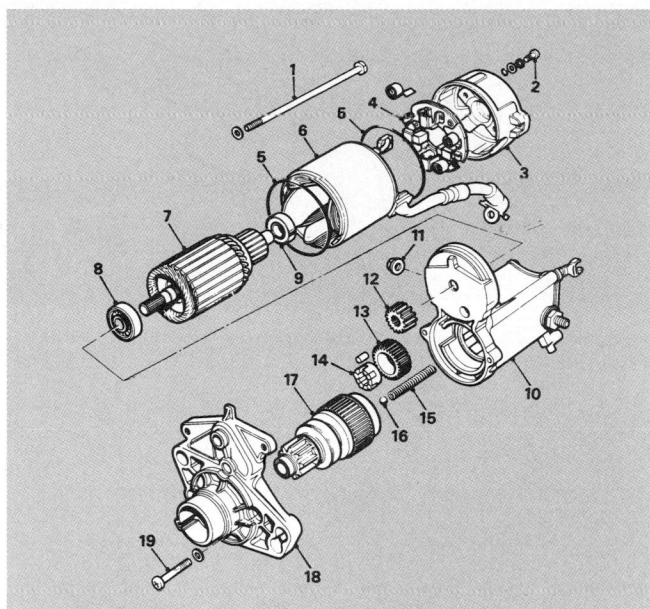

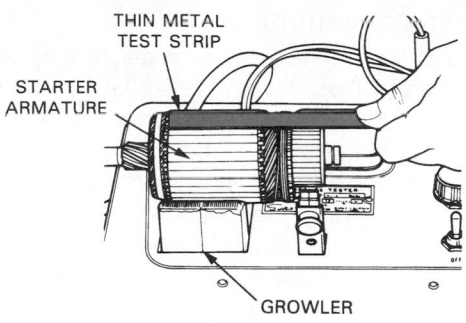

Figure 26-42. Using a growler to test the starter armature for short circuits. (Chevrolet)

Figure 26-40. One type of starter employing a solenoid-actuated overruning clutch drive. 1—Motor through-bolt. 2—Brush holder screw. 3—End cover. 4—Brush holder. 5—Ring seal. 6—Yoke. 7—Armature. 8—Gear housing bearing. 9—End cover bearing. 10—Solenoid housing. 11—Terminal nut. 12—Pinion gear. 13—Idler gear. 14—Roller bearings and cage. 15—Plunger spring. 16—Steel ball. 17—Overrunning clutch. 18—Gear housing cover. 19—Solenoid screw. (Sterling)

has passed beneath the strip. If a short circuit exists, the strip will vibrate when the shorted section passes under it. Do not operate the growler when the armature is not in place.

Checking the Armature for Grounds

Place one test prod (110 V test unit) on the armature core, **Figure 26-43.** Touch each commutator segment with the other prod. If the armature is grounded, the test lamp will light. Discard grounded or shorted armatures.

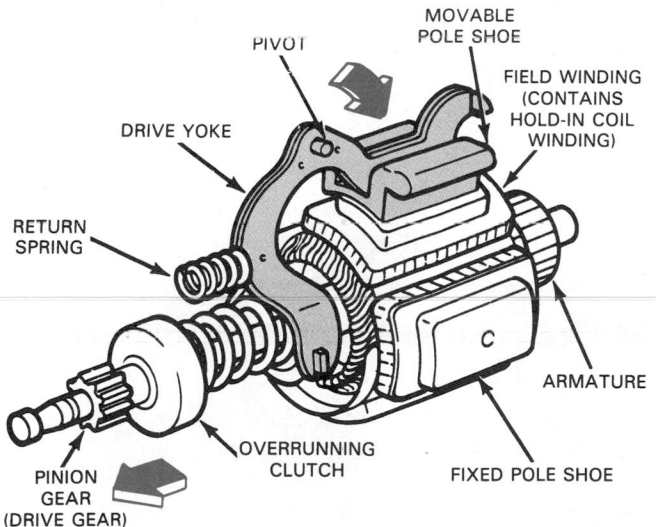

Figure 26-41. This starter uses a movable pole shoe device to actuate the starter drive gear. (Chrysler)

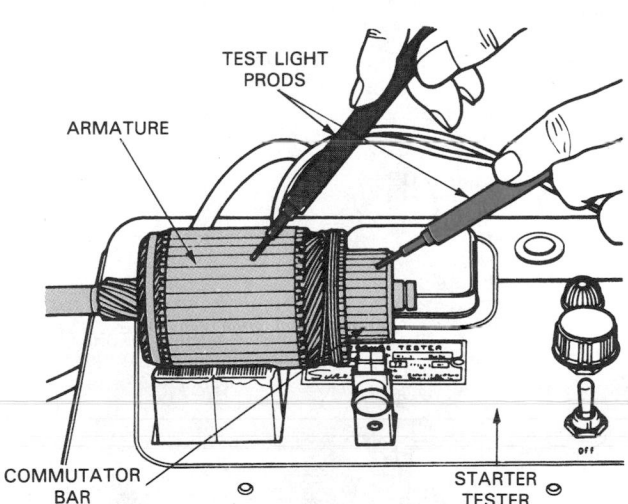

Figure 26-43. Checking a starter armature for grounds. (Chevrolet)

Testing the Armature for Short Circuits

Place the **armature** in a growler as in **Figure 26-42.** Make sure the brush and copper dust are removed from between the commutator segments when the mica has been undercut.

Hold a thin steel strip (hacksaw blade is fine) loosely on the top of the armature (tip one edge up). Turn on the growler. Turn the armature until the entire armature core

Inspecting the Commutator Bars for Opens

Prolonged cranking may overheat the starter and cause the solder on the **commutator bars** (conductor-to-commutator segment connections) to melt and be thrown off. Inspect the joints for missing solder. Also, inspect the segments (especially trailing edges) for signs of burning that could indicate an open circuit. Refer to **Figure 26-44.**

If the bars are not too badly damaged, resolder the connections and turn the commutator. Check the commutator for runout (should not exceed .003-.005". or 0.08-0.13 mm) and scoring, **Figure 26-45.**

Turning the Commutator

Support the armature in a proper holding fixture or a lathe. Be certain that the armature shaft is centered properly. Remove only enough copper from the commutator to clean up scoring, burning, or runout.

Although undercutting the mica (insulation between bars) is not generally required on starter motors, some manufacturers do recommend that it be done. In such cases, follow all manufacturer's instructions. Sand lightly with No. 400 sandpaper when finished. Do not use emery cloth. See **Figure 26-46.**

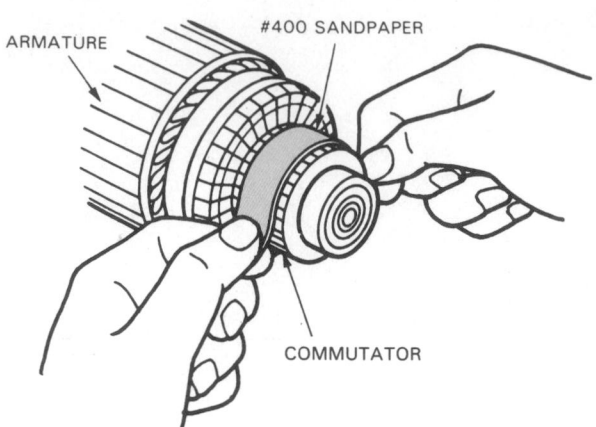

Figure 26-46. Sand the commutator with No. 400 sandpaper and clean it thoroughly when finished. (Chevrolet)

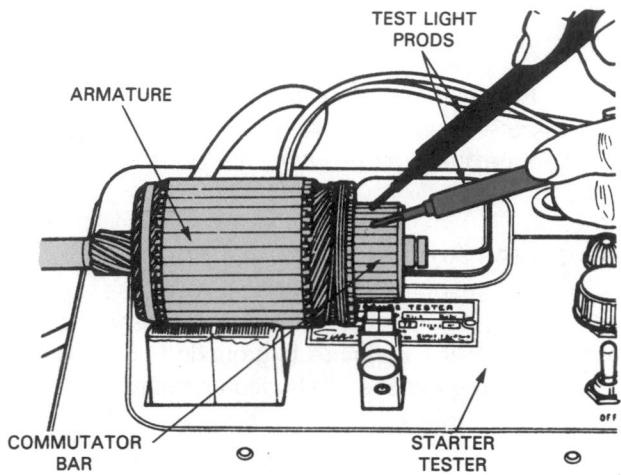

Figure 26-44. Testing armature coils for continuity (opens). (Chrevrolet)

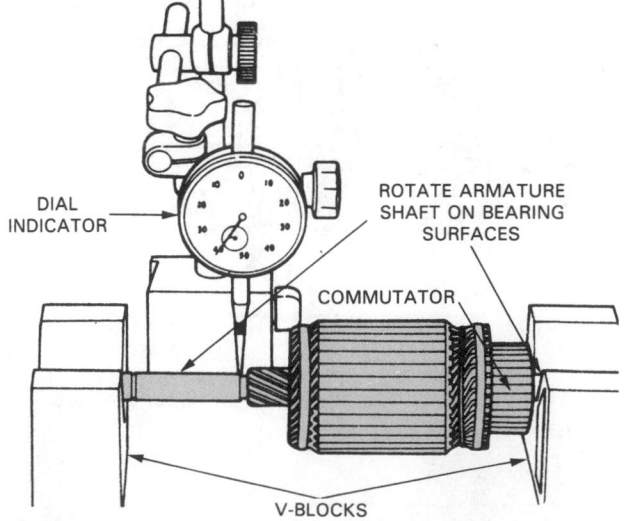

Figure 26-45. Checking a starter shaft for runout. A dial indicator will also be moved to the commutator surface to check it for runout. (Chevrolet)

Test Field Coils for Opens

The starter *field coils* should be checked with an ohm-meter. Use a 110-volt test light. Be careful to avoid shocks. Place one test prod on the coil terminal stud or on the connector from the solenoid, **Figure 26-47.** Place the other prod on the insulated brush lead. This, in effect, places a

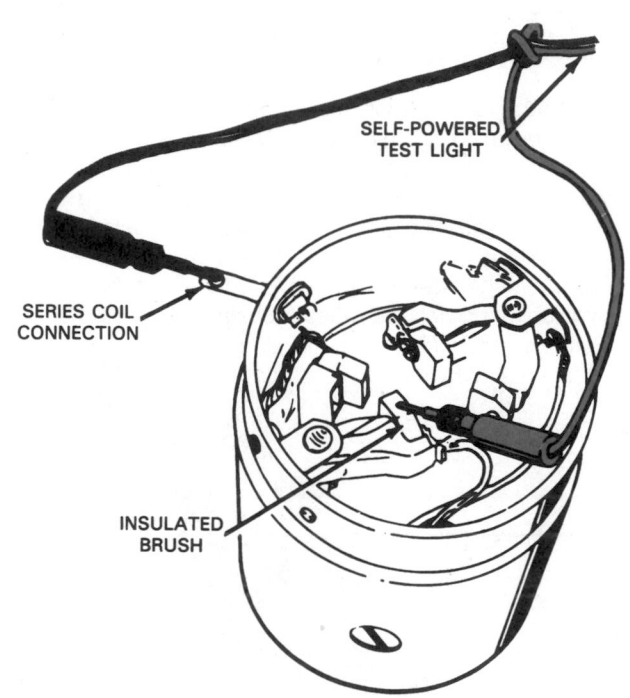

Figure 26-47. Testing starter field coils for opens. (Buick)

prod on each end of the field coils. The test lamp should light. No light indicates an open circuit.

Test Field Coils for Grounds

Use a 110-volt test light. Place one prod on the field coil connector and the other on the frame. The lamp should not light. A lighted lamp indicates a ground. Be certain that no part of the field circuit, brushes, or connectors are touching the frame. If the starter uses a shunt coil, disconnect the shunt before making the test. See **Figure 26-48.**

Check Brushes

Brushes should be replaced when they are worn to within one-half of their original length or if they are oil soaked. If the starter is dismantled for another reason, replace the brushes regardless of their length. When

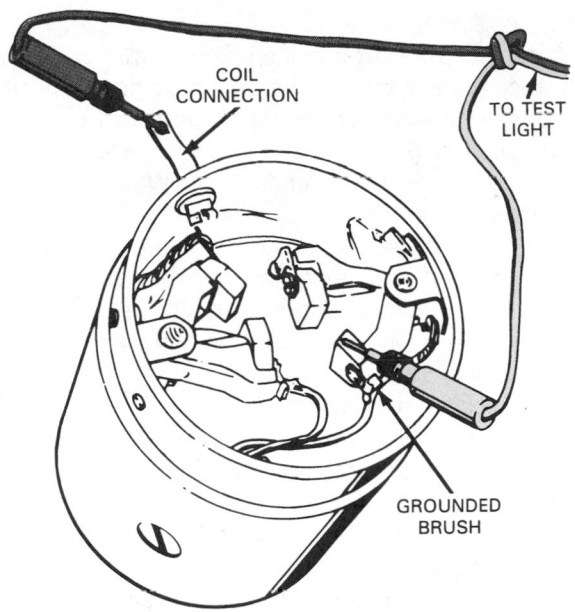

Figure 26-48. Testing starter field coils for grounds. (Buick)

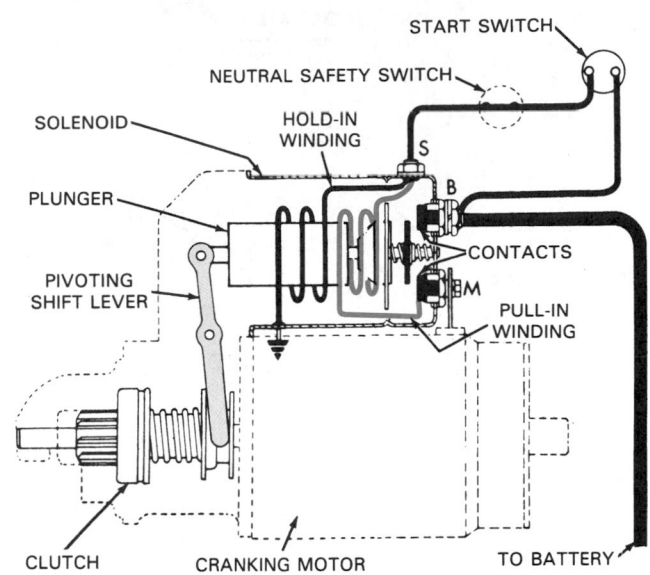

Figure 26-50. Typical starter solenoid. Note the winding arrangement. (GM)

soldering is required, make certain that the solder joint is sound. Use high-temperature solder.

Check the insulated brush holders for grounds, **Figure 26-49.** Make sure the brushes slide freely. If fastened to movable arms, the arms should be free and in alignment.

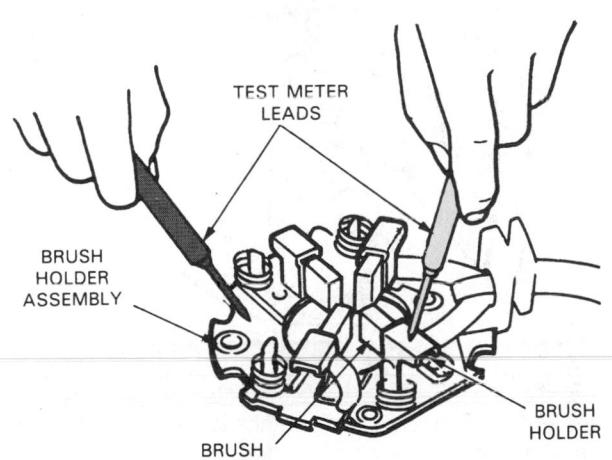

Figure 26-49. Testing the starter insulated brush holders for ground with a test meter. (Geo)

Testing the Starter Solenoid

In addition to a clean, functional set of contacts, proper solenoid operation requires sound pull-in and hold-in windings. Study the typical starter solenoid winding circuit in **Figure 26-50.**

The test in **Figure 26-51** is used to test the pull-in winding, and the test in **Figure 26-52** is used to test the hold-in winding. To make these tests, leave the solenoid in place on the starter, but remove all leads. Depending on which winding is to be tested, make the hookups as indicated. With the switch on, adjust the carbon pile to produce the manufacturer's specified voltage. Check the ammeter reading.

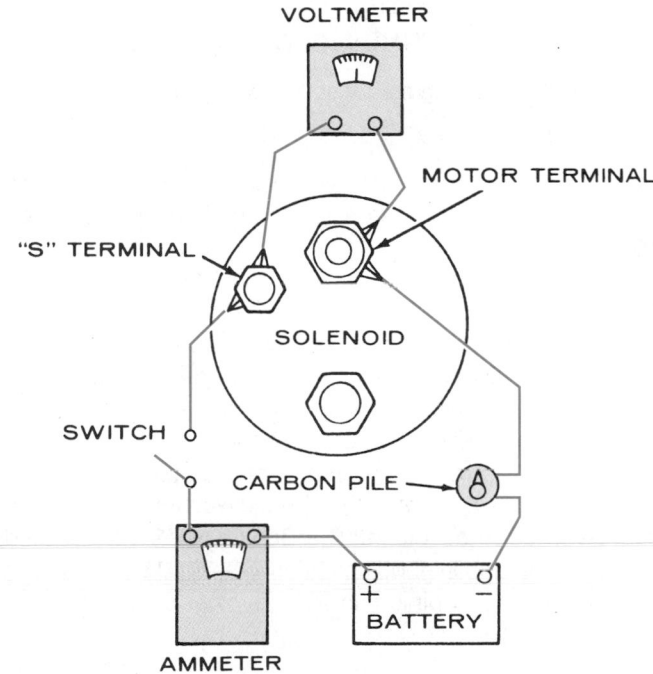

PULL-IN WINDING TEST CONNECTIONS

Figure 26-51. Testing starter solenoid pull-in winding circuits. (GM)

If the ammeter reading exceeds specified levels, it indicates a grounded or shorted circuit. A low reading is caused by excessive resistance. If no ammeter reading is apparent, the circuit is open.

 Caution: When testing a pull-in winding, do not leave the circuit energized for longer than 15 seconds. This will prevent overheating. Keep in mind that as the circuit heats up, resistance increases and current draw decreases.

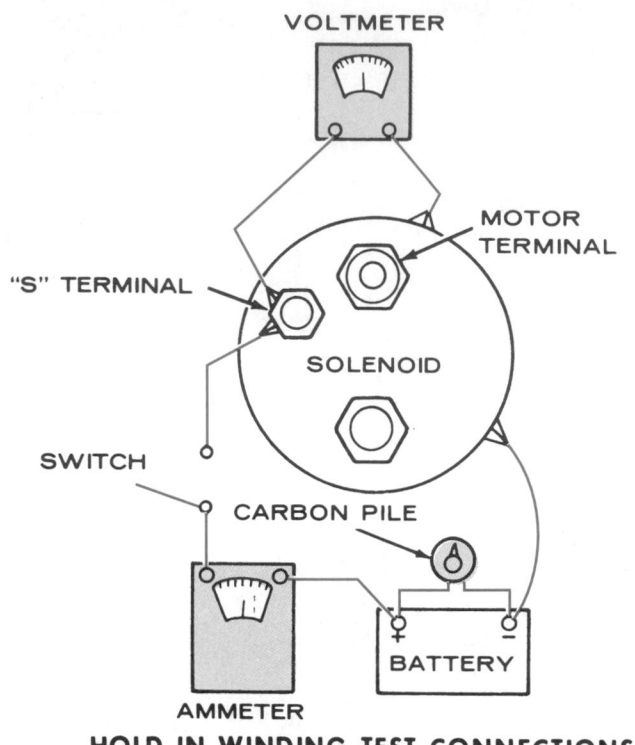

HOLD-IN WINDING TEST CONNECTIONS

Figure 26-52. Testing starter solenoid hold-in winding circuits. (GM)

As with all tests, use a test procedure and specifications for the exact unit.

Other Starter Checks

Inspect the bushings and replace them if excessive wear is present. Check brush spring tension, **Figure 26-53.** Inspect both pinion and flywheel gear teeth for any evidence of chipping, milling, cracking, or improper engagement pattern. The overrunning drive must turn freely in the coast direction and lock tightly in the drive direction. Thrust washers and spacers must be in good condition. The Bendix drive, where used, must be clean and in good condition. Check all soldered connections. Check the pinion housing for signs of cracking.

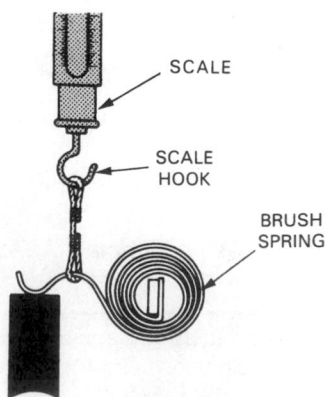

Figure 26-53. Testing starter brush spring tension with a spring scale. (Geo)

Starter Assembly

Assemble the starter in the reverse order of disassembly. If necessary, lubricate the two bushings with several drops of recommended lubricant. Wipe a thin coat of light lubricant on the armature shaft splines. Never lubricate unless specified by the manufacturer. Where soldering is required, use rosin core solder only.

Some starters use a sealer in some locations to prevent the entry of dust and water. When assembling the parts, apply a nonhardening sealer. Where grommets are used, they must be in good condition and properly inserted.

Torque the through-bolts to specifications. Check the overrunning clutch pinion clearance by either forcing (where possible) the solenoid arm to the fully applied position or by energizing the starter solenoid. When energizing the solenoid, ensure that the starter motor cannot turn. The solenoid motor terminal can be connected to ground to help prevent starter rotation.

When the solenoid has moved the pinion to the fully applied position, measure the clearance between pinion and pinion stop. Look at **Figure 26-54.** Pinion clearance is adjustable on some starters. On many units, however, clearance cannot be adjusted. When it is wrong, it must be corrected by installing new parts.

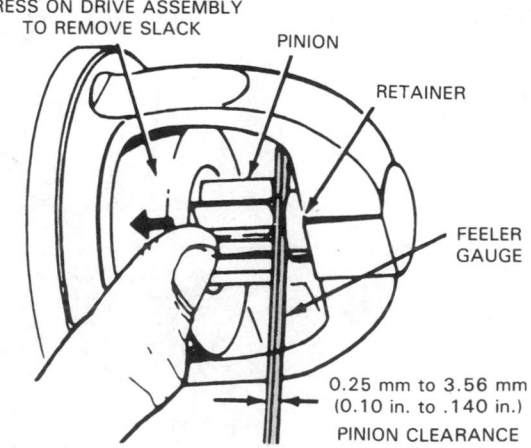

Figure 26-54. Pinion gear clearance is checked with a feeler gauge. (Pontiac)

Testing the Starter

When assembly is complete, give the starter a no load and stall torque test before attaching it to the engine. If the solenoid is installed on the engine, make sure that the solenoid linkage moves the pinion gear.

Installing the Starter

Disconnect the battery ground strap. Clean the mounting flange or pad until it is spotless. This is necessary for proper electrical ground and for accurate mechanical alignment. Install the starter and torque the fasteners.

Some starter setups permit measuring flywheel-to-pinion clearance. **Figure 26-55** illustrates the use of a wire gauge to determine such clearance on one setup.

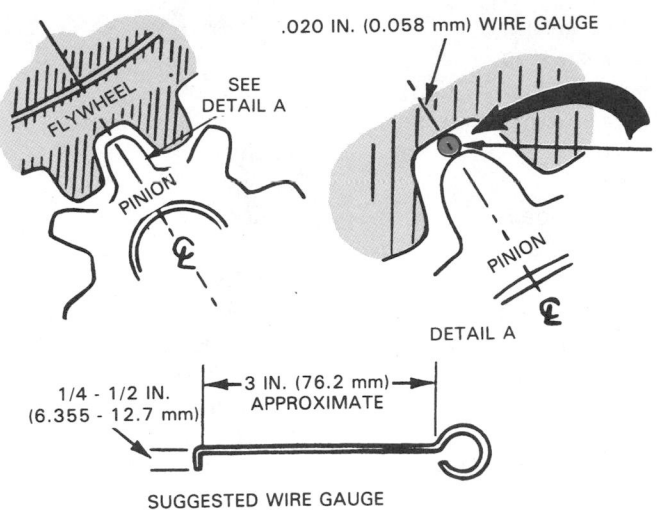

.020 IN. (0.058 mm) WIRE GAUGE

SEE DETAIL A

FLYWHEEL

PINION

PINION

DETAIL A

1/4 - 1/2 IN.
(6.355 - 12.7 mm)

3 IN. (76.2 mm)
APPROXIMATE

SUGGESTED WIRE GAUGE

Figure 26-55. Checking flywheel-to-pinion clearance. (Pontiac)

If the pinion-to-flywheel clearance is incorrect, it is often possible to bring it within the specified range by using mounting shims to tip the starter slightly. This must be done carefully. Make a final clearance check after tightening. Connect the wiring. Connect the battery ground strap. Try the starter. Remember that all splash and/or heat shields, sealing gaskets, and brackets must be in good condition and in place.

Tech Talk

Suppose you are in New York City and want to get to Chicago in a hurry. You go to the airport and are told that to get to Chicago, you must go first to Boston, Atlanta, Miami, New Orleans, and St. Louis. How would you feel about such a roundabout method of getting from one place to another? Do you think an airline that routes its planes in this way would be in business very long?

Many automotive technicians take a similarly inefficient route when trying to figure out what is wrong with a vehicle. They go all over the map to get from the problem to the solution, trying one thing after another instead of isolating the problem and investigating the causes.

For instance, when confronted with a car that will not start, many technicians simply change the battery, only to have the car back in a few days with a brand new, dead battery. When they determine that the new battery is dead, they charge the battery, replace the alternator, and return the vehicle to its owner. A few days later, the car is back in the shop and the owner is very angry. It must be embarrassing to find out that the problem is a grounded circuit, draining the battery.

Technicians are always being asked to get from New York to Chicago by the most efficient route. In other words, they are asked to find out what is really wrong with a vehicle and fix it. It is up to you to learn the most efficient way to determine what is wrong and what to do about it.

Summary

Batteries can explode. Be careful! Wear gloves and goggles when handling electrolyte. Keep the battery hold-down snug, cable connections clean and tight, and electrolyte up to the proper level. Use distilled water unless tap water has been tested and found to be acceptable.

Where possible, specific gravity should be checked with a hydrometer. Correct the reading to temperature. Where a battery is of sealed construction, the state of charge can be determined by either studying the built-in hydrometer "eye" or by using suitable test instruments. Charge batteries that are less than 75% charged.

Battery open circuit voltage can be determined with a low-reading voltmeter. Cell voltage should be 2.06 volts or more. Cell variation should not exceed about 0.5 volts.

Batteries may be recharged either by slow charging or by fast charging. Slow charging is preferable when time permits. Wet batteries may be kept charged in storage by trickle charging. Be careful to avoid overcharging. Store in a cool area. Store dry-charged batteries in a cool, dry spot.

When activating a dry-charged battery, fill it with the specified electrolyte. Fast charge the battery until the specific gravity is at least 1.240 and the electrolyte temperature is 80°F (27°C) or above. A replacement battery should equal or exceed the original in ampere-hour capacity. Three popular battery electrical load ratings are cold cranking amps, cranking amps, and reserve capacity.

When installing the battery, be sure to ground the correct terminal. Current U.S. vehicles ground the negative terminal. The negative post is smaller in diameter than the positive post and may have a NEG, N, or (–) stamped on the top. A voltmeter may be used to check for battery drain.

When using jumper cables to connect a booster battery, connect the booster positive to vehicle battery positive and booster negative to the vehicle frame or engine.

Charging system problems can involve the alternator, regulator, wiring, battery, or any combination of these items. When repairing or replacing one unit, check the others also.

Always disconnect the battery ground strap before making test connections or removing any part of the charging system. Check the charging system for excessive resistance by measuring field circuit resistance, alternator-to-battery positive terminal resistance, and alternator-to-battery ground resistance. Check the alternator output against specifications.

When working on alternator regulators, observe all the normal alternator system cautions. Many electronic regulators are nonadjustable and must be replaced if malfunctioning.

Clean all alternator parts except rotor, stator, and brush assemblies in solvent. Do not wash sealed bearings. Replace alternator brushes during an overhaul.

Test the rotor for opens, shorts, and grounds. Test the alternator diodes with a special tester, an ohmmeter, or a test light. Protect diodes from excessive heat and from mechanical shock. Use a press to remove and replace the diodes. Check stator windings for opens, shorts, and grounds. Inspect the slip rings for signs of scoring and burning. If needed, turn and polish with No. 400 sandpaper. Test the alternator radio capacitor.

Before condemning the starter, check the battery condition. Check the battery cables, the connections, and the entire starter system wiring for high resistance. Clean and tighten connections and replace wiring where indicated.

When conducting starter tests, do not operate the starter for any longer than 20-30 seconds. Allow a two minute cooling off period before resuming cranking. Check solenoids, switches, and relays for excessive resistance, shorting, and mechanical faults. The starter no-load test, the load test, and the stall torque test may be used as required to check starter performance and current draw. Clean all starter parts except the armature, field coils, commutator, bushes, and where used, the overrunning clutch in solvent.

Test the armature for short circuits and grounds. Check the commutator bars for indication of an armature open. Check the commutator for run out, burning, and scoring. Turn and polish with No. 400 sandpaper when required. Do not use emery cloth. When turning the commutator, remove only enough copper to clean it up. Undercut the mica if recommended by the manufacturer.

Test the field coils for opens and grounds. Check the brush holders for grounds. Inspect soldered connections. When using 110-volt test equipment, be careful to avoid shocks. Replace the starter brushes during overhaul.

Check the starter bushings and armature shaft bearing area. Inspect the pinion gear and the Bendix or overrunning clutch drive unit. Check the pinion housing for cracks.

Lubricate the starter bushings with a few drops of 20W oil during starter assembly. Coat the armature shaft splines with a light coat of Lubriplate. If a Bendix drive is used, oil it lightly. Check pinion clearance. Install all grommets snugly. Use nonhardening sealer where required. Torque all through-bolts. Clean the starter mounting pad and torque the mounting fasteners. Replace the heat shields and brace brackets. Test the starter function.

Know These Terms

Battery	Electrical load test
Electrolyte	Battery charger
Sulfuric acid	Slow charging
Open circuit voltage test	Fast charging
Percentage of charge	Trickle charging
Specific gravity	Dry-charged batteries
Hydrometer	Battery groups
Surface charge	Battery rating
Cold cranking amps (CCA)	Electronic regulator
Cranking amps (CA)	Electro-mechanical
Reserve capacity (RC)	regulator
Battery temperature sensor	Resistance
Polarity	Brushes
Shorts	Diodes
Parasitic loads	Starter solenoid
Jump started	Neutral safety switch
Booster battery	Load test
Jumper cables	No-load test
Alternator regulator	Stall torque
Voltage regulator	Starter drives
Overcharging	Armature
Undercharging	Commutator bars
Amperage	Field coils
Voltage	

Review Questions—Chapter 26

Do not write in this book. Write your answers on a separate sheet of paper.

1. Battery electrolyte is made up of _____ and _____.
2. When mixing or adding electrolyte to batteries, always protect your _____.
   (A) hands
   (B) eyes
   (C) skin
   (D) All of the above.
3. Wash skin with _____ to remove battery acid.
4. Battery corrosion may be readily removed with a solution of _____ and water.
   (A) baking soda
   (B) sulfuric acid
   (C) chalk
   (D) milk
5. When the electrolyte level is low, bring it up by adding _____.
   (A) a solution of water and sulfuric acid
   (B) sulfuric acid only
   (C) water only
   (D) Either A or B.
6. Use only _____ water or approved tap water for battery service.
7. Which of the following instruments is used to test electrolyte specific gravity?
   (A) Voltmeter.
   (B) Hydrometer.
   (C) Ammeter.
   (D) Specificometer.
8. Average full charge specific gravity would be about _____.
   (A) 1.260 -1.280
   (B) 1.110 - 1.130
   (C) 1.400 -1.450
   (D) 1.200 - 1.220

9. Specific gravity readings must be corrected for _____.

10. A battery should be recharged when the state of charge is reduced to _____ percent.
    (A) 50
    (B) 25
    (C) 75
    (D) Any of the above.

11. When installing a battery, always connect the _____ cable last.

MATCHING

Match the battery voltage with the type of vehicle in which it is used.

12. Late-model cars and light trucks.   (A) 6 volt
13. Large trucks and construction equipment.   (B) 12 volt
14. Old American cars.   (C) 24 volt
                                                (D) 36 volt

15. How is the battery positive post or terminal identified?
    (A) It is wider than the negative post.
    (B) It is painted red.
    (C) A (+) or POS is stamped on the post.
    (D) Any of the above, depending on manufacturer.

16. When connecting a booster battery to a dead battery in a vehicle, hook the booster positive to the vehicle battery _____ and booster negative to the vehicle battery _____.

17. List the three things that determine battery group.

18. Cold cranking amps (CCA) are measured at a battery temperature of _____.
    (A) –17°F (-27°C)
    (B) 0°F (–17°C)
    (C) 32°F (0°C)
    (D) 80°F (26.5°C)

19. Reserve capacity (RC) is measured in _____.
    (A) amperes
    (B) volts
    (C) minutes
    (D) degrees F

20. Name four alternator parts that must *not* be cleaned in solvent.

21. When overhauling an alternator, new _____ should be installed if they show any signs of wear or damage.
    (A) brushes
    (B) bearings
    (C) stator windings
    (D) All of the above.

22. List ten precautions regarding service work on alternator charging systems.

23. Always _____ the battery before connecting or disconnecting any unit in the alternator system.
    (A) recharge
    (B) discharge
    (C) disconnect
    (D) remove

24. Diodes may be tested with a(n) _____.
    (A) ohmmeter
    (B) special diode tester
    (C) test lamp
    (D) All of the above.

25. Electronic regulators have _____ set(s) of points
    (A) one
    (B) two
    (C) no
    (D) Varies with manufacturer.

26. Check the starter circuit for _____, and if it is discovered, clean and tighten connections as required.

27. Never operate starter continuously for more than _____.
    (A) 1 minute
    (B) 20-30 minutes
    (C) 20-30 seconds
    (D) 5 seconds

28. If the starter solenoid clicks when energized but the starter does not operate, the problem is in the _____.
    (A) starter
    (B) internal solenoid contacts
    (C) ignition switch
    (D) Either A or B.

29. List three starter parts that should *not* be cleaned in solvent.

30. Test the starter field coils for _____ and _____.

ASE-Type Questions

1. Technician A says that battery efficiency is improved by cold weather. Technician B says that battery specific gravity indicates cold cranking amps (CCA). Who is right?
    (A) A only.
    (B) B only.
    (C) Both A & B.
    (D) Neither A nor B.

2. Technician A says that when time is available, slow charging is better than fast charging. Technician B says that open-circuit voltage should be checked immediately after charging a battery. Who is right?
    (A) A only.
    (B) B only.
    (C) Both A & B.
    (D) Neither A nor B.

3. Technician A says that a 12-volt battery will work fine in a 6-volt system. Technician B says that replacing the original equipment battery with a smaller battery will save wear and tear on the charging system. Who is right?
    (A) A only.
    (B) B only.
    (C) Both A & B.
    (D) Neither A nor B.

4. Technician A says that a discharged battery will not affect charging system readings. Technician B says that when a defective battery is found, it can be assumed

that the rest of the starting and charging system is satisfactory. Who is right?

(A) A only.
(B) B only.
(C) Both A & B.
(D) Neither A nor B.

5. All of the following can cause a short in the electrical system EXCEPT:

(A) pinched wiring.
(B) defective solenoid.
(C) high battery cable resistance.
(D) stuck relay.

6. Technician A says that electronic regulators are not adjustable. Technician B says that alternator rotor and stator windings should be checked for opens, shorts, and grounds. Who is right?

(A) A only.
(B) B only.
(C) Both A & B.
(D) Neither A nor B.

7. Efficient starter operation is most dependent upon

_____.

(A) a fully charged battery.
(B) proper engine oil.
(C) a well-oiled starter drive.
(D) a dust free armature.

8. Technician A says that starter brushes should be replaced when they are worn to within one-half of their original length. Technician B says that starter brushes should be replaced if they are oil soaked or any time that the starter is dismantled for another reason. Who is right?

(A) A only.
(B) B only.
(C) Both A & B.
(D) Neither A nor B.

9. Technician A says that starter pinion-gear-to-pinion-stop clearance is automatic and cannot be adjusted. Technician B says that starter pinion-gear-to-flywheel-gear clearance is automatic and cannot be adjusted. Who is right?

(A) A only.
(B) B only.
(C) Both A & B.
(D) Neither A nor B.

10. All of the following statements about testing starter armatures are true, EXCEPT:

(A) the armature can be checked with a growler and hacksaw blade.
(B) a grounded armature can be turned to repair it.
(C) prolonged cranking may melt the solder on the commutator bars.
(D) the commutator can be turned in a lathe.

Suggested Activities

1. Draw a simple electrical schematic showing a workable starting and charging system. The schematic should include the battery, starter, alternator, ignition switch, solenoid, and related wiring (external voltage regulator optional).

2. Remove, clean, and reinstall the terminals of a battery. List the electronic devices (such as the clock) that must be reset when the battery cables are removed.

3. Use a battery charger to recharge a battery in a vehicle. Demonstrate the proper method of isolating the battery and charger from the rest of the vehicle electrical system and the correct way of connecting the charger cables to the battery.

4. Using shop test equipment, test the battery in a vehicle. Also make a hydrometer test if possible. Compare the two readings to determine the state of charge of the battery. If the battery is not fully charged, perform Activity 5 to determine the reason.

5. Using the shop equipment, check the electrical values (amperage and voltage) of a vehicle's starting and charging systems. Perform tests during cranking and as the running engine charges the battery. If the readings are not correct, try to find the reason.

27

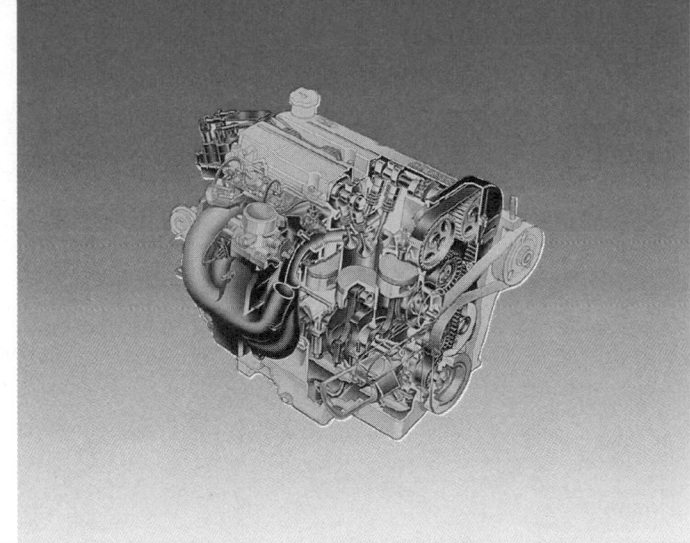

Chassis Electrical Service

After studying this chapter, you will be able to:
- Identify and define chassis wiring and related components.
- Explain the differences between chassis wiring and engine wiring.
- Identify chassis electrical components.
- Troubleshoot and replace chassis electrical components.
- Work safely on vehicles equipped with air bag systems.
- Troubleshoot and service air bag systems.

Although many vehicle electrical systems are directly related to engine operation, they are not the only systems that you will be called on to service. Many vehicle electrical components are not directly connected with the vehicle engine or drive train operation. Examples include safety devices such as vehicle lights, horns, and windshield wipers as well as entertainment and comfort items such as radios, electronic compasses, power windows, and door locks. This chapter will cover electrical components and their associated wiring that are used on the vehicle body and chassis.

Chassis Wiring

Chassis wiring consists of all of the wiring not directly connected with the engine and drive train. This wiring extends throughout the vehicle. Wiring to devices which will not be operated except when the vehicle is being driven, such as the windshield wipers and radio is routed through the ignition switch. Wiring to the vehicle lights or other systems which can be operated at any time is powered directly from the vehicle battery.

Almost all vehicle wiring is installed as part of a *wiring harness.* Wiring harnesses are groups of wires wrapped together for ease of installation. A typical harness is shown in **Figure 27-1.** Wiring harnesses have molded electrical connectors which can be attached to other harnesses or directly to electrical components. Some vehicles use a *printed circuit* for at least part of their wiring needs, usually at the dashboard. The printed circuit shown in **Figure 27-2** is a vinyl plastic sheet with the circuits etched or printed on it.

All chassis wires are *color-coded* to make identification of individual wires easy. Color codes can be single wire colors, or colors with contrasting stripes or bands. The use of stripes and bands makes hundreds of color combinations possible. The technician should carefully check wire colors, since many wires in a harness may have similar colors.

Using Wiring Schematics

Wiring *schematics* are used to trace out vehicle wiring systems. A schematic is a pictorial diagram of electrical wiring throughout the vehicle. Wire colors are given on the schematic, making identification of needed wires easy. Some schematics show the exact flow of electricity, such as **Figure 27-3,** while others show the general process of a particular system, such as the computer control schematic shown in **Figure 27-4.** Note that the schematic does not show the return flow of electricity. This is because the current flow is assumed to return to the battery's negative terminal through the vehicle's body and frame.

Schematics are often included in the vehicle service manual or may be supplied separately. Tracing the flow of electricity through a schematic is similar to reading a road map. The flow of current can traced out from its starting point to the component experiencing problems. Conversely, the flow of current can be traced backwards from the inoperable component through switches, control relays, and other components back to the battery.

Fuses, Fusible Links, and Circuit Breakers

To protect the chassis wiring from damage, *fuses* are used in the electrical system. These were discussed in detail in Chapter 9. Almost all factory installed fuses are installed in the *fuse block,* usually located under the dashboard. A few fuses may be installed at the device which they protect. When an electrical accessory, such as foglights is installed, an *in-line fuse* may be installed in the wiring leading to the device.

Also used are *fusible links,* **Figure 27-5,** which are lengths of wire calibrated to melt when current flow exceeds a certain value. Most fusible links are located near the battery positive cable. They can be attached to the positive terminal

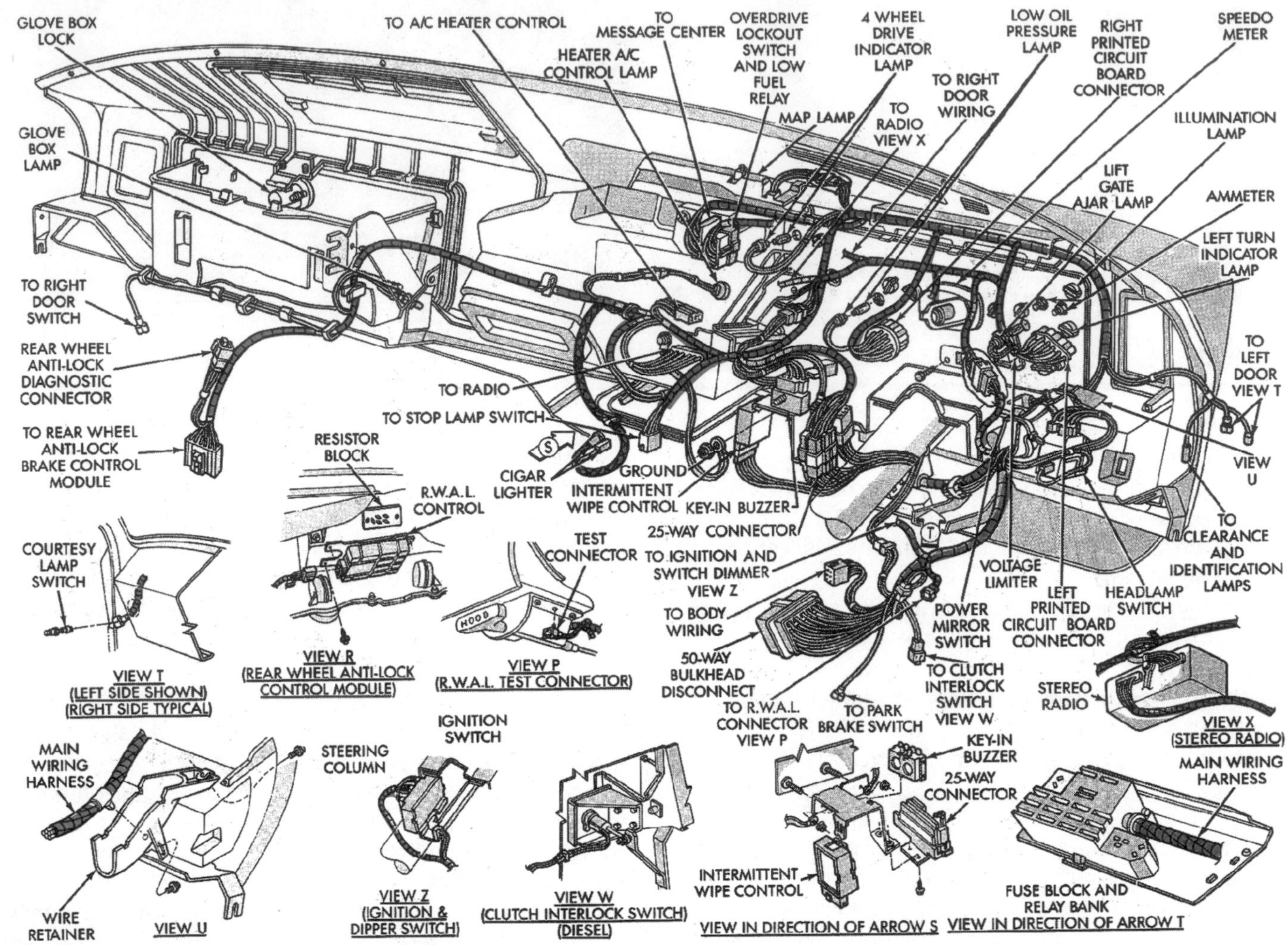

Figure 27-1. One particular instrument panel wiring harness with connectors going to the various components. Without this type of "road map," you will quickly become lost in a maze of wires. (Dodge)

clamp, a body mounted junction block, or at the starter solenoid when it is mounted on the inner fender.

Circuit breakers are excess current protection devices which will automatically reset. The advantage of the circuit breaker is that it will automatically reset when current flow stops and it has time to cool off. Circuit breakers are used on systems vital to vehicle safety, such as the headlights and in high current motors used in tailgate windows and convertible tops. The headlight circuit breaker is located in the headlight switch, while other circuit breakers are installed in the fuse block or at the protected motor.

Chassis Wiring Service

The most common problem encountered in electrical service is **blown** (melted) **fuses.** Sometimes fuses overheat or vibrate apart after long service. However, the most common cause of blown fuses is a short in the wiring or an electrical device or an overload in an electric motor. Fusible links can also melt and stop carrying current. A melted link can be spotted by insulation that is discolored or burned off completely. Pull gently on the ends of the fusible link, since they often melt at the end connections where the break is

not visible. If the fusible link wire can be pulled apart or feels springy, the wire has probably come apart inside of the insulation. Simply replacing a blown fuse or fusible link may not solve the problem. Always find out why the fuse or fusible link has blown or circuit breaker has opened and correct the problem.

> **Caution: Do not replace any fuse or circuit breaker with a metal slug or other non-fused connection. This can cause melted wires, destroyed components, or a vehicle fire. For the same reason, do not replace a fusible link with regular wire.**

Other wiring problems include bad connections at plug-in connectors caused by dirt, grease, corrosion, overheating, or short circuits. Wires can also short inside of the harness due to vibration or from being pinched between vehicle parts. In many cases, careful inspection of the wiring will reveal the damaged section. To check wiring problems that are not obvious, start the engine. With the affected electrical unit operating, wiggle, twist, tap, and generally flex all underhood electrical connectors as you observe the operation of the device. If the device quits

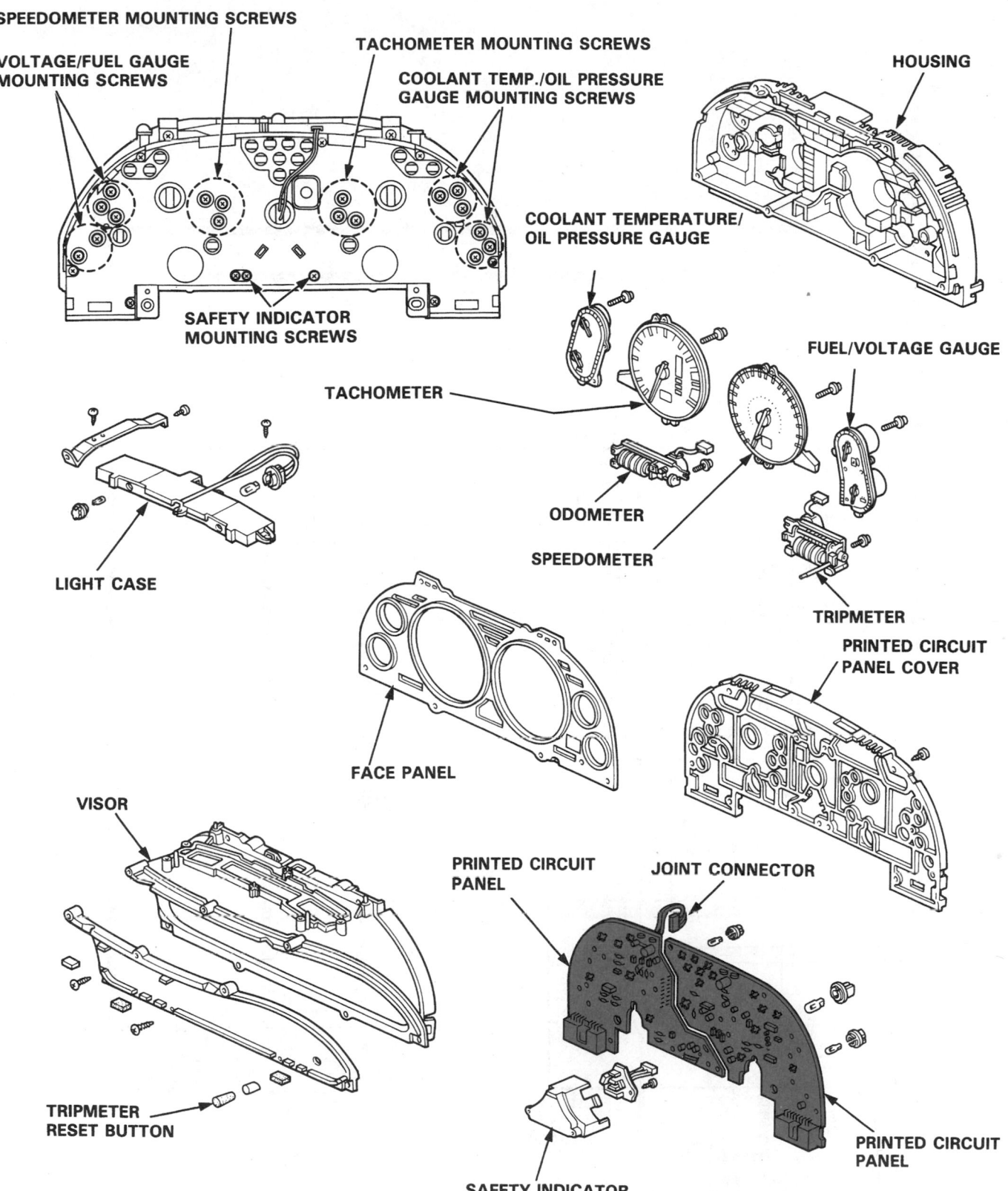

SPEEDOMETER MOUNTING SCREWS

VOLTAGE/FUEL GAUGE MOUNTING SCREWS

TACHOMETER MOUNTING SCREWS

COOLANT TEMP./OIL PRESSURE GAUGE MOUNTING SCREWS

HOUSING

SAFETY INDICATOR MOUNTING SCREWS

COOLANT TEMPERATURE/ OIL PRESSURE GAUGE

TACHOMETER

FUEL/VOLTAGE GAUGE

ODOMETER

SPEEDOMETER

LIGHT CASE

TRIPMETER

PRINTED CIRCUIT PANEL COVER

FACE PANEL

VISOR

PRINTED CIRCUIT PANEL

JOINT CONNECTOR

TRIPMETER RESET BUTTON

PRINTED CIRCUIT PANEL

SAFETY INDICATOR

Figure 27-2. An instrument panel gauge assembly using printed circuit panels (boards). Handle terminals and circuit panels with care. (Honda)

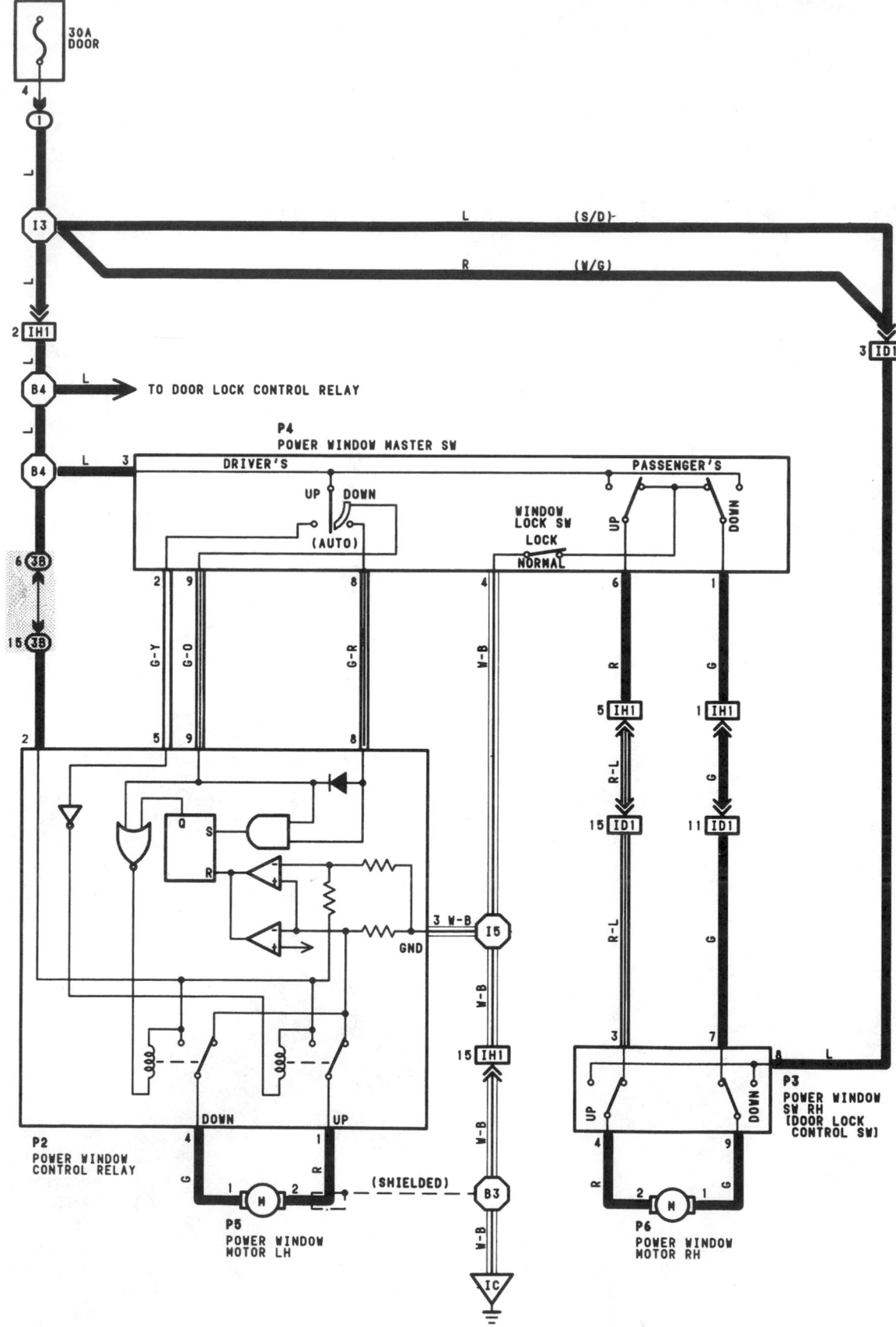

Figure 27-3. A wiring schematic for a power window circuit. Trace the circuit from the switches to the power window motors. (Toyota)

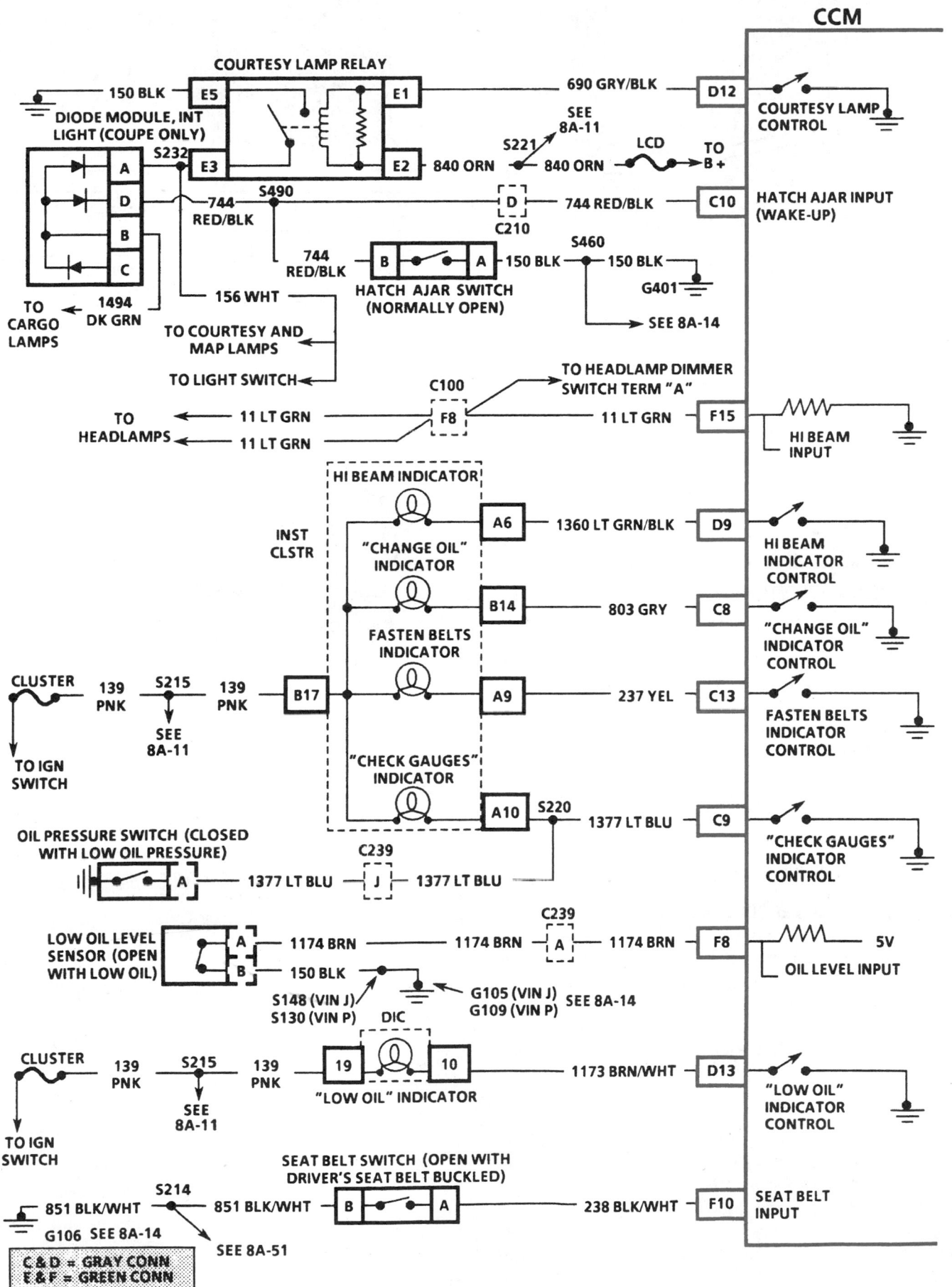

Figure 27-4. Study this computer control module (CCM) wiring schematic carefully. (Chevrolet)

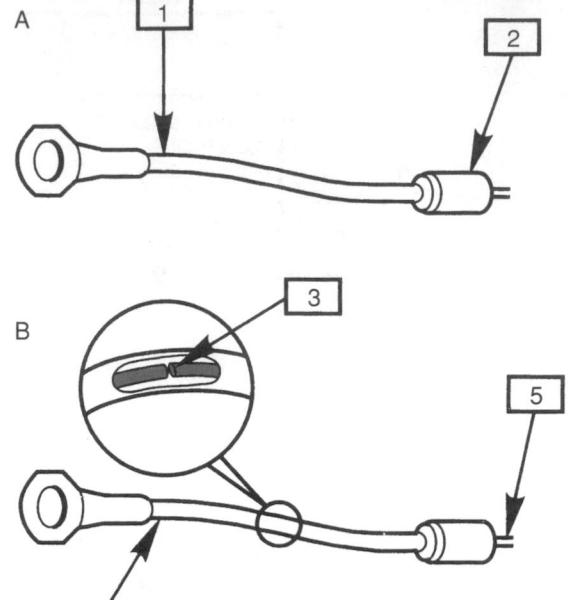

	FUSIBLE LINK BEFORE SHORT CIRCUIT
1	FUSIBLE LINK BEFORE SHORT CIRCUIT
2	CONNECTOR COVERING
3	BROKEN CIRCUIT BENEATH INSULATION
4	FUSIBLE LINK AFTER SHORT CIRCUIT
5	CUT WIRE HERE

Figure 27-5. A—A good fusible link. B—This fusible link has melted apart after a short circuit. When replacing fusible link, always use the correct length and gauge. (Geo)

working, works intermittently, or operation drastically changes when a connector is flexed, the connector should be taken apart for further inspection.

Vehicle Lights and Switches

Vehicle lights consist of two major groups, safety lighting and convenience lighting. Safety lighting devices are the headlights, taillights, marker lights, dashboard lights, brake lights, turn signal lights, and backup lights. Convenience lighting consists of interior lights and courtesy lights as well as trunk lights, underhood lights, and glove compartment lights.

Safety Lights

Headlights are operated by the driver through the headlight switch. **Figure 27-6** shows an older knob type headlight switch while **Figure 27-7** shows the newer rocker headlight switch. The headlight switch also operates the taillights and marker lights. The headlight switch also contains a *rheostat* which is used to adjust the brightness of the dashboard lights and may also be used to operate the interior lights when the doors are closed. Most headlight switches contain a circuit breaker for the headlights instead

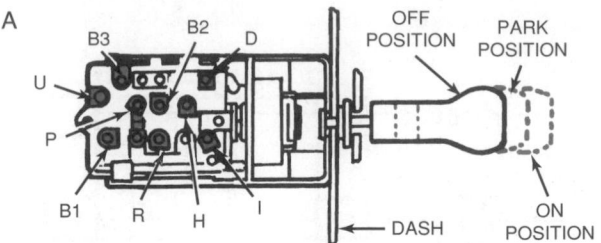

SWITCH POSITION	CONTINUITY BETWEEN
OFF	B1 to P OPTICAL HORN
PARK	B1 to P OPTICAL HORN B2 to R PARK LAMPS B3 to U HEADLAMPS ON WARNING CIRCUIT
ON	B1 to P OPTICAL HORN B1 to H HEADLAMPS B2 to R PARK LAMPS B3 to U HEADLAMPS ON WARNING CIRCUIT

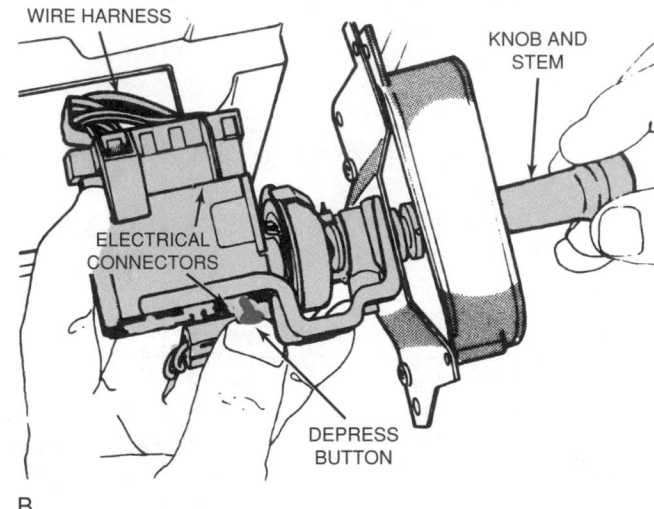

Figure 27-6. Study this push-pull style headlight switch. A—Switch position and continuity. B—Complete switch and wiring harness. Note that depressing the button with your finger allows the knob and stem to pull out of the switch itself for removal from the dash. (Dodge)

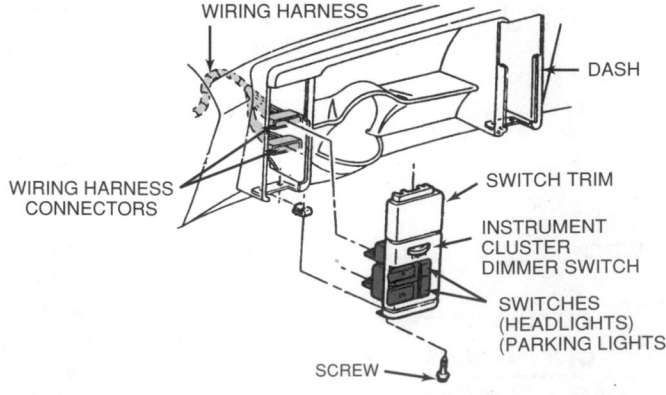

Figure 27-7. A rocker style, dash-mounted headlight/parking light switch with wiring harness and connectors. (General Motors)

of a fuse. After passing through the headlight switch, the headlight wiring passes through a dimmer switch, which allows the driver to select high or low headlight beams. The dimmer switches on older vehicles were located on the floorboard by the drivers left foot, but late-model vehicles have the dimmer installed on the turn signal lever.

Headlights on older vehicles are known as *sealed beams.* Sealed beams are a complete sealed headlight assembly with a heavy glass lens and mirrored interior surfaces to reflect the light produced by the *filament* (light producing element). The sealed beams used on vehicles with two headlights and the outer lights on four headlight systems contain two filaments, one each for low and high beams. The inner lights on four headlight systems contain only one high beam filament. **Figure 27-8** shows the older round type sealed beam and the more current rectangular sealed beam.

Newer vehicles use *halogen* headlights. Some vehicles are equipped with halogen headlights in the form of a sealed beam unit. However, most late model vehicles are equipped with composite headlights. Instead of a complete sealed beam unit, the composite uses a halogen bulb with a separate filament, **Figure 27-9.** This halogen gas-filled bulb can be replaced without removing the entire headlight assembly. The bulb is installed from the rear of the capsule

headlight assembly. The halogen gas allows the filament to be much brighter than older sealed beam designs with about the same service life.

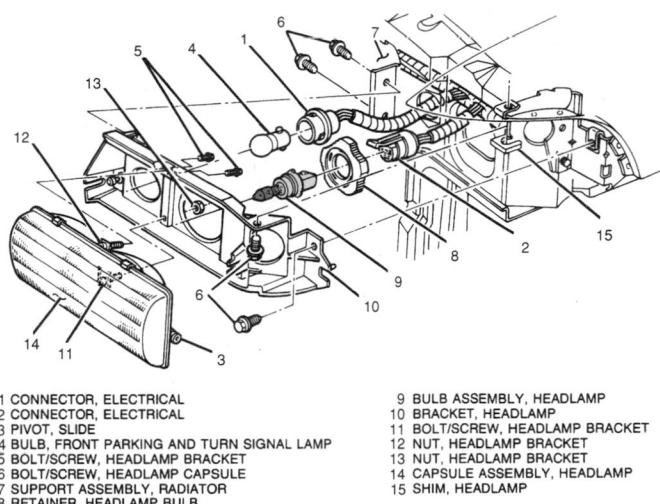

1 CONNECTOR, ELECTRICAL	9 BULB ASSEMBLY, HEADLAMP
2 CONNECTOR, ELECTRICAL	10 BRACKET, HEADLAMP
3 PIVOT, SLIDE	11 BOLT/SCREW, HEADLAMP BRACKET
4 BULB, FRONT PARKING AND TURN SIGNAL LAMP	12 NUT, HEADLAMP BRACKET
5 BOLT/SCREW, HEADLAMP BRACKET	13 NUT, HEADLAMP BRACKET
6 BOLT/SCREW, HEADLAMP CAPSULE	14 CAPSULE ASSEMBLY, HEADLAMP
7 SUPPORT ASSEMBLY, RADIATOR	15 SHIM, HEADLAMP
8 RETAINER, HEADLAMP BULB	

Figure 27-9. One type of headlight composite assembly. This unit uses a halogen headlight bulb which is removable. (General Motors)

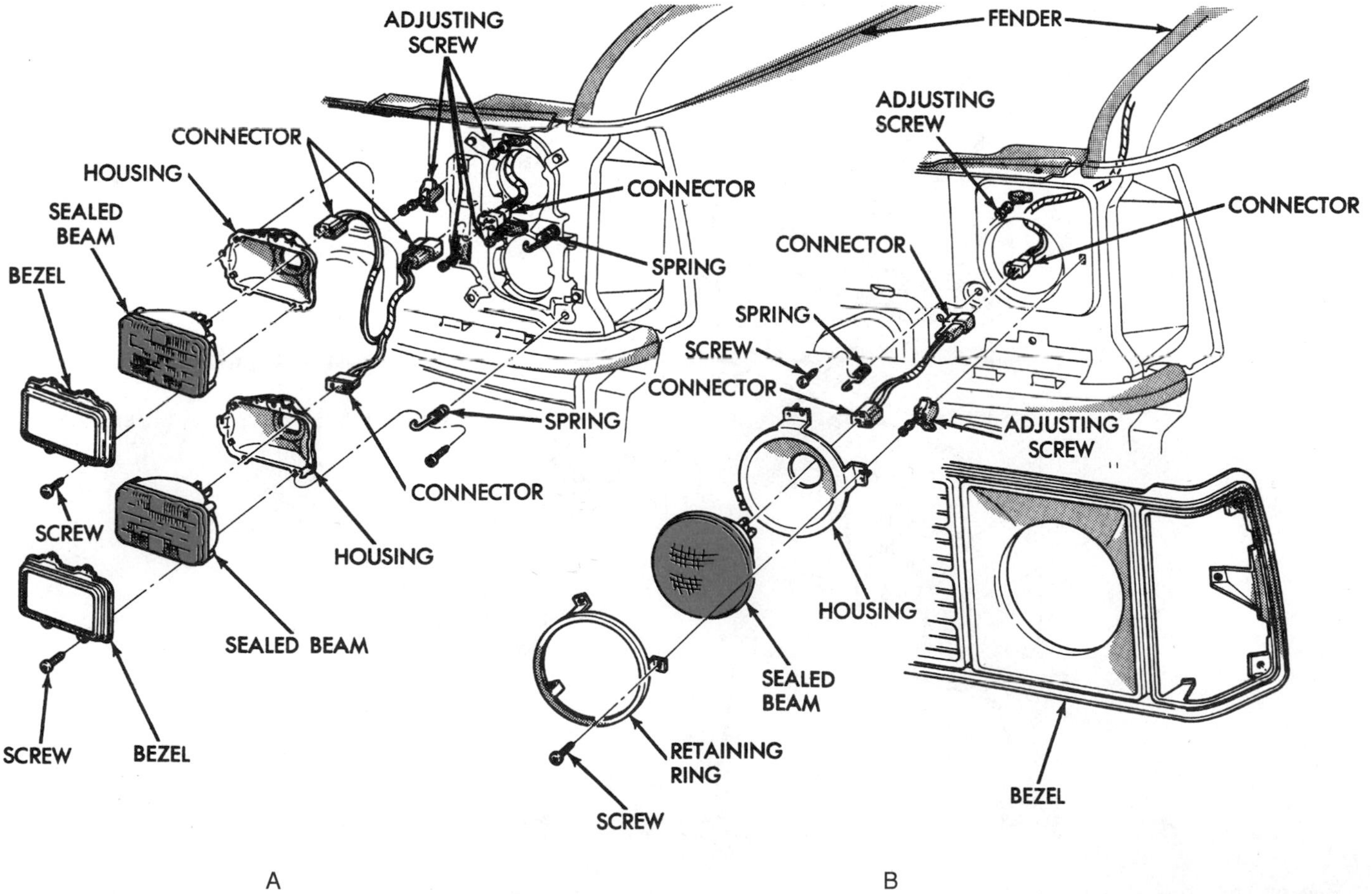

A

B

Figure 27-8. These are two typical sealed beam headlight assemblies. A—Rectangular shape. B—Round style. (Chrysler)

Tail and marker lights are simple filament light bulbs which are similar to the light bulb found in homes. Some taillight bulbs contain two filaments, one for the taillights and one brighter filament for the brake and turn signal lights. Many front marker bulbs also contain two filaments, one for the marker lights and a bright filament for the turn signals. Modern practice however, is to have separate bulbs for each function. Backup light switches are usually located on the transmission linkage and operate when the vehicle is placed in reverse gear. Backup lights are single filament bulbs, with no connection to the other light assemblies.

Brake Lights and Switches

Brake lights are either single or dual filament light bulbs operated by a switch attached to the brake pedal. The switch is a simple on-off type. Older **brake light switches** are pressure switches, operated by hydraulic pressure in the brake system. Newer brake light switches are mechanical. These switches are usually installed on the brake pedal and energized when the brake pedal is pressed. On some older vehicles, the brake light wiring passes through the turn signal assembly so that the brake lights are bypassed when the turn signal is being used. Modern vehicles usually have separate bulbs for the brake and turn signals.

Turn Signals, Flasher Lights, and Switches

Turn signals are operated by the vehicle driver. The selector lever contains a set of contacts which send current to the turn signal lights on the left or right side of the vehicle, as well as left-right indicators on the dashboard. The turn signal wiring contains a **flasher unit** which causes the lights to turn on and off rapidly, **Figure 27-10.** The turn signal flasher unit is usually installed on the fuse block or in a special holder under the vehicle dashboard.

The turn signal filament is usually in the same bulb as the brake light filament. At one time, however, the turn signals and brake lights used the same filament, usually in the same bulb as the taillight filament. The **emergency flasher switch** contains contacts which send current to the turn signal lights on both sides of the vehicle. The emergency flasher is separate from the turn signal flasher and is usually installed on the fuse block or under the vehicle dashboard.

Dashboard Lights

There are two classes of dashboard lights. The first, illuminating lights, light up the speedometer, gauges, and the wiper, headlight, and heater-air conditioner controls. The second group, indicator lights, warn of engine problems such as charging system problems, overheating and low oil pressure.

The illuminating lights are controlled through the headlight switch, which uses a rheostat to vary their brightness. There are usually several lights, although some modern vehicles use only a few bulbs and distribute their light through a **fiber optic** (light carrying) harness. Indicator

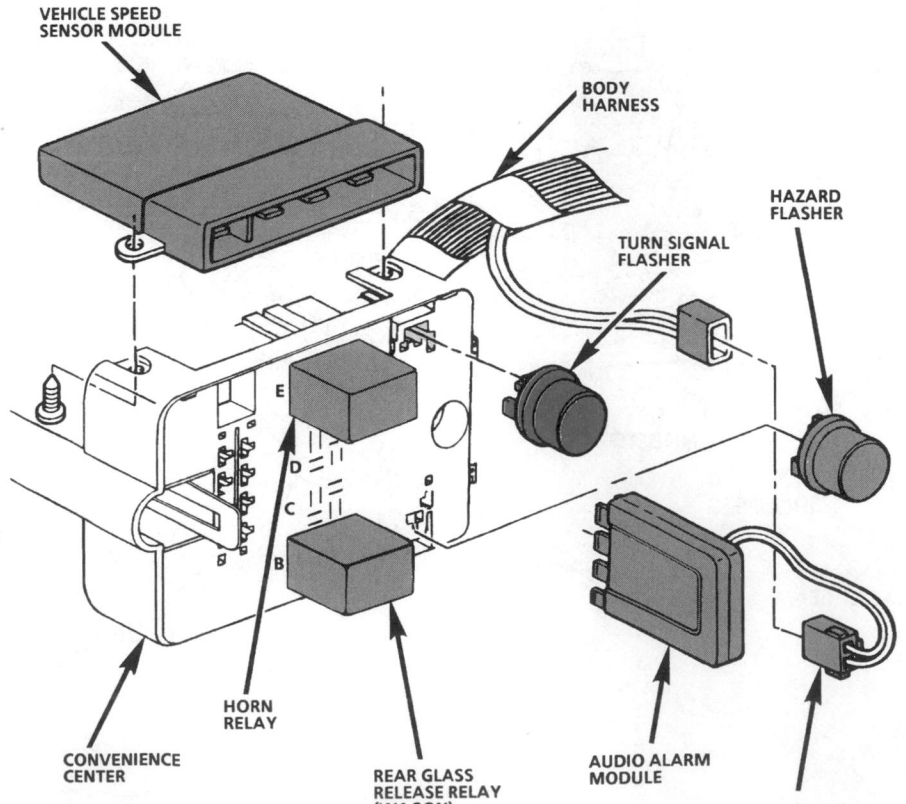

Figure 27-10. Turn signal flasher unit along with the convenience center where it is usually mounted. These are normally pushed in or pulled out of the socket for testing or replacement. (General Motors)

lights are installed on the dashboard and operated by senders. Typical indicator lights monitor engine temperature, oil pressure, and charging system condition. Indicator light senders are simple on-off switches, operated by temperature or pressure changes. The charging system light is usually operated by the alternator voltage regulator. Some indicator lamps, such as the check engine and anti-lock brake indicators, are operated by a external control module.

Gauges

Some vehicles use *gauges* to record oil pressure, engine temperature, and charging system operation. Every vehicle has a fuel gauge. The basic pressure or temperature gauge circuit consists of the gauge unit and a *sender* installed on the engine. Charging system gauges are usually voltmeters which measure the charging system voltage. Fuel gauge senders consist of a variable resistor attached to a float in the tank. Gauge design and service procedures vary between manufacturers. The operation of many gauges can be checked by disconnecting the sender and observing gauge movement. Some gauges can be further tested by grounding the sender terminal and observing gauge operation.

Convenience Lights

This group of lights includes all of the lights that are not required for vehicle safety, but are installed to illuminate the passenger sections of the vehicle. The vast majority of these lights are single filament lights operated by on-off switches installed in the door jams or glove compartment, or auxiliary switches in the vehicle's interior or trunk.

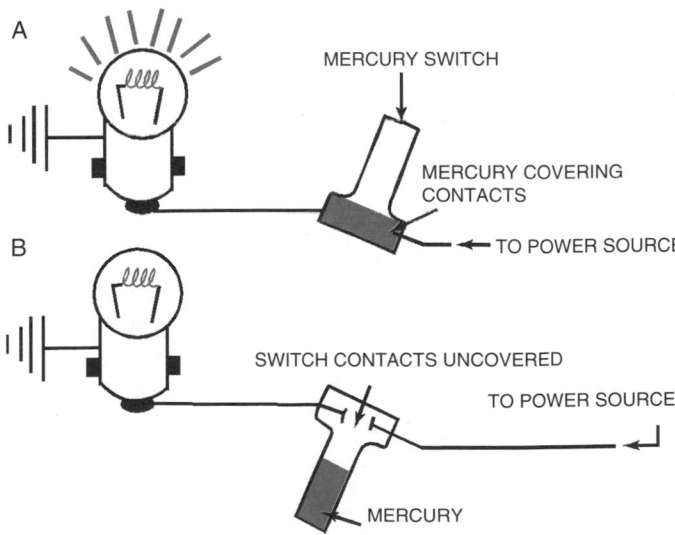

Figure 27-11. A—Hood open, mercury switch turns underhood light on. B—When the hood is closed, the mercury has flowed away from the switch, turning the light off.

Some courtesy lights are operated by a *mercury switch*, **Figure 27-11.** Examples are the trunk and underhood lights. The mercury in the bulb will not make contact when the trunk or hood is down. However, when the hood or trunk lid is raised, the mercury flows into contact with the electrical connectors, completing the circuit

Vehicle Light Service

The most common problem in the vehicle light circuit is a burned out bulb. However, other problems can cause a light to fail to illuminate. Many problems are caused by defective switches. On older vehicles, a wire often becomes disconnected, or a connector plug develops high resistance. This is especially common with tail and marker lights where the connector is exposed to water and dirt.

On older systems that use two-filament bulbs, one filament can burn out while the other continues to operate. It is also possible for the burned out filament to contact the other filament, causing electrical feedback. An example of this would be the front marker lights coming on when the brakes are applied. If a light bulb is broken, the base can usually be removed with pliers.

 Caution: When changing halogen lightbulbs (composite), be extremely careful not to touch the bulb surface with your hands. Halogen bulbs are coated with a special substance, and the oil from your hands can cause premature bulb failure. In some cases, the bulb can shatter with considerable force.

Adjusting Brake Light Switches

Pressure switches are not adjustable and should be replaced when they are defective. After the switch is replaced, the brakes should be bled, as explained in Chapter 34. Mechanical switches are adjusted so that only a small amount of brake pedal movement is required to operate the switch. **Figure 27-12** shows the adjustment distance for one specific installation. After installing the switch on

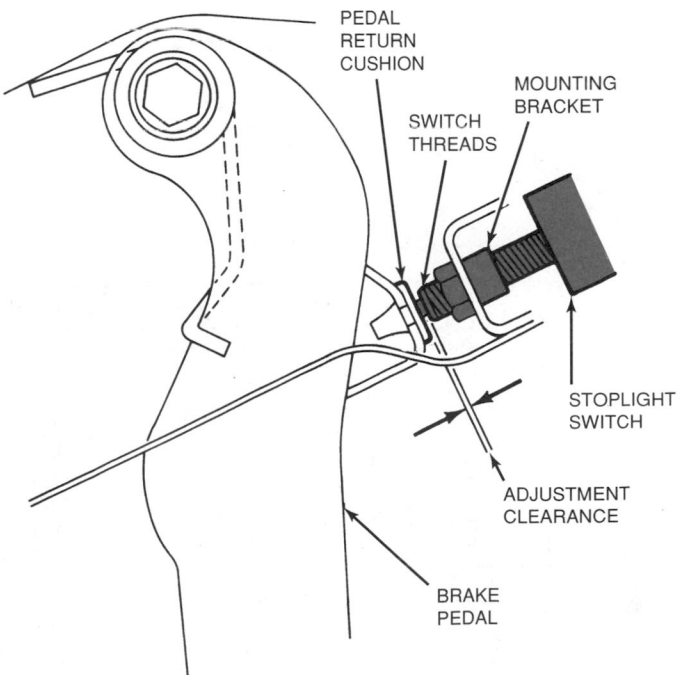

Figure 27-12. One stoplight switch arrangement. (Geo)

most vehicles, pull back on the brake pedal. This is to ensure that the stoplight switch does not prevent the brake pedal from returning to the fully released position. Some brake light switches adjust automatically.

Chassis Mounted Motors

Chassis mounted motors include the windshield wiper motor, power windows and vent windows, tailgate windows, and sunroof motors, as well as motors which operate convertible tops and power antennas. The modern vehicle may have as many as ten small dc motors to operate various systems. Except for the windshield wiper motor, switches used to control these motors are spring loaded so they return to the off position when the operator's hand is removed. This prevents accidental operation of the motor, with resulting motor overheating and damage.

Windshield Wiper Motors and Controls

Windshield wiper motors are high torque motors, capable of overcoming the binding effects of ice on the wiper blades and mechanisms, **Figure 27-13.** For this reason, wiper motors are durable in normal service, requiring relatively little maintenance. Windshield wiper motors have special *park mechanisms,* which cause the wiper blades to

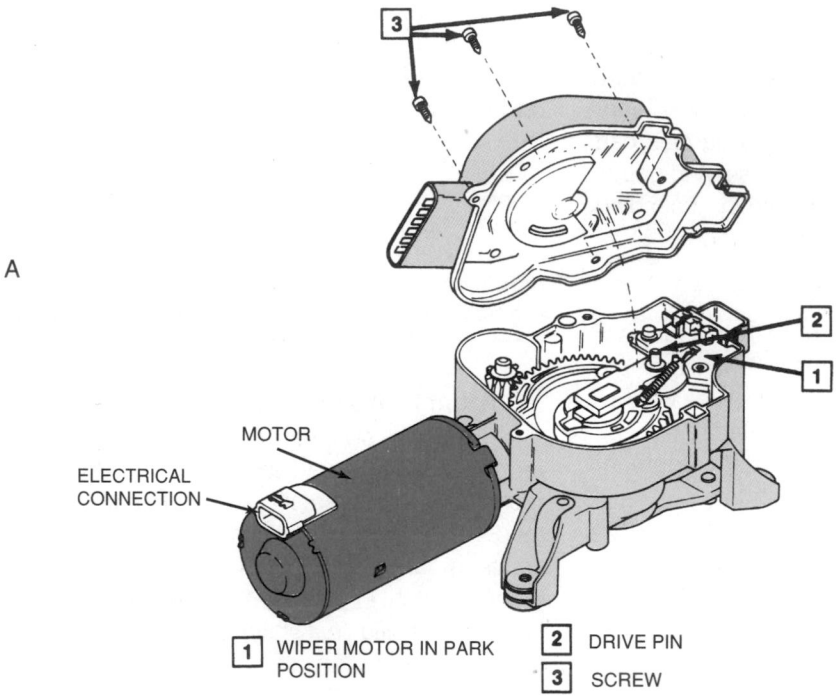

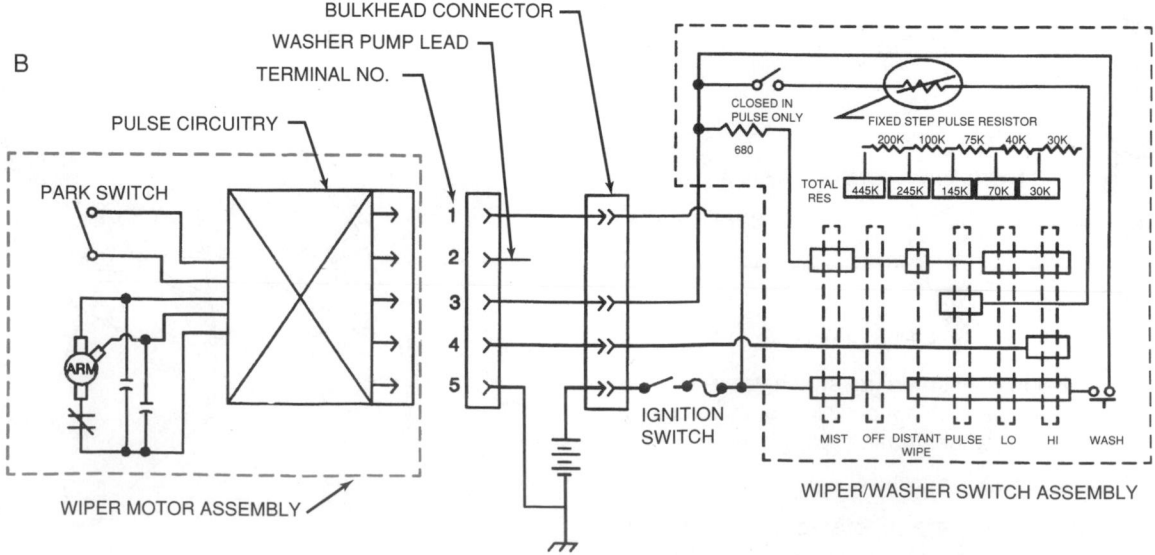

Figure 27-13. A—Wiper motor and gear assembly. B—Wiring schematic for an intermittent (pulse) wiper system. Trace the various circuits until you are familiar with each. (Pontiac)

return to the fully down position when the wipers are turned off. Some older wiper motors were equipped to operate the windshield washer pump, but most modern designs use a separate pump located in the washer reservoir.

Power Window, Tailgate, Convertible Top, and Sunroof Motors

These are generally high torque motors which are able to overcome the drag of dry or tight operating mechanisms and glass channels. Most of these motors have built-in overload switches or circuit breakers to prevent overheating damage. The convertible top motor is unique in that, instead of working directly to raise and lower the top, it is used to

drive a hydraulic pump which powers hydraulic cylinders that operate the top. The majority of these motors are operated by on-off switches located on the vehicle dashboard, door, or console. See **Figure 27-14.**

Power Antenna Motors and Switches

Power antenna motors are simple in construction and are usually operated through an automatic relay or by a manual three-position switch. The relay is energized when the radio is turned on or when the ignition switch is turned on when the radio is already on. The manual switch allows for positioning the antenna in any position that best suits the driver.

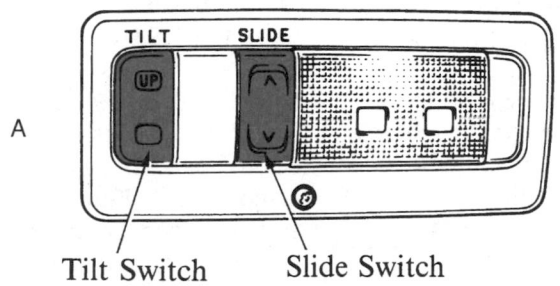

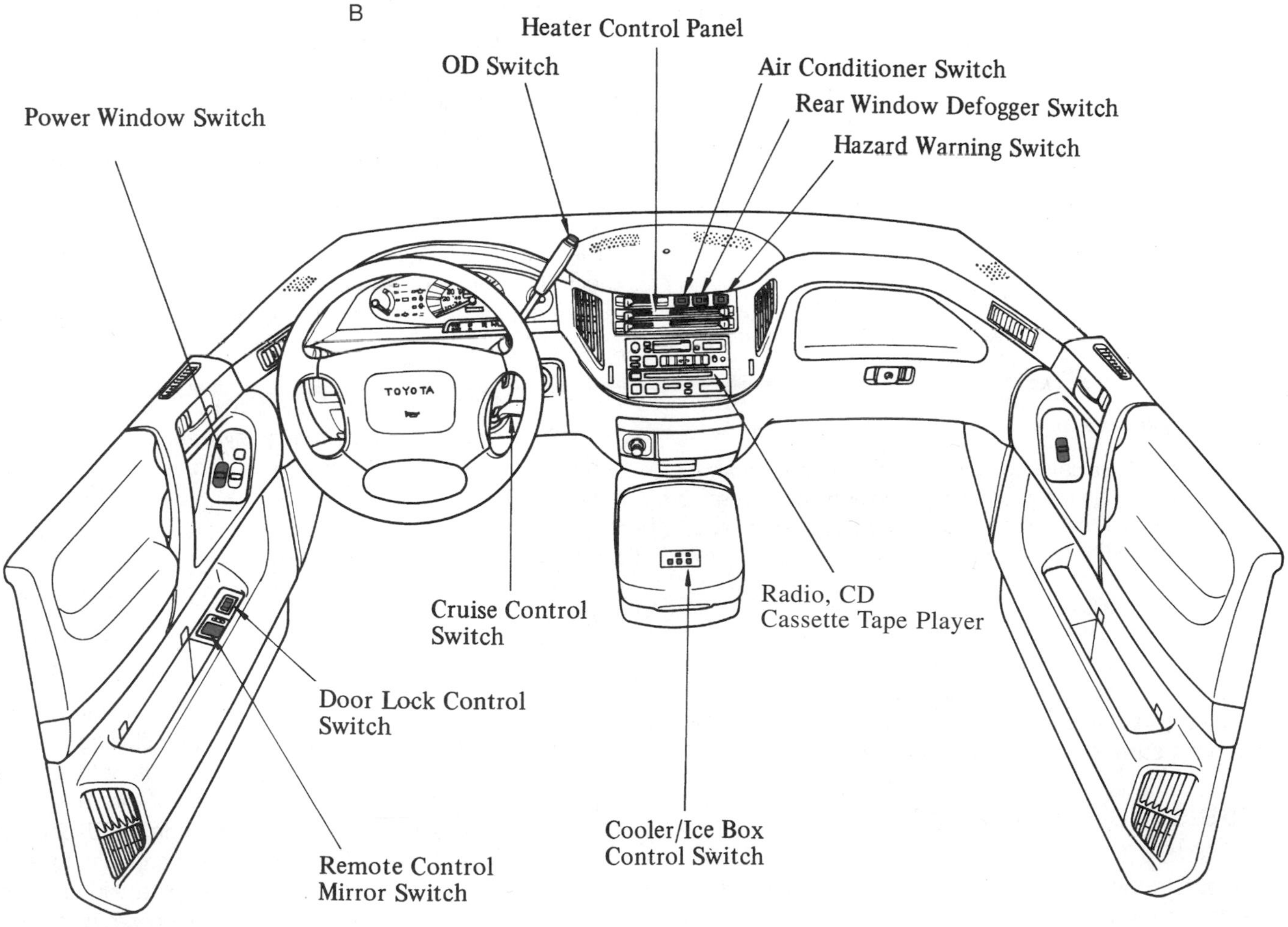

Figure 27-14. A—Sunroof tilt and slide switches. B—Vehicle control switches in their various locations as used by one manufacturer. (Toyota)

Electric Motor Service

Electrical motor service in the average vehicle is confined to ensuring that the motor is at fault and replacing it. Sometimes the entire assembly is replaced when the motor goes bad, for example power antennas. Most of the small electric motors used in these applications are exchanged for rebuilt units.

To check out a vehicle electric motor, bypass the controls (switches, relays) with a fused jumper wire. If the motor operates, the problem is in the control switches or wiring. If the motor does not work, it is defective. Most electric motors are replaced easily. Remove the electrical connectors first, and then remove the mounting bolts or other fasteners. Some power window motors require that holes be drilled in the door frame to remove the motor attaching hardware. **Figure 27-15** shows a typical window motor installation.

 Caution: Some motor operated devices, such as door or tailgate glass, may drop when the motor is removed. Always consult the manufacturer's service manual, and block the mechanism in place if necessary.

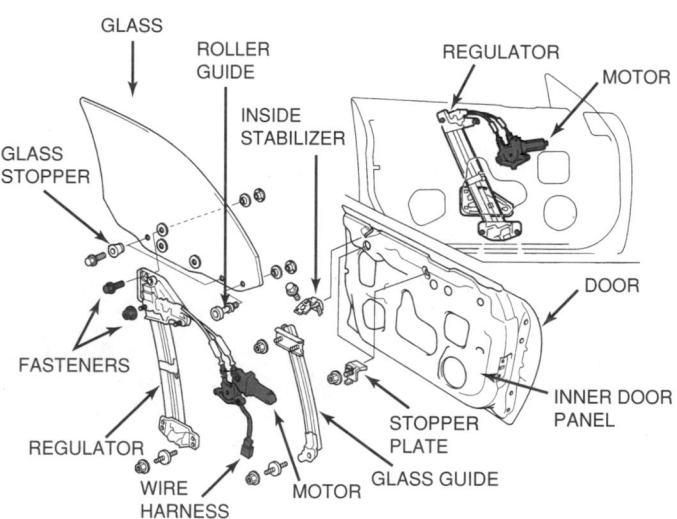

Figure 27-15. A typical power window assembly using an electric motor to cycle the window glass up and down. The motor and regulator mechanism are held to the inner door panel with nuts and bolts. (Honda)

Some motors, such as those used on windshield wipers and door motors, may require special positioning or aligning when they are reinstalled to ensure that the mechanism stops in the correct place. When reinstalling any motor, make sure ground straps, if any, are in place.

Chassis Mounted Solenoids and Relays

Chassis mounted solenoids are similar in construction to the solenoids used to energize the vehicle starter. They are used to operate door locks and trunk releases. *Relays* are a type of solenoid which close electrical contacts,

instead of operating a mechanical device. They are used to direct large current flows that might damage a switch. Switches used to control most solenoids are spring-loaded to return to the off position, preventing accidental operation of the solenoid.

Power Door Lock Solenoids and Switches

Power door lock solenoids are two position solenoids. The solenoids have two windings, allowing them to move a control rod in two directions. When the control switch is moved in one direction, the solenoid moves the door lock to the unlocked position. When the switch is moved in the other direction, the solenoid moves the door lock to the locked position. Wiring is usually straightforward, with separate circuits for the locked and unlocked solenoid positions. See **Figure 27-16.**

Trunk Release Solenoids

Trunk release solenoids are single position solenoids operated by a switch installed in the vehicle glove compartment, **Figure 27-17.** Power to the trunk release switch passes through the ignition switch. This keeps unauthorized persons from opening the trunk.

Solenoid Service

Although an ohmmeter can be used to check the solenoid windings, the simplest way to check out a solenoid is to bypass the control switch with a jumper wire. If the solenoid operates, the problem is in the control switch or wiring. If the solenoid does not work, it is defective. Occasionally an inoperative solenoid is caused by sticking, misaligned, or bent linkage on the device to which it is attached. Always check this possibility before replacing the solenoid. The easiest method is to disconnect the solenoid and then check its operation. Solenoids cannot be repaired and are replaced after ensuring that the solenoid is the cause of the problem.

Remote Keyless Entry System

The *remote keyless entry system* permits locking and unlocking of the vehicle's doors and/or trunk lid using a hand-held radio transmitter. These battery-operated transmitters are electronically coded to each vehicle. When replacing the transmitter's battery or working on the system, follow the manufacturer's instructions to prevent part or system damage.

Control Relays

Control relays are similar to starter solenoids. A small current flow energizes a magnetic winding, closing a set of contact points which send a heavy current flow to another unit, such as a motor or heating coil. Use of the relay eliminates having to pass heavy current through the dashboard controls, possibly overheating them and consuming extra electricity fighting the resistance of the extra wiring. Many relays used on late-model vehicles are power transistors with no moving parts. This cuts down on electricity consumption and is more reliable. Relays are used to operate

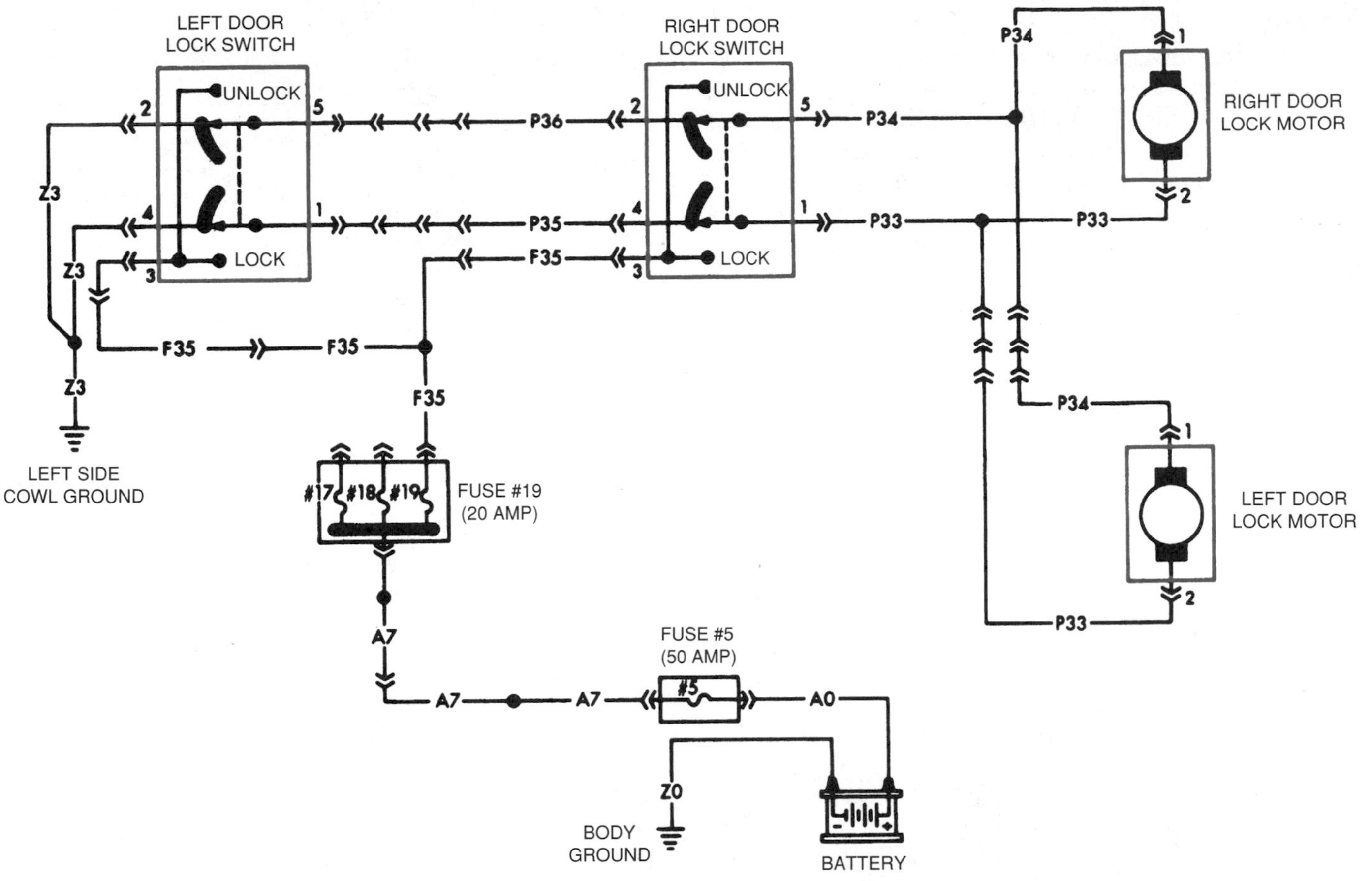

Figure 27-16. A wiring schematic for one power door lock circuit. This system uses reversible motors to actuate the linkage. (Dodge)

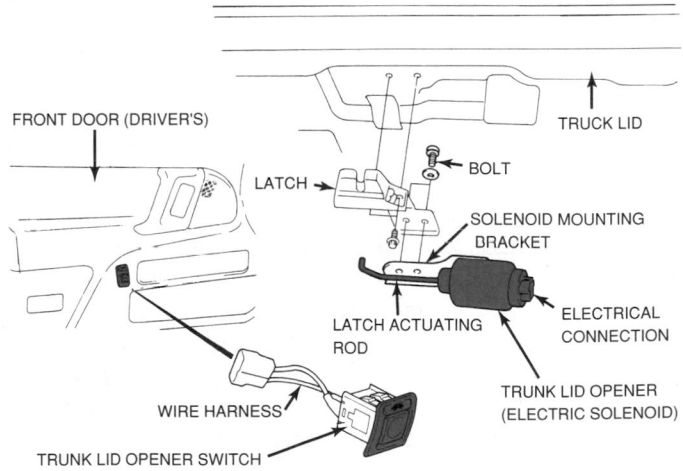

Figure 27-17. A trunk release solenoid and the solenoid operating switch. (Hyundai)

many heavy current consuming electrical devices on the modern vehicle. Relay service is confined to verifying that the relay is not functioning and replacing it.

Radios and Sound Systems

The repair of radios and related equipment, such as cassette tape and compact disc players is beyond the scope of this text. These units are best serviced by a qualified electronics shop. However, some simple checks which can be made before removing the unit for service are explained below.

Diagnosing Radio Problems

If the unit does not come on at all, check the fuse. On aftermarket units, check for the presence of any in-line fuses. Also check for any broken or disconnected input and ground wires. Also check that the antenna cable is plugged into the radio and antenna. Check that the wires to the speakers are not disconnected and that the speakers are grounded. If the radio has static, the source can be difficult to find. Often, the problem is simple to correct once it is located.

Check that there is no defect in the ignition system or charging system by operating the radio with the key on, but without starting the engine. If the static is only present when the engine is running, unplug the alternator with the engine running. If the noise stops, the stator or diodes are causing the static. Check the plug wires, rotor, cap, and other sources of ignition noise. Make sure that the plugs and wires are radio suppression types. Check for a crack in one of the speaker diaphragms. Check all ground straps on the radio, dashboard, antenna, and engine. If these checks do not locate the problem, the radio must be removed for repair.

Horns

The horn uses a diaphragm with a make and break contact. When energized, the horn diaphragm flexes, or vibrates, creating noise. As it flexes, it breaks the electrical contact inside of the horn body, causing current flow to stop. The loss of current causes the diaphragm to return to its original position, where it is reenergized. This flexing of the diaphragm occurs many times per second, creating a continuous noise.

Horns are operated by steering wheel contacts which energize a relay. The relay directs heavy current to the horns themselves. A few horn circuits ground the horn circuit directly through the steering column, eliminating the relay. Typical steering wheel contacts are shown in **Figure 27-18.** In some vehicles equipped with air bags, the horn contacts are incorporated with the air bag inflator module.

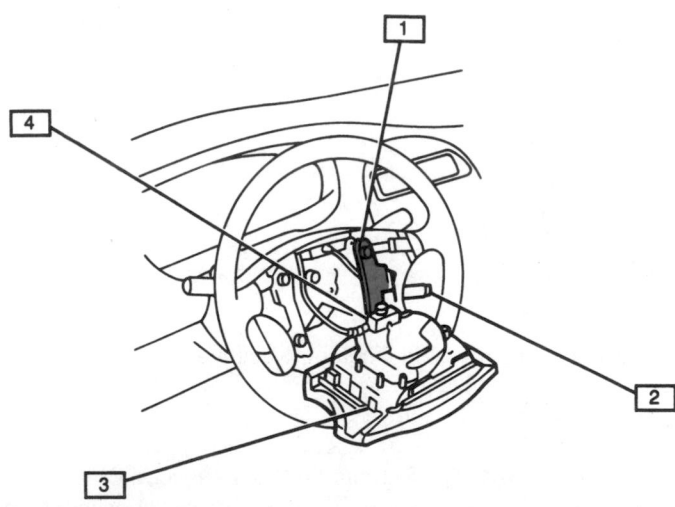

Figure 27-18. 1—Horn switches on the steering wheel. 2—Cruise control switch. 3—Air bag inflator module. 4—Upper steering column connector. (Geo)

Most horn problems are caused by defects in the steering wheel contacts. If they do not close, the horn will not blow. If they stick closed, the horn will blow continuously. Servicing the steering wheel contacts usually means at least partially disassembling the steering column. If pressing the horn contacts causes the relay to click, but the horn does not operate, the problem is in the horn, the horn ground, or the relay contacts.

Rear Window and Mirror Defrosters

These devices consist of a heater **grid** (a series of fine wires) applied to the glass surface of the rear window or mirror, **Figure 27-19.** The grid material has a calibrated resistance which opposes current flow. As current flows through the grid, it produces heat to melt any ice or snow. The temperature flow through the grid is kept constant by a load sensing device. Most glass defrosters are controlled by a dashboard switch working through a relay. Most defroster service consists of locating breaks in the heating grid wires. Breaks can be fixed without removing the grid from the

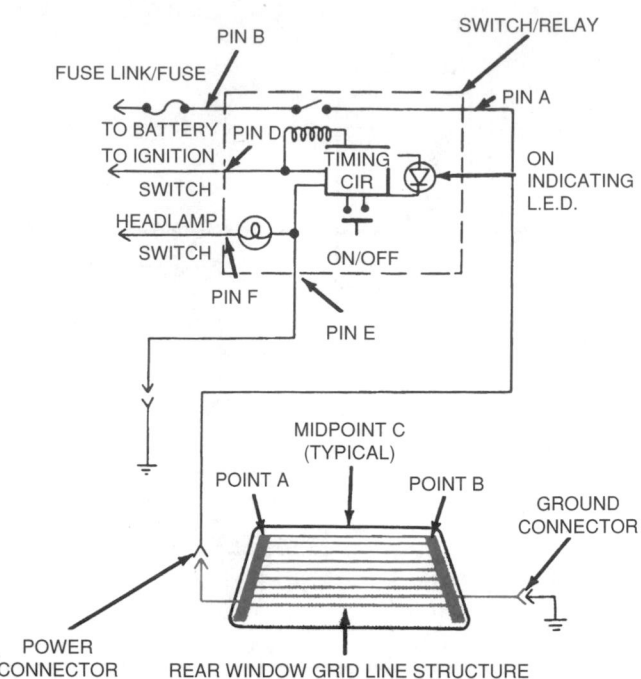

Figure 27-19. Rear window defogger grid with wiring and control schematic. Use caution when cleaning these grids. Razor blades and other sharp objects can easily damage the fine grid wires. (Chrysler)

glass. Refer to the manufacturer's service manual for repair procedures. Relays and switches can also be defective and should be checked according to manufacturers specifications.

Body Computer Systems

The remainder of this chapter will deal with **body computer systems.** A body computer system controls any function that does not affect engine operating conditions. The sensors, control units, and actuators used in body computer systems are similar to those found in computerized engine control systems. Typical systems controlled by body computers include air bag systems and cruise control systems, which are covered here. In addition, many heater and air conditioning systems, radio, anti-lock brake systems, traction controls, and active suspension systems are also controlled by body computers. They will be discussed in the chapters where they apply. Other body computers can control trip odometers, compasses, and other displays.

Air Bag Systems

Air bag systems, or **supplemental restraint systems,** are becoming standard on most modern vehicles. These systems are designed to deploy when a vehicle is involved in a frontal collision of reasonable force. Most air bag systems consist of several common components, **Figure 27-20,** which include:

- Diagnostic control module.
- Front impact sensors.
- Coil assembly.
- Inflator module.

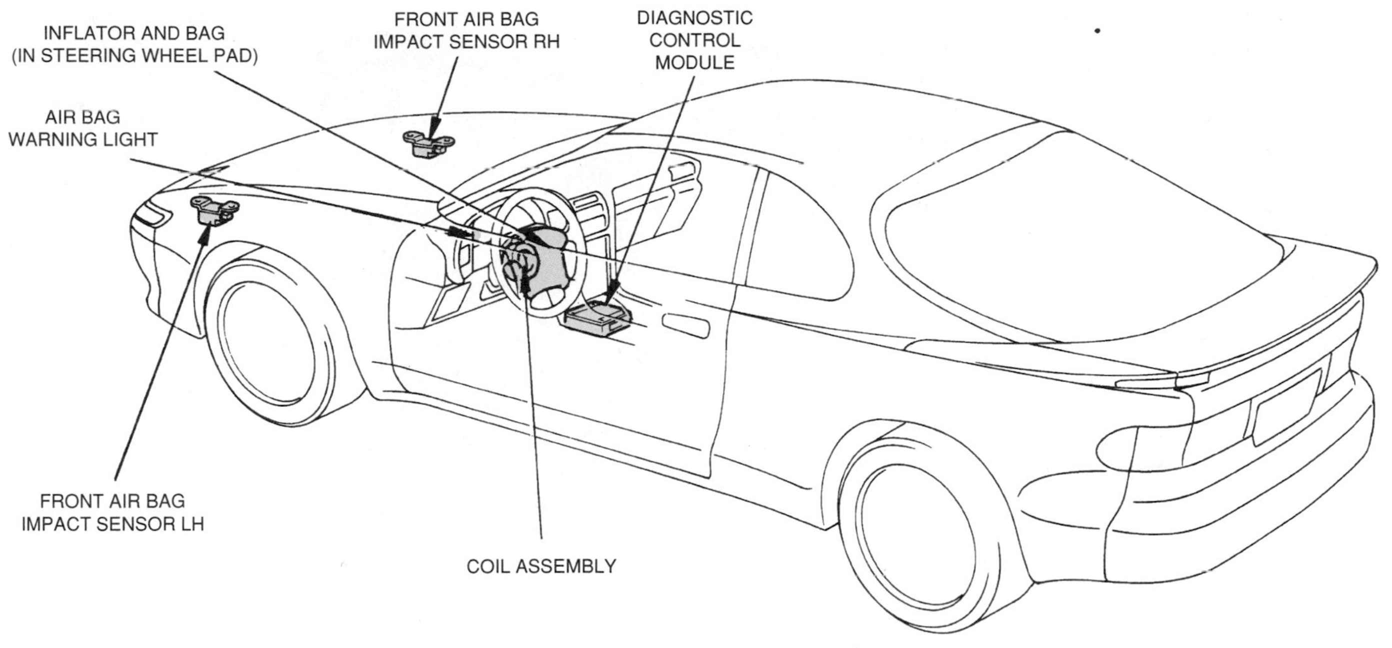

INFLATOR AND BAG
(IN STEERING WHEEL PAD)

FRONT AIR BAG
IMPACT SENSOR RH

DIAGNOSTIC
CONTROL
MODULE

AIR BAG
WARNING LIGHT

FRONT AIR BAG
IMPACT SENSOR LH

COIL ASSEMBLY

Figure 27-20.   Typical air bag system components. Note the location of the front impact sensors and inflator module. (Toyota)

These components work together to fully **deploy** (inflate) the air bag within 50 milliseconds after a frontal impact. After deployment, the air bag will deflate in approximately 100 milliseconds.

Diagnostic Control Module

The **diagnostic control module** performs several functions in the air bag system, **Figure 27-21.** The module serves as a monitoring system for the air bag components, warns the driver of system malfunctions by activating the air bag indicator light, and stores trouble codes which are used during system diagnosis. If battery voltage is lost in an accident, most diagnostic control modules provide the air bag system with an alternate source of power. The diagnostic

control module also contains a special safing sensor designed to prevent accidental deployment. This sensor must close simultaneously with one of the impact sensors to trigger the air bag system. The safing sensor prevents a faulty front impact sensor from activating the air bag system, **Figure 27-22.**

Impact Sensors

The **impact sensors** are usually located on the front section of a vehicle's frame or on each side of the radiator housing. An impact sensor is an open switch, which is designed to close when an impact provides a velocity change that is severe enough to warrant air bag deployment. See **Figure 27-22.**

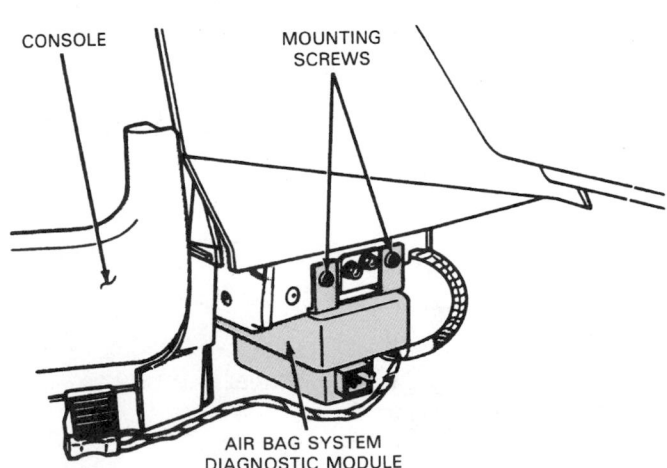

CONSOLE

MOUNTING
SCREWS

AIR BAG SYSTEM
DIAGNOSTIC MODULE

Figure 27-21.   Typical air bag diagnostic module. Note that this unit is mounted under the dash and near the center console. (Chrysler)

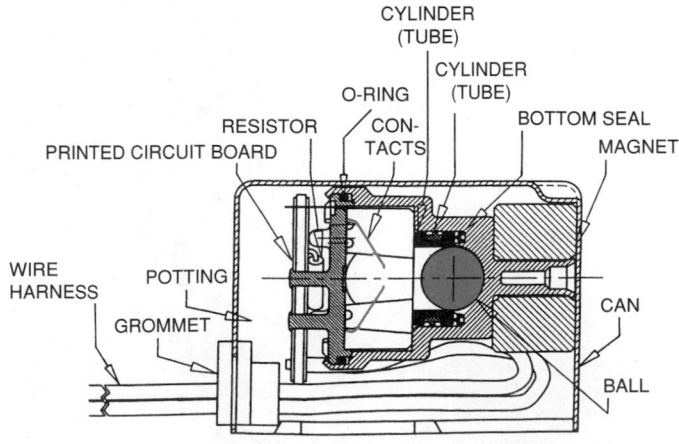

CYLINDER
(TUBE)

CYLINDER
(TUBE)

O-RING

BOTTOM SEAL

RESISTOR

CON-
TACTS

MAGNET

PRINTED CIRCUIT BOARD

WIRE
HARNESS

POTTING

GROMMET

CAN

BALL

Figure 27-22.   One type of impact sensor. If the vehicle is involved in a collision, the ball will break free of the magnet field and close the contacts, triggering the air bag system. (Breed Technologies, Inc.)

Coil Assembly

The **coil assembly** consists of two current carrying coils which are attached to the vehicle's steering column. As the steering wheel is rotated, these coils maintain a continuous electrical connection between the inflator module and diagnostic module. The coil assembly is sometimes referred to as a clock spring. A typical coil assembly is illustrated in **Figure 27-23.**

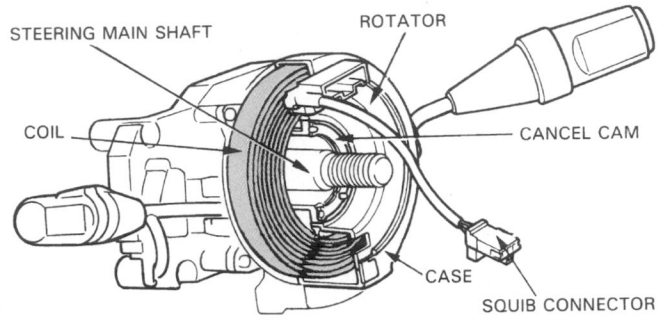

Figure 27-23. Cutaway view of a typical coil assembly. Note the squib connector which connects the coil assembly to the inflator module. (Toyota)

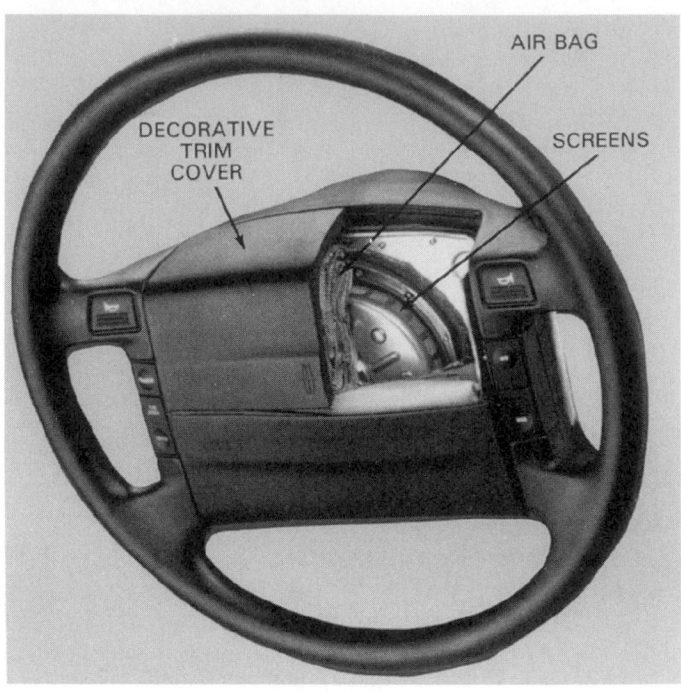

Figure 27-24. Cutaway view of an inflator module housed in a steering wheel assembly. Note the air bag folded under the decorative trim. (Ford)

Inflator Module

The **inflator module** is located in the center of the steering wheel in driver's side air bag systems. This module contains the inflatable fabric air bag, an initiator squib, and an inflator (gas generating material). The inflator module is usually covered with a decorative trim piece, **Figures 27-24** and **27-25.** In addition to a driver's side air bag, some vehicles are equipped with a passenger side air bag. Passenger side inflator modules are usually mounted above the glove box on the passenger side of the vehicle. A passenger side inflator module is shown in **Figure 27-26.**

Air Bag Operation

When a vehicle is involved in a collision that is severe enough to warrant air bag deployment, the impact sensors close. If at least one impact sensor and the safing sensor in the diagnostic module close, a signal is sent to the initiator squib. When signaled, the squib generates a thermal reaction which ignites the gas generating material (sodium azide-based propellant) in the inflator, **Figure 27-27.** This material releases a large amount of harmless gas, which quickly fills the air bag.

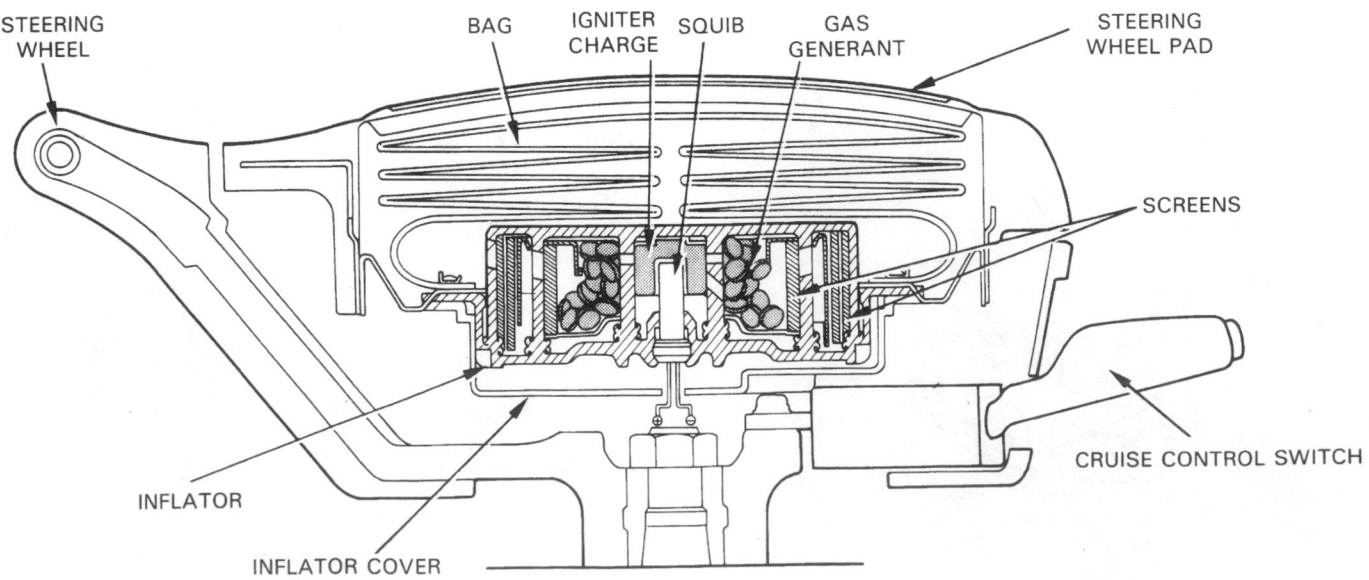

Figure 27-25. One type of air bag inflator module. Note the screens that allow gas from the generant to enter the bag. (Toyota)

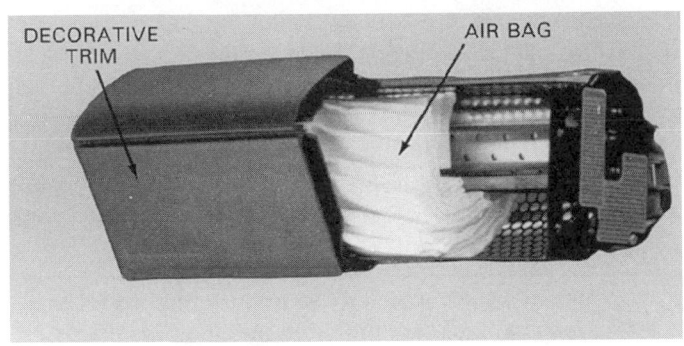

Figure 27-26. Cutaway view of a passenger side inflator module. (Ford)

Troubleshooting Air Bag Systems

 Warning: To avoid possible deployment, consult the proper service manual before attempting to troubleshoot air bag systems. Most manufacturers require the use of special testing equipment when servicing an air bag system. Using incorrect testing procedures can cause an accidental deployment.

The self-diagnostic system should be used when troubleshooting air bag systems. Since procedures for accessing trouble codes vary, consult an appropriate manual before attempting to trigger the diagnostic system. Most manufacturers produce a scan tool to retrieve codes. Many components in an air bag system are not serviceable. If the trouble codes indicate a faulty component, it must be replaced, **Figure 27-28.** To prevent accidental deployment, always disable the air bag system before attempting repair procedures. Most manufacturers simply recommend disconnecting battery voltage. Some, however, require the initiator squib to be disconnected. This disables the diagnostic module's alternate power source.

Caution: The diagnostic control module in some systems can retain power well after the battery has been disconnected. Follow the manufacturer's recommendations for disabling the air bag system. Static electricity can also cause an accidental deployment. Make sure you are well grounded before touching any part of the air bag system.

DIAGNOSTIC CODES

CODE NO.	DIAGNOSIS	TROUBLE AREA
11	Short circuit in squib wire harness (to ground)	• Wire harness
	Front air bag sensor turned on at all times	• Front air bag sensor • Wire harness
	Center air bag sensor system turned on at all times	• Center air bag sensor assembly
12	Short circuit in squib wire harness (to +B)	• Wire harness
13	Short in squib circuit	• Squib • Wire harness
14	Open in squib circuit	• Squib • Wire harness
15	Open in front air bag sensor wire harness	• Wire harness
22	Open in air bag warning light system	• Bulb • Wire harness
31	Internal malfunction of center air bag sensor assembly	• Center air bag sensor assembly
41	Malfunction stored in memory	

Figure 27-28. Trouble code chart for a specific air bag system. Always check for diagnostic codes before attempting to service an air bag system. (Toyota)

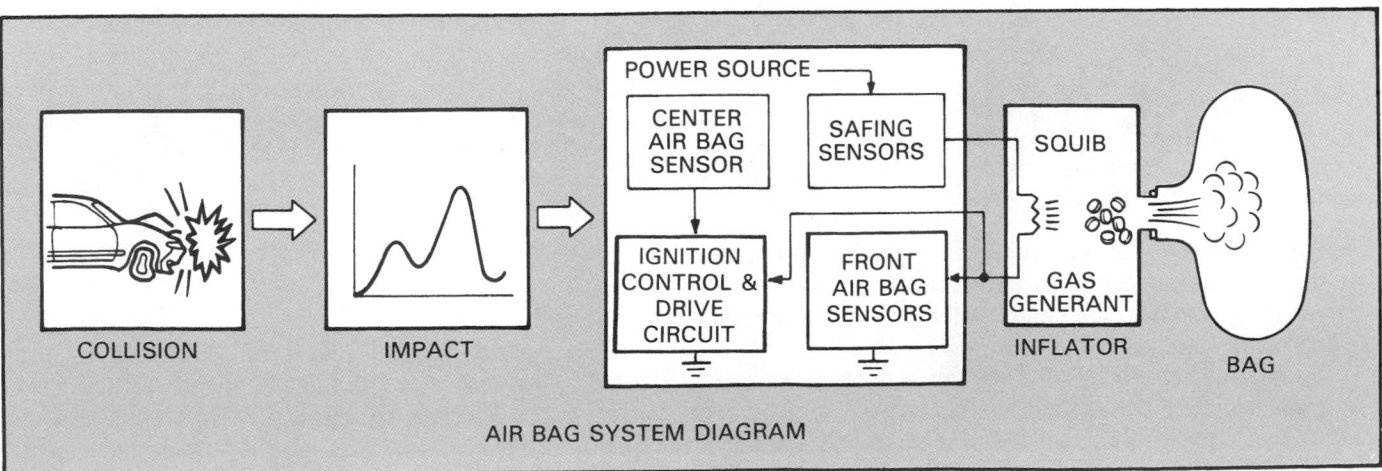

Figure 27-27. Study this air bag activation sequence. Note that the safing sensor and front impact sensors must both be triggered to cause deployment. (Toyota)

Servicing a Deployed Air Bag

When an air bag is deployed, the process will release sodium hydroxide powder into the vehicle's interior. This powder can cause irritation of the skin, eyes, nose, and throat. Wear rubber gloves and safety glasses when removing the deployed bag. After the bag has been removed, vacuum the interior thoroughly to remove residual powder. Make sure to vacuum the heater and air conditioner outlets, **Figure 27-29.** If residue remains, wipe down the interior surfaces with a damp cloth. Follow manufacturer's recommendations for proper disposal.

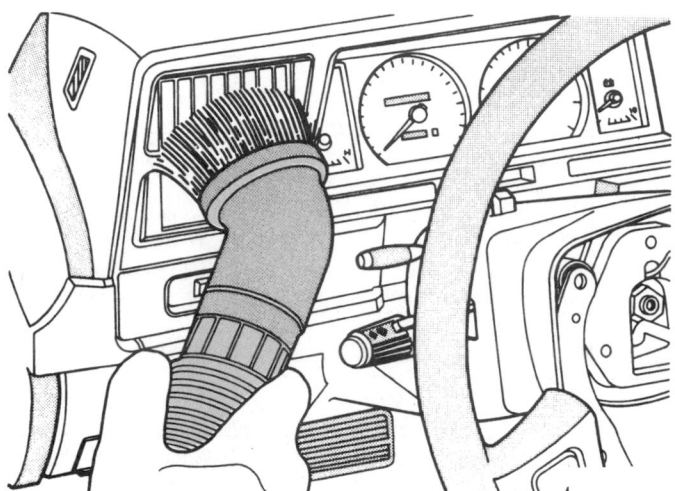

Figure 27-29. After air bag deployment, be sure to vacuum the vehicle's interior to remove any sodium hydroxide powder, which can irritate the skin, eyes, nose, and throat. (Chrysler)

Following air bag deployment, most manufacturers recommend replacement of all related parts. Some only require the replacement of the inflator module and the initiator squib. Always replace all items listed in the service manual. In some systems, reusing sensors and diagnostic modules can cause unprovoked deployment of the air bag system. Some air bag systems require the use of a scan tool to reset the system after a deployment.

Air Bag Service Precautions

When working on air bag systems, there are certain precautions that should be taken to reduce the risk of damage to the system and injury to the passengers. These precautions include the following:

- Always disable the air bag system before attempting to service any component on or near the system (steering column, dashboard, or the front of the engine compartment).
- Never subject the inflator module to temperatures greater than 175°F (79.4°C).
- If any part of the air bag system is accidentally dropped, the component should be replaced.
- Never test air bag components with electrical test equipment unless instructed by manufacturer.

Care should be taken when handling live (not deployed) inflator modules. When carrying a live module, point the bag and trim cover away from you. This will minimize the chance of injury in the case of accidental deployment. When placing a live inflator module on a bench, always face the bag and trim cover up. This will allow the air bag to expand freely in the event of accidental deployment.

> **Note:** If you replace a live inflator module for any reason, it is recommended that the old inflator module be deployed before it is discarded. Consult the manufacturer's service manual for the recommended disposal procedure.

Cruise Control

Cruise control systems were formerly operated by various electromechanical devices. However, the latest cruise control systems are operated by body computers. Cruise control systems consist of several common components, **Figure 27-30.** These components include:

- Vehicle speed sensor.
- Operator controls.
- Control module.
- Throttle actuator.

Vehicle Speed Sensor

The **vehicle speed sensor** uses a rotating magnet to generate a small electrical signal. It is usually mounted on the drive shaft or is driven by the transmission or transaxle governor assembly. It sends a speed signal to the control module. The speed sensor may also send a signal to the engine control computer.

Operator Controls and Control Module

The operator controls are used to set the desired speed. Control location varies between manufacturers, but is usually mounted on the turn signal lever. The operator can set the speed, and can also make minor adjustments to speed as necessary. Another operator control is the brake pedal release switch, usually mounted on the brake pedal bracket. When the operator presses on the brake pedal, the switch sends a signal to the cruise control module which disengages the cruise control. The control module pro-cesses the inputs from the operator controls and the speed sensor and produces an output signal to the throttle actuator.

Throttle Actuator

The throttle actuator opens and closes the vehicle throttle to maintain the operator set speed. Throttle actuators can be electric motors directly operated by the control module. In most cases, however, the throttle actuator is a vacuum diaphragm servo connected to a vacuum controller. The module operates the vacuum controller, which in turn operates the vacuum diaphragm.

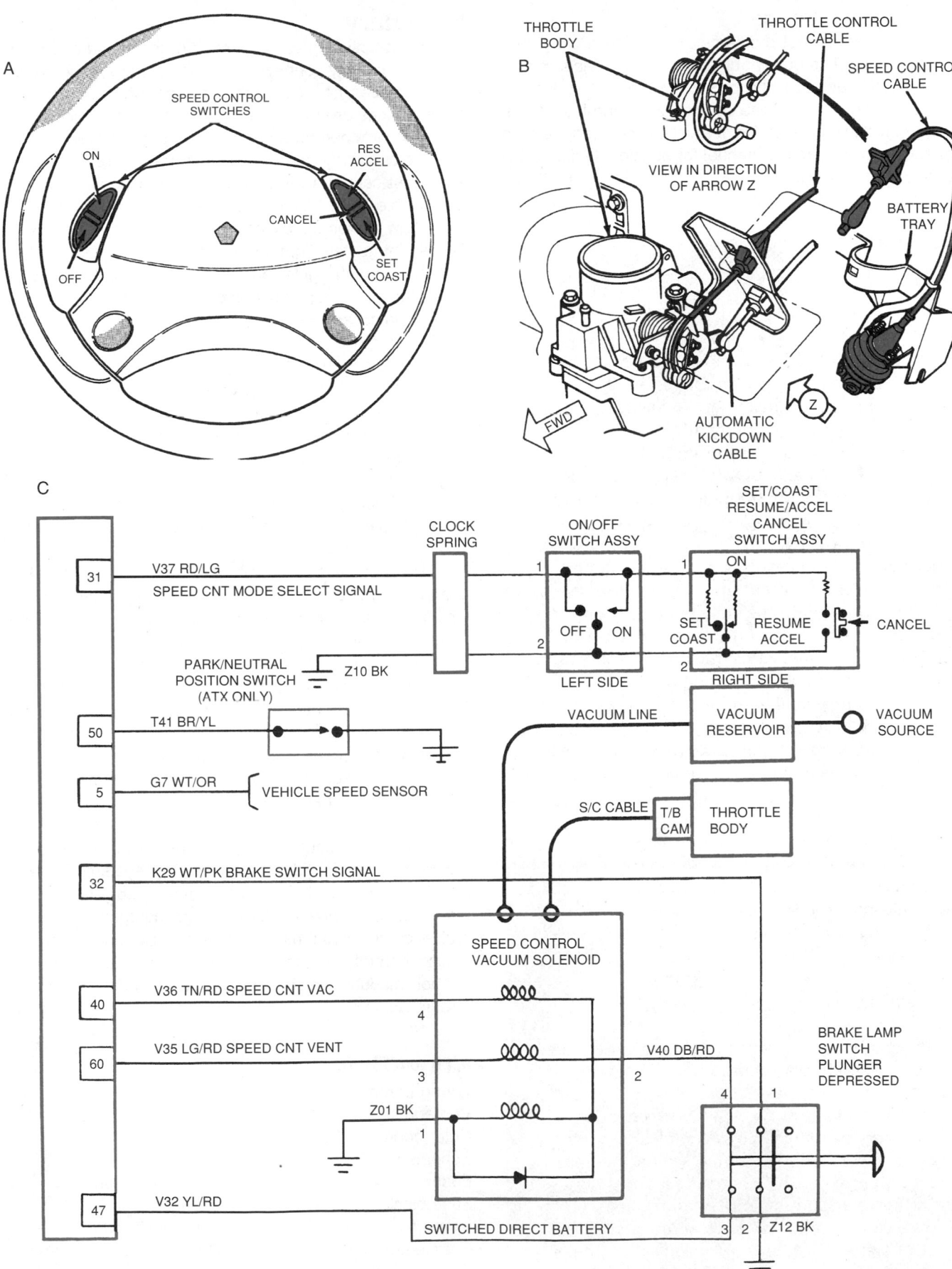

Figure 27-30. A cruise control system as used by one manufacturer. A—Speed control switches are located in the steering wheel. B—Mechanical schematic of the system. C—Cruise control circuit schematic. (Chrysler)

Cruise Control Service

Most cruise control problems are not electrical. Either the throttle linkage is out of adjustment or the vacuum system develops a defect. If the problem appears to be in the electrical system of the cruise control, check the fuse first. If the control module is defective, it must be replaced. Refer to the manufacturer's service manual for additional information on cruise control service.

Tech Talk

Often, the technician will be asked to add gauges to a vehicle. Although warning lights are sufficient for most driving situations, some special cases make gauges useful. For instance, if a vehicle is being used to tow a trailer or boat, it is a good idea to add an engine or transmission temperature gauge. Oil pressure gauges are often added to give the driver a better idea of engine condition when the vehicle is operated at high RPM. If a vehicle has extra electrical equipment, an ammeter or voltmeter can be added to let the driver know exactly what is going on in the electrical system. Tachometers are used to warn of engine overspeeding or to indicate shift points. Sometimes, a vacuum gauge is added to let the driver know about the state of engine tune and for driving at the most economical speeds and engine loads. In many cases, the owner just wants to know what is going on in the engine.

Gauges are available individually or in sets of two, three, or four. It is a relatively simple job to add engine oil pressure, temperature, RPM, vacuum, or amperage/voltage gauges to a vehicle. The major tasks are:

- Installing the sender unit on the engine.
- Running a wire from the sender to the gauge.
- Running a wire from the gauge to a power source that is hot only when the ignition is on.
- Finding a convenient place to install the gauge, in a location that will be visible to the driver.
- Connecting the gauge illumination light to the instrument panel lighting.

Instead of using a sender, vacuum gauges are installed by running a vacuum line directly to the gauge. Some older oil pressure and temperature gauges are mechanical types, with tubes to direct oil pressure into the gauge. However, most modern gauges have an engine-mounted sender that is electrically connected to the gauge. A sender is not used with tachometers, ammeters, or voltmeters. These gauges receive a signal directly from the vehicle's electrical system. Installing a transmission temperature gauge is similar to installing an engine temperature gauge, with the obvious difference that the sensor is installed on the transmission.

Summary

Chassis wiring consists of all of the wiring and components not directly connected with the engine and drive train. Some devices are routed through the ignition switch while other devices are powered directly from the vehicle battery. Wiring is wrapped together into wiring harnesses.

Color coding and schematics make wire tracing easy. The most common problem in wire service is blown fuses and fusible links. Overload relays can open when the current draw becomes excessive. Vehicle light systems are divided into safety lighting devices, such as the headlights, taillights, marker lights, dashboard lights, brake lights, turn signal lights, backup lights; and convenience lights, such as interior lights and courtesy lights, trunk lights, underhood lights, and glove compartment lights.

Chassis mounted motors include the windshield wiper motor, power window, tailgate motors, sunroof motors, convertible top motors and power antenna motors. Solenoids are used to operate door locks and trunk releases. Relays are a type of solenoid used to direct large current flows that might damage a switch. Radios, cassette tape, and CD players should be repaired by a qualified electronics shop. Some simple tests can be made before removing a radio for service.

The horn uses a diaphragm with a make and break contact. They are operated by steering wheel contacts which energize a relay. Rear window and mirror defrosters consist of a heater grid applied to the glass surface of the rear window or mirror. A body computer system controls any function that does not affect engine operating conditions. Typical body computer systems include air bag systems and cruise control systems. Most body computer systems have self-diagnostic capabilities. Service procedures will vary among manufacturers. Consult the appropriate service manual before attempting to service body computer systems.

Special precautions should be taken when working on vehicles equipped with an air bag system. To reduce the risk of injury, always disable the system before working on or near any air bag system components. Modern cruise control systems are operated by body computers. Cruise control systems consist of speed sensors and a control module which operates a vacuum or electrical throttle actuator.

Know These Terms

Wiring harness	Filament
Printed circuit	Halogen
Color code	Brake light switch
Schematic	Flasher unit
Fuse	Emergency flasher
Fuse block	switch
In-line fuse	Fiber optic
Fusible link	Gauge
Circuit breaker	Sender
Blown fuse	Mercury switch
Rheostat	Park mechanism
Sealed beam	Relay

Remote keyless entry
Grid
Body computer systems
Air bag systems
Supplemental restraint
  systems
Deploy

Diagnostic control module
Impact sensors
Coil assembly
Inflator module
Cruise control
Vehicle speed sensor

Review Questions—Chapter 27

Do not write in this book. Write your answers on a separate sheet of paper.

1. Vehicle wiring is installed as part of a _____.
2. Most fusible links are mounted near the battery _____ cable.
3. The rheostat is used to adjust the brightness of _____ lights.
   (A) tail
   (B) marker
   (C) dashboard
   (D) courtesy
4. The sealed beams used on older vehicles have two filaments in which of the following vehicle headlight arrangements?
   (A) Two headlights only.
   (B) The outer lights on four headlight systems.
   (C) The inner lights on four headlight systems.
   (D) Both A & B.
5. The backup lights are connected to which other light assemblies?
   (A) Taillights.
   (B) Turn signal lights.
   (C) Dashboard lights.
   (D) None of the above.
6. List the two classes of dashboard lights.
7. A mercury switch is often used in the _____ or _____.
8. Door or tailgate glass may drop when the _____ is removed.
   (A) motor
   (B) solenoid
   (C) relay
   (D) wiring
9. Always _____ the air bag system before attempting to service any component on or near the system's components.
10. Cruise control throttle actuators can be _____ or _____.

ASE-Type Questions

1. All of the following statements about body wiring are true, EXCEPT:
   (A) Chassis wiring extends throughout the vehicle.
   (B) Wires in a wiring harness are not color-coded.
   (C) Some wiring is attached directly to battery voltage.
   (D) Some wiring is routed through the ignition switch.

2. Technician A says that some schematics show the exact flow of electricity. Technician B says that some schematics show the general process of a system. Who is right?
   (A) A only.
   (B) B only.
   (C) Both A & B.
   (D) Neither A nor B.
3. Which of the following will automatically reset when it cools off?
   (A) Fuse block.
   (B) Fusible link.
   (C) Circuit breaker.
   (D) In-line fuse.
4. Technician A says that replacing a blown fuse may not solve the electrical problem. Technician B says that fusible links can be replaced with regular wire. Who is right?
   (A) A only.
   (B) B only.
   (C) Both A & B.
   (D) Neither A nor B.
5. Replacing a fuse with a non-fused connection could cause all of the following, EXCEPT:
   (A) melted wires.
   (B) battery overcharging.
   (C) ruined electrical components.
   (D) a vehicle fire.
6. Technician A says that the rheostat in the headlight switch circuit is used to control headlight brightness. Technician B says that the dimmer switch in the headlight switch circuit is used to control dashboard light illumination. Who is right?
   (A) A only.
   (B) B only.
   (C) Both A & B.
   (D) Neither A nor B.
7. Technician A says that the windshield washer can be part of the wiper motor assembly. Technician B says that the windshield washer may be located in the washer reservoir. Who is right?
   (A) A only.
   (B) B only.
   (C) Both A & B.
   (D) Neither A nor B.
8. All of the following could cause an inoperative solenoid, EXCEPT:
   (A) defective solenoid winding.
   (B) excessive voltage.
   (C) sticking linkage.
   (D) blown fuse.
9. Technician A says that body computer systems control the ignition timing and the air-fuel ratio. Technician B says that the impact sensors in an air bag system are located on the vehicle's fire wall. Who is right?
   (A) A only.
   (B) B only.
   (C) Both A & B.
   (D) Neither A nor B.

10. All of the following statements about the sodium hydroxide powder used in air bags are true, EXCEPT:
    (A) when an air bag is deployed, sodium hydroxide is released into the vehicle's interior.
    (B) sodium hydroxide powder is harmless.
    (C) wear rubber gloves and safety glasses when removing a deployed air bag.
    (D) if any sodium hydroxide residue remains, wipe down the interior surfaces with a damp cloth.

Suggested Activities

1. Draw an electrical schematic showing a vehicle horn, horn relay, battery, and horn button (on steering wheel). Explain how the components work together to operate the horn.
2. Without referring to a service manual, write a step-by-step procedure for testing the operation of the parking brake warning light from the driver's seat. Compare your procedure with the procedure outlined in the service manual.

3. Use a test light to test a chassis electrical component and/or wiring. Determine what is happening when the light does or does not come on and make a chart of your findings. See if you can develop this chart into a troubleshooting chart for the component and wiring.
4. Use a multimeter or VOM to test a chassis electrical component and/or wiring. Tests should include measuring voltage drop across the components in a live circuit, checking the resistance of deenergized components, and measuring amperage draw of a working circuit.
5. Measure the resistance in a circuit and use Ohm's law to find the amperage draw of the circuit. For instance, if battery voltage is 12 volts, and the circuit resistance is 4 ohms, the amperage draw will be 3 amps. After making the calculation, measure amperage draw with the shop equipment. Do the actual and calculated resistances agree? If they do not, can you think of a reason why? Write a report summarizing your conclusions.

The automotive technician commonly uses diagnostic analyzers when diagnosing driveability problems. (OTC Tools)

28

Driveability

After studying this chapter, you will be able to:
- Identify driveability.
- Explain the differences between tune-ups and driveability diagnosis.
- Explain the modern use of the term tune-up.
- List the basic steps for a maintenance tune-up.
- Summarize important preliminary tests.
- Do road and dynamometer tests.
- Explain engine system problem diagnosis.

This chapter will enable you to understand and contrast the tune-up and driveability needs of the older engine with the needs of the modern engine. Knowing the difference will help you to explain to your customers what service is really needed. This will reduce misunderstandings and allow you to proceed with the correct repair procedures.

Tune-up Versus Driveability Diagnosis

One of the major changes brought about by the use of computer-controlled engine systems is the change in *tune-ups*. Years ago, restoring performance and smoothness, in what is now called *driveability,* required a tune-up. Today a tune-up is considered to be a preventive maintenance service. Restoring performance and smoothness now requires troubleshooting the affected system instead of replacing suspected parts. In the past, engine efficiency was restored by the tune-up. Today, engine efficiency is restored by driveability diagnosis and service. Years ago, a tune-up could be described as the periodic process of inspecting, testing, adjusting, cleaning, repairing, or replacing certain components to restore engine performance, (horsepower, torque, mileage, smoothness of operation, and emission levels) to that normally expected from an engine in good operating condition. A tune-up in the past could involve any service short of an engine overhaul.

The concept of the tune-up has changed greatly in the last few years. The modern tune-up is a maintenance procedure which involves changing spark plugs, inspecting ignition components, and changing fuel and air filters. If required, the ignition timing may be set and the carburetor idle speed adjusted. However, the tune-up should not be expected to restore performance any more that an oil change would. When confronted with a problem that used to be corrected with a tune-up, the technician must determine which parts, if any, are really defective and if they are causing the complaint.

Maintenance Tune-up

This section will cover the procedures for a *maintenance tune-up.* The maintenance tune-up is sometimes called an *emissions tune-up* and consists of changing the spark plugs and the air, fuel, and emissions filters. These tune-ups are often done in response to an *emission flag* or *light* which appear on the dashboard instrument clusters of some cars and light trucks at certain time or mileage intervals.

Specifications and Quality Parts

Specifications such as spark plug gap, engine idle speed, and ignition timing must apply to the exact engine and year model being tuned. Even though the engine may have remained basically unchanged for years, there may be minor changes that can affect specifications. **Figure 28-1** shows some common tune-up specifications. The parts usually replaced in a maintenance tune-up are the spark plugs and various filters. Other parts which may be replaced are the distributor cap and rotor, if the vehicle has a distributor, and plug wires. Occasionally a fuel injector or carburetor vacuum diaphragm will also be replaced. When replacement is required, use top quality parts that will fit properly, function correctly, and provide adequate service life.

Solicit Owner Comments

Before starting a tune-up, ask the owner for any comments regarding engine starting or performance. A set of prepared questions may be used to make sure all important areas are discussed. If the answers to your questions indicate that a maintenance tune-up will not solve the problem, explain this to the customer before proceeding. By doing this, you will be able to provide a proper diagnosis that will correct the vehicle's problem.

Service Records

On all service jobs, document the customer's complaint, the cause of the complaint, and what action you took

ENGINE TUNE-UP SPECIFICATIONS

Displacement Litres/C.I.D.	Cyl.	VIN Code	Produced In²	Division Usage	Type Carb./Fuel Inj.	Bbls.	AC Type Number	Gap Inches	Magnetic Probe[1]	Timing Light M.T.	Timing Light A.T.	Curb (Slow) RPM M.T.	Curb (Slow) RPM A.T.	Fast (Cold) RPM M.T.	Fast (Cold) RPM A.T.	Cam Step	Pressure P.S.I.	Volume Pint/Sec.
GENERAL MOTORS																		
1.0/61 Geo Metro	3	6	J	1	EFI (TBI)	1	R42XLS	.043	–	4	4	4	4	–	–	–	–	–
1.5/90 Geo Spectrum	4	7	J	1	Stromberg/ Nippon	2	R42XLS	.043	–	15°	10°	750	1000	2400	2400	First	4.5[5]	–
1.6/98 Geo Prizm DOHC	4	5	J	1	Multi-Port EFI	–	R43XLS	.043	–	4	4	4	4	–	–	–	–	–
1.6/98 Geo Tracker	4	U	J	1	EFI (TBI)	1	R43XLS	.040	–	4	–	4	–	–	–	–	–	–
1.6/98 LeMans	4	6	K	2	EFI (TBI-700)	1	R44XLS6	.060	–	12	12	600[13]	500[13]	13	13	–	9-13	0.5/15
2.0/121 OHC	4	K	B	2	EFI (TBI-700)	1	R44XLS	.045	9.5°	8°	8°	13	13	13	13	–	9-13	0.5/15
2.0/121 OHC Turbo	4	M	B	2	Multi-Port EFI	–	R42XLS	.035	9.5°	8°	5°	13	13	13	13	–	40.5-47[6]	0.5/15
2.0/121 OHV H.O.	4	1	U	1,4	EFI (TBI-700)	1	R44LTSM	.035	9.5°	17	17	13	13	13	13	–	9-13	0.5/15
2.3/138 Quad-4 H.O.	4	A	U	2,3	Multi-Port EFI	–	FR3LS	.035	9.5°	17	17	13	13	13	13	–	40.5-47[6]	0.5/15
2.3/138 Quad-4	4	D	U	2,3,4	Multi-Port EFI	–	FR3LS	.035	9.5°	17	17	13	13	13	13	–	40.5-47[6]	0.5/15
2.5/151	4	R	U	1,2,3,4	EFI (TBI-700)	1	R43TS6	.060	9.5°	17	17	13	13	13	13	–	26-32	0.5/15
2.5/151	4	U	U	2,3,4	EFI (TBI-700)	1	R43TS6	.060	9.5°	17	17	13	13	13	13	–	9-13	0.5/15
2.8/173	V6	S	M	1,2	Multi-Port EFI	–	R43TSK	.045	9.5°	17	17	13	13	13	13	–	40.5-47[6]	0.5/15
2.8/173	V6	W	U,C,M	1,2,3,4	Multi-Port EFI	–	R43LTSE	.045	9.5°	17	17	13	13	13	13	–	40.5-47[6]	0.5/15
3.1/192	V6	T	C,M	2,3,4	Multi-Port EFI	–	R43LTSE	.045	9.5°	17	17	–	13	–	13	–	40.5-47[6]	0.5/15
3.1/192 Turbo	V6	V	U	2	Multi-Port EFI	–	R42LTS	.045	9.5°	17	17	–	13	–	13	–	40.5-47[6]	0.5/15
3.3/204 "3300"	V6	N	U	3,4	Sequential Port EFI	–	R44LTS6	.060	9.5°	–	17	–	13	–	13	–	40.5-47[6]	0.5/15
3.8/238 "3800"	V6	C	U	2,3,4	Sequential Port EFI	–	R44LTS6	.060	9.5°	–	17	–	13	–	13	–	40.5-47[6]	0.5/15
3.8/238 Trans Am Turbo	V6	7	U	2	Sequential Port EFI	–	R42LTS	.035	9.5°	–	17	–	13	–	13	–	40.5-47[6]	0.5/15
4.3/262	V6	Z	U	1	EFI (TBI-220)	2	R45TS	.035	9.5°	–	TDC	–	13	–	13	–	9-13	0.5/15

Figure 28-1. Some common tune-up specifications as used by one vehicle manufacturer. These specifications cover three-, four-, and six-cylinder engines. (AC Delco)

to correct the complaint. Keep an accurate record of all repairs, any parts repaired or replaced, and the date and mileage at the time of installation. These records can be helpful in diagnosing trouble at some future date. The life span of many parts may be gauged in time or in miles. Accurate *documentation* is essential in handling guarantee work and for service billing. When the customer returns for service, check the service records for the length of time or mileage since the last service. Note the mileage since the last service. **Figure 28-2** shows a typical service repair order.

Engine Mechanical Condition

Before performing any part of the tune-up, check the compression in all cylinders. If the compression (or cylinder leakage) test indicates a problem, be sure to inform the owner of the need for internal repairs before proceeding with the tune-up. There will be cases where, even though the mechanical condition of the vehicle is poor, the owner will want to go ahead with basic tune-up to keep the vehicle running. If the engine fails the compression test, perform a cylinder leakage test to determine where the problem lies and document your findings. Compression testing, cylinder leakage tests, and vacuum testing are covered in Chapter 11.

Other Preliminary Checks

After checking engine mechanical condition, several important preliminary checks must be made before starting

the tune-up. Failure to check these items until later may invalidate the work preceding them. The items involved in these preliminary checks, if dirty, loose, disconnected, or misadjusted, can produce a variety of apparent faults in other related units. Failure to make these preliminary checks can result in time wasted chasing faults that are actually nonexistent. The following checks are the minimum which should be performed. Any other problems which come to light should be investigated further and corrected.

- Check all drive belts for condition and tension.
- Check heat control valve for free operation.
- Clean or replace PCV and EGR valves. Recheck valve operation after they are installed.
- On engines with adjustable valves, reset the valve adjustment to manufacturer's specifications.
- Check battery terminals for corrosion and tighten connections as needed.
- Check the amount and condition of the engine oil and radiator coolant. If fluid levels are low, check for obvious leaks or other problems.
- Observe all electrical leads and tighten if necessary. Pay particular attention to engine and body ground straps.
- Tighten intake manifold and carburetor fasteners. If needed, torque head bolts.
- Tighten fuel system fittings and ensure that all vacuum lines are secure.

13879

Since... ...1912
HARPER MOTORS
4800 NORTH HIGHWAY 101 • EUREKA, CALIFORNIA 95501
PHONE: 707-443-7311
"CROSS OVER THE BRIDGE"

BAR # AA001724
EPA # CAD 983595489
P & A CODE: 07755-0

FORD QUALITY CAR CARE

SERVICE HRS. MON-FRI
7:30 A.M. - 5:30 P.M.

Hazardous Waste Disposal Fee:
Used Motor Oil and/or Used Anti-freeze are regu-lated **Hazardous Waste** & are being legally trans-ported, stored and recycled.

TERMS		ORIGINAL ESTIMATE (PARTS & LABOR)	AUTHORIZED ADD'L REPAIRS	ADD'L REPAIRS OK'D BY	PHONE
	☐ CASH			DATE	TIME
	☐ CREDIT CARD	$	$		
ALL PARTS ARE NEW UNLESS SPECIFIED OTHERWISE		REVISED ESTIMATE (PARTS & LABOR)	AUTHORIZED ADD'L REPAIRS	ADD'L REPAIRS OK'D BY	PHONE
		$	$	DATE	TIME

ALL PARTS WILL BE DISCARDED UNLESS INSTRUCTED OTHERWISE ☐ SAVE

I ACKNOWLEDGE NOTICE AND ORAL APPROVAL OF ANY INCREASE IN THE ORIGINAL ESTIMATED PRICE AND RECEIPT OF A COPY HEREOF.
PLEASE READ REVERSE SIDE.
CUSTOMER SIGNATURE X *Rebecca Stockel*

(CHECK (✓) APPROPRIATE BOX)

CLAIMS REVIEW	AUTHORIZATION TO SUBMIT CLAIM	PARTS SCRAP OUT
$	$	$
PARTS	LABOR	TOTAL

Authorized Signature And Date

ON BEHALF OF SERVICING DEALER, I HEREBY CERTIFY THAT THE INFORMATION CONTAINED HEREON IS ACCURATE UNLESS OTHERWISE SHOWN. SERVICES DESCRIBED WERE PERFORMED AT NO CHARGE TO OWNER. THERE WAS NO INDICATION FROM THE APPEARANCE OF THE VEHICLE OR OTHERWISE THAT ANY PART REPAIRED OR REPLACED UNDER THIS CLAIM HAD BEEN CONNECTED IN ANY WAY WITH ANY ACCIDENT, NEGLIGENCE OR MISUSE. RECORDS SUPPORTING THIS CLAIM ARE AVAILABLE FOR (1) YEAR FROM THE DATE OF PAYMENT NOTIFICATION AT THE SERVICING DEALER FOR INSPECTION BY REPRESENTATIVES OF FORD

(SIGNED)   DEALER, GENERAL MANAGER, OR AUTHORIZED PERSON   (DATE)

```
RO: 024594-9        ADV: BOB    7325  TAG:              RO: 024594
CUST:    18992                        VIN:
                                        F 91    EXPLORER
                                        RED
                                      STK:          SLD:
HOME:                                 LICENSE:
                                      DATE/TIME IN:              14:03
PAY METHOD: CASH                      MILES IN:    26670
PRINTED ON
PROGRAM CODE: 93B15  COMMITMENT CODE:      APPROVAL CODE: D
---------------------***CUSTOMER INVOICE***---------------------

REPAIR: 1  TYPE: W  CONCERN CODE:

CUSTOMER CONCERN : PROGRAM #93B15           BATTERY CONCERN

        PART              DESCRIPTION    CC   LIST    PRICE  QTY   TOTAL
 65650                                   79           .00   0
 F3TZ,10A687,A         COVER ASY-BATTERY           15.61   1

                              PARTS AMOUNT - REPAIR 1:      WARRANTY

   OPERATION          DESCRIPTION        TECH    SSN    TIME        TOTAL
 B15A            PROGRAM 93B19           23    4835    1.0

                              LABOR AMOUNT - REPAIR 1:      WARRANTY


 TECHNICIAN DIAGNOSIS/REPAIR COMMENTS
    PROGRAM COMPLETED
    INSTALLED BATTERY COVER

                              TOTAL AMOUNT - REPAIR 1:      WARRANTY

GAS: QTY    SALE       OIL: QTY    SALE       GREASE: QTY    SALE
---------------------------------------------------------------------

                            WARRANTY
                     LABOR SALES        52.15
                     PARTS W&P CLAIM    15.61
                     W&P RECEIVE        67.76
```

GPD-103821   **LIMITED WARRANTY-ALL WORK GUARANTEED 90 DAYS OR 4,000 MILES WHICHEVER COMES FIRST.** PAGE 1
(END OF REPAIR ORDER)

Figure 28-2. Note this vehicle service repair order. Always document any repairs made on a vehicle, no matter how minor they may seem. This repair order is for a manufacturer's warranty recall. (Harper Motors)

Checklist for Maintenance Tune-ups

The following checklist shows the tests, adjustments, and other operations commonly performed during a maintenance tune-up. The steps are listed in the general order in which they should be done. Always use a checklist to avoid duplication and to make sure nothing of importance is overlooked.

- Check the vehicle's prior service record and question owner regarding vehicle performance.
- Clean and tighten battery terminals. Tighten battery hold-down.
- Operate the starter to make certain engine cranks over rapidly enough to perform an accurate compression test. If not, check the starting and charging system and recommend repairs.
- Check oil, coolant, and all other fluid levels.
- Remove spark plugs (gasoline) or nozzles and glow plugs (diesel).
- Check engine compression. If compression readings indicate an internal engine problem, conduct further tests and discuss results with the customer before proceeding.
- Gap new spark plugs and install.
- Check drive belts, PCV valve, valve clearance, and heat control valve as needed.
- Inspect all emission control devices.

 Note: Some emission control systems are closely tied in with both fuel and ignition systems. They should be checked and adjusted in the order specified by the manufacturer.

- Replace air, fuel, PCV, and vapor canister filters as needed.
- Check distributor wiring (primary and secondary) for condition, connections, and routing.
- Inspect rotor and replace if needed. Lubricate wick under rotor where used.
- Clean and inspect distributor cap. Replace if needed.

 Note: If the cap is replaced, replace the rotor also. If the rotor is replaced, replace the cap.

- Lubricate distributor as needed.
- Reconnect all fittings and reinstall the air cleaner.
- Start engine.
- Check automatic choke for correct setting and action (if used), and test operation of the thermostatic air cleaner.
- Test distributor vacuum advance (if used).
- Test distributor centrifugal advance (if used).
- Check and adjust ignition timing if adjustable.

 Note: Follow timing setting procedure on underhood emission control label.

- Check charging voltage and isolate any charging system problems.
- Check and adjust carburetor or fuel injection idle speed and mixture.
- Analyze combustion gases.

 Note: Make certain vehicle exhaust emission levels comply with federal and state requirements.

- Check radiator and heater hoses, freeze plugs, and transmission cooling lines for leakage.
- Road test vehicle.
- Perform a final inspection for leaks.
- Remove any grease from the vehicle's interior and body.
- Fill out vehicle service record.
- Deliver the vehicle to its owner.
- Answer any questions the owner may have.

Road Testing

No tune-up is complete until the vehicle has been *road tested.* Use the road test to check for smooth, responsive, ping-free acceleration. Vehicle operation must be smooth (no missing, bucking, or loping) at low, medium, and high speed. Engine should not stall following a fast stop. Check the dash instruments for proper operation. Upon returning to the shop, inspect the vehicle for water, fuel, or oil leaks.

In addition to checking all engine systems, the road test offers an opportunity to check the brakes, transmission, steering, clutch, and rear axle. Although repairs to these areas are not within the realm of a tune-up, call the owner's attention to any such work needed. Many shops also test the horn, headlights, brake lights, backup lights, and signal lights before delivery. This takes little time and helps build customer goodwill. For road testing, select an area where the vehicle may be driven at various speeds, accelerated rapidly, and braked abruptly. Be careful and obey all traffic laws. Treat the customer's vehicle as though it were your own—remember that you are responsible for it until delivered.

Chassis Dynamometer Road Test

The use of a *chassis dynamometer* instead of a regular road test on the streets has some advantages. It saves time, reduces the possibility of accidents, and allows you to check actual torque and speedometer accuracy. These checks may not be possible during an actual road test. It will also permit the use of diagnostic instruments while the engine is driving the vehicle.

In making a dynamometer test, the vehicle is parked on the dynamometer with the drive wheels resting on rollers. See **Figure 28-3.** The controls are connected to the engine. The engine is started, the transmission is placed in gear, and the drive wheels begin to spin the rollers. The rollers place a load on the engine as though the vehicle were actually on the road. The chassis dynamometer provides a handy and accurate method of quickly and thoroughly road testing a vehicle right in the shop.

Figure 28-3.   A vehicle performing a dynamometer test. Note that the drive wheels are on the rollers. An engine cooling fan (not shown) is sometimes placed in front of the vehicle to help aid in engine cooling. (Chrysler)

 Warning: When using a dynamometer, make sure that the area is well-ventilated. This will prevent the buildup of carbon monoxide. Also make sure that the vehicle is securely on the dynamometer and that safety stops and other restraint devices are used. Failure to do so could allow the vehicle to accidentally leave the dynamometer, which could result in injuries and property damage.

Driveability Diagnosis

Isolating and curing a driveability problem involves many procedures. Some procedures consist of finding out what is wrong, while other procedures correct what is wrong. The basic steps in driveability diagnosis are similar to performing a tune-up, but with more emphasis on diagnosis. Follow these steps when performing any diagnosis:

- Check the operation of vehicle systems to determine the problem areas.
- Determine which parts could be the cause of the problem.
- Check the condition and operation of the suspected parts.
- Repair or replace any suspected parts.
- Recheck vehicle operation.

These will be covered in more detail later. Keep in mind that it is easy to change a part or make a simple adjustment to restore vehicle driveability. The hard part is finding out which part requires adjustment or replacement. This process is the heart of *diagnosis,* or *troubleshooting.* This ability to find the cause of a problem and its solution is what separates the professional automotive technician from the parts changer.

To become an expert at diagnosis, the technician must know how internal combustion engines and their related systems operate. In the other chapters in this book, you learned how the various engine systems work together to create an efficient engine. You also learned how to make various tests of the engine, ignition, and fuel systems and how to repair or replace defective components. Now that you have this knowledge, you will need to develop the ability to approach a problem in a calm and logical manner, no matter how mysterious or frustrating the problem.

Basic Principles of Diagnosis

Some of the basic principles of diagnosis are detailed in the next paragraphs. Although most of them could be called common sense and hardly worth mentioning, they are often forgotten when a problem occurs.

Determine the Exact Problem

When presented with a driveability or any other automotive problem, start by determining the exact cause of the problem. The information that you are given, either by the driver or your own testing, can sometimes be misleading. The driver's description may not really describe the problem. Take the vehicle on a road test with the driver and ask the driver about the problem. Sometimes the description and diagnosis is correct. Always take the time to double-check.

Try to relate any driver comments to a definite condition, such as hard starting, poor acceleration, or missing. Also make sure that you find out the following conditions under which the problem occurs: vehicle speed, throttle position, transmission gear, engine temperature, and weather conditions. Find out when and how often the problem occurs, are there sounds or vibrations associated with the problem, and whether any recent work was done to the vehicle.

Be sure that you correctly interpret the information that you get from test equipment, **Figure 28-4.** If you find that the idle speed was set too low on a vehicle that has begun stalling at lights, do not assume that increasing the idle speed will cure the condition. The low idle speed may be caused by a dead cylinder, vacuum leak, incorrect timing or advance mechanism, inoperative idle speed solenoid, or a dozen other problems. If you reset the idle, the engine might quit stalling, but it could leave your shop with the real problem uncorrected.

Also make sure that the presumed problem source is not being caused by another vehicle system. If you concentrate on one area because that is where the problem usually occurs, or should occur, you may miss an obvious

Figure 28-4. The use of up-to-date diagnostic equipment is a must for correctly diagnosing today's sophisticated vehicles. (Snap-on Tools)

defect in another system and waste valuable hours of diagnosis time. Understanding the function and possible defects in every part of the vehicle will allow you to consider all of the possibilities.

Remember that the engine systems are not the only source of driveability trouble. Driveability problems can be mistaken for problems in the manual clutch, automatic transmission shift system, lockup torque converter, air conditioner, starting and charging systems, and even in the front end, steering, and brakes. Brief checking procedures will enable you to isolate the real source of driveability problems.

Visual Inspection

Always perform a *visual inspection* before conducting diagnostic tests. Check the simple things first; It will save a lot of time and trouble to check all of the visibly obvious possibilities before going on to complex testing procedures that require a lot of equipment and time. For example, do not try to solve a driveability problem by working on the fuel or ignition systems until after you are positive that all of the manifold vacuum hoses are in place and in good condition. Knowing that all of the simple things are OK will allow you to zero in on the hard things. **Figure 28-5** shows some simple checks which can be made.

Avoid Guessing

Always avoid snap judgments about the cause of the problem. Sometimes you will hear of making an ***educated***

guess. However an educated guess is not a guess at all, but a reasonable decision, based on experience, testing, and the process of elimination. Once these reasonable decisions are reached, they are verified by a visual inspection and testing. Uneducated guessing or jumping at the first possible cause that comes to mind is a dangerous way of diagnosing problems. Unfortunately, it can quickly become a habit, done over and over no matter how many times it causes unnecessary work and aggravation.

Remain Calm

One of the hardest principles of diagnosis is to remain calm, no matter how much you would like to scream and throw things. Controlling your emotions is often the hardest part of the job, especially if you meet with a series of dead ends while looking for a problem. However, it is a necessary skill which must be developed and maintained. Nothing will be accomplished by losing your composure. If you have a tendency to overreact to situations, you will have to unlearn this behavior and teach yourself to remain calm. In the meantime, try to present an outward appearance of calm, at least to avoid upsetting anyone else, especially the customer. Many times, this will also help you to calm yourself.

Using Service Literature

Service literature is vital when diagnosing a problem. ***Service manuals*** provide detailed information on testing procedures. Wiring schematics allow you to trace circuits to arrive at a defective part or connection. Troubleshooting charts give a summary of possible problem causes, making the diagnostic process quicker. Always treat service literature carefully since you will want to reuse it. ***Technical service bulletins,*** which are usually released by the vehicle's manufacturer, can give clues to solving difficult or unusual driveability or other automotive problems.

Using Test Equipment

Various test equipment can be used to check engine systems. Vacuum gauges can be used to check overall engine mechanical condition as well as the condition and timing of the ignition system and valve train. A timing light can be used to check the ignition timing and the timing advance systems. Exhaust gas analyzers are used to check the air-fuel ratio and proper operation of the carburetor or fuel injectors. An oscilloscope will determine the condition of the ignition system components and can also be used to check the alternator for proper operation. Multimeters can check the operation of the oxygen sensor and engine control module as well as the operation of various other input and output devices. The fuel pressure tester will check the system pressure of both carbureted engines and fuel injection systems.

Steps in Driveability Diagnosis

The following steps in driveability diagnosis are the simplest way to determine just where the problem is, what it consists of, and how to correct it. Following these steps instead of guessing at the problem will pay off in the long run.

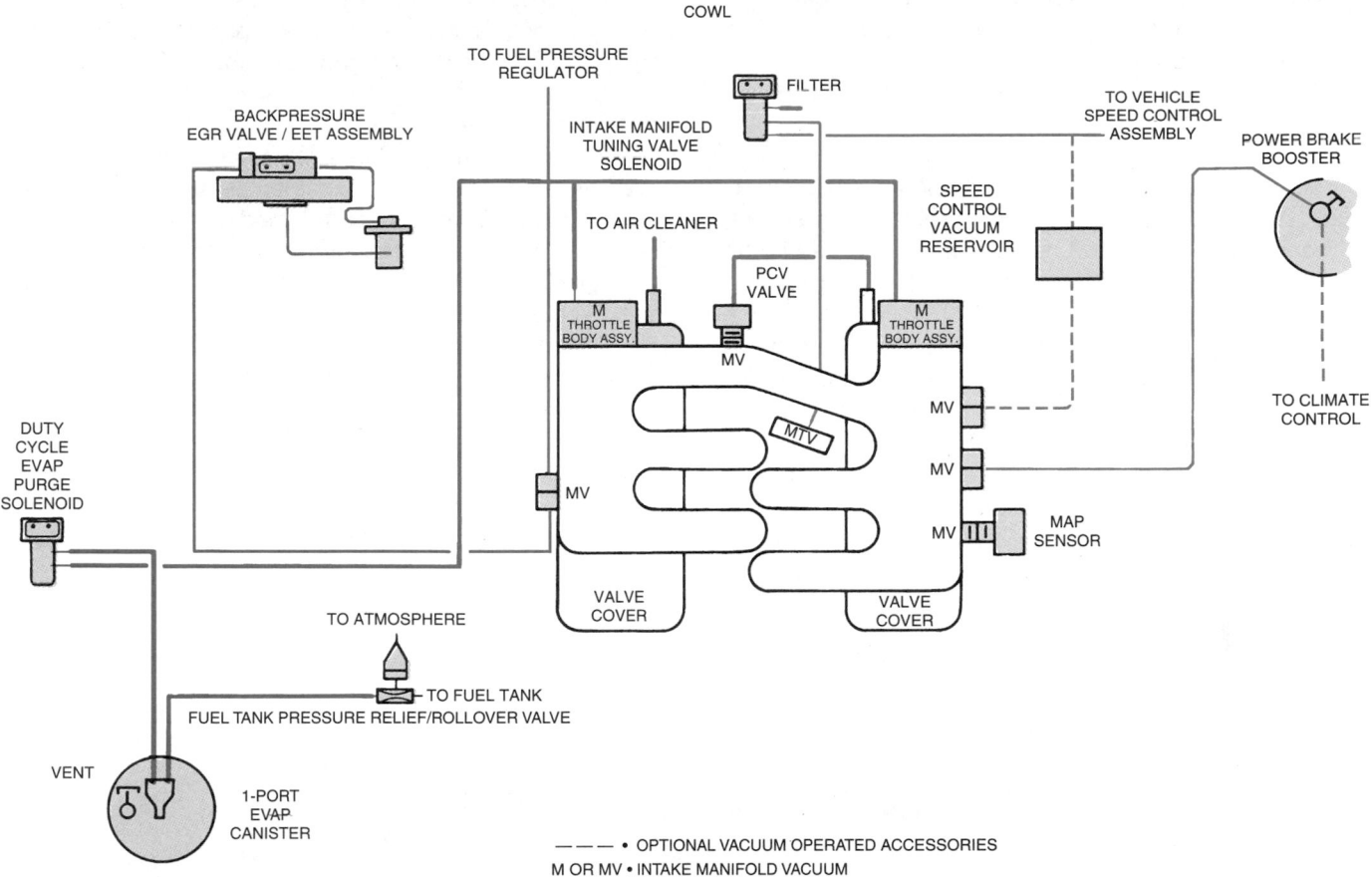

COWL

TO FUEL PRESSURE REGULATOR

FILTER

BACKPRESSURE EGR VALVE / EET ASSEMBLY

INTAKE MANIFOLD TUNING VALVE SOLENOID

TO AIR CLEANER

TO VEHICLE SPEED CONTROL ASSEMBLY

POWER BRAKE BOOSTER

SPEED CONTROL VACUUM RESERVOIR

PCV VALVE

M THROTTLE BODY ASSY.

M THROTTLE BODY ASSY.

MV

MTV

MV

MV

TO CLIMATE CONTROL

DUTY CYCLE EVAP PURGE SOLENOID

MV

MV

MAP SENSOR

TO ATMOSPHERE

VALVE COVER

VALVE COVER

TO FUEL TANK

FUEL TANK PRESSURE RELIEF/ROLLOVER VALVE

VENT

1-PORT EVAP CANISTER

— — — • OPTIONAL VACUUM OPERATED ACCESSORIES
M OR MV • INTAKE MANIFOLD VACUUM
MTV • INTAKE MANIFOLD TUNING VALVE

Figure 28-5.   One particular engine vacuum schematic. Check all the connections for tightness and check all lines for kinks, breaks, splits, and correct routing. (Chrysler)

Verifying the Complaint

To determine the problem areas, it is best to begin by checking systems rather than individual parts. The checking procedure could be as simple as a road test, or as complex as checking the vehicle with an oscilloscope or computer analyzer. The point is to determine which system is causing the problem. While performing this step, remember to look for obvious problems and retrieve computer trouble codes.

Determining the Cause of the Complaint

The step above should have given you some sort of clue as to what the problem could be. Using a process of deduction, determine which parts of the engine, fuel system, ignition, or other vehicle part could cause the problem. This is the step where logical thought processes play a part. Continue checking the vehicle; remember you are looking for a logical cause for the problem. Once you have determined that a particular part could be at fault, proceed to check that part. The part could be checked by observing its physical condition, by electrical or vacuum testers, or by observing how the part operates. By whatever means, be sure to thoroughly check the part.

Correcting the Problem

Some parts can be adjusted or repaired while other parts must be replaced as a unit. To keep from making the original problem worse or replacing it with another problem, always follow the manufacturers' directions for any adjustment, repair, or replacement procedure. The vehicle should be road tested to determine whether the problem has been fixed. It may be necessary, or easier, to check the vehicle using an oscilloscope or other analyzer. The purpose is to determine whether repairs have been successful, and whether any other problems require attention.

Computers and Driveability Diagnosis

Computer-controlled systems makes vehicles run much more efficiently, but can also make troubleshooting more difficult. On the other hand, a control module's **self-diagnostic capability** can make troubleshooting much easier. Before beginning diagnosis on any computer-controlled vehicle, thoroughly check all non-computer systems. Many driveability problems on computer-controlled vehicles can be caused by vacuum leaks, ignition secondary problems, lack of filter maintenance, and other non-computer problems. For example, the EGR valve and control system are a common source of problems such as pinging, rough idle, surging, hesitation, and stalling. Defective input sensors are a major cause of computer system problems. A good way to check the system is to check the sensors and wiring first and then check the output devices. Check the control module last. There are three exceptions to this rule:

- When a part is visually observed to be defective.
- When the non-electronic checking procedure has uncovered a problem.
- When a check of system performance has pinpointed the problem area.

In these cases, first check the components most likely to cause the problem. Also note that problem in a sensor, output device, or the control module may be stored in the control module's memory section as a trouble code, as explained below. If the check engine light or service engine light is on, retrieve the trouble codes before proceeding further. The stored codes may quickly pinpoint the trouble area. Once the trouble codes are identified, make further tests as identified in the manufacturer's service manual. In some cases, the defective component is identified by the trouble code. In other cases, a vehicle subsystem is isolated, and the entire subsystem must be diagnosed. On older computer systems without the self-diagnosis feature, defects must be checked out by a process of elimination.

Test each part in the suspected system. Determine if parts which cannot be tested, such as the ignition module and/or engine control module, are good or bad.

Retrieving Trouble Codes

Before performing any involved diagnostic routines on a vehicle with an on-board computer, always check for **trouble codes** from the control module's memory. If the dashboard or computer-mounted indicator light is on when the engine is running, trouble codes are present in the computer memory. The dashboard light is usually yellow and is marked "check engine" or "service engine soon." Typical indicator light locations are shown in **Figure 28-6.** A light mounted directly on the computer is usually a red **LED (light emitting diode)**. Always check the control module's memory for trouble codes, since some codes may be stored even if the light is not on. Trouble codes can be obtained from the computer by a two-part process. All methods of trouble code retrieval are variations of this two-part process:

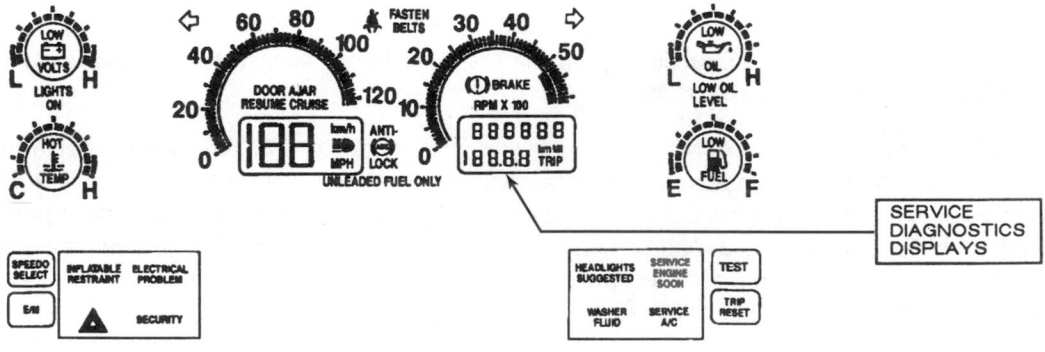

Figure 28-6. A—Digital instrument cluster with a "Service Engine Soon" indicator light. B—Analog (needle type) instrument cluster with a "Check Engine" light. (General Motors)

- Grounding a terminal to place the computer in self diagnosis mode.
- Reading the codes that the computer displays.

Accessing Codes without a Retrieval Tool

Accessing trouble codes without a special retrieval tool is done by one of two methods. The most common method is to ground one terminal of the diagnostic connector and observe a series of flashes from a diagnostic light. The light may be the dashboard service warning light, or it may be an LED (light emitting diode) installed on the computer housing. The sequence of light flashes forms a numerical code. The factory service manual contains instructions for correctly reading the light flashes. The trouble code numbers can be written down for later comparison with the corresponding numbers in the service manual to identify the faulty component or system.

Another common method of reading trouble codes is to connect an analog (needle type) voltmeter to the proper leads of the diagnostic connector, **Figure 28-7.** Another connector terminal is grounded and the trouble code output is read as a series of pulsations of the voltmeter needle. Always follow the manual procedure exactly, since the wrong sequence of steps can erase the trouble codes or possibly set incorrect codes.

 Note: Write down any trouble codes for reference when consulting the service manual.

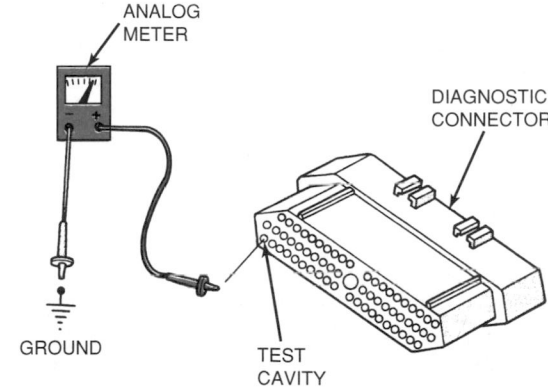

Figure 28-7. An analog meter can be used to retrieve trouble codes by grounding one meter probe and placing the other probe in the correct diagnostic connector test cavity. (Simpson Electric Co., Chrysler)

On a few vehicles, the trouble codes are displayed on the digital readout of the radio or air conditioner controls. Code accessing is similar to other vehicles, but the code numbers can be read directly from the digital screen.

Using a Scan Tool

A special electronic device called a **scan tool** can simplify the code retrieval process. Different types of scan tools are shown in **Figure 28-8.** It is far easier to use a scan tool

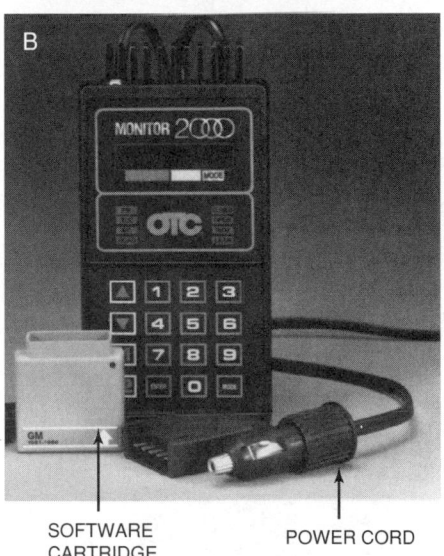

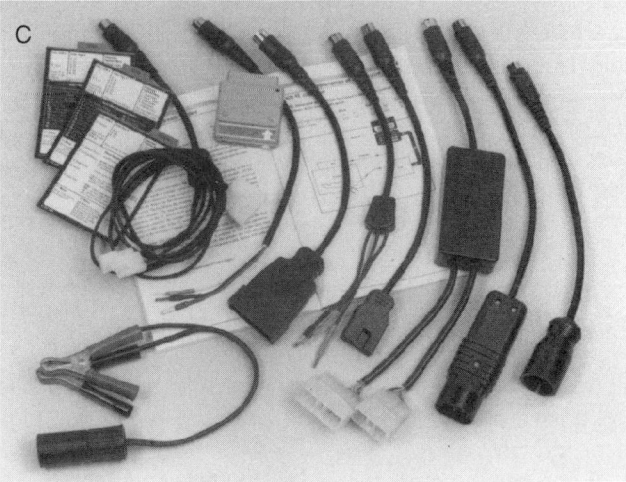

Figure 28-8. Diagnostic scan tools and connectors. A—Hand-held vehicle diagnostic scan tool. B—Hand-held computer scan tool with power cord and vehicle information software cartridge. C—Diagnostic scan tool connectors and software. Always handle these tools with care and return them to their protective cases when not in use. (OTC Tools)

than to perform the procedures explained above. Scan tools display the code numbers on a screen. Some scan tools can store the trouble codes for future reference. They also perform the grounding step to place the control module in the diagnostic mode. A typical tool is shown attached to the vehicle's diagnostic connector in **Figure 28-9.** Most scan tools also provide engine and vehicle information that can be useful in diagnosis. Always follow the manufacturer's directions exactly when installing the tool and retrieving the codes.

INSTRUMENT PANEL

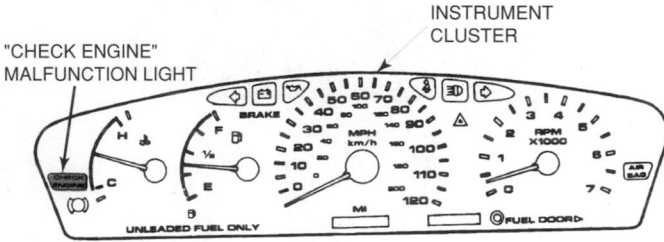

DIAGNOSTIC CONNECTOR

DATA LINK CONNECTOR

"CHECK ENGINE" MALFUNCTION LIGHT

INSTRUMENT CLUSTER

Figure 28-9. Accessing a trouble code by grounding the correct diagnostic connector lead and observing the "flashes" of the instrument cluster "Check Engine" light. Follow all scan tool or vehicle manufacturer's instructions carefully. Carelessness can be costly in time and destroyed components. (Chrysler)

Interpreting Trouble Codes

Trouble codes indicate one of two things:

- An engine problem is causing one of the sensors to transmit a voltage signal that is out of range (too high or too low).
- A part of the computer control system is defective.

Sometimes the same trouble code can be caused by either of these two problem areas; therefore, it is vital to correctly interpret the trouble codes. Each trouble code is displayed as a number which corresponds to a specific

problem. Once the trouble codes are retrieved, they can be compared against the trouble code information in the service manual. Once the problem area has been identified, you can proceed to concentrate on that area. If the trouble code indicates that the problem is a defective output device or system, you will be able to go to the specific part and determine whether the problem is a disconnected or defective part, a mechanical problem with the part, or a wiring problem. In the case of a out-of-range sensor reading, you can proceed to determine whether the problem is a defective sensor or another engine condition that is causing the out-of-range reading.

Hard and Intermittent Codes

Two types of codes are stored in the computer memory. They are generally called permanent, or **hard codes,** and temporary, or **intermittent codes.** Hard codes will indicate an ongoing problem that still exists on the vehicle. They are the easiest to track down. Intermittent codes are set by problems that occur occasionally or only one time and are usually harder to isolate.

Separating Hard and Intermittent Codes

A hard code will keep the indicator light illuminated whenever the engine is running and will sometimes come back almost immediately if an attempt is made to clear it. Intermittent codes will activate the light while the problem is occurring, after which the light will go out. To diagnose most computer systems, the technician must separate hard codes from intermittent codes by first recording all codes. Then, the codes are removed from the control module using the method specified in the service manual. Next, restart the engine and allow it to run for a specific period of time. After the engine has been running for enough time, stop it and re-enter the diagnostic mode. Codes that have been reset are hard codes. Codes that have not reset are intermittent codes.

In many cases, an intermittent code indicating a defective sensor may not indicate that the sensor is defective, only that it is responding to another problem. An example is an intermittent trouble code for a rich oxygen sensor reading. Although the oxygen sensor may be defective, it is more common for another component, such as a leaking fuel injector or defective airflow sensor to cause the rich mixture problem. Problems that set hard codes can usually be tracked down quickly, while problems causing intermittent codes may take longer to diagnose.

Clearing Trouble Codes

After obtaining the codes and making repairs, you should erase any trouble codes from the control module's memory. After erasing the trouble codes, operate the vehicle for at least ten minutes to ensure that the control module can compensate for any changes in vehicle operation, then re-enter the diagnostic mode to ensure that none of the trouble codes have been reset.

Tech Talk

The top technician arrives at work on time and is absent only for good reasons. If absence is necessary, the technician will immediately notify the employer so that customer commitments and work loads may be adjusted.

Good technicians invariably are hard workers. During any periods when they may not have work assignments, they will clean tools, maintain equipment, sweep the work station, or help fellow technicians. They take pride in their work and pride in the business. They know that by helping the business to prosper, they too will prosper.

Top technicians devote time and energy toward the betterment of the trade. They gladly share their knowledge with apprentices. They conduct themselves, at all times, in a way that brings credit to the automotive service profession.

mine the exact problem, check the simple things first, avoid guessing, and remain calm.

Before beginning diagnosis on any computer-controlled vehicle, thoroughly check all non-computer systems. Retrieve trouble codes and separate the hard and intermittent codes. Always clear the trouble codes from the control module once repairs are completed.

Know These Terms

Tune-up
Driveability
Maintenance tune-up
Emissions tune-up
Emissions flag
Emissions light
Specifications
Documentation
Road test
Chassis dynamometer
Diagnosis

Troubleshooting
Visual inspection
Educated guess
Service manuals
Technical service bulletins
Self-diagnostic capacity
Trouble codes
LED (light emitting diode)
Scan tool
Hard codes
Intermittent codes

Summary

In the past, restoring performance and smoothness required a tune-up, replacing parts known to be worn out. Today a tune-up is a preventive maintenance service. Restoring performance and smoothness now requires troubleshooting the systems affecting driveability.

The parts usually replaced during a maintenance tune-up are the spark plugs and various filters. Other parts which may be replaced are plug wires, distributor cap and rotor, and occasionally a fuel injector or carburetor vacuum diaphragm. Follow a tune-up checklist to avoid duplication and possible omission of important steps. Keep records showing parts installed, date, mileage, etc. Use any available prior service records to help you before starting the tune-up. Be sure to document all repairs and any problems that remain.

Engine mechanical condition should be checked before performing the tune-up. If the engine checks out OK, perform the preliminary checks on the drive belts, PCV and EGR valves, valve clearance, electrical connections, fasteners, and fittings before starting the tune-up. Always road test a vehicle following a tune-up. If available, a chassis dynamometer may be used instead of actual road testing. Be certain to check out all emission control devices for proper operation. Check exhaust emission levels for compliance with emission regulations.

Isolating and correcting a driveability problem involves troubleshooting procedures as well as repair and service operations. Complete diagnosis includes checking the operation of vehicle systems to determine problem areas, determining which parts could be the cause of the problem, checking the condition and operation of the suspected parts, repairing or replacing the suspected parts and rechecking vehicle operation. Always remember to deter-

Review Questions—Chapter 28

Do not write in this book. Write your answers on a separate sheet of paper.

1. If a maintenance tune up does not solve a vehicle driveability problem, what should the technician do?
2. Owner comments or answers to questions are often helpful in _____.
   (A) locating trouble spots
   (B) determining the exact problem
   (C) deciding how much to charge
   (D) Both A & B.
3. Service records are useful when _____.
   (A) diagnosing trouble at a future date
   (B) handling guarantee work
   (C) service billing
   (D) All of the above
4. List eight important preliminary checks that should be made before the tune-up is started.
5. Following a tune-up, the vehicle should always be _____.
6. The _____ is a handy tool to check the fuel system at all speeds.
7. The hardest part of driveability service is to _____.
   (A) diagnose the problem
   (B) repair a part
   (C) adjust a part
   (D) replace a part
8. Name five common pieces of test equipment that can be used to diagnose driveability problems.
9. For future reference, _____ should be written down once retrieved.
10. A trouble code which resets after the computer has been disconnected and reconnected is a _____ code.

ASE-Type Questions

1. Technician A says that a maintenance tune-up, if properly done, will guarantee satisfactory engine performance. Technician B says that specifications for a certain model and engine are good for other years as long as the engine remains basically the same. Who is right?
   (A) A only.
   (B) B only.
   (C) Both A & B.
   (D) Neither A nor B.

2. Compression tests and cylinder leakage tests are used to determine_____ condition.
   (A) fuel system
   (B) ignition system
   (C) engine mechanical
   (D) all of the above

3. Technician A says that a road test enables the technician to determine whether the tune-up was satisfactory. Technician B says that while road testing, the technician should ignore any other vehicle problem and concentrate on the engine. Who is right?
   (A) A only.
   (B) B only.
   (C) Both A & B.
   (D) Neither A nor B.

4. Technician A says that a chassis dynamometer is preferable to driving the vehicle on the streets. Technician B says that the engine should be cold for accurate tune-up work. Who is right?
   (A) A only.
   (B) B only.
   (C) Both A & B.
   (D) Neither A nor B.

5. Technical service bulletins are usually released by
   _____.
   (A) vehicle manufacturers
   (B) aftermarket parts suppliers
   (C) independent testing organizations
   (D) consumer protection groups

6. Technician A says that an oscilloscope can be used to determine whether the computer control system is properly advancing the ignition timing. Technician B says that a multimeter can be used to check the condition of spark plug wires. Who is right?
   (A) A only.
   (B) B only.
   (C) Both A & B.
   (D) Neither A nor B.

7. Technician A says that a pressure test will reveal a faulty fuel injector on a multiport system. Technician B says that a faulty multiport fuel injector can often be checked by listening with a stethoscope or similar tool. Who is right?
   (A) A only.
   (B) B only.
   (C) Both A & B.
   (D) Neither A nor B.

8. Technician A says that a non-electronic part is never the source of a driveability problem. Technician B says that when a part is visually observed to be defective, it should be replaced without further checking. Who is right?
   (A) A only.
   (B) B only.
   (C) Both A & B.
   (D) Neither A nor B.

9. All of the following are ways to retrieve trouble codes, EXCEPT:
   (A) ground one terminal of the diagnostic connector and observe the flashes from a dashboard warning light.
   (B) ground the dashboard warning light and observe the pulses on a voltmeter.
   (C) ground one terminal of the diagnostic connector, and observe the pulses on a voltmeter.
   (D) use a code retrieval tool to access and display the codes.

10. Which of the following could cause a trouble code to set?
    (A) A disconnected or defective sensor.
    (B) A wiring problem.
    (C) An out-of-range condition caused by the engine.
    (D) All of the above.

Suggested Activities

1. Make a list of all of the engine and drive train systems which could cause driveability problems, such as fuel, ignition, emission controls, transmission, and air conditioning. See how many individual components you can list under each system. Compare your list with those of the other class members.

2. Using the factory service manual, obtain the procedure for retrieving computer trouble codes for an assigned vehicle with computer engine controls. Retrieve the trouble codes and use the service manual troubleshooting charts to determine the problem. If your instructor permits, create trouble codes by disconnecting wires or hoses. Retrieve these codes and compare them with the created problem.

3. Diagnose a vehicle driveability problem using logical diagnosis procedures and one or more of the following pieces of test equipment:

   - scan tool (code retrieval tool).
   - multimeter.
   - vacuum gauge.
   - compression tester.
   - oscilloscope.

4. Discuss the procedures used in the above activity and your conclusions with your instructor and the other members of your class.

29

Clutch and Flywheel Service

After studying this chapter, you will be able to:
* Explain the construction, operation, and service of diaphragm spring clutches.
* Describe the construction, operation, and service of coil spring clutches.
* Adjust different types of clutch linkages.
* Summarize clutch break-in procedures.
* Diagnose clutch problems and suggest possible corrections.

Although the majority of new vehicles are sold with automatic transmissions or transaxles, a significant percentage of vehicles on the road have manual transmissions. Every vehicle with a manual transmission or transaxle has a clutch, and every clutch eventually wears out. Therefore, the technician must be familiar with clutch service. This chapter will cover the service of automotive clutches and flywheels.

Clutch Service

The clutch is a simple friction device that connects and disconnects the engine from the transmission or transaxle. Modern clutches are all the single-plate type, with one *friction disc* installed between the flywheel and pressure plate surfaces. Servicing the clutch is usually confined to making linkage adjustments or replacing the clutch components. These procedures are explained below.

Asbestos Warning

Clutch friction materials contain *asbestos*—a known carcinogen (substance that can cause cancer). Grinding clutch friction materials, cleaning clutch assemblies, etc., can produce small airborne particles of asbestos. These are easily inhaled by the technician. Breathing these asbestos particles may cause cancer. When some exposure to asbestos might be unavoidable, wear an approved respirator. Never use compressed air to blow clutch assemblies clean. Use a vacuum source or flush with water.

Clutch Design and Operation

The modern, single-plate, dry-disc clutch uses either individual, direct-pressure *coil springs* or a *diaphragm spring* to apply force to the *pressure plate.* A direct-pressure, coil-spring-loaded clutch is illustrated in **Figure 29-1.** The diaphragm spring clutch is pictured in **Figure 29-2.**

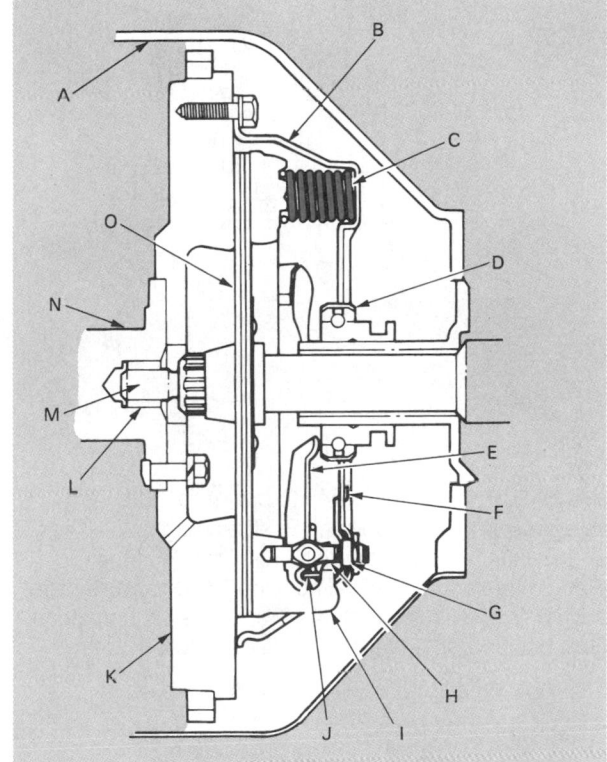

Figure 29-1. With this clutch, force is applied to pressure plate by coil springs. A—Bell housing. B—Pressure plate clutch cover. C—Coil spring. D—Clutch release bearing. E—Release lever. F—Anti-rattle spring. G—Adjustment nut. H—Eyebolt. I—Pressure plate. J—Strut. K—Flywheel. L—Pilot bearing. M—Transmission input shaft. N—Crankshaft. O—Drive disc. (Chevrolet)

Determine Reason for Clutch Failure

Before repairing a damaged clutch, it is a good idea to study the various parts to determine the cause of the failure. Merely replacing the worn or damaged parts is an invitation to trouble. Common clutch problems, their causes, and cures are covered in the problem diagnosis chart in Chapter 41.

Before condemning the clutch, check for correct pedal free play as explained later in this chapter. Inspect the linkage for wear and binding. Check and tighten the engine mounts. Tighten the rear spring clamp or U-bolt assemblies.

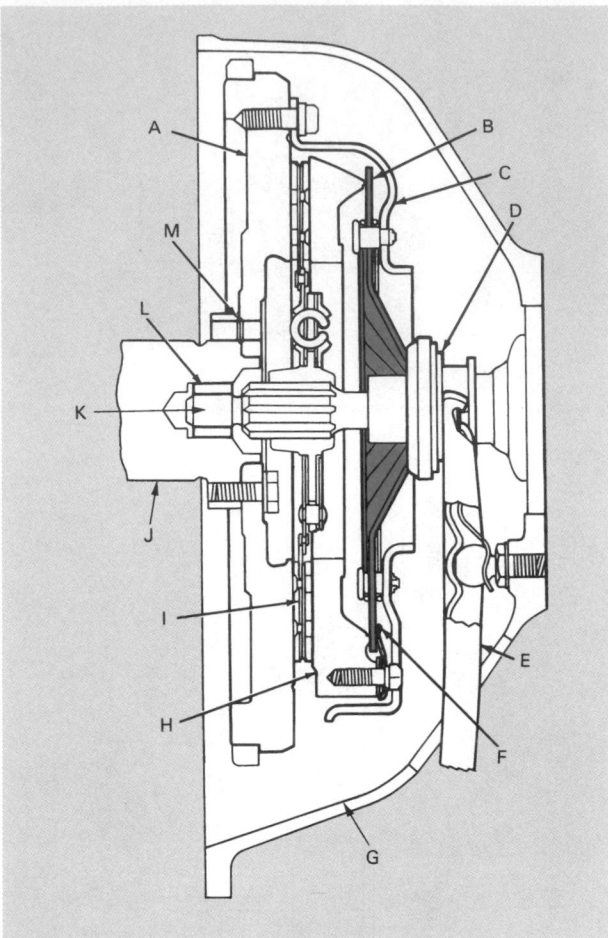

Figure 29-2. Force is supplied to pressure plate by diaphragm spring. A—Flywheel. B—Diaphragm. C—Pressure plate. D—Clutch release bearing. E—Throw-out fork. F—Retracting spring. G—Bell housing. H—Pressure plate. I—Drive disc. J—Crankshaft. K—Transmission input shaft. L—Pilot bushing. M—Dowel hole. (Chevrolet)

Clutch Removal

 Warning: Before proceeding, disconnect the battery ground strap to prevent the engine from being cranked while working on the clutch.

Using suitable tools and equipment, remove the transmission or transaxle. Chapter 30 contains specific instructions for removing manual transmissions and transaxles.

Mark the Pressure Plate and Flywheel

Use a sharp prick punch to mark both the pressure plate and the flywheel. If the pressure plate assembly is reused, it should be installed in exactly the same position. This is necessary so the balance of the flywheel-clutch assembly will not be thrown off. See **Figure 29-3**.

Remove the Pressure Plate

When the transmission or transaxle has been removed, pull the ***throw-out bearing*** out of the ***throw-out fork.*** If working clearance is needed, disconnect the clutch linkage from the fork. The fork may then be tipped back or removed.

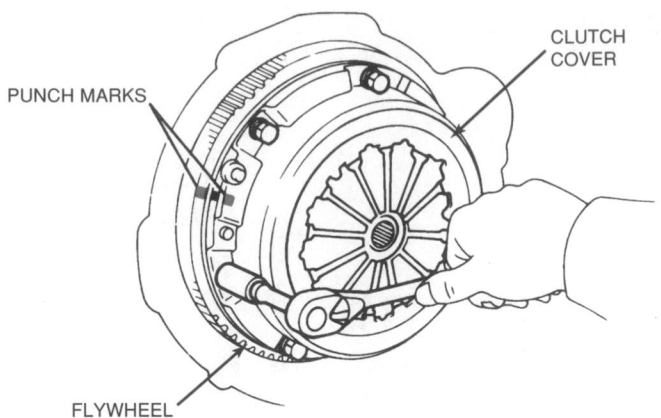

Figure 29-3. Mark pressure plate and flywheel before removing pressure plate.

In some instances, the clutch assembly can be exposed for removal by removing a sheet metal splash pan. Other designs require the removal of the entire flywheel housing. Remove only those parts required.

Loosen each pressure-plate-to-flywheel fastener one turn at a time. Continue around the fasteners until all have been loosened. This permits removing the pressure of the coil springs or diaphragm spring evenly and prevents twisting or warping of the pressure plate.

If desired, a clutch disc ***pilot shaft*** can be inserted through the clutch disc hub and into the crankshaft pilot bearing. This will hold the disc in position until the pressure plate fasteners are removed. A used transmission input (clutch) shaft can be used in place of a pilot shaft. See **Figures 29-4** and **29-5**.

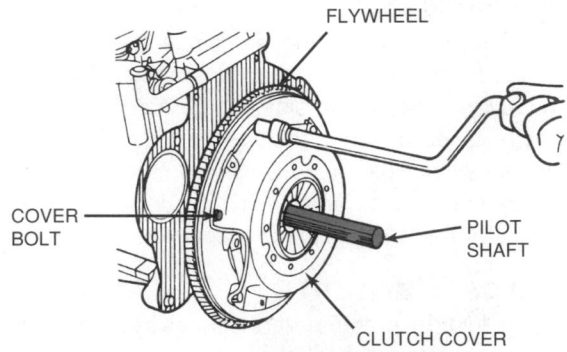

Figure 29-4. Using transmission input shaft to hold clutch disc in position while removing the pressure plate fasteners. The input shaft may also be used to align the disc with the pilot bearing during pressure plate installation. (Chrysler)

Remove all but one pressure plate fastener. While holding the pressure plate assembly up and in, remove the final fastener. Remove the pressure plate and clutch disc. Do not touch the pressure plate, clutch disc, or flywheel clutch surface with greasy fingers. Refer to **Figure 29-6**.

Cleaning Parts

Clean the flywheel face and pressure plate assembly in a nonpetroleum-based cleaner. Brake or electrical winding cleaner is ideal for this purpose. Both units must be

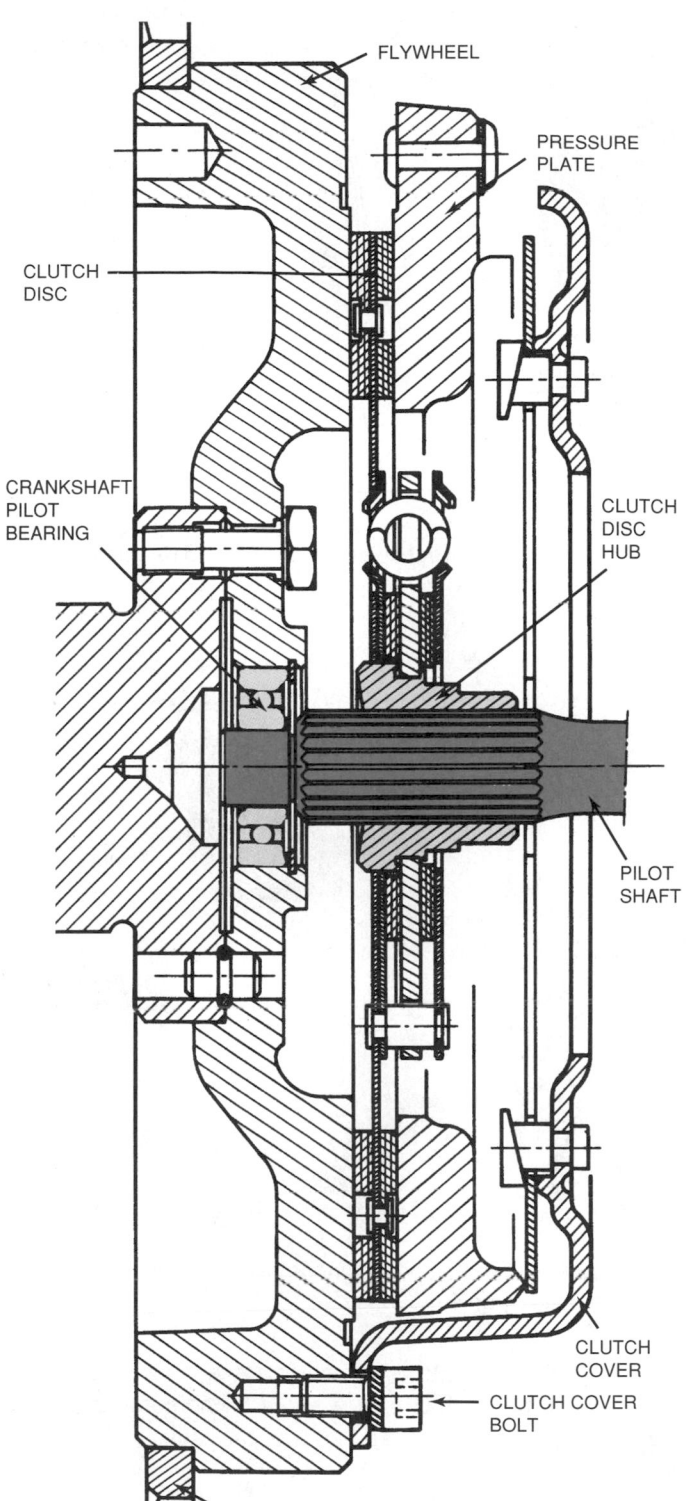

Figure 29-5. A pilot shaft has been inserted through the clutch disc hub and into the crankshaft pilot bearing. This will properly align the parts as the fasteners are secured.

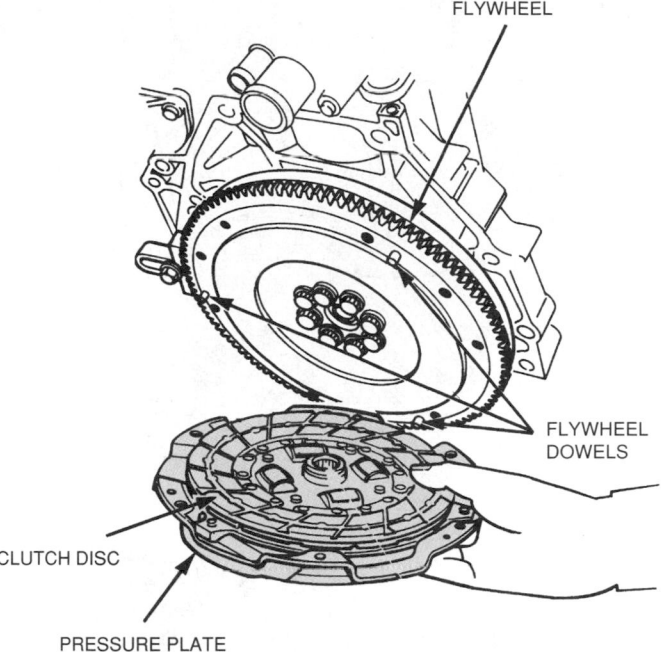

Figure 29-6. Removing the clutch disc and pressure plate. (Honda)

spotlessly clean and absolutely free of oil or grease. Once cleaned, use care to prevent contamination.

Never wash the throw-out bearing in any kind of solvent. The throw-out bearing is packed with grease and sealed. Washing it would remove or dilute the lubricant. The throw-out bearing may be wiped with a clean cloth moistened with solvent.

Sand Clutch Friction Surfaces

Use medium-fine emery cloth or equivalent aluminum oxide paper to sand the friction surfaces of the flywheel and the pressure plate. Sand so that the sanding scratch marks run across the surface. Sand lightly until the surfaces are covered with fine scratch lines.

This will break the **glaze** (coating of shiny, hardened metal) on these surfaces and remove any carboned oil deposits. The new clutch disc will seat smoothly and quickly against the sanded surfaces.

 Note: If the surfaces of the flywheel and pressure plate cannot be restored by sanding, they must be machined with special equipment to remove any heat marks or grooves (usually called turning).

Flywheel-to-Clutch Friction Surface

The flywheel-to-clutch friction surface must be clean, dry, lightly sanded, and free of heavy **heat checking** (cracking). It must also be free of scoring and warpage. Do not expect a clutch disc and pressure plate to work properly when assembled on a glazed, dirty, rough, or warped flywheel surface.

Checking Flywheel Runout

To check flywheel runout, set up a dial indicator and rotate the flywheel. Force the flywheel in one direction while turning to prevent end play from affecting the reading. Determine runout by reading the indicator. Check both the clutch disc contact surface and the rim edge. Replace the flywheel or have the friction surface reground if required. **Figure 29-7** shows a flywheel clutch surface being checked for warpage with a dial indicator.

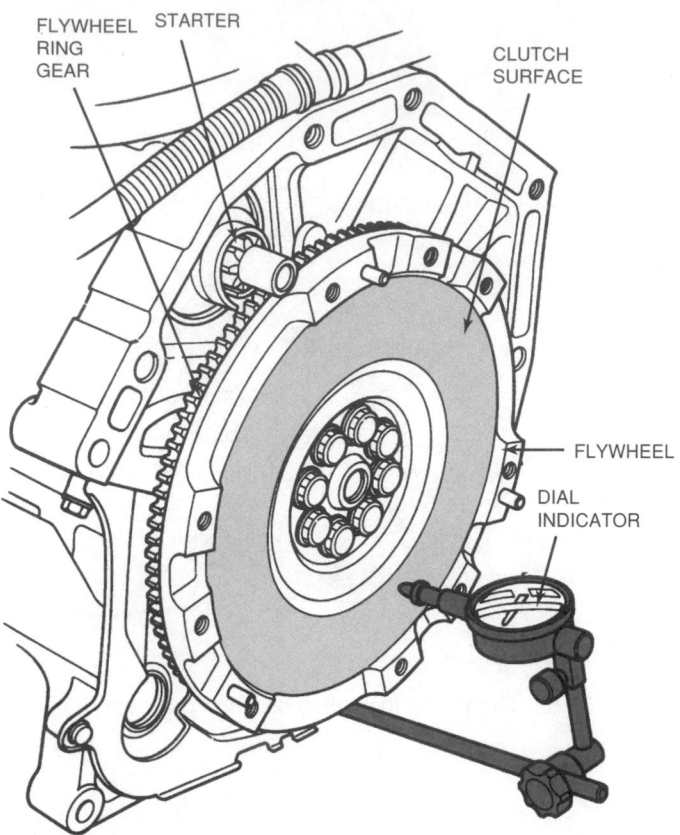

Figure 29-7. Using a dial indicator to check the flywheel face for warpage. (Honda)

Flywheel Mounting

The flywheel crankshaft flange surface must be clean and true. If dowel pins are used, align the flywheel. Install cap screws and torque them to specifications. If required, coat the cap screw threads with oil-resistant sealer. When needed, use lock washers or a lock plate. Some flywheels use a hardened plate that is intended to protect the flywheel against damage from the cap screw heads, **Figure 29-8.** If the clutch disc contact face is scored or wavy, it must be reground, **Figure 29-9.**

Flywheel Ring Gear Removal

Flywheel **ring gears** are placed on the outside of the flywheel and contact the starter teeth during cranking. Some ring gears are heated and placed in position. Upon cooling, they shrink and grasp the flywheel tightly. Others are welded or bolted in position.

If the ring gear is welded to the flywheel, begin removal by cutting the welds. Next, heat the old gear and drive it from the flywheel. Ring gears utilizing a shrink fit can also be heated (keep heat away from flywheel) and removed. If necessary, the ring gear can also be drilled almost through and a chisel can be used to spread the gear for removal. When driving the gear off, do not strike the flywheel.

Ring Gear Installation

If a shrink fit is used, the gear should be heated (do not exceed 450°F, or 232°C). A controlled temperature oven

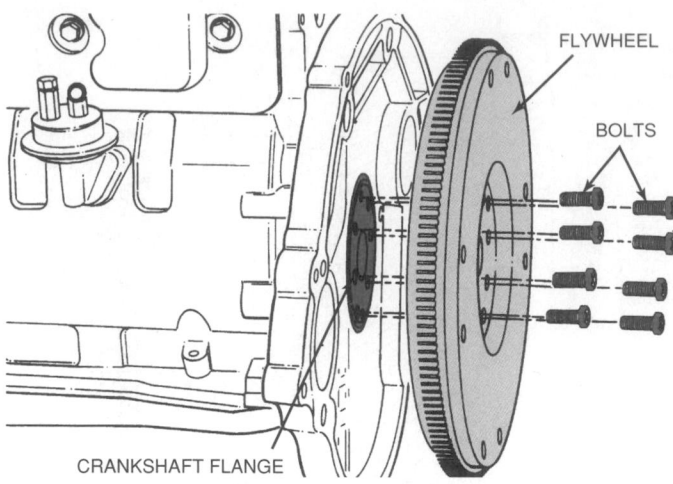

Figure 29-8. This flywheel uses a hardened metal plate to protect the flywheel from cap screw (bolt) head damage when the bolts are tightened. (Cummins Engine Co.)

Figure 29-9. Using a special grinder to resurface the clutch pressure plate. (VanNorman)

is ideal for this purpose. If this type of oven is not available, the gear can be heated in oil. Use a thermometer and keep the gear from touching the bottom of the tank.

 Caution: Cover the tank while heating to avoid fire.

When the ring is hot, quickly place it over the flywheel contact surface and immediately drive it into place. Chilling the flywheel helps. Be sure the ring is placed so the relieved edged of the teeth (if so designed) face in the desired direction, **Figure 29-10.**

Another installation method involves placing the gear on a fire brick surface and heating it with an acetylene torch. Move the flame around the ring. Wire solder (50/50 or 40/60 type) is touched against the ring frequently as the

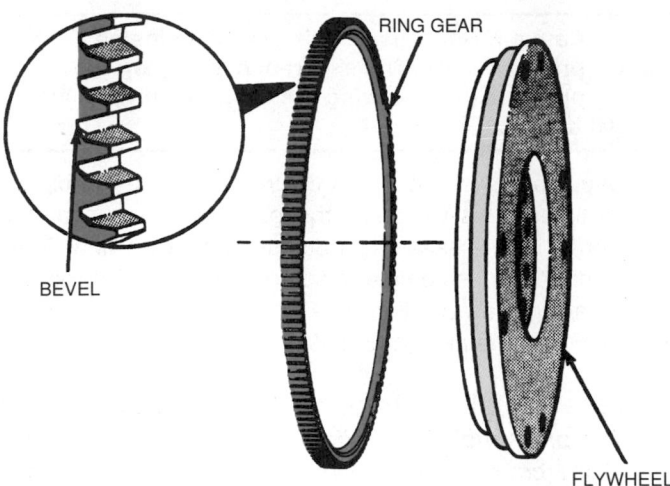

Figure 29-10.   A correctly positioned, beveled-edge ring gear that is ready to be installed on the flywheel. (Dodge)

temperature is raised. When the solder starts to melt when touched firmly against the ring, the temperature is high enough. The 50/50 (50% tin, 50% lead) melts at 414°F (212°C). The 40/60 (40% tin, 60% lead) melts at 460°F (238°C).

 Caution: Do not overheat the ring, as the teeth will be softened.

When installing a ring gear that is arc welded to the flywheel, add as little weld material as necessary to maintain flywheel balance.

Pressure Plate Assembly

Inspect the pressure plate for excessive burning, heat checking, warpage, and scoring. Check the coils or diaphragm spring for evidence of cracking, loss of temper (overheating), and looseness. Check the ends of the release levers (where they contact the throw-out bearing) for wear. In the case of the diaphragm spring, check the ends of the release fingers. See **Figures 29-11** and **29-12.**

As with the flywheel, the pressure plate friction surface must be clean, dry, lightly sanded, and free of scoring, warpage, and heavy checking. Pressure plate assemblies should be rebuilt or replaced unless they are satisfactory in all respects.

Rebuilding a Pressure Plate Assembly

Many shops use rebuilt or reconditioned pressure plate assemblies instead of rebuilding the units in their own shops. Unless proper tools are available and the technician is thoroughly skilled in clutch rebuilding, it is advisable to use a factory rebuilt unit.

If rebuilding is required, mark the pressure plate parts so that all the parts can be reassembled in the same relative position. Place the assembly on a special base plate fixture or set it up in a hydraulic press. When using a hydraulic press, insert the spacer blocks under the pressure

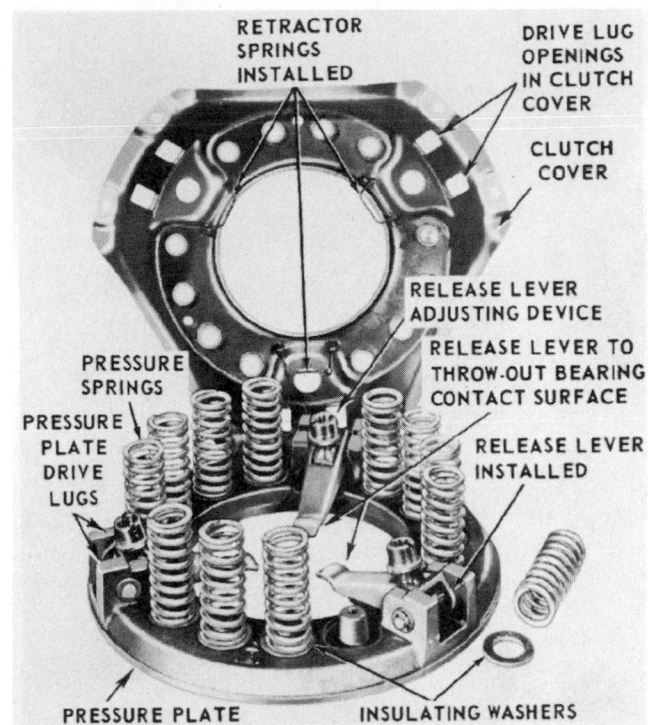

Figure 29-11.   Coil spring type pressure plate check points. (GM)

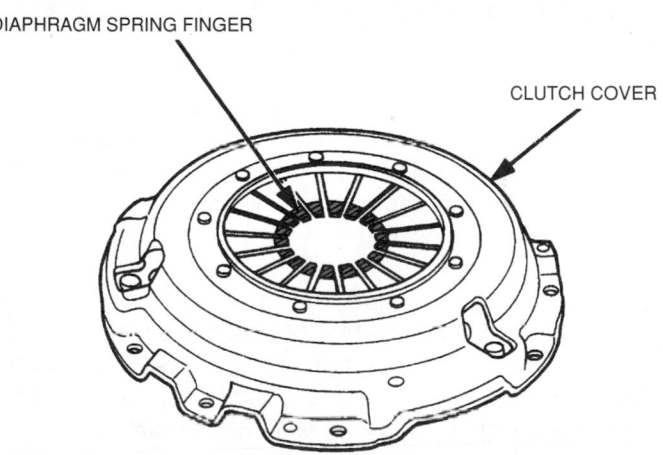

Figure 29-12.   Pressure plate check points. This shows the diaphragm spring fingers. (Honda)

plate so the pressure plate can move downward when pressure is applied.

Apply pressure to the pressure plate while loosening the adjustment nuts. When the adjustment nuts have been removed, release the pressure and allow the cover to move upward and off.

Check all pressure plate parts for cracking, wear, overheating, and other damage, **Figure 29-13.** Check coil spring tension. The pressure plate can be resurfaced if it is not badly damaged.

Reassemble all pressure plate parts in their correct order. Align the marks. Use new or reconditioned parts as required. Check the clearance between the pressure plate drive lugs and the openings in the pressure plate. Apply

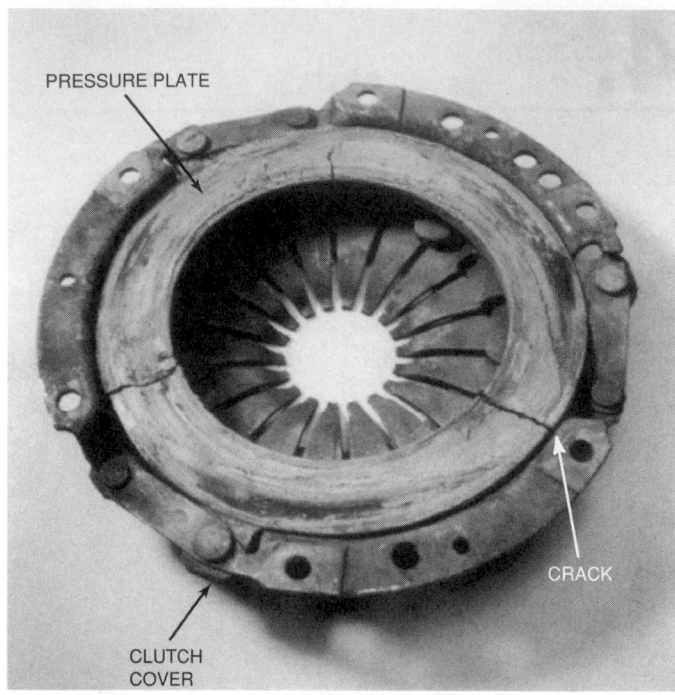

Figure 29-13. Pressure plate showing damage. (Luk Automotive)

lithium (high-temperature) grease to the lug-to-pressure-plate contact areas.

Adjusting Clutch Release Fingers

It is important that the pressure plate be withdrawn an equal amount around the entire circumference when the release fingers are depressed. This will permit complete disengagement for shifting and smooth engagement when the clutch is reapplied.

After installing the pressure plate and clutch disc on the flywheel, place a straightedge across the pressure plate and measure the distance from each release finger. Carefully adjust each finger to the specified distance by tightening or loosening the adjusting nuts. See **Figure 29-14.**

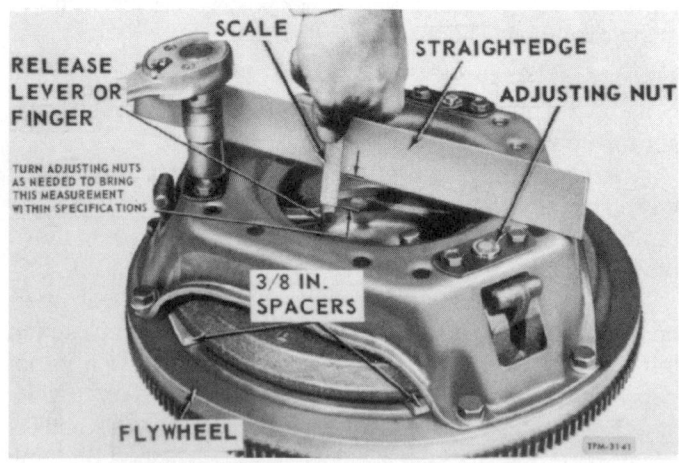

Figure 29-14. Checking the clutch release finger or lever adjustment. Turn the lever adjusting nuts as required. (GM)

Caution: Never use an air wrench to install a pressure plate. The air wrench may warp the pressure plate, leaving the actuating fingers at unequal heights.

Use a press or the clutch fixture to actuate the clutch several times. This will allow the parts to seat. Following actuation, check release finger adjustment for the final time. When adjustment is complete, some manufacturers recommend staking the adjusting nuts so they will not loosen in service. Stake the nuts in at least two places.

Replace the Clutch Pilot Bushing or Bearing

The **pilot bushing** or **pilot bearing** is installed in the rear of the crankshaft and aligns and supports the transmission/transaxle input shaft. It is good practice to always install a new clutch pilot bushing (or bearing in some cases) when doing a clutch job. Worn pilot bushings can cause clutch chatter, spot burning, and transmission/transaxle input gear damage. The pilots are relatively inexpensive and are easily changed.

An expandable finger or a threaded puller can be used to pull the pilot bushing or bearing, **Figure 29-15.** Sometimes the pilot bushing can be removed by packing the recess with heavy grease and using a tight-fitting punch to strike the inside of the bushing. The force will be transferred through the grease and push the bushing out. See **Figure 29-16.**

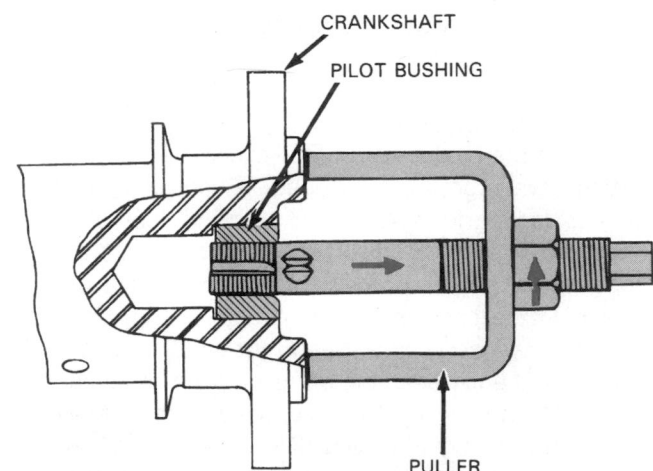

Figure 29-15. Using a threaded tip puller to remove the clutch pilot bushing. If a ball bearing is used, an expandable finger tip puller should be used. (Oldsmobile)

Clean out the pilot bushing recess in the end of the crankshaft. Wipe the outside of the new pilot with a light film of high-temperature grease. Place the pilot on a driver (chamfered inner hole end facing outward) and drive the bushing into place. When driving a bearing, use a driver that contacts the outer race only. Look at **Figure 29-17.** Where retainers are used to secure the bearing or bushing, install them as specified.

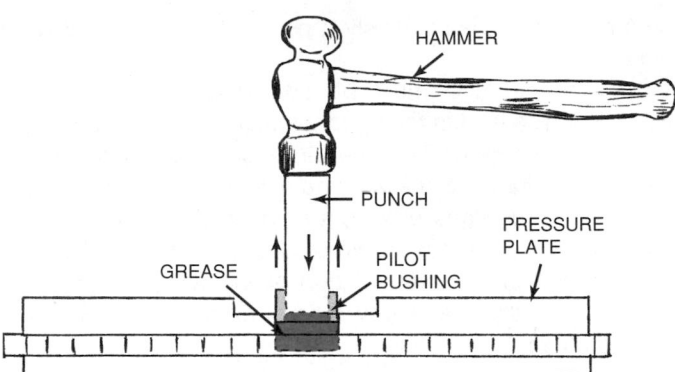

Figure 29-16. Forcing the pilot bushing from its bore housing in the pressure plate using grease and a snug fitting punch. The punch tries to displace the grease, which in turn, forces the pilot bushing up and out.

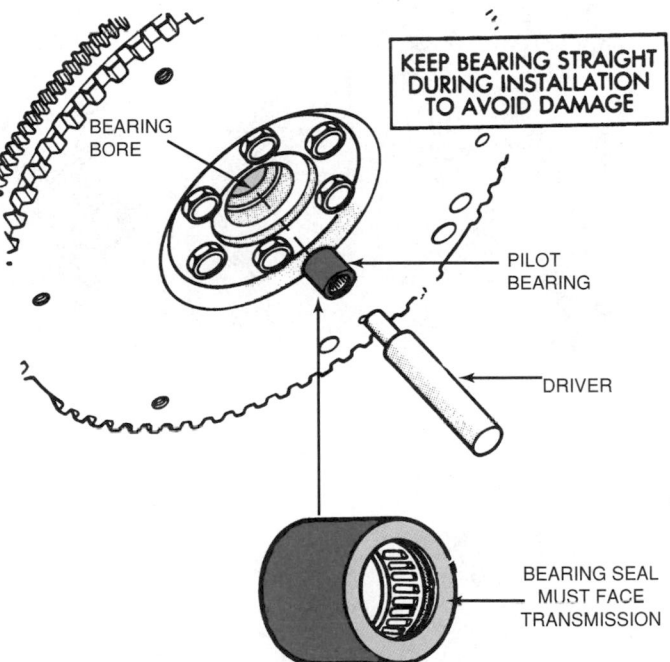

Figure 29-17. Installing a pilot bearing with a special driver tool. Start and drive the bearing squarely. (Dodge)

When installing a pilot bearing, install it with the open side of the bearing facing inward (seal end facing the transmission/transaxle). Apply a thin film of high-temperature grease to the inside of the bushing. Never over lubricate the bushing, as the excess grease will find its way onto the clutch disc facing, causing clutch chatter and grabbing.

Clutch Housing Must Be Aligned

The portion of the clutch housing to which the transmission or transaxle is attached must be properly aligned with the crankshaft centerline.

In instances where short throw-out bearing life, clutch chatter, early input shaft bearing failure, and jumping out of gear indicate possible housing misalignment, both the housing bore and face runout should be checked. If the clutch

housing has been removed, it is good practice to check the alignment after installation.

Checking Clutch Housing Face and Bore Runout

Set up a dial indicator as shown in **Figure 29-18.** Check for clutch housing bore runout. Make certain the indicator stem rides against the machined bore surface. The indicator mounting bar must also be firmly affixed to the flywheel. The stem must be at right angles to the bore.

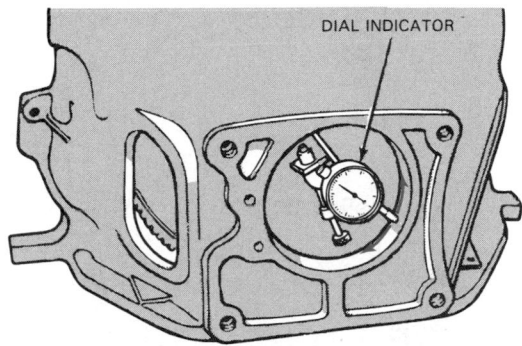

Figure 29-18. Checking clutch housing bore runout. (Chrysler)

Zero the indicator and slowly turn the flywheel until the indicator stem has traveled completely around the bore. Watch the indicator needle throughout the stem travel. The total needle travel (amount needle moved from both sides of the zero mark) represents double the actual runout. For example, if the total needle travel is .018″ (0.46 mm), actual runout would be .009″ (0.23 mm).

To check housing face runout, adjust the dial indicator so that the stem end rides against the machined face of the housing. The stem should be at right angles to the face. Turn the housing one complete turn while noting the total needle travel, **Figure 29-19.**

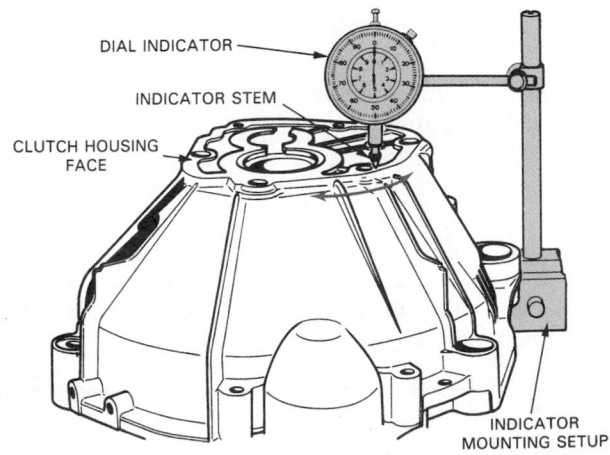

Figure 29-19. Checking clutch housing face runout with a dial indicator. The housing is turned in a circle, keeping the dial indicator stem in contact with the mounting face (surface).

If either bore or face runout exceeds specifications, the situation must be corrected by using thin shims between the housing and the engine block. Some manufacturers provide offset dowel pins that can be used to correct bore runout. When the offset dowels are used, shims must be employed to correct face runout. The use of offset dowel pins is shown in **Figure 29-20.** Whenever a correction for bore runout has been made, face runout should be rechecked. When face runout has been changed, bore runout must be rechecked.

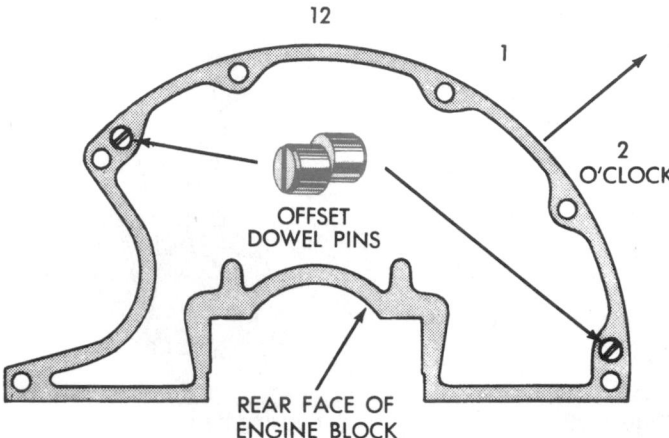

Figure 29-20. Offset dowel pins may be used to correct bore runout. (Plymouth)

Make careful adjustments and keep checking runout until it is brought within limits. If bore or face runout cannot be brought within limits, or if an excessive shim thickness is required, the clutch housing must be replaced.

Installing the Clutch Disc and Pressure Plate Assembly

Installation of the clutch disc and pressure plate assembly is a relatively easy task. However, the job is often ruined or the service life seriously shortened by careless handling of the parts, improper tightening, and disc damage during transmission or transaxle installation. Use care and follow the directions given in this section.

Check for Oil Contamination

Oil leaking from the transmission or transaxle, flywheel bolts, or rear main seal can quickly ruin the friction material on a new clutch disc. Always check these two potential trouble spots carefully before installation of the clutch assembly. Repair as needed.

 Note: Oil leaks that flow into the clutch area must be stopped.

Use a New Clutch Disc

It is advisable to install a new clutch disc when the clutch has been disassembled. When you consider the cost of a new disc compared to the overall costs and the assurance of proper operation and extended service life offered

by a new disc, it is obviously a poor practice to reinstall an old disc.

If the old disc must be considered for installation, check the disc friction facing for signs of looseness, glazing, wear, or oil soaking. Examine the hub torsional coil springs (cushion springs) to make certain they are not broken or loose. Look for signs of warpage or cracking. Hub splines must be free of excessive wear. Generally, 0.03″ (0.8 mm) is the maximum amount of hub spline wear allowable. If the disc is faulty in any way, it must be discarded. Refer to **Figure 29-21.**

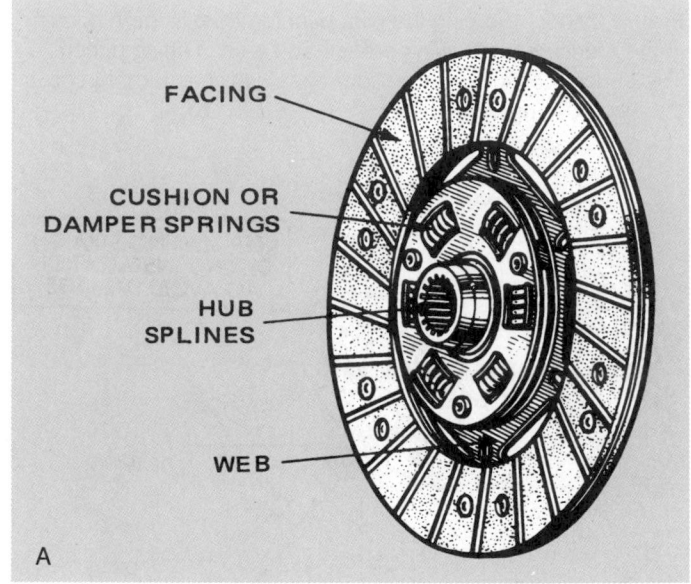

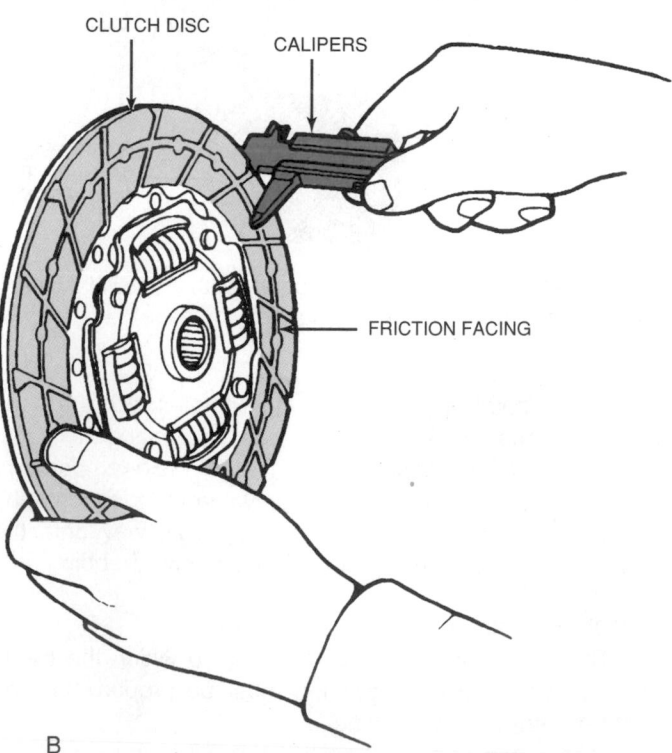

Figure 29-21. A—If the old clutch disc must be reinstalled, check these areas to determine serviceability. Remember, it is good practice to install a new clutch disc. B—Checking the friction material for thickness with a caliper. (Honda)

Install the Clutch Disc with the Correct Side Facing the Flywheel

Examine the clutch disc friction facing. If one side is marked "flywheel," place that side toward the flywheel. If neither side is marked, place the disc against the flywheel so that the hub and hub cushion or damper spring assembly will clear both the flywheel and the pressure plate.

By careful study of the clutch and disc design, the correct side to place against the flywheel will become obvious. Note that the long side of the hub faces away from the flywheel in **Figure 29-22.** It faces toward the flywheel in the setups pictured in **Figures 29-2** and **29-23.**

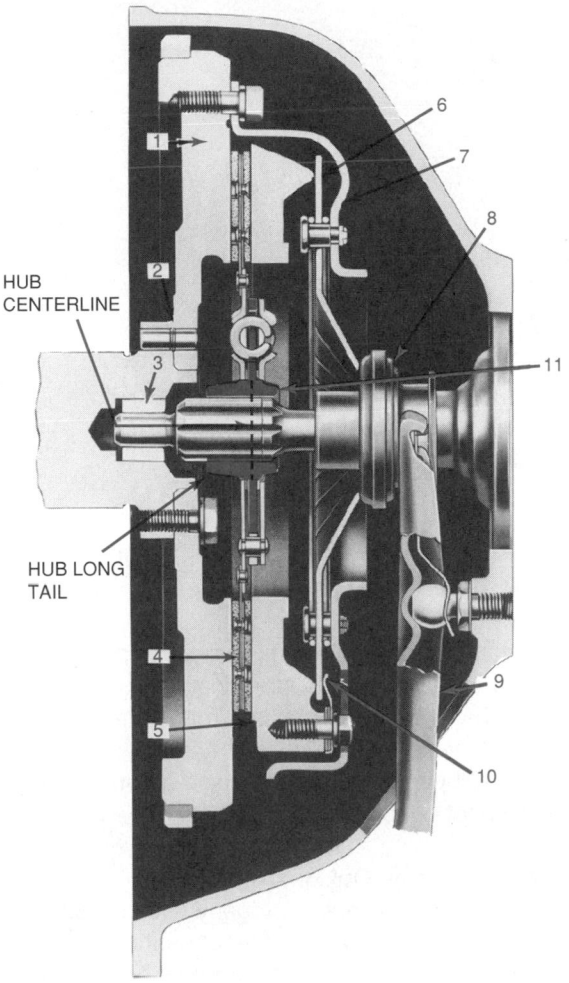

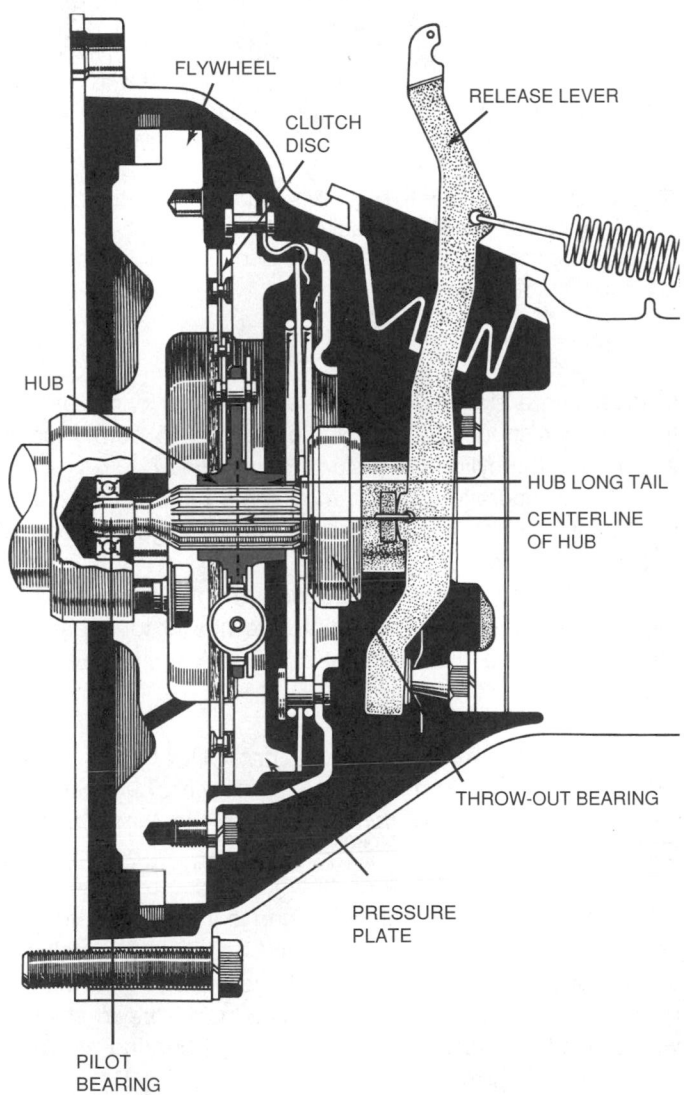

Figure 29-22.   A clutch disc with the hub long tail facing away from the flywheel. (Toyota)

Figure 29-23.   A clutch disc with the hub long tail facing the flywheel. 1—Flywheel. 2—Dowel. 3—Pilot bushing. 4—Clutch disc. 5—Pressure plate. 6—Diaphragm spring. 7—Clutch cover. 8—Throw-out bearing. 9—Release fork. 10—Retracting spring. 11—Clutch disc hub. (Ford)

Use a Clutch Disc Pilot Shaft

While holding the clutch disc and pressure plate assembly against the flywheel, pass a used transmission input shaft or a pilot shaft through the disc hub and into the pilot bearing. See **Figures 29-24** and **29-25.**

The use of the pilot shaft will align the disc hub with the clutch pilot bearing. This will hold the parts in alignment while the pressure plate is attached.

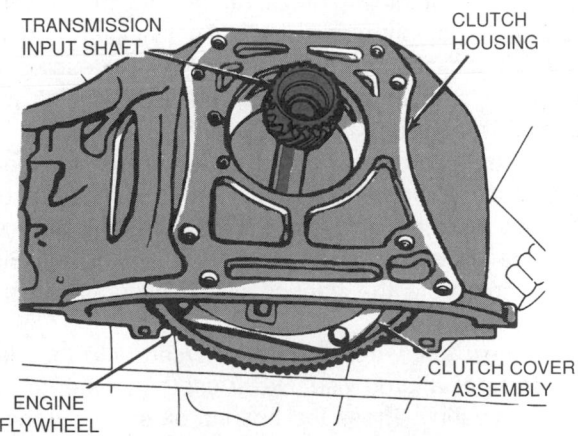

Figure 29-24.   Transmission drive pinion (input shaft) being used to hold pressure plate and clutch disc to flywheel. (Dodge)

Start all the pressure plate fasteners. Use lock washers. Tighten each fastener one turn. Continue around the fasteners, one turn per fastener, until the pressure plate is

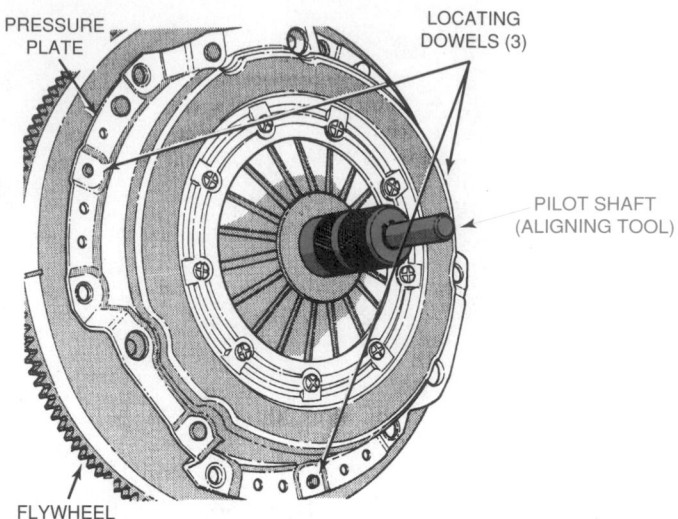

Figure 29-25. Using a pilot or clutch disc aligning tool to hold pressure plate and clutch disc to the flywheel. (Plymouth)

snug against the flywheel. At this time, use a torque wrench and tighten the fasteners to specifications.

After the pressure plate is torqued, remove the pilot shaft. When the transmission or transaxle is installed, the input shaft will pass through the disc hub and into the pilot bearing without difficulty.

Install a New Throw-Out Bearing

A properly installed and properly used clutch will last a long time. Even though the throw-out bearing appears to be good, it is good practice to install a new bearing whenever the clutch is overhauled. Failure to do this may result in bearing failure long before the clutch is worn out.

If, for some reason, the reuse of the old throw-out bearing must be considered, inspect it carefully. The bearing should spin freely but with enough drag to indicate the presence of grease. Press the bearing against a flat surface. While maintaining pressure, revolve the bearing. It should turn smoothly, with no sign of catching or roughness.

In some cases, there are provisions for greasing. If the bearing is mechanically sound, the addition of proper grease will render it fit for further service.

On some throw-out bearing assemblies, the bearing may be pressed from the sleeve. This allows the use of the old sleeve by merely pressing a new bearing into place. Other sleeve designs, such as the one pictured in **Figure 29-26,** incorporate the bearing as an integral part of the sleeve.

If a new throw-out bearing is forced onto the sleeve, use a press or a large vise. Never use a hammer to seat a throw-out bearing. Press the bearing on squarely and until fully seated.

Pack the inner groove of the throw-out sleeve with high-temperature grease. Also, coat the throw-out fork groove with a *thin* coating of the same lubricant.

Hydraulic Throw-Out Bearing Assembly

Some systems employ a hydraulic throw-out bearing assembly, which combines a throw-out bearing and a slave

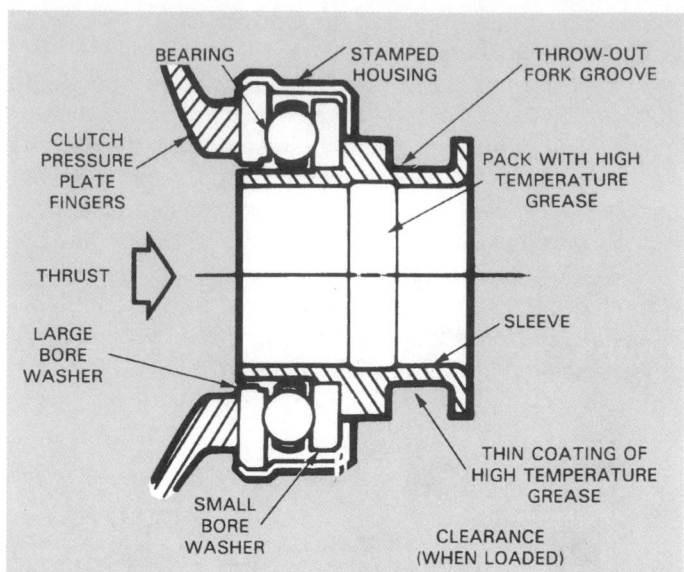

Figure 29-26. In this throw-out bearing assembly, the bearing is an integral part of the sleeve. Note the use of high-temperature grease inside the sleeve and on the throw-out fork groove. (Federal-Mogul)

cylinder into a single unit. The slave cylinder encircles the transmission input shaft, and the bearing is permanently attached to the cylinder's piston, **Figure 29-27.**

During operation, piston movement causes the throw-out bearing to travel in a linear direction, engaging or disengaging the pressure plate.

The hydraulic throw-out bearing and the slave cylinder must be serviced as an assembly. Do not try to disassemble the unit. The hydraulic lines will leak if they are disturbed.

Lubricate and Install the Clutch Throw-Out Fork

Lubricate the throw-out fork pivot with Lubriplate or similar grease. Wipe a *thin* coating on the throwout fork fingers.

Install the fork. Make certain it is secured to the pivot and that any internal retracting spring is in place. If the fork fingers are held to the throw-out bearing with retaining springs or clips, make certain the fingers are in their proper positions and the clips are in place. Install the dust boot where used. A typical throw-out fork and bearing setup is illustrated in **Figure 29-28.**

Do Not Depress Clutch Pedal until Installation Is Complete

After the throw-out fork and throw-out bearing have been installed, avoid depressing the clutch pedal before the transmission or transaxle is fully in place. To do so will exert pressure on the clutch release fingers, causing them to pull the pressure plate away from the disc. This would release the disc and allow it to drop down, preventing the transmission input shaft from passing through the disc hub and into the pilot bearing. Transmission installation would be impossible without disc realignment.

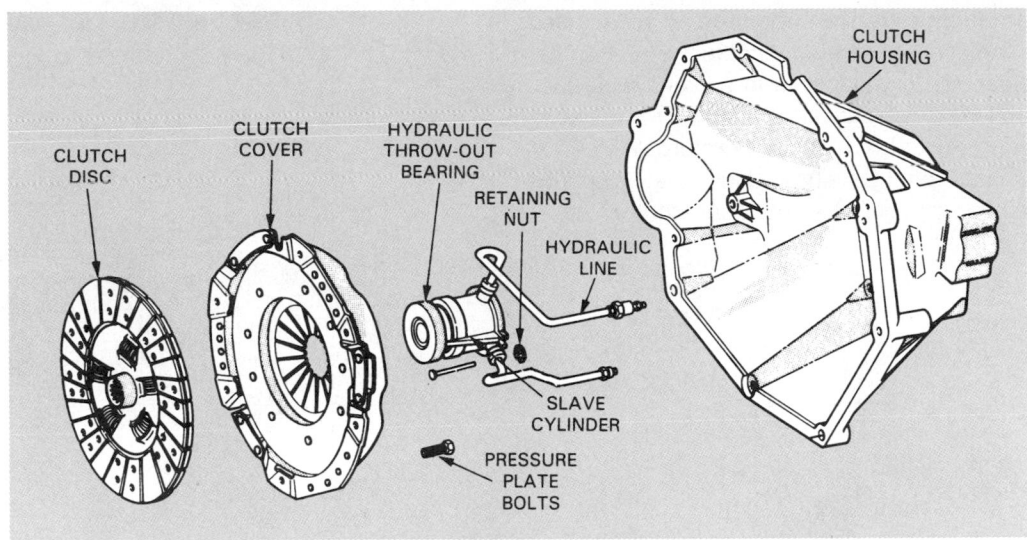

Figure 29-27. Overall view of a hydraulic throw-out bearing assembly. (Jeep)

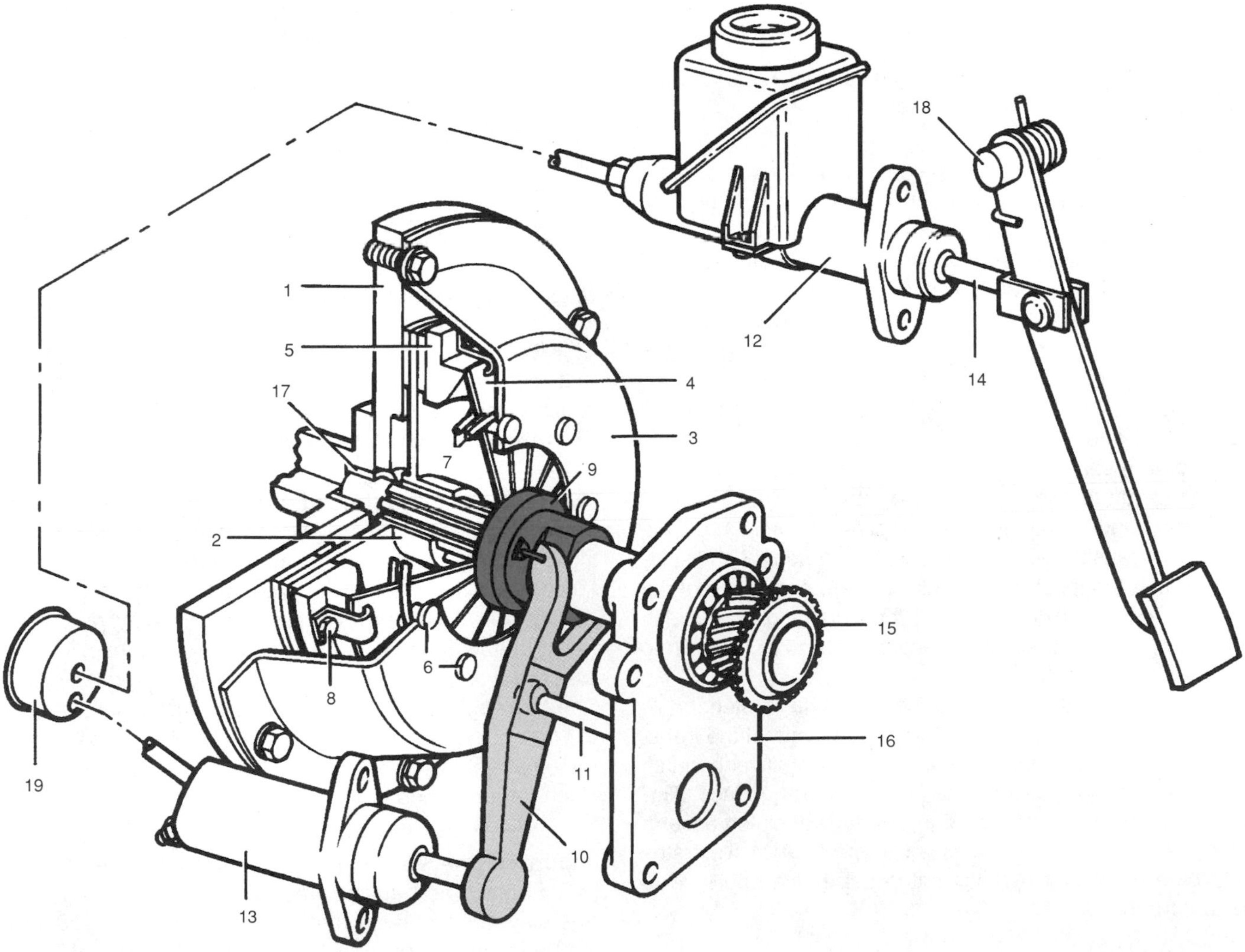

Figure 29-28. A cutaway view of a throw-out fork and hydraulic system. 1—Flywheel. 2—Disc hub. 3—Clutch cover. 4—Spring finger. 5—Pressure plate. 6—Rivets. 7—Springs. 8—Bolt. 9—Throw-out bearing. 10—Throw out fork. 11—Fork pivot. 12—Master cylinder. 13—Slave cylinder. 14—Push rod. 15—Transmission input shaft. 16—Input shaft retaining plate. 17—Pilot bushing. 18—Clutch pedal. 19—Hydraulic damper. (Land Rover)

Use Care when Installing the Transmission or Transaxle

Tighten the input shaft bearing retainer. See **Figure 29-29.** Using a clean rag dampened with solvent, wipe the input shaft until absolutely clean. Dry the shaft with a clean cloth. Apply a very thin coat of high-temperature grease to the portion of the input shaft bearing retainer that supports the throw-out bearing sleeve. Do not lubricate the input shaft.

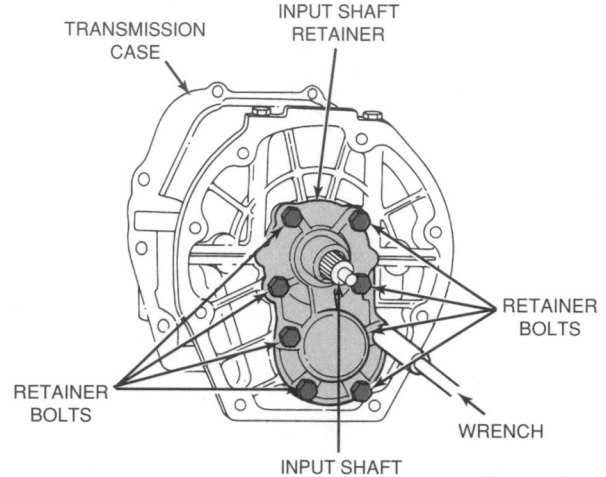

Figure 29-29.   Tightening the transmission input shaft bearing retainer bolts. Torque bolts to specifications. (Geo)

If the transmission or transaxle shows signs of oil leakage through the input shaft bearing, correct the leak before installation.

Place the transmission or transaxle on a suitable stand and align it with the engine crankshaft centerline. Place the transmission/transaxle in gear. Pass the input shaft and front bearing retainer through the throw-out bearing sleeve. When the input shaft splines strike the disc hub, turn the output shaft to turn the input shaft. This will align the splines on the shaft and the hub. Push inward on the transmission as the output shaft is turned. When the splines are aligned, force the shaft through the hub and into the pilot bearing.

If the shaft resists entering the pilot, carefully move the rear of the transmission or transaxle up and down and sideways. When the input shaft is fully seated, both sides of the transmission/transaxle front will be touching the clutch housing or engine block. Install fasteners and bring them to proper torque.

Never use the transmission/transaxle fasteners to draw the unit into place. Never allow the weight of the transmission or transaxle to hang on the input shaft and clutch disc Keep it supported until the fasteners are in place. **Figure 29-30** shows a cross section of a typical clutch assembly with the transmission installed. **Figure 29-31** illustrates an exploded view of a clutch setup used with one type of manual transaxle.

Attach the Clutch Linkage

Connect the clutch linkage assembly. Install all springs, washers, cotter pins, etc. Lubricate where required.

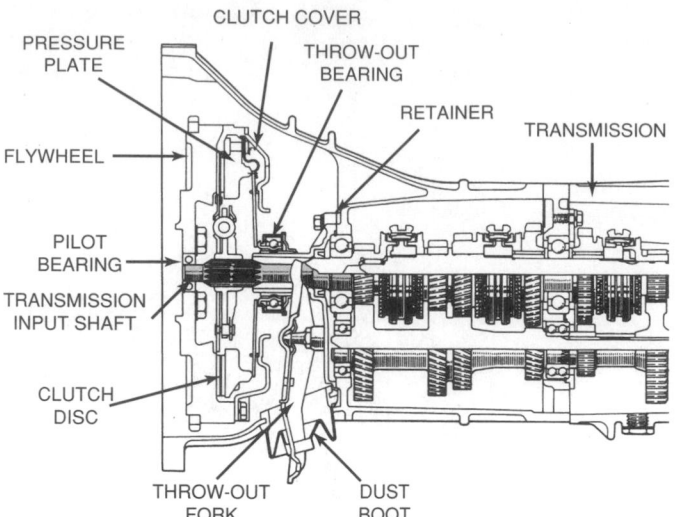

Figure 29-30.   A cross-sectional view of a typical clutch assembly with the transmission attached. (Mazda)

Operate the clutch pedal several times to check linkage operation. Adjust pedal free play as explained below. Replace the dust boot (where used) if cracked or torn.

Pedal Free Play

The throw-out bearing should touch the clutch release fingers only when the clutch pedal is depressed.

 Note: One clutch assembly utilizes an automatic self-adjuster that removes pedal free play and keeps the throw-out bearing in contact with the release fingers at all times.

Most clutch release assemblies must be adjusted so that the throw-out bearing moves away from the whirling clutch release fingers when the clutch pedal is released. This allows the throw-out bearing to stand still, prolonging its service life.

From the fully released position, the clutch pedal must be depressed a certain distance before the throwout bearing is forced against the clutch release fingers. This distance is called clutch pedal *free play,* or free travel. See **Figure 29-32.** Failure to adjust the free play properly can result in severe damage. If the free play is insufficient, the clutch will slip and overheat, resulting in short clutch life. The throwout bearing will be in constant motion, causing it to wear out quickly. If the free play is excessive, the clutch may not release completely, causing hard shifting, gear clash, and damage to the gear teeth.

Important Checks before Adjusting Pedal Free Play

Some clutch assemblies have provisions for only the free play adjustment. Others however, provide adjustments for pedal height and total pedal travel. When this is the case, both pedal height and total travel should be checked before adjusting pedal free play. Clutch return action should also be observed.

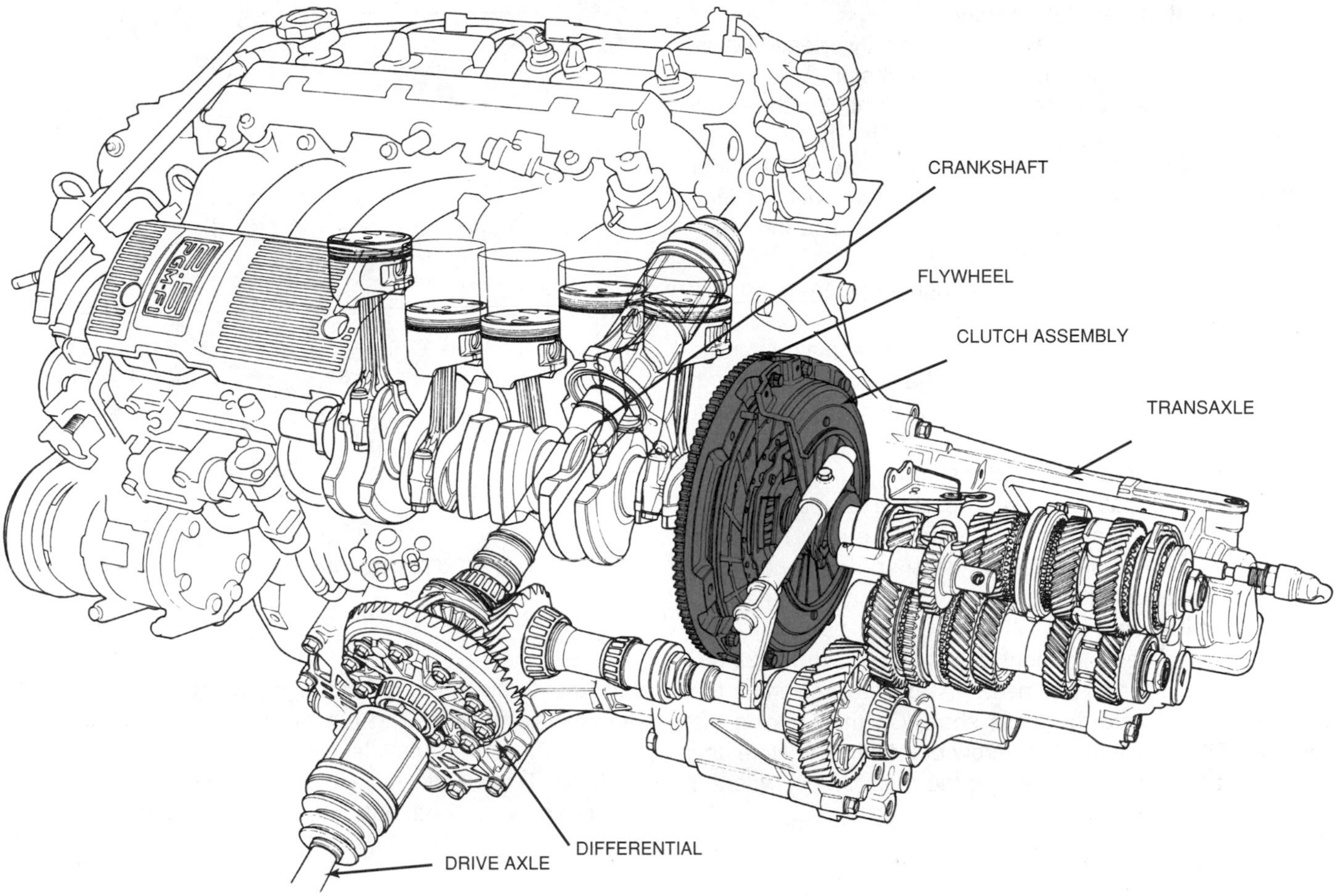

CRANKSHAFT

FLYWHEEL

CLUTCH ASSEMBLY

TRANSAXLE

DRIVE AXLE

DIFFERENTIAL

Figure 29-31. A cutaway view of one particular clutch setup that is used with a manual transaxle. (Honda)

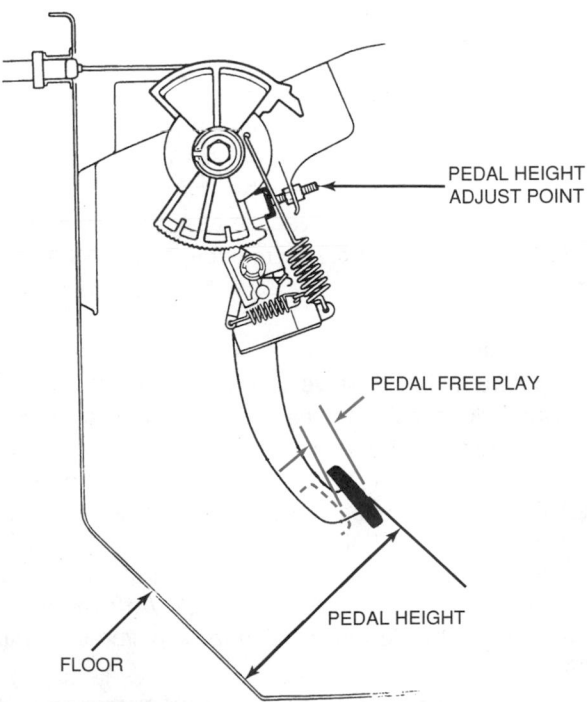

PEDAL HEIGHT
ADJUST POINT

PEDAL FREE PLAY

PEDAL HEIGHT

FLOOR

Figure 29-32. Clutch pedal free travel and pedal height for one particular vehicle. Free play for this assembly is 0.08″ to 1.10″ (2 mm to 28 mm). (Toyota)

Clutch Pedal Height

Where adjustment is possible, check the pedal height against specifications. Height measurement is usually determined by checking the distance from the pedal to a specific spot. It may also be checked by comparing clutch pedal height to that of the brake pedal. Adjust the pedal stop as required.

Clutch Pedal Total Travel

Where required, check pedal total travel by measuring the distance the clutch pedal moves in traveling from the fully released position to the fully extended position. Adjust as needed.

Clutch Pedal Return Action

Check the clutch pedal return action. The pedal should return until firmly against the stop. If the pedal sticks or catches, check for binding, interference, or a weak return spring. In the event that the pedal does not fully return, check the return spring or springs. Replace or adjust as required.

Never adjust the clutch linkage in an endeavor to force the clutch pedal to return the full distance. To do so will remove free play and will ruin the throwout bearing and possibly the entire clutch.

Adjusting Clutch Pedal Free Play

Make sure the clutch pedal is in the fully released position and that it is firmly against the pedal stop. Use a couple of fingers to depress the clutch pedal until the throw-out bearing engages the release fingers. The pedal should move (from the fully released position) downward under moderate finger pressure. When the throwout bearing engages the release fingers, a sharp increase in the resistance to downward movement will be felt.

The measured distance the pedal moves from the fully extended position to the point at which the release fingers are engaged represents the amount of free play. Average free play is about 1″ (25.4 mm). Check specifications. If pedal free play does not meet specifications, adjust the linkage as needed.

There are numerous linkage setups. Study the action as the clutch pedal is depressed. Find the adjustment device and move it as required to provide proper free play. Tighten the locknuts and replace the snap rings and cotter pins after the adjustment is made. Check pedal free play and readjust if necessary.

One linkage arrangement is pictured in **Figure 29-33.** On this setup, pushing the pedal (A) downward forces the pushrod (B) to rotate the cross shaft (C), thus forcing the pushrod (D) to actuate the throw-out fork (E). Note the adjustment threads on the end of the pushrod (D) where it passes through the swivel.

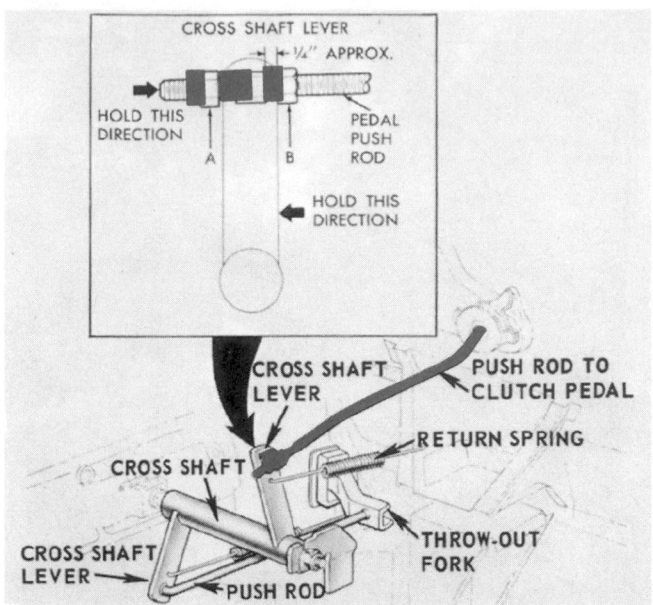

Figure 29-34.   Clutch pedal free travel adjustment setup.

until the throw-out bearing engages the release fingers. Hold in this position and run the nut (B) up to within 1/4″ (6.35 mm) of the shaft lever. Release the lever and the pushrod. Tighten the nut (A) until the cross shaft lever is secured between both nuts. Check the pedal for correct free play.

Self-Adjusting Clutch Linkage

When a self-adjusting linkage is used, check the clutch cable for kinks, cuts, and pinched areas. Be sure the self-adjusting clutch mechanism is clean and lightly lubricated, **Figure 29-35.** Check for damaged parts on the self-adjusting mechanism, such as worn pawl and detent (quadrant) teeth or a loose mounting bracket.

Operate and check that the clutch releases fully. If equipped, be sure that the neutral start switch is properly secured and adjusted. Follow the manufacturer's recommendations for the specific vehicle at hand. **Figures 29-36** and **29-37** show typical clutch release mechanisms. Study them closely.

Hydraulic Linkage

Where a hydraulic slave cylinder is used to actuate the throw-out fork, check the master cylinder fluid level. Add fluid if required. Flush the system if the fluid is old or contaminated. (See Chapter 34 on brakes for servicing hydraulic units.) Check the master cylinder, slave cylinder, line, and connections for leaks if the fluid level is low.

Adjust pedal free play to specifications. A typical slave cylinder setup is shown in **Figure 29-38.** An overall view of one type of hydraulic clutch linkage is pictured in **Figure 29-39.**

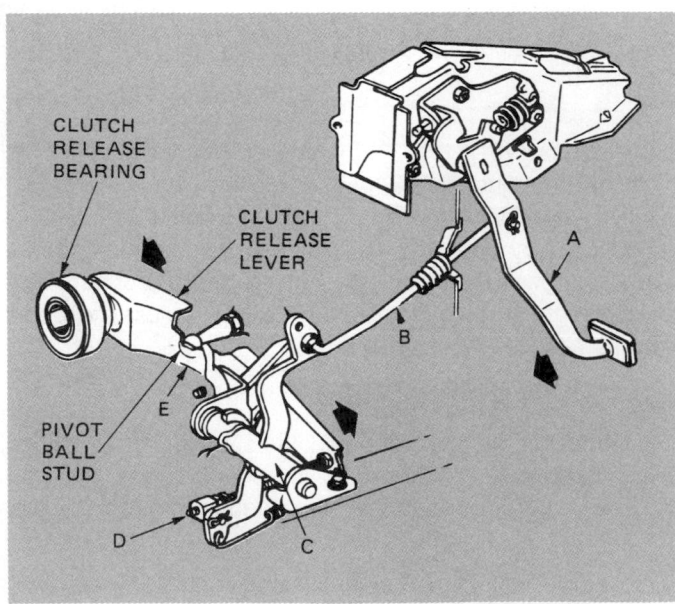

Figure 29-33.   Clutch pedal linkage arrangement. (Federal-Mogul)

A somewhat similar linkage arrangement is pictured in **Figure 29-34.** Note that the adjustment threads are on the upper pushrod end. To set pedal free play on this setup, run both nuts (A) and (B) away from the swivel. Force the pushrod end toward the fire wall while pushing the cross shaft lever in the opposite direction. Move the shaft lever

---

 Caution: Use the proper type of brake fluid only. Motor oil, transmission fluid, or any kind of petroleum-based oil will damage rubber parts.

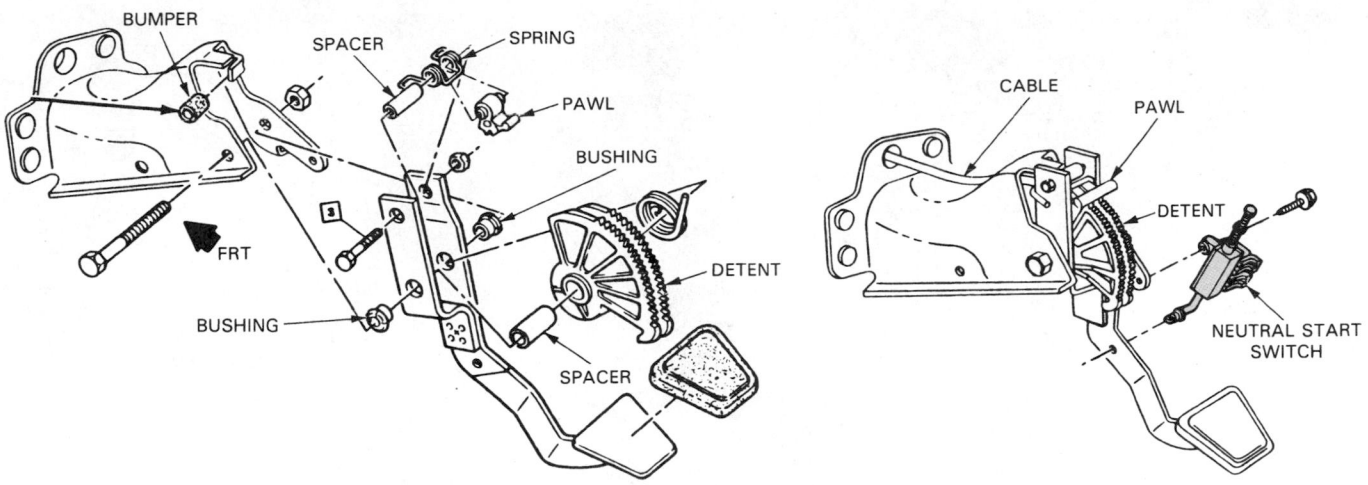

Figure 29-35. Exploded view of a self-adjusting clutch pedal assembly. Note the neutral start switch and its location. (Buick)

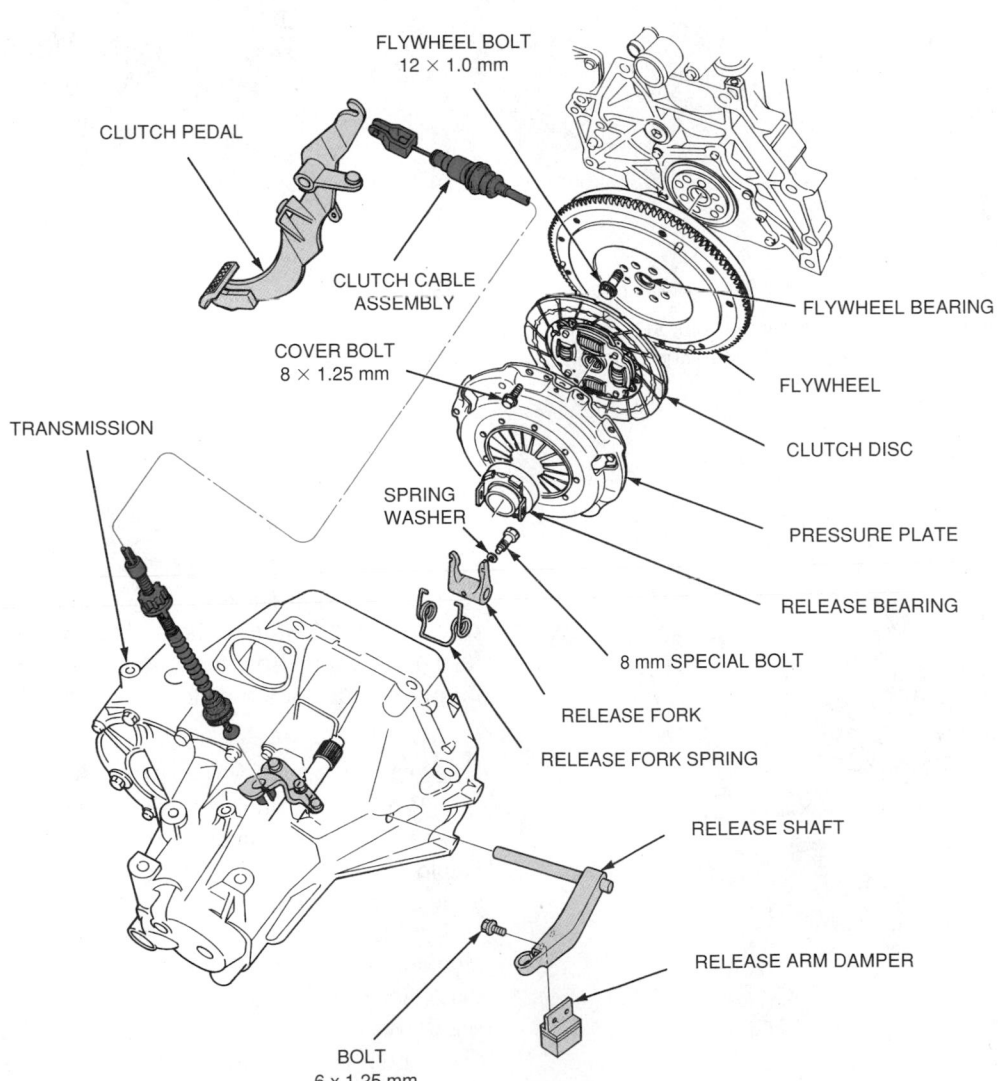

Figure 29-36. An exploded view of a transaxle clutch and release linkage assembly. This unit uses an adjustable cable to transfer clutch pedal movement to the release shaft and fork. (Honda)

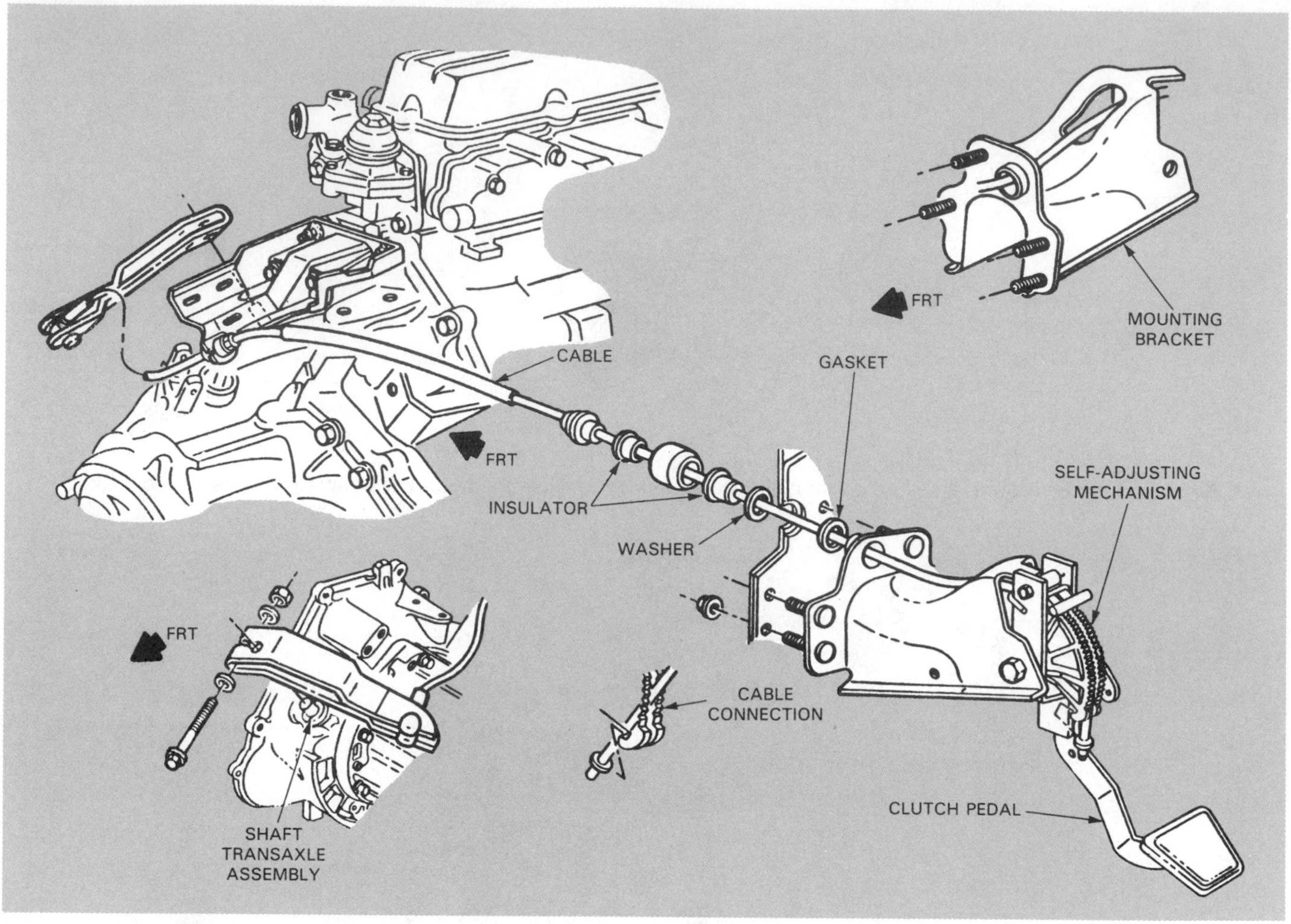

Figure 29-37.   Overall view of one particular clutch mounting bracket and cable assembly. The use of a cable greatly simplifies linkage location and routing. Note the self-adjusting mechanism used to take up part wear and cable stretch. (Chevrolet)

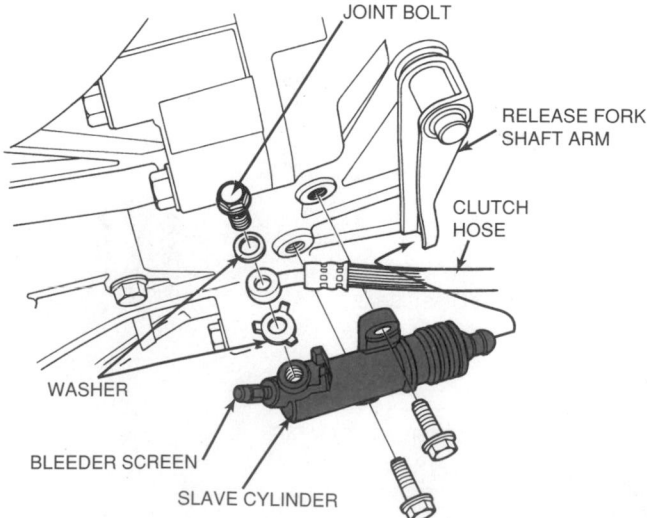

Figure 29-38.   A hydraulic slave cylinder with related parts. (Honda)

Clutch Break-In

It is good practice to subject the newly installed clutch disc to around twenty starts. This will wear off the friction facing "fuzz" and seat the disc properly. Following this initial break-in, recheck the clutch pedal free play.

Steam Cleaning Precautions

When the engine and clutch housing are steam cleaned, a certain amount of moisture enters the housing. Rapid heating of the housing by the steam blast will also cause condensation.

If the clutch is not used for some time following steam cleaning, corrosion may form on the clutch unit. The clutch disc facing tends to absorb moisture, which can cause enough corrosion to literally "freeze" the flywheel, clutch disc, and pressure plate together. If this happens, the clutch assembly must be disassembled in order to separate the units.

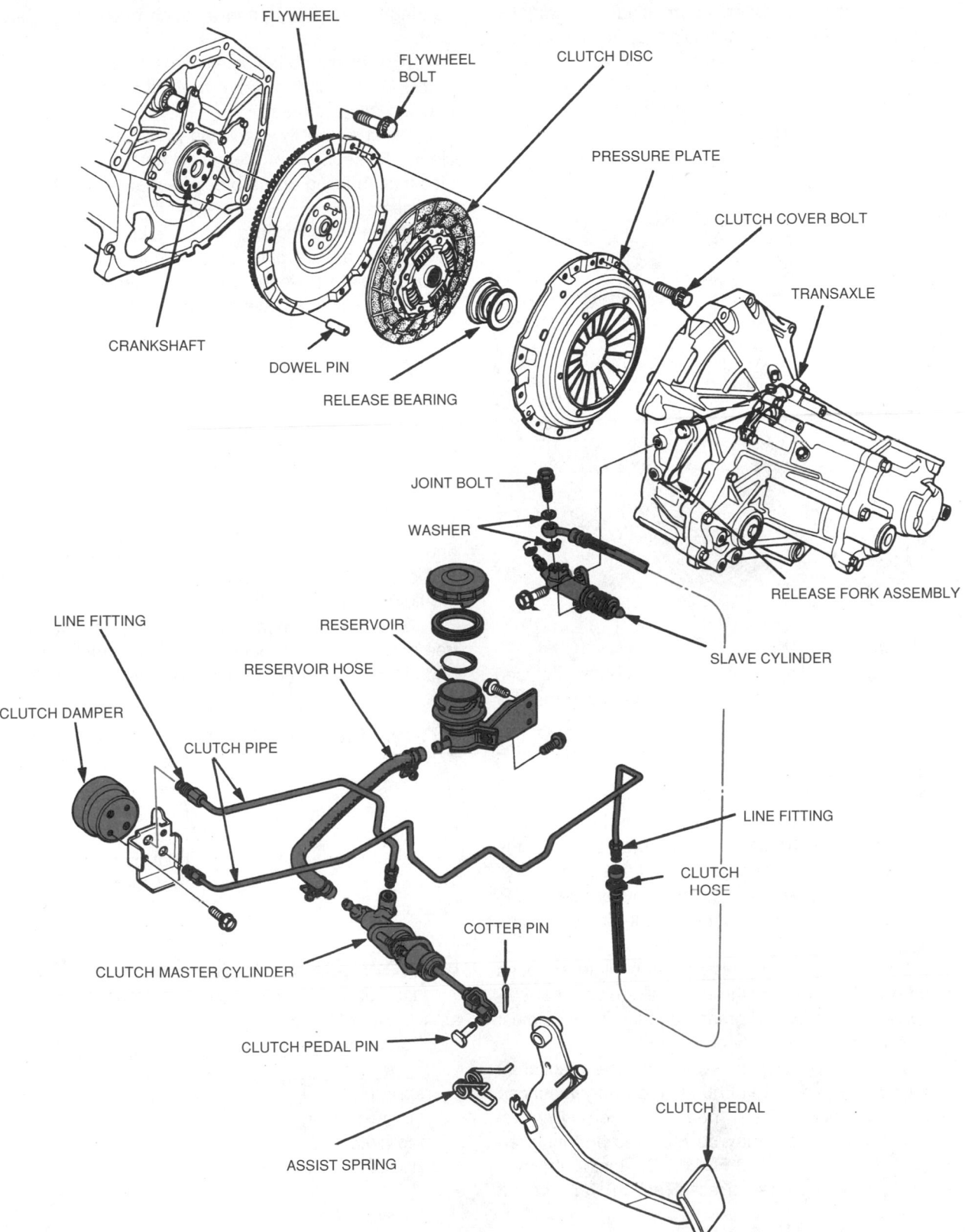

Figure 29-39. An overall view of one particular hydraulic clutch linkage assembly for a manual transaxle. Note the clutch damper. A diaphragm helps absorb hydraulic fluid shock, smoothing the clutch engagement.

To prevent corrosion after steam cleaning, start the engine, set the brakes, and shift the transmission into high gear. Run the engine at a moderate speed and slowly let the clutch pedal out until the engine tries to drive the car forward. Hold the pedal at this point and allow the clutch to "slip" for about five or six seconds. This will heat up the clutch enough to dry it.

Tech Talk

There may come one day in your career as a technician where you are having a difficult or insufficient time to perform a job on a customer's vehicle. If the part or adjustment is not in direct sight and will not adversely affect the vehicle's performance, you may be tempted to charge the customer for it any way as the customer might never know the difference. This is referred to as "smoking" by technicians, but is simply another name for stealing. If you are caught intentionally "smoking" a repair, you will lose your job and could possibly face criminal prosecution. The best remedy for this is not to do it at all, no matter how strong the temptation.

Summary

Coil springs or a diaphragm spring is commonly used to apply force to the pressure plate. Always study the disassembled parts in an attempt to determine what caused the clutch trouble. Be sure to disconnect the battery ground strap when working on the clutch.

The pressure plate and flywheel should be marked before removal to ensure correct balance during reassembly. Loosen each pressure plate fastener one turn at a time to prevent warping the pressure plate during removal.

Do not clean the clutch disc or the throw-out bearing in solvent. Use a non-petroleum cleaner on the pressure plate and flywheel.

Sand both the flywheel and pressure plate surfaces with fine emery cloth to break the mirror-like glaze. For satisfactory service, flywheel and pressure plate surfaces must not be warped, scored, or badly checked.

The flywheel mounting surface and the crankshaft flange must be clean and free of burrs. Torque flywheel cap screws and use locks where needed. Check flywheel runout. Flywheel ring gears may be removed and installed by heating. Never exceed 450°F (232°C). Install the ring with the teeth pointing in the correct direction. Tack weld if required.

If the pressure plate assembly is to be rebuilt, mark the pressure plate release fingers and the pressure plate to ensure assembly in the same relative positions. The pressure plate and flywheel friction surface, if not ruined, may be reground.

When reassembling the pressure plate, check the fit of the pressure plate drive lugs (where used) in the pressure plate. Adjust the release fingers. Always install a new pilot

bearing or bushing during a clutch overhaul. Lubricate the pilot.

If problems so indicate, check the clutch housing alignment. Shims and offset dowel pins are used to correct housing misalignment.

Be sure the flywheel and pressure plate surfaces are clean. To keep them clean, do not touch the new clutch disc friction lining or the pressure plate and flywheel friction surfaces.

When installing the clutch, align the pressure plate. Align the pressure plate and flywheel marks. Tighten each pressure plate fastener a little at a time until the pressure plate touches the flywheel. Torque the fasteners. Always use a new clutch disc and install a new throw-out bearing during a clutch overhaul.

Once the clutch, throw-out bearing, and fork have been installed, do not depress the clutch pedal until the transmission or transaxle is in place. Support the transmission or transaxle while installing. Never let it hang on the input shaft.

Attach the clutch linkage, lubricate, and check alignment and action. Check the clutch pedal height, total travel, and free play. Check the hydraulic linkage master cylinder and slave cylinder for leaks. Flush the hydraulic system if the fluid is dirty.

Give the clutch a quick break-in and recheck pedal free play. Readjust if needed. Slip the clutch for a few seconds following steam cleaning to prevent corrosion.

Know These Terms

Asbestos	Glaze
Coil spring	Heat checking
Diaphragm spring	Ring gear
Pressure plate	Pilot bushing
Throw-out bearing	Pilot bearing
Throw-out fork	Free play
Pilot shaft	

Review Questions—Chapter 29

Do not write in this book. Write your answers on a separate sheet of paper.

1. Force is applied to the pressure plate by either _____ springs or a _____ spring.

2. List two safety precautions for dealing with asbestos in the clutch assembly.

3. Before removing the pressure plate fasteners, always _____.

    (A) wipe them off
    (B) block the flywheel
    (C) prick punch the pressure plate and flywheel
    (D) check for disc warpage

4. Name the clutch parts which should be replaced whenever the clutch is serviced.

5. Align the clutch disc hub with the _____ by using a clutch aligning arbor or a used transmission input shaft.

6. What should you check the flywheel-to-clutch friction surface for?

7. When installing a new flywheel ring gear, never heat it above _____.
   (A) 200°F (93°C)
   (B) 900°F (482°C)
   (C) 650°F (343°C)
   (D) 450°F (232°C)

8. Name some indications of a worn clutch pilot bushing?

9. To prevent clutch corrosion following steam cleaning, the technician should _____.
   (A) allow the car to stand for several hours before running
   (B) start the engine and slip the clutch
   (C) raise the rear end and spin the wheels
   (D) oil the clutch disc facing

10. Name the three ways in which the clutch linkage can be operated.

ASE-Type Questions

1. What is the first thing that should be removed when replacing a clutch?
   (A) Transmission.
   (B) Inspection cover.
   (C) Battery cable.
   (D) Clutch linkage.

2. Technician A says that each pressure plate fastener should be removed completely before proceeding to the next one. Technician B says that the pressure plate fasteners should be tightened before installing the pilot shaft. Who is right?
   (A) A only.
   (B) B only.
   (C) Both A & B.
   (D) Neither A nor B.

3. Technician A says that the pressure plate or flywheel friction surfaces can be sanded to restore them to service. Technician B says that pressure plate assemblies can be rebuilt satisfactorily in some cases. Who is right?
   (A) A only.
   (B) B only.
   (C) Both A & B.
   (D) Neither A nor B.

4. When installing the pressure plate assembly to the flywheel, always _____.
   (A) align the prick punch marks
   (B) install the top fastener first
   (C) use a C-clamp to secure the unit
   (D) tighten each fastener fully before starting on the next one

5. On most vehicles, clutch pedal free play is adjusted by

   _____.
   (A) placing shims under the pressure plate
   (B) adjusting the clutch linkage
   (C) bending the pedal stop
   (D) aligning the clutch housing

6. Technician A says that flywheel runout is preset and does not require checking. Technician B says that some flywheel ring gears are secured by short arc welds. Who is right?
   (A) A only.
   (B) B only.
   (C) Both A & B.
   (D) Neither A nor B.

7. Insufficient pedal free play can cause _____.
   (A) clutch slipping
   (B) excessive throw-out bearing wear
   (C) rapid clutch disc wear
   (D) All of the above.

8. Excessive pedal free play can cause all of the following, EXCEPT:
   (A) hard shifting.
   (B) fast throw-out bearing wear.
   (C) gear clash when shifting.
   (D) transmission gear damage.

9. Technician A says that when replacing a clutch, it is advisable to install a new pilot bearing or bushing. Technician B says that to assist in forcing the input shaft into the pilot bearing, it is permissible to tighten the transmission to clutch housing fasteners. Who is right?
   (A) A only.
   (B) B only.
   (C) Both A & B.
   (D) Neither A nor B.

10. If the clutch pedal sticks or catches, the technician should do all of the following, EXCEPT:
    (A) check for linkage binding or interference.
    (B) check for a weak return spring.
    (C) adjust the clutch linkage to remove free play.
    (D) replace worn parts when found.

Suggested Activities

1. Inspect several different used clutch parts and determine why each one failed. Be sure to follow the asbestos precautions listed earlier.

2. Obtain the necessary measuring equipment and measure the runout of a flywheel. If out of specifications, try to determine if the problem is in the friction surface or the flywheel itself.

3. Take a vehicle with a manual transmission on a road test and perform all of the checks you learned in this chapter.

4. Give complete estimates for replacing the worn clutch parts you studies earlier. Include all applicable parts, reconditioning, and labor prices.

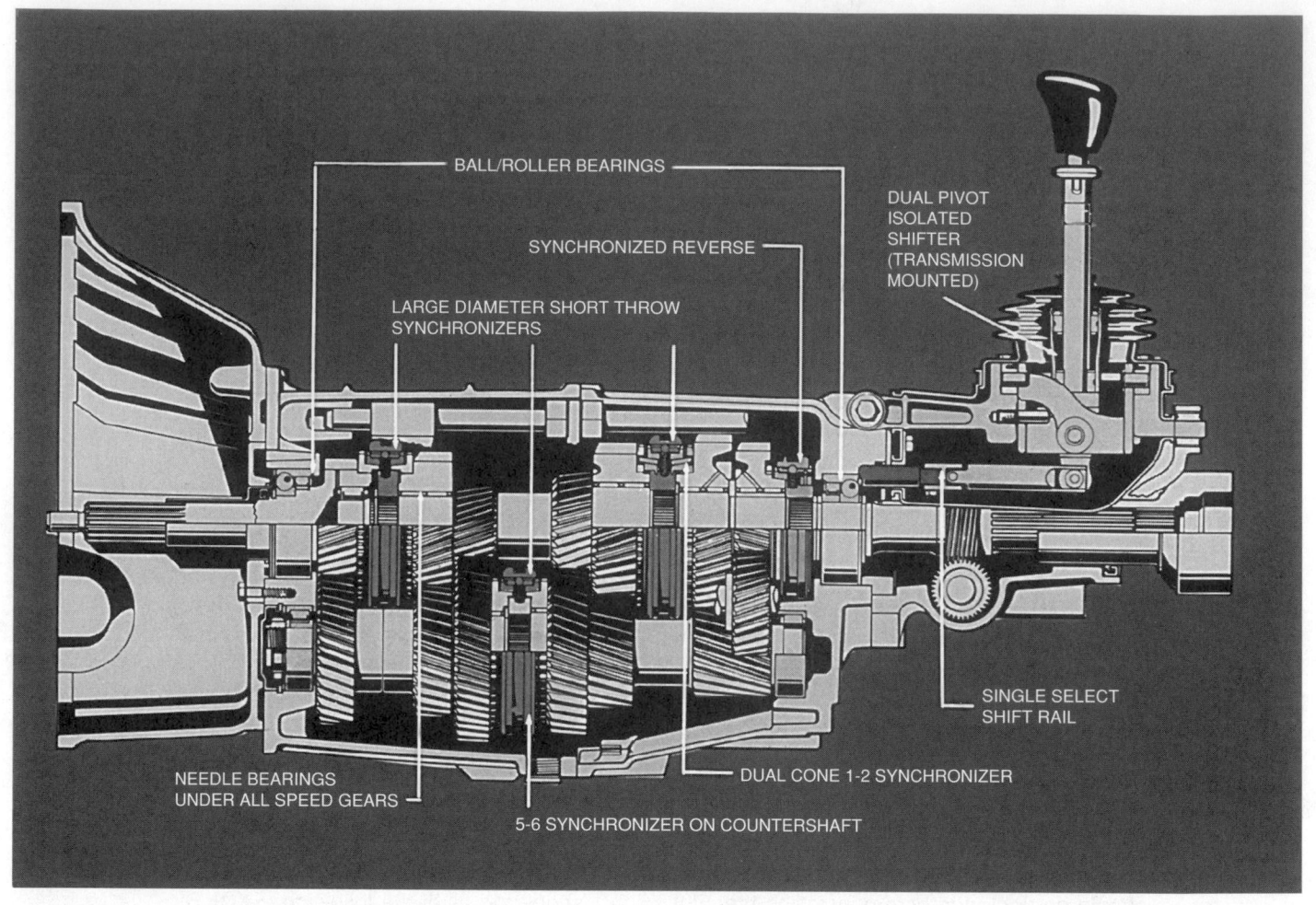

BALL/ROLLER BEARINGS

SYNCHRONIZED REVERSE

LARGE DIAMETER SHORT THROW
SYNCHRONIZERS

DUAL PIVOT
ISOLATED
SHIFTER
(TRANSMISSION
MOUNTED)

SINGLE SELECT
SHIFT RAIL

NEEDLE BEARINGS
UNDER ALL SPEED GEARS

DUAL CONE 1-2 SYNCHRONIZER

5-6 SYNCHRONIZER ON COUNTERSHAFT

Cutaway of a six-speed manual transmission. Study the location of the major components. (Chevrolet)

30

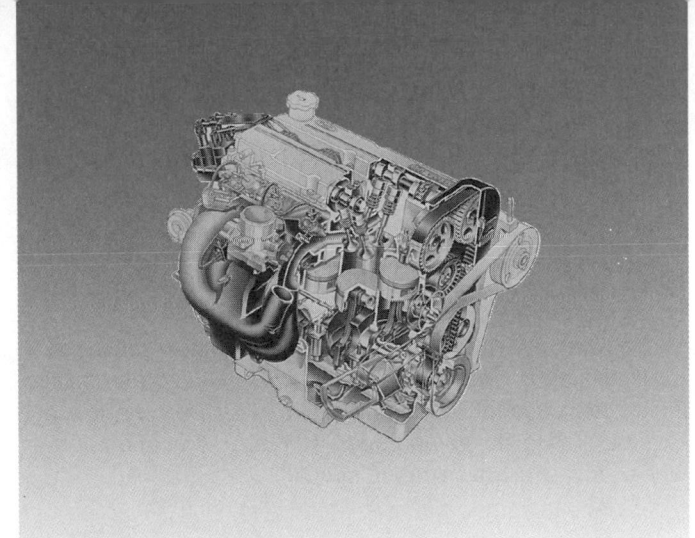

Manual Transmission and Transaxle Service

After studying this chapter, you will be able to:
- Explain manual transmission construction and operation.
- Explain manual transaxle construction and operation.
- Disassemble, check parts, and reassemble a manual transmission.
- Disassemble, check parts, and reassemble a manual transaxle.
- Diagnose manual transmission and transaxle problems.

This chapter will cover the design of manual, or standard, transmissions and transaxles. The manual transmission or transaxle gears are selected by the driver and are always used with a manual clutch.

Transmission and Transaxle Designs

A *transmission* is always used on vehicles with front engines and rear-wheel drive. The parts layout of all manual transmissions is similar. A *transaxle* is used on vehicles with front engines and front-wheel drive. In some cases, transaxles are used on vehicles with rear engines and rear-wheel drive.

The gears in all manual transmissions and transaxles are *sliding gears,* which are moved in and out of engagement by the driver through *shift linkage.* Modern manual transmissions and transaxles usually have *synchronized gears,* with special internal clutches to prevent gear clash when shifting in all forward speeds. The four main classes of transmission/transaxle gears are reduction, direct drive, overdrive, and reverse, **Figure 30-1.** The following sections explain the workings of various manual transmissions and transaxles.

Manual Transmission Types

Manual transmissions in modern rear-wheel drive vehicles can have three, four, five, or six forward speeds. The transmission is installed on the clutch housing. A drive shaft connects the transmission to the rear axle and differential assembly.

The three-speed transmission is being replaced by transmissions with more gears. However, many three-speeds are still being used, especially in older full-size cars

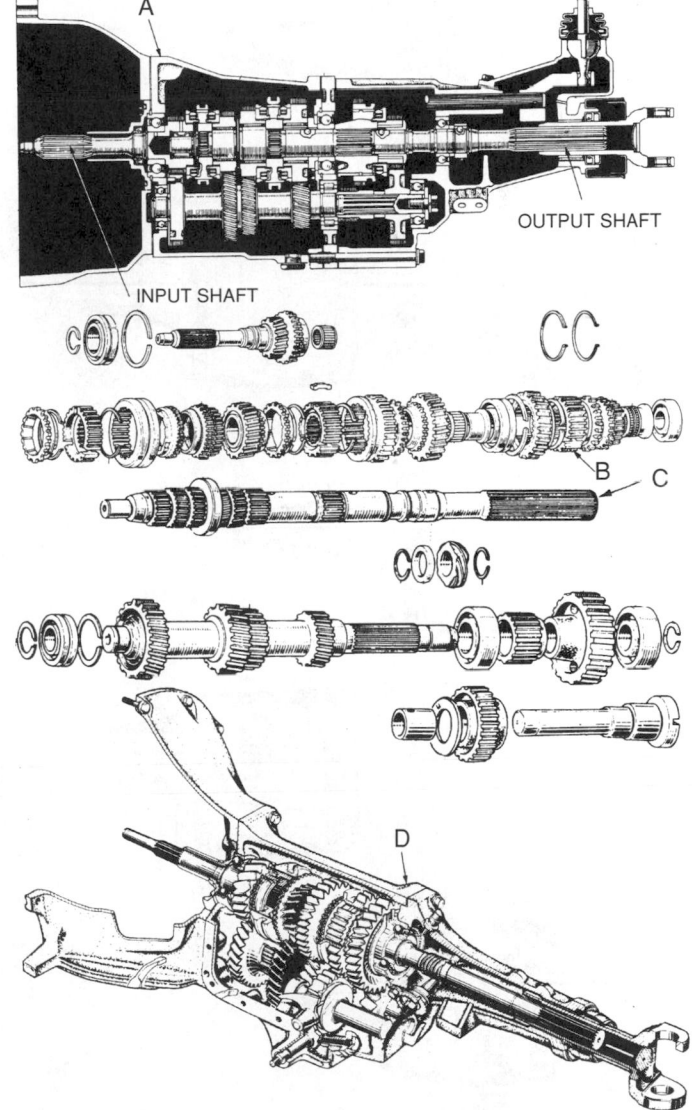

Figure 30-1. Overdrive transmissions. A—Five-speed transmission in which fifth gear is an overdrive gear. The input shaft turns about one-third slower than the output shaft in fifth gear. B—Input shaft, gears, synchronizers, bearing, etc. C—Output shaft and cluster gear and idler assembly. D—Four-speed transmission in which fourth gear is an overdrive gear. Can you identify the overdrive gear in each transmission? (Toyota and Dodge)

and light trucks. The three-speed transmission provides drive ratios of approximately 2.79 to 1 in first gear (input shaft turns 2.79 times to rotate the output shaft once); 1.70 to 1 in second gear, and 1 to 1 in third gear. Gear, or drive, ratios vary, depending on vehicle weight, engine horsepower, and other factors.

Power flow through the gears of a typical three-speed transmission is pictured in **Figure 30-2**. Study the positioning of the second and high synchronizer and the low and reverse sliding sleeve and gear. The operation of other rear-wheel drive transmissions is similar.

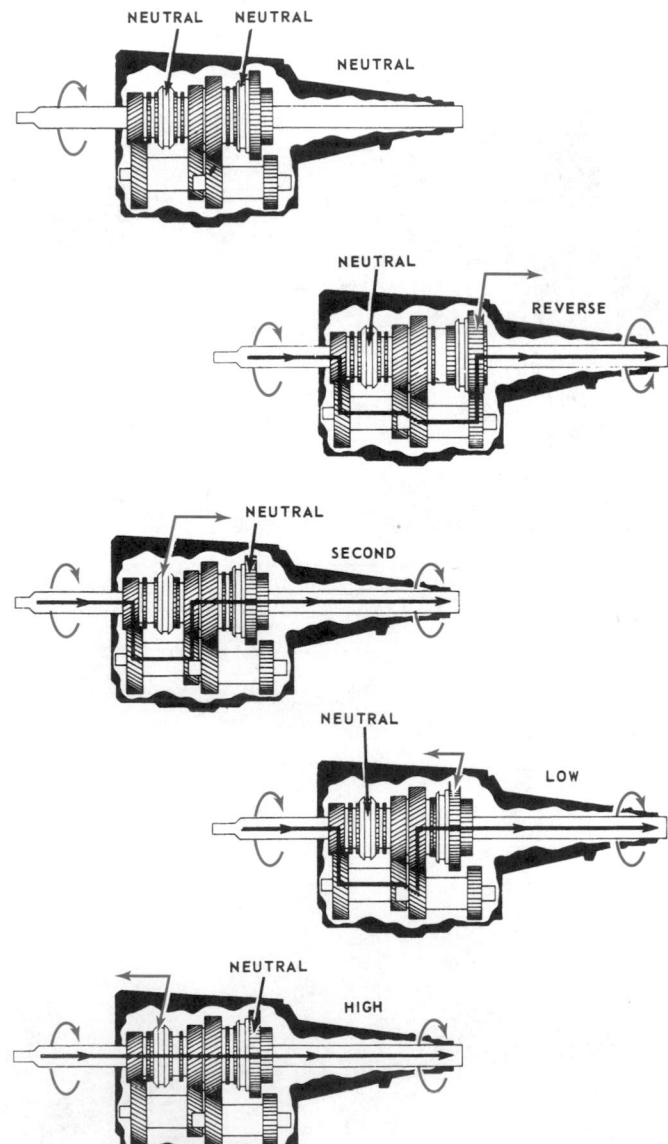

Figure 30-2. Gear drive relationship in various speeds. Note shift movement indicated by the arrows. (Pontiac)

The first gear ratio of four-, five-, and six-speed transmissions is similar to that of the three-speed transmission. The extra gears in these transmission give the driver a wider latitude in selecting an appropriate gear for a given situation.

Typical ratios for a four-speed transmission are around 2.78 to 1 for first gear, 1.93 to 1 for second, 1.36 to 1 for third, and 1 to 1 for fourth, or high, gear. As with a three speed, these ratios vary. Study the working parts in the four-speed transmission shown in **Figure 30-3**. Note that all forward gears are synchronized.

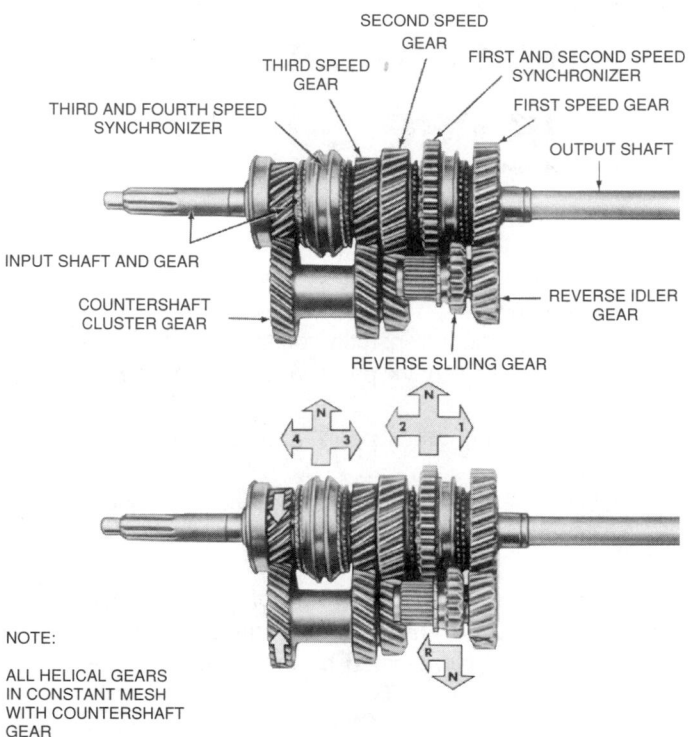

NOTE:

ALL HELICAL GEARS
IN CONSTANT MESH
WITH COUNTERSHAFT
GEAR

Figure 30-3. Working parts of a typical four-speed, synchronized transmission. (Ford)

On many four- and five-speed transmissions, the highest gear (fourth and fifth) is an overdrive gear, such as 1 to 0.7. On some five- and six-speed transmissions, both upper gears are overdrives. Study the transmissions in **Figures 30-4** and **30-5**. These transmissions are diagnosed, serviced, and repaired in the same way as manual transmissions in which the top gear is direct (1 to 1). Refer to the manual transmission section of this chapter for service and repair information. Refer to the diagnosis section for problem solving.

Manual Transaxle Types

On front-wheel drive vehicles, the transmission and differential assemblies are installed in a single housing. This construction is commonly referred to as a transaxle. Transaxles operate in the same way as rear-drive transmissions and rear axle differentials, but all parts are housed together. The manual transaxle has the same kinds of gears, synchronizers, and shifting mechanisms as a manual transmission. The number of forward gear ratios varies from three to five.

The major differences between a transaxle and a transmission are the shape of the case and the placement

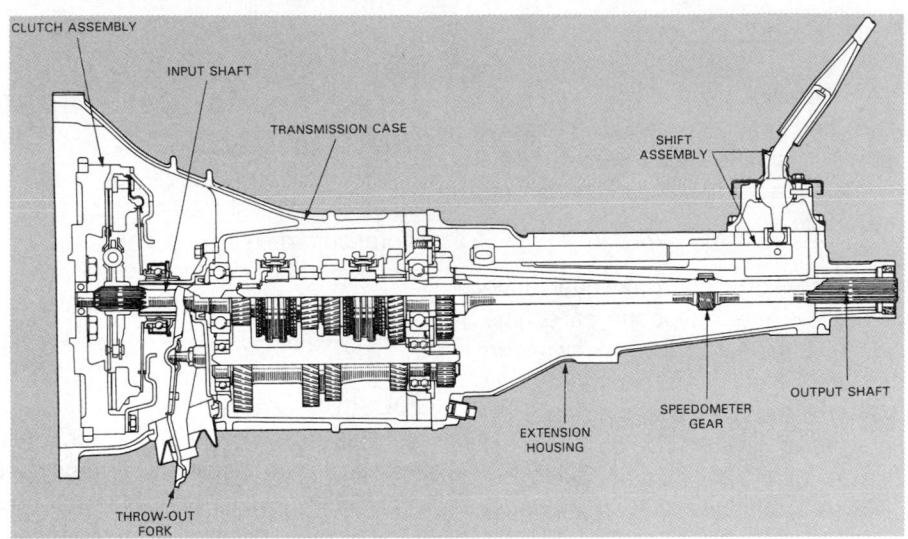

Figure 30-4. Cross-sectional view of a four-speed transmission. (Mazda)

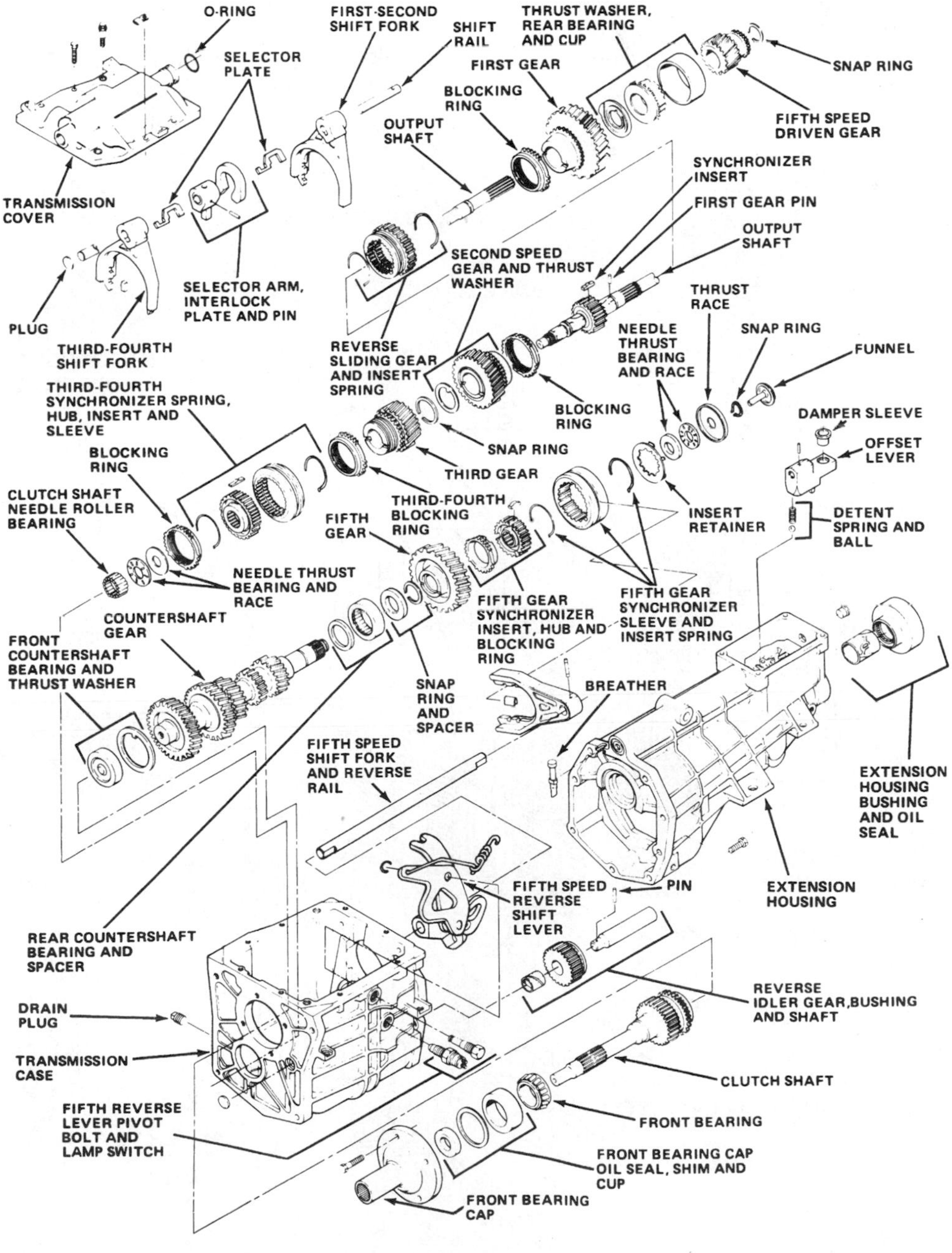

Labels in Figure 30-4:
CLUTCH ASSEMBLY
INPUT SHAFT
TRANSMISSION CASE
SHIFT ASSEMBLY
OUTPUT SHAFT
SPEEDOMETER GEAR
EXTENSION HOUSING
THROW-OUT FORK

Labels in Figure 30-5:
O-RING
SELECTOR PLATE
FIRST-SECOND SHIFT FORK
SHIFT RAIL
THRUST WASHER, REAR BEARING AND CUP
FIRST GEAR
BLOCKING RING
SNAP RING
FIFTH SPEED DRIVEN GEAR
OUTPUT SHAFT
TRANSMISSION COVER
SYNCHRONIZER INSERT
FIRST GEAR PIN
OUTPUT SHAFT
SECOND SPEED GEAR AND THRUST WASHER
THRUST RACE
PLUG
SELECTOR ARM, INTERLOCK PLATE AND PIN
REVERSE SLIDING GEAR AND INSERT SPRING
NEEDLE THRUST BEARING AND RACE
SNAP RING
FUNNEL
THIRD-FOURTH SHIFT FORK
DAMPER SLEEVE
OFFSET LEVER
THIRD-FOURTH SYNCHRONIZER SPRING, HUB, INSERT AND SLEEVE
BLOCKING RING
SNAP RING
THIRD GEAR
BLOCKING RING
INSERT RETAINER
DETENT SPRING AND BALL
BLOCKING RING
CLUTCH SHAFT NEEDLE ROLLER BEARING
FIFTH GEAR
THIRD-FOURTH BLOCKING RING
NEEDLE THRUST BEARING AND RACE
COUNTERSHAFT GEAR
FIFTH GEAR SYNCHRONIZER INSERT, HUB AND BLOCKING RING
FIFTH GEAR SYNCHRONIZER SLEEVE AND INSERT SPRING
FRONT COUNTERSHAFT BEARING AND THRUST WASHER
SNAP RING AND SPACER
BREATHER
EXTENSION HOUSING BUSHING AND OIL SEAL
FIFTH SPEED SHIFT FORK AND REVERSE RAIL
EXTENSION HOUSING
REAR COUNTERSHAFT BEARING AND SPACER
FIFTH SPEED REVERSE SHIFT LEVER
PIN
DRAIN PLUG
REVERSE IDLER GEAR, BUSHING AND SHAFT
TRANSMISSION CASE
CLUTCH SHAFT
FIFTH REVERSE LEVER PIVOT BOLT AND LAMP SWITCH
FRONT BEARING
FRONT BEARING CAP OIL SEAL, SHIM AND CUP
FRONT BEARING CAP

Figure 30-5. Exploded view of a five-speed transmission. This unit uses an aluminum case, extension housing, and cover. Note the various parts and their relationship to each other. (Jeep)

of the parts within the case. Additionally, the transaxle contains the differential gears and may use a drive chain or two gears to transfer power inside of the transaxle. The most obvious external difference is the presence of two axles connecting the transaxle to the front wheels. See **Figure 30-6.**

There are two basic variations of front-wheel drive transaxle construction. The type used depends on engine placement in the vehicle. An engine can face sideways in the vehicle, or it can face forward. An engine that is mounted sideways is called a transverse engine, and an engine that is mounted forward is called a conventional engine. A manual transaxle with a transverse engine is shown in **Figure 30-7.** Power flow takes place in a straight line, without any change in the angle once it leaves the engine.

Figure 30-8 shows the power flow through a transaxle on a vehicle with conventional engine placement. In this design, the output shaft drives the ring and pinion gear in the differential. This ring and pinion gear is a hypoid type, like the ones used on rear wheel drive vehicles. The design of the ring and pinion causes the power to make a 90° turn. This type of transaxle more closely resembles the rear-wheel drive manual transmission.

Servicing Manual Transmissions and Transaxles

Service procedures for the internal components of manual transmissions and transaxles are similar. The major differences are in removing the unit from the vehicle. Always obtain and refer to the correct manufacturer's service manual. The service manual procedures should be followed exactly.

Question Owner

Talk to the owner about observations and complaints regarding transmission or transaxle operation. Ask questions to help pinpoint possible trouble areas. Make a list of possible problems based on the owner's statements. Chapter 41 contains troubleshooting charts for manual transmissions and transaxles.

Check Clutch and Shift Linkage

If the owner complains of hard shifting, gear clash, or jumping out of gear, check the clutch and shift linkage operation and adjustment before road testing.

The clutch pedal free travel must be within specifications. Excessive free travel will prevent full withdrawal of the

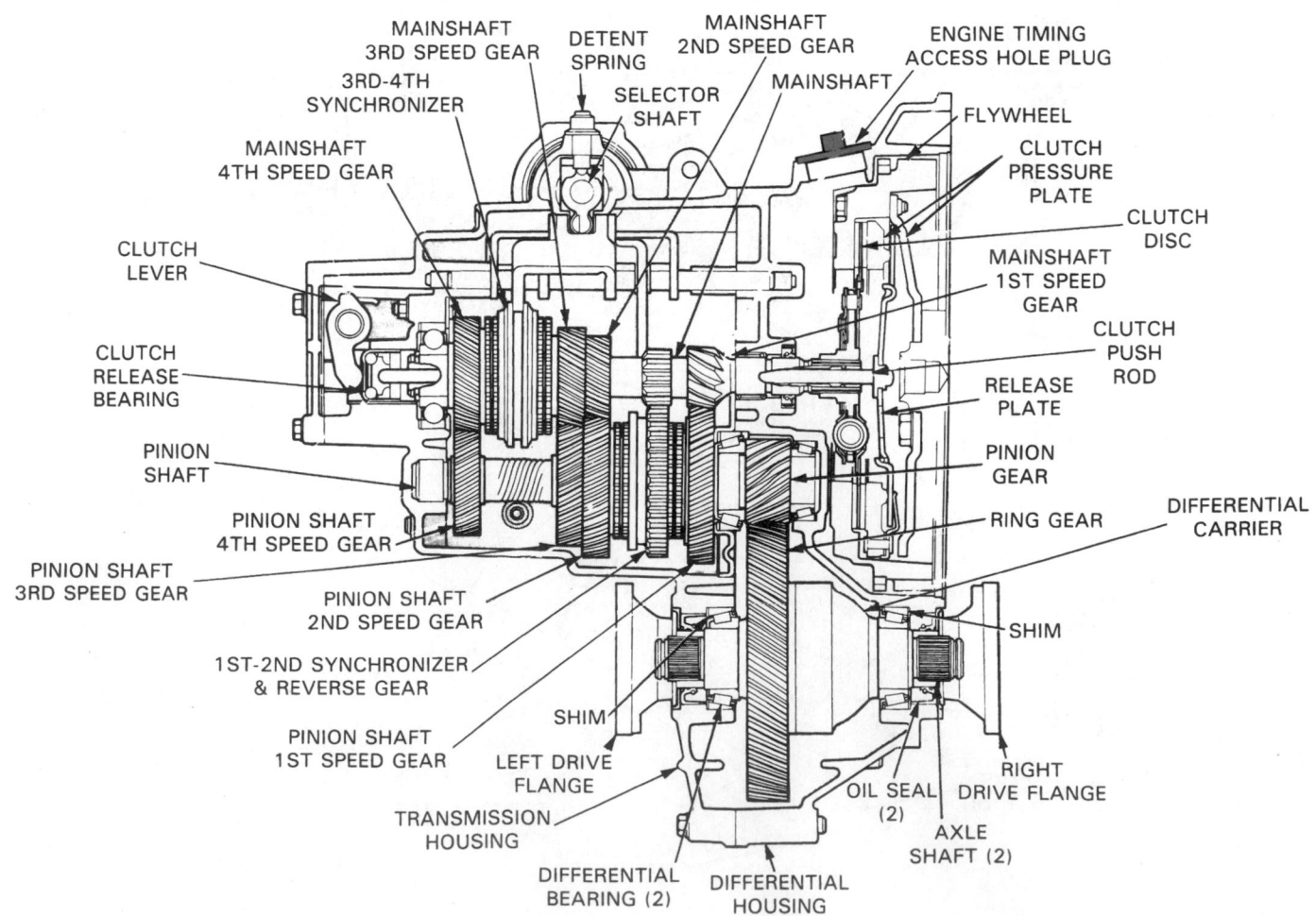

Figure 30-6.   Cross section of a four-speed manual transaxle. Note the timing access hole plug. (Chrysler)

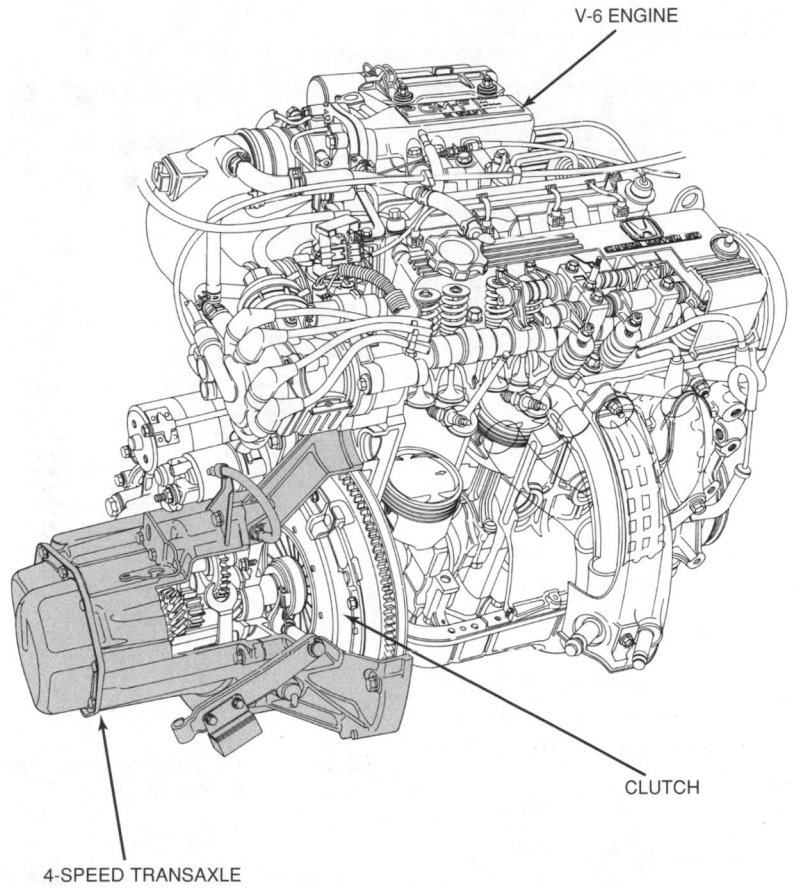

Figure 30-7. Cutaway of a transverse-mounted engine and a four-speed manual transaxle assembly. How many different parts can you correctly identify. (Honda)

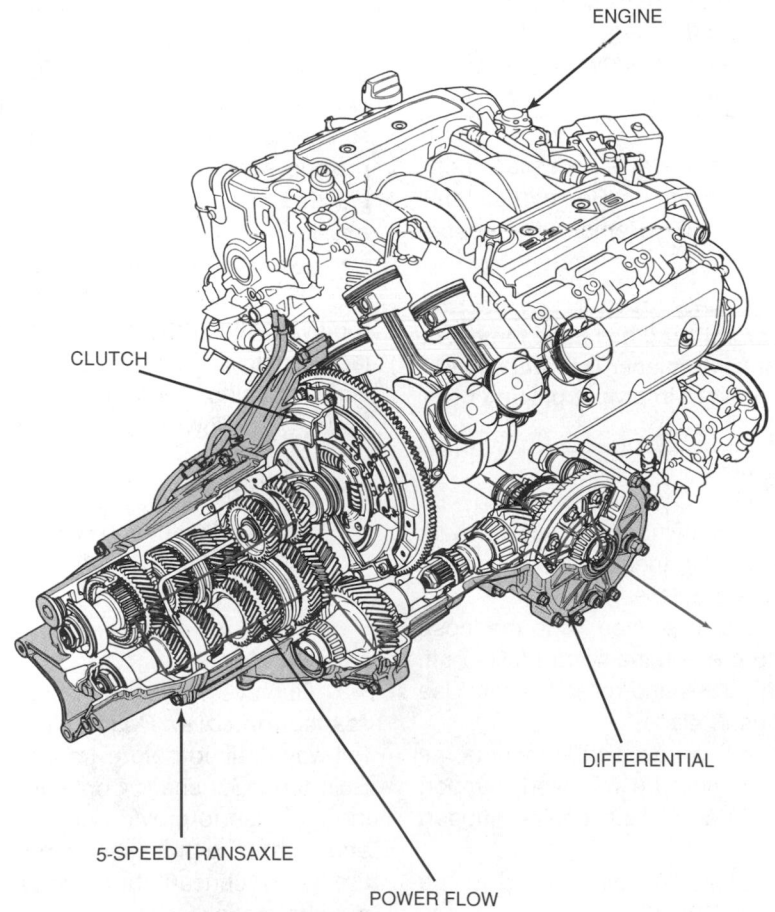

Figure 30-8. Cutaway of a 5-speed transaxle with an inline, V-6 engine. (Honda)

pressure plate from the clutch disc. This will cause the transmission or transaxle input shaft to continue turning, making shifting difficult and noisy. Clutch adjustments were covered in Chapter 29.

The shift linkage must operate smoothly and must be adjusted so the transmission or transaxle is shifted fully into gear. Failure to provide full shift engagement can cause the transmission or transaxle to jump out of gear. Linkage adjustments are covered later in this chapter.

Road Test when Possible

Whenever possible, the vehicle should be road tested. Some discretion must be used. Check the transmission or transaxle lubricant level before road testing. If a road test is performed, it should include some heavy acceleration and deceleration. Operate the vehicle at various speeds. When possible, the route should include some bumpy sections and a hill.

Check closely for abnormal noise, jumping out of gear, vibration, hard shifting, gear clash during shifting, and leaks. Note the gear (reduction, direct drive, overdrive) in which any problem was most evident.

Transmission or Transaxle Removal

 Note: Before removing the transmission, make sure that removal is necessary. Some transmission or transaxle repairs can be performed with the transmission or transaxle in the vehicle. A few of these include shift linkage adjustment, shift cover overhaul, cover gasket replacement, and output shaft oil seal replacement.

If transmission or transaxle removal is necessary, raise the vehicle and drain the transmission oil. Remove the shift linkage (mark to facilitate assembly). Remove the speedometer cable.

 Note: Once a cable or shift rod has been removed, put the fasteners back into place. This will speed up reassembly and prevent improper placing of fasteners.

Disconnect the drive shaft or CV drive axles and wire them out of the way. Before removing the shaft(s), mark them so they can be reassembled in their original positions. See the Chapter 33 for complete details.

If the U-joint is a cross-and-roller type, tape the loose roller bearings to the cross to prevent them from falling off. **Figure 30-9** shows a typical cross-and-roller U-joint. Use tape to hold the roller bearings in place.

Remove the transmission or transaxle mounts as needed. If a support member must be removed, support the engine with either a jack stand or an engine support strap.

If the engine must be raised to gain access to the transmission mounts, be careful to avoid damage to any

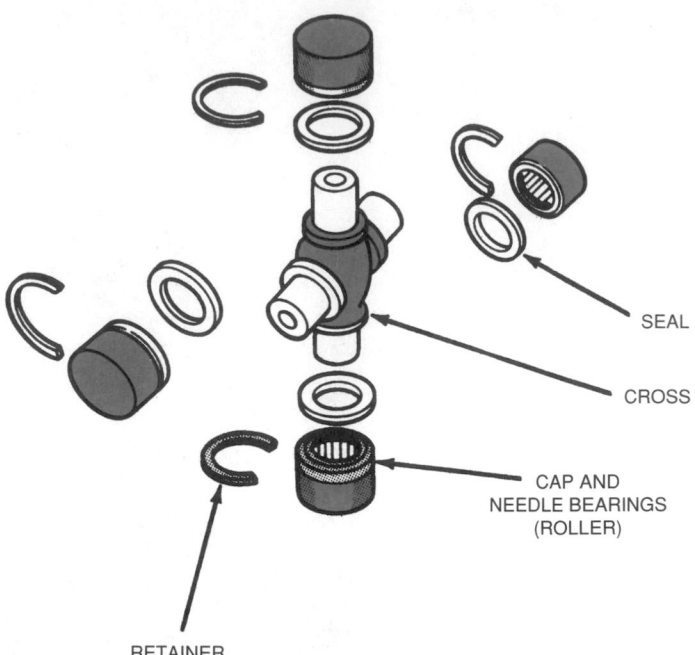

Figure 30-9. Exploded view of a typical cross-and-roller universal joint. (Chrysler)

attached parts. If pushing upward on the oil pan, place a wide block of wood between the pan and the jack.

Use a Transmission Jack or Pilot Bolts

If the transmission or transaxle is of a size that can be easily handled, remove either the two upper or two lower transmission-to-clutch-housing fasteners. Install *pilot bolts* (which can be made by cutting the heads from two correct size bolts) in their places. Pilots should be long enough to provide support until the input shaft is clear of the clutch disc hub. Remove the remaining fasteners. Slide the transmission (or transaxle) away from the clutch housing. When free, lower the transmission to the floor.

If desired, a *transmission jack* can be used for removal. Attach the transmission or transaxle firmly to the jack. Remove the fasteners holding the transmission to the clutch housing. Then, guide the transmission away from the housing and lower it to the floor.

Clean Exterior

Before beginning disassembly, clean the outer surfaces of the transmission or transaxle thoroughly. This will permit disassembly with a minimum amount of contamination.

Flush Interior

Remove the transmission or transaxle *shift plate* or *inspection cover.* Pour a pint of clean solvent into the case (oil was drained before transmission or transaxle removal). Spin the input shaft. Continue turning the shaft while rocking the case to provide additional agitation. Drain the case and repeat the process. This flushing will remove enough of the heavy lubricant that a visual inspection of the gear teeth may be made.

Inspect Gears, Shafts, Synchronizers, and Other Parts

Before disassembling the transmission or transaxle, remove the top or side covers, if used. Turn the gears over slowly while carefully inspecting the teeth for chipping, galling, and excessive wear. Rock the gears on the shaft to determine approximate clearance. Check end play of the cluster gear, reverse idler gear, and input and output shafts. Inspect the synchronizer units for excessive looseness. Check the condition of the teeth engaged by the synchronizer clutch sleeve.

 Note: This step is not possible on transmissions or transaxles without top or side covers. In these cases, the transmission/transaxle must be entirely or partly disassembled to check internal parts.

This initial inspection will help to indicate the location and extent of the problem. Refer to **Figure 30-10.**

Disassembly Procedure Varies

Although basic transmission or transaxle designs are similar, disassembly procedures vary widely among the different makes and models.

Some transmissions require that the extension housing and output shaft be removed first. Some permit the removal of the input shaft first, while others require that the cluster shaft be lowered to the bottom of the case for removal of the output shaft and gears. Some transmissions are designed with two aluminum end castings that are attached to a central support. The end castings must be removed to gain access to the gears and shafts.

Some transaxles require the removal of the differential assembly before beginning repairs. Other transaxles must be split to expose the internal gears. On other designs, both CV axle housings must be removed before repairs can be made. Where one design may require input shaft removal by passing the shaft into the case and out the cover hole, another may permit the shaft to be pulled directly from the case. In all cases, the differential assembly must be removed, either as part of the transaxle (transverse engines), or as a separate unit (conventionally placed engines).

Due to space limitations, it is obvious that the disassembly procedure for all transmissions or transaxles cannot be covered in this text. Therefore, one typical method of removal and installation will be shown. Instead of dwelling on a specific disassembly procedure, the transmission or transaxle parts will be covered separately. General inspection techniques will also be discussed.

Use Manufacturer's Service Manual

The technician should obtain a service manual covering the specific transmission or transaxle to be overhauled. Disassembly and assembly order and technique will be shown. Exploded views will assist in the correct positioning of all parts, and specifications will be given.

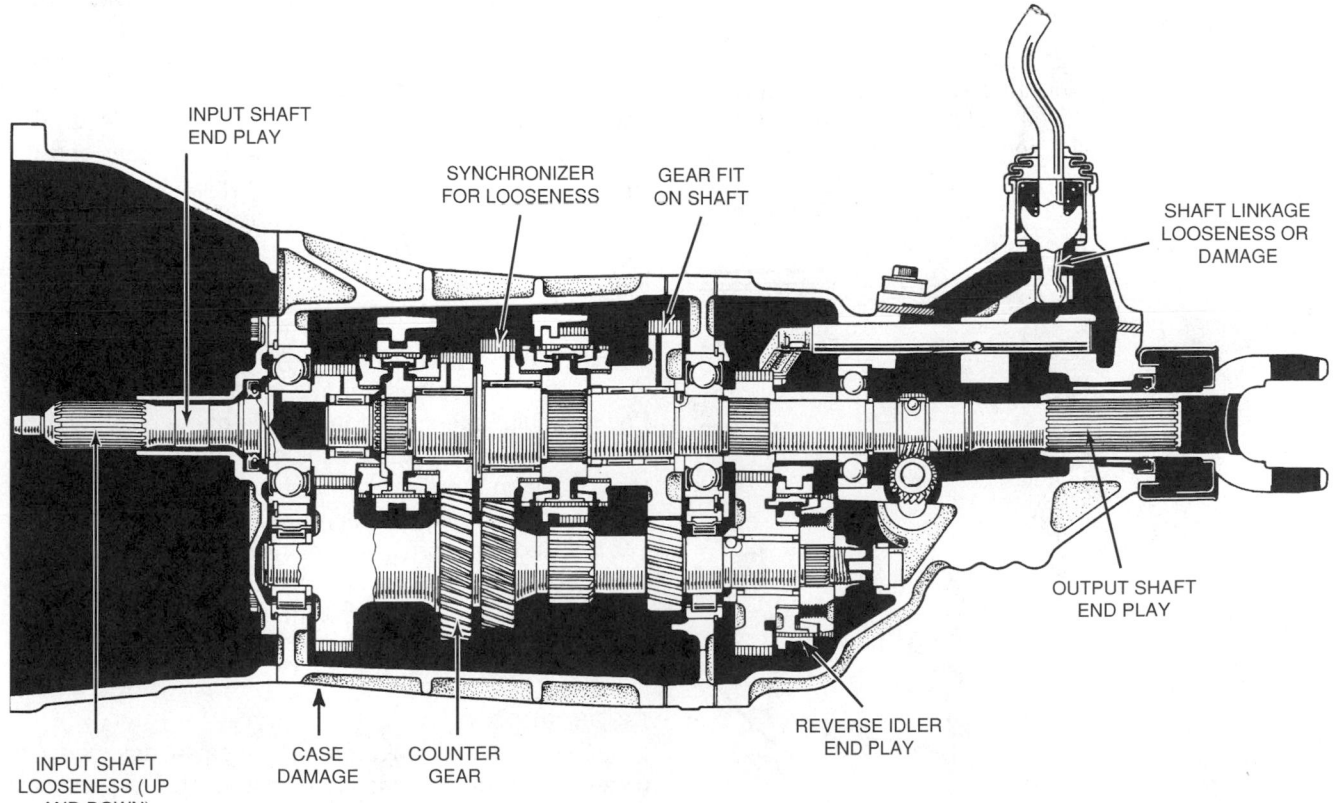

Figure 30-10. Inspect gears, shafts, synchronizers, bearings, and other parts before disassembling the transmission or transaxle. (Toyota)

General Disassembly Procedures

Place the transmission or transaxle in a suitable stand, **Figure 30-11.** Follow the manufacturer's recommended order of part removal. If no manual is available, study the method of construction. This will provide clues as to which part should be removed first, second, etc. Careful study will also usually indicate how the parts must be removed. Be sure to place *alignment marks* on the transmission or transaxle housing and any extension or CV axle housings before beginning disassembly. See **Figure 30-12.**

If used, the input shaft bearing retainer may be removed. On a rear-drive transmission, remove the exten-

sion housing fasteners and pull the housing. This will usually allow either the output shaft or the input shaft to be pulled far enough to determine the exact removal procedure.

On some transmissions and transaxles, lowering the cluster gear to the bottom of the case is required to permit shaft removal. Proceed with the disassembly, being careful to avoid excessive hammering. Where a hammer is required, use a lead, plastic, brass, or rawhide hammer. A drift punch, when used, should be brass or soft steel.

 Note: Use care to avoid distorting snap rings in case they must be reused. Always use new snap rings during assembly when possible.

Remove each synchronizer unit as one part. Be certain to keep the cones or blocking rings with the unit and on the same side as originally installed. Be careful not to lose any roller or needle bearings used in the transmission or transaxle.

In some transmissions and transaxles, the shift rails operate in the case rather than in a separate shift cover. See **Figure 30-13.** This design generally necessitates shift fork and rail removal. Be careful to avoid losing any of the detent springs, detents, interlocks, or setscrews. The cluster gear will usually contain a number of needle bearings. Do not lose them.

 Caution: Avoid excessive pounding to loosen parts. Handle parts carefully to avoid chipping and nicking. Place all the small parts (loose needles and rollers, detent springs, and detent plugs or balls) in a separate container to prevent loss.

Remove all the parts from the case, including the input and output shaft bearings. Drive the reverse idler shaft free of the case and remove the reverse idler gear and thrust washers. **Figure 30-14** illustrates a typical four-speed transmission. **Figure 30-15** illustrates a typical transaxle. It is completely disassembled. Study the part names, positioning, and relationships.

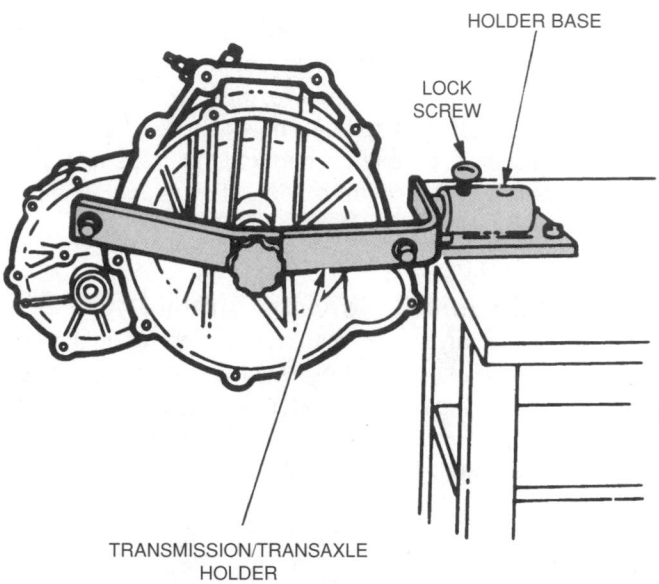

Figure 30-11. A transmission/transaxle holding fixture makes service faster and easier. The holder base allows the holder to be rotated and locked in many convenient working locations. (Chevrolet)

Clean All Parts Thoroughly

Clean all gears, bearings, and shafts until spotless. Pay particular attention to the inside of the case and extension housing. Any tiny particles of chipped teeth or bearing that remain in a crevice or hard to reach spot will be loosened by the new lubricant and will eventually find their way into the moving parts, where they will cause accelerated wear or even broken gear teeth. The quality of automotive repair is closely related to the thoroughness of cleaning—be meticulous in all cleaning.

Inspecting Parts

Once the transmission or transaxle has been completely disassembled and cleaned, the internal parts can be inspected. In the following sections, internal parts are grouped by major assemblies below. Keep in mind that many minor variations are possible.

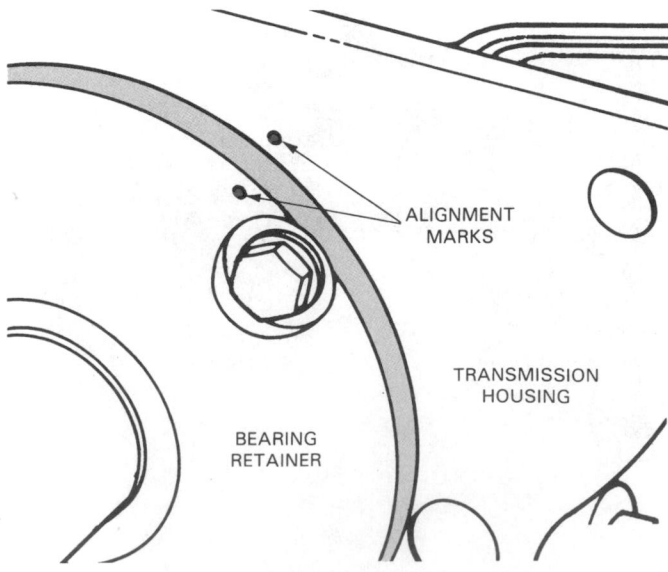

Figure 30-12. Bearing retainer-to-transmission case alignment marks. (Chevrolet)

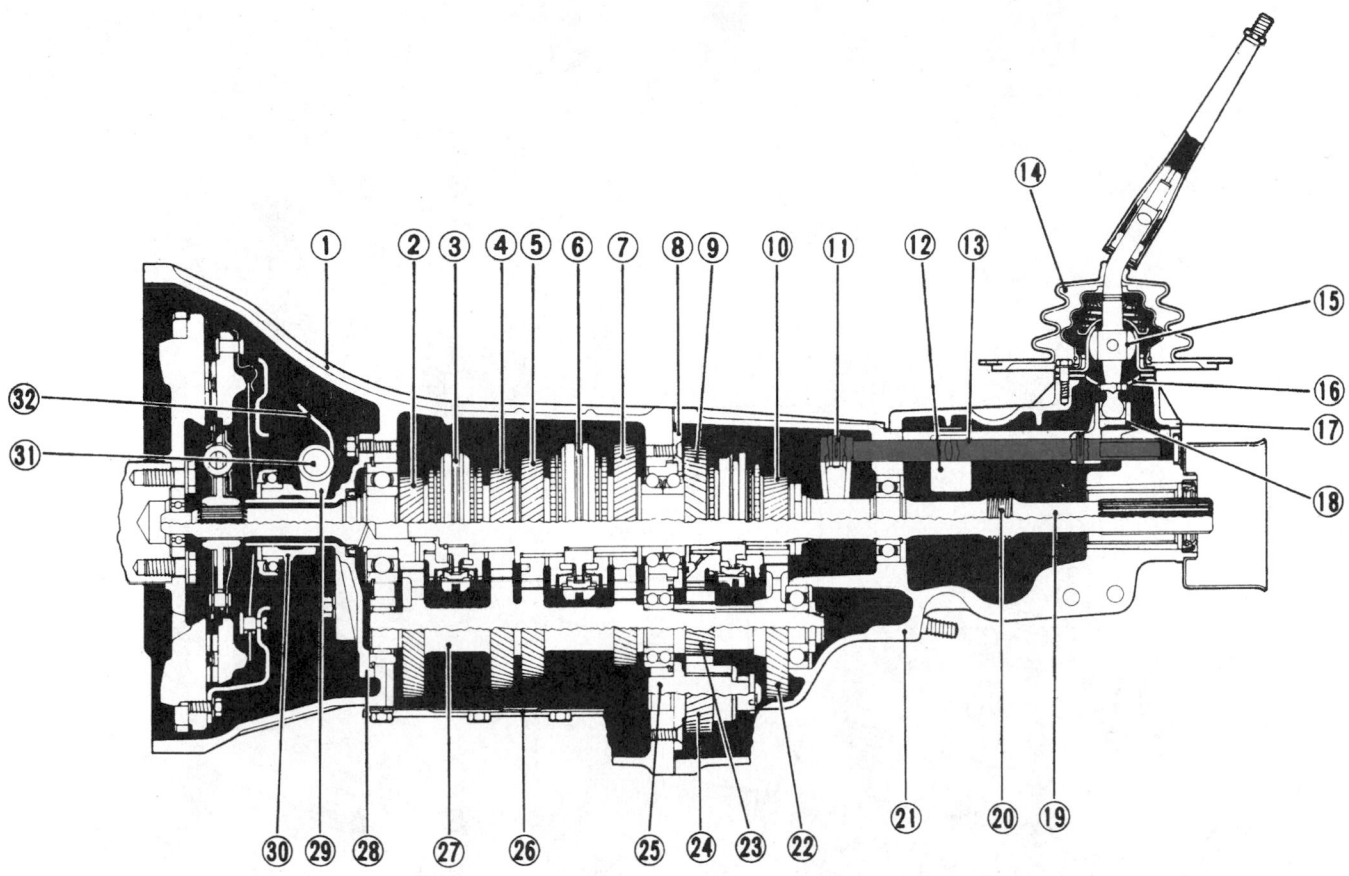

Figure 30-13. A shift rail that operates in the case. 1—Transmission case. 2—Main drive pinion. 3—3-4 synchronizer. 4—Third gear. 5—Second gear. 6—1-2 synchronizer. 7—First gear. 8—Bearing retainer. 9—Overdrive synchronizer assembly. 10—Overdrive gear. 11—Control finger. 12—Neutral return finger. 13—Control shaft. 14—Control lever cover. 15—Control lever assembly. 16—Stopper plate. 17—Control housing. 18—Change shifter. 19—Mainshaft. 20—Speedometer. 21—Extension housing. 22—Counter overdrive gear. 23—Counter reverse gear. 24—Reverse idler gear. 25—Reverse idler gear shaft. 26—Under cover. 27—Counter gear. 28—Front bearing retainer. 29—Clutch shift arm. 30—Release bearing carrier. 31—Clutch control shaft. 32—Return spring. (Chrysler)

Inspecting Input Shaft

The *input shaft* connects the other internal transmission parts to the clutch. Check the clutch pilot bearing end for wear and scoring. Examine the shaft splines where they contact the clutch disc splines. They must be smooth and free of excessive wear. Inspect the drive gear for wear, galling, pitting, and chipping. The drive gear synchronizer clutch teeth must be free of wear. Check the clutch teeth closely for tapering. The end of each clutch tooth is normally chamfered for easy engagement with the clutch sleeve. The remaining portion of the tooth body, however, must not be tapered. Taper or excessive wear can cause the transmission to jump out of gear.

Rotate each roller bearing while watching for signs of chipping or flaking. Check the condition of the roller bearing contact surface in the end of the shaft. The blocking ring (shift cone) contact surface must be true and smooth.

Examine the input shaft bearing for wear or other damage. The bearing contact surface on the shaft must be of full diameter with no sign of wear caused by the inner race turning on the shaft. **Figure 30-16** shows the various areas and parts of the input shaft that require inspection.

Replace Input Shaft Bearing Retainer Oil Seal

Always replace the bearing retainer oil seal, **Figure 30-17.** Wipe a coat of sealer around the outside of the new seal and drive it into place. Make sure the seal is driven squarely, to the proper depth, and with the seal lip facing the transmission or transaxle.

Inspect Extension Housing or CV Axle Housing

Check the bushings in the *extension housing* or *CV axle housings* (where the CV axles enter the transaxle) and replace them if necessary. Always replace the housing rear oil seal, **Figure 30-18.** Clean the housing and drive in a new bushing if required. Coat the outer edge of the new oil seal with sealer. With the seal lip facing inward, drive the seal squarely into the housing. Make sure the seal is driven to the proper depth. Refer to **Figure 30-19.**

Inspect Output Shaft and Gears

Inspect the *output shaft* bearing surfaces. They should be perfectly smooth with no evidence of galling. Try the gears on the shaft. They should turn smoothly without excessive rocking. Where gears are splined, check for excessive play.

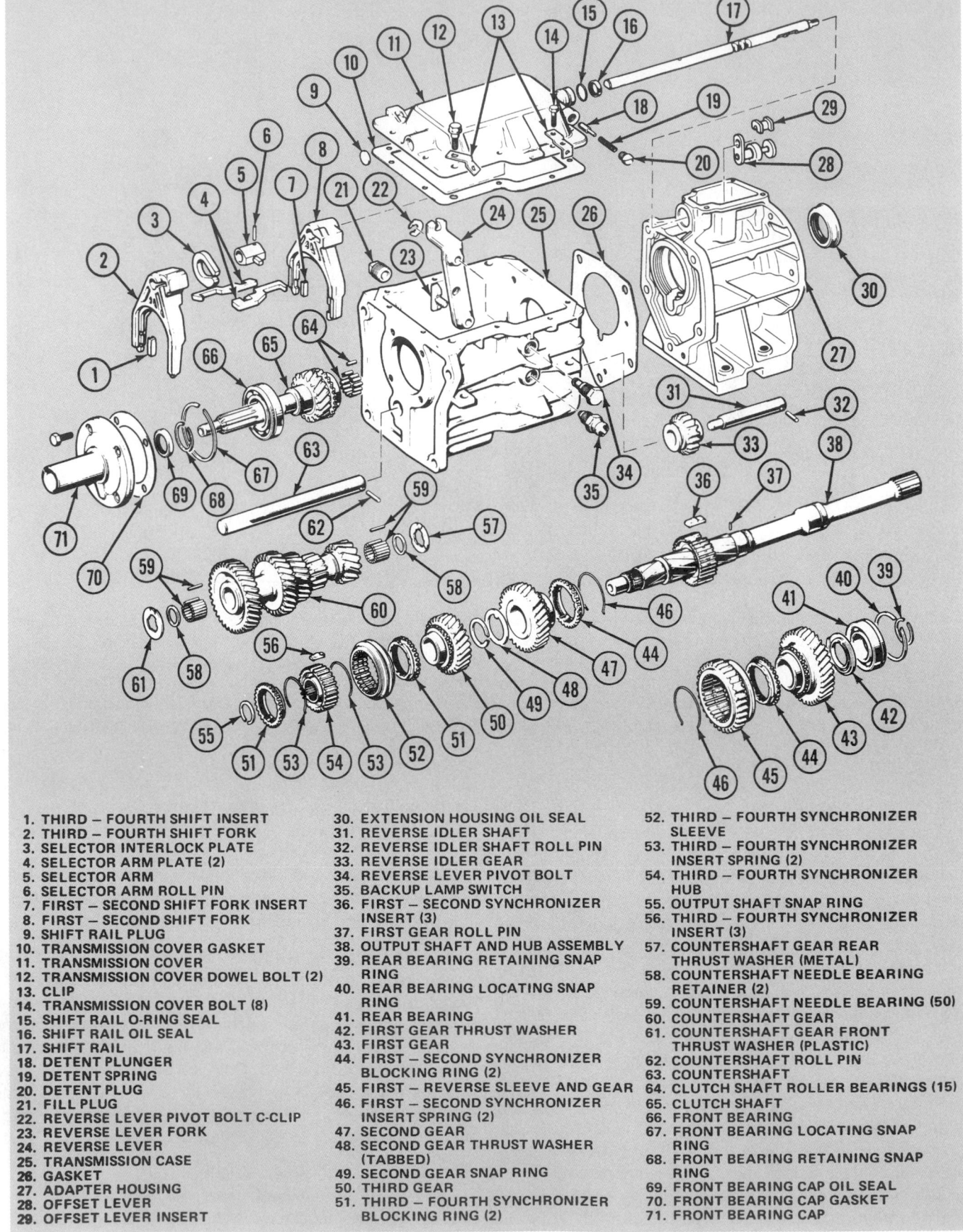

1. THIRD – FOURTH SHIFT INSERT
2. THIRD – FOURTH SHIFT FORK
3. SELECTOR INTERLOCK PLATE
4. SELECTOR ARM PLATE (2)
5. SELECTOR ARM
6. SELECTOR ARM ROLL PIN
7. FIRST – SECOND SHIFT FORK INSERT
8. FIRST – SECOND SHIFT FORK
9. SHIFT RAIL PLUG
10. TRANSMISSION COVER GASKET
11. TRANSMISSION COVER
12. TRANSMISSION COVER DOWEL BOLT (2)
13. CLIP
14. TRANSMISSION COVER BOLT (8)
15. SHIFT RAIL O-RING SEAL
16. SHIFT RAIL OIL SEAL
17. SHIFT RAIL
18. DETENT PLUNGER
19. DETENT SPRING
20. DETENT PLUG
21. FILL PLUG
22. REVERSE LEVER PIVOT BOLT C-CLIP
23. REVERSE LEVER FORK
24. REVERSE LEVER
25. TRANSMISSION CASE
26. GASKET
27. ADAPTER HOUSING
28. OFFSET LEVER
29. OFFSET LEVER INSERT

30. EXTENSION HOUSING OIL SEAL
31. REVERSE IDLER SHAFT
32. REVERSE IDLER SHAFT ROLL PIN
33. REVERSE IDLER GEAR
34. REVERSE LEVER PIVOT BOLT
35. BACKUP LAMP SWITCH
36. FIRST – SECOND SYNCHRONIZER INSERT (3)
37. FIRST GEAR ROLL PIN
38. OUTPUT SHAFT AND HUB ASSEMBLY
39. REAR BEARING RETAINING SNAP RING
40. REAR BEARING LOCATING SNAP RING
41. REAR BEARING
42. FIRST GEAR THRUST WASHER
43. FIRST GEAR
44. FIRST – SECOND SYNCHRONIZER BLOCKING RING (2)
45. FIRST – REVERSE SLEEVE AND GEAR
46. FIRST – SECOND SYNCHRONIZER INSERT SPRING (2)
47. SECOND GEAR
48. SECOND GEAR THRUST WASHER (TABBED)
49. SECOND GEAR SNAP RING
50. THIRD GEAR
51. THIRD – FOURTH SYNCHRONIZER BLOCKING RING (2)

52. THIRD – FOURTH SYNCHRONIZER SLEEVE
53. THIRD – FOURTH SYNCHRONIZER INSERT SPRING (2)
54. THIRD – FOURTH SYNCHRONIZER HUB
55. OUTPUT SHAFT SNAP RING
56. THIRD – FOURTH SYNCHRONIZER INSERT (3)
57. COUNTERSHAFT GEAR REAR THRUST WASHER (METAL)
58. COUNTERSHAFT NEEDLE BEARING RETAINER (2)
59. COUNTERSHAFT NEEDLE BEARING (50)
60. COUNTERSHAFT GEAR
61. COUNTERSHAFT GEAR FRONT THRUST WASHER (PLASTIC)
62. COUNTERSHAFT ROLL PIN
63. COUNTERSHAFT
64. CLUTCH SHAFT ROLLER BEARINGS (15)
65. CLUTCH SHAFT
66. FRONT BEARING
67. FRONT BEARING LOCATING SNAP RING
68. FRONT BEARING RETAINING SNAP RING
69. FRONT BEARING CAP OIL SEAL
70. FRONT BEARING CAP GASKET
71. FRONT BEARING CAP

Figure 30-14.   An exploded view of a four-speed transmission. Study the parts carefully. (Jeep)

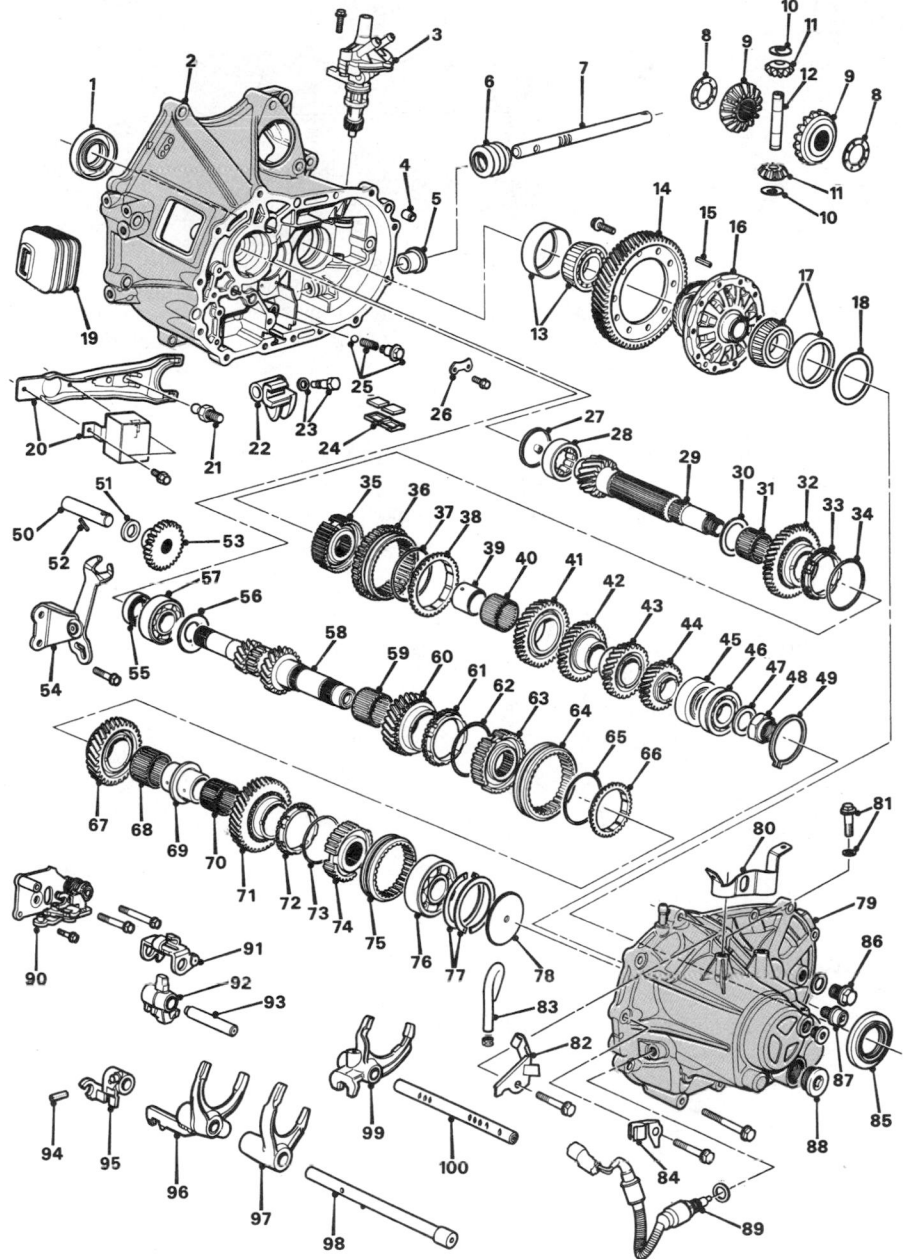

35. SYNCHRO HUB—1ST/2ND GEAR
36. SYNCHRO SLEEVE—1ST/2ND GEAR
37. SYNCHRO SPRING
38. SYNCHRO RING—2ND GEAR
39. SELECTIVE COLLAR—2ND GEAR END FLOAT
40. NEEDLE ROLLER BEARING—2ND GEAR
41. 2ND GEAR
42. 3RD GEAR
43. 4TH GEAR
44. 5TH GEAR
45. ROLLER BEARING—COUNTERSHAFT
46. BALL BEARING—COUNTERSHAFT
47. WASHER
48. COUNTERSHAFT NUT—L.H. THREAD
49. SNAP RING
50. REVERSE IDLER SHAFT
51. THRUST WASHER—REVERSE IDLER SHAFT
52. ROLLER PIN—REVERSE IDLER SHAFT
53. REVERSE IDLER GEAR
54. REVERSE FORK
55. OIL SEAL—MAINSHAFT
56. BELVILLE WASHER—MAINSHAFT END THRUST
57. BALL BEARING—MAINSHAFT
58. MAINSHAFT
59. NEEDLE ROLLER BEARING—3RD GEAR
60. 3RD GEAR
61. SYNCHRO RING—3RD GEAR
62. SYNCHRO SPRING
63. SYNCHRO HUB 3RD/4TH GEARS
64. SYNCHRO SLEEVE 3RD/4TH GEARS
65. SYNCHRO SPRING
66. SYNCHRO RING—4TH GEAR
67. 4TH GEAR
68. NEEDLE BEARING—4TH GEAR
69. DISTANCE COLLAR—4TH/5TH GEARS
70. NEEDLE BEARING—5TH GEAR
71. 5TH GEAR
72. SYNCHRO RING
73. SYNCHRO SPRING
74. SYNCHRO HUB—5TH GEAR
75. SYNCHRO SLEEVE—5TH GEAR
76. BALL BEARING—MAINSHAFT
77. SELECTIVE SNAP RINGS—MAINSHAFT END
    THRUST
78. OIL GUIDE PLATE
79. TRANSMISSION CASING
80. LIFTING EYE
81. REVERSE IDLER SHAFT BOLT AND WASHER
82. BREATHER PIPE
83. BREATHER PIPE BRACKET
84. REVERSE LIGHT SWITCH HARNESS BRACKET
85. OIL SEAL—DIFFERENTIAL
86. FILLER/LEVEL PLUG
87. DRAIN PLUG
88. ACESS PLUG—COUNTERSHAFT BEARING
    SNAP RING
89. REAR LIGHT SWITCH
90. SHIFT ARM ASSEMBLY
91. INTERLOCK
92. SHIFT ARM GUIDE
93. SHIFT SHAFT
94. ROLL PIN—5TH/REVERSE GEAR SELECTOR
95. GEAR SELECTOR—5TH/REVERSE GEARS
96. SELECTOR FORK—3RD/4TH GEARS
97. SELECTOR FORK—5TH GEAR
98. SELECTOR SHAFT—5TH/REVERSE GEARS
99. SELECTOR FORK—1ST/2ND GEARS
100. SELECTOR SHAFT—1ST/2ND GEARS

1. OIL SEAL—DIFFERENTIAL
2. DIFFERENTIAL HOUSING
3. SPEED SENSOR—INSTRUMENTS AND
   POWER STEERING
4. DOWEL
5. OIL SEAT—SELECTOR ROD
6. BOOT
7. SELECTOR ROD
8. THRUST WASHER—SUN GEAR
9. SUN GEAR
10. THRUST WASHER—PLANET PINION
11. PLANET PINION
12. PINION SHAFT
13. TAPER ROLLER BEARING—DIFFERENTIAL
14. FINAL DRIVE GEAR
15. ROLL PIN—DIFFERENTIAL PINION SHAFT
16. DIFFERENTIAL CASING
17. TAPER ROLLER BEARING—DIFFERENTIAL
18. SELECTIVE SHIM—DIFFERENTIAL PRE-LOAD

19. BOOT
20. CLUTCH THROWOUT ARM AND DAMPER
21. PIVOT—CLUTCH THROWOUT ARM
22. SELECTOR ROD GUIDE
23. DOWEL BOLT AND WASHER
24. MAGNET
25. DETENT CAP BOLT, BALL AND SPRING—
    SELECTOR ROD
26. RETAINER PLATE—COUNTERSHAFT BEARING
27. OIL GUIDE PLATE
28. PARALLEL ROLLER BEARING—
    COUNTERSHAFT
29. COUNTERSHAFT
30. SELECTIVE THRUST WASHER—1ST GEAR
    END CLEARANCE
31. NEEDLE ROLLER BEARING—1ST GEAR
32. 1ST GEAR
33. SYNCHRO RING—1ST GEAR
34. SYNCHRO SPRING

Figure 30-15.   A disassembled view of a five-speed manual transaxle assembly. (Sterling Motor Cars)

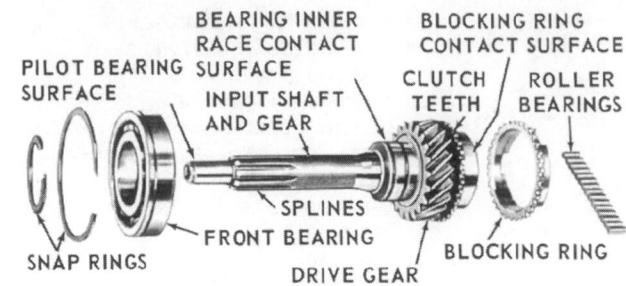

Figure 30-16. Check these areas and parts of the input shaft assembly. (Ford)

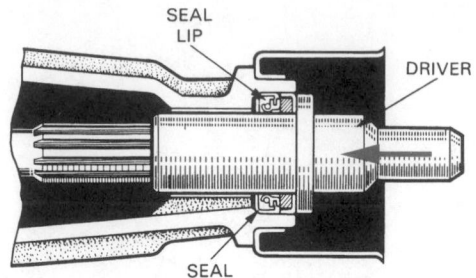

Figure 30-19. Installing a new oil seal into the extension housing. Note that the seal lip is facing inward (toward transmission). (Toyota)

Look over every tooth on every gear. There must be no signs of chipping, galling, or wear. If the gear has a blocking ring surface, it must be smooth. Look at **Figure 30-20.** Check the inboard pilot bearing surface of the shaft. This, too, must be perfectly smooth.

All snap ring grooves must have sharp, square shoulders. Thrust washers must be smooth. Thickness must meet specifications. Inspect the output shaft rear bearing.

The outboard splines should be in good condition. Synchronizer inspection will be covered later in this chapter. A typical output shaft assembly is shown in **Figure 30-21.**

Check the shafts (input and/or output) for runout with a dial indicator. The shaft assembly should be supported on each end with V-blocks. The dial indicator is placed against the shaft at a specified point. The dial is set to zero. The

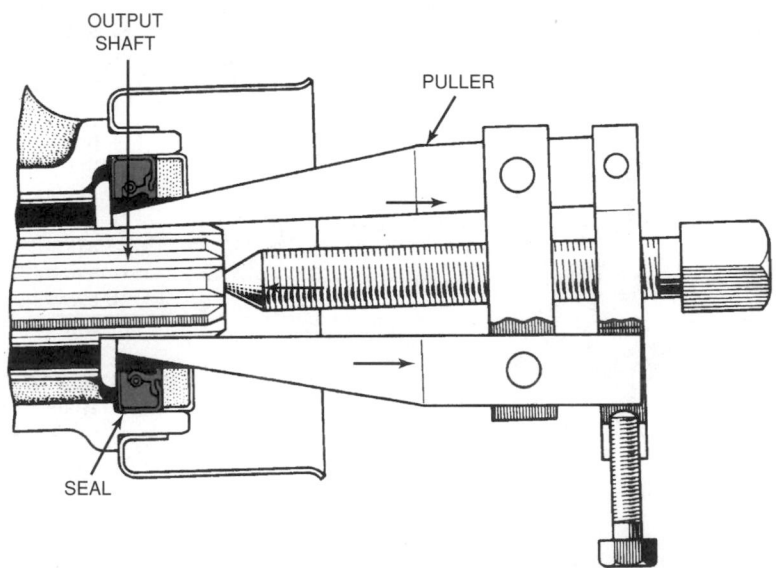

Figure 30-17. Removing a seal with a special two-leg puller. Be careful not to damage the seal bore or output shaft. (Toyota)

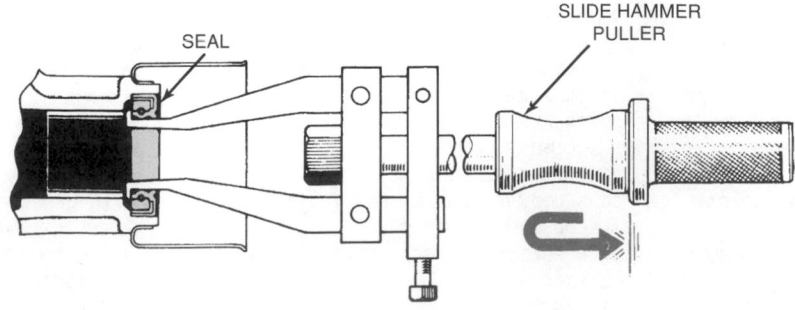

Figure 30-18. Removing an extension housing oil seal with a slide hammer puller. (Toyota)

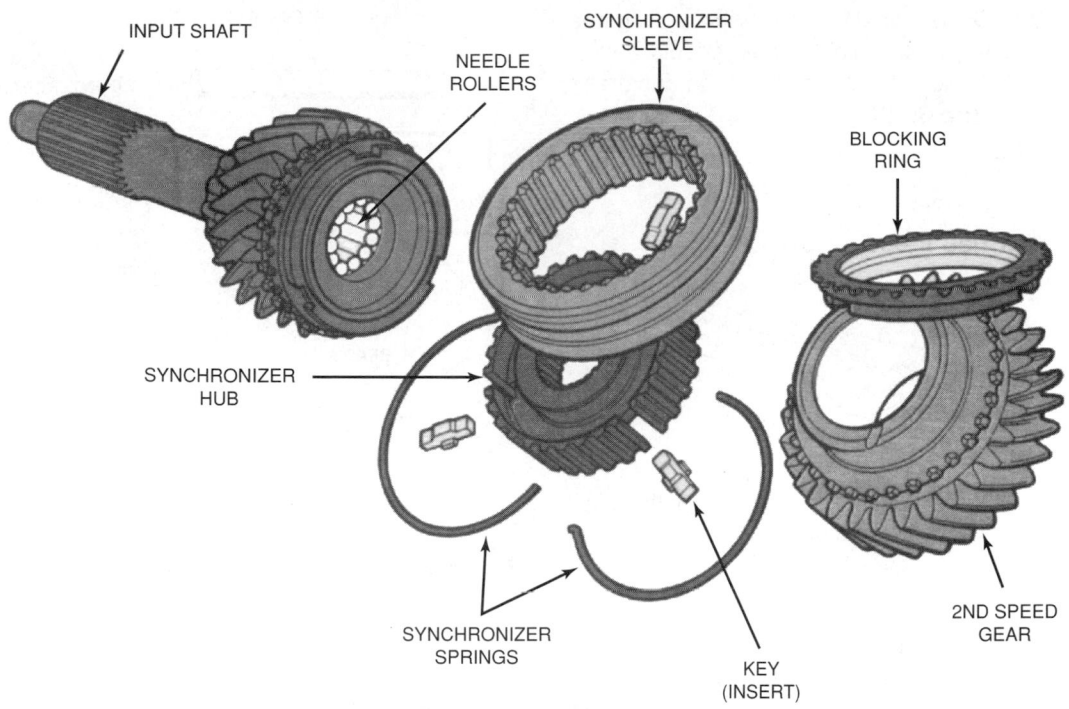

Figure 30-20. A blocking ring and related components. (Borg-Warner)

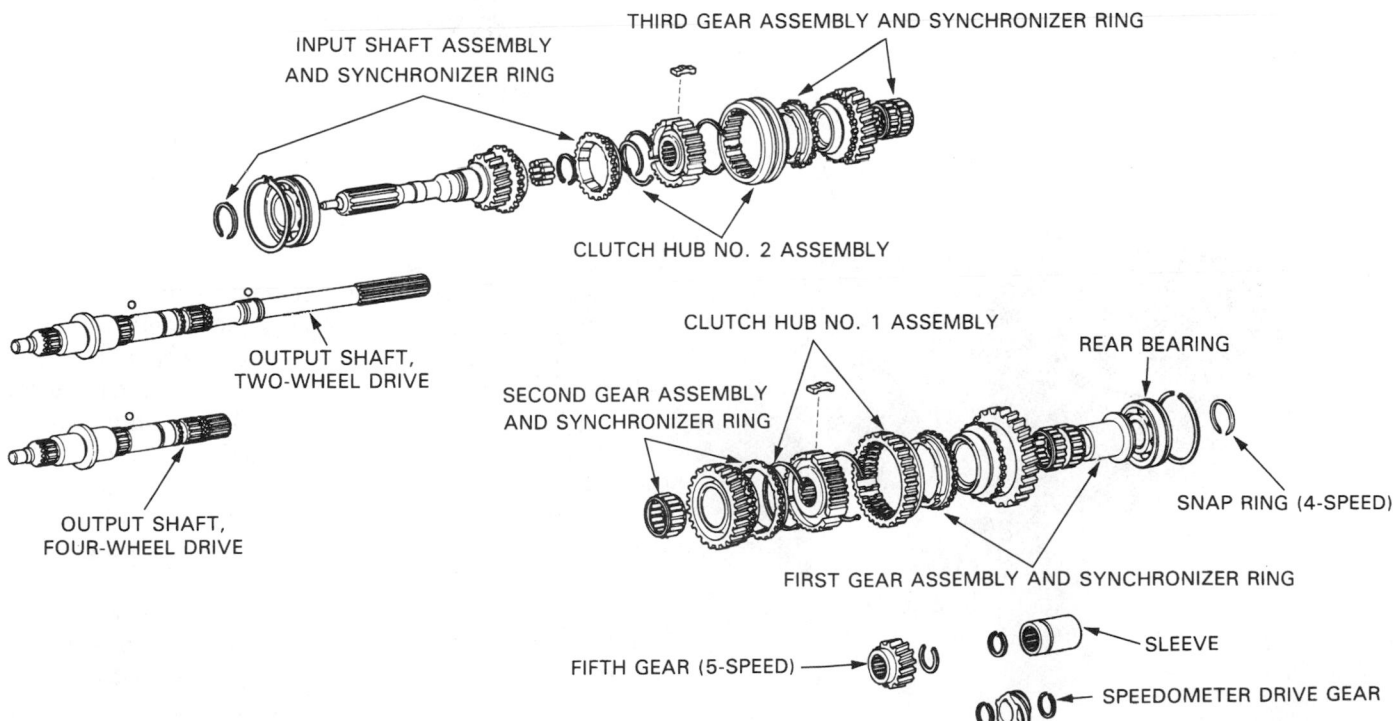

Figure 30-21. Exploded view of an output shaft assembly. Note the difference between the two-wheel and four-wheel drive shafts. (Toyota)

shaft is then rotated (in either direction) while noting the maximum runout reading on the dial. Runout should generally noft exceed .002″ (0.06 mm). Follow the manufacturer's specifications. See **Figure 30-22.**

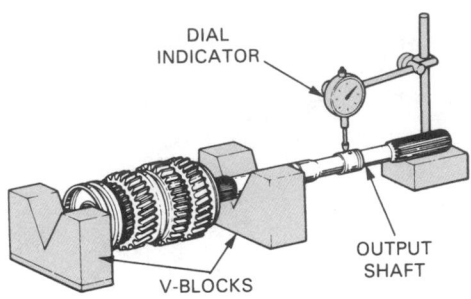

Figure 30-22. Checking an output shaft for runout with a dial indicator. Note the V-blocks, which accurately support the shaft. (Toyota)

Inspect Countershaft and Gears

Lift the **countershaft** from the case and retrieve any needle bearings that have fallen to the bottom of the case. Clean the shaft, gears, needle bearings, thrust washers, and other parts. Inspect the teeth of all gears. Examine the needle bearings and the countershaft. Check the thrust washers, spacers, and retainer washers.

If the countershaft is equipped with an **antilash plate** (prevents normal backlash from causing rattle), check the teeth and springs. The antilash plate in **Figure 30-23** is riveted to the countershaft and should not be removed. Replace the gear and plate as a unit. Some antilash plates are removable. One type of countershaft assembly is illustrated in **Figure 30-24.**

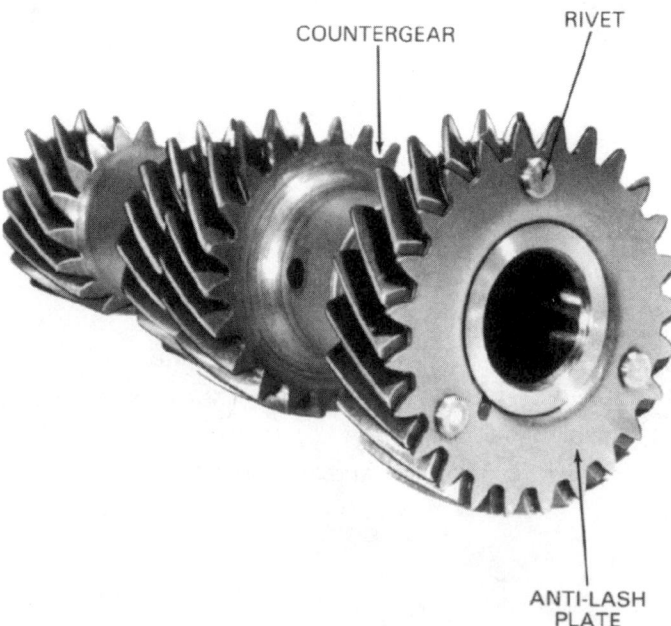

Figure 30-23. Countergear anti-lash plate. This plate and gear must be replaced as a unit. (Oldsmobile)

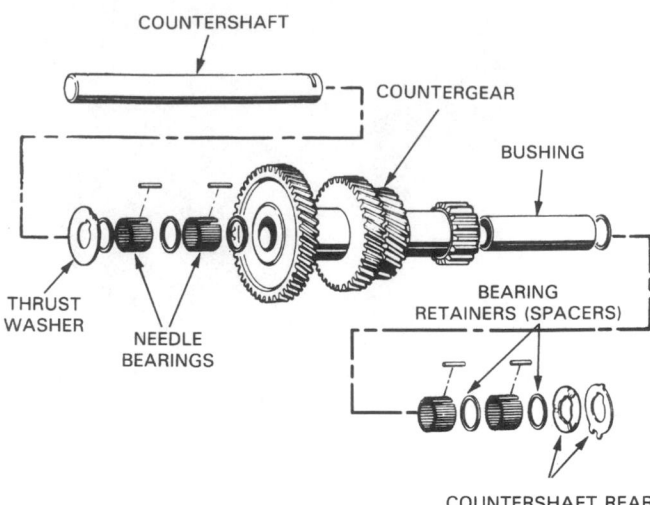

Figure 30-24. Typical countergear (cluster gear), shaft, and bearings. (Jeep)

Inspect Reverse Idler Gear

Examine the **reverse idler** shaft. Inspect the idler gear bushings (some transmissions and transaxles use needle bearings) and thrust washers. Check the gear teeth carefully. Try the gear on the shaft and test it for wear. A reverse idler gear unit is shown in **Figure 30-25.**

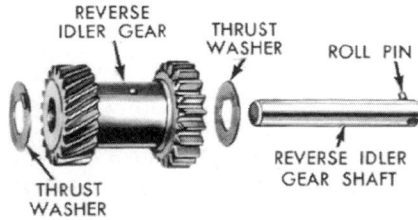

Figure 30-25. One type of reverse idler gear assembly. This gear uses bronze bushings.

Inspect Synchronizers

Since the synchronizers prevent gear clash, they should be carefully checked for damage. All defective parts should be replaced. Scribe (mark) each blocking ring and the hub so that rings can be returned to their original side. If the clutch sleeve and hub are not marked, **Figure 30-26,** scribe them so that the sleeve and hub may be reassembled in the same position.

Slide the clutch sleeve from the clutch hub. Remove the inserts and insert springs. Clean all parts. **Figure 30-27** shows a widely used type of synchronizer.

Check the inserts and insert springs for excessive wear. Slide the sleeve on the hub (marks aligned) and test play. Inspect the hub inner splines. The sleeve clutch teeth must not be battered or tapered. Pay particular attention to the blocking rings. The inside should still show fine grooves and the teeth should be in good shape. The notched sections (that fit over inserts) should not be battered and worn.

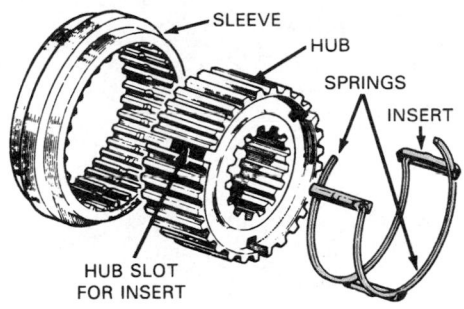

Figure 30-26. Correct position of insert springs in this particular installation. When installed, the springs are inside the hub, one on each end, with the inserts in the hub slots.

The **cone surface** of the gears engaged by the synchronizer should be smooth. **Figure 30-28** shows a synchronizer clutch sleeve (inserts and springs are shown, hub is not shown), blocking rings, and the two gears served by the synchronizer. Note the smooth gear cone surfaces and the grooves in the inner section of the blocking rings.

Assemble Synchronizer

To assemble the synchronizer shown in **Figure 30-29**, lubricate with transmission or transaxle lube. Place one of the insert springs in the hub so that the humped portion rests in one of the hub insert slots. Align the hub and sleeve marks and start the sleeve on the hub. Be sure the sleeve is facing in the correct direction.

Install the three inserts and push the sleeve into place. Install the second spring on the opposite side of the hub in exactly the same manner as the first. Make sure that the clutch sleeve and hub marks are aligned and that the insert springs are securely in place behind the lips or tabs on the ends of the inserts. Install each blocking ring.

Insert spring installation varies. Follow the manufacturer's instructions. Note how the springs are installed in **Figure 30-30.** The bent tip on each spring is installed in the same insert.

Some synchronizers are easily installed by placing the springs in the hub, installing the inserts, and then placing a compressing tool around the hub. This holds the inserts down so that the hub can be installed. Refer to **Figure 30-31.**

Inspect Transaxle Chain and Sprockets or Gears

Closely inspect the **drive chain** and **drive sprockets** of the chain drive assembly for wear or damage. Check the chain for slack and worn pins. If the transmission uses two

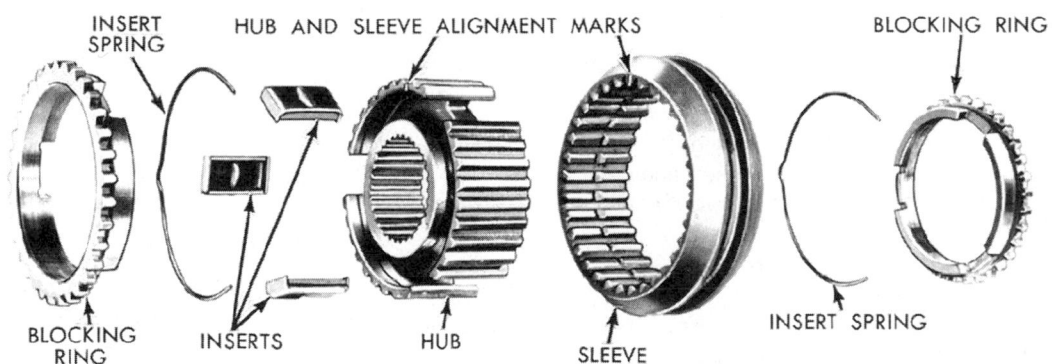

Figure 30-27. Disassembled synchronizer. Note the alignment marks on the sleeve and hub.

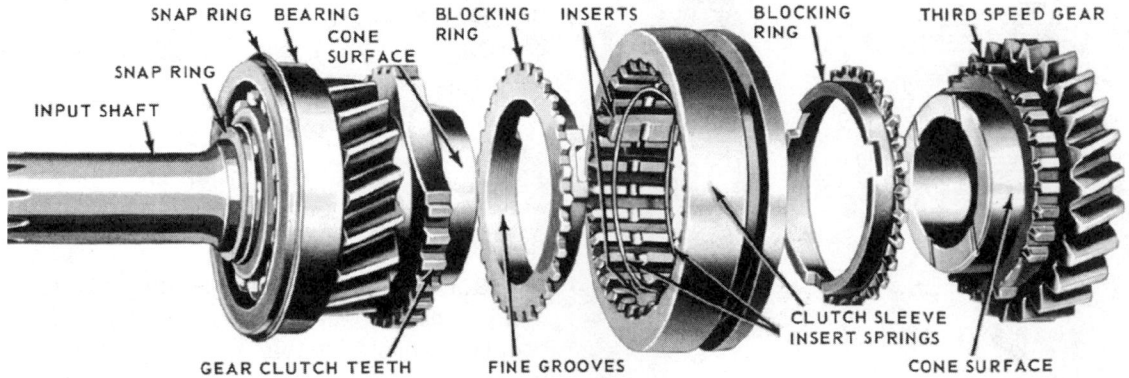

Figure 30-28. Synchronizer (minus hub) and the gears it serves. (GMC)

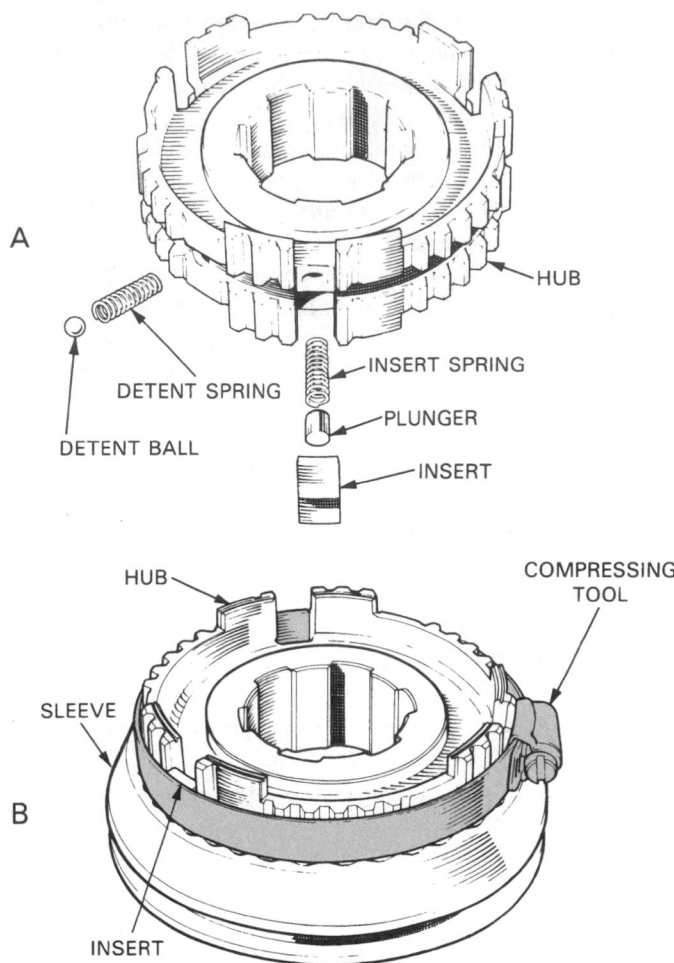

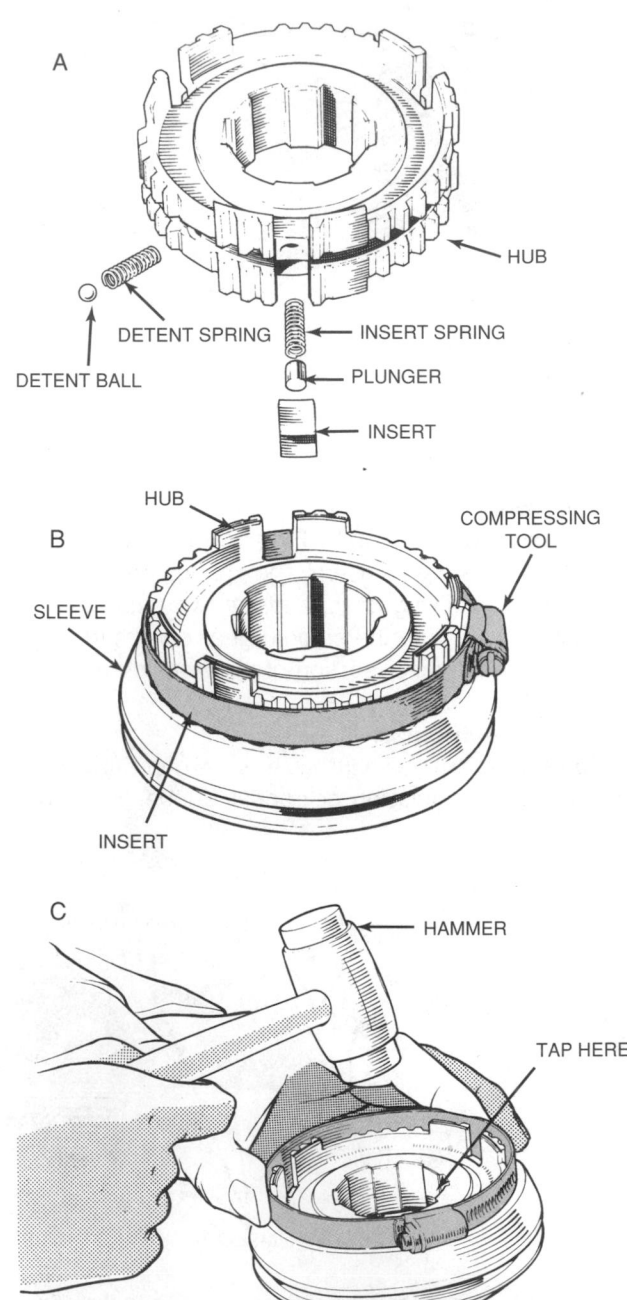

Figure 30-29. A—Synchronizer hub with insert spring, insert plunger, and insert. Note the detent ball and spring. B—The compressing tool is being used to secure the insert and detent assemblies while the hub is slipped into the sleeve. (British-Leyland)

Figure 30-31. A—Synchronizer hub with insert, insert plunger, and insert spring. Note the detent ball and spring. B—The compressing tool is being used to hold the insert and detent units. C—The hub is being gently tapped into position with a plastic hammer.

large gears for power transfer, check them for chipping, wear, and loose fit on the shaft splines.

Inspect Transaxle Differential Unit

Closely inspect the *differential unit* for wear or damage. Differential gears are checked in the same manner as the gears in the transmission. The hypoid-type differential assembly can be checked following the procedures outlined in Chapter 33.

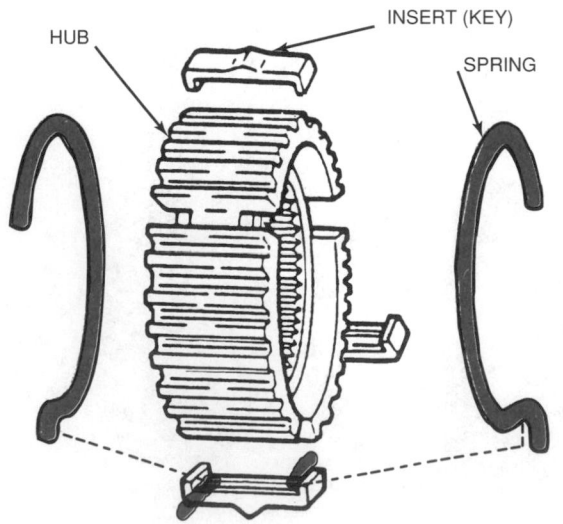

Figure 30-30. Insert springs with bent tips. Note that both bent tips go into the same insert. (Borg-Warner)

Check Case and Other Housings for Cracks and Burrs

Inspect the front bearing retainer, transmission or transaxle case, and any extension or CV axle housings for signs of cracking. Look carefully, especially around bolt holes and shaft and bearing openings.

On aluminum cases, check for porous areas (slight flaws in aluminum when cast), which allow gear lubricant to seep to the outside. Follow transmission or transaxle manufacturer's recommendations for repair.

Also check all shift covers, inspection covers, and other sheet metal parts for dents and warping that could prevent them from sealing properly. Carefully straighten any damaged areas or replace the part.

Check the extension-to-case and the case-to-clutch-housing surfaces for any burrs that could cause misalignment. If burrs are found, remove them with a fine mill file. Look at **Figure 30-32.** If the transmission or transaxle has a vent, make sure it is open.

Obtain and Check New Parts

When a part is unfit for service, new parts must be obtained. Always check the new part against the old for design, size, and shape. Try the part in the transmission or transaxle to make sure it fits properly.

Use New Snap Rings, Thrust Washers, and Gaskets

To prevent future problems, use new **snap rings** whenever available. New **thrust washers** will provide proper end play. New gaskets (use gasket cement) are a must. Some transmission and transaxle cases use RTV (room temperature vulcanizing) sealer in place of gaskets. Always use the recommended sealer. An inferior seal can cause a complete loss of lubricant, leading to transmission or transaxle failure. If drive-in expansion plugs were removed, install new plugs. Use the recommended sealer on all plugs and pins.

Caution: Parts must be absolutely clean and well lubricated before assembly.

After cleaning and inspection, all parts should be oiled and placed in clean containers. Before installation, every part should be heavily lubricated with transmission oil or transmission fluid as recommended by the manufacturer.

Seal and Stake Pins

Where pins pass through the outer wall of the case, apply sealer to the hole so that the pin will not leak oil. Drive the pin slightly below the surface of the case and stake to prevent loosening.

Check for Cracks Where Indicated

When a transmission or transaxle has suffered heavy gear damage (teeth shattered), use crack detection chemicals on the remaining gears. Crack detection was covered in Chapter 6. Check the shafts and shaft openings in the case also. Discard all parts showing the slightest sign of cracking. Replace the bearings, even if they appear to be good.

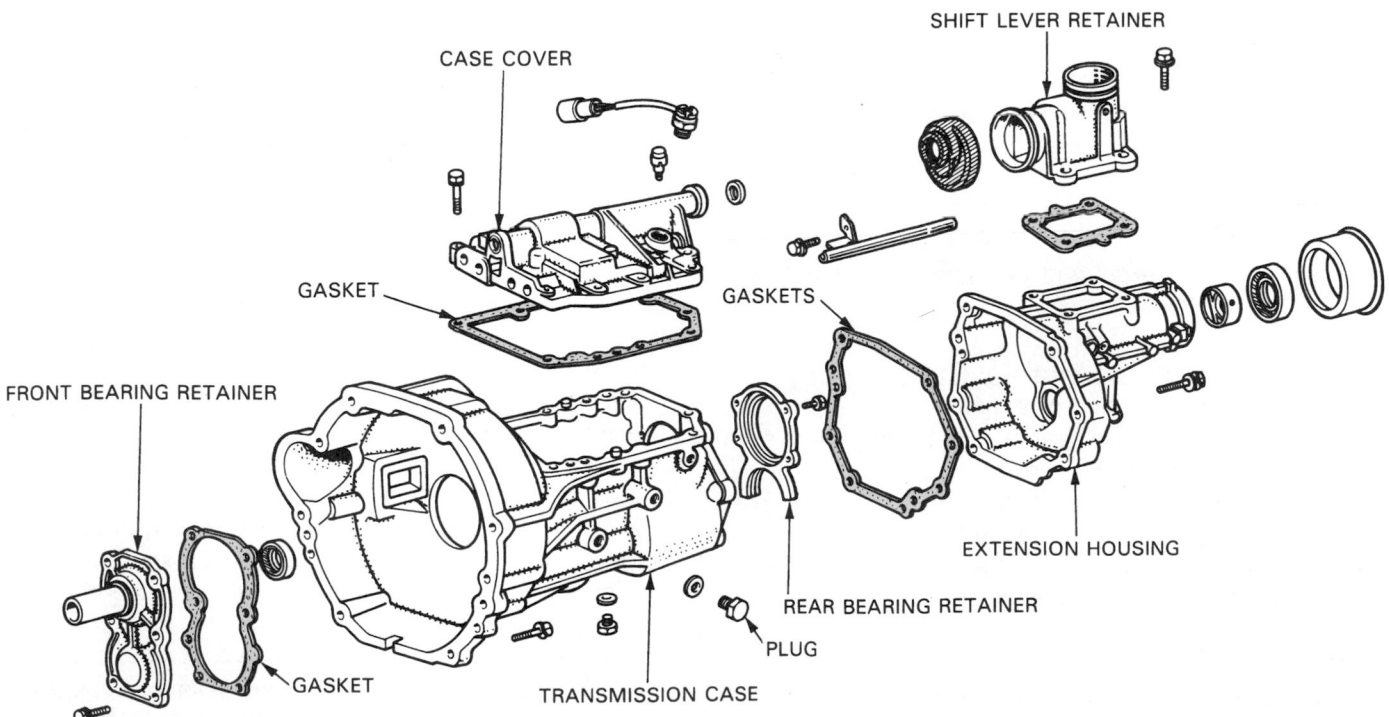

Figure 30-32. Transmission case and gasket assembly. Check the case, extension housing, bearing retainer, and cover for cracking, porosity, and other damage. (Toyota)

Transmission or Transaxle Assembly

Basically, the transmission or transaxle is reassembled in the reverse order of disassembly. All parts must be lubricated and properly installed. Make frequent use of the manufacturer's service manual to ensure that all parts are reinstalled correctly.

General Internal Part Installation Procedures

Lubricate all bushings and shafts with transmission oil before beginning assembly. To install thrust washers, place a coating of soft grease on each end of the gear and press the thrust washers into the grease. Make sure they face in the right direction. The grease will hold the washers in place as the gear is installed.

 Note: Any assembly lube/grease used to hold internal parts in place must be compatible with, and dissolve readily in, the normal oil or transmission fluid used in the transmission or transaxle.

If any gears, such as the counter gear or the reverse idler gear, use needle bearings, the bearings may be held in place with a *dummy shaft.* A dummy shaft is a wooden or metal shaft that is the same diameter as the regular shaft but only as long as the gear and thrust washer thickness. The gear is then placed in the case with the needle bearings and thrust washers are installed. When the regular shaft is pushed through the case opening and into the gear, the dummy is forced out the other side. This procedure provides proper alignment and holds the needles, spacers, and thrust washers in line.

If a counter gear must be lowered to install the output or input shaft, place it into the case but do not install it until the main shafts are in place.

Never use excessive force to make a part fit. If some part does not slide into position as it should, stop and check for the source of difficulty.

Spin all gears after they have been installed. They must turn freely. Use a dial indicator or feeler gauge to check the end play of all units for which an end play specification is given. A typical end play checking procedure is shown in **Figure 30-33.**

Lubricate Assembled Internal Parts

When the transmission or transaxle internal parts are fully assembled, pour fresh gear oil over the gears and shaft through the cover opening. Use the recommended oil viscosity. Some units use automatic transmission fluid. Turn the input shaft while shifting through the gears. The shafts and gears should turn freely with no catching. Check shaft end play if it was not checked earlier.

Installing Shift Cover

To install the shift cover, place the transmission or transaxle in neutral. Place the shift fork levers in the neutral position. Hold the cover in line with the cover hole. The shift

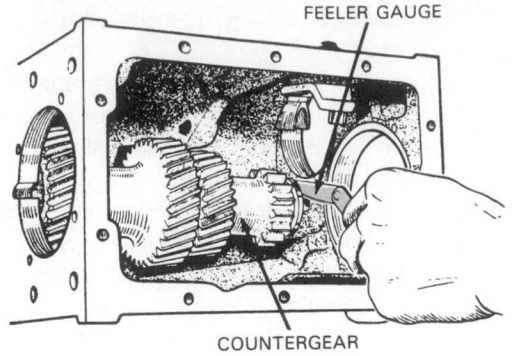

Figure 30-33. Checking countergear end play with a feeler gauge. (British-Leyland)

forks must align with the clutch sleeve and gear fork grooves.

Using a new gasket and cement, guide the shift forks into their grooves. Insert the cover fasteners and tighten them to specifications. Try the shift mechanism for proper operation, **Figure 30-34.**

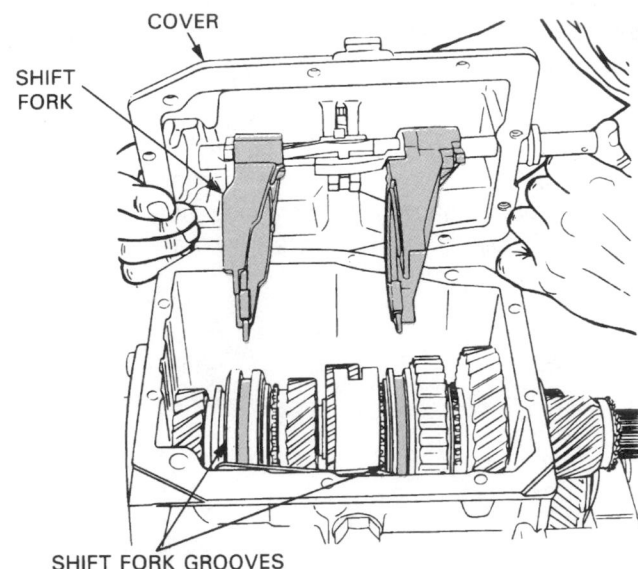

Figure 30-34. Installing the shift cover. Shift forks must align with the shift fork grooves. Do not force the cover into position! (Chevrolet)

Transmission or Transaxle Installation

Wipe the clutch housing and transmission or transaxle face clean. Check for burrs. Using guide pins or a transmission or transaxle jack, raise the transmission or transaxle into alignment with the engine and insert the input shaft through the clutch throwout bearing, through the disc hub, and into the pilot bearing.

 Caution: Never let the transmission or transaxle hang with all of its weight supported by the input shaft.

Install and torque the fasteners holding the transmission or transaxle to the clutch housing or engine. Install the drive line components, speedometer cable, shift linkage, and other parts.

Adjusting Shift Linkage

Disconnect the shift rods at the transmission or transaxle (or at column shift levers if used). Place the transmission or transaxle shift levers in neutral. If the linkage has slotted adjustment holes, loosen the adjustment nuts and leave the shift rods connected.

With the transmission or transaxle shift levers in neutral, place the shift levers in neutral. Adjust the levers, stop block, etc., **Figure 30-35**. It may be necessary to pass an aligning pin through the levers or to use a special tool as shown in **Figure 30-36**. Tighten the linkage adjustment nuts.

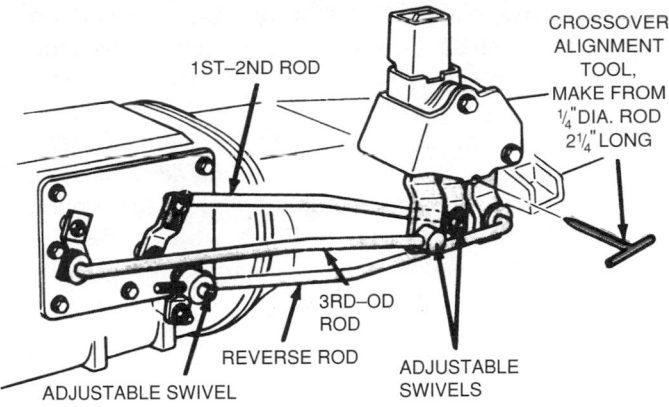

Figure 30-36. Adjusting shift linkage on a floor shift transmission. Note the use of an alignment pin to hold the gearshift in the correct position during adjustment.

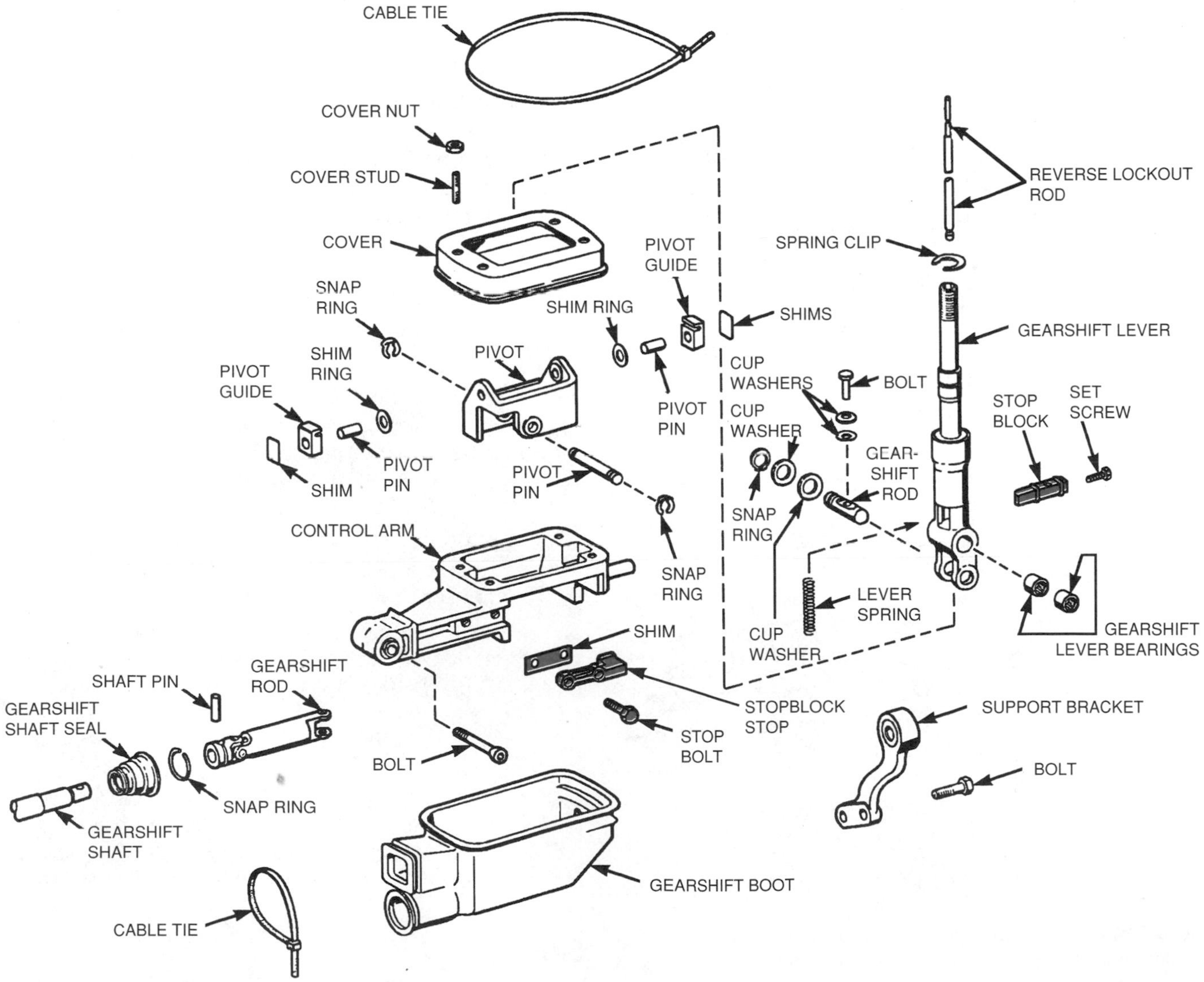

Figure 30-35. Exploded view of one type of adjustable shift linkage for a six-speed transmission. Note the adjustable stop blocks, which control linkage movement. (GM)

If the linkage is the type that was disconnected, adjust the linkage length so that the rods just reach from the transmission or transaxle to the column shift levers. Insert and secure the linkage.

A typical floor shift is illustrated in **Figure 30-37.** To adjust this linkage, loosen the shift linkage adjustment nuts. Place the gear shift lever in neutral and pass the alignment pin through the aligning holes. Place the transmission or transaxle shift levers in neutral. Tighten the adjustment nuts. Finally, remove the pin.

Fill Transmission or Transaxle

Fill the transmission or transaxle to the level of the filler plug with the recommended gear oil or automatic transmission fluid. Fill slowly so the oil will have time to flow. If the differential assembly of the transaxle is a separate unit, fill it properly with clean gear oil of the correct viscosity and type. See **Figure 30-38.**

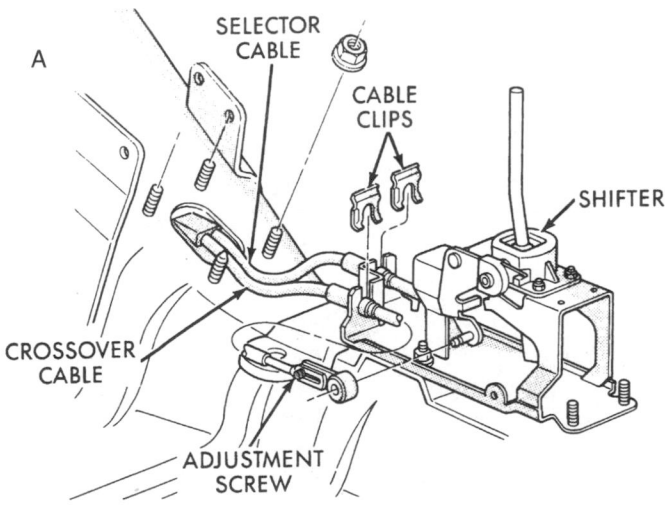

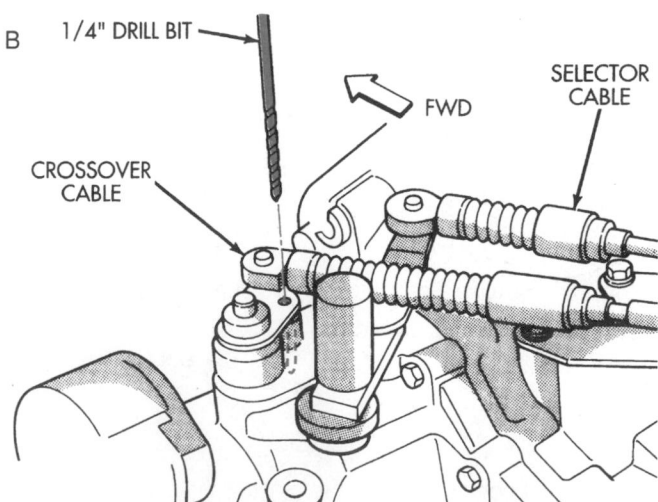

Figure 30-37. A—Shift (crossover) cable assembly with adjustment screw. B—Alignment pin (drill bit used here) being placed into aligning holes to provide the correct linkage alignment before and during tightening of the adjustment screw. (Chrysler)

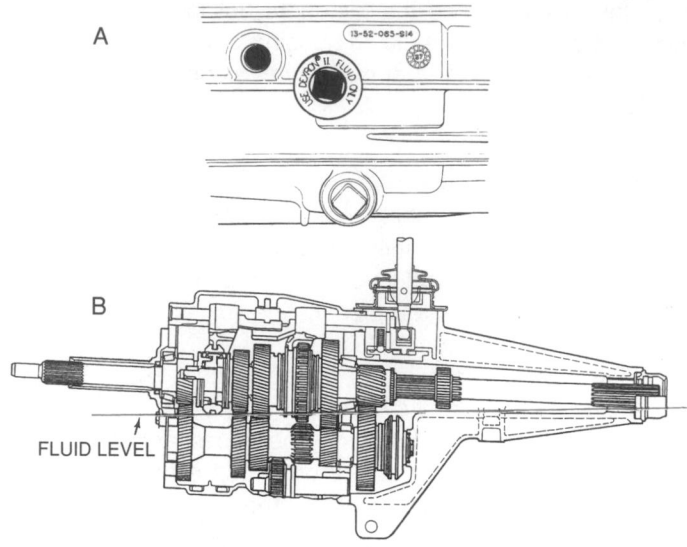

Figure 30-38. A—Be sure to use the correct type of transmission lubricant. B—A proper lubricant fill (full) level for one particular five-speed transmission. (Borg-Warner)

Road Test

Road test the vehicle. The transmission or transaxle should operate quietly and smoothly. Shifting should be smooth and positive with no jumping out of gear. Shift up and down to test the synchronizers. When back at the shop, check the transmission or transaxle for leaks and recheck the lubricant level.

Tech Talk

One of the most frustrating jobs in manual transmission or transaxle work is installing the spring-loaded detent balls that hold the internal linkage pieces in position. It seems that there is never enough room to reach in and place the ball properly. You will probably drop the balls several times before you are finished—if the springs don't launch them across the shop.

An easy way to install detent balls involves using an old hacksaw blade. Bend the blade so that one end will reach into the recesses of the transmission. Place the detent ball on the hole in the end of the blade with a little grease. The hole will hold the ball in place while you position it against its spring. Then, install the levers or rails over the ball and the hacksaw blade. After everything is in position, carefully slide the blade out, leaving the ball in place.

Summary

Vehicle transmissions and transaxles are of three-, four-, five-, and six-speed design. Current practice is toward full synchronization for all forward speeds. An overdrive may be incorporated. Transaxles are used on front-wheel drive vehicles.

Remove the transmission or transaxle only when necessary. To remove a transmission or transaxle, drain the transmission oil. Remove all controls, wires, etc. Drop the drive shaft or shafts. Remove the fasteners holding the housing to the transmission or transaxle and pull transmission or transaxle back. Use pilot bolts or a jack. Do not allow the transmission or transaxle to hang on the input shaft at any time.

Clean the outside of the transmission or transaxle before disassembly. Flush the inside of the transmission or transaxle and examine the gear teeth. Make any needed end play and clearance checks before disassembly.

General disassembly requires dropping the countergear to the bottom of the case (use a dummy shaft) and then removing either the input or output shaft. A manufacturer's service manual should be available for reference.

Place the transmission or transaxle on a stand. If hammering is required, use a soft-face type. Keep all synchronizer parts together. Be careful to avoid losing roller or needle bearings, snap rings, springs, or detent balls. Place them in a separate container. All parts must be thoroughly cleaned.

Inspect all synchronizer parts for excessive wear, chipping, galling, and cracking. Check synchronizer clutch sleeve teeth and the corresponding gear clutch teeth. Teeth should not be chipped, tapered, or excessively worn.

Synchronizer blocking rings should show some sign of fine tooling lines on the inside tapered surface. When reassembling synchronizers, make certain the hub and clutch sleeve marks are aligned and that the inserts and springs are correctly installed.

Always install new seals. Use new gaskets and apply gasket cement. In some cases, RTV sealer or O-rings are used. When lock pins pass through the case, use sealer and stake the pins. Use new thrust washers and snap rings. Lubricate all parts as they are installed. Avoid using heavy force to make parts fit.

Compare new parts with used parts for size, shape, and operation. Where heavy damage was incurred. check the case, gears, and shaft for cracking.

Use soft grease to hold roller and needle bearings in place during assembly. Do not plug lubricant entry holes. Use grease that readily dissolves in oil. Make certain snap rings are properly seated. Use a dummy shaft to install the countergear in the case.

Make certain that the fasteners are of the proper length. Seal threads on fastener holes that pass through the transmission or transaxle case. When assembled, check for correct end play on all parts. All moving parts must turn freely and without catching. Check shifting action.

Align the shifter forks carefully when installing the shift cover. Install the transmission or transaxle. Slowly fill with recommended lubricant. Make all necessary connections. Check the shift linkage adjustment. Road test the vehicle and recheck the lubricant level.

Know These Terms

Transmission	CV axle housings
Transaxle	Output shaft
Sliding gears	Countershaft
Shift linkage	Antilash plate
Synchronized gears	Reverse idler
Pilot bolts	Cone surface
Transmission jack	Drive chain
Shift plate	Drive sprockets
Inspection cover	Differential unit
Alignment marks	Snap rings
Input shaft	Thrust washers
Extension housing	Dummy shaft

Review Questions—Chapter 30

Do not write in this book. Write your answers on a separate sheet of paper.

1. A _____ has only one output shaft, while a _____ has two output shafts.
2. A transverse engine is installed _____ in the vehicle.
3. Before road testing, always check the _____ in the transmission or transaxle.
4. List five defects that should be checked for during a road test of a manual transmission or transaxle.
5. After cleaning, check the transmission or transaxle case and extension housing for _____.
6. List six inspection points for the input shaft assembly.
7. Always check the case-to-clutch-housing surfaces for any burrs that could cause _____.
8. A dummy shaft is the same _____ as the regular shaft, but it is not as _____.
9. The transmission or transaxle should be filled to the bottom of the _____ _____ with the recommended type and grade of lubricant.
10. When removing or installing a transmission or transaxle, never allow the weight of the unit to hang on the _____ _____.

ASE-Type Questions

1. Technician A says that an average ratio for first gear in a transmission or transaxle is 5.69 to 1. Technician B says that a four-speed transmission or transaxle has a much lower first gear ratio than does a three-speed transmission. Who is right?
   (A) A only.
   (B) B only.
   (C) Both A & B.
   (D) Neither A nor B.
2. Modern manual transmissions in rear-wheel drive vehicles can have _____ forward gears.
   (A) four
   (B) five
   (C) six
   (D) All of the above.

3. Technician A says that clutch adjustment can affect transmission or transaxle shifting. Technician B says that synchronizer condition can affect transmission or transaxle shifting. Who is right?
   (A) A only.
   (B) B only.
   (C) Both A & B.
   (D) Neither A nor B.

4. All of the following should be replaced any time the transmission or transaxle is disassembled, EXCEPT:
   (A) snap rings.
   (B) seals.
   (C) bearings.
   (D) gaskets.

5. A gear should never be reused if the teeth show any signs of _____.
   (A) chipping
   (B) galling
   (C) excessive wear
   (D) Any of the above.

6. Technician A says that some antilash plates are removable. Technician B says to replace the antilash plate and corresponding gear as a unit if worn. Who is right?
   (A) A only.
   (B) B only.
   (C) Both A & B.
   (D) Neither A nor B.

7. When assembling synchronizers, you should do all of the following EXCEPT:
   (A) lubricate the synchronizers.
   (B) align the hub and clutch sleeve marks.
   (C) make sure the sleeve is facing in the correct direction.
   (D) separate the insert springs from the synchronizers.

8. Some transmissions and transaxles use _____ as a lubricant.
   (A) gear oil
   (B) automatic transmission fluid
   (C) brake fluid
   (D) Both A & B.

9. Grease used to hold internal parts in place must dissolve in _____.
   (A) parts cleaning solvent
   (B) normal grade oil or transmission fluid
   (C) kerosene
   (D) alcohol

10. Before adjusting the length of the shift linkage rods, both the shift lever and the transmission or transaxle must be in _____.
   (A) neutral
   (B) first
   (C) third
   (D) any gear

Suggested Activities

1. Do a survey at your school to determine what percentage of the faculty, staff, and students owns vehicles with manual transmissions. How do your figures compare with the national average of about 10%?

2. Using the appropriate service manual, check and, if necessary, adjust the linkage on a manual transmission/transaxle.

3. Tear down a manual transmission or transaxle and list all needed parts for a rebuild.

4. Calculate the cost of repairing the above transmission by the following process:
   a. Use a flat rate manual to find the prices of the needed parts.
   b. Use a flat rate manual to find the labor times for replacing needed parts.
   c. Decide if the clutch will be replaced and add the clutch parts and labor to the list.
   d. Total the labor times and multiply them by the average labor rate for your area.
   e. Add the total of parts and labor.
   f. Add other charges, such as supplies (rags, cleaners, and oil absorbent) and outside services (machine shop work) for a grand total of what it would cost to repair this transmission.

5. Discuss your price calculations with the other members of your class. Ask if there is anything you missed. Determine whether the cost of the repair is greater or less than the cost of a replacement transmission.

31

Four-Wheel Drive Service

After completing this chapter, you will be able to:
- Explain four-wheel drive construction and operation.
- Define part-time and full-time four-wheel drive.
- Disassemble, check parts, and reassemble a transfer case.
- Disassemble, check parts, and reassemble a typical locking hub assembly.
- Diagnose four-wheel drive problems.

This chapter will cover the design and operation of four-wheel drive systems with emphasis on the transfer case. This chapter will also detail the differences between part-time and full-time four-wheel drive systems. Front wheel locking hubs are also discussed. Service procedures for the transfer case and locking hubs are also covered.

Four-Wheel Drive Components

Modern four-wheel drive systems may be used with either a manual or an automatic transmission. All four-wheel drive systems use a *transfer case* between the transmission output end and the system drive shafts. The purpose of the transfer case is to divide the power flow so that both the front and rear wheels are driven by engine power. All four-wheel drive systems have two drive shafts. Some systems that are engaged at all times make use of special internal components to compensate for the differences in wheel distance traveled during turns.

Transfer Case

The transfer case is needed to apply transmission output shaft torque to the front and rear drive shafts. Engine power enters the transfer case from the transmission output shaft. Power is transmitted to each drive shaft through a set of gears or a chain and sprockets. A differential assembly or a viscous coupling is used to compensate for changes in front and rear axle speeds. **Figure 31-1** illustrates a four-wheel drive setup with a transfer case. Note how both drive shafts are attached to the transfer case. Transfer cases can be either *part-time* of *full-time* units.

Part-Time Transfer Case Operation

On modern part-time transfer cases, the driver can select one of three different drive modes by operating a lever on the vehicle console or floor:

- Two-wheel drive—high range.
- Four-wheel drive—high range.
- Four-wheel drive—low range.

Although it would be possible to operate in the two-wheel drive—low range, the transfer case shift linkage does not allow selecting this mode, **Figure 31-2.** Trace the power flow starting with the transmission output shaft. The output shaft is splined to and drives the transfer case main drive gear. The main drive gear is in constant mesh with the idler cluster gear. The idler cluster turns freely in needle bearings on the idler shaft. Note that the idler cluster is made up of two gears, one large (high range) and one small (low range). These gears are in constant mesh with the output gears. Both output gears turn freely in bushings on the transfer case output shaft.

The *sliding clutch* is splined to the output shaft. In the neutral position (shown), it is centered between, but not engaging the output gears. Low range (high engine RPM, low wheel RPM) is engaged when the sliding clutch is shifted into engagement with the low-range output gear. High range (low engine speed RPM, high drive wheel RPM) is engaged when the sliding clutch is moved into engagement with the high-range output gear. The output gear that is engaged with the clutch turns the sliding clutch. Since the clutch is splined to the output shaft, the shaft also turns.

Two-Wheel, Four-Wheel Drive Action

The transfer case output shaft is made of two parts, **Figure 31-2.** The long section is driven by the sliding splined clutch. This long output shaft section, in turn, will drive the rear drive shaft. The shorter front section is connected to the long section only when the four-wheel drive sliding splined clutch (which is splined to and constantly turned by the long section) is moved into engagement with the splined end of the short shaft. When two-wheel drive is desired, the short output shaft is disconnected by moving the four-wheel sliding clutch out of engagement. The long shaft will then drive the rear drive shaft, but will not apply torque to the front. Four-wheel drive mode is accomplished by merely moving the four-wheel clutch into engagement with the short shaft. Torque will then be applied to both front and rear drive shafts.

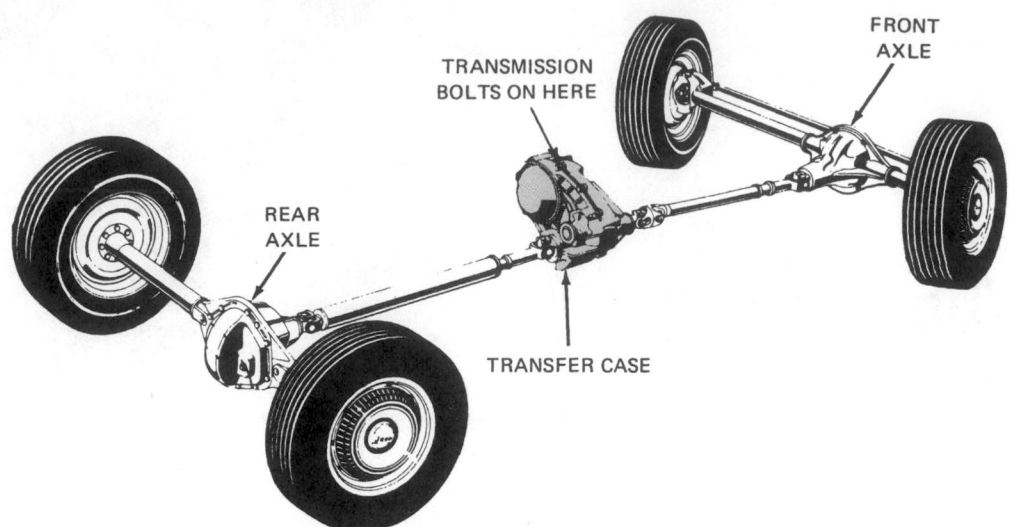

Figure 31-1. Typical four-wheel drive setup. Note how the transfer case drives both front and rear drive shafts. (Jeep)

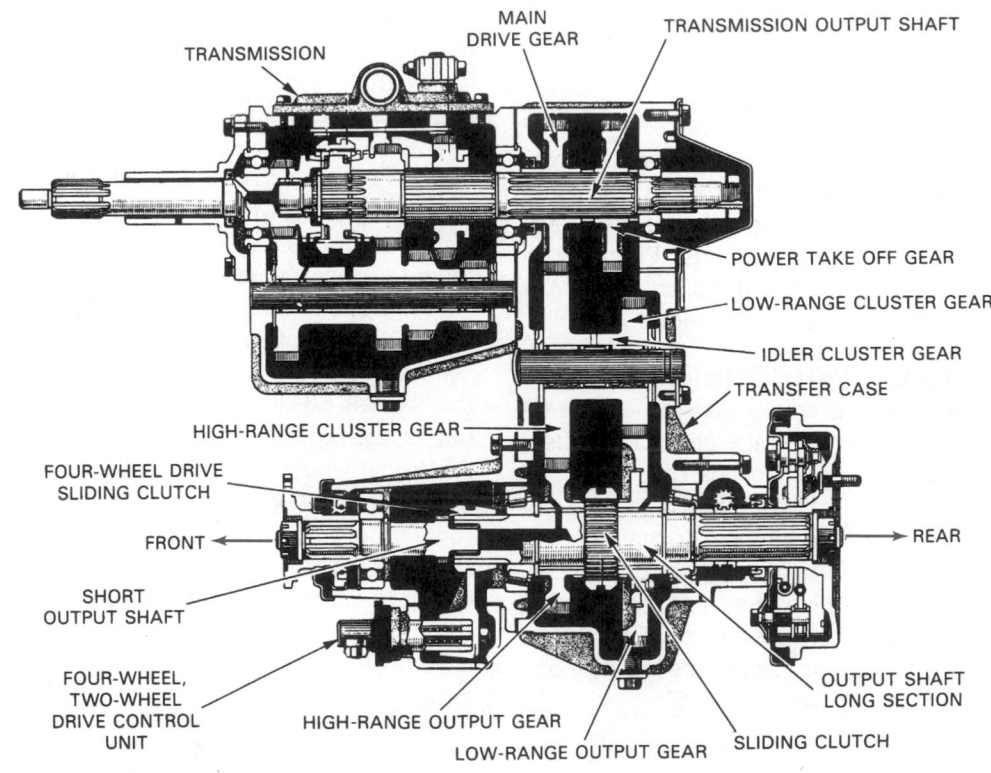

Figure 31-2. One type of transfer case used on a part-time four-wheel drive system. (Toyota)

Vehicles equipped with this type of transfer case must never be operated in four-wheel drive on dry, hard-surfaced roads. The vehicle's front wheels rotate slightly faster, because they follow a more curved path than the rear. As a result, *windup,* or internal stresses between the front and rear axle parts builds up in the entire drive train until something breaks. Either the tires will break loose or slip on the pavement or a drive train part will be damaged. Since it is very difficult for the tires to break loose on hard, dry road surfaces, the vehicle will probably be damaged. On another type of transfer case, the front drive shaft and ring gear assembly is driven at all times. A vacuum motor is used to

disconnect the front wheels from the front axle, **Figure 31-3.** The vacuum motor operates a shift collar installed in the front drive axle, which is similar to the collar used with a manual transmission synchronizer.

Full-Time Four-Wheel Drive

Some transfer cases permit the vehicle to constantly operate in four-wheel drive on any road surface. These units make use of a *differential assembly* or a *viscous clutch* to allow for differences in front and rear axle speeds. Although these assemblies work in different ways, they both accomplish the same thing. They are discussed in detail below.

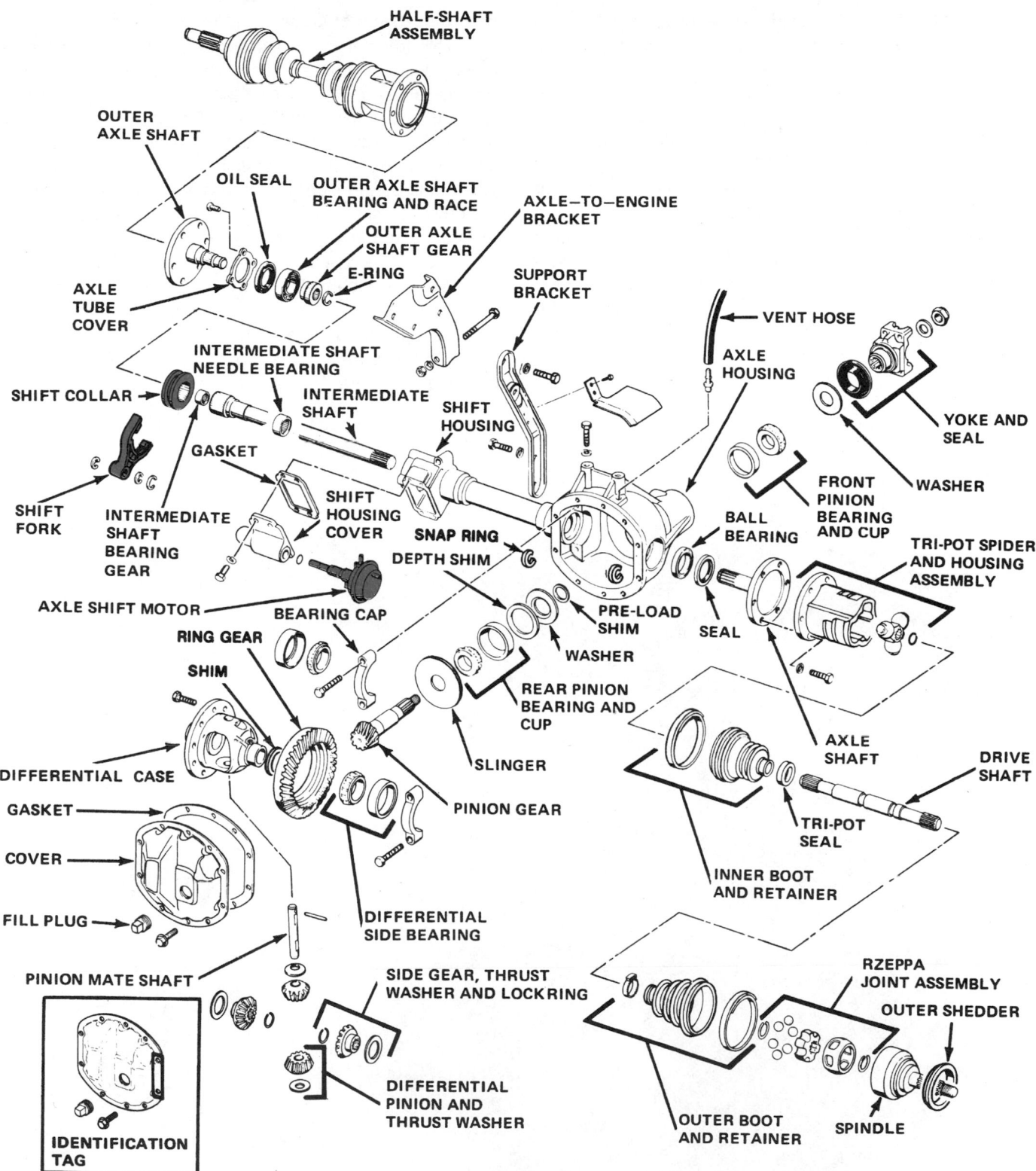

Figure 31-3. One type of front axle assembly that is driven continuously by the transfer case. The axle is shifted in and out of four-wheel drive with a vacuum axle shift motor and shift fork unit. (Jeep)

Full-Time Transfer Case with Differential Unit

One manufacturer's full-time transfer case is shown in **Figure 31-4.** Note that the drive chain transmits power from the drive sprocket to the differential case sprocket. A differential unit inside the case applies driving torque to

both the front and rear transfer case output shafts. The differential allows the front and back shafts to rotate at different speeds while still applying power. This keeps drive train windup from damaging parts and permits constant use in four-wheel drive. This unit employs a limited-slip differential that will provide some drive to either the front or rear axle if one wheel is spinning. For very severe traction situations, the unit has a mechanism to lockout (stop) the differential action. This provides drive to both front and rear drive shafts. Never use lockout control on dry, hard roads. Use only when stuck or under very poor traction situations.

An exploded view of the transfer case is illustrated in **Figure 31-5.** This transfer case is available with or without a low range reduction unit. Another type of full-time transfer case is pictured in **Figure 31-6.** It uses a chain drive and a standard (nonlimited-slip) differential unit. Low and high range is accomplished through gearing. This unit may be locked out when wheel spin is experienced. The lockout must be disengaged whenever the vehicle is driven on dry paved roads.

Full-Time Transfer Case with Viscous Coupling

This transfer case operates somewhat like the differential-equipped transfer case. The basic difference being the viscous coupling used in place of the mechanical limited-slip differential. See **Figure 31-7.** The viscous coupling contains a special silicone fluid that acts as a torque biasing, limited-slip unit. The coupling is attached to the front drive shaft by the side gear and drive sprocket. These turn the drive sprocket and front output shaft. The two sprockets are connected with a drive chain. The rear drive shaft is attached to the viscous coupling through the rear output shaft side gear teeth. These teeth are meshed with the differential pinions.

During normal operation, the viscous coupling does not operate. When excessive wheel spin is present, the coupling transfers torque to the axle having the best

Figure 31-4. Cutaway of a full-time transfer case. Note the use of a chain to drive the differential unit. This case is also equipped with a planetary gear, low-range assembly. (Warner Gear)

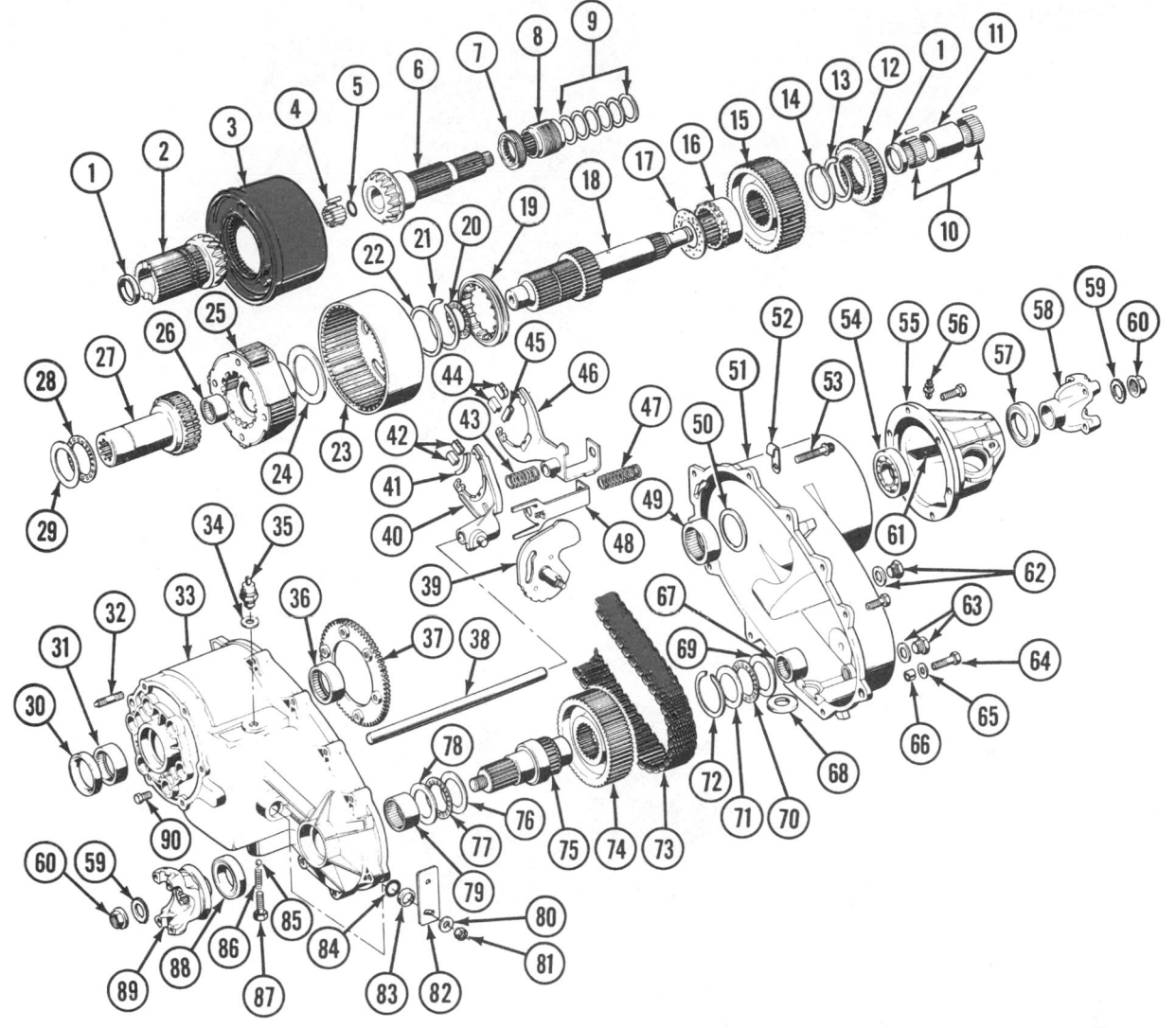

1. **MAINSHAFT REAR BEARING SPACER—SHORT (2)**
2. **SIDE GEAR**
3. **VISCOUS COUPLING AND DIFFERENTIAL ASSEMBLY**
4. **MAINSHAFT REAR PILOT ROLLER BEARINGS (15)**
5. **MAINSHAFT O-RING**
6. **REAR OUTPUT SHAFT**
7. **OIL PUMP**
8. **SPEEDOMETER GEAR**
9. **DIFFERENTIAL END PLAY SHIMS**
10. **MAINSHAFT NEEDLE BEARINGS (82)**
11. **MAINSHAFT REAR BEARING SPACER**
12. **CLUTCH GEAR**
13. **CLUTCH GEAR LOCATING RING**
14. **DRIVE SPROCKET LOCATING RING**
15. **DRIVE SPROCKET**
16. **SIDE GEAR CLUTCH**
17. **MAINSHAFT THRUST WASHER**
18. **MAINSHAFT**
19. **CLUTCH SLEEVE**
20. **MAINSHAFT THRUST BEARING**
21. **ANNULUS GEAR RETAINING RING**
22. **ANNULUS GEAR THRUST WASHER**
23. **ANNULUS GEAR**
24. **PLANETARY THRUST WASHER**
25. **PLANETARY ASSEMBLY**
26. **MAINSHAFT FRONT PILOT BEARING**
27. **INPUT GEAR**
28. **INPUT GEAR THRUST BEARING**
29. **INPUT GEAR THRUST BEARING RACE**
30. **INPUT GEAR OIL SEAL**
31. **INPUT GEAR FRONT BEARING**

32. **FRONT CASE MOUNTING STUD (6)**
33. **FRONT CASE**
34. **LOCK MODE INDICATOR SWITCH GASKET**
35. **LOCK MODE INDICATOR SWITCH**
36. **INPUT GEAR REAR BEARING**
37. **LOW-RANGE LOCKPLATE**
38. **SHIFT RAIL**
39. **RANGE SECTOR**
40. **RANGE FORK**
41. **RANGE FORK INSERT**
42. **RANGE FORK PADS**
43. **MODE FORK SPRING**
44. **MODE FORK PADS**
45. **MODE FORK INSERT**
46. **MODE FORK**
47. **SHIFT RAIL SPRING**
48. **MODE FORK BRACKET**
49. **REAR OUTPUT SHAFT BEARING**
50. **REAR OUTPUT SHAFT BEARING SEAL**
51. **REAR CASE**
52. **WIRING CLIP**
53. **SPLINE BOLT**
54. **REAR OUTPUT BEARING**
55. **REAR RETAINER**
56. **VENT**
57. **OUTPUT SHAFT OIL SEAL**
58. **REAR YOKE**
59. **YOKE SEAL WASHER**
60. **YOKE LOCKNUT**
61. **VENT CHAMBER SEAL**
62. **FILL PLUG AND GASKET**
63. **DRAIN PLUG AND GASKET**
64. **REAR CASE BOLT**
65. **WASHER (2)**

66. **CASE ALIGNMENT DOWEL**
67. **FRONT OUTPUT SHAFT REAR THRUST BEARING**
68. **MAGNET**
69. **FRONT OUTPUT SHAFT REAR THRUST BEARING RACE (THICK)**
70. **FRONT OUTPUT SHAFT REAR THRUST BEARING**
71. **FRONT OUTPUT SHAFT REAR THRUST BEARING RACE (THIN)**
72. **DRIVEN SPROCKET RETAINING SNAP RING**
73. **DRIVE CHAIN**
74. **DRIVEN SPROCKET**
75. **FRONT OUTPUT SHAFT**
76. **FRONT OUTPUT SHAFT FRONT THRUST BEARING RACE (THIN)**
77. **FRONT OUTPUT SHAFT FRONT THRUST BEARING**
78. **FRONT OUTPUT SHAFT FRONT THRUST BEARING RACE (THICK)**
79. **FRONT OUTPUT SHAFT FRONT BEARING**
80. **WASHER**
81. **LOCKNUT**
82. **OPERATING LEVER**
83. **RANGE SECTOR SHAFT SEAL RETAINER**
84. **RANGE SECTOR SHAFT SEAL**
85. **DETENT BALL**
86. **DETENT SPRING**
87. **DETENT RETAINING BOLT**
88. **FRONT OUTPUT SHAFT SEAL**
89. **FRONT YOKE**
90. **LOCKPLATE BOLTS**

Figure 31-5. Exploded view of a full-time transfer case. (Jeep)

625

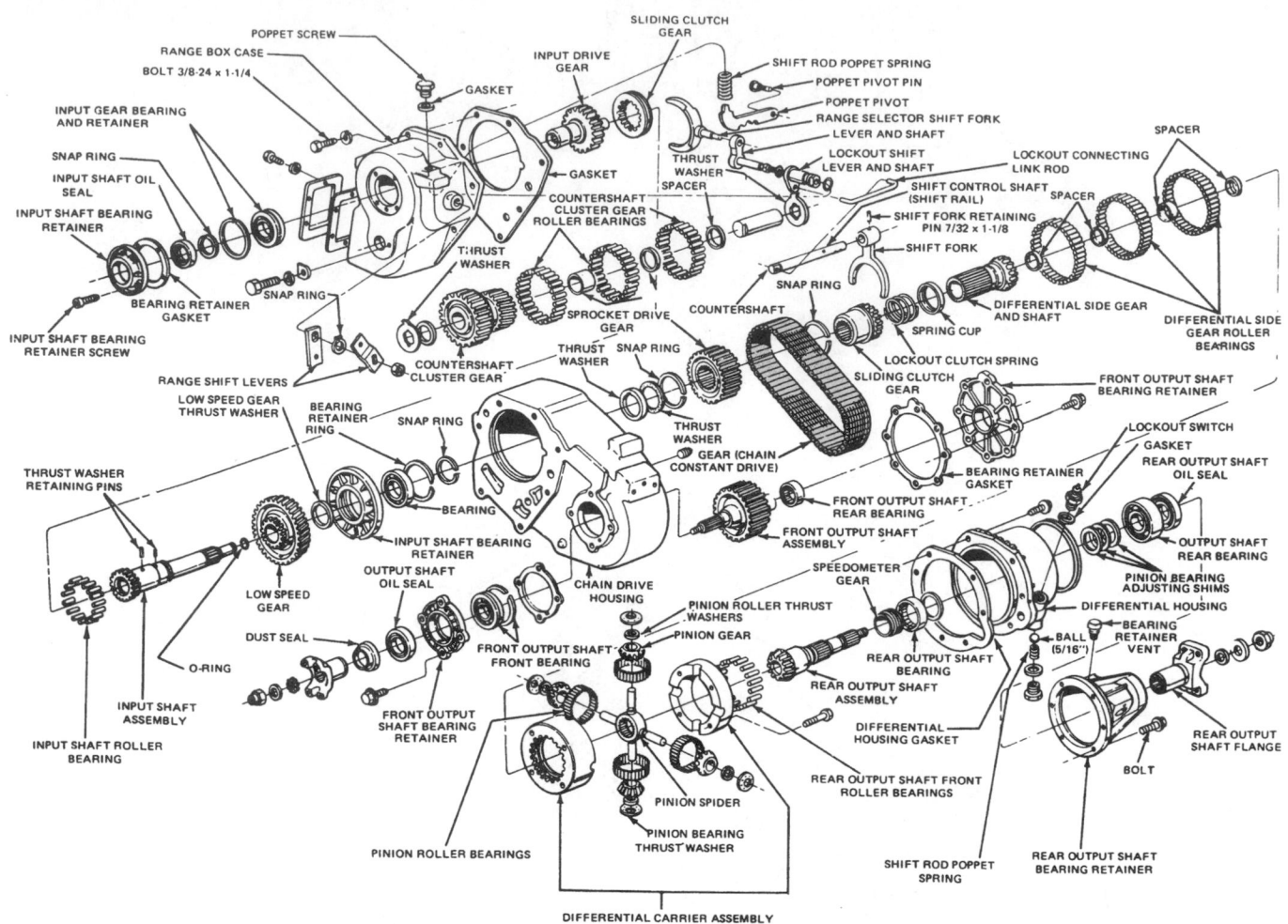

Figure 31-6. Exploded view of a transfer case that uses a chain to drive the differential unit. It does not employ a limited-slip feature in the differential. It does not use planetary gears to achieve low range. Conventional gearing is used. (Ford)

traction, either front or rear. The silicone fluid in the coupling is very thick, or viscous, and will not thin due to heat. As one axle overspeeds because of wheel slippage, the coupling rotational speed also increases. As the coupling rotational speed increases, the fixed clutch plates are forced to rotate in the silicone fluid as they increase in speed. As fluid is forced between the clutch plates and displaced, it expands, creating friction and more resistance to higher input speed. The coupling does not lock the axles together, it controls the amount of slipping. At the same time, it sends maximum torque to the slower moving axle. Transfer case power flow is shown in **Figure 31-8.**

> ⚠ **Caution: The viscous coupling and pinion assembly are not serviceable as a unit. They are sealed together and the silicone fluid is not replaceable. If the coupling and/or pinions are damaged, replace the entire unit with a new one.**

Transfer Case Service

The following sections detail the service procedures for typical transfer cases. These procedures are general due to

the many types of four-wheel drive systems in service. Always obtain and use the proper manufacturer's service manual. Follow the manufacturer's directions for transfer case lubricant type and viscosity. Check the lubricant level and do not overfill. If periodic changes are recommended, be sure to use the correct type of fluid. Any transfer case using a limited-slip differential requires a special lubricant or lubricant additive. Talk to the owner about observations and complaints regarding transfer case operation. Ask questions to help pinpoint possible trouble areas. Make a list of possible problems based on the owner's statements. Chapter 42 contains troubleshooting charts for four-wheel drive transfer cases.

Whenever possible, the vehicle should be road tested. Check the transfer case lubricant level before road testing. If the unit has a viscous coupling, check that the coupling is not leaking by inspecting the transfer case oil. Leaking silicone will appear as globules of silicone fluid in the transfer case oil. When making the road test, include some heavy acceleration and deceleration. Operate the vehicle at various speeds. The route should include, when possible, some bumpy sections and a hill. Check closely for abnormal noise, jumping out of gear, vibration, hard shifting, gear clash during shifting, and

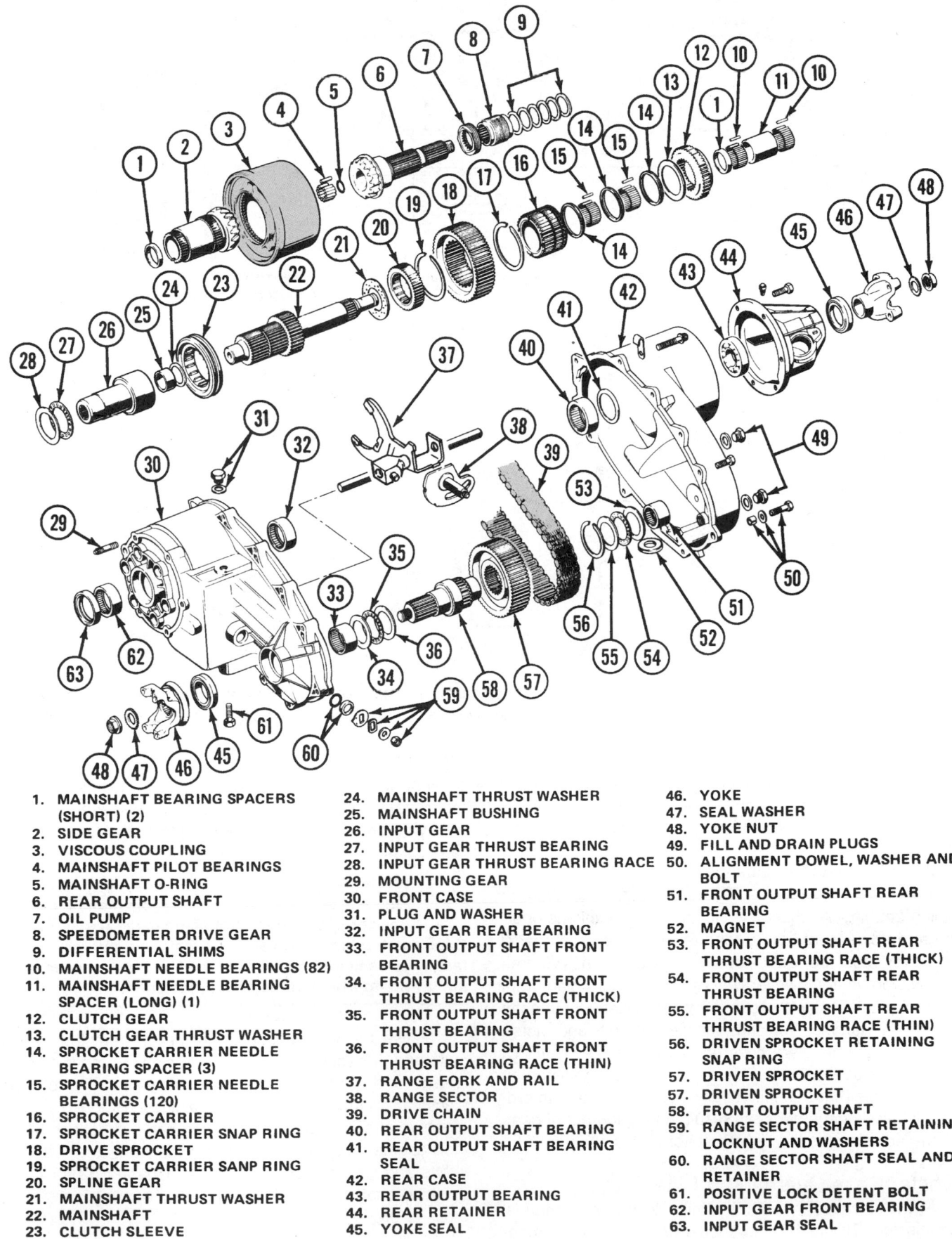

1. **MAINSHAFT BEARING SPACERS (SHORT) (2)**
2. **SIDE GEAR**
3. **VISCOUS COUPLING**
4. **MAINSHAFT PILOT BEARINGS**
5. **MAINSHAFT O-RING**
6. **REAR OUTPUT SHAFT**
7. **OIL PUMP**
8. **SPEEDOMETER DRIVE GEAR**
9. **DIFFERENTIAL SHIMS**
10. **MAINSHAFT NEEDLE BEARINGS (82)**
11. **MAINSHAFT NEEDLE BEARING SPACER (LONG) (1)**
12. **CLUTCH GEAR**
13. **CLUTCH GEAR THRUST WASHER**
14. **SPROCKET CARRIER NEEDLE BEARING SPACER (3)**
15. **SPROCKET CARRIER NEEDLE BEARINGS (120)**
16. **SPROCKET CARRIER**
17. **SPROCKET CARRIER SNAP RING**
18. **DRIVE SPROCKET**
19. **SPROCKET CARRIER SANP RING**
20. **SPLINE GEAR**
21. **MAINSHAFT THRUST WASHER**
22. **MAINSHAFT**
23. **CLUTCH SLEEVE**

24. **MAINSHAFT THRUST WASHER**
25. **MAINSHAFT BUSHING**
26. **INPUT GEAR**
27. **INPUT GEAR THRUST BEARING**
28. **INPUT GEAR THRUST BEARING RACE**
29. **MOUNTING GEAR**
30. **FRONT CASE**
31. **PLUG AND WASHER**
32. **INPUT GEAR REAR BEARING**
33. **FRONT OUTPUT SHAFT FRONT BEARING**
34. **FRONT OUTPUT SHAFT FRONT THRUST BEARING RACE (THICK)**
35. **FRONT OUTPUT SHAFT FRONT THRUST BEARING**
36. **FRONT OUTPUT SHAFT FRONT THRUST BEARING RACE (THIN)**
37. **RANGE FORK AND RAIL**
38. **RANGE SECTOR**
39. **DRIVE CHAIN**
40. **REAR OUTPUT SHAFT BEARING**
41. **REAR OUTPUT SHAFT BEARING SEAL**
42. **REAR CASE**
43. **REAR OUTPUT BEARING**
44. **REAR RETAINER**
45. **YOKE SEAL**

46. **YOKE**
47. **SEAL WASHER**
48. **YOKE NUT**
49. **FILL AND DRAIN PLUGS**
50. **ALIGNMENT DOWEL, WASHER AND BOLT**
51. **FRONT OUTPUT SHAFT REAR BEARING**
52. **MAGNET**
53. **FRONT OUTPUT SHAFT REAR THRUST BEARING RACE (THICK)**
54. **FRONT OUTPUT SHAFT REAR THRUST BEARING**
55. **FRONT OUTPUT SHAFT REAR THRUST BEARING RACE (THIN)**
56. **DRIVEN SPROCKET RETAINING SNAP RING**
57. **DRIVEN SPROCKET**
57. **DRIVEN SPROCKET**
58. **FRONT OUTPUT SHAFT**
59. **RANGE SECTOR SHAFT RETAINING LOCKNUT AND WASHERS**
60. **RANGE SECTOR SHAFT SEAL AND RETAINER**
61. **POSITIVE LOCK DETENT BOLT**
62. **INPUT GEAR FRONT BEARING**
63. **INPUT GEAR SEAL**

Figure 31-7. Exploded view of a viscous coupling transfer case assembly. This case can be shifted manually or with vacuum motors. (Chrysler)

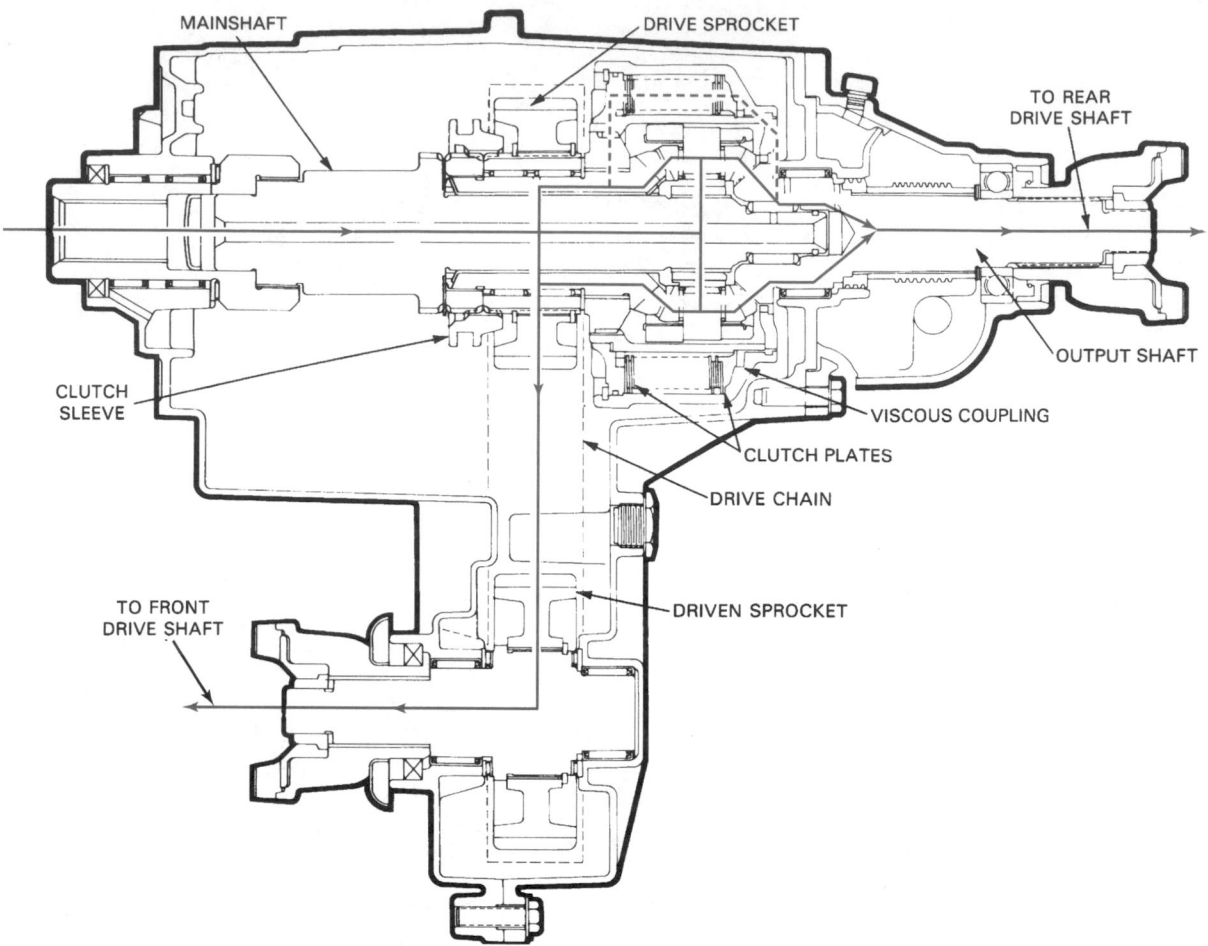

Figure 31-8. Power flow schematic of a viscous coupling transfer case. The solid line is the flow of power to the front and rear axles. The dotted line represents power flow through the coupling when excessive wheel spin (loss of traction) is encountered. (Chrysler)

leaks. Note the transfer case position (two-wheel drive—high range, four-wheel drive—high range, four-wheel drive—low range) in which any problem was most evident.

Check Clutch and Shift Linkage

If the owner complains of hard shifting, gear clash, or jumping out of gear, check the clutch and shift linkage operation and adjustment before road testing. The clutch pedal free travel must be within specifications. Excessive free travel will prevent full withdrawal of the pressure plate from the clutch disc. This will cause the transfer case input shaft to continue turning, making shifting difficult and noisy. Clutch adjustments were covered in Chapter 29. The shift linkage must operate smoothly and should be adjusted so that the transfer case is shifted fully into gear. Failure to provide full shift engagement can result in jumping out of gear. Linkage adjustments are covered later in this chapter.

Transfer Case Overhaul

Transfer case overhaul is similar to that of a manual transmission. The technician should obtain a service manual covering the specific transfer case to be overhauled and refer to it as the unit is disassembled. Disassembly and assembly order, specifications, and techniques will be shown. Exploded views will assist in the correct positioning

of all parts. Although basic transfer case designs are similar, disassembly procedure and order of disassembly varies widely among the different makes and models.

 Note: Some transfer case repairs, such as shift linkage adjustment and seal replacement, can be performed with the transfer case in the vehicle. Once an attaching part has been removed, put the fasteners back into place. This will facilitate reassembly and avoid improper placement of fasteners.

Raise the vehicle and drain the oil from the transfer case and, if necessary, the transmission. Remove the shift linkage and mark it to facilitate reassembly. Remove any electrical connectors and vacuum lines. Before removing the drive shafts, mark them so they can be reassembled in their original positions. Disconnect the front and rear drive shafts and wire out of the way. See Chapter 33 for details on drive shaft service. Tape the roller bearing caps to the cross to prevent them from falling off.

 Caution: The transfer case is very heavy and awkward. Get someone to help you support and lower the transfer case from the vehicle.

Remove the transfer case mounts as needed. If a support member must be removed, support the engine and transmission assembly with a jack stand or other support. If pushing upward on the engine or transmission oil pan, place a wide block of wood between the pan and jack. A transmission jack should be used for removal. Attach the transfer case firmly to the jack. Then remove the fasteners holding the transfer case to the transmission, slide the transfer case away from the transmission and lower the transmission jack. If the transfer case is of a size and weight that can be easily handled, pilot bolts can be used to facilitate removal. Remove all but two of the transfer case-to-transmission housing fasteners. Install the pilot bolts in two mounting holes. The pilot bolts should be long enough to provide support until the transfer case input shaft is clear of the transmission output shaft. With the help of an assistant, slide the transfer case away from the transmission and lower it to the floor.

General Disassembly Procedures

To aid in locating external fasteners, clean the transfer case outer surfaces thoroughly before beginning disassembly. This will also minimize contamination of internal parts. Some transfer cases are designed with two aluminum end castings attached to a central support. The end castings must be removed to gain access to the gears and shafts. Other transfer cases must be split to expose the internal gears. Due to space limitations, it is obvious that a text such as this one cannot cover the disassembly procedure for all transfer cases. Instead of discussing specific disassembly procedure and order, the transfer case parts will be covered separately and general inspection techniques will be discussed.

Place the transfer case on a clean workbench or in a suitable stand, if available. Follow the manufacturer's recommended order of part removal. If no manual is available, study the method of construction. This will provide clues as to which part should be removed first, second, etc. Careful study will also usually indicate how the parts must be removed. Be sure to place alignment marks on the transfer case housing before beginning disassembly. Two common transfer cases are shown in **Figures 31-9** and **31-10**. Note that one is driven by gears, while the other case uses a chain drive. If the transfer case has internal shift forks, remove

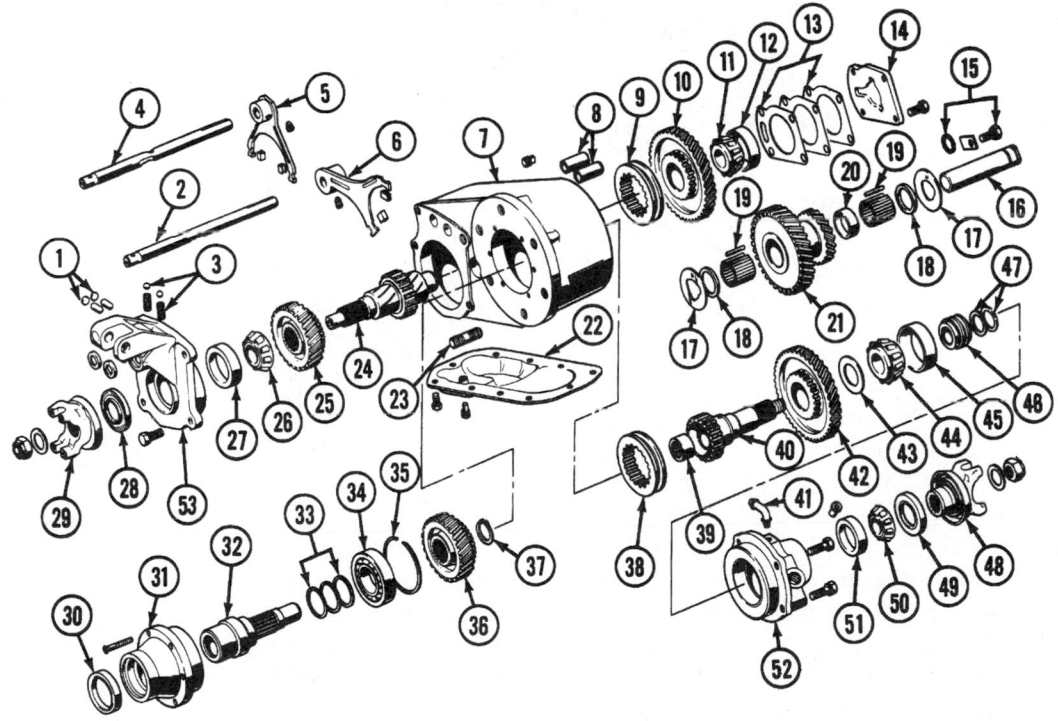

1. INTERLOCK PLUGS AND INTERLOCKS	13. END PLAY SHIMS – FRONT OUTPUT SHAFT	27. FRONT OUTPUT SHAFT BEARING RACE	41. VENT
2. SHIFT ROD – REAR OUTPUT SHAFT FORK	14. COVER PLATE	28. OIL SEAL	42. CLUTCH GEAR – REAR OUTPUT SHAFT
3. POPPET BALLS AND SPRINGS	15. LOCK PLATE, BOLT AND WASHER	29. FRONT YOKE	43. THRUST WASHER
4. SHIFT ROD – FRONT OUTPUT SHAFT FORK	16. INTERMEDIATE GEAR SHAFT	30. SEAL	44. BEARING – REAR OUTPUT SHAFT FRONT
5. FRONT OUTPUT SHAFT SHIFT FORK	17. THRUST WASHER	31. SUPPORT – INPUT SHAFT	45. RACE – REAR OUTPUT SHAFT BEARING
6. REAR OUTPUT SHAFT SHIFT FORK	18. BEARING SPACER (THIN)	32. INPUT SHAFT	46. SPEEDOMETER DRIVE GEAR
7. TRANSFER CASE	19. INTERMEDIATE GEAR SHAFT NEEDLE BEARINGS	33. SHIMS	47. END PLAY SHIMS
8. THIMBLE COVERS	20. BEARING SPACER (THICK)	34. INPUT SHAFT BEARING	48. REAR YOKE
9. CLUTCH SLEEVE – FRONT OUTPUT SHAFT	21. INTERMEDIATE GEAR	35. INPUT SHAFT BEARING SNAP RING	49. REAR OUTPUT SHAFT OIL SEAL
10. CLUTCH GEAR – FRONT OUTPUT SHAFT	22. BOTTOM COVER	36. REAR OUTPUT SHAFT GEAR	50. BEARING – REAR OUTPUT SHAFT REAR
11. BEARING – FRONT OUTPUT SHAFT REAR	23. STUD (CASE-TO-TRANS.)	37. SNAP RING	51. BEARING RACE
12. RACE – FRONT OUTPUT SHAFT BEARING	24. FRONT OUTPUT SHAFT	38. CLUTCH SLEEVE – REAR OUTPUT SHAFT	52. REAR BEARING CAP
	25. FRONT OUTPUT SHAFT GEAR	39. INPUT SHAFT REAR BEARING (NEEDLE) (OR PILOT BEARING)	53. FRONT BEARING CAP
	26. FRONT OUTPUT SHAFT BEARING (FRONT)	40. REAR OUTPUT SHAFT	

Figure 31-9. Exploded view of a part-time, gear-driven transfer case. Study the parts carefully. (Jeep)

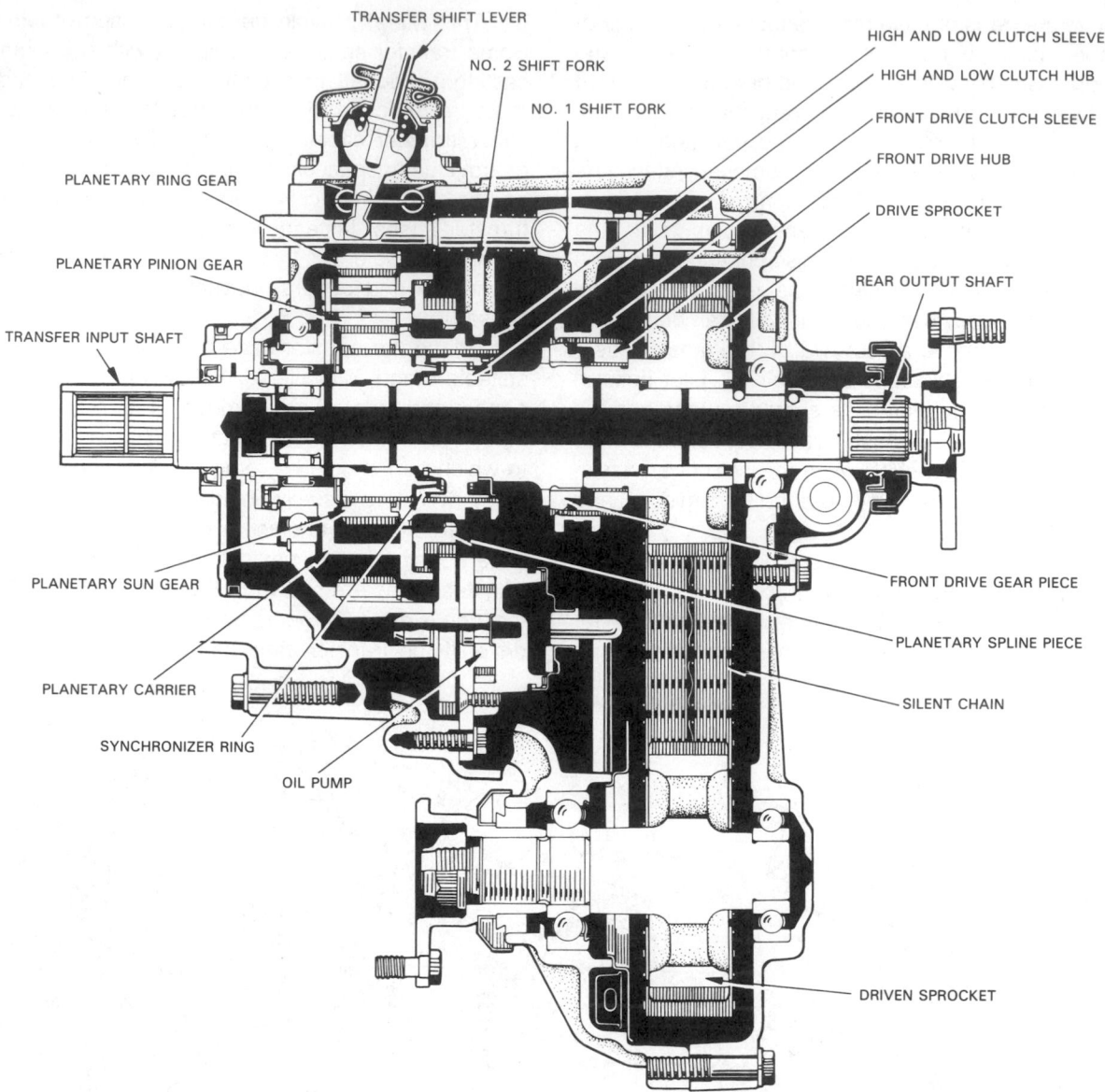

TRANSFER SHIFT LEVER

NO. 2 SHIFT FORK

NO. 1 SHIFT FORK

PLANETARY RING GEAR

PLANETARY PINION GEAR

TRANSFER INPUT SHAFT

PLANETARY SUN GEAR

PLANETARY CARRIER

SYNCHRONIZER RING

OIL PUMP

HIGH AND LOW CLUTCH SLEEVE

HIGH AND LOW CLUTCH HUB

FRONT DRIVE CLUTCH SLEEVE

FRONT DRIVE HUB

DRIVE SPROCKET

REAR OUTPUT SHAFT

FRONT DRIVE GEAR PIECE

PLANETARY SPLINE PIECE

SILENT CHAIN

DRIVEN SPROCKET

Figure 31-10. Cutaway view of a two-speed, part-time transfer case. This case uses a planetary gear reduction setup, along with a drive chain. Low range reduction is 2.566:1. (Toyota)

them first. Do not lose any of the detent springs, detents, interlocks, or setscrews. Then remove all the parts from the case, including all bearings. The internal gears may use individual needle bearings. Retrieve all of these bearings and check the service manual to ensure that you have the proper count. Place any small parts (loose needles and rollers, springs, fasteners) into a separate container to prevent loss. Avoid distorting snap rings in case they must be reused. Lay out all parts in order so that the transfer case can be reassembled simply by reversing the order of disassembly.

⚠ **Caution: Avoid excessive use of a hammer to loosen parts. Use a brass hammer if necessary. Handle parts carefully to avoid chipping and nicking. If possible, use new snap rings for reassembly.**

Cleaning and Inspecting Parts

Clean all internal parts, especially gears, bearings, and shafts. Thoroughly clean the inside of the case. Any tiny particles of chipped teeth or bearing material that remain will be loosened by the new lubricant and will eventually find their way into the moving parts where they will cause damage. Once the transfer case has been completely disassembled and cleaned, the internal parts can be inspected. Keep in mind that many variations in part construction and layout are possible, depending on:

- Transfer case manufacturer.
- Variations in the vehicle body type, engine, and transmission.
- Whether the unit is from a full-time or part-time four-wheel drive system.
- Whether the forward drive mechanism uses gears or a chain and sprockets.

When a transfer case has suffered heavy gear damage such as shattered teeth, use crack detection chemicals on the remaining gears. Crack detection was covered in Chapter 14. Check the shafts and shaft openings in the case also. Discard all parts showing the slightest sign of cracking. Replace the bearings, even if they appear to be good.

Inspect Transfer Case Housing

Inspect the transfer case for signs of cracking. Look carefully, especially around bolt holes and shaft and bearing openings. On aluminum cases, check for porous areas or other flaws in the case. Also check all sheet metal covers for dents and warping which would prevent them from sealing properly. Carefully straighten any damaged areas or replace the part. Check the transfer case mating surfaces for any burrs that could cause misalignment or leaks. Remove any burrs with a fine mill file. If the transfer case has a vent, make sure it is open. Check the bushings in the transfer case housing (if used) and replace if necessary. Always replace any external transfer case oil seals, such as those shown in **Figure 31-11.**

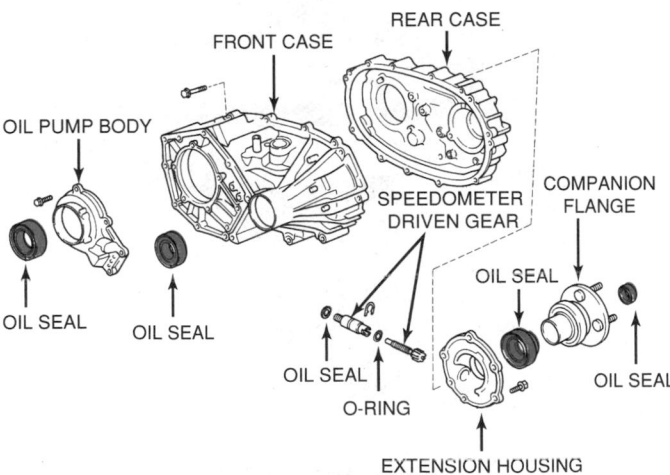

Figure 31-11. Replace transfer case external seals as needed during inspection and repair. (Toyota)

Inspect All Shafts and Gears

Inspect all shaft bearing surfaces. They should be smooth with no evidence of wear or damage. Place the gears on the shaft. They should turn smoothly without excessive rocking. Where gears are splined, check for excessive play. Look over every tooth on every gear. There must be no signs of chipping, galling, or wear. All snap ring grooves must have sharp square shoulders. Thrust washers must be smooth and not worn appreciably. Thrust washer thickness should be measured with a micrometer. Inspect all shaft support bearings and internal shaft or gear bushings. Replace any that are not in good condition. Check the synchronizers if the transfer case uses them. A typical transfer case shaft and gear assembly is shown in **Figure 31-12.** Closely inspect the drive chain and drive sprockets of the chain drive assembly for wear or damage. Check the chain for slack and worn pins, **Figure 31-13.** If the transfer case uses two large gears for power transfer, check them for chipping, wear, and loose fit on the shaft splines.

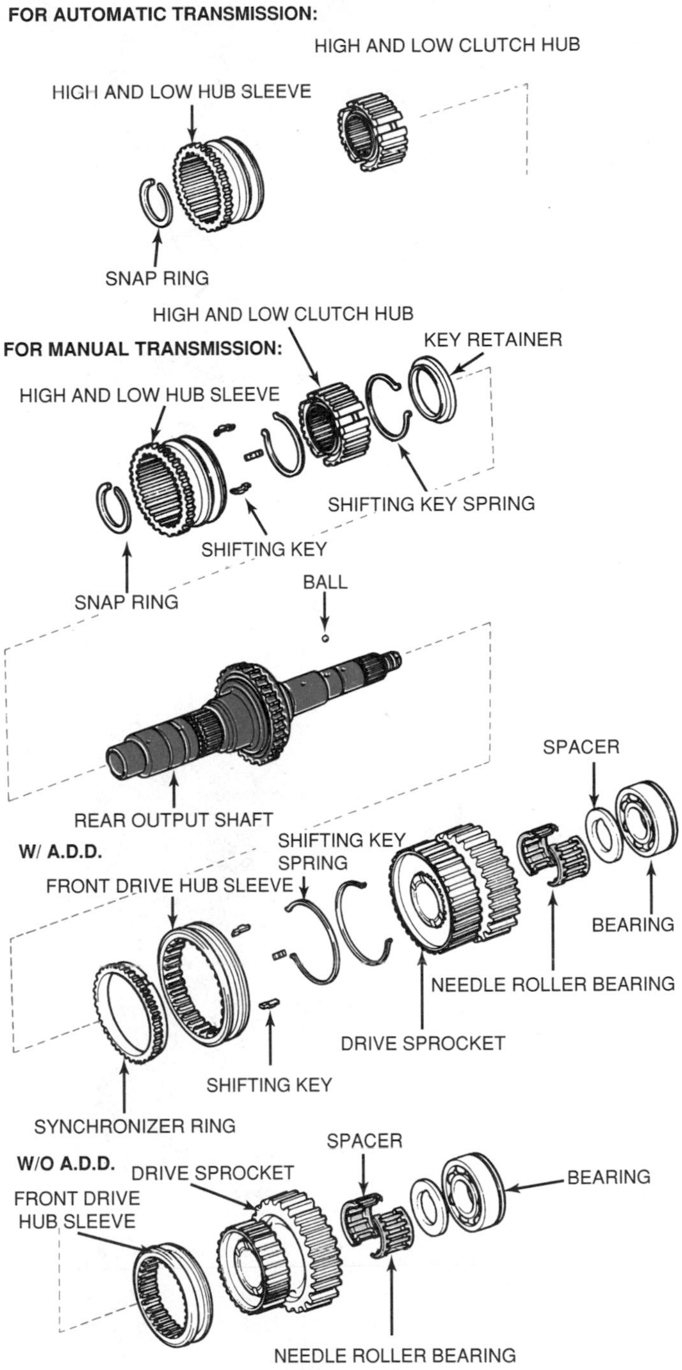

FOR AUTOMATIC TRANSMISSION:

FOR MANUAL TRANSMISSION:

Figure 31-12. Typical transfer case shaft and gear assemblies with related components. Note the two-piece needle roller bearings. (Toyota)

Inspect Transfer Case Pump, Differential Unit, and Viscous Coupling

If the transfer case has an internal lubrication pump, such as the one in **Figure 31-14,** check it for wear and proper clearances. Replace the pump if it shows any signs of wear or if clearances are excessive. Closely inspect the differential unit or viscous coupling for wear or damage. Differential gears are checked in the same manner as the gears inspected earlier. The viscous coupling should be checked for leakage, which will appear as globules of silicone in the transfer case oil. Replace any suspected coupling. A viscous coupling is shown in **Figure 31-15.**

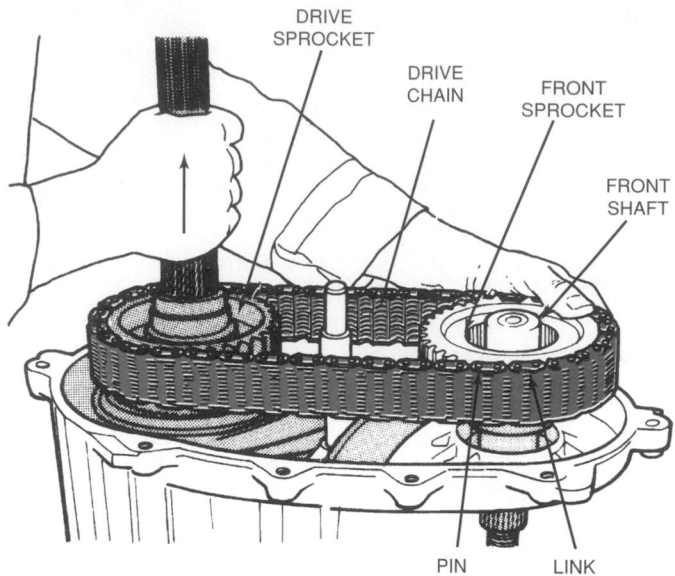

Figure 31-13. Remove the drive chain and sprockets. Check the chain for excessive wear and broken or missing links and pins. (Dodge)

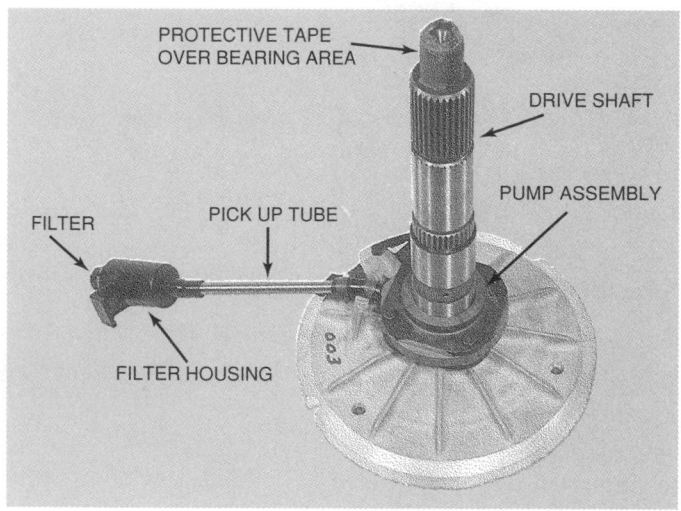

Figure 31-14. A transfer case internal lubrication pump assembly, pickup tube, filter, and filter housing. (Borg-Warner)

 Note: The viscous coupling cannot be disassembled for repairs. Replace the entire unit when defective.

Obtain New Parts

When a transfer case component is worn or damaged, replace the defective parts. Considering the difficulty of removing and disassembling the transfer case, any suspect part should be replaced. Always check the new part against the old for design, size, and shape. Try the part on the associated shaft or in the transfer case to make sure it fits properly. Use new snap rings whenever they can be obtained. New thrust washers will provide proper end play. New gaskets and seals are a must. Some transfer cases

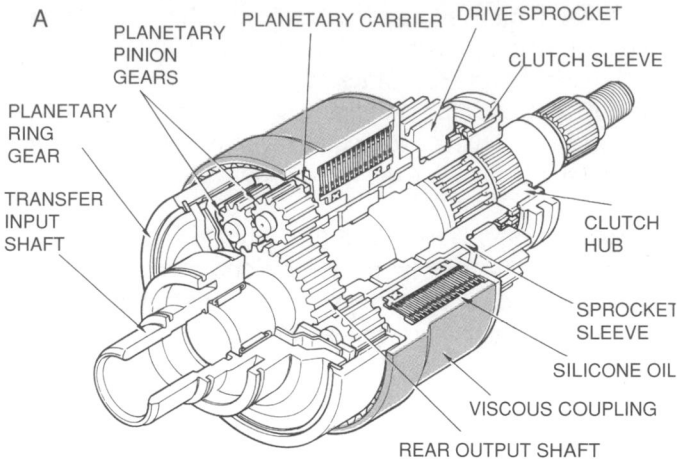

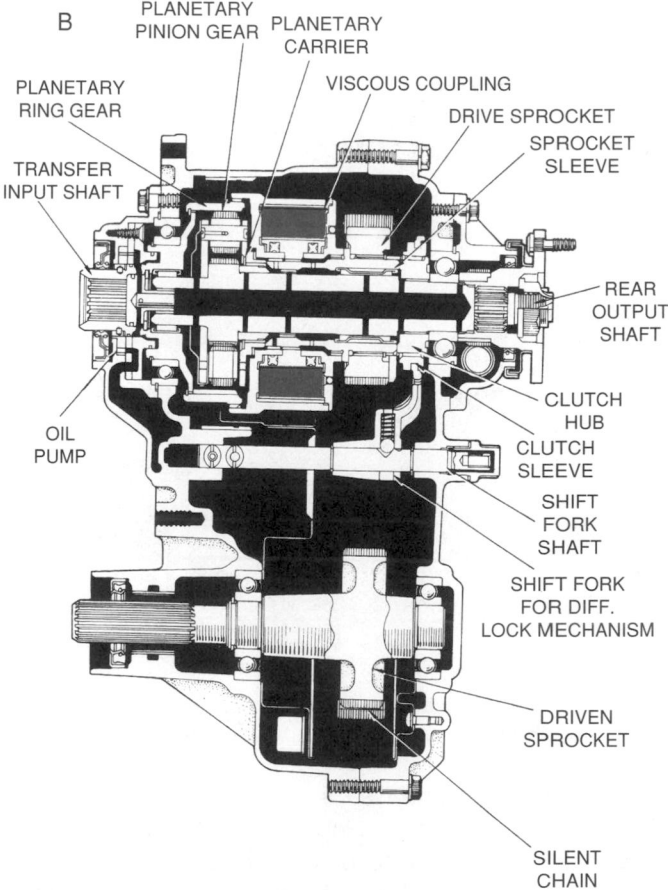

Figure 31-15. A—A cutaway of one particular type of transfer case viscous coupling. The inside of the coupling is filled with silicone oil. The unit slips to allow for torque build up without damaging the drive train. B—Cross-sectional view of a transfer case that incorporates a viscous clutch. (Toyota)

use RTV (room temperature vulcanizing) or anaerobic sealer in place of gaskets. Always use the recommended sealer. An inferior seal can cause a complete loss of lubricant, leading to transfer case failure.

 Caution: Parts must be absolutely clean and well lubricated before assembly.

Following cleaning and inspection, all parts should be oiled and placed in clean containers. Before installation, every part should be heavily lubricated with gear oil or automatic transmission fluid as recommended by the manufacturer.

Transfer Case Reassembly

The transfer case is reassembled in the reverse order of disassembly. All parts must be lubricated, properly positioned, and secured before installation. Make frequent use of the proper manufacturer's service manual to ensure that all parts are reinstalled correctly. Never use excessive force to make a part fit. If a part does not slide into position as it should, stop and check for the source of difficulty. Lubricate all bushings and shafts with transmission oil before beginning assembly. To install thrust washers, place a coating of soft grease on each end of the gear and press the thrust washers into the grease. Make sure they face in the right direction. The grease will hold the washers in place as the gear is installed.

 Note: Any grease used to hold internal parts in place must be compatible with and dissolve readily in the normal oil or transmission fluid used in the transfer case.

Check all shafts and gears after reassembly. There should be no binding or hard to turn parts. If any parts are binding, disassemble and determine the cause. Check the end play of all units where an end play specification is given, using a dial indicator or feeler gauge as needed. A typical end play checking procedure is shown in **Figure 31-16.** When the transfer case internal parts are fully assembled, pour fresh gear oil over the gears and shaft through the cover opening. Use the recommended gear oil and correct viscosity. Turn the input shaft while shifting through the gears. The shafts and gears should turn freely with no binding. Check shaft end play, if not checked earlier. After all checks have been made, install the shift mechanism, if applicable.

Transfer Case Installation

Wipe the clutch housing and transfer case face clean and check both for burrs. Using pilot bolts or a transmission jack, raise the transfer case into alignment with the engine and align the case input shaft with the transmission output shaft. Then carefully push the transfer case into position at the rear of the transmission.

⚠️ **Caution: Never let the transfer case hang with all of its weight supported by the shafts. Damage to the transfer case and transmission will result. Also, the transfer case could slip off of the transmission, resulting in damage and/or injuries if it hits someone.**

Install and torque the fasteners holding the transfer case to the transmission. Reinstall all transmission and transfer case mounts. Install the selector linkage (if used), electrical and vacuum lines, and other parts. Install the front

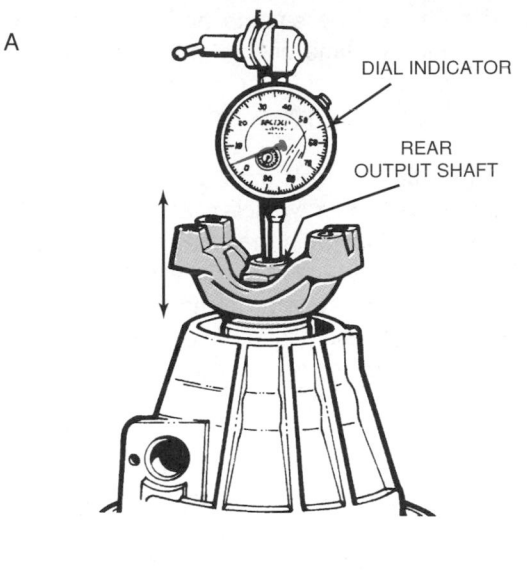

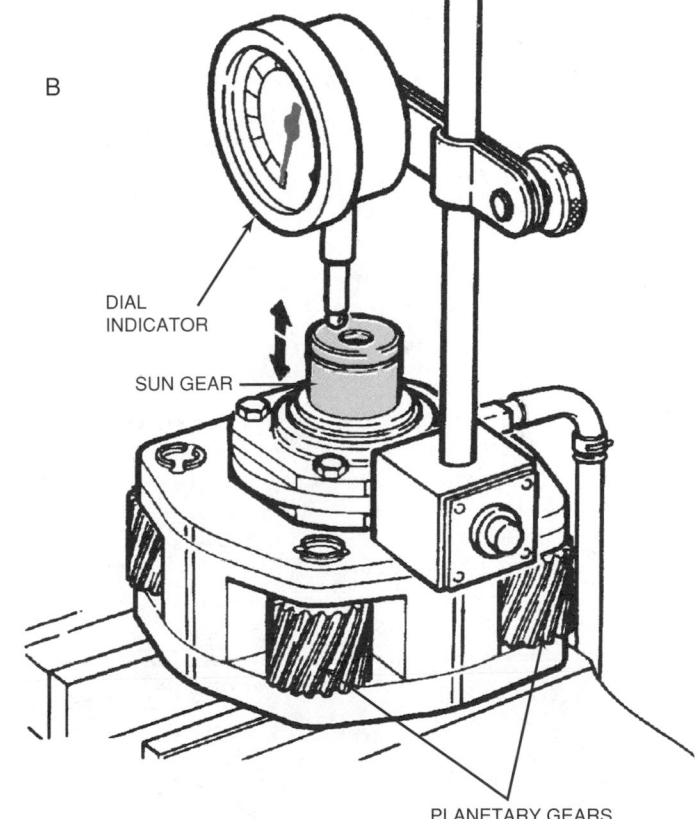

Figure 31-16. A—Checking rear output shaft end play with a dial indicator. B—Checking the clearance between the sun gear and the planetary gear set with a dial indicator. (Ford and Range Rover)

and rear drive shafts, being careful to match the alignment marks. Adjust the selector linkage as necessary. Fill the transfer case to the level of the filler plug with the recommended lubricant. Fill slowly so the oil will have time to flow into all moving parts.

Road Test

Road test the vehicle. The transfer case should operate quietly and smoothly. On part-time units, shifting between all ranges should be should be smooth and positive with no jumping out of gear. Full-time units should operate quietly and without any unusual feel. After returning to the shop, check for fluid leakage and recheck the lubricant level.

Locking Hubs

Some four-wheel drive vehicles use front **locking hubs** to engage and disengage the front wheels and front drive axle. This type of arrangement is a component of a part-time four-wheel drive system, but is not controlled by internal parts in the transfer case. The locking hub is a device which locks the front wheels to the front axle at the wheel hub.

Some locking hubs are engaged and disengaged automatically by the use of one-way, or **overrunning clutches** in the front drive axles. These one-way clutches will transfer power in one direction but will freewheel, or overrun, if power is applied in the other direction. These clutches lock up whenever the engine is driving the front wheels through the transfer case and unlock when the transfer case is returned to 2-wheel drive operation. Other locking hubs can be automatically released by moving the transfer case to the two-wheel position and backing up the vehicle for a few feet. A typical manual locking hub is shown in **Figure 31-17.**

Locking Hub Service

Locking hubs are simple in construction and are relatively simple to repair. However, locking hubs must be carefully cleaned and checked for corrosion since they are much more likely to become contaminated with water and dirt. Seals and gaskets must be in perfect shape to protect the internal parts. See **Figure 31-18.** To begin removal of the locking hub assembly, lift the vehicle at the affected axle and remove the wheel. Most locking hub components are held in place by a snap ring. Remove the front hub cover and the wheel bearing nut first. Then remove the snap ring and slide the hub parts from the axle shaft. Disassemble the locking hub on a clean workbench. Check all parts carefully for signs of wear, corrosion, and dirt. Typical locking hubs are shown in **Figures 31-19** and **31-20.**

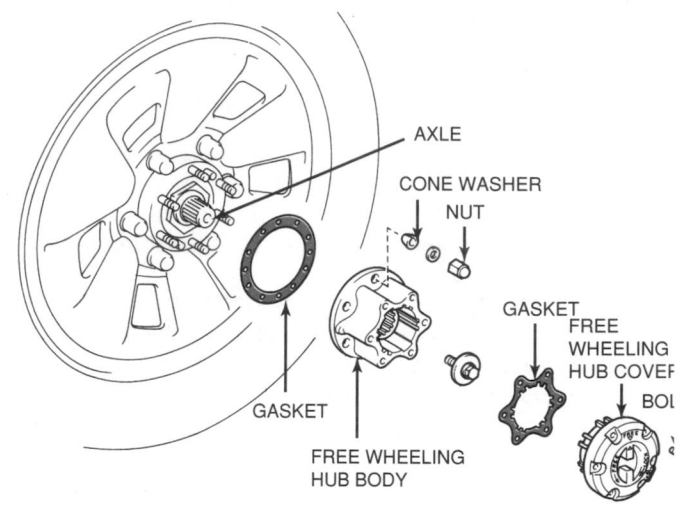

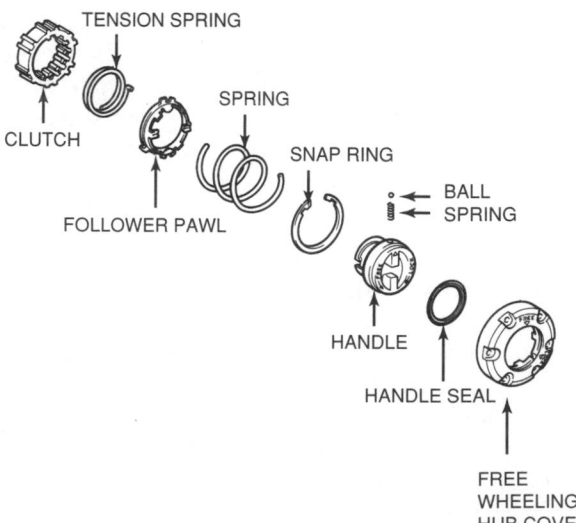

Figure 31-18. Exploded view of a manual locking hub assembly. Always replace seals, gaskets, and O-rings when servicing the hub and/or bearings. (Toyota)

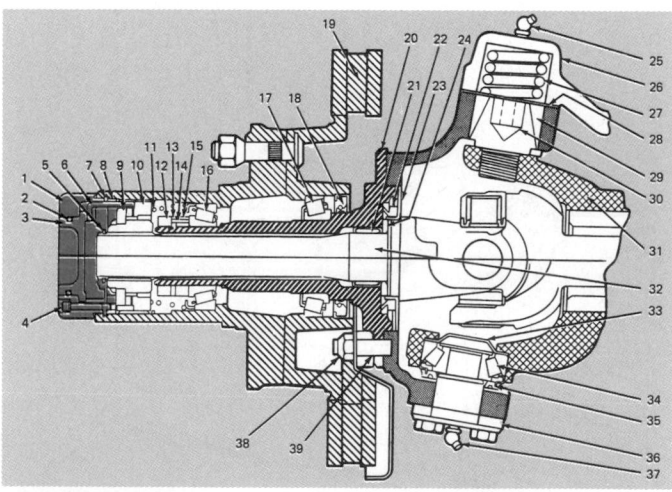

1. RETAINING PLATE
2. O-RING
3. ACTUATOR KNOB
4. RETAINING PLATE BOLT
5. AXLE SHAFT SNAP RING
6. ACTUATING CAM BODY
7. INTERNAL SNAP RING
8. OUTER CLUTCH RETAINING RING
9. AXLE SHAFT SLEEVE AND CLUTCH RING
10. INNER CLUTCH RING
11. SPRING
12. LOCK NUT
13. LOCK-ADJ. NUT
14. PIN-ADJ. NUT
15. ADJUSTING NUT
16. OUTER WHEEL BEARING
17. INNER WHEEL BEARING
18. SEAL
19. HUB-AND-DISC

20. SPINDLE
21. SPINDLE BEARING
22. SEAL
23. DEFLECTOR
24. SPACER
25. LUBE FITTING
26. UPPER BEARING CAP
27. PRESSURE SPRING
28. GASKET
29. BUSHING, KING-PIN
30. KING-PIN
31. YOKE
32. OUTER AXLE SHAFT
33. GREASE RETAINER
34. LOWER BEARING
35. SEAL
36. BEARING CAP
37. LUBE FITTING
38. SPINDLE ATTACHING NUT
39. SPINDLE ATTACHING BOLT

Figure 31-17. A cutaway view of a manually locking hub assembly as used by one manufacturer. (GMC)

 Note: Carefully check the seals and gaskets for any damage which would permit the entry of water or loss of lubricant. This is extremely important when servicing locking hubs, since they are often submerged in water and mud during off-road operation.

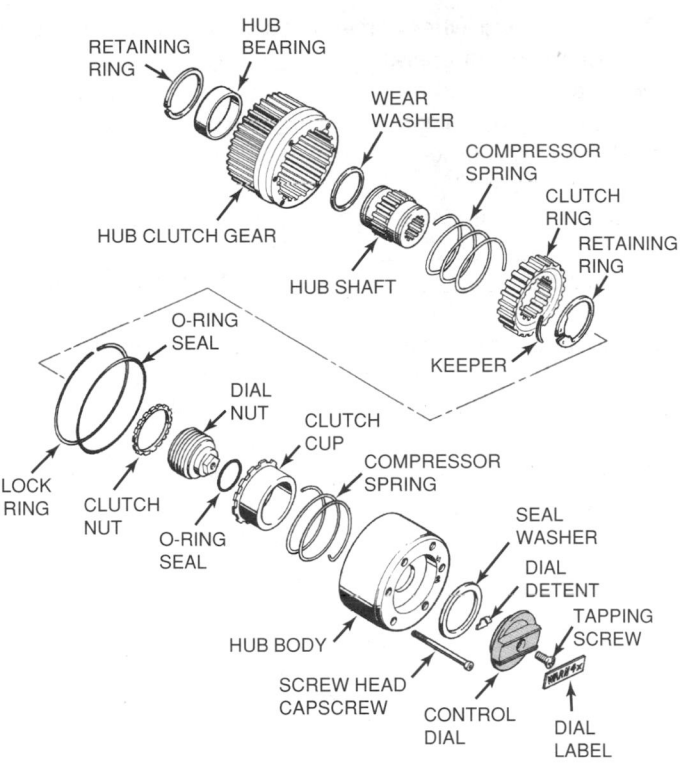

Figure 31-19. Exploded view of a manual locking hub. (Jeep)

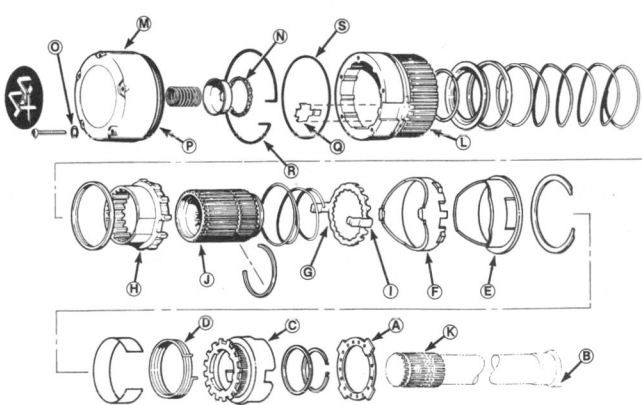

Figure 31-20. Study this exploded view of a automatic locking hub assembly. Note the names of each part. A—Drag sleeve retainer washer. B—Axle housing. C—Drag sleeve. D—Brake band. E—Steel inner cage. F—Plastic outer cage. G—Cam follower. H—Clutch gear. I—Cam follower. J—Hub sleeve. K—Axle shaft. L—Clutch housing. M—Hub outer cover. N—Bearing assembly. O—Cover seal O-ring. P—Cover sealing O-ring seal groove. Q—Seal bridge retainer. R—Wire retaining ring. S—Cover sealing O-ring. (Chevrolet)

Install new parts as needed, being careful to coat all parts with the correct type of lubricant. Ensure that sufficient grease has been installed in the hub cavity. If the front hub assembly has adjustable wheel bearings, adjust them as outlined in Chapter 38.

Vacuum Motor Service

On those front wheel drive assemblies having a *vacuum motor,* the front wheels may fail to drive if the vacuum motor is inoperative or the linkage is stuck. If the shift collar in the axle shift collar assembly is stuck, the front axle may be engaged at all times. Check the vacuum motor with a vacuum pump to ensure that the diaphragm is not leaking. If the motor is defective, it can be replaced.

To service the vacuum motor and linkage, remove the differential inspection cover and vacuum motor as a unit. The shift fork and linkage will also be attached to the cover, **Figure 31-21.** Check all parts for wear and ensure that the shift collar is not stuck or damaged. See **Figure 31-22.** Replace any worn parts as necessary. If the shift collar must be removed, refer to Chapter 33 on axle service. When reassembling the vacuum motor and cover to the axle, make sure that the shift fork engages the shift collar. Refill the axle with the correct lubricant and recheck system operation.

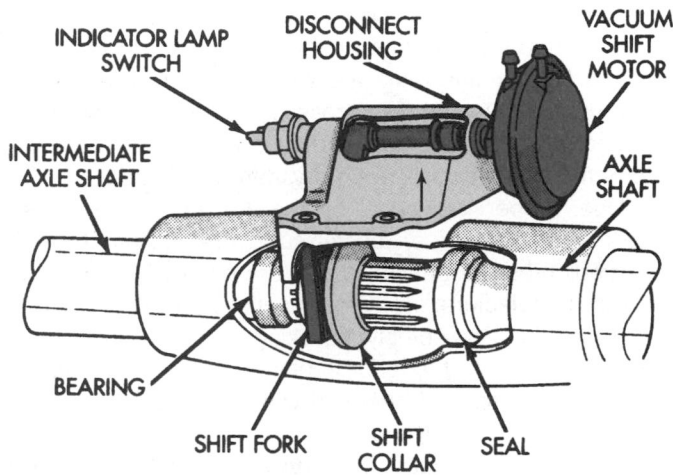

Figure 31-21. Remove the vacuum motor, cover, and shift fork assembly after removing all fasteners, wiring, and vacuum hoses. Cover the opening with a clean shop towel to prevent dirt or small parts from entering the housing. (Dodge)

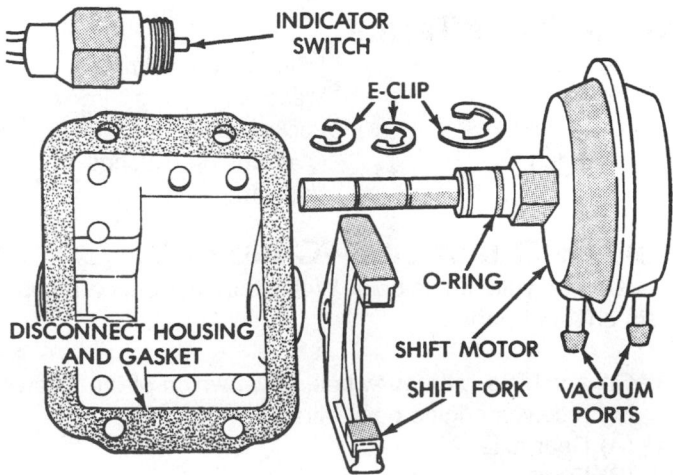

Figure 31-22. Check all shift motor parts carefully for signs of binding, excessive wear, water damage, breakage, etc. Repair or replace as necessary. (Dodge)

Tech Talk

Transfer cases may not seem very heavy, but they are oddly shaped and awkward to handle. If you try to lift a transfer case into position by yourself, it is likely to slip and fall, crushing your hand or foot. If it does not hurt you, the case will be damaged when it hits the floor.

The best way to install a transfer case or any heavy underbody component is with a transmission jack. Always strap the unit to the jack with the retaining chain. If a transmission jack is not available, make sure that you have at least one other person to help you. Tell the other person exactly how you intend to lift and place the transfer case.

Summary

Transfer cases are either part-time or full-time units. Never operate the part-time unit in four-wheel drive on dry, hard roads. Full-time units are always in four-wheel drive, with a differential assembly or viscous coupling to allow for differences in axle speeds. Full-time units must not be operated in the lockout position on dry, hard road surfaces.

Use proper lubricant for the transfer case. When removing or installing a transfer case, use the proper handling equipment as transfer cases are heavy. For overhaul, use the manufacturer's service manual and follow instructions carefully. Disassembly, checking, and cleaning procedures are similar to those for transmissions and transaxles. Parts requiring special attention when used are the differential and viscous coupling.

Locking hubs should be serviced carefully, since they are exposed to extremes of operation in dirt and water. Front wheel bearings should be adjusted when necessary. Vacuum motors can be serviced by removing the inspection cover and motor from the axle assembly as a unit. Check all parts for damage or wear and make sure that the shift collar is not stuck. Recheck four-wheel drive operation after reassembly.

Know These Terms

Transfer case	Differential assembly
Part-time	Viscous coupling
Full-time	Locking hubs
Sliding clutch	Overrunning clutches
Windup	Vacuum motor

Review Questions—Chapter 31

Do not write in this book. Write your answers on a separate sheet of paper.

1. On a vehicle with four-wheel drive, which of the following receives engine power first?
   (A) Rear axle.
   (B) Front axle.
   (C) Front driveshaft.
   (D) Transmission.

2. Full-time four-wheel drive vehicles should be driven in "lockout" when operating _____.
   (A) on dry paved roads
   (B) in muddy fields
   (C) on snow or ice
   (D) Both B & C.

3. One type of transfer case uses a viscous coupling filled with _____.

4. Drive train _____ can damage the transfer case, drive shafts, or other drive train parts.

5. Name three factors affecting the exact design of a transfer case.

6. Warps and dented areas in sheet metal covers can be repaired by _____ or by replacing the part.

7. Name two transfer case repairs which can be performed with the transfer case installed in the vehicle.

8. Check for chipping, galling, and wear on every _____ of every _____.

9. Most locking hub parts are held to the axle shaft with _____.

10. To service the vacuum motor and linkage, remove the _____ and vacuum motor as a unit.

ASE-Type Questions

1. All modern four-wheel drive systems have of the following parts, EXCEPT:
   (A) two drive shafts.
   (B) a transfer case.
   (C) a viscous coupling.
   (D) front and rear drive axles.

2. Technician A says that full-time four-wheel drive systems drive the rear wheels at all times. Technician B says that part-time four-wheel drive systems drive the front wheels at all times. Who is right?
   (A) A only.
   (B) B only.
   (C) Both A & B.
   (D) Neither A nor B.

3. Technician A says that a part-time four-wheel drive unit uses a differential or viscous clutch. Technician B says that a part-time four-wheel drive unit uses a sliding clutch. Who is right?
   (A) A only.
   (B) B only.
   (C) Both A & B.
   (D) Neither A nor B.

4. All of the following statements about a differential unit installed inside of the transfer case are true EXCEPT:
   (A) the differential unit applies driving torque to the front output shaft only.
   (B) the differential allows front and rear drive shafts to be driven at different speeds.
   (C) the differential keeps drive train windup from damaging parts.
   (D) the differential allows constant operation in four-wheel drive.

5. Technician A says that the front axles of a part-time four-wheel drive systems may be disengaged by locking hubs. Technician B says that the front axles of a part-time four-wheel drive systems may be disengaged by a vacuum motor. Who is right?
   (A) A only.
   (B) B only.
   (C) Both A & B.
   (D) Neither A nor B.
6. If the owner complains of hard shifting or gear clash, check the _____ first.
   (A) driveshafts and U-joints
   (B) clutch adjustment
   (C) transfer case shift linkage
   (D) oil level
7. If any transfer case shafts appear to be binding the transfer case should be _____.
   (A) installed and driven until loose
   (B) disassembled and the problem located
   (C) replaced with a new transfer case
   (D) Either A or B.
8. If a hammer is being used to loosen parts, be sure to use a _____ hammer.
   (A) large
   (B) steel
   (C) claw
   (D) brass
9. Which of the following is the LEAST likely to become damaged by dirt or water entry?

(A) Viscous clutch.
(B) Internal shaft and gear bearings.
(C) Locking hubs.
(D) Transmission output shaft.
10. While tearing down a transfer case with a viscous clutch, a few globules of silicone were found. Technician A says to replace the viscous clutch. Technician B says that since only a few globules of silicone were found in the old oil, it is OK to reuse the viscous clutch. Who is right?
    (A) A only.
    (B) B only.
    (C) Both A & B.
    (D) Neither A nor B.

Suggested Activities

1. Draw a schematic of a typical part-time four-wheel drive unit. Label the major components and show power flow in both two- and four-wheel drive modes.
2. Do a survey at your school to determine what percentage of the faculty, staff, and students owns vehicles with four-wheel drive systems. Also, ask whether the systems are full time or part time.
3. Write a short report explaining why you think four-wheel drive vehicles are becoming more popular.
4. Obtain some damaged four-wheel drive parts and discuss the possible causes of the damage with your classmates.

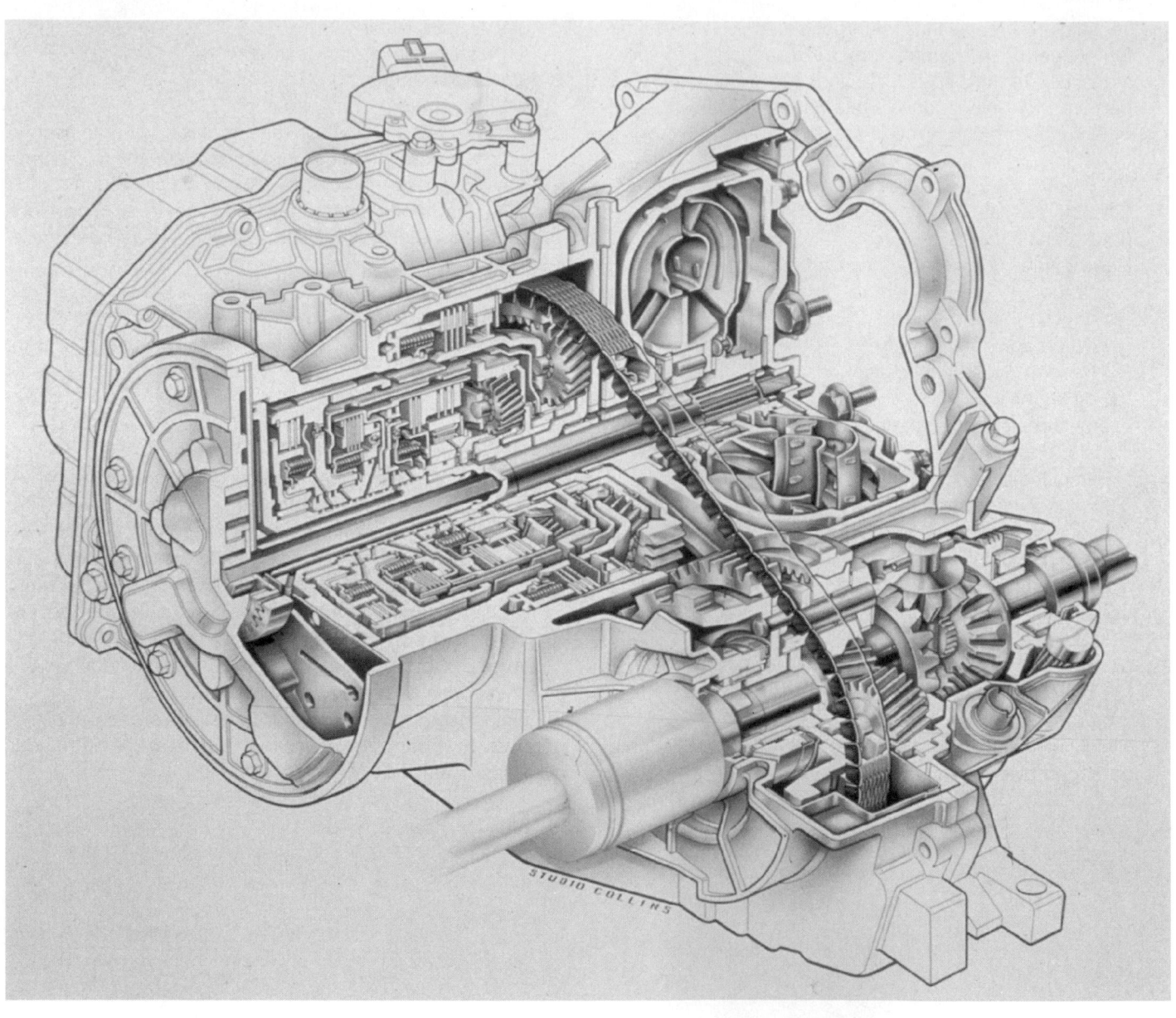

Cutaway of an electronically controlled four-speed transaxle. The electronic controls provide smooth, consistent shifting through the entire range of operating conditions. (Ford)

32

Automatic Transmission and Transaxle Service

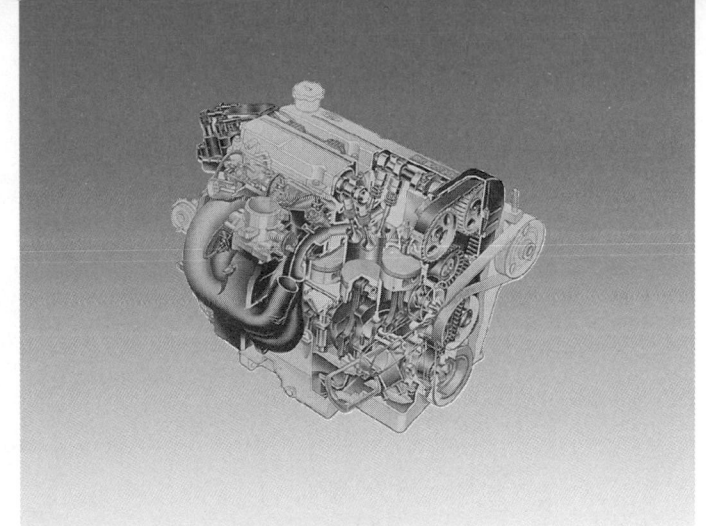

After studying this chapter, you will be able to:
- Explain automatic transmission and transaxle in-vehicle service and diagnosis.
- Explain towing procedures for vehicles with automatic transmissions and transaxles.
- Summarize the adjustment of automatic transmission and transaxle linkage.
- Explain automatic transmission and transaxle shift linkage and band adjustment.
- Describe common automatic transmission/transaxle testing tools and equipment.
- Summarize automatic transmission and transaxle removal and installation.
- List common automatic transmission and transaxle problems and corrections.
- Road test an automatic transmission or transaxle.

Automatic transmission and transaxle operating principles and service procedures are relatively complicated. The increased reliance on electronic controls, overdrive units, and yearly changes all combine to further complicate service. It is not within the scope of this text to cover complete automatic transmission and transaxle service and repair. Hundreds of pages would be needed to provide complete overhaul, test, and adjustment details for the various types and models of transmissions. This chapter will cover the in-vehicle service (service that can be performed while the transmission is in the vehicle) of modern automatic transmissions and transaxles. Transmission removal and installation will also be covered.

Automatic Transmission and Transaxle Design

Modern automatic transmissions and transaxles are usually either a three or four speed unit. They contain a *torque converter,* one or more *planetary gearsets,* multiple sets of holding members (clutches and bands), and a *hydraulic control system.*

Torque Converter Design

Torque converters use the movement of transmission fluid to transfer power. Since the power transfer is through the fluid, there is no mechanical connection between the engine and road. This allows the engine to continue running when the transmission is in gear and stopped. Modern torque converters utilize a hydraulically-operated clutch, called a *lockup clutch,* **Figure 32-1.** This clutch is applied to lock up internal parts of the converter to prevent slippage. The converter lockup clutch may apply in any gear other than low and reverse. The locking action provides direct, no-slip drive for increased fuel economy.

Planetary Gearsets and Holding Members

All transmissions and transaxles use planetary gearsets to provide different gear ratios. By holding different parts of the planetary gearset and driving others, many different ratios are possible from the same set of gears. The range of gears available from a typical planetary gearset is shown in **Figure 32-2.** To obtain additional gear ratios, more than one gearset may be used. Gearsets may be combined, sharing some common members. *Holding members* are used to apply and drive various parts of the planetary gearsets. Typical holding members are *bands,* multiple disc *clutch packs,* and *one-way* or *overrunning clutches.* The action of the various holding members is controlled by the hydraulic system.

Hydraulic Control System

The hydraulic control system depends on pressure developed by a transmission *oil pump.* The pump creates hydraulic pressure which is controlled by *spool valves.* The spool valves control hydraulic pressure and use it to fill the torque converter and obtain different gears as needed. The major valves which are contained in all automatic transmissions are:

- The *main pressure regulator,* which monitors the pump output to control the overall system hydraulic pressure. The main pressure regulator valve setting is controlled by the preset tension on a spring acting on the valve.
- The *manual valve* is operated by the driver to engage the transmission in park, reverse, neutral, drive, manual second or low, and other available gears.

STATOR
IMPELLER
TRANSMISSION INPUT SHAFT
TURBINE
CLUTCH APPLY PISTON
TORSIONAL ISOLATOR SPRINGS
CLUTCH FRICTION SURFACE
LOCK-UP CLUTCH
INPUT
OUTPUT
NON LOCK-UP POSITION (PISTON RELEASED)
INPUT
OUTPUT
LOCK-UP POSITION (PISTON ENGAGED)

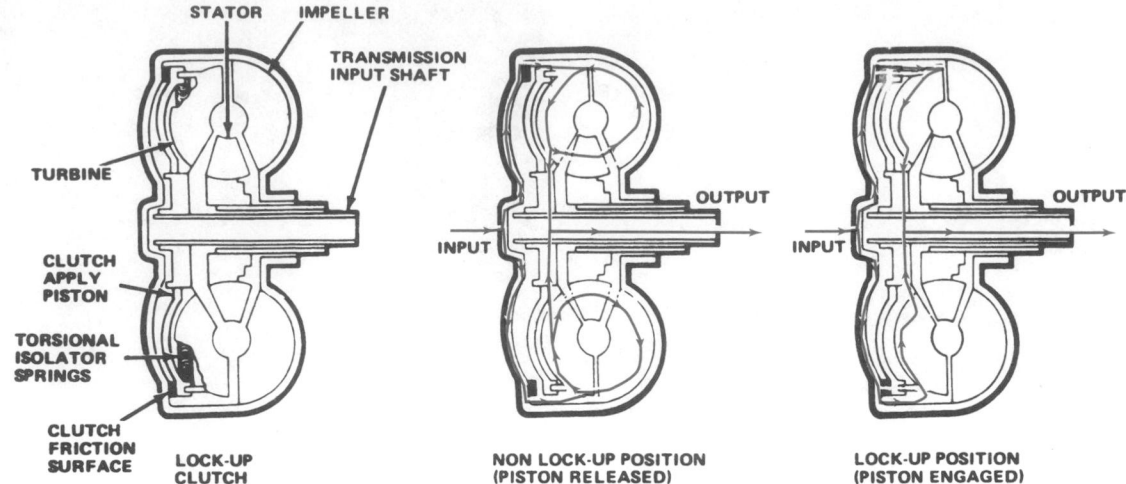

Figure 32-1. Operation of one type of lockup converter. When in lockup position, the converter acts as a solid drive unit. (Chrysler)

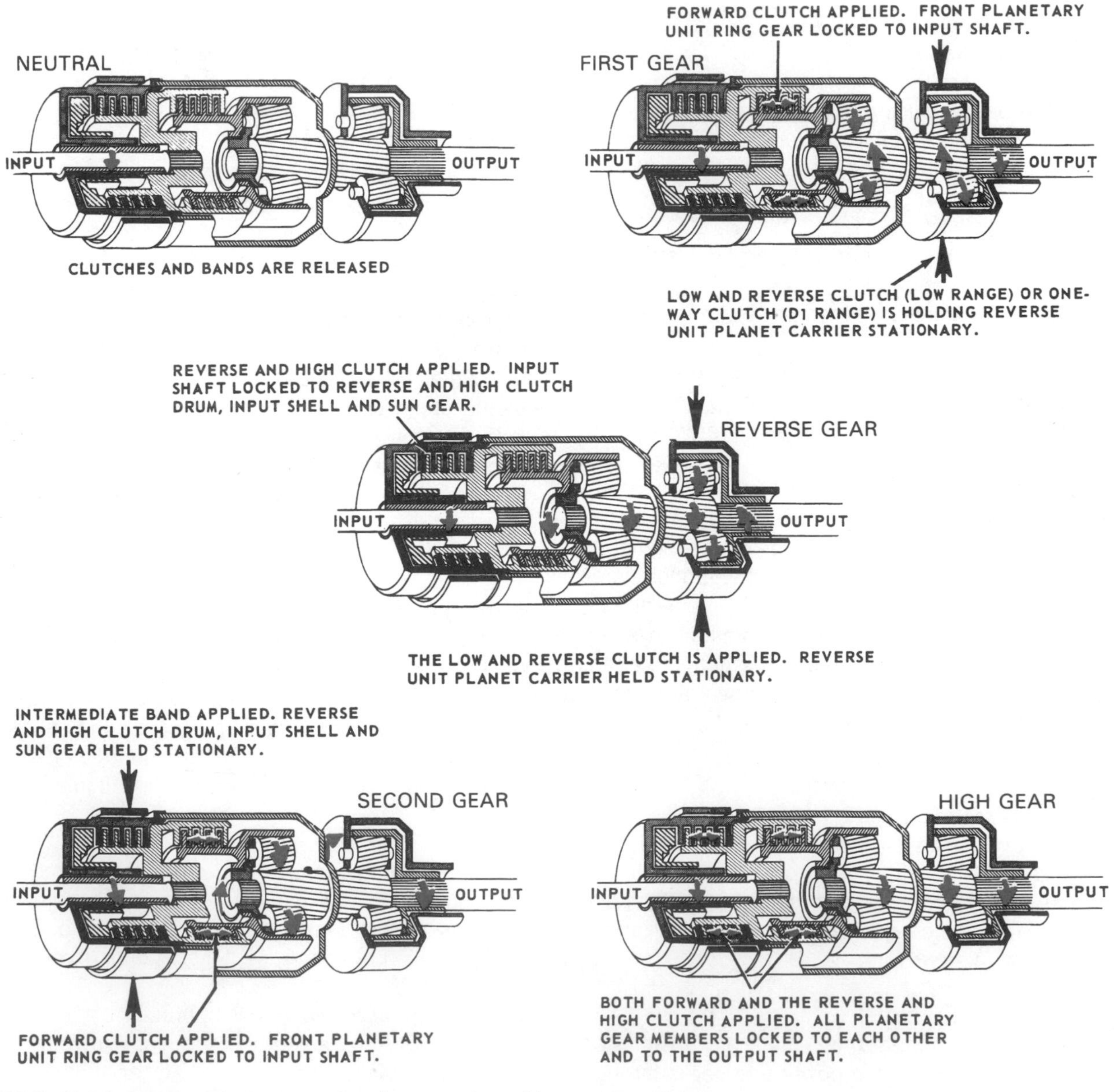

NEUTRAL
INPUT
OUTPUT
CLUTCHES AND BANDS ARE RELEASED
FORWARD CLUTCH APPLIED. FRONT PLANETARY UNIT RING GEAR LOCKED TO INPUT SHAFT.
FIRST GEAR
INPUT
OUTPUT
LOW AND REVERSE CLUTCH (LOW RANGE) OR ONE-WAY CLUTCH (D1 RANGE) IS HOLDING REVERSE UNIT PLANET CARRIER STATIONARY.
REVERSE AND HIGH CLUTCH APPLIED. INPUT SHAFT LOCKED TO REVERSE AND HIGH CLUTCH DRUM, INPUT SHELL AND SUN GEAR.
REVERSE GEAR
INPUT
OUTPUT
THE LOW AND REVERSE CLUTCH IS APPLIED. REVERSE UNIT PLANET CARRIER HELD STATIONARY.
INTERMEDIATE BAND APPLIED. REVERSE AND HIGH CLUTCH DRUM, INPUT SHELL AND SUN GEAR HELD STATIONARY.
SECOND GEAR
INPUT
OUTPUT
FORWARD CLUTCH APPLIED. FRONT PLANETARY UNIT RING GEAR LOCKED TO INPUT SHAFT.
HIGH GEAR
INPUT
OUTPUT
BOTH FORWARD AND THE REVERSE AND HIGH CLUTCH APPLIED. ALL PLANETARY GEAR MEMBERS LOCKED TO EACH OTHER AND TO THE OUTPUT SHAFT.

Figure 32-2. Clutch, band, and gearset action during various drive ranges. (Ford)

- The **shift valves** redirect hydraulic pressure to the holding members to obtain different gears in drive range. These valves are moved by other valves, as explained below.
- The **throttle valve** is controlled by linkage from the engine throttle plates, or by a vacuum modulator operated by engine manifold vacuum. The throttle valve tries to move the shift valve to the downshifted (lower gear) position. The more the throttle is depressed, the higher the throttle pressure.
- The **governor valve** is mounted on or driven by the output shaft. As governor pressure rises, it tries to move the shift valve to the upshifted (higher gear) position. The higher the shaft speed, the higher the governor pressure.

Some other components of the hydraulic system include **servos,** which operate the bands, **clutch pistons** which operate the multiple disc clutches, and **accumulators** which cushion the application of the holding members. Another important part of the hydraulic system is the **filter,** which removes dirt and metal from the transmission fluid. Many of the valves and other components are installed in a **valve body** attached to the bottom of the transmission case. **Figure 32-3** shows the layout of a simple automatic transmission hydraulic system. Note the relationship of the valves just discussed. Other valves are used to cushion shifts, provide detent shift for passing, and control the lockup torque converter.

Increasingly, the hydraulic control system of modern automatic transmissions and transaxles are computer-

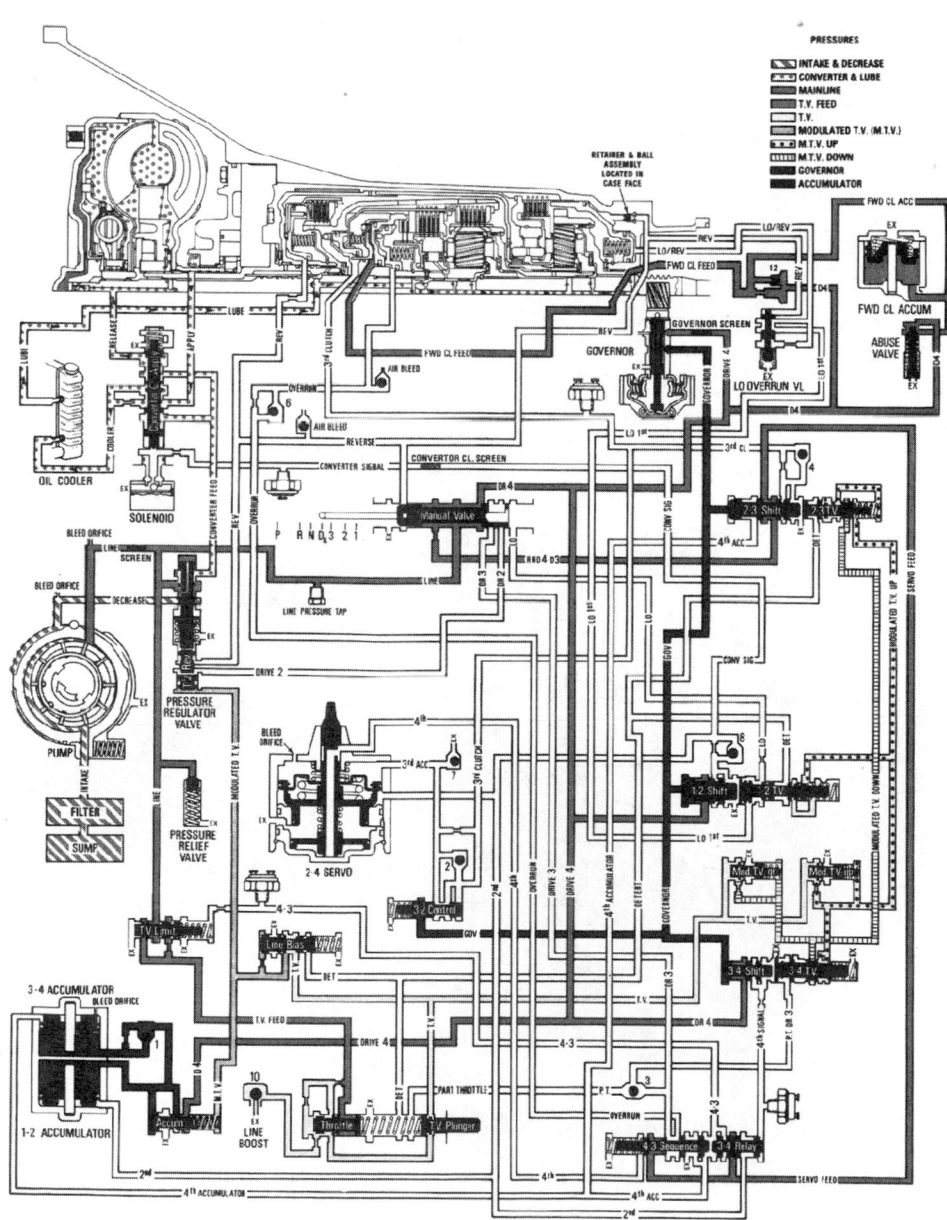

Figure 32-3.   A hydraulic circuit layout for one four-speed automatic transmission. The circuit illustrates control while in first gear. (General Motors)

controlled. Shift points, system pressures, and the operation of the lockup torque converter are operated by computer-controlled solenoids. The modern automatic transmission also contains speed sensors and pressure switches which produce input signals to the control module. On many modern automatic transmissions and transaxles, the hydraulic system is completely controlled by a body computer or powertrain control module.

Transmission and Transaxle Designs

Transmissions are always found on vehicles with front engines and rear wheel drive. The parts layout of all automatic transmissions is similar. From the torque converter, the input shaft passes through the hydraulic pump to mate with the clutch drums, planetary gears, and output shaft, **Figure 32-4.**

Automatic transaxles are used on vehicles with front engines and front wheel drive and vehicles with rear engines and rear wheel drive. Parts layout of transaxles may vary slightly, since the power flow must be split. Compare the transaxle in **Figure 32-5** with the transaxle in

Figure 32-6. Note that in the first design engine power flows from the torque converter, through a drive chain, and then into the clutch drums, planetary gearsets, and differential assembly. In the second design, power flows from the torque converter, through the input shaft, and into the clutch drums and planetary gears. From the planetaries, it flows into two large drive gears and then into the output shaft and differential gears. Transaxles can be placed **transversely** (sideways in the vehicle) or **conventionally** (facing the vehicle front). The transverse mounting is more common, but many conventional placements are found. Compare **Figures 32-7** and **32-8.**

In-Vehicle Service and Problem Diagnosis

Many transmission problems can be solved by a simple adjustment or repair. As stated earlier, this chapter discusses typical in-vehicle transmission service and problem diagnosis. For information relating to a specific unit, always refer to the manufacturer's service manual. The manual will

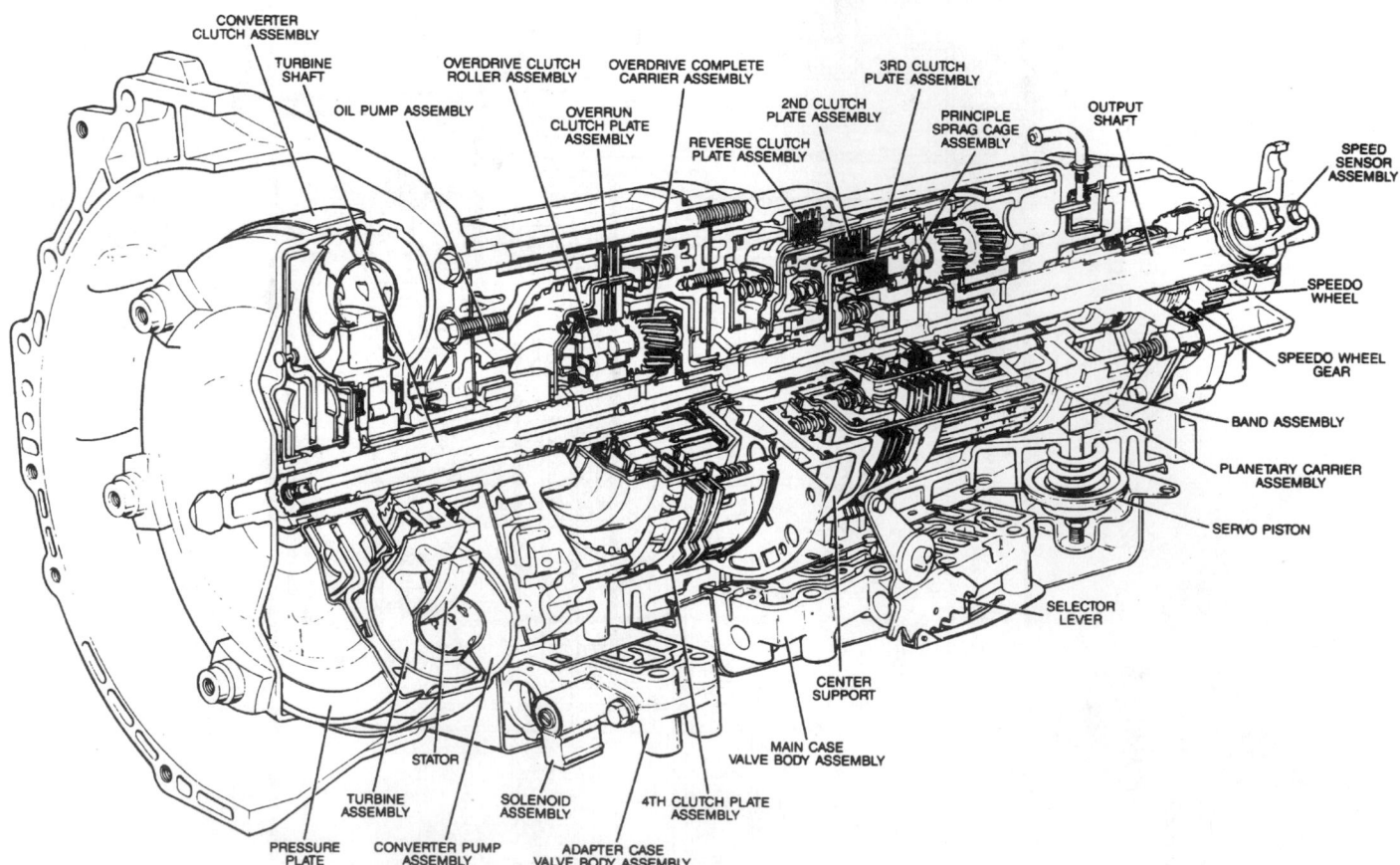

Figure 32-4. Cutaway of an electronically controlled, four-speed automatic transmission. The overdrive ratio is 0.723:1. Study the parts closely. (Hydra-Matic Division of General Motors)

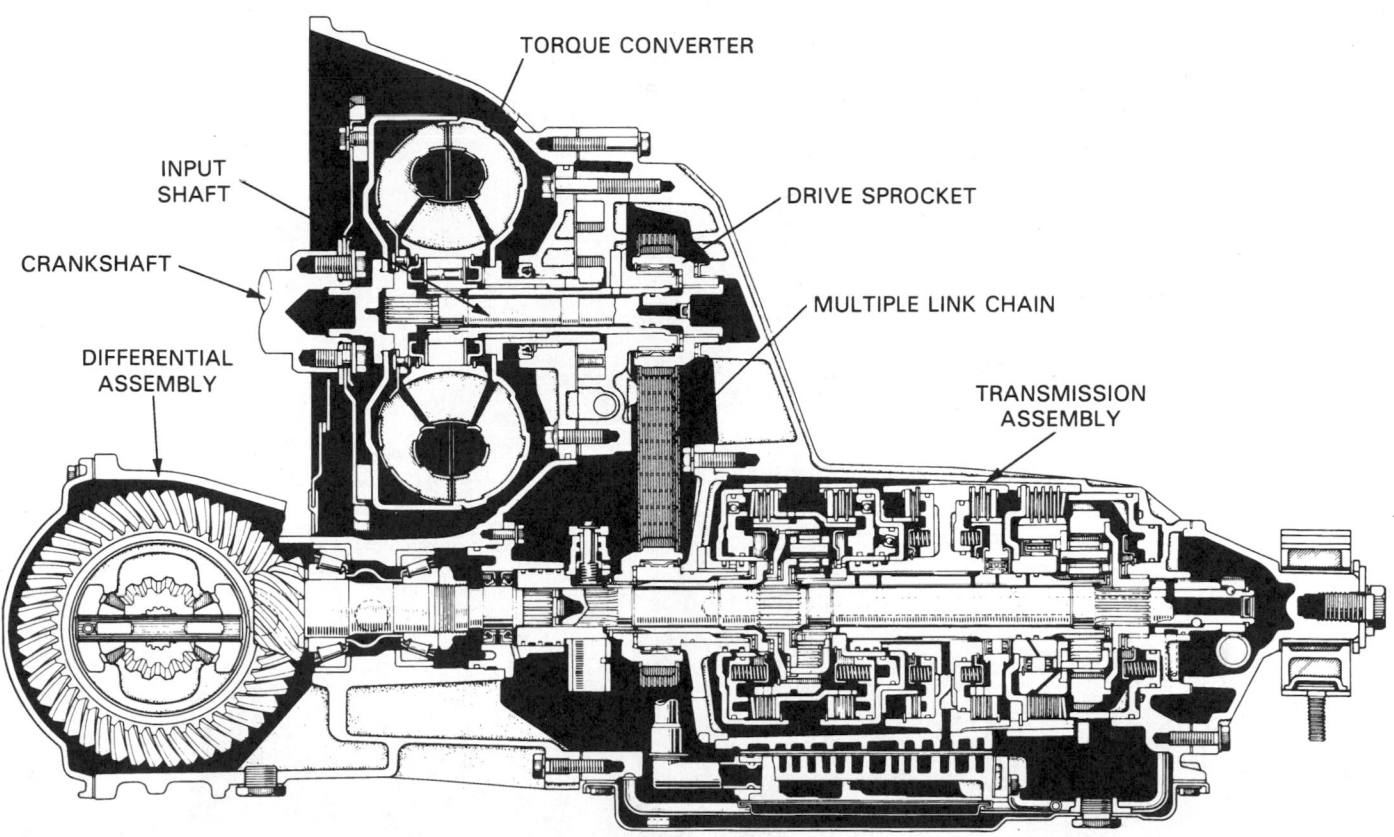

Figure 32-5. One type of automatic transaxle arrangement. Note that torque from the converter is transmitted to the transmission by a multiple link chain. (Toyota)

provide complete disassembly, inspection, and assembly details. Manufacturers' service manuals contain exploded views and illustrations covering the disassembly, parts inspection, and reassembly of the transmission or transaxle.

Transmission Service Basics

Vehicles with automatic transmissions cannot be push-started. If the vehicle will not start by cranking with the starter, determine the starting or charging system problem, and correct it. Charging and starting system service was covered in Chapter 26. If the rear end, drive shaft, and transmission in a rear wheel drive vehicles are in sound condition, the vehicle may be towed in neutral at a nominal speed. Generally, do not exceed 45 mph (72 kph) for a distance not greater than 50 miles (80 km). Be sure to release the parking brake. Some manufacturers caution against towing for distances exceeding 12 to 15 miles (24 to 80 km). Check the transmission fluid level before towing. When the transmission or drive line components are inoperative, the vehicle must be towed from the rear end. The vehicle may be towed without raising the rear wheels by removing

the drive shaft at the differential end. If you use this method, be sure to tie the shaft up out of the way securely.

Front-wheel drive vehicles should have the driving wheels raised off the road or placed in wheel dollies to tow. Four-wheel drive vehicles require that a drive line be removed on some units or that the wheels must be placed in dollies. Others can be towed with all four wheels on the road by placing the transmission in park and the transfer case in neutral. Towing speed is generally around 30 mph (48 kph) with a distance of around 15 miles (24 km). Remember that whenever a vehicle has drive line, wheel bearing, drive shaft, or transmission problems, use wheel dollies or lift the affected end so that towing does not cause additional damage. The best method of towing a disabled vehicle is a platform towing vehicle, often called a skid truck. Always follow the vehicle manufacturer's recommended towing method. Do not use the ignition lock mechanism in the steering column to hold the wheels in a straight ahead position. Damage to the lock and steering column is likely. Use an approved steering wheel clamping tool. Always use a safety chain or strap. **Figure 32-9** illustrates a

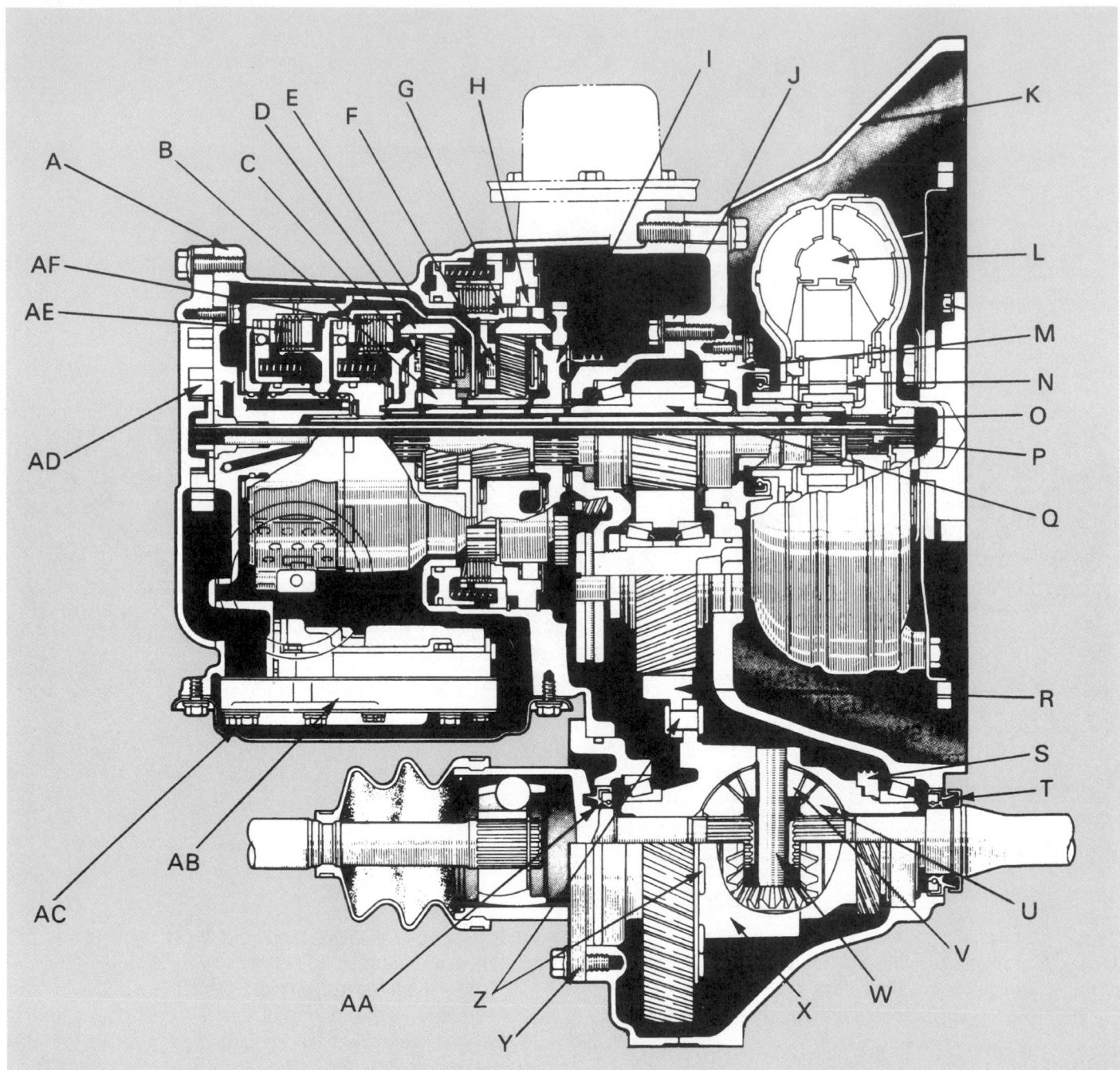

Figure 32-6. Cutaway of a three-speed automatic transaxle. Gear ratios are: First—2.841:1; Second—1.541:1; Third—1.000:1; and Reverse—2.400:1. Note that the ring gear (R) is secured to differential gear case with rivets (Z). A—Transmission. B—Sun gear. C—Planetary carrier. D—Rear clutch hub assembly. E—Connection shell (clutch housing). F—Planetary carrier. G—One-way clutch. H—One-way clutch. I—Drum hub assembly. J—Bearing housing. K—Torque converter housing. L—Torque converter. M—Bearing cover. N—Oil seal. O—Turbine shaft. P—Oil pump shaft. Q—Output gear. R—Ring gear. S—Speedometer drive gear. T—Oil seal. U—Side gear. V—Pinion gear. W—Pinion shaft. X—Differential gear case. Y—Side bearing housing. Z—Rivets. AA—Oil seal. AB—Control valve. AC—Oil pan. AD—Oil pump. AE—Front clutch. AF—Rear clutch. (Mazda)

typical tow truck attaching method for the front and rear of the same vehicle. Do not allow passengers to ride in the towed vehicle.

Transmission Service Tools

To properly adjust bands, check throttle linkage or make other adjustments, a set of tools designed for the purpose should be available. In addition to the basic set, special purpose tools must be acquired to service specific transmissions. **Figure 32-10** shows some of the special tools needed for transmission in-vehicle adjustments. A 0-300 PSI (0-2068 kPa) pressure gauge should also be included. Major repair jobs will require many more standard and specialized tools.

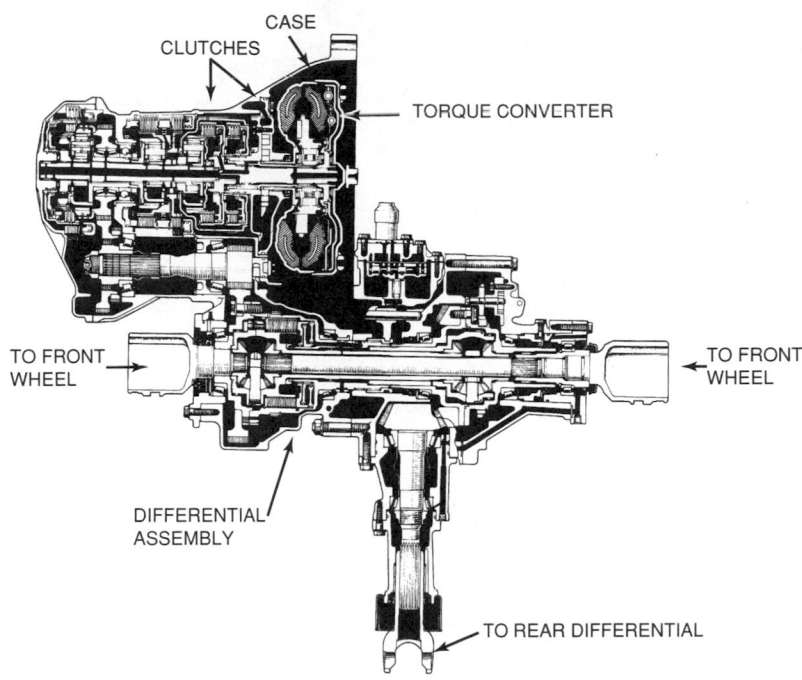

Figure 32-7. A four-speed electronically controlled transaxle used with a transverse mounted engine. The differential assembly setup is for an all-traction, four-wheel drive system. Gear ratios are: 1st.—2.81:1, 2nd.—1.549:1, 3rd.—1.00:1, 4th.—0.734:1, and Reverse—2.296:1. (Toyota)

Figure 32-8. Cutaway of a front wheel drive electronically controlled, four-speed overdrive automatic transaxle, which is used with a longitudinally mounted engine. Gear ratios are: 1st.—2.84:1, 2nd.—1.57:1, 3rd.—1.00:1, and 4th.—0.69:1. (Eagle Division of Chrysler)

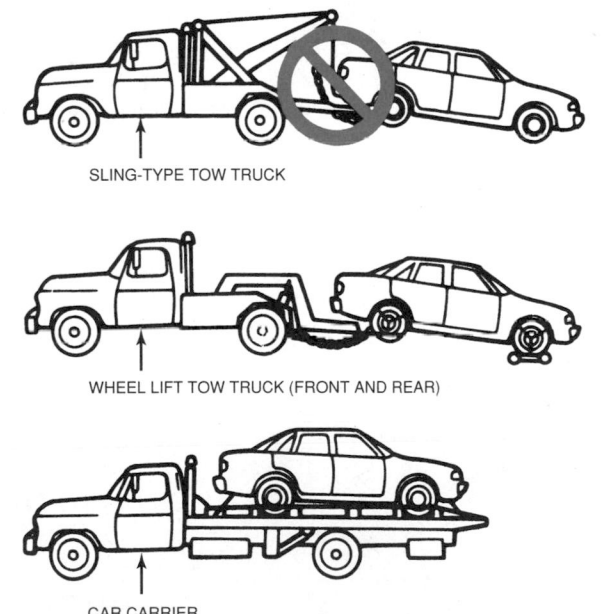

Figure 32-9. Several common towing methods for vehicles. Follow all the vehicle manufacturer's towing recommendations to prevent damage. (Geo)

Fluid Level

Transmission fluid level is very important. The level should be checked at least once a month, or whenever a transmission problem is suspected. Always check the fluid level before conducting any other transmission or transaxle tests. Hydraulic system operation can be affected by either a high or low fluid level. A high fluid level (above the full mark) will cause foaming with fluid *aeration* (filling oil with tiny air bubbles) resulting. When aerated oil is pumped throughout the transmission, faulty clutch and band operation, erratic shifts, overheating, cavitation noise (noise caused by the pump or torque converter operating in aerated oil), and other problems can result. A low fluid level can cause overheating, slipping in all gears, erratic shifts, suction noises as the pump draws in air, and other operational malfunctions.

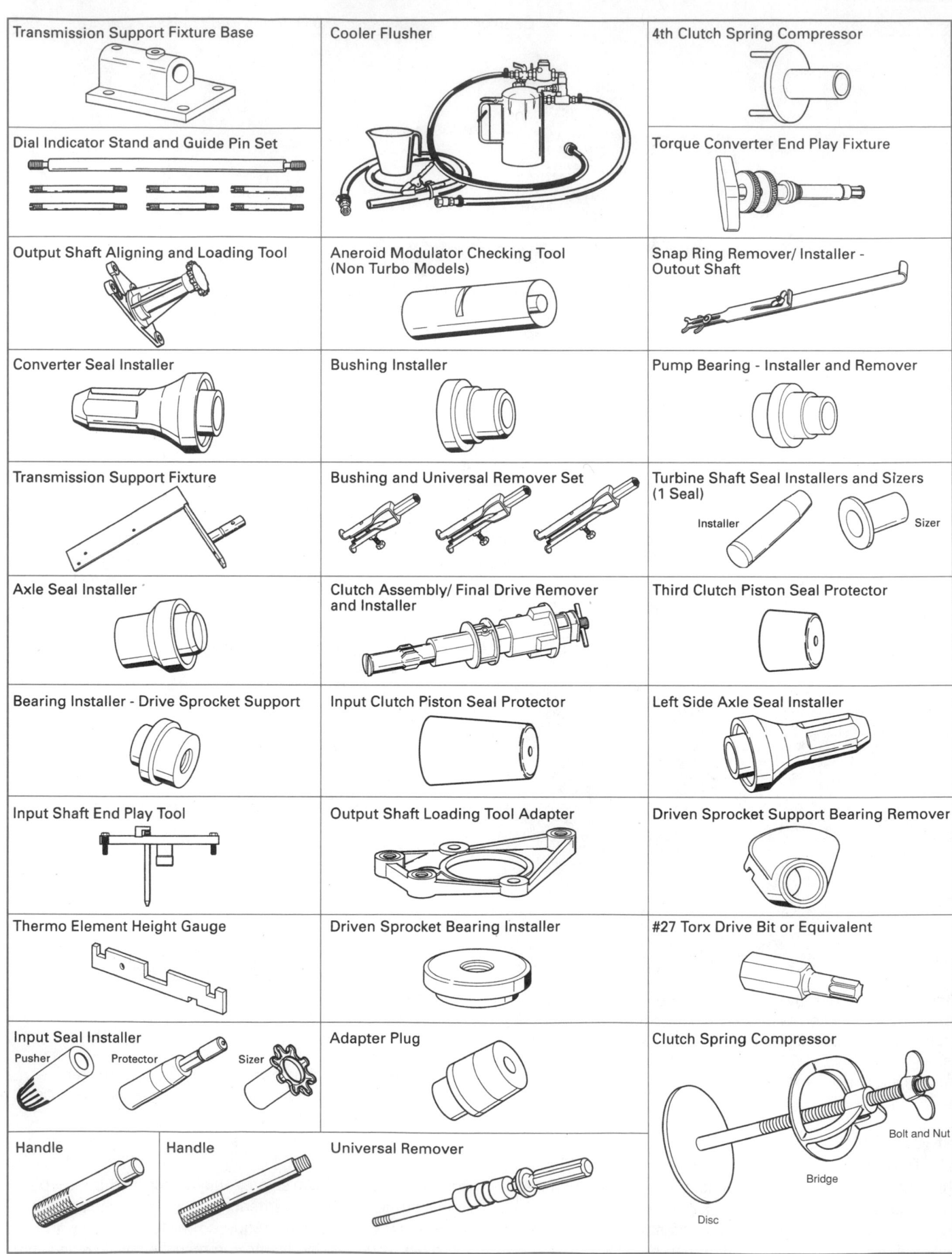

Transmission Support Fixture Base	Cooler Flusher	4th Clutch Spring Compressor
Dial Indicator Stand and Guide Pin Set		Torque Converter End Play Fixture
Output Shaft Aligning and Loading Tool	Aneroid Modulator Checking Tool (Non Turbo Models)	Snap Ring Remover/ Installer - Outout Shaft
Converter Seal Installer	Bushing Installer	Pump Bearing - Installer and Remover
Transmission Support Fixture	Bushing and Universal Remover Set	Turbine Shaft Seal Installers and Sizers (1 Seal) Installer Sizer
Axle Seal Installer	Clutch Assembly/ Final Drive Remover and Installer	Third Clutch Piston Seal Protector
Bearing Installer - Drive Sprocket Support	Input Clutch Piston Seal Protector	Left Side Axle Seal Installer
Input Shaft End Play Tool	Output Shaft Loading Tool Adapter	Driven Sprocket Support Bearing Remover
Thermo Element Height Gauge	Driven Sprocket Bearing Installer	#27 Torx Drive Bit or Equivalent
Input Seal Installer Pusher Protector Sizer	Adapter Plug	Clutch Spring Compressor Bolt and Nut Bridge Disc
Handle	Handle Universal Remover	

Figure 32-10. Several special tools are needed to properly service and repair automatic transmissions and transaxles. Always use the correct tools. (Cadillac)

Checking Transmission Fluid Level

Before checking the fluid level, the transmission fluid must be brought to normal operating temperature (170°-200°F or 77°-93°C). Four or five miles of driving, including frequent stops and starts, will usually produce normal fluid temperature. Also operating the vehicle at a fast idle with the gear select lever in park or neutral and the wheels blocked and parking brake set may be used to heat up the fluid. If the end of the dipstick is almost too hot to touch, the transmission is at operating temperature. Before checking the fluid, shift the transmission or transaxle through all of the ranges before returning it to park or neutral. Make sure that:

- The vehicle is in a level position.
- Fluid temperature is normal.
- Engine is idling.
- Shift lever is in neutral or park as required.

 Note: Never check the oil level with the transmission or transaxle in any drive range unless specifically recommended by the manufacturer.

With the engine idling, wipe off the dipstick cap and the end of the filler tube. Remove dipstick. Wipe it clean. Then insert it back into the filler tube. Make certain that the dipstick enters to the full depth. Remove the dipstick and observe the fluid level. The fluid level (transmission/transaxle at operating temperature, shift lever in N or P as needed) should be between the add and full marks on the dipstick. See **Figure 32-11.** Add fluid if needed. Under no circumstances must the level move above the full mark. If the transmission fluid level is above full, drain off the required amount. Unless you are positive that the fluid is hot, do not add fluid to bring the level to the full mark. By keeping the level just under full, when the fluid does reach operating temperature, it will not be overfull. Look at **Figure 32-12.**

Check Fluid Condition

Factory-installed fluid generally contains a red dye which makes finding leaks easier. The fluid in these cases normally has a reddish hue. When examining the fluid level on the dipstick, check the oil for discoloration and a burned smell. Such a condition indicates damaged bands or clutches. Also check the dipstick for deposits of varnish, which indicate that the transmission fluid has repeatedly overheated.

If any antifreeze or water has entered the transmission through the oil cooler, or by driving through very high water, the fluid will look milky. Any appreciable amount of water entry will raise the fluid level. If any antifreeze or water is found, check the transmission oil cooler for an internal leak. A cooler leak must be fixed immediately and the transmission flushed, or the antifreeze will severely damage the holding members. Air bubbles indicate aeration or an air leak in the pump suction (usually in the filter).

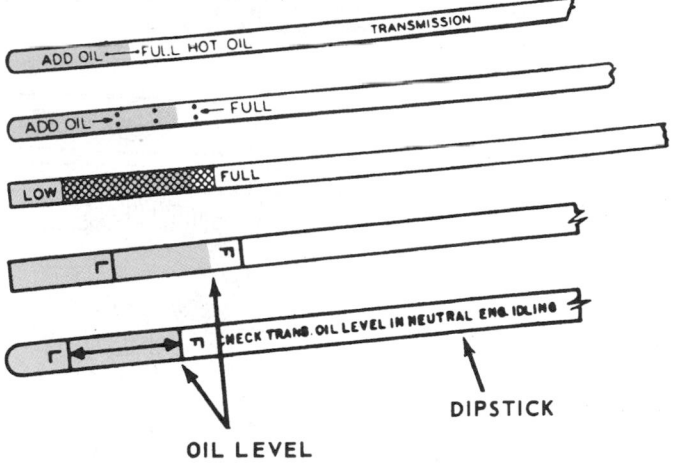

Figure 32-11. Transmission fluid level must be between the ADD and FULL mark on the dipstick. Some of the dipsticks illustrated show a one quart range from add to full, others show one pint. (Standard Oil)

Fluid Type

When adding fluid to any modern automatic transmission or transaxle, use fluids marked **Dexron III/Mercon** only. Dexron III is a new fluid which replaces Dexron II, which has been in use in automatic transmissions for many years. Some import manufacturers, such as Honda, specify a different type of fluid. Follow manufacturer's recommendations. If called for by the manufacturer, Type F fluid may be used in some older vehicles. Use care when checking the fluid level or adding fluid to prevent dirt from entering the transmission.

 Caution: Do not use fluid marked with the letters AQ-ATF. This is obsolete Type A, Suffix A fluid, which is not suitable for modern vehicles. Also, do not use Dexron II in transmissions that use Dexron III.

Transmission/Transaxle Identification

Before any service work can be performed, the type of transmission that is in the vehicle must be determined. On most vehicles, simply noting the shape of the transmission pan is all that is needed. On others, a code or date is sometimes required. These are usually either on a label in the vehicle or stamped on the transmission case. Make certain that you have correctly identified the type of transmission/transaxle that is in the vehicle. Double check your identification by consulting the manufacturer's service manual. This will ensure that you have the correct information when ordering parts.

Aluminum Transmission Parts

Automatic transmission and transaxle cases and other parts are made of aluminum. While quite suitable for this purpose, aluminum parts require care in handling to avoid nicking, scratching, or burring machined surfaces. Threads are soft and easily stripped. Always use a torque wrench to prevent stripping the threads. To prevent galling, dip the fas-

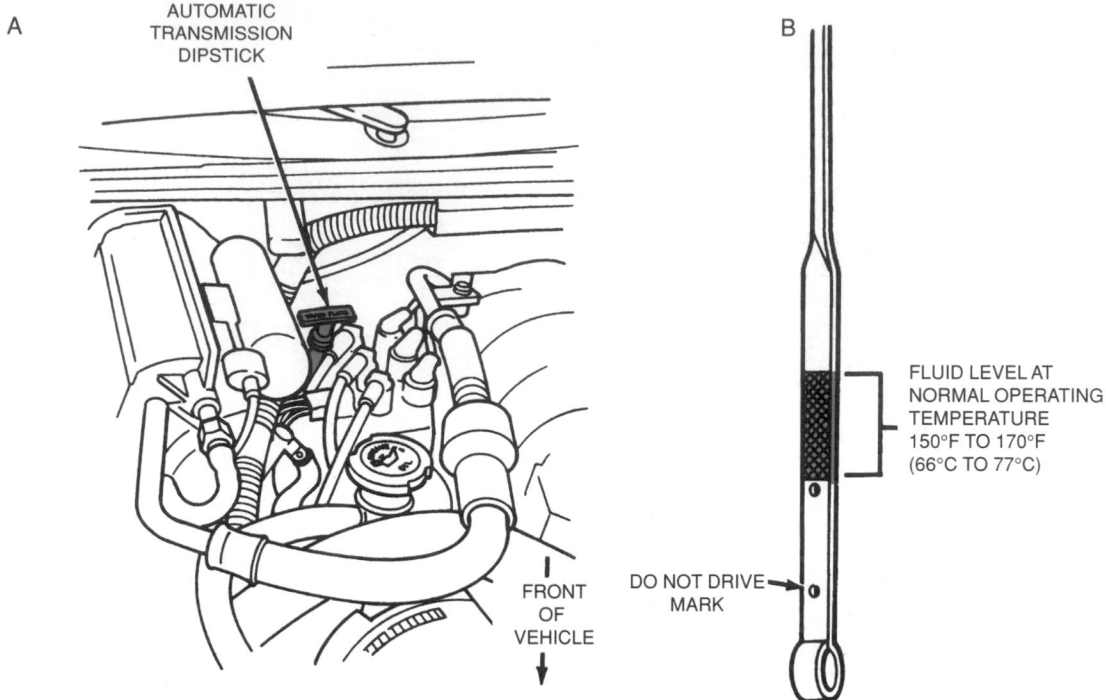

Figure 32-12. A—Dipstick location on one vehicle. B—Dipstick fluid level indicator marks. Follow manufacturer's exact fluid level checking procedures. (Ford)

tener threads in transmission fluid. If a thread is stripped, use a Heli-Coil to make a repair. Thread repair was discussed in Chapter 7.

Transmission Fluid and Filter Change Cycles

Most vehicle manufacturers recommend periodic transmission or transaxle fluid and filter changes. Intervals vary from around 12,000 to 100,000 miles (19,300 to 160,000 km), depending upon the type of service and transmission being serviced. Some manufacturers do not recommend changing the fluid and filter.

Some manufacturers recommending changing the fluid and filter more often under severe conditions, such as trailer towing and use in heavy traffic, or severe service such as found in police cars and taxicabs. Under these conditions, it is better to change the fluid and filter too often than take a chance on transmission or transaxle damage. If the vehicle operating conditions are causing the fluid to be overheated often, an *add-on transmission cooler* should be installed, **Figure 32-13.** The cooler will greatly extend fluid and transmission life. Add-on transmission coolers are generally located in front of the radiator.

Fluid and Filter Service Procedures

Before beginning the draining process, make sure that the transmission fluid is at normal operating temperature to ensure proper draining. Some transmissions and transaxles require draining both the converter and oil pan. Other transmissions require draining the oil pan only. Since most modern transmission and transaxle pans do not contain a drain plug, loosen the fasteners to permit draining. Usually removing all but the last four fasteners at the rear of the pan

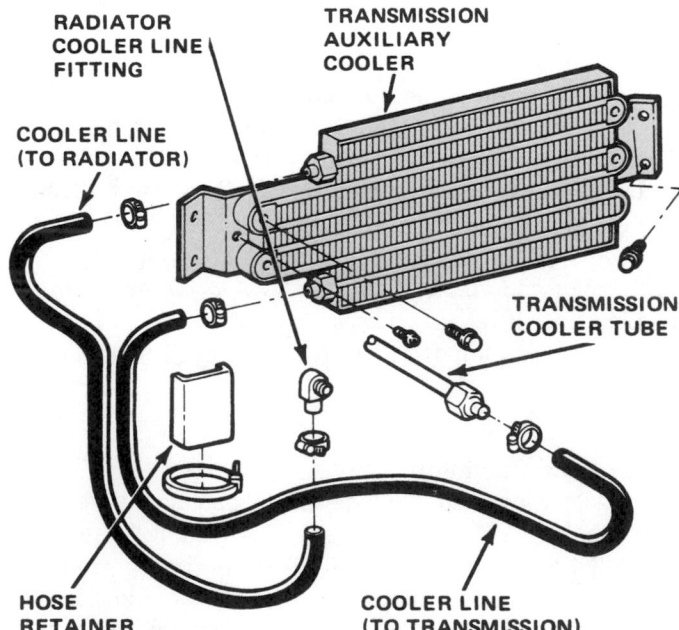

Figure 32-13. An auxiliary transmission oil cooler. Note how hoses connect between radiator cooler line fitting and transmission cooler tube. (Jeep)

will allow the fluid to drain out into a container with a minimum of spilled oil. If the fill tube attaches to the side of the pan, remove the tube to permit draining. See **Figure 32-14.** Be careful when draining. The fluid may be hot enough to produce serious burns. Remove the oil pan and clean it thoroughly. Remove the old fluid filter and any filter gaskets or seals. Some filters are used to retain check balls,

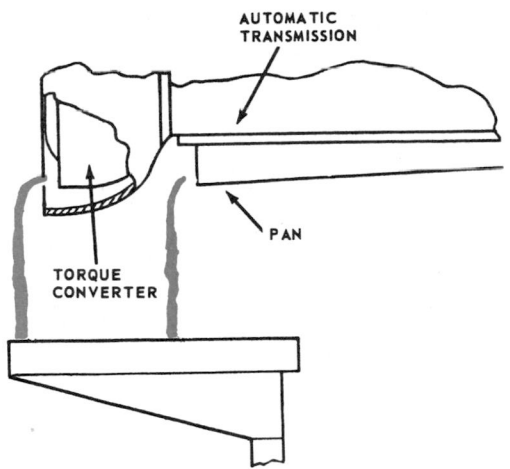

Figure 32-14. Drain both converter and transmission pan when required.

springs, or valves, which can drop out of the valve body when the filter is removed. Note their positions and reinstall when the filter is replaced. Install the new filter using a new gasket or seal as necessary. Clean the pan and case sealing surfaces thoroughly. Some pans contain a small magnet that aids the filter in removing metal particles from the fluid. Be sure to clean and reinstall the magnet.

> **Note: If the oil pan contains heavy deposits of sludge and burned material, be sure to inform the owner that the unit will probably need an overhaul soon. Often, the new fluid installed in a transmission or transaxle in poor shape will loosen sludge deposits and cause the unit to fail quickly. If the oil pan must be removed to make band adjustments, make the adjustments before reinstalling the pan. Refer to the next section for band adjustment procedures.**

Reinstall the pan using a new gasket or RTV silicone, **Figure 32-15.** Replace the fill pipe if removed. Add the amount of fluid specified by the manufacturer to the transmission. Start the engine and check the fluid level. Add more fluid as needed.

 Caution: Work quickly to add sufficient fluid. The pump or converter can be damaged if they are operated for any period without fluid.

Band Adjustment

Some transmissions require periodic **band adjustments** to compensate for normal wear. Other designs in which the band is subjected to moderate wear do not require adjustment at periodic intervals. In many cases, the band cannot be adjusted except when it is disassembled for overhaul. These bands are adjusted by adding or subtracting shims inside of the servo assembly or by replacing the servo apply pin. When you are making band adjustments, make certain the specifications relate to the transmission at hand. Follow specifications exactly. Failure to do so may cause serious transmission damage.

Some external band adjustments on older vehicles are reached through the floor pan after turning the mat to one side, **Figure 32-16.** Others are accessible from beneath the vehicle, **Figure 32-17.** Some require removal of the transmission oil pan, **Figure 32-18.** The typical external adjustment consists of an adjusting screw passing through the case and engaging one end of the band. A locking nut is provided to secure the adjusting screw.

General adjusting procedure requires loosening the locknut several turns, tightening the adjustment screw to an exact torque and then backing the screw off an exact number of turns. The screw is held in this position while the locknut is tightened. Remember this is a critical adjustment and must be done exactly as specified. In **Figure 32-19,** a technician is using a torque wrench to tighten the adjusting screw.

In using the tool shown in **Figure 32-20,** the locknut is loosened with the socket and the adjusting screw is brought to the recommended torque with a regular torque wrench. The dial counter is then set to zero. As the adjusting screw is backed out, the counter will record the exact number of turns. When the correct number is reached, the adjustment screw is held stationary and the locknut is tightened. When band adjustments are difficult to reach, an extension, such

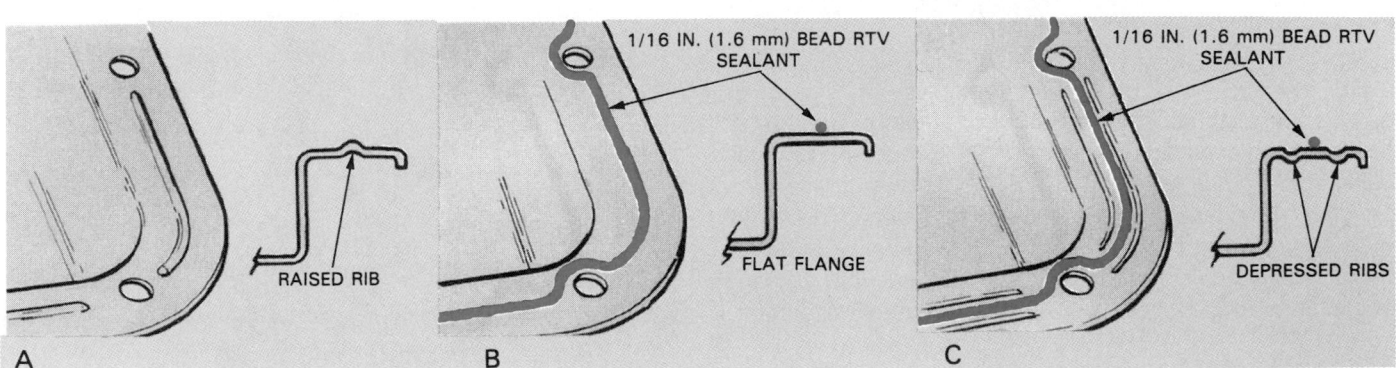

Figure 32-15. Three different transmission oil pan mounting flange designs. A—Raised center rib. It should only be used with a conventional gasket. B—Flat flange. Use RTV sealer or gasket, C—Depressed ribs. Use RTV sealer or gasket. Note positioning of RTV sealer on inside of holes to prevent oil leakage past fasteners. (Chevrolet)

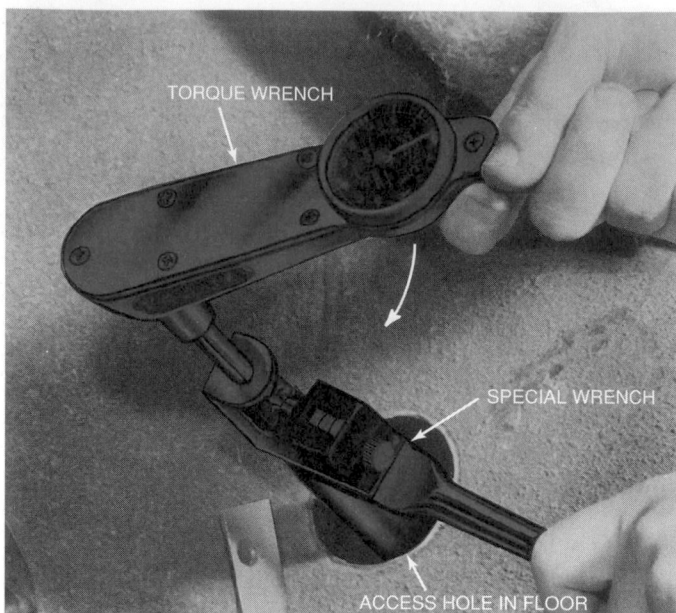

Figure 32-16.   Using a special wrench and torque wrench to properly adjust a transmission band through an access hole in the floor pan. This is generally done on older vehicles. (Oldsmobile)

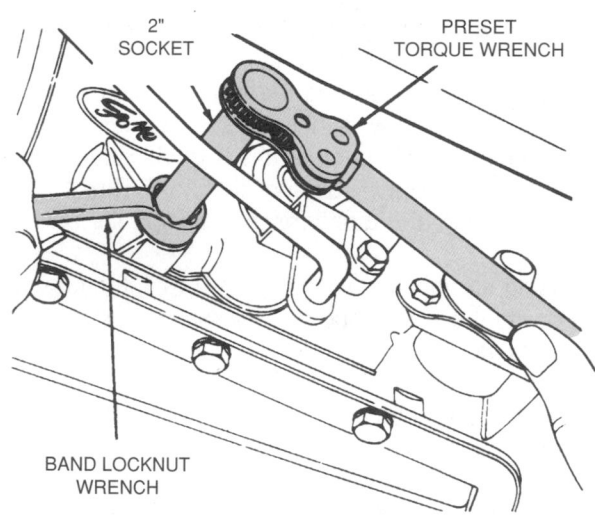

Figure 32-17.   Tightening band adjusting screw from under the vehicle with preset torque wrench.

as the one pictured in **Figure 32-21** is helpful. Remember that when an extension is used with the torque wrench, indicated torque (dial reading) is less than actual torque. See Chapter 7 on torque wrenches and fasteners. The transmission shown in **Figure 32-22** requires removal of the oil pan to make one of the band adjustments. Following band adjustment, road test the vehicle for proper shift operation.

Manual Shift Linkage Adjustment

The position of the manual valve in the valve body is controlled by an internal *detent assembly.* Even if the external linkage is misadjusted, the internal manual valve

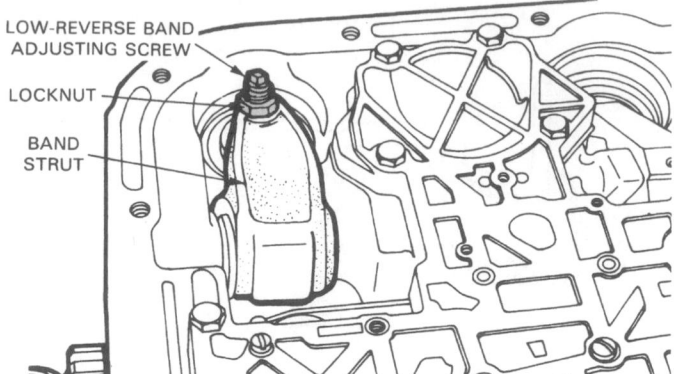

Figure 32-18.   This transmission requires the removal of the oil pan to adjust the low-reverse band. (Chrysler)

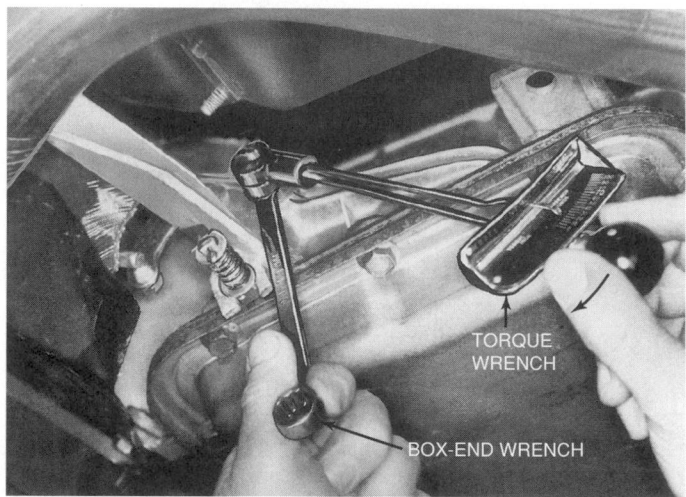

Figure 32-19.   Technician using a torque wrench (beam type) and a box-end wrench to correctly adjust a band screw. (Chevrolet)

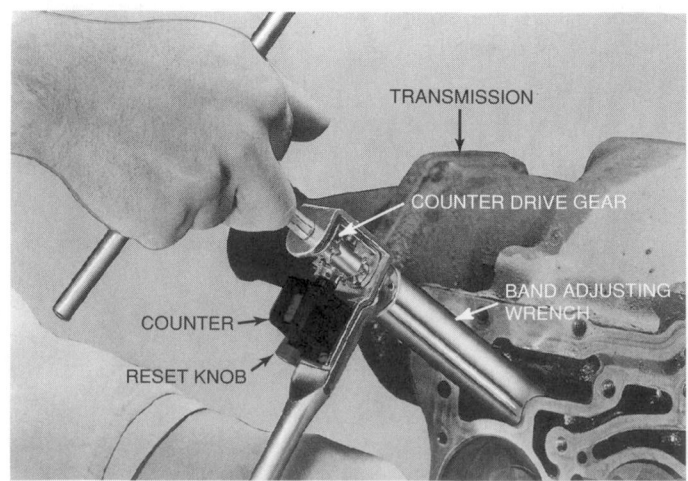

Figure 32-20.   A special tool with a "counter meter" used to count wrench revolutions while adjusting this transmission band. (Snap-On Tools)

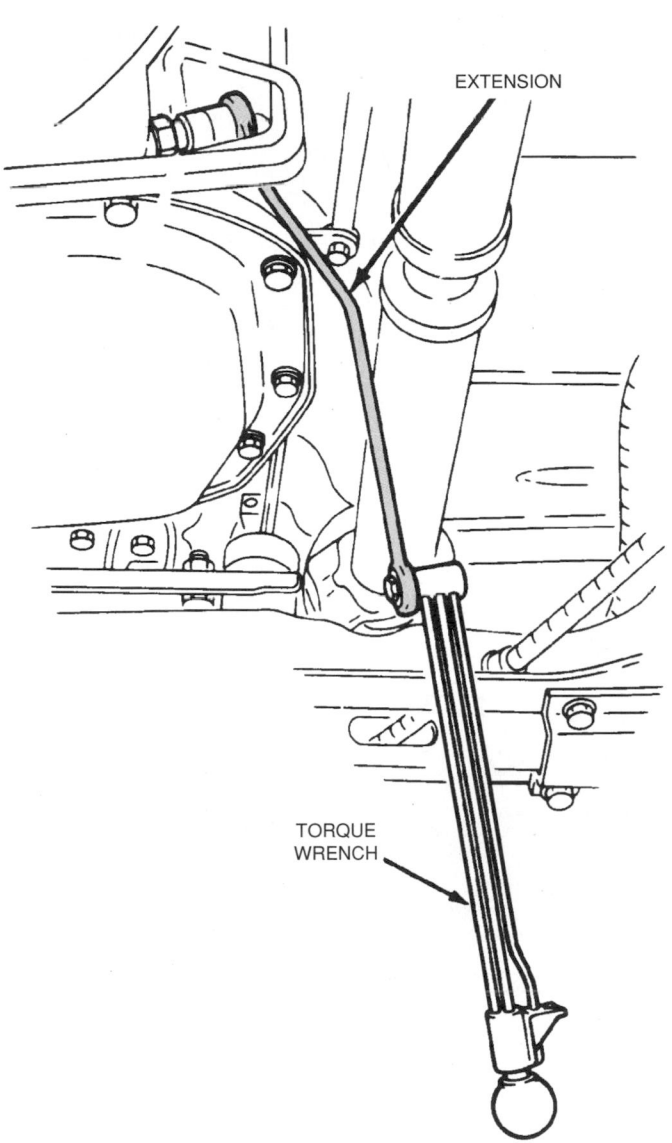

Figure 32-21. An extension makes this adjustment screw easy to torque. (Jeep)

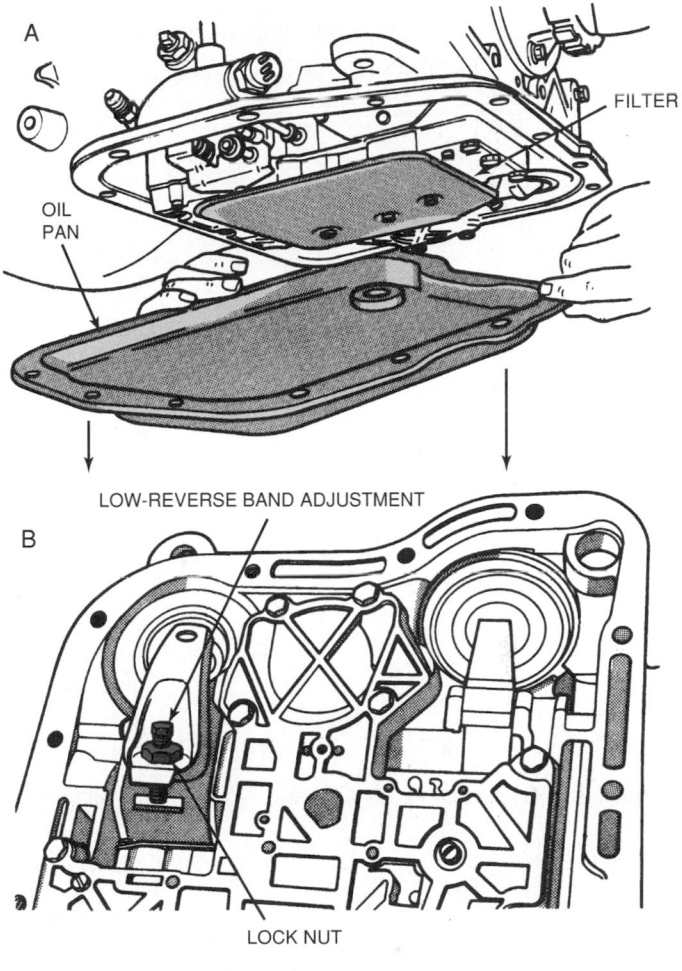

Figure 32-22. A—Removing the transmission oil pan and filter to provide access to the low-reverse band adjustment screw and locknut shown in B. (Dodge)

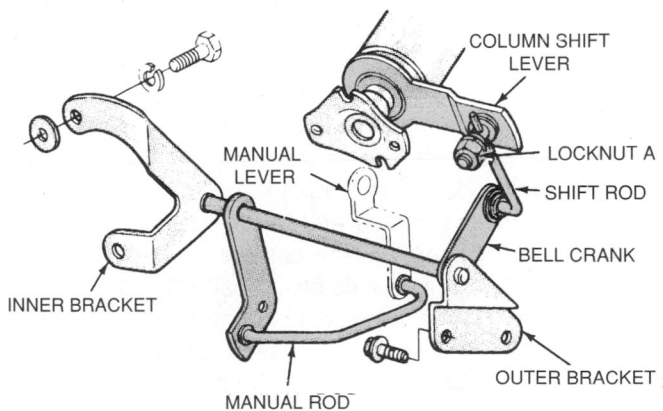

Figure 32-23. One type of column shift arrangement. (Ford)

will be positioned correctly. However, the exterior linkage can become so misadjusted that the driver will be unable to tell what gear is being selected. Most external linkage adjustments are to ensure that when the shift lever quadrant indicates a specific drive range, the transmission shift lever is actually in that position.

Even though the linkage was initially set correctly, wear, loosening of locknuts, and deterioration of engine mounts can alter the setting enough to cause trouble. If the engine mounts are damaged, do not adjust the linkage until new mounts are installed. The old mounts could allow further shifting of the engine and transmission which will throw the linkage out of adjustment again. The linkage setup pictured in **Figure 32-23** is typical.

To adjust this particular linkage, loosen locknut A until the shift rod slides in the swivel clamp (trunnion) freely. Move the manual lever into the park position (second from rear). Place gearshift selector lever in the park position. When both the transmission manual lever and the gearshift

lever are in the park positions, tighten the locknut. Move the shift lever through all ranges and check for operation and alignment. Modern vehicles use a cable instead of a linkage system for manual shifting. The floor shift in **Figure 32-24** adjusts in much the same way. Adjust the shift linkage or cable carefully as accuracy is a must. Make certain parking pawl lock functions correctly.

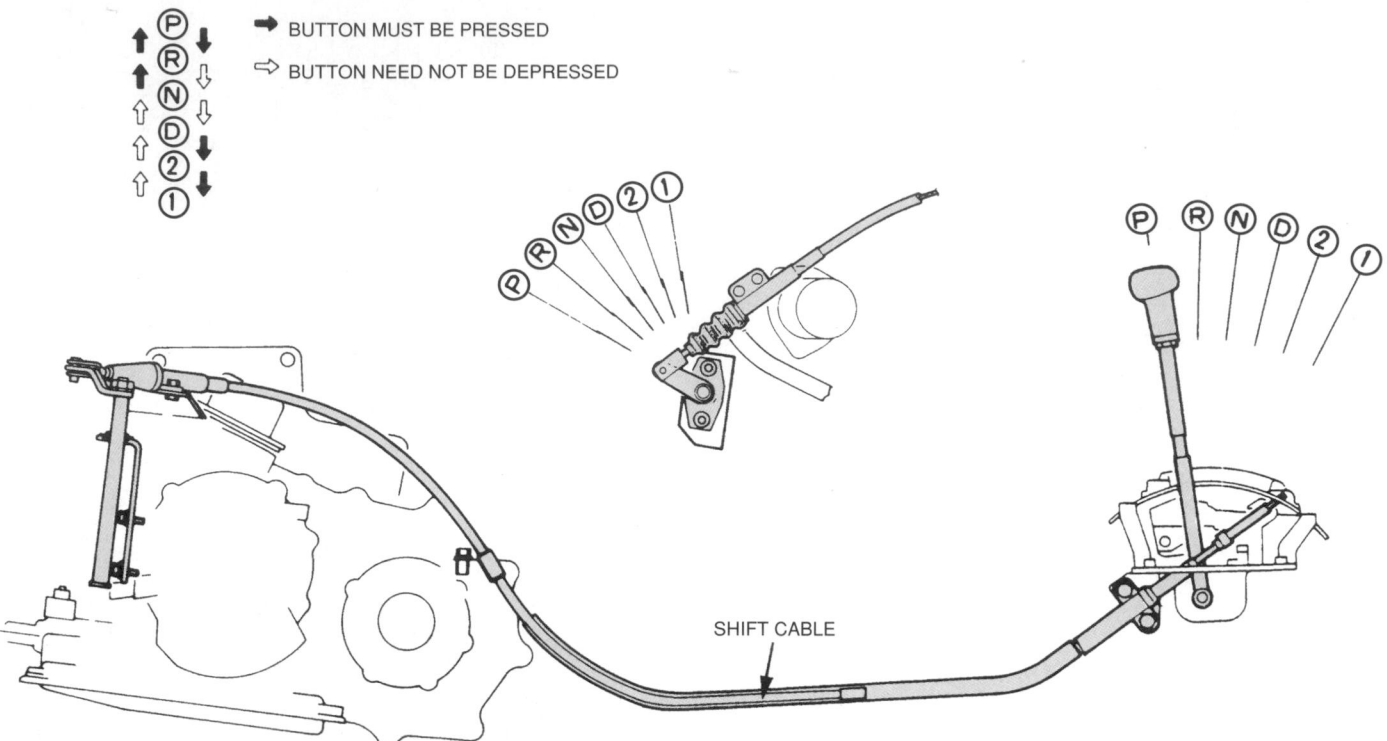

Figure 32-24. One floor shift linkage arrangement with shift cable. (Mazda)

Throttle Linkage (TV) Adjustment

The throttle linkage is usually called the *TV,* or *throttle valve* cable or linkage. TV adjustment is critical. The relationship between the carburetor or fuel injector throttle opening and the position of the throttle valve controls the transmission shift points. On most transmissions, the throttle valve affects the operation of the main pressure regulator, and therefore, affects the overall transmission hydraulic pressures. Faulty adjustment can result in incorrect shift points and internal pressures and can cause transmission or transaxle failure. Any movement of the accelerator pedal must produce a corresponding change in the positioning of the carburetor or fuel injection throttle plates and in the throttle valve position. Some automatic transmissions have a TV rod connected on one end to the throttle valve lever. The other end connects to the carburetor or throttle body linkage. Any change in throttle plate positioning will cause a corresponding change in the lever. Many modern transmissions and transaxles use a TV cable to produce the same result. **Figure 32-25** illustrates the TV cable arrangement of a common transmission.

Adjusting Throttle Valve Rods and Cables

Most throttle valve rods can be adjusted by pressing the accelerator pedal to the floor. Then check that the throttle plates are completely open and that the throttle lever is completely bottomed against its stop inside of the transmission. To adjust most TV cables, press the accelerator to the floor. Then loosen the cable stop (located at the top of the engine) and pull the TV cable all the way forward, **Figure 32-26.** Some TV cables are self-adjusting. Pull the cable all

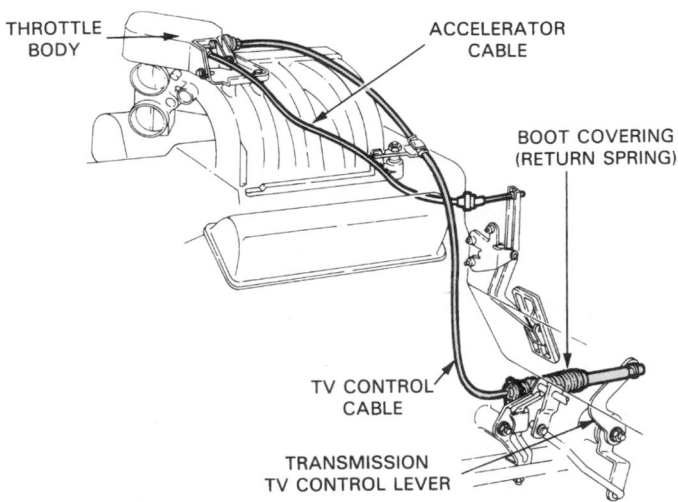

Figure 32-25. Throttle valve (TV) cable attaches to throttle body linkage on one end and to transmission TV lever on other. (Ford)

the way forward, then step hard on the accelerator pedal. This will adjust the cable. Recheck shift operation to ensure that the adjustment is correct.

Vacuum Modulator

Many transmission and transaxles have a *vacuum modulator.* On many transmissions, the modulator replaces the TV linkage to operate the throttle valve. On other transmissions, the modulator controls transmission pressures while a separate rod or cable controls upshift speeds. The modulator contains a vacuum diaphragm assembly with a

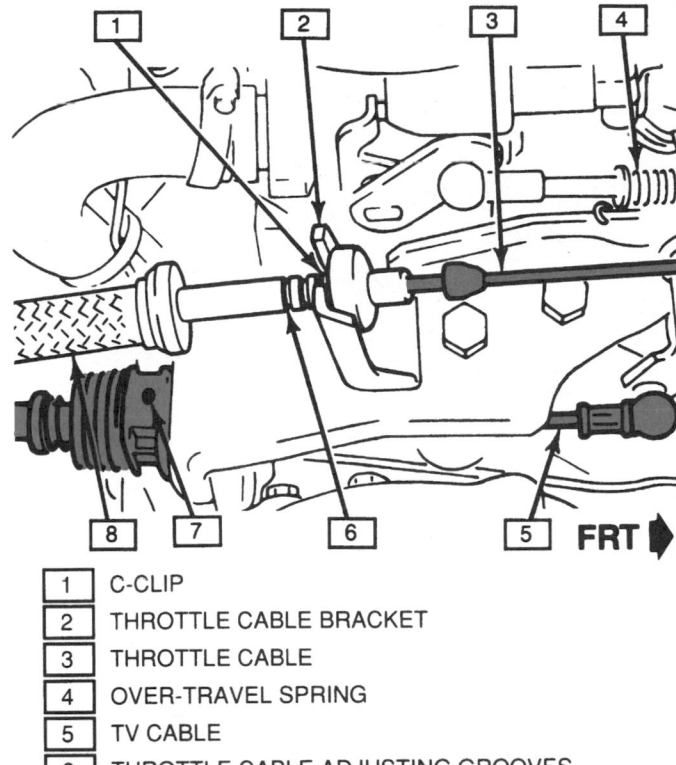

1	C-CLIP
2	THROTTLE CABLE BRACKET
3	THROTTLE CABLE
4	OVER-TRAVEL SPRING
5	TV CABLE
6	THROTTLE CABLE ADJUSTING GROOVES
7	TV CABLE ADJUSTING PIN
8	THROTTLE CABLE BOOT

Figure 32-26. One particular TV cable adjustment arrangement. (Pontiac)

hose attached to intake manifold vacuum. Manifold vacuum operating on the diaphragm alters the positioning of the throttle valve in accordance with engine vacuum, which corresponds to engine load. An additional refinement incorporates an evacuated bellows. It provides diaphragm action and adjusts pressure to the valve in accordance with changes in barometric pressure. **Figure 32-27** illustrates an altitude-compensating vacuum modulator.

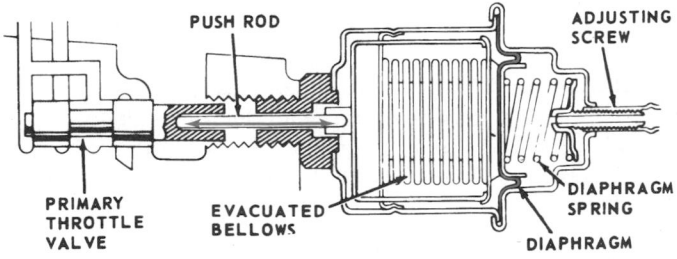

Figure 32-27. Vacuum controlled primary throttle valve. Note use of barometric pressure sensitive bellows. (Ford)

When shift points are too high or low, the vacuum modulator should be visually checked for a bent neck and for vacuum leakage. To check for leakage apply a controlled vacuum to the unit. The vacuum should read the same with the unit attached as with the hose pinched off. Also check for a plugged, split, or disconnected modulator vacuum line.

Transmission control pressure can be altered by adjusting the vacuum control, **Figure 32-28.** All adjustments must be correlated with engine vacuum and barometric pressure. Most modulators no longer have adjusting screws.

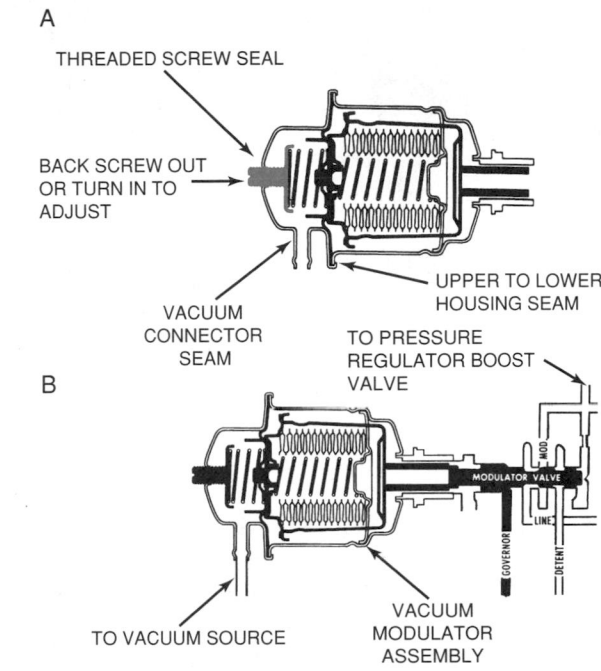

Figure 32-28. A—Cutaway view of an adjustable vacuum modulator unit. B—The vacuum modulator valve assembly in the detent position. (General Motors)

Downshift (Detent) Adjustment

Some transmissions are equipped with a vacuum modulator to control normal up and down shifts and a mechanical linkage to control forced downshifting, usually called a *detent rod* or *detent cable.* The detent should be adjusted carefully to ensure that the transmission will downshift in accordance with manufacturer's specifications and engine demand. Detent rod linkage is pictured in **Figure 32-29.** Detent downshifts can be accomplished by using a solenoid controlled by a downshift switch. Where such an arrangement is used, the switch must be properly adjusted. Note the gauge rod and test light to check the adjustment of the downshift switch in **Figure 32-30.**

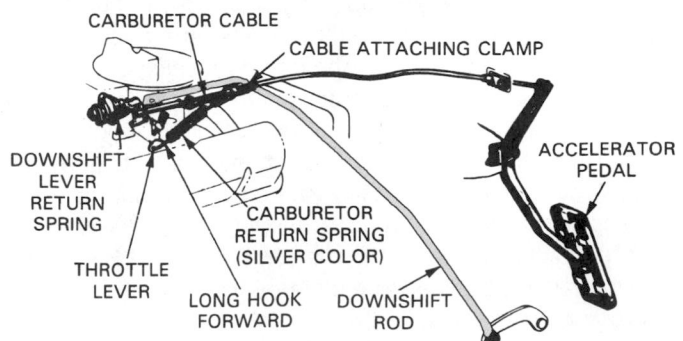

Figure 32-29. A downshift rod assembly and its location on one particular setup and engine that uses a carburetor.

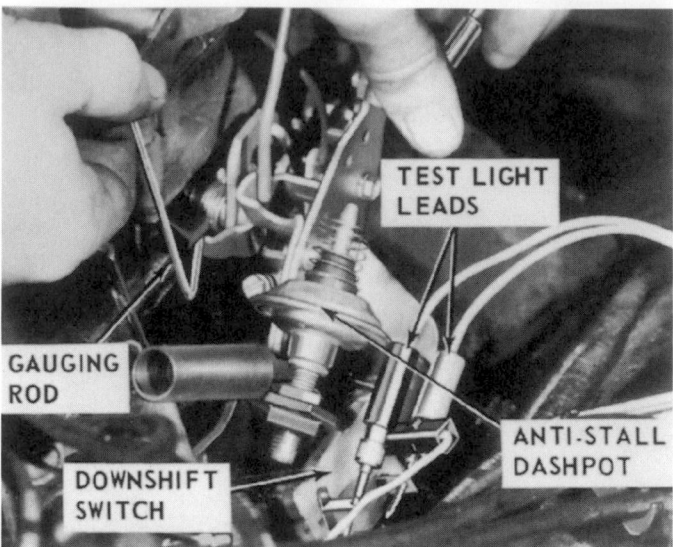

Figure 32-30. Checking downshift switch adjustment. (Cadillac)

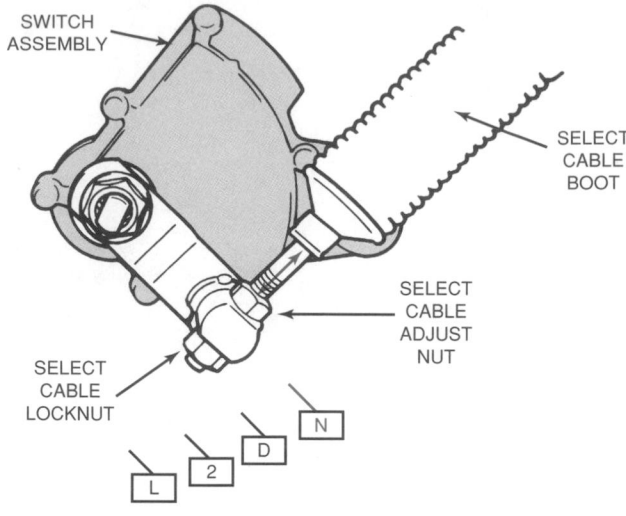

Accelerator Pedal Height and Linkage Action

Many throttle linkage adjustment specifications indicate a definite distance between the bottom of the accelerator pedal and the floor mat. With this measurement as specified, the engine hot idle speed must be correct as well as the adjustment of the throttle valve linkage or cable, and detent rod, cable, or electric detent switch. When the accelerator is fully depressed, the carburetor throttle valves must be in the wide open position. The linkage action must be smooth and free of binding. Lubricate as needed.

Neutral Safety Switch

Always check the neutral safety starting switch for proper operation. The engine should crank with the selector lever in either the neutral or park position. The engine should not crank with the selector lever in any other position. Adjust or replace the neutral safety switch as needed. The switch may be located on the steering column or on the floor shift console. In some cases, the switch is located on or in the transmission itself. Refer to **Figure 32-31.**

Leak Detection

When you have to add fluid frequently, it indicates a leak somewhere in the system. There are a number of potential leak areas such as the pan or housing gaskets, oil filler or manual valve seal, front pump seal or O-ring, rear seal, converter neck, drain or pressure plugs, cooling line connections, and cooler. In rare cases, a leak may be caused by a crack or porosity in the transmission case. At road speed, wind passing under the vehicle body will cause fluid to flow back toward the rear of the vehicle. For example, it is quite possible for engine oil from a leaking rocker arm cover to flow back to the end of the transmission extension housing. At first glance, this might appear to be a leaking rear transmission seal. Other leaking areas can be misleading in the same manner.

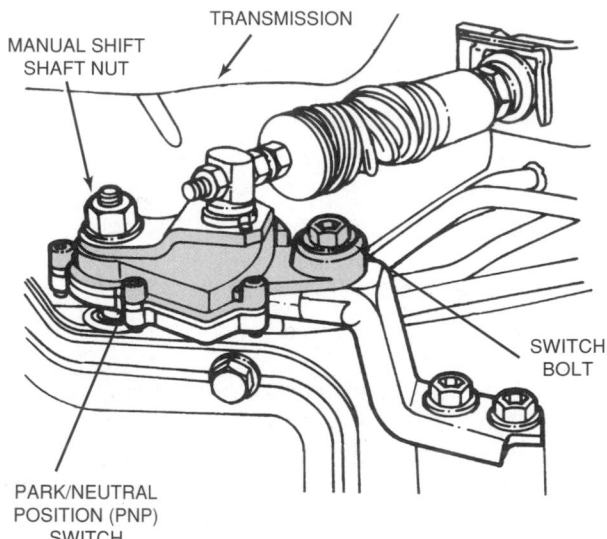

Figure 32-31. A park/neutral position (PNP) safety switch and the select cable. Follow the vehicle manufacturer's adjustment recommendations. The switch must be correctly aligned with the various positions—low, second, drive, neutral, etc. (Geo)

 Note: A leaking vacuum modulator will allow transmission fluid to be drawn into the engine and burned. There will be no external sign of a leak.

Identify Leaking Fluid

Do not assume that the fluid dripping from the rear of the transmission or from the converter housing is transmission fluid. It may be engine oil, coolant, brake fluid, or power steering fluid. Transmission fluid is generally dyed red and can usually be identified by the color. Refer to **Figure 32-32.** A black light is very helpful in determining the type of fluid. Compare the appearance of the leaking fluid to that on the engine, power steering, and transmission dipsticks. If needed, a special fluorescent dye may be added to the

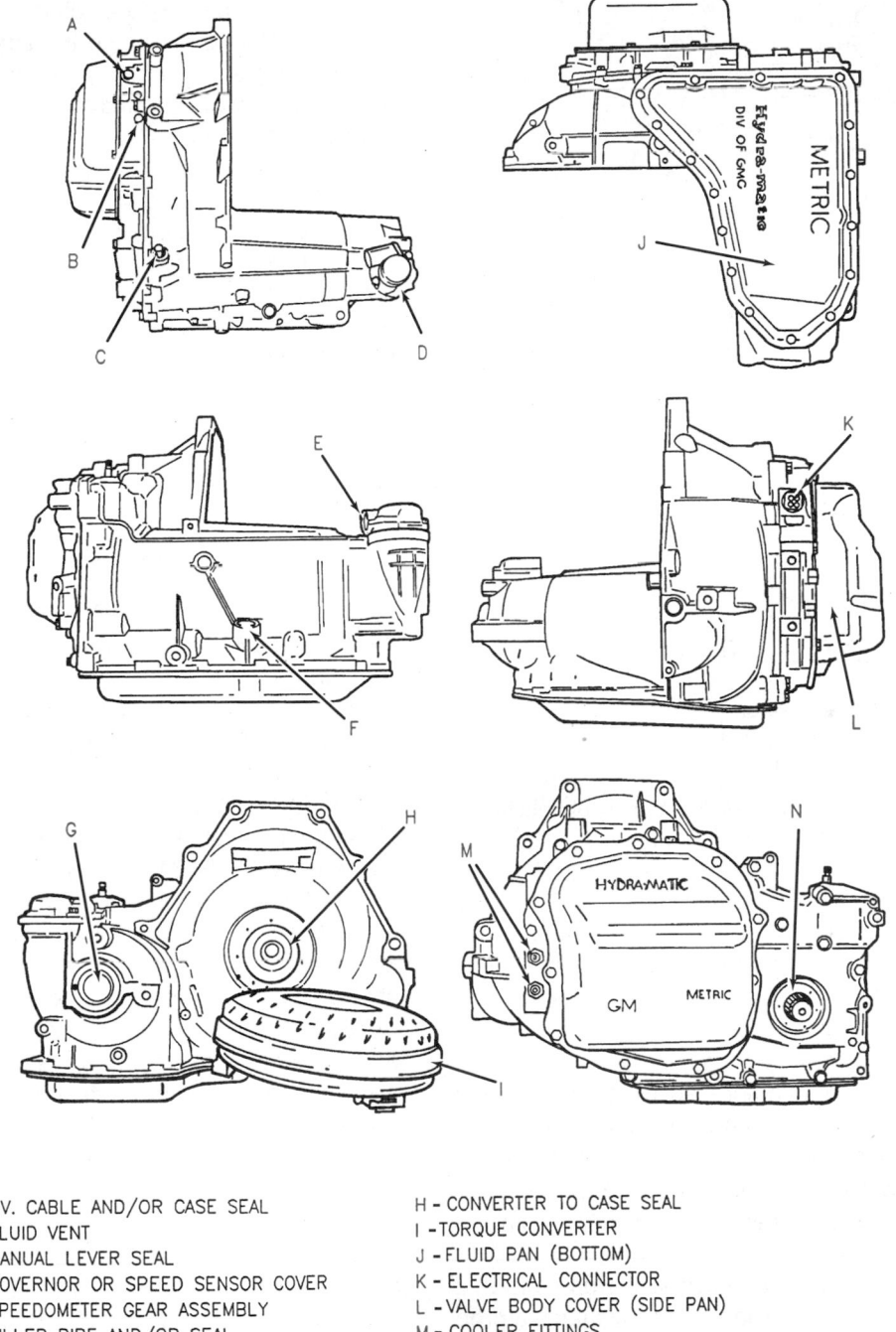

A - T.V. CABLE AND/OR CASE SEAL
B - FLUID VENT
C - MANUAL LEVER SEAL
D - GOVERNOR OR SPEED SENSOR COVER
E - SPEEDOMETER GEAR ASSEMBLY
F - FILLER PIPE AND/OR SEAL
G - AXLE SEAL (R.H.)

H - CONVERTER TO CASE SEAL
I - TORQUE CONVERTER
J - FLUID PAN (BOTTOM)
K - ELECTRICAL CONNECTOR
L - VALVE BODY COVER (SIDE PAN)
M - COOLER FITTINGS
N - AXLE SEAL (L.H.)

Figure 32-32. A few possible transmission fluid leak points on one particular automatic transaxle. (Chevrolet)

transmission fluid for positive identification. It is very difficult to pinpoint the source of a leak when the parts are covered with dirt and oil. Clean the engine, converter housing, and transmission. Blow dry with air. Remove the converter housing inspection pan and clean the converter. Clean the inside of the housing. Blow dry.

Following cleaning, operate the engine at a fast idle to bring the transmission fluid to normal operating temperature. Stop the engine, place the vehicle on a lift, and restart the engine. Examine the engine and transmission for leaks. Shifting the transmission through all drive ranges will help in starting any existing leak. Watch carefully for

the first sign of a fluid leak. If no leaks are apparent, operate the vehicle on the road for several miles, with frequent starts and stops. Place the vehicle on a lift and recheck for leaks. When fluid flows from the converter housing, it could mean a loose converter drain plug, leaking converter, defective front seal, housing-to-case fastener leak, or similar defect. **Figure 32-33** illustrates possible leakage points and flow of fluid in a typical converter-housing assembly.

Diagnosing Transmission Problems

The following section covers methods to detect some minor transmission problems and how to determine whether

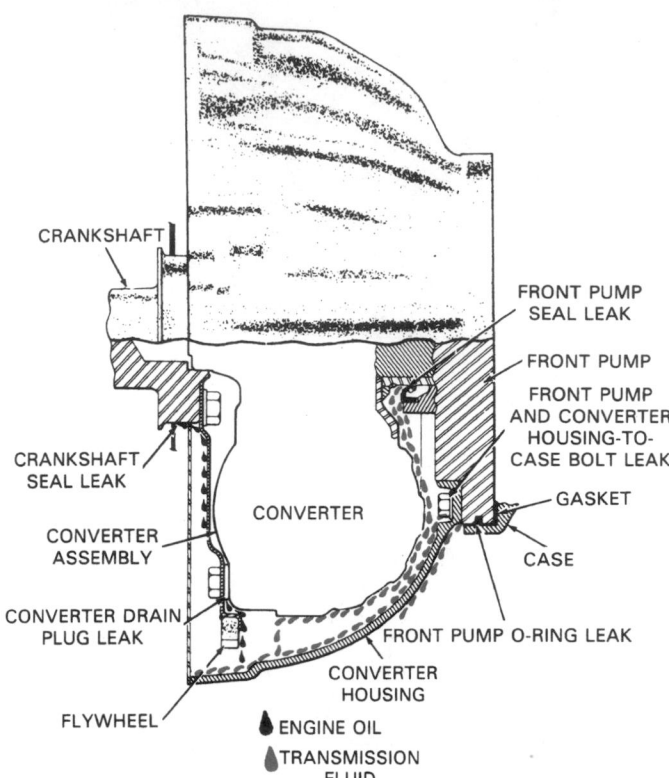

CRANKSHAFT

FRONT PUMP
SEAL LEAK

FRONT PUMP

FRONT PUMP
AND CONVERTER
HOUSING-TO-
CASE BOLT LEAK

CRANKSHAFT
SEAL LEAK

CONVERTER

GASKET

CONVERTER
ASSEMBLY

CASE

CONVERTER DRAIN
PLUG LEAK

FRONT PUMP O-RING LEAK

CONVERTER
HOUSING

FLYWHEEL

ENGINE OIL

TRANSMISSION
FLUID

Figure 32-33. Possible leakage points and flow of fluid in typical converter-housing assembly. (Ford)

further checking is needed. The variety of transmission types and models coupled with yearly modifications make it impractical to formulate a generalized diagnosis chart of significant value. As with service techniques and procedures, the use of the manufacturer's service manual is recommended. It will contain a comprehensive diagnosis chart or guide that applies to the transmission concerned. Whenever possible, talk to the owner regarding transmission performance. It is a good idea to have the owner present during the road test. This will enable the owner to point out exact symptoms.

The **troubleshooting chart,** such as the one shown in **Figure 32-34,** allows the technician to quickly match a problem condition with the possible causes and corrections. In many cases the "problem" is actually a normal condition. This is especially true of newer transmissions and transaxles which shift more firmly that older transmissions. In such cases, a tactful explanation of transmission operation will be all the repair needed. **Band and clutch application charts** indicate which holding members are applied in which gear. This makes it easy to determine what band or clutch is defective when the transmission slips in a particular gear.

Do not attempt to diagnose transmission or transaxle problems until the engine has been determined to be in sound mechanical condition and properly tuned. The idle speed must be correct. The engine should accelerate from a standing start to any desired speed without missing, hesitation, or lack of power. Locate and correct any

engine problems before checking the transmission or transaxle. Both engine and transmission/transaxle must be at operating temperature prior to testing. If the transmission is electronically controlled, retrieve any trouble codes before proceeding.

Road Test

A road test can help to determine the exact transmission or transaxle problem. Some shops employ the use of road test charts such as that pictured in **Figure 32-35.** The use of such a chart ensures that all pertinent checks are made. It also provides the technician with a written record that is helpful for diagnostic purposes. Shift points and shift patterns obviously must relate to the transmission being tested. Perform each check or adjustment carefully. An error, even though small, can often seriously upset transmission performance. Remember that in a series of diagnostic steps, the accuracy of each check and adjustment can be completely dependent on the preceding steps.

Shift Point Check

Shift points are a good indicator of internal and external transmission or transaxle problems. Bring the unit to the normal operating temperature. Move the selector lever from neutral through all drive ranges (engine at normal idle RPM). These initial holding member engagements should be smooth. Harsh engagements can indicate either excessive engine idle RPM or incorrect control pressures.

Road test the vehicle. From a standing start with normal acceleration, the transmission should make all shifts within a reasonable range. Check the service manual for the exact shift points. Specified shift points (road speed or engine RPM at which transmission shifts) depend upon such things as engine size, tire size, and rear axle ratios. If the unit uses a lockup torque converter, the converter apply might feel like an extra shift. If the converter lockup is hard to detect or to separate it from a gearshift, attach a tachometer to the engine. Converter lockup apply will cause a smaller RPM drop than gear changes. On some computer-controlled automatic transmissions, a scan tool (if available with the correct software) can also detect when lockup occurs.

Automatic shifts should go from lowest to highest. Coasting downshifts should be smooth. Part throttle and detent downshifts should occur when the accelerator pedal is depressed. Engagement at each shift should be smooth, yet positive with no sign of slippage. If the transmission has a lockout feature for first gear (vehicle starts in second to provide better traction for slippery roads), place the selector in the low gear lockout (D2 or 2) range. Vehicle should start out in second gear.

Pressure Checks

Checking oil pressure is a good way to determine the condition of the hydraulic system, including the pump, valves, pressure regulator, and internal seals. Since oil pressures, check points, and methods of checking vary, always consult the manufacturer's service manual. Begin by ensuring that the transmission is at normal operating tem-

Remedial Steps If Oil Pressure Is Not Normal

Trouble symptom	Probable cause	Remedy
1. *Line pressures are all low (or high). NOTE *"Line pressures" refers to oil pressures 2, 3, 4 and 5 in the "Standard oil pressure table" on the previous page.	a. Clogging on oil filter b. Improper adjustment of oil pressure (line pressure) regulator valve c. Sticking of regulator valve d. Looseness of valve body tightening part e. Improper oil pump discharge pressure	a. Visually inspect the oil filter; replace the oil filter if it is clogged. b. Measure line pressure ② (kickdown brake pressure); if the pressure is not the standard value, readjust the line pressure, or if necessary, replace the valve body assembly. c. Check the operation of the regulator valve; repair if necessary, or replace the valve body assembly. d. Tighten the valve body tightening bolt and installation bolt. e. Check the side clearance of the oil pump gear; replace the oil pump assembly if necessary.
2. Improper reducing pressure	a. Improper line pressure b. Clogging of the filter of the reducing-pressure circuit c. Improper adjustment of the reducing pressure d. Sticking of the reducing valve e. Looseness of valve body tightening part	a. Check the ② kickdown brake pressure (line pressure); if the line pressure is not the standard value, check as described in item 1 above. b. Disassemble the valve body assembly and check the filter; replace the filter if it is clogged. c. Measure the ① reducing pressure; if it is not the standard value, readjust, or replace the valve body assembly. d. Check the operation of the reducing valve; if necessary, repair it, or replace the valve body assembly. e. Tighten the valve body tightening bolt and installation bolt.
3. Improper kickdown brake pressure	a. Malfunction of the D-ring or seal ring of the sleeve or kickdown servo piston b. Looseness of valve body tightening part c. Functional malfunction of the valve body assembly	a. Disassemble the kickdown servo and check whether the seal ring or D-ring is damaged. If it is cut or has scratches, replace the seal ring or D-ring. b. Tighten the valve body tightening bolt and installation bolt. c. Replace the valve body assembly.

Figure 32-34. Example of a troubleshooting chart from one manufacturer. It lists the trouble, probable cause, and remedy (correction) for several improper transmission fluid pressures. (Hyundai)

perature and checking the fluid level. Clean dirt from around the pressure taps (plugs). Remove the tap and connect a suitable pressure gauge. Gauge hose should be long enough to reach the driver's compartment for road testing. A typical gauge, 0-300 PSI (0-2068 kPa) is shown connected to the check point in **Figure 32-36.** Note the use of a long hose.

If needed, attach a tachometer to provide accurate RPM check points, **Figure 32-37.** Drive the vehicle at the recommended road speeds. Check the pressure in the specified drive range. Closely watch the gauge during shifts to determine whether a particular servo or clutch seal is leaking. Other pressure tests can be performed in the shop. Be careful to place the transmission in the correct drive

ROAD TEST SYMPTOM CHART

Numbers in chart below correspond with those indicated in Trouble-shooting charts. (Located in proper service manual for vehicle being tested.)

Range	Operation	Code	ROUGH	SHIFT TIMING [Mark km/h (MPH)]	NO SHIFT	SHIFT SLIPPAGE	VEHICLE WON'T MOVE	CRUISE SLIPPAGE	POOR POWER/ACCELERATION	NOISY	ENGINE WON'T START	VEHICLE WON'T STAND STILL	NO ENGINE BRAKING	COMMENTS
PARK RANGE	ENG. START										A			
	HOLDING									B		C		
"R" RANGE	Man. shift (Vehicle at halt)	P-R					U			V				
	REVERSE						E·U	E	E	V				
"N" RANGE	Man. shift (Vehicle at halt)	R-N								V				
	ENG. START										A			
	N									B		D		
"D" RANGE	Man. shift	N-D	F				G·U			V				
	1st						G·U		I	V				
	Auto shift	1-2	L		J	N				V				
	2nd								P	V				
	Auto shift	2-3	M		K	O				V				
	3rd in lock-up "OFF"								P	V				
	Auto shift Lock-up "OFF" (3) → Lock-up "ON" (3)				A2	A3				V				
	3rd in Lock-up "ON"								P	V				
	Auto shift Lock-up "ON" (3) → Lock-up "OFF" (3)									V				
	Decel.	3-2			Q	T				V				
	Kickdown	3-2			Q·S	T				V				
	Decel.	2-1			R					V				
	Kickdown	2-1			R					V				
"2" RANGE	Man. shift (Vehicle in operation)	D-2			W		H·U			V				
	1st						H·U		I	V				
	Auto shift	1-2	L		J	N				V				
	2nd								P	V				
	Decel.	2-1			R					V				
	Kickdown	2-1			R					V				
"1" RANGE	Man. shift (Vehicle in operation)	2-1	A1		R·Z					V				
	Man. shift (Vehicle in operation)	D-1			R·X					V				
	Acceleration						H·U		I	V				
	"1" Engine Braking									V			Y	

Figure 32-35. One form of transmission road test chart. Use one for exact transmission being tested. (Nissan)

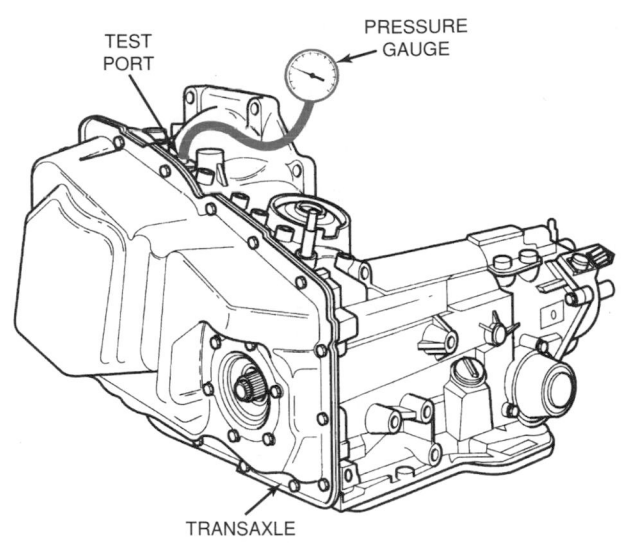

Figure 32-36. A hydraulic fluid test gauge connected to the automatic transaxle to obtain a pressure check. (Cadillac)

range and operate at the exact RPM. Compare gauge readings with those specified.

A vacuum gauge (in addition to a pressure gauge and tachometer) is required to check control oil pressure on transmissions with a vacuum modulator. The vacuum modulator test setup shown in **Figure 32-38** uses a hand-held vacuum pump in place of engine vacuum. Manufacturers provide specifications showing the correct control pressure at a given engine vacuum. If an altitude-compensating vacuum unit is used, be sure to make allowance for the barometric pressure during the test. Vacuum gauge readings will

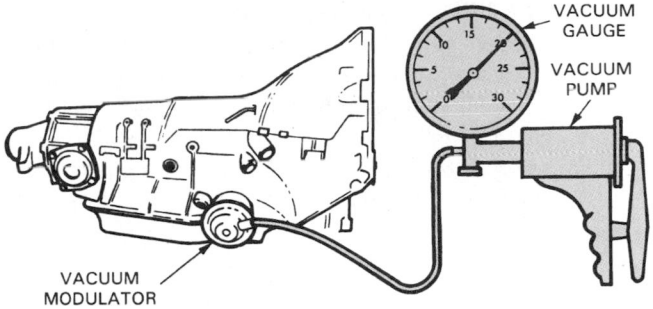

Figure 32-38. Vacuum gauge and pump combination being used to check vacuum modulator. (Chevrolet)

be about 1 inch lower for every 1000 feet (305 meters) rise in elevation. Barometric pressure can also be affected by weather conditions, but usually not enough to seriously affect pressure readings.

Stall Testing

The ***stall test*** is used on some transmissions to determine the condition of the disc clutches, bands, one-way clutch, and other parts. To stall test a transmission, bring the engine to its normal operating temperature. Connect a tachometer so that it may be read from the driver's seat. Apply both the parking and service brakes. Place the selector lever in the recommended stall test position (drive, low, reverse, etc.). While holding the brakes on with great force, push the throttle to the recommended throttle position. Do not go beyond full throttle into the kickdown position unless so recommended.

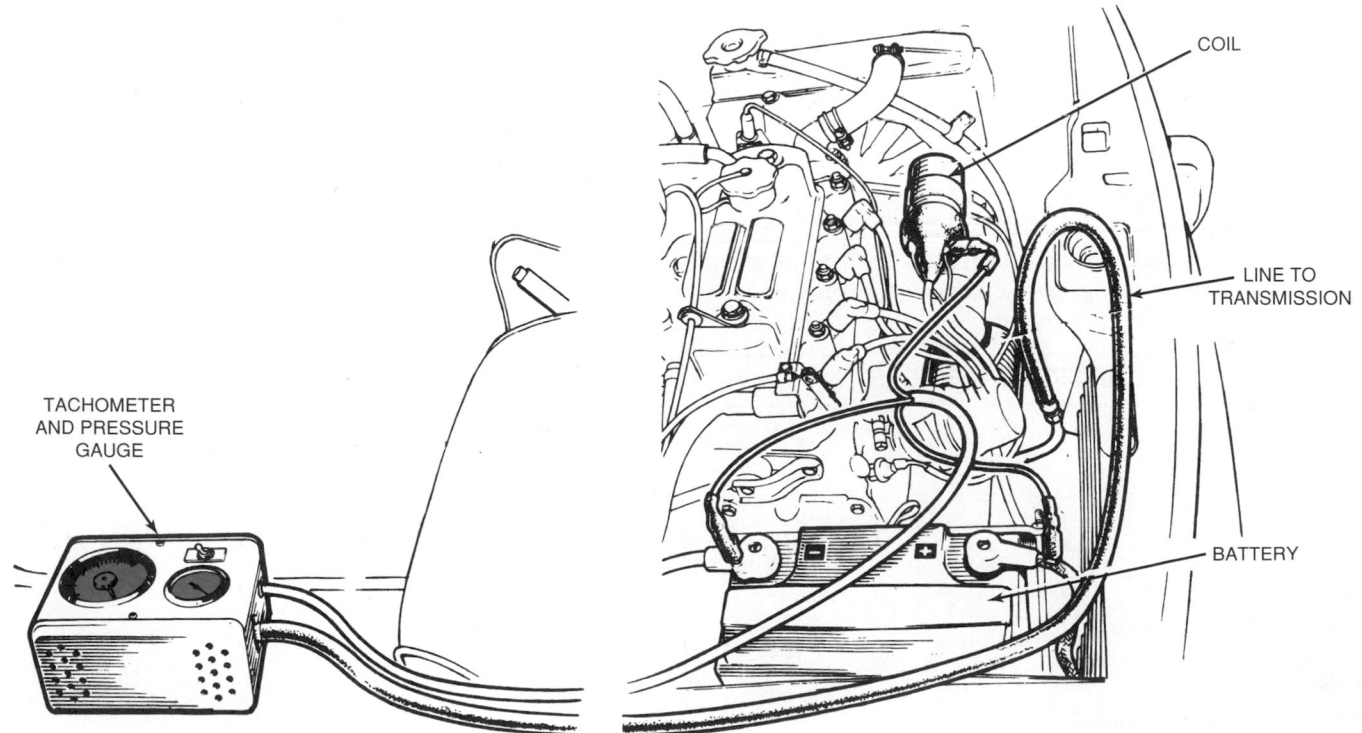

Figure 32-37. Attaching a tachometer and pressure gauge tool to check for correct shift RPM ranges and transmission operating fluid pressure. (Automotive Products Co.)

Note the RPM indicated while operating at full throttle. If engine speed is below specifications, it can indicate engine or converter stator problems. RPM above the manufacturer's specifications can mean slipping bands or clutches. When stall testing, never keep the accelerator pedal in the full throttle position for longer than five seconds. To do so will overheat the transmission. Return the selector lever to the neutral position and operate the engine at around 1200 RPM for a minute or two before stall testing a different drive range. If the engine RPM exceeds stall specifications during the stall test, release the accelerator immediately. Make certain the brakes are firmly applied and keep people out of the way.

 Caution: Some transmissions must not be stall tested. Follow manufacturer's instructions.

In-Vehicle Repairs

The following repair operations are designed to be performed with the transmission or transaxle installed in the vehicle. Always consult the manufacturer's service manual for the exact procedures.

Casting Repair

If a fluid leak is the result of a porous casting or a small crack, a satisfactory repair can often be made by using an epoxy resin. Operate the vehicle until the transmission reaches full operation temperature. Clean the case thoroughly and mark the leakage area. Apply several coats of nonflammable solvent to the leak and surrounding areas. Blow dry each time. Immediately following a final scrubbing, apply air until dry. Mix a batch of epoxy resin following the epoxy manufacturer's directions. Apply a heavy coating to the case. The case should still be hot. Allow to cure for a minimum of three to four hours before starting the vehicle. Following the waiting period, road test and recheck for leaks.

External Seal Replacement

There are many seals, O-rings, and gaskets on the average automatic transmission or transaxle. Most of them can be changed by removing any parts which interfere with

access. Most seals can be pried out and a new seal carefully driven into place. Note the following precautions:

- Ensure that the shaft and seal bore are free of nicks and dents.
- Clean the seal area of the transmission.
- Coat the outside of the new seal with sealer.
- Coat the lips with transmission fluid before installation.
- Use a suitable installation tool.
- Ensure that the seal lip faces toward the inside of the transmission.

Replacing O-rings is similar to replacing seals. The sealing surfaces should be carefully cleaned and checked for damage. The new O-ring should be oiled and placed into the bore, or on the separate part as specified. Install all fasteners and check for leaks. When gaskets are replaced, all of the old gasket material should be removed. Use gasket cement only if called for by the gasket manufacturer. After installing the new gasket, carefully torque the fasteners to the proper torque. The table in **Figure 32-39** indicates whether the transmission or transaxle must be removed from the vehicle to service a particular seal.

Transmission Electrical Device Replacement

Many late model transmissions and transaxles have solenoids and pressure sensors installed as part of the computer control system. To change any of these devices, the oil pan must be removed. Then remove the electrical connector from the device to be changed. Remove the old device and install the new part. Reinstall the electrical connector and reinstall the oil pan. Always recheck the operation of the engine and the transmission or transaxle after replacing an electrical device.

Governor Assembly Replacement

The valves in the governor assembly are operated by centrifugal force and are prone to sticking. Therefore, it is often necessary to remove the governor for cleaning or replacement. Some governors are mounted on the output shaft. These governors can only be accessed by removing the extension housing (transmissions) or the oil pan and

TRANSMISSION IN-VEHICLE	TRANSMISSION MUST BE REMOVED
Extension housing seal	Front pump seal
Manual shaft seal	Front pump O-ring
Governor seals	Front pump gasket
Governor cover gasket	Clutch piston seals
Speedometer gear seal and O-ring	Side pan gasket (transaxles)
Accumulator O-rings	
Servo piston O-rings	
Pan gasket	
Valve body gasket	
Extension housing gasket	
Filler tube seal	

Figure 32-39. In-vehicle and out-of-vehicle transmission service and repair procedures.

valve body (some transaxles). On other transmissions or transaxles, the governor is installed on the side of the case and can be accessed by removing a cover plate. Some extension housings have a cover plate for governor access. Once the governor is removed, check it for sticking and dirt. Check all valves for free movement. If the governor is case-mounted, carefully check the drive gear for damage and the governor bore for wear. Carefully check the governor springs. A weak or misplaced spring will affect shift points. Thoroughly clean the governor and oil it before reinstalling. Always recheck transmission shift speeds after changing the governor.

Valve Body Replacement

The valve body assembly is removed by pulling the pan and removing the valve body-to-transmission fasteners. Before removing the fasteners, remove the filter, linkage, and electrical connectors as necessary. When removing the valve body, be sure to remove it slowly in order to catch any valves, servo and accumulator springs or pistons, check balls, or linkage parts that may fall free. An exploded view of a typical valve body is shown in **Figure 32-40.** With the

valve body on the bench, check it for metal particles and sludge. Check every valve for free movement. If any valve is sticking, it can be carefully removed and cleaned. Also check the valve bore for sludge or metal. If the valve cannot be made to work properly, replace the valve body.

Check the valve body for proper placement of all valves and springs. Reversed valves or misplaced springs will affect valve body operation. Check the condition of the sheet metal spacer plate and any check balls. Thoroughly clean the valve body and oil it before reinstalling. Be sure to install any check balls, accumulator or servo pistons and springs, and linkage. Do not use gasket cement when replacing the valve body. Torque the valve body bolts from the inner bolts outward. Install a new filter and reinstall the pan. Always recheck transmission operation after servicing the valve body.

Clutch and Band Operation

Once the valve body has been removed, **_air pressure checks_** can be made. This procedure consists of applying air pressure to check clutch and band operation. The transmission in **Figure 32-41** has had the control valve body

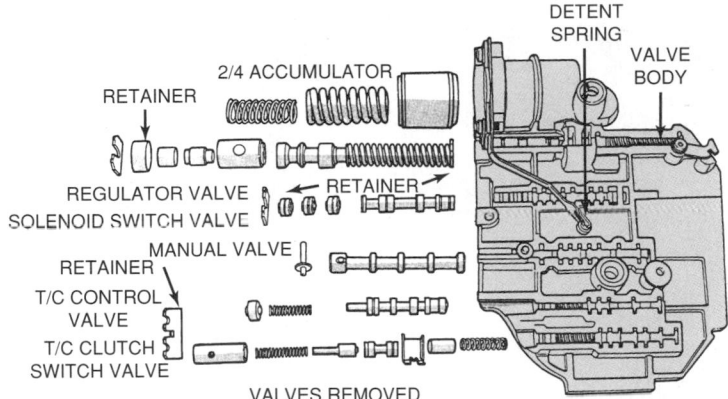

Figure 32-40. Exploded view of one type of valve body. This valve body is used with a four-speed automatic transaxle. (Chrysler)

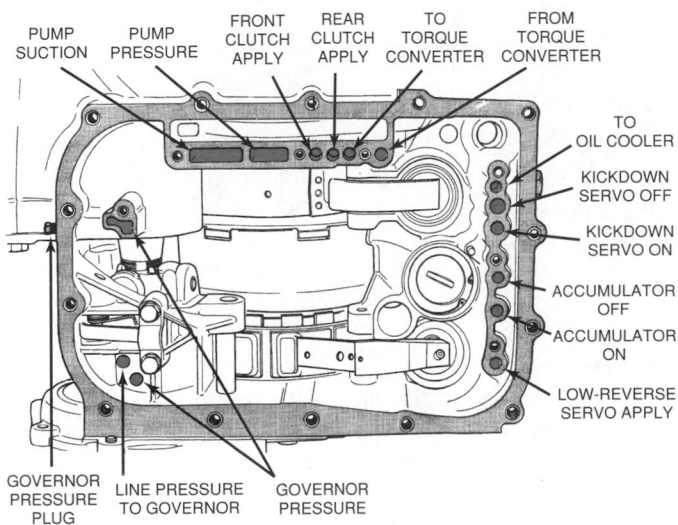

Figure 32-41. Transmission case internal oil passages have been exposed by removing the oil pan and valve body assembly. (Chrysler)

removed. Note the case oil passageways. Clutch action is being checked in **Figures 32-42** and **32-43.** When air is applied, a distinct thump can be heard or felt if the clutch piston is functioning. The application of air to the band servo apply passageways will cause the band to tighten. Application of air to the servo release passage will cause the band to loosen. Use clean, dry air only. Nozzle must be clean. Be sure to use air on correct passageways and do not exceed manufacturer's recommended maximum testing air pressures.

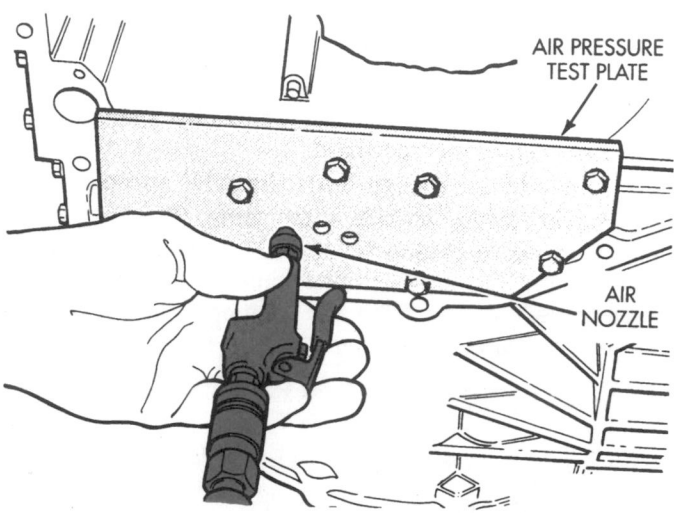

Figure 32-42. Applying air pressure to check clutch action. Note the air pressure test plate, which exposes the correct test holes and seals the holes not used. Use clean, moisture-free air and do not exceed the recommended test pressure. Wear your safety glasses. (Chrysler)

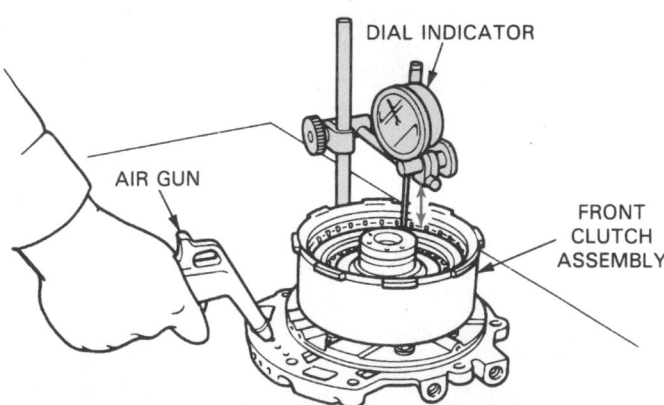

Figure 32-43. Front clutch unit being checked with air gun. This particular clutch has been removed from transmission for checking. Note dial indicator being used to measure clutch clearance (travel). (Mazda)

Other In-Vehicle Checks and Repairs

Depending upon transmission design, a number of other tests and repairs can often be performed with the transmission in the vehicle. The vacuum modulator, modulator valve, servo, and park-lock device can often be removed, inspected, and replaced without pulling the transmission. Follow manufacturer's recommendations.

Transmission or Transaxle Removal

To begin transmission or transaxle removal, disconnect the battery ground strap. Remove the starter unless it is needed to rotate the engine to remove the bolts or nuts holding the converter to the flywheel or drive plate.

 Note: Do not pry on the ring gear teeth to rotate the engine and converter. This can damage the ring gear. Special *flywheel turners* are available. Some manufacturers recommend using a ratchet and socket to turn the crankshaft balancer nut, Figure 32-44.

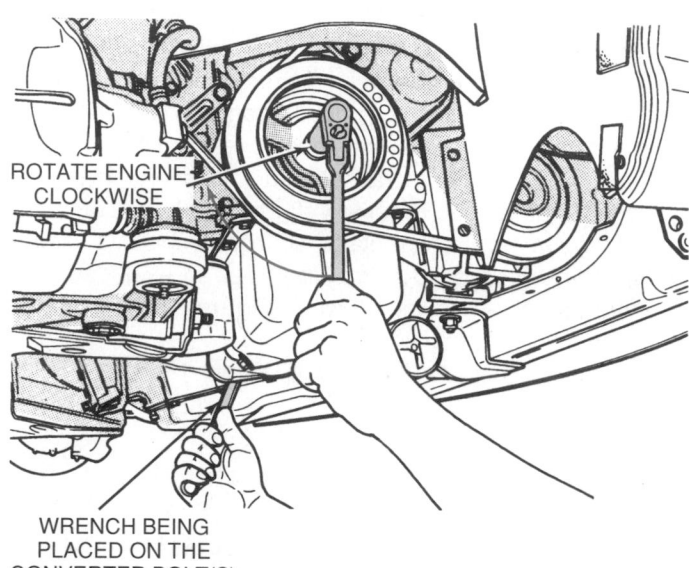

Figure 32-44. An engine is rotated clockwise so that the next converter bolt can be accessed. If you are rotating the engine using this method, disconnect the battery to prevent accidental starter engagement. (Chrysler)

Remove the converter-to-flywheel fasteners, Also remove wires, coolant lines, shift rod, vacuum line, downshift rod, filler tube, speedometer cable, and other parts. Disconnect the drive shaft or CV drive axles and wire out of the way. Before removing the shafts, mark them so they can be reassembled in their original positions. See Chapter 33 for complete details. If the U-joint is a cross and roller type, tape the loose roller bearings to the cross. Remove the transmission or transaxle mounts as needed. If a support member must be removed, support the engine with either a jack stand or an engine support strap or fixture. If the engine must be raised to gain access, be careful to avoid damage to any attached parts. If pushing upward on the oil pan, place a wide block of wood between the oil pan and jack.

Use a Transmission Jack

Automatic transmissions and transaxles are heavy and a transmission jack should be used for removal. Whenever a transmission or transaxle is being removed, get someone to help you stabilize the unit as it is lowered. Attach the transmission or transaxle firmly to the jack. Then remove the fasteners holding the transmission or transaxle to the engine. Guide the transmission or transaxle away from the engine and lower.

 Note: The transmission/transaxle and converter should always be removed as an assembly. The retaining bar will prevent the converter from dropping off during removal. See Figure 32-45.

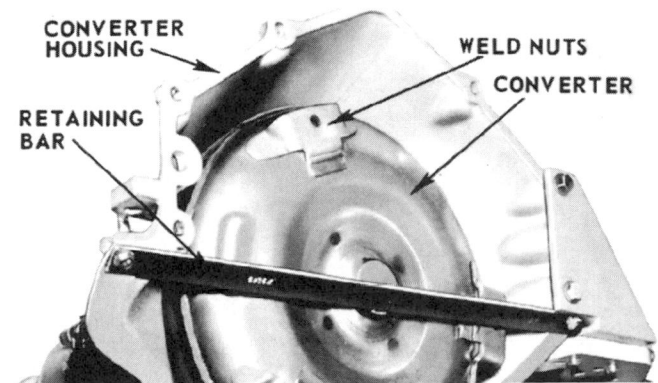

Figure 32-45. Always use retaining bar or strap to prevent converter from falling off during transmission removal or installation. (GMC)

Torque Converter Cleaning

After the torque converter has been removed and thoroughly drained, which usually takes about 15 minutes, purge any remaining fluid with air pressure. Put approximately 2 quarts (2.2 liters) of recommended cleaning solvent into converter and shake vigorously. Drain again and use compressed air to blow dry.

Most converters may be pressure cleaned and drained with a special cleaning machine. One is pictured in **Figure 32-46.** The converter is bolted to a mounting plate and the proper hoses are connected. The converter is rotated at 20 RPM while cleaning solvent is passed through it. Air is injected into the solvent to aid cleaning action through agitation. After installing the converter, transmission, and related parts in the vehicle, add the required amount and proper type of new fluid before starting the engine. Start the engine and move the shift lever through all drive ranges and back to park. Allow the vehicle to idle to heat up the fluid. Check the transmission fluid level when hot. Add more fluid if needed and check for leaks.

Flushing Oil Cooler

To avoid the possibility of damage to a new or rebuilt transmission, the oil cooler and lines should be thoroughly *flushed* to remove any metal particles or other material. Use clean solvent and a pressure gun. Reverse flush until the solvent comes out clean. Flush out the solvent (in normal direction of flow) with automatic transmission fluid. Pass fluid through the lines until all the solvent is removed. Cap the lines until ready to reconnect.

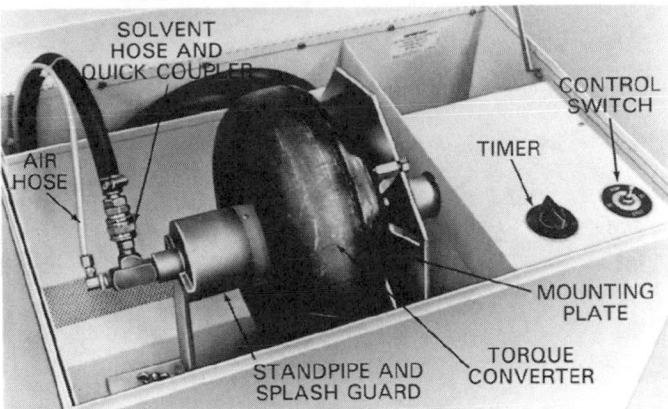

Figure 32-46. One type of torque converter cleaner. This unit helps remove harmful contaminants (metal particles, sludge, etc.) that can circulate into transmission, plugging filter screens and valve bodies. This unit can also be used for flushing transmission oil coolers. (Owatonna Tool Co.)

 Caution: Oil cooler hydraulic pressures are low, usually about 10 PSI (68.9 kPa). Do not use air pressure in excess of normal hydraulic pressures.

A flushing unit, such as that pictured in **Figure 32-47,** does a good job of flushing the cooler. Follow manufacturer's recommendations for the correct flushing procedure. After flushing, check all connections. If the oil flow through the lines seems impeded, check for dents or a pinched section. Replace line if damaged. Be extremely careful with plastic cooler lines and connectors. Keep away from sharp or hot areas. Replace the radiator if the cooler is clogged and cannot be cleaned. **Figure 32-48** shows two typical cooler line arrangements.

Flushing may also be done by installing the transmission and filling with the recommended amount of fluid. Connect the transmission oil outlet line only. Place the inlet end in a container. Start the engine, move the gear selector through the various ranges and return to neutral. Allow about one quart of fluid to pump through the lines. Stop the engine and add another quart of fluid. Continue this process until the fluid coming out the return pipe is clear and clean. Reconnect line and add transmission fluid.

Transmission Installation

Install the transmission in the reverse order of removal. Always install the transmission and torque converter as an assembly. Make sure the converter is installed into the front pump properly and to the full depth. See **Figure 32-49.** Use a retaining strap to keep the converter from falling out. Align converter and drive plate or flywheel marks and be certain the converter hub or pilot enters the recess in the crankshaft.

 Caution: Do not allow the weight of the transmission to hang on the drive plate or flywheel. Avoid prying on the drive plate.

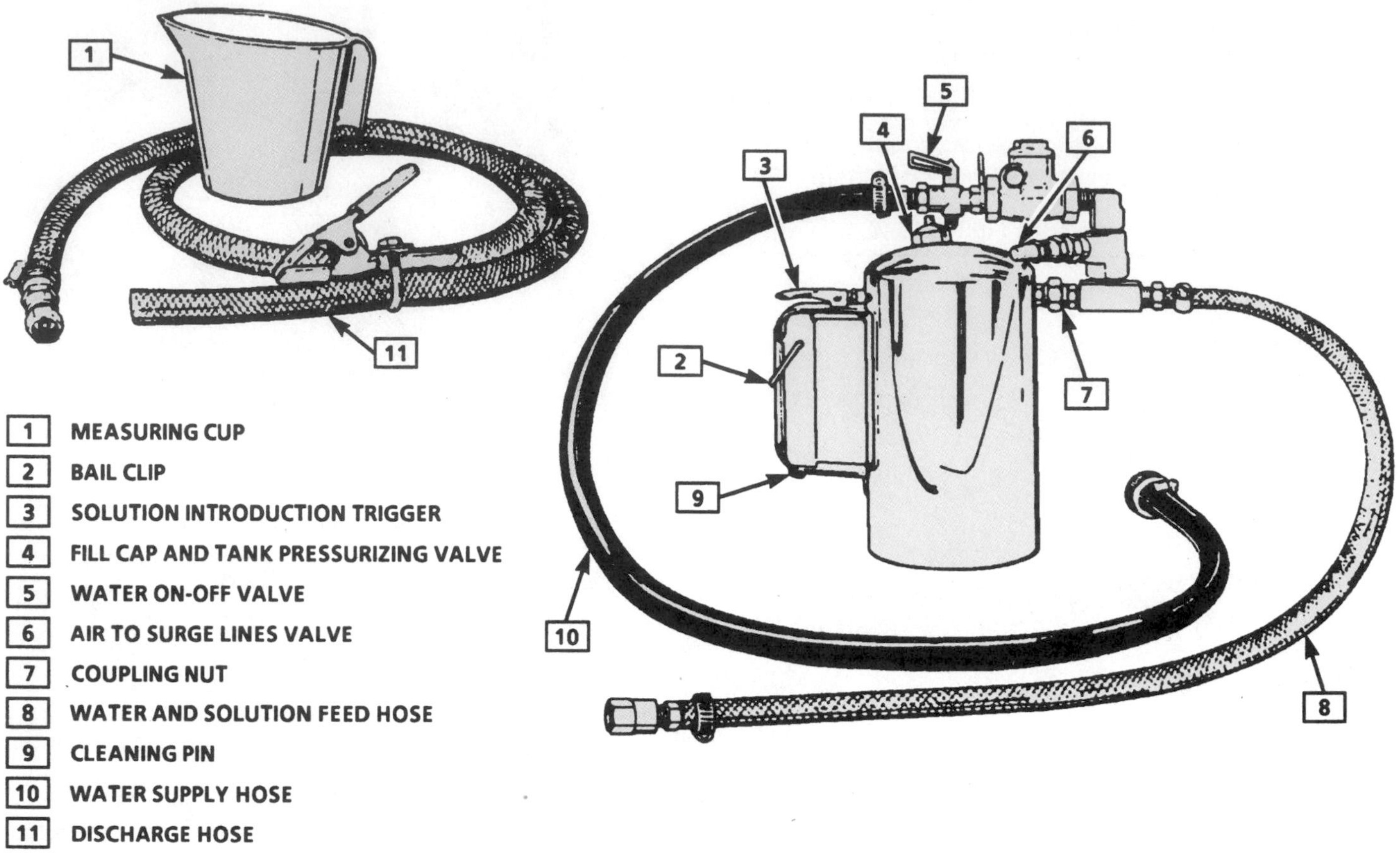

1 MEASURING CUP
2 BAIL CLIP
3 SOLUTION INTRODUCTION TRIGGER
4 FILL CAP AND TANK PRESSURIZING VALVE
5 WATER ON-OFF VALVE
6 AIR TO SURGE LINES VALVE
7 COUPLING NUT
8 WATER AND SOLUTION FEED HOSE
9 CLEANING PIN
10 WATER SUPPLY HOSE
11 DISCHARGE HOSE

Figure 32-47. An oil cooler and fluid line flushing tool. When using this tool with shop compressed air, the air line should be equipped with a oil/water filter unit. Never exceed the vehicle manufacturer's recommended fluid flushing pressure. (General Motors)

OIL COOLER INSIDE RADIATOR SIDE TANK
GASOLINE
DIESEL

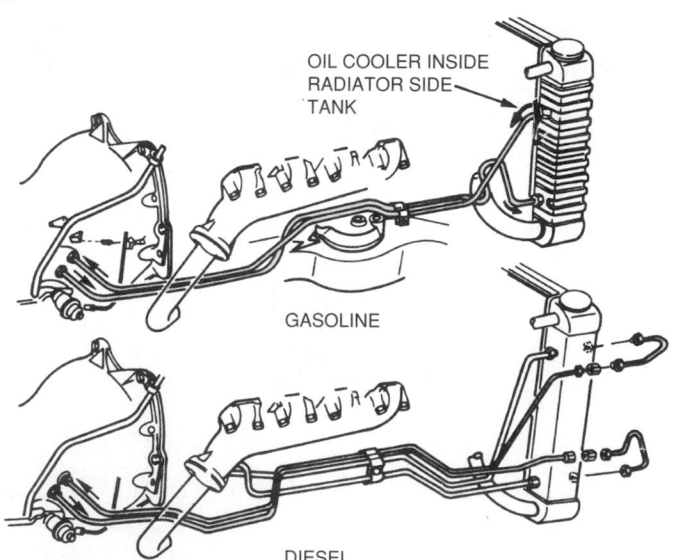

Figure 32-48. Typical transmission oil cooler line arrangements for a gasoline and for a diesel engine. (Buick)

BELL HOUSING
A
TORQUE CONVERTER WELD NUT
RULER
STRAIGHTEDGE

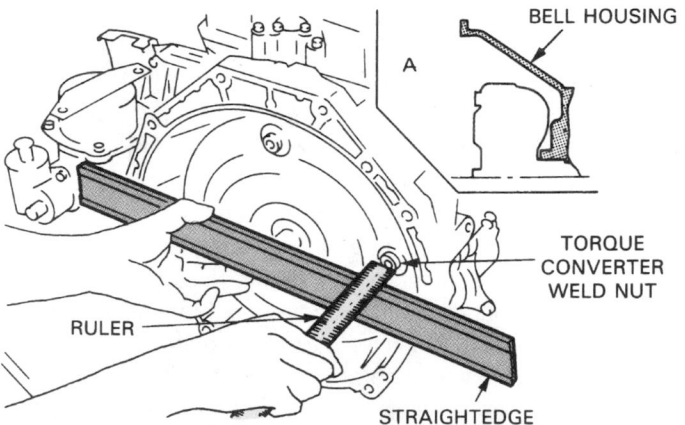

Figure 32-49. By placing a straightedge across front of bell housing and measuring to torque converter weld nut, you can confirm that converter is fully seated. (Chrysler)

After installing the transmission or transaxle on the engine, make sure that the converter can turn after the engine-to-transmission/transaxle housing bolts are tight. If the converter cannot be turned, find out why and correct the problem before proceeding. If the converter can be turned, install it to the drive plate or flywheel. When completely installed and all lines, wires, linkage, and other parts are connected, add the amount of fluid as specified by the manufacturer. Start the engine and move the selector through the gears, recheck the fluid level and add more if required. Bring to normal operating temperature, check for leaks, and road test. Make final adjustments and another check for leakage.

Tech Talk

One of the most controversial areas of automotive service is whether or not to use chemical additives. There are many of these additives available. Engine oil additives are available to reduce oil burning and noises, clean the engine, reduce wear, or free sticking valve lifters. Cooling system chemicals are often used to clean the system, reduce corrosion, or seal leaks. Other additives clean the fuel injectors, remove water from the gas tank, raise octane, or seal the power steering system. If used as maintenance items, some of these additives may reduce deposit buildup, wear, and corrosion, and possibly seal some minor leaks. Oil viscosity improvers (thickeners) can reduce—although not eliminate—oil burning, blowby, and noises. However, many additives are sold as cures for vehicle problems that can only be solved by major repairs. As cures, it can only be said that they probably will not make the problem worse.

Additives are frequently used in automatic transmissions. Many transmission additives claim to seal leaks, stop slipping, and free sticking valves. Using these products usually results in disappointment. No additive can repair burned clutches or bands or broken parts. Any solvent strong enough to free sticking transmission valves is strong enough to damage the seals, friction materials, and plastic parts. Occasionally, using an additive will seal a minor leak, but in most cases, the only permanent cure is to replace the seal or gasket. Too much of the seal swelling solvent can make the leak worse and cause other external and internal seals to start leaking.

Some transmission additives are advertised as transmission "tune-up" products. While these may be of some help, the best tune-up for a transmission is to change the oil and filter regularly and to make band adjustments when necessary.

If you are tempted to use some kind of additive to solve an automatic transmission problem, do not be disappointed if it does not work. Since additives are relatively cheap, it might be worthwhile to try a can for a minor oil leak. But if the leak does not stop, it is time to change the seal or gasket. Adding more than one can may overexpand other seals, causing additional leaks.

Summary

A large percentage of transmission and transaxle problems can be solved by in-vehicle service procedures. Modern transmissions and transaxles are either three or four speed automatic units utilizing a standard or lockup torque converter, compound planetary gearset, holding members, and a hydraulic control system. On many late model transmissions and transaxles, the hydraulic system is computer-controlled.

The torque converter drives the transmission directly. The converter drives the transaxle directly through a multiple link chain or with gears. Transmissions vary from year to year and from model to model. Always use manufacturer's service manual for exact repair and adjustment procedures. When towing, tow in neutral. Do not exceed 45 mph (72 kph) or distance recommended by maker, usually around 50 miles (80 km). If transmission or drive components are inoperative, raise the drive wheels for towing. The technician should have the tools required to perform accurate transmission diagnosis, adjustment, and repair.

Fluid level is critical. Overfilling can cause aeration, leaking, and poor operation. A low fluid level can cause overheating and slipping. When checking fluid level, make certain that the vehicle is level and the shift lever is in neutral or park, the fluid is at operating temperature, the engine is idling, and the dipstick enters to full depth. Move the selector through all ranges and check fluid level again. Do not allow dirt to enter the fill pipe. Check fluid for odor, discoloration, aeration, and signs of water.

Use care when running the engine with the vehicle in gear. Apply both the emergency and service brakes. When idling with lever in park or neutral, set the emergency brake and block wheels. Some manufacturers recommend periodic draining of fluid while others do not. When draining fluid, it should be at operating temperature. Be careful to avoid burns. Some transmission designs require periodic band adjustments. Adjust bands very carefully and exactly as specified by the manufacturer. Improper band adjustment can cause serious damage.

Shift linkage must be adjusted accurately. Engine mounts must be in good condition to prevent altering linkage adjustment. Accelerator pedal height, throttle plate, TV, and downshift linkage adjustment must be exact. Adjust downshift switch if needed. Check operation of neutral safety switch. Adjust or replace as needed. To detect leaks, clean off the transmission and converter housing. Allow the engine to idle and check for evidence of a transmission fluid leak. A black light is helpful in locating leaks. Some leaks may be repaired without transmission removal. Porous castings can often be repaired with epoxy resin.

The engine must be in good condition and properly tuned before diagnosing transmission problems. Shift points must occur at recommended speeds and should be smooth and positive. Transmission fluid must be at operating temperature before conducting pressure tests. The RPM, drive range, and road speed are important in determining pressure. When conducting a stall test, apply both parking and service brakes. Do not operate at full throttle for longer than five seconds. Operate engine in neutral to cool fluid between stall test periods. Some governors may be exposed by removing the extension housing while others are covered with a removable plate. The control valve body may be removed by draining the fluid and dropping the pan. Band and clutch action can be checked with air pressure on some transmissions. Use clean, dry air.

When removing a transmission, be careful to avoid springing the drive plate. Secure the transmission to the jack. Get someone to help you when removing or installing a transmission. Remove the converter and transmission as an assembly. Some front-wheel drive vehicles require the removal of the engine with the transmission. Others must have the engine properly supported before transmission removal. Use a retaining bar or clip to prevent the converter from dropping off. Mark the drive plate and converter. Always flush the oil cooler and lines before connecting to a new or repaired transmission. Reverse flush with clean solvent followed with transmission fluid. Use care to align marks and avoid damage to the drive plate during transmission installation. Torque all fasteners. Dip fastener threads in fluid before installing. Repair stripped threads with Heli-Coils.

Know These Terms

Torque converter	Transversely
Planetary gearset	Conventionally
Hydraulic control system	Aeration
Lockup clutch	Dexron III/Mercon
Holding member	Add-on transmission cooler
Band	Band adjustment
Clutch pack	Detent assembly
One-way clutch	TV
Overrunning clutch	Throttle valve
Oil pump	Vacuum modulator
Spool valve	Detent rod
Main pressure regulator	Detent cable
Manual valve	Troubleshooting chart
Shift valve	Band and clutch application
Throttle valve	chart
Governor valve	Shift point
Servos	Stall Test
Clutch pistons	Air pressure check
Accumulators	Flywheel turner
Filter	Flushed
Valve body	

Review Questions—Chapter 32

Do not write in this book. Write your answers on a separate sheet of paper.

1. Transmission fluid level should be kept _____.
   (A) on the full mark
   (B) between the add and the full marks
   (C) slightly below the add mark
   (D) slightly above the full mark
2. Most modern automatic transmissions require a special fluid called _____.
   (A) DEXRON III/MERCON
   (B) TYPE F
   (C) DEXRON II
   (D) AQ-ATF
3. Drain transmission fluid while it is _____.
4. Transmission fluid installed at the factory is usually _____ in color.
   (A) yellow
   (B) green

   (C) red
   (D) clear
5. Sagging engine mounts can alter the _____.
   (A) TV rod adjustment
   (B) downshift rod adjustment
   (C) selector rod adjustment
   (D) All of the above.
6. A detent _____ is sometimes used in preference to a downshift rod.
7. Name three gaskets which can be replaced without removing the transmission or transaxle from the vehicle.
8. A porous casting can often be repaired by cleaning and covering the leaking area with _____.
9. When stall testing, never maintain the full throttle position for longer than _____ seconds.
   (A) 5
   (B) 15
   (C) 45
   (D) 60
10. The oil pressure gauge used for transmission or transaxle oil pressure checks should read from zero to _____ PSI or _____ kPa.
11. Which two valves operate the shift valve to control shift points?
12. Always use a _____ to secure the transmission to the jack.
13. Never allow the weight of the transmission and converter to rest on the _____.
14. Before installing a new or repaired transmission, the _____ and _____ should be flushed.
15. The converter lockup clutch may apply in any gear other than _____ and _____.

ASE-Type Questions

1. Technician A says that most transmissions are of the same design. Technician B says that most transmission problems require transmission removal for correction. Who is right?
   (A) A only.
   (B) B only.
   (C) Both A & B.
   (D) Neither A nor B.
2. All of the following statements about pushing and towing vehicles with automatic transmissions are true, EXCEPT:
   (A) when trying to start a vehicle, it is better to tow it.
   (B) modern vehicles with automatics cannot be started by pushing.
   (C) front wheel drive vehicles can towed with the front wheels off of the ground.
   (D) when the transmission is inoperative, the vehicle should be towed with the drive wheels off of the ground.
3. Check fluid level when the fluid temperature is _____.
   (A) cold
   (B) slightly warm

(C) at normal operating temperature

(D) overheated

4. Technician A says that all automatic transmissions should be drained about every 24,000 miles (38 600 km). Technician B says that all periodic changing of transmission fluid requires that the converter be drained also. Who is right?

(A) A only.

(B) B only.

(C) Both A & B.

(D) Neither A nor B.

5. Linkage adjustments are important to maintain

_____.

(A) proper upshift points

(B) proper downshift points

(C) transmission service life

(D) All of the above.

6. Before checking transmission or transaxle operation, which of the following should be checked first?

(A) Oil level.

(B) Engine condition.

(C) Idle speed.

(D) All of the above.

7. Milky fluid indicates the presence of _____ in the transmission or transaxle.

(A) sludge

(B) varnish

(C) water or coolant

(D) motor oil

8. Technician A says that some bands do not require periodic adjustments. Technician B says that air pressure checking will locate an out-of-adjustment band. Who is right?

(A) A only.

(B) B only.

(C) Both A & B.

(D) Neither A nor B.

9. A transmission slips when shifting, but not when taking off from a stop. Technician A says that the problem is a defective governor. Technician B says that the problem is a worn forward clutch. Who is right?

(A) A only.

(B) B only.

(C) Both A & B.

(D) Neither A nor B.

10. When removing the transmission, always remove the converter _____.

(A) with the transmission

(B) before the transmission

(C) after the transmission

(D) the converter can be left on the engine

Suggested Activities

1. Check the fluid level of at least three automatic transmissions or transaxles. Also inspect the dipstick for signs of fluid overheating. Write a short report summarizing the process and describing any special precautions that must be taken (such as allowing some transaxles to warm up before checking the level).

2. Draw a simple diagram showing how the governor and throttle valves work on the shift valve in an automatic transmission oil circuit. Explain how extra valves could be added to obtain more gears.

3. Use a set of planetaries and shafts from a scrap transmission to get various gears. Other class members can hold various parts of the geartrain to get reduction, direct, overdrive, and reverse. Try to figure out which parts to hold and drive to get the same number of gears as the transmission had originally.

4. Change the oil and filter of an automatic transmission or transaxle. Inspect the bottom of the pan for the presence of metal or sludge. After servicing the transmission/transaxle, check the hydraulic pressures according to the service manual procedures. Make a chart showing how the pressure changes in different gearshift positions.

5. Tear down an automatic transmission or transaxle and list all needed parts to rebuild it. Calculate the cost of repairing the unit by finding the prices of parts and labor using a flat rate manual. Total the labor times and multiply them by the average labor rate for your area. Add the total of parts and labor. After determining other charges, such as supplies and outside services, calculate a grand total of what it would cost to repair this transmission.

6. Discuss your price calculation in Activity 5 with the other members of your class. Ask if there is anything that you missed. Determine whether the cost of repair is greater or less than the cost of a replacement transmission or transaxle.

Cutaway of a late-model rear-wheel drive automobile. What type of driveline components would you find in this vehicle? (Ford)

33

Axle and Driveline Service

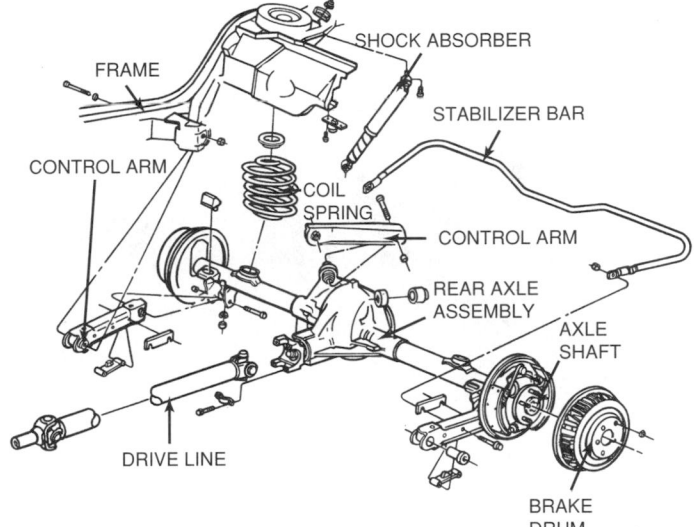

After studying this chapter, you will be able to:
- Explain the construction and operation of one- and two-piece Hotchkiss drive shafts.
- Service one- and two-piece drivelines.
- Describe cross-and-roller universal joints.
- Service cross-and-roller universal joints.
- Diagnose driveline and universal joint problems.
- Explain the construction and operation of front-wheel drive CV axles.
- Explain the construction and operation of CV joints.
- Service CV axles, joints, and boots.
- Explain the construction, operation, and service of axle housings.
- Compare drive axle types.
- Describe the construction, operation, and service of differentials.
- Diagnose differential and axle problems.

This chapter will cover the operating principles and service of drive shafts and universal joints found on rear-wheel drive vehicles. The service of front and rear drive axles is also covered. Information on the removal and replacement of rear wheel drive ring and pinion and differential units is also presented.

Rear Wheel Drive Shaft Service

Modern drivelines use an open drive shaft. This design is commonly called the **Hotchkiss** design. Drive force and axle housing windup are handled by leaf springs or by control arms. A typical Hotchkiss drive assembly is pictured in **Figure 33-1.**

The drive shaft may consist of one or more pieces. A one-piece drive shaft is illustrated in **Figure 33-2.** Note the **slip yoke,** which allows lengthwise movement between the transmission and the rear axle housing. The slip yoke slides onto the splined transmission output shaft. The end yoke is attached to the differential pinion shaft or to the pinion shaft flange, depending on the design. Modern long-wheelbase pickup trucks and a few older cars utilize two-piece drive shafts. This application requires the use of a **center support bearing.** Study the center support bearing arrangement in **Figure 33-3.**

Figure 33-1. Exploded view of a Hotchkiss-type rear axle and driveline assembly. (GM)

Cross-and-Roller Universal Joint

The **cross-and-roller universal joint** is used on rear wheel drive shafts. Needle bearings are used to reduce friction. An exploded view of the cross-and-roller joint is shown in **Figure 33-4.** The cross-shaped piece in the center is called a **trunnion.** The **bearing caps** in this design are retained by snap rings set into the yoke at the outer ends of the bearing caps. Other U-joints are held in place by U-bolts passing around the bearing cap and through the yoke or by injection-molded nylon rings. When this type of joint is disassembled, removing the caps shears the nylon ring. Conventional bearing caps with snap ring retainers are used for replacement.

Constant Velocity Universal Joint

A **constant velocity universal joint** causes both the input and output sides of the joint to rotate at the same speed throughout the full 360° of rotation. It is made by connecting two single cross-and-roller joints with a center yoke and using a centering socket yoke and socket support yoke.

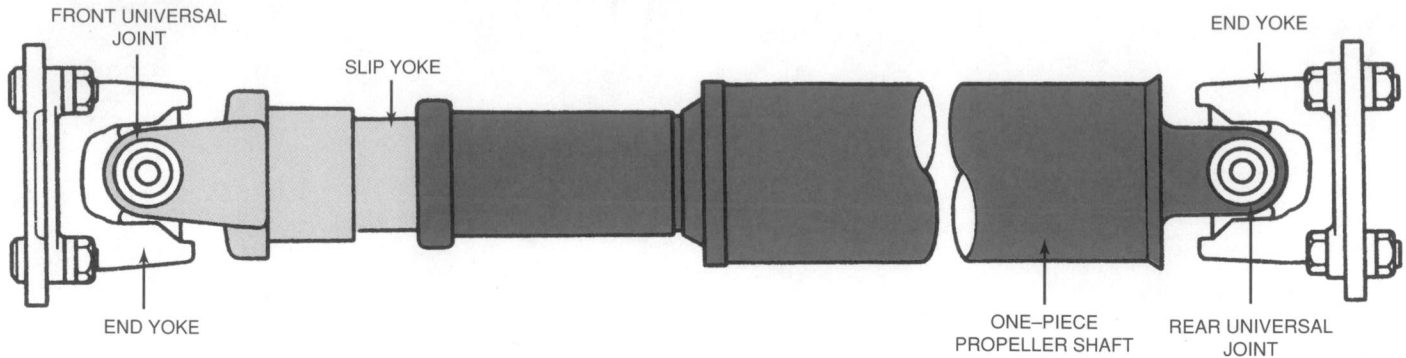

Figure 33-2. A one-piece drive shaft. (Toyota)

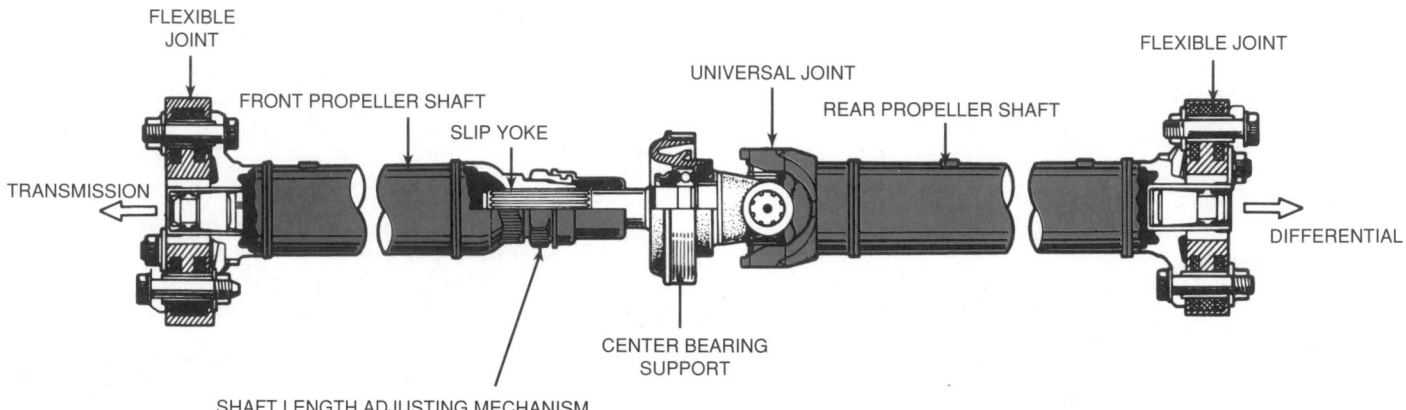

Figure 33-3. A two-piece drive shaft. Note the use of a center support bearing. (Toyota)

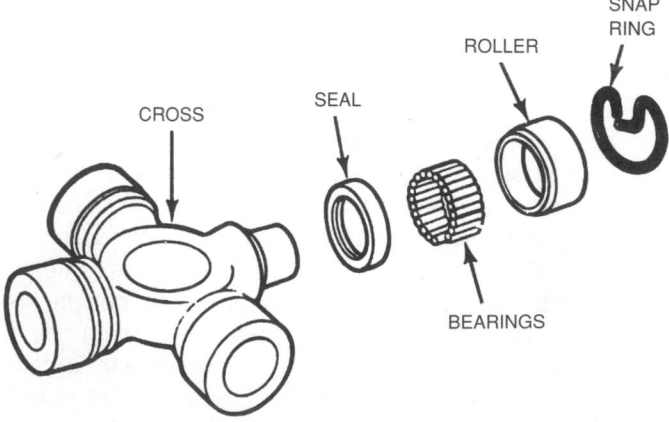

Figure 33-4. A basic cross and bearing cap universal joint. Bearing caps are retained by snap rings. (Spicer)

The centering socket between the joints forces each half of the unit to rotate on a plane forming one half of the total angle between the drive shaft and the transmission or differential pinion shaft. See **Figure 33-5.** The use of a constant velocity joint produces a very smooth flow of power, even over fairly acute driving angles. One or more constant velocity joints may be used.

Removing Rear Drive Shaft

Before disassembling a U-joint and removing the drive shaft, mark the drive shaft, slip yoke, flange yoke, and companion flange. Then, the parts may be reassembled in exactly the same relative positions. The yokes at both ends of the drive shaft must be in the same plane. The yokes in **Figure 33-6A** are correctly aligned so that both will operate in the same plane. The yokes in **Figure 33-6B** are incorrect. When the yokes are permanently affixed to the ends of the shaft, do not be concerned about yoke alignment.

Disassemble the rear U-joint and remove the shaft from the rear axle pinion flange. See **Figure 33-7.** Some shafts employ flange yokes on one or both ends. In these cases, merely remove the flange fasteners.

Do Not Drop Bearing Caps

If the bearing caps are not retained on the cross with a thin strap, tape them on. This will keep them from dropping and possibly losing the needle bearings.

Support Drive Shaft

After disassembling the rear U-joint, let the shaft end down carefully. Do not allow the shaft to fall. Do not allow the shaft to hang supported by one U-joint. Never force the shaft to flex the U-joint beyond its capacity to swivel. Careless

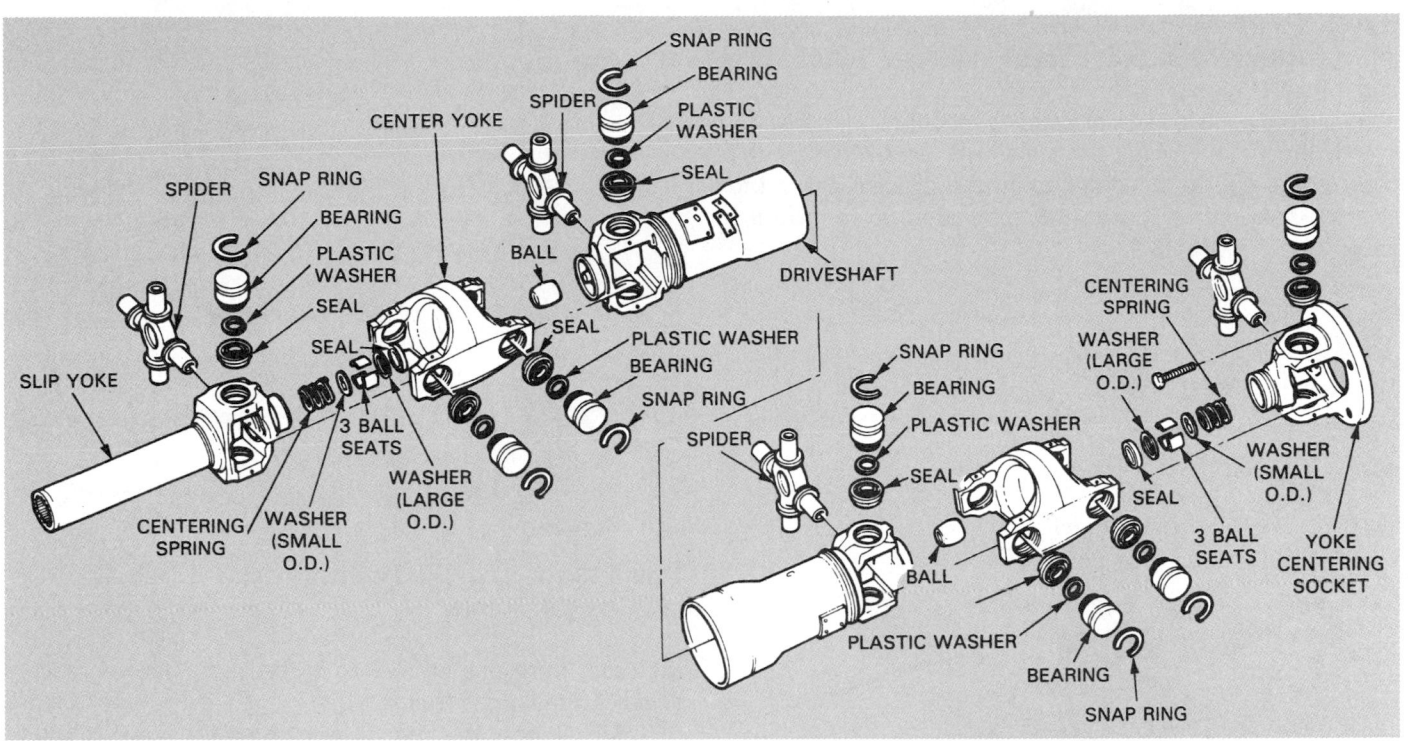

Figure 33-5.   Exploded view of a drive shaft and two constant velocity universal joints. Study the part names and their locations. (Ford)

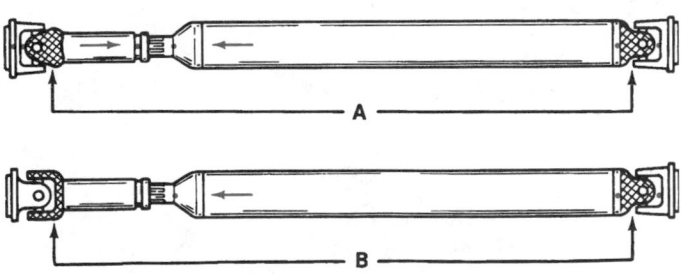

Figure 33-6.   Yoke alignment is critical. The yokes in A are aligned. The yokes in B are not and vibration, damage, etc., will occur.

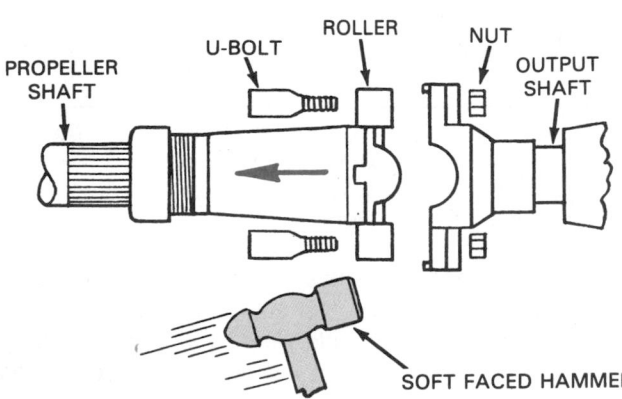

Figure 33-7.   Breaking a universal joint so the drive shaft may be removed.

handling can cause severe damage to the shaft and joints. When the shaft is long and clumsy, have another technician help during shaft removal and installation.

Two-Piece Shaft and Center Support Bearing

If a two-piece shaft is employed, the center support bearing must be removed to permit shaft withdrawal. Check between the support and the frame for the presence of shims. If used, replace the shims when installing the center support. Always check the condition of the center support bearing before reinstalling it.

When a slip joint is placed between the shaft and one of the U-joints, it is possible to enter the splined stub shaft into the slip yoke in a number of positions.

 Caution: Engage the stub shaft with the slip yoke so that both yokes are in the same plane. If the yokes are misaligned, joint phasing will be out and serious vibration can result.

Protect Slip Yoke Surface

If the front shaft slip yoke engages the transmission output shaft, cover the slip yoke with cardboard or several layers of rags. This will protect the yoke from dirt and nicks. When needed, place a spare yoke or special plug in the transmission to prevent fluid leakage while the shaft is removed.

Repairing Cross-and-Roller U-Joints

Clamp the solid portion of the U-joint in a vise. If the yoke must be clamped, clamp it lightly. Avoid clamping the tube portion of the drive shaft. All drive shafts (aluminum, composite, or steel) are thin and can be easily damaged. This damage can cause shaft failure during operation. Support the drive shaft according to the manufacturer's recommendations.

If the bearing caps are held with snap rings at the outer edge, tap the bearing cap inward a small amount to free the snap ring, **Figure 33-8.** Use pliers to remove the snap rings, **Figure 33-9.**

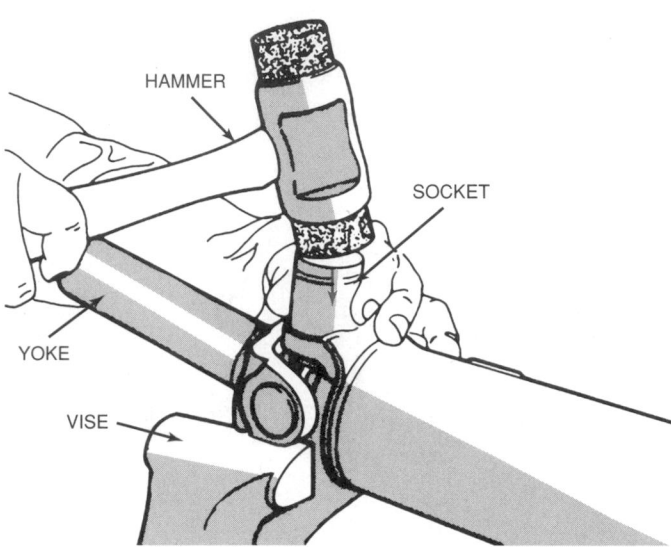

Figure 33-8. Tap the bearing cap inward a small amount to free the snap ring. (Dodge)

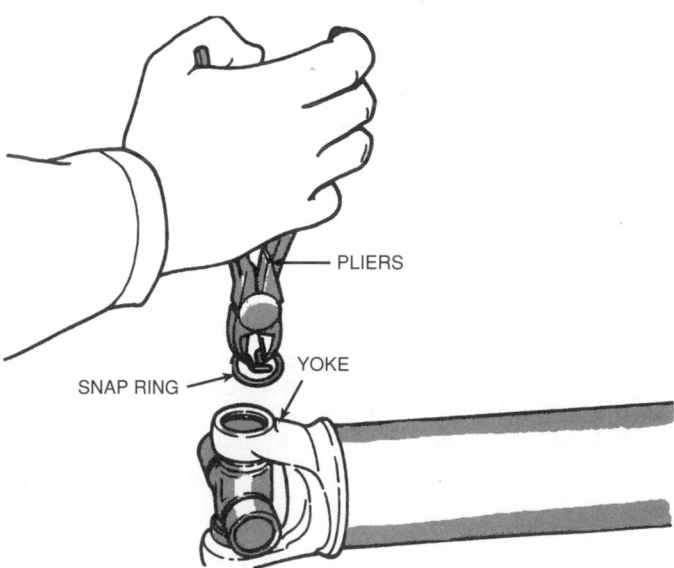

Figure 33-9. Removing a snap ring with pliers after the bearing cap has been tapped inward. (Dodge)

When the bearing caps are secured with snap rings that engage the cap on the inner side, tap the bearing cap inward a small amount and drive the snap rings out with a thin punch or screwdrivers, **Figure 33-10.**

Place the yoke between the jaws of a heavy vise. Adjust the jaws so that the yoke is just free to move. Rest

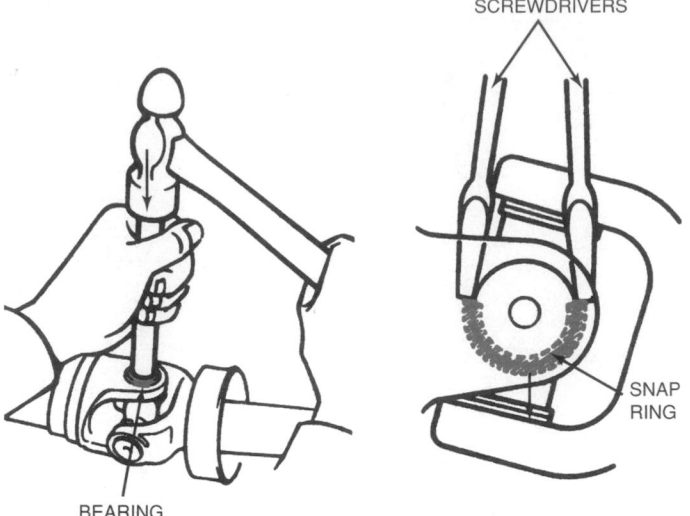

Figure 33-10. Using screwdrivers to remove snap rings from bearing caps. (Toyota)

the cross trunnions on the top of the jaws. Use jaw covers to protect the cross trunnions.

Strike the yoke smartly with a lead, brass, or plastic hammer. This will drive the yoke downward, causing the cross to force the bearing cap partially out of the yoke lug. Look at **Figure 33-11.**

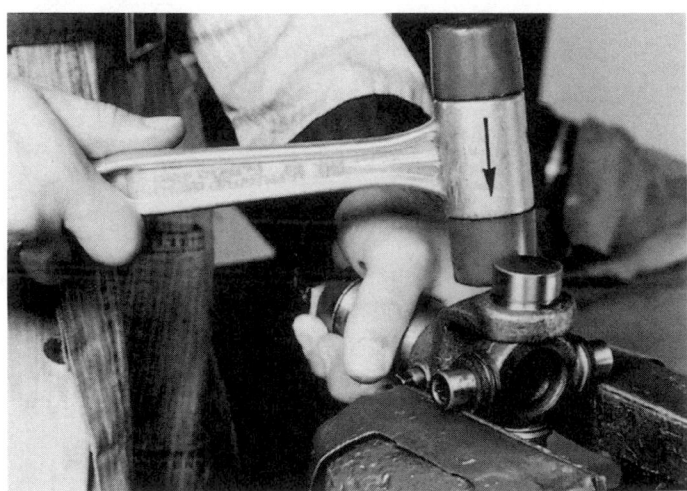

Figure 33-11. Driving the yoke downward to remove the bearing cap. (Dana Corp.)

 Note: If the bearing caps are held by injection-molded plastic, heat the yoke with a torch to soften the plastic. While the yoke is still hot, drive the bearing caps from the unit.

A vise may also be used as a press by placing a small socket against one bearing cap and a large socket against the yoke on the opposite side. As the vise is closed, the small socket will force the cross to push the opposite bearing cap partially into the large socket.

When the bearing cap is forced out, grasp the cap and strike the yoke to complete removal. Some bearing caps can also be removed (after loosening) with pliers. Do not spill the needle bearings when the bearing cap is free.

Force the cross in the opposite direction to remove the other bearing cap. The cross may then be forced against one lug, tipped outward, and removed. Refer to **Figure 33-12.**

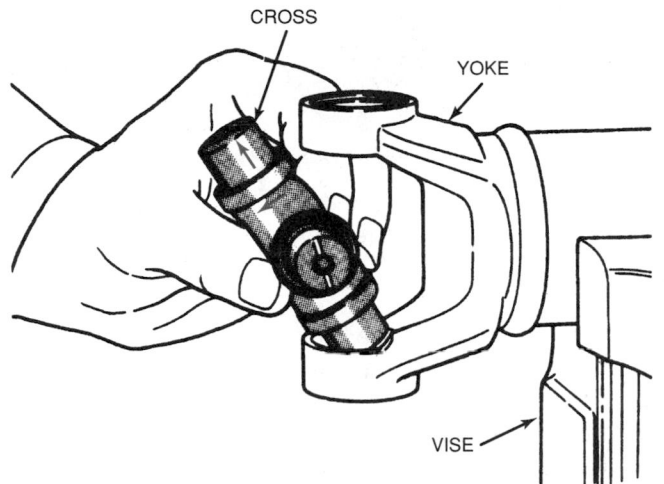

Figure 33-12. Tip the cross and remove it from the yoke. (Dodge)

Universal Joint Cleaning and Inspection

Wipe off the cross trunnions. If they are worn, discard the cross, bearing caps, and snap rings. A U-joint repair kit will be needed. If the trunnions look good, clean the cross thoroughly. Blow out the grease passages. Check the condition of the lug holes.

Wash the bearing caps and needles. Blow them dry. If the inside of the bearing caps and the trunnion bearing surface is free of corrosion and grooving, the parts may be reused. Check all needles for signs of chipping or breakage. Try the bearing caps on the trunnions for evidence of looseness.

A universal joint repair kit is relatively inexpensive. If the old joint shows the slightest sign of wear, install a repair kit. If either the bearing caps or the cross is worn, replace both. Never install new bearing caps on an old cross or vice versa.

Assembling a Universal Joint

If new seal retainers are needed, drive them into place with a punch designed for the purpose. The retainer must be driven on the cross with the open side of the retainer facing outward, toward the end of the trunnion. Make certain that the retainers are on squarely and to the full depth.

Pack the bearing cap bearings with the recommended lubricant. If the bearing is of the sealed type (no provision for greasing following installation), pack the grease reservoirs at the ends of the trunnions. Pack carefully to eliminate trapped air. Install seals.

Start one of the bearing caps in a yoke lug. Insert it from the bottom with the open side of the bearing cap up to

prevent the loss of needles. Make sure that each bearing cap contains the specified number of needles. Insert one of the cross trunnions into the bearing cap. Start the other bearing cap, making certain it slips over the trunnion.

When partially seated, place the two bearing caps between the vise jaws. Squeeze until the bearing caps are flush with the yoke. Stop tightening when the caps are flush; do not overtighten. Tap one of the bearing caps. Use a soft-faced punch that is the full width of the bearing cap. Tap in until the cap is slightly below the snap ring groove in the lug. In the event of an inner side snap ring arrangement, tap through the lug until the snap ring can be inserted. Insert a new snap ring, **Figure 33-13.** Make certain that the snap ring is seated to its full depth.

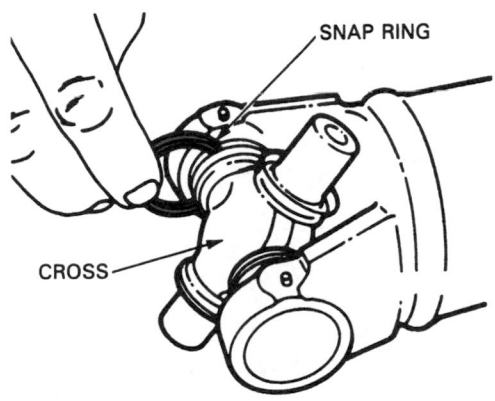

Figure 33-13. Inserting a snap ring into bearing cap groove. (Chevrolet)

Some joints require measuring snap ring-to-yoke groove clearance to be sure the fit is correct. After assembling the universal joint and the installing snap rings, place the joint in a vise. Force the cross to one side. With a feeler gauge, measure ring-to-yoke groove distance as shown in **Figure 33-14.** If the measurement is not within manufacturer's specs, replace the snap rings with thinner or thicker ones until the recommended clearance is obtained. All snap rings should have the same thickness for proper drive shaft balance.

 Caution: Using an excessive amount of grease when rebuilding a U-joint can prevent bearing caps from seating fully. This will give a false snap ring fit reading.

Support the cross and strike the yoke to force the bearing cap into firm contact with the snap ring. With an inner snap ring, this will force the snap ring against the inner face of the yoke. Always seat the bearing cap in this fashion to prevent improper centering of the cross. Refer to **Figure 33-15.** Install the other snap ring or rings and seat the bearing caps against rings.

If a grease fitting is used, force universal joint grease into the joint slowly until it starts to show at the seals. Use a low-pressure hand grease gun or a power gun equipped with a pressure relief valve. Never use a high-pressure gun

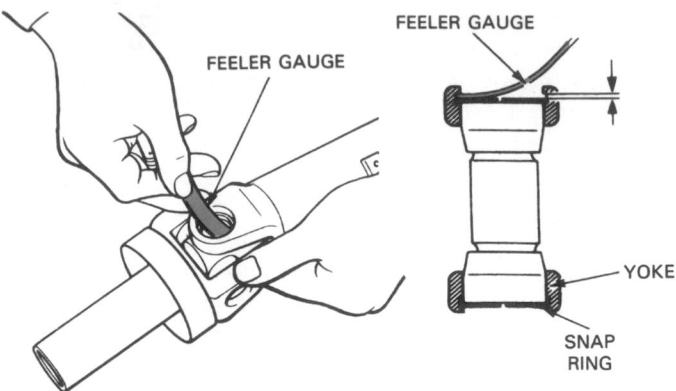

Figure 33-14. Measuring snap ring-to-groove clearance with a feeler gauge. Note how the gauge is inserted between the top of snap ring and the groove. (Chrysler)

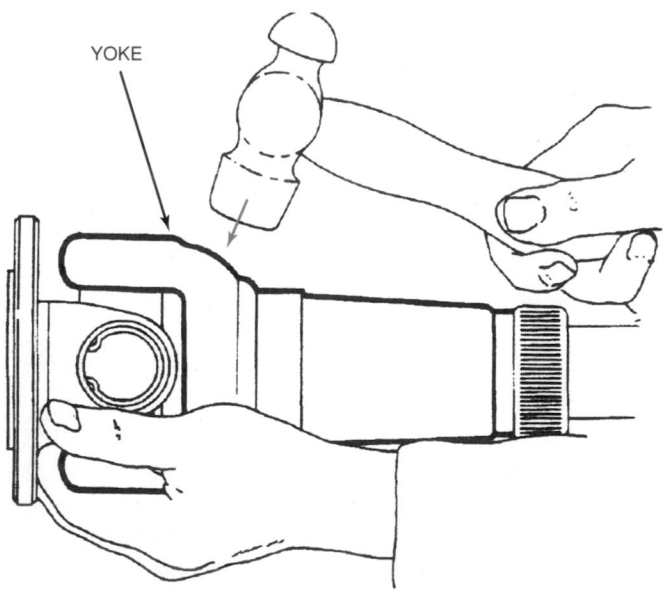

Figure 33-15. Striking the yoke to seat the bearing cap snugly against the snap ring and groove. (British-Leyland)

without this adapter, as it is possible to blow the bearing caps out of the yokes with the tremendous pressure. Seals may be damaged, too.

Test the action of the assembled joint. It should move throughout its range without binding. If a slight bind exists, rap the yoke lugs with a soft hammer. This will usually free the joint. If it does not, disassemble the joint and check for the source of the bind.

Repairing Rear-Wheel Drive Constant Velocity Universal Joints

The constant velocity U-joint is literally two cross-and-bearing cap joints attached by a center yoke. Mark the center yoke, slip yoke, and shaft yoke so that all parts are reassembled in the same order. Mark crosses if they will be reused so that grease fittings will be accessible, **Figure 33-16.**

Remove the snap rings and force the bearing caps from one end. A special bearing cap remover can be used to force the bearing caps partially from the yoke. The bearing cap

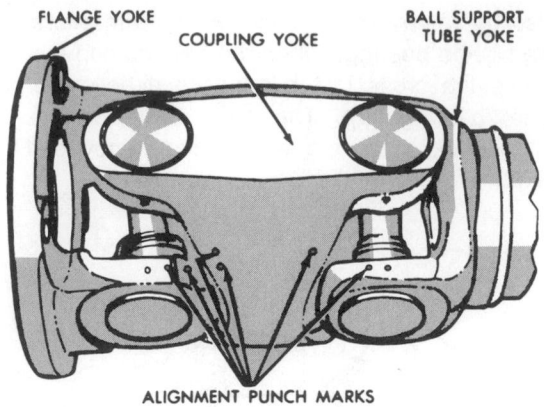

Figure 33-16. Constant velocity joint marked before disassembly. Note the double marks on the left side. This prevents mixing the ends. (Chrysler)

is then grasped in the vise, and the center yoke is driven upward to complete pulling of the bearing cap. The bearing caps are lifted from the center socket yoke, and the cross is tipped and removed.

The tool is then used to force out the bearing caps in the other end of the center yoke. Avoid forcing the center yoke too far to one side. Stop when the slinger ring just touches. Grasp the bearing caps and remove them.

Reassemble the joint in the reverse order of disassembly. Use new parts where required. Lubricate the centering device. When assembled, remove the grease plugs, lubricate, and replace the plugs, **Figure 33-17.** When reassembling a sealed joint, lubricate all parts before reassembly.

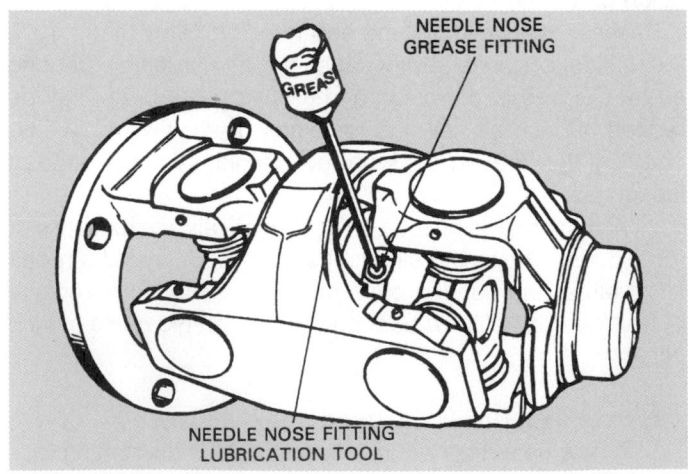

Figure 33-17. Lubricating a constant velocity universal joint. Note the needle nose grease fitting. (GMC)

Drive Shaft Installation

Check joints to make sure all marks are aligned. Cover the slip yoke with cardboard or rags. Position the shaft in the vehicle. Support the shaft during installation to prevent damage to the U-joints.

Remove the covering from the slip yoke and lubricate the outside surface as recommended. Some installations use grease; others use transmission fluid. The inner splined surface may be lubricated with transmission fluid. The unit may also require grease as in **Figure 33-18**. The oil seal on the output shaft prevents automatic transmission fluid from entering the splines. This type of joint must be greased.

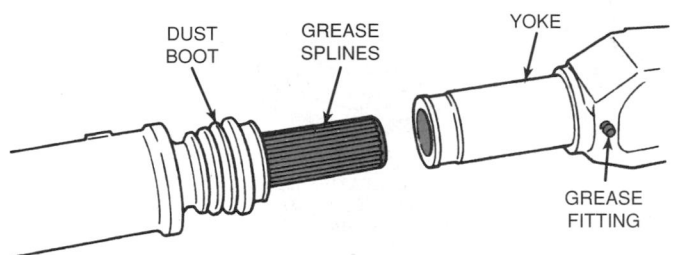

Figure 33-18. This slip yoke setup requires greasing the inner spline surface. Note the grease fitting. (Suzuki)

When connecting the U-joint, make certain that the marks on the shaft yoke and flange yoke are aligned. Check the flange for nicks or burrs.

In cases where a drive shaft has a splined stub, make certain the arrows (factory balance marks) or punch marks on the shaft and slip yoke are aligned.

If U-bolts are used to connect bearing caps to the flange yoke, torque the U-bolt nuts as specified. Excessive tightening will distort the bearing caps and cause shaft shudder and short life.

Before tightening U-bolts, make certain the bearing cap heads are underneath the locating tang. After torquing, rap the joint with a soft hammer and retorque the fasteners. If a strap is used on the cross, make certain that it fits into the pockets provided in the yoke, **Figure 33-19**.

Inspect the driveline to make sure all fasteners are secured. If a center support bearing is used, torque the mounting fasteners. Where specified, check the clearance between the end of transmission extension housing and the front slip yoke face. Grasp the shaft and shake it sideways. There should be no discernible movement. Road test the vehicle to check for quiet operation.

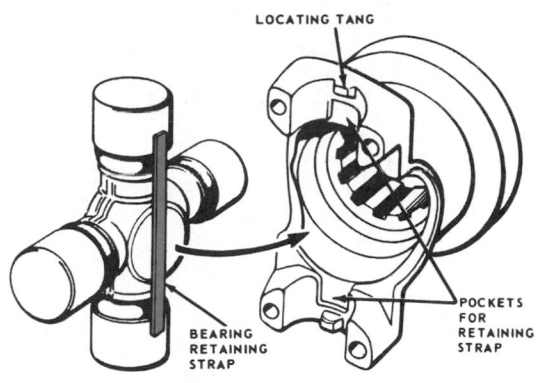

Figure 33-19. The retaining strap, when used, must fit into the yoke pockets. (Ford)

Drive Shaft Balance

The drive shaft turns at engine RPM in high gear. This requires that the shaft be accurately *balanced.* If the shaft is bent or badly dented, it should be replaced. Proper straightening and balance are beyond the capabilities of a regular shop.

If the vehicle is being undercoated, keep the shaft and U-joints covered. Undercoating on the shaft may cause serious vibration.

The shaft can be checked for runout in the vehicle by using a dial indicator. Mount the indicator to some rigid spot and place the stem on the driveline near one end. Turn a back wheel to rotate the drive shaft. Note the indicator reading. Move indicator to other end and then to the center.

When noting the indicator reading, do not count sudden changes from a weld, flat spot, or minor tube out-of-roundness. **Figure 33-20** illustrates typical measuring points on one- and two-piece drivelines. Total indicator reading (TIR) at these points should generally not exceed .030″ (0.76 mm). Follow the manufacturer's recommendations for your particular driveline.

Minor shaft unbalance can occasionally be corrected by using hose clamps (Whittek type). The clamps are attached to the shaft and rotated around until the shaft is balanced. See **Figure 33-21**.

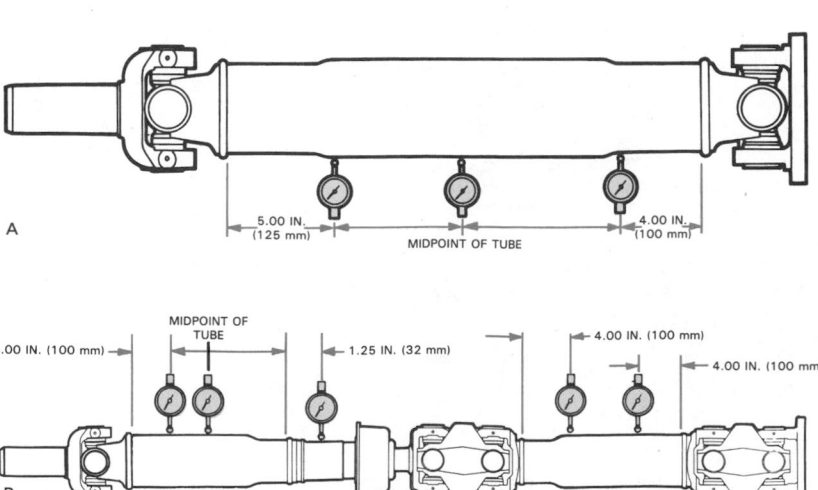

Figure 33-20. Check points to be used for obtaining runout. A—One-piece driveline. B—Two-piece driveline. (Cadillac)

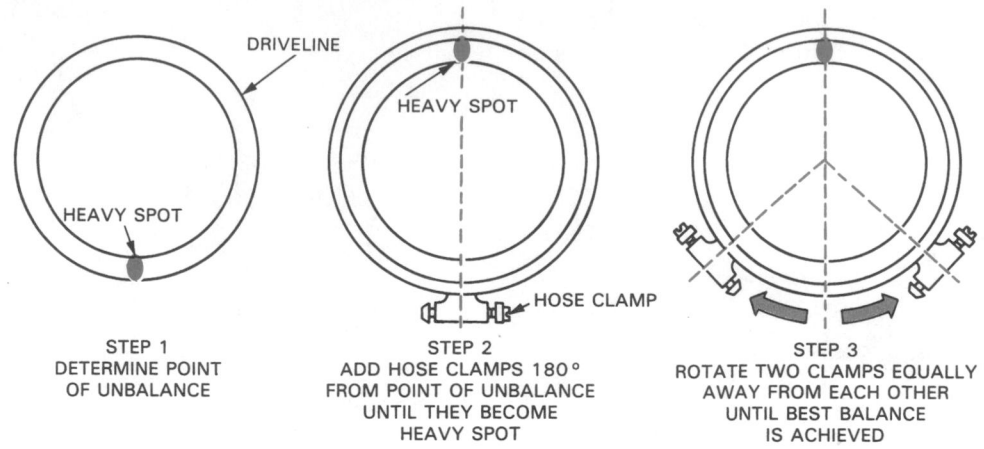

Figure 33-21. Eliminating driveline unbalance with Whittek (screw) type hose clamps. (Buick)

If everything checks out all right but vibration persists, disconnect the rear U-joint. Turn the pinion flange 180° and reconnect the joint. If the vibration is still present, disconnect the front slip yoke. Rotate the yoke 180° and reconnect it.

Drive Shaft Angle

If the *drive shaft angle* (angle formed between the front and rear U-joints) is too great, driveline vibration is likely to occur at cruising speeds. This is due to the design of the cross-and-roller U-joint, which can cause great variations in drive shaft speed when angles are too great. When shaft vibration is present, check the angle formed between the centerline of the drive shaft and the differential pinion shaft.

A special gauge is shown in **Figure 33-22.** The gauge is placed on the front universal joint and drive shaft. The pointer indicates shaft-to-joint angle. The vehicle must be level and at normal curb weight (no passengers or luggage; gas tank full). Use a drive-on or axle-engagement lift. Do not use a frame contact lift, as this will allow the axle housing to hang down and alter the drive angle. The gauge can also be used to check the rear universal joint angle. The gauge is attached to the yokes and not the crosses.

A spirit level gauge can also be used to check the drive shaft drive angle. The gauge is adjusted by centering the

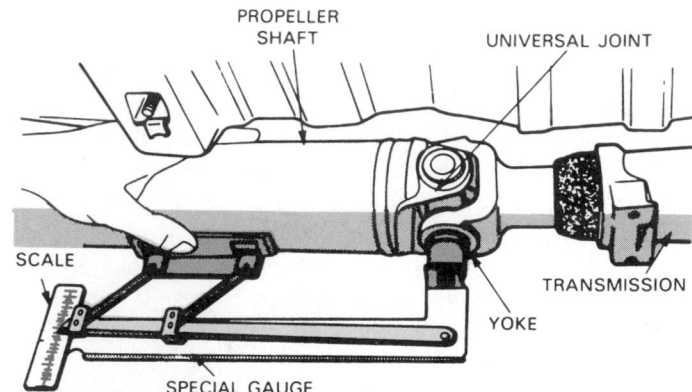

Figure 33-22. Using special gauge to measure the front universal joint angle. Keep the gauge firmly in position while measuring. (Plymouth)

level bubble while holding it on the differential carrier housing. The gauge is then held against the drive shaft, and bubble position is checked against specifications.

A third technique for checking drive angle is illustrated in **Figure 33-23.** This requires that the measuring device be placed at three different locations: the front drive shaft, the

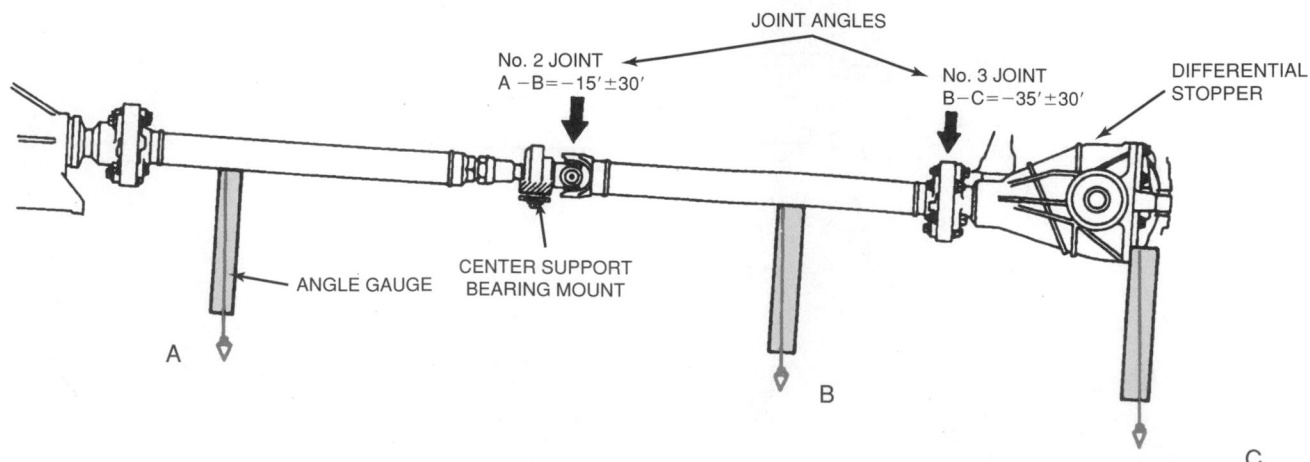

Figure 33-23. Measuring drive shaft angle in three spots with angle gauges. Follow tool and vehicle manufacturers' specifications. (Toyota)

rear drive shaft, and the rear axle housing. The measurements at all three places must match the specifications given in the service manual.

If driveline angles are not within the recommended range, the drive shaft drive angle must be adjusted. On some vehicles, the transmission extension can be raised or lowered by using shims. The rear axle housing may be tilted by adjusting the control arms. If the arms are not adjustable, new arms must be installed. When rear leaf springs are used, tapered wedges may be inserted between the spring and the axle spring pad.

If the thick portion of the wedge faces the rear of the vehicle, the pinion shaft companion flange will be tilted downward. To raise the flange, insert the wedge so that the thick side faces the front. See **Figure 33-24.**

The usual drive angle adjustment involves the axle housing only. Many vehicles do not provide for transmission mount adjustments.

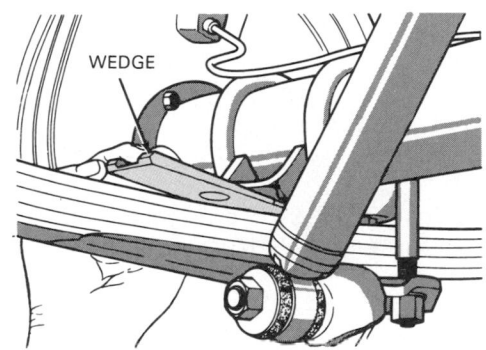

Figure 33-24. Inserting a tapered wedge between the rear spring and the axle housing to change the drive shaft "drive" angle. (Chrysler)

Front-Wheel Drive CV Axle Service

Constant velocity joints, or CV joints, are used on most modern front-wheel drive vehicles and on some rear-wheel drive vehicles with independent rear suspensions. Their design produces less vibration than the conventional cross-and-roller U-joint. This is important when the possibility of transmitting driveline vibration is great, such as when drive shafts (axles) are located in the front of the vehicle. One particular front-wheel drive CV joint and axle assembly is shown in **Figure 33-25.** The one- or two-piece front-wheel drive axles are usually equipped with inboard (inside) and outboard (outside nearest wheel) CV joints. See **Figure 33-26.**

There are two basic CV joint types: *tripod joints* and *Rzeppa joints* (also called ball and channel). The Rzeppa joint is by far the most common. **Figure 33-27** pictures both the tripod and Rzeppa units.

CV joints are protected by a *CV boot.* CV boots are bellows-shaped covers that completely seal the interior parts of the CV joint. Typical boots can be seen in **Figure 33-27.** CV joints will usually last the life of the vehicle if they are not damaged. If the boot becomes torn, all of the CV joint lubricant will be thrown out, dirt and water will enter, and the joint will fail quickly. Therefore, CV boots must be inspected frequently. Damaged boots should be replaced immediately.

Removing CV Axles

The following is a general procedure for removing CV axles. Follow manufacturer's recommendations for your vehicle. Remove the battery negative cable. The vehicle should be elevated with a jack and placed on jack stands or with a floor lift. This will provide the necessary work space.

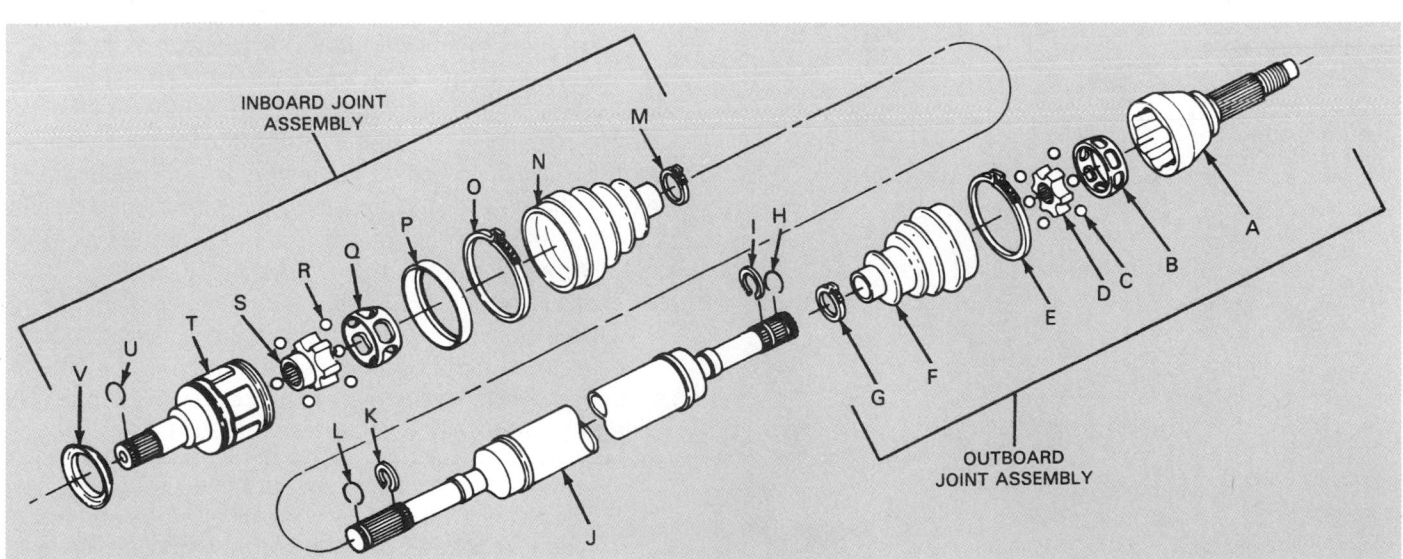

Figure 33-25. Exploded view of one type front-wheel drive axle and universal joint assembly. A—Outer bearing race and stub shaft assembly. B—Bearing cage. C—Ball bearings. D—Inner bearing race. E—Boot clamp (large). F—Boot. G—Boot. H—Circlip. I—Stop ring. J—Interconnecting shaft. K—Stop ring. L—Circlip. M—Boot clamp (small). N—Boot. O—Boot-clamp (large). P—Bearing retainer. Q—Bearing cage. R—Ball bearings. S—Inner bearing race. T—Outer bearing race and stub shaft assembly. U—Circlip. V—Dust deflector. (Ford)

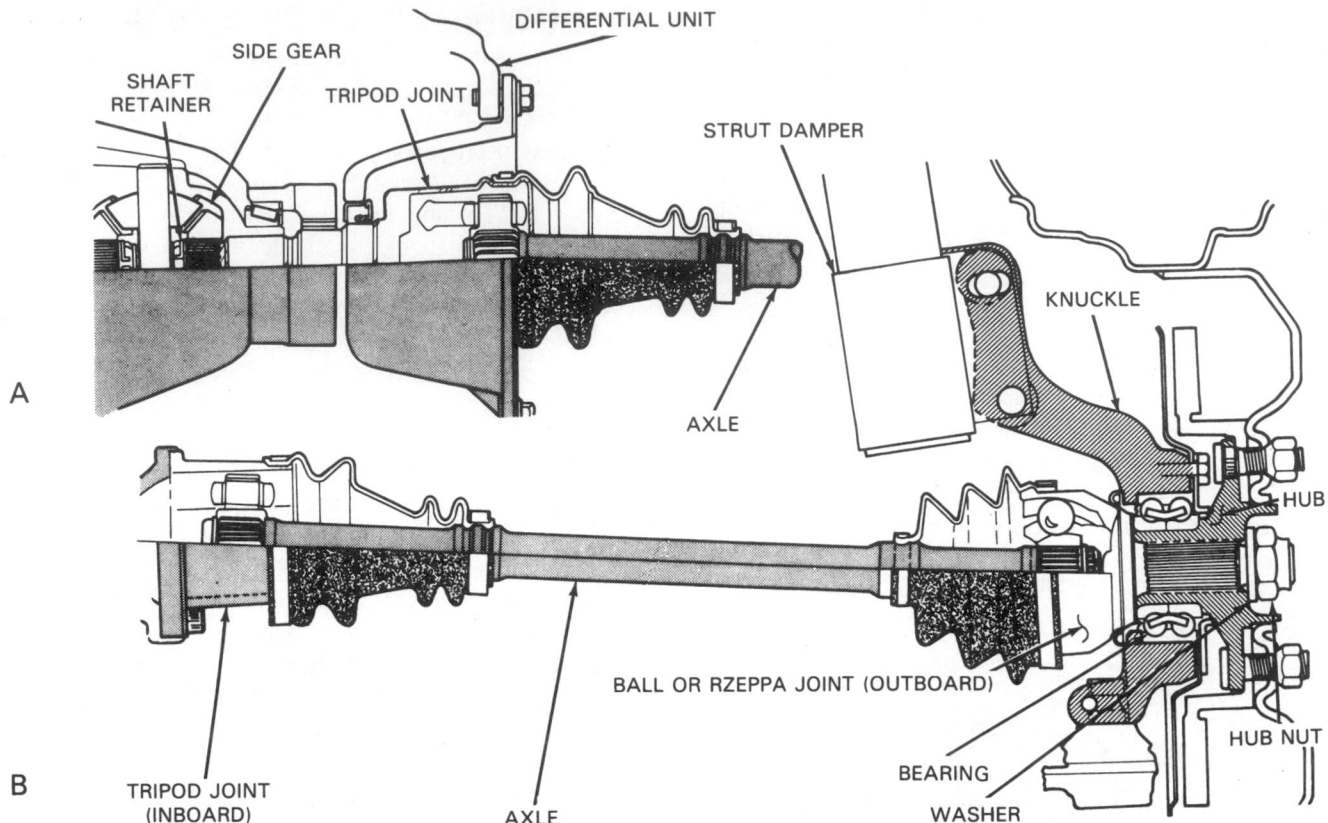

Figure 33-26. One front-wheel drive axle and universal joint setup. Joints used on this unit are of constant velocity tripod and ball type. Note somewhat different inboard joint attachment methods. A—Automatic transmission. B—Manual transmission. (Chrysler)

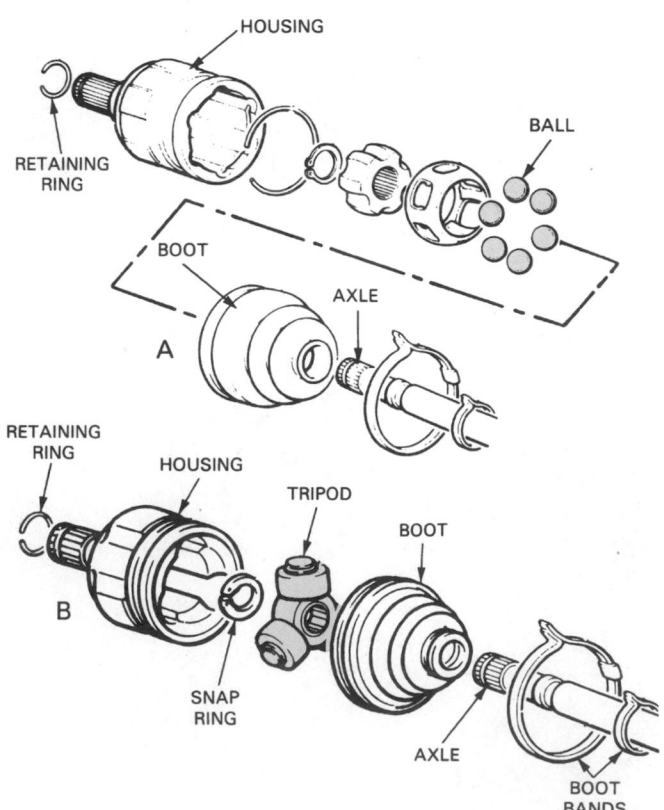

Figure 33-27. A—Exploded view of a ball (Rzeppa) joint. B—Tripod joint. Note that the tripod setup is similar to a ball and trunnion universal joint. (Chrysler)

Remove the front wheels on the side of the axle to be removed. Remove the hub nut and loosen the axle from the front wheel bearing located in the *steering knuckle.*

> **Note: Some axles must be pressed from the wheel bearing and steering knuckle assembly. Consult the manufacturers' service manual.**

Next, remove any part that restricts access to the CV joint fasteners. Some vehicles require the partial or complete removal of the steering knuckle assembly to allow for CV axle removal. If so, remove the fasteners holding the steering knuckle to the lower control arm, **Figure 33-28.** Remove the tie rod end and strut rod mounting, if necessary. Slide the steering knuckle assembly off the CV axle shaft and wire it out of the way. The inner end of most CV axle shafts is held to the transaxle by an internal snap ring, and the axle can be removed with a sharp pulling motion. Some CV axles must be removed with a special tool. Others are removed by carefully prying between the inner CV joint and the transaxle case, **Figure 33-29.**

> **Note: A few CV axles are held to the transaxle output shaft flange by bolts or by studs and nuts. Remove these fasteners before removing the axle.**

CV Joint Disassembly

Begin disassembly of either a tripod and Rzeppa joint by removing the *straps* holding the CV boot, **Figure 33-30.**

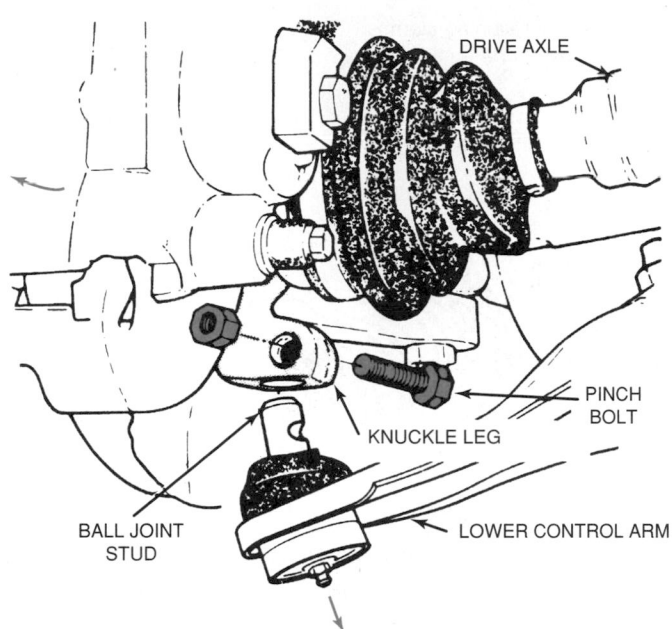

Figure 33-28.   Removing the pinch bolt to separate the lower control arm and steering knuckle. Use caution if the parts are under tension. (Driveshaft Technology, Inc.)

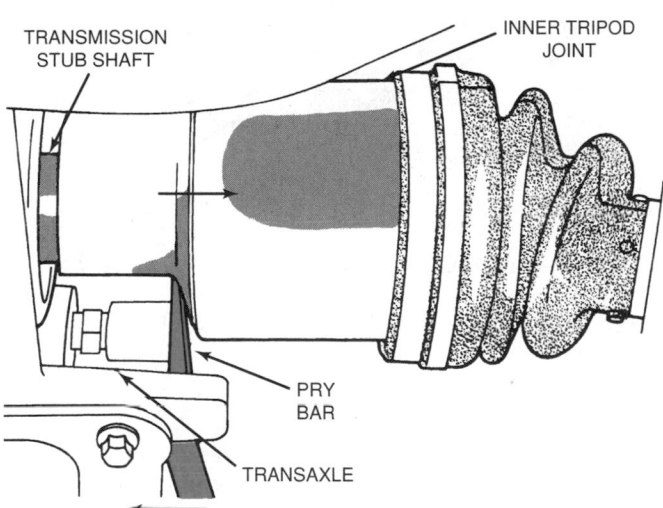

Figure 33-29.   Removing the CV axle and joint from the transaxle stub shaft with a pry bar. Do not damage parts. (Chrysler)

The boot can then be either cut off or slid out of the way to gain access to the CV joint.

Next, remove any snap rings, **Figure 33-31,** and carefully separate the joint. If the joint will not come apart easily, tap it lightly with a hammer.

 Caution: Be sure that all snap rings have been removed before striking the CV joint with a hammer.

Clean all external parts except rubber boot thoroughly in solvent. Disassemble the joint and inspect all internal parts for wear or damage. Tripod joints will slide apart to gain access to internal parts. The balls in Rzeppa joints

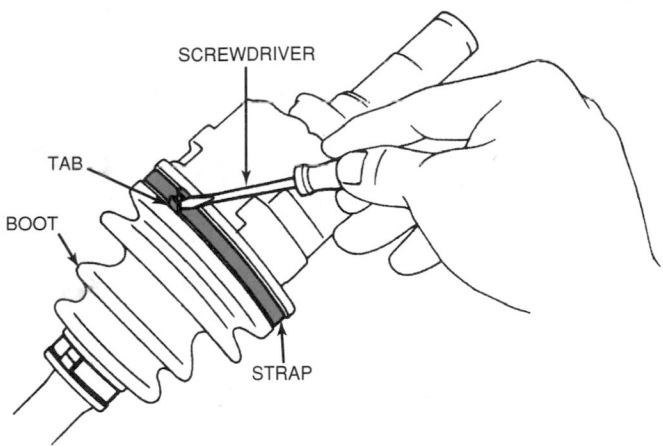

Figure 33-30.   Removing boot straps by bending up and releasing the strap tab with a screwdriver. If the boot is going to be reused, do not damage it during removal. (Toyota)

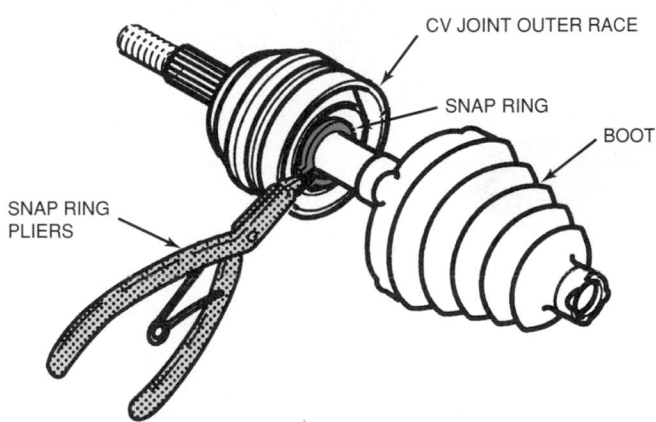

Figure 33-31.   Removing a snap ring so the joint may be disassembled. Work in a *neat* and *clean* area. (Cadillac)

are contained in a cage. The cage must be tilted inside of the housing to remove the balls. **Figure 33-32** illustrates a tripod CV joint being disassembled after boot removal. **Figure 33-33** shows a disassembled Rzeppa joint. Once the CV joint is apart, clean it thoroughly.

 Note: If the boot only is being changed, install the new boot and reverse the removal steps to complete the job. Be sure to clean the CV joint and check it for wear before reassembly. Thoroughly grease the joint before reinstalling the boot.

CV Joint Reassembly

Replace internal CV joint parts as required. Although replacement parts are available, many technicians prefer to replace the entire CV joint.

CV joints are usually assembled in the reverse order of disassembly. Be sure to replace all defective parts.

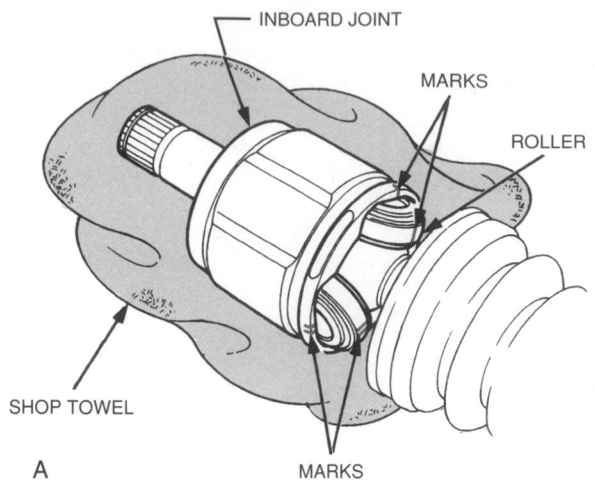

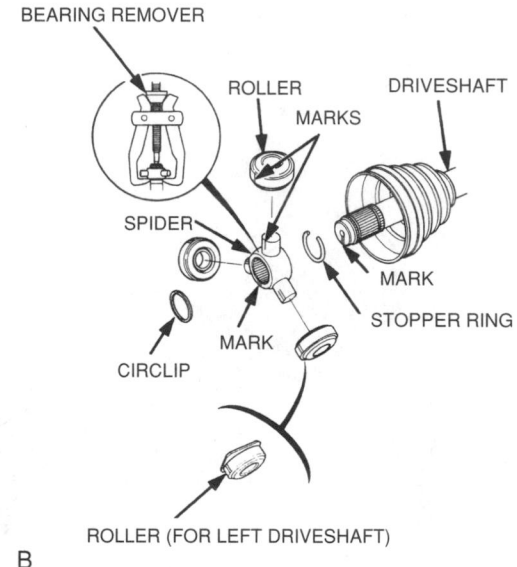

Figure 33-32. Disassembling a tripod CV joint. A—Mark components before disassembly. B—Remove parts as shown. (Honda)

Lubricate where required using the special CV joint lubricant provided. Align any scribe marks. Follow the manufacturer's procedures for reassembly.

 Note: Install a new CV joint boot whenever the CV joint is disassembled. Pack any remaining CV joint lubricant into the boot before replacing the boot seal straps.

There are several methods of retaining the CV boot straps, **Figure 33-34.** If the straps are not properly installed, centrifugal force will throw all of the lubricant out of the CV joint.

CV Axle Installation

Reverse the removal procedure. Align the scribe marks. Lubricate where necessary. Be sure to follow the manufacturer's instructions carefully.

1. Cut seal retaining clamps.
2. Remove parts as shown.

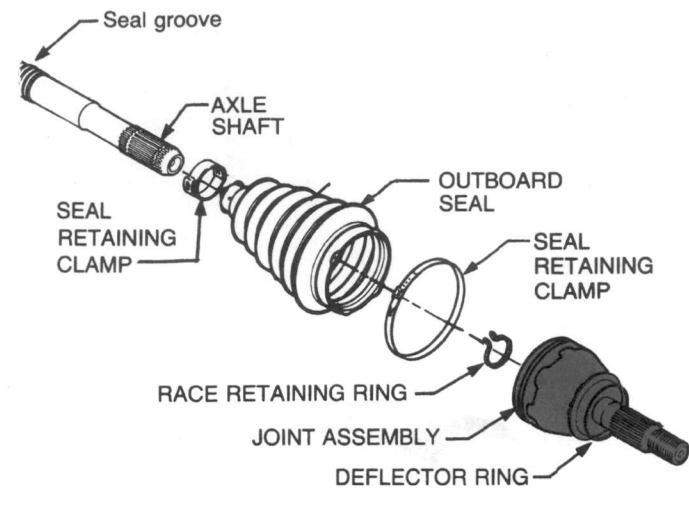

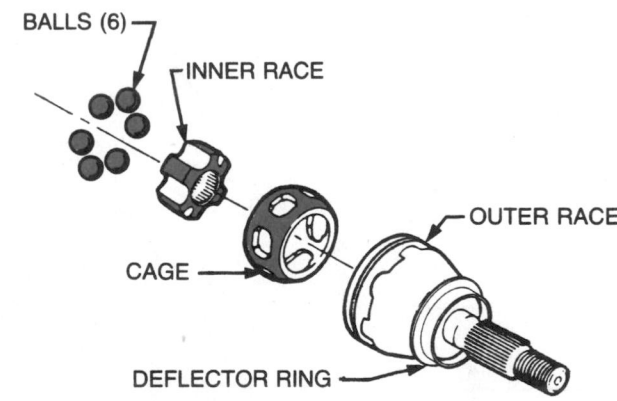

Figure 33-33. Disassembling a Rzeppa CV joint. (Saginaw Division of GM)

 Caution: Be sure to torque all fasteners and double-check all areas. A failure in this area can lead to loss of vehicle control and occupant injury.

Servicing Axle Shafts

This section will cover the servicing of the side axles of rear-wheel drive rear axle assemblies. The information presented here will also apply to solid axles used on four-wheel drive vehicles.

Modern Side Axles

The modern side axle assembly is a *semifloating* design in which the axle drives, retains, and supports the wheel. A single ball or bearing cap wheel bearing is used at the outer end of each axle housing. The axle can be retained in the housing by a retainer plate or by axle shaft locks on the inner ends of the axles. These types of axles are also used on the front axle assembly of a four-wheel drive vehicle.

The differential carrier may be of the integral type (permanent part of the axle housing), **Figure 33-35.** It may also be a removable type, sometimes called a chunk or pumpkin. See **Figure 33-36.**

An exploded view of one type of independent front axle assembly for a four-wheel drive vehicle is shown in **Figure 33-37.** A cutaway of an assembled drive axle is pictured in **Figure 33-38.** Study part names and relationships.

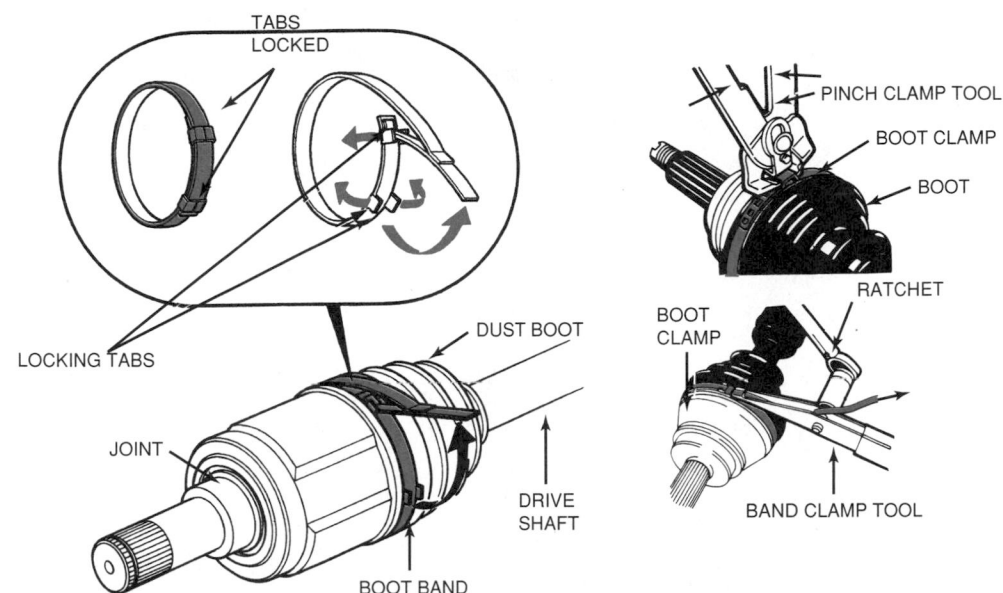

Figure 33-34.   Installing and restraining boot straps with a special strap (band) and pinch tools. (Perfect Circle & Honda)

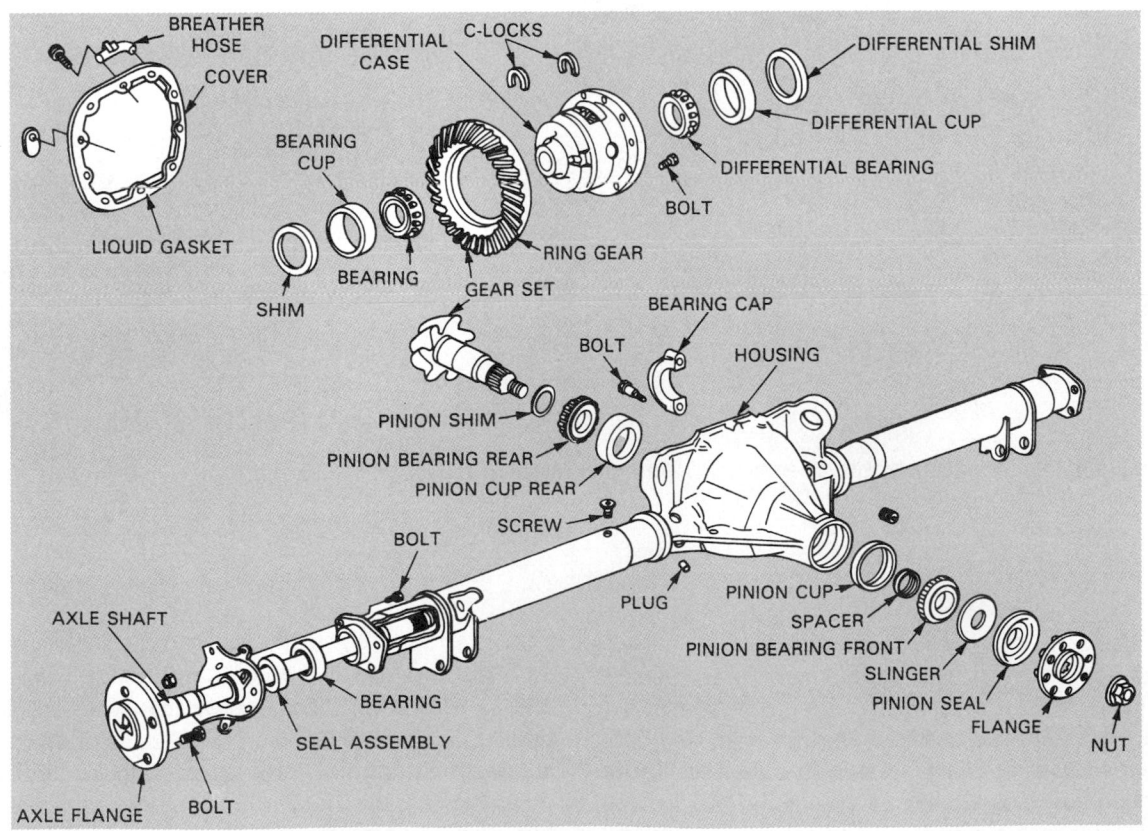

Figure 33-35.   Exploded view of a rear drive axle assembly. Study the different parts and relationships. (Ford)

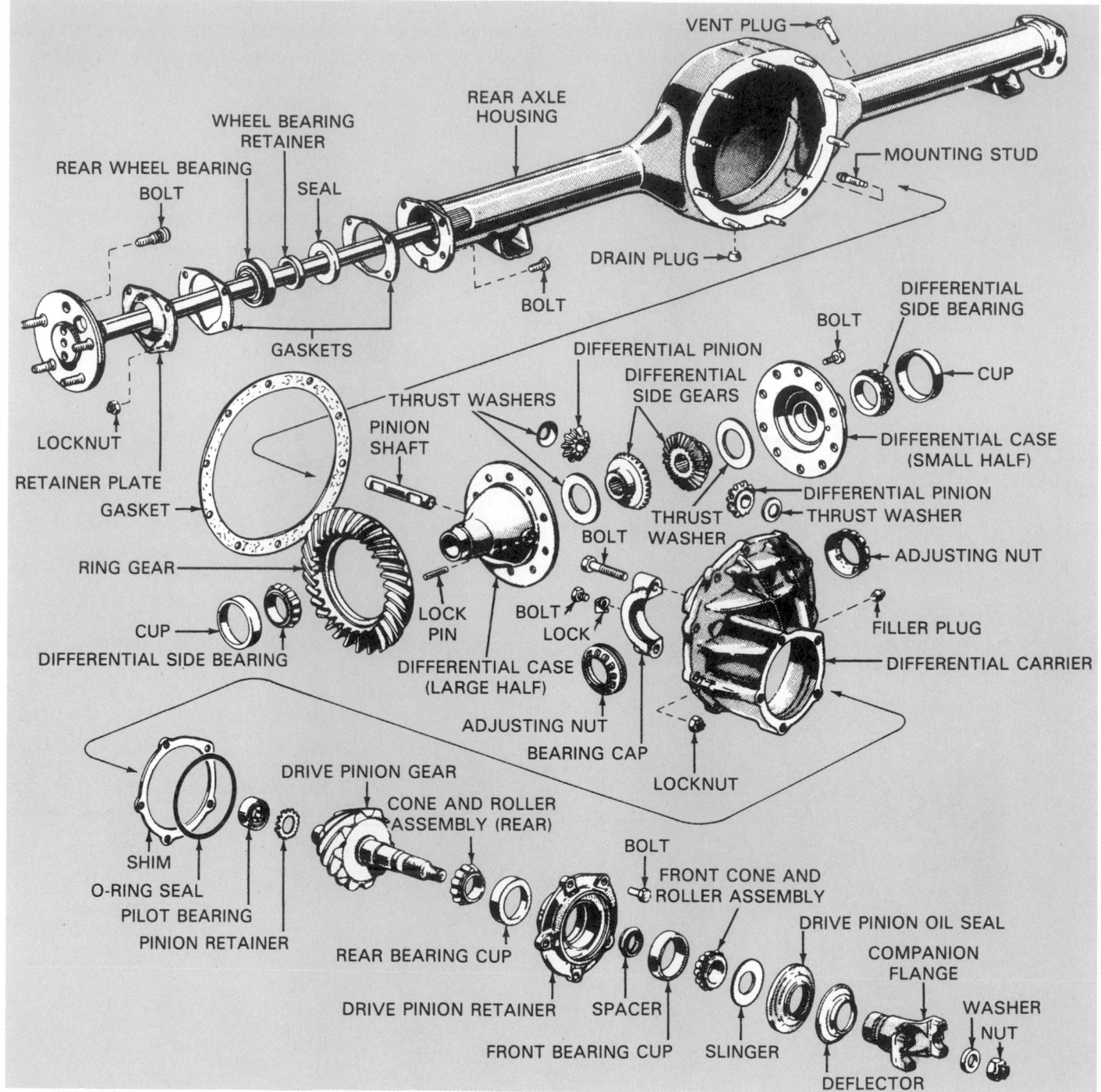

Figure 33-36. Drive axle assembly with a removable differential carrier. (Ford)

Axles for Independent Rear Suspensions

The rear axles used with independent rear suspensions resemble small drive shafts. The axle shafts are attached to the differential assembly output shaft and contain U-joints or CV joints. A typical joint is shown in **Figure 33-39.** Service for these axles is the same as for the Hotchkiss and CV axles discussed earlier in this chapter.

Flanged End Side Axle Removal

The *flanged end axle* is shown in **Figures 33-35** and **33-36.** To pull an axle, remove the wheel. Pull the brake drum off after unscrewing the small drum-retaining cap screw or the flat nuts threaded over the lug bolts.

Remove the nuts from the bearing retainer plate. If the design permits, pull the retainer plate outward far

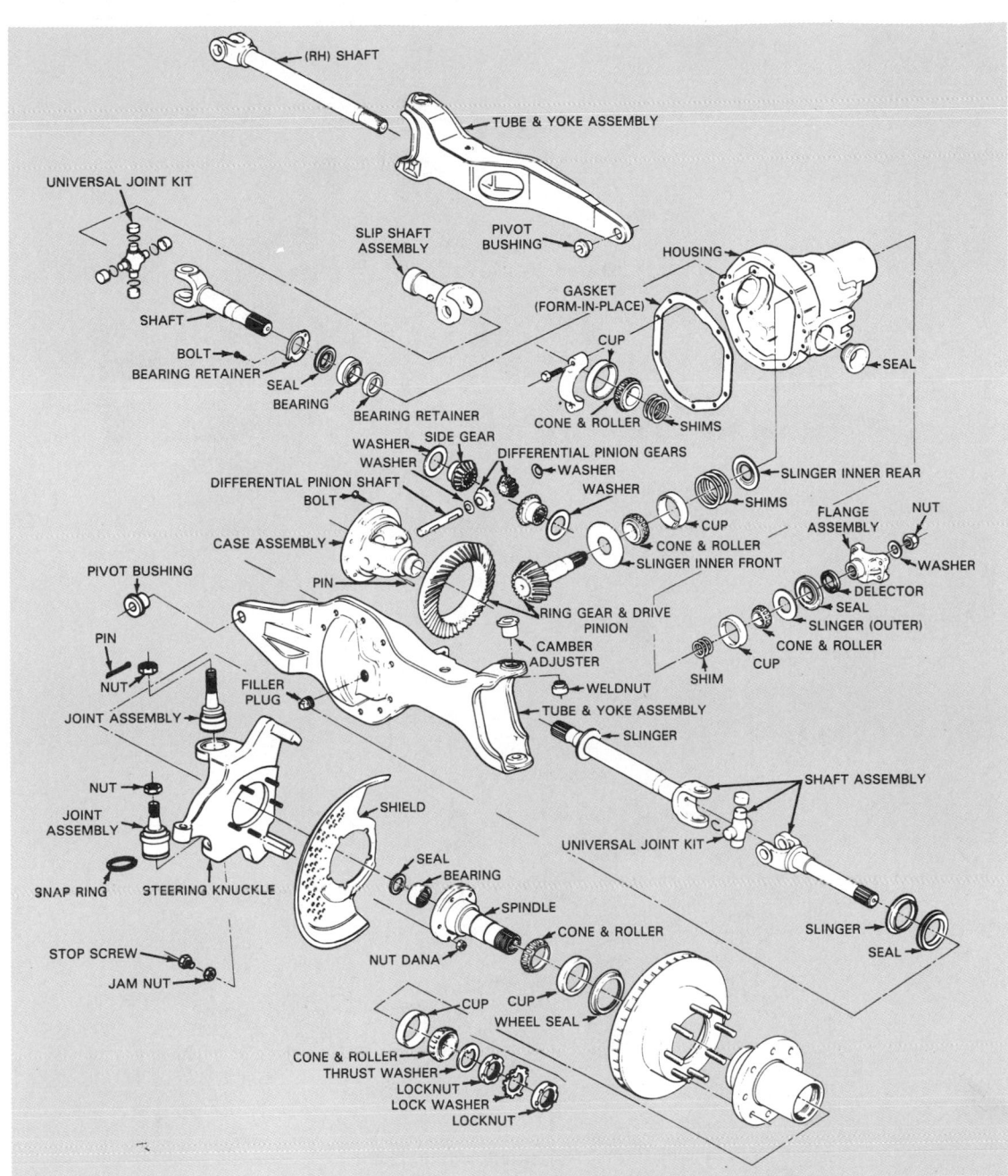

Figure 33-37. An exploded view of an independent suspension, front drive axle assembly used on one four-wheel drive vehicle. (Ford)

enough to reinstall one nut to hold the brake backing plate in place.

Attach a slide hammer puller to the axle flange. With a few sharp blows, pull the axle bearing free of the housing. Remove the tool and slide the axle from the housing. Refer to **Figure 33-40.**

If a nut was not placed on one backing plate bolt before axle removal, make certain that the backing plate is not disturbed when the axle is pulled. Place a nut in position as soon as the axle is out. This is very important as the brake line can be bent, kinked, or weakened if the backing

plate is moved. A typical housing end backing plate and axle assembly is illustrated in **Figure 33-41.**

C-Lock Axle Removal

On some rear axles, the axle is retained with an inner end lock, which is often called a **C-lock.** To remove such an axle, pull the wheel and brake drum. Drain the differential housing and remove the inspection plate. Remove the differential pinion shaft (not the drive pinion shaft). Push the axle inward as far as it will go. This will free the C-lock from the recess in the axle side gear. Remove the C-lock. Withdraw the axle. See **Figure 33-42.**

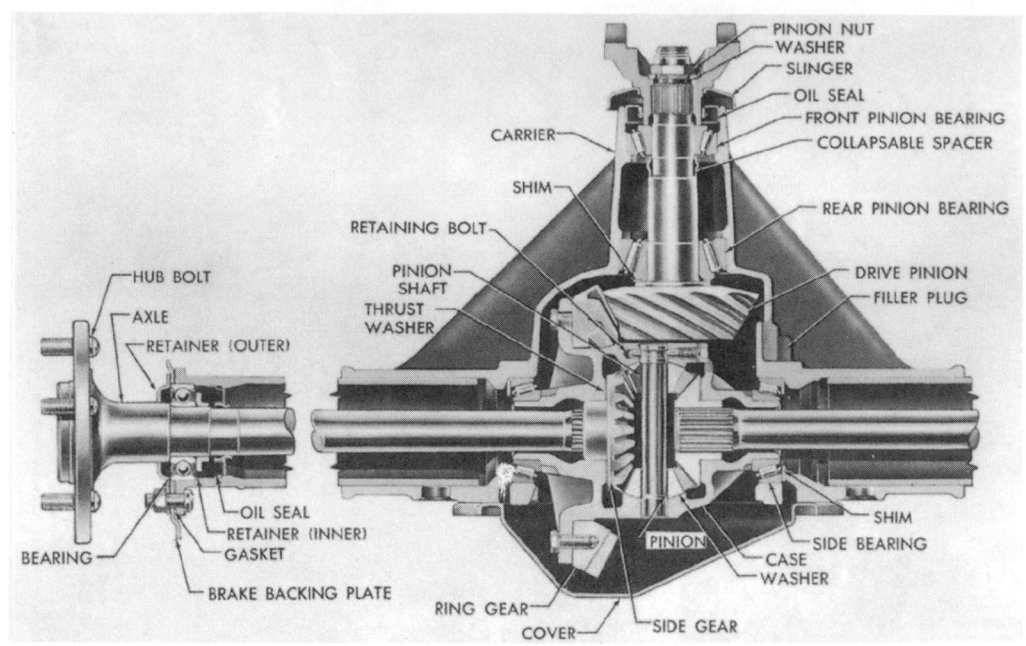

Figure 33-38. Assembled view of a drive axle. (Oldsmobile)

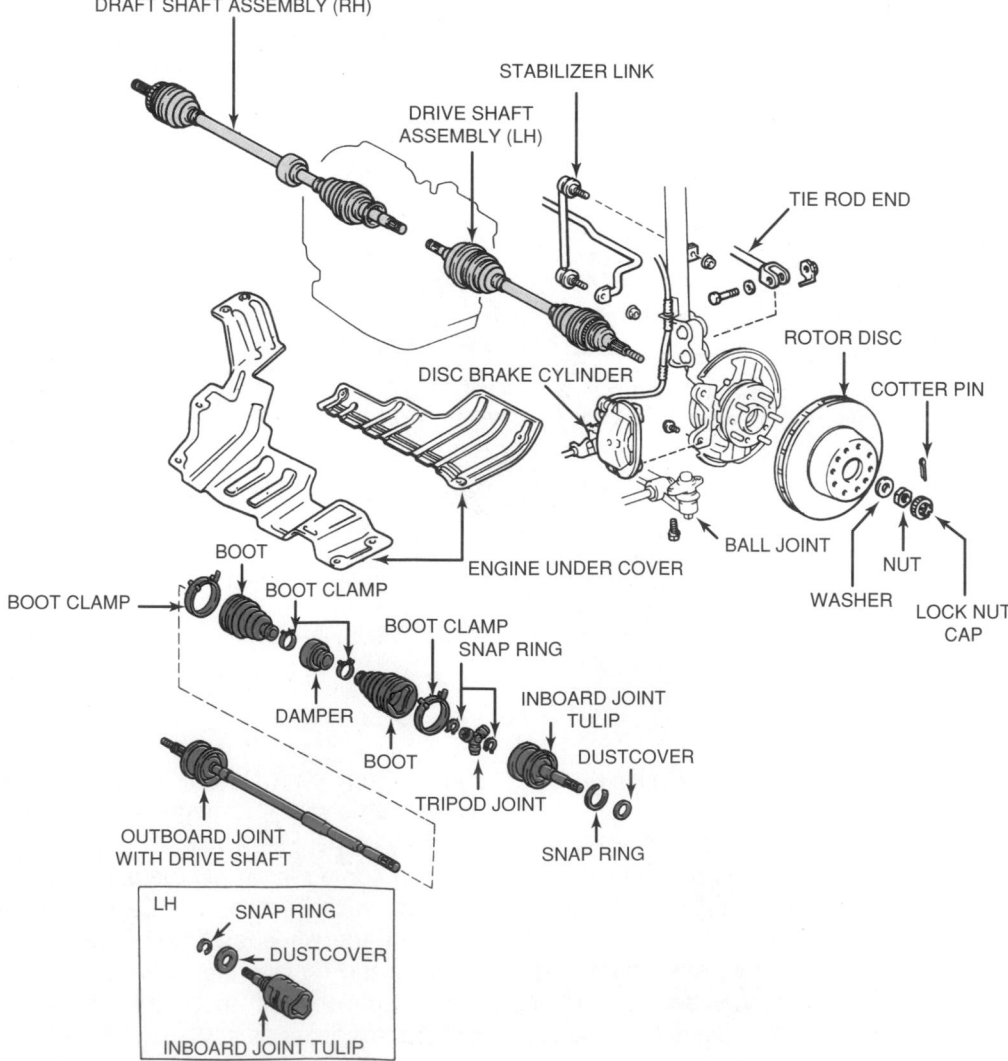

Figure 33-39. Exploded view of a rear-wheel drive, independent suspension drive axle arrangement. Study the axle and CV joint construction. (Toyota Motor Corp.)

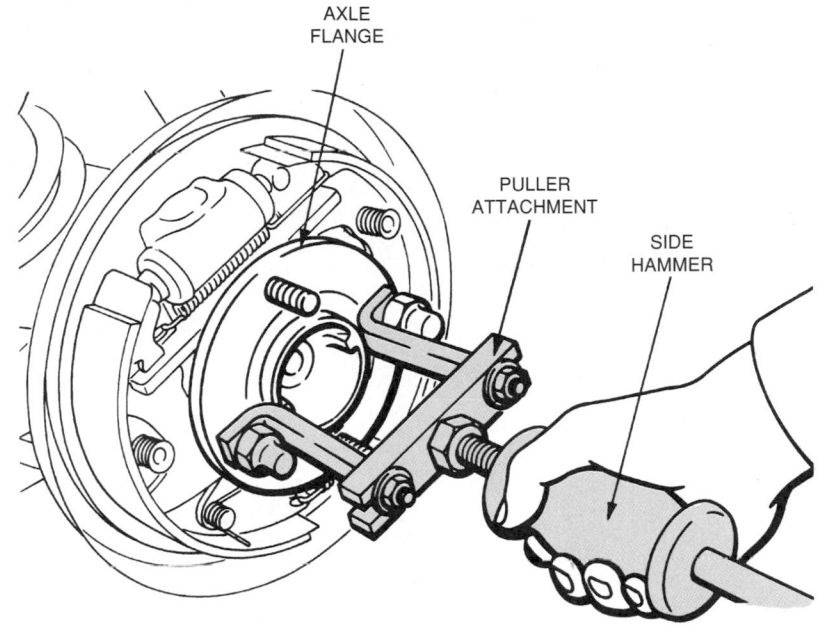

Figure 33-40. Using a slide hammer and puller attachment to remove a rear axle. (Chrysler)

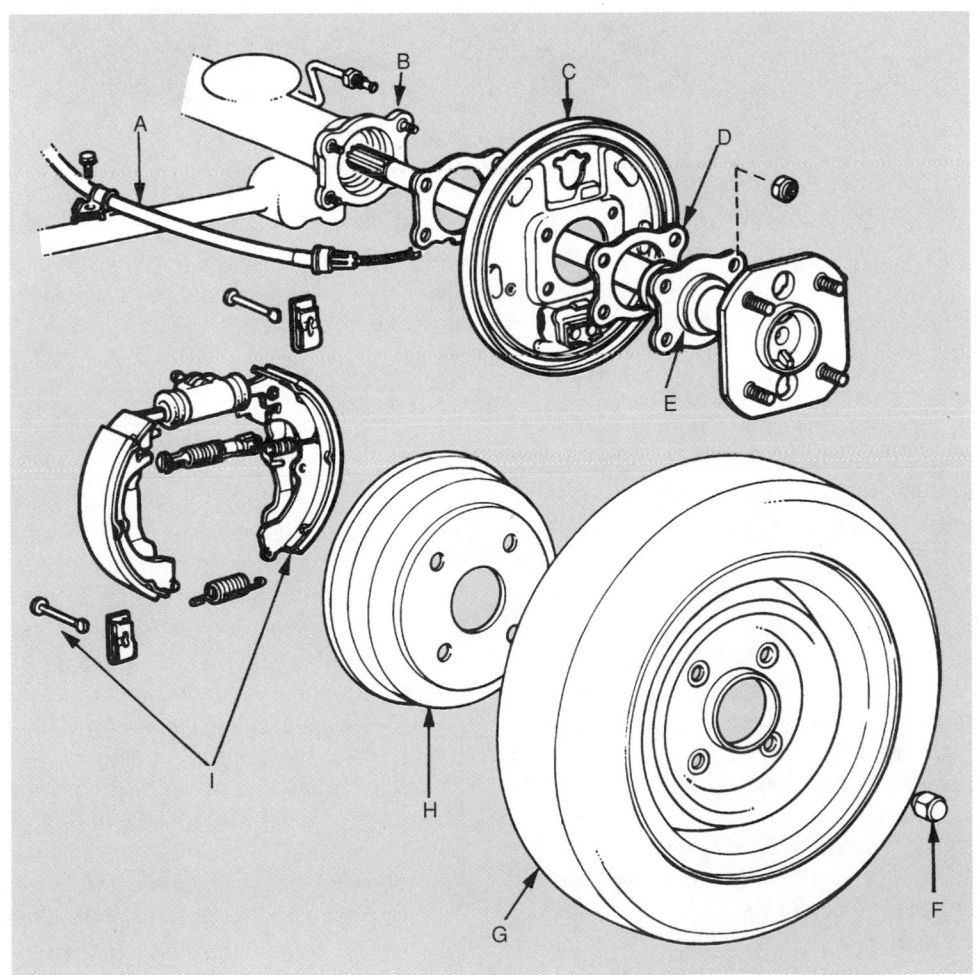

Figure 33-41. Typical rear axle assembly. A—Parking brake cable. B—Axle housing end. C—Backing plate. D—Axle shaft. E—Axle bearing. F—Wheel nut. G—Wheel and tire. H—Brake drum. I—Brake shoe assembly. (Toyota)

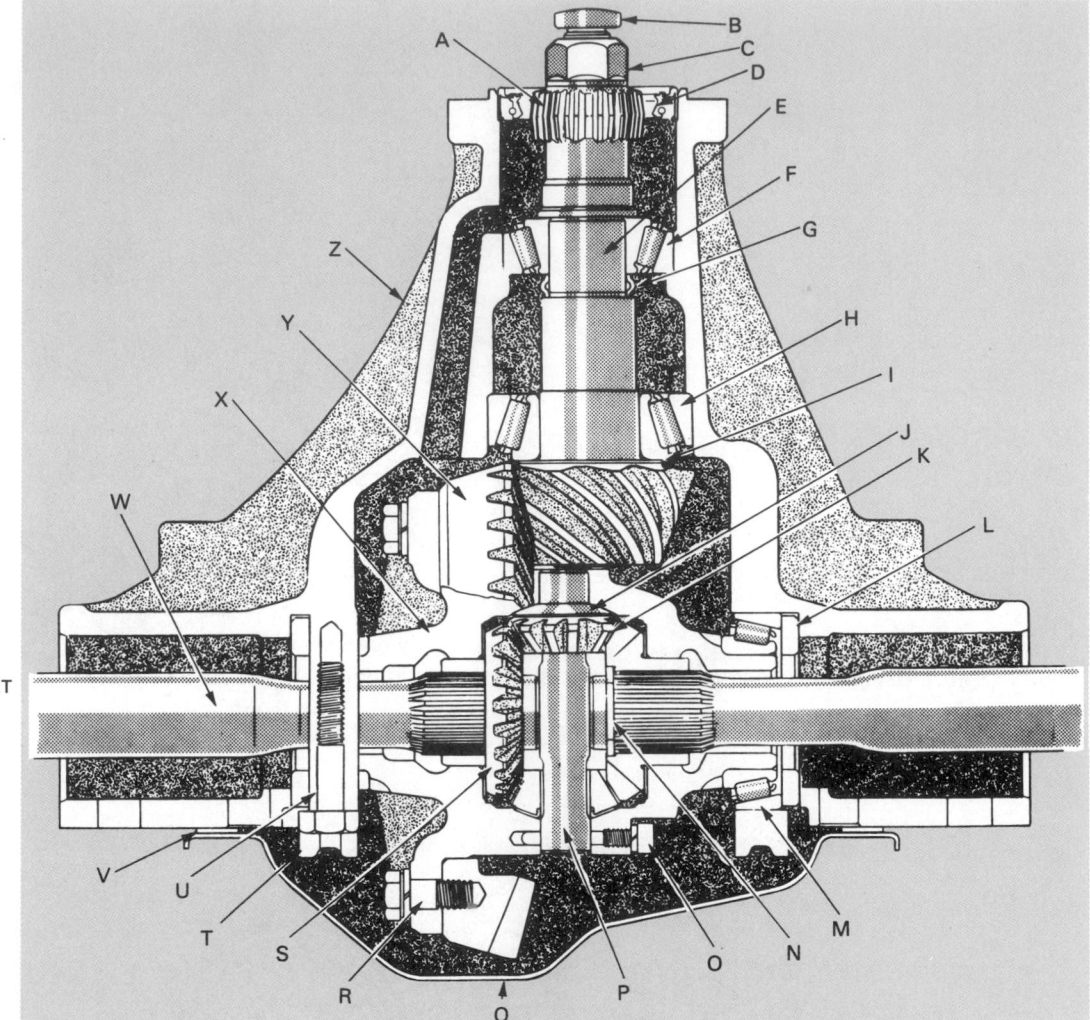

A. DRIVE COUPLING
B. THRUST WASHER
C. LOCK NUT
D. OIL SEAL
E. DRIVE PINION
F. PINION FRONT BEARING
G. PRELOAD SPACER
H. PINION REAR BEARING
I. PINION DEPTH SHIM
J. THRUST WASHER
K. PINION GEAR
L. SHIM/SPACER
M. DIFFERENTIAL BEARING
N. AXLE SHAFT C-LOCK
O. LOCK SCREW
P. PINION SHAFT
Q. DIFFERENTIAL COVER
R. RING GEAR BOLT
S. SIDE GEAR
T. BEARING CAP
U. BEARING CAP BOLT
V. DIFFERENTIAL COVER GASKET
W. AXLE SHAFT
X. DIFFERENTIAL CASE
Y. RING GEAR
Z. DIFFERENTIAL CARRIER

Figure 33-42. These axles are retained by C-locks (N) on the axle shaft inner ends. Note how the differential pinion shaft (P) keeps the axle ends in the outward position, thus forcing the C-locks into the recesses in the side gears (S). Also note the special drive coupling (A) used with the extension housing (torque tube) setup. (Chevrolet)

Tapered End Axle Removal

On some older vehicles, the wheel hub or hub-drum assembly is attached to the axle by means of a taper and key, **Figure 33-43,** or by a taper, key and splines, **Figure 33-44.** This requires the use of a heavy-duty puller to remove the hub.

Broken Axle Removal

When an axle has broken in service, a short piece or stub may be left in the housing. This section can often be retrieved by using a powerful magnet on a long handle, a tapered spring spiral on a handle (spring is turned and climbs up on broken section), or some other special tool.

Examine the break carefully by placing the broken ends together. If the break is clean (no missing pieces), drain and flush the housing thoroughly.

If small pieces are missing from the break, clean and flush the housing until all particles are removed. In some cases, complete disassembly of the differential and

drive pinion assembly is required. Remember that a very tiny particle of axle shaft metal can ruin bearings and gears.

Axle Shaft Inspection

When an axle is removed, it should be carefully washed and blown dry. Do not wash sealed bearings. Inspect the splines for evidence of wear. Look carefully for indications of twisting. See **Figure 33-45.** Check the oil seal contact surfaces. Polish off any burrs.

The shaft may be placed on V-blocks or between centers to check for runout, bending, or other problems. **Figure 33-46** illustrates the use of V-blocks and a dial indicator to check an axle for runout. **Figure 33-47** shows the axles being held between centers while checking for bends and flange runout with a dial indicator.

Inspect wheel lugs (on flange type axles) and replace any that are broken or stripped. Use a press, **Figure 33-48.** Discard shafts showing signs of twisting, excessive wear, or runout beyond specifications.

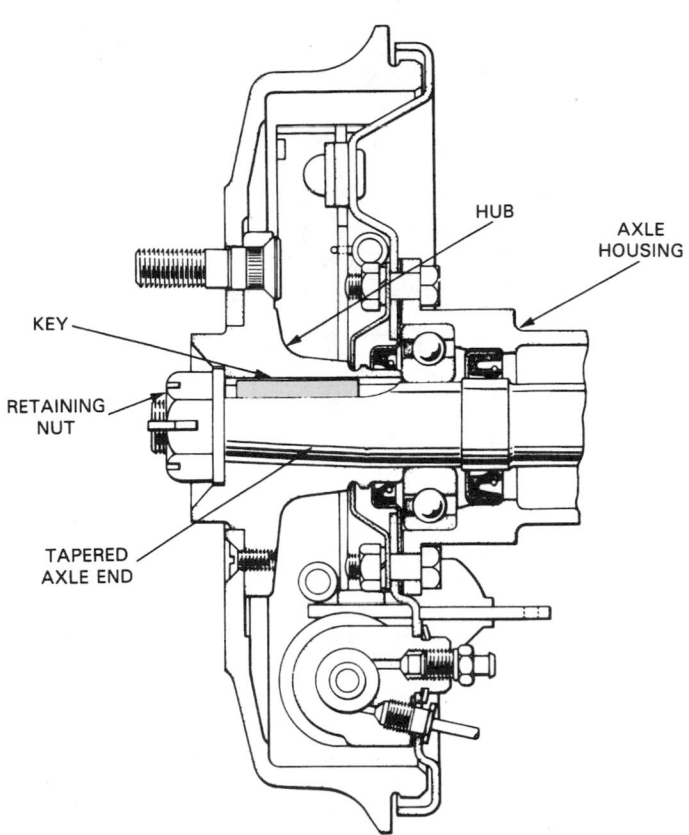

Figure 33-43.   This hub is attached to the axle with a tapered end axle and key. The retaining nut holds the hub firmly against the taper and key. (British-Leyland)

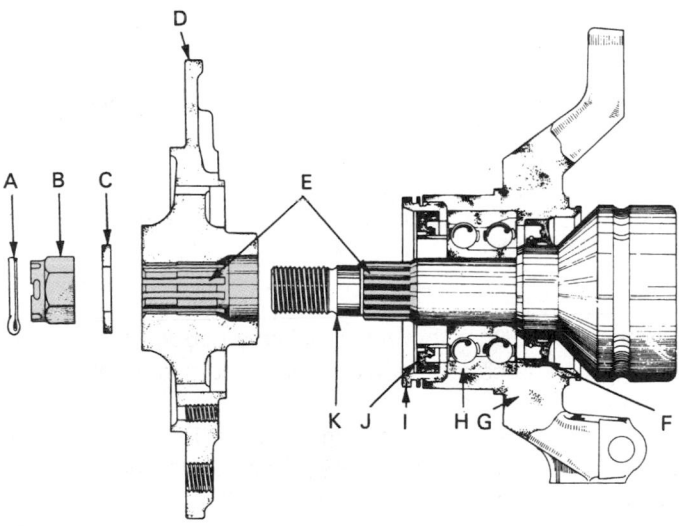

Figure 33-44.   This hub is secured to the axle with splines and a retaining nut. A—Cotter pin. B—Castle retaining nut. C—Washer. D—Hub. E—Splines. F—Seal. G—Steering knuckle housing. H—Double row ball bearing. I—Nut. J—Seal. K—Axle (drive). (Saab)

Axle Oil Seal Replacement

Following axle removal, always install new oil seals. Some installations utilize two oil seals—one on the inside of the bearing and the other on the outside. The bearing is

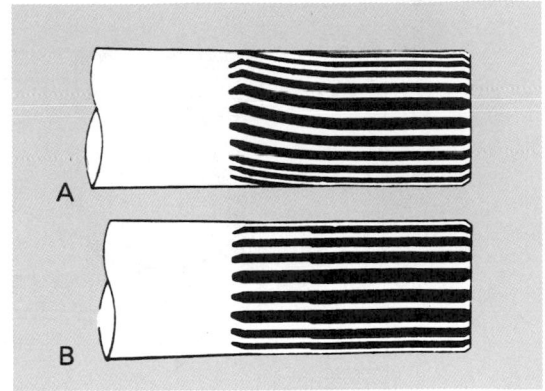

Figure 33-45.   Axle damage. A—Axle has been twisted. B—Splines have step wear (worn thin where axle engages gears). (Isuzu)

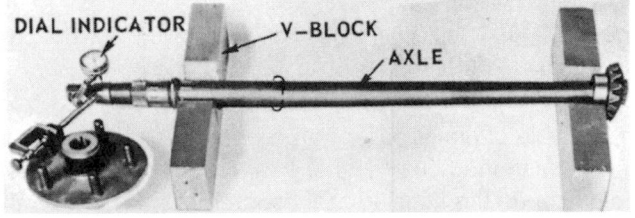

Figure 33-46.   Using V-blocks and a dial indicator to check an axle for runout. (Chrysler)

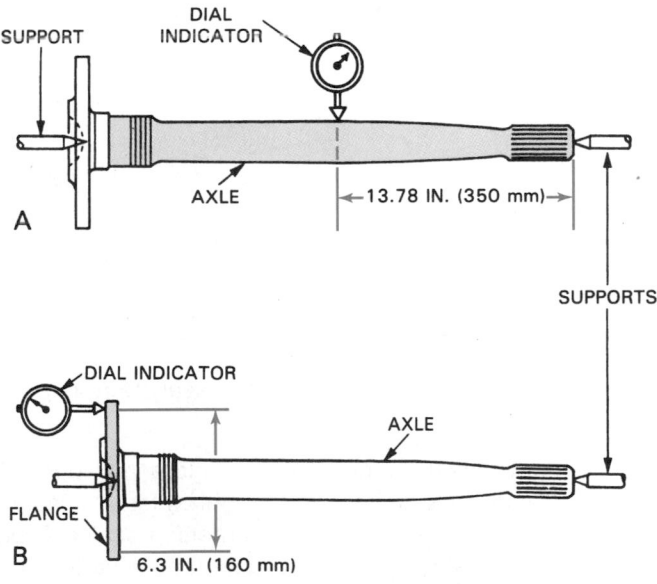

Figure 33-47.   A—Checking axle for bend with a dial indicator. B—The indicator is placed against the flange to measure flange runout. Note that the axles are supported on tapered centers. (Chevrolet)

either sealed for life or it depends upon periodic applications of wheel bearing grease. When the wheel bearing is lubricated by the differential lubricant, only an outer seal is used.

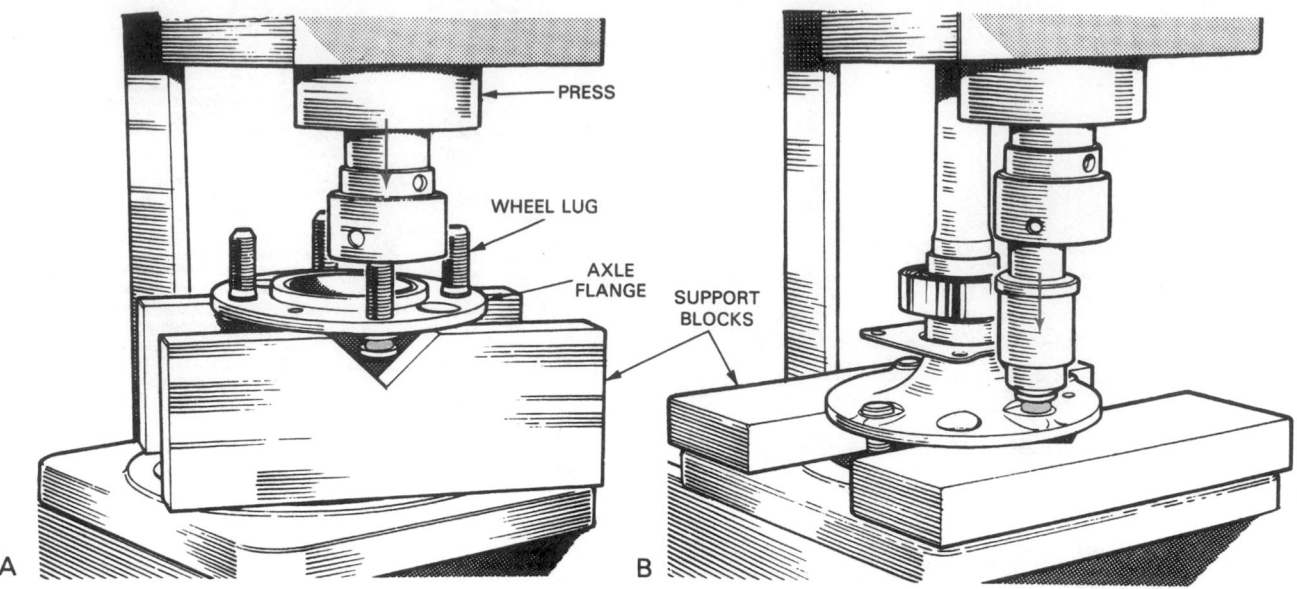

Figure 33-48. Replacing a damaged wheel lug. A—The press is forcing the lug from the flange. B—A new lug is pressed into position. (Chrysler)

A slide hammer puller with a hook nose is very handy for removing the housing inner seal. When pulling the seal, avoid scoring the housing seal counterbore, **Figure 33-49.**

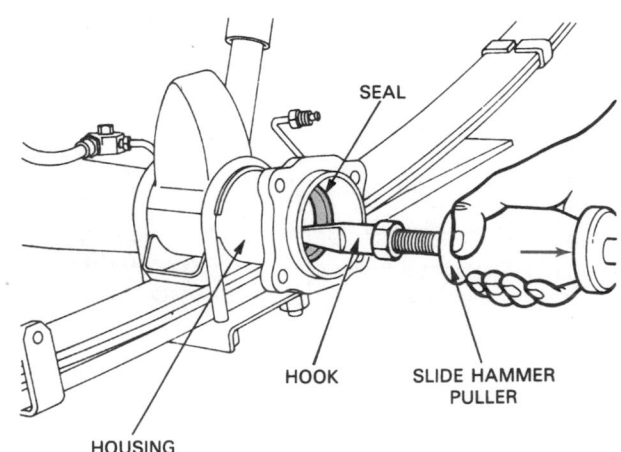

Figure 33-49. Pulling an axle housing oil seal. (Chrysler)

Clean seal counterbore. Remove nicks and burrs. If the seal is made of leather, soak it in light oil for 30 minutes. Coat the outer seal edge with nonhardening sealer. Apply gear oil to the seal lip. Using a suitable tool, drive the seal into place. The seal lip must face inward. Drive the seal squarely and to proper depth. See **Figure 33-50.**

The outer seal may be built into the bearing itself. It may also be incorporated in the oil seal retainer.

Rear Wheel Bearing Replacement

Where a **bearing retainer ring** is used, place the axle so that the ring rests on a solid support, such as a vise. Slide a protective sleeve up to the ring. Notch the ring with a grinder and break it away with a hammer and chisel. See

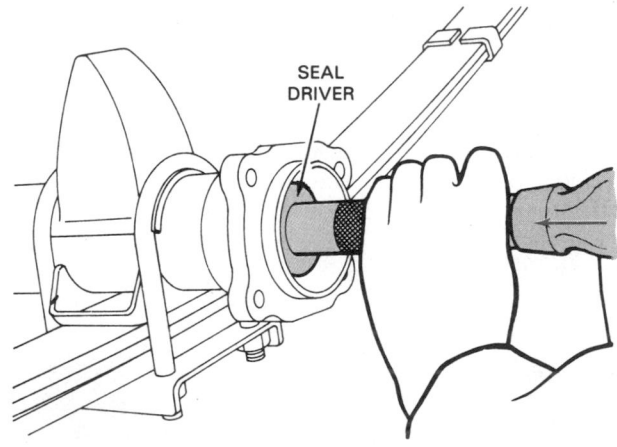

Figure 33-50. Driving an axle seal into position with a seal driver. (Chrysler)

Figure 33-51. Do not grind completely through the ring, as this would damage the axle. Make certain a protective sleeve is used.

Slide the retainer ring from the shaft. Set the axle up in a press (a puller can also be used) so that the bearing may be grasped while the axle is forced through the bearing. Grasp the bearing, not the retainer plate. Make certain the axle flange is clear of the puller and press.

 Note: Use a bearing cover, Figure 33-52. Also use protective goggles to prevent injury from flying parts in the event the bearing explodes under pulling pressure.

Clean the axle and coat the bearing face and retaining ring contact surface with a film of lubricant. Use the type used for ball joints.

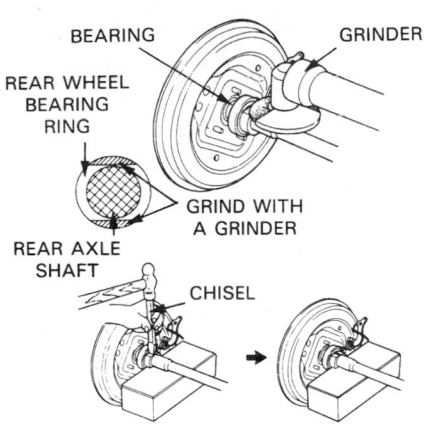

Figure 33-51. Notch the bearing ring with grinder. Then, crack the ring with a hammer and chisel.

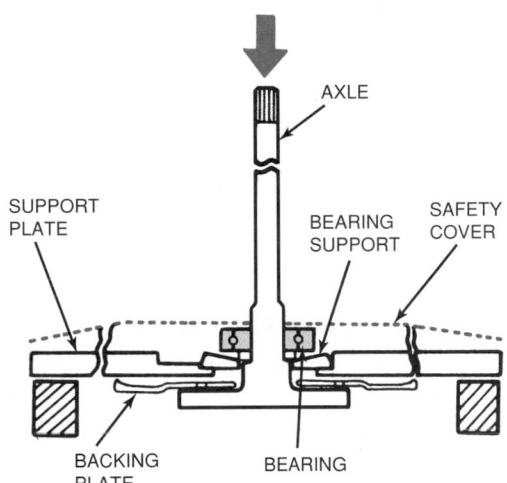

Figure 33-52. Axle bearing being removed. Support the bearing to prevent damage. Place a safety cover or shield over the bearing to protect yourself and others. Bearings under pressure can fracture and come apart with great force! (Mazda)

Put the retaining flange into position on the axle. Slide the new bearing on the axle. The bearing must face in the direction specified. Set the axle up in a press so that the bearing inner race is supported. Do not install the bearing by exerting pressure on the outer race.

Before pressing the bearing into place, check the retainer plate for proper positioning and the bearing for correct installation. Press the bearing on the shaft as specified. The bearing is pressed on a specific distance from the flange surface.

Slide the retaining ring into position. It must face as recommended. Set the axle in the press so that the retaining ring is well supported. Support the ring around its full circumference, not in just two spots. Force the axle through the ring until the ring just contacts the bearing. See **Figure 33-53.** Never try to press the bearing and retaining ring on at the same time. Always use a new retaining ring.

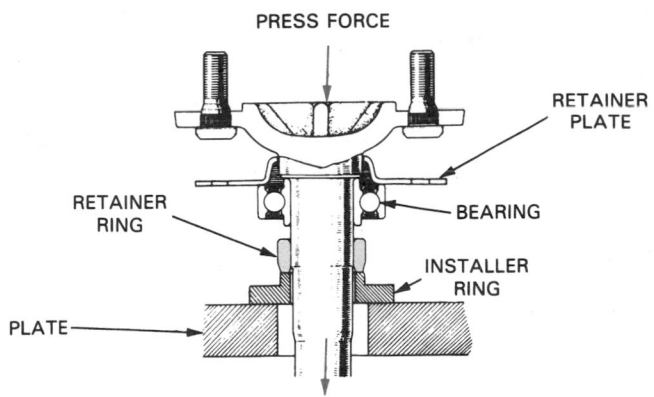

Figure 33-53. Pressing a bearing retaining ring into position. Note how the installer ring supports the retainer ring. (Toyota)

One axle setup has the retainer plate so close to the bearing that the bearing cannot readily be grasped for pulling. When this is the case, cut off the roller cage outer section. Grind off a section of the inner race. Use a sleeve to protect the axle. Then, remove the rollers one at a time.

Cut out the remaining portion of the cage and pull the outer race from the axle. The inner race may now be grasped for pulling. Some bearings are retained with a locknut. Remove the bearing carefully on these to avoid possible thread damage.

Axle Installation

An axle must be clean. If the wheel bearings were damaged, clean and flush the housing. Place a new gasket on the housing end. Place a new O-ring gasket on the bearing outer face.

Coat the length of the axle with clean gear oil. Lubricate the bearing counterbore in the housing. Lubricate the bearing if required. Slide the axle into the housing. Pass the splined end and axle length through the oil seal very carefully to avoid damage.

As the shaft is passed into the housing, support its weight. Engage the splined end in the axle side gear. Align the bearing and start it into the housing counterbore. Sometimes the axle is longer on one side than the other. Make sure axle is installed on the correct side.

Align the retainer plate so that the oil drain section, **Figure 33-54,** is over the drain hole in the backing plate. The gasket must be aligned to expose the oil drain hole. Do not plug the hole with sealer. If the oil drain is not aligned, oil leakage past the bearing will pass into the brake assembly. Oil can then reach the shoes and drum or pads and rotor, ruining the linings.

When installing an axle with a tapered roller bearing and shims, make certain that the shims are clean and in the proper position. Use gaskets and sealer where required. On axles with the hub attached to a tapered end, install the shims, backing plate, and an outer seal. Use new gaskets and coat with sealer. Tighten the fasteners. Attach the brake lines and bleed the brakes (see Chapter 34, Brake Service).

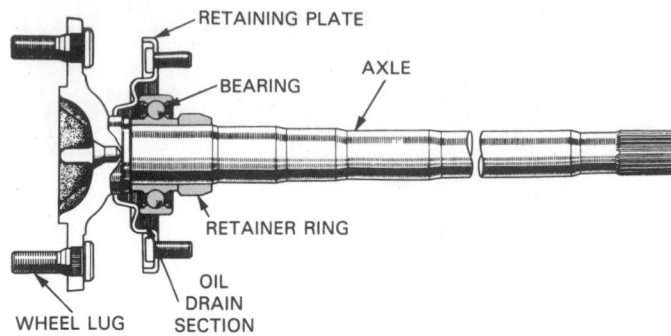

Figure 33-54. Bearing and retainer ring installed properly on the axle. Note the position of the oil drain section. (Toyota)

Check Axle End Play

After the axle retainer plate fasteners are torqued, check the axle for proper **end play.** Attach a dial indicator firmly to the axle flange and adjust the indicator stem against the backing plate. Pull the axle in and out and note the total reading. This will be the axle end play.

Some axles are designed so that end play is controlled by the play in the wheel bearings (ball type), by shims (tapered roller), or by an adjusting nut on one end of the axle housing (tapered roller bearings). Follow the manufacturer's specifications. See **Figure 33-55.**

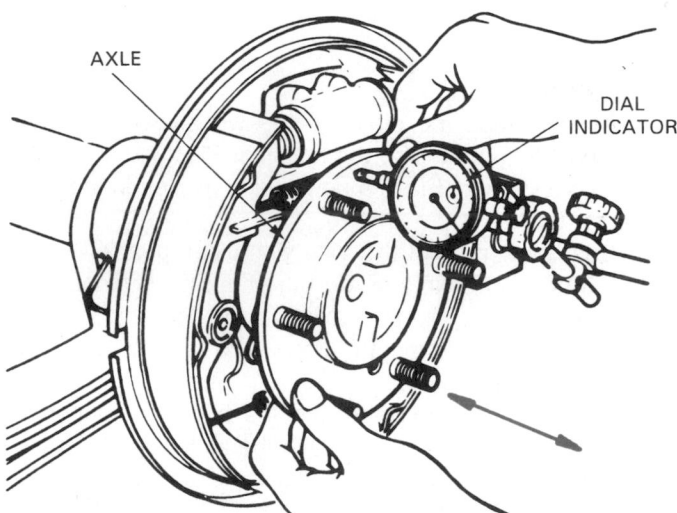

Figure 33-55. Checking axle end play. Move the axle back and forth while watching the indicator. (Nissan)

Ring and Pinion, Differential Unit Service

The **ring gear** and **pinion gear** used in modern rear axle assemblies are referred to as **hypoid gears.** This refers to the placement of the pinion gear below the center of the ring gear. This is done to reduce the height of the driveline and to allow for a lower driveline hump in the floor of the passenger compartment. In addition to the ring and pinion, the rear axle assembly contains the **differential gears,** which are used to allow for different amounts of side wheel travel when making turns.

The following sections detail the basic troubleshooting and repair of the rear axle assembly, including ring and pinion removal and replacement and setting of pinion depth, gear backlash, and ring gear-pinion tooth pattern. The information here also applies to the front wheel axles used on four-wheel drive vehicles.

Troubleshooting

Drive axle sounds can be among the hardest to isolate and cure. Many other sounds can be mistaken for noise in the rear axle assembly. Certain body types, such as station wagons, may transmit more noise to the passenger compartment.

Road Testing

Before road testing for drive axle assembly problems, check the lubricant level. Add lubricant if required. Check the tires for a saw-tooth wear pattern or for a mud and snow tread design. Both can produce distinct rumbles, growls, or other noises. Bring the tire pressure to specifications.

Drive the vehicle far enough to warm the lubricant. Then check action during drive (acceleration), cruise (engine driving enough to maintain vehicle speed), float (engine neither driving nor holding back; vehicle speed will slowly decrease), and coast (accelerator released; engine on compression) conditions.

Noises Often Mistaken for Drive Axle Sounds

If the tires are suspected, inflate both front and back tires to 50 psi (345 kPa). If the tires are responsible, the noise should be noticeably altered. Reduce pressure to the recommended level immediately following road test.

Worn or improperly adjusted front wheel bearings can produce sounds similar to those caused by a defective rear axle. Raise the front end and shake wheel to detect looseness. Spin to test for roughness. During the road test, noise produced by the front wheel bearings can usually be reduced or altered by pressing on the brake while maintaining vehicle speed.

Certain road surfaces produce distinct sounds. By driving on a different surface, these sounds can be quickly identified. The transmission can also produce noises easily confused with typical drive axle problems.

Engine noise is occasionally mistaken for rear axle sounds. With the vehicle standing still, operate the engine at the approximate RPM at which the sound was noticed during the road test. If the sound is again heard, it will obviously not be the drive axle.

Check the drive shaft for possible unbalance or wear. When road testing, sounds produced by tires, front wheel bearings, road surface, or drive shaft unbalance will not change when the vehicle is switched from drive to coast (or vice versa).

Relating Drive Axle Sounds to Specific Parts

Bearing sounds tend to produce a low-pitched whine or growl that is fairly constant in pitch and extends over a wide range of road speeds.

Sounds produced by gears are apt to be of variable pitch and most pronounced in specific speed ranges or pull (drive, cruise, float, coast) conditions.

Defective rear wheel bearings will produce a continuous growl that is the same in all pull conditions. Sudden turns to the right or left will increase or decrease the load on a given bearing and will alter the sound somewhat. Jack up rear of the vehicle and turn the wheels slowly while "feeling" for any signs of roughness. Chipped bearings can produce a clicking sound.

Ring and pinion noise will usually be related to a specific pull condition. If it shows during drive, it will probably disappear during coast.

Differential pinion and side gear noise will be noticeable on turns, as there is little movement of these gears in straight ahead driving. Pinion bearing noise is low pitched and continuous.

When drive pinion bearings or differential case side bearings are worn, the ring and pinion backlash and tooth contact pattern is altered. This can produce a compound noise made up of bearing growl and gear whine.

A low-speed squeal can be caused by the pinion oil seal. A clanking sound occurring during acceleration or deceleration may be caused by worn universal joints, worn transmission, excessive ring and pinion backlash, worn pinion and axle side gear teeth, or worn drive pinion shaft.

Service Operations

The following sections cover the servicing of various rear axle and differential assembly parts.

Replacing Pinion Shaft Seal and/or Flange

Disconnect the drive shaft as explained above and move it out of the way. If required, measure the pinion shaft bearing preload by using an inch-pound torque wrench.

With the rear wheels free and the emergency brake released, tap the brake backing plates to free the brake shoes from the drum. Spin each wheel several times to make certain there is no drag. One method of ensuring complete freedom from brake drag is to remove both rear wheels and brake drums.

Use a torque wrench with the proper socket to turn the drive pinion shaft through several complete revolutions. Note the inch-pound reading during turning. Write this down, **Figure 33-56.**

Scribe Shaft, Nut, and Flange

Scribe a line starting on the pinion shaft end and running along the threads up to and part way across the end of the nut. Prick punch the companion flange in line with the scribe mark. Note the number of threads exposed beyond the nut. This procedure will ensure correct reassembly of all parts. If a new companion flange will be installed, it will be unnecessary to scribe and punch the mark.

Use a Special Holding Tool

Use a pinion companion flange holding tool to keep the flange from moving while the retaining nut is removed.

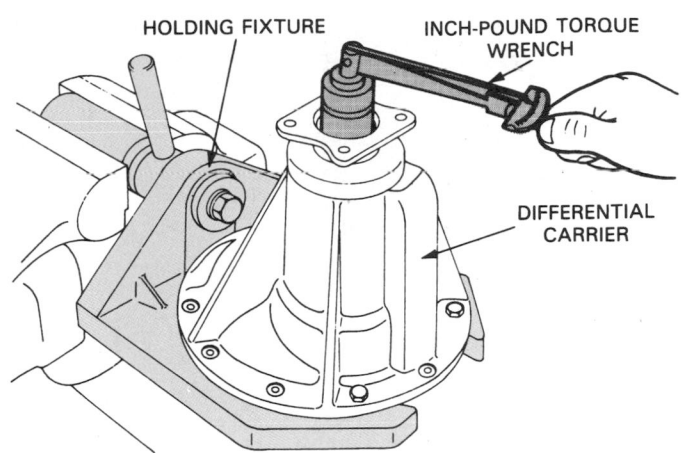

Figure 33-56. Measuring the torque required to turn the pinion shaft. Note the carrier holding fixture. (Chrysler)

Do not try to use a pry bar or a large crescent wrench to hold the flange. To prevent damage, use a tool designed for the job, **Figure 33-57.** Following pinion nut removal, use a pinion flange puller to remove the flange. One such puller is pictured in **Figure 33-58.** Do not try to pound the flange off.

Seal Removal and Installation

Remove the pinion oil seal by prying it out of the carrier or by using a threaded puller as in **Figure 33-59.** Before removing, note the depth to which seal is seated.

Wipe out the seal recess thoroughly. Wipe off the outer diameter of the seal and coat the seal with a thin layer of nonhardening sealer. Make certain that the new seal is of the correct size and type. With a proper seal installer, drive the seal (lip facing inward) into place. Drive the seal squarely and to the correct depth. Some manufacturers recommend installing the seal with a special installer that forces the seal into position by tightening the pinion nut. This eliminates hammering and the possibility of distorting the seal.

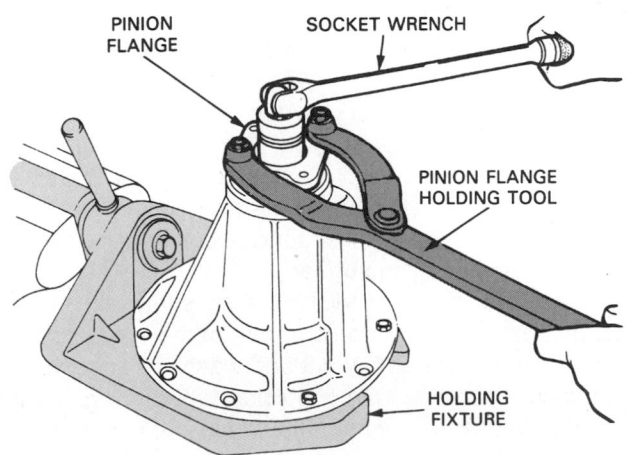

Figure 33-57. Using a pinion flange tool to prevent flange rotation while removing the retaining nut with a socket wrench. (Chrysler)

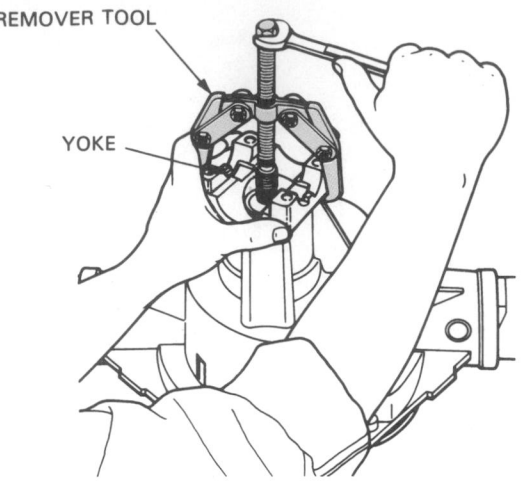

Figure 33-58. Using a puller to remove the differential pinion yoke or flange. (Ford)

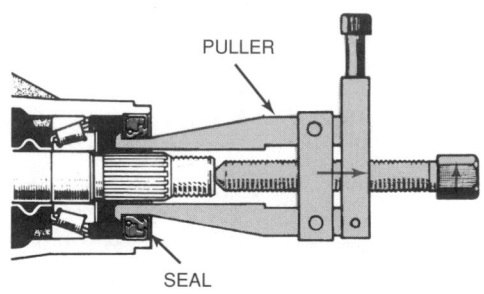

Figure 33-59. Removing the pinion oil seal with a special puller. (Toyota)

Check the Pinion Flange

If the old pinion shaft flange is to be reused, wash it and blow it dry. Inspect the seal contact surface. If necessary, remove any nicks or burrs. If the seal surface is worn or if the splines show evidence of wear, discard the flange. When a new flange will be installed, check for nicks and burrs. Also make sure it is the proper size and shape.

Install the Pinion Flange

Lubricate the seal lip, the flange seal contact surface, and the splines with gear oil. Align the punch mark on the flange with the scribe mark on the shaft. Start the flange into place. If a new flange is used, alignment is not required. If difficulty is experienced in getting the flange on far enough to start the retaining nut, use a puller. Never pound on the flange, as it can inflict serious damage to the bearings and/or ring and pinion gear.

Install the washer and the pinion shaft nut. Place a small amount of lubricant on the face of the washer and on the nut threads. Use a new nut and washer if specified.

Grasp the flange with a holding tool and tighten nut. When the nut starts to tighten the flange in place, rotate the pinion shaft a few times to make sure the bearings are seated. Then, check **preload** as outlined in the rear axle overhaul section.

 Note: Pinion bearing preload must be correct. Follow the manufacturer's specifications.

Connect the universal joint. Inspect the lubricant level in the axle housing.

Ring and Pinion, Differential Removal

Drain the housing. Remove both axle shafts. Disconnect the drive shaft. Check drive pinion shaft preload. If the differential carrier is of the removable type, unscrew the fasteners and remove the carrier. Watch out; it is heavy. Place the carrier in a repair stand, **Figure 33-60.**

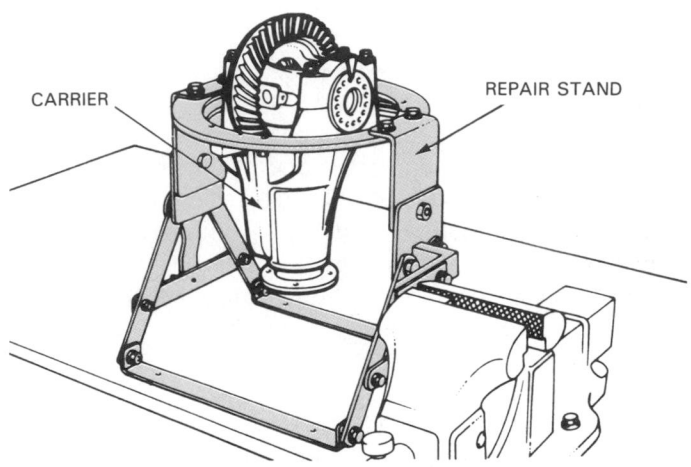

Figure 33-60. Differential carrier bolted to a repair stand.

If the carrier is of the integral type, it may be necessary to remove the entire housing. Check the manufacturer's manual. Repair stands designed to handle the entire housing are available.

Mark Parts before Removal

Before removing the differential case side bearing caps, make certain each cap and adjusting nut (where used) is marked. The caps and carrier are factory marked in **Figure 33-61.** If no marks are visible, mark the caps and carrier with a scribe or prick punch. See **Figure 33-62.**

It is also good practice to check the backlash between the ring and pinion gears before differential case removal (see section on adjusting backlash later in this chapter). Tooth contact pattern and bearing preload can also be checked.

Remove the case bearing cap fasteners and caps. Rap the caps to remove. Do not mar the cap parting surface. If they are the mechanically adjustable type shown in **Figure 33-63,** the differential case will lift out readily.

If the shim is of the adjusted preload type, use a couple pinch bars or a differential puller to force the case out of the housing while in the repair stand. Tie each shim pack together and identify. Do not interchange shims or shift them from one side to the other, **Figures 33-64.** Do not

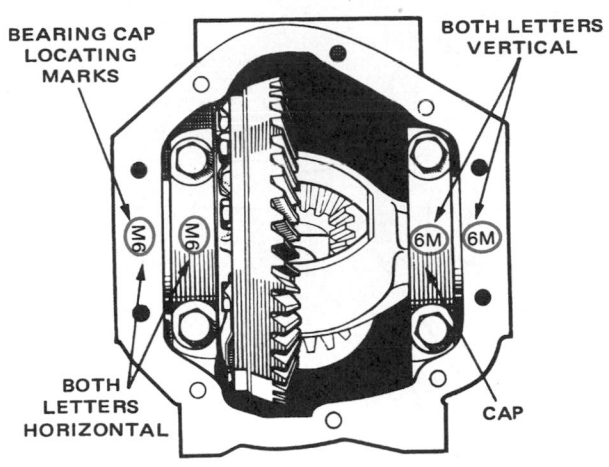

Figure 33-61. These differential case side bearing caps are factory marked for proper positioning.

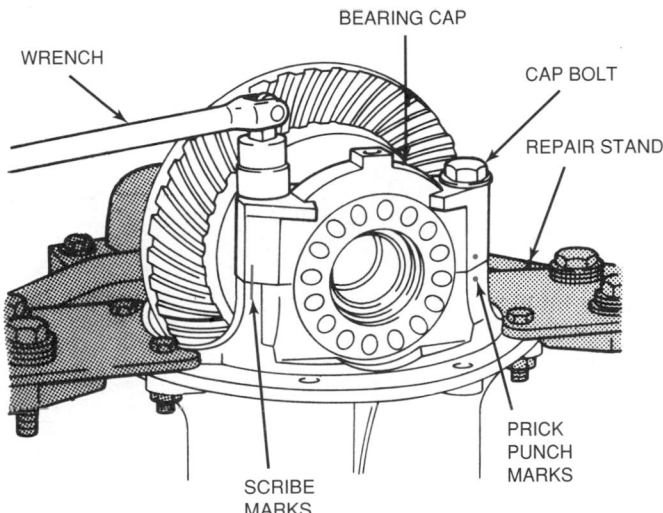

Figure 33-62. Mark the caps or carrier *before* removing the caps. (Geo)

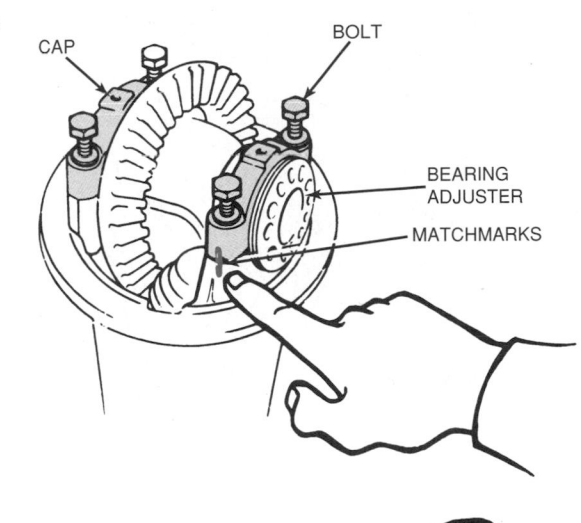

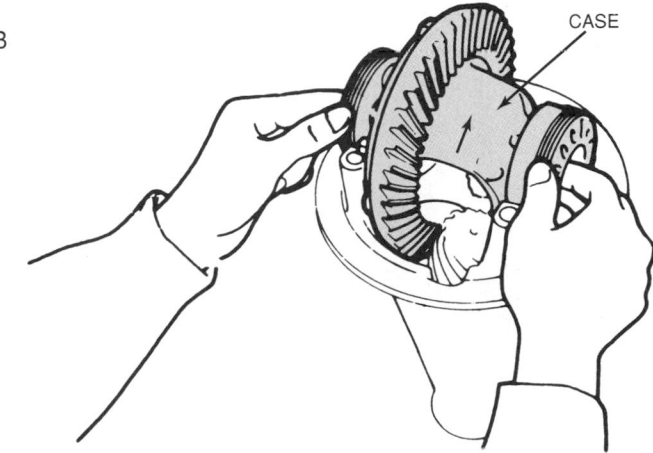

Figure 33-63. A—Placing match marks on the housing and bearing caps before removal. Loosen the bolts and remove with caps. B—The differential case and bearing should lift right out. (Toyota)

drop the side bearing outer races. Identify the races to prevent mixing them.

A special adapter is sometimes attached by means of two ring gear cap screws. A slide hammer puller is then connected to the adapter. The case is withdrawn with a series of sharp blows.

Another technique involves using a differential housing spreader, **Figure 33-65.** The spreader is installed as directed, and the turnbuckle is expanded. Never expand the housing more than specified. Consider a .020″ (0.51 mm) expansion the absolute limit. Following expansion, remove the case and immediately release the spreader.

Differential Disassembly, Inspection, and Repair

Use a suitable puller to remove the differential case side bearings (if required), **Figure 33-66.** Tie the side bearings to the outer races or cups. Free the ring gear by removing the fasteners. Tap the gear free of the case. Drive out the pinion gear lock pin and remove the pinion shaft, **Figure 33-67,** or remove the pinion shaft lock screw, **Figure 33-68.**

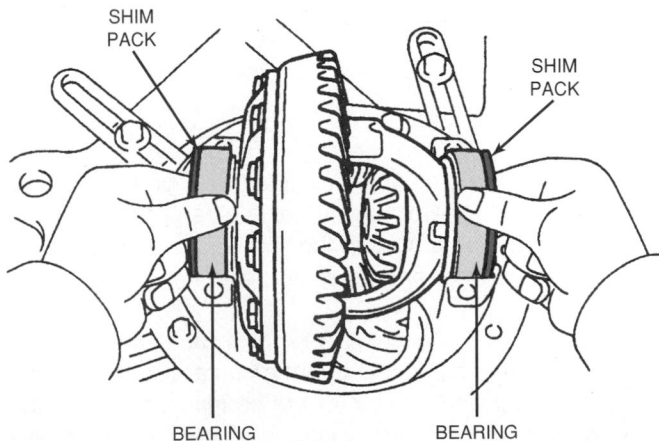

Figure 33-64. Keep the shim packs from each side with the bearings as you remove the case. Tie the shim packs and bearings from each side together. Mark them *left* and *right*. (Toyota)

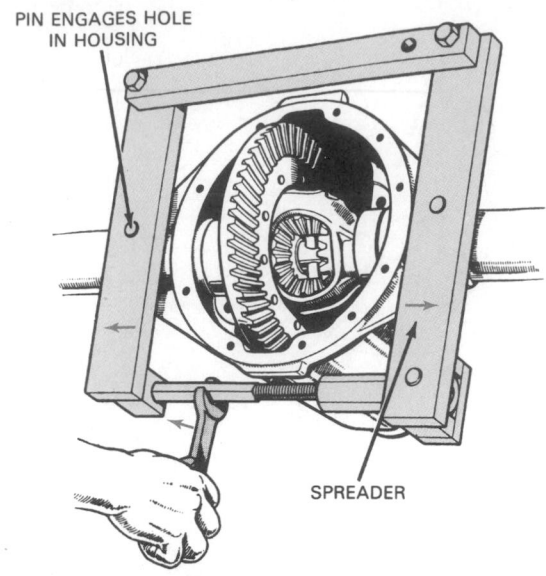

Figure 33-65. Using a housing spreader. Never expand housing more than .020″ (0.51 mm).

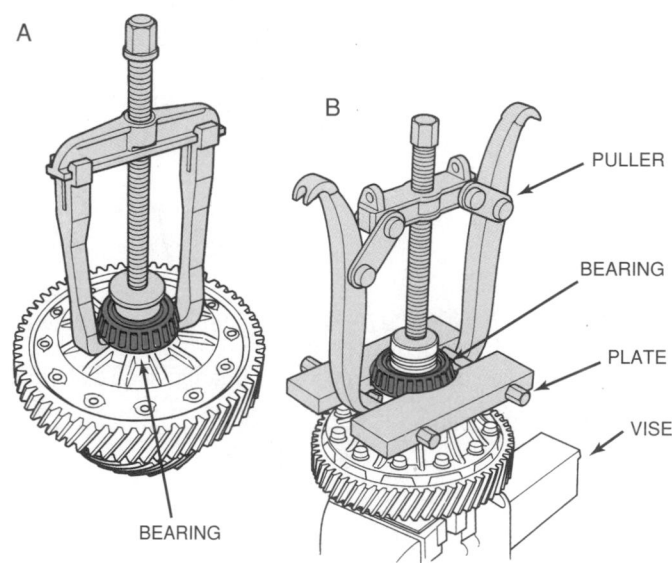

Figure 33-66. Removing the differential case side bearings. A—Using a two-leg puller. B—Using a two-leg puller and plate. (Honda)

Remove the pinion gears. Wash all parts and blow them dry. Inspect the pinion and axle side gears for excessive wear or chipping. Check the ring and drive pinion gear for scoring, chipping, and other damage.

Check Differential Case for Wear and Runout

Examine the case side bearing contact surfaces. They must be perfect with no sign of the bearing inner race having turned on them. Thrust washer surfaces inside the case must be smooth and free of excessive wear.

Place the case in a set of V-blocks and check the ring gear flange attaching surface with a dial indicator. Runout must be within specifications, **Figure 33-69.** If new side bearings are required, lubricate the case contact surface.

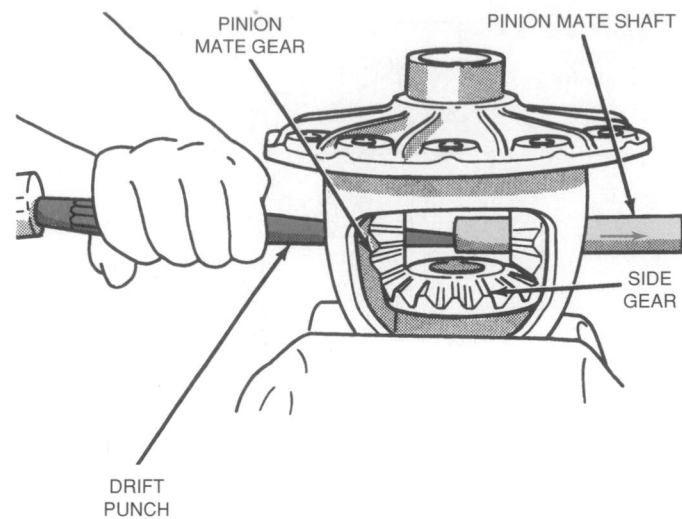

Figure 33-67. Removing the pinion mate shaft with a hammer and punch. (Dodge)

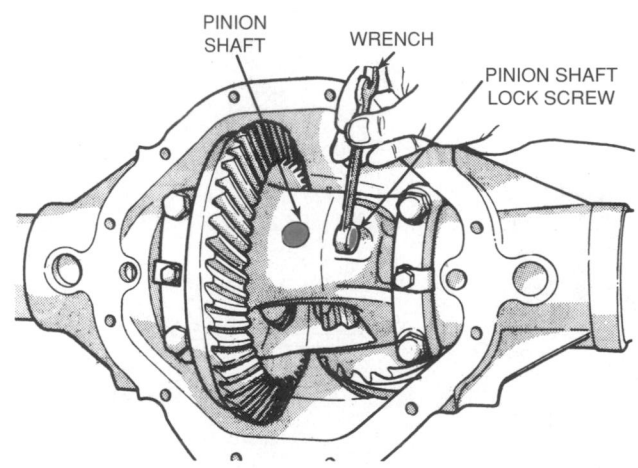

Figure 33-68. Removing the pinion shaft lock screw with a wrench. (Dodge)

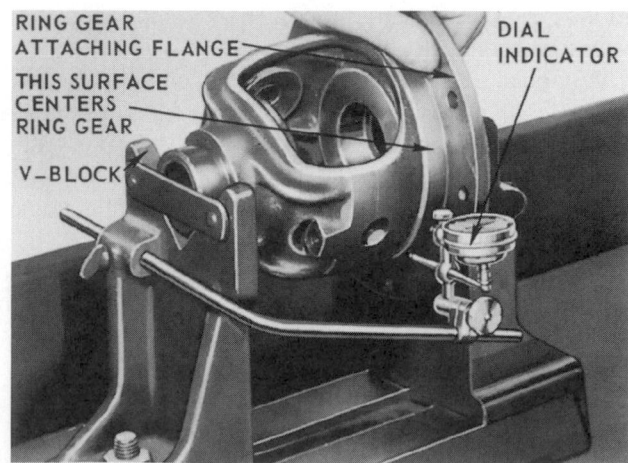

Figure 33-69. Checking ring gear centering surface runout. The attaching flange must also be checked. (GMC)

Install shims if used between the case and the bearing. Drive or press the bearings into position. Apply force to the inner cone—not to the rollers, **Figure 33-70.**

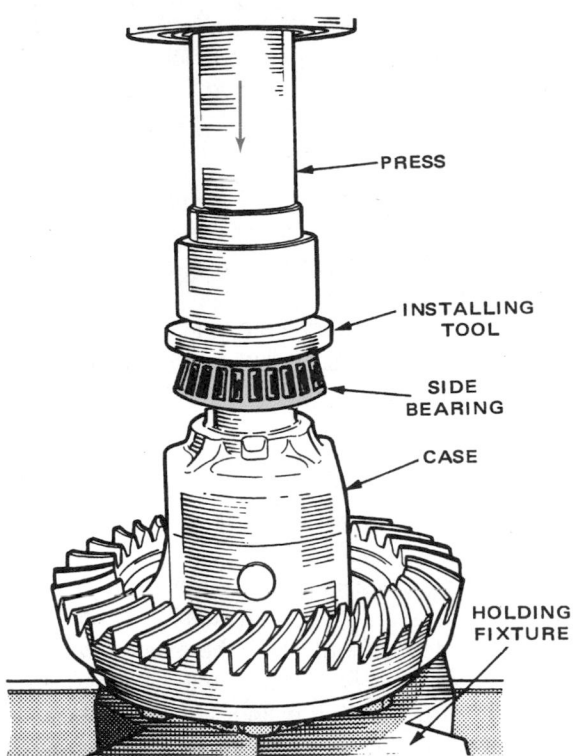

Figure 33-70. Installing a new differential side bearing. The installing tool must apply force to the *inner race only!* (Plymouth)

When new side bearings are used, use new outer cones also. Lubricate the case, thrust washers, pinions, and axle side gears. Place the side gears and washers into position in the case. "Walk" the pinion gears around the axle side gears until aligned with the shaft hole. Insert the pinion shaft spacer block and the lock pin.

Rotate the gears a few times. Then check clearance between the side gear and the thrust washer, **Figure 33-71.**

 Note: Where inner axle end C-locks are used, it will be necessary to remove the pinion shaft and spacer block to install the axles.

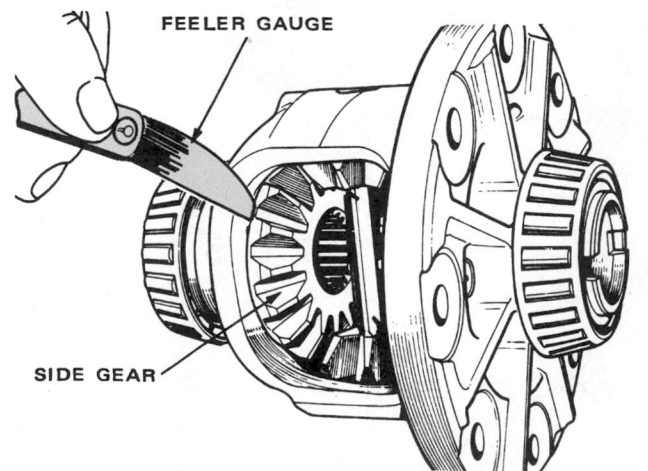

Figure 33-71. Method of checking clearance between the axle side gear and the thrust washer. (Plymouth)

New Ring Gear Installation

When either a new ring gear or a pinion drive gear is required, both gears must be replaced. Never change one without the other. Always check the new ring and pinion to make certain that they are a matched set. The match number on the pinion must be the same as the number on the ring. Note the numbers on the ring and pinion in **Figure 33-72.** The number 4 appears on both the ring and the pinion, thus indicating they are a matched set. The + 1/2 is a marking to indicate the variation from a standard pinion depth setting. This number is needed to determine the thickness of the pinion shaft shim pack. This will be discussed under pinion drive gear installation.

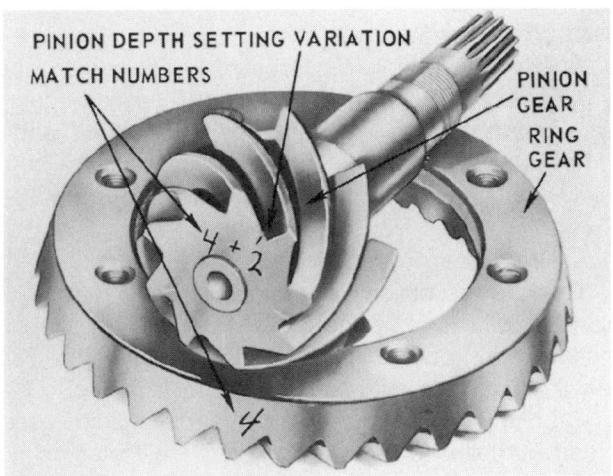

Figure 33-72. Typical ring and pinion gear markings to indicate a matched set.

Check the case flange and the attaching surface of the ring gear for the slightest sign of burring, dirt, and other problems. The two contact surfaces must be spotlessly clean.

Insert several guide studs in the ring gear to provide accurate alignment with the differential case. Position the ring gear. Lubricate all attaching cap screws. Start the cap screws into ring gear and run them up alternately until the ring gear just touches the case. Remove the guide studs and run up the remaining fasteners.

Tighten the ring gear fasteners alternately, first on one side and then on the other. Bring the fasteners to one-half recommended torque the first time around. Go over the fasteners a second time, bringing them to full torque. If guide studs are not available, run a cap screw into each side of the ring. Pull up on the ring to align the ring with the case.

 Note: Use ring gear fasteners only. Do not use regular cap screws in place of ring gear fasteners. Fasteners must be lubricated. Fasteners must be a snug fit in both the case and the ring gear. Do not use lock washers unless used in the original installation. Some cap screws require the use of a liquid adhesive. Follow the manufacturer's recommendations.

Some ring gear setups require the gear to be brought to a specified temperature before installation. Use a special heating oven or oil bath heater. Never attempt to heat the ring gear with an acetylene torch, as this can remove the tempering.

Gear Ratio Must Be Correct

The new ring and pinion set must have the correct number of teeth so that the desired **gear ratio** (number of times the pinion gear turns during each drive ring turn) is maintained. If the ratio is to be changed, make certain that the new set is adaptable to the differential case. On some installations, different cases are used, depending on the gear ratio.

Check Ring Gear Runout

After the differential is mounted in the carrier, check the **runout** of the ring gear. If runout is beyond specified limits, remove the ring gear. Check for nicks, burrs, and dirt on the contact surfaces. Reassemble and check runout again. Runout must be within specified limits, **Figure 33-73.**

Pinion Drive Gear Removal

Remove the pinion flange retaining nut. Remove the pinion flange (see replacing pinion shaft seal and/or pinion flange in first part of chapter). With differential case removed, tap the pinion shaft inward until it is free.

On one type of pinion arrangement, the pinion assembly can be pulled off the carrier after the fasteners have been removed, **Figure 33-74.**

Be careful to save all shims. Tie individual shims in the pack together and identify as to location. Measure the thickness of each shim and write it down in case shims are lost. Wash all parts of the assembly and blow them dry. Inspect parts for wear, chipping, and scoring.

Installing New Pinion Bearings

Remove both front and rear bearing cups from the carrier. Do not mar the surface of the counterbore during removal. **Figure 33-75** shows the use of a puller in removing a bearing cup.

Check the bores. Lubricate and install new cups. Drive the cups in squarely to the correct depth. If adjusting shims are used beneath the inner cup, be certain they are spotlessly clean and in place. If a new pinion gear is being installed, adjust the shim pack as required.

The pinion assembly in **Figure 33-76** uses shims for positioning the pinion gear. Preload is controlled by a collapsible spacer.

Remove the pinion shaft inner bearing. Lubricate the pinion shaft. Install a spacer or shim, if used. Drive the bearing firmly into position. Place the pinion gear against a soft, clean surface. Apply pressure to the inner cone—not to the rollers, **Figure 33-77.** If pinion depth must be checked, do not install the collapsible spacer on the pinion shaft until the depth check is made.

Checking and Adjusting Pinion Depth

Pinion gear depth (distance from face of pinion gear to centerline of ring gear) is critical. Each matched ring and pinion set is tested at the factory for the relationship between the ring gear and pinion that will produce the best tooth contact pattern. This relationship (actual pinion depth)

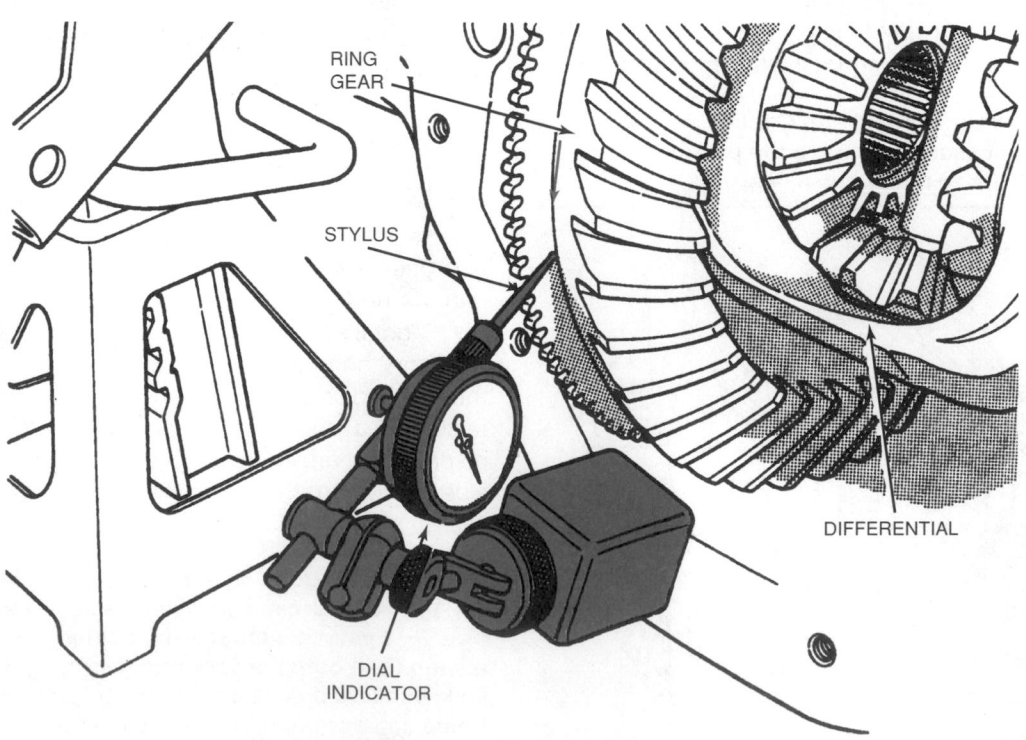

Figure 33-73. Measuring ring gear runout with a dial indicator. (Dodge)

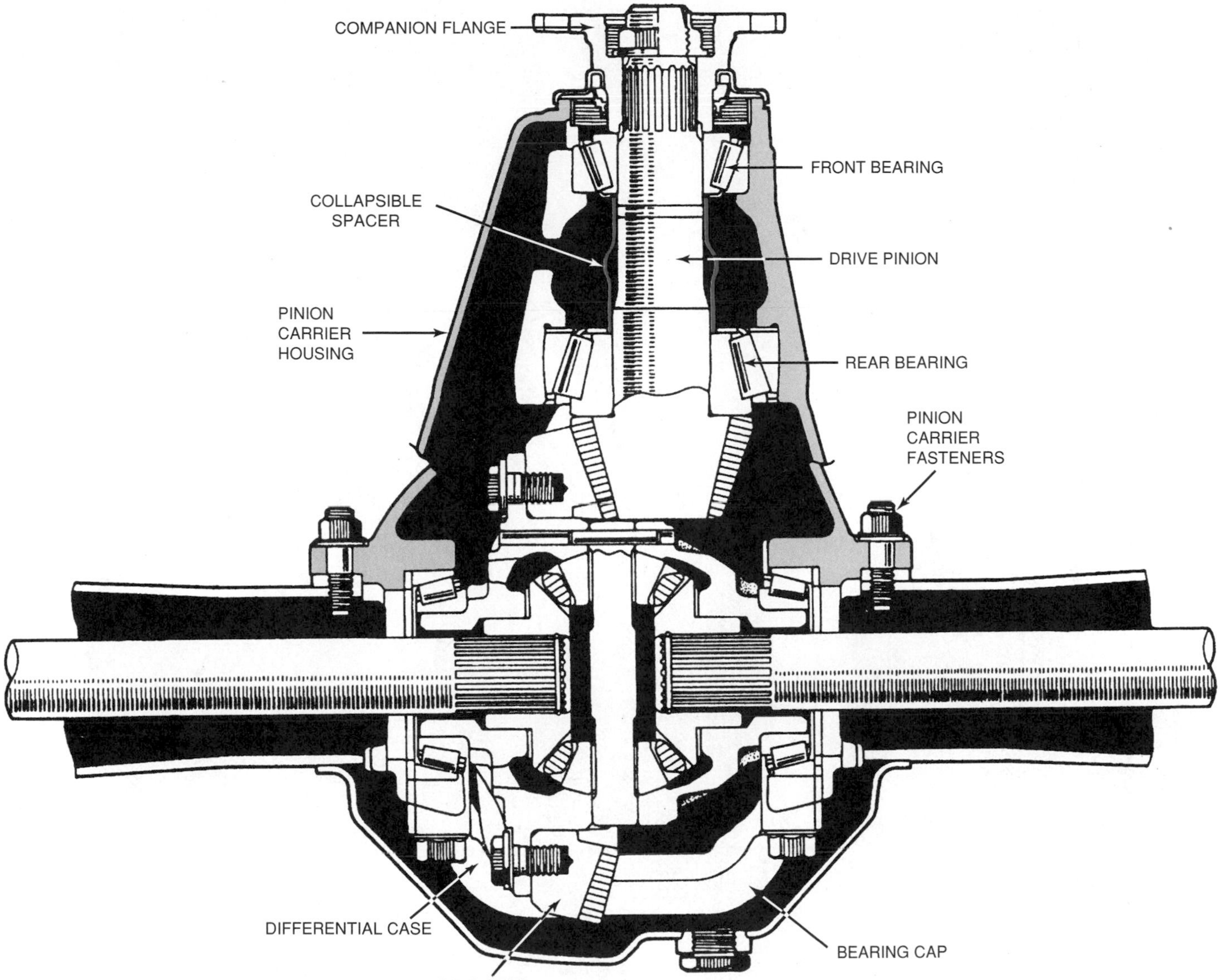

COMPANION FLANGE

FRONT BEARING

COLLAPSIBLE
SPACER

DRIVE PINION

PINION
CARRIER
HOUSING

REAR BEARING

PINION
CARRIER
FASTENERS

DIFFERENTIAL CASE

BEARING CAP

RING GEAR

Figure 33-74.   Removable pinion carrier housing. Note the collapsible spacer. (Toyota)

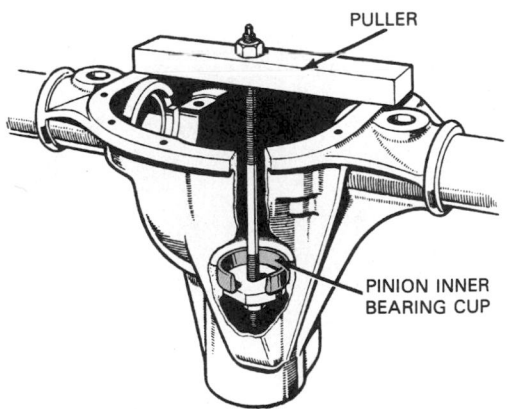

PULLER

PINION INNER
BEARING CUP

Figure 33-75.   Pulling the pinion inner bearing cup from the carrier.

is compared to a nominal (standard) pinion depth. The difference is marked on the pinion gear.

If the actual pinion depth is such that the pinion is closer to the ring gear centerline, the amount in thou-

sandths marked on the pinion is preceded by a - (minus) sign. If the pinion depth is such that the pinion is a greater distance from the centerline, the amount is preceded by a + (plus) sign. The position of the pinion in relation to the ring gear centerline for a + (plus) and a - (minus) pinion marking is pictured in **Figure 33-78.**

Pinion depth is controlled by placing shims between the pinion gear and the bearing, **Figures 33-76, 33-77, 33-78;** between the inner bearing outer race or cup and the carrier; or between the pinion retainer and the carrier face, **Figure 33-74.**

As illustrated in **Figure 33-78,** shims must be added for pinions marked with a minus and removed for pinions marked with a plus. An exception to this is the Ford pinion illustrated in **Figure 33-74.** In this design, the addition of shims is required for a plus marking. Pinion depth should be checked with special gauges when a new ring and pinion set, new pinion bearings, or a new carrier is installed.

If the original ring and pinion, inner bearing, and carrier will be reused, the original shim pack will give the proper

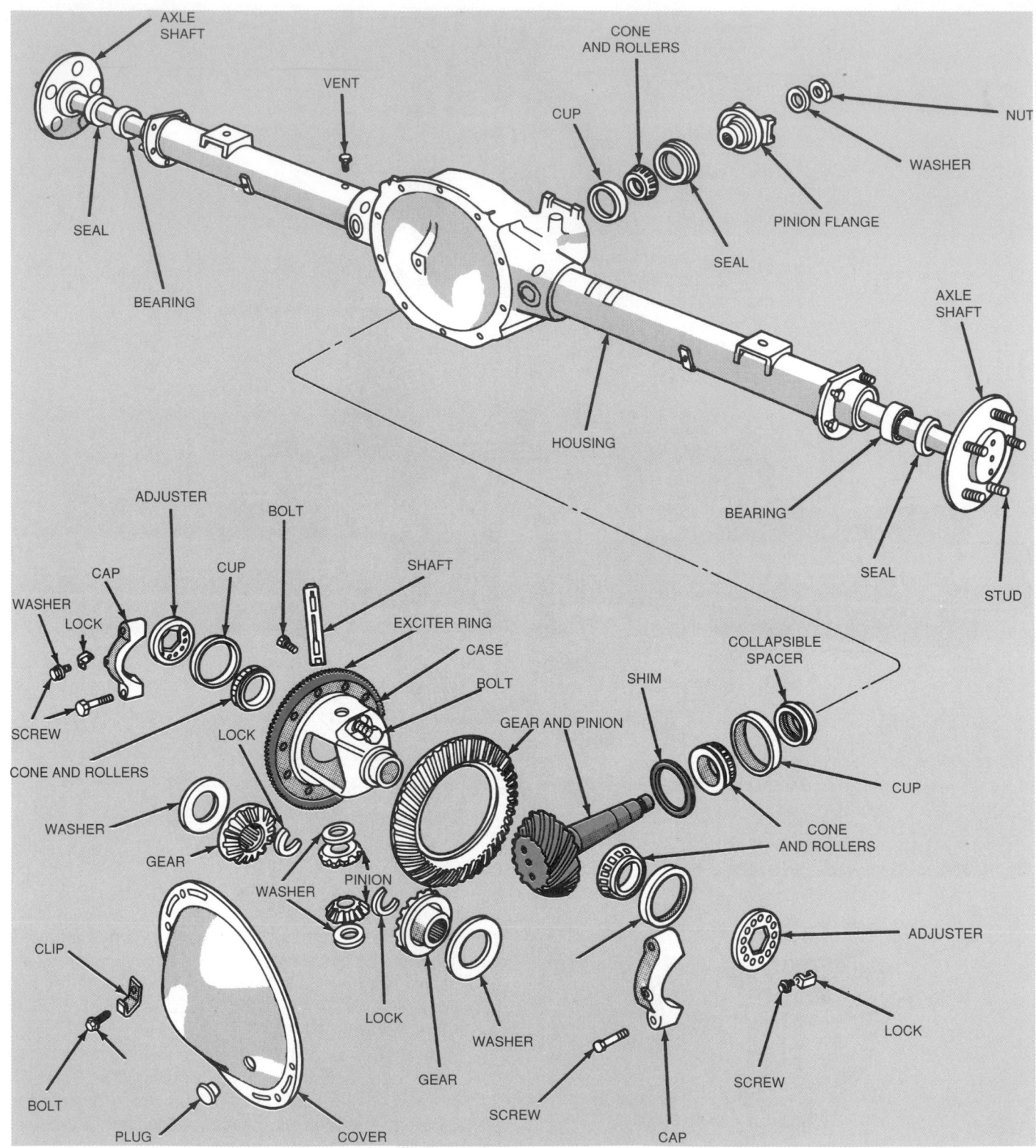

Figure 33-76. Exploded view of a differential assembly that uses shims for positioning the pinion gear. Note the rear wheel anti-lock brake sensor exciter ring. (Dodge)

depth. To set the pinion depth, use a special gauge designed for that purpose. There are numerous types available.

One type of setting gauge is shown in **Figure 33-79.** The bearings are lubricated and held in position while the

gauge plate and clamp plate are secured with the clamp screw. Note the gauge body resting in the case side bearing bores.

The clamp screw is tightened until the bearings are preloaded to 20 inch-pounds (2.26 N·m). Place the gauge

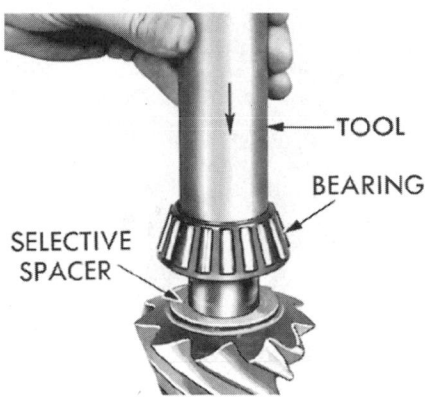

Figure 33-77. Driving a pinion shaft bearing. Note that the pinion depth spacer is in position. (Dodge)

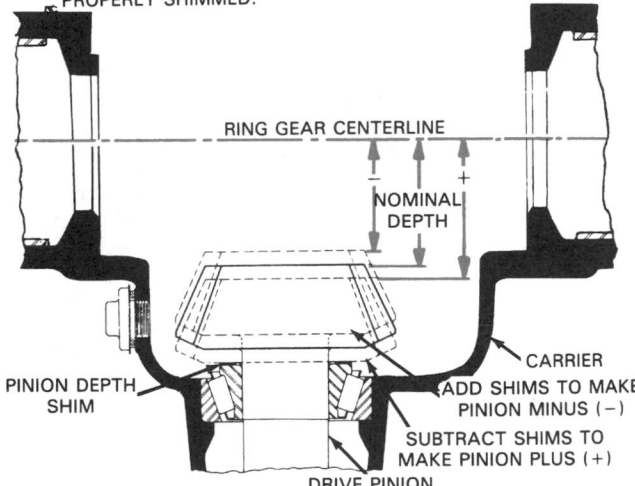

PINION DEPTHS MARKED "−" (MINUS), NOMINAL DEPTH, AND "+" (PLUS) ILLUSTRATE THE RELATIVE POSITION EACH PINION WOULD SET IN RELATION TO THE CENTER-LINE OF THE RING GEAR AFTER BEING GAUGED AND PROPERLY SHIMMED.

Figure 33-78. Relative distance from the ring gear centerline for a pinion marked with a minus (−), a plus (+), and a nominal (0). (Pontiac)

body in the case side bearing bores. The bores and the gauge must be clean.

Mount a dial indicator on the gauge body. The indicator stem must contact the body plunger. Swing the gauge body so that the plunger is clear of the gauge plate. Set the indicator to zero. Swing the gauge body in the bores so that the plunger moves across the gauge plate. Swing it back and forth until the highest reading is noted.

Another type of gauging device is being used in **Figure 33-80.** A special gauge block is inserted in the pinion bearings and brought to specified torque. The arbor is held in place by hand or with bearing cups. Selective thickness spacers are tried between the face of the gauge block and the arbor. When a spacer that will just fit is found, write down the thickness. Examine the pinion for a plus or minus amount. If the chosen spacer is marked .094 and the pinion is marked minus 2, add .002 in. (0.05 mm) to the thickness

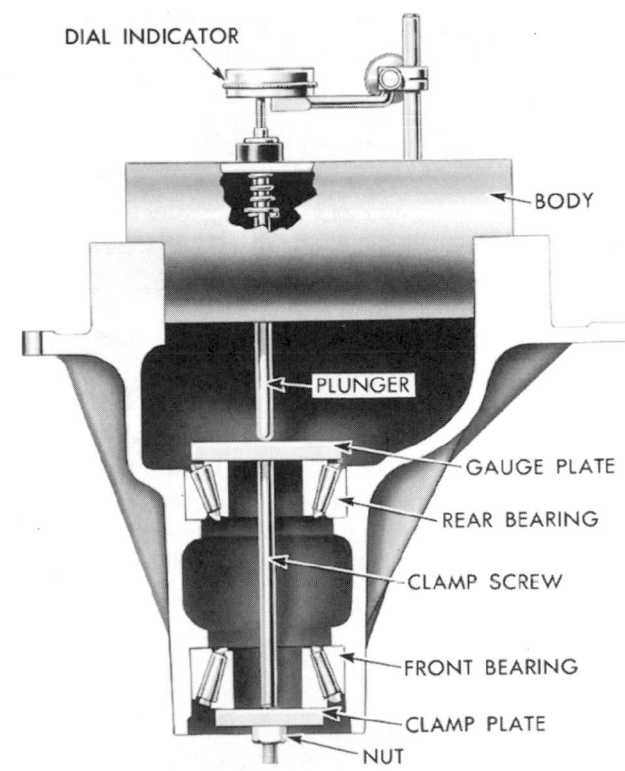

Figure 33-79. One type of pinion setting gauge.

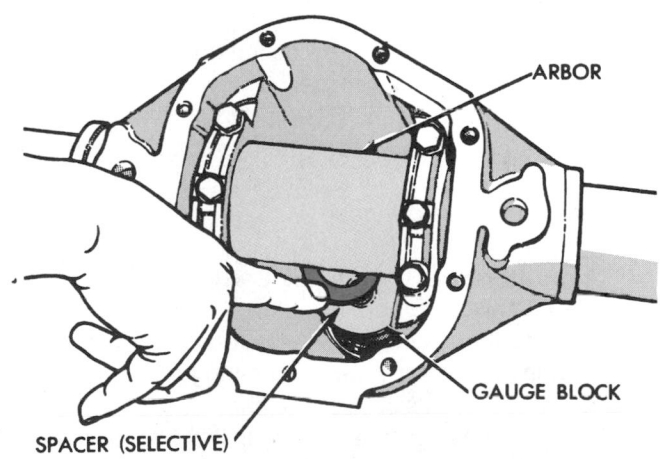

Figure 33-80. Measuring a housing for correct pinion shim thickness with a special gauge block tool. (Dodge)

of the chosen .094 in. (2.38 mm) spacer. The correct spacer to place between the pinion gear and bearing will then be .094 + .002 = .096 in. (2.38 + 0.05 = 2.43 mm).

If a new pinion gear is being used in the same carrier and with the original bearings, adjust the original shim pack by the plus or minus amount marked on the pinion.

 Note: When the pinion is marked with a plus number, subtract this amount from the shim pack. When a minus number is used, add this amount to the thickness of the shim pack. The Ford pinion in Figure 33-74 is an exception. For this specific setup, reverse the procedure.

Install the pinion after determining the correct depth setting shim pack. Lubricate all parts before assembly. Parts must be clean and free of burrs.

Pinion Preload Must Be Correct

To prevent the pinion gear from moving away from the ring gear under load, the pinion bearings must be properly preloaded. If preload shims are used, add or subtract shims until the preload is correct when the pinion flange nut is brought to the specified torque.

When the pinion flange retaining nut is torqued, turn the pinion shaft several turns to allow the bearings to seat before checking preload.

When preload shims and a solid spacer are used, manufacturers may recommend tightening the pinion nut to a specified torque. Follow the manufacturer's instructions. When a collapsible preload spacer is used, the directions may call for bringing the nut up to the original mark (old flange being used) plus an additional amount such as 1/8 turn or 1/32" (0.79 mm).

Another technique involves gradually tightening the retaining nut to a specific bearing preload. Preload is measured with an inch-pound torque wrench. It should be equal to the preload before disassembly. Check preload frequently during the tightening process to avoid exceeding recommended preload. A few additional inch-pounds may be recommended. This method will work with either a new or used flange.

If the bearing preload is exceeded on designs employing a collapsible preload spacer, a new spacer must be installed. Do not try to correct by backing off the pinion nut to obtain the correct preload. When preload is exceeded, the spacer is collapsed to the point where the ring and pinion contact pattern is disturbed.

Installing Differential Case in the Carrier (Threaded Adjuster Type)

Lubricate the differential side bearings and place cups on the bearings. Lubricate the side bearing bores in the carrier to allow easy cup side movement.

Place the case in the carrier. If the ring and pinion gearset is of the nonhunting type (any one pinion gear tooth contacts only a certain number of ring gear teeth), make certain that the marked ring and pinion teeth are meshed. See **Figure 33-81.** Hunting-type gearsets (any one pinion gear contacts all ring gear teeth) will not be marked and may be meshed in any position.

Move the assembly in the bores until a small amount of *backlash* (play between ring and pinion gear) is present. Then, install the threaded adjusters snugly against the bearing cups. Adjusters must be installed with about the same number of threads showing on the outside of each adjuster.

Install the bearing caps so that the marks are aligned. Insert the cap fasteners and bring them to the correct torque. Check for smooth operation of the adjusters as the fasteners are torqued. If binding is experienced, remove and check for dirt, burrs, and nicks. Following full torquing, loosen the fasteners and retorque to around 25 foot-pounds

Figure 33-81. The nonhunting gearset marking should be aligned when meshing the ring to the pinion. (Ford)

(33.90 N·m). Some manufacturers recommend loosening the fasteners and then torquing one fastener on each cap to full torque.

Loosen the right-hand adjuster (or pinion side of ring gear) and tighten the left-hand adjuster (on back side of ring gear) until no backlash is present. Rotate the ring gear while tightening the left-hand adjuster. **Figure 33-82** illustrates how the adjusters are moved using spanner wrenches.

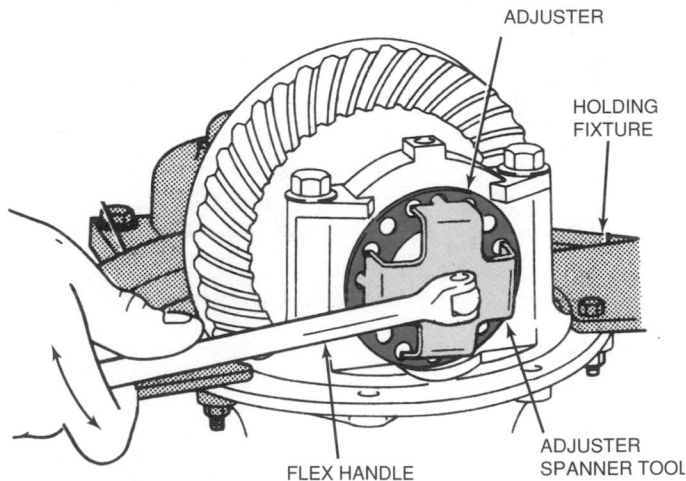

Figure 33-82. Adjusting bearing backlash with an adjuster spanner tool and a flex handle. (Geo)

Tighten left-hand bearing cap fasteners to full torque. Turn the right-hand adjuster in until the left-hand bearing is in firm contact with the left-hand adjuster. Loosen the right-hand adjuster and retighten. At this point, the case bearings are just snug with no end play or preload. There is no backlash between the ring and pinion.

Set up a dial indicator to check backlash. The indicator stem must be in line with the direction of tooth travel. Look at **Figure 33-83.**

After bringing the right-hand cap fasteners to full torque, turn the right-hand adjuster in two or three notches. This will preload the bearings and should give the specified backlash.

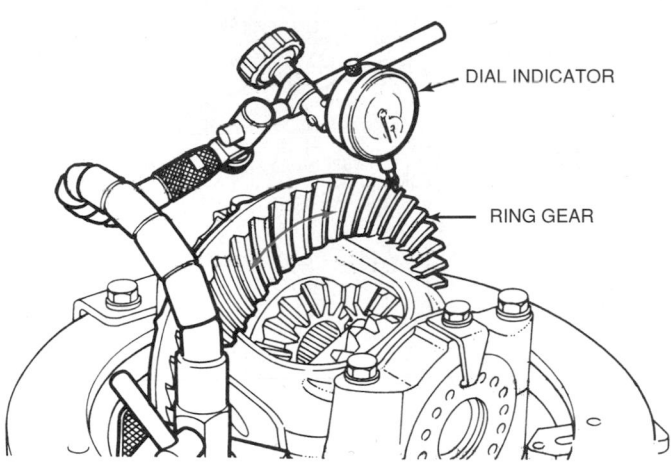

Figure 33-83. A dial indicator set up to measure gear backlash. (Chrysler)

Check the backlash at four different spots around the ring. Leave the ring in the position producing the smallest amount of backlash. If backlash is as specified (around .006-.008 in. or 0.15-0.20 mm), insert the adjuster locks. Torque the lock fasteners.

If backlash varies at the different points more than the specified allowable variation (around .002 in. or 0.05 mm), check the ring gear for runout. If necessary, the ring must be removed, cleaned, reassembled, and rechecked. Check case flange runout also, **Figure 33-84.**

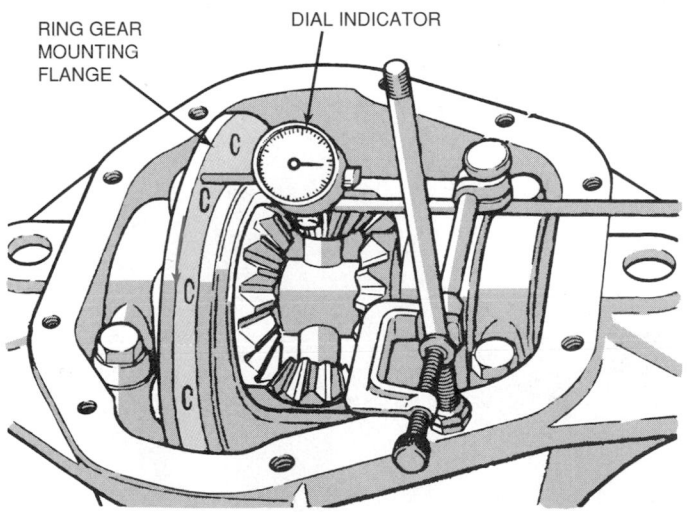

Figure 33-84. Checking the ring gear mounting flange for runout with a dial indicator. (Dodge)

If backlash is not quite as specified, loosen one adjuster and tighten the other until backlash is correct. Bearing cap fasteners must be at full torque during these adjustments.

When moving the adjusters, move the adjuster that is being loosened *two* notches. Move the adjuster that is being tightened one notch. Then tighten the adjuster that was loosened one notch. This procedure assures that solid contact is made. It will prevent loosening in service.

Another method that is sometimes specified for preloading differential side bearings involves bringing the adjusters up so that no end play exists in the bearings. With no backlash between the ring and pinion, a dial indicator is used to measure the carrier spread as the right-hand adjuster is tightened. When the carrier spread (distance between side bearing bores being increased due to bearing preloading) reaches the specified amount, the backlash should be close to specifications. If not, adjust by loosening one adjuster and tightening the other.

Installing the Differential Case in the Carrier— Shim Preload Adjustment

Clean the side bearing carrier bores. Lubricate the bearings and install the cups. If old bearings are being used, use the original shim packs. Place shims on each end of the bearing cups. Start the case into the carrier bores.

If a new case, new carrier, or new bearings are used, the original shim packs will not guarantee the correct preload. In these instances, it will be necessary to determine the proper thickness shim pack.

In general, the selection of shims involves placing enough shims or spacers on each side to remove all side play (just snug, no preload). Refer to **Figure 33-85.**

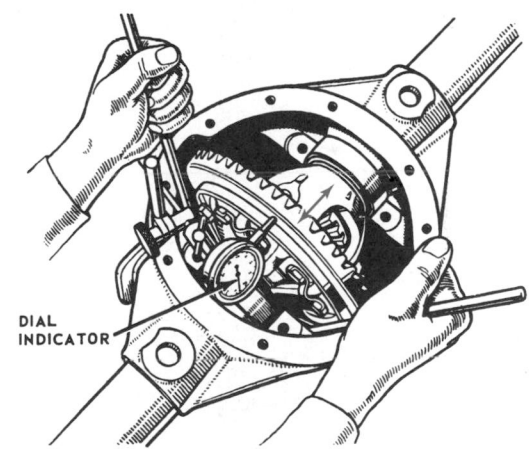

Figure 33-85. Checking side play in the differential case bearings. Add shims until the backlash just disappears.

The manufacturer will usually require that a spacer of a certain thickness be placed on one side to start with. This will aid in having the ring and pinion backlash within workable measurements when the side play is removed.

Shims may then be moved from one side to the other until the backlash is correct. See **Figure 33-86.**

When the backlash is correct (check in four places at 90° intervals around the ring gear) and there is no existing end play or preload, add two shims of equal thickness, one on each side. Use the thickness specified by the manufacturer.

Use a carrier spreader, if needed, to permit the installation of preload shims. Lubricate the shims and avoid undue pounding. Light tapping on the shims with a soft hammer is permissible.

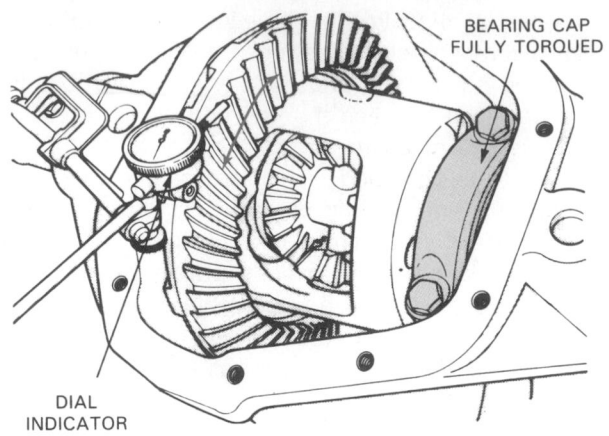

Figure 33-86.   Checking backlash between the ring and pinion gears. Caps should be in place and fully torqued. (Chrysler)

There are some differential assemblies that place the side bearing shims between the carrier and the bearing inner cone. Look at **Figure 33-87**. Some production side bearing spacers or shims cannot be reused. They must be replaced with steel service spacers and shims.

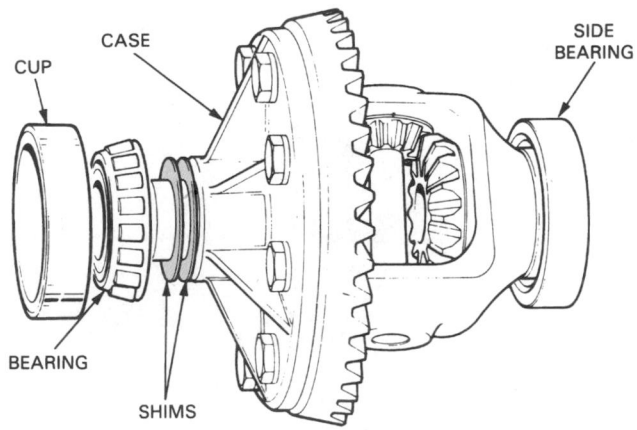

Figure 33-87.   This differential carrier uses shims between the case and the side bearing cones.

Some manufacturers specify that a specific preload adjustment check be made by using a torque wrench on one side of the ring gear fasteners or on the pinion shaft. When preload and backlash adjustments are as specified, recheck the torque on the bearing cap fasteners. Rap the top of the fasteners with a hammer and retorque.

Checking the Tooth Contact Pattern

The relationship between the ring and pinion gears must be adjusted to produce the correct *contact pattern.*

To check the contact pattern, (preload and backlash must be correct) cover all the ring gear teeth with a light coating of hydrated ferric oxide or some other suitable compound. Some new gear sets come with a special compound for this purpose. Apply the compound to the teeth with a reasonably stiff paint brush. See **Figure 33-88**.

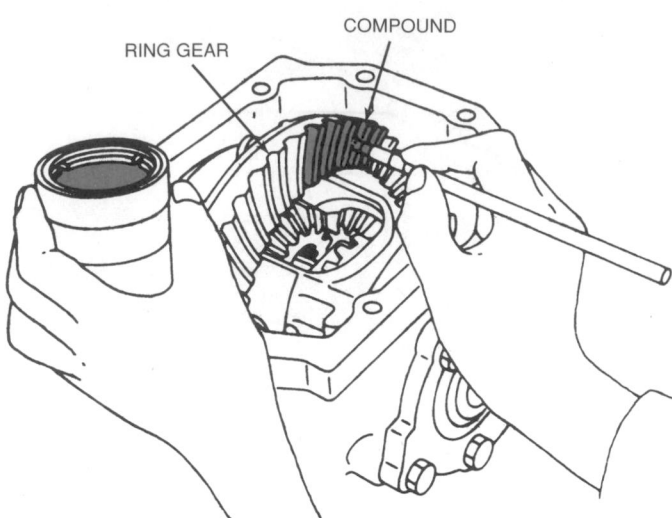

Figure 33-88.   Applying a special pattern compound to the gear teeth with a brush. The compound will show the tooth contact pattern when the gears are rotated. Incorrect tooth contact can produce noise and/or a short gear life span. (Infiniti)

Using a wrench, turn the pinion shaft in the normal forward drive direction while creating a drag on the ring gear. The technician in **Figure 33-89** is using a brass drift to bind the ring gear. Continue turning the pinion until the ring gear has made one full turn. This will produce a *drive pattern.* The drive pattern is produced by the pinion gear driving the ring gear, **Figure 33-90**.

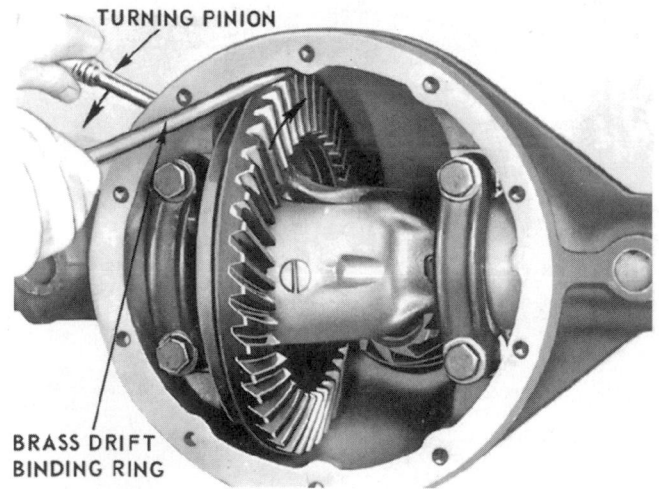

Figure 33-89.   Cranking (turning) the pinion while binding the ring gear to produce a drive pattern.

Turn the pinion in the opposite direction while binding the ring to produce a *coast pattern.* This is the pattern produced when the ring gear drives the pinion gear.

There is no exact pattern that must be formed. The pattern shape varies, depending on gear set design, wear, and load. In general, however, the pattern (contact area) should be even around the ring. Unevenness indicates excessive ring runout.

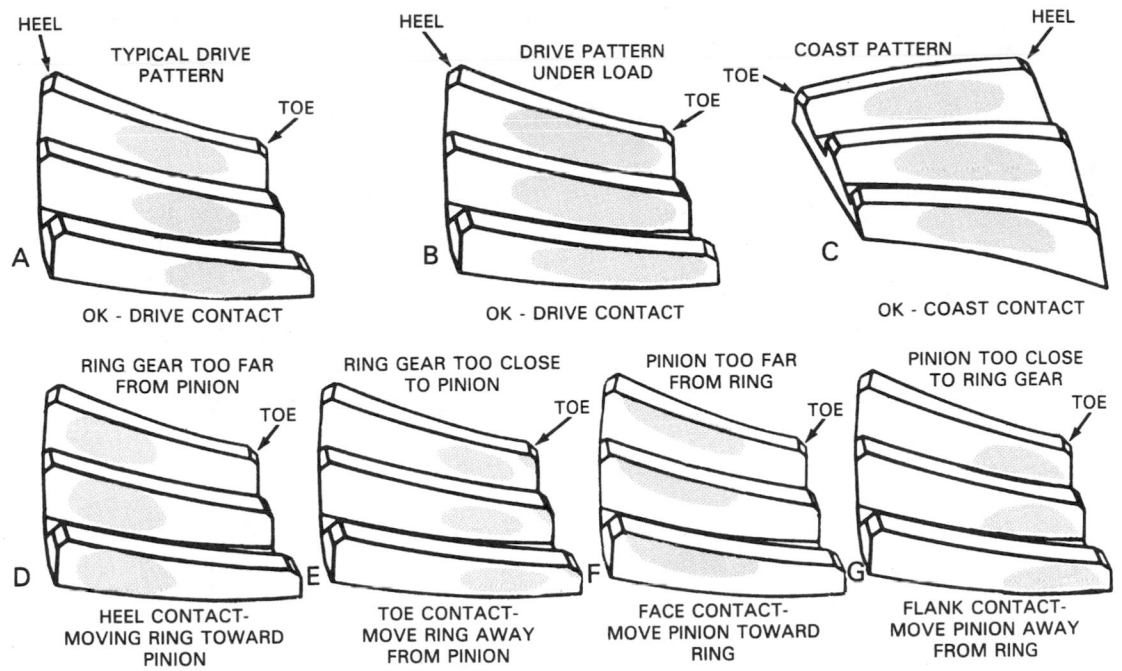

Figure 33-90.   Typical ring gear tooth contact patterns.

The drive pattern should be centrally located between the top and bottom of the tooth. It can be somewhat closer to the toe. Under increased loading, the pattern spreads out and tends to move towards the heel of the tooth. When the point of heavy loading is reached (pulling, hills, or rapid acceleration), the pattern may extend almost the full distance from toe to heel. The drive side of a ring gear tooth is the convex side. The coast side of a ring gear tooth is the concave side. Note the gear tooth nomenclature in **Figure 33-91.**

The coast pattern should also be centralized between the top and bottom of the tooth. In some cases, it may be a little longer and closer to the toe. Examine the pattern closely for the presence of thin, hard pressure lines that indicate an area of narrow contact that will produce unusually high localized pressure. Such lines should not be present.

A heel contact pattern is caused by excessive backlash. It is corrected by moving the ring towards the pinion. Toe contact indicates insufficient backlash. To correct this problem, move the ring away from the pinion. Face contact indicates the pinion is set too far from the ring. To correct, move the pinion toward the ring. Flank contact requires moving the pinion away from the ring gear.

When moving either the ring or the pinion to correct the contact pattern, move in small amounts. Make certain that the bearings are properly preloaded, the cap fasteners are fully torqued, and the backlash is within specifications before rechecking the pattern.

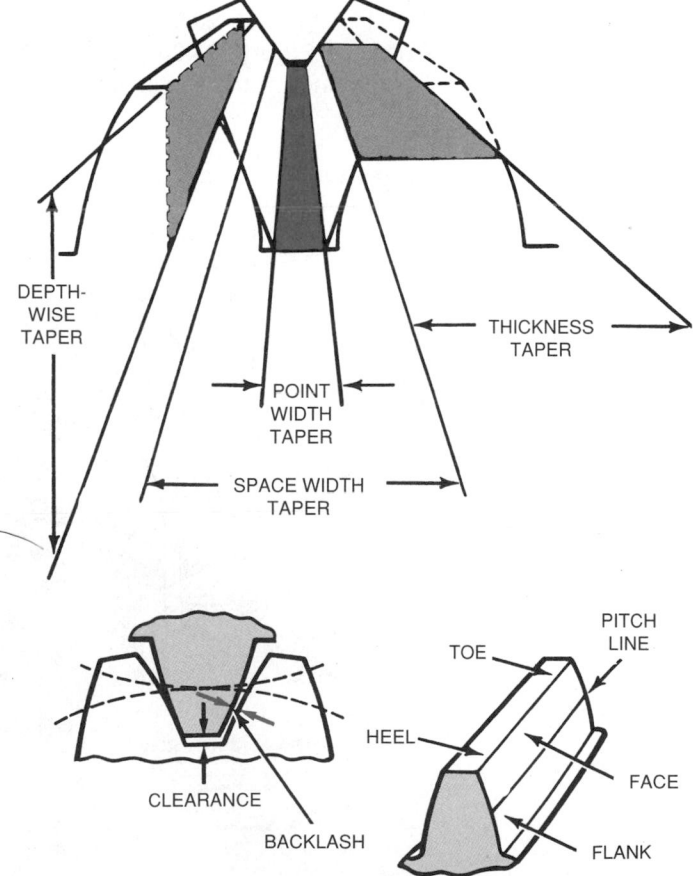

Figure 33-91.   Common gear tooth nomenclature. (GM)

Limited Slip Differential Service

The *limited slip* (also called Sure Grip, No-Spin, Anti-Spin, Positive Traction) type of traction differential uses friction members (cone or disc clutch). When one wheel attempts to spin, driving force will still be applied to the non-spinning wheel by the differential. See **Figure 33-92.**

In the conventional, nontraction differential, when one wheel spins, no driving force is applied to the other. A trac-

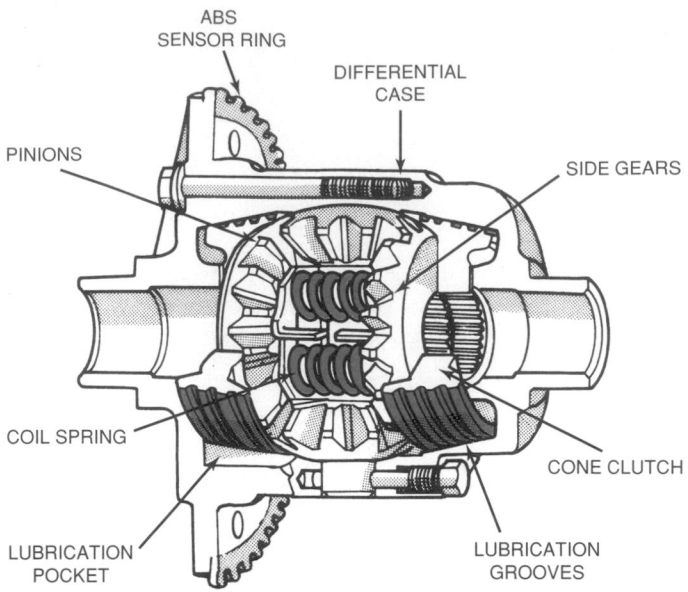

Figure 33-92. Cross-sectional view of a traction-type differential that incorporates coil springs. Note the anti-lock brake system sensor (excitor) ring. (Chrysler)

tion differential, which uses a clutch pack on either side of axle side gears, is pictured in **Figure 33-93.**

In the Sure Grip design, **Figure 33-93,** two pinion shafts are used. Note that the ends of the shafts are wedge shaped. They operate in V-shaped ramps. When a driving force is applied to the ring gear, the pinion shafts slide up the V-ramps and compress both clutch packs. This results in a mechanical connection between both axles.

When rounding a corner, the outside axle turns faster than the inner axle. This causes the pinion shaft on the outer side to slide down its ramp. This releases the clutch pack on that side and allows normal differential action.

If one wheel spins, the clutch pack on that side is released. The pack on the slower-turning wheel causes it to remain clutched to the differential case. It will thus receive turning force despite differential action. **Figure 33-94** depicts a cross section view of a traction differential that has a preload springs instead of V-shaped ramps found in the Sure Grip type.

A somewhat different type of traction differential is illustrated in **Figure 33-95.** This unit uses cone clutch brakes, one on each side of the axle side gears, to provide traction.

Normal differential action causes clutches to slip. When one wheel starts spinning, the slower-moving axle still remains clutched to the differential case and will therefore receive some driving force.

Cone brakes are kept preloaded to the case by means of preload springs. The normal tendency for the side gears to move away from the pinions under load also increases the cone loading. See **Figure 33-95.**

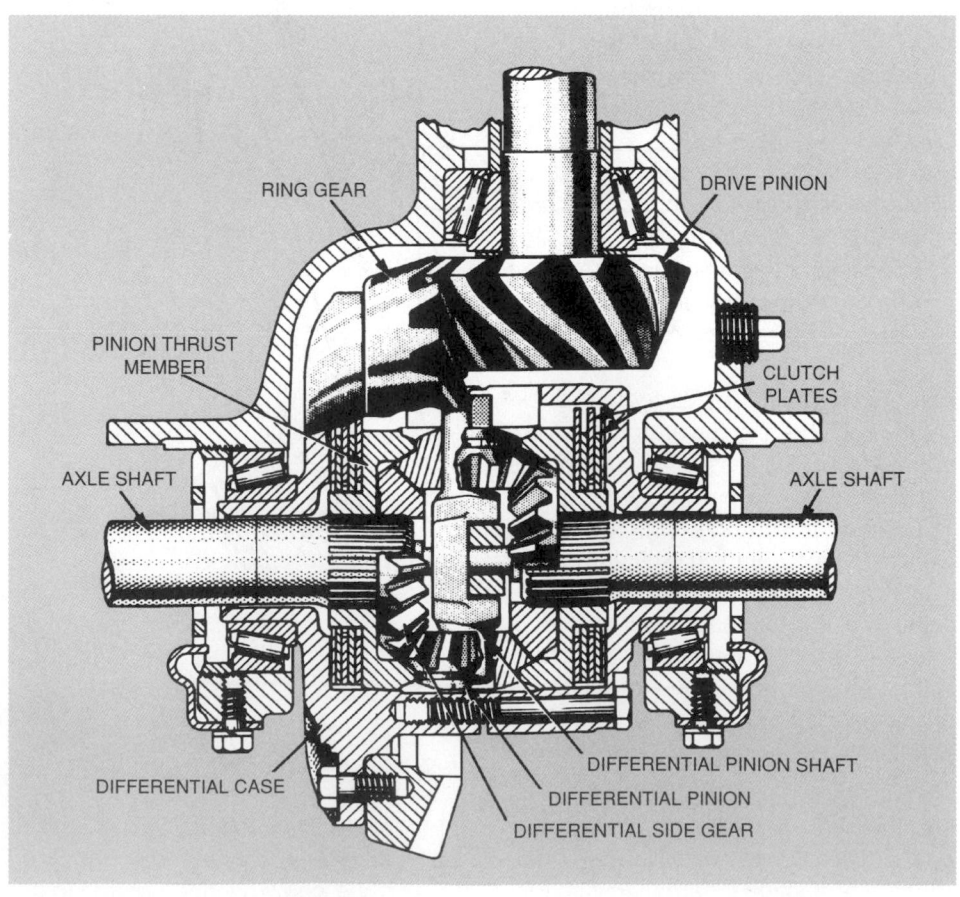

Figure 33-93. Cross section of a Sure Grip differential.

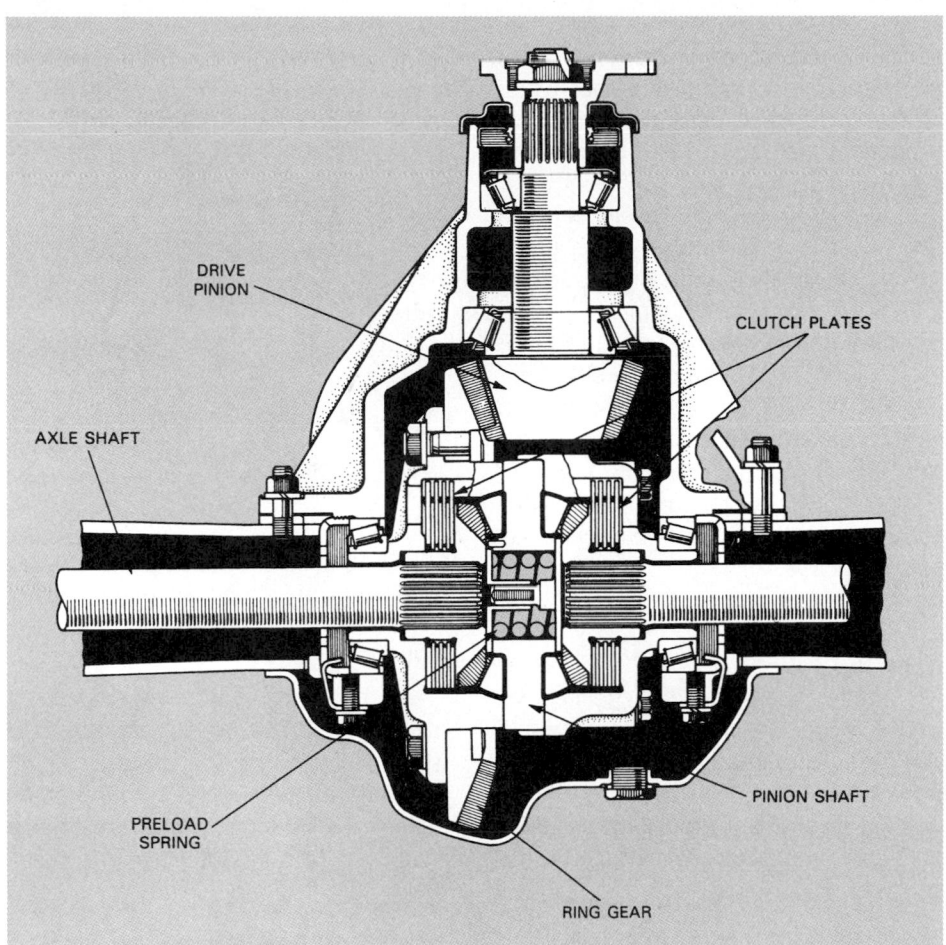

Figure 33-94. This limited slip traction-type differential uses a single preload spring. Note the clutch plates. (Toyota)

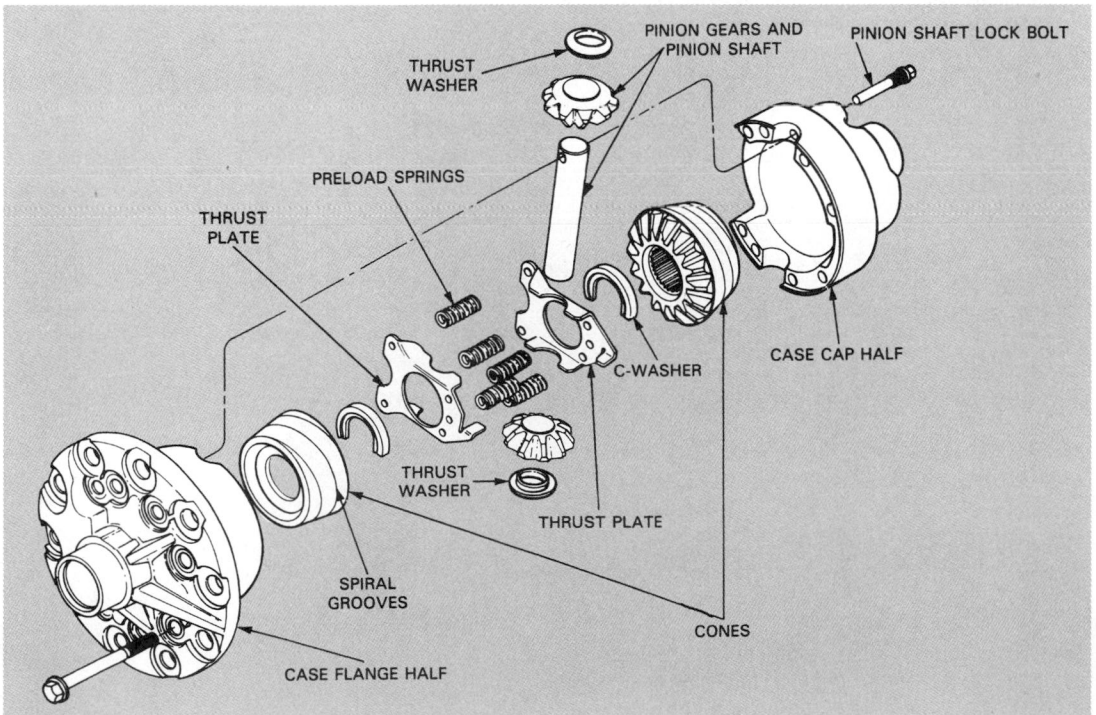

Figure 33-95. Exploded view of a cone-type positive traction differential. Note the spiral grooves on the cones. These grooves provide lubrication passages. (Ford)

One particular positive action type traction differential uses a governor assembly. The purpose of the governor is to positively lock both rear axles (wheels) together when one wheel spins more than 100 RPM faster than the other during slow vehicle operation. **Figure 33-96** shows an exploded view of this unit.

Lockup takes place through the use of flyweights in the governor, cam system, and the multiple-disc clutch units. The flyweights move outward to engage the latching bracket as one axle turns faster than the other.

This retards the camform side gear. In turn, this compresses the multiple-disc clutch unit, locking one side gear to the case. Equal driving torque is then transmitted to each wheel. When axle (wheel) speed difference drops below 100 RPM or road speed of vehicle is 20 mph (32 km/h) or faster, the differential operates as a standard (nonpositive traction) type. Service of this unit is basically the same as for other types using clutch plates.

Testing Traction Differential Action

Traction-type differential action may be checked by raising *one* wheel free of the floor. Place the transmission in neutral, block the wheel remaining in contact with the floor, and release the parking brake.

Use an adapter similar to that shown in **Figure 33-97** to provide a means of attaching a torque wrench to the

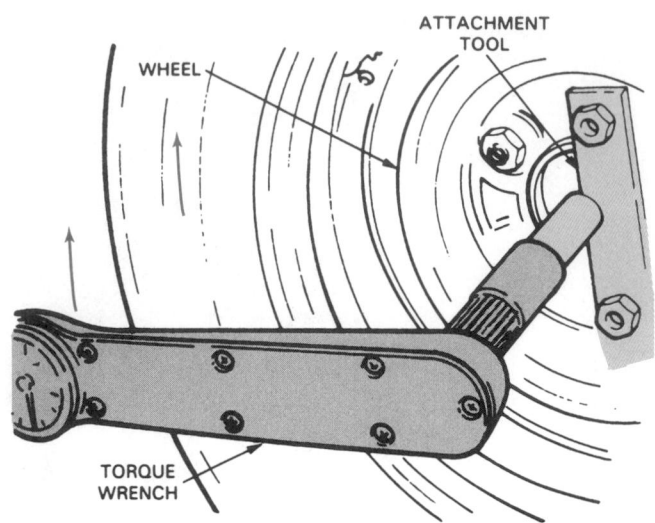

Figure 33-97. Checking traction differential action by measuring torque required to turn raised (off ground) wheel. Note attachment tool to connect and center torque on wheel. (Ford)

raised wheel. The wrench head must be in the center of the wheel.

Turn the wheel and note the amount of torque required to keep the wheel moving. Check this amount against specifications. Torque specifications will vary, depending on

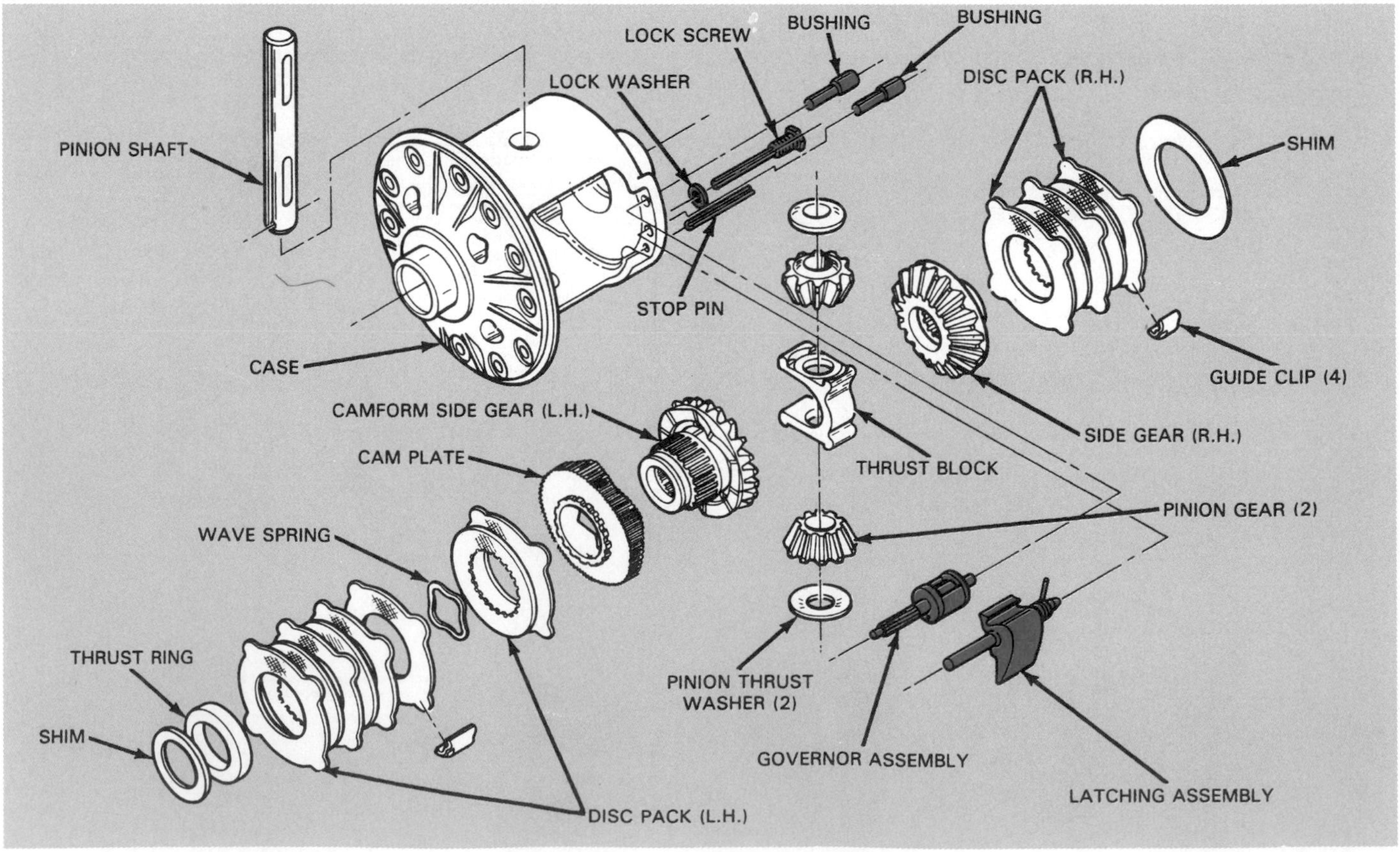

Figure 33-96. Exploded view of a positive traction differential. Note the governor assembly. (Chevrolet)

design. Some positive action differential units can be tested while they are out of the axle housing. They can be held in a vise with a special tool and rotated (in the direction of normal travel) with a torque wrench. See **Figure 33-98.** The initial break-away (when unit begins to slip under force) torque is then recorded. Use the manufacturer's torque reading for your specific unit. Some traction differentials use only gears instead of cones or clutch plates. They generally do not require special lubricants.

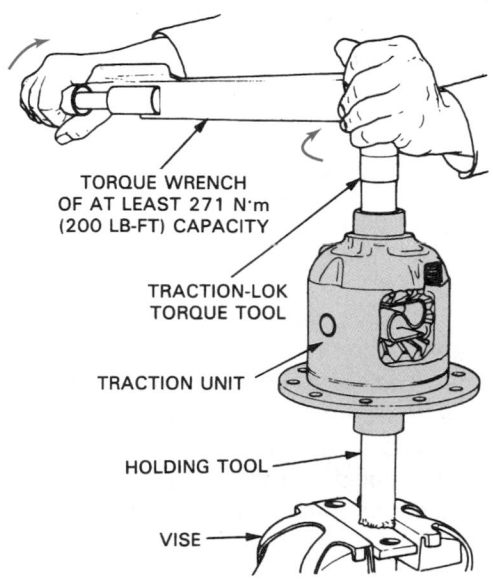

Figure 33-98. Testing a traction differential unit out of the carrier. Use proper tools and mounting procedures for an accurate reading. (Ford)

Traction Differential Service

Other than the clutch packs, cone brakes, and springs that make up the limited slip action, service on the traction differential is much like that for the conventional unit already discussed.

If the differential case is split (made in two pieces), make certain the two halves are marked before disassembly. See **Figure 33-99.** After disassembly, clean and inspect all parts. If brake cones will be reused, do not reverse positions. If one half of the case is damaged, replace both halves.

Before reassembly, lubricate all parts thoroughly with special traction differential lubricant. Use the axles to align the side gears and cone brakes or pinion thrust blocks while the case is bolted together.

Install the differential in the axle housing. If the axle end thrust blocks are of the type that can fall out of position, check that they are in place before installing the axles.

Drive Axle Lubrication

For conventional differentials, the use of a hypoid or a multipurpose gear lubricant is generally specified. Use the recommended viscosity. Most traction-type differentials

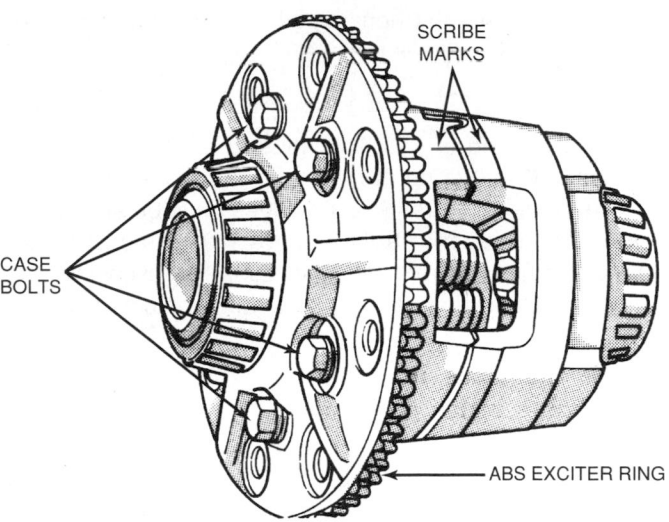

Figure 33-99. A two-piece (split) differential case. Mark both halves *before* disassembly. Keep all parts in their correct order. (Chrysler)

require a special lubricant. Never use anything but the specified oil.

Maintain the oil level in the housing so that if checked warm, the level is in line with the bottom of the filler hole. If cold, the level can be up to 1/2 in. (12.70 mm) below the hole. Wipe off the filler plug and the surrounding area before plug removal. Wipe off the filler gun nozzle. Under no circumstances must any foreign material enter the housing. See **Figure 33-100.**

Keep Vent Open

The axle housing is vented by means of a small hole, a tiny capped pipe, or a hose. The vent prevents a buildup

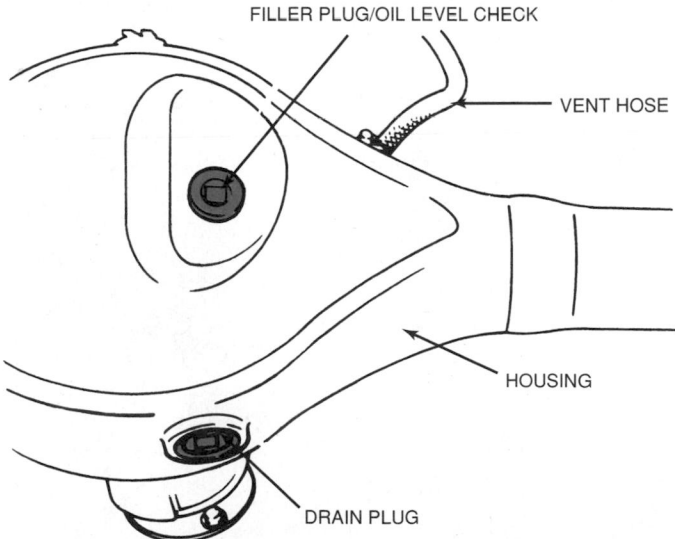

Figure 33-100. Lubricant drain and fill plugs in one particular differential housing. Always refill to the specific level recommended by the manufacturer with the correct lubricant. (Geo)

of pressure within the housing as the lubricant warms up. Make certain the vent is open.

Housing Alignment

One method of checking housing alignment is shown in **Figure 33-101.** The flanges on the axle ends must be clean and free of burrs. Straight edges must be straight and held in firm contact with the flanges during measurement. See the manufacturer's specifications for allowable misalignment. Check in both horizontal and vertical positions.

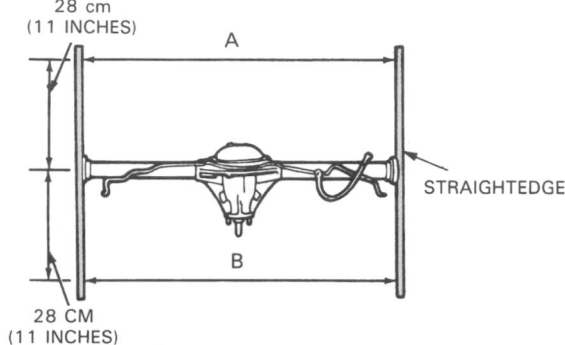

Figure 33-101. Checking housing alignment. For this particular housing, the difference between measurement A and B should not exceed 3/32" (2.38 mm). Check in a vertical plane and a horizontal plane. (Chrysler)

Tech Talk

CV joints will outlast the rest of the vehicle if they are properly lubricated. The lubricant is good for the life of the CV joint and does not have to be changed. Often, however, CV axles fail due to a lack of lubricant. The prime reasons for CV joint failure are a damaged boot and failure to use the proper lubricant during service. Both of these problems are easy to prevent.

Whenever a front-wheel drive vehicle is on the rack, check the CV joint boots for damage. A torn boot is usually easy to spot, and the stationary parts near the joint will be covered with grease. If the boots are damaged, advise the owner to replace them immediately and to check the CV joint for wear and corrosion.

Whenever you replace a defective CV joint or boot, always clean the interior of the joint thoroughly and repack it with the correct replacement lubricant. New boots and CV joints generally come with the correct lubricant, which is usually packaged in a plastic bag. Use as much of this lubricant as you can squeeze out of the bag. If a new joint or boot does not come with lubricant, do *not* substitute chassis grease. The CV joint will fail quickly. When you reassemble the joint, make sure that the boot retaining straps are correctly positioned and tightened to prevent lubricant loss.

Summary

Modern vehicles use the open shaft Hotchkiss drive shaft. Drive shafts can be made of one or more pieces. The cross-and-roller universal joint is commonly used by modern vehicles. The cross-and-roller joint consists of two yokes connected by a cross. Bearing caps, containing needle bearings, reduce friction. The bearing caps may be retained by snap rings, U-bolts, cap screws, or other means.

Before disconnecting a U-joint to remove the shaft, mark the shaft, joint, and drive flange to preserve balance. Yokes on both ends of the shaft must be in the same plane.

Support the shaft during removal. Cover the slip yoke. Avoid bending sharply at the U-joint. Do not allow the shaft to hang supported by a U-joint. Tape the bearing caps to the cross to prevent dropping off during shaft removal. Never tighten vise jaws on the drive shaft tube. Support the free end of the shaft while the other end rests in a vise. Use jaw covers on the vise.

Remove the snap rings and dismantle the joint. Clean and inspect. If the cross or bearing caps are worn, replace both. Use new seals and snap rings. Lubricate with universal joint grease. Use a low-pressure gun and fill the joint slowly. On sealed types, lubricate before assembly. After the joint is assembled and snap rings are installed, strike the yokes to seat the bearing caps against the snap rings. Joint action should be smooth.

When installing a drive shaft, cover the slip yoke to prevent entry of dirt and damage from contact with vehicle underbody parts. Support the shaft. Lubricate the slip yoke. Yokes must be in the same plane. All marks must be aligned. Torque the joint U-bolts or cap screws. Tap the joint and retorque. Crimp the locking tabs against the cap screws. Check all fasteners. Shake the shaft to detect looseness. Road test for proper operation.

If shaft vibration is present, check the shaft for runout, presence of undercoating, misaligned marks, or improper drive shaft angle. Replace sprung or badly dented shafts. Drive shaft angle may be checked by various methods, including special gauges, levels, protractors, and plumb bobs. The vehicle must be level and at curb weight for drive angle check. Tilt the rear axle housing to provide the correct drive angle by adjusting the control arms (coil springs) or by using tapered wedges (leaf springs). Some vehicles require adjusting the transmission height also. Others are nonadjustable.

Constant velocity (CV) joints are used on most modern front-wheel drive vehicles and on some rear-wheel drive vehicles. The two main types of CV joints are the tripod joint and the Rzeppa joint. Torn CV boots are a common source of CV joint failure. Removing the CV axle often requires that the steering knuckle be removed. CV joints can be disassembled and worn parts replaced, but many technicians prefer to replace the entire joint when defective.

The typical drive axle assembly contains the ring and pinion gears and the differential assembly. Axles are retained in the housing with a retainer plate or with C-locks.

Before road testing, check the lubricant level, tire pressure, and tread pattern. Check action during drive, cruise, float, and coast conditions. Road surface, tire tread, front wheel bearings, transmission, and other factors can make noises easily mistaken for drive axle problems. Check carefully before pulling the axle apart.

Check bearing preload. Scribe a line on the pinion shaft, retaining nut, and flange before loosening retaining nut. Hold the companion flange with special wrench while loosening the flange nut. Use a puller to remove the flange. Clean the pinion seal recess. Soak the new seal if required. Coat the outer diameter of the new seal with cement. Install, lip in, to correct depth.

Inspect the pinion flange for nicks and burrs. Lubricate before installation. Draw the flange on with a nut. Never pound on the pinion flange or pinion shaft. Tighten the pinion flange nut as required. If preload is exceeded, install a new collapsible spacer (where used).

Pull axles by removing retainer plates or inner end C-locks. On front-wheel drive units, remove universal joints and/or the spindle assembly. Use a slide hammer puller on conventional axles. Do not disturb the backing plate unless necessary. If the backing plate must be pulled, disconnect the brake line. If an axle was broken or if other damage occurred, flush the housing thoroughly. Check the axle for twists and bends.

Do not wash sealed wheel bearings. Always install new oil seals following axle removal. Notch bearing retainer rings to remove. When pressing new wheel bearings into place, apply pressure to the inner race only. Press a new retaining ring into firm contact with the bearing. Do not press the ring and bearing on at the same time. The bearing must face in the correct direction and must be pressed on to the proper position.

When installing axles, do not damage the seals. The retainer plate must be positioned so that the oil drain hole will function. Where axle and end play shims are used, install in their original positions. Check axle end play. Where a tapered end axle is used, make certain the drive key is in place when the hub is attached to the axle. Use a new cotter pin to secure the hub retaining nut.

Some carriers are removable, others are an integral part of the housing. Mark differential case bearing adjusters and bearing caps before disassembly. Check backlash and tooth contact pattern before removing the case. Use a puller or pry the case out of the carrier. Mark and save all shims. A spreader may be required. Generally, do not spread housings more than .020″ (0.51 mm).

Clean and inspect the differential case and parts. Replace as needed. When case side bearings must be replaced, use new outer cups. The ring and pinion must be replaced as a matched pair. The ring and pinion must have matching numbers. Mark ring and pinion gears before disassembly if they are of the nonhunting type.

Check the ring gear flange for runout. Attach the ring gear with special fasteners. Contact surfaces of the ring and pinion must be spotless. Lubricate ring gear fasteners or coat with recommended liquid adhesive before assembly.

Fasteners must be a snug fit in the ring and flange. When removing the pinion shaft, mark and save shims. Do not damage the bearing counterbore during the removal of pinion outer races.

Set proper pinion depth by using a special setting gauge. When using a new drive pinion, correct the depth setting by allowing for the plus or minus amount marked on the pinion. Shims must be clean and of the proper thickness to provide exact pinion depth. When installing the pinion, preload must be as specified. Use a new seal.

Before installing the differential case, lubricate the entire assembly thoroughly. If the ring and pinion gear set is of the nonhunting type, mesh the marked teeth during case assembly. Adjust the case side bearing preload as specified. Check ring and pinion backlash. Check the ring and pinion tooth contact pattern by coating the ring gear with a special compound. Load the ring gear and turn the pinion until the ring makes one full turn. Do this in both drive and coast directions. The contact pattern should be centralized between bottom and top of the tooth. The pattern may be slightly toward the toe.

Correct faulty pattern by adjusting the pinion in or out by moving the ring toward or away from the pinion. Traction-type differentials utilize clutch packs or cone brakes to provide power to both axles, even when one wheel is spinning.

Traction differentials may be tested in the vehicle by measuring the torque required to turn the raised wheel. The other wheel must contact the floor. The transmission and/or transfer case must be in neutral, with emergency brake off. Lubricate all traction differential parts with recommended lubricant upon assembly. Fill differential housing to within 1/4″ to 1/2″ (6.35 to 12.70 mm) of the filler plug or as recommended by the manufacturer. Use multipurpose gear lubricant for conventional differentials and a special lubricant for traction type units if required. Do not allow dirt to enter the housing when checking lubricant level or when filling. The axle vent must be open.

Know These Terms

Hotchkiss	Flanged end axle
Slip yoke	C-lock
Center support bearing	Bearing retainer ring
Cross-and-roller universal joint	End play
	Ring gear
Trunnion	Pinion gear
Bearing cap	Hypoid gear
Constant velocity universal joint	Differential gear
	Preload
Balanced	Gear ratio
Drive shaft angle	Runout
Constant velocity joint	Pinion gear depth
Tripod joint	Backlash
Rzeppa joint	Contact pattern
CV boot	Drive pattern
Steering knuckle	Coast pattern
Straps	Limited slip
Semifloating	

Review Questions—Chapter 33

Do not write in this book. Write your answers on a separate sheet of paper.

1. The two-piece drive shaft utilizes a _____ bearing.

2. The bearing caps in the cross and bearing cap joint are retained by _____.
   (A) snap rings
   (B) U-bolts
   (C) cap screws
   (D) One or more of the above, depending on manufacturer.

3. To allow driveline length to change, a _____ is installed in the drive shaft.

4. What portion of a drive shaft is easily damaged by clamping in a vise?

5. If the bearing caps are held in place by injection-molded plastic, what should be done before they are removed?
   (A) Heat them in a oil bath.
   (B) Heat them with a torch.
   (C) Chill them with dry ice.
   (D) Strike them hard with a brass hammer.

6. The _____ on each end of the drive shaft should be in the same plane.

7. Before removing a drive shaft, it is important that the shaft and pinion flange or yoke be _____ to preserve shaft _____.

8. List the two basic types of CV joints?

9. Some CV axles are held to the transaxle by an internal _____.

10. Most drive axles found on cars and light trucks are of the _____ design.
    (A) full-floating
    (B) three-quarter floating
    (C) semifloating
    (D) non-floating

11. Most axles are retained in the housing by using a _____ plate or by using _____ on the axle inner ends.

12. List three things that can make noises that can be mistaken for drive axle problems.

13. A rear axle noise that varies during sudden turns to the left or right is probably caused by _____.
    (A) axle bearings
    (B) front wheel bearings
    (C) rear axle gears
    (D) worn U-joint(s)

14. Before removing a pinion flange, check the bearing _____.

15. Hold the pinion flange with a _____ while loosening the retaining nut.
    (A) crescent wrench
    (B) pipe wrench
    (C) large screwdriver
    (D) special tool

16. If the differential carrier is the integral type, it may be necessary to remove the _____ to service the internal components.

17. When tightening a pinion flange retaining nut on installations using a collapsible spacer, what must be done if the preload is exceeded?
    (A) Install a new spacer.
    (B) Back off the nut until preload is correct.
    (C) Back off the nut past correct preload and tighten until preload is correct.
    (D) Leave preload alone.

18. Axle wheel bearing retainer rings may be removed from the axle after _____.
    (A) heating
    (B) chilling
    (C) notching with a chisel
    (D) cutting with a torch

19. The wheel hub on a tapered end axle is kept from turning by a _____.

20. Pinion depth is adjusted by placing shims between the _____ and _____.
    (A) bearing, case
    (B) gear, bearing cone
    (C) case, gear
    (D) either A or B, depending on the design

21. Proper ring and pinion tooth contact pattern is important. The pattern should generally be _____.
    (A) centralized on the tooth
    (B) centralized between top and bottom of the tooth but closer to the toe
    (C) centralized between top and bottom of the tooth but closer to the heel
    (D) near the top of the tooth and extending over the entire length

22. In the hunting-type ring and pinion gear set, any one tooth on the pinion will contact _____ on the ring.
    (A) all teeth
    (B) certain teeth
    (C) one other tooth
    (D) either A or B, depending on the design

23. When checking backlash between the ring and pinion, place the dial indicator stem against one of the _____ gear teeth.

24. Tooth contact pattern is adjusted by moving either the _____ or the _____.

25. When one rear wheel is spinning, the limited slip differential unit applies power to the wheel that _____.
    (A) is spinning
    (B) is not spinning
    (C) has the most traction
    (D) Both B & C.

ASE-Type Questions

1. The Hotchkiss-type drive shaft is sometimes called a(n) _____ design.

(A) closed
(B) open
(C) hypoid
(D) semifloating

2. Technician A says that if the cross is in good condition but the bearing caps are not, it is permissible to replace the bearing cap only. Technician B says that some U-joints are sealed and must be lubricated before assembly. Who is right?
   (A) A only.
   (B) B only.
   (C) Both A & B.
   (D) Neither A nor B.

3. Technician A says that minor drive shaft imbalance can sometimes be corrected with hose clamps. Technician B says that a newly assembled U-joint should have a rather stiff action until broken in. Who is right?
   (A) A only.
   (B) B only.
   (C) Both A & B.
   (D) Neither A nor B.

4. All of the following are the result of a torn CV boot, EXCEPT:
   (A) CV joint grease will be thrown out.
   (B) dirt and water will enter the CV joint.
   (C) the CV axle will be bent.
   (D) the CV joint will wear out.

5. Technician A says that front-wheel drive axles can be of a one- or two-piece design. Technician B says that rear wheel drive shafts can be of a one- or two-piece design. Who is right?
   (A) A only.
   (B) B only.
   (C) Both A & B.
   (D) Neither A nor B.

6. A rear axle noise that varies between drive and coast is probably caused by _____.
   (A) axle bearings
   (B) front wheel bearings
   (C) rear axle gears
   (D) worn U-joint(s)

7. All of the following statements about axle replacement are true, EXCEPT:
   (A) always install a new oil seal whenever an axle has been removed.
   (B) when removing or installing bearings, use the proper equipment to protect against flying parts, as bearings can explode.
   (C) the brake backing plate must always be removed before pulling an axle.

   (D) whenever an axle has broken or other damage has occurred, always inspect the housing thoroughly.

8. Technician A says that differential side bearing shims may be mixed and used on either side. Technician B says that ring and pinion gears must be replaced as matched sets. Who is right?
   (A) A only.
   (B) B only.
   (C) Both A & B.
   (D) Neither A nor B.

9. Technician A says that pinion depth can be set satisfactorily by measuring from the pinion gear to the axle centerline with an accurate ruler. Technician B says that a pinion gear marked + 2 must be shimmed so that it will operate .002″ closer to the ring gear centerline than a pinion marked 0. Who is right?
   (A) A only.
   (B) B only.
   (C) Both A & B.
   (D) Neither A nor B.

10. Technician A says that the limited slip-clutch on the wheel that is spinning is released. Technician B says that limited slip differentials should always be lubricated with regular multipurpose gear lubricant. Who is right?
    (A) A only.
    (B) B only.
    (C) Both A & B.
    (D) Neither A nor B.

Student Activities

1. Draw a sketch showing the differences between one- and two-piece drivelines used on rear-wheel drive vehicles. Illustrate the center support bearing on the two-piece design.

2. Inspect a rear-wheel drive shaft for dry, loose U-joints and/or damage to the shaft. Make a report for your instructor.

3. Inspect a front CV axle shaft for loose CV joints and leaking boots. Make a report for your instructor.

4. Replace a U-joint or CV joint. Write a report listing the replacement procedures in the proper order, and the tools and supplies needed.

5. Calculate the axle ratio on a vehicle by turning one wheel (other wheel stationary) and counting the revolutions of the driveshaft. Does this agree with the published specifications for the vehicle? Discuss the results with your instructor and the other members of your class.

This on-vehicle brake lathe is set up to true a front brake rotor on a four-wheel drive pickup truck. (Hunter)

34

Brake Service

After studying this chapter, you will be able to:
- Explain drum brake construction, operation, and service.
- Summarize disc brake construction, operation, and service.
- Explain the operation and service of power brakes.
- Explain the operation and service of anti-lock brake system.
- Describe master cylinder operation, construction, and service.
- Diagnose brake hydraulic system problems.
- Diagnose brake friction system problems.
- Diagnose power brake system problems.

This chapter will cover the operation and servicing of modern brake systems. This includes both the hydraulic system (master cylinder, wheel cylinders, calipers, lines and hoses, and valves) and the friction system (brake shoes and drums; disc brake rotors and pads). Power brakes will also be covered.

Safety in the Shop

Before beginning hands-on brake service, note this possible on-the-job hazard to your health. Brake friction materials contain *asbestos*—a known *carcinogen* (a substance that can cause cancer). Removing brake drums, cleaning brake assemblies, and other operations can produce small airborne particles of asbestos. These are easily inhaled by the technician. Breathing these particles may cause cancer.

Observe the Following Rules to Prevent Breathing Asbestos
1. Never use compressed air to blow brake assemblies clean. Use a vacuum source or flush with water.
2. Equip all brake service equipment with an efficient dust removal system. Turn on the system whenever the equipment is in operation.
3. When some exposure might be unavoidable, wear an approved filter mask.

General Brake Cautions
1. Use care when removing wheel to avoid damage to caliper external brake lines.
2. Reject any drums or rotors that do not meet thickness specifications.
3. Turn drums and rotors in axle pairs. Variations in thickness between right and left sides should meet minimum specifications.
4. Replace fluids siphoned from the master cylinder in order to retract pistons.
5. Pump up brakes to bring pads into contact with the disc before operating the vehicle.
6. Do not separate caliper halves unless so specified.
7. When removing the caliper to pull the rotor, place cardboard or another suitable block between the pads to prevent the pistons from working out of the cylinders.
8. Tap the master cylinder, wheel cylinders, and calipers during bleeding to help dislodge trapped air.
9. "Riding" the brake will quickly ruin the brakes.
10. If the caliper mounting bolts are the prevailing torque type, replace them with new ones.
11. When fitting either oversize or offset wheels, make certain they clear the caliper assembly.
12. Adjust the front wheel bearings to remove play.

Brake Inspection

Periodic brake inspections are a must for safe and efficient brake operation. The inspection should be thorough. It is best to develop a checklist so that no important area is overlooked. Specific instructions concerning various brake system components are presented below.

Brake Pedal and Master Cylinder

Check the brake pedal free play. Check the total pedal travel. There should be ample travel remaining when the brakes are fully applied. The pedal should be firm with no spongy feeling that could indicate air in the system. The pedal, when held firmly applied, must remain at one point and should not move slowly toward the floor. Pedal action should be smooth and quiet.

Check the fluid level in the reservoir. If equipped with power brakes, exhaust the vacuum reservoir (engine off) by repeated brake applications. Hold the brake pedal down firmly while starting the engine. As soon as the engine starts, the brake pedal will move downward if the vacuum booster is functioning. Check for signs of leakage.

Brake Light Switch and Bulbs

Check switch operation by inspecting brake lights while brake is being applied. Lights should come on quickly, even with very mild brake pressure. If service is needed, refer to Chapter 27.

Wheel Cylinders and Brake Shoe Assemblies

A periodic inspection generally involves pulling a wheel and drum. If any trouble is indicated (brake lining wear, fluid leakage, part scoring), all wheels should be removed.

Check the wheel cylinders for leakage by pulling back the lip of the dust boots. Any fluid, other than normal dampness in the boot, indicates a leak. The shoe lining should have ample wear remaining and should be free of oil or grease. Inspect retracting springs, shoe hold-downs, automatic adjusting device, and shoe contact pads on the backing plate. Backing plate and shoe anchors must be tight.

Brake Drums

Check drums for out-of-round or tapered condition. The drums must be free of scoring, cracking, grease, and oil.

Disc Brakes

Check brake pads for wear. Check rotor or disc for scoring, cracking, uneven wear, or warping. Caliper pistons should show no signs of leakage.

Seals

Oil and grease seals must be in good condition with no visible signs of leakage. Seals should be changed whenever the bearings are removed.

Parking Brake

The parking brake should hold the vehicle securely. When the brake is firmly applied, there must still be ample pedal travel remaining. Check for missing cotter pins, frayed cables, rust, etc.

Brake Lines and Hoses

Inspect all hoses for cracking, softening, or swelling. Check lines for leakage, damage from contact with moving parts, and vibration. All line clips, hold-down assemblies, and other fasteners must be in place.

Chassis

The brake inspection must also include a check for loose wheel bearings, worn ball joints, worn steering parts, defective shock absorbers, broken struts, and worn springs. These parts can affect braking action.

Road Test

Following the above checks, drive the vehicle to test brake action. The vehicle should stop quickly and smoothly. There must be no tendency to dive or to pull to one side or the other. Inspection points for a typical brake system are illustrated in **Figure 34-1.**

Full information on the inspection and servicing of all of the brake components will be given in this chapter.

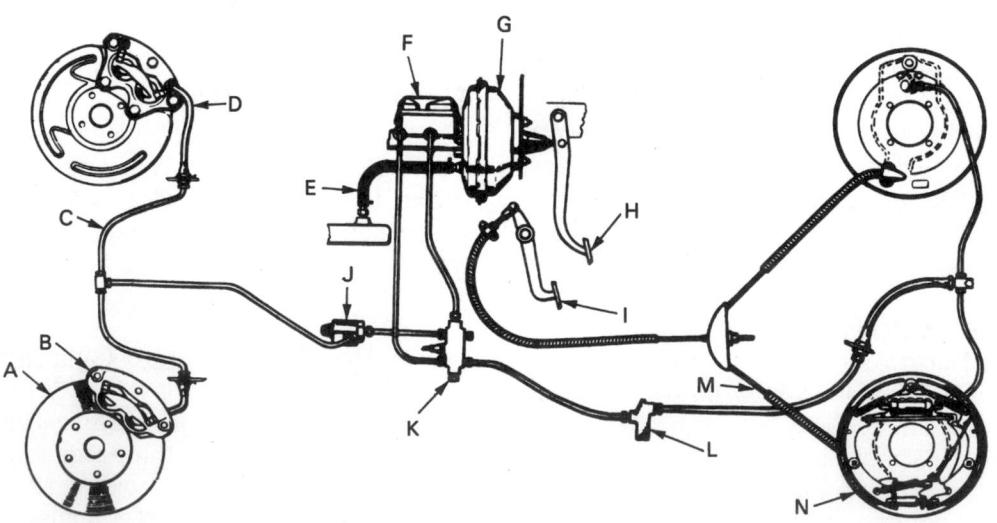

Figure 34-1. Inspection points. A—Disc. B—Caliper. C—Line. D—Flex hose. E—Vacuum line. F—Master Cylinder. G—Power booster. H—Brake Pedal. I—Parking brake. J—Metering valve. K—Brake warning light. L—Proportioning valve. M—Parking brake cable system. N—Brake shoe assembly. (Bendix)

Warning: The brakes, when needed, must work and must work right. Make every inspection thorough. Perform all brake work carefully and to the highest standards. Use only quality parts. Refuse to do any "half-way" jobs. Remember that every time the pedal is depressed, the lives of a number of people can depend upon your skill, knowledge, and care. Do not let them down.

Brake Hydraulic System Operation

The hydraulic brake system uses a master cylinder to develop hydraulic pressure. The master cylinder may be power (vacuum or hydraulic) assisted. Pressure is transmitted to each caliper and wheel cylinder through steel tubing and flexible hoses.

Brake Fluid

Use only top-quality, DOT (Department of Transportation) approved brake fluid. The latest brake fluid is marked **DOT 3.** Alcohol-based fluid, where available, can be used, but most manufacturers recommend the newer **silicone brake fluid.** The fluid must have a boiling point of at least 284°F (140°C). Do not reuse old brake fluid. Keep fluid in clean, tightly sealed, well marked containers. Protect it from contamination with dust, water, and oils. Do not mix regular and silicone fluids.

Brake Fluid Will Ruin Paint

Do not spill brake fluid on the vehicle's paint. If fluid gets on a painted surface, wipe it off and immediately wash the surface with mild soap and water. Although the newer silicone brake fluid is harmless to paint, some brake systems may contain some older alcohol-based fluid. Remember that most brake fluids (other than pure silicone) can ruin the finish.

Flushing the System

If necessary, the brake system may be flushed with new brake fluid. It can also be flushed with alcohol or an approved brake cleaning solvent and rinsed with brake fluid. This procedure should be performed only if the master cylinder, calipers, and wheel cylinders are to be reconditioned. Flushing should always be done prior to repairs.

Master Cylinder Operation

The **master cylinder** converts the pressure on the brake pedal into hydraulic pressure in the brake system. When master cylinder is in released position, **Figure 34-2,** there is no pressure in the lines.

 Note: On drum brakes only, a low static pressure remains in the lines due to a special check valve.

The brake shoe retracting springs pull the shoes away from the brake drum and force the wheel cylinder pistons inward. This action causes fluid to flow through the lines toward the master cylinder. The fluid will lift the **check valve** from its seat and flow into the master cylinder **reservoir.**

When pressure in the lines has dropped to the point where it is less then the force developed by the check valve spring, the check valve will be returned to its seat. This maintains residual line pressure. Some systems do not use residual check valves. They depend on wheel cylinder cup design or cup expanders to keep air from leaking into the system.

Figure 34-2 shows the braking system (on one wheel only) when brakes are released. Note that the master cylinder piston is released to the point where the **primary cup** clears the **compensating port.** This allows fluid to move into the reservoir.

When the brake pedal is depressed, the master cylinder piston is forced into the cylinder. As soon as the primary cup passes the compensating port, the fluid ahead of the piston is trapped. Any further piston movement will force the fluid to flow through the brake lines.

Single-Piston Master Cylinder

Older vehicles (before 1967) may be equipped with **single-piston master cylinders.** Because they had only one operating piston, a faulty unit or a fluid leak could cause brake system failure. For this reason, single piston master cylinders are no longer used.

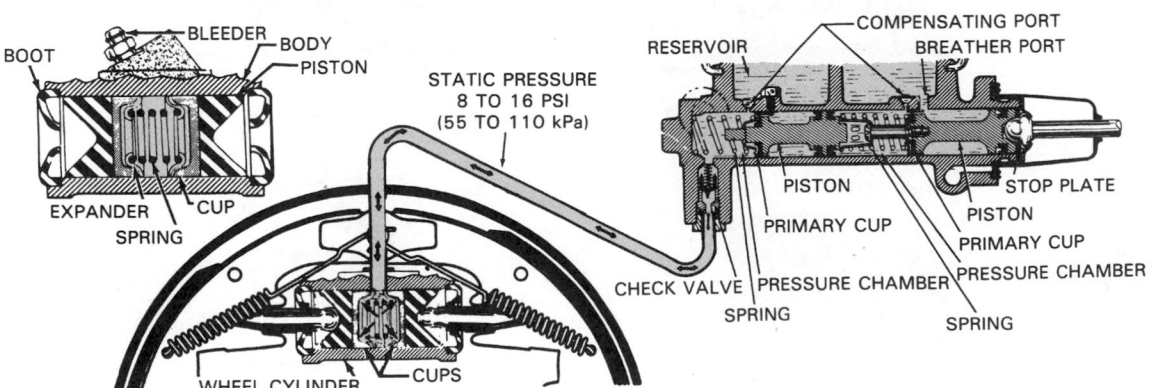

Figure 34-2.   Drum brake system with brakes released. (Buick)

A cross-sectional view of a single-piston master cylinder is shown in **Figure 34-3.** Note that this type of master cylinder has only one brake fluid reservoir.

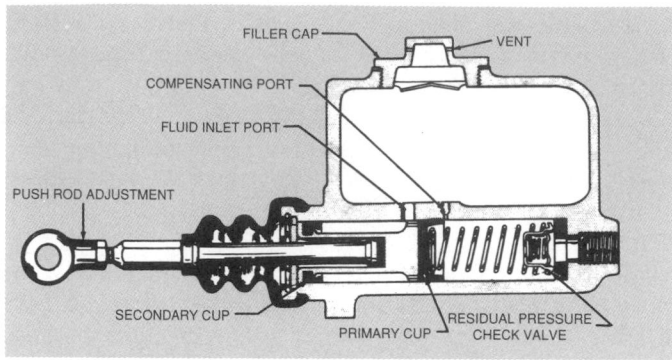

Figure 34-3.   Typical single-piston master cylinder.

Dual-Piston Master Cylinder

The ***double-piston master cylinder*** (also called dual piston or split system) was developed so that the hydraulic systems for the front and rear wheels could be completely separated. With such a separation, a failure or leak in the front system would not affect the rear and vice versa. The chance of both failing at once is unlikely.

One type of dual piston master cylinder is shown in **Figure 34-4.** When the master cylinder push rod is forced inward, the primary piston moves toward the ***floating piston*** (also called secondary piston) until the compensating port is closed. Further movement of the primary piston is then transmitted to the floating piston. As the floating piston is forced forward by the hydraulic fluid separating it from the primary piston, it closes off the other compensating port. Further movement of the primary piston builds up pressure in both outlet systems (one to the front brakes and the other to the rear brakes).

Figure 34-5 illustrates the action of the dual piston master cylinder in protecting against complete brake failure. In **Figure 34-5A,** the master cylinder push rod is in the released position. In **Figure 34-5B,** the push rod has forced the primary and floating pistons to build up pressure in both front and rear hydraulic systems. In **Figure 34-5C,** the front brake line has ruptured, allowing the primary piston to move in until the floating piston struck the end of the cylinder. Pressure is still maintained to the rear wheels. In **Figure 34-5D,** the rear wheel brake line has moved inward until it bumped the floating piston, thus maintaining pressure to the front wheel system.

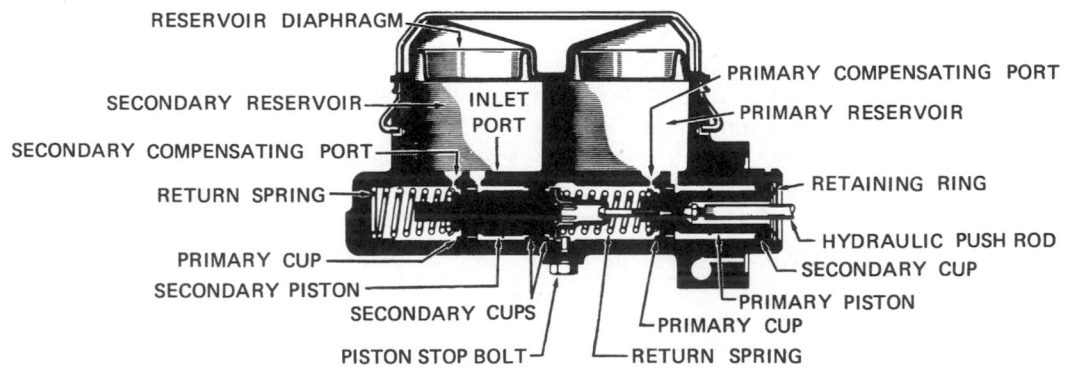

Figure 34-4.   Typical tandem (dual) master cylinder. (Bendix)

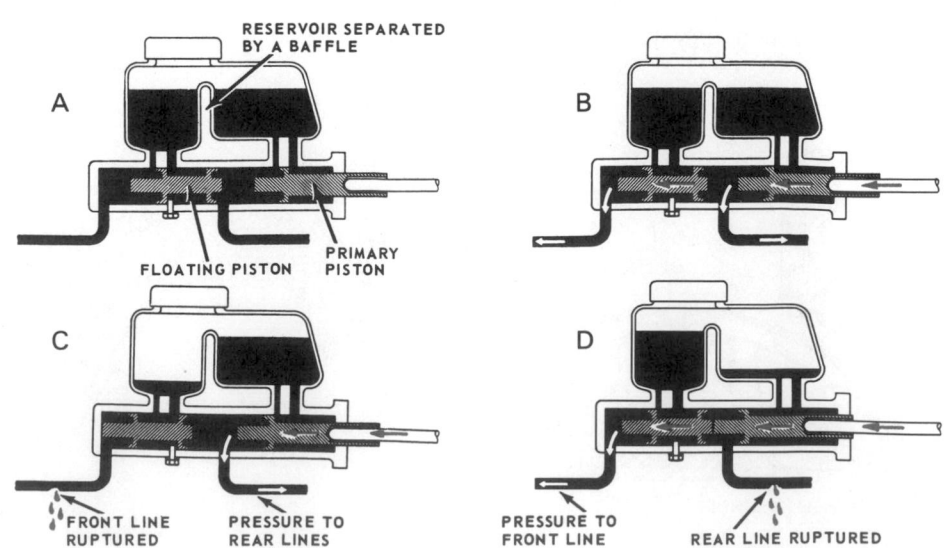

Figure 34-5.   Action of a tandem master cylinder in the event of either front or rear brake system failure. (Mercedes-Benz)

Failure of either the front or rear system will be evidenced by a sudden increase in the brake pedal travel required to apply the brakes. A pressure differential safety switch is used to activate a warning light. **Figure 34-6** also illustrates a dual master cylinder. Note the location of the residual check valves in this unit. Some dual piston master cylinders have completely separate reservoirs, **Figure 34-7.** Others merely use a baffle to form two reservoirs. Look at **Figure 34-8.**

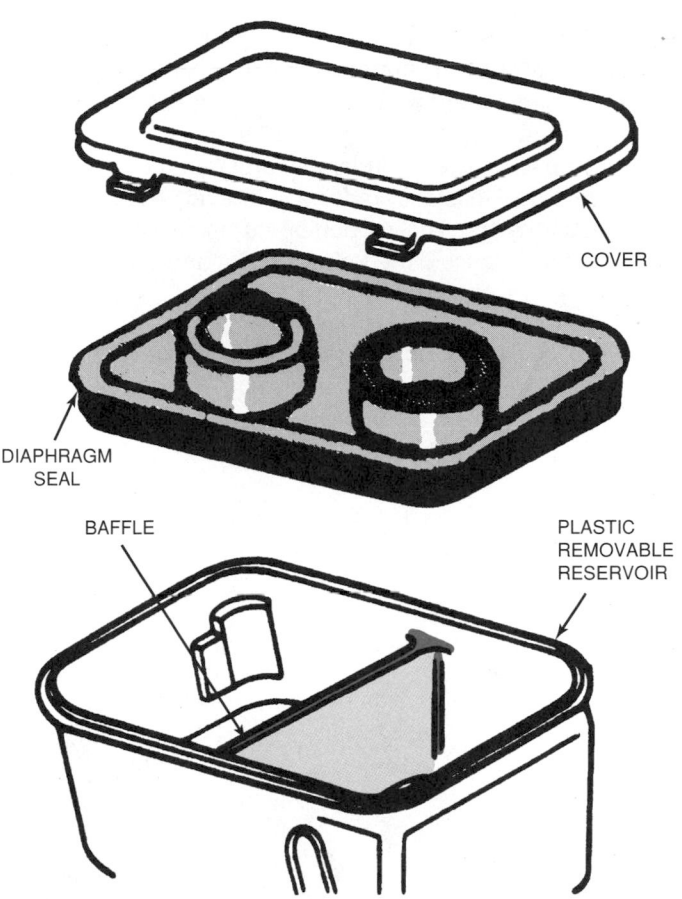

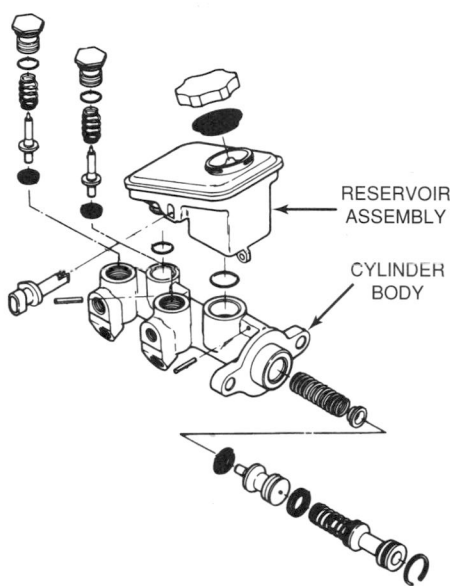

Figure 34-6. Exploded view of a compact master cylinder assembly. Note the plastic reservoir assembly and aluminum cylinder body. (Pontiac)

Figure 34-8. A plastic, removable master cylinder reservoir that has an internal "baffle" to create two reservoir chambers. (Chrysler Corp.)

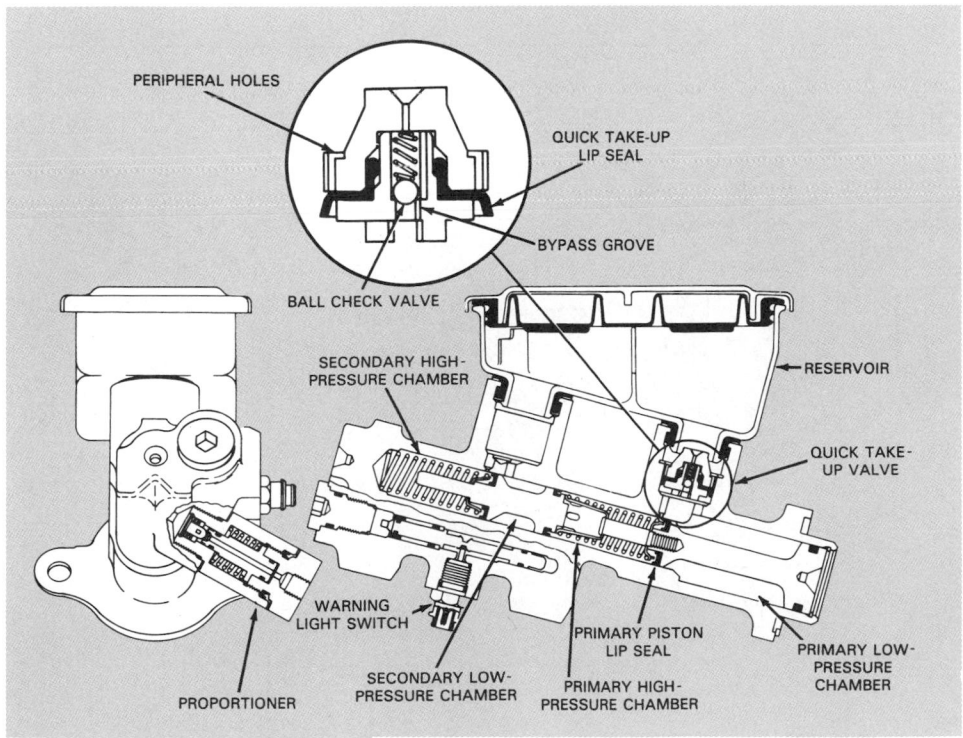

Figure 34-7. Cutaway view of a quick take-up master cylinder. Note that this unit also has a warning light switch and a proportioner attached to the cylinder body. (Delco)

Compact Master Cylinder

The compact master cylinder is a composite design (plastic reservoir and aluminum body) that is used in diagonally split brake systems, **Figure 34-9.**

Compact master cylinders incorporate the functions of a standard dual master cylinder, a fluid level sensor, and integral proportioners. The proportioners are used to improve front-to-rear balance during heavy brake applications.

Quick Take-Up Master Cylinder

The quick take-up master cylinder is designed to be used with low-drag disc brake calipers. The quick take-up

feature is designed to supply a large volume of low-pressure fluid to the brakes during the start of application. This low-pressure fluid rapidly supplies the increased fluid displacement needs caused by the no-drag caliper pistons.

There are four separate outlet ports on the cylinder housing. Each feeds an individual brake assembly. See **Figure 34-10.** A proportioning valve and warning light switch are housed in an integral bore located on the bottom of the cylinder.

During the start of brake application, more fluid is displaced in the low-pressure primary chamber than the high-pressure chamber. This displacement is created because

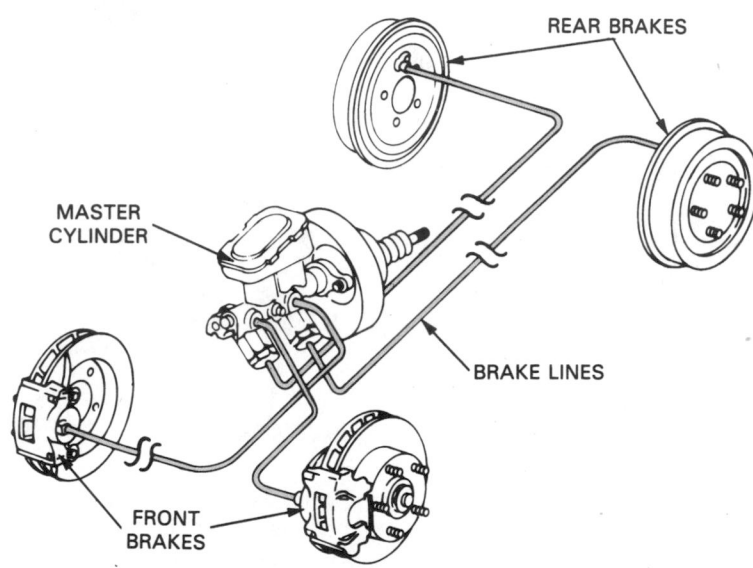

Figure 34-9. Schematic of a diagonally split braking system. Each brake line has its own attachment point on the master cylinder. (Bendix)

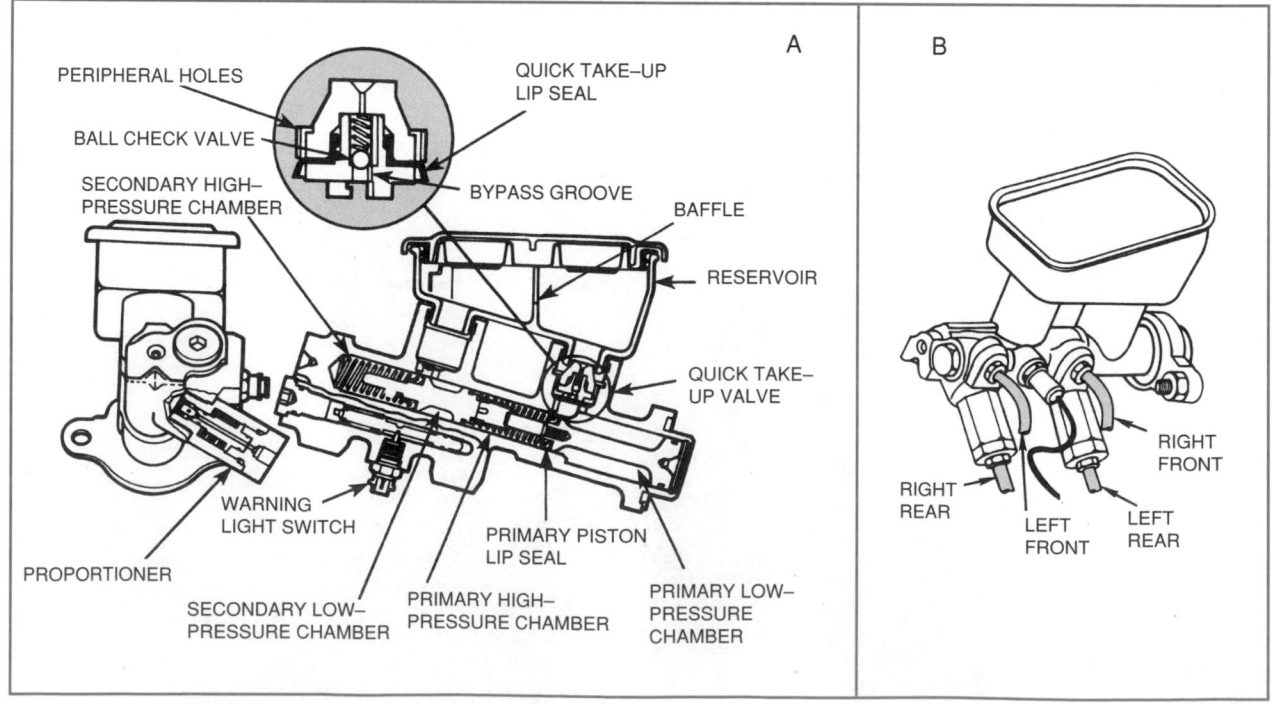

Figure 34-10. A—Cross-sectional view of a quick take-up master cylinder with a proportioning valve and warning light switch. B—Four brake line connection points. (Bendix)

the low-pressure chamber has a larger diameter than the high-pressure chamber.

As continued application occurs, brake fluid is forced around the outer edge of the primary piston lip seal. From there it goes into the high pressure chamber and on to the braking units at the wheels. Look at **Figure 34-11A.**

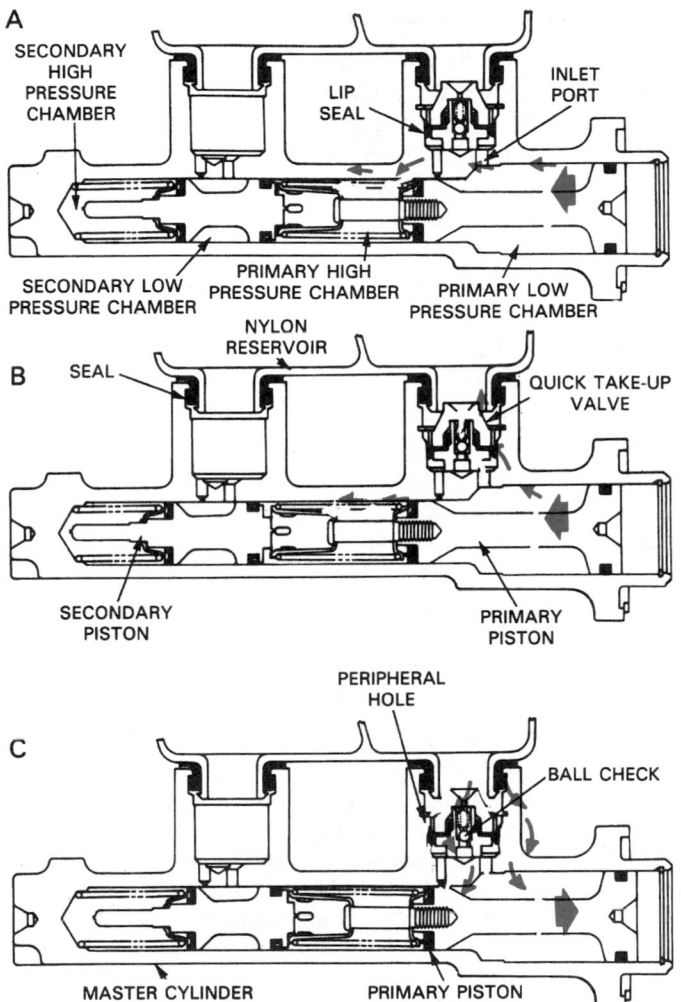

Figure 34-11. Operation sequence of a quick take-up master cylinder. A—Start of quick take-up application. Note fluid flowing around primary piston cup. B—Primary piston and secondary piston now have equal pressure. Cylinder now operates as a conventional unit. Note fluid flow through quick take-up valve into reservoir. C—Releasing. (Delco)

To create equal pressure and displacement in both systems, the primary piston travels a lesser amount than the secondary piston. At a preset pressure, the quick take-up valve "ball check" opens. This allows excess fluid in the larger primary chamber to flow into the reservoir. See **Figure 34-11B.** Once the primary piston lip seal has passed the quick take-up valve port, high pressure is built up ahead of each piston. The master cylinder functions like a conventional unit.

When the brakes are released, the master cylinder piston springs return the pistons faster than the returning fluid

can travel. A vacuum is then generated in both the high- and low-pressure chambers. If the vacuum were not relieved, fluid would pass around the piston seal cup lips in an effort to eliminate the vacuum, **Figure 34-11C.**

To stop this vacuum from forming, the primary chamber vacuum is compensated by the bypass groove in the quick take-up valve. The primary piston is compensated by fluid traveling from the reservoir through small-diameter holes in the quick take-up valve. The secondary piston chamber vacuum is relieved by fluid traveling from the reservoir through the compensating port and bypass hole.

Checking Master Cylinder

The master cylinder fluid level can be easily checked. Refer to **Figure 34-12.** After thoroughly cleaning the cover(s) and the surrounding area, remove the cover to expose the fluid. Fluid level should be around 1/4″ (6.35 mm) from the top of the reservoirs, G. Fluid must be clean and free of discoloration. Make sure that the cover vent, C, a tiny hole, is open to prevent pressure buildup in reservoir. Check the condition and placement of the reservoir seal diaphragm, F. The bail wire, D, must snap on tightly.

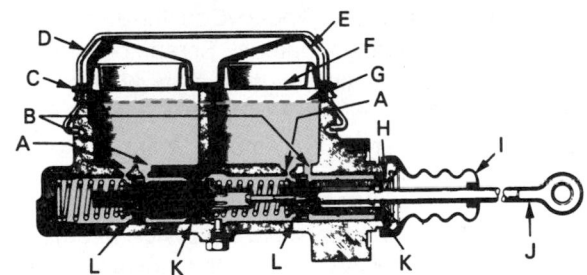

Figure 34-12.   Master cylinder check points. A—Compensating ports. B—Inlet ports. C—Vent. D—Bail. E—Reservoir cover. F—Diaphragm reservoir seal. G—Fluid level. H—Push rod retainer. I—Dust boot. J—Push Rod. K—Secondary cups. L—Primary cups. (Bendix)

Inspect beneath the **_dust boot,_** I, for evidence of fluid leakage past the secondary cup, K. Check primary cups, L, by applying the brakes firmly. Hold pressure. The pedal should not move inward. If it does, it indicates that one or both primary cups could be allowing fluid to escape. A leak elsewhere in system will also cause the pedal to fall away.

The compensating ports, A, must be open when the pedal is released. If it is closed by dirt, corrosion, a swollen primary cup, or improper linkage adjustment, it can cause a pressure buildup in the lines that will keep the brakes applied.

Nylon reservoirs are usually equipped with molded-in (thin area) windows that are used to view the fluid level. See **Figure 34-13.**

Residual check valves, where used (drum brakes only), must function properly to maintain a static pressure in the lines. A faulty check valve can cause excessive pedal travel before the brakes apply. Worn linings or

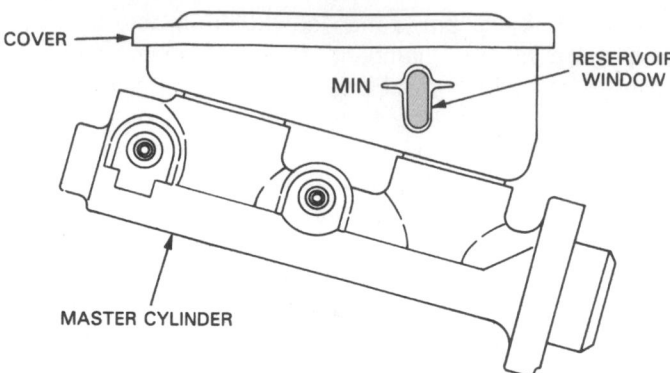

Figure 34-13. Master cylinder reservoir window. Cover does not have to be removed to check fluid level. (Pontiac)

improperly centered shoes can also cause excessive pedal travel.

The check valve can be tested by applying and releasing the brakes and then cracking open a wheel cylinder bleed screw. If residual pressure is present, a brief spurt of fluid will occur.

Master Cylinder Repair

Remove the master cylinder. Cap the brake lines to prevent the entry of foreign material. Scrape off exterior dirt. Wash the exterior in approved brake system solvent. Remove the push rod where used. (In some designs, the stop plate or retainer must be removed first.)

 Caution: Some stop plate retaining rings can fly out with great force. Hold the piston in until the snap ring is removed. Withdraw pistons, springs, and other parts.

If residual check valves are used, remove the valves by pulling the tube seats. This is done by threading a screw into the seat and prying up on the screw, **Figure 34-14.**

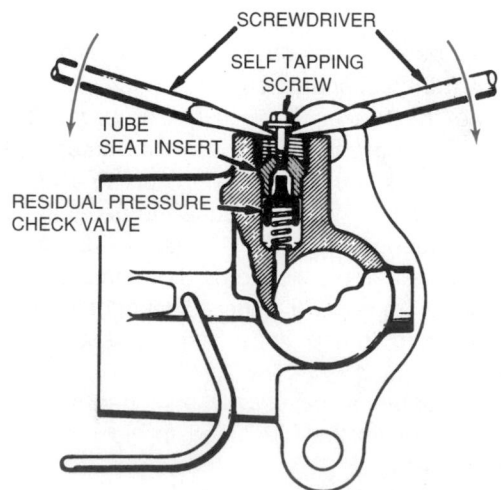

Figure 34-14. Pulling tube seat insert to free the check valve for removal.

Use Special Solutions for Cleaning

 Caution: Clean all parts in a recommended brake cleaning solution or brake fluid. Never allow brake system rubber parts to contact gasoline, kerosene, oil, or any type of petroleum-based cleaner. Never touch rubber parts with oily or gasoline-soaked fingers. Wash your hands with soap and water before handling parts.

If exceptionally dirty, it is permissible to wash the disassembled cylinder body, head nut, push rod, and reservoir cap in fresh petroleum-based solvent provided the parts are blown dry, rinsed in approved brake solvent or alcohol, blown dry again, rinsed again in brake solvent or alcohol, and blown dry a third time.

When all parts are clean, inspect the cylinder surface. Hold it up to a good light. Scoring, pitting, or heavy corrosion will require discarding entire master cylinder. Minor (very light) scratches and corrosion can be removed with crocus cloth. Do not use emery cloth or sandpaper.

The cylinder, in some cases, can be honed to remove minor scratches. The hone stones must be true, clean, and extremely smooth. Hone as little as possible. Use brake fluid as a hone lubricant. Place crocus cloth over the hone stones for a final smoothing.

Some manufacturers diamond bore the master cylinder to a very smooth finish and then roll the surface to produce a glassy finish. Honing this type of cylinder during service will destroy the glassy finish and, therefore, is not recommended. Do not attempt to remove scratches, pits, or corrosion from aluminum master cylinder bores. This removes the protective anodized surface. If any scratches or pits show or if aluminum can be seen through the anodizing, the cylinder must be replaced.

 Note: Do not try to salvage a master cylinder unless the cylinder is in excellent condition. Trying to save a few pennies can cost dearly.

When the cylinder has been cleaned, scrub the bore with a clean, lint-free cloth dipped in approved brake solvent. Repeat the flushing process two more times. Compressed air must be oil free.

Ports Must Be Open and Free of Burrs

Check the compensating and inlet or breather ports. They must be clean and open. The compensating port may be cleaned by passing a thin (.020″ or 0.508 mm), smooth, copper wire through the opening. Do not pass square or rough-tipped steel wires through the port.

If a burr is present at the port, remove it with a deburring tool. The slightest burr will cut the primary cup and cause leakage. Remove all burrs. Give all parts a final rinse with brake cleaning fluid and blow dry.

Lubricate with Brake Fluid

Coat the cylinder wall with brake fluid. Dip the piston and rubber cups in clean brake fluid. Assemble in the reverse order of disassembly.

Cylinders, cups, and pistons must be coated with brake fluid before assembly. Parts assembled dry can cause sticking and scoring. Use a repair kit if the cylinder is in excellent condition. Never install old parts. Make certain that the piston stop plate lock ring is properly engaged. **Figure 34-15** illustrates the parts of a typical master cylinder. All parts should be carefully inspected during service.

Bleed Master Cylinder before Installing

Attach bleeder tubes, **Figure 34-16.** Add the recommended brake fluid to the reservoir until the fluid level is above the ends of the bleeder tubes. Force the pistons in and out several times until all air is dispelled from the cylinder. Maintain the reservoir level while bleeding. Remove the bleeder tubes. Install the cover to prevent fluid contamination. Plugs or a special bleeding syringe can be used in place of the bleeder tubes. Follow the manufacturer's recommendations. See **Figures 34-17** and **34-18.**

 Caution: Avoid spraying brake fluid. Wear safety goggles.

Install the cylinder and connect the lines. At this time, it is good practice to crack each master cylinder line connection open a small amount. Wrap a rag around the connection. Depress the brake pedal gently to force the remaining air out of the master cylinder. Tighten the connection before releasing. Adjust the brake pedal. Bleed the brakes (discussed later in this chapter). Fill the master cylinder to the proper level and install the cap and seal.

Adjusting Brake Pedal Height

If the pedal has an adjustable stop, measure the distance from the floorboard to the bottom of the pedal. Check against specifications and adjust if needed, **Figure 34-19.**

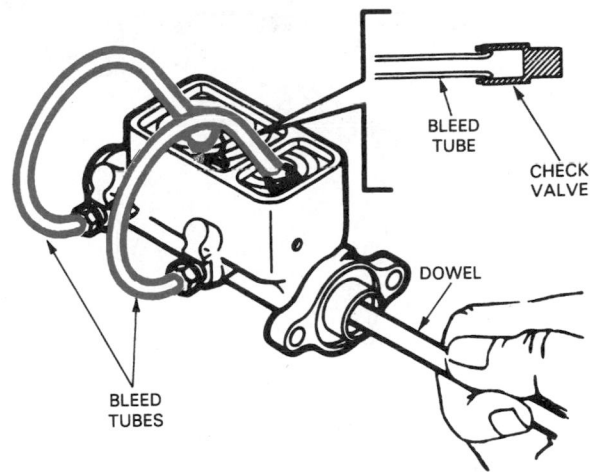

Figure 34-16. Bench bleeding a master cylinder before installation. Note the bleeder tubes. Operate the pistons until air is expelled. (Chrysler)

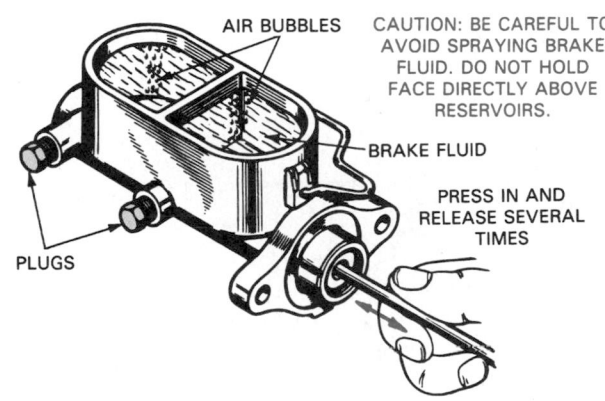

Figure 34-17. Bleeding a master cylinder with the aid of plugs. Force the piston in and out until air bubbles stop. Install the cylinder. (Bendix)

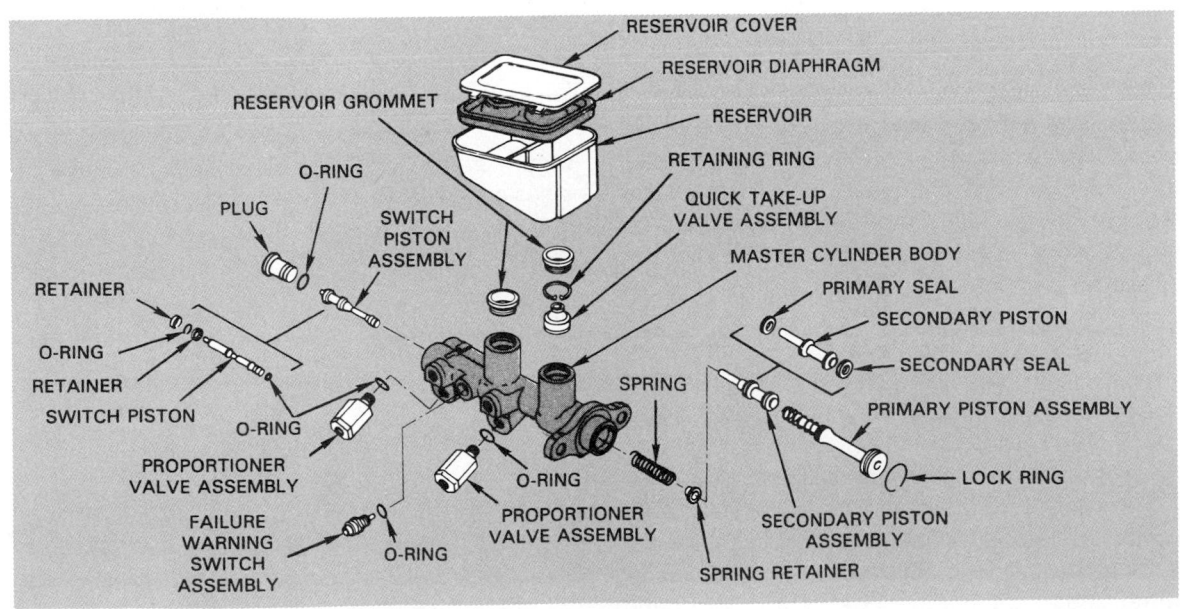

Figure 34-15. Exploded view of one type master cylinder. Carefully inspect *all* parts during service. Follow the manufacturer's overhaul procedures carefully. (Bendix)

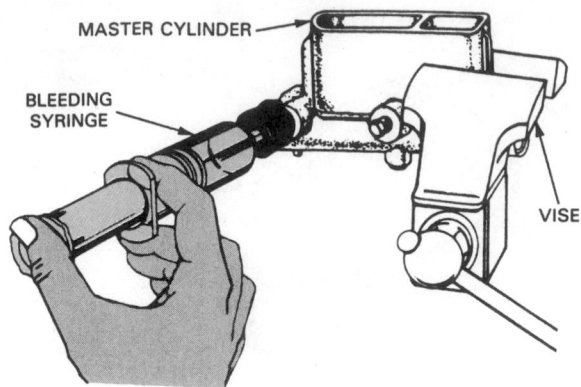

Figure 34-18.   Master cylinder being bled with a special syringe. Plug the outlet holes. Fill the cylinder with fluid (about half full). Remove a plug. Depress the syringe plunger fully. Place it firmly against an outlet. Pull the plunger out until the syringe is half full. Remove the syringe. Point it straight up. Expel air until fluid squirts out. Put the syringe (with fluid) on the same outlet and depress the plunger. When air bubbles in the reservoir stop, remove the syringe and plug the outlet. Repeat this procedure on the other outlets. Plug the outlets firmly. (EIS)

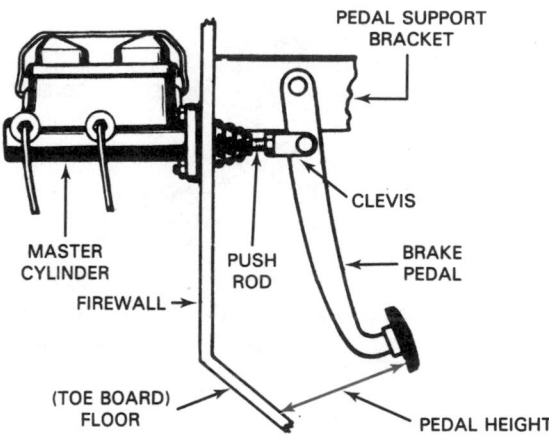

Figure 34-19.   Brake pedal height should be as specified.

Adjusting Brake Pedal Free Travel

Brake pedal *free travel* is the distance the pedal moves before the push rod engages the cylinder piston. Free travel is needed to ensure that the piston will not be applied when the pedal is in the released position.

Free travel is automatically set on some cylinders when the brake pedal height is correctly adjusted by lengthening or shortening the push rod clevis. See **Figure 34-20.**

Other types utilize a separate pedal stop. The push rod is adjusted until the correct free travel exists. **Figure 34-21** illustrates pedal free travel.

On some vehicles with power brakes, the technician must check the distance from the push rod to the face of the vacuum booster. Use a special gauge and adjust as needed before mounting the cylinder, **Figures 34-22** and **34-23.** Proper free travel for manual (non-power) brakes is around 1/4″ to 1/2″ (6.35 to 12.70 mm). For power-assisted brakes, free travel ranges from 1/8″ to 3/8″ (3.18 to 9.53 mm).

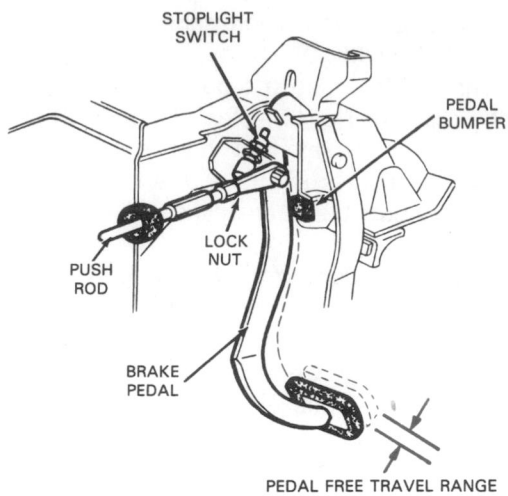

Figure 34-20.   Brake pedal free travel.

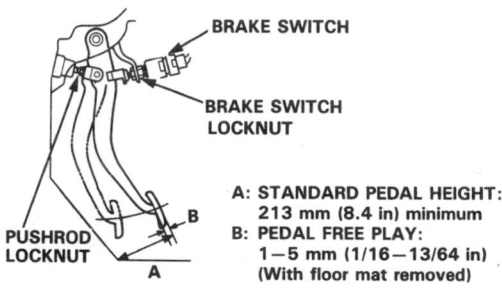

A: STANDARD PEDAL HEIGHT: 213 mm (8.4 in) minimum
B: PEDAL FREE PLAY: 1–5 mm (1/16–13/64 in) (With floor mat removed)

Loosen the pushrod locknut and screw the pushrod in or out with pliers until the standard pedal height from the floor is 213 mm (8.4 in). After adjustment, tighten the locknut firmly.

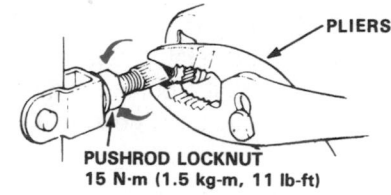

PUSHROD LOCKNUT
15 N·m (1.5 kg-m, 11 lb-ft)

Screw in the brake switch until its plunger is fully depressed (threaded end touching the pad on the pedal arm). Then back off the switch 1/2 turn and tighten the locknut firmly.

Figure 34-21.   Obtaining brake pedal free travel by pushrod adjustment on one particular setup. If necessary, adjust the brake light switch *after* pushrod adjustment. (Honda)

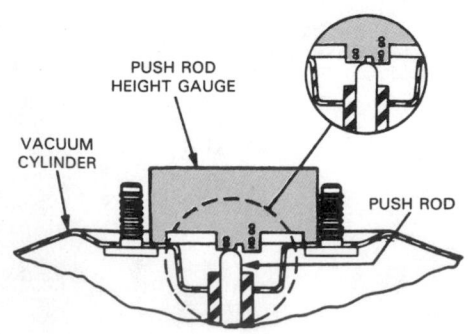

Figure 34-22.   Checking the distance that the master cylinder push rod protrudes from the vacuum booster unit. (Pontiac)

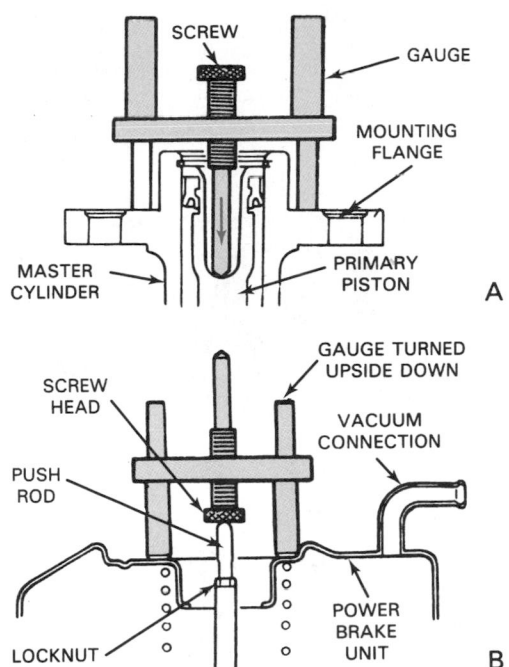

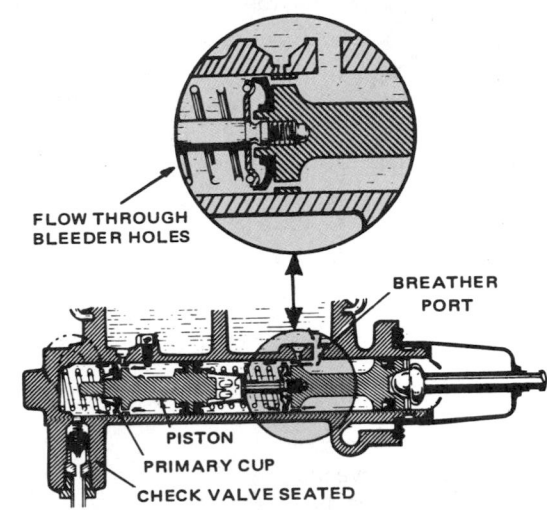

instant piston release until the check valve can move from its seat. The primary cup lips are forced away from the cylinder wall by the passage of fluid through tiny bleeder holes in the head of the piston. See **Figure 34-25.**

Figure 34-25. Master cylinder operation at start of fast release. (Buick)

As the piston continues to release, fluid forces the check valve off its seat and flows into the cylinder. When the piston releases to the point where the compensating port is uncovered, excess fluid will flow into the reservoir. Look at **Figure 34-26.**

Types of Wheel Cylinders

Three typical wheel cylinders are shown in **Figure 34-27.** Shown in A, the single end type is used one per brake shoe, or in some cases, only one per wheel where one shoe is allowed to apply the other. The stepped cylinder, in B, is used to apply a different force to each brake shoe. The most widely used cylinder, C, uses two pistons in a straight cylinder. One other type employs a pierced baffle between the pistons to retard the return of one of the pistons.

Wheel Cylinder Service

Always remove, disassemble, and clean wheel cylinders when the brakes are relined. Relining the brakes, in

Figure 34-23. Special adjustment gauge being used to measure and set push rod length. A—Gauge set on master cylinder mounting flange. Screw is turned in until it just touches the primary piston. B—Gauge is turned upside down and place on the power brake unit. Loosen the locknut and turn the push rod until it just touches the screw head. Tighten the locknut. Proper push rod clearance is now set. (Mazda)

Wheel Cylinder Operation

Pressure from the master cylinder is delivered to the **wheel cylinder** by lines and hoses. This pressure moves the wheel cylinder pistons outward until the brake shoes contact the drum. Any increase in brake pedal pressure beyond this point will cause a corresponding increase in shoe-to-drum contact. **Figure 34-24** shows the system with brakes being applied. Since the brake drum is attached to the axle, contact with the brake shoes causes the drum and axle to stop turning.

When the brake pedal is released, the brake shoe retracting springs force fluid to flow backward into the master cylinder. Tiny holes in the piston prevent vacuum action that could draw air into the cylinder. The holes also permit

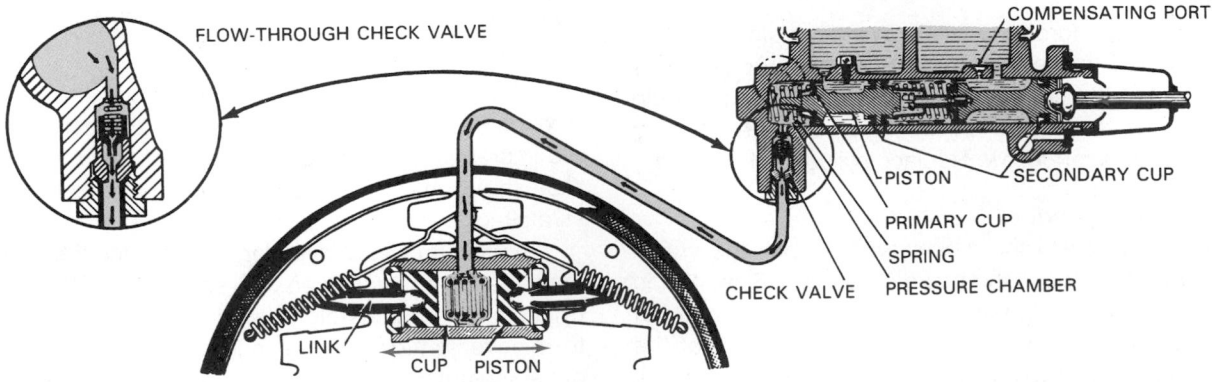

Figure 34-24. Drum brake system with brakes applied. (Buick)

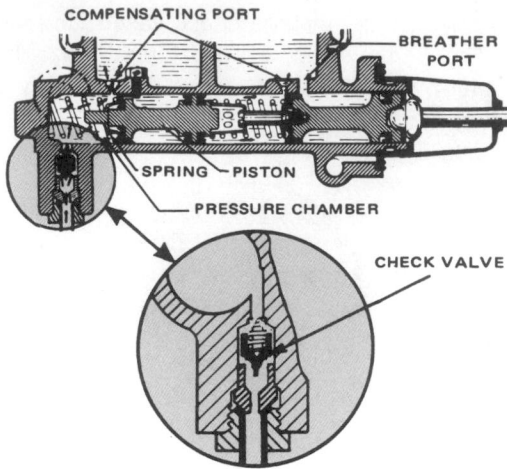

Figure 34-26. Master cylinder operation during finish of fast release. (Buick)

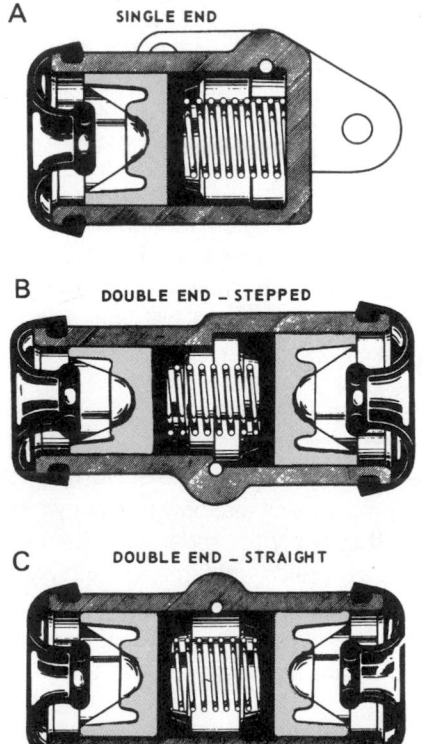

Figure 34-27. Typical wheel cylinders. (Bendix)

some designs, can force the wheel cylinder pistons deeper into the cylinder. In the event corrosion, rust, or gum has formed between the cups, forcing the pistons inward would cause the cups to operate on the rough surface. Scoring and leakage will soon follow. Replace cylinders if needed.

Remove Wheel Cylinder

To gain access to the wheel cylinder, pull the wheel and brake drum. Remove the brake shoes (see Brake Shoe Removal in this chapter). Loosen the brake line flare nut at the wheel cylinder. Do not bend the brake line out of the way. This can damage the line and make alignment difficult during installation. Remove the wheel cylinder-to-backing plate fasteners. Remove the cylinder. See **Figure 34-28.**

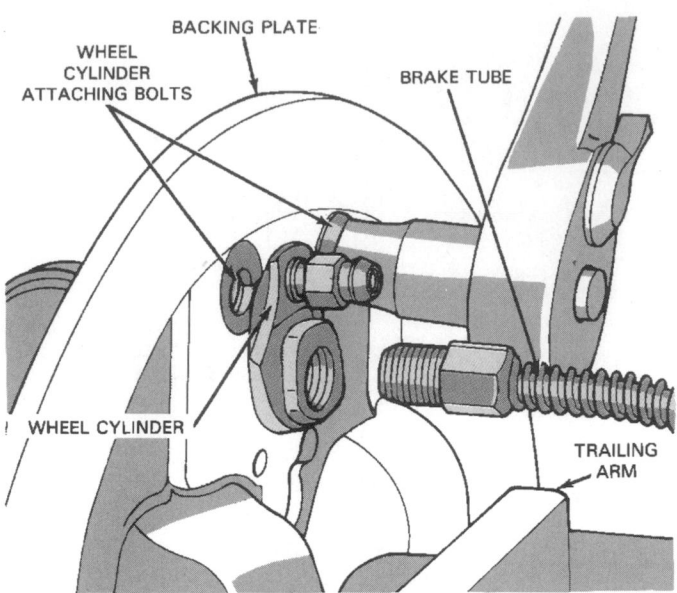

Figure 34-28. Removing the wheel cylinder attaching bolts so the cylinder can be removed from the backing plate. (Chrysler)

Observe Cautions

When disassembling, repairing, and assembling any wheel cylinder, keep rubber parts away from oil and grease. Wash hands with soap and water before handling rubber parts. Use approved (non-petroleum based) brake cleaning solvents or denatured alcohol for cleaning. Lubricate parts with brake fluid before reassembly.

Wheel Cylinder Repair

Pull the rubber boots free of the cylinder and push the pistons, cups, and spring from the cylinder. Use air on single end cylinders to force the piston free. See **Figure 34-29.**

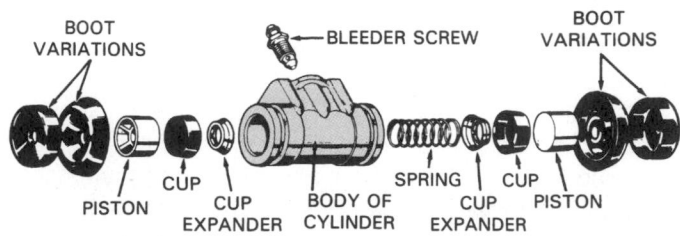

Figure 34-29. Typical wheel cylinder. (Bendix)

Wash all parts in approved brake solvent or denatured alcohol. Some wheel cylinder pistons are made of iron and are impregnated with lubricant. Do not wash these pistons; wipe them off. Pistons should not be reused if pitted or scratched.

Aluminum wheel cylinder bodies should be replaced if they are pitted, corroded, or scratched. Clean cast iron cylinders with crocus cloth and inspect. If crocus cloth fails to remove scratches or pitting, light honing (with very fine grit stones) may be used. Use brake fluid for stone lubrication, **Figure 34-30.** If the wheel cylinder has a special glassy, rolled finish, do not attempt honing.

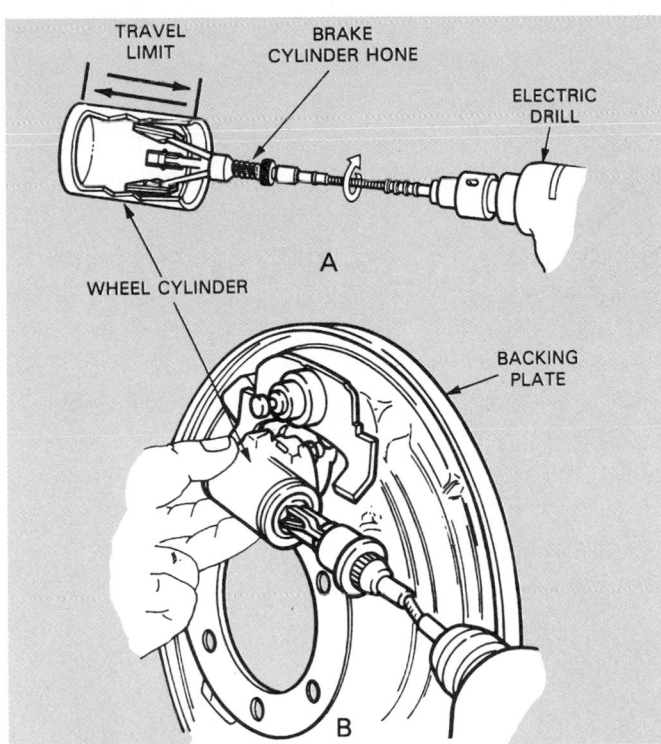

Figure 34-30. Honing a wheel cylinder. A—Hone in place. Note stone travel limit. *Do not* push stones all the way through or pull them completely out while they are turning. Compress spring-loaded fingers and insert them before starting to turn the hone. B—Wheel cylinder being honed while mounted on the backing plate. (Niehoff)

Following honing or the use of crocus cloth, scrub the cylinder with a rag soaked in brake cleaner. Rinse at least two times and blow dry.

 Note: The compressed air used to blow cylinders dry must be dry and free of oil. If it is not, allow parts to air dry.

Inspect the cylinder. The finish must be free of scoring and pitting. A slight pitting in the very center of the cylinder is permissible as long as it is not on that part of the cylinder that engages the rubber cups. If doubtful, discard the cylinder.

Many shops will not overhaul wheel cylinders. They feel that the cost of the labor involved, along with a possible reduction in the service life of used cylinders, does not warrant such work. When a cylinder is defective, it is replaced with a new one.

Check the clearance between the piston and cylinder wall. It must not exceed .005″ (0.127 mm) for cylinders 1″ (25.4 mm) or less in diameter, or .007″ (0.178 mm) for cylinders exceeding 1″ (25.4 mm) in diameter. Use a No-Go gauge or a feeler gauge. Pistons must be free of corrosion, scoring, and flat spots. If the pistons pass this test, coat the cylinder, new cups, and pistons with brake fluid and assemble. See **Figure 34-31.**

Note: Make certain that the cup lips face inward. If cup expanders are used, they must be in place. Do not damage cups when starting them into the cylinder. Do not force the cups over the center ports.

Snap the end boots into place to hold the pistons in the cylinder. Use a cylinder clamp if needed. Install the cylinder on the backing plate. Connect the brake line. Install the shoes and drum. Bleed the brakes. A typical wheel cylinder installation is illustrated in **Figure 34-32.**

Disc Brake Caliper Service

Disc brakes utilize a heavy disc, called a rotor, instead of a conventional brake drum. The disc is bolted to the wheel hub. A **brake caliper,** bolted to the spindle, surrounds the disc. When the brake is applied, hydraulic pressure from the master cylinder forces the **caliper piston** outward, forcing friction pads against the revolving disc. This will stop the disc.

Disc brakes are highly resistant to fade (loss of friction from overheating). A typical disc brake assembly is pictured in **Figures 34-33** and **34-34.** The friction pads are self-adjusting and operate with very little clearance between the lining and disc. One design actually allows the pads to rub the disc very lightly at all times.

Disc Brake Caliper

A caliper utilizing two hydraulic pistons on each side is illustrated in **Figure 34-35.** This particular caliper may

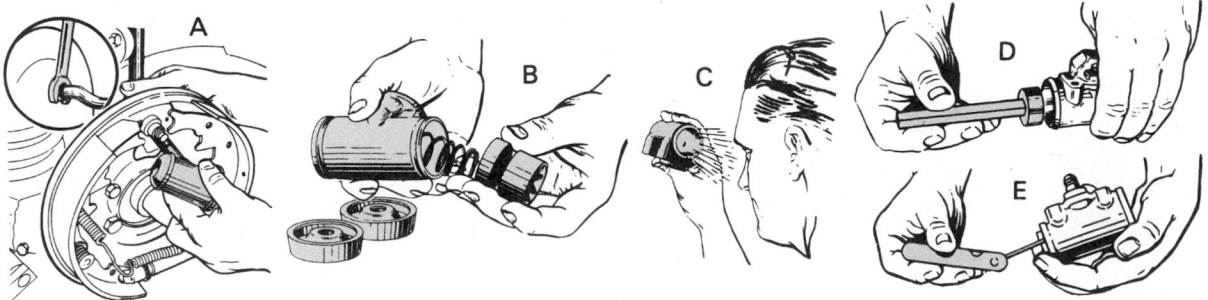

Figure 34-31. Some major steps in wheel cylinder reconditioning. A—Remove cylinder. B—Disassemble and clean. C—Inspect cylinder. D—Checking cylinder with No-Go gauge. E—Checking cylinder-to-piston clearance with a feeler gauge. (Wagner)

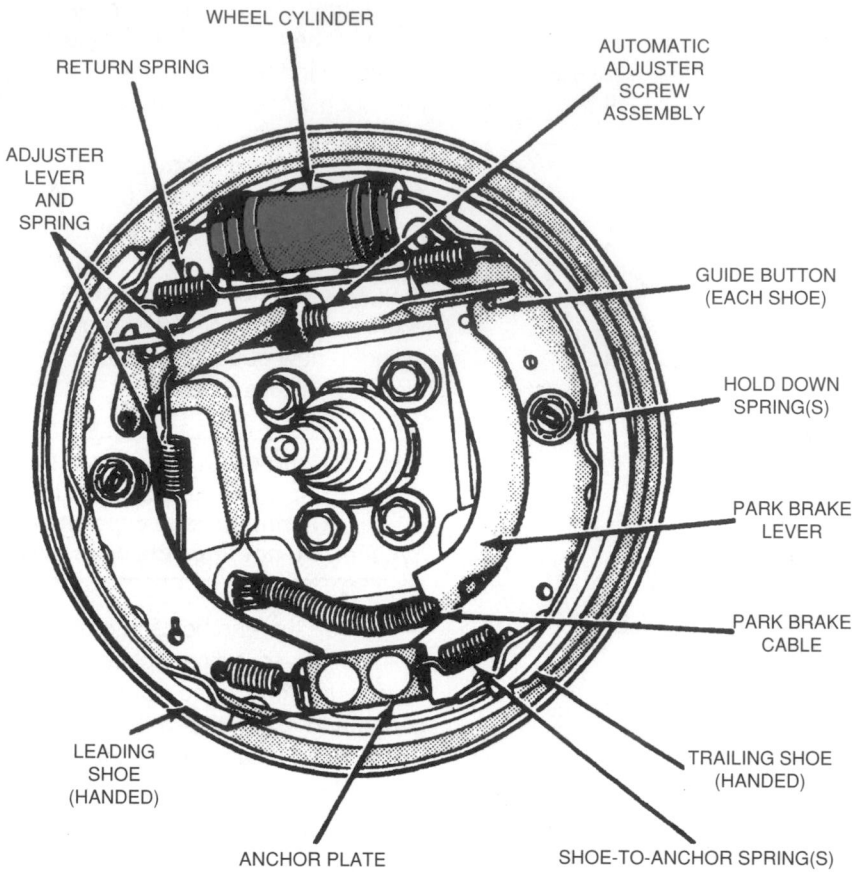

WHEEL CYLINDER

RETURN SPRING

AUTOMATIC
ADJUSTER
SCREW
ASSEMBLY

ADJUSTER
LEVER
AND
SPRING

GUIDE BUTTON
(EACH SHOE)

HOLD DOWN
SPRING(S)

PARK BRAKE
LEVER

PARK BRAKE
CABLE

LEADING
SHOE
(HANDED)

TRAILING SHOE
(HANDED)

ANCHOR PLATE

SHOE-TO-ANCHOR SPRING(S)

Figure 34-32   A typical wheel cylinder installation. This is from the left side of the vehicle. (Chrysler)

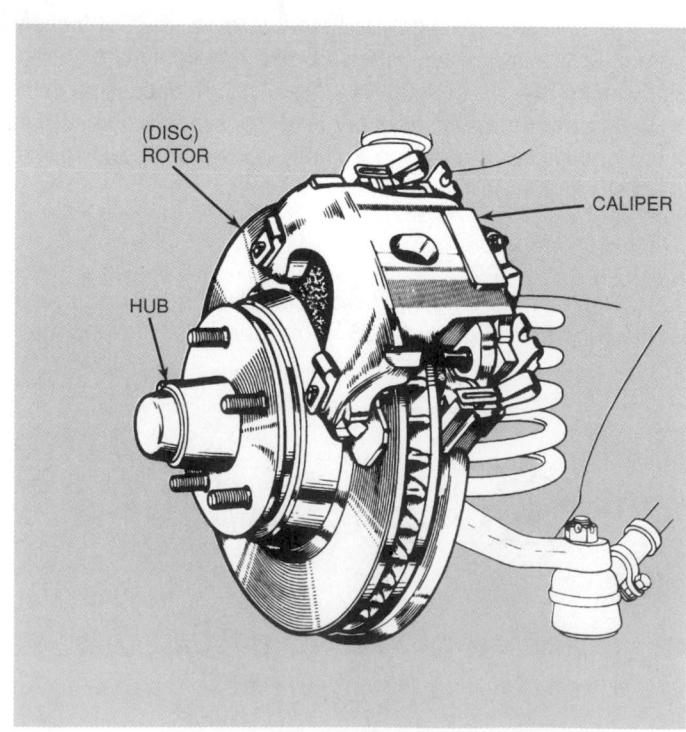

(DISC)
ROTOR

CALIPER

HUB

Figure 34-33.   Typical disc brake assembly. (Bendix)

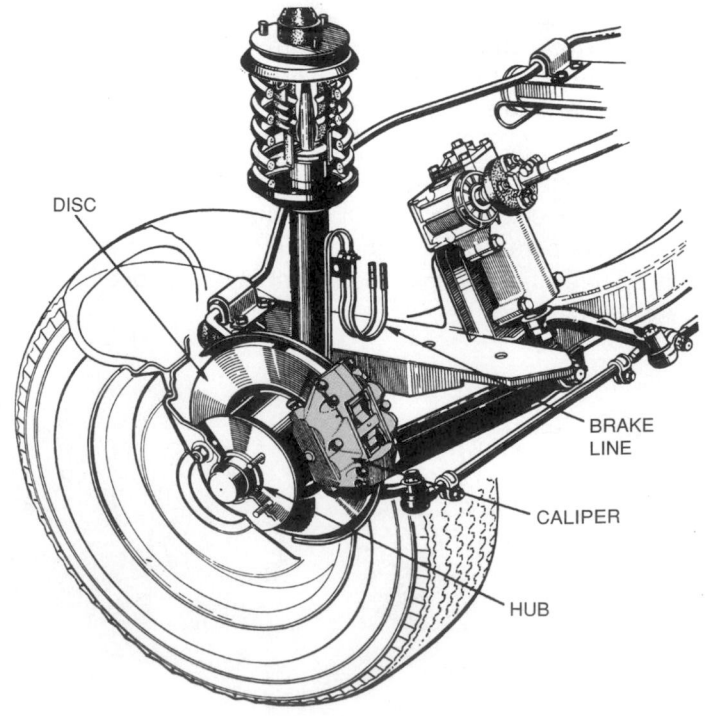

DISC

BRAKE
LINE

CALIPER

HUB

Figure 34-34. Typical front disc brake setup. (BMW)

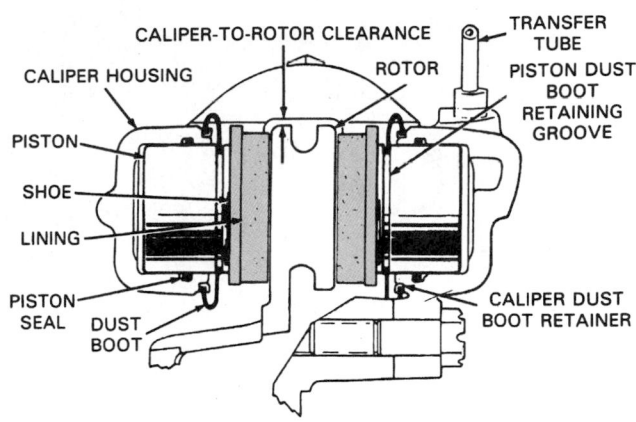

Figure 34-35. Exploded view of a disc brake caliper using two pistons in each half. (Chrysler)

Figure 34-37. One type of caliper pad and piston design.

have the two halves separated for repair. New seal rings must be used when bolting the halves back together. Some calipers must not have the halves separated. The technique used to maintain pad clearance in the caliper shown in **Figure 34-36** is simple and effective.

When the piston is forced outward to apply the disc, the piston seal stretches slightly to the side, **Figure 34-36A.** When the pedal is released, the seal straightens up and draws the piston back far enough for the pad to clear the disc, **Figure 34-36B.** In addition to the withdrawal action of the seal, any slight runout in the disc also helps to push the pad away.

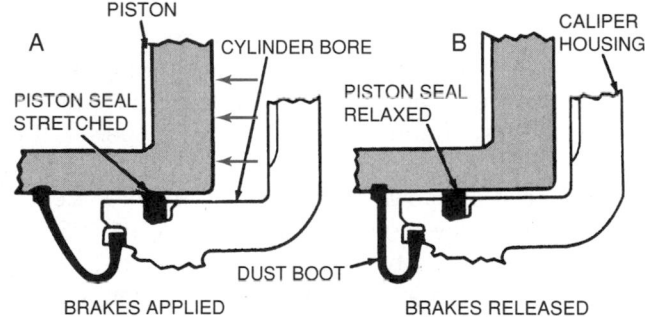

Figure 34-36. Seal action maintains proper pad-to-disc clearance. A—Brakes applied, seal forced sideways. B—Brakes released, seal pulls piston back.

Fixed and Floating Calipers

Some caliper assemblies are held rigidly in place. These are called *fixed calipers* and require the use of at least one piston on each side to force the pads against the disc. **Figure 34-37** illustrates one arrangement.

The *floating caliper* uses one piston and is free to slide sideways. As the piston is forced out, it first shoves the brake pad it contacts against the disc. When all movement in this direction is taken up, the caliper itself slides away from the piston. This draws the other pad (installed in outboard side of caliper) against the disc or rotor. Further piston travel merely applies pressure to both pads.

Actual movement is very small as the pads barely clear the disc after the brakes have been released. **Figure 34-38** shows the various parts of the common single piston, floating caliper assembly. Modern vehicles often have disc

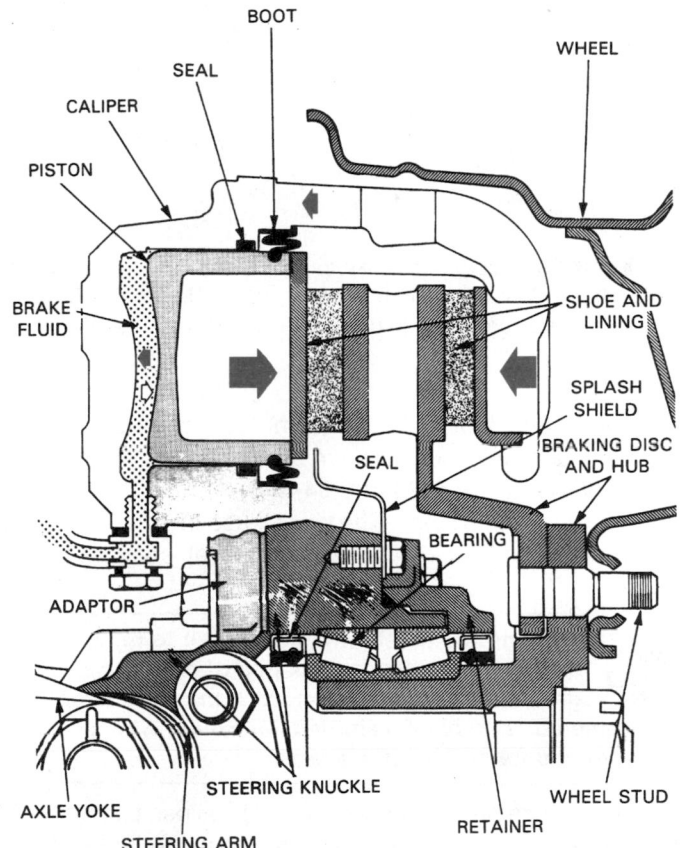

Figure 34-38. Cross section of a single piston, floating caliper disc brake as used on one particular front-wheel drive vehicle. (Dodge)

brakes on the front, with drum brakes on the rear. Some vehicles have disc brakes on both front and rear. The hydraulic system action is essentially the same for all system configurations.

Servicing Disc Brake Calipers

When the caliper is removed, check carefully for any aligning shims. Tag as to proper location. If the caliper halves can be separated, **Figure 34-37,** do so. Then, continue disassembly. See **Figure 34-39A.** Remove the piston

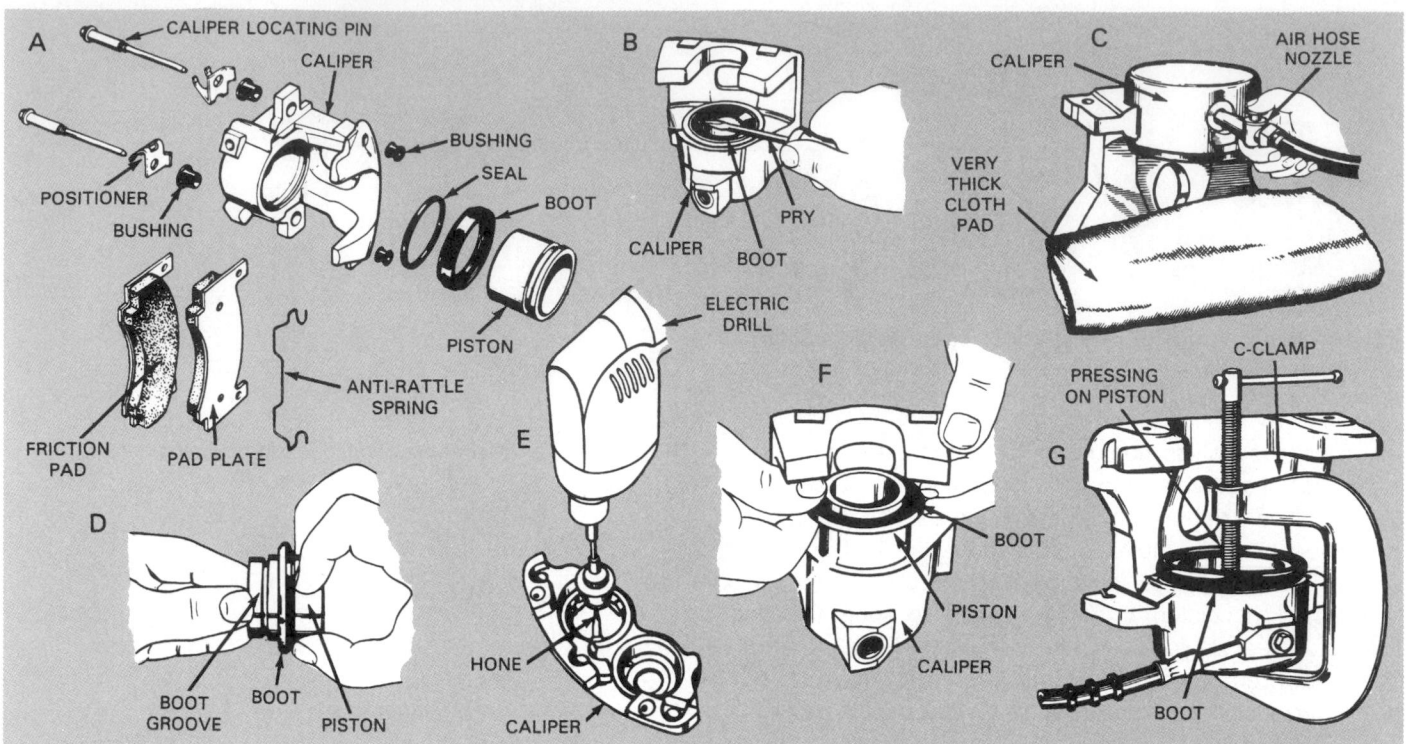

Figure 34-39. Common brake caliper overhaul operations. A—Exploded view of a single piston floating caliper. B—Removing piston boot. C—Use of air to remove piston. *Be careful!* D—Installing boot on cleaned and lubricated piston. E—Honing cylinder bore. F—Inserting piston in clean, lubricated bore. G—Forcing piston all the way in with a small C-clamp. (Bendix)

dust boots (or boot on single piston caliper). Use care (a fiber or plastic pry stick helps) to avoid scratching either the piston or cylinder wall, **Figure 34-39B.**

Remove the pistons. The careful use of an air hose, as shown in **Figure 34-39C,** makes removal easy on some calipers.

STOP Warning: Be careful when using air to remove the caliper piston. Use a thick pad of cloth. Apply air gradually with little pressure. If the piston does not come out, remove the air. Rap the caliper with a soft hammer and try air pressure again.

Do not remove phenolic (plastic) caliper pistons with air pressure. They require more force to move in their bore than the cast iron type. They can come out with enough force to damage the piston. Remove these with system hydraulic pressure before the brake lines are disconnected from the calipers.

Pad with cloth to avoid piston damage. Keep fingers clear, as the piston can come out very fast. Turn unit away from face and body. Keep other personnel away and cover the whole assembly with a heavy shield cloth.

Remove the cylinder seal. Use a nonmetallic pry tool. When the caliper assembly is stripped, as in **Figure 34-39A,** clean all parts in brake cleaner and blow them dry. Make certain that the air source is oil free. If in doubt, blow the parts dry, give them a final rinse in clean brake cleaner or alcohol, and let them air dry. Be careful with alcohol—it is very flammable.

Check caliper cylinders carefully for scoring or corrosion. Some assemblies require that a feeler gauge be used between the piston and bore to check for proper fit. If the bore is in relatively poor condition, discard it. If it is in fair condition, hone as shown in **Figure 34-39E.** Bore size must not be increased by more than around .001″ (0.025 mm). Use brake fluid on the hone. Stones must be fine.

A cylinder bore in quite good condition can often be cleaned by hand, using crocus cloth. Following honing (or use of crocus cloth), the entire unit must be thoroughly cleaned in brake cleaner or alcohol. Brush out boot and seal grooves with a nonmetallic brush. Thoroughly blow out the grooves and all passageways. Repeat cleaning several times.

Coat the new piston seal with special lubricant and place it into the groove in the cylinder. Use your fingers only. Lubricate the bore. Make sure the seal is seated.

Check the condition of the piston(s) and replace them if the plating is scored, corroded, or worn. If the caliper contains more than one piston, always replace them in pairs. Check phenolic (plastic) pistons for cracks, gouges, or chips.

Thoroughly clean the piston and groove. Coat the new boot with special lubricant. Slide the boot over the piston, **Figure 34-39D.** Some pistons require the use of a special silicone sealer in the dust boot groove. Install it before the boot is placed on the piston. This is shown in **Figure 34-40.** Slide the boot into its groove.

Make certain that the cylinder bore and piston are coated with brake fluid. Place the piston in the bore and

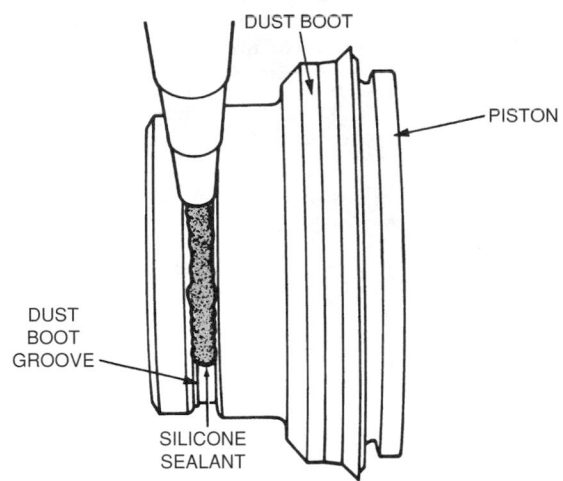

Figure 34-40.   Placing special silicone sealer in the dust boot groove before the boot is installed. (Bendix)

press inward, **Figure 34-39F.** If needed, a C-clamp may be used against piston. See **Figure 34-39G.** The clamp will hold piston down while the edge of the boot is snapped into place in the caliper boot groove.

When using a C-clamp with plastic pistons, place a smooth piece of metal or wood across the piston. Do not place the C-clamp in direct contact with the piston, or damage to the piston may result. Use a blunt tool. Do not puncture the boot. If you do, replace the boot.

Install the brake pads. Some calipers permit installation after the caliper is mounted. Secure as needed. Lubricate any recommended surfaces. Never get lubricant on the pad or disc. Install the caliper as recommended.

 Note: Do not switch calipers from side to side. Mounting the calipers on the opposite side will often place the bleeder screw in a position that makes it impossible to completely bleed the brakes.

Bleed and actuate the brakes to make sure the caliper pads are in full contact with the disc. The above techniques are common, but variations in calipers might call for a slightly different installation method. Use recommended procedures.

Servicing Brake Lines and Hose

Brake lines must be in excellent condition, free of rust, dents, kinks, and abraded areas. They must be supported to prevent vibration. Hoses must be free of cracking, kinking, swelling, and cuts. Hoses must not contact any moving parts. When replacing brake lines, use only double-wrapped, coated steel tubing.

 Warning: Never use copper tubing for brake lines.

Use double-lap flares on the tubing ends. See Chapter 8 for complete instructions on flaring, cutting, and bending. **Figure 34-41** illustrates the formation of a dou-

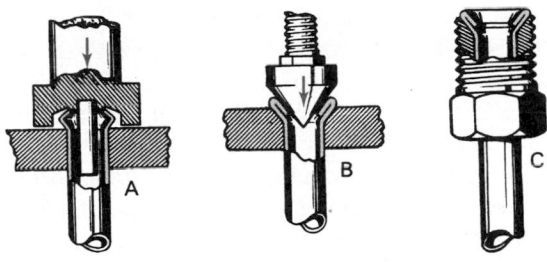

Figure 34-41.   Steps involved in forming a double-lap flare, A—Forming single lap. B—Forming double lap. C—Finished double-lap flare with fitting. (Bendix)

ble-lap flare. **Figure 34-42** pictures an I.S.O. (International Standards Organization) type flare. These are not interchangeable.

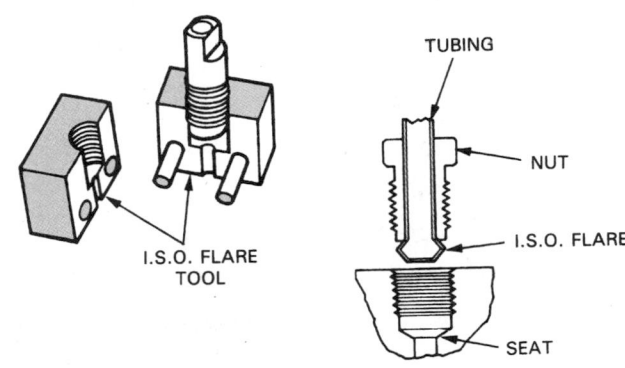

Figure 34-42.   Cutaway view of an I.S.O. (International Standards Organization) flare and seat. Note the special tool required to form this flare. Follow the tool manufacturer's instructions. *Do not* use this flare with a single-lap or double-lap flare arrangement. (Bendix)

Servicing Brake System Hydraulic Valves

To provide even braking and warn of problems, the brake hydraulic system of modern vehicles contains many valves. The most common valves are the proportioning valve, the metering valve, and the pressure differential switch. These valves are sometimes installed in a single housing, called a combination valve.

Proportioning Valve

A *proportioning valve* is used in brake systems using disc brakes in the front and drum brakes in the rear. Under mild stops, braking effort is about equal to the front and rear. As pedal pressure is increased, the proportioning valve controls (and finally limits) pressure to the rear wheels. This reduces the possibility of rear-wheel lockup during heavy braking. The proportioning valve can be a separate unit or it can be incorporated into a combination valve.

Dual Proportioning Valve

Some vehicles utilize a diagonally split brake system with a dual proportioning valve. The master cylinder is connected directly to the valve. From there, the system is divided diagonally.

Height-Sensing Proportioning Valve

The *height-sensing proportioning valve* uses a variable pressure range feature, which increases the pressure to the rear brakes as the vehicle's weight (cargo) increases. This pressure will diminish as the vehicle's weight decreases. Most valves are located on the vehicle's chassis and are connected to the rear axle with a calibrated tension spring or a rod-type linkage. See **Figure 34-43**.

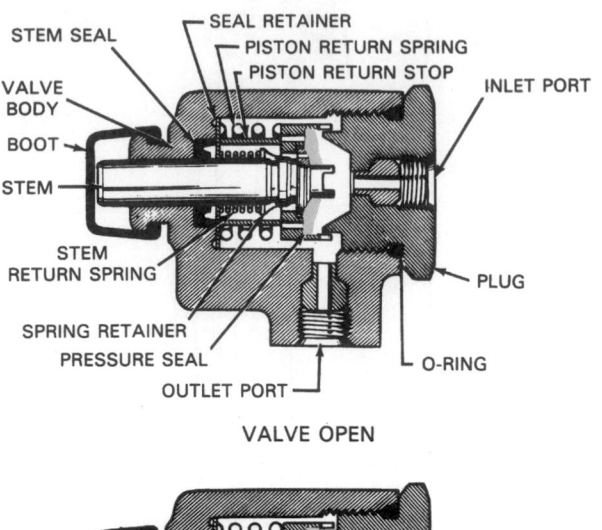

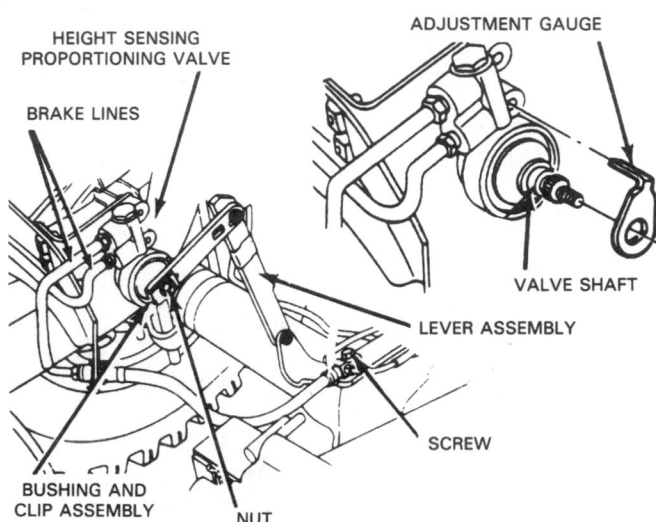

Figure 34-43. Height-sensing proportioning valve assembly. This unit is adjustable; others are not. Some require special bleeding procedures. Follow the manufacturer's service recommendations. (Fram)

Figure 34-44. Typical metering valve operation. (Chevrolet)

Vehicle weight transfer during a stop will cause chassis height-to-axle distance to change. The spring or rod linkage will also change in length. This, in turn, adjusts the valve, limiting pressure to the rear brakes. Loading the vehicle (wood in the bed of a truck, for example) will also actuate the valve.

 Warning: Do not alter vehicle riding height with air shocks or springs when equipped with this type of proportioning valve. Unsafe braking action could result.

Disc Brake Metering Valve

Vehicles with front disc and rear drum brakes require the use of a *metering valve*. See **Figure 34-44**. The metering valve closes off pressure to the front disc brakes until a specified pressure level is generated in the master cylinder. This allows pressure to force the back brake shoes to overcome retracting spring pressure and move into contact with the drum. Pressure beyond this opens the metering valve, and both front and rear brakes receive pressure.

Pressure Differential Switch

All dual brake systems use a *pressure differential switch* to warn the driver that one-half of the split brake

system has failed. A small piston "floats" in a cylinder separating two pressure chambers. One side of each chamber is connected to one side of the master cylinder. The piston is centered by a spring on each end. An electrical switch is placed in the center of the piston. The switch will be grounded whenever the piston moves to one side. This completes an electrical circuit through the dashboard-mounted brake warning light.

Figure 34-45 illustrates one type of differential pressure switch. It is in the normal "Light Out" position. Each side has equal pressure and the piston remains centered. When one side of the system develops a leak, the pressure drops on that side of the valve. The piston is forced toward the low pressure side. It then touches the electrical plunger and provides the ground needed to light the warning light.

Combination Valve

Combination valves contain either one or two of the valves discussed above. They are called the two-function valve and the three-function valve. The two-function valve combines the metering valve and the brake warning light switch in one unit, **Figure 33-46A**. Some units may contain a proportioning valve instead of the metering valve.

The three-function valve houses the metering valve, the proportioning valve, and the brake warning light switch, **Figure 34-46B**. These valves cannot be adjusted or repaired. If they are defective, the entire unit must be replaced.

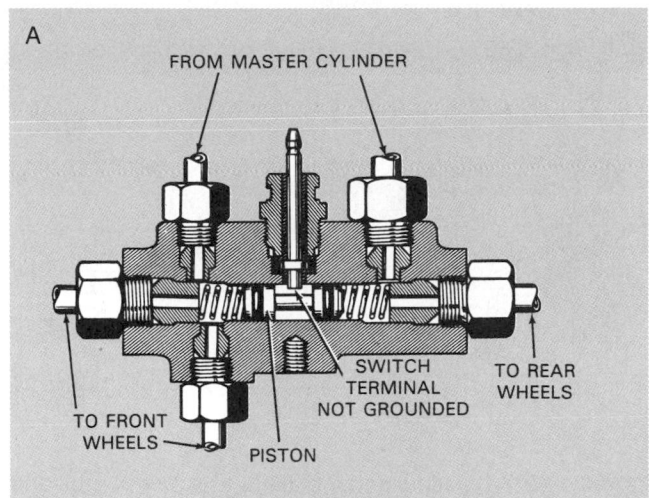

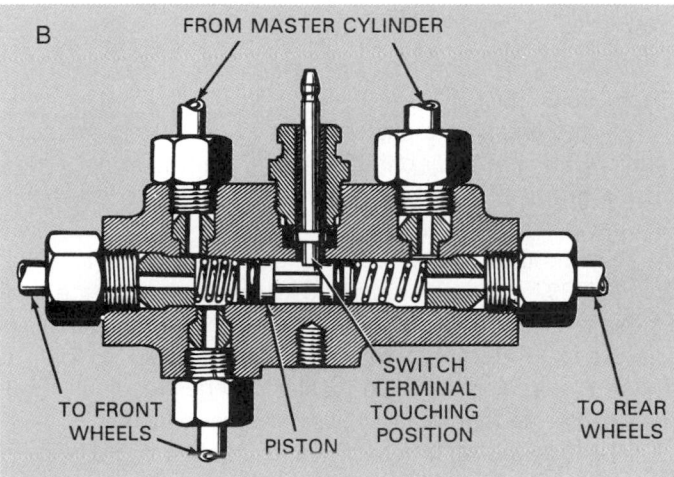

Figure 34-45. A—Pressure differential brake warning switch in normal position (no brake failure). The switch terminal is not touching the piston. B—Pressure differential brake warning switch with one side of system faulty. Note how the piston is forced toward the faulty side, grounding the switch terminal. The warning light would come on. (Chevrolet)

Bleeding the Brakes

Bleeding the brakes means removing air from brake system. Air can enter in a number of ways: a low fluid level in the master cylinder, a disconnected system component, or leaky wheel or master cylinder cups. Air in the system causes a springy or spongy feel when braking.

Bleeding consists of pumping fresh fluid throughout the system. This forces air out through the wheel cylinder or caliper bleeder valves. Brakes can be bled by manual or pressure means.

Manual Bleeding

Manual bleeding will require an assistant to pressurize the brake system by pressing on the brake pedal. Clean all wheel cylinder or caliper bleeder screws. Remove the cap or plug from the bleeder screw, if used. Attach a bleeder hose to the bleeder screw farthest from the master cylinder. Place the free end in a clear glass jar partially filled with brake fluid. Look at **Figure 34-47.**

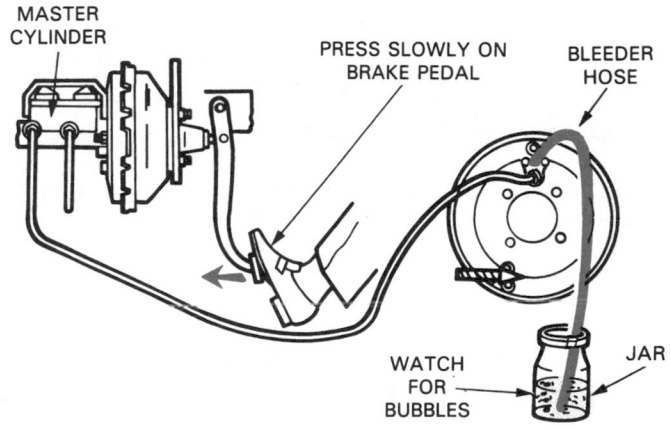

Figure 34-47. Manually (by foot) bleeding a rear wheel cylinder. Be sure to place the bleeder hose in a brake fluid jar. (Niehoff)

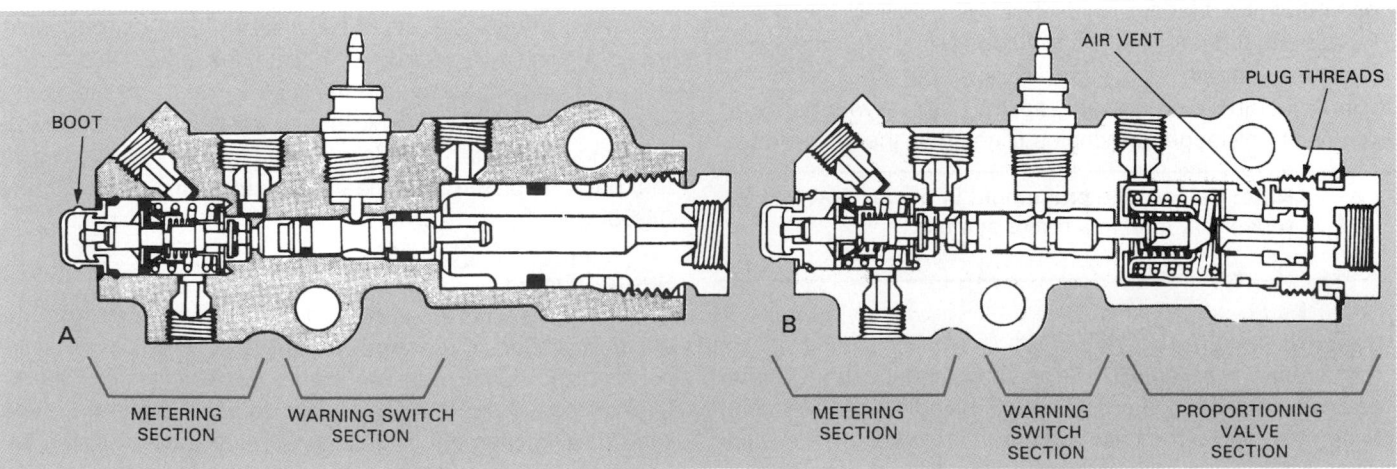

Figure 34-46. The two types of combination valves are the two-function valve (A) and the three-function valve (B). When servicing the brakes, always inspect these valves for leakage inside the boot and around the fittings. (Bendix)

Note: If the master cylinder is equipped with a bleeder screw, bleed the master cylinder first.

Clean the master cylinder reservoir cap and the surrounding area. Fill the reservoir almost to the top. Open the bleeder screw 3/4 turn. The free end of the hose must be submerged in the jar of fluid. Press the brake pedal slowly to the floor. This will force air and fluid from the wheel cylinder. Release pedal slowly. Repeat this process (keep reservoir filled at all times) until fresh brake fluid, with no air bubbles, flows into the jar. See **Figure 34-48.**

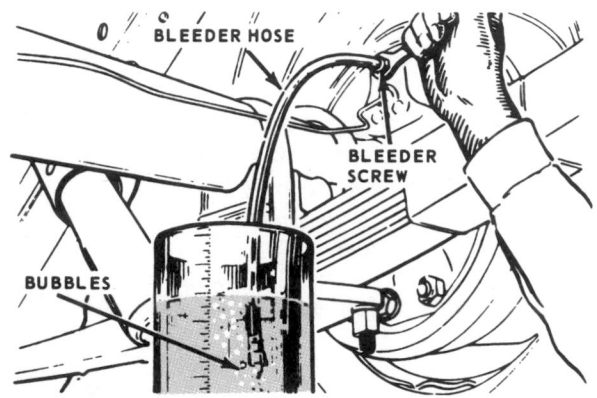

Figure 34-48. Bleed the cylinder until clear fluid, with *no* air bubbles, flows from the hose. Note bubbles still being forced from this system.

Tighten the bleeder screw. Remove the hose and move the setup to the wheel on the opposite side of the vehicle. Bleed the remaining cylinders or calipers in the same manner.

If desired, instead of letting up the brake pedal slowly, the bleeder screw may be closed after the pedal is depressed but before releasing. This requires an assistant. The pedal may then be released swiftly. Press the pedal down and reopen the bleeder. When the pedal reaches the floor, shut the bleeder again before releasing the brake. Repeat this process until clear fluid, with no air, enters jar.

Make certain all bleeder screws are shut off firmly. When bleeding disc brakes, rap the caliper with a plastic hammer to dislodge air bubbles clinging to the caliper wall.

Note: Discard the brake fluid in the jar. Never reuse this fluid in a brake system.

Pressure Bleeding

Pressure bleeding is faster than manual bleeding and requires only one person. Manual bleeding requires one person to operate the brake and another to watch the wheel area. A pressure tank, partially filled with brake fluid, is attached to the master cylinder reservoir. **Figure 34-49** illustrates a typical pressure bleeding hookup.

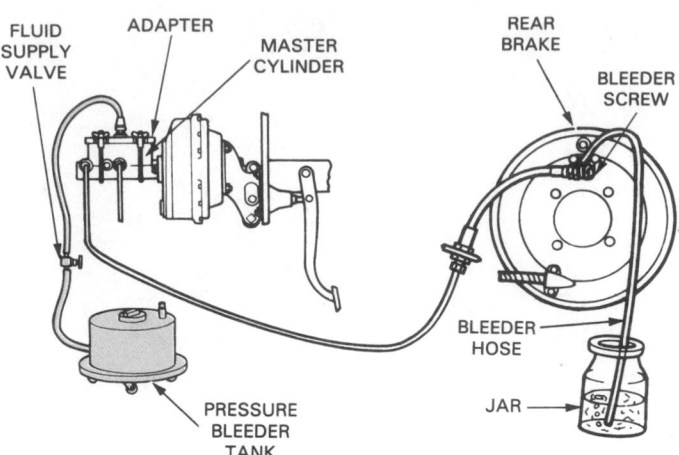

Figure 34-49. Bleeding a rear brake with a pressure bleeder tank and adapter. This method is generally recommended over manual bleeding. (Niehoff)

Pressure Bleeding Tank

Some pressure tanks separate the fluid from the compressed air with a diaphragm. If the tank does not use a diaphragm, only clean, dry, oil free, compressed air should be used.

Fill the tank to the specified level and charge to 20-30 psi (138-207 kPa) with an air hose. Avoid shaking the tank as this tends to form air bubbles. Keep the tank at least 1/3 full. Bleed the tank as required. Then, use an adapter to attach the tank to the filled master cylinder reservoir. Both the adapter and the master cylinder must be clean.

Turn on the tank hose valve to admit fluid pressure to the master cylinder. Attach a bleeder hose. Open the bleeder and allow fluid to flow from the cylinder until clean and free of air bubbles. Close the bleeder securely. Repeat this process on the remaining wheels. Shut off the pressure tank and remove it. Siphon off enough fluid to lower the master cylinder fluid level to 3/8″ (9.53 mm) from the top.

Bleeding Systems with Dual Master Cylinder

If the master cylinder has two caps but a common reservoir, attach the pressure bleeder tank to one hole. Insert a blind (no vent hole) cap in the other. If separate reservoirs are used, attach the tank to one and bleed that side. Then, attach the tank to the other side. When bleeding tandem master cylinders, bleed the wheels served by the primary piston (not floating piston) first. See **Figure 34-50.**

Surge Bleeding

In cases where it is difficult to remove the air from the wheel cylinder, try *surge bleeding.* Attach a pressure bleeder and admit pressure to the master cylinder. Open a bleeder screw and have a helper depress the brake pedal with a fast movement. Release the pedal slowly. Wait a few seconds and repeat. Continue until air is expelled. On the last downstroke of the brake pedal, close the bleeder screw quickly.

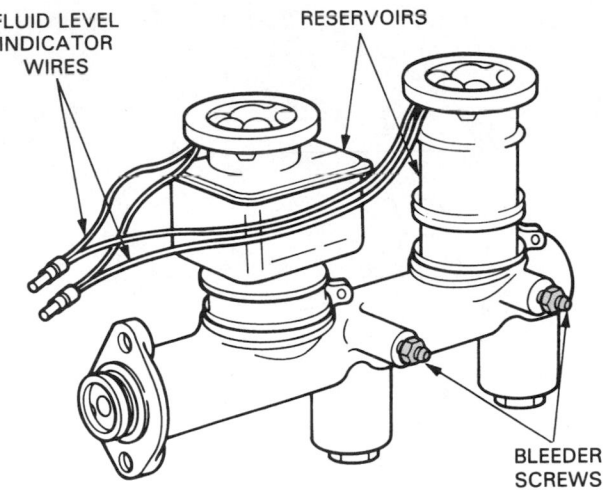

Figure 34-50. Master cylinder bleeder screws. Note the separate reservoirs and the use of fluid level indicators and wires. (Niehoff)

Bleeding Disc Brake Systems

When front disc brakes are used, the metering valve must be blocked open. A spring-like hold-open tool is recommended to prevent valve damage. Some installations require the removal of the pressure differential warning light switch terminal and plunger to prevent switch damage during bleeding.

Bleeding Power Brakes

Bleed power brakes as already described. When the brakes are being pumped to bleed them, it is helpful to start the engine and allow the booster to help apply the brakes. Close the bleeder before releasing the pedal when bleeding power units.

Bleeding Anti-Lock Brake Systems

Anti-lock brake systems do not operate at speeds under 6 to 10 MPH. Therefore, the bleeding procedure for a stationary anti-lock-equipped vehicle is the same as for a vehicle without anti-lock brakes. However, procedures for bleeding anti-lock brake systems vary among manufacturers. Always consult the vehicle's service manual and follow the recommendations carefully.

 Warning: The working pressure of some boost systems can reach 2600 psi (1 793 kPa). These systems must be pumped down to relieve pressure before the lines can be loosened. Failure to do so can result in serious injury.

Brake Friction Member Service

Friction members are the devices that stop the vehicle by the use of friction. Friction members include brake shoes and drums, and disk brake pads and rotors. These service of these units is covered below.

Servo Brake Shoe Design

Brake shoes can be arranged so that one shoe helps to apply the other. This setup is referred to as a **servo brake.** A servo brake arrangement is shown in **Figure 34-51.** Note that when shoes are forced into contact with the drum, the primary (P) shoe is carried around with the drum. This jams the secondary shoe(s) against the drum and anchor pin.

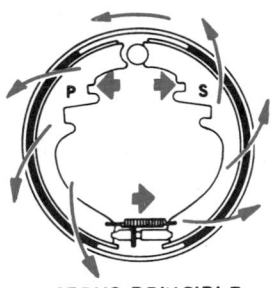

Figure 34-51. Single-anchor, self-energizing, servo brake arrangement.

These shoes are also **self-energizing.** The shoe free end is forced into contact with the revolving drum. The free end moves toward the anchored end of the shoe, creating friction that tends to force the shoe even tighter against the drum.

Figure 34-52 illustrates a uniservo brake with one single-end wheel cylinder. This arrangement is referred to as uniservo. **Figure 34-53** shows the same setup as in **Figure 34-51,** except the springs and wheel cylinder have been added. This is called a duo-servo, self-energizing brake arrangement.

Figure 34-52. A uni-servo brake with one single-end wheel cylinder.

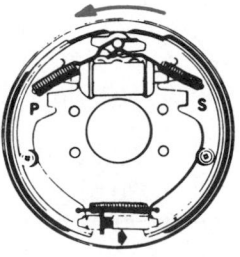

Figure 34-53. A duo-servo brake assembly.

Non-Servo Brake

Since each shoe in **Figure 34-54A** is anchored, it is impossible for one shoe to assist in the application of the

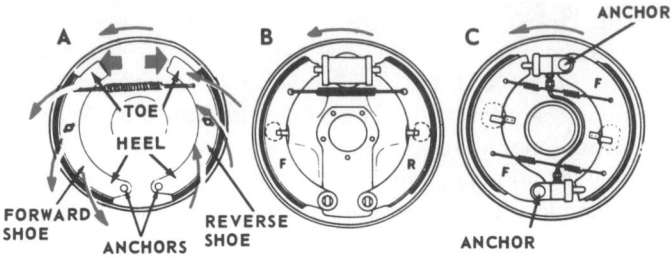

Figure 34-54. Double-anchor, non-servo brake design.

other. This brake is called a **non-servo brake.** The forward shoe is self-energizing; the reverse shoe is not (drum turning in direction of arrow). **Figure 34-54B** shows the same setup, but the wheel cylinder and spring have been added. **Figure 34-54C** uses a single-end cylinder for each shoe. Note that both shoes are self-energizing. Both B and C are double-anchor, non-servo brakes. **Figure 34-55** illustrates three other non-servo action brake shoe and anchor arrangements.

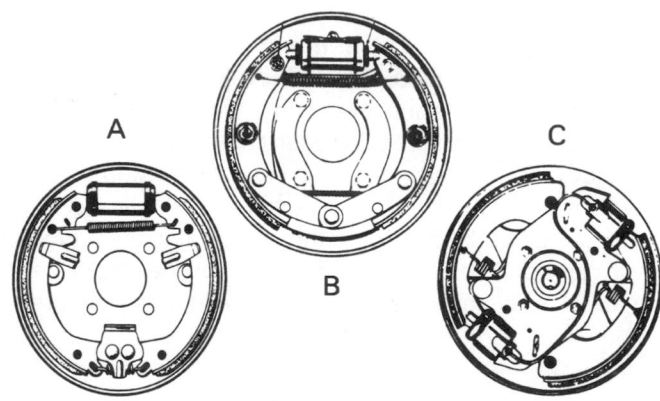

Figure 34-55. Other brake types. In that the anchored ends of these shoes are free to move up and down, they are all self-centering. (Wagner)

Self-Centering Brakes

Some brake shoes are **self-centering,** that is, they will center themselves in the drum when applied. To do this, they must be free to move up and down as well as outward. Double-anchor brakes are not self-centering. Single-anchor brakes, **Figure 34-56,** are self-centering because the anchored ends are free to move up or down.

Most Common Drum Brake Design

The drum brake design in wide use today is the single-anchor, duo-servo. The anchor is fixed (cannot be moved), and bottom is free to move. This automatically centers the shoes. The use of a ratcheting device makes the brake self-adjusting, **Figure 34-56.**

Brake Shoe Removal

Pull the wheel and drum. The parking brake must be off to remove rear drums. If the brake shoes are too tight to pull the drum, back off the adjustment. On self-adjusting brakes, pass a thin screwdriver through the adjustment slot

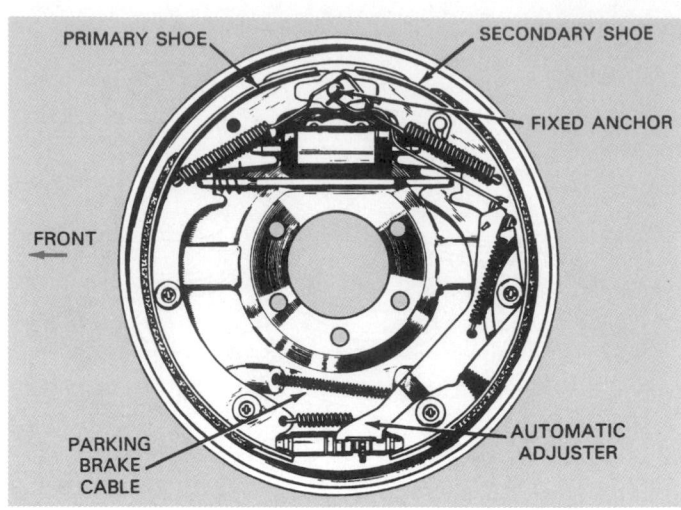

Figure 34-56. Fixed single-anchor, duo-servo, self-adjusting brake design. (Bendix)

in the backing plate. Hold the adjuster lever free while loosening the adjuster wheel (star wheel). If adjustment is through a slot in the brake drum, a hook may be used to pull the adjuster lever free, **Figure 34-57.**

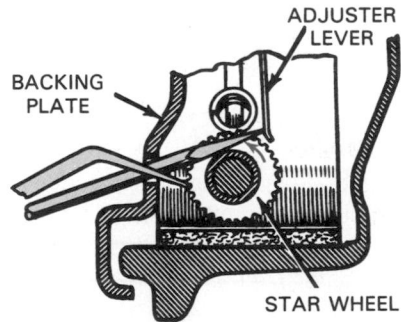

BACKING OFF ON ADJUSTING SCREW
(ACCESS SLOT IN BACKING PLATE)

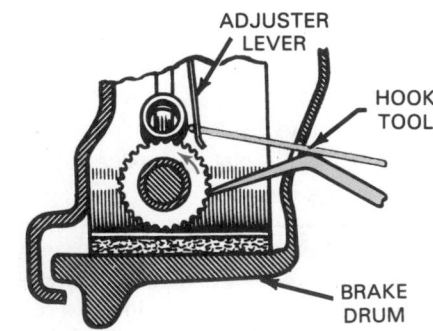

BACKING OFF ON ADJUSTING SCREW
(ACCESS SLOT IN BRAKE DRUM)

Figure 34-57. Adjuster lever must be held out of the way to back off the adjuster star wheel.

Study the Parts Arrangement

Before attempting to remove the shoes, study the arrangement of the brake parts. Note the color of the springs, where the springs are connected, in what order the springs are connected, how hold-downs are installed, etc. This procedure will help during assembly.

Clamp the Wheel Cylinder

Install a wheel cylinder clamp to prevent the pistons from popping out of the cylinder. Leave the clamp in place until the shoes are reinstalled. See **Figure 34-58.**

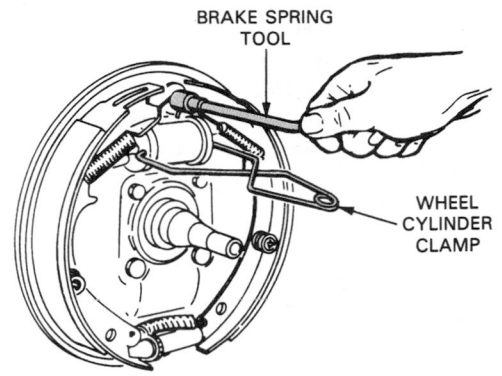

Figure 34-58. Brake spring tool being used to remove shoe return springs. Note the cylinder clamp. (FMC)

Remove the Shoes

Use a brake spring tool to remove the *retracting springs,* as shown in **Figure 34-58.** A number of spring arrangements for single-anchor, duo-servo brakes are shown in **Figure 34-59.**

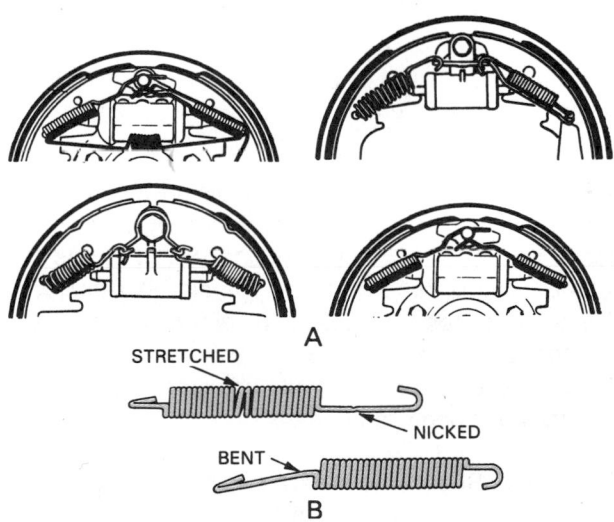

Figure 34-59. A—Single-anchor, duo-servo shoe retracting spring arrangements. B—These retracting springs are unsuitable for further use.

Remove the shoe *hold-downs,* **Figure 34-60.** If the shoes are fixed to anchors, remove anchors or fasteners as needed. As parts are removed, lay them out in proper order. Keep the parts for each wheel in one group. Clean and inspect all parts.

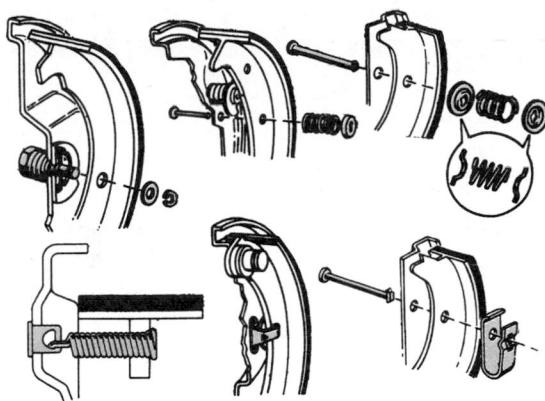

Figure 34-60. Various types of brake shoe hold-downs.

Warning: See the cautions about breathing asbestos at the beginning of this chapter.

Check springs carefully to make certain they are in good condition. Damaged springs may be recognized by discoloration, stretched areas, nicks, and deformed end hook openings. See **Figure 34-59.**

Installing Brake Shoes

Clean the backing plate and torque plate mounting fasteners. Sand the shoe pads (raised portions of backing plate used to support shoes). Coat with a film of high-temperature grease, **Figure 34-61.** Clean and back off the *self-adjuster mechanism.* This will allow the drum to clear the new, thicker lining, **Figure 34-62.**

Place a small amount of high-temperature grease on the adjuster screw threads and on the ends where they contact the brake shoes. Lubricate the area between the hold-down and the shoe surface and the area where the wheel cylinder links or push rods contact the shoes. Use special brake high-temperature lubricant and use it sparingly. Never use oil or other greases.

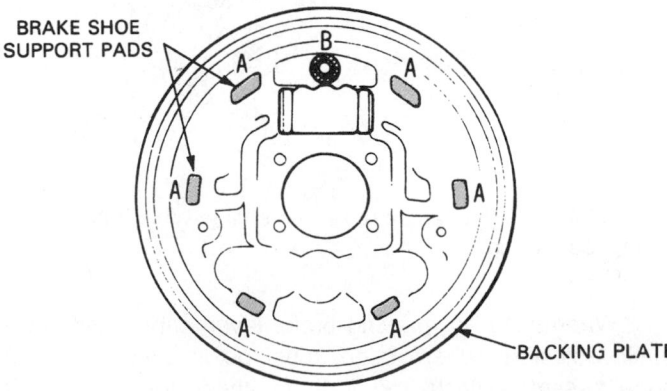

Figure 34-61. A—Clean and lubricate the brake shoe support pads. B—Lightly grease the anchor if recommended. (Plymouth)

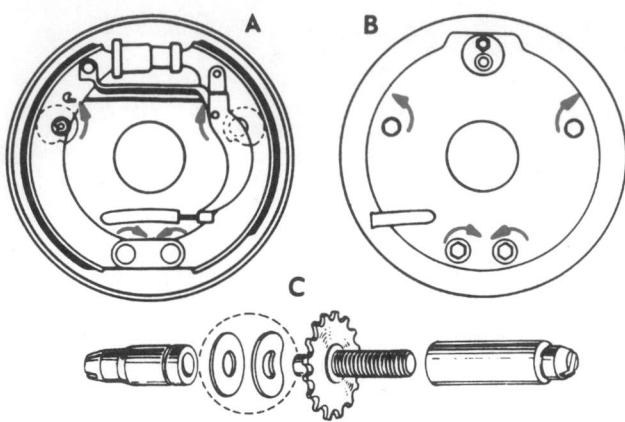

Figure 34-62. Back off the adjuster cams (A and B) to provide the clearance required to install the brake drum. Clean, lubricate, and collapse the adjuster type shown in C. (Wagner)

⚠ **Caution: Keep grease and oil away from lining. Avoid touching the lining with your fingers as much as possible. Keep your hands free of grease and oil. Remember that even the slightest bit of oil on the lining will ruin the brake job.**

Install the shoes, being careful to place the primary and secondary shoes in their proper positions. On single-anchor, duo-servo applications, the primary shoe will have the shortest lining and will face the front of the vehicle. The primary shoe will be the first shoe encountered moving away from the wheel cylinder in the direction of forward wheel rotation.

Install hold-downs and retracting springs. Make certain that the springs are in the correct position and hooked in the proper spot, **Figures 34-59 and 34-60.** Use a brake spring tool to avoid damage to the spring, **Figure 34-63.**

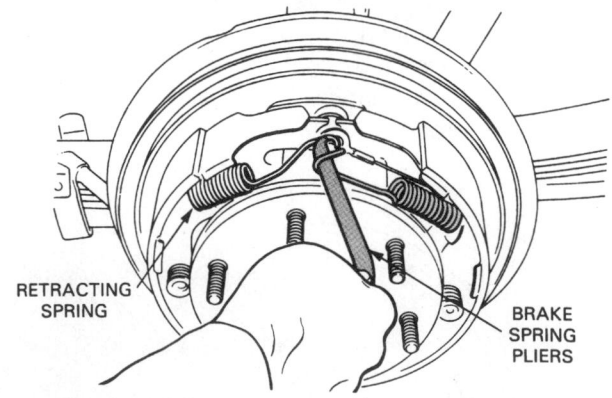

RETRACTING SPRING

BRAKE SPRING PLIERS

Figure 34-63. Mounting a retracting spring with a brake spring tool. (Dodge)

When installed (parking brake lever, cable, and automatic adjusters, where used, must be in place), rap the shoe assembly back and forth to check for freedom of movement. Recheck the entire assembly. Install the brake drum and adjust the shoes.

Parts Must Be in Correct Position

The shoes must be in their correct positions. The star wheel must face the adjustment slot in the backing plate. Self-adjusters must be installed on the correct side of the vehicle.

Using Gauge to Make Initial Shoe Adjustment

Brakes with self-adjusting shoes need only an initial adjustment following the installation of new shoes. Normally, the automatic adjuster will then maintain proper lining-to-drum clearance for the life of the lining.

Release the parking brake and slack off the cable so that both shoes are in firm contact with the anchor pin. Using a special gauge, **Figure 34-64,** adjust to brake drum diameter. Lock the gauge securely.

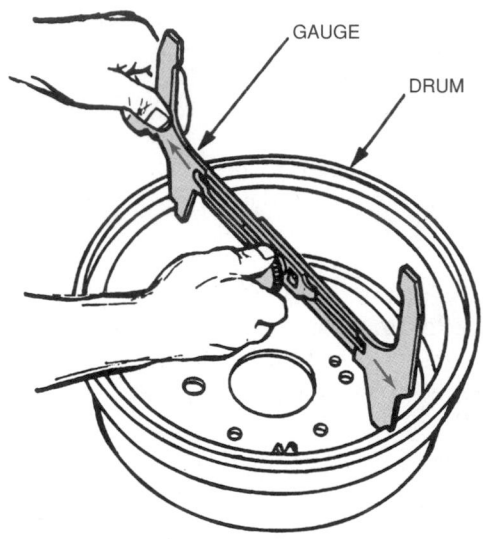

GAUGE

DRUM

Figure 34-64. Adjusting a special gauge to fit inside the brake drum diameter. Lock the gauge securely. (Bendix)

Expand the shoes outward (hold lever free of star wheel to prevent burring wheel) until they just fit in the opposite side of the adjusting gauge. See **Figures 34-65 and 34-66.** Install the drums and wheels. Start the vehicle and make a series of stops in reverse. This causes the brake shoes to stick to the drum and follow it around far enough to activate the automatic adjuster. Repeat reverse stops until a full pedal is attained.

Making Initial Shoe Adjustment by Hand

If no setting gauge is available, install the drum. With the wheel free of the ground and the parking brake disconnected, remove the star wheel adjustment slot cover. It may be in the backing plate or drum. While holding the adjuster lever out of the way, **Figure 34-67,** back off the star wheel about 30 notches. Make reverse stops until a full pedal is secured.

With a brake adjusting tool, turn the adjusting star wheel in the direction that will expand the shoes. While turning the wheel, revolve the tire in the direction of forward

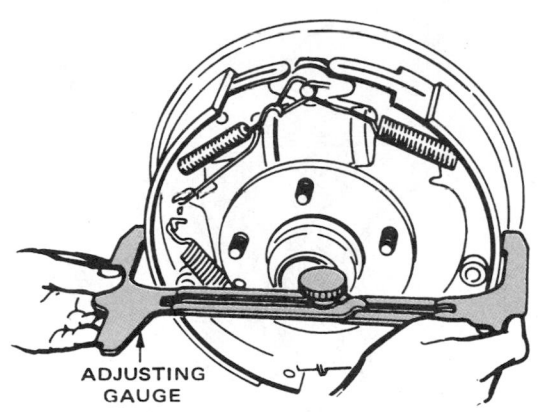

Figure 34-65. Adjusting the shoes to the gauge. Check in several directions. (Bendix)

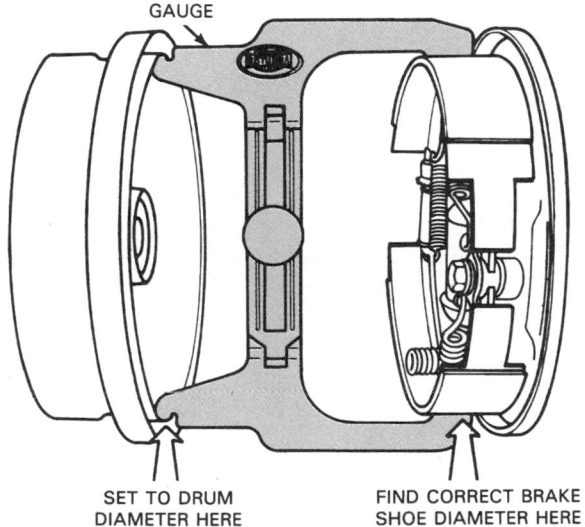

Figure 34-66. Brake shoe adjusting gauge. Set the gauge to the drum. Then adjust the shoes to fit. (Ford)

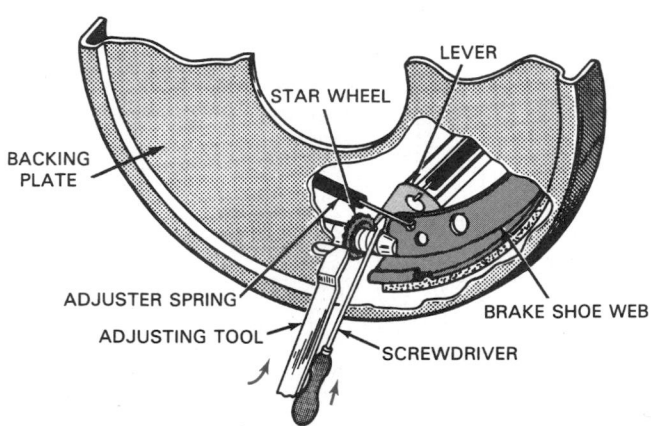

Figure 34-67. Holding the adjuster lever out of the way while turning the star wheel. (Chrysler)

travel. Continue turning the star wheel until a firm drag is felt when attempting to rotate the tire.

> **Note: Some cars do not have an opening in front of the star wheel. Careful inspection will reveal a slug (metal still in opening) that must be punched out to form the opening. These slugs can be in the backing plate or in the face of the brake drum itself. When finished with adjustment, fill slot with a recommended slot plug.**

> **Caution: If the slug is knocked out with wheel and drum installed, remove wheel and drum and discard slug. Never leave it inside.**

Changing Disc Brake Pads

In some cases, the *disc brake pads* are equipped with small metal tabs that contact the rotor when the pads become excessively worn. The tabs will make a shrill noise every time the brakes are applied. Regardless of the wear determining device, pads should be changed when worn to within 1/8″ (3.18 mm) of their bases. Refer to **Figure 34-68.**

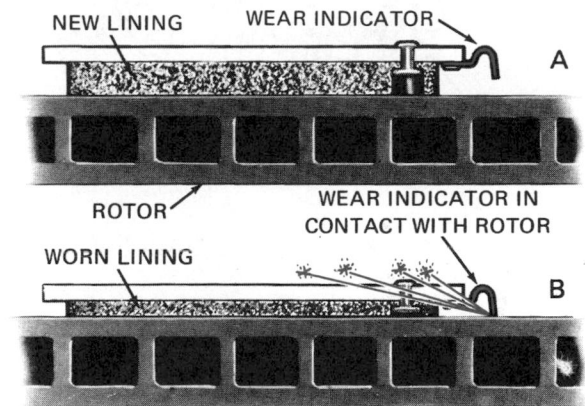

Figure 34-68. Warning wear indicator tab action. A—New pad. The indicator does not touch the disc. B—Pad worn. The indicator strikes the disc and alerts the driver of a worn pad. (Oldsmobile)

Before forcing the piston back, siphon off brake fluid from the master cylinder disc brake reservoir (until it is about one third full) to make room for that displaced when the piston is forced inward. Failure to do this will result in flooding the master cylinder. See **Figure 34-69.**

If necessary, remove the caliper. Do not allow the caliper to hang from the brake hose (or sensor wire). Use a C-clamp to force the pistons back into the bore. This will free the pads from the disc, **Figure 34-70.**

When the pads are moved away the full distance (this bottoms pistons in their bores), the pads may be withdrawn, **Figure 34-71.** Some pads are positioned with pins.

When the pads are removed, check the pistons and boots for leakage, corrosion, and gumming. If necessary, disassemble and clean (See Caliper Repair). Check the disc for excessive scoring and oil or grease contamination.

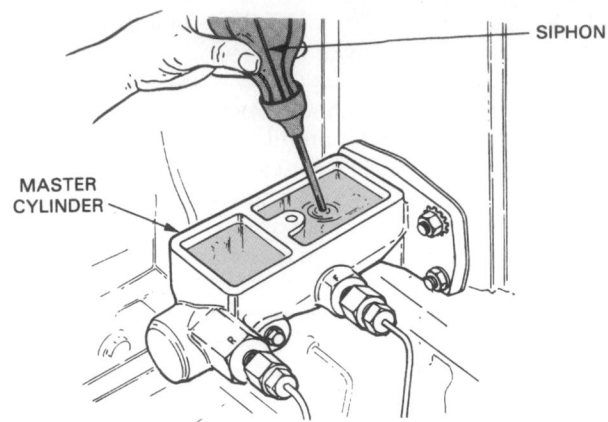

Figure 34-69. Removing brake fluid from the reservoir with a siphon. Do not reuse old fluid. (FMC)

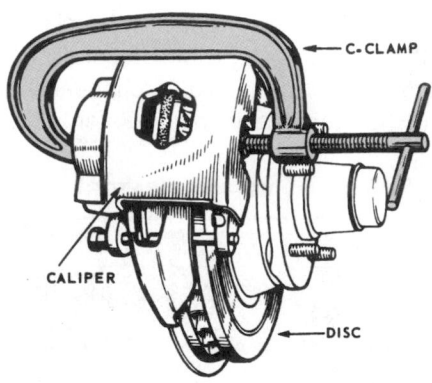

Figure 34-70. Using a clamp to force a brake piston back into its bore to free the brake pads. (Bendix)

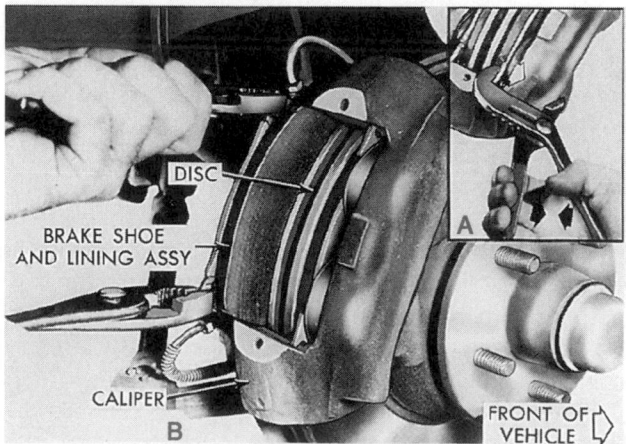

Figure 34-71. Pulling friction pads from the caliper. A—Pushing piston back. B—Removing pad. (Plymouth)

Caliper Alignment

Check (if needed) to make certain that the caliper is centrally located over the disc (not required with floating calipers), **Figure 34-72.**

Check that the pads are parallel with the disc surface. See **Figure 34-73.** If alignment error exceeds specifications,

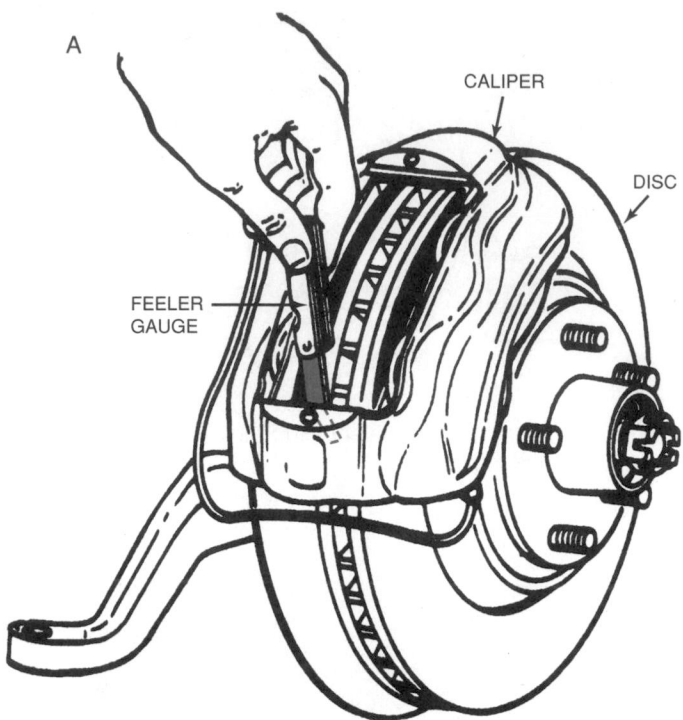

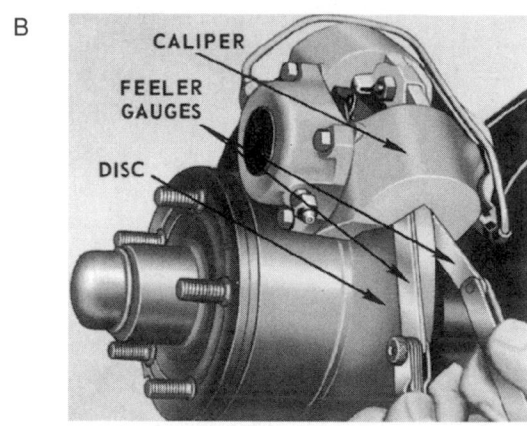

Figure 34-72. A—Checking a fixed caliper for rotor-to-caliper clearance. B—Checking a fixed caliper for proper centering on the brake disc. Because these calipers cannot move, correct clearance is a *must!* (Wagner and Bear)

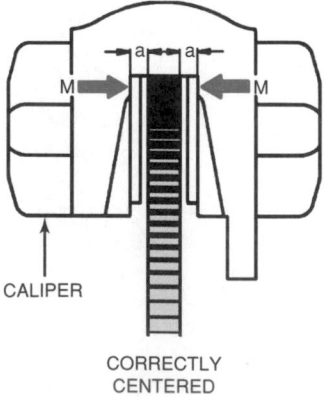

Figure 34-73. Checking a fixed caliper to make certain it is parallel with the disc. (Mercedes-Benz)

check for missing or wrongly placed shims, front end damage, or incorrect installation. **Figure 34-74** shows correct and incorrect caliper-to-disc alignment.

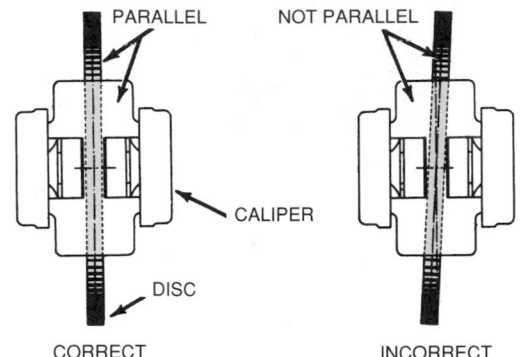

Figure 34-74.   Correct and incorrect caliper-to-disc alignment. (Mercedes-Benz)

Insert new pads. Lubricate (as recommended) any sliding metal surfaces with special grease (such as moly-disulfide). Install the splash shield or any other pad-holding device. Always use appropriate fasteners.

Pump the brake pedal to force the pads out against the disc. Bring the master cylinder to the correct level. Do not attempt to drive the vehicle until a full pedal is obtained by pumping the pedal until the pads are against the disc. The brakes will not function on the first application of the pedal if this is not done.

Breaking in a New Set of Brake Linings or Brake Pads

Following the installation of new brake linings or pads, it is important that they be given the proper **break-in.**

When road testing following the completion of a brake job, make eight to ten mild stops from around 25 mph (40.2 km/h). Make the same number of stops from around 45 mph (72.4 km/h) at one mile (1.6 km) intervals. Stops must be mild.

Caution the owner to avoid severe use of the brakes for several hundred miles. This will seat the linings properly and lengthen service life.

Brake Drum and Rotor Service

The **brake drums** and **rotors** are as important as the pads and shoes to proper brake operation. The drums and rotors should be carefully checked for damage as outlined below. Correct repair and refinishing procedures are vital.

Brake Drum Service

Wash the brake dust from the drum. If grease or oil is present, remove with cleaning solvent. Blow dry. Wipe drum braking surface with a clean, alcohol-soaked rag. Wipe again with a dry rag. Repeat this process until the drum is spotless.

Inspect Brake Drum

Inspect the brake drum for scoring, cracking, heat checking, bell-mouth wear, and barrel-shape wear. Refer to **Figure 34-75.** Scoring, bell-mouth, and barrel wear may be

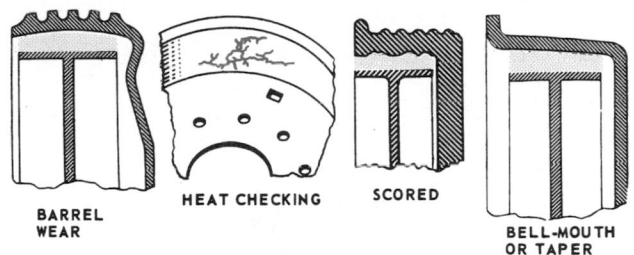

Figure 34-75.   Brake drum wear patterns. (Wagner)

removed by turning if the damage is not too deep. Heat checking can also be minimized and often removed by turning the drum. Use a brake drum micrometer to check for out-of-roundness. Measure in 45° increments around the drum.

 Warning: Destroy any drum that is actually cracked. Never try to weld a cracked drum.

Although some specifications call for less runout, any drum measuring more than .010″ (0.254 mm) out-of-round or showing more than .005″ (0.127 mm) taper should be trued by turning or grinding. Drums that measure over .060″ (1.524 mm) above standard should be destroyed. This does not apply to truck drums. Some vehicle drums cannot exceed .030″ (0.762 mm). Check the manufacturer's specifications.

If the drum appears serviceable without turning, polish it with fine emery cloth as shown in **Figure 34-76.** This will remove the glassy surface that can cause poor brake action with new shoes. Most shops prefer to lightly turn drums, no matter how good they look. **Figure 34-77** shows a special micrometer being used to check for drum out-of-roundness.

Turn Drums in Pairs

Although brake drums can differ slightly in diameter between the front and rear, the front drums must be the same diameter (within .010″ [0.254 mm] of each other). The rear drums must also be the same diameter. When a drum on one side needs turning, turn the one on the other side to the same diameter.

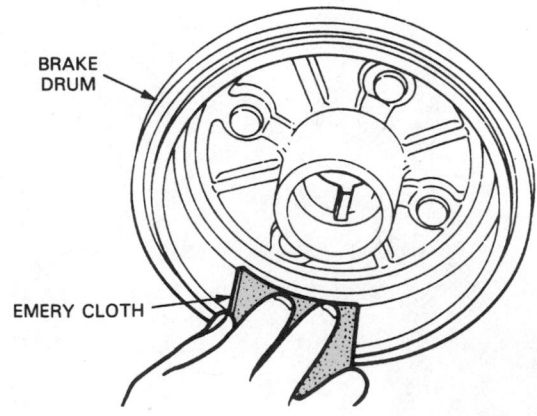

Figure 34-76.   Using emery cloth to clean and deglaze the brake drum lining contact surface. Clean thoroughly when finished. (Mazda)

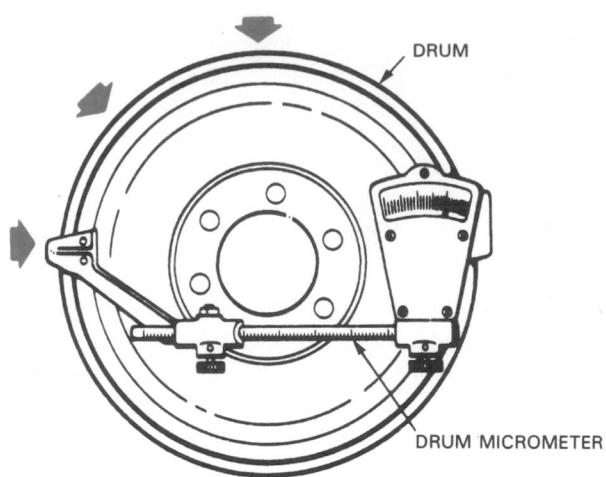

Figure 34-77. A drum micrometer is used to check the brake drum for out-of-roundness. Check in several spots. (Wagner)

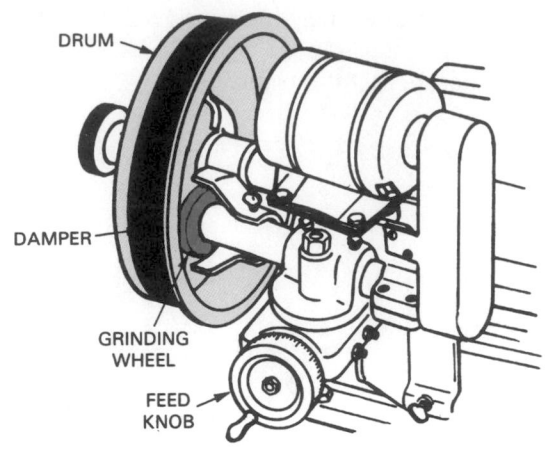

Figure 34-79. Grinding a brake drum with a special grinder. *Wear safety goggles!* (FMC)

Remove as Little Metal as Possible

Because the drum is made thinner by turning, remove only enough metal to true the drum. Never increase the standard drum diameter by more than .060″ (1.524 mm). The removal of too much drum metal can cause overheating, checking, and failure.

Using a Drum Lathe or Grinder

Drums may be trued by **turning** (using a cutter bit) or by **grinding** (passing a high-speed grinding wheel across a revolving drum). Many shops use only turning. Some turn and then dress very lightly with the grinder. Others use only the grinder.

If the tool is sharp, the cut is light, and the feed is slow, the turned finish will be satisfactory. It can be slightly more resistant to squeal and chatter than the ground surface. **Figure 34-78** illustrates a brake drum lathe. Note the tool bit.

Figure 34-79 shows a drum grinder in action. The drum must be accurately mounted. The cut must be light

and the feed slow to produce a satisfactory finish. Be sure to place a damper on the drum to prevent chatter marks. Follow the tool manufacturer's directions.

After truing, clean the drum braking surface with a scrub brush and hot, soapy water. Rinse with hot water and dry immediately. Wipe off with a clean, alcohol-soaked rag.

Clean New Drums

New drums are usually given a protective coating to guard against rust. Remove the coating and clean the braking surface with alcohol. Some coatings require lacquer thinner for removal.

Metallic Lining

To use **metallic brake shoe lining,** the drum must be honed to a 20 micro-inch finish. Special heat-resistant brake springs must also be used.

Figure 34-80 illustrates one of the bonded metallic shoe pads. Each pad consists of a top friction facing with a bottom section of bonding material. If shoe pads are worn,

Figure 34-78. Turning a drum in a brake lathe. (Ammco)

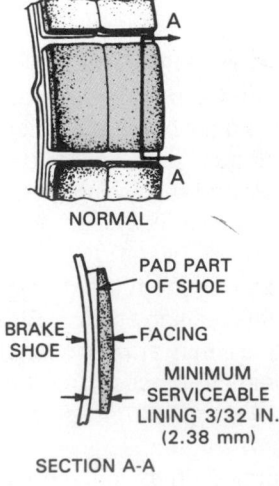

Figure 34-80. Cross section of a metallic brake lining. (Chevrolet)

the facing area will be greatly reduced. Replace these shoes when either end of the pad measures under 3/32″ (2.38 mm). See **Figure 34-81.**

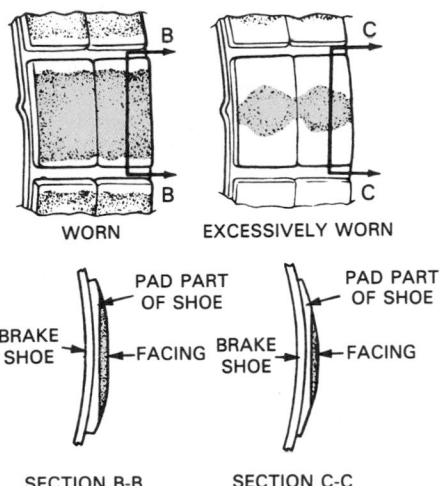

Figure 34-81. Metallic brake lining wear patterns. (Chevrolet)

Disc Rotor Service

The brake disc (rotor) should be free of excessive or heavy scoring. Some scoring is natural as the disc is not completely protected against the elements. Scoring up to around .015″ (0.38 mm) deep, as long as the disc is smooth, is permissible. Clean up minor roughness with fine emery cloth. Look at **Figure 34-82.**

Check the disc for lateral runout (side-to-side wobble). Before checking, set front wheel bearing clearance to just remove any end play.

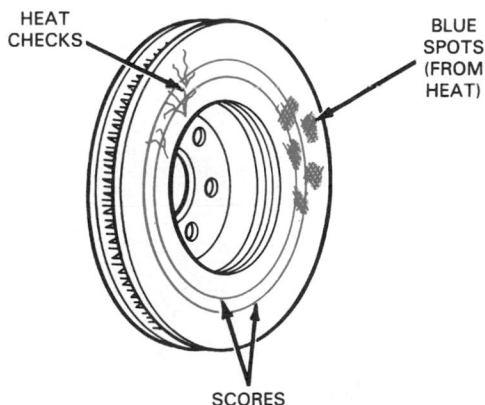

Figure 34-82. Disc problems. Blue spots and minor scoring can be removed. A crack or a series of cracks requires disc replacement. (Niehoff)

Mount a dial indicator to a solid surface. Place the indicator anvil in about 1″ (25.4 mm) from the wear surface outer edge. Slowly rotate the disc and read the dial. Maximum runout should not exceed .003-.004″ (0.076-0.102 mm). Refer to **Figure 34-83.**

Also check the disc for parallelism (same disc thickness all the way around). Using a micrometer, check the

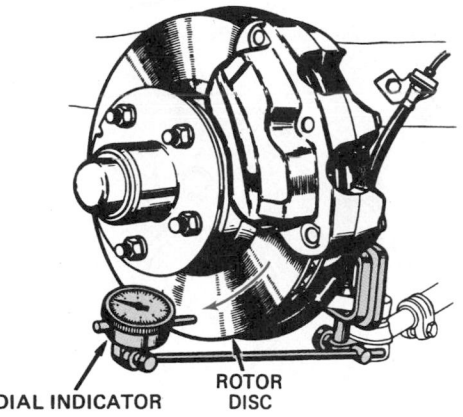

Figure 34-83. Checking disc (rotor) runout with a dial indicator. (Bendix)

disc thickness (in from wear edge about an inch or 25.4 mm) in six or eight spots around the disc. Carefully record each measurement.

The maximum difference in readings should not exceed .0005″ (0.013 mm). This may seem like a small amount, but anything more than this causes a pulsating brake pedal and possible brake shudder or chatter. A few manufacturers call for even smaller maximums, such as .00025″ (.0064 mm).

Disc Minimum Thickness

When wear has reduced disc thickness beyond the recommended minimum, the disc should be discarded. This minimum thickness is generally marked on the disc assembly. See **Figure 34-84.** Never reduce to this thickness by grinding—this is the wear limit. Minimum grinding thickness must leave more material.

Truing Disc

Measure the disc with a micrometer at 6-8 different locations around the braking surface to check for parallelism (thickness variations). See **Figure 34-85.** If not worn beyond turning or truing thickness (different than minimum wear thickness), the disc may be turned on a disc refinishing machine. This is shown in **Figure 34-86A.** This tool cuts both sides of the disc at once, thus reducing the chance of chatter.

Remove only enough stock to clean up the disc surface on both sides. Do not reduce the thickness beyond recommendations. Follow all machine manufacturer's directions. This is a precision operation.

Upon completion of the turning operation, the disc surfaces should be given a nondirectional, crosshatch finish using the proper grinding attachments. The surface should run between 20-80 micro inches with 50 micro inches being about average. A typical crosshatching attachment is shown in **Figure 34-86B.**

Never resurface one disc. Discs must be done in pairs to ensure smooth, even braking. When installing a disc, all contact surfaces must be spotless to prevent runout.

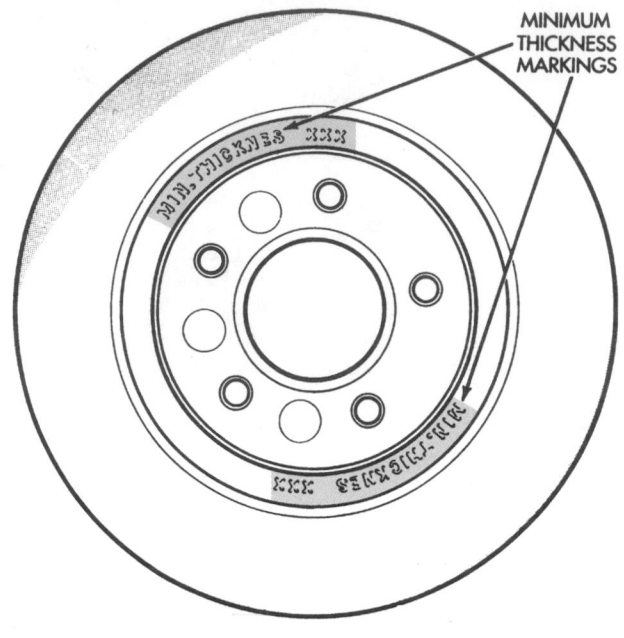

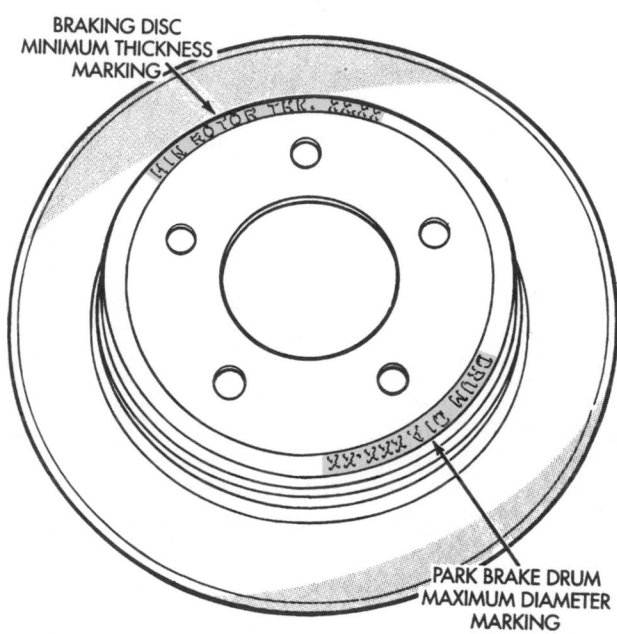

Figure 34-84. Wear limits showing minimum thickness as marked on a front and rear brake disc. Note that the rear disc also provides a wear limit for the parking brake drum minimum thickness. (Chrysler)

Parking Brake Adjustments

The *parking brake* adjustment is more important than most technicians realize. If the parking brake is set too loose, it will not hold properly. If the parking brake is set too tight, the brakes will drag when the vehicle is moving. This will overheat and ruin the brakes.

Adjusting Rear Wheel Parking Brake

Apply the parking brake around 3 notches (about 1 3/4″ or 44.5 mm travel). Adjust the equalizer nut until a slight drag is noticeable at the rear wheels. Refer to **Figure 34-87.**

Release the brake. The wheels should turn freely. Parking brake cables must operate freely. Lubricate if needed.

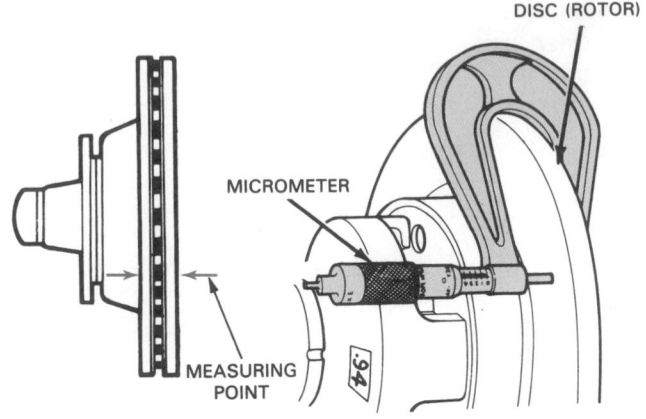

Figure 34-85. Measuring disc parallelism with a micrometer. Measure at twelve equally spaced locations around the braking surface. (Niehoff)

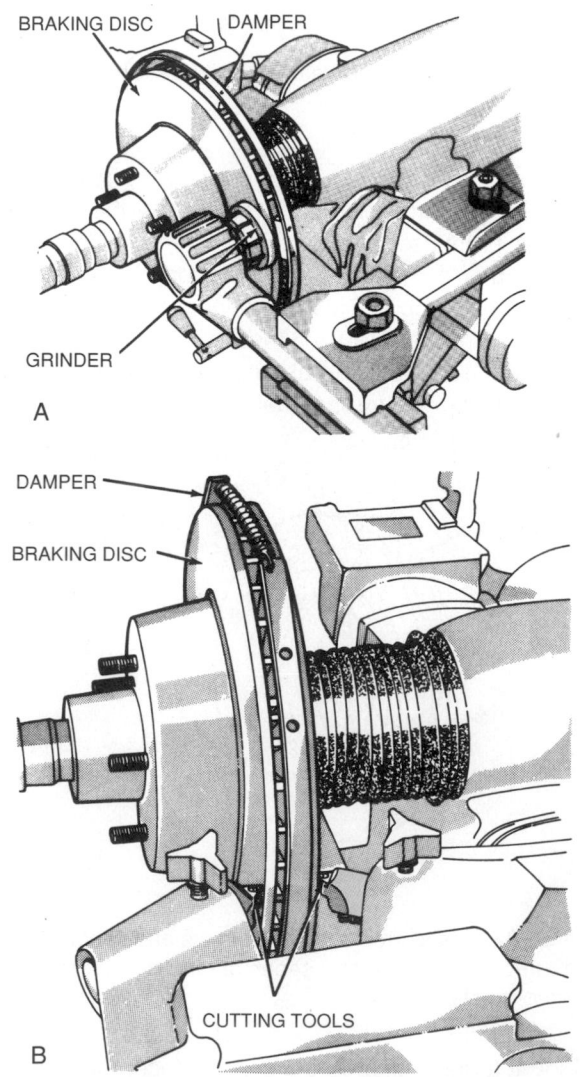

Figure 34-86. A—Disc refacing (sanding) machine attachment. This sander will give the disc a 50 micro-inch surface and nondirectional hatch marks. B—Disc refinishing tool. This particular tool has a cutter on each side (straddle cutter) and resurfaces both faces of the disc at the same time. Use extreme caution and be sure to keep the machine clean. *Always wear safety goggles!* (Dodge)

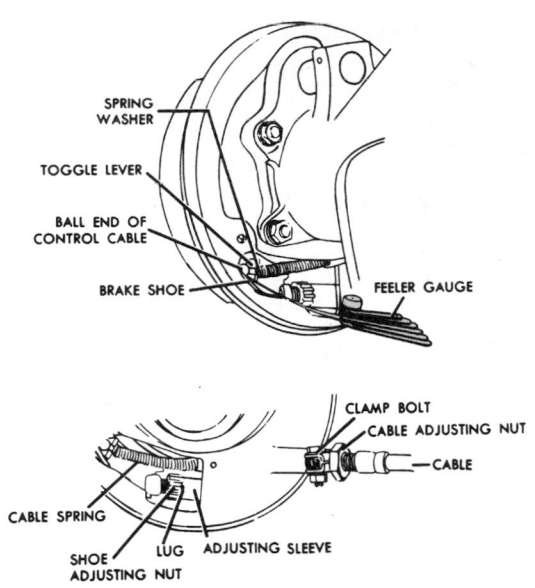

Figure 34-87. One type of internal parking brake. (World-Bestos)

⚠️ **Note: The parking brake must release fully. If the brake is set too tight, it can cause the automatic adjuster to malfunction. It can also ruin the lining from overheating. The service brakes should be properly adjusted before adjusting the parking brake.**

Adjusting Disc Brake Type Parking Brake

Vehicles with disc brakes in the rear require a somewhat different procedure for adjustment of the parking brake mechanism. There are two basic types: the internal expanding shoe-and-drum type and a screw-actuated unit that is an integral part of the caliper. See **Figures 34-88** and **34-89.**

To adjust the disc (drum) type, **Figure 34-90,** rotate the star wheel by placing an adjusting tool through an opening generally located in the face of the rotor-drum.

If parking brake shoes require replacement, disconnect the caliper and back off the star wheel (if necessary). Remove the rotor-drum unit. The shoes are serviced in the same manner as the servo-type service brake.

To compensate for new shoes or cable wear, engage the parking brake pedal or hand lever one notch. Adjust cable for slack at the equalizer.

For adjustment of the screw-actuated unit, all that is generally necessary is adjustment of the cable. This too, is performed at the equalizer. Check all parts for freedom of movement. Follow the manufacturer's service procedures.

Power Brake Service

Power brakes consist of a power booster used with a regular master cylinder to reduce required pedal travel and to produce needed hydraulic pressures with a relatively small amount of foot pressure.

Most power brakes operate by engine vacuum and atmospheric pressure acting on a vacuum diaphragm to apply pressure directly to the master cylinder pistons, **Figure 34-91.** A typical *vacuum power booster* is pictured in **Figure 34-92.**

A booster is shown in the released position in **Figure 34-93.** Note that engine vacuum exists on both sides of the

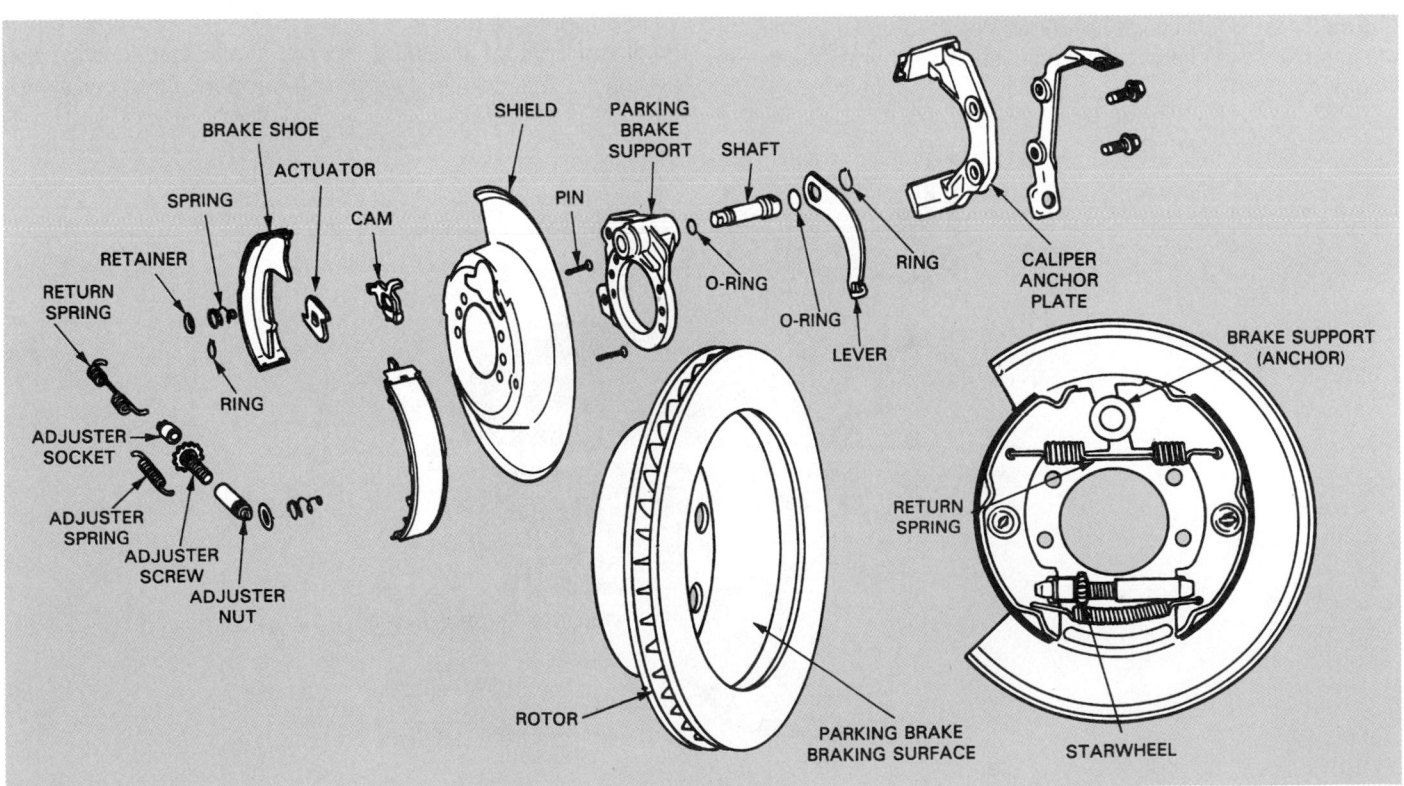

Figure 34-88. Rotor-drum parking brake assembly. Study the part names and relationships. (FMC)

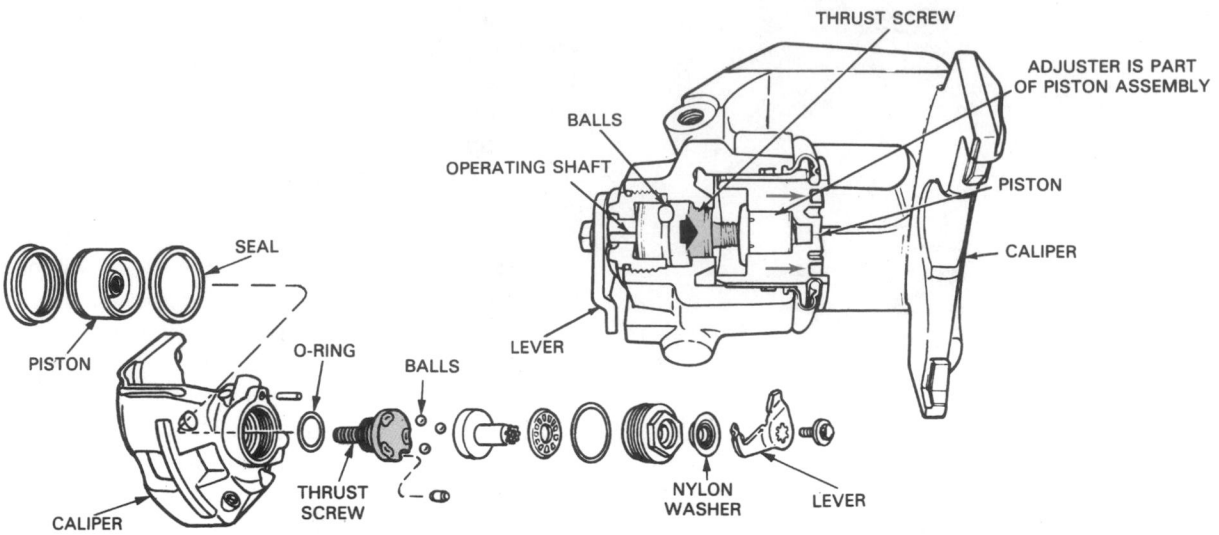

Figure 34-89. Cutaway and exploded views of a screw-actuated disc brake parking brake assembly. As the thrust screw is turned by the lever, the piston firmly clamps the rotor between the pads. (FMC)

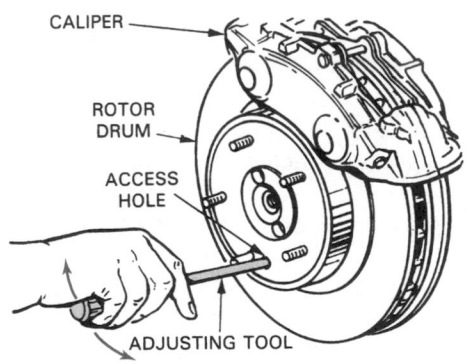

Figure 34-90. Adjusting a rotor-drum parking brake. Rotating the internal star wheel provides adjustment of shoe-to-drum clearance. (FMC)

diaphragm. When the brake pedal forces the push rod inward, the vacuum port is closed and the atmospheric port is opened, admitting atmospheric pressure to one side of the diaphragm. This moves diaphragm assembly, causing the master cylinder push rod to actuate the master cylinder pistons and build up hydraulic pressure in the system. Other boosters, some containing two diaphragms for increased pressure, are also used.

Checking Power Brake Operation

With the engine stopped, exhaust the vacuum in the vacuum tank by making several brake applications. While holding firm foot pressure on the brake pedal, start the engine. If the unit is functioning properly, the pedal will

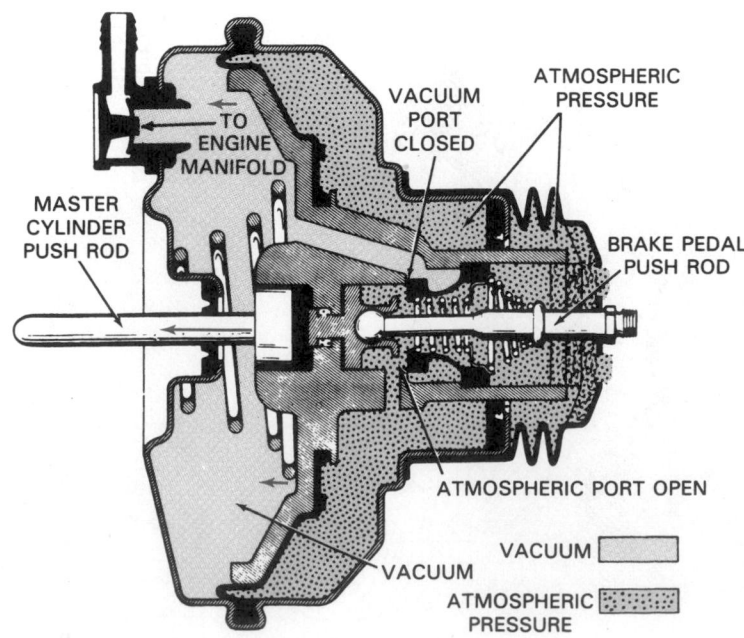

Figure 34-91. Power booster in the applied position. Note how atmospheric pressure acting on the diaphragm forces the push rod toward the master cylinder. (Chevrolet)

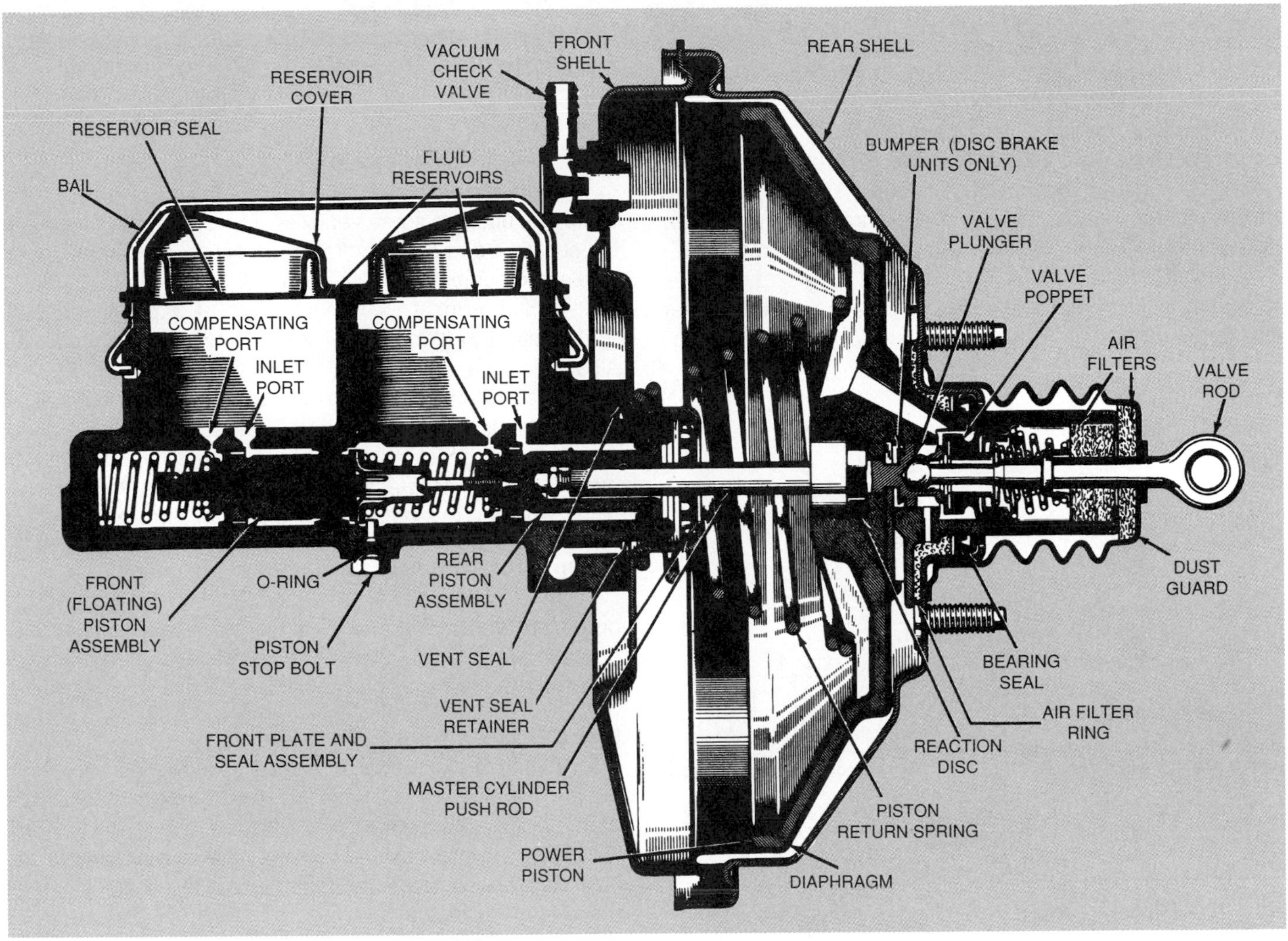

Figure 34-92. Typical power brake setup. Note how a diaphragm is used to seal between the housing and the power piston. (Pontiac)

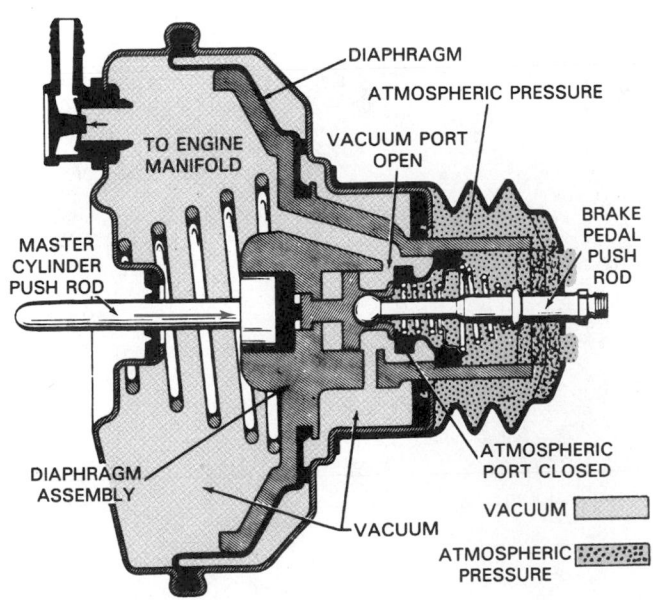

Figure 34-93. Power booster in the released position. (Chevrolet)

move downward when the engine starts. If it does not, check the a mount of vacuum at the booster vacuum inlet. It should be the same as existing engine vacuum.

Power Booster Maintenance

Periodic inspection of the vacuum lines should be performed. Replace any cracked, soft, or otherwise defective lines. A few older power brake boosters call for cleaning the inlet air filter.

The engine should be in sound mechanical condition so that a proper vacuum is created. Check for vacuum leaks. When the engine is shut off, the vacuum should remain in the lines. Loss of vacuum indicates a leak.

Clean or replace the atmospheric air filter. Some booster units require periodic lubrication with booster oil. Do not lubricate boosters unless specified and then only with the correct oil.

If the power unit needs repair, exhaust the static vacuum in the lines by pressing on the brake pedal several times. On some units the booster can be removed without disturbing the hydraulic lines to the master cylinder. On others, the entire assembly must be removed.

Disassemble the vacuum booster. Clean all rubber parts in alcohol. Check parts for wear and replace as needed. The power piston (sliding type) cylinder wall must be free of rust and dents.

Assemble the unit, using care to place all parts in the correct position. Use special lubricant where required. Use new gaskets. Use sealer where needed. Check the length of the master cylinder push rod. Be sure to stake the tab socket if required by the manufacturer. See **Figure 34-94.**

Install booster. Hook up the lines. Bleed the brakes and test. An exploded view of a double-diaphragm power booster is pictured in **Figure 34-95.**

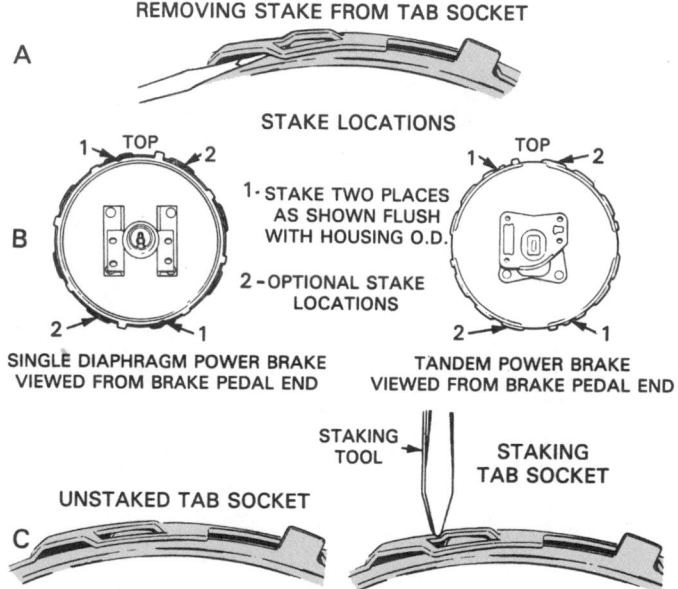

Figure 34-94. A—Removing stake from the tab socket. B—Various stake locations on a single and dual diaphragm power brake unit. C—Unstaked socket being staked. (Chevrolet)

 Note: Many shops do not perform power booster overhaul. They prefer to install new or rebuilt units.

Hydraulic Power Booster

A **hydraulic power booster** (also called "Hydro-Boost") is used on some vehicles. The power steering pump is used as a source of hydraulic pressure. Other belt-driven or electric pumps may also be used.

A Hydro-Boost system consists of a pump, booster, and master cylinder. **Figure 34-96** shows one type of overall system.

Like the vacuum booster, the hydraulic booster is attached to the master cylinder. Depressing the brake pedal actuates the booster valves. This causes the booster to apply pressure to the master cylinder primary piston. An exploded view of a booster is pictured in **Figure 34-97.**

Hydro-Boost in Released Position

While in the released position, fluid flow is through the booster power section and on to the power steering gear. No operating pressure is built up in the booster at this time. A booster in the released position can be seen in **Figure 34-98.**

Hydro-Boost in Applied Position

As the brake pedal is depressed, the booster input push rod and piston are moved forward, toward the master cylinder. This causes the spool valve to also move forward. This allows more fluid to flow into the cavity behind the power piston. As pressure builds behind the power piston, it moves forward actuating the master cylinder. **Figure 34-99** illustrates a power booster in the applied position.

Hydro-Booster Failure

Most hydraulic booster units use an accumulator. This unit can contain a spring and/or gas under pressure. The accumulator is filled with hydraulic fluid each time the

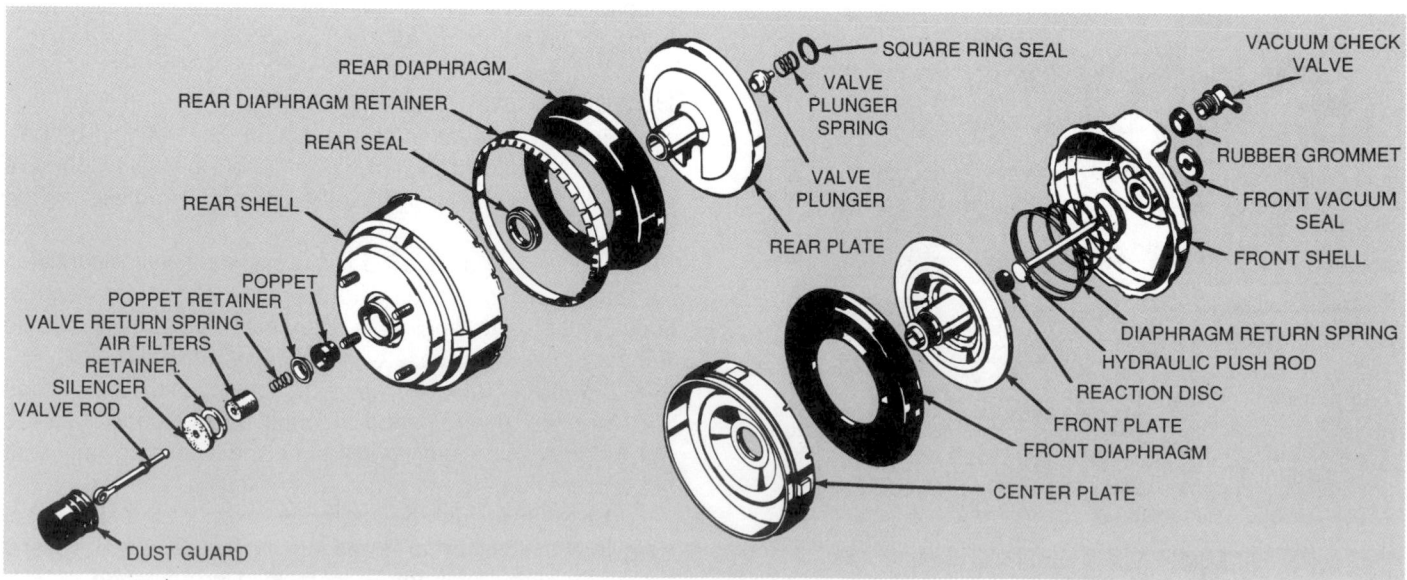

Figure 34-95. Exploded view of a double diaphragm power booster. (Pontiac)

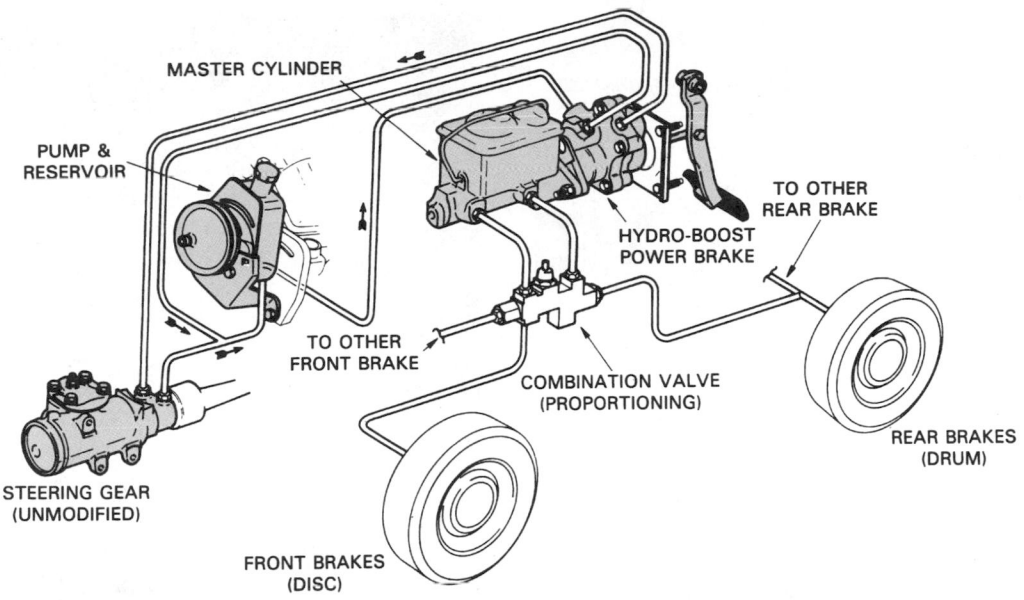

Figure 34-96. Overall Hydro-Boost system layout. Note hydraulic fluid flow arrows (black). (Bendix)

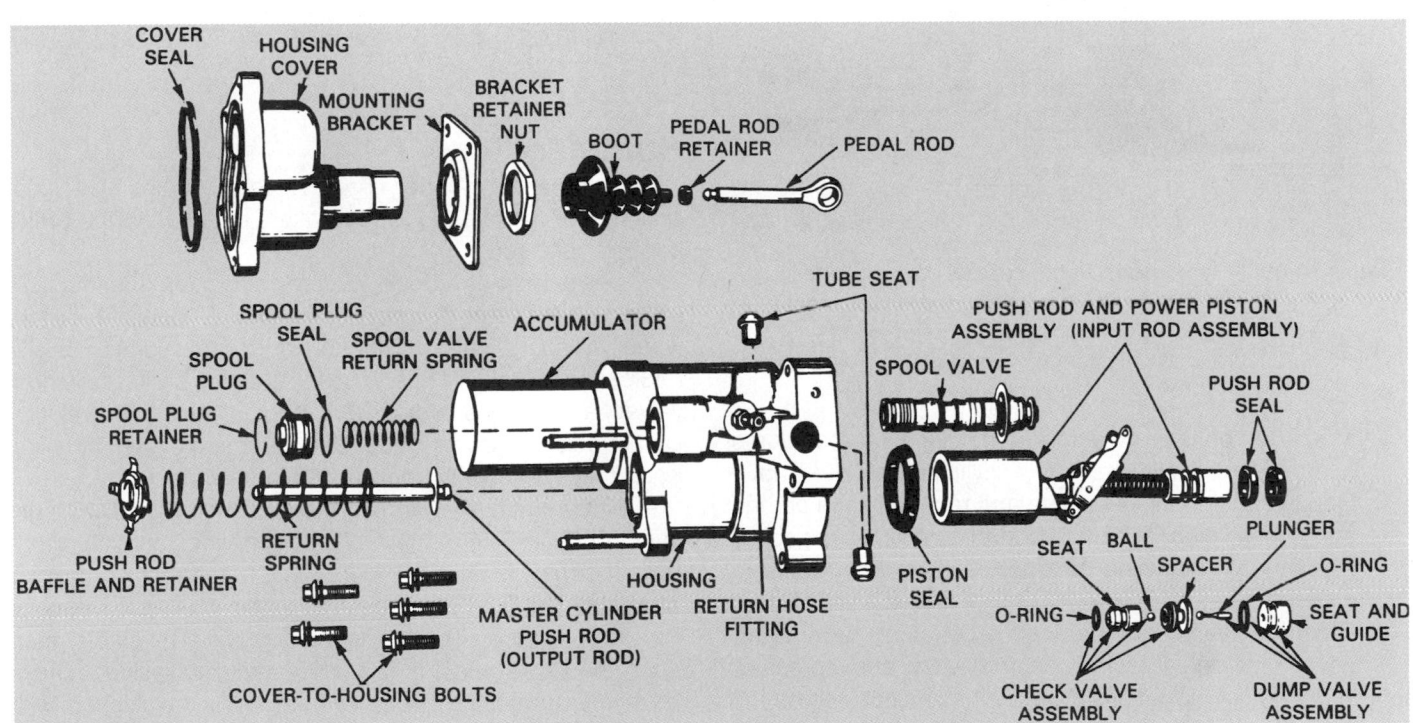

Figure 34-97. Exploded view of a Hydro-Boost unit. Study the parts and their locations. (Bendix)

brakes are applied. If the hydraulic power source fails for some reason, the accumulator will provide around three pressure assisted stops. Brakes can also be operated with no power assist, but will require a much firmer pedal pressure.

> ⚠ **Caution: Accumulators contain strong springs and pressurized gas. They can come apart with lethal force. Do not apply heat. Follow the manufacturer's recommendations for correct disposal. Do not attempt accumulator service without the proper training and tools.**

A common problem with hydraulic brake boosters is belt squeal when the brake is applied. This is often caused by a loose belt or a defective accumulator. In some cases, the brake pedal travel is excessive, placing an extra load on the hydraulic system.

Hydro-Boost Service

The following general service steps are for a Hydro-Boost unit. Always follow the manufacturer's procedures.

1. Remove the Hydro-Boost from vehicle—with or without the master cylinder connected. Do not bend or kink steel brake lines.

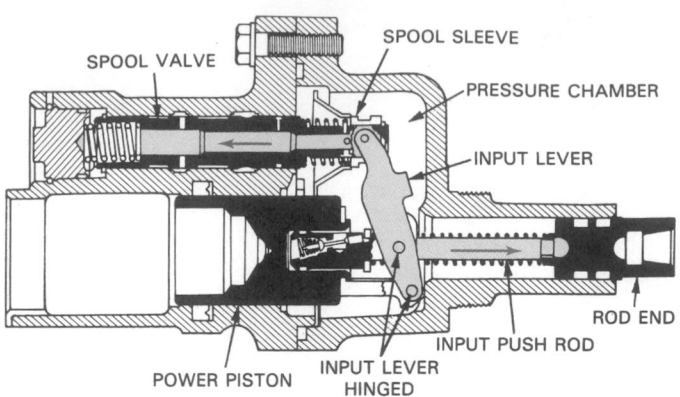

Figure 34-98. Cross sectional view of one particular Hydro-Boost unit. The booster is in the fully released position. (FMC)

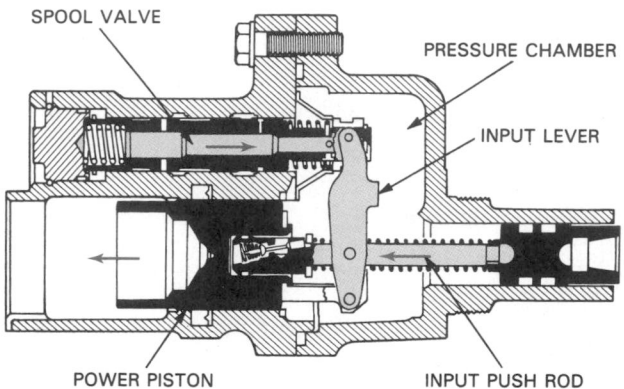

Figure 34-99. Hydro-Boost in the applied position. The input lever has moved the spool valve, allowing more pressure in the pressure chamber. The power piston is forced forward, applying pressure to the master cylinder. (FMC)

2. Mount the booster on a special holding fixture or clamp it in a vise. Usually, the master cylinder end goes up.
3. Remove the spool valve plug and retainer. Take out the spool valve plug, O-ring(s), spring, and other parts.
4. Remove all remaining parts. Be sure to keep them in order.
5. Clean all parts in denatured alcohol or new, clean power steering fluid. Check the valve and bores for scratches or indications of wear. If scratches can be felt with your fingernail, the booster unit should be replaced. These units maintain extremely close tolerances and parts are not interchangeable.
6. Reassemble in the reverse order of disassembly. Replace all seals and O-rings. Lubricate all parts with clean power steering fluid as you reassemble.

Tech Talk

The most common cause of disc brake repair comebacks is noise. While the squeals from brake systems will not cause damage or loss of braking ability, they can drive the owner and technician up the wall.

Semi-metallic brake linings are the noisiest, but all types of brake linings can act up.

Most brake noises right after overhaul are caused by vibrations set up by the action of the moving rotor against the stationary pads. There is always some vibration during braking, but most of it at a higher or lower frequency than the average human ear can hear. Unfortunately, these vibrations can also occur at frequencies that can be heard, especially by the vehicle owner.

When overhauling the brakes, you should do everything possible to eliminate or dampen these vibrations. Begin with the basics: machine the rotor as smooth and flat as you can and use high-quality brake linings. Use all anti-squeak shims or compounds furnished by the manufacturer. These shims or compounds are placed on the backs of the pads. Additional anti-squeak compounds are available and can be used as needed. As a simple final precaution, make sure the wear indicator is not bent and touching the rotor.

Summary

The master cylinder check valve maintains a residual pressure in the lines to drum brakes, even when the brake pedal is released.

Use a complete checklist when doing a brake inspection. Inspect the master cylinder, brake pedal, stoplight switch, wheel cylinders, calipers, brake lining, brake drums, brake rotors, seals, brake lines and hoses, parking brake, switches, valves, and chassis components. Also, road test the vehicle. Do not perform halfway jobs. Use approved brake fluid only. Keep brake fluid away from car's painted surfaces.

Modern master cylinders are usually the double piston (tandem) type. The tandem cylinder provides an extra measure of safety. Master cylinders must not leak, externally or internally. The fluid level must be within 3/8″ (9.53 mm) of the reservoir top. The compensating port must be open when the brake pedal is fully released. The residual check valve must function. Brake systems may be flushed with approved brake solvent (bleed until all solvent is removed) and then filled with fresh brake fluid.

Master cylinders can often be repaired by cleaning and installing a repair kit. Use non-petroleum-based solvents for cleaning master cylinders, wheel cylinders, and calipers. Use crocus cloth to clean up minor corrosion and scratches in the master cylinder, wheel cylinders, and calipers. Do not use crocus cloth or sandpaper on aluminum master cylinders or wheel cylinders. If damaged, they must be replaced. Light honing (not on aluminum components), followed by polishing with crocus, is possible in many cases. Use brake fluid on the hone stones. Clean the cylinder thoroughly to remove abrasive.

Always disassemble and rebuild or replace wheel cylinders at every brake reline job. Discard cylinders showing more than .005″ (0.127 mm) clearance between cylinder wall and piston or that show pitting, corrosion, or scratches that are not removed during the honing process. Remove burrs from cylinder ports. Before assembling cylinders, coat pistons and cups with fresh brake fluid. If there is the slightest doubt as to the advisability of repairing a cylinder, throw it away. Air used to blow brake cylinders dry must be free of water and oil. If it is not, finish the cylinders with an alcohol rinse and allow them to air dry.

When removing wheel assemblies from disc brakes, use care to avoid damage to caliper brake lines. Some disc brake caliper halves must not be separated. Some calipers require removal to change the friction pads. Others do not. Siphon fluid from the master cylinder reservoir before forcing pad pistons inward.

When replacing a brake line, use double-wrapped, coated steel tubing only. Use double-lap or I.S.O. flares only. Protect tubing from vibration. Avoid sharp bends. Keep the tubing away from moving parts and heat.

Do not attempt overhaul of the metering valve, differential pressure switch, proportioning valve, or either type of combination valve. If any of the above valves are defective, replace them.

Bleed the cylinder farthest from the master cylinder first. If the master cylinder has a bleeder valve, bleed it first. On split systems (tandem cylinders), bleed the wheel cylinders served by the primary piston first. Brakes may be bled manually or with a pressure bleeder. Bleed until clear fluid with no air bubbles appears. Never reuse fluid. Anti-lock brake systems require special bleeding techniques. Brake pedal height and free play must be correct. Check operation of power booster where used.

Install new grease seals at every brake reline. The brake design in wide use today is the self energizing, duo-servo, single-fixed anchor, self-adjusting type. The forward, or primary, shoe is the first shoe from the wheel cylinder in the direction of forward rotation. This is generally the front shoe. The reverse, or secondary, shoe is generally the rear shoe (faces toward rear of car). On duo-servo brakes, the primary shoe will have a shorter section of lining.

Study the wheel brake shoe assembly before removal. Keep all parts together. Use proper tools. Clamp the wheel cylinder. When installing shoe assemblies, clean and lubricate the shoe support pads. Lubricate the push rod-to-shoe, adjuster, adjuster-to-shoe, and hold-down areas. Lubricate sparingly and only with special high-temperature grease.

Install shoes in their correct locations. Install springs, hold-downs, and other parts. Springs must be in good condition and in the proper position. Keep shoe lining free of oil and grease.

Never adjust brakes too close. Some anchor pins are adjusted by rotating (eccentric type) or by moving up and down (slotted type). Shoes must be properly centered in the drum. Self-adjusting brakes need only an initial adjustment following relining. They will then maintain correct clearance for the life of the lining. Adjustment slots for moving the star wheel may be in the backing plate or in the brake drum.

If a caliper is removed, check for mounting shims. Never replace one-half of a caliper. If caliper cylinders cannot be cleaned with crocus cloth, discard the caliper. When installing a caliper, use shims in their original locations. Check the caliper for proper centering over the disc. The caliper must also be parallel to the disc.

Brake drums must be free of cracking, excessive scoring, and heavy heat checking. Drum should not be more than .010″ (0.254 mm) out-of-round. Taper should not exceed .005″ (0.127 mm).

Drums may be trued by turning or grinding. Remove only enough metal to clean up the drum. Never remove more than .060″ (1.524 mm). When a drum on one side needs truing, turn the drum on the other side to the same size.

Drums turned to .030″ (0.762 mm) or larger oversize require the use of thicker lining or shim stock under the lining. Clean drums thoroughly after turning or grinding. Metallic brake lining requires heat resistant springs and a 20 micro-inch drum finish.

Check the disc for excessive scoring, wear, and runout. After installing new pads, pump up the brakes to force the pads against the disc before driving the vehicle. The pedal should be firm. Keep front wheel bearings adjusted to the manufacturer's "specs." Wheel bearing adjustment is especially critical on disc brake jobs.

Keep the parking brake adjusted. Do not set it too tight. Adjust the parking brake only after adjusting the service brakes.

Efficient booster operation depends on a sound unit and a normal vacuum or hydraulic source, depending upon booster type. Check lines for leaks.

Know These Terms

Asbestos	Pressure differential switch
Carcinogen	Combination valve
DOT 3	Bleeding
Silicone brake fluid	Manual bleeding
Master cylinder	Pressure bleeding
Check valve	Surge bleeding
Reservoir	Brake shoe
Primary cup	Servo brake
Compensating port	Self energizing
Single-piston master	Non-servo brake
cylinder	Self-centering
Double-piston master	Retracting spring
cylinder	Hold-down
Floating piston	Self-adjuster mechanism
Dust boot	Disc brake pad
Free travel	Break-in
Wheel cylinder	Brake drum
Brake caliper	Brake rotor
Caliper piston	Turning
Fixed caliper	Grinding
Floating caliper	Metallic brake shoe lining
Proportioning valve	Parking brake
Height-sensing	Power brake
proportioning valve	Vacuum power booster
Metering valve	Hydraulic power booster

Review Questions—Chapter 34

Do not write in this book. Write your answers on a separate sheet of paper.

1. Residual pressure in the brake lines is maintained by the _____.
   - (A) proportioning valve
   - (B) master cylinder check valve
   - (C) master cylinder compensating port
   - (D) slight pressure on brake pedal

2. List five important items to be checked during a brake inspection.

3. A dual master cylinder _____.
   - (A) provides greater braking power
   - (B) applies pressure to separate front and rear systems
   - (C) works the clutch also
   - (D) has two cylinders, one on top of the other

4. When the brake pedal is fully released, the _____ in the master cylinder must be open to relieve pressure buildup in the system.

5. Use _____ cloth to remove slight corrosion and scratches in wheel and master cylinders.

6. The maximum allowable clearance between a brake cylinder piston and its cylinder wall is _____.
   - (A) .010″ (0.254 mm)
   - (B) .050″ (1.270 mm)
   - (C) .005″ (0.127 mm)
   - (D) .001″ (0.025 mm)

7. Brake fluid containing _____ will ruin the paint on a vehicle.
   - (A) alcohol
   - (B) silicone
   - (C) oil
   - (D) either A or B

8. The brake design commonly used today is the
   _____.
   - (A) duo-servo, fixed anchor, self-adjusting
   - (B) non-servo, single adjustable anchor
   - (C) self-energizing, duo-anchor, self-centering
   - (D) single servo

9. Brake shoes and pads must be kept free of _____ and _____.

10. When replacing a brake line, use _____.
    - (A) copper tubing
    - (B) brass tubing
    - (C) double-wrapped steel tubing
    - (D) single-wall steel tubing

11. After installing new pads, always pump the brakes to force the _____ out against the _____ before driving the vehicle.

12. The safest way to remove phenolic (plastic) pistons from calipers is by the use of _____.
    - (A) a large screwdriver
    - (B) special pliers
    - (C) air pressure
    - (D) brake system pressure

13. The Hydro-Boost unit receives necessary operating pressure from the _____.

14. The _____ proportioning valve incorporates a variable pressure range feature to prevent brake lockup.

15. A dual proportioning valve is used on a _____.
    - (A) single master cylinder
    - (B) Hydro-boost unit
    - (C) diagonal split brake system
    - (D) None of the above.

ASE-Type Questions

1. Technician A says that wheel cylinders should be rebuilt or replaced when the brake shoes are replaced. Technician B says that the master cylinder should be rebuilt or replaced when the brake shoes are replaced. Who is right?
   - (A) A only.
   - (B) B only.
   - (C) Both A & B.
   - (D) Neither A nor B.

2. The primary brake shoe faces _____.
   - (A) the back of the vehicle
   - (B) the front of the vehicle
   - (C) to the front on the left side and to the rear on the right side
   - (D) in either direction, depending on the manufacturer

3. Technician A says that brake springs are all alike and may be installed at random. Technician B says that a cracked brake drum can be salvaged by welding. Who is right?
   - (A) A only.
   - (B) B only.
   - (C) Both A & B.
   - (D) Neither A nor B.

4. When a drum on the front left of a vehicle is turned .030 inch (0.762 mm), the drum on the front right should be turned _____.
   - (A) .010″ (0.254 mm)
   - (B) .030″ (0.762 mm)
   - (C) .060″ (1.524 mm)
   - (D) .300″ (7.620 mm)

5. Always adjust the parking brake before _____.
   - (A) adjusting the brake shoes
   - (B) turning the drums
   - (C) bleeding the brakes
   - (D) None of the above.

6. Start the brake bleeding process by bleeding the wheel cylinder or caliper that is _____.
   - (A) closest to the master cylinder
   - (B) on the same side as the master cylinder
   - (C) farthest away from the master cylinder
   - (D) on the left front side

7. Technician A says that pressure bleeding requires two people. Technician B says that fluid bled from the system can be used again if it is strained. Who is right?
   - (A) A only.
   - (B) B only.

(C) Both A & B.
(D) Neither A nor B.

8. The disc brake caliper does *not* have to be removed to perform any of the following tasks, EXCEPT:
   (A) changing pads.
   (B) bleeding the caliper.
   (C) replacing caliper piston seals.
   (D) changing a brake hose.

9. The quick take up master cylinder supplies a large volume of _____ fluid at the start of brake application.
   (A) cool
   (B) reverse-flow
   (C) high-pressure
   (D) low-pressure

10. Technician A says that after the brakes are overhauled, the technician should make 8 or 10 stops from high speed to seat the linings. Technician B says that aluminum wheel cylinders may be honed. Who is right?
    (A) A only.
    (B) B only.
    (C) Both A & B.
    (D) Neither A nor B.

Student Activities

1. Make a diagram of a front disc brake/rear drum brake hydraulic system. Explain the operation and interaction of the hydraulic and mechanical components.

2. Draw a wheel cylinder and a single piston caliper on the blackboard and explain how the hydraulic force is turned into movement of the shoes and pads.

3. Draw a pressure differential valve on the board and explain the differences in fluid flow in each of the following modes:

   • Normal operation.
   • Pressure loss at the rear (or right front-left rear of a split system).
   • Pressure loss at the front (or left front-right rear of a split system).

4. Check the fluid level in at least three vehicle master cylinders. Explain how to determine what type of fluid should be added.

5. Bleed the brakes of a vehicle without ABS. Write a short report summarizing the bleeding procedures.

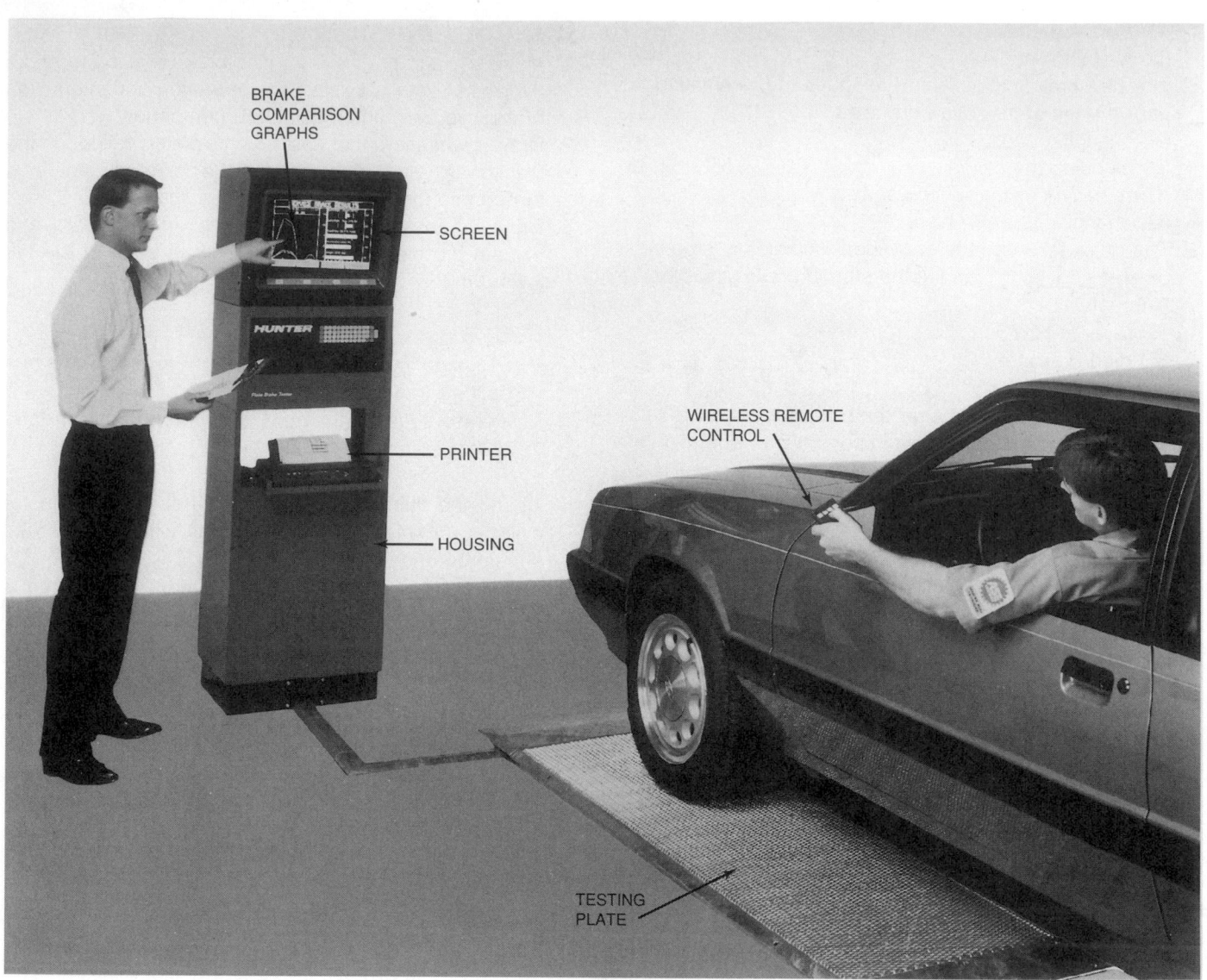

BRAKE
COMPARISON
GRAPHS

SCREEN

HUNTER

PRINTER

HOUSING

WIRELESS REMOTE
CONTROL

TESTING
PLATE

These technicians are using a brake testing system to accurately check brake performance. The testing system measures braking force, vehicle deceleration, and side slip. The brake at each wheel is checked as the vehicle is driven onto the testing plates. (Hunter)

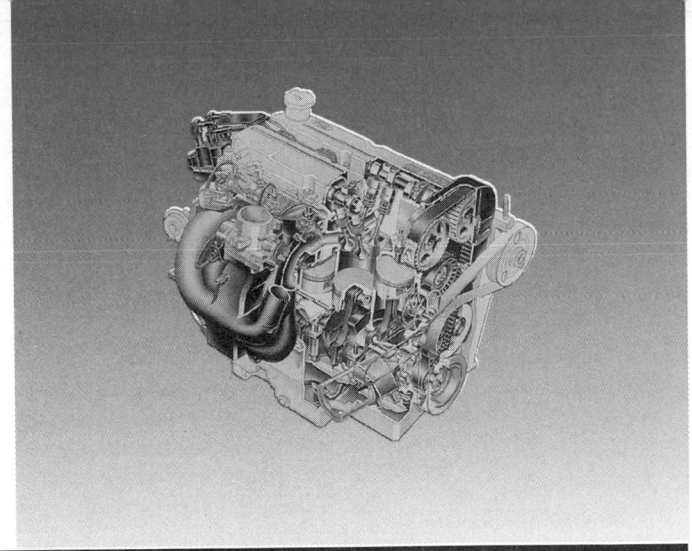

35

Anti-Lock Brake and Traction Control System Service

Upon completion of this chapter you will be able to:
- Explain anti-lock brake system operation.
- Identify anti-lock brake system components.
- Diagnose anti-lock brake system problems.
- Explain traction control system operation.
- Identify traction control system components.
- Diagnose traction control system problems.

This chapter will cover the principles of anti-lock brakes and traction controls. Both are similar in that they use electronic components to control the brake hydraulic system. The hydraulic system, in turn, controls the application of the brake friction elements. The major differences between the systems include the ultimate purpose of each system and the fact that the traction control system also affects the engine output on some vehicles. On many new vehicles, the anti-lock brakes and the traction control system are operated by a single electronic/hydraulic control system.

Anti-Lock Brake Systems

Many vehicles are now being equipped with **anti-lock brake systems,** often referred to as **ABS** systems. Most ABS systems used on automobiles are similar to the one shown in **Figure 35-1** and control all four wheels. The ABS systems used on most light trucks and a few small cars control only the rear wheels, **Figure 35-2.** All ABS systems, whether two- or four-wheel systems, use electronic and hydraulic components to help prevent wheel lockup during hard braking. Anti-lock brakes allow the driver to maintain directional control while providing maximum braking efficiency.

Always Obtain a Service Manual

Anti-lock brake systems are made by many vehicle and parts manufacturers. These systems, while similar, require different troubleshooting and service procedures. The same system may be installed on different makes of

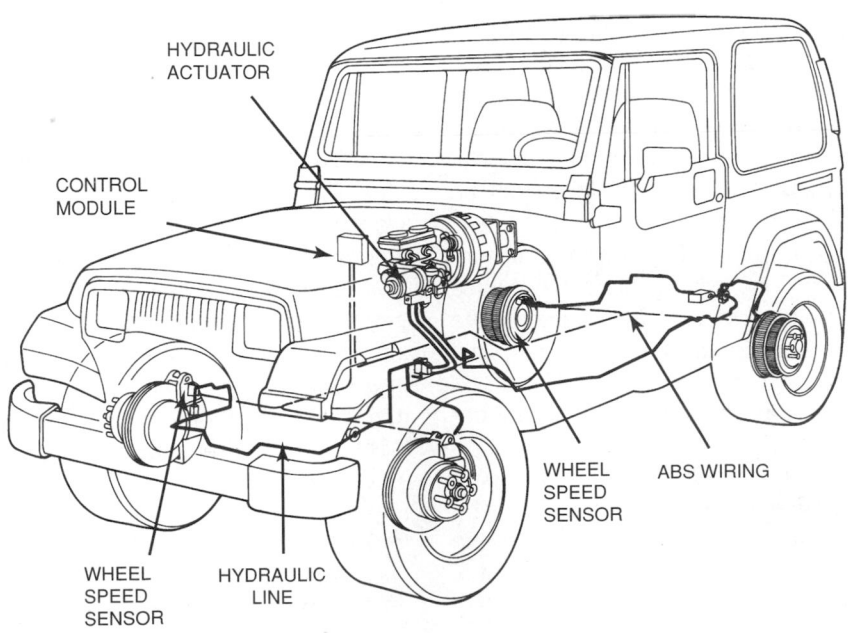

Figure 35-1. A vehicle equipped with a four-wheel anti-lock braking system. Study the various systems and parts. (Jeep)

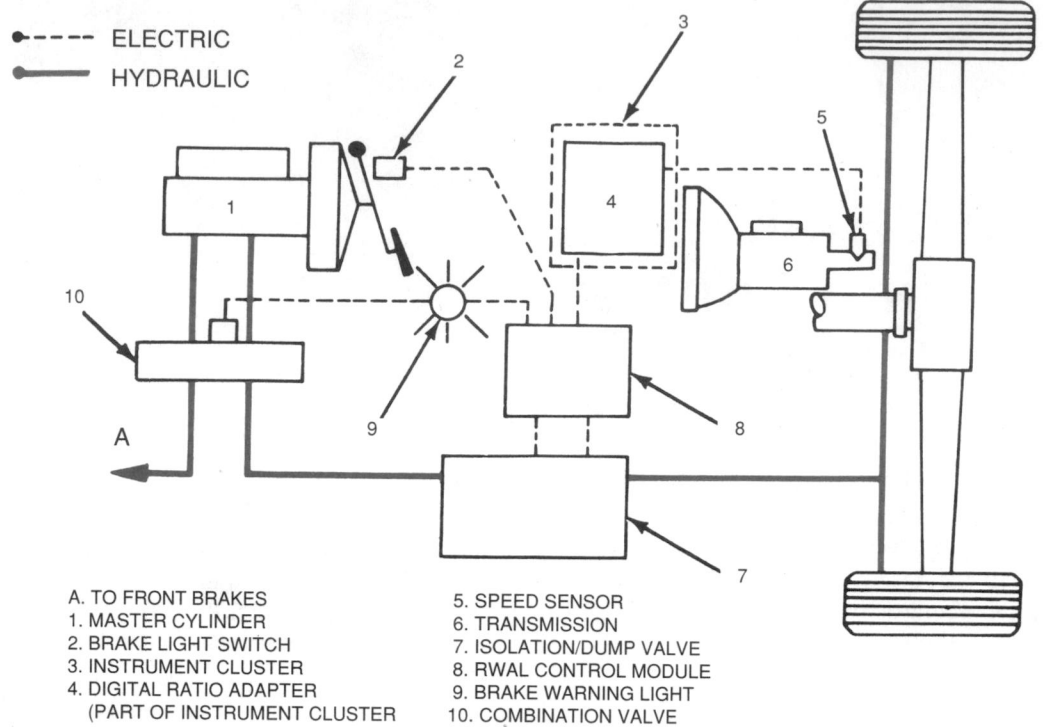

A. TO FRONT BRAKES
1. MASTER CYLINDER
2. BRAKE LIGHT SWITCH
3. INSTRUMENT CLUSTER
4. DIGITAL RATIO ADAPTER
   (PART OF INSTRUMENT CLUSTER

5. SPEED SENSOR
6. TRANSMISSION
7. ISOLATION/DUMP VALVE
8. RWAL CONTROL MODULE
9. BRAKE WARNING LIGHT
10. COMBINATION VALVE

Figure 35-2. A rear wheel anti-lock brake system. Study the electrical and hydraulic circuits and various components. (GM)

vehicles, and the same line of vehicles may have two or more brands of anti-lock brake systems. Therefore, it is important to refer to the correct service manual before beginning any repairs on an anti-lock brake system.

The Reason for Anti-Lock Brakes

When a situation calling for a quick stop arises, the average driver tends to apply the brakes as hard as possible. Although this is a natural reaction, it is the wrong thing to do in most situations. Applying the brakes as hard as possible causes one or more wheels to lock up, causing a skid. Skidding tires cannot contribute to slowing the vehicle. If any one of the tires is skidding, the vehicle cannot be steered effectively.

On wet or icy pavement, the tires slip on the moisture on the road. When the road is dry, locking the wheel causes the tire rubber to begin melting. Melting is caused by the tremendous friction from the stationary tire rubbing against the pavement. The tire then slips on the melted rubber. Skid marks commonly seen on roads are actually melted rubber from a panic stop.

Safety experts recommend avoiding skids by pumping the brakes. Pumping the brakes means alternately applying and releasing the brake pedal as quickly as possible during a panic stop. While this will help prevent wheel lockup, it is hard for many drivers to remember. Additionally, it is very difficult to pump the brakes fast enough to have any real effect.

The force of the brake pedal is transmitted to the brakes by hydraulic pressure developed in the master cylinder. Therefore, modulating (alternately reducing and increasing) the brake hydraulic pressure between the master cylinder and the wheel calipers or wheel cylinders can prevent lockup. The ABS system pumps the brakes at a much faster rate than any driver could. Since the anti-lock brake system only operates during very hard stops, normal braking is unaffected by an ABS system.

Advantages of Anti-Lock Brake Systems

The major advantage of anti-lock brakes is, of course, the elimination of wheel lockup under hard braking. Preventing wheel lockup reduces the chances of skidding and improves vehicle control during panic stops.

The other advantage of anti-lock brake systems is the reduction of tire wear and flat spotting caused by panic stops. If the wheel is not turning as the vehicle continues to move, friction will melt a flat spot in the bottom of the tire. On wet roads, there is still some friction that will grind a flat spot onto the tire. If the wheel can be kept turning as the vehicle is stopped, tire wear will be even.

Anti-Lock Brake System Components

Anti-lock brake systems use an electronic control system to modify the operation of the brake hydraulic system. The electronic and hydraulic components work together to prevent wheel lockup during periods of hard braking. Most anti-lock brake systems, no matter who manufacturers them, contain several common components. These components include wheel speed sensor units, an anti-lock control module, and a hydraulic actuator. See **Figure 35-1.**

Note that the brake friction components (shoes and pads), most of the hydraulic components (wheel cylinders, caliper pistons, master cylinder, and hydraulic lines), and the power brake system components are the same as those used on vehicles without ABS. When discussing ABS systems, the standard friction and hydraulic components are referred to as the *foundation brakes* or the *base brakes.*

Wheel Speed Sensor Units

Anti-lock brake systems use *speed sensor* units to determine the rate of wheel rotation. Most wheel speed sensor units consist of a toothed rotor, or wheel, and a sensing unit, **Figure 35-3.** The toothed rotor is attached to the vehicle's axle or brake rotor and rotates at the same speed as the wheel and tire. As the rotor spins, it creates a magnetic field in the sensing unit. The sensing unit converts the magnetic field into a pulsating voltage signal, which is sent to the control module. The strength and frequency of this signal varies in relation to the speed of the wheel.

Some anti-lock brake systems have wheel-speed sensing units that are mounted at each wheel. Other systems use speed sensors mounted on the rear axle housing or in the transmission, **Figure 35-4.** Axle and transmission-mounted sensors are commonly used on two-wheel ABS systems and are found on some four-wheel ABS systems.

G-Force Sensor

Some systems contain a *G-force sensor,* which measures the rate of deceleration by comparing the vehicle tilt during braking to the normal ride position. The G-force sensor is often installed in the passenger compartment. G-force sensor input, along with wheel sensor readings, is used by the control module to develop outputs to the hydraulic system. See **Figure 35-5.** Some ABS systems use a form of the G-force sensor called a *lateral accelerometer* to sense cornering speed.

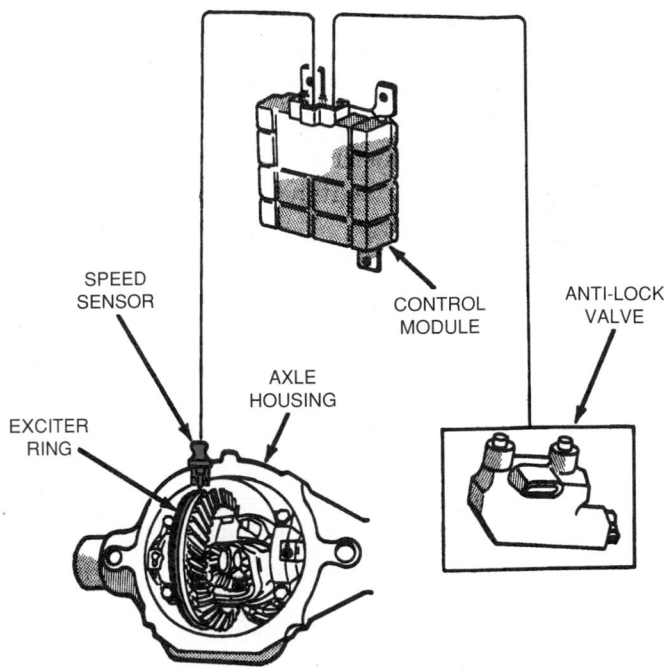

Figure 35-4.   A speed sensor that is mounted in the rear axle housing. Note the toothed exciter ring, which is fastened to the ring gear. (Dodge)

Control Module

The *control module* uses the signals produced by the wheel sensors to determine when the anti-lock system should be activated. When a wheel is nearing a lockup condition, the control module signals the hydraulic actuator to regulate fluid pressure to that wheel. The control module processes inputs and delivers outputs using the same general process as the engine control computers discussed in earlier chapters. A typical anti-lock control module is shown in **Figure 35-6.**

Most control modules are equipped with self-diagnostic capabilities. The control module will illuminate an *ABS warning light* on the vehicle dashboard if there is a malfunction in the ABS system. The light also comes on during and shortly after starting as a bulb and wiring check. This

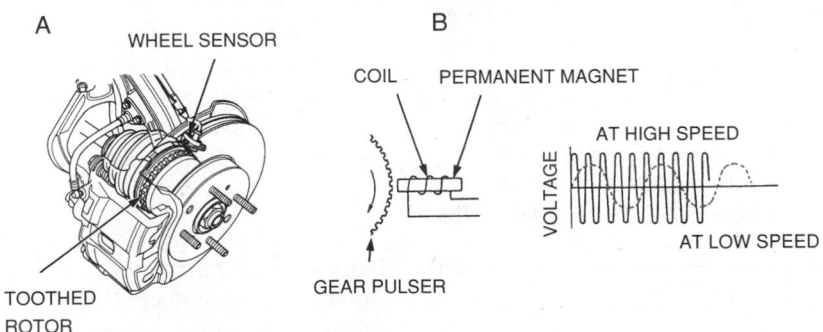

Figure 35-3.   A—A wheel speed sensor and toothed rotor. B—When the toothed rotor turns, the magnetic flux around the coil in the wheel sensor alternates, producing voltages with a frequency in proportion to the speed of the rotating wheel. These pulses are sent to the anti-lock control module to identify wheel speed. (Honda)

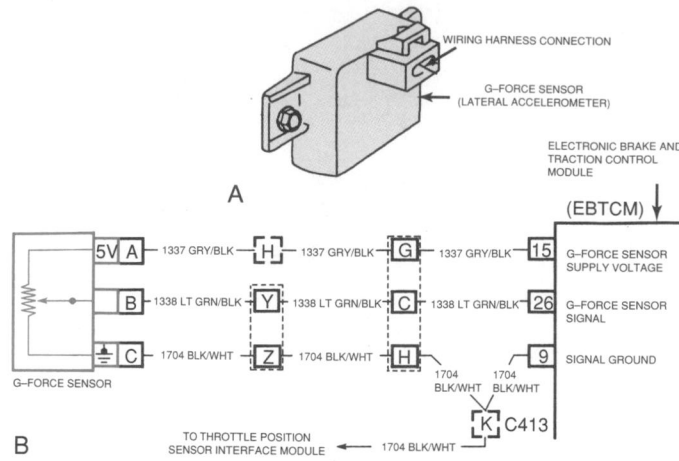

Figure 35-5. A—Typical G-force sensor (lateral accelerometer). B—G-force sensor and wiring going to the electronic brake control module. The G-force sensor cannot be repaired and must be replaced as a complete assembly. Handle these sensors with care; they are easily damaged! (Chevrolet)

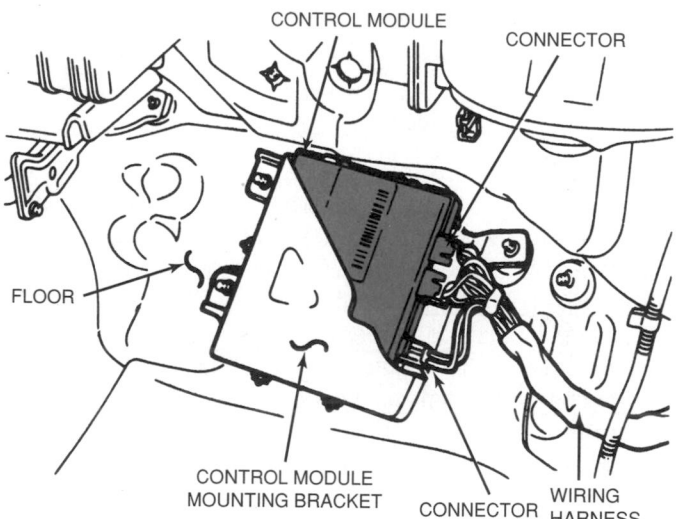

Figure 35-6. Anti-lock brake control module, mounting bracket, and wiring harness. (Geo)

light can be used on some systems to retrieve trouble codes.

 Note: Do not confuse the ABS warning light with the *brake system warning light* that is used on all vehicles. The ABS light is usually amber. The brake warning light is red. Typical lights are shown in Figure 35-7. In some cases, both lights are operated by the control module.

Hydraulic Actuator

The ***hydraulic actuator*** is the unit that regulates the pressure delivered to the brakes based on commands it receives from the control module. The actuator usually consists of two or four ***solenoid valves,*** a ***hydraulic pump,***

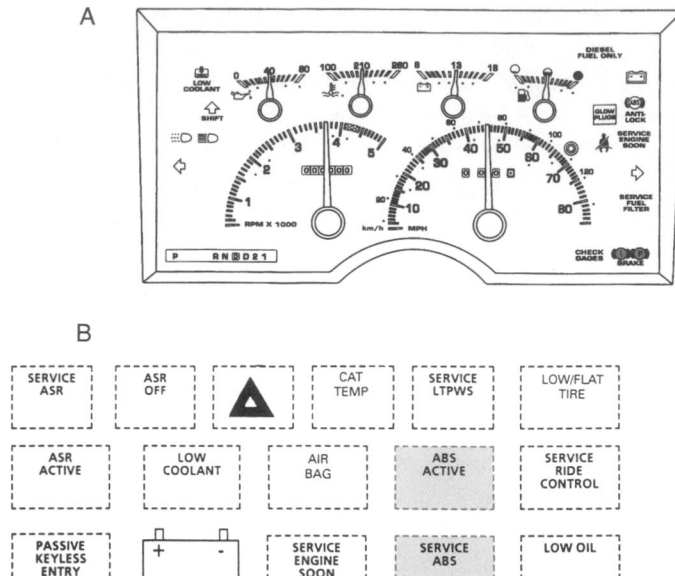

Figure 35-7. A—An instrument cluster with ABS and brake warning lights. B—A driver information center with ABS active and service lights. (GM)

and an ***accumulator.*** All of the above components may be housed in a single casing or may be separately mounted and connected by high-pressure hoses. See **Figure 35-8.** The actuator on a two-wheel ABS system will have two solenoid valves, and the actuator on a four-wheel ABS system will have four solenoid valves. Some systems use three solenoid valves—one for each front wheel and a single solenoid to operate both rear wheels. No matter how many solenoids there are, they control the hydraulic system in the same way.

The solenoid valves control the hydraulic pressures by two methods, depending on the system and the severity of the lockup position:

- When the lockup condition is slight, the ABS solenoids are positioned to seal the passage between the master cylinder and brakes lines so no additional pressure can reach the affected wheel cylinder or caliper.
- When the lockup condition is severe, the ABS solenoids will be positioned to dump small amounts of hydraulic fluid back to the reservoir, the accumulator, or the hydraulic pump intake. This fluid removal reduces, or bleeds off, hydraulic pressure going to the individual wheel cylinder or piston.

These processes occur many times per second, causing the slight ***pulsation*** that can be felt in the brake pedal during ABS operation. This pulsation is caused by the ABS system alternately pumping the brakes to give maximum braking power without wheel lockup. Note that the hydraulic actuator controls the brake hydraulic system pressure during ABS operation, no matter what degree of pressure is applied to the brake pedal by the driver.

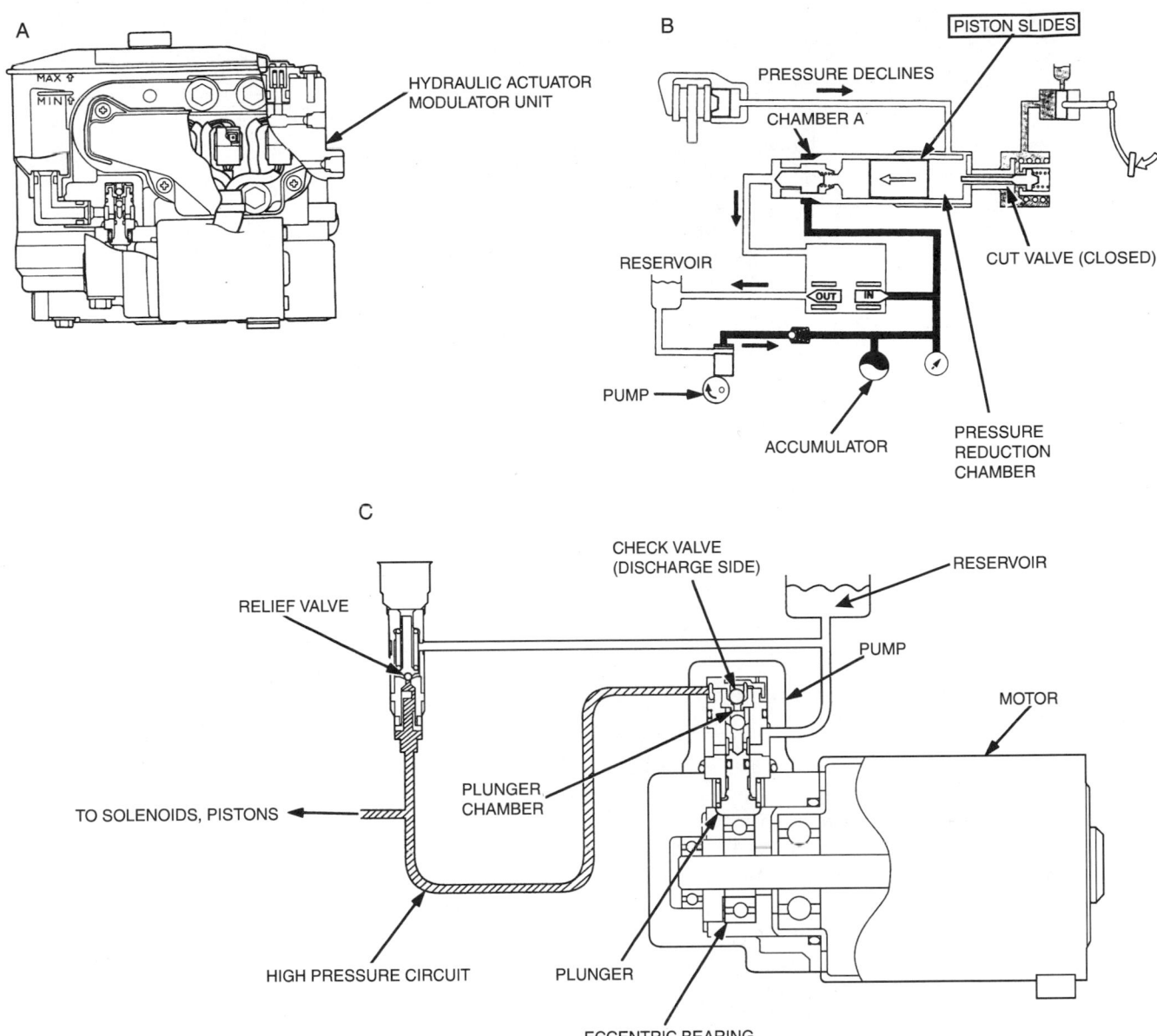

Figure 35-8. A—Hydraulic actuator. B—Anti-lock brake system operation schematic. C—Cutaway view of the electric motor, pump, and the relief valve. (Honda)

During ABS operation, hydraulic system pressure is constantly being bled off and then reapplied to provide maximum braking without wheel lock. Therefore, if the ABS is used for long periods, the original pressure applied may not be sufficient to operate the brakes. The hydraulic actuator pump is used to provide makeup pressure to the hydraulic system. The intake of some hydraulic pumps is piped through the solenoids and used to quickly draw off pressure when a particular wheel must be depressurized quickly. This process is controlled by the solenoids.

An accumulator is also installed in the hydraulic actuator or between the master cylinder and the actuator. It absorbs extra fluid when the actuator valves are bleeding off pressure. The accumulator also holds fluid pressure in reserve to allow for brake operation if the pump is unable to keep up with pressure demands.

Piston-Operated Hydraulic Actuator

One variation of the hydraulic actuator uses moveable pistons instead of a hydraulic pump to produce hydraulic pressure. The pistons are operated by small electric motors through reduction gears. This actuator is called a ***hydraulic modulator.*** The hydraulic modulator regulates the pressure delivered to the brakes in a manner similar to the conventional hydraulic actuator. However, the solenoids used in the hydraulic modulator have only one function—to isolate, or seal, the passage between the master cylinder and the affected wheel cylinder or caliper. If additional pressure control is needed, the pistons are moved to increase or reduce the hydraulic pressure to a particular circuit.

A cutaway view of the hydraulic modulator is shown in **Figure 35-9.** Notice that the pistons are operated by motor-driven screw assemblies called ***ball screws.*** The ball screws

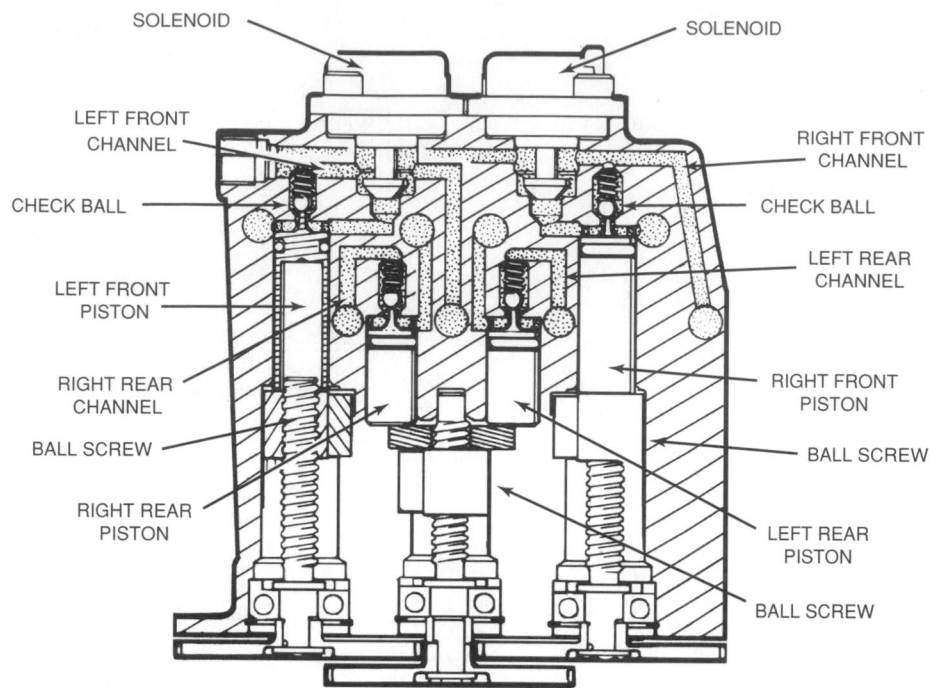

Figure 35-9. A cutaway view of a hydraulic modulator assembly.

operate by moving up or down on threaded rods. Note that each front wheel piston has a separate ball screw, while the rear pistons are both operated by single ball screw.

The pistons can be driven forward to increase pressure or backward to reduce pressure. In addition, the pistons can be held in position to maintain a certain pressure. The pistons serve as accumulators for extra pressure. The piston position can be precisely controlled by extremely close tolerances in the ball screws and reduction gears, and by the use of brakes on the drive motors. The brakes

can be electromagnetic brakes or expansion spring brakes. A typical drive motor and brake assembly is shown in **Figure 35-10.**

Pedal Travel Switch

Some ABS systems are equipped with a *pedal travel switch,* which is mounted on the brake pedal assembly. The pedal travel switch is electrically connected to the control module. The signal from the pedal travel switch alerts the control module when pedal pulsation

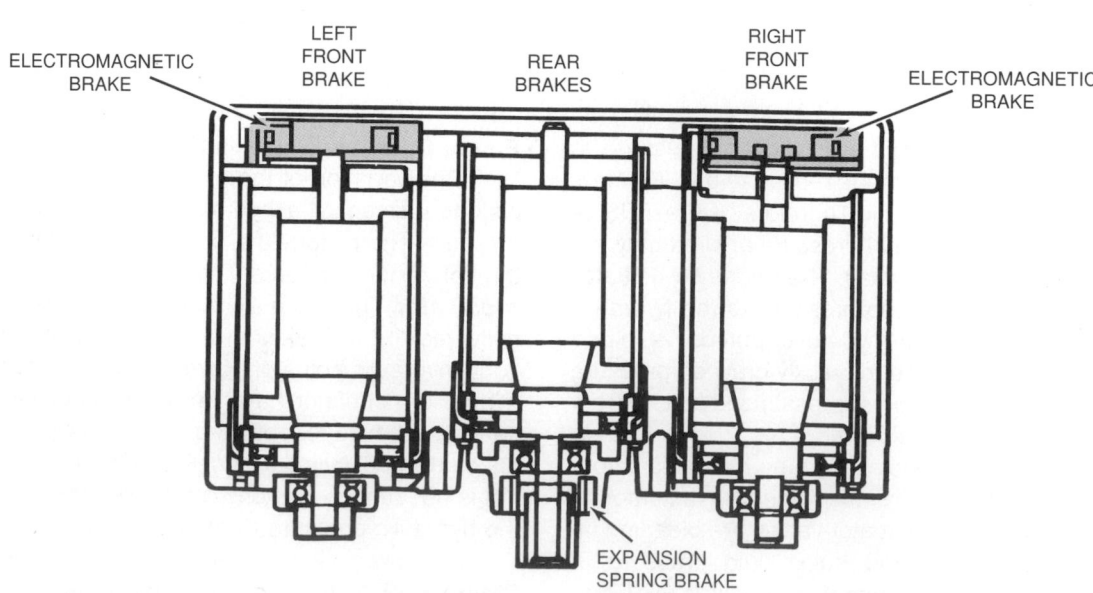

Figure 35-10. Cutaway of an electric drive motor and electromagnetic brake (EMB) assembly.

becomes excessive during ABS operation. The control module then modifies the action of the hydraulic actuator solenoid valves to reduce pulsation.

Anti-Lock Brake Operation

Under normal light braking conditions, the anti-lock portion of the brake system does not operate. The sensors continuously monitor wheel rotation and send signals to the anti-lock control module. When the brake pedal is pressed, fluid flows from the master cylinder, through the hydraulic actuator, and into the wheel cylinder or caliper, **Figure 35-11**. Basic hydraulic brake operation was discussed in Chapter 34.

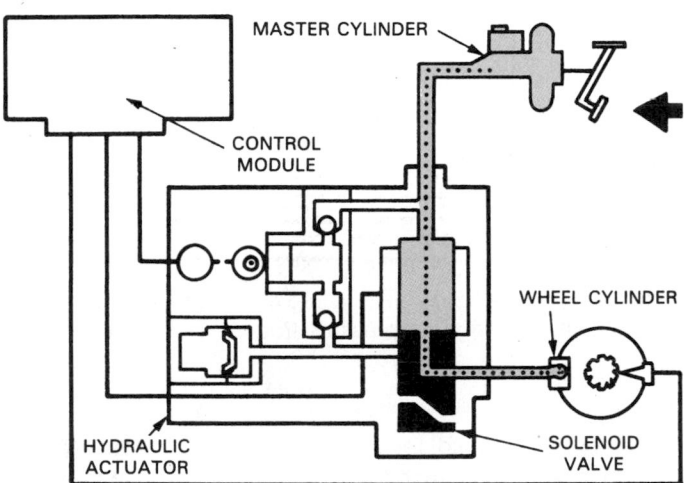

Figure 35-11. Anti-lock brake system operation during normal braking. Hydraulic fluid flows directly through the solenoid into the wheel cylinder.

When the control module senses that a wheel is nearing a lockup condition, it signals the solenoid valve in the hydraulic actuator to block the fluid passage between the master cylinder and the wheel cylinder. When this occurs, pressure is trapped between the wheel cylinder and the hydraulic actuator. Master cylinder fluid pressure cannot flow through the solenoid valve, and the brake pressure at the affected wheel is held constant, **Figure 35-12.**

If the control module detects a complete lockup, it will command the hydraulic actuator to decrease pressure to the affected wheel cylinder. To accomplish this, the solenoid valve in the actuator moves to cut off fluid pressure from the master cylinder and to allow brake fluid at the caliper to flow into the accumulator, reservoir, or pump intake, **Figure 35-13.** When this occurs, pressure at the wheel is decreased.

On the piston-type hydraulic modulator, the solenoid valves isolate the circuit from the master cylinder and the pistons are moved to reduce pressure. **Figure 35-14** shows the solenoid and piston operation to control the front brakes.

When all the wheels are rotating normally, the solenoid valves in the actuator return to their original positions

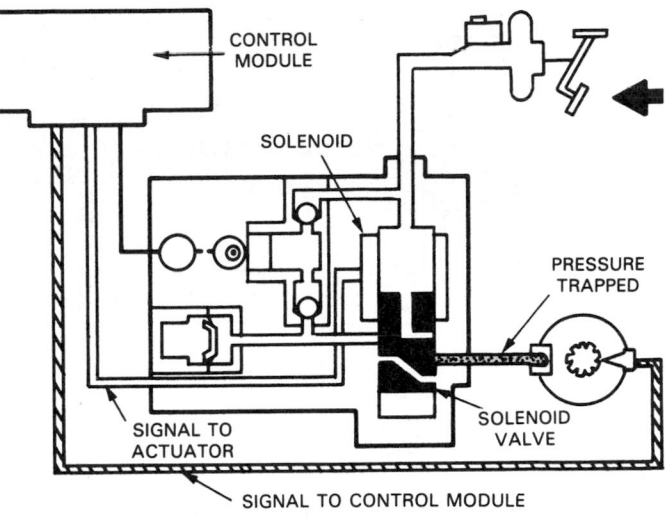

Figure 35-12. When the electronic control unit senses a potential wheel lockup, it instructs the solenoid to block hydraulic fluid to the wheel cylinder.

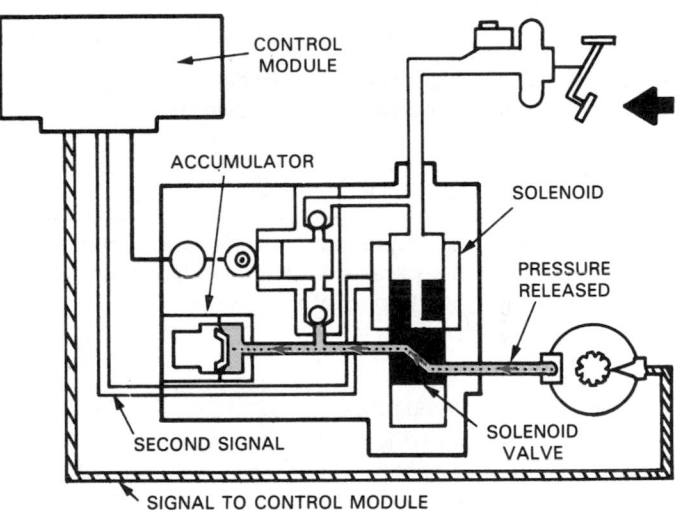

Figure 35-13. If a wheel locks up, the solenoid is instructed to release hydraulic pressure at the affected wheel. Note the fluid flowing back into the accumulator.

and the foundation braking system takes over. At the same time, the actuator pump delivers any excess fluid in the accumulator back to the master cylinder. If necessary, a typical anti-lock system can repeat this cycle up to 15 times a second.

Anti-Lock Brake System Maintenance

No specific ABS maintenance is needed. The wheel sensors should be periodically checked for damage. Check the toothed rotors for contamination with dirt, grease, or road debris. Check the level in the brake master cylinder as you would with a non-ABS brake system. Add fluid as necessary. If the fluid level seems excessively low, check for leaks in the system. Other brake system checks can be made according the information in Chapter 34.

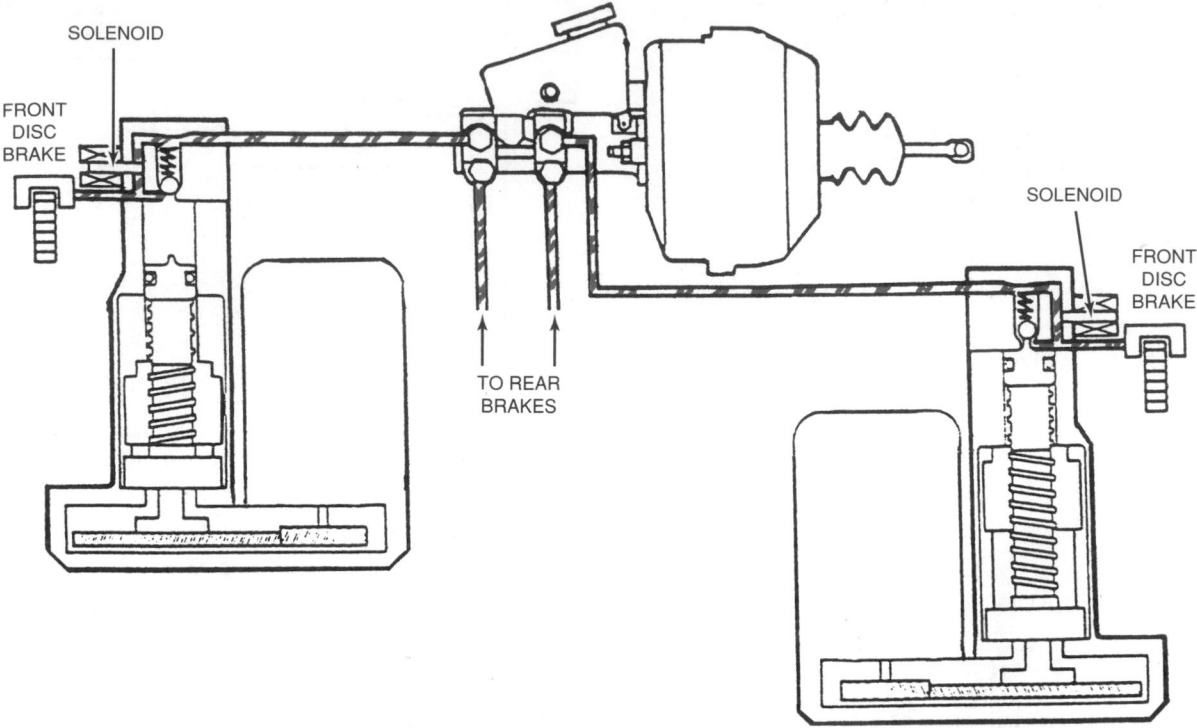

Figure 35-14. Anti-lock brake system decreasing hydraulic pressure to the front brake system to help prevent wheel lockup. The piston and the ball screw have moved down. This permits the check ball to seat, isolating fluid pressure from the front brake.

 Note: Check the manufacturer's requirements before adding brake fluid. Many ABS systems are not designed to accept silicone brake fluid.

Troubleshooting Anti-Lock Brakes

Under hard braking, the brake pedal will pulsate slightly. This is a normal condition when the anti-lock brake system is operating. If no pulsation is felt, the anti-lock system may not be operating. Another sign of trouble is when the brakes lock up above 6 to 10 mph (9.7-16.1 km/h). Below 6-10 mph, the system is deactivated and lockup may occur. An obvious sign of trouble is when the ABS warning light stays on after the vehicle has been operating for a few minutes, or when the light flickers during vehicle operation. It is normal for the light to be on for several seconds after the vehicle is started.

 Caution: Be sure to observe all traffic rules when testing the anti-lock brake system. Perform all ABS road testing in a safe area, away from other vehicles.

Making Preliminary Checks

Many ABS systems require the use of special testers, such as the one shown in **Figure 35-15,** to pinpoint internal system troubles. However, many preliminary checks can be made visually or with simple test equipment and hand tools. If ABS trouble is suspected, or if the ABS light is on, start by checking for the following problems:

- Low brake fluid level in the master cylinder—A low fluid level will cause the ABS light to come on and may also trigger the red brake warning light. See the fluid caution above before adding fluid to the reservoir.
- External fluid leaks—External leaks will cause erratic pressure application and low level in the master cylinder. Leaks may also trigger the ABS light.
- Worn disc brake pads and rotors or worn and maladjusted shoes and drums—Excessive wear or maladjustment will force the hydraulic system to provide more fluid to the caliper piston or wheel cylinder, upsetting hydraulic pressure development.
- Problems in the power brake booster—A defect in the booster can cause a hard pedal or slow brake application, either of which can cause ABS problems.
- Stuck parking brake cable—A stuck parking brake cable will cause partial application of the parking brakes, resulting in hydraulic system or sensor malfunction.
- Incorrect charging system voltage—Low voltage will cause the ABS computer to operate incorrectly. Charging system service was covered in Chapter 29.
- Blown fuses in the ABS input—There may be several fuses supplying power to various circuits in the ABS system, **Figure 35-16.**
- High resistance or disconnected control wiring—Check carefully at connections under the vehicle. Also check for disconnected or corroded ground wires.
- Defective relays—As shown in **Figure 35-17,** there may be several relays operated by or delivering power to the ABS system. Check that these relays are not

A

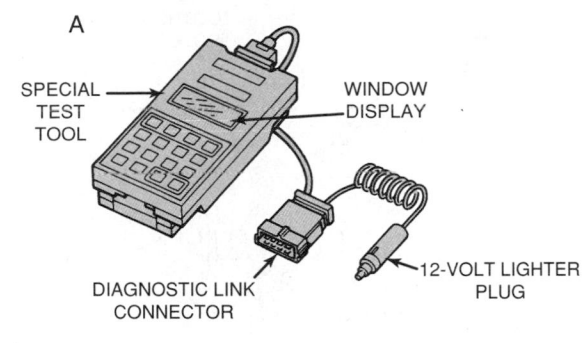

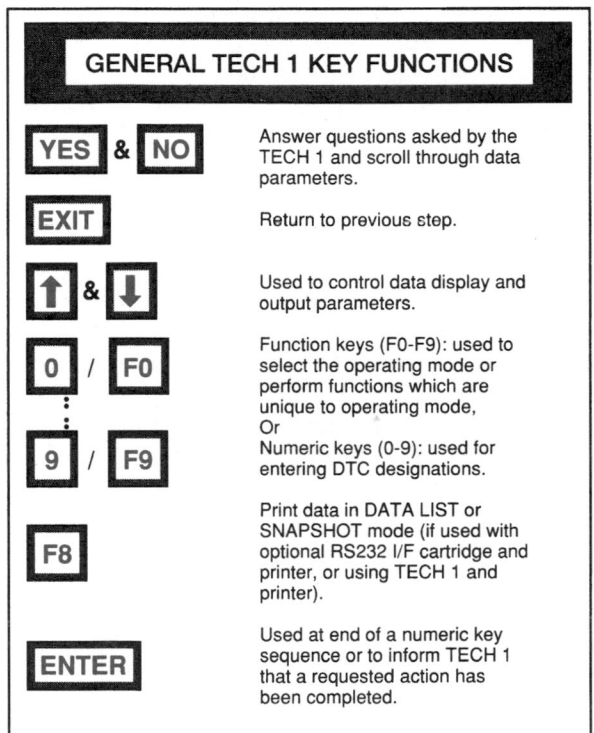

Figure 35-15. A—Special anti-lock brake system electrical testing tool. B—Testing tool keys and their functions. This tool attaches to the ABS brake diagnostic link connector (DLC) and is powered by a 12-volt lighter outlet. (GM)

loose or disconnected. Also check that the sockets are not overheated, corroded, or otherwise damaged.

- Mismatched tires—All tires on a vehicle equipped with ABS should be the same size and type. The tires should always be the same height as the original equipment.

Retrieving Trouble Codes

Most anti-lock brake systems have self-diagnostic capabilities. If no problems are uncovered during the above checks, retrieve the trouble codes stored in the control module's memory. Recovery procedures are similar to those for the engine control computer. Refer to Chapters 25 and 28.

Some ABS trouble codes can be located by going through a series of code retrieval steps and watching a series of flashes from the dashboard-mounted ABS trouble light. Another retrieval process involves using a voltmeter to

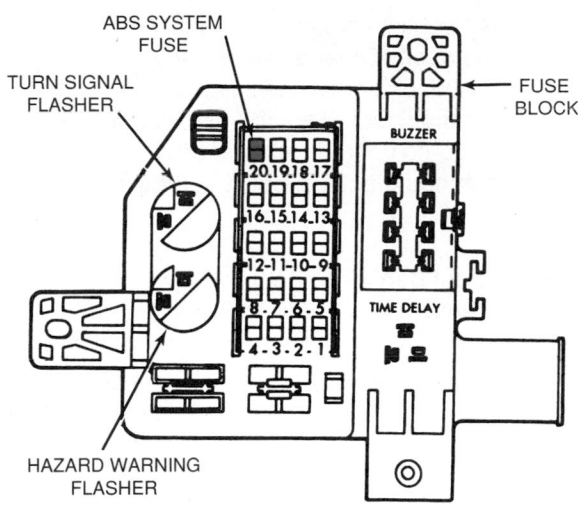

Figure 35-16. One particular fuse block that contains an anti-lock brake system fuse. (Chrysler)

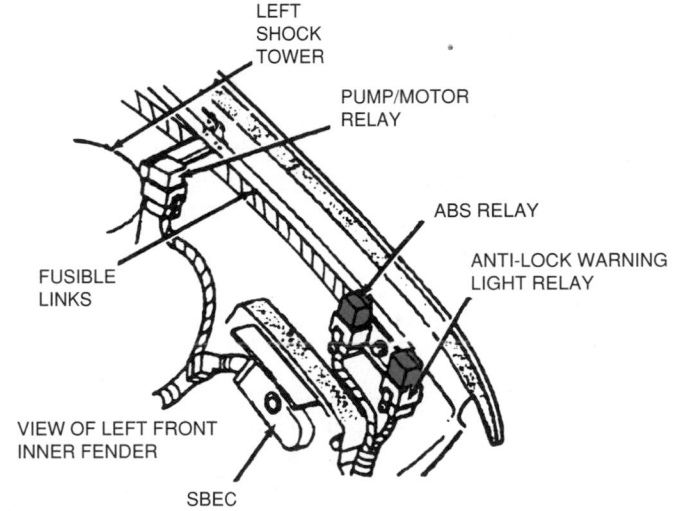

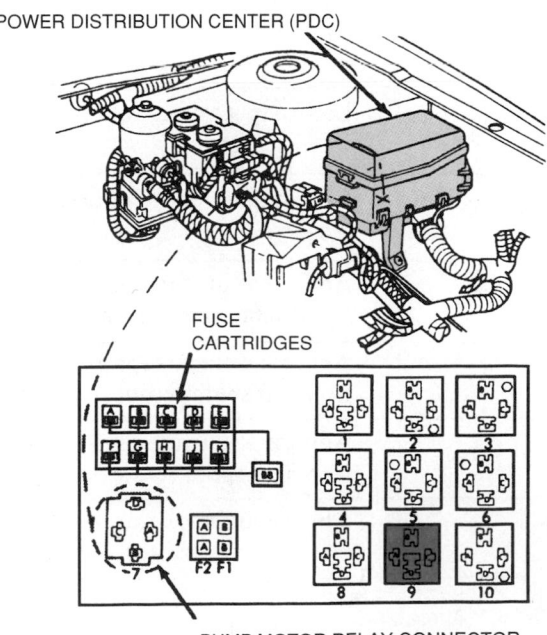

Figure 35-17. ABS relay locations. (Chrysler)

observe voltage pulses created by the control module in the self-diagnosis mode. Other systems require that a special scan tool be used to retrieve codes. Always consult the vehicle's service manual for the appropriate method. The trouble codes should be compared to the appropriate trouble code chart to determine potential problems, **Figure 35-18.**

Checking Wheel Sensors

Wheel sensors are a common source of ABS problems. They should be inspected for signs of physical damage. A buildup of dirt or grease between the rotor teeth can cause the control module to set a trouble code. Many manufacturers recommend checking wheel sensors with an ohmmeter to determine their resistance. If the reading does not fall within specifications, the sensor should be replaced.

If possible, check the air gap between the sensor and the rotor teeth. A gap that is too wide or too small will cause erratic readings. A typical gap checking procedure is shown in **Figure 35-19.** While not specifically called for on some systems, using a brass feeler gauge will result in a more accurate reading.

Some systems do not have gap specifications. When this is the case, make sure that the sensor assembly is mounted in exactly the same position as the old sensor. Make sure that all fasteners are correctly torqued.

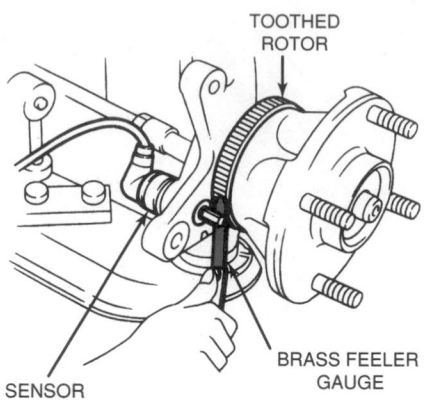

Figure 35-19.   Checking the air gap between the speed sensor and the toothed rotor. Set this gap (when adjustable) to the vehicle manufacturer's specifications. (Nissan)

Always make sure that the wiring from the sensor is routed correctly. A sensor wire passing too close to a source of heat or strong magnetic fields can cause the wiring to provide false information to the control module. Wires should, therefore, be kept away from the exhaust system and ignition wires. Also check that the wiring is retained by the proper clips to reduce the possibility of cutting a wire during turns or braking.

DIAGNOSTIC CODE (Sensor Check Mode)

Code No.	Diagnosis	Malfunctioning Area
Normal	All speed sensors and sensor rotors are normal	
71	Low output voltage of front right speed sensor	• Front right speed sensor • Sensor installation
72	Low output voltage of front left speed sensor	• Front left speed sensor • Sensor installation
73	Low output voltage of rear right speed sensor	• Rear right speed sensor • Sensor installation
74	Low output voltage of rear left speed sensor	• Rear left speed sensor • Sensor installation
75	Abnormal fluctuation in output voltage of front right speed sensor	• Front right sensor rotor
76	Abnormal fluctuation in output voltage of front left speed sensor	• Front left sensor rotor
77	Abnormal fluctuation in output voltage of rear right speed sensor	• Rear right sensor rotor
78	Abnormal fluctuation in output voltage of rear left speed sensor	• Rear left sensor rotor

Figure 35-18.   A trouble code chart for one specific anti-lock brake system. This chart only contains trouble code information for the wheel speed sensors. (Toyota)

Another cause of improper speed sensor readings is a physical problem at the wheel. A common problem is a warped rotor or drum caused by overtorquing the lug nuts. The sensor rotor may also become warped, causing an erratic signal to be produced by a good sensor. If the sensor rotors were overheated, dropped, or hammered into place on the hub, they may lose their magnetic properties. Loose wheel bearings, CV joints, or suspension and steering system parts can also cause erratic speed sensor readings.

Checking Control Module

If a trouble code indicates that the anti-lock control module is faulty, check the input voltage to the unit. If the control module does not receive sufficient voltage, it will not operate properly. Check the wiring to the control module. Make sure all connections are clean and secure. Verify the operation of all related anti-lock system components before condemning the control module.

> **Caution: Do not try to make ohmmeter checks to the control module unless they are specifically called for by the manufacturer. The electronic circuitry inside the module can be destroyed by ohmmeter current.**

Some scan tools can operate the control module by inputting test signals. If the control modulator will not provide the proper outputs based on the inputs of the scan tool, it can be assumed that the module is defective. Follow the scan tool manufacturer's instructions to perform these tests. In most cases, the internal components of the control module cannot be serviced. The module must be replaced if it is defective.

Checking Hydraulic Actuator

If a faulty hydraulic actuator is suspected, it should be tested according to the manufacturer's recommendations. Some manufacturers specify ohmmeter tests to determine the condition of the solenoid valves and motor in the actuator. Another test, shown in **Figure 35-20**, checks for proper hydraulic pressures at the actuator under various conditions. Some hydraulic actuators can be disassembled to check for internal problems.

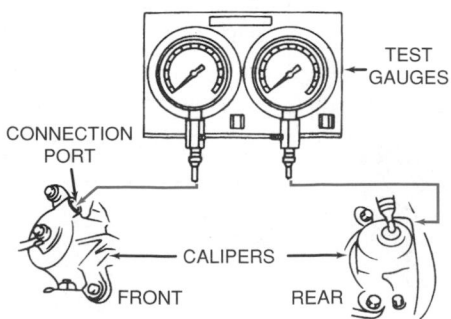

Figure 35-20. Checking hydraulic pressures at the front and rear brake calipers with a special gauge. (Nissan)

Replacing ABS Parts

Most ABS parts, such as the wheel speed sensors, control module, and hydraulic actuator, are not field repairable. They should be replaced if they are defective. Note that most of the hydraulic system and friction elements are similar to those on units without ABS. Refer to Chapter 34 for service on all non-ABS components. Before replacing any part of the ABS system, refer to the cautions below.

- Make sure that the ignition key is off before disconnecting any ABS electrical connector. Some manufacturers recommend removing the battery cable.
- Depressurize the brake system before beginning any repairs to the hydraulic system. Pumping the brake pedal a minimum of 40 times will discharge the accumulator. Also make sure that the ignition key is off, since the hydraulic actuator motor may attempt to recharge the accumulator if pressure is removed when the key is on.
- If repair procedures require the replacement of any hydraulic hoses or lines, make sure that the correct replacement lines are used. Hydraulic pressures are high in an ABS hydraulic system, and a standard brake hose may rupture.
- Be sure that the ignition switch remains in the *off* position while bleeding ABS system brakes. The system may attempt to repressurize itself if the ignition is turned on during bleeding.

Speed Sensor

To replace a speed sensor mounted on the axle, begin by removing the wheel and tire. Then remove the fasteners holding the sensor to the steering knuckle or axle housing. Pull the speed sensor out of the housing or knuckle and disconnect the electrical connector. See **Figure 35-21**. After reinstalling, be sure to recheck the sensor-to-rotor gap. Reinstall the wheel assembly and check ABS operation.

To replace a speed sensor mounted on the differential assembly or transmission, raise the vehicle and remove the fasteners holding the sensor to the transmission or differential, **Figure 35-22**. Pull the speed sensor out of the mounting bracket and disconnect the electrical connector. Install the new sensor, making sure that all wiring is clipped in place properly. Adjust the gap if possible and recheck ABS operation.

Toothed Rotor

The toothed rotor is sometimes bolted to the rear of the brake rotor or axle assembly. In some cases, it is pressed on. Some rotors are not removable, and must be replaced by replacing the entire brake rotor or axle assembly. In almost all cases, the brake rotor or axle must be removed to gain access to the toothed rotor. Follow the manufacturer's directions.

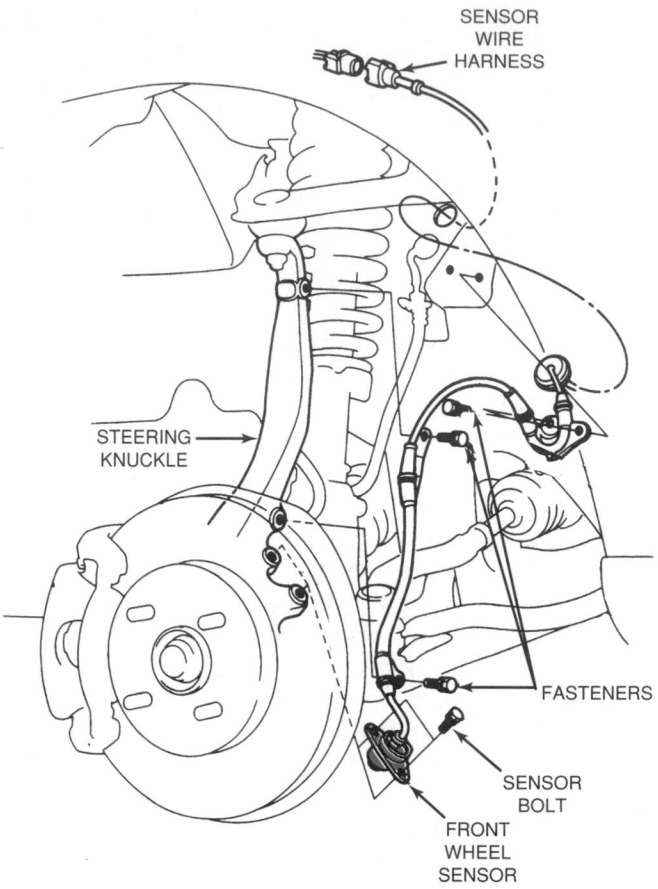

Figure 35-21. Removing a speed sensor that is attached to the steering knuckle. (Honda)

 Caution: The replacement rotor must never be hammered into position or dropped. The magnetic properties of the rotor may be destroyed.

G-Force Sensor

The G-force sensor is usually mounted in the passenger compartment, **Figure 35-23.** To remove the sensor, remove any covering trim or carpet and remove the wiring harness. Loosen the bracket fasteners and remove the sensor. Reverse the removal process to install the new sensor.

Caution: The G-force sensor measures vehicle tilt to determine G-forces. The replacement sensor must be mounted in exactly the same position as the old sensor, or the readings will be inaccurate.

Control Module

Make sure the ignition switch is off or the battery is disconnected as applicable. Then, remove the control module electrical connectors. Remove the module bracket fasteners and remove the module from the vehicle. The location of a typical module is shown in **Figure 35-24.**

Note: A few modules are attached to the hydraulic actuator and master cylinder. The entire assembly must be removed to gain access to the module.

Install the new module and tighten the bracket fasteners. Reconnect the electrical connectors and check ABS operation.

Hydraulic System Components

Hydraulic system components include the hydraulic actuator, pump and motor, and accumulator. These components may be housed in a single unit, or they may be separate units connected by high-pressure hoses. **Figures 35-25** and **35-26** show some typical hydraulic system components and locations. Due to the variations in hydraulic system design, general service procedures will be outlined below.

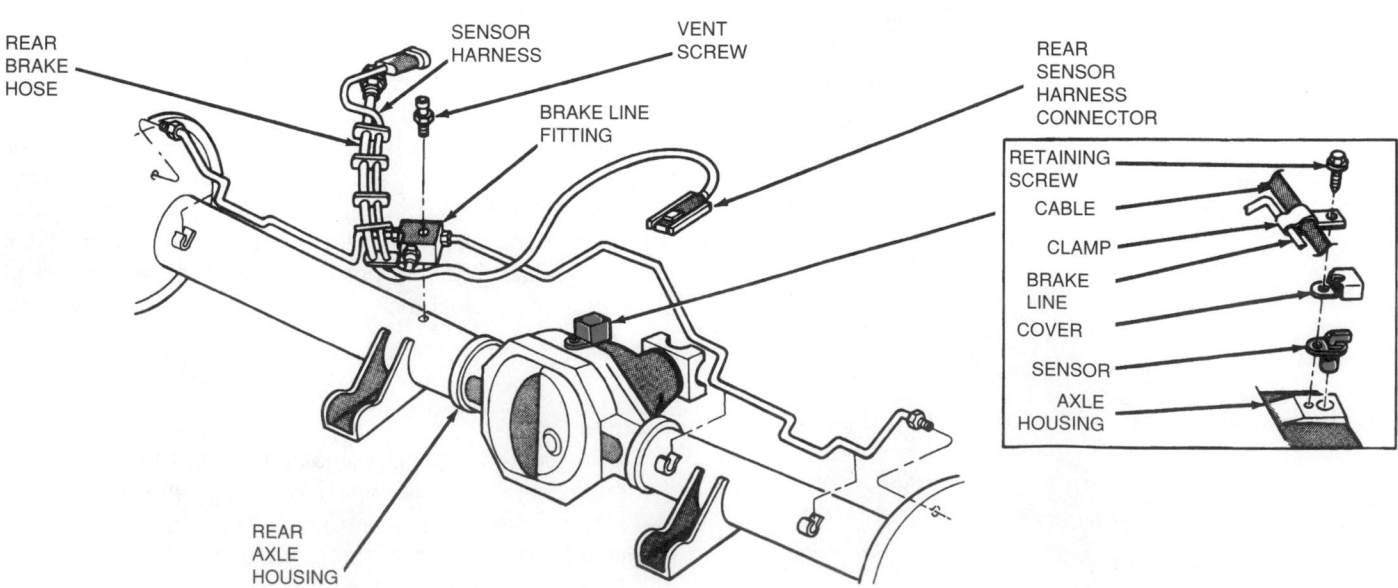

Figure 35-22. Removing a speed sensor from the rear axle housing. Clean around the sensor before removing to prevent dirt from entering the axle housing. (Chrysler)

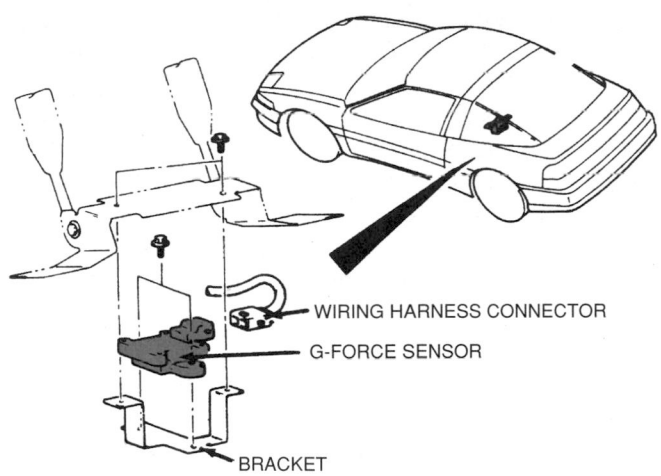

Figure 35-23. A typical G-force sensor and its location inside one particular vehicle. (Geo)

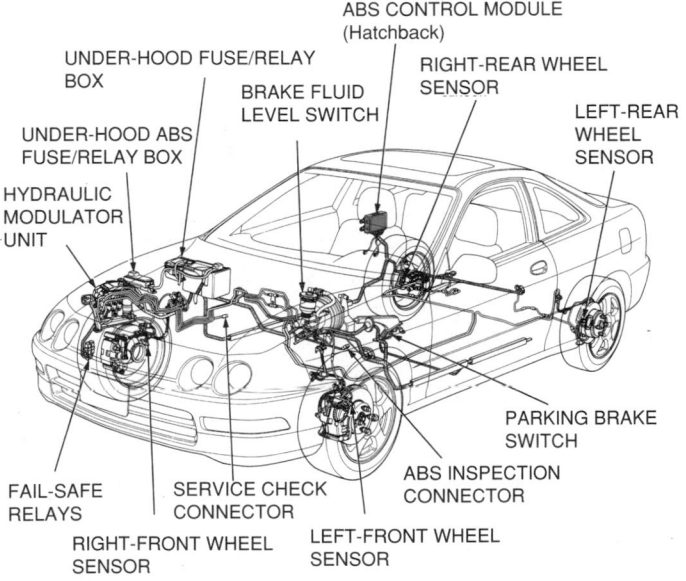

Figure 35-24. Location of the control module in a specific vehicle. Module location varies from vehicle to vehicle. (Honda)

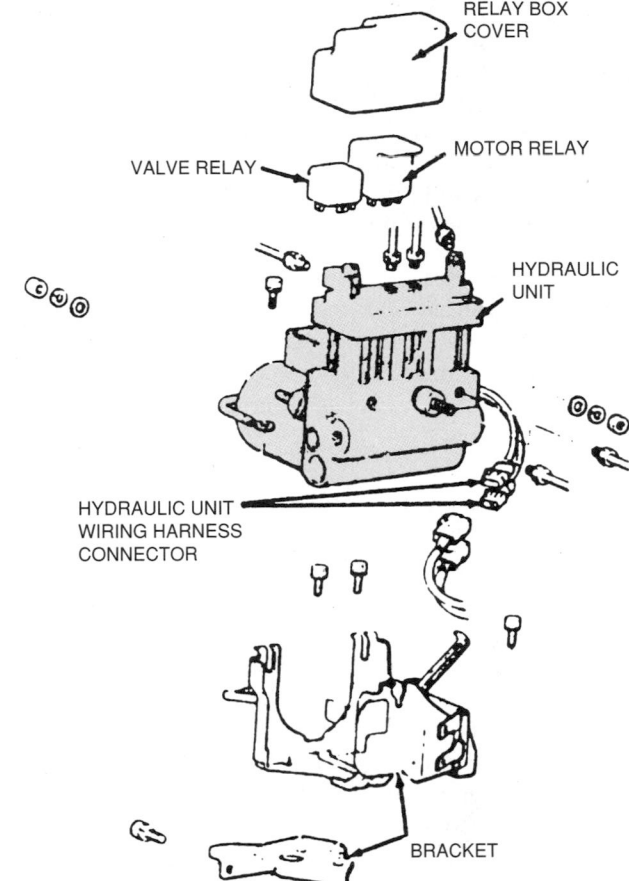

Figure 35-25. A hydraulic actuator and its related components. (Chrysler)

Begin hydraulic system component service by depressurizing the hydraulic system according to manufacturer's instructions. If necessary, remove any electrical connections; then remove the defective component. Many of the ABS hydraulic components are attached to the master cylinder. Therefore, the master cylinder may have to be removed. If the defective component must be disassembled, follow the manufacturer's instructions carefully. Clean all parts in the recommended cleaner and lay them out on a clean workbench before beginning reassembly.

Begin reassembly by rebuilding all subassemblies. If a repair kit is used to overhaul a specific component or its subassembly, use all the new parts, even if the old ones seem good. This is especially true of seals and gaskets. Lubricate all new seals with clean brake fluid before installation. Make all possible bench tests before reinstallation to ensure that the component will operate properly on the vehicle.

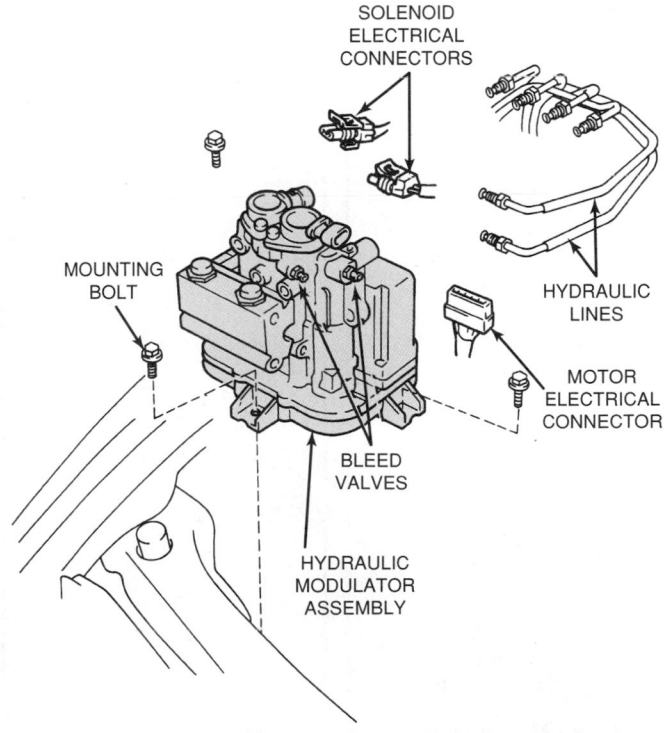

Figure 35-26. A hydraulic modulator assembly. (Geo)

Install the new or overhauled component. Use new gaskets and seals as needed. Tighten all fasteners to the correct torque and use new fasteners where called for by the manufacturer. Reattach the electrical connectors and bleed the brakes according to the manufacturer's instructions.

 Note: Do not turn the ignition switch on until the bleeding procedure is completed.

Start the vehicle and check ABS operation. The ABS warning light may remain on for a few minutes, until the system has repressurized. After correct operation has been verified, recheck the hydraulic system for leaks and sufficient reservoir level.

Traction Control Systems

To reduce wheel spin when accelerating on slippery surfaces, some vehicles are equipped with *traction control systems.* These systems reduce engine power and operate the brake system to increase vehicle acceleration and stability on low-friction or uneven road surfaces, **Figure 35-27.** Traction control systems also provide higher levels of cornering performance.

The traction control system has the ability to apply the brakes on the drive axles. On a two-wheel drive system, it will control only the two driving wheels. On a full-time four-wheel drive system, it can apply any one of the four brakes.

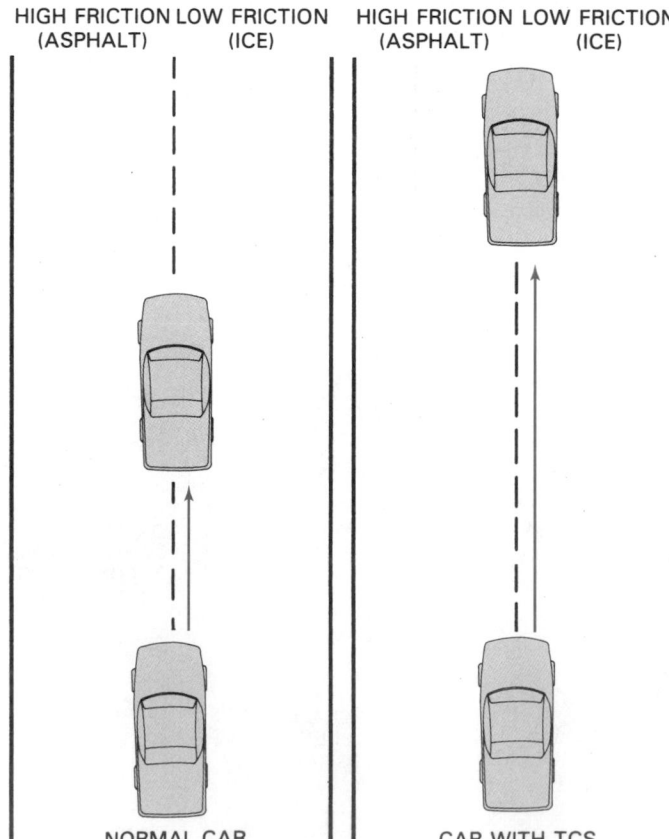

Figure 35-27. Vehicles equipped with a traction control system accelerate efficiently on low-friction surfaces.

If the system detects one drive wheel spinning at a faster rate than the others, it will apply the appropriate amount of braking force to slow the wheel to the correct speed.

If the system determines that both (or all) drive wheels are spinning excessively, it can close the throttle or briefly retard ignition timing to prevent further spinning. Most vehicles with traction control also have an anti-lock brake system. On many new vehicles, the anti-lock brake system and the traction control system are controlled by a single electronic control module. A system with one electronic module may have one or two hydraulic actuators. See **Figure 35-28.**

Traction Control System Components

Most traction control systems have several common components. Typical systems consist of the following parts:

- *Wheel sensors*—Monitor wheel speed and send signals to the control module. Often, they are the same sensors used in the anti-lock brake system.
- *Control module*—Receives signals from the sensors and decides on outputs to control the hydraulic brake actuators and throttle motor or ignition timing control.
- *Throttle motor*—Moves the throttle plate as instructed by the control module.
- *Hydraulic actuator*—Varies the amount of brake pressure at the drive wheels based on signals from the control module.
- *Indicator lamp*—Alerts the driver when the traction control system is operating. On some systems, there are separate lights to indicate when the traction control system is operating and when a system malfunction has occurred.

Traction Control System Maintenance

No specific traction control system maintenance is needed. The wheel sensors should be checked for damage and contamination with dirt, grease, or road debris whenever the vehicle is on a lift. The engine control section of the system should only be checked if trouble develops. Periodically check the fluid level in the brake master cylinder.

Troubleshooting Traction Control Systems

Most traction control systems are equipped with self-diagnostic capabilities. Methods for retrieving trouble codes for these systems vary from manufacturer to manufacturer. Refer to the appropriate service manual for proper diagnostic and service techniques.

Replacing Traction Control System Components

Most traction control components are similar to anti-lock brake components. Replacement procedures are similar. Refer to the engine section of the proper service manual for engine component replacement.

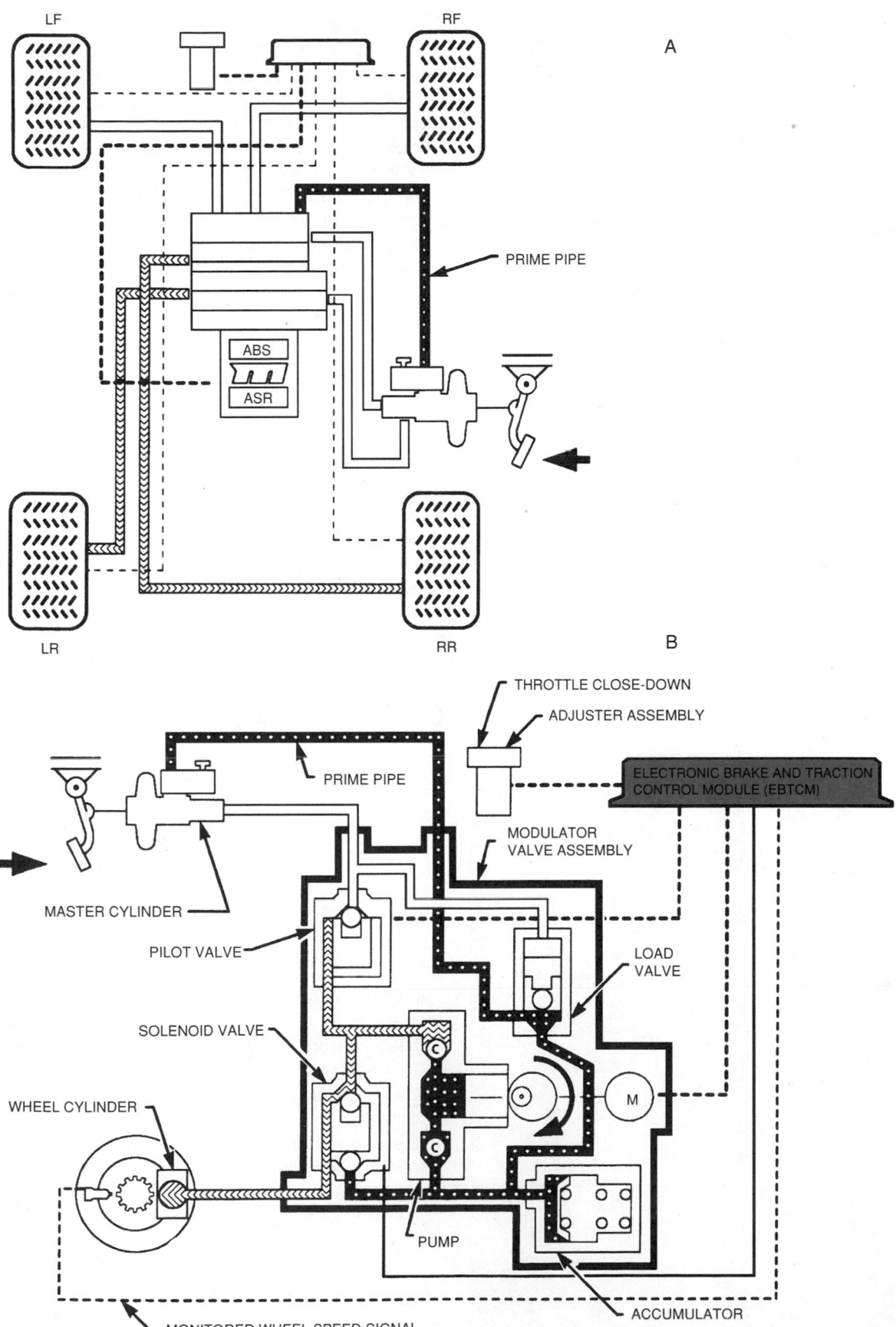

Figure 35-28. A—Traction control system schematic. This particular system is called an automatic slip regulation (ASR) system. B—Traction control operation schematic. Note that both the anti-lock brake system and the traction control system are controlled by the electronic brake and traction control module. (Chevrolet)

Warning: Traction control hydraulic components are under pressure. Pump the brake pedal at least 40 times to remove residual pressure before servicing any hydraulic system component.

Performing a Brake Job on a Vehicle with ABS or Traction Control

Many common brake service procedures, such as pad and shoe replacement, rotor and drum service, and wheel bearing replacement, are not affected by the presence of ABS or traction controls. If the replacement procedures involve the wheel speed sensors, treat them gently and recheck the gap where applicable. Remember not to drop or hammer on the sensor rings. Never use the sensor rings to pry on other components.

Hydraulic components on ABS and traction control vehicles are serviced in the same manner as conventional systems. However, all replacement parts must be able to withstand higher pressures than standard components. Make sure that all hoses, lines, fittings, rebuilt components, and wheel cylinder and caliper kits are designed for the system on which you are working.

Make sure that the hydraulic system has been depressurized before disconnecting any hydraulic system part. Also, make sure that the ignition key remains off until the hydraulic system is completely reassembled and bled.

Tech Talk

In earlier chapters, you learned to check all non-electronic engine components before investigating a problem in the electronic control unit or other electronic components. The same procedures apply to ABS systems as well. Always keep in mind that the basic principles of brake system operation are the same for vehicles with ABS as they are for non-ABS vehicles. The ABS system only operates during very hard braking, and does not affect the normal operation of the wheel brake assemblies. Worn out friction materials or hydraulic leaks will cause the same problems on ABS and non-ABS systems.

When beginning to diagnose an ABS problem, make sure that all of the non-ABS components are in good condition. Check the condition of all brake pads, shoes, rotors, and drums. Check the brake calipers and wheel cylinders for leaks or binding, and, when they are used, check the metering, proportioning, and pressure differential valves for proper operation. The only exception to this is when the ABS trouble codes indicate a definite problem in the ABS system itself. If your checks reveal that the non-ABS brake components are not the source of the problem, only then should you proceed to check the ABS components.

Summary

Anti-lock brake systems use electronic and hydraulic components to help prevent wheel lockup during hard braking. Anti-lock brake systems used on automobiles control all four wheels. Light truck ABS systems operate only the rear wheels. The basic principle of all ABS systems is that they control the brake hydraulic system to pulse the brakes on and off, preventing wheel lockup. The components and operation of all anti-lock brake systems are similar, but enough differences exist to make it necessary to carefully read the manufacturer's service manual.

Common ABS components include the wheel speed sensors, control module, and hydraulic actuator. Other components that can be used are the G-force sensor and brake travel switch. All anti-lock brake systems have an amber warning light, in addition to the red brake warning light used on all vehicles.

ABS troubleshooting may involve the use of special testers. However, many ABS checks can be made with standard tools and test equipment. Most anti-lock brake service can be performed without special tools. Due to the high pressures created by anti-lock brake systems, safety precautions should always be followed. Always depressurize the hydraulic system before doing any work on the ABS hydraulic components.

Traction control systems increase vehicle acceleration and stability on slippery or uneven road surfaces. They reduce engine power output and apply the brakes on the drive wheels to maximize traction.

Normal brake service operations, such as pad or shoe replacement and caliper or wheel cylinder rebuilding, are similar to those on vehicles without ABS or traction controls. However, the system must be depressurized before doing any work on the hydraulic system.

Know These Terms

Anti-lock brake systems	Hydraulic pump
ABS	Accumulator
Foundation brakes	Pulsation
Base brakes	Hydraulic modulator
Speed sensor	Ball screw
G-force sensor	Pedal travel switch
Lateral accelerometer	Traction control system
Control module	Wheel sensor
ABS warning light	Control module
Brake system warning light	Throttle motor
Hydraulic actuator	Hydraulic actuator
Solenoid valve	Indicator lamp

Review Questions—Chapter 35

1. ABS systems used on most automobiles are used to control lockup on _____ _____ wheels.
   (A) the front
   (B) the rear
   (C) all four
   (D) All of the above, depending on manufacturer.

2. Name the three main components used by both the anti-lock braking and traction control systems.

3. Most anti-lock brake systems have _____ capabilities.

4. Pulsation in the brake pedal during ABS operation is a sign of _____.
   (A) low fluid level
   (B) a defective sensor
   (C) a defective actuator
   (D) normal system operation

5. On a piston-operated hydraulic actuator (hydraulic modulator), the pistons take the place of the _____.
   (A) hydraulic pump
   (B) accumulator
   (C) solenoids
   (D) Both A and B.

6. If an ABS equipped vehicle has a pull to one side when braking, which of the following is the most likely cause?
   (A) Hydraulic modulator.
   (B) Sticking caliper.
   (C) Restricted brake hose.
   (D) All of the above.

7. When the wheel lockup condition is severe, the solenoids in the ABS hydraulic actuator will be positioned to dump small amounts of hydraulic fluid back to the _____.
   (A) reservoir
   (B) accumulator
   (C) hydraulic pump intake
   (D) All of the above, depending on the manufacturer.

8. Name ten things that should be checked before retrieving the ABS system trouble codes.

9. When bleeding the brakes on an ABS system, do not turn the _____ on until bleeding is completed.

10. Most brake service procedures for ABS and traction control brake systems are _____ to normal brake system service.

ASE-Type Questions

1. ABS wheel speed sensors can be installed at all of the following places on the vehicle, EXCEPT:
   (A) flywheel.
   (B) brake rotor.
   (C) transmission.
   (D) differential.

2. Technician A says that the amber ABS warning light illuminates only when the system is malfunctioning. Technician B says that the traction control system may have two indicator lights. Who is right?
   (A) A only.
   (B) B only.
   (C) Both A & B.
   (D) Neither A nor B.

3. Technician A says that some scan tools can read ABS trouble codes from the control module. Technician B says that some scan tools can send input signals to the control module to test for the correct outputs. Who is right?
   (A) A only.
   (B) B only.
   (C) Both A & B.
   (D) Neither A nor B.

4. On many ABS systems, a scan tool can be used to _____.
   (A) check voltages
   (B) check hydraulic pressures
   (C) retrieve trouble codes
   (D) bleed the hydraulic system

5. Many manufacturers recommend checking wheel sensors with _____.
   (A) a voltmeter
   (B) an ohmmeter
   (C) a test light
   (D) All of the above.

6. All of the following can cause the ABS controller to set a trouble code EXCEPT:
   (A) leaking accumulator.
   (B) faulty wheel speed sensor.
   (C) low fluid level.
   (D) an out-of-round drum.

7. An ABS equipped vehicle has a pedal pulsation during light braking. Technician A says that the pedal pulsation means that the ABS system is working normally. Technician B says that the pedal pulsations during light braking indicates that the ABS system is defective. Who is right?
   (A) A only.
   (B) B only.
   (C) Both A & B.
   (D) Neither A nor B.

8. Technician A says that the ABS accumulator must be depressurized before the electronic control unit can be replaced. Technician B says that static electricity can ruin an electronic control unit. Who is right?
   (A) A only.
   (B) B only.
   (C) Both A & B.
   (D) Neither A nor B.

9. Pumping the brake pedal at least _____ times will discharge the accumulator.
   (A) 20
   (B) 40
   (C) 60
   (D) 80

10. In operation, the traction control system controls the operation of the brake hydraulic system and the _____.
    (A) engine
    (B) transmission and torque converter
    (C) positraction differential
    (D) four-wheel drive system

Suggested Activities:

1. Draw a sketch showing the relationship of the ABS hydraulic and electronic control components to the

base brake system. Explain how the ABS hydraulic system operates to control the base brake hydraulic system. Also explain how the electronic components control the operation of the hydraulic components.

2. Locate a vehicle with an anti-lock brake system and study the ABS code retrieval procedure and troubleshooting charts in the appropriate manufacturer's service manual. Retrieve and list any ABS trouble codes that may be stored based on the information obtained.

3. Check the sensor-to-wheel air gaps of the vehicle wheel speed sensors. If available, check a vehicle that has a drive train speed sensor. Perform other tests listed in the service manual.

4. Bleed an anti-lock brake system according to manufacturers specifications.

36

Suspension System Service

After studying this chapter, you will be able to:
- Explain the construction, operation, and service of conventional front suspensions.
- Explain the construction, operation, and service of conventional rear suspensions.
- Describe the function of coil springs, torsion bars, and leaf springs.
- Describe the function of load-carrying and following ball joints.
- Explain the construction, operation, and service of MacPherson strut suspensions.
- Describe the function of control arms, strut rods, and sway bars.
- Describe the function of shock absorbers and MacPherson strut dampers.
- Summarize the operating principles and service of front and rear suspensions.
- Diagnose problems in suspension systems.

This chapter is intended to familiarize you with the various types of front and rear suspension systems found on modern vehicles. The variety of suspension designs is great, but all have a common purpose of absorbing shocks while keeping the wheels in contact with the road surface. All suspension systems contain many of the same components, such as springs, control arms, and ball joints. Some systems have strut rods, stabilizer or sway bars, shock absorbers, or MacPherson struts.

STOP Warning: All suspension systems contain parts under spring tension. Be sure to identify all parts under spring tension and remove this tension before disassembling any part. Failure to do so can result in part or equipment damage and/or a severe or even fatal injury.

Front Suspension Systems

This section will cover the service of various components on the two major types of front suspension systems, the *conventional* and the *MacPherson strut.* Differences and similarities between the two types are called out.

Conventional Suspensions

Modern conventional front suspension systems are equipped with *coil springs* or *torsion bars.* Most coil springs are mounted between the vehicle frame and the lower control arm, as shown in **Figure 36-1.** Some older vehicles, however, used coil springs that were mounted between the upper control arm and vehicle body. A torsion bar is a long spring steel rod which takes the place of a conventional spring. An example of a torsion bar front suspension system is shown in **Figure 36-2.** When the lower arm moves upward, it twists the torsion bar. Another torsion bar arrangement called transverse mounting is illustrated in **Figure 36-3.** The bars go across the width of the chassis and back to the control arms.

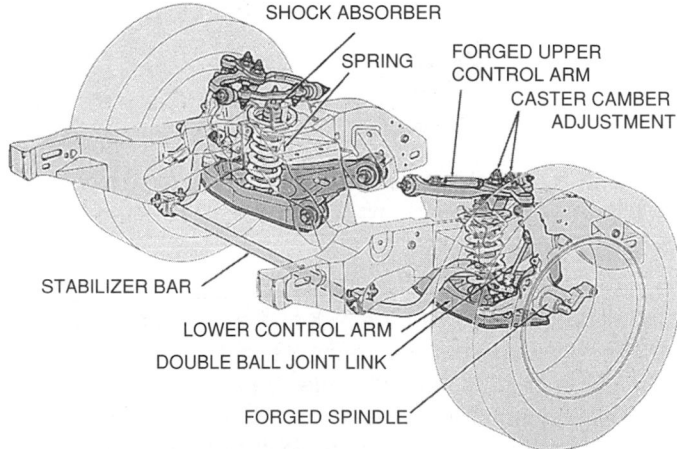

Figure 36-1. One type of conventional front suspension system as used on a rear-wheel drive car. (Ford)

Front Coil Spring Service

Raise the vehicle and place jack stands under the frame. Remove the wheel and tire assembly. Disconnect the stabilizer bar and remove the shock absorber. Disconnect the lower arm tie strut, if used. Attach a safety chain. Place a jack under the lower control arm so that it is parallel to the arm. This allows the jack to roll forward or backward to follow the movement of the control arm free end. Remove the lower ball joint stud as recommended under

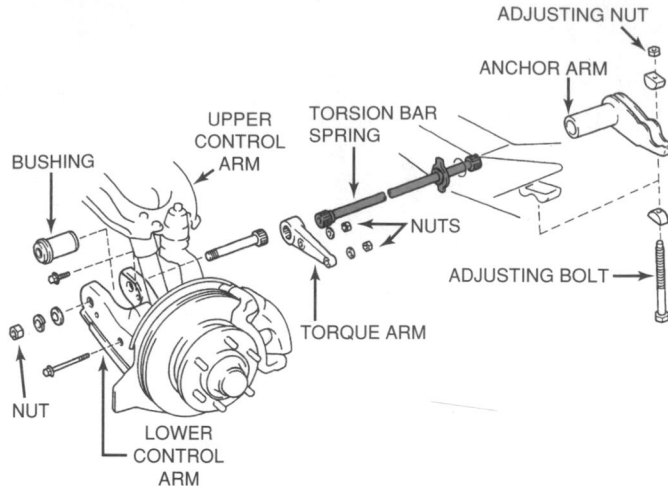

Figure 36-2. A torsion bar front suspension setup. This is how most torsion bar suspensions are arranged. (Toyota)

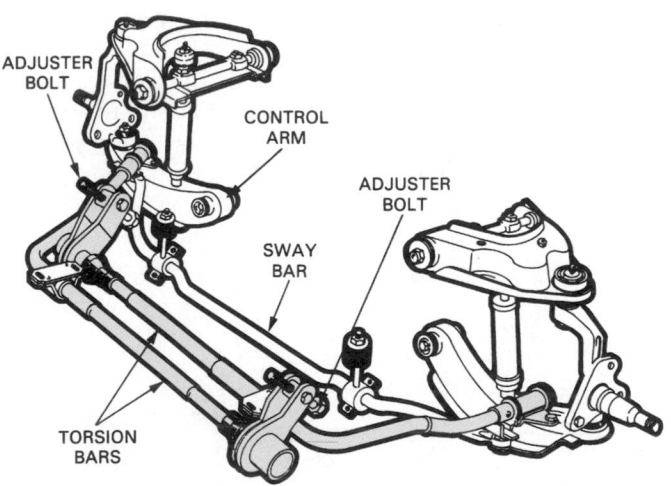

Figure 36-3. Torsion bars arranged in a transverse manner. Note that each bar has its own adjustment bolt. (Moog)

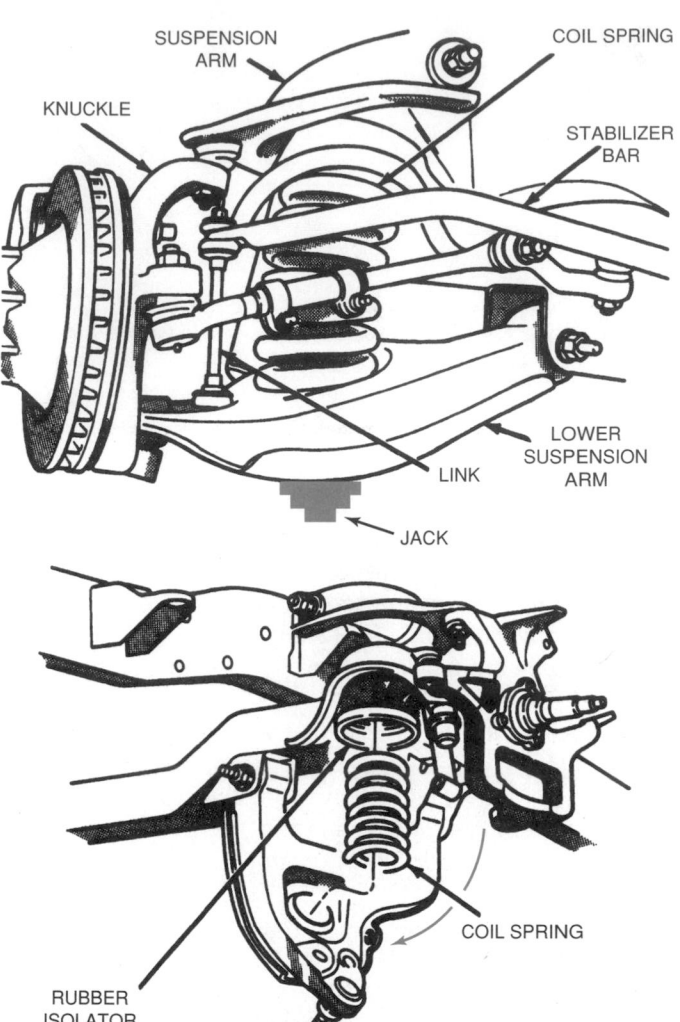

Figure 36-4. Lowering the lower control arm while it is still under coil spring tension, with a jack. *Be careful!* (Dodge)

ball joint removal. Lower the jack and control arm until pressure is removed from the spring. Remove the spring carefully. If it is slightly loaded (under pressure), it could snap out violently. See **Figure 36-4.**

To install a spring, reverse the above procedure. Make certain that any spring insulators used are in place and that the spring is correctly installed. Specifications usually call for the spring end to be in a certain location. **Figure 36-5** illustrates the correct spring end location for one vehicle. When the control arm is raised, make sure that the spring does not rotate out of position. Raise the arm until the ball joint stud passes through the spindle body. You may have to guide the spindle onto the ball joint stud. Install the stud nut, torque, and insert a cotter pin. Install the shock absorber, stabilizer bar, and tie strut where used. Use extreme care when removing and installing springs. Carelessness can result in a serious accident.

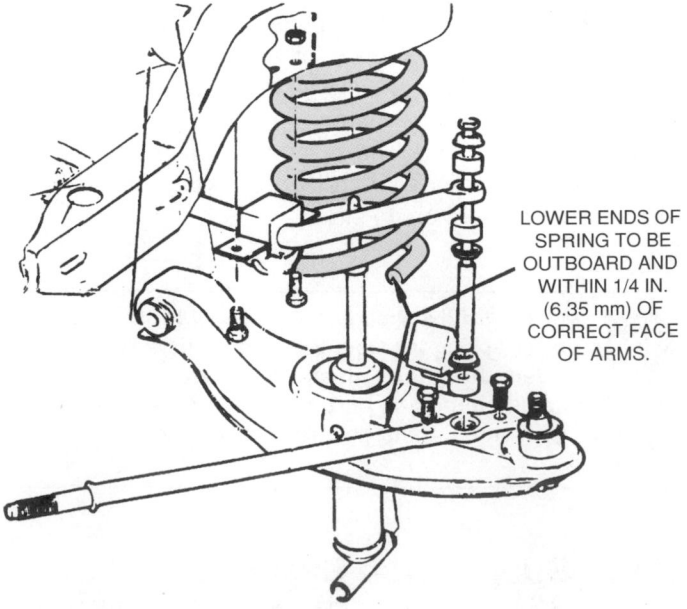

Figure 36-5. Correct spring end location for one vehicle. (Buick)

Spring Compressors

Some coil springs cannot be removed or installed without the use of a **spring compressor.** The compressor is inserted into the spring and the draw bolt tightened. This pulls the coils together to both shorten and unload the spring, making removal possible. **Figure 36-6** illustrates one type of spring compressor in position. Make sure the compressor is installed correctly and that the draw bolt is secure.

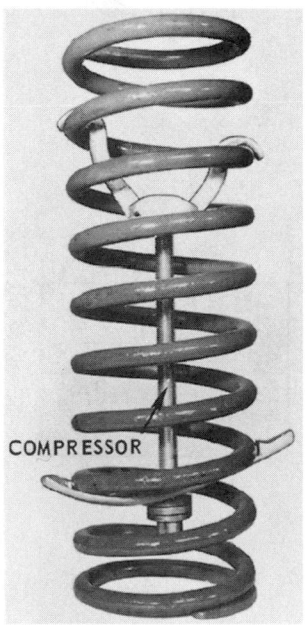

Figure 36-6. One type of spring compressor in position. Always use care when compressing any spring. (Branich)

Torsion Bar Service

To service a torsion bar, first raise the vehicle by the frame until the front control arms are in the full rebound (down) position. On some vehicles, the rubber rebound bumper must be removed to permit the upper arm to reach the full rebound position. Turn the torsion bar anchor bolt to unload the torsion bar. Mark the torsion bars to indicate the right and left side in order to avoid confusion and ease installation. **Figure 36-7** illustrates a typical adjustable torsion bar rear support. A torsion bar, rear support, upper and lower control arms, and strut rod are shown in **Figure 36-8.**

A detailed view of one method of attaching the torsion bar to the lower control arm is shown in **Figure 36-9.** Disengage the lock ring and plug from the rear anchor or support. Clean the torsion bar ahead of the seal, **Figure 36-10.** Disengage the seal from the anchor and carefully slide the seal partially up the bar. Slide the bar backward far enough to disengage the front hex from the control arm. Pull the bar to one side and then remove from the front. Some installations permit sliding the bar backwards out through the rear anchor.

If the bar is stuck in the anchors, use a special clamp-on striking pad to avoid denting or nicking the surface. The

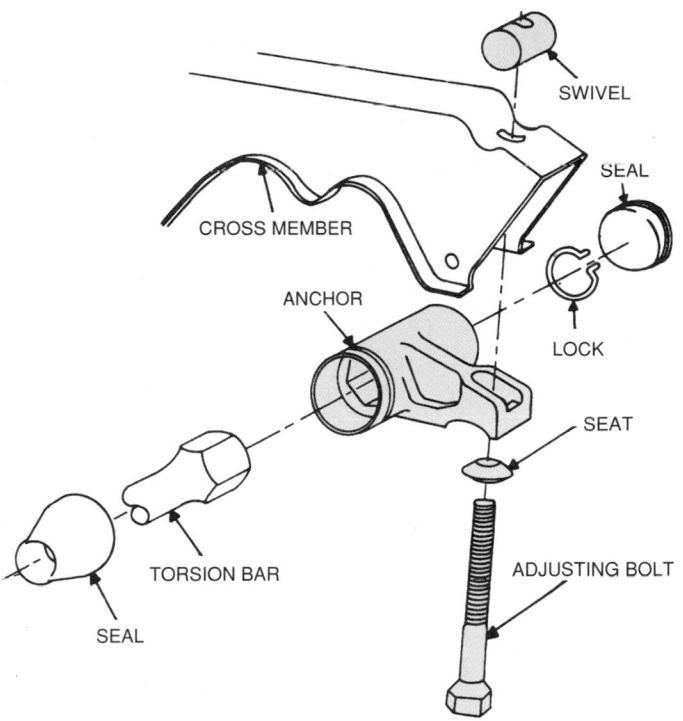

Figure 36-7. One type of adjustable torsion bar rear support. (Chrysler)

pad is clamped to the bar and struck with a hammer to loosen the bar. Never use heat on the bar or on the front and rear anchors. Do not hammer on the bar or use a pipe wrench. Clean and inspect the bar. Remove any small nicks or burrs by filing and polishing with fine emery cloth. Paint the polished sections with rust resistant primer. Like all springs, a torsion bar can crack if nicked. Clean, inspect, and lubricate the rear anchor swivel and adjusting bolt. Replace if needed. Clean front and rear bar anchor hex holes.

Make sure the bars are installed on their designated sides. The bar must be clean before installation. Slide the bar through the rear anchor and slip a new seal over the bar. Coat both ends of the torsion bar with multipurpose grease. Insert the bar front hex end into the lower control arm. Install the rear anchor lock ring and plug. Fill the opening around the front of the rear anchor with multipurpose grease and carefully position the seal. Load the bar a small amount with the adjusting screw. Place the vehicle on the floor and adjust front ride height by turning the torsion bar adjusting bolt. Bounce vehicle vigorously and recheck height. **Figure 36-11** illustrates the measuring points for checking the front and rear control height for a specific vehicle equipped with an independent front and rear suspension.

MacPherson Strut Service

A MacPherson strut assembly is shown in **Figure 36-12.** The compact design of the MacPherson strut eliminates the need for an upper control arm and other suspen-

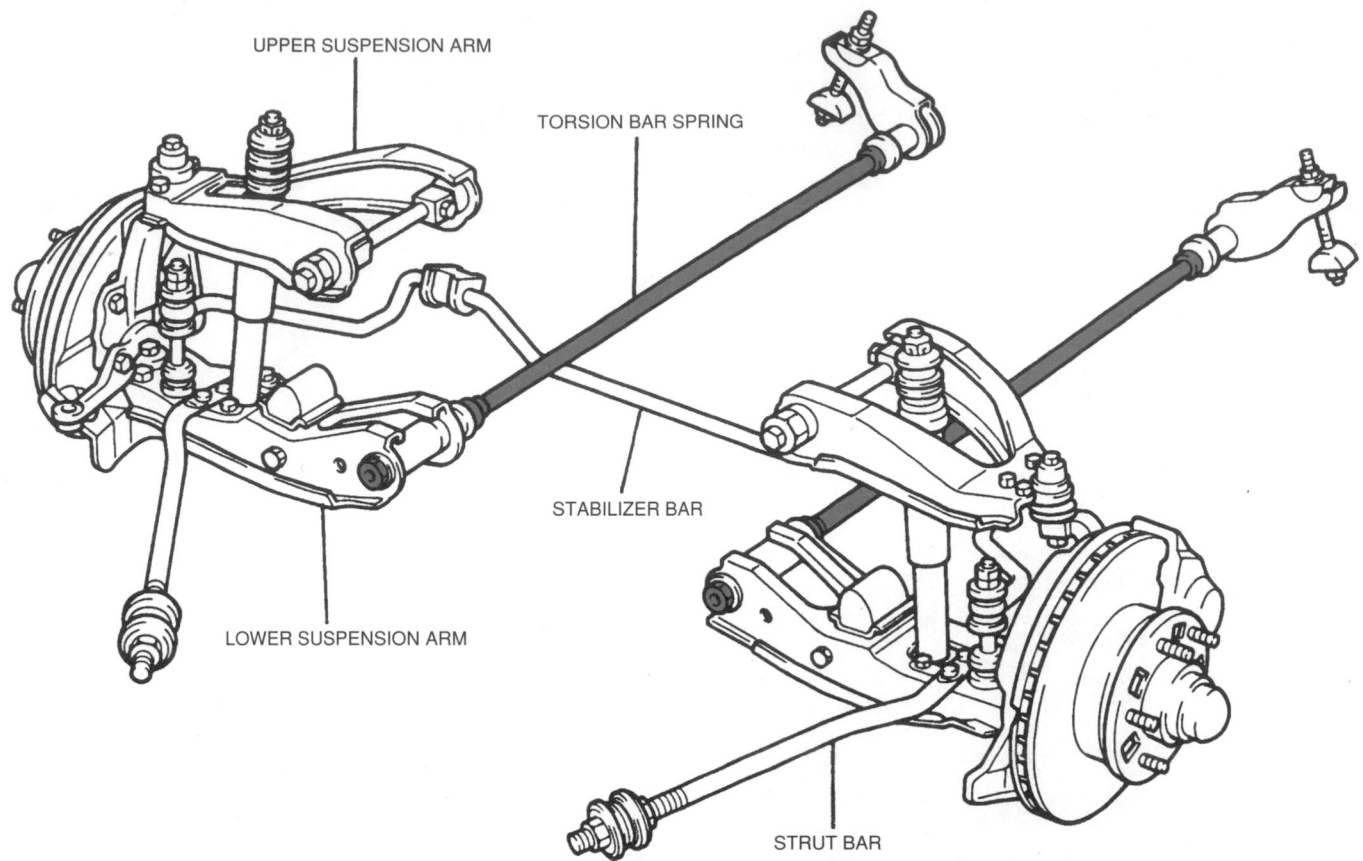

Figure 36-8.   A torsion bar arrangement. Note that the torsion bars are connected to the lower control arms. (Toyota)

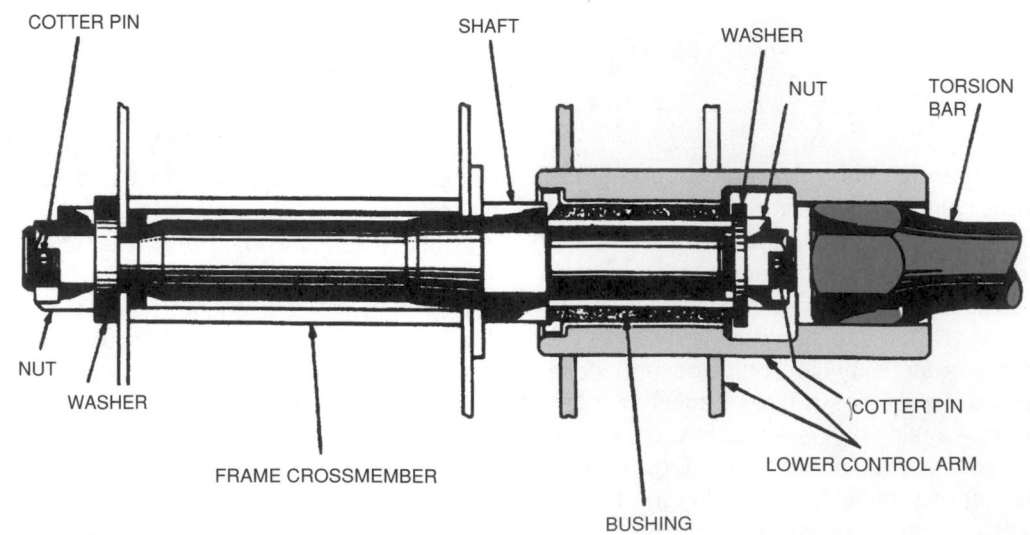

Figure 36-9.   This is a cross-section of the torsion bar pivot shaft section in a lower control arm. Note how the hexagonal head of the torsion bar fits into the lower suspension control arm.

sion components. Note that the MacPherson strut suspension usually contains a coil spring. There are two basic MacPherson strut coil spring arrangements. One type uses the coil spring mounted on the lower control arm, **Figure 36-13.** The most common type (which will be covered here)

mounts the coil spring so that it surrounds the strut damper or shock. Look at **Figure 36-14.**

To remove the MacPherson strut, place the vehicle on a hoist or jack stands. Raise the hood in order to access the strut bolts (generally three) on each inner fender well at the

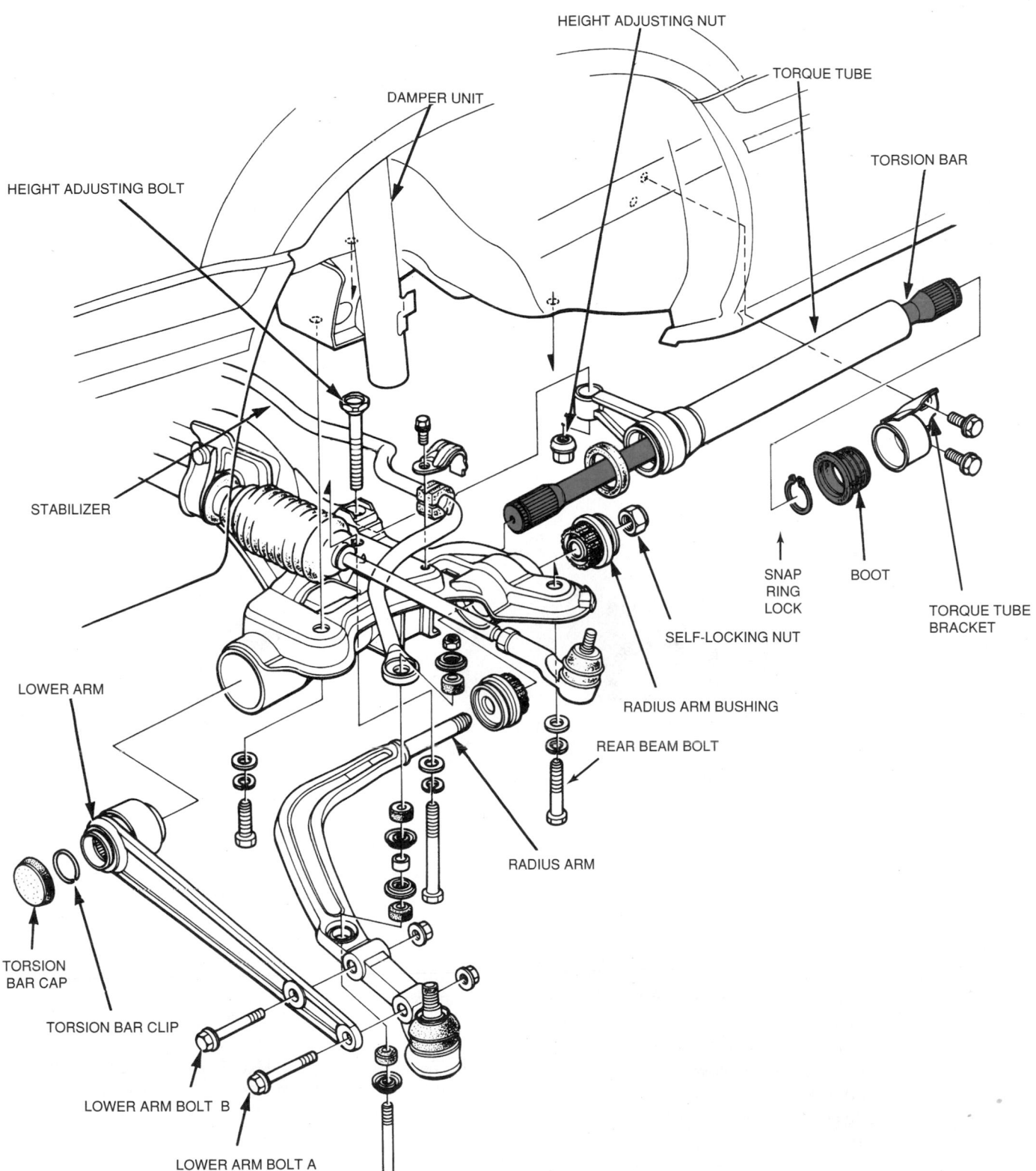

HEIGHT ADJUSTING NUT

TORQUE TUBE

DAMPER UNIT

TORSION BAR

HEIGHT ADJUSTING BOLT

STABILIZER

SNAP RING LOCK

BOOT

TORQUE TUBE BRACKET

SELF-LOCKING NUT

LOWER ARM

RADIUS ARM BUSHING

REAR BEAM BOLT

RADIUS ARM

TORSION BAR CAP

TORSION BAR CLIP

LOWER ARM BOLT B

LOWER ARM BOLT A

Figure 36-10. Exploded view of one torsion bar assembly. (Honda)

top. Mark one bolt on each side of the vehicle. Leave at least one bolt or nut attached until the bottom of the strut is disconnected. Remove the tire and wheel. Disconnect the lower mounting bolts or ball joint depending on the attachment method used. Disconnect the brake assembly and/or line and any wiring or brackets. Support the strut so it will

not fall. Remove the nut or bolt which was left connected on the fender well. Remove the strut and mount it in a special holding fixture or vise. See **Figure 36-15.**

Attach a coil spring compressor. Compress the spring until tension is removed from the spring retainer, rebound bumper, and other parts. Loosen the strut rod nut while

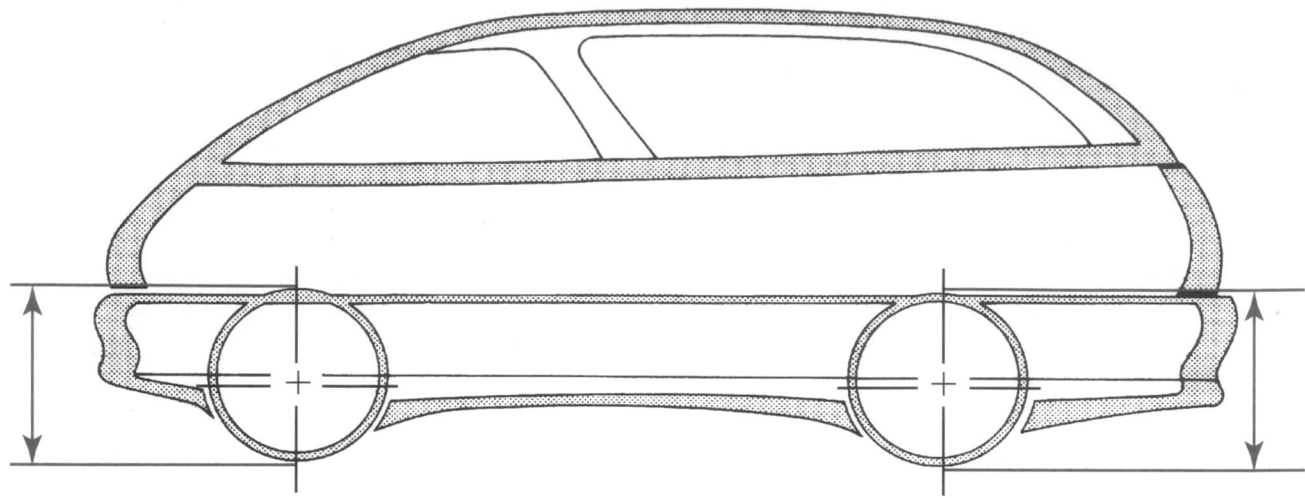

Figure 36-11. Measuring points for checking control height of a minivan. (Toyota)

Figure 36-12. One type of front-wheel drive, MacPherson strut front suspension. (Cadillac)

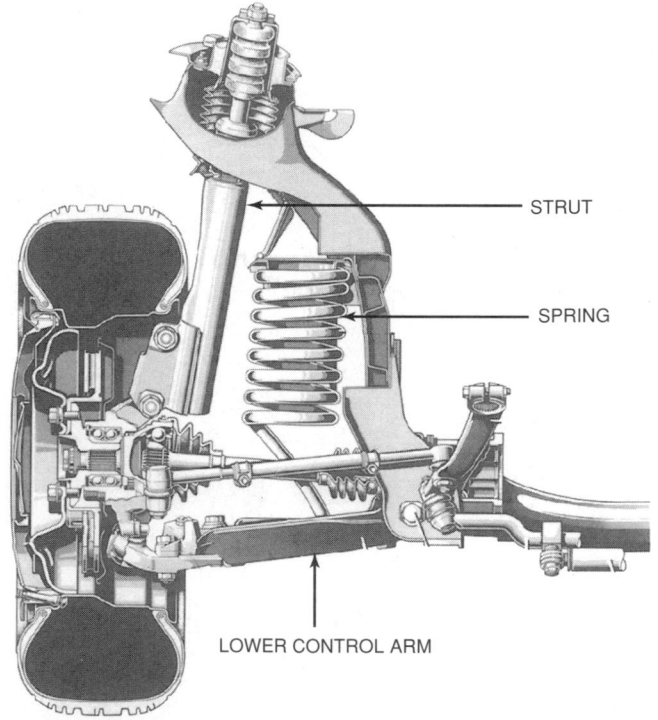

Figure 36-13. One type of MacPherson strut type front suspension that locates springs between the frame and lower control arm. (Mercedes-Benz)

holding the strut rod, **Figure 36-16.** Pull off the rebound bumper, spring retainer, and other parts. Lift off the coil spring. Be sure to mark the spring top and bottom (if different). Also label which side of the vehicle it was removed from. If the spring requires replacement (sagging, bent, broken), carefully relieve compressing tool tension. Remove the spring and discard it. Place the new spring in the tool and compress. Reinstall parts in reverse order of disassembly. Torque all fasteners to specifications. Reconnect brake lines and bleed if necessary. Align the suspension and road test.

 Warning: As with all springs under tension, be extremely careful. They can fly off with lethal force.

Shock Absorber Service

Shock absorbers are hydraulic units which absorb spring oscillations to provide a steady, smooth ride. The shock absorbers must be in good condition. When a shock

is operating properly, it will control spring oscillation, spring rebound, and rate of spring compression. When mounted at an angle or straddle-mounted, body sway and lean are also minimized. **MacPherson strut dampers** are also considers shock absorbers, since they perform the same function that a shock absorber does in a conventional system.

The commonly used shock is of the telescopic or airplane type. Typical telescopic shock action is illustrated in **Figure 36-17.** Note the extended shock in **Figure 36-17(1).** The rebound stroke pulls the piston upward, forcing fluid in A through the valve in the piston to compartment B. Vacuum

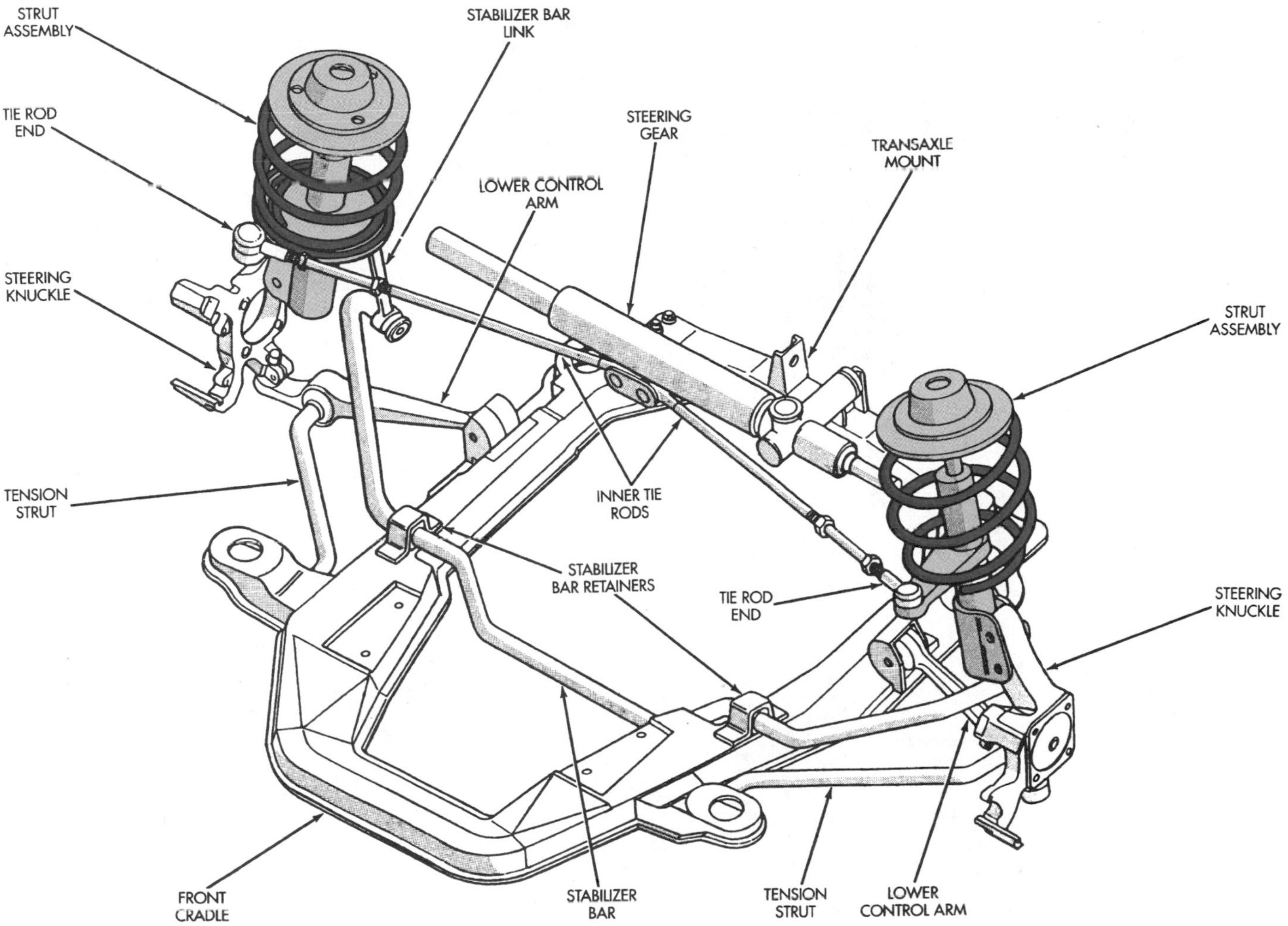

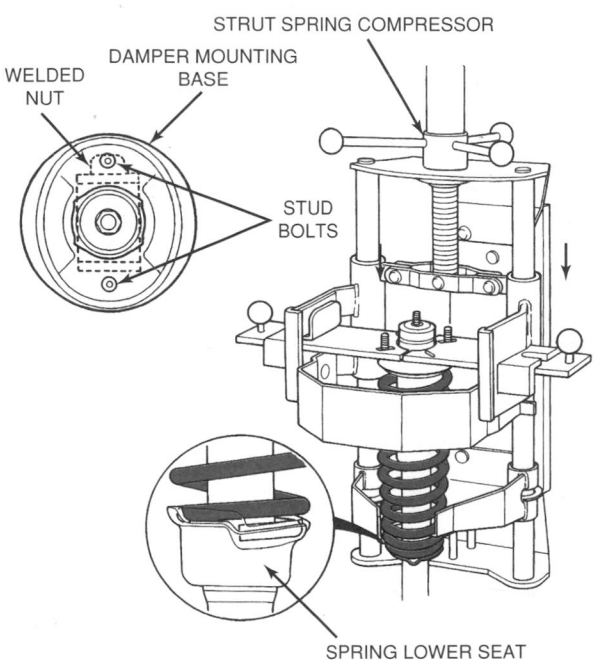

Figure 36-14.   A coil spring/strut type front suspension assembly. (Chrysler)

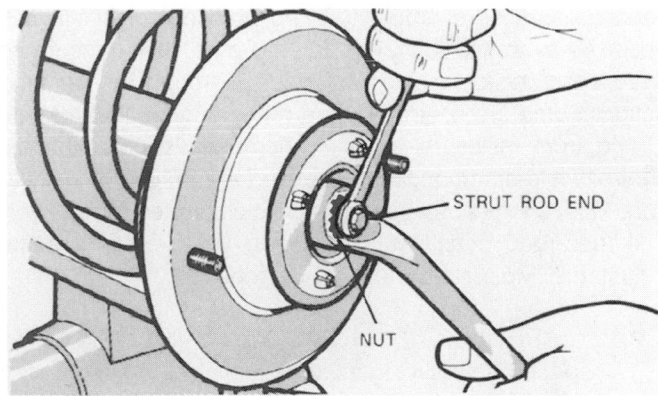

Figure 36-16.   Removing strut rod nut while holding strut rod. Be sure spring tension *has been relieved* before completely removing nut.

Figure 36-15.   A strut spring compressor and holding fixture. When compressing a strut spring, make sure you follow the same safety precautions that apply to conventional springs. (Honda)

action draws fluid through the base valve from reservoir C. **Figure 36-17(2)** shows the action during the compression stroke. The piston is forced downward. This causes fluid to be forced through the piston valve into compartment A, and through the base valve into reservoir C. Area D is air space above the fluid.

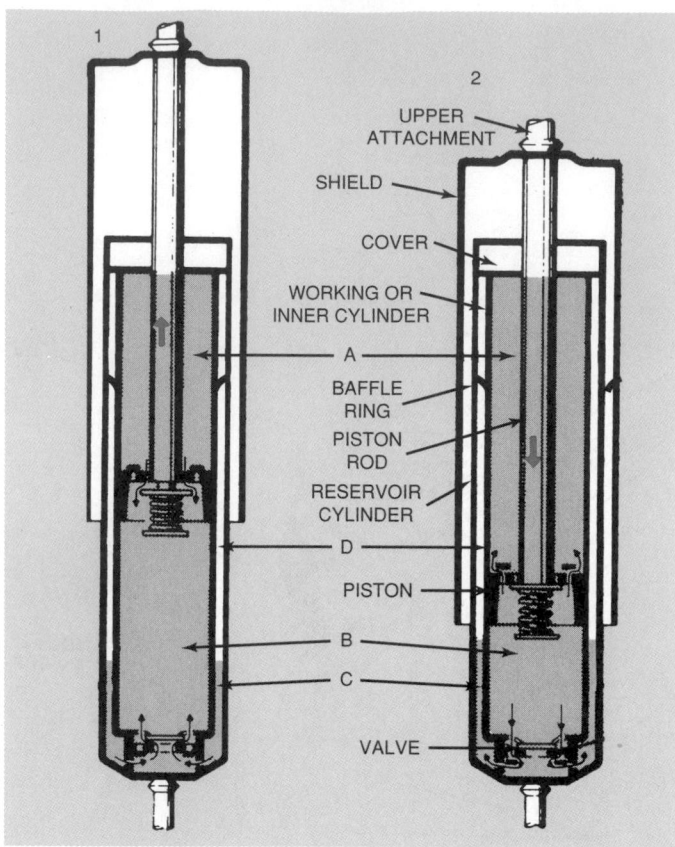

Figure 36-17. Normal action or a double-acting shock absorber. (Volvo)

The fluid passing through the various valves or orifices slows down the movement of the piston, thus placing a damping action on the movement of the springs. Most shock absorbers made today are *gas charged.* This type uses a gas-filled chamber to keep pressure on the shock absorber hydraulic fluid at all times. Some shock absorbers have adjusting devices to control the amount of damping action. Some are controlled by a manual valve that may be turned from inside the vehicle. Some have an automatic control while others must be adjusted at the time of installation. Most shock absorber valves are calibrated for an average load-road condition for a given vehicle and are not adjustable. Most shocks cannot be repaired.

Checking Shock Absorbers and Strut Dampers

Inspect each shock absorber or MacPherson strut damper for signs of fluid leakage. Replace them if leaks are found. Check the condition of the rubber bushings. Shocks or dampers can rattle, pound, and cause poor control if the mounting bushings are worn or missing. Also inspect mounting brackets and fasteners. Grasp shock or damper and try to shake sideways and up and down. Compare shock action by bouncing each corner of the vehicle vigorously and quickly releasing at the bottom of the down stroke. Shocks or dampers in good condition will allow about one free bounce and will then stop any further movement. If shock action is doubtful, service or replace.

Replacing Shock Absorbers

Modern gas-filled shock absorbers will expand to their full length when not installed, and may need to be compressed slightly to fit the attachment points. Use new rubber bushings with new shocks. Install bushings and washers in the correct order. Make certain that any stone guards face in the correct direction. Tighten the shock mounting bolts with the vehicle at normal curb height (weight on wheels) to prevent placing the bushing under a strain. Do not over-tighten fasteners. Typical shock absorber mounting at the front of the vehicle is illustrated in **Figure 36-18.** Follow the shock manufacturer's installation guidelines.

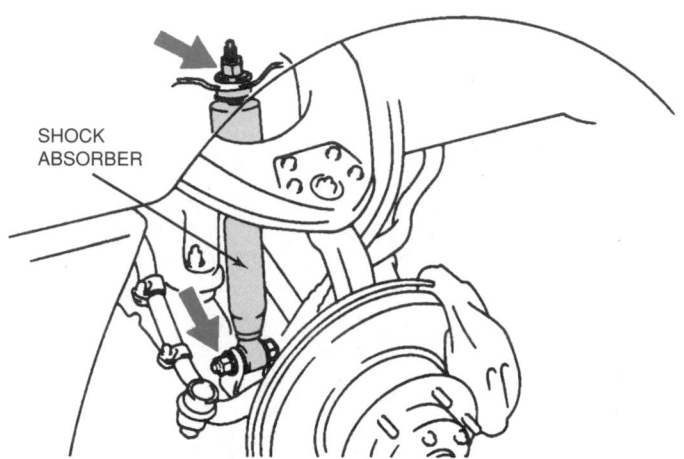

Figure 36-18. Inspect all shock absorbers, dampers, and mounts for wear, leaks, damage, etc. (Toyota)

Replacing Strut Dampers

The procedure for replacing the strut damper assembly is identical in most cases to that given for MacPherson strut spring replacement discussed earlier in this chapter. Some strut dampers can be replaced as a cartridge while others require replacement of the entire strut. To replace a strut damper cartridge, remove the spring as outlined in the spring replacement section. Be sure to use an adequate spring compressor when needed. Unscrew the nut holding the paper to the housing and pull the cartridge from the housing. Add fresh oil to the bottom of the housing (if required) and install the new damper assembly. Finally, reinstall the spring. A cutaway of a cartridge type strut damper is shown in **Figure 36-19.**

Ball Joint Service

All modern vehicles, whether they are equipped with conventional or MacPherson strut assemblies use *ball joints.* The function of the ball joint is to carry the vehicle load to the wheels while still allowing relative movement between the wheel assembly and vehicle body. The ball joint which carries the majority of the vehicle weight is called the *load-carrying ball joint.* **Figure 36-20** shows one that is *preloaded* by a coil spring or rubber pressure ring. This preloading will keep the joint bearing surfaces in constant contact, **Figure 36-21.** Depending upon arrangement, both ball joints can be placed under either **tension-**

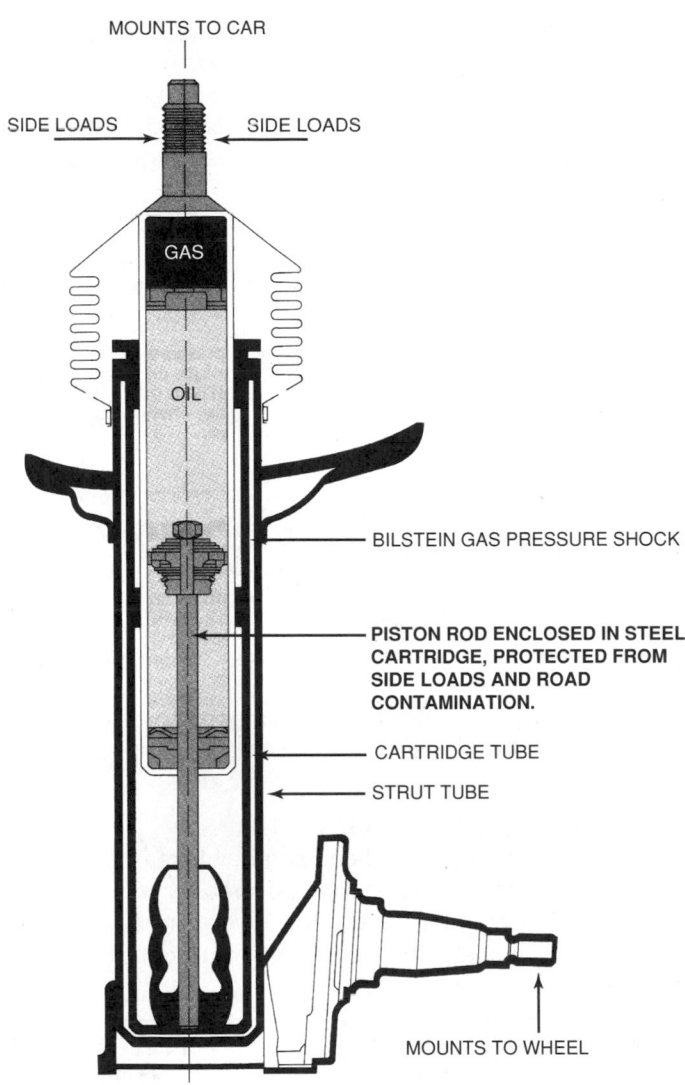

MOUNTS TO CAR

SIDE LOADS   SIDE LOADS

GAS

OIL

BILSTEIN GAS PRESSURE SHOCK

PISTON ROD ENCLOSED IN STEEL CARTRIDGE, PROTECTED FROM SIDE LOADS AND ROAD CONTAMINATION.

CARTRIDGE TUBE

STRUT TUBE

MOUNTS TO WHEEL

Figure 36-19. Cutaway view of a cartridge type strut damper. Not all struts use replacement cartridges. (Bilstein)

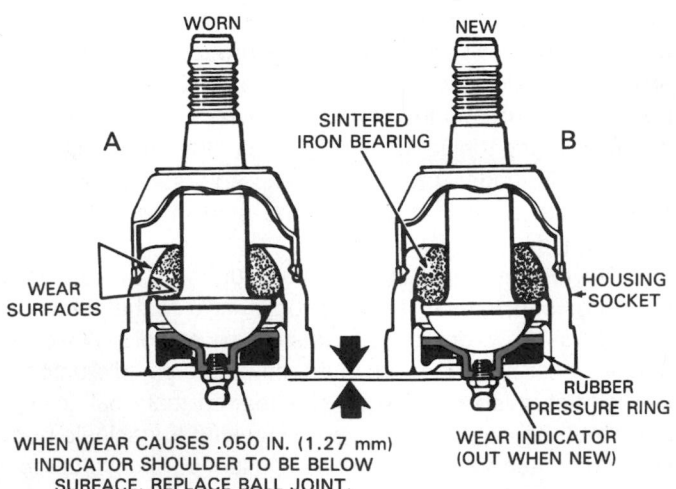

WORN   NEW

A   SINTERED   B
           IRON BEARING

WEAR
SURFACES
                                    HOUSING
                                    SOCKET

WHEN WEAR CAUSES .050 IN. (1.27 mm)   RUBBER
INDICATOR SHOULDER TO BE BELOW   PRESSURE RING
SURFACE, REPLACE BALL JOINT.
                          WEAR INDICATOR
                          (OUT WHEN NEW)

Figure 36-20. One type of load-carrying ball joint. Note wear indicator. (Oldsmobile)

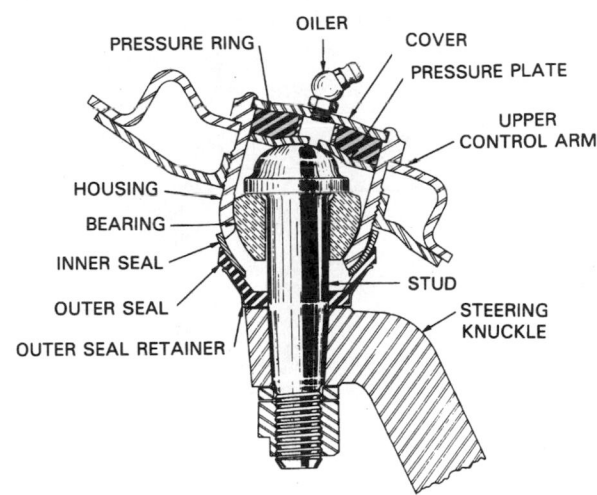

PRESSURE RING   OILER   COVER
                          PRESSURE PLATE
                          UPPER
                          CONTROL ARM
HOUSING
BEARING
INNER SEAL
OUTER SEAL   STUD
OUTER SEAL RETAINER   STEERING
                       KNUCKLE

Figure 36-21. Typical follower (non load-carrying ball joint). Note rubber pressure ring used to provide constant loading.

loading (forces attempt to pull joint apart) or ***compression-loading*** (forces attempt to compress joint).

A second arrangement tension loads the follower joint (upper joint in this case) and compression loads the main load-carrying joint (lower joint in this case). Note that the coil spring is between the lower control arm and frame in **Figures 36-22** and **36-23**.

Ball Joint Wear

Excessive ball joint wear will alter wheel alignment and can cause hard steering, shimmy, and tire wear. Although the follower joint does wear, the load-carrying joint will usually wear out first so check both joints. If the follower shows any discernible looseness, replace it. The

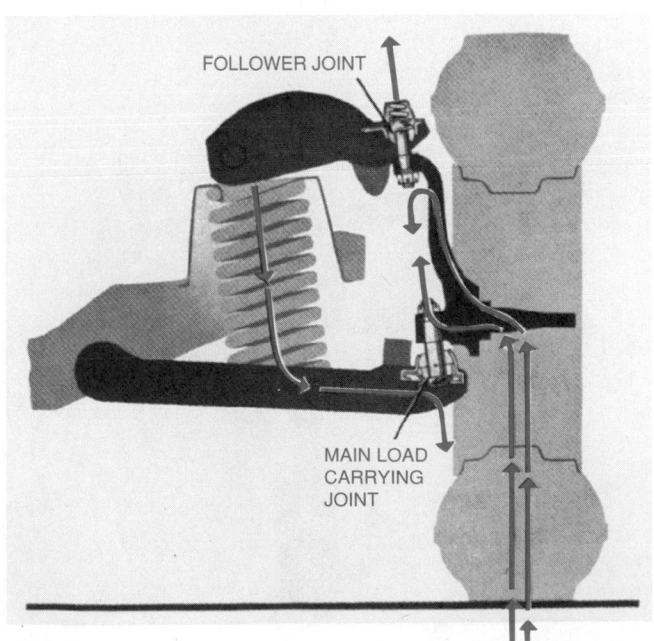

FOLLOWER JOINT

MAIN LOAD
CARRYING
JOINT

Figure 36-22. This suspension arrangement tension loads either ball joint. Main load-carrying joint is at the bottom. (Moog)

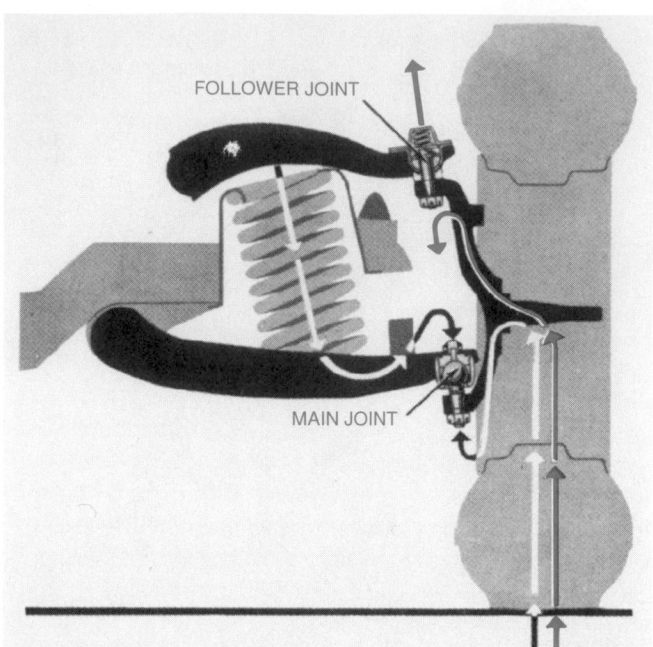

Figure 36-23. This suspension arrangement tension loads the follower joint and compression loads the main joint. (Moog)

main joint clearance or play should not exceed manufacturer's specifications.

To check ball joints for wear, they must be properly unloaded (pressure removed). When the coil spring is located between the lower control arm and the frame, **Figure 36-24,** place the jack under the lower control arm. When the jack is raised high enough to provide clearance between the tire and floor, the ball joints will be unloaded.

After properly unloading the ball joint, the amount of wear may be determined in one of two ways. Some manu-

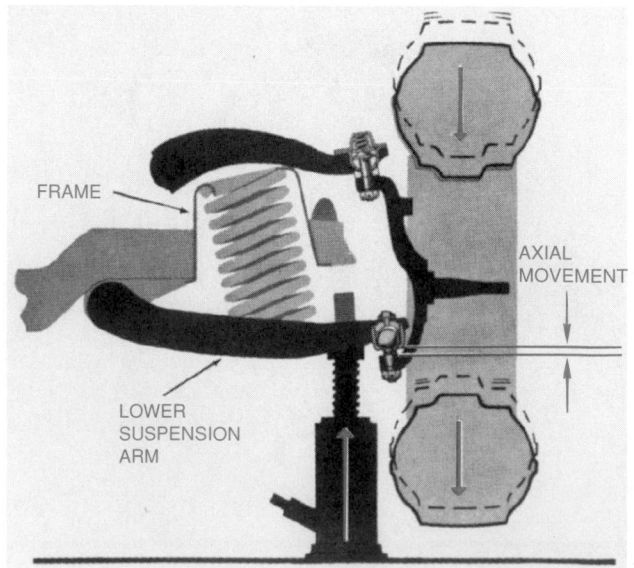

Figure 36-24. Unloading ball joints. When coil spring is mounted between lower suspension arm and frame, place a jack under *lower suspension arm. Be careful!*

facturers recommend checking joint play by measuring the axial movement. Axial movement is the up and down movement of the wheel and tire assembly. See **Figure 36-25A.** Other manufacturers specify testing for excessive clearance by measuring tire sidewall movement. See **Figure 36-25B.** Follow manufacturer's specifications, as they can vary for what constitutes excessive ball joint play, depending upon joint design.

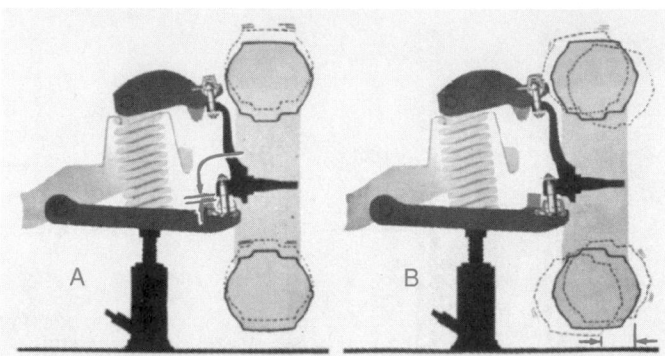

Figure 36-25. Two methods of measuring ball joint wear. A—Axial movement. B—Tire sidewall movement.

Load-Carrying Ball Joint Service

When replacing a load-carrying ball joint, you will use some of the procedures that were covered earlier. Raise the vehicle and place a jack under the lower control arm if the coil spring is mounted between the lower control arm and the frame or body, **Figure 36-24.**

STOP **Warning: Always place a jack beneath the lower control arm when the coil spring is mounted between the lower arm and the frame. Unless a jack is in place against the lower control arm, removal of either the upper or lower ball joint will allow the spring to propel the lower control arm downward with lethal force.**

Remove the cotter key from the ball joint stud nut. Loosen the stud nut several turns. In some cases, the regular castle nut is removed and a standard hex nut is placed on the stud to within two or three threads of the steering spindle or knuckle. A special removal tool may be placed between the ends of the upper and lower stud ends, **Figure 36-26.** Turn the tool to apply pressure to the ball stud. When the stud is under pressure, strike the steering spindle sharply with a hammer to free the stud in the spindle or knuckle body.

Never try to force the ball stud out of the spindle body by using heavy pressure with a tool similar to that shown in **Figure 36-26.** To do so would distort the spindle. While the stud is under moderate pressure, strike the spindle until the ball joint stud is free. The tension-loaded main ball joint in **Figure 36-27** is being removed by striking the spindle body with a hammer. When the ball stud is loose, remove the tool and stud nut. Make certain the lower arm is securely supported. Lower the control arm slowly until the ball joint is clear. The jack should be parallel with the control arm, as in

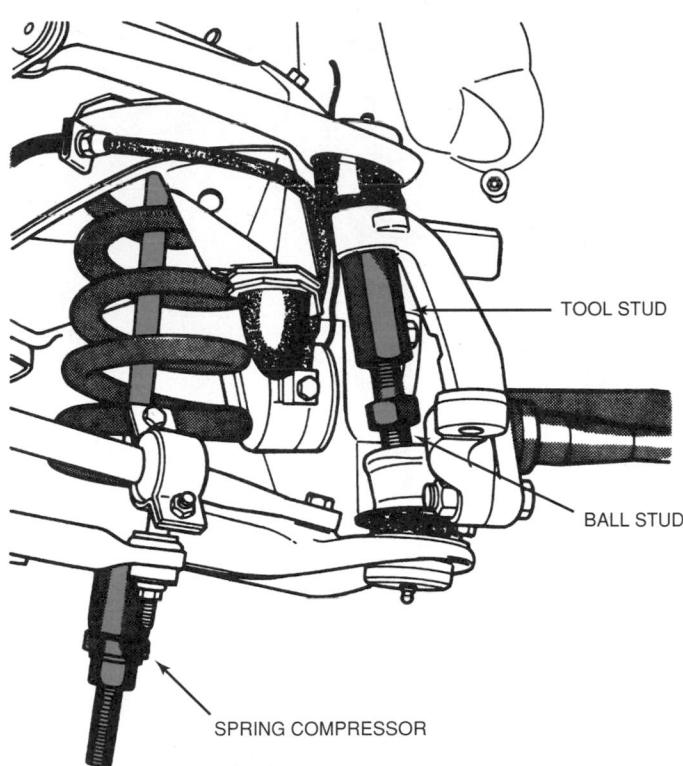

Figure 36-26.   Applying ball stud removal pressure with a stud tool. (Dodge)

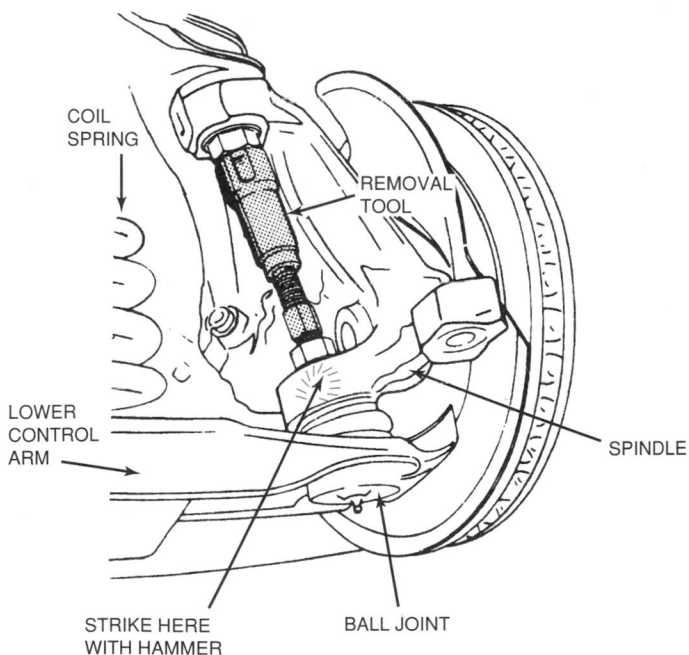

Figure 36-27.   Removing a ball joint stud by hammering spindle body. Be careful not to damage any drive axles or anti-lock brake sensors that may be present. (General Motors)

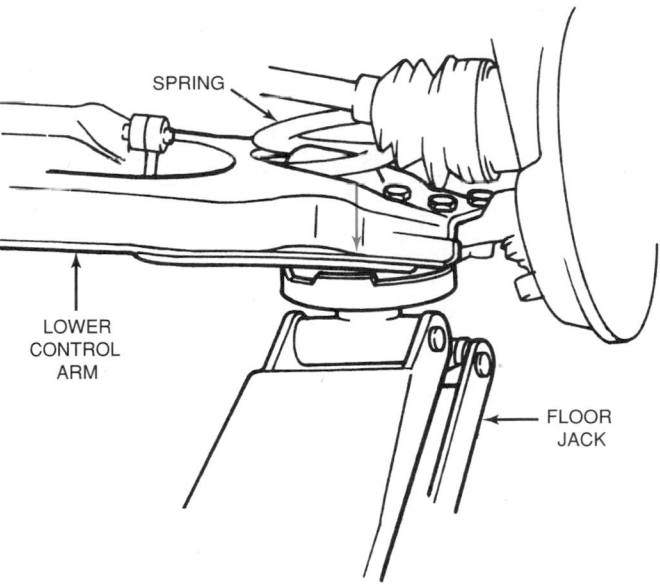

Figure 36-28.   Supporting lower control arm with a floor jack. Make sure the jack plate is securely under the control arm before unloading spring pressure. (GEO)

Figure 36-28. If necessary, disconnect the lower control arm pivot shaft and remove the arm.

Some ball joints are screwed in place while others may be riveted, pressed, bolted, or welded. Where threaded, remove joint by unscrewing. Clean both the arm and threads completely. Install the new joint and torque to specifications. If the joint is riveted to the arm, drill through the rivets with the specified size drill bit. Cut off the rivet heads and drive rivets out. A power chisel makes rivet head removal easy. Some manufacturers recommend drilling off the rivet heads that secure the joint. This procedure is illustrated in **Figure 36-29.** Clean arm thoroughly and install the ball joint. Instead of inserting new rivets, use the special bolts supplied specifically for mounting the ball joints. Torque bolts to specifications.

Figure 36-30 illustrates the removal and installation of a ball joint that is pressed into place. Clean the spindle body ball stud hole and ball joint stud. If removed, replace control arm. With coil spring properly in place, raise arm with jack until ball stud passes through spindle body. Install retaining nut and torque. Install cotter pin and lubricate joint. If a camber eccentric is incorporated in the upper ball stud, check and adjust camber as covered in Chapter 39.

Follower Ball Joint Service

The general procedure involved in removing and installing a follower ball joint is quite similar to that described for the main load-carrying joint. When the coil spring is mounted between the lower control arm and frame, **Figure 36-31,** support the lower arm. Do not allow spring pressure to slam down the control arm when the follower joint stud is removed. Some follower joints are welded to the control arm. When worn, the entire assembly must be replaced.

Steering Knuckle

The steering knuckle is mounted between the two ball joints in a conventional suspension system and at one end the damper in a MacPherson strut suspension. The knuckle allows the suspension system to turn the front wheels while retaining the wheel and brake assembly. The steering

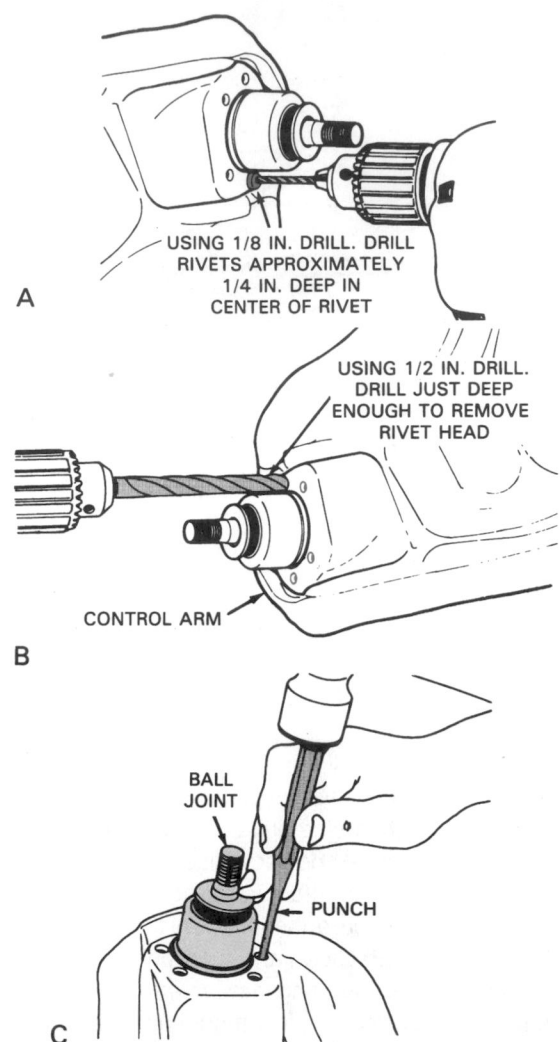

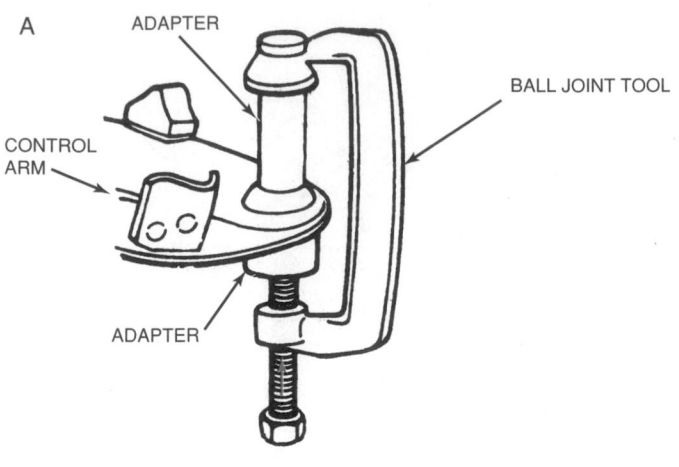

Figure 36-29. Removing a ball joint by drilling off rivets. A—Drilling a 1/8″ (3.16 mm) hole 1/4″ (6.35 mm) deep in rivet center. B—Rivet heads have just been drilled off using a 1/2″ (12.7 mm) bit. *Do not* drill into the control arm itself. C—Using a punch to drift out rivets, freeing the ball joint. (Buick)

knuckle on most conventional suspensions has a spindle cast into it. This spindle provides a smooth surface for wheel bearings to turn.

Control Arm Removal

The **control arm** must be removed when it becomes damaged or to replace the **control arm bushings.** Disconnect the shock absorber, stabilizer bar, tie strut, and other parts as needed. Block the lower control arm with a jack. Remove the ball joint stud from the steering knuckle. When removing the control arm mounting shaft, mark the location of camber and caster shims, position of bushings, or other alignment components to assist in rough resetting of camber and caster. When removing the tie strut (where used), do not move the rear locknut (nut on lower arm side of the rubber strut bushing). **Figure 36-32** illustrates a typical upper control arm completely disassembled.

Control Arm Bushings

Always replace both control arm bushings even if only one is worn. When installing a new inner shaft, use new

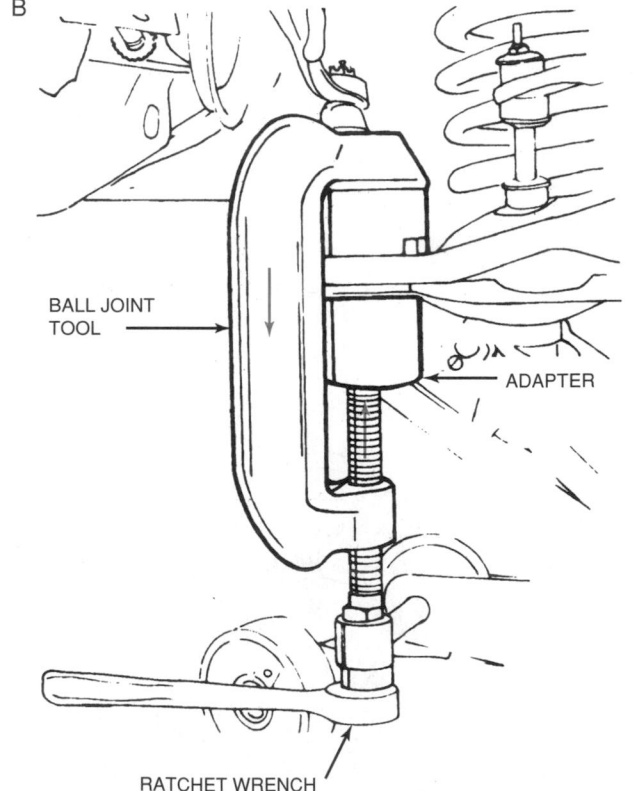

Figure 36-30. A—Removing a pressed-in ball joint. B—Installing a pressed-in ball joint. (General Motors)

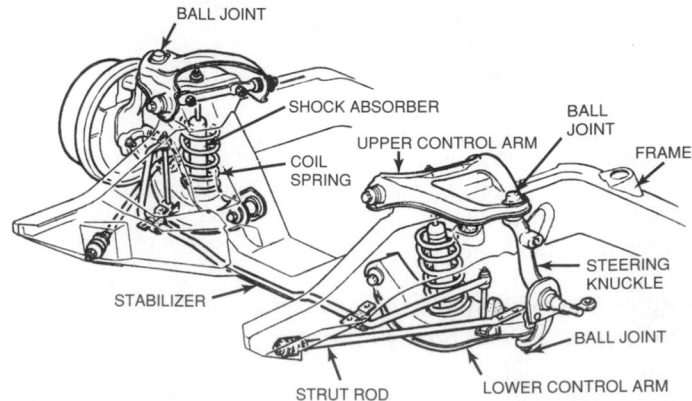

Figure 36-31. One coil spring suspension setup showing ball joint locations. (General Motors)

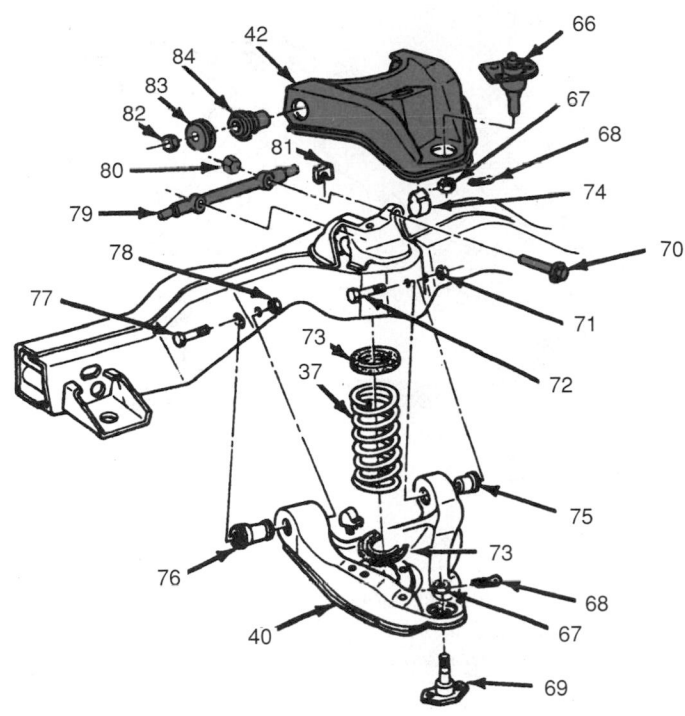

Figure 36-32. Upper and lower control arm shown in a disassembled view. Study all the parts and locations. 37—Coil spring. 40—Lower control arm. 42—Upper control arm. 66—Upper ball joint. 67—Nut. 68—Cotter pin. 69—Lower ball joint. 70—Bolt. 71—Nut. 72—Bolt. 73—Insulator. 74—Bumper. 75—Bushing. 76—Bushing. 77—Bolt. 78—Nut. 79—Shaft. 80—Nut. 81—Shim. 82—Nut. 83—Retainer. 84—Bushing. (General Motors)

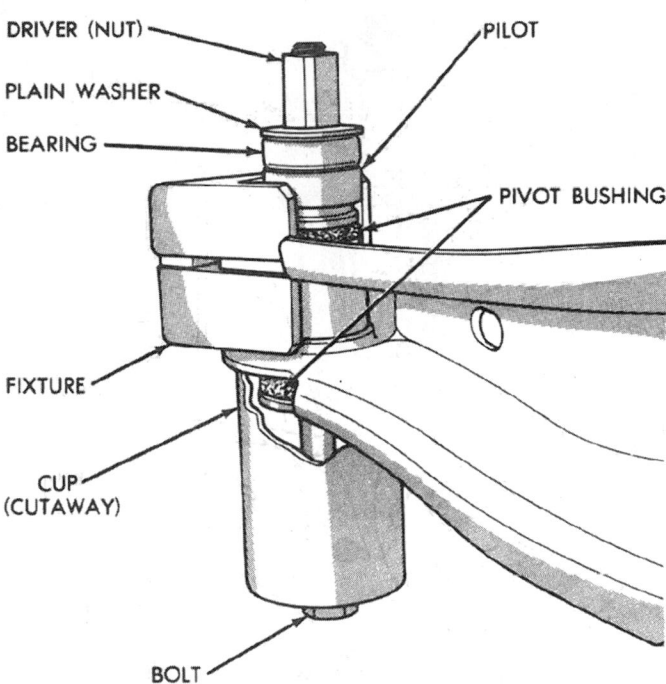

Figure 36-33. Removing a pressed-in control arm bushing. (Chrysler)

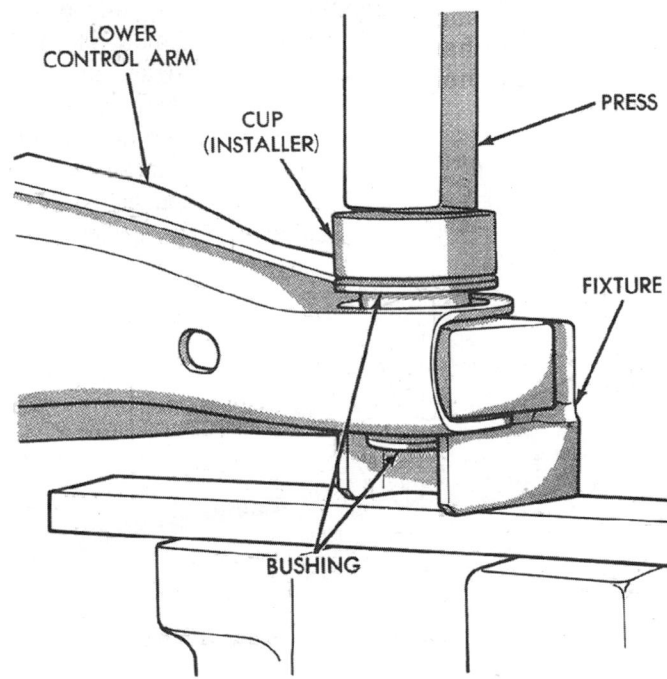

Figure 36-34. Replacing a control arm bushing using a special tool. (Chrysler)

bushings. Remove the fasteners and washers from the end of the bushings. Apply penetrating oil around the bushing. To facilitate bushing removal, bolt on a tool similar to that shown in **Figure 36-33.** Note that several tools are used in this setup.

Set the arm up in a vise and press the bushing out by turning the nut on the press while holding the receiving cup on the other end. Reverse the arm and remove the other bushing. If threaded type bushings are used, they may be removed by unscrewing. Clean the control arm and check for cracks, heavy dents, springing, and other problems. Check the inner shaft for excessive wear.

To install new bushings, place an install tool on the bushing, making sure the bushings are on the correct ends. Install a stiffener tool to prevent the arm from being bent, **Figure 36-34.** Set the arm up in a press and start the new bushings into place. Using the bushing pressing tools, force the bushings into place, **Figure 36-34.** Install outer washers and fasteners. Torque to specifications. If threaded bushings are used, make certain the inner shaft is correctly centered in the arm. In the case of the lower control arm that utilizes a tie strut, there is only one inner bushing. Note how a small spacer tube is used to prevent arm distortion while removing the lower arm bushing, **Figure 36-35.** The spacer, when required, should also be used when installing the bushing.

Strut Rods and Bushings

If the vehicle is equipped with *strut rods,* disconnect them from the control arms and frame, **Figure 36-36.** In most cases it will not be necessary to remove any other parts. If the strut rods are threaded for caster adjustment, count the number of threads on one side and reinstall the rod in the same position. This will make alignment easier. Install the replacement rods and torque to specifications.

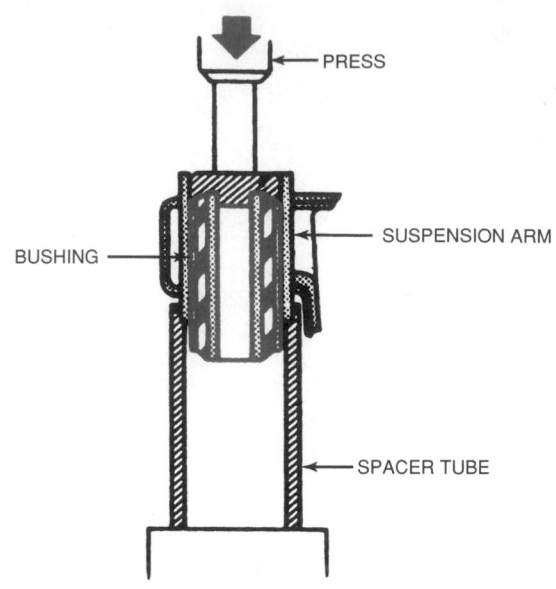

Figure 36-35. Removing a suspension arm bushing with a press. Note the use of a special tool to assist in bushing removal. (Nissan)

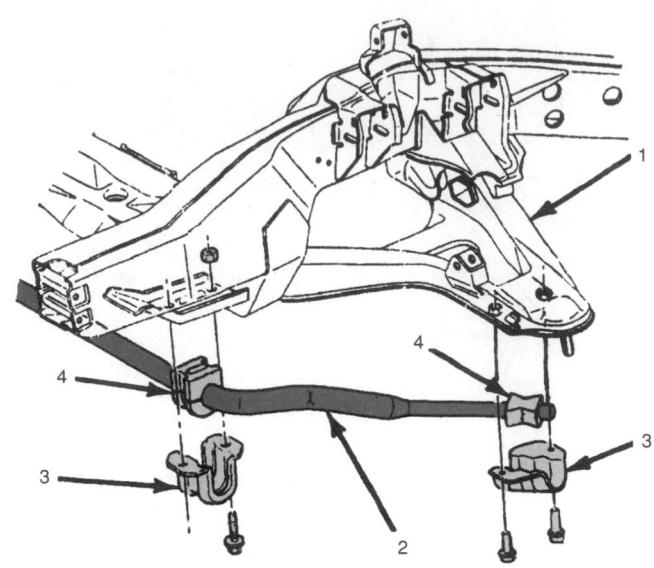

Figure 36-37. Stabilizer bar bushing assemblies. 1—Lower control arm. 2—Stabilizer bar. 3—Bushing clamps. 4—Bushings. (General Motors)

Stabilizer Bar Bushings

To replace *stabilizer bar bushings,* disconnect the stabilizer bar rod at the control arm. Remove the long bolt and remove the bushings. Reinstall the assembly with new bushings, being sure to properly assemble all bushings, washers, and spacers in their original position. Install the long bolt in its original position and tighten the nut. **Figure 36-37** shows a typical stabilizer bar bushing assembly.

The bar bushings can be replaced by unbolting the bar brackets and removing the bushings. The bushings are split, allowing them to be slipped over the bar. Installation is the reverse of removal.

Rear Suspension Systems

Most vehicles generally use either coil, leaf spring, or MacPherson strut suspension systems. When coils are employed, control arms (also called control links or control struts) must be used to provide proper rear axle housing alignment. **Figure 36-38** illustrates a typical control arm setup. A coil spring rear suspension system is

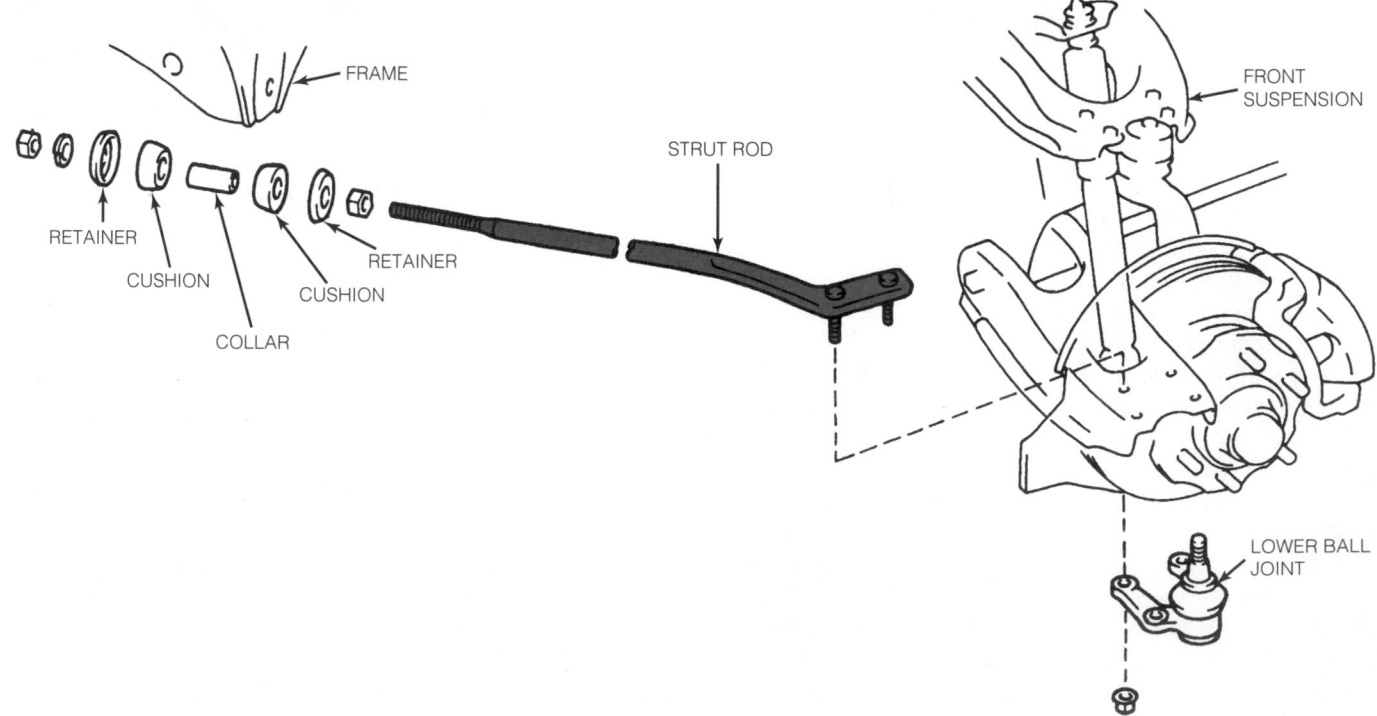

Figure 36-36. Exploded view of a strut rod assembly. (Toyota)

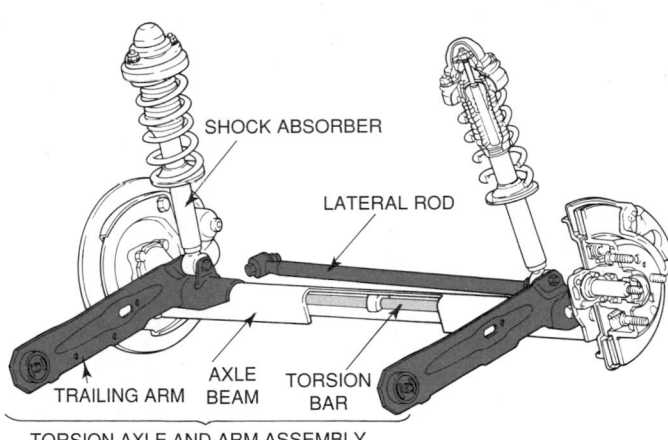

Figure 36-38. One type of rear axle suspension. Note the use of a torsion bar. (Hyundai)

shown in **Figure 36-39.** Note how the upper control arm is placed at an angle. These arms also function as the conventional track bar. A coil spring rear suspension, as used with one particular front-wheel drive, is illustrated in **Figure 36-40.**

Figure 36-41 shows a different form of rear suspension using leaf springs. The independent rear suspension system in **Figure 36-42** uses a single multiple-leaf spring mounted in a transverse position. Another similar rear suspension has a single leaf spring made of fiberglass. Removal and replacement procedures for coil springs and MacPherson strut assemblies are similar to those given in the front suspension section.

Rear Leaf Spring Service

The most common *leaf spring* failure point is the front and rear bushings. Some leaf spring bushings are best removed and installed by using a suitable puller as illustrated in **Figure 36-43.** Following removal of the old bushing, clean the spring eye thoroughly.

Coat with a suitable lubricant before pulling new bushing into position. Allow the weight of the vehicle to rest on the bushings before torquing shackle bolts. Replace any broken spring leaves. Use inserts between the spring leaves (where required). The spring center bolt must be tight. Be sure to torque spring U-bolts. All spring rebound clips must be in place. Be careful when removing or replacing a fiberglass spring. Nicks, chips, or other damage from rough handling can lead to spring failure.

Replacing Rear Suspension Control Arms and/or Bushings

When replacing rear suspension control arms or control arm bushings, it is important that the vehicle be at its normal standing height. The weight of vehicle must be on the rear wheels before tightening the control arm pivot bolts. This procedure applies to track bars as well. By allowing the vehicle to return to its normal standing height, the rubber bushings will be at rest (no twisting strain on them) while tightening the control arm bolts. This will allow them to flex in either direction from normal without damage to the bushings.

 Caution: Rubber bushings should be lubricated with rubber lube only. Never lubricate with engine oil, grease, or kerosene.

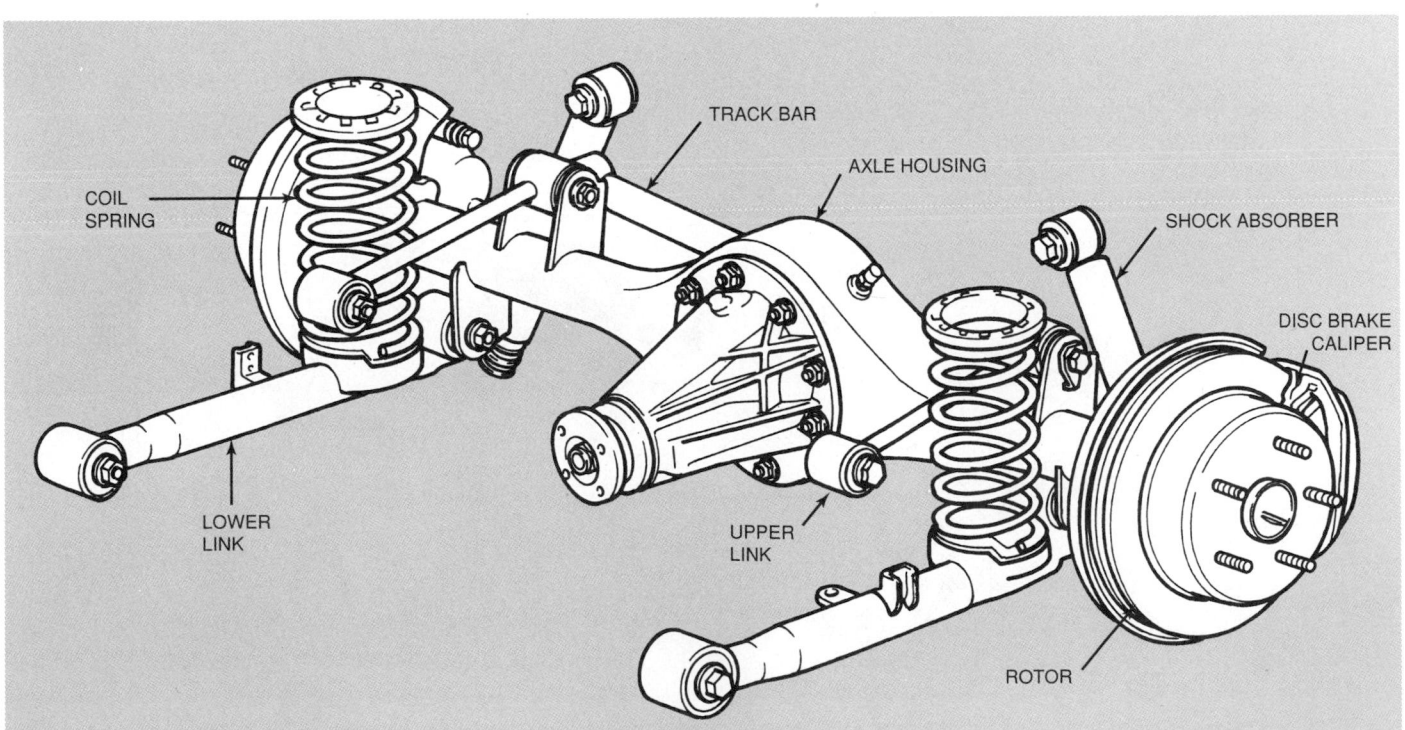

Figure 36-39. A coil spring rear suspension used on a rear-wheel drive vehicle. (Toyota)

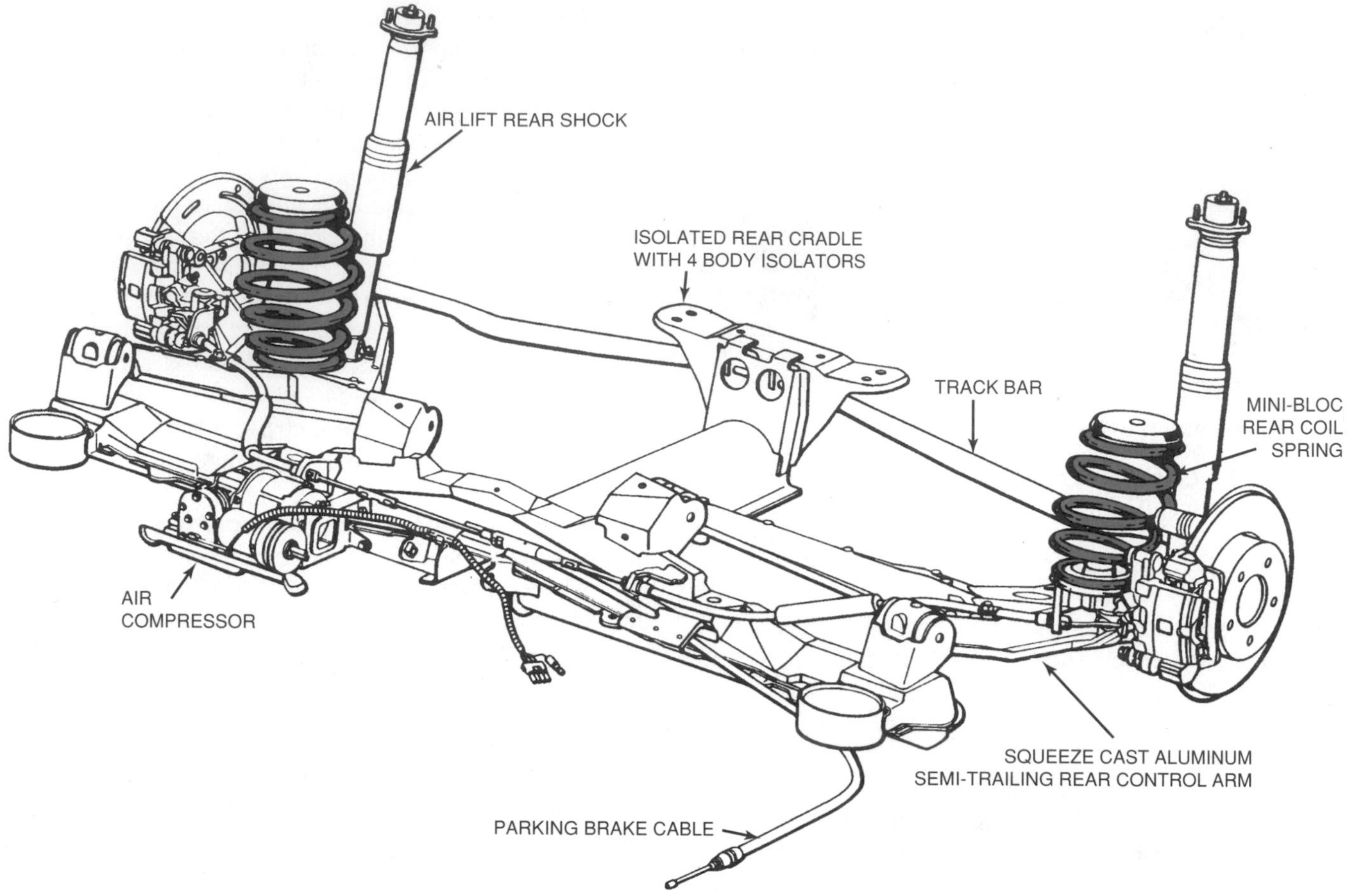

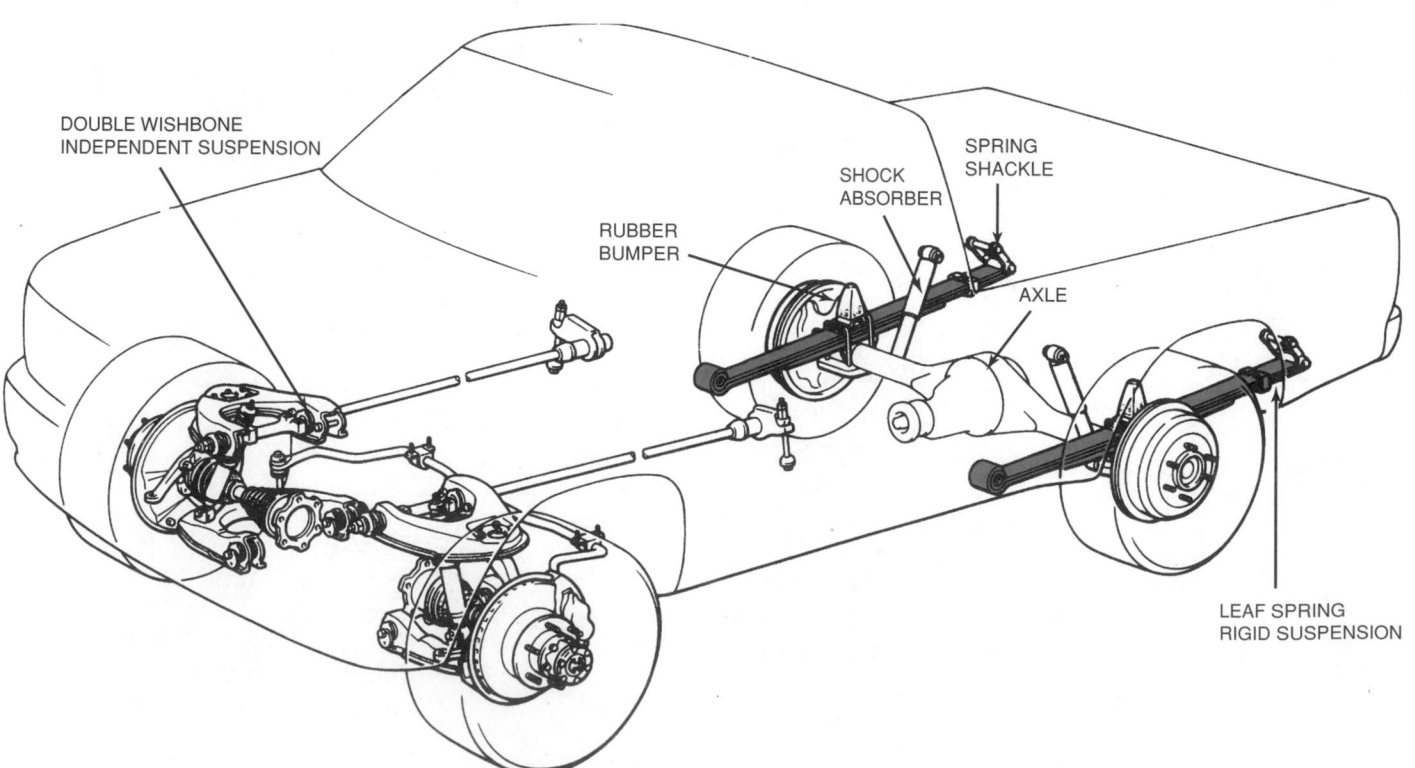

Figure 36-40.   A coil spring rear suspension with air lift shock absorbers. (General Motors)

Figure 36-41.   A four-wheel drive vehicle using torsion bar front suspension and leaf spring rear suspension. (Toyota)

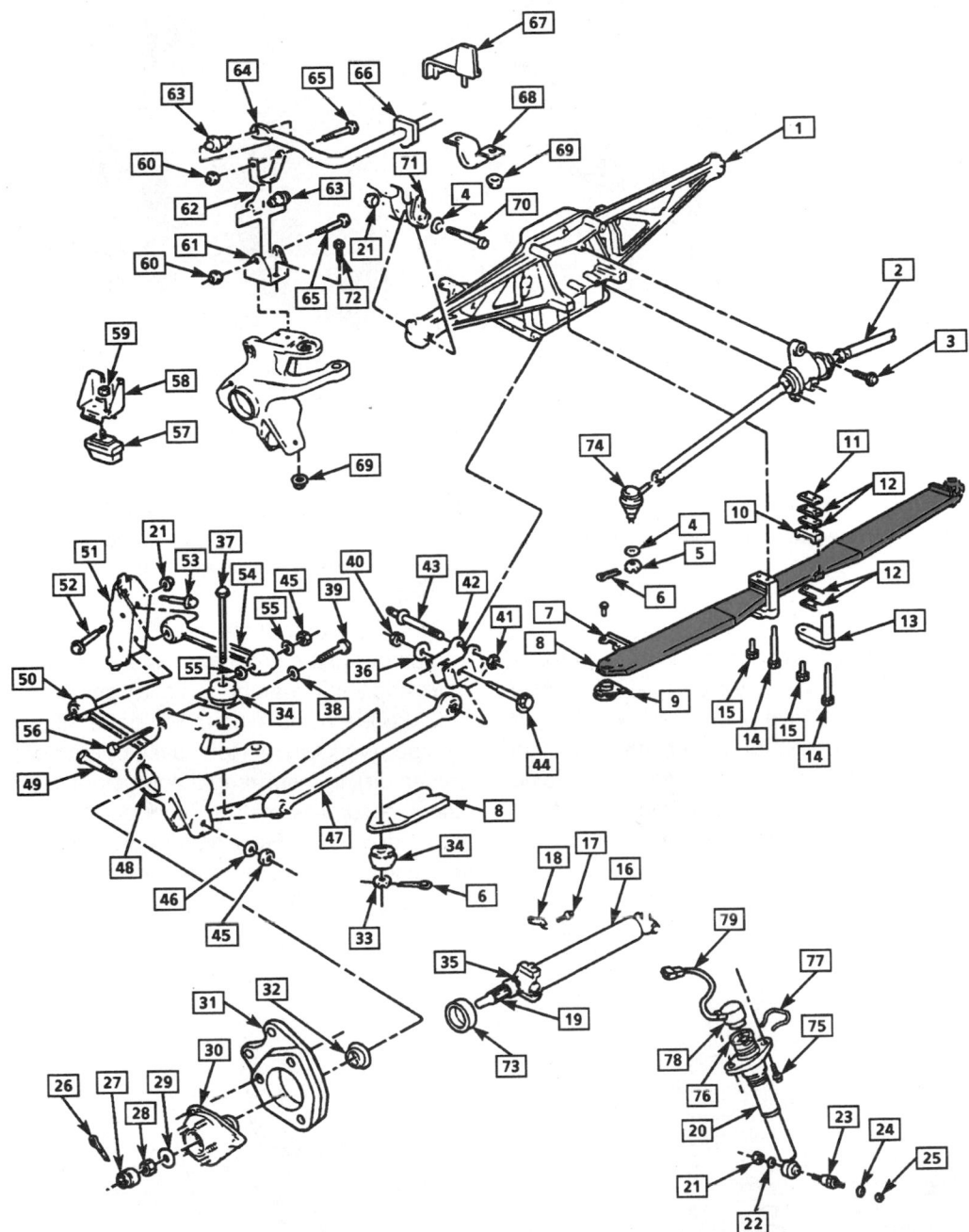

Figure 36-42. An independent rear suspension using a single fiberglass leaf spring. Do not nick, cut, or scratch these springs. *Complete spring failure may result!* 1—Differential carrier. 2—Axle tie rod. 3—Axle tie bolt. 4—Tie rod washer. 5—Axle tie rod nut. 6—Cotter pin. 7—Spring upper retainer. 8—Rear spring. 9—Spring lower retainer. 10—Spring cushion. 11—Spring insulator. 12—Spring spacer. 13—Spring anchor plate. 14—Hex flanged head bolt. 15—Hex flanged head bolt. 16—Axle shaft. 17—Drive U-joint shaft retainer bolt. 18—U-joint shaft retainer. 19—Wheel spindle. 20—Selective ride control shock absorber. 21—Hex nut. 22—Shock absorber washer. 23—Shock absorber stud. 24—Shock absorber washer. 25—Hex nut. 26—Cotter pin. 27—Wheel nut retainer. 28—Spindle nut. 29—Spindle washer. 30—Wheel hub. 31—Caliper mounting plate. 32—Wheel spindle washer. 33—Slotted spring nut. 34—Spring insulator. 35—Anti-lock brake tooth ring. 36—Spindle rod adjustment cam. 37—Spring bolt. 38—Washer. 39—Wheel hub bolt. 40—Spindle rod adjustment nut. 41—Hex nut. 42—Spindle rod bracket. 43—Spindle rod bracket stud. 44—Wheel spindle rod adjustment bolt. 45—Hex nut. 46—Spindle rod washer. 47—Spindle rod. 48—Suspension knuckle. 49—Hex bolt. 50—Wheel spindle lower control rod. 51—Spindle control rod bracket. 52—Wheel spindle rod bolt. 53—Hex bolt. 54—Wheel spindle upper control rod. 55—Spindle rod washer. 56—Spindle rod bolt. 57—Suspension bumper. 58—Suspension bumper bracket. 59—Hex nut. 60—Stabilizer shaft link nut. 61—Stabilizer shaft link bracket. 62—Stabilizer shaft link. 63—Stabilizer shaft link insulator. 64—Stabilizer shaft. 65—Stabilizer shaft link bolt. 66—Stabilizer shaft insulator. 67—Stabilizer shaft bracket support. 68—Stabilizer shaft bracket. 69—Hex flanged nut. 70—Differential carrier bolt. 71—Differential carrier member. 72—Hex bolt. 73—Wheel hub bearing seal. 74—Axle outer socket. 75—Shock absorber bracket bolt. 76—Cup assembly retainer. 77—Actuator retaining cup. 78—Shock absorber electrical actuator. 79—Actuator electrical connector. (Chevrolet)

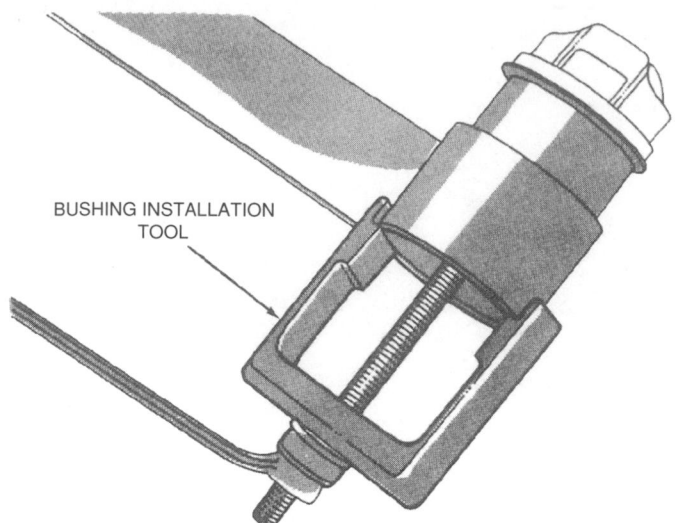

Figure 36-43. Installing a new leaf spring pivot bushing. (Chrysler)

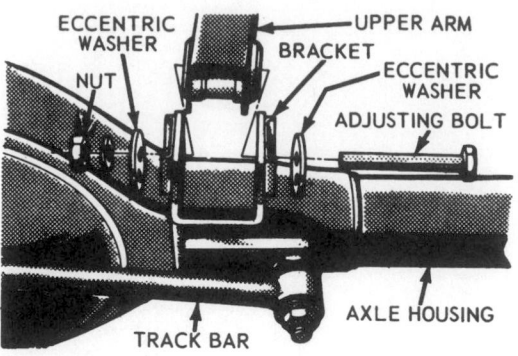

Figure 36-45. This rear axle housing may be tilted to adjust pinion drive angle by varying the upper control arm length. Length may be altered by eccentric washer setup.

Automatic Level Control

Some vehicles are equipped with an *automatic level control* system. This system is used to compensate for the weight of passengers or cargo. It can maintain normal curb height at the rear of the vehicle as measured from the frame or bumper to the ground. Most systems will level the vehicle with additional weight of up to approximately 500 pounds (227 kg.). A basic system will generally include an air compressor (vacuum or electrically-operated air pump), air tank (reservoir), pressure regulator, height control sensor, special shock absorbers or struts, connecting wire, tubing, hose, and an air dryer. See **Figure 36-46.** A hydraulic level control system using an oil pump is shown in **Figure 36-47.**

Be very careful to place the control arms on the proper side, **Figure 36-44.** Check the drive angle of the differential pinion and adjust as needed. Drive angle may be changed by adjusting the length of the control arm or arms. Note in **Figure 36-45** that the upper control arm frame-to-rear axle housing distance may be varied through the use of an eccentric washer. For complete details on differential pinion angle adjustment, see Chapter 33.

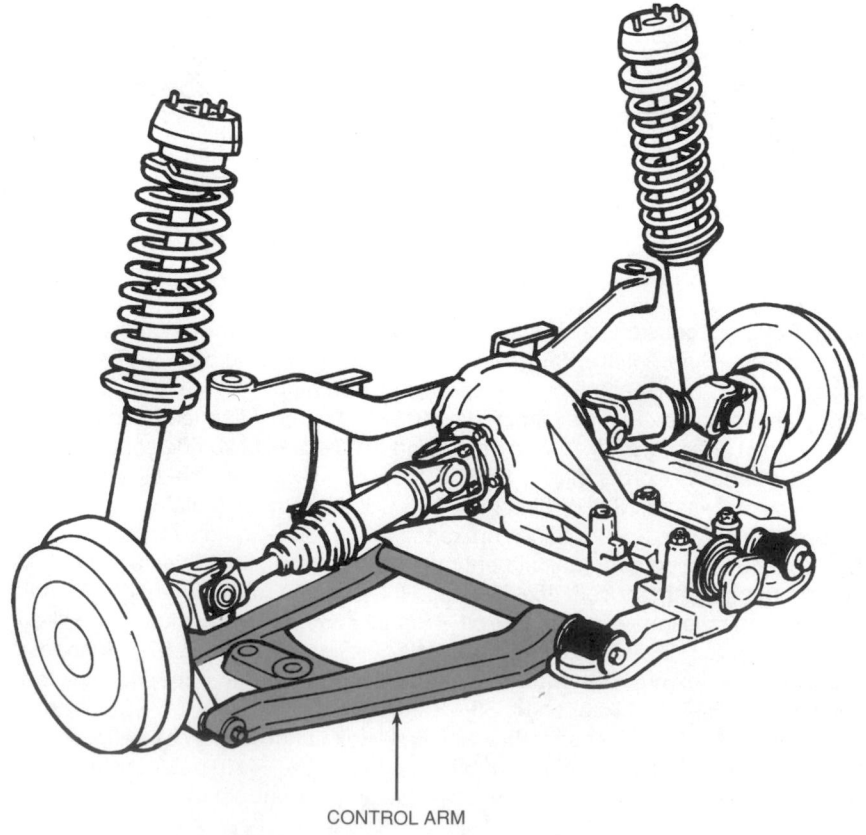

Figure 36-44. Be careful to always replace control arms to the proper side. (Moog)

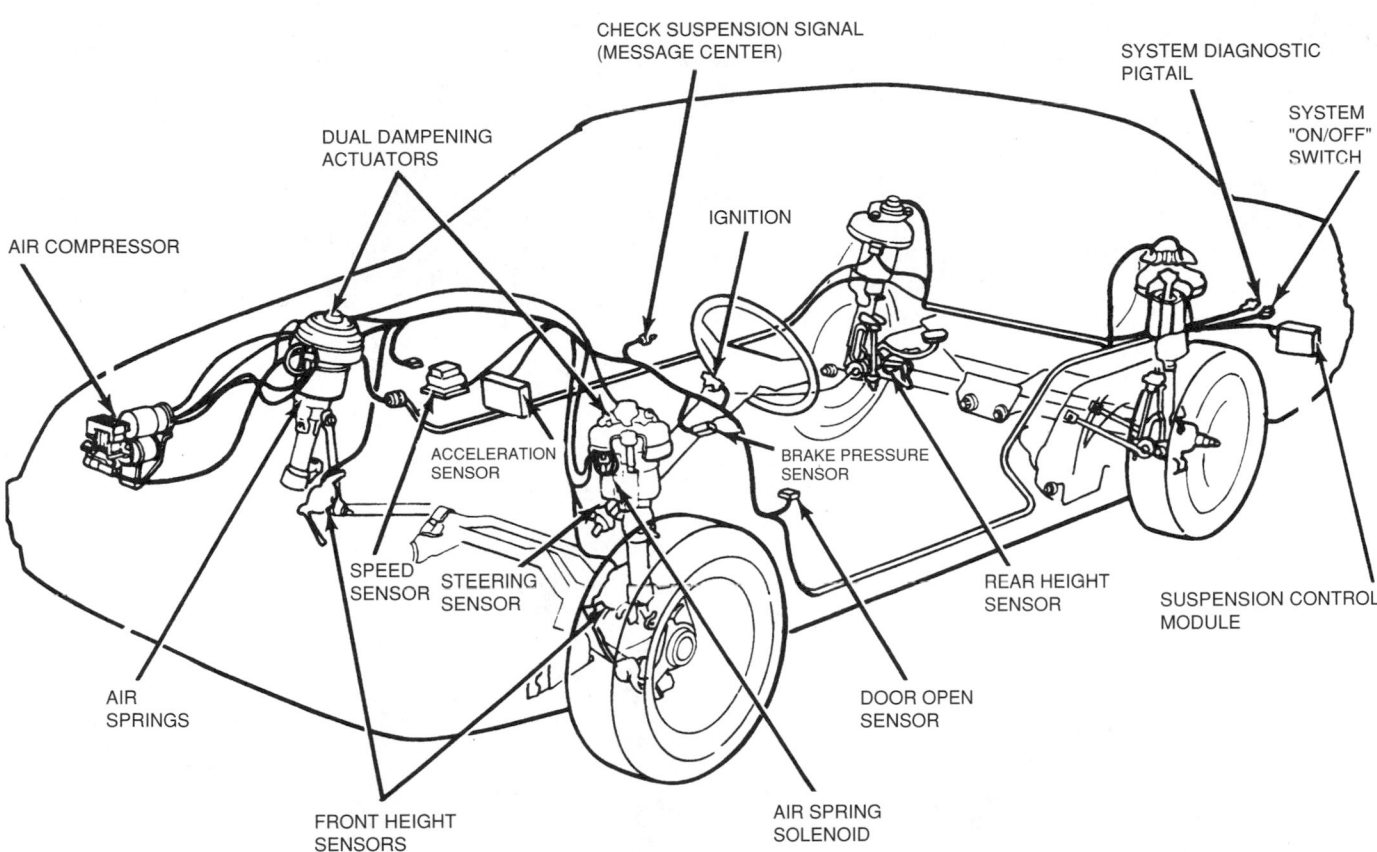

Figure 36-46.   Vehicle with an automatic level control system. Carefully study the overall system. (Ford)

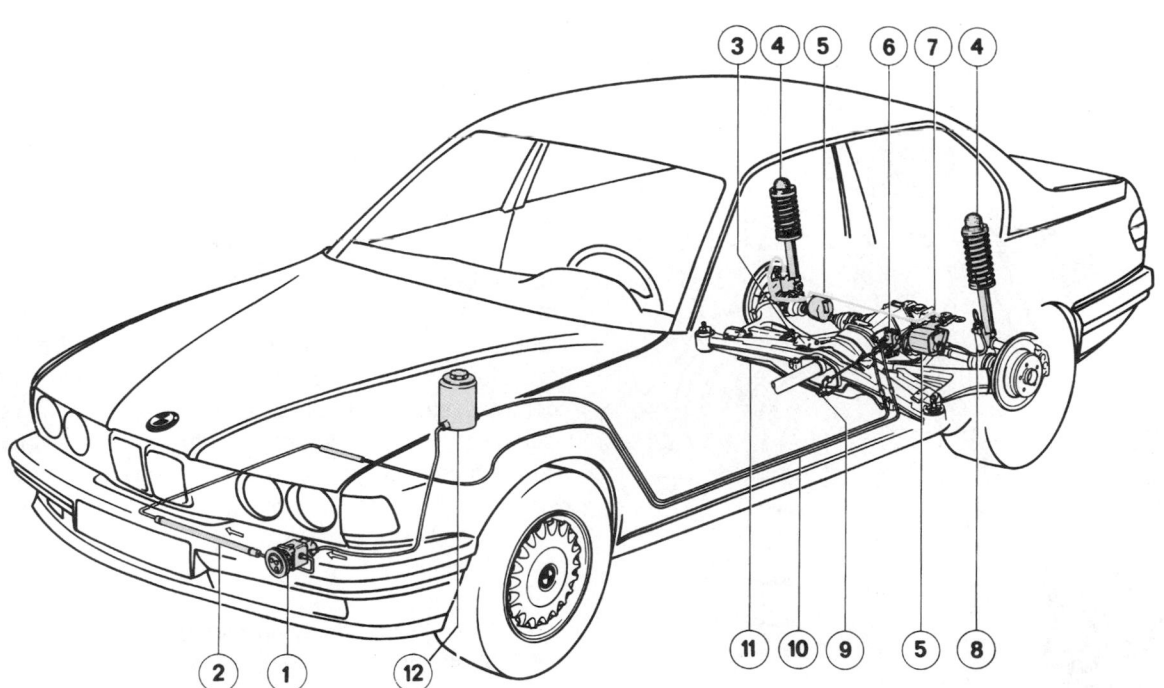

Figure 36-47.   One type of load leveling system that uses a hydraulic power steering pump. Note the wheel camber switch, which triggers an instrument cluster light when overloading of the vehicle produces excessive wheel camber. 1—Pump. 2—Expansion hose. 3—Wheel camber warning switch. 4—Spring strut. 5—Pressure reservoir. 6—Regulating valve. 7—Branch. 8—LAD (load absorbing dependent). 9—Regulating linkage mount with regulating rod. 10—Feed and return lines. 11—Stabilizer. 12—Fluid reservoir. (BMW)

Height Control Sensor

A *height control sensor* or *valve* detects any distance changes between the frame and suspension by an overtravel lever (actuating arm). The unit is attached to the vehicle frame and is connected to a suspension arm or the rear axle housing. As the distance changes, the overtravel lever will cause the control valve to admit more air to the shocks or exhaust some, either mechanically by moving valves or electrically by starting the compressor. **Figure 36-48** illustrates an electric height control sensor with linkage.

Air-Operated Struts and Shocks

The automatic level control system generally uses two air-operated struts or shock absorbers. The struts are hydraulically damped and operate in the conventional manner with the added benefit of being able to extend or decrease their operating range length with an air chamber, rubber boot, and fittings. A cutaway of an air-hydraulic strut is illustrated in **Figure 36-49**.

Automatic Level Control Service

The following is a general service procedure to be used before other checks are made. Determine the vehicle recommended *curb height,* or trim height. Start the engine and run it for 15-30 seconds. Place two people in the rear

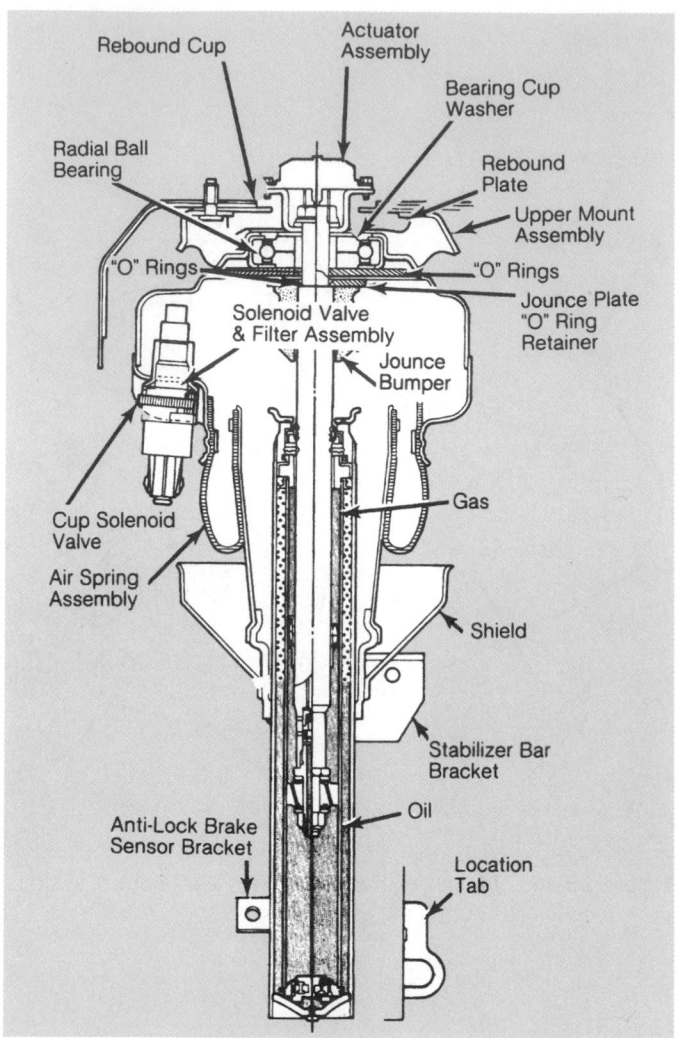

Figure 36-49. Cutaway view of an electronically controlled, air-operated strut. (Ford)

seat or the equivalent weight in the trunk and turn the ignition on. There should be a delay of 8-14 seconds with most systems before the vehicle begins to raise.

The height obtained when the compressor shuts off should be within 3/4" (19.1 mm) of the specified curb height at the beginning of the test. Remove the people or equivalent weight from the vehicle. There should be an 8-14 second delay before the vehicle begins to lower. If the level control system fails this preliminary test, consult the vehicle manufacturer's service manual for any specific tests. Follow all diagnosis and repair steps exactly. Areas of inspection should include the following:

- Compressor.
- Height sensor.
- Tubing and hose and connections.
- Air shocks.
- Electrical connections and wire.
- Electric relays.
- Fuses.
- Pressure regulator.
- Exhaust solenoid.

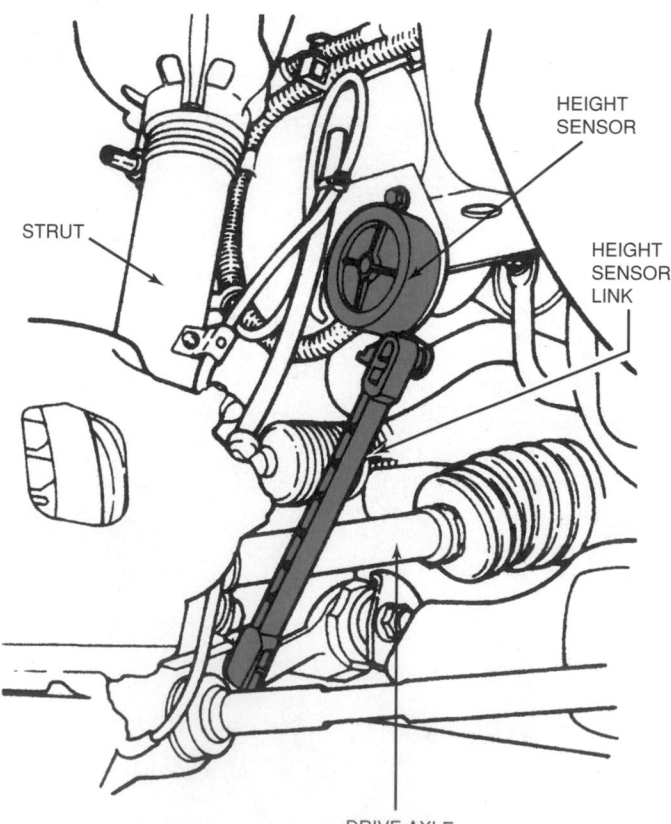

Figure 36-48. An electrically operated height control sensor with linkage. (Ford)

Computerized Ride Control Systems

Computerized ride control systems, also called *active suspensions,* are computer-controlled electronic suspension systems which can adapt to specific driving conditions, **Figure 36-50.**

Under normal driving conditions, a driver can pick the ride best suited for handling and comfort. For example, if a vehicle is being driven on a winding road, the driver can pick a firm setting. In this mode, the ride control module will signal actuators to close valves on the adjustable shocks. This will produce a stiff ride and the vehicle will be able to corner better. If the vehicle is being driven on a highway, however, the driver can switch to a soft mode. In this setting, the valves in the adjustable shocks are opened and a soft, comfortable ride is produced.

Under certain driving conditions, the control module will override the driver's selection. During periods of hard braking, a brake sensor signals the control module to close the valves on the adjustable front shocks. This stiffens the front shocks and minimizes front-end diving.

Under heavy acceleration, the acceleration sensor signals the control module to stiffen the adjustable rear shocks, preventing rear-end squatting, **Figure 36-51.** When the driver steers the vehicle into a sharp turn, a steering sensor sends an appropriate signal to the control module. The module signals the actuators to increase shock pressure on the outside of the vehicle. This action decreases vehicle leaning in turns. Other systems also provide programmed ride control. Typical ride control systems consist of the following components:

* Control module (uses signals from the steering and brake sensors to control actuators).
* Steering sensor (monitors the direction and speed of steering wheel rotation).
* Brake sensor (monitors brake system applications).
* Acceleration signal sensor (monitors rate of acceleration).
* Mode select switch (allows driver to adjust ride control system).
* Actuators (control the flow of hydraulic fluid in the adjustable shock absorbers).

Ride Control System Troubleshooting

Troubleshooting procedures for ride control systems vary among manufacturers. Consult the appropriate service manual for proper instructions. Most ride control systems have self-diagnostic capabilities which simplify the troubleshooting process. The ride control module is usually located in the vehicle passenger compartment. It continuously monitors data sent by the various sensors and controls the output circuits of the appropriate systems. Diagnostic system functions are also controlled by this unit.

If the computer recognizes a problem in one of the input or output devices, it will alert the driver by triggering a trouble indicator light on the dashboard. A trouble code will be stored to aid the technician in making proper repairs. Always follow the manufacturer's recommendations when accessing diagnostic codes and servicing the system. A suspension control system check sheet is shown in **Figure 36-52.**

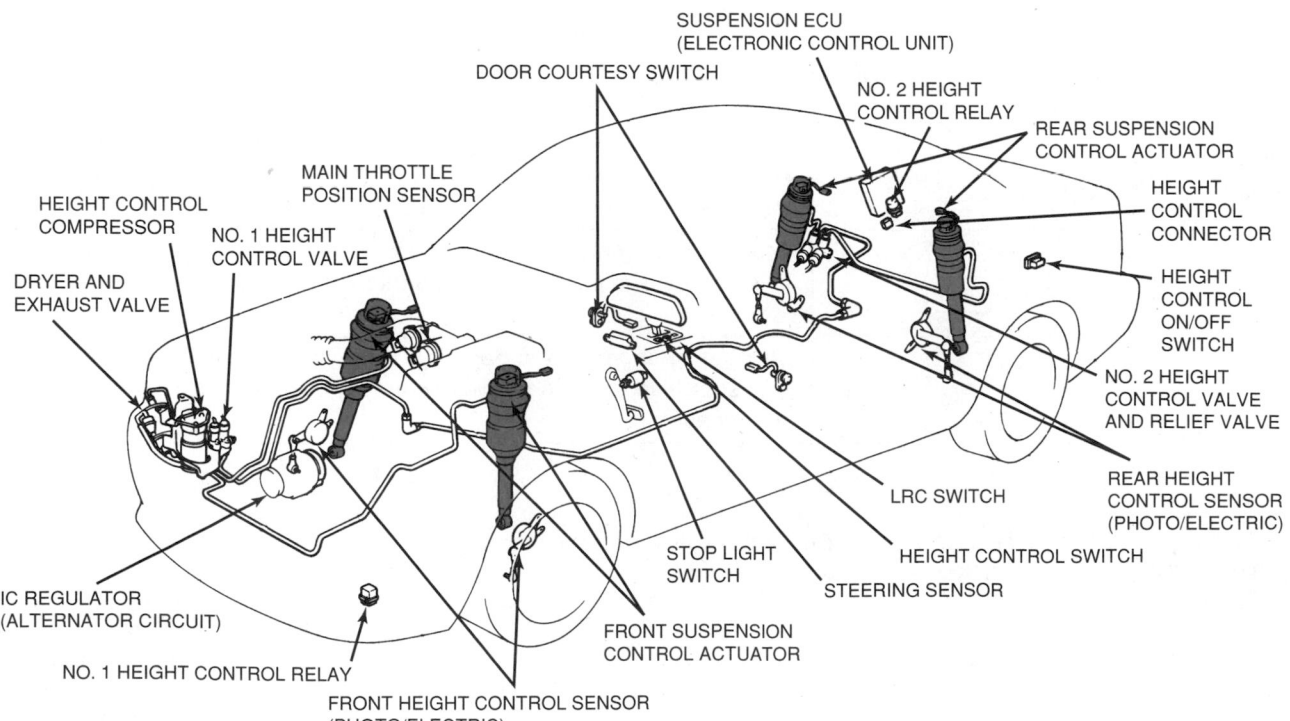

Figure 36-50. A computerized ride control "active suspension" system. Study all the parts. (Toyota)

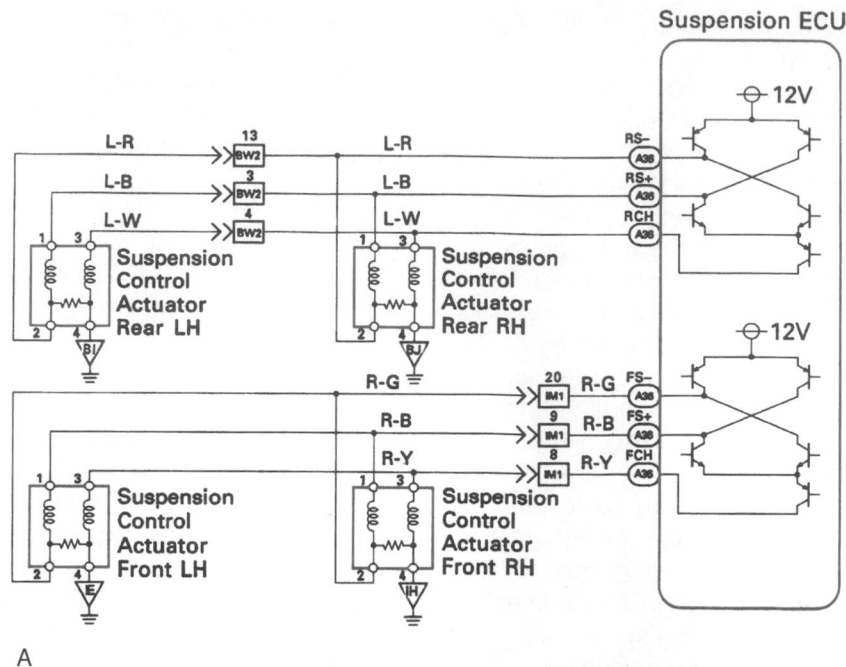

A

	Control	Function
Anti-Roll Control		Changes spring rate and damping force to ''firm'' mode. This control suppresses rolling and minimizes change of the vehicle posture improving controllability.
Anti-Dive Control		Changes spring rate and damping force to ''firm'' mode. This control suppresses nose diving of the vehicle during braking and minimizes changes of the vehicle posture.
Anti-Squat Control		Changes spring rate and damping force to ''firm'' mode. This control suppresses squatting of the vehicle during acceleration and minimizes change of the vehicle posture.
High Speed Control		Changes spring rate to ''firm'' and damping force to ''medium'' modes respectively. This control improves driving stability and controllability at high speeds.
Rough Road Control		Changes spring rate and damping force to ''medium'' or ''firm'' mode as needed to suppress bottoming of the vehicle and thus riding comfort when driving on uneven roads.
Pitching Control		Changes spring rate and damping force to ''medium'' or ''firm'' mode. This suppresses pitching of the vehicle when running over uneven road.
Bouncing Control		Changes spring rate and damping force to ''medium'' or ''firm'' mode. This suppresses up and down bouncing of the vehicle when running over uneven road.

B

Figure 36-51. A—Active suspension electronic control unit and system electrical schematic. B—Chart illustrating control and function of the system depending upon vehicle position. (Lexus)

SUSPENSION CONTROL System Check Sheet

TECHNICIAN'S
NAME

Customer's Name		Registration No.	
		Registration Year	/ /
		Frame No.	
Date Vehicle Brought In	/ /	Odometer Reading	km Mile

Date of Problem Occurrence		/ /
Frequency of Problem Occurrence		☐ Constant ☐ Sometimes (times per day, month) ☐ Once only
Conditions at Time of Problem Occurrence	Weather	☐ Fine ☐ Cloudy ☐ Rainy ☐ Snowy ☐ Various/Others
	Outdoor Temperature	☐ Hot ☐ Warm ☐ Cool ☐ Cold (Approx. °F(°C))
	Place	☐ Highway ☐ Suburbs ☐ Inner City ☐ Hill (☐ Up, ☐ Down) ☐ Rough Road ☐ Others ( )

Problem Symptom	☐ Malfunction in damping force and spring rate control.	☐ Cannot be changed by operating LRC switch. ☐ Anti-roll control does not operate. ☐ Anti-squat control does not operate. ☐ Anti-dive control does not operate. ☐ High speed control does not operate. ☐ Others ( )
	☐ Malfunction in vehicle height control	☐ Vehicle height cannot be changed by operating the height control switch. ☐ High speed control does not operate. ☐ Ignition Switch OFF Control does not operate. ☐ Others ( )
	☐ Others	

Diagnostic Trouble Code Check	1st Time	☐ Normal Code ☐ Malfunction Code (Code)
	2nd Time	☐ Normal Code ☐ Malfunction Code (Code)

Figure 36-52.   One type of suspension control system check sheet used to question the owner and test. (Lexus)

Tech Talk

Many automotive students dream of working for a racing team. While this would be a fun way to make a living, the chances that you will actually do this are slim. Out of the millions of automotive technicians, no more than a few thousand have paying jobs in the auto racing industry. The odds are at least 100,000 to 1 that you will ever collect a paycheck from a racing organization. It is far more likely that you will be repairing the vehicles of people who barely drive the speed limit than race cars.

There is nothing wrong with having an interest in working on high performance vehicles. However, chances are that you will only work on race cars in your spare time, and make a daily living repairing the engines, brakes, front suspensions, automatic transmissions, or air conditioners of standard production vehicles. Therefore, it is to your advantage to know how to service these systems, not just how to build high performance vehicles.

Summary

Front suspension systems use coil springs, torsion bars, MacPherson struts, or a combination of each. Ball joints are used to allow up and down as well as swivel action of the spindle body. One ball joint is loaded (main load-carrying joint) while the other is non-loaded (follower joint). Ball joint may be tension or compression-loaded.

Some conventional and MacPherson strut front suspension coil springs must be compressed for removal or installation. Others may be unloaded by slowly lowering the lower suspension arm. Be careful, loaded coil springs have tremendous force. Use a jack to lower the suspension arm.

Be sure to reinstall spring insulators where required. Position spring end as specified. Do not nick or dent springs. Spring sagging (broken or weak) may be detected by measuring vehicle curb height. Remove torsion bar by unloading front suspension arms and then backing off bar tension anchor. The torsion bar must be free of nicks and burrs. Lubricate both ends of the torsion bar before installing. Never heat a torsion bar or bar anchors. Set the vehicle standing height by turning torsion bar adjusting bolt.

Shock absorbers and strut dampers must function well to provide safe handling and a comfortable ride. Check shock operation by bouncing vehicle or by bench testing shocks. Most modern shocks are gas-filled for better control. Some shocks are adjustable. If a stone shield is used, place in correct direction. Do not overtighten shock bushing fasteners.

To check ball joint wear, the joints must be unloaded. When a coil spring is between lower arm and frame, unload the joint by placing a jack beneath the lower control arm. When a coil spring is between the upper suspension arm and body, place the jack beneath the frame. In some cases,

a wedge must be placed between the underside of the upper arm and the frame. Check ball joint wear by measuring either axial (up and down) movement or side to side movement of the tire.

The use of a suitable puller eases ball joint removal. Striking the spindle with a hammer also helps. Always use great care when removing ball joints to prevent the coil spring from being released violently. When bolting new ball joints to suspension arms, use special bolts supplied for the purpose. When the joint is welded to the arm, both the arm and joint should be replaced as an assembly.

When removing control arms, note the number and location of camber and caster shims or other adjusting devices. When pressing suspension arm bushings out or in, use a stiffener tool to prevent the arms from distorting. Rear suspension systems commonly use either leaf or coil springs. Replace sagged rear coil springs and weak or broken leaf springs. Place the weight of the vehicle on the spring shackle bushings before tightening bushing fasteners. When installing rear axle control arms, check the differential pinion shaft drive angle. Place the vehicle at its normal standing height before tightening the control arm bushing bolts. Use rubber lubricant only on rubber bushings.

Some vehicles are equipped with automatic level control. This system keeps curb height correct when the vehicle has additional weight or passengers. The system uses an air compressor, valves, tubing and hose, height sensor, and air shocks or struts. Some vehicles employ an air-operated, electronically controlled shock absorber active suspension at all wheels.

Know These Terms

Conventional suspension	Tension-loading
MacPherson strut suspension	Compression-loading
	Control arm
Coil springs	Control arm bushings
Torsion bars	Strut rods
Spring compressor	Stabilizer bar bushings
Shock Absorber	Leaf spring
MacPherson strut damper	Automatic level control
Gas charged	Height control sensor
Ball joints	Height control valve
Load-carrying ball joints	Curb height
Preloaded	Active suspensions

Review Questions—Chapter 36

Do not write in this book. Write your answers on a separate sheet of paper.

1. Torsion bars _____ to absorb road shocks.
   (A) bend
   (B) compress
   (C) twist
   (D) expand

2. Front suspension ball joints can be _____ or _____ loaded.

3. Name three results of excessive ball joint wear.

4. Before checking ball joint wear, the joint must be _____.

5. Allowable wear tolerances for ball joints vary between
_____.
(A) makes of vehicles
(B) upper and lower joints
(C) cars and trucks
(D) all of the above

6. When placing a jack under the lower suspension arm to lower the arm following ball joint stud removal, place the jack _____ to the length of the lower arm.

7. To avoid distorting the suspension arm when pressing out bushings, use a _____.
(A) stiffener tool
(B) vise
(C) new bushing
(D) small hammer

8. What important rear axle angle can be adjusted by altering the length of rear control arms? _____

9. Bouncing the vehicle is one way to test shock general condition. After releasing the vehicle, If the shocks are good, how many bounces (oscillations) should the vehicle make before stopping?
(A) 1
(B) 2
(C) 3
(D) 4

10. Which of the following is the best description of a gas charged shock absorber?
(A) A shock absorber containing pressurized gas instead of hydraulic fluid.
(B) A shock absorber containing pressurized gas and hydraulic fluid.
(C) A shock absorber filled with compressed air from a vehicle mounted compressor.
(D) A shock absorber filled with compressed air from an outside source.

ASE-Type Questions

1. Technician A says that MacPherson strut suspensions have only one ball joint per wheel. Technician B says that on systems having two ball joints per wheel, one of the ball joints is the main load-carrying joint while the other acts as a follower or guide. Who is right?
(A) A only.
(B) B only.
(C) Both A & B.
(D) Neither A nor B.

2. Technician A says that all suspensions contain parts under spring tension. Technician B says that all suspensions contain coil springs, either at the front or rear. Who is right?
(A) A only.
(B) B only.
(C) Both A & B.
(D) Neither A nor B.

3. Technician A says that lowering the lower arm to release coil spring tension can be dangerous if done incorrectly. Technician B says that a spring compressor is always needed to remove front suspension system coil springs. Who is right?
(A) A only.
(B) B only.
(C) Both A & B.
(D) Neither A nor B.

4. Vehicle standing height (vehicle equipped with torsion bars) can be changed by adjusting _____.
(A) torsion bar length
(B) torsion bar anchor tension
(C) rear leaf spring height
(D) rear leaf spring length

5. All of the following statements about hydraulic fluid leakage at the MacPherson strut damper are true, EXCEPT:
(A) excessive leakage means that the damper should be replaced.
(B) slight leakage is a normal condition.
(C) leakage is usually the result of seal failure.
(D) when the damper is replaced, the spring should be replaced also.

6. Technician A says that all MacPherson strut assemblies incorporate a coil spring around the strut damper. Technician B says that the action of MacPherson strut dampers is the same as that of conventional shock absorbers. Who is right?
(A) A only.
(B) B only.
(C) Both A & B.
(D) Neither A nor B.

7. The procedure for replacing a MacPherson strut damper assembly and a MacPherson strut spring in most cases is _____.
(A) identical
(B) similar
(C) completely different
(D) dependent on the manufacturer

8. When replacing a front MacPherson strut assembly, the technician must gain access to the upper strut bolts by _____.
(A) removing the wheel
(B) opening the hood
(C) pulling up the front carpet
(D) removing the inner fenders

9. Technician A says that a common service procedure performed on leaf springs is bushing replacement. Technician B says that a common service procedure performed on control arms is bushing replacement. Who is right?
(A) A only.
(B) B only.
(C) Both A & B.
(D) Neither A nor B.

10. All of the following are true statements about computer ride control systems, EXCEPT:
(A) under certain driving conditions, the control module will override the driver's selection.
(B) in the soft mode, the vehicle will corner well.
(C) most ride control systems have self-diagnostic capabilities.
(D) during sharp turns, the actuators increase shock pressure on the outside of the vehicle.

Suggested Activities

1. Write a report listing the differences between conventional and MacPherson strut suspensions.
2. Obtain the vehicle's specifications and measure vehicle ride height. Determine whether the ride height can be adjusted. If the ride height is adjustable, correct improper ride height. If the ride height is not adjustable, determine which parts must be replaced to restore the correct ride height.
3. Inspect suspension components for wear. The check should include all ball joints, and control arm bushings, and the strut rod and stabilizer bushings if used. Demonstrate the checking procedure to other members of the class.
4. Replace shock absorbers on a conventional suspension system. Make a list of the tools that you needed to perform the job.
5. Replace a MacPherson strut assembly, including removal disassembly, parts replacement, reassembly, and reinstallation on the vehicle. Write a short report, listing the tools that you needed to perform the job and explaining why the vehicle must be aligned after strut replacement.

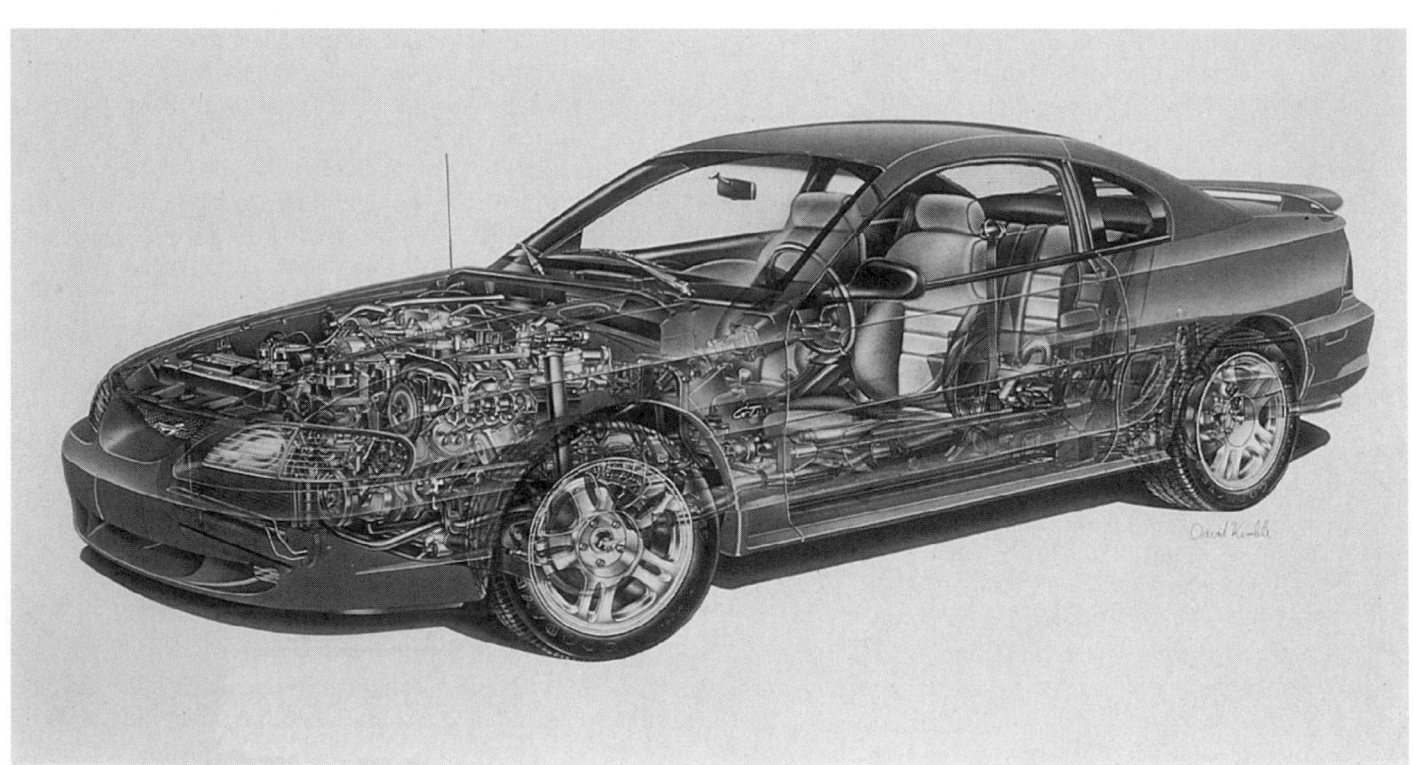

Phantom view of a rear-wheel drive automobile. This vehicle is equipped with a power-assisted rack and pinion steering system. (Ford)

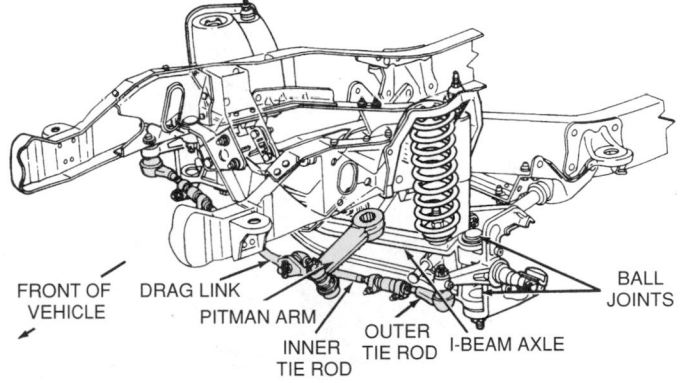

37

Steering System Service

After studying this chapter, you will be able to:
- Explain the differences between conventional and rack and pinion steering systems.
- Identify the components of conventional steering systems.
- Identify the components of rack and pinion steering systems.
- Diagnose problems in conventional and rack and pinion steering systems.
- Summarize the construction, operation, and service of steering linkage components.

Steering systems, though varying in design, all contain the same basic elements. They consist of a steering wheel, steering shaft, steering gearbox or rack and pinion assembly, steering arms, and steering knuckle assemblies. This chapter will cover both conventional and rack and pinion steering systems.

STOP **Warning: When working on a vehicle equipped with a supplemental restraint system (air bag), always follow the manufacturer's service, repair, and handling instructions. Failure to do so can result in personal injury caused by the unintentional activation of the system. Neglecting the manufacturer's precautions can also prevent the air bag from inflating during an accident, resulting in occupant injury or death. For more information on air bag systems, see Chapter 27.**

Types of Steering Systems

The two most common types of steering systems are the *conventional*, or parallelogram steering system, and the *rack and pinion steering system*. A typical conventional steering system is shown in **Figure 37-1,** and a rack and pinion steering system is illustrated in **Figure 37-2.**

Steering Column and Steering Wheel

Because of the number or steering column designs, a general discussion of steering columns and steering wheel removal and installation is presented here. Squeaks, roughness, binding, and other steering system problems can be caused by worn, dirty, or dry *steering shaft* bearings in the steering column. Column looseness or misalignment also

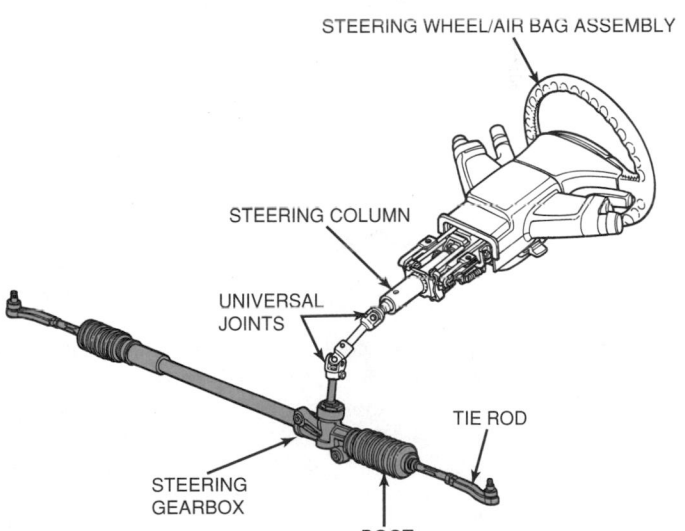

Figure 37-1. Conventional steering system components. (Ford)

FRONT OF VEHICLE — DRAG LINK — PITMAN ARM — INNER TIE ROD — OUTER TIE ROD — I-BEAM AXLE — BALL JOINTS

STEERING WHEEL/AIR BAG ASSEMBLY
STEERING COLUMN
UNIVERSAL JOINTS
TIE ROD
STEERING GEARBOX
BOOT

Figure 37-2. Manual rack and pinion steering assembly. (Hyundai)

can cause trouble. **Figure 37-3** is an exploded view of a typical steering column. An exploded view of a tilt steering column assembly is illustrated in **Figure 37-4.** Consult the manufacturer's service manual for specific service procedures for each steering column. If the steering wheel is mounted on the steering shaft so that marks are in alignment, the spoke position, if incorrect, must be altered by moving the tie rod adjuster sleeves. For complete details on

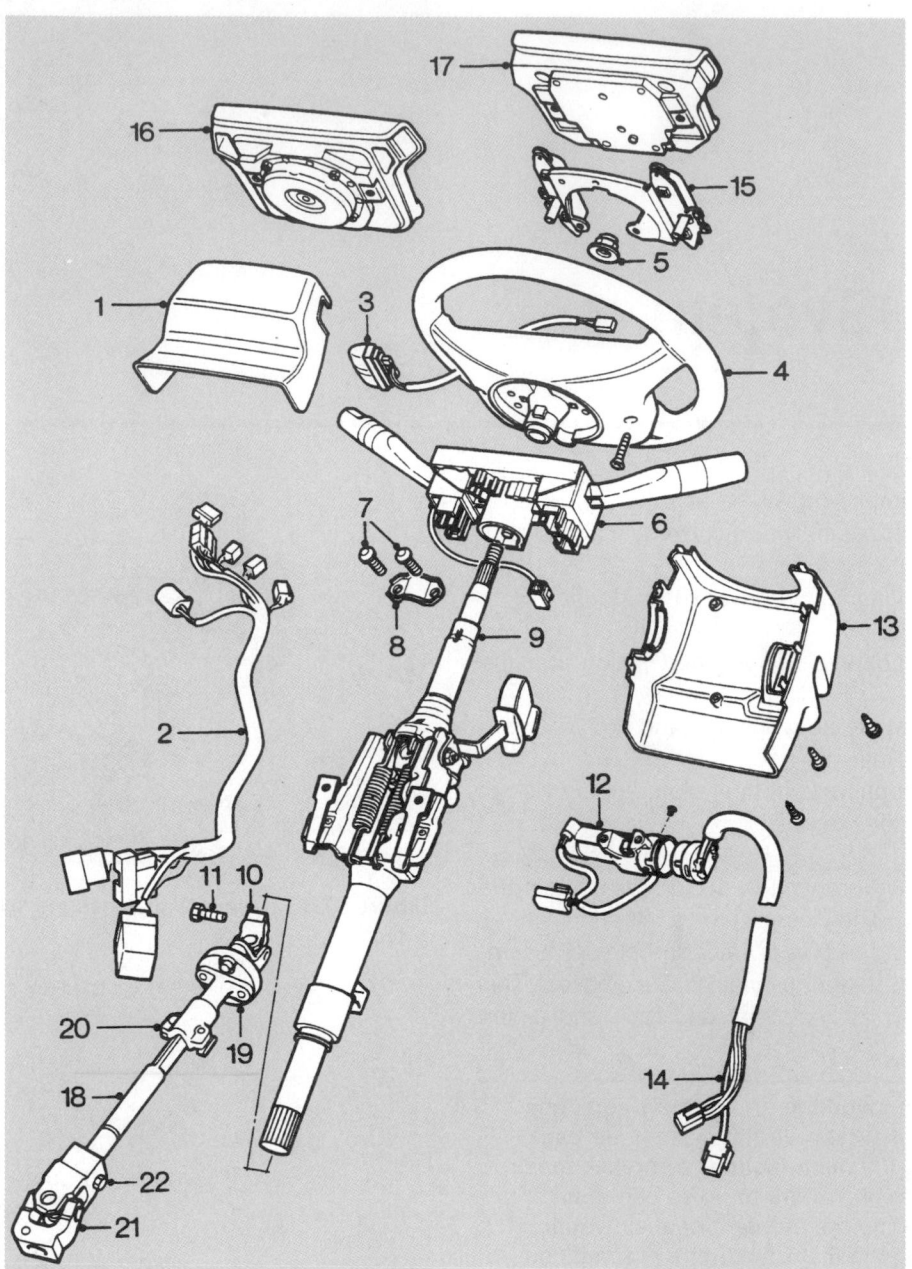

Figure 37-3. An exploded view of a typical steering column. 1—Upper cover. 2—Wiring harness. 3—Cruise control harness. 4—Steering wheel. 5—Nut. 6—Turn signal and wiper control assembly. 7—Bolt. 8—Column bracket. 9—Steering shaft. 10—Pinch collar. 11—Pinch bolt. 12—Ignition lock cylinder. 13—Lower cover. 14—Ignition wiring harness. 15—Support plate. 16—Horn pad. 17—Inflator module. 18—Intermediate steering shaft. 19—Steering collar. 20—Pinch collar. 21—Stub shaft pinch collar. 22—Pivot joint. (Land Rover)

this operation, see the toe-in and steering wheel position adjustment in Chapter 39.

Steering Wheel Service

If the vehicle is equipped with an air bag system, be sure to disable it according to the manufacturer's recommended procedure. Remove the steering wheel center cap or inflator module and any other parts required to expose the steering wheel retaining nut. Some columns are fitted with a safety retaining ring that snaps into a groove above the nut. Remove the ring and the nut carefully. Check the steering wheel and shaft for alignment marks. If none are

used and if the wheel is to be replaced in the same position, mark the steering wheel and shaft. Use a suitable puller to remove the wheel. Refer to **Figure 37-5.** Never hammer on the end of the steering shaft. Damage to the column, steering shaft, and/or collapsible joint can occur.

Install the parts that precede the steering wheel in the reverse order in which they were removed. Install the wheel on the steering shaft, aligning the marks to ensure proper positioning. See **Figure 37-6.** If no aligning marks are used, center the steering gear and mount the wheel with the spokes in proper position for straight driving. Make sure any wiring for the horns, air bag, and steering wheel controls, (if

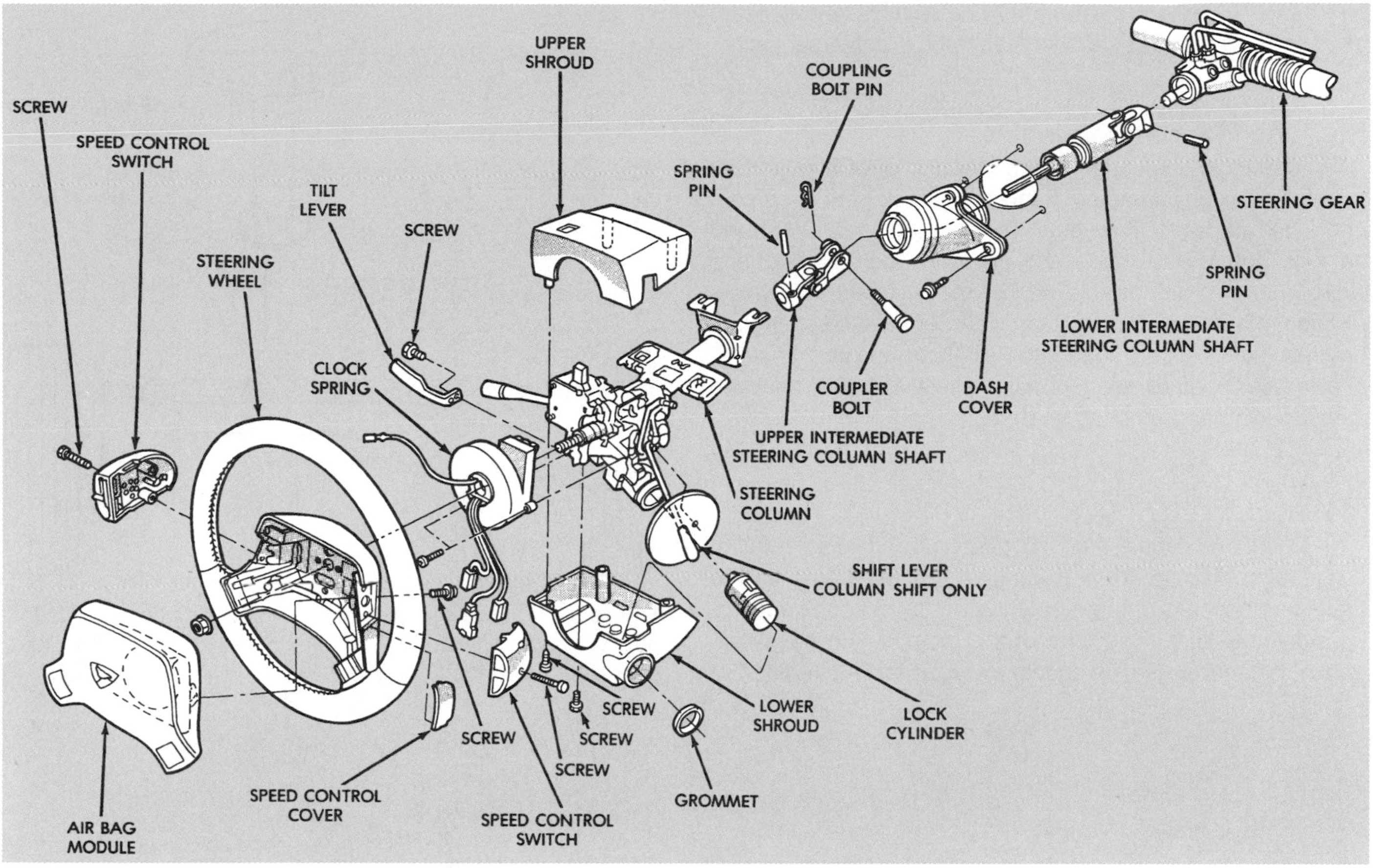

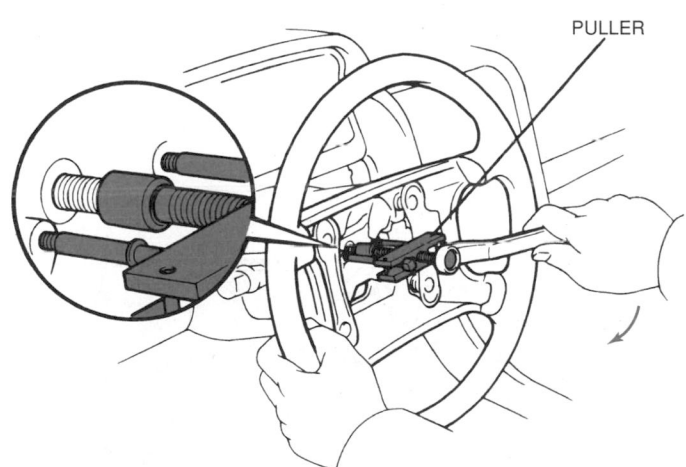

Figure 37-4. Exploded view of a tilt steering column. Note the air bag module. (Chrysler)

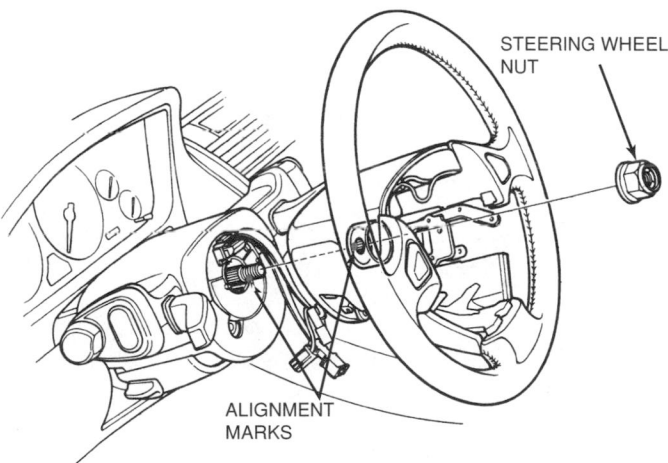

Figure 37-5. Using a puller to remove a steering wheel. Be careful not to damage the steering shaft threads. (Lexus)

Figure 37-6. When replacing the steering wheel, be sure to align the alignment marks. (Honda)

used) is not chafed or pinched as the wheel is installed. Coat the steering shaft threads with locking compound to hold the nut in place. Install the washer and wheel retaining nut. Torque the retaining nut to factory specifications. Reinstall all remaining components and enable the air bag system, if equipped.

Conventional Steering Gears

This section covers the steering gears used in most older vehicles and many current cars and light trucks. The steering gear must turn the rotation of the steering wheel into side to side motion at the steering linkage. Conventional steering gears use the *recirculating ball* design. The gearbox is attached to the frame and is usually connected to the steering shaft by a shock absorbing universal joint.

Steering Gear Inspection

A periodic inspection of the steering gear is important to safety as well as ease of handling. Check gear alignment and lubricant level. Turn gear from full left to full right and back to detect any roughness or binding. Shake steering wheel as much as possible without moving the front wheels (engine off) to check for gear wear or misadjustment. If needed, adjust worm shaft thrust preload and pitman shaft over-center preload. Inspect the flexible coupling between gear housing and steering shaft. See **Figure 37-7.**

Manual Steering Gear

Common manual steering gears use the recirculating ball design. The gearbox is attached to the frame and is usually connected to the steering shaft by a shock absorbing universal joint. One form of the recirculating ball worm and nut steering gear is shown in **Figure 37-8.** A different

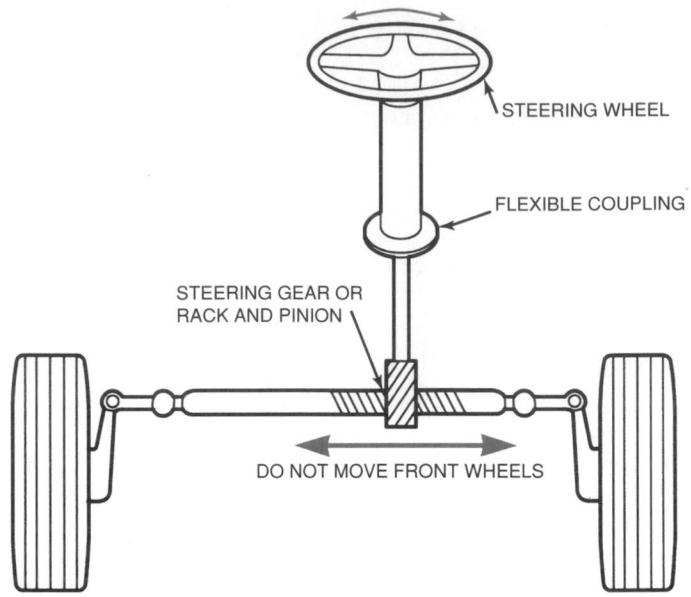

Figure 37-7. Shaking the steering wheel slightly to check for gear wear and adjustment. Do not turn the steering wheel far enough to move the front wheels. (Saginaw Division of GM)

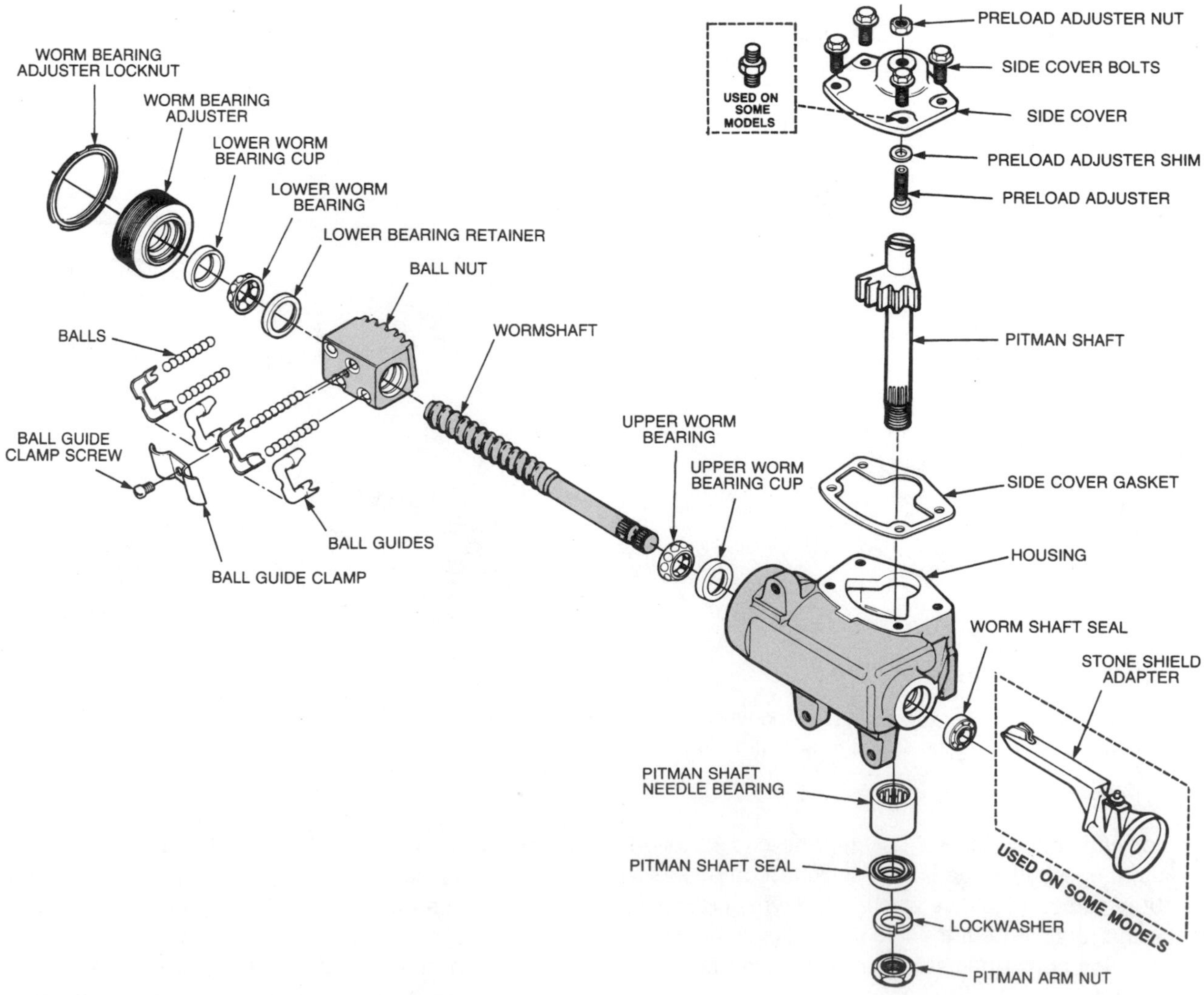

Figure 37-8. Exploded view of a gear housing, ball nut, and worm shaft assembly. (Saginaw Division of GM)

recirculating ball worm and nut steering gear is illustrated in **Figure 37-9.** Note how the pitman arm is attached to the pitman shaft (cross shaft, sector shaft, etc.). A rack and pinion gearbox is illustrated in **Figure 37-10.**

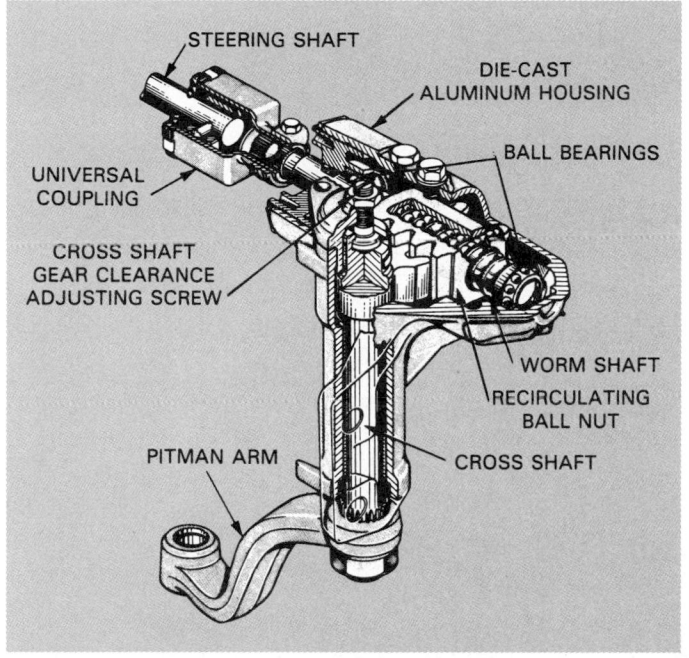

STEERING SHAFT

DIE-CAST
ALUMINUM HOUSING

BALL BEARINGS

UNIVERSAL
COUPLING

CROSS SHAFT
GEAR CLEARANCE
ADJUSTING SCREW

WORM SHAFT

RECIRCULATING
BALL NUT

PITMAN ARM

CROSS SHAFT

Figure 37-9. Another type of recirculating ball worm and nut steering gear. (Plymouth)

Checking Manual Steering Gear Lubricant Level

Clean off the filler plug and surrounding area. Remove the filler plug to check the level of the gear lubricant. Note the steering gearbox filler plug and lubricant level shown in **Figure 37-11.** If needed, fill the gearbox to the indicated level using lubricant recommended by the vehicle's manufacturer. Some steering gears do not have regular filler plugs. One such gearbox is shown in **Figure 37-12.** To check the fluid level in this type of gear, remove the two cover attaching bolts. Fill gearbox at fastener hole A until lubricant appears at hole B. Always use the correct lubricant. Multipurpose gear lubricant is often specified. Occasionally, a soft, extreme pressure (E.P.) multipurpose chassis lubricant is used as a manual steering gear lubricant. Unless the oil is contaminated, there is no need for periodic steering gear oil changes.

Manual Steering Gear Adjustments

There are two adjustments on the majority of steering gears, worm bearing preload and over-center adjustment, which is the clearance between the ball nut and sector teeth with the gear in the center of its travel. Before making these adjustments, make sure that any binding is not caused by gearbox and steering column misalignment.

 Caution: Adjust the worm shaft bearing preload first with the gear in an off-center position. Make the over-center adjustment last with the gear in the center of its travel.

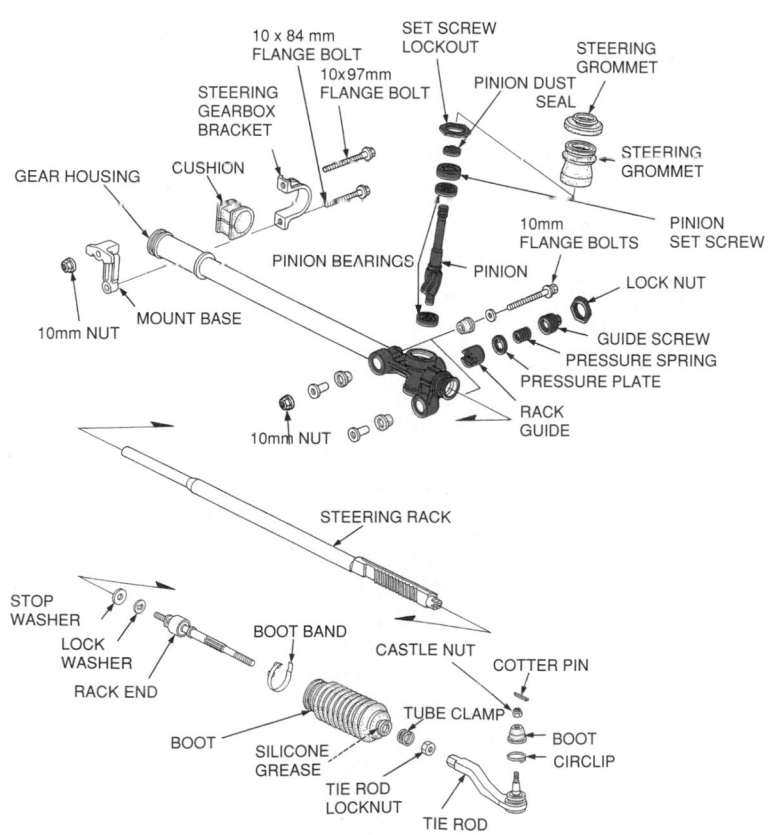

10 x 84 mm
FLANGE BOLT

SET SCREW
LOCKOUT

STEERING
GROMMET

10x97mm
FLANGE BOLT

PINION DUST
SEAL

STEERING
GEARBOX
BRACKET

STEERING
GROMMET

GEAR HOUSING

CUSHION

PINION
SET SCREW

10mm
FLANGE BOLTS

PINION BEARINGS

PINION

LOCK NUT

MOUNT BASE

GUIDE SCREW

10mm NUT

PRESSURE SPRING

PRESSURE PLATE

RACK
GUIDE

10mm NUT

STEERING RACK

STOP
WASHER

LOCK
WASHER

BOOT BAND

CASTLE NUT

COTTER PIN

RACK END

TUBE CLAMP

BOOT

BOOT

SILICONE
GREASE

CIRCLIP

TIE ROD
LOCKNUT

TIE ROD

Figure 37-10. Exploded view of a rack and pinion gearbox and related components. (Honda)

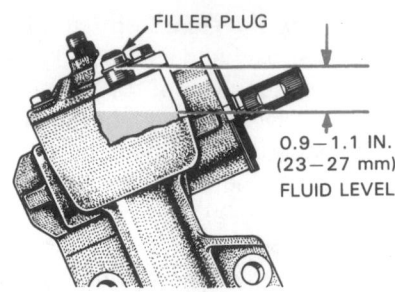

Figure 37-11. Maintain the steering gear lubricant at the manufacturer's specified level. (Toyota)

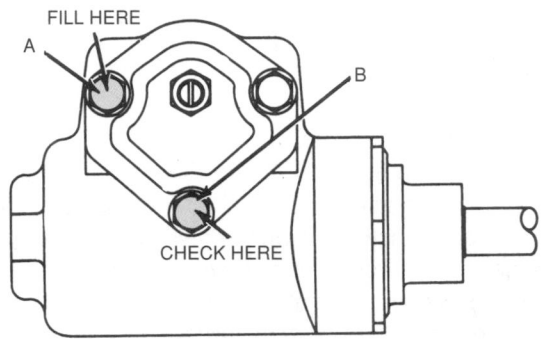

Figure 37-12. Remove the gear cover fasteners to check and adjust the lubricant level. (Chevrolet)

Worm Bearing Preload Adjustment

To make the **worm bearing preload** adjustment, remove the pitman arm from the shaft, which is discussed later in this chapter. Loosen the pitman shaft adjusting screw locknut. Back off the adjusting screw two or three turns. See **Figures 37-13** and **37-14.** Remove any steering system load on the worm gear by turning the steering wheel the specified number of turns away from the center position. Do not turn the steering wheel until it strikes the stops as this will damage the gearbox. Always turn the steering wheel slowly if the pitman arm is disconnected.

Use an inch-pound torque wrench to turn the steering wheel toward the center position, **Figure 37-15.** Note the reading when the steering wheel is moving the specified

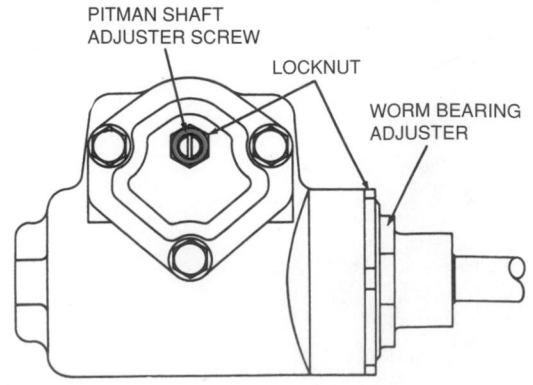

Figure 37-13. Loosen the locknut and unscrew the pitman shaft adjuster screw. (Chevrolet)

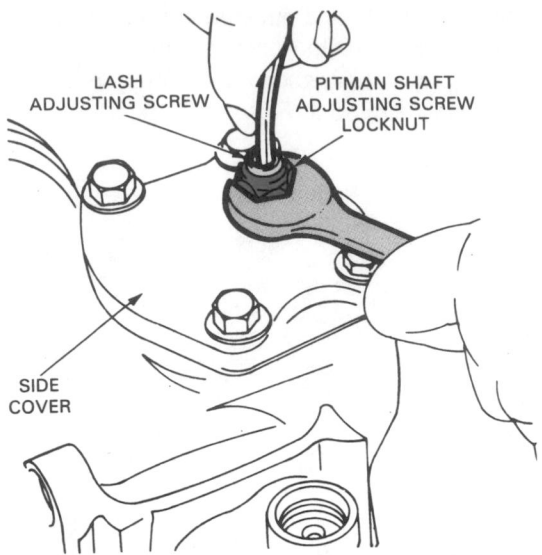

Figure 37-14. Turning the pitman shaft lash adjusting screw. Note: Some locknuts have left-hand threads. (Jeep)

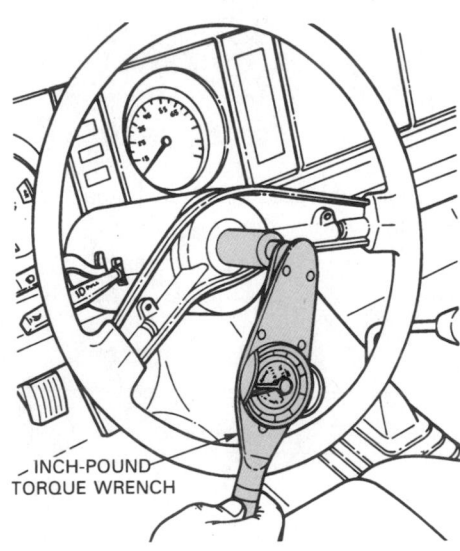

Figure 37-15. Using an inch-pound torque wrench to check worm shaft preload. Try to maintain a constant turning speed with the wrench for the most accurate reading. (Ford)

distance either side of center. Compare with factory specifications. If any adjustment is required, loosen the worm shaft bearing adjuster locknut. Turn bearing adjuster as required to produce the specified worm shaft bearing preload. Tighten the locknut securely and recheck turning torque, **Figure 37-16.** The wheel should turn freely from stop to stop without binding or roughness. If roughness is present, the worm bearings may be worn and must be replaced. When worm shaft bearing preload adjustment is complete, proceed with the over-center mesh adjustment.

Pitman Shaft Over-Center Adjustment

To make the **over-center adjustment**, which is the depth of gear mesh at the center of its travel, determine the

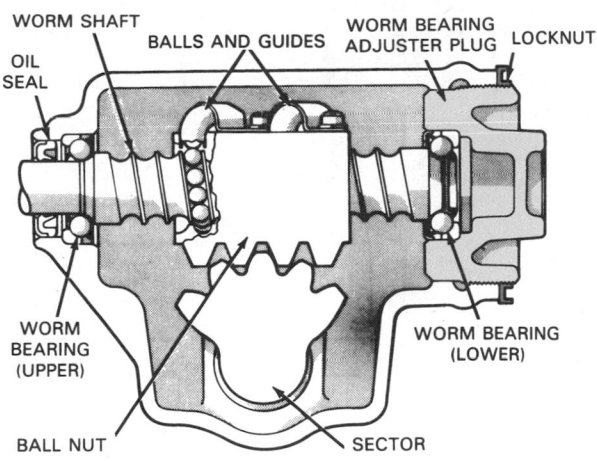

Figure 37-16. After loosening the locknut, the worm shaft bearing adjuster plug is turned until bearing preload is set to specs. (Chrysler)

exact center of the steering gearbox travel. Then turn the pitman shaft lash adjuster screw clockwise until all play is removed. Tighten adjuster screw locknut. Check the pull required to move the steering wheel through the center high point with an inch-pound torque wrench. To do this, first center the gear. Move the wheel an additional one-half turn to the left. Then pull the steering wheel one full turn to the right. Note the highest reading and compare with manufacturer's specifications.

Loosen the locknut and move the pitman shaft lash adjuster screw as required. Tighten the locknut securely and recheck over-center adjustment. The pull required represents the original worm preload plus the over-center load, **Figure 37-17.** Note how the clearance between the pitman shaft sector gear teeth and the ball nut teeth can be reduced by forcing the pitman shaft inward with the lash adjuster screw. The tapered ball nut teeth make this possible, **Figure 37-18.** Some manufacturers specify the use of a spring scale on the steering wheel in place of a torque wrench. If a scale is used, it must be accurate. Attach as shown in **Figure 37-19.** Pull on the scale. Keep it in line with the direction of wheel travel.

Manual Steering Gear Overhaul

Remove the pitman arm. Remove the worm shaft-to-steering shaft universal joint. Remove the housing-to-frame fasteners and remove the gearbox. Some cars require removal of the steering wheel or the entire steering column to facilitate gearbox removal. Clean the exterior of the housing thoroughly. Disassemble the gearbox according to manufacturer's instructions. Generally, the pitman shaft cover should be removed to gain access to the pitman shaft. After the pitman shaft is removed from the housing, remove the steering shaft and ball nut assembly. When withdrawing the worm shaft and ball nut assembly, hold it in a horizontal position.

Disassemble and clean the worm shaft and all other parts as detailed in the manufacturer's service manual. Inspect bearings, cups, and worm shaft bearing surfaces for

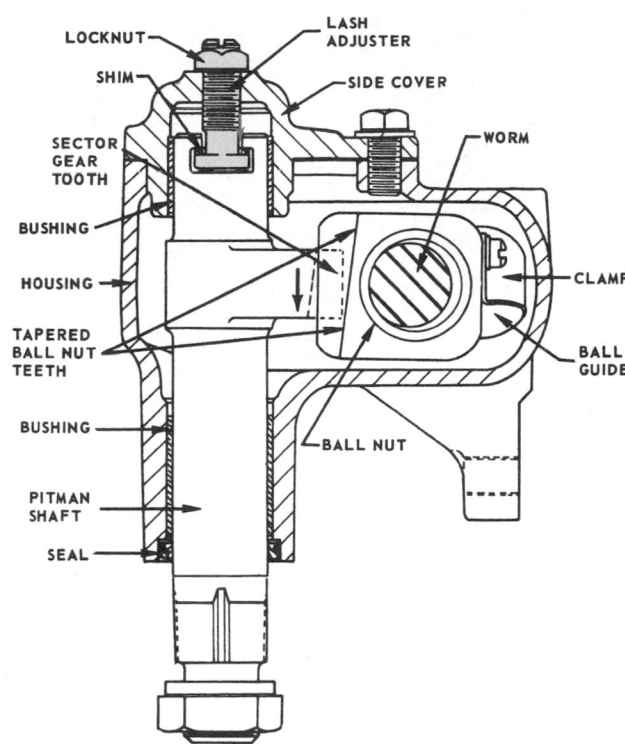

Figure 37-17. When the lash adjuster screw forces the pitman shaft inward, the pitman sector gear moves into closer mesh with the tapered ball nut teeth. (Buick)

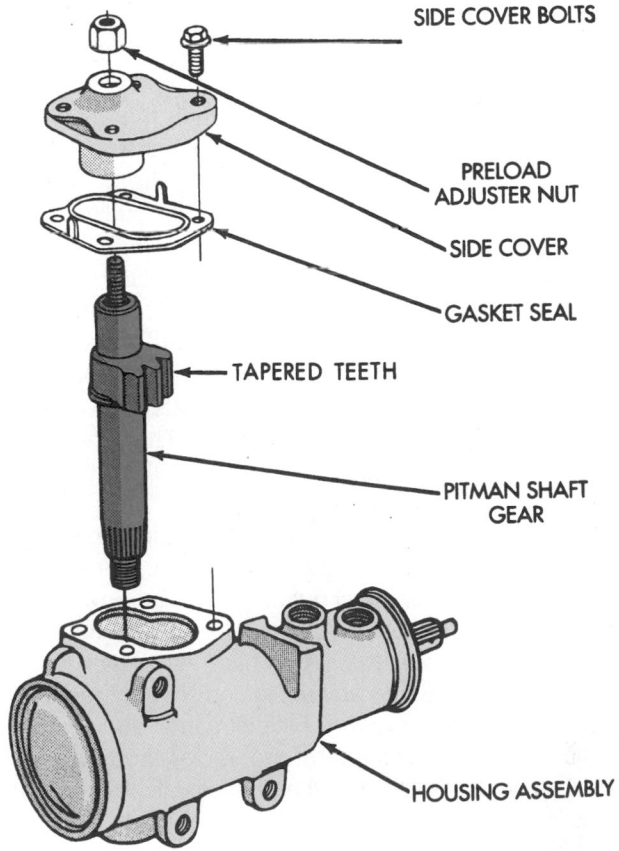

Figure 37-18. A pitman shaft gear with tapered teeth. (Dodge)

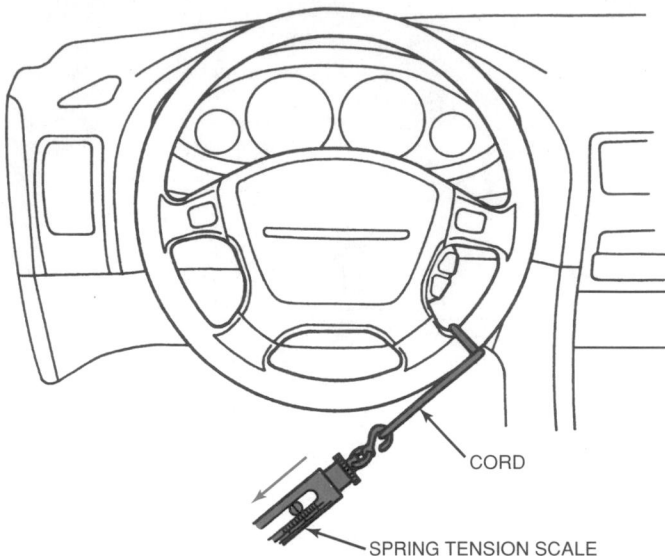

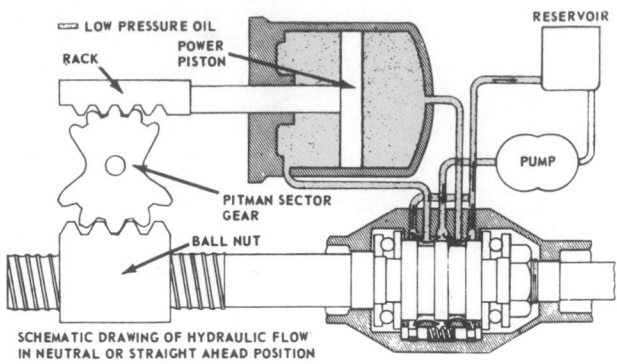

Figure 37-20. Offset type internal power steering gear. (Oldsmobile)

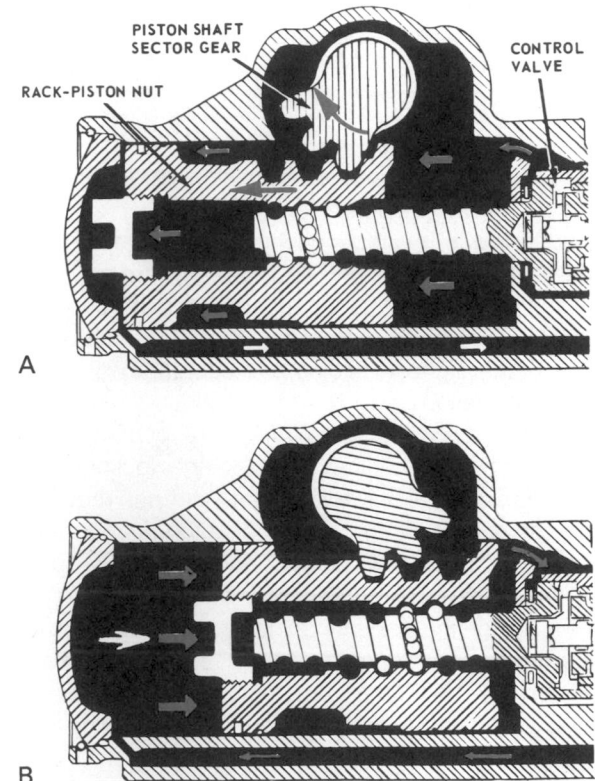

Figure 37-21. A—Action of an inline power steering gear during a left turn. B—Action of an inline power steering gear during a right turn.

Figure 37-19. Checking steering gear adjustment with an accurate spring tension gauge (scale).

pitting, galling, and wear. Check the worm shaft, sector teeth, ball nut, and ball nut bearing surfaces. Inspect the pitman shaft for wear, scoring, and galling. Replace parts as needed. Make sure that new gaskets and seals are used.

 Warning: The steering gear condition is very important to the safe operation of the steering system. Replace all parts showing signs of damage or noticeable wear.

Reassemble the internal parts of the gearbox. Install the ball nut onto the worm shaft so that when the assembly is placed in the gear housing, the deep side of the nut teeth will face the cover. Replace the worm gear in the gearbox and install the pitman shaft and cover. Readjust as outlined earlier.

Conventional Power Steering Service

The conventional power steering gear uses an integral *power cylinder*. The power cylinder is part of the steering gear and is geared to the pitman shaft. A *control valve* is also used in the housing. Internal power steering gears are of two general types, offset and inline. The offset power steering gear connects the power piston to the pitman shaft as illustrated in **Figure 37-20.**

The inline design, so named because the ball nut-power piston, worm shaft, and control valve are all in line, utilizes the recirculating ball nut as part of the power piston. The action of the inline type during a left turn is illustrated in **Figure 37-21A.** Note how the control valve has admitted fluid under pressure (red arrows) to one side of the rack-piston nut. This causes it to move the pitman shaft sector gear. The fluid being displaced by the rack-piston nut (white arrows) flows back through the control valve to the pump reservoir.

When the steering wheel is turned hard enough in the other direction to activate the control valve, fluid under pressure (red arrows) is admitted to the opposite side. This

forces the rack-piston nut to reverse the direction of the pitman shaft sector gear. See **Figure 37-21B.** The steering gear shown in **Figure 37-22** is of the inline type and utilizes a torsion bar operated spool valve. The rack-piston nut utilizes the recirculating ball principle for low friction operation. **Figure 37-23** illustrates another type of power steering gear.

Power Steering Gear Adjustments

The inline power steering gear has three basic adjustments, *thrust bearing preload, worm to rack-piston preload*, and *pitman shaft over-center preload*. These adjustments, unless specified otherwise, can be made while the gearbox is in the car. If disassembly is required, consult the manufacturer's service manual.

SECTOR
WORM SHAFT
PRESSURE
RETURN
SPOOL VALVE
PISTON
BALLS
HOUSING
TORSION BAR
INPUT SHAFT

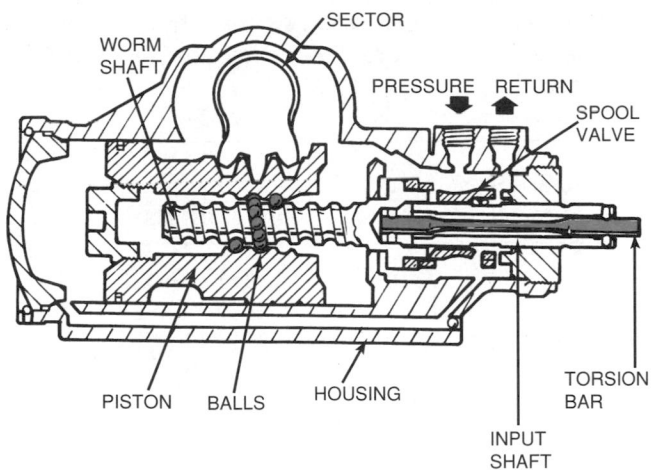

Figure 37-22. Cutaway of a typical inline, torsion-bar-operated, spool valve power steering gear. (Moog)

Thrust Bearing Preload

Thrust bearing preload may be checked with the gearbox in the car. Adjustment, however, requires removal in some instances. Remove the pitman arm and back off the pitman shaft lash adjuster if specified. Also, if required, disconnect the fluid return line from the pump reservoir and drain the gearbox by turning it from right to left several times. Turn the steering wheel to the extreme right or left and back the specified amount. Using a torque wrench or a spring scale, measure the pull required to move the steering wheel a specified distance. This will indicate the thrust bearing preload only. **Figure 37-24** shows how one power steering gear thrust bearing preload is adjusted. Turn gear stub shaft the specified amount from the center position. Loosen the pitman shaft lash adjuster screw. Attach an inch-pound torque wrench and turn the stub shaft through a specified arc. Tighten or loosen adjuster plug as needed to produce the correct preload.

SPANNER WRENCH
12- POINT SOCKET
TORQUE WRENCH

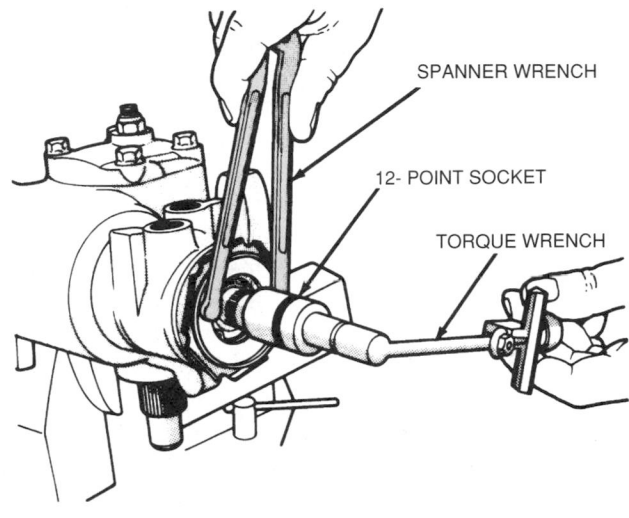

Figure 37-24. Using a spanner wrench to move the adjuster plug until the torque wrench indicates correct thrust bearing preload. (Chrysler)

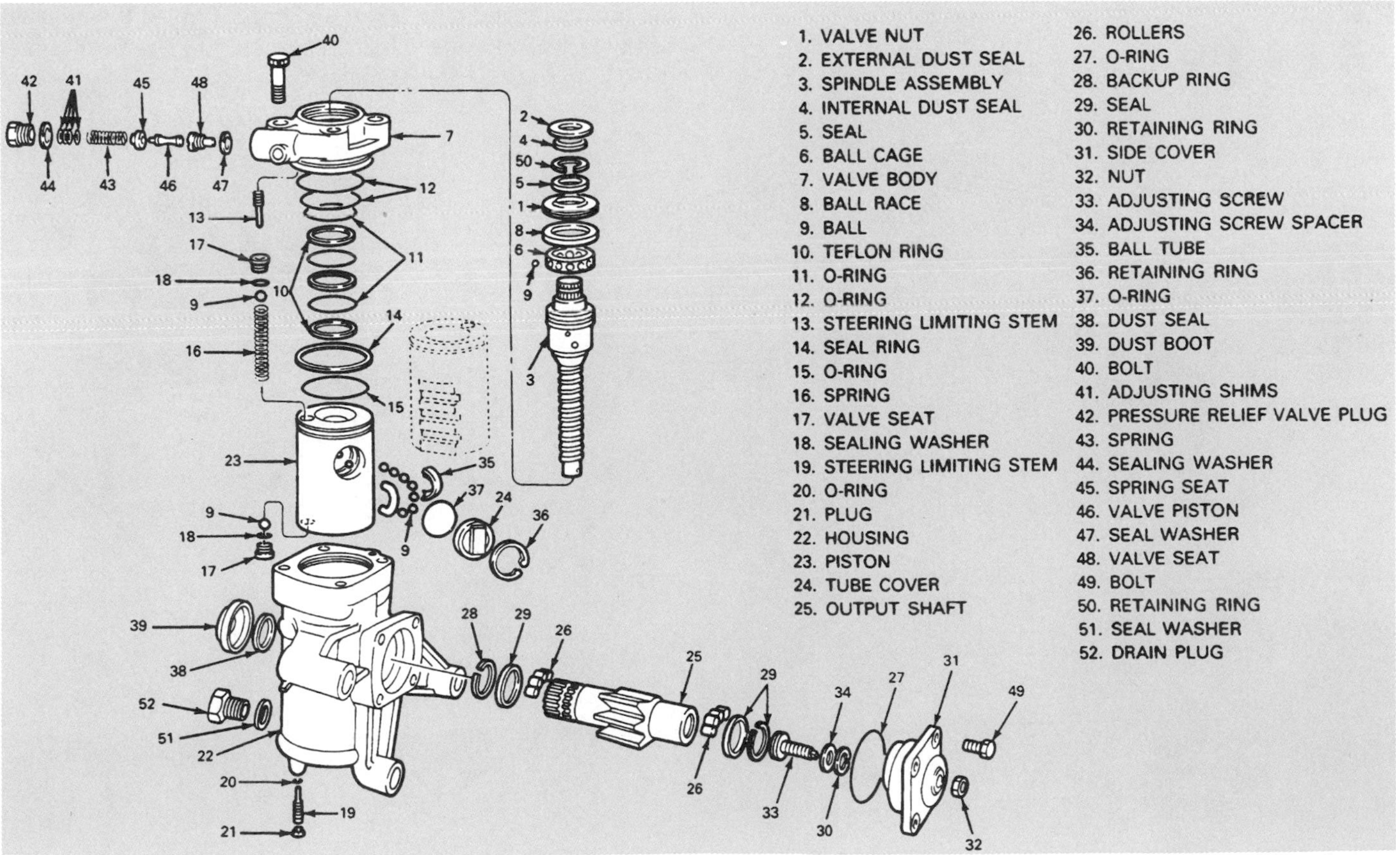

1. VALVE NUT
2. EXTERNAL DUST SEAL
3. SPINDLE ASSEMBLY
4. INTERNAL DUST SEAL
5. SEAL
6. BALL CAGE
7. VALVE BODY
8. BALL RACE
9. BALL
10. TEFLON RING
11. O-RING
12. O-RING
13. STEERING LIMITING STEM
14. SEAL RING
15. O-RING
16. SPRING
17. VALVE SEAT
18. SEALING WASHER
19. STEERING LIMITING STEM
20. O-RING
21. PLUG
22. HOUSING
23. PISTON
24. TUBE COVER
25. OUTPUT SHAFT
26. ROLLERS
27. O-RING
28. BACKUP RING
29. SEAL
30. RETAINING RING
31. SIDE COVER
32. NUT
33. ADJUSTING SCREW
34. ADJUSTING SCREW SPACER
35. BALL TUBE
36. RETAINING RING
37. O-RING
38. DUST SEAL
39. DUST BOOT
40. BOLT
41. ADJUSTING SHIMS
42. PRESSURE RELIEF VALVE PLUG
43. SPRING
44. SEALING WASHER
45. SPRING SEAT
46. VALVE PISTON
47. SEAL WASHER
48. VALVE SEAT
49. BOLT
50. RETAINING RING
51. SEAL WASHER
52. DRAIN PLUG

Figure 37-23. Exploded view of one type of internal piston power steering gear unit. (Ford)

Worm to Rack-Piston Preload

With the pitman arm removed and the pitman shaft lash adjuster loosened, move the steering wheel to a position about one-half turn from the center. Pull the wheel through a very short arc (about 1″ or 25.4 mm) and note the torque or scale reading. The reading should be slightly higher than the thrust bearing preload reading. The gearbox must be dismantled to adjust the worm rack-piston preload. You may want to consider overhauling the gearbox if an adjustment is needed. A general procedure for power steering gear overhaul is covered later in this chapter.

The worm groove is ground with a high point in the center. When the rack-piston passes this point, a mild preload is produced. With the steering gear disassembled, clamp the rack-piston lightly in a vise. Make sure to protect the rack-piston with jaw covers. With the valve assembly in place on the worm, rotate the worm until the required distance is obtained from the end of the rack-piston to the thrust bearing face. This locates the rack-piston on the high point of the worm.

With an inch-pound torque wrench, rotate the stub shaft in both directions covering an overall arc of about 60°. Note the torque reading in both directions. Average the two highest readings and compare your results with the manufacturer's specifications. Look at **Figure 37-25.** If the preload is lower than required, it may be brought to specifications by replacing the balls with the next larger size.

Service replacement ball sizes, as used by one manufacturer, are shown in **Figure 37-26.** Note the very small size differences.

Size Code	Mean Diameter	Size Range of Ball
6	.28117″	.28112″ – .28122″
7	.28125″	.28120″ – .28130″
8	.28133″	.28128″ – .28138″
9	.28141″	.28136″ – .28146″
10	.28149″	.28144″ – .28154″
11	.28157″	.28152″ – .28162″

Figure 37-26. Replacement ball size chart from one manufacturer.

Pitman Shaft Over-Center Preload

The pitman shaft over-center preload is perhaps the most critical as far as vehicle handling is concerned. This adjustment can usually be made with the steering gear in the vehicle. Center the steering gear. Using either a torque wrench or spring scale, measure the amount of pull required to move the wheel through the over-center position. Perform the test several times and average the readings. If the over-center preload must be adjusted, first center the steering gear. Move the pitman shaft lash adjuster screw until the torque reading is as specified when the gear is moved over about a 20° arc. Tighten the adjuster screw locknut. **Figure 37-27** illustrates how the over-center

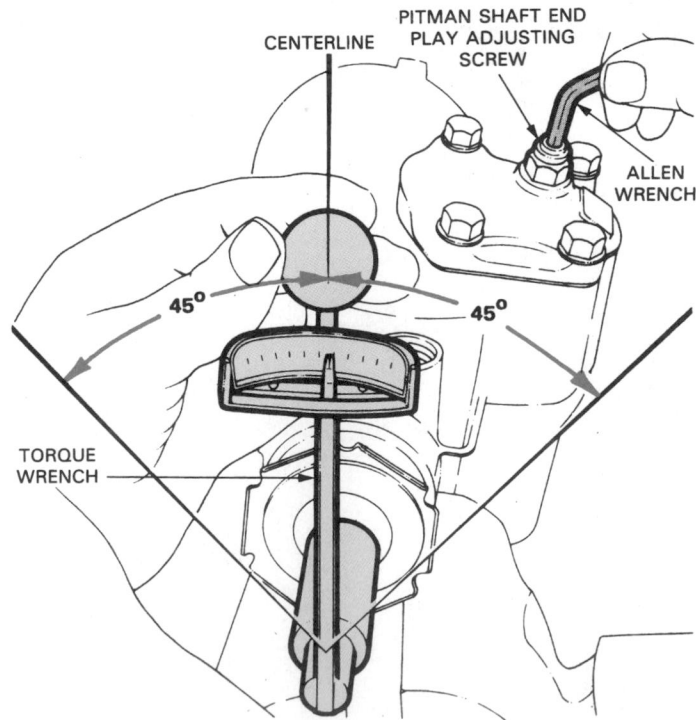

Figure 37-25. Checking worm-to-rack-piston preload with a torque wrench.

Figure 37-27. Using a torque wrench and an Allen wrench to properly adjust pitman shaft over-center preload. (Chrysler)

preload is adjusted on the bench. The procedure is basically the same when the gearbox is on the car. The pitman arm must be disconnected.

Power Steering Gear Overhaul

Begin the overhaul by disconnecting the pressure and return hoses from the steering gear. Elevate and cap the line fittings. Plug the housing openings. Remove the pitman arm and mark the pitman shaft and steering shaft coupling for correct reinstallation. Remove the coupling fastener and steering gear fasteners. Remove and drain the gearbox. Cycle the rack-piston by turning the stub shaft lock-to-lock several times. This will assist in draining the gearbox. Plug hose fitting openings. Clean the exterior of the gear thoroughly and disassemble it as needed. Clean and inspect all parts and replace where required. Install new seals, O-rings, gaskets, rack-piston ring, and other parts as needed. Complete rebuilding kits, such as illustrated in **Figure 37-28,** are available.

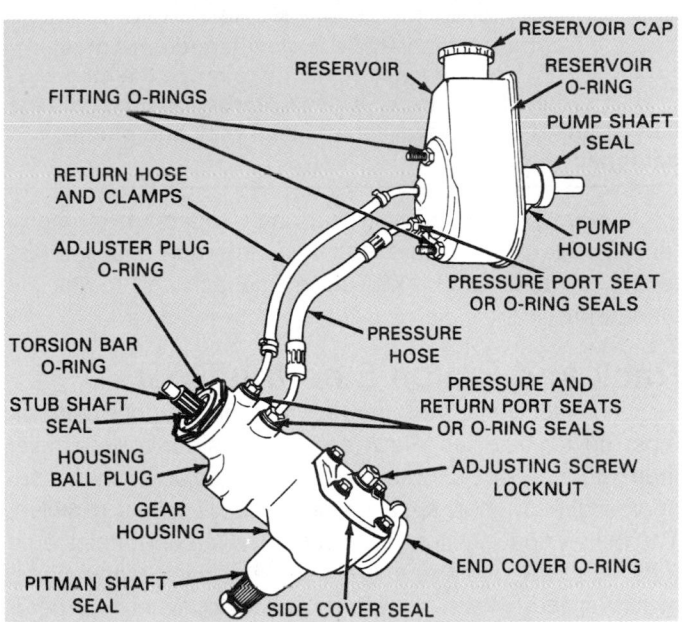

Figure 37-29. Possible power steering fluid leak points on the pump and gear. (Chrysler)

Figure 37-28. A power steering rebuild/service set. (McCord)

Assemble in reverse order of disassembly and make necessary adjustments. **Figure 37-29** shows typical power steering system leakage points. Clean all parts thoroughly and handle parts carefully to avoid nicking, burring, or distorting. Keep your work area, tools, and hands clean. Remember that dirt, even in very small amounts, can ruin the power steering gear, pump, control valve, power cylinder, and test instruments. Never strike or hammer the housings. Do not steam clean unless specified by the manufacturer.

Steering Gear Alignment

When reinstalling the steering gear, check for proper alignment with the steering shaft. Misalignment can cause bindings and premature wear. The steering gear, when in the exact center of travel, should be attached to the steering shaft. Make certain the steering wheel spokes are in the correct position. All alignment marks should be in line. **Figure 37-30** shows the alignment marks on one gear

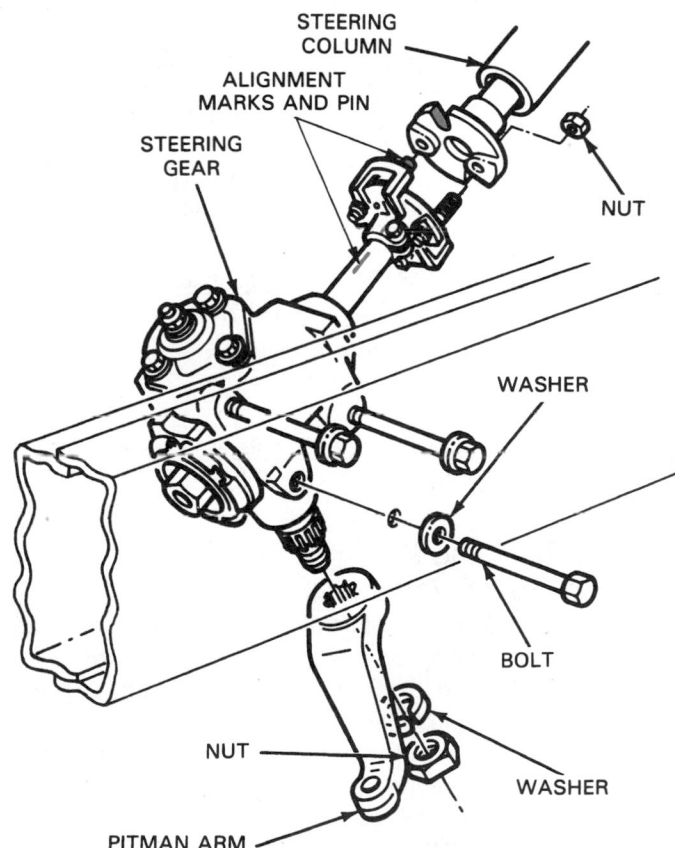

Figure 37-30. Be sure to align all witness (alignment) marks and pins when reassembling the steering gear shaft and coupling. (Ford)

installation. After proper gear housing alignment, the steering wheel should turn through its full travel smoothly without roughness or binding.

⚠ **Caution:** If the vehicle is elevated, do not grasp a front tire and twist it quickly to move the steering wheel to full lock. Severe steering column damage can occur. This is especially true with rack and pinion equipped vehicles.

Gear housing and steering shaft alignment is important. Check to make sure gear fasteners and coupling fasteners are torqued to specifications. Attach and torque the pitman arm.

Rack and Pinion Steering Gears

This section covers the rack and pinion gear used on most newer vehicles. Rack and pinion steering is simpler than other systems, with the steering column shaft connected directly to a *sector shaft*, usually called a pinion. The pinion operates the rack section, which operates the tie rods, and therefore the steering knuckles. Many parts, including the linkage system used with conventional gearboxes, are eliminated by this system. **Figure 37-31** shows a typical rack and pinion steering system.

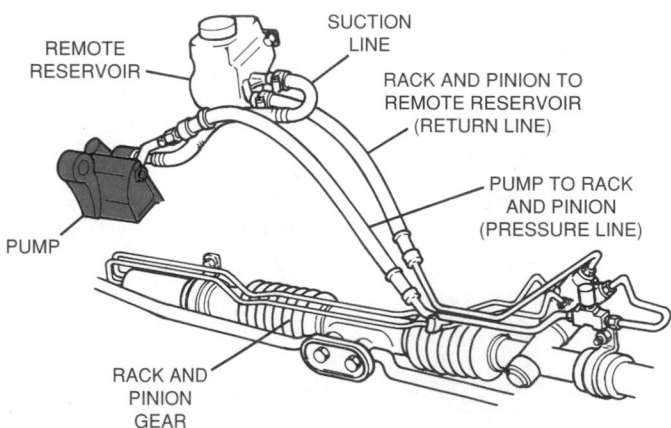

Figure 37-31. Power rack and pinion steering system. This pump uses a remote fluid reservoir. (Moog)

Manual Rack and Pinion Steering Gear Overhaul

Ideally, a rack and pinion steering gear should be replaced when leaking or malfunctioning. However, if an overhaul is preferred or desirable, begin by marking the location of the steering shaft coupling on the pinion shaft. Then remove the bolt securing the coupling to the shaft. Remove the tie rod ends. Unbolt the rack assembly from the frame cross member. On some vehicles, the rack is secured to the vehicle's body. Carefully remove the rack assembly from the vehicle. Do not catch and tear the rubber dust boots. Be sure to secure any shims. See **Figure 37-32.**

Mount the rack in a special holding fixture or gently grip with a vise. Obtain a reassembly toe setting by measuring from the center of the tie rod end to the boot retaining groove on both sides. Record these measurements; they will be used during reassembly. Next, remove the tie

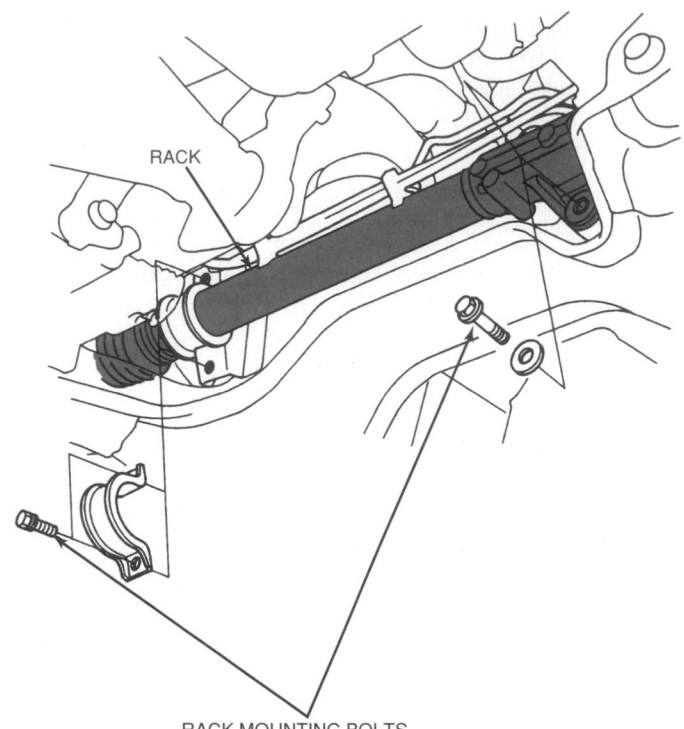

Figure 37-32. Removing the rack assembly from the vehicle. Use care to avoid part damage. Keep shims and other parts in the correct order. (Honda)

rods, dust boots, and clamps. Tie rod removal is explained later in this chapter. Some units will require new clamps as the old ones must be cut off. New boots should always be used. Depending upon the rack type, remove the retaining pin or the claw washer. See **Figure 37-33.**

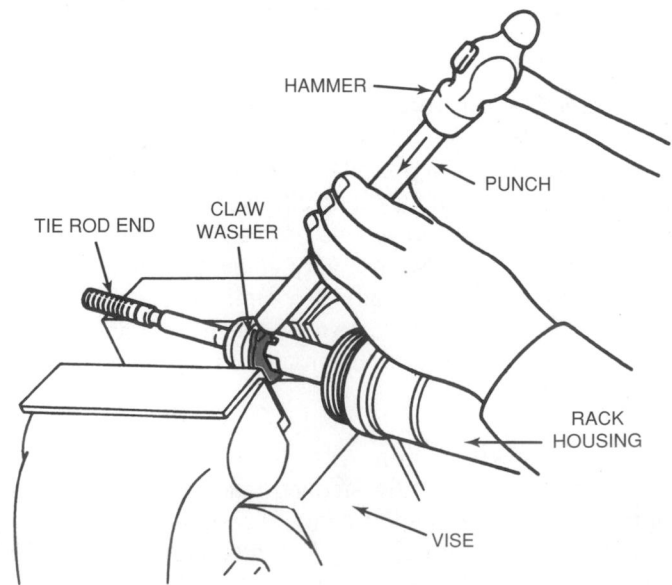

Figure 37-33. Unstaking a claw washer with a hammer and punch before attempting to remove the tie rod end. (Geo)

Caution: If the rack has worn or damaged threads, scoring in the housing bores (especially in aluminum housings), or more than two retaining pin holes in it, a new steering gear assembly must be installed.

Remove the steering gear locknut, adjuster plug, spring, and rack bearing guide. Take off dust cover. Unscrew pinion bearing cap and remove pinion shaft locknut, snap ring, and pinion. Disconnect any remaining fasteners and pull the rack from its housing. Thoroughly clean all metal parts in solvent. Check for wear, cracks, scoring, missing teeth, and damaged seals. An exploded view of a rack and pinion assembly is illustrated in **Figure 37-34.** Reassembly is basically a reversal of disassembly procedures. Follow manufacturer's recommendations for the unit being serviced.

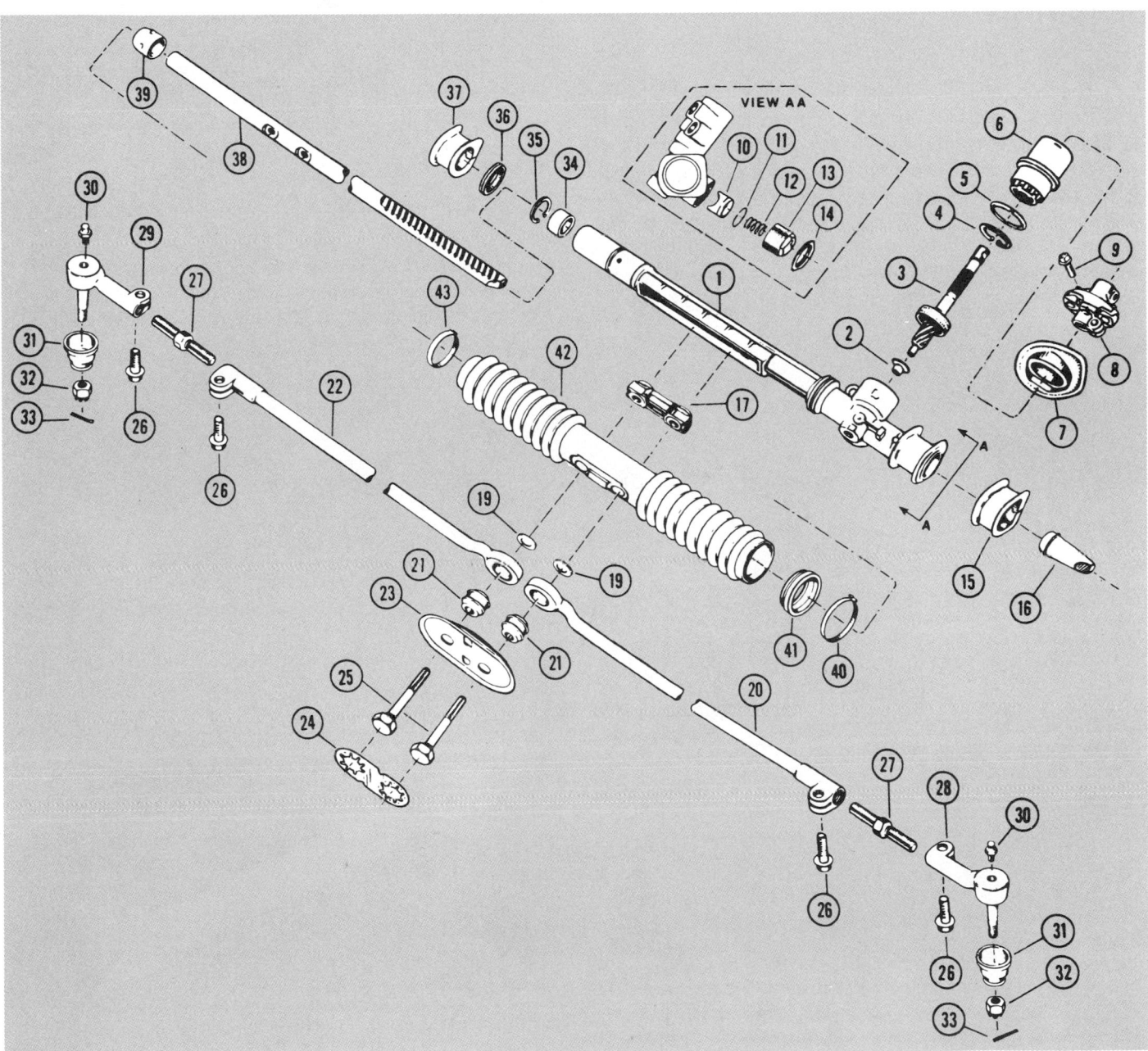

Figure 37-34.   An exploded view of a rack and pinion assembly. 1—Rack and pinion housing. 2—Roller bearing assembly. 3—Bearing and pinion assembly. 4—Retaining ring. 5—Dust seal. 6—Damper assembly. 7—Dash seal. 8—Steering coupling assembly. 9—Pinch bolt. 10—Bearing. 11—O-ring seal. 12—Spring. 13—Adjuster plug. 14—Lock nut. 15—Mounting grommet. 16—Housing end cover. 17—Rack guide. 19—Washer. 20—Inner tie rod. 21—Inner pivot bushing. 22—Inner tie rod. 23—Bolt support plate. 24—Lock plate. 25—Inner tie rod bolt. 26—Bolt. 27—Tie rod adjuster. 28—Outer tie rod assembly. 29—Outer tie rod assembly. 30—Lubrication fitting. 31—Tie rod seal. 32—Hex nut. 33—Cotter pin. 36—Retaining bushing. 37—Mounting grommet. 38—Steering rack. 39—Housing end cover. 40—Boot clamp. 41—Retaining bushing. 42—Rack and pinion boot. 43—Boot clamp. (Saginaw Division of GM)

Torque all fasteners to specifications and double-check all connections.

Rack and Pinion Power Steering

The power rack and pinion system uses a rotary control valve to regulate the fluid coming from the pump. It routes the fluid to the appropriate side of the rack piston, **Figure 37-35.** The piston converts hydraulic pressure to a linear movement. This movement is transmitted to the steering arms by the tie rods.

Control Valves

The control valve directs the flow of power steering fluid from one side of the rack piston to the other, **Figure 37-36.** As the steering wheel is turned, the resistance created by the vehicle's front tires causes the valve's torsion rod to twist. The twisting action causes a difference in the degree of rotation between the valve and the spool. As this occurs, the passages in the control valve change. Fluid can no longer flow directly through the valve and back into the reservoir. Instead, it must pass through the passages of the power cylinder.

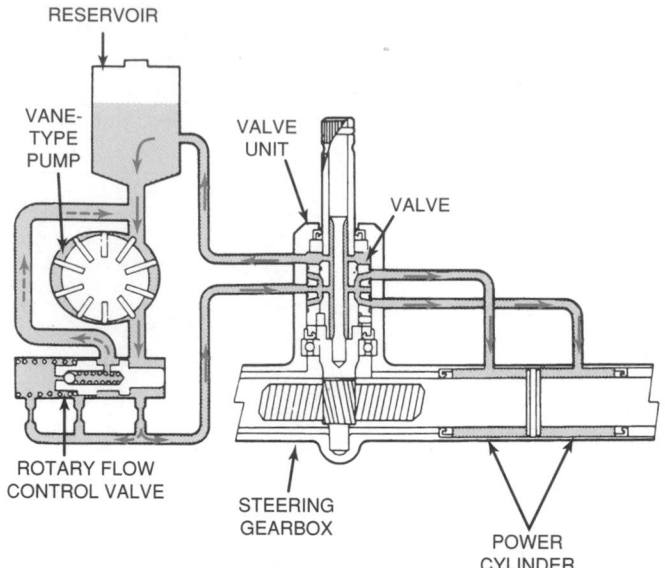

Figure 37-35. Cutaway view of a power rack and pinion steering system. Note the rotary flow control valve, which regulates the fluid traveling from the pump. (Honda)

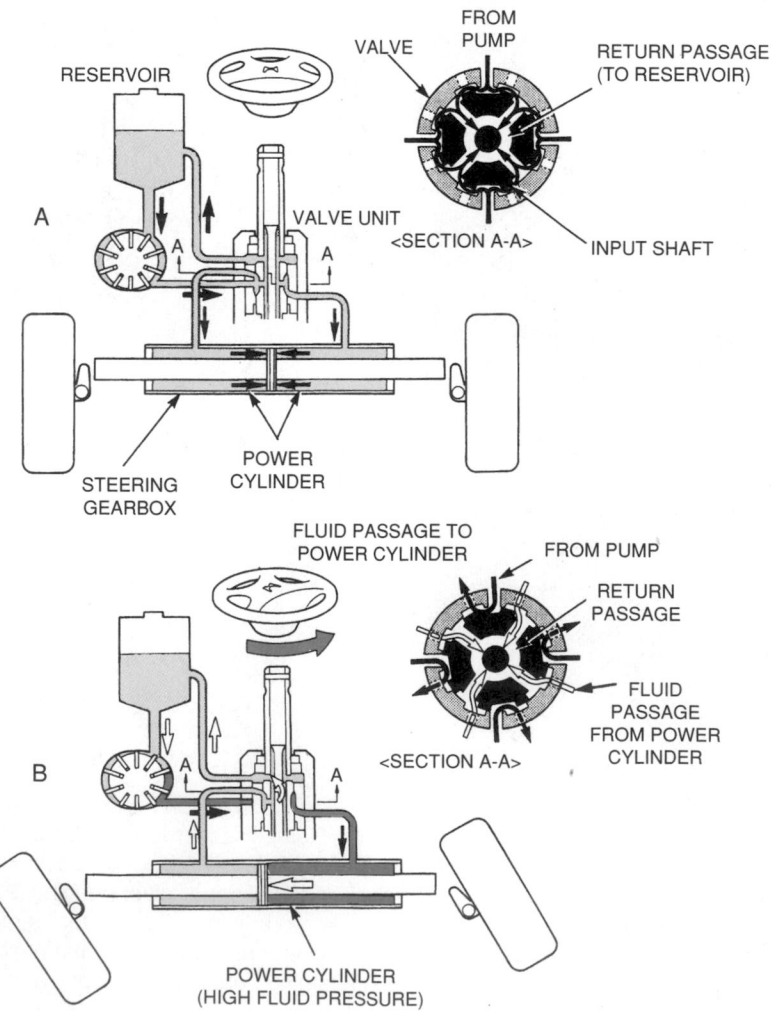

Figure 37-36. Control valve operation. A—Steering straight ahead. B—Turning left. (Honda)

For a right turn, a circuit is opened that allows the fluid to be pumped through the spool's top radial groove and into the right side of the power cylinder. At the same time, fluid is discharged from the left side of the power cylinder by the spool's bottom radial groove. This fluid flows back into the valve chamber above the spool and is routed into the reservoir. The opposite circuit is opened for a left turn. As long as the torsion rod is twisted, hydraulic pressure will act on the rack. The amount of force on the rod will be reduced when the fluid acts on the rack. This reinforces the action of the pinion. The moment the force on the torsion rod is released, the valve's return passage is opened and the fluid will flow directly back into the reservoir.

Power Cylinder

The power cylinder is an integral part of the rack housing, **Figure 37-37.** There are two power steering fluid lines that run between the cylinder and the control valve. The lines are connected on the left and right side of the piston. When turning right, fluid is pumped to the right side of the power cylinder, forcing the piston and rack to the left. The fluid is then discharged from the left section of the power cylinder. Simultaneously, the boot on the left side is distended and the boot on the right side is compressed. This causes air to flow through a capillary tube between the boots, keeping the air pressure constant.

Movement of the rack is transferred to the steering members by the tie rods. When an overhaul of the power rack and pinion system is necessary, follow all of the manufacturer's recommendations carefully. Disassembly procedures are similar to those for manual rack and pinion systems. Remember, steering is critical. Perform only top-notch work.

Power Steering Pumps

Power steering systems utilize fluid under pressure to provide most of the turning force to the front wheels. These systems assist both front and rear wheels on vehicles equipped with four-wheel steering. All units use a pump to provide hydraulic pressure to the control valve.

Power steering pumps, **Figures 37-38** to **37-43,** usually are **vane**, **slipper**, or **roller** types. All use a ring with a

cam-shaped inner opening. A rotor turns inside the cam ring. The rotor may employ vanes to form a seal between the rotor and cam. **Figure 37-38** illustrates a typical vane-type

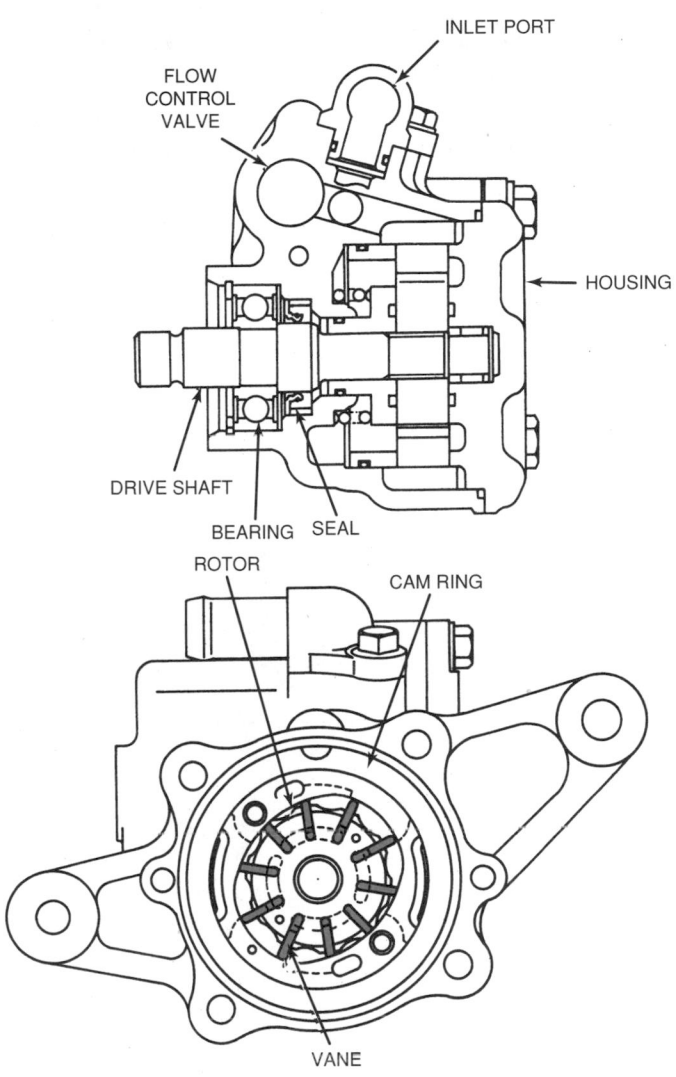

Figure 37-38. A belt-driven, vane-type power steering pump. Note that this pump uses ten vanes to help smooth fluid pulsations. (Honda)

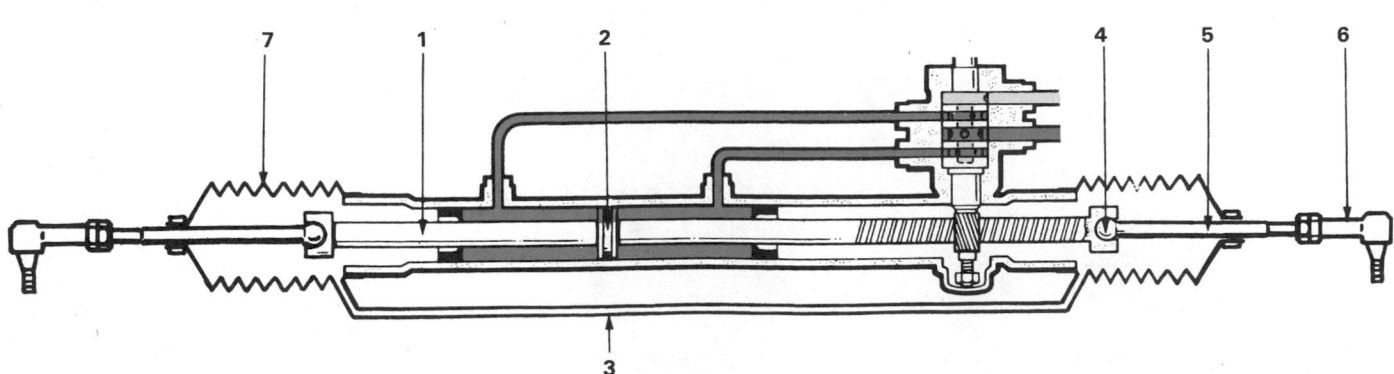

Figure 37-37. A power cylinder cutaway. 1—Rack. 2—Piston. 3—Pressure-equalizing tube. 4—Inner ball joint. 5—Tie rod. 6—Tie rod joint. 7—Boot. (SAAB)

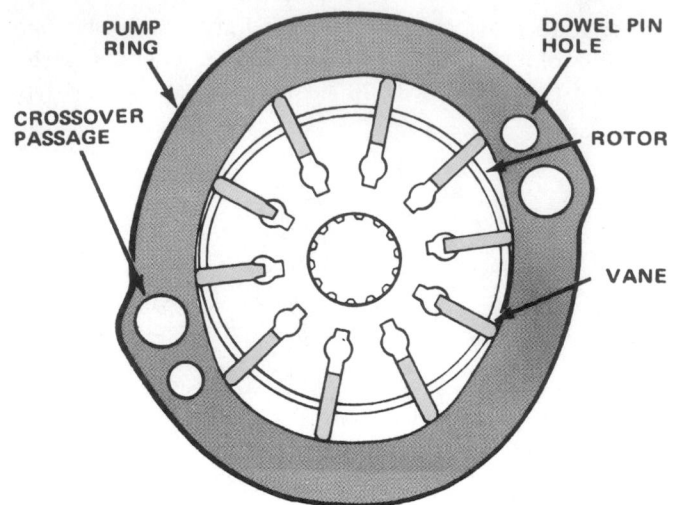

Figure 37-39. Vane-type power steering pump. Note the relationship of the rotor and vanes to the pump ring. (Chrysler)

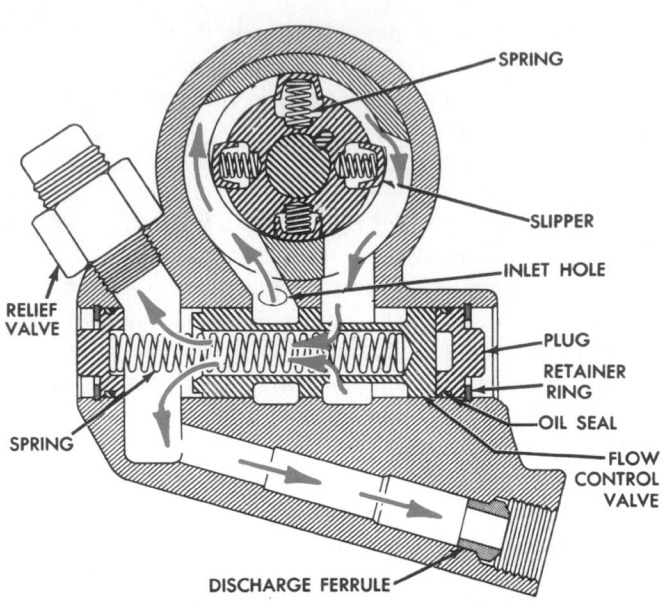

Figure 37-41. Slipper-type power steering pump. (Dodge)

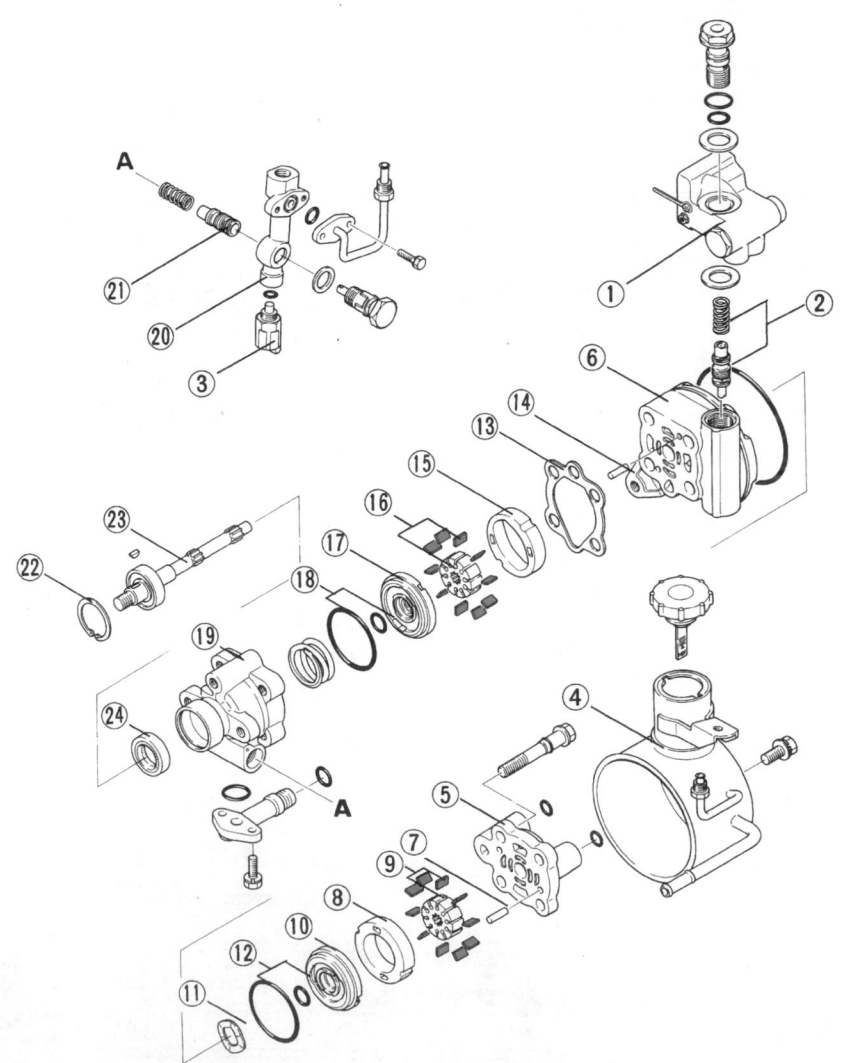

Figure 37-40. An exploded view of a power steering pump. 1—Top pump housing. 2—Flow control valve. 3—Pressure sensor. 4—Reservoir housing. 5—Rear pump housing. 6—Main pump housing. 7—Dowel pin. 8—Pump rotor. 9—Rotor housing and vanes. 10—Pressure plate. 11—Pressure plate spring. 12—Seal. 13—Gasket. 14—Bracket. 15—Pump rotor. 16—Rotor housing and vanes. 17—Pressure plate. 18—Seal. 19—Forward pump housing. 20—Pressure sensor housing. 21—Pressure control valve. 22—Snap ring. 23—Drive shaft. 24—Drive shaft seal. (Mazda)

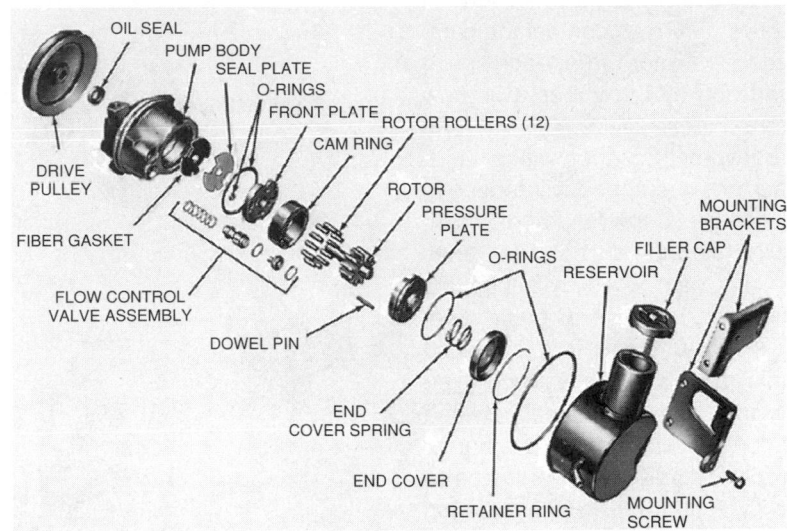

Figure 37-42.   Exploded view of a roller-type power steering pump. Note the location of the rotor rollers. (Chrysler)

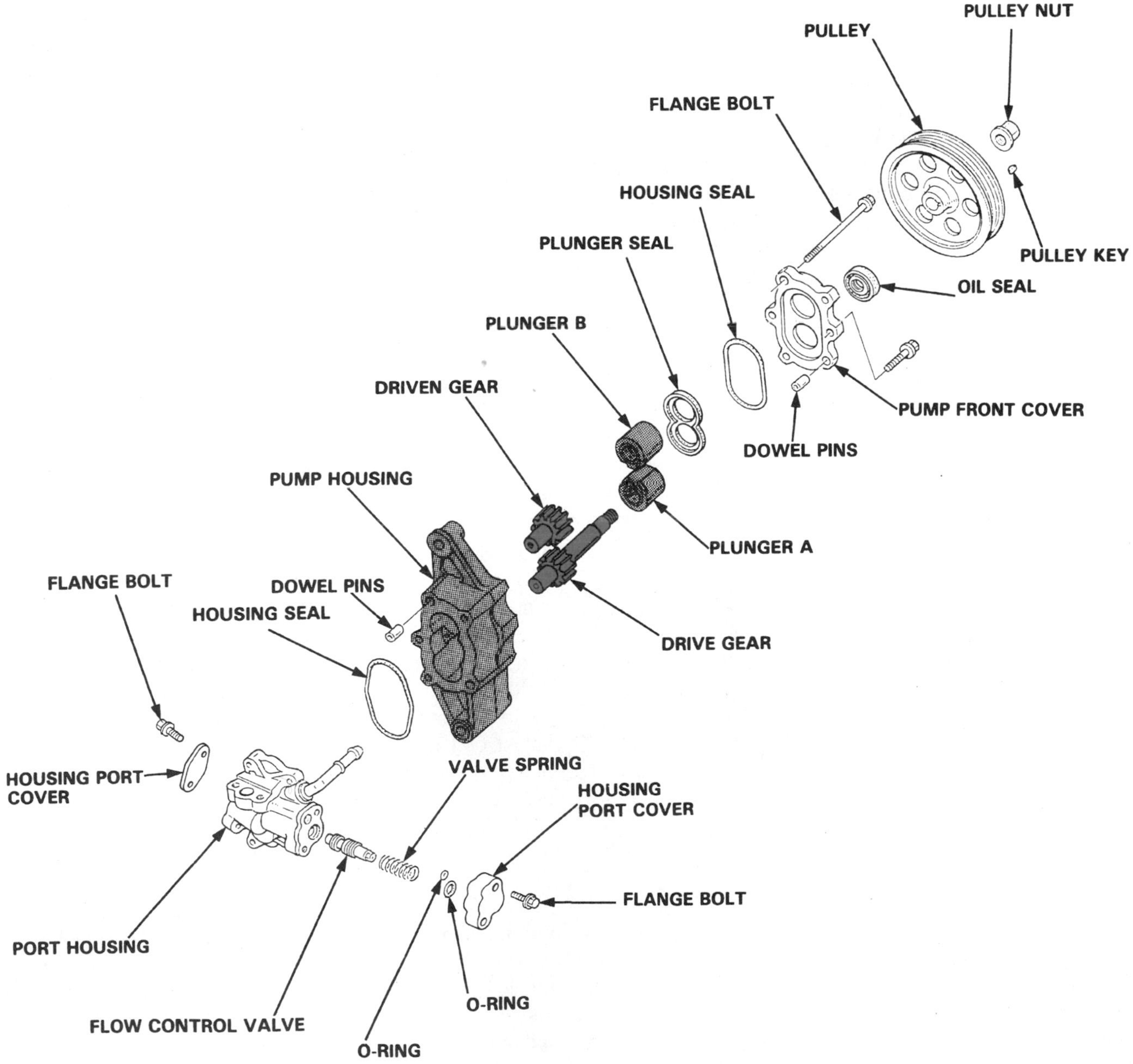

Figure 37-43.   Exploded view of a gear-type power steering pump assembly. (Honda)

power steering pump. Note how the vanes contact the cam-shaped pump ring inside. When the rotor turns, each space formed between the rotor and ring by the vanes, will grow from a small size to a large size, **Figure 37-39.** This will form a vacuum and fill the space between the vanes with oil.

As the rotor continues to turn, the space will reduce in size, **Figure 37-39.** This will compress the fluid and force it through the outlet of the power steering pump. The vanes are kept in contact with the ring cam walls by centrifugal force and by fluid pressure fed to the base of each vane. The pump design in **Figure 37-40** gives it a balanced pumping action. The pump in **Figure 37-41** is a slipper-type pump. It uses spring-loaded slippers to form a seal between the rotor and ring. Note the flow of fluid through the pump. The roller pump utilizes a series of rollers in preference to vanes or slippers, **Figure 37-42.** A gear-type power steering pump is illustrated in **Figure 37-43.**

Power Steering Pump Belt

Most installations utilize one or two V-belts or a serpentine belt to drive the power steering pump. The belt or belts can operate from the engine crankshaft pulley. See **Figure 37-44. Figure 37-45** illustrates a typical power steering arrangement that employs a single belt drive. Note that the fluid reservoir is separate from the pump on this setup. Carefully inspect power steering belts for glazing, rotting, cracking, or swelling and replace as needed. If excessive belt squeal occurs during sharp turning of the front wheels, the belt is probably loose and should be adjusted. Adjustment may be checked by using a belt tension gauge. Replace or adjust belt as needed.

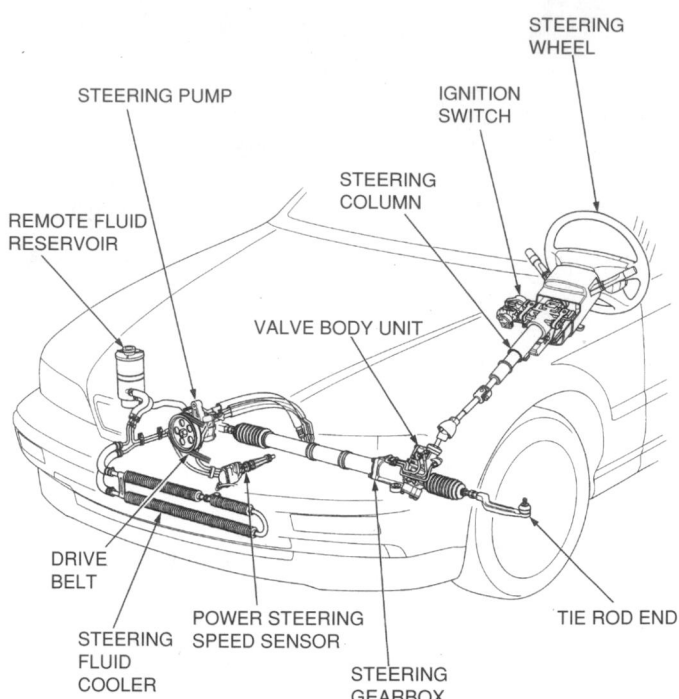

Figure 37-45. Overall power rack and pinion steering setup that uses a belt-driven pump and a remote fluid reservoir. (Honda)

Power Steering Service

If a vehicle does not use a serpentine belt with an automatic self-adjuster, belt tension may be checked using a torque wrench, belt deflection, or a strand tension gauge. The torque wrench method calls for adjusting the belt tension until a certain torque is required to turn the power steering pump pulley. The belt deflection method requires pressing inward on a certain spot and measuring the resulting amount of belt deflection. The strand tension gauge is the most accurate method of testing belt tension. The instrument is slipped around the belt and the pump moved in or out until the tension gauge reads as specified.

If the belt needs adjustment, loosen the pump attaching fasteners. Move the pump outward as needed and tighten fasteners. Be careful when prying on pumps to adjust belt tension. Pry only on the heavy section. If the pump is equipped with a special wrench tab, use it. Never pry on the reservoir or filler neck. Some pumps are equipped with an adjusting bolt, which eliminates the need to pry on the pump body, **Figure 37-46.**

To replace the belt or belts, loosen fasteners. Rotate pump inward to slack and remove belts. Install new belts and tension as specified. See **Figure 37-47.** New belts are tightened somewhat more than used belts to compensate for initial stretching and seating. When removing and installing belts, disconnect the battery ground terminal to prevent injury.

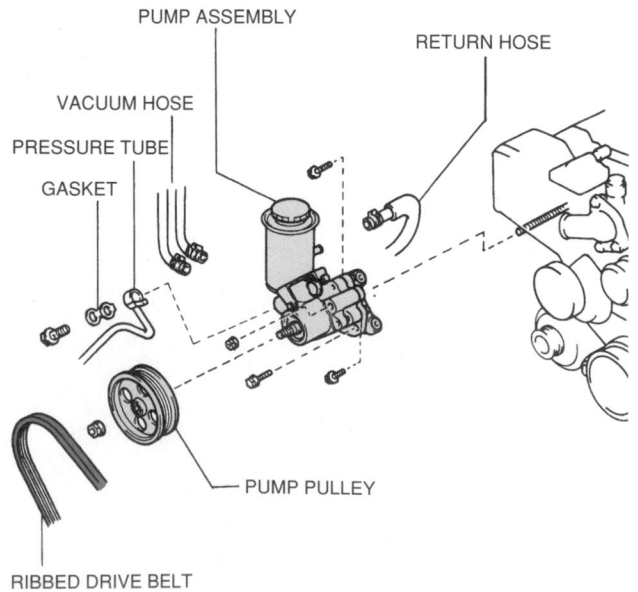

Figure 37-44. Most power steering pumps are belt driven. (Toyota)

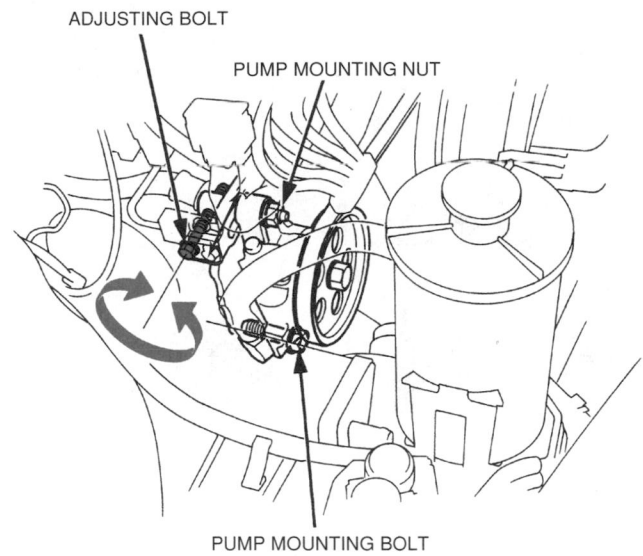

Figure 37-46. Adjusting power steering pump belt tension with an adjusting bolt setup that is an integral part of the pump housing. (Honda)

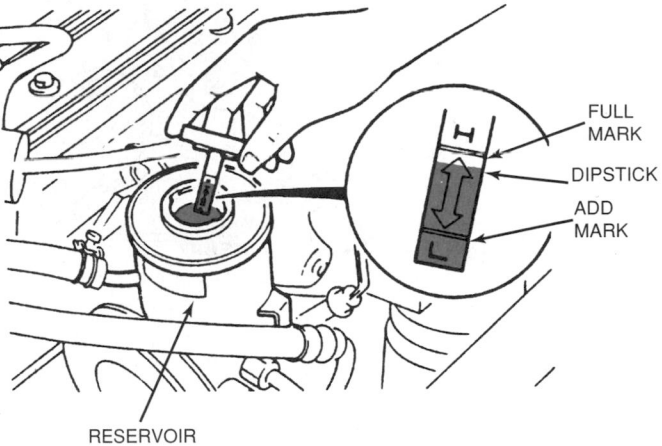

Figure 37-48. Keep the power steering pump filled to the proper level. In this system, a dipstick is used to check fluid level. (Mazda)

Power Steering Fluid Level

Check the *fluid level* in the power steering pump reservoir. Fluid should be between add and full marks. Check with fluid at operating temperature. The reservoir illustrated in **Figure 37-48** has a dipstick to make checking easy. Clean top before removal to prevent dirt entry into reservoir. If the fluid level is low, inspect entire system for leaks. See **Figures 37-49** and **37-50**. If fluid must be added, always use power steering fluid intended for the system being worked on. Modern vehicles are designed to use special power steering fluid, not automatic transmission fluid. Always check manufacturer's specifications.

Power Steering System Pressure Test

By conducting a power steering system *pressure test*, problems can be easily identified as to origin. Pressure problems may be found in the pump itself or in the hose or gear system. There are three major precautions for making an accurate pressure test, proper test connections, correct engine RPM, and specified fluid temperature. Before conducting a pressure test, belt tension must be checked. If needed, adjust the belts. Fluid level must be as specified.

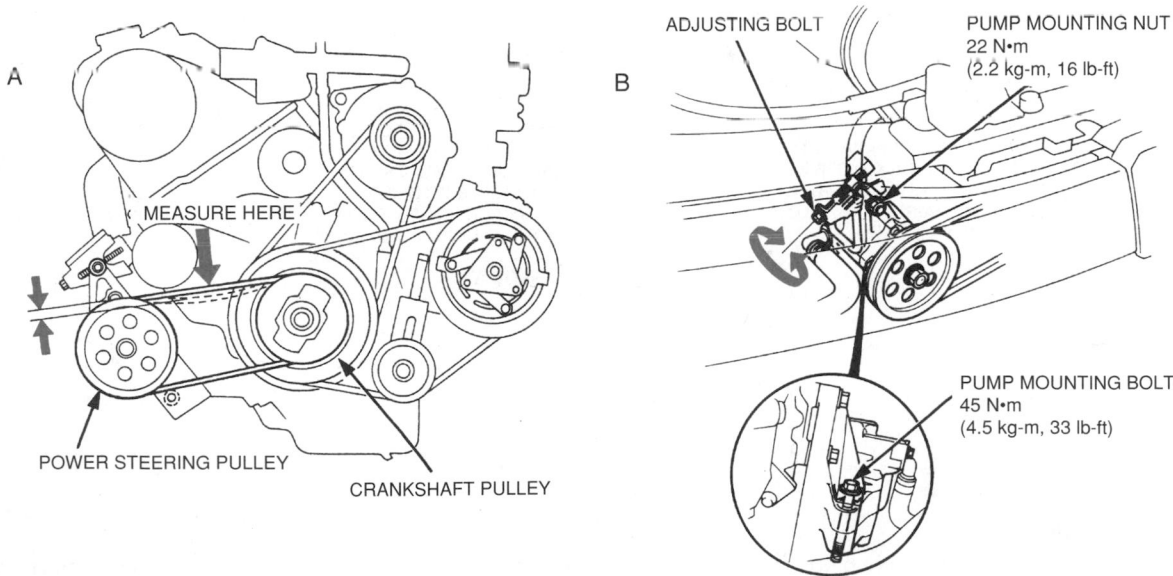

Figure 37-47. A—New power steering belt has been installed. B—Belt tension is adjusted by turning the power steering pump adjusting bolt. Follow the manufacturer's recommendations for the correct tension. Too much tension can damage the pump bearings. Too little tension will cause belt slippage and poor overall pump output. (Honda)

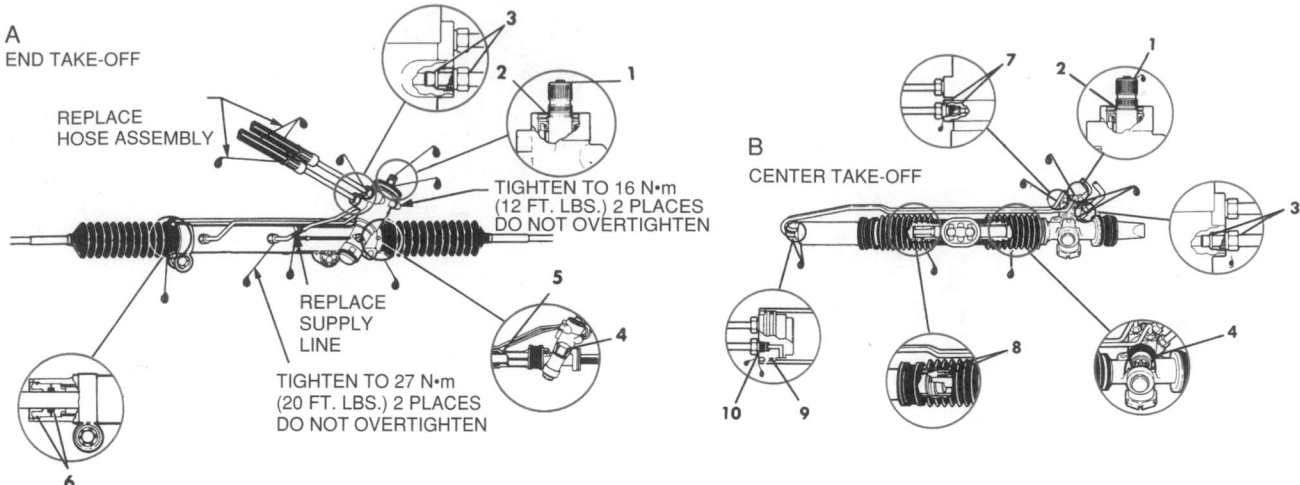

Figure 37-49.   Rack and pinion system leakage points on end take-off (A) and center take-off (B) types. 1—Seepage between the torsion bar and stub shaft. 2—Replace the dust and shaft seals. 3—Torque fittings. 4—Replace the pinion shaft seal. 5—Replace the inner rack seal. 6—Replace the O-ring and lip seal. 7—Torque fittings, replace O-rings, repair threads, or replace the housing. 8—Replace the piston rod guide seal and the O-ring seal. 9—Replace the O-ring seal. 10—Torque the cylinder fittings, replace the O-ring seal, repair the threads, or replace the bulkhead. (Saginaw Division of GM)

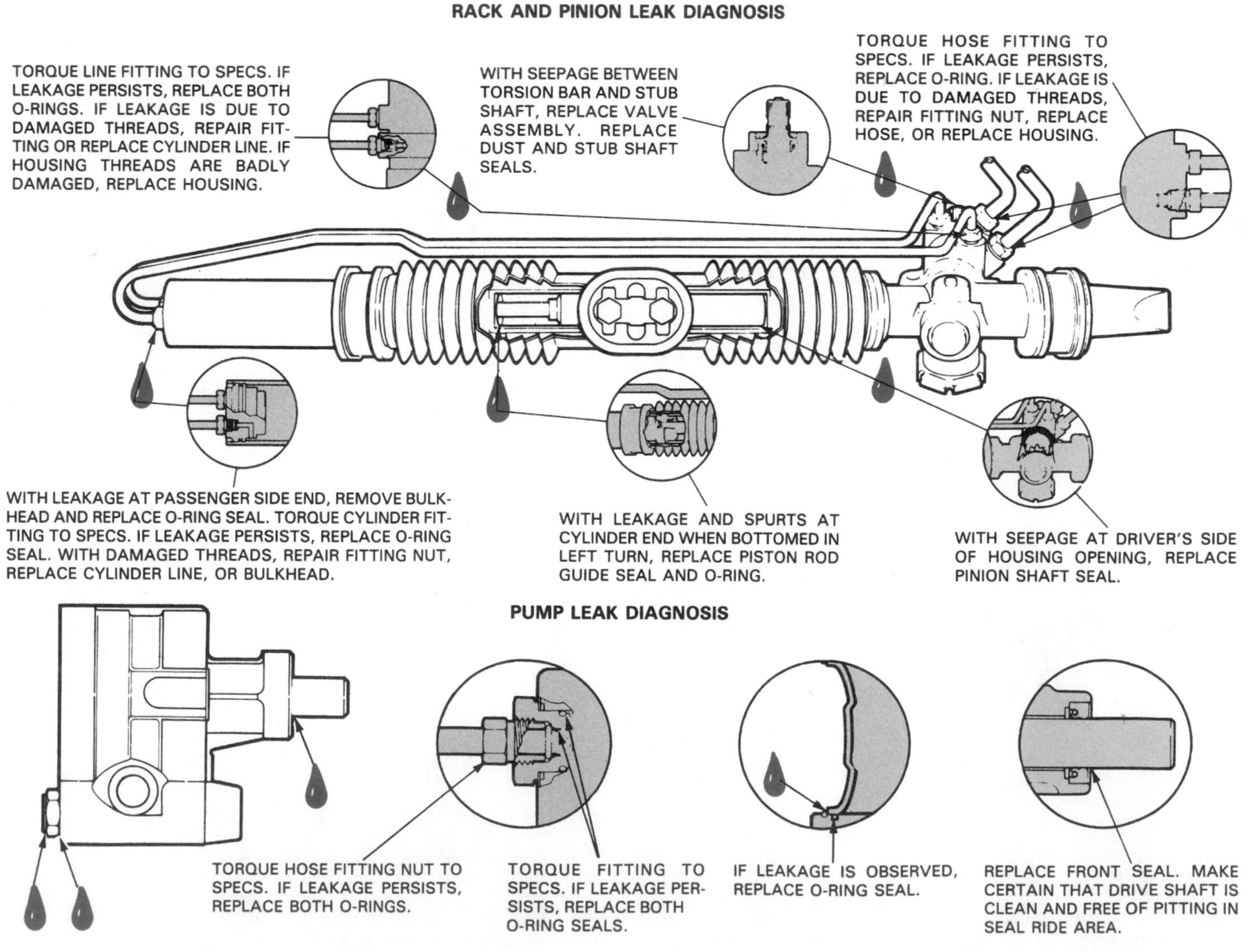

RACK AND PINION LEAK DIAGNOSIS

TORQUE LINE FITTING TO SPECS. IF LEAKAGE PERSISTS, REPLACE BOTH O-RINGS. IF LEAKAGE IS DUE TO DAMAGED THREADS, REPAIR FITTING OR REPLACE CYLINDER LINE. IF HOUSING THREADS ARE BADLY DAMAGED, REPLACE HOUSING.

WITH SEEPAGE BETWEEN TORSION BAR AND STUB SHAFT, REPLACE VALVE ASSEMBLY.   REPLACE DUST AND STUB SHAFT SEALS.

TORQUE HOSE FITTING TO SPECS. IF LEAKAGE PERSISTS, REPLACE O-RING. IF LEAKAGE IS DUE TO DAMAGED THREADS, REPAIR FITTING NUT, REPLACE HOSE, OR REPLACE HOUSING.

WITH LEAKAGE AT PASSENGER SIDE END, REMOVE BULK-HEAD AND REPLACE O-RING SEAL. TORQUE CYLINDER FIT-TING TO SPECS. IF LEAKAGE PERSISTS, REPLACE O-RING SEAL. WITH DAMAGED THREADS, REPAIR FITTING NUT, REPLACE CYLINDER LINE, OR BULKHEAD.

WITH LEAKAGE AND SPURTS AT CYLINDER END WHEN BOTTOMED IN LEFT TURN, REPLACE PISTON ROD GUIDE SEAL AND O-RING.

WITH SEEPAGE AT DRIVER'S SIDE OF HOUSING OPENING, REPLACE PINION SHAFT SEAL.

PUMP LEAK DIAGNOSIS

TORQUE HOSE FITTING NUT TO SPECS. IF LEAKAGE PERSISTS, REPLACE BOTH O-RINGS.

TORQUE FITTING TO SPECS. IF LEAKAGE PER-SISTS, REPLACE BOTH O-RING SEALS.

IF LEAKAGE IS OBSERVED, REPLACE O-RING SEAL.

REPLACE FRONT SEAL. MAKE CERTAIN THAT DRIVE SHAFT IS CLEAN AND FREE OF PITTING IN SEAL RIDE AREA.

Figure 37-50.   Rack and pinion and pump leak diagnosis for one particular manufacturer. Note the recommended correction with each leak area. (Buick)

Remove the high pressure outlet hose from the pump. Insert a 0-2000 psi (0-13,790 kPa) gauge and shutoff valve between the disconnected hose and the pump outlet. The gauge must be between the shutoff valve and the pump, **Figure 37-51.** Torque the fittings and open the gauge fully. If the manufacturer's specifications call for an exact RPM and fluid temperature, install a thermometer in the pump reservoir and connect a tachometer, **Figure 37-52.** Bleed the system by starting the engine and turning the steering wheel from full right to left and back several times. Check fluid level and add if needed. Operate the engine until fluid temperature reaches indicated level. The shutoff valve must be open. Raise the engine RPM to factory test specifications and note system pressure with the valve open (wheels in straight ahead position).

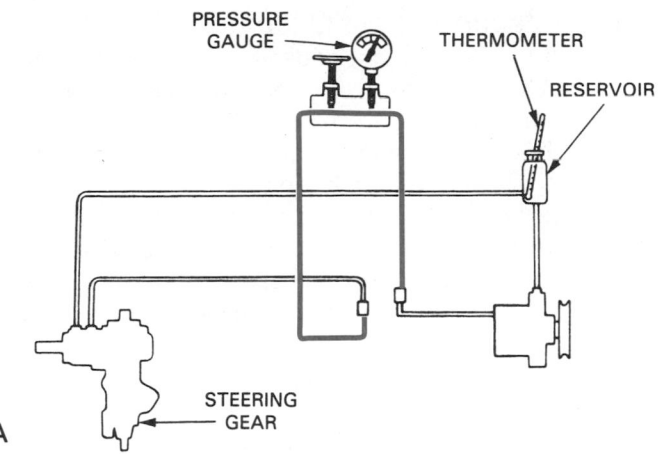

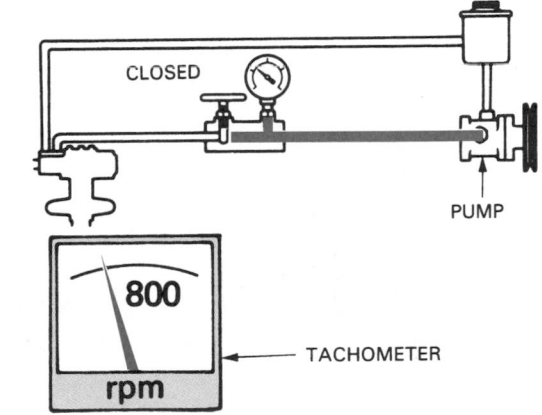

Figure 37-52. A—Some pressure tests call for the use of a thermometer and pressure gauge. B—A tachometer and pressure gauge may also be needed. Do not shut the gauge off (closed) for more than about five seconds to prevent system damage. (Chrysler, Toyota)

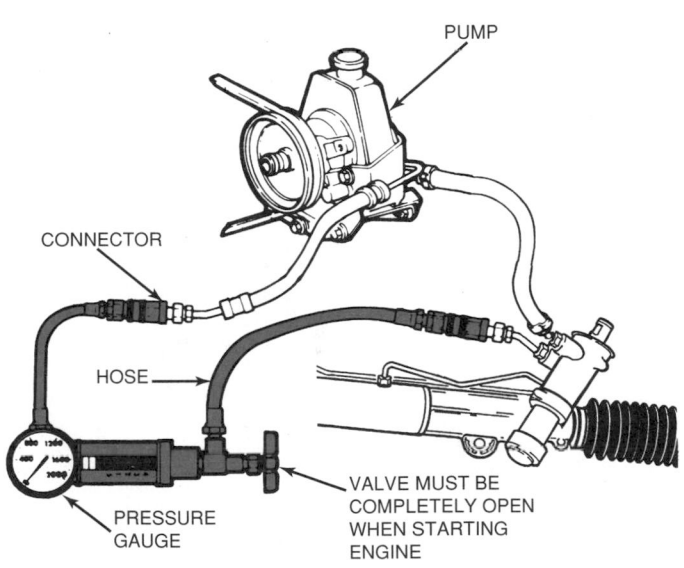

Figure 37-51. Setup used for obtaining power steering pressure. Follow the manufacturer's direction carefully. Wear goggles! (Saginaw Division of GM)

With the weight of the car on its wheels, turn the steering wheel to the right or left until the stop is reached. Hold the wheel hard against the stop and read the maximum pressure developed. Never hold the wheels hard against the stops for longer than five seconds. This will cause a rapid rise in fluid temperature and damage the pump. Check pressure against specifications. Pressure specifications generally call for somewhat over 1000 psi (6895 kPa). If the pressure is below an acceptable level, slowly close the shutoff valve by returning the steering wheel to the straight ahead position. If the pressure rises to the proper level with the valve off, the pump is working properly and the pressure drop is in the hoses or gear system. If the system pressure does not rise, the pump is at fault. Never leave the shutoff valve in the closed position longer than five seconds. To do so would cause a rapid fluid temperature rise resulting in pump damage. Some manufacturers call for checking maximum pressure by using the shutoff valve only.

Bleeding Steering System

When a hydraulic steering system has been repaired, an accurate fluid level reading cannot be obtained unless **bleeding** is performed to remove trapped air from the system. A basic bleeding procedure is as follows:

1. Fill the reservoir with the correct type of fluid.
2. Start the engine and allow it to run for about one minute. Do not turn the wheels.
3. Shut off the engine and allow the vehicle to sit for about two minutes. This allows tiny air bubbles and foam to form larger, more easily expelled bubbles.
4. Refill the reservoir.
5. Start the engine and let it idle for about two minutes.
6. Check the fluid level and add if necessary.
7. Check the repaired part of the system for leaks.
8. Road test the vehicle. Check for abnormal steering function, noise, and leaks.
9. Recheck the fluid level and add if necessary.

Note: Do not overfill the reservoir.

Power Steering Pump Overhaul

Leaking seals or worn or damaged parts require pump disassembly and repair. When removing the pump pulley, use a puller. Never try to hammer the pulley off. Look at **Figure 37-53.** Some pumps have fiberglass or nylon reservoirs which can be damaged by prying or hammering. Clean pump exterior before disassembly. Drain as much power steering fluid from the pump as possible. Obtain a service manual and refer to it during the overhaul. Disassemble the pump as required, using care to avoid excessive force. Clean all parts and lay out on a clean table. **Figure 37-54** shows a typical vane-type pump completely disassembled. Carefully inspect all parts for excessive wear. Check for galling, nicks, or other physical damage. Check flow control valve. Replace damaged or worn parts.

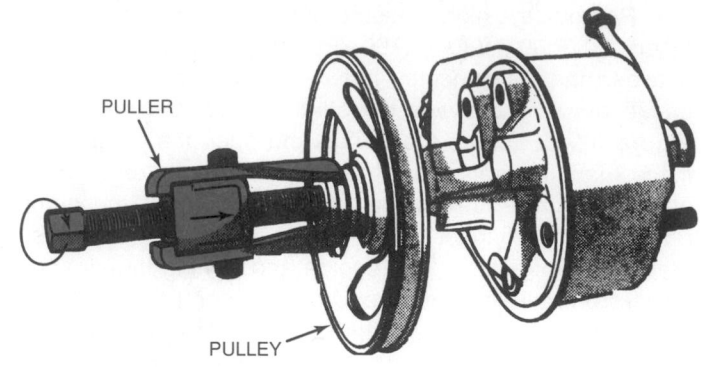

Figure 37-53. Removing the pulley from a power steering pump with a special puller. (Dodge)

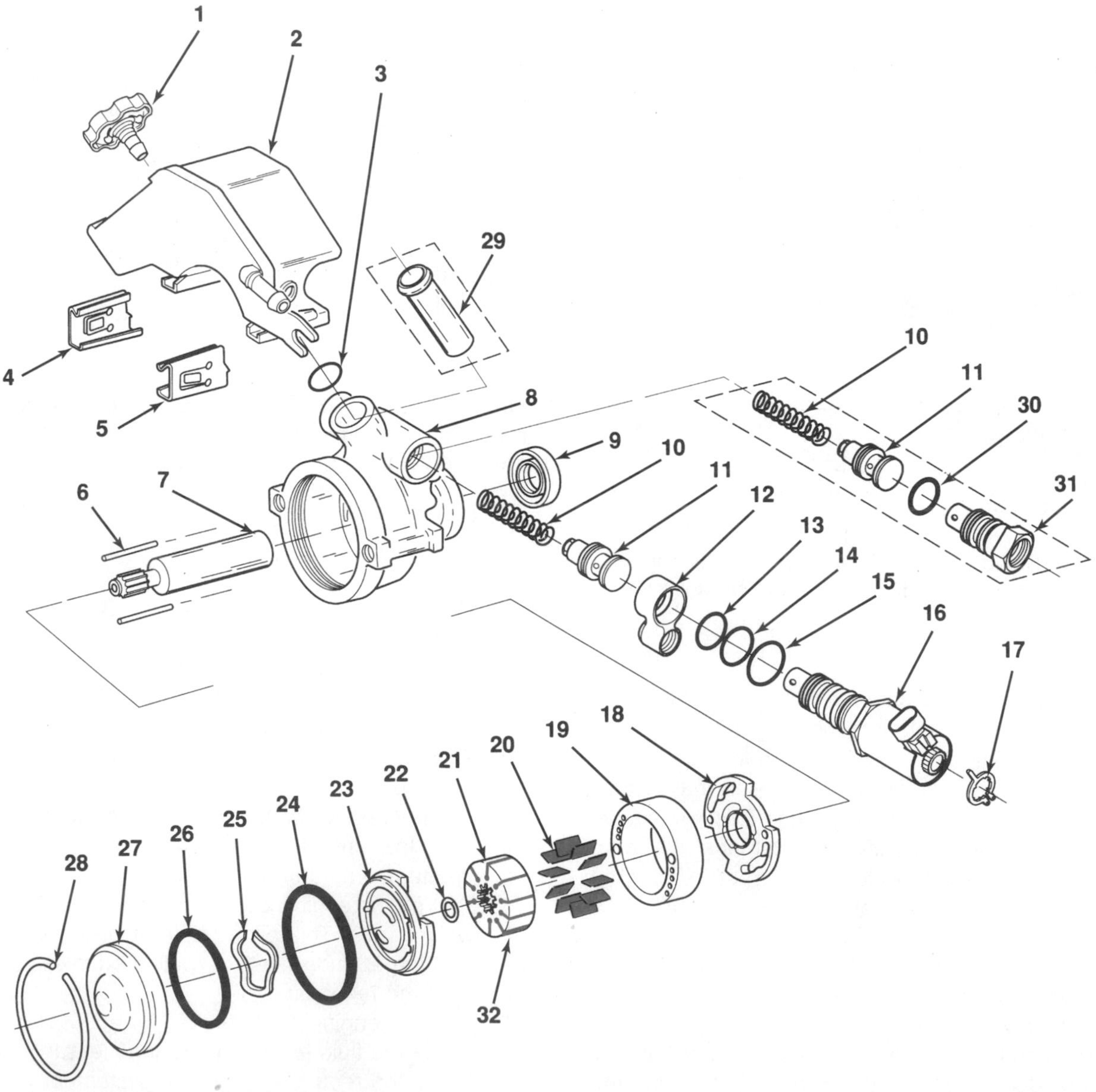

Figure 37-54. A rotor vane steering pump completely disassembled. 1—Reservoir cap. 2—Reservoir. 3—O-ring. 4—Retaining clip. 5—Retaining clip. 6—Dowel pin. 7—Drive shaft. 8—Housing assembly. 9—Drive shaft seal. 10—Spring. 11—Flow control valve. 12—Adaptor housing. 13—O-ring. 14—Seal. 15—Seal. 16—Power steering sensor. 17—Lock ring. 18—Thrust plate. 19—Pump ring. 20—Vanes (10). 21—Pump rotor. 22—Shaft retaining ring. 23—Pressure plate. 24—O-ring. 25—Pressure plate spring. 26—Seal. 27—End cover. 28—Retaining ring. (Saginaw Division of GM)

When assembling, lubricate all parts. Most modern vehicles call for special power steering fluid instead of automatic transmission fluid. Always use the exact fluid specified by the manufacturer. Vane rounded ends must ride against the cam ring. To facilitate proper installation of parts without damage to the O-rings, use a coating of petroleum jelly. Install new seals, O-rings, and gaskets. Protect the shaft seal when inserting the rotor drive shaft. **Figure 37-55** illustrates the use of a shaft seal protector. If the pressure plate is spring-loaded, use a press to hold the end plate while inserting the retaining (snap) ring, **Figure 37-56.** Make certain the flow control valve springs are not distorted, nicked, or damaged. Install springs and valve correctly.

Install pulley using a special installation tool and mount the pump on the engine. Make certain pulley drive key is in place. Adjust belt tension as described earlier in this chapter. If a leaking drive shaft seal is the only trouble, it can often be replaced without removing the pump from the car. The first step in on-the-car seal replacement is to remove the drive belt and pulley. Next, pry out the old seal. Then drive in a new seal using a suitable driving tool, **Figure 37-57.**

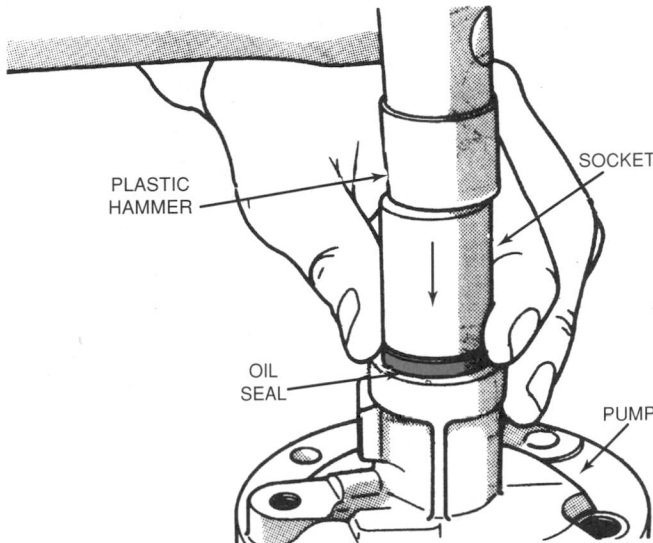

Figure 37-57. Installing a new pump shaft seal. To prevent a leak, be sure the seal is facing the proper direction before installation. (Dodge)

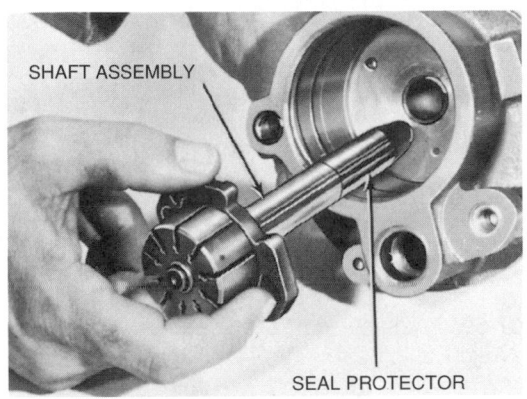

Figure 37-55. By using a seal protector, the shaft can be passed through the seal without damage.

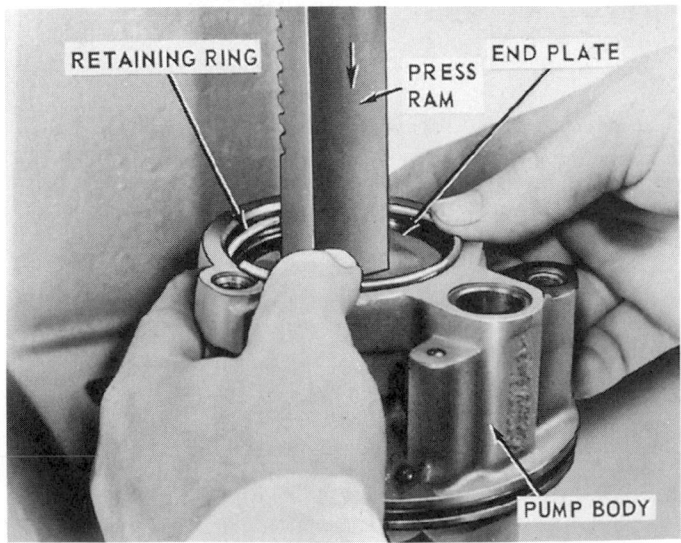

Figure 37-56. Using a press to facilitate pump end plate retaining ring installation.

Power Steering Hoses

Power steering hose is subjected to very high hydraulic system pressures. Carefully inspect each hose for softness, swelling, cracking, abrasion, etc. Inspect hose fittings for cracking and looseness and replace where needed. Power steering hose replacement is relatively simple. Remove hose or hoses from the steering pump and cap the pump outlets. Tip the hose end down into a container to drain. Remove the fitting from the power steering gear or from the power piston control valve. Install the new hose and tighten fittings to specifications. Use only quality replacement hose, do not use remanufactured hose. Install high pressure hose on the pump outlet-to-gear circuit.

Power Steering Coolers and Switches

Most **power steering coolers** are simply extra lengths of tubing placed where air can flow over them. They are usually part of the low-pressure return circuit. If the car is equipped with a power steering cooler, check it for leakage. If necessary, clean the cooler surface. See **Figure 37-58.** A leaking cooler should be replaced. Some manufacturers incorporate a **pressure sensing switch** into the power steering pump. This switch protects the engine from overloading by controlling idle speed. It can also cycle the air conditioning compressor on and off. This switch can be replaced by unscrewing it and installing a replacement.

Steering Linkage

The **steering linkage** consists of the various parts that connect the steering gear to the wheels. It is vital to the

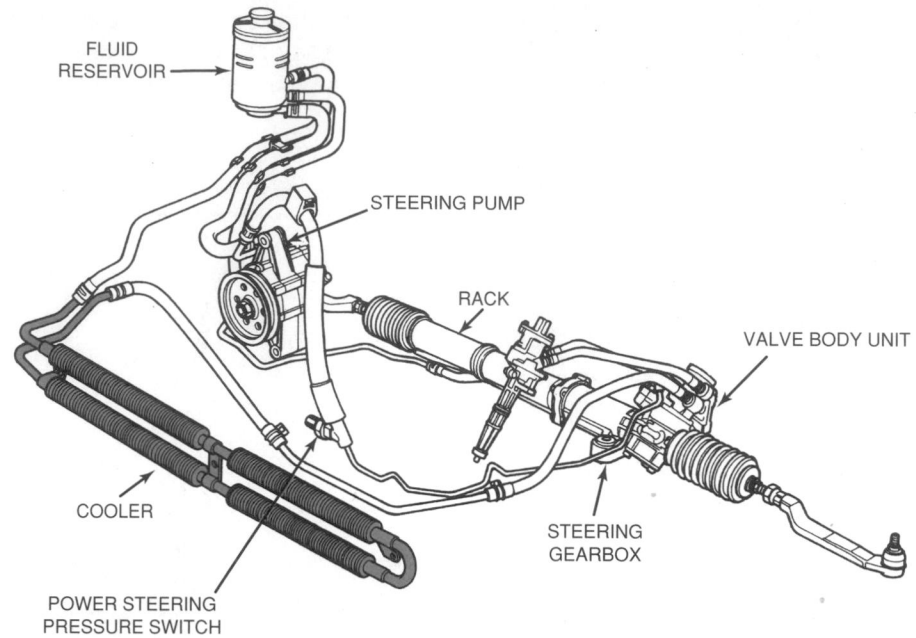

Figure 37-58. One type of power steering pump cooler. Check the cooler pipe for kinks, cracks, loose hose connections, and debris. Air passing over the tubing and the fins reduces the fluid temperature. (Honda)

operation of the overall steering system. There are many places where the steering linkage can become worn, damaged, or bent. Steering linkage arrangements vary depending upon need and basic design. One typical conventional steering system is illustrated in **Figure 37-59.** A rack and pinion system is shown in **Figure 37-60.** Note that they contain some of the same parts, such as tie rod ends.

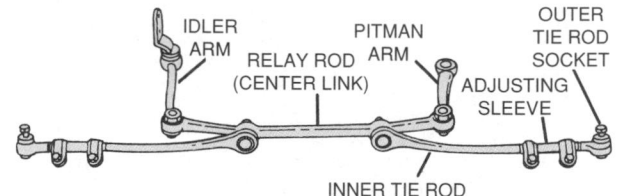

Figure 37-59. A parallelogram steering linkage arrangement. (Monroe Auto Equipment)

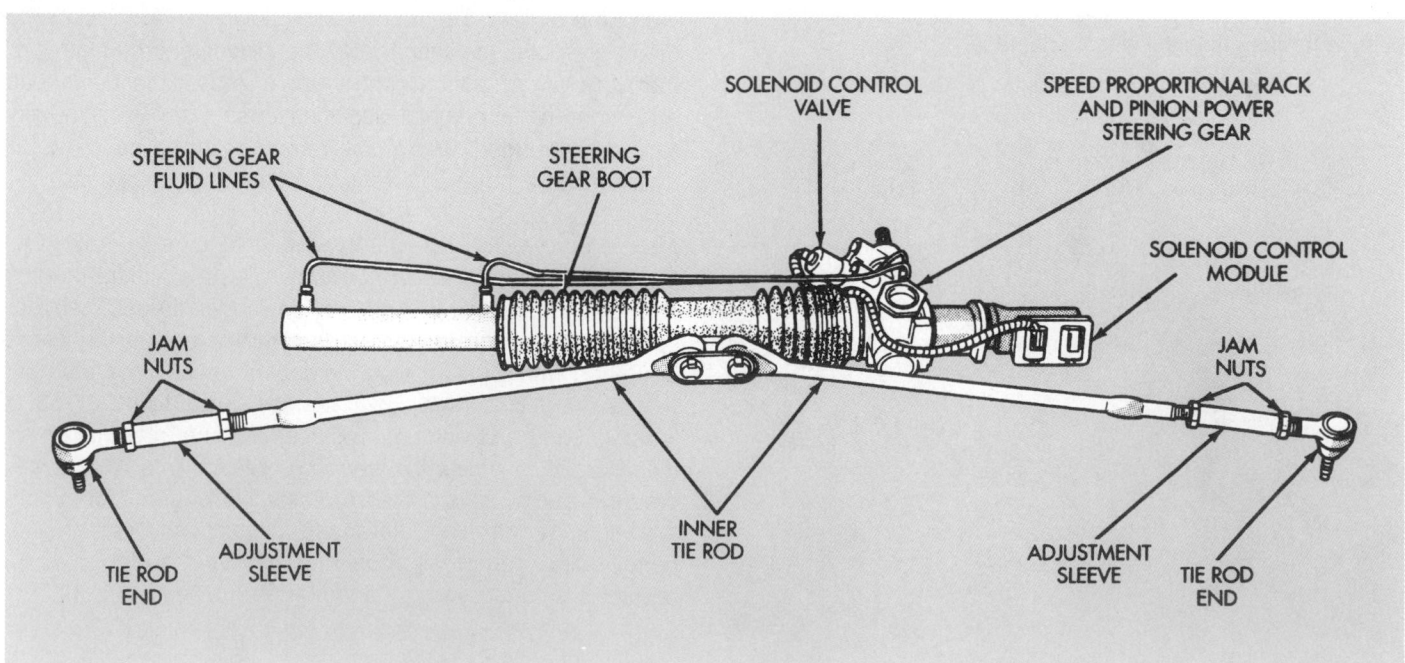

Figure 37-60. A rack and pinion, variable assist, speed sensing (proportional) steering gear setup. (Chrysler)

Note: See Chapter 41 for information on steering system lubrication (greasing) as part of preventive maintenance.

Steering Linkage Service

Raise the car and inspect all steering linkage connections. Check ball sockets for looseness by shaking the center link and tie rods. Check idler arm mounting fasteners. Check pitman arm retaining nut tension. Inspect tie rod sleeve adjusters and sleeve clamp bolts. Check steering arm fasteners. All nuts and cotter pins should be in place. Tighten loose fasteners and replace worn joints and leaking grease seals. Check for bent parts. Review the section on tie rod end replacement later in this chapter. Repair or replace as needed.

Pitman Arms

Pitman arms are used on conventional steering systems only. Remove the pitman arm-to-pitman shaft retaining nut. Install a suitable puller. Tighten puller until pitman arm pulls free. Protect pitman shaft and threads. Do not hammer on the end of the puller or on the end of the pitman shaft. Hammering could damage the steering gear. See **Figure 37-61.** To remove the pitman arm from the drag link or from the center link ball socket stud, see the section on tie rod end removal.

To install the pitman arm, clean the end of the pitman shaft thoroughly. Lubricate the splined area of the pitman shaft. Install the pitman arm on the shaft. Be certain to align

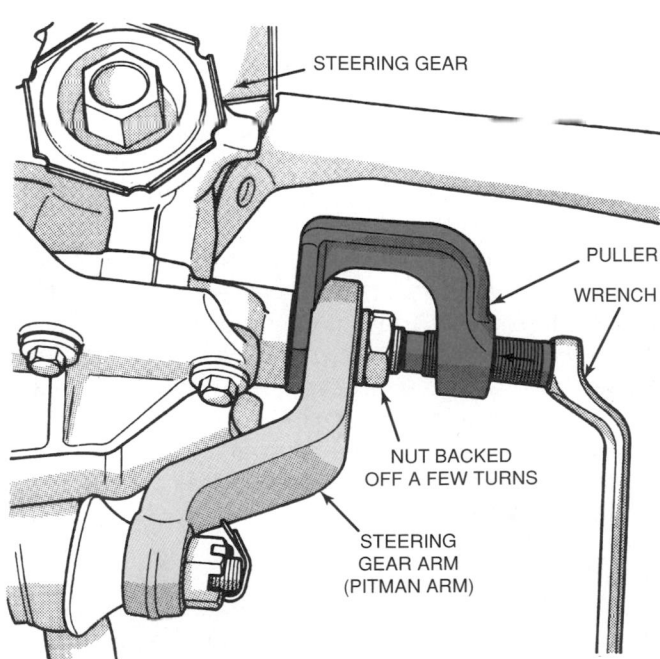

Figure 37-61. Using a special puller to remove the pitman arm from the steering gear. (Dodge)

arm and shaft correctly, **Figure 37-62.** Install lock washer and retaining nut. Torque nut to specifications. Support one side of the pitman arm. With a heavy hammer, strike the other side with a sharp blow. Never hammer on the retaining nut or against the end of the shaft. Torque the nut again. The sharp blow will assist in proper seating of the pitman arm on the shaft. Stake the nut to prevent loosening.

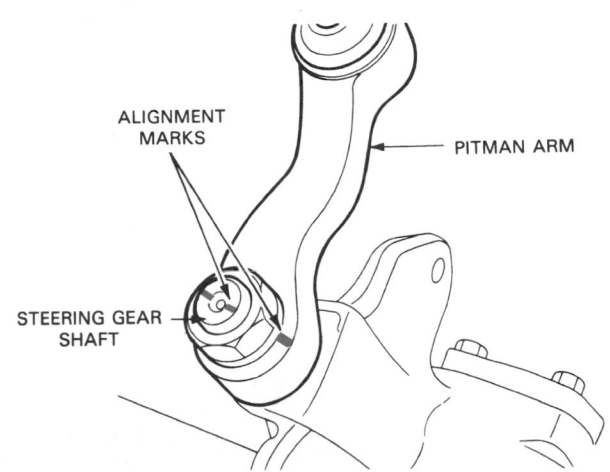

Figure 37-62. Alignment marks on a pitman arm and steering gear shaft. (Plymouth)

Idler Arms

Idler arms are found only on conventional steering systems. Remove the bolts and nuts holding the idler arm to the frame. Then remove the idler arm from the center link stud as applicable. To install the new idler arm, place the arm on the drag link or center link ball socket stud as applicable. Then install and tighten the idler arm-to-frame bolts and nuts. After all fasteners are in place, tighten the ball socket fastener and install a new cotter pin if necessary.

Tie Rod Ends

All steering systems contain *tie rod ends.* If a tie rod end is found to be worn by checking deflection (looseness), it should be discarded. See **Figure 37-63. Figure 37-64** illustrates typical tie rod ball socket construction. In **Figure 37-64A,** the half-ball type is shown while **Figure 37-64B** employs the full ball design. Note that a plug is used to allow periodic lubrication. In most tie rod designs, a fitting is normally installed in place of a plug. Removal and replacement procedures are the same for either type.

Note: For ease of reassembly, count the number of exposed threads on the old tie rod where it threads into the rest of the steering linkage. Install the new part with the same number of threads showing. This will simplify alignment.

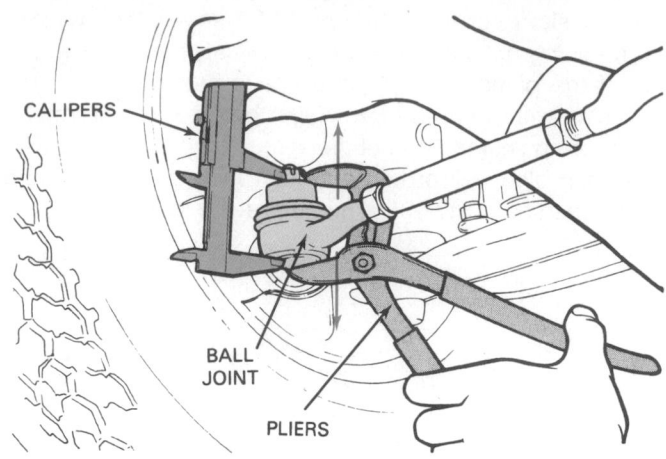

Figure 37-63. Grip the ball joint with pliers, compress it fully, and measure the compressed joint. The service limit (allowable wear) for this joint is .060″ (1.5 mm). (Chrysler)

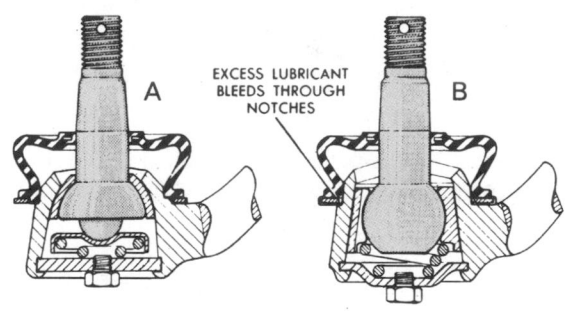

Figure 37-64. Tie rod end (ball socket) construction. (Chrysler)

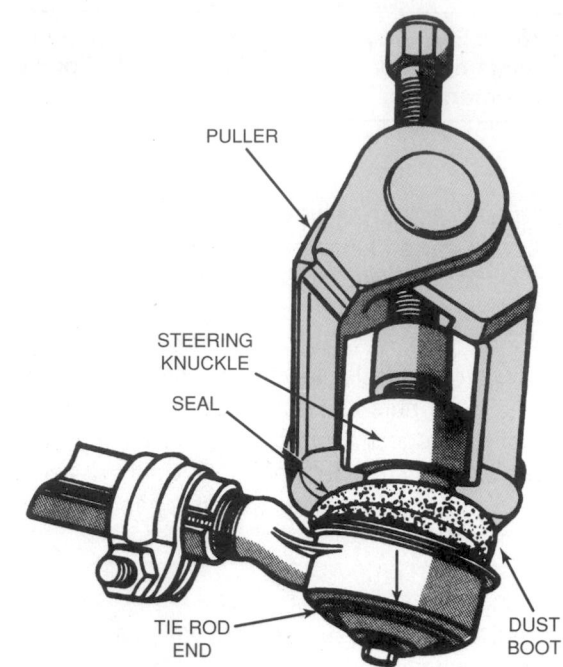

Figure 37-65. Removing a tie rod end from the steering knuckle with a puller. (Chrysler)

Remove the cotter pin and retaining nut. The stud is held in place by a taper fit which must be broken or loosened. A special removing tool, such as shown in **Figure 37-65,** may be used to break the taper. This tool will remove the tie rod end without damage to the seal or to the socket. If a puller is not available, the tie rod stud can be removed by striking the steering arm sharply several times with a hammer while supporting it with a heavy block of steel. When installing the tie rod ball stud, clean the stud and the tapered hole into which it fits. Wipe stud with a thin coat of oil. Insert stud and install the retaining nut. Torque to specifications and insert a new cotter pin.

Tie Rod Adjuster Sleeve

The **adjuster sleeves** on conventional systems are threaded into the inner and outer tie rod ends. Turning the sleeves lengthens or shortens the overall tie rod assembly to adjust the toe. Clean the tie rod, tie rod end threads, and the adjuster thoroughly. Lubricate adjuster sleeve threads. Force the tie rod and tie rod end against the adjuster sleeve while turning the sleeve. Continue turning the sleeve until toe is correct. The tie rod and tie rod end should have about the same number of threads turned into the adjusting

sleeve. Position the adjuster sleeve clamps over the threaded portion of the tie rod in the sleeve. The sleeve slot and clamp opening should be correctly aligned. Torque clamp bolts to specifications. **Figure 37-66** illustrates a typical linkage system. Note tie rod end construction, clamp arrangement, and other parts.

Rack and Pinion Tie Rods

Rack and pinion tie rod removal is similar to removal on a conventional system. Remove the cotter pin and retaining nut. Then loosen and remove the stud by breaking the taper with a power removing tool or puller. To remove the tie rod, remove the tie rod end from the shaft of the tie rod. Remove the bellows (boot) over the end of the rack and pinion assembly and remove the tie rod retaining pin. Consult the manufacturer's service manual to determine whether the retainer must be unscrewed, drilled, or driven out of the tie rod end. Then, using a special tool such as the one shown in **Figure 37-67,** unscrew the tie rod. Some vehicles have a crimped sleeve to hold the tie rod end in place. This must be ground or chiseled off and a new sleeve crimped into place. Using the removal tool, install the new tie rod and a new retaining pin. Replace the bellows and tie rod end and align the vehicle.

Center Links

The procedure for replacing **center links**, or drag links, is similar to the procedure for tie rod ends. Remove the cotter pin and nut from any tie rod ends which need removal, and break the taper with a power tool or puller. Reverse the removal procedure to install the new link. Be sure to use a new cotter pin.

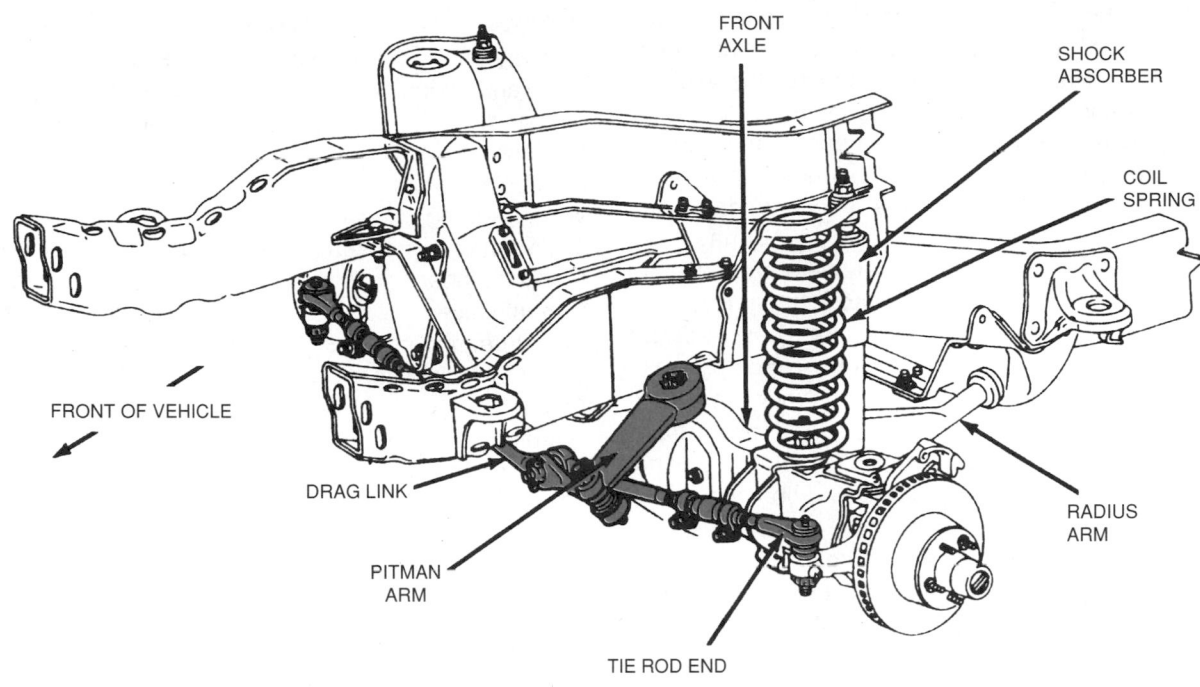

FRONT
AXLE

SHOCK
ABSORBER

COIL
SPRING

FRONT OF VEHICLE

DRAG LINK

PITMAN
ARM

RADIUS
ARM

TIE ROD END

NOTE: TO PREVENT INTERFERENCE
WITH OTHER COMPONENTS.

VERTICAL

FRONT OF
VEHICLE

+45°   −45°

AFTER SETTING TOE, THE TWO CLAMP BOLTS/NUTS ON EACH
ADJUSTING SLEEVE MUST BE POSITIONED WITHIN A LIMIT OF
45 DEGREES (PLUS/MINUS) AS SHOWN WITH THE THREADED END OF
THE BOLTS ON THE LEFT-HAND SLEEVE POINTING TOWARDS THE
FRONT OF THE VEHICLE AND THE BOLTS ON THE RIGHT-HAND
SLEEVE FACING REARWARD.

Figure 37-66. A steering linkage arrangement used on a four-wheel drive vehicle. Study this arrangement carefully. The pitman arm transfers the steering gear movement through the drag link and tie rods to the spindles. (Ford)

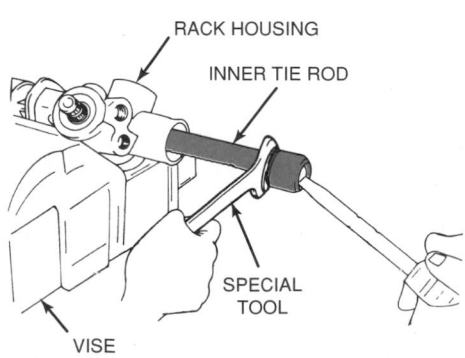

RACK HOUSING

INNER TIE ROD

SPECIAL
TOOL

VISE

Figure 37-67. Removing a rack and pinion tie rod end by unscrewing it with a special wrench. (Hyundai)

Tech Talk

It is vital that you correctly repair or replace front end components. Some types of improper or careless repairs simply result in a dissatisfied customer, additional work, or at worst, replacing parts that were damaged by the incorrect repair. However, any problem that causes loss of steering control will almost always result in an accident.

Summary

Steering systems consist of a steering wheel, steering shaft, steering gearbox or rack and pinion assembly, pitman arm, linkage, steering arms, and steering knuckle assemblies. Steering systems can be conventional, or parallelogram systems, or rack and pinion systems. All steering system work is critical to the safe operation of the vehicle. Steering wheels should be carefully aligned to center them.

The most common type of steering gear is the recirculating ball worm and nut. Check lubricant level in manual steering gear periodically and use the recommended lubricant when adding. Manual steering gears usually have two adjustments, worm bearing preload and over-center adjustment. Make the worm bearing preload adjustment first. The conventional power steering gear has three basic adjustments, thrust bearing preload, worm to rack-piston preload, and pitman shaft over-center preload. When repairing power steering gears, use care to keep dirt away from parts. Avoid denting or nicking parts. Do not force parts together. Use new seals and gaskets. Lubricate parts before assembly. Steering gear must be properly aligned with the steering shaft. Adjust steering wheel spoke position by turning the tie rod adjusting sleeves. Steering wheel hub and shaft marks must be aligned. When installing a steering wheel, align marks and torque the retaining nut.

Power steering pumps can be of the vane, slipper, roller, or gear types. Steering pumps are generally belt driven. When overhauling power steering pumps, use care to avoid nicking parts. Clean all parts thoroughly. Use new seals and gaskets and lubricate parts before assembly. Replace soft, cracked, or abraded power steering hose. Use quality replacement hose. Torque all connections. Bleed air from hose, gear, and pump by turning steering wheel from one side to the other several times (engine running).

The steering system should have a thorough inspection at regular intervals. Inspection should cover linkage connections, tie rod adjuster sleeve clamps, all system fasteners, steering arms, pitman arm, steering gear, power steering pump lubricant level, power steering pump belts, power steering hose, and cooler (where used). Road test vehicle for proper steering.

Tension a new belt slightly tighter than a used belt to allow for initial belt stretch. When adjusting, removing, or installing belts, remove battery ground strap. Before conducting a power steering pressure test, check belt tension and reservoir fluid level. Use a 0-2000 psi (0-13,800 kPa) gauge. Never close the pressure test shutoff valve or hold the steering wheel hard against the stops for a period exceeding five seconds. When adjusting pump belt tension, pry on a heavy section (not filler pipe or reservoir) of the pump or use the notch for a wrench in the mounting bracket.

When removing or installing the pitman arm, never hammer on the end of the pitman shaft or the end of the puller. When installing the pitman arm, align it on the shaft correctly. Torque pitman arm retaining nut. Loose idler arms must be replaced. Tie rod adjuster sleeves must be installed with an equal number of threads engaged on each end. Position sleeve clamps over threaded area and turn to specified angle.

Know These Terms

Conventional steering system
Rack and pinion steering system
Steering shaft
Recirculating ball
Worm bearing preload
Over-center adjustment
Power cylinder
Control valve
Thrust bearing preload
Worm to rack-piston preload
Pitman shaft over-center preload
Sector shaft

Vane pump
Slipper pump
Roller pump
Fluid level
Pressure test
Bleeding
Power steering cooler
Pressure sensing switch
Steering linkage
Pitman arm
Idler arm
Tie rod end
Adjuster sleeve
Center link

Review Questions—Chapter 37

Do not write in this book. Write your answers on a separate sheet of paper.

1. Worn, dirty, or dry steering column shaft bearings can cause what kind of steering system problem?
   (A) Squeaks.
   (B) Roughness.
   (C) Binding.
   (D) All of the above.
2. Conventional steering gears use the _____ design.
3. When checking manual steering gear lubricant level, the filler plug and surrounding area should be _____.
4. The typical manual steering gear has two basic adjustments, _____ and _____.
5. Which of the two adjustments in question 5 is done first?
6. Name the three types of power steering pumps.
7. A squealing sound when turning the steering wheel against the stops usually indicates a loose power steering _____.
8. Name three important considerations for making an accurate test of power steering system pressure.
9. To disconnect two steering parts that are held by a taper, the taper must be broken (loosened), usually by _____.
   (A) striking it with a hammer
   (B) heating it cherry red with a torch
   (C) cooling it with dry ice
   (D) the taper will come loose when the attaching nut is removed
10. Some idler arms can be repaired by installing new _____.
    (A) bushings
    (B) seals
    (C) grease fittings
    (D) All of the above.

ASE-Type Questions

1. Technician A says that the steering gear must be correctly aligned with the steering shaft when it is reinstalled. Technician B says that it is OK to adjust steering wheel spoke position by removing the wheel and relocating it on the steering shaft. Who is right?
   (A) A only.
   (B) B only.
   (C) Both A & B.
   (D) Neither A nor B.

2. The lubricant in a manual steering gearbox should be changed every _____.
   (A) two years
   (B) 30,000 miles
   (C) each spring and fall
   (D) the lubricant does not require periodic changing

3. Technician A says that conventional steering gear adjustments are usually checked by using a torque wrench or spring scale. Technician B says that there are no adjustments to be made on a power steering conventional steering gear box. Who is right?
   (A) A only.
   (B) B only.
   (C) Both A & B.
   (D) Neither A nor B.

4. When overhauling any hydraulic unit, one of the most important rules is _____.
   (A) working fast
   (B) painting the exterior
   (C) cleanliness
   (D) use of labor saving tools

5. All of the following statements about correctly checking power steering fluid level are correct, EXCEPT:
   (A) The fluid must be cold to make an accurate check.
   (B) Some power steering reservoir caps have dipsticks.
   (C) Some power steering reservoirs have level marks on the reservoir body.
   (D) Always top off with special power steering fluid when recommended.

6. Technician A says that the power steering system is bled using bleeder fittings located on the high pressure side of the gearbox. Technician B says that the power steering system is bled using bleeder fittings located on the low pressure side of the gearbox. Who is right?
   (A) A only.
   (B) B only.
   (C) Both A & B.
   (D) Neither A nor B.

7. All of the following statements about power steering hoses are true, EXCEPT:
   (A) High pressure hoses are used between the pump outlet and the gearbox.
   (B) Power steering coolers are usually installed in the high pressure circuit.
   (C) Hoses should be replaced if they show any swelling or cracks.
   (D) Hose replacement is simple, but results in draining some of the fluid.

8. When conducting a power steering pressure test, never leave the shutoff valve closed for longer than _____.
   (A) five minutes
   (B) five seconds
   (C) twenty seconds
   (D) one minute

9. Technician A says that the pitman shaft can be heated to remove the pitman arm. Technician B says that using a pickle fork-type tie rod separator can damage the seal. Who is right?
   (A) A only.
   (B) B only.
   (C) Both A & B.
   (D) Neither A nor B.

10. Technician A says that tie rod adjuster sleeve clamps can be tightened in any handy position. Technician B says that removing the inner tie rod end on a rack and pinion steering system requires a special tool. Who is right?
    (A) A only.
    (B) B only.
    (C) Both A & B.
    (D) Neither A nor B.

Suggested Activities

1. Inspect two vehicles with a conventional steering system and a rack and pinion steering system. Determine the difference between each system and write a short report explaining the differences. Add simple sketches to improve the report.

2. Inspect steering components for wear. The inspection should include all tie rod ends, idler arm, and pitman arm if used. Demonstrate the inspection procedure to other members of the class.

3. Replace a tie rod end, center (drag) link, or idler arm on a conventional steering system. Make a list of the tools that you need to perform the job.

4. Replace a tie rod and/or bellows boot on a rack and pinion system. Make a list of the tools that you needed to perform the job. Explain how the lubricant is added to the unit.

5. Replace a conventional steering box and a rack and pinion unit. Make a list of the tools that you needed to perform each job.

This late-model vehicle is equipped with all-weather steel-belted radial tires and chrome-plated alloy wheels. (Lexus)

38

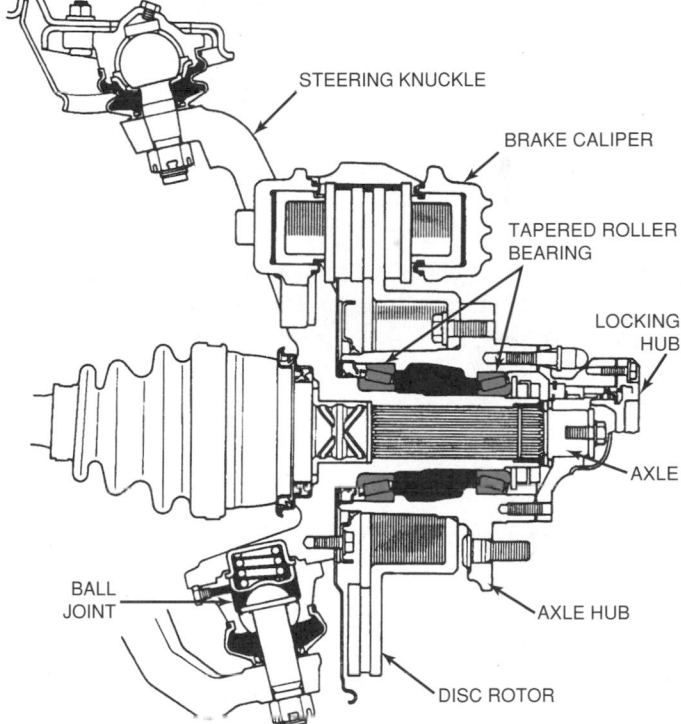

Wheel and Tire Service

After studying this chapter, you will be able to:
- Describe the construction, operation, and service of wheel bearings.
- Explain tire and wheel construction and service.
- Summarize tire size, type, and quality ratings.
- Diagnose common wheel bearing and tire related problems.

This chapter will cover the design and service procedures for wheel bearings, wheel rims, and tires. This chapter provides basic information about tire and wheel service. Tire repair, wear problems, mounting, and balancing are discussed.

Wheel Bearings

The following sections cover the servicing of wheel bearings found on front and rear-wheel drive vehicles. These bearings form the connection between the rotating wheel and brake assemblies and the nonrotating wheel spindles. The drive and nondrive axles of a vehicle are supported by bearings. Three main types of bearings are used on modern vehicles:

- *Tapered roller bearings,* **Figure 38-1.**
- *Straight roller bearings.*
- *Ball bearings,* **Figure 38-2.**

Tapered roller bearings can be cleaned, regreased, and adjusted. The straight roller and ball bearings used on most modern vehicles cannot be serviced and are replaced as a unit. A few older vehicles use ball bearings that can be regreased in the front axles. The first part of this section covers the service of tapered roller bearings. The following section covers the service of sealed roller and ball bearings.

 Note: Rear wheel bearings used in the axle assemblies of rear-wheel drive vehicles are covered in Chapter 33.

Tapered Roller Bearing Service

Rear-wheel drive vehicles have tapered roller bearings in the front wheels, **Figure 38-1.** Some front-wheel drive

Figure 38-1. A cutaway view of a four-wheel drive front axle and hub assembly that uses tapered roller bearings. (Toyota)

Labels in figure: STEERING KNUCKLE, BRAKE CALIPER, TAPERED ROLLER BEARING, LOCKING HUB, AXLE, AXLE HUB, DISC ROTOR, BALL JOINT

vehicles may use tapered roller bearings in the rear axle hub assembly. The tapered roller bearing consists of the *rollers* and *cage* and the inner and outer *races.* To remove the bearings, other wheel components must be removed. Begin by prying off the wheel cover, being careful to avoid springing it out of shape. Pry a little at a time, moving around the cap.

 Note: Some wheel covers are held on by *wheel cover locks,* as shown in Figure 38-3. Other vehicles with custom wheels have *wheel rim locks,* Figure 38-4. The key to these locks is in the vehicle and must be located to remove the wheel covers. After using the wheel lock key, replace it in the vehicle. Without the key, the driver will not be able to remove the wheel and tire in an emergency.

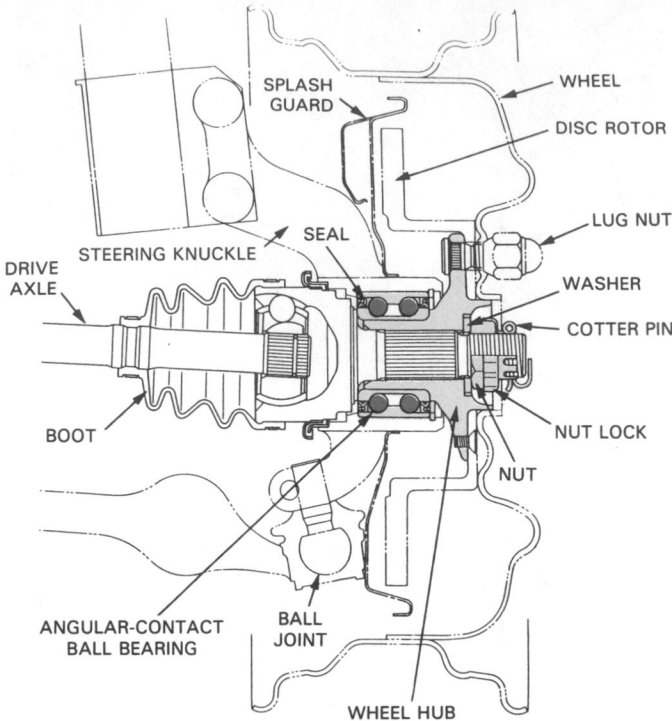

Figure 38-2. One type of front-wheel drive hub and bearing assembly. This particular arrangement uses angular-contact ball bearings. (Daihatsu)

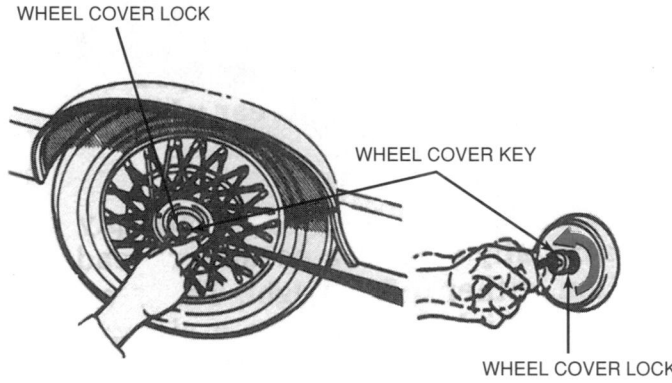

Figure 38-3. One type of wheel cover lock arrangement.

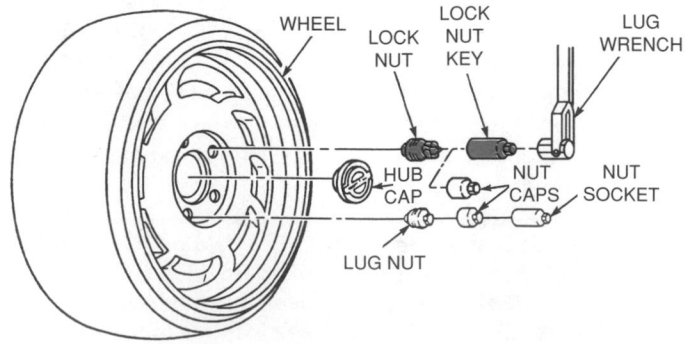

Figure 38-4. Special light alloy (aluminum) wheel locking nut. These replace one standard nut per wheel. Note the unique pattern on the nut head. A special key with a corresponding pattern fits over the nut head for removal. (GM)

Tapered Roller Bearing Removal

After removing the wheel cover, remove the wheel lug nuts and remove the wheel and tire. Remove the bearing dust cap. Straighten the cotter pin and remove it, then unscrew the adjusting nut. Note that some vehicles use a left-hand thread nut on the rear wheels. If the vehicle has front disc brakes, remove the caliper. Caliper removal was discussed in Chapter 34. Also remove the anti-lock brake (ABS) sensor if applicable.

 Caution: The drum or rotor may be hot. Use a rag, if necessary, to protect your hands.

Remove the washer from the steering knuckle, or **spindle,** and shake the drum or rotor from side to side or pull it outward a short distance. Then push it back on. This will move the outer bearing so it can be grasped and removed from the hub. Remove the outer bearing and place in a clean container. Then grasp the drum or rotor firmly and pull it straight off the spindle. Be careful that the inner bearing and seal are not dragged across the spindle threads. See **Figure 38-5.** If the brake shoes drag and make wheel assembly removal difficult, back off the brake shoe adjustment (see Chapter 34). Lay the drum or rotor over a clean rag or piece of paper. Use a long, soft steel drift to engage the inner bearing race. Do not strike the roller cage. Tap the inner bearing from the hub. Tap a little at a time, moving the drift around the race. This will remove the bearing and grease seal. Discard the old grease seal. Always use a new grease seal following bearing or brake service. See Chapter 10 for complete instructions on bearing cleaning and checking. Important points to remember are:

- Use a final rinse of clean solvent.
- Never spin the bearing with air pressure.
- Examine each roller and race.
- Pack bearings with lubricant and store in a clean container until ready to use.
- Discard bearings showing the slightest signs of chipping, galling, or wear.
- If any part of the bearing is damaged, replace the entire bearing.
- A used roller assembly must always be installed in the original race.

Thoroughly clean and flush out the inside of the hub. Do not allow solvent and grease to contact the brake drum or disc surfaces. Wipe the hub dry with a clean cloth and inspect the bearing races. If damaged, or if either the inner or outer roller bearing assembly is damaged, remove the corresponding race, **Figure 38-6.** Use a brass or soft steel drift. If the hub is slotted, place the drift on the exposed edge of the outer race at the slot. If slots are not provided, place the drift on the thin exposed race edge. Tap the race from the hub. Move the drift around so that the race is forced out without excessive tipping. Tipping the race can

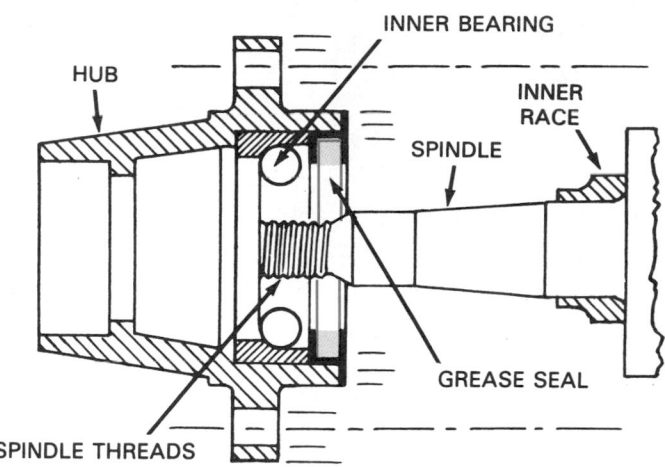

Figure 38-5. Support the wheel when removing or installing it to prevent the inner bearing and grease seal from dragging over the spindle threads.

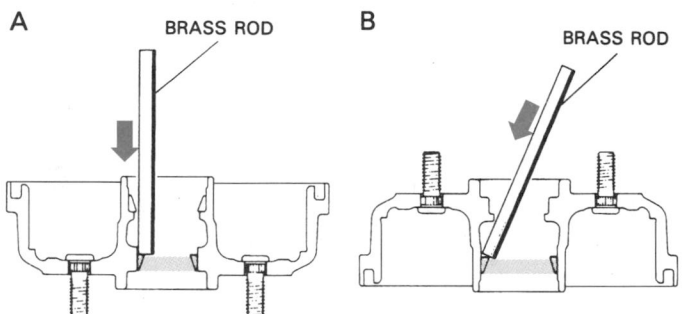

Figure 38-6. A—Driving the outer bearing race from the hub. B—Driving the inner race from the hub. (Mitsubishi)

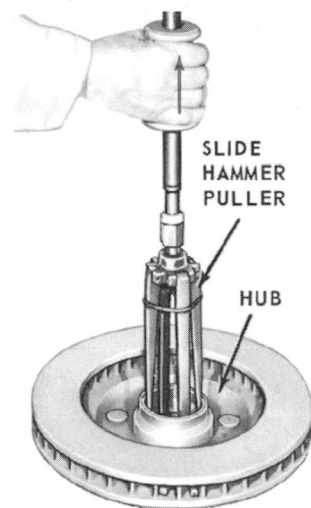

Figure 38-7. Using a slide hammer puller to remove the hub bearing race. (Ford)

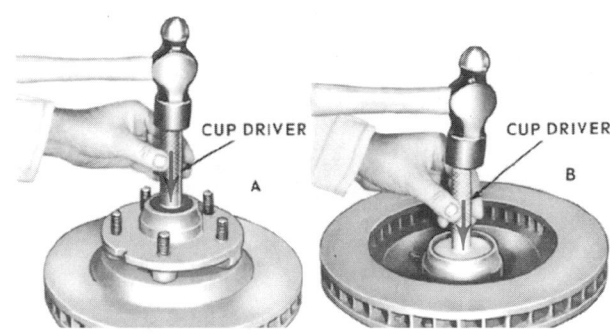

Figure 38-8. A—Installing an outer bearing race. B—Installing an inner bearing race. Note the use of the race driver tool.

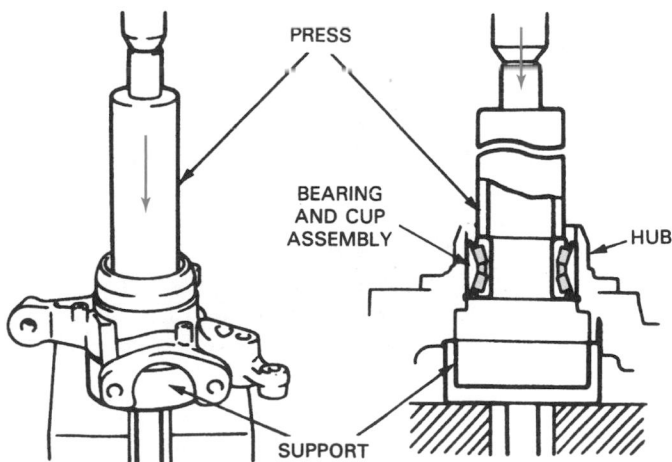

Figure 38-9. Using a press to install the bearing and race assembly in the hub. *Wear your safety glasses!* (Toyota)

distort the hub. Use care to avoid damaging the hub with the drift. A puller, as in **Figure 38-7,** will remove the hub races easily and will avoid tipping.

Wipe the hub recess clean. Lubricate new bearing race and place in position over recess. Make certain that the race faces in the correct direction. Using a driver, drive the race inward until seated firmly against stop. Refer to **Figure 38-8.** The race may be pressed into place if such equipment is available. See **Figure 38-9.** If a drift punch is used, tap a little at a time. Move the punch around the race to avoid cocking or tipping. Use a soft steel drift. Never use a hardened punch.

Packing Wheel Bearings

Never repack a bearing with any kind of grease without first removing all of the original grease from both bearings and the hub. Many types of grease are not compatible and should never be mixed. Use only high temperature grease on a modern vehicle, since all modern brake systems operate at high temperatures. Using a bearing packer or your hands, pack each bearing with the specified wheel bearing grease. Make sure each bearing is fully packed and that a generous amount of grease is applied to the outside of the rollers. Never apply grease to an oily bearing as the grease

will not adhere properly. Bearing must be clean and dry before packing.

To prevent rust from moisture condensation and grease runoff from the bearings, both the hub, race surfaces, and dust cap interior should be given a coating of grease. The coating in the cap can be relatively light. Coat the hub inner cavity to a depth that will bring the grease level up to the inner edge of the bearing races. Never pack the hub full of grease. Pack as illustrated in **Figure 38-10.**

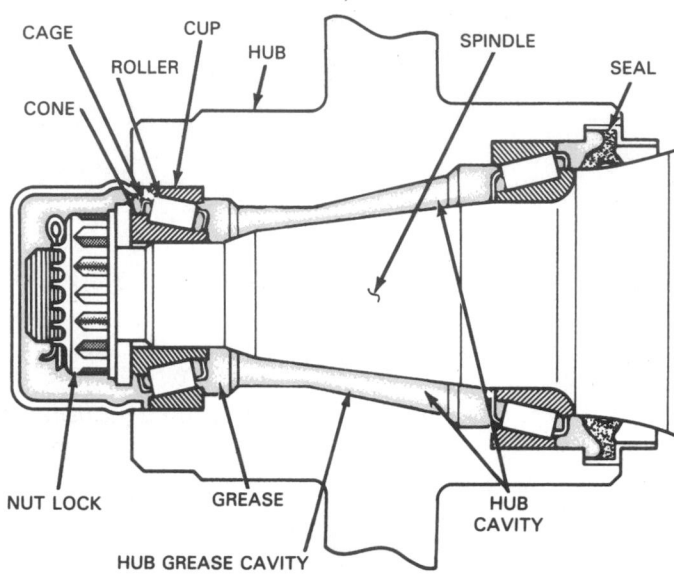

Figure 38-10.   Fill the hub grease cavity to the depth shown. Also, place a light film of grease inside the dust cap. Follow the vehicle manufacturer's recommendations for the type and amount of grease used. (Plymouth)

Insert the packed inner bearing into the hub. The neoprene seal lips should be lubricated with a small amount of wheel bearing grease. Then wipe out the seal recess in the hub and place the seal on the hub with the sealing lip facing inward. Using a seal driver, drive the seal to the proper depth. Do not drive the seal in so deeply that it engages the bearing. Seals are usually driven in until flush with the top surface of the hub. Refer to **Figure 38-11.** If a punch or hammer must be used to seat the seal, strike the seal outer edge only. The inner portion is unsupported and a blow there will destroy the seal. Wipe off any grease on the outside of the seal or on the hub.

Brake Assembly and Spindle

Cover the spindle with a clean cloth. Clean off the brake assembly with approved equipment. Do not apply a direct blast of cleaning fluid, as the dust and dirt could be forced into the wheel cylinders or calipers. Clean the spindle thoroughly with a cloth dampened with solvent. Wipe dry with a clean cloth. Brake cleaning was discussed in Chapter 34.

 Warning: Do not use compressed air to clean or dry brake parts as they can contain asbestos. Review the asbestos warning in Chapter 34.

Examine the spindle carefully for signs of cracking, wear, or scoring. If the vehicle has considerable mileage or is used in heavy service, the spindle should be tested for

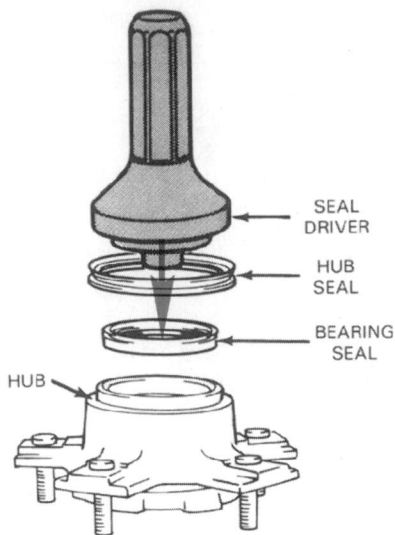

Figure 38-11.   Using a seal driver to install the hub and bearing seal. Be sure the seals are facing in the proper direction.

cracks. The inner race is designed to move on the spindle. This movement exposes a constantly changing portion of the race to the heaviest pressure from the rollers which increases bearing life. To ensure proper race movement, the inside of the race and the area of the spindle which touches the race must be very smooth and coated with a film of grease. If rusty or at all rough, polish the race contact areas of the spindle with crocus cloth. Wipe the spindle clean and lubricate it with a light coat of wheel bearing grease to prevent rusting and to facilitate race motion.

Installing Tapered Wheel Bearings

Check the brake shoes and drum or rotor and pads for grease and fingerprints. Clean them with a nonpetroleum solvent if necessary. Support the drum or rotor and slide straight on spindle, **Figure 38-12.** Do not drag the grease seal over spindle threads. When the drum or rotor is in position, insert the outer bearing, safety thrust washer, and locknut. Do not forget to install the pronged safety washer (if used). To avoid interference by brake friction pads, do not reinstall the caliper until the bearing adjustment is complete.

Wheel Bearing Adjustment

Proper wheel bearing adjustment is very important. Improper adjustment can cause poor brake performance, wheel shake, poor steering, or rapid bearing wear. See **Figure 38-13.** Each manufacturer specifies a particular adjustment procedure. There are several methods that may be used for adjusting wheel bearings. Two of the most accurate and widely recommended are the torque wrench method and the dial indicator method.

Bearing Adjustment—Torque Wrench

In this method, the locknut is tightened to a specified torque while spinning the wheel in the direction of tightening. This heavier initial torque seats the bearings. The nut is then loosened until it can be rotated by hand. Then the nut

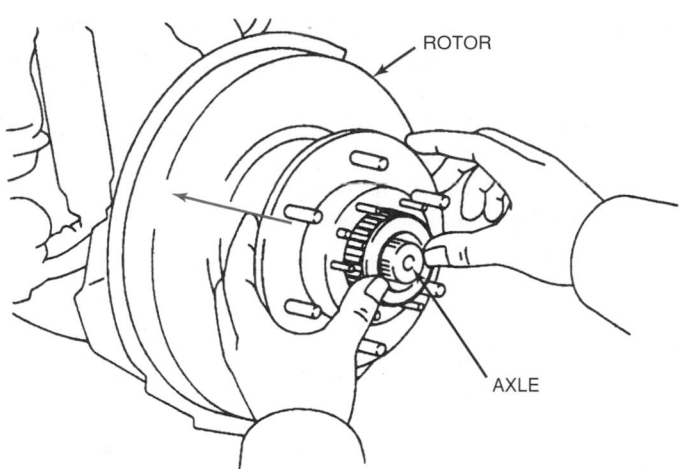

Figure 38-12.   Installing a hub on the spindle. Be careful not to damage the grease seal by dragging it over the end of the axle or spindle threads. (Toyota)

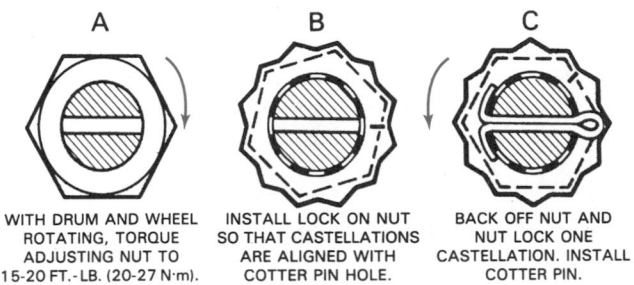

Figure 38-13.   Adjusting the wheel bearing using a stamped adjustment nut. (Ford)

is once again torqued, this time to a lower value. The nut is then backed up until the cotter pin will pass through the nearest hole in the spindle and one of the slots in the nut. See **Figure 38-14.** Some vehicles use a stamped nut lock that fits over the regular nut. This provides a finer adjustment in that more combinations of nut position and alignment with the cotter pin holes are available, **Figure 38-15.**

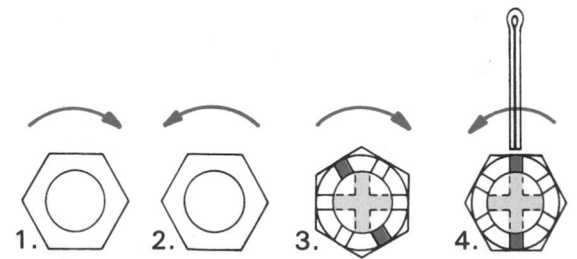

1—ROTATE WHEEL AND SEAT BEARING BY TIGHTENING NUT TO 10-16 FT.-LB. (13.5-21.6 N·m) TORQUE.
2—LOOSEN NUT UNTIL FREE.
3—RETIGHTEN NUT 20-25 IN.-LB. (2.3-2.8 N·m) TORQUE.
4—LOOSEN NUT UNTIL NEAREST HOLE IN SPINDLE LINES UP WITH A SLOT IN NUT. INSERT COTTER PIN.

Figure 38-14.   One wheel bearing adjustment procedure that involves the use of a torque wrench. (Pontiac)

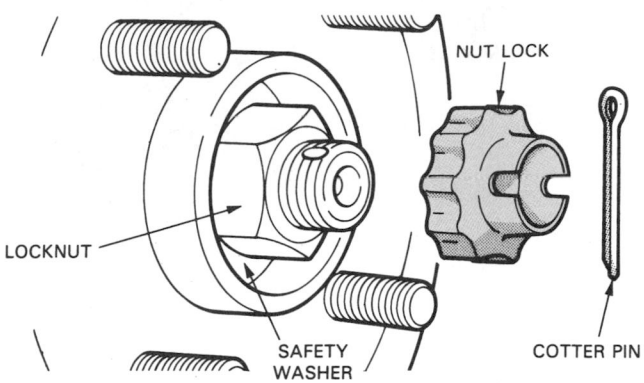

Figure 38-15.   By using a stamped adjustment nut lock, fine wheel bearing adjustment is possible. (Chrysler)

This special lock cap is compared with other nut types in **Figure 38-16.** Note that the nut may be adjusted as little as 1/24 turn. Another technique employing a torque wrench when the special stamped locking nut is used is illustrated in **Figure 38-17.** The adjusting nut is tightened to around 20 ft.-lb. (27 N·m) while spinning the wheel. The stamped locknut is then tried over the adjusting nut until one of the slots is aligned with the cotter pin hole in the spindle. The adjusting nut and locknut are then carefully loosened by one slot. The cotter pin is then inserted. Some vehicles use a special staked nut in place of a cotter pin. Look at **Figure 38-18.** When the staked nut is removed, it must be discarded. The nut has an integral, thin lip that is forced into a groove cut in the axle stub shaft with a special tool. Do not use a screwdriver or other sharp edged tool for staking.

SIX SLOTS IN ADJUSTING NUT
ONE HOLE IN SPINDLE

ADJUSTMENT CAN BE LOCKED AT
INTERVALS OF 1/6 TURN OF NUT

EIGHT SLOTS IN ADJUSTING NUT
ONE HOLE IN SPINDLE

ADJUSTMENT CAN BE LOCKED AT
INTERVALS OF 1/8 TURN OF NUT

SIX SLOTS IN ADJUSTING NUT
TWO HOLES IN SPINDLE

ADJUSTMENT CAN BE LOCKED AT
INTERVALS OF 1/12 TURN OF NUT

EIGHT SLOTS IN 12-POINT LOCK CAP
INSTALLED OVER ADJUSTING NUT
ONE HOLE IN SPINDLE

ADJUSTMENT CAN BE LOCKED AT
INTERVALS OF 1/24 TURN OF NUT

Figure 38-16.   Various front wheel locknut types.

Bearing Adjustment—Dial Indicator

Tighten the adjusting nut firmly with a medium size adjustable wrench while spinning the wheel. Loosen the adjusting nut up slowly until just finger free. Attach a dial indicator so that the indicator stem just contacts the machined

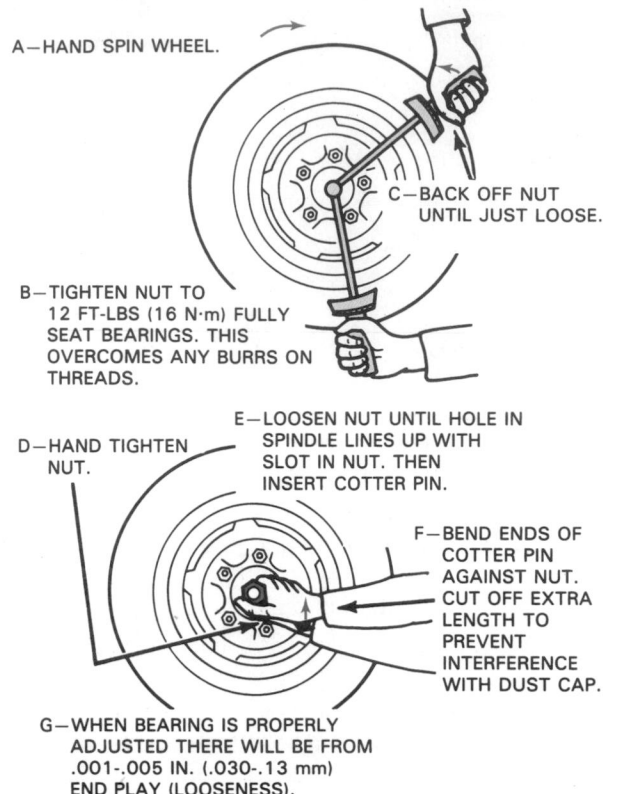

A—HAND SPIN WHEEL.

B—TIGHTEN NUT TO 12 FT-LBS (16 N·m) FULLY SEAT BEARINGS. THIS OVERCOMES ANY BURRS ON THREADS.

C—BACK OFF NUT UNTIL JUST LOOSE.

D—HAND TIGHTEN NUT.

E—LOOSEN NUT UNTIL HOLE IN SPINDLE LINES UP WITH SLOT IN NUT. THEN INSERT COTTER PIN.

F—BEND ENDS OF COTTER PIN AGAINST NUT. CUT OFF EXTRA LENGTH TO PREVENT INTERFERENCE WITH DUST CAP.

G—WHEN BEARING IS PROPERLY ADJUSTED THERE WILL BE FROM .001-.005 IN. (.030-.13 mm) END PLAY (LOOSENESS).

Figure 38-17. One method of wheel bearing adjustment with the tire and wheel on the vehicle. (Cadillac)

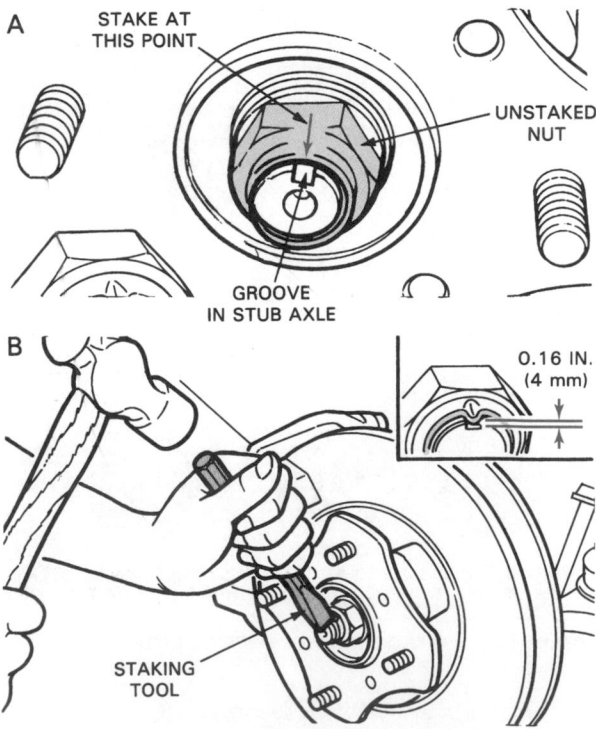

A   STAKE AT THIS POINT

UNSTAKED NUT

GROOVE IN STUB AXLE

B

0.16 IN. (4 mm)

STAKING TOOL

Figure 38-18. Staking the wheel nut to prevent rotation. A—An unstaked nut. Note the groove in the stub axle. B—A staking tool being used to force the nut lip into the axle groove. Note the proper staking depth. (Mazda)

end (outer side) of the hub, **Figure 38-19.** Grasp the sides of the rotor or the tire and pull straight in and out. Read gauge for amount of end play. Adjust nut until end play is within manufacturer's specifications. The dial indicator may be mounted to the spindle nut with the indicator touching the hub end. It may also be mounted to a wheel stud with the indicator stem contacting the end of the spindle.

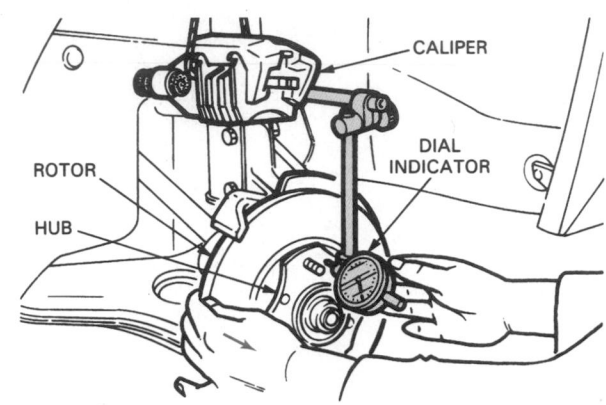

CALIPER

ROTOR

HUB

DIAL INDICATOR

Figure 38-19. A dial indicator being used to check bearing play. Note that the caliper has been removed. This makes accurate measuring easier. (Mazda)

Regardless of the technique used, the wheel will spin smoothly, freely, and with no appreciable lateral play (side shake) when the adjustment is correct. Do not confuse ball joint or suspension arm bushing wear with wheel bearing looseness. If in doubt, mount a dial indicator as described and check actual end play. For most tapered roller wheel bearings, adjust so that end play ranges from .001″ to .005″ (0.025 to 0.127 mm). Bearing service is illustrated in **Figure 38-20.** If disc brakes are used, up to .001″ (0.025 mm) end play is normally acceptable. Excessive end play will allow the disc to wobble.

Tap the head of the cotter pin firmly into the nut slot. Cut the pin to a length that will permit bending the ends, **Figure 38-21.** If a static collector is used in the dust cap, make certain the end of the pin bent over the spindle is short enough so that it will not hit the collector prong. The cotter pin may be installed as pictured in **Figure 38-22.** Regardless of the technique used for bending the pin ends, always use a new cotter pin. Use the thickest cotter pin that can be passed easily through the hole. Make certain the pin is tight after the ends are bent. A loose pin can break from vibration. Use new O-ring or sealer where required. Always make a final check before installing the dust cap to make certain that the safety washer, cotter pin, and staked nut (if used) are properly installed.

Sealed Ball and Roller Bearings

Many front-wheel drive vehicles use sealed straight roller or ball bearings, **Figure 38-23.** The rear axle bearings of some front-wheel drive vehicles are sealed. Sealed bearings must be replaced when they are defective or have damaged grease seals.

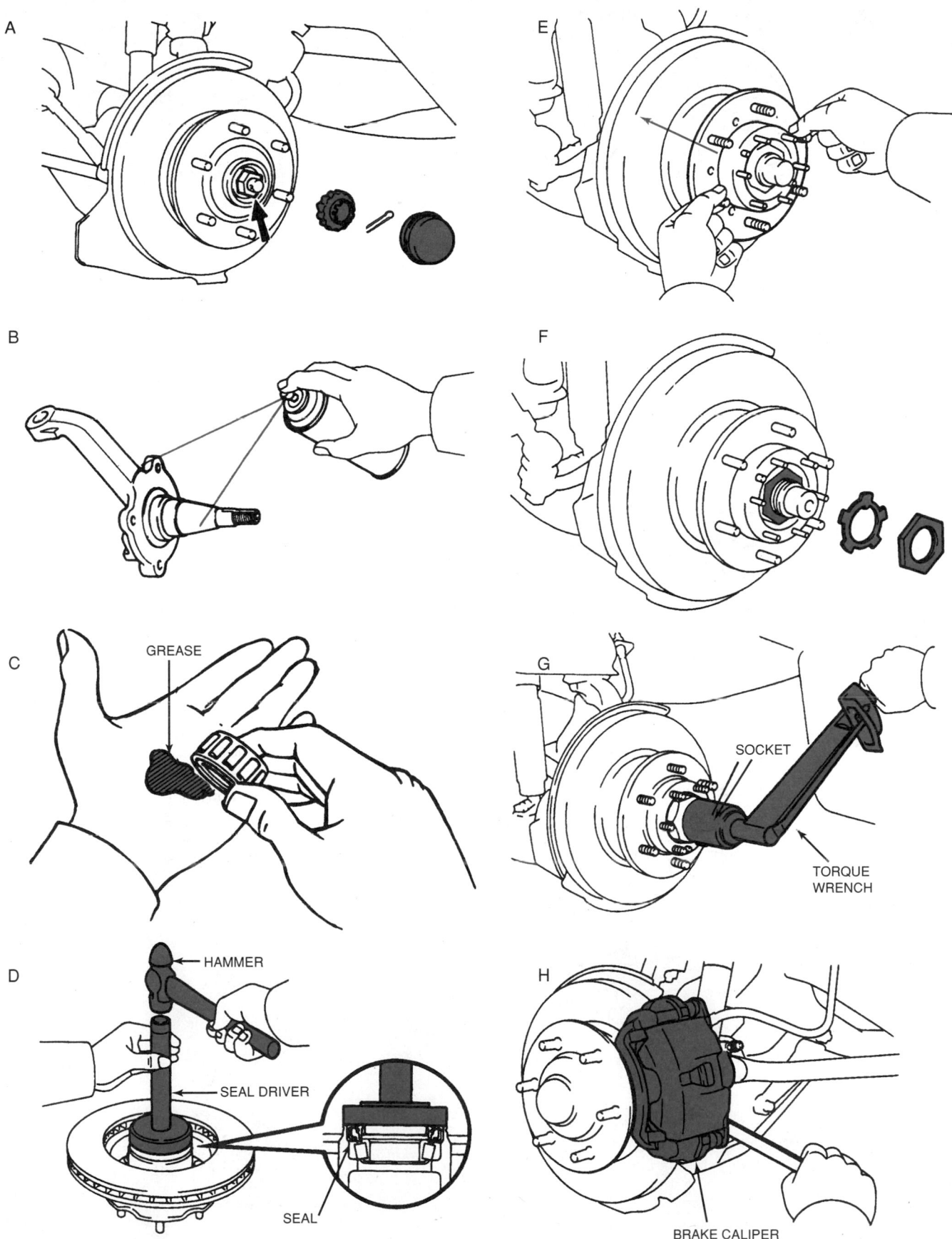

Figure 38-20. Some steps involved in wheel bearing service. A—Remove the dust cap, cotter pin, adjustment cap, and nut. B—Clean the spindle and check for damage. C—Clean the hub and bearings. Inspect for damage. Repack with grease. D—Install new seals. E—Install the hub and bearings onto the spindle. F—Replace lockwashers and nut. G—Torque adjustment nuts to specifications. H—Reinstall the brake caliper. (Toyota)

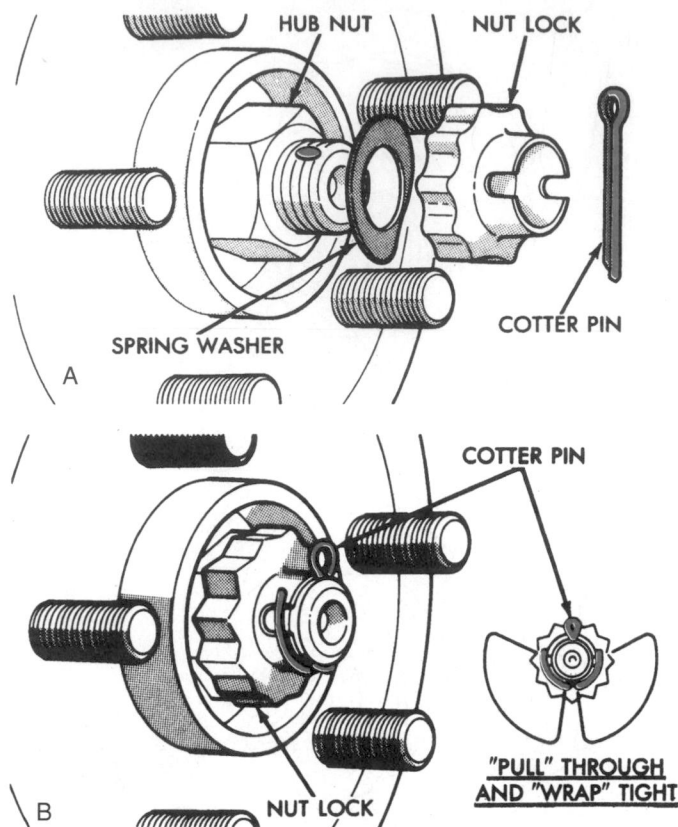

Figure 38-21. A—Installing the spring washer, nut lock, and cotter pin into a hub nut. B—The parts are installed, and the cotter pin is properly positioned and bent. (Chrysler)

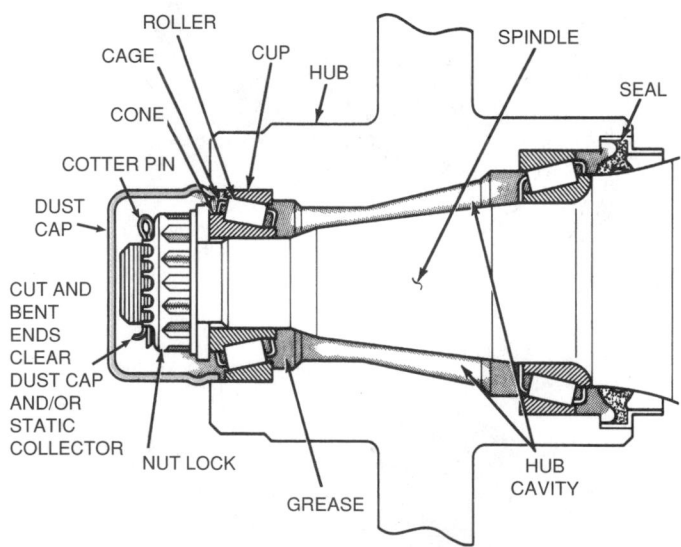

Figure 38-22. A properly installed cotter pin. Note how the ends of the pin are cut and bent to clear the dust cap sides and front. *Never* reuse the old cotter pin or one that does not fit the hole snugly. (Plymouth)

Sealed Bearings—Front-Wheel Drive Axles

Removal of most sealed front bearings require pressing out the bearing. This requires the removal of the steering knuckle assembly from the vehicle. A few bearings will

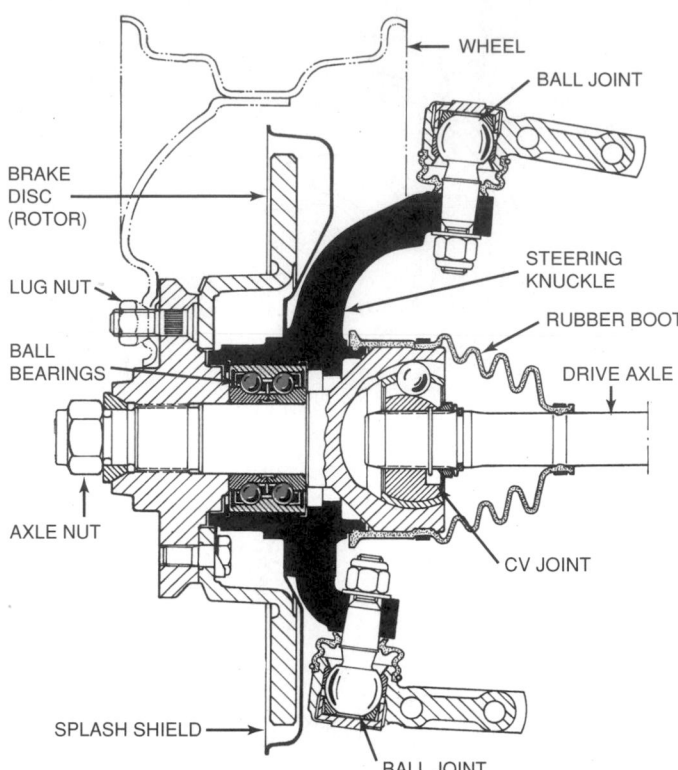

Figure 38-23. Front-wheel drive hub assembly that incorporates sealed ball bearings. (Saab)

slide out of the steering knuckle after the knuckle is removed from the vehicle and a snap ring removed. Some bearings are simply bolted to the steering knuckle and are replaced along with the hub as an assembly, **Figure 38-24.** Some bearings can be serviced only by replacing the complete steering knuckle assembly. Therefore, the following removal process is a general procedure. Consult the manufacturer's service manual for the exact procedure for each vehicle. Begin by taking off the wheel cover and removing the wheel and tire as explained earlier. Remove the cotter pin, nut lock (when used), hub nut, and washer.

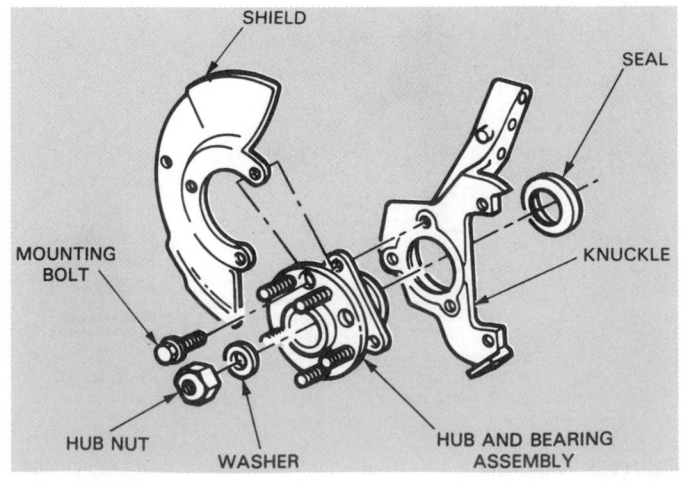

Figure 38-24. Exploded view of one type of wheel hub and bearing assembly. (Pontiac)

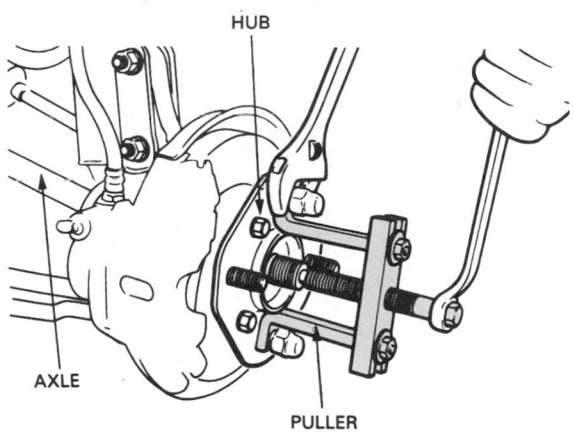

Figure 38-26. Using a puller to remove the hub. Do not use heat. (Dodge)

Pressed-in Bearing Replacement

To remove the pressed-in bearing, first remove any snap rings or dustcovers in the steering knuckle and place the knuckle on a suitable press. Press the bearing out of the steering knuckle using the correct adaptors, **Figure 38-27.** Note the position of any bearing spacers or other internal parts. Refer to Chapter 10 for additional information on bearing pressing techniques. Clean and inspect the steering knuckle and all parts which will be replaced. If the knuckle has any cracks or wear spots, replace it. Replace any dented or worn dustcovers or wear plates. Carefully position all parts of the bearing assembly over the steering knuckle. Using the correct adaptors, press the new bearing into the steering knuckle. Install any snap rings or dustcovers in their correct positions.

Reinstalling Steering Knuckle

Replace the steering knuckle on the vehicle, sliding the CV axle shaft into the bearing opening. Reinstall and torque all MacPherson strut and ball joint fasteners. Replace the nut holding the CV axle shaft into place and tighten to specifications. Install the cotter pin or deform the staked nut as required, **Figure 38-28.** Replace the brake caliper, ABS sensor and harness (if equipped), wheel, and wheel cover.

> **Note: After removing and reinstalling the steering knuckle on the vehicle, front end alignment must be checked. See Chapter 39.**

Replacing Sealed Bearings— Rear Nondriving Axles

Most sealed bearings used on rear wheel, nondriving axles are replaced as a unit. No other bearing service is possible. Many manufacturers recommend checking bearing play and preload in a method similar to the tapered bearing check discussed previously. Check the manufacturer's service manual for exact methods and specifications. Begin the replacement procedure by removing the wheel cover, then remove the wheel and tire. Remove the cotter pin or nut lock as applicable, hub nut, and washer. Remove

> **Note: The staked nut or cotter pin should always be replaced with new units. Some sealed bearing assemblies contain anti-lock brake wheel speed sensors. Replace the bearing, hub, and sensor as a unit if defective. They are not field serviceable.**

Remove the brake caliper and brake rotor. Support the caliper with a wire hook. Never depend on the brake hose to support the caliper. Loosen and remove the anti-lock brake wiring harness and sensor (if equipped), hub mounting bolts, and splash shield. Carefully observe the position of all parts so they can be reassembled in the correct position. An exploded view of hub components is shown in **Figure 38-25.** Some vehicles require that a puller be attached to push the CV drive axle out of the bearing. Do not use a hammer or heat the assembly to aid removal. See **Figure 38-26.** The steering knuckle can be removed from the suspension by removing the outer tie rod end, ball joint, and MacPherson strut attaching bolts. See Chapter 36 for more detailed removal procedures.

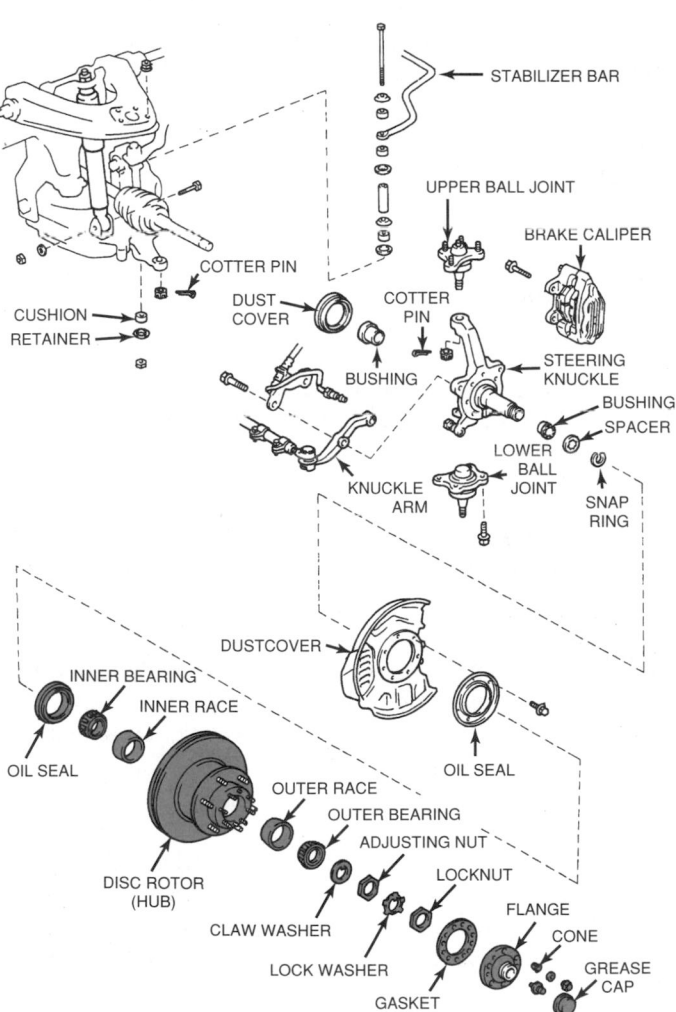

Figure 38-25. Exploded view of a four-wheel drive front hub and its related parts. (Toyota)

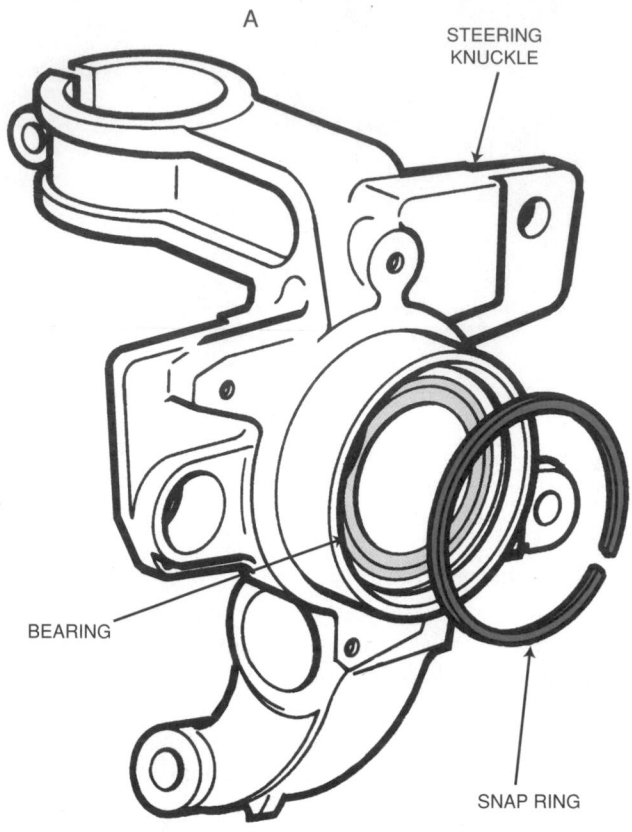

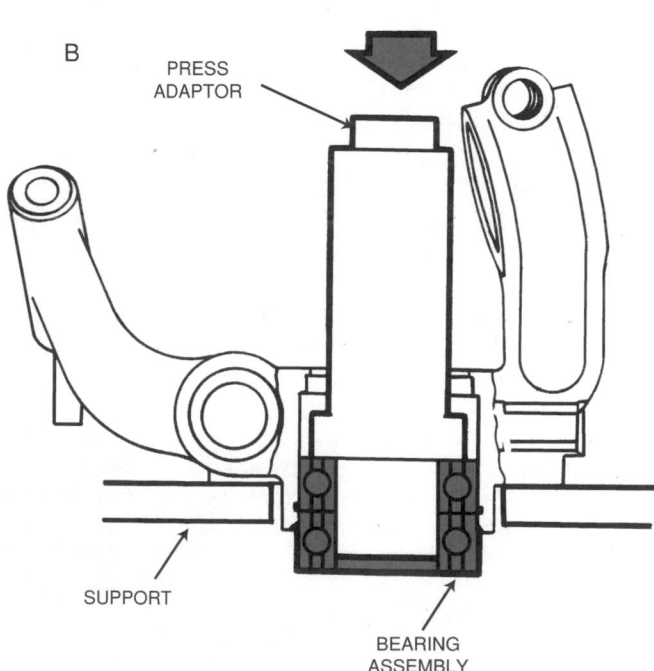

Figure 38-27. A—Remove the snap-ring and place the steering knuckle in a press. Support the knuckle properly. B—Remove the bearing from the steering knuckle with an arbor press and a special bearing adaptor tool. (Sterling)

and support the brake caliper, and remove the brake rotor. If the rear axle has drum brakes, remove the drum. If the vehicle is equipped with anti-lock brakes, remove the sensor and/or sensor connector.

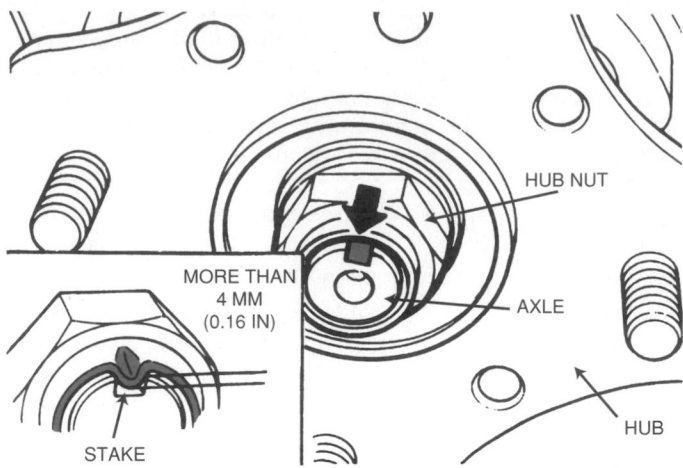

Figure 38-28. Hub nut on an axle showing the proper staking position and stake depth. If staked improperly, the nut may come off, allowing the hub to separate from the axle. (Mazda)

 Caution: Make sure that the brake assembly is supported before removing the bearing hub. Damage could result if the brake assembly is left to hang.

Loosen and remove the bearing hub mounting bolts and remove the hub. Carefully observe the position of all parts for reassembly. If the hub is being reused, install a new bearing in the hub. Reinstall the hub and bearing assembly. If any alignment shims were behind the hub assembly when it was removed, make sure they are reinstalled in their original location. Install the rotor and caliper or drum as applicable. Install and tighten the axle nut. Recheck axle play if necessary. Reinstall the wheel and tire assembly and wheel cover.

 Note: Where used, the staked nut or cotter pin should always be replaced with new hub bearing units.

Vehicle Wheel Rims

In the past, factory supplied vehicle *wheel rims* (the assembly on which the tire is mounted) were all made of stamped steel, painted to match the car color, or simply painted black. The only way to obtain any other type of wheel in the past was from an aftermarket supplier. Today, however, *custom wheels* are available as original equipment from vehicle manufacturers. In addition, aluminum, aluminum alloy, composite (graphite or plastic), and chromed steel wheels are available from many aftermarket manufacturers. Some wheels are solid aluminum, while others have a steel core covered with aluminum. Alloy wheels are usually a mixture of aluminum and magnesium. Wire wheels are also available. **Figure 38-29** shows some common custom wheels.

Wheel Rim Size

Rim size is determined by three measurements: rim width, rim diameter, and flange height. Rim width and

Figure 38-29. Selection of custom wheels. A—One-piece cast aluminum wheels. B—Wire spoke wheels. C—Steel wheels. Use care when working with custom wheels to prevent damage. (Appliance Wheels)

diameter are measured in inches. Flange height is identified by letters such as J or K. The letters indicate a definite flange height. For example, a K rim flange is 0.77″ (19.5 mm) high. See **Figure 38-30.** These measurements apply to rims made of any material.

Wheel Torquing

When the wheel rims are made of aluminum, or a composite of aluminum and steel, proper torque is critical. Always torque to the manufacturer's specifications. Do not use an impact wrench on any aluminum or alloy wheel unless it is equipped with a *torque stick,* **Figure 38-31A.** Torque sticks are flexible extensions which limit the output of the impact wrench to a preset value. This is accomplished by the flexing action built into the torque stick. When a certain torque value is reached, the stick will flex instead of transmitting further torque. They are available in several common torque settings. Although correct torque is not as

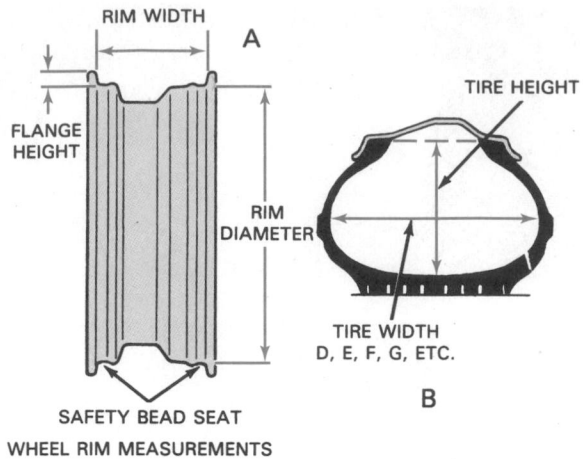

RIM WIDTH

A

TIRE HEIGHT

FLANGE HEIGHT

RIM DIAMETER

TIRE WIDTH D, E, F, G, ETC.

B

SAFETY BEAD SEAT

WHEEL RIM MEASUREMENTS

Figure 38-30. A—Rim size is identified by rim width, rim diameter, and flange height. Note the safety bead seats. These are used to keep the tire on the rim in the event of tire failure. B—The relationship between tire height and tire width determines the aspect ratio. If the tire height is 78% of the tire width, the aspect ratio would be 78. (Dodge, Firestone)

important with steel rims, the front disc brake rotors on most modern vehicles can be deformed by over-torquing. If torque sticks are not available, use a torque wrench to tighten the rim, **Figure 38-31B.**

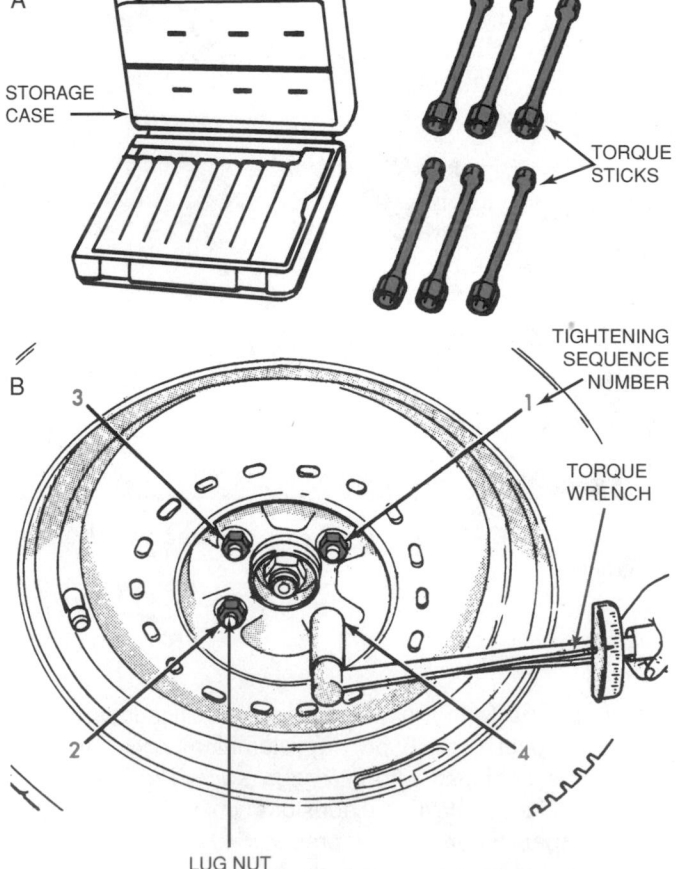

A

STORAGE CASE

TORQUE STICKS

B

TIGHTENING SEQUENCE NUMBER

TORQUE WRENCH

3

1

2

4

LUG NUT

Figure 38-31. A—Torque sticks. B—Torque wrench being used to set the lug nuts to a specific torque. (Chrysler, GM)

Checking for Wheel Damage

Check all rims for cracking, elongated mounting holes, and bent mounting flanges. Slight leakage of a steel rim can be corrected by welding or brazing without compromising rim safety. A porous aluminum rim can be repaired with an epoxy sealer. This wheel repair is similar to the automatic transmission porous casing repair described in Chapter 32. Aluminum rims should not be welded for any reason. Excessive runout can be checked as outlined in the tire balancing section.

Wheel Lug Service

Wheel lugs are pressed into the bearing hub. *Lug nuts* are used with the lugs to hold the wheel to the hub. Lug nuts should be tightened to the proper torque and in the sequence shown in **Figure 38-31B.** This will prevent wheel or hub distortion and will protect the lug from damage. If the wheel lugs are difficult to remove, they should be coated with anti-seize compound to prevent damage.

If a lug nut is damaged or missing, it should be replaced as soon as possible. Always replace broken lug nuts or bolts with the correct size and type. Most lugs can be knocked out of the wheel hub after the wheel rim and the brake drum or rotor are removed, **Figure 38-32.** The new lug can be installed by using a press or by drawing the lug through the hub using a wheel nut, **Figure 38-33.** Lubricate all parts thoroughly before installation. If the lug will not press solidly into the hub, replace the hub.

Vehicle Tires

Tires are a vital, but often overlooked part of overall vehicle performance. Improper handling, braking, and ride quality may result from defective tires or tires that are wrong for the vehicle. Serious handling problems can be caused by something as simple as underinflation. The following

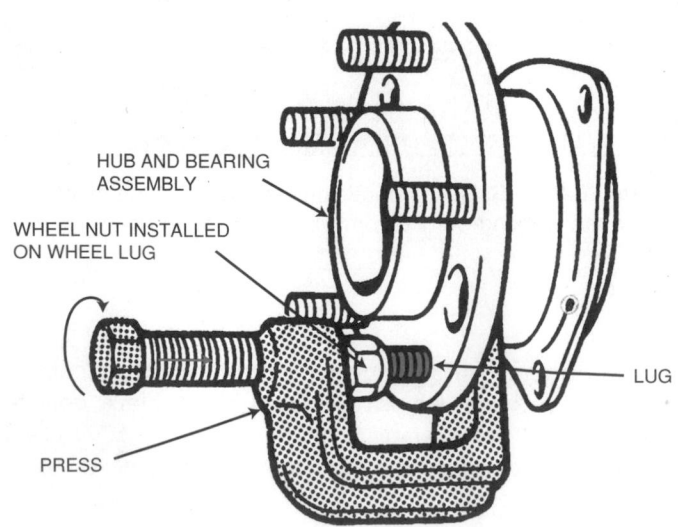

HUB AND BEARING ASSEMBLY

WHEEL NUT INSTALLED ON WHEEL LUG

LUG

PRESS

Figure 38-32. Removing a damaged lug bolt with a special press. (GM)

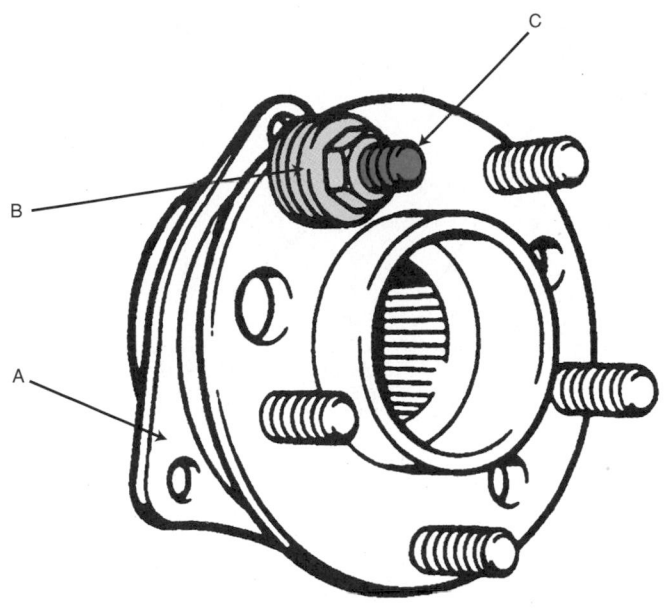

A—HUB AND BEARING ASSEMBLY
B—INSERT WASHERS OVER WHEEL LUG
C—TIGHTEN NUT TO DRAW WHEEL LUG INTO
    CORRECT POSITION

Figure 38-33.   Installing a new lug bolt into the hub by using washers and a lug nut. As the lug nut is tightened, the lug bolt will be drawn into position. (GM)

section covers modern tire grading, selection, and installation techniques.

Tire Cord Construction

Many older tires were constructed using two or four **plies** (layers of cord material) laid at an angle to the tire centerline. Look at **Figure 38-34A.** This is termed **bias** construction. Another method of arranging the plies is illustrated in **Figure 38-34B.** This is called a **bias-belted** cord arrangement. Note the difference in cord angles between **Figures 38-34A** and **38-34B.**

The third type of construction is **radial,** in which the body cords cross the tire centerline almost at right angles to the belts, **Figure 38-34C.** Radial tires may also be belted. Today, radial tires are almost universally used for all applications, including retrofitting older vehicles that originally came with bias tires. Rayon, nylon, polyester, aramid, Kevlar, and fiberglass are used as cord materials. Steel wire is often used in the belt section of radial tires. Other materials are also being tested and evaluated.

> **Caution: Manufacturers do not advise mixing radial and bias tires on the same vehicle. Poor vehicle handling will result. If radial and bias tires must be used on the same vehicle, ensure that the bias tires are placed on the front axle.**

Tire Rating Information

Tire ratings are determined by a system of numbers and letters which are molded on the side of the tire or listed in the vehicle owner's manual. The rating system identifies the tire size, rim size, and type of construction, as well as the maximum speed and load handling capabilities. A typical modern tire might have the series of letters and numbers shown in **Figure 38-35** on its sidewall.

The letter P indicates the tire is designed for a passenger vehicle, such as a car or light truck. Other possible tire designations are T for temporary, such as a space saver tire, LT for light trucks, and C for commercial or large trucks. This letter may be absent on some tires. The number 225 represents the tire's section width in millimeters, measured at the tire's widest point. This is the actual tire size. Tire size can range from 145 to 315, with most sizes from about 185 to 235. The higher the number, the larger the tire. The number 70 is the aspect ratio (relationship of a tire's cross-sectional height to its width). Other common aspect ratios are 60, 65, 75, 78, and 80. The higher the aspect ratio, the taller the tire. Low aspect ratios provide more traction, while high aspect ratios give better mileage. The letter H is the speed

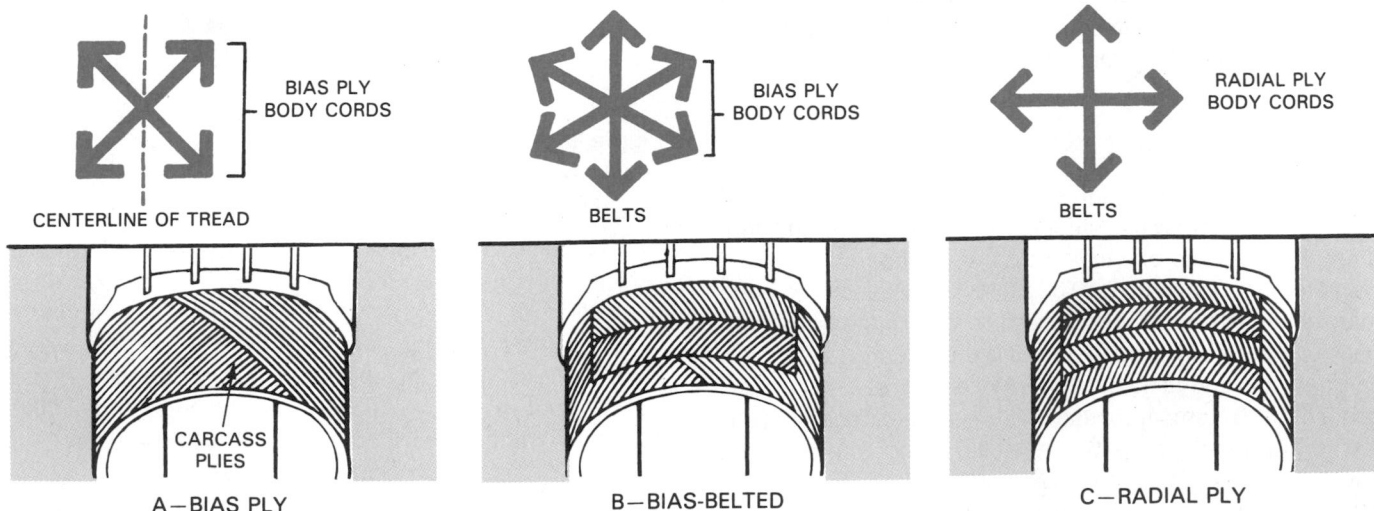

Figure 38-34.   Three methods of arranging tire cords. Note the arrows above each ply method. These indicate the direction of the ply cords. (Goodyear Tire and Rubber Co.)

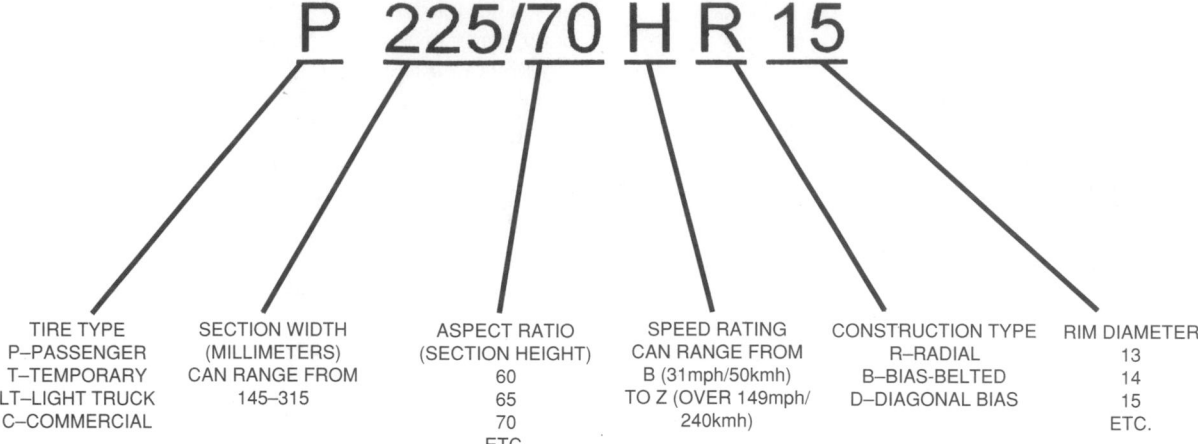

TIRE TYPE	SECTION WIDTH	ASPECT RATIO	SPEED RATING	CONSTRUCTION TYPE	RIM DIAMETER
P–PASSENGER	(MILLIMETERS)	(SECTION HEIGHT)	CAN RANGE FROM	R–RADIAL	13
T–TEMPORARY	CAN RANGE FROM	60	B (31mph/50kmh)	B–BIAS-BELTED	14
LT–LIGHT TRUCK	145–315	65	TO Z (OVER 149mph/	D–DIAGONAL BIAS	15
C–COMMERCIAL		70	240kmh)		ETC.
		ETC.			

Figure 38-35. Typical tire rating information.

rating. The speed rating gives the maximum speed at which the tire can be operated. This ranges from *B* (31 mph or 50 kmh) to *Z* (over 149 mph or 240 kmh). The letter *R* indicates radial ply construction. A bias ply tire will be marked *B*. Almost all passenger car and light truck tires made today are radial tires. The number *15* is the rim diameter in inches. Modern wheel rims range from 12 inches (rare) to 17 inches (also rare). The most common rim sizes are 13, 14, and 15 inches.

Tire Quality Grading

All passenger and light truck vehicle tires now being produced are graded by the Department of Transportation (DOT) **uniform tire quality grading** system. The quality grading system is applicable to the following three areas:

The **temperature resistance** rating has three letter-grade levels: A, B, and C. "A" offers the greatest resistance to heat generation. "C" provides the least. All tires must meet the "C" rating. Tire **traction** is also graded on three levels: A, B, and C. "A" offers the best traction (wet roads), while "C" offers the smallest amount. Tire **tread wear** is graded by using a set of numbers ranging from 100 to about 500. A tire that has a tread wear grade of 150 should supply approximately 50% more mileage than a tire with a tread wear rating of 100.

Special Service Tires

Many safety and high-speed tires are available. High speed tires generally use steel wires in the outer ply and tread area. Steel resists expansion from centrifugal force, which helps to control distortion. They also resist punctures better than fabric belts. Most vehicles are now equipped with a compact, or **space saver** spare tire. It is designed to take up less cargo space and is lighter than a normal tire. The compact spare tire is for temporary use only. Use it to replace a flat until the normal tire is repaired or replaced. Do not rotate a space saver tire in with the other tires. When replacing this tire, mount only on a special wheel designed for its use. Do not use hub caps or wheel covers on the rim. Possible tire damage could result. Keep inflated to recommended pressure. A compact spare tire is pictured in **Figure 38-36**.

Figure 38-36. A compact spare tire compared to a tire of normal size. (Goodyear Tire and Rubber Co.)

Tire Selection

A tire load information label can be found on most vehicles. It is generally located on the driver's door, on the door pillar, or inside the glove box. The load information label contains specific information on maximum vehicle load, tire size including the spare tire, and inflation pressures. Older vehicles with obsolete grading systems can be equipped with modern tires by the use of interchange charts, such as the one in **Figure 38-37**.

Tire Pressure

All tires must be inflated to the recommended pressure. An underinflated tire will cause the sidewalls to flex excessively and will quickly generate damaging heat. In

P-METERIC SIZE **(35 psi max. pressure)	IF VEHICLE TIRE PLACARD SPECIFIES A P-METERIC TIRE SIZE, THE FOLLOWING ARE ACCEPTABLE SUBSTITUTE SIZES: Use inflation pressure specified on vehicle tire placard.
P215/60R16	P225/55R16, P235/50R16
P225/60R16	P255/50R16
P205/55R16	P225/50R16
P225/55R16	P215/60R16, P235/50R16
P225/50R16	P215/60R16, P225/55R16, P235/50R16
P235/50R16	P215/60R16, P225/55R16
P245/50R16	P225/60R16
P255/50R16	P265/50R16
P265/50R16	P275/50R16
P275/50R16	(NONE)
P245/40R17	(NONE)
P275/40R17	P315/35R17
P315/35R17	P275/40R17

*The letters H, S, V, or Z may be included in the tire size designation of P-metric and other metric sizes preceding the "R"
**For 'standard load' tires

ALPHA-NUMERIC SIZE* ON VEHICLE PLACARD (32 PSI MAX. PRESSURE)	IF VEHICLE TIRE PLACARD SPECIFIES AN ALPHA-NUMBERIC TIRE SIZE, THE FOLLOWING ARE ACCEPTABLE SUBSTITUTE SIZES IMPORTANT: Add 3 PSI above the pressure specified on the vehicle the placard to assure adequate load capacity.
AR78-13	P165/80R13, P175/75R13, P185/70R13, P195/60R13, P215/50R13, 185/70R13
BR 78-13	P175/80R13, P185/75R13, P195/70R13, P195/65R13, P205/60R13
CR78-13	P185/80R12, P195/70R13, P215/60R13, P235/50R13
BR78-14	P175/75R14, P185/70R14, 185/70R14
CR78-14	P185/75R14, P195/70R14, P205/65R14, P215/60R14, P195/70R14
DR78-14	P185/80R14, P195/75R14, P205/70R14, P205/65R14, P215/60R14, P245/50R14
ER78-14	P195/75R14, P205/70R14, P255/60R14, P245/50R14
FR78-14	P205/75R14, P215/70R14, P235/60R14, P265/50R14
GR78-14	P215/75R14, P225/70R14, P245/60R14 P255/55R14, P265/50R14
HR78-14	P225/75R14, P235/70R14
BR78-15	P165/80R15, P175/75R15, P185/70R15
ER78-15	P195/75R15, P215/65R15, P245/50R15
FR78-15	P205/75R15, P215/70R15, P215/65R15, P235/60R15, P245/50R15
GR78-15	P215/75R15, P215/70R15, P235/60R15, P255/55R15, P265/50R15
HR78-15	P225/75R15, P235/70R15, P255/60R15, P275/50R15
JR78-15	P225/75R15, P235/70R15, P255/60R15
LR78-15	P235/75R15, P245/70R15, P255/65R15, P265/60R15, P295/50R15

Figure 38-37.   One type of tire size interchange chart.

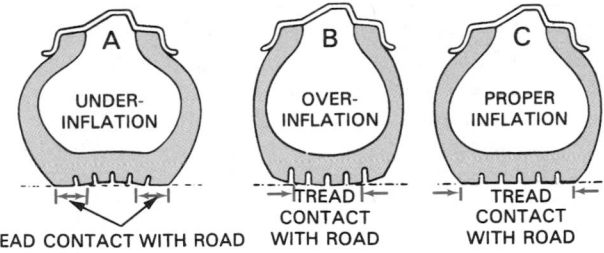

Figure 38-38.   The effect of inflation pressure on the tire-to-road contact. (Rubber Mfg. Association)

ered cold after standing out of direct sunlight for three or four hours. When tires are driven, their temperature rises. The amount of temperature increase will depend upon speed, load, road smoothness, and prevailing temperature. A cold tire at 24 psi (165 kPa) will build up pressure to about 29 psi (200 kPa) after 4 miles (6.4 km) at speeds over 40 mph (64.4 kmh). When checking hot tires, pressure will exceed cold specifications. Never let air out of hot tires to get specified cold pressure. For heavy loads or sustained high speed driving, many manufacturers recommend increasing cold pressure 4 psi (25 kPa).

Tire Rotation

Tire life can be extended by periodic tire rotation. The front tires are placed at the rear before any front wheel misalignment can cause serious tire imbalance or tire wear. Rotate tires about every 5000 miles (8000 km). **Figure 38-39** shows popular methods of rotation, using both conventional and radial tires.

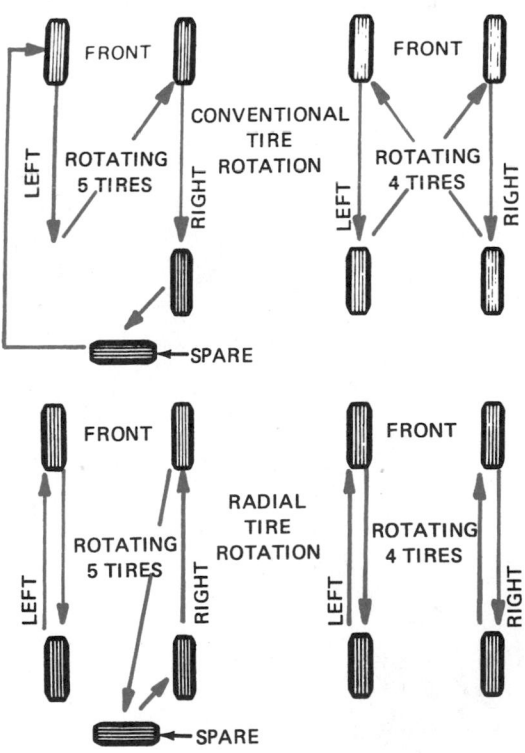

Figure 38-39.   Tire rotation chart for both conventional and radial tires. Follow the specific rotation pattern recommended by the vehicle or tire manufacturer. (Chrysler)

addition, the center section of the tread will buckle up away from the road, causing rapid wear on the tire edges. See **Figure 38-38A.** Overinflation will make the tire ride hard and will also make it more susceptible to ply breakage. Note how the overinflated tire in **Figure 38-38B** bulges in the center, thus pulling the edges of the tire away from the road. This produces rapid wear in the center. To provide proper steering, ride, wear, and dependability, keep the tire pressure within the manufacturer's recommended range. Note how the full tread width of the correctly inflated tire in **Figure 38-38C** contacts the surface of the road.

Inflate tires to recommended pressure when cold (at prevailing atmospheric temperature). A tire may be consid-

Caution: Some manufacturers do not recommend radial tire rotation. Other radial tire manufacturers recommend that radial tires be rotated so they always turn in the same direction, Figure 38-39D. Do not rotate in the compact (space saver type) spare tire. Space saver spares are for emergency driving only.

Tire Demounting and Mounting

Use the proper equipment to demount and mount tires. Use care to avoid damaging the bead sealing surfaces. Always use an approved rubber lubricant before demounting and mounting. Otherwise, you may tear the sealing surface and/or cause excessive strain on the bead wire. Refer to **Figure 38-40.** Before mounting a tire on a wheel, clean off the rim sealing area with coarse steel wool. File off nicks and burrs. Straighten any dented area on the sealing flanges (edges). If the rim has any cracks or splits, discard it. See **Figure 38-41.**

 Note: When mounting oversize tires, make sure the wheel is approved for their use.

Repairing a Punctured Tire

If a tire is suspected of having a leak, first fill it with air. Place the tire and wheel in a drum filled with water. A hose can also be used. Look for air bubbles forming on the tire

Figure 38-41. Clean the rim and check for cracks, dents, and old wheel weights *before* mounting the tire. (Rubber Mfg. Association)

surface and at the bead. Also check the wheel rim and valve stem for leakage. When the leak is located, mark it with crayon or chalk. All tires have repairable and nonrepairable areas. Never repair a tire with:

- Ply separation.
- Damaged bead wires.
- Tread separation.
- Loose cords.
- Cuts or cracks that extend into the tire cord (fabric) material.
- Tread wear indicators showing.
- Sidewall punctures, bulges, or damage.
- Punctures larger than 0.5″ (13 mm).

In the past, punctures were repaired by inserting a rubber plug in the puncture hole without demounting the tire. However, due to safety concerns, this method of repair is no longer recommended. The use of plugs without demounting the tire can result in sudden tire failure.

To repair a puncture properly, demount the tire and remove the puncturing object, noting the angle of penetration. Clean the puncture area with a special tool. A correct puncture repair must fill the damage area and patch the inner liner. A **plug** or **liquid sealer** is used to fill the puncture hole from the inside of the tire. If a plug is used, cut it off slightly above the tire's inside surface. After filling the hole, scuff the puncture area well beyond the actual damage. Then apply cement to the scuffed area. Apply a **patch** that will cover the puncture well beyond the damaged area according to the manufacturer's directions. A tool called a **stitcher** is used to help bond the patch tightly to the tire's inner liner. See **Figure 38-42.** Allow sufficient time for drying.

Figure 38-40. Demounting a tire. *Use caution and wear safety goggles!* (Hunter Engineering Co.)

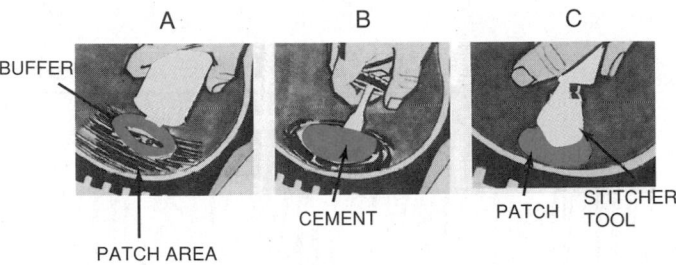

Figure 38-42. Installing a tire patch. A—Buff an area slightly larger than the patch and clean the buffed area thoroughly. B—Apply the cement with a brush (allow for recommended drying time). C—Install the patch. Use the stitcher tool to firmly roll the patch into contact with the cement. Roll over the entire surface of the patch. (Goodyear Tire and Rubber Co.)

Tire Inflation Following Mounting

When mounting the tire, use a liberal amount of rubber lubricant. Do not use silicone. Use a clip-on air chuck to attach the air hose to the valve stem. Back away from the tire while inflating. Never exceed a pressure of 40 psi (276 kPa) in an endeavor to force the beads out against the rim flanges. If difficulty is experienced, deflate the tire and check for the source of trouble. Stay away from the tire while seating the beads. Reduce air pressure following bead seating. Look at **Figure 38-43.** On some tires, the use of a *bead expander* or seal ring will help trap sufficient air to inflate a tubeless tire. Remove expander before tire pressure exceeds 10 psi (69 kPa).

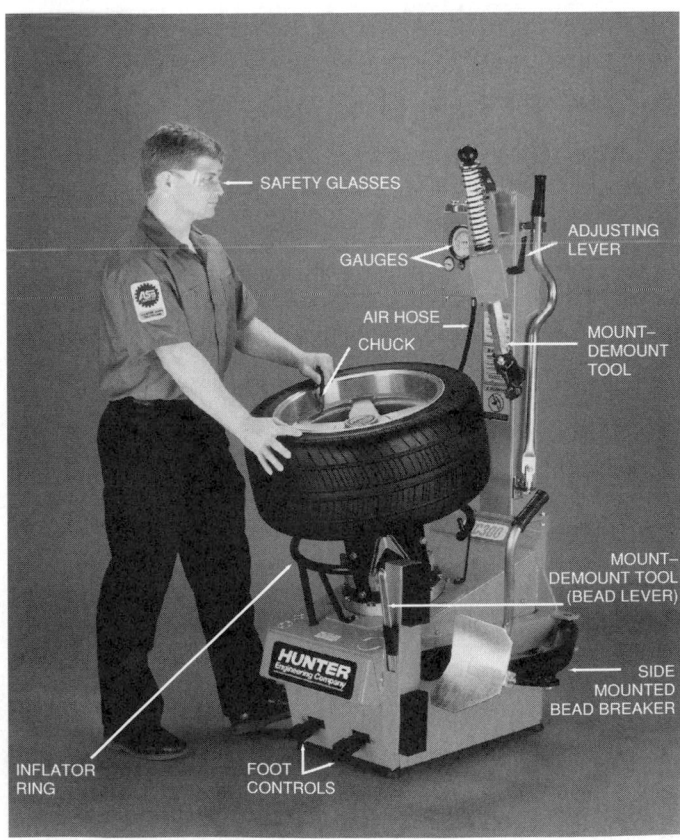

Figure 38-43. Inflating a newly mounted tire. (Hunter Engineering Co.)

The tire and rim can explode with extreme force if too much air is applied. When a tire bead is forced into place, it can cock to one side and bind. If air pressure is allowed to exceed 40 psi (276 kPa), the wire bead can snap. This can allow the bead edge to explode outward against the rim flange with such force that the flange is sheared off. Never exceed maximum bead seating pressure. Do not inflate tires with air that is contaminated with oil, gasoline, or cleaning solvents because tire damage or explosion can occur.

Tire Wear Patterns

An important part of tire service is inspecting the tire treads for unusual wear patterns. Although worn suspension parts or poor alignment can be responsible for rapid or uneven tire wear, underinflation, overinflation, toe, camber, and cornering wear are the most common causes. Refer to **Figure 38-44.**

Underinflation can cause rapid edge or shoulder wear, **Figure 38-44A.** Overinflation can wear out the center of the tread, **Figure 38-44B.** Excessive toe-in or toe-out will cause extremely rapid wear and will be evidenced by feathered edges as in **Figure 38-44E.** Improper camber angle will wear only one side of the tread, **Figure 38-44D.** Excessive speed around corners will generally cause a rounding of the outside shoulder. There are certain similarities to toe wear in some cases. A combination of causes can produce numerous wear patterns. One common symptom of combination wear is a series of cupped out spots around the tire, **Figures 38-44F** and **38-44G.** This pattern is also common when toe is off on a rear tire. When a vehicle's tires show wear patterns as illustrated in **Figure 38-44,** corrective measures are needed.

Wheel and Tire Balance

Irregularities in construction, shifting of the cords and weight mass from tread wear, and other problems can cause the tire and wheel assembly to become unbalanced. At highway speeds, even a slight imbalance can cause *wheel tramp* (tire and wheel hopping up and down) or *wheel shimmy* (shaking from side to side). Wheel assemblies must be in both static and dynamic balance.

> **Caution: If the tire is defective or the rim is damaged, do not try to correct the problem by balancing. Replace the affected tire or rim.**

Static Balance

To be in *static balance,* the weight mass must be evenly distributed around the axis of rotation. See **Figure 38-45A.** A wheel in static balance will remain balanced in any position, whereas static imbalance will cause the heavy side to rotate to the bottom. The wheel is brought into static balance by clipping weights to the rim opposite the heavy side. If more than 2 ounces (56 g) of weight is required, the weight should be split by adding one-half of the required amount to the inside of the rim and the remainder to the outside. By placing half of the weight on each side, dynamic balance will not be disturbed. Look at **Figure 38-45B.**

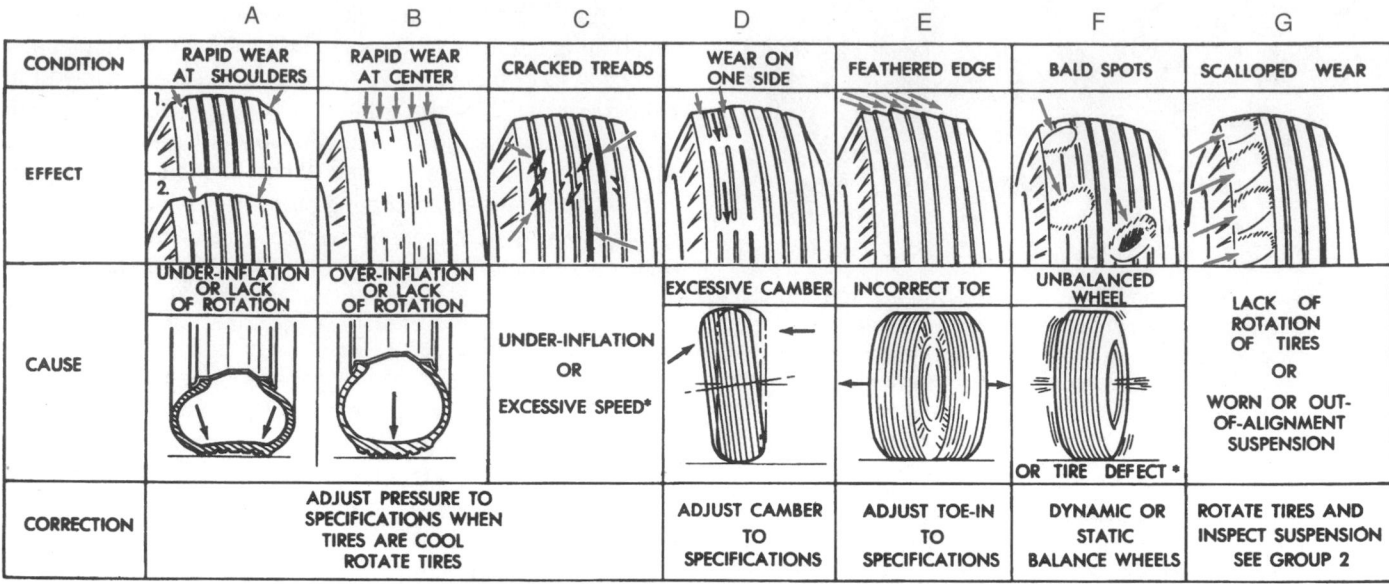

CONDITION	A RAPID WEAR AT SHOULDERS	B RAPID WEAR AT CENTER	C CRACKED TREADS	D WEAR ON ONE SIDE	E FEATHERED EDGE	F BALD SPOTS	G SCALLOPED WEAR
EFFECT							
CAUSE	UNDER-INFLATION OR LACK OF ROTATION	OVER-INFLATION OR LACK OF ROTATION	UNDER-INFLATION OR EXCESSIVE SPEED*	EXCESSIVE CAMBER	INCORRECT TOE	UNBALANCED WHEEL OR TIRE DEFECT *	LACK OF ROTATION OF TIRES OR WORN OR OUT-OF-ALIGNMENT SUSPENSION
CORRECTION	ADJUST PRESSURE TO SPECIFICATIONS WHEN TIRES ARE COOL ROTATE TIRES			ADJUST CAMBER TO SPECIFICATIONS	ADJUST TOE-IN TO SPECIFICATIONS	DYNAMIC OR STATIC BALANCE WHEELS	ROTATE TIRES AND INSPECT SUSPENSION SEE GROUP 2

Figure 38-44. Some abnormal tire wear patterns. Note the *cause,* the *effect,* and the *correction.* (Dodge)

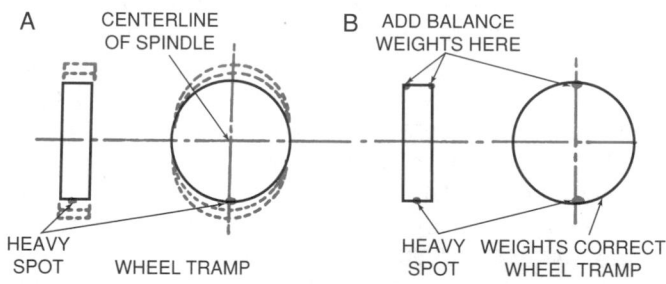

Figure 38-45. A wheel brought into static balance by adding proper size balance weights to the light side. Note how the weights are split, with one-half placed on each side of the wheel. (Pontiac)

Dynamic Balance

To be in *dynamic balance,* the centerline of the weight mass must be in the same plane as the centerline of the wheel. **Figure 38-46** shows a wheel and tire assembly that is dynamically imbalanced. Note how the weight mass centerline fails to coincide with the plane of the wheel centerline. When the wheel rotates, centrifugal force attempts to force the weight mass to align with the wheel centerline. Since the direction of this force is one way on one side of the assembly and the other is on the opposite side, **Figure 38-46A,** it causes the wheel to shimmy, **Figure 38-46B.** Dynamic imbalance is corrected by adding wheel balance weights in amounts sufficient to bring the weight mass and wheel centerlines into the same plane. To be in dynamic balance, the assembly must also be in static balance. **Figure 38-47** pictures a dynamically balanced wheel and tire assembly. Note how the wheel and weight mass centerlines coincide, **Figure 38-47A.** When the wheel rotates, there is no shimmy, **Figure 38-47B.**

Measuring Wheel and Tire Runout

A wheel and tire assembly with excessive lateral or radial runout cannot be balanced properly. Modern tires

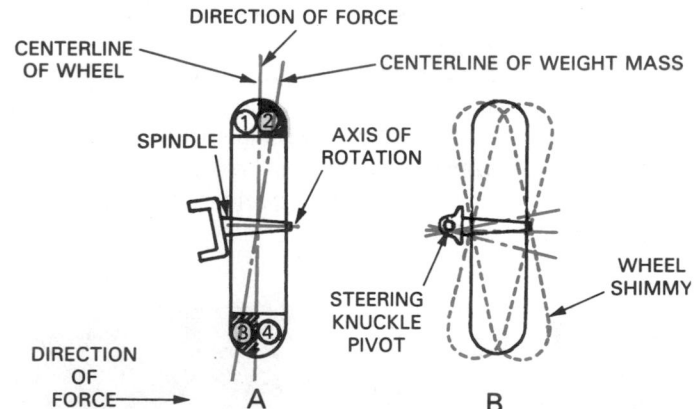

Figure 38-46. A dynamically unbalanced wheel and tire assembly. (Plymouth)

often develop tread separations, which result in excessive runout. Such tires cannot be balanced and should be discarded. Always check tire runout before balancing. Check runout at the points indicated in **Figure 38-48.**

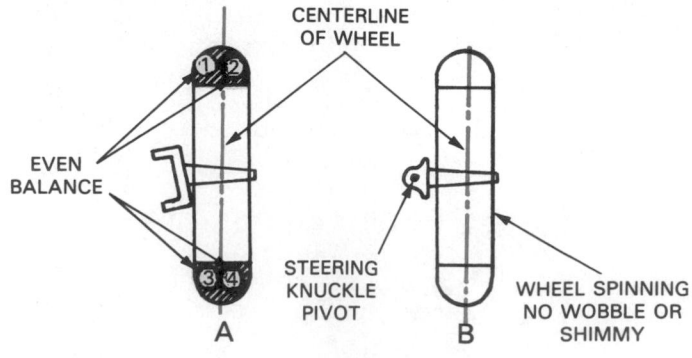

Figure 38-47. A dynamically balanced tire and wheel assembly.

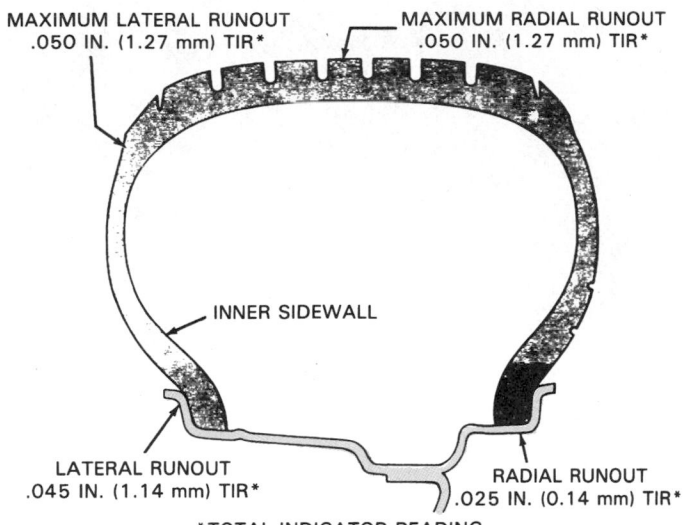

Figure 38-48. Check the wheel and tire at these points with a dial indicator. (Cadillac)

Generally, tire radial and lateral runout should be kept within the figures shown in **Figure 38-48.** When possible, use a dial indicator setup as shown in **Figure 38-49.** Follow manufacturer's specifications. If tire runout is excessive, check wheel rim runout. It may be possible to bring tire runout within specs by shifting the tire on the rim until the point of maximum tire runout is opposite the point of maximum wheel runout. Runout may be checked by using a dial indicator or a special indicator. This is shown in **Figure 38-49.** The indicator stand must be heavy enough to hold the instrument in a fixed position. Raise the wheel and position the indicator. Slowly rotate the wheel and note the reading. The tire must be warm to avoid any flat spots from sitting in one place for a long time.

Balancing Techniques

Modern radial tires must have both static and dynamic balance. The tire should be balanced statically first and then balanced dynamically. Tire and wheel assemblies may be balanced on the vehicle or off the vehicle. An off-car balancer is pictured in **Figure 38-50.** Follow manufacturer's instructions. An on-car balancer is shown in **Figure 38-51.**

> 🛑 **STOP** Warning: Front-wheel drive vehicles should have the front wheels spun by the engine, not with an on-car balancer. The suspension should not be allowed to hang unsupported while spinning the wheels. Driving constant velocity joints at extreme angles can cause excessive vibration and part damage.

Limit wheel speed to around 35 mph (56.3 kmh), as indicated on speedometer. Remember that the speedometer indicates only one-half of the actual wheel speed when one wheel is spun and the other is stopped. Extreme speed can cause the tire to disintegrate. It can also cause possible differential or transaxle damage.

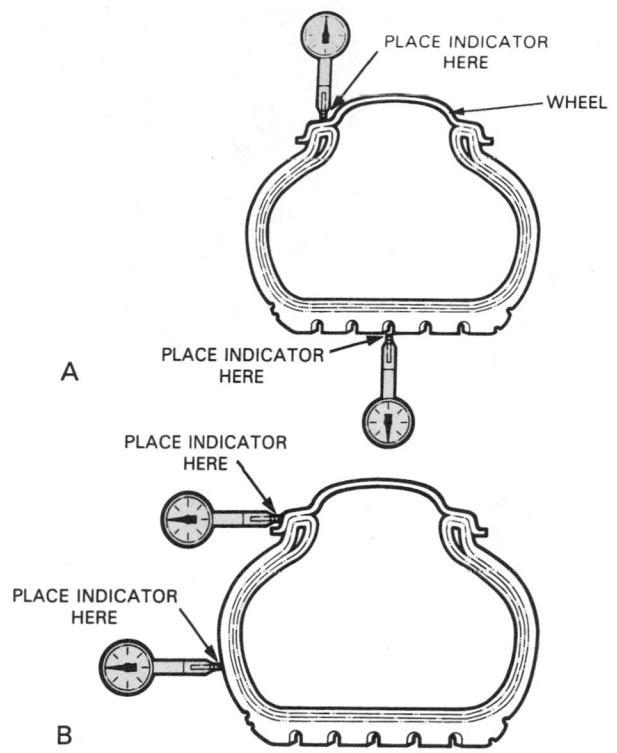

Figure 38-49. A—Checking tire and rim radial runout. B—Checking lateral runout with a dial indicator. (B.F. Goodrich)

Balancing Rear Wheels

The rear wheel and tire assemblies should also be balanced. When a standard differential is used, jack up one side only. When balanced, lower the vehicle to the floor. Raise the other wheel and balance. Do not try this on the limited-slip type differential as it will move the vehicle forward. When using an on-car balancer on vehicles equipped with a limited-slip differential, raise both wheels from the floor. Remove one wheel and replace a couple of the lug nuts to hold the drum in place. Balance the side with the wheel in place. Once that side is balanced, the other wheel should be reinstalled and balanced. It is not necessary to remove the wheel already balanced. Make certain the vehicle is secure on jack stands. Keep personnel out from in front of the vehicle.

> ⚠️ Caution: When balancing the rear wheels, if one wheel is on the floor and the other is free to turn, the revolving wheel will turn twice as fast as the speedometer indicates. Do not exceed a speedometer reading of around 40 mph (64 kmh). This will produce a wheel speed of about 80 mph (129 kmh).

With the limited-slip differential setup (both sides free of floor), wheel speed will be that indicated by the speedometer. Use quality equipment in top shape and follow the manufacturer's instructions. Always clean the wheel of mud and grease and pick out rocks and other debris stuck in the tread before balancing.

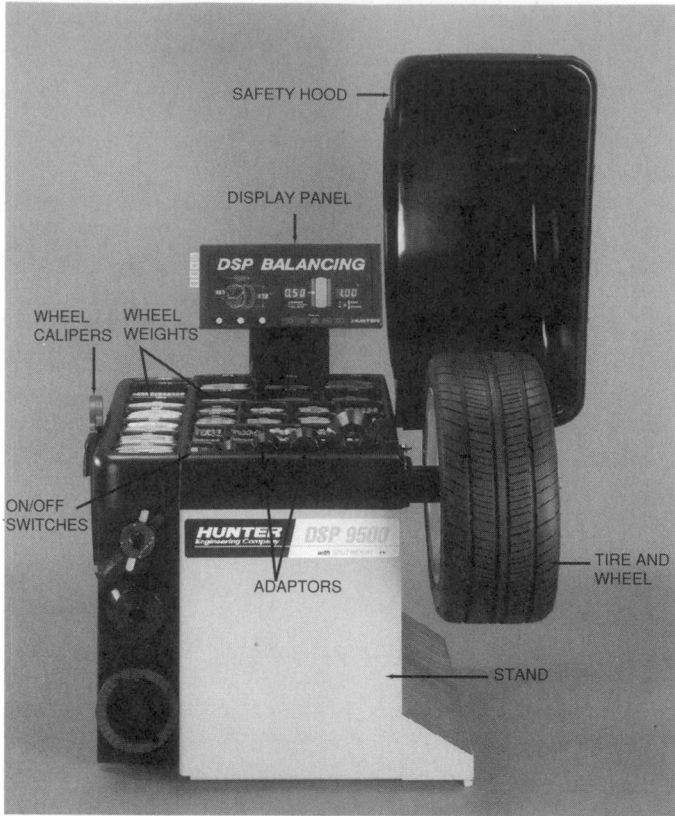

Figure 38-50. One type of electronic, off-vehicle wheel balancer. (Hunter Engineering Co.)

Figure 38-51. An on-vehicle electric wheel balancer. Follow the equipment and/or vehicle manufacturer's specific balancing procedures. (Hunter Engineering Co.)

Tech Talk

Specialization (concentrating on one area of the vehicle) is the trend in most modern automotive shops. It is common to work for one of the many shops that specialize in exhaust systems, brakes, alignment, transmissions, air conditioning, or driveability. Even shops where you will be expected to perform many different types of work will have their specialists in alignment, air conditioning, transmissions, and other areas. This is a natural result of the increasing complexity of modern cars and trucks.

However, you must still have knowledge of all of the systems of modern vehicles, or you may be stuck on a problem that is caused by a system outside of your area of expertise, or destroy a part related to the system you are working on. For instance, a front end vibration that is caused by a faulty torque converter clutch will never be solved by a front end specialist who does not know anything about automatic transmissions. An air conditioning specialist may never find out that the reason the compressor clutch will not engage is because of a diagnostic code or other problem in the electronic control unit. Even changing a battery can become a nightmare if you do not know that disconnecting the battery will wipe out any stored information in the engine control computer, ABS system, radio, and other systems.

Therefore, it is vital that you have at least a working knowledge of all of the systems of a modern vehicle, not just those you are working on at the moment. Try to keep up with all developments in motor vehicles, since almost all changes will somehow affect your job.

Summary

Most front wheel bearings are tapered roller designs. Front wheel bearings may be the ball or straight roller design. Clean, pack, and adjust tapered roller wheel bearings on a mileage schedule as recommended by the manufacturer. Pack the hub recess and coat the spindle and dust cap with wheel bearing grease. Adjust roller bearings to produce up to .003″ (0.076 mm) end play. Ball bearings should have a mild preload. Use a new cotter pin or staked nut following adjustment. Be sure to bend cotter pin ends open so that the pin is tight. A loose cotter pin can break. Always check to make sure the safety washer and nut lock (if used) are in place. Use a new grease seal when repacking wheel bearings. Keep grease off of the brake linings, drums, pads, and rotors. When a bearing must be replaced, replace the bearing outer and inner race. Never exchange bearings from one wheel to another. Do not mix wheel bearing lubricants.

Many kinds of wheel rims are available today. Wheel rim size is determined by flange height, width between flanges, and the diameter across the rim. Wheel lugs are critical to vehicle operation and should be replaced when broken. Tire size is determined by the diameter across beads when mounted and cross-sectional width. Rayon, nylon, polyester, fiberglass, aramid, Kevlar, and steel are widely used in tire manufacture. The tire fabric or cord may be applied in diagonal, radial, or a combination of these two patterns. Tires are rated according to a system which determines size, load, and speed ratings. Tires are graded for temperature resistance, traction, and tread wear by the Department of Transportation (DOT). Tire pressure must be correct. Check pressure when cold. Rotate tires about every 5000 miles (8000 km).

Use rubber lubricant when demounting or mounting tires. Clean the rim and check for dents, burrs, and cracks before mounting a tire. Punctures can only be repaired by patching and filling the hole. When seating tire beads against the rim flanges, stand back and do not exceed 40 psi (276 kPa) pressure. Reduce to normal running pressure when seated.

Tire wear patterns can often indicate the cause of wear. Both front and back wheel and tire assemblies must be statically and dynamically balanced. Clean the wheel and tire before balancing. Check tire radial and lateral runout before balancing. Check wheel lug torque and tighten in the proper sequence. Static balance should be corrected first, then dynamic balance.

On-car or off-car balancing equipment may be used. Some front-wheel drive vehicles should use the engine to spin the tires when using an on-car balancer. When balancing back wheels with on-car equipment, do not exceed 35-40 mph (56.3-64.4 kmh) speedometer reading. In cases where a limited-slip differential is used, on-car balancing requires raising both sides. Remove one wheel and balance the remaining one. Replace the first wheel and then balance it.

Know These Terms

Tapered roller bearings
Straight roller bearings
Ball bearings
Roller
Cage
Race
Wheel cover lock
Wheel rim lock
Spindle
Wheel rim
Custom wheels
Torque stick
Wheel lug
Lug nut
Plies
Bias

Bias-belted
Radial
Uniform tire quality grading
Temperature resistance
Traction
Tread wear
Space saver
Plug seal
Liquid sealer
Patch
Stitcher tool
Bead expander
Wheel tramp
Wheel shimmy
Static balance
Dynamic balance

Review Questions—Chapter 38

Do not write in this book. Write your answers on a separate sheet of paper.

1. Where are tapered roller bearings usually used?
   (A) The front axles of rear-wheel drive vehicles.
   (B) The rear axles of front-wheel drive vehicles.
   (C) The rear axles of rear-wheel drive vehicles.
   (D) Both A & B.
2. When a vehicle is equipped with wheel cover locks, where is the removal key usually located?
   (A) On the wheel.
   (B) In the vehicle.
   (C) At the manufacturer's headquarters.
   (D) At the dealer's service department.
3. When is it okay to pack a bearing hub with grease?
4. Explain why high temperature wheel bearing grease should be used to repack wheel bearings on modern vehicles?
5. Rotate tires every _____ miles or _____ km.
6. _____ should always be used to ease bead seating.
7. The aspect ratio refers to the relationship between the tire _____, and _____.
8. Wheel tramp is caused by _____ imbalance.
9. Wheel shimmy is caused by _____ imbalance.
10. List the three grades used in the Uniform Tire Quality Grading System.

ASE-Type Questions

1. Technician A says that a torque stick should be used when tightening an aluminum or composite wheel rim with an impact wrench. Technician B says that over-torquing a steel wheel could warp the brake rotor. Who is right?
   (A) A only.
   (B) B only.
   (C) Both A & B.
   (D) Neither A nor B.
2. All of the following statements about wheel lugs are true, EXCEPT:
   (A) A damaged lug nut should be replaced as soon as possible.
   (B) Lug nuts should be tightened in the proper sequence.
   (C) A damaged lug can be knocked out of the hub.
   (D) If a new lug will not press solidly into the hub, a larger lug should be used.
3. Technician A says that sealed ball bearings can be repacked if care is taken. Technician B says that all old grease should be removed from tapered roller bearings before repacking. Who is right?
   (A) A only.
   (B) B only.
   (C) Both A & B.
   (D) Neither A nor B.
4. Before driving the dustcover into place, _____.
   (A) apply a thin coat of grease to cover inside
   (B) make certain cotter pin is in place

(C) make sure safety washer is in place

(D) All of the above.

5. An old outer bearing race may be used with the
_____.

   (A) the original bearing assembly

   (B) a new bearing assembly

   (C) the old bearing assembly from the other side of the vehicle

   (D) All of the above.

6. Technician A says to always replace the cotter pin when packing or replacing wheel bearings. Technician B says that a staked nut may be reused if it is not badly bent. Who is right?

   (A) A only.

   (B) B only.

   (C) Both A & B.

   (D) Neither A nor B.

7. If you drive on wet roads, which of the following traction grades would give the best traction?

   (A) A.

   (B) B.

   (C) C.

   (D) These grades do not apply to wet pavement conditions.

8. Technician A says that a leak in a tire's sidewall can be patched. Technician B says that a leak in a tire's sidewall should not be repaired under any circumstances and that the tire should be replaced. Who is right?

   (A) A only.

   (B) B only.

   (C) Both A & B.

   (D) Neither A nor B.

9. Technician A says that both front and rear tire and wheel assemblies should be balanced. Technician B says that a tire in dynamic balance will also be in static balance. Who is right?

   (A) A only.

   (B) B only.

   (C) Both A & B.

   (D) Neither A nor B.

10. Extreme wear on the outside on both sides of the tire tread indicates _____.

   (A) overinflation

   (B) underinflation

   (C) incorrect toe

   (D) bent rim

Suggested Activities

1. Obtain the correct measuring tools to check wheel rim runout. After checking several rims, determine the average runout.

2. Service (remove, clean, repack, reinstall, adjust) a tapered roller wheel bearing assembly. Refer to the manufacturer's service manual for the proper type of grease and for bearing tightening procedures.

3. Remove and replace a tire installed on a steel rim.

4. Remove and replace a tire installed on an aluminum or other custom rim. List the differences between servicing this type of rim and a steel rim.

5. List the reasons that a leak in a tire may not be repairable. Consult your instructor as necessary. Patch a tire after determining that it is repairable.

39

Wheel Alignment

After studying this chapter, you will be able to:
- Explain the importance of wheel alignment.
- Summarize wheel alignment procedures.
- Explain the difference between two-wheel and four-wheel alignment.
- Diagnose common alignment-related problems.

This chapter will cover the purpose and methods of wheel alignment. It is intended as a brief overview of the various angles involved in front end alignment. Different alignment methods for front- and rear-wheel drive vehicles, and the principle of two-wheel and four-wheel alignment will be covered also. After completing this chapter, you will have a good basis for a thorough study of the principles of front end and steering geometry.

Defining Wheel Alignment

Wheel alignment refers to the process of measuring and correcting the various angles formed by the front and rear wheels, spindles, and steering arms. Correct alignment is vital. Improper alignment can cause hard steering, pulling to one side, wandering, noise, and rapid tire wear.

Major Alignment Angles

The various alignment angles, (caster, camber, toe, steering axis inclination, and toe-out on turns) are all related. A change in one can alter the others. Some of the angles, such as caster, camber, and toe-in, are adjustable. Others, such as steering axis inclination and toe-out on turns are built in and can only be adjusted by changing parts or bending the vehicle frame.

Caster

Caster is the tilting of the spindle support centerline from a true vertical line as viewed from the side of the vehicle. The spindle support centerline is an imaginary line drawn through the center of the upper and lower ball joints, or the ball joint and upper strut bearing on MacPherson strut suspensions. When the tire support centerline intersects the roadway at a point ahead of the tire, the caster is positive. Tilting the spindle so that the support centerline strikes the road behind the tire support centerline produces negative caster.

Both positive and negative caster angles are illustrated in **Figure 39-1**. Positive or negative caster is measured in

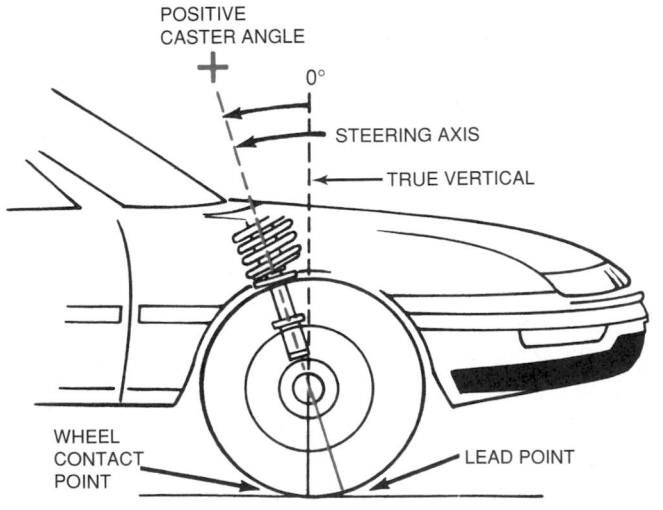
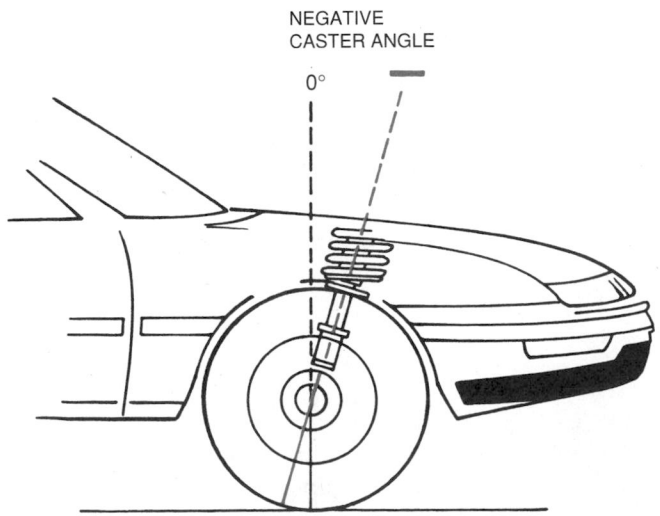

Figure 39-1. Positive and negative caster in relation to true vertical. (Perfect Equipment Corp.)

degrees from true vertical. Positive caster tends to assist the wheels in maintaining a straight ahead position. A negative caster setting can make turning the wheels easier. Incorrect caster can cause hard steering, wandering, high speed instability, and pull to the side with less caster. Improper caster angles will not cause tire wear.

Camber

Camber is the tilting of the wheel centerline away from a true vertical line as viewed from the front of the vehicle. When the top of the wheel is tilted outward from the vehicle, camber is positive. When the top of the wheel is tilted inward, camber is negative. Both positive and negative camber are illustrated in **Figure 39-2.** Camber angles are usually small, usually no more than 1° positive or negative from zero. Too much variation in camber will cause pulling. Excessive camber, whether positive or negative, will cause tire wear.

When adjusting front wheel camber, the left wheel can be set with about 0.25° to 0.5° more positive camber to compensate for *road crown.* Since the vehicle will tend to pull toward the side with greater positive camber, setting the left front wheel camber more positive will offset the pull effect of the crowned road. It is not necessary to set the rear wheel camber (when adjustable) to compensate for road crown.

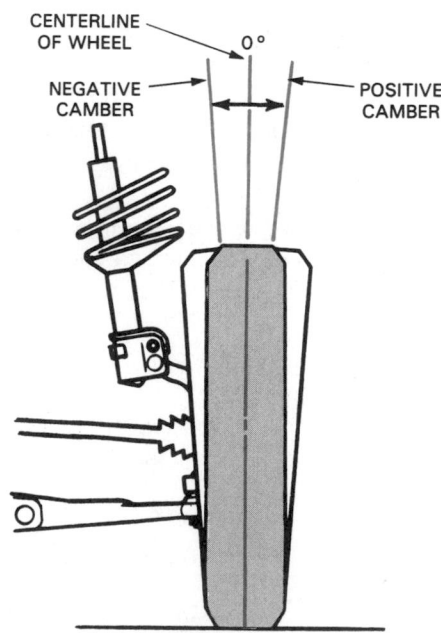

Figure 39-2. Positive and negative camber on one front-wheel drive arrangement. (Buick)

Steering Axis Inclination

Steering axis inclination or SAI, is the imaginary line formed by tilting the top ball joint or strut mount inward. This angle is measured in degrees from true vertical, **Figure 39-3.** Steering axis inclination helps to place vehicle load on the tire-road contact patch, which provides

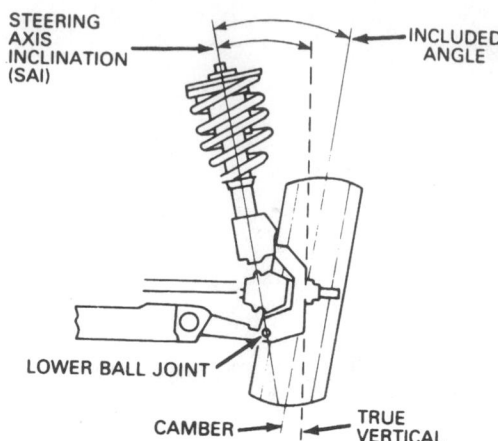

Figure 39-3. Steering axis inclination (SAI) is formed by tilting the strut upper mount and lower ball joint as viewed from the front of the vehicle. This setting is normally negative on front-wheel drive vehicles. Note the included angle. This is the sum of the camber angle and the steering axis inclination (General Motors)

better tracking and easier steering. Steering axis inclination is nonadjustable. If the vehicle's SAI is incorrect, check for a bent spindle, frame, strut, or other problem and replace parts as needed. If the incorrect SAI reading is a result of a bent frame, it may be necessary to have the frame straightened at a body shop. The average steering axis inclination will vary greatly depending on the manufacturer. The total of the SAI and the camber on any one wheel is referred to as the *included angle.* The included angle can be determined by adding the SAI and camber together.

Setback

Setback is a condition in which one front wheel spindle is positioned behind the spindle on the opposite side. This condition can also be present in rear wheel assemblies. Setback is usually caused by collision damage. One indication of setback is a caster reading that varies by more than 1° from one side of the vehicle to the other. Many types of alignment equipment cannot measure setback. Severe setback can sometimes be detected by measuring between the rear of each tire and the wheel opening.

Toe

Toe is the relative positions of the front and rear of a tire in relation to the tire on the other side of the vehicle. Look at **Figure 39-4.** Note that the distance at the back of the tires is greater than the distance in the front. Rear-wheel drive vehicles are toed in to compensate for the natural tendency of road-to-tire friction to force the wheels apart. On some front-wheel drive vehicles, the front tires are toed out. This is done to offset the force created by the drive axles which tends to drive or throw the tires inward during operation. The toe setting compensates for this and allows the front tires to run parallel to one another while rolling straight down the road.

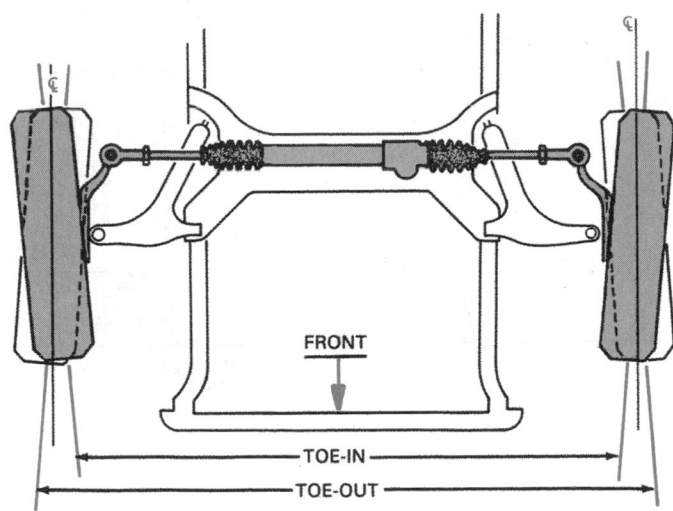

Figure 39-4. Toe-in and toe-out. Note that the wheels are closer together at the front than at the back, with toe-in. (Chrysler)

Toe-Out on Turns

When the vehicle rounds a corner, the front wheel on the inside of the turn is forced to follow a smaller arc than the outer wheel. If the wheels remained parallel during the turn, the tires would be forced to slip. Note that the steering arms in **Figure 39-5** are parallel to the centerline of the vehicle. With such an arrangement, the front wheels remain parallel when making a turn. This can cause tire slip, **Figure 39-5.**

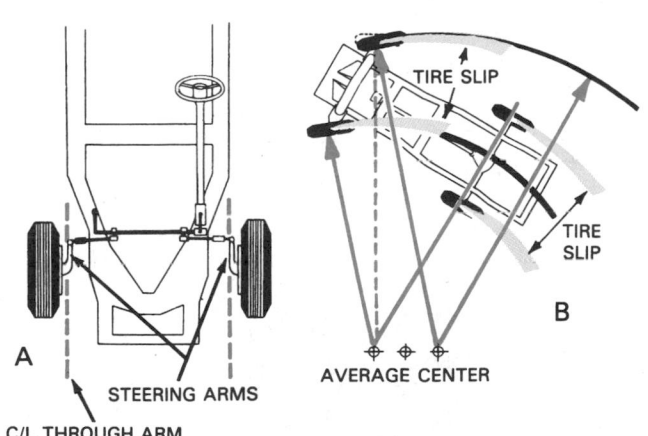

Figure 39-5. When steering arms are parallel (red lines) as in A, front wheels remain parallel during turns, thus causing tire slip, B. (Hunter Engineering Co.)

Tire slip on turns is avoided by angling the steering arms, as in **Figure 39-6.** When the front wheels are turned, the inner wheel will be forced to turn more sharply, increasing the **toe-out on turns.** This allows all wheels to turn from the same center, thus eliminating tire slip. In effect, the actual toe-out is small. The specification for toe-out on turns may call for the outer wheel to be at a certain angle when the inner wheel is turned to exactly 20°, or a certain angle for the inner wheel when the outer wheel is turned to 20°.

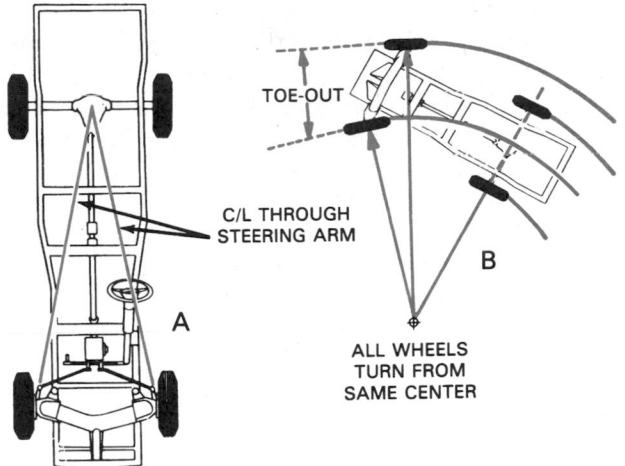

Figure 39-6. A—Angling steering arms causes toe-out to occur on turns. B—This allows tires to roll about their respective arcs without slipping.

Although specifications vary, they usually call for around a 1°-3° difference between the inner and outer wheel turning angles. See **Figure 39-7.**

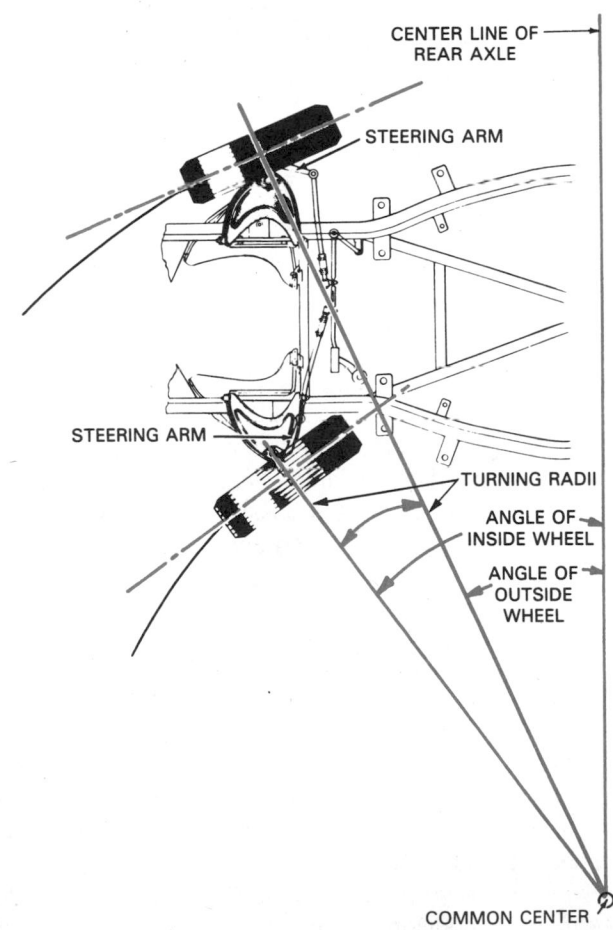

Figure 39-7. Toe-out on turns must be specified. Wheels turn about a common center determined by wheelbase of vehicle. Note that with respect to common point, inside wheel is ahead of outside wheel and makes a sharper angle than the outer one. (Bear)

Tire Scrubbing

Tire scrubbing (sideslip) is generally a result of either toe-in or toe-out. It may also be caused by incorrect camber, incorrect caster, or worn or broken parts. A wheel will normally try to run in the direction of its toe angle. However, because the wheel is fastened to the vehicle, it will be forced to travel straight ahead (when driving in that direction). A tire scuffing action occurs, which is similar to dragging the tire sideways on the road surface. A toe problem that is severe will quickly wear a tire.

Wheel Tracking

Wheel tracking is the ability of a vehicle's rear wheels to follow directly behind the front wheels. If the rear wheels are not tracking correctly, the vehicle will not travel in a straight line unless the front wheels are turned to compensate for the misalignment. This condition is often referred to as *dog-tracking,* **Figure 39-8.**

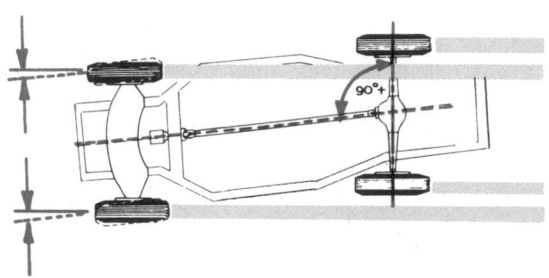

Figure 39-8.   Dog-tracking occurs when the rear wheels do not follow directly behind the front wheels. (Hunter Engineering Co.)

Tracking is set by aligning the vehicle's *thrust angle* with its geometric centerline, **Figure 39-9.** Ideally, the thrust angle should cover the centerline. This would result in perfect tracking. Manufacturer's tolerances, accident damage, and normal wear, however, make perfect alignment rare. Vehicles with front-wheel drive, four-wheel drive, and four-wheel steering also complicate thrust angle alignment. The technician must strive to align the thrust angle and the geometric centerline as closely as possible. Tire wear, poor fuel economy, and incorrect handling can result if the vehicle's thrust angle is not properly set.

Types of Wheel Alignment

In the past, the only type of wheel alignment performed was the *two-wheel alignment,* or front-wheel alignment. The rear wheels were attached to a solid rear axle assembly which could not be adjusted and was rigid enough to stay in reasonable alignment. Today, the *four-wheel alignment,* in which the alignment of the front and rear wheels are checked and adjusted, is commonly performed. Most front-wheel drive vehicles have provisions for adjusting the rear wheels. In addition, many rear-wheel drive vehicles are equipped with independent rear suspensions, which also must be adjusted. Modern solid rear axles and suspension systems are lighter than on earlier cars and can be knocked out of adjustment easily.

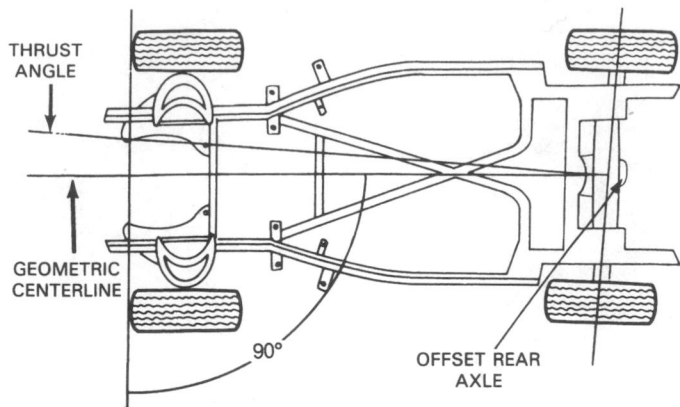

Figure 39-9.   Relationship between vehicle's thrust angle and centerline. Note that rear axle is offset and angle is greater than 90°. (Sun Electric)

Adjustable settings on the front wheels are caster, camber, and toe. Nonadjustable settings are steering axis inclination and toe-out on turns. The rear wheel settings which can be made on many vehicles are camber and toe. Modern practice is to check both front and rear wheel alignment. Checking all four wheels also makes it possible to set the thrust angle to ensure perfect wheel tracking.

Wheel Alignment Equipment

Wheel alignment equipment varies greatly, from simple mechanical gauges to computerized devices. To do any kind of alignment, the technician must have equipment capable of checking all of the alignment angles listed above. Simple camber and caster checking devices held by magnets to the wheel hub will allow fairly accurate checking, **Figure 39-10.** Toe can be checked by trammel bars, **Figure 39-11,** a drive-over plate, **Figure 39-12,** or even a tape measure. However, to do an accurate four-wheel alignment on a modern vehicle, more elaborate equipment is needed.

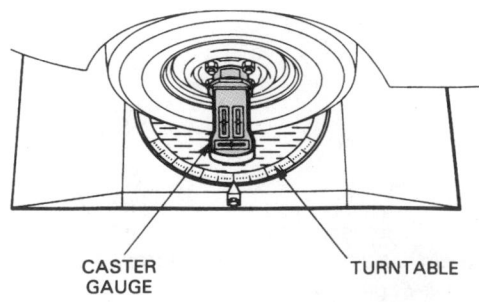

Figure 39-10.   One setup for checking caster angle.

The basic alignment rack will be equipped with *turning plates* to allow the front wheels to be turned for measuring caster and to allow the vehicle suspension to settle into its normal riding position after being raised. The ideal alignment rack will be high enough, or have a pit deep enough to permit easy access to the underside of the vehicle. The best alignment racks are attached to a hydraulic

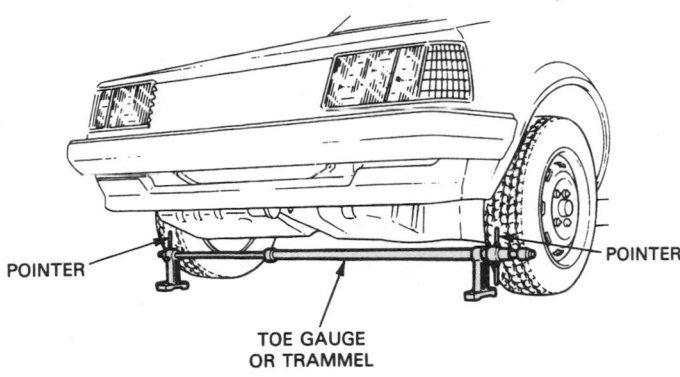

Figure 39-11. Checking the toe with a trammel. (Mazda)

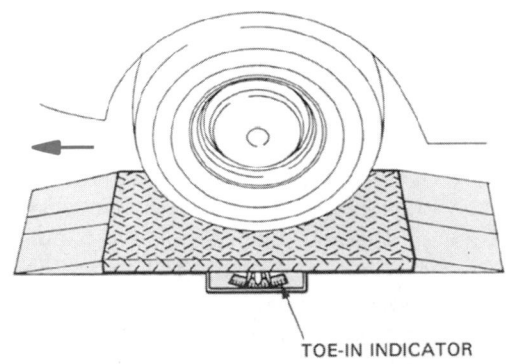

Figure 39-12. Vehicle being driven over one particular toe-in indicator setup. (Toyota)

Figure 39-13. Vehicle set up to have toe-out on turns checked. As wheel is turned, light beam cross will move on the chart. (Hunter Engineering Co.)

lift, so they may be lowered to drive the vehicle on and raised to gain access to the underside of the vehicle for extended periods.

The alignment machine itself should be able to accurately measure all of the alignment angles. Modern alignment machines must be capable of measuring the rear-wheel alignment as well as front-wheel alignment. This necessitates the use of rear-wheel sensing devices. The wheel mounted sensing devices used on modern alignment machines are usually called *heads.* Many alignment machines use wheel mounted light beam generators to measure the alignment angles, **Figure 39-13.** The latest alignment machines use wheel mounted electronic sensors and a computer to provide readouts on a screen, **Figure 39-14.** There are many manufacturers of alignment equipment. Obtain and study the user manuals to familiarize yourself with the alignment equipment's operation. When checking and adjusting wheel alignment, use quality equipment that is in good condition. Wheel alignment is a precision operation; both equipment and techniques must be perfect.

Performing Wheel Alignments

The following procedures will apply to both conventional and MacPherson strut assemblies. Alignment angles are designed to produce the same results no matter what type of suspension, steering, or drive train are used. If possible, road test the vehicle before beginning the wheel alignment. Check the vehicle for handling problems, noises, and

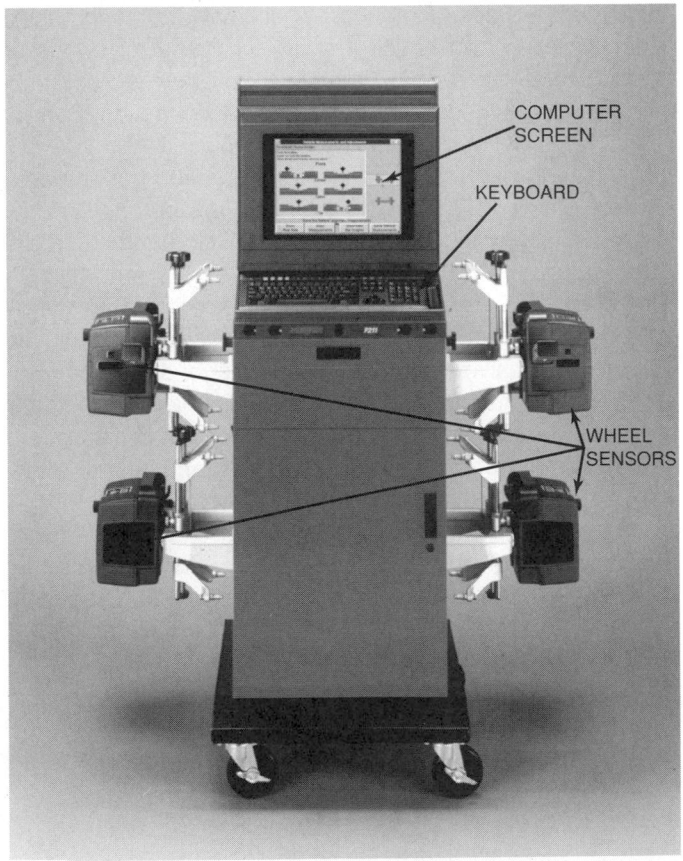

Figure 39-14. Computerized alignment machine. The sensors are mounted on the vehicle's wheels, and alignment readings are displayed on the screen. (Hunter Engineering Co.)

other factors which might be the cause of problems. If possible, talk to the customer and find out why the vehicle is being brought in for an alignment. Then perform the prealignment checks listed in the following section.

 Note: When road testing part-time four-wheel drive vehicles, make sure the transfer case is in the two-wheel high range.

Prealignment Checks

Begin by driving the vehicle on the alignment rack. The vehicle must be driven on as straight as possible. Many complaints of improper wheel alignment can be traced to wear, part damage, problems in the tires, brakes, wheel bearings, or other nonrelated areas or items. Do not attempt to align a vehicle that has worn or damaged parts. Check the suspension and steering parts in the front and rear of the vehicle for wear or damage as explained in Chapters 36 and 37.

Suspension parts to be checked include: ball joints, upper and lower control arm bushings, stabilizer bar bushings, strut rod bushings, and shock absorbers or struts. In addition, check all suspension parts for bends, kinks, and other damage. Steering parts to check include the gearbox or rack and pinion, pitman arm, idler arm, tie rods, and center link. Be especially careful to check the gearbox play and gearbox-to-frame fasteners. Check for wear, improper adjustment, or loose fasteners. Check power steering operation. Also carefully check the vehicle frame for bends or twists. Correcting a bent frame requires the services of a body shop equipped to perform frame straightening. Correct all problems before proceeding.

Place the vehicle on a level surface and bounce both ends of the vehicle from the center of the bumpers. Allow the vehicle to come to its normal rest position and check the *ride height,* or curb height, **Figure 39-15.** If the ride height is incorrect, look for broken or sagged springs. Replace all defective springs. Check the passenger compartment and trunk for excessive weight such as luggage, sales samples, tools, sporting goods, and other items. Remove any excess weight. On some vehicles with torsion bar suspensions, the ride height can be adjusted. Check the manufacturer's service manual.

Inspect the tires for wear, bulging, or other damage. Carefully note any tire conditions, as discussed in Chapter 38, which might indicate an alignment problem. Tire size and pressure must be as specified on all four wheels. Never attempt to align a vehicle with mismatched tires or when one of the tires on an axle is worn and the other has good tread. Check the front wheel bearings for damage or excessive play. Spin the wheels and check for bent rims, dragging brakes, and loose wheel lugs.

Final Preparation for Wheel Alignment

After all needed repairs have been made, final preparations for alignment can be made. To ensure accurate alignment checks and adjustments, the vehicle must be at

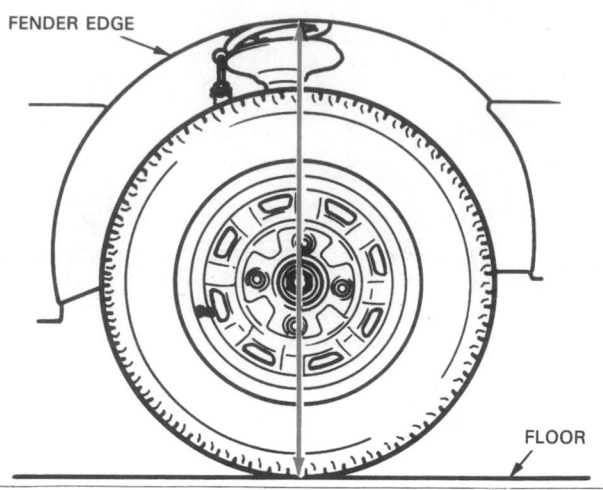

Figure 39-15. Checking the trim height on a vehicle with MacPherson strut front suspension. (Geo)

curb weight. Curb weight is the weight of the vehicle with all normal accessories and a full tank of gas, but without the driver or passengers. Many manufacturers specify bouncing both the front and rear of the vehicle at the center of the bumpers. This allows the vehicle to come to its normal rest position before making alignment checks. See **Figure 39-16.**

 Note: Some import vehicle manufacturers specify that weights be placed in the vehicle to simulate an average weight of passengers and luggage. **Refer to the manufacturers' specifications for exact weight and placement.**

Figure 39-16. Bounce the front and rear of the vehicle. Allow it to come to normal curb height before making alignment checks. With this method, no alignment spacers are used. (Jeep)

Alignment Specifications

One of the most important parts of performing a wheel alignment is obtaining the correct specifications. All vehicle manufacturers publish and regularly update alignment specifications for current and older models. Always look up the most current alignment specifications for the vehicle before beginning the alignment. Do not guess at specifications.

Alignment Setup

Be sure to set up the alignment equipment as specified by the manufacturer. If the equipment is attached to the wheel hub or the wheel rim, **Figure 39-17,** the wheel cover must be removed. Many modern wheel covers are held to the rim by wheel cover locks or by the lug nuts themselves. Custom wheels are secured by wheel locks, **Figure 39-18.** The key to these locks is located in the vehicle and must be used to remove the wheel covers. Many modern wheel rims are made of aluminum or chrome plated steel, and special precautions must be taken to prevent scratching the rim. Refer to the manufacturers' service literature.

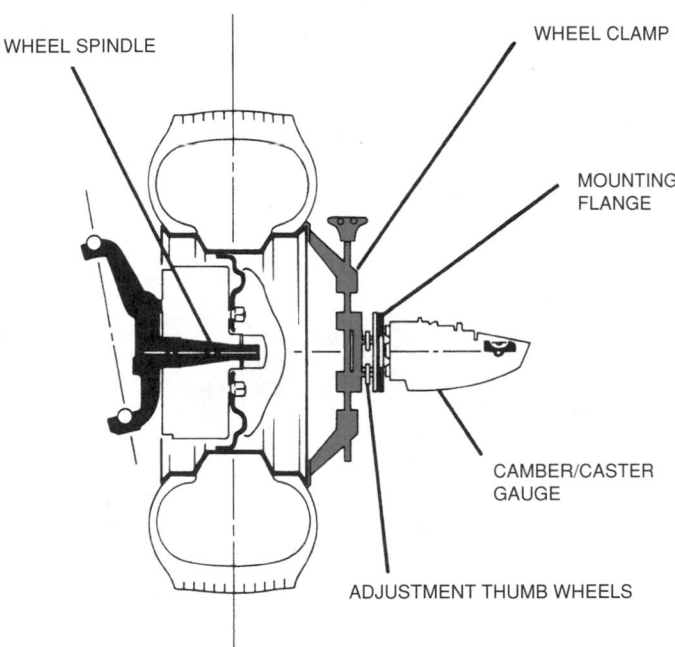

Figure 39-17.   Alignment tool attached to the wheel. Be sure to connect the tool safety strap (not shown) if used. Handle these tools with care. (Ammco Tools)

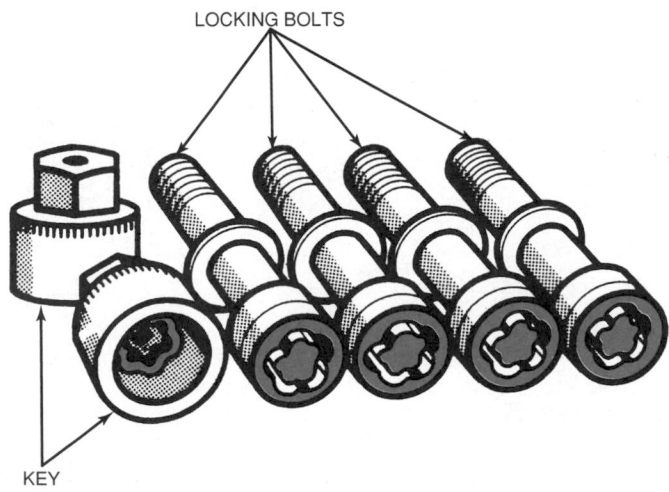

Figure 39-18.   Wheel locking bolts and removal key. These bolts are for use with alloy wheels. The styles vary. (Mercedes-Benz)

 Note: After using the wheel lock key, replace it in the vehicle. Without it the driver will not be able to remove the tire in an emergency. Be sure to attach any safety straps to the rim to prevent damage to the head if it falls off the rim.

Runout Compensation

Wheel rims always have some distortion or ***runout.*** Even a new rim has some runout. If the alignment heads are installed on the edges of the rims, this runout must be accounted for or it will cause false readings. To compensate for runout, attach the alignment equipment to the rim and raise the wheels from the rack. On front-wheel drive vehicles, apply the parking brake and place the transmission in neutral. Perform runout compensation as recommended by the operator's manual for the alignment equipment. Repeat this procedure for each wheel, then lower the vehicle.

Turn the steering wheel from side to side several times to equalize any play in the steering system. If the vehicle has power steering, the engine should be running. Then center the steering wheel, **Figure 39-19,** and lock it in place with a special wheel locking tool. Turn the engine off if applicable. To prevent excessive wheel movement during the caster check, lock the brakes by using a brake pedal depressor, as shown in **Figure 39-20.** Make sure the parking brake is applied and shift an automatic transmission into park.

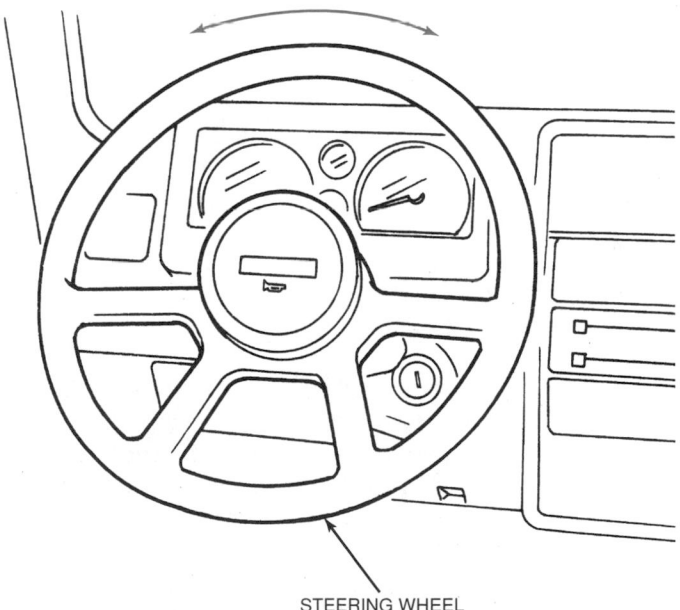

Figure 39-19.   Centering the steering wheel by turning it from side-to-side several times to equalize any play. (Suzuki)

Measuring, Recording, and Adjusting Alignment

The first step in adjusting alignment is to measure and record all alignment readings. If the vehicle is receiving a four-wheel alignment, start by measuring, recording, and

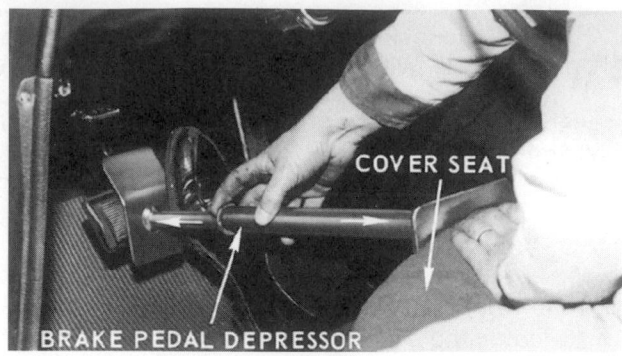

Figure 39-20. Use a brake pedal depressor when checking steering axis inclination. Protect the seat surface. (Ammco)

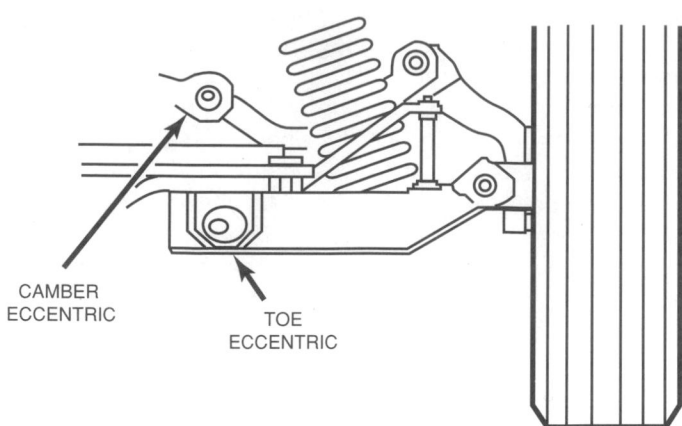

Figure 39-21. Using eccentric cams to properly adjust rear chamber. (Hunter Engineering Co.)

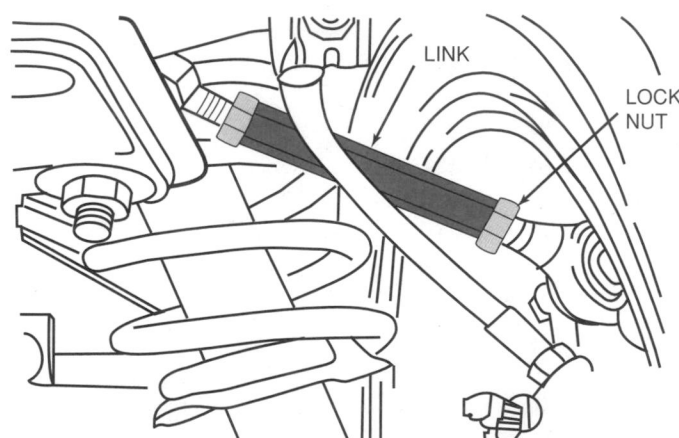

Figure 39-22. Using a threaded rod to adjust rear camber. (Hunter Engineering Co.)

adjusting the rear camber and toe. If the vehicle is receiving a two-wheel alignment, start with the front wheel measurement section later in this chapter. In many cases, it is advisable to check and record the rear wheel alignment, even if the rear cannot be aligned. An example would be when the steering wheel cannot be centered, or when rear tire wear is excessive. Specific methods of using the various types alignment equipment are not discussed, due to the great number and variety of alignment devices currently available. Always consult the manufacturers' service information for the recommended type of alignment equipment.

 Note: Always adjust vehicle toe last. Toe is affected by other adjustment, and will need readjustment if adjusted first.

Rear Wheel Adjustment

Since the rear wheels do not affect steering, the most common effects of improper settings are tire wear and noise. However, if the rear toe is off, the steering wheel may be difficult to center. Note that there is no adjustment for caster on the rear wheels, since this is a factor that affects steering and is not needed on the rear.

Rear Camber

There are several methods of setting rear camber. **Figure 39-21** shows some methods of adjusting the camber using egg-shaped cams called *eccentrics.* Another method of adjusting the camber by using *threaded rods* is illustrated in **Figure 39-22.** Other designs provide for loosening the rear strut bolts, pushing or pulling the wheel into position, and retightening the bolts. All alignment settings must be within the manufacturer's specified range.

Rear Toe

Rear toe can be set by one of several methods depending on the manufacturer. Like rear camber, rear toe can be set by either eccentric cams or threaded rods. On some vehicles, toe is adjusted by loosening a lock bolt or jam nut and pushing or pulling the suspension part into position, **Figure 39-23.** The lock bolt is then retightened. **Figure 39-24** illustrates a method of setting toe by rotating the tie rod.

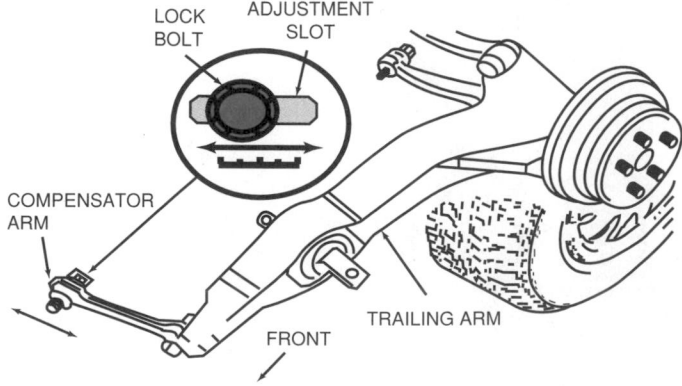

Figure 39-23. Adjusting rear toe by loosening the lock bolt and sliding the suspension into the correct position. (Hunter Engineering Co.)

 Note: On some older alignment machines, toe is measured in inches. This is also true if you are using a trammel bar to set front toe-in.

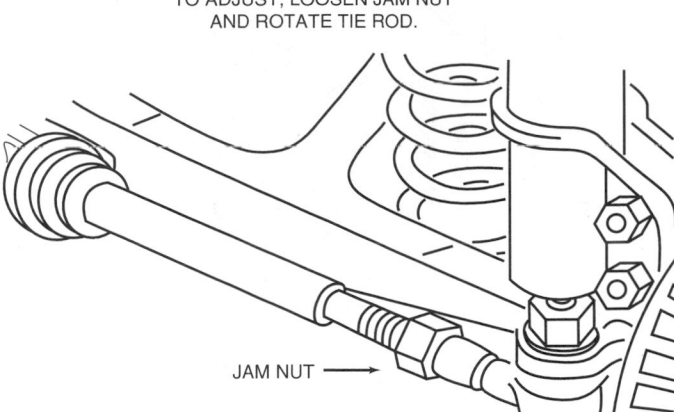

TO ADJUST, LOOSEN JAM NUT
AND ROTATE TIE ROD.

JAM NUT →

Figure 39-24. Lengthening or shortening the strut rod to set rear toe to specifications. (Hunter Engineering Co.)

Some vehicles with **four-wheel steering** (the rear wheels turn with the front wheels) must have the rear toe set by a different method than that used by vehicles with two-wheel steering. To make this adjustment, the technician must have a special tool to lock the rear steering gearbox. The tool is installed to lock the gearbox before setting the rear camber and toe, removed to set the front caster and camber, and reinstalled to set the front toe. Refer to the manufacturer's service manual for the exact procedures and specifications.

Setting Rear Alignment Using Shims

On many late model vehicles, there are no adjusting devices for setting camber and toe. A method of adjusting alignment using **shims** has been devised. Shims can also be used on the rear axles of some vehicles in which the factory adjustment is insufficient. Rear axle shims are round metal or plastic discs that are thicker on one side than the other, as seen in **Figure 39-25.** The amount of needed caster and toe change is determined by recording

the actual readings and looking up the factory specifications. The type of shim and its exact placement is then calculated, **Figure 39-26.**

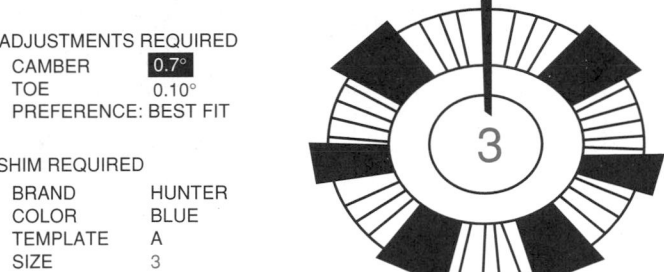

LEFT REAR

ADJUSTMENTS REQUIRED
CAMBER   0.7°
TOE   0.10°
PREFERENCE: BEST FIT

SHIM REQUIRED
BRAND   HUNTER
COLOR   BLUE
TEMPLATE   A
SIZE   3
ANGLE   191°

Figure 39-26. Camber/toe adjustments required, along with the correct shim. Dark areas show where shim must be cut to provide mounting bolt clearance. (Hunter Engineering Co.)

The rear brake drum or rotor must be removed and the bearing housing separated from the rear axle. The shim is then placed between the rear bearing and axle, as in **Figure 39-27.** This tilts the bearing, and therefore the wheel in the correct direction to give the proper camber and toe specifications. This procedure must be done carefully to ensure that the final reading is correct and that all rear axle parts are reinstalled in their original positions. The rear wheel bearings must be properly adjusted and a new cotter pin must be used. This procedure was discussed in Chapter 38.

Front Wheel Alignment

After measuring, recording, and setting rear wheel alignment, proceed to check the front alignment. On many vehicles, either the caster or camber is not adjustable. On other vehicles, only the toe can be adjusted. Be sure to check the manufacturer's specifications to determine what

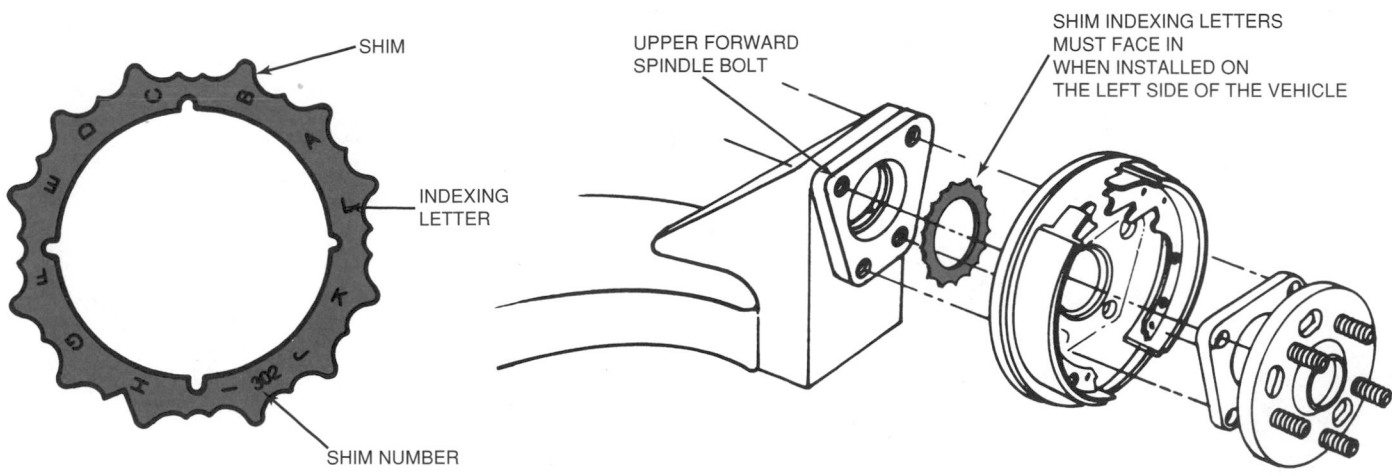

SHIM

INDEXING
LETTER

SHIM NUMBER

UPPER FORWARD
SPINDLE BOLT

SHIM INDEXING LETTERS
MUST FACE IN
WHEN INSTALLED ON
THE LEFT SIDE OF THE VEHICLE

Figure 39-25. Setting the rear alignment to specs with one type of round metal shim. If needed, two shims may be used together to obtain the most accurate adjustment. (Perfect Equipment Co.)

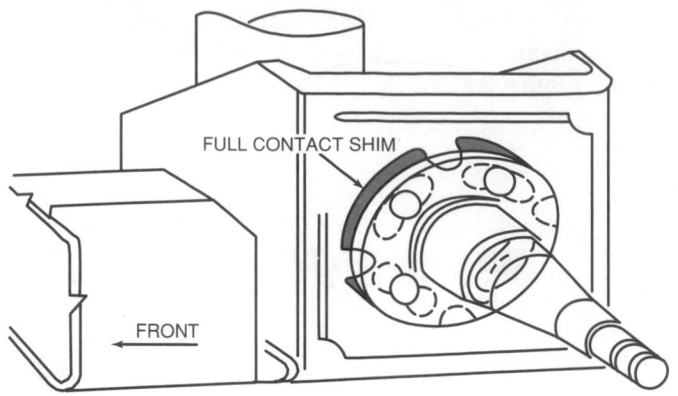

Figure 39-27. Camber and toe being set by using a full contact type shim. (Hunter Engineering Co.)

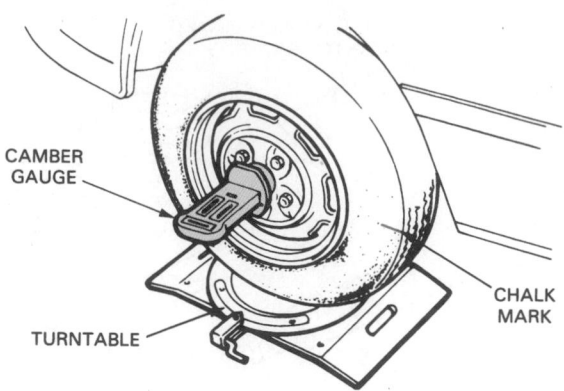

Figure 39-28. Camber gauge attached to the wheel. Be sure wheel is aimed straight ahead. Lock the turntable. (Mazda)

can be adjusted. On many vehicles, adjusting caster will affect camber and vice versa. For this reason, caster and camber are usually adjusted and checked together. Many methods are provided for adjusting caster and camber with the same adjustment.

 Caution: Never attempt to make non-factory adjustments by bending or welding suspension or steering parts. In some cases, aftermarket parts are available to make caster or camber adjustments which cannot be made by following factory procedures. Check with local parts suppliers for the availability of these parts.

Front Caster

Unlock the steering wheel and carefully check the caster angle by following the equipment manufacturer's instructions. Repeat the caster check on the other wheel. **Figure 39-28** illustrates the use of one form of caster gauge. Always set caster exactly as specified. Make certain both sides are alike within 0.5°. Remember that handling is often improved on crowned roads by deliberately setting the driver's side caster up to 0.5° more negative than the passenger's side. Regardless of setting variation to compensate for road crown, set-

tings must be within the manufacturer's specified range and with no more than 0.5° difference between sides.

Caster is adjusted on many modern vehicles by moving the lower strut rod in or out, **Figure 39-29. Figure 39-30** illustrates how caster is adjusted on some vehicles with MacPherson strut suspensions by loosening the nuts holding the top of the strut tower and sliding the tower forward or backward. Sometimes, the strut tower mounting holes may have to be cut or filed to obtain enough movement.

Front Camber

Before checking the camber, make sure that the wheels are in the straight ahead position. Use equipment as directed by the manufacturer. **Figure 39-31** shows one type of camber checking tool. Remember that it is acceptable to set the camber slightly more positive on the left wheel to compensate for road crown.

Figures 39-32A and **39-32B** show one common way of moving the camber by loosening the nuts holding the top of the strut tower and sliding the tower in or out. Another method, moving an eccentric attached to the lower control arm, is shown in **Figure 39-33**. In **Figure 39-34**, the camber is adjusted by moving an eccentric located on the top or

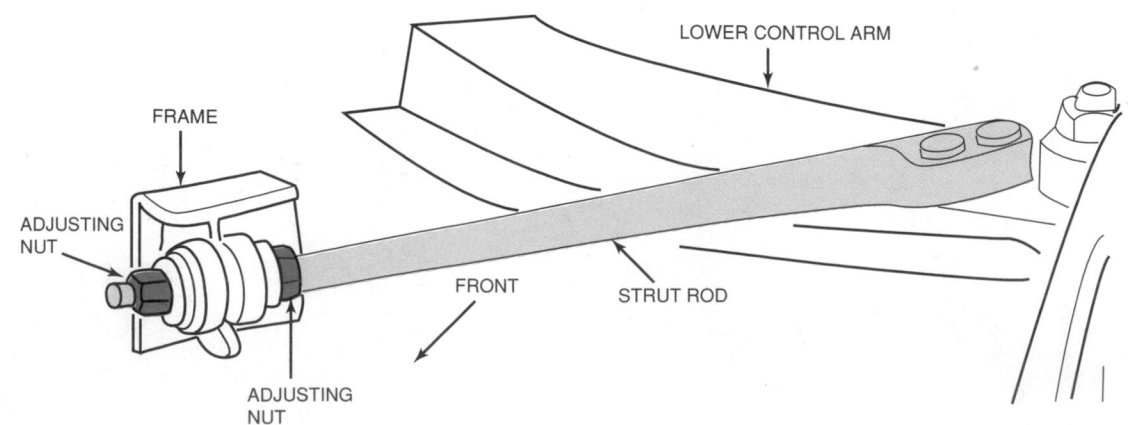

Figure 39-29. Caster adjustment is made by moving the strut rod with adjusting nuts. On this setup, increase caster by shortening the strut rod or decrease caster by lengthening the strut rod. (Hunter Engineering Co.)

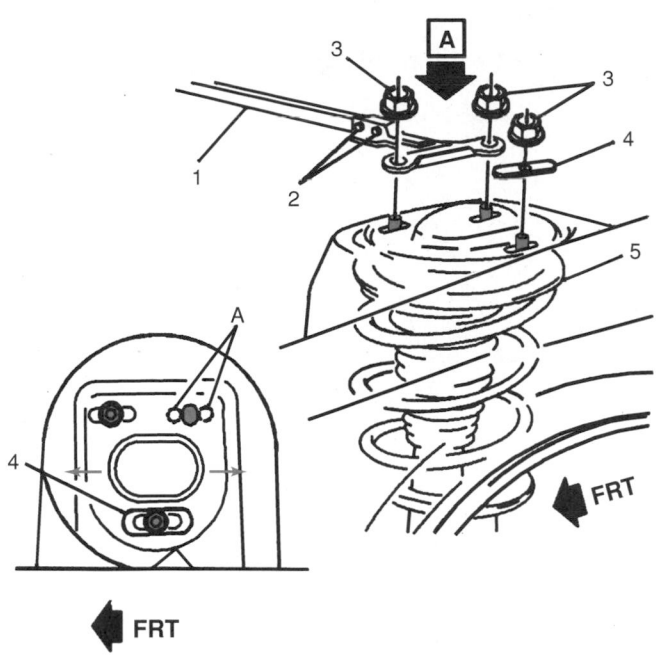

A DRILL 11/32 IN. HOLES
1 STRUT HOUSING TIE BAR
2 THROUGH-BOLTS, 37 N•m (27 FT.–LB.)
3 NUT, 24 N•m (18 FT.–LB.)
4 WASHER
5 STRUT

Figure 39-30. One type of caster adjustment with a MacPherson strut suspension setup. (Pontiac)

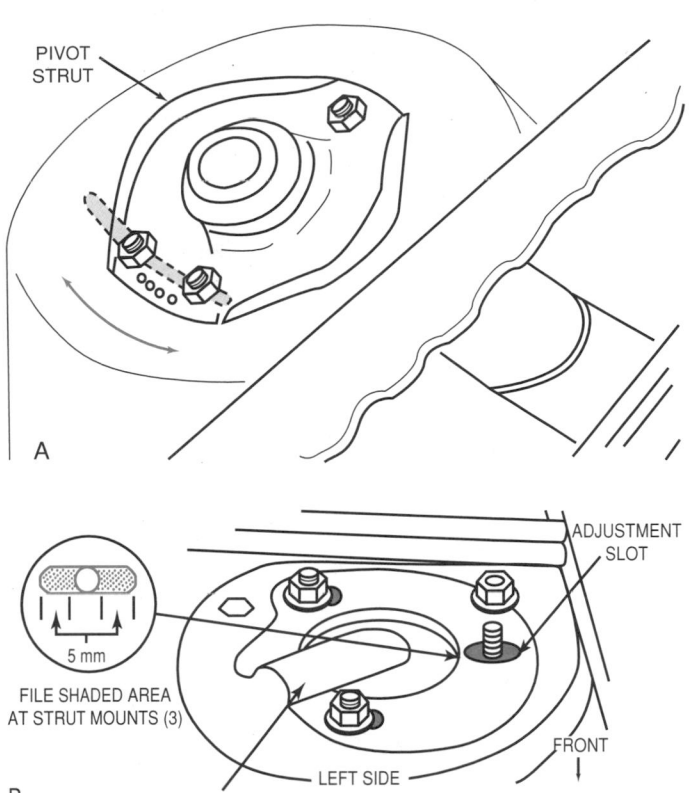

Figure 39-32. Camber adjustment methods. A—By pivoting the strut. B—By sliding the strut sideways. (Hunter Engineering Co.)

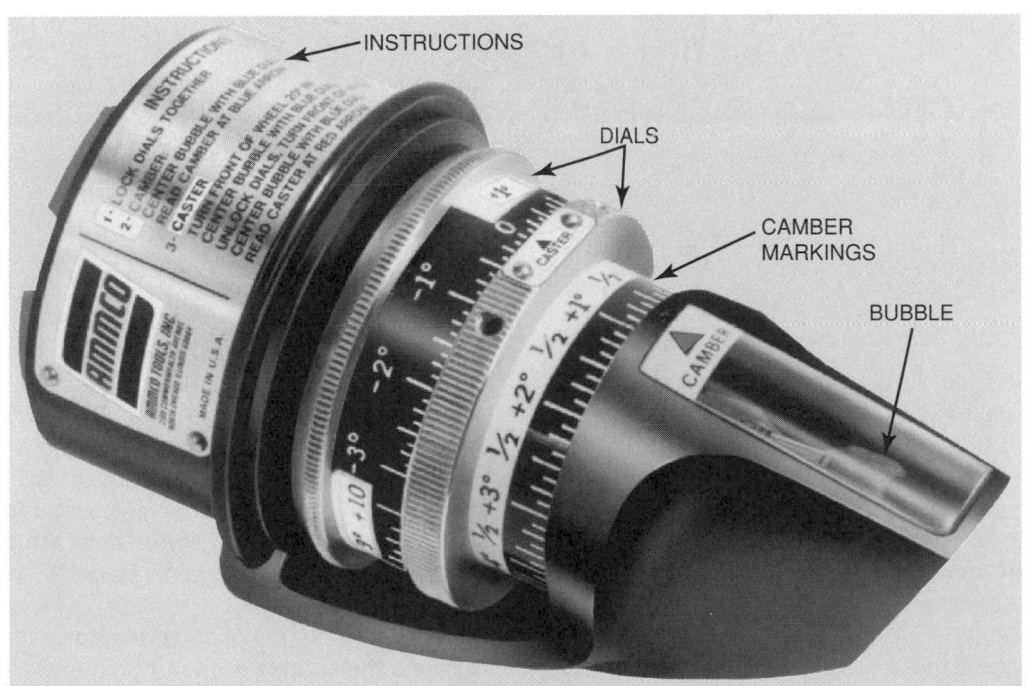

Figure 39-31. One particular camber checking tool. Use the tool as directed by the manufacturer. (Ammco Tools)

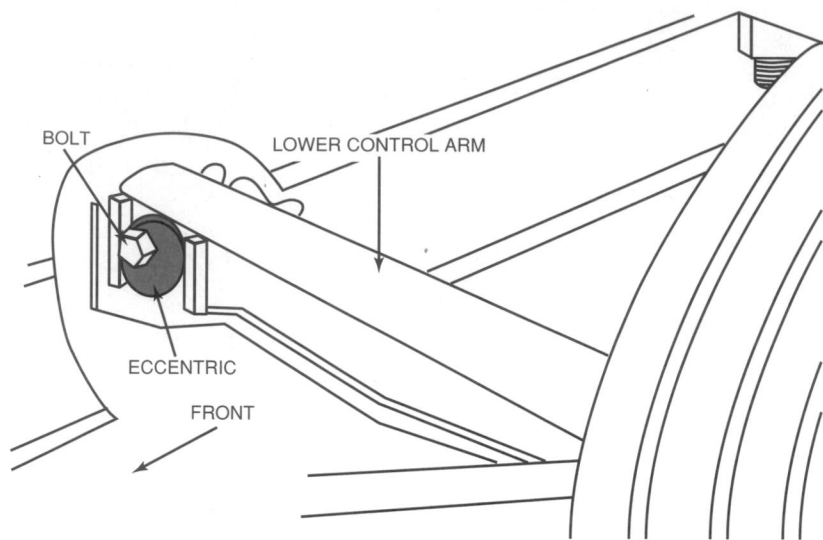

Figure 39-33. Lower control arm moved by rotating the adjusting eccentric.

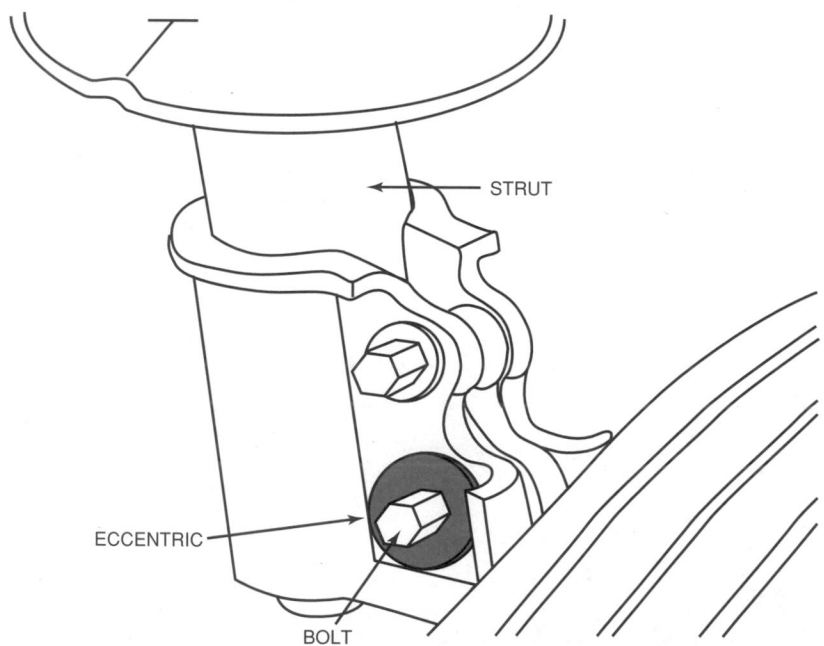

Figure 39-34. Rotate the eccentric (cam) on the strut to set correct camber. (Hunter Engineering Co.)

bottom bolt holding the strut assembly to the spindle. On other designs, camber is adjusted by loosening the strut bolts, pushing or pulling the wheel into position, and then retightening. The strut rod mounting slots may require filing or cutting to allow enough movement.

Other Methods of Adjusting Caster and Camber

There are a number of other methods used for caster and camber adjustment. On many older vehicles and current light trucks and large rear-wheel drive domestic cars, shims are used at both sides of the upper control arms, **Figure 39-35A.** Another method uses slotted holes in the vehicle frame or control arm, **Figure 39-35B.** Eccentrics on the upper or lower control arm bushings may be used to make adjustments, **Figure 39-35C** and **39-35D.** In another design, the spot welds or rivets holding the top of the strut tower to the body are drilled out or chiseled off, and the tower moved to the desired position, **Figure 39-35E.** On some vehicles, the strut tower nuts are removed and the strut assembly lowered and rotated to obtain the correct reading, **Figure 39-35F.**

When using any of these methods, the technician must calculate the change made to both caster and camber. For instance, adding a shim to the rear of the upper control arm in **Figure 39-35A** will move the upper ball joint backward and increase positive caster, but it will also move the ball

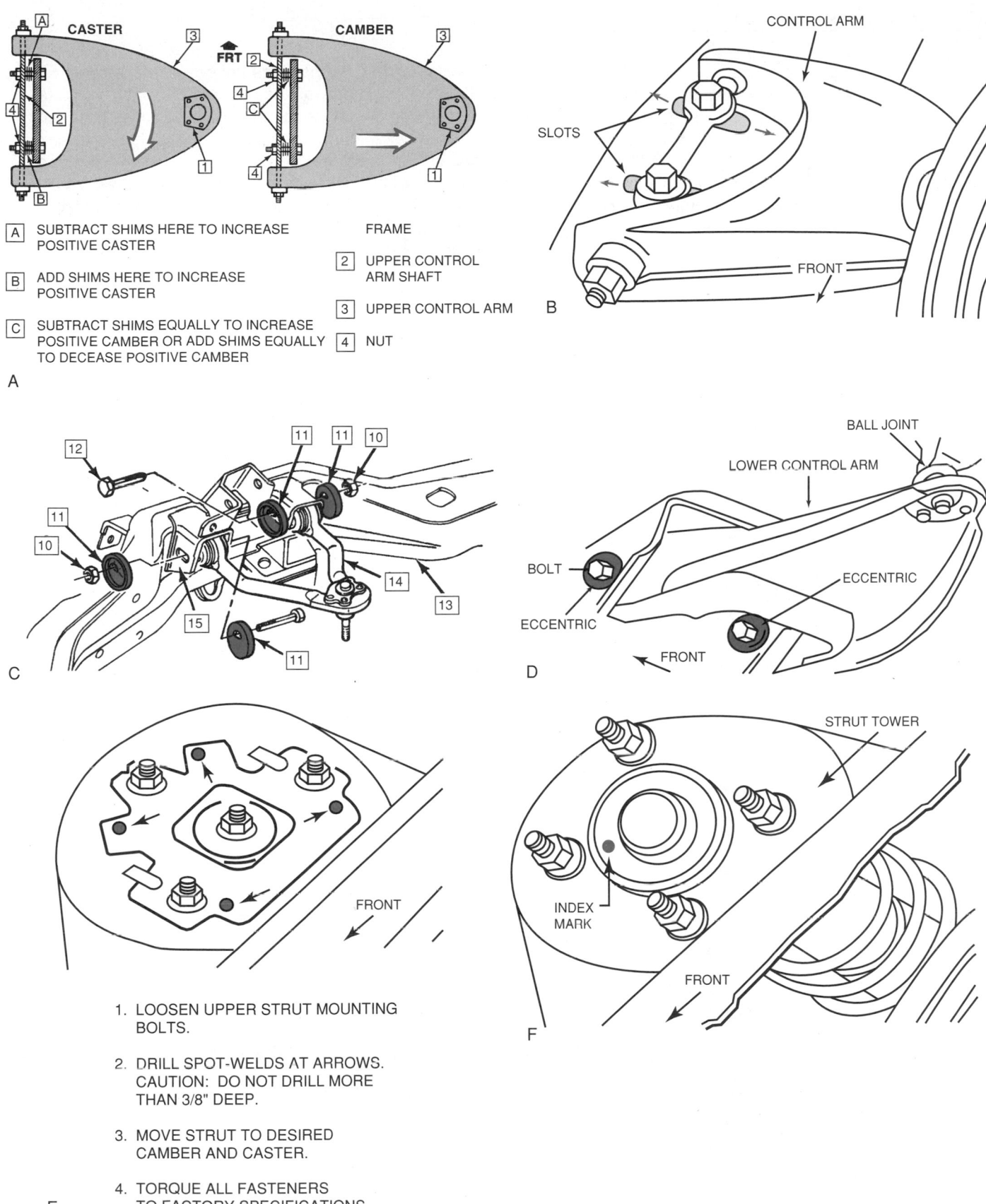

A

A	SUBTRACT SHIMS HERE TO INCREASE POSITIVE CASTER
B	ADD SHIMS HERE TO INCREASE POSITIVE CASTER
C	SUBTRACT SHIMS EQUALLY TO INCREASE POSITIVE CAMBER OR ADD SHIMS EQUALLY TO DECEASE POSITIVE CAMBER

	FRAME
2	UPPER CONTROL ARM SHAFT
3	UPPER CONTROL ARM
4	NUT

1. LOOSEN UPPER STRUT MOUNTING BOLTS.

2. DRILL SPOT-WELDS AT ARROWS. CAUTION: DO NOT DRILL MORE THAN 3/8" DEEP.

3. MOVE STRUT TO DESIRED CAMBER AND CASTER.

4. TORQUE ALL FASTENERS TO FACTORY SPECIFICATIONS.

Figure 39-35. A—Adding or removing shims to obtain the correct caster and camber adjustment. B—Camber/caster adjustment by moving control arm in or out in the provided slots. C—Rotate the eccentric cams to set caster and camber on this particular control arm. 10-Nut. 11-Eccentric cams. 12-Cam bolt. 13-Frame. 14-Control arm. 15-Frame bracket. D—Adjustment eccentrics located on the lower control arm. E—Drilling the spot welds so the strut can be adjusted for camber/caster. F—Remove the strut tower nuts. Lower tower and rotate to align the index mark. Replace fasteners and torque to specifications. (Chevrolet, Hunter Engineering Co.)

joint inward, making camber more negative. Certain control arms are designed with the ball joint off center, as in **Figure 39-36.** Adjusting one end will have more effect on the camber, while adjusting the other end will have more effect on the caster. With experience, you will be able to dictate how much any one adjuster can be moved to get the desired caster and camber. Even after you develop that experience, always recheck both caster and camber when making any adjustments.

Adjusting Caster and Camber using Eccentric Bushings

Caster and camber are not adjustable using conventional adjusting devices on many light trucks having a solid front axle. To adjust caster and camber on these vehicles,

special *eccentric bushings* have been developed, **Figure 39-37.** To use one of these bushings, first calculate the amount by which caster and camber must be changed. Then select the proper bushing using a chart similar to the one shown in **Figure 39-38.** To install the bushing, remove the upper ball joint from the axle. Remove the old bushing, which is completely round, and install the eccentric bushing in its place, **Figure 39-39.** Be sure that the eccentric bushing is turned to where it will make the proper change. Reinstall the ball joint and wheel and recheck caster and camber.

Checking Steering Axis Inclination

Although steering axis inclination cannot be adjusted, it should be checked whenever another cause cannot be

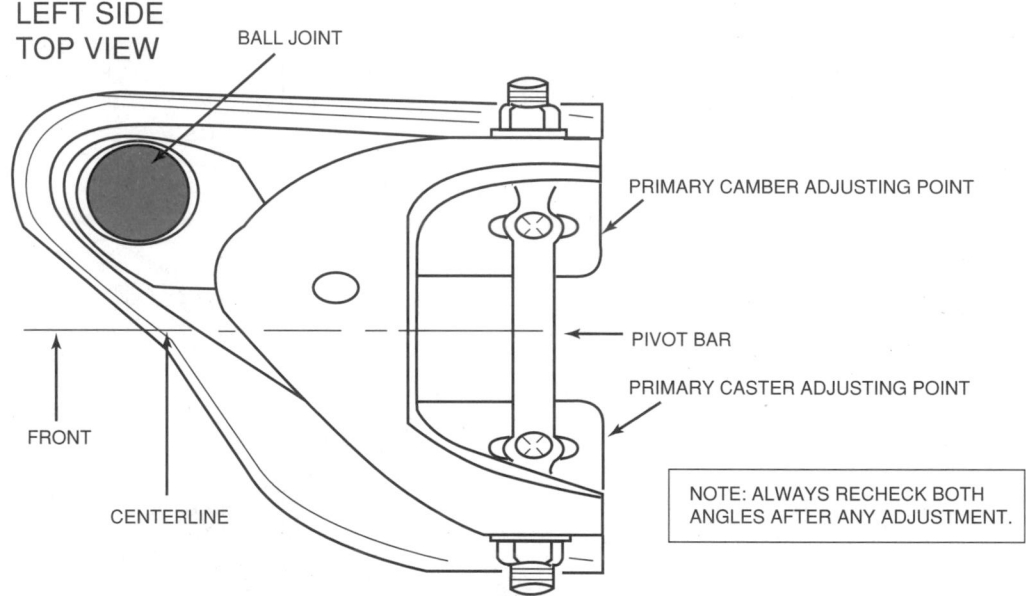

Figure 39-36.   A control arm with the ball joint mounted off center. (Hunter Engineering Co.)

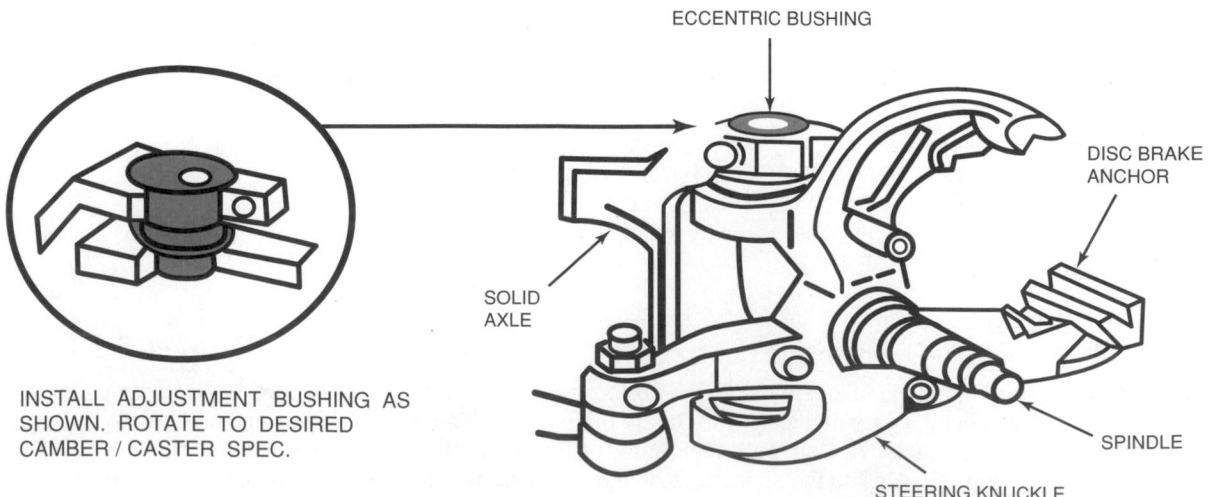

Figure 39-37.   A solid front axle having camber/caster adjustment made with an eccentric bushing. (Hunter Engineering Co.)

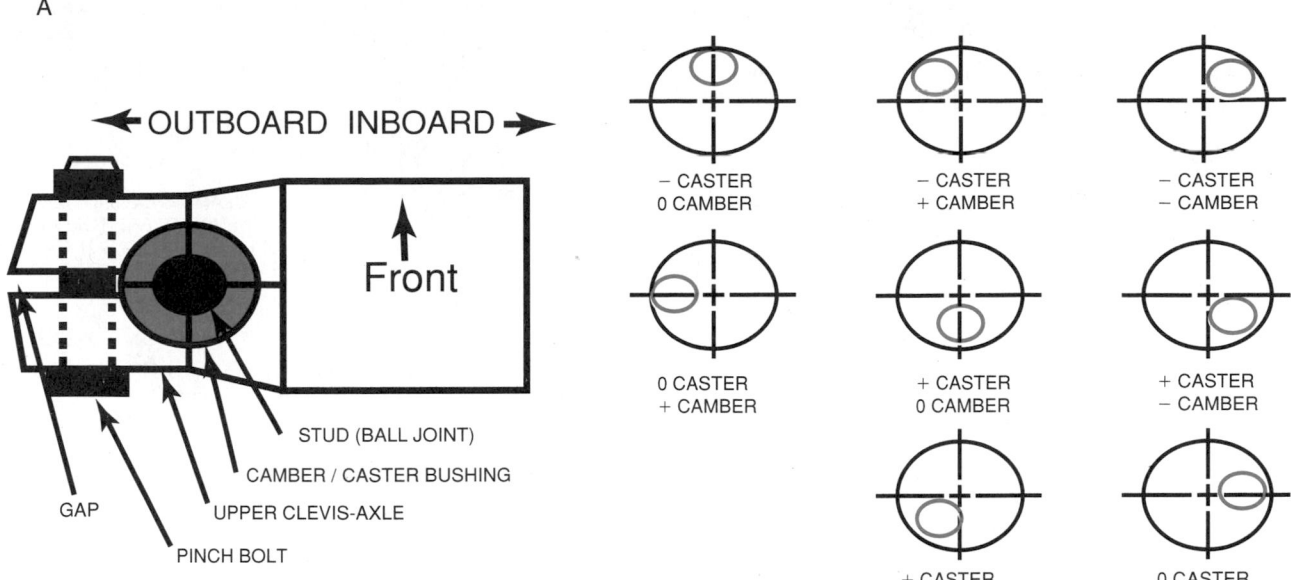

A

B

ON HIGHER DEGREE BUSHINGS IT MAY BE NECESSARY TO WIDEN THE GAP OF THE PINCH BOLT ASSEMBLY SLIGHTLY FOR EASE OF INSTALLATION.

2WD & 4 WD Applications	Bushing I.D. Number	+ or - Degrees of Adjustment			
		2WD		4 WD	
		Max. Camber or Caster	Combined Camber & Caster	Max. Camber or Caster	Combined Camber & Caster
FORD 2WD	HR-1/4	.25 (1/4)	.2 (3/16)	.2 (3/16)	.1 (1/8)
87 & Up F150, F250, & F350 89-90 Bronco II 91 & Up Explorer 89 & Up Ranger	HR-1/2	.50 (1/2)	.3 (5/16)	.4 (3/8)	.2 (1/4)
	HR-3/4	.75 (3/4)	.5 (1/2)	.6 (5/8)	.4 (3/8)
	HR-1	1.00 (1)	.7 (11/16)	.7 (3/4)	.5 (1/2)
FORD 4 WD	HR-1¼	1.25 (1¼)	.9 (7/8)	.9 (7/8)	.6 (5/8)
Mid 90 Bronco II 90 & Up Explorer Mid 90 & Up Ranger *(All three with pinch bolt style axle)*	HR-1½	1.50 (1½)	1.1 (1-1/16)	1.0 (1)	.7 (3/4)
	HR-1¾	1.75 (1¾)	1.2 (1-3/16)	1.2 (1-3/16)	.9 (7/8)
	HR-2	2.00 (2)	1.4 (1-3/8)	1.4 (1-3/8)	1.0 (1)
MAZDA 4 WD	EX -1¾	DO NOT INSTALL		1.75 (1-3/4)	1.1 (1-1/8)
91 & Up Navajo	EX-2	DO NOT INSTALL		2.00 (2)	1.3 (1-1/4)

Figure 39-38. A—Caster/camber bushing adjustment positions. B—One type of bushing selection chart for both two- and four-wheel drive vehicles. (Hunter Engineering Co.)

found for a handling or tire wear problem. When checking, make certain that the camber angle is taken into consideration in that a change in camber will also affect steering axis inclination. Keep the brakes locked while checking inclination. Camber, caster, and steering axis inclination are illustrated in **Figure 39-40.**

Checking Toe

Start the engine if the vehicle has power steering, turn the steering wheel from side to side, then center it. Stop the engine and lock the steering wheel in the centered position. Then loosen the tie rod adjusting sleeve clamp bolts (conventional steering, **Figure 39-41**) or locknuts (rack and pinion steering, **Figure 39-42**). Adjust toe by turning the sleeves or rods to obtain exactly half of the needed toe on each wheel. Some vehicles have only one sleeve in which case the steering wheel cannot be centered. Unlock the steering wheel and turn it from side to side, then recenter it. Recheck the toe on each side and readjust as needed.

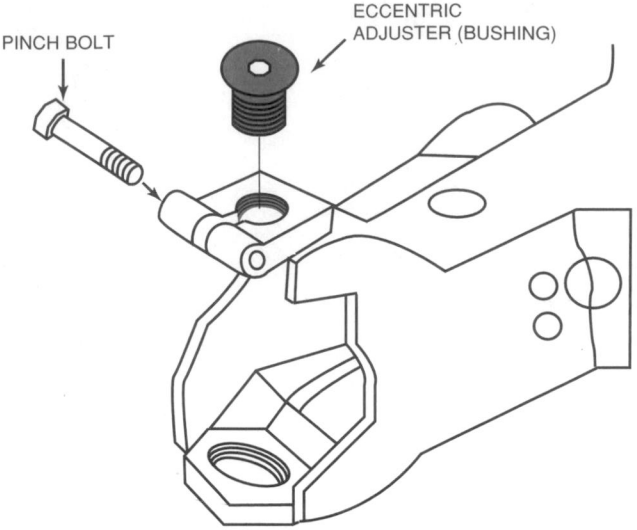

Figure 39-39. Installing an eccentric adjuster bushing into correct position before reinstalling the ball joint. (Hunter Engineering Co.)

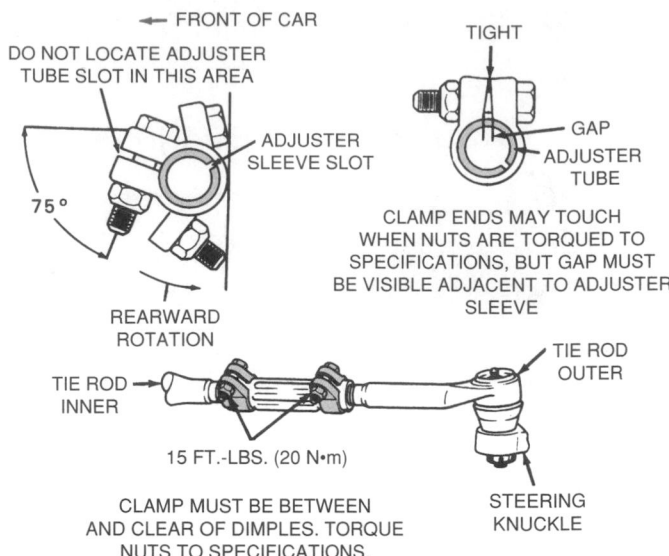

Figure 39-41. Proper positioning of one particular tie rod adjusting sleeve clamp. (Oldsmobile)

Caution: On some vehicles with conventional steering, the tie rod adjusting sleeve clamp bolts must be in a specific location in relation to the tie rod top or front surface to prevent interference with other parts. The toe-in adjustment is critical. An improper toe-in setting can severely wear the tire tread in a very short period of driving.

Follow the manufacturer's recommendations for proper clamp positioning. If none are available, study the steering linkage and be certain no interference is possible. **Figure 39-41** illustrates the proper positioning for one particular setup. Sleeve clamps must be over the threaded rods and must be torqued. The sleeve should be centered over the tie rod and tie rod socket shaft.

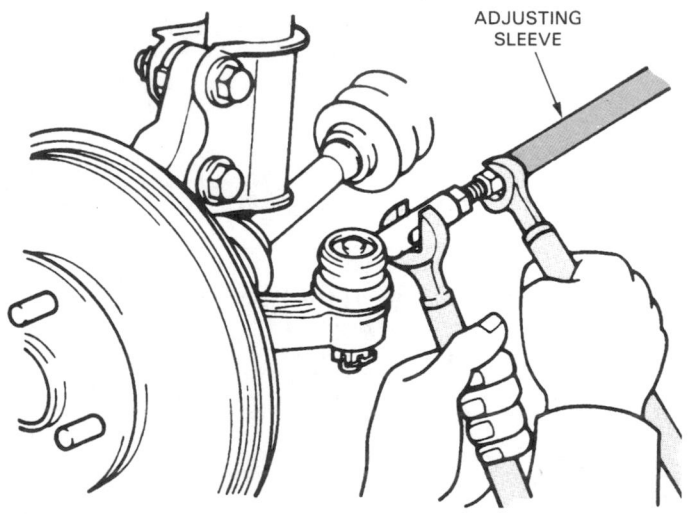

Figure 39-42. Adjusting front toe-in. Turn the adjusting sleeve as specified in the service manual. (Geo)

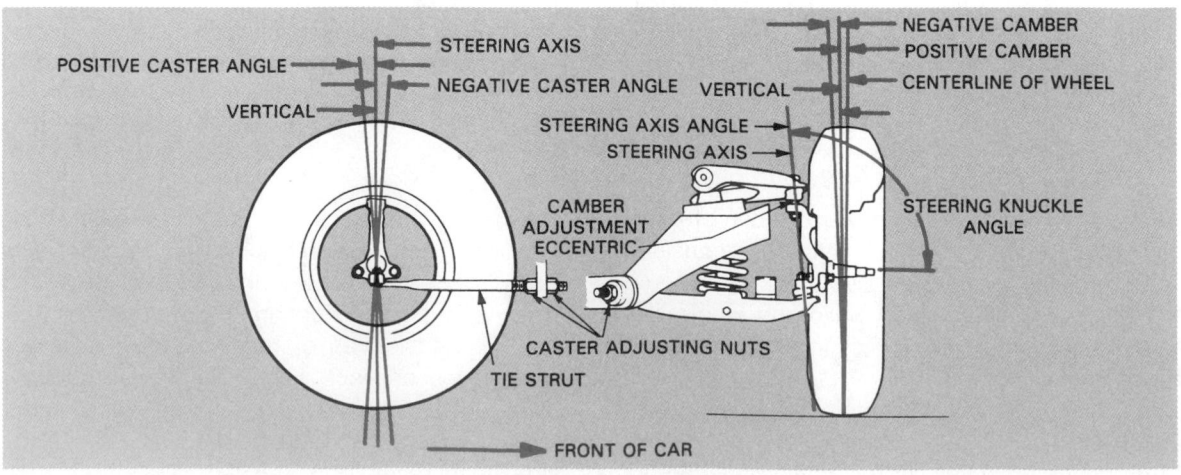

Figure 39-40. Camber, caster, and steering axis inclination (angle). Note how the camber and caster are adjusted on this setup. (Cadillac)

STOP **Warning: A loose tie rod sleeve, an improperly positioned clamp, a loose fastener, or a poorly centered sleeve can cause an accident. Double check all fasteners and the position of all parts.**

When the toe-in is adjusted correctly, the steering wheel should be straight with the wheels in the straight ahead position. If the steering wheel is off center, it may be straightened by turning both tie rod sleeves in the same direction until the steering wheel is aligned. Wheel spoke positioning for one vehicle is shown in **Figure 39-43.** When properly aligned, the steering wheel should be in the correct plane with the front wheels in the straight ahead position. Both front wheels should be at the same angle to a centerline drawn lengthwise through the vehicle and with the steering gear on the center point of travel. Look at **Figure 39-44.**

Checking Toe-Out on Turns

Leave the brake pedal depressor applied. Turntables must be set at 0° with the locking pins removed. Wheels should be in the straight ahead position. Turn the front of the right wheel inward until the turntable dial reads exactly 20°. Read the indicator on the left wheel. This reading is the angle of toe-out for the left wheel. It should be slightly more than 20°.

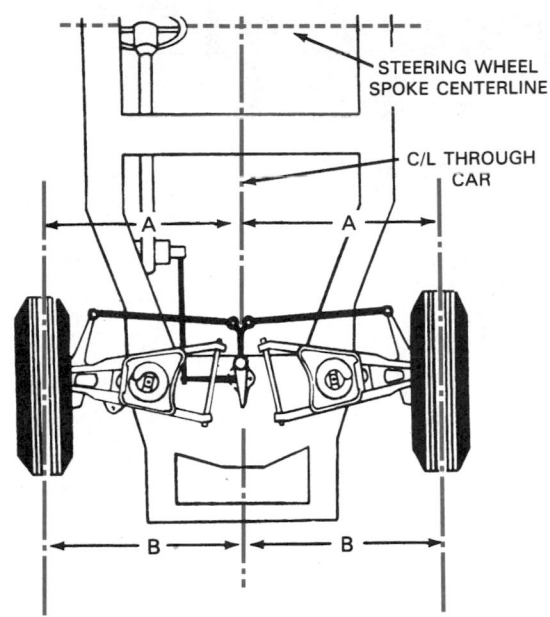

Figure 39-44.   Center point steering. Steering wheel in correct plane, wheels forming equal angles to the centerline (C/L) with wheels in the straight ahead position. Both A dimensions are equal, as are both B dimensions.

Turn the front of the left wheel inward 20° and read the indicator on the right wheel turntable. This is the angle of toe-out for the right wheel. Compare with specifications. Turning radius or angle of toe-out is built into the steering arms. If the angles are not according to specifications, the steering arms are bent and must be replaced. **Figure 39-45** illustrates the use of a turntable in checking turning radius. **Figure 39-46** illustrates a vehicle set up to be checked for toe-out on turns with a computerized alignment machine.

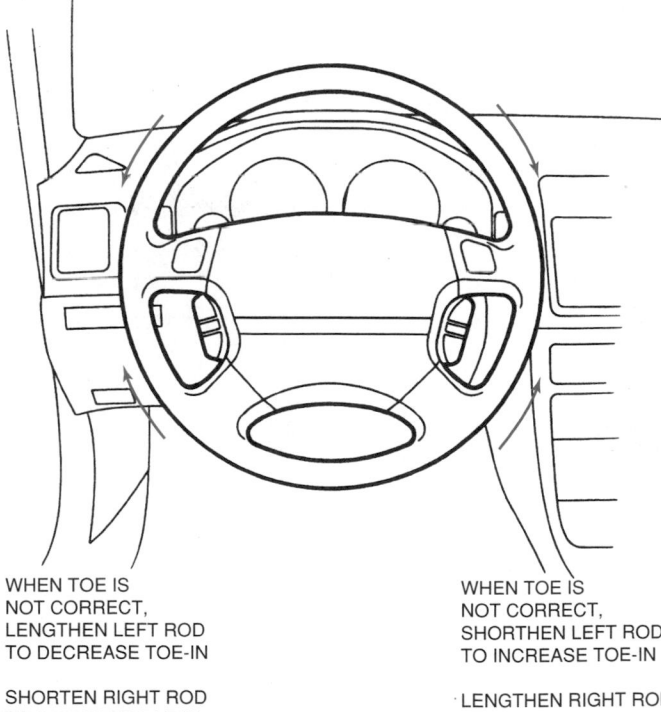

WHEN TOE IS CORRECT, TURN BOTH CONNECTING ROD SLEEVES DOWNWARD TO ADJUST SPOKE POSITION

WHEN TOE IS CORRECT, TURN BOTH CONNECTING ROD SLEEVES UPWARD TO ADJUST SPOKE POSITION

WHEN TOE IS NOT CORRECT, LENGTHEN LEFT ROD TO DECREASE TOE-IN

WHEN TOE IS NOT CORRECT, SHORTHEN LEFT ROD TO INCREASE TOE-IN

SHORTEN RIGHT ROD TO INCREASE TOE-IN

LENGTHEN RIGHT ROD TO DECREASE TOE-IN

ADJUST BOTH RODS EQUALLY TO MAINTAIN NORMAL SPOKE POSITION

Figure 39-43.   Correcting the steering wheel spoke positioning by adjusting tie rods. (Honda)

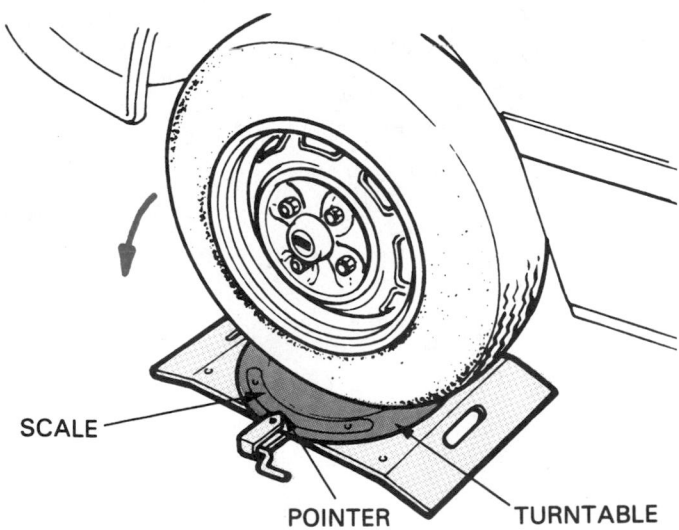

SCALE

POINTER   TURNTABLE

Figure 39-45.   Turning radius is being checked by placing vehicle on a turntable. The reading is obtained with the pointer and scale. (Mazda)

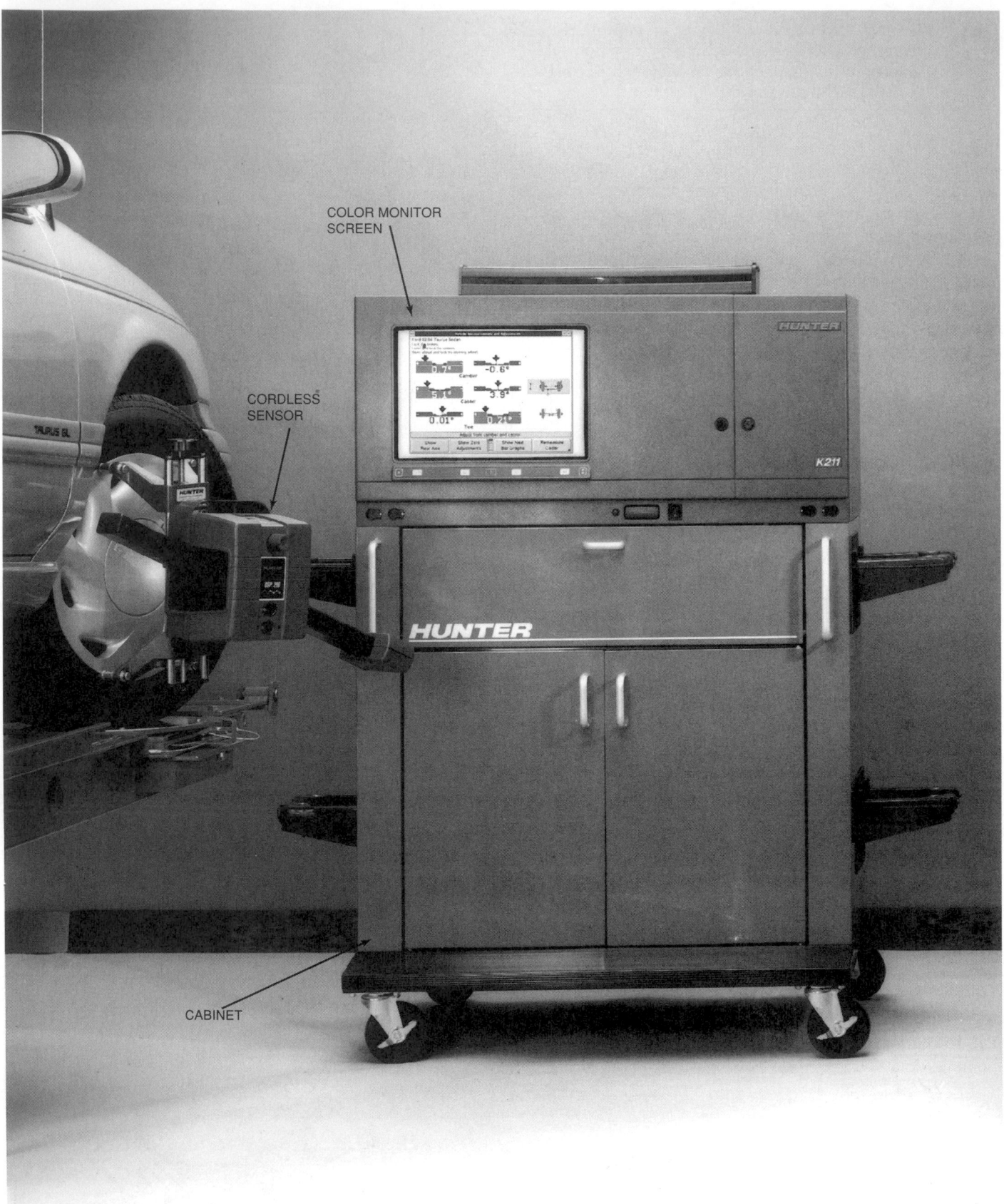

COLOR MONITOR
SCREEN

CORDLESS
SENSOR

CABINET

Figure 39-46. A vehicle being checked for toe-out with a computerized alignment machine. Follow the manufacturer's operating instructions. Use care when handling the machine. (Hunter Engineering Co.)

Final Alignment Check

In addition to repeating the prealignment inspection, make certain that vehicle curb height is as specified, **Figure 39-47A.** Check that caster, **Figure 39-47B,** and camber, **Figure 39-47C,** are correct. Check that the toe-in, **Figure 39-47D,** is correct. Check that the steering axis inclination is as required, **Figure 39-47E,** and that toe-out on turns meets specifications, **Figure 39-47F.** Be sure that all fasteners are tight after the alignment is complete. Road test the vehicle after any wheel alignment. If the vehicle is aligned correctly, it will not pull to the right or left and will not wander excessively. The steering wheel will be straight when driving straight forward.

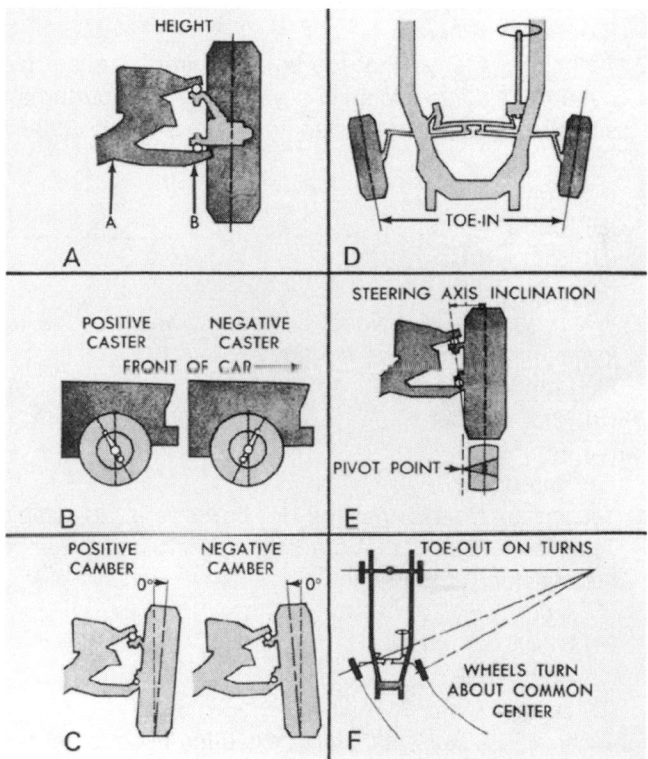

Figure 39-47. To ensure the proper steering and handling characteristics, all of these wheel alignment factors must be as specified. (Plymouth)

Tech Talk

In most cases, it is not obvious that a vehicle has been aligned. The vehicle will probably handle about the same as it did when it was brought in. Sometimes, the customer may not believe that you actually aligned the vehicle. Even worse, you may get blamed for a problem elsewhere on the vehicle or, in a large shop with many alignment technicians, someone else's incorrect alignment.

After making alignment adjustments, always place a mark on the front suspension, always in the same general location. A can of paint in an unusual color or mechanic's crayon will work well. This will let you know that you worked on the vehicle the next time that it is in the shop. Also write down all alignments readings for that particular vehicle—before and after alignment adjustments. A small stenographer's notebook can be kept out of the way in your toolbox. This information will help you diagnose a comeback problem.

Finally, always check that the steering wheel is straight during the road test, and straighten it if it is crooked. Most drivers have no idea what was done to align the suspension of their vehicle, but they can't help but notice a crooked steering wheel.

Summary

Wheels must be properly aligned to produce good steering, handling, and tire wear. Alignment angles are caster, camber, toe-in, steering axis inclination, and toe-out on turns. Wheels must also track correctly.

Caster (top ball joint forward or backward or bottom) may be specified as negative (tipped to front) or positive (tipped to rear). Camber (top of wheel in or out) may be specified as negative (tipped inward) or positive (tipped outward). Toe (relative position of front and rear of tires) is used to compensate for looseness in the steering system. Toe may be in or out depending on the vehicle. Toe is critical to proper tire wear. It must be carefully checked and corrected. Toe-out on turns allows the inner wheel to turn more sharply than the outer so that it may move about a smaller radius without the tires scrubbing. Toe-out on turns is determined by the angle of the steering arms. Steering axis inclination (tipping top ball joint inward) places the load nearer the tire-road contact area. This makes for easier steering and reduces the need for excessive camber. Steering axis inclination is not adjustable.

Many types of alignment checking equipment are available. A modern alignment machine must be used to perform a four-wheel alignment. Before checking wheel alignment, make the recommended prealignment inspections. Check for worn or damaged parts and replace any that are not up to specifications. Check vehicle ride height and curb weight. Tires must be in good condition, and must match by type, amount of wear, and size. Air pressure must be correct.

Vehicle manufacturers have devised many methods to adjust caster and camber. Never heat or bend suspension or steering parts to make changes. Special shims and bushings are available to make extra adjustments. More positive camber may be adjusted into the left front wheel to compensate for road crown. Caster can also be varied in the left wheel to handle the normal road crown. Use quality aligning equipment in proper condition. Make all checks and adjustments carefully and to exact specifications.

When the alignment is complete, all angles should match factory specifications. The steering gear must be at midpoint in its travel. The steering wheel spokes should be in the proper position. Always road test the vehicle before and after a wheel alignment. If the vehicle is aligned correctly, it will not pull to the right or left, and will not wander excessively. The steering wheel will be straight when driving straight forward.

Know These Terms

Wheel alignment	Two-wheel alignment
Caster	Four-wheel alignment
Camber	Turning plates
Road crown	Heads
Steering axis inclination	Ride height
Included angle	Curb weight
Setback	Runout
Toe	Eccentrics
Toe-out on turns	Threaded rods
Tire scrubbing	Four-wheel steering
Wheel tracking	Shim
Dog-tracking	Eccentric bushing
Thrust angle	

Review Questions—Chapter 39

Do not write in this book. Write your answers on a separate sheet of paper.

1. Camber can be changed by _____.
   (A) tipping the top ball joint in or out
   (B) tipping the top of the tire in or out
   (C) tipping both the ball joints inward
   (D) Both A & B.

2. Performing a four-wheel alignment will reduce the chance of _____.

3. Curb _____ and ride _____ should be as specified before aligning front wheels.

4. Vehicles with front-wheel drive or independent rear suspension systems require _____ and _____ checks at the rear wheels.

5. The pull created by road crown is best offset by _____.
   (A) running the left tire with less pressure
   (B) increasing negative camber in the left front wheel
   (C) increasing positive camber in the left front wheel
   (D) increasing toe-in

6. Steering and suspension parts must never be _____.
   (A) bent
   (B) welded
   (C) heated
   (D) All of the above.

7. Steering axis inclination and camber are added together to form the _____.

8. Vehicle toe must be set _____.
   (A) in
   (B) out
   (C) at zero
   (D) Any of the above, depending on the vehicle.

9. When doing a four-wheel alignment, which of the following angles must be set last?
   (A) Front camber.
   (B) Rear camber.
   (C) Front toe.
   (D) Rear toe.

10. Compensating the heads removes the effect of runout in the _____.
    (A) bearings
    (B) control arms
    (C) wheel rim
    (D) All of the above.

ASE-Type Questions

1. Technician A says that caster angle involves tipping the top of the tire in or out. Technician B says that caster is an imaginary line through the wheel spindle. Who is right?
   (A) A only.
   (B) B only.
   (C) Both A & B.
   (D) Neither A nor B.

2. Technician A says that toe-in is required to offset toe-out on turns. Technician B says that toe-out on turns is adjusted by altering the length of the tie rods. Who is right?
   (A) A only.
   (B) B only.
   (C) Both A & B.
   (D) Neither A nor B.

3. When doing a four-wheel alignment, which of the following angles must be set first?
   (A) Front camber.
   (B) Rear camber.
   (C) Front toe.
   (D) Rear toe.

4. Technician A says that toe-out on turns is adjustable. Technician B says that steering axis inclination cannot be adjusted. Who is right?
   (A) A only.
   (B) B only.
   (C) Both A & B.
   (D) Neither A nor B.

5. Technician A says that shims are often used to set rear toe. Technician B says that moving the lower strut rod is a common method of setting front caster. Who is right?
   (A) A only.
   (B) B only.
   (C) Both A & B.
   (D) Neither A nor B.

6. A vehicle has a shimmy (vibration) that can be felt in the steering wheel at 45 MPH (72 kph). Technician A says that the problem could be caused by an improper caster setting. Technician B says that the problem could be caused by a worn tie rod end. Who is right?
   (A) A only.
   (B) B only.
   (C) Both A & B.
   (D) Neither A nor B.

7. All of the following methods are used to set front caster and camber on modern vehicles, EXCEPT:
   (A) shims at the control arm mounting.
   (B) eccentrics on the control arm bushings.
   (C) bending the control arm.
   (D) rivets removed and strut tower moved into position.

8. When shimming a rear axle, the shim is placed between the rear wheel bearing housing and the _____.
   (A) brake drum or rotor
   (B) axle
   (C) wheel rim
   (D) brake backing plate

9. All of the following statements about a vehicle that has been properly aligned are true, EXCEPT:
   (A) the vehicle will pull slightly to the left.
   (B) the vehicle will not wander.
   (C) the tire wear will be minimal.
   (D) the steering wheel will be straight when driving straight forward.

10. Technician A says that, when centering the steering wheel on a vehicle with power steering, the engine should be running. Technician B says that the brake pedal lock will prevent excessive movement when checking caster. Who is right?
    (A) A only.
    (B) B only.
    (C) Both A & B.
    (D) Neither A nor B.

Suggested Activities

1. Inspect at least three vehicles and determine the alignment adjustment devices. Then refer to the service manual to determine whether you found all of the adjusters. Write a report to the other members of your class on the things to look for when searching out alignment devices.

2. Look up alignment specifications for a particular make of vehicle over the last 10 years in a manual and determine the range of settings, from highest to lowest. Be sure to include the following:

   - Caster in degrees.
   - Camber in degrees.
   - Toe in fractions of an inch.

   Also include the following, if applicable:

   - Rear camber in degrees.
   - Rear toe in fractions of an inch.

3. Perform a two-wheel alignment on a rear-wheel drive vehicle. Write a short report on how you aligned the vehicle, and what adjustments were needed. Also write down the alignment readings before and after and how you obtained the correct specifications and what adjustments were needed.

4. Perform a complete four-wheel alignment on a front-wheel drive vehicle. Write a short report on how you aligned the vehicle, the alignment readings before and after, and what adjustments were needed.

5. Research aftermarket (non-factory) devices which can provide additional alignment adjustment, and report to the other members of your class on how these devices are used to gain additional adjustment on front and rear wheels.

Refrigerant recovery equipment, such as the units shown above, must be used when discharging air conditioning systems. (Robinair Div., SPX Corp.)

40

Air Conditioning and Heater Service

After studying this chapter, you will be able to:
- Explain basic refrigeration theory.
- Identify major air conditioning system components.
- List the safety rules for air conditioning service.
- Inspect an air conditioning system for problems.
- Recover, evacuate, and recharge an air conditioning system.
- Service air conditioning and heater parts.
- Install air conditioning system parts.
- Service refrigerant oil.
- Diagnose air conditioning and heating problems.

Originally, automobile air conditioners and heaters were separate from each other and were manually controlled by the vehicle's occupants. On modern vehicles, the air conditioner and heater are combined into one system that provides air at whatever temperature is desired. Some systems automatically respond to changes in outside temperature, humidity, and sunload. This chapter will cover the principles of both air conditioning and heating.

> Note: The air conditioning service procedures in this chapter are general in nature. Before starting work on any air conditioning system, be sure to obtain a service manual for the vehicle you are working on. You should also review all up-to-date materials regarding tools, refrigerant handling, and service procedures.

Principles of Air Conditioning

Air conditioning is a process in which air entering the vehicle is cooled, cleaned, and dehumidified. The parts of a typical basic air conditioning system are shown in **Figure 40-1.** The various parts of the system are connected by tubing and flexible hose. The system contains a charge of *refrigerant*, which provides the actual cooling effect. The job of the air conditioning system is to vary pressures so that the refrigerant will change from a liquid to a vapor (boil) at one place in the system and condense from a vapor to a liquid in another part of the system.

Types of Refrigerant

A refrigerant is a chemical compound of such elements as chlorine, hydrogen, fluorine, and carbon that is able to change *state* from a liquid to a vapor or from a vapor to a liquid. By undergoing this change in state, a refrigerant can give a considerable cooling effect by absorbing large amounts of heat in relation to its volume. The refrigerant's *boiling point*, or temperature at which it will change into a vapor, can be varied by pressure changes in the air conditioning system.

There are two types of refrigerant used in modern vehicle air conditioning systems. Older systems use *R-12*, which is sometimes referred to as CFC-12. However, R-12 has been suspected of contributing to the depletion of the ozone layer, which protects the earth from harmful radiation. R-12 is being replaced by *R-134a*, also called HFC-134a, which is less damaging to the earth's ozone layer and has a low global warming impact. Although these two refrigerants have different chemical compositions and boiling points, service procedures for systems using either type are similar.

> Caution: Always follow all rules regarding proper handling of refrigerant. Do not discharge refrigerant into the atmosphere. This is a violation of federal and state laws. R-12 and R-134a refrigerants, their oils, and most of their service tools are not interchangeable, Figure 40-2. Always use the correct refrigerant, oil, and tools designed for the system that you are working on.

Refrigerant is used over and over in the system and will maintain its efficiency indefinitely unless contaminated with dirt, water, or air. It is colorless in both the vapor and liquid state. Refrigerant is nonpoisonous, except when in direct contact with an open flame. Unless combined with moisture, it is noncorrosive. It is heavier than air and will become a vapor when released into the atmosphere.

> Warning: Do not use any other refrigerant as a substitute for R-12 or R-134a. Many substances sold as replacements may contain butane or propane gas. Both of these gases are highly explosive and flammable. Some substances sold as replacements contain blends of refrigerants used in commercial air conditioning. These blended refrigerants can cause damage to an automotive air conditioning system.

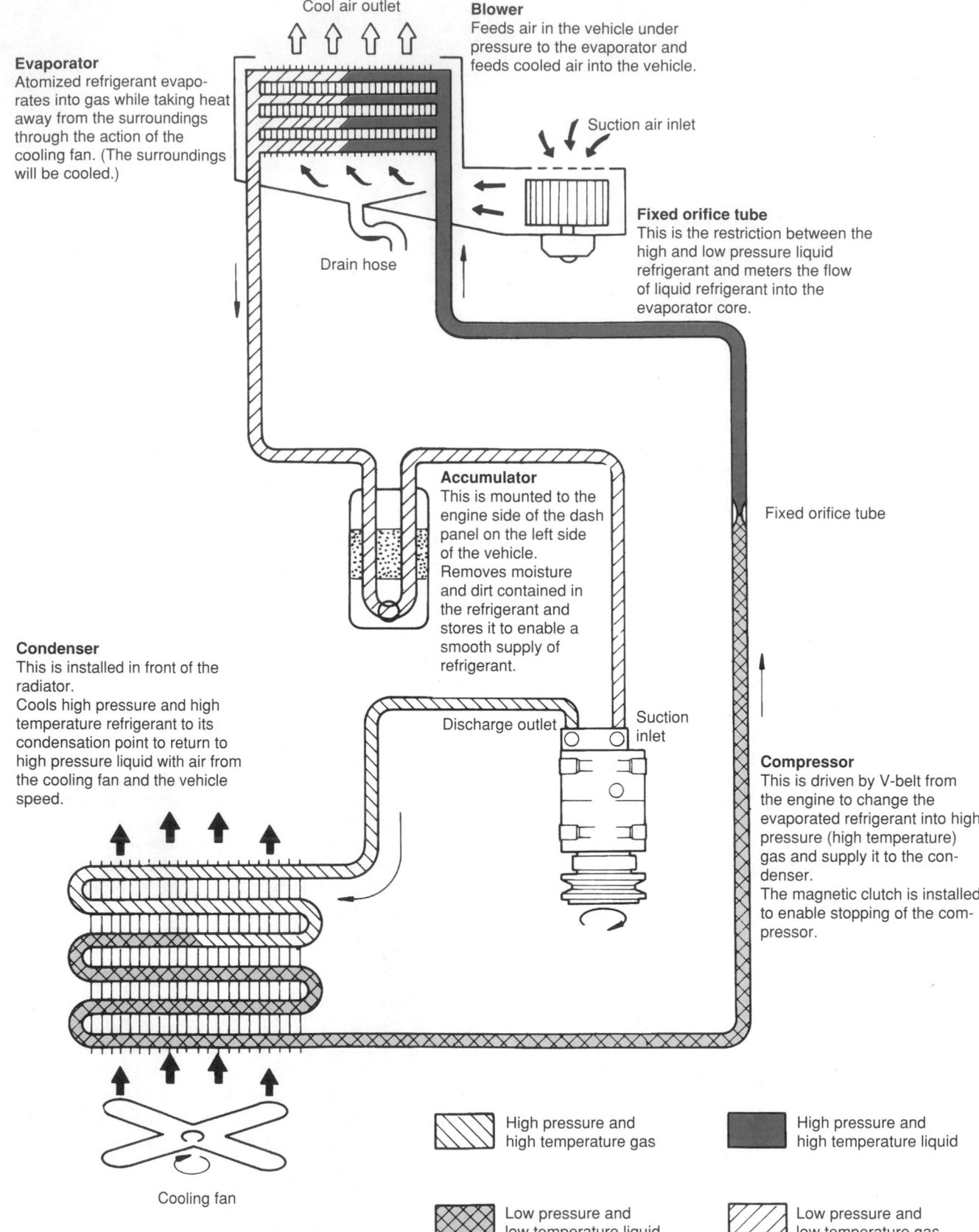

Cool air outlet

Blower
Feeds air in the vehicle under pressure to the evaporator and feeds cooled air into the vehicle.

Evaporator
Atomized refrigerant evaporates into gas while taking heat away from the surroundings through the action of the cooling fan. (The surroundings will be cooled.)

Suction air inlet

Fixed orifice tube
This is the restriction between the high and low pressure liquid refrigerant and meters the flow of liquid refrigerant into the evaporator core.

Drain hose

Fixed orifice tube

Accumulator
This is mounted to the engine side of the dash panel on the left side of the vehicle. Removes moisture and dirt contained in the refrigerant and stores it to enable a smooth supply of refrigerant.

Condenser
This is installed in front of the radiator.
Cools high pressure and high temperature refrigerant to its condensation point to return to high pressure liquid with air from the cooling fan and the vehicle speed.

Discharge outlet

Suction inlet

Compressor
This is driven by V-belt from the engine to change the evaporated refrigerant into high pressure (high temperature) gas and supply it to the condenser.
The magnetic clutch is installed to enable stopping of the compressor.

Cooling fan

High pressure and high temperature gas

High pressure and high temperature liquid

Low pressure and low temperature liquid

Low pressure and low temperature gas

Figure 40-1. The automotive refrigeration cycle. Note the refrigerant state in various parts of the system. (Hyundai)

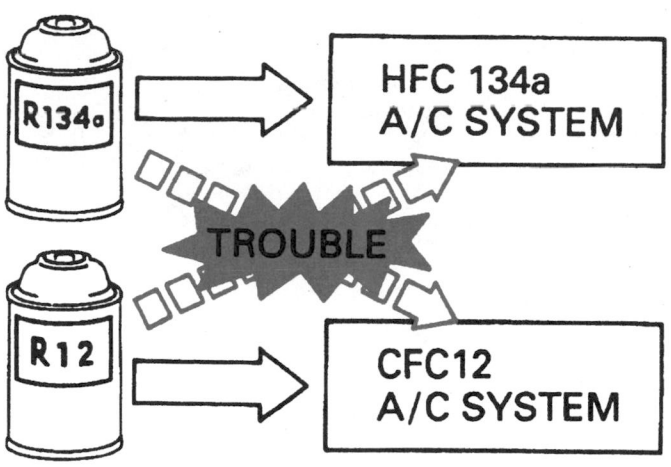

Figure 40-2. Never mix different refrigerants or put them in the wrong system. (Toyota)

Air Conditioning Cycle

There is a distinct **pressure-temperature relationship** for refrigerants. When the system pressure is lowered, the refrigerant boiling point lowers, turning liquid refrigerant into a vapor. As the pressure is increased, the boiling point rises and vaporized refrigerant returns to a liquid state. Pressure-temperature charts for R-12 is shown in **Figure 40-3** and R-134a in **Figure 40-4**.

R-12 PRESSURE - TEMPERATURE RELATIONSHIP

The table below indicates the pressure of R-12 at various temperatures. For instance, a drum of Refrigerant at a temperature of 26.6°C (80°F) will have a pressure of 579.9kPa (84.1psi). If it is heated to 51.6°C (125°F), the pressure will increase to 1,154.9 kPa (167.5 psi). It also can be used conversely to determine the temperature at which R-12 boils under various pressures. For example, at a pressure of 207.5 kPa (30.1 psi), R-12 boils at 0°C (32°F).

°C	°F	kPa	PSIG	°C	°F	kPa	PSIG
-29.8	21.7	0	Atmos-	12.7	55	358.5	52.0
			pheric	15.5	60	397.8	57.7
			Pressure	18.3	65	439.2	63.7
-28.8	-20	16.5	2.4	21.1	70	482.7	70.1
-23.3	-10	31.0	4.5	23.8	75	530.2	76.9
-20.5	-5	46.9	6.8	26.6	80	579.9	84.1
-17.7	0	63.4	9.2	29.4	85	632.3	91.7
-15.0	5	81.4	11.8	32.2	90	686.7	99.6
-12.2	10	101.4	14.7	35.0	95	745.3	108.1
- 9.4	15	122.0	17.7	37.7	100	806.0	116.9
- 6.6	20	145.5	21.1	40.5	105	870.2	126.2
- 3.8	25	169.6	24.6	43.3	110	937.7	136.0
- 1.1	30	196.5	28.5	46.1	115	1010.1	146.5
0	32	207.5	30.1	48.8	120	1083.2	157.1
1.6	35	224.8	32.6	51.6	125	1154.9	167.5
4.4	40	255.1	37.0	54.4	130	1234.2	179.0
7.2	45	287.5	41.7	60.0	140	1410.0	204.5
10.0	50	322.0	46.7				

Figure 40-3. R-12 pressure-temperature relationship chart. (Chevrolet)

R-134a PRESSURE - TEMPERATURE RELATIONSHIP

This table indicates the pressure of R-134a at various temperatures. For instance, a drum of refrigerant at a temperature of 27°C (80°F) will have a pressure of 609 kPa (88 psi). If it is heated to 52°C (126°F), the pressure will increase to 1298 kPa (188 psi).

TEMPERATURE		BAROMETRIC PRESSURE		TEMPERATURE			
°C	°F	kPa	PSIG	°C	°F	kPa	PSIG
-9	(16)	106	(15)	38	(100)	857	(124)
-8	(18)	115	(17)	39	(102)	887	(129)
-6	(22)	134	(19)	40	(104)	917	(133)
-4	(24)	144	(21)	41	(106)	948	(137)
-3	(26)	155	(22)	42	(108)	980	(142)
-2	(28)	166	(24)	43	(110)	1012	(147)
-1	(30)	177	(26)	44	(112)	1045	(152)
0	(32)	188	(27)	46	(114)	1079	(157)
1	(34)	200	(29)	47	(116)	1114	(162)
2	(36)	212	(31)	48	(118)	1149	(167)
3	(38)	225	(33)	49	(120)	1185	(172)
4	(40)	238	(35)	50	(122)	1222	(177)
7	(45)	272	(40)	51	(124)	1260	(183)
10	(50)	310	(45)	52	(126)	1298	(188)
13	(55)	350	(51)	53	(128)	1337	(194)
16	(60)	392	(57)	54	(130)	1377	(200)
18	(65)	438	(64)	57	(135)	1481	(215)
21	(70)	487	(71)	60	(140)	1590	(231)
24	(75)	540	(78)	63	(145)	1704	(247)
27	(80)	609	(88)	66	(150)	1823	(264)
30	(85)	655	(95)	68	(155)	1948	(283)
32	(90)	718	(104)	71	(160)	2079	(301)
35	(95)	786	(114)	74	(165)	2215	(321)
				77	(170)	2385	(342)

Figure 40-4. A pressure-temperature relationship chart for R-134a refrigerant. (General Motors)

Figure 40-5 illustrates the refrigerant state in various parts of the system during the air conditioning cycle. With the system operating, high pressure liquid refrigerant collects on the high pressure side of the system. The refrigerant moves through a restriction into the evaporator. The restriction causes the liquid refrigerant to enter the evaporator at low pressure. The lowered pressure decreases the refrigerant's boiling point.

In the evaporator, the refrigerant is warmed by air forced through the coils by the **blower motor**. As more heat from the air is absorbed, the refrigerant begins to boil, turning into a vapor. By the time it reaches the evaporator outlet, the refrigerant is completely vaporized. The cooled air is then returned to the passenger compartment. From the evaporator, refrigerant vapor is drawn into the compressor, which results in an increase in vapor pressure and a rapid rise in temperature. The vapor is pumped to the condenser under high pressure, sometimes as much as 400 psi (2400 kPa). This raises the boiling point of the refrigerant to a temperature higher than the outside air.

In the condenser, the hot, high pressure refrigerant vapor gives up its heat to the air stream moving over the

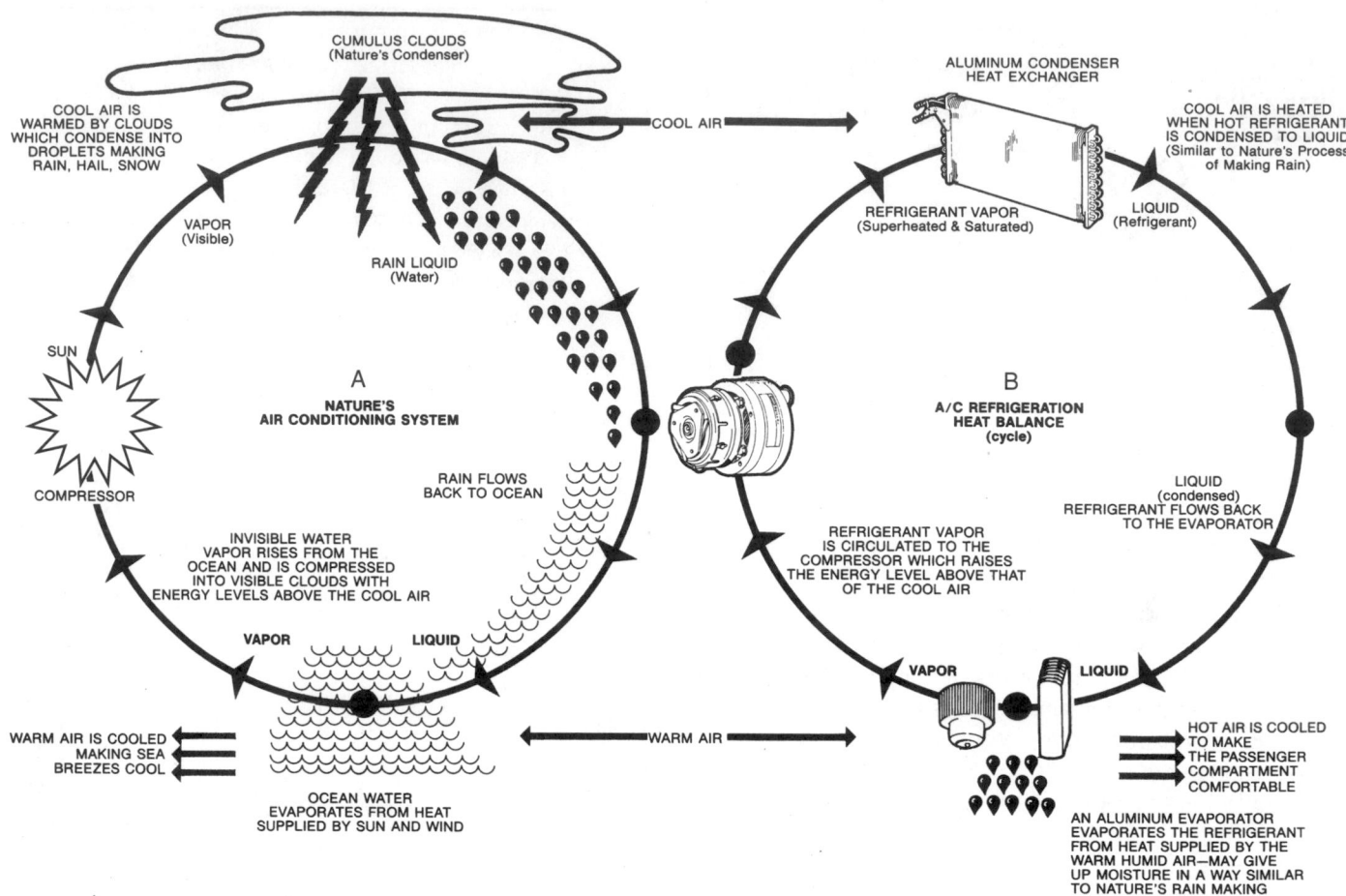

Figure 40-5. The process which takes place during the refrigeration cycle. Compare nature's air conditioning system A, to the automotive air conditioning refrigeration cycle in B. (Harrison Radiator)

condenser fins. Air is forced through the condenser by vehicle movement, or by the radiator cooling fan when the vehicle is stationary. The change in temperature causes the refrigerant to condense, or return to its liquid state. Still under pressure from the compressor, the liquid refrigerant flows to the restrictor for another cycle through the air conditioning system.

Types of Air Conditioning Systems

There are two major types of air conditioning systems. They are classified by the type of restrictor used between the condenser and evaporator. One system uses an *thermostatic expansion valve*, or *TXV*, **Figure 40-6.** In this system, the entrance of liquid refrigerant into the evaporator is controlled by varying the opening of the expansion valve, depending on the temperature at the evaporator outlet.

The restrictor opening in orifice tube systems is not variable and the flow of refrigerant is varied by controlling the operation of the compressor. On some orifice systems, the compressor is turned on and off. This is called a *cycling clutch orifice tube* or CCOT system, as in **Figure 40-7.** On other systems, the pumping capacity of the compressor is varied as needed. These are termed *variable displacement orifice tube* (VDOT) systems.

Major Components of the Air Conditioning System

All automotive air conditioning systems can be broken down into their basic parts. The following list contains the parts common to all air conditioning systems:

- Compressor
- Condenser
- Restrictor
- Evaporator
- Lines and hoses

If any one of these parts should fail, the air conditioning system will not work. In addition, some air conditioners, depending on the system, contain the following components:

- Receiver-drier
- Accumulator
- Evaporator pressure control
- Sight glass
- Pressure switches
- Mufflers

Other parts are not vital to overall air conditioner operation. However, they increase air conditioner efficiency, durability, and operational quality.

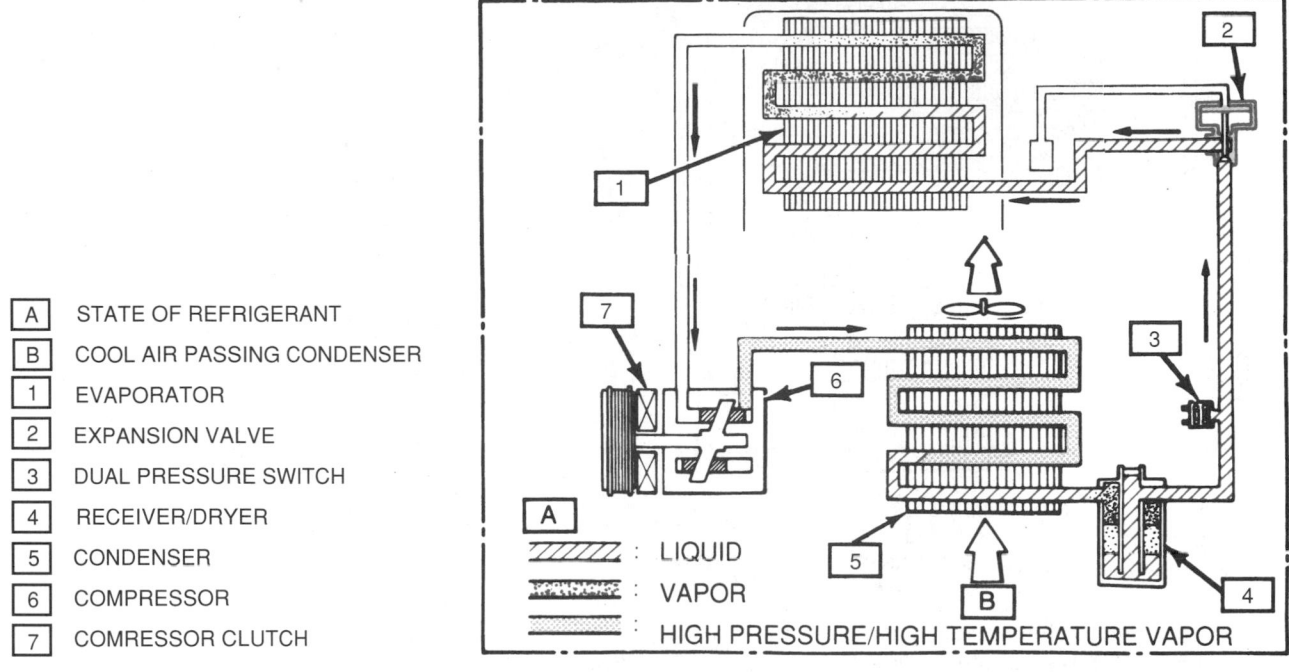

A	STATE OF REFRIGERANT
B	COOL AIR PASSING CONDENSER
1	EVAPORATOR
2	EXPANSION VALVE
3	DUAL PRESSURE SWITCH
4	RECEIVER/DRYER
5	CONDENSER
6	COMPRESSOR
7	COMRESSOR CLUTCH

Figure 40-6. Overall view of a refrigeration system which incorporates an expansion valve (2). Study the system carefully. (Geo)

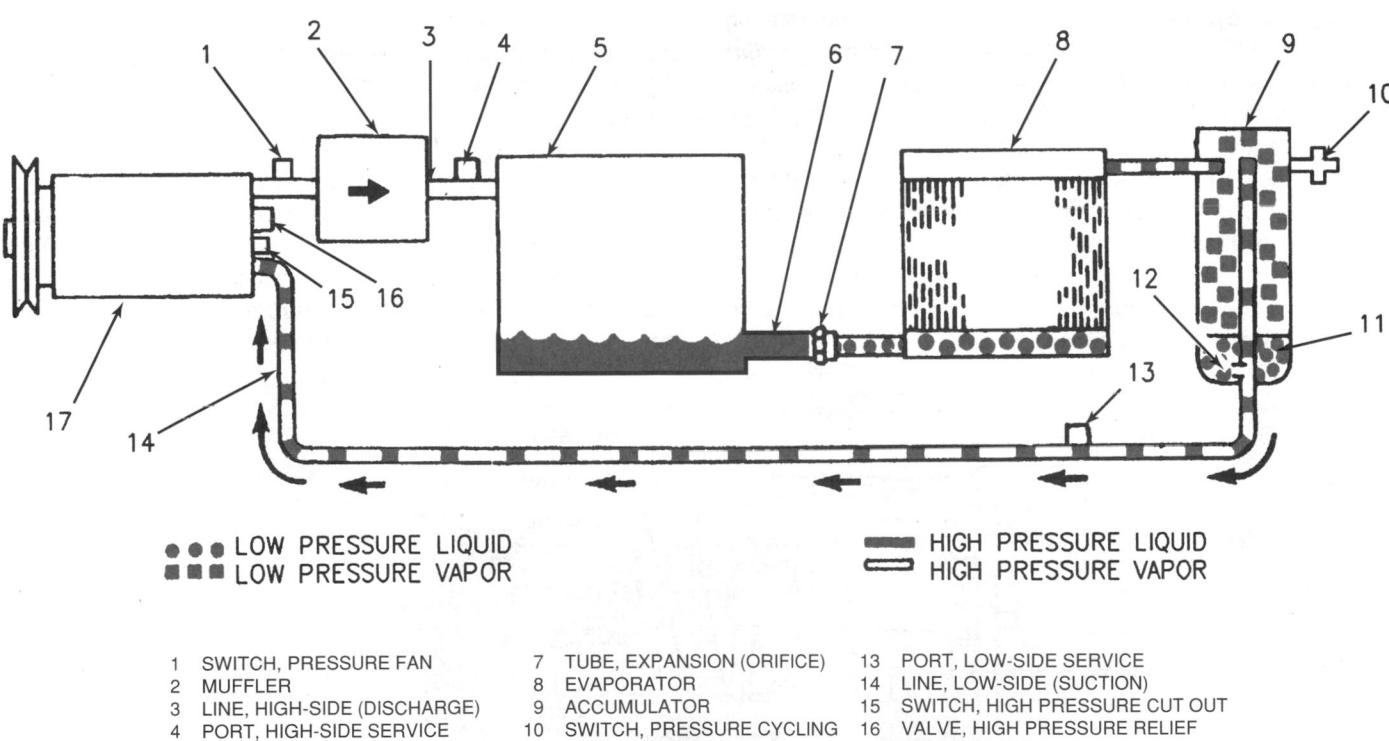

1 SWITCH, PRESSURE FAN	7 TUBE, EXPANSION (ORIFICE)	13 PORT, LOW-SIDE SERVICE
2 MUFFLER	8 EVAPORATOR	14 LINE, LOW-SIDE (SUCTION)
3 LINE, HIGH-SIDE (DISCHARGE)	9 ACCUMULATOR	15 SWITCH, HIGH PRESSURE CUT OUT
4 PORT, HIGH-SIDE SERVICE	10 SWITCH, PRESSURE CYCLING	16 VALVE, HIGH PRESSURE RELIEF
5 CONDENSER	11 DESICCANT	17 COMPRESSOR
6 LINE, LIQUID	12 HOLE, OIL BLEED	

Figure 40-7. A cycling clutch orifice tube (CCOT) refrigeration system schematic. (General Motors)

Compressor

The refrigerant leaves the evaporator as a low pressure vapor and travels to the *compressor* through the flexible low pressure vapor line. Look at **Figure 40-8.** The compressor draws in the vapor and forces it through the high pressure vapor line to the condenser. The compressor is used to both move and pressurize the refrigerant.

Basic Compressor Designs

Most automotive refrigerant compressors are piston types. Internally they resemble small engines. Many older air conditioning systems use two-cylinder compressors. These compressors are either V-type compressors or in-line designs, **Figure 40-9.** The pistons in these compressors are attached to a rotating crankshaft in the same manner as an

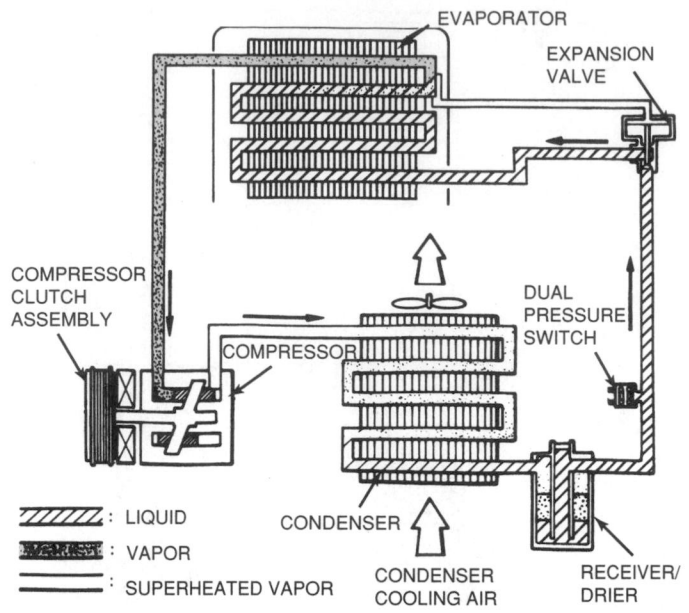

Figure 40-8. Schematic of refrigeration portion of a typical air conditioning system. Arrows indicate the flow of refrigerant. (Geo)

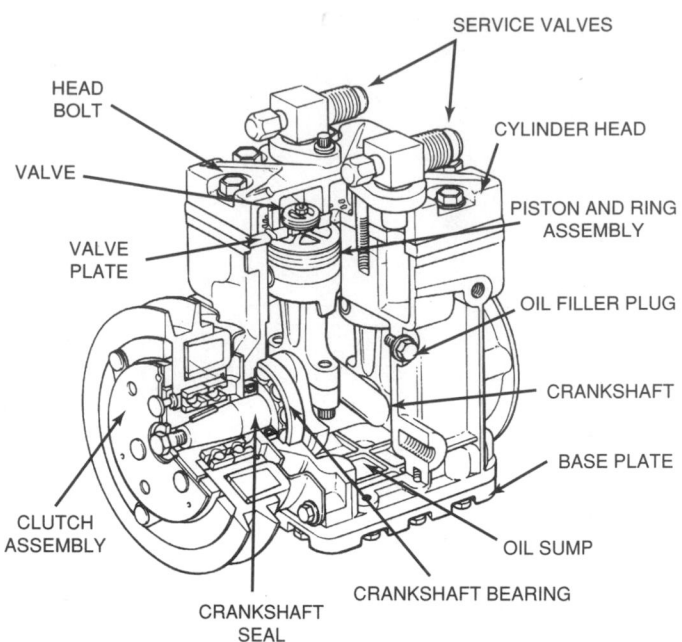

Figure 40-9. A cutaway view of a two-cylinder air conditioning compressor. (Nissan)

engine. The cylinders are at right angles to the rotating crankshaft. Other air conditioning systems employ *radial* compressors, **Figure 40-10.** The radial type also uses a type of crankshaft to operate the pistons. Note that these pistons are also at right angles to the crankshaft.

Another common type of compressor is the *axial* type. In the axial type the pistons are parallel to the rotating input shaft. The pistons are forced to move back and forth in an axial direction by the action of a rotating swash or wobble plate. On a typical compressor, there may be three double end pistons operating in six separate cylinders. This would

be referred to as a six-cylinder compressor. In addition to the piston compressors, a few units are rotary types, **Figure 40-11,** compressing the refrigerant by the use of rotary vanes.

Variable Displacement Compressors

Some compressors are designed with internal valves to allow their pumping capacity to be varied. This variation in compressor output is used to control evaporator temperature to prevent icing. While *variable displacement compressors* are usually used with fixed orifice air conditioning

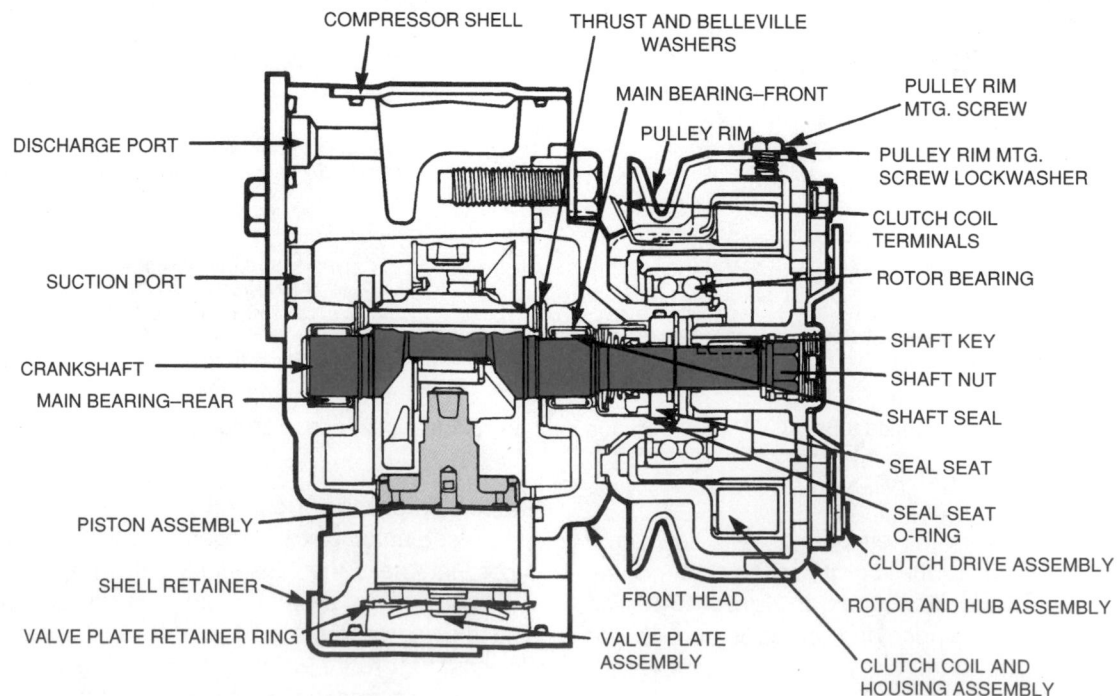

Figure 40-10. A cross-sectional view of a radial type air conditioning compressor. Study the construction. (Harrison Radiator)

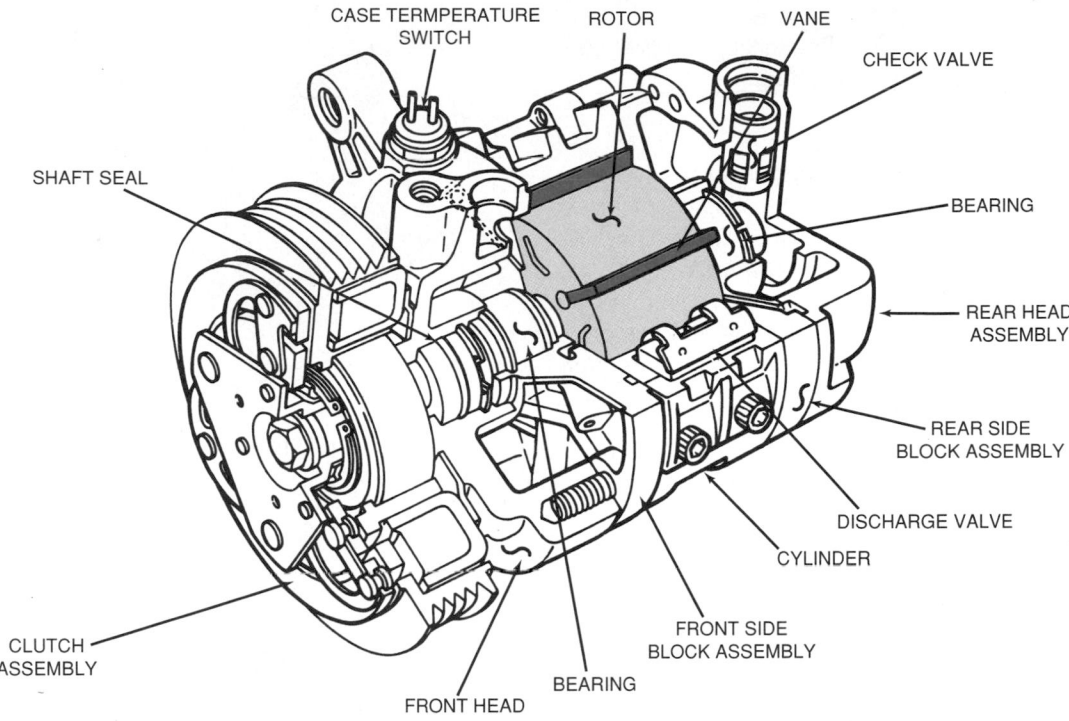

Figure 40-11. A cutaway view of a rotary 5-vane compressor. (Geo)

systems, they are sometimes used on systems with expansion valves. A five-cylinder, variable displacement compressor is shown in **Figure 40-12.** Note the internal valve which varies compressor capacity according to system pressure variations. This compressor can meet all air conditioning needs without cycling on and off.

The compressor's internal intake valve reduces the refrigerant output whenever the evaporator pressure becomes too low. This reduces the load on the engine,

reducing the amount of fuel used to operate the air conditioning system. The internal valve is moved by pressures in the evaporator, and changes the piston displacement to either reduce or increase refrigerant output.

Pressure Relief Valve

Some compressors are equipped with a **pressure relief valve.** Under unusual conditions, the compressor pressure may exceed safe limits. If this happens, the relief

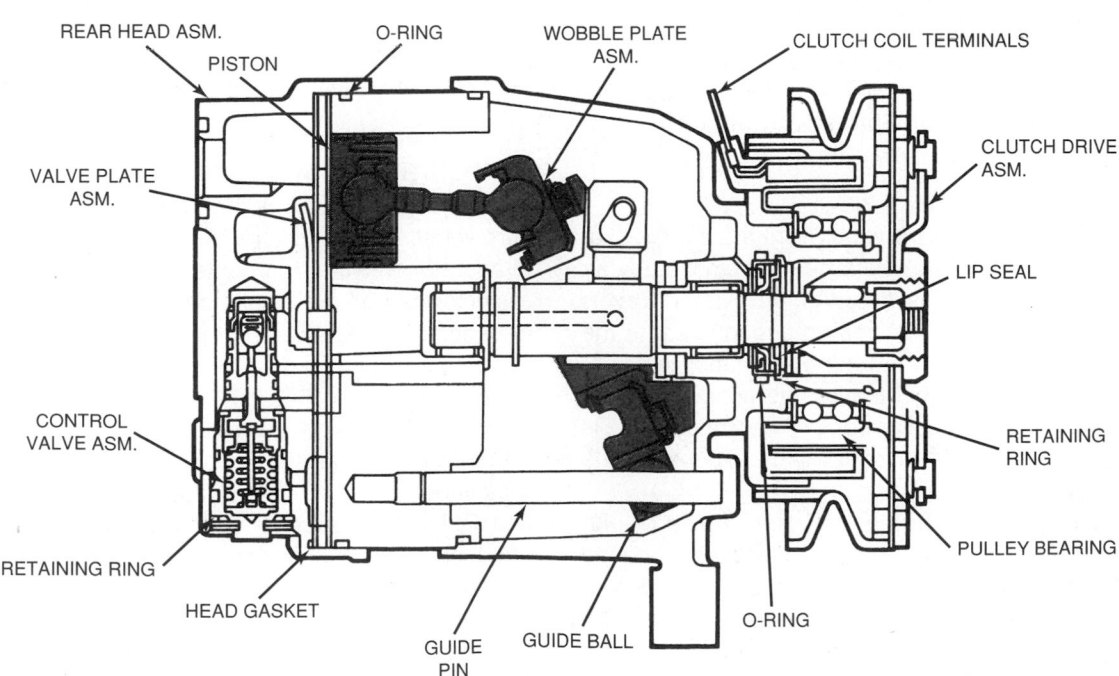

Figure 40-12. A cutaway view of a V-5 compressor. Note the piston and wobble plate assembly. (AC Delco)

valve will open and reduce pressure to a safe level. If the relief valve has opened, a possible restriction or other condition is present and should be corrected.

Compressor Clutch

The **compressor clutch** is energized to place the air conditioning system into operation. The clutch coil is an electromagnet which draws the clutch hub inward, locking the revolving pulley to the compressor shaft. On some systems, the compressor clutch is applied whenever the air conditioner is on. On cycling clutch systems, the compressor is turned on and off to control evaporator pressure. Various designs are used for magnetic clutches. One type is shown on the compressor in **Figure 40-13.**

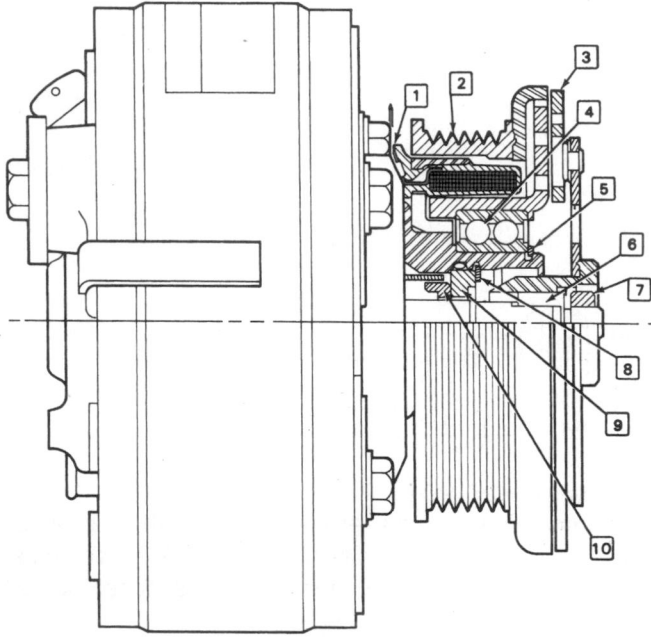

Figure 40-13. Cutaway of a magnetic clutch assembly as used on one particular radial compressor. 1—Clutch coil. 2—Pulley rotor. 3—Clutch drive assembly. 4—Rotor bearing. 5—Bearing retainer. 6—Shaft Key. 7—Shaft nut. 8—Seal seat retainer. 9—Shaft seal seat. 10—Shaft seal. (Chevrolet)

Condenser

The heated, high pressure vapor from the compressor is forced into the **condenser,** where heat is removed by air passing over the condenser fins. As the vapor travels through the condenser coils, it gives up enough heat to the passing air stream to cause the refrigerant vapor to return to its liquid state. As the liquid leaves the condenser, it is stored in the receiver-dehydrator. The condenser is mounted in front of the radiator so it will be exposed to the stream of incoming air.

Condensers and evaporators are often made of aluminum. During system operation, condenser pressures and temperatures are both high. Condensers are mounted in front of the radiator, as shown in **Figure 40-14.** Follow the path of the high pressure vapor from the compressor as it travels through the condenser, **Figure 40-15.**

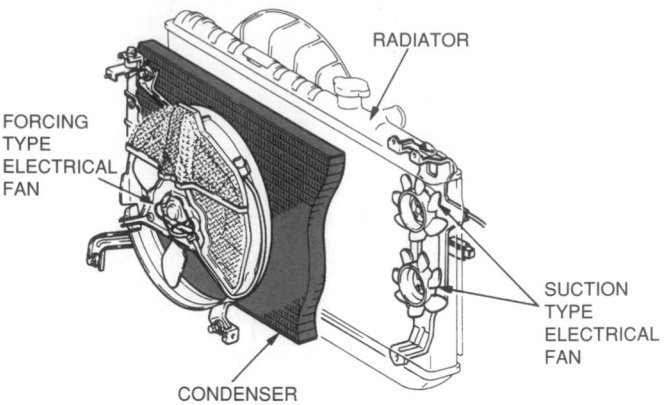

Figure 40-14. A condenser mounted in front of the radiator. Note the three electric cooling fans and their mounting locations. (Toyota)

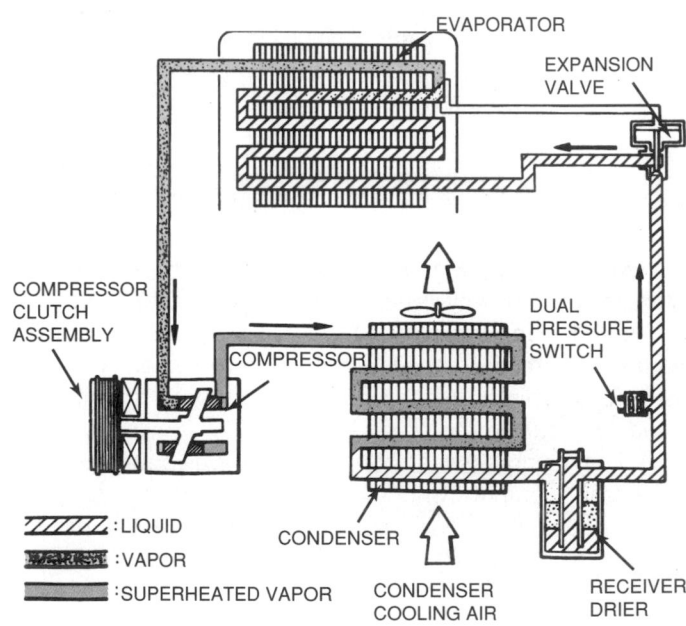

Figure 40-15. Refrigeration system schematic. Note the flow of refrigerant to the condenser. (Geo)

Refrigerant Flow Restrictor

Refrigerant reaches the **flow restrictor** as a high pressure liquid. The restrictor causes the refrigerant to enter the evaporator in small amounts, reducing its pressure. The restrictor can be an expansion valve or a fixed orifice tube, depending on the system design.

Expansion Valve

The expansion valve admits a metered amount of refrigerant into the evaporator. The refrigerant moves into the evaporator as a relatively low temperature, low pressure liquid. The temperature sensitive power element bulb is attached to the evaporator outlet. A capillary tube (length of tubing of small diameter which acts as a throttle on refrigerant) connects the bulb to the expansion valve.

As the temperature of the evaporator outlet rises, the expansion valve is opened, admitting a greater amount of refrigerant. When the temperature drops, the valve begins to close. The action of the valve is also affected by spring and by evaporator pressure. **Figure 40-16** is a cutaway view of a thermostatic expansion valve. Expansion valve servicing is usually limited to replacing the screen and tightening of any connections which leak because of insufficient torque.

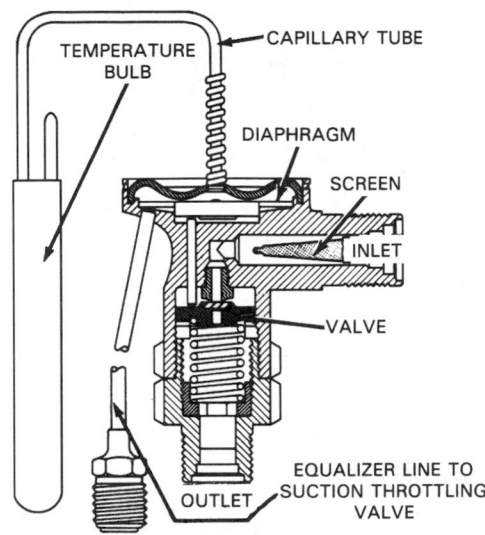

Figure 40-16. A typical thermostatic expansion valve. Study the construction carefully. (Chevrolet)

Fixed Orifice Tube

Some systems utilize a *fixed orifice tube* as an expansion valve. The plastic or metal tube houses a fine screen and a small fixed orifice through which a metered flow of liquid refrigerant can pass, **Figure 40-17.** The orifice tube is placed in a line that travels from the condenser outlet to the evaporator inlet. The fixed orifice diameter restricts the flow of liquid refrigerant into the evaporator. This provides a low pressure liquid flow to the evaporator.

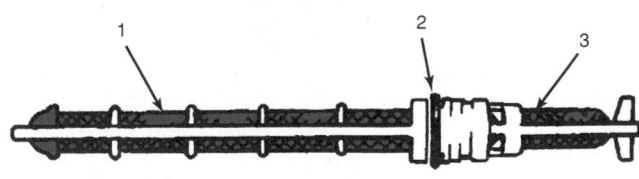

EXPANSION (ORIFICE) TUBE
1 LONG SCREEN END (INLET)
2 O-RING
3 SHORT SCREEN END (OUTLET)

INSTALL WITH SHORTER SCREEN END TOWARD
EVAPORATOR AND USE NEW O-RING SEAL

Figure 40-17. An expansion (orifice) tube. (General Motors)

A typical system using an fixed orifice tube is shown in **Figure 40-18.** To control the flow of refrigerant through the evaporator, a cycling clutch compressor is used. The sys-

tem shown in **Figure 40-18** uses a thermostatic cycling switch to turn the compressor clutch on or off. The system also has a compressor low pressure switch to de-energize the compressor clutch if system pressure drops to 25 psi (172 kPa). This provides compressor protection in event the system refrigerant charge is lost. It also prevents system operation when the ambient air temperature is below freezing. Fixed orifice tube service is limited to replacement.

Evaporator

The *evaporator* transfers heat from the incoming air to the refrigerant. As the low pressure liquid refrigerant enters the evaporator from the expansion valve, it begins to vaporize. This vaporizing action absorbs heat from the evaporator's tubes and cooling fins. Air passing over the cold tubes and fins gives up heat to the core and a stream of cooled air enters the vehicle, **Figure 40-19.**

When the air strikes the cold fins, it is dehumidified as some of the moisture in the air condenses and drains off the core. Particles of dust and pollen in the air tend to stick to the wet fins and drain off with the water, reducing the amount of pollutants entering the vehicle. Some evaporators have a line placed at the bottom of the housing and connected to the suction side of the compressor. This line returns any refrigerant oil which may have settled to the bottom of the evaporator to the compressor.

The evaporator contains no moving parts and is usually not subject to internal clogging. However, driving in very dusty areas or long use will occasionally cause the evaporator surface to become clogged. A missing intake air screen can allow leaves and other debris to clog the evaporator surface and case. Evaporators can develop refrigerant leaks, usually due to excess moisture in the system freezing in the bottom of the evaporator.

Lines and Hoses

To connect the parts of the air conditioning system, *lines and hoses* are used. Connections between parts that are solidly mounted on the body, such as the condenser and evaporator, are often connected by metal lines made of aluminum or steel. Connections between parts that have relative movement, such as the engine-mounted compressor and the body-mounted condenser, use flexible hoses.

Muffler

A small *muffler* is often placed between the compressor and the condenser to reduce pumping noise. The muffler is sometimes part of the hose itself and is usually referred to as a muffler hose. A muffler may also be used to reduce line vibrations. Always install mufflers with the outlet side down so that refrigerant oil will not be trapped.

Receiver-Drier

The *receiver-drier* is used only on air conditioning systems with expansion valves and is located between the condenser and restrictor. It is a reservoir for liquid refrigerant after it has been condensed, **Figure 40-20.** The receiver-drier contains a desiccant which filters and removes mois-

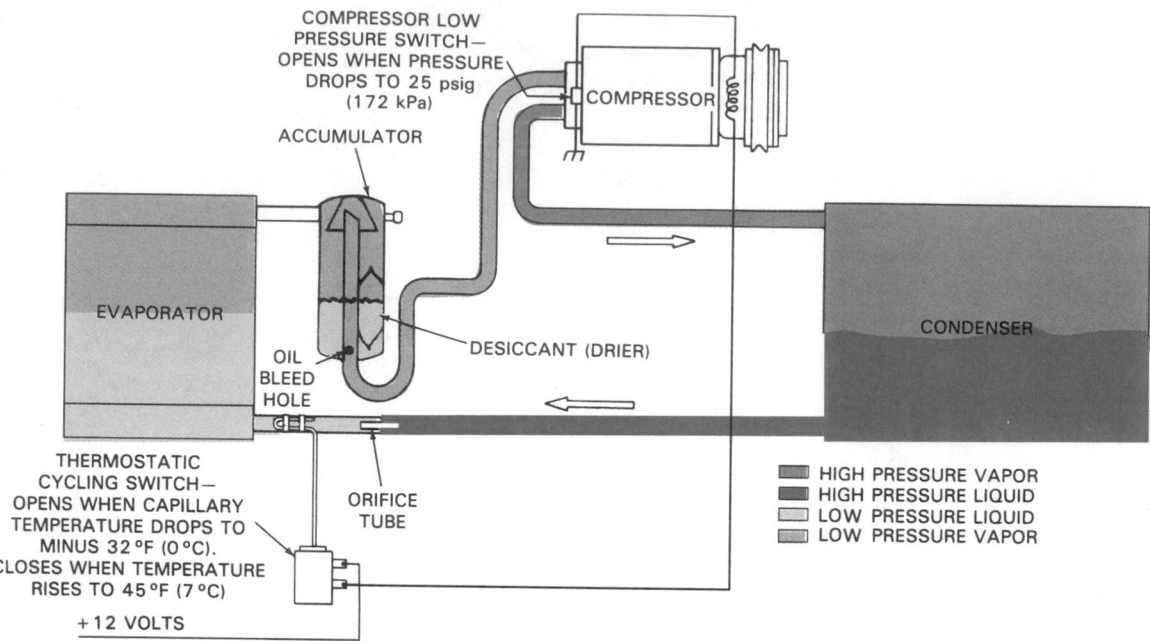

COMPRESSOR LOW PRESSURE SWITCH—OPENS WHEN PRESSURE DROPS TO 25 psig (172 kPa)

ACCUMULATOR

COMPRESSOR

EVAPORATOR

CONDENSER

OIL BLEED HOLE

DESICCANT (DRIER)

THERMOSTATIC CYCLING SWITCH—OPENS WHEN CAPILLARY TEMPERATURE DROPS TO MINUS 32°F (0°C). CLOSES WHEN TEMPERATURE RISES TO 45°F (7°C)

ORIFICE TUBE

+12 VOLTS

HIGH PRESSURE VAPOR
HIGH PRESSURE LIQUID
LOW PRESSURE LIQUID
LOW PRESSURE VAPOR

Figure 40-18. Air conditioning system using an orifice tube expansion valve. (Geo)

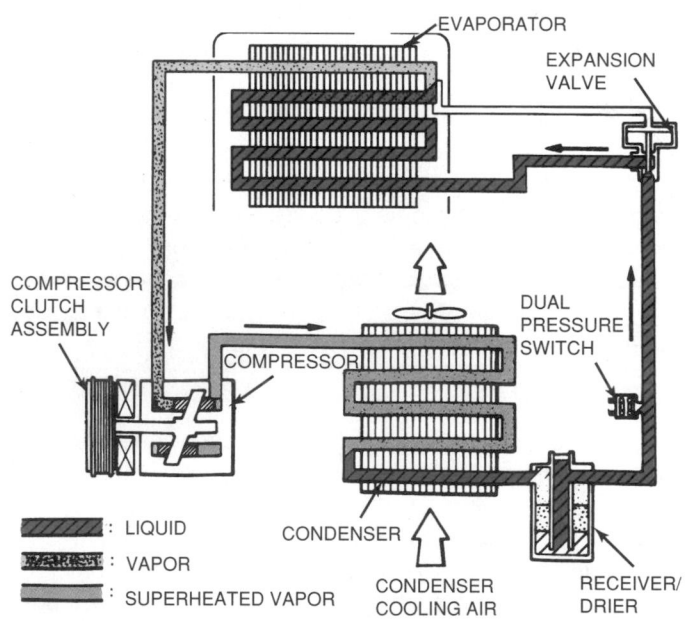

EVAPORATOR

EXPANSION VALVE

COMPRESSOR CLUTCH ASSEMBLY

COMPRESSOR

DUAL PRESSURE SWITCH

: LIQUID

: VAPOR

: SUPERHEATED VAPOR

CONDENSER

CONDENSER COOLING AIR

RECEIVER/ DRIER

Figure 40-19. A schematic of the refrigeration portion of a typical air conditioning system. Note the flow of refrigerant from the condenser to the evaporator. (Geo)

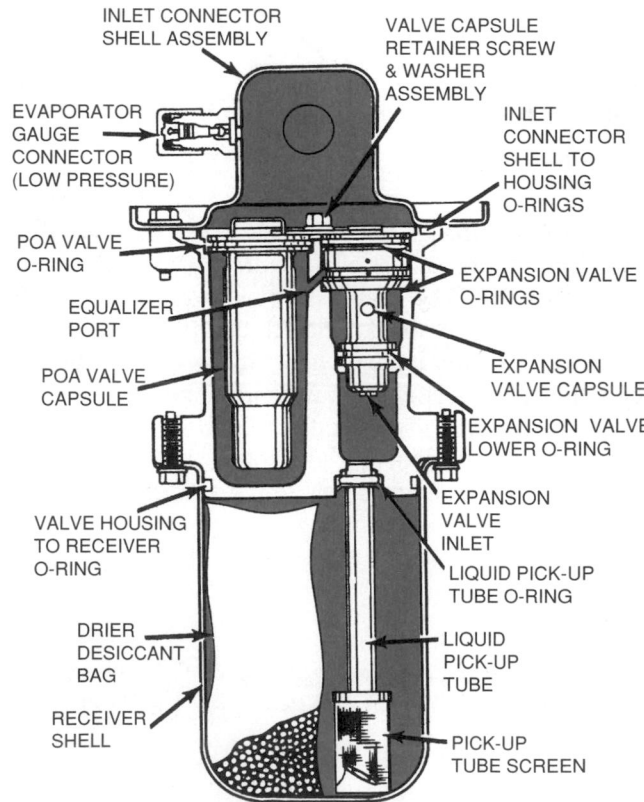

INLET CONNECTOR SHELL ASSEMBLY

VALVE CAPSULE RETAINER SCREW & WASHER ASSEMBLY

EVAPORATOR GAUGE CONNECTOR (LOW PRESSURE)

INLET CONNECTOR SHELL TO HOUSING O-RINGS

POA VALVE O-RING

EQUALIZER PORT

EXPANSION VALVE O-RINGS

POA VALVE CAPSULE

EXPANSION VALVE CAPSULE

EXPANSION VALVE LOWER O-RING

VALVE HOUSING TO RECEIVER O-RING

EXPANSION VALVE INLET

DRIER DESICCANT BAG

LIQUID PICK-UP TUBE O-RING

RECEIVER SHELL

LIQUID PICK-UP TUBE

PICK-UP TUBE SCREEN

Figure 40-20. Cutaway view of a valve-in-receiver unit. Study the construction. (Sun Electric)

ture from the refrigerant. It is often the location of the sight glass, when one is used.

The receiver-drier may contain a fusible safety plug which releases pressure when refrigerant temperature exceeds a specified point (about 212°F or 100°C). The receiver drier is often the site for one or more low pressure Schrader valve fittings. When more than one Schrader valve fitting is used, a pressure-cycling switch is usually installed on one of them. When the receiver-drier becomes inoperative (plugged or moisture laden), it is usually replaced.

Sight Glass

A *sight glass* may be installed in the receiver-drier or in a high pressure liquid line. The sight glass is used to inspect the refrigerant for the presence of bubbles or foam. One type of sight glass construction is shown in **Figure 40-21.** Use of the sight glass is covered under system ser-

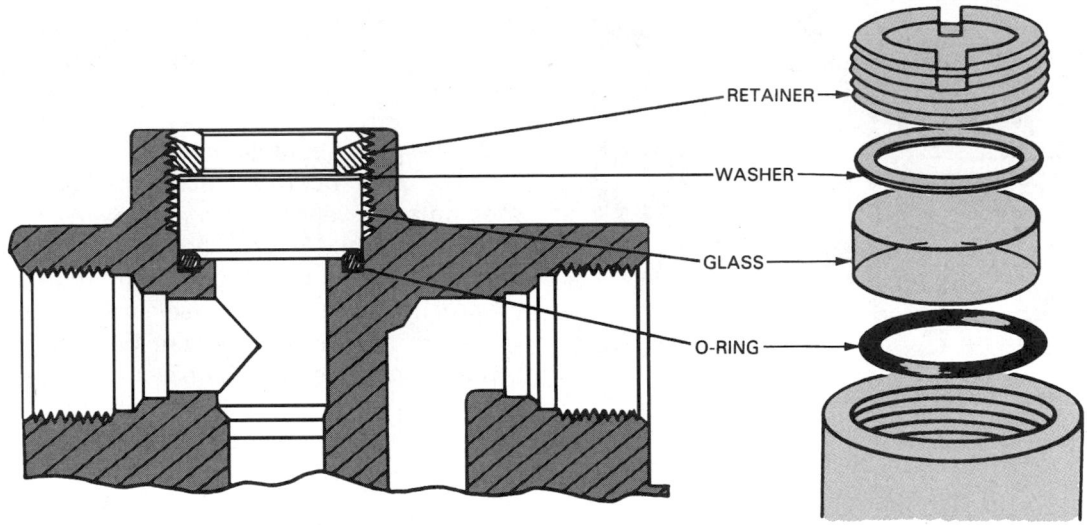

Figure 40-21. An exploded view of sight glass construction. (Chevrolet)

vice later in this chapter. Some systems, especially those with cycling clutches, do not have a sight glass.

Accumulator

Accumulators are used only on vehicles with fixed orifice air conditioning systems. The accumulator is installed between the evaporator and compressor suction line. The design of the accumulator allows it to act as a reservoir for pressurized refrigerant vapor, by causing any liquid refrigerant to fall to the bottom of the accumulator body, where it evaporates before it is drawn into the compressor. This prevents damage to the compressor as it cycles on and off. The accumulator also contains the desiccant for moisture removal.

An accumulator containing a filter screen, liquid bleed hole, desiccant, and pressure switch fitting is shown in **Figure 40-22.** Some accumulators used on older vehicles may also incorporate a pressure control valve, expansion valve, and a service fitting. When the accumulator becomes clogged or moisture laden, some models require replacement of the entire unit, while the desiccant and filter screen can be replaced on others.

Evaporator Pressure Controls

Evaporator temperature generally will run from 33° to 60°F (1° to 16°C). If the evaporator temperature drops to freezing (32°F or 0°C), condensation on the core will freeze and block off the airflow. Pressure in the evaporator must be controlled to prevent freezing. If pressure can be held between 29 and 30 psi (200 and 207 kPa), freezing will be eliminated. There are several types of *evaporator pressure controls.*

Hot Gas Bypass Valve

A *hot gas bypass valve* was used on some older vehicles. The valve was placed in the outlet side of the evaporator and metered high pressure, hot refrigerant from the compressor into the evaporator. This maintained the

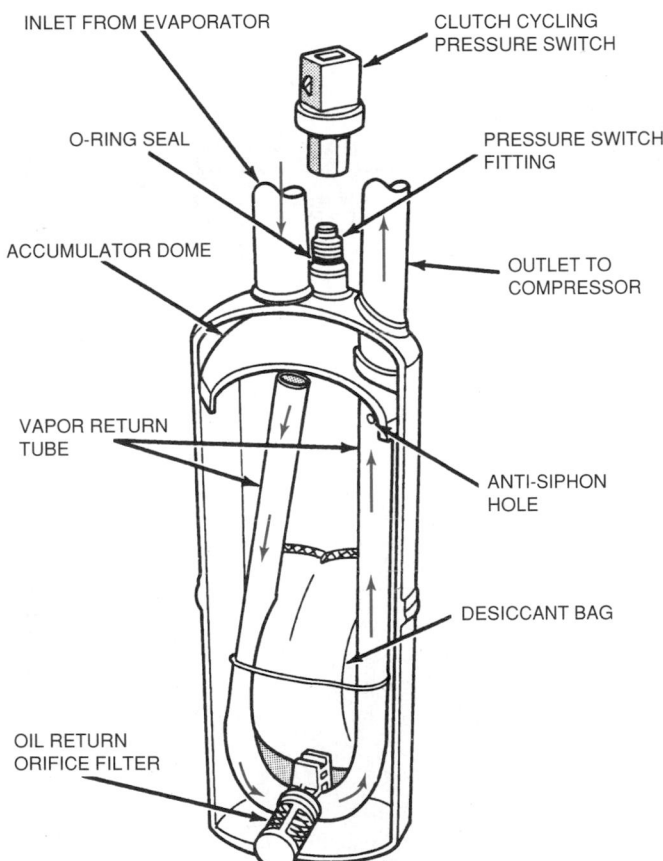

Figure 40-22. A cutaway view of one type of receiver-drier unit. Note the clutch cycling pressure switch. (Dodge)

evaporator pressure at a point high enough to prevent icing. A hot gas bypass valve is illustrated in **Figure 40-23.**

Suction Throttling Valve

The *suction throttling valve* was also used on older vehicles. It was placed at the evaporator outlet. When evaporator pressure rises, the valve releases pressure into the

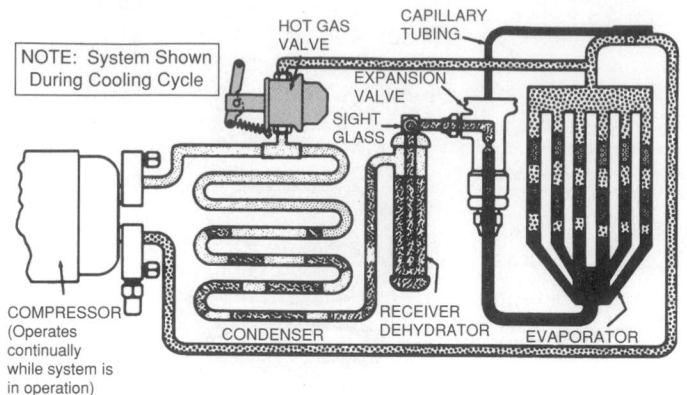

Figure 40-23. Evaporator icing controlled with a hot gas bypass valve.

low pressure vapor line to the compressor. If the pressure drops down, the valve restricts the flow, raising evaporator pressure.

Pilot Operated Absolute Valve

The *pilot operated absolute valve*, or POA, was used on a few vehicles until recently. A POA valve is illustrated in **Figure 40-24A**. The bellows assembly shown in **Figure 40-24A** is under a vacuum. The bellows operates the pilot needle valve. The needle valve, by opening or closing, alters the relative pressure between the compressor and evaporator sides of the piston. This causes the piston to open and close the cylinder ports and maintain a constant evaporator pressure. The system in **Figure 40-24B** uses a POA valve.

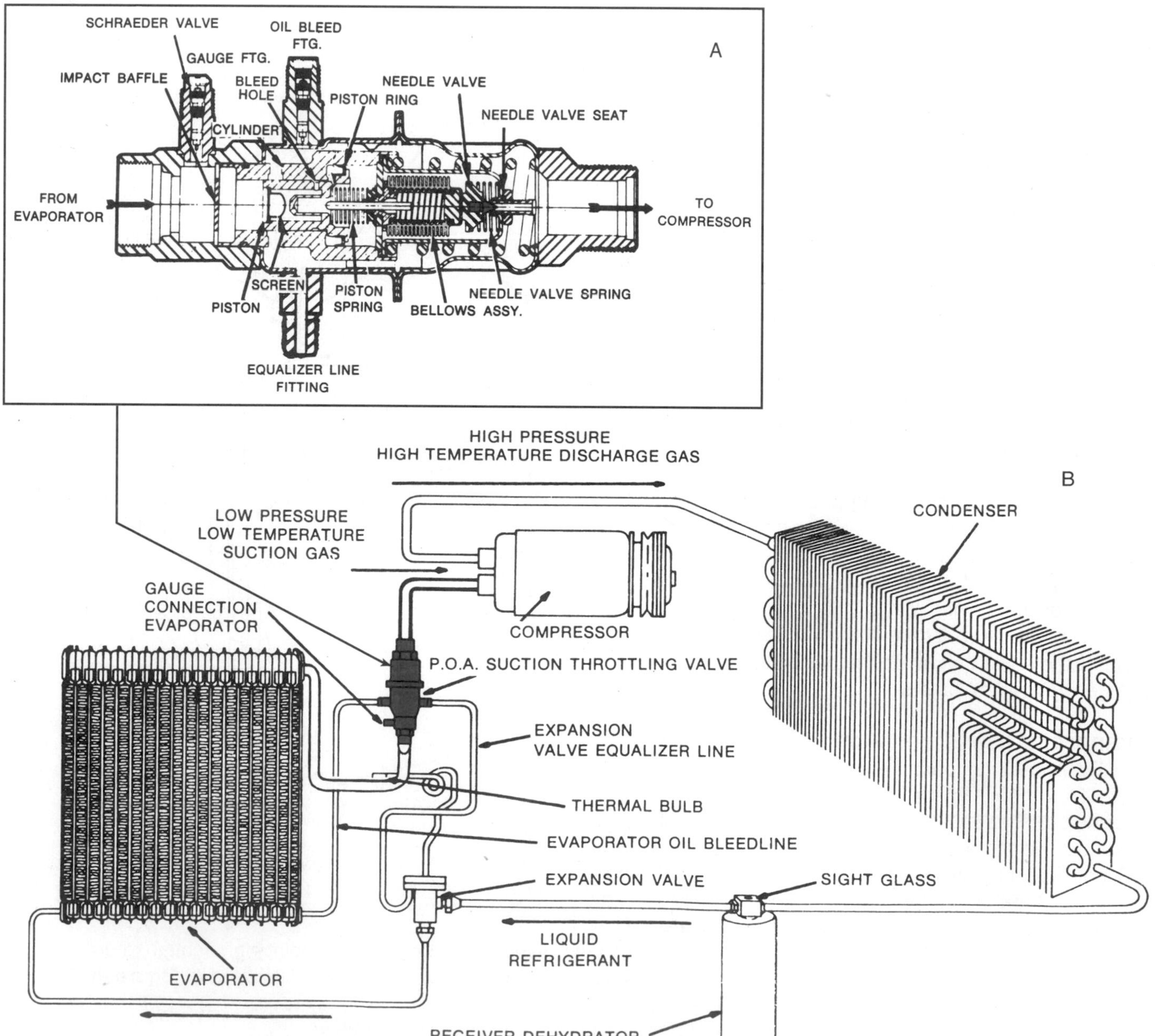

Figure 40-24. A—A cross-sectional view of a Pilot Operated Absolute (POA) valve. B—The pilot operated absolute valve and its location in an air conditioning system. (Harrison Radiator)

Compressor Cutout Switch

The method of preventing evaporator icing on most newer vehicles is a *thermostatic switch* that disengages the compressor when evaporator core temperature drops to a specific point. It does this by de-energizing the compressor magnetic clutch. When the temperature rises to a set level, the switch engages the compressor. The magnetic clutch is energized and the compressor is again driven. This on and off action of the compressor prevents evaporator core freezing. Refer to **Figure 40-25** for a system using a compressor cutout switch.

Electrical Switches

The air conditioning system may have several electrical switches. These switches control various functions in the system, or prevent damage. Some compressors are equipped with a *low pressure switch* to prevent compressor damage in the event the system charge is lost. If system pressure approaches zero, the switch contacts open, de-energizing the magnetic clutch.

 Note: Some electronic control systems on newer cars are designed to set a diagnostic trouble code that will prevent compressor clutch engagement if the low pressure switch senses a low system charge. Be sure to clear any codes from the control module before beginning any compressor or leak tests and after service work is completed.

The compressor magnetic clutch can also be de-energized by a *full throttle cut-out switch.* This switch eliminates compressor drag when the vehicle is being accelerated at full throttle. It is attached to the throttle linkage. Another throttle control device related to the air conditioner is the anti-dieseling switch, which momentarily energizes the compressor clutch when the ignition is switched off. This loads the engine and reduces the chance of dieseling. Idle speed-up solenoids are designed to improve engine operation by raising engine idle speed when the air conditioner is turned on. Other solenoids close the throttle plates when the ignition is turned off. Refer to Chapter 21.

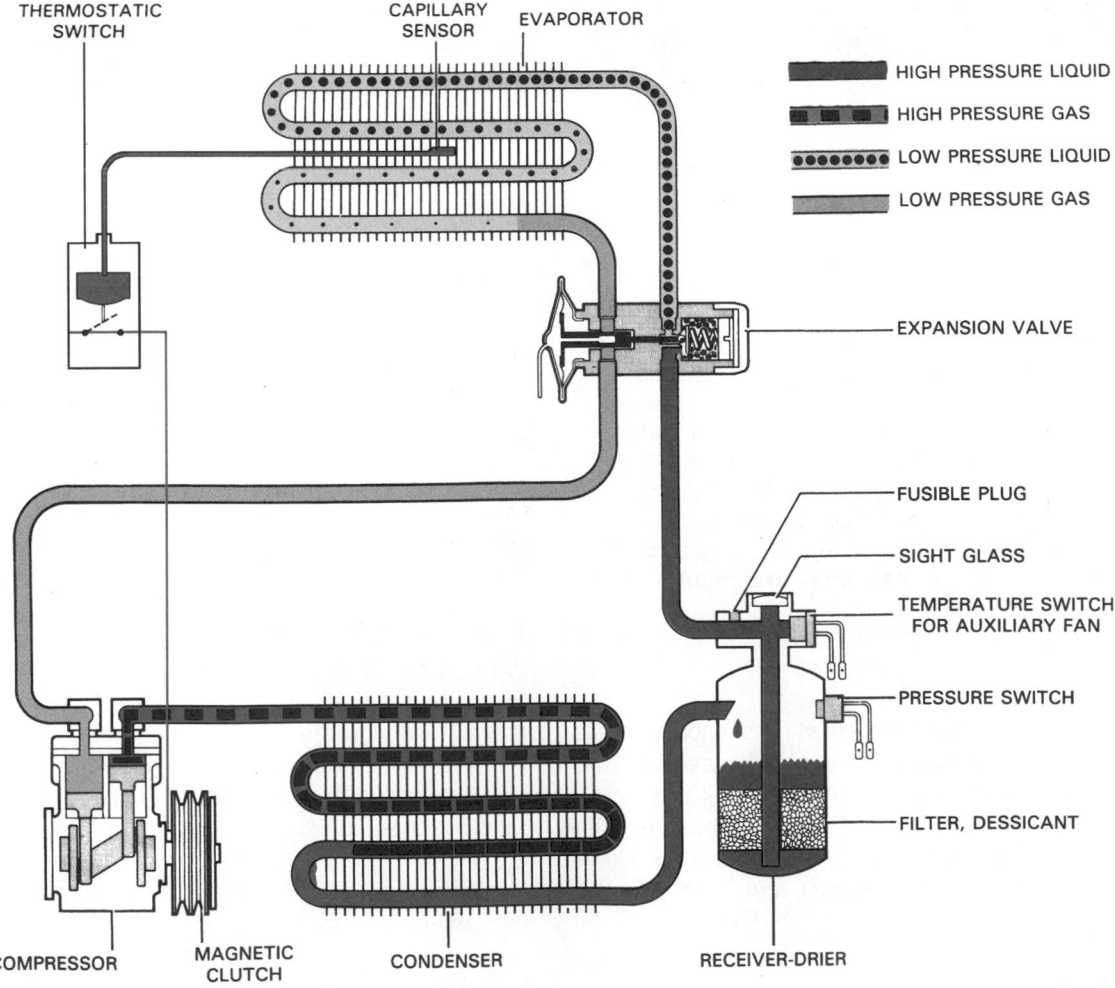

Figure 40-25.   Evaporator icing in this system is controlled by a thermostatic switch that cycles the compressor on and off. (Mercedes-Benz)

On most fuel injected cars, the idle speed and compressor operation are controlled by an electronic control unit (ECU), or powertrain control module (PCM). When the ECU determines that the engine accessory load should be reduced, it will send an electrical signal to de-energize the compressor clutch relay. This generally takes place under high power steering loads, full throttle conditions, etc.

Air Conditioning System Service

For the remainder of this chapter, we will be concerned with common air conditioning service procedures. Most of the procedures will apply to all systems, regardless of manufacturer or vehicle model. Refrigerant can be extremely dangerous. Study the following safety rules concerning the air conditioning system. Memorize and observe all of these precautions. **Figure 40-26** illustrates two safety tools that can help prevent painful and serious injury. Typical system service tools are shown in **Figure 40-27.**

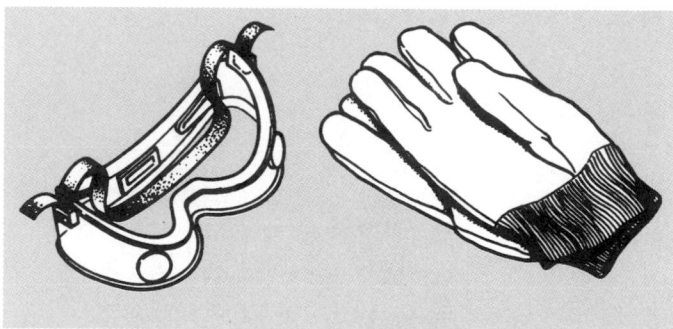

Figure 40-26.   An air conditioning technician's "best friends." Use them! (Jaguar)

🛑 **STOP**   **Warning: When working on a vehicle equipped with a supplemental restraint system (air bag), always follow the manufacturer's service, repair, and handling instructions. Failure to do so can result in personal injury and vehicle damage caused by the unintentional activation of the system. Neglecting the manufacturer's precautions can also prevent air bag deployment, which can result in occupant injury or death in an accident. See Chapter 27 for more information on air bag systems.**

Safety Rules

Always wear protective goggles when servicing the air conditioning system. When refrigerant is released into the atmosphere, it will evaporate so fast that it will freeze the surface of most objects it contacts. If it strikes the eyes, this rapid freezing action can cause serious eye injury or blindness. If refrigerant is allowed to contact your eyes, take the following steps:

1. Do not panic.
2. Splash large amounts of water (90° to 100°F or 32° to 38°C) into the eyes to raise temperature. *Do not rub.*

3. Apply several drops of sterile mineral oil to each eye.
4. Consult an eye specialist immediately—even if the pain has passed.

Keep refrigerant away from the skin. If refrigerant contacts your skin, treat it in the same manner recommended for the eyes. When opening fittings or connections, wear a pair of protective gloves and cover the fitting with a loose cloth.

Never discharge refrigerant directly into the atmosphere. Not only is this illegal, it can be deadly. Keep the service area well ventilated. Refrigerant gas is heavier than air and if discharged into a small area without proper ventilation, it can displace the air and cause suffocation. There is also the possibility it may contact an open flame and produce poisonous *phosgene gas*. Never breathe the smoke produced when refrigerant contacts a flame. Never subject the air conditioning system to high temperatures by steam cleaning, welding, or baking body finishes on or near the system. To do so can cause a dangerous rise in system refrigerant pressure.

Do not subject refrigerant cylinders or small cans to excessive heat. Dangerous internal pressures can be reached quickly if they are subjected to excessive heat, causing the can or cylinder to burst. If it is necessary to heat a cylinder or can during system charging, never heat with anything but warm water or warm wet rags (not over 125°F or 52°C). Never use a torch or stove. Never leave refrigerant cylinders uncapped. The refrigerant cylinder valve and safety plug is protected with a screw cap. This cap should be replaced on the cylinder immediately after use. Keep the cap in place when the cylinder is in storage or is being moved.

When filling a small cylinder from a larger one, do not completely fill the cylinder. Allow ample space for refrigerant expansion due to heating. A full cylinder is extremely dangerous. Never connect a refrigerant container to the system high pressure side. Refrigerant can flow back from the system into the container, causing it to explode violently. When transporting refrigerant containers, place them in the car's trunk or pickup bed. Never place refrigerant containers in a vehicle's passenger compartment. If the container is in a open truck bed, protect the container from the sun to prevent overheating.

Preventing Air Conditioning System Contamination

The air conditioning system will not tolerate dirt, air, or moisture. The system must be chemically stable (contains only pure refrigerant and a small quantity of pure refrigerant oil) to function as designed. The presence of air, dirt, or moisture can cause sludging, corrosion, freezing of the expansion valve, and other problems. In order to ensure the chemical stability of the system, always observe the following general service precautions:

• Plan the work and lay out parts so the system will be open for as short a period of time as possible to prevent the entry of moisture.

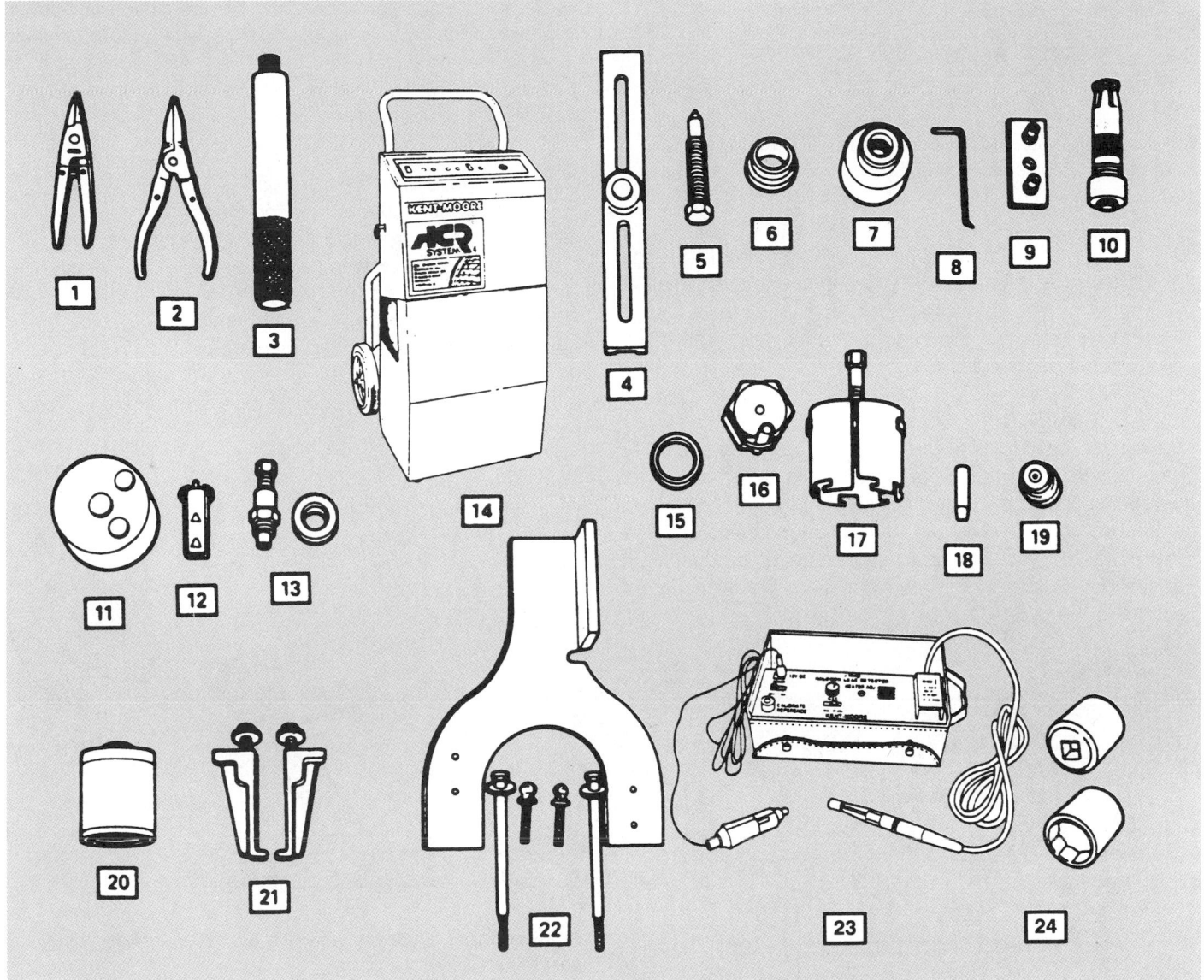

Figure 40-27. A small selection of many specialty tools which are necessary for air conditioning system service and repair. 1—Snap ring pliers. 2—Snap ring pliers. 3—Driver handle. 4—Puller bar. 5—Forcing screw. 6—Bearing remover. 7—Bearing installer. 8—O-ring remover. 9—Pressure testing connector. 10—Seat seal remover and installer. 11—Support block. 12—O-ring installer. 13—Hub and drive plate remover and installer. 14—Refrigerant recovery and recycling machine. 15—Pulley and bearing assembly installer. 16—Bearing staking tool. 17—Pulley puller. 18—Shaft seal protector. 19—Pulley pilot. 20—Clutch coil installer adapter. 21—Clutch coil puller legs. 22—Compressor holding fixture. 23—Electronic leak detector. 24—Special nut socket. (Pontiac)

- Service tools should be spotlessly clean and dry.
- Before disconnecting any fitting, clean around it thoroughly.
- Refrigerant lines should be close to room temperature before disconnecting. This will help prevent condensation from forming inside the line.
- As soon as a line or part is disconnected, cap it to prevent the entry of oil, dirt, moisture, or other foreign material. See **Figure 40-28.**
- If parts have become contaminated and flushing is indicated, flush with dry nitrogen or other approved flushing agent.

- Replacement lines and parts should be at room temperature before removing sealing caps to prevent moisture contamination.
- Do not remove sealing caps from lines or parts until ready to connect into the system.
- Avoid keeping the system open (part or line disconnected) for longer than five minutes.
- Connect the receiver-drier into the system last. This will ensure maximum moisture protection.
- Keep compressor oil free of moisture. When using a container for compressor oil, the container must be clean and dry. Compressor oil containers should be

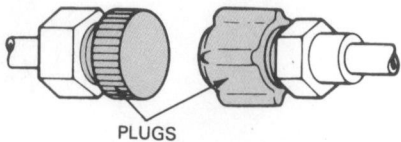

PLUGS

Figure 40-28. When lines are opened, immediately close with plugs or caps such as these. These will keep out dirt and moisture. (Nissan)

kept capped. Do not open the oil container until ready to use. Cap immediately following use to prevent entry of dirt or moisture.

- Always evacuate the system to remove air and moisture before charging the system.

Gauge Manifold

An air conditioning **gauge manifold** is needed for charging a system, checking system pressure, and other operations. It consists of two gauges set in a manifold containing two gauge valves and three outlet connections. See **Figure 40-29.** The low pressure gauge is graduated in pounds per square inch in one direction and in inches of vacuum in the other.

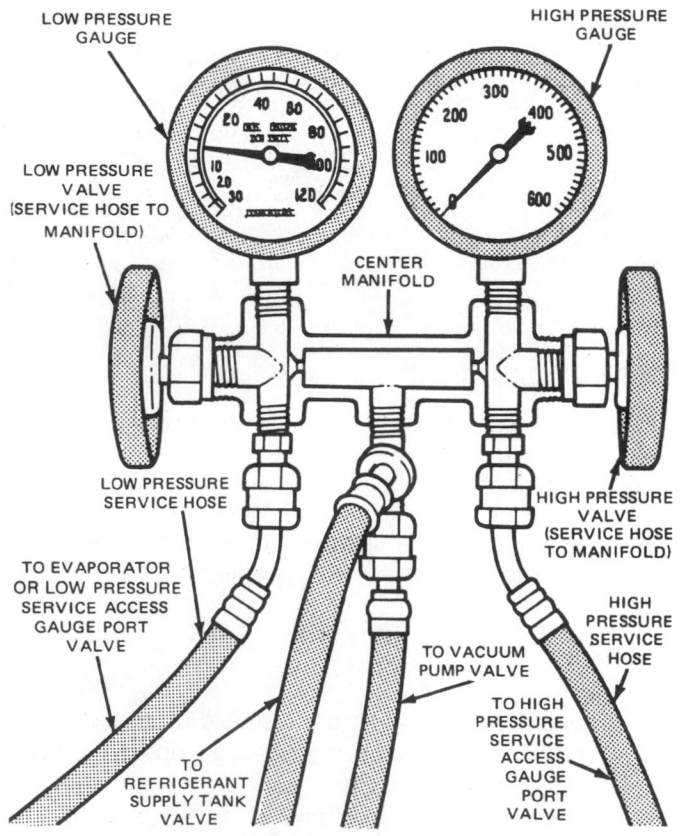

Figure 40-29. A manifold gauge set. Handle with care. (Ford)

The center manifold connection is common to both valves. It is used for attaching a hose for charging with refrigerant, attaching to a vacuum pump for system evacuation, or for injecting oil into the system. Note in **Figure**

40-29, that the center connection can be closed or opened to either of the side connections by opening (counterclockwise) or closing (clockwise) the valves. Also note that even with the valves shut, the gauges are always open to pressure from the side connections.

Schrader Valve Service Fittings

A **Schrader valve** is a spring-loaded valve that permits the connection of gauge lines into a system not using service fittings equipped with hand-operated valves. A cutaway view of a Schrader valve is shown in **Figure 40-30.** Schrader valve locations vary by vehicle. They may be on the compressor, condenser, evaporator, accumulator, or in the connecting lines. However, there will almost always be only one fitting on the suction side and one on the discharge side.

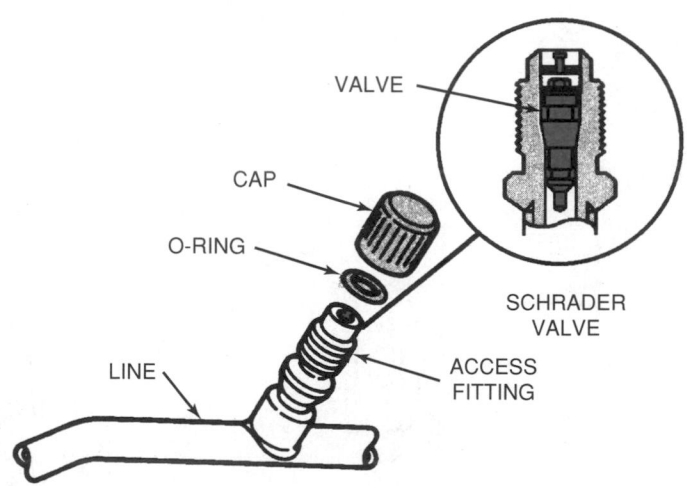

Figure 40-30. Cutaway view of a Schrader service valve assembly. (General Motors)

Special adapters are required to connect the gauge manifold hose ends to the Schrader valves. Some adapters are threaded onto the fitting, while others are quick-disconnect push-on types. When connecting gauge lines to Schrader valves, use a piece of heavy cloth to divert any refrigerant that may escape. Wear gloves and goggles.

 Note: On most late-model vehicles, the high side Schrader valve fitting has a different thread pattern which requires a special adapter.

Connect the low pressure compound gauge to the valve in the low pressure side of the system. Connect the high pressure valve line to the discharge or high pressure side Schrader valve. Manifold valves must be off (turned fully clockwise) before connecting gauge lines to Schrader valves. When finished, replace Schrader valve protective caps. Tighten the caps finger tight only to prevent damage to the sealing surface of the valve.

Caution: When disconnecting gauge lines from Schrader valves, disconnect any adapters from the vehicle's Schrader valve fitting first, then remove the adapter from the gauge line. Do not remove the charging hose from the gauge set or refrigerant source until the gauge set is completely disconnected from the vehicle's service fittings.

R-134a Service Fittings

Systems using R-134a refrigerant have a special SAE (Society of Automotive Engineers) connection fitting. This fitting is a different shape from the Schrader valve fitting. This helps to prevent cross-contamination as R-12 service fittings cannot be easily connected.

 Caution: Never attempt to adapt R-12 fittings to an R-134a system. Cross-contamination with severe system damage will result.

Hand Shutoff Valves

Service fittings equipped with a *hand shutoff valve* permits the gauge lines to be attached to the service fittings without using a Schrader valve. These hand valves are found on R-12 systems only. A typical shutoff valve service fitting is shown in **Figure 40-31**. Note that the valve has three positions.

In **Figure 40-31A,** the valve is shown in the fully closed, clockwise position, also referred to as front-seated. This closes the system line to the compressor port. In **Figure 40-31B,** the valve is shown in the fully opened (back-seated) position. This fully counterclockwise position is used for normal operation. Note that the gauge line service port is closed. When the valve is half open (mid-positioned), this leaves both ports open so that a gauge may be used to read system pressure. This is also the position for discharging, evacuating, and charging the system, **Figure 40-31C.**

To attach the gauge lines to the service fitting gauge connections, the valves should be in the full-opened position, **Figure 40-31B.** Remove the gauge line connection cap slowly. When any pressure is exhausted, remove the cap. Attach gauge line. Wear goggles and gloves.

 Note: Manifold gauge valves should be in the off position before connecting gauge lines to service fittings.

Connect the low pressure gauge line to the compressor low (suction) side. Connect the high pressure gauge line to the compressor high (discharge) side. Open both service valves halfway, **Figure 40-31C.** Instructions for attaching the manifold center connection to the refrigerant container or vacuum pump will be found in the sections dealing with discharging, evacuation, and charging.

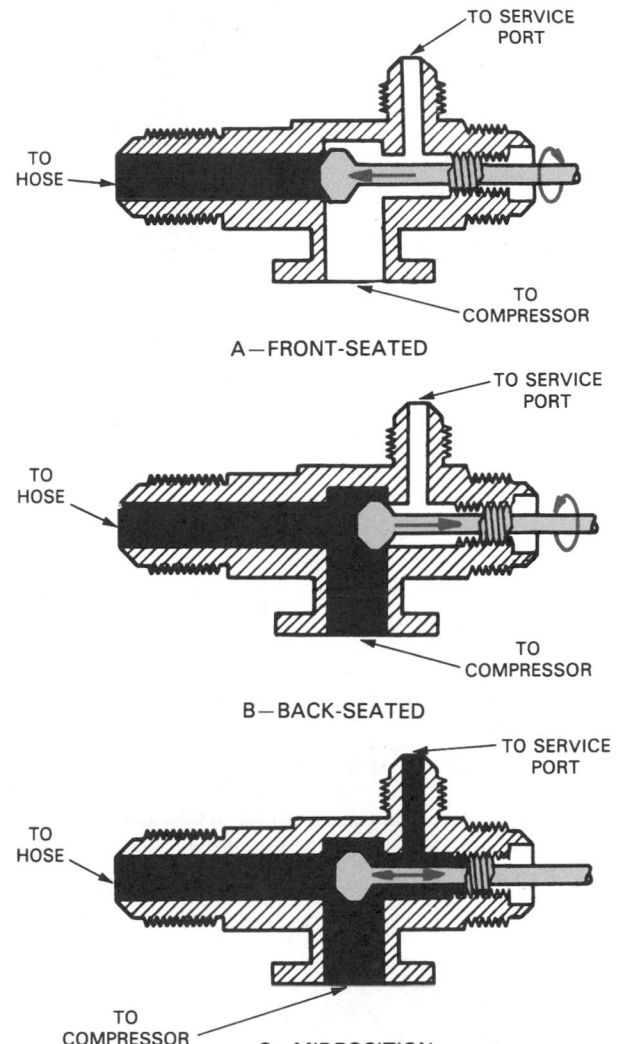

Figure 40-31.   Service fitting hand valve operating positions.

Leak Detectors

There are several types of leak detectors used in air conditioning service work. A *liquid leak detector* may be used to detect large leaks. The liquid is placed in contact with the joints being checked. Using a strong light, carefully inspect for signs of bubbles or foam which indicate a leak. A leak detection method that was commonly used for many years employed a tool called a *halide torch*, **Figure 40-32**. It is strongly recommended that halide torches no longer be used. The halide torch flame, whenever it contacts escaping refrigerant, produces dangerous phosgene gas. The efficient and safe *electronic leak detector* should be used instead, **Figure 40-33**.

Red and fluorescent dyes were used for leak detection in the past, but are no longer recommended. Some dyes are not chemically stable with the refrigerants and can clog the expansion valve and/or compressor. The dye can also stain hands, paint, and clothing, as well as contaminating the refrigerant.

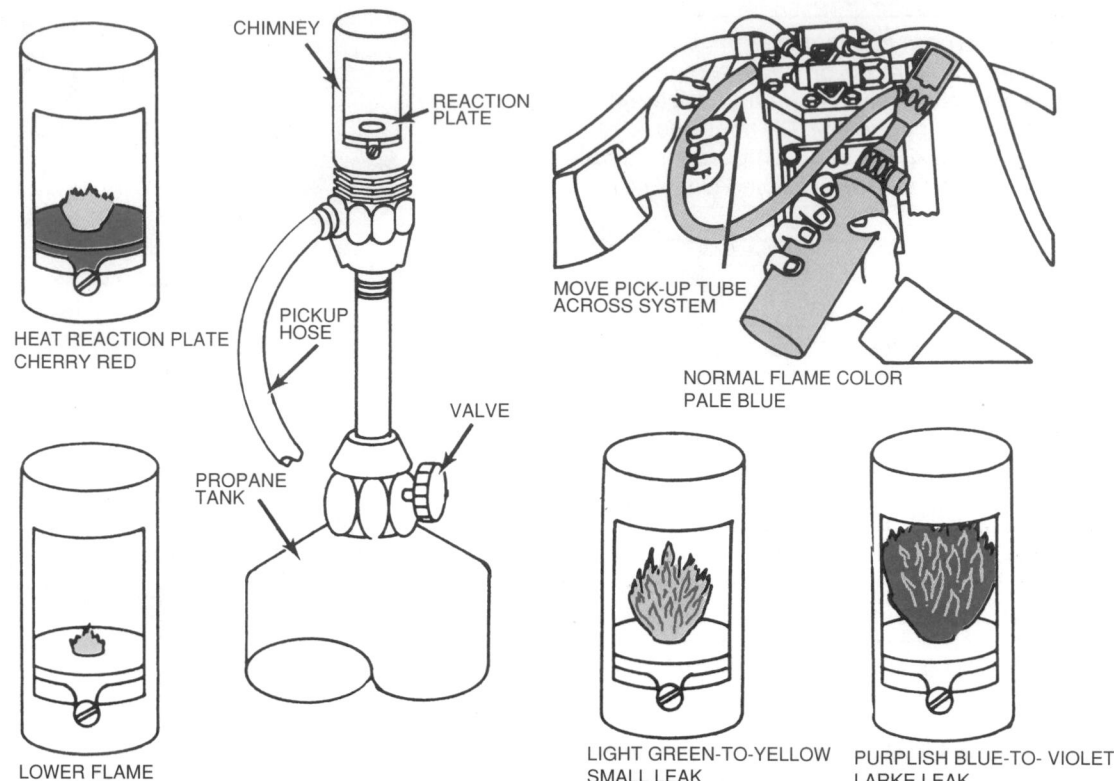

CHIMNEY

REACTION PLATE

HEAT REACTION PLATE CHERRY RED

PICKUP HOSE

VALVE

PROPANE TANK

LOWER FLAME

MOVE PICK-UP TUBE ACROSS SYSTEM

NORMAL FLAME COLOR PALE BLUE

LIGHT GREEN-TO-YELLOW SMALL LEAK

PURPLISH BLUE-TO- VIOLET LARKE LEAK

Figure 40-32. A Halide (propane) torch leak detector tool. This torch should not be used unless no other type of leak detector is available. Use an electronic leak detector whenever possible! (Sun Electronics)

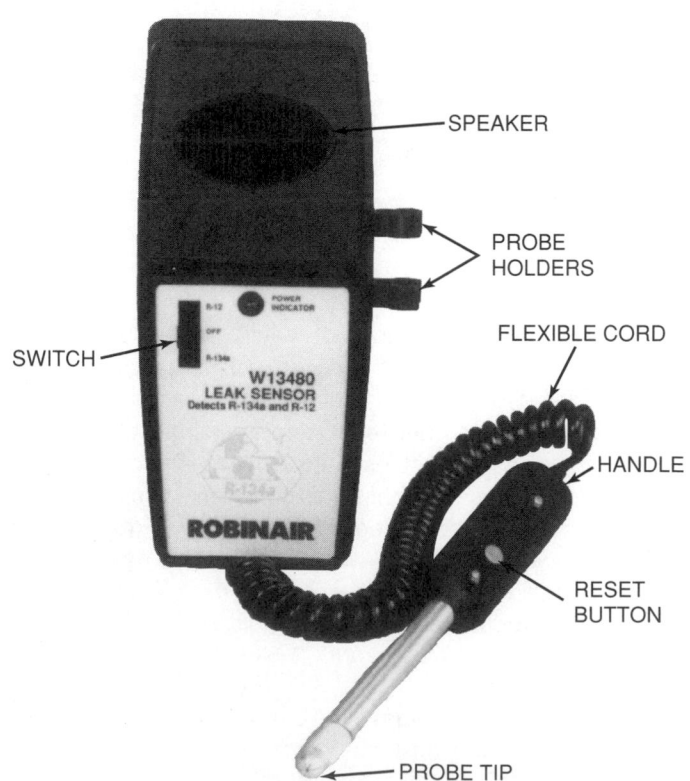

SPEAKER

PROBE HOLDERS

SWITCH

FLEXIBLE CORD

HANDLE

RESET BUTTON

PROBE TIP

Figure 40-33. One type of electronic leak detector tool. The tool indicates a refrigerant leak with indicator lights and an audible beeper. This tool may be used with both R-12 and R-134a refrigerants. (Robinair Div., SPX Corp.)

Preparing the System for Leak Detection

It is good practice to leak test the entire system, even if a obvious leak is detected, before any repairs are performed. By leak testing the entire system, if more than one leak is found, they may be repaired at the time the system is open. If the entire system is not leak tested prior to making initial repairs, a subsequent leak test may disclose additional leaks that will require reopening the system to correct. Also, leak testing the entire system will prevent harmful air and moisture from being drawn in when evacuating the system prior to charging. If the system has become discharged, it must be partially charged (see charging the system) before testing for leaks.

When a leak is suspected, torque all connections. Never overtighten to try to stop a leak. If a connection leaks after it has been torqued to specifications, disassemble the joint to determine the cause. Wipe off joints to remove any excess oil that may have absorbed refrigerant to prevent false readings. Use a stream of compressed air to clear away any refrigerant vapors. Make certain that the area has sufficient ventilation to keep the air clean. Operate the air conditioning system for a few minutes to build up pressure in the high side. Do not operate the engine while leak testing.

 Note: Never operate a discharged air conditioning system.

Shut off the engine and test the high pressure side for leaks. Wait a few minutes for the pressure to equalize between the high and low pressure sides and then test the low side for leaks. A gauge manifold may be connected into the system and the low pressure side tested under refrigerant cylinder pressure. This is higher than the normal low side pressure and will disclose leaks more readily.

Using Halide Torch Leak Detector

 Warning: As mentioned earlier, refrigerant forms phosgene gas when burned by a flame. It is strongly recommended that an electronic leak detector be used. In the event that a halide torch tool must be used, observe the following instructions carefully. Never breathe fumes or black smoke produced by the torch flame when the search hose is placed near a leaking joint. Keep a fire extinguisher at hand in the event the torch flame should start a fire.

Check all connections, joints, and parts. Make sure the surrounding air is not contaminated with refrigerant vapor. Before testing, blow away any vapors with compressed air or a large fan. While testing, the surrounding air should be relatively still. Open the torch valve until a slight hiss of gas is heard, then light the torch. The flame should be small, which makes the tool more sensitive to leaks, and an almost colorless, pale blue.

When the torch flame is adjusted, place the end of the search hose near the various joints. Hold the hose near the bottom of each joint for several seconds. While the search hose is in position, watch the flame carefully. If a small leak exists, the flame will turn yellow-green. A medium size leak will turn the flame blue, while a large leak will cause it to turn purple.

Electronic Leak Detector

When using an electronic leak detector, it is very important to follow the tool manufacturer's instructions exactly. When this is done, the electronic detector is a very sensitive and reliable tool. Many models emit both visual and audible signals to alert the operator to the presence of refrigerant.

 Note: Some electronic leak detectors can sense the presence of only one type of refrigerant. Make sure the leak detector can be used to detect refrigerant leaks from the system at hand and is set up properly. Read the manufacturer's operation manual before using the leak detector.

After setting up the detector as recommended by the manufacturer, pass the probe tip over the system components. In **Figure 40-34,** a technician is checking the compressor. Keep the probe close to the suspected leak. Move the probe slowly, around 1″ (25.4 mm) per second. Circle the probe completely around the fittings, paying particular attention to the bottom areas. Refrigerant is heavier than air and tends to settle downward. Study the probe movement recommendations of one manufacturer in **Figure 40-35.** Common leak check points for one system are illustrated in **Figure 40-36.**

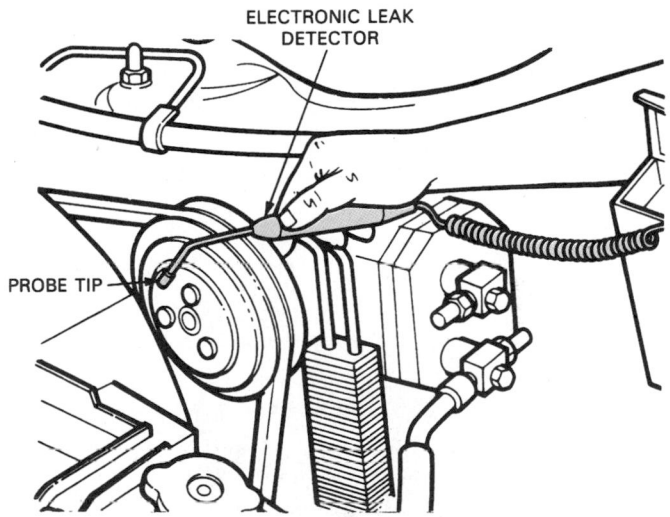

Figure 40-34. Using an electronic leak detector. When the probe tip nears an area with a refrigerant leak, the tool will emit a load signal. (Ford)

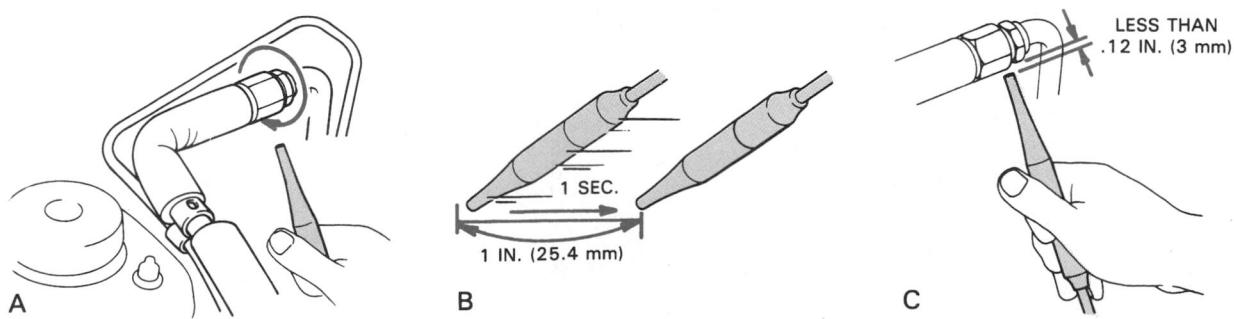

Figure 40-35. Electronic leak detector probe tip being used as recommended by one manufacturer. A—Move the probe completely around the suspected leak area. B—Move the probe tip slowly, about 1″ (25.4 mm) per second. C—Keep the probe tip close to the leak area. (Toyota)

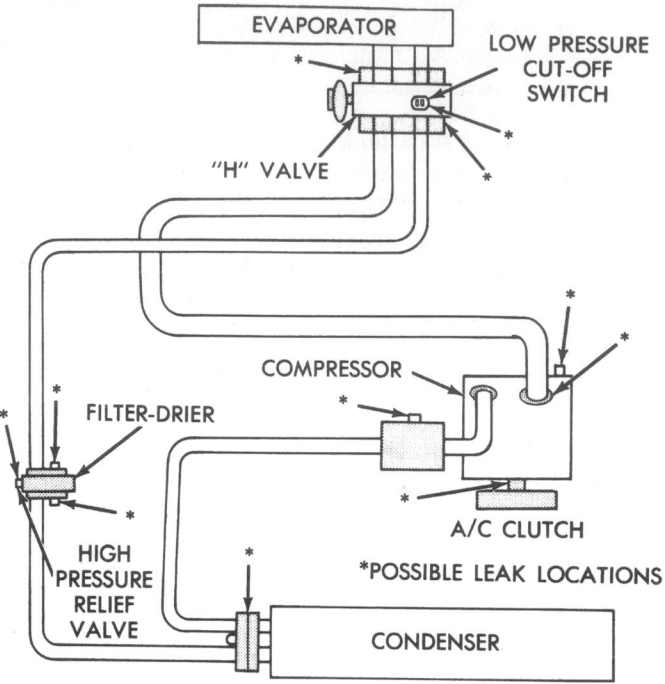

Figure 40-36. Some common refrigerant leak check points on one system. (Dodge)

Discharging the System

The only recommended procedure for *discharging* (removing the refrigerant from) the air conditioning system is to recover all of the refrigerant using a *refrigerant recovery unit*, **Figure 40-37.** Follow manufacturers directions when recovering the refrigerant. Do not mix different types of refrigerant in the recovery equipment. Remember that the refrigerant will be reused when the system is recharged.

Always check the system for leaks before recovering the refrigerant. The system charge must be recovered prior to the replacement of any part containing refrigerant. The only exception to this would be the compressor when it is equipped with hand-operated service valves. When the service valves on the compressor are fully closed, the compressor will be isolated from the rest of the system. Once the compressor is isolated, open the gauge fitting cap a very small amount to relieve the pressure in the compressor. The compressor may then be removed.

The recovery unit will filter the refrigerant and remove any sludge or acids before returning it to the system. Also, a considerable amount of oil will be drawn out, especially during a fast refrigerant recovery. It is very important that the amount of oil removed be measured so that the same amount of fresh oil can be returned to the system. Many

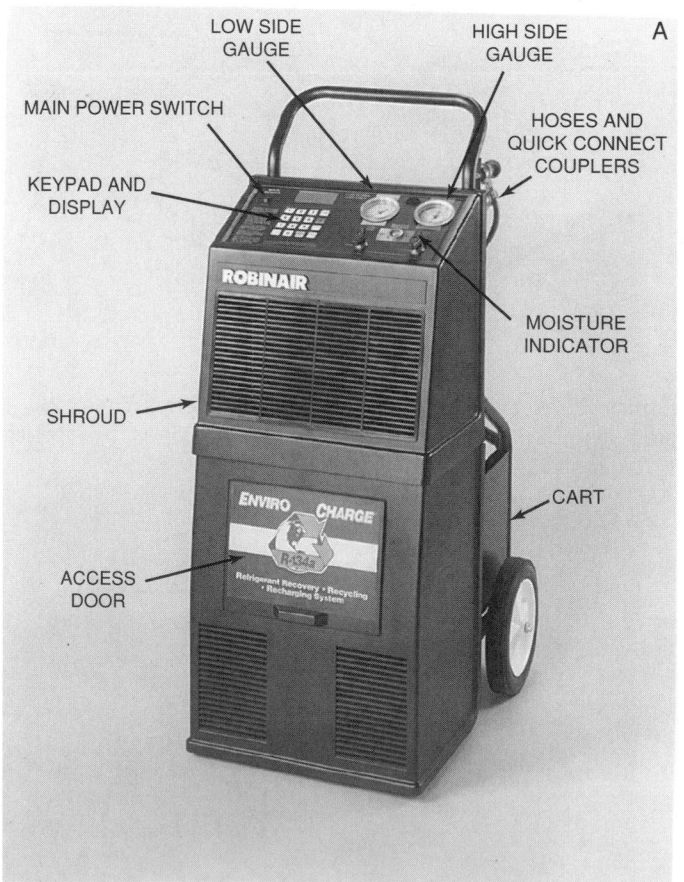

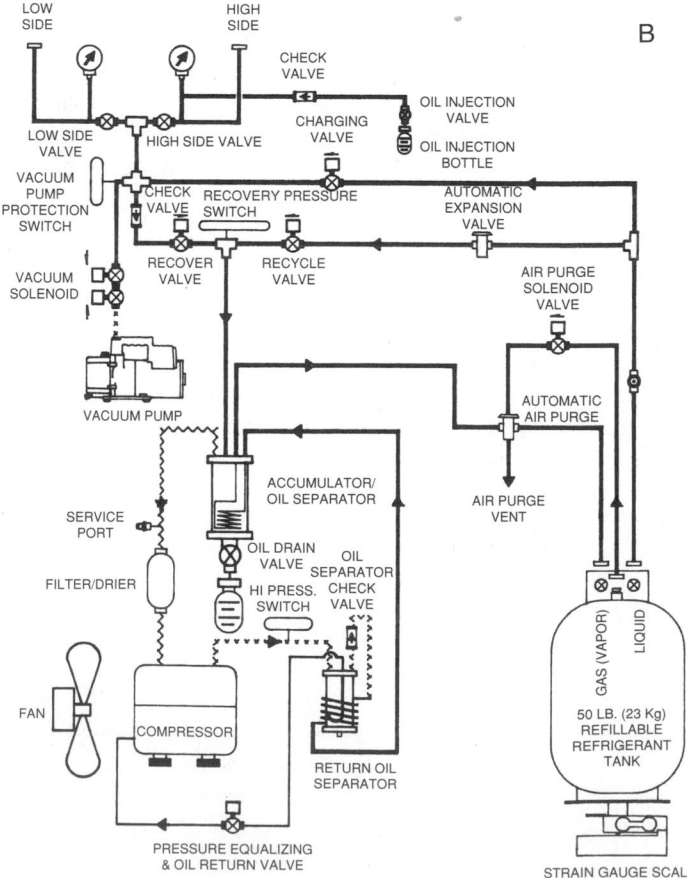

Figure 40-37. A—One type of refrigerant recovery unit. Always follow the tool manufacturer's operating procedures. B—The recovery unit's system schematic. (Robinair Div., SPX Corp.)

recovery units will automatically remove and reinstall any oil which leaves with the refrigerant. When connecting the recovery unit to the vehicle, always wear goggles and gloves.

Evacuating the System

Evacuating the system means attaching a **vacuum pump** to remove air and moisture. This is absolutely vital before recharging. Any air in the system will cause reduced operating efficiency. Water vapor carried in with the air will cause severe corrosion of internal parts as well as oil sludging.

Begin by attaching the manifold gauge set. Both gauge valves must be off. Attach a vacuum pump to the manifold gauge set center connection. The refrigerant cylinder valve must be closed. **Figure 40-38** illustrates one type or setup for evacuating a system. The same setup will be used for charging. Where hand-operated service valves are used instead of Schrader valves, they must be in mid-position.

Many refrigerant recovery units have provisions for evacuating the system before the refrigerant is reinstalled. This eliminates the separate gauge manifold, vacuum pump, refrigerant cylinder, and lines which must be hooked up each time.

Open the high pressure manifold gauge valve slowly to relieve any pressure buildup. Close the high pressure valve and start the vacuum pump. Slowly open both the high and low pressure manifold gauge valves. If there is a manual valve in the vacuum line, open it. Open vacuum pump shut-off valve slowly to prevent oil from being drawn out of the pump.

Run the vacuum pump until the low pressure gauge (vacuum portion) indicates 29″ (711 mm) of vacuum at sea level. The vacuum pump, in proper condition, should draw a vacuum of 29″ (711 mm) at sea level. Subtract 1″ (25.4 mm) for every thousand feet (304 M) of elevation. For example: At 5,000 feet (1 520 M), the pump should draw 24″ (29″ minus 5″) or 584 mm (711 mm minus 127 mm) of vacuum.

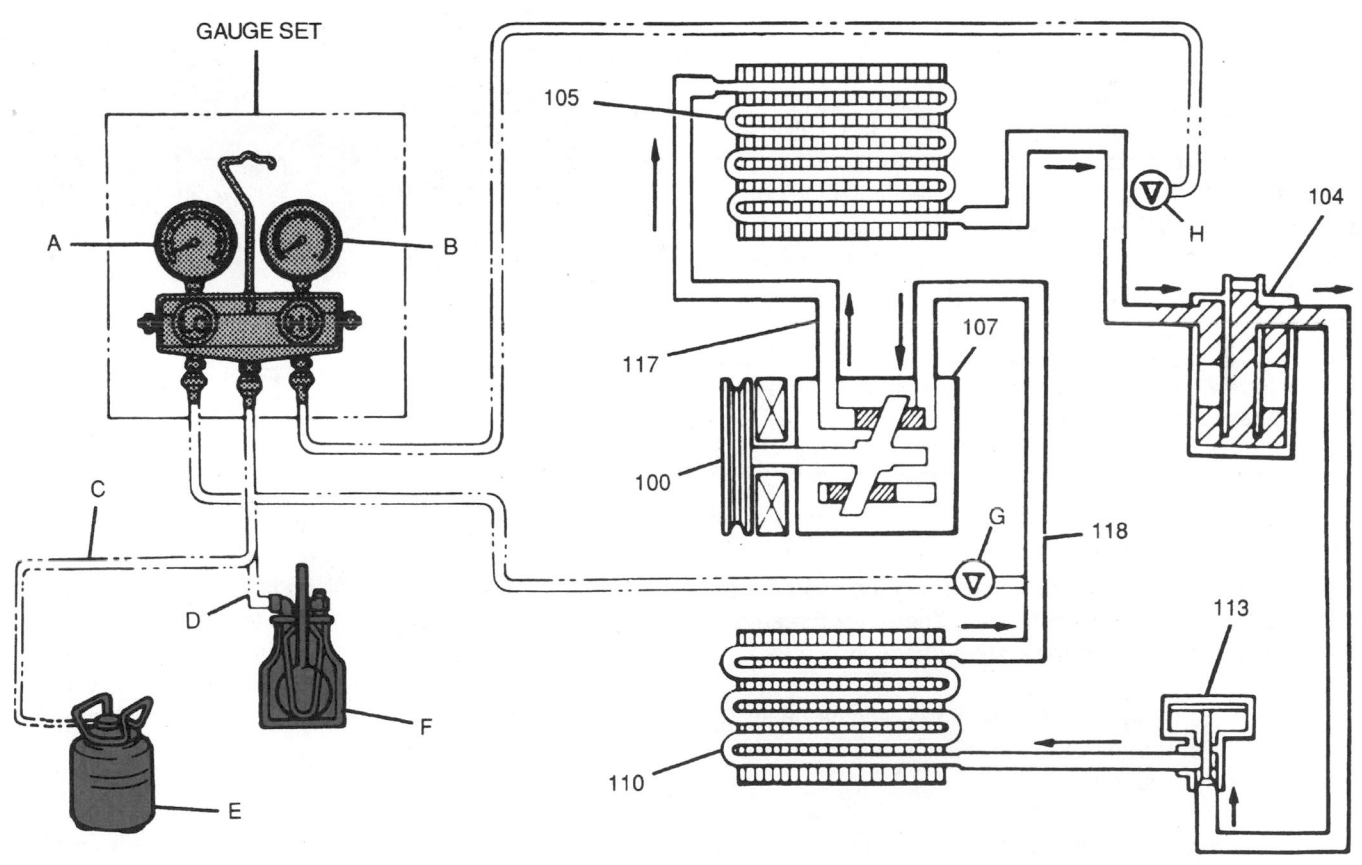

A	LOW-SIDE GAUGE	G	LOW-SIDE SERVICE VALVE
B	HIGH-SIDE GAUGE	H	HIGH-SIDE SERVICE VALVE
C	USED WHEN CHARGING	100	A/C COMPRESSOR CLUTCH
D	USED WHEN EVACUATING	104	RECEIVER/DRYER
E	REFRIGERANT DRUM	105	CONDENSER
F	VACUUM PUMP	107	COMPRESSOR

110	EVAPORATOR
113	EXPANSION VALVE
117	COMPRESSOR DISCHARGE PIPE
118	COMPRESSOR SUCTION PIPE

Figure 40-38. Study this setup for system evacuating. Always follow the procedure recommended by the manufacturer. (Geo)

Note: Some of the latest air conditioning systems and service equipment may call for measuring vacuum in microns. If a conversion chart is not provided, the system should be evacuated until a reading of 300 microns is reached.

If the vacuum cannot be drawn to 29″ (711 mm) at sea level, either the pump is defective, the desiccant contains excessive moisture, or there is a leak in the system or hookup lines. When the gauge reads 29″ (711 mm) of vacuum, run the pump for an additional 15 minutes. Then shut off both the high and low pressure gauges. Shut off the valve in the vacuum line (if equipped) and stop vacuum pump. System should hold vacuum with no more than a 2″ (51 mm) drop in five minutes.

Adding Refrigerant for Leak Testing

A partial charge can be added for the purpose of leak testing if the system is low or has lost its charge completely. If a charging station is being used, meter out the recommended amount of refrigerant into the charging cylinder (the amount recommended by the manufacturer for a partial charge for leak test purposes).

With the engine off, slowly open the high pressure gauge valve. Open the charging cylinder top valve and allow the specified amount of refrigerant to enter the system. Close the high pressure gauge valve. Close the charging cylinder valve. When the partial charge has entered the system, leak test as recommended earlier. If leaks are found, recover the system charge and make repairs before proceeding.

 Note: Be sure to recover the partial charge before disassembling the system.

Refrigerant Charging

Once all repairs have been made and the system has been evacuated, it can be recharged. There are three possible sources of refrigerant for system charging:

- The original refrigerant charge in the recovery unit.
- A cylinder of refrigerant.
- A 1 pound disposable can.

The refrigerant cylinder is often used with a recovery unit or a **charging station**, which meters the exact amount of refrigerant into the system, **Figure 40-39.** These cylinders are available in 15, 30, and 50 pound sizes. The 1 pound disposable can is becoming harder to find because of federal regulations concerning recycling and handling of refrigerants. All work equally well. Be certain to follow manufacturer's recommendations for system charging. Above all, wear goggles and gloves and observe all safety rules regarding storage, handling, and use of refrigerant.

Figure 40-39. A typical charging station. It may be used for refrigerant recovery, evacuation and charging. (Robinair Div., SPX Corp.)

There are several recommended charging techniques. One method charges the low side with refrigerant vapor while the engine is running. Another charges the high side with refrigerant liquid with the engine off. As with recovery, always follow the exact directions for the method employed. Remember, when charging into the low side with the engine operating, refrigerant vapor must be used as liquid refrigerant may damage the compressor. Before charging, the system should be evacuated, filled with a partial charge, and leak tested.

Using Charging Station or Recovery Unit

If a charging station or recovery unit, such as shown in **Figure 40-40** is being used, fill the charging cylinder with the amount of liquid refrigerant specified for a full charge. If a recovery unit is being used, set the controls to the proper amount of charge. The amount varies according to the system but will often range from around 1.95 to 4 lb. (0.88 to 1.8 kg).

With the charging station or recovery unit ready, engine off, open the high pressure gauge fully. The low pressure gauge valve must be closed. Open valve at top of

Figure 40-40. A refrigerant recovery, recycling, recharging station. Follow the tool manufacturer's operating instructions. (Robinair Div., SPX Corp.)

the charging cylinder and allow refrigerant to flow into the high pressure side of the system. When refrigerant stops flowing into the recovery system, shut off the high pressure gauge valve. Start the engine and operate at 1500 RPM. Set the air conditioner controls for maximum cold. Open the low pressure gauge valve so the suction side of the system will draw in the remaining refrigerant.

When all of the refrigerant has entered the system, close all valves, shut off the engine, and disconnect the charging station from the system. If the charging station lines are attached to service fittings with hand valves, open them fully to seal off the gauge line connection. Replace all service valve caps. Turn on the air conditioning system to maximum cooling and check for proper operation.

Weighing Method

With the engine off, connect the manifold gauge set to the system. Evacuate, partial charge, leak test, and evacuate the system. Gauge valves should both be closed. Connect the refrigerant cylinder to the manifold gauge center connection. With both valves off, open the refrigerant cylinder valve. Open the cylinder hose connection at the manifold for a few seconds to allow the refrigerant to purge air from the hose. Tighten hose connection. Place the cylinder on an accurate scale. Note the exact weight of the cylinder. See **Figure 40-41.**

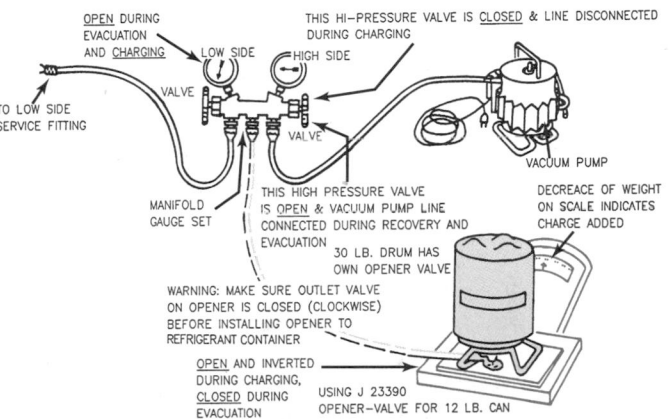

Figure 40-41. A setup used for charging a system with refrigerant using a tank and scale method. (General Motors)

Open the high pressure gauge valve so a charge of liquid refrigerant will enter the high pressure side of the system. The low pressure valve must be closed. Liquid refrigerant may be obtained by drawing from the bottom of the cylinder or by turning the cylinder upside-down. Allow the liquid refrigerant to flow into the system until the desired amount has entered. Check the scale frequently during the operation. If sufficient liquid refrigerant will not enter the system, close the high pressure gauge valve.

Turn the cylinder right side up or draw from the top of the cylinder so that refrigerant vapor will be available. Start the engine and operate at 1500 RPM. Turn air conditioner on and set to maximum cold. Open the low pressure gauge valve and allow refrigerant vapor to flow into the low side of the system until the required charge has entered. Shut off low pressure gauge valve. Stop the engine and close the refrigerant cylinder valve. Disconnect the charge setup from system. Restart the engine and air conditioning system and check for proper operation.

 Caution: Unless specifically recommended, never allow liquid refrigerant to enter the low pressure side of the system. Charge the high pressure side with liquid. Charge the low pressure side with vapor. Remember that when the refrigerant container is upright, it will discharge vapor. When container is upside down or on its side, it will discharge liquid refrigerant.

Low Pressure Side Charging

For the low pressure charging method to work, the engine and air conditioner must be operating. Before charging, the system must be evacuated, filled with a partial charge, and leak tested. Then proceed with the low pressure side charging.

If a charging station is being used, fill the charging cylinder with the amount of liquid refrigerant needed for a full charge. If a recovery unit is being used, set the controls to the proper amount of charge. Attach the hoses and open the low side valve. Ensure that the high side valve is closed. Turn on the charging station or recovery unit, and allow refrigerant to flow into the low side for about one minute.

Close the low side valve, start the engine and operate at 1500 RPM. Turn the compressor on and set to maximum cold and high blower speed. Open the low pressure gauge valve and allow refrigerant vapor to flow into the low side of the system until the required charge has entered. Close the low pressure valve and shut off the engine. Shut off the charging station or recovery unit. Disconnect the charge setup from the vehicle. Restart the engine and air conditioner and check for proper operation.

Using One Pound Cans

Attach the low pressure gauge to the accumulator (low pressure side of system). The high pressure gauge should be connected to the vacuum pump. Attach gauge set center hose to the one pound can dispenser fitting. Following proper system evacuation, close high side gauge valve and leave closed. With the air conditioning controls off, start the engine and operate at normal hot idle speed.

Invert cans to allow liquid to flow. Open one can and allow it to flow into the system via the low pressure fitting. When one pound has entered the system, shut off the valve for that can and turn the compressor on. Repeat the charging procedure using a second can. Continue idling engine until the recommended charge has entered the system. Shut off the manifold valve and continue engine operation for around 30 seconds. This will clear the lines and gauge manifold.

> **STOP** **Warning: When using one pound cans, do not open the high side service valve as the can will explode from system pressure backing up into it.** Never remove the charge hose until the gauge manifold hoses are first removed completely from the vehicle's service fitting as this may result in the complete loss of the refrigerant charge.

If less than one pound is called for, open the can valve. When the frost line on the outside of the can reaches the halfway mark, shut off the valve. Before shutting off the engine, remove the low pressure hose fitting from the accumulator service fitting. When removing the hose fitting, unscrew quickly to prevent excessive loss of refrigerant. Cap service fittings and shut engine off. Remember to check the system for leaks and for proper operation. The

cans are used just as if they were regular refrigerant tanks. Cautions pertaining to tanks also apply to cans.

Air Conditioning Component Service

Most service of air conditioning system components involves the replacement of parts. When the air conditioning system must be opened for part removal and replacement, the following steps must be taken in the order listed:

- Check system for leaks, add partial charge if necessary.
- Recover system charge.
- Remove and replace part.
- Evacuate system.
- Charge system.
- Recheck system for leaks.

Service Precautions

The following are general rules for removing and replacing air conditioning system components. Always recover the system's refrigerant charge before opening a connection. Clean connections before opening them. If any pressure is evident, allow it to seep out slowly before completely separating the connection. Cap or plug lines and parts as soon as they are disconnected. Remove caps from either new or used components just before installation.

Use new O-rings when replacing parts. Make certain the new O-rings are of the correct size and properly positioned. Coat both the fittings and O-rings with refrigerant oil before assembly. If a connection is made without applying refrigerant oil, it will probably leak. The connection must be properly aligned, clean, and free of nicks or burrs. See **Figures 40-42** through **40-44.** Torque all connections to specifications. Remember that aluminum and copper connections require less torque than steel connections. If one end of the connection is steel and the other is aluminum or copper, torque to aluminum or copper specifications only.

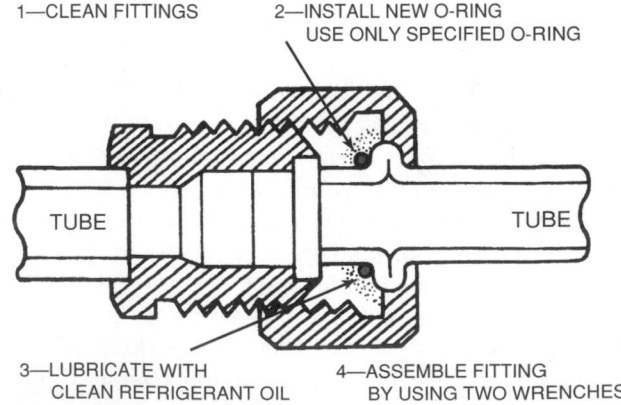

1—CLEAN FITTINGS   2—INSTALL NEW O-RING
                     USE ONLY SPECIFIED O-RING

TUBE   TUBE

3—LUBRICATE WITH   4—ASSEMBLE FITTING
   CLEAN REFRIGERANT OIL   BY USING TWO WRENCHES

Figure 40-42. A cutaway view of one particular line fitting which uses an O-ring seal. When servicing lines, fittings, etc., always use new seals. (Hyundai)

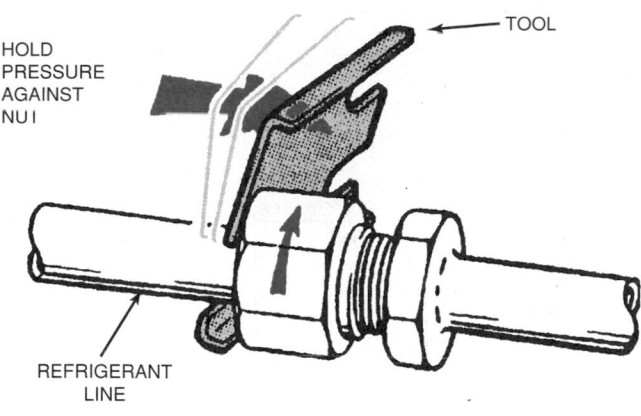

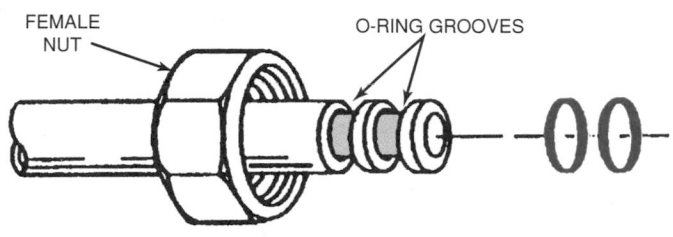

* USE NONMETALLIC TOOL TO REMOVE O-RINGS

Figure 40-43. One type of dual O-ring joint. Note the special tool required to disassemble and assemble the joint. (Pontiac)

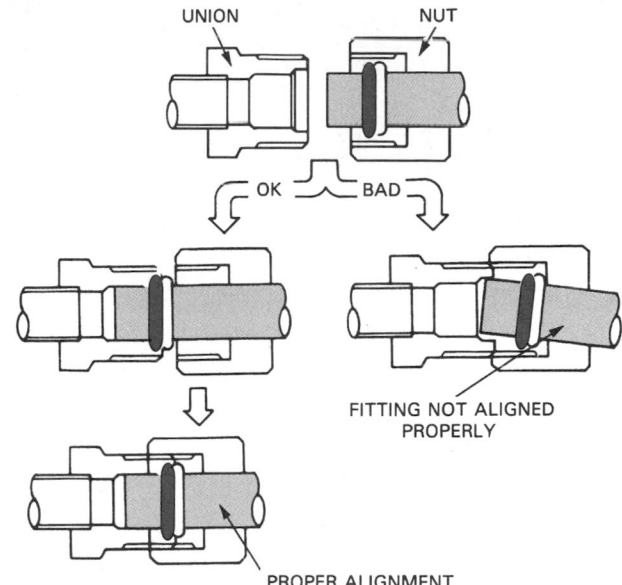

Figure 40-44. Fittings must be properly aligned or they will leak. (Nissan)

Replacing Hose and Tubing

One of the most common air conditioning service procedures is the replacement of leaking hoses. When replacing the hose, avoid sharp bends. General practice calls for hose bends with a bend radius from five to ten times the diameter of the hose, depending on hose construction.

Keep hose at least 3″ (80 mm) away from the exhaust system unless special heat shields are used. To pull a hose attached with a hose clamp, remove the clamp and make an angular cut as shown in **Figure 40-48A.** The hose may then be pulled. Do not nick the fitting with the knife.

When installing hose utilizing a clamp, coat the hose and tube with refrigerant oil. Then slide the hose over the tube sealing beads and up to the locating bead, **Figure 40-48B.** Position the clamp, **Figure 40-48B,** as shown in **Figure 40-48C.** Note how the locating bead in **Figure 40-48C** is used to position the clamp. The clamp screw is then torqued. Following the first 1000 miles (1 610 km) of operation, torque the clamp screws again.

A typical torque table used by one company is shown in **Figure 40-45.** Note that the table is based on the tube material as well as diameter. Recommended torque values in one specific system for the various connections using O-rings is shown in **Figure 40-46.** When tightening or loosening connections, always use two wrenches to avoid twisting the tubing. Note that **Figure 40-47** shows one nut being held with an open end wrench while the other nut is being tightened with a torque wrench. A flare-nut wrench will hold better than an open end and will be less likely to deform the nut.

HEX FITTING SIZE (mm)	CONNECTION	B/U HEX FITTING SIZE (mm)	TORQUE (N·m)
24	A/C Cond. Hose to Cond. Inlet		27.5 +/- 7.5
24	Evap. Tube to Cond. Outlet		27.5 +/- 7.5
22	Evap. Tube to Module	20	27.5 +/- 7.5
32	A/C Accum. to Module	27	45.0 +/- 7.0
27	A/C Comp. Hose to A/C Accum.	N/A	45.0 +/- 7.0
32	Aux. Comp. Hose (Female) to A/C Comp. Hose (Male Brazed)	27	45.0 +/- 7.0
24	Aux. Evap. Hose (Female) to Evap. Tube (Male Brazed)	20	27.5 +/- 7.5
22	Aux. Evap. to Aux. Module	16	16.5 +/- 1.5
26	Aux. Comp. to Aux. Module	22	32.0 +/- 4.0

Figure 40-45. A metric fitting torque table. (Chevrolet)

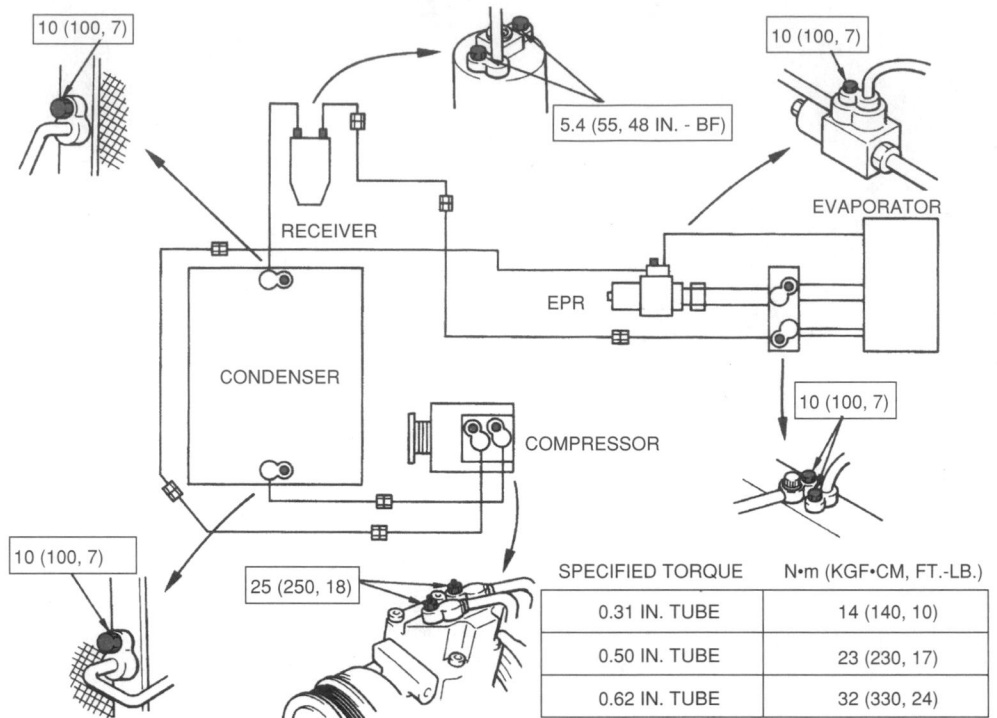

SPECIFIED TORQUE	N•m (KGF•CM, FT.-LB.)
0.31 IN. TUBE	14 (140, 10)
0.50 IN. TUBE	23 (230, 17)
0.62 IN. TUBE	32 (330, 24)

Figure 40-46. A recommended torque valve schematic for the various O-ring connectors on one vehicle. (Lexus)

Figure 40-47. Use two wrenches when loosening a connection. Use a torque wrench when tightening. (General Motors)

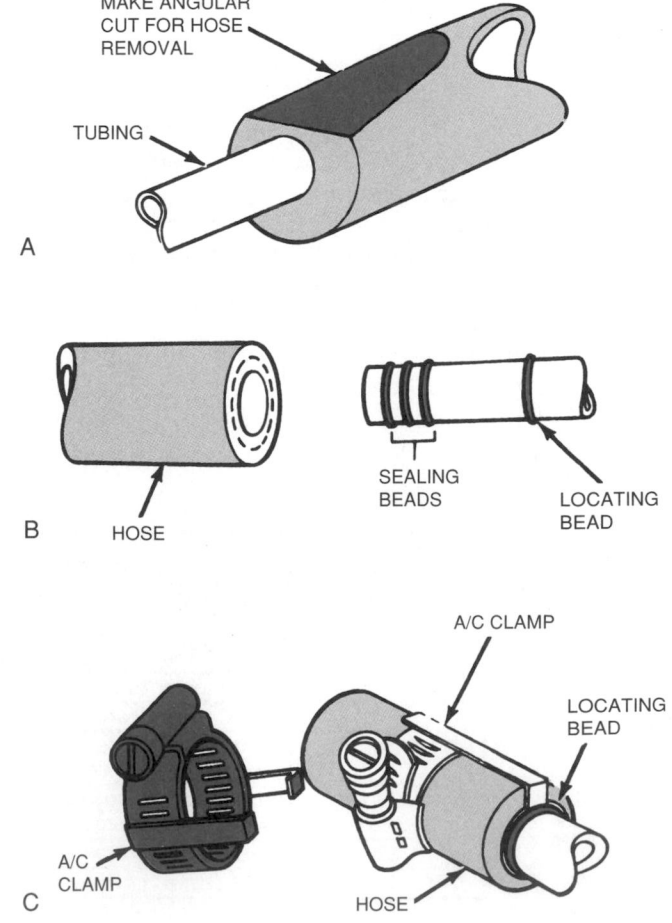

Figure 40-48. Air conditioning line clamp connections. (AC Delco)

Some hoses are assembled with sleeves. **Figure 40-49** illustrates the repair procedure involved in hose replacement on such a setup. To replace a defective fitting on a sleeve arrangement, cut off the hose directly behind the sleeve. Lubricate a new service fitting with refrigerant oil and insert into hose. Install a hose clamp, position, and tighten to specifications. Look at **Figure 40-49.**

Other setups may employ a spring lock coupling. This type holds the two parts together through the use of a garter spring that snaps over a flare on the female fitting end. O-rings seal against leakage. The separation of these spring lock couplings requires the use of a special removal tool. **Figure 40-50** illustrates the spring lock coupling and correct technique used to either connect or disconnect it. When replacing a hose, be sure to use a specified type hose for air conditioning systems. Reinstall all hose clamps, tubing clamps, and insulators to prevent vibration and other damage.

Be careful in the selection of tape when taping hoses to prevent vibration or to hold away from hot areas. Some plastic tapes are not compatible with certain hose compounds. If used, they will cause serious deterioration of the

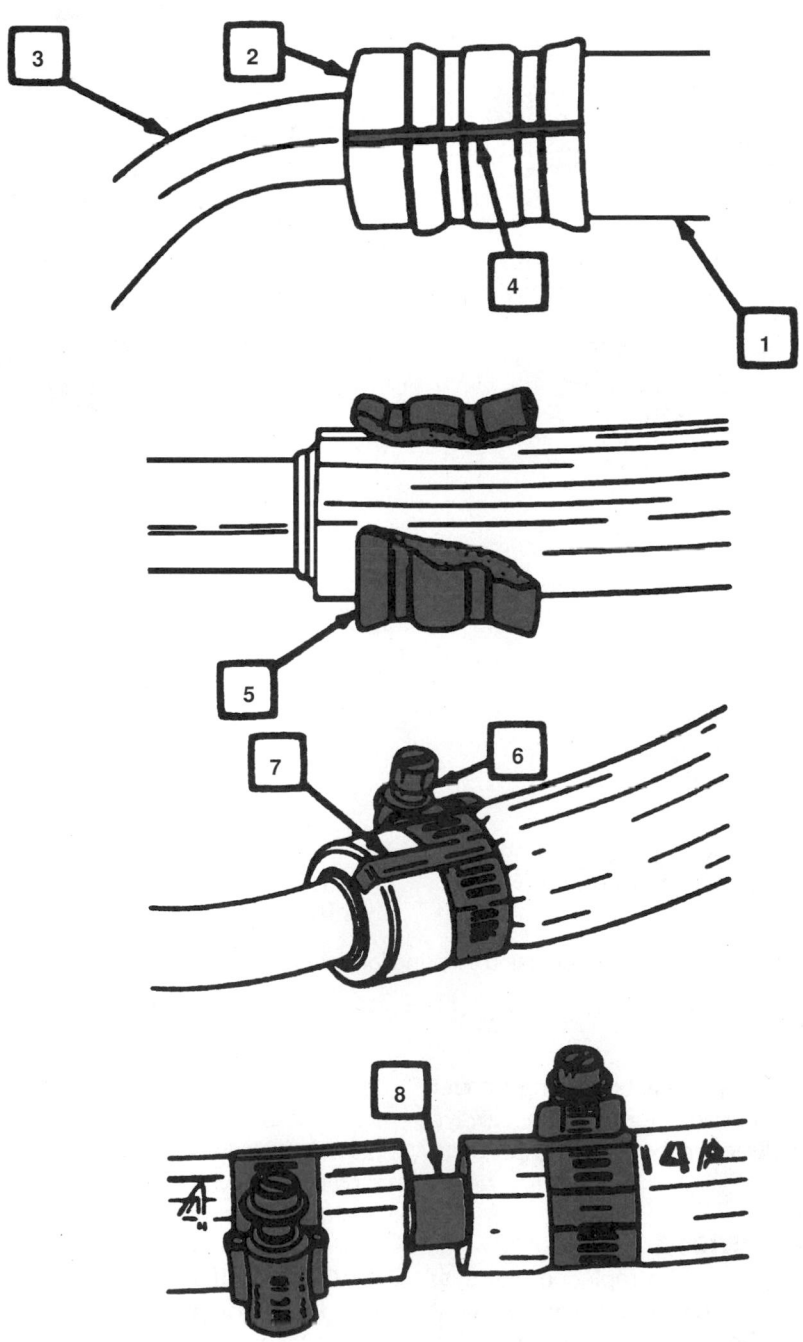

Figure 40-49.   Sleeved hose fitting repair procedures. 1—Hose. 2—Sleeve. 3—Tube. 4—Cut in sleeve made by a fine tooth hacksaw. 5—Removing the sleeve. 6—Screw clamp. 7—Screw clamp locating lug. 8—Spliced fitting. (Buick)

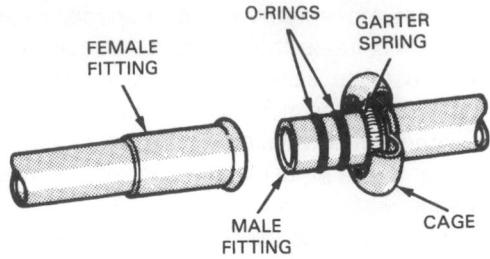

NOTE PARTS OF SPRING LOCK COUPLING.

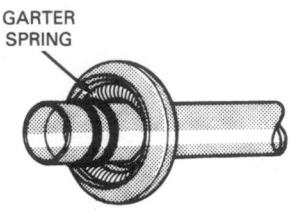

BEFORE CONNECTING, CHECK FOR MISSING OR
DAMAGED GARTER SPRING. REMOVE DAMAGED
SPRING WITH SMALL HOOKED WIRE. INSTALL NEW
SPRING IF DAMAGED OR MISSING.

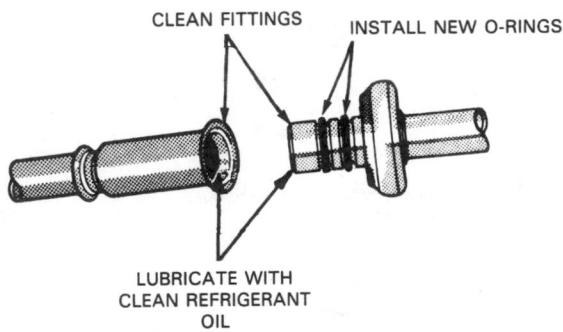

ASSEMBLE FITTING BY PUSHING WITH A SLIGHT
TWISTING MOTION.

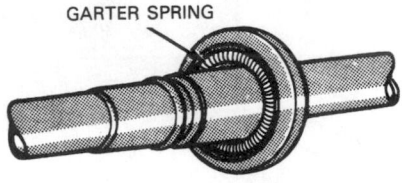

TO ENSURE COUPLING ENGAGEMENT, CHECK TO BE
SURE GARTER SPRING IS OVER FLARED END OF
FEMALE FITTING.

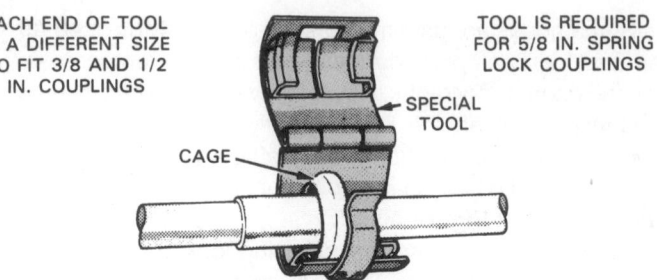

TO DISCONNECT COUPLING, FIT TOOL TO COUPLING
SO THAT TOOL CAN ENTER CAGE TO RELEASE
GARTER SPRING.

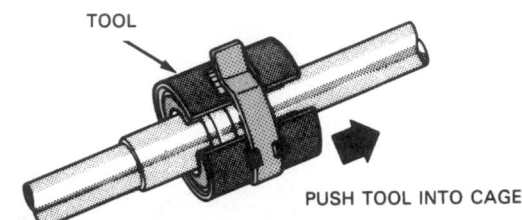

CLOSE TOOL AND PUSH THE TOOL INTO THE CAGE
OPENING TO RELEASE THE FEMALE FITTING FROM
THE GARTER SPRING.

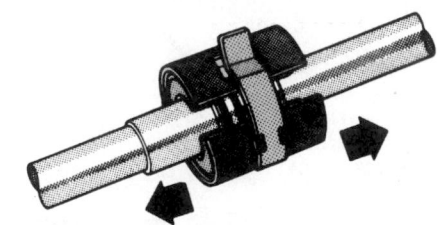

PULL COUPLING MALE AND FEMALE FITTINGS
APART.

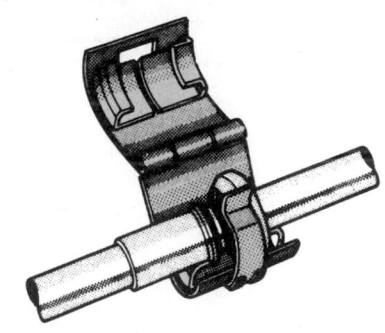

REMOVE TOOL FROM DISCONNECTED SPRING LOCK
COUPLING.

Figure 40-50.   Inspecting, connecting, and disconnecting a spring lock connector. Note use of special coupling removal tool.
(Ford)

hose. If tubing must be bent, use a suitable tubing bender to avoid kinks. Do not try to rebend a formed line. Always check all connections for leaks after the system has been charged.

Component Replacement

When a major component must be replaced, the system's refrigerant charge must be recovered. Replacement procedures for such units as the condenser, receiver-drier, and compressor are usually straightforward. Remember to use new O-rings when reconnecting fittings. Evaporator replacement, however, can be lengthy and complex. In many cases, the heater core, ductwork, and some dash and passenger compartment components must be removed to replace an evaporator. Always obtain the proper service manual and follow all procedures exactly.

Compressor Clutch Replacement

If the compressor clutch is inoperative, weak, or the clutch faces are worn, the clutch and magnetic coil can be replaced without discharging the system. Some systems require a special tool to remove the pulley, while others can be removed by loosening a large bolt on the front of the compressor shaft. Reinstallation is the reverse of removal. Refer to **Figure 40-51.**

> **Caution: Do not install the clutch assembly without checking the clearance between the drive and driven plates. This specification, and the method of checking, are given in the appropriate service manual.**

Compressor Overhaul

Usually, a compressor is simply replaced when it has seized or no longer functions properly. However, it is sometimes more desirable to overhaul the compressor, rather

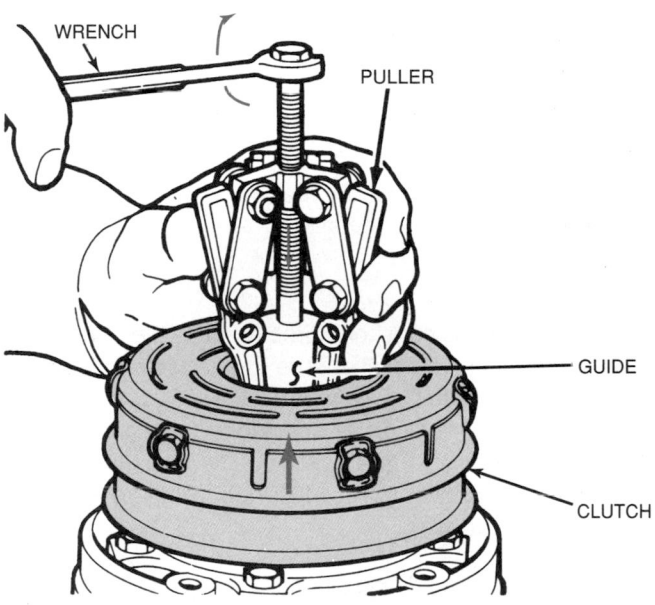

Figure 40-51. Removing a compressor clutch assembly with a puller and guide tool. (General Motors)

than replace it. When overhauling a compressor, always use the manufacturer's service manual. Cleanliness should be emphasized. Follow overhaul instructions carefully for the exact unit being worked upon.

Use a holding fixture if available. Clean all parts thoroughly. Inspect all parts, bearings, and sealing surfaces. Replace worn or damaged components. Use new seals and gaskets. Lubricate selected parts with clean, fresh refrigerant oil of the correct type and viscosity. Always use proper tools to ensure correct disassembly and reassembly without part distortion or seal damage. Tighten all fasteners with a torque wrench. Add the recommended amount of new refrigerant oil.

The compressor can be bench tested for external seal leakage prior to installation. Look at **Figure 40-52.** After the compressor is installed, evacuate and charge the system. With the engine running, operate the air conditioning controls to cycle the compressor on and off a number of times. This will burnish the clutch plates and provide better initial torque transfer.

Additional Filtration Devices

Air conditioning systems will not tolerate foreign materials. When a compressor has been badly damaged, a liquid line filter should be installed to remove contamination from the system, **Figure 40-53.** Adding the extra filter will eliminate the need to flush the system following compressor repairs.

Expansion Valve and Orifice Tube Service

Most expansion valves and orifice tubes have small screens installed ahead of them. These screens often become plugged with metal particles or other debris. The system charge must be recovered to clean or replace the screen. If system diagnosis indicates that the screen is restricted, replacement may be necessary. If the particles

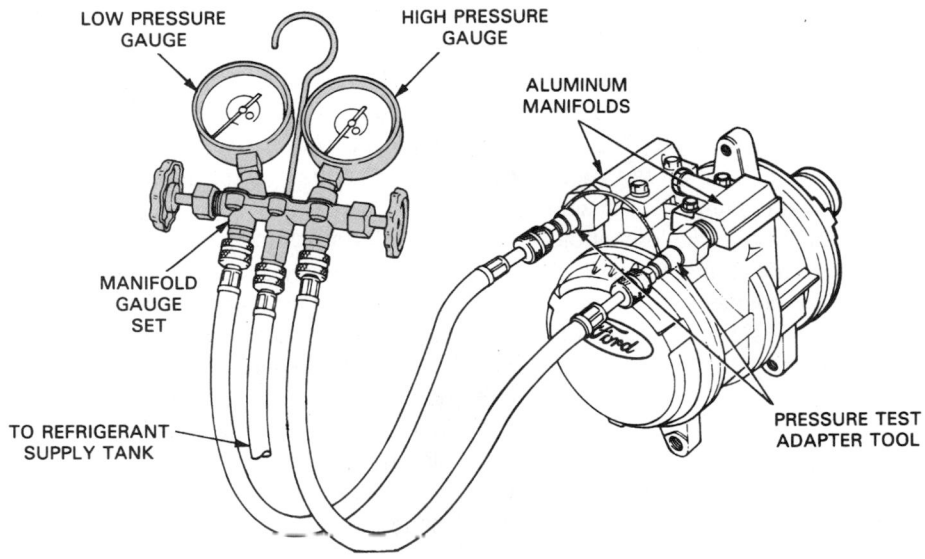

Figure 40-52. Using a manifold gauge set to test a compressor for external leaks. An electronic leak detector may also be used. (Ford)

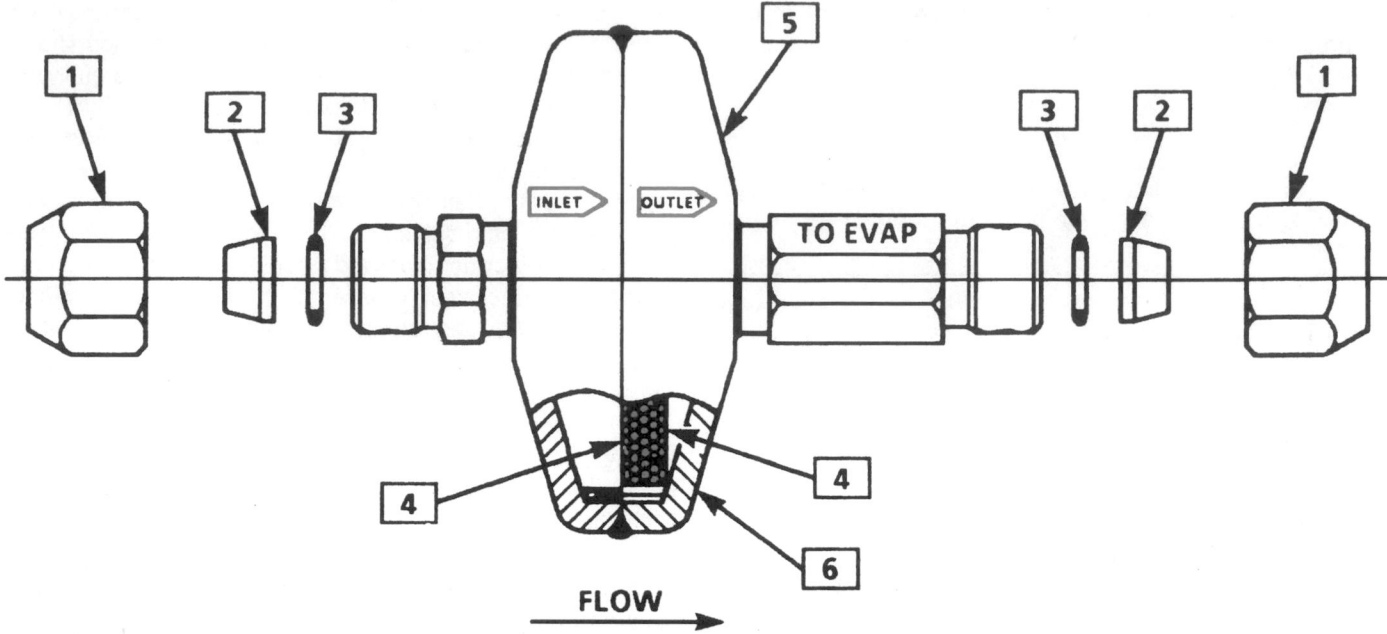

Figure 40-53. This liquid line filter eliminates the need to flush the line following repairs. Follow the manufacturer's installation instructions. 1—Nut. 2—Ferrule. 3—O-ring. 4—Screen. 5—Filter housing. 6—Filtering pad. (General Motors)

are fine and gritty, they can be flushed. Follow the manufacturer's recommendations for specific cleaning instructions. Expansion valves and orifice tubes are not repairable. If either one is clogged or defective, it must be replaced as a unit.

System Lubrication

A specific amount (varies with system size) of **refrigerant oil** is placed in the system when assembled at the factory. The oil is used to provide lubrication for the compressor. The type of oil will vary with the type of refrigerant that is used.

R-12 systems use a **mineral oil** based lubricant in most applications. In R-134a systems, an **ester** or **polyalkylene glycol** or **PAG** oil is used. These oils mix easily with the refrigerant and is circulated throughout the system. The remainder stays in the compressor. Never mix different types of oil as they are not compatible.

Too little oil will ruin the compressor, too much will reduce system efficiency. Consult the manufacturer's service manual for recommended amounts of replacement oil. This initial amount of oil is all that the system needs. It will remain in the system until a leak develops or the system is opened for part replacement. If the system is functioning properly and there are no leaks, the oil supply is known to be adequate.

Methods of Oil Loss

Oil can be lost by a leak in the system, careless discharging (discharging too fast), or when replacing a part. For example, when a evaporator is replaced, a certain amount of the system's oil supply remains in the evaporator. When installing the new evaporator, add the specified amount of replacement oil directly into the evaporator before installation. This will ensure the correct amount of oil is in the system. When an evaporator, receiver, condenser, or compressor is replaced, a specific amount of oil should be added to replenish the system. The expansion valve, suction throttling valve, fixed orifice tube, and lines may be replaced without adding oil.

Checking Compressor Oil Level

If the system has been leaking and an oil film is evident, the oil level should be checked. Some compressors have a small oil level valve near the bottom of the compressor body. If so equipped, operate the system for 15 minutes at maximum cooling. Shut off the engine and air conditioning system and wait 5 minutes. Open the valve cap slightly. If oil drips out, tighten the cap. Wait a few moments and reopen. If oil comes out in a steady stream, sufficient oil is present. If refrigerant vapor hisses out, the oil level is low. Leak test the system and make repairs.

Checking Compressor Oil Level Using a Dipstick

A number of compressors have provisions for checking the oil level by using a dipstick. A typical oil checking procedure is completed as follows. Operate the engine at 1500 RPM with the air conditioning system at maximum cooling for 15 minutes. Shut the engine and system off. Isolate the compressor from the system by fully closing both service fitting hand valves.

With the valves closed, loosen the high pressure gauge fitting cap. Let the pressure escape from within the compressor. The cap must be loosened slowly and only a small amount. Remove the oil filler plug. Pass a clean flattened 1/8″ (3.18 mm) steel rod through the filler hole and down to the bottom of the sump. It may be necessary to turn the compressor shaft a small amount to clear the rod. Withdraw the rod and measure the oil depth. Compare with manufacturer's specifications.

Add or remove oil as needed. Check and replace the O-ring, if needed, and replace the filler plug. Evacuate the compressor by drawing a vacuum on the high pressure fitting gauge connection. Shut the vacuum pump line valve and fully open both service fitting hand valves. Remove vacuum line and replace gauge connection cap. Replace caps on both valve stems. **Figure 40-54** shows a dipstick used on one type of radial compressor.

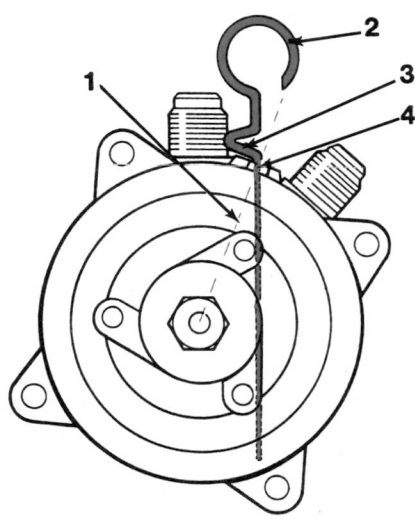

MOUNTING ANGLE IN DEGREES	ACCEPTABLE OIL LEVEL IN INCREMENTS
0	2-4
10	4-5
20	5-6
30	6-7
40	7-9
50	9-10
60	10-12
90	12-13

Figure 40-54. Compressor mounting angles will produce different oil levels on the dipstick. (Jaguar)

Checking Oil Level after Compressor Removal

Many compressors must be removed to check the oil level. Run the air conditioning system for 15 minutes at maximum cooling (unless an excessive amount of oil has escaped from the system). Recover the system's refrigerant charge, remove the compressor, and cap lines. With the compressor in a horizontal position (oil sump down), drain the oil into a clean, graduated container. Carefully measure the oil removed to determine the exact number of fluid ounces. Examine the condition of the oil. If metal chips, water, sludge, or other debris is present, the system should be flushed. If the oil is OK, install the correct amount of new oil.

Adding Oil by Injection

Some systems may have oil added without discharging the system by using a special injection device. The injector is connected to the low pressure gauge manifold connection, **Figure 40-55.** The center manifold connection is capped. The gauge set is connected into the system. The lines, gauges, and injector connections are purged. The system is then operated with the gauge valves open and with the service fitting hand valves opened halfway. This will draw the oil into the suction side of the compressor. Following oil injection, recheck the oil level in the compressor, if possible.

> **Caution:** When charging oil by injection, do not draw oil directly out of the oil container.
> Contamination and/or system overcharging may result. Always use a oil injection tool.

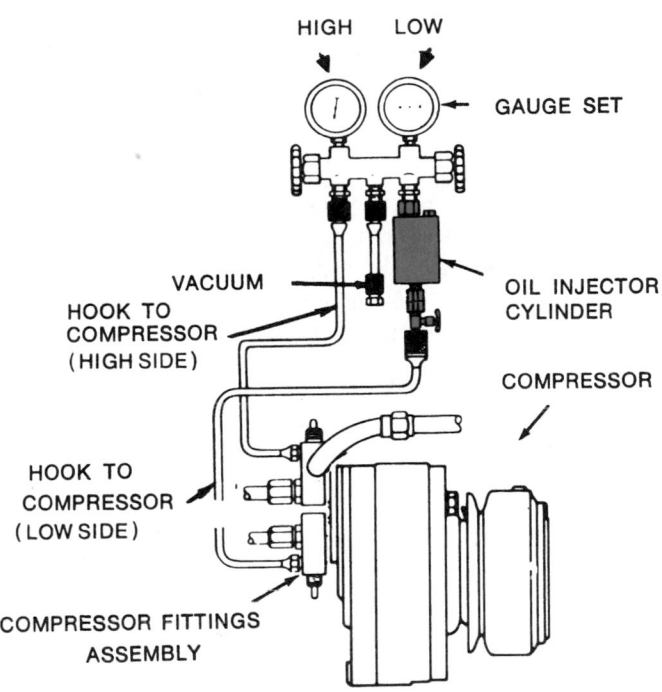

Figure 40-55. Adding oil to a charged system with an oil injector cylinder setup. (General Motors)

Flushing

If a compressor seizes or an internal compressor part fails, small metal particles are usually distributed throughout the system. To remove these particles, it is necessary to clean the system by *flushing.* When flushing parts to remove contamination, wear goggles, gloves, and protective clothing. Use a recommended flushing agent (nitrogen is often specified) and tools. Only closed type flushing tools should be used. Flushing should be done outside, or in a controlled ventilation area built for this type of service.

Performance Complaints

When the owner complains of poor air conditioning performance, do not start on an elaborate, full-scale system analysis. Make a few simple checks first. These quick checks may unmask the trouble.

Proper System Operation

Ask the owner to operate the system. Observe how he or she sets the controls. You will discover that occasionally the driver either sets the controls wrong or operates the system with one or more windows open. Advise the driver as to proper operation of the system. Explain that cooling efficiency will vary with ambient (moving) air temperature and humidity. On a hot or humid day, the system may fail to cool the vehicle to the point to which it is normally capable. Inspect the compressor drive belt for looseness, excessive wear, or breakage. Adjust or repair as needed.

Compressor Operation

Check the compressor for proper operation. Check the operation of the compressor magnetic clutch to make certain the compressor is being driven. The compressor clutch should not cycle excessively. The compressor should not be excessively noisy. Check the compressor drive belt for proper tension.

Sight Glass

Start the system and operate for at least 5 minutes with controls set for maximum cooling. Examine the refrigerant flow through the sight glass. If the ambient air temperature is above 70°-75°F (21°-24°C), there usually should not be any foam or bubbles visible. Bubbles, when the temperature is below 70°F (21°C), are normal. If bubbles or foam show in the glass, the system may be low on refrigerant. Exceptionally high temperatures can occasionally cause the appearance of foam or bubbles.

When the system is empty, no foam or bubbles will be visible. When the system is empty, however, the sight glass will have an oily look and will not be as clear as it would be with the system charged. If loss of refrigerant is suspected, check for leaks. **Figure 40-56** shows a chart, used by one manufacturer, with various sight glass conditions, their meanings, and causes.

Inspect Lines and Hoses

Examine hoses and lines to make certain they are not kinked or flattened. Restrictions will often cause cold or frosty spots just beyond the point of restriction. Bulges or bubbles are signs that a hose is defective. Leaking hoses will usually be evident by oil at the leak site.

Air Distribution System

Inspect blower motor for proper operation. Check operation of air blending doors (mixes heater air with evaporator air in varying proportions). The air system should be free of obstructions and leaks. Evaporator drain must be open. The air output should be consistent and even from all vents and free of odors.

Condenser and Radiator

Check the front and rear surfaces of both the radiator and condenser for signs of clogging from insects, dirt, and other debris. Remove any material that may impede airflow. If the vehicle is equipped with air dams used to direct air flow, make sure that are in place and in good condition. The use of bug screens mounted in front of the radiator and condenser can cause problems. If the vehicle has an electric cooling fan, make sure it is in good condition and operating properly.

Item to check	Adequate	Insufficient	Almost no refrigerant	Too much refrigerant
State in sight glass	CLEAR Air bubbles sometimes appear when engine speed is increased or decreased.	FOAMY or BUBBLY Air bubbles always appear.	FROSTY Frost appears.	NO FOAM No air bubbles appear.
Temperature of high and low pressure lines	High-pressure side is hot while low-pressure side is cold. (A big temperature difference between high and low-pressure side.)	High-pressure side is warm and low-pressure side is slightly cold. (Not so large a temperature difference between high and low-pressure side.)	There is almost no temperature difference between high and low-pressure side.	High-pressure is hot and low-pressure side is slightly warm. (Slight temperature difference between high and low-pressure side.)
Pressure of system	Both pressures on high and low-pressure sides are normal.	Both pressures on high and low-pressure sides are slightly low.	High-pressure side is abnormally low.	Both pressure on high and low-pressure sides are abnormally high.

Figure 40-56. This chart shows several sight glass refrigerant conditions. (Infiniti)

Testing System Performance

It is sometimes difficult to determine just how well the system is functioning by merely depending upon the driver's opinion (based on physical reaction to temperature inside vehicle). As mentioned, temperature and humidity affect system efficiency. To gain a true picture of system efficiency, it is essential that it be performance tested. Performance testing generally involves checking system operating pressures (low and high side), and the temperature of the air being discharged into the vehicle.

The pressure and temperature readings are then related to the ambient air temperature and relative humidity to determine system efficiency under ideal operating conditions. Test techniques and specifications vary with the different makes and models. Follow manufacturer's specifications, **Figure 40-57.**

System Diagnostic Charts

Many vehicle manufacturers provide very helpful diagnostic charts covering all aspects of their systems. One such chart is shown in **Figure 40-58.** When available, use these charts as they provide tests and other procedures that are helpful in pinpointing specific problems quickly and accurately. A diagnostic chart for air conditioning problems is located in Chapter 42. Always obtain and use the diagnostic charts in the vehicle's service manual.

System Service Following Collision

When a vehicle has been involved in an accident that could have damaged the air conditioning system, the system should be checked as soon as possible. Examine compressor and compressor clutch pulley for damage. Remove the compressor clutch energizing wire before the vehicle is operated, if damage to the compressor or other air conditioning system parts is apparent. Replace any air conditioning parts that were damaged. Do not attempt to repair parts by welding, soldering, or other means. If the system was damaged to the point that the refrigerant charge was lost, replace the receiver-drier.

Retrofitting

As the supply of R-12 diminishes, it will become necessary to adapt older air conditioning systems to use R-134a. This procedure is called *retrofitting.* As long as R-12 is available, use it to recharge these systems. If a vehicle requires a major repair, such as a compressor or evaporator replacement, the option to retrofit may be given to the customer.

Each manufacturer publishes guidelines for retrofitting their vehicles. When retrofitting an air conditioning system, follow the manufacturer's procedures closely. Failure to do this can result in system damage, poor system performance, and/or refrigerant release.

RELATIVE HUMIDITY (%)	AMBIENT AIR TEMP		MAXIMUM LOW SIDE PRESSURE		ENGINE SPEED (rpm)	MAXIMUM RIGHT CENTER AIR OUTLET TEMPERATURE		MAXIMUM HIGH SIDE PRESSURE	
	°F	°C	PSIG	kPaG		°F	°C	PSIG	kPaG
20	70	21	32	221	2000	43	6	175	1207
	80	27	32	221		44	7	225	1551
	90	32	32	221		50	10	275	1896
	100	38	33	228		51	11	275	1896
30	70	21	32	221	2000	45	7	190	1310
	80	27	32	221		47	8	235	1620
	90	32	34	234		54	12	290	2000
	100	38	38	262		57	14	310	2137
40	70	21	32	221	2000	46	8	210	1448
	80	27	32	221		50	10	255	1758
	90	32	37	255		57	14	305	2103
	100	38	44	303		63	17	345	2379
50	70	21	32	221	2000	48	9	225	1551
	80	27	34	234		53	12	270	1862
	90	32	41	283		60	16	325	2241
	100	38	49	338		69	21	380	2620
60	70	21	32	221	2000	50	10	240	1655
	80	27	37	255		56	13	290	2000
	90	32	44	303		63	17	340	2344
	100	38	55	379		75	24	395	2724
70	70	21	32	221	2000	52	11	255	1758
	80	27	40	276		59	15	305	2103
	90	32	48	331		67	19	355	2448
80	70	21	36	248	2000	53	12	270	1862
	80	27	43	296		62	17	320	2206
	90	32	52	356		70	21	370	2551
90	70	21	40	276	2000	55	13	285	1965
	80	27	47	324		65	18	335	2310

Figure 40-57.   An air conditioning performance test chart as used by one vehicle manufacturer. (Pontiac)

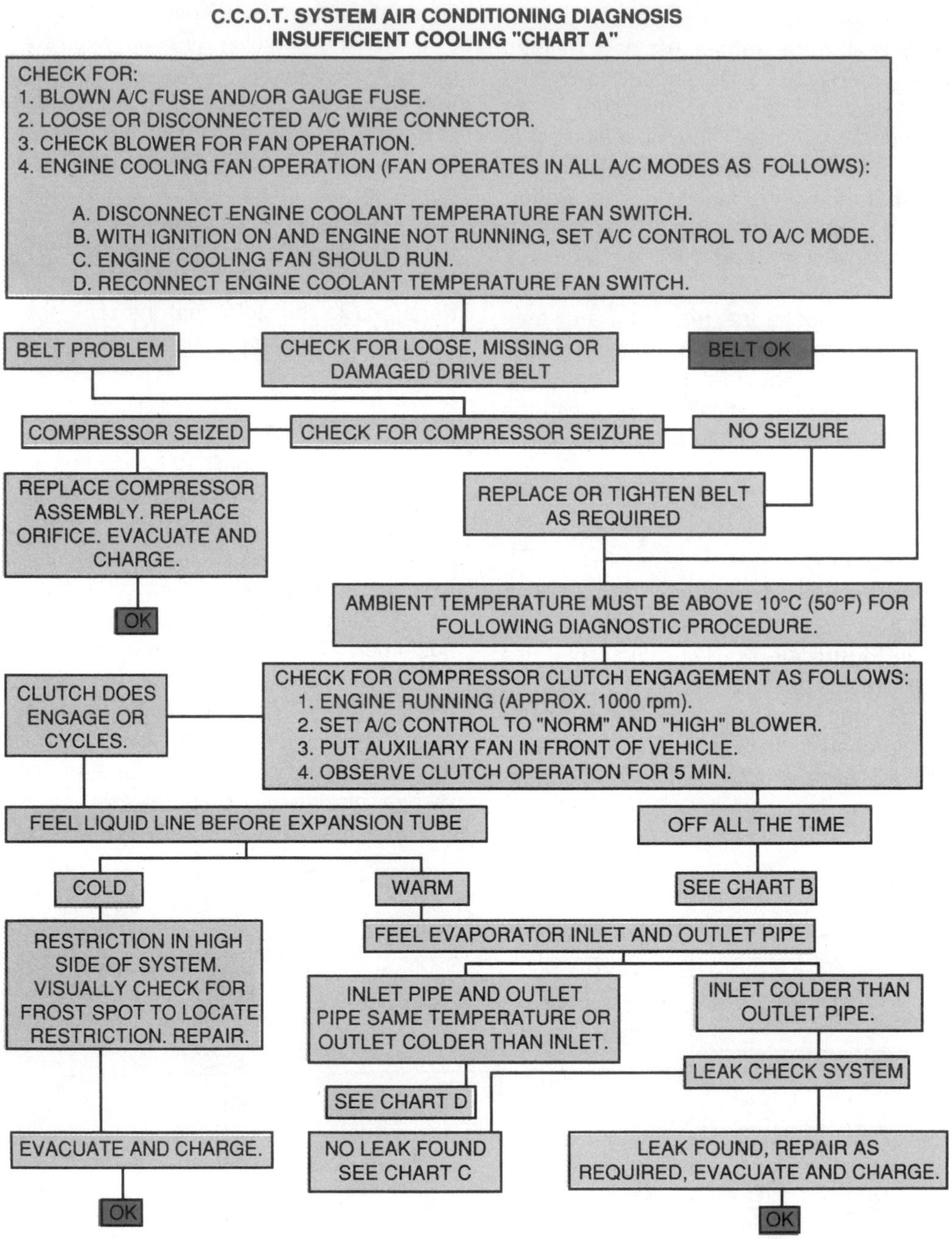

C.C.O.T. SYSTEM AIR CONDITIONING DIAGNOSIS
INSUFFICIENT COOLING "CHART A"

CHECK FOR:
1. BLOWN A/C FUSE AND/OR GAUGE FUSE.
2. LOOSE OR DISCONNECTED A/C WIRE CONNECTOR.
3. CHECK BLOWER FOR FAN OPERATION.
4. ENGINE COOLING FAN OPERATION (FAN OPERATES IN ALL A/C MODES AS FOLLOWS):

   A. DISCONNECT ENGINE COOLANT TEMPERATURE FAN SWITCH.
   B. WITH IGNITION ON AND ENGINE NOT RUNNING, SET A/C CONTROL TO A/C MODE.
   C. ENGINE COOLING FAN SHOULD RUN.
   D. RECONNECT ENGINE COOLANT TEMPERATURE FAN SWITCH.

| BELT PROBLEM | CHECK FOR LOOSE, MISSING OR DAMAGED DRIVE BELT | BELT OK |

| COMPRESSOR SEIZED | CHECK FOR COMPRESSOR SEIZURE | NO SEIZURE |

REPLACE COMPRESSOR ASSEMBLY. REPLACE ORIFICE. EVACUATE AND CHARGE.

REPLACE OR TIGHTEN BELT AS REQUIRED

OK

AMBIENT TEMPERATURE MUST BE ABOVE 10°C (50°F) FOR FOLLOWING DIAGNOSTIC PROCEDURE.

CLUTCH DOES ENGAGE OR CYCLES.

CHECK FOR COMPRESSOR CLUTCH ENGAGEMENT AS FOLLOWS:
1. ENGINE RUNNING (APPROX. 1000 rpm).
2. SET A/C CONTROL TO "NORM" AND "HIGH" BLOWER.
3. PUT AUXILIARY FAN IN FRONT OF VEHICLE.
4. OBSERVE CLUTCH OPERATION FOR 5 MIN.

| FEEL LIQUID LINE BEFORE EXPANSION TUBE | | OFF ALL THE TIME |

| COLD | WARM | SEE CHART B |

RESTRICTION IN HIGH SIDE OF SYSTEM. VISUALLY CHECK FOR FROST SPOT TO LOCATE RESTRICTION. REPAIR.

FEEL EVAPORATOR INLET AND OUTLET PIPE

| INLET PIPE AND OUTLET PIPE SAME TEMPERATURE OR OUTLET COLDER THAN INLET. | INLET COLDER THAN OUTLET PIPE. |

LEAK CHECK SYSTEM

SEE CHART D

| EVACUATE AND CHARGE. | NO LEAK FOUND SEE CHART C | LEAK FOUND, REPAIR AS REQUIRED, EVACUATE AND CHARGE. |

OK   **OK**

Figure 40-58. An air conditioning diagnostic flow chart for insufficient cooling. Use these charts to quickly diagnose automotive problems. (AC Delco)

 Caution: Never attempt to convert an R-134a system to use R-12. Severe system damage will result.

Heater System

The heater depends on hot engine coolant flowing through a metal core to provide heat to the passenger compartment. On modern vehicles, the *heater core* is integrated into the overall air conditioning system, **Figure 40-59.** On vehicles without air conditioning, the heater system consists of a heater core, blower motor, and associated ductwork. One type of heater and blower system is shown in **Figure 40-60.**

Checking Heater Operation

When possible, question the owner as to apparent problem, any unusual sounds, or other symptoms. Inspect

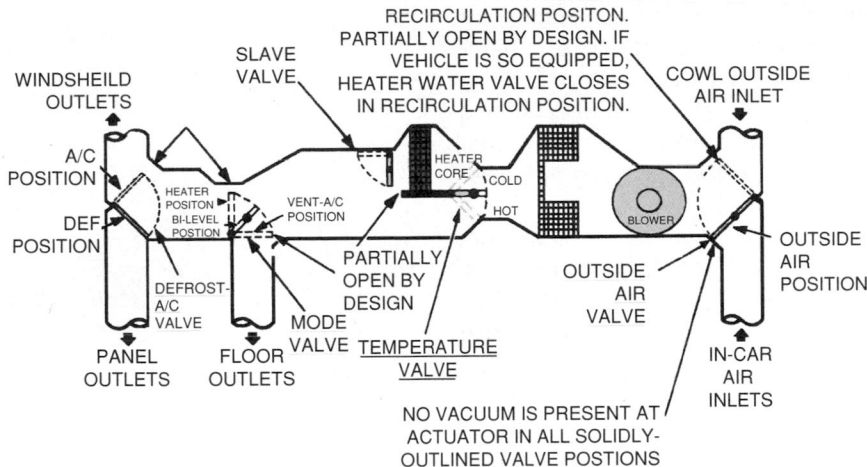

Figure 40-59. One heater-air conditioning system assembly showing the heater core location in relation to other parts. (General Motors)

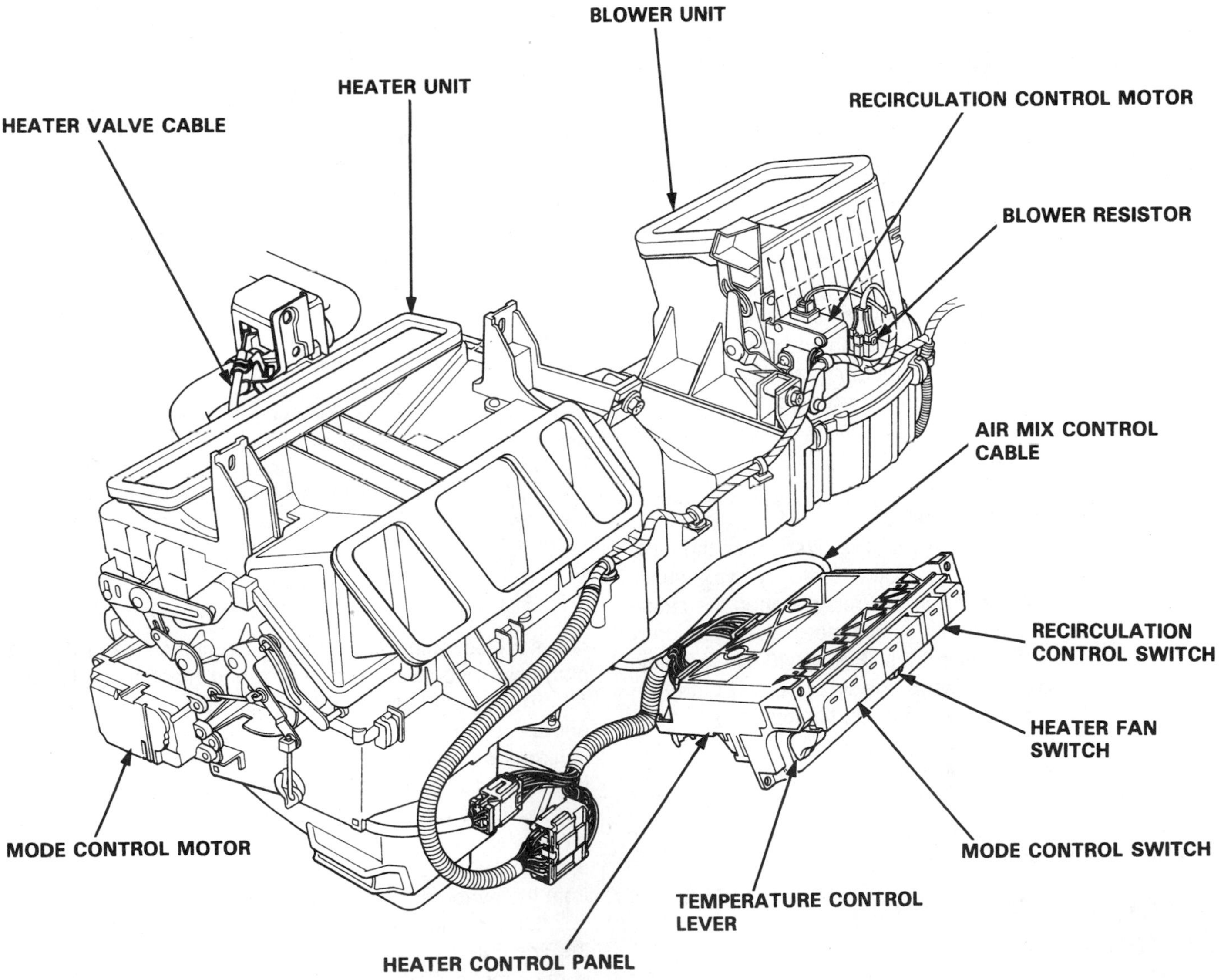

HEATER VALVE CABLE

HEATER UNIT

BLOWER UNIT

RECIRCULATION CONTROL MOTOR

BLOWER RESISTOR

AIR MIX CONTROL CABLE

RECIRCULATION CONTROL SWITCH

HEATER FAN SWITCH

MODE CONTROL SWITCH

MODE CONTROL MOTOR

TEMPERATURE CONTROL LEVER

HEATER CONTROL PANEL

Figure 40-60. Overall view of a typical heater system. Study the part names and relationships. (Honda)

the entire cooling system as well as the heater system, for leakage. Check hoses for softening, cracking, kinks, or hardening. Inspect air intake for clogging or bent or loose ducting. Bring the engine to its normal operating temperature and operate the heater controls while checking for proper response. Check heat control valve operation, blower speeds, defroster, and vent operation.

As required, check blower fuse, operation of vacuum motors, and mechanical controls. For further diagnostic information, see the heater section in Chapter 42. See Chapter 22 for more on hoses, antifreeze, and other cooling system related information.

Heater Shut-Off Valve

Many heater systems are equipped with a *shut-off valve*, which stops the flow of engine coolant through the heater core when heating is not needed. If the heater blows cold air, check the operation of the shut-off valve by operating the external linkage. If the heater begins working when the linkage is moved to the opposite of its original position, the valve was stuck. Check for cooling system debris in the valve, or a defective vacuum diaphragm where used. On cable operated shut-off valves, check for misadjustment or a broken cable.

Heater Core Service

If the heater core is suspected of leaking, conduct a cooling system pressure test. Make certain that there are no leaks at the hose-to-core attachment points. If the heater core is clogged, output will be low when the engine is at normal operating temperature. The heater core is usually located under the dashboard, with its outlets passing through the vehicle firewall. Replacement procedures are somewhat similar to evaporator core replacement and may involve removing parts of the ductwork and other underdash components. Always obtain the proper service manual and follow all procedures exactly.

Blower Motor Service

If the blower motor is inoperative, first check the fuse. If the fuse is OK, check the blower motor relays, usually located on the engine firewall. The relay is often the cause of an inoperative blower at some speed settings. Many vehicles use resistor assemblies, **Figure 40-61,** to obtain various blower speeds. Always check for burned out resistors, especially if the blower works on some speeds but not others. Check any electronically controlled blower motor circuits using procedures outlined in the appropriate service manual. If all other components are good, test the blower motor for voltage and amperage draw. Perform all tests as specified by the manufacturer.

Air Distribution and Control System Service

Modern heating and air conditioning systems have elaborate control systems using electrical switches and

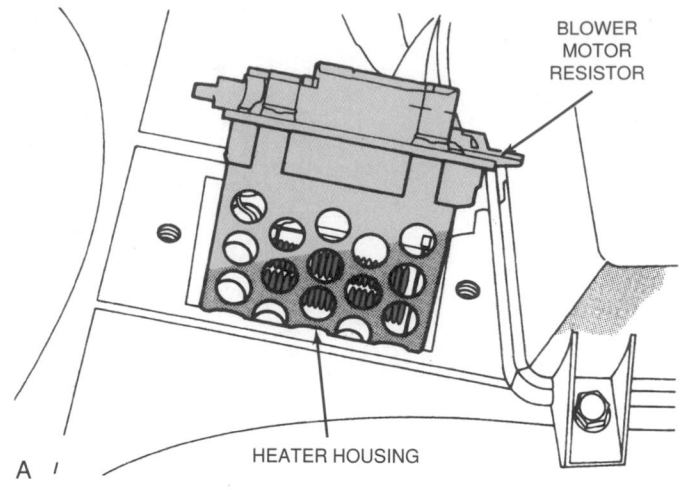

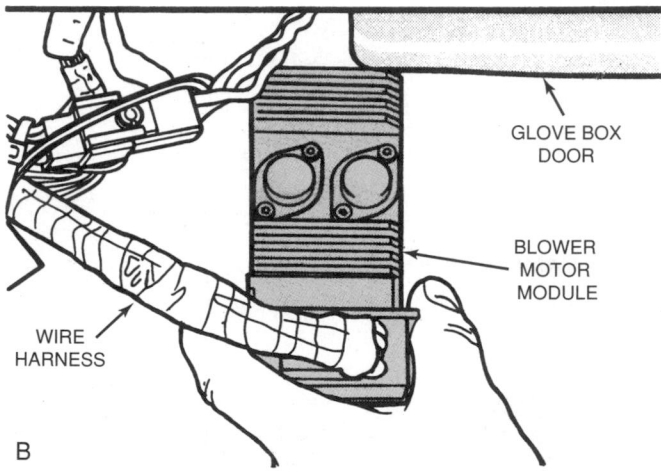

Figure 40-61. A—One type of blower motor resistor assembly located in the heater housing, and used with a non-automatic temperature control system. B—A blower motor module located in the heater housing, and used with an automatic temperature control system. This module receives control signals from the body control module (BCM). The power module varies the voltage traveling to the blower motor. This unit provides fourteen different speeds. (Chrysler)

relays, electronic sensors and controls, vacuum diaphragms, reservoirs, and hoses, and mechanical linkage. All of these controls work together to operate the heating and air conditioning system and control air distribution. The control system operates the blower motor, as well as doors in the air distribution system. The doors are built into the ductwork and direct air flow to the vents, floor, or windshield as needed. A separate door, usually called a *blend door*, controls the temperature of the incoming air by blending air from the evaporator and heater core.

Modern auto air conditioning systems, especially in the computerized versions have complex wiring and vacuum control systems. Manual control systems are operated by the vehicle occupants through a series of vacuum and electrical switches, cables and/or levers. In an automatic system, a central computer or control module, controls the air distribution system based on inputs from thermistors (temperature sensitive resistors, usually referred to as sensors), and pressure sensors, as well as the temperature settings made by the passengers. Any one of these devices can cause trouble.

Air Distribution Wiring and Vacuum Circuits

The air mixture or blending abilities of an air flow control system, permits a discharge of temperature regulated air into the vehicle. In hot weather, this blending system will permit the evaporator to operate constantly near the freezing point, thus permitting full efficiency. In colder weather, the controls can be adjusted to produce warm air from the same ducts. When the weather is cold and humid, the system can be adjusted to use the evaporator to remove humidity from the incoming air and the heater core to warm it. This air is then directed to the windshield to reduce fogging.

Basic checks of the control system consist of making sure that all vacuum hoses are in position, and that linkage cables are correctly adjusted. Also check for blown fuses and disconnected wiring. More complex checking will require using the vehicle's service manual. **Figures 40-62** and **40-63** illustrate a system analysis wiring diagram and a system analysis vacuum diagram.

Air Distribution System Ductwork

The system ductwork must be in place for the blending abilities of the air distribution system to be fully utilized. Check all ductwork for damage or misalignment. Also check any gaskets and seals for damage. One often overlooked area is the intake ductwork at the front cowl. This often becomes clogged with dirt and leaves, reducing the ability of the blower to pull in air.

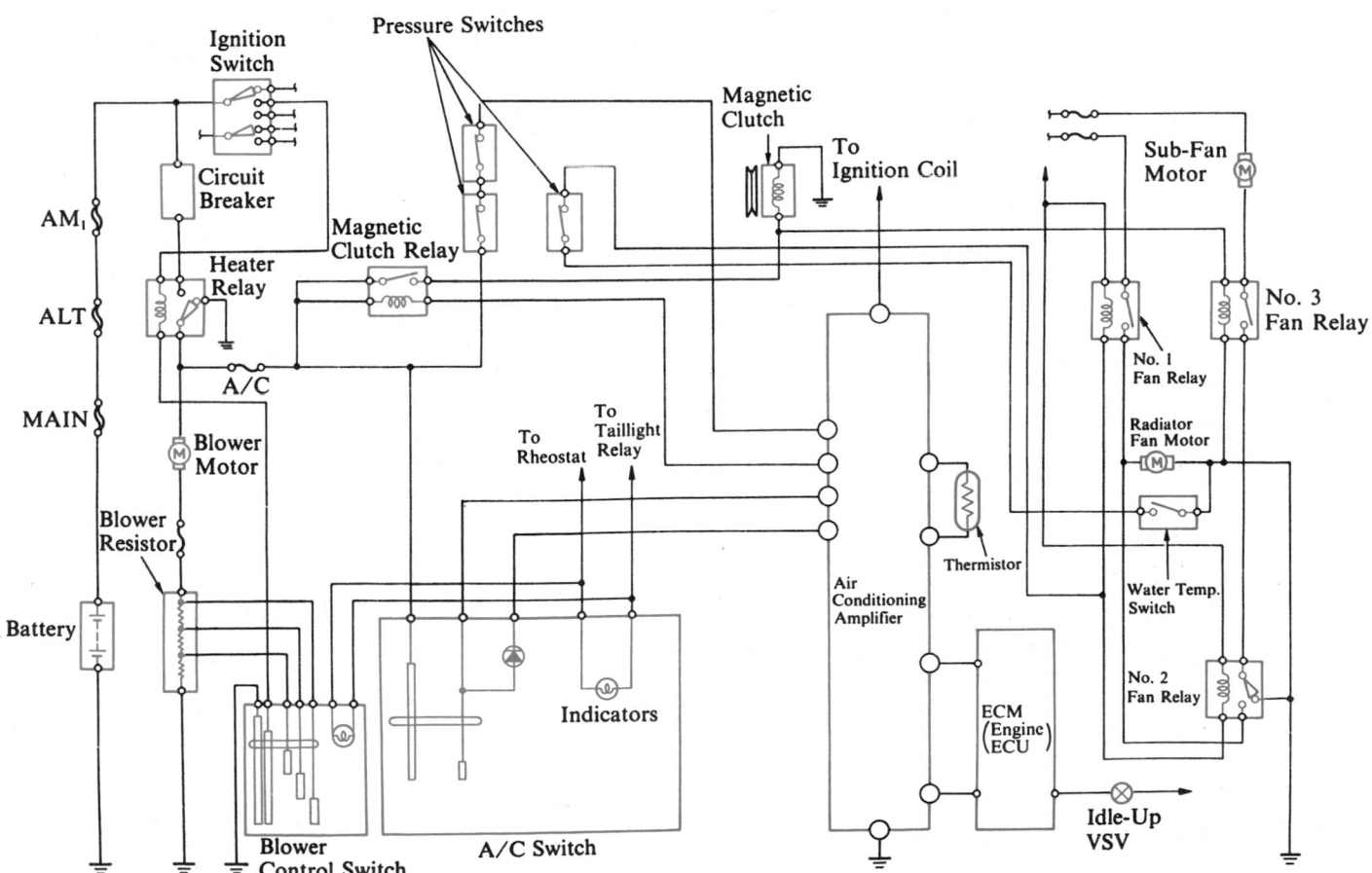

*ECM: Engine Control Module

Figure 40-62. An air conditioning system wiring schematic. These are a must for proper diagnosis. (Toyota)

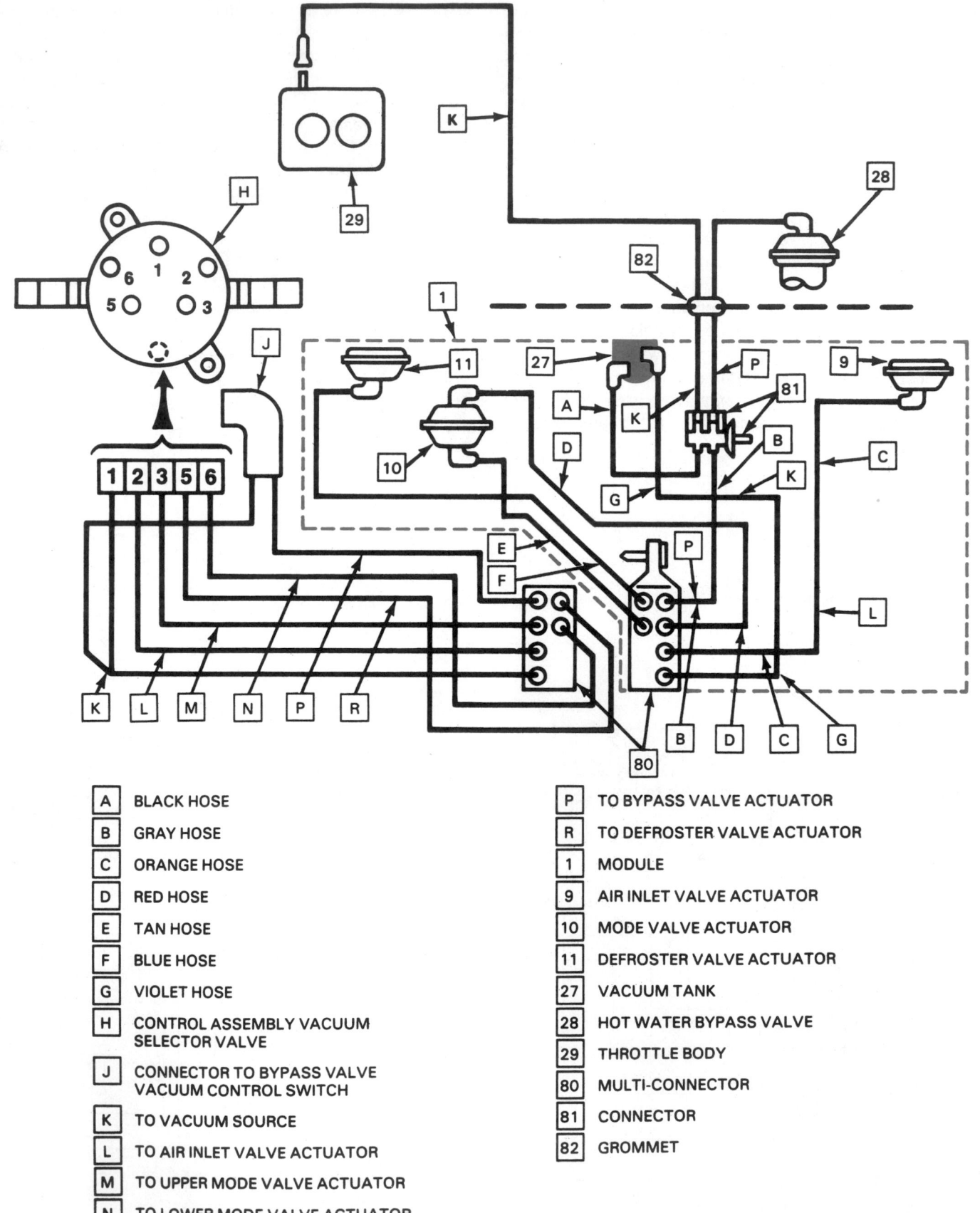

6 1 **2**
5 **3**

1 2 3 5 6

K L M N P R

A	BLACK HOSE		P	TO BYPASS VALVE ACTUATOR
B	GRAY HOSE		R	TO DEFROSTER VALVE ACTUATOR
C	ORANGE HOSE		1	MODULE
D	RED HOSE		9	AIR INLET VALVE ACTUATOR
E	TAN HOSE		10	MODE VALVE ACTUATOR
F	BLUE HOSE		11	DEFROSTER VALVE ACTUATOR
G	VIOLET HOSE		27	VACUUM TANK
H	CONTROL ASSEMBLY VACUUM SELECTOR VALVE		28	HOT WATER BYPASS VALVE
J	CONNECTOR TO BYPASS VALVE VACUUM CONTROL SWITCH		29	THROTTLE BODY
K	TO VACUUM SOURCE		80	MULTI-CONNECTOR
L	TO AIR INLET VALVE ACTUATOR		81	CONNECTOR
M	TO UPPER MODE VALVE ACTUATOR		82	GROMMET
N	TO LOWER MODE VALVE ACTUATOR			

Figure 40-63. A vacuum hose diagram for one specific vehicle. (General Motors)

Tech Talk

Improper disposal of refrigerant is a serious concern. Whether or not you believe that refrigerants can damage the ozone layer, there is one overriding reason to recycle refrigerants: if you do not, you are breaking the law. Improper refrigerant disposal is covered by federal and, in some cases, state laws.

Not too long ago, a local salvage yard sold an air conditioner compressor from a wrecked vehicle. When the owner of the salvage yard removed the compressor, he simply opened the refrigerant lines, discharging the refrigerant to the atmosphere. Unfortunately, the compressor buyer was an agent of the Environmental Protection Agency, investigating just this sort of activity. In the end, the owner agreed to pay a substantial fine to stay out of jail. You do not want this to happen to you.

Also, replacing wasted refrigerants costs money. For instance, R-12 refrigerant costs over seven times as much as it did just a few years ago. R-12 has not been manufactured since January 1, 1996. As supplies of R-12 decrease, the price will become very high. Once R-12 is no longer available, the air conditioner will require a retrofit to accept another type of refrigerant. It makes good economic and environmental sense to recover and reuse refrigerants.

Summary

Air conditioning systems may be either manually or electronically controlled. The automatic system cleans, dehumidifies, and adjusts the temperature of the incoming air. The air is first cooled and then, if needed, heated to the desired level. Air conditioning involves using a refrigerant (R-12 or R-134a) to vaporize (boil) and condense when pressures change. The air conditioning system uses this change in pressures to remove heat from air entering the passenger compartment and transfer it to the outside air.

Modern air conditioners can be classified according to whether they have a variable or fixed restrictor. Variable restrictors are called expansion valves, while fixed restrictors are called fixed orifices. All air conditioning systems contain some similar components, while other components are used only on some systems. The compressor pumps and compresses the incoming refrigerant vapor. The condenser changes the refrigerant vapor into a liquid. The restrictor allows the refrigerant to enter the evaporator at low pressures. The evaporator causes the refrigerant to boil, removing heat from the incoming air. The evaporator also dehumidifies and cleans the incoming air. The entire system is connected by lines and hoses.

The receiver-drier acts as a storage cylinder for high pressure liquid when located between the condenser and evaporator. The accumulator holds excess refrigerant on the low side of the system. It prevents the entry of liquid refrigerant into the compressor. It also cleans and removes moisture.

On many systems, evaporator pressure is controlled by a valve placed between the evaporator and compressor. On newer vehicles, either a pressure or temperature switch is used to cycle the compressor on and off to control evaporator icing. The system is protected from excessive pressure by a safety valve. One or more mufflers may be used to quiet system noises. A sight glass may be used to view the stream of liquid refrigerant.

Always follow safety rules dealing with air conditioning service. Always wear goggles and gloves when servicing the system and keep the area well ventilated. Do not discharge refrigerant directly into the service area, if can form phosgene gas if it contacts a flame. Do not subject the system to high temperatures. Never leave a refrigerant cylinder uncapped. Do not overheat or fill a cylinder completely. Never connect refrigerant containers to the system high side. Never transport refrigerant containers in the passenger compartment of a vehicle.

Observe recommended service precautions to prevent system contamination. Remember the enemies of air conditioning systems are dirt, water, and air. Recover the system's charge before opening any connection. The manifold gauge set is connected to the system by means of Schrader or SAE valves. Gauge valves must be in the closed position before connecting set. Use only electronic leak detection tools. Detector probe should be used slowly and close to test area. Set up and use as directed by manufacturer. Always use a refrigerant recovery unit. The system must be evacuated for the recommended length of time at 29" of vacuum. Evacuation removes air and moisture from the system.

Charge the system with a partial charge following evacuation and test for leaks. Then charge the system with the specified amount of refrigerant. Before removing any part for service, follow the series of steps given in the text. Always use new O-rings. Protect hose and tubing from vibration, kinks, sharp bends, and heat. Torque all connections.

The amount of compressor oil in the system is critical. It may be checked by measuring the level in the compressor. In others, the compressor must be removed and the oil drained and measured. When an evaporator, condenser, receiver, or other part is replaced, a specific amount of oil must be added to the new unit to replace oil that remains in the old part. The oil level need not be checked in a system in which no leaks are present. Some systems permit oil to be injected into the system without discharging.

A number of simple checks will often disclose the trouble in a malfunctioning system. Performance testing involves comparing system pressure and discharge air temperature with specified pressures and temperatures related to ambient air temperature and humidity. Inspect the system as soon as possible following collision damage.

Know These Terms

Air conditioning	Evaporator pressure
Refrigerant	controls
State	Hot gas bypass valve
Boiling point	Suction throttling valve
R-12	Pilot operated absolute
R-134a	valve
Pressure-temperature	Thermostatic switch
relationship	Low pressure switch
Blower motor	Full throttle cut-out switch
Thermostatic expansion	Phosgene gas
valve	Gauge manifold
TXV	Schrader valve
Cycling clutch orifice tube	Hand shutoff valve
Variable displacement orifice	Liquid leak detector
tube	Halide torch
Compressor	Electronic leak detector
Radial	Discharging
Axial	Refrigerant recovery unit
Variable displacement	Evacuating
compressor	Vacuum pump
Pressure relief valve	Charging station
Compressor clutch	Refrigerant oil
Condenser	Mineral oil
Flow restrictor	Ester
Fixed orifice tube	Polyalkylene glycol
Evaporator	PAG
Lines and hoses	Flushing
Muffler	Retrofitting
Receiver-drier	Heater core
Sight glass	Shut-off valve
Accumulator	Blend door

Review Questions—Chapter 40

Do not write in this book. Write your answers on a separate sheet of paper.

1. Name three things that the air conditioning system does to the air entering the vehicle.
2. Name the two types of air conditioning system restrictors.
3. The condenser performs which of the following?
   (A) Changes refrigerant vapor into liquid.
   (B) Changes liquid refrigerant into vapor.
   (C) Controls the evaporator temperature.
   (D) Removes moisture from the air entering the vehicle.
4. The sight glass permits _____.
   (A) viewing liquid refrigerant
   (B) viewing refrigerant vapor
   (C) checking refrigerant for icing
   (D) checking oil level in compressor
5. List ten safety rules regarding working with, on, or around air conditioning systems.
6. Describe the first aid procedure involved when refrigerant gets in the eyes.
7. When torquing a connection that uses aluminum for one end and steel for the other, use the torque values given for _____.

8. The gauge manifold assists in _____.
   (A) checking system pressures
   (B) evacuating the system
   (C) recovering the refrigerant
   (D) All of the above.
9. Some R-12 system have different high and low side _____ valve fittings.
10. Before connecting the manifold gauge set into the system, the gauge valves must be in the _____ position.
11. When a part is to be replaced in the system, list in the correct order the six steps that should be taken regarding system evacuation, charging, etc.
12. To evacuate the system properly, the system must be subjected to a vacuum of around _____.
    (A) 8″
    (B) 29″
    (C) 48″
    (D) 58″
13. Performance testing involves checking _____.
    (A) discharge air temperature
    (B) system pressures
    (C) ambient air temperature and humidity
    (D) All of the above.
14. Name the door that is used to control air output temperature.
15. List four things that should be checked when inspecting the air distribution system.

ASE-Type Questions

1. Refrigerant-12 is gradually being replaced for use in air conditioners with _____.
   (A) butane
   (B) nitrogen
   (C) R-134a
   (D) R-22
2. Technician A says that refrigerant will eventually wear out from endless cycles through the system and should be replaced at specified intervals. Technician B says that, as the pressure is increased on refrigerant, the boiling point goes up. Who is right?
   (A) A only.
   (B) B only.
   (C) Both A & B.
   (D) Neither A nor B.
3. The receiver-drier performs all of the following functions, EXCEPT:
   (A) Stores liquid refrigerant.
   (B) Removes debris and dirt from the refrigerant.
   (C) Causes the refrigerant to condense into a liquid.
   (D) Removes moisture from the refrigerant.
4. Technician A says that the evaporator changes refrigerant vapor back into liquid refrigerant. Technician B says that the pilot operated absolute (POA) valve controls evaporator pressure. Who is right?
   (A) A only.
   (B) B only.
   (C) Both A & B.
   (D) Neither A nor B.

5. On a fixed orifice system, cycling the compressor clutch does all of the following, EXCEPT:
   (A) Controls compressor speed.
   (B) Prevents evaporator icing.
   (C) Keeps evaporator temperature from becoming too low.
   (D) Keeps evaporator pressure from becoming too low.

6. Refrigerant leaves the compressor as a _____.
   (A) cold, high pressure vapor
   (B) hot, high pressure vapor
   (C) cold, low pressure vapor
   (D) hot, high pressure liquid

7. Technician A says that moisture can cause corrosion of the internal air conditioning system parts. Technician B says that moisture can cause refrigerant oil sludging. Who is right?
   (A) A only.
   (B) B only.
   (C) Both A & B.
   (D) Neither A nor B.

8. Phosgene gas is created when refrigerant comes in contact with _____.
   (A) moisture
   (B) refrigerant oil
   (C) flame
   (D) dirt

9. Technician A says that some systems require complete discharging in order to check compressor oil level. Technician B says that a high quality polyalkylene glycol (PAG) oil is satisfactory for use in all air conditioning systems. Who is right?
   (A) A only.
   (B) B only.
   (C) Both A & B.
   (D) Neither A nor B.

10. When charging a system, never add liquid refrigerant to the _____ unless specifically required.
   (A) system high side
   (B) system low side
   (C) evaporator
   (D) Any of the above.

Suggested Activities

1. Draw a sketch showing the flow of refrigerant through a simple air conditioning system. Indicate major parts and how the system controls refrigerant flow.

2. From the drivers' seat of a vehicle, perform an operational check on the heating and air conditioning system. Use a thermometer to check air conditioner output. Perform two tests, one in the shop and one outside.

3. Attach gauges to an air conditioning system and check system pressures.

4. Using the procedure in the appropriate service manual, check adjustment of the various doors in the blower case.

With proper maintenance, this late-model four-cylinder engine will provide many years of trouble-free operation. (Buick)

41

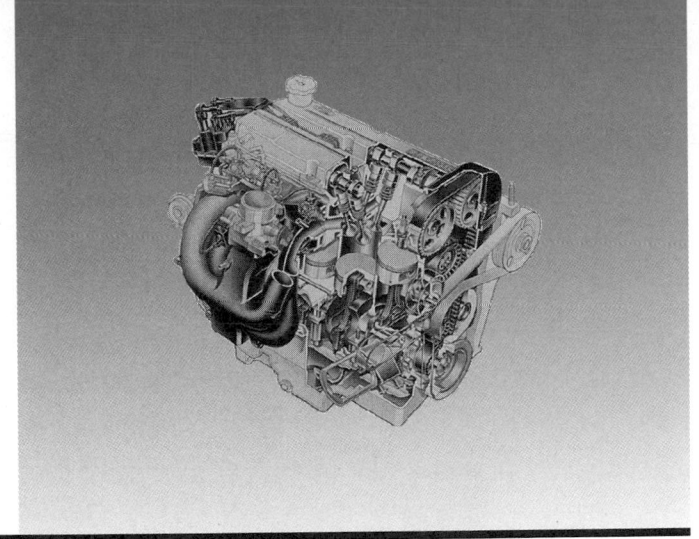

Preventive Maintenance

After studying this chapter, you will be able to:
* Describe the purpose of preventive maintenance.
* List the basic parts of a lubrication system.
* Explain oil filtration systems and their service.
* Describe oil classifications.
* Explain how to change engine oil and filter.
* Explain how to lubricate front suspension fittings.
* Describe other preventive maintenance procedures.

This chapter will cover basic preventive maintenance procedures. Most of the material will be concerned with changing the engine oil and filter and lubricating the front suspension fittings, but other vital maintenance procedures will also be covered.

Protecting the Engine Lubrication System

The importance of a properly functioning engine lubrication system cannot be overemphasized. An ample supply of clean oil of the correct type must reach all bearing surfaces. The best way to protect the lubrication system is to regularly change the engine oil and filter.

The basic parts of the lubrication system are the oil sump or pan, oil pickup, oil pump, relief valve, distribution lines, filter, bypass valve, and oil pressure sending unit. The path of the oil from the sump to the various moving parts in a typical lubrication system is shown in **Figure 41-1.** Trace the flow.

Oil Filtration Systems

In the past, some oil filtration systems allowed unfiltered oil to reach the moving parts of the engine. This was done to minimize the effects of a clogged filter. The disadvantage of these systems is that the moving parts can be damaged by dirt or metal particles in the unfiltered oil.

All modern vehicles use the **full-flow** system. In this system, all the oil must pass through the filter before reaching the bearings. The filter contains an internal pressure relief valve to ensure that the engine receives oil if the filter element clogs.

Figure 41-2A shows a full-flow lubrication system. The pump provides oil under pressure. The pressure regulating valve controls maximum pressure. The check valve in the

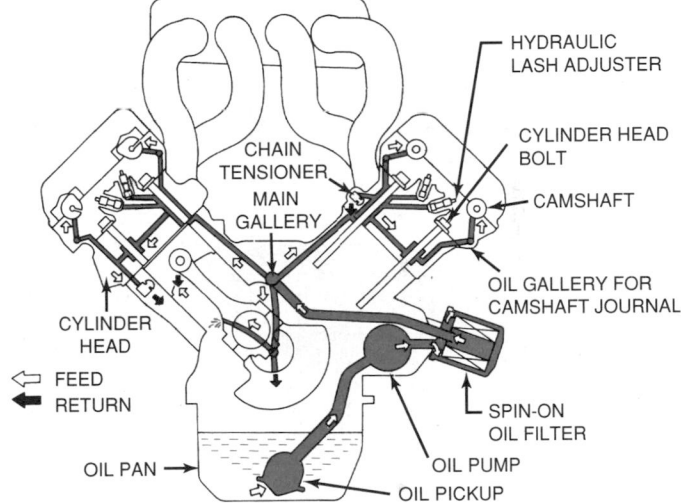

Figure 41-1. A typical lubrication system for one dual overhead camshaft engine. (Nissan)

filter closes when the engine is stopped, preventing the filter from draining. A low-pressure **bypass valve** is used to bypass the filter completely when the filter clogs and pressure on the bearing side drops. Compare this with the partial-flow filtering system in **Figure 41-2B**.

When the filter element in the full-flow system becomes clogged, the bypass opens. Unfiltered oil, which may contain chunks of sludge, travels to the bearing side. For this reason, it is vitally important that oil filter elements be changed at intervals determined by engine condition, use, and conditions of operation.

Modern Oil Filters

Most modern filter elements are known as **surface** filters. They utilize treated paper, folded accordion style, to block the passage of particles. The particles accumulate on the surface of the paper. **Figure 41-3** shows a typical surface filter.

Some filters are the **depth** type, **Figure 41-4**. The filtering medium is composed of a number of different fibers that have different filtering abilities. The particles are trapped at different layers in the filtering material.

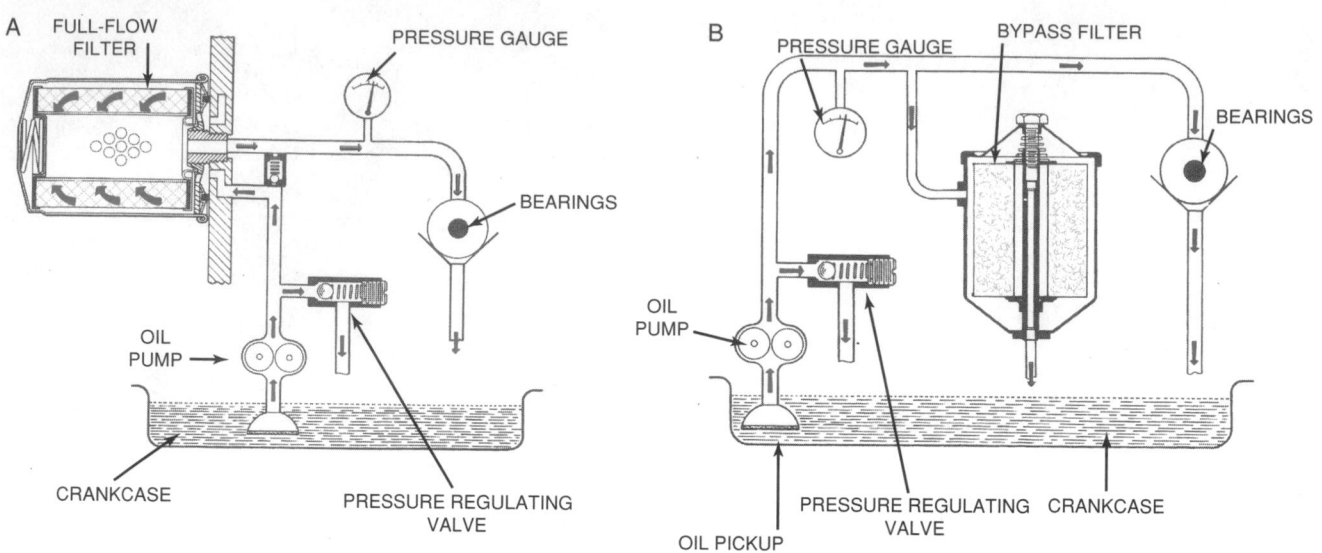

Figure 41-2. A—Schematic of a full-flow lubrication system. B—A partial-flow oil filtering system. Compare the two systems. Note that in the full-flow system, all oil is filtered before reaching the bearings. (Wix)

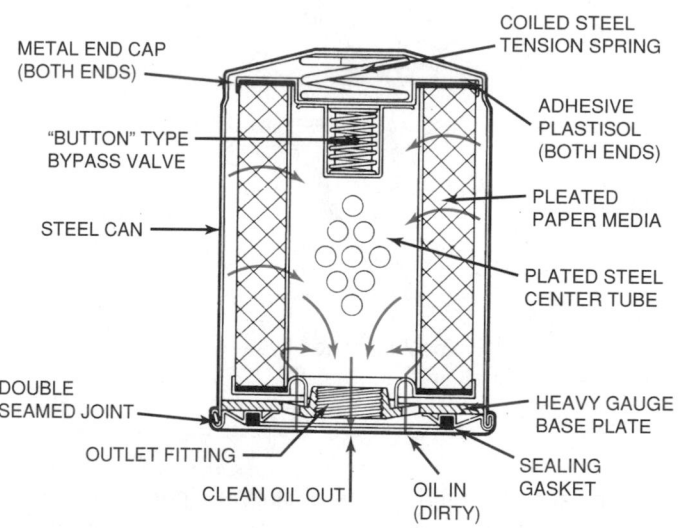

Figure 41-3. A cross-section of a surface filtering oil filter element. Note the bypass valve. (Wix)

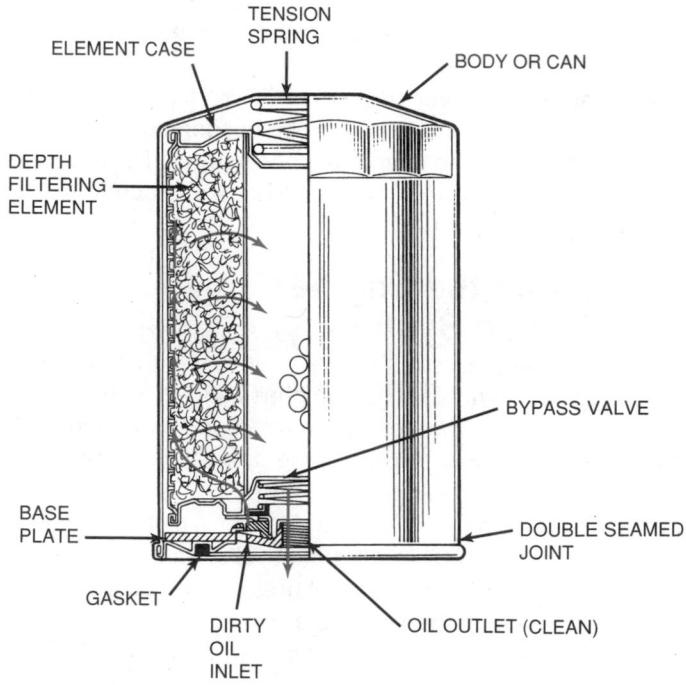

Figure 41-4. Cutaway view of a depth-type oil filter. (Wix)

In older vehicles, the filter assembly often consists of a *filter element* enclosed in a separate housing, as in **Figure 41-5.** The element is replaced, and the housing is reused. The replacement filter element usually comes with the gaskets or O-rings needed to reseal the housing. This type of filter is still used on large trucks, construction equipment, and agricultural equipment. A filter element used on some late-model automobiles is installed in the oil pan, **Figure 41-6.**

The majority of modern cars and light trucks use the *spin-on filter,* **Figures 41-3** and **41-4.** In this type of filter, the element and housing are a single unit. The entire unit is replaced periodically. Although these filters may vary in size, they are all of the same basic design.

Even the best filters will not remove all impurities (water, acids, microscopic abrasive dirt and metal particles). In addition, as filters begin to load up (clog), they become less efficient. The better the job of filtration an oil filter does, the sooner it will need replacement. Therefore, oil filters should be changed whenever the oil is changed.

Engine Oils

Engine oil must provide good lubrication under a large range of engine temperatures and speeds. It must be thin enough to allow the starter to crank the engine and heavy enough to protect the engine under heavy loads and high temperatures. Oil must also carry away heat and keep impurities in suspension until they can be trapped by the oil filter. In addition, oil must seal the gap between the piston

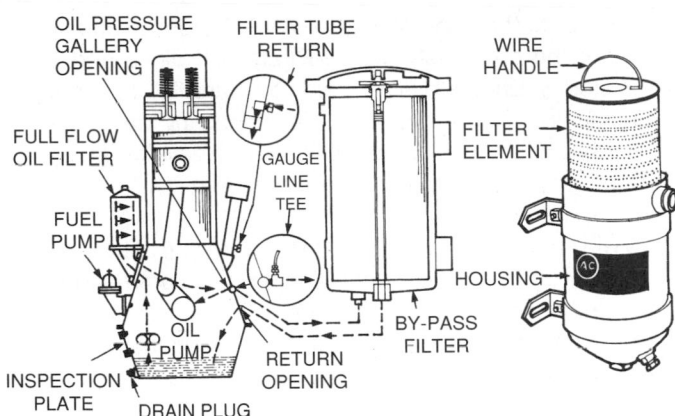

Figure 41-5. A housing-style (canister) bypass oil filtering system. Note that the filter element lifts out of the housing with a wire handle. (AC)

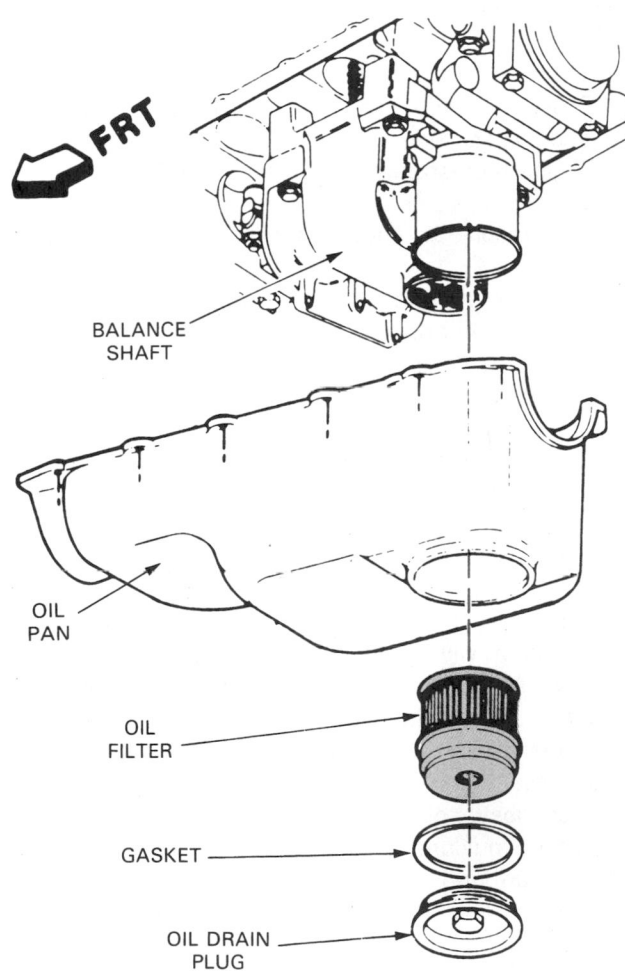

Figure 41-6. In this lubrication system, the oil filter is located in the oil pan. (Buick)

ring and cylinder wall to prevent compression loss. The selection of the proper oil to do all of these jobs is critical. The sections below discuss some of the standards for modern engine oils.

Viscosity

Modern engine oils are classified according to several criteria. The most commonly recognized classification is *viscosity,* or *weight.* Viscosity is an oil's resistance to flow. An oil that flows readily is commonly referred to as thin or light. One that flows slowly is called thick or heavy. Engine oils are graded according to their viscosity by *SAE* (Society of Automotive Engineers) *numbers* ranging typically from 5 (lightest) to 50 (heaviest). Most modern oils are *multi-grade* oils. All vehicle manufacturers recommend multi-grade oils for normal use. Single weight oils should be used only when temperatures will be above freezing.

Multi-grade oils meet the viscosity requirements of two or more SAE grades. Typical multi-grade oils are marked 5W-30, 10W-30, 10W-40, 20W-40, or 20W-50. The W stands for winter, and the number before the W is the viscosity of the oil at low temperatures. The number without a W is the weight at normal engine operating conditions. **Figure 41-7A** shows the SAE weight marking on a typical engine oil. Note that **Figure 41-7B** shows a range of temperatures for particular oil weights. Always consult the owner's manual for more information on the proper oil weight.

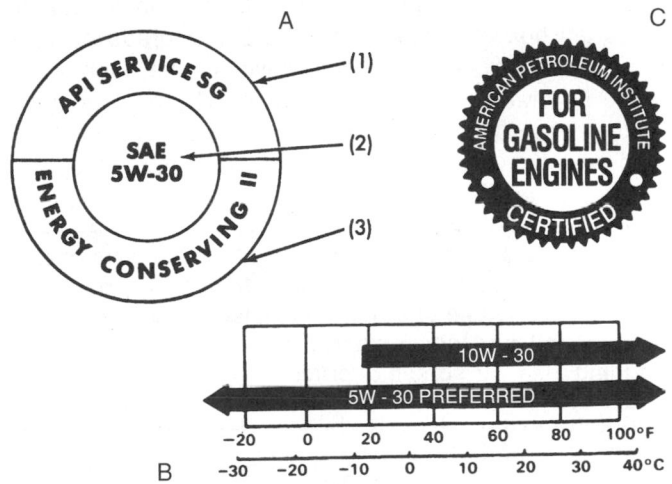

Figure 41-7. A—A typical engine oil container with markings showing viscosity (5W-30) and service classification (SG). B—Oil temperature range chart. C—API "starburst" symbol. This symbol is can be found on both conventional and synthetic oils. (Chrysler, Honda)

While heavier oils give some extra protection to worn bearings and other loose engine parts, lighter oils are better for engines in good condition. Lighter oils actually reduce friction because they can flow more easily. This improves both fuel efficiency and engine life.

Oil Grades

At the present time, there are eight oil *service grades* for automotive gasoline engines. The API (American Petroleum Institute) has classified these oils as SA, SB, SC, SD, SE, SF, SG, and SH. The letter "S" indicates the oil is for use in *spark* ignition (gasoline) engines. **Figure 41-7C** illustrates the API marking found on many oils intended for gasoline engines. This marking signifies that the oil meets the American Petroleum Institute standards for gasoline-fueled engines.

The API has classified oils for use in diesel engines as CA, CB, CC, CD, and CE. The "C" indicates that the oil is for use in **compression ignition** (diesel) engines. The second letter indicates the amount of anti-wear additives, oxidation stabilizers, and detergents. The eight current gasoline engine oil grades are discussed below.

SA and SB oils were the first engine oils to be classified by the API. They are recommended for light loads, moderate speeds, and clean conditions. They generally contain no additives and, therefore, are known as **non-detergent oils**. These oils are still available for use in very old engines. Additionally, they are sometimes called for in gearboxes and for use in two-cycle engines. They should never be used in late-model vehicle engines.

In 1964, **detergent oils** were introduced. Detergent oils have special additives that hold contaminants, such as dirt, water, and acids, in suspension until they can be trapped by the oil filter. The first detergent oil was grade SC, followed over the years by grades SD, SE, SF, SG, and SH. The latest oil designation is SH. This oil can also be used in place of all former oil classifications. Most manufacturers do not bother to put the earlier grade designations on their oil, as these designations have been superseded by grade SH. CE is the latest oil grade for diesel engines and supersedes CA, CB, CC, and CD oils. CD oil is still widely available and can be used in all but the latest diesel engines.

> **Note: If non-detergent oils (SA or SB) have been used in an engine for a long time, it may be inadvisable to switch to a detergent oil. The detergent oil may loosen internal engine deposits, clogging the filter screen or engine oil passages. See Figure 41-8.**

Figure 41-8. A badly clogged oil pickup screen. (Chrysler)

Refer to the chart in **Figure 41-9.** Note the relationship between the previously used API classifications and those in use today. Engine oils may also be classified according to manufacturer's specifications (developed by some engine makers) and to military specifications (developed by the U.S. military for oils to be used by them).

Determining When Oil Should Be Changed

Car and engine manufacturer's recommended oil change intervals range from 2,000 to 7,500 miles (3 200 to 12 000 km), depending on operating conditions. There are so many variables that an exact recommendation would be unwise. Engine type (gasoline, diesel, etc.), engine load, trip length, operating speed, temperature, and dust all effect the useful life of engine oil.

The following conditions can be considered near ideal, and if the engine is operated under them, the oil change interval can be extended to the maximum recommended by the car manufacturer:

- Engine is mechanically sound.
- Engine is operated for reasonably long periods each time it is started.
- Engine temperature is at 180°- 200°F (82.3°-93.3°C) or higher.
- Carburetion or fuel injection system is properly adjusted.
- Intake air is properly filtered (clean, undamaged filter).
- Oil filter is in good condition.
- Crankcase ventilation system is functioning properly.
- Engine speeds kept from moderate to reasonably high.
- Engine is operated under clean environmental conditions.
- Engine is not overloaded, such as when pulling a heavy trailer.

If, however, operating conditions are not ideal, the oil change interval will be shortened. In fact, under the worst conditions, such as dust storms, prolonged idling, constant stops and starts, or operation in cold weather, the change interval can be as little as 500 to 1000 miles (805 to 1600 km).

Since most engines are not operated under either ideal or extreme conditions, it is important to know the general conditions surrounding the use of the engine in question.

A reasonable oil change interval is somewhere between the extremes listed above. At no time should the manufacturer's recommended maximum interval be extended. Also, keep in mind that diesel engine oil change intervals are shorter than the recommended intervals for gasoline engines.

Changing the Oil and Filter

> **Note: Refer to Chapter 1 for important information about disposing of used oil and filters. Do not pour used oil on the ground or into drains.**

REFERENCE CHART

	NEW API ENGINE SERVICE CLASSIFICATIONS	PREVIOUS API ENGINE SERVICE CLASSIFICATIONS	RELATED DESIGNATIONS MILITARY AND INDUSTRY
GASOLINE ENGINES	SA	ML	Straight Mineral Oil
	SB	MM	Inhibited Oil
	SC	MS (1964)	1964 MS Warranty Approved, M2C101-A
	SD	MS (1968)	1968 MS Warranty Approved, M2C101-B, 6041 (Prior to July, 1970)
	SE	None	1972 Warranty Approved, M2C101-C, 6041-M (July 1970)
	SF	None	1980 Warranty Approved
	SG	None	1987 Warranty Approved
	SH	None	1993 Warranty Approved
DIESEL ENGINES	CA	DG	MIL-L-2104A
	CB	DM	Supp. 1
	CC	DM	MIL-L-2104B
	CD	DS	MIL-L-45199B, Series 3
	CE		

Figure 41-9.   API (American Petroleum Institute) service classification chart. (Valvoline)

Change the oil when the engine is at its normal operating temperature. Place an appropriate container under the oil pan to catch the used oil. Remove the drain plug and allow the oil to drain completely from the oil pan. Clean the drain plug and reinstall it. Use a new gasket if the old gasket has been damaged.

To change a spin-on oil filter, use a suitable wrench to remove the old filter. See **Figure 41-10.** Wipe the engine filter base clean, **Figure 41-11A.** Rub a thin film of engine oil (not grease) on the new filter seal ring, **Figure 41-11B.** Run the filter up until the seal ring engages the base, **Figure 41-11C,** and then give it another half turn, **Figure 41-11D.** In tightening, follow the manufacturer's specifications. Do not overtighten the filter. Overtightening may split the gasket, distort the filter, and make removal difficult.

 Note: Some filters must be filled with oil before installation.

On vehicles with cartridge-type filters, remove and discard the old filter element. Clean the filter housing, center bolt, and related parts. Obtain new gaskets. Lightly oil the housing gasket during assembly. Be sure the filter element is the correct length and that it fits the center bolt snugly. A filter that is too long will be crushed. One that is too short

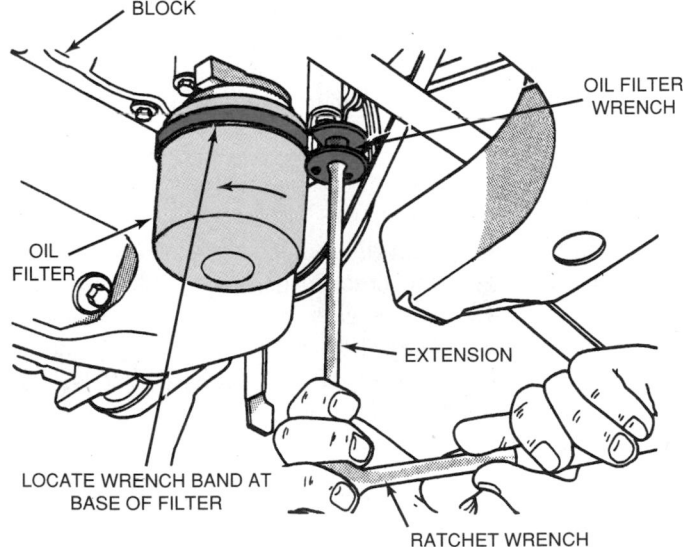

Figure 41-10.   Removing a spin-on oil filter element with a strap wrench. (Chrysler)

will not be secured. Some disposable elements are located inside the oil pan. See **Figure 41-6.**

After changing the filter, fill the crankcase with oil of correct grade and viscosity (as recommended by manufacturer).

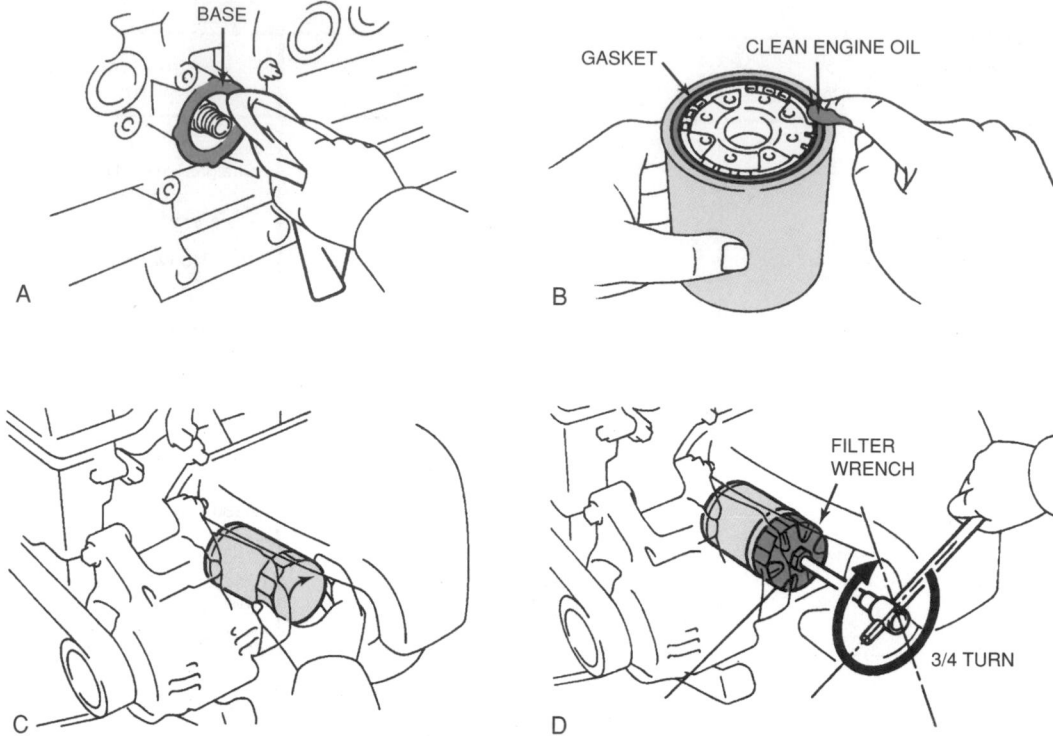

Figure 41-11. Changing a spin-on oil filter. (Toyota)

If the filter was changed, add extra oil. Most new filters require anywhere from one-half quart to one quart of additional oil. Before starting the engine, check the oil level on the dipstick.

Run the engine for a few minutes and then turn it off. Check for leaks around the drain plug and the filter. Recheck the oil level.

> **Caution: Use care while draining the oil, as it may be hot enough to cause painful burns. Avoid skin contact. Prolonged skin contact with oil has been shown to cause skin disorders and possibly skin cancer.**

Check the Oil Cooler

If an engine uses an *oil cooler,* check the lines and fittings for leaks. Replace cracked hoses. Check the cooler for the presence of dirt, leaves, or other debris that may interfere with the cooling action. One type of engine oil cooler is pictured in **Figure 41-12.** The oil cooler is often connected to the lubrication system through an adapter at the oil filter, **Figure 41-13.**

Other Services during Oil and Filter Change

It is important that several other vehicle systems be lubricated or checked for proper operation when the oil is changed. Some of the most common services are listed below. Consult the vehicle service and owner's manuals for other maintenance services.

Lubricate Front Suspension and Steering Linkage

Front end steering and suspension parts should be checked for *grease fittings,* **Figure 41-14.** Typical parts

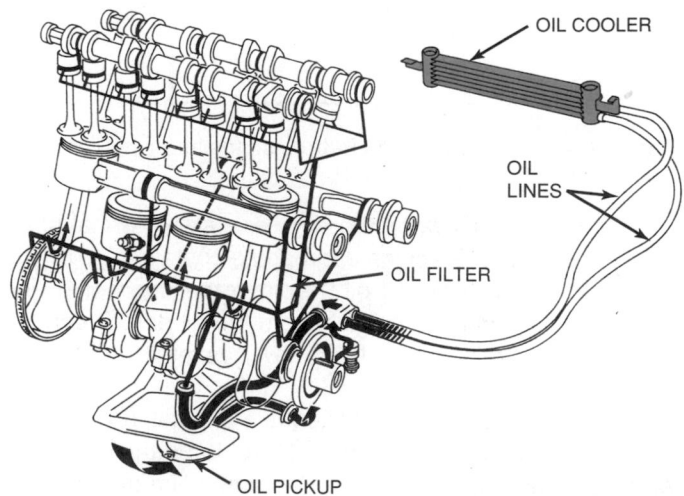

Figure 41-12. Engine oil cooler and lubrication system schematic. (Saab)

with grease fittings are the inner and outer tie rod ends, idler arm, pittman arm, drag (center) link, and ball joints. On some vehicles, the control arm bushings have grease fittings. Many companies publish charts showing the lubrication points for specific vehicles, **Figure 41-15.**

If fittings are present, the parts should be lubricated on a regular basis, usually between 2,000 and 8,000 miles (3218 to 12872 km). Check the manufacturer's specifications for exact lubrication intervals. Some suspension parts have *plugs* instead of fittings. If plugs are installed, the technician must replace them with grease fittings, **Figure 41-16.** After greasing is completed, the plugs can be

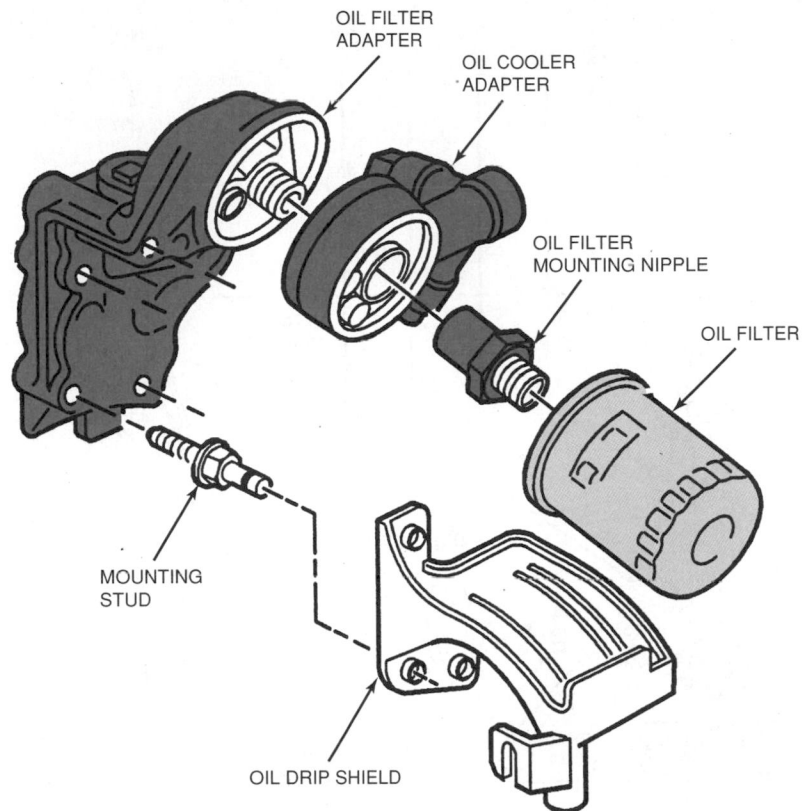

Figure 41-13. Oil cooler adapter location. (GM)

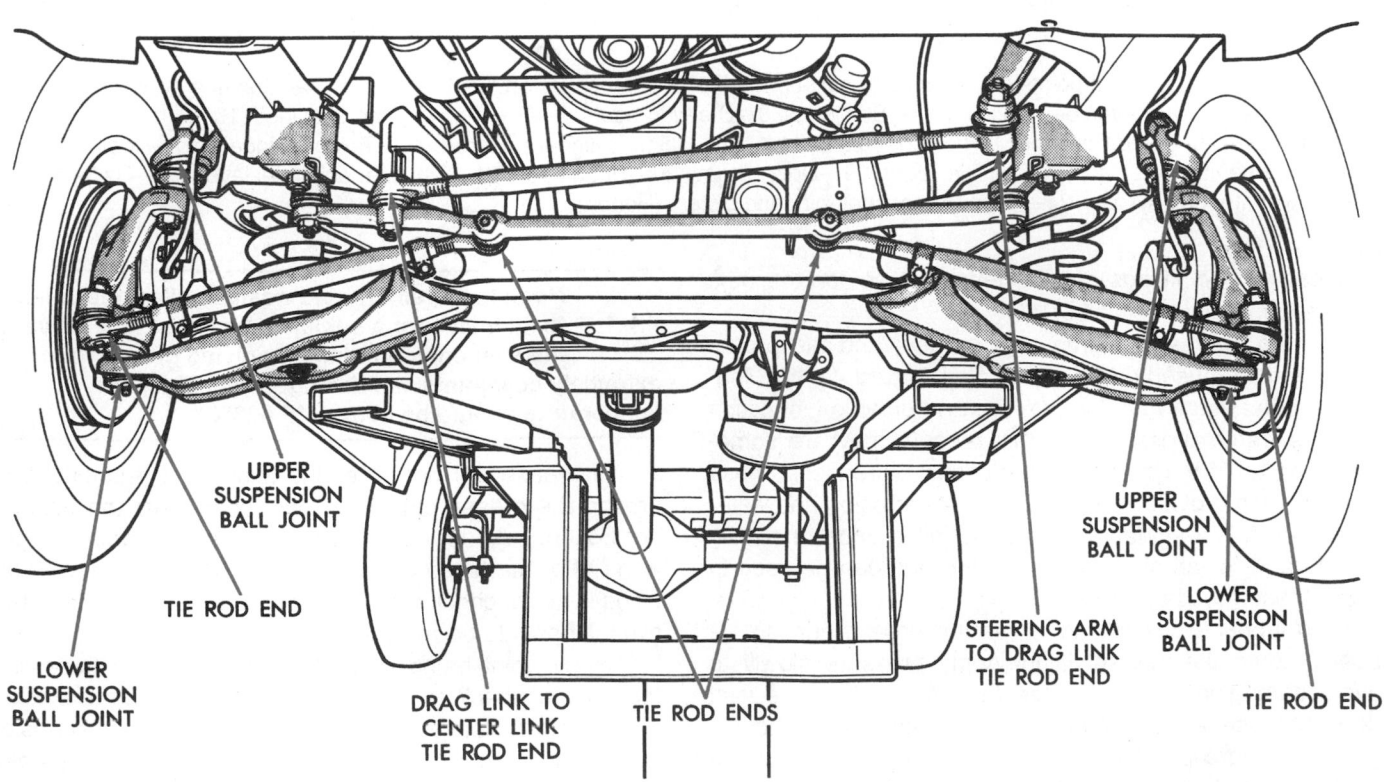

Figure 41-14. Grease fittings on one particular vehicle front suspension and steering assembly. (Dodge)

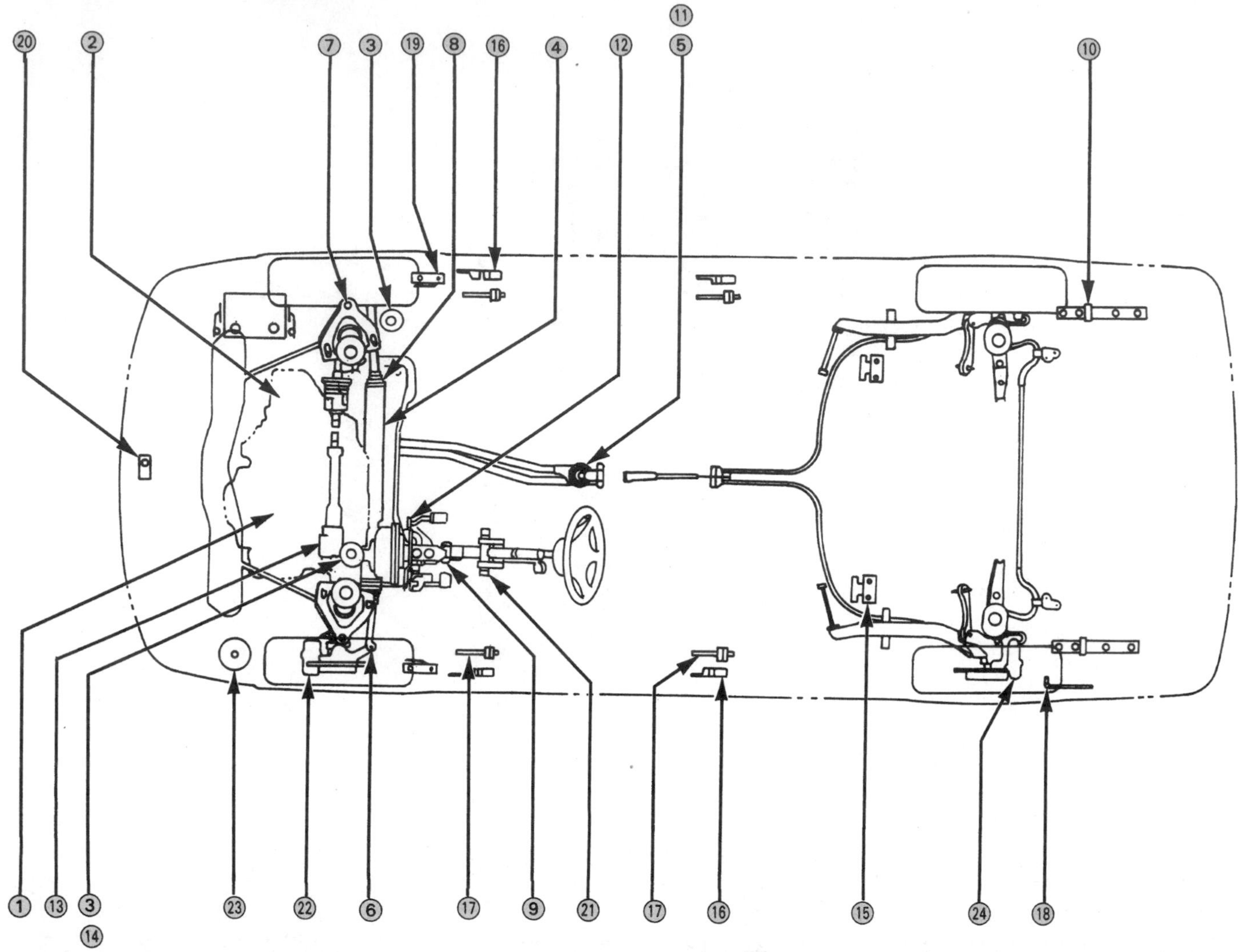

Figure 41-15. Lubrication points on a particular car. 1—Engine. 2—Transmission. 3—Brake parts. 4—Steering gearbox. 5—Transmission shift lever. 6—Ball joints. 7—Ball joints. 8—Steering boots. 9—Steering column bushings. 10—Trunk hinges. 11—Shift lever. 12—Pedal linkage. 13—Intermediate shaft. 14—Master cylinder pushrod. 15—Tailgate hinges. 16—Door hinges. 17—Door opening detents. 18—Fuel filler door. 19—Door hinges. 20—Hood latch. 21—Tilt steering wheel lever. 22—Caliper. 23—Power steering system. 24—Caliper dust seal, pin, and piston. (Honda)

replaced or the fittings can be left in place for the next lubrication.

There are several grades of grease, and the proper type should be used on the fitting. See **Figure 41-17.** Modern greases usually contain *lithium* and provide lubrication under extreme pressure. For this reason, they are sometimes called *EP* (for extreme pressure) greases. These greases also provide protection against corrosion and water entry, which is important to fittings installed under the vehicle. A hand- or an air-operated grease gun can be used to apply these greases.

To lubricate the fittings, press the grease gun nozzle straight onto the grease fitting. Apply pressure slowly to avoid damaging the seals. See **Figure 41-18.** If the joint does not use a *sealed boot,* apply grease until the old grease is forced from the joint. If the joint has as a sealed boot, apply grease until the boot begins to bulge slightly.

Note: In extremely cold weather, allow the vehicle to sit inside for a sufficient length of time to warm the suspension fittings. Applying grease to extremely cold joints can damage them. The joint temperature should be above 0°F (-33°C).

If grease will not enter the joint, or if it squirts from around the grease gun and fitting, check that the fitting is not frozen. In most cases, the fitting has become clogged with dirt or hardened grease and should be replaced. If the fitting is good, check for a damaged or frozen joint. A defective joint should be replaced.

If the joint being greased seems to have excessive movement, check for a worn or loose part. Do not allow the vehicle to leave the shop with an unsafe suspension system. More information on checking and servicing steering and suspension parts is given in Chapters 36, 37, and 39.

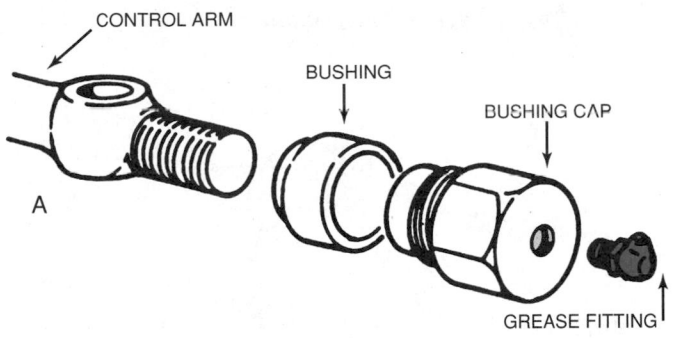

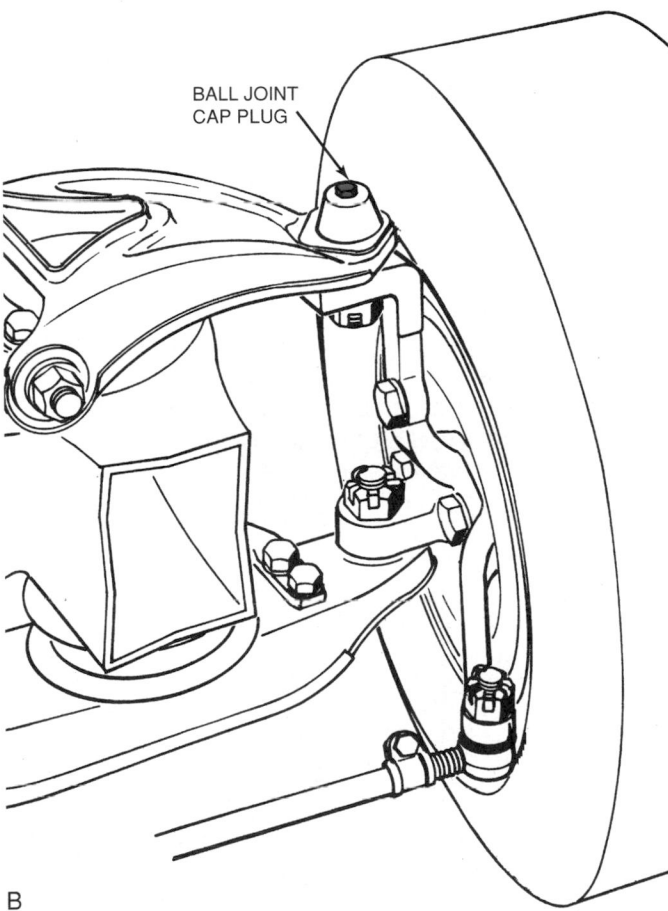

Figure 41-16. A suspension system that incorporates plugs in place of grease fittings. The plugs must be removed and replaced with grease fittings for lubrication. (Moog)

Lubricate Driveline

When servicing rear-wheel drive vehicles, check for grease fittings on the drive shaft U-joints, **Figure 41-19,** and lubricate if necessary. U-joints can use the same EP lithium grease as front end parts. It may be necessary to turn the drive shaft to reach the fittings. U-joints require a very small amount of grease, and excess grease will damage the seals. On front-wheel drive vehicles, check the CV axle boots for damage. See Chapter 33, Axle and Drive Service.

Check Crankcase Ventilation System

It pointless to change the oil and filter if the positive crankcase ventilation (PCV) system is not removing

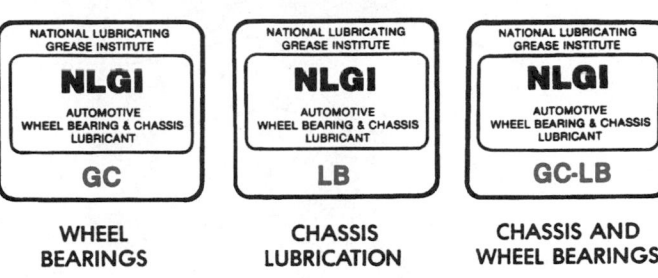

Figure 41-17. National Lubrication Grease Institute (NLGI) symbols. The letter "G" indicates wheel bearing grease. The letter "L" indicates chassis grease. These symbols appear on all approved grease. (Chrysler)

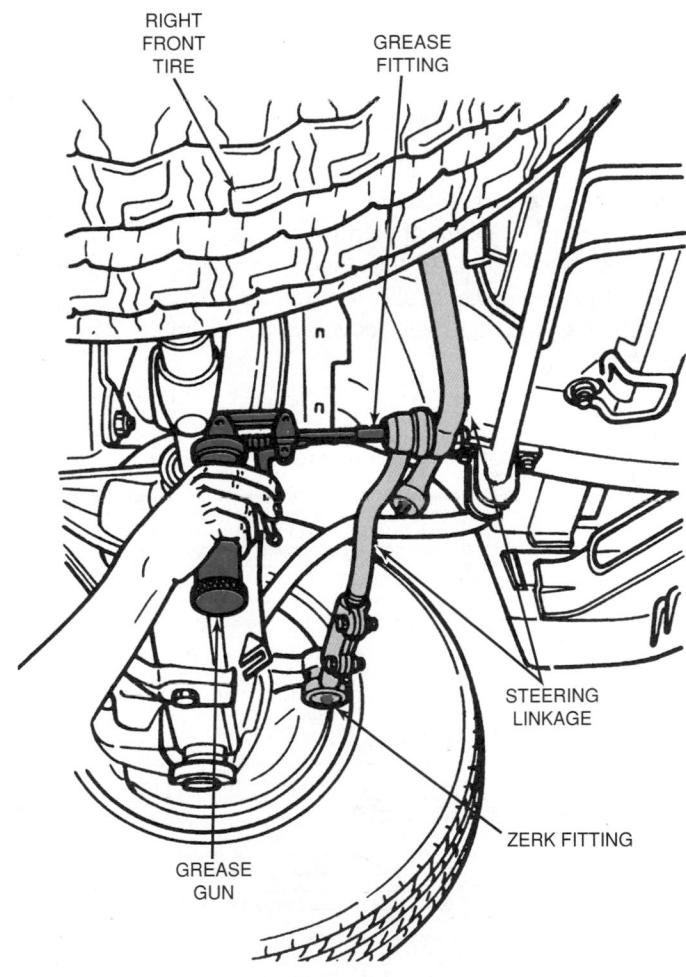

Figure 41-18. Lubricating the steering linkage with a hand-operated grease gun. Always clean the grease fittings before lubricating. This will help prevent dirt from being forced into the fitting and joint. (Ford)

crankcase vapors. An inoperative PCV system will permit a rapid buildup of sludge, water, and acids that will shorten the life of the engine. PCV problems will have a negative effect on mileage and emissions. Always check the valve and hoses at every oil change. For complete details on the construction, operation, and service of the PCV system, refer to Chapter 24, Emission System Service.

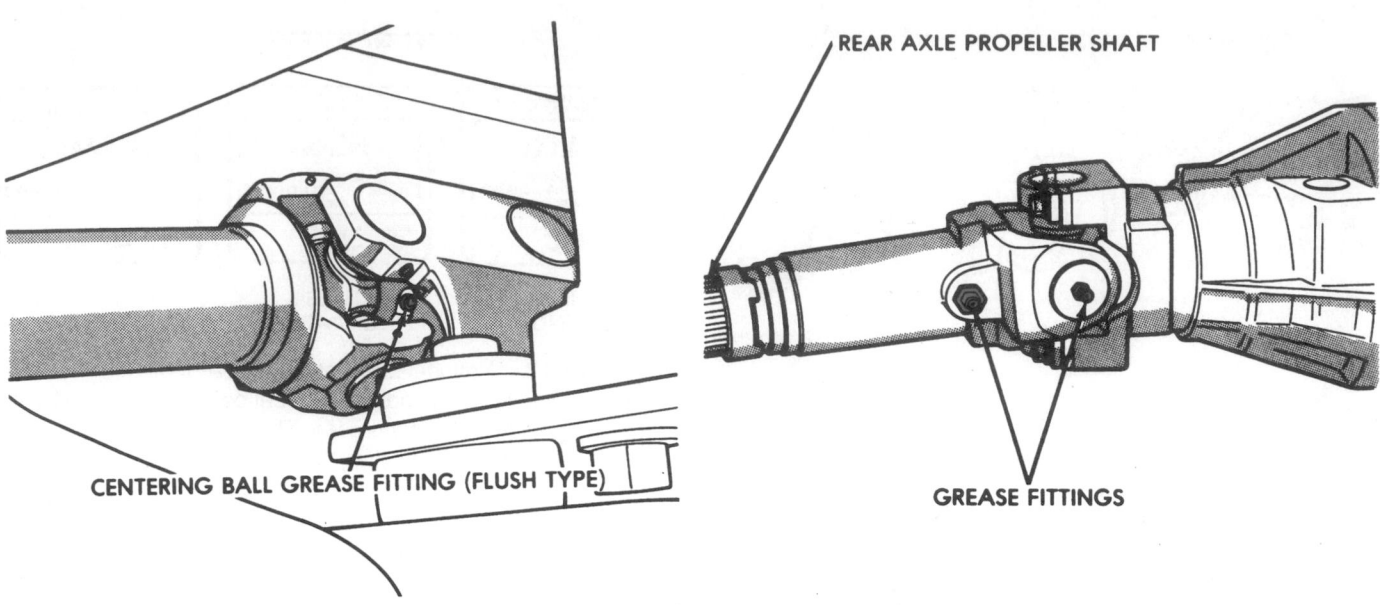

CENTERING BALL GREASE FITTING (FLUSH TYPE)

REAR AXLE PROPELLER SHAFT

GREASE FITTINGS

Figure 41-19. Several driveline joint grease fittings and their locations. (Dodge)

Check Air and Fuel Filters

Air and fuel filters should be checked at regular intervals and changed when they show any sign of restriction. Fuel filters were discussed in Chapter 19, Fuel Delivery. Air cleaner service was covered in Chapter 20, Fuel Injection.

Check Fluid Levels

Whenever the oil is changed, be sure to check the fluid levels in the manual transmission or transaxle, transfer case, and rear axle assembly, if equipped. Refer to Chapters 30, 31, and 33 as necessary. Remember that some front-wheel drive vehicles have a separate differential

MAINTENANCE SCHEDULE B — NORMAL DRIVING CONDITIONS
Ranger/Explorer 2.3L 4-Cylinder, 2.9L, 3.0L and 4.0L 6-Cylinder Engines
B —Required for all vehicles.
b — Required for 49 States vehicles (all States except California); recommended, but not required, for California and Canada vehicles.
(b) — This item not required to be performed. However, Ford recommends that you also perform maintenance on items designated by a "(b)" in order to achieve best vehicle operation.
Failure to perform this recommended maintenance will not invalidate the vehicle emissions warranty or manufacturer recall liability.

MAINTENANCE OPERATION	MILES (Thousands)	7.5	15	22.5	30	37.5	45	52.5	60	67.5	75	82.5	90	97.5	105	112.5	120
NORMAL DRIVING SERVICE INTERVALS — PERFORM AT THE MONTHS OR DISTANCES SHOWN, WHICHEVER OCCURS FIRST.	KILOMETERS (Thousands)	12	24	36	48	60	72	84	96	108	120	132	144	156	168	180	192
EMISSION CONTROL SYSTEMS																	
Change engine oil and oil filter — every 6 months OR		B	B	B	B	B	B	B	B	B	B	B	B	B	B	B	b
Replace spark plugs — standard					B				B				B				b
platinum type (3.0L)									B								b
Replace coolant — every 36 months OR					B				B				B				b
Check cooling system, hoses and clamps (1)							ANNUALLY										
Replace air cleaner filter					B				b				b				b
Check/clean idle speed control air bypass valve (2.3L) (1)									(b)								(b)
Check/clean throttle body (1)									(b)								(b)
Replace PCV valve (3)									b								b
Replace spark plug wires									b								b
Inspect drive belt condition and tension — 2.3L									b								b
OTHER SYSTEMS																	
Check wheel lug nut torque (2)		B	B	B	B	B	B	B	B	B	B	B	B	B	B	B	B
Rotate tires		B		B		B		B		B		B		B		B	
Check clutch reservoir fluid level		B	B	B	B	B	B	B	B	B	B	B	B	B	B	B	B
Inspect and lubricate automatic transmission shift linkage (cable system)		B	B	B	B	B	B	B	B	B	B	B	B	B	B	B	B
Inspect and lubricate front wheel bearings					B				B				B				B
Inspect disc brake system and lubricate caliper pins			B		B		B		B		B		B		B		B
Inspect drum brake linings, lines and hoses			B		B		B		B		B		B		B		B
Inspect exhaust system for leaks, damage or loose parts					B				B				B				B
Inspect and remove any foreign material trapped by exhaust system shielding		B	B	B	B	B	B	B	B	B	B	B	B	B	B	B	B
Lubricate driveshaft U-joints if equipped with grease fitting		B	B	B	B	B	B	B	B	B	B	B	B	B	B	B	B
Inspect parking brake system for damage and operation			B		B		B		B		B		B		B		B
Lubricate throttle/kickdown lever ball stud					B				B				B				B
Lubricate rear driveshaft double cardan joint centering ball (Ranger SWB 4×4)		B	B	B	B	B	B	B	B	B	B	B	B	B	B	B	B
Lubricate front drive axle R.H. axle shaft slip yoke (4×4)					B				B				B				B
Inspect spindle needle bearing spindle thrust bearing lubrication (4×4)					B				B				B				B
Inspect hub lock lubrication (4×4)					B				B				B				B
Change transfer case fluid (4×4)									B								B
Lubricate steering linkage joints if equipped with grease fittings		B	B	B	B	B	B	B	B	B	B	B	B	B	B	B	B

(1) Check means a function measurement of system's operation (performance, leaks or conditions of parts). Correct as required.
(2) Wheel lug nuts must be retightened to proper torque specifications at 500 miles/800 km of new vehicle operation. See your Owner Guide for proper torque specifications. Also retighten to proper torque specification at 500 miles/800 km after (1) any wheel change or (2) any other time the wheel lug nuts have been loosened.
(3) At 60,000 miles/96 000 km, your dealer will replace the PCV valve at no cost on 2.3L, 2.9L, 3.0L and 4.0L engines except California and Canada vehicles.
Note: Change rear axle lubricant at 100,000 miles (160 000 km) or if the rear axle has been submerged in water. Otherwise, the rear axle lubricant should not be checked or changed unless a leak is suspected or repair is required.

Figure 41-20. A maintenance schedule for one particular vehicle. This schedule is to be followed when the vehicle is operated under *normal* driving conditions. (Ford)

Maintenance Task	Chapter
Check cooling system	22
Check exhaust system condition	23
Check emission control device operation	24
Check battery charge and electrolyte level	26
Check clutch adjustment	29
Change automatic transmission fluid	32
Check brake operation and brake fluid level. Inspect brake system for leaks	34
Repack wheel bearings	10,38
Check tire pressure and condition	38
Check air conditioner/heater operation	40

Figure 41-21.   Some common maintenance tasks and the chapters in which they are discussed.

assembly. Check the fluid level in the automatic transmission as covered in Chapter 32, Automatic Transmission and Transaxle service.

Also check the fluid levels in the coolant recovery tank, power steering reservoir, windshield washer, and brake master cylinder. Refill as needed and, except for the windshield washer fluid, determine the reason for the low level.

Lubricate Parking Brake Cable

In many cases, the parking brake is never used. Instead, the vehicle driver uses the transmission park position to hold the vehicle in place. The brake cable often rusts and becomes sticky in its sheath. When the parking brake finally is used, it often sticks in the *on* position, preventing vehicle movement or severely damaging the brakes.

The parking brake cable should be cleaned and lubricated whenever the oil and filter are changed. Use a combination of lubricant and penetrating oil on the cable sheath under the vehicle and a small amount of engine oil on the cable where it extends out of its sheath under the dashboard. Operate the parking brake a few times to distribute the lubricant.

Lubricate Body Hinge Pivots and Lock Mechanisms

The body hinge points include the door and hood hinges. These points are subject to wear and rust and should be lightly lubricated with oil or white grease whenever the oil and filter are changed. The door locking mechanisms and the hood lock cables should also be lightly lubricated.

 Caution: Do not use chassis grease on the door lock mechanisms, as this type of grease will stain clothing if the door lock is accidentally contacted by a person entering the vehicle.

Door or trunk locks can be lubricated with dry graphite. Do not use oil on the lock cylinder, since oil will clog the cylinder mechanism.

Other Maintenance Procedures

Many other preventive maintenance procedures should be performed as needed. These tasks will vary, depending on the manufacturer's time and mileage recommendations and the condition of the system being serviced, **Figure 41-20. Figure 41-21** identifies some common maintenance tasks and the chapters in which they are discussed.

Tech Talk

It is almost impossible to overemphasize the importance of proper vehicle maintenance. However, some technicians develop pet maintenance procedures and services which may not really accomplish anything. While these pet procedures will not cause harm, they may lead the technician to forget about other necessary maintenance procedures. There is the story of the technician who put the vehicle on the lift, drained the oil, and got so interested in cleaning out the body drain holes that he forgot to put the oil drain plug back in.

The only way to avoid this sort of problem is to develop a set maintenance routine, beginning with consulting the factory service manual for the exact maintenance procedures needed. Then follow the procedures exactly. Obviously, the engine oil will be changed, and other fluid levels checked. The other procedures should be performed in order so that nothing is overlooked.

This does not mean that you ignore other, obvious maintenance needs. What it means is that you must always perform the required factory service procedures as a bare minimum. After these procedures are performed, you can investigate the need for other vehicle maintenance services.

Summary

The correct grade and viscosity of engine oil must be supplied in ample quantities to all moving engine surfaces. Oil filtration systems can be full flow or partial flow types.

Filter elements are of the surface type or the depth type. Filters should be changed before they become clogged. Replacement intervals vary with engine wear, vehicle use, and driving conditions.

Use the recommended oil for all late-model engines. It will provide the type of lubrication needed by the modern engine, which is highly stressed and operates at high temperatures. The use of quality oil of the correct viscosity and changing it at regular intervals is a must.

Replacement filters must be the correct size and type. Spin-on filters must be replaced at recommended intervals. After removing the old filter, clean the filter mounting base. If necessary, check the mounting nipple tightness. Apply clean oil to the new filter seal, fill the filter with oil (if recommended), and install the filter. Tighten the filter to the manufacturer's specifications. Fill the crankcase with the correct type and amount of oil. Start the engine and check for oil leakage.

At each oil change, PCV system operation should be checked. An inoperative PCV system can cause sludging, rapid wear, poor mileage, and stalling. Lubricate the front-end components if specified. Check fluid levels and grease the driveline, parking brake cable, and body hinges where indicated. Other maintenance procedures are given in other chapters of this book.

Know These Terms

Full-flow oil filter	Spark ignition
Bypass valve	Compression ignition
Surface filter	Non-detergent oil
Depth-type filter	Detergent oil
Filter element	Oil cooler
Spin-on filter	Grease fitting
Viscosity	Plug
Weight	Lithium grease
SAE numbers	EP grease
Multi-grade	Sealed boot
Service grade	

Review Questions—Chapter 41

Do not write in this book. Write your answers on a separate sheet of paper.

1. Oil viscosity refers to the oil's _____.
   (A) color
   (B) flow rate, or resistance to flow
   (C) quality
   (D) number of additives
2. When discussing oil classification, what does the letters S and C denote?
3. A spin-on filter should be tightened about _____ turn(s) after contacting the base.
   (A) 2
   (B) 1 1/2 to 1 3/4
   (C) 1/2 to 3/4
   (D) 3
4. A new filter usually requires about _____ additional quart(s) of oil.
   (A) 1
   (B) 2
   (C) 3
   (D) 5

5. Drain the oil when the engine is _____.
6. Name five steering and suspension parts that can be equipped with grease fittings.
7. Name 8 vehicle units that require a fluid level check during an oil change.
8. Parking brakes usually stick in the _____ position.
9. Door hinges should be lubricated with what type of lubricant?
10. What type of lubricant should be used on lock cylinders?

ASE-Type Questions

1. The most commonly used type of oil filtration system is the _____.
   (A) shunt
   (B) bypass
   (C) splash
   (D) full-flow
2. When the filter in a full-flow system clogs up, the oil _____.
   (A) cannot reach the bearings
   (B) is shunted into the pan
   (C) is bypassed directly to the bearings
   (D) forces a hole through the filter element
3. Technician A says that most modern oil filters are the spin-on type. Technician B says that a depth filter stops all the dirt on the surface of the element. Who is right?
   (A) A only.
   (B) B only.
   (C) Both A & B.
   (D) Neither A nor B.
4. All of the following statements about API service grades for engine oil are true, EXCEPT:
   (A) there are now eight oil grades for gasoline engines.
   (B) the "C" in the service grade means that the oil can be used in a diesel engine.
   (C) SH oil can be used to replace non-detergent (SA or SB) oil.
   (D) SH oil is a detergent oil.
5. An inoperative PCV system will _____.
   (A) permit a rapid buildup of sludge in the engine
   (B) cause emissions and mileage problems
   (C) shorten engine life
   (D) All of the above.
6. All of the following statements about front-end lubrication are true, EXCEPT:
   (A) some suspension parts have plugs instead of grease fittings.
   (B) pressure should be applied slowly to avoid damaging seals.
   (C) if plugs are installed, the part cannot be greased.
   (D) if the joint has as a sealed boot, grease until the boot begins to bulge slightly.
7. Technician A says that all fluid should be checked during an oil change. Technician B says that if the vehicle records show that it is normally brought in for service, only the most vital fluids need to be checked. Who is right?

(A) A only.
(B) B only.
(C) Both A & B.
(D) Neither A nor B.

8. Technician A says that grease should be added to the universal joints until it seeps out of the seals. Technician B says that universal joints can use the same grease as other suspension parts. Who is right?
   (A) A only.
   (B) B only.
   (C) Both A & B.
   (D) Neither A nor B.

9. Technician A says that the parking brake cables should be lubricated with a combination or lubricant and penetrating oil. Technician B says that the parking brake should be actuated a few times after lubrication. Who is right?
   (A) A only.
   (B) B only.
   (C) Both A & B.
   (D) Neither A nor B.

10. All of the following can be used to lubricate door hinges EXCEPT:
    (A) white lithium grease.
    (B) lightweight oil.
    (C) wheel bearing grease.
    (D) dry graphite.

Suggested Activities

1. Write a short report listing the consequences of poor or no maintenance on a modern car or truck.

2. Check the fluid levels in a vehicle's engine, cooling system, transmission, brake master cylinder, power steering reservoir, windshield washer reservoir, and rear differential (if applicable).

3. Perform preventive maintenance on a vehicle which includes changing the engine oil and filter, greasing the suspension, and checking fluid levels in the radiator, transmission, master cylinder, and power steering reservoir. Also check the air filter, tire pressure, exterior lights, and other vehicle systems.

This technician is using a computerized information and diagnostic system to diagnose a driveability problem. Always follow the vehicle manufacturer's recommendations when diagnosing problems. (Ford)

42

Problem Diagnosis Charts

After studying this chapter, you will be able to:
- Read a troubleshooting chart.
- Use a troubleshooting chart to compare a problem with its probable cause and correction.

This chapter will allow you to look up the causes and corrections of various vehicle problems. These problems are grouped by major vehicle systems and have been discussed in the chapters which address the service of each system.

Troubleshooting charts are a quick and thorough method of determining all of the possible causes of a prob-

lem. They are a reference source of troubleshooting information. Studying this chapter will allow you to become familiar with the layout and uses of troubleshooting charts. The troubleshooting charts in this chapter are general. Always consult a service manual for the exact troubleshooting charts for each vehicle.

 Note: Engine mechanical diagnosis and troubleshooting charts are contained in Chapter 11.

Cooling System Problem Diagnosis

Problem: Overheating

Possible cause	Correction
1. Coolant level low.	1. Add coolant and check for leaks.
2. Drive belt loose.	2. Adjust belt tension.
3. Drive belt broken.	3. Replace belt.
4. Drive belt glazed or oil-soaked.	4. Replace belt.
5. Thermostat stuck closed.	5. Replace thermostat.
6. Radiator pressure cap inoperative.	6. Replace pressure cap.
7. Bugs, leaves, other debris on radiator core.	7. Flush with water from back to front.
8. Rust scale clogging radiator.	8. Flush radiator and install rust inhibitor.
9. Rust scale clogging in block.	9. Flush cooling system and install rust inhibitor.
10. Valve timing off.	10. Reset valve timing.
11. Air leaks into system.	11. Pressure test and repair leaks.
12. Coolant hoses clogged.	12. Replace hoses.
13. Coolant hose collapsed.	13. Replace hose.
14. Low antifreeze boiling point.	14. Change antifreeze or thermostat.
15. Late ignition timing.	15. Adjust timing.
16. Leaking cylinder head gasket.	16. Replace gasket. Check block and head surfaces.
17. Water pump impeller slipping or broken.	17. Replace water pump.
18. Brakes dragging.	18. Adjust brakes.
19. Vehicle overloaded.	19. Advise driver.
20. Manifold heat valve stuck or broken.	20. Loosen or repair.
21. Fan speed slow—improper pulley size.	21. Install larger diameter pulley.
22. Low engine oil level.	22. Add oil to full mark.
23. Frozen coolant.	23. Thaw and add antifreeze.
24. Exhaust system back pressure.	24. Change muffler or open up dented pipe.
25. Lean carburetor mixture.	25. Clean carburetor. Install proper size jets.
26. Wrong cylinder head gasket.	26. Install correct head gasket.
27. Ignition timing retarded.	27. Advance ignition timing.
28. Defective electric fan motor.	28. Replace fan motor.
29. Defective spark delay valve.	29. Replace valve.
30. Core sand in head or block.	30. Clean or replace.
31. Inoperative fan fluid coupling (fan clutch).	31. Replace fan clutch.
32. Aftermarket (add-on) air conditioner on vehicle equipped with a standard cooling system.	32. Install heavy duty cooling system parts.

33. Defective electric fan ambient temperature switch.
34. Clogged catalytic converter(s).
35. Lean fuel mixture.

33. Replace fan switch.
34. Replace catalytic converter(s).
35. Adjust fuel mixture.

Problem: Overcooling and/or slow warmup

Possible cause
1. Thermostat stuck open.
2. Weather extremely cold.
3. No thermostat.
4. Low temperature thermostat.

Correction
1. Replace thermostat.
2. Cover a portion of the radiator.
3. Install a thermostat.
4. Install a high temperature thermostat.

Problem: Apparent overheating or overcooling

Possible cause
1. Faulty temperature sender.
2. Faulty temperature gauge.
3. Faulty gauge wiring.
4. Complete unit faulty (bulb type).
5. Improper fan size, type, or speed.

Correction
1. Replace gauge sender.
2. Replace gauge.
3. Check and repair any breaks or loose connections.
4. Replace entire unit—gauge, tubing, and bulb.
5. Replace with correct unit.

Problem: Belt squeal upon acceleration

Possible cause
1. Belt loose.
2. Belt glazed.
3. Excessive friction in belt-driven accessory.

Correction
1. Adjust belt tension.
2. Replace belt.
3. Repair defective unit.

Problem: Belt squeal at idle

Possible cause
1. Belt loose.
2. Pulleys misaligned.
3. Uneven pulley groove.
4. Foreign material on belt.
5. Belt width not uniform.
6. Belt tensioner loose or broken.

Correction
1. Adjust belt tension.
2. Align all pulleys.
3. Replace pulley.
4. Clean or replace belt.
5. Replace belt.
6. Tighten or replace.

Problem: Belt jumps from pulley or rolls over in pulley groove

Possible cause
1. Belt loose.
2. Pulleys misaligned.
3. Broken cords (internal).
4. Mismatched belts.
5. Eccentric pulley.
6. Loose pulley.

Correction
1. Adjust belt tension.
2. Align all pulleys.
3. Replace belt.
4. Install matched set of belts.
5. Replace.
6. Tighten or replace.

Problem: Noisy water pump

Possible cause
1. Bearing worn and rough.
2. Seal noisy.
3. Loose impeller.

Correction
1. Repair or replace pump.
2. Add inhibitor-water pump lube mixture to system.
3. Rebuild or replace pump.

Problem: Buzzing radiator cap

Possible cause
1. Coolant boiling.

Correction
1. Shut engine off and correct cause of overheating.

Problem: Coolant loss

Possible cause
1. Leaking radiator.
2. Leaking hose.
3. Cracked hose.
4. Overheating.
5. Overfilling.
6. Air leak at bottom hose.

Correction
1. Repair leak or replace radiator.
2. Tighten clamp or replace hose.
3. Replace hose.
4. Correct cause.
5. Fill to correct level.
6. Tighten clamps or replace hose.

7. Blown head gasket.
8. Water pump seal leaking.
9. Heater core leaking.
10. Cracked block or head.
11. Radiator pressure cap inoperative.
12. Leaking block freeze plugs.
13. Improper cylinder head tightening.
14. Leak at temperature sender.
15. Leaking surge tank.
16. Leak at fasteners that enter water jacket.
17. Cracked water jacket or thermostat housing.
18. Damaged coolant recovery bottle.
19. Leaking petcock.

7. Replace gasket and check mating surfaces.
8. Replace seal or entire pump.
9. Replace heater core.
10. Repair or replace.
11. Replace radiator cap.
12. Replace freeze plugs.
13. Torque as recommended.
14. Tighten or replace sender.
15. Repair leak or replace tank.
16. Remove fasteners, cement, and reinstall.
17. Repair or replace.
18. Replace recovery bottle.
19. Tighten or replace petcock .

Fuel System Problem Diagnosis

Problem: No fuel delivery

Possible cause
1. No fuel.
2. Tank vents clogged.
3. Tank filter clogged.
4. Fuel lines kinked or clogged.
5. Vapor lock.

6. Fuel pump inoperative.
7. Fuel filter or filters clogged.
8. Frozen fuel line.
9. Air leak between fuel pump and tank.
10. Carburetor float valve stuck shut.
11. Clogged injectors.
12. Inoperative injection pump (diesel).

Correction
1. Add fuel to the tank.
2. Open fuel tank vents.
3. Replace tank filter.
4. Straighten or clean fuel lines.
5. Cool fuel lines. Change to less volatile gas. Protect fuel lines from heat.
6. Rebuild or replace pump.
7. Clean or replace filters.
8. Thaw and remove water from the fuel system.
9. Repair air leak.
10. Loosen and clean float valve.
11. Clean or replace injectors, locate source of deposits.
12. Repair or replace pump.

Problem: Insufficient fuel delivery

Possible cause
1. Tank vent partially clogged.
2. Tank filter partially clogged.
3. Gas lines kinked or clogged.
4. Vapor lock.

5. Air leak between fuel pump and tank.
6. Fuel filter partially clogged.
7. Fuel pump check valves worn.
8. Stretched, cracked, or perforated fuel pump diaphragm.
9. Fuel pump-to-block gasket too thick.
10. Weak fuel pump spring.
11. Wrong pump.
12. Worn pump linkage.
13. Worn pump link actuating cam or eccentric.
14. Fuel pump loose.
15. Fuel pump body screws loose.
16. Clogged injection pipes.
17. Defective injectors.
18. Faulty injection pump (diesel).
19. Fuel injection pulse width incorrect.
20. Mass airflow sensor malfunction.
21. Defective oxygen sensor.

Correction
1. Open tank vent.
2. Replace tank filter.
3. Straighten or clean fuel lines.
4. Cool fuel lines. Change to less volatile gas. Protect fuel lines from heat.
5. Repair air leak.
6. Clean or replace filter.
7. Install new pump.
8. Install new pump.
9. Reduce gasket thickness.
10. Install new pump.
11. Install correct pump.
12. Install new pump.
13. Replace cam or eccentric.
14. Tighten pump fasteners.
15. Tighten pump body screws.
16. Clean or replace pipes.
17. Clean or replace injectors.
18. Rebuild or replace pump.
19. Check control module and sensors. Replace as needed.
20. Replace mass airflow sensor.
21. Replace oxygen sensor.

Problem: Excessive fuel delivery or pressure

Possible cause
1. Fuel pump diaphragm over-tensioned.
2. Fuel pump diaphragm spring too strong.
3. Seized pump link (no free play).
4. Incorrect pump.
5. Fuel injection pulse width excessive.
6. Fuel injection pressure regulator malfunctioning.
7. Engine control module defective.

Correction
1. Loosen body screws; adjust diaphragm and tighten screws.
2. Install proper spring.
3. Free pump link.
4. Replace pump.
5. Check control module and sensors. Replace as needed.
6. Adjust or replace pressure regulator.
7. Replace control module.

8. Mass airflow sensor malfunction.
9. Defective oxygen sensor.

8. Replace mass airflow sensor.
9. Replace oxygen sensor.

Problem: Carburetor flooding

Possible cause
1. Defective inlet needle valve.
2. Float level too high.
3. Dirty inlet needle valve.
4. Excessive fuel pressure.
5. Float sunk.
6. Float binding.
7. Heavy fuel flow pulsations.
8. Internal circuit leakage.

Correction
1. Replace inlet needle valve and seat.
2. Adjust float level.
3. Clean needle valve, fuel lines, and filters.
4. Reduce pressure.
5. Reset float level or replace float.
6. Align float.
7. Install or replace pulsation damper.
8. Repair or replace carburetor.

Problem: Improper choke operation

Possible cause
1. Choke thermostatic spring tension adjusted wrong.
2. Choke vacuum break inoperative or improperly adjusted.
3. Choke stove tube clogged.
4. Choke unloader adjustment incorrect.
5. Choke plate shaft or linkage binding.
6. Engine warmup too slow.
7. Clogged exhaust crossover passage.
8. Choke clean air tube clogged.
9. Choke vacuum piston inoperative.
10. Owner fails to depress accelerator to allow choke plate to close.
11. Air cleaner or cleaner gasket binds choke plate to close.
12. Faulty thermostatic spring.
13. Choke assembled improperly.
14. Defective cold start valve.
15. Loose choke linkage.

Correction
1. Adjust spring tension.
2. Adjust or replace vacuum break.
3. Clean stove tube.
4. Correct unloader adjustment.
5. Clean and align linkage.
6. Check cooling system.
7. Clean crossover passage.
8. Clean tube.
9. Clean and open line.
10. Advise driver.
11. Install cleaner and gasket correctly.
12. Replace thermostatic spring.
13. Assemble choke correctly.
14. Replace cold start valve.
15. Adjust and secure linkage.

Problem: Stalling and/or rough idling

Possible cause
1. Idle speed too slow.
2. Fast idle speed too slow.
3. Throttle return dashpot inoperative.
4. Throttle dashpot improperly adjusted.
5. Fuel level in bowl too high.
6. Fuel level in bowl too low.
7. Idle mixture screw or screws improperly adjusted.
8. Idle system clogged.
9. Choke set too rich.
10. Choke set too lean.
11. Carburetor flooding.
12. Clogged air cleaner.
13. Vacuum leak.
14. Ruptured vacuum power jet diaphragm.
15. Idle mixture needles grooved.
16. Carburetor icing.
17. PCV system clogged.
18. Hot idle compensator (air valve) inoperative.
19. Bowl vent clogged.
20. Idle air bleeds clogged.
21. Choke valve binding.
22. Choke linkage sticking.
23. Defective choke coil.
24. Vacuum diaphragm for choke opening incorrectly adjusted.
25. Defective float needle valve.
26. Exhaust heat valve stuck open.
27. Incorrect distributor vacuum advance.
28. Inoperative canister purge valve.
29. Restricted air cleaner and/or exhaust.
30. Secondary throttle sticking open.
31. Fast idle solenoid inoperative.
32. Defective glow plug system (diesel).

Correction
1. Increase idle speed.
2. Increase fast idle speed.
3. Replace dashpot.
4. Adjust dashpot correctly.
5. Lower fuel level.
6. Raise fuel level.
7. Adjust mixture screws.
8. Clean carburetor.
9. Lean choke setting.
10. Enrich choke setting.
11. See *Carburetor flooding*.
12. Clean or replace air cleaner.
13. Repair leak.
14. Replace power jet diaphragm.
15. Replace needles (screws).
16. Warm engine and carburetor and take corrective action.
17. Clean PCV system.
18. Replace air valve.
19. Open vent.
20. Clean carburetor.
21. Repair choke valve.
22. Free linkage.
23. Replace choke coil.
24. Adjust to manufacturers specifications.
25. Replace needle valve.
26. Free heat valve or replace.
27. Adjust to specifications.
28. Replace valve or canister.
29. Repair restriction or replace restricted part.
30. Free throttle.
31. Replace solenoid.
32. Repair glow plug system.

33. Injection pump timing off (diesel).	33. Correct timing.
34. Air in injection lines (diesel).	34. Bleed off air.
35. Low compression.	35. Determine reason and repair.
36. Faulty injection pump (diesel).	36. Repair or replace pump.
37. Malfunctioning injection nozzles.	37. Repair or replace nozzles.
38. Contaminated fuel.	38. Flush system. Add fresh, clean fuel.
39. EGR vacuum hoses misrouted.	39. Correct as required.
40. Defective EGR valve.	40. Replace EGR valve.

--------------------- Problem: Idle speed varies ---------------------

Possible cause

1. Defective or improperly adjusted throttle return dashpot.
2. Loose or defective power valve.
3. Throttle linkage dirty.
4. Throttle return spring weak.
5. Accelerator pedal sticking.
6. PCV valve sticking.
7. Fuel inlet valve sticking.
8. Loose or inoperative spark control valve.
9. Fast idle cam sticking.
10. Defective air cleaner vacuum motor.
11. Dirty or malfunctioning fuel injectors.
12. Injector control malfunction.

Correction

1. Replace or adjust dashpot.
2. Tighten or replace power valve.
3. Clean linkage.
4. Replace with stronger spring.
5. Clean and lubricate accelerator cable and/or linkage.
6. Replace PCV valve.
7. Clean or replace valve.
8. Tighten or replace spark control valve.
9. Free cam linkage.
10. Replace motor.
11. Clean or replace fuel injectors.
12. Replace injector control or control module.

--------------------- Problem: Poor acceleration ---------------------

Possible cause

1. Accelerator pump linkage disconnected.
2. Accelerator pump linkage improperly adjusted.
3. Accelerator pump diaphragm ruptured.
4. Accelerator pump piston worn or cracked.
5. Accelerator pump check valve dirty or defective.
6. Accelerator jets clogged.
7. Fuel level in bowl too low.
8. Accelerator pump follow through spring too weak.
9. Exhaust manifold heat control valve stuck.
10. Power valve inoperative.
11. Low fuel pump pressure.
12. Main fuel passage clogged.
13. Air leaks.
14. Defective secondary diaphragm.
15. Secondary throttle plates stuck.
16. Clogged air cleaner.
17. Faulty fuel injectors.
18. Engine control module defective.
19. Plugged catalytic converter.
20. Clogged muffler.
21. Bent tail pipe.
22. Clogged fuel filters.
23. Defective injection pump (diesel).
24. Defective injection nozzles (diesel).

Correction

1. Connect linkage.
2. Adjust correctly.
3. Replace diaphragm.
4. Replace piston.
5. Clean or replace check valve.
6. Clean jets.
7. Raise fuel level.
8. Replace spring.
9. Free heat control valve.
10. Clean or replace power valve.
11. Replace fuel pump.
12. Clean carburetor.
13. Repair air leaks.
14. Replace diaphragm.
15. Free throttle plates.
16. Clean or replace air filter.
17. Clean or replace fuel injectors.
18. Replace control module.
19. Replace catalytic converter.
20. Replace muffler.
21. Replace tail pipe.
22. Clean or replace filters.
23. Rebuild or replace pump.
24. Replace nozzles.

--------------------- Problem: Lean mixture at cruising speeds ---------------------

Possible cause

1. Low float setting.
2. Low fuel volume or pressure.
3. Bowl vent clogged.
4. Main discharge jet too small.
5. Metering rod or valve inoperative.
6. Air leaks.
7. Exhaust heat control stuck.
8. Vacuum passage to distributor clogged.
9. Defective spark control valve.
10. Main discharge jet clogged.
11. Incorrect carburetor jet size.
12. Defective injection pump (diesel).
13. Fuel injection system control malfunction.
14. Dirty or defective injector nozzles (diesel).

Correction

1. Raise float setting.
2. See insufficient fuel delivery.
3. Clean bowl vent.
4. Install proper jet.
5. Repair metering rod or valve.
6. Repair air leaks.
7. Free control valve.
8. Clean carburetor.
9. Replace spark control valve.
10. Clean carburetor.
11. Replace jets with correct size.
12. Repair or replace pump.
13. Adjust, repair, or replace.
14. Clean or replace nozzles.

Problem: Rich mixture at cruising speeds

Possible cause
1. Air cleaner clogged.
2. Leaking float.
3. Float level too high.
4. Float inlet valve dirty.
5. Excessive fuel pressure.
6. Fuel flow pulsations.
7. Main discharge jet too large.
8. Choke sticking on.
9. Engine running too cold.
10. Power valve diaphragm ruptured.
11. Air bleeds clogged.
12. Faulty fuel injection pump.
13. Malfunctioning fuel injection control system.

Correction
1. Clean or replace air filter.
2. Replace float.
3. Adjust float level.
4. Clean valve and lines.
5. Reduce fuel pressure.
6. Install pulsation damper.
7. Install correct size jet.
8. Free and adjust choke.
9. Check cooling system.
10. Replace power valve.
11. Clean carburetor.
12. Rebuild or replace pump.
13. Adjust, repair, or replace affected parts.

Problem: Low top speed

Possible cause
1. Incorrect throttle linkage adjustment.
2. Clogged air cleaner.
3. Choke sticking on.
4. Low or high float level.
5. Fuel pressure too low or high.
6. Air leak.
7. Secondary throttle valves inoperative.
8. Improper secondary throttle adjustment.
9. Main jet too small.
10. Main jet clogged.
11. Obstruction under accelerator pedal.
12. Engine operating too cold or hot.
13. Clogged catalytic converter.
14. Pinched exhaust pipe.
15. Clogged muffler.
16. Faulty injection pump (diesel).
17. Plugged injection nozzles (diesel).
18. Fuel injection system control malfunction.
19. Low compression.
20. Incorrect (small) tire size.
21. Incorrect final drive ratio.

Correction
1. Adjust linkage correctly.
2. Clean or replace air cleaner.
3. Clean and adjust choke.
4. Adjust float level.
5. Adjust fuel pressure.
6. Repair air leak.
7. Clean and rebuild carburetor.
8. Adjust throttle correctly.
9. Install proper size jet.
10. Clean carburetor.
11. Remove obstruction.
12. Check cooling system.
13. Repair or replace converter.
14. Replace pipe.
15. Replace muffler.
16. Adjust, repair, or replace pump.
17. Clean or replace nozzles.
18. Repair, adjust, or replace affected unit(s).
19. Repair engine.
20. Install correct size tires.
21. Install correct ratio gears.

Problem: Hard starting when cold

Possible cause
1. Choke inoperative or improperly adjusted.
2. Flooding from excessive use of accelerator pump or rich choke.
3. Failure to depress throttle to allow choke valve to close.
4. Air leak.
5. Clogged air cleaner.
6. Fuel level in bowl incorrect.
7. Bowl vent clogged.
8. No fuel delivery.
9. Stale or contaminated fuel.
10. Gasoline not sufficiently volatile.
11. Incorrect grade of diesel fuel.
12. Vacuum leaks.
13. Defective ignition components.
14. Incorrect timing.
15. Discharged or defective battery.
16. Corroded or loose battery and starter connections.
17. Defective starter motor.

Correction
1. Clean and adjust choke.
2. Hold throttle in wide open position and crank engine. Advise driver.
3. Advise driver.
4. Repair air leak.
5. Clean or replace air cleaner.
6. Adjust fuel level.
7. Clean bowl vent.
8. Check tank and delivery system.
9. Drain tank. Flush system. Fill with fresh fuel.
10. Change to more volatile fuel.
11. Use correct grade fuel.
12. Locate and repair.
13. Locate, clean, adjust, or replace.
14. Set to specifications.
15. Charge or replace battery.
16. Clean and tighten connections.
17. Rebuild or replace starter.

Problem: Hard starting when hot

Possible cause
1. Flooding from excessive use of choke or accelerator pump.
2. Vapor lock.

Correction
1. Hold throttle wide open and crank until engine starts.
2. Cool lines. Change to less volatile fuel and protect lines from heat.

3. Bowl vent clogged.
4. Air leak.
5. Clogged air cleaner.
6. Fuel level incorrect.
7. No fuel delivery.
8. Stale or contaminated fuel.
9. Overheated engine.
10. Exhaust heat control valve stuck.
11. High elevation.
12. Improper choke unloader adjustment.
13. Vacuum hoses split, kinked, or loose.
14. Incorrect ignition timing.
15. Fuel vapor boil over.
16. Overheated carburetor.
17. Malfunctioning fuel injection system control.

3. Clean bowl vent.
4. Repair air leak.
5. Clean or replace air filter.
6. Adjust fuel level.
7. Check delivery system.
8. Drain tank and fuel system. Fill with fresh fuel.
9. Check cooling system.
10. Free control valve.
11. Change to less volatile fuel.
12. Adjust properly.
13. Replace and secure connections.
14. Set to specifications.
15. Hold throttle full open while cranking.
16. Check for proper heat shield and/or insulator installation.
17. Repair, adjust, or replace affected parts.

—————————————————— Problem: Excessive fuel consumption ——————————————————

Possible cause
1. Excessive speed.
2. Rapid acceleration.
3. Heavy loads or trailer towing.
4. Low tire pressure.
5. Dragging brakes.
6. Stop and start driving.
7. Fuel leaks (external).
8. Clogged air cleaner.
9. Choke on.
10. Main jets too large.
11. Accelerator pump stroke adjusted wrong.
12. Low grade or stale gasoline.
13. Exhaust heat control valve stuck.
14. Fuel level in bowl too high.
15. Leaking carburetor float.
16. Faulty inlet valve or seat.
17. Metering rod worn.
18. Fuel pressure excessive.
19. Power valve stuck open.
20. Heavy fuel pulsations.
21. Front wheel alignment out.
22. Exhaust system clogged.
23. Transmission slipping.
24. Wrong axle gear ratio.
25. Incorrect tire size.
26. Malfunctioning fuel injection system control.
27. Faulty fuel injector pump (diesel).
28. Injector pump timing incorrect (diesel).
29. Incorrect grade of diesel fuel.
30. Torque converter lockup inoperative.

Correction
1. Caution owner to reduce speed.
2. Accelerate moderately.
3. Normal.
4. Inflate tires to proper level.
5. Adjust brakes.
6. Normal.
7. Repair leaks.
8. Clean or replace cleaner.
9. Clean and adjust choke.
10. Reduce jet size.
11. Adjust accelerator pump stroke.
12. Use higher grade fuel. Use fresh fuel.
13. Free valve.
14. Lower fuel level.
15. Replace float.
16. Replace both valve and seat.
17. Replace metering rod.
18. Lower fuel pressure.
19. Replace power valve.
20. Install pulsation damper.
21. Align front wheels.
22. Replace muffler and/or tail pipe.
23. Adjust or overhaul transmission.
24. Change to factory ratio.
25. Install proper size tires.
26. Repair, adjust, or replace affected control.
27. Repair, adjust, or replace pump.
28. Set to specifications.
29. Use correct grade.
30. Repair or replace lockup solenoid, converter, or control module.

Ignition System Problem Diagnosis

—————————————————— Problem: No spark ——————————————————

Possible cause
1. Breaker points defective or misadjusted (point ignition).
2. Distributor pickup defective or misadjusted (electronic ignition)
3. Defective condenser.
4. Discharged battery.
5. Faulty coil or primary circuit resistor.
6. No primary current to points.
7. Defective coil high tension lead.
8. Defective rotor and/or distributor cap.
9. Defective plug wires.
10. Moisture in distributor cap and on points.
11. Breaker plate not grounded.
12. Defective ignition control module.
13. Loose, corroded, or open electronic control module ground lead.
14. Loose, corroded, or disconnected primary connections.

Correction
1. Install new points.
2. Replace or adjust as needed.
3. Replace condenser.
4. Charge battery.
5. Replace coil or resistor.
6. Check ignition switch, coil, resistor, wiring.
7. Replace lead.
8. Replace cap and rotor.
9. Replace plug wires.
10. Dry cap and points.
11. Replace or tighten ground wire.
12. Replace ignition module.
13. Tighten, clean, or connect as needed.
14. Clean, cover with special, protective grease and shove firmly into distributor.

15. Defective distributor electronic pickup.
16. Trigger wheel positioned too high.
17. Incorrect trigger wheel-to-pickup air gap.
18. Defective cam or crankshaft sensor.

15. Replace pickup unit.
16. Reposition correctly.
17. Set correctly. Use nonmagnetic feeler gauge.
18. Replace defective sensor.

Problem: Weak or intermittent spark

Possible cause
1. Breaker points defective (where used).
2. Defective condenser (where used).
3. Point dwell set incorrectly.
4. Discharged battery.
5. Loose or dirty primary wiring connections.
6. Weak coil.
7. Defective primary circuit resistor.
8. Burned rotor and cap contacts.
9. Defective resistance spark plug wires.
10. Insufficient system voltage.
11. Weak breaker spring pressure (point ignition only).
12. Worn distributor bushings or bent shaft.
13. Worn distributor cam (point ignition only).
14. Breaker arm sticking (point ignition only).
15. Loose spark plug wires.
16. Defective distributor electronic pickup.
17. Trigger wheel pin sheared.
18. Shorted primary wiring.
19. Loose wiring harness connectors.

Correction
1. Install new points.
2. Install new condenser.
3. Set dwell correctly.
4. Charge or replace battery.
5. Clean and tighten connections.
6. Replace coil.
7. Replace resistor.
8. Replace cap and rotor.
9. Replace resistance wires.
10. Adjust regulator.
11. Increase spring pressure.
12. Replace bushings or shaft.
13. Replace cam.
14. Free and lubricate bushing.
15. Clean and tighten connections.
16. Replace pickup.
17. Replace pin.
18. Replace wire and relocate.
19. Tighten connections.

Problem: Missing at idle or low speed

Possible cause
1. Weak or intermittent spark at plugs.
2. Fouled spark plugs.
3. Spark plug gaps too narrow.
4. Improper plug heat range.
5. Damaged plugs.
6. Defective distributor electronic pickup.
7. Loose harness connections.
8. Discharged battery.
9. Coil polarity incorrect.

Correction
1. See *Weak or intermittent spark.*
2. Clean or replace plugs.
3. Adjust gaps to specifications.
4. Install proper heat range.
5. Replace plug or plugs.
6. Replace pickup unit.
7. Clean and tighten connections.
8. Charge or replace battery.
9. Reverse coil primary leads.

Problem: Missing during acceleration

Possible cause
1. Weak spark.
2. Plugs damp.
3. Fouled plugs.
4. Plug gap too wide.
5. Damaged plug.
6. Incorrect trigger wheel-to-pickup air gap.
7. Defective vacuum advance.
8. Incorrect coil polarity.
9. Crossfiring.
10. Weak ignition coil.

Correction
1. See *Weak or intermittent spark.*
2. Dry plugs.
3. Clean or replace plugs.
4. Gap as specified.
5. Replace plug.
6. Set gap to specifications.
7. Repair or replace vacuum advance.
8. Reverse coil primary leads.
9. Rearrange ignition secondary wires.
10. Replace ignition coil.

Problem: Missing during cruising and high-speed operation

Possible cause
1. Weak spark.
2. Improper heat range plug (too hot).
3. Crossfiring.
4. Fouled plug.
5. Plug gap incorrect.
6. Damaged plug.
7. Ignition timing incorrect.
8. Defective distributor.
9. Loose or corroded wire connections.
10. Defective spark plug wires.
11. Weak ignition coil.

Correction
1. See *Weak or intermittent spark.*
2. Install proper heat range plug.
3. Arrange wires properly. If needed, install new wires.
4. Clean or replace plugs.
5. Gap to specifications .
6. Replace plug.
7. Reset timing.
8. Repair or replace distributor.
9. Clean and tighten connections.
10. Replace wires.
11. Replace ignition coil.

Problem: Missing at all speeds

Possible cause
1. Weak spark.
2. Fouled spark plugs.
3. Damaged plug.
4. Crossfiring.
5. Plug gap too wide or too narrow.
6. Plugs and/or distributor damp.
7. Improper plug heat range.
8. Defective distributor.
9. Defective spark plug wires.
10. Distributor trigger wheel pin sheared or missing.
11. Burned or corroded breaker points.
12. Defective condenser.

Correction
1. See *Weak or intermittent spark.*
2. Clean or replace plugs.
3. Replace plug.
4. Arrange wiring correctly and if needed, install new wires.
5. Adjust gap as needed.
6. Dry distributor and plugs.
7. Change to correct heat range.
8. Repair or replace distributor.
9. Replace plug wires.
10. Install new pin.
11. Replace and gap points.
12. Replace condenser.

Problem: Short point life (point-type distributors only)

Possible cause
1. Oil on points.
2. Excessive system voltage.
3. Primary ballast resistor bypassed.
4. Incorrect primary circuit ballast resistor.
5. Defective condenser.
6. Incorrect capacity condenser.
7. Dirt on points.
8. Defective coil.
9. Worn distributor shaft or bushings.
10. Defective ignition switch.
11. Points improperly aligned.
12. Points improperly gapped.

Correction
1. Clean and remove source of oil.
2. Adjust voltage regulator.
3. Run coil circuit through resistor.
4. Install correct resistor.
5. Install new condenser.
6. Install condenser of correct capacity.
7. Clean points.
8. Replace coil.
9. Rebuild or replace distributor.
10. Replace switch.
11. Align points.
12. Gap points as specified.

Problem: Coil failure

Possible cause
1. Carbon tracking on tower.
2. Excessive system voltage.
3. Oil leak in coil.
4. Engine heat damage.
5. Physical damage.

Correction
1. Replace coil and wire nipple.
2. Adjust voltage regulator.
3. Replace coil.
4. Replace coil. Relocate or baffle against heat.
5. Replace coil.

Problem: Short spark plug life

Possible cause
1. Incorrect plug heat range (too hot—burns).
2. Incorrect plug heat range (too cold—fouls).
3. Mechanical damage during installation.
4. Loose spark plug (overheats and burns).
5. Incorrect plug reach (too short—fouls).
6. Incorrect plug reach (too long—strikes piston).
7. Worn engine—oil fouling.
8. Bending center electrode.
9. Detonation.

10. Preignition.

11. Lean mixture.

Correction
1. Install correct (cooler) heat range.
2. Install correct (hotter) heat range.
3. Install correctly.
4. Tighten plugs to proper torque.
5. Install plugs with correct reach.
6. Install plugs with correct reach.
7. Switch to hotter plugs or overhaul engine.
8. Bend side electrode only.
9. Adjust timing. Change to higher octane gas and/or remove carbon buildup.
10. Remove carbon buildup, install valves with full margin, install cooler plugs.
11. Adjust air-fuel ratio.

Problem: Preignition

Possible cause
1. Overheated engine.
2. Glowing pieces of carbon.
3. Spark plugs overheating.
4. Sharp valve edges.
5. Glowing exhaust valve.

Correction
1. Check cooling system.
2. Remove carbon.
3. Change to cooler plugs.
4. Install valves with full margin.
5. Check for proper tappet clearance, for sticking, and air leaks.

Problem: Detonation

Possible cause
1. Ignition timing advanced.
2. Engine temperature too high.
3. Carbon buildup is raising compression ratio.
4. Low octane fuel.
5. Exhaust heat control valve stuck.
6. Excessive block or head metal removed to increase compression.

Correction
1. Retard timing.
2. Check cooling system.
3. Remove carbon.
4. Switch to high octane fuel.
5. Free valve.
6. Use thicker gasket, change head, or true warped head or block surface.

Problem: Backfiring in intake manifold

1. Intake valve not properly seating.
2. Lean mixture.
3. Crossfiring.
4. Plug wires installed wrong.
5. Carbon tracking in distributor cap.
6. Insufficient choke when engine is cold.
7. Incorrect ignition timing.

1. Check for broken spring, valve clearance, sticking, seat condition.
2. Adjust mixture.
3. Arrange plug wires or install new wires if needed.
4. Connect wires to proper plugs.
5. Replace cap and rotor.
6. Adjust choke.
7. Set timing to specifications.

Problem: Backfiring in exhaust system

Possible cause
1. Turning key off and on while vehicle is in motion.
2. Current flow interruption in primary circuit.
3. Coil-to-distributor cap secondary wire shorting or coil itself shorting.
4. Faulty points or condenser.
5. Weak or intermittent spark.
6. Incorrect valve timing.
7. Air injection system diverter or diverter valve inoperative.

Correction
1. Advise driver to avoid this practice.
2. Check circuit for loose connections and shorts.
3. Replace wire or coil.
4. Replace points and condenser.
5. See *Weak or intermittent spark*.
6. Correct timing.
7. Replace valve.

Problem: Engine kicks (attempts to run backward) during cranking

Possible cause
1. Ignition timing too far advanced.
2. Plug wires installed incorrectly.
3. Carbon tracking.

Correction
1. Retard ignition timing.
2. Attach wires to proper plugs.
3. Replace distributor cap and rotor.

Starting System Problem Diagnosis

Problem: Starter will not crank engine

Possible cause
1. Dead battery.
2. Loose or dirty battery connections.
3. Defective starter switch.
4. Defective starter solenoid.
5. Defective or improperly adjusted neutral safety switch.
6. Starter terminal post shorted.
7. Defective starter.
8. Engine bearings seized.
9. Engine bearings too tight.
10. Piston-to-cylinder wall clearance too small.
11. Water pump frozen.
12. Insufficient ring clearance.
13. Hydrostatic lock (water in combustion chamber).
14. Starter drive pinion jammed into flywheel teeth.

15. Starter armature seized.

Correction
1. Charge or replace battery.
2. Clean and tighten connections.
3. Replace starter switch.
4. Replace solenoid.
5. Replace or adjust switch.
6. Replace insulation.
7. Rebuild or replace starter.
8. Grind crankshaft. Replace bearings.
9. Install correct bearings.
10. Fit pistons correctly.
11. Thaw. Place antifreeze in cooling system.
12. Install correct rings.
13. Remove water and repair leak.
14. Remove starter. Install new pinion and replace starter ring gear if needed.
15. Rebuild or replace starter.

Problem: Starter cranks engine slowly

Possible cause
1. Low battery state of charge.
2. Loose or dirty battery cable connections.
3. Battery capacity too small.
4. Dirty or burned switch contacts.
5. Excessively heavy engine oil.
6. Starter motor defective.

Correction
1. Charge battery.
2. Clean and tighten connections.
3. Install larger capacity battery.
4. Replace switch.
5. Drain and install lighter oil.
6. Rebuild or replace starter.

7. Engine bearings, pistons, or rings fitted too close.
8. Cold, heavy oil in manual transmission.
9. Extreme cold weather.

7. Provide proper clearance.
8. Hold clutch in while cranking.
9. Preheat engine prior to cranking.

Problem: Starter makes excessive noise

Possible cause
1. Starter-to-flywheel housing mounting fasteners loose.
2. Dragging armature.
3. Dragging field pole shoes.
4. Dry bushings.
5. Chipped pinion teeth.
6. Chipped flywheel ring gear teeth.
7. Bent armature shaft.
8. Worn drive unit.
9. Loose starter through-bolts. Loose end frame bolts.
10. Flywheel ring gear misaligned.

Correction
1. Tighten mounting fasteners.
2. Replace armature and/or bushings.
3. Tighten pole shoes.
4. Lubricate bushings.
5. Replace pinion.
6. Replace ring gear.
7. Replace armature.
8. Replace starter drive unit.
9. Tighten all starter and frame cap bolts.
10. Install new ring gear.

Problem: Starter cranks but will not engage flywheel ring gear

Possible cause
1. Broken spring or bolt (Bendix type).
2. Dirty drive unit.
3. Sheared drive key.
4. Stripped or sheared pinion teeth.
5. Section of ring gear teeth stripped.
6. Defective or dry overrunning clutch drive unit.
7. Snapped armature shaft.
8. Broken spring (overrunning clutch type).

Correction
1. Replace spring or bolt.
2. Clean or replace unit.
3. Replace drive key.
4. Replace drive unit.
5. Install new ring gear.
6. Replace drive unit.
7. Replace armature.
8. Replace drive unit.

Problem: Starter drive pinion releases slowly or not at all

Possible cause
1. Dirty Bendix drive sleeve.
2. Drive pinion binds on drive sleeve splines (mechanical bind).
3. Starter switch defective.
4. Dirty pinion sleeve.
5. Disengagement linkage (overrunning clutch type) binding.
6. Linkage retracting spring weak or broken.
7. Actuating solenoid sticking.
8. Centrifugal pinion release pin sticking.
9. Insufficient drive pinion-to-ring gear clearance.

Correction
1. Clean drive sleeve.
2. Replace drive unit.
3. Replace starter switch.
4. Clean pinion sleeve.
5. Clean, align, and adjust linkage.
6. Install new spring.
7. Clean solenoid.
8. Replace drive unit.
9. Adjust clearance or replace linkage.

Charging System Problem Diagnosis

Problem: No charge

Possible cause
1. Alternator drive belt loose or broken.
2. Voltage regulator fusible link blown.
3. Sticking or worn commutator brushes.
4. Loose or corroded connection.
5. Rectifiers open.
6. Charging circuit open.
7. Open circuit in stator winding.
8. Field circuit open.
9. Defective field relay.
10. Defective voltage regulator.
11. Open isolation diode.
12. Open resistor wire.
13. Drive pulley slipping.
14. Brushes oil soaked.
15. Corroded or loose brush connections.
16. Seized bearings.

Correction
1. Tighten or replace belt.
2. Install new fusible link.
3. Free or replace brushes.
4. Clean and solder connections.
5. Correct cause and replace rectifiers.
6. Correct as needed.
7. Replace stator.
8. Test and correct as required.
9. Replace relay.
10. Replace voltage regulator.
11. Replace diode.
12. Replace resistor wire.
13. Install new key and tighten.
14. Replace brushes.
15. Clean and tighten connections.
16. Replace bearings. Check shaft for damage.

Problem: Low or erratic rate of charge

Possible cause
1. Loose drive belt.
2. Open stator; grounded or shorted turns in stator windings.

Correction
1. Tighten belt.
2. Replace stator.

3. High resistance in battery terminals.
4. Charging circuit resistance excessive.
5. Engine ground strap loose or broken.
6. Loose connections.
7. Voltage regulator points oxidized.
8. Voltage regulator setting too low.
9. Defective rectifier.
10. Dirty, burned slip rings.
11. Grounded or shorted turns in rotor.
12. Brushes worn. Brush springs weak.

3. Clean and tighten terminals.
4. Repair cause of high resistance.
5. Tighten or replace strap.
6. Tighten connections.
7. Clean and adjust or replace regulator if required.
8. Increase regulator setting.
9. Replace rectifier.
10. Turn slip rings.
11. Replace rotor.
12. Replace brushes and/or springs.

Problem: Excessive rate of charge

Possible cause
1. Voltage regulator setting too high.
2. Voltage regulator ground defective.
3. Defective voltage regulator.
4. Alternator field winding grounded.
5. Open rectifier.
6. Loose connections.

Correction
1. Lower regulator setting.
2. Ground properly.
3. Replace regulator.
4. Repair grounded field winding.
5. Replace rectifier.
6. Tighten connections.

Problem: Noise

Possible cause
1. Drive belt slipping.
2. Drive pulley loose.
3. Drive pulley misaligned.
4. Mounting bolts loose.
5. Worn bearings.
6. Dry bearing.
7. Open or shorted rectifier.
8. Sprung rotor shaft.
9. Open or shorted stator winding.
10. Alternator fan dragging.
11. Excessive rotor end play.
12. Out-of-round or rough slip rings.
13. Hardened brushes.

Correction
1. Tighten belt.
2. Tighten pulley.
3. Align pulley.
4. Tighten mounting bolts.
5. Replace bearings.
6. Lubricate or replace as required.
7. Replace rectifier.
8. Install new rotor.
9. Test. Replace stator as needed.
10. Adjust fan clearance.
11. Adjust for correct end play.
12. Turn slip rings.
13. Replace brushes.

Problem: Regulator points oxidized, pitted or burned

Possible cause
1. Incorrect regulator connections.
2. Rotor coil windings shorted.
3. Regulator setting too high.
4. Poor ground.
5. Brush leads touching each other.
6. Air gap incorrect.
7. Point gap incorrect.
8. Oil on points.
9. Filings or other abrasive particles between points.
10. Use of emery cloth.

Correction
1. Replace regulator. Connect properly.
2. Replace rotor.
3. Reduce regulator setting.
4. Correct ground.
5. Separate leads.
6. Adjust air gap.
7. Adjust point gap.
8. Clean points. Replace if needed.
9. File or sand. Clean thoroughly.
10. Replace regulator. Never use emery cloth to clean points.

Problem: Undercharged battery

Possible cause
1. No charge or low charge rate.
2. Excessive use of starter.
3. Defective battery.
4. Excessive resistance in charging circuit.
5. Defective alternator.
6. Defective regulator.
7. Low regulator setting.
8. Electrical load exceeds alternator rating.
9. Electrical draw in system.
10. Excessive starter motor draw.
11. Water level low in battery cells.

Correction
1. See *No charge* or *Low or erratic rate of charge*.
2. Tune engine for faster starting.
3. Replace battery.
4. Test and remove resistance.
5. Rebuild or replace alternator.
6. Replace regulator.
7. Raise regulator setting.
8. Reduce load or install higher capacity alternator.
9. Test. Remove source of electrical draw.
10. Rebuild or replace starter motor.
11. Bring electrolyte up to proper level.

Problem: Overcharged battery

Possible cause
1. Excessive resistance in voltage regulator circuit.
2. Voltage regulator setting too high.
3. Upper (double-contact) voltage regulator points stuck.
4. Regulator-alternator ground wire loose or open.
5. Defective battery.
6. Voltage regulator coil open.
7. Current regulator setting too high.
8. Other defective regulator parts.

Correction
1. Clean and tighten connections.
2. Lower voltage regulator setting.
3. Replace regulator.
4. Tighten or replace wire.
5. Replace battery.
6. Replace regulator.
7. Reduce current regulator setting.
8. Replace regulator.

Problem: Excessive use of water or loss of electrolyte

Possible cause
1. Battery case cracked.
2. Voltage regulator setting too high.
3. Excessive charge rate from other causes.
4. Battery subjected to excessive heat.
5. Battery sealing compound loose.

Correction
1. Replace battery.
2. Lower voltage regulator setting.
3. See *Excessive rate of charge* and *Overcharged battery*.
4. Change battery location or insulate battery against heat.
5. Replace battery.

Engine and Accessory Noise Diagnosis

Problem: Combustion knocks

Sound Identification: When the fuel charge is fired before the spark plug fires (preignition) or when a double-flame front is produced that creates a uncontrolled burning of the fuel charge (detonation), a sharp metallic pinging sound is created. This pinging is most noticeable during heavy acceleration.

Possible cause
1. Carbon buildup.
2. Spark plugs too hot—wrong heat range.
3. Spark plugs loose.
4. Ignition timing advanced too far.
5. Low octane gasoline.
6. Overheated valve edge.
7. Lean fuel mixture.

Correction
1. Remove carbon.
2. Change to cooler plugs.
3. Tighten plugs to proper torque.
4. Retard ignition timing.
5. Change to higher octane.
6. Install valve with sufficient margin.
7. Adjust fuel mixture.

Problem: Other engine noises

Sound Identification: The various accessory units such as the water pump, alternator, power steering pump, and air conditioning compressor can produce a variety of squealing, grinding, thumping, and howling noises. They may be quickly checked by disconnecting the accessory drive belts.

Engine mounts can cause heavy metallic noises if they are too tight or too loose.

Exhaust pipes, mufflers, and tail pipes can also be responsible for various thumps, clangs, and rattles.

Exhaust Emission Controls Diagnosis

Problem: Air pump noisy

Possible cause
1. Loose belt.
2. Bearing defective.
3. Vane bearings defective.
4. Carbon seals or shoes defective.
5. Air leak in hose.
6. Loose hose connection.
7. Defective relief valve.
8. Air cleaner air leak.
9. Pump bracket loose.
10. Vanes striking housing bore when pump is new.
11. Hoses touching other parts of the vehicle.
12. Vacuum differential valve defective.
13. Bypass valve defective.
14. Pump failure.
15. Filter plugged.
16. Seized pump.
17. Loose pulley.

Correction
1. Adjust belt tension.
2. Replace bearing.
3. Replace vane assembly.
4. Replace seals or shoes.
5. Replace hose.
6. Tighten hose connection.
7. Replace relief valve.
8. Tighten air cleaner.
9. Tighten bracket fasteners.
10. Normal. With some driving, "chirping" sound should soon stop.
11. Align and secure hoses.
12. Replace valve.
13. Replace valve.
14. Replace pump.
15. Clean or replace.
16. Replace pump.
17. Tighten to specifications. Replace pulley if damaged.

Problem: Air injection system inoperative

Possible cause
1. Drive belt loose or broken.
2. Pump seized or frozen.
3. Pump relief valve stuck open.
4. Hose connection loose.
5. Hose disconnected or broken.
6. Hose kinked.
7. Check valve stuck shut.
8. Air distribution manifold or injection tubes clogged.
9. Air cleaner clogged.
10. Diverter valve inoperative.

Correction
1. Adjust tension or replace.
2. Replace pump.
3. Replace relief valve.
4. Tighten connection.
5. Attach and tighten or replace.
6. Replace hose. Align and secure.
7. Replace check valve.
8. Clean or replace.
9. Replace air cleaner.
10. Replace diverter valve.

Problem: System hose burned or baked

Possible cause
1. Check valve stuck open.

Correction
1. Replace check valve.

Problem: Exhaust system burned

Possible cause
1. Relief valve in air injection pump stuck shut.

Correction
1. Replace relief valve.

Problem: Engine backfires through exhaust system

Possible cause
1. Diverter valve vacuum line leaking, kinked, or disconnected.
2. Defective diverter valve.
3. Excessive engine idle RPM.
4. Choke setting too rich.
5. Defective choke.
6. Air pump inoperative.

Correction
1. Replace line.
2. Replace valve.
3. Adjust idle speed.
4. Lean out choke setting.
5. Clean and adjust or replace.
6. See *Air injection system inoperative.*

Problem: Engine backfires through intake manifold

Possible cause
1. Improper ignition timing or distributor dwell angle.
2. Choke improperly adjusted.
3. Accelerator pump faulty or set too lean.

Correction
1. Adjust dwell and set timing as recommended.
2. Adjust choke.
3. Repair, replace, or adjust as needed.

Problem: Engine surges at all speeds

Possible cause
1. Carburetor defective or misadjusted.
2. Defective diverter valve.

Correction
1. Repair, replace, or adjust carburetor.
2. Replace valve.

Problem: Rough engine idle

Possible cause
1. Defective diverter valve or PCV valve.
2. Diverter valve vacuum line leaks.
3. Carburetor defective or misadjusted.
4. Improper ignition timing.
5. Defect in ignition system.
6. Faulty EGR valve operation.
7. EGR hoses misrouted.
8. EGR valve gasket defective.
9. Improper EGR vacuum at idle.
10. Defective early fuel evaporation (EFE) valve.
11. Defective altitude compensator
12. No vacuum to early fuel evaporation valve.

Correction
1. Replace defective valve.
2. Replace line or repair connection.
3. Repair, replace, or adjust carburetor.
4. Reset timing.
5. See Chapter 18, Ignition System Service.
6. Clean or replace unit. Check vacuum and vacuum lines.
7. Correct as required.
8. Replace gasket.
9. Check vacuum source. Replace or repair as required.
10. Replace EFE valve.
11. Replace compensator.
12. Repair as required.

Problem: Engine hesitates on acceleration

Possible cause
1. Defective diverter valve.
2. Diverter valve vacuum line leaks.
3. Air outlet to intake manifold, from diverter valve, leaking.
4. Defective early fuel evaporation valve.

Correction
1. Replace diverter valve.
2. Repair connections or replace hose.
3. Repair connections or replace hose.
4. Replace valve.

5. Malfunctioning EGR valve.
6. EGR hoses misrouted.

5. Replace EGR valve.
6. Route EGR hoses correctly.

Problem: EGR valve does not open

Possible cause
1. Defective EGR valve.
2. Dirty EGR valve.
3. Loose or damaged hose
4. Stem frozen into position
5. Defective coolant temperature switch.
6. No vacuum to EGR valve.

7. Defective thermal control valve.
8. Defective control system—plugged passageways.

Correction
1. Replace EGR valve.
2. Clean EGR valve.
3. Connect or replace.
4. Clean or replace valve.
5. Replace switch.
6. Check EGR vacuum solenoid, EGR vacuum switch, vacuum regulator valve, vacuum pump, and hoses. Repair as required.
7. Replace valve.
8. Clean out deposits.

Problem: Excessive exhaust emission levels

Possible cause
1. Fouled catalytic converter.
2. Rich fuel mixture.
3. Faulty air injection system.
4. Stuck or inoperative EGR valve.
5. Ignition timing off.

6. Inoperative or malfunctioning thermostatic air cleaner system.
7. Faulty early fuel evaporation system.
8. Faulty electronic control module.
9. Emission control units missing.
10. Thermal vacuum sensor defective.
11. Defective spark plugs.
12. Air leakage at idle.
13. Defective PCV valve.
14. Defective air control valve.
15. Defective oxygen sensor.

Correction
1. Replace catalyst or entire unit.
2. Check and correct cause.
3. Check system. Adjust or repair as needed.
4. Clean or replace.
5. Check coolant temperature override switch action. Check transmission-controlled spark advance. Check other spark advance units and control devices.
6. Check system operation.
7. Check system operation. Check thermal switch action.
8. Replace ECM if faulty. Check wiring and connectors.
9. Replace with proper units. Retest.
10. Replace thermal vacuum sensor.
11. Replace spark plugs.
12. Locate and correct.
13. Replace PCV valve.
14. Replace valve.
15. Replace oxygen sensor.

Exhaust System Diagnosis

Problem: Exhaust odor enters vehicle during highway operation

Possible cause
1. Leaking exhaust system connections.
2. Holes in muffler or pipe system.
3. Tail pipe does not protrude far enough to rear or side.
4. Oil drips on hot exhaust system.
5. Holes in body or fire wall.
6. Operating vehicle with back window down.

Correction
1. Tighten connections. Repair or, if needed, replace units.
2. Replace defective units.
3. Install correct length of pipe or an extension.
4. Repair oil leaks.
5. Locate and seal holes.
6. Inform owner.

Problem: Engine lacks power

Possible cause
1. Clogged muffler.
2. Clogged or kinked exhaust or tail pipe.
3. Muffler or pipes too small for vehicle.
4. Catalytic converter clogged or crushed shut.

Correction
1. Replace muffler.
2. Replace pipe.
3. Install muffler and pipes of the correct size and type.
4. Replace with new converter.

Problem: Excessive exhaust system noise

Possible cause
1. Holes in muffler or pipes.
2. System connections leaking.
3. Exhaust manifold or pipe gaskets blown.
4. Muffler of incorrect design.
5. Muffler burned inside.
6. Carbon build-up in straight-through design muffler.
7. Hole in catalytic converter.

Correction
1. Replace defective units.
2. Repair connections.
3. Replace gaskets.
4. Replace with correct muffler.
5. Replace muffler.
6. Replace muffler.
7. Replace converter.

Problem: Exhaust system mechanical noise

Possible cause
1. System improperly aligned.
2. Support brackets loose, bent, or broken.
3. Incorrect muffler or pipes.
4. Baffle loose in muffler.
5. Manifold heat control valve rattles.
6. Engine mounts worn.
7. Damaged or defective catalytic converter.

Correction
1. Align system.
2. Tighten.
3. Install correct muffler or pipes.
4. Replace muffler.
5. Replace thermostatic spring.
6. Replace engine mounts.
7. Repair or replace converter.

Clutch Problem Diagnosis

Problem: Clutch slips

Possible cause
1. Insufficient pedal free travel.
2. Disc facing soaked with oil or grease.

3. Broken or weak pressure plate spring or springs.
4. Clutch disc facing worn.
5. Hydraulic or mechanical linkage sticking.

Correction
1. Adjust free travel.
2. Clean clutch and pressure plate, replace disc. Correct source of oil contamination.
3. Rebuild or replace pressure plate.
4. Replace clutch disc.
5. Clean, align, and lubricate where needed.

Problem: Clutch chatters and/or grabs

Possible cause
1. Clutch disc facing oil or grease soaked.
2. Burned clutch disc facing.
3. Warped or worn clutch disc.
4. Pressure plate warped.
5. Pressure plate or flywheel surface scored.
6. Pressure plate fingers bind.
7. Clutch housing-to-transmission surface out of alignment with crankshaft centerline.
8. Sticking linkage.
9. Pilot bearing worn.
10. Pressure plate release fingers improperly adjusted.
11. Engine mounts loose or worn.
12. Transmission loose.
13. Rear spring shackles or axle housing control arms loose.
14. Worn splines or transmission input shaft.
15. Faulty throw-out bearing.

Correction
1. Replace clutch disc. Correct source of leak.
2. Replace clutch disc.
3. Replace clutch disc.
4. Grind or replace.
5. Grind or replace.
6. Free fingers.
7. Align or replace housing.

8. Free linkage.
9. Install new pilot bearing.
10. Adjust fingers.
11. Tighten or replace mounts.
12. Tighten fasteners.
13. Tighten shackles or replace control arm insulators and tighten.
14. Replace shaft.
15. Replace throw-out bearing.

Problem: Clutch will not release properly

Possible cause
1. Excessive pedal free travel.
2. Warped clutch disc.
3. Clutch facing torn loose and folded over.
4. Warped pressure plate.
5. Clutch housing misaligned.
6. Clutch disc hub binding on transmission input shaft.
7. Pilot bearing worn.
8. Faulty throw-out bearing.
9. Throw-out fork off pivot.
10. Clutch disc is frozen (corroded) to flywheel and pressure plate.
11. Excessive idle speed.

Correction
1. Adjust pedal travel.
2. Replace clutch disc.
3. Replace clutch disc.
4. Grind or replace.
5. Align housing.
6. Free hub.
7. Replace pilot bearing.
8. Replace throw-out bearing.
9. Install fork properly.
10. Replace disc and clean flywheel and pressure plate.
11. Adjust idle speed.

Problem: Clutch is noisy when pedal is depressed—engine running

Possible cause
1. Dry or worn throw-out bearing.
2. Worn pilot bearing.
3. Excessive total pedal travel.
4. Throw-out fork off pivot.
5. Clutch housing misaligned.
6. Crankshaft end play excessive.

Correction
1. Replace bearing.
2. Replace pilot.
3. Adjust pedal travel.
4. Install fork correctly.
5. Align housing.
6. Correct end play.

Problem: Clutch is noisy when pedal is depressed—engine not running

Possible cause
1. Dry, sticking linkage.
2. Dry or scored throw-out bearing sleeve.
3. Pressure plate drive lugs rubbing clutch cover.

Correction
1. Lubricate and align linkage.
2. Lubricate or replace.
3. Lubricate with high temperature grease.

Problem: Clutch noisy when pedal is fully released—engine running

Possible cause
1. Insufficient pedal free travel.
2. Clutch disc worn.
3. Clutch disc springs broken.
4. Clutch housing misaligned.
5. Worn clutch disc hub splines.
6. Worn input shaft splines.
7. Sprung input shaft.
8. Input shaft transmission bearing worn.

Correction
1. Adjust free travel.
2. Replace clutch disc.
3. Replace clutch disc.
4. Align housing.
5. Replace clutch disc.
6. Replace input shaft.
7. Replace input shaft.
8. Replace transmission bearing.

Problem: Excessive pedal pressure

Possible cause
1. Linkage needs lubrication.
2. Pressure plate release fingers binding.
3. Linkage misaligned.
4. Throw-out bearing sleeve binding on transmission bearing retainer.
5. Sticking linkage in master or slave cylinder.

Correction
1. Lubricate.
2. Free and lubricate.
3. Align linkage.
4. Free and lubricate retainer.
5. Clean or replace as needed.

Problem: Rapid clutch disc wear

Possible cause
1. Insufficient pedal free travel.
2. Scored flywheel or pressure plate.
3. Driver "rides" the clutch (rests foot on clutch while driving).
4. Driver races engine and slips clutch excessively during starting.
5. Driver holds vehicle on hill by slipping clutch.
6. Weak pressure plate springs.

Correction
1. Adjust free travel.
2. Resurface or replace.
3. Advise driver.
4. Advise driver.
5. Advise driver.
6. Rebuild or replace pressure plate assembly.

Manual Transmission/Transaxle Problem Diagnosis

Problem: Shifts hard—all gears

1. Excessive clutch pedal free travel.
2. Worn or defective clutch.
3. Failure to fully depress clutch pedal when shifting.
4. Shift cover loose.
5. Shift fork, shafts, levers, or detents worn or loose.
6. Improper shift linkage adjustment.
7. Linkage needs lubrication.
8. Linkage binding, bent, or loose.
9. Wrong transmission lubricant.
10. Insufficient lubricant.
11. Excess amount of lubricant.
12. Transmission misaligned.
13. Input shaft bearing retainer loose or cracked.
14. Synchronizer worn, damaged, or improperly assembled.

1. Adjust free travel.
2. Replace worn parts.
3. Advise driver.
4. Tighten cover.
5. Tighten or replace.
6. Adjust linkage.
7. Lubricate linkage.
8. Free, straighten, or tighten as needed.
9. Drain and fill with recommended lubricant.
10. Add lubricant to filler plug level.
11. Drain excess lubricant.
12. Correct transmission alignment.
13. Tighten or replace retainer.
14. Replace or reassemble synchronizer.

Problem: Gear clash during downshifting

Possible cause
1. Synchronizer worn, damaged, or improperly assembled.
2. Shifting too fast (ramming into lower gear).
3. Shifting to a lower gear when vehicle speed is excessive.
4. Clutch not releasing properly.
5. Excessive output shaft end play.

Correction
1. Replace or reassemble synchronizer.
2. Force into gear with a smooth, slower shift.
3. Slow down to appropriate speed before shifting.
4. Adjust or repair as needed.
5. Adjust end play.

Note: See *Hard shifting—all gears.*

Problem: Jumps out of gear

Possible cause
1. Transmission loose or misaligned.
2. Clutch housing loose or misaligned.
3. Shift linkage improperly adjusted.
4. Shift rail detents worn or detent springs weak.
5. Synchronizer clutch sleeve teeth worn.
6. Loose shifter cover.
7. Shift fork, shaft, or levers worn.
8. Worn clutch teeth on input shaft or other gears.
9. Worn gear teeth.
10. Worn countergear bearings and/or thrust washers.
11. Worn reverse idler gear bushing or bearings.
12. Worn output shaft pilot bearing.
13. Input shaft bearing retainer loose.
14. Other parts striking shift linkage.
15. Worn input or output shaft bearings.
16. Worn input shaft bushing in flywheel.
17. Bent output shaft.

Correction
1. Tighten or align transmission.
2. Tighten or align clutch housing.
3. Adjust linkage.
4. Replace rail detents and/or springs.
5. Replace synchronizer.
6. Tighten shifter cover.
7. Replace worn part.
8. Replace input shaft or gears.
9. Replace gears.
10. Replace countergear shaft, bearings, and washers.
11. Replace gear, bearings, and shaft.
12. Replace rollers. Replace shafts if necessary.
13. Tighten bearing retainer.
14. Make adjustments to provide clearance.
15. Replace bearings.
16. Replace input shaft bushing or bearing.
17. Replace output shaft.

Problem: Noise in all gears

Possible cause
1. Insufficient lubrication.
2. Worn or damaged bearings.
3. Worn or damaged gears.
4. Wrong lubricant.
5. Excessive synchronizer wear.
6. Defective speedometer drive gears.
7. Transmission misaligned.
8. Excessive input or output shaft and/or countergear end play.
9. Contaminated lubricant.

Correction
1. Fill to filler plug.
2. Replace bearings.
3. Replace gears.
4. Drain and fill with recommended lubricant.
5. Replace synchronizer.
6. Replace speedometer drive gears.
7. Correct alignment.
8. Adjust end play.
9. Disassemble clean and repair transmission.

Problem: Noise in neutral with engine running

Possible cause
1. Worn or damaged input shaft bearing.
2. Worn or damaged gears.
3. Lack of lubrication.
4. Countershaft bearings worn or damaged.
5. Output shaft pilot bearing worn or damaged.
6. Countergear anti-lash plate worn or damaged.
7. Lubricant contaminated with broken metal.

Correction
1. Replace input shaft bearing.
2. Replace gears.
3. Fill transmission to the proper level.
4. Replace bearings, countergear, and shaft.
5. Replace all rollers.
6. Replace plate or countergear as required.
7. Disassemble, clean, and repair transmission.

Problem: Noise in direct-drive gear

Possible cause
1. Defective input shaft bearing.
2. Defective output shaft bearing.
3. Defective synchronizer.
4. Defective speedometer drive gears.

Correction
1. Replace input shaft bearing.
2. Replace output shaft bearing.
3. Replace synchronizer.
4. Replace speedometer drive gears.

Problem: Noise in reduction or overdrive gear

Possible cause
1. Countergear rear bearings worn or damaged.

2. Defective synchronizer
3. Constant mesh gear loose on shaft.
4. Constant mesh gear teeth worn or chipped.

Correction
1. Replace countergear bearings. Replace shaft and countergear if needed.
2. Replace synchronizer.
3. Replace gear and/or shaft.
4. Replace second speed gear.

Problem: Noise in reverse

Possible cause
1. Reverse idler bushings worn.
2. Reverse idler gear worn or damaged.
3. Countergear reverse gear worn or damaged.
4. Defective reverse sliding gear (synchromesh low gear).

Correction
1. Replace idler gear or bushings.
2. Replace reverse idler gear.
3. Replace countergear.
4. Replace reverse sliding gear.

Problem: Sticks in gear

Possible cause
1. Insufficient lubricant
2. Synchronizer clutch sleeve teeth burred.
3. Sticking shift rails.
4. Synchronizer blocking ring stuck to mating gear.
5. Shift linkage defective.
6. Insufficient clutch pedal free travel.
7. Transmission misaligned.

Correction
1. Fill to filler plug.
2. Replace synchronizer.
3. Free and lubricate.
4. Free, lubricate, or replace blocking ring or mating gear.
5. Repair or replace linkage.
6. Adjust clutch pedal free travel.
7. Correct alignment.

Problem: Gear clash when shifting from neutral to low or reverse

Possible cause
1. Insufficient clutch pedal free travel.
2. Wrong lubricant.
3. Engine RPM too high.
4. Insufficient time between depressing clutch and shifting.
5. Sticking input shaft clutch pilot bearing.

Correction
1. Adjust free travel.
2. Drain and fill with correct lubricant.
3. Set to correct idle RPM.
4. Advise driver.
5. Replace pilot bearing.

Problem: Loss of lubricant

Possible cause
1. Cover loose.
2. Cover gasket loose or defective.
3. Input shaft bearing retainer loose, broken, or gasket defective.
4. Input shaft bearing retainer seal defective.
5. Output shaft seal worn.
6. Countershaft loose in case.
7. Lubricant level too high.
8. Shaft expansion plugs loose in case.
9. No sealer on bolt threads.
10. Damage shift shaft seal.
11. Vent plugged.
12. Wrong lubricant.
13. Cracked case or extension housing.
14. Drain or filler plug loose.

Correction
1. Tighten cover.
2. Tighten cover and/or replace gasket.
3. Tighten retainer, replace gasket or retainer.
4. Replace retainer seal.
5. Replace shaft seal.
6. Replace case.
7. Drain to level of filler plug.
8. Replace plugs. Use sealer.
9. Place sealer on bolt threads.
10. Replace shift shaft seal.
11. Open vent.
12. Drain and refill with recommended lubricant.
13. Replace case or housing.
14. Tighten filler plug.

Transfer Case (Part-Time Drive) Problem Diagnosis

Problem: Jumps out of gear in two-wheel drive

Possible cause
1. Shift lever detent spring weak or broken.
2. Sliding clutch spline engaging surface worn or tapered.

Correction
1. Replace spring.
2. Replace worn parts.

Problem: Jumps out of gear in four-wheel drive

Possible cause
1. Shift lever interference with floor pan.
2. Excessive transfer case movement.
3. Sliding clutch engaging surfaces tapered or worn.
4. Bent shift fork.
5. Shift rod detent spring weak or broken.
6. Shift lever torsion spring (where used) not holding.
7. Worn bearings, gear teeth, or shafts.

Correction
1. Provide proper clearance.
2. Check and replace transfer case mounts.
3. Replace worn parts.
4. Replace shift fork.
5. Replace detent spring.
6. Replace torsion spring.
7. Overhaul unit.

Problem: Noise

Note: Transfer cases using a gear drive produce considerable gear whine, which is normal.

Possible cause
1. Worn bearings, splines, chipped gears, or worn shafts.
2. Low lubrication level.
3. Loose or broken mounts.

Correction
1. Rebuild unit.
2. Fill to proper level.
3. Tighten or replace mounts.

Transfer Case (Full-Time) Diagnosis

Problem: Noisy operation

Possible cause
1. Low lubrication level.
2. Operating in "lockout" on hard, dry surface roads.
3. Improper lubricant.
4. "Slip-stick" condition ("Quadra-Trac" type). Makes a grunting, pulsating, rasping sound.

5. Excessive wear on gears, chains, or differential unit.
6. Loose or deteriorated mounts.

Correction
1. Fill to correct level.
2. Shift out of "lockout." Advise driver.
3. Drain and fill with recommended lubricant.
4. Normal if vehicle has not been driven for a week or two. Should stop after some usage. If it persists, drain fluid and refill. Use special additive if required. Make certain tire sizes are the same and pressures are equal.
5. Rebuild as needed.
6. Tighten or replace.

Problem: Jumps out of low range and/or is hard to shift into or out of low range

Possible cause
1. Shift linkage improperly adjusted, bent, or broken.
2. Shift rails dry or scored.
3. Improper driver operation.
4. Reduction unit parts worn or damaged.

Correction
1. Adjust correctly. Straighten or replace.
2. Clean, polish, or lubricate or replace as needed.
3. Follow shift procedure recommended by manufacturer.
4. Repair as needed.

Problem: Lockout will not engage

Possible
1. Lockout parts damaged
2. Defective vacuum control. Loose or damaged vacuum lines ("Quadra-Trac").
3. Defective shift linkage.

Correction
1. Repair as needed.
2. Replace control. Replace or connect vacuum hoses.

3. Repair or replace.

Problem: Will not engage in two-wheel drive

Possible cause
1. No vacuum. Loose or broken hoses.
2. Defective shift motor (axle).
3. Defective shift motor (transfer case).

Correction
1. Replace hoses. Secure all loose connections.
2. Replace shift motor.
3. Replace shift motor.

Problem: Will not engage in four-wheel drive

Possible cause
1. No vacuum. Loose or broken hoses.
2. Defective axle shift motor.
3. Binding or broken transfer case shift linkage.
4. Defective axle shift linkage.
5. Damaged transfer case.

Correction
1. Replace hoses. Secure all loose connections.
2. Replace shift motor.
3. Repair or replace shift linkage.
4. Repair or replace shift linkage.
5. Repair or replace transfer case.

Problem: Loss of lubricant

Possible cause
1. Clogged breather vent in transmission and/or transfer case.
2. Lubricant level too high in transmission and/or transfer case.
3. Improper lubricant or viscosity.
4. Defective seals, worn bearings, and/or shaft.
5. Porous case area.
6. Transfer case-to-transmission bolts loose.

Correction
1. Open clogged breather vent.
2. Drain lubricant to the correct level.
3. Drain and fill with proper lubricant.
4. Replace worn parts as needed.
5. Clean and repair area per manufacturer's instructions.
6. Tighten. Replace seal if necessary. Check lubricant level.

Problem: Vehicle wanders when driving straight ahead

Possible cause
1. Improperly matched tire size.
2. Uneven tire pressure.

Correction
1. Use a matched set of tires.
2. Adjust air pressure to recommended levels.

Automatic Transmission and Transaxle Diagnosis

——— Problem: Fluid leaks ———

Possible cause
1. Defective gaskets or seals
2. Loose bolts
3. Porous or cracked case.
4. Leaking vacuum modulator diaphragm
5. Overfilled transmission.

Correction
1. Replace defective parts.
2. Tighten bolts.
3. Repair or replace case.
4. Replace vacuum modulator.
5. Reduce fluid level.

——— Problem: Slipping in gear ———

Possible cause
1. Low fluid level
2. Clogged filter
3. Stuck valve.
4. Burned holding members
5. Misadjusted bands (when used).
6. Internal leaks.

Correction
1. Add fluid and check for leaks.
2. Replace filter.
3. Remove valve body and free sticky valves.
4. Disassemble transmission, replace burned holding members.
5. Adjust bands, recheck operation.
6. Disassemble transmission and correct leaks.

——— Problem: No up or downshifts ———

Possible cause
1. Linkage misadjusted.
2. Governor stuck.
3. Stuck valves.
4. Defective or disconnected vacuum modulator (when used).
5. Internal leaks.

Correction
1. Readjust linkage.
2. Remove and free sticky governor or replace.
3. Remove valve body and free sticky valves.
4. Replace modulator, check vacuum lines.
5. Disassemble transmission and correct leaks.

——— Problem: Noises ———

Possible cause
1. Clogged filter.
2. Pump or torque converter defective.
3. Defective gears.

Correction
1. Replace filter.
2. Replace pump or torque converter.
3. Replace gears.

Drive Line Problem Diagnosis

——— Problem: Noisy operation ———

Possible cause
1. U-joint fasteners (U-bolts, cap screws) loose.
2. Lack of lubricant in U-joints.
3. Worn U-joint.
4. Worn center support bearing.
5. Loose center support.
6. Joint or shaft striking some part of vehicle underbody.

7. Worn CV joint (front wheel drive)

Correction
1. Tighten fasteners.
2. Lubricate U-joints.
3. Replace U-joint.
4. Replace support bearing.
5. Tighten support fasteners.
6. Shim, tighten, or replace center mount. Check for debris in frame tunnel and for worn mounts.
7. Replace CV joint.

——— Problem: Propeller shaft vibration or shudder ———

Possible cause
1. U-joint fasteners loose.
2. Worn U-joint.
3. Shaft sprung or dented.
4. Undercoating on shaft.
5. Joint flange surface nicked or burred.
6. Worn slip joint splines.
7. Dry slip joint.
8. Shaft yokes out of phase (not aligned).
9. Shaft yoke and slip yoke assembled wrong.
10. Shaft yoke and pinion flange yoke assembled wrong.
11. Cross not centered in yoke.

Correction
1. Tighten U-joint fasteners.
2. Replace U-joint.
3. Replace drive shaft.
4. Remove undercoating.
5. Disassemble. File off burrs.
6. Replace slip yoke and/or stub shaft.
7. Clean and lubricate.
8. Align yokes as required.
9. Disconnect slip yoke. Rotate 180° and reconnect.
10. Disconnect flange yoke. Rotate 180° and reconnect.
11. Strike yoke to move rollers out against snap rings.

12. U-joints tight.
13. Roller U-bolts over tightened.
14. Drive angle wrong.
15. Loose center support.
16. Center support rubber insulator deteriorated.
17. Worn center support bearing.
18. Loose rear spring U-bolts.
19. Loose rear axle housing control arm bolts.
20. Loose pinion companion flange retaining nut.
21. Weak springs.
22. Rear spring center bolt sheared, axle housing shifted.

12. Strike yoke lugs to free. Replace joint if needed.
13. Loosen and torque properly.
14. Check and adjust as required.
15. Tighten center support.
16. Replace center support bearing.
17. Replace support bearing.
18. Torque bolts.
19. Tighten bolts. Replace bushings if worn.
20. Tighten nut.
21. Replace springs.
22. Realign axle housing (if needed) and replace center bolt.

─────────── Problem: CV axle shaft vibration or shudder ───────────

Possible cause
1. Worn CV joint.
2. Bent CV axle shaft.
3. Worn front wheel bearings.

Correction
1. Replace CV joint.
2. Replace shaft.
3. Replace bearings.

Rear Axle Problem Diagnosis

─────────── Problem: Noise during straight ahead driving ───────────

Possible cause
1. Insufficient lubricant.
2. Improper lubricant.
3. Differential case bearings worn.
4. Drive pinion shaft bearings worn.
5. Ring and pinion worn.
6. Excessive backlash.
7. Insufficient backlash.
8. Excessive ring and pinion backlash.
9. Insufficient ring and pinion backlash.
10. Pinion shaft or differential case bearings not preloaded.
11. Excessive ring gear runout.

12. Ring gear fasteners loose.
13. Ring and pinion not matched.
14. Differential case bearing cap fasteners loose.
15. Warped housing.
16. Pinion shaft companion flange retaining nut loose.
17. Tooth (ring and pinion) contact pattern incorrect.
18. Loose wheel.
19. Wheel hub loose on tapered axle.
20. Wheel hub key (on tapered axle) sheared.
21. Wheel (axle) bearing worn.
22. Bent axle.
23. Wheel hub or axle keyway worn.
24. Dry pinion shaft seal.
25. Loose universal joint retainers.
26. Damaged universal joint.
27. Worn or broken front-wheel drive front suspension parts.
28. Worn or broken transaxle unit.

Correction
1. Fill housing to correct level.
2. Drain. Flush and fill with correct lubricant.
3. Replace bearings.
4. Replace pinion bearings.
5. Replace ring and pinion.
6. Adjust backlash.
7. Adjust backlash.
8. Adjust backlash.
9. Adjust backlash.
10. Preload as specified by the manufacturer.
11. Remove ring, clean, and check flange runout. Reinstall and check runout. Replace ring or case as needed.
12. Torque fasteners.
13. Install a matched ring and pinion set.
14. Torque fasteners.
15. Replace housing.
16. Torque flange nut.
17. Adjust as needed.
18. Tighten wheel lugs.
19. Inspect, if not damaged, torque retaining nut.
20. Install new key.
21. Replace axle bearing and seal.
22. Replace axle.
23. Replace axle or hub as needed.
24. Replace pinion shaft seal.
25. Tighten universal joint retainers.
26. Replace universal joint.
27. Repair or replace as necessary.
28. Repair or replace as needed.

─────────── Problem: Noise when rounding a curve ───────────

Possible cause
1. Differential pinion gears worn or broken.
2. Differential pinion shaft worn.
3. Axle side gears worn or broken.
4. Excessive axle side gear or pinion gear end play.
5. Excessive axle end play.
6. Improper type of lubricant.
7. Loose or broken suspension parts (front-wheel drive).
8. Loose or broken universal joints.

Correction
1. Replace gears.
2. Replace pinion shaft.
3. Replace side gears.
4. Install new thrust washers or replace case and/or gears.
5. Adjust end play.
6. Drain. Flush and fill with correct lubricant.
7. Repair or replace parts as needed.
8. Tighten or replace universal joints.

─────── Problem: Clunking sound when engaging clutch, accelerating, or decelerating ───────

Possible cause
1. Excessive ring and pinion backlash.
2. Excessive end play in pinion shaft.
3. Axle side gears and pinions worn.
4. Differential bearings worn.
5. Side gear thrust washers worn.
6. Differential pinion shaft loose in case or pinions.
7. Axle shaft splines worn.
8. Wheel hub or axle keyway worn.
9. Loose wheel or hub.
10. Loose or broken universal joints.

Correction
1. Adjust backlash.
2. Preload bearings.
3. Replace worn gears.
4. Replace bearings.
5. Replace thrust washers.
6. Replace pinion shaft, gears, or differential case.
7. Replace axle.
8. Replace hub or axle.
9. Tighten fasteners.
10. Tighten or replace universal joints.

─────── Problem: Axle leaking lubricant ───────

Possible cause
1. Breather clogged.
2. Worn seals.
3. Carrier-to-housing or inspection cover loose.
4. Carrier or inspection cover gasket damaged.
5. Lubricant level too high.
6. Wrong type of lubricant.
7. Porous housing (standard and transaxle).
8. Stripped fill plug threads.
9. Cracked housing (standard and transaxle).

Correction
1. Open breather.
2. Install new seals.
3. Tighten fasteners.
4. Install new gasket or sealer.
5. Drain lubricant to proper level.
6. Drain. Flush and install correct lubricant.
7. Repair or replace housing.
8. Repair or replace as needed.
9. Repair or replace housing.

─────── Problem: Noises that may be confused with drive axle assembly ───────

Possible cause
1. Low air pressure in tires.
2. Road surface.
3. Transmission.
4. Bent propeller shaft.
5. Loose U-joints.
6. Engine.
7. Front wheel bearings.
8. Tire tread.
9. Dragging brakes.
10. Excessive front wheel end play.

Correction
1. Inflate tires to proper pressure.
2. Test on several different road surfaces.
3. Check transmission.
4. Replace shaft.
5. Tighten of replace U-joints.
6. Check engine.
7. Replace bearings.
8. Inflate temporarily to 50 psi (34.5 kPa) for road test only.
9. Adjust brakes.
10. Adjust wheel bearings.

─────── Problem: Rear axle overheating ───────

Possible cause
1. Wrong type of lubricant.
2. Insufficient lubricant.
3. Overloading (pulling heavy trailer).
4. Gears worn.
5. Bearing preload too great.
6. Insufficient backlash between ring and pinion.

Correction
1. Drain, flush, and fill with correct lubricant.
2. Fill lubricant to proper level.
3. Reduce vehicle load. Advise driver.
4. Replace gears.
5. Adjust preload as specified.
6. Adjust backlash.

Brake Problem Diagnosis

─────── Problem: No brakes ───────

Possible cause
1. Broken line, hose, or other leak.
2. Air in system.
3. Lining and/or pads worn.
4. Master cylinder cups leaking.
5. Low fluid level in master cylinder.
6. Brake pedal linkage disconnected.
7. Automatic shoe adjusters not functioning.
8. Vaporized fluid from excessive braking.
9. Caliper seal or piston damage.

Correction
1. Repair source of leak.
2. Bleed system. Repair source of air entry.
3. Adjust or reline brakes.
4. Rebuild or replace master cylinder.
5. Fill reservoir and bleed system.
6. Reconnect brake pedal.
7. Repair or replace adjusters. Adjust shoes.
8. Allow to cool. Install super heavy-duty fluid. Advise driver.
9. Repair or replace caliper as needed.

Problem: Spongy pedal

Possible cause
1. Air in system.
2. Shoes not centered in drum.
3. Drums worn or too thin.
4. Soft hose.
5. Shoe lining wrong thickness.
6. Cracked brake drum.
7. Brake shoes distorted.
8. Insufficient brake fluid.
9. Bent pads.

Correction
1. Bleed system. Repair source of air entry.
2. Adjust anchors to center shoes.
3. Replace drums.
4. Replace hose.
5. Install correct lining.
6. Replace drum.
7. Replace shoes.
8. Bleed system. Fill with fluid.
9. Replace pads.

Problem: Hard pedal (excessive foot pressure required)

Possible cause
1. Incorrect lining.
2. Linings contaminated with grease or brake fluid.
3. Brake shoes not centered.
4. Primary and secondary shoes reversed.
5. Brake linkage binding.
6. Master or wheel cylinder pistons frozen.
7. Linings hard and glazed.
8. Lining ground to wrong radius.
9. Brake line or hose clogged or kinked.
10. Power booster unit defective.
11. No vacuum to power booster.
12. Engine fails to maintain proper vacuum to booster.
13. Pads worn excessively thin.
14. Seized caliper piston(s).
15. Heat-checked or blued rotor.
16. Faulty proportioning valve.
17. Quick take-up valve center orifice clogged.

Correction
1. Install proper lining.
2. Replace or reline shoes. Repair source of leak.
3. Center brake shoes.
4. Install shoes in correct location.
5. Free and lubricate.
6. Rebuild or replace cylinder.
7. Sand lining with medium grit sandpaper.
8. Grind lining as specified.
9. Repair or replace line or hose.
10. Repair or replace power booster.
11. Replace clogged, soft lines. Repair vacuum leaks.
12. Tune or overhaul engine.
13. Replace pads.
14. Repair or replace.
15. Replace rotor.
16. Replace valve.
17. Replace master cylinder.

Problem: Brakes grab (one or more wheels)

Possible cause
1. Grease or brake fluid on lining and/or pads.
2. Lining charred.
3. Lining loose on shoe.
4. Loose wheel bearings.
5. Defective wheel bearings.
6. Loose brake backing plate.
7. Defective drum.
8. Sand or dirt in brake shoe assembly.
9. Wrong brake lining.
10. Primary and secondary linings or shoes reversed.
11. Loose caliper.
12. Defective power brake booster.
13. Uneven tire pressure.

Correction
1. Replace lining and/or pads.
2. If mild, sand. If severe, replace.
3. Replace brake shoes.
4. Adjust wheel bearings.
5. Replace bearings.
6. Torque backing plate fasteners.
7. Resurface or replace drum.
8. Disassemble and clean linings and drum.
9. Install correct lining.
10. Install correctly.
11. Tighten to specifications.
12. Repair or replace.
13. Inflate to specifications.

Problem: Brakes fade

Possible cause
1. Poor quality shoes and/or pads.
2. Excessive use of brakes.
3. Overheated brake fluid.
4. Improper lining-to-drum contact.
5. Thin brake drums.
6. Dragging brakes.
7. "Riding" the brake pedal.
8. Excessively thin rotors.

Correction
1. Replace shoes and/or pads.
2. Use lower gears, reduce speed or load.
3. Flush. Install super heavy-duty fluid.
4. Adjust shoes or resurface drum.
5. Install new drums.
6. Adjust or repair other cause of dragging.
7. Advise driver to keep foot off brake pedal unless needed.
8. Replace rotors.

Problem: Brakes pull vehicle to one side

Possible cause
1. One wheel grabbing.
2. Shoes not centered or adjusted properly.
3. Different lining on one side or shoes reversed on one side.

Correction
1. See *Brakes grab*.
2. Center and adjust lining-to-drum clearance.
3. Replace lining or install shoes in proper position.

4. Plugged brake line or hose.
5. Uneven tire pressure.
6. Front end misaligned.
7. Sagged, weak, or broken spring. Weak shock absorber or strut.
8. Wheel cylinder bore diameter different on one side.
9. Pads contaminated with grease or brake fluid.
10. Caliper or backing plate loose.

4. Clean or replace brake line.
5. Use same pressure on both sides.
6. Align front end.
7. Install new spring, shocks or struts.
8. Install correct size cylinder.
9. Replace pads.
10. Tighten backing plate retainers to specifications.

─────── Problem: Brakes drag ───────

Possible cause
1. Parking brake adjusted too tight.
2. Clogged hose or line.
3. Master cylinder reservoir cap vent clogged.
4. Brake pedal not fully releasing.
5. Insufficient pedal free travel.

6. Brakes adjusted too tight.
7. Brakes not centered in drum.
8. Master cylinder or wheel cylinder cups soft and sticky.
9. Loose wheel bearing.
10. Parking brake fails to release.
11. Shoe retracting springs weak or broken.
12. Out-of-round drum.
13. Defective power booster.
14. Seized caliper piston.
15. Sliding caliper bound.

16. Rotor thickness out of specifications.
17. Loose caliper bolts.
18. Bent pads.
19. Improper or contaminated brake fluid.

Correction
1. Adjust properly.
2. Clean or replace brake line.
3. Open vent in cap.
4. Adjust brake pedal.
5. Adjust pedal free travel so that compensating port will be open when brake is released.
6. Adjust correctly.
7. Center shoes in drum.
8. Rebuild or replace cylinders. Flush system.
9. Adjust wheel bearings.
10. Clean and lubricate parking brake linkage.
11. Replace shoe springs.
12. Resurface drum.
13. Rebuild or replace booster.
14. Rebuild or replace caliper.
15. Free caliper. Clean sliding surfaces and lubricate if required by manufacturer.
16. Replace rotor.
17. Tighten to specifications.
18. Replace pads.
19. Repair as necessary.

─────── Problem: "Nervous" pedal (pedal moves rapidly up and down when applying brakes) ───────

Note: This is a normal operating condition on vehicles equipped with anti-lock brakes.

Possible cause
1. Brake drums out-of-round.
2. Excessive disc runout.
3. Loose wheel bearings.
4. Drums loose.
5. Rear axle bent.
6. Brake assembly attachments loose or missing.

Correction
1. Resurface drums.
2. Resurface or replace disc.
3. Adjust wheel bearings.
4. Tighten wheel lugs, adjust brakes.
5. Replace axle.
6. Repair as necessary.

─────── Problem: Brakes chatter ───────

Possible cause
1. Weak or broken shoe retracting springs.
2. Defective power booster.
3. Loose backing plate.
4. Loose or damaged wheel bearings.
5. Drums tapered or barrel shaped.
6. Bent brake shoes.
7. Dust on lining.
8. Lining glazed.
9. Drum damper spring missing.
10. Grease or fluid on linings.
11. Shoes not adjusted properly.
12. Incorrect brake pads.
13. Damaged brake pads.
14. Damaged rotors.

Correction
1. Replace springs.
2. Rebuild or replace booster.
3. Tighten fasteners.
4. Adjust or replace bearings.
5. Resurface drums.
6. Replace brake shoes.
7. Sand linings and clean.
8. Sand linings and clean.
9. Install damper spring.
10. Repair source of leak and reline brakes.
11. Center and adjust shoes.
12. Install correct pads.
13. Replace pads.
14. Replace or resurface rotors.

─────── Problem: Brakes squeal ───────

Possible cause
1. Glazed or charred shoes and/or pads.
2. Dust or metal particles imbedded in lining.
3. Lining rivets loose.

Correction
1. Sand or replace shoes and/or pads.
2. Sand lining and clean.
3. Replace pads or shoes.

4. Wrong type of lining.
5. Shoe hold-down springs weak or broken.
6. Drum damper spring missing.
7. Shoes improperly adjusted.
8. Shoes bent.
9. Bent backing plate.
10. Shoe retracting springs weak or broken.
11. Drum too thin.
12. Lining saturated with grease or brake fluid.
13. Pad wear sensors contacting rotor.
14. Rotor contacting caliper.

15. Loose outboard pads.

4. Install pads or shoes with the correct lining.
5. Replace hold-down springs.
6. Install damper spring around drum.
7. Adjust shoes.
8. Replace shoes.
9. Replace backing plate.
10. Replace springs.
11. Replace drum.
12. Replace lining. Repair leak.
13. Replace pads. Resurface rotor if necessary.
14. Check for loose fasteners, missing shims, and other problems. Correct as required.
15. Bend tabs to tighten. Replace if tabs are broken.

Problem: Shoes click

Possible cause
1. Shoe is pulled from backing plate by following tool marks in drum.
2. Shoe bent.
3. Shoe support pads on backing plate grooved.

Correction
1. Smooth drum braking surface.
2. Replace shoes.
3. Smooth and lubricate pads or replace backing plate.

Problem: Red brake warning light comes on

Possible cause
1. Air in system.
2. Malfunctioning master cylinder.
3. Worn out brake lining.
4. Defective shoe adjusters.
5. Contaminated or improper brake fluid.

Correction
1. Check for reason and bleed system.
2. Repair or replace as necessary.
3. Replace pads or shoes.
4. Adjust or replace as necessary.
5. Repair as necessary.

Problem: Amber anti-lock brake (ABS) light comes on

Possible cause
1. Anti-lock brake system malfunction.

Correction
1. Refer to manufacturer's diagnosis and service recommendations.

Problem: Automatic shoe adjusters will not function

Possible cause
1. Adjuster wheel (star wheel) rusty or dirty.
2. Parts installed wrong.
3. Adjuster lever dirty and sticky.
4. Star wheel notches burred.
5. Adjuster lever bent.

Correction
1. Clean threads. Lube with high temperature grease.
2. Install adjuster correctly.
3. Clean and lube adjuster.
4. Install new adjuster.
5. Install new adjuster lever.

Wheel Balance and Alignment Problem Diagnosis

Problem: Wheel tramp

Possible cause
1. Brake drum, rotor, wheel, or tire out of static balance.
2. Wheel or tire out-of-round (excessive radial runout).
3. Defective shock absorbers.
4. Bulge on tire.
5. Defective front stabilizer.
6. Loose or worn wheel bearings.
7. Defective MacPherson strut.

Correction
1. Balance assembly statically and dynamically.
2. Change tire position on wheel or discard tire or wheel as needed.
3. Replace shocks.
4. Replace tire.
5. Replace stabilizer.
6. Adjust or replace bearings.
7. Replace strut.

Problem: Wheel shimmy

Possible cause
1. Wheel and tire assembly out of dynamic balance.
2. Tire pressure uneven.
3. Worn or loose front wheel bearings.
4. Defective shock absorbers or struts.
5. Improper or uneven caster.
6. Excessive tire or wheel runout.
7. Abnormally worn tires.
8. Improper toe-in.
9. Defective stabilizer bar.

Correction
1. Balance assembly statically and dynamically.
2. Inflate both front tires to same pressure.
3. Adjust or replace bearings.
4. Replace shocks or struts.
5. Adjust caster angle.
6. Correct by moving tire on rim or replace defective parts.
7. Move to rear if still serviceable.
8. Adjust to specifications.
9. Replace stabilizer.

10. Tire pressure too low.
11. Loose wheel lugs.
12. Front end misaligned.
13. Bent wheel.

10. Inflate tires to correct pressure.
11. Tighten lugs.
12. Align front end.
13. Replace wheel.

Problem: Poor recovery following turns and/or hard steering

Possible cause
1. Low tire pressure.
2. Lack of lubrication.
3. Front wheels misaligned.
4. Bent spindle assembly.

Correction
1. Inflate to proper pressure.
2. Lubricate steering system.
3. Align front wheels properly.
4. Replace spindle assembly.

Problem: Vehicle pulls to one side

Possible cause
1. Uneven tire pressure.
2. Improper toe-in.
3. Incorrect or uneven caster.
4. Incorrect or uneven camber.
5. Improper rear wheel tracking.
6. Tires not same size.
7. Bent spindle assembly.
8. Worn or improperly adjusted wheel bearings.
9. Dragging brakes.

Correction
1. Inflate both front tires to same pressure.
2. Adjust toe-in to specifications.
3. Adjust caster angle.
4. Adjust camber angle.
5. Align rear axle assembly.
6. Install same size tires on both sides.
7. Replace spindle.
8. Adjust or replace bearings.
9. Adjust brakes.

Problem: Vehicle wanders from side to side

Possible cause
1. Low or uneven tire pressure.
2. Toe-in incorrect.
3. Improper caster.
4. Improper camber.
5. Worn or improperly adjusted front wheel bearings.
6. Vehicle overloaded or loaded too much on one side.
7. Bent spindle assembly.

Correction
1. Inflate tires to recommended pressure.
2. Adjust toe-in.
3. Adjust caster angle.
4. Adjust camber angle.
5. Replace or adjust wheel bearings.
6. Advise owner regarding vehicle load limits.
7. Replace spindle.

Problem: Tire squeal on corners

Possible cause
1. Low tire pressure.
2. Toe-out on turns incorrect.
3. Excessive cornering speed.
4. Bent spindle assembly.
5. Improper front end alignment.

Correction
1. Inflate to recommended pressure.
2. Replace bent steering arm.
3. Advise driver.
4. Replace spindle.
5. Align front wheels.

Problem: Loose, erratic steering

Possible cause
1. Loose front wheel bearings.
2. Loose wheel lugs.
3. Wheel out of balance.

Correction
1. Replace or adjust.
2. Tighten lugs.
3. Balance wheel assembly.

Problem: Hard riding

Possible cause
1. Excessive tire pressure.
2. Improper tire size.
3. Heavy-duty shock absorbers installed.

Correction
1. Reduce pressure to specifications.
2. Install correct size.
3. Advise driver and/or change shocks.

Problem: Improper wheel tracking

Possible cause
1. Frame sprung.
2. Rear axle housing sprung.
3. Broken leaf spring.
4. Broken spring center bolt; spring shifted on axle housing.
5. Wheels misaligned.

Correction
1. Straighten frame.
2. Replace or straighten housing.
3. Replace spring.
4. Install new spring center bolt.
5. Align all wheels.

Problem: Noise from front or rear wheels

Possible cause
1. Wheel lugs loose.
2. Defective wheel bearings.
3. Loose wheel bearings.
4. Lack of lubrication.
5. Lump or bulge on tire tread.
6. Rock or debris stuck in tire tread.
7. Cracked wheel.
8. Wheel hub loose on axle taper (where used).
9. Wheel bearing worn or defective.

Correction
1. Tighten lugs.
2. Replace wheel bearings.
3. Adjust wheel bearings.
4. Lubricate bearings.
5. Replace tire.
6. Remove rock or debris.
7. Replace wheel.
8. Inspect and tighten.
9. Replace wheel bearing.

Problem: Tires lose air

Possible cause
1. Puncture.
2. Bent, dirty, or rusty rim flanges.
3. Loose wheel-rim rivets.
4. Leaking valve core or stem.
5. Striking curbs with excessive force.
6. Flaw in tire casing.
7. Excessive cornering speed especially with low tire pressure.
8. Porous wheel rim.

Correction
1. Repair puncture.
2. Clean or replace wheel.
3. Peen rivets.
4. Replace as needed.
5. Advise driver.
6. Repair or replace tire.
7. Advise driver.
8. Repair porous wheel rim.

Problem: Tire wears in center

Possible cause
1. Excessive pressure.

Correction
1. Reduce tire pressure to specifications.

Problem: Tire wears on one edge

Possible cause
1. Improper camber.
2. High speed cornering.

Correction
1. Align camber angle.
2. Advise driver.

Problem: Tire wears on both sides

Possible cause
1. Low pressure.
2. Overloading vehicle.

Correction
1. Inflate tires to specifications.
2. Advise driver.

Problem: Tire scuffing or feather edging

Possible cause
1. Excessive toe-out (inside edges).
2. Excessive toe-in (outside edges).
3. Excessive cornering speed.
4. Improper tire pressure.
5. Wheel shimmy.
6. Improper toe-out on turns.
7. Excessive runout.
8. Improper camber.
9. Bent spindle assembly.

Correction
1. Correct toe-out.
2. Correct toe-in.
3. Advise driver.
4. Inflate tires to specifications.
5. Balance wheels statically and dynamically.
6. Replace bent steering arm.
7. Correct or replace tire or wheel.
8. Adjust camber angle.
9. Replace spindle.

Problem: Tire cupping

Possible cause
1. Uneven camber.
2. Bent spindle assembly.
3. Improper toe-in.
4. Improper tire pressure.
5. Excessive runout.
6. Wheel and tire assembly out of balance.
7. Worn or improperly adjusted wheel bearings.
8. Grabby brakes.

Correction
1. Correct camber angle.
2. Replace spindle.
3. Adjust toe-in.
4. Inflate tires to specifications.
5. Correct or replace wheel or tire.
6. Balance both statically and dynamically.
7. Replace or adjust wheel bearings.
8. Repair brakes.

Problem: Heel and toe wear

Possible cause
1. Grabby brakes.
2. Heavy acceleration.

Correction
1. Repair brakes.
2. Advise driver.

Manual and Power Steering Systems Diagnosis

Problem: Hard steering and poor recovery following turns

Possible cause	Correction
1. Tire pressure low.	1. Inflate to correct pressure.
2. Power steering pump defective.	2. Repair or replace pump.
3. Power steering pump fluid level low.	3. Add fluid to reservoir.
4. Manual steering gear lubricant level low.	4. Add lubricant.
5. Incorrect front wheel alignment.	5. Align front wheels.
6. Ball joints dry.	6. Lubricate ball joints.
7. Steering linkage sockets dry.	7. Lubricate linkage.
8. Linkage binding.	8. Relieve binding.
9. Damaged suspension arms.	9. Replace arms.
10. Steering gear adjusted too tight.	10. Adjust gear correctly.
11. Steering shaft bushing dry.	11. Lubricate bushings.
12. Steering shaft bushing or coupling binding.	12. Align shaft or coupling.
13. Excessive caster.	13. Adjust caster.
14. Sagged front springs.	14. Replace springs.
15. Bent spindle body.	15. Replace spindle.
16. Steering wheel rubbing steering column jacket.	16. Adjust jacket, check for steering shaft damage.
17. Steering gear misaligned.	17. Align gear.
18. Sticky valve spool.	18. Clean or replace spool valve.
19. Steering pump belt loose.	19. Adjust belt tension.
20. Power steering hose kinked or clogged.	20. Replace hose.
21. Different size front tires.	21. Install correct size tires on both sides.
22. Malfunctioning steering gear pressure port poppet valve.	22. Repair or replace.
23. Rack and pinion adjusted incorrectly.	23. Adjust to specifications.
24. High internal leakage of rack and pinion assembly.	24. Repair leaks or replace gear.
25. Rack and pinion mountings loose, causing binding.	25. Tighten mountings to specifications.
26. Defective steering stabilizer.	26. Replace stabilizer.

Problem: Vehicle pulls to one side

Possible cause	Correction
1. Uneven tire pressure.	1. Equalize pressure.
2. Brakes dragging.	2. Adjust brakes.
3. Improper front end alignment.	3. Align front end.
4. Wheel bearings improperly adjusted.	4. Adjust bearings.
5. Damaged or worn steering valve assembly.	5. Replace steering valve assembly.
6. Tire sizes not uniform.	6. Install tires of the same size.
7. Broken or sagged spring.	7. Replace spring.
8. Rear axle housing misaligned.	8. Align rear housing.
9. Bent spindle.	9. Replace spindle.
10. Frame sprung.	10. Straighten frame.
11. Radial tire problem.	11. Switch front tires. If vehicle now pulls in the other direction, tires are defective.

Problem: Vehicle wanders from side to side

Possible cause	Correction
1. Weak shock absorber or strut.	1. Replace shocks or struts.
2. Loose steering gear.	2. Torque mounting fasteners.
3. Loose rack and pinion mountings.	3. Tighten to specifications.
4. Ball joints and steering linkage need lubrication.	4. Lubricate suspension.
5. Steering gear not on high point.	5. Adjust steering gear properly.
6. Broken or missing stabilizer bar or link.	6. Replace stabilizer or link.
7. Rack and pinion improperly adjusted.	7. Adjust to specifications.
8. Tie rod end loose.	8. Tighten. Replace if worn.

Problem: Sudden increase in steering wheel resistance

Possible cause	Correction
1. Pump belt slipping.	1. Adjust belt tension.
2. Internal leakage in gear.	2. Overhaul or replace gear.
3. Fluid level low in pump.	3. Add fluid.
4. Engine idle too slow.	4. Adjust idle.
5. Air in system.	5. Bleed system.
6. Low tire air pressure.	6. Inflate to recommended level.
7. Insufficient pump pressure.	7. Test and repair or replace as required.
8. High internal leakage in rack and pinion.	8. Repair leaks or replace gear.
9. Defective steering stabilizer.	9. Replace stabilizer.

Problem: Steering wheel action jerky during parking

Possible cause
1. Loose pump belt.
2. Oily pump belt.
3. Defective flow control valve.
4. Insufficient pump pressure.

Correction
1. Adjust belt tension.
2. Replace belt. Clean pulleys. Repair source of leak.
3. Replace flow control valve.
4. Test and repair.

Problem: No effort required to turn wheel

Possible cause
1. Steering gear torsion bar broken.
2. Broken tilt column U-joint.
3. Steering wheel hub-to-shaft key missing. Splines stripped. Loose nut.

Correction
1. Replace spool valve and shaft assembly.
2. Replace U-joint.
3. Replace key, shaft, or wheel. Tighten nut to specifications.

Problem: Excessive wheel kickback and play

Possible cause
1. Steering linkage worn.
2. Air in system.
3. Front wheel bearings improperly adjusted.
4. Gear over-center adjustment loose.
5. Worm gear not preloaded.
6. No worm to rack-piston preload.
7. Loose pitman arm.
8. Loose steering gear.
9. Steering arms loose on spindle body.
10. Excessive play in ball joints.
11. Defective rotary valve.
12. Worn steering shaft universal joint.
13. Extra large tires.

14. Defective steering stabilizer.

Correction
1. Replace worn linkage components.
2. Bleed and add fluid if needed.
3. Adjust front wheel bearings.
4. Make correct over-center adjustment.
5. Preload worm gear.
6. Install larger set of rack piston balls.
7. Torque pitman arm nut.
8. Tighten mounting fasteners.
9. Tighten arm fasteners.
10. Replace ball joints.
11. Replace rotary valve.
12. Replace joint and/or shaft.
13. Advise owner. Install a steering stabilizer or replace with a larger stabilizer.
14. Replace stabilizer.

Problem: No power assist in one direction

Possible cause
1. Defective steering gear.

Correction
1. Overhaul or replace gear as needed.

Problem: Steering pump pressure low

Possible cause
1. Pump belt loose.
2. Belt oily.
3. Pump parts worn.
4. Relief valve springs defective or stuck open.
5. Low fluid level in reservoir.
6. Air in system.
7. Defective hose.
8. Flow control valve stuck open.
9. Pressure plate not seated against cam ring.
10. Scored pressure plate, thrust plate, or rotor.
11. Vanes incorrectly installed.
12. Vanes sticking in rotor.
13. Worn or damaged O-rings.

Correction
1. Adjust belt.
2. Clean pulleys. Replace belt. Correct source of leak.
3. Overhaul pump.
4. Repair or replace as needed.
5. Add fluid.
6. Correct source of leak. Bleed system.
7. Replace hose.
8. Clean or replace valve.
9. Repair or replace cam ring and pressure plate.
10. Replace damaged parts and flush system.
11. Install vanes correctly.
12. Free vanes. Clean thoroughly.
13. Replace O-rings.

Problem: Steering pump noise

Possible cause
1. Air in system.
2. Loose pump pulley.
3. Loose belt.
4. Glazed belt.
5. Hoses touching splash shield.
6. Low fluid level.
7. Clogged or kinked hose.
8. Scored pressure plate.
9. Scored rotor.
10. Vanes installed wrong.
11. Vanes sticking in rotor.
12. Defective flow control valve.

Correction
1. Correct leak and bleed system.
2. Tighten pulley.
3. Tension belt correctly.
4. Replace belt.
5. Reroute hose to prevent contact.
6. Add fluid, check for leaks.
7. Replace hose.
8. Polish. Replace if badly scored.
9. Polish. Replace if badly scored.
10. Install vanes correctly.
11. Free vanes and clean thoroughly.
12. Replace flow control valve.

13. Loose pump.
14. Reservoir vent plugged.
15. Dirty fluid.
16. Pump bearing worn.
17. Chirp type noise.
18. Whine or growl.

13. Tighten pump mounting fasteners.
14. Clean vent.
15. Drain, flush, and refill.
16. Overhaul as needed.
17. Tighten loose belt.
18. Low fluid. Fill to proper level.

Problem: Steering gear dull rattle or chuckle

Possible cause
1. Gear loose on frame.
2. Loose over-center adjustment.
3. No worm shaft preload.
4. Insufficient or improper lubricant (manual gear).

Correction
1. Tighten gear mounting fasteners.
2. Make correct over-center adjustment.
3. Adjust preload.
4. Fill with specified lubricant.

Problem: Hissing sound in gear

Possible cause
1. Normal sound when turning wheel when vehicle is standing still or when holding wheel against stops.
2. Gear loose.
3. Noisy pressure control valve.
4. Intermediate shaft rubber plug missing.

Correction
1. Normal condition, advise driver.
2. Tighten mounting fasteners.
3. Replace valve.
4. Replace plug.

Problem: Tire squeal on turns

Possible cause
1. Excessive speed.
2. Low air pressure.
3. Faulty wheel alignment.
4. Excessive load.
5. Rack and pinion mountings loose.

Correction
1. Advise driver.
2. Inflate to correct pressure.
3. Align wheels.
4. Advise driver.
5. Tighten mountings to specifications.

Problem: External fluid leaks

Possible cause
1. Defective hose.
2. Loose hose connections.
3. Cracked hose connections.
4. Pitman shaft seal in gear defective.
5. Gear housing end cover O-ring seal leaking.
6. Gear torsion bar seal leaking.
7. Adjuster plug seals leaking.
8. Side cover gasket.
9. Pump too full.
10. Pump shaft seal defective.
11. Scored shaft in pump.
12. Oil leaking out of reservoir from air contamination.
13. Pump assembly fasteners loose.
14. Leaking power cylinder (linkage type).
15. Rack and pinion housing cracked.
16. Extreme cam ring wear.
17. Scored pressure plate, rotor, or thrust plate.
18. Vanes incorrectly installed.
19. Reservoir cracked.
20. Pump reservoir cap leaking.
21. Defective rack and pinion stub shaft seal.
22. Defective rack and pinion rotary valve.
23. Pinion shaft seal leaking.
24. Rack and pinion bulkhead seal defective.

Correction
1. Replace hose.
2. Tighten to proper torque.
3. Replace hose.
4. Replace seal. Check bearing for excessive wear.
5. Replace seal.
6. Replace valve and shaft assembly.
7. Replace seals.
8. Replace gasket.
9. Reduce fluid level.
10. Replace shaft seal.
11. Replace shaft.
12. Correct source of air leak.
13. Torque fasteners.
14. Overhaul as needed.
15. Replace steering gear.
16. Replace parts. Flush system.
17. Replace parts. Flush system.
18. Install pump vanes properly.
19. Replace reservoir.
20. Repair or replace cap.
21. Replace stub shaft seal.
22. Replace rotary valve.
23. Replace shaft seal.
24. Replace seal.

Air Conditioning System Diagnosis

Problem: Excessive high side pressure

Possible cause
1. Air in system.

2. Overcharge of refrigerant.
3. Engine overheating.
4. Fan belt slipping.

Correction
1. Leak test. Recover and correct leak. Evacuate and charge system.
2. Recover. Evacuate and charge with correct amount.
3. Correct cause of overheating.
4. Adjust or replace belt.

5. Clogged condenser core.
6. Excessive oil in system.
7. Restriction in lines, condenser, or receiver-dehydrator.
8. Expansion valve superheat setting too low.
9. Filters or screens plugged.

5. Remove bugs, leaves, dirt, and other debris.
6. Remove excess oil.
7. Remove part and clean or replace as needed.
8. Replace unit.
9. Remove and clean or replace as needed.

Problem: Insufficient high side pressure

Possible cause
1. Insufficient refrigerant charge.
2. Defective compressor valves.
3. Expansion valve or evaporator pressure valve stuck open.

Correction
1. Charge system with recommended amount or refrigerant.
2. Replace valves or compressor.
3. Replace valve.

Problem: Excessive low side pressure

Possible cause
1. Defective expansion valve.
2. Insufficient oil in system.
3. Expansion valve thermal bulb not in good contact with evaporator.
4. Defective evaporator pressure control valve.
5. Expansion valve frozen.
6. Compressor clutch slipping.
7. Restricted suction line.
8. Slipping compressor drive belt.
9. Defective compressor valves.
10. Moisture in system.

Correction
1. Replace expansion valve.
2. Add oil.
3. Clean connection and tighten. Insulate outlet pipe as required.
4. Replace control valve.
5. Replace receiver-dehydrator. Recharge system.
6. Repair or replace clutch.
7. Clean or replace suction line.
8. Adjust or replace belt.
9. Replace valves or compressor.
10. Repair leaks. Replace receiver-drier. Evacuate and recharge system.

Problem: Insufficient low side pressure

Possible cause
1. Insufficient charge.
2. Insufficient airflow.
3. Defective evaporator pressure control valve.
4. Defective expansion valve.
5. Liquid line clogged.
6. Restricted suction line, receiver-drier, or expansion valve.
7. Temperature control thermostat does not cut out.
8. Compressor clutch will not disengage.

Correction
1. Charge with recommended amount of refrigerant.
2. Clean evaporator core. Check blower operation.
3. Repair. Adjust or replace as needed.
4. Replace expansion valve.
5. Replace line.
6. Replace line, receiver-dehydrator, or expansion valve.
7. Replace thermostat.
8. Repair or replace compressor clutch.

Problem: Water discharged with airflow

Possible cause
1. Clogged evaporator drain.

Correction
1. Clean evaporator drain.

Problem: System noisy

Possible cause
1. Compressor mounting loose.
2. Compressor belt slipping.
3. Refrigeration system lines vibrating.
4. Blower motor defective.
5. Loose air ducts.
6. Excessive oil in system.
7. Blower blades striking housing.
8. Obstructions in airflow system.
9. Defective compressor.
10. Defective expansion valve.

Correction
1. Tighten mounting fasteners.
2. Adjust belt tension.
3. Install clamps and insulators.
4. Replace blower motor.
5. Tighten air ducts.
6. Drain and install correct amount of oil.
7. Adjust for clearance.
8. Remove obstructions.
9. Repair or replace as required.
10. Replace expansion valve.

Problem: Airflow contains objectionable odor

Possible cause
1. Odor-producing material on evaporator core.
2. Outside odors drawn in by airflow system.

Correction
1. Clean evaporator core, add disinfectant.
2. Advise driver as to reason.

─────────────── **Problem: Insufficient airflow** ───────────────

Possible cause
1. Defective blower.
2. Clogged ducts.
3. Evaporator core icing.
4. Loose duct hose connections.
5. Shut-off valves in air discharge outlets closed.
6. Dirty evaporator core.
7. Airflow system control doors malfunctioning.
8. Blower disconnected or circuit fuse blown.

Correction
1. Replace blower.
2. Clean ducts.
3. Replace control valve or thermostatic switch.
4. Attach flexible hose securely.
5. Advise driver as to proper operation.
6. Clean core.
7. Check vacuum or electronic control system.
8. Connect or replace fuse.

─────────────── **Problem: Evaporator icing** ───────────────

Possible cause
1. Defective or improperly adjusted evaporator pressure valve.
2. Defective thermostatic switch.
3. Compressor clutch will not disengage.
4. Thermostat capillary tube not in proper contact with evaporator

Correction
1. Adjust or replace valve.
2. Replace switch.
3. Repair clutch.
4. Place tube in proper contact with core.

─────────────── **Problem: No or insufficient cooling** ───────────────

Possible cause
1. Defective thermostatic switch.
2. Defective evaporator pressure valve.
3. Broken or slipping compressor belt.
4. Compressor defective.
5. Compressor clutch inoperative.
6. Defective expansion valve.
7. Insufficient refrigerant charge.
8. Excessive oil in system.
9. Expansion valve screen clogged.
10. Bugs, leaves, other debris on condenser.
11. Fan belt slipping or broken.
12. Excessive refrigerant charge.
13. Moisture in system.
14. Air in system.
15. Evaporator core dirty.
16. Clogged or kinked lines.
17. Clogged receiver-dehydrator.
18. Engine overhearing.
19. Clogged evaporator drain.
20. Evaporator icing.
21. Clogged orifice tube.

Correction
1. Replace switch.
2. Replace valve.
3. Replace or adjust tension.
4. Replace compressor.
5. Repair clutch.
6. Replace expansion valve.
7. Charge system.
8. Drain system and add correct amount.
9. Clean screen or replace valve.
10. Clean condenser.
11. Adjust tension or replace belt.
12. Charge correctly.
13. Repair leaks. Install new receiver-dehydrator and charge.
14. Repair leaks. Evacuate and charge.
15. Clean core.
16. Clean or replace lines.
17. Install new receiver-dehydrator.
18. Correct cause.
19. Clean drain.
20. See *Evaporator icing*.
21. Replace orifice tube.

Air Distribution System Diagnosis

─────────────── Problem: Blower does not operate correctly ───────────────

Possible cause
1. Blown fuse.
2. Defective motor.
3. Faulty blower resistor.
4. Defective switch.
5. Loose connections.
6. Faulty wiring.

Correction
1. Replace fuse. Fix short if needed.
2. Replace motor.
3. Replace resistor.
4. Replace switch.
5. Clean and tighten.
6. Repair wiring.

─────────────── Problem: Inadequate heating ───────────────

Possible cause
1. Faulty blower motor.
2. Heat valve control inoperative.
3. Defective heat control valve.
4. Clogged air inlet.
5. Bent, kinked inlet ducting.

Correction
1. Replace blower motor.
2. Free control and make certain valve control functions.
3. Replace heat control valve.
4. Clean air inlet, replace screen if missing.
5. Straighten or replace.

6. Debris on heater core.
7. Control doors inoperative.
8. Faulty controls
9. Faulty heater operation.
10. Faulty engine thermostat.
11. Plugged or kinked heater hoses.
12. Low engine coolant level.
13. Clogged heater core.

6. Clean heater core.
7. Free and make certain they operate properly.
8. Adjust or replace as needed.
9. Advise owner as to proper operation.
10. Replace thermostat.
11. Straighten or replace hoses.
12. Add coolant and check for leaks.
13. Reverse flush or replace heater core.

Problem: Inadequate defrost

Possible cause
1. Defective blower switch.
2. Defective or inoperative blower motor.
3. Defroster ducts are disconnected.
4. Improper control door operation.
5. Clogged defroster outlets.

Correction
1. Replace switch.
2. Repair or replace.
3. Connect ducts.
4. Free, adjust, and check control door.
5. Clean outlets.

Problem: Defrost causes windshield fogging

Possible cause
1. Leaking heater core.
2. Loose hose to core fitting.
3. Water (from rain or washing) entering system.

Correction
1. Replace heater core.
2. Tighten fitting.
3. Check seals for leaks.

Problem: Excessive heat

Possible cause
1. Faulty operation of controls.
2. Controls loose or stuck.

Correction
1. Advise driver in correct use.
2. Connect and check for proper operation.

Tech Talk

When diagnosing a problem, always check the easy, obvious causes first. This includes making visual checks and looking into known failure points of a particular vehicle. However, when you locate a failed component, do not simply replace it. Always try to figure out why it failed. There may be an underlying problem that will destroy the replacement component.

While you should listen to customer complaints and gather as much information as possible from other sources, always make your own tests and draw your own conclusions about the problem. Do not trust the information or test results provided by anybody else, whether it is the owner or a fellow technician.

When using the factory diagnostic sequences, follow them exactly. At the very least, this will tell you what the problem is not. Using the factory diagnostic sequences will allow you to deal with one problem at a time. Do all possible troubleshooting before disassembling or replacing any components. Be sure that replacement parts are correct and of good quality. If your chain of diagnosis does not work, start again from the beginning.

Review Questions—Chapter 42

Do not write in this book. Write your answers on a separate sheet of paper.

1. List the possible causes of belt squealing when the engine is accelerated.
2. Noise caused by a worn water pump bearing can be fixed by _____.
   (A) adding water pump lube to the cooling system
   (B) replacing the pump
   (C) adjusting the drive belt
   (D) Either A or B.
3. Which of the following defects could cause low charging system output?
   (A) Loose belt.
   (B) Worn alternator brushes.
   (C) Worn alternator bearings.
   (D) Either A or B.
4. A clogged exhaust system will cause what driveability problem?
5. What effect would very heavy engine oil have on the operation of the starter?
6. Name three driver actions that could cause rapid clutch wear.
7. Name five noises that may be confused with noises in the rear axle assembly.

8. What could cause the amber ABS light to come on?
   (A) ABS electronic system malfunction.
   (B) A base brake hydraulic malfunction.
   (C) A low fluid level in the master cylinder.
   (D) All of the above.

9. If there is no power assist in one direction only, what could be the cause?
   (A) Low pressure in one tire.
   (B) Stuck brake caliper on one side.
   (C) Defective power steering gear.
   (D) Defective power steering pump.

10. If a blower motor keeps blowing fuses, what could be the problem?

ASE-Type Questions

1. All of the following can cause slow engine warmup EXCEPT:
   (A) missing thermostat.
   (B) slipping water pump belt.
   (C) thermostat stuck open.
   (D) improper tenperature themostat.

2. Technician A says that rough idle could be caused by a vacuum leak. Technician B says that rough idle could be caused by excessive idle speeds. Who is right?
   (A) A only.
   (B) B only.
   (C) Both A & B.
   (D) Neither A nor B.

3. All of the following could cause detonation (pinging), EXCEPT:
   (A) retarded timing.
   (B) low octane fuel.
   (C) overheated engine.
   (D) excessive compression pressures.

4. A carbon track in the distributor cap could cause all of the following, EXCEPT:
   (A) backfiring.
   (B) missing.
   (C) preignition.
   (D) kicking back during cranking.

5. Technician A says that the EGR valve will remain open if it does not receive vacuum. Technician B says that the EGR valve will remain closed if it does not receive vacuum. Who is right?
   (A) A only.
   (B) B only.
   (C) Both A & B.
   (D) Neither A nor B.

6. Technician A says that noise in a manual transmission reduction gear may be in the countergear. Technician B says that noise in a manual transmission reduction gear may be caused by a problem with the constant mesh gear. Who is right?
   (A) A only.
   (B) B only.
   (C) Both A & B.
   (D) Neither A nor B.

7. All of the following could cause U-joint noise, EXCEPT:
   (A) Worn joint internals.
   (B) Loose fasteners.
   (C) Lack of lubrication.
   (D) Overlubrication.

8. An out-of-round drum could cause brake _____.
   (A) pulsation
   (B) fading
   (C) grabbing
   (D) Both A & C.

9. A vehicle has a complaint of a hard ride. Technician A says that the tires could be underinflated. Technician B says that heavy-duty shock absorbers could have been installed. Who is right?
   (A) A only.
   (B) B only.
   (C) Both A & B.
   (D) Neither A nor B.

10. Too much heat from the heating system is a sign of

    _____.
    (A) a defective blower
    (B) low coolant level
    (C) misadjusted controls
    (D) a clogged heater core

Suggested Activities

1. Use the diagnosis charts in this chapter to determine the causes of an engine miss at high speeds. List them in the order that you think they should be checked.

2. Use the diagnosis charts in this chapter to determine the causes of transmission slippage. List them in the order that you think they should be checked.

3. Use the diagnosis charts in this chapter to determine the causes of loose steering. List them in the order that you think they should be checked.

4. Consult the diagnosis charts in a service manual to determine the causes of high engine oil consumption. Note the order that they should be checked.

5. Consult the diagnosis charts in a service manual to determine the causes of a vibration when the brakes are applied. Note the order that they should be checked.

6. Consult the diagnosis charts in a service manual to determine the causes of no heat from the vehicle heater. Note the order that they should be checked.

Cutaway of a late-model four wheel drive vehicle. Before servicing any vehicle, the service writer or technician should fill out a repair order. (Chevrolet)

43

Repair Orders and Cost Estimates

After studying this chapter, you will be able to:
- Explain the purpose of repair orders.
- Fill out a repair order.
- Explain the purpose of cost estimates.
- Complete a cost estimate.

This chapter explains the use of repair orders and cost estimates. Repair orders tell the technician about a vehicle's problem and the needed repair. They also provide a record for billing the customer. The technician must be able to prepare cost estimates so that the customer can have a basis for determining whether or not a repair should be performed.

 Note: This is an important chapter. It will help you develop important skills needed for many positions in the auto repair industry. Study it carefully.

Repair Orders

A *repair order,* also called a shop work order, is used to keep a record of the services performed on a particular vehicle. It is used to determine the final bill and may be used to determine the technician's pay for work performed. If the vehicle service will be paid for by the customer, the repair order is termed a **customer pay order.** If the service is covered by a warranty or guarantee, the repair order is called a **warranty order.** Many repair orders contain both customer pay and warranty work. See **Figures 43-1** and **43-2.**

The repair order is initiated by the service manager, service writer, or shop manager. This person fills in the customer's name, address, and telephone number, and completes the vehicle information, such as the make, model, year, mileage, and number of cylinders.

The vehicle's problem is also listed on the repair order to aid the technician. If the customer complained of a cold start driveability problem, for example, this will provide the technician with a starting point for diagnosis. If the vehicle is in for routine maintenance services, there will be no problem listed.

 Note: It is the job of the person who initiates the order to determine the actual problem area. If, for instance, the customer comes in wanting a "tune-up," the actual vehicle performance or driveability complaint should be determined.

An estimate of the anticipated repair costs (explained below) is shown to the customer. If he or she agrees to the cost, the repair order is then given to a technician to be used for diagnosing, testing, and correcting the problem. If costs will exceed the estimate, the customer should be notified. The customer should give permission for the increased cost before the job is completed.

At the beginning of the repair job, the technician will write or punch in the time started and will do the same when finished, allowing for time off for lunch, breaks, or other jobs. When the defective parts are replaced, they are listed in the space provided on the repair order. The part number, description, and price are also included. In some cases, it will be necessary to state whether the part is new, used, or rebuilt.

After the repair is complete, the labor cost is computed. Then, the part prices, the costs of outside repair services, and the prices of other supplies are added to the order. All prices are totaled and sales tax is added. This is the customer's total bill. The calculation of prices will probably be the job of the service manager or the shop cashier. No matter what you are required to fill in on the repair order, make all necessary additions neatly and correctly. This provides that added "professional look" to your overall work. In many cases, the repair order will be used to calculate your pay. Accuracy and legibility are critical.

One or two copies of the repair order are given to the customer. The remaining copies are retained by the shop for records. Warranty repair orders are similar to standard repair orders and usually use the same order form. The customer also receives a copy of this order, but is not billed for repairs covered under the warranty.

Determining Labor Costs

Most shops use one of two methods to determine correct labor costs. In the first method, labor costs are

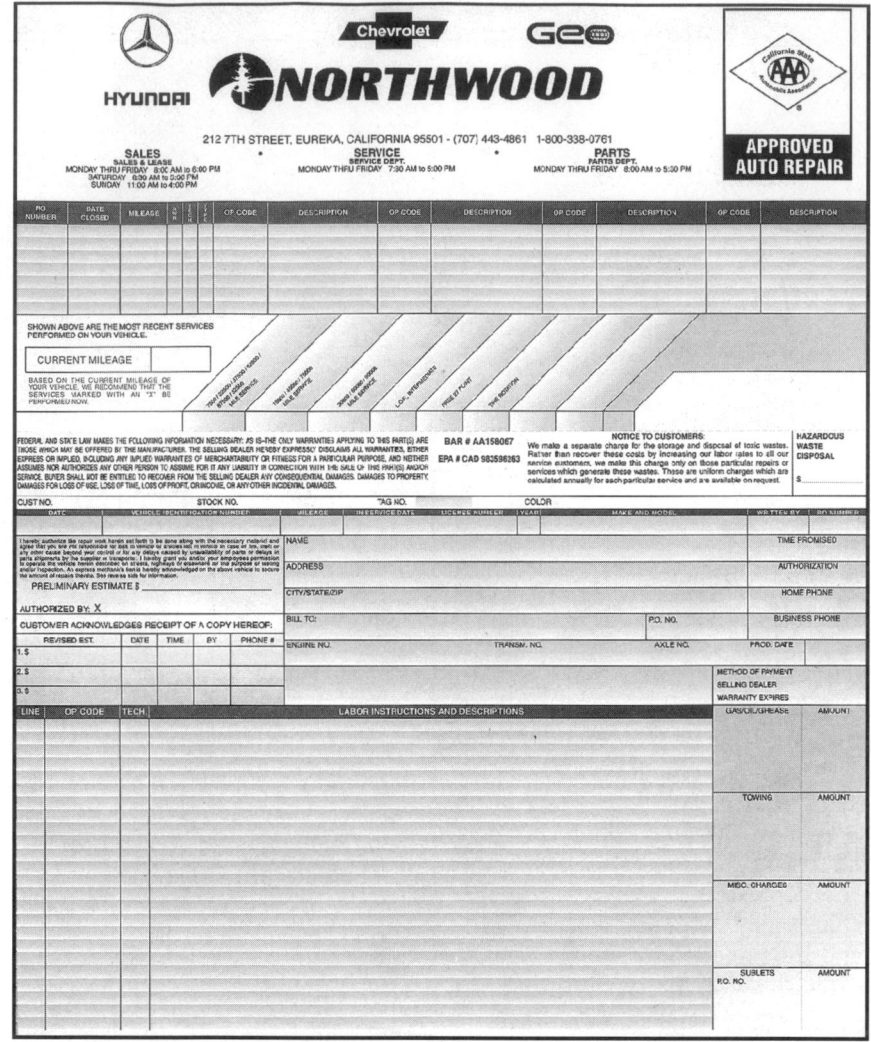

Figure 43-1. One type of shop repair order. Study the various sections carefully. Note the section for labor instructions and the box for the hazardous waste disposal fee. (Northwood Auto Plaza)

calculated using an **hourly rate** (amount charged per hour of technician's time). The time actually spent working on the vehicle multiplied by the labor rate is equal to labor cost. If, for example, the repair took two hours and the hourly rate is $50.00, the bill would be $100.00 ($50.00 × 2 hours).

The other method involves the use of a **flat rate manual.** This manual gives an estimate of how much time the technician should need to complete certain repairs. If the technician is to replace a set of spark plugs, he or she simply looks up plug replacement for the engine being serviced. The manual may indicate one hour for the job. Again, the number of hours multiplied by the labor rate will give the cost (1 hour × $50.00 = $50.00). If unexpected problems arise and the plug replacement takes two hours, the customer is only required to pay the flat rate amount. This prevents overcharging.

In addition to the regular hourly wage, some shops pay their technicians the difference between flat rate time and actual repair time if actual repair time is less than the quoted flat rate. This allows a fast technician to earn more per hour.

Determining Part Costs

When calculating part costs on a repair order, a percentage increase, or **markup,** is generally added to the **wholesale,** or **jobber,** price of each part. Wholesale prices will vary, depending on suppliers, brand names, and whether the part is new, rebuilt, or used. The percentage is added to cover the shop's cost for handling the part, paperwork, and margin of profit. If, for instance, the markup at your shop is 20% and the wholesale price of the part is $45.00, multiply the part cost by the percentage:

$$\$45.00 \times .20 = \$9.00$$

Then add the markup to the wholesale price of the part:

Wholesale Price:	$45.00
Markup:	+$ 9.00
Total:	$54.00

Some rebuilt parts have a **core charge.** The core charge is a deposit on the old part, which must be turned in for rebuilding. When the old part is returned to the parts

Figure 43-2. One type of body shop customer pay order.

outlet, the core charge is refunded to the shop. Therefore, the customer should not pay the core charge.

Determining Outside Service Costs

Certain repairs require the services of an outside repair facility, such as a machine shop or radiator repair shop. In some cases, outside service personnel come to the shop to perform the repairs directly on the vehicle. Examples are windshield repairs and installing custom radios or other electronic equipment. These costs have to be added to the repair order. The shop may or may not mark up the services of the outside facility.

Other Charges

Some shops charge an extra amount for supplies, such as rags, solvents, or lubricants. This may be a percentage of the total bill or a flat dollar amount. Some shops are required to charge a **disposal fee** to cover the costs of

disposing of such waste as used motor oil or scrap tires. Again, this may be a flat amount or a percentage of the total bill. Such fees are usually turned over to local or state government agencies to cover the costs of waste disposal, and the shop must remember to get the fee from the customer.

Calculating Sales Tax

Sales tax is levied almost everywhere. Taxes must be paid by the automotive repair shop, even if the shop does not charge the customer. Therefore, it is very important to add the sales tax to the bill. In some places, the sales tax applies to parts but not labor. Some of your customers, such as agencies of the Federal government, churches, or charitable organizations, may be tax exempt. Check with your local taxing agencies to determine the exact tax application.

To compute the sales tax, multiply the tax rate by the total of parts and labor costs. For example, if the total parts and labor cost is $75.00 and the sales tax rate is 6%, multiply $75.00 by .06:

$$\$75.00 \times .06 = \$4.50$$

Then, add the tax to the parts and labor total:

Parts and Labor:	$75.00
Tax:	+$ 4.50
Total:	$79.50

The final total for the job is $79.50. When making these computations, add any other applicable sales or use taxes (city and state) that may apply in your area.

Cost Estimates

A **cost estimate** is similar to a repair order, but is written to show the vehicle owner what a repair is expected to cost. It is always good practice to give the customer an estimate on all work to be done.

 Caution: Do not assume that the vehicle owner will always want the work done. Some owners may prefer to trade in the vehicle, shop for a better price, or simply leave the problem uncorrected.

Preparing a cost estimate involves diagnosing the vehicle problem and determining what needs to be done to correct the problem. The needed parts and time to make repairs must be determined to the best of the technician's ability. In many cases, the shop manager or service manager will determine the cost of the parts and labor. In other situations, the technician must determine the total price.

Estimating Labor

Begin by determining exactly what service operations will need to be performed to complete the job. Do not forget related operations that must be performed to complete the job. An example would be discharging the air conditioner to gain access to the heater core. This would mean that the additional work of evacuating and recharging the air conditioner should be added to the total labor cost.

After all labor operations have been determined, consult a flat rate manual to determine the total labor time. Multiply this time figure by your shop labor rate to determine the total labor cost.

Estimating Parts Prices

Determine what parts will be needed to complete the job. Do not forget related parts and supplies, such oil and coolant, that will be used to finish the job. Also determine the need for outside services as outlined above.

After the needed parts have been determined, refer to a flat rate manual to obtain parts prices or call local parts outlets to get the latest prices. Also, call outside service suppliers to obtain their prices for needed work that cannot be performed in your shop. When listing parts and outside services on the estimate, do not forget to add the normal shop markup.

Adding Other Costs

As mentioned previously, there may be extra charges for supplies, disposal fees, and sales taxes. Do not forget to add them to your estimate.

Tech Talk

One of the best automotive technicians that the authors knew was one of the worst at communicating with vehicle owners. He figured that they were as familiar with what could go wrong with any part. He would always say that a failed part was "toast." While this is a snappy line in action movies, it totally fails to communicate what is wrong with an automotive part. More witty customers would always reply "Toast? I didn't know it was ever bread." This would make the technician mad, and things would go downhill from there.

Failure to communicate properly is probably the biggest cause of conflict between technicians and customers. When talking to customers, try to describe the problem exactly. Don't use words like "shot," or "wasted." Simply describe the problem, explaining that a part is loose, scored, shorted, grounded, misaligned, or came apart. Even "burned out" or "broken" is better than "toast."

Remember, communication is a two-way process. Listen closely when your customer tells you about the problem. Ask about any sounds, at what speed and transmission gear the problem happens, and whether the problem happens when accelerating or decelerating. Also ask about the weather conditions when it happens (approximate temperature and humidity). Ask whether the problems occurs occasionally or all the time. And most definitely ask about any recent work done on the vehicle, and even if they have changed brands or grades of gasoline.

Be sure that you and the owner agree on what is wrong with the vehicle: engine stalling, hard starting, transmission or clutch slipping, or another definite problem. Also, before starting any repairs, make sure that the customer knows what the repairs will be and what they will cost.

Summary

Repair orders are used to keep a record of services performed on vehicles. Repair orders are used for billing and to determine the technician's pay. The repair order is begun by listing the customer and vehicle information and a brief description of the problem to be corrected.

After the technician completes the repairs, he or she fills out the repair order, listing the labor times and parts used. This information is used to bill the customer. The price of the labor and parts, the cost of outside services and supplies, and sales taxes are added to create the final bill.

Labor costs are determined by multiplying the actual time taken (or the time listed in the flat rate manual) by the shop labor rate. Parts costs are determined by adding the standard shop markup to the wholesale, or jobber, price. Charges for outside services, supplies, and sales taxes, are added to the total of parts and labor.

A cost estimate is similar to a repair order. It is used to show the owner what a repair is expected to cost. To prepare a cost estimate, the technician must diagnose the vehicle problem and determine what needs to be done to correct it. The needed parts and labor must be determined accurately. Do not assume that the vehicle owner will always want the work done.

Always bill customers accurately and honestly. The finest advertisement for any shop—and any technician—is scrupulous honesty at all times.

Know These Terms

Repair order	Wholesale price
Customer pay order	Jobber price
Warranty order	Core charge
Hourly rate	Disposal fee
Flat rate manual	Sales tax
Markup	Cost estimate

Review Questions—Chapter 43

Do not write in this book. Write your answers on a separate sheet of paper.

1. If the flat rate manual says that a job should take 3 hours and the shop labor charge is $35.00 per hour, the labor cost of the job is _____.
   (A) $35.00
   (B) $70.00
   (C) $105.00
   (D) $350.00

2. If the shop markup on parts is 25% and the wholesale price of a part is $18.00, what is the price to the customer?
   (A) $4.50
   (B) $13.50
   (C) $22.50
   (D) $24.50

3. If the labor cost to install the part in Question 4 is $22.00, a $2.50 supply charge is added, and the local sales tax is 5%, what is the total bill?
   (A) $25.72
   (B) $49.35
   (C) $55.35
   (D) $235.00

4. If an alternator belt cannot be replaced without removing the air conditioner and power steering belts, the estimate for alternator belt replacement would include labor for removing and replacing _____.
   (A) all three belts
   (B) the air conditioner and alternator belts only
   (C) the power steering and alternator belts only
   (D) the alternator belt only

5. Sales taxes are paid to the shop by the customer. What does the shop do with the collected sales taxes?
   (A) Keeps them to pay for disposal fees.
   (B) The shop pays state or local sales tax.
   (C) Uses them to pay its income taxes.
   (D) Returns them to the customer at the end of the year.

ASE-Type Questions

1. All of the following statements about repair orders are true, EXCEPT:
   (A) repair orders are used to keep a record of services performed on a vehicle.
   (B) repair orders may be used to pay the technician for work performed.
   (C) repair orders are used for warranty jobs only.
   (D) repair orders are sometimes called shop work orders.

2. All of the following statements about core charges are true EXCEPT:
   (A) the core charge is refunded when the core is returned to the parts store.
   (B) the core charge is made on parts that can be reconditioned.
   (C) core charges are typically applied to alternators, water pumps, and brake shoes.
   (D) the core charge will be refunded even if the part is too badly damaged to rebuild.

3. Technician A says that the customer should pay the core charge on a rebuilt part. Technician B says that the core charge is refunded when the old part is turned in. Who is right?
   (A) A only.
   (B) B only.
   (C) Both A & B.
   (D) Neither A nor B.

4. Technician A says that the vehicle problem must be diagnosed before preparing a cost estimate. Technician B says that the vehicle owner will always want the work done. Who is right?
   (A) A only.
   (B) B only.
   (C) Both A & B.
   (D) Neither A nor B.

5. Technician A says that flat rate manuals give the approximate time needed to make a specified repair. Technician B says that flat rate manual times must be multiplied by the shop labor rate to obtain the actual labor price. Who is right?
   (A) A only.
   (B) B only.
   (C) Both A & B.
   (D) Neither A nor B.

Suggested Activities

1. List some of the things that should be placed on a repair order or cost estimate. Compare your list with an actual repair order.

2. Fill out a repair order, listing out the following information:

- Owners name and address.
- Owners home and work telephone numbers.
- Vehicle identification number (VIN #).
- Body style.
- Number of doors.
- License plate number.
- Color.
- Engine size and manufacturer.
- Transmission type and manufacturer.
- Tire size.
- Whether the vehicle is equipped with air conditioning, power steering, or power brakes.
- Owners complaint or work to be done.

3. With other class members, conduct a role playing session concerning dealing with a customer complaint. Take turns playing the technician and the dissatisfied customer.
4. Write five estimates for repair of different vehicle components. Be sure to include parts prices and appropriate labor time. Total the combined parts and labor as if you were going to sell the work to a customer.

44

ASE Certification

After studying this chapter, you will be able to:
* Explain why technician certification is necessary.
* Explain the process of registering for ASE tests.
* Explain how to take the ASE tests.
* Identify typical ASE test questions.
* Explain what is done with ASE test results.

This chapter will explain the reasons for the National Institute for Automotive Service Excellence (ASE) certification and the advantages of being ASE certified. This chapter also explains how to apply for and take the ASE tests. When you have finished studying this chapter, you will know the purposes of ASE and the ASE tests. You will also have a good understanding of the test methods and the test results.

Reasons for ASE Tests

The concept of setting standards of excellence for skilled jobs is not new. Many ancient societies had associations of skilled workers who set standards and enforced rules of conduct. Many modern labor unions are descended from early associations of skilled workers. Certification processes for aircraft mechanics, aerospace workers, and electronics technicians have existed since the beginnings of these industries.

Due to the fragmented, decentralized nature of the automotive repair industry, standards for the automotive repair industry were difficult to establish and enforce. Anyone could claim to be an automotive technician, no matter how unqualified. A large segment of the public came to regard technicians as dishonest, unintelligent, or both.

The *National Institute for Automotive Service Excellence,* now called *ASE,* was established in 1975 to provide a *certification* process for automobile technicians. ASE is a non-profit corporation formed to encourage and promote high standards of automotive service and repair. ASE does this by providing a series of written tests on various subjects in the automotive repair, heavy truck repair, auto body/paint, and engine machinist areas.

These tests are called *standardized tests,* which means that the same test in a particular subject is given to everyone throughout the United States. Any person passing one of these tests and meeting certain experience requirements, is certified in the subject covered by that test. If a technician can pass all of the tests in the automotive or heavy truck areas, he or she is certified as a *master technician* in that area.

The ASE certification test program identifies and rewards skilled and knowledgeable technicians. Periodic recertification provides an incentive for updating skills and also provides guidelines for keeping up with current technology. The test program allows potential employers and the driving public to identify good technicians and helps the technician advance his or her career. The program is not mandatory on a national level, but many employers now hire only ASE certified technicians. Over 500,000 persons are now ASE certified in one or more areas.

Other ASE activities are undertaken to encourage the development of effective automotive service training programs, conduct research on the best methods of performing instruction, and publicize the advantages of technician certification. ASE is managed by a board made up of persons from the automotive and truck service industries, motor vehicle manufacturers, state and federal government agencies, schools and other educational groups, and consumer associations.

The ASE certification program has brought many advantages to the automotive industry, including increased respect and trust of automotive technicians, at least of those who are ASE certified. This has resulted in better pay and benefits for technicians and increased standing in the community. Because of ASE, automotive technicians are taking their place next to other skilled artisans.

Applying for the ASE Tests

Anyone may apply for and take any ASE test. However, the applicant must have two year's work experience as an automobile, truck, auto body, or paint technician or as an engine machinist to become certified. In some cases, training programs or courses, an apprenticeship program, or time spent performing similar work may be substituted for all or part of the work experience.

ASE tests are given twice each year, in the spring and fall. Tests are usually held during a two-week period at night during the work week. The tests are given by a separate organization called *ACT.* ACT is a nonprofit organization experienced in administering standardized tests. The tests are given at designated test centers in over 300 places in the United States. If necessary, special test centers can be set up in remote locations. However, there must be enough potential applicants for the establishment of a special test center to be practical. To apply for the ASE tests, begin by obtaining an *application form* like the one shown in **Figure 44-1.** To obtain the most current application form, contact ASE at the following address:

National Institute for Automotive Service Excellence
13505 Dulles Technology Drive
Herndon, VA 22071-3415

ASE will send the proper form inside a *registration booklet,* which explains how to complete the form. When you get the booklet, fill the form out carefully, recording all needed information. You may apply to take as many tests as are being given, fewer tests, or only one test if desired.

Proof of work experience, or qualified substitutes, should also be included, according to the instructions in the latest registration booklet. If there is any doubt about what should be placed in a particular space, consult the registration booklet. Determine the closest test center and record its number in the appropriate space. Most test centers are located at local colleges, high schools, or vocational schools. In addition to the application, you must include a check, money order, or credit card number to cover all necessary fees. A fee is charged to register for the test series, and a separate fee is charged for each test to be taken. See the latest registration booklet for the current fee structure. In some cases, your employer may pay the registration and test fees. Check with your employer before sending in your application.

To be accepted for either the Spring or Fall ASE tests, your application and payment must arrive at ASE headquarters by the registration deadline, which is at least one month before the first test date. To ensure that you can take

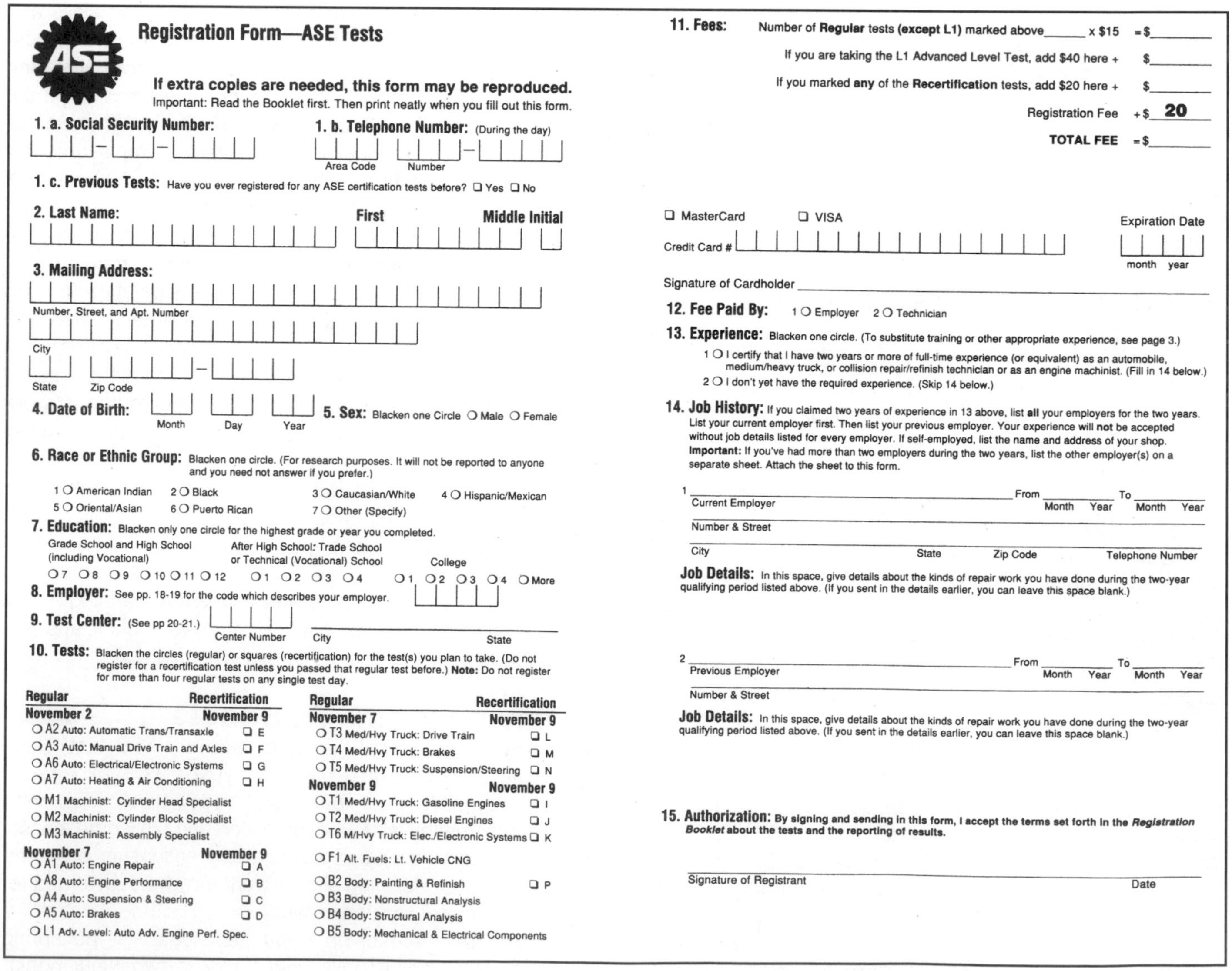

Figure 44-1. A typical registration form for the National Institute for Automotive Service Excellence. (ASE)

the test at the test center of your choice, send in the application as early as possible. After sending the application and fees, you will receive an **admission ticket** to the test center. This should arrive by mail within two weeks of sending the application. If your admission ticket has not arrived, and it is less than two weeks before the first test date, contact ASE using the phone number given in the registration booklet. If the desired test center is filled when ASE receives your application, you will be directed to report to the nearest center that has an opening. If it is not possible to go to the alternate test center that was assigned, contact ACT immediately using the phone number given in the latest ASE registration booklet.

Taking the ASE Tests

Be sure to bring your admission ticket with you when reporting to the test center. When you arrive at the test center, you will be asked to produce the admission ticket and a driver's license or other photographic identification. In addition to these items, bring some extra number 2 pencils. Although pencils will be made available at the test center, some extra pencils may save you time if the original pencil breaks. After you enter the test center and are seated, listen to and follow all instructions given by the test administrators. During the actual test, carefully read all test questions before making a decision as to the proper answer. The ASE tests are designed to measure your knowledge of three things:

* Basic information on how automotive systems and components work.
* Diagnosis and testing of systems and components.
* Repairing automotive systems and components.

Each ASE test will contain between 40 and 80 test questions, depending on the subject to be tested. All test questions are **multiple-choice,** with four possible answers. These types of multiple choice questions are similar to the multiple-choice questions used in this textbook. Questions can be in one or two parts. Samples of these types of test questions are given below.

One-Part Question

1. The cooling system part that allows the engine to warm up quickly is the _____.
   (A) water pump
   (B) coolant recovery reservoir
   (C) thermostat
   (D) radiator

Notice that the question calls for the best answer out of all of the possibilities. The thermostat is the part that remains closed to prevent coolant flow through the radiator until the engine warms up. Therefore, "C" is correct.

Two-Part Question

1. Technician A says that the ignition coil changes high voltage into low voltage. Technician B says that the distributor pickup coil produces a low voltage signal. Who is right?
   (A) A only.
   (B) B only.
   (C) Both A and B.
   (D) Neither A nor B.

This question asks you to read two statements and decide if they are true. Both statements can be true, both can be false, or only one of them can be false. In this case, the statement of technician A is wrong, since the ignition coil produces high voltage from low voltage. The statement of technician B is correct, since the pickup coil does produce a low voltage signal. Therefore, the correct answer is "B."

Negative Questions

Some questions are called **negative questions.** These questions ask you to identify the wrong answer. They will usually have the word "except" in the question.

1. Low oil pressure could be caused by all of the following problems, EXCEPT:
   (A) Low oil level.
   (B) Worn oil pump.
   (C) Clogged oil screen.
   (D) Tight bearing clearances.

Since tight bearing clearances would not cause low oil pressure, while the other defects listed could, the correct answer is "D."

A variation of the negative question will use the word "least," such as the one below.

1. The computer-controlled engine of a late model car knocks during acceleration. Which of these defects is the LEAST likely cause?
   (A) Incorrect timing.
   (B) Defective knock sensor.
   (C) Plugged fuel filter.
   (D) Low octane gasoline.

In this case, the least likely cause of engine knocking was a plugged fuel filter, which is much more likely to cause engine stalling or poor performance instead of knocking. Therefore, the correct answer is "C."

Incomplete Sentence Questions

Some test questions are **incomplete sentences,** with one of the four possible answers correctly completing the sentence. An example of an incomplete sentence question is given below.

1. The coolant temperature sensor is used to measure _____ temperature.
   (A) exhaust gas
   (B) engine
   (C) incoming air
   (D) ambient (outside) air

Once again the question calls for the best answer. The coolant temperature sensor measures the temperature in the engine by monitoring coolant temperature, so "B" is correct.

After completing all the questions in a particular test, recheck all of your answers one time to ensure that you did not miss anything that would change your answer, or that you did not make a careless error on the answer sheet. In most cases, rechecking your answers more than once is unnecessary and may lead you to change correct answers to incorrect ones. The time allowed for each test session is about four hours. Take as long as you need on any one test but work as quickly as you can. You may leave after completing you last test and handing in all test material.

Test Results

ACT requires six to eight weeks to process the tests from the various centers and mail the results. You will receive a confidential report of your performance on the tests. The report will show your score on the test and whether this score is sufficient for certification. The test questions are also subdivided into general areas to help you determine any skill areas in which you may require further study. For instance, the engine performance test questions will be divided into such subsections as ignition, fuel, starting and charging, engine mechanical, and computer controls. Also included with the report is a certificate of certification for all of the tests that you have passed, an ASE shoulder patch, and a pocket card listing all of the areas that you are certified in. See **Figure 44-2.**

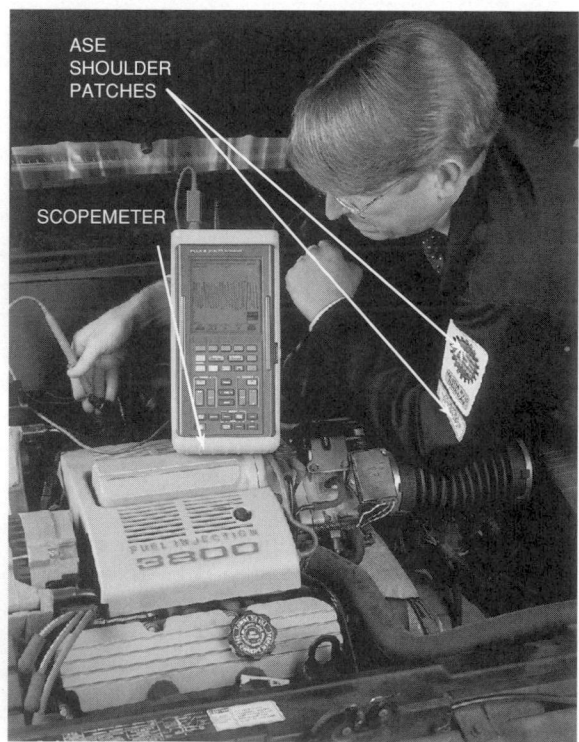

Figure 44-2. An ASE certified master auto technician, with specialized training in advanced automobile engine performance using a state-of-the-art scopemeter. (Fluke)

ASE takes the position that all test results are confidential information and provides them only to the person who took the test. This is done to protect your privacy. The only test information that ASE will release is to confirm to an employer that you are certified in a particular area. Test results will be mailed to your home address and will not be provided to anyone else. This is true even if your employer has paid the test fees. If you wish your employer to know exactly how you performed on the tests, you must provide him or her with a copy of your test results.

If you fail a certification test, you can retake it again as many times as you would like. However, you (or your employer) must pay all of the applicable registration and test fees again. You should study all available information in the areas where you did poorly. A copy of the ASE Test Preparation Guide may be helpful to sharpen your skills in these areas. The ASE Test Preparation Guide is free, and can be obtained by filling out the coupon at the back of the registration booklet. Other preparation books are available at bookstores and through mail order.

Other ASE Tests

There are three ASE test areas other than the well known battery of tests for automotive technicians. ASE now offers an advanced level test in engine performance. This specialty test is designed to comply with amendments to the Clean Air Act for emission inspection and maintenance. Previous certification in regular automobile engine performance is required to take this test. A test in alternative fuels specializing in light vehicle compressed natural gas (CNG) is also available. Engine machinists can become certified in three separate skill areas.

Recertification Tests

Once you have passed the certification test in any area, you must take a ***recertification test*** every five years to keep your certification. This assures that you have kept up with current technology. The process of applying to take the recertification tests is similar to that for the original certification tests. Use the same form and enclose the proper recertification test fees. If you allow any of your certifications to lapse, you must take the regular certification test to regain your certification.

Tech Talk

School may frustrate you, but don't give it up. The fact that you are not great in math or language classes does not mean that you lack ability. It just means that you have aptitudes in different areas. Many automotive technicians are not very good with pencil and paper, even though they may be great at diagnosis and repair.

Modern vehicles, however, require a level of reading ability that was not needed in the past. Factory service manuals and technical service bulletins must be read and understood to troubleshoot computer controls and locate driveability problems. The ASE tests are another example. Instead of proving your knowledge by actually working on a vehicle, you must read and comprehend a series of questions to pass the tests. In addition, these materials inevitably include technical terms that will be even harder to comprehend if you are still having trouble with the non-technical words. This is why it is important to increase your reading ability as much as possible.

So what do you do to increase your reading ability? The answer is to read. Practice in anything, especially reading, improves your ability. You don't have to read great works of literature. General reading sources are your local newspaper, news magazines, and a vast array of novels, biographies, histories, and reference books. There are many sources of interesting reading material related to cars, trucks, and service including a large number of automotive magazines devoted to every possible part of the automotive culture. There are also various automotive technical and marketing publications, service manuals, and training materials.

Summary

The automotive industry was one of the few major industries that did not have testing and certification programs. This lack of professionalism in the automobile industry led to poor or unneeded repairs and decreased status and pay for automobile technicians. The National Institute for Automotive Service Excellence, or ASE, was started in 1975 to overcome these problems. ASE tests and certifies automotive technicians in major areas of automotive repair. This has increased the skill level of technicians, resulting in better service and increased benefits for technicians.

ASE tests are given in the Spring and Fall. Anyone can register to take the tests by filling out the proper registration form and paying the registration and test fees. The registrant must also select the test center that he or she would like to go to. To be considered for certification, the registrant must have two years of hands-on experience. About three weeks after applying for the test, the technician will receive a test entry ticket which he or she must bring to the test center.

The actual test questions will test your knowledge of general system operation, diagnosing problems, and repair techniques. All of the questions are multiple choice questions. The questions must be read carefully. The entire test should be gone over one time only to catch any mistakes.

Test results will arrive within six to eight weeks after the test session. Results are confidential and will be sent only to the home address of the person who took the test. If a test was passed, and the experience requirement has been met, the technician will be certified in that skill area for five years. Anyone who fails a test can take it again in the next session. Tests can be taken as many times as necessary. Recertification tests can be taken at the end of the five year certification period.

Know These Terms

National Institute for
   Automotive Service
   Excellence
ASE
Standardized tests
Master technician
ACT
Application form

Registration booklet
Admission ticket
Multiple choice question
Negative question
Incomplete sentence
   question
Recertification test

Review Questions—Chapter 44

Do not write in this book. Write your answers on a separate sheet of paper.
1. Name all of the categories of ASE Tests.
2. If a technician can pass all of the tests in the automotive or heavy truck areas, he or she is certified as a
   _____.
   (A) trainee
   (B) general technician
   (C) master technician
   (D) knowledgeable technician
3. List the optional tests now administered by ASE to automotive technicians.
4. You can take the ASE tests, but you will not be certified by ASE until you fulfill what requirement?
5. You should begin to register for the ASE test by obtaining a _____.
6. If your admission ticket has not arrived and there is less than two weeks before the first test date, who should you contact?
7. ASE tests are designed to measure your knowledge of what three things?
8. ASE test questions resemble the ones in _____.
   (A) college level courses
   (B) essay-type tests
   (C) verbal examinations
   (D) this book
9. ASE provides test results to _____.
   (A) the technician who took the test.
   (B) whoever paid for the test.
   (C) the technician's employer.
   (D) Both A & C.
10. An ASE certification is good for _____.

ASE-Type Questions

1. Technician A says that ASE encourages high standards of automotive service and repair by providing a series of written tests. Technician B says that ASE encourages high standards of automotive service and repair by providing a series of hands-on tests. Who is right?
   (A) A only.
   (B) B only.
   (C) Both A & B.
   (D) Neither A nor B.

2. In some cases, all of the following may be substituted for all or part of the work experience, EXCEPT:
   (A) training programs or courses.
   (B) a promise to work in the automotive field for two years minimum.
   (C) time spent performing similar work.
   (D) an apprenticeship program.

3. The advantages that ASE certification has brought to automotive technicians include all of the following, EXCEPT:
   (A) increased respect.
   (B) better working conditions.
   (C) lower pay scales.
   (D) increased standing in the community.

4. ASE tests are given _____ each year.
   (A) once
   (B) twice
   (C) four times
   (D) twelve times

5. ASE tests are held _____.
   (A) during normal working hours
   (B) at night during the work week
   (C) on national holidays
   (D) any time

6. A technician who is not certified in any area may take all of the following ASE tests EXCEPT:
   (A) Engine Performance.
   (B) Advanced Engine Performance.
   (C) Light Vehicle, Compressed Natural Gas.
   (D) Engine Repair.

7. A technician can retake any certification test _____.
   (A) two times
   (B) four times
   (C) five times
   (D) any number of times

8. Technician A says that the ASE test session lasts about four hours. Technician B says that anyone can leave as soon as they are done and all test materials are turned in. Who is right?
   (A) A only.
   (B) B only.
   (C) Both A & B.
   (D) Neither A nor B.

9. When taking ASE tests, you should do all of the following EXCEPT:
   (A) arrive at the test center early.
   (B) work quickly, but carefully.
   (C) bring several number 2 pencils.
   (D) check your answers at least three times.

10. Technician A says that all ASE test scores are confidential information and can only be released with the technician's permission. Technician B says that if the technican's employer pays for the tests, they are entitiled to a copy of the test results from ASE. Who is right?
    (A) A only.
    (B) B only.
    (C) Both A & B.
    (D) Neither A nor B.

Suggested Activities

1. Obtain an ASE registration booklet and determine the dates on which each of the eight regular automotive tests is offered. List those tests that you think you could pass.

2. Determine where the nearest ASE test center has been located in the past and whether it is likely to be used as a test center again.

3. Make a copy of the ASE test application form and fill it out, indicating your actual experience as if you were applying for certification.

4. Take the sample test in the ASE registration booklet and use the results to identify areas where you are weak. Discuss with your instructor what should be done to raise your skill and knowledge levels in these areas.

45

Career Opportunities in the Automotive Field

After studying this chapter, you will be able to:
- List general classes of jobs in automobile service and repair.
- List areas of specialization in automobile service and repair.
- Explain job working conditions and salaries.
- List addresses of various organizations that offer information on automotive careers.

In this chapter, we will discuss various jobs in automotive maintenance and repair and explain how to obtain these jobs.

General Classes of Jobs

The sections below list general classes of jobs available in the automotive service industry. Note that some of these jobs allow you to start out with a minimum of experience and, as you gain that experience, move into more complex, well-paying positions.

Cleaning

In cleaning, you will steam clean engines and other large assemblies. In some cases, the underbody portion of the vehicle must be steam cleaned. You will wash and often wax exterior finishes. Vacuuming, window washing, and upholstery cleaning might be part of your job.

Part of your day may be spent moving and delivering vehicles. Occasionally, you might assist technicians, parts specialists, or other personnel. Your work in the cleaning department will allow you to demonstrate your ability as a hard working, responsible person. There will be plenty of chances to observe work in other areas. These opportunities, coupled with additional study, will help prepare you for advancement. When ready, you may move from the cleaning department to the lubrication department.

Lubrication

Lubrication involves lubricating the working parts of the vehicle and checking the oil level in the engine, transmission, differential, and transfer case. It includes inspection of the battery, master cylinder, radiator, steering system, brake system, and other parts critical to the safe operation of the vehicle.

Work in this area will provide you with an opportunity to learn a great deal about the various systems on the vehicle. It will pave the way to advancement toward more complicated mechanical service.

Light Repair Technician

The **light repair technician** performs minor jobs, such as shock absorber installation, muffler and exhaust part installation, cooling system service, and other basic adjustments and repairs. Part of the work as a light repair technician consists of checking out new vehicles before delivery. You will go over the entire vehicle to make certain that all systems are functioning and are in proper adjustment.

Training in this job is invaluable. It will prepare you for the more complicated heavy repair work or for work in a specialty area, such as drivetrain or brake service.

Heavy Repair Technician

As a **heavy repair technician,** you will disassemble, check, repair, and reassemble major components, such as engines, transmissions, differentials, and transfer cases. This job will require a great deal of study, practice, and experience.

At first, you will probably work under a qualified, experienced technician in this area. Your success will depend upon your aptitude (natural ability), interest, and ambition. Once you master the work involved, you will be a valuable asset in any automotive shop and will be in a good position for advancement. See **Figure 45-1.**

Areas of Specialization

Modern automobiles and light trucks are constantly being improved with the addition of electronic engine and drivetrain controls, anti-lock brakes, air bags, electronic steering, ride and traction controls, and other new devices and features. It is becoming more and more difficult for a technician to master the service and repair of the entire vehicle. If the volume of work permits, specialization in one area will provide the customer with faster and more efficient service. The technician handling the job will specialize in that particular area. He or she will have advanced training and experience in a chosen specialty. Full-time work in one area will help the specialist become highly proficient.

Figure 45-1. This heavy repair technician is installing a crankshaft in an engine block.

Driveability Technician

The **driveability technician** will handle jobs involving diagnosing and isolating engine problems and servicing the ignition system, fuel system, and many other engine and vehicle systems. A thorough understanding of the electronic engine controls is a must. Alternator and starter diagnosis and repairs may also be required.

Driveability work requires a high level of competency and at least a general understanding of almost every part of the vehicle. It is a good paying job and will provide an excellent chance for further advancement, **Figure 45-2.**

Figure 45-2. This driveability technician is checking for an engine problem with a hand-held diagnostic tool.

Brake Technician

The **brake technician** does such work as disc and drum turning; shoe adjustment; caliper, master cylinder, and wheel cylinder repair; bleeding; and line replacement, **Figure 45-3.** Special training in brake trouble diagnosis, power brake units, and anti-lock brakes is required.

Figure 45-3. A brake technician using an on-car brake lathe to true a front rotor. (Hunter Engineering Co.)

Transmission/Transaxle Technician

The **transmission/transaxle technician** must be able to work on both standard and automatic units. This technician will also service electronic transmission/transaxle control systems. Necessary skills include testing, diagnosis, disassembly, checking, repair, and reassembly of transmissions and transaxles. The transmission/transaxle technician must have a thorough background in the fundamentals, as well as special training in this field.

Front End Technician

The **front end technician** performs wheel balancing and wheel alignment. See **Figure 45-4.** This technician also works on the steering gearbox, steering linkage, spindles, springs, ball joints, shocks, struts, and control arms. It is the front end technician's duty to see that the vehicle steers and handles easily and safely, and that the tires run smoothly and wear properly.

To be a successful front end technician, you must have a thorough understanding of rack and pinion steering, MacPherson struts, power steering systems, modern alignment equipment and adjusters, and electronic and pneumatic ride controls.

Electrical Technician

The modern vehicle makes wide use of electrical units. The electrical technician will handle work on radios, tape and CD players, electric seats, window operating devices,

Figure 45-4. This front-end technician is attaching an alignment sensor assembly to the front wheel of a vehicle. (Hunter Engineering Co.)

instruments, alternators, regulators, and starters. Knowledge of wiring and lighting is also needed.

The job of *electrical technician* requires an extensive knowledge of electricity and electronics, as well as the repair and adjustment procedures for all electrical units.

Air Conditioning Technician

The *air conditioning technician* checks, adjusts, and repairs the vehicle air conditioning system. There are many jobs for technicians with special training in this area.

Success in this area requires a knowledge of the various types of refrigerants used and methods of recovering and reusing them. You must also know about heating systems, control systems, automatic controls, and ductwork.

Body and Fender Technician

Body and fender work, although separate from mechanical repair, is an important area of automotive service. The *body and fender technician* will repair damage to the vehicle's metal structure, the upholstering, and the inside trim. The body and fender technician will install glass and repair locks, handles, and various trim pieces.

This job requires proficiency in cutting, welding, metal bumping, filling, priming, and painting. Painting is becoming a specialty within the field of body and fender work.

Supervisory Positions

Most technicians entering a particular field look forward to advancement in pay and position. Advancement is dependent on your knowledge and skill, as well as a demonstration of your ability to cope with the problems of the position.

Shop Supervisor

The *shop supervisor* is in charge of the technicians in the repair department. The supervisor is held directly responsible for the work turned out by the technicians. This position calls for a highly competent technician who is familiar with and able to perform all the jobs that enter the shop.

In larger repair facilities, the supervisor's time will be spent directing the technicians, checking their work, giving suggestions, and in general, seeing that the shop runs smoothly and efficiently. In a small shop, the supervisor may spend part of the day doing repair work, with the remainder of the time devoted to supervision.

Service Manager

The *service manager* holds a very responsible position. This title is held by the person in charge of the overall service and repair operation. The service manager must see that customers get prompt, efficient, fairly priced service. Customers must be pleased, and the technicians in the department must be satisfied.

The service manager's job usually includes the handling of employee training programs. This requires close cooperation with factory representatives to see that the latest and best service techniques are employed.

The service manager must have insight into the job itself. This calls for leadership ability, a good personality, training, knowledge, and the ability to work with others. Being a service manager is not an easy job, but it certainly is a worthwhile ambition. Various jobs found in the modern shop are shown on the dealer organization chart, **Figure 45-5.**

What to Expect from Service Facilities

The service facility of today is a far cry from the crowded, dark, cold, and poorly ventilated garage of yesterday. The modern shop is well-lighted, roomy, and properly ventilated. Even the smallest shops have provided for the comfort and satisfaction of their employees.

Working Conditions

Many repair facilities have lunchrooms, showers, and individual lockers for their employees. Hydraulic lifts and power tools are used to eliminate much of the heavy labor involved in automotive repair and provide easy access to various parts of the vehicle.

Most technicians work inside, and modern shops are usually heated in the winter. When a job requires roadside repair, the technician may be faced with varying weather conditions.

Wages

It is difficult to say how much money you will make as an automotive technician. Much depends on the type of work performed, the geographical location of the job, the employer, the prevailing business conditions, and the job

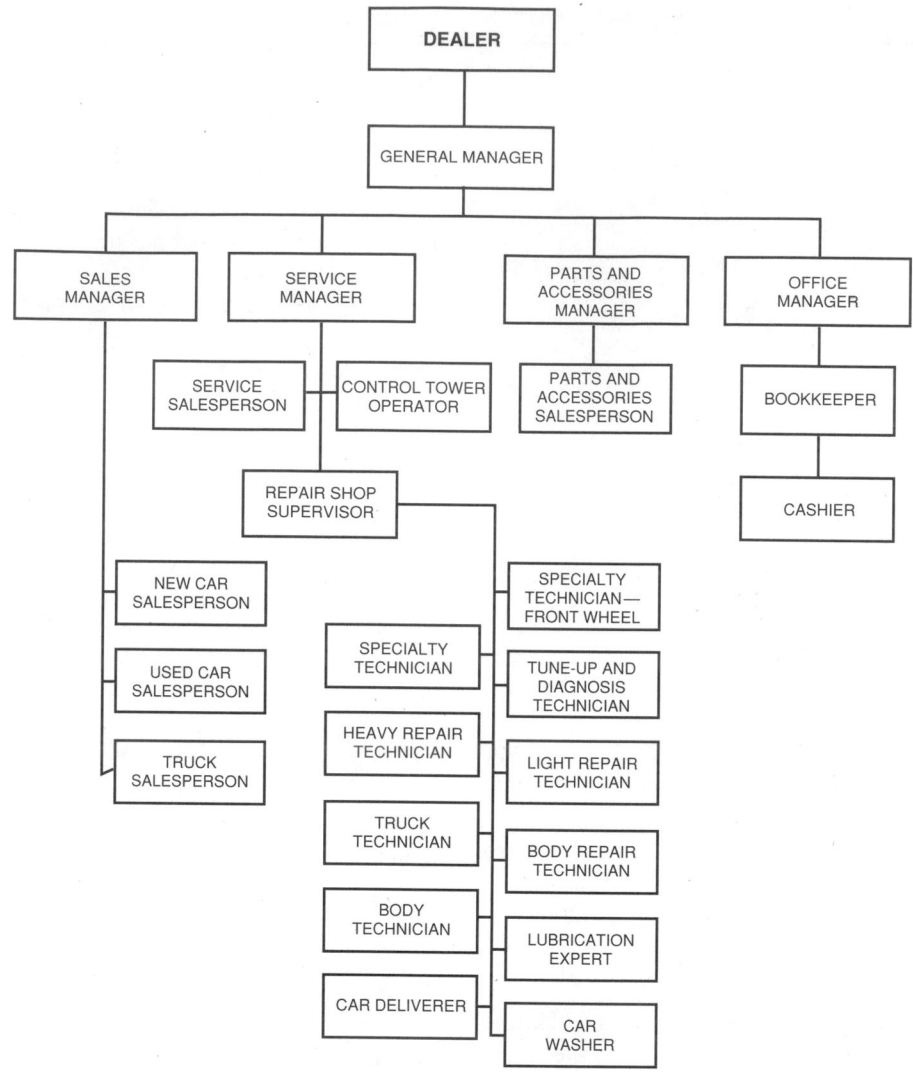

Figure 45-5.   This chart illustrates the organization of one specific automobile dealership.

supply and demand. All have a definite influence on a technician's earnings.

Pay can be based on an hourly wage, or it can be based on commission. Under the wage system, the technician is paid by the number of hours he or she is actually at the shop, no matter what the work load. Under the commission system, amount the technician is paid depends on what work comes in and how fast he or she can complete it. Many auto technicians receive a certain percentage of the customer labor charge. As the rates for various jobs are fixed, the skilled technician will be able to do more jobs in one day than the unskilled technician and, as a result, will earn more money.

Most technicians earn a good living. Many shops pay by a combination of an hourly wage and commission, and most shops offer a package of benefits, such as paid insurance, vacation, and a pension or profit sharing setup. Wages and commissions are competitive between shops in the same area. The earnings of most automotive technicians are in line with the earnings of individuals employed in other technical jobs.

Availability of Employment

The increasing use of vehicles and the addition of more complex items on vehicles have created a lucrative field for qualified technicians. If you really learn the trade and are a hard working, conscientious person, you should be able to readily find employment.

About a third of all technicians work in new and used vehicle dealer service departments. Another third work in repair shops that specialize in a single aspect of automotive repair, such as body and fender work; driveability; brake, front end, radiator work; and other areas. Many technicians work in service stations that perform light repairs or in small, privately owned shops that perform a variety of repairs. Other technicians work for large fleet owners, such as utility companies, dairies, produce companies, and federal, state, county, and city organizations.

Would You Do Well and Would You Be Satisfied in This Field?

If you are sincerely interested in all types of vehicles, enjoy working on and studying about them, and are in relatively good health, the chances are good that you will like the automotive repair field and will do well in it.

How Does a Person Become an Automotive Technician?

A person develops into a good auto technician by study, observation, instruction, and experience. High schools, trade schools, the armed forces, and apprentice programs offer excellent opportunities to acquire the training necessary to gain employment in this field.

The following vehicle manufacturers and importers may be able to furnish you with educational booklets, brochures, manuals, etc. Some items may be offered free of charge, while others may carry a nominal fee. For materials of this type, direct your request to the manager of educational publications.

Training program and job placement information may also be offered. For this type of information, address your request to the personnel manager or the manager of the training department.

BMW of North America, Inc.
300 Chestnut Ridge Road
Woodcliff Lake, NJ 07675

Chrysler Corporation
College Graduates:
College Recruitment Services
Personnel Department
Chrysler Corporation
Chrysler Center
12000 Chrysler Drive
Highland Park, MI 48288-1919
High School /Vocational School Graduates:
Manager, Personnel Department
Chrysler Corporation
Chrysler Center
12000 Chrysler Drive
Highland Park, MI 48288-1919

Ford Motor Company
Placement and College Recruitment
Ford Motor Company
The American Road
Dearborn, MI 48121

General Motors Corporation
Salaried Placement Personnel
General Motors Corporation
General Motors Building
3044 W. Grand Blvd.
Detroit, MI 48202

Honda Motor Co., Inc.
1919 Torrance Blvd.
Torrance, CA 90501-2746

Mazda Motor Of America, Inc.
7755 Irvine Center Drive
Irvine, CA 92630

Mercedes-Benz Of North America, Inc.
P.O. Box 350
One Mercedes Drive
Montvale, NJ 07645-0350

Mitsubishi Motor Sales Of America, Inc.
6400 Katella Avenue
Cypress, CA 90630

Nissan Motor Manufacturing Co., USA
P.O. Box 191
18501 South Figueroa Street
Carson, CA 90248-0191

Porsche Cars North America, Inc.
100 W. Liberty Street
Reno, NV 89501

Saab Cars USA, Inc.
4405-A Saab Drive
P.O. Box 9000
Norcross, GA 30091

Subaru of America, Inc.
P.O. Box 6000
Subaru Plaza
Cherry Hill, NJ 08034-6000

Toyota Motor Sales USA, Inc.
19001 S. Western Avenue
Torrance, CA 90509

Volkswagen of America, Inc.
3800 Hamlin Road
Auburn Hills, MI 48236

Volvo Cars of North America, Inc.
P.O. Box 913
One Volvo Drive
Rockleigh, NJ 07647

Additional Information

The following automobile industry related associations may also provide interesting and informative materials.

A good collection of pamphlets, brochures, training manuals, and other materials will form the basis for a very useful library. Remember that today, as always, learning and earning go hand in hand.

American Petroleum Institute (API)
1220 L Street NW
Washington, DC 20005

Automotive Safety Foundation
1776 Massachusetts Avenue NW
Washington, DC 20036

Battery Council International (BCI)
401 N. Michigan Avenue
Chicago, IL 60611

Equipment and Tool Institute (ETI)
1806 Johns Drive
Glenview, IL 60025-1657

Mechanic's Education Association (MEA)
1805 Springfield Avenue
Maplewood, NJ 07040-2910

Motor and Equipment Manufacturers Association (MEMA)
P.O. Box 13966
Research Triangle Park, NC 27709-3966

Motor Vehicle Manufacturers Association of the U.S., Inc.
300 New Center Building
Detroit, MI 48202

National Automobile Dealers Association (NADA)
8400 Westpark Drive
McLean, VA 22102

Professional Mechanics Association (PMA)
P.O. Box 840
Stewartstown, PA 17363-0840

Rubber Manufacturers Association (RMA)
1400 K Street NW, Suite 900
Washington, DC 20005

Know These Terms

Light repair technician
Heavy repair technician
Driveability technician
Brake technician
Transmission/transaxle
    technician

Front end technician
Electrical technician
Air conditioning technician
Body and fender technician
Shop supervisor
Service manager

Tech Talk

A career in the automotive field is just like any other career choice. You can get out of your career as much as you want, but you are going to have to put in some effort to further it. One way to further your career is to increase your knowledge by continuing to attend some sort of school or training.

Examples of further education that a technician might look to receive would be to attend technical training classes sponsored by tool and vehicle manufacturers. These are usually held at local community colleges, high schools, or trade schools. These classes will expand your technical expertise and will make you more valuable to your employer. You could obtain skills that can help you in your automotive work. Take some classes in welding as this is a vital skill in any automotive shop. With the increased use of computers to diagnose and repair vehicle systems, a few classes in computer usage will not only help you understand and operate these high-tech tools of the trade, but they will also help you in the fast changing, computer oriented world.

If you continue your education, it can open doors that you may not be aware of. Many engineers working for vehicle and parts manufacturers started in the automotive business as technicians. Some service managers started as technicians. With education, your own expectations are the limit.

Summary

There are many jobs available in the automobile service industry. General job classifications include cleaning, lubrication, light repair, and heavy repair. Cleaning jobs involve steam cleaning engines, washing and waxing vehicle exteriors, and cleaning interiors. Lubrication involves lubricating the vehicle and checking fluid levels in the engine, transmission, differential, etc. Light repair technicians perform minor jobs, such as exhaust system service and cooling system service. Heavy repair technicians service major components, such as engines and transmissions.

Because late-model vehicles are so complex, it is difficult for a technician to master the service and repair of the entire vehicle. Therefore, many technicians specialize in one or two specific areas. Specialty areas include driveability, brakes, transmissions/transaxles, front ends, electrical systems, and air conditioning.

Technicians can advance to a variety of supervisory positions, such as shop supervisor or service manager. The shop supervisor is in charge of the technicians in the repair department. The service manager is responsible for the overall operation of the service and repair facility.

Modern repair shops are pleasant places to work. They are generally well lighted, roomy, and well ventilated. Many repair facilities have lunchrooms, showers, and lockers.

The wages an automotive technician can expect to earn depend on the type of work performed, the geographic location of the job, and the prevailing business conditions. Pay can be based on an hourly rate, or it can be based on commission.

The growing number of vehicles on the road and the increased complexity of late-model vehicles have created a lucrative field for hard-working, conscientious automotive technicians.

Review Questions—Chapter 45

Do not write in this book. Write your answers on a separate sheet of paper.

1. Which of the following shop employees checks new vehicles before delivery?
   (A) Shop manager.
   (B) Light repair technician.
   (C) Heavy repair technician.
   (D) Parts counter person.
2. Why is specialization becoming commonplace in most shops?
3. The driveability technician must know a great deal about _____.
   (A) ignition systems
   (B) fuel injection
   (C) carburetors
   (D) All of the above.
4. Radios, cassette tape and CD players are all components serviced by the _____.
5. Technicians are paid _____.
   (A) an hourly wage
   (B) by commission
   (C) a combination of an hourly wage and commission
   (D) All of the above.

ASE-Type Questions

1. Examples of government agencies which hire automotive technicians include all of the following EXCEPT:
   (A) US Post Office.
   (B) Western Auto.
   (C) City Transit Authorities.
   (D) State Highway Departments.
2. Technician A says that in larger shops, the shop supervisor may spend part of the day doing repair work, with the remainder of the time devoted to supervision. Technician B says that in a small shop, all of the shop supervisor's time will be spent directing the technicians and seeing that the shop runs efficiently. Who is right?
   (A) A only.
   (B) B only.
   (C) Both A & B.
   (D) Neither A nor B.
3. All of the following statements about franchise operations are true, EXCEPT:
   (A) the local franchise is operated by the local owner.
   (B) the national franchising operation allows the local owner to use its name.
   (C) the national franchising operation controls the day-to-day operation of the local shop.
   (D) the technicians are paid by the local owner.

4. Montgomery Ward, Sears, and K-Mart are examples of _____.
   (A) franchise operations
   (B) national chains
   (C) government agencies
   (D) small shops
5. All of the following statements about modern repair facilities are true, EXCEPT:
   (A) hydraulic lifts and power tools have removed much of the heavy labor.
   (B) most automotive technicians work inside.
   (C) the service facility of today is crowded, dark, cold, and poorly lighted.
   (D) many modern repair facilities have lunchrooms and showers.

Suggested Activities

1. Visit three or four different repair shops in your area. Note the condition of the work areas, the appearance of the technicians and other personnel, and what types of jobs were being performed. Prepare a report for the class on your findings.

 Note: Be sure to get permission from the shop owner or manager, do not walk into the shop unescorted.

2. Contact a few of the vehicle manufacturers and/or industry associations listed earlier. Ask them for information on training programs as well as the types of qualifications each one looks for in an applicant. Share your findings and any pamphlets, catalogs, or brochures you might receive with the class.
3. Go to the library and research the career opportunities for automotive technicians in your area. Find the average salary for a technician in your area.
4. Obtain a job application from a local repair shop. Make a copy of it and fill it out. Make sure to fill in all relative information as well as any work experience (even experiences unrelated to automotive technology).

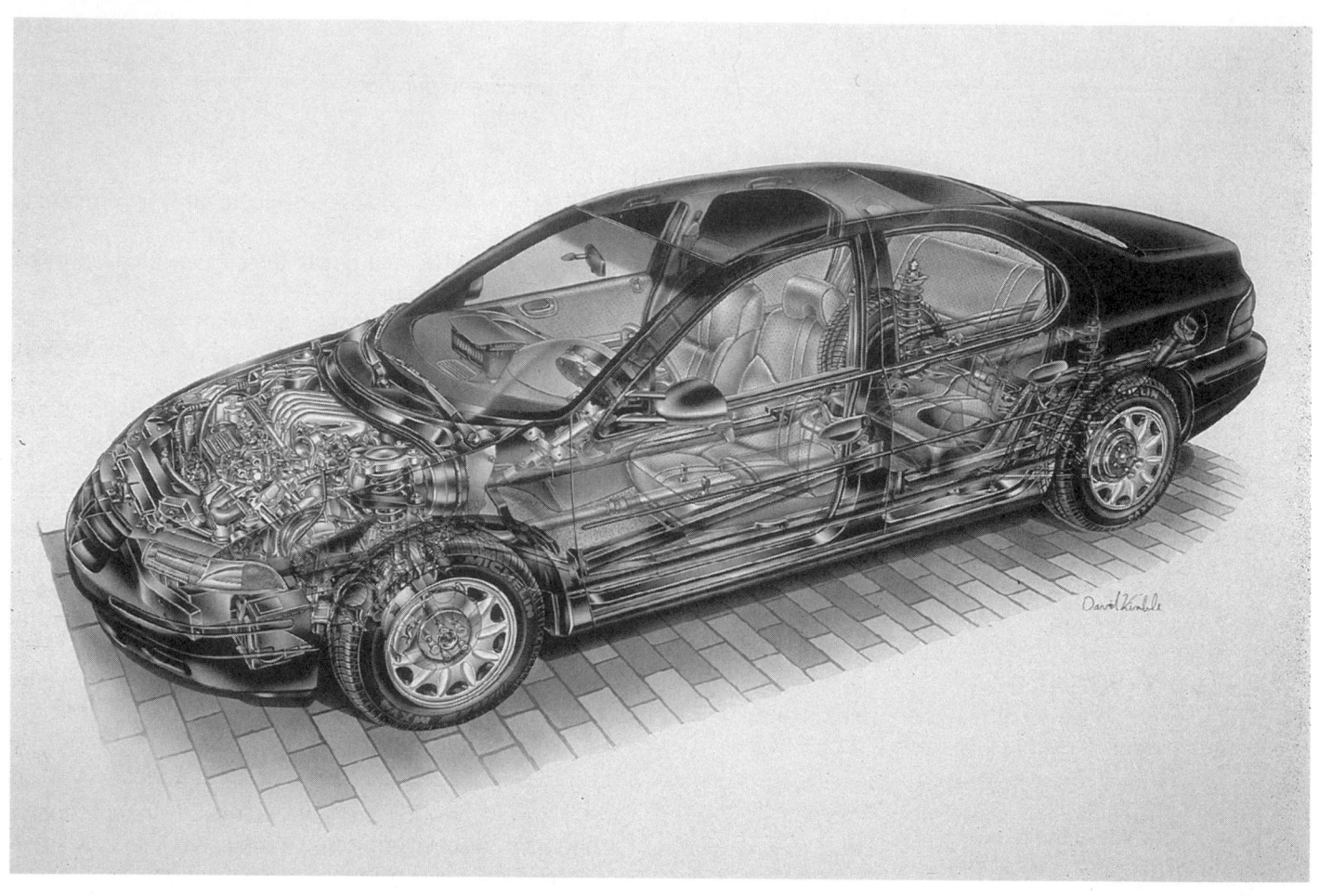

Phantom view of a late-model front-wheel drive automobile. How many components can you identify? (Dodge)

Appendix

SOME COMMON ABBREVIATIONS			
U.S. CUSTOMARY		**METRIC**	
UNIT	ABBREVIATION	UNIT	ABBREVIATION
inch	in.	kilometer	km
feet	ft.	hectometer	hm
yard	yd.	dekameter	dkm
mile	mi.	meter	m
grain	gr.	decimeter	dm
ounce	oz.	centimeter	cm
pound	lb.	millimeter	mm
teaspoon	tsp.	cubic centimeter	cm^3
tablespoon	tbsp.	kilogram	kg
fluid ounce	fl. oz.	hectogram	hg
cup	c.	dekagram	dkg
pint	pt.	gram	g
quart	qt.	decigram	dg
gallon	gal.	centigram	cg
cubic inch	in^3	milligram	mg
cubic foot	ft^3	kiloliter	kL
cubic yard	yd^3	hectoliter	hL
square inch	in^2	dekaliter	dL
square foot	ft^2	liter	L
square yard	yd^2	centiliter	cL
square mile	mi^2	milliliter	mL
Fahrenheit	F	square kilometer	km^2
barrel	bbl.	hectare	ha
fluid dram	fl. dr.	are	a
board foot	bd. ft.	centare	ca
rod	rd.	tonne	t
dram	dr.	Celsius	C
bushel	bu.		

MEASURING SYSTEMS

U.S. CUSTOMARY	METRIC

LENGTH

U.S. CUSTOMARY	METRIC
12 inches = 1 foot	1 kilometer = 1000 meters
36 inches = 1 yard	1 hectometer = 100 meters
3 feet = 1 yard	1 dekameter = 10 meters
5,280 feet = 1 mile	1 meter = 1 meter
16.5 feet = 1 rod	1 decimeter = 0.1 meter
320 rods = 1 mile	1 centimeter = 0.01 meter
6 feet = 1 fathom	1 millimeter = 0.001 meter

WEIGHT

U.S. CUSTOMARY	METRIC
27.34 grains = 1 dram	1 tonne = 1,000,000 grams
438 grains = 1 ounce	1 kilogram = 1000 grams
16 drams = 1 ounce	1 hectogram = 100 grams
16 ounces = 1 pound	1 dekagram = 10 grams
2000 pounds = 1 short ton	1 gram = 1 gram
2240 pounds = 1 long ton	1 decigram = 0.1 gram
25 pounds = 1 quarter	1 centigram = 0.01 gram
4 quarters = 1 cwt	1 milligram = 0.001 gram

VOLUME

U.S. CUSTOMARY	METRIC
8 ounces = 1 cup	1 hectoliter = 100 liters
16 ounces = 1 pint	1 dekaliter = 10 liters
32 ounces = 1 quart	1 liter = 1 liter
2 cups = 1 pint	1 deciliter = 0.1 liter
2 pints = 1 quart	1 centiliter = 0.01 liter
4 quarts = 1 gallon	1 milliliter = 0.001 liter
8 pints = 1 gallon	1000 milliliter = 1 liter

AREA

U.S. CUSTOMARY	METRIC
144 sq. inches = 1 sq. foot	100 sq. millimeters = 1 sq. centimeter
9 sq. feet = 1 sq. yard	100 sq. centimeters = 1 sq. decimeter
43,560 sq. ft. = 160 sq. rods	100 sq. decimeters = 1 sq. meter
160 sq. rods = 1 acre	10,000 sq. meters = 1 hectare
640 acres = 1 sq. mile	

TEMPERATURE

FAHRENHEIT		CELSIUS
32° F	Water freezes	0° C
68° F	Reasonable room temperature	20° C
98.6° F	Normal body temperature	37° C
173° F	Alcohol boils	78.34° C
212° F	Water boils	100° C

USEFUL CONVERSIONS

WHEN YOU KNOW:	MULTIPLY BY:	TO FIND:
TORQUE		
pound-inch pound-foot	0.11298 1.3558	newton-meters (N•m) newton-meters
LIGHT		
foot candles	1.0764	lumens/meters^2 (lm/m^2)
FUEL PERFORMANCE		
miles/gallon	0.4251	kilometers/liter (km/L)
SPEED		
miles/hour	1.6093	kilometers/hr (km/h)
FORCE		
kilogram ounce pound	9.807 0.278 4.448	newtons (n) newtons newtons
POWER		
horsepower	0.746	kilowatts (kw)
PRESSURE OR STRESS		
inches of water pounds/sq. in.	0.2491 6.895	kilopascals (kPa) kilopascals
ENERGY OR WORK		
btu foot-pound kilowatt-hour	1055.0 1.3558 3600000.0	joules (J) joules joules

CONVERSION TABLE
METRIC TO U.S. CUSTOMARY

WHEN YOU KNOW ⬇	MULTIPLY BY: * = Exact		TO FIND ⬇
	VERY ACCURATE	APPROXIMATE	
LENGTH			
millimeters	0.0393701	0.04	inches
centimeters	0.3937008	0.4	inches
meters	3.280840	3.3	feet
meters	1.093613	1.1	yards
kilometers	0.621371	0.6	miles
WEIGHT			
grains	0.00228571	0.0023	ounces
grams	0.03527396	0.035	ounces
kilograms	2.204623	2.2	pounds
tonnes	1.1023113	1.1	short tons
VOLUME			
milliliters	0.20001	0.2	teaspoons
milliliters	0.06667	0.067	tablespoons
milliliters	0.03381402	0.03	fluid ounces
liters	61.02374	61.024	cubic inches
liters	2.113376	2.1	pints
liters	1.056688	1.06	quarts
liters	0.26417205	0.26	gallons
liters	0.03531467	0.035	cubic feet
cubic meters	61023.74	61023.7	cubic inches
cubic meters	35.31467	35.0	cubic feet
cubic meters	1.3079506	1.3	cubic yards
cubic meters	264.17205	264.0	gallons
AREA			
square centimeters	0.1550003	0.16	square inches
square centimeters	0.00107639	0.001	square feet
square meters	10.76391	10.8	square feet
square meters	1.195990	1.2	square yards
square kilometers		0.4	square miles
hectares	2.471054	2.5	acres
TEMPERATURE			
Celsius	*9/5 (then add 32)		Fahrenheit

CONVERSION TABLE
U.S. CUSTOMARY TO METRIC

WHEN YOU KNOW ⬇	MULTIPLY BY: * = Exact		TO FIND ⬇
	VERY ACCURATE	APPROXIMATE	
LENGTH			
inches	* 25.4		millimeters
inches	* 2.54		centimeters
feet	* 0.3048		meters
feet	* 30.48		centimeters
yards	* 0.9144	0.9	meters
miles	* 1.609344	1.6	kilometers
WEIGHT			
grains	15.43236	15.4	grams
ounces	* 28.349523125	28.0	grams
ounces	* 0.028349523125	.028	kilograms
pounds	* 0.45359237	0.45	kilograms
ton	* 0.90718474	0.9	tonnes
VOLUME			
teaspoons	* 4.97512	5.0	milliliters
tablespoons	* 14.92537	15.0	milliliters
fluid ounces	29.57353	30.0	millilitres
cups	* 0.236588240	0.24	liters
pints	* 0.473176473	0.47	liters
quarts	* 0.946352946	0.95	liters
gallons	* 3.785411784	3.8	liters
cubic inches	* 0.016387064	0.02	liters
cubic feet	* 0.028316846592	0.03	cubic meters
cubic yards	* 0.764554857984	0.76	cubic meters
AREA			
square inches	* 6.4516	6.5	square centimeters
square feet	* 0.09290304	0.09	square meters
square yards	* 0.83612736	0.8	square meters
square miles	* 2.589989	2.6	square kilometers
acres	* 0.40468564224	0.4	hectares
TEMPERATURE			
Fahrenheit	* 5/9 (after subtracting 32)		Celsius

DIMENSIONAL AND TEMPERATURE CONVERSION CHART

INCHES			DECIMALS	MILLI-METERS	INCHES TO MILLIMETERS		MILLIMETERS TO INCHES		FAHRENHEIT & CELSIUS			
					in.	mm	mm	in.	°F	°C	°C	°F
	1/32	1/64	.015625	.3969	.0001	.00254	0.001	.000039	-20	-28.9	-30	-22
			.03125	.7937	.0002	.00508	0.002	.000079	-15	-26.1	-28	-18.4
1/16		3/64	.046875	1.1906	.0003	.00762	0.003	.000118	-10	-23.3	-26	-14.8
			.0625	1.5875	.0004	.01016	0.004	.000157	-5	-20.6	-24	-11.2
	3/32	5/64	.078125	1.9844	.0005	.01270	0.005	.000197	0	-17.8	-22	-7.6
			.09375	2.3812	.0006	.01524	0.006	.000236	1	-17.2	-20	-4
1/8		7/64	.109375	2.7781	.0007	.01778	0.007	.000276	2	-16.7	-18	-0.4
			.125	3.1750	.0008	.02032	0.008	.000315	3	-16.1	-16	3.2
	5/32	9/64	.140625	3.5719	.0009	.02286	0.009	.000354	4	-15.6	-14	6.8
			.15625	3.9687	.001	.0254	0.01	.00039	5	-15.0	-12	10.4
3/16		11/64	.171875	4.3656	.002	.0508	0.02	.00079	10	-12.2	-10	14
			.1875	4.7625	.003	.0762	0.03	.00118	15	-9.4	-8	17.6
	7/32	13/64	.203125	5.1594	.004	.1016	0.04	.00157	20	-6.7	-6	21.2
			.21875	5.5562	.005	.1270	0.05	.00197	25	-3.9	-4	24.8
1/4		15/64	.234375	5.9531	.006	.1524	0.06	.00236	30	-1.1	-2	28.4
			.25	6.3500	.007	.1778	0.07	.00276	35	1.7	0	32
	9/32	17/64	.265625	6.7469	.008	.2032	0.08	.00315	40	4.4	2	35.6
			.28125	7.1437	.009	.2286	0.09	.00354	45	7.2	4	39.2
5/16		19/64	.296875	7.5406	.01	.254	0.1	.00394	50	10.0	6	42.8
			.3125	7.9375	.02	.508	0.2	.00787	55	12.8	8	46.4
	11/32	21/64	.328125	8.3344	.03	.762	0.3	.01181	60	15.6	10	50
			.34375	8.7312	.04	1.016	0.4	.01575	65	18.3	12	53.6
3/8		23/64	.359375	9.1281	.05	1.270	0.5	.01969	70	21.1	14	57.2
			.375	9.5250	.06	1.524	0.6	.02362	75	23.9	16	60.8
	13/32	25/64	.390625	9.9219	.07	1.778	0.7	.02756	80	26.7	18	64.4
			.40625	10.3187	.08	2.032	0.8	.03150	85	29.4	20	68
7/16		27/64	.421875	10.7156	.09	2.286	0.9	.03543	90	32.2	22	71.6
			.4375	11.1125	.1	2.54	1	.03937	95	35.0	24	75.2
	15/32	29/64	.453125	11.5094	.2	5.08	2	.07874	100	37.8	26	78.8
			.46875	11.9062	.3	7.62	3	.11811	105	40.6	28	82.4
1/2		31/64	.484375	12.3031	.4	10.16	4	.15748	110	43.3	30	86
			.5	12.7000	.5	12.70	5	.19685	115	46.1	32	89.6
	17/32	33/64	.515625	13.0969	.6	15.24	6	.23622	120	48.9	34	93.2
			.53125	13.4937	.7	17.78	7	.27559	125	51.7	36	96.8
9/16		35/64	.546875	13.8906	.8	20.32	8	.31496	130	54.4	38	100.4
			.5625	14.2875	.9	22.86	9	.35433	135	57.2	40	104
	19/32	37/64	.578125	14.6844	1	25.4	10	.39370	140	60.0	42	107.6
			.59375	15.0812	2	50.8	11	.43307	145	62.8	44	112.2
5/8		39/64	.609375	15.4781	3	76.2	12	.47244	150	65.6	46	114.8
			.625	15.8750	4	101.6	13	.51181	155	68.3	48	118.4
	21/32	41/64	.640625	16.2719	5	127.0	14	.55118	160	71.1	50	122
			.65625	16.6687	6	152.4	15	.59055	165	73.9	52	125.6
11/16		43/64	.671875	17.0656	7	177.8	16	.62992	170	76.7	54	129.2
			.6875	17.4625	8	203.2	17	.66929	175	79.4	56	132.8
	23/32	45/64	.703125	17.8594	9	228.6	18	.70866	180	82.2	58	136.4
			.71875	18.2562	10	254.0	19	.74803	185	85.0	60	140
3/4		47/64	.734375	18.6531	11	279.4	20	.78740	190	87.8	62	143.6
			.75	19.0500	12	304.8	21	.82677	195	90.6	64	147.2
	25/32	49/64	.765625	19.4469	13	330.2	22	.86614	200	93.3	66	150.8
			.78125	19.8437	14	355.6	23	.90551	205	96.1	68	154.4
13/16		51/64	.796875	20.2406	15	381.0	24	.94488	210	98.9	70	158
			.8125	20.6375	16	406.4	25	.98425	212	100.0	75	167
	27/32	53/64	.828125	21.0344	17	431.8	26	1.02362	215	101.7	80	176
			.84375	21.4312	18	457.2	27	1.06299	220	104.4	85	185
7/8		55/64	.859375	21.8281	19	482.6	28	1.10236	225	107.2	90	194
			.875	22.2250	20	508.0	29	1.14173	230	110.0	95	203
	29/32	57/64	.890625	22.6219	21	533.4	30	1.18110	235	112.8	100	212
			.90625	23.0187	22	558.8	31	1.22047	240	115.6	105	221
15/16		59/64	.921875	23.4156	23	584.2	32	1.25984	245	118.3	110	230
			.9375	23.8125	24	609.6	33	1.29921	250	121.1	115	239
	31/32	61/64	.953125	24.2094	25	635.0	34	1.33858	255	123.9	120	248
			.96875	24.6062	26	660.4	35	1.37795	260	126.6	125	257
		63/64	.984375	25.0031	27	690.6	36	1.41732	265	129.4	130	266

CAPACITY CONVERSION U.S. GALLONS TO LITERS

Gallons	0	1	2	3	4	5
	Liters	Liters	Liters	Liters	Liters	Liters
0	00.0000	3.7853	7.5707	11.3560	15.1413	18.9267
10	37.8533	41.6387	45.4240	49.2098	52.9947	56.7800
20	75.7066	79.4920	83.2773	87.0626	90.3480	94.6333
30	113.5600	117.3453	121.1306	124.9160	128.7013	132.4866
40	151.4133	155.1986	158.9840	162.7693	166.5546	170.3400

MILLIMETER CONVERSION CHART

mm in.								
15 = .5905	30 =1.1811	45 =1.7716	60 =2 3622	75 =2.9527	90 =3.5433	105 =4.1338	120 =4.7244	
.25=.0098	15.25=.6004	30.25=1.1909	45.25=1.7815	60.25=2.3720	75.25=2.9626	90.25=3.5531	105.25=4.1437	120.25=4.7342
.50=.0197	15.50=.6102	30.50=1.2008	45.50=1.7913	60.50=2.3819	75.50=2.9724	90.50=3.5630	105.50=4.1535	120.50=4.7441
.75=.0295	15.75=.6201	30.75=1.2106	45.75=1.8012	60.75=2.3917	75.75=2.9823	90.75=3.5728	105.75=4.1634	120.75=4.7539
1 =.0394	16 =.6299	31 =1.2205	46 =1.8110	61 =2.4016	76 =2.9921	91 =3.5827	106 =4.1732	121 =4.7638
1.25=.0492	16.25=.6398	31.25=1.2303	46.25=1.8209	61.25=2.4114	76.25=3.0020	91.25=3.5925	106.25=4.1831	121.25=4.7736
1.50=.0591	16.50=.6496	31.50=1.2402	46.50=1.8307	61.50=2.4213	76.50=3.0118	91.50=3.6024	106.50=4.1929	121.50=4.7885
1.75=.0689	16.75=.6594	31.75=1.2500	46.75=1.8405	61.75=2.4311	76.75=3.0216	91.75=3.6122	106.75=4.2027	121.75=4.7933
2 =.0787	17 =.6693	32 =1.2598	47 =1.8504	62 =2.4409	77 =3.0315	92 =3.6220	107 =4.2126	122 =4.8031
2.25=.0886	17.25=.6791	32.25=1.2697	47.25=1.8602	62.25=2.4508	77.25=3.0413	92.25=3.6319	107.25=4.2224	122.25=4.8130
2.50=.0984	17.50=.6890	32.50=1.2795	47.50=1.8701	62.50=2.4606	77.50=3.0512	92.50=3.6417	107.50=4.2323	122.50=4.8228
2.75=.1083	17.75=.6988	32.75=1.2894	47.75=1.8799	62.75=2.4705	77.75=3.0610	92.75=3.6516	107.75=4.2421	122.75=4.8327
3 =.1181	18 =.7087	33 =1.2992	48 =1.8898	63 =2.4803	78 =3.0709	93 =3.6614	108 =4.2520	123 =4.8425
3.25=.1280	18.25=.7185	33.25=1.3091	48.25=1.8996	63.25=2.4901	78.25=3.0807	93.25=3.6713	108.25=4.2618	123.25=4.8524
3.50=.1378	18.50=.7283	33.50=1.3189	48.50=1.9094	63.50=2.5000	78.50=3.0905	93.50=3.6811	108.50=4.2716	123.50=4.8622
3.75=.1476	18.75=.7382	33.75=1.3287	48.75=1.9193	63.75=2.5098	78.75=3.1004	93.75=3.6909	108.75=4.2815	123.75=4.8720
4 =.1575	19 =.7480	34 =1.3386	49 =1.9291	64 =2.5197	79 =3.1102	94 =3.7008	109 =4.2913	124 =4.8819
4.25=.1673	19.25=.7579	34.25=1.3484	49.25=1.9390	64.25=2.5295	79.25=3.1201	94.25=3.7106	109.25=4.3012	124.25=4.8917
4.50=.1772	19.50=.7677	34.50=1.3583	49.50=1.9488	64.50=2.5394	79.50=3.1299	94.50=3.7205	109.50=4.3110	124.50=4.9016
4.75=.1870	19.75=.7776	34.75=1.3681	49.75=1.9587	64.75=2.5492	79.75=3.1398	94.75=3.7303	109.75=4.3209	124.75=4.9114
5 =.1968	20 =.7874	35 =1.3779	50 =1.9685	65 =2.5590	80 =3.1496	95 =3.7401	110 =4.3307	125 =4.9212
5.25=.2067	20.25=.7972	35.25=1.3878	50.25=1.9783	65.25=2.5689	80.25=3.1594	95.25=3.7500	110.25=4.3405	125.25=4.9311
5.50=.2165	20.50=.8071	35.50=1.3976	50.50=1.9882	65.50=2.5787	80.50=3.1693	95.50=3.7598	110.50=4.3504	125.50=4.9409
5.75=.2264	20.75=.8169	35.75=1.4075	50.75=1.9980	65.75=2.5886	80.75=3.1791	95.75=3.7697	110.75=4.3602	125.75=4.9508
6 =.2362	21 =.8268	36 =1.4173	51 =2.0079	66 =2.5984	81 =3.1890	96 =3.7795	111 =4.3701	126 =4.9606
6.25=.2461	21.25=.8366	36.25=1.4272	51.25=2.0177	66.25=2.6083	81.25=3.1988	96.25=3.7894	111.25=4.3799	126.25=4.9705
6.50=.2559	21.50=.8465	36.50=1.4370	51.50=2.0276	66.50=2.6181	81.50=3.2087	96.50=3.7992	111.50=4.3898	126.50=4.9803
6.75=.2657	21.75=.8563	36.75=1.4468	51.75=2.0374	66.75=2.6279	81.75=3.2185	96.75=3.8090	111.75=4.3996	126.75=4.9901
7 =.2756	22 =.8661	37 =1.4567	52 =2.0472	67 =2.6378	82 =3.2283	97 =3.8189	112 =4.4094	127 =5.0000
7.25=.2854	22.25=.8760	37.25=1 4665	52.25=2.0571	67.25=2.6476	82.25=3.2382	97.25=3.8287	112.25=4.4193	
7.50=.2953	22.50=.8858	37.50=1.4764	52.50=2.0669	67.50=2.6575	82.50=3.2480	97.50=3.8386	112.50=4.4291	
7.75=.3051	22.75=.8957	37.75=1.4862·	52.75=2.0768	67.75=2.6673	82.75=3.2579	97.75=3.8484	112.75=4.4390	
8 =.3150	23 =.9055	38 =1.4961	53 =2.0866	68 =2.6772	83 =3.2677	98 =3.8583	113 =4.4488	
8.25=.3248	23.25=.9153	38.25=1.5059	53.25=2.0965	68.25=2.6870	83.25=3.2776	98.25=3.8681	113.25=4.4587	
8.50=.3346	23.50=.9252	38.50=1.5157	53.50=2.1063	68.50=2.6968	83.50=3.2874	98.50=3.8779	113.50=4.4685	
8.75=.3445	23.75=.9350	38.75=1.5256	53.75=2.1161	68.75=2.7067	83.75=3.2972	98.75=3.8878	113.75=4.4783	
9 =.3543	24 =.9449	39 =1.5354	54 =2.1260	69 =2.7165	84 =3.3071	99 =3.8976	114 =4.4882	
9.25=.3642	24.25=.9547	39.25=1.5453	54.25=2.1358	69.25=2.7264	84.25=3.3169	99.25=3.9075	114.25=4.4980	
9.50=.3740	24.50=.9646	39.50=1.5551	54.50=2.1457	69.50=2.7362	84.50=3.3268	99.50=3.9173	114.50=4.5079	
9.75=.3839	24.75=.9744	39.75=1.5650	54.75=2.1555	69.75=2.7461	84.75=3.3366	99.75=3.9272	114.75=4.5177	
10 =.3937	25 =.9842	40 =1.5748	55 =2.1653	70 =2.7559	85 =3.3464	100 =3.9370	115 =4.5275	
10.25=.4035	25.25=.9941	40.25=1.5846	55.25=2.1752	70.25=2.7657	85.25=3.3563	100.25=3.9468	115.25=4.5374	
10.50=.4134	25.50=1.0039	40.50=1.5945	55.50=2.1850	70.50=2.7756	85.50=3.3661	100.50=3.9567	115.50=4.5472	
10.75=.4232	25.75=1.0138	40.75=1.6043	55.75=2.1949	70.75=2.7854	85.75=3.3760	100.75=3.9665	115.75=4.5571	
11 =.4331	26 =1.0236	41 =1.6142	56 =2.2047	71 =2.7953	86 =3.3858	101 =3.9764	116 =4.5669	
11.25=.4429	26.25=1.0335	41.25=1.6240	56.25=2.2146	71.25=2.8051	86.25=3.3957	101.25=3.9862	116.25=4.5768	
11.50=.4528	26.50=1.0433	41.50=1.6339	56.50=2.2244	71.50=2.8150	86.50=3.4055	101.50=3.9961	116.50=4.5866	
11.75=.4626	26.75=1.0531	41.75=1.6437	56.75=2.2342	71.75=2.8248	86.75=3.4153	101.75=4.0059	116.75=4.5964	
12 =.4724	27 =1.0630	42 =1.6535	57 =2.2441	72 =2.8346	87 =3.4252	102 =4.0157	117 =4.6063	
12.25=.4823	27.25=1.0728	42.25=1.6634	57.25=2.2539	72.25=2.8445	87.25=3.4350	102.25=4.0256	117.25=4.6161	
12.50=.4921	27.50=1.0827	42.50=1.6732	57.50=2.2638	72.50=2.8543	87.50=3.4449	102.50=4.0354	117.50=4.6260	
12.75=.5020	27.75=1.0925	42.75=1.6831	57.75=2.2736	72.75=2.8642	87.75=3.4547	102.75=4.0453	117.75=4.6358	
13 =.5118	28 =1.1024	43 =1.6929	58 =2.2835	73 =2.8740	88 =3.4646	103 =4.0551	118 =4.6457	
13.25=.5217	28.25=1.1122	43.25=1.7028	58.25=2.2933	73.25=2.8839	88.25=3.4744	103.25=4.0650	118.25=4.6555	
13.50=.5315	28.50=1.1220	43.50=1.7126	58.50=2.3031	73.50=2.8937	88.50=3.4842	103.50=4.0748	118.50=4.6653	
13.75=.5413	28.75=1.1319	43.75=1.7224	58.75=2.3130	73.75=2.9035	88.75=3.4941	103.75=4.0846	118.75=4.6752	
14 =.5512	29 =1.1417	44 =1.7323	59 =2.3228	74 =2.9134	89 =3.5039	104 =4.0945	119 =4.6850	
14.25=.5610	29.25=1.1516	44.25=1.7421	59.25=2.3327	74.25=2.9232	89.25=3.5138	104.25=4.1043	119.25=4.6949	
14.50=.5709	29.50=1.1614	44.50=1.7520	59.50=2.3425	74.50=2.9331	89.50=3.5236	104.50=4.1142	119.50=4.7047	
14.75=.5807	29.75=1.1713	44.75=1.7618	59.75=2.3524	74.74=2.9429	89.75=3.5335	104.75=4.1240	119.75=4.7146	

METRIC – INCH EQUIVALENTS

INCHES (FRACTIONS)	INCHES (DECIMALS)	MILLIMETERS	INCHES (FRACTIONS)	INCHES (DECIMALS)	MILLIMETERS
	.00394	.1	15/32	.46875	11.9063
	.00787	.2		.47244	12.00
	.01181	.3	31/64	.484375	12.3031
1/64	.015625	.3969	1/2	.5000	12.70
	.01575	.4		.51181	13.00
	.01969	.5	33/64	.515625	13.0969
	.02362	.6	17/32	.53125	13.4938
	.02756	.7	35/64	.546875	13.8907
1/32	.03125	.7938		.55118	14.00
	.0315	.8	9/16	.5625	14.2875
	.03543	.9	37/64	.578125	14.6844
	.03937	1.00		.59055	15.00
3/64	.046875	1.1906	19/32	.59375	15.0813
1/16	.0625	1.5875	39/64	.609375	15.4782
5/64	.078125	1.9844	5/8	.625	15.875
	.07874	2.00		.62992	16.00
3/32	.09375	2.3813	41/64	.640625	16.2719
7/64	.109375	2.7781	21/32	.65625	16.6688
	.11811	3.00		.66929	17.00
1/8	.125	3.175	43/64	.671875	17.0657
9/64	.140625	3.5719	11/16	.6875	17.4625
5/32	.15625	3.9688	45/64	.703125	17.8594
	.15748	4.00		.70866	18.00
11/64	.171875	4.3656	23/32	.71875	18.2563
3/16	.1875	4.7625	47/64	.734375	18.6532
	.19685	5.00		.74803	19.00
13/64	.203125	5.1594	3/4	.7500	19.05
7/32	.21875	5.5563	49/64	.765625	19.4469
15/64	.234375	5.9531	25/32	.78125	19.8438
	.23622	6.00		.7874	20.00
1/4	.2500	6.35	51/64	.796875	20.2407
17/64	.265625	6.7469	13/16	.8125	20.6375
	.27559	7.00		.82677	21.00
9/32	.28125	7.1438	53/64	.828125	21.0344
19/64	.296875	7.5406	27/32	.84375	21.4313
5/16	.3125	7.9375	55/64	.859375	21.8282
	.31496	8.00		.86614	22.00
21/64	.328125	8.3344	7/8	.875	22.225
11/32	.34375	8.7313	57/64	.890625	22.6219
	.35433	9.00		.90551	23.00
23/64	.359375	9.1281	29/32	.90625	23.0188
3/8	.375	9.525	59/64	.921875	23.4157
25/64	.390625	9.9219	15/16	.9375	23.8125
	.3937	10.00		.94488	24.00
13/32	.40625	10.3188	61/64	.953125	24.2094
27/64	.421875	10.7156	31/32	.96875	24.6063
	.43307	11.00		.98425	25.00
7/16	.4375	11.1125	63/64	.984375	25.0032
29/64	.453125	11.5094	1	1.0000	25.4001

Dictionary of Automotive Terms

A

AAA: American Automobile Association.

ABDC: After Bottom Dead Center.

ABS: Anti-lock Braking System.

ABS warning light: Amber indicator lamp mounted in the instrument cluster. Illuminates when there is a problem with the anti-lock brake system.

Absolute zero: A state in which no heat is present. Believed to be −459.7°F or −273.16°C.

AC: Alternating current.

ACT: American College Testing program.

Accelerator: Floor pedal used to control, through linkage, throttle valve in carburetor.

Accelerator pump: Small pump, located in carburetor, that sprays additional gasoline into air stream during acceleration.

Accident: An unplanned event that results in damage and/or injury.

Accumulator (Air conditioning): Receiver-dehydrator combination.

Accumulator (Brake): Gas-charged cylinder or chamber used to store brake fluid. Normally used in anti-lock brake systems.

Accumulator piston (Automatic transmission): Unit designed to assist the servo to apply brake band quickly, yet smoothly.

Acetone: A very flammable, volatile solvent. Mixes with water.

Acetylene: Gas commonly used in welding or cutting operations.

Acid core (Solder): Wire solder with a central core containing an acid flux.

Ackerman principle: Bending outer ends of steering arms slightly inward so that when car is making a turn, inside wheel will turn more sharply than outer wheel. This principle produces toe-out on turns.

Actuator: Device that converts electrical signals into physical actions. Most actuators are classified as motors, solenoids, or relays.

Additive: Solution, powder, etc., added to gasoline, oil, grease, etc., in an endeavor to improve characteristics of original product.

Add-on transmission cooler: Heat exchanger installed in front of the radia-

tor to provide extra cooling for an automatic transmission.

Adjustable pilot (Valve grinding): An expandable device used to position and guide either cutter or stone mandrels (sleeve) for valve grinding.

Advance (Ignition timing): To set ignition timing so a spark occurs earlier or more degrees before TDC.

AERA: Automotive Engine Rebuilders Association.

Aeration: Process of mixing air into a solution such as engine coolant.

AFBMA: Antifriction Bearing Manufacturers Association.

Agitation (Cleaning): Shaking or vibration applied to a cleaning solution to assist cleaning process.

Air bag system: Restraint system that uses an inflatable bag to protect occupants during a severe frontal or side collision.

Air bleed: An orifice or small passageway designed to allow a specific amount of air to enter a moving column of liquid (such as fuel).

Air cleaner: Device used to remove dust, abrasive, etc., from the air being drawn into engines, compressors, power brakes, etc.

Air conditioning: System used to control the temperature, movement, cleanliness, and humidity of air in a vehicle.

Air conditioning specialist: Person highly trained and knowledgeable in the field of automotive air conditioning.

Air cooled: An object cooled by passing a stream of air over its surface.

Air dam: A device placed beneath the front bumper to reduce amount of air turbulence or direct air to the radiator.

Air drill: Drill operated by pneumatic pressure.

Air filter: A device through which air is drawn to remove dust, dirt, etc.

Airflow sensor: Device to measure volume and speed of air moving into intake manifold.

Air-fuel ratio: Ratio (by weight or by volume) between air and gasoline that makes up engine fuel mixture.

Air gap (Regulator): Distance between contact armature and iron core that when magnetized, draws armature down.

Air gap (Spark plugs): Distance between center and side electrodes.

Air horn (Carburetor): Top portion of air passageway through carburetor.

Air horn (Accessory): Warning horn operated by compressed air.

Air injection reaction (AIR): An emission control system used to lower levels of carbon monoxide and hydrocarbon emissions. Accomplished by injecting a stream of air into exhaust stream near exhaust valve.

Air operated: Press, lift, etc., operated by compressed air as opposed to a fluid.

Air pollution: Contamination of earth's atmosphere by various natural and manufactured pollutants such as smoke, gases, dust, etc.

Air pressure check (Automatic transmission): Using compressed air to check clutch and band operation.

Air spring: Container and plunger separated by air under pressure. When container and plunger attempt to squeeze together, air compresses and produces a spring effect. Air spring has been used on some suspension systems.

Align: To bring various parts of unit into correct positions in respect to each other or to a predetermined location.

Aligning bar (Crankshaft): A precision tool (bar) used to check engine main bearing alignment.

Aligning punch: Punch with a long, gradual taper that may be passed through holes in two objects, thus aligning the holes for insertion of fasteners, etc.

Alloy: Mixture of two or more materials.

Alnico magnet: Magnet using (Al) aluminum, (Ni) nickel, and (Co) cobalt in its construction.

Alpha numeric (Tire): Tire size designation using letters to indicate load carrying capacity. Example: GR 78-15. The letter G = load/size relationship. R = radial construction. 78 = height to width ratio. 15 = rim diameter in inches.

Alternator: Device that produces AC current. The AC is rectified before reaching car's electrical system.

Alternating current (AC): Electric current that first flows one way in circuit and then other. Type normally used in homes.

Altitude compensation: Altering the adjustment, tension, position, etc., of some unit such as a carburetor, vacuum modulator, etc., so that unit operation will be in conformance to that required at any specific elevation.

Aluminum oxide (Abrasive): An abrasive (sanding) paper coated with particles of aluminum oxide.

Aluminum oxide beads: Beads, made of aluminum oxide used in construction of catalytic converters.

AMA: Automobile Manufacturers Association.

Amalgamate: A mixture of two or more materials or compounds—such as solder, which is made up basically of tin and lead.

Ambient temperature: Temperature of air surrounding an object.

Ammeter: Instrument used to measure rate of current flow in amperes.

Ampere: Unit of measurement used in expressing rate of current flow in a circuit.

Ampere hour capacity: Measurement of storage battery ability to deliver specified current over specified length of time.

Aneroid: A device, such as a barometer bellows, that neither contains nor uses a liquid.

Aneroid barometer: A device to measure atmospheric pressure. It utilizes an aneroid capsule (bellows) that expands and contracts with differences in pressure.

Angular contact (Bearing): An antifriction bearing, such as a ball bearing, designed to carry both radial and thrust loads.

Anneal: To remove hardness from metal. Heat steel to a red color, then allow it to cool slowly. Unlike steel, copper is annealed by heating, and then plunging it immediately into cold water.

Annealed stainless steel: Stainless steel that has been heat treated to remove stress and to soften.

Annular groove: A groove, such as used for bearing oil distribution, snap ring installation, etc., that runs completely around a bearing, shaft, etc.

Annulus gear: A ring shaped gear such as the internal tooth ring (annulus) gear used in some overdrive units.

Anode: In an electric circuit—the positive pole.

Antibackfire valve: Valve used in air injection reaction (exhaust emission control) system to prevent backfiring during period immediately following sudden deceleration.

Antifreeze: Chemical added to cooling system to prevent coolant from freezing in cold weather.

Antifriction bearing: Bearing containing rollers or balls plus an inner and outer race. Bearing is designed to roll, thus minimizing friction.

Antiknock (Fuel): Indicates various substances, that can be added to gasoline to improve its resistance to knocking (spark knock, preignition, or detonation).

Antilash plate: A plate designed to maintain constant and intimate contact between two gears. This removes "play" or "backlash".

Anti-lock brakes: Computerized brake system that prevents wheel lock-up by pulsating fluid pressure to affected wheel(s).

Antipercolator: Device for venting vapors from main discharge tube, or well, of a carburetor.

Antiseize compound: A compound designed to prevent galling, sticking, or seizing of fastener threads.

Antistall dashpot (Carburetor): A diaphragm operated unit designed to retard final closing of throttle valve to prevent stalling.

API: American Petroleum Institute.

Apply servo (Transmission): The hydraulically operated pistons used to apply bands in an automatic transmission.

APRA: Automotive Parts Rebuilders Association.

Apprentice program: Educational program designed to teach a trade through on-the-job training and study.

Arbor press: A stout press, often hand operated, used to insert or remove bearings, bushings, collars, etc.

Arc or electric welding: Welding by using electric current to melt both metal to be welded and welding rod or electrode that is being added.

Arcing: Electricity leaping the gap between two electrodes.

Armature (Relay, regulator, horn, etc.): The movable part of the unit.

Armature (Starter or generator): The portion that revolves between the pole shoes, made up of wire windings on an iron core.

Asbestos: Heat resistant and nonburning fibrous mineral widely used for brake shoes, clutch linings, etc. Do not inhale asbestos fibers or dust as it can cause cancer.

Asbestos wick seal: Bearing oil seal constructed of woven asbestos fibers.

ASME: American Society of Mechanical Engineers.

Aspect ratio (Tire): Ratio between height and width of a tire.

ASTM: American Society of Testing Materials.

Asymmetric tire tread: Tire tread with a non-symmetrical (uneven) pattern. Designed to reduce tire vibration and noise.

ATA: American Trucking Association.

ATDC: After Top Dead Center.

Atmosphere: Layer of gases (referred to as air) surrounding earth.

Atmospheric pressure: Pressure exerted by atmosphere on all things exposed to it. Around 14.7 pounds per square inch or 101 kPa at sea level.

Atom: Tiny particle of matter made up of electrons, protons, and neutrons. Atoms or combinations of atoms make up molecules. Electrons orbit around center or nucleus made up of protons and neutrons.

Atomize: To break a liquid into tiny droplets.

Automatic choke: A carburetor choke device that automatically positions itself in accordance with carburetor needs.

Automatic leveling control: Pressure system which maintains proper body height with changes in load.

Automatic transmission: A transmission that shifts itself. Shift range and points are determined by road speed, quadrant position, engine loading, etc.

Automatic transmission fluid (ATF): Special lubricating fluid designed for use in automatic transmissions.

AWG: American Wire Gauge. United States standard for measurement of nonferrous wires, sheet material, and rods.

AWL (Tire): Sharp pointed steel tool used to probe cuts, nail holes, etc., in tires.

Axial: Direction parallel to shaft or bearing hole.

Axial compressor: An air conditioning compressor in which a series of pistons are moved in an axial direction by a swash plate.

Axis: The line about which a revolving object rotates.

Axle (Full-floating): Axle used to drive rear wheels. It does not hold them on nor support them.

Axle (Semi or one-quarter floating): Axle used to drive wheels, hold them on, and support them.

Axle (Three-quarter floating): Axle used to drive rear wheels as well as hold them on. It does not support them.

Axle end gears: Two gears, one per axle, that are splined to the inner ends of drive axles. They mesh with and are driven by "spider" gears.

Axle end play: Axle shaft "play" or movement in an endwise direction.

Axle housing: Enclosure for axles and differential. It is partially filled with differential fluid (oil).

Axle ratio: Relationship or ratio between the number of times the propeller shaft must revolve to turn the axle drive shafts one turn.

Axle retainer: Device such as a nut, collar, C-lock, etc., designed to secure axle in place.

Axle side gear: Gear on drive axle inner end. It mates with differential pinion gears. In turn, through the pinion shaft, it connects axles to differential case.

B

Babbitted bearing: A bearing in which bearing material, in this case babbit, is bonded directly to bearing housing.

Backfire (Intake system): Burning of fuel mixture in intake manifold. May be caused by faulty timing, crossed plug wires, leaky intake valve, etc.

Backfire (Exhaust system): Passage of unburned fuel mixture into exhaust system where it is ignited and causes an explosion (backfire).

Backhand welding: A method of oxy-acetylene welding in which torch tip faces into puddle, AWAY from direction of welding.

Backlash: Amount of "play" between two parts. In case of gears, it refers to how much one gear can be moved back and forth without moving gear into which it is meshed.

Back pressure: Resistance to flow of exhaust gases through exhaust system.

Back pressure transducer valve (BPV): A valve, sensitive to engine exhaust system back pressure, that adjusts or modulates action of EGR (Exhaust Gas Recirculation) valve.

Backup lights: White lights attached to the rear of a vehicle. Lights are turned on whenever transmission is placed in reverse. Provides illumination for backing at night.

Baffle: Obstruction used to slow down or divert the flow of gases, liquids, sound, etc.

Balance (Tire): See *Static Balance* and *Dynamic Balance*.

Balance point (Lifting): The point or location at which an object may be lifted while retaining proper balance (equal weight on both sides of lift point).

Balance weight: A weight that is added to a rotating shaft, wheel, etc., so as to bring object into balance to prevent vibration.

Balk ring: Ring attached to balk gear hub in overdrive unit. It lets gear rotate while ring is stationary.

Ball and trunnion: Type of universal joint using needle bearing mounted balls which swivel inside sockets.

Ball bearing (Antifriction): Bearing consisting of an inner and outer hardened steel race separated by a series of hardened steel balls.

Ball joint: Flexible joint utilizing ball and socket type of construction. Used in steering linkage setups, steering knuckle pivot supports, etc.

Ball joint rocker arms: Rocker arms that instead of being mounted on shaft, are mounted upon ball-shaped device on end of stud.

Ball joint steering knuckle: Steering knuckle that pivots on ball joints instead of on a kingpin.

Ball nut (Steering gear): That portion of a steering gear riding on the worm shaft (on a series of steel balls) and meshed with pitman shaft sector gear.

Ball peen hammer: A steel hammer with round peen head on one end. Useful for general striking and for peening pins, rivets, etc.

Ball race: That portion of a ball bearing (inner and outer) that contains and bears against bearing balls.

Ball stud (Valve train): The stud upon which rocker arm pivot ball is affixed.

Ballast resistor: Resistor constructed of special type wire, properties of which tend to increase or decrease voltage in direct proportion to heat of wire.

Band: Holding member in an automatic transmission. Used to stop clutch rotation during certain transmission gear ranges.

Band and clutch application chart: Diagnostic chart used to identify transmission member operating conditions in each gear range.

Barometric pressure: Atmospheric pressure as determined by a barometer.

Barometric pressure sensitive bellows: An evacuated (air removed) bellows that expands or contracts with changes in atmospheric pressure.

Barrel wear (Brakes): A brake drum wear pattern in which wear is greater in center of shoe contact area.

Barrier plate (Friction bearing): A very thin plating between copper layer and tin overplate on a precision insert bearing. It prevents tin in overplate from entering copper.

Base brakes: The hydraulic and friction members of the automotive brake system. Does not include any boosters or ABS components.

Base circle: As applied to camshaft—lowest spot on cam. Area of cam directly opposite lobe.

Base metal: Metal underneath a coating or plate. Can refer to metal of parts being welded as opposed to filler metal being added.

Bastard file: A file in which cutting edges are somewhat coarser than those employed by a second cut file.

Battery: Electrochemical device for producing electricity.

Battery capacity: Rating of current output of battery. Determined by plate size, number of plates, and amount of acid in electrolyte.

Battery charging: Process of renewing battery by passing electric current through battery in reverse direction.

Battery—maintenance-free: A battery so designed as to not need any additional water during its normal service life.

Battery rating: Standardized measurement of battery's ability to deliver electrical energy under specified conditions.

Battery reserve capacity: Measurement (in minutes) of battery's ability to supply electrical system energy in event generating system is inoperative.

Battery reserve capacity rating: The measure of number of minutes a full charged battery at 80°F (26.7°C) can be discharged at 25 amperes and still maintain a minimum voltage of 1.75 volts per cell.

Battery shedding: Grids losing active materials that fall off and settle in bottom of battery case.

Battery state of charge: Electrical energy available from a given battery in relation to that which would be normally available if battery were fully charged.

Battery temperature sensor: Sensor installed in some batteries to control overcharging.

Battery voltage: Determined by the number of cells. Each cell has 2.1V. Three cells will produce a 6V battery and six cells a 12V battery.

BBDC: Before Bottom Dead Center.

BCI: Battery Council International.

BDC: Bottom Dead Center.

Bead (Tire): Steel wire reinforced portion of tire that engages the wheel rim.

Bead expander: A device used to expand tire beads out against rim flange to permit inflation of tubeless tire.

Bead wire (Tire): Steel wire used in tire bead area to prevent bead expansion.

Bearing: Area of unit in which contacting surface of a revolving part rests.

Bearing axis: A line through center of a bearing, parallel to length of shaft upon which bearing operates.

Bearing bore: Center opening in a bearing inner cone or ring. Bore diameter determines shaft, spindle, etc., size applicable to a given bearing.

Bearing cap: Removable portion of a split (two piece) friction bearing. May contain either an insert or integral bearing surface.

Bearing cap cross bolt: A strengthening bolt passed through engine crankcase and main bearing cap. When secured, adds rigidity to main bearing cap.

Bearing clearance: Amount of space left between shaft and bearing surface. This space is for lubricating oil to enter.

Bearing cone creep: Slow rotational movement of the antifriction bearing inner cone or ring around shaft, spindle, etc.

Bearing contact area: That area contacted by sliding or rolling elements of a bearing.

Bearing crush: In a precision insert bearing, having bearing ends protrude a very small distance above bearing parting surface. When cap is drawn up, bearing halves are "crushed" into tight contact with bore.

Bearing journal: That portion of a shaft engaging a friction bearing surface.

Bearing oven: A special oven designed to heat and expand antifriction bearing inner cone to aid installation.

Bearing packer: A device used to inject grease into an antifriction bearing.

Bearing preload: Placing a bearing, by means of adjustment, under an initial load. This helps prevent bearing and part misalignment when unit is subjected to normal load stresses.

Bearing spread: In a precision insert bearing, having bearing parting surface diameter slightly larger (positive spread) than bore diameter. This allows bearing to "snap into place" and holds halves in place during assembly.

Belleville clutch: A traction differential clutch disc and plate assembly constructed so as to impart friction producing pressure when assembled.

Bell housing (Clutch housing): Metal covering around flywheel and clutch, or torque converter assembly.

Belted bias: Tire plies crisscrossed; belts beneath tread area.

Belt slack: A measured amount of belt "looseness" or deflection.

Belt tension: Amount of contact pressure produced between pulley and belt when belt is tightened. Determined by measuring belt deflection or slack.

Bench bleeding (Master cylinder): Removing air from brake master cylinder before installing new or rebuilt unit on the vehicle.

Bench grinder: Abrasive wheel bolted to a work bench.

Bench vise: A vise bolted to a work bench.

Bending spring (Tubing): A special spring that is placed over a section of tubing to permit bending without kinking.

Bendix type starter drive: A self-engaging starter drive gear. Gear moves into engagement when starter starts spinning and automatically disengages when starter stops.

Bevel edge rule: A rigid steel rule with one or both edges beveled to permit more precise edge viewing and placement.

Bevel gear: Gear in which teeth are cut in a cone shape, as found in axle end gears.

Bevel spur gear: Gear in which teeth are cut in a cone shape. Teeth are aligned with cone centerline, as found in some differential gears.

Bezel: Crimped edge of metal that secures glass face to an instrument.

BHP: Brake horsepower. Measurement of actual power produced by engine.

Bias-belted tire: A tire in which sidewall plies are cross-biased at an angle to tire centerline and tread area belts are of radial design. A cross between bias and radial design.

Bias ply: Tire plies crisscross; belts not used under tread area.

Bias tire: A tire in which body cord plies are arranged in a cross-biased pattern at an angle to tire centerline.

Black light: Instrument used in detecting leaks, cracks, etc. Emits invisible (ultraviolet) light that when directed on fluorescent materials, causes them to glow.

Bleeder screw: A screw, that when loosened, opens a small hole to permit escape of air trapped in a wheel cylinder, brake cylinder, etc.

Bleeding: Removing air, pressure, fluid, etc., from a closed system, as in air conditioning.

Bleeding the brakes: Refers to removal of air from hydraulic system. Bleeder screws are loosened at each wheel cylinder, (one at a time) and brake fluid is forced from master cylinder through lines until all air is expelled.

Blend door: Door installed in the air conditioning blower case. Controls temperature of the air going to the passenger compartment.

Block: Part of engine containing cylinders.

Block distortion: Twisting, bending, etc., of the engine block. Can be caused from overheating, improper fastener torque, internal stress, etc. Can cause cylinder bore, crank bearing bore, etc., distortion, and misalignment.

Block guide pin: Smooth headed pins that are inserted into cylinder block to provide proper block-to-gasket and cylinder head alignment.

Blow-by: Refers to escape of exhaust gases past piston rings.

Blower: Supercharger.

Blowholes: Voids in weld metal caused by improper welding technique, settings, filler rod, etc.

Blowtorch: A small torch often incorporating an integral fuel tank that is pressurized, via a hand pump, to force fuel under pressure to the torch tip. Useful for heating large soldering coppers, soldering pipes, melting lead, etc.

Blueprinting (Engine): Dismantling engine and reassembling it to exact specifications.

BMEP: Brake Mean Effective Pressure.

Body putty: Material designed to smooth on dented body areas. Upon hardening, putty is dressed down and area painted.

Boiling point: Exact temperature at which a liquid begins to boil.

Bolt length: A measurement taken from end of bolt to underside of bolt head.

Bolt-on eccentric: An eccentric (cam shaped) device bolted to camshaft, etc. Converts rotary motion into reciprocating motion to operate fuel pump, vacuum pump, etc.

Bonded brake lining: Brake lining that is attached to brake shoe by adhesive.

Booster: Device incorporated in car system (such as brakes and steering), to increase pressure output or decrease amount of effort required to operate or both.

Booster battery: An extra battery, connected in parallel to regular vehicle battery. Used as an emergency measure to provide additional cranking capacity when regular battery is damaged, discharged, or of insufficient size.

Bore: May refer to cylinder itself or to diameter of the cylinder.

Bore alignment: An indication of how well true centerline of each one of a series of bores (such as camshaft bearing bores) align with a common centerline through them all. A misaligned bore can be either off-center, out-of-round, or tipped.

Bore diameter: Diameter of cylinders.

Bore face: Surface area surrounding open end of a cylinder or bearing bore.

Bore misalignment: A condition existing when true centerline of two or more bores do not coincide with their common centerline. Can also refer to bore true centerline not being in

desired alignment with some other part.

Boring: Renewing cylinders by cutting them out to a specified size. Boring bar is used to make cut.

Boring bar (Cylinder): Machine used to cut engine cylinders to specific size. As used in garages, to cut worn cylinders to a new diameter.

Boss: A rib or enlarged area designed to strengthen a certain portion or area of an object.

Bottled gas: LPG (Liquefied Petroleum Gas) gas compressed into strong metal tanks. When confined in tank under pressure, gas is in liquid form.

Bound electrons: Electrons in inner orbits around nucleus of atom. They are difficult to move out of orbit.

Bourdon tube: Circular, hollow piece of metal used in some instruments. Pressure on hollow section causes it to attempt to straighten. Free end then moves needle on gauge face.

Bowed crankcase: A condition in which engine block warpage or distortion has actually bent crankcase, thus throwing crank bearing bores out of alignment.

Bowl vent: A small hole near top of a carburetor float bowl. Used to allow air to move in or out as pressures dictate. Prevents formation of either pressure or vacuum above bowl fuel.

Boxed frame: A frame in which two channel shaped rails are welded together (open side to open side) forming a box shape providing great strength.

Boxed rod: Connecting rod in which I-beam section has been stiffened by welding plates on each side of the rod.

Braided cover: A woven shielding placed around a wire, hose, etc., to provide additional strength, resistance to abrasion, etc.

Brake anchor: Steel stud upon which one end of brake shoes is either attached to or rests against. Anchor is firmly affixed to backing plate.

Brake anti-roll device: Unit installed in brake system to hold brake line pressure when car is stopped on upgrade. When car is stopped on upgrade and brake pedal released, anti-roll device will keep brakes applied until either clutch is released or accelerator is depressed.

Brake backing plate: Rigid steel plate upon which brake shoes are attached. Braking force applied to shoes is absorbed by backing plate.

Brake band: Band, faced with brake lining, that encircles a brake drum. Used on several parking brake installations.

Brake bleeding: See *Bleeding the Brakes*.

Brake cones: Tapered cones used to center brake drums and discs for refinishing on a brake grinder or lathe.

Brake cylinder: See *Wheel Cylinder*.

Brake—disc type: Braking system that instead of using conventional brake drum with internal brake shoes, uses steel disc with caliper type lining application. When brakes are applied, section of lining on each side of spinning disc is forced against disc thus imparting braking force. This type is very resistant to brake fade.

Brake drum: Cast iron or aluminum housing, bolted to wheel, that rotates around brake shoes. When shoes are expanded, they rub against machined inner surface of brake drum and exert braking effect upon wheel.

Brake drum lathe: Machine to refinish inside of a brake drum.

Brake fade: Reduction in braking force due to loss of friction between brake shoes and drum. Caused by heat buildup.

Brake feel: Discernible relationship between the amount of brake pedal pressure and the actual braking force being exerted. Special device is used in power brake installations to give driver this feel.

Brake fluid: Special fluid used in hydraulic brake systems. Never use anything else in place of regular fluid.

Brake flushing: Cleaning brake system by flushing with alcohol or brake fluid. Done to remove water, dirt, or any other contaminant. Flushing fluid is placed in master cylinder and forced through lines and wheel cylinders where it exits at cylinder bleed screws.

Brake horsepower (bhp): Measurement of actual usable horsepower delivered at crankshaft. Commonly computed using an engine on a chassis dynamometer.

Brake hose: Flexible hose which connects brake lines to wheel cylinders. It allows suspension movement without damage.

Brake line: Steel tubing which carries brake fluid from master cylinder to wheel cylinders.

Brake lining: Friction material fastened to brake shoes. Brake lining is pressed against rotating brake drum, stopping car.

Brake—parking or emergency: Brake used to hold car in position while parked. One type applies rear brake shoes by mechanical means and other type applies brake band to brake drum in drive train.

Brake pedal height: A measurement of distance between top face of brake pedal and floor.

Brake—power: Conventional hydraulic brake system that utilizes either engine vacuum or hydraulic pressure to operate a power piston. Power piston applies pressure directly to master cylinder piston. This reduces amount of pedal pressure driver must exert to stop car.

Brake shoe heel: End of brake shoe adjacent to anchor bolt or pin.

Brake shoe toe: Free end of shoe, not attached to or resting against an anchor pin.

Brake shoes: Part of brake system, located at wheels, upon which brake lining is attached. When wheel cylin-

ders are actuated by hydraulic pressure, they force brake shoes apart.

Brake specialist: A person highly trained and experienced in field of brake diagnosis, service, and repair.

Brakes—System Warning Light: Red light mounted in the instrument cluster. Indicates a hydraulic system malfunction in the brake system.

Brakes—power booster (Hydraulic): Brake booster employing hydraulic pressure from the power steering system to apply force to master cylinder.

Brass drift punch: Punch, made of brass, used to drive shafts, pins, etc., in or out of their respective bores without damage.

Brass hammer: Hammer made of brass. Useful for striking jobs in which a steel hammer could damage work.

Braze: To join two pieces of metal together by heating edges to be joined and then melting drops of brass or bronze on area. Unlike welding, this operation is similar to soldering, only a higher melting point material is used.

Brazing flux: A powder or liquid used in brazing, that tends to remove scale and oxidization, allowing brazing metal to both flow and bond readily.

Brazing rod: Bronze, manganese bronze, silver alloy, etc., rods used in braze welding. Melts at a lower temperature than base metal.

Breakaway torque: When tightening a fastener, measurement of twisting force (torque) required to start a stuck or already tightened fastener turning. This torque is not a true indication of actual fastener torque as it will be higher than that used in initial tightening and higher than that required to keep it moving.

Break-in: Period of operation between installation of new or rebuilt parts and time in which parts are worn to the correct fit. Driving at reduced and varying speed for a specified mileage to permit parts to wear to the correct fit.

Break-in coating: A special oil, additive, compound, etc., used on a new part to prevent scoring, overheating, seizing, etc., during the break-in period.

Break-over angle: Included angle that a vehicle can cross over without dragging underneath center section. Break-over angle is determined by vehicle ground clearance and wheelbase.

Breaker (Tire): Rubber or fabric (or both) strip placed under tread to provide additional protection for main tire carcass.

Breaker arm: Movable arm upon which one of breaker points is affixed.

Breaker points (Ignition): Pair of movable points that are opened and closed to break and make the primary circuit.

Breather pipe: Pipe opening into interior of engine. Used to assist ventilation. Pipe usually extends downward to a point just below engine so

passing air stream will form a partial vacuum thus assisting in venting engine.

Breather port (Master cylinder): A small hole in master cylinder cap or cover that allows air to move in or out of reservoir. This prevents either vacuum or pressure forming above reservoir brake fluid.

Brinelling (Bearing): A condition in which an antifriction bearing race or ring has a series of dents or grooves worn in bearing surface.

Brinell test: A test to determine relative hardness of a given material, such as steel. A hardened steel ball of a specific size (1 centimeter) is pressed into material under a specific pressure and surface area of resulting dent is determined, divided into load force, and indicated as a Brinell number.

Bristle brush: A brush used for general cleaning. May use steel, brass, plastic, etc., bristles depending on type.

Broach: Bringing metal surface to desired shape by forcing multiple-edged cutting tool across surface.

Bronze: An alloy basically consisting of tin and copper.

Brush: Pieces of carbon, or copper, that rub against the commutator on generator and starter motor.

B&S gauge (Brown and Sharpe): Standard measure of wire diameter.

BTDC: Before Top Dead Center.

BTU (British thermal unit): Measurement of the amount of heat required to raise temperature of one pound of water, one degree Fahrenheit.

BUDC: Before Upper Dead Center. Same as BTDC.

Bulkhead union: A pipe union (connector) designed to connect two pipes on opposite sides of a bulkhead (divider) such as an engine compartment fire wall.

Buna: Synthetic (manufactured) rubber.

Bunsen burner: Small gas (propane, natural) burner, as commonly used in laboratories.

Burnish: To bring a surface to a high shine by rubbing with hard, smooth object.

Burnished to size: Bringing an object such as a bushing, to its final size by rubbing with a very hard, smooth tool.

Burnishing tool: A very smooth, hard surfaced tool used to rub a metal surface to produce a dense, extremely smooth finish.

"Burn oil": An expression used to indicate process of an engine leaking oil past rings into combustion chamber where it is burned.

Bushing: Bearing for shaft, spring shackle, piston pin, etc., of one piece construction which may be removed from part.

Butane: Petroleum gas that is liquid, when under pressure. Often used as fuel in trucks.

Butt connector (Electrical): An insulated connecting device (either crimp or solder type) used to join ends of two wires together.

Butterfly valve: Valve in carburetor that is so named due to its resemblance to insect of same name.

Butt weld: Joining two pieces of metal by placing them edge to edge and welding along junction line.

Bypass: To move around or detour regular route or circuit taken by air, fluid, electricity, etc.

By-pass filter: Engine oil filter that constantly filters portion of oil.

By-pass valve: Valve that can open and allow fluid to pass through in other than its normal channel.

C

CAFE: Corporate Average Fuel Economy.

Cage (Bearing): An enclosure, often stamped steel, that retains, separates, and spaces bearing balls or rollers.

Calibrate: As applied to test instruments—adjusting dial needle to correct zero or load setting.

Caliper (Brake): Disc brake component which forms cylinder and houses piston and brake pads (linings). It produces clamping action on rotating disc to stop car.

Caliper alignment: Refers to brake caliper alignment in relation to brake disc (rotor). Caliper pistons-brake pads must be at right (90°) angles to disc braking surface and on fixed calipers, centered over disc.

Calipers (Inside and outside): Adjustable measuring tool placed around or within an object and adjusted until it just contacts. It is then withdrawn and distance measured between contacting points.

Calorie (Gram): A unit of heat. Amount of heat required to raise the temperature of one gram of water 1 deg. centigrade.

Calorific value: Measurement of the heating value of fuel.

Calorimeter: Measuring instrument used to determine amount of heat produced when a substance is burned; also friction and chemical change heat production.

Cam: Offset portion of shaft that will, when shaft turns, impart motion to another part such as valve lifters.

Cam angle or dwell (Ignition): Number of degrees breaker cam rotates from time breaker points close until they open again.

Camber: Tipping top wheel centerline outward produces positive camber. Tipping wheel centerline inward at top produces negative camber. When camber is positive, tops of tires are further apart than bottom.

Cam flank (Camshaft): That portion of a cam lobe between cam nose and point at which opening action occurs or closing action stops.

Cam ground: Piston ground slightly egg-shaped. When heated, it becomes round.

Cam lobe lift (Camshaft): A measurement of amount of travel cam will

impart to lifter from full closed (lifter on base circle) to full open (lifter on tip of cam nose).

Cam nose (Camshaft): Tip or highest point on a cam lobe.

Camshaft: Shaft with cam lobes (bumps) used to operate valves.

Camshaft end play: A measurement of longitudinal (end to end) movement of camshaft.

Camshaft gear: Gear that is used to drive camshaft.

Camshaft runout: A measurement of amount of bend existing in a camshaft.

Camshaft sprocket: Toothed device attached to camshaft and meshed with drive chain or belt.

Camshaft thrust plate: A flat plate designed to control thrust force and amount of end movement or play.

Candela: A unit of measure for light intensity.

Candle power: Measurement of light producing ability of light bulb.

CAP: Cleaner Air Package System of reducing amount of unburned hydrocarbons in automobile exhaust.

Capacitance: Property of condenser that permits it to receive and retain an electrical charge.

Capacitor: See Condenser.

Capillary action: Movement of liquid along surface of a solid. Caused by state of surface tension (attraction) existing between molecules of liquid and solid.

Capillary tube: A very fine tube with a tiny hole. Capillary action (liquid movement into tube) can take place.

Cap parting edges (Bearing): That portion of a bearing cap that presses against other bearing half when cap is installed.

Cap screw: A headed fastener that passes through one part and threads into another. When cap screw is tightened, parts are drawn together. No nut is required.

CARB: California Air Resources Board.

Carbon: Used to describe hard or soft black deposits found in combustion chamber, on plugs, under rings, on and under valve heads, etc.

Carbon arc: Flow of electricity across a gap between two electrodes one of which must be made of carbon.

Carbon dioxide (CO_2): A tasteless, odorless, colorless gas. Used in carbonated drinks, some fire extinguishers, etc.

Carbonize: Building up of carbon on objects: spark plugs, pistons, heads, etc.

Carbon monoxide (CO): Deadly, colorless, odorless, and tasteless gas found in engine exhaust. Formed by incomplete burning of hydrocarbons.

Carbon pile: Refers to amperage or voltage regulator utilizing a stack of carbon discs in its construction.

Carbon solvent: A cleaning solvent especially formulated to loosen and remove carbon deposits.

Carbon tracking (Electrical): Carbon trail along a path of electrical current flashover such as is formed by cur-

rent flow between insulated terminals of a distributor cap.

Carburetor: Device used to mix gasoline and air in correct proportions.

Carburetor adapter: Adapter used to fit or place one type of carburetor on an intake manifold that may not be originally designed for it. Also used to adapt four-barrel carbs to two-barrel manifolds.

Carburetor circuits: Series of passageways and units designed to perform a specific function—idle circuit, full power circuit, etc.

Carburetor icing: Formation of ice on throttle plate or valve. As fuel nozzles feed fuel into air horn, it turns to a vapor. This robs heat from air and when weather conditions are just right (fairly cold and quite humid), ice may form.

Carburizing flame: Welding torch flame with an excess of acetylene.

Carcass ply: Tire main body plies.

Carcinogen: Any substance, such as asbestos or carbon tetrachloride, that can cause cancer.

Cardan joint: Type of universal joint.

Carrier bearings: Bearings upon which differential case is mounted.

Case-hardened: Piece of steel that has had outer surface hardened while inner portion remains relatively soft.

Caster: Tipping top of kingpin either forward or toward the rear of car. When tipped forward, it is termed negative caster. When tipped toward rear, it is positive caster.

Casting: Pouring metal into a mold to form an object.

Castle or castellated nut: Nut having series of slots cut into one end. Cotter pin may be passed through to secure nut.

Catalytic converter: Device used in exhaust system to reduce harmful emissions. Catalyst in converter may be coated with palladium, platinum, and rhodium. Catalyst may be of oxidizing and/or reducing design.

Cathode: In electric circuit—the negative pole.

Caustic: Compound, solution, etc., that will cause burning and corrosion.

CCS: Controlled Combustion System of reducing unburned hydrocarbon emission from engine exhaust.

CEC: Combination Emission Control.

Cell (Battery): Individual (separate) compartments in battery which contain positive and negative plates suspended in electrolyte. Six-volt battery has three cells, twelve-volt battery has six cells.

Cell connector: Lead strap or connection between battery cell groups.

Celsius: A temperature scale based on the freezing point of water as 0° and boiling point as 100°.

Centering sleeve: Sleeve passed over engine crankshaft front portion to align timing cover prior to tightening fasteners.

Centering socket (U-joint): Central socket of a constant speed universal joint. It tends to keep both halves of joint operating in a plane that forms one-half of operating angle.

Centerline: Imaginary line drawn lengthwise through center of an object.

Center link: Also called relay rod or connecting link, it transfers motion from pitman arm to tie rods.

Center of gravity: Point in object through which, if an imaginary pivot line were drawn, would leave object in balance. In car, the closer the weight to the ground, the lower the center of gravity.

Center punch: A sharp nosed punch used to form a small "V" shaped depression so as to properly align a drill bit prior to actual drilling.

Center steering linkage: Steering system utilizing two tie rods connected to steering arms and to central idler arm. Idler arm is operated by drag link that connects idler arm to pitman arm.

Center support bearing (Propeller shaft): A bearing used for central support of long, two-piece propeller shafts.

Centrifugal advance (Distributor): Unit designed to advance and retard ignition timing through action of centrifugal force.

Centrifugal clutch: Clutch that utilizes centrifugal force to expand a friction device on driving shaft until it is locked to a drum on driven shaft.

Centrifugal force: Force which tends to keep moving objects traveling in straight line. When moving car is forced to make a turn, centrifugal force attempts to keep it moving in straight line. If car is turning at too high a speed, centrifugal force will be greater than frictional force between tires and road and the car will slide off the road.

Ceramic filter: Filtering device utilizing po-rous ceramic as filtering agent.

Ceramic substrate: A ceramic material, covered with aluminum oxide, that forms base upon which palladium, platinum, etc., are applied. Used in one type of catalytic converter construction.

Cetane number: Measurement of diesel fuel performance characteristics.

CFM: Cubic feet per minute. A measure of air flow.

Chain hoist: A lifting device employing an endless chain running through two or more chain sheaves.

Chain link pin: Pin passing through engine timing chain link sections.

Chain slack: A measurement of amount of "play" or looseness in a timing chain. Generally determined by measuring chain deflection.

Chain tensioner: A device used to reduce slap and flutter from a timing chain by removing slack. Device can be either fixed or spring-loaded.

Chamfer: To bevel (or a bevel on) edge of an object.

Change of state: Condition in which substance changes from a solid to a liquid, a liquid to a gas, a liquid to a solid, or a gas to a liquid.

Charcoal canister: Emission control device containing activated charcoal granules. Used to store gasoline vapors from tank and carburetor. When engine is started, stored vapors are drawn into cylinders and burned.

Charge (Air conditioning): A given or specified (by weight) amount of refrigerant.

Charge (Battery): Passing electric current through battery to restore it to active (charged) state.

Charge rate: Electrical rate of flow, in amperes, passing through the battery during charging.

Charging (Air conditioning): Inserting the specified charge (amount) of refrigerant into the air conditioning system.

Charging station: A complete portable setup refrigerant tank, gauges, hoses, etc., that is used to service automotive air conditioning systems.

Chase: To repair damaged threads.

Chassis: Generally, chassis refers to frame, engine, front and rear axles, springs, steering system, and gas tank. In short, everything but body and fenders.

Chassis dynamometer: See *Dynamometer*.

Chatter (Tool): A vibrating, bouncing motion. When applied to cutting tools, tool will leave an uneven surface made up of fine ridges.

Check valve: Valve that opens to permit passage of fluid or air in one direction and closes to prevent passage in opposite direction.

Chilled iron: Cast iron possessing hardened outer skin.

Chloride flux: An acid (hydrochloric) type soldering flux. Do not use on wiring.

Choke: Butterfly valve located in carburetor used to enrichen mixture for starting engine when cold.

Choke "break": A device, electrical or vacuum operated, designed to partially open carburetor choke when the engine starts.

Choke stove: Heating compartment in or on exhaust manifold from which hot air is drawn to automatic choke device.

CID: Cubic Inch Displacement.

Circuit (Electrical): Source of electricity (battery), resistance unit (headlight, etc.) and wires that form path for flow of electricity from source, through unit and back to source.

Circuit breaker (Lighting system): Protective device that will make and break flow of current when current draw becomes excessive. Unlike fuse, it does not blow out but vibrates on and off thus giving driver some light to stop by.

Circular mil: A unit of measurement equal to cross-sectional area of a circle one mil in diameter. One mil equals 0.001 in. Used to indicate wire size.

Class (Bolt): A description of thread fit between bolt and nut. Of three classes (1, 2, and 3), class 1 is quite loose, class 2 normal fit as used on automotive applications, and class 3 is very close.

Clearance: Given amount of space between two parts—between piston and cylinder, bearing and journal, etc.

Clevis pin: A pin passing through each side of clevis (yoke) open end.

Clinch joint (Bearing): A bearing made by rolling steel backing into a round tube with a dovetail protrusion locking mating edges together.

Clockwise: Rotation to right as that of clock hands.

Closed cooling system: Type of system which uses an overflow tank.

Closed loop fuel system: A fuel system in which air-fuel ratio is constantly adjusted in relationship to hydrocarbon content of exhaust. An oxygen sensor in exhaust, working through an electronic control unit, alters either carburetor jet size or fuel injection system pulse width.

Cluster or counter gear: Cluster of gears that are all cut on one long gear blank. Cluster gears ride in bottom of transmission. Cluster provides a connection between transmission input shaft and output shaft.

Clutch: Device used to connect or disconnect flow of power from one unit to another.

Clutch arbor: A round steel shaft, one end of which is slipped into flywheel clutch pilot bearing or bushing. Diameter of remainder fits inside of clutch disc splines. Arbor aligns disc with flywheel friction surface while pressure plate is installed.

Clutch cover: That portion of clutch that surrounds and secures pressure plate assembly. Cover bolts to flywheel.

Clutch diaphragm spring: Round dish-shaped piece of flat spring steel. Used to force pressure place against clutch disc in some clutches.

Clutch disc: Part of clutch assembly splined to transmission clutch or input shaft. Faced with friction material. When clutch is engaged, disc is squeezed between flywheel and clutch pressure plate.

Clutch disc damper spring: A series of coil springs located between disc hub and disc proper. Springs soften impact to clutch shaft when disc is seized between pressure plate and flywheel.

Clutch disc hub: Central splined portion of clutch disc.

Clutch explosion: Clutches have literally flown apart (exploded) when subjected to high rpm. Scatter shield is used on competition cars to protect driver and spectators from flying parts in event clutch explodes.

Clutch friction surface: Refers to areas of clutch that rub against disc friction facing.

Clutch housing or bell housing: Cast iron or aluminum housing that surrounds flywheel and clutch mechanism.

Clutch linkage: Mechanism which transfers movement from clutch pedal to throw-out fork.

Clutch pedal free travel: Specified distance clutch pedal may be depressed before throw-out bearing actually contacts clutch release fingers.

Clutch pedal height: A measurement from top face of pedal to floor mat.

Clutch pilot bearing: Small bronze bushing, or in some cases ball bearing, placed in end of crankshaft or in center of flywheel depending on car, used to support outboard end of transmission input shaft.

Clutch pressure plate: Part of a clutch assembly that through spring pressure, squeezes clutch disc against flywheel thereby transmitting driving force through the assembly. To disengage clutch, pressure plate is drawn away from flywheel via linkage.

Clutch release fingers: Steel fingers on pressure plate assembly that, when depressed by throw-out bearing, pull pressure plate away from clutch disc.

Clutch semi-centrifugal release fingers: Clutch release fingers that have a weight attached to them so that at high rpm release fingers place additional pressure on clutch pressure plate.

Clutch throw-out fork: Device or fork that straddles throw-out bearing and used to force throw-out bearing against clutch release fingers.

Coast pattern (Ring and pinion): Contact pattern (area of contact between differential ring and pinion gear) when vehicle is coasting (car driving engine).

Coil (Ignition): Used to step up battery voltage to point necessary to fire spark plugs.

Coil core: Multilayered mass of iron around which coil windings are wrapped. Some designs place core outside of windings.

Coil polarity: Refers to ignition coil (Neg. or Pos.) primary connection hookup. Battery and coil polarity must be same. When battery negative is grounded, coil negative must be connected to ground through distributor.

Coil spring: Section of spring steel rod wound in spiral pattern or shape. Widely used in both front and rear suspension.

Cold: Little or no perceptible heat.

Cold bending: Bending a part without heating it first.

Cold clearance setting (Valves): Adjusting valve lash or clearance when engine is at room temperature.

Cold cranking rating (Battery): Measurement of cranking amperes that a battery can deliver over a period of 30 seconds at 0°F (−17.8°C) and still maintain a minimum cell voltage of 1.2 volts.

Cold expanding (Piston): Expanding an engine piston by mechanical means and without use of heat.

Cold flow (Gasket): Excessive fastener torque causing gasket to flatten and extrude outward.

Cold patching: Repair method used to seal leaks in plastic fuel tanks.

Cold soak cleaning: Immersing parts in a cold cleaner bath for recommended time period to help loosen and remove carbon, dirt, grease, etc.

Cold solder: An electrical joint that has had solder applied to it before it reached proper soldering temperature. Characteristics include clumping of solder on the joint.

Cold start injector: Fuel injector which sprays additional fuel for cold engine starting.

Cold start valve (Fuel Injection): A valve used on certain gasoline fuel injection systems. Valve supplies additional flow of fuel during cold starting conditions.

Collapsed (Piston): Piston whose skirt diameter has been reduced due to heat and forces imposed upon it during service.

Collapsible preload spacer: A special spacer as used between bearings on some differential drive pinion shafts. When nut is torqued to specs, spacer will collapse a specified amount and will thus provide an initial (before torque loading) load (preload) on bearings.

Collector ring (Alternator): Rings (also called "slip" rings) mounted on rotor. Brushes rub against collector rings and "collect" electrical current produced by alternator.

Color coding (Wiring): Using various colors to identify specific wiring circuits. Wiring diagrams show circuits and specify color.

Combination valve (Brakes): A dual purpose valve that can combine proportioning, metering, and pressure differential warning functions.

Combustion: Process involved during burning.

Combustion chamber: Area above piston with piston on TDC. Head of piston, cylinder, and head form the chamber.

Combustion chamber volume: Volume of combustion chamber (space above piston with piston on TDC) measured in cc (cubic centimetres).

Commutator: Series of copper bars connected to armature windings. Bars are insulated from each other and from armature. Brushes (as in generator or starter) rub against whirling commutator.

Commutator segment or bar (Starter): Copper bars connecting armature windings to brushes.

Compensating port: Small hole in brake master cylinder to permit fluid to return to reservoir.

Compensator valve (Automatic transmission): Valve designed to increase pressure on brake band during heavy acceleration.

Compound: Two or more ingredients mixed together.

Compound planetary gearset: Refers to use of combination of two or more planetary gearsets in a single assembly.

Compressibility: Ability of a material to be flattened by applying pressure. Compressibility of steel is low, cork is high.

Compression: Applying pressure to a spring, or any springy substance, thus causing it to reduce its length in direction of compressing force. Applying pressure to gas, thus causing reduction in volume.

Compression check: Testing compression in all cylinders at cranking speed. All plugs are removed, compression gauge placed in one plug hole, throttle cracked wide open, and engine cranked until gauge no longer climbs. Compression check is a fine way in which to determine condition of valves, rings, and cylinders.

Compression connection (Tubing): A flareless tubing fitting using a tapered edge sleeve that, when squeezed between the fitting body and nut, pinches tubing to produce a seal. Another type uses sleeve function as an integral nose on nut.

Compression gauge: Gauge used to test compression in engine cylinders.

Compression loading (Ball joint): A front suspension ball joint arrangement that, when under loading forces, causes ball joint parts to be compressed together. Tension loading attempts to pull ball out of socket.

Compression ratio: Relationship between cylinder volume (clearance volume) when piston is on TDC and cylinder volume when piston is on BDC.

Compression ring groove (Piston): Groove cut into piston head to accept a compression ring.

Compression rings: Top piston rings, generally two, designed to seal between piston and cylinder to prevent escape of gas from combustion chamber.

Compression stroke: Portion of piston's movement devoted to compressing the fuel mixture trapped in engine's cylinder.

Compression tester: Gauge used to check engine compression pressure.

Compressor (Air conditioning): Device using a series of pistons to raise pressure of refrigerant in system. Also causes refrigerant to flow through system.

Compressor protection switch (Air conditioning): A heat and/or pressure sensitive switch to protect compressor from damage caused by loss of oil and overheating.

Computerized diagnostic unit: An electrical diagnostic unit that receives input from numerous sensors and then automatically, through pre-programming, determines possible problems. Advanced units detect problems, and suggest possible corrections and/or further tests. Some provide printout sheets.

Computerized ignition: Ignition system using sensors which feed electrical information to computer. Computer then controls ignition system and sometimes other functions (carburetor, fuel injection, transmission) for maximum efficiency.

Computerized ride control (Active suspension): Advanced suspension system that can adapt to specific driving conditions.

Concentric: Two or more circles so placed as to share common center.

Concentric grinding (Brakes): Grinding brake lining (mounted on shoe) contour so that it matches that of brake drum. Gives full contact between drum and shoe.

Condense: Turning vapor back into liquid.

Condenser (Ignition): Unit installed between breaker points and coil to prevent arcing at breaker points. Condenser has ability to absorb and retain surges of electricity.

Condenser (Refrigeration): Unit in air conditioning system that cools hot compressed refrigerant and turns it from vapor into liquid.

Condensation: Moisture, from air, deposited on a cool surface.

Conduction: Transfer of heat from one object to another by having objects in physical contact.

Conductor: Material forming path for flow of current.

Cone clutch: Clutch utilizing cone-shaped member that is forced into a cone-shaped depression in flywheel, or other driving unit, thus locking two together. Although no longer used on cars, cone clutch finds some applications in small riding tractors, heavy power mowers, etc.

Connecting rod: Connecting link between piston and crankshaft.

Connecting rod aligner: Tool designed to check rod for twist and bend.

Connecting rod bearings: Inserts which fit into connecting rod and ride on crankshaft journals.

Connecting rod bend: A condition in which centerlines of rod pin bore and big end bearing bore are not parallel—as viewed from edge of an upright rod.

Connecting rod cap: Lower removable part of rod which holds lower bearing insert.

Connecting rod journal: That portion of crankshaft riding in and contacting connecting rod bearing.

Connecting rod side play: Amount of sliding movement determined by measuring distance rod can be moved from full forward to full rearward position.

Connecting rod spit hole: Small hole drilled through upper portion of connecting rod big end. Allows oil to squirt or spurt out to lubricate a specific area, such as cylinder, camshaft, etc.

Connecting rod straightener: Tool used to remove connecting rod twist, bend, or offset.

Connecting rod twist: A condition in which centerline of rod pin bore is turned either to left or right, as related to centerline of rod big end bore—as viewed looking downward on an upright rod.

Constant drive overdrive: An overdrive unit that, when engaged, is constantly connected to drive wheels and will not permit freewheeling (coasting).

Constant mesh gears: Gears that are always in mesh with each other.

Constant velocity universal joint: Universal joint so designed as to effect smooth transfer of torque from driven shaft to driving shaft without any fluctuations in speed of driven shaft.

Contact points also called breaker points: Two removable points or areas that when pressed together, complete circuit. These points are usually made of tungsten, platinum, or silver.

Continuity (Electrical): Refers to an electrical circuit in which all contacting parts are clean and tight, so as to permit desired current flow.

Continuous fuel injection: A fuel injection system in which injectors are always open and as such, feed fuel constantly. Amount of fuel delivered can be determined by an airflow sensor.

Contraction (Thermal): Reduction in size of object when cooled.

Control arm (Suspension): a pivoting arm that maintains alignment of an axle, steering knuckle assembly, etc., while permitting needed movement.

Control module: Small computer used to control specific systems within an automobile. Control modules are generally used to govern the air bag and anti-lock brake systems.

Control rack: Toothed rod inside mechanical injection pump which rotates pump plunger to control quantity of injected fuel.

Control valve: A movable valve in an air, fluid, etc., line, that is designed to start, stop, or alter movement, speed, volume, direction, etc.

Convection: Transfer of heat from one object to another when hotter object heats surrounding air and air heats other object.

Coolant: Liquid in cooling system.

Coolant temperature override switch (CTO): Coolant controlled vacuum switch that cuts off engine vacuum to EGR valve when engine temperature is below a specified point.

Cooling system: System, air or water, designed to remove excess heat from engine.

Cooling system scale: A coating of rust, mineral, etc., deposited in both engine coolant jacket and radiator. If heavy, interferes with coolant flow and causes overheating.

"Copper" (Soldering): A soldering iron utilizing a relatively heavy copper block attached to a metal shaft with insulated handle. Tinned copper is placed in a flame for heating.

Core: When referring to casting—sand unit placed inside mold so that when metal is poured, core will leave a hollow shape.

Core hole plug: A metal plug (sometimes called "freeze" plug) pressed into holes in engine water jacket casting sand core holes.

Corona (Electrical): Luminous discharge of electricity visible near surface of an electrical conductor under high voltage.

Corrode: Removal of surface material from object by chemical action.

Cotter key (Pin): A split pin that is inserted through a hole in a shaft, bolt, etc. Ends are spread apart to prevent key from falling out. Used to secure nuts, clevis pins, shafts, etc.

Counterbalance: Weight attached to some moving part so part will be in balance.

Counterbore: Enlarging hole to certain depth.

Counterclockwise: Rotation to the left as opposed to that of clock hands.

Countershaft: Intermediate shaft that receives motion from one shaft and transfers it to another. It may be fixed (gears turn on it) or it may be free to revolve.

Countersink: To make a counterbore so that head of a screw may set flush, or below the surface.

Counterweight: A weight, integral or attached, affixed to a part such as a crankshaft, to bring revolving mass into balance.

Coupling: Connecting device used between two objects so motion of one will be imparted to other.

Coupling point: This refers to point at which both pump and turbine in torque converter are traveling at same speed. The drive is almost direct at this point.

Cowl: Part of car body between engine firewall and front of dash panel.

"Crack" a fitting: To slowly open a fitting a small amount.

Crack detection: Using X ray, chemical solution, magnetic field, etc., to locate otherwise unseen fractures or cracks in a metal part.

Crack pinning: Repairing a crack, such as in a cylinder head, by installing a series of overlapping threaded pins. They are cut off and filed flush with surface.

Crankcase: Part of engine that surrounds crankshaft. Not to be confused with the pan which is a thin steel cover that is bolted to crankcase.

Crankcase dilution: Accumulation of unburned gasoline in crankcase. Excessively rich fuel mixture or poor combustion will allow some of gasoline to pass down between pistons and cylinder walls.

Crankcase ventilation: Process of drawing clean air through interior of engine to remove blow-by gases and other fumes.

Crankcase web: A thin, reinforcing wall cast as integral part of the crankcase to provide rigidity for main bearing bores.

Crank grinder: A machine used to grind crankshaft journals to highly accurate dimensions.

Cranking motor: Starter. Device to revolve engine crankshaft to start engine. Works through a gear engaging another gear on flywheel.

Cranking vacuum test: An engine test that determines basic engine (piston, ring, cylinder, valve) condition by measuring amount of vacuum developed in engine cylinders during cranking.

Crankshaft: Shaft running length of engine. Portions of shaft are offset to form throws to which connecting rods are attached. Crankshaft is supported by main bearings.

Crankshaft gear: Gear mounted on front of crankshaft. Used to drive camshaft gear.

Crankshaft micrometer: A micrometer designed to measure crankshaft main bearing journal diameter while the crankshaft is in place (main cap off).

Crankshaft sprocket: Timing chain sprocket attached to one end of crankshaft.

Crankshaft throw: Offset part of crankshaft where connecting rods fasten.

Crankshaft thrust face: Precision ground portion of crankshaft, at right angles to ends of main bearing journal, that operates against main bearing thrust surface. Controls end play.

Crimped terminal: An electrical connector into which wire is inserted. Connector body is then forced inward at one or more points, thus gripping wire tightly.

Crocus cloth: A very fine abrasive cloth using a coating of iron oxide particles.

Cross and roller: Type of universal joint using a center cross (spider) mounted in needle bearings.

Cross bolt spacer (Crankshaft): On engines employing a transverse stiffening bolt through both main bearing cap and crankcase, spacer is used between two sides of cap and crankcase walls. Prevents crankcase damage when tightening bolt.

Cross firing: A condition in which firing of a given spark plug fires an additional plug. Caused by voltage from one wire being imparted to another by poor insulation or by improper routing of plug wires.

Cross shaft (Steering): Shaft in steering gearbox that engages steering shaft worm. Cross shaft is splined to pitman arm.

Crosshatch finish (Cylinder): Pattern left in an engine cylinder bore by honing. Fine, visible circumferential scratch line cross one another at an angle. Angle depends upon hone rpm and number of up and down strokes in a given period of time.

Cross-threading: Mismating of screw threads caused by engaging threads when their respective centerlines are not aligned. Will cause threads to jam and continued turning will ruin one or both threads.

Cross union (Pipe): A four-way pipe connector in which any given connection is at right angles to adjacent connections.

Crude oil: Petroleum in its raw or unrefined state. It forms the basis of gasoline, engine oil, diesel oil, kerosene, etc.

Cubes: Cubic inches, or cubic inch displacement of an engine.

Cu. In. (C.I.): Cubic inch.

Cuno filter: Filter made up of a series of fine discs or plates pressed together in a manner that leaves very minute space between discs. Liquid is forced through these openings to produce straining action.

Cup driver (Bearing): A tool designed to install bearing cups (outer ring) in axles, front wheel bearing housing, etc.

Cup raceway (Bearing): That portion of bearing cup (ring) designed to operate against bearing balls or rollers.

Curb height: Indicates height of an automobile without passengers but with full fuel load. Measured from roadway surface to a specified location on car undercarriage.

Curb weight: Full operating (oil, coolant installed) weight of a vehicle without passengers but including a full tank of fuel.

Current: Movement of free electrons through conductor.

Current draw: Amount of current flow through a given electrical device when connected to a circuit.

Cushion spring (Clutch): A series of coil springs located between clutch disc hub and clutch disc. Springs soften shock when clutch is engaged.

Cutout (Regulator): Device to connect or disconnect generator from battery circuit. When generator is charging, cutout makes circuit. When generator stops, cutout breaks circuit. Also referred to as cutout relay and circuit breaker.

Cycle: Reoccuring period during which series of events take place in definite order.

Cylinder: Hole, or holes, in cylinder block that contain pistons.

Cylinder balance test: Process of checking engine rpm and vacuum while operating engine on selected pairs of cylinders at a time. Do not use this test on catalytic converter equipped vehicles.

Cylinder block: See *Block*.

Cylinder bore: See *Bore*.

Cylinder dial gauge: A dial gauge measuring instrument designed to check engine cylinder bore diameters.

Cylinder head: Metal section bolted on top of block. Used to cover tops of cylinders. In many cases cylinder head contains the valves. Also forms part of combustion chamber.

Cylinder hone: Tool that uses an abrasive to smooth out and bring to exact measurement items such as engine cylinders, wheel cylinders, bushings, etc.

Cylinder leakage tester: A special test tool used to check cylinder, ring, piston, valve, etc., condition by pressurizing a given cylinder (piston TDC on compression) to a given point with compressed air. Gauge then checks percentage of leakage.

Cylinder liner: See *Cylinder Sleeve*.

Cylinder sleeve: Replaceable cylinder. It is made of a pipe-like section that is either pressed or pushed into the block.

Cylinder stroke: See *Stroke*.

D

Damper: A unit or device designed to remove or reduce vibration, oscillation, etc., of a moving part, fluid, air, etc.

Damper spring (Valve): A coil spring, installed inside regular valve spring, that helps to reduce spring vibration.

Dashboard: Part of body containing driving instruments, switches, etc.

Dashpot: Unit utilizing cylinder and piston, or cylinder and diaphragm, with small vent hole, to retard or slow down movement of some part.

DC (Electrical): Direct Current.

DC (Piston position): Dead Center. Piston at extreme top or bottom of its stroke.

Dead axle: Axle that does not rotate but merely forms base upon which to attach wheels.

Dead center (Engine): Point at which piston reaches its uppermost or downmost position in cylinder. Rod crank journal would be at 12 o'clock UDC or 6 o'clock LDC.

Deceleration: Process of slowing down in rotational speed, forward speed, etc.

Deceleration valve: It feeds air into intake manifold to prevent backfiring during deceleration.

Decibel: A unit of measurement used to indicate a sound level or to indicate the difference in specific sound levels.

Deep groove ball: A ball bearing in which balls engage a rather deep groove in both inner and outer rings. Bearing will handle heavy radial and moderate thrust loads.

Deflection rate (Springs): Measurement of force, in lbs., required to compress leaf spring a distance of one inch.

Deglazer: Abrasive tool used to remove glaze from cylinder walls so a new set of rings will seat.

Degree (Circle): 1/360 part of a circle.

Degree wheel: Wheel-like unit attached to engine crankshaft. Used to time valves to a high degree of accuracy.

Dehumidify: Act of removing a certain amount of moisture from air.

Dehydrate: To dry out. Remove moisture.

Demagnetize: Removing residual magnetism from an object.

Deploy: Term used to describe the activation of an air bag system.

Depolarize: Removal of residual magnetism thereby destroying or removing the magnetic poles.

Depth type filter (Engine oil): An engine oil filter utilizing a relatively thick layer of fibrous materials to filter out dirt, metal particles, etc. Entire layer acts as a filter with particles lodging at different depths.

Desiccant: Material, such as silica-gel, placed within a container to absorb and retain moisture.

Detent ball and spring: Spring loaded ball that snaps into a groove or notch to hold some sliding object in position.

Detergent: Chemical added to engine oil to improve its characteristics (sludge control, nonfoaming, etc.).

Detonation: Fuel charge firing or burning too violently, almost exploding.

Developer solution (Fluorescent penetrant): Solution used to draw fluorescent crack detection penetrant to surface so that the application of black light will make presence of any cracks readily visible.

Dexron III/Mercon: Automatic transmission fluid that replaces Dexron II, which was in use for many years.

Diagnosis: Process of analyzing certain symptoms, readings, etc., in order to determine underlying reason for trouble at hand.

Diagnostic control module: Electronic computer that controls the air bag system. Also referred to as an Diagnostic Energy Reserve Module (DERM).

Diagnostic link: A built-in electrical connector used to attach a diagnostic test instrument.

Dial gauge or indicator: Often used precision micrometer type instrument that indicates exact reading via needle moving across dial face.

Diamond bored: Surface of cylinder has been brought to size by removal of material with a diamond faced cutting tool.

Diamond tipped dresser: A stone dresser using a small piece of diamond attached to tip. Used to smooth and reface grinding stones.

Diaphragm: Flexible cloth-rubber sheet stretched across an area thereby separating two different compartments.

Diaphragm spring (Clutch): A clutch pressure plate spring device that, instead of using several coil springs, employs a single, cone-shaped piece of sheet spring steel. Depressing cone center lifts outer edge removing pressure. Release center and outer circumference pushes on pressure plate.

Dichlorodifluoromethane: Refrigerant-12 used in air conditioning system.

Die (Forming): One of a matched pair of hardened steel blocks that are used to form metal into a desired shape.

Die (Thread): Tool for cutting threads.

Die casting: Formation of object by forcing molten metal, plastic, etc., into die.

Dielectric: A material, such as glass, rubber, etc., that resists flow of electricity. An insulator.

Diesel engine: Internal combustion engine that uses diesel oil for fuel. True diesel does not use an ignition system but injects diesel oil into cylinders. Piston compresses air so tightly that air is hot enough to ignite diesel fuel without spark.

Diesel injector: A nozzle device for spraying diesel fuel into precombustion chamber.

Diesel fuel grade: Classification of diesel fuel operating characteristics, 1-D is for cold weather and 2-D is for normal conditions.

Diesel injection pump: Mechanically operated fuel pump which develops high pressure to force fuel out of injectors and into combustion chambers.

Dieseling: Condition in which engine continues to run after ignition key is turned off. Also called "running on."

Differential: Unit that will drive both rear axles at same time but will allow them to turn at different speeds in turns.

Differential case (Carrier): Steel unit to which the ring gear is attached. Case drives spider gears and forms an inner bearing surface for axle end gears.

Differential winding: A secondary winding in an electrical device that is wound in a reverse manner as related to the primary (main) windings.

Digital EGR valve: EGR valve that can be operated by the vehicle's engine ECU.

Dimmer switch: Foot or hand operated switch for headlight low and high beams.

Diode: Unit having ability to pass electric current readily in one direction but resisting current flow in the other.

Dipstick: Metal rod that passes into oil sump. Used to determine quantity of oil in engine.

Direct current (DC): Electric current that flows steadily in one direction only.

Direct drive: Such as high gear when crankshaft and drive shaft revolve at same speed.

Direct fuel injection: Fuel is sprayed into combustion chamber.

Direct ignition system: A type of computer-controlled ignition system similar to the distributorless system, but does not use spark plug wires.

Directional stability (Steering): Ability of car to move forward in straight line with minimum of driver control.

Dirt wear: (Antifriction bearing): Bearing wear caused by abrasive action of dirt.

Discharging (air conditioning): Procedure for draining a vehicle's air conditioning system of its refrigerant charge.

Discharge (Battery): Drawing electric current from battery.

Discharge pressure (Air conditioning): Pressure of refrigerant as it leaves compressor.

Discharge side (Air conditioning): The high pressure section of the air conditioning system extending from the compressor to the expansion valve.

Disc wheel: Wheel constructed of stamped steel.

Displacement: Volume of air displaced by piston traveling from BDC to TDC.

Distillation: Heating a liquid and then catching and condensing the vapors given off by heating process.

Distilled water: Water from which all impurities have been removed through an evaporative process.

Distortion: Altering shape or size of something through application of heat, pressure, motion, etc.

Distribution block (Tubing): A multiple outlet tubing (pipe) fitting that is connected to an air, gas, water, etc., supply line so as to provide outlet connections for two or more branch lines.

Distribution tubes (Cooling system): Tubes used in engine cooling area to guide and direct flow of coolant to vital areas.

Distributor (Ignition): Unit designed to make and break the ignition primary circuit and to distribute resultant high voltage to proper cylinder at correct time.

Distributor cap (Ignition): Insulated cap containing central terminal with series (one per cylinder) of terminals that are evenly spaced in circular pattern around central terminal . Secondary voltage travels to central terminal where it is then channeled to one of outer terminals by the rotor.

Distributorless ignition system: A type of computer-controlled ignition system that eliminates the distributor by using a sensor mounted on the crankshaft to provide timing.

Diverter valve: A device used in the air injection system to divert air away from the injection nozzles during periods of deceleration. Prevents "backfiring."

DOHC: Refers to an engine with double (two) overhead camshaft.

DOT: Department of Transportation.

Documentation: Repair orders or other means used to record work performed on a vehicle.

Dog tracking: Condition where the rear wheels of a vehicle are not aligned with the front wheels.

Double compression fitting: A tubing fitting in which, upon tightening, nose of the nut is forced tightly against tubing by a corresponding angle on fitting body. This provides seal.

Double flare: End of tubing, especially brake tubing, has a flare so made that flare area utilizes two wall thicknesses. This makes a much stronger joint and from safety standpoint, it is a must.

Double post lift: Vehicle lift utilizing two lifting rams. Can be of suspension type (front and back ram) or frame type (side to side rams) design.

Dowel pin: Steel pin, passed through or partly through, two parts to provide proper alignment.

Downdraft carburetor: A carburetor in which air passes downward through carburetor into intake manifold.

Downshift: Shifting to lower gear.

Downshift switch: A switch that actuates an electrical solenoid that causes automatic transmission to downshift when throttle valve reaches a predetermined angle.

Drag link: A steel rod connecting pitman arm to one of steering knuckles. On some installations drag link connects pitman arm to a center idler arm.

Drain cock: A faucet-like fitting used to drain water, fuel, etc., from engine, radiator, fuel tank, etc.

Drain plug: A plug that can be removed to drain oil pan, differential, transmission, etc.

Draw (Electrical): Amount of electrical current required to operate electrical device.

Draw (Forming): To form (such as wire) by pulling wire stock through series of hardened dies.

Draw (Temper): Process of removing hardness from a piece of metal.

Draw-filing: Passing file, at right angles, up and down length of work.

Drier (Receiver-drier): Tank, containing desiccant, inserted in air conditioning system to absorb and retain moisture.

Drill: Tool used to bore holes.

Drill gauge: A flat metal gauge used to check twist drill lip angle and width. Useful for accurate sharpening.

Drill press: Nonportable machine used for drilling.

Drive axle: A steel shaft used to transmit driving force (torque) from differential to driving wheels. May be of single or multiple piece construction.

Drive-fit: Fit between two parts when they must be literally driven together.

Driveability: The process of diagnosing, troubleshooting, isolating, and repairing a problem on a vehicle. Term normally used when describing a repair of an engine performance problem.

Driveline: Propeller shaft, universal joints, etc., connecting transmission output shaft to axle pinion gear shaft.

Drive or propeller shaft safety strap: A metal strap or straps, surrounding drive shaft to prevent shaft from falling to ground in event of a universal joint or shaft failure.

Drive pattern (Gear teeth): Contact area between driving and driven gear tooth under driving (engine driving car) conditions—as opposed to coast (car driving engine) conditions.

Drive ratio: Numerical ratio indicated by number of turns a driving gear must revolve to turn driven gear one full revolution. For example, if differential pinion must turn four times to turn ring gear once, differential ratio is 4 to 1.

Drive shaft: Shaft connecting transmission output shaft to differential pinion shaft.

Drive train: All parts that generate power (engine) and transmit it to road wheels (transmission, clutch, drive shaft, differential, drive axles).

Driving lights: Auxiliary headlights, often very bright, that can be used to increase amount of illumination provided by regular headlights.

Drop center rim: Center section of rim being lower than two outer edges. This allows bead of tire to be pushed into low area on one side while the other side is pulled over and off the flange.

Drop forged: Part that has been formed by heating steel blank red hot and pounding it into shape with a powerful drop hammer.

Dropped axle: Front axle altered so as to lower the frame of car. Consists of

bending axle downward at outer ends. (Solid front axle.)

Dry air: Compressed air that does not contain water in form of suspended droplets.

Dry cell or dry battery: Battery (like flashlight battery) that uses no liquid electrolyte.

Dry charged battery: Battery with plates charged but lacking electrolyte. To be placed in service, electrolyte is added.

Dry disc clutch: A clutch design in which clutch disc friction surface operates without lubrication of any type.

Dry friction: Resistance to movement between two unlubricated surfaces.

"Dry" setting (Carburetor): A carburetor float level setting (adjustment for fuel level) made without fuel being in fuel bowl.

Dry sleeve: Cylinder sleeve application in which sleeve is supported in block metal over its entire length. Coolant does not touch sleeve itself.

Dry sump: Instead of letting oil throw-off drain into a regular oil pan sump, system collects and pumps this oil to a remote (separate) container or sump.

Dry weight: Weight of vehicle without fluid (oil, fuel, water) in various units.

Dual brakes: Tandem or dual master cylinder to provide separate brake system for both front and rear of car.

Dual breaker points (Ignition): Distributor using two sets of breaker points to increase cam angle so that at high engine speeds, sufficient spark will be produced to fire plugs.

Duals: Two sets of exhaust pipes and mufflers—one for each bank of cylinders.

Dummy shaft: A temporary shaft that is inserted through bearings, bushings, parts, etc., to hold them in proper alignment while regular shaft is inserted.

Dust boot: A flexible cloth, rubber, neoprene, etc., cover over a joint, connector, etc., to prevent entry of water or dirt into the unit.

Dwell: See Cam Angle.

Dye penetrant (Crack detection): A special penetrating dye used in crack detection. Dye flows into even tiny, invisible cracks. When surface is cleaned and developer applied, dye is drawn from cracks and spreads over surface far enough to make crack area very visible.

Dynamic balance: When centerline of weight mass of a revolving object is in same plane as centerline of object, that object would be in dynamic balance. For example, weight mass of the tire must be in the same plane as centerline of wheel.

Dynamometer: Machine used to measure engine horsepower output. Engine dynamometer measures horsepower at crankshaft and chassis dynamometer measures horsepower output at wheels.

Dynamometer break-in: Running a new or rebuilt engine, for a specific length of time, while engine is

attached to a dynamometer. This permits controlled loading and careful monitoring of engine performance to ensure proper break-in.

E

Early fuel evaporation (EFE): System that passes hot exhaust gases over a certain portion of intake manifold to provide better fuel atomization during engine warm-up.

Earth (Electrical): British term for ground.

Earth wire: British term for ground wire.

Eccentric (Off center): Two circles, one within the other, neither sharing the same center. A protrusion on a shaft that rubs against or is connected to another part.

Eccentric grinding (Brakes): Grinding contact surface of brake lining to a different contour (smaller radius) than that of brake drum. When applied, center of shoe contacts before ends. Additional braking pressure springs shoe so that entire lining surface contacts drum.

Economizer valve: Fuel flow control device within carburetor.

EEC: Evaporative Emission Control.

EGR: Exhaust Gas Recirculation.

Elasticity: That property of a material that allows it to stretch, compress, bend, without breaking and still return to its original size and shape. Rubber possesses great elasticity.

Elastic limit: A measurement of how far material can be bent, stretched, compressed, etc., and still return to exact size, position, etc., when disturbing force is removed.

Elbow (Pipe): A curved pipe fitting designed to produce a change in line direction. Common angles are 90° and 45°.

Electrical conductive residue: Any material left following a process, such as soldering, in which residue itself can form a path for electrical current.

Electrical pitting (Bearing): Erosion of a bearing surface caused by a flow of electricity through a revolving bearing. Tiny electrical arcs between moving parts burn pinholes in bearing surface.

Electric arc: A flow of electricity across an air gap between two conductors. When voltage is high enough, air becomes ionized and then will conduct electrical current.

Electric assist choke: A choke utilizing an electric heating unit to speed up its opening time.

Electric fuel pump: Fuel pump operated by electric motor. Normally mounted in or near fuel tank.

Electrochemical: Chemical (battery) production of electricity.

Electrode (Spark plug): Center rod passing through insulator forms one electrode. The rod welded to shell forms another. They are referred to as center and side electrodes.

Electrode (Welding): Metal rod used in arc welding.

Electrode holder (Arc welding): In arc welding, handle device that grasps welding electrode.

Electrolyte: Sulphuric acid and water solution in battery.

Electromagnet: Magnet produced by placing coil of wire around steel or iron bar. When current flows through coil, bar becomes magnetized and will remain so as long as current continues to flow.

Electromagnetic: Magnetic (generator) production of electricity.

Electron: Negatively charged particle that makes up part of the atom.

Electron theory: Accepted theory that electricity is flow of electrons from one area to another.

Electronic: Refers to electrical circuits or units employing transistors, magnetic amplifiers, computers, etc.

Electronic control: Using an electronic device, such as a computer, to operate or control action of some part or system.

Electronic control unit (ECU): A group of electronic components such as transistors, diodes, thermistors, resistors, etc., that are wired into a unified circuit in such a manner to produce specific electrical signals in response to external sensor inputs.

Electronic fuel injection: An electric solenoid type injector, engine sensors, computer, etc., used to control fuel spray into engine.

Electronic ignition: Ignition system with no conventional breaker points. Primary circuit is broken by magnetic pickup and electronic control unit.

Electronic leak detector (Air conditioning): An electrically operated instrument used to test air conditioning system for R-12 leakage.

Electroplate: Process of depositing gold, silver, chrome, nickel, etc., upon an object by placing object in special solution and then passing an electric current through solution. Object forms one terminal, special electrode the other. Direct current is used.

Element (Battery): Group of plates. Three elements for a six volt and six elements for a twelve volt battery. The elements are connected in series.

Elliot type axle: Solid bar front axle on which ends span or straddle steering knuckle.

Elongate: Lengthening or stretching a material by application of some force such as heat, pressure, motion, etc.

Emergency drive lockout (4-wheel drive): A device, as employed on some fulltime four-wheel drive vehicles, used to lock up transfer case differential so as to provide direct mechanical torque transfer to both front and rear drive differentials.

EMF: Electromotive force. (Voltage.)

Emissions: Byproducts of automotive engine combustion that are discharged into atmosphere. Major pollutants are oxides of nitrogen, carbon monoxide, hydrocarbons, and various particulates. Term also includes vapor (hydrocarbon) loss from fuel tank and carburetor.

Emissions information label: Label normally located in the engine compartment that gives timing, idle speed, and vacuum hose routing information.

Emissions tune-up: See *Maintenance tune-up.*

End lift: A lifting device designed to elevate one end of vehicle.

End play: Amount of axial (lengthwise) movement between two parts.

Energy (Physics): Capacity for doing work.

Engine (Auto): Device that converts heat energy into useful mechanical motion.

Engine adapter: Unit that allows a different engine to be installed in a car—and still bolt up to original transmission.

Engine block: Main engine casting that contains cylinders, piston and crankshaft assemblies. Head bolts to top. Oil sump or pan bolts to bottom.

Engine centerline: A line, equidistant from top, bottom, and sides, running through engine in a direction parallel to crankshaft.

Engine displacement (Size): Volume of space through which head of piston moves in full length of its stroke—multiplied by number of cylinders in engine. Result is given in cubic inches.

Engine mounts: Pads made of metal and rubber which hold engine to frame.

Engine sequence tests: Laboratory engine tests to determine how well a specific engine oil will prevent scuffing, corrosion, oxidation, wear, etc. Also referred to as "Car Manufacturer's Sequence Tests."

Engine stand: A holding fixture for engine so that disassembly, repair, etc., is made easier by having engine at standing height and capable of being turned to different positions.

EP lubricant (Extreme pressure): Lubricant compounded to withstand very heavy loads imposed on gear teeth.

EPA: Environmental Protection Agency. This is a Federal agency.

Equalizer line (Air conditioning): On air conditioning systems employing a POA suction throttling valve, a tube connecting this valve to spot underneath expansion valve control diaphragm. This modulates expansion valve action.

Ermeto fitting: A tubing fitting designed for high pressure application. A special compression sleeve cuts into tubing and forces it against body seat. Often used on heavy walled tubing that is hard to flare.

ESC: Electronic Spark Control.

Etching (Bearing): Dulling or corroding of bearing surface through action of water (rusting) or presence of a corrosive substance. Bearings that are inactive for prolonged periods are particularly susceptible.

Ethylene glycol: Chemical solution added to cooling system to protect against freezing.

Evacuating (air conditioning): Process of removing oxygen from an air conditioning system by pumping air out of the system, creating a vacuum.

Evaporation: Process of a liquid turning into a vapor.

Evaporation control system: Emission control system designed to prevent gasoline vapors from escaping into atmosphere from tank and carburetor.

Evaporator: Unit in air conditioning system used to transform refrigerant from a liquid to a gas. It is at this point that cooling takes place.

Excite: To pass an electric current through a unit such as field coils in generator.

Exhaust cutout: Y-shaped device placed in exhaust pipe ahead of muffler. Driver may channel exhaust through muffler or out other leg of the Y where exhaust passes out without going through the muffler.

Exhaust gas analyzer: Instrument used to check exhaust gases to determine combustion efficiency.

Exhaust gas recirculation: Admitting a controlled amount of exhaust gas into intake manifold during certain periods of engine operation. This lowers combustion flame temperature, thus reducing level of nitrogen oxides emission.

Exhaust manifold: Connecting pipes between exhaust ports and exhaust pipe.

Exhaust pipe: Pipe connecting exhaust manifold to muffler.

Exhaust sensor: A device in exhaust stream to measure oxygen content. It can, through an electronic control unit, be used to alter air-fuel ratios, engine timing, etc.

Exhaust stroke: Portion of piston's movement devoted to expelling burned gases from cylinder.

Exhaust system: Parts which carry engine exhaust to rear of car—exhaust manifold, pipes, muffler, and catalytic converter.

Exhaust valve (Engine): Valve through which burned fuel charge passes on its way from cylinder to exhaust manifold.

Expansion tank: A tank, connected to cooling system, into which water can enter or leave as needed during coolant heating (expansion) or cooling (contraction).

Expansion valve (TVX) (Air conditioning): Device used to reduce pressure and meter flow of refrigerant into evaporator.

Extension housing: A housing attached to rear of a transmission so as to render its length suitable to available space.

Extension jack: A lifting jack with a very long, adjustable stem making it suitable for supporting from floor to engine, transmission, etc., while vehicle is in air on a lift.

Eye bolt: A bolt with threads on one end and a round loop (eye) on other. Useful for engine removal from car.

F

°F: Temperature measurement in degrees Fahrenheit.

Fabric ply (Tire): A layer of fabric (nylon, rayon, polyester, etc.) making up one of plies (layers) involved in construction of a tire. May refer to either sidewall or to tread plies.

Face (Engine valve): That portion of intake or exhaust valve that contacts valve seat.

Face indented wear (Engine valve): A grooved wear area on valve face. Caused by wear and pounding action of valve face slamming against valve seat.

Face shield: A clear, protective shield that covers entire face for protection during grinding, striking, etc., operations.

Fahrenheit: Thermometer on which boiling point of water is 212° and freezing point is 32°.

Fan: A device designed to create a moving stream of air. Generally employed for cooling purposes.

Farad: Unit of capacitance; capacitance of condenser retaining one coulomb of charge with one volt difference of potential.

Fast charging: Charging a battery by passing a relatively heavy current through it. This will restore battery charge reasonably well in one to two hours.

Fast idle: Engine idle rpm when throttle is held partially open by a fast idle cam or solenoid during cold engine idle conditions.

Feeder wire: A wire supplying current to several circuits—such as the feeder wire to a terminal block to which several other circuit wires connect.

Feeler gauge: Thin strip of hardened steel, ground to an exact thickness, used to check clearances between parts.

Fender cover: A protective pad that is laid over car fender area to prevent marring paint while leaning over to work on underhood areas.

Fender skirt: Plate designed to cover portion of rear fender wheel opening.

Ferromagnetic: That property of certain metals, such as steel, iron, nickel, etc., that cause it to form molecular alignment within magnetic domains when material is magnetized. A material that is magnetic, capable of being magnetized, or that responds to a magnetic field.

Ferrous metal: Metal containing iron or steel.

F-head engine: Engine having one valve in the head and the other in the block.

Fiber gear: A gear constructed of resin impregnated fibers that are compressed and hardened. Generally provide quiet operation.

Fiberglass: Mixture of glass fibers and resin that when cured (hardened) produces a very light and strong material. Used to build boats, car bodies, repair damaged areas, etc.

Fiber optic: A path for electricity or data transmission in which light acts as the carrier.

Field: Area covered or filled with a magnetic force.

Field coil: Insulated wire wrapped around an iron or steel core. When current flows through wire, strong magnetic force field is built up.

Field frame: That portion of an electrical generator or motor upon which field coil is wound.

Filament: Fine wire inside light bulb that heats to incandescence when current passes through it. The filament produces the light.

Filler metal (Welding): Molten metal added to base metal during welding or brazing process.

Fillet: Rounding joint between two parts connected at an angle.

Fillet radius: Degree of curve (radius) involved in a curved edge or corner such as used on crankshaft journals where journal end meets crankshaft sides. Fillet prevents corner cracking better than a sharp right angle corner. Indicates size of fillet.

Fillet weld: A weld in which filler metal is placed in corner where two metal pieces join at angles to each other.

Filter: Device designed to remove foreign substances from air, oil, gasoline, etc.

Final drive ratio: Overall gear reduction (includes transmission, overdrive, auxiliary transmission, etc., gear ratio as well as rear axle ratio) at rear wheels.

Finishing stone (Hone): Fine stone used for final finishing during honing.

Fire wall: Metal partition between driver's compartment and engine compartment.

Firing order: Order in which cylinders must be fired—1, 5, 3, 6, 2, 4, etc.

Fit: Contact area between two parts.

Fixed caliper (Brake): A disc brake design in which caliper body is rigidly attached and thus is unable to move in any direction. It cannot, as is done in a sliding caliper, center itself over disc or rotor.

Flame arrestor vent plug (Battery): A battery filler plug designed to reduce possibility of an open flame igniting hydrogen gas present in battery cells. If gas hovering above battery is ignited, plug prevents flame from passing into battery.

Flange: A flared, collar-like section formed on a shaft, pipe, beam, etc. Often located on end to facilitate fastening sections together or to provide a base for affixing some other part.

Flanged end axle: A drive axle with outer end formed into a flange to mount wheel.

Flange height (Wheel): A distance determined by measuring from bottom of wheel bead to top of flange. Flange retains tire bead.

Flare angle (Tubing): The angle formed when end of tubing is spread (flared) open for use in a flare fitting.

Flare connection: A tubing connection that both secures and seals by gripping flared end of tubing between two similar angled areas formed in fitting body and nut.

Flaring cone: A tapered cone that is forced into open end of a piece of tubing to produce a flared end suitable for use in a flare fitting.

Flaring tool: Tool used to form flare connections on tubing.

Flashback (Oxyacetylene welding): A condition in which oxygen has entered acetylene hose or vice versa and due to failure to correctly purge both lines, a combustible mixture exists in hoses. Upon lighting torch, flame, instead of burning just at tip, moves inside and a fire starts burning in hoses.

Flashover (Electrical): A condition in which electrical current, instead of moving through an intended conductor, jumps across an open space or moves along surface of an insulator, such as a coil tower, distributor cap, etc., either directly to ground or to some other circuit.

Flash point: The point in the temperature range at which a given oil will ignite and flash into flame.

Flat head: Engine with all the valves in block.

Flat spot: Refers to a spot experienced during an acceleration period where the engine seems to "fall on its face" for a second or so and will then begin to pull again.

Flexible drive plate (Automatic transmission): A thin, bendable drive plate attached both to crankshaft and transmission torque converter. Drives torque converter.

Flint: Stone-like material that is used in a spark lighter for welding torches. The flint, when scratched across a rough, hardened metal surface, gives off a heavy shower of sparks.

Float: Unit in carburetor bowl that floats on top of fuel. It controls inlet needle valve to produce proper fuel level in bowl, can be of hollow metal, plastic, or cork.

Float bowl: The part of the carburetor that acts as a reservoir for gasoline and in which the float is placed.

Float circuit: That portion of the carburetor devoted to maintaining a constant level of fuel in carburetor. Consists of float bowl, float, inlet valve, etc.

Float drop: A measurement of distance a carburetor fuel bowl float moves from full up to full down positions (no fuel in bowl). Can also indicate a specified distance from a specific spot on float to a specific spot on carburetor, with float in full down position.

Floating caliper (Brakes): A disc brake in which caliper assembly is mounted on pins (rods) to allow some lateral (side) movement. This permits caliper to automatically maintain a centralized position over disc or rotor.

Floating insert (Bearing): A precision insert friction bearing that has bearing material on both inner and outer surfaces. Bearing slides against both journal and bore surfaces. It is seldom used.

Float level: Height of fuel in carburetor float bowl. Also refers to specific float setting that will produce correct fuel level.

Flooding: Condition where fuel mixture is overly rich or an excessive amount has reached cylinders. Starting will be difficult and sometimes impossible until condition is corrected.

Flow meter: Sensing device which measures flow of air or liquid.

Fluid coupling: Unit that transfers engine torque to transmission input shaft through use of two vaned units (called a torus) operating very close together in a bath of oil.

Fluid drive fan: A cooling fan that uses a liquid, such as silicone oil, to permit a controlled amount of slippage to limit maximum fan speed. Also controls fan speed, through thermostatic valve action, in relation to engine temperature requirements.

Fluorescent penetrant: A crack detection solution that penetrates into even minute cracks. When surface is wiped clean, a developer will draw penetrant to surface where it will spread out wider than crack. When subjected to black light, penetrant glows, disclosing crack.

Flute: Groove in cutting tool that forms a passageway for exit of chips removed during the cutting process.

Flux (Magnetic): Lines of magnetic force moving through magnetic field.

Flux (Soldering, brazing): Ingredient placed on metal being soldered or brazed, to remove and prevent formation of surface oxidation which would make soldering or brazing difficult.

Flux core wire solder: Wire solder with a hollow center that is filled with either rosin or acid flux.

Flywheel: Relatively large wheel that is attached to crankshaft to smooth out firing impulses. It provides inertia to keep crankshaft turning smoothly during periods when no power is being applied. It also forms a base for starter ring gear and in many instances, for clutch assembly.

Flywheel ring gear: Gear on outer circumference of flywheel. Starter drive gear engages ring gear and cranks engine.

Flywheel runout: Measured amount of either side to side (lateral) movement or radial (up and down) movement present in a revolving flywheel.

Fog lights: Amber or clear lamps specially designed to provide better visibility in fog. Are usually mounted as close to the road as is feasible.

Foot-pound: Measurement of work involved in lifting one pound one foot.

Foot-pound (Tightening): One pound pull one foot from center of an object.

Force: Pressure (pull, push, etc.) acting upon body that tends to change state of motion, or rest, of the body.

Force-fit: Same as drive-fit.

Forehand welding: An oxyacetylene welding technique in which torch tip is aimed slightly away from molten puddle and towards direction of welding.

Forge: To force piece of hot metal into desired shape by hammering.

Four banger, six banger, etc.: Four cylinder, six cylinder engine, etc.

Four bolt main: A crankshaft main bearing employing two fasteners on each side.

Four-on-the-floor: Four-speed manual transmission with floor mounted shift.

Four-stroke cycle engine: Engine requiring two complete revolutions of crankshaft to fire each piston once.

Four-wheel alignment: Process in which all the wheels on a vehicle are aligned with each other.

Four-wheel drive: Vehicle in which front wheels, as well as rear, may be driven.

Four-wheel steering: System used to provide limited steering for the rear wheels. Operates in relation to the front wheels.

Fractional drill: A twist drill, size of which is indicated in fractions (1/16, 1/8, 3/16, etc.) of an inch.

Frame: Portion of automobile upon which body rests and to which engine and springs are attached. Generally constructed of steel channels.

Frame (Conventional): Strong, steel members run from front to rear of body.

Frame (Integral): Car body serves as portion or all of frame.

Frame rails: Structural sections of the car frame. Often specifically used to refer to two outside longitudinal sections.

Free electrons: Electrons in outer orbits around nucleus of atom. They can be moved out of orbit fairly easily.

Free play: Amount of unimpeded movement, radial, lateral, longitudinal, etc., that exists between two parts.

Freewheel: Usually refers to action of car on downgrade when overdrive overrunning clutch is slipping with resultant loss of engine braking. This condition will only occur after overdrive unit is engaged but before balk ring has activated planetary gearset.

Freezing: When two parts that are rubbing together heat up and force lubricant out of area, they will gall and finally freeze or stick together.

Frequency: Rate of change in direction, oscillation, cycles, etc., in given time span.

Fretting (Bearing): Corrosive-like surface damage to bearing face or to outer ring, outer surface or inner ring, inner surface. These are portions of bearing touching bore walls and shaft surface. There is little, or in some cases, no movement between these surfaces.

Friction: Resistance to movement between any two objects when placed in contact with each other. Friction is not constant but depends on type of surface, pressure holding two objects together, etc.

Friction bearing: Bearing made of babbitt, bronze, etc. There are no moving parts and shaft that rests in bearing merely rubs against friction material in bearing.

FTC: Federal Trade Commission.

Fuel: Combustible substance that is burned within (internal) or outside (external) an engine so as to impart motion to pistons, vanes, etc.

Fuel accumulator: Spring loaded diaphragm device which dampens fuel pressure pulsations, muffles noise, and helps maintain residual pressure with engine off.

Fuel bowl: Storage area in carburetor for extra fuel.

Fuel distributor: Device which meters fuel to injectors at correct rate of flow for engine conditions.

Fuel filter: A device that removes dirt, rust particles, and in some cases, water from fuel before it moves into carburetor or fuel injection system.

Fuel gauge: A device to indicate the approximate amount of fuel in tank.

Fuel injection: Fuel system that uses no carburetor but sprays fuel either directly into cylinders or into intake manifold just ahead of cylinders.

Fuel level (Carburetor): Normal working level or height of fuel in carburetor fuel bowl. Level is determined by float setting.

Fuel level "wet" setting: Checking or adjusting carburetor fuel level by measuring actual working height of gasoline in fuel bowl.

Fuel line: That portion of the fuel system, consisting of tubing and hose, that carries fuel from tank to carburetor or injection system.

Fuel mixture: Mixture of gasoline and air. An average mixture, by weight, would contain 14.7 parts of air to one part of gasoline.

Fuel pulsation: Fuel pressure variations due to fuel pump action.

Fuel pump: Vacuum device, operated either mechanically or electrically, that is used to draw gasoline from tank and force it into carburetor.

Fuel pump pressure: Pressure, in pounds per square inch or kilopascals, developed by a fuel pump.

Fuel pump vacuum: Amount of vacuum, in inches of mercury, developed by a fuel pump.

Fuel pump volume: Amount of fuel a pump will deliver in a specified period of time, at a specified rpm (where engine driven).

Fuel rail: In an electronic gasoline injection system, hollow pipe that is connected to and supplies fuel for injectors. Can also refer to a common feeder pipe for multi-carburetor installation.

Fuel tank: A large tank of steel or plastic, used to store a supply of fuel aboard vehicle.

Fulcrum: Support on which a lever pivots in raising an object.

Full-floating axle: Rear drive axle that does not hold wheel on nor does it hold wheel in line or support any weight. It merely drives wheel. Used primarily on trucks.

Full-floating piston pin: A piston pin that is free to turn in both piston and rod. Pin is secured by snap rings at each end.

Full-flow lubrication system: An engine lubrication system in which all engine oil from oil pump must first pass through a filter before reaching bearings. If filter clogs, a bypass permits oil to reach bearings.

Full-flow oil filter: Oil filter that filters all of oil passing through engine—before it reaches the bearings.

Full house: Engine that is fully modified and equipped for all-out performance.

Full pressure system: Type of oiling or lubrication system using an oil pump to draw oil out of a sump and force it through passages in engine.

Full rebound (Suspension): In a suspension system, position of a spring or shock at precise time that frame (or body) is separated from axles (or control arms) the maximum distance.

Full-time four-wheel drive: Setup in which all four wheels are driven—all the time—off road or on. Addition of a third differential, located at transfer case, permits front and rear wheels to operate at different speeds.

Full-time transfer case: Four-wheel drive transfer case that drives all four wheels all the time. Two-wheel drive is not possible. Such systems permit four-wheel drive on dry, hard surfaced roads by incorporating a differential in transfer case unit.

Fuse: Protective device that will break flow of current when current draw exceeds capacity of fuse.

Fuse block: A central block or area for various circuit fuses.

Fusible link: A special wire inserted into a circuit to provide protection in event of overloading, shorts, etc. Overloads will melt wire and break circuit. Unlike a regular fuse, fusible link will permit overloading for a short time before melting.

Fusion: Two metals reaching the melting point and flowing or welding themselves together.

G

Gal: Gallon.

Galled (Bearing): Bearing surface damage caused by lack of lubrication, overheating, improper lubrication, etc. Metal surface in numerous high spots literally melts from heat and attempts to weld together, thus pulling out and smearing small chunks of metal. Advanced galling will cause bearing seizure.

Galvanometer: Instrument used to measure pressure, amount of, and direction of an electric current.

Gap bridging (Spark plug): A buildup of carbon, lead, etc., on spark plug electrodes. Buildup can advance to point gap is completely filled (bridged) and plug becomes inoperative.

Gas: A nonsolid material. It can be compressed. When heated, it will expand and when cooled, it will contract. (Such as air.)

Gas burner or gasser: Competition car with engine set up to operate on standard pump gasoline instead of an alcohol, nitro, etc., mixture.

Gaseous shield (Welding): Shield of inert gases produced when arc welding with coated electrodes or T.I.G., M.I.G., etc., welding setup. Gases shield molten metal being welded from air, thus preventing oxidization of weld metal.

Gasket: Material placed between two parts to insure proper sealing.

Gasket—multiple layer: A gasket utilizing two or more layers of different material, such as asbestos center, steel top and bottom.

Gasket—neoprene: A gasket constructed of manufactured rubber. Impervious to most automotive oils, greases, solvents.

Gasket shellac: A shellac sealing compound placed on certain gasket installations to assist in sealing and often, as an aid in positioning gasket during part assembly.

Gasohol: Automotive engine fuel made up of around 90% gasoline and 10% ethanol alcohol.

Gasoline: Hydrocarbon fuel used in the internal combustion engine.

Gassing: Small hydrogen bubbles rising to top of battery electrolyte during battery charging.

GAWR: See Gross axle weight rating.

Gear: Circular object, usually flat edged or cone-shaped, upon which a series of teeth have been cut. These are meshed with teeth of another gear and when one turns, it also drives the other.

Gear backlash: Amount of measured movement between mating gear teeth when one gear is held and other is moved to limit of travel, first one way then, then the other.

Gear pump: A pump, utilizing two meshed gears, that draw in and force out oil, fuel, etc. Capable of building high pressure.

Gear ratio: Relationship between number of turns made by driving gear to complete one full turn of driven gear. If driving gear turns four times to turn driven gear once, gear ratio would be 4 to 1.

Gear runout: A measured amount of either gear lateral movement (side to side wobble) or radial (up and down) movement that exists when a gear is revolved.

Generator: Electromagnetic device for producing electricity.

Glass: Term used for the material "Fiberglass."

Glass pack muffler: Straight through (no baffles) muffler utilizing fiberglas packing around perforated pipe to deaden exhaust sound.

Glaze: Highly smooth, glassy finish on cylinder walls.

Glaze breaker or deglazer: Abrasive tool used to remove glaze from cylin-

der walls prior to installation of new piston rings.

Glazed surface (Cylinder): A cylinder surface that has worn to a bright, glass-like finish. This glaze must be removed by honing to insure proper seating of new piston rings.

Glow plug: A heating device placed in a diesel engine precombustion chamber to facilitate cold engine starting. When engine is cold, an electric current is passed through plug causing it to glow red hot. This helps ignite compressed fuel.

GMC: General Motors Corporation.

Governor: Device designed to automatically control speed or position of some part.

GPM: Gallons Per Minute.

Gradient: Angle of hill. A 20% gradient would be a hill that would rise two feet for every ten forward feet of travel. This is determined by rise as a percentage of forward travel.

Grid: Lead screen or plate to which battery plate active material is affixed.

Grind: Remove metal from object by means of revolving abrasive wheel, disc, or belt.

Grommet: A rubber, plastic, etc., doughnut shaped object, with a slot cut around outer edge. Used to snap into holes in sheet metal to provide protection for a wire, tube, etc., passing through hole.

Gross axle weight rating: Total load carrying capacity of a given axle (front or back) setup. Weight rating can be expressed as rating at springs (total load on springs) or at ground (total load measured where tire meets ground). Weight at ground rating includes weight of tires, wheels, axle, and springs.

Ground (Battery): Terminal of battery connected to metal framework of car. In this country, negative terminal is grounded.

Ground clamp (Welding): Clamp on end of ground wire. Must be attached to work to complete a circuit when arc welding.

Growler: Instrument used in testing starter and generator armature.

Gudgeon pin: British term for piston or wrist pin.

Gum (Fuel system): Oxidized portions of fuel that forms deposits in fuel system or engine parts.

Gusset: A metal piece, usually of flat plate, used to strengthen a joint between two parts such as frame rails. Usually welded or riveted into place.

Gut: To strip the interior of car. May also refer to removing internal baffles from muffler.

GVW: Gross Vehicle Weight. Total weight of vehicle including vehicle passengers, load, etc. Used as indicator of how heavy vehicle can be loaded (GVW minus vehicle curb weight equals payload).

GVWR: Gross Vehicle Weight Rating. See GVW.

H

Hacksaw: Hand operated metal cutting saw. Can use various blade lengths and tooth configurations.

Half-hard copper (Tubing): Copper tubing that has not been fully annealed (softened).

Half-moon key: Driving key serving same purpose as regular key but it is shaped somewhat like a half circle.

Halide torch: A gas torch used to detect R-12 leaks in air conditioning systems.

Halogen bulb: Light bulb in which tungsten filament is surrounded by a halogen gas such as iodine, bromine, etc. Bulb glass is quartz to withstand intense heat.

Hand brake: Hand operated brake which prevents vehicle movement while parked by applying rear wheel brakes or transmission brake.

Hand drill: A drill, either manual or electric, that is held in hands to operate.

Hardening sealant: A sealant material that upon full curing, becomes hard.

Harmonic balancer: See *Vibration Damper.*

HC: Symbol for hydrocarbon.

Headlights: Main driving lights used on front of vehicle.

Head marking (Bolt): Marks placed on a bolt, capscrew, etc., to indicate fastener grade (material strength).

Head mating surface (Block): That portion of engine cylinder block that mates (contacts) with cylinder head.

Head pressure: See *Discharge Pressure.*

Heat baffle: A shield placed around or next to some pipe, hose, wire, etc., to protect it from a heat source such as an exhaust manifold.

Heat checking (Brake): Small surface cracks in brake drums or brake discs (rotors) caused from heat generated during braking.

Heat control valve (Manifold): A valve in exhaust manifold that directs a portion of hot exhaust gases to a selected area of intake manifold to provide heat for improved cold engine operation. Controlled by vacuum motor or thermostatic spring. Also called "heat riser," "early fuel evaporation valve," etc.

Heat crossover (V-type engine): Passage from one exhaust manifold up, over, and under carburetor and on to other manifold. Crossover provides heat to carburetor during engine warmup.

Heat discoloration: Metal surface coloring that is caused by application of heat, either from friction or from an outside heat source.

Heat engine: Engine operated by heat energy released from burning fuel.

Heat exchanger: Device, such as radiator, either used to cool or heat by transferring heat from one object to another.

Heat range (Spark plugs): Refers to operating temperature of given style plug. Plugs are made to operate at different temperatures depending upon thickness and length of porcelain insulator as measured from sealing ring down to tip.

Heat riser: Area, surrounding portion of the intake manifold, through which exhaust gases can pass to heat fuel mixture during warmup.

Heat-shrink tubing: Plastic tube used to insulate electrical solder joints.

Heat sink: Device used to prevent overheating of electrical device by absorbing heat and transferring it to atmosphere.

Heat stove: Sheet metal housing around a portion of exhaust manifold. An intake pipe from housing provides hot air to carburetor air cleaner when needed. Can also mean a small shrouded depression in exhaust manifold from which hot air may be drawn to automatic choke housing.

Heat transfer: Movement of heat from one object to another by convection, conduction, or radiation. Can also refer to movement of heat through a given object—by conduction.

Heat treatment (Metal): Application of controlled heat to metal object to alter its characteristics (toughness, hardness, etc.).

Heavy repair: Generally refers to shop work involving complete dismantling, rebuilding, replacement, etc., of major items such as engine, transmission, etc.

Heel (Brake): End of brake shoe which rests against anchor pin.

Heel (Gear tooth): Wide end of tapered gear tooth such as found in differential gears.

Hg: Abbreviation for the word mercury. Vacuum is measured in inches of mercury.

Helical: Spiraling shape such as that made by a coil spring.

Helical gear: Gear that has teeth cut at an angle to centerline of gear.

Heli-coil: A coil spring insert used to create new threads (same diameter and thread as original) in a hole with stripped threads.

Hemi: Engine using hemispherical-shaped (half of globe) combustion chambers.

Hemispherical combustion chamber: A round, dome-shaped combustion chamber that is considered by many to be one of the finest shapes ever developed. Hemispherical-shape lends itself to use of large valves for improved breathing and suffers less heat loss than other shapes.

Herringbone gears: Two helical gears operating together and so placed that angle of the teeth form a "V" shape.

Hex nipple (Pipe): A pipe nipple with center section hexagonal (six sided) shape.

High compression heads: Cylinder head with smaller combustion chamber area thereby raising compression. Head can be custom built or can be a stock head milled (cut) down.

High flash point: A liquid such as cleaning solution, oil, etc., that must be heated to fairly high temperatures before vapors will spontaneously ignite.

High pressure lubricant: A lubricant containing special additives that provide great resistance to film rupture under heavy contact pressure, such as is found in some traction type differentials.

High-pressure spray cleaning: Cleaning process employing a solution under heavy pressure, that is discharged at high velocity from a spray nozzle.

High range (4-wheel drive): The upper gear (more road speed, less torque) of a two speed (high-low) transfer case as used in four-wheel drive applications.

High reach jack: A lifting jack in which the lift arm, ram, etc., can move over a very long range making it capable of raising objects to a considerable height.

High-rise manifold: Intake manifold designed to mount carburetor or carburetors, considerably higher above engine than is done in standard manifold. Done to improve angle at which fuel is delivered.

High side (Air conditioning): In an air conditioning system, that portion of system that operates under considerable pressure (between compressor and expansion valve).

High tension: High voltage from ignition coil. May also indicate secondary wire from the coil to distributor and wires from distributor to plugs.

Hoist: See *Chain Hoist.*

Hold-down clip: A metal or plastic device (clip) used to secure a wire, pipe, hose, etc., so as to prevent movement, vibration, etc.

Holding jig: A device for holding an object while grinding, bending, machining, etc.

Hole saw: Metal cutting saw made in shape of a tube, one end has cutting teeth, other a drive tang. Used for cutting round holes in sheet metal, wood, etc.

Hone: To remove metal with fine grit abrasive stone to precise tolerances.

Honed to size: A bearing bore, bushing, etc., brought to final finished size by honing (removal of a small amount of metal with an abrasive material such as a stone).

Honing machine: Machine used to bring bearing bores, bushings, etc., to accurate, smooth finished size, by removing a small amount of metal stock with abrasive stones.

Honing oil: Special oil used in honing process. Flushes stones to assist in cutting and reduces heat buildup.

Hood pins: Pins designed to hold hood closed.

Hooke's law: Law stating that amount of distortion (bending, twisting, lengthening, etc.) caused in a solid, as long as it is kept within elastic limits of material, will be directly proportional to applied force.

Hook rule: Small, short (6 in.) flat steel rule with a hook attached to scale starting end.

Hopping up: Increasing engine performance through various modifications.

Horizontal-opposed engine: Engine possessing two banks of cylinders that are placed flat or 180 deg. apart.

Horsepower: Measurement of engine's ability to perform work. One horsepower is defined as ability to lift 33,000 pounds one foot in one minute. To find horsepower, total rate of work in foot pounds accomplished is divided by 33,000. If a machine was lifting 100 pounds 660 feet per minute, its total rate of work would be 66,000 foot pounds.

Dividing this by 33,000 foot pounds (1 horsepower) you find the machine is rated as 2 horsepower (hp).

Horsepower (Brake): See Brake horsepower.

Horsepower (Frictional): Amount of horsepower lost to engine friction.

Horsepower (Gross): Maximum horsepower developed by engine without a fan, air cleaner, alternator, exhaust system, etc.

Horsepower (Net): Maximum horsepower developed by engine equipped with fan, air conditioning, air cleaner, exhaust system, and all other systems and items normally present when engine is installed in car.

Horsepower—weight factor: Relationship between total weight of car and horsepower available. By dividing weight by horsepower, number of pounds to be moved by one horsepower is determined. This factor has a great effect on acceleration, gas mileage, and all around performance.

Hose clamps: Devices used to secure hoses to their fittings.

Hoses: Flexible rubber tubes for carrying water, oil, air, and other fluids.

Hotchkiss drive: Method of connecting transmission output shaft to differential pinion by using open drive shafts. Driving force of rear wheels is transmitted to frame through rear springs or through link arms connecting rear axle housing to frame.

Hot idle: Engine idle speed during normal operating temperature range. It is slower than that of "cold idle" (fast idle).

Hot patch (Tire): Application of a sealing patch to a tire or tube through use of heat and pressure.

Hot spot: Localized area in which temperature is considerably higher than surrounding area.

Hot tank: Tank filled with a hot, caustic solution (often alkaline based). Used for heavy duty cleaning of radiators, engine blocks, etc.

Hot wire: Wiring around key switch so as to start car without key. Wire connected to battery or some part of electrical system in which a direct connection to battery is present. A current-carrying wire.

Housing spreader (Differential): A tool used to spread differential housing a small amount to permit removal or installation of differential case and bearing assembly.

Hp: Horsepower.

Hub (Wheel): Unit to which wheel is bolted.

Hunting gearset (Differential): A ring and pinion gearset in which the same teeth on pinion and ring mesh every so many revolutions. Even ratios such as 3 to 1, 2.5 to 1, etc., bring this about. By using a ratio of 3.11 to 1, 2.53 to 1, etc., this would not occur and the gearset would then become "nonhunting."

Hyatt roller bearing (Antifriction): Similar to conventional roller bearing except that rollers are hollow and are split in a spiral fashion from end to end.

Hydraulic: Refers to fluids in motion. Hydraulics is science of fluid in motion.

Hydraulic brakes: Brakes operated by hydraulic pressure. Master cylinder provides operating pressure transmitted via steel tubing to wheel cylinders or pistons that apply brake shoes to brake drums and/or discs.

Hydraulic floor jack: A low hydraulic jack, equipped with wheels for easy moving, used for lifting front, side, or rear of car.

Hydraulic hand jack: A compact, powerful, portable hydraulic jack consisting of base, reservoir, and short ram.

Hydraulic lifter: Valve lifter that utilizes hydraulic pressure from engine's oiling system to keep it in constant contact with both camshaft and valve stem. They automatically adjust to any variation in valve stem length.

Hydraulic press: A press with a large, suspended hydraulic cylinder and ram. Ram is actuated by pressure generated in a small cylinder and transmitted through a connecting pipe to large cylinder. Used for applying force to remove or install bearings, collars, bushings, etc.

Hydraulic puller: A pulling device utilizing a hydraulic cylinder to generate force required.

Hydraulics: The science of liquid in motion.

Hydro-boost: Name for one type of hydraulically operated (steering pump pressure) brake booster.

Hydrocarbon—unburned: Hydrocarbons that were not burned during the normal engine combustion process. Unburned hydrocarbons make up about 0.1 percent of engine exhaust emission.

Hydrocarbons (HC): Combination of hydrogen and carbon atoms. All petroleum based fuels (gasoline, kerosene, etc.) consist of hydrocarbons.

Hydrometer: Float device for determining specific gravity of electrolyte in a battery. This will determine the state of charge.

Hydropneumatic suspension: Suspension system using both a liquid (oil) and compressed air for springing.

Hygroscopic: Ability to absorb moisture from air.

Hypoid gearing: System of gearing wherein pinion gear meshes with ring gear below centerline of ring gear. This allows a somewhat lower drive line thus reducing hump in the floor of car. For this reason hypoid gearing is used in differential on many cars.

I

ICEI: Internal Combustion Engine Institute.

Icing: Formation of ice (under certain atmospheric conditions) on throttle plate, air horn walls, etc., caused by lowering of fuel mixture temperature as it passes through air horn.

ID: Inside diameter.

Idle: Indicates engine operating at its normal slow speed with throttle closed.

Idle mixture: Air-fuel mixture delivered to engine during idle.

Idler arm: Steering system part that supports one end of center link.

Idler gear: A gear, between two other gears, that is driven by one and drives other. This permits both driving and driven gear to rotate in same direction with no change in gear ratio.

Idler sprocket: An additional sprocket, generally used on long runs of timing chain, that takes up excess chain slack to prevent harmful chain flap or distortion.

Idle screw (Carburetor): Adjusting screw (now fixed at factory) used to control amount of and/or ratio of fuel and air delivered to engine during idle.

Idle speed screw: A screw used to adjust carburetor throttle plate position to secure desired idle rpm.

Idle valve or idle needle: Needle used to control amount of fuel mixture reaching cylinders during idling. It, or they, may be adjusted by turning the exposed heads.

Ignition: Lighting or igniting fuel charge by means of a spark (gas engine) or my heat of compression (diesel engine).

Ignition switch: Key operated switch in driver compartment for connecting and disconnecting power to ignition and electrical system.

Ignition system: Portion of car electrical system, designed to produce a spark within cylinders to ignite fuel charge. Consists basically of battery, key switch, resistor, coil, distributor, points, condenser, spark plugs, and necessary wiring.

Ignition timing: Refers to relationship between exact time a plug is fired and position of piston in degrees of crankshaft rotation.

I-head engine: Engine having both valves in the head.

IHP: Indicated Horsepower.

IMEP: Indicated Mean Effective Pressure.

IMI: Ignition Manufacturer's Institute.

Impact sensors: An open switch used in air bag systems. The switch is designed to close when vehicle is involved in a severe frontal impact.

Impact wrench: An air or electrical driven wrench that tightens or loosens nuts, cap screws, etc., with series of sharp, rapid blows.

Impeller: Wheel-like device upon which fins are attached. It is whirled to pump water, move and slightly compress air, etc.

In.: Inch.

Inch-gram: Metric unit of measure indicating amount of twisting or turning force being applied to something such as a fastener, shaft, etc.

Inch-ounces: U.S. customary unit of measure indicating amount of twisting or turning force being applied to something such as a fastener, shaft, etc. Equivalent to one-twelfth inch-pound.

Inch-pounds: English unit of measure indicating amount of twisting or turning force being applied to something such as a fastener, shaft, etc. Equivalent to 12 inch-ounces.

Included angle (Steering): Angle formed by centerlines drawn through steering axis (kingpin inclination) and center of wheel (camber angle) as viewed from front of car. Combines both steering axis and camber angles.

Independent suspension: A suspension system that allows each wheel to move up and down without undue influence on other wheels.

Indicated horsepower (ihp): Measure of power developed by burning fuel within cylinders.

Induction: Imparting of electricity into one object, not connected, to another by the influence of magnetic fields.

Inertia: Force which tends to keep stationary object from being moved, and tends to keep moving objects in motion.

Inertia switch: An electrical switch designed to be operated by a sudden movement, such as that caused by a collision.

Inflator module: Air bag system component that houses the inflatable bag, initiator, and gas generating material.

Inhibited cleaning solution: A caustic cleaning solution that has been weakened to prevent surface erosion of aluminum parts while soaking.

Inhibitor: Substance added to oil, water, gas, etc., to prevent action such as foaming, rusting, etc.

Injector: Refers to valve mechanism (used in fuel injection system) that squirts or injects measured amount of gasoline into intake manifold in vicinity of intake valve. In diesel engine, fuel is injected directly into combustion chamber.

Injector pump (Diesel): A mechanical pump that forces diesel fuel, under high pressure, to and through injector nozzles. Pump provides proper injection timing.

Injector timing (Diesel): Relationship between instant of fuel injection in any one cylinder, to position of piston in degrees of crankshaft rotation.

In-line engine: Engine in which all cylinders are arranged in straight row.

In-line fuse: A fuse placed directly in an individual circuit wire. Installed as close to electrical source as possible.

In-line injector pump (Diesel): An injector pump utilizing a number of plungers operating in cylinders. Plunger-cylinder assemblies (one per engine cylinder) are positioned in a straight line and are operated by a single camshaft.

Inner flame cone (Oxyacetylene): Small cone of flame visible at tip opening.

Input shaft: Shaft delivering power into mechanism. Shaft from clutch into transmission is transmission input shaft.

Insert bearing: Removable, precision made bearing which insures specified clearance between bearing and shaft.

Insert recess cutter (Valve): A cutting tool used to counterbore head to install a valve seat insert. Removes integral seat and leaves a precise recess to accept insert.

Insert removal plug (Valve): A tool used to grasp underside of a valve seat insert so that it may be pulled out.

Inside caliper: A precision measuring tool designed to measure inside diameter of cylinders, bearing bores, etc.

Insulation: Material used to reduce transfer of noise (sound insulation), heat (heat insulation), electricity (electrical insulation).

Insulator (Electrical): Material that will not (readily) conduct electricity.

Intake manifold: Connecting tubes between base of carburetor and port openings to intake valves.

Intake stroke: Portion of piston's movement devoted to drawing fuel mixture into engine cylinder.

Intake valve (Engine): Valve through which fuel mixture is admitted to cylinder.

Integral: Part of. (The cam lobe is an integral part of camshaft.)

Integral carrier: A drive axle differential assembly in which carrier (supports differential case) is constructed as an integral part of housing and as such, cannot be removed as a separate unit.

Integral guide (Valve): A valve guide machined right in head metal itself.

Integral seat (Valve): Valve seat cut right in head metal itself.

Interference angle (Valve): Approximate one degree difference in angle between valve face and valve seat, used to produce an interference fit.

Interference fit (Valve): A valve face-to-valve seat contact in which either valve face or valve seat is ground to a slightly different angle (around 1°) than other. Aids in quick seating.

Intermediate bearing: A bearing on a multiple bearing shaft, such as camshaft, crankshaft, etc., that is located between two end bearings.

Intermediate gear: Any gear in auto transmission between 1st and high.

Intermittent: Not constant but occurring at intervals.

Intermittent codes: Computer diagnostic code that does not return immediately after it has been cleared.

Internal combustion engine: Engine that burns fuel within itself as means of developing power.

Internal gear: A gear with teeth cut on an inward facing surface. Example: outer gear is a planetary gearset. Teeth face inward towards center.

Inverted Flare: A tubing 45° angle flare fitting in which nut (male threads) threads into body (female).

Ion: Electrically charged atom or molecule produced by electrical field, high temperature, etc.

Ionize (Air): To convert wholly or partly, into ions. This causes air to become a conductor of electricity.

I.S.O. flare: A tubing flare that looks somewhat like a regular double-lap flare following initial belling operation. Belled end section is compressed between nut and body producing a secure seal.

J

Jab saw: A special hacksaw used for cutting in restricted areas. Consists of a handle and rigid section to secure a short section of hacksaw blade.

Jackshaft: A shaft used between two other shafts.

Jack stand: A fixed or adjustable height, metal stand placed under a raised vehicle. Prevents car from falling in event of jack failure or slippage.

Jam nut: Two nuts securely tightened against each other on a stud. A wrench can then be placed on lower nut to remove stud or top nut to install. Can also be used to prevent a nut from loosening.

Jet: Small hole or orifice used to control flow of gasoline or air in various parts of carburetor.

Joule: Meter-kilogram-second (mks) unit of energy or work equal to a force of 1 newton applied through a distance of 1 meter. Joule is the equivalent of 0.737324 foot-pounds.

Journal: Part of shaft prepared to accept a bearing. (Connecting rod, main bearing.)

Journal polishing: Removing minute sharp edges following grinding of a camshaft, crankshaft, etc., bearing journal(s). Leaves extremely smooth finish (around 7 micro inches).

Journal taper: Condition in which one end of a bearing journal is smaller in diameter than other. Difference in two readings indicates amount of taper.

Jumper cables: Two large diameter (8 gage or heavier) insulated cables with clamps. Used to temporarily connect a charged battery to a discharged one to provide extra cranking capacity. Use caution!

Jumper wire: A length of automotive wire, used for bypassing a defective circuit, testing a bulb, etc.

Jump starting: Starting a vehicle with a discharged battery by using jumper battery or vehicle with a charged battery. Batteries are connected with jumper cables. Connect in parallel. Follow safety rules!

Junction block: A connection point (block) for a number of wires. Can also contain receptacles for fuses. Generally incorporates a nonconducting base for mounting.

K

Keen-sert: A hollow type plug with internal and external threads. Used to bring a threaded, stripped hole back to a usable condition, diameter, etc.

Kerf: Name commonly given to the cut (slot) made with an oxyacetylene cutting torch.

Kerosene: Flammable hydrocarbon oil produced from distilling petroleum. Uses include fuel, lamp oil, etc.

Key: Parallel-sided piece inserted into groove cut part way into each of two parts, which prevents slippage between two parts.

Keyway: Slot cut in shaft, pulley hub, wheel hub, etc. Square key is placed in slot and engages a similar keyway in mating piece. Key prevents slippage between two parts.

Kickdown switch: electrical switch that will cause transmission, or overdrive unit, to shift down to lower gear. Often used to secure fast acceleration.

Kill switch: Special switch designed to shut off ignition in case of emergency.

Kilometer: Metric measurement equivalent to 5/8 of mile.

Kilopascals (kPa): Metric equivalent to English psi (pounds per square inch).

Kingpin: Hardened steel pin that is passed through the steering knuckle and axle end. The steering knuckle pivots about the kingpin.

Kingpin or steering axis inclination: Tipping the tops of the kingpins inward towards each other. This places the centerline of steering axis nearer centerline of tire-road contact area.

Knife file: A file which has a blade that tapers to a sharp edge on one side. End view resembles a "drawn out" triangle shape.

Knocking (Bearing): Noise created by part movement in a loose or worn bearing.

Knocking (Fuel): Condition, accompanied by audible noise, that occurs when gasoline in cylinders burns too quickly. Also referred to as detonation.

Knuckle: A part utilizing a hinge pin (kingpin, swivel pin) that allows one part to swivel around another part. An example is a steering knuckle.

Knurl: To roughen surface of piece of metal by pressing series of crosshatched lines into the surface and thereby raising area between these lines.

L

Lacquer (Paint): Fast drying automotive body paint.

Laminated: Something made up of many layers.

Land: Metal separating a series of grooves.

Lands (Ring): Piston metal between ring grooves.

Lap: One complete trip around race track or route laid out for racing.

Lap or lapping: To fit two surfaces together by coating them with abrasive and then rubbing them together.

Latent heat: Amount of heat (btu's) beyond boiling or melting point, required to change liquid to a gas, or a solid to a liquid.

Latent heat of evaporation: Amount of heat (btu's) required to change a liquid to a vapor state without elevating vapor temperature above that of the liquid.

Lateral movement: Side to side movement (wobble or runout) such as may be exhibited by side surface of a revolving flywheel, tire, pulley, etc. Movement is in a direction nearly parallel to centerline of the shaft, hub, spindle, etc., object is attached to.

Lb.: Pound.

Lead burning: Connecting two pieces of lead by melting edges together.

Leaded gasoline: Gasoline containing tetraethyl lead, an antiknock additive. It must not be used in vehicles with catalytic converters.

Lead hammer: A striking tool using a head made of lead to prevent marring object being struck.

Leaf spring: Suspension spring made up of several pieces of flat spring steel. Varying numbers of leaves (individual pieces) are used depending on intended use. One car uses single leaf in each rear spring.

Lean mixture (Fuel): Mixture with an excessive amount of air in relation to fuel.

Leakdown rate: Rate at which a gas or fluid, under pressure, escapes from container. In an engine hydraulic valve lifter, how long it takes to collapse lifter a specified distance under a specified pressure.

Left-hand thread: A thread that is cut so that fastener must be turned counterclockwise to tighten, clockwise to loosen.

Letter drills: Series of drills in which each drill size is designated by letter of alphabet—A, B, C, etc.

Lever: A rigid bar or shaft pivoting about a fixed fulcrum (shaft, pin, etc.). It is used to increase force or to transmit or change motion.

Lever bender (Tubing): A mechanical, hand operated tubing bender using a lever arm to form a smooth bend in tubing.

Leverage: Increasing force by utilizing one or more levers.

L-head engine: Engine having both valves in block and on same side of cylinder.

Lift saddle: That portion of a lift designed to engage vehicle frame, axle, etc., for lifting.

Lift strap: A strap specifically designed for engine removal. Has an adjustable, non-slip pull point attachment.

Lightened valves: Valves in which all possible metal has been ground away to reduce weight. This will allow higher rpm without valve float.

Light repair: Automotive repair work involving ignition, cooling, fuel, charging, electrical, etc., systems. Work in which parts are relatively small and easily portable.

Limited-slip differential: Differential unit designed to provide superior traction by transferring driving torque, when one wheel is spinning, to wheel that is not slipping.

Line boring: Boring a series of holes, bushings, etc., so that all are accurately aligned with a common centerline.

Linkage: Movable bars or links connecting one unit to another.

Liquid charging (Air conditioning): Charging air conditioning system with liquid refrigerant instead of refrigerant vapor.

Liquid line (Air conditioning): High-pressure liquid refrigerant line between receiver-dehydrator and expansion valve.

Liquid traction: Special liquid applied to tires of drag racers to provide superior traction.

Liquid-vapor separator: Tank which prevents liquid fuel from entering vapor line.

Liquid withdrawal (LPG): Drawing LPG from bottom of tank to insure delivery of liquid LPG. Withdrawal from top of tank will deliver LPG in the gaseous state.

Liter: Metric measurement of capacity—equivalent to 2.11 pints. Five litres equals 1.32 gallon.

Live axle: Axle upon which wheels are firmly affixed. Axle drives the wheels.

Live wire: See *Hot wire*.

Load range (Tire): Letter system (A, B, C, etc.) used to indicate specific tire load and inflation limit.

Lobe: Projection (hump-like portion) of a cam, such as on engine camshaft, that extends beyond base circle.

Locating lug (Bearing): A small projecting tab, lip, etc., on a precision insert bearing that holds it in place to prevent either insert rotation or end movement.

Locking plate: A metal plate, one section of which is affixed to part and other to a nut, capscrew, etc., to prevent fastener loosening.

"Lock Up" torque converter: A torque converter equipped with a hydraulically operated clutch that, when applied, locks impeller (pump) and turbine together, thus eliminating fluid slippage.

Lockwasher: A washer, either split or with locking tabs, placed between a fastener and part. When fastener is tightened, washer cuts into both fastener and part and prevents loosening.

Lockwasher—external: A thin, flat lockwasher with bent friction tabs around outer edge. Tabs prevent fastener loosening.

Lockwasher—internal: A thin, flat lockwasher with friction tabs around edge of hole. Tabs cut into fastener and part to prevent loosening.

Log manifold: Special intake manifold generally designed to accept four or more carburetors. Each side has bases for carburetors set on a pipe-like log area.

Long and short arm suspension: Suspension system utilizing upper and lower control arm. Upper arm is shorter than lower. This is done so as to allow wheel to deflect in a vertical direction with a minimum change in camber.

Longitudinal leaf spring: Leaf spring mounted parallel to length of car.

Louver: Ventilation slots such as sometimes found in hood of automobile.

Low brake pedal: Condition where brake pedal approaches too close to floorboard before actuating the brakes.

Low flash point: That property of a liquid that will allow vapors given off during heating to ignite spontaneously at a relatively low liquid temperature.

Low lead fuel: Gasoline containing not much more than 0.5 grams of tetraethyl lead per gallon.

Low pivot swing axle: Rear axle setup that attaches differential housing to frame via a pivot mount. Conventional type of housing and axle extend from differential to one wheel. The other side of differential is connected to other driving wheel by a housing and axle that is pivoted at a point in line with differential to frame pivot point.

Low pressure adapter (Lubrication): An adapter that is placed on a high pressure lube gun that reduces pressure to prevent universal joint seal and bearing retainer damage. Used on other low pressure applications also.

Low pressure line (Air conditioning): Low pressure refrigerant line between evaporator outlet and compressor.

Low pressure spray cleaning: Part cleaning through use of an air stream that, passing through nozzle, draws in cleaning solution. Solution then leaves nozzle in form of a spray.

Low range (Transfer case): Lower gear range in a typical two-speed (high-low) four-wheel drive transfer case. Provides more torque and less road speed.

Low side (Air conditioning): That portion of an air conditioning system that is subjected to low pressure refrigerant. Extends from expansion valve (evaporator) to suction side of compressor.

LPG: Liquefied petroleum gas.

Lubricant: Any material, usually of a petroleum nature such as grease, oil, etc., that is placed between two moving parts in an effort to reduce friction.

Lubrication: Reducing friction between parts by coating them with oil, grease, etc.

Lubrication passage: A hole, channel, groove, etc., designed to permit flow of lubricant.

Lug (Engine): To cause engine to labor by failing to shift to a lower gear when necessary.

Lumen: A measurement of light intensity.

M

Machine screw: A nontapered screw, using a standard screw thread. May utilize a round, flat, oval, fillister, hex, etc., head. Head may be formed to accept an Allen, Phillips, Fluted, Clutch, etc., wrench or driver.

Macpherson strut: Front end suspension system in which wheel assembly is attached to a long, telescopic strut. Strut permits wheels to pivot and move up and down. Strut also acts as a shock absorber.

Magnaflux: Special chemical process used to check parts for cracks.

Magnet (Permanent): Piece of magnetized steel that will attract all ferrous material. Permanent magnet does not need electricity to function and will retail its magnetism over a period of years.

Magnetic clutch (Air conditioning): Electromagnetic clutch that engages or disengages air conditioning compressor pulley.

Magnetic field: Area encompassed by magnetic lines of force surrounding either a bar magnet or electromagnet.

Magnetic pulse distributor: An electronic (no breaker points) distributor that makes and breaks coil primary circuit through means of a magnetic pickup assembly that is triggered by an armature (reluctor, trigger wheel) tooth passing close by. Induced current (pulse) triggers a transistor thus breaking the circuit.

Mags or mag wheel: Lightweight, sporty wheels made of magnesium. Term mag is often applied to aluminum, and aluminum and steel combination wheels.

Maintenance tune-up: Tune-up that includes replacing the spark plugs and air, fuel, and emissions filters.

Main bearing bore: Cylindrical hole in which precision insert crankshaft main bearings are placed.

Main bearing cap: Removable section (cap) that contains lower half of crankshaft main bearing insert.

Main bearings (Engine): Bearings supporting crankshaft in cylinder block.

Main bearing supports: Steel plate installed over main bearing caps to increase their strength for racing purposes.

Main discharge tube: Carburetor fuel passage from bowl to air horn.

Main journal gauge: A gauge designed to check crankshaft main bearing journals for size, taper, and out-of-roundness, while crank is still mounted in block.

Major diameter (Thread): Diameter of a fastener threaded area, as determined by distance from top of one thread, at right angles through center of fastener, to top of a corresponding thread.

Mandrel: Round shaft used to mount stone, cutter, saw, etc.

Manifold: Pipe or number of pipes connecting series of holes or outlets to common opening. See *Exhaust manifold* and *Intake manifold*.

Manifold absolute pressure sensor (MAP): A sensing device that determines intake manifold pressure as a factor of engine speed and load changes. Sensor sends appropriate electrical signals to an electronic control module. Control module adjusts fuel injector pulse width accordingly.

Manifold air temperature sensors (MAT): Computer sensor used to measure the temperate of the air coming into the intake manifold.

Manifold gauge set (Air conditioning): A manifold assembly containing two pressure gauges (one high, one low), two gauge valves, and three outlet connections. Used to service (discharge, charge) air conditioning system.

Manifold heat control valve: Valve placed in exhaust manifold, or in exhaust pipe, that deflects certain amount of hot gas around base of carburetor to aid in warmup.

Manometer: Instrument to measure pressure (vacuum).

Manual choke: Carburetor choke operated by hand.

Manual control valve (Transmission): Hand (linkage) operated valve which controls oil flow and transmission gear selection.

Mass airflow sensor (MAF): Computer sensor used to measure the amount of air entering the intake manifold. Also called an airflow meter.

Master cylinder: Part of hydraulic brake system in which pressure is generated.

Master rod (Radial engine): Primary or main connecting rod to which other connecting rods are attached.

Material Safety Data Sheet (MSDS): Information on a chemical or material that must be provided by the material's manufacturer. Lists potential health risks and proper handling procedures.

Mating surface: A surface upon an object that is placed in contact with a surface on another object. Can also refer to a specific area being used as a contact surface.

Matter: Substance making up physical things occupying space, having weight, and perceptible to the senses.

Maximum wear: Generally refers to greatest amount of wear (cylinders, journals, etc.) that can be tolerated before part must either be rebuilt or replaced. Can also refer to a section of a cylinder, shaft, etc., that has greatest amount of wear.

Mechanical brakes: Service brakes that are actuated by mechanical linkage connecting brakes to brake pedal.

Mechanical efficiency: Engine's rating as to how much potential horsepower is wasted through friction within moving parts of engine.

Mechanical fuel injection: A mechanically driven pump forces fuel into engine.

Mechanical fuel pump: Engine mounted pump operated by eccentric.

Mechanical lifter (Valve): A nonhydraulic valve lifter. Does not self-adjust and requires a specific clearance (tappet clearance) that must be adjusted periodically.

Mechanical puller: A nonhydraulic pulling device utilizing either a screw thread, lever, or hammer blow as a means of developing pulling pressure.

Megohm: 1,000,000 ohms.

Melting point: Temperature point at which a material changes from a solid into a liquid.

MEMA: Motor and Equipment Manufacturers' Association.

MEP: Mean Effective Pressure. Pressure of burning fuel (average) on power stroke subtracted by average pressure on other three strokes. Pressure is in pounds per square inch or kilopascals.

Mesh: To engage teeth of one gear with those of another.

Metal fatigue: Crystallizing of metal due to vibration, twisting, bending, etc. Unit will eventually break. Bending a piece of wire back and forth to break it is a good example of metal fatigue.

Metal shot: Very small, metallic balls that are projected, by means of an air blast, against an object so as to remove rust, paint, etc. May also be used for light surface peening to relieve surface tension.

Metering rod: Movable rod used to vary opening area through carburetor jet.

Metering valve (Brakes): Valve in brake line that limits fluid pressure to disc brakes. This assures that the rear (drum) brakes apply at about the same time as front (disc) brakes.

Metric size: Units made to metric system measurement.

Metric system: A decimal system of measurement based on meter (length, area, volume), liter (capacity), and gram (weight and mass).

Mica: Insulation material used between commutator segments in starter motors.

Micro: When the word "micro" precedes measurement units, such as watt, ampere, etc., it means one-millionth of that unit.

Micro inch: A linear measurement unit equivalent to one millionth of an inch. Often used in describing relative smoothness of a metal surface finish as measured in micro inches.

Microfarad: 1/1,000,000 farad.

Micrometer (Inside and outside): Precision measuring tool that will give readings accurate to within fraction of one thousandth of an inch.

Micrometer—anvil: That portion of a micrometer that is engaged by tip of spindle if micrometer is closed. It forms one area that is held in contact with work to be measured. Spindle tip forms other. Reading indicates distance between anvil and tip.

Micrometer depth gauge: A micrometer specially designed to measure hole, spline, slot, etc., depth.

Micrometer—inside: A straight-line micrometer designed to measure inside diameter of cylinders, bores, etc.

Micrometer interchangeable anvil: An anvil designed to be used on a micrometer that features measurement coverage exceeding normal 1 in. range. A single outside micrometer can be made to read objects from 0 to 6 in., for example, by merely inserting proper length anvil. Inside micrometers use interchangeable rods.

Micrometer locknut: Locking nut used to secure a setting by preventing accidental turning of thimble during handling.

Micrometer—multiple range: A single micrometer used over a wide range of measurement by either using interchangeable anvils of different lengths (outside micrometer) or interchangeable rods (inside micrometer).

Micrometer—outside: A micrometer designed to read outside diameters of pistons, journals, pins, etc.

Micrometer rachet: A small ratcheting knob on end of micrometer thimble. Operator may use knob to tighten spindle on workpiece. Upon reaching a predetermined pressure (torque), knob ratchet will slip. Provides even thimble tensioning for each setting.

Micrometer sleeve long line: Reference line drawn length of sleeve. Forms edge line for sleeve numbers and reference line for thimble marks.

Micrometer sleeve numbers: Division line numbers along sleeve long line. Numbers indicate each .100 in. of spindle travel—from .000 to 1.000 in.

Micrometer spindle (outside micrometer): Sliding rod portion that is moved either in or out by rotating thimble. Workpiece is positioned between anvil and spindle tip.

Micrometer thimble: Knurled handle portion of micrometer that is turned to adjust micrometer to workpiece.

Micrometer vernier scale: An additional set of longitudinal scale lines drawn on sleeve. Used in conjunction with thimble edge marks, these vernier lines enable operator to make readings accurate to .0001 in. (one ten thousandth).

MIG: A metal inert gas welding procedure in which inert gas is used to shield weld metal from atmosphere.

Mike: Either refers to micrometer or to using micrometer to measure an object.

Mill: Often used to refer to engine.
    To remove metal through use of rotating toothed cutter.

Mill file: A general purpose single-cut, flat file available in different lengths and cuts.

Millimeter: Metric measurement equivalent to .039370 of an inch.

Milling machine: Machine that uses variety of rotating cutter wheels to cut splines, gears, keyways, etc.

Miniature fuse: A very compact, plug-in type fuse. Uses two prongs connected by a wire-like element designed to melt when circuit loading exceeds a specified level (amperage).

Minimum wear: Can be used to indicate a small amount of wear that leaves part in serviceable condition. Can also be used to indicate, for example, that portion of a shaft, bore, etc., showing least amount of dimensional change from wear.

Minor diameter (Thread): Diameter as determined by measuring from bottom of one thread "V", at right angles through the center of fastener, to bottom of "V" of the corresponding thread.

Misfire: Fuel charge in one or more engine cylinders which fails to fire or ignite at proper time.

Mixing handle (Gas welding): Handle, of an oxyacetylene welding torch, that contains both an acetylene and an oxygen control valve. Valves adjust flow and mixing occurs in handle area.

Modulator (Transmission): Pressure control or adjusting valve used in hydraulic system of automatic transmission.

Mold: Hollow unit into which molten metal is poured to form a casting.

Molecule: Smallest portion that matter may be divided into and still retain all properties of original matter.

Monoblock: All cylinders cast as one unit.

Monolithic substrate (Catalytic converter): A ceramic honeycomb mass, surface areas of which can be treated with platinum, palladium, and rhodium. Used in one type of catalytic converter.

Motor: Electrically driven power unit (electric motor). Term is often incorrectly applied to internal combustion engine.

Motor (Generator): Attaching generator to battery in such a way it revolves like an electric motor.

Mounting bullet (Seal): A thin, smooth, round nose cap placed over nose of a shaft so that it may be passed through a seal without damage to seal lip.

Movable pole shoe starter: A starter (cranking motor) design with a movable pole shoe attached, through linkage, to starter drive pinion assembly. When starter is energized, magnetic field forces movable shoe to actuate linkage, thus engaging starter drive pinion.

MPH: Miles per hour.

Muffler (Air conditioning): Device which reduces pumping noise and vibration in system.

Muffler (Exhaust): Unit through which exhaust gases are passed to quiet sounds of running engine.

Multiport injection: Fuel injection system in which there is one injector per cylinder.

Multiple disc clutch: Clutch utilizing several clutch discs in its construction.

Multiple link chain: Drive chain employing, in addition to outside links, additional inner links. Permits use of a wide chain for great strength and good wear characteristics.

Multiple-ply hose: A hose using two or more layers or reinforcing fabric.

Multiple row bearing: A bearing containing two or more rows of balls, rollers, or needles.

Multi-viscosity oils: Oils meeting SAE requirements for both low temperature requirements of light oil and high temperature requirements of heavy oil. Example: (SAE 10W-30).

Mushroom valve lifter: A valve lifter in which bottom is wider (a collar-like section) than main body that rides in lifter guide. Mushroom lifter requires removal of camshaft to withdraw lifter.

Mutual induction: Creating voltage in one coil by altering current in another nearby coil.

MVMA: Motor Vehicle Manufacturers Association.

N

NADA: National Automobile Dealers' Association.

NATTS: National Association of Trade and Technical Schools.

NBFU: National Board of Fire Underwriters.

NC threads: National Coarse thread sizes.

Needle Bearing (Antifriction): Roller type bearing in which rollers have very narrow diameter in relation to their length.

Needle nose fitting (Lubrication): A grease fitting, such as used in some universal joints, that requires use of a needle nose (thin, pointed) tip on grease gun.

Needle valve: Valve with long, thin, tapered point that operates in small hole or jet. Hole size is changed by moving needle valve in or out.

NF threads: National Fine thread sizes.

Negative spread (Bearing): A two-piece insert bearing with diameter across outside of parting edges slightly smaller than bearing bore diameter. When inserted in the cap, insert will touch bottom but sides at parting edges will have some clearance.

Negative terminal: Terminal (such as on battery) from which current flows on its path to positive terminal.

Neoprene: Synthetic rubber. Highly resistant to oils, grease, ozone, etc.

Neutral flame: An oxyacetylene flame in which proportion of acetylene and oxygen are such that flame is neither reducing (carburizing—excess acetylene) nor oxidizing (excess oxygen).

Neutralize: To stop or destroy some force or chemical action, such as by applying baking soda solution to stop action of battery acid.

Neutral safety switch: A switch that opens (disconnects) starter circuit when transmission is in gear.

Neutron: Neutral charge particle forming part of an atom.

Newton-metres: A unit of force, as used in metric system, to indicate torque.

Newton's law: For every action there is an equal and opposite reaction.

NHRA: National Hot Rod Association.

NHTSA: National Highway Traffic Safety Administration.

NIASE (ASE): National Institute for Automotive Service Excellence.

Nitrogen oxides: In combustion process, nitrogen from air combines with oxygen to form nitrogen oxides.

NLGI: National Lubricating Grease Institute.

Nonferrous metals: All metals containing no iron—except in very minute quantities.

Nonflammable: A substance that will not burn.

Nonhardening sealant: A sealant, that when fully cured, remains in a soft, pliable state.

Nonhunting gearset (Differential): A ring and pinion gearset in which same teeth on ring and pinion do not mesh on a regular basis every so many revolutions. Brought about by using uneven ratios such as 3.21 to 1, 4.11 to 1, etc. Nonhunting feature improves wear characteristics.

Nonreinforced hose: Hose that uses no wires, fabric, etc., to strengthen it.

Nonseparable bearing: An antifriction bearing that cannot be taken apart.

Non-serviceable: A part or device whose design and construction does not permit rebuilding. Can also be used to indicate a part of device that is no longer fit for use.

Nonservo brake: A brake design in which each shoe (primary and secondary) works independently and as such, neither one assists in application of other.

Normalizing regulator: Process of operating charging system for a specified period of time to bring regulator up to normal operating temperature.

North pole (Magnet): Magnetic pole from which lines of force emanate; travel is from north to south pole.

Nozzle: Opening through which fuel mixture is directed into carburetor air stream.

NSC: National Safety Council.

Number drills: Series of drills in which each size is designated by number (0-80).

Nut—castle: A nut with slots out through a reduced size top section. Slots accept cotter pins. Looks like a "castle."

Nut—hex: Six sided (hexagonal) nut.

Nut—pal: Thin, stamped nut that is turned tightly against regular nut to prevent loosening.

Nut—slotted: A hexagonal nut with slots cut through top section to accept cotter pins.

Nut—speed: A thin, flat spring steel nut used for rapid fastener installation where great strength is not required.

Nut—wing: A nut with two wing-like projections to permit turning with fingers. Also called "thumb nut."

Nylon: A synthetic thermoplastic made up of long-chain polymeric amide molecules.

O

Octane rating: Rating that indicates a specific gasoline's ability to resist detonation.

OD: Outside diameter.

Odometer: Device used to measure and register number of miles traveled by car.

OEM: Original Equipment Manufacturer.

Off-road vehicle: Vehicle designed to operate in rough country (hills, sand, mud, etc.) without benefit of regular roads.

Offset dowel pin: A locating steel dowel pin in which around one-half of cylindrical body is offset somewhat from other. Following insertion in, for example, the rear face of block, they can be turned either direction to correct clutch housing bore to crankshaft misalignment. Fasteners are then tightened.

Ohm: Unit of measurement used to indicate amount of resistance to flow of electricity in a given circuit.

Ohmmeter: Instrument used to measure amount of resistance in given unit or circuit. (In ohms.)

Ohm's law: Formula for calculating electrical values in a circuit.

Oil baffle: A thin plate or diaphragm (often steel) arranged to restrict, direct, control, etc., oil movement from one area to another. Often used in oil pan sump to prevent oil slosh and pump starvation during engine steep angle operation.

Oil bath air cleaner: Air cleaner that utilizes a pool of oil to insure removal of impurities from air entering carburetor.

Oil burner: Engine that consumes an excessive quantity of oil.

Oil classification CA, CB, CC, CD, CE: Classification for oil designed for use in diesel engines.

Oil classification SA, SB, SC, SD, SE, SF, SG, SH: Classification for oil designed for use in automotive gasoline engines.

Oil clearance (Bearing): Amount of operating clearance (between bearing and journal) needed to provide proper lubricating oil circulation.

Oil—combination splash and pressure system: Engine oiling system that uses both pressure and splash oiling to accomplish proper lubrication.

Oil control ring (Piston): A piston ring designed to prevent excessive oil consumption by scraping excess oil from cylinder. Usually lower (furthest down in cylinder) ring or rings.

Oil cooler: Device used to remove excess heat from engine and/or transmission oil. Can be air or water cooled design.

Oil dipstick: See Dipstick.

Oil filter: Device used to strain oil in engine thus removing abrasive particles.

Oil—full pressure system: Engine oiling system that forces oil, under pressure, to moving parts of engine.

Oil gallery: Pipe or drilled passageway in engine used to carry engine oil from one area to another.

Oil gauge: A dash mounted device that indicates engine oil pressure in pounds per square inch (psi) or kilopascals (kPa). Can be of electrical or Bourdon tube design.

Oil nozzle: A short section of pipe or nozzle used to direct a stream of oil against some moving part such as timing chain, gear, etc.

Oil pan: See *Pan*.

Oil pickup: Connects to oil pump and extends into bottom of oil pan. Oil is drawn through pickup into pump.

Oilproof paper: A special paper used to wrap greased antifriction bearings for long term storage. Prevents leaching of lube from bearings.

Oil pump: Device used to force oil, under pressure, to various parts of the engine. It is driven by gear on camshaft.

Oil pumping: Condition wherein an excessive quantity of oil passes piston rings and is consumed in combustion chamber.

Oil ring: Normally bottom piston ring which scrapes excess oil off cylinder wall.

Oil seal: Device used to prevent oil leakage past certain area.

Oil seal—double lip: An oil seal employing two sealing lips for added control.

Oil seal—garter spring: Continuous spring that maintains seal lip pressure against shaft.

Oil seal—single lip: An oil seal employing one seal lip.

Oil slinger: Device attached to revolving shaft so any oil passing that point will be thrown outward where it will return to point of origin.

Oil soaked (Clutch, brakes): A condition in which friction surfaces, as used in dry clutches, brake lining, etc., become contaminated with oil. Discard such linings!

Oil—splash system: Engine oiling system that depends on connecting rods to dip into oil troughs and splash oil to all moving parts.

Oil strainer (Engine): A fine wire mesh screen through which oil entering oil pump is drawn. It will remove larger particles of dirt or other abrasives.

Oil sump: That portion of oil pan that holds supply of engine oil.

One-way clutch: Locks shaft in one direction and allows rotation in other.

Open circuit: Circuit in which a wire is broken or disconnected.

Open circuit voltage (Battery): Cell voltage when battery has no completed circuit across posts and is not receiving or delivering energy.

Open windings (Electrical): A winding circuit that has been broken, thus stopping current flow.

Organic flux (Soldering): A soldering flux somewhat less corrosive than acid flux. Should never be used for electrical connections—always use rosin or resin flux!

Orifice: A small hole or restricted opening used to control flow of gasoline, air, oil, etc.

Orifice tube expansion valve (Air conditioning): A form of air conditioning system expansion valve that utilizes a fixed orifice (hole) to control flow rate of refrigerant to evaporator. Compressor clutch is cycled on and off to start and stop refrigerant flow.

O-ring: A round ring, often of neoprene, that is used as a seal.

O-ring connector (Tubing): A tubing fitting that uses an O-ring to produce a seal between tubing and fitting.

Oscillating action: Swinging action such as that in pendulum of a clock.

Oscillating piston pin: A piston pin secured to rod and thus forced to oscillate (rotate back and forth) in piston.

Oscilloscope: Testing unit which projects visual reproduction of the ignition system spark action onto screen of cathode-ray tube.

Otto cycle: Four-stroke cycle consisting of intake, compression, firing, and exhaust strokes.

Out-of-round: A piston, shaft, journal, etc., in which diameter is greater in one direction than another, thus forming an egg shape.

Output shaft: Shaft delivering power from within mechanism. Shaft leaving transmission, attached to propeller shaft, is transmission output shaft.

Outside Caliper: An instrument used to check outside diameter of an object. Caliper leg tips are carefully adjusted to workpiece then removed. Distance between tips is measured with a steel rule.

Outside Diameter: Diameter of a cylinder, circle, etc., as measured in a straight line from outside surface on one side, through center, to outside surface on other side.

Overcenter adjustment (Steering gear): Adjustment between pitman shaft gear sector teeth and ball nut teeth in straight ahead (center) position. Adjustment made by testing torque required to turn wormshaft from one side of straight ahead position, through straight ahead position (overcenter) on other side.

Overdrive: Unit utilizing planetary gearset so actuated as to turn drive shaft about one-third faster than transmission output shaft.

Overdrive stages: Locked-out; direct, freewheeling; and overdrive.

Overdrive transmission: A transmission in which highest gear utilizes a ratio that drives output shaft faster than input, thus allowing reduced engine rpm.

Overhead camshaft: Camshaft mounted above the head, driven by long timing chain or belt.

Overhead valves: Valves located in head.

Overheating: A condition in which any part, fluid, system, etc., has attained a temperature considered excessive.

Overplate (Friction bearing): A very thin layer, such as a tin-lead mix, applied over another layer of different material on a precision insert bearing.

Overrunning clutch: Clutch mechanism that will drive in one direction only. If torque is removed or reversed, clutch slips.

Overrunning clutch starter drive: Starter drive that is mechanically engaged. When engine starts, overrunning clutch operates until drive is mechanically disengaged.

Oversize bore (Engine cylinder): A cylinder that has been bored out to a size that is larger than normal. Requires appropriate oversize piston.

Oversize pin: A piston pin that is larger in diameter than one of standard size. Used to compensate for pin boss, rod, or bushing wear.

Oversize valve stem: An engine valve with a stem that is larger in diameter than one of standard size. Used to compensate for valve guide wear.

Oversquare engine: Engine in which bore diameter is larger than length of stroke.

Oversteer: Tendency for car, when negotiating a corner, to turn more sharply than driver intends.

Oxidation: Surface of a material, such as steel, combining with oxygen in air, thus forming a very thin layer of oxide.

Oxides of nitrogen (NO_x): Undesirable exhaust emission, especially prevalent when combustion chamber flame temperatures are high.

Oxidize (Metal): Action where surface of object is combined with oxygen in air to produce rust, scale, etc.

Oxidizing flame: Welding torch flame with an excess of oxygen. Free or unburned oxygen tends to burn molten metal.

Oxyacetylene welding: Welding in which required heat is produced by a torch burning a mixture of oxygen and acetylene.

Oxygen: Gas, used in welding, made up of colorless, tasteless, odorless, gaseous element oxygen found in atmosphere.

Oxygen sensor (Emission control): A oxygen sensitive sensor placed in engine exhaust stream. Electrical signals, varying with oxygen content of exhaust, are sent from sensor to electronic control module. Using these signals, along with others, control unit can adjust carburetor air-fuel mix, ignition timing, etc.

P

Pads (Brake): Another term for disc brake "shoe and lining" assembly.

Palladium: Rare metallic element (Pd) often used as a catalyst coating in catalytic converters.

Pan: Thin stamped cover bolted to bottom of crankcase, forms a sump for engine oil and keeps dirt, etc., from entering engine.

Pancake engine: Engine in which cylinders are on a horizontal plane. This reduces overall height and enables them to be used in spots where vertical height is restricted.

Paper air cleaner: Air cleaner that makes use of special paper through which air to carburetor is drawn.

Parabolic reflector: A light reflector (concave mirror) that emits parallel light rays. Bulb filament must be located at focal point of parabola.

Parallel circuit: Electrical circuit with two or more resistance units so wired as to permit current to flow through both units at same time. Unlike series circuit, current in parallel circuit does not have to pass through one unit to reach the other.

Parallelogram steering linkage: Steering system utilizing two short tie rods connected to steering arms and to a long center link. The link is supported on one end on an idler arm and the other end is attached directly to pitman arm. Arrangement forms a parallelogram shape.

Parasitic load: Normal electrical load from the ECU, radio, and other electrical components placed on a vehicle's battery when the engine is not operating.

Parking brake: Hand operated brake which prevents vehicle movement while parked by locking rear wheels, or transmission output shaft.

Parking lights: Small lights on sides, front, and rear of vehicle. Usually red or amber color in rear and amber in front. Used so that vehicle will be more visible during dark hours. Lights are turned on whenever headlight switch is operated.

Parking pawl: A plunger or toothed segment that engages a notched gear to lock up (Prevent rotation) transmission output shaft when placed in "park." Prevents car from rolling when automatic transmission is in park.

Particulates (Lead): Tiny particles of lead found in engine exhaust emissions when leaded fuel is used.

Parting edge (Bearing): That edge or surface that forms a juncture (connecting line) between upper and lower halves of a friction bearing.

Parting surface: Surface forming a juncture (connecting point) between two parts. When two parts are disassembled, they will separate at parting surfaces.

Parts washer: A device (spray, soak, etc.) used to clean parts.

Part-time four-wheel drive: A four-wheel drive system that can be operated in either a two-wheel or four-wheel drive mode. This setup cannot be operated in four-wheel drive on dry, hard surfaced roads.

Part-time transfer case: Four-wheel drive transfer case that permits either four-wheel or two-wheel drive.

Pascal's law: "When pressure is exerted on confined liquid, it is transmitted undiminished."

Paste state: That state in which a material, such as solder, is neither solid or liquid but is soft and plastic-like.

Pawl: Stud or pin that can be moved or pivoted into engagement with teeth cut on another part—such as parking pawl on automatic transmission that can be slid into contact with teeth on another part to lock rear wheels.

Payload: Amount of weight that may be carried by vehicle. Computed by subtracting vehicle curb weight from GVW.

PCV (Positive Crankcase Ventilation): System which prevents crankcase vapors from being discharged directly into atmosphere.

Pedal "free travel": Distance that a fully released brake or clutch pedal can be readily depressed before linkage actuates either master cylinder or clutch release fingers. Free travel insures that brake or clutch is fully released.

Pedestal grinder: A grinder mounted atop a somewhat slender column to place grinder at a convenient working height.

Peen: To flatten out end of a rivet, etc., by pounding with round end of a hammer.

Penetrating oil: Special oil used to free rusted parts so they can be removed.

Periphery: Outside edge or circumference.

Permanent magnet: Magnet capable of retaining its magnetic properties over very long period of time.

Petrol: Gasoline.

Petroleum: Raw material from which gasoline, kerosene, lube oils, etc., are made. Consists of hydrogen and carbon.

Phillips head screw: Screw having a fairly deep cross slot instead of single slot as used in conventional screws.

Phosgene gas: A very toxic (poisonous) gas. Can be formed when refrigerant is exposed to an open flame.

Phosphate coating: A thin coating of phosphate applied to surface of metal. Sometimes applied to camshafts to aid in proper break-in. Often applied to other metallic surfaces to prevent corrosion.

Phosphor-bronze: Bearing material composed of tin, lead, and copper.

Photochemical: Relates to branch of chemistry where radiant energy (sunlight) produces various chemical changes.

Photochemical smog: Fog-like condition produced by sunlight acting upon hydrocarbon and carbon monoxide exhaust emissions in atmosphere.

Pickup (Oil): Screened unit that either floats on, or is submerged in, engine oil sump oil. Oil for pump enters through pickup.

Pickup (Vehicle): A light duty (1/2, 3/4, 1 ton) open bed truck.

Pickup coil: Device in electronic type distributor which senses engine speed (distributor rotation) and sends electrical pulses to control unit.

Piezoelectric ignition: System of ignition that employs use of small section of ceramic-like material. When this material is compressed, even a very tiny amount, it emits a high voltage that will fire plugs. This system does not need a coil, points, or condenser.

Pilot bearing (Clutch): A small bearing (either antifriction or bushing type) located in center of flywheel or crankshaft end. Bearing aligns and supports flywheel end of clutch shaft (transmission input shaft).

Pilot operated absolute (POA): A modified form of a suction throttling valve. Used in air conditioning system to control evaporator pressure so as to allow low evaporator temperatures without freezing (icing).

Pilot shaft: Dummy shaft placed in a mechanism as a means of aligning parts. It is then removed and regular shaft installed.

Pin boss: That section of engine piston that aligns and supports piston (wrist) pin.

Pin fitting: Process involved in honing piston or rod pin bores until a correct pin fit is attained.

Pinging: Metallic rattling sound produced by the engine during heavy acceleration when ignition timing is too far advanced for grade of fuel being burned.

Pinion carrier: Part of rear axle assembly that supports and contains pinion gear shaft.

Pinion (Gear): Small gear either driven by or driving a larger gear.

Pinion flange (Differential): Unit (flange) splined to outer end of differential pinion gear shaft. Used as an attaching point for propeller shaft universal joint.

Pinion shaft (Differential): Shaft that supports, aligns, and drives differential pinion gear.

Pin knock: Sound (sharp, double-knock) produced by excessively worn piston pins and/or bearings.

Pin punch: A punch with a long, narrow, nontapered nose. Used to drive pins from their holes.

Pintle: A round pin about which some part pivots.

Pintle valve (EGR valve): Diaphragm controlled valve used to control flow of exhaust gas through exhaust gas recirculation valve.

Pipes: Exhaust system pipes.

Piston: Round plug, open at one end, that slides up and down in cylinder. It is attached to connecting rod and when fuel charge is fired, will transfer force of explosion to connecting rod then to crankshaft.

Piston boss: Built-up area around piston pin hole.

Piston collapse: Reduction in diameter of piston skirt caused by heat and constant impact stresses.

Piston displacement: Amount (volume) of air displaced by piston when moved through full length of its stroke.

Piston expansion: Increase in diameter of piston due to normal piston heating.

Piston head: Portion of piston above top ring.

Piston lands: Portion of piston between ring grooves.

Piston pin or wrist pin: Steel pin that is passed through piston. Used as base upon which to fasten upper end of connecting rod. It is round and is usually hollow.

Piston ring: Split ring installed in a groove in piston. Ring contacts sides of ring groove and also rubs against cylinder wall thus sealing space between piston and wall.

Piston ring (Compression): Ring designed to seal burning fuel charge above piston. Generally there are two compression rings per piston and they are located in two top ring grooves.

Piston ring (Oil control): Piston ring designed to scrape oil from cylinder wall. Ring is of such design as to allow oil to pass through ring and then through holes or slots in groove. In this way oil is returned to pan. There are many shapes and special designs used on oil control rings.

Piston ring end gap: Distance left between ends of the ring when installed in cylinder.

Piston ring expander: See *Ring expander.*

Piston ring groove: Slots or grooves cut in piston head to receive piston rings.

Piston ring side clearance: Space between sides of ring and ring lands.

Piston skirt: Portion of piston below rings. (Some engines have an oil ring in skirt area.)

Piston skirt expander: Spring device placed inside piston skirt to produce an outward pressure which increases diameter of skirt.

Piston skirt expanding: Enlarging diameter of piston skirt by inserting an expander, by knurling outer skirt surface, or by peening inside of piston.

Piston slap: Slamming side to side (tipping) movement of piston when piston-to-cylinder clearance is excessive. Can produce a very audible hollow, clattering sound.

Piston thrust pressure: Pressure applied to cylinder wall by one side of piston. During compression stroke, piston is thrust against one side of cylinder and during firing stroke, against other.

Pitch (Thread): Distance from center of one screw thread to center of adjacent (next to) thread. Pitch determines number of threads per inch.

Pitman arm: Short lever arm splined to steering gear cross shaft. Pitman arm transmits steering force from cross shaft to steering linkage system.

Pitman shaft (Steering): Steering gearbox shaft upon which pitman arm is attached.

Pits: Area at a race track for fueling, tire changing, making mechanical repairs, etc.

Pit stop: A stop at the pits by racer, for fuel, tires, repairs, etc.

Pivot: Pin or shaft about which a part moves.

Planet carrier: Part of a planetary gearset upon which planet gears are affixed. Planet gears are free to turn on hardened pins set into carrier.

Planet gears: Gears in planetary gearset that are in mesh with both ring and sun gear. Referred to as planet gears in that they orbit or move around central or sun gear.

Planetary gearset: Gearing unit consisting of ring gear with internal teeth, sun or central pinion gear with external teeth, and series of planet gears that are meshed with both the ring and the sun gear.

Plastic range: Temperature range over which a material, such as solder, remains in plastic state (soft, not liquid or solid).

Plastigage: A soft plastic, in wire form, used to measure bearing clearance.

Plates (Battery): Thin sections of lead peroxide or porous lead. There are two kinds of plates—positive and negative. The plates are arranged in groups, in an alternate fashion, called elements. They are completely submerged in the electrolyte.

Platinum: Precious metal sometimes used in the construction of breaker points. It conducts well and is highly resistant to burning.

Play: Movement between two parts.

Plexiglas: Trade name for an acrylic plastic, made by the Rhom and Haas Co.

Pliers: A tool with two pincer-like handles pivoted together, with various shaped jaws. Used for cutting, grasping, bending, etc.

Pliers—chain nose: Pliers with short tapered jaws.

Pliers—diagonal: Pliers with full length cutting jaws. Used to cut wires, cotter pins, etc.

Pliers—electrician: Pliers with jaws that provide a flat gripping surface on front area along with a short cutting section on one side. Widely used by electricians.

Pliers—ignition: Very small pliers designed for use on ignition distributors.

Pliers—needle nose: Pliers with rounded, long, thin, tapered jaws designed for use in close quarters.

Pliers—rib joint: Pliers with a series of interlocking ribs that allow pliers to be adjusted over a very wide working range.

Pliers—slip joint: Pliers in which pivot pin can be moved (slipped) from one of two holes to other to provide two distinct working ranges (amount of jaw opening).

Pliers—vise grip: Pliers that can be adjusted so that when handles are squeezed together, a special over-center arrangement allows jaws to exert extremely heavy pressure. Continued handle closing allows handles to move overcenter, thus locking themselves into position while maintaining pressure.

Plies (Tire): Layers of rubber impregnated fabric that make up carcass or body of tire.

Plug gapping: Adjusting side electrode on spark plug to provide proper air gap between it and the center electrode.

Plug weld: A welding technique in which one steel plate, containing one or more holes, is placed in contact with another. They then are joined by applying weld metal in holes, thus fusing both parts together.

Ply rating (Tires): Indication of tire strength (load carrying capacity). Does not necessarily indicate actual number of plies. Two-ply four-ply rating tire would have load capacity of a four-ply tire of same size but would have only two actual plies.

P-metric (Tire): Tire size designation based on international standards. Example: P 155/80R13. P = passenger car use. 155 = section width in millimeters. 80 = height to width ratio. R = radial construction. 13 = wheel rim diameter in inches.

Pneumatic: Pertaining to air. Operated by air pressure.

Pocket tape: A flexible, retracting measuring tape, available in different lengths, designed to be carried in pocket.

Polarity (Battery terminals): Indicates if the battery terminal (either one) is positive or negative (plus or minus) (+ or −).

Polarity (Generator): Indicates if pole shoes are so magnetized as to make current flow in a direction compatible with direction of flow as set by battery.

Polarity (Magnet): Indicates if end of a magnet is north or south pole (N or S).

Polarizing (Generator): Process of sending quick surge of current through field windings of generator in direction that will cause pole shoes to assume correct polarity. This will insure that the generator will cause current to flow in same direction as normal.

Pole (Magnet): One end, either north or south, of a magnet.

Pole shoes: Metal pieces about which field coil windings are placed. When current passes through windings, pole shoes become powerful magnets. Example: pole shoes in a generator or starter motor.

Polyalkylene glycol (PAG): Oil used in air conditioning systems that have R-134a as a refrigerant.

Polyethylene: Thermoplastic resin. Used for its flexible, tough, oil resistant and insulation properties as wire insulation, tubing, etc.

Pony car: Small, sporty car along the lines of the Mustang, Firebird, Camaro, etc.

Poppet: A spring-loaded ball engaging one or more indentations. Used to hold one object in position in relation to another.

Poppet valve: Valve used to open and close valve port to engine cylinders.

Porcelain (Spark plug): Material used to insulate center electrode of spark plug. It is hard and resistant to damage by heat.

Porosity: Small air or gas pockets, or voids, in metal.

Porous bronze: A material made by compressing tiny particles of bronze, under extremely high pressure, until they form a rigid but porous (full of holes) mass. Useful as a filter, oil retaining bushing, etc.

Port: Openings in engine cylinder blocks for exhaust and intake valves and water connections.

To smooth out, align, and somewhat enlarge intake passageway to the valves.

Portable crane: A hydraulic, electric, or manual lifting device equipped with wheels to facilitate moving about.

Portable steam cleaner: A relatively small steam cleaner equipped with wheels for easy portability.

"Ported" spark advance: A distributor vacuum advance unit connected to a hole or "port" located a specified distance above carburetor throttle valve when in closed position. As throttle is opened, port will be uncovered and vacuum applied to advance unit.

Positive terminal: Terminal (such as on battery), to which current flows.

Post (Battery): Round, tapered lead posts protruding above top of battery to which battery cables are attached.

Potential: An indication of amount of available energy.

Potentiometer: Variable resistor with three connections. One connection (called wiper) slides along resistive unit. Can be used as a voltage divider.

Pour point: Lowest temperature at which fluid will flow under specified conditions.

Power: Time rate at which energy is converted into work.

Power booster (Brakes): Engine vacuum or power steering fluid operated device on fire wall which increases brake pedal force on master cylinder during stops.

Power brakes: A brake system in which a vacuum or hydraulic booster is used to greatly multiply foot pressure to master cylinder.

Power drill: An electric or pneumatic tool designed to hold and rotate twist drills. Can also be used for wire brushing, polishing, etc., operations with correct accessories.

Power plant (Auto): The vehicle engine.

Power steering: Steering system utilizing hydraulic pressure to increase the driver's turning effort. Pressure is utilized either in gearbox itself or in hydraulic cylinder attached to steering linkage.

Power steering pump: Belt driven pump which produces pressure for power steering system.

Power or firing stroke: Portion of piston's movement that transmits power of burning fuel mixture to crankshaft.

Powertrain control module (PCM): Computer that controls the operation of the engine and transmission/transaxle shift points.

PPM (Parts-Per-Million): Term used in determining extent of pollution existing in given sample of air.

Practical efficiency: Amount of horsepower delivered to drive wheels.

Precision insert bearing: Very accurately made replaceable type of bearing. It consists of an upper and lower shell. The shells are made of steel to which a friction type bearing material has been bonded. Connecting rod and main bearings are generally of precision insert type.

Preheat flame (Cutting torch): Ring of small flames emitted at tip of an oxy-acetylene cutting torch. They are used to heat metal to a red heat so as to facilitate cutting with a central jet of oxygen.

Preheating: Application of some heat prior to later application of more heat. Cast iron is preheated to avoid cracking when welding process is started. A coil (ignition) is preheated prior to testing.

Preheating (Metal): Process of raising temperature of metal to specific level before starting subsequent operations such as welding, brazing, etc.

Preignition: Fuel charge being ignited before proper time.

Preloading: Adjusting antifriction bearing so it is under mild pressure. This prevents bearing looseness under a driving stress.

Prelubricator (Engine): A pressurized, oil-filled tank used to force lubricating oil through engine lubrication system prior to actually starting engine. Lubes all bearings and prevents possible delay in pressure buildup following first starting of a rebuilt engine.

Press-fit: Condition of fit (contact) between two parts that requires pressure to force parts together. Also referred to as drive or force fit.

Pressure bleeder: Device that forces brake fluid, under pressure, into master cylinder so that by opening bleeder screws at wheel cylinders, all air will be removed from brake system.

Pressure cap: Special cap for radiator. It holds a predetermined amount of pressure on water in cooling system. This enables water to run hotter without boiling.

Pressure differential switch: Hydraulic switch in brake system that operates brake warning light in dashboard.

Pressure plate (Clutch): Circular plate, driven by flywheel, that forces clutch disc friction surface tightly against flywheel. When clutch is disengaged, pressure plate releases clutch disc.

Pressure regulator valve (Fuel system): A valve, used in some gasoline injection systems, that maintains a predetermined level or pressure on fuel passing to fuel injectors.

Pressure relief valve: Valve designed to open at specific pressure. This will prevent pressures in system from exceeding certain limits.

Pressure tester (Cooling): A hand operated air pump used to pressurize cooling system to check for leaks. Can also be used to check pressure cap for proper opening pressure and sealing leaks.

Prestart pressurization (Engine): See Prelubricator.

Prick punch: A sharp, pointed steel punch used to place a small dot-like mark on a part. Has a sharper point (less included angle) than a center punch.

Primary circuit (Ignition system): Low voltage (6 or 12 volt) part of ignition system.

Primary, forward, or leading brake shoe: Brake shoe installed facing front of car. It will be a self-energizing shoe.

Primary winding (Coil): Low voltage (6 or 12 volt) winding in ignition coil. The primary winding is heavy wire; secondary winding uses fine wire.

Primary wires: Wiring which serves low voltage part of ignition system. Wiring from battery to switch, resistor, coil, distributor points.

Printed circuit: Electrical circuit made by connecting units with electrically conductive lines printed on a panel. This eliminates actual wire and task of connecting it.

Probe (Mechanical): A thin, long necked tool that is often expandable. Used to reach into relatively inaccessible areas. May utilize a magnet or movable fingers for part insertion or removal or a mirror for viewing blind areas.

Progressive linkage: Carburetor linkage designed to open throttle valves of multiple carburetors. It opens one to start and when certain opening point is reached, it will start to open others.

Prony brake: Device utilizing friction brake to measure horsepower output of engine.

Propane (LPG): Petroleum product, similar to and often mixed with butane, useful as engine fuel. May be referred to as LP-Gas.

Propeller shaft: Shaft connecting transmission output shaft to differential pinion shaft.

Proportioning valve (Brakes): Valve in brake line which keeps rear wheels from locking up during rapid stops.

Proton: Positive charge particle, part of atom.

Prussion blue: A deep blue pigment (dye) mixed with a grease-like carrier. By spreading a thin film on one part and then placing other part firmly in position, then removing, it is possible to check contact surfaces for high and low spots.

PSI: Pounds per square inch.

PTO: Power take off. A spot or place on transmission or transfer case from which an operating shaft from another unit (such as a winch) can be driven. Usually consists of a removable plate that exposes a drive gear.

Puddle (Welding): Area of base metal that is brought to molten state by electric arc or by oxyacetylene flame. Where required, filler rod is melted into puddle.

Puller bar: A rigid steel bar to which puller arms or jaws are attached. Bar allows different positioning of jaws to provide wide range of adjustment.

Puller strap (Engine): A length of cable or chain with attachment device at each end, used to pull (raise) engines.

Pull it down (Engine): Term often used in reference to dismantling and overhauling an engine.

Pull point (Engines): When lifting engines, that point, in relation to static balance, at which lifting hook is attached to puller strap or bar. Pull point must be secure and located to keep engine properly balanced and at correct angle while lifting.

Pulsation damper: Device to smooth out fuel pulsations or surges from pump to carburetor.

Pulse air injection: Emission control system which feeds air into exhaust gases by using pressure pulsations of exhaust system.

Pulse width: Often used to describe length of time a fuel injector is held open. Pulse being electric current applied to the injector winding and width being length of time current is allowed to flow. The wider the pulse, the more fuel delivered.

Pulsed fuel injection: Fuel system in which injectors are only open for a short period and remain closed the rest of the time. The amount of fuel delivered is controlled by how long the injector is open.

Pump: A device designed to cause movement of water, fuel, air, etc., from one area to another.

Pump diaphragm (Fuel pump): A thin layer of flexible material (often neoprene coated fabric) stretched over a sealed compartment containing an inlet and an outlet check valve. By flexing diaphragm up and down, a pumping action is obtained.

Pumping the gas pedal: Forcing accelerator up and down in an endeavor to provide extra gasoline to cylinders. This is often cause of flooding.

Purge: Removing impurities from system. See Bleeding.

Push rod: Rod that connects valve lifter to rocker arm. Used on valve-in-head installations.

Push rod runout (Valve train): A measurement of amount of bend present in push rod. By placing each end in a V-block and then rotating with a dial indicator contacting the center area, exact amount of runout is determined.

Push rod seat (Valve train): That portion of both valve lifter and rocker arm engaged by their respective ends of push rod.

Pylon: Marker for controlling traffic.

Q

Quadrant (Gearshift): A gear position indicator often using a shift lever actuated pointer. Can be marked PRND21 (3-speed), PRND321 (4-speed), etc.

Quadra-trac: See Full time four-wheel drive.

Quenched (Flame): Flame front in combustion chamber being extinguished as it contacts colder cylinder walls. This sharply elevates hydrocarbon emissions.

Quenching: Dipping heated object into water, oil, or other substance, to quickly reduce temperature.

Quicksilver: Metal mercury. Often used in thermometers.

Quick take-up master cylinder: A brake master cylinder that supplies a large amount of fluid (under low pressure) during first part of brake application. This supplies extra fluid needed to quickly return no-drag type brake caliper pistons so pads engage disc (rotor).

R

R-12 (CFC-12): Refrigerant used in older air conditioning systems. Gradually being replaced by R-134a in newer vehicles. Also called dichlorodifluoromethane.

R-134a (HFC-134a): Refrigerant used in the air conditioning systems of most vehicles manufactured after 1992. Replaced R-12 due to environmental concerns.

Race (Bearing): Inner or outer ring that provides a contact surface for balls or rollers in bearing.

Race camshaft: Camshaft, other than stock, designed to improve performance by altering cam profile. Provides increased lift, faster opening and closing, earlier opening and later closing, etc. Race camshafts are available as semi-race or street grind, three-fourths race or full race. Grinds in between these general categories are also available.

Racing slick: Type of tire used in "drag racing" as well as some "stock car" applications. Tread surface of tire is completely smooth, for maximum rubber contact with track surface.

Rack and pinion gearbox (Steering): Steering gear utilizing pinion gear on end of steering shaft. Pinion engages long rack (bar with teeth along one edge). Rack is connected to steering arms via rods.

Rack piston (Steering): In recirculating ball type of power steering gear, large piston that rides on worm. One side of piston has a series of teeth (called rack) that engage pitman shaft sector gear teeth. When worm is turned, rack piston slides (does not rotate), thus rotating pitman shaft.

Radial (Direction): Line at right angles (perpendicular) to shaft, cylinder, bearing, etc., centerline.

Radial compressor: A small air conditioning compressor using reciprocating pistons working at right angles to shaft and spaced around shaft in radial fashion.

Radial engine: Engine possessing various numbers of cylinders so arranged that they form circle around crankshaft centerline.

Radial loading (Bearing): A load (pressure) placed on a bearing in a direction that would be at right angles to shaft centerline.

Radial movement: Up and down movement (runout) such as that exhibited by outer surface of a revolving tire, wheel, shaft, etc. Movement is at right angles to axis of rotation.

Radial pressure: Pressure on an object applied at a right angle to its centerline.

Radial runout: Rotating shaft, wheel, pulley, etc., runout (up and down movement) as measured at a right angle to centerline of shaft, axle, etc.

Radial tire: Plies parallel and at right angle to tread, belts under tread area.

Radiation: Transfer of heat from one object to another when hotter object sends out invisible rays or waves that, upon striking colder object, cause it to heat.

Radiator (Engine cooling): A device used to remove heat from engine coolant. It consists of a series of finned passageways. As coolant moves through passages, heat is conducted to fins where it transfers to a stream of air forced through fins.

Radiator cap: Pressure cap that fits on radiator neck. It keeps coolant from boiling.

Radius: Distance (in a straight line) from center of a circle or circular motion, to a point on edge (circumference).

Radius rods: Rods attached to axle and pivoted on frame. Used to keep axle at right angles to frame and yet permit an up and down motion.

Rail: Dragster built around a relatively long pipe frame. Often the only body panels used are around the driver's cockpit area.

Ram (Hydraulic): A round steel shaft, one end attached to a piston operating in a sealed cylinder. Other end passes out of cylinder and is placed against workpiece. When hydraulic pressure is applied to piston, ram exerts pressure on workpiece. Used in hydraulic jacks, presses, etc.

Ram air: Air "scooped" up by an opening due to vehicle forward motion.

Ram induction: Using forward momentum of car to scoop air and force it into carburetor via a suitable passageway.

Ram intake manifold: Intake manifold that has very long passageways that at certain speeds aid entrance of fuel mixture into cylinders.

Rasp cut file: A file utilizing rows of relatively large sharp, tooth-like projections. Used for woodwork, filing soft metals, such as solder, brass and aluminum.

Raster pattern: On an oscilloscope, a display of all engine cylinders, one above other, with number one cylinder at bottom of screen.

Ratchet handle: Socket wrench handle with a ratcheting head to allow short back and forth handle movement without disengaging socket from fastener. Can be set to drive in either direction.

Rated horsepower (Engine): Indication of horsepower load that may safely be placed upon engine for prolonged periods of time. This would be somewhat less than the engine maximum horsepower.

Ratio: Fixed relationship between things in number, quantity, or degree. For example, if fuel mixture contains one part of gas for fifteen parts of air, ratio would be 15 to 1.

Rawhide hammer: A striking tool with a head formed of rawhide (untanned animal hide). Used for lighter striking on objects that would be damaged by a regular steel hammer.

Rayon braid (Hose): A woven rayon reinforcing layer, either in hose or applied to outside.

Reactor: See Stator.

Ream: To enlarge or smooth hole by using round cutting tool with fluted edges.

Reamed finish: A finished surface in a bore, bushing, etc., produced by a reamer.

Reamer: A cylindrical cutting tool with a series of longitudinal fluted cutting edges (fixed or adjustable). Used to enlarge, bring to size, or finish a bore, bushing, etc.

Reamer—nonadjustable: A reamer that is of a fixed size.

Reamer—spiral flute: A reamer in which longitudinal fluted cutting edges, instead of paralleling tool centerline, are spiraled (like stripes on a barber pole). Tends to produce smoother cutting with less chatter.

Reamer—straight flute: Reamer in which longitudinal fluted cutting edges are straight and are parallel to the reamer centerline.

Rear axle (Banjo type): Rear axle housing from which differential unit may be removed while housing remains in place on car. Housing is solid from side to side.

Rear axle housing (Split type): Rear axle housing made up of several pieces and bolted together. Housing must be split apart to remove differential.

Rebabbitting: Process of casting a new babbitt liner in a bearing. Babbitt (mix of lead, tin, copper, etc.) is firmly bonded to bearing bore.

Rebore (Engine): To bore out engine cylinders to a larger size. New pistons will be required.

Receiver-drier: See Drier.

Reciprocating action: Back-and-forth movement such as action of pistons.

Recirculating ball worm and nut: Very popular type of steering gear. It utilizes series of ball bearings that feed through and around and back through grooves in worn and nut.

Rectifier: Device used to change AC (alternating current) into DC (direct current).

Red line: Top recommended engine rpm. If a tachometer is used, it will have a mark (Red line) indicating maximum rpm.

Reducing flame: Welding flame in which there is an excess of acetylene.

Reduction (Gear): A gear that increases torque by reducing rpm of a driven shaft in relation to that of driving shaft.

Refrigerant: Liquid used in refrigeration systems to remove heat from evaporator coils and carry it to condenser.

Refrigerant oil: Special oil which lubricates air conditioning compressor.

Refrigerant recovery unit: Electronic station that combines a refrigerant storage tank, vacuum pump, gauges, and service valves. Used to recover, recycle, and recharge refrigerant in automotive air conditioning systems.

Refrigeration cycle: Series of events or actions that take place in air conditioning system as refrigerant moves through system.

Reground: Refers to a crankshaft, camshaft, etc., on which bearing journals have been resurfaced by grinding. Unless built up before grinding, reground journals will have a smaller diameter.

Regulator (Electrical): Device used to control voltage and current output.

Regulator (Gas or liquid): Device used to reduce and control pressure.

Relative humidity: Actual amount of moisture in a given sample of air compared to total amount that sample could hold (at same temperature).

Relay: Magnetically operated switch used to make and break flow of current in circuit. Also called "cutout, and circuit breaker."

Relief valve: A spring-loaded valve designed to open and relieve pressure when pressure exceeds certain limits.

Relieve: Removing, by grinding, small lip of metal between valve seat area and cylinder—and removing any other metal deemed necessary to improve flow of fuel mixture into cylinder. Porting is generally done at same time.

Reluctor: A component in electronic ignition system distributor. It is affixed to the distributor shaft and triggers magnetic pickup. This, in turn, triggers control unit which breaks coil primary circuit causing coil to "fire."

Remote choke (Carburetor): A bimetallic choke device, usually set in a choke stove well, located some distance from carburetor. Linkage connects choke to carburetor choke valve.

Remote keyless entry: Electronic system that is added to some vehicles to enable the vehicle's owner to lock and unlock the doors and open the trunk using a key fob transmitter.

Replaceable guide (Valve): An engine valve guide that can be removed and replaced with a new guide.

Residual magnetism: Magnetism remaining in an object after removal of any magnetic field influence.

Residual tension: A pulling force or strain that remains constantly applied to some object even though other major forces have been removed.

Resistance (Electrical): Measure of conductor's ability to retard flow of electricity.

Resistance wire: A wire designed to provide a carefully calculated resistance to electrical current flow. Can be used to limit current flow and to reduce voltage.

Resistor: Device placed in circuit to lower voltage. It will also decrease flow of current.

Resistor spark plug: Spark plug containing resistor designed to shorten both capacitive and inductive phases of spark. This will suppress radio interference and lengthen electrode life.

Resonator: Small muffler-like device that is placed into exhaust system near end of tail pipe. Used to provide additional silencing of exhaust.

Resurfacing (Block, head): Process of grinding or planing the engine block to cylinder head contact surfaces. Done to eliminate warpage, physical damage, etc., and in some cases, to increase compression.

Retard: (Ignition timing): To set the ignition timing so that spark occurs later or less degrees before TDC.

Retorque: Following initial torquing, a second torquing of fasteners to compensate for gasket crush between parts, loosening caused by vibration, etc.

Retrofitting: Process of converting an air conditioning system that uses R-12 to handle R-134a refrigerant.

Reverse-Elliott type axle: Solid bar front axle on which steering knuckles span or straddle axle ends.

Reverse flush: Cleaning cooling system by pumping a powerful cleaning agent through system in a direction opposite to that of normal flow.

Reverse idler gear: Gear used in transmission to produce a reverse rotation of transmission output shaft.

Reverse polarity (Welding): In arc welding, when electrode is connected to machine positive terminal, ground wire to negative terminal.

Rheostat: A variable type resistor used to control current flow.

Rhodium: A metallic element (Rh), sometimes employed as a catalyst in catalytic converters.

Ribbed belt: A flexible, fabric reinforced belt that uses a series of longitudinal "V" shaped ribs that mesh with corresponding grooves in pulleys.

Rich mixture (Fuel): Mixture with an excessive amount of fuel in relation to air.

Riding the clutch: Riding the clutch refers to driver resting a foot on clutch pedal while car is being driven.

Rifle brush: A cylindrical bronze, steel, etc., bristle brush as used in cleaning bore of a firearm or small holes in parts.

Right angle: An angle of 90° (one quarter of a circle).

Rigid hone: A honing tool in which stone holders, although capable of in and out adjustment, cannot spring inward, tip, or flex. Stones thus remain parallel at all times.

Rim: (Tire): The outer portion of a wheel upon which tire is mounted.

Ring: (Chrome): Ring on which the outer edge has a thin layer of chrome plate.

Ring: (Pinned): Steel pin, set into piston, is placed in space between ends of ring. Ring is thus kept from moving around in groove.

Ring break-in: Wearing-in process involved following installation of new piston rings. Tiny ridges on both rings and cylinder wall quickly wear off producing a smooth and proper fit.

Ring—compression: Piston ring designed to seal against leakage past piston. Compression rings are located above oil ring.

Ring compressor: A tool designed to force piston rings inward in their grooves so that piston and rings can be inserted into engine cylinder bore.

Ring expander: Spring device placed under rings to hold them snugly against cylinder wall.

Ring float: That situation in which piston rings are not fully pressed against cylinder wall. Caused by excessive cylinder bore taper. Ring is squeezed in at bore bottom and piston travels to top and before ring can fully expand, returns to bottom.

Ring gap: Distance between ends of piston ring when installed in cylinder.

Ring gap spacing: Locating ring gaps equidistant around piston. By spacing them so they do not line up, gas leakage through gaps is reduced and vertical wear pattern in cylinder is avoided. Also applies to gaps in a single, multiple piece ring.

Ring gear: Large gear attached to differential carrier or to outer gear in planetary gear setup.

Ring gear centerline: A line that would, if drawn across face of gear, pass through exact center of gear.

Ring gear runout: Measured amount of wobble (side to side movement) produced when a ring gear is rotated through one full turn.

Ring groove cleaner: A scraping tool designed to remove carbon from piston ring grooves.

Ring groove gauge: A measuring device (gauge) used to check piston ring groove depth to insure depth is compatible with replacement rings.

Ring groove reconditioning tool: A tool, hand or power driven, used to cut a piston ring groove to a wider size, thus removing tapered, battered sides. A thin spacer is then inserted into top of recut groove returning it to proper size.

Ring grooves: Grooves cut into piston to accept rings.

Ring groove spacer: A thin spacer ring that is inserted in a groove cut on top side of a piston ring groove. Ring takes place of battered material machined from damaged groove and

produces a groove of proper shape and size.

Ring job: Reconditioning cylinders and installing new rings.

Ring—oil control: A slotted piston ring, often of multiple piece construction, used to prevent excessive oil flow past piston into combustion chamber. Scrapes oil from cylinder wall and returns it to crankcase.

Ring ridge: Portion of cylinder above top limit of ring travel. In a worn cylinder, this area is of smaller diameter than remainder of cylinder and will leave ledge or ridge that must be removed.

Ring ridge reamer: A tool used to cut away narrow band of unworn cylinder wall (ring ridge) found between top of cylinder and highest point of ring travel.

Ring side clearance: That space existing between the side of piston ring and groove in which it operates.

Ring—taper face: A piston ring on which ring face (side towards piston) is tapered when at rest, only a portion on ring face contacts wall.

Ring tipping: A condition in which a piston ring operating in a badly tapered groove, tips from one side to other depending on forces (firing, compression, etc.) exerted upon it.

Ring travel: The total distance a ring moves in cylinder from BDC to TDC. Ring travel and length of piston stroke are same.

Rivet: Metal pin used to hold two objects together. One end of the pin has head and other end must be set or peened over.

Rivet—countersunk: A rivet, such as used on brake lining, in which head is sunk beneath lining surface to prevent rivet from striking drum, disc, etc.

Rivet—pop: A rivet useful for fastening two pieces together when rivet hole is accessible from one side only. Rivet is pushed through both pieces. When tool handles are compressed, a tapered pin is drawn back partly through rivet, thus expanding and tightening rivet in "blind" hole.

RMA: Rubber Manufacturer's Association.

Road crown: Roads are not level. They are raised in center so that water will run off readily. This "crown" or angled surface is termed road camber.

Road feel: Feeling imparted to steering wheel by wheels of car in motion. This feeling can be very important in sensing and predetermining vehicle steering response.

Road test: Process of driving vehicle upon road for purpose of diagnosing problems, checking efficiency of repairs, testing overall operation, etc.

Rocker arm: Arm used to direct upward motion of push rod into a downward or opening motion of valve stem. Used in overhead valve installations.

Rocker arm cover: Stamped steel or plastic covering or shroud fastened to engine cylinder head so as to cover valve operating mechanisms.

Rocker arm shaft: Shaft upon which rocker arms are mounted.

Rocker panel: Section of car body between front and rear fenders and beneath doors.

Rockwell hardness: Measurement of the degree of hardness of given substance.

Rod: Refers to a car, driving a car hard, or to a connecting rod.

Rod cap: Lower removable half of connecting rod big end.

Rodding the radiator: Top and sometimes the bottom tank of the radiator is removed. The core is then cleaned by passing a cleaning rod down through tubes. This is done when radiators are quite clogged with rust, scale, and various mineral deposits.

Rod heater: A device used to heat connecting rod small end to facilitate installation of piston pin.

Roll bar: Heavy steel bar that goes from one side of frame, up and around in back of the driver, and back down to the other side of frame. It is used to protect driver in the event that the car rolls over.

Roll cabinet: A portable tool cabinet on small wheels or casters to facilitate moving about. Tool chest of drawers often is placed atop cabinet.

Roller bearing: Bearing utilizing a series of straight, cupped, or tapered rollers engaging an inner and outer ring or race.

Roller clutch: Clutch, utilizing series of rollers placed in ramps, that will provide drive power in one direction but will slip or freewheel in the other direction.

Roller lifter (Valve): A valve lifter incorporating a small roller on bottom end. Roller engages camshaft and allows lifter operation with a minimum of friction between lifter and cam lobe.

Roller tappets or lifters: Valve lifters that have roller placed on end contacting camshaft. This is done to reduce friction between lobe and lifter. They are generally used when special camshafts and high tension valve springs have been installed.

Roller-vane pump: A vane pump, such as some fuel injection pumps, utilizing round rollers as operating vanes.

Rolling contact: Contact between moving parts, such as a roller against bearing race, where one part, instead of sliding, is rolling against other.

Rolling friction: Resistance to movement (friction) created by two moving objects in contact with each other— when one of the units is rolling across other. Will be less than sliding friction.

Rolling radius: Distance from road surface to center of wheel with vehicle moving under normal load. Rolling radius is dependent on tire size.

Rollover valve: Valve in fuel delivery line to prevent escape of raw fuel during an accident in which car is upside down.

Room temperature: An enclosed space air temperature of around 68–72°F (20.1–22.2°C).

Room temperature vulcanizing (RTV) silicone: A silicone sealing compound used as a gasket. Will set up or harden (vulcanize) at normal room temperature.

Rosin core (Soldering): A wire solder with a hollow center filled with rosin flux. Used for soldering electrical connections.

Rotary engine: Piston engine in which the crankshaft is fixed (stationary) and in which cylinders rotate around crankshaft.

Rotary engine (Wankel): Internal combustion engine which is not of a reciprocating (piston) engine design. Central rotor turns in one direction only and yet effectively produces required intake, compression, firing, and exhaust strokes.

Rotary flow (Torque converter): Movement of oil as it is carried around by pump and turbine. Rotary motion is not caused by oil passing through pump, to turbine, to stator, etc., as is case with vortex flow. Rotary flow is at right angles to centerline of converter whereas vortex flow is parallel (more or less depending on ratio between speeds of pump and turbine).

Rotary injection pump (Distributor type): A diesel injection pump one type of which uses a single pumping unit (two radial opposed pistons) to generate pressure for fuel distribution to all injectors. Fuel from pump passes through a distributor unit for proper injector delivery.

Rotary motion: Continual motion in circular direction such as performed by crankshaft.

Rotary valve (Steering): A power steering gear valve, that instead of moving back and forth, is rotated by steering gear shaft to open appropriate ports for hydraulic assist control.

Rotor (disc) lateral runout (Brakes): The amount of wobble or side to side (lateral) movement present when brake disc (rotor) is turned through one full revolution.

Rotor (disc) parallelism (Brakes): Relates to how well one side of brake disc or rotor aligns (parallel) with other. Perfect parallelism is present when rotor thickness is constant at all points around rotor.

Rotor (Distributor): Cap-like unit placed on end of distributor shaft. It is in constant contact with distributor cap central terminal and as it turns, it will conduct secondary voltage to one of the other terminals.

Rotor pump: A pump, fuel, oil, etc., employing a multiple lobe roller operating inside of a rotating ring with corresponding rotor recesses. Liquid is trapped, carried around and squeezed out by enlargement and then reduction of spaces between inner and outer rotor.

Roughing stone (Hone): Coarse stone used for quick removal of material during honing.

RPM: Revolutions per minute.

Rubbing block (Distributor): Insulated block attached to movable distributor point arm. Arm rubs against distributor cam and opens and closes points.

Run-down torque: That torque required to turn fastener before it exerts closing pressure to parts. Caused by friction between fastener threads (dirt, battered threads, etc.).

Running-fit: Fit in which sufficient clearance has been provided to enable parts to turn freely and to receive lubrication.

Running on: See *Dieseling*.

Runout: Rotating object, surface of which is not revolving in a true circle or plane. Runout can be measured in a radial (at right angles to centerline of object) direction or in a lateral (lengthwise to centerline) direction.

S

SAE: Society of Automotive Engineers.

SAE or rated horsepower: A simple formula of long standing is used to determine what is commonly referred to as the SAE or Rated Horsepower. The formula is:

$$\frac{\text{Bore Diameter}^2 \times \text{Number of Cylinders}}{2.5}$$

This formula is used primarily for licensing purposes and is not too accurate a means of determining actual brake horsepower.

Safe edge (File): A file in which one or more surface areas are smooth (no cutting edges at all). This allows filing one particular surface without danger of accidentally cutting an adjacent area.

Safety factor: Providing strength beyond that needed, as an extra margin of insurance against part failure.

Safety hubs: Device installed on the rear axle to prevent wheels from leaving car in event of a broken axle.

Safety rim: Rim having two safety ridges, one on each lip, to prevent tire beads from entering drop center area in event of a blowout. This feature keeps tire on rim.

Safety valve: Valve designed to open and relieve pressure within a container when container pressure exceeds predetermined level.

Safety wire: Soft wire used to secure fasteners to prevent unscrewing from vibration, temperature changes, etc.

Sal ammoniac: A mineral (ammonium chloride), often used in block form upon which to rub a soldering copper to assist in proper tinning (getting a covering of solder on copper tip).

Sand blast: Cleaning by the use of sand propelled at high speeds in an air blast.

Saybolt viscometer: Instrument used to determine fluidity or viscosity (resistance to flow) of an oil.

Scale (Cooling system): Accumulation of rust and minerals within cooling system.

Scan tool: A diagnostic tool used to extract trouble codes from an automobile's computer.

Scatter shield: Steel or nylon guard placed around bell or clutch housing to protect driver and spectator from flying parts in event of part failure at high rpm. Such a shield is often placed around transmissions and differential units.

Scavenging: Referring to a cleaning or blowing out action in reference to the exhaust gas.

Schrader valve: Valve, similar to spring loaded valve used in tire stem, used in car air conditioning system service valves.

Score: Scratch or groove on finished surface.

Scored piston: A piston with vertical grooves and deep scratches in piston to cylinder contact surface. Caused by lack of lubrication, abrasive material such as hard carbon, fractured ring particles, etc.

Scoring: Producing deep scratches and grooves in a piston, bearing, etc., contact surface. Caused by insufficient lubrication, abrasive particles, etc.

Screw clamp (Hose): A hose clamp that is tightened by means of a threaded screw.

Screwdriver—clutch: A screwdriver with a tip shaped somewhat like an hourglass. Used for clutch head screws.

Screwdriver—offset: A screwdriver in which tip is bent at an angle (usually 90 degrees) so as to turn screws in which there is little room between screw head and some other surface.

Screwdriver—Phillips: A screwdriver with a tip shaped somewhat like a cross in which cross arms are same width for their full length.

Screwdriver—Reed & Prince: A screwdriver in which tip is shaped somewhat like a cross in which cross arms are wider at outer edge and taper almost to a point where they intersect at center.

Screwdriver—standard: A screwdriver with a blade tip in which blade edge is same width across diameter of screwdriver. Used in all screws with a single, straight slot.

Screwdriver—stubby: A very short screwdriver for use in cramped or restricted areas.

Screw extractor: Device used to remove broken bolts, screws, etc., from holes.

Screw pitch gauge: See *Thread gauge*.

SCS: Speed Control Switch. (Speed sensitive spark advance control.)

Scuffing: Very similar to scoring in many respects. Caused by lack of lubrication, improper clearance, etc. Metal particles are torn from one contact surface such as piston, and deposited on other, such as cylinder. Contact surfaces often discolored by heat produced.

Seal: Device which prevents oil leakage around moving part.

Seal driver: A tool used to install seals.

Sealed beam headlight: Headlight lamp in which lens, reflector, and filament are fused together to form single unit.

Sealed bearing: Bearing that has been lubricated at factory and then sealed. It cannot be lubricated during service.

Sea level: Elevation as measured at ocean surface level. To avoid change in height caused by rise and fall of tide, middle (mean) level between high and low levels is used.

Seat: Surface upon which another part rests or seats. Example: Valve seat is matched surface upon which valve face rests.

Seat (Rings): Minor wearing of piston ring surface during initial use. Rings then fit or seat properly against the cylinder wall.

Secondary circuit (Ignition system): High voltage part of ignition system.

Secondary piston (Master cylinder): In a brake system dual master cylinder, that piston actuated by pressure generated by primary piston. Primary is actuated by either brake pedal linkage or power booster rod.

Secondary, reverse, or trailing brake shoe: Brake shoe that is installed facing rear of car.

Secondary wires: High voltage wire from coil to distributor central tower and from outer towers to spark plugs.

Second cut file: A file with medium size (roughness) cutting edges.

Section height (Tire): Distance, at right angles, from center of inside surface of tread area to a line intersecting (crossing through) two bead bottom edges. Calculated with tire mounted and at normal pressure.

Section modulus: Relative structural strength measurement of member (such as frame rail) that is determined by cross-sectional area and member shape.

Section width (Tire): Measurement of a tires' inside width at widest point between two sidewalls, when mounted and at normal pressure.

Sector gear: A partial gear, such as used on a steering gear pitman shaft, that is actually only a portion (pie shaped slice) of normal 360° gear. Gear can only be operated through a limited arc.

Sector shaft (Steering gear): Another term for pitman shaft. Has a sector gear (partial gear) on one end and pitman arm attached to other.

Sediment: Accumulation of matter which settles to bottom of a liquid.

Seize: See *Freezing*.

Seized: A term describing condition of a bearing, shaft, pin, etc., that due to insufficient clearance, lack of lubrication, etc., has overheated. Through scuffing and galling, it is stuck fast and is thus unable to turn or slide.

Self-adjusting: A mechanism, linkage, series of related parts, etc., in which a required clearance is automatically maintained without need for periodic manual adjustment.

Self-aligning bearing: A bearing that is secured in such a manner that it is free to pivot or swivel, thus permitting a certain amount of shaft lateral movement without binding bearing.

Self-centering brakes: Wheel brake design in which both brake shoe assemblies "float" and are free to move about so that when applied, center themselves in relation to brake drum.

Self-diagnostics: The ability of a computer to continuously monitor the operation of a specific system and send warning signals when an abnormal condition is detected.

Self-energizing: Brake shoe (sometimes both shoes) that when applied develops wedging action that actually assists or boost braking force applied by wheel cylinder.

Self-induction (Electromagnetic): Creation of voltage in a circuit by varying current in circuit.

Self-locking: A fastener utilizing built-in thread friction produced by tight threads, plastic plugs, neoprene rings, etc., so that when tightened it will not loosen under normal use.

Self-starting rod (Arc welding): An electric arc welding rod that utilizes a special flux coating that makes it very easy to get arc started and tends to automatically maintain proper rod to work distance as rod is consumed.

Self-tapping: Fastener designed to cut its own thread as it is turned into hole.

SEMA: Specialty Equipment Manufacturer's Association.

Semi-elliptical spring: Spring, such as commonly used on truck rear axles, consisting of one main leaf and number of progressively shorter leaf springs.

Semifinished insert (Bearing): An insert bearing that following installation, must be machined to proper size by removing a certain amount of bearing material.

Semifloating (Drive axle): A drive axle in which drive shaft secures, aligns, and drives wheel. Supports weight of vehicle.

Sensor: A device used to detect a change in heat, pressure, exhaust emissions, speed, etc., and to emit a suitable signal to a control unit.

Separable bearing: A bearing capable of being disassembled.

Separators (Battery): Wood, rubber, or plastic sheets inserted between positive and negative plates to prevent contact.

Sequence of assembly: Recommended order of operations involved in assembly of a transmission, starter, etc.

Series circuit: Circuit with two or more resistance units so wired that current must pass through one unit before reaching other.

Series-parallel circuit: Circuit of three or more resistance units in which a series and a parallel circuit are combined.

Serviceable: A part or unit whose design and construction permit disassembly for purposes of rebuilding. Can also be used to indicate a part or unit whose condition is such that it can still be used.

Service classification (Oil): A listing indicating ability of a specific oil to provide proper lubrication under specific engine operating conditions.

Service manager: Person in shop who greets customers, determines their needs, and assigns mechanics as required. Prepares cost estimates, handles service complaints, and in general, coordinates shop activity.

Service valve (Air conditioning): A valve (hand or Schrader type) used to open sealed air conditioning system to perform discharge, charge, etc., operations.

Service writer: Person who greets customer, determines their needs, and writes up necessary information (customer name, address, description of apparent trouble, etc.). As opposed to a service manager, service writer is primarily concerned with paperwork involved. Beyond this point, other persons take over.

Servo (Transmission): Oil operated device used to push or pull another part—such as tightening the transmission brake bands.

Servo action: Brakes so constructed as to have one end of primary shoe bearing against end of secondary shoe. When brakes are applied, primary shoe attempts to move in the direction of the rotating drum and in so doing applies force to the secondary shoe. This action, called servo action, makes less brake pedal pressure necessary and is widely used in brake construction.

Setscrew: A screw threaded through one part until it jams solidly against another, thus locking them together—such as a pulley to a shaft.

Shackle: Device used to attach ends of a leaf spring to frame.

Shaft drive angle (Propeller shaft): Angle formed between center lines of propeller shaft and differential pinion shaft.

Shaft runout: Amount of radial (up and down) movement that takes place during one complete revolution of shaft.

Shave: Removal of some chrome or decorative part.

Shave (Engine): Removal of metal from contact surface of cylinder head or block.

Shift forks: Devices that straddle slots cut in sliding gears. Fork is used to move gear back and forth on shaft.

Shift mechanism: Device for changing transmission gear range.

Shift point: Point, either in engine rpm or road speed, at which transmission should be shifted to next gear.

Shift rails: Sliding rods upon which shift forks are attached. Used for shifting the transmission (manual).

Shift range (4-wheel drive): Used to refer to two speed transfer case gear position. Case can be shifted into high range (no gear reduction) or low range (around two to one reduction).

Shim: A thin piece of brass, steel, etc., inserted between two parts so as to adjust distance between them. Sometimes used to adjust bearing clearance.

Shim pack: A bearing shim made up of numerous thin (.001—.002 in.) laminations (layers). Bearing can be adjusted by removing a layer at a time until specified clearance is obtained.

Shock absorber: Oil filled device used to control spring oscillation in suspension system.

Shop supervisor: Person responsible for overall shop operation. Checks progress and quality of work, observance of safety rules, utilization and condition of shop, coordination between various departments, customer relations, etc.

Short or short circuit: Refers to some "hot" portion of the electrical system that has become grounded. (Wire touching a ground and providing a completed circuit to the battery.)

Short block: Engine block complete with crankshaft and piston assemblies.

Shorting harness: An arrangement of wires that are used to short out (ground) spark plugs so as to perform engine cylinder balance test.

Shot peening: A process utilizing a blast of small metal or plastic shot that is directed against surface of some part. Can be used for cleaning, piston expansion, relieving part surface tension, etc.

Shrink-fit: Fit between two parts which is so tight, outer or encircling piece must be expanded by heating so it will fit over inner piece. In cooling, outer part shrinks and grasps inner part securely.

Shroud: Metal enclosure around fan, engine, etc., to guide and facilitate airflow.

Shunt: An alternate or bypass portion of an electrical circuit.

Shunt lubrication system: An engine lubrication system that passes oil from pump through both filter and shunt (bypass) at all times. Oil from both then merges and passes to bearings.

Shunt winding: Wire coil forming an alternate or by-pass circuit through which current may flow.

Side-draft carburetor: Carburetor in which air passes through carburetor into intake manifold in a horizontal plane.

Sidewall: Part of tire between tread and bead, has size and rating information.

Sight glass: Clear glass window in air conditioning line which lets mechanic check refrigerant for air bubbles (low refrigerant) and moisture (pink color).

Silver solder: Similar to brazing except that special silver solder metal is used.

Single-barrel, double-barrel, and four-barrel carburetors: Number of throttle openings or barrels from the carburetor to the intake manifold.

Single cut file: A file utilizing a single row of angled cuts that are all parallel.

Single lap flare: A tubing flare in which a single layer of tubing is secured between fitting body and nut seal angles.

Single plate clutch: A clutch utilizing a single clutch disc secured between flywheel and pressure plate.

Single post frame lift: A vehicle lift utilizing one centrally located ram.

Sintered bronze: Tiny particles of bronze pressed tightly together so that they form a solid piece. The piece is highly porous and is often used for filtering purposes.

Sintering: Process involved in forming a part, such as a bushing, by heating (no melting involved) a compressed mass of copper, bronze, iron, etc., powder.

Sipe: Small slits in tire tread designed to increase traction. Also called kerfs.

Siphon: Process of removing liquid from container by use of atmospheric pressure and gravity acting on a column of liquid in a hose, pipe, etc. One end of hose, pipe, etc., is submerged in liquid and other (discharge end) is held at a point below level of liquid in container.

Skid plate: Stout metal plate or plates attached to underside of vehicle to protect oil pan, transmission, fuel tank, etc., from damage caused by "grounding out" on rocks, curbs, and road surface.

Skirt collapse (Piston): Condition in which diameter across piston skirt area has been reduced through action of heat and shock.

Skirt thrust surface (Piston): That portion of piston skirt at right angles to piston pin when viewing piston from top.

Skiving: Cutting away a portion of tire tread to correct out-of-round problem.

Skiving hose: Removing one or more outer layers of hose rubber so that skived section can be pushed into a hose fitting. Usually involves removal of rubber down to first fabric layer.

Skiving knife: A special knife used to skive hose prior to insertion in fitting.

Slag (Welding): Accumulation of hardened and burned flux left on weld area following brazing or arc welding in which flux was used.

Slag inclusions (Welding): A weld in which weld metal contains particles of slag.

Slant engine: In-line engine with cylinder block tilted from vertical plane.

Slave cylinder (Hydraulic): In a hydraulic system, a cylinder containing a piston (such as a brake wheel cylinder) that is forced to move by pressure generated in another (connected) cylinder (such as brake master cylinder).

Sleeve (Cylinder): See *Cylinder sleeve*.

Sleeve puller: Tool used to withdraw and install engine cylinder sleeves.

Slide hammer: A pulling device that utilizes a sliding weight that can be hammered against a portion of handle to generate pulling force.

Sliding fit: See *Running-fit*.

Sliding friction: Friction (resistance to movement) between two parts in which surface of one is sliding over surface of other.

Sliding gear: Transmission gear splined to the shaft. It may be moved back and forth for shifting purposes.

Slip angle: Difference in actual path taken by a car making a turn and path it would have taken if it had followed exactly as wheels were pointed.

Slip joint: Joint that will transfer driving torque from one shaft to another while allowing longitudinal movement between two shafts.

Slipper pump: A pump using spring-loaded, slipper-like vanes riding in grooves in a rotor. Rotor operates inside a cam-shaped ring.

Slingshot: Form of dragster using rather long thin frame with a very light front axle and wheel assembly.

Slitting file: A four surfaced file with a parallelogram cross section.

Slotted anchor: A wheel brake design in which brake shoe anchor is passed through a slotted opening in backing plate, thus allowing anchor to be moved for accurate shoe-to-drum centering.

Slow charging (Battery): Recharging a battery by passing a low current (5 to 7 amps) through it for a relatively long period (14 to 24 hours).

Slow idle: Normal hot engine idle speed.

Sludge: Black, mushy deposits throughout interior of the engine. Caused from mixture of dust, oil, and water being whipped together by moving parts.

Small hole gauge: A device used to measure inside diameter of small holes. Gauge is adjusted to hole and gauge is then measured with an outside micrometer.

Smog: Fog made darker and heavier by chemical fumes and smoke.

Snap ring: Split ring snapped into a groove in a shaft or in a groove in a hole. It is used to hold bearings, thrust washers, gears, etc., in place.

Snubber: Device used to limit travel of some part.

Soaking tank: A cleaning tank in which parts are submerged for a recommended period in some type of cleaner.

Socket adapter: A device used to allow a socket with one particular drive size to be used with another different drive size (1/4 in., 3/8 in., etc.) handle ratchet, etc.

Socket—six-point (Wrench): A socket with a hexagonal (six sided) shaped hole. Grips fastener flats across entire surface. Has six inside corners.

Socket—twelve-point (Wrench): Socket with twelve inside corners that produce twelve short gripping areas. Engages only a portion of each fastener flat.

Socket—swivel (Wrench): A socket with an integral swivel drive unit.

Socket—universal joint: A swivel type device that allows socket to be operated at various angles.

Sodium valve: Valve in which stem has been partially filled with metallic sodium to speed up transfer of heat from valve head, to stem and then to guide and block.

"Soft" water: Water containing a minimum amount of minerals such as calcium, magnesium, etc.

SOHC: Engine with single overhead camshaft.

Soldered on (Terminal): A wire terminal that is attached to wire by soldering.

Soldering: Joining two pieces of metal together with lead-tin mixture. Both pieces of metal must be heated to ensure proper adhesion of melted solder.

Soldering flux: A cleaning agent (rosin or acid type) that is placed on parts to be soldered. Prevents oxidization of surface and greatly assists in solder flow and adhesion.

Soldering gun: Electrically heated soldering iron shaped somewhat like a pistol. Trigger switch sends current through copper tip, raising it to soldering heat. Usually used for light soldering such as done on wiring.

Solenoid: Electrically operated magnetic device used to operate some unit. Movable iron core is placed inside of coil. When current flows through coil, core will attempt to center itself in coil. In so doing, core will exert considerable force on anything it is connected to.

Solid axle: Single beam runs between both wheels. May be used on either front or rear of car.

Solid state: An electrical device, such as a regulator, that has no moving parts. Such units use transistors, diodes, resistors, etc., to perform all electrical functions.

Solvent: Liquid used to dissolve or thin other material. Examples: Alcohol thins shellac; gasoline dissolves grease.

Spade terminal: A male electrical connector with a single, slotted, flat blade.

Spalling (Bearing): A condition in which tiny areas of bearing surface have flaked off. As flaking accelerates, large craters can be formed.

Spark: Bridging or jumping of a gap between two electrodes by current of electricity.

Spark advance: Causing spark plug to fire earlier.

Spark arrestor: Device used to prevent sparks (burning particles of carbon) from being discharged from exhaust pipe. Usually used on off-road equipment to prevent forest fires.

Spark gap: Space between center and side electrode tips on a spark plug.

Spark knock: See Preignition.

Spark lighter (Welding): A flint and steel device used to produce sparks with which to light an oxyacetylene torch.

Spark plug: Device containing two electrodes across which electricity jumps to produce a spark to fire fuel charge.

Spark plug heat range: An indication of how fast plug transfers heat from insulator tip, through insulator to shell and into head and atmosphere. Longer or narrower insulator, produces hotter plug.

Spark plug oil fouling: Buildup of oil deposit caused by worn valve guides, leaking rings, etc., allowing an excessive amount of oil to enter combustion chamber.

Spark plug reach: Distance from plug-to-head contact surface (gasket or taper) to end of threaded nose section.

Spark plug size: Relates to outside diameter (major thread diameter) of threaded nose section.

Spark plug type: Refers to plug construction, such as resistor, nonresistor, single electrode, etc.

Specialization: Mechanic concentrated in one particular area of auto repair—brakes, tune-up, transmission, engines.

Specific gravity: Relative weight of a given volume of specific material as compared to weight of an equal volume of water.

Speed: Time rate of motion without regard to direction. Forward speed (mph or km/h) of a vehicle, rotational speed (rpm) of an engine, etc.

Speed density: Method of determining the amount of air going into the intake manifold by monitoring sensor input and calculating the amount of airflow based on the sensor readings.

Speed handle: A socket hand tool with an offset (crank) area that permits rapid and full rotation of socket.

Speedometer: Instrument used to determine forward speed of an auto in miles per hour or kilometres per hour.

Spherical roller (Bearing): A bearing roller in which center outside diameter exceeds that of either end giving roller a convex (barrel shape).

Spider gears: Small gears mounted on shaft pinned to differential case. They mesh with, and drive, the axle end gears.

Spindle (Wheel): Machined shaft upon which inside races of front wheel bearings rest. Spindle is an integral part of steering knuckle.

Spin-on filter: An engine oil filter that is a complete unit (case and filter) in itself. It is attached by merely threading it onto a short section of pipe. Cannot be disassembled for cleaning.

Spiral bevel gear: Ring and pinion setup widely used in automobile differentials. Teeth of both ring and pinion are tapered and are cut on a spiral so that they are at an angle to centerline of pinion shaft.

Spirit level: A leveling device using a floating "bubble" visible inside a glass tube.

Spline: metal (land) remaining between two grooves. Used to connect parts.

Splined joint: Joint between two parts in which each part has splines cut along contact area. Splines on each part slide into grooves between splines on other part.

Split keepers (Valve): Valve spring retainer lock made up of a two piece tapered cone that wedges between retainer and valve stem grooves.

Split manifold: Exhaust manifold that has a baffle placed near its center. An exhaust pipe leads out of each half.

Spongy pedal: When there is air in brake lines, or shoes that are not properly centered in drums, brake pedal will have a springy or spongy feeling when brakes are applied. Pedal normally will feel hard when applied.

Spool balance valve (Automatic Transmission): Hydraulic valve that balances incoming oil pressure against spring control pressure to produce a steady pressure to some control unit.

Spool valve: Hydraulic control valve shaped somewhat like spool upon which thread is wound.

Sports car: Term commonly used to describe a relatively small, car with a high performance engine.

Spot weld: Fastening parts together by fusing, at various spots. Heavy surge of electricity is passed through the parts held in firm contact by electrodes.

Sprag clutch: Clutch that will allow rotation in one direction but that will lock up and prevent any movement in the other direction.

Spring (Main leaf): Long leaf on which ends are turned to form an "eye" to receive shackle.

Spring booster: Device used to "beef" up sagged springs or to increase the load capacity of standard springs.

Spring capacity at ground: Total vehicle weight (sprung and unsprung) that will be carried by spring bent or deflected to its maximum normal loaded position.

Spring capacity at pad: Total vehicle sprung weight that will be carried by spring bent or deflected to its normal fully loaded position.

Spring free length (Valve): Overall length of a coil spring when all compression forces are removed.

Spring loaded: Device held in place, or under pressure from a spring or springs.

Spring oscillation: Rapid compression and rebound movement that exists in a coil spring following a sudden change in loading pressure.

Spring rebound: Reverse direction spring movement following sudden compression (loading). Spring attempts to return to its original position.

Spring scale: A weighing device using a coil spring that is stretched as pressure is applied. Stretching is indicated by a needle moving along a scale.

Spring skirt expander (Piston): A spring steel device inserted inside a piston to apply outward (expansion) pressure to skirt thrust surfaces.

Spring squareness (Valve spring): Refers to angle of spring ends as related to spring centerline. Should be perfectly square (90°).

Spring steel: Heat treated steel having the ability to stand a great amount of deflection and yet return to its original shape or position.

Spring windup: Curved shape assumed by rear leaf springs during acceleration or braking.

Sprocket: Toothed wheel used to drive chain or cogged belt.

Sprung weight: Weight of all parts of car that are supported by suspension system.

Spur gear: Gear on which teeth are cut parallel to shaft.

Spurt or squirt hole: Small hole in connecting rod big end that indexes (aligns) with oil hole in crank journal. When holes index, oil spurts out.

Square engine: Engine in which bore diameter and stroke are of equal dimensions.

Sq. ft.: Square Foot.

Sq. in.: Square Inch.

Stabilizer bar: Transverse mounted spring steel bar that controls and minimizes body lean or tipping on corners.

Staked insert (Valve): A valve seat insert that is held in recess by extruding some of head metal over seat edge by hammering metal with a special punch.

Staked nut: Nut held in position by staking (forcing a part of nut into a groove, hole, etc., in other part).

Staking: Holding a nut, pin, etc., into place by hammering a portion of part into a groove, cutout, etc., in mating part. This prevents turning, sliding, etc., movement. A staking punch, with an appropriate nose, is needed.

Stall: To stop rotation or operation.

Stall test (Automatic transmission): Testing torque converter-transmission action by applying full engine load (wide open throttle) with transmission in gear and brakes firmly applied. Must be very brief test (5 seconds). Engine rpm is noted at full stall.

Stall torque (Starter): Full torque developed by starter motor when pinion is prevented from turning.

Stamping: Sheet metal part formed by pressing between metal dies.

Starter (Engine): Electric motor which uses a geardrive to crank (spin) engine for starting.

Starter pinion gear: Small gear on end of starter shaft that engages and turns large flywheel ring gear.

Starter solenoid: Large electric relay that makes and breaks the electrical connection between the battery and starting motor.

Starting punch: A punch, with a tapered nose, used to start pins out of their holes.

Starting system: Parts (starter motor, gear drive, switch, solenoid, wires, battery, etc.) used to crank car for starting.

Star wheel (Brakes): A small brake shoe adjusting wheel with a series of radial prongs that can be engaged by tip of a screwdriver so as to turn wheel.

State of charge (Battery): Refers to amount of potential electrical energy present in battery at time of testing. Indicated by specific gravity of electrolyte.

Static balance: When a tire, flywheel, crankshaft, etc., has an absolutely even distribution of weight mass around axis of rotation, it will be in static balance. For example, if front wheel is jacked up and tire, regardless of where it is placed, always slowly turns and stops with the same spot down, it would not be in static balance. If, however, wheel remains in any position in which it is placed, it would be in static balance. (Bearings must be free, no brake drag, etc.)

Static electricity: Electricity generated by friction between two objects. It will remain in one object until discharged.

Static pressure (Brakes): Pressure that always exists in brake lines—even with brake pedal released. Static pressure is maintained by a check valve.

Static radius: Distance from road surface to center of wheel with vehicle normally loaded, at rest.

Static suppression: Removal or minimizing of unwanted electromagnetic waves that cause radio static interference (hissing, crackling, etc.).

Stator: Small hub, upon which series of vanes are affixed in radial position, that is so placed that oil leaving torque converter turbine strikes stator vanes and is redirected into pump at an angle conducive to high efficiency. Stator makes torque multiplication possible. Torque multiplication is highest at stall when the engine speed is at its highest and the turbine is standing still.

Steam cleaning: Cleaning by using a jet of steam directed against surface to be cleaned.

Steel drift: A steel bar, heavy punch, etc., that is placed against an object so that it can be moved by hammering against drift.

Steel pack muffler: Straight-through (no baffles) muffler utilizing metal shavings surrounding a perforated pipe. Quiets exhaust sound.

Steering arms: Arms, either bolted to, or forged as an integral part of steering knuckles. They transmit steering force from tie rods to knuckles, thus causing wheels to pivot.

Steering axis inclination: See *Kingpin inclination*.

Steering gear: Gears, mounted on lower end of steering column, used to multiply driver turning force.

Steering geometry: Term sometimes used to describe various angles assumed by components making up front wheel turning arrangement, camber, caster, toe-in, etc.

Also used to describe related angles assumed by front wheels when car is negotiating a curve.

Steering knuckle: Inner portion of spindle affixed to and pivoting on either a kingpin or on upper and lower ball joints.

Steering knuckle angle: Angle formed between steering axis and centerline of spindle. This angle is sometimes referred to as Included Angle.

Steering linkage: Various arms, rods, etc., connecting steering gear to front wheels.

Steering system: All parts (steering wheel, shaft, gears, linkage, etc.) used in transferring motion of steering wheel to front wheels.

Stellite: Extremely hard metal (mix of chromium, tungsten, cobalt, etc.) often used for exhaust valve seats, valve face, etc., on heavy duty engines.

Stethoscope: Device (as used by doctors) to detect and locate abnormal engine noises. Handy tool for troubleshooting.

Stick shift: Transmission that is shifted manually through use of various forms of linkage. Often refers to upright gearshift stick that protrudes through floor.

Either floor or steering column mounted manual shift device for transmission.

Stock car: Car as built by factory.

Stoichiometric fuel mixture: A fuel mixture in which proportions of air and fuel are such as to permit complete burning. The ideal mixture for any given engine and set of conditions.

Stone dresser: A device used to cut a new surface on a grinding wheel or stone. May be diamond tipped or mechanical star wheel type.

Stone sleeve (Valve): Cylindrical unit upon which engine valve seat grinding stone is attached. Sleeve slips over and is guided by pilot. Also termed "mandrel."

Stone sleeve pilot (Valve): Rigid metal rod that is twisted into valve guide with upper protruding portion acting as a guide or pilot for grinding stone sleeve.

Stone truing (Valve): Cutting a fresh, correct surface on a grinding stone by passing a diamond tipped dresser across stone at correct angle.

Stoplight: Warning lights, red in color, attached to rear of vehicle. Stoplights come on whenever brake pedal is depressed.

Storage battery: Another term for car battery. See *Battery*.

Straightedge (Steel): Long, flat, relatively thin, steel strip with perfectly straight edges. Used for drawing straight lines, checking surfaces for warpage, etc.

Straight polarity (Welding): In DC arc welding, having current flow from machine negative terminal (rod holder cable attached to negative terminal) through electrode to work and then on through ground cable to machine positive terminal.

Straight roller (Bearing): A bearing roller in which roller outside diameter is constant from one end to other.

Stranding (Wire): Center current carrying portion of an insulated wire. Can be of copper, aluminum, etc., and can be of one piece or multi-wire construction. Automotive wire is of multi-strand construction for great flexibility without breakage.

Street rod: Slightly modified rod that will give good day-to-day performance on the streets.

Stress: To apply force to an object. Force or pressure an object is subjected to.

Striking an arc (Welding): Scratching arc welding electrode along workpiece to establish an arc producing current flow.

Striping tool: Tool used to apply paint in long narrow lines.

Stroboscope: See *Timing light*.

Stroke: Distance piston moves when traveling from TDC to BDC.

Stroked crankshaft: Crankshaft, either special new one or stock crank reworked, that has connecting rod throws offset so that length of stroke is increased.

Stroker: Engine using crankshaft that has been stroked.

Stud: Metal rod with threads on both ends.

Stud puller: Tool used to install or remove studs.

Sub-specialist: A person specializing within a speciality—such as a person handling fuel injection pumps exclusively, even though fuel injection pumps would be under general area of a fuel system specialist.

Suction: See *Vacuum*.

Suction line: See *Low pressure line*.

Suction throttling valve: Valve placed between air conditioning evaporator and compressor which controls evaporator and compressor which controls evaporator pressure to provide maximum cooling without icing evaporator core.

Sulfation: Formation of lead sulphate on battery plates.

Sulphuric acid (Battery): Acid (36%) that is mixed with water (64%) to form battery electrolyte. A powerful acid; wear goggles and rubber gloves.

Sump: Part of oil pan that contains oil.

Sun gear: Center gear around which planet gears revolve.

Supercharger: Unit designed to force air, under pressure, into cylinders. Can be mounted between carburetor and cylinders or between carburetor and atmosphere.

Superheat switch: See *Compressor protection switch*.

Supplemental restraint systems: See *Air bag system*.

Sure-grip differential: High traction differential which causes both axles to rotate under power.

Surface type filter: A filter in which filtering medium traps dirt, abrasives, etc., on surface. A paper filter (without additional depth filtering material) would be a surface type filter.

Surge bleeding (Brakes): Rapid stroke of brake pedal (with pressure bleeder attached to master cylinder reservoir and wheel bleed screw open) to cause a violent surge of fluid into wheel cylinder in order to remove trapped air.

Suspension height: A specified distance from one or more suspension components (such as suspension lower arm) to either floor or to some spot on body. This will establish correct suspension arm, spring, etc., heights and/or angles in relation to vehicle frame or body.

Suspension lift: A lift that raises vehicle by engaging only front and rear suspension systems (such as front, lower suspension arms and rear axle housing).

Swaged insert (Valve): An engine valve seat insert that is held in its recess by swaging (rolling pressure that forces metal to flow or extrude), thus locking seat by forcing head metal over a chamfer cut on seat outside diameter.

Sway bar: See *Stabilizer bar*.

Sweating: Joining two pieces of metal together by placing solder between them and then clamping them tightly together while heat, sufficient to melt the solder, is applied.

Swing axle: Independent rear suspension system in which each driving wheel can move up or down independently of other. Differential unit is bolted to frame and various forms of linkage are used upon which to mount wheels. Drive axles, utilizing one or more universal joints, connect differential to drive wheels.

Switch (Electric): A device to make (complete) or break (interrupt) flow of current through a circuit.

Synchromesh transmission: Transmission using device (synchromesh) that synchronizes speeds of gears that are being shifted together. This prevents "gear grinding." Some transmissions use synchromesh on all shifts, while others synchronize second and high gearshifts.

Synchronize: To bring about a timing that will cause two or more events to occur simultaneously; plug firing when the piston is in correct position, speed of two shafts being the same, valve opening when piston is in correct position, etc.

Synchronize (Transmission): A friction device to bring two transmission gears to same rotational speed before meshing. Avoids clashing gears.

T

Tachometer: Device used to indicate speed of engine in rpm.

Taillight: Lights, usually red or amber, attached to rear of vehicle. Lights operate in conjunction with headlights.

Tail pipe: Exhaust piping running from muffler to rear of car.

Tank gauge unit: Variable resistor device in fuel tank. It operates fuel gauge in dashboard.

Tap: To cut threads in a hole, or can be used to indicate fluted tool used to cut threads.

Tap and die set: Set of taps and dies for internal and external threading—usually covers a range of the most popular sizes.

Tap—bottoming: Internal thread cutting tool designed to cut full threads completely to bottom of a hole.

Tapered end axle: Axle using a tapered end upon which wheel hub is secured by means of a key and attaching nut.

Tapered roller (Bearing): Cone shaped bearing roller.

Tapered roller bearing (Antifriction): Bearing utilizing series of tapered, hardened steel rollers operating between an outer and inner hardened steel race.

Tappet: Screw used to adjust clearance between valve stem and lifter or rocker arm.

Tappet clearance: On non-hydraulic lifter setups, operating clearance that exists in valve train to prevent valve from being held open when parts heat up and elongate.

Tappet noise: Noise caused by lash or clearance between valve stem and rocker arm or between valve stem and valve lifter.

Tap—pipe: An internal thread cutting tool that cuts threads suitable for pipe fittings.

Tap—plug: An internal thread cutting tool with a slight nose taper—between a taper and bottoming tap.

Tap—taper: Internal thread cutting tool on which first few threads have been ground to form a tapered nose shape. This permits tap nose to enter partway into hole, making it easier to start cutting threads.

Tap water: Water as drawn from a typical household faucet. Depending upon source, can be either "hard" or "soft."

TCS: Transmission Controlled Spark.

TDC: Top Dead Center.

Technical service bulletins (TSB): Information published by vehicle manufacturers in response to vehicle conditions, problems, etc. that may not be diagnosed by normal methods.

Teflon: Plastic with excellent self-lubricating (slippery) bearing properties.

Telescoping gauge: Measuring tool consisting of a spring loaded collapsible rod affixed at right angles to a locking handle. Used to measure inside diameter of holes.

Temper: To effect a change in physical structure of piece of steel through use of heat and cold.

Temperature gauge: Dash mounted instrument to indicate temperature of engine coolant. May be operated electrically or by Bourdon tube.

Tensile strength: An indication of how much stretching force a material can withstand before it breaks.

Tension: Pulling or stretching stress applied to an object.

Tension loading: Placing a load, in such a manner, as to apply a pulling or stretching force to an object. A torqued fastener is under tension loading.

Terminal: Connecting point in electric circuit. When referring to battery, it would indicate two battery posts.

Terminal block (Electrical): A central distribution block that receives current from one wire and through means of a bus bar, conducts it to a number of others.

Test lamp: A light bulb wired in series with a battery and two test wire leads. Used to check circuits, grounds, opens, etc.

T-fitting: A T-shaped fitting that may be inserted into a line for purpose of attaching an additional line at same point.

T-handle: Socket wrench extension with a round rod handle passed through it at right angles at one end. Other end has square socket drive connection tip.

T-head engine: Engine having intake valve on one side of cylinder and exhaust on other.

Thermal bulb: A temperature sensitive device consisting of a hollow bulb filled with liquid, connected by means of a capillary tube to a control unit, dial, etc.

Thermal efficiency: Percentage of heat developed in burning fuel charge that is actually used to develop power determines thermal efficiency. Efficiency will vary according to engine design, use, etc. If an engine utilizes great deal of heat to produce power, its thermal efficiency would be high.

Thermal sensor: A temperature sensitive sensor.

Thermal time switch (Carburetion): A time controlled switch that is also temperature sensitive. Used with some fuel injection system cold start valves.

Thermistor: Resistor that changes its resistance in relation to temperature.

Thermostat: Temperature sensitive device used in cooling system to control flow of coolant in relation to temperature.

Thermostatically controlled air cleaner (TAC): An emission control device used to control temperature of air entering air cleaner. Cleaner receives heated air during engine warmup.

Thermostatic Spring: A heat sensitive, bimetallic (two kinds of metal) spring that winds or unwinds as temperature changes take place.

Thermostatic switch: A switch that is actuated by temperature changes.

Third brush (Generator): Generator in which a third, movable brush is used to control current output.

Thread length: A measurement of length of threaded area on a bolt, capscrew, etc.

Thread-pitch gauge: A gauge used to determine number of threads per inch on a fastener. Consists of many leaves, each with a specific thread cut on one edge.

Three-quarter floating (Axle): A drive axle that secures, aligns, and drives wheel. Does not support vehicle weight.

Three-quarter race camshaft: Description of custom camshaft indicating type of lobe grinding which, in turn, dictates type of use. Other grinds are one-quarter race, full-race, street-grind, etc.

Three-way catalytic converter: Converter, sometimes called dual converter, that combines both an oxidizing and reducing catalyst. Controls NOx, CO, and HC emissions.

Throttle body: Throttle plate assembly that contains sensors and vacuum connectors. Used in place of a carburetor throttle plate on fuel injected vehicles.

Throttle body injection: Fuel injection system that uses one or more fuel injectors mounted above or in the throttle body itself.

Throttle return dashpot: Carburetor device which slows throttle closing and prevents stalling.

Throttle valve: Valve in carburetor. It is used to control amount of fuel mixture that reaches cylinders.

Throttle valve sensor and throttle position sensor: Sensor which measures amount of throttle valve opening and provides information for fuel injection computer.

Throttle valve (Transmission): Valve in automatic transmission which controls oil flow to regulator plug.

Throw: Offset portion of crankshaft designed to accept connecting rod.

Throwing a rod: When an engine has thrown a connecting rod from crankshaft, major damage is usually incurred.

"Throw off" oil: Lubricating oil that is thrown outward from rotating parts.

Throw-out bearing (Clutch): Bearing that is forced against clutch throw-out fingers to release clutch.

Throw-out lever (Clutch): Pivoted lever that actuates clutch throw-out bearing.

Throw-out sleeve (Clutch): Sliding sleeve upon which clutch throw-out bearing is mounted. Actuated by throw-out lever.

Thrust: A pushing or shoving force exerted against one body by another.

Thrust angle: Imaginary lines of force that cross lengthwise through vehicle's tires.

Thrust bearing: Bearing designed so as to resist side pressure.

Thrust flange: A shoulder on a shaft that rides against a thrust bearing to control end play and thrust forces.

Thrust loading: Load force applied parallel to crankshaft, camshaft, etc., centerline.

Thrust surface: That portion (surface) of a part that either receives or transmits a force from or to another part.

Thrust washer: Bronze or hardened steel washer placed between two moving parts. The washer prevents longitudinal movement and provides a bearing surface for thrust surfaces of parts.

Tie rod: Rod, or rods, connecting steering arms together. When tie rod is moved, wheels pivot.

TIG: Gas tungsten arc welding (tungsten inert gas).

Tightening sequence: Order in which fasteners should be tightened or torqued to prevent part distortion.

Time fuel injection: Fuel injection is timed to occur when intake valve opens.

Timing: The act of coordinating two or more separate events or actions in relation to each other. Example: Timing the firing of plug to piston position on compression stroke.

Timing belt: A flexible, toothed belt used to rotate camshaft.

Timing chain: Drive chain that operates camshaft by engaging sprockets on camshaft and crankshaft.

Timing cover: Cover over front of engine. Houses timing chain or gear mechanism and front crankshaft oil seal.

Timing gears: Both the gear attached to the camshaft and the gear on the crankshaft. They provide a means of driving the camshaft.

Timing light: Stroboscopic unit that is connected to secondary circuit to produce flashes of light in unison with firing of specific spark plug. By directing these flashes of light on whirling timing marks, marks appear to stand still. By adjusting distributor, timing marks may be properly aligned, thus setting timing.

Timing marks (Ignition): Marks, usually located on vibration damper, used to synchronize ignition system so plugs will fire at precise time.

Timing marks (Valves): One tooth on either the camshaft or crankshaft gear will be marked with an indentation or some other mark. Another mark will be found on other gear between two of teeth. Two gears must be meshed so that marked tooth meshes with marked spot on other gear.

Timing sprockets: Chain or belt type sprockets on crankshaft and camshaft.

Tinning: Coating piece of metal with a very thin layer of solder.

Tin-plated: Covered with a very thin coating of tin.

TIR (Total Indicator Reading): Dial indicator needle reading amount from lowest to highest reading produced by a complete rotation of a gear, shaft, etc.

Tire balance: In that tires turn at relatively high speeds, they must be carefully balanced both for static balance and for dynamic balance.

Tire bead: Portion of tire that bears against rim flange. Bead has a number of turns of steel wire in it to provide great strength.

Tire casing: Main body of tire exclusive of tread.

Tire inflation pressure: Recommended maximum tire air pressure as given on tire sidewall.

Tire plies: Layers of nylon, rayon, etc., cloth used to form casing. Many car tires are two ply with a four ply rating. Two ply indicates two layers of cloth or plies.

Tire rotation: Moving front tires to rear and rear to front to equalize any wear irregularities.

Tire sidewall: Portion of tire between tread and bead.

Tire size: Given on tire sidewall as coded letter-number designation of size, section height, and diameter across bead.

Tire tread: Part of tire that contacts road.

Toe-in: Having front of wheels closer together than back (front wheels). Difference in measurement across front of wheels and the back will give amount of toe-in.

Toe-out: Having front of wheels further apart than the back.

Toe-out on turns: When car negotiates a curve, inner wheel turns more sharply and while wheels remain in this position, a condition of toe-out exists.

Toggle switch: Switch actuated by flipping a small level either up and down or from side to side.

Tolerance: Amount of variation permitted from an exact size or measurement. Actual amount from smallest acceptable dimension to largest acceptable dimension.

Tooth contact pattern: Refers to shape, size, and location of actual contact area between two mating gear teeth.

Tooth heel (Differential ring gear): Wider outside end of tooth.

Tooth toe (Differential ring gear): Narrower inside end of tooth.

Top off: Fill a container to full capacity.

Torque: Turning or twisting force such as force imparted on drive line by engine.

Torque arm: An arm or lever attached to some part to control amount and direction of movement caused by torque (twisting) forces.

Torque bar or rod: An articulated bar between frame and drive axle housing designed to relieve leaf springs of axle torque (twisting) strain. Prevents axle windup and/or hop during heavy acceleration or braking. Also called traction bar.

Torque converter: Unit, quite similar to fluid coupling, that transfers engine torque to transmission input shaft. Unlike fluid coupling, torque converter can multiply engine torque.

This is done by installing one or more stators between torus members. Driving torus is referred to as "pump" and driven torus as "turbine."

Torque (Gross): Maximum engine torque developed by engine without fan, air cleaner, alternator, exhaust system, etc.

Torque (Net): Maximum torque developed by engine equipped with fan, air cleaner, exhaust system, and all other systems or units present when engine is installed in vehicle.

Torque multiplication (Automatic transmission): Increasing engine torque through the use of a torque converter.

Torque stick: Calibrated tool used with an impact wrench to remove wheel lug nuts.

Torque tube drive: Method of connecting transmission output shaft to differential pinion shaft by using an enclosed drive shaft. Drive shaft is enclosed in torque tube that is bolted to rear axle housing on one end and is pivoted through a ball joint to rear of transmission on other. Driving force of rear wheels is transferred to frame through torque tube.

Torque wrench: Wrench used to draw nuts, cap screws, etc., up to specified tension by measuring torque (turning force) being applied.

Torquing sequence: See *Tightening sequence.*

Torsional vibration: Twisting and untwisting action developed in shaft. It is caused either by intermittent applications of power or load.

Torsion bar: Long spring steel rod attached in such a way that one end is anchored while other is free to twist. If an arm is attached at right angles to free end, any movement of arm will cause rod or bar to twist. Bar's resistance to twisting provides a spring action. Torsion bar replaces both coil and leaf springs in some suspension systems.

Torsion bar suspension: Suspension system that makes use of torsion bars in place of leaf or coil spring.

Torus: Fluid coupling rotating member. There are two—driving and driven torus.

Tote board: Portable board or rack containing a series of tools such as pullers and accessories.

Tote tray: Portable tray for tools. May be hand carried to work area.

Toxic: Poisonous.

TPC: Tire Performance Criteria.

Track: Distance between front wheels or distance between rear wheels. They are not always the same.

Traction bar: Articulated bar or link attached to frame and rear axle housing to prevent spring windup during heavy acceleration or braking.

Traction control: Computerized system that governs engine throttle and brake system operation to increase vehicle traction on low-friction surfaces.

Traction differential: See *Limited-slip differential.*

Traction (Tire): Frictional force generated between tire and road. Necessary for braking, steering, and driving.

Trammel: Steel bar or rod with adjustable, sliding indicator arms. Used to check measurements between parts. Often used for checking wheel and tire toe-in.

Transaxle: Drive setup in which transmission and differential are combined into a single unit.

Transducer: Vacuum regulator actuated or controlled electrically. A device that converts an input signal (electrical) into an output signal (diaphragm movement) of a different form.

Transfer case: Gearbox, driven by transmission, that will provide driving force to both front and rear propeller shafts on four-wheel drive vehicle.

Transformer: Electrical device used to increase or decrease voltage. Car ignition coil transforms voltage from 12 volts to upward of 30,000 volts.

Transistor: Electrical device made of semi-conducting material and using at least three electrical connections. Often used as a switching device.

Transistor Ignition: Form of ignition system utilizing transistors and a special coil. Conventional distributor and point setup is used. With transistor unit, voltage remains constant, thus permitting high engine rpm without resultant engine "miss." Point life is greatly extended as transistor system passes a very small amount of current through points.

Transistorized: Electronic device employing transistors. Can also refer to electronic, as opposed to mechanical, control or operation of some function, such as making and breaking ignition primary circuit.

Transmission: Device that uses gearing or torque conversion to effect a change in ratio between engine rpm and driving wheel rpm. When engine rpm goes up in relation to wheel rpm, more torque but less speed is produced. Reduction in engine rpm in relation to wheel rpm produces a higher road speed but delivers less torque.

Transmission adapter: A unit that allows a different make or year transmission to be bolted up to original engine.

Transmission (Automatic): Transmission that automatically effects gear changes to meet varying road and load conditions. Gear changing is done through series of oil operated clutches and bands.

Transmission (Standard or Conventional): Transmission that must be shifted manually to effect a change in gearing.

Transverse leaf spring: Leaf spring mounted at right angles to length of car.

Transverse mounted: Mounted crosswise or at right angles to vehicle centerline.

Traps: Area over which car is raced for timing purposes.

Tread: Distance between two front or two rear wheels.

Tread (Tire): Portion of tire which contacts roadway.

Tread ply (Radial tire): Reinforcing plies lying beneath tread area. These are in addition to body plies that also pass under tread.

Tread width (Tire): Distance between outside edges of tread as measured across tread surface.

Trickle charging: Maintaining a charge in a stored battery by passing a constant, but very low current, through the battery.

Trip odometer: Auxiliary odometer that may be reset to zero at option of driver. Used for keeping track of mileage on trips up to one thousand miles.

Trouble codes: Numerical value that represents an abnormal operating condition as detected by a self-diagnostic system. These codes are usually extracted from the computer's memory during service.

Troubleshooting: Diagnosing engine, transmission, etc., problems by various tests and observations.

Troubleshooting chart: Diagnostic flow chart that provides step-by-step procedures to test automotive systems.

TRS: Transmission Regulated Spark.

Trunnion: One of two pivots, bearings, etc., placed opposite to each other so as to permit a swiveling or tilting action of some part. Example: Universal joint trunnion (yoke bearings) that allow cross to swivel.

Tube cutter: Tool used to cut tubing by passing a sharp wheel around tube.

Tubeless (Tire): Tire constructed for use without inner tube, valve stem snaps into and seals in wheel rim.

Tune-up: Process of checking, repairing, and adjusting carburetor, spark plugs, points, belts, timing, etc., in order to obtain maximum performance from engine.

Tune-up specialist: Person highly trained and skilled in area of engine tune-up. Checks operation of and corrects problems in ignition, fuel, charging, cooling, cranking, etc., systems.

Turbine: Wheel upon which series of angled vanes are affixed so moving column of air or liquid will impart a turning motion to wheel.

Turbine engine: Engine that utilizes burning gases to spin a turbine, or series of turbines, as a means of propelling the car.

Turbocharger: Exhaust powered supercharger.

Turbulence: Violent, broken movement or agitation of a fluid or gas.

Turning radius: Diameter of circle transcribed by outer front wheel when making a full turn.

TV: Throttle valve rod or cable that extends from foot throttle linkage to throttle valve in automatic transmission.

TVS: Thermostatic Vacuum Switch.

Twist drill: Metal cutting drill with spiral flutes (grooves) to permit exit of chips while cutting.

Two-stoke cycle engine: Engine requiring one complete revolution of crankshaft to fire each piston once.

U

UAW: United Auto Workers.

U-bolt (Spring): A horseshoe shaped bolt, with threads on each end, that passes around axle housing to secure leaf spring.

Umbrella seal (Valve): A cover placed over valve stem end and extending out over valve spring. Directs dripping oil away from stem and guide area to minimize oil leakage past valve guides.

UNC (Thread): Unified National Coarse thread sizes.

Undercoating: Soft deadening material sprayed on underside of car, under hood, trunk lid, etc.

Under-square engine: Engine in which bore diameter is smaller than length of stroke.

Understeer: Tendency for car, when negotiating a corner, to turn less sharply than driver intends.

UNEF (Thread): Unified National Extra Fine thread sizes.

UNF (Thread): Unified National Fine thread size.

Unit body: Car body in which body itself acts as frame.

Unit loading: Applying a loading force to very specific area or part, such as is done by adding a crimp, wire, etc., to a gasket to increase pressure around an opening, etc.

Universal joint: Flexible joint that will permit changes in driving angle between driving and driven shaft.

Unleaded gasoline: Gasoline not containing tetraethyl lead. Must be used with vehicles equipped with a catalytic converter.

Unsprung weight: All parts of car not supported by suspension system; wheels, tires, etc.

Updraft Carburetor: Carburetor in which the air passes upward through the carburetor into the intake manifold.

Upset: Widening of diameter through pounding.

Upshift: Shifting to a higher gear.

UTQGS: Uniform Tire Quality Grading System.

V

Vacuum: Enclosed area in which air pressure is below that of surrounding atmospheric pressure.

Vacuum advance (Distributor): Unit designed to advance and retard ignition timing through action of engine vacuum working on a diaphragm.

Vacuum amplifier: A device used to increase force or action produced by a vacuum.

Vacuum booster: Small diaphragm vacuum pump, generally in combination with fuel pump, used to bolster engine vacuum during acceleration so vacuum operated devices continue to operate.

Vacuum gauge: Gauge used to determine amount of vacuum in a chamber.

Vacuum modulator: Device which uses engine vacuum to control throttle valve in automatic transmission.

Vacuum motor: A device, utilizing a vacuum operated diaphragm, which causes movement of some other unit.

Vacuum pump: Diaphragm type of pump used to produce vacuum.

Vacuum runout point: Point reached when vacuum brake power piston has built up all the braking force it is capable of with vacuum available.

Vacuum switch (Electric): An electrical switch that is operated by vacuum.

Vacuum tank: Tank in which vacuum exists. Generally used to provide vacuum to power brake installation in event engine vacuum cannot be obtained. Tank will supply several brake applications before vacuum is exhausted.

Valve: Device used to either open or close an opening. There are many different types.

Valve body (Automatic transmission): Unit containing various shifter valves, springs, passageways, etc. Used to control transmission shift operation.

Valve clearance (Engine): Space between end of valve stem and actuating mechanism (rocker arm, lifter, etc.)

Valve duration: Length of time, measured in degrees of engine crankshaft rotation, that valve remains open.

Valve face: Outer lower edge of valve head. The face contacts the valve seat when the valve is closed.

Valve face angle: See Face angle.

Valve float: Condition where valves in engine are forced back open before they have had a chance to seat. Brought about (usually) by extremely high rpm.

Valve grinding: Renewing valve face area by grinding on special grinding machine.

Valve guide: Hole through which stem of poppet valve passes. It is designed to keep valve in proper alignment. Some guides are pressed into place and others are merely drilled in block or in head metal.

Valve head (Engine): Portion of valve above stem.

Valve-in-head engine: Engine in which both intake and exhaust valve are mounted in the cylinder head and are driven by push rods or by an overhead camshaft.

Valve keeper or valve key or valve retainer: Small unit that snaps into a groove in end of valve stem. Designed to secure valve spring, valve spring retaining washer, and valve stem together. Some are of split design and some are horseshoe shaped.

Valve lash: Valve tappet clearance or total clearance in the valve operating train with cam follower on camshaft base circle.

Valve lift: Distance a valve moves from full closed to full open position.

Valve lifter or cam follower: Unit that contacts end of valve stem and camshaft. Follower rides on camshaft. Cam lobes move it upward to open valve.

Valve margin: Width of edge of valve head between top of valve and edge of face. Too narrow a margin results in preignition and valve damage through overheating.

Valve oil seal: Neoprene rubber ring placed in groove in valve stem to prevent excess oil entering area between stem and guide. There are other types of these seals.

Valve overlap: Certain period in which both intake and exhaust valve are partially open. (Intake is starting to open while exhaust is not yet closed.)

Valve port: Opening, through head or block, from intake or exhaust manifold to valve seat.

Valve rotator: Unit that is placed on end of valve stem so that when valve is opened and closed, the valve will rotate a small amount with each opening and closing. This gives longer valve life.

Valve seat: Area onto which face of poppet seats when closed. Two common angles for this seat are forty-five and thirty degrees.

Valve seat grinding: Renewing valve seat area by grinding with a stone mounted upon a special mandrel.

Valve seat insert: Hardened steel valve seat may be removed and replaced.

Valve seat runout: A measurement of valve seat out-of-roundness (concentricity). Also provides an indication of seat squareness with valve guide centerline.

Valve spring: Coil spring used to keep valves closed.

Valve spring compressor: Tool used to collapse valve spring so that retainer may be removed.

Valve stem (Engine): Portion of valve below head. The stem rides in the guide.

Valve stem clearance: Clearance between stem and guide.

Valve tappet: Adjusting screw to obtain specified clearance at end of valve stem (tappet clearance). Screw may be in top of lifter, in rocker arm, or in the case of ball joint rocker arm, nut on mounting stud acts in place of a tappet screw.

Valve timing: Adjusting position of camshaft to crankshaft so that valves will open and close at the proper time.

Valve train: Various parts making up valve and its operating mechanism.

Valve umbrella: Washer-like unit placed over end of the valve stem to prevent entry of excess oil between stem and guide. Used in valve-in-head installations.

Vane: Thin plate affixed to rotatable unit to either throw off air or liquid, or to receive thrust imparted by moving air or liquid striking the vane. In the first case it would be acting as a pump and in the second case as a turbine.

Vane pump: Pump using two or more spring loaded vanes (flat, rectangular strips) operating in slots in a rotor. As rotor spins, vane ends rotate and rub against pump walls. Rotor is offset in relation to pump walls.

Vapor: Gaseous state of a substance usually a liquid or solid. Example: Steam.

Vapor charging: Charging air conditioning system with refrigerant vapor.

Vaporization: Breaking gasoline into fine particles and mixing it with air.

Vapor-liquid separator: A device used to separate liquid from a vapor—such as can be used in an engine PCV system to prevent engine oil being drawn out of engine along with crankcase vapors.

Vapor lock: Boiling or vaporizing of the fuel in the lines from excess heat. Boiling will interfere with movement of the fuel and will in some cases, completely stop the flow.

Vapor separator: A device used on cars equipped with air conditioning to prevent vapor lock by feeding vapors back to the gas tank via a separate line.

Variable pitch stator: Stator that has vanes that may be adjusted to various angles depending on load conditions. Vane adjustment will increase or decrease efficiency of stator.

Variable venturi: A carburetor venturi whose opening size can be varied to meet changing engine speed and load.

Varnish: Deposit on interior of engine caused by engine oil breaking down under prolonged heat and use. Certain portions of oil deposit themselves in hard coatings of varnish.

V-belt: V shaped belt commonly used to spin alternator, water pump, power steer-ing pump, and air conditioning com-pressor.

V-block: A block of steel with a deep "V" groove cut in one or more spots. Can be used in pairs to support a shaft while it is turned to check for runout, support round work for drilling, etc.

Velocity: Time rate of motion. Speed with which an object moves as measured in feet per second, miles per hour, etc.

Venturi: That part of a tube, channel, or pipe so tapered as to form a smaller or constricted area. Liquid, or a gas, moving through this area will speed up and as it passes narrowest point, a partial vacuum will be formed. Taper facing flow of air is much steeper than taper facing away from flow of air. Venturi principle is used in carburetor.

Vibration damper: Round weighted device attached to front of crankshaft to minimize torsional vibration.

Viscosimeter: Device used to determine viscosity of a given sample of oil. Oil is heated to specific temperature and then allowed to flow through set orifice. Length of time required for certain amount of flow determines oil's viscosity.

Viscosity: Measure of oil's ability to pour.

Viscosity index: Measure of oil's ability to resist changes in viscosity when heated.

Viscosity rating: A rating of how "thick" or "thin" a sample of oil may be. This refers to how fast a given amount will flow through a specific size hole at a given temperature.

Viscous coupling: A nondirect coupling (driving unit) between two drive components that utilizes a fluid (such as silicone) to produce transfer of power. Allows for some slippage.

Volatile: A substance that evaporates (turns to vapor) easily. Example: Gasoline.

Volatility: Property of gasoline, alcohol, etc., to evaporate quickly and at relatively low temperatures.

Volt: Unit of electrical pressure or force that will move a current of one ampere through a resistance of one ohm.

Voltage: Difference in electrical potential between one end of a circuit and the other. Also called EMF (electromotive force). Voltage causes current to flow.

Voltage drop: Lowering of voltage due to excess length of wire, undersize wire, etc.

Voltage regulator: See Regulator (Electrical).

Voltmeter: Instrument used to measure voltage in given circuit. (In volts.)

Volume: Measurement, in cubic inches, cubic feet, etc., of amount of space within a certain object or area.

Volumetric efficiency: Comparison between actual volume of fuel mixture drawn in on intake stroke and what would be drawn in if cylinder were to be completely filled.

Vortex: Mass of whirling liquid or gas.

Vortex flow (Torque converter): Whirling motion of oil as it moves around from pump, through turbine, stator and back into pump and so on.

V-type engine: An engine with cylinders arranged in two separate banks (rows) and set at an angle (V-shape) to each other.

Vulcanization: Process of heating compounded rubber to alter its characteristics—making it tough, resilient, etc.

W

Wandering (Steering): Condition in which front wheels tend to steer one way and then another.

Wankel engine: Rotary combustion engine having one or more three-sided rotors mounted on drive shaft operating in specially shaped chambers. Rotor turns constantly in one direction yet produces an intake, compression, firing, and exhaust stroke.

Warpage: Bending or twisting of an object caused by heat, improper fastener torque, etc.

Water detector: Sensor in diesel fuel system which warns driver of water contamination of fuel.

Water jacket: Area around cylinders and valves that is left hollow so that water may be admitted for cooling.

Water pump: The pump, usually a centrifugal type, used to circulate coolant throughout cooling system.

Water sensor (Diesel): A device in a diesel fuel system to detect presence of water in fuel.

Watt (Electrical): A unit of electrical power amounting to one joule per second.

Waveform or pattern (Oscilloscope): Visible pattern produced on an oscilloscope screen.

Wedge: Engine using wedge-shaped combustion chamber.

Wedge combustion chamber: Combustion chamber utilizing wedge shape. It is quite efficient and lends itself to mass production and as a result is widely used.

Weight (Curb): Weight of vehicle (no passengers) with all systems (fuel, cooling, lubrication) filled.

Weight (Shipping): Basic vehicle weight including all standard items but without fuel or coolant.

Weight (Sprung): See *Sprung weight*.

Weight distribution: Percentage of total vehicle weight as carried by each axle (front and rear).

Welch plug: Another term for engine sand casting core hole plug. Also called "freeze plug."

Weld: To join two pieces of metal together by raising area to be joined to point hot enough for two sections to melt and flow together. Additional metal is usually added by melting small drops from end of metal rod while welding is in progress.

Weld bead: Layer of metal deposited during a welding operation.

Wet friction: Resistance to movement between two lubricated surfaces.

Wet sleeve: Cylinder sleeve application in which water in cooling system contacts a major portion of sleeve itself.

"Wet" steam: Steam containing heavier water droplets that have not been fully vaporized.

Wheel aligner: Device used to check camber, caster, toe-in, etc.

Wheel alignment: Refers to checking or adjusting various angles involved in proper placement or alignment of both front and rear wheels.

Wheel balancer: Machine used to check wheel and tire assembly for static and dynamic balance.

Wheelbase: Distance between center of front wheels and center of rear wheels.

Wheel bearing: Ball or roller bearings on which wheel hub rotates.

Wheel brake: A brake operating at wheel, either drum or disc design.

Wheel cylinder: Part of hydraulic brake system that receives pressure from master cylinder and in turn applies brake shoes to drums.

Wheel dolly: A wheeled device used to elevate and install heavy truck wheel and tire assemblies.

Wheel hop: Hopping action of rear wheels during heavy acceleration.

Wheel hub: That unit upon which wheel is fastened.

Wheelie bars: Short arms attached to rear of a drag racer to prevent front end from rising too far off ground during heavy acceleration. Arms are usually of spring material and have small wheels attached to ends that contact ground.

Wheel lug or lug bolt: Bolts used to fasten wheel to hub.

Wheel rim locks: Locking lug nuts or bolts used to deter theft of custom wheels.

Wheel sensor: Magnetic speed sensor used in an anti-lock brake system to measure wheel speed.

Wheel shimmy: Lateral (side-to-side) vibration of a tire and wheel assembly.

Wheel tracking: Ability of the rear wheels to follow directly behind the front wheels.

Wheel tramp: Hopping (up and down) vibration of a tire and wheel assembly.

Wide treads, wide oval, etc.: Wide tires. Tire height (bead to tread surface) is about 70 percent of tire width across outside of carcass.

Winch: An electrically or mechanically driven drum that will wind in a length of cable. Used to remove vehicles from mud, ascend very steep slopes, pull logs, etc.

Windscreen: British term for windshield.

Wire gauge: A steel plate with a number of various size openings. Used to determine wire diameter and thickness of sheet metal.

Wire loom: A woven covering through which one or more wires can be passed. Secures and protects wires.

Wire wheel: A vehicle wheel using a series of wire (round steel rods) spokes. May also refer to a cleaning wheel made up of wire bristles.

Wiring diagram: Drawing showing various electrical units and wiring arrangement necessary for proper operation.

Wiring harness: A series of wires bound together to form a handy, compact, and protected unit. Often sheathed in a protective covering.

Witness marks: Punch marks used to position or locate some part properly.

Wobble plate: A round, flat plate with a shaft passing through its center. Plate is affixed to shaft at an angle to shaft centerline. When shaft turns, plate rotates and also wobbles from side to side. Used on axial air conditioning compressor to operate pistons.

Woodruff key: A half round key inserted in a circular slot in a shaft. Protrudes above shaft into a part keyway to prevent turning.

Work: A force applied to a body causing body to move.

Work hardening: Hardening of a material by bending, pounding, vibration, etc.

Worm and roller: Steering gear utilizing a worm gear on steering shaft. A roller on one end of cross shaft engages worm.

Worm and sector: Type of steering gear utilizing worm gear engaging sector (a portion of a gear) on cross shaft.

Worm and taper pin: Steering gear utilizing worm gear on steering shaft. End of cross shaft engages worm via taper pin.

Worm gear: A long, cylindrical gear containing a continuous spiral tooth (thread-like). Gear centerline is at right angles to centerline of worm wheel.

Worm shaft (Steering): Steering gear shaft upon which a worm gear is formed. Turns pitman shaft.

Wrench—adjustable: A wrench in which two parallel jaws may be adjusted open or closed by action of a small worm gear. Often called "Crescent wrench."

Wrench—Allen: A hexagonal shaped wrench used to turn Allen screws.

Wrench—box end: Double-end wrench with six or twelve point opening at each end.

Wrench—combination: Double-end wrench with a box end on one end and an open end on other.

Wrench—flare nut: Wrench, similar to a box end but with a section of box cut away. Used to turn tubing nuts.

Wrench—flex head: Wrench with a swivel socket on each end.

Wrench—fluted: Wrench, similar to an Allen wrench but with a series of flutes (grooves) that fit into a corresponding hole in fastener.

Wrench—open end: Double-end wrench with fixed, parallel jaws.

Wrench—pipe (Inside and outside): Wrench with toothed jaws designed to bite into pipe to prevent slipping.

Wrench—ratchet box end: Wrench with a box end arrangement that is free to ratchet. Allows wrench to be moved back and forth without removing it from fastener.

Wrench—stud: Wrench designed to grasp stud shank for insertion or removal.

Wrist pin: See *Piston pin*.

Y

Yield strength (Elastic limit): Maximum force (in pounds per square inch) that can be sustained by given member and have that member return to its original position, length, shape, etc., when force or pressure is removed.

Yoke: Slotted or split end of an object that straddles and is fastened to another, such as a universal joint yoke straddles cross or spider.

Z

Zener diode: A silicone diode that serves as a rectifier (allows electrical current flow in ONE direction only) until voltage being applied to diode attains a certain level (called Zener voltage) at which point diode becomes conductive.

Zero defects: In manufacturing, taking extreme care to make something so well that there will be no failures caused by faulty workmanship or parts.

Zinc: A metal used in plating steel panels, parts, etc., to help prevent rusting and corrosion.

Acknowledgments

The production of a book of this nature would not be possible without the cooperation of the automotive industry. In preparing the manuscript for **Auto Service and Repair**, the industry has been most cooperative. The authors acknowledge the cooperation of these companies with great appreciation:

Accurate Products, Inc.; AC Spark Plug Div. of General Motors Corp.; Aeroquip Corp.; Aimco; Air Lift Co.; Air Reduction; Al-Beck Forbes, Inc.; Albertson and Co.; Alemite Div. of Stewart-Warner; Alfa Romeo Cars, Allen Test Products; All-Lock Co., Inc.; Alondra, Inc.; Aluminum Co. of America; A.L.C. Co.; Amco Mfg. Corp.; American Brake Shoe Co.; American Bosch Arma Corp.; American Hammered Automotive Replacement Div.; American Iron and Steel Institute; American Manufacturers Assn.; American Optical Co.; American Petroleum Institute; American-Standard; American Standards Assn., Inc.; Amerimac, Inc.; Ammco Tools, Inc.; Anti-Friction Bearing Manufacturers Assn., Inc.; AP Parts Corp.; Appleton Electric Co.; Armstrong Patents Co., Ltd.; Armstrong Tire & Rubber; Armstrong Tool Co.; Arnolt Corp.; Aro Corp.; Audi; Ausco Co.; Automotive Electric Assn.; Automotive Products, Inc.; Automotive Service Industry Assn.; Baldwin, J. A., Mfg. Co.; Band-it Company; Barbee Co., Inc.; Battery Council International; Beach Precision Parts Co.; Bear Mfg. Co.; Beckman Instruments, Inc.; Belden Mfg. Co.; Bendix Automotive Service Div. of Bendix Corp.; Benwil Industries; Bethlehem Steel Co.; BF Goodrich; Big Four Industries, Inc.; Binks Mfg. Co.; Black and Decker Mfg. Co.; Blackhawk Mfg. Co.; B & M Automotive Products; Bonney Forge and Tool Works; Borg & Beck; Bilstein Corp. of America; Borg Warner Corp.; Bosch, Robert, Corp.; Bowes Mfg., Inc.; Branick Mfg. Co., Inc.; Breeze Corp., Inc.; Bremen Bearing Co.; British-Leyland Motors, Inc.; British Motor Corp.—Hambro, Inc.; Brown and Sharpe, Indus. Prod. Div.; Cadillac Div. of General Motors Corp.; Buick Div. of General Motors Corp.; Bundy Tubing; Burke Co.; Carter Div. of ACF Industries, Inc.; Cedar Rapids Eng. Co.; Central Tool Co.; Champion Pneumatic Machinery Co.; Champion Spark Plug Co.; Chevrolet Div. of General Motors Corp.; Chicago Rawhide Mfg. Co.; Chief Industries, Inc.; Chrysler Plymouth Div. of Chrysler Corp.; Citroen Cars Corp.; Clayton Associates, Inc.; Cleveland Graphite; Bronze Div. of Clevite Corp.; Clevite Service Div. of Clevite Corp.; Cole-Hersee Co.; Colt Industries; Continental Air Tools; Continental Motors Corp.; Cooper Tire and Rubber Co.; Corbin Co.; Cornell, William Co.; Corning, Cox Instrument; CPI Engineering Services, Inc.; CRC Chemicals; Cummins Engine Co., Inc.; Dana Corp.; Deere & Co.; Delco-Remy Div. of General Motors Corp.; Detroit Diesel Allison; Duetz Corp.; DeVilbiss Co.; Dodge Div. of Chrysler Corp.; Dole Valve Co.; Doug Nash Equipment; Dover Corp.; Dow Corning Corp.; Dual Drive, Inc.; Duff-Norton; Dunlop Tire Company; Dura-Bond Engine Parts Co.; Duralcan USA; Durke - Atwood Co.; Easco Tools; Eaton Corp.; Echlin Mfg. Co.; Edelmann, E., and Co.; E.I. du Pont de Nemours and Co.; EIS Automotive Corp.; Electrodyne; ESB Brands, Inc.; Environmental Systems Products, Inc.; Ethyl Corp.; Eutectic Welding Alloys Corp.; Everco Industries, Inc.; Exxon Company USA; Fafnir Bearing Co.; FAG Bearing, LTD.; Federal-Mogul Corp.; Fel-Pro, Inc.; Ferrari Cars; Fiat; Firestone Tire and Rubber Co.; Fiske Brothers Refining Co.; Fletch/Air Inc.; Fluke Corp.; FMC Corp; Ford Div. of Ford Motor Co.; Fox Valley Instrument; Fram Corp.; Gates Rubber Co.; Gatke Corp.; General Electric; General Instrument Corp.; General Tire & Rubber Co.; Geo Division of GM; G.H. Meiser & Co.; Girling Ltd.; GKN Automotive, Inc.; Glassinger & Company; Globe Hoist Co.; GMC Truck and Coach Div. of General Motors Co.; Goodall Mfg. Co.; Goodrich Co.; Goodyear Tire and Rubber Co.; Gould Inc.; Graco, Inc.; Gray Co., Inc.; Graymills Corp.; Grey-Rock Div. of Raybestos-Manhattan, Inc.; Guaranteed Parts Co.; Guide Lamp Div. of General Motors; Gulf Oil Corp.; Gunite Foundries Div. of Kelsey-Hayes Co.; Gunk Chemical Div. of Radiator Specialty Co.; Halibrand Eng. Corp.; Hamilton Test Systems; Harrison Radiator Div. of General Motors; Hastings Mfg. Co.; Hayden, Inc.; H.E. Dreyer, Inc.; Hein-Werner Corp.; Heli-Coil Products; Helm, Inc.; Hickok Automotive Group; H.K. Porter, Inc.; Holley Carburetor Div. of Colt Industries; Homestead Industries, Inc.; Honda; Hub City Iron Co.; Huck Mfg. Co., Hyundai Motor America; Hunter Eng. Co.; Hydramatic Div. of General Motors; Ideal Corp.; Ignition Manufacturers Inst.; Imperial Eastman Corp.; Ingersoll-Rand; Inland Mfg. Co.; International Harvester Co.; International Mfg. Co.; Iskenderian Racing Cams; Isuzu of

America, Inc.; ITT Automotive; Jaguar Cars, Ltd.; Jeep Div. of American Motors Corp.; Johnson Bronze Co.; Johns-Manville; Kal-Equip. Co.; K-D Mfg. Co.; Kelly-Springfield Tire Co.; Kelsey-Hayes Co.; Kem Manufacturing, Inc.; Kent Moore Org.; Kester Solder Co.; KIA Motors; Kleer-Flo Co.; K.O. Lee Co.; Koni America, Inc.; Kwik-Way Mfg. Co.; Land-Rover; Lear Siegler, Inc.; Leece-Neville Co.; Lenroc Co.; Libby-Owens-Ford Co.; Lincoln Electric Co.; Lincoln Eng. Co.; Lincoln-Mercury Div. of Ford Motor Co.; Lisle Corporation; Littlefuse, Inc.; Loctite Corporation; Lucas, Joseph, Ltd.; Lufkin Rule Co.; Mack Trucks, Inc.; MacMillan Petroleum Corp.; Magnaflux Corp.; Mansfield Tire & Rubber Co.; Maremont Corp.; Marquette Corp.; Martin Senour Paints; Marvell-Schebler Products Div. of Borg-Warner Corp.; Maserati; Master Pneumatic-Detriot Inc.; Mazda; McCartney Manufacturing Co., Inc.; McCord Corp.; McCreary Tire & Rubber Corp.; Meco, Inc.; Mercedes-Benz; Merit Industries, Inc.; Meyer Hydraulics; Midland-Ross Corp.; Mobil Oil Corp.; Monitor Manufacturing; Monroe Auto Equipment Co.; Moog Industries, Inc.; Morton-Norwich Products, Inc.; Motorcraft; Motorola Automotive Products, Inc.; Motor Wheel Corp.; Murray Corp.; Muskegon Piston Ring Co.; Mustang Dynamometers; Napa-Belden; Micro Test; National Board of Fire Underwriters; National Engines Co.; Nice Ball Bearing Co.; Nicholson File Co.; Nissan; Nugier, F.A., Co.; Oakite Products, Inc.; Oldsmobile Div. of General Motors Corp.; Omega Mfg. Co.; Owatonna Tool Co.; Packard Electric; P and G Mfg. Co.; Parker Fluid Connectors; Paxton Products; Pennsylvania Refining Co.; Perfect Circle Corp.; Perfect Equipment Corp.; Permatex Co., Inc.; Peugeot Inc.; Phillips Temco, Inc.; Pontiac Div. of General Motors Corp.; Porsche; Porter, H.K., Inc.; Prestolite Co.; Pro-Cut International; Proto Tool Co.; P.T. Brake Lining Co., Inc.; Purolator Products, Inc.; Pyroil Co.; Quaker State Corp.; Questor; Raybestos Div. of Raybestos-Manhattan, Inc.; Realmarket Associates; Rexnord; Rinck-McIlwaine, Inc.; Renault; Robertshaw Controls Co.; Robinair Division of SPX Corp.; Rochester Div. of General Motors; Rockford Clutch Div. of Borg-Warner Corp.; Rockwell International; Rodac Corp.; Rootes Motors, Inc.; Rottler Boring Bar Co.; RTI Technologies, Inc.; Rubber Manufacturers Assn.; Ruger Equipment Co.; Saab-Scania of America, Inc.; Saginaw Steering Gear; Salisbury Corp.; Schrader Div. of Scovill Mfg. Co., Inc.; Sealed Power Corp.; Semperit of America, Inc.; Shell Oil Co.; Sherwin-Williams Co.; Shim-A-Line Inc.; Simpson Electric Co.; Sioux Tools Inc.; SKF Industries, Inc.; Skil; Slep Electronics; Snap-on Tools Corp.; Society of Automotive Eng., Inc.; Solex Ltd.; Sornberger Equip. Sales; South Bend Lathe, Inc.; Spicer; Standard Motor Products; Standard Oil Co. of Calif.; Standard-Thomson Corp.; Stant Mfg. Co., Inc.; Star Machine and Tool Co.; Starrett, L.S., Co.; Stemco Mfg. Co.; Stewart-Warner; Storm-Vulcan, Inc.; Straza Industries; Sturtevant, P.A., Co.; Subaru; Sun Electric Corp.; Sunnen Products Co.; Takata Total Safety Systems; Testing Systems, Inc.; Texaco, Inc.; The Aluminum Association; Thexton Mfg. Co., Inc.; Thompson Products Replacement Div. of Thompson-Ramo-Wooldridge, Inc.; Thor Power Tool Co.; 3-M Company; Timken Roller Bearing Co.; Torrington; Tomco Coupler; Toyota; Traction Master Co.; Trucut (Frank Wood and Co.); TRW, Inc.; Ultra-Violet Products, Inc.; Union Carbide Corp.; Uniroyal, Inc.; United Parts Div. of Echlin Mfg. Co.; UOP, Inc.; United Tool Processes Corp.; U.S. Chemicals; U.S. Cleaner Corp.; Utica-Herbrand Div. of Kelsey-Hayes Co.; Vaco Products Co.; Valvoline Oil Co.; Van Norman Machine Co.; Vellumoid Co.; Vetronix Vehicle Electronics; Victor Mfg. and Gasket Co.; Volkswagen of America, Inc.; Volvo of America Corp.; Voss Inc.; Wagner Electric Corp.; Walbro, Walker Mfg. Co.; Warner Gear-Warner Motive; Weatherhead Co.; Weaver Mfg. Div. of Dura Corp.; Werther International; Wessels Company; Westberg Mfg. Co.; Wheelabrator-Frye Inc.; Whitaker Cable Corp.; White Engine Co.; Williams, J.H., and Co.; Wilton Corp.; Wix Corp.; Woodhill Permatex; World Bestos Div. of the Firestone Tire and Rubber Co.; Wright-Austin Co.; Wudel Mfg. Co.; Young Radiator Co.

Portions of the materials contained in this text have been reprinted with the permission of General Motors Corporation, Service Technology Group.

Index

A

Accelerator pump, 409, 418
Accelerator pump checks and adjustment, 418-420
Accidents, avoiding, 13, 14
Accumulators, 641, 756, 881
Acid core, 159
ACT, 969
Active suspensions, 791
Add-on transmission cooler, 648
Adhesives and sealants, 125, 126
Adjustable stand, 205
Adjuster sleeves, 822
Adjusting disc brake type parking brake, 743
Adjusting rear wheel parking brake, 742, 743
Adjusting valve lash (hydraulic lifters), 311-314
  cam lobe base circle, 312
  plunger at top of travel, 312
Adjusting valve lash (mechanical lifters), 312-314
Aeration, 645
Air bag operation, 560
Air bag service precautions, 562
Air bag systems, 558-560
Air bag systems, troubleshooting, 561
Air cleaner assembly, 377
Air cleaner elements, 403
Air cleaner service, 403-405
Air conditioning and heater service, 871-911
  blower motor service, 906
  component replacement, 898-903
  retrofitting, 903
Air conditioning cycle, 873, 874
Air conditioning principles, 871-874
Air conditioning system,
  compressor, 875-878
  condenser, 878
  electrical switches, 883, 884
  evaporator pressure controls, 881-883
  major components, 874
  types, 874

Air conditioning system contamination, preventing, 884-886
Air conditioning system diagnosis, 957-959
Air conditioning system service, 884-898
  component service, 894-898
  discharging the system, 890, 891
  evacuating the system, 891, 892
  gauge manifold, 886, 887
  leak detectors, 887-891
  preventing contamination, 884-886
  refrigerant charging, 892-894
  safety rules, 884
Air conditioning technician, 977
Air control valve, 478
Air distribution and control system service, 906-908
Air distribution system diagnosis, 959, 960
Air distribution system ductwork, 907
Air distribution wiring and vacuum circuits, 907
Airflow sensors, 499
Air gap, 339
Air guide, 474
Air induction system, 377
Air injection system, 474
Air pump, 474
Air-cooled engines, 449
Air-fuel ratios, 375
Air-operated struts and shocks, 790
Alignment angles, major, 849-852
Alignment marks, 606
Alignment setup, 855
Alignment specifications, 854
Alternator, 526
Alternator disassembly and overhaul, 529-533
Alternator output, checking, 527, 528
Alternator service precautions, 527
Altitude compensating device, 422
Ammeter, 59, 163
Amperage, 527
Amperes, 152
Aneroid, 422